Reference Guide to

Russian Literature

Reference Guide to

RUSSIAN LITERATURE

Editor

NEIL CORNWELL

Associate Editor

NICOLE CHRISTIAN

FITZROY DEARBORN PUBLISHERS
LONDON • CHICAGO

FITZROY DEARBORN PUBLISHERS
70 East Walton Street
Chicago, Illinois 60611
USA

or

11 Rathbone Place
London W1P 1DE
England

British Library Cataloguing in Publication Data
Reference guide to Russian literature
1. Russian literature 2. Russian literature – History and criticism
I. Cornwell, Neil
891.7'09

ISBN 1–884964–10–9

First published in the USA and UK 1998

Typeset by Tradespools Ltd., Frome, Somerset
Printed in Great Britain by the Bath Press

Cover illustration: *The Moscow Kremlin* by Aleksei Kravchenko, 1923

Cover design by Philip Lewis

CONTENTS

EDITOR'S NOTE

The *Reference Guide to Russian Literature* aims to be a wide-ranging guide to the main writers of Russian literature and to their best-known works. We therefore include entries on some 273 writers and 293 works. The *Guide* covers, albeit selectively, the entirety of Russian literature, from the Kievan period to the post-communist writing of the Russian Federation, although there is an unashamed bias towards the 19th and 20th centuries and, to some extent, towards contemporary authors.

The writer entries are arranged in alphabetical order (A to Z in the western alphabet). Many of the entries on writers are accompanied by essays on individual works of literature, placed chronologically after the appropriate writer entry. Anonymous works can be found in the alphabetical sequence under the English-language title of the work (cross-references are provided for alternative titles).

The basic brief to contributors was to provide essays of approximately 1000 words, both for writers (from Pushkin down to the lesser known) and for single works. Some, particularly those on a few of the most important figures, are up to half as long again; some are a little shorter. The entry for each writer consists of a biographical sketch of the subject, plus a list of the writer's primary works in chronological order and grouped by genre where applicable, including translations into English, and a selected list of bibliographies and critical studies on the author. While there is a certain near-uniformity intended in the length of both writer and work entries, there is considerable variation in the scale of the Publications lists, which are designed, as far as possible, to reflect the publishing profile, status, and critical reception of the figure concerned. Priority has normally been given to secondary sources in English, or in English-language editions, where these are available.

The Publications lists include separately published books, including translations into English. On-going editions are indicated by a dash after the date of publication. Dates refer to the first publication (often in journals) unless indicated otherwise. The first mention of a title in the text is followed by an English translation in parenthesis. In cases where there are no published translations a literal translation is provided within square brackets.

A further word should be said on the choice of entries, which was based on the recommendations of the advisers (listed on page xi). As far as writers are concerned, selection has been limited to Russian (as opposed to other Slavs, or citizens of the former Soviet Union), and to non-Russian writers writing in Russian. Thus Vasil Bykov, who writes in Belorussian, is omitted, whereas Chingiz Aitmatov, a Kirgiz writing predominantly – latterly at least – in Russian, is included, as is Fazil' Iskander (an Abkhazian who writes in Russian) and Gennadii Aigi (a Chuvash Russian-language poet). Critics and thinkers have not been included, unless they are also well known as creative literary figures (thus Chernyshevskii and Herzen are in, but not Dobroliubov or Rozanov; Solov'ev and Tynianov, but not Bakhtin or Lotman). A single exception is made in the case of Belinskii, whose prominence is such that any *Reference Guide to Russian Literature* was felt to be unthinkable without his presence. Normally we have been prepared to include only leading exponents of creative writing (or *khudozhestvennaia literatura*); in the 20th century, however, we are persuaded that the genre of memoir literature has assumed such an importance that Nadezhda Mandel'shtam, Evgeniia Ginzburg, and Lidiia Ginzburg had to be accommodated. The declared preference for a generous inclusion of "new" writers has necessitated the leaving out of a number of figures well known in the Soviet period whose reputation is no longer, and whose importance seems no longer, what it once was: writers for whom space might certainly have been found had a volume such as this been compiled ten or 20 years ago. In any case, of course, debate around the margins on who should or should not have been included can never be fully legislated for.

Our policy regarding Russian-language writing means that Vladimir Nabokov is, perforce, included, but he is represented as far as work entries are concerned by selections from that portion of his *oeuvre* written originally in Russian (we therefore include for instance *The Defence* and *The Gift*, but not *Pale Fire* or *Lolita*). Regarding work entries otherwise, Chekhov has the highest number (the four main plays, together with four of his stories); other major figures are restricted to a maximum of seven; many have fewer and quite a number of writers featured have no additional work entries. It may be considered that a number have been adequately characterized in their writer entry. Some may not have produced any single "outstanding" work; others may be known only for their output of short lyric poems or prose miniatures: we chose not to commission 1000-word essays on a single lyric poem and did not feel it desirable to include a range of much shorter additional entries. Essays on individual works have normally been devoted to more substantial compositions: novels, plays, narrative poems, collections or cycles of short stories or of lyric poetry. Authors whose publishing profile does not conform to such a pattern may have suffered accordingly. Preference has normally been given to works of a general cultural, as well as purely literary, significance and frequently – but by no means exclusively – to works known in English-language translation.

The main editorial thrust of this volume is to provide readable and informative essays, plus an essential bibliographical guide, on the main writers and works of Russian literature for the student and the general reader. The publications lists are selective, rather than aspiring to be exhaustive.

The *Reference Guide* includes 13 Introductory Essays, which give coverage to most periods, topics, and genres of Russian literature. These essays provide a context and serve in sum as a comprehensive introduction to the body of writer and work entries that follows. One Russian writer – namely Pushkin (as the "father of Russian literature") – has here been singled out for more detailed treatment: an essay having been commissioned on him and the inspiration he drew from English literature, in the shape of the works of Byron and Shakespeare.

Also provided is a historical Chronology, a Glossary of more specialized terms, and a General Reading List of anthologies, histories and other works of reference, and general (or non-single-author-based) studies in English. The book concludes with a Title Index to the Publications lists, which contains titles in the original language and in English translation.

Dates of births and deaths are given in New Style (Russia having changed to the Gregorian calendar only after the Revolution). Well-known older historical dates are given in Old Style (such as 14 December 1825, the date of the Decembrist uprising against Nicholas I; and reference to the February and October Revolutions – which would have meant using the unfamiliar March and November respectively, according to the New Style).

The opinions expressed in this volume are those of the individual contributors alone and do not reflect any views or policy of the editors or the publisher.

Acknowledgments

The editors are grateful to the advisory panel for their valuable counsel and assistance in compiling the lists of writers and works for inclusion and their help in locating contributors. Many others helped in a similar fashion at various stages; in particular, thanks are due to Sibelan Forrester, Valentina Polukhina, Barry Scherr, and Gerald Smith. Special thanks are due our proof-reader, Radojka Milevic, and the splendid support of our in-house editor, Lesley Henderson. The main thanks, though, must go to our 180 contributors, without whose efforts, it goes without saying, this volume, which has been some four years in the making, would not have been possible and could not have been brought to fruition. The contributors range from far and wide (Europe, Russia and Australasia, as well as North America and the British Isles) and they feature emeritus professors and a wide range of leading active academic Slavists, as well as junior lecturers, independent scholars, and graduate students – many of whom should be academic stars in the future; our contributors also include several contemporary writers. We also gratefully acknowledge both the patience and the at times vital participation of our colleagues in the Department of Russian Studies at the University of Bristol.

NEIL CORNWELL *Editor*
NICOLE CHRISTIAN *Associate Editor*
University of Bristol, 1998

Note on Transliteration

The system of transliteration from Cyrillic used in this volume is that of the Library of Congress, without diacritics. Representation of the soft sign is omitted from place names (unless they appear in transliterated titles or quotations); English forms of the most common place names are used (such as, Moscow, St Petersburg, Yalta, Sebastopol, Archangel). Names of people and characters (except perhaps when featured in translated titles) follow Library of Congress transliteration (thus "Fedor Dostoevskii" and "Lev Tolstoi"). Anglicized name-forms are used for tsars (thus "Alexander I", but "Aleksandr Pushkin"). Exceptions are made too for a small number of well-known figures who retain their accustomed spelling, or something closer thereto (Beria, Herzen, Tchaikovskii, Yeltsin), and in the case of Russian émigrés who have established a particular spelling though residence and publishing in the west (D.S. Mirsky). Cross-references of names are provided in the body of the book. The overall aim has been to attain a very large measure of consistency, without total subjection to pedantry.

ADVISERS

A.D.P. Briggs
Ellen Chances
Anna Lisa Crone
Catriona Kelly
Arnold McMillin
Robin Milner-Gulland
Kathleen Parthé

CONTRIBUTORS

Robin Aizlewood
Joe Andrew
Anthony Anemone
Carolyn Jursa Ayers
Joy H. Bache
Lewis Bagby
Gilda Baïkovitch
Radha Balasubramanian
Henryk Baran
Andrew Barratt
Rosamund Bartlett
Michael Basker
Michael Beresford
David M. Bethea
Birgit Beumers
Charles Bland
Craig Brandist
A.D.P. Briggs
Angela Brintlinger
Gary Browning
Diana Lewis Burgin
Neil Carrick
Philip Cavendish
Ellen Chances
Nicole Christian
Katerina Clark
Roger Cockrell
Julian W. Connolly
Olga Cooke
Neil Cornwell
Jane Costlow
Anna Lisa Crone
Anthony Cross
Nicholas Crowe
J.A.E. Curtis
S. Dalton-Brown
Pamela Davidson
Martin Dewhirst
Laszlo Dienes
Daša Šilhánková Di Simplicio
Peter Doyle
Elena Dryzhakova
Milton Ehre
Frank Ellis
John Elsworth
Herman Ermolaev
Michael Falchikov
Rachel S. Farmer
I.P. Foote
Sibelan Forrester
Peter France
Simon Franklin
Richard Freeborn
Jacqueline French
Paul Friedrich
Jehanne M. Gheith
David Gillespie
John Goodliffe
Helena Goscilo
Knut Grimstad
Richard B. Grose
Joan Delaney Grossman
Jane Gary Harris
Peter Henry
Anthony Hippisley
Katharine Hodgson

Michael J. de K. Holman
David M. Holohan
D.L.L. Howells
Stephen Hutchings
Gerald J. Janecek
D. Barton Johnson
Malcolm V. Jones
W. Gareth Jones
Andrew Kahn
George Kalbouss
Catriona Kelly
Sonia I. Ketchian
R.J. Keys
Michael Kirkwood
Shoshana Milgram Knapp
A.V. Knowles
Viktor Krivulin
Danuše Kšicova
Robert Lagerberg
Ronald Lane
Boris Lanin
Alla Latynina
Eric Laursen
Robert Leach
W.J. Leatherbarrow
C. Nicholas Lee
Jennifer Lonergan
Nathan Longan
Lev Loseff
Stephen Lovell
David A. Lowe
Christopher Luck
Nicholas Luker
Rosalind McKenzie
Arnold McMillin
John McNair
Gordon McVay
Cynthia Marsh
Rosalind Marsh
David W. Martin
Amanda Metcalf
Priscilla Meyer
Miroslav Míkulašek
Lesley Milne
Robin Milner-Gulland
Marilyn Minto
Michael Molnar
Joseph P. Mozur, Jr.
James Muckle
A.B. Murphy
Elizabeth B. Neatrour
Catharine Theimer Nepomnyashchy
Michael Nicholson
Katherine Tiernan O'Connor
Derek Offord
Patrick O'Meara
Donna Tussing Orwin
Michael O'Toole
Temira A. Pachmuss
Neil Parsons
Maria Pavlovszky
Richard Peace
Thomas Pedrick
Anna Pilkington
Igor Pilshchikov
Valentina Polukhina
Robert Porter
Ivo Pospišil
Michael Pursglove
Michael Pushkin
Avril Pyman
Michael Ransome
Donald Rayfield
Robert Reid
Andrew Reynolds
Graham Roberts
Ekaterina Rogachevskaia
Andrei Rogachevskii
Peter Rollberg
Judson Rosengrant
Wendy Rosslyn
Robert Russell
Linda Hart Scatton
John Schillinger
Marian Schwartz
Olga Sedakova
Igor Shaitanov
Mikhail Sheinker
Svetlana Shnitman-McMillin
Alexandra Smith
Melissa T. Smith
Ruth Sobel
Elena Sokol
Karla Thomas Solomon
Sven Spieker
John Sullivan
Arch Tait
Margaret Tejerizo
Francis J. Thomson
R.D.B. Thomson
Helen L. Tilly
Roman Timenchik
Andrew Baruch Wachtel
David N. Wells
Willem G. Weststeijn
Claire Whitehead
Faith Wigzell
Gareth Williams
James Woodward
A. Colin Wright
Barbara Wyllie
Gleb Žekulin
Zinovii Zinik
Irene Zohrab

ALPHABETICAL LIST OF WRITERS AND WORKS

ALPHABETICAL LIST OF WORKS

CHRONOLOGICAL LIST OF WRITERS

fl. 11th century	Ilarion of Kiev
1053–1125	Vladimir Monomakh
c.1056–after 1113	Nestor
c.1130–1182	Kirill of Turov
c.1360–1419(?)	Epifanii Premudryi
1400s–before 1472	Afanasii Nikitin
c.1470–1555	Maxim the Greek
1530–1584	Ivan IV
1620–1682	Avvakum
1628/29–1680	Simeon Polotskii
1703–1769	Vasilii Trediakovskii
1708–1744	Antiokh Kantemir
1711–1765	Mikhail Lomonosov
1717–1777	Aleksandr Sumarokov
1734–1792	Mikhail Chulkov
1735–1770	Fedor Emin
1740–1791	Iakov Kniazhnin
1743–1810	Ekaterina Dashkova
1743–1816	Gavrila Derzhavin
1745–1792	Denis Fonvizin
1749–1802	Aleksandr Radishchev
1758–1823	Vasilii Kapnist
1766–1826	Nikolai Karamzin
1769–1844	Ivan Krylov
1769–1816	Vladislav Ozerov
1774–1829	Anna Bunina
1777–1846	Aleksandr Shakhovskoi
1780–1825	Vasilii Narezhnyi
1783–1866	Nadezhda Durova
1783–1852	Vasilii Zhukovskii
1787–1855	Konstantin Batiushkov
1787–1836	Antonii Pogorel'skii
1789–1852	Mikhail Zagoskin
1791–1859	Sergei Aksakov
1792–1878	Petr Viazemskii
1795–1829	Aleksandr Griboedov
1795–1826	Kondratii Ryleev
1796–1846	Nikolai Polevoi
1797–1846	Vil'gel'm Kiukhel'beker
1797–1837	Aleksandr Marlinskii
1798–1831	Anton Del'vig
1799–1837	Aleksandr Pushkin
1800–1844	Evgenii Baratynskii
1800–1870	Aleksandr Vel'tman
1802–1839	Aleksandr Odoevskii
1803–1847	Nikolai Iazykov

1803–1863	Koz'ma Prutkov
1803–1873	Fedor Tiutchev
1804–1860	Aleksei Khomiakov
1804–1869	Vladimir Odoevskii
1804–1855	Mariia Zhukova
1805–1827	Dmitrii Venevitinov
1807–1893	Karolina Pavlova
1809–1852	Nikolai Gogol'
1809–1842	Aleksei Kol'tsov
1811–1848	Vissarion Belinskii
1812–1891	Ivan Goncharov
1812–1870	Aleksandr Herzen
1812–1858	Evdokia Rostopchina
1813–1877	Nikolai Ogarev
1813–1882	Vladimir Sollogub
1814–1842	Elena Gan
1814–1841	Mikhail Lermontov
1815–1892	Evgeniia Tur
1817–1875	A.K. Tolstoi
1818–1883	Ivan Turgenev
1819–1893	Avdot'ia Panaeva
1820–1892	Afanasii Fet
1821–1881	Fedor Dostoevskii
1821–1878	Nikolai Nekrasov
1821–1881	Aleksei Pisemskii
1822–1900	Dmitrii Grigorovich
1823–1886	Aleksandr Ostrovskii
1823–1884	Nadezhda Sokhanskaia
1824–1864	Aleksandr Druzhinin
1824–1889	Nadezhda Khvoshchinskaia
1826–1889	Mikhail Saltykov-Shchedrin
1828–1889	Nikolai Chernyshevskii
1828–1910	Lev Tolstoi
1829–1865	Mikhail Mikhailov
1831–1895	Nikolai Leskov
1835–1863	Nikolai Pomialovskii
1843–1902	Gleb Uspenskii
1853–1921	Vladimir Korolenko
1853–1900	Vladimir Solov'ev
1855–1909	Innokentii Annenskii
1855–1888	Vsevolod Garshin
1856–1937	Ekaterina Letkova
1860–1904	Anton Chekhov
1861–1928	Anastasiia Verbitskaia
1862–1887	Semen Nadson
1863–1949	Aleksandr Serafimovich

1863–1927	Fedor Sologub
1865–1941	Dmitrii Merezhkovskii
1866–1949	Viacheslav Ivanov
1866–1907	Lidiia Zinov'eva-Annibal
1867–1942	Konstantin Bal'mont
1868–1936	Maksim Gor'kii
1869–1945	Zinaida Hippius
1869–1905	Mirra Lokhvitskaia
1870–1953	Ivan Bunin
1870–1938	Aleksandr Kuprin
1871–1919	Leonid Andreev
1872–1952	Aleksandra Kollontai
1872–1936	Mikhail Kuzmin
1872–1952	Teffi
1873–1924	Valerii Briusov
1873–1954	Mikhail Prishvin
1877–1901	Ivan Konevskoi
1877–1957	Aleksei Remizov
1877–1932	Maksimilian Voloshin
1878–1927	Mikhail Artsybashev
1880–1934	Andrei Belyi
1880–1921	Aleksandr Blok
1880–1932	Aleksandr Grin
1881–1972	Boris Zaitsev
1882–1969	Kornei Chukovskii
1883–1945	Dem'ian Bednyi
1883–1958	Fedor Gladkov
1883–1945	A.N. Tolstoi
1884–1937	Nikolai Kliuev
1884–1937	Evgenii Zamiatin
1885–1922	Velimir Khlebnikov
1885–1933	Sofiia Parnok
1886–1957	Mark Aldanov
1886–1921	Nikolai Gumilev
1886–1939	Vladislav Khodasevich
1886–1968	Aleksei Kruchenykh
1887–1938/39	Benedikt Livshits
1887–1964	Samuil Marshak
1887–1941	Igor' Severianin
1888–1982	Marietta Shaginian
1889–1966	Anna Akhmatova
1889–1963	Nikolai Aseev
1889–1954	Lidiia Seifullina
1890–1960	Boris Pasternak
1891–1940	Mikhail Bulgakov
1891–1967	Il'ia Erenburg
1891–1926	Dmitrii Furmanov
1891–1938	Osip Mandel'shtam
1891–1952	Mariia Shkapskaia
1892–1977	Konstantin Fedin
1892–1968	Konstantin Paustovskii
1892–1960	Anna Prismanova
1892–1941	Marina Tsvetaeva
1893–1930	Vladimir Maiakovskii
1894–1940	Isaak Babel'
1894–1958	Georgii Ivanov
1894–1938	Boris Pil'niak
1894–1943	Iurii Tynianov
1895–1934	Eduard Bagritskii
1895–1925	Sergei Esenin
1895–1963	Vsevolod Ivanov
1895–1958	Mikhail Zoshchenko
1896–1958	Evgenii Shvarts
1897–1937	Il'ia Il'f
1897–1986	Valentin Kataev
1897–1962	Anatolli Mariengof
1898–1959	Iurii Libedinskii
1898–1937	Nikolai Oleinikov
1899–1994	Leonid Leonov
1899–1980	Nadezhda Mandel'shtam
1899–1977	Vladimir Nabokov
1899–1960	Iurii Olesha
1899–1951	Andrei Platonov
1899–1934	Konstantin Vaginov
1900–1970	Nikolai Erdman
1901–1976	Anna Barkova
1901–1993	Nina Berberova
1901–1956	Aleksandr Fadeev
1901–1924	Lev Lunts
1902–1990	Lidiia Ginzburg
1902–1989	Veniamin Kaverin
1903–1971	Gaito Gazdanov
1903–1942	Evgenii Petrov
1903–1958	Nikolai Zabolotskii
1904–1977	Evgeniia Ginzburg
1904–1936	Nikolai Ostrovskii
1904–1941	Aleksandr Vvedenskii
1905–1964	Vasilii Grossman
1905–1942	Daniil Kharms
1905–1973	Vera Panova
1905–1984	Mikhail Sholokhov
1907–1996	Lidiia Chukovskaia
1907–	Irina Grekova
1907–1982	Varlam Shalamov
1908–	Natal'ia Baranskaia
1909–1978	Iurii Dombrovskii
1910–1975	Ol'ga Berggol'ts
1910–1971	Aleksandr Tvardovskii
1911–	Semen Lipkin
1911–87	Viktor Nekrasov
1911–	Anatolii Rybakov
1913–	Sergei Zalygin
1915–1979	Konstantin Simonov
1918–	Vladimir Dudintsev
1918–	Aleksandr Solzhenitsyn
1919–1977	Aleksandr Galich
1919–	Aleksandr Granin
1919–1986	Boris Slutskii
1920–1983	Fedor Abramov
1920–1994	Iurii Nagibin
1920–1990	David Samoilov
1922–	Aleksandr Zinov'ev
1923–	Grigorii Baklanov
1923–1996	Boris Mozhaev
1923–1984	Vladimir Tendriakov
1924–	Viktor Astaf'ev
1924–	Iurii Bondarev
1924–1997	Bulat Okudzhava
1924–1997	Vladimir Soloukhin
1925–1988	Iulii Daniel'

1925–1997	Andrei Siniavskii
1925–1991	Arkadii Strugatskii
1925–1981	Iurii Trifonov
1927–1982	Iurii Kazakov
1928–	Chingiz Aitmatov
1929–	Iuz Aleshkovskii
1929–	Fazil' Iskander
1929–1974	Vasilii Shukshin
1930–1995	Vladimir Maksimov
1931–	Anatolii Pristavkin
1931–	Georgii Vladimov
1932–	Vasilii Aksenov
1932–	Vasilii Belov
1932–	Vladimir Voinovich
1933–	Evgenii Evtushenko
1933–	Boris Strugatskii
1933–	Andrei Voznesenskii
1934–	Gennadii Aigi
1934–	Nina Katerli
1935–	Anatolii Gladilin
1935–	Evgenii Rein
1936–	Dmitrii Bobyshev
1936–	Natal'ia Gorbanevskaia
1936–	Aleksandr Kushner
1937–	Bella Akhmadulina
1937–	Andrei Bitov
1937–	Mark Kharitonov
1937–	Lev Loseff
1937–	Vladimir Makanin
1937–	Valentin Rasputin
1937–	Viktoriia Tokareva
1937–1972	Aleksandr Vampilov
1938–	Leonid Borodin
1938–	Oleg Chukhontsev
1938–1990	Venedikt Erofeev
1938–	Liudmila Petrushevskaia
1938–1980	Vladimir Vysotskii
1939–	Mikhail Kuraev
1940–1996	Iosif Brodskii
1940–	Dmitrii Prigov
1940–	Iuliia Voznesenskaia
1941–1990	Sergei Dovlatov
1943–	Leonid Ioffe
1943–	Eduard Limonov
1943–	Sasha Sokolov
1944–	Viktor Krivulin
1944–	Anatolii Kurchatkin
1944–	Sergei Stratonovskii
1945–	Zinovii Zinik
1946–	Arkadii Dragomoshchenko
1946–	Viacheslav P'etsukh
1946–	Evgenii Popov
1947–	Viktor Erofeev
1948–	Mikhail Aizenberg
1948–	Elena Shvarts
1948–	Ivan Zhdanov
1949	Ol'ga Sedakova
1951–	Tat'iana Tolstaia
1954–	Aleksei Parshchikov
1954–	Irina Ratushinskaia
1955–	Timur Kibirov
1955–	Vladimir Sorokin
1962–	Viktor Pelevin

GENERAL READING LIST

General Histories and Encyclopedias

Auty, Robert and Dimitri Obolensky (editors). *An Introduction to Russian Language and Literature*, *Companion to Russian Studies*, vol. 2, Cambridge and New York, Cambridge University Press, 1977.

Benn, Anna and Rosamund Bartlett. *Literary Russia: A Guide*, London, Papermac, 1997.

Bristol, Evelyn. *A History of Russian Poetry*, Oxford and New York, Oxford University Press, 1991.

Brown, William Edward. *A History of Seventeenth-Century Russian Literature*, Ann Arbor, Ardis, 1980.

Brown, William Edward. *A History of 18th Century Russian Literature*, Ann Arbor, Ardis, 1980.

Brown, William Edward. *A History of Russian Literature of the Romantic Period*, 4 vols, Ann Arbor, Ardis, 1986.

Čiževskij, Dmitrij. *History of Russian Literature from the Eleventh Century to the End of the Baroque*, The Hague, Mouton, 1960.

Čiževskij, Dmitrij. *History of Nineteenth-Century Russian Literature*, 2 vols, translated by Richard Noel Porter, Nashville, Vanderbilt University Press, 1974.

Fennell, John and Antony Stokes. *Early Russian Literature*, Berkeley, University of California Press, and London, Faber, 1974.

Hare, Richard. *Russian Literature from Pushkin to the Present Day*, London, Methuen, 1947; Freeport, New York, Books for Libraries Press, 1970.

Harkins, William E. *Dictionary of Russian Literature*, New York, Philosophical Library, 1956; London, Allen and Unwin, 1957.

Kasack, Wolfgang. *A Dictionary of Russian Literature since 1917*, translated by Maria Carlson and Jane T. Hedges, New York, Columbia University Press, 1988.

Kelly, Catriona. *A History of Russian Women's Writing, 1820–1992*, Oxford and New York, Clarendon Press, 1994.

Kuskov, Vladimir. *A History of Old Russian Literature*, translated by Ronald Vroon, Moscow, Progress, 1980.

Lavrin, Janko. *A Panorama of Russian Literature*, London, University of London Press, and New York, Barnes and Noble, 1973.

Ledkovsky, Marina, Charlotte Rosenthal, and Mary Zirin. *Dictionary of Russian Women Writers*, Westport, Connecticut, Greenwood Press, 1994.

Likhachev, D.S. *A History of Russian Literature 11th–17th Centuries*, Moscow, Raduga, 1989.

Lindstrom, Thaïs S. *A Concise History of Russian Literature*, 2 vols, London, University of London Press, and New York, New York University Press, 1966 and 1978.

Lvov-Rogachevsky, L. *A History of Russian Jewish Literature*, edited and translated by Arthur Levin, Ann Arbor, Ardis, 1979.

Mirsky, D.S. *A History of Russian Literature*, edited by Francis J. Whitfield, New York, Knopf, and London, Routledge, 1949.

Moser, Charles (editor). *The Russian Short Story: A Critical History*, Boston, Twayne, 1986.

Moser, Charles (editor). *The Cambridge History of Russian Literature*, Cambridge and New York, Cambridge University Press, 1989; revised edition, 1992.

Pyman, Avril. *A History of Russian Symbolism*, Cambridge and New York, Cambridge University Press, 1994.

Slonim, Marc. *The Epic of Russian Literature from Its Origins Through Tolstoy*, New York, Oxford University Press, 1950.

Terras, Victor (editor). *Handbook of Russian Literature*, New Haven, Yale University Press, 1985.

Terras, Victor. *A History of Russian Literature*, New Haven, Yale University Press, 1991.

Weber, Harry B. *et al.* (editors). *The Modern Encyclopedia of Russian and Soviet Literature*, Gulf Breeze, Florida, Academic International Press, vols 1–10, 1977–91; thereafter Rollberg, Peter (editor), *The Modern Encyclopedia of East Slavic, Baltic and Eurasian Literatures*, vols 11–12, and forthcoming.

General Studies

Anderson, Roger and Paul Debreczeny (editors). *Russian Narrative and Visual Art: Varieties of Seeing*, Gainesville, University Press of Florida, 1994.

Andrew, Joe (editor). *The Structural Analysis of Russian Narrative Fiction*, Keele, Essays in Poetics Publications, [1984].

Baring, Maurice. *Landmarks in Russian Literature*, London, Methuen, and New York, Macmillan, 1910.

Barta, Peter I. *et al.* (editors). *Russian Literature and the Classics*. Amsterdam, Harwood Academic, 1996.

Bethea, David M. *The Shape of Apocalypse in Modern Russian Fiction*, Princeton, Princeton University Press, 1989.

Brodskii, Iosif. *Less than One: Selected Essays*, New York, Farrar Straus Giroux, and London, Viking, 1986; Harmondsworth, Penguin, 1987.

Brooks, Jeffrey. *When Russia Learned to Read: Literacy and Popular Literature, 1861–1917*, Princeton, Princeton University Press, 1985.

Brostrom, Kenneth N. (editor). *Russian Literature and American Critics: In Honor of Deming B. Brown*, Ann Arbor, Michigan, Department of Slavic Languages and Literatures, 1984.

Chances, Ellen. *Conformity's Children: An Approach to the*

Superfluous Man in Russian Literature, Columbus, Ohio, Slavica, 1978.

Clyman, Toby W. and Diana Greene (editors). *Women Writers in Russian Literature*, Westport, Connecticut, Greenwood Press, 1994.

Cornwell, Neil. *James Joyce and the Russians*, London, Macmillan, 1992.

Davie, Donald (editor). *Russian Literature and Modern English Fiction*, Chicago, University of Chicago Press, 1965.

Erlich, Victor. *The Double Image: Concepts of the Poet in Slavic Literatures*, Baltimore, Johns Hopkins Press, 1964.

Field, Andrew (editor). *The Complection of Russian Literature*, London, Allen Lane, and New York, Atheneum, 1971.

Frank, Joseph. *Through the Russian Prism: Essays on Literature and Culture*, Princeton, Princeton University Press, 1990.

Freeborn, Richard (editor). *Russian Literary Attitudes from Pushkin to Solzhenitsyn*, London, Macmillan, and New York, Barnes and Noble, 1976.

Freeborn, Richard. *The Russian Revolutionary Novel: Turgenev to Pasternak*, Cambridge and New York, Cambridge University Press, 1982.

Freeborn, Richard and Jane Grayson (editors). *Ideology in Russian Literature*, New York, St Martin's Press, and London, Macmillan, 1990.

Friedberg, Maurice. *Russian Classics in Soviet Jackets*, New York, Columbia University Press, 1962.

Garrard, John (editor). *The Russian Novel from Pushkin to Pasternak*, New Haven, Yale University Press, 1983.

Gasparov, Boris *et al.* (editors). *Christianity and the Eastern Slavs*, vol. 3, *Russian Literature in Modern Times*, Berkeley, University of California Press, 1995.

Gifford, Henry. *The Novel in Russia: From Pushkin to Pasternak*, London, Hutchinson, 1964; New York, Harper and Row, 1965.

Heldt, Barbara. *Terrible Perfection: Women and Russian Literature*, Bloomington, Indiana University Press, 1987.

Jones, Malcolm V. and Robin Feuer Miller (editors). *The Cambridge Companion to the Classic Russian Novel*, Cambridge, Cambridge University Press, 1998.

Kelly, Catriona *et al.* (editors). *Discontinuous Discourses in Modern Russian Literature*, London, Macmillan, and New York, St Martin's Press, 1989.

Kornblatt, Judith Deutsch. *The Cossack Hero in Russian Literature*, Madison, University of Wisconsin Press, 1992.

Lotman, Yury. *Analysis of the Poetic Text*, edited and translated by D. Barton Johnson, Ann Arbor, Ardis, 1976.

Lotman, Ju. M. and B.A. Uspenskij. *The Semiotics of Russian Culture*, edited by Ann Shukman, Ann Arbor, University of Michigan, 1984.

McMillin, Arnold (editor). *From Pushkin to "Palisandriia": Essays on the Russian Novel in Honour of Richard Freeborn*, London, Macmillan, and New York, St Martin's Press, 1990.

Mandelker, Amy and Roberta Reeder (editors). *The Supernatural in Slavic and Baltic Literature: Essays in Honor of Victor Terras*, Columbus, Ohio, Slavica, 1988.

Marsh, Rosalind (editor). *Gender and Russian Literature: New Perspectives*, Cambridge and New York, Cambridge University Press, 1996.

Mathewson, Rufus W., Jr. *The Positive Hero in Russian Literature*, New York, Columbia University Press, 1958; revised edition, Stanford, Stanford University Press, 1975.

Mihajlov, Mihajlo. *Russian Themes*, translated by Marija Mihajlov, New York, Farrar Straus and Giroux, and London, Macdonald, 1968.

Morson, Gary Saul (editor). *Literature and History: Theoretical Problems and Russian Case Studies*, Stanford, Stanford University Press, 1986.

O'Toole, L. Michael. *Structure, Style and Interpretation in the Russian Short Story*, New Haven, Yale University Press, 1982.

Phelps, Gilbert. *The Russian Novel in English Fiction*, London, Hutchinson, 1956.

Poggioli, Renato. *The Poets of Russia, 1890–1930*, Cambridge, Massachusetts, Harvard University Press, 1960.

Popkin, Cathy. *The Pragmatics of Insignificance: Chekhov, Zoshchenko, Gogol*, Stanford, Stanford University Press, 1993.

Rabinowitz, Stanley (editor and translator). *The Noise of Change: Russian Literature and the Critics (1891–1917)*, Ann Arbor, Ardis, 1986.

Rancour-Lafferrière, Daniel (editor). *Russian Literature and Psychoanalysis*, Amsterdam and Philadelphia, Benjamins, 1989.

Reeve, F.D. *The Russian Novel*, New York, McGraw-Hill, 1966; London, F. Muller, 1967.

Rosenthal, Bernice Glatzer (editor). *The Occult in Russian and Soviet Culture*, Ithaca, Cornell University Press, 1997.

Scherr, Barry. *Russian Poetry: Meter, Rhythm, and Rhyme*, Berkeley, University of California Press, 1986.

Semeka-Pankratov, Elena (editor). *Studies in Poetics. Commemorative Volume: Krystyna Pomorska (1928–1986)*, Columbus, Ohio, Slavica, 1995.

Slonim, Marc. *Russian Theater, from the Empire to the Soviets*, Cleveland, World, 1961.

Stacy, Robert H. *Russian Literary Criticism: A Short History*, Syracuse, New York, Syracuse University Press, 1974.

Wachtel, Andrew Baruch. *The Battle for Childhood: Creation of a Russian Myth*, Stanford, Stanford University Press, 1990.

Wachtel, Andrew Baruch. *An Obsession with History: Russian Writers Confront the Past*, Stanford, Stanford University Press, 1994.

Wigzell, Faith (editor). *Russian Writers on Russian Writers*, Oxford, Berg, 1994.

Worrall, Nick. *The Moscow Art Theatre*, London and New York, Routledge, 1996.

Ziolkowski, Margaret. *Hagiography and Modern Russian Literature*, Princeton, Princeton University Press, 1988.

Zholkovsky, Alexander. *Text Counter Text: Rereadings in Russian Literary History*, Stanford, Stanford University Press, 1994.

18th and 19th Centuries

Andrew, Joe. *Writers and Society During the Rise of Russian Realism*, London, Macmillan, and Atlantic Highlands, New Jersey, Humanities Press, 1980.

Andrew, Joe. *Russian Writers and Society in the Second Half of the Nineteenth Century*, London, Macmillan, and Atlantic Highlands, New Jersey, Humanities Press, 1982.

Andrew, Joe. *Women in Russian Literature, 1780–1863*, London, Macmillan, and New York, St Martin's Press, 1988.
Andrew, Joe. *Narrative and Desire in Russian Literature, 1822–1849*, London, Macmillan, and New York, St Martin's Press, 1993.
Beaudoin, Luc J. *Resetting the Margins: Russian Romantic Verse Tales and the Idealized Woman*, New York, Peter Lang, 1997.
Cockrell, Roger and David Richards (editors). *The Voice of a Giant: Essays on Seven Russian Prose Classics*, Exeter, University of Exeter, 1985.
Cornwell, Neil (editor), *The Society Tale in Russian Literature: From Odoevskii to Tolstoi*, Amsterdam, Rodopi, 1998.
Cross, A.G. (editor). *Russian Literature in the Age of Catherine the Great: A Collection of Essays*, Oxford, Meeuws, 1976.
Donchin, Georgette. *The Influence of French Symbolism on Russian Poetry*, The Hague, Mouton, 1958.
Drage, C.L. *Russian Literature in the Eighteenth Century*, London, published by the author, 1978.
Fennell, John (editor). *Nineteenth-Century Russian Literature: Studies of Ten Russian Writers*, London, Faber, and Berkeley, University of California Press, 1973.
Finke, Michael C. *Metapoesis: The Russian Tradition from Pushkin to Chekhov*, Durham, North Carolina, Duke University Press, 1995.
Freeborn, Richard. *The Rise of the Russian Novel: Studies in the Russian Novel from "Eugene Onegin" to "War and Peace"*, Cambridge, Cambridge University Press, 1973.
Garrard, J.G. (editor). *The Eighteenth Century in Russia*, Oxford, Clarendon Press, 1973.
Gifford, Henry. *The Hero of His Time: A Theme in Russian Literature*, London, Edward Arnold, and New York, Longmans Green, 1950.
Gutsche, George and Lauren G. Leighton (editors). *New Perspectives on Nineteenth-Century Russian Prose*, Columbus, Ohio, Slavica, 1982.
Hingley, Ronald. *Russian Writers and Society in the Nineteenth Century*, 2nd revised edition, London, Weidenfeld and Nicolson, 1977.
Ingham, Norman W. *E.T.A. Hoffmann's Reception in Russia*, Würzburg, Jal, 1974.
Karlinsky, Simon. *Russian Drama from Its Beginnings to the Age of Pushkin*, Berkeley, University of California Press, 1985.
Katz, Michael R. *Dreams and the Unconscious in Nineteenth-Century Russian Fiction*, Hanover, New Hampshire, University Press of New England, 1984.
Layton, Susan. *Russian Literature and Empire: Conquest of the Caucasus from Pushkin to Tolstoy*, Cambridge and New York, Cambridge University Press, 1994.
Leighton, Lauren G. *Russian Romanticism*, The Hague, Mouton, 1975.
Leighton, Lauren G. *The Esoteric Tradition in Russian Romantic Literature: Decembrism and Freemasonry*, University Park, Pennsylvania State University Press, 1994.
Levitt, Marcus C. *Russian Literary Politics and the Pushkin Celebration of 1880*, Ithaca, Cornell University Press, 1989.
Maegd-Soep, Carolina de. *The Emancipation of Women in Russian Literature and Society*, translated by the author and Jos Coessens, Ghent, Ghent State University, 1978.
Mersereau, John, Jr. *Russian Romantic Fiction*, Ann Arbor, Ardis, 1983.
Moser, Charles A. *Antinihilism in the Russian Novel of the 1860's*, The Hague, Mouton, 1964.
Moser, Charles A. *Esthetics as Nightmare: Russian Literary Theory, 1855–1870*, Princeton, Princeton University Press, 1989.
Nabokov, Vladimir. *Lectures on Russian Literature*, edited by Fredson Bowers, New York, Harcourt Brace Jovanovich, 19881; London, Weidenfeld and Nicolson, 1982; London, Picador, 1983.
Nilsson, Nils Åke (editor). *Russian Romanticism: Studies in the Poetic Codes*, Stockholm, Almqvist & Wiksell, 1979.
Offord, Derek (editor). *The Golden Age of Russian Literature and Thought*, London, Macmillan, and New York, St Martin's Press, 1992.
Passage, Charles E. *The Russian Hoffmannists*, The Hague, Mouton, 1963.
Reid, Robert (editor). *Problems of Russian Romanticism*, Aldershot, Hampshire, and Brookfield, Vermont, Gower, 1986.
Simpson, Mark S. *The Officer in Nineteenth-Century Russian Literature*, Washington, DC, University Press of America, 1981.
Terras, Victor. *Belinskij and Russian Literary Criticism: The Heritage of Organic Aesthetics*, Madison, University of Wisconsin Press, 1974.
Todd, William Mills III. *The Familiar Letter as a Literary Genre in the Age of Pushkin*, Princeton, Princeton University Press, 1976.
Todd, William Mills III (editor). *Literature and Society in Imperial Russia, 1800–1914*, Stanford, Stanford University Press, 1978.
Todd, William Mills III. *Fiction and Society in the Age of Pushkin: Ideology, Institutions and Narrative*, Cambridge, Massachusetts, Harvard University Press, 1986.
Von Gronicka, André. *The Russian Image of Goethe*, 2 vols, Philadelphia, University of Pennsylvania Press, 1968 and 1985.
Welsh, David J. *Russian Comedy, 1765–1823*, The Hague, Mouton, 1966.

20th Century

Avins, Carol. *Border Crossings: The West and Russian Identity in Soviet Literature, 1917–1934*, Berkeley, University of California Press, 1983.
Beaujour, Elizabeth Klosty. *Alien Tongues: Bilingual Russian Writers of the "First" Emigration*, Ithaca, Cornell University Press, 1989.
Beumers, Birgit. *Yury Lyubimov at the Taganka Theatre: 1964–1994*, Amsterdam, Harwood Academic, 1997.
Booker, M. Keith. *Bakhtin, Stalin, and Modern Russian Fiction: Carnival, Dialogism and History*, Westport, Connecticut, Greenwood Press, 1995.
Brandist, Craig. *Carnival Culture and the Soviet Modernist Novel*, London, Macmillan, and New York, St Martin's Press, 1996.
Brown, Deming. *Soviet Russian Literature since Stalin*, Cambridge and New York, Cambridge University Press, 1978.

Brown, Deming. *The Last Years of Soviet Russian Literature: Prose Fiction, 1975–1991*, Cambridge and New York, Cambridge University Press, 1993.

Brown, Edward J. *The Proletarian Episode in Russian Literature, 1928–1932*, New York, Columbia University Press, 1953.

Brown, Edward J. (editor). *Major Soviet Writers: Essays in Criticism*, London and New York, Oxford University Press, 1973.

Brown, Edward J. *Russian Literature since the Revolution*, revised and enlarged edition, Cambridge, Massachusetts, Harvard University Press, 1982.

Chung, Hilary and Michael Falchikov (editors). *In the Party Spirit: Socialist Realism and Literary Practice in the Soviet Union, East Germany and China*, Amsterdam and Atlanta, Rodopi, 1996.

Clark, Katerina. *The Soviet Novel: History as Ritual*, Chicago, University of Chicago Press, 1981; 2nd edition, 1985.

Clowes, Edith W. *Russian Experimental Fiction: Resisting Ideology after Utopia*, Princeton, Princeton University Press, 1993.

Cornwell, Neil. "Through the Clouds of Soviet Literature", *The Crane Bag*, 7/1 (1983), 17–33; reprinted in *The Crane Bag Book of Irish Studies*, vol. 2 (1982–1985), Dublin, Blackwater Press, 1987.

Crouch, Martin and Robert Porter (editors). *Understanding Soviet Politics Through Literature*, London, Allen and Unwin, 1984.

Dewhirst, Martin and Robert Farrell (editors). *The Soviet Censorship*, Metuchen, New Jersey, Scarecrow Press, 1973.

Doherty, Justin. *The Acmeist Movement in Russian Poetry: Culture and the Word*, Oxford, Clarendon Press, and New York, Oxford University Press, 1995.

Dunham, Vera S. *In Stalin's Time: Middleclass Values in Soviet Fiction*, enlarged and updated edition, Durham, North Carolina, Duke University Press, 1990.

Elsworth, John (editor). *The Silver Age in Russian Literature*, London, Macmillan, and New York, St Martin's Press, 1992.

Epstein, Mikhail N. *After the Future: The Paradoxes of Postmodernism and Contemporary Russian Culture*, Amherst, University of Massachusetts Press, 1995.

Erlich, Victor. *Russian Formalism: History, Doctrine*, 1955; revised edition, The Hague, Mouton, 1965; New Haven, Yale University Press, 1981.

Erlich, Victor (editor). *Twentieth-Century Russian Literary Criticism*, New Haven, Yale University Press, 1975.

Erlich, Victor. *Modernism and Revolution: Russian Literature in Transition*, Cambridge, Massachusetts, Harvard University Press, 1994.

Ermolaev, Herman. *Censorship in Soviet Literature, 1917–1991*, Lanham, Maryland, Rowman and Littlefield, 1997.

Eshelman, Raoul. *Early Soviet Postmodernism*, Frankfurt, Peter Lang, 1997.

France, Peter. *Poets of Modern Russia*, Cambridge and New York, Cambridge University Press, 1982.

Frankel, Edith Rogovin. *Novy Mir: A Case Study in the Politics of Literature, 1952–1958*, Cambridge and New York, Cambridge University Press, 1981.

Gibian, George. *Interval of Freedom: Soviet Literature During the Thaw, 1954–1957*, Minneapolis, Minnesota University Press, 1960.

Gibian, George and H.W. Tjalsma (editors). *Russian Modernism: Culture and the Avant-Garde, 1900–1930*, Ithaca, Cornell University Press, 1976.

Gillespie, David. *The Twentieth-Century Russian Novel: An Introduction*, Oxford, Berg, 1996.

Goscilo, Helena. *Dehexing Sex: Russian Womenhood During and After Glasnost*, Ann Arbor, University of Michigan Press, 1996.

Graffy, Julian and Geoffrey A. Hosking. *Culture and Media in the USSR Today*, London, Macmillan, 1989.

Graham, Sheelagh Duffin (editor). *New Directions in Soviet Literature*, London, Macmillan, and New York, St Martin's Press, 1992.

Harris, Jane Gary (editor). *Autobiographical Statements in Twentieth-Century Russian Literature*, Princeton, Princeton University Press, 1990.

Hayward, Max and Edward L. Crowley (editors). *Soviet Literature in the Sixties: An International Symposium*, New York, Praeger, 1964; London, Methuen, 1965.

Hayward, Max. *Writers in Russia, 1917–1978*, edited by Patricia Blake, London, Harvill Press, and San Diego, Harcourt Brace Jovanovich, 1983.

Hingley, Ronald. *Russian Writers and Soviet Society, 1917–1978*, New York, Random House, and London, Weidenfeld and Nicolson, 1979.

Hodgson, Katharine. *Written with the Bayonet: Soviet Russian Poetry of World War Two*, Liverpool, Liverpool University Press, 1996.

Hosking, Geoffrey. *Beyond Socialist Realism: Soviet Fiction since "Ivan Denisovich"*, London, Granada, and New York, Holmes and Meier, 1980.

James, C. Vaughan. *Soviet Socialist Realism: Origins and Theory*, London, Macmillan, and New York, St Martin's Press, 1973.

Lakshin, Vladimir. *Solzhenitsyn, Tvardovsky and "Novy Mir"*, edited and translated by Michael Glenny, Cambridge, Massachusetts, MIT Press, 1980.

Lawton, Anna (editor). *Russian Futurism Through Its Manifestoes, 1912–1928*, Ithaca, Cornell University Press, 1988.

Loseff, Lev. *On the Beneficence of Censorship: Aesopian Language in Modern Russian Literature*, Munich, Sagner, 1984.

Lowe, David. *Russian Writing since 1953: A Critical Survey*, New York, Ungar, 1987.

Luker, Nicholas (editor). *After the Watershed: Russian Prose, 1917–1927: Selected Essays*, Nottingham, Astra Press, 1996.

McMillin, Arnold (editor). *Under Eastern Eyes: The West as Reflected in Recent Russian Émigré Writing*, London, Macmillan, 1991; New York, St Martin's Press, 1992.

McMillin, Arnold (editor). *Symbolism and After: Essays on Russian Poetry in Honour of Georgette Donchin*, London, Bristol Classical Press, 1992.

Maguire, Robert A. *Red Virgin Soil: Soviet Literature in the 1920's*, Princeton, Princeton University Press, 1968.

Markov, Vladimir. *Russian Futurism: A History*, Berkeley, University of California Press, 1968.

Markov, Vladimir. *Russian Imagism, 1919–1924*, 2 vols,

Giessen, Wilhelm Schmitz, 1980.
Marsh, Rosalind J. *Soviet Fiction since Stalin: Science, Politics and Literature*, London, Croom Helm, and Totowa, New Jersey, Barnes and Noble, 1986.
Marsh, Rosalind. *Images of Dictatorship: Portraits of Stalin in Literature*, London and New York, Routledge, 1989.
Marsh, Rosalind. *History and Literature in Contemporary Russia*, London, Macmillan, and New York, New York University Press, 1995.
Maryniak, Irena. *Spirit of the Totem: Religion and Myth in Soviet Fiction, 1964–1988*, Leeds, W.S. Maney, 1995.
Matich, Olga and Michael Heim (editors). *Third Wave: Russian Literature in Emigration*, Ann Arbor, Ardis, 1984.
Muchnic, Helen. *From Gorky to Pasternak*, New York, Random House, 1961; London, Methuen, 1963.
Nilsson, Nils Åke (editor). *Art, Society, Revolution: Russia, 1917–1921*, Stockholm, Almqvist & Wiksell, 1979.
Nilsson, Nils Åke (editor). *Studies in 20th Century Russian Prose*, Stockholm, Almqvist & Wiksell, 1982.
Parthé, Kathleen. *Russian Village Prose: The Radiant Past*, Princeton, Princeton University Press, 1992.
Peterson, Nadya L. *Subversive Imagination: Fantastic Prose and the End of Soviet Literature*, Boulder, Colorado, Westview Press, 1997.
Pike, Christopher (editor). *The Futurists, the Formalists, and the Marxist Critique*, London, Ink Links, 1979.
Pomorska, Krystyna. *Russian Formalist Theory and Its Poetic Ambiance*, The Hague, Mouton, 1968.
Porter, Robert. *Four Contemporary Russian Writers*, Oxford, Berg, 1989.
Porter, Robert. *Russia's Alternative Prose*, Oxford, Berg, 1994.
Proffer, Carl R. (editor). *Modern Russian Poets on Poetry*, Ann Arbor, Ardis, 1976.
Proffer, Carl R. *The Widows of Russia and Other Writings*, Ann Arbor, Ardis, 1987.
Richardson, William. *"Zolotoe Runo" and Russian Modernism, 1905–1910*, Ann Arbor, Ardis, 1986.
Roberts, Graham. *The Last Soviet Avant-Garde: OBERIU – Fact, Fiction, Metafiction*, Cambridge and New York, Cambridge University Press, 1997.
Rühle, Jürgen. *Literature and Revolution: A Critical Study of the Writer and Communism in the Twentieth Century*, edited and translated by Jean Steinberg, London, Pall Mall Press, and New York, Praeger, 1969.
Russell, Robert. *Russian Drama of the Revolutionary Period*, London, Macmillan, and Totowa, New Jersey, Barnes and Noble, 1988.
Russell, Robert and Andrew Barratt (editors). *Russian Theatre in the Age of Modernism*, London, Macmillan, and New York, St Martin's Press, 1990.
Ryan-Hayes, Karen L. *Contemporary Russian Satire: A Genre Study*, Cambridge and New York, Cambridge University Press, 1995.
Scott, H.G. (editor). *Soviet Writers' Congress 1934: The Debate on Socialist Realism and Modernism in the Soviet Union*, London, Lawrence and Wishart, 1977 (first published 1935).
Segel, Harold B. *Twentieth-Century Russian Drama: From Gorky to the Present*, revised edition, Baltimore, Johns Hopkins University Press, 1993.
Seton-Watson, Mary. *Scenes from Soviet Life: Soviet Life Through Official Literature*, London, BBC Publications, 1986.
Seyffert, Peter. *Soviet Literary Structuralism: Background, Debate, Issues*, Columbus, Ohio, Slavica, 1983.
Shentalinsky, Vitaly. *The KGB's Literary Archive*, translated by John Crowfoot, London, Harvill Press, 1995.
Shepherd, David. *Beyond Metafiction: Self-Consciousness in Soviet Literature*, Oxford, Clarendon Press, and New York, Oxford University Press, 1992.
Shneidman, N.N. *Soviet Literature in the 1970's: Artistic Diversity and Ideological Conformity*, Toronto, University of Toronto Press, 1979.
Shneidman, N.N. *Soviet Literature in the 1980's: Decade of Transition*, Toronto, University of Toronto Press, 1989.
Shneidman, N.N. *Russian Literature, 1988–1994: The End of an Era*, Toronto, University of Toronto Press, 1995.
Sicher, Efraim. *Jews in Russian Literature After the October Revolution*, Cambridge, Cambridge University Press, 1995.
Simmons, Ernest (editor). *Through the Glass of Soviet Literature: Views of Russian Society*, New York, Columbia University Press, 1953.
Slonim, Marc. *Soviet Russian Literature: Writers and Problems, 1917–1977*, 2nd revised edition, London and New York, Oxford University Press, 1977.
Smith, Gerald S. *Songs to Seven Strings: Russian Guitar Poetry and Soviet "Mass Song"*, Bloomington, Indiana University Press, 1984.
Steiner, Peter. *Russian Formalism: A Metapoetics*, Ithaca, Cornell University Press, 1984.
Struve, Gleb. *Russian Literature Under Lenin and Stalin, 1917–1953*, Norman, University of Oklahoma Press, 1971.
Svirski, Grigori. *A History of Post-War Soviet Writing: The Literature of Moral Opposition*, edited and translated by Robert Dessaix and Michael Ulman, Ann Arbor, Ardis, 1981.
Tait, Arch. "The Awarding of the Third Russian Booker Prize", *Modern Language Review*, 92/3 (1997), 660–77.
Thomson, Boris. *The Premature Revolution: Russian Literature and Society, 1917–1946*, London, Weidenfeld and Nicolson, 1972.
Thomson, Boris. *Lot's Wife and the Venus of Milo: Conflicting Attitudes to the Cultural Heritage of Modern Russia*, Cambridge and New York, Cambridge University Press, 1978.
Vishevsky, Anatoly. *Soviet Literary Culture in the 1970s: The Politics of Irony*, Gainesville, Florida University Press, 1993.
Williams, Robert C. *Artists in Revolution: Portraits of the Russian Avant-Garde, 1905–1925*, Bloomington, Indiana University Press, 1977.

Anthologies

Aksenov, Vasilii *et al.* (editors). *Metropol: A Literary Almanac*, New York, Norton, 1982.
Andrew, Joe (editor). *Russian Women's Shorter Fiction: An Anthology, 1835–1860*, Oxford, Clarendon Press, and New York, Oxford University Press, 1996.
Atarov, Nikolai (editor). *Anthology of Soviet Short Stories*, 2 vols, Moscow, Progress, 1976.
Bannikov, Nikolai (editor). *Three Centuries of Russian Poetry*, Moscow, Progress, 1980.
Bethell, Nicholas and Barry Rubin (editors). *Kontinent I: The*

Alternative Voice of Russia and Eastern Europe, London, André Deutsch, and New York, Anchor, 1976.
Blake, Patricia and Max Hayward (editors). *Dissonant Voices in Soviet Literature*, New York, Pantheon, 1962; London, Allen and Unwin, 1964.
Blake, Patricia and Max Hayward (editors). *Half-way to the Moon: New Writing from Russia*, New York, Holt Rinehart and Winston, and London, Weidenfeld and Nicolson, 1964.
Bochkarev, Yuri (editor). *Soviet Russian Stories of the 1960's and 1970's*, Moscow, Progress, 1977.
Bowra, C.M. (editor). *A Book of Russian Verse*, translated by various hands, London, Macmillan, 1943; Westport, Connecticut, Greenwood Press, 1971.
Brown, Clarence (editor). *The Portable Twentieth-Century Russian Reader*, New York and Harmondsworth, Penguin, 1985.
Chukhontsev, Oleg (editor). *Dissonant Voices: The New Russian Fiction*, London, Harvill Press, 1991.
Collins, Christopher and Gary Kern (editors). *The Serapion Brothers: A Critical Anthology*, Ann Arbor, Ardis, 1975.
Cooper, Joshua (translator). *Four Russian Plays*, Harmondsworth, Penguin, 1972.
Erofeev, Viktor and Andrew Reynolds (editors). *The Penguin Book of New Russian Writing: Russia's "Fleurs du mal"*, Harmondsworth and New York, Penguin, 1995.
Fen, Elisaveta (editor and translator). *Modern Russian Stories*, London, Methuen, 1943.
Fetzer, Leland (editor and translator). *Pre-Revolutionary Russian Science Fiction: An Anthology (Seven Utopias and a Dream)*, Ann Arbor, Ardis, 1982.
Field, Andrew (editor). *Pages from Tarusa: New Voices in Russian Writing*, Boston, Little Brown, 1964; London, Chapman and Hall, 1965.
Gerenstein, Grigori (editor). *The Terrible News: Russian Stories from the Years Following the Revolution*, London, Black Spring Press, 1990.
Ginsburg, Mirra (editor and translator). *The Fatal Eggs and Other Soviet Satire, 1918–1963*, New York, Macmillan, 1963; London, Quartet, 1993.
Ginsburg, Mirra (editor and translator). *The Ultimate Threshold: A Collection of the Finest in Soviet Science Fiction*, New York, Holt Rinehart and Winston, 1970; Harmondsworth, Penguin, 1978.
Glad, John and Daniel Weissbort (editors). *Russian Poetry: The Modern Period*, Iowa City, University of Iowa Press, 1978.
Glenny, Michael (editor). *Three Soviet Plays*, Harmondsworth and Baltimore, Penguin, 1966; as *The Golden Age of Soviet Theatre*, Harmondsworth and New York, Penguin, 1981.
Goscilo, Helena (editor). *Balancing Acts: Contemporary Stories by Russian Women*, Bloomington, Indiana University Press, 1989.
Goscilo, Helena (editor). *Lives in Transit: A Collection of Recent Russian Women's Writing*, Dana Point, California, Ardis, 1995.
Goscilo, Helena and Byron Lindsey (editors). *Glasnost: An Anthology of Russian Literature under Gorbachev*, Ann Arbor, Ardis, 1990.
Goscilo, Helena and Byron Lindsey (editors). *The Wild Beach and Other Stories*, Ann Arbor, Ardis, 1992.
Graham, Stephen (editor). *Great Russian Short Stories*, London, Benn, 1929; New York, Liveright, 1959.
Green, Michael (editor and translator). *The Russian Symbolist Theater: An Anthology of Plays and Critical Texts*, Ann Arbor, Ardis, 1986.
Houghton, Norris (editor). *Great Russian Short Stories*, New York, Dell, 1958.
Jacobson, Helen Saltz (translator). *New Soviet Science Fiction*, New York, Macmillan, and London, Macmillan, 1979.
Johnson, Kent and Stephen M. Ashby (editors). *Third Wave: The New Russian Poetry*, Ann Arbor, University of Michigan Press, 1992.
Kagal, Ayesha and Natasha Perova (editors). *Present Imperfect: Stories by Russian Women*, Oxford and Boulder, Colorado, Westview Press, 1996.
Kelly, Catriona (editor). *An Anthology of Russian Women's Writing, 1777–1992*, Oxford and New York, Oxford University Press, 1994.
Kommissarzhevsky, Victor (editor). *Nine Modern Soviet Plays*, Moscow, Progress, 1977.
Korovin, Valentin (editor). *Russian 19th-Century Gothic Tales*, Moscow, Raduga, 1984.
Langland, Joseph, Tamas Aczel, and Laszlo Tikos (editors and translators). *Poetry from the Russian Underground: A Bilingual Anthology*, New York, Harper and Row, 1973.
Leighton, Lauren G. (editor). *Russian Romantic Criticism: An Anthology*, New York, Greenwood Press, 1987.
Luker, Nicholas (editor and translator). *An Anthology of Russian Neo-Realism: The "Znanie" School of Maxim Gorky*, Ann Arbor, Ardis, 1982.
Luker, Nicholas (editor). *From Furmanov to Sholokhov: An Anthology of the Classics of Socialist Realism*, Ann Arbor, Ardis, 1988.
MacAndrew, Andrew R. (translator). *Four Soviet Masterpieces*, New York, Bantam, 1965.
McLaughlin, Sigrid (editor and translator). *The Image of Women in Contemporary Soviet Fiction: Selected Stories from the USSR*, New York, St Martin's Press, and London, Macmillan, 1989.
Magidoff, Robert (editor). *Russian Science Fiction, 1969: An Anthology*, New York, New York University Press, and London, University of London Press, 1969.
Mikhailova, Alla (editor). *Classic Soviet Plays*, Moscow, Progress, 1979.
Milner-Gulland, Robin and Martin Dewhirst (editors). *Russian Writing Today*, Harmondsworth, Penguin, 1977.
Minto, Marilyn (editor and translator). *Russian Tales of the Fantastic*, London, Bristol Classical Press, 1994.
Montagu, Ivor and Herbert Marshall (editors). *Soviet Short Stories, 1942–1943*, London, Pilot Press, 1943.
Mortimer, Peter and S.J. Litherland (editors). *The Poetry of Perestroika*, translated by Carol Rumens and Richard McKane, Cullercoats, Iron Press, 1991.
Moss, Kevin (editor). *Out of the Blue: Russia's Hidden Gay Literature, an Anthology*, San Francisco, Gay Sunshine, 1997.
Newnham, Richard (editor). *Soviet Short Stories/Sovetskie rasskazy*, London, Dobson, and Baltimore, Penguin, 1963.
Obolensky, Dimitri (editor). *The Penguin Book of Russian*

Verse, Harmondsworth, Penguin, 1965; as *The Heritage of Russian Verse*, Bloomington, Indiana University Press, 1976.

Pachmuss, Temira (editor and translator). *Women Writers in Russian Modernism*, Urbana, University of Illinois Press, 1978.

Pomorska, Krystyna (editor). *Fifty Years of Russian Prose: From Pasternak to Solzhenitsyn*, 2 vols, Cambridge, Massachusetts, MIT Press, 1971.

Proffer, Carl R. (editor). *From Karamzin to Bunin: An Anthology of Russian Short Stories*, Bloomington, Indiana University Press, 1969.

Proffer, Carl R. (editor). *Russian Romantic Prose: An Anthology*, Ann Arbor, Translation Press, 1979.

Proffer, Carl R. and Ellendea Proffer (editors). *The Ardis Anthology of Recent Russian Literature*, Ann Arbor, Ardis, 1975.

Proffer, Carl R. and Ellendea Proffer (editors). *The Silver Age of Russian Culture: An Anthology*, Ann Arbor, Ardis, 1975.

Proffer, Carl R. and Ellendea Proffer (editors). *Contemporary Russian Prose*, Ann Arbor, Ardis, 1982.

Proffer, Carl and Ellendea Proffer (editors). *The Barsukov Triangle, The Two-Toned Blond and Other Stories*, Ann Arbor, Ardis, 1984.

Proffer, Carl R. *et al.* (editors). *Russian Literature of the Twenties: An Anthology*, Ann Arbor, Ardis, 1987.

Proffer, Ellendea and Carl R. Proffer (editors). *The Ardis Anthology of Russian Futurism*, Ann Arbor, Ardis, 1980.

Reavey, George and Marc Slonim (editors and translators). *Soviet Literature: An Anthology*, London, Wishart, 1933; New York, Covici Friede, 1934.

Reddaway, Peter (editor). *Soviet Short Stories: Volume 2/Sovetskie rasskazy 2*, Harmondsworth, Penguin, 1968.

Reeve, Franklin D. (editor and translator). *Contemporary Russian Drama*, New York, Pegasus, 1968.

Richards, David (editor). *The Penguin Book of Russian Short Stories*, Harmondsworth and New York, Penguin, 1981.

Rodker, John (editor). *Soviet Anthology*, London, Jonathan Cape, 1943.

Rydel, Christine (editor). *The Ardis Anthology of Russian Romanticism*, Ann Arbor, Ardis, 1984.

Rzhevsky, Nicholas (editor). *An Anthology of Russian Literature from Earliest Writings to Modern Fiction: Introduction to a Culture*, Armonk, New York, M.E. Sharpe, 1996.

Senelick, Laurence (translator). *Russian Comedy of the Nikolaian Era*, Amsterdam, Harwood Academic, 1996.

Shkarovsky, Arthur (translator). *Everything but Love: Science-Fiction Stories*, Moscow, Mir, 1973.

Smith, Gerald S. (editor and translator). *Contemporary Russian Poetry: A Bilingual Anthology*, Bloomington, Indiana University Press, 1993.

Soviet Women Writing: Fifteen Short Stories, New York, Abbeville Press, 1990; London, John Murray, 1991.

Struve, Gleb (editor). *Russian Stories*, New York, Bantam, 1961; as *Russian Stories: A Dual-Language Book*, New York, Dover, 1990.

Townsend, R.S. (translator). *Russian Short Stories*, London, Dent, and New York, Dutton, 1924.

Weissbort, Daniel (editor). *Post-War Russian Poetry*, Harmondsworth, Penguin, 1974.

Zalygin, Sergei (editor). *The New Soviet Fiction: Sixteen Short Stories*, New York, Abbeville Press, 1989.

Zenkovsky, Serge A. (editor and translator). *Medieval Russia's Epics, Chronicles, and Tales*, revised and enlarged edition, New York, Dutton, 1974.

Journals (of or including literature in translation)

Glas: New Russian Writing, Moscow, Birmingham and Somerville, Massachusetts, 1991 –

Russian Literature Triquarterly [*RLT*], Ann Arbor, 1–24, 1971–91.

Soviet Literature, Moscow, 1946–91.

Additional Useful Sources

Biblioteka literatury drevnei Rusi, 20 vols. St Petersburg, 1997–

Kratkaia literaturnaia entsiklopediia, vols 1–9, Moscow, 1962–78.

Lewanski, Richard C. *The Literature of the World in English Translation*, vol. 2, *The Slavic Literatures*, New York, New York Public Library, 1967.

Moody, Fred (editor). *10 Bibliographies of 20th Century Russian Literature*, Ann Arbor, Ardis, 1977.

Muratova, K.D. (editor). *Istoriia russkoi literatury deviatnadtsatogo veka: Bibliograficheskii ukazatel'*, Leningrad, 1962.

Muratova, K.D. (editor). *Istoriia russkoi literatury kontsa XIX–nachala XX veka: Bibliograficheskii ukzatel'*, Leningrad, 1963.

Nikolaev, P.A. (editor). *Russkie pisateli, 1800–1917: Biograficheskii slovar'*, 3 vols, Moscow, 1989–94.

Proffer, Carl R. and Ronald Meyer. *Nineteenth-Century Russian Literature in English: A Bibliography of Criticism and Translation*, Ann Arbor, Ardis, 1990.

Russkie sovetskie pisateli – Poety: Bibliograficheskii ukazatel', vols 1–15, Moscow, 1977–91; thereafter *Russkie pisateli – Poety (Sovetskii period): Bibliograficheskii ukazatel'*, vols 16–18, St Petersburg, 1991–95.

Stepanov, V.P. and Iu. Stennik (editors). *Istoriia russkoi literatury XVIII veka: Bibliograficheskii ukazatel'*, Leningrad, 1968.

Tarasenkov, An. *Russkie poety XX veka, 1900–1955: Bibliografiia*, Moscow, 1966.

Terry, Garth M. *East European Languages and Literatures*, vol. 1, Oxford, Clio Press, 1978; vols 2–6, Nottingham, Astra Press, 1982–94.

CHRONOLOGY

c.860
Invention of the Cyrillic alphabet

c.882
Union of Novgorod and Kiev

988
Vladimir of Kiev allows establishment of episcopal see in Rus'

1108
City of Vladimir founded

1113
Vladimir II (Monomakh) (ruled 1113–25)

1125
Russian territories divided into conflicting principalities. "Period of Feudal Partition", with Vladimir-Suzdal dominant under the reigns of Iurii Dologorukii (1149–57) and Andrei Bogoliubskii (1157–74)

1156
Founding of Moscow

1221
Founding of Nizhnii Novgorod

1223
Mongols (Tartars) defeat Galician, Volhynian, and Polovtsian forces at the battle of Kalka

1240
Destruction of Kiev, resulting in establishment of Mongol control

1242
Defeat of Teutonic Knights by Aleksandr Nevskii

c.1260
New Sari (near present day Volgograd) becomes new capital

1325
Ivan I (ruled 1325–41)

1380
Battle of Kulikovo in which the Tartars are defeated by Prince Dmitrii Donskoi, Grand Prince of Moscow

1382
Moscow recaptured by Tartars

1392
Moscow annexes Suzdal and Nizhnii Novgorod

1410
Battle of Tannenberg

1425
Civil war for the throne of Moscow (1425–50)

1462
Ivan III ("The Great") ruled 1462–1505

1512–22
Russo-Polish war

1533
Ivan IV ("The Terrible") becomes first tsar (ruled 1533–84)

1555
Building of St Basil's cathedral in Moscow begins (completed 1560)

1564
Printing of the first book in Moscow

1584
Founding of Archangel

1598
Boris Godonov (ruled 1598–1605)

1605–13
Time of the Troubles

1610–12
Moscow under Polish control

1613
Mikhail (ruled 1613–45) establishes Romanov dynasty

1645
Aleksei (ruled 1645–76)

1682
Peter I ("The Great") and Ivan V rule. Peter I sole tsar (1696–1725)
Archpriest Avvakum martyred

1687
Slav-Greek-Latin Academy established in Moscow

1697–98
Peter's Great Embassy to England and Holland

1703
Founding of St Petersburg
First Russian newspaper

1712
Government transferred to St Petersburg

1721
Peace of Nystad ends the Great Northern War
Abolition of Patriarchate
Creation of the Table of Ranks, defining a hierarchy for all in state service

1722
Peter I redesignates the tsardom of Muscovy as the Empire of All Russias and becomes the first Emperor

1723
Treaty of St Petersburg

1725
Catherine I (ruled 1725–27)
Academy of Sciences founded in St Petersburg

1727
Peter II (ruled 1727–30)

1731
Corps of Cadets for training the nobility created

1755
Moscow University founded

1757
Russia joins the Seven Years' War against Prussia
Academy of Arts founded in St Petersburg

1762
Catherine II ("The Great") comes to the throne (ruled 1762–96)

1765
Free Economic Society founded to modernise agriculture and finance

1782
Denis Fonvizin's *The Minor* produced in St Petersburg

1790
Aleksandr Radischev's *A Journey from St Petersburg to Moscow*

1796
Paul I (ruled 1796–1801)

1801
Paul I assassinated
Alexander I (ruled 1801–25)
Georgia joins the Empire

1805
Russian forces defeated by Napoleon at the Battle of Austerlitz

1812
Napoleon invades Russia

1818
Nikolai Karamzin's *History of the Russian State* (1818–29)

1825
Decembrist Uprising (14 December, Old Style)
Nicholas I (ruled 1825–55)

1833
Aleksandr Pushkin's *Evgenii Onegin* (written 1823–31)

1836
Sovremennik (1836–66 and 1911–15) founded by Pushkin

1837
Death of Pushkin

1840
Mikhail Lermontov's *A Hero of Our Time*

1842
Nikolai Gogol's *Dead Souls*

1844
Vladimir Odoevskii's *Russian Nights*

1852
Death of Gogol'

1853
Crimean War (1853–56) ends with Russia's defeat

1855
Alexander II (ruled 1855–81)
Aleksandr Herzen's *My Past and Thoughts* (1855–69)

1859
Ivan Goncharov's *Oblomov*

1860
Founding of Vladivostok

1861
Emancipation of the Serfs

1862
Ivan Turgenev's *Fathers and Sons*

1863
Lev Tolstoi's *War and Peace* (1863–68)

1865
Fedor Dostoevskii's *Crime and Punishment*

1873
First "To the People" Populist movement (1873–74)
Lev Tolstoi's *Anna Karenina* (1873–77)

1876
Land and Freedom Party founded

1877
Russo-Turkish War (1877–78)

1879
People's Will Group established after split within the Land and Freedom Party
Fedor Dostoevskii's *The Brothers Karamazov* (1879–80)

1881
Alexander II assassinated by activists of the People's Will
Alexander III (ruled 1881–94)
Death of Fedor Dostoevskii

1882
Peasants Land Bank established
Inspectorate of labour conditions established

1891
Construction begins on the Trans-Siberian railway
Franco-Russian alliance signed

1894
Nicholas II (ruled 1894–1917)

1897
Russia joins the gold standard
Moscow Arts Theatre founded

1898
Social Democrat Party founded

1901
Socialist Revolutionary Party founded
Anton Chekhov's *Three Sisters*

1903
2nd Social Democrat Party Congress in Brussels and London: Party splits into Bolshevik (majority) and Menshevik (minority) factions

1904
Death of Anton Chekhov

1905
Russo-Japanese War (1904–05) ends in Russia's defeat
Marchers to Nicholas II's Winter Palace shot by troops
"First Revolution", general strike, and the formation of the St Petersburg Soviet

1906
First Duma

1907
Gor'kii's *The Mother*

1909
Apollon (1909–17) founded by Nikolai Gumilev and Sergei Makovskii

1910
Death of Lev Tolstoi

1912
First issue of *Pravda*

1913
Andrei Belyi's *Petersburg*

1914
Germany declares war on Russia (August 1914)
St Petersburg renamed Petrograd

1916
Rasputin, the royal favourite, murdered

1917
February Revolution
Nicholas II abdicates and is placed under arrest
Soviets set up in Petrograd and Moscow
Provisional Government under Aleksandr Kerenskii assumes control
October Revolution: Lenin seizes power
Cheka (secret police) formed

1918
Red Army formed, led by Trotskii
Russia withdraws from World War I by accepting the Treaty of Brest-Litovsk
Nicholas II and his family executed in Ekaterinburg, ending the Romanov dynasty
"Red Terror" follows attempt on Lenin's life
Civil War (1918–21)

1919
Evgenii Zamiatin's *We* (written 1919–20)

1921
Revolt at the Kronstadt Naval Base crushed
Beginning of NEP (New Economic Policy)

1922
Central censorship office, Glavlit, created
Establishment of the Union of Soviet Socialist Republics (USSR)
Boris Pil'niak's *The Naked Year*

1924
Death of Lenin
Petrograd renamed Leningrad
Stalin becomes leader

1925
Tsaritsin renamed Stalingrad
Mikhail Bulgakov's *The White Guard*
Novyi mir established as organ of the Soviet Writers' Union

1927
Iurii Olesha's *Envy*

1928
End of NEP
First Five-Year Plan
Mikhail Sholokov's *Quiet Flows the Don* (1928–40)

1929
Trotskii deported to Turkey
Collectivisation of agriculture and policy of liquidation of the Kulak class begins

1930
Suicide of Vladimir Maiakovskii

1932
Soviet Writers' Union founded; all other groupings dissolved

1933
Ivan Bunin awarded the Nobel Prize for Literature

1934
Assassination of Kirov
Beginning of the Great Purges
First Congress of Soviet Writers' Union at which the policy of socialist realism is promulgated

1936
Stepping up of purges (1936–39)
Death of Gor'kii

1937
Vladimir Nabokov's *The Gift*

1939
Finland invaded and conquered (1940)

1940
Trotskii murdered in Mexico City by NKVD agent

1941
Germany invades the Soviet Union: beginning of the Great Patriotic War (1941–45)
Leningrad is blockaded, Kiev taken, and Moscow under threat

1945
Soviet Union declares war on Japan

1946
Beginning of "Zhdanov era". Ideological orthodoxy re-imposed on arts and sciences (1946–48), followed by renewed purges (1948–52)

1948–49
Soviet blockade of Berlin

1953
Death of Stalin
L.P. Beria (Soviet secret police chief) tried for treason and executed
Nikita Khrushchev General Secretary of the Communist Party (1953–64)
First Thaw (1953–54)

1954
Second Congress of the Soviet Writers' Union
Beginning of literary rehabilitations

Il'ia Erenburg's *The Thaw*

1956
Hungarian Uprising crushed by Soviet forces
Second Thaw (1956–59)

1957
Soviet Union launches the world's first space satellite, Sputnik I

1958
Boris Pasternak's *Doctor Zhivago*. Pasternak awarded the Nobel Prize for Literature, but is forced to refuse it

1961
Iurii Gagarin becomes the first man to orbit the Earth
Building of the Berlin Wall
Stalingrad renamed Volgograd

1962
Cuban Missile Crisis: Khrushchev withdraws the weapons
Khrushchev attacks modern art at the Manezh Gallery
Aleksandr Solzhenitsyn's *One Day in the Life of Ivan Denisovich*

1964
Khrushchev removed from office
Soviet Union under collective leadership of Leonid Brezhnev, Aleksei Kosygin, and Nikolai Podgornii (1964–68)

1965
Mikhail Sholokhov awarded the Nobel Prize for Literature
Iulii Daniel' and Andrei Siniavskii imprisoned for "anti-Soviet" publications

1966
Mikhail Bulgakov's *The Master and Margarita* published in abridged form, 1966–67 (written 1928–40)

1968
Invasion of Czechoslovakia
Samizdat publications flourish
Aleksandr Solzhenitsyn's *Cancer Ward*

1969
Solzhenitsyn expelled from the Soviet Writers' Union

1970
Solzhenitsyn awarded the Nobel Prize for Literature

1972
Beginnings of policy of détente: SALT I (1972) and SALT II (1979) arms limitation talks with the United States
President Nixon visits the Soviet Union
Iosif Brodskii "invited" to leave the Soviet Union: signals beginning of the "Third Wave" of emigration

1974
Solzhenitsyn deported to Frankfurt following the publication in Paris of *The Gulag Archipelago*

1975
Vladimir Voinovich's *The Life and Extraordinary Adventures of Private Ivan Chonkin* published in Paris

1979
Soviet invasion of Afghanistan. Second "Cold War" begins
Promulgation of *Metropol'* almanac

1980
Vasilii Aksenov's *The Burn* published in the United States

1981
Death of Iurii Trifonov

1982
Death of Leonid Brezhnev
Iurii Andropov (leader 1982–84) begins social and economic reforms

1984
Konstantin Chernenko (leader 1984–85)

1985
Mikhail Gorbachev (leader 1985–91)
Policies of glasnost and perestroika introduced

1986
Andrei Sakharov and his wife Elena Bonner rehabilitated
Glasnost reaches the Soviet Writers' Union
Boris Yeltsin becomes Moscow Party leader

1987
Iosif Brodskii awarded the Nobel Prize for Literature
Publication of previously banned works (soon becomes unlimited)

1988
Pasternak's *Doctor Zhivago* and Zamiatin's *We* published in Russia for the first time

1989
The last Soviet forces withdraw from Afghanistan (February)
Protesters killed by Soviet troops in Tbilisi, Georgia (April)
Fall of the Berlin Wall heralds the collapse of the Soviet-backed regimes of central and eastern Europe, and the reunification of Germany: the USSR does not intervene
First complete Russian translation of James Joyce's *Ulysses* published

1991
Boris Yeltsin elected President of the Russian Federation
Gorbachev elected President by the Supreme Soviet
Attempted KGB-sponsored coup (August) fails. Gorbachev resigns in December.
Ukraine and Belarus issue declaration that the USSR has ceased to exist (8 December) and create the Commonwealth of Independent States (CIS): of the former Soviet republics only the Baltic states and Georgia refuse to join.
Leningrad renamed St Petersburg

1992
Russian Booker Prize for fiction established

1994
Solzhenitsyn returns to Russia

1996
Yeltsin wins presidential re-election
Death of Iosif Brodskii

1997
Russia accepted at the meeting of the "G7" economic powers
Death of Andrei Siniavskii

GLOSSARY

Acmeism Post-Symbolist poetic grouping of the 1910s, striving for the "acme" of expression

Bylina Russian traditional Heroic poem

Cheka Extraordinary Commission for Combating Counter-Revolution and Sabotage: Soviet State secret police (1917–22), forerunners of the KGB

Conceptualism Postmodernist tendency in late 20th-century Russian literature

Decembrists Participants in the failed uprising against Nicholas I, St Petersburg, 14 December (Old Style), 1825

Dol'nik An accentual verse metre (term coined by Briusov, early 20th century)

Fellow Traveller [*Poputchik*] Sympathiser with the general aims of socialist construction in the years of consolidation of the Bolshevik-Soviet state

Five-Year Plans Forced industrialization for economic development; introduced by Stalin, 1928

Formalism Name (originally pejorative) given to close-reading and technical approach to literary analysis conducted by group of critics headed by Viktor Shklovskii, 1910s–20s

Futurism Iconoclastic avant-garde movement of 1910s

Glasnost Policy of "openness" in public and artistic expression, introduced by Gorbachev (from 1985)

Golden Age Flowering of Russian literature (especially poetry), coinciding with the "Age of Pushkin" (1820s, 1830s)

Gosizdat Officially published material by State publishing house in the Soviet period

Goslitizdat State publishing house of the first half of the Soviet period

Izbrannoe Selected Works

KGB Committee for State Security: Soviet State security organs from 1953

Kolkhoz Collective farm (Soviet period), initially under "collectivization", from late 1920s

Kulak [Literally "fist"] Richer peasant farmer, singled out for dispossession under "collectivization"

LEF Left Front of Arts: revolutionary artistic grouping of the 1920s, headed by Vladimir Maiakovskii

Litfond Hardship fund for needy writers, established in the 19th century; subsequently administered by Union of Soviet Writers (see Writers' Union below)

Liubomudry Society of Wisdom Lovers: philosophical-literary grouping of the early 1820s, basing itself on German Romantic philosophy and headed by V.F. Odoevskii

NEP New Economic Policy: limited re-introduction of market economy, following the Civil War, 1921–27 (succeeded by Five-Year Plan for construction of a socialist economy)

NKVD People's Commissariat for Internal Affairs: Soviet State security organs, predecessors of the KGB

OBERIU (Oberiuty) Association of Real Art (and its members): avant-garde artistic movement operating in Leningrad, late 1920s–early 1930s, headed by Daniil Kharms and Aleksandr Vvedenskii

OGPU Unified State Political Directive: Soviet secret police (1922–34)

Perestroika Policy of "reconstruction" of the economy and institutions, brought in under Gorbachev (1985–91)

Poema Long, or narrative, poem

Polnoe sobranie sochinenii Complete Works

Populism "Narodniki" (agrarian socialist) movement of 1870s

Povest' Longer story; novella; novel written to a limited time-frame

Proletkult Proletarian Culture: radical movement for culture and literacy in the immediate post-revolutionary years of the Soviet state (1917–21)

RAPP Russian Association of Proletarian Writers: vanguard movement promoting hegemony of proletarian literature from mid-1920s to its closure in 1932

Rasskaz Short story; tale

Roman Novel; romance (literary or amorous)

Samizdat [Literally "self-publishing"] Illegal distribution of unpublishable material in the post-Thaw Soviet period

Serapion Brothers Literary grouping of early 1920s, based in St Petersburg, headed by Lev Lunts. (Its name was taken from collective of story-tellers composing frame-tale work by E.T.A. Hoffmann)

Silver Age Renewed flowering of Russian literature (especially poetry) in the "Symbolist" period, late 19th and early 20th centuries (cf. "Golden Age")

Skaz First-person narrative style or discourse

Skazka Fairy tale

Slavophile [*Slavianofil*] Adherent of 19th-century movement proposing Russian (or Pan-Slavic) solution to the problem and development of Russian state, economy, and culture

SMERSH Acronym (from "death to spies") for Soviet counter-intelligence force during World War II

Sobranie sochinenii Collected Works

Stikhotvoreniia (Stikhi) Poetry (verses)

Symbolism *Fin de siècle* artistic movement, based on "dualist" and neo-Romantic principles, partly inspired by French Symbolism

Taktovik A Russian verse form

Tamizdat [Literally "there-publishing"]. Illegal overseas/ western publication of material unpublishable in the post-Thaw Soviet period

Thaw The period (c.1953–64) (or sub-periods) of relative cultural relaxation that followed the death of Stalin, tentatively encouraged by Khrushchev's policy of "de-Stalinization"

VAPP Immediate precursor to RAPP

Village Prose Sub-genre of Russian fiction of the 1960s–70s, concentrating on rural themes

Westernizer [*Zapadnik*] Proponent of "western" solutions to Russia's political and cultural problems

Writers' Union Up to 1932: one of the Russian writers' association formed in the early Soviet period; post 1932 (literally Union of Soviet Writers) – the official and unitary literary organization imposed by the Soviet state

INTRODUCTORY ESSAYS

Old Russian Literature

In the eyes of the world Russian literature is perhaps the chief glory of Russian culture. What the world knows, above all, is the classic Russian novel, whose great age was amazingly brief – a mere quarter century, all within the reign of Alexander II (1855–81), which saw the publication of the best works of Tolstoi, Dostoevskii, Turgenev, and Goncharov. Those with a deeper interest might extend their knowledge back to the time of Pushkin and Lermontov in the early 19th century, and forward to Chekhov and the modernist Silver Age – around a century altogether – so becoming aware that Russian literature has more to it than blockbuster narratives: in particular an intensely-developed poetic tradition. Few outsiders (and not all Russians) understand, however, how deeply *literaturnost'* ("literariness") has been ingrained in Russian cultural consciousness over the thousand years since the Conversion, or realize that what is usually called Old Russian literature forms part of a distinctive tradition whose effects are far from being exhausted yet. Of course the forms of sophisticated literature, like the forms of upper-class behaviour, were changed radically and forcibly after Peter the Great's Westernizing measures, but many underlying older principles remained intact, to be revealed in numerous ways as time went on.

Analogous situations are obviously to be seen in the other sophisticated art-forms: painting, sculpture, architecture, and music. In each, wholesale innovations of form, genre, and purpose apparently swept away "medieval" artistic systems. It may be, however, that literature, embedded as it must be in practices of language, is less susceptible than other arts to the sudden and complete imposition of new methods. Whatever the reasons, mid-18th-century writers such as Vasilii Trediakovskii and Mikhail Lomonosov, themselves propagators of western literary forms, had considerable interest in the literary tradition they were engaged in remodelling, an interest redoubled at the turn of the century with the generation of Aleksandr Radishchev, the Decembrists, and subsequently of Pushkin and his contemporaries, when the issue of "Russianness" in literature came into sharp focus. It was then, too, that a growing antiquarian and historical interest in the manuscript heritage of Old Russia was galvanized by the sensational discovery (c.1795) of a complex, subtle, and highly original work thought to date from the 12th century, *Slovo o polku Igoreve* (*The Lay of Igor's Campaign*), raising questions about the nature and aesthetic qualities of Old Russian literature that have been with us ever since.

To discuss this literature in any detail would take a volume or several volumes. The purpose of this treatment is to fit it into the larger picture of Russian literary and cultural history: so I intend chiefly to give a fresh (if necessarily generalized) view of the diachronic nature of the literary experience in Russia.

First, some preliminary observations have to be made. The term Old Russian Literature, near-universal in scholarly usage, needs to be employed with caution. It (with its variants Early or Medieval Russian literature) is a temporal designation, tying literary development to historical periodization. Taken as implying that literature of the Old Russian period (i.e. up to Peter the Great's reforms) is qualitatively separate from what came afterwards, the term is misleading. Modern literary forms (i.e. like those of the baroque elsewhere) are observable in Russian literature at least from the early 17th century (even if they do not lead to masterpieces of European quality), within a still largely medieval literary system, whose after-effects, as suggested above, in turn long outlive the end of Old Russia itself. I propose instead the coinage Russian Traditional Literature as a conceptual rather than periodic term.

There is far more traditional (or Old) Russian literature than is usually thought, as plenty of it remains unpublished. Two works from the time of Ivan IV (ruled 1533–84) have more than 20,000 pages each in manuscript. More significantly, there are literally thousands of chronicles from the early 12th to the 18th century originating from a large number of local centres, often small or remote; hundreds of versions of oral epic poems have been transcribed; and we must not forget the hundreds or thousands of translated religious and learned works, mostly of Byzantine origin, that were the bedrock of sophisticated traditional literature. Despite the large quantity of works that remain, we also know for certain of some that have not survived, and can postulate the former existence of many other lost works. There are probably still significant rediscoveries to be made: several important early works have been discovered in single copies in modern times. As for the durability of traditional Russian literature, one may mention as a curiosity the fact that there are still so-called Old Believer communities in out-of-the-way areas where a manuscript tradition of religious polemics in an essentially 17th-century vein has persisted to the present. More significantly, the guru of modernist Russian poetics, Velimir Khlebnikov (1885–1922), could claim to be the culminating "Old" Russian writer (to the extent that he purged from his work all vocabulary of west European origin). The poet Osip Mandel'shtam wrote admiringly of him that "he cannot distinguish which is nearer, the railway bridge or *The Lay of Igor's Campaign*." Khlebnikov's followers, a group that extends to the present generation (such as Viktor Sosnora), have shown the continuing vitality of his example, and his influence has rippled outwards to affect much modern Russian writing. Even had Khlebnikov never lived, through Aleksei Remizov and other writers the older Russian traditions of "literariness" would have been revived and given credibility for the 20th century, and doubtless beyond.

The next general point that must be made about traditional Russian literature is that it existed in two great complementary spheres: the "visible" and the "invisible", in other words the written and the oral. Historians, for obvious reasons, concentrate on the former, admitting the latter only when (as with oral epics, the so-called *byliny*) it achieved permanent "visible" embodiment by being written down – often in confusing multiple variants and probably several centuries after the work first arose. Early Russians perceived, it seems, the distinctiveness, but also the complementary nature of each of these spheres, allotting them separate roles (so that, for example, lyric poetry is absent from written literature until the 17th century, though evidently abundant in the Russian experience in the form of folk-song). It would be tempting, but wrong, to equate these two spheres, written and oral, with the "sacred" and "profane" respectively. Although the written word often carried overtones of sacredness it was also used for entirely humdrum practical purposes (and the boundary between the literary and the non-literary is particularly hard to draw in a pre-modern age). Unwritten, oral literary creativity, by contrast, derives in direct descent from pre-Christian Rus', and never ceased to carry undertones of "pagan" folk belief – though, as the centuries passed, it also acquired a multitude of Christian motifs, often strangely metamorphosed and "folkified". So while to some extent a sacred/profane, or more profoundly, a Christian/pagan dichotomy can be observed in Russian traditional literariness, it cannot wholly or permanently be equated with the written/unwritten spheres. In fact the conceptual world of oral literature subtly and significantly penetrated the writing in Christianized Rus', and lent a specifically Russian colouration to some of its best monuments: whether, for example, through turns of speech, proverbs or epic fragments in the early chronicles, through the stylized evocation of pagan divinities in *The Lay of Igor's Campaign*; through the wit and wordplay of *Molenie Daniila Zatochnika* [The Petition of Daniil the Exile]; the ecstatic transformation of peasant lamentation in Epifanii's *Zhitie Stefana Permskogo* [The Life of St Stephen of Perm]; the overtones of heroic epos in various military tales; the "folkishness" of many aspects of Avvakum's autobiography; the chilling evocation and personification of the popular conception of human destiny in *Gore-Zlochastie* [Tale of Woe-Misfortune]; or the fairy-tale motifs of *Povest' o Petre i Fevronii* (*Peter and Fevronia of Murom*). More generally, many stylistic features – types of antithesis and parallelisms, paratactic structures, riddling formulations, stock epithets – enter even sophisticated traditional literature from the folk sphere. The question of reverse influence, from the written to the oral, is harder to assess: but such influence was probably to some degree felt at least in the last century of Old Russia and indeed the first after Peter the Great: as Dmitrij Čiževskij writes, in the baroque age "The novel turns into a fairy-tale in short-story form, the love poem into a popular song, the religious lyric into a 'spiritual song.'"

A corollary to my suggested way of perceiving traditional Russian "literariness" is that literature is no longer to be regarded as simply the business of the literate segment of society. Much scholarly ingenuity has gone into trying to establish what proportion of the Old Russian population could read and write (in 16th-century Muscovy it may have been below five per cent, but much higher, for example in pre-Tartar Novgorod). Such figures, even if they could be reliably established, would not have any readily-ascertainable cultural significance. The written sphere of literature – at least its dominant religious component – was suffused even among the illiterate through readings in churches, in monastic refectories, and in princely courts; oral literature – whether through folk-tales and songs, oral epos, the performance of itinerant minstrels (*skomorokhi*) – would have reached the entire population of pre-modern Russia without exception, however much it may have been frowned upon by the authorities and the Church.

The last, and largest, of these general observations concerns the most fundamental and individual aspect of the world of Russian traditional literature, that of its language. It has already been mentioned that the arrival of Christianity in Rus' was accompanied by the new religion's inseparable concomitant, a fully-fledged literary language known to us as Old Church Slavonic. The "Apostles to the Slavs", Cyril and Methodius, with their assistants, devised Old Church Slavonic as a written language to express the conceptual world of the Bible, the Church Fathers, theology, and late-antique "high culture" generally (through complex structures and a large abstract vocabulary, for example), basing this language on the South Slav speech of the hinterland of Thessaloniki, from which they came. At the time (mid-9th century) the south, west, and east Slav dialects, later each to give birth to several distinct languages, were sufficiently close to be mutually comprehensible, and the apostles' translations (and, soon, original texts) were of equal use in Moravia – for which they were first commissioned – Bulgaria and, over a century later, Russia. Thus the written language for religious and translated literature generally was not exclusive to Rus': it constituted, in Likhachev's phrase, a "Byzantine-Slav cultural milieu", "a sort of common culture for the southern and eastern Orthodox Slav lands that evolved simultaneously as a single totality in various Slavonic countries as a result of the transplantation of Byzantine culture into them ... a supra-national cultural milieu". Riccardo Picchio and others have called this community *Slavia Orthodoxa*, "Orthodox Slavdom".

How did Church Slavonic relate to the spoken and eventually written language of the east Slavs, progenitor of Russian, Ukrainian, and Belorussian? At the time of the Conversion they still had large areas of vocabulary, phonology, and morphology in common, while such differences as existed were of a regular and easily-comprehended nature. Syntactically, Old Church Slavonic was partly based on the Greek from which most of its literature was derived. But while over the centuries Old Russian evolved in syntax and vocabulary, shedding some complexities of its grammar, Church Slavonic, fixed in the forms established in the canonical religious texts, underwent no significant changes. At the end of the Old Russian period, Ludolf's pioneering grammar of Russian (published in Oxford in 1696) could state in a famous formulation that "loquendum est Russice & scribendum est Slavonice" (Russian is for speaking and Slavonic for writing), going on to point out that nowhere in the world was Slavonic actually a spoken language.

Ludolf's dictum, together with the modern perception of Russian and Church Slavonic as separate languages, can lead to a serious misunderstanding of the subtle and idiosyncratic linguistic situation in Rus'. In most European countries the early-medieval language of religion and scholarship was the international medium of Latin; vernacular literatures emerged only slowly and haphazardly towards the end of the Middle Ages (save where, as in some Nordic lands, oral epos and similar folk-works were transcribed in written versions). The role of Church Slavonic in Russia and other Orthodox Slav lands looks similar to that of Latin in the parts of Europe dominated by the patriarchate of Rome (the Papacy); but the resemblance is superficial. From its pre-Christian past, Latin carried the weighty baggage of the largest and most diverse literature the world had ever seen (leaving aside the socio-political pretensions wrapped up in this baggage): it was a fully-developed linguistic system usable in a multitude of registers from the poetic and rhetorical to the colloquial and legalistic. Church Slavonic, by contrast, was created to be a written language with the express purpose of transmitting the sacred Word to the Slavs. It proved in practice a flexible instrument for the creation of new words as well as the translation of pre-existing material, not all overtly religious. But it remained in its essence a sacred language, occasioning awe, respect, and considerable pride among the Orthodox Slavs – their main highway to salvation. Unlike Latin among west and central Europeans, it was not sensed by its users as "other". Specialists often still write as if an "Old Russian literary language" existed side-by-side with Church Slavonic, the two available for use as the writer's choice or the task to be fulfilled dictated. But this would have astonished an early Russian, who did not even have the term Church Slavonic at his disposal. Far from being linguistically alien to him, what we call Church Slavonic was perceived as the time-hallowed, lofty register of Russian – its "bookish" (without modern pejorative connotations) version.

The contemporary scholar Boris Uspenskii has brilliantly analysed the fundamental "diglossia" that characterized this linguistic situation, at any rate until the mid-17th century when the modern attitude that gave rise to Ludolph's comment became widespread. Until then diglossia meant that translation (and parody) was impossible between Russian and Church Slavonic: they fulfilled functionally different roles within what was felt to be a single language. That does not mean, however, that the distinction between them was not powerfully felt: after all, the "bookish" language had to be learnt, had fixed and "correct" forms, was a microcosm of the divine order, while Russian vernacular language forms were unstable, unregulated, "undivine", and hence potentially pagan or devilish. As Uspenskii puts it: "The specific character of the Russian linguistic, and more broadly cultural consciousness consists for the most part in the fact that here – in the functioning of diglossia as a linguistic and cultural mechanism – there exists no zone that is semantically neutral and which does not make reference to the sacred sphere. Hence, an absence of a connection with the sacred, the Divine, basically signifies a connection with its opposite, with the world of the Devil." Uspenskii gives some startling and thought-provoking examples (in Russian folk-tradition, we learn, the Devil loves to be called *chert*, the Russian word for him, and dreads the Slavonic term *bes*). None the less there were perfectly legitimate areas for the use of written vernacular Russian: for practical purposes (decrees, laws, letters, ambassadorial messages etc.) and – from the point of view of literary development most interestingly – in contexts where it is mixed to a greater or lesser degree with Slavonicisms. Sometimes this mixing is well-demarcated: thus in Epifanii's *Zhitie Stefana Permskogo,* basically written in Slavonic, the Permian sorcerer who figures in its climactic scene speaks Russian (Uspenskii likewise cites Russophone Chaldeans in the "mystery play", derived from the Book of Daniel, that was performed in cathedrals). Often, though, such stylistic mixing could be more complicated with subtler purposes: thus stylistically-marked Slavonicisms can achieve lofty effects or suggest biblical reminiscences in chronicles or military tales whose language is fundamentally the Russian vernacular; the author who calls himself Daniil the Exile deliberately combines popular and learned (Slavonic) language to dazzle his audience with his wit; many other instances could be adduced, involving some of the most interesting and idiosyncratic Old Russian works and genres.

In the later 17th century the diglossia that has been described began to be questioned: vernacular Russian had moved far enough away from Church Slavonic for them to be perceived as distinct languages. Yet neither then, nor even in the 18th century, when in the wake of Peter the Great's reforms the entire west European literary system was imported piecemeal to Russia, did the Russian language turn its back on its Church Slavonic heritage. Following similar attempts in France, Germany, and elsewhere, the most influential mid-18th-century theorist, Mikhail Lomonosov, codified what to 18th-century taste seemed the chaotic literary language into three stylistic levels – "high", "middle", and "low" – suitable for various genres. For Lomonosov the defining factor was to be the quantity and nature of the Slavonicisms in the vocabulary employed at each level (Church Slavonic elements that had become incomprehensible to Russians on the one hand, and crudely colloquial or dialect forms on the other, were excluded from the system altogether). Though Lomonosov's system was too fiddly and cumbersome to be a practical guide for long – and was alien to the spirit of simplicity and spontaneity that characterized the early-romantic age that followed that of the baroque in Russia as elsewhere – its principles were not unsound. In Pushkin's age there were still "archaists" for whom the Slavonic component was the truly literary element in Russian, and could be made a bulwark against the flood of west Europeanism (in vocabulary, syntax, and style) that inundated Russia from Peter's time onwards; needless to say, questions of national identity were closely linked with the language question. The further history of the problematics of the literary language shows, very briefly, that the general 19th-century attempt to produce a neutral, middle-of-the-road, internationally-based and homogenized all-purpose language was continually liable to be subverted by a Russian partiality for folk-elements (including semi-literate speech) on the one hand, and the continuing vitality of its Slavonic component on the other. The latter was indeed strengthened by a great deal of new abstract vocabulary, Slavonic in form and derivation. The modern scholar Boris Unbegaun was tempted to speculate in print as to whether the Russian literary language is Russian or Slavonic in essence, coming down in favour of the latter.

This problem cannot really be resolved. All one can say is that modern written Russian is a hybrid, whose "grandparents" are normalized Russian, folk and dialect Russian, west European imports, and Church Slavonic elements. Juggling the balance between them has given modern Russian literature an extraordinary richness of texture; the reader even of classic 19th-century writers such as Gogol' and Dostoevskii will miss much by not appreciating it – and in translation such things can all too easily be missed. In the 20th century a host of writers – Belyi, Remizov, Babel', Platonov, and Zoshchenko are merely among the outstanding names – play brilliantly and wittily with linguistic possibilities that are, after all rooted in the age-old Russian tradition of "literariness".

Early Russia did not produce any of the select group of independently-standing masterpieces that have entered the canon of "great works" of medieval literature, accessible in theory to readers of all cultures such as *The Divine Comedy*, *The Decameron*, *The Canterbury Tales*, the lyric poems of Dafydd ap Gwilym or Li Po, the Icelandic sagas, or the *Niebelungenlied*. As far as Russia is concerned, only *The Lay of Igor's Campaign* seems to have been occasionally promoted to such status, and it fills the role rather awkwardly, despite its undeniable individuality and poetic richness. The failure of this literature to engage the world's consciousness would seem to have distinctive causes that are not really to do with intrinsic literary merit or the lack of it. The problem is that there is something curiously ungraspable about Russian traditional literature and about the individual works within it. The boundaries between "literary" and "unliterary" texts are even more blurred than is usual in early literatures. Indeed, in my view, the chief masterpiece of early Russian literature, *Povest' vremennykh let* (*Primary Chronicle*), is a work whose literary, "shaped" qualities are often ignored altogether. Many of these texts are extremely unstable, and in the versions that have come down to us are clearly the result of multiple editing or rewritings; they can appear in such different guises that even identifying and naming them as separate works is a contentious business. This textual instability, incidentally, is a result of the purposes and methods of literary production in pre-modern Russia, and not merely of scribal sloppiness. By contrast, canonical religious works, whose wording carried divine authority, were copied and recopied through the centuries with few, if any, changes. When the ancient norms of Church Slavonic seemed in danger of being forgotten or ignored around the late 14th–15th centuries a powerful (though not always well-informed) movement for the restoration of its correct orthographic and other principles spread through the Orthodox Slavs, starting in the Balkans – hence cumbersomely known to Russian literary historians as the "Second South Slavonic Influence" (the first having been in the aftermath of the Conversion), but really part of, paradoxically, a great movement of cultural renewal in the Orthodox lands, still poorly understood in its totality.

The biggest problem in the appreciation of traditional Russian literature is that of contextualizing the works in question. An out-and-out "new critical" or indeed Formalist approach, concentrating exclusively on the text alone, can be of little help to our understanding. It takes a conscious effort for most westerners to enter into the civilizational context of early Russia; for Russians themselves the difficulties are much less, and Russians are often familiar with their own pre-modern literature – particularly the *Primary Chronicle* and *The Lay of Igor's Campaign* – to a degree that seems to be matched in English only from the age of Shakespeare and the "Authorized Version" of the Bible onwards.

Our cursory survey of the traditions of Russian literature would be incomplete without a brief attempt to indicate how some of its characteristics have lived on to become determinants within the apparently very different circumstances of post-Petrine – and in particular 20th-century – Russian literary culture. I make no claim, of course, that the points listed represent all the significant features of Russia's specific "literariness", or indeed that they are exclusive to Russia, or add up to some fully-integrated picture, or are very profound. But in each case they seem to me to relate both to pre- and post-Petrine literature; if we take them all together (and there are no doubt others that could be added), we may find that collectively they help us to map out a phenomenology or "conceptosphere" of Russian literature in its *longue durée*: something that seems seldom if ever to have been attempted. I start from rather large, perhaps banal points and move on first to others that have a more specific connection with literariness and its embodiments, then to some underlying "psycholiterary" factors.

Implicit in much early and subsequent Russian literature is the creation of landscapes that are really mental maps or chronotopes of Rus' (and of its boundaries, physical or mental, with outsiders). Note, too, the many "idealized landscapes" of Russian literature, whether in the *Slovo o pogibeli russkoi zemli* (*Orison on the Downfall of Russia*), Avvakum's *Zhitie* (*Life*) or Goncharov's "Oblomovka". Complementing this, there has been a pervasive historical concern that is really rooted in "mythistoricism" – the creation, often spontaneous, of national myth; but by the 19th century, often involving its ironic or tragic juxtaposition with "real life". Just as characteristic is a sort of dialogue between the competing claims of history and literature for the source material. No reader of *War and Peace* can be unaware of this, but it is equally pervasive in Pushkin, Solzhenitsyn, and much other literature, and is found as far back as early saints' lives and the *Primary Chronicle*.

The ideological saturation of much Russian literature ("ideology" is to be taken in the broad, Bakhtinian sense of a world-view; patriotic and political as much as religious) is particularly obvious in the pre-Petrine and Soviet periods, but is scarcely less apparent in the 18th and 19th centuries. This may not be unsubtle or monological. Bakhtin, for example, powerfully argued a view of Dostoevskii's mature novels (and more generally of the post-Dostoevskian novel) as a polyphony of incompatible ideologized voices.

Related to this point is a frequent concern with "great questions" (in Russian often termed *prokliatye*, "accursed" questions!) that may be of a moral or Existential kind but are, perhaps, at their most interesting when they concern identity ("who/ where/ what are we?", see, for example, the first lines of the *Primary Chronicle*). Of course there has been a reaction, explicit or implicit, against this all-too-obvious trait of Russian literature among some 20th-century writers (such as Pasternak's remarks through the mouth of Doctor Zhivago on Pushkin and Chekhov as opposed to Gogol', Tolstoi, and Dostoevskii) – but it shows no sign of abating.

Unexpectedly perhaps, Russian literature has at all stages of its history been remarkably open to outside influences, or ready to absorb large numbers of translated works. This absorption has not been indiscriminate however, and the "life" led by translated texts (whether, for example, the Byzantine Greek history of George Hamartolos, the Orthodox *Philokalia*, Alexander Pope's *Essay on Man*, the long poems of Byron, or the stories of H.G. Wells) can have a very different significance in a Russian context, where they fulfil new cultural needs, from their original existence.

The diglossia between the Old Russian and the Slavonic elements within the written Russian language has led to tensions, uncertainties (particularly in the 18th century) and great expressive possibilities for Russian writers, a peculiarly Russian situation that readers of Russian literature in other countries have not always understood. The consequent omnipresent awareness of the very materials of literature has often led to a sense of "the word" itself being the real hero of the literary work (whether, to take a few examples, the pre-Tartar Petition of Daniil the Exile, in large medieval rhetorical works, in Gogol', the Futurists, Khlebnikov or Platonov).

A strong awareness of what Likhachev calls "literary etiquette", of the "behaviour" of literature *vis-à-vis* the reader, is perhaps related to the above. It is not quite the same as conventionality, though (particularly in Old Russia) it can manifest itself through commonplaces or stereotypes, and it can for instance make the forms of 20th-century Russian poetry look curiously conventional to the western eye. Not surprisingly, disruption of literary etiquette, especially among some 20th-century writers, can seem highly subversive – just as using not quite the right diction and phraseology in Soviet speech could do.

By contrast, there has always been instability and mixing of genre in Russian writing. Much Old Russian literature, especially where influenced by oral folkloric models, hovers tantalizingly on the boundary between prose and poetry (this is notoriously evident in *The Lay of Igor's Campaign*, irreducible to poetic metres yet sometimes included in anthologies of verse). The literature of the 19th and 20th centuries is ostensibly well-defined generically, yet such definition is often skin-deep (even Gogol''s *Mertvye dushi* (*Dead Souls*), his only "novel", is subtitled "epic poem"! – while by contrast Pushkin's *Evgenii Onegin* is a "novel in verse"; 20th-century writers such as Khlebnikov and Kharms no longer try to conceal their freedom from generic constraints). Indeed this erasure of boundaries operates on a larger scale still. Russian writing has always had difficulty coping with the notion that clear distinctions can be made between the literary and non-literary use of language, and many of its most characteristic works seem (by western standards) awkwardly poised between "literature" and "non-literature" (the Chronicles, Avvakum's autobiography, Radishchev's *Puteshestvie iz Peterburga v Moskvu* [*A Journey from St Petersburg to Moscow*], *War and Peace*, Herzen's *Byloe i dumy* [*My Past and Thoughts*] are just a few examples.) The "practical" orientation of much Russian literature has a distinctly medieval feel.

Literature has always been open to cross-fertilization and co-operation with the other arts. The remarkable development of Russian opera from the early 19th century, to take one example, is neither "literature-led" nor "music-led" but a real partnership of music, text, and spectacle. In the Pre-Petrine period, sacred literature, art, architecture, and music tended towards a single totalizing iconic vision.

Narrative structure in Russian literature of all periods is often weak, or at least as seen from the viewpoint of the western preference for neat plot structures and the rigorous operation of causality. Originality of plot seems often to have been regarded as less important than the realization of mythic or archetypal situations (Katerina Clark has compared the "quest" motif of the typical Soviet novel to folk-tales and saints' lives). The structural tendency is for *nanizivanie*, the stringing-together of plot elements, and the very language, particularly in the early period, favours paratactic structures (that can cause insuperable problems for translators of Old Russian literature). Comparisons can again be made with Russian music and even such sophisticated 19th-century composers as Musorgskii and Tchaikovskii avoided sonata form, preferring the "stringing-together" of thematic variations. Agglomerative works tend to be the result. It is significant that the first major "novel" in Russia, Lermontov's *Geroi nashego vremeni* (*A Hero of Our Time*), is called by its narrator "my chain of tales"; it also happens to be a remarkable generic mixture. Again we can cite Radishchev's *Journey* and Herzen's *My Past and Thoughts*, together with one of the longest and most memorable of all "agglomerative" works, Dostoevskii's *Brothers Karamazov*, a ragbag of tales and tales-within-tales. Pre-Petrine folk and sophisticated literature (not only chronicle-writing) is essentially episodic and agglutinative.

A further consequence is the "open-endedness" of much Russian literature, with its admission of apparently extraneous material and "unfinalized", even Existentialist feel. Chekhov, in his mature plays and some late stories, is the obvious exemplar here. One recalls with astonishment in this context a historical novel to which the author, Solzhenitsyn, appended a note inviting readers to send him material that might serve to correct the text. The reader is a direct participant in the literary process (*A Hero of Our Time* with its two Prefaces is also relevant here); Bakhtin's principle of "dialogism" in the best modern literature appears nakedly. This characteristic may well be a necessary corrective to the "ideological saturation" mentioned earlier. In Old Russian literature, "unfinishedness" is a normal feature of the text: new material can always be added.

There has always been in Russian literature a tendency towards large forms. At its simplest this may be a story (or lyric) cycle. More innovatively, it can mean the *sverkhpovest'* ("supertale") – a term devised by Khlebnikov – whose building-blocks are diverse ordinary poems or tales, "like a sculpture made from different coloured blocks of different stone". Again the novels of Dostoevskii and Tolstoi ("great baggy monsters", in Henry James's well-known formulation) can be cited. In Old Russian literature, the *Primary Chronicle* is an evident predecessor of the "supertale", but it should also be noted that virtually every early Russian literary work that we consider independent came down to us as a component part of a larger manuscript, a miscellany comprising other texts; little scholarly work on the principles of compilation of such miscellanies appears yet to have been done.

Certain literary modes and forms have acquired a special colouration in Russia from early times onwards, for example lyric forms have tended towards lamentation, epic towards celebration. The role of literary humour has been particularly significant – the "laughter world" of Rus' as Likhachev and Panchenko called it in a famous study. Laughter can be threatening, a form of "anti-behaviour", associated for example, with carnivalistic excesses and topsy-turveydom, the "unmasking" absurdities of holy fools, or Ivan the Terrible's corrosive and theatrical sarcasm. This dangerous aspect of laughter is never far away in Gogol', Dostoevskii, or successors in the 20th century such as Belyi (*Petersburg*), and once again was analysed by Bakhtin, who saw it as deriving from the ancient genre of "Menippean Satire" – though in Russia it clearly also has folkloric roots. As a milder phenomenon, laughter is often a mixed emotion in Russian literature (the characteristic "laughter through tears" of Chekhov's plays and Goncharov's *Oblomov*); but the most typical vein of humour, going back to Old Russian, is inventive paronomasia and similar word-play, assisted by the varied and unstable registers and the notorious diglossia of the Russian language.

Self-consciousness about the literary process has often led Russian authors to "metafiction" – the examination of the literary process itself within the literary work. We may cite as examples the self-questioning of the bard of *The Lay of Igor's Campaign* as to the best mode in which to recount his story, the obsessive interest of the narrator of *A Hero of Our Time* in his position *vis-à-vis* his readers, Shklovskii's remarkable pseudo-18th-century (but very "modern") novel *Zoo. Pis'ma ne o liubvi, ili tret'ia Eloiza* (*Zoo, or Letters Not about Love*).

"Publication" of literature in Russia has never meant exclusively the printing and dissemination of books through commercial channels. Naturally in Old Russia (even after printing was introduced in the mid-16th century) written literature existed almost exclusively in the form of manuscripts that were copied *ad hoc* and usually collected into miscellanies. Texts other than those considered sacred would be revised, shortened, conflated with others, modernized for whatever reasons patrons and copyists thought fit. This kind of manuscript tradition has actually continued to modern times, for polemical purposes, among some remote Old Believer communities. But *samizdat* ("self-publishing") for a limited circle of readers, in manuscript or typescript form remained a characteristic aspect of Russian literary production through the 18th, 19th, and 20th centuries. Actual copyings and recopyings could reach almost the entire educated public quite quickly as happened in the 19th century with Griboedov's play *Gore ot uma* (*Woe from Wit*), and in the later Soviet period with many works. While clearly such "self-publishing" in post-Petrine times was primarily a means of bypassing censorship, it is also a signal of a Russian view of literature less as the production of a commodity, more as the intense dialogue of a literate class (sometimes disaffected from authority) with itself.

Perhaps because of this quality of literature as dialogue, an autonomous realm of debate, there is a powerful element of intertextuality – implicit or explicit reference to other writings the reader can be assumed to recognize – in modern Russian literature; after all, as Nabokov used to point out, the whole of classic Russian literature can be housed on a few bookshelves and be familiar to the average reader. But intertextuality was a vitally important feature of Old Russian literature too. The frequent quotations from the Bible (particularly the Psalms) and writings of the Church Fathers, even in works that we might consider primarily secular in orientation, do not represent mere padding or general edification, but are generally carefully chosen to provide an eternal context to counterpoint transitory events. Within the field of Old Russian writing itself there are intertextual echoes of, for example, Ilarion's *Slovo "O zakone i blagodati"* (*Sermon on Law and Grace*) in many subsequent works; while an astonishing example is the dependence of the various works known collectively as *Zadonshchina* (about Dmitrii Donskoi's defeat of the Tartar Mamai, 1380) on the pre-Tartar *The Lay of Igor's Campaign*.

There is equally a reliance on subtextuality, as much in Old Russian as in 20th-century Russian writing. Modern scholars such as Picchio have shown how hidden, as well as explicit, biblical references constitute "thematic clues" that may determine the proper reading of early texts (such clues are normally placed near the text's opening). Late medieval literature in particular is fond of intricate puzzles, allegories, codes, of the riddling method (so well known too from folk-song) of periphrasis, of *not* naming the object directly: features that readers of "difficult" modern writers such as Khlebnikov will readily recognize.

A deep and widespread subtext to all Russian literature is that of Russian folk-belief, manifest even in explicitly Christian writers such as Gogol', Dostoevskii, Kharms or Soviet writers such as Zabolotskii and Platonov. Concern with the connected concepts of *dolia* (fate, lot) and *volia* (free will, liberty), with *onnyi svet*, the realm of the dead and its relation to that of the living is especially frequent.

Finally, an enduringly persistent tradition in Russian literature, whether ancient or modern, written or oral, is that of the word as magical – note that in Old Russia "word", *slovo*, had a broader reference than in English, implying also "discourse" or "piece of literature". The opening of St John's gospel, supposedly the first item to be translated in the missionary project of St Cyril and St Methodius, is of course "In the beginning was the Word", immediately equating the Word with the divinity and divine order. Church Slavonic, which as we have seen was an inalienable element in the diglossia of Old Russian writing, was regarded as sacred in itself, and Russia as having been made holy after its adoption. But before Christianity (and persisting after it) there were the *zagovory*, magical spells or prayer – equivalents within folk-belief. Note also the magical significance of the Scandinavian runes known to Russia's early Viking rulers. Silence, too, had a sacred significance (particularly after Hesychasm, "quietism", was adopted as Orthodox church doctrine in the 14th century) – see Dostoevskii's "Legend of the Grand Inquisitor" in *The Brothers Karamazov*. It is striking how modernists such as the Russian Futurists gave "the word" (often the "self-valid" or "self-sufficient word", *samotsennoe/samovitoe slovo*) an almost supernatural significance. Maiakovskii's last poem, opening "I know the power of words, I know the tocsin of words", is an extraordinary example, while Kharms noted in the 1930s "I know four kinds of word-machines: poems, prayers, songs and spells". It is not too much to suggest that the obsessive attention paid by the Soviet authorities to verbal expression derived from a deep-seated fear of the word's magic power.

ROBIN MILNER-GULLAND

Pre-Revolutionary Russian Theatre

In the late 17th century, when the French professional theatre was at its zenith and England and Spain looked back over several generations to the heyday of their theatre, drama in Russia first tottered into official existence. Wishing to please his new wife and mark the birth of their first child (the future Peter the Great), Tsar Alexei ordered the court performance of a play, the biblical story of Esther, entitled *Artaxerxes*. This was the same tsar who, in 1648, had decreed the destruction of all musical instruments and theatrical properties, with severe punishment for anyone using them. Now, in 1672 (when Paris was watching the premiere of Racine's *Bajazet*), the stilted, day-long play received royal approval, and the German producer Johann Gregorii (1631–75), was encouraged to form a small Court Theatre. The enterprise began well, extolling the Monarchy and glorifying the Christian Church as instructed, but it staged only nine productions and fizzled out in less than three years. This miserable false start, ill-conceived, artificial and un-Russian as it was, typifies the desultory beginnings of the Russian theatre, which would not achieve any real stature or permanence for nearly another century. Its early story is one of sporadic outbursts in various directions, followed by persecution, indifference or uncontainable competition from foreigners.

The earliest sources of Russian theatre are similar to those in other countries, deriving from either folk arts or both pagan and liturgical ceremony. Peripatetic entertainers – minstrels, clowns, animal-trainers, puppeteers, musicians and the like – were in demand from the earliest times of Russian history to perform at holidays and festivals, weddings and funerals. (The Russian *skomorokh* combined many of these functions.) Despite their natural popularity with ordinary Russians, they were distrusted by both Monarchy and Church, cruelly persecuted and driven to the outer regions of the country. Ecclesiastical drama, while more acceptable, failed to develop in any meaningful direction. One or two morality pieces became established in annual performances, particularly "The Fiery Furnace", an adaptation of the famous third chapter of Daniel, in which three youths are rescued at the last moment from death in the flames as punishment for refusing to worship the Golden Calf. Church schools also borrowed from abroad, imitating first Byzantine religious drama and then the theatrical practices of Jesuit schools in Poland, which even permitted diverting interludes (usually improvised) to enliven the familiar morality pieces. From this sub-genre emerged at least one or two 17th-century plays written in Russian that have a modest claim to interesting characters and stories, the best of them generally considered to be *Komediia pritchi o bludnom syne* [Prodigal Son] by Simeon Polotskii (1628/29–80). These separate streams, however, never fed into each other to produce an early current of indigenous drama, and all the attempts to assimilate western theatrical culture petered out after 1676, when Alexei died and the small court theatre was closed. Three decades of indifference ensued.

Early in the 18th century Peter the Great, seeing the propaganda potential of drama, made some attempts to institute a popular theatre using secular materials. His coercive measures brought in some hundreds of spectators but killed off any genuine enthusiasm; attention reverted to the court where imported ballet and opera became fashionable in Moscow and even in the newly-constructed St Petersburg. Some historical plays were written and produced by Feofan Prokopovich (1681–1736), but the actors were always non-Russian, and the spirit of the age – strictly moral when prescribed by the Church and flippant within the royal precincts – discouraged new theatrical practices. Once again a halting start came to nothing much.

The next beginning was a real one. Several factors came together by the middle of the century to initiate a truly Russian theatrical tradition. A professional company was created by royal edict in 1756, its chief performer being Fedor Volkov (1729–63), a celebrated young actor-manager whose reputation had been made in the provinces (Iaroslavl); his impact was such that Belinskii would one day describe him as "the father of the Russian theatre". He put money, talent, and effort into the company, eventually becoming its director and leaving it, when he died, in good health. His arrival coincided with the mature work of Russia's first serious playwright, Aleksei Sumarokov (1717–77), the author of a dozen derivative comedies and nine more substantial tragedies, which provided good roles for Volkov. Apart from an interesting adaptation of *Hamlet*, which transformed the play into a political allegory with a happy ending, the most striking of his plays was *Dmitrii samozvanets* (*Dmitrii the Imposter*) 1771, the Russian subject-matter of which won immediate popularity and also invited imitation, notably by Iakov Kniazhnin (1740–91) in *Vadim Novgorodskii* [Vadim of Novgorod] (1789). For the first time Russian plays were being well performed by Russian actors. Along with the serious plays a wide range of entertainment through comedy and opera also became available, much of it along lines dictated by France and Germany. The Empress herself, Catherine the Great (1729–96), contributed numerous works, now regarded as undistinguished, but some of them imaginative enough to break with the ruling Neoclassical tradition and involve the adaptation of Shakespeare. This age also produced one dramatist of enduring significance, Denis Fonvizin (1745–92), whose satirical comedies posed serious questions about the responsibilities of the landowning class. His first original play was *Brigadir* (*The Brigadier*) 1780, an entertaining satire directed against the over-Frenchified manners of polite Russian society; the characters speak an absurd language half-way between French and Russian, coining ludicrous gallicisms in every other sentence to avoid the ostensible vulgarity of their native language. His masterpiece, *Nedorosl'* (*The Minor*) 1782, creates a group of amusingly negative characters not far removed from the archetypes of Molière but recognizably Russian; this is the earliest Russian play that is still performed in the 20th century.

By the end of the century Russia had created a theatrical tradition which, for all its old-fashioned spirit, consisted of original Russian works, well-written and ably performed by Russian actors. The strongest development of all was in the theatre itself, which had grown rapidly in popularity at all levels of society. Encouragement came from the top. Catherine herself had ordered the beginning of a Grand Theatre, later called the Bolshoi, in 1773, and six years later she founded the Imperial Theatre School. All of this involved much expenditure, which Catherine may be credited with underwriting for good artistic reasons as well as for the possibilities of autocratic control that naturally ensued. At the same time, all the major provincial towns now wanted to introduce and encourage this new medium; many did so successfully without subsidy. Privately owned theatres also flourished, serf companies proliferating both in the mansions of Moscow and on the landowners' country estates. Wealthy neighbours sought to outdo each other in the lavishness of provision and production; the buying and selling of serf artists, sometimes *en masse*, has produced legendary stories of exploitation and excess. Standards of achievement must have varied from rustic enthusiasm to a high degree of metropolitan professional expertise; large numbers of people were involved in the performances, and still larger ones enjoyed watching them. In this way a broad theatrical infrastructure was laid down during a few short decades, in buildings and boards, artistic texts and commercial expertise, but also in the Russian mentality. When the 19th century dawned Russia at last possessed the potential for rich development and serious achievement. So appealing was the theatre now that most of Russia's greatest literary artists, as well as many less gifted, would soon want to write for it.

Not that the national investment paid immediate dividends. Conservative tastes prevailed for a couple of decades, the most popular dramatists looking back to the examples of their predecessors. Historical drama enjoyed a popularity beyond its intrinsic merits as purveyed by Russian writers. The plays of Vladislav Ozerov (1769–1816), for instance, packed the theatres past the limits of safety and ran for years to thunderous applause. Written in creaky hexameters and declaimed with a brash pomposity, they nevertheless captured the contemporary imagination that was more concerned with national pride than artistic niceties, cultural innovation or profound ideas. *Edip v Afinakh* [Oedipus in Athens] (1804), began and ended with a rousing tribute to the tsar; *Dmitrii Donskoi* [Dmitrii of the Don] (1806) presented historical characters who could be easily translated into their modern counterparts, Napoleon, Alexander I and his aides, so that the audience could cheer the triumphs of Old Russia and at the same time invoke new ones. More extreme still were the offerings of an outright chauvinist, Nestor Kukol'nik (1809–68), whose drama *Ruka Vsevyshnego otechestvo spasla* [The Hand of the Almighty Has Saved Our Fatherland] (1832) lavished praise on the Romanov dynasty for their historic role as saviours of Russia. The author even "improved" his text by incorporating a list of amendments proposed by Nicholas I. Writers of successful plays like these were raised to wealth and short-lived glory; their works are read now only by devoted specialists.

Russia has no great tradition of classical, tragic or historical drama able to claim unalloyed quality and international renown. It was in the flourishing field of Russian comedy that artistic advances were soon made and then multiplied. Comedy came in many different forms; light opera, *comédie larmoyante*, satirical drama, melodrama, vaudeville, and every kind of comic translation or adaptation all enjoyed their hours on the Russian stage of the early 19th century. Vaudeville was especially popular. This theatrical hybrid, born of light opera and French comedy, began as a one-act play and gathered some complexity as the years went by, adding acts and increasing the amount of improvisation. With interpolated songs and dances, it was an agreeable form of relaxation, light-hearted, gently satirical, and not without the odd touch of naughtiness. It could even accommodate a mild form of political and social criticism, though it never so much as brushed against subversiveness or sedition. A close eye was kept on everything said or done on stage, Nicholas I exercising personal control over the repertory and even the casting of plays. In vaudeville what mattered more than ideas, music or character-portrayal was the speedy storyline with its stream of jokes and the inevitable snappy ending. Musical quality was not a priority. Many hundreds of vaudevilles were enjoyed over several decades, ranging in quality from dire vulgarity to a polished style that has kept one or two of them alive still in the modern repertory. The father of the genre was Aleksandr Shakhovskoi (1777–1846), a name to conjure with in the annals of Russian theatre. Having written Russia's first vaudeville, *Kazak-stikhotvorets* [The Cossack Poet], in 1812, he went on to serve as impresario, director, theatre manager, talent-spotter, and eventually elder-statesman of the profession. His versatile career spanned five decades, beginning under Catherine, seeing the Russian theatre through to full maturity, and leaving its own legacy of well over a hundred plays. His early masterpiece *Urok koketkam, ili Lipetskie vody* [A Lesson for Coquettes, or Lipetsk Spa] (1815), for all its old-fashioned appearance, was strikingly modern in action, story, characters, and especially language, the verse medium permitting for perhaps the first time plausible-sounding conversation. The modernization of the Russian literary language, for which Pushkin is usually given exclusive credit, was initiated by Shakhovskoi and a handful of similar writers, the stage being an important vehicle for its implementation.

The new age soon began to produce a dynasty of famous actors and actresses, as well as the first Russian plays of real consequence. By mid-century Aleksandr Griboedov (1795–1829), Aleksandr Pushkin (1799–1837), Nikolai Gogol' (1809–52), and Ivan Turgenev (1818–83) had each written a play of such quality that, in one form or another, it still appears on the national, even the international, stage. Griboedov's *Gore ot uma* (*Woe from Wit*) 1825, was a satirical verse comedy in four acts, using free iambic lines. The satire was acerbic and direct, contemporary manners in St Petersburg being castigated by the sullen, anti-social hero Chatskii, whose pungent diatribes are among the most memorable declamatory pieces in the language. Without naming names they left no doubt in the audience's mind; everyone could identify, for instance, the brutish plutocrat who was rumoured to have swapped some of his long-serving serf retainers for four borzois. All Russians acknowledge the striking quality of the language of this play; Pushkin's famous prophecy that half of its lines would become Russian proverbs was rapidly vindicated. Pushkin's own play, *Boris Godunov* (1831), was conceived as nothing less than an epoch-making innovation in historical drama. Away went the conventions and artificialties of the Neoclassical stage; the author turned to his beloved Shakespeare in a deliberate search for historical authenticity and, above all, psychological consistency. Written in a curious form of blank verse (with a French-style caesura after the fourth syllable of every line), the play may have been originally conceived as a five-act tragedy, but the author chose to do away with divisions into anything other than 23 varied tableaux. These attempts to create distance from the English master have done the play a disservice, emphasizing a fault that already exists; in its keenness to look original it appears like a collage of brilliant scenes that fail to cohere into a proper piece of theatre. Despite containing many examples of Pushkin's most effective poetry in the grand style,

Boris Godunov is now best-known in its simplified operatic version (1874) by Musorgskii. Similarly, *Woe from Wit*, for all its qualities, has never succeeded abroad, not even on the London stage in 1993 with the most excellent of translators and staging.

This is not true of the plays by Gogol' and Turgenev. The former's *Revizor* (*The Government Inspector*) 1836, is hilariously successful wherever it is performed. This work, in four acts of modern (if provincial) prose, has no serious rival for acceptance as Russia's greatest play. A penniless opportunist, Khlestakov, takes advantage of a misunderstanding to pass himself off as a Government Inspector in a scruffy backwoods town, whose tatty officials scurry round in one silly antic after another in order to ingratiate themselves with him. The wonderful processions of tawdry supplicators, the dramatic irony that builds a succession of amusing crises, the wide range of comedy from slapstick-pantomime upwards – all of this gives the play a universal appeal that has little to do with the dreadful state of particular institutions of rural Russia. The many attempts at imposing deep meanings on this play – moral, sexual, political – are best discounted. This is comedy at its purest, far transcending the satirical purpose from which it first grew.

Turgenev's play *Mesiats v derevne* (*A Month in the Country*), well-known though it may be, is a more substantial achievement than most people realize. Written at the very point of mid-century, it belongs really to the following century, demonstrating how much ground had been traversed since the days of Ozerov and Kukol'nik. The action takes place on a country estate. A young tutor, Beliaev, turns the head of the mistress, Mme Islaeva, and also her 17-year-old ward, Vera. The older woman is a *tour de force* of theatrical characterization. Neglected by a busy husband and conscious (at 29) of the first signs of ageing, she permits her lower instincts of self-interest to prevail over everything else in a ruthless attempt to gain favour with the young man. There is little overt action and no outright catastrophe results from her selfish conduct, but the destinies of a dozen characters have been changed, mostly for the worse, by the end of the play. Turgenev has demonstrated his pessimistic vision (deriving from personal experience) of the power of Eros to disrupt and ruin ordinary lives. This apparently light comedy – there is much amusement in it – prefigures psychological drama by at least a generation, which is why the play was undervalued by everyone (including the diffident author himself) in its day. It is a most accomplished work, ever popular around the world, and the unacknowledged debt owed to this work by Anton Chekhov is only now coming to full acknowledgement; the borrowings, general and particular, are remarkable. Turgenev's play therefore enjoys a double distinction; celebrated in its own right, it is also the founder of a famous tradition in Russian drama.

These four plays show how far Russian theatre was able to progress in the first half of the 19th century. The rise of Russian actors was equally impressive. By the 1840s a cult of personality had been spun effectively around several accomplished performers; the names of Karatygin (1802–53), Mochalov (1800–48), and Shchepkin (1788–1863) became legendary. The first two were polar opposites, professional-classical versus amateur-romantic; the handsome and dedicated Karatygin acted impressively, deploying meticulous and dependable skills, whereas the stooping, impulsive Mochalov worked by instinct and emotion, sometimes attaining sublime heights of inspiration but often sinking back into dull recitation. Russia was lucky to have them both at the same time, and sometimes (as in *Woe from Wit*) they performed together. Mikhail Shchepkin, who was born more than a decade before them and outlived them by a similar period, in some ways combined their qualities and rose to even greater popularity, particularly in the 1860s. His acting career began in the late 18th-century manner, with a strong declamatory style of acting accompanied by emphatic gesticulation. Convinced of the ineffectiveness of such artificial strutting about the stage, he worked consciously to evolve a style of acting that would parallel the "natural school" affected by literature itself in the early 19th century. Realism became the order of his day, based on close observation and detailed imitation of actual people. Empathy and intelligence were brought to bear on each role, along with the most scrupulous preparation. It is not difficult to discern the beginnings of the Stanislavskii method in these mid-century preparations for what we now know as modern drama.

The career of Aleksandr Ostrovskii (1823–86) thoroughly exemplifies the new sense of realism. He is unique among front-rank Russian playwrights in writing for the theatre alone, his 50 plays constituting a broad study of contemporary Russian life centred on the middle class, such as it was, or on classless people. Owners of small businesses are well represented and this new capitalist community turned attention repeatedly to the subject of money. Ostrovskii's other main preoccupation is of a more general kind: the nasty tendency for some small-minded people blessed with a little power to misuse it by oppressing less fortunate individuals. The petty tyrant (often a woman) who operates only on a domestic or local scale but with cruel and tragic consequences for his or her dependants, known to Russians as a *samodur*, appears in a number of Ostrovskii's plays, notably in his best-known work, *Groza* (*The Storm*) 1859 (the subject of Janáček's opera *Katia Kabanova*). Here the oppressive Kabanikha impels her son into grovelling obedience and her daughter-in-law into a brief love affair followed by repentance, confession, and suicide. This pessimistic play ruthlessly exposes family despotism against a background of demeaning Russian provincialism. The socio-political implications of Ostrovskii's work have emerged with some clarity, but to the detriment of his overall reputation, which depends excessively on his being defined as a realist. It is a mystery why he has so far not proved amenable to export through translation, unlike many of his compatriots, though this is unlikely to be redressed until the broad universality of his themes is properly substantiated in criticism and new translations recommend themselves to modern directors. Ostrovskii's habilitation on the world stage is long overdue.

Other mid-century Russian dramatists of significance include Aleksei Pisemskii (1821–81), whose peasant tragedy *Gor'kaia sud'bina* (*A Bitter Fate*), shared a national prize for excellence in the theatre with *The Storm* in 1859, and Aleksandr Sukhovo-Kobylin (1817–1903), whose personal problems (including a long-standing threat of indictment for murder) long overshadowed his work, to the temporary detriment of a powerful trilogy, *Svad'ba Krechinskogo* (*Krechinskii's Wedding*), *Delo* (*The Case*), and *Smert' Tarelkina* (*The Death of Tarelkin*) 1854–69, which spirals down through the dark depiction of administrative corruption in the provinces to a kind of early black comedy in a St Petersburg strongly reminiscent of

Gogol'. Towards the end of the century two different Tolstois came to prominence in the theatre. First, A.K. Tolstoi (1817–75) completed a historical trilogy in blank verse: *Smert' Ioanna Groznogo* (*The Death of Ivan the Terrible*) 1866, *Tsar' Fedor Ioannovich* (1868), and *Tsar' Boris* (1870). Not for the first time his sense of timing was out; having, earlier in the century, written a historical novel just when the genre itself was going out of favour, now he presented further historical materials that were not particularly wanted by the public, nor were they immediately acceptable to the establishment, since they seemed to adopt an anti-monarchical stance. Performance was delayed until the 1890s. Along with Pushkin's version of *Boris Godunov*, Tolstoi's plays are considered to be the outstanding representatives of Russian historical drama. The more famous Lev Tolstoi made at least ten attempts to write for the stage, producing one drama of remarkable strength and quality, *Vlast' t'my* (*The Power of Darkness*) 1888, in which the obvious didactic spirit is, fortunately, overwhelmed by a disturbing story, which involves nothing less than infanticide on stage. The mature writer also makes careful use of closely-studied peasant language, as well as showing a true sense of both characterization and construction; a strong impression of reality derives from the origin of this tragedy in real-life events.

Apart from these writers, and a good number of minor figures, the Russian theatre in the second half of the 19th century sustained itself on many translations and adaptations from abroad. Also from the west came the impetus for a brilliant new start to theatrical life in Russia. Impressed by the forces of naturalism that were sweeping across the continent, and aware of naturalist tendencies already maturing in their own country, two great figures came together to form what would soon become one of Russia's most celebrated cultural institutions, the Moscow Arts Theatre. Konstantin Stanislavskii (1863–1938) joined with Vladimir Nemirovich-Danchenko (1858–1943) under the auspices of the amateur Society for Art and Literature, and within a short time their new ideas were bearing rich fruit. It is still a cause for astonishment for us to contemplate the originality and sheer quality that went into the production of their fifth offering, a revival of Chekhov's unsuccessful play *Chaika* (*The Seagull*) in 1898. Ol'ga Knipper (soon to be the author's wife), Stanislavskii himself, and the up-and-coming, imaginative Vsevolod Meierkhol'd (1874–1940) all took part, and the remarkable innovation was that not one of them could be regarded as a star. Personality was submerged in a sense of communal contribution and achievement; what mattered now was the total effect of verisimilitude conveyed at a slow pace by the steady build-up of atmosphere as opposed to remarkable incidents, all of this sustained by the closest attention to production detail. Chekhov would stage his last three dramas, *Diadia Vania* (*Uncle Vania*), *Tri sestry* (*The Three Sisters*), and *Vishnevyi sad* (*The Cherry Orchard*), at the Moscow Arts Theatre, and the two main directors, especially Stanislavskii, would soon rise to lasting celebrity with their assiduous writings on the training and direction of actors and plays. The "Stanislavskii Method" became a byword for professionalism and excellence in the modern theatre. As to Chekhov, he has become everyone's favourite, enduringly popular in all countries. His great success was to remove the last vestiges of artificiality from the stage, blurring the distinction between tragedy and comedy, so that his plays cannot be forced into either category. It had now become less interesting to see someone struck down by the gods than worn down by the gentle abrasion of everyday existence and the growing awareness that time has moved faster than might seem possible, taking with it many lost possibilities. There is some oblique criticism of contemporary Russia in all of this, but Chekhov's aimless or misdirected characters do not belong to a single nation. The sadness of unfulfilled opportunity, misapplied effort, recurrent ill-fortune and empty existence, as well as the difficulty of intimate communication with other people – this mood of melancholic disappointment is recognizable to all audiences, as is the call for a renewal of strength that is also implicit in Chekhov's plays.

One other important new Russian play was produced by the Moscow Arts Theatre in 1905, when Gor'kii's remarkable tragedy of the dosshouse, *Na dne* (*The Lower Depths*), with all its striking political undertones, rose to instant fame before going off around the world on a tide of popularity that has yet to run its full course. Like Chekhov's work this play may be seen as a piece of contemporary social criticism, and one that happened to get off to a good start by being so well-presented. In fact it has more quality than any such narrow judgement might suggest, dealing as it does with universal concepts such as the nature of truth and the immorality of misjudging people by surface appearances. Like Tolstoi's *The Power of Darkness*, from which it partly derives, this play achieves its broad didactic purpose by dissolving it in strongly interesting language, characters, and situations. The delicacy of this achievement is borne out by the lack of any such subtlety in Gor'kii's other half-dozen plays, which by comparison seem tendentious in their treatment of too-obvious political content. Another playwright of the period, Leonid Andreev (1871–1919), began his career in a similarly Neorealistic manner with *K zvezdam* (*To the Stars*) in 1905, but soon developed a taste for a more rhetorical style and allegorical range of meanings. One or two of his later plays, particularly *Tot, kto poluchaet poshchechinu* (*He Who Gets Slapped*) 1915, found short-lived success at home and even abroad, though a rapid decline in his popularity (applying also to his reputation as a story writer) was never arrested. Andreev now rests in obscurity and his plays are unlikely to be revived.

By the end of the century, the country had entered a period of economic and social turmoil that would culminate in the violent political events of 1905 and 1917. The cultural scene reflected the same spirit of instability, uncertainty, and yearning for change. In theatrical circles a new tendency arose, more diffuse and much less successful in box-office terms than Neorealism, towards a broader expressiveness supposedly achieveable through new experiments with symbol, enchanting or mystifying language, and the representation of a greater reality than that which the five senses crudely perceive. Meierkhol'd first attempted to stage Symbolist works at the Moscow Arts Theatre, in the hope that the challenging ideas of Maeterlinck might catch on; when they did not he transferred his attentions to St Petersburg, working with the famous actress Vera Kommisarzhevskaia (1864–1910) in the theatre that she had founded. Typical of his more successful work there was the startling triumph of a poetic drama by a young poet, Aleksandr Blok (1880–1921), entitled *Balaganchik* (*The Puppet Show*) and described as a "mystical satire". A puzzling work, this story of Pierrot and Columbine appears to relate both love and death to a transcendent reality, or perhaps to ridicule writers who try to do this sort of thing. Wildly controversial in its day, it achieved a *succès de scandale*, making the poet's name as well as confirming the director in his role as the country's leading theatrical experimentalist.

For many people novelty was the order of the day. Valerii Briusov (1873–1924) and Nikolai Evreinov (1879–1953), among other less well-known theoreticians and directors, condemned the Stanislavskii school as narrow-minded, backward-looking, and stultifying. Taking over from Meierkhol'd at Kommisarzhevskaia's theatre in 1908, Evreinov advanced the anti-realist cause still further in his writings, adaptations, and many productions. He also directed a small experimental theatre called "The Crooked Mirror" that captivated rapturous, if sometimes bemused, audiences from 1908 to 1918. Elsewhere up and down the country theatrical experimentation, often overlapping with avant-garde poetry readings, flowed out from small private theatres into cafés, night-clubs, cabaret rooms, parks, and other public places. The Futurists were shocking the bourgeoisie and everyone else with their crazy stunts and outrageous manifesto pronouncements, bringing iconoclasm, insult, and self-advertisement to a fine art. The poetry readings of Vladimir Maiakovskii (1893–1930) were memorable theatrical performances in themselves and some of his works were plays more than poems. His *Vladimir Maiakovskii: tragediia* (*Vladimir Maiakovskii: A Tragedy*) carried on where Blok's *The Puppet Show* had left off; performed in Luna Park, St Petersburg, in December 1913, it began with an open statement by the poet-actor-director that no one was going to understand what was about to happen, and few did. It is possible retrospectively to view this piece as a "monodrama of suffering" in which the poet emerges as a scapegoat for the sins of mankind, but contemporary audiences, lacking the hindsight that we now enjoy, were left bemused. Alternating with *Vladimir Maiakovskii* was *Pobeda nad solntsem* [Victory Over the Sun], a kind of opera written by the Futurist most committed to "transrational" language, Aleksei Kruchenykh (1886–1968), with a prologue by Khlebnikov, music by Matiushin, and sets by Malevich; when the Futurists caught the sun and dragged it down from the sky the onlookers may have been able to take this as a satirical thrust against the Symbolists, but the words and details of the piece must have bewildered them.

Most people, enjoying the spectacle and scandal, did not mind the obscurity; many were conscious of witnessing significant experiments that could only enrich the cultural achievement of their country. Everyone could feel the intensity of the new theatrical experience; travelling companies took the experimental words out into the far provinces. The nation was shocked, puzzled, disturbed, and impressed by turns; no one could remain indifferent. A kind of excitement bordering on hysteria had taken over the Russian cultural scene, reflecting and prefiguring the apocalyptic political changes about to engulf the nation and its art. The outside world knew about this. Along with Russian art and music (especially ballet), the late-coming theatre of that country, standing now for high professionalism on the one hand and amazing creativity on the other, had risen to such prominence that it had captured the world's imagination, delivering a confident challenge to Europe and America. Then came the Revolution.

A.D.P. Briggs

Russian Literature in the 18th Century

At the beginning of the 18th century, Russia had no secular literary culture to compare with that of western Europe. There were no acknowledged authors. Consequently there were no readers and no publishers and presses to cater for their needs. There was a lack not only of a literary Russian language, but even of a modern typography. By the end of the century the situation had been transformed. Russia now possessed a vibrant literary culture that was part of Europe's and would produce and sustain a literary genius destined to become her national poet. Significantly Aleksandr Pushkin was born in the closing year of the 18th century on 6 June 1799.

What accounted for this remarkable transformation? The prime mover was Peter the Great who took over the government in 1694 with a mission to Westernize his Empire and make it an equal of the most advanced states of Europe. Peter himself was no writer – unlike his later successor Catherine the Great – and few literary works appeared during his reign. His policy of rapid westernization, however, inevitably led to the emergence of a literary culture modelled on that of Europe and recognizable as "European". That process determined the particular development of Russian literature in the 18th century.

The Russia inherited by Peter had not been immune to western influence. Earlier in the 17th century Catholic Poles had occupied Moscow during the Time of Troubles, and the Protestant Swedish armies of Charles XII had marched through Russian lands at the beginning of Peter's reign. It was the foreign colony of western craftsmen, merchants, and mercenaries established in Moscow's Nemetskaia Sloboda (Foreign Quarter) that nurtured Peter's own enthusiasm for western ways. Peter regained for his Empire extensive areas of traditional Russian lands in today's Belarus and Ukraine that had been deeply influenced by Catholic and Latin culture during long years of Polish domination.

What have come to be recognized as "Petrine" reforms had certainly been under way before Peter's accession. But it was Peter who was acknowledged by both the contemporary opponents of his reform and its supporters to have made a decisive break with the past.

During his reign there was little evidence of the birth of a new literature. But by obliging the influential upper classes to dress in western style, attend social assemblies and acquaint themselves with western mores, Peter sought to change their outlook. By ordering the boyars to shave off their beards, Peter altered the very appearance of Russian faces. Likewise he changed the appearance of the traditional typeface used by the Russian Orthodox Church: in 1708 he created the new *grazhdanskii shrift* (civil typography) which could be used not only for technical and didactic works, but, in principle, for secular, entertaining literature. A new typeface was not the sole fundamental requirement supplied by Peter for a literary culture: other rudiments were basic education and the translation of standard textbooks. He encouraged the transformation of the Moscow Academy, previously a Church school, into a modern academy based on the one in Kiev with its tradition of teaching the classical languages and philosophy.

Russian literature developed not only under the press of these reforms but also in response to the towering personality of Peter himself, which was to act as a focus for Russian writers until the end of the century and beyond. "Grant health, power, peace, security! / Grant this to Tsar Peter, crowned by Thee, /And to his most loyal chieftain, Ivan!" was the concluding chorus of Feofan Prokopovich's *Vladimir*, a five-act tragi-comedy on the Christianization of the Russian lands in the 10th century. Performed at the Kiev Academy in July 1705, in the presence of Peter the Great's henchman Ivan Mazeppa, *Vladimir* was a major literary *tour de force* by a young 24-year-old cleric with modern, Westernizing views. Some of its salient features would remain characteristic of Russian literature throughout the century. In form, it imitated an European exemplar; in this case it drew on the established Jesuit tradition of school drama. In content, it combined eulogy of an active, reforming tsar and his supporters with a satirical attack on those obscurantist backsliders who opposed reform. Prokopovich's *Vladimir* railed against the superstitious, ignorant, drunken, and gluttonous pagan priests of pre-Christian Russia, but these also manifested the failings of the Orthodox clerics of contemporary Russia; consequently *Vladimir* had a distinct anti-clerical and secular bias. The play, therefore, was political in its thrust, as much of 18th-century Russian literature would prove to be. Significantly Prokopovich's outlook had been determined by his background and education. Born in Kiev in 1681, he had received his early education at the city's Academy that had long been subject to Latinate influences. Like other brilliant students, he then pursued his studies at Jesuit colleges in Polish territory before being sent to Rome; here he completed in 1701 three years of study at the "Greek College", where the Vatican trained men for its mission in eastern Europe. He returned to Kiev to re-embrace Orthodoxy, critical of the Papacy yet deeply influenced by western ways of thought and committed to support for the Petrine plans for modernizing Russia to enable her to rank alongside other European nations.

The pattern of Prokopovich's upbringing and education was repeated in the lives of the other prominent and influential Russian writers in the next generation. Also coming from the periphery of the Russian Empire with ready access to the outside world, they would spend a vital, shaping period of their life in western Europe. These were Antiokh Kantemir (1708–44), Vasilii Trediakovskii (1703–69), and Mikhail Lomonosov (1711–65).

Kantemir was the son of a Moldavian prince, Dmitrii Kantemir, a renowned scholar who had written a Latin history of the Ottoman Empire and had come to Moscow as a political émigré. Naturally gifted, nurtured in a cultured home and acquainted with classical Greek and Latin literature, Antiokh Kantemir was exceptional enough to be sent first to London in 1732 as Russian envoy, and then as Ambassador to Paris in 1738. Trediakovskii was the son of a priest in Astrakhan on the Caspian Sea where Italian Capuchins had established a Catholic mission. It was from them that he received his early education, a grounding in Greek and Latin and exposure to western culture. After two years in Moscow at the Slavo-Greco-Latin Academy, he went abroad in 1725 to study first at The Hague and then from 1726–30 at the University of Paris. Here he came to know and even participated in French literary life, an experience that would be crucial not only for his personal career but for the development of Russian literature. Lomonosov, like Trediakovskii, was born in a place with ready access to sea routes that brought western influence to bear on Russians. His home was a village near Archangel on the Severnaia Dvina river that ran into the White Sea. Like Trediakovskii, Lomonosov used the Slavo-Greco-Latin Academy as a staging post on a journey that would lead to European universities, first at Marburg and then at Freiburg. Although his mission was to study chemistry and mining, his acquaintance with the literary life of Germany enabled him to make a crucial contribution to Russian letters after his return to St Petersburg's Academy of Sciences in 1741.

If direct acquaintanceship with European literary life was one experience that Prokopovich, Kantemir, Trediakovskii, and Lomonosov shared, another feature common to all four was that they were not rooted in the traditional noble families of Russia. Their families were either displaced or belonged to social strata of low esteem. Consequently, the young men recognized that their ambition could be best sustained by Petrine values that exalted talent, merit, and devotion to the strengthening of the state above birth and inherited station. Literature was used by them, as it had been used by Prokopovich with his *Vladimir*, as a political weapon to defend the Petrine reforms by praising their author and to attack the reactionaries who attempted after Peter's death to undermine the advances made under his reign.

It is not Peter's own epoch that saw the emergence in print of a secular European-style literature in Russia. The 1730s was the decade that witnessed the flowering of a literature consciously modelled on European exemplars. Kantemir wrote six satires between 1729 and 1731 in response to the danger he saw coming from obscurantist clerics and backwoods noblemen who rejected Peter's inheritance, particularly the introduction of modern science and technology and the encouragement of European classical Latin education at the expense of the traditional Greek-orientated learning of Muscovite Orthodoxy. But his negative satire was balanced by his attempt in 1730 to write an epic poem on Peter, his *Petrida*. The *Petrida*, like other attempts by Russian 18th-century poets to compose epics, remained unfinished. The eulogy of Petrine values was more commonly conveyed in the Russian solemn ode, developed in particular by Lomonosov, which remained the most esteemed poetic genre until the end of the century.

Both satire and ode were poetic forms for which classical and French Neoclassical models were readily available. At this early stage in the establishment of modern secular Russian literature, reliance on such well-defined canonical models was essential. The new literature would be based on western technique and methods, as surely as the technology and procedures of the reformed army and administration would be founded on those of Europe. Kantemir indeed drew attention to the technical sources of his satires by accompanying his verse with copious notes to explain in detail what he was about and whose example he was following. The Latin satirists Juvenal, Persius, and Horace were all acknowledged as precursors in his fourth satire, but it was the supreme legislator of French 17th-century Neoclassicism, Nicolas Boileau, who was indicated as Kantemir's main mentor and guide. Whenever Kantemir directly copied from these satirists, the source of his "imitations" was dutifully registered in the accompanying reference. The opening note of Kantemir's fifth satire confessed that a previous version had all been taken from Boileau's eighth satire. It was Boileau's *Odes* too that served as models for their Russian imitators. Trediakovskii's "Oda torzhestvennaia o sdache goroda Gdanska" [Solemn Ode on the Surrender of the City of Gdansk] (1734), which he claimed in an afterword to be the very first ode in Russian, was in places a direct translation of Boileau's *Ode sur la prise de Namur* (*Ode on the Capture of Namur*) 1693, and the *Rassuzhdenie ob ode voobshche* [Discourse on the Ode in General], which constituted the afterword, was a reworking of Boileau's *Discours sur l'ode* that had introduced his own ode. Lomonosov's 1739 "Oda na vziatie Khotina" [Ode on the Capture of Khotin] in turn followed the pattern of Boileau's *Ode sur la prise de Namur*, although another western exemplar also made its presence felt – Johann Christian Günther's German ode on the peace of Passowitz between the Austrian and Ottoman Empire in 1718.

It was the metre of Günther's ode, the accentual iambic tetrameter, which accounted for the depth of its imprint on that of Lomonosov. The latter's "Pis'mo o pravilakh rossiiskogo stikhotvorstva" [A Letter on Russian Versification] (1739), had been composed in Freiburg and sent to the Russian Academy of Sciences in St Petersburg together with the "Oda na vziatie Khotina", which served as an example of the new form of versification that he proposed. The establishment of a system of versification, generally acceptable and which has lasted to this day, was one of the most important achievements of the 18th century. Since the late 17th century, the dominant system of prosody used by Russians in their writings was syllabic verse, a method borrowed from Polish poetry. In syllabic verse there were rhymed pairs of lines with a fixed number of syllables in each line. It was a system well suited to a language, such as Polish, with its regular penultimate stress on words. Russian, however, with its characteristic mobile stress was unsuited to verse organized in this way. Nevertheless Kantemir's satires had been written according to the rules of Polish syllabic verse with an obligatory penultimate stress in each line mimicking the penultimate stress automatically produced by a Polish word ending a line. Trediakovskii also composed his early verse, including the "Oda torzhestvennaia o sdache goroda Gdanska", in accord with the syllabic system, but he grew uneasy at its inadequacy for the Russian language. Lacking the musical attributes of "measure and cadence", argued Trediakovskii, syllabic verse did not sing to the Russian ear and deserved to be called "mere prose". Consequently he wrote a treatise, *Novyi i kratkii sposob k slozheniiu rossiiskikh stikhov* (*A New and Brief Method for Composing Russian Verse*) 1735, which proposed a new rhythmical principle, a regular alternation of stressed and unstressed syllables that was appropriate to a language such as Russian with its mobile but very marked stress.

As in other fields, Trediakovskii was a trail-blazer who hacked away at outworn tradition in order to show the way forward, but it was often others who strode out boldly along the new path. Lomonosov's *Pis'mo o pravilakh rossiiskogo stikhotvorstva* seemed to present a more thoroughgoing reform as it expanded greatly the possibilities of accentual verse but it relied essentially on Trediakovskii's radical break with the prevailing system. Eventually a comprehensive theory of Russian syllabo-tonic prosody was produced by Trediakovskii, in 1752, in his revised *Sposob k slozheniiu rossiiskikh stikhov*, which drew on the experience of Russian poets in using the new metrics in the preceding decade.

Not only Russian metrics were refined by the combined efforts of Trediakovskii and Lomonosov but the literary language itself. One of the effects of Peter the Great's stress on secular reforms was that Church Slavonic was fast losing its role as the vehicle of literature and culture. Peter himself used as simple and direct a colloquial language as possible in his own writings, but his spoken Russian was incoherent, invaded by new military and administrative terms of foreign origin. There was no court nor cultural centres and salons to cultivate a polite society language on the basis of this clumsy vehicle of everyday intercourse. For the generation of writers who appeared after Peter, however, with their new conception of literature and new techniques, the forging of a complementary new literary language was essential. Trediakovskii had returned to Russia in 1730 from Paris anxious to introduce to his fellow countrymen the light-hearted fiction and lyrical love poetry of French *galant* literature. While abroad, he had translated Paul Tallemant's *Voyage de L'Isle d'Amour* and his realization of a new kind of literary Russian was made plain in his preface:

> I humbly beg you not to be angry with me for not translating this book into Church Slavonic but into almost the most ordinary Russian such as we speak among ourselves. I have done this for the following reasons: firstly, Church Slavonic is for us an ecclesiastical language, whereas this is a secular book; secondly, Church Slavonic in the present age is for us very obscure and many of us cannot read it, whereas this is a book about sweet love which should be understood by everybody; thirdly, ... Church Slavonic sounds harsh to my ears.

His practice, unfortunately, could not match the clarity of his theory. Sweet love was rendered not only by simple, colloquial speech, "such as we speak among ourselves"; it was mingled with bureaucratic officialese, strange-sounding Gallicisms and Slavonicisms, and the lexical muddle was further deformed by a clumsy syntax and dislocated word order. Trediakovskii nevertheless contributed to the elaboration of a literary language indirectly by his conscious transplantation of the generic system of French Neoclassical literature into Russia. As Russians were initiated into a hierarchy of genres – epic, ode, elegy, satire, eclogue, lyric, *précieux* romances, comedies, epigrams, and songs – they realized that gradations of language might best suit each genre. The practice and taste of Russian writers in the 1730s and 1740s ensured that lines of demarcation would begin to emerge in the mass of Church Slavonic and Russian vocabulary. The "high style", reserved for epic and ode, was marked by a large admixture of Slavonicisms which, however, had to be understandable to Russians. The "low style", shunning all Slavonicisms, could embrace vulgar colloquialisms. The "middle style", drawing on the vocabulary stock common to both Church Slavonic and Russian, was allowed a discreet tinge of Slavonicisms. It was this growing refinement of usage that was reflected in Lomonosov's theory of the three styles expressed in his *Ritorika* [Rhetoric] (1748), *Rossiiskaia grammatika* [Russian Grammar] (1755), and in his 1757 essay "O pol'ze knig tserkovnykh v rossiiskom iazyke" [On the Usefulness of Church Books in the Russian Language]. This "theory of the three styles" was not original; it adopted the current conventional linguistic theory of France to the Russian situation that Lomonosov observed. But the effect of his essays on his contemporaries was beneficial in that it gave theoretical justification to what was happening in practice. He enabled writers in the second half of the 18th century to align their writings consciously with a neutral, middle style.

Initially, the foundations of a Russian literary culture had been laid by talented individuals who strove to impose European criteria on their countrymen. They laboured almost in isolation, relying on a coterie of like-minded enthusiasts for their readership. That audience, however, was significantly broadened by the enthusiastic patronage bestowed by Empress Elizabeth during her reign (1741–62) on the theatre. A degree of compulsion was still necessary to turn Russians into theatregoers: Elizabeth made attendance at her court theatre mandatory for her courtiers. Equally indicative of the progress in spreading the appeal of Russia's literary culture was the success of an amateur troupe of actors in the provincial city of Iaroslavl led by a merchant's son, Fedor Volkov. After ordering Volkov's company to St Petersburg to give a command performance at court, Empress Elizabeth decided to polish the provincial enthusiasm by enroling them in the Kadetskii korpus, a state school for privileged young noblemen.

It was from this establishment that the third prominent Russian poet of the time had graduated. Aleksandr Sumarokov (1717–77) ranked himself alongside his senior contemporaries Trediakovskii and Lomonosov, whose disciple he had originally been. Between 1747 and 1751 he wrote five tragedies, all constructed according to the dictates of the Neoclassical form of drama, derived from Racine and Corneille and still acknowledged as the only way of composing serious drama by contemporaries such as Voltaire in France and Gottsched in Germany. *Khorev*, *Hamlet*, *Sinav i Truvor*, *Artistona*, and *Semira* were to be the kernel of the Russian theatrical repertoire for a generation. Formulaic in plot – the relationship between a pair of lovers close to a sovereign is subverted by a clash between social duty and personal passion, and then resolved – the plays nevertheless had a novel appeal in their portrayal on stage of human emotions. Sumarokov's *Khorev* was one of the four plays performed by Volkov for Elizabeth at her court, and when the Empress instituted a public theatre in St Petersburg in 1756 from Volkov's men who had been sufficiently refined at the Kadetskii korpus, Sumarokov was appointed its director. He thus became the first in a long line of Russian noblemen to devote himself exclusively to a profession of literature. Confident of his superiority as a writer, he accepted as completely justified the title bestowed on him of the Russian Racine. It was partly this sense of being guardian of a high European tradition that prompted him to return to the writing of Neoclassical tragedies in the late 1760s in response to the vogue for the new sentimental bourgeois drama of France that he deplored. A feature of these later tragedies, best exemplified by his *Dmitrii samozvanets* (*Dmitrii the Imposter*) 1771, was their intention, in deference to Voltaire's example, to preach civic virtue and warn of the dangers of private passion.

The didactic impulse that was reinforced by the growth of the bourgeois drama in contemporary France was also apparent in the Russian comedies and sentimental drama that flourished in Catherine the Great's reign (1762–96). Play-writing then enjoyed particular prestige since Catherine herself, aided by her literary secretaries, was a prolific composer of comedies whose satirical targets were social misdemeanours such as gossiping and hypochondria, although her sights were occasionally raised to attack parental tyranny and religious bigotry. Her distaste for any religious enthusiasm was further manifested in a group of comedies she wrote in 1785–86 directed against exponents of Russian Freemasonry.

One of Catherine's collaborators was Ivan Elagin (1725–94) who replaced Sumarokov as director of the Imperial Theatres in 1766, and encouraged young disciples who would make their mark on Russian drama, such as Denis Fonvizin (1745–92), Vladimir Lukin (1737–94), and Bogdan Elchaninov (1744–70). Lukin's *Shchepetil'nik* [The Haberdasher] (1765), based on Robert Dodsley's *The Toy-Shop* (1735), was an example of his policy of "adapting to our customs" foreign plays. In his dramas Lukin attempted to Russianize characters, situations, surroundings, and social relationships while, at the same time, transferring to the Russian context the overt social moralizing and sermonizing of his European sources. It was on the pioneering foundations of Lukin and Elchaninov that Fonvizin was able to compose *Brigadir* (*The Brigadier*) in 1769, which became one of the most acclaimed Russian 18th-century comedies mainly because of its masterly portrayal of society and the naive, long-suffering, comically humble Russian woman in the role of the Brigadier's wife. In 1781 Fonvizin completed his masterpiece, *Nedorosl'* (*The Minor*), the only 18th-century play that has retained a permanent place in the Russian theatrical repertoire. In *The Minor* a group of *raisonneurs*, spokesmen for Petrine and enlightened values, prevail against a motley of provincial boors and ignoramuses who, nevertheless, with their crude energy and ripe colloquial parlance form the abiding dramatic interest.

The butts of Fonvizin's satire were not new. They had been paraded in most of the comedies of the previous two decades, including the plays composed by Catherine the Great. The satirical targets had also been set up in the moral weeklies that were a crucial stage in the creation of Russian prose literature. Again Catherine herself took the initiative by launching in 1769 a weekly paper, *Vsiakaia vsiachina* [All Sorts], modelled on the renowned English journals of Joseph Addison and Richard Steele, *The Spectator* and *The Tatler*.

Literature for Catherine was a means of furthering her policy of encouraging the Russian nobility to become agents of Enlightenment. So in 1768 she established her Society for the Translation of Foreign Books that gave a stamp of approval to modern writers such as Montesquieu, Voltaire, Diderot, D'Alambert, Blackstone, Swift, Fielding, Gellert, and Goldoni. Enlightenment thought had already been distilled in translation into the famous *Nakaz*, or Instruction, to the deputies summoned to a legislative commission in 1767. The assembly itself, only suspended on the outbreak of hostilities with Turkey two years later, formed a rudimentary public opinion and was a demonstration of how the freedom of thought, speech and the press – all prerequisites for a flourishing literary culture – had been expanded.

The moral weeklies were another demonstration of the concept of freedom of expression promulgated in the *Nakaz*. *Vsiakaia vsiachina* called on other writers to join with it in satirizing the anti-Enlightenment elements that still frustrated Peter the Great's objective of transforming Russian society, and several new journals sprang up in response to the imperial summons. The most successful by far was *Truten'*, edited by Nikolai Novikov (1744–1818) who followed it with the equally impressive *Zhivopisets* (1772–73) and *Koshelek* (1774). Not content with being editor of these moral weeklies, Novikov became a historiographer and published sketches of leading Russian writers in his *Opyt istoricheskogo slovaria o rossiiskikh pisateliakh* [An Essay on the Historical Dictionary of Russian Writers] (1772), reflecting the extent of the emergence of a distinctive Russian literary culture. From 1779 to 1789 he held the lease of Moscow University Press and, benefiting from Catherine the Great's 1783 decree permitting independent presses, he became Russia's leading publisher.

That Novikov had sufficient material to feed his presses in the 1780s was due, to a great extent, to the impetus given to prose writing by his own satirical journals of 1769–74. In them he was able – in letters, pen-portraits, dialogues, and stories – to practise a literary prose style that proved adequate to express the concerns of his age. Travel sketches from supposed "correspondents" foreshadowed the vogue for travel literature, closely linked with the epistolary mode, that flourished towards the close of the 18th century. The fashion gave rise to some of the most significant Russian prose works of the century: Fonvizin's letters from abroad during his journeys of 1777–78 and 1784–85; the radically critical *Puteshestvie iz Peterburga v Moskvu* (*A Journey from St Petersburg to Moscow*) by Aleksandr Radishchev (1749–1802); and *Pis'ma russkogo puteshestvennika* (*Letters of a Russian Traveller*) by Nikolai Karamzin (1766–1826).

Editors of some of the 1769–74 moral weeklies such as Fedor Emin (1735–70) and Mikhail Chulkov (1734–92) made the first attempts at producing extended prose fiction. Emin, editor of *Adskaia pochta*, as well as translating romances from Spanish, Italian, and Portuguese, tried his hand at novel writing and is credited with the first original Russian novel with *Nepostoiannaia fortuna* [Inconstant Fortune] (1763). It initiated a short but productive period of novel writing: further novels by Emin, Chulkov, Popov and a series of Neoclassical and allegorical novels by Mikhail Kheraskov (1733–1807) whose cultivation of a wide array of genres, both within and without the Neoclassical canon, and role in organizing and inspiring young literary talent made him an outstanding figure of Catherine's reign. One of the most distinguished novels of the 18th century was Chulkov's *Prigozhaia povarikha, ili Pokhozhdenie razvratnoi zhenshchiny* [The Comely Cook] 1770, with its rumbustious narrative of contemporary life and manners. Russian fiction, however, had a hard struggle to make any headway against the stream of translated novels available to the Russian reader in the last third of the century: Fanny Burney, Henry Fielding, Madame de Genlis, Oliver Goldsmith, Samuel Richardson, Jean-Jacques Rousseau, Laurence Sterne, and Jonathan Swift eclipsed the earnest pioneers of Russian fiction.

It was not until the last decade of the century that a Russian writer of prose fiction appeared whose work could stand comparison with that of his European contemporaries. This was Nikolai Karamzin, whose first novella *Evgenii i Iuliia* [Eugene and Julia] appeared in 1789 in Russia's first magazine for children. Soon his original fiction filled the pages of literary journals and almanacs founded and edited by him. The first Russian Sentimental story, *Bednaia Liza* (*Poor Liza*), published in 1792, enjoyed outstanding success and signalled a new stage in Russian literature. In 1794–95 the almanac *Aglaia* carried the stories "Ostrov Borngol'm" [The Island of Bornholm] and "Sierra Morena". The success of the journals won for Karamzin the right to be called Russia's first modern journalist. Prose fiction, inspired by European Sentimentalism, and journalism were not the only fields in which Karamzin indicated fresh paths for Russian literature to follow. Prompted by the growing enthusiasm for Shakespeare in Germany, Karamzin was the first to reveal the genius of Shakespeare to the Russian reader with his translation from the original of *Julius Caesar* and preface that sought to explain the particular qualities of the Shakespearean drama. Another prompt to which Karamzin responded was the vogue for the poetry of Ossian, the Gaelic bard of antiquity that James Macpherson had claimed to have translated. Karamzin's poetry, hinting at folk-song and singing of the pure emotions of the human heart, anticipated the romantic lyricism of the following century. New themes were accompanied by daring technical playfulness, such as his teasing use of near rhymes and blank verse. In his verse, as in his supple prose, are heard the colloquial intonations and lucid syntax with which Karamzin transformed literary Russian at the close of the century. No theoretical treatises on the nature of Russian, however, were left by him; his Russian was based on his own personal appreciation of the sound and significance of living speech, the fittingness of words and expressions from common parlance or foreign borrowings.

Above all, Karamzin was guided in all that he did by his conviction of the standing of the individual author. It is worth comparing Karamzin's self-image as an author with that of his contemporary Gavrila Derzhavin (1743–1816), the greatest poet before Pushkin. Throughout his work, Derzhavin had demonstrated unrivalled creative inventiveness and independence. Not shackled by the dictates of Neoclassical canons, by playfully mixing light satire and lyricism into the pattern of the Lomonosovian solemn ode, he produced dazzling hybrids. His bold innovation was evident in the mock ode "Felitsa" (1782), a lightly veiled allusion to Catherine the Great, that established his renown. Derzhavin went on to write poems of genius in which his own personality, his exuberance in the richness of life's pleasures and anguish at the brevity of his own span were manifested in brilliantly innovative verse. Yet Derzhavin retained the modest view of his own poetry as an adjunct to the more important service he could render his sovereign as a high official in the Russian administration.

For Karamzin, however, the calling of author was the highest possible and had no need to be buttressed by other services outside literature. Dedicated to the sole profession of author, he did not limit himself to poetry alone, but played his part in all possible fields – fiction, drama, philosophical essays, poetry – and as editor and publisher as well as writer. While acknowledging the role that Catherine the Great had played in enhancing the prestige of writers, Karamzin drew pointed attention to the essentially amateur nature of her own pastimes with her pen. What distinguished the truly committed professional writer in Karamzin's eyes was his gift of being a unique vessel to hold genius. A writer's personality should be projected in his works, not out of vanity, but as a focus for genius. Behind that confident assertion of the writer's standing in society lay all the strivings to establish foundations of a national Russian literature in the 18th century.

The influence now exercised by the individual author on his society had its darker side. The last decade of the century, it is true, would be known as Karamzin's period in recognition of his intellectual and moral leadership. Those closing years would also be remembered as the time when the Russian state, in the person of Catherine the Great, alarmed by the French Revolution of 1789, moved to silence authors suspected, however unjustly, of being threats to the established political order. Radishchev, whose *A Journey from St Petersburg to Moscow* might well have been welcomed by Catherine earlier in her reign as an argument in favour of enlightenment, was exiled to Siberia for publishing a book now perceived as seditious. Novikov, whose whole career had been devoted to succouring Catherine's enlightened literary enterprises, was sentenced in 1792 to 20 years' incarceration in the Schlüsselburg fortress, and suspect publications impounded in his presses and bookshops were condemned to be burnt in 1793–94.

As the new century dawned, Russian literature already possessed its martyrs, casting a dark shadow on the triumphal achievements of those pioneers who had discovered a supple literary language, new literary forms, and a confidence to break free from the restraints of foreign Neoclassical models. Russian literature had revealed the power of the individual conscience in the Russian writer.

W. Gareth Jones

Aleksandr Pushkin: From Byron to Shakespeare

It is something of a textbook topos that different national literatures have their own quite different national poets – father figures who are considered seminal or originary (the "origin without origin") to the nation's culture and world-view. What is less easily explained is how and why a certain national poet should appear on the scene precisely when he does. Why, for example, should Dante epitomize Italian Catholic culture in the 13th–14th centuries, Shakespeare Anglo-Saxon culture in the 16th–17th centuries, and Goethe German culture in the 18th–19th centuries? Clearly, the problem is more complicated than the serviceable apophthegm of genius "being in the right place at the right time", for what we are dealing with in these special instances is the combination (two-way, mutually interpenetrating) of an individual and a culture/national identity both coming of age, and knowing or sensing, they are coming of age, at the same time. The young man who may have been involved in a libellous deer-poaching incident or the wealthy senior citizen who mysteriously wills his wife a "second-best bed" becomes Shakespeare, going to his grave, as a recent biographer phrases it, "not knowing, and possibly not caring, whether *Macbeth* or *The Tempest* or *Antony and Cleopatra* ever achieved the permanence of print" (S. Schoenbaum). Great contemporaries such as Spenser or Jonson become instead, on the scales of history, foils of genius – Laertes to the Hamlet whose play-within-the-play contains them, rather than the other way around.

One ingredient in this coming-of-age formula is the awareness of the necessity of a mature inside/outside perspective: what is "ours", beginning with a national poetic tradition, has sufficient internal dignity and grandeur that it can, now for the first time, take on the challenge of the larger, supranational context (here European high culture, the classical and Judaeo-Christian traditions, and so on) as an equal. Poised on this inside/outside, ours/theirs seam, the culture, through the creations of this gifted individual, comes to value its own unique character in a manner that seems not parochial but universal. (This is what Dostoevskii was alluding to with reference to universal *otzyvchivost'*, "responsiveness", in his famous Pushkin speech.) A poet's "source material", broadly defined, including historical personages and famous characters from literature, plots, genre conventions, rules of style, rhyme schemes and metres, are no longer simply "imitated" or copied (the relation of the lesser to the greater), but are borrowed freely and boldly and reworked in accordance with this new mature outlook. Shakespeare uses Holinshed respectfully but creatively; Pushkin uses his teacher Karamzin in precisely the same way.

The present essay is an attempt to place Russia's national poet in a correct alignment along this inside/outside seam. My argument, in brief, will be that for Pushkin, Byron and Shakespeare, as creative writers and personalities, represented a crucial choice in the period 1824–26; and furthermore, that being English, these figures offered the "Frenchman" (his nickname at the Lycée) Pushkin a choice of romantic personality (*lichnost'*) versus "romantic" art, but romantic art defined in a special, non- or anti-Byronic way. Pushkin needed the Byronic personality up to a point to define his emerging authorial "I", and in a real sense he never stopped being interested in that personality and never stopped, in his typically masked, indirect way, applying the lessons of that personality to his own life and artistic career. However, at a rather precise juncture, by now pored over by literary historians, Pushkin turned from Byron to Shakespeare, and he did so not only because Byron had by then died (1824). There were other reasons, ones that had to do with Pushkin's own beginnings and points of orientation. The names of Byron and Napoleon had become inevitably linked in the young poet's mind (and indeed in those of his entire generation) since the early 1820s: the first exercising a mythical authority in the sphere of art, and the second an equally mesmerizing authority on the stage of history. Here the core text was the third canto of *Childe Harold*, where the "self-exiled" hero broods on the defeat ("thou fatal Waterloo!") of the great man "whose spirit, antithetically mixt ... [was] extreme in all things", and "quenchless evermore, preys upon high adventure". "The joining of himself [Byron] with Napoleon appealed to his self-esteem", writes Pushkin of the author-hero dynamics of *The Corsair*, and of that work's otherwise inexplicable success ("On Olin's Tragedy *Korser*" [1827, unpublished]). Pushkin had begun his career by celebrating Russia's victory over Napoleon in "Vospominaniia v Tsarskom Sele" [Reminiscences in Tsarskoe Selo] (1814), yet throughout these early years the myth of the *muzh sudeb* ("man of fate"), whose success on the battlefield coexisted in the schoolboy's mind with the prestige of 18th-century French literary models and tastes that had informed his first reading, continued to cast a powerful spell. With the death of the *echt*-romantic personality in history and art came the simultaneous urge to "de-Gallicize" his own work and its tradition and to find an inside/outside path that better accorded with the Russian language and with Russian history, thought, and culture.

Pushkin came to Byron and Shakespeare primarily through the French, and this, for a creative personality as linguistically sensitive as his, was immensely problematic. As he wrote to his friend Prince Viazemskii apropos possible linguistic indiscretions in his Byronic poem *Bakhchisaraiskii fontan* (*The Fountain of Bakhchisaray*) in December 1823, on the verge of his transition away from Byron and toward Shakespeare: "I hate to see in our primitive language traces of European affectation and French refinement. Rudeness and simplicity are more becoming to it. I preach from internal conviction, but as is my custom I write otherwise." Here we find the always independent Pushkin chafing not only at the lacquered *bon goût* of his first teachers Voltaire and Parny, but also at the salon-inspired speech, with its "feminine" circumlocutions, of the Karamzinian school, among whose senior members numbered the poet's own relatives (his francophile uncle Vasilii L'vovich, for example), and whose most brilliant graduate he was. The young poet wanted, in short, to find a way to practise what he preached.

Various Soviet Pushkin scholars, including Tomashevskii, Alekseev, and Levin, have studied aspects of the poet's "Shakespearism" with great philological care and insight. The one thing persistently missing in their treatments, however is what Pushkin felt personally, in terms of his own challenges and anxieties, as he took on first Byron and then, more crucially, Shakespeare, perhaps the central figure in the western canon. Because Pushkin is, as the famous cliché goes, "our everything" (*nashe vse*), there is the unavoidable tendency to treat him as an invulnerable god who enters into these sub- and con-textual tugs-of-war with nothing to lose. Indeed, according to Soviet "philological" argument, he borrows and makes his own effortlessly, with little or no personal investment. However, I here suggest that Pushkin consciously and a times even hotly, plays Shakespeare off the French and, in so doing, he creates an analogous niche for himself along the Russo-French cultural axis.

Pushkin and Byron

Pushkin was introduced to European romanticism largely through Byron, his older contemporary. Traditionally it has been argued that the "naive" phase of Pushkin's infatuation with Byron coincided with his southern exile (1820–24): it was in these years that the impressionable poet modeled certain aspects of his political and amorous behaviour on the cult of the alienated Byronic hero; that he wrote his narrative poems, especially the hugely popular *Kavkazskii plennik* (*The Prisoner in the Caucasus*), published in 1822, and *The Fountain of Bakhchisaray* (1824), as Russian versions of Byron's oriental tales (*The Giaour*, *The Bride of Abydos*, *The Corsair*, etc.); and that this infatuation grew increasingly complex until *Tsygany* (*The Gypsies*) 1827 – Pushkin's last *poema* based on "early" Byronic models of characterization – where the treatment of the central hero becomes so ambiguous and ironic as to lead commentators to conclude that the poet has now passed beyond Byron, and developed a polemical as opposed to pupilary relationship to him.

Much evidence to support this view can be gleaned from Pushkin's biography and from his correspondence. On the one hand, Byron was obviously the *kumir* ("idol") during this period when Pushkin, in forced physical exile (Byron's was ultimately voluntary), challenged social norms with politically incendiary verse and reputedly stormy liaisons with married women (Amalia Riznich, Karolina Sobańska, and Elizaveta Vorontsova). On the other hand, Viktor Zhirmunskii in his classic work (*Bairon i Pushkin: iz istorii romanticheskoi poemy*, 1924) has shown how Pushkin learned a great deal from the form of the Byronic verse tale: its fragmentariness (*otryvochnost'*), its creation of exotic/oriental setting, its rapid transitions and plot dynamics, its fluid relationship between hero and narrator, its telescoping of sexual conquest and military exploits – all became, *mutatis mutandis*, aspects of Pushkin's southern *poemy*. But even here Pushkin never follows Byron completely: in *The Fountain of Bakhchisaray* his female characters (Zarema and Mariia) are more complex than Byron's; and in *The Captive in the Caucasus* the narrator shows a strange, un-Byronic tendency to paint the natural beauty of the "others" (the Circassians) within the story, but to celebrate Russia's imperial right to conquer such indigenous peoples in the epilogue. By the same token, and despite the famous "Don Juan list", the small and ugly (or, as he liked to think, "satyr-like") Pushkin was an imprecise replica of the dashing Byronic lover: too trusting, too hot-tempered and given to fits of jealousy, he could be (in his own recounting) manipulated by cunning rivals or, just as likely, by the beautiful women who took pleasure in tormenting him.

As mentioned, Byron's life, like Napoleon's, had left an enduring impression on Pushkin. He needed to see that life as a finished secular *vita* ("the life of the poet"), as something he could feel himself outside or beyond, before he could move on. The nearest the reader comes to seeing Pushkin speak candidly about Byron's life is not in his correspondence, where he tends to wrestle with a friend or contemporary (Petr Viazemskii, Aleksandr Marlinskii) over the great man's significance in a kind of sibling rivalry, but in an 1835 draft of a biographical article he had planned to write based on Byron's memoirs (*Letters and Journals of Lord Byron*), published by Thomas Moore in 1830 and cited by Pushkin in their French edition. This draft is fascinating because in it Pushkin speaks warmly about aspects of the biography that are almost self-referential – that is, the parallels are so clear that the author must, at some level, be speaking about himself. (Typically, Pushkin is most self-revealing when he discusses a privileged other, and most guarded when he talks directly about himself.) For example, not only is the age and historical significance of the Byron family noteworthy, but so, more importantly, is the fact that "Byron valued his genealogy more than his literary works. A completely understandable feeling! The brilliance and the hereditary honours of his ancestors elevated the poet, while his own acquired [literary] fame brought him petty insults, ones that often humiliated the noble lord and yielded his name up to the whim of gossip." Here the Pushkin of "Moia rodoslovnaia" [My Genealogy] (1830) is both describing a former hero's struggle with his own social context from the point of view of that hero's nobility (Byron's *blagorodtsvo* [nobility], a spiritual quality related to its proud past; see Pushkin's famous line about "leaving the hero [Napoleon] his heart" in his poem "Geroi" [The Hero] 1830), and thinking about his own similar difficulties – an ancient noble family fallen on hard times, subject to gossip, intrigue, the petty insults of his *kameriunkerstvo* [his court position as "the gentleman of the bedchamber"], and so on.

Likewise, Byron's unhappy childhood and family life (mention of which would be too "humiliating" to include in one's published writing); his desultory record as a student but his love of athletics, games, and competitions; his "playful, hot-tempered, grudge-bearing" (*rezvyi, vspyl'chivyi i zlopamiatnyi*) character; his passion for the "severe beauties" of Scottish nature and his eerily unattainable first love (see Pushkin's famous *potaennaia liubov'*); and his distinguished and eccentric naval ancestors. All these biographical details are not random to Pushkin, but selected and commented on because they resonate powerfully with his own past and sense of *amour-propre*. Even the discussion in the draft of Byron's eccentric grandfather, who isolated himself in Newstead Abbey with only his housekeeper and servant for company and who whiled away the time "feeding and instructing" crickets (Pushkin's Arzamasian nickname ironically being *sverchok*, "cricket") seems almost foreordained, playfully suggestive of Pushkin's own creation Ivan Petrovich Belkin, himself a humorous *alter ego* for the poet holed away in Boldino. Last but not least, there is poetic justice to the fact that Pushkin ends this draft with reference to Byron's "wounded pride" (*iazvlennoe samoliubie*), to his fatal combination of "magnanimity" (*velikodushie*) and "unbridled passions" (*neobuzdannye strasti*), and to the limp, his physical mark of Cain, an accident of birth that he blamed on his highly-strung mother and with which she hurt him by calling him once, in a scornful tone, a "lame boy" (*khromoi mal'chishka*). Pushkin himself did not suffer any such obviously symbolic physical defect, but he was ugly and unloved as a child in ways that left their own mark of Cain. The defiant last sentence of this abandoned homage to Byron's life is as close as Pushkin will ever come to explaining his own will to succeed and turn adversity to advantage: "This very defect [of the club foot] increased [the boy's] desire to distinguish himself in all exercises demanding physical strength and agility." Within months of writing these lines Pushkin would be dying in terrible pain with D'Anthès's bullet lodged in his abdomen; when Dal', the doctor-friend overseeing the patient's last hours, suggested he cry out to relieve the agony, the poet answered, "It would be ridiculous to allow this trifle to overpower me!"

But this was Byron's *life*. Its rebellious heroism could be bracing and inspiring, a way to measure one's own actions with an eye to their place in history, but not necessarily a means of understanding the world outside oneself. "I want to understand you, / I search for meaning in you", Pushkin writes in his famous insomnia poem "Stikhi, sochinennye noch'ia vo vremia bessonitsy" ("Lines Written at Night During Insomnia") 1830. Ultimately the Byronic hero, the product of words, whether he be Childe Harold or Conrad or Manfred, did not leave Pushkin and his emerging tradition enough to work with. Indeed, the life appears to have obstructed the work, so that by approximately 1828 when Pushkin's English was sufficient to read both Byron and Shakespeare in the original, he seems to have become much more interested in the figure whose life will permanently remain in the shadows, whose every recorded action will always be contested by scholars, and whose greatest works exist in a relationship of permanent mystery to their creator's biography. To borrow a distinction first made by the Milton scholar Douglas Bush, "alienation" is a distinctly modern concept, while "isolation" is the only possible status for the outlaw hero of Renaissance drama. Macbeth is "isolated", and deservedly so, from the society whose laws he has traduced; Manfred also has terrible crimes on his conscience, but the grandeur of his titanic personality is supposed to counterbalance, if not ultimately outweigh, the cost of alienation. To put it crudely, society itself has to be sufficiently advanced and secularized in order to produce the notion of "alienation" in the first place.

Despite his remarkable sophistication, Pushkin grew impatient with the Byronic model and its magnificent egotism. Without knowing it, he sensed that Russian literature, and the world that literature reflected, would be better served by the lessons Byron's younger colleague Keats first associated with the name of Shakespeare and gathered under another heading: "At once it struck me, what quality went to form a Man of Achievement especially in Literature and which Shakespeare possessed so enormously – I mean *Negative Capability*, that is when man is capable of being in uncertainties, mysteries, doubts, without any irritable reaching after fact and reason." Pushkin could have used Keats's term when he said, in another letter to Viazemskii (June 1824) describing his hero's Achilles' heel:

> I see that ... you are sad about Byron, but I am very glad of his death, as a sublime theme for poetry. Byron's genius paled with his youth. In his tragedies, not excluding even *Cain*, he is no longer that flaming demon who created *The Giaour* and *Childe Harold*. The first two cantos of *Don Juan* are superior to the following ones. His poetry noticeably changed. He was created completely topsy-turvy; there was no gradualness in him, he suddenly matured and attained manhood, sang his song, and fell silent; and his first sounds did not return to him again.

In 1824 Pushkin could hardly have read Byron in the original with any serious understanding; moreover, it is not at all clear how carefully he has read the other cantos of *Don Juan* that he here so summarily dismisses. Even so, he has caught a fatal lack of development ("there was no gradualness in him") in all the shimmering variety. As the narrator hastens to tell the reader in the first chapter of *Evgenii Onegin*, he, as opposed to Byron, "the poet of pride" (*gordosti poet*), "can write tales in verse about something other than oneself" ("Pisat' poemy o drugom, / Kak tol'ko o sebe samom").

It has been suggested more than once that Byron's *sprezzatura* ease and brilliance, his love of "chatter" and action-delaying digression, his urbanity and even complaisant cynicism, and above all his deployment of a stanzaic form designed to give his mercurial genius free rein, were adopted by Pushkin and put to use in the greatest work of his middle phase, *Evgenii Onegin* (written 1823–31). Pushkin did not hesitate to make use of certain formal features characteristic of the later Byron of *Beppo* and *Don Juan*: his most ambitious work is named after a peripatetic hero, it is organized in a loosely expandable canto/chapter format, the narrator has a playfully foregrounded role, and so on. Pushkin did, therefore, have his eye on *Don Juan* when he first started working on his *roman v stikhakh* ("novel in verse"). But the likeness abruptly stops at the level of character/personality. Byron, particularly after 1824, is useful to Pushkin only on a comedic level (compare the links between *Beppo* and *Domik v Kolomne* [The Little House in Kolomna] 1830, also written in *ottava rima*). As Pushkin says in his correspondence, *Evgenii Onegin* is more unalike *Don Juan* than alike, its universalizing irony – a tantalizing "hovering" between the poetic and the prosaic, wonder and disappointment – veers away from Byronic satire. Likewise, the Onegin stanza is much more flexible than *ottava rima* in English (it is in effect a quicksilver combination of Petrarchan and Elizabethan sonnet), has virtually none of the latter's "burlesque" effect (poetry, especially rhymes, making fun of their doggerel sounds), and can be genuinely lyrical or *bel canto*. Onegin himself does have Byronic tendencies, beginning with an arrested personality, but is far from celebrated for them by his narrator, while Tat'iana is neither Donna Julia nor Haidée, but a genuine muse figure created out of provincial everyday life who comes to occupy a central, rather than episodic, place in the story. In sum, Byron could be of no use to Pushkin in the creation of serious, much less tragic, portraits (not even knowing English well, Pushkin sensed, as we can tell from the aforementioned quotation, how weak Byron's verse tragedies were) or in his turn toward history, broadly defined. Here his guide would have to be Shakespeare.

Pushkin and Shakespeare

Pushkin freely adopted, with breathtaking virtuosity and almost always with a playfulness that underscored the self-conscious nature of the gesture, the formal features and narrative strategies of the major literary figures of his time or of the past, such as Voltaire, Ariosto, Anacreon, Chénier, Parny, Byron, Ovid, Scott, Dante, Goethe, Batiushkov, Zhukovskii, Bogdanovich, Karamzin, and Derzhavin. But in this group Shakespeare occupies a special position, for it is my hypothesis that Pushkin's mature aspiration was to become nothing less than the Shakespeare of Russian culture. By the mid-1820s his correspondence is increasingly punctuated by admiring references to "our father Shakespeare":

> Verisimilitude of situations and truth of dialogue – here is the real rule of tragedy. (I have not read Calderón or Vega) but what a man this Shakespeare is! I can't get over it. How paltry is Byron as a tragedian in comparison with him! This Byron who never conceived but one sole character ... this Byron, then, has parceled out among his characters such-and-such a trait of his own character; his pride to one, his hate to another, his melancholy to a third, etc., and thus out of one complete, gloomy, and energetic character he has made several insignificant characters – there is no tragedy in that.
>
> (Letter to N.N. Raevskii *fils*, July 1825)

In a draft of the same letter Pushkin writes: "Read Sh[akespeare] ... he never fears compromising his hero/character [*deistvuiushchee litso*]; he has him speak with all the naturalness of life [*so vseiu zhiznennoi neprinuzhdennost'iu*] because he is certain that at the appropriate time and place he can make that hero find a language consistent with his character".

As already suggested, however, these first ecstatic comments about Shakespeare were mediated by their French source: the 1821 Paris edition (Chez Ladvocat) of the *Oeuvres complètes de Shakespeare*. This popular edition, based on the 18th-century prose translations of Letourneur that François Guizot and Amedée Pichot had recently revised, came supplied with a 150-page essay by Guizot on Shakespeare's life and times that Pushkin studied thoroughly as he proceeded to read the poetry and plays. As the Guizot essay was Pushkin's first and most immediate introduction to Shakespeare and his historical-literary context, its importance as a document can not be overstated. (There were other sources that Pushkin used to become better acquainted with Shakespeare, including a French translation of August Schlegel's *Vorlesungen über dramatische Kunst und Literatur* (*A Course of Lectures on Dramatic Art and Literature*) and Madame de Staël's *De la littérature considérée dans ses rapports avec les institutions sociales* (*The Influence of Literature upon Society*). The focus here is on Guizot and the "La Harpe/Voltaire" tradition of French Shakespeare criticism represented by him.) This is the same historian Guizot, author of *Histoire générale de la civilisation en Europe* (1828), that Pushkin would take issue with in his 1830 review(s) of Nikolai Polevoi's *Istoriia russkogo naroda* [A History of the Russian People] (1829–33): by slavishly following Guizot and the latter's notion of historical determinism leading inevitably to "European" (read French-dominated) Enlightenment and the emergence of the *tiers-état*, Polevoi (himself a commoner) not only insulted the memory of a better historian (Karamzin, who taught first and foremost respect for one's past), but fatally misread the unique, saving difference of Russian history – its *sluchainost'* (its "chance" or unpredictable, random quality) – that which distinguishes it from the neat French model. It was these same Euro- and Franco-centric assumptions about the shape of history and national genius in Guizot's otherwise informative and admiring essay on Shakespeare that must have made Pushkin pause to contemplate his own fate, during his northern exile in Mikhailovskoe (1824–26). Buried in the woods, looked after only by his ageing nanny and the "oak groves", he again made a virtue of necessity – the thoughts of flight abroad that had been his farewell to the south (for example the watery escape route and Byronic and Napoleonic heroics of "K moriu" [To the Sea] 1824) became his figurative greeting to the Russian historical imagination, the Shakespeare- and Karamzin-inspired "romantic tragedy" *Boris Godunov* (written 1824–25, published 1831).

Guizot's essay came with its own cultural bias, which the "responsive" (*otzyvchivyi*) Pushkin would have noticed immediately, and seen as turned on himself, the "barbarous"

Russian. Not only would he have to find the "real" Shakespeare through the Gallicizing prism, he would in his own work have to project a "Russianness" that was smart enough, and self-aware enough to stave off such reductionist thrusts. Guizot writes, for example, that "We live in the time of civilization and foresight, in which everything has its place and its order, in which the destiny of each individual is determined by circumstances more or less imperious". This must have sounded absolutely absurd (and condescending) to Pushkin, who in his own position would have felt very far from a society and history "where everything has its place". Furthermore, Guizot goes on to explain the phenomenon of Shakespeare by alluding to two types of poet – the one who develops logically, as an extension of this orderly civilization: "A poet begins by being a poet; he who is to become one knows it almost from his infancy"; and the one who develops "in difficult and the most vulgar of times", as an extension of nature, or as Guizot seemed to be saying, a brute, uncivilized man ("the poet that forms the only nature"). Shakespeare – and Pushkin himself – clearly belong to the second group with its raw, unpredictable genius and its "fougueuse [impetuous] imagination". Lacking "the universal and profound imprint of Roman civilization", Great Britain became a melting pot of non-distinguishable conqueror and conquered (Saxons, Danes, Normans, and so on) – all "également barbares"; and whereas the Franks found in Gaul a well-established Roman Catholic clergy capable of modifying the institutions, ideas, and way of life of the victors, the Christian priest of the Saxons "was Saxon himself, long since vulgar and barbarous, like his congregation".

The point, as one imagines Pushkin reading such lines, is not that Great Britain (or Russia for that matter) *is* civilized by European standards during these early centuries prior to the appearance of its national genius, but that its "lack" cannot be judged from the vantage of French "fullness" (romantic historiography, clichés about elemental genius, and so on). The following lines in particular can be perceived as a challenge to a great Russian writer who also happens to possess a "native" command of French: "Thus the young civilization of the North grows, in England, in simplicity as well as with the energy of its own nature, independent of borrowed forms and of the foreign vitality received elsewhere from the old civilization of the South". Pushkin, representing another "civilisation du Nord", would use Shakespeare to show not only how "unsimple" was his own genius, but also how it could borrow the forms of other European cultures, including the French, in a way that was by no means "natural" or unconscious. Many of the arguments that Guizot makes in his long essay would be taken up by Pushkin precisely as a challenge – how to turn these potential anomalies or "defects" of Shakespearean dramaturgy (such as the shattering of classical unities, the mixing of "pure" comedic and tragic genre expectations, the undermining of consistent character "types") into the productive principle of a new *Russian* theatre liberated from French Neoclassical principles. Guizot, however, would see the hypocritical essence ("la fourberie menaçante de l'hypocrite") of Molière's *Tartuffe* as confirmation of its classical heritage and a source of national pride. Pushkin would point out the artificiality, and the lack of verisimilitude in that notion of character:

> In Molière the hypocrite [Tartuffe] chases after the wife of his benefactor, while acting the hypocrite; takes the estate under protection, while acting the hypocrite; asks for a glass of water, while acting the hypocrite. In Shakespeare the hypocrite [Angelo in *Measure for Measure*] pronounces sentence with vainglorious severity, but fairly; justifies his cruelty with the profound reasoning of a statesman; seduces innocence with powerful, attractive sophistries, not a ridiculous combination of piety and cheap charm [*volokitstvo*].
>
> ("Table-Talk")

In short, while Guizot has many positive things to say about Shakespeare, his tone and his ready-made juxtapositions (such as French-English, classical-popular, orderly-chaotic) continue in a lesser key the earlier generalizations of La Harpe, who in commenting about Letourneur's translations seemed perplexed that a people having such exemplars as Corneille, Racine, and Voltaire could take seriously the works of "un auteur barbare" whose "monstrous" plays are, despite patches of talent, bereft of common sense and plausibility. It was presumably not only the more notorious statements of La Harpe (and Voltaire) but also those of Guizot that Pushkin had in mind when he wrote, in a note of 1832, that "It is well-known that the French are the most anti-poetic people". What he meant by this was that Shakespeare was the essence both of true "poetry" (imaginative empathy) and true "historical" consciousness, that the French tendency to find an elegant, abstracting argument or "plot" (*vymysel*) for everything was inadequate to explain Shakespeare (and hence "unpoetic", in the sense of ungifted, imperceptive), and that, as far as Russia's troubled history was concerned, including the 1825 Decembrist Uprising, Pushkin would try to approach it, as he urged his friend Anton Del'vig to do, "with the glance of Shakespeare".

The extent to which Shakespeare informs the works of the second half of Pushkin's career, beginning with *Boris Godunov*, is truly astonishing: naming only those with an obvious Shakespeare connection, one finds *Graf Nulin* (*Count Nulin*), *Arap Petra Velikogo* (*The Blackamoor of Peter the Great*), *Poltava*, *Malen'kie tragedii* (*The Little Tragedies*), *Povesti Belkina* (*The Tales of Belkin*), and *Andzhelo*. Three aspects of Pushkin's mature "borrowing" of Shakespeare are noteworthy for our purposes. First, the life itself, although gleaned by Pushkin from Guizot and other sources, seems to have been of limited interest, as opposed to the case of Byron. Where certain parallels could be used and where the poetic narrator (subject) and romantic hero (object) formed a seam that was the essence of romantic irony ("life is a work of art and the poet its creator"), Shakespeare could not be "got at", and this turned out to be liberating. What was, in modern and postmodern terms, a theatrical metaphor in Byron, something originating in the words and role-playing of the speaker, was in Shakespeare nothing more or less than a fact of life. "All the world's a stage", yes, but that stage was not perceived as a figure of speech. There was no way to join up, other than through sheer speculation, the voice inside the poems (too hermetic) or inside the plays (too much belonging to the "voice zones" of individual characters) with the voice (virtually unrecorded) and the actions outside them. Second, Pushkin is principally interested in the lessons of Shakespearean character, especially verisimilitude and the "unpredictability" of life, but what is striking is that this newly flexible, utterly un-Byronic notion of character coexists with a powerful appreciation of "classical" form (here Pushkin's roots in 18th-century French culture would never be fully transcended). And third, the oppositions of poetry/prose and history/fiction, so crucial to Pushkin's later works, would now be filtered through a Shakespearean lens as well: Shakespeare's magical ability to blend, within the covers of one play, the antithetical stylistic registers of a Master Elbow and an Angelo/Isabella as well as the forms of poetry and prose (metre, rhyme, etc.), all of which had been lost in the Letourneur translations, would find an analogue in some of Pushkin's greatest poems, stories, and plays.

Of all the works that demonstrate Pushkin's new-found admiration for Shakespeare, perhaps none is more bold, more "epochal" in its inspiration, than *Boris Godunov*. The play is a goldmine of reinvented and thoroughly "russified" Shakespearean characters, episodes, vying levels of diction, genre telescoping (tragedy and history), and spirited dialogue with sources (especially Karamzin's 10th and 11th volumes of *Istoriia gosudarstva rossiiskogo* [The History of the Russian State], which had appeared in March 1824). Pushkin the poet clearly knew what he was doing:

> Being completely certain that the outmoded forms of our theatre were in need of reshaping, I organized my tragedy according to the system of Our Father Shakespeare, and I sacrificed at his altar two of the classical unities [time and place], while barely preserving the third [action]. In addition to these famous three unities there is another, that of style [*edinstvo sloga*], about which the French critical literature is silent (probably because they assume its necessity cannot be contested) ... [Here too] I followed this very seductive example [of Shakespeare].

(Draft Letter to the publisher of *Moskovskii vestnik*, 1828). Thus, in Boris's staged rejection of the crown one can readily see echoes of *Julius Caesar* and *Richard III*; in the cynical comments of Shuiskii and Vorotynskii that open Pushkin's drama against the backdrop of the artificially wailing *narod*, a recasting of the tribunes Flavius and Marullus and the benighted commoners of *Julius Caesar*; in the Pretender's light-hearted ability to recreate himself anew in different roles and with different addressees, a play on the Hal character of *Henry IV* Parts 1 and 2, just as his disarmingly sound, saddle-cradling sleep on the losing field of battle is a playful inversion of Richard III's famous "A horse! a horse! my kingdom for a horse!"; and in the famous love scene between the Pretender and Marina Mniszek at the fountain, a return to the balcony scene of *Romeo and Juliet*, but with this powerfully ironic difference – Marina is not a swooning, innocent Juliet, but a scheming, utterly cool Lady Macbeth, and so on. The connections are rich and almost endlessly multiplying. As Pushkin brought these characters to life from the pages of Karamzin, he looked at them all "with the glance of Shakespeare" – he did not hold them to an overarching plot (the dramatist's idea of how history "exfoliated"), but made them all full-blooded personalities, with often conflicting motivations, and with words that constantly shifted their meanings depending on the *Realpolitik* of context.

But not even Pushkin could create the equivalent of Shakespearean drama in a vacuum. That he used the French as a negative point of departure, but still used them, is the real marvel of this new invention of Russian "romantic tragedy". For what Pushkin achieved, for all his sincere statements about dispensing with the unities, was a remarkably classical concept of form played off against a dynamic new Shakespearean understanding of character. With regard to the formal aspects of the play, Pushkin was typically self-concealing while appearing to be self-revealing: he says in the same draft letter quoted above that "I replaced the honourable alexandrine with blank verse, I demeaned myself in several scenes with despised prose, and I did not divide my tragedy into acts." However, as a recent scholar, I. Ronen, has posited following D. Blagoi and others, the play is constructed in an elegant mirror symmetry, with the themes (Russia/Poland, east/west, secular love/primitive patriarchy, legitimacy/imposture, death of children/dynastic succession, and so on), characters (Boris/Pretender), and episodes of its first ten scenes lined up, pyramid-like, with those of the last ten (14–23), leaving the scenes 11–13, those involving Poland and culminating with the Pretender's declaration of love to Marina at the fountain – as the peak of the pyramid and the point at which all fortunes turn. But this numbering has to be added by the reader: it is not there in the text. In other words, Pushkin has consciously removed those formal markers of the historical tragedy, such as mention of large and small divisions (acts/scenes) or listing of dramatis personae, that draw attention to their artificialty, their *staged* quality. Why? Because he is bringing history to life, actually not metaphorically – the ultimate Shakespearean magic. At the same time, however, his work is subtly structured within a framework of homeostatic tensions and releases that reveals the strength of an opposing tradition – the French Neoclassical.

The centre of Pushkin's play and the height of its romantic tension is the fountain scene, where the Pretender is forced by circumstances to decide between two roles – the resilient Hal who is Henry V *in statu nascendi* and the pining Romeo who longs to hear words of love from the lips of his Juliet. This is indeed the juncture where the love plot and the political plot come together and vie for supremacy, where issues of erotic role-playing and "power" blur into those of martial prowess and legitimate right to govern. This is also the point where Pushkin's understanding of Shakespearean disinterestedness or "negative capability" comes most to the fore. "Thanks to the French", writes Pushkin in the previously cited draft letter, "we do not understand how a dramatic author can reject his own mode of thought [*obraz myslei*] in order to transpose himself to the age that he imagines." Thus the genuinely romantic is not the filtering through the thought patterns of intervening generations and cultures (here the French), but the attempt to shed those patterns in order to come as close as possible to re-entering the still "open" and future-laden experiences of a former age. Historical personages are not actors on some dramatist's or director's stage; at the time they speak and act, there is no denouement, other than their own fears and desires, pulling them forward into the future.

In this respect, the fountain scene has been both brilliantly read and, in my opinion, misread by recent critics of a postmodern stance. Monika Greenleaf, for example, argues for a provocative homology between Hal's "theatrical talent", where his "princely assumption" is that "everything is as counterfeit to his own behaviour", and the Pretender's "understanding of the contingency of his being" – "There *is* no referential basis for Dmitry's language ... His pure verbal invention is their [the Pretender's and Marina's] entrée into history". Likewise, Juliet's famous "What's in a name?" becomes the deadly ironic play with the Pretender's different names in this erotic duel. However, where Greenleaf and the postmoderns err is in their treatment of the theatrical imagery and role-playing as metaphorical *tout court*, as linguistic habiliments that can be donned risk-free – worn (thus the emphasis on "fashion") for the duration of the performance and then placed calmly among the other costumes and stage decorations. But Pushkin and Shakespeare lived in worlds where life and language were continually filled with risk. In the fountain scene Pushkin was not only embedding some of his own very vulnerable feelings about strong, calculating women who use their beauty to gain power outside the domestic sphere; he was also showing the full romantic potential of the Pretender's character, who becomes a kind of "poet in life/ history". When the Pretender finally understands the limits of the crisis he has cast himself into by trying to reach Marina through the "truth", self-exposure, and "honest" love, he gathers himself together and makes his most powerful speech: "The shade of [Ivan] the Terrible adopted me, / Named me Dimitrii from the grave, / Incited people around me / And doomed Boris to be sacrificed to me / – I am the Tsarevich". Two things draw attention away from a postmodern (or "post-Byronic") reading and towards a "Shakespearean" one: first, the Pretender breaks into rhymed verse (*usynovíla + nareklá + vozmutíla + obreklá + tsarévich ia*) as he declares these lines – these are the formal markers of his sudden rising in grandeur in Marina's and the audience's eyes, and Pushkin never questions the ontological reality of language, its ability to say what it means; and second, for the only time in the scene, the voice "proudly" (*gordo*) delivering these words is named as "Dmitrii", and not as the *Samozvanets* ("Pretender"). In other words, at this point the Pretender fully assumes the identity of the Tsarevich, not on a stage he can walk away from but in life, in history, with all the risks attendant on that move (one day in the future his ashes will be shot from the Kremlin back in the direction of Poland). And when he does this, Marina backs down for now she respects and fears him, which is her condition (since she understands that her beauty and his "love" are worth nothing in the abstract) for any amorous reciprocity in the first place. If Pushkin has not shown how this erotic battle actually happened (if it ever did), he has shown how it could have happened, and he has shown brilliantly how the different "Pretenders" ("lover", "fugitive monk", "tsarevich", and so on) can coexist fully in one very tense and pivotal "historical" situation.

In conclusion, this Shakespearean notion of disinterestedness in character portrayal coupled with a powerful, though never foregrounded, appreciation of inhering form, stayed with Pushkin throughout the remainder of his career. On the level of character, for example, we find the Othello-Desdemona situation in Mariia's inexplicable and ultimately self-destructive passion for the older Mazepa in *Poltava* (a theme that the author of course knew in his family history – see for example *The Blackamoor of Peter the Great*, and his own choice of bride). Likewise, several of the characters and situations in *The Little Tragedies* suggest Shakespearean sources and transpositions: in "Skupoi rytsar'" ("The Avaricious Knight") Pushkin has split Shylock's trade and passion between the parodic Jew (*zhid*) and the noble baron, just as in "Motsart i Sal'eri" ("Mozart and Salieri") he has given us an Iago figure in the deeply and mysteriously offended Salieri, but one transferred from the sphere of martial skill (Iago is angered because he has been passed over by Othello for Cassio – "mere prattle without practice is all his soldiership") to that of art. So too might one see the central plot device of "Kamennyi gost'" ("The Stone Guest") – Don Juan's most "impossible" (and thus maximally arousing) suit yet, that of the pious widow Donna Anna, whose husband he has slain – as a reprise of the great wooing scene in *Richard III*, when Richard, Duke of Gloucester offers the weapon and bares his breast to the newly widowed Anne, whose feelings, because she believes the villain's ploy ("Your beauty was the cause of that effect [the killing of her husband Edward]"), go from fierce invective to the beginnings of love in the space of a single scene. One might even go so far as to speculate that Pushkin's famous "descent to prose" in *The Tales of Belkin* is a playful reversal, or "de-tragification", of several of the most famous Shakespearean plots: the outer limits of revenge in "Vystrel" ("The Shot") [*Othello*]; a storm-induced case of mistaken identity among young lovers and a strangely magical fate in "Metel'" ("The Blizzard") [*The Tempest*]; graveside humour and metapoetic thoughts involving Eros and Thanatos in "Grobovshchik" ("The Coffin-Maker") [*Hamlet*]; a beloved daughter who "betrays" a proud and vulnerable father in "Stantsionnyi smotritel'" ("The Stationmaster") [*King Lear*], and a feud between two families whose children are carrying on a secret romance in "Baryshnia-Krest'ianka" ("The Peasant Lady") [*Romeo and Juliet*]. The essence of all these various inversions, however, is that human potential is always greater than the ability of any pre-ordained plot to contain it. Thus, in the "Little Tragedies", at the centre of whose title page Pushkin sketched the head of Shakespeare, we are constantly confronted with the contradictions: a knight (noble) who is covetous (ignoble), a guest (a human presence invited in) that is stone (immobile, inhuman), and so on. By the same token, as Pushkin shifted to prose and the language of everyday life, he wanted to focus on those characters who step out of the roles assigned to them by the "plots" of western literature – the "eternally fortunate" count of "The Shot" must now live with a sense of guilt and dishonour (he has taken an unearned shot against Silvio); the "prodigal daughter" Dunia of "The Stationmaster" does succeed at escaping her biblically-imposed destiny, but at the cost of hurting her father, whose death she comes to mourn at the end.

Last but not least, the Angelo that Guizot and his tradition saw as flawed and inconsistent is in Pushkin's work of the same name one of the greatest, and psychologically realistic, characters in world literature. That this epitome of justice, rectitude, and the law could "fall" for Isabella's virtue, just as Isabella's passionate chastity could in the end "rise" to make a case for mercy on behalf of her tormentor, seemed to Pushkin the very essence human plot potential: neither honour nor mercy has meaning outside the other. One can easily imagine, for example, the poet who urged the new tsar (Nicholas) to be lenient toward his Decembrist friends in "Stansy" [Stanzas] (1826), and who named as one of his singular virtues in his great valedictory poem "Ia pamiatnik sebe vozdvig nerukotvornyi" [I have erected a monument not made by hand] (1836) the fact that he "called for mercy toward the fallen", remembering the eloquent pleas for mercy delivered by Isabella and her sister character Portia from *The Merchant of Venice*. It was not by chance that a brave virgin (Masha Mironova), whose "honour" is at stake at various points in the story and whose call for mercy before the Empress Catherine on behalf of a tainted loved one (Petr Grinev) saves the day, becomes the prosaic muse figure of Pushkin's last major work, the Scottian historical romance *Kapitanskaia dochka* (*The Captain's Daughter*) 1836. It was precisely this exceptional gesture of mercy, from a position of moral and/or political authority, that broke the predictable form of justice and thereby gave it vitality. By the end of his life Pushkin had left a Russian legacy of Shakespearism never to be duplicated but which took time to be understood and appreciated. He had borrowed without imitating; he had written of imagined others without speaking "only about himself"; he had passed beyond Byron to a salutary self-consciousness that would, as the "origin without origins", feed his tradition indefinitely.

DAVID M. BETHEA

The Classic Russian Novel

The classic Russian novel comprises the major Russian novels published between 1830 and 1880. They form a body of writing in the genre that can be shown to have certain specific characteristics that we nowadays think of as "Russian". These works are classic not in the sense of any "classic-romantic" opposition, but in the straightfoward sense of being accepted as standard or definitive both within the framework of Russian literature and in terms of its influence. They are the works of Turgenev, Tolstoi, and Dostoevskii and their immediate predecessors, or near-contemporaries, Pushkin, Lermontov, Gogol', and Goncharov. In short, barely more than half-a-dozen men of outstanding genius, born in the 30 years between 1799 and 1828, created what we can now regard as the Russian novel. In the case of Tolstoi and Dostoevskii their achievement has become traditionally so associated with perfection in the genre that it has earned the Russian novel the distinction of being considered in relation to classical norms of the Homeric, of Attic Tragedy, of Menippean satire, the medieval mystery play, and so on. Their novels have come to be regarded with the same esteem as the classical works of world literature and for this reason alone deserve to be treated as classics in their own right.

It has been a commonplace of criticism to talk about "realism" in relation to the Russian novel. Soviet treatments tended to stress such "realism" in a socio-political *dirigiste* spirit to the exclusion of practically any other kind of approach. Undoubtedly valuable for its historicity, such a blinkered treatment found difficulty dealing with the greatest works of Russian literature, such as Dostoevskii's major novels and the religious, anti-revolutionary ideas, not to mention the aberrant human behaviour, contained in them. Restricted by the official tenets of socialist realism, scholarly Soviet treatments of the Russian novel were usually so uninspired that they left plenty of room for other approaches to flourish in the non-Soviet world.

Curiously enough, this led to a diktat of an opposite kind. Emphasis came to be placed on such issues as polyphonism (*pace* Bakhtin) in a spirit that tended to regard the polyphonic or "multi-voiced" novel as somehow superior to the single-voiced novel, with its obvious authorial presence. Formalist considerations, concentration on specific features of the Tolstoian or Dostoevskian novel, quasi-structuralist approaches, no doubt valuable and illuminating in their own right, tended to be as limited in their appraisal of the Russian novel as the politically prescriptive emphasis on "realism".

There is no doubt that the novel in its Russian context reflected social issues, portrayed heroes and heroines characteristic of Russian society, and came to play a more important role than its European counterparts in giving expression to a range of substantive moral issues and choices facing the society of its time. It existed and evolved in a climate of official government censorship largely unknown in the west. Yet it passed through the crucible of that censorship and emerged so strengthened and assertive of its own right to govern opinion that it made censorship seem a futile official irrelevancy.

It is worth pointing out that the creators of the classic Russian novel were for the most part privileged members of Russian society who were not in any radical sense anti-establishment. They were all patriots. They all enjoyed the right to travel, whether in Russia (excluding, naturally, the enforced travel of exile) or in Europe (with the exception of Pushkin and Lermontov); and the freedom to travel in Europe was vitally enriching to Gogol', Turgenev, and Goncharov, if for very different reasons, whereas for Dostoevskii and Tolstoi it had a profound influence in stimulating and defining their work and their attitudes. Intellectually and culturally all those who helped to create the classic Russian novel wrote as Russians, both deeply conscious of being part of a European heritage and aware that they wrote for a Europeanized, if not for a specifically European, readership.

They wrote to justify as well as to expose. They were concerned more with portraiture than plotting, more with ideas than adventure narratives. They made reality seem strange or "defamiliarized" (as in Tolstoi's case) or explored metaphysical reality (as in Dostoevskii's epileptic "penetration of the real") by a propensity for assuming, above all, that fact and fiction need not be distinct entities.

The classic Russian novel asserted detachment as its prerogative from the very start. This was Pushkin's gift to Russian literature. Though always urged in one or another direction by partisan critics, the greatest of the Russian 19th-century novelists asserted a freedom to bear their own witness. A prophetic role may gradually have obtruded, lending the classic Russian novel near-biblical powers of moral edification; yet its penetrative honesty and its humanistic concerns are the ultimate touchstone by which its greatness is to be judged.

Pushkin's novel in verse *Evgenii Onegin* (written 1823–31) has to be regarded as the first Russian novel and is thematically of a classic simplicity. Pushkin, as narrator and first-person participant, may never be absent from his work but he contrives throughout to maintain a historian's detachment in telling the simple story of his hero Onegin's relationship with his heroine, Tat'iana. Places, seasons, foods, pastimes, and activities seem to have a verifiable contemporary authenticity.

As a novel in verse, inspired by Byron's *Don Juan*, *Evgenii Onegin* must seem derivative; yet it achieved a uniquely formulaic role in determining the evolution of the classic Russian novel. Concerned principally with portraiture, through the medium of Pushkin's delightful stanzas that have such a beautifully sustained, dance-like vitality, the novel opens with an elaborate picture of Onegin's daily life as a typical St Petersburg dandy. He is exceptional only in suffering from Byronic disillusionment. He therefore leaves St Petersburg and moves to the country, a stranger to its ways. Here he encounters the pensive, impressionable Tat'iana. She falls in love with him, apparently confusing him with the hero of a romantic novel, and he, in rejecting her love, reveals himself as cold, superfluous, and dangerous.

After killing his close friend, the young poet Lenskii, in a duel, Onegin departs on travels that eventually bring him back to St Petersburg four years later where he finds Tat'iana married and an admired adornment of the *beau monde*. After falling desperately in love with her, he is humiliated to learn that she, having discovered so much about him and his world, can speak with a definitive authority about her own duty of fidelity as a wife and in so doing assert a morality clearly superior to the norm prevailing in high society.

The last meeting between hero and heroine provides both a dramatic climax and a final moral test of the hero's worth. In so doing it establishes the classic Russian novel as one characterized by dramatic encounters in which the truth of people's lives is suddenly laid bare.

In the prose work *Geroi nashego vremeni* (*A Hero of Our Time*) 1840, Lermontov used his dramatic sense to explore a similar kind of Byronic portraiture but in a manner that was less detached, more subjective than Pushkin's; the "novel", comprising the linked short stories "Bela", "Maksim Maksimych", "Taman", "Princess Mary", and "The Fatalist", was termed a "chain of stories" by its author. The hero Pechorin was intended as a successor to Onegin but has much in him that might be ascribed directly to Lermontov himself. The autobiographical impulse, though, is cleverly concealed by the use of three narrators; and the work falls into two parts: the first two stories offer a portrayal of Pechorin seen through others' eyes; the final three stories comprise Pechorin's "journal" and aspire to give a private picture.

A discernible air of irony and mystification surrounds this "hero of our time" despite Lermontov's claim that it is a portrait "composed of the vices of our entire generation in their full development". Though supposedly offering such a generalized portrayal of a Byronic type, the work diagnoses the dilemma of its hero at a much deeper level. Man as the plaything of fate or master of his destiny is the issue that forms the psychological and ideological focus of Pechorin's activity. Crippled morally – or so he claims – he compensates with a defiance of law and convention that pits him against society and against fate.

Clearly a psychological study, and full of intriguing complexities, particularly in its chronology, Lermontov's "novel" has little coherence beyond its purpose as portraiture. The enfranchising of the ordinary, the non-Byronic, in the Russian novel, its "democratizing" in a loose sense, occurred first through the comic, word-rich genius of Gogol'. *Mertvye dushi* (*Dead Souls*) 1842, can lay claim to be the first true prose novel in Russian literature even though Gogol' entitled it a "poem" (partly for censorship reasons).

A picaresque work, in that it describes the travels of its hero, Chichikov, in search of "dead souls" (that is, the serfs still subject to poll tax though they had died since the last census), the novel owes much to theatrical principles of presentation in depicting the essentially comic encounters between the hero and the respective serf-owners. Each encounter occurs within a grotesquely detailed setting, a miniature world of incongruously characterizing possessions, and the humour largely derives from ignorance of the visitor's intentions. It is a classic work of comedy, often deviously satirical, both in its characterization and in its tendency to digressions and extended metaphors.

Suggestively, as if in the corners of its Bosch-like vision of rural Russia, the novel enfranchises hosts of partially glimpsed characters. But the foreground grotesques – Korobochka, Manilov, Nozdrev, Sobakevich, Pliushkin, the serf-owners whom the hero visits – have a dreadful ordinariness and *poshlost'* (Pushkin's definition of them, so Gogol' claimed, meaning vulgar acquisitiveness). None is more evidently characteristic of this than Chichikov himself, even though he may be mistaken for Antichrist, Napoleon or a certain mysterious Captain Kopeikin.

Gogol' himself might also be mistaken for a great comic genius, but he wished to be mistaken for a prophet of a new, morally rejuvenated Russia. So at the magnificent climax of *Dead Souls*, Chichikov in his carriage drawn by a troika of horses is transformed into a vision of Russia racing into the future. At this point the classic Russian novel came of age and acquired purpose as well as stature.

During the 1840s prose became the dominant medium in Russian writing. The purpose prescribed for it by the leading critic of the decade, Vissarion Belinskii – to offer an exposure and diagnosis of the ills of society (of which serfdom was the most conspicuous and the most proscribed by the censorship) – found reflection in only two works that could be seriously called finished novels: Aleksandr Herzen's *Kto vinovat?* (*Who is to Blame?*) and Ivan Goncharov's *Obyknovennaia istoriia* (*A Common Story*) both of 1847. Herzen's *Who is to Blame?* is a study of the superfluous intellectual and the damage such a type can inflict. Of greater literary value is Goncharov's sardonic, understated portrait of an ordinary young nobleman from the provinces, callow in his romanticism, who receives a lesson in the harsh realities of life from his uncle, a prominent St Petersburg bureaucrat and learns it so well that he ends up more self-seeking and cynical even than his mentor.

In the immediate post-Crimean War period the writer most responsible for enlarging the scope of the Russian novel was Ivan Turgenev. Although he had made his name initially through his famous sketches of rural life, *Zapiski okhotnika* (*Sketches from a Hunter's Album*), it was after being exiled to his country estate for the publication of his work in a separate edition (1852) that he turned to writing novels. *Rudin* (1856), his first work in the genre, portrayed an eloquent intellectual, a so-called "superfluous man" of the 1840s, who fails to live up to his words when faced by the strong-minded young heroine Natal'ia. Rudin is portrayed, for all his weakness, as gifted with an enthusiasm for ideas. In 1860 Turgenev added an epilogue in which his "eternal wanderer" of a hero dies the death of a revolutionary on a Paris barricade in 1848.

The novel has theatrical antecedents and is so composed that each of the principal characters is introduced with an explanatory biography of some sort and placed in a particular setting. The only unknown quantity is the hero who arrives (like Onegin) as a stranger from outside. As portraiture, the novel explores the hero's meaning in socio-political terms: as a cosmopolitan advocate of western ideas, and also in terms of his emotional fallibility.

As a conjuror of atmosphere Turgenev had no equal. He succeeded in evoking the world of the Russian country estate so perfectly that no other writer has surpassed him. In his second novel, *Dvorianskoe gnezdo* (*A Nest of the Gentry*) 1859, he produced a picture of a summer idyll as backdrop to the sad story of Lavretskii's return to his gentry home after a self-imposed exile in Europe and the failure of his love for Liza, a religious heroine who may be said to epitomize a spiritual ideal that Turgenev, ever the agnostic, could admire but never share.

The purposeful role of the classic Russian novel found expression in Turgenev's case as a chronicle of the Russian intelligentsia. In Goncharov's second novel, his masterpiece, *Oblomov* (1859), the portrait of the hero epitomized the indolence and stagnation of the nobility against which the intelligentsia had to struggle. Immured more firmly in his theatrically elaborate setting than any Gogolian character, coddled in his St Petersburg apartment by his ineptly devoted servant and the self-delusion of his patrician idleness, Oblomov is a masterly – not to say loving – study of a disease, diagnosed by the radical critic Nikolai Dobroliubov as "Oblomovism" (his famous critique "Chto takoe Obmolovshchina?" ["What is Oblomovism?"]). Although in part a love-story, the novel is chiefly memorable as the greatest monument to sloth in literature. The efforts of the ostensible "positive" hero, Shtolts, to persuade Oblomov to lead a fuller life seem ultimately meaningless when compared with the child-like purity of heart and soul that Oblomov succeeds in retaining to the end.

But the critical clamour for positive images in literature could not be ignored. Turgenev responded in his third novel, *Nakanune* (*On the Eve*) 1860 – the title anticipates the Emancipation of the Serfs scheduled for 1861 – by portraying his heroine Elena as unable to choose between her two Russian suitors since neither is sufficiently positive for her. She finally chooses a Bulgarian patriot and accompanies him to Venice where he dies. Less satisfactory in structure than his previous novels, it offered the first major study of a heroine capable of renouncing her heritage and liberating herself even if the consequences were tragic.

The image of the liberated woman became central to the seminal propagandist novel *Chto delat'?* (*What is to Be Done?*) 1863, by Nikolai Chernyshevskii, a work exemplifying the need for literature (and art generally) to be a "textbook on life" and therefore to serve a recognizable civic purpose. Banned immediately after publication, the novel's Utopian socialist vision of a humanity liberated through co-operative work may seem comic in its earnestness, but it undoubtedly concentrated minds by projecting an image of revolutionary change.

Turgenev picked up on such an image in his greatest novel, *Ottsy i deti* (*Fathers and Sons*) 1862, in which he created the figure of the nihilist Bazarov. Bazarov may not be the portrait of a revolutionary in a strictly political sense. He is radical only in his cast of mind and social attitude as one who abrogates everything that is not justifiable according to the laws of the natural sciences. The figure of Bazarov has never ceased to arouse controversy. A series of different settings serve as a means of gradually revealing important facets of the hero, his ideological significance, for instance, his romanticism and, in the end, his flawed humanity. Though a materialist, an extrovert, Quixotic in his desire for action, he is forced to acknowledge an introspective, Hamlet-like quality in himself when he falls in love with a wealthy widow. Returning eventually to his parental home once his attempts to find love have failed, he dies from typhus poisoning contracted after performing an autopsy.

Bazarov, representative of the younger generation, proves victorious in a ridiculous duel with his older opponent, Pavel Kirsanov, a dandyish anglicized Russian of Turgenev's generation. Even though his own destiny was to be that of a tragic hero who dies with his potential unrealized, Bazarov's outspoken, plebeian honesty contains a Promethean arrogance in the name of science that could imply root-and-branch Jacobinism as well as disdain for the established order. His nihilism might seem ultimately to contain a challenge to divine justice in the name of human freedom.

No Russian novelist was more conscious of this aspect of nihilism than Fedor Dostoevskii. His major novels explore it as an obsessive pathology afflicting the Russian intelligentsia, yet always in the light of a dramatic debate between opposed ideas *pro* and *contra*.

His first treatment of these issues took the form of a monologue attributable to an "underground man" (in Part I of *Zapiski iz podpol'ia* [*Notes from Underground*] 1864). The author of this profoundly paradoxical work asserts that man is not naturally inclined to act rationally in his own best interests and that he demonstrates his individuality by the exercise of his caprice or free will.

The *Notes from Underground* open the way, ideologically speaking, to Dostoevskii's first important achievement as a novelist, the portrayal of the drop-out student Raskol'nikov, hero of his first masterpiece, *Prestuptenie i nakazanie* (*Crime and Punishment*) 1866. During some two weeks of a hot St Petersburg summer Raskol'nikov murders a shrewish old moneylender and her sister and succeeds in evading suspicion until an examining magistrate puts pressure on him and the young prostitute, Sonia, who loves Raskol'nikov and eventually persuades him to confess.

Why did he commit murder? The novel analyzes his motives and for the purpose makes dramatic use of a unity of time, place, and action in the novel form through Raskol'nikov's own sick, hallucinatory apprehension of reality. There is no doubt that this is a crowded, fetid, urban ant-heap of a world, packed with "voices" and given a baroquely detailed authenticity. But the "crime" is what excites and horrifies. It is a planned, deliberate killing committed for what superficially appears to be a two-fold motivation: altruistically to rid society of the moneylender's malign influence; egotistically to prove that he, Raskol'nikov, is a latter-day Napoleon, one of the "extraordinary" men who can usurp the place of God in the moral universe.

Such a Promethean ideal is parodied in the figure of Svidrigailov, who demonstrates the ultimately nihilistic meaning of such supposed free will by committing suicide. In the course of revealing what Dostoevskii called "the psychological process of the crime", Raskol'nikov realizes that his motives were all flawed. But whether or not he abandons his satanic arrogance must remain in doubt.

Profoundly complex and multifaceted, *Crime and Punishment* established new standards of psychological portraiture and ideological debate in the Russian novel. The world it depicted was essentially in flux; even notions of the real were imperilled; and divine judgement, like any obvious authorial moral, was absent. It was unique as an example of detective fiction, but equally unique, if in a quite different genre, was the work during the 1860s of Dostoevskii's great contemporary, Lev Tolstoi. In the course of the decade he created the greatest historical novel ever written, *Voina i mir* (*War and Peace*) 1869.

As a historical narrative this epic work deals with Russia's two main confrontations with Napoleon (Austerlitz in 1805 and Borodino in 1812), but in other respects it may be considered a family chronicle novel devoted to the two main families of Bolkonskiis and Rostovs. The ideological meaning of the work is personalized through the lives and evolving ideas of its two main heroes, Prince Andrei Bolkonskii and his friend Pierre Bezukhov.

The apparently seamless way in which history and fiction coalesce, the range of episode and social scene are all facets testifying to Tolstoi's genius for evoking character and suggesting, in a pictorial sense, an active, vital replica of reality. Sometimes, however, a moral colouration is given to events through the way the observer-narrator's candid eye "defamiliarizes" what is seen, as in the famous example of Natasha Rostov's visit to the opera.

Although an epic novel about violent events and the "swarm life" of human beings stricken by war, in its fundamental assumptions *War and Peace* ultimately stresses the role of the Russian nobility as a mainstay of the status quo. The major heroines become matriarchs, and their husbands, family men, given only to oblique thoughts about political change.

In terms of personal ideas the novel is about the search for God. If, for Prince Andrei, God is finally identified with love as an eternal unifying source to which he will return at his death, for Pierre, under the influence of the only peasant figure in the novel, Platon Karataev, life itself, in all its multiplicity, is a manifestation of the divine. In historical terms, the novel is concerned with debunking the Napoleonic myth and nowhere is this more obvious than in the second epilogue where Tolstoi argues a case for assuming that power in history rests less with the so-called leaders than with those who participate directly in events.

Russia's relationship with Europe was of paramount importance for Turgenev at this time. In 1867, for example, in his fifth novel *Dym* (*Smoke*), set in Baden-Baden, he urged the need for Russia to become more civilized and European. To Dostoevskii, on the other hand, this was anathema. Driven into exile in Europe by his creditors, he now saw his native country as in need of a new image of Christ to protect it from European influences.

He conceived such an image in his second great novel *Idiot* (*The Idiot*) of 1868 in the figure of the epileptic Prince Myshkin. Plunged into a mill-race of events upon his return to Russia, Myshkin encounters a metropolitan world of financial greed, nihilism, and hysteria. The image of the beautiful Nastasia Filippovna is the most memorable in a striking array of female figures attracted to him; she is also the ultimate victim of the murderous world of St Petersburg avarice surrounding her. Among several brilliantly executed scenes in the novel the most outstanding is the final one when Myshkin and Nastasia's murderer, Rogozhin, spend a nightmarish wake beside her corpse.

In a publicistic sense *The Idiot* attempts too much. Sub-plots and secondary issues have a clogging effect. The message of the "positively beautiful man", Prince Myshkin, changes from that of the world redeemed by beauty to the anti-Catholic notion of a Russian Christ destined to bring salvation to a corrupt Europe.

In his third great novel *Besy*, translated as *The Devils* or *The Possessed*, European ideas can be seen to have entered into sections of the Russian intelligentsia on the pattern of the story from St Luke's gospel about the man possessed of devils. Set in a small Russian provincial town and ostensibly filtered through the observations of a know-all narrator, the novel describes how Stavrogin, a young scion of the local nobility originally tutored by an elderly liberal, Verkhovenskii, returns after a period abroad to renew his acquaintance with his "disciples", Shatov and Kirillov. The central theme of the novel is derived from the notorious affair of Nechaev (1847–82) who, in 1869, organized the murder of a member of a revolutionary cell to guarantee other members' loyalty.

A loose familial relationship of ideas can be seen to exist between Stavrogin's "disciples". Shatov, paradoxically uncommitted in his beliefs, advocates the notion of a people or nation as God-bearing, while Kirillov is obsessed with suicide as a means of overcoming the fear of death and ensuring for mankind the freedom of man-godhood. Both "disciples" die – Shatov as the victim of a plot like Nechaev's, designed by Verkhovenskii's son, Petr, to guarantee loyalty to his revolutionary cell, and Kirillov by his own hand after signing a false confession to Shatov's murder. Stavrogin, the "father" of their ideas, is cast by Petr in the role of revolutionary leader but eventually is proved impotent, both sexually and ideologically, and hangs himself.

A sinister, very dark novel, manifestly anti-revolutionary in intent, *The Devils* nevertheless contains some of the funniest scenes in Dostoevskii's *oeuvre*. It also originally contained a horrific chapter (unpublished in Dostoevskii's lifetime) in which Stavrogin confesses to the rape of a young girl who subsequently kills herself from shame.

Violence, mayhem, murder, and suicide, the strong ingredients of Dostoevskii's fiction, reflected an increasing malaise in Russian society during the 1870s. As the younger intelligentsia gradually united under the banner of "freedom for the people" or Populism (*Narodnichestvo*) and resorted finally to terrorism in the struggle against the autocracy, the leading novelists treated the incipient unrest as posing a serious danger above all to the family and the moral health of the nation.

Dostoevskii's first contribution in this respect was his novel of 1875, *Podrostok* (translated as *A Raw Youth* and as *An Accidental Family*). Generally acknowledged to be the least successful of his major novels, it describes a young man's attempt to establish his legitimacy as the member of an "accidental family" of the Russian nobility. The cause of family breakdown in this instance was attributed largely to intelligentsia free-thinking, personified by the father, Versilov. In Mikhail Saltykov-Shchedrin's relentlessly harsh satire *Gospoda Golovlevy* (*The Golovlevs*), published serially 1875–80, the focus is on the greed of the mother and the hypocrisy of the son. So far as the politics of the decade were concerned, the only novel to offer an understanding picture of revolutionary Populism was Turgenev's *Nov'* (*Virgin Soil*) of 1877, but its lukewarm appraisal of the revolutionaries' aims while celebrating their self-sacrifice made it seem ambiguous and dated.

The age of the classic Russian novel concludes with two masterpieces, Tolstoi's *Anna Karenina* (1875–77), and Dostoevskii's *Brat'ia Karamazovy* (*The Brothers Karamazov*) 1880. Both reflect closely the dominant issues of the decade – in Tolstoi's case, the emancipation of women, the new role of the landowning nobility, the threat posed by the urban to the rural, the Russo-Turkish War; in Dostoevskii's, the issue of justice, faith versus free will, the power of money, the incipient terrorism – all within the framework of the damage done to the moral fibre of society and particularly to the family.

Anna Karenina may seem a triumph of authorial detachment in a technical sense, though there is no denying that the famous epigraph "Vengeance is mine and I will repay" presupposes some degree of authorial judgement. This does not mean that Anna's is not a portrait of deeply engaging vitality, and her tragedy the more poignant for that reason. Her high-society world has an equally strong allure. Driven by a need for love in her infatuation with Vronskii and turned into a social pariah by her husband's refusal of a divorce, she is seen moving brilliantly through her world, deserving better than its superficiality and yet never able to achieve a spiritual focus. Her suicide can seem as inevitable in its tragedy as the railway lines on which she immolates herself, but it is also all-too-humanly understandable in its futility and despair.

Structurally a novel of twin strands divided into eight parts, Anna's story is complemented by the parallel story of Konstantin Levin, which clearly enough reflects the author's own spiritual quest. Insufferably opinionated and serious-minded though Levin is, he possesses a truthful eye and can see Anna for what she is on the only occasion they meet – a vital, beautiful woman consumed by the tragedy of her loveless situation. His own marriage, if uneven, at least permits him the security of love and the chance to reach beyond rational causes to a belief in the popular wisdom that one should live for one's soul, thereby discovering a concept of God that can reconcile all men. His discovery, set as it is against the background of the Russo-Turkish War of 1877–78, the first so-called "War of Liberation", has a pacifist appeal no doubt suited to its time; it lacks, however, the contentious challenge that Dostoevskii brought to his classic study of the meaning of justice.

The Brothers Karamazov, though conceived much earlier, sprang from Dostoevskii's attendance at the trial of the terrorist Vera Zasulich in 1878 and has as its climax the trial of Dmitrii Karamazov for the killing of his father. Pronounced guilty by the jury, Dmitrii is shown in the first three parts of this four-part novel to be the victim of a miscarriage of justice. The reasons are explored in a supposedly narrated account of what actually happened in the three days immediately preceding the parricide.

Set in a small town suspiciously like Staraia Russa (Dostoevskii's vacation resort not far from Novgorod) and at a remove of 13 years before the supposed time of writing, the novel challenges notions of the real, and of truth and justice in many complex ways. On one level, it is about money. At a deeper level, it is about the choices facing Russia. These take two principal forms in the opposed ideas of Dmitrii's brothers, Ivan and Alesha.

Ivan seeks to liberate mankind from God and his unjust world by decrying the notion of a hell for evil-doers and offering a brilliant critique of Christ's teaching (in the famous chapter "The Grand Inquisitor"). He ends with the nihilistic assertion that there is no virtue and "all is permissible". Ironically Smerdiakov, his illegitimate brother, acts on such permissiveness to commit the parricide. The irony is compounded when Ivan is confronted on the eve of Dmitrii's trial by his personal devil who challenges him to tell the truth. But Ivan, for whom truth has become so deeply penetrated by paradox, cannot do more at the trial than declare that "We all desire our father's death", and a miscarriage of justice becomes inevitable.

Alesha, studying to be a monk at a local monastery, offers the teaching of his spiritual father, Zosima, as an antidote to Ivan. He advocates a Christian responsibility for all other men's sins. The killing of the father, however reprobate, becomes in this context a heinously nihilistic act that destroys both the unity of generations and the idea of justice as inseparable from universal responsibility for sin.

The ideas must seem incomplete, as the novel was incomplete, but in their boldness, as in the exploration of the tenuous line between the real and the unreal, the rational and irrational, Dostoevskii expanded the limits of the novel as a genre. His legacy of the ideological novel was the summit of achievement in the classic Russian novel. No other half-century of novel-writing in any literature has been able to match it.

RICHARD FREEBORN

The Superfluous Man in Russian Literature

The "superfluous man" (*lishnii chelovek*) is a term that, since the mid-19th century, has been applied to a particular type of character in Russian literature. Ivan Turgenev's work of 1850, *Dnevnik lishnego cheloveka* (*The Diary of a Superfluous Man*), popularized the term "superfluous man", which came to be used to identify literary characters of an earlier period of the 19th century as well as those in the middle years of the century and beyond, into the 20th century. Often, the end of the tradition of "superfluous men" was earmarked as the mid-19th century, with characters such as the eponymous Oblomov in Ivan Goncharov's novel, many of Turgenev characters, including Chulkaturin, in *The Diary of a Superfluous Man*, and Bazarov, in *Ottsy i deti* (*Fathers and Sons*).

Although the idea of the superfluous man is specific to Russia, it is also part of a broader phenomenon in terms of the ways in which cultures, past and present, have viewed nonconformists and conformists. Whether we examine a southern woman writer from the United States, Kate Chopin, in her novel, *The Awakening* (1899); or the German writer, Friedrich Schiller, in his play, *Die Räuber* (*The Robbers*) 1871; or the French director Eric Rohmer, in his film, *L'Amour l'après-midi* [Chloë in the Afternoon] 1972, like the Russian writers we shall explore in the superfluous man tradition, these artists, disparate in time and place, have created works in which, explicitly or implicitly, conformity to the status quo is presented as a virtue. Certain writers, from different cultures, weave the same patterns, often portraying those who dare to be different as literal or spiritual losers. Characters who submit to the status quo, who conform to social or religious values, are often portrayed as the moral victors.

Sometimes the nonconformist can be seen as a noble, tragic figure, but sometimes he or she can be seen as being explicitly or implicitly condemned. The authorial disapproval of nonconformist behaviour, or an ambivalent attitude toward nonconformity, marks the life and art of diverse cultures.

The psychologist Erich Fromm, in *Escape from Freedom* (1941), observed that a desire for freedom coexists with a desire for submission. Psychological experiments, by Stanley Milgram and Solomon Asch, have shown that people think that they support individualism more than they do. This pattern fits the Russian superfluous man tradition in that certain writers, hailed as individualists, actually reflect, in their works, an ambivalent attitude toward their nonconformist protagonists.

The late 18th-century Bildungsroman taught the importance of learning to reconcile oneself to society. Both rugged individualism and a will to conform have been observed as distinctive features of the culture of the United States. A children's book by the American writer Gertrude Crampton, *Tootle*, stars a young train who loves going off the tracks to romp and play in a flower-filled meadow. The final message conveyed to young readers is that the train must never go off the tracks.

In Russia, we see that Boris and Gleb, the first saints to be canonized by the Russian Church, were admired for their refusal to rebel. In Russian Orthodoxy, human beings are viewed more as an integral part of a larger community rather than as individuals. The collective is emphasized. Salvation is attained by remaining within the community rather than by individual effort. The concept of "universality" (*sobornost'*) emphasizes the collective nature of the human being's life and religion. Russian Orthodoxy condemns the human being's attempts to lead an isolated or independent existence.

These values were reflected in the beliefs of the Slavophiles, a group of the 19th-century intellectuals who believed that the path to Russia's salvation lay in the values of the simple Russian people, in the ideal of communality, Russian religion, the irrational, and the peasant commune with its communal ownership of property. Others among the educated, the Westernizers, felt that Russia's salvation resided in the adoption of west European laws, innovations, and values such as individualism and rational thought. The experience of the Westernized Russians, who often studied in western Europe and then returned to their homeland, was indirectly reflected in portrayals of the superfluous man. Here were people who, because of their western education, felt that they did not fit into Russia, yet in western Europe, they felt they were Russians who did not fit into Europe.

Just who were the superfluous men who inhabited so many works of Russian literature? Let us first turn to a general description of the literary type. As I have written elsewhere, the superfluous man has been described "as an ineffectual aristocrat at odds with society", "as 'dreamy, useless', as an 'intellectual incapable of action', an 'ineffective idealist', 'a hero who is sensitive to social and ethical problems, but who fails to act, partly because of personal weakness, partly because of political and social restraints on his freedom of action'". (Ellen B. Chances, *Conformity's Children: An Approach to the Superfluous Man in Russian Literature*, 1978). A typical description of the type appeared in a Soviet literary encyclopedia, where the superfluous man's essence was described as his "alienation from his environment, eventually leading to a complete break from and falling out with it" (*Literaturnaia entsiklopediia*, vol. 6, 1932).

Often, this type of weak outsider misfit man was juxtaposed to a strong woman who did fit into society, who could act, and who could become involved in the life around her. Accounts frequently turn to the juxtaposition of the weak, ineffectual Evgenii Onegin, protagonist of Aleksandr Pushkin's novel in verse, *Evgenii Onegin*, and Tat'iana, the novel's strong, effective heroine. Sometimes, like Onegin, the superfluous men came from the "tainted", false atmosphere of the city, often from the westernized city of St Petersburg. Conversely, the female foils, like Tat'iana, had strong roots in and ties to the Russian countryside.

The term "superfluous man" was most commonly used to refer to certain characters, beginning with Pushkin's *Evgenii Onegin* and extending to Turgenev's *The Diary of a Superfluous Man*. Critical evaluation of such characters sometimes focused on them as tragic or romantic heroes, unsuccessful because of society's inability to respect or to understand the individualist who is an outsider on account of his superior qualities. Consequently the writers themselves could be seen as favouring their alienated, outsider figures by pointing to the flaws within society that led to this alienation of such talented "superfluous" characters.

Examples of this kind of structure include one of the earliest depictions of the superfluous man in Russian literature, the character of Chatskii in Aleksandr Griboedov's play, *Gore ot uma* (*Woe from Wit*). Chatskii is shown to have a strong moral compass, a feature that makes him stand out in the society in which he lives. He is an utter misfit, but his qualities are those that are shown to be worthwhile, in spite of the fact that society considers him to be crazy.

Another example of the virtues of the misfit being upheld is in a novel that comes much later, but which fits into the tradition of the romantic hero. Boris Pasternak's *Doktor Zhivago* (*Doctor Zhivago*) features an epomymous hero whose "superfluity" to society is hailed by the author as being a positive characteristic. His difference from most members of society, his individualism, and his independent thinking are qualities to be admired. All of this is something that the world needs, according to Pasternak, in order to maintain and uphold the most important values of human life. Iurii Zhivago is able therefore, to tap into his own inner talents and create powerful, lasting poems. Even though Zhivago sacrifices his life, Pasternak makes it clear, by the end of the novel, that Zhivago's poetry will continue to live.

Here Pasternak, in creating his superfluous man, reflects the 19th- and 20th-century tradition of the Russian intelligentsia. In describing his misfit hero, Pasternak is drawing upon the strong tradition, within the 19th century, of the special calling of the Russian writer. The writer is regarded as someone who is different from the rest of society, but who is more noble. This is a tradition whose roots can be found in the 19th-century romantic attitude ennobling the artist. It is a tradition that lasted longer in Russia and the Soviet Union than in western Europe, perhaps, paradoxically, precisely because the Soviet Union, with its Iron Curtain and its isolation from the rest of the world, "froze" in place many features of 19th-century culture.

Pasternak's description of Iurii Zhivago, the poet, resonates with Pushkin's depiction of the poet in his famous poem of the 1820s, "Prorok" ("The Prophet"). In Pushkin's poem, an angel appears to a man, touches his eyes and ears, and substitutes the tongue of a wise serpent for his own tongue. The angel takes out the man's heart and instead inserts flaming coal. God then instructs him to burn people's hearts with His Word. In Pasternak's novel, Zhivago, the doctor, spiritually heals people with the words of his poetry.

Pushkin's poem about the special calling of the poet continued to live in Russian culture well into the 1980s. For example, the film director Andrei Tarkovskii quoted Pushkin's poem in his book *Zapechatlennoe vremia* (*Sculpting in Time*) 1981, to explain the role of the artist, and "The Prophet" appeared in an article written by the protagonist of Andrei Bitov's novel, *Pushkinskii dom* (*Pushkin House*).

In his novel, Bitov speaks of Russian literature from the 18th century to the early pre-revolutionary years of the 20th century as still being in place in the 1960s and early 1970s, preserved like a "nature preserve", precisely because of the rupture that Stalin had caused in social and cultural life. Moreover, Bitov himself, in *Pushkin House*, offers the reader a character, Modest Platonovich Odoevtsev, whose virtues are shown to be his independence of spirit and his individualism in the face of pressures to conform to the demands of the Soviet system. Odoevtsev's grandson, Leva Odoevtsev, is criticized for his dependence on the system, for the fact that he does not even know how dependent he is on the system, for the fact that, even if he were set free from the system, he himself would ask to return.

Most depictions of superfluous men in the 19th and 20th centuries differed from those one might observe in Griboedov's play or in the novels of Pasternak and Bitov. While Griboedov, Pasternak, and Bitov praised their misfit protagonists for daring to challenge the dictates of society, a close examination of *Evgenii Onegin* reveals the fact that Pushkin has an ambivalent attitude towards his hero. He implicitly and explicitly criticizes him precisely because he is a nonconformist. And Tat'iana's virtues are praised precisely because, by the end of the novel, she submits to the flow of life and does not rebel against the status quo. At the beginning of the novel, Tat'iana is a nonconformist. She prefers reading to passing her time with the empty upper-crust society set of the countryside. Describing Tat'iana after she moves to St Petersburg, Pushkin praises her for having learned how to live according to the dictates of society. In his depiction of his heroine, Pushkin has chosen to praise the characteristics of submission to society rather than those of the individualist. Onegin is described as fitting nowhere, neither in St Petersburg society nor in the countryside, and this quality, the reader surmises, is a negative one. Pushkin is ambivalent in his attitude towards the conformist in that while he praises Tat'iana for finally conforming to society, he criticizes her sister Ol'ga for her failure to distinguish herself from the majority.

Another early depiction of the superfluous man, Mikhail Lermontov's *Geroi nashego vremeni* (*A Hero of Our Time*) 1840, offers a negative attitude toward Pechorin, the "hero" of his time. Lermontov's Pechorin, a Byronic, romantic figure, a rebellious loner, is constantly shown as a disruptive force, wherever he goes. In contrast, another character in the novel, Maksim Maksimich, a kindly, straightforward man, is shown as a positive force. Maksim Maksimich does not question fate, as Pechorin does. He accepts whatever life doles out to him. Quite simply, Lermontov praises Maksim Maksimich and condemns Pechorin.

In Pushkin's and Lermontov's early depictions of superfluous men, we can discern patterns that will continue to appear in later novels containing the same types of protagonists. *Evgenii Onegin* contains a character, Onegin, who rebels against society. *A Hero of Our Time* describes a character, Pechorin, who is a metaphysical rebel. (It is no coincidence that the French writer Albert Camus, a century later, chose a quotation from Lermontov's novel as the epigraph to his Existential novel, *La Chute* [*The Fall*], about a metaphysical rebel.) From this time on, many Russian writers who described superfluous men wrote about social or metaphysical outsiders.

Aleksandr Herzen's *Kto vinovat?* (*Who is to Blame?*) is a social novel, describing the origins of a Russian social dreamer type. Herzen's protagonist, Bel'tov, is shown to have been brought up on large doses of literature, cut off from real life. What Herzen has done is to take the type of dreamer common in German romanticism (such as E.T.A. Hoffmann's Anselmus in "Der goldene Topf" ["The Golden Pot"]), in which characters prefer (and are praised for preferring) the realm of imagination to the less colourful, bland routines of daily living. In the creation of his superfluous man, a Russian social dreamer, Herzen cross-breeds a German romantic dreamer hero, following the models of romanticism, with the hero of a social novel, following the models of novels by French urban social writers like Balzac and Russian writers of naturalist works. Critics have pointed out that Herzen was so impressed with Gogol''s naturalistic setting in *Mertvye dushi* (*Dead Souls*) that he chose his own locale with Gogol''s example in mind. In addition, Herzen had as precedents the misfit types of Pechorin and Onegin.

Herzen's contribution to the tradition of the superfluous man lay in his combination of all these models, which led him to create a superfluous man who wants to help society in some way. By placing a dreamer in a social novel, by describing a dreamer type who wants to help change society, Herzen had put forward a Russian "social dreamer", a character who is transformed into a superfluous man with socio-political overtones. He is an outcast from society because he wants to, but cannot, play an active role in changing society. Thus Bel'tov, like many real-life Russian aristocrats, wishes to play a political role in society.

In spite of the steps Herzen had taken in defining a new type of superfluous man, his portrayal of Bel'tov is remarkably similar to that of Pushkin and Lermontov, in that Bel'tov's inability to act is blamed not on society, but on Bel'tov himself. Bel'tov's isolation from society and his escape into a world of books and ideas are blamed for his inability to adapt to life. Herzen analyses the figure as a sociological type. Moreover, he casts his superfluous man character in terms that match his discussions in articles, which bring to mind the German philosopher Friedrich Schelling's *Naturphilosophie*. Thus just as human beings are cut off from nature, Bel'tov is cut off from society as a whole.

Herzen's novel, though hardly a literary masterpiece, is essential to a study of the superfluous man. By casting his superfluous man in ideological terms, he nudged the tradition in directions that were soon followed by Dostoevskii and Tolstoi. He therefore played a key role in the history of the superfluous man.

Also key to the tradition are the novels of Ivan Turgenev, a contemporary of Dostoevskii, Tolstoi, and Herzen. Like Bel'tov, the eponymous hero of Turgenev's *Rudin* lives in the world of abstract ideas. He is the social outcast who, because of his nonconformity, cannot live a normal life. He uses his idealism as an excuse to dodge responsibility to other human beings. In the process he causes unhappiness and pain to those who are close to him. A lonely wanderer, Rudin sacrifices his life on the barricades in Paris in 1848. Even in death he remains an outsider. The French insurgents incorrectly identify him as a Pole. In contrast, a conformist figure, Lezhnev, is shown to be happy and successful in human relations and in life.

Whereas Rudin fits into the tradition of social misfits, the superfluous men who inhabit Turgenev's other novels are metaphysical outsiders who do not fit into the cycle of nature. *The Diary of a Superfluous Man*, the short novel that, as we know, bears responsibility for popularization of the term "superfluous man", serves as a case in point. In his diary, the main character Chulkaturin writes, "Nature, obviously, did not count on my arriving and consequently, treated me like an unexpected and uninvited guest." In fact, in social terms, Chulkaturin does not differ from those who, like the prince, Bazmenkov, surround him. He feels superfluous, but the only evidence he presents, his loss of Liza, his loved one, to another man, is merely a case of loss in love, not a case of true superfluity. Chulkaturin is superfluous because he has made himself so. He feels cut off from nature as a whole. He even quotes a Pushkin poem, "Brozhu li ia vdol' ulits shumnykh" ("Whether I wander along noisy streets"), that confirms these feelings of the human being's aloneness and the cyclical quality of nature. Chulkaturin recalls fond childhood memories of feeling at one with nature and, at death, yearns to recapture this state. Even his diary entries demonstrate his lack of oneness with the cycles of nature, for the entries, from March to April, document the time during which nature moves towards spring, towards the awakening of new life, whereas Chulkaturin's comments make it obvious that he is in the dying phase of his own life. In this portrayal of the superfluous man, nature, rather than society, is triumphant.

In Turgenev's *Fathers and Sons*, the nonconformist is treated as social misfit, outsider to nature's cycle, and rebel against God's order. *Fathers and Sons* reflects the historical realities of its age. The novel is often interpreted as a fictional representation of the clash between the generation of fathers, men of the 1840s, liberals, for evolution; and the generation of sons, men of the 1860s, radicals, for revolution. Analyses of the novel have often concentrated on its socio-political dimensions or its aesthetic qualities. Depending on critics' political leanings, arguments have been made that the main character, the nihilist Bazarov, is drawn positively or negatively. (One of the best essays ever written on this aspect of *Fathers and Sons* is Isaiah Berlin's "Fathers and Children" in his book *Russian Thinkers*, 1978.) Critics who have wanted to wrest the novel from political interpretations have insisted on Turgenev's concentration on art itself.

Yet what we notice is that the real victors in the novel are those characters from each generation – Nikolai Kirsanov; his son Arkadii; and Arkadii's love, Katia – who submit to the natural unfolding of life. The losers from each generation – Nikolai Kirsanov's brother Pavel; Bazarov; and Odintsova, the woman he loves – are those who do not conform to the natural order. Turgenev emphasizes Bazarov's superfluity by drawing him alone, structurally and sociologically. Turgenev makes him a member of the emerging *raznochintsy* (Russian intellectuals not of noble birth) middle class, neither aristocrat nor lower class. As a nihilist, Bazarov rebels against the established order. Turgenev emphasizes Bazarov's isolation. Even at the beginning of the novel, he is made to sit alone in a coach, while his friend Arkadii and Arkadii's father sit together in a carriage. He is often shown arriving or departing. In addition, almost all the other characters, with the exception of Bazarov and Pavel Kirsanov, ideological opponents, belong somewhere and are paired. By the end of the novel, we are left with Bazarov alone and Pavel Kirsanov alone, each having refused to let life flow naturally. Arkadii, unlike Bazarov, has understood that people should accept the forces of life and death. Implicit in Turgenev is the belief that submission to life is a virtue. The issue, therefore, is not only fathers versus sons, but submission versus rebellion. Those who do not belong are condemned, and those who do, thrive.

Goncharov's novel *Oblomov* is about a landowner of the old generation who is so lazy that it takes him approximately one-third of the book to get out of bed. In contrast Oblomov's childhood friend Shtolts, half German and half Russian in origin, who believes in action, progress, and new ideas. Turgenev's Bazarov, with his new ideas, was superfluous because he did not fit into the life of the country gentry. Oblomov, with his old ideas of the country gentry, does not fit into the life of the new society. We see an example, in *Oblomov*, almost of superfluity in reverse, in comparison with some of the works examined in this essay. Bel'tov, Turgenev's Rudin and Bazarov, and Chatskii do not fit into society because of their *new* ideas. Oblomov is almost a parody of this because he has *no* ideas. He wants to be left alone to contemplate the life of a bygone era, to live in dreams of the idyllic past. Like other superfluous men, Oblomov does not fit into conventional society. Since he does not want to go forward or to be active or to rush around, he is the social deviant. What Goncharov has done here is to abstract Oblomov's personal problem to the level of old Russia's not fitting into new Russia. Oblomov wants to halt the passage of time. He refuses to leave his house or his bed. He runs away from actions that would lead him to maturity. Rather than marrying Ol'ga, the woman he loves, he buries himself in the protective coating of his dressing gown. Oblomov would prefer to keep life as it was when he was a child. As with other superfluous men, Oblomov is condemned.

He chooses as a wife not Ol'ga, his love, but another relic of the past, Agaf'ia Matveevna. The problem is that the past has no part in the present. Those who do not fit into the present are condemned, defeated by change. Shtolts, on the other hand, can change and adapt to life in the new Russia. He accomplishes good, keeping his own estate and Oblomov's in working order. He is not scared by an adult love relationship and wins O'lga's hand.

Dostoevskii and Tolstoi built upon the tradition of the superfluous man by casting their depictions in ideological terms. For Dostoevskii, superfluity is represented as the Russian intelligentsia being cut off from the "people" (*narod*). Those who belong to the intelligentsia, who deviate from the norms of the simple people, are attacked as incomplete, warped, in some other way chastised. Those who are invested with the characteristics of the people are praised.

In the Pushkin speech that Dostoevskii gave near the end of his life, he declared that the Russian intelligentsia were cut off from the "soil" (*pochva*). Pushkin was, for Dostoevskii, important in allowing Russian society to be resurrected if it were to form a close bond with the "people's truth". Dostoevskii sees this in Pushkin's Tat'iana, for she embodies the Russian soul, whereas Europeanized characters like Onegin do not.

These ideas reflect Dostoevskii's ideology of "concept of the soil" (*pochvennichestvo*) which, during the 1860s, he set forth on the pages of *Vremia* and *Epokha*, political-literary journals that he co-edited and to which he contributed. Dostoevskii, with his *pochvennichestvo*, wanted to synthesize the Westernizer and Slavophile approaches to Russian culture. He believed that the reforms of Peter the Great had been correct, but that Russians should not blindly worship the west. He maintained that the virtues of Russia, its religion, and particular identity were important, but that the Westernizing reforms of Peter the Great should not be rejected out of hand. The Westernized heroes in Dostoevskii's fiction, therefore, have to take a journey through doubt and rational thought in order to come to an acceptance of Russian spiritual values.

In the early 1860s the "concept of the soil" supported the political reforms introduced by Tsar Alexander II. Dostoevskii, for a variety of reasons, then lost his confidence in the capacity of political reform to change society. The reforms of Alexander II had not been far-reaching enough. Russian radicals began to use terrorist tactics rather than just discussing new ideas. Dostoevskii's visit to western Europe in 1862–63 convinced him that adherence to rational laws alone will not change people. Instead he concluded that change was possible only by the irrational, spontaneous spiritual love of one human being for another.

Ideological depictions of the superfluous man, wedded to his own particular ideology of "concept of the soil" are typical of Dostoevskii's fictional works. In the case of *Zapiski iz podpol'ia* (*Notes from Underground*) 1864, the consequences of the underground man's adoption of European forms is his utter paralysis, his inability to cope with reality. For example, the underground man says that the groans of an educated man differ from those of others in that they are the moans of a man "'who has cut himself off from the soil and the people', as the saying goes today". The underground man lives in books and daydreams and therefore cannot deal with life. Juxtaposed to him is Liza, from Riga, but with Russian parents. She acts spontaneously, naturally, with compassion. *Notes from Underground* fictionally reproduces the tenets of "the concept of the soil". The man who is plagued by the rational, abstract ideas of the west does not fit into Russia. The Russian intelligentsia is a misfit, is morally ill, does not fit into the real authentic Russia of the simple people, with their irrational Christian spontaneous love of one human being for another. The underground man is an ideological nonconformist. He is diseased because he is distorted by Westernized artificial thinking. He is even from the Westernized city of St Petersburg, "the most premeditated and artificial city" in the world.

Prestuplenie i nakazanie (*Crime and Punishment*) tells the story of Raskol'nikov, whose very name comes from the Russian word for "schism". He is split off from himself and from Russian spiritual values because he has the disease of the western ideas of egoism and self-interest. Dostoevskii transforms his diseased protagonist, superfluous to the life-affirming forces of Russia, into a criminal, into a murderer. Joseph Frank, in his *Dostoevsky: The Miraculous Years, 1865–1871* (1995), explains that in *Crime and Punishment* Dostoevskii is showing the literal dead end of the ideas of the Russian radicals of the 1860s. In contrast to Raskol'nikov, Russian Orthodox Christianity infuses the life of Sonia Marmeladova, whose example leads Raskol'nikov to abandon the ideas of western individualism and adopt those of Russian Christianity.

Here too, then, we see the influence of Dostoevskii's "concept of the soil" as he paints the picture of his superfluous man, Raskol'nikov, superfluous to Russian society and values, and to human society. We see Sonia's natural spiritual love as she submits unquestioningly to God.

Dostoevskii's other major works also present portrayals of superfluous men. In *Besy* (*The Devils* or *The Possessed*), Dostoevskii concludes that it is not just St Petersburg, but Russia itself that is crippled because it has lost its attachment to the values of the people. Dostoevskii sets his novel in the provinces. He documents the way in which characters are "possessed" by west European ideas and therefore cut off from their native roots. Westernized Russia itself is superfluous. Byronic Stavrogin, radical Petr Verkhovenskii, and Stepan Verkhovenskii, a man of the 1840s, have lost their way. By the end of the novel, Stepan Verkhovenskii literally returns to the earth, through his understanding of the lessons of Christianity.

Prince Myshkin, the main character of *Idiot* (*The Idiot*) 1868, is drawn by Dostoevskii as the positively good individual, who, because of his goodness, is superfluous to the everyday world of corruption. A society filled with suspicion cannot accept the pure person. Myshkin even states: "I am superfluous in society". Myshkin is the outcast because, in his meekness, honesty, and Christ-like manner, he defies the mores of conventional society.

Dostoevskii's final novel, *Brat'ia Karamazovy* (*The Brothers Karamazov*) 1881, outlines two paths open to people. One is marked by western rational thought, isolation, individualism, egoism, and literal or spiritual death. This is the path followed by Ivan Karamazov, who questions the very structure of God's universe. Ivan is uprooted from the Russian soil. His thought, Dostoevskii points out, leads to a world in which "everything is permitted". The other path is followed by his brother, Alesha, who ultimately does not rebel against God's order, who accepts the world as it is, who conforms to God's community. His path is marked by unconditional love and by an "everyone is responsible for everyone else" approach to life. Dostoevskii points out that spiritual outcasts, superfluous men like Ivan or the bible-questioning, France-worshipping Smerdiakov, will literally or figuratively die. On the other hand, those who conform to God's law, like Alesha or his spiritual father, Father Zosima, or, by the end of the novel, Kolia Krasotkin, will yield more links to other people, in the unending chain of everyone being linked to everyone.

Tolstoi is not usually considered as a creator of superfluous men, yet in *War and Peace* and *Anna Karenina* we see the same kind of configuration of ideological conformists and nonconformists as we do in Dostoevskii's works. For Tolstoi, in *War and Peace*, the superfluous people are those who do not conform to or who rebel against the laws of history. In *The Brothers Karamazov*, Dostoevskii's heroes conformed to God's laws. The idea of superfluity was linked to religious factors. In *War and Peace*, Tolstoi also connects superfluity with a theory of history, rather than just with a religious doctrine. Those who suffer disaster are those who try to defy, who refuse to conform to the flow of, the laws of history. Tolstoi points out that Napoleon, in believing that history can be made by the will of one individual, is wrong. He wants to control what cannot be controlled. He fails to understand that it is necessary to submit to the laws of history because history is made of the wills of many individuals. Russia's General Kutuzov was a hero, in Tolstoi's eyes, because he knew that there are no heroes. He understood that history consists of the interrelationship of many factors.

Characters other than historical figures are portrayed according to the same dichotomy. Andrei is abstract, cerebral, intellectual, and admires Napoleon. Intellect comes between him and life. He is superfluous to life because he wants to control it. Pierre learns to accept things as they are, through the lessons of Platon Karataev, a simple Russian peasant who teaches him about the connection to God's designs for the universe. In this novel, Tolstoi praises those who conform and who submit to historical destiny. Submission to historical destiny is connected to religion.

In *Anna Karenina*, Tolstoi shows us that conformity to life is praiseworthy if it is attached to genuine religious faith. Levin discovers, by mowing hay with peasants, that the meaning of life is life itself. Anna Karenina, like Levin, acts spontaneously. She is condemned because, as a married woman, she has dared to transgress God's laws by having an affair with a man who is not her husband. Tolstoi even describes Anna as "superfluous" in the nursery. In fact she is superfluous because she has refused to conform to God's laws. Levin deviates from the norms of high society, but he holds true to the path of God's laws.

In the novels of Dostoevskii and Tolstoi, the further away the characters are from the soil and from the religious beliefs that grow there, the more problems are created. If characters remain close to the Russian soil, they can discern the importance of submitting to the order of things. Levin tills the earth. A simple Russian peasant reveals the meaning of life to him. Platon Karataev plays a similar role with Pierre. Dostoevskii's Sonia Marmeladova and Alesha Karamazov are in harmony with Russian Christianity. Anna Karenina, Stavrogin, Petr Verkhovenskii, Ivan Karamazov, and the underground man rebel against God's order. Andrei fails to submit to the laws of history. All of these characters are superfluous because they are nonconformists to some metaphysical order.

In Russian literature of the turn of the century, a direct dealing with the theme of the superfluous man is abandoned. In some of Chekhov's works, though, we see the familiar pattern of society's rejection of the person who thinks differently. One example is in the story "Palata No. 6" ("Ward Six"), whose protagonist, Andrei Ragin, is deemed mad because he finds the inmate of a mental institution more interesting to talk to than the boring people in society at large. Most of Chekhov's works deal with superfluity in a different way, though. For many of Chekhov's characters, people feel superfluous and isolated not because they are different, but because they are human. In previous depictions of the superfluous man, with the exception of Turgenev's Chulkaturin, characters felt like misfits because there was an objective difference between them and their environment. With Chekhov's misfits, there is a sense of the universality of isolation. One such case is the story entitled "Lishnii chelovek" ("The Superfluous Man"), where the main character feels superfluous to his wife's circle of friends.

With the Soviet period, and with the advent of socialist realism in the 1930s, it might be argued that the theme of the superfluous man disappeared. After all, writers were urged to depict positive heroes helping to build socialism. Furthermore, one can, I believe, paradoxically, discern ways in which portrayals of superfluous heroes in the mainstream works of the 19th century made their presence felt in the literature of the new Soviet state. First of all, there were those works by fellow traveller writers like Iurii Olesha, which depicted people who could not fit into the new structures of Soviet life. Olesha's *Zavist'* (*Envy*) 1927, follows the adventures of two men, Kavalerov and Ivan Babichev, who cannot adapt to the new life. This pattern is vaguely reminiscent of Oblomov, who did not want to keep pace with the rhythms of change. (Kavalerov, however, would like to participate, but he is incapable of conforming). Juxtaposed to Kavalerov is Andrei Babichev, who participates fully in the new society. Olesha does not take sides, for he shows both the flaws of those who conform and those who do not.

Second, there were works that directly urged the building of the new Soviet state. Fedor Gladkov's novel *Tsement* (*Cement*) 1925, a prototype of the Soviet industrial novel, shows the importance of adhering to the collective, of adhering to the Soviet system. Gleb comes home from the front, and his wife Dasha shows that working towards the future of communism is more important than expressing personal feelings to particular individuals. Sacrificing oneself to the masses is more important than living one's personal life. Gleb learns that his intimate relationship with his wife is to be subordinated to their common goal of building socialism. By the end of the novel, Gleb learns to shed his personal concerns in the name of the common goal of the workers' building of the new society. Often, in these novels, the outsider becomes the insider. The heroes become actively involved with socialism.

Paradoxically, this tradition had deep affinities with that of the 19th-century superfluous man. The person who is different is cast as a villain. The one who conforms is the hero. Accordingly the works of Soviet socialist realism, with their heroes of the Soviet system and their villains rebelling against the system, are tied, in terms of the approach to the conformist and the nonconformist, to the main line of Russian literature of the 19th century.

In a 1988 interview in a French literary magazine, Andrei Bitov was asked about his views on the superfluous man today. He explained that the superfluous man tradition still exists, but that it has changed since the 19th century. Nineteenth-century conceptions of the superfluous man, explained Bitov, located him within a particular social context. Now, Bitov continued, it makes sense to view the superfluous man within a global context. Bitov asked, "To what end does Man exist, to what extent is he indispensable (or useless) in relation to his environment, to the system that governs life?" ("Bitov: l'energie de l'erreur", *Magazine littéraire*, March 1988, 40–41).

Bitov's novel, *Ozhidanie obez'ian* (*The Monkey Link*), published in 1995, addresses the same question he posed in the interview of the purpose of the human being: "Is the human being superfluous to nature?" What is the relationship of the human being to other biological species? What is the role of human beings *vis-à-vis* other human beings? To this day, the superfluous man tradition continues to live.

ELLEN CHANCES

Women's Writing in Russia

Russian women have been writing, in the broadest sense, if not producing literature, for many centuries. Female signatures have been found on some of the earliest documents in the Russian language yet discovered – the letters written on birchbark by inhabitants of Novgorod in the 11th, 12th, and 13th centuries. Another "private" genre of writing practised by women (though much more rarely) was autobiography. But the ecclesiastical and political nature of much pre-Petrine writing (sermons, hagiography, chronicles) meant that women were largely excluded from the public tradition, and that the named "bookmen" (*knizhniki*) of the medieval period included no women whatever.

The exclusion of women from public *pis'mennost'* (writing) in medieval times delayed their entry into the literary world, once that had been established in Russia. It was not until the second half of the 18th century that women began contributing to the secular, westernized, tradition of literature as such – that is, writing as more than purely functional communication – which had then been established in Russia for about a hundred years. However, from the 1750s various factors combined positively to encourage women's participation in literature. The importation of western treatises of moral education and good breeding, such as François Fénelon's *De L'Éducation des filles* (*Instruction for the Education of a Daughter*) of 1687, meant that reading was now accepted as an important part of young women's intellectual development. The curriculum of Catherine's model school for "young noblewomen", Smol'nyi Institute, included western and Russian literary classics, and the cultivation of the women in Catherine's court was to be remarked on by foreign visitors during the late 18th century.

Accordingly, in the late 18th and early 19th centuries a number of women, mostly well-educated aristocrats, did indeed begin contributing to the development of Russian letters. Several of them were the sisters, daughters or wives of male writers. Ekaterina Sumarokova (1746–97) was the daughter of the poet and playwright Aleksandr Sumarokov; Elizaveta Kheraskova (c.1740–1809) and Ekaterina Urusova (1747–c.1817) the wife and cousin respectively of Mikhail Kheraskov, author of the epic *Rossiiada*. The connections of these and comparable women, such as the Svin'ina sisters and Mar'ia Sushkova (1752–1803), facilitated their entrée to literary journals, some of which, for example *Priiatnoe i poleznoe preprovozhdenie vremeni* (A Pleasant and Instructive Manner of Passing the Time), and Nikolai Karamzin's *Aonidy*, published a number of original texts and translations by women, in keeping with the Sentimentalist cult of the "fair sex" as the arbiters of virtue and taste.

Though some late 18th- and early 19th-century women poets were no more than dilettante rhymesters, some, for example Urusova and Kheraskova, and later Aleksandra Murzina and Aleksandra Magnitskaia (active in the 1790s), Mar'ia Pospelova (1780–1805) and Anna Volkova (1781–1834), were genuinely talented individuals, the best of whose work displays intelligence, wit, and technical facility. The most determined, the most prolific, as well as probably the most talented was Anna Bunina (1774–1829), the first woman writer to live by her pen. Though lacking the social advantages of Urusova and Kheraskova, Bunina by sustained effort turned herself into an erudite Neoclassical poet, the author of epics as well as lyric verse, whose work includes some of the earliest genuinely autobiographical poetry by Russian writers of either gender. Another remarkable figure was the short-lived, but prodigious Elisaveta Kul'man (1808–25), who had a command of classical languages as well as several modern ones, and who was the author of interesting Neoclassical verse, including a tribute to the Greek poet Corinna, much of it written in unrhymed "Pindaric" stanzas.

Besides poetry, women writers produced didactic drama (Elizaveta Titova as well as the late 18th century's most famous woman writer, Catherine II), and fiction. A good deal of the latter was feeble indeed, consisting of sprawlingly-plotted novels and didactic *contes*; typical was the work of Mariia Izvekova (1790s–1830), author, among other works, of *Milena, ili redkii primer velikodushiia* [Milena, or A Rare Example of Magnanimity] (1806), whose titles bespeak their sentimental and moralistic content. However, Russian nationals writing in French also produced some more distinguished works, notably Julie (or Juliane) de Krüdener's *Valérie* (1803), famous in its day throughout Europe.

The rise of Pushkinian romanticism in the 1820s had contradictory effects on women's writing. The new understanding of "genius" as an extraordinary individual talent, rather than the individual guiding spirit of every human being, led to questioning of whether a woman could be a "genius". In his review of Mariia Zhukova's first collection of stories in 1838, Belinskii argued that women were by nature unfitted for the composition of great imaginative works. Such arguments inhibited the writing of romantic poetry by women; only when romanticism had become a marginal trend, in the 1840s, when the hegemony of realism began, could the notion of "genius" be appropriated by women. Karolina Pavlova (1807–93), the outstanding poet of the 1840s and 1850s, made full use of her new opportunities in poems such as "Zovet nas zhizn'" [Life Calls Us] (1846) and "Tri dushi" [Three Souls] (1845), and also in the remarkable prose and verse tale *Dvoinaia zhizn'* (*A Double Life*) 1848, reminiscent of Christina Rossetti's *Maud* (also written in the late 1840s, though not published until 1897). However, in the 1820s and 1830s, a good deal of women's poetry consisted of melodious but not very original confessions of love, static meditations on nature, and other kinds of salon verse. Yet some writers, such as Nadezhda Teplova (1814–48), were able to manipulate salon stereotypes in order to produce more distinguished work, which questioned the notion that women's primary task was to inspire men, and included self-conscious evocations of the act of writing.

The correlate of the idea that women were naturally limited in imaginative sweep was the notion that they were particularly fitted for the composition of prose. The years after 1820, therefore, led to an upsurge of prose writing by women. From the late 1830s in particular, writers such as Elena Gan (1814–42), Evdokiia Rostopchina (1812–58), and Mariia Zhukova (1804–55) used the "marginal hero" conventions of the romantic "society tale" in order to articulate resentment about the unequal status of women in Russian society – a fiercely held feeling since the late 18th century – in a way that was less abstract and schematic than before, and which gave closer attention to the fates of women from outside the metropolitan aristocracy. The rise of prose also fostered the development of an interesting tradition among women poets that one could describe as "prose in verse". Poets such as Iuliia Zhadovskaia (1824–83) and Rostopchina, again, wrote first-person confessional poetry that employed obvious masks, and (in the case of Rostopchina's "Neizvestnyi roman" [An Unknown Romance]) adopted a narrative frame such as was used in the romantic novella, in order to distance and ironize the sentiments expressed.

After the emigration of Karolina Pavlova from Russia in 1853, poetry went into a decline lasting nearly four decades. Though genres such as "prose in verse" (see above), political poetry (the minor poet Anna Barykova [1839–93] was the author of some fine satires), and religious verse (whose main exponent was the prolific Elizaveta Shakhova [1822–99]) saw some activity, the years between 1850 and 1890 were very much the "age of prose" for women writers, and of politically committed prose at that.

In the early 1840s, Russian radicals, following in the wake of French Utopian socialism, had begun taking an interest in the "woman question". The domination of these radicals of the "thick journals", literary and political monthlies, the key forums for political debate, meant that issues such as education for women and the liberation of wives and daughters from the shackles of male domination in the family began to play an even greater role in women's writing than before. With few exceptions, women tended to express their views on the "woman question" in literature and reviews rather than in essays, which gave much of their work a strong didactic bent. Perhaps the most popular type of narrative in the 1850s and 1860s was a "provincial tale", in which an unmarried young girl from a middling country gentry background struggles against the restricted future conventional expectation has in mind for her, sometimes with the help of a sympathetic man who lends her books and counsel. In one of the most striking of such tales, *Pansionerka* [The Schoolgirl] (1861), by Nadezhda Khvoshchinskaia (1824–89), the heroine, Lelen'ka, is successful in her fight against intellectual fossilization. Repudiating both the old-fashioned education offered at her school, the minor civil servant chosen as a husband for her by her appalling mother, she departs to celibacy and a life of self-sufficient labour in St Petersburg. Not all narratives offered such stirring models of self-betterment: in some, such as *Zhenskaia dolia* [A Woman's Lot] (1862) by Avdot'ia Panaeva (1819–93) or "Istoriia Poli" [Polly's Story] (1866), and "Eshche razbitoe serdtse" [Another Broken Heart] (1862) by Sof'ia Soboleva (1840–84), the weight of convention proves too strong for rebellion to be successful. But the association of education and work with liberation was seldom questioned, and, following the canons of didactic prose established in the 18th century, the heroine was usually directly contrasted with her negative counter-image, a frivolous and coquettish sister or friend relentlessly pursuing the conventional feminine reward – marriage to a single man of good fortune. Overwhelmingly, it was young unmarried women, rather than middle-aged ones with family responsibilities, that interested women writers, though in the work of Evgeniia Tur (1815–92), such as "Antonina" (1851), the problems of maternity were sometimes considered as well.

Besides such narratives of women's liberation, women writers of the day also produced some outstanding pieces of regional prose (especially notable here were Nadezhda Sokhanskaia [1823–84], also the author of a superb confessional autobiography, and Aleksandra Kobiakova [1823–92], writer of interesting stories about provincial merchant women). The tradition of adopting masculine pseudonyms espoused by many writers in the 1850s and 1860s also allowed women, if they wanted, to raise their voices in the debate about topical questions that had nothing to do with the "woman question" as such, including serf emancipation (Sof'ia Khvoshchinskaia [1828–65] in her "Domashniaia idilliia ne nashego vremeni" [A Domestic Idyll of Olden Times] 1863), and monasticism (Anna Korvin-Krukovskaia [1843–87] in her "Mikhail" 1864).

The development from the 1860s of women's liberation groups organized by women did not have a strong direct impact on women's writing, though some of the realist writers of the 1890s, such as Ol'ga Shapir (1850–1916), were feminist activists, and others, such as Ekaterina Letkova (1856–1937), sympathetic to at least some of its aims. However, participants in the women's movement rarely figured in the writings of these or of other women authors. Much more significant as a force in women's fiction was Populism, whose effects began to be felt from the late 1870s: the "positive heroines" of didactic narratives were now often women of peasant or working-class stock, with neurotic upper- or middle-class ladies sometimes acting as foils. One of the earliest examples of the new trend was the story "Akhmetkina zhena" [The Turkish Soldier's Wife] (1881) by Valentina Dmitrieva (1859–1947), of peasant origin herself. In the 1890s, Sof'ia Smirnova (1852–1921), Iuliia Iakovleva, pseudonymously "Bezrodnaia" (1858–1910), and Anastasiia Verbitskaia (1861–1928), besides Shapir and Letkova, were all to produce interesting examples of such stories about working women, downtrodden or resilient. Now that employment opportunities had expanded, stories about professional women were another popular genre; the fact that women's employment often remained low-status and unfulfilling was confronted, for example, in Letkova's story "Otdykh" [The Holiday] (1896), in which an unfulfilled white-collar worker puts an end to her life during a river cruise. The prevalence of suicide, murder, and other extreme events often gave work by women naturalists (as with their male contemporaries) a melodramatic colouration, which was also observable in the many narratives in which questions of sexual liberation were explored. A key text of the 1890s was Mariia Krestovskaia's anti-*Kreutzer Sonata* novel *Artistka* [The Actress] (1891), which showed a heroine torn between fulfilment as an artist and as a sexual being. The novel was the forerunner to such notorious early 20th-century bestsellers as Verbitskaia's *Kliuchi schast'ia* [The Keys to Happiness] (1909–13) and *Gnev Dionisa* [The Anger of Dionysus] (1910) by Evdokiia Magrodskaia (1866–1930).

Another vehicle for debates on professionalism, if less often on sexuality, in the 1880s and 1890s was the memoir. Some women who had achieved outstanding success in their professions, such as Sof'ia Kovalevskaia, pioneering woman mathematician (1850–91), left memoirs of their lives which, while not explicitly "feminist" in orientation, were all the same remarkable works of female self-assertion.

An entirely contrary trend in the 1890s was represented by the incipient Decadent movement in Russia. Like her male counterpart, the Decadent heroine jettisoned the Russian intelligentsia's treasured ideals of self-sacrifice to the collective good in favour of self-fulfilment, often of a sexually hedonistic kind. Mariia Bashkirtseva, a budding painter whose diary was posthumously published in 1887, three years after her death at the age of 26, became famous all over Europe. Translated from the original French into Russian in 1892, the diary had an enormous impact on at least two generations of Russian women; those influenced or inspired by it included the young Marina Tsvetaeva. Echoes of Bashkirtseva's neurotic self-aggrandisement can also be heard in the powerful verse of Mirra Lokhvitskaia (1869–1905), who expressed a bold sexuality new to Russian women's poetry. But the towering woman writer of Russian decadence was Zinaida Hippius (1869–1945), whose artful and disturbing poetry of moral transgression pioneered the liberating androgyny that was to become fashionable among most early 20th-century women poets. Posing now as an egotistical man, now as a demonic woman, Hippius was also one of the first woman poets to exploit Russian Symbolism's new interest, after 1900, in specifically feminine prophetic voices – the oracle, the soothsayer, the wise woman. Besides poetry, she was the author of interesting, often distinctly Gothic, stories, and of perhaps the first major dramatic works by a Russian woman writer. *Makov tsvet* [The Red Poppy] (1908) and *Zelenoe kol'tso* (*The Green Ring*) 1914 (staged by Meierkhol'd in 1915) are powerful evocations of the claustrophobic atmosphere in the early 20th-century Russian intelligentsia, in which armed uprisings, intellectual disputation, and romantic outpouring alike prove futile and redundant, and fond hopes in the capacity of the "younger generation" to jettison the past are the only consolation for disillusioned observers in their middle years.

Hippius was the first swallow of what was to prove a remarkable summer for women writers. Between 1900 and 1920, countless women took up the pen as poets, prosaists, memoirists, and occasionally dramatists. The Symbolist cult of the "eternal feminine" could pose dangers in that it supposed the "feminine" to exist for the delight or edification of a contemplating male. But the more intelligent women writers, such as Adelaida Gertsyk (1874–1925), Liubov' Stolitsa (1884–1934), Poliksena Solov'eva (1867–1924), and Liudmila Vil'kina (pseudonym of Izabella Vil'ken, 1873–1920), were fully aware of the threats, and wore their "eternal feminine" masks ironically and self-consciously. Women's capacity for ironic distance was enhanced by the so-called "crisis of Symbolism" (1910–13), in which young representatives of would-be post-Symbolist schools attacked what had by then become the literary establishment for the stereotypicality of its themes and the poverty of its stylistic apparatus. Though women poets were relatively poorly represented in the various Futurist movements, some (for example Elena Guro, 1877–1913) were encouraged by the new taste for primitivism in poetry and painting to publish work in an original vein of childish naivety (see particularly *Nebesnye verbliuzhata* [*The Little Camels of the Sky*] 1914.) Among the Acmeists, emphasis on the centrality of (judiciously aestheticized) everyday experience led to a revival of "prose in verse", of which Anna Akhmatova soon proved an outstandingly talented practitioner. Whatever the passing fashions in types of prose and theme, the new emphasis everywhere on "the word as such" (*slovo kak takovoe*) was helpful to women poets, whose historical weakness, as a group, had been the all too artless outpouring of feeling. A particularly impressive example of a poet who benefited from the new emphasis on "the word as such" was Sofiia Parnok (1885–1933).

The new stress on the importance of craftsmanship was not without significance in the quite different tradition of realist prose, where writers such as Liubov' Gurevich (1866–1940), Lidiia Avilova (1864–1943), and Varvara Tsekhovskaia (writing as "Ol'nem", 1872–1941) worked with more innovative techniques than their predecessors, such as stream-of-consciousness and mixed perspective. In the early stories of Ol'ga Forsh (1873–1961), populist subjects appeared to radically novel effect through the employment of material from folklore and folk-beliefs ("Za zhar-ptitsei" [Hunting the Fire-Bird] 1910). But perhaps the most original writer was Lidiia Zinov'eva-Annibal (1866–1907), whose extraordinary short-story cycle, *Tragicheskii zverinets* [The Tragic Menagerie] (1907), the first-person narrative of a coldly observant, calculating, and self-indulgent adolescent girl, suggests that the author might have developed, had she lived, into one of Russia's foremost modernist writers.

For various reasons, the Bolshevik Revolution in 1917, while by no means stifling women writers' activities, did not always nurture the promising traditions that had developed in the three decades before its occurrence. The "bourgeois feminist" movement – an insulting catch-all term used to denote all the various non-socialist groupings, ignoring considerable differences between these – was one casualty of the Bolsheviks' action against oppositional political groupings of all kinds. The women's liberation agenda was not set according to the Bolsheviks' own programme of legal and economic reform and political consciousness-raising. Responsibility for the latter was assigned in particular to the women's section of the Party, which was founded in 1919 and came to be known as the *Zhenotdel*. Its determined organizers, unlike their feminist predecessors, made themselves felt in fiction as well as in life; one of them was, for example, given a leading role in a 1927 production novel, *Lesozavod* [The Saw Mill], by Anna Karavaeva (1893–1979). The "new woman", a socially and sexually emancipated individual in sympathy with revolutionary ideals, if not invariably a Party official, also figured widely, most famously in *Liubov' pchel trudovykh* (*Love of Worker Bees*) 1923, a collection of short stories by Aleksandra Kollontai (1872–1952), Commissar for Social Welfare from 1917 to 1922 and politically the most powerful woman writer in Russian history, with the exception of Catherine II. Like pre-revolutionary realism, the new fiction of women's liberation was often openly didactic, and the "new woman" had her negative counterpart in the "backward" bourgeois or peasant woman, hostile to communist ideology and self-servingly attached to her children, husband, lover, personal appearance, religious beliefs, or other such reprehensible object. No wonder that the more adventurous writers, such as Lidiia Seifullina (1889–1954), often preferred to adopt a masculine viewpoint in their work.

After 1930, when Stalin declared the "woman question" solved, and closed down the *Zhenotdel*, its activists disappeared from fiction, but the "new woman" continued to be a popular figure until the mid-1930s, when increasing disapproval of extramarital intercourse and other such "promiscuous" behaviour meant that fiction, like ideology, began to place a new emphasis on women's duties as wives and mothers. In the late 1930s and the 1940s, the main characters of factory-and-collective-farm novels by writers such as Karavaeva, Antonina Koptiaeva (b. 1909), Galina Nikolaeva (real name Volianskaia, 1911–63), and Vera Panova (1905–73) were often women in full-time employment and taking an active role in Party business who none the less managed to work the "second shift" of domestic duties smilingly and uncomplainingly. Though equality of women continued to be proclaimed as a Soviet achievement, the new emphasis on rigidly defined gender roles in the home now made the proclamations ring hollow. Wartime propaganda and fiction briefly revived a feistier kind of heroine (for example, the partisan fighter Zoia Kosmodemianskaia), but in a manner that made clear the enormity and "unfemininity" of such behaviour. Ironically, one of the most important texts produced by a woman in the post-revolutionary period, and published in 1930–31 just before the imposition of socialist realism, was the autobiographical trilogy, *Kaftanchik* [The Little Caftan], *Liakh* [The Polack], and *Otryv* [The Break] by Vera Gedroits (1876–1932). So far from observing traditional boundaries in these books, Gedroits, who wrote using the male first name Sergei, suggested that conventional sex dominations might be wholly illusory (after her brother's death, the heroine, Vera, "becomes" Sergei). The trilogy, which the publisher's reviewer, the writer Konstantin Fedin, compared to Pasternak's autobiographical writing, is one of the outstanding achievements in women's prose writing of any period.

In poetry, cultural centralization had still more unfortunate effects. During the early 1920s, a certain limited pluralism was in evidence, with "bourgeois" writers such as Anna Akhmatova or Sofiia Parnok, or, before her emigration, Marina Tsvetaeva (1892–1941), as well as many less prominent figures, able to publish their work with hindrance, either in Russia or abroad. But attacks on such poetry as "backward" were frequent (for example, in Trotskii's *Literatura i revoliutsiia* [*Literature and Revolution*] of 1923). Furthermore, the new order did not generate any significant tradition of revolutionary poetry by women. With rare exceptions, such as Anna Barkova's *Zhenshchina* [Woman] (1922), a collection of poems about revolutionary female types whose callow romanticism later embarrassed a Barkova grown wise and cynical about revolutionary blood-letting, women made no contributions to the development of proletarian poetry. And Mariia Shkapskaia (1891–1952), while committed to the revolutionary cause from the start, produced, in her poetry, fierce critiques of Civil War violence, rather than comfortable endorsements of Bolshevik policy; in "Iav'" [Reality] (1923), for example, she offers a representation of a political execution that only external evidence (the place and date of composition) indicates must be a White atrocity, rather than a Red one. All this, as well as women's under-representation in key organizations such as RAPP (Association of Proletarian Writers), meant that women poets were particularly vulnerable after cultural centralization began. Akhmatova, Parnok, Anna Radlova (1891–1949), Elizaveta Polonskaia (real name Movshezon, 1890–1969), Mariia Shkapskaia, and Anna Barkova represent only the better-known instances of talented poets who stopped publishing, and in some cases writing, poetry in the late 1920s. The pity was the greater in that officially-published poetry by women was generally undistinguished in formal and intellectual terms. In the 1930s, poets such as Ol'ga Berggol'ts (1910–1975) and Margarita Aliger (1915–92) published some energetic, if rather inchoate, poems about the life of the "new woman". However, their efforts were quickly overtaken by the policy changes of the mid-1930s, which made motherhood the proper subject of poetry as much as prose. Though the war allowed some women poets (Vera Inber [1890–1972], as well as Ol'ga Berggol'ts) respite from the duty to represent heroines of monolithic socialist virtue, the effect of cultural centralization was to push most serious women's poetry underground. Even talented poets, such as Vera Zviagintseva (1894–1972), published mostly mediocre verse in the Stalin period.

Most of the better work by Soviet women poets came from the "internal emigration": it was done by writers such as Akhmatova, Barkova, Parnok, Mariia Petrovykh (1908–79), and Elena Tager (1895–1964), writing without hope of immediate publication. During the late 1920s and early 1930s, Parnok produced some of her best poems, including some unique celebrations of lesbian love. In the 1930s, 1940s, and early 1950s, some remarkable poetry was composed in prison camps by incarcerated writers, including Tager and Barkova; a selection has now appeared in the series "Poety – uzniki Gulaga" (Prisoner Poets of the Gulag), put out by the Vozvrashchenie organization in Moscow. Literary distinction was also achieved by many of the poets living in actual, physical, emigration from Russia, in Paris, Berlin, Helsinki, and other centres of the Russian diaspora. Undoubtedly the pivotal figure was Marina Tsvetaeva, the best of whose work, including superb narrative poems and plays as well as lyric verse, dates from her early years in emigration, 1921–26.

But there were also a number of other talented women poets in the diaspora, among them Raisa Blokh (1899–1943), Vera Bulich (1898–1954), Sofiia Pregel' (1902–72), Alla Golovina (1909–87), and Anna Prismanova (1892–1960), all of whom produced well-crafted and original verse that eschewed the tendency, rather marked among other émigrées, to offer more or less well-composed reassortments of Akhmatovian themes and images. In prose, émigrées were less remarkable by force of numbers but two writers in particular did interesting work. Teffi (1872–1952), a very popular humourist before the Revolution, lost some of her light-heartedness in emigration, and embarked on a series of poignant, satirical, and sometimes bitter portraits of life in exile that are among the most interesting prose produced in the Russian diaspora. Nina Berberova (1901–93), while at most a mediocre poet, was a talented prose writer whose work includes elegant novellas of émigré society and an accomplished autobiography, *Kursiv moi* (*The Italics Are Mine*) 1969. Less distinguished in literary terms were the autobiographies of Irina Odoevtseva (real name Iraida Geinike, 1895–1990), *Na beregakh Nevy* [On the Banks of the Neva] (1967) and *Na beregakh Seny* [On the Banks of the Seine] (1983), which, however, offer striking impressions of literary life during the first years of Soviet rule in the Paris emigration.

Given the peculiar restrictions that socialist realism had imposed on women writers, there was a certain historical justice in the fact that several of them played a prominent part in de-Stalinizing the Writers' Union after 1953. At the Union's 2nd Congress in 1954, Ol'ga Forsh acted as symbolic figurehead, while Ol'ga Berggol'ts made a memorable speech denouncing the pompous inhumanity of Soviet literature. Women also made notable contributions to the recovery of history that began with Khrushchev's assaults on Stalin's crimes at the 20th Party Congress in 1956. Two central works were Evgeniia Ginzburg's *Krutoi marshrut* (translated into English as *Journey into the Whirlwind* and *Within the Whirlwind*) and Nadezhda Mandel'shtam's *Vospominaniia* (translated into English as *Hope Against Hope* and *Hope Abandoned*), both written in the early 1960s, which circulated widely in manuscript prior to their publication in the west (the first volumes came out in 1967 and 1970 respectively). These were followed by Lidiia Chukovskaia's justly famous diary-biography *Zapiski ob Anne Akhmatovoi* (*The Akahmatova Journals*) 1976–80. All these works appeared for the first time in their author's native country during the late 1980s, when Mikhail Gorbachev's policy of glasnost also gave opportunities to previously unpublished women memoirists. A 1989 collection edited by S. Vilenskii, *Dodnes' tiagoteet* [The Pain Lasts], contained accounts, many very powerful, by more than 30 women of life in Stalin's camps. During the 1980s and 1990s, women who spent the Stalin years in more fortunate circumstances, such as Raisa Orlova and Elena Bonner, have offered striking chronicles of growing up under the leader's rule, while Larisa Vasil'eva's popular biography *Kremlevskie zheny* [The Kremlin Wives] (1992), was both a luridly readable bestseller and a pioneer in a genre new to Russian literary culture.

Though by no means all women writers wholeheartedly welcomed de-Stalinization (the veteran Marietta Shaginian [1888–1982] being among those who urged caution), women writers were notable participants in the revival of critical realism that was ushered in by the Thaw. Khrushchev's announcement in 1956 that discrimination against women was still a problem was crucial, since it allowed the "woman question" to be posed once more. Issues such as women's struggles at work, and especially their need to work the "double shift" as housekeepers and carers, were explored by writers such as Irina Grekova (pseudonym of Elena Ventsel', b. 1907), Maiia Ganina (b. 1927), and Natal'ia Baranskaia (b. 1908). Baranskaia's "Nedelia kak nedelia" ("A Week Like Any Other"), a refreshingly honest account of an ordinary working mother's week, created a furore when first published in 1969. Critical realism has remained a central genre for women writers, though some, particularly Liudmila Petrushevskaia (b. 1938), have become more ambitious in their formal approach. Petrushevskaia, who is also a major playwright, makes extensive use of internal monologue in her fiction, and in stories such as *Vremia noch'* (*The Time: Night*) 1992, employs devices such as the "found text" in a way that clouds the transparency, and problematizes the accessibility to which women's realism has so often pretended. The realism of the 1960s and 1970s has sometimes expressed nostalgia for the "traditional" femininity supposedly "destroyed" by communist rule, but here too Petrushevskaia is an innovator, suggesting – for example in "Svoi krug" ("Our Crowd") 1988 – that women's much-celebrated role as carers for others often turns them into downtrodden drudges, self-serving manipulators, or bullies. Another interesting and innovative realist is Nina Katerli (b. 1934), who makes free use of fantasy in works such as *Chudovishche* ("The Monster") 1983; *Polina* (1984) has attracted a good deal of interest among western feminists because of its imaginative revision of the Soviet ideal of maternity. Katerli is also the author of stimulating essays, including a dramatic account of her indictment for libel by right-wing nationalists.

The 40 years since 1956 have also witnessed a tremendous renaissance in women's poetry, in which the rediscovery of Akhmatova's work was a significant moment. Though Akhmatova's commemoration of the Great Terror, *Rekviem* (*Requiem*) written 1935–43, remained unacceptable to Soviet officialdom until 1987, the cycle, like the memoirs of Ginzburg or Mandel'shtam, was circulated privately before being published in the west in 1963. *Requiem* apart, a good number of Akhmatova's lyric poems did see the light of day in the late 1950s and early 1960s, most significantly in the substantial collection *Beg vremeni* [The Flight of Time] (1965). Contemporaneously, Marina Tsvetaeva's poetry also started reaching the Soviet public for the first time; a landmark was the publication of a critical edition of her work, *Stikhotvoreniia i poemy* [Lyric and Narrative Poems] in 1965. The reappearance of these two "ancestors" strengthened the emerging talents of such young poets as Bella Akhmadulina (b. 1937), Novella Matveeva (b. 1934), and Iunna Morits (b. 1937), who have all since established themselves as major writers. Since the 1960s and especially since the 1970s, women's poetry has been a significant and recognized force in Russian literature, with such outstanding 1970s debutantes as Elena Shvarts (b. 1948) and Ol'ga Sedakova (b. 1949) now joined by promising younger writers such as Mariia Avvakumova and the religious poet Oles'ia Nikolaeva (b. 1955).

On the whole, poets since the Thaw have been more adventurous, in technical terms, than their contemporaries working in prose; they have also been more attracted to metaphysical dimensions of reality. However, the 1980s saw a revival of such "poetic" directions in prose too. As with anti-realism in recent Russian prose generally, the silencing of the early 20th-century avant-garde has sometimes led to a curious conservatism in more recent experimental writing. The controversial work of Valeriia Narbikova (b. 1958), for example, has much in common with the writing of Gertrude Stein. The ornamentalist prose of Tat'iana Tolstaia (b. 1951) looks to Nabokov and Bunin, the short stories of Nina Sadur (b. 1950) to Daniil Kharms. Compared with some of their western counterparts, such as Angela Carter, Monique Wittig, Louise Erdrich, Candia McWilliam, or Toni Morrison, and indeed with some Russian women poets, some younger-generation Russian women prosaists can seem more promising in their intentions than in their achievements. However, the prose writers are in no sense weighed down by their influences, and there is no doubt that Sadur, Tolstaia or Narbikova, along with "hyper-realists" such as Svetlana Vasilenko (b. 1956) and Larisa Vaneeva (b. 1953), are producing some of the most innovative work coming out of Russia today.

This short survey of Russian women's writing has done no more than mention the best-known names, all of them producing "literature" in the most conventional sense. It should be noted, though, that women writers have also made notable contributions to various para-literary or non-literary genres for writing. As in other countries, children's writing has attracted numerous talents: after the Revolution, these included writers who might have had trouble placing their work under the new system, such as the poets Elizaveta Dmitrieva (better known under her pseudonym Cherubina de Gabriak) and Elizaveta Polonskaia. Women have worked with distinction as literary critics (Mariia Tsebrikova, Liubov' Gurevich, Alla Latynina, Natal'ia Ivanova), as literary historians (Lidiia Ginzburg, Emma Gershtein), as journalists (Evgeniia Tur, Anna Volkova, Tat'iana Bogdanovich, Mariia Shkapskaia), as biographers (Lidiia Chukovskaia), as cultural theorists (Ol'ga Freidenberg), and as film scenarists (Natal'ia Riazantseva, Mariia Khmelik). All of these are areas urgently requiring the detailed consideration that has now begun to be given to women's prose, poetry and autobiography, which, until the early 1980s, themselves attracted little serious study, whether in Russia or abroad.

CATRIONA KELLY

Russian Literary Theory: From the Formalists to Lotman

Literary theory in Russia was not the exclusive concern of literary theorists and critics. Just as in England writers as varied as Alexander Pope, T.S. Eliot, and David Lodge have theorized about literary form and language, about the place of literature in culture and in relation to the other arts, so in Russia Mikhail Lomonosov in the 18th century, Aleksandr Pushkin and Lev Tolstoi in the 19th, and Andrei Belyi, Vladimir Maiakovskii, and Boris Pasternak in the 20th century made not only radical experiments with form in poetry and prose fiction, but also original and significant theoretical statements.

The main focus of this essay is on the Russian Formalist critics of the 1910s and 1920s and their contemporaries Mikhail Bakhtin (1895–1975) and Vladimir Propp (1895–1970), and the leaders of the Tartu semiotics school in the 1960s to 1980s who have also had a major influence on literary theory outside Russia. Here again, however, theory was not divorced from the practice of writing. Two of the leading Formalists, Viktor Shklovskii (1893–1984) and Iurii Tynianov (1894–1943), wrote fascinating novels and biographies, while Shklovskii and Osip Brik (1888–1945) experimented with film scenarios and scripts.

The material of which literary works are made is, ultimately, language, so it is no accident that the two young organizations that united to form the Russian Formalists in 1914 were the Moscow Linguistic Circle and the St Petersburg-based Society for Poetic Language (OPOIAZ). Shklovskii, one of the founders of OPOIAZ, insisted that the first object of literary study should be form: "The literary work is pure form, it is neither thing, nor material, but a relationship of materials." This kind of statement fitted in, of course, with the materialist philosophy of the early Soviet period. However, the Formalist theorists were at odds with what they regarded as the "naive sociologizing" of the typical Marxist critics of the 1920s, who only looked to literature for reflections of the social structure and manners of its age. This conflict with the hardline Marxists led to the enforced demise of the Formalist movement.

In the early Formalist pronouncements, however, the main enemy was traditional literary history, criticism, and teaching. Roman Jakobson (1896–1982) contrasted its faults with the approach of a true science of literature in 1921 in a typically picturesque way:

> The subject of literary science is not literature, but literariness, i.e. that which makes a given work a literary work. Up till now, however, historians of literature have mostly behaved like the police who, when they want to arrest someone, take in everyone and everything found in the apartment and even chance passers-by. Historians of literature have in the same way felt the need to take in everything – everyday life, psychology, politics, philosophy. Instead of a science of literature we have fetched up with a conglomeration of cottage industries.

The keys to the new literary science were system and function. Every literary text involves choices from systems of possible options that are typical of the genre to which that text belongs: a narrative has a plot structure (complication – crisis – denouement) which is typical of a certain kind of story or novel; it has typical characters (heroes, villains, helpers, witnesses) and characteristic settings for the action. All of these are chosen, like ingredients in a recipe, from the available systems of plot-structure, character-type, and setting-frame that the writer's literary culture makes available. Similarly, a lyric poem creates a particular "I–you" relationship and a particular sound structure with selections from systems of grammar, imagery, metre, rhythm, rhyme, assonance, alliteration, and so on. But the scientific aspect of literary form does not stop with these systems of choice. They do not operate in isolation from each other in the work. Each chosen element has a function within the whole; it interacts with the other elements to produce a complex play of forces and meanings. Take something as simple as a rhyme in a poem: at first glance – or hearing – it merely sets up a sound echo with the final word or phrase in a preceding line. But the rhyming words are different, they mean different things, they may belong to different grammatical categories, and the context of both grammar and meaning of the lines in which they occur is quite different. The rhyme may also point outwards from the poem to other poems, "intertextually", or may even be a kind of comment by the poet on himself, on the nature of poetry, or on his readers. It may have all these functions at once and interact with other functioning elements such as metre, the interplay of grammatical and metrical units, or may highlight a clash of imagery.

Peter Steiner, an American commentator, has instructively highlighted and compared what he calls "the three metaphors of Russian Formalism": the machine, the organism, and the system. Certain Formalists were mainly preoccupied with the components of a literary work and their articulation, like cogs in a machine; others saw a literary work as having more in common with a living organism, each organ, each cell, each nerve functioning in a complex and self-balancing interaction that guaranteed life to the organism; others focused on the notion of the individual work as a system of choices and interactions, and even on the whole of literature as a complex, self-balancing system, whose very evolution could be described in systemic terms. Steiner chooses to see these three metaphors as distinguishing different phases of Formalism dominated in turn by different theorists. But the scientific nature of the enterprise stressed by Shklovskii and Jakobson involved all three metaphors from the start.

The first article of Formalist theory by Viktor Shklovskii, "Voskreshenie slova" ("The Resurrection of the Word"), was published in 1914. His complex notion was much discussed in the following decade. In the first place "the word" – language – is the very material from which literature is constructed; theories of literature must resurrect an interest in this material. Second, language is different in a literary text from other contexts; one important definition of "literariness" is that the literary text rescues words from the stale, clichéd usage of everyday discourses, reanimates their meaning, makes their form palpable. But this was not just a technical matter for Shklovskii; it becomes an ethical issue. One reason why we should take literature very seriously indeed is that it refreshes and renews our vision of reality; it resurrects not just "the word", *but the world*:

> As they become habitual, actions are automatized ... This is a process ideally typified by algebra, where objects are replaced by symbols ... Through this algebraic mode of thinking we grasp things by counting them and measuring them; we do not see them, but merely recognize them by their primary features. The thing rushes past us, prepacked, as it were; we know that it is there by the space that it takes up, but we see only its surface. This kind of perception shrivels a thing up, first of all in the way we perceive it, but later this affects the way we handle it too ... Life goes to waste as it is turned into nothingness. Automatization corrodes things, clothing, furniture, one's wife and one's fear of war ... And so that a sense of life may be restored, that things may be felt, so that stones may be made stony, there exists what we call art.

Shklovskii called the main literary device for this kind of renewal of our vision "making strange". This is sometimes translated by the more technical-sounding words "defamiliarization" or "de-automatization", that is, opposing the process of automatization described in Shklovskii's quotation. But "making strange" is a better term. Lev Tolstoi, reputedly one of the world's great "realist" writers, has everyday social customs observed through the eyes of a naive character, and they are "made strange" for us too: all the charades and pretences involved in an opera or a church service are unmasked by the innocent gaze – and, of course, by the innocent language – of a child or an uneducated person. The most extreme example of this device occurs in Tolstoi's story "Kholstomer" ("Strider"), which is told from the point of view of a horse. The behaviour of people with each other and towards animals – indeed, the whole concept of private property – is subjected to the ruthlessly naive gaze of the horse.

Shklovskii shows, however, that this trick is not confined to literary fiction, because he sees it as one of the key mechanisms of the erotic riddle where locks and keys or rings and marlinspikes provide the metaphors for female and male sexual organs and their interplay. This move on Shklovskii's part to link the use of a device in complex literary genres with its use in simple and even "disreputable" folk genres is characteristic of the Formalists' lively thinking across established categories and of their desire to shake up categorized thinking about the institution of literature. It is reminiscent of the anecdote told by the great Russian film director and theorist Sergei Eisenstein (1898–1948), who was a contemporary and friend of the Formalists, about how an erotic folk-tale (about a fox – a vixen – getting trapped and raped by a hare) gave him the inspiration for the turning-point in his great historico-political recreation of the defeat of the Teutonic Knights in *Aleksandr Nevskii* (1938).

All of the Formalists were keen to loosen the boundaries between the literature that is officially sanctioned and taught in school and the other forms of discourse, like the joke, the riddle, the proverb, the folk-tale, which are typical creative forms of non-literate people's culture. To this extent they were in tune with the aspirations of the Russian Revolution and the subsequent drive for the re-evaluation of popular culture with which they coincided. On the other hand, much of their work was aimed at elucidating exactly what is "literariness" and involved contrasting speech in literature with speech in "everyday genres", such as news reports, scientific papers or official announcements. One of the determinative devices of the literary text, Shklovskii claimed, was its tendency to "lay bare the device", and this too became a Formalist slogan. A novel like *Don Quixote* or *Tristram Shandy* does not stop at "making strange" the worlds of medieval knights or married couples – it shows off the devices that make this defamiliarization possible: in *Tristram Shandy* Laurence Sterne drags out trivial actions, constantly interrupts the progress of the narrative, shifts chapters around, mixes rows of asterisks or drawings with verbal text, and, moreover, shows off in doing so.

For the Formalists this had both psychological and ethical implications. They were not convinced by Herbert Spencer's widely popular notion that art works psychologically, according to the principle of greatest efficiency with least effort. On the contrary, Shklovskii asserted, art works deliberately through "form made difficult"; our perceptions are deliberately "slowed down" through a whole variety of technical ploys: in narrative, the normal order of events may be inverted, or digressions introduced; in poetry, sequences of sounds may be deliberately hard to pronounce, or fresh images or startling rhymes or puns or grammatical distortions may force us to stop and read again or reflect. Only the "automatized" forms of everyday speech flow seamlessly and aim to achieve the most with the least effort. Ethically, this deliberate "putting the brakes on" perception is part of the "resurrection of the word" and the revival of moral awareness.

Most of Shklovskii's programmatic and memorable theoretical pronouncements related to literary prose. We should note, however, that most of the other Russian Formalists between 1917 and 1929 were equally interested in poetry and prose: Boris Eikhenbaum (1886–1959) wrote on "Verse Melody" and the poetry of Anna Akhmatova as well as on the prose of Gogol' and Tolstoi; Boris Tomashevskii (1890–1957)'s book *O stikhe* [On Verse] 1929, was as significant as his *Teoriia literatury* [Theory of Literature] 1925, which dealt mainly with narrative; Iurii Tynianov explored the relationship between systems and functions equally thoroughly in his books *Problema stikhotvornogo iazyka* (*The Problem of Verse Language*) 1924, and *Gogol' i Dostoevskii K teorii parodii* [Gogol' and Dostoevskii. Towards a Theory of Parody] (1921). The three other most prominent theorists of the heyday of Russian Formalism, Roman Jakobson, Osip Brik, and Viktor Zhirmunskii (1881–1971), wrote almost exclusively about poetry. In many ways all of these writers opened up areas of poetic theory and analysis that have been explored in depth outside Russia relatively recently. Yet their work is hardly known outside circles of Russian specialists. The reasons are fairly obvious: the argument is untranslatable. In order to illustrate patterns of word-choice, rhythm, stress, sound patterning and so on in Russian poetry you have to use the Russian words and patterns. The only satisfactory way to translate Osip Brik's concepts of "Sound Repetitions" from Pushkin and Lermontov, for instance, would be to rewrite his paper in terms of comparable patterns in two comparable English poets, say, Byron and Coleridge. But none of the poetic devices is isolated; they interact in different ways linguistically in the two languages, and culturally in the two poetic traditions. Even the fact that most educated Russian readers know their greatest poets by heart, while the English do not, makes a difference to the way the theory is taken up.

The lack of awareness outside Russia of the high quality of the Formalists' theories and analyses of poetry (except, at second-hand, through Victor Erlich's excellent book *Russian Formalism: History, Doctrine*, first published in 1955) has reduced appreciation of just how scientific their "science of literature" could be. There is something so intense about short poetic forms like the verse lyric that it becomes much easier to show the choices that are being made from the systems of metre, rhythm, verse structure, rhyme, alliteration, assonance, enjambment, grammatical units, and so on, than is the case with the larger and more diffuse forms of the novel and short story or dramatic genres. Jakobson was able to show that Pushkin's most famous two-stanza poem "Ia vas liubil" ("I Loved You Once") achieves its emotional power from the interplay of grammatical structures with rhythm and sound patterning and depends hardly at all on imagery, which for most earlier critics had been the touchstone of lyric poetry. Moreover, the function of each choice – say, a rhyme or a change of rhythm – in the overall texture of a poem is also more easily determined than the function of analogous choices – a pair of characters who are foils for each other or a change of setting – in a novel.

Ia vas liubil: liubov' eshche, byt' mozhet
V dushe moei ugasla ne sovsem;
No pust' ona vas bol'she ne trevozhit;
Ia ne khochu pechalit' vas nichem.

Ia vas liubil bezmolvno, beznadezhno,
To robost'iu, to revnost'iu tomim;
Ia vas liubil tak iskrenno, tak nezhno,
Kak dai vam Bog liubimoi byt' drugim.

I loved you: it may be that love has not completely died in my soul; but let it not trouble you any more; I do not wish to sadden you in any way.

I loved you silently, hopelessly, tormented now by diffidence and now by jealousy; I loved you so truly, so tenderly as God may grant you to be loved by another.

(Prose Translation by Dimitri Obolensky)

It was mainly in relation to poetry that the Formalists evolved many of their most significant ideas and methods of analysis. One key idea was the concept of "foregrounding": a literary text foregrounds particular features, while others keep the "automatized" functions they have in ordinary language. Thus, "making strange" is one variety of foregrounding. An obvious example in verse would be the pairs of matching adverbs or instrumentals in successive lines of the second stanza of Pushkin's poem: *bezmolvno – beznadezhno* (silently – hopelessly), *to robost'iu – to revnost'iu* (now by diffidence – now by jealousy), *tak iskrenno – tak nezhno* (so truly – so tenderly). We note that these not only relate to each other in both meaning and grammatical form, but each has a marker of its match at the beginning: *bez-*, *to-*, *tak*. This is a heavy degree of foregrounding of parallelism: we tend not to utter such heart-felt pairs of words in everyday language. Part of its function, however, is to set up a kind of automatism within the stanza (Jakobson compared the rhythms involved to heartbeats) which is shattered by the shock of the direct appeal on behalf of the beloved in the last line, where the grammar is much more complex and difficult to process ("form made difficult") and the only parallel is the implied one between *drugim* (another) and the poet.

There was a further dimension to foregrounding, however, which emerged quite early in the writings of Jakobson, Eikhenbaum, and Tynianov, and that was the concept of the dominant, which has implications for all literary theories that involve close study of the text. In 1927 Iurii Tynianov wrote:

> The work is a system of correlated factors. Correlation of each factor with the others is its *function* in relation to the whole system. It is quite clear that every literary system is

> formed not by the peaceful interaction of all the factors, but by the supremacy, the foregrounding, of one factor (or group) that functionally subjugates and colours the rest. This factor bears the name that has already become established in Russian scholarly works of the *dominant* ...

Tynianov went so far as to claim that this complex functioning of the dominant was the defining characteristic of literature: "Since a system is not a free interplay of equal elements but presupposes the foregrounding of one group of elements ('a dominant') and the deformation of others, a work becomes literature and acquires its literary function through just this dominant." The implications of this assertion were developed a decade later by Jan Mukařovský of the Prague School of Structuralism and in the 1970s by Zholkovskii and Shcheglov, whose work will be mentioned later. In a non-Slavonic context they have contributed to "systemic-functional" approaches to literary stylistics.

Linked to the untranslatability of theoretical writing about poetry mentioned earlier is the fact that the first translation of "Formalist" writing to reach English-speaking readers was Vladimir Propp's *Morfologiia skazki* (*Morphology of the Folktale*), originally published in 1928 and published in English translation in the United States in 1958. Propp was an anthropologist who did not belong to the Formalist movement, yet he pioneered the "morphological" method of analysing the structure of a narrative genre by assigning a consistent set of "functions" to stages of the plots of a large range of Russian folk-tales. The value of this work was immediately recognized in a lengthy review by Claude Lévi-Strauss, the influential French structural anthropologist, and the fame and influence of Propp's work in the west was assured. Theories of literary characters as "actants" whose roles relate to their designated plot-functions were developed by French Structuralists such as Roland Barthes, Claude Bremond, and A-J. Greimas. "Proppian" analyses have flourished in literary and semiotic courses in universities worldwide and have been tested on such diverse texts as "Little Red Riding Hood" and Alfred Hitchcock's film *North by North-West*.

The other Russian contemporary of the Formalists, who did not count himself a Formalist but who has had a major influence on literary scholarship, cultural studies, and film studies in our own time, was Mikhail Bakhtin. His early work on Dostoevskii and the long tradition of "dialogic" discourse in the novel broke new ground in Russia when it was published in 1929; in France, when it was recognized and developed by Julia Kristeva in the late 1960s; and in the English-speaking world, when it finally appeared in translation, along with many of Bakhtin's other writings, in the 1970s and 1980s. According to Bakhtin and his close colleague, Voloshinov, every utterance, all speech used in natural contexts, is "dialogic", that is, it presupposes the point of view and possible reactions of a listener. In much of the early Dostoevskii this "dialogism" becomes an obsession as the paranoid heroes of *Bednye liudi* (*Poor Folk*) or *Dvoinik* (*The Double*) constantly speak "glancing over their shoulder" at possible contradictions or criticisms. But Bakhtin goes further. He claims that Dostoevskii is unique among 19th-century novelists in making this dialogism a constructional principle: not only do all his characters speak dialogically, but the narrator himself is dialogic and never resolves the conflict represented by the competing voices of his characters. Bakhtin's concept led to certain other important ideas such as intertextuality (the dialogic relations between one literary text and other implied texts) and the chronotope (the way in which time and space are often collapsed into a single frame in the modern novel). Bakhtin himself developed these concepts in some depth in his later writings and they have been explored by a wide range of literary theorists and analysts since they were first published in English in 1981.

With the concept of "carnival" Bakhtin projected the notion of dialogue from the "micro-level" of the speech situation (in novels and in discourse in general) to the "macro-level" of the socio-political arena. In an extended analysis of the writings of Rabelais, Bakhtin argued that the medieval carnival, with its buffoonery, inversions of norms, and generally "scandalous" character and language, was the "dialogic" response of the lower classes to the secure ideology and monologic pronouncements of those in power. Since the appearance in English of *Rabelais and His World* in 1968 this concept has had a major influence on theories of literature, film, theatrical performance, cultural studies, and sociology.

One of Bakhtin's closest colleagues, Pavel Medvedev, published what purported to be a major critique of Russian Formalist theory in 1928, *Formal'nyi metod v literaturovedenii* (published in English in 1978 as *The Formal Method in Literary Scholarship*). This came at the end of a decade in the new Soviet Union in which life got progressively more difficult for Shklovskii and his colleagues. The early years following the Revolution of 1917 had opened up exciting prospects for writers, artists, filmmakers, and even literary theorists, with the new regime's drive for universal education, for experimentation with new structures in art and literature as well as in society and politics, its concern for the common man (hence Formalist interest in folk literature), and its cult of the machine (reflected in the Formalist preoccupation with "devices" and "mechanisms"). But by the mid-1920s education was becoming social engineering, experimentation was giving way to extreme conventionalism, respect for the common man had become the "dictatorship of the proletariat", and the State under Stalin was turning itself into a machine that would crush all free thought and all opposition.

Russian intellectual life, even in times of trouble – perhaps particularly in times of trouble – has always involved lively and combative exchanges. The debates between the Formalists and their sympathizers and the sociologically-minded ultra-Marxist critics raged on the pages of the many new literary journals, in committees of writers and scholars, and on the platforms of public meetings, but the tide gradually turned against the Formalists. Shklovskii, who in 1927 had called an article *V zashchitu sotsiologicheskogo metoda* [In Defence of the Sociological Method] (arguing for a synthesis of formal analysis and social interpretation), by 1930 had capitulated with *Pamiatnik nauchnoi oshibke* [A Monument to Scientific Error]. The other Formalists did not take recantation this far, but they all steered away from theory and busied themselves with traditional and unchallenging scholarly activity such as editing or writing biographies and memoirs. In any case, apart from the personal attacks on individual theorists and the group, the possibilities for publishing either original theory or original poetry and prose were dwindling as the doctrine of socialist realism was enforced. Only Roman Jakobson, who had moved to Prague in 1921, was able to continue his wide-ranging theorizing and became a founding member of the Prague School of Structuralists, who continued many of the best initiatives of the Russian Formalist theorists – until they too were driven out or underground by another totalitarian regime, that of Hitler.

Medvedev, then, published his detailed account of Formalist theory at precisely the time when the cultural powers-that-be required a critique and rebuttal of such lively and innovative thinking. But Russians under authoritarian rulers often resort to the "Aesopian" ploy of dressing up a positive account as if it were a fierce critique, and Medvedev's readers would have learned from his book a great deal about the virtues of the "formal method", as well as some of its extremes and vices. Even this publicity was, however, short-lived, because by the early 1930s all mention of the Formalists (and the literary and artistic movements of Futurism, Acmeism, Constructivism, Suprematism, and so on) was banned: they were not even history.

A revival of interest in Russian Formalism and the work of Bakhtin, Voloshinov, Propp and the other theorists of the 1920s began in the 1960s under the philistine but more benign, regime of Nikita Khrushchev. It may have been helped by Victor Erlich's monumental treatise and the appearance of translations in the west of Propp, Shklovskii, Eikhenbaum, Tomashevskii and – eventually – Bakhtin and Medvedev. In 1967 two young literary theorists in Moscow, Aleksandr Zholkovskii and Iurii Shcheglov, published a paper from the Tartu Summer School on Sign Systems entitled – in true Aesopian style – "From the Prehistory of Soviet Work on Structural Poetics". This was an appreciation of the pioneering work of the Formalists and an appeal for the resurrection of some of their principles and methods. In the 1970s these same scholars pioneered their own "generative model" of the literary text that developed further several key aspects of Formalist theory. They called it a "Theme <Expressiveness Devices> Text Model" and it involved postulating an underlying theme for a work – which might be as short as a maxim or as long as a novel – and then generating the ultimate text through successive stages of elaboration. The "devices" (a very Shklovskian word) were such general psychological-textual mechanisms as parallelism, contrast, augmentation, concretization, and so on (mechanisms recognised also by the Formalists). The model involved a very coherent and consistent engagement with the details of the literary text and was tested on drama (Molière) and film (Eisenstein), as well as on poetry and prose forms of literature. The authors both emigrated to North America in the late 1970s, however, and their method was not adopted by other Russian theorists. It tended to get lost in the welter of "post-structuralist" theorizing that by this time was the dominant mode in the west.

It is instructive that the "centre" for the revival of Russian structural poetics and semiotics from the late 1960s to the early 1990s was Tartu, a small city in Estonia on the Baltic periphery of the Soviet Union. Established academics and officialdom alike mistrusted or feared "theory", so it was only tolerated in isolated departments of literature and discreetly organized and published summer schools. However, the interest generated worldwide by the Tartu group and its regular collections of "Papers on Sign Systems" made a mockery of their marginalization in Russian scholarship – indeed, it showed up the inadequacy of most of the mainstream literary scholarship going on in the Soviet Union during this period, which was reminiscent of the "conglomeration of cottage industries" criticized by Jakobson back in 1921.

The central organizing genius of this group was Iurii Lotman (1922–93), who held the Chair of Russian Literature at Tartu University. He not only organized and published the summer schools with a dedicated group of colleagues, but himself wrote and published a series of books and articles that were widely read and used in courses on literary theory in the west. The best-known of these were *Struktura khudozhestvennogo* (*The Structure of the Artistic Text*) 1970 and *Analiz poeticheskogo teksta* (*Analysis of the Poetic Text*) 1972, which extended many of the concepts and methods of the Formalists and Prague School Structuralists. At the same time, Lotman and his closest colleagues were evolving theories of cultural semiotics that explored far beyond the boundaries of officially recognized literature and pioneered recent movements in cultural studies and critical ethnography. In Moscow Boris Uspenskii, a senior and active member of the "Tartu" group, explored in his 1970 book *Poetika kompozitsii* (*A Poetics of Composition*) not only the play with point-of-view in literary and other verbal texts, but its significance in the analysis of pictorial texts such as medieval Russian icons.

With Lotman's untimely death in 1993, much of the drive has gone out of the Tartu School, and in most countries the precise formal study of the literary text has given way to the looser, more contextual, more intuitive approaches of Marxist, feminist, psychoanalytical, and cultural theorizing. Politically, too, the times have been changing in Russia. The openness made possible by Gorbachev's policy of glasnost has made it possible for all intellectual movements to be heard. But Russian literary theory has generally thrived in conditions of isolation and intellectual overheating. The economic plight of many intellectuals and writers in Russia, coupled with a new freedom to travel, has led many of the most original and best-known theorists to live and work abroad where their work has to take its chances in the over-stocked "open market" of ideas and approaches. The intense and open-minded theorizing about literature and the other arts that flourished so paradoxically in the "closed society" of Soviet communism in the 1920s and 1970s may succumb to the chill winds of "economic rationalism". It is to be hoped that the achievements of Russian literary theory will be kept alive by students of Russian literature until it is ready for rediscovery and development at some time in the 21st century.

MICHAEL O'TOOLE

Post-Revolutionary Russian Theatre

The Bolshevik Revolution had an enormous impact on cultural life in general, but particularly on the theatre, which was quickly perceived as a possible tool for "agitation" among the masses and the propagation of socialist ideas. Many theatre directors supported the Revolution, and were themselves supported in turn by the People's Commissar for Enlightenment, Anatolii Lunacharskii. Vsevolod Meierkhol'd (1874–1940), who had staged rather grandiose pre-revolutionary productions at the Aleksandrinskii Theatre in St Petersburg, immediately dedicated his art to the Revolution, and from 1918 to 1921 he was in charge of the Moscow Theatre Section of the Commissariat. During this time, commonly known as the "Theatrical October", he demanded a complete break with theatrical traditions: the theatre should become exclusively a tool for State and Party propaganda. Along with the young directors Sergei Eisenstein, Nikolai Evreinov, and Nikolai Okhlopkov, Meierkhol'd favoured mass spectacles, such as Evreinov's *Vziatie zimnego dvortsa* [Storming of the Winter Palace], performed on 7 November 1920 for 100,000 spectators with 8,000 participants commanded by the director with the help of a field phone. A celebration of the Revolution, the spectacle underlined at the same time a theatricalization of life (based on real events), and a politicization of art. Both directors and playwrights sought to politicize themes and theatricalize form in the years immediately after the Revolution. Vladimir Maiakovskii's *Misteriia-Buff* (*Mystery-Bouffe*) 1918 (revised 1921), was the first "Soviet" play, specifically written in compliance with these demands. While thematically showing the triumph of the proletariat, Maiakovskii commented in the prologue of the play on the need to break down the fourth wall and openly attacked the verisimilitude of Stanislavskii's realism.

While Stanislavskii had aimed at creating an illusion of reality on stage, and wished the theatre to mirror reality, Meierkhol'd perceived the function of theatre as that of a magnifying glass, which would enhance certain fragments or episodes of reality. Meierkhol'd therefore restructured plays into fragments and episodes that would rouse the audience rationally rather than (as in Stanislavskii's method) emotionally. The sets were Constructivist in style, the costumes resembled factory wear, and leaflets were distributed to the audience as if at a political meeting; all these features were designed to bring art closer to the worker. Meierkhol'd perceived theatre as having a social function; he went out to factories to perform plays, and closely monitored audience response in order to heighten the comical and agitational elements in his productions. Calling for the collaboration of all aesthetic disciplines, he aspired towards a synthesis of the arts. He worked with renowned artists such as Liubov' Popova, Aleksandr Rodchenko, and Varvara Stepanova in his Constructivist productions of *Zori* [Dawns] (1920), *Velikodushnyi rogonosets* [The Magnanimous Cuckold] (1922) and *Smert' Tarelkina* [Tarelkin's Death] (1922). Meierkhol'd's use of placards for locations served to stylize rather than to create reality on stage, and documentary evidence and cinematic devices such as screens, slogans, and projections enhanced parallels to real life, making the spectator aware of being in a theatre that sought to "agitate". His actors trained in biomechanics, so that movements on stage would be choreographed and paced, rather than motivated by psychological identification. Words were less important than the body language, characters became types, lacking in psychological depth: his was a theatre of demonstration rather than of identification and experience.

Despite his political engagement for the revolutionary cause, Meierkhol'd came under attack from Proletcult, an organization deprecating professionalism in the arts, and claiming that only workers should be creative in the artistic realm. Although this claim was not endorsed officially – in fact, Lenin defied its proponent Kerzhentsev by arguing that high standards must be maintained in culture and Lunacharskii called for a "return to Ostrovskii" and his critical realism – it was realism that would be favoured over formal innovation in the late 1920s. The prevalence of realism is obvious from the dramatic writing of the 1920s, and its treatment of the Revolution and the Civil War. Initially, recent history was presented in foreign settings as in Sergei Tret'iakov's *Rychi, Kitai!* [Roar, China!] and *Slyshish', Moskva?!* [Are You Listening, Moscow?!] (the latter set in Germany); later it was set in Russia, as for example in Vsevolod Vishnevskii's *Optimisticheskaia tragediia* (*Optimistic Tragedy*). Such writing lent itself for the purposes of propaganda of the official "historical truth" and was therefore supple enough to fit within the parameters of socialist realism, such as the plays of Bill-Belotserkovskii, Boris Lavrenev, Lidiia Seifullina, Aleksandr Afinogenov, Nikolai Pogodin, and others. Konstantin Trenev's *Liubov' Iarovaia* is a play whose eponymous heroine denounces her husband to the Reds; it enjoyed great success at the Malyi Theatre in 1926. Vsevolod Ivanov's *Bronepoezd 14-69* (*Armoured Train 14-69*), in which a Red officer is so devoted to the cause of the Revolution that he seizes a train of Whites which is about to leave the country, was staged at the Moscow Arts Theatre in 1927. Both productions were hailed by the realists.

Satire was prominent as a genre in the 1920s, inspired largely by the incongruities of life during the New Economic Policy (NEP), introduced by Lenin in 1921. Mikhail Bulgakov's *Zoikina kvartira* (*Zoya's Apartment*) and Nikolai Erdman's *Mandat* (*The Mandate*) and *Samoubiitsa* (*The Suicide*) are as scathing towards NEP as are Maiakovskii's later plays, written specifically for Meierkhol'd's theatre, *Bania* (*The Bathhouse*) and *Klop* (*The Bedbug*). Censorship, exercized by the Central Repertoire Board (*Glavrepertkom*), established in 1922, prevented this genre from flourishing. Satirical and grotesque elements informed the productions at the Vakhtangov Theatre, which had developed a style of fantastic realism for which Bulgakov's *Zoya's Apartment*, with its dream sequences, provided ideal material. Evgenii Vakhtangov (1883–1922), one of Stanislavskii's favourite pupils, had led the Third Studio at the Moscow Arts Theatre, which in 1926 became the Vakhtangov Theatre. Vakhtangov reconciled the formal innovations of Meierkhol'd with the psychological depth of Stanislavskii, while emphasizing the need for an imaginative reading of the text (rather than an obsession with the word, or a restructuring of the text into episodes) and enhancing the grotesque element of reality that came as a result of his preoccupation with the theme of death. His approach is best captured in his 1922 production of *Princess Turandot*. Vakhtangov died prematurely, leaving no direct successor, although his tradition was continued at the theatre by Ruben Simonov (1899–1968), and inspired the work of Aleksei Popov (1892–1961).

Aleksandr Tairov (1885–1950) founded and headed the Kamerny Theatre (1914–49). Tairov remained unpolitical after the Revolution, drawing on the classical heritage of western and eastern theatre. He relied heavily on the actor to "master his instrument" – to control voice, gesture, movement – yet without turning him into an acrobat as Meierkhol'd did. His productions were choreographed and depended on rhythm set by musical scores, while formally relying on the expressivity of gesture (mime). In order to allow for more movement in space, he used Constructivist sets and collaborated with leading artists and designers (Aleksandra Ekster, the Stenberg Brothers). His Soviet masterpiece was the production of Vishnevskii's *Optimistic Tragedy* in 1933, based on the Kronstadt rebellion, in which he underlined the dialectic forces of life and death, harmony and chaos.

The purges of the late 1930s had a tragic and devastating effect on the diversity of artistic expression: Mikhail Chekhov had emigrated, and the Second Studio of the Moscow Arts Theatre, founded by him, was closed in 1936; Nikolai Okhlopkov was removed from the Realistic Theatre (which was merged with the Kamerny) in 1937; the playwright Sergei Tret'iakov was arrested and shot in 1939; Meierkhol'd's theatre was closed in 1938, and Meierkhol'd was arrested and shot in 1940; his actress wife Zinaida Raikh was murdered in the same year. From the pantheon of Russian directors of the 20th century Tairov alone survived, but he was removed from the Kamerny Theatre in 1949, a late victim of the *Zhdanovshchina* (hardline cultural policies that held sway under the aegis of Andrei Zhdanov). Stanislavskii's theory was canonized in 1938 (following his death), and the psychological realism of the Moscow Arts Theatre, which had been elevated to an Academic Theatre, was the only tolerated style. However, Stanislavskii left no successor at the Moscow Arts Theatre; it was headed for almost 30 years by groups of actors and directors who preserved the productions largely in their original shape, and turned what was an innovative theatre at the turn of the century into a museum piece.

Socialist realism dominated dramatic writing during the 1930s. Nikolai Arbuzov's *Tania* (1938) is archetypal: when she gets married Tania leaves medical school for her husband's sake, but he sees in this act a lack of devotion to socialism, and eventually leaves her for another woman who takes part in the transformation of society. Tania undergoes a change, and realizes her potential as doctor before she can find happiness. The theme of transformation (or elimination) of those who do not work for social goals made this play comply with socialist realism, while it is structurally overloaded with coincidences and seems contrived. The characters, however, are portrayed as psychologically convincing. Arbuzov was to make a more important contribution to theatre and drama in a different way, though. In 1938, together with the director Valentin Pluchek, he set up a studio for young actors and dramatists, with whom he worked in a "joint stock" method on a socialist theme, the construction of the city of Komsomolsk on the Amur. The play *Gorod na zare* [City of the Dawn] (1941), was published under his name, but with no reference to its collaborators. The studio's activities came to a halt with the war. After Zhdanov's return to Moscow in 1946 the arts suffered from his attempt to tighten control in the cultural sector. The "theory" of conflictless drama postulated that socialist realist drama cannot contain a conflict (other than between good and better or good and perfect). This led to a total stagnation in dramatic writing – conflict being the most vital ingredient in a dramatic structure – and consequently to a crisis in the theatre arts with an absence of good contemporary drama and the conforming of theatres to the model of the Moscow Arts Theatre.

The Thaw remedied this crisis. First, an editorial in *Pravda* on 7 April 1952 attacked the drama-without-conflict "theory" and called for playwrights to express the truth and to strike against any negative aspects of Soviet life, thereby enabling dramatists to write again. Second, the theatre arts were affected directly when an editorial in *Kommunist* in 1955 favoured diversity and deprecated the levelling and uniformity in the arts. The rehabilitation of Meierkhol'd led to a revival of some of his productions, and the Stanislavskii system that had dominated Soviet theatre was challenged by Boris Zakhava and Ruben Simonov, who called for a synthesis of the acting methods of emotional experience (*perezhivanie*) and representation (*predstavlenie*).

Under the Soviet regime, theatre had functioned as a tool for propaganda and a platform for ideological debate. As such, the theatre was subjected to Party and State control. The immediate responsibility for theatres lay with the Moscow City Council, which controlled the repertoire, allocated budgets, gave preliminary consent to each new play for its inclusion in the repertoire and a final consent to the stage production in the form of a licence. In 1953 *Glavrepertkom* was abolished in order to introduce decentralization so that the expanding media system could be covered; matters relating to theatre were henceforth referred to the newly formed USSR Ministry of Culture. It received its directives both from the Council of Ministers and from the Central Committee of the Communist Party.

The Thaw affected the theatre in a variety of ways: first, a new generation of playwrights emerged with Leonid Zorin, Viktor Rozov, Aleksandr Shtein, and others. Second, young and promising directors were appointed to head prestigious theatres: Mariia Knebel, a pupil of Mikhail Chekhov, was appointed to the Central Children's Theatre in Moscow. Meierkhol'd's pupil Nikolai Okhlopkov was put in charge of the Maiakovskii Theatre, while Valentin Pluchek was appointed to head the Satire Theatre. Most significant for the future were the appointments of Georgii Tovstonogov to the Bolshoi Drama Theatre in Leningrad; Anatolii Efros to the Lenin Komsomol Theatre, Moscow; and Iurii Liubimov to the "Taganka" Theatre of Drama and Comedy, Moscow. Third, for the first time in many years, new theatres were founded, such as the Sovremennik (Contemporary) in Moscow, headed by Oleg Efremov.

The plays of Viktor Rozov (b. 1913) provided the impulse for young directors to explore further the psychological realism of Stanislavskii. Rozov's plays focus on "young boys", children on the way to adulthood, and therefore appealed to a theatre that wanted to create a hero with whom both actor and audience could easily identify psychologically. His plays became the main source for the repertoire of Anatolii Efros and Oleg Efremov. In Rozov's *V poiskakh radosti* [In Search of Joy] (1957) the hero demolishes a piece of furniture, symbol of the petty bourgeoisie, with his father's sabre; the gesture accompanying this act became symbolic for the break with tradition. The Sovremennik started as a studio from the Moscow Arts Theatre school under Oleg

Efremov, opening in 1957 with Rozov's *Vechno zhivye* (*Alive Forever*). Efremov had begun acting at a time when monumental realism was receding. He did not aim at outward verisimilitude, and consciously combined a stylized, abstract set with an authentic way of life (the everyday realism of "kitchen drama"). For Efremov psychological realism did not require that the actor's personality should merge with that of the character. Apart from Rozov's dramatic writing, the work of other new playwrights also found their way onto the stage of the Sovremennik, such as by Aleksandr Volodin, who, in his plays, criticized the interference of personal motives with the achievement of higher social goals, exposing the negative aspects that were obstacles on the road to communism. Efremov was often criticized for including too many contemporary plays in the repertoire. The Sovremennik also staged historical plays, such as Leonid Zorin's *Dekabristy* [The Decembrists], Aleksandr Svobodin's *Narodnovol'tsy* and Mikhail Shatrov's *Bol'sheviki* [The Bolsheviks], a trilogy investigating the psychological motivation of revolutionary figures from the Decembrist uprising to the Bolshevik Revolution. Efremov left the Sovremennik to become chief artistic director at the Moscow Arts Theatre in 1970. There he successfully introduced a generation of young dramatists into the repertoire, such as Aleksandr Gelman and Mikhail Roshchin, whose plays dealt with the inner conflicts of contemporary men resulting from work. In his often controversial productions Efremov investigated work ethics in relation to the individual conscience. He was also the first director to stage successfully the plays of Aleksandr Vampilov. When the theatre had to move to its new building on the Tverskoi Boulevard, the bond with the audience, so vital for Efremov's approach, was broken, and the Moscow Arts Theatre ossified.

Anatolii Efros had gained most of his experience working on contemporary drama, and at the Theatre of the Lenin Komsomol he continued staging plays by Viktor Rozov, Aleksei Arbuzov, and Eduard Radzinskii. He developed a repertoire almost entirely based on contemporary drama. In Rozov's *V den' svad'by* [On the Day of the Wedding] (1964) the revolt of the heroine against her arranged marriage was represented formally by her breaking free from the set, which consisted of tables and chairs arranged for a wedding party. Efros started to work with the concept of "psycho-physics", where movement has the function of making inner psychological changes visible. Radzinskii's *104 stranitsy pro liubov'* [104 Pages about Love] (1964), opposing the rationalism (of the "Scientific-Technological Revolution") to emotional behaviour, and explicitly talking about sexual relationships, met with many objections from the censoring body. Radzinskii's *Snimaetsia kino* [A Film is Being Shot] (1965) was equally criticized for outspoken sexuality, a taboo subject on the Soviet stage. Arbuzov's *Moi bednyi Marat* [The Promise or My Poor Marat] (1965), about a woman choosing her husband out of duty rather than love (she marries him after he has been injured during the Leningrad blockade), saw love triumph at the end. Objections were made to Efros's concern with failure rather than success. Most controversial were Efros's interpretations of two classics: Chekhov's *Chaika* (*The Seagull*) in 1966 and *Tri sestry* (*Three Sisters*) in 1967. Both productions were condemned as an unorthodox interpretation of Chekhov in terms of "lack of communication", perceiving Chekhov as a predecessor of the western Theatre of the Absurd (with no equivalent in the Soviet Union, since a socialist society knew no absurdity). Efros was removed from the Lenin Komsomol Theatre and transferred to an inferior post at the Malaia Bronnaia Theatre where he worked mainly on classical drama, enhancing the tragic dimensions in comic texts (such as Gogol''s *Zhenit'ba* [*The Marriage*]). Efros developed his method of structural analysis for the exploration of character psychology and his concept of the necessity for the psychological motivation of movement on stage, "psycho-physics". Efros perfected his method of structural analysis for a clear-cut image of character and externalization of psychological motivation while teaching at the Theatre Institute (GITIS).

In 1956, Georgii Tovstonogov (1913–89) was appointed chief artistic director of the Bolshoi Drama Theatre in Leningrad. Tovstonogov merged the approaches of Stanislavskii and Meierkhol'd, mixed stylization with authenticity, and combined figurativeness with psychological analysis. Tovstonogov's was an actor's theatre in which the director did not impose an idea on the actor, but had a concept of the production as a whole. Tovstonogov's use of theatrical devices was balanced and purposeful. His productions showed a harmony between historical and contemporary meaning, between the objective and the subjective, the historical and the personal, which created a sense of ambivalence. Tovstonogov's repertoire included contemporary plays by Volodin and Rozov, Gelman and Radzinskii; the classics of Gor'kii and Chekhov; prose adaptations of Sholokhov, Tolstoi, and Dostoevskii. A remarkable production of this decade was the adaptation of Tolstoi's "Kholstomer" ("Strider"). The set was made of sack-cloth, which was draped around the stage. The costumes were made of the same material, and the actors playing horses wore leather straps around their head and body as a harness, thus imprisoning the body. Tovstonogov used cinematic devices, such as the reading by a disembodied voice of an essay by Tolstoi. Similarly, he maintained the narrative stance through the voice of an actor who assumed the narrator function for the dream sequences. Tovstonogov interpreted the condition of the horse as a tragic metaphor for human life, creating at the same time an allegory for the deformation of nature by claiming it as human property. His concern rested with the universal and the general rather than with explicit social criticism, and thus Tovstonogov was not a controversial figure in Soviet theatre.

The opposite is true for the *enfant terrible*, Iurii Liubimov (b. 1917). Liubimov had noticed the dangerous uniformity in Soviet theatre and abhorred the use of make-up, costume, and decorative props. With his acting class he staged in 1963 Bertolt Brecht's *Der gute Mensch von Sezuan* (*The Good Person of Szechwan*) in which he successfully came to terms with the Brechtian epic theatre. Liubimov was subsequently put in charge of the Taganka Theatre. *The Good Person of Szechwan* was set on a bare stage; posters decorated the sides, panels indicated locations; songs were used for comment, and a musical rhythm set the pace of the production; choreographed movement replaced verbal action. These elements, drawn from Brecht and Meierkhol'd, characterized Liubimov's style of the 1960s, and the message of the production – the individual must be in solidarity with the people to be successful in his actions – enhanced the strong socio-political stance of the theatre. The range of theatrical devices was fully explored in the initial years, but especially vividly in *Ten Days that Shook the World* (1965), based on John Reed's account of the Revolution. Liubimov drew heavily on the devices of circus, shadow play, folk theatre, agitational theatre, and documentary theatre to create a revolutionary spectacle. The integration of the audience into the festive revolutionary atmosphere served to deprive history of its magnificence and private life of its seclusion. Like many other directors, Liubimov staged prose adaptations and poetic montages to establish a repertoire in the absence of genuinely good drama. Liubimov's theatre is, therefore, an "author's theatre" (*avtorskii teatr*): the director composes or adapts texts and imposes his personal interpretation on the production. In Liubimov's theatre, the actor is an executor of the director's will. A perfect symbiosis between director and designer was reached when Liubimov collaborated with David Borovskii, who worked only with natural material and authentic objects, an approach that ideally matched Liubimov's concept that there should be nothing "false" on stage. A preoccupation with image and form dominated Liubimov's approach to the theatre. A central metaphor concentrated the contents of the literary material in a formal image.

Censorship interfered heavily with the creation of new repertoires in the late 1960s: during the 23rd Party Congress in 1966, several critical and controversial productions were banned (Tvardovskii's *Terkin na tom svete* [Terkin in the Other World]; Radzinskii's *Snimaetsia kino*); and Efros was dismissed for "ideological shortcomings" in 1967. Cultural policy continued along a reactionary line in the 1970s. The 25th Party Congress of 1976 promoted the "production theme" in drama, compelling playwrights to show the hero at work. Since such plays were not very attractive, the theatres instead proceeded to adapt prose works. Young directors, however, started to work under the auspices of the established theatres, which opened so-called "small stages" in the late 1970s for experimental work, allowing also for a more intimate contact with the audience.

After 1986 Russian theatre benefited greatly from Gorbachev's reforms. The theatres supported the course of glasnost and perestroika actively and with great determination. The reforms were brought in gradually and they affected both the organization of theatre, transforming State plans into a market-orientated management, and artistic standards.

Gorbachev replaced the hardliners in key positions in the cultural sector of State and Party and encouraged a process of liberalization in the arts. The All-Russian Theatre Society (VTO) was disbanded at the initiative of Oleg Efremov and reorganized into the Theatre Workers' Union (STD), which removed the power of control over theatres from the Moscow City Council. At the same time the Artistic Councils (advisory boards) of theatres were endowed with substantial power, which led to the split of the Moscow Arts Theatre in 1987 into the Chekhov-Moscow Arts Theatre headed by Oleg Efremov, and the Gor'kii-Moscow Arts Theatre led by Tati'ana Doronina – an early side-effect of the attempts at gradual democratization.

An experiment allowing theatres to run their own budgets proved beneficial to the studio theatres. They were able to obtain official status and claim subsidy from the local authorities; consequently, their number grew rapidly. The studios enjoyed enormous popularity during the initial years of glasnost and perestroika, almost outdoing the established theatres. From 1991 new conditions of management were introduced by law: funds for the running of theatres were created and alternative sources of financing were encouraged, while the subsidies remained fixed. A variety of forms of ownership became possible: theatres could be municipal or state enterprises, falling into the state sector; or they could go entirely into the private sector. A contract system was introduced whereby only essential staff would be kept on the payroll. Producers' agencies were established to finance productions.

Audiences have changed over the past years, for two reasons: first, the real show was happening on the political stage; second, ticket prices went up and made it almost impossible for the former "intelligentsia" to frequent the theatres. Theatres are still in the process of redefining their roles in the changed political climate.

During the first years of reform the repertoires included a number of old, formerly banned productions, and plays both of the western Theatre of the Absurd, and of the Russian *oberiuty* Daniil Kharms and Aleksandr Vvedenskii. Their absurd and non-representational plays were not performed in the 1920s because of censorship, with the long-term implication that Soviet theatre suffered throughout the century from a lack of the absurd tradition, both in dramatic writing and in theatre practice. A multitude of plays and adaptations of western and émigré playwrights and authors appeared on the playbills. New dramatists were also quickly absorbed into the repertoire, the most popular being Liudmila Razumovskaia, Nina Sadur, Liudmila Petrushevskaia; Aleksandr Galin, Nikolai Koliada, and Aleksei Shipenko.

Directors responded with reluctance. The great directors of the 1960s and 1970s had disappeared from the stage: Iurii Liubimov had been exiled; Anatolii Efros and Georgii Tovstonogov had died, with none leaving successors. Most directors who have emerged with perestroika are pupils of theatre theorists rather than of practitioners, and many of today's directors teach at the State Theatre Institute RATI (GITIS). Petr Fomenko (b. 1932) had worked in Moscow during the 1960s and, following the ban of several productions in 1968 such as *Smert' Tarelkina*, he moved to the Comedy Theatre in Leningrad. It was not until the 1980s that he returned to Moscow and became a teacher at GITIS. His work with his students as a pedagogue is as outstanding as are his productions in the professional theatre. He has set up a workshop, the Fomenko Studio, where he directs or allows one of his students to direct. At the Vakhtangov Theatre he staged Ostrovskii's *Bez viny vinovatye* (*More Sinned Against than Sinning*).The play is not set on the stage – the first act takes place in the foyer, the second in the buffet so as to remove the action from the theatrical environment – to underline the human element of the fate of the main characters of the play, which is itself set in a theatrical context. Although Fomenko's strength is his work with the actor, he creates wonderful images for the core of a scene rather than the entire production. Anatolii Vasil'ev (b. 1942), a pupil of Maria Knebel, had revived the Stanislavskii Theatre artistically when he joined it in 1977. Vasil'ev uses the actor like wax in his hands, creating a psychologically and physically real character on stage, behind which the personality of the actor is effaced. His production of Viktor Slavkin's *Vzroslaia doch' molodogo cheloveka* [A Young Man's Grown-Up Daughter] (1979) was spectacular because of its use of jazz music, condemned in the 1950s and 1960s as decadent. The play is about the meeting of old university friends, now in their forties, who were once jazz fans and *stiliagi* ("teddy boys"). Two levels of time are contrasted: the present of the 1970s with the past of the 1950s, which is expressed through jazz music. As a result of internal quarrels Vasil'ev had to leave the Stanislavskii Theatre and was offered the small stage at the Taganka Theatre, where for several years he rehearsed Slavkin's next play, *Cerceau*. This was premiered in 1985 and has been acclaimed as the best production of the 1980s. The 40-year old "Rooster" invites some colleagues, neighbours, and accidental acquaintances for a weekend at a dacha. All the characters lead their own lives without revealing their true feelings. After a series of excursions into the past, the tragic isolation of each of them becomes apparent, and yet they are incapable of sharing more of their lives with each other. In 1987 Vasil'ev set up his own theatre, the School of Dramatic Art. He has since been interested in the process of rehearsal, rather than the result (i.e. performance), and therefore has not completed any production in Moscow since 1987. Initially experimenting with improvisation, he later worked on dialogue structures in Thomas Mann and philosophical treatises. His main concern is the expression of ideas and the relationship of the idea to the speaker. Vasil'ev is without doubt one of the most influential people in terms of the theory of acting and analysis. As a practitioner, though, he has failed.

Mark Zakharov (b. 1933) came to the Theatre of the Lenin Komsomol in 1973 and developed a wide-ranging repertoire, including musical productions, political documentaries, contemporary plays, and classics given a modern interpretation. He has created a reputation for himself by his political engagement in the early stage of perestroika when he was one of the first to catch the spirit of reform, challenging in his articles the interference of bureaucrats. In his productions, he tackled historical issues with a hitherto unknown openness, as in Mikhail Shatrov's *Diktatura sovesti* [The Dictatorship of Conscience], which for the first time mentions figures such as Bukharin and Trotskii, who had been blotted out of Soviet history books. He catches the spirit of the time, attracting young audiences with productions such as the rock-opera *Iunona i Avos'* (*Perchance*) by Voznesenskii and Rybnikov (1981).

Lev Dodin has created a fine repertoire at the Malyi Theatre, Leningrad, mainly adapting prose for the stage. He staged a trilogy based on Fedor Abramov's Village Prose, and has adapted Iurii Trifonov, William Golding, and more contemporary writers such as Sergei Kaledin for the stage. His style is much influenced by Liubimov, and often devices echo those from the Taganka's productions. In his more recent work, though, greater emphasis has been placed on character and psychology.

The studio theatres are numerous, but transient. Only those that existed before 1986 have sustained their reputation. These have, however, made a powerful impact on the Russian theatre scene in that they have revived the notion of collective responsibility and have restored intimacy with the audience as opposed to the unconvincing psychologism of the Arts Theatre style in a huge auditorium.

Recent "sensations" include *Lysyi briunet* [The Bald Brunette], a non-play by Dana Gink, starring the rock star Petr Mamonov. The bald and the brunette are two facets of one person, who communicate with the past by means of a wardrobe. The language is constructed on accidental alliteration and associative chains, and is nonsensical and illogical. There is no dramatic development, and the play is altogether a slap in the face of public taste. Nevertheless, it proved to be the most popular recent production for young theatre audiences. There is also the director Roman Viktiuk, who established his reputation with a most controversial production of *The Maids* by Jean Genet. Sharing with Genet homosexual inclinations, Viktiuk cast men for the parts of the maids and produced a show influenced by dance-theatre and using elaborate choreographic scores. He founded his own commercial theatre and relies on star names and titles to attract audiences.

In the absence of censorship and control, directors are for the first time since the Revolution free to experiment, and to return both artistically and economically to pre-revolutionary structures, enriched by the contributions of Soviet directors and influences from the west.

BIRGIT BEUMERS

Experiment and Emigration: Russian Literature, 1917–1953

In the first few years after the 1917 October Revolution, more than three million Russians were beyond the rapidly diminishing geographical borders of the Russian Empire. There were those who were simply swept along by the wind of the proletarian revolution, but in the main the exodus comprised the intelligentsia and the officer class – the potential readership of the literature of the Russian emigration. Thus a new mass readership came spontaneously into being, with an abundance of writers and works on which to feast. The diaspora contained representatives of the most diverse styles and trends: among the realists were Ivan Bunin, Aleksei Tolstoi, and Ivan Shmelev; the modernists included Andrei Belyi (temporarily) and Aleksei Remizov, and were later joined by Evgenii Zamiatin; the Symbolists were represented by Konstantin Bal'mont, Dmitrii Merezhkovskii, Zinaida Hippius, and Viacheslav Ivanov – the latter subsequently becoming head of the Vatican library in Rome; of the Acmeists there were Georgii Ivanov and Nikolai Otsup; the Futurist contingent comprised Igor' Severianin and

David Burliuk; others included the writers of popular fiction Ivan Nazhivin and Aleksandr Artsybashev, and important figures such as Leonid Andreev, Irina Odoevtseva, Boris Zaitsev, Aleksandr Kuprin, and many other lesser names. In emigration they shared the general politicization of their environment, a nostalgia for a vanished world, and the desire to come to a new understanding of their sharply altered literary status. Many of them considered it their duty to combine their literary pursuits with political engagement by exposing the vices of the Soviet regime and continually drawing world attention to what they saw as its evils. Among these artistically weak, but publicistically powerful, works can be included Ivan Bunin's *Okaiannye dni* [The Cursed Days] (1935), Ivan Shmelev's *Solntse mertvykh* [The Sun of the Dead] (1926), Aleksei Remizov's *Vzvikhrennaia Rus'* [Russia in the Whirlwind] (1927), and Mikhail Osorgin's *Sivtsev Vrazhek* (*Quiet Street*) 1928.

The political views of many writers had hardened even before they left Russia. If Vladimir Maiakovskii welcomed the Revolution and embraced it, then writers in the opposing camp rejected it utterly. Examples of anti-Bolshevik activities include Aleksandr Kuprin as editor of General Iudenich's army newspaper *Prinevskii krai*, Gleb Struve's editorship of the Rostov newspaper *Velikaia Rossiia*, and Ivan Bunin and Academician Kondakov as editors of the Odessa newspaper *Iuzhnoe slovo*. Others, such as Roman Gul', Antonii Ladinskii, and Ivan Lukash, actively took part in the Civil War on the side of the Whites.

If literary life in Russia was characterized by creeping censorship and the closure of privately owned publishing houses during the 1920s, then the picture in emigration was different. In Europe, China, and the United States many new publishing outlets, newspapers, and journals emerged. In 1920 130 Russian newspapers were published, the next year 250, and in 1922 more than 350. The most popular of these were the Paris-based *Poslednie novosti* (1920–40); and *Obshchee delo* and *Vozrozhdenie* (1925–40), *Rul'* (1920–31), *Segodnia* and *Za svobodu*, which operated, respectively, from Berlin, Riga, and Warsaw. The leading literary journals included *Griadushchaia Rossiia* (Paris), *Russkaia mysl'* (Sofia-Prague-Paris, 1921–27), edited by P.B. Struve, *Volia Rossii* (Prague), and the famous *Sovremennye zapiski* (Paris, 1920–40). In 1942, with the second wave of Russian emigration, *Novyi zhurnal* began to be published in New York. Important publishing houses were set up in Paris and Berlin. In Berlin Z.I. Grzhebin and I.V. Gessen established outlets, and others worthy of mention are Mysl' and Petropolis. In Paris the publishers Russkaia zemlia, Sovremennye zapiski, and Vozrozhdenie were founded. Elsewhere Bibliofil in Revel, Russkaia biblioteka in Belgrade, Severnye ogni in Stockholm, Gramatu draugs in Riga, Plamia in Prague, Rossiia-Bolgariia in Sofia, and many others contributed to what was a vibrant and active literary community.

The years 1921–23 saw Berlin as the capital of Russian emigration, uniting both Soviet writers and émigrés. It was in Berlin that the journals *Russkaia kniga* (after 1922 it became *Novaia russkaia kniga*), and Andrei Belyi's *Epopeia* were published, as well as *Beseda*, founded by Gor'kii and orientated towards Soviet Russia even though it was banned there. The literary situation in Berlin was unique because émigrés were published side by side with Soviet writers, so-called fellow-travellers. Some writers who were resident in Berlin at this time decided to return to Soviet Russia, including Belyi, Gor'kii, Aleksei Tolstoi, Ivan Sokolov-Mikitov, Viktor Shklovskii, and Il'ia Erenburg.

Berlin was not, however, the only centre of Russian émigré literary activity. The printing presses in Paris and then New York were also busy. The poet Igor' Severianin lived out the rest of his days in Estonia. The Riga-based newspaper *Segodnia* was read throughout the Baltic republics and Poland. The publishing house Salamandra produced the daily newspaper *Slovo* and the illustrated journal *Perezvony* (1925–29), whose literary section was run by Boris Zaitsev. *Perezvony* was responsible for publishing works by Bunin, Shmelev, Konstantin Bal'mont, Teffi, Mark Aldanov, and Georgii Adamovich.

In Warsaw the Taverna poetov was run by Professor A.L. Bem, before he left for Prague (he was arrested and executed there in 1945 by the Red Army). In Harbin the journal *Rubezh* flourished between 1927 and 1945. Its most frequent contributor was the notable poet Arsenii Nesmelov, who was to die in prison after his return to the USSR. Shanghai was the birthplace of the journal *Russkie zapiski* (1937–39), as well as *Shankhaiskaia zaria*, *Slovo*, *Novyi put'*, *Russkii avangard*, *Russkoe znamia*, *Emigrantskaia mysl'*, *Putevoi znak*, *Svet*, *Dal'nevostochnyi vestnik*, several daily and weekly newspapers, and some publishing houses.

Nashe znanie, based in Tientsin, published the crude anti-communist novels of N.N. Breshko-Breshkovskii (*Korol' pulemetov* [King of the Machine-Guns], *Pod plashchom satany* [Beneath the Cloak of Satan], and *Vzdyblennaia Evropa* [Europe Aroused]). A.I. Serebriakov's publishing house in Tientsin established some sort of record by producing Ivan Nazhivin's Collected Works in 40 volumes.

Yugoslavia became first and foremost the military centre of Russian emigration, although Belgrade was the home of the newspaper *Novoe vremia*, founded by M.A. Suvorin, son of the eminent Russian journalist and publisher. The Yugoslav king gave funds to émigré writers, and the publishing house Russkaia biblioteka was attached to the Serbian Academy of Sciences. Belgrade also hosted in September 1928 the first (and last) Congress of Writers and Journalists. Among those who took part were Aleksandr Kuprin, Dmitrii Merezhkovskii, Zinaida Hippius, Vasilii Nemirovich-Danchenko (the brother of Vladimir, founder of the Moscow Arts Theatre), and Boris Zaitsev.

One of the most important centres was Prague, the home of the satirist and journalist Arkadii Averchenko until his death in 1925. There existed here a Union of Russian Writers and Journalists, and literary discussions and soirées were organized around readings of works by Bunin, Vladimir Nabokov, and Mikhail Osorgin. The Free Russian University held seminars on literature, including modern literature.

When the cream of Russian philosophy was expelled from Russia in 1922, and with the consequent pressure exerted by the Soviet regime towards its intellectuals, the atmosphere in Berlin changed for the worse. No longer was dialogue and co-operation between Soviet and émigré writers possible. The capital of the first wave of the Russian emigration switched to Paris, which in the early 1920s was already the home of Aldanov, Bal'mont, Bunin, Hippius, Teffi, Dmitrii Merezhkovskii, and others.

Sovremennye zapiski emerged as the leading journal of the emigration. One of its editors was I.I. Bunakov-Fondaminskii, whose organizational capabilities attracted some of the leading lights of the emigration. It was also largely thanks to Bunakov-Fondaminskii that, despite straitened circumstances, 70 issues in all were published. Bunakov-Fondaminskii maintained close relations with Hippius and Merezhkovskii, whom he had known before the Revolution, Aleksei Tolstoi and his wife Nataliia Krandievskaia, Bunin, and Nabokov. Aleksei Tolstoi published the first (and best) version of his novel *Khozhdenie po mukam* (*Road to Calvary*) in *Sovremennye zapiski* (1920–21).

Bunakov-Fondaminskii also founded, together with Fedor Stepun and Georgii Fedotov, the journal *Novyi Grad* (1931–39). As a Jew, Bunakov-Fondaminskii was sent to a concentration camp in the aftermath of the Nazi occupation of France. He was killed in 1942 in Auschwitz. *Sovremennye zapiski* was closed down on the eve of the Nazi invasion of France in 1940. In its time it had published such leading lights as Andrei Belyi, Maksimilian Voloshin, Zamiatin, Remizov, Bunin, Gaito Gazdanov, Vladislav Khodasevich, Marina Tsvetaeva, Boris Poplavskii, and many others.

In ideological terms the political life of the emigration revolved around the Socialist Revolutionaries. In 1921 the collection *Smena vekh* [Changing Landmarks], edited by Iu.V. Kliuchnikov, S.S. Luk'ianov, and N.V. Ustrialov, put forward the idea of accommodation with the Bolsheviks, and from this idea the newspaper *Nakanune* was born. Together with the Berlin journal *Novaia russkaia kniga*, it published works by both émigré and Soviet writers. The literary section of *Nakanune* was edited by Count Aleksei Tolstoi, and was so popular in the Soviet Union that works written by Moscow authors were sent to Berlin via the diplomatic bag! Soviet writers who were published here included Konstantin Fedin, Sergei Esenin, Valentin Kataev, and Mikhail Bulgakov. Unfortunately, the real nature of the Soviet regime became clear later to the leaders of the *smenovekhovtsy* (the "Changing Landmarks" group of émigré intellectuals, seeking rapprochement with the USSR), for on their return to Soviet Russia many of them were repressed.

Another trend that flirted with Bolshevism was Eurasianism. It emphasized Russia's links with Asia and the East, and saw Russia's geographical position between Europe and Asia as a "third path" of development. Leading representatives were the philosophers Nikolai Trubetskoi and Georgii Florovskii. Between 1926 and 1928 the Eurasian journal *Versty*, edited by D.P. Sviatopolk-Mirskii, P.P. Suvchinskii, and S.Ia. Efron, was published in Paris. The ideas of Eurasianism even found reflection in Soviet literature, in the work of Boris Pil'niak and Vsevolod Ivanov. The leaders of the Eurasian movement met with representatives of the Soviet leadership, including General Tukhachevskii, unaware that they were being set up as part of a political intrigue. The Eurasian movement was later destroyed through the machinations of the NKVD.

If the Eurasians and the *smenovekhovtsy*, and the writers who supported them, advocated some rapprochement with the Bolsheviks, then the followers of the "White idea" categorically rejected any such compromise. Through their Paris-based newspaper *Vozrozhdenie*, edited from 1925 to 1927 by P.B. Struve, the White movement developed a coherent anti-communist programme and a whole political ideology.

The literary section of *Vozrozhdenie* was edited by Vladislav Khodasevich. One of its central figures was Ivan Bunin, since 1920 one of the spiritual leaders of the White movement, and the chairman of the Union of Russian Writers and Journalists. The Russian literary emigration gained the recognition it craved in 1933, when Bunin became the first Russian to win the Nobel Prize for Literature.

A place where writers could meet was the social centre "Pravoslavnoe delo" (Orthodox Cause) in Paris, founded by Elizaveta Skobtseva, née Pilenko (Kuz'mina-Karavaeva by her first marriage), otherwise known as Mat' Mariia. Her two-volume book on the lives of the saints, entitled *Zhatva dukha* [Harvest of the Spirit], came out in 1927, and her *Stikhi* [Poems] was published in 1937. She died in the Nazi concentration camp at Ravensbrück in 1945, and her posthumous collection *Stikhotvoreniia* [Poems] came out in 1947.

Any real literary process is impossible to envisage without the interaction of different generations of writers. The younger generation of émigré writers was disenchanted with the liberal ideas of their fathers, as a result of which two organizations were established. Molodaia Rossiia (Young Russia) accommodated both monarchists and National Bolsheviks-cum-Fascists, and in 1934 called itself the "second Soviet Party" in far-left opposition to the Bolsheviks. They worked with the journal *Novyi grad*, founded by Bunakov-Fondaminskii, Stepun, and Fedotov. During the War "Molodaia Rossiia" fought against the Nazis. A far more durable organization was the National Labour Union, which has survived to this day. Basing its ideology on the philosophy of Sergei Levitskii and Roman Redlikh, the Union saw Soviet totalitarianism in the same light as that later described by George Orwell in his novel *1984*. In 1946 the Posev publishing house was set up, its name deliberately symbolic (i.e. sowing the seeds of enlightenment). Posev published books by both the first and subsequent waves of emigration. It also still runs two journals: *Posev*, which is inclined to social and political debate; and *Grani*, which is more of a literary journal. *Grani* was the first émigré journal permitted by the Soviet government to gain subscribers on the territory of the USSR, in 1988. Today its editorial offices are situated in Russia, in the town of Ramenskoe, near Moscow.

The younger generation of émigrés in Paris gathered around Vladislav Khodasevich and Georgii Adamovich. Indeed, these elder statesmen played the same role in the emigration that Zamiatin played in Soviet Russia in the early 1920s, and which was later taken up by Gor'kii. Finally, many young writers of the emigration were associated with the Russian Christian Movement Abroad, which also included such luminaries as the philosophers Father Sergei Bulgakov and Nikolai Berdiaev, and the literary scholar Konstantin Mochul'skii.

The emigration's fidelity to the traditions of classical Russian literature became not just a protest against their profanation in the Soviet literary process – suffice it to mention here the numerous comparisons of Aleksandr Fadeev with Lev Tolstoi – but also a separate theme. Full-length studies of the Russian classical heritage include, apart from those by Berdiaev, Bunin's *Osvobozhdenie Tolstogo* [Tolstoi's Liberation] (1937), and his unfinished "O Chekhove" [About Chekhov], published in 1955; Boris Zaitsev's *Zhizn' Turgeneva* [The Life of Turgenev] (1932), *Zhukovskii* (1954), and *Chekhov* (1954); Khodasevich's novel *Derzhavin* (1931), and his critical works *Poeticheskoe khoziaistvo Pushkina* [Pushkin's Poetic Economy] (1924) and *O Pushkine* [On Pushkin] (1937).

One of the features of émigré literature that made it distinct from Soviet literature was the unfettered evolution of its religious motifs. One of the most prominent Orthodox writers in the diaspora was Boris Zaitsev, who developed the religious themes already evident in his *oeuvre* in such works as *Prepodobnyi Sergii Radonezhskii* [The Life of St Sergius of Radonezh] (1926), *Strannoe puteshestvie* [Strange Journey] (1924), *Afon* [Athos] (1928), and *Valaam* (1936). The same themes are evident in his secular writings, such as his four-volume autobiographical *Puteshestvie Gleba* [Gleb's Journey] (1937–53).

Ivan Shmelev moved from anti-Bolshevik tirades in the 1920s to books infused with religious feeling. These include *Bogomol'e* (*Pilgrimage*) 1935, *Leto Gospodne* (*The Summer of Our Lord*) 1933–48, and *Puti nebesnye* [Heavenly Ways] 1937–48.

The literature of the Russian emigration retained its links with the literary past, but was inwardly free, under no pressure from State diktat, and did not have to look nervously over its shoulder for the censor or the secret police. In this, of course, it is markedly different from the literature of the Soviet Union, which depended on the arbitrary whim of the censor and which was subject to editorial interference. Soviet writers *en masse* willingly compromised themselves, and submitted to self-censorship in their artistic and philosophical reflections. Only a handful (Anna Akhmatova, Osip Mandel'shtam, Evgenii Zamiatin, and a few others) were able to distance themselves from the approaching totalitarian onslaught. For those outside the country, inner freedom was perhaps the only compensation for being torn from their land and their roots.

The first wave of the literary emigration was formed during the Civil War, but its numbers continued to increase in subsequent years. One of the most important prose writers of the 20th century, Evgenii Zamiatin, was among the growing number of later émigrés. Zamiatin's run-in with the Bolshevik authorities was occasioned by his novel *My* (*We*), written in 1920. It is typically anti-Utopian in form, with its heretical lone hero who stands in opposition to the regime. In the 1920s and 1930s Zamiatin was no dissident wanting fundamentally to change the structures of power (all the more so as these structures had not yet taken shape in the form in which we know them today). Above all he was concerned with questions of the writer's freedom to create. His 1921 article "Ia boius'" [I Fear] was prophetic in this respect, for in it he asserted that "Russian literature has but one future – its past". Zamiatin's own subsequent career in his native land was to be ample proof of that.

Zamiatin wrote to Stalin requesting permission to emigrate (although on reading the letter one could be forgiven for thinking that he actually demanded permission to emigrate). In November 1931 Zamiatin left Russia, and never returned. He was accompanied to the railway station by another "heretic", Mikhail Bulgakov, who was to remain in Russia. Zamiatin remained a Soviet citizen to the end of his days, and at international conferences he spoke as the representative of the Soviet delegation.

In emigration Zamiatin developed his career in other areas, for instance in writing screenplays (notably for Jean Renoir's adaptation of Gor'kii's *Na dne* (*The Lower Depths*) as *Les Bas-Fonds*) and literary criticism. He published articles on Soviet literature in *Novyi zhurnal* and the French journal *Marianne*, and in 1931 gave a lecture in Prague on the contemporary Russian theatre. His most important publications in his émigré period, though, remain works of fiction. His novel *Bich Bozhii* [Scourge of God], about Attila the Hun, was written between 1928 and 1935, and a collection of miscellaneous writings appeared in New York in 1955. Other notable works by Zamiatin include *Chudesa* [Miracles] and *Rus'* [Russia], which are reminiscent of works by Nikolai Leskov, Aleksei Remizov, and Anatole France. However, although Remizov, despite the vagaries of his chosen subject, expressed himself to the point of self-parody, Zamiatin in *Chudesa* remains ironically detached, even erotic, and rejects the possibility of returning to the past.

Zamiatin had much in common with the Formalists in his emphasis on the importance of style and composition, rhythm and syntax. It is therefore not fortuitous that it was Viktor Shklovskii, the last surviving Formalist, who campaigned for Zamiatin's publication in the Soviet Union in the early 1980s. Like the Formalists, Zamiatin spoke of the art of discourse, and for him a poetic work was something akin to a musical composition or an architectural monument constructed from words. His views on the poetic and narrative technique of Boris Pil'niak echo the Formalist thesis of making reality "strange" (*ostranenie*) in a literary work. (Both Pil'niak and Zamiatin were subjected to harsh ideologically-based persecution in 1929.) In his 1920 lecture "O iazyke" [On Language] Zamiatin announced that a writer must create his own language, with its own laws and its own lexis. The lexis must be wide-ranging, from dialect to archaisms to terms from contemporary science. The narrative must be built around a meticulous selection of images. In "Zakulisy" [Behind the Scenes] Zamiatin also said that the writer must forget about the technical side of writing to allow his characters to take on their own life within his consciousness.

Zamiatin's lectures laid the groundwork for the emergence of other literary groupings in the 1920s, in particular the Serapion Brothers. This group contained many young writers, such as Vsevolod Ivanov, Nikolai Tikhonov, Konstantin Fedin, Mikhail Zoshchenko, Nikolai Nikitin, Mikhail Slonimskii, Veniamin Kaverin, Lev Lunts, the critic I. Gruzdev, and others. The theoretician and unofficial leader of the Serapion Brothers was the brilliant Lev Lunts, who died at the tragically young age of 23. He wrote the manifesto "Pochemu my Serapionovy Brat'ia?" ("Why Are We Serapion Brothers?") 1922, and the article "Ob ideologii i publitsistike" ("Ideology and Publicistic Literature") 1923. On 27 February 1922 the Communist Party Central Committee decided to support the Serapionovy brat'ia publishing house on condition that the members of the group did not publish in other "reactionary" publications.

The Serapion Brothers regarded Zamiatin as their literary "uncle". The subsequent erasing of his name from the literary annals naturally produced a distorted picture of the nature of the post-revolutionary literary process. Zamiatin was indefatigable and transformed the House of Art, where he delivered his lectures, into something of a literary academy. The writer and artist Iurii Annenkov notes that it was impossible to calculate the number of lectures Zamiatin gave to his class, all accompanied by readings from the works of the Serapion Brothers and informed discussion of them.

Another leading figure of the 1920s who refused to buckle before the onslaught of left-wing criticism and state coercion was Mikhail Bulgakov. Real debate that would be impossible in the succeeding decades raged around his 1926 play *Dni Turbinykh* (*The Days of the Turbins*) and the novel on which it was based, *Belaia gvardiia* (*The White Guard*) 1925. After clashes with the censor, Bulgakov wrote his celebrated "Pis'mo sovetskomu pravitel'stvu" ("Letter to the Soviet Government"), in which he asserted it as his duty as a writer to fight censorship in all its forms. It was in this spirit that he wrote the plays *Bagrovyi ostrov* (*The Crimson Island*), *Beg* (*Flight*), and *Poslednie dni* (*The Last Days* (*Pushkin*)), the dystopian novella "Rokovye iaitsa" ("The Fatal Eggs"), and the prose work *Zhizn' gospodina de Mol'era* (*The Life of Monsieur de Molière*). Nevertheless, Bulgakov gained some ideological insurance by writing the pro-Stalin play *Batum*. Having survived the terrible years of the 1930s, Bulgakov died in 1940 of sclerosis of the kidneys.

Among the most important names in Russian literature of the 1920s and 1930s were Andrei Platonov and Boris Pil'niak. Platonov depicted Marxism as a new religion, totalitarianism as the destruction of culture, machinery, and technology as the new symbols of life. Pil'niak, on the other hand, saw the Revolution as an elemental upsurge of energy. Pil'niak began work on his novel *Golyi god* (*The Naked Year*) in the summer of 1917, and completed it on 25 December 1920. He realized that the Revolution was history being made before his very eyes, and he tried to convey the colossal scale of events in his novel. Thus the image of the storm, with its elemental fury, plays a vital role. The novel is episodic in structure, built around a montage of conflicting themes that express the author's basic idea of post-revolutionary Russia as torn asunder and worn down by life's redundant details.

The publication in 1926 of *Povest' nepogashennoi luny* (*Tale of the Unextinguished Moon*), based on the death of the legendary military commander Mikhail Frunze after an unnecessary operation that Stalin forced him to have, brought Pil'niak to the attention of the secret police. His novel *Krasnoe derevo* (*Mahogany*), which he himself called his "harshest anti-Soviet work", was published abroad in 1929, and Pil'niak, alongside Zamiatin, was subjected to bitter attacks. Among those demanding their exclusion from the writers' federation were Valentin Kataev, Efim Zozulia, Eduard Bagritskii, and Mikhail Kol'tsov.

Pil'niak wrote the essay "Che-Che-O" with Andrei Platonov in 1928. Further works include *Volga vpadaet v Kaspiiskoe more* (*The Volga Falls to the Caspian Sea*), an attempt to obey the "social command" of literature, *Sozrevanie plodov* [The Ripening of Fruit] and *O'kei: Amerikanskii roman* [OK: An American Novel]. Even this latter, a favourite of Stalin's, was not enough to save him from arrest in 1937 and execution in 1938. Despite his posthumous rehabilitation in 1956, it was only in 1976 that the first book edition of his works appeared.

Leonid Dobychin (1896–1936) wrote very little: two volumes of short stories and the short novel *Gorod En* [The City of N]. Dobychin's experimentalism was not understood by his contemporaries, as it adhered neither to the dictates of socialist realism nor imitated the ornamental prose of Pil'niak and Zamiatin, and he remained on the periphery of Russian literary life. *Gorod En* runs counter to the ideological tendentiousness of much Russian literature of the time, with its world of phantasmagoria and travesty in which nothing has a name. Dobychin was accused by the Leningrad Writers' Union of Formalism and naturalism, as a consequence of which he disappeared. His body was fished out of the Neva several months later.

One of the most important developments in the emigration was Maksim Gor'kii's departure from Russia in 1921. This act may have been occasioned by the increasing clampdown on the literary intelligentsia, but may also owe something to the fact that he was not elected head of the Writers' Union in either the Moscow or Petrograd branches. Instead, Boris Zaitsev was elected head of the Moscow branch, and his deputies were Mikhail Osorgin and Nikolai Berdiaev. It is now obvious that after the Revolution, and after his anti-Leninist *Nesvoevremennye mysli* (*Untimely Thoughts*) 1918, the quality of his literary output declined. In these years Gor'kii wrote the cycle *Po Rusi* (*Through Russia*), the plays *Somov i drugie* [Somov and Others] (written 1930–31), *Egor' Bulychov i drugie* (*Yegor Bulychov and Others*) (written 1931), *Dostigaev i drugie* (*Dostigaev and Others*) 1934, and the novels *Delo Artamonovykh* (*The Artamonov Business*) 1925 and *Zhizn' Klima Samgina* (*The Life of Klim Samgin*) 1925–36. After he returned permanently to Russia in 1933 he was declared the "founder of socialist realism".

The Life of Klim Samgin is an important work, embracing Russian history over four decades. But his rewriting of *Vassa Zheleznova* in 1935, his protracted work on *Klim Samgin* and its artificial ending all speak of the creative crisis brought about by Gor'kii's absolute capitulation to Stalinism. He not only worked with the tyrant, but also supported him with both his own moral authority and his writings, in which he disparaged the intelligentsia and glorified the dictatorship of the proletariat. To the young writers who looked to him as their mentor he affirmed that a writer was first and foremost "the eyes, ears, and voice of his class".

Gor'kii's attitude towards the reality around him continues to arouse controversy. He justified the Solovki concentration camp after his trip there in 1929, as well as the White Sea canal constructed entirely by Gulag slave labour, and even the regime's repression of its political opponents (the Industrial Party, for instance). He furthermore shut his eyes to the brutality of collectivization, which led to tens of millions starving to death. Also, aspects of his life in emigration have yet to be clarified. For instance, was Gor'kii or his milieu involved in NKVD operations, or was Gor'kii's residence in the west used as a cover for Soviet espionage activities? Was Gor'kii involved in exporting and selling Russian cultural artefacts in order to buy grain for the Soviet Union to offset the calamitous consequences of collectivization? To what extent did the regime subsidize his various newspapers and journals, and encourage his acquaintance with those western writers and journalists it deemed tolerable?

A particular genre in the literature of this time, especially in emigration, was autobiography. There were a number of works devoted to the nostalgia of childhood in the "golden age", where the child's view of the world is complemented by that of the adult author/narrator. Among such works are Bunin's *Zhizn' Arsen'eva* (*The Life of Arsen'ev*) 1930–39; Gor'kii's trilogy *Detstvo* (*My Childhood*); *V liudiakh* (*My Apprenticeship*), and *Moi universitety* (*My Universities*) 1913–23; Zaitsev's *Puteshestvie Gleba*, 1937–53; Kuprin's *Iunkera* [The Junkers] 1928–32; Aleksei Tolstoi's *Detstvo Nikity* (*Nikita's Childhood*) 1945; and Ivan Shmelev's *The Summer of Our Lord*, 1933–48 and *Pilgrimage*, 1935.

There were some writers whose talent blossomed in the emigration. Among these were Roman Gul', writer of prose, memoirs and screenplays, literary scholar and publisher, and one of the most colourful figures in Russian literature of the 20th century. He fought on the side of the Whites during the Civil war, and began writing his first book, *Ledianoi pokhod* [Campaign of Ice], in a German camp for displaced persons. An extract appeared in V.B. Stankevich's Berlin-based journal *Zhizn'* in 1920, and the book as a whole was published in 1921. Gul''s own experience of emigration and the stories of other émigrés formed the basis of three further books: *Zhizn' na fuksa* [A Life on Good Luck] (1927), *V rasseianii sushchie* [The Dispersed Community] (1923), and *Belye po Chernomu* [Whites on Black] (1928).

In 1929 Gul''s novel *General BO*, subsequently renamed *Azef*, appeared. Its main characters are the *agent provocateur* Azef and the terrorist B. Savinkov (in 1949 Albert Camus was to base his play *Les Justes* on this novel). This was followed by the novel *Skif* [The Scythian], which Gul' called a "historical chronicle", whose main characters are Tsar Nicholas I and the anarchist Mikhail Bakunin. In 1932 his book *Tukhachevskii. Krasnyi marshal* [Tukhachevskii. The Red Marshal] was published in Berlin, and remains one of Gul''s best psychological studies. This was followed a year later by *Krasnye marshaly. Voroshilov, Budennyi, Bliukher, Kotovskii* [The Red Marshals. Voroshilov, Budennyi, Bliukher, Kotovskii].

In *General BO* Gul' is interested in Russian terrorism as a struggle for power. His 1936 book *Dzerzhinskii (Menzhinskii, Peters, Latsis, Iagoda)* discusses those Bolsheviks in whose hands terror became a weapon of power, and shows the history of communist terror beginning in 1918.

Gul' miraculously survived a 21-day incarceration in a Nazi concentration camp in 1933. He was profoundly affected by the refined tortures inflicted on the camp's inmates, although he himself was not tortured, and wrote about it in his book *Orianenburg. Chto ia videl v gitlerovskom kontsentratsionnom lagere* [Orianenburg. What I Saw in One of Hitler's Concentration Camps] (1937). After the war Gul' helped many displaced Soviet people in western Europe, setting up the democratic group Rossiiskoe narodnoe dvizhenie and publishing the journal *Narodnaia pravda* in 1948. In 1950 he moved to New York, where he continued to publish *Narodnaia pravda* for another two years. He then became involved with *Novyi zhurnal*, conceived by its founders Mark Aldanov and M. Tsetlin as a successor to *Sovremennye zapiski*, and he edited it until his death in 1986. Gul' published the book *Odvukon'* [Relay Rider] in 1973, followed by *Odvukon'* 2 in 1982. He wrote about his own life at least three times: in *Kon' ryzhii* [The Chestnut-Coloured Steed] (1952), *Moia biografiia* [My Biography] (1986), and the three-volume *Ia unes Rossiiu. Apologiia emigratsii* [I Carried Russia Away With Me. An Apologia for the Emigration] (1981–84). This trilogy became one of the most important and authoritative works on the history of 20th-century Russian literature in both Soviet and émigré letters.

Vladimir Nabokov was born on 23 April 1899 (he was actually born on 22 April, but, after 1900, his birthday became the 23 April), and thus liked to boast that he was born on the same day as Shakespeare, and a century after Pushkin. His first literary efforts were published under the pseudonym V. Sirin. In emigration since 1919, he graduated from Trinity College, Cambridge in 1922. His first works of the 1920s, *Mashen'ka* (*Mary*); *Korol', dama, valet* (*King, Queen, Knave*); and *Zashchita Luzhina* (*The Defence*) were all marked by their stylistic virtuosity as well as their adherence to the Russian classical tradition. Whereas the official literature of socialist realism emphasized "reality", Nabokov gave free rein to the play of myth, parody, and imagination.

One of the main themes of his 1932 novel, *Podvig* (*Glory*), Russia itself, as it was to be in his autobiographical *Drugie berega* (*Speak Memory*) more than 20 years later. The theme of *Priglashenie na kazn'* (*Invitation to a Beheading*) 1935–36, is the separation of body and soul, as in Zamiatin's *We*. He continued his stylistic experimentation in his 1937 novel *Dar* (*The Gift*), with its ferocious parody of Nikolai Chernyshevskii. Nabokov also wrote a number of plays, the most famous of which is the 1938 *Izobretenie val'sa* (*The Waltz Invention*).

Nabokov left Europe for the United States in 1940, after which time his literary language became English. His novels *Bend Sinister* (1947), *Lolita* (1955), and *Pnin* (1957) were written during his stay in America. In 1959 he returned to Europe, where he wrote *Pale Fire* (1962) and *Look at the Harlequins* (1974), as well as translating Pushkin's *Evgenii Onegin*. He died in Switzerland on 2 July 1977.

It was in emigration that the talent of Mark Aldanov flourished. Aldanov was already approaching middle age when he developed a taste for the historical novel. There followed *Sviataia Elena, malen'kii ostrov* (*Saint Helena, Little Island*) 1923, the tetralogy *Deviatoe termidora* (*The Ninth Thermidor*) 1923, *Chortov Most* (*The Devil's Bridge*) 1925, and *Zagovor* [The Conspiracy] 1927. Aldanov's approach to history was fundamentally at odds with that of the prevailing Soviet class-based ethos, as he aimed to explore the inner life of his dramatis personae, and shows the close interaction of the individual and his time. Among his other novels are those about the Russian Revolution and its roots: *Istoki* (*Before the Deluge*), *Kliuch* (*The Key*), *Begstvo* (*The Escape*), and *Peshchera* [The Cave].

A word should be reserved for the poet Aleksandr Vertinskii, the first and most important of the Russian balladeers. He left Russia in November 1920, returning to the Soviet Union in the winter of 1943. He was enormously popular in Russia, and gave rise to a whole new generation of bards that includes Bulat Okudzhava, Aleksandr Galich, and Vladimir Vysotskii.

The year 1941 placed the first Russian emigration in a dilemma: should they support the Nazis fighting communism, or should they stand by the beloved motherland? On 22 June 1941, the day after the German invasion, Dmitrii Merezhkovskii spoke on the radio of his support for the Nazis. Many émigrés, especially those who had been in the military, were ready to take up arms against the Soviet Union, seeing the German attack as tantamount to the destruction of the communist regime. One of the commanders of General Vlasov's Russian Liberation Army was the ageing Cossack leader Petr Krasnov, the author of more than 20 novels. He was handed over to the Red Army after his surrender to the Allies, and in 1945 was hanged with piano wire in the Lubianka prison.

Other literary émigrés, however, fought against the Germans, including Gaito Gazdanov, Zinaida Shakhovskaia, and Georgii Adamovich. Many others who did not fight, even the vehement anti-Bolshevik Bunin, supported the Red Army.

The New York-based *Novoe russkoe slovo* became the main literary outlet of what had now become two waves of emigration. The new literature of emigration brought with it experience of the camps, and differed from the literature of the first wave both in terms of style and theme. Notable works include Nikolai Narokov's *Mnimye velichiny* (*The Chains of Fear*) 1952, Sergei Maksimov's *Denis Bushuev* (1949), the novels of Leonid Rzhevskii (editor of the journal *Granii*), and the poetry of Ivan Elagin from the early 1950s until his death in 1987.

With the onset of glasnost in 1987 all the various strands of Russian literature – Soviet literature, socialist realism, the literature of the emigration, *tamizdat* and *samizdat* – came together, enabling the whole of 20th-century Russian literature to be studied as an integrated whole, regardless of where a particular writer lived. Nevertheless, if in the Soviet Union émigré literature was always regarded as self-enclosed and inward-looking, émigrés themselves always emphasized the unity of Russian literature. The words of the critic Vladimir Weidlé here are characteristic: "There were Stalin and Lenin Prizes, there was Soviet rubbish, but on our side there was also rubbish. But there did not exist two literatures, there has always been only one Russian literature in the 20th century."

BORIS LANIN
translated by David Gillespie

Socialist Realism in Soviet Literature

Socialist realism was the official literary "method" or "theory" of Soviet literature virtually until the breakup of the Union in 1991. After Stalin died, however, in 1953, writers began to dismantle the tradition, pushing the limits of the possible. This process continued until, by the late decade or so of Soviet rule, most literary practice had strayed a long way from what, in the 1930s and 1940s, might have been accepted as socialist realism. Yet, at the same time, the conventions of socialist realism had become so ingrained as habits of composition that in the first decades of the post-Stalin period even dissident writers rarely broke out of its formal, as distinct from ideological, mould (the legacy of socialist realism can be found, for example, in the early novels of Solzhenitsyn). This essay, however, will discuss socialist realism only in its most classical, Stalinist version and will not treat the successive layers of complexity that accrued to the tradition in the post-Stalin years.

Not all Soviet literature is socialist realist. Not even all Stalinist, non-dissident literature is socialist realist. When discussing Soviet literature, one has to draw a distinction between at least three categories of works: those that exemplify socialist realism, those that are read as non- or anti-Soviet but which happen to have been published in the Soviet Union, and a third category, those that are representative of Soviet literature but not specifically socialist realist. Many in the latter category are (or were) even officially promoted (in, for example, the Writers' Union's "Golden List" of around 100 classics of Soviet literature).

Socialist realism as such did not exist until the Bolshevik Revolution of 1917 was almost 15 years old, or more precisely until after a decree as promulgated in April 1932 abolishing all independent writers' organizations and forming the single Union of Soviet Writers. The term itself was not presented to the Soviet public until 17 May 1932, in a speech made by Gronskii, the president of the new Writers' Union's Organizational Committee (legend has it that the term "socialist realism" had been thought of by Stalin in a meeting in Maksim Gor'kii's study).

Having coined the term, those in power in Soviet literature had to decide what it meant. Gor'kii (the First Secretary of the Writers' Union) and other authoritative figures began to clarify this in articles and speeches of 1932–34 and the First Plenum of the Organizational Committee, held in October 1932, was devoted to the topic. It was not, however, until August 1934, when the First Congress of the Writers' Union was held, that socialist realism acquired a canonical formulation in two keynote addresses to the Congress, one by Gor'kii, and the other by Andrei Zhdanov, the chief representative of the Party's Central Committee. Thereafter, these two speeches functioned as *the* canonical source for the definition, together with Lenin's 1905 article "Party Organization and Party Literature" (see below) and Gor'kii's articles in the book *O literature* [On Literature], published in 1933 (and in later redactions of the same book).

These sources identify a number of features that socialist realism should contain. Many of the stipulations are in effect taboos which, in that they have been fairly rigorously enforced over the decades, have ensured that socialist realism has, both aesthetically and thematically, been a conservative and even somewhat puritanical literature. For example, writers were enjoined to expunge from their work any trace of bald "physiologism" (read mention of sex and other such bodily functions). They were also to avoid all approaches and language that might not be accessible to the masses. This injunction has meant that socialist realism is not highbrow, but lowbrow, or at best middlebrow. Effectively, it also put an end to the literary experimentalism and modernist trends that had flowered in the 1920s.

The language to be used in socialist realism was circumscribed. There were to be no sub-standard locutions, no dialecticisms, no scatology, and no abstruse or long-winded expressions – let alone the neologisms and trans-sense language that had been favoured by the Russian avant-garde. In consequence, most socialist realist writers used only a somewhat *comme il faut* version of standard Russian, resulting often in stilted dialogue (this was one of the trends that was reversed in the post-Stalin era, starting from the late 1950s).

Other proscriptions were more ideological in nature. For example, there was to be no "obscurantism" – no infusion of religious or mystical sentiment, no positive account of the occult. Needless to say, a socialist realist work was *not* to espouse the views of any political group that rivalled the Bolsheviks, whether of the left or of the right. Instead, literature was to serve the ideological position and policies of the Bolshevik Party, and in so doing should be "optimistic" and forward-looking (that is, it should intimate the great and glorious future).

These ideological prescriptions were contained in the doctrine of mandatory *partiinost'*, the cornerstone or *sine qua non* of socialist realism. *Partiinost'* – a term that is generally and somewhat barbarously translated into English as "party-mindedness" – is, then, ostensibly a quality inherent in a socialist realist work. It might be more accurately described, however, as a code word signalling the radical reconception of the role of the writer that is so central to socialist realism. If, before, the writer (and this was largely true even of the politically committed writer) saw himself as an original creator of texts, once socialist realism was instituted his role became much more instrumental, as is implicit in Zhdanov's famous characterization of the Soviet writer (in his speech to the First Writers' Congress) as an "engineer of human souls". Literature was now viewed in a utilitarian way (even more so than before) in terms of how it might "engineer" certain habits of thinking in the populace. Indeed, the writer was seen as rather like a trained professional, working for the government, who was to implement certain assignments or elaborate certain themes that were given to him either explicitly or implicitly (in either case, often through official speeches, articles in *Pravda*, and so on). Even then, he was not to fulfil these assignments in a freehanded way. The socialist realist writer did not really have autonomy over his own texts, which would often be rewritten several times before publication; sometimes he reworked them himself under prompting; sometimes another writer reworked them, and at other times it might be an editor at the publishing house. Such rewritings could at times be without the author's knowledge or permission.

The many injunctions contained in the official speeches to the First Congress of the Writers' Union and other authoritative sources, which determined the ultimate shape of socialist realism, do not fully define the heart of the tradition or establish its unique qualities. This is even true of the doctrine of mandatory *partiinost'* which, though it signals a purely service role for the writer, does not, after all, specify much about the kind of writing he will produce. The injunctions to the writer found in the canonical sources for socialist realism set out the parameters in which he was to operate, but provide only sketchy guidelines for what was to become a highly conventionalized literary tradition. The socialist realist writer was, in practice, not just to be politically correct; as an "engineer of human souls", he was expected to adhere to a particular code of construction.

The principal function of the Soviet socialist realist writer was to provide legitimizing myths for the state, to "show the country its heroes". In consequence, the second cornerstone of socialist realism, together with *partiinost'*, was the "positive hero", an emblematic figure whose biography was to function as a model for readers to emulate. Thus socialist realism is a version of heroic biography. Small wonder the novel, the most popular biographical genre of the modern period, became the central genre of socialist realism. The heroic conventions that were established in the socialist realist novel were used to a greater or lesser extent in most other literary genres, and in other media, such as film.

The particular conventions that define the socialist realist tradition were themselves established by exemplars. Ever since 1932, when the Writers' Union was formed and socialist realism was declared the sole method appropriate for literature, most official pronouncements on literature, and especially the addresses that opened every Writers' Congress, contained a short list of exemplars to guide the writers in their future work. Each new version of the list contained at its core the official classics of socialist realism, plus a few recently published works. No two lists were exactly the same, and those recently published works added to a given list were often omitted in subsequent lists. There is, however, a core of novels that were cited with sufficient regularity to be considered a canon. They include: Dmitrii Furmanov's *Chapaev* (1923); Aleksandr Fadeev's *Razgrom* (*The Rout*) 1927 and *Molodaia gvardiia* (*The Young Guard*) originally published in 1946, but the rewritten redaction of 1951 is the canon text; Fedor Gladkov's *Tsement* (*Cement*) 1925; Maksim Gor'kii's *Zhizn' Klima Samgina (*written 1925–36); Iurii Krymov's *Tanker "Derbent"* [The Tanker Derbent] (1937–38); Nikolai Ostrovskii's *Kak zakalialas' stal'* (*How the Steel Was Tempered*) 1934; Aleksandr Serafimovich's *Zheleznyi potok* (*The Iron Flood*) 1924; Mikhail Sholokhov's *Tikhii Don* (*Quiet Flows the Don*) 1928–40 and *Podniataia tselina* (*Virgin Soil Upturned*) 1932–60.

These canonical works have been a crucial factor in determining the shape of all socialist realist works, but particularly of the novel. There was a good deal of external stimulus for following these exemplars besides the mere fact that they were advanced by authoritative voices. In the early 1930s, a literary institute was set up to train writers to follow the models. A preferential scale of royalty payments and other attractions such as dachas and visits to Houses of Creativity in idyllic locations were dangled before the writer as positive inducements to follow the developing official traditions of the Soviet novel. In other words, when authoritative voices cried out "Give us more heroes like X [the hero of some model novel]", the cry did not fall on entirely deaf ears.

As a result, the business of writing novels soon became comparable to the procedure followed by medieval icon painters. Just as the icon painter looked to an "original" to find the correct angle for a given saint's hands, the correct colours for a given theme, and so on, the Soviet writer could copy the gestures, facial expressions, actions, and symbols used in texts already pronounced canonical.

The Soviet writer did not merely copy isolated tropes, characters, and incidents from the exemplars. He organized the entire plot structure of his novel on the basis of patterns present in them. From the mid-1930s on, most novels were *de facto* written to a single masterplot that itself represents a synthesis of the plots of several model novels (primarily Gor'kii's *Mother* and Gladkov's *Cement*).

This shaping of the plot does not, however, account for everything in a given socialist realist novel. Despite the frequent western charge that these novels are clichéd and repetitive, it is not true that every novel is nothing more than the reworking of a single formula. In any given novel one must distinguish between, on the one hand, its overarching plot or macrostructure and, on the other, the microstructures, the smaller units that are threaded together by this shaping formula – the digressions, subplots, and so on. If a novel is looked at in terms of these smaller units, much of it will be found to be somewhat journalistic and topical; it may, for instance, be geared to praising a recent Soviet achievement or to broadcasting or rationalizing a new decree.

The overarching plot of a given novel is not tied, as are these smaller units, to the particular point in time when it was written (such as to celebrating a recent decree that may be revoked subsequently). If its plot were stripped of all references to a particular time or place, or to a particular theme of the novel, it could be distilled to a highly generalized essence. The abstract version of a given novel's plot is the element that is, in effect, shaped by the masterplot.

Not all Soviet novels follow the masterplot. Not even all novels in the canon follow it completely. One will note, for example, that many of the canonical exemplars were published in the 1920s, or even earlier (like Gor'kii's *Mother*), namely, before socialist realism *per se* existed. They may from a *post*-1932 standpoint, however, be seen as embryonically socialist realist. In practice, once socialist realism had been instituted, aspects of earlier works that did not become conventional for socialist realism, or perhaps were even proscribed in canonical formulations of it, either became, as it were, "non-aspects" in that they were totally ignored in the criticism, or they were written out in subsequent redactions (one example of this can be found in the first, 1925 redaction of Gladkov's *Cement*, in which an apparently positive character, Badin, is a rapist!). More remarkably, one of the official classics of Soviet literature, Sholokhov's *Quiet Flows the Don*, shows only occasional traces of the masterplot, and primarily in connection with lesser characters. Statistically, however, a detectable (though hypothetical) masterplot has been followed to a greater or lesser degree in the overwhelming majority of Soviet novels from the 1930s and 1940s. Its status as a defining trait of socialist realism does not depend on the actual percentage of novels patterned on it, for the masterplot is not random or arbitrary; it illustrates major tenets of Marxism-Leninism.

The use of a formulaic plot suggests that socialist realism might be compared with other varieties of popular formulaic literature, such as detective stories and serial romances. Such comparisons have their limits, however, because the socialist realist novel is not intended to be "mere entertainment". From at least 1932–34, the time when the canon was instituted, its main function was to serve as the repository of official state myths. It had a mandatory allegorical function in that the biography of its hero was expected to stand in for the great myths of national identity.

Stalinist political culture centred on two major, and interrelated, myths of national identity, the myth (or master metaphor) of the "Great Family", and the myth of Moscow. The Great Family of Stalinist myth is essentially the Stalinist state. As a "family", it is contrasted with the "little", or nuclear, family to which individuals are expected to pay allegiance only to the extent that this nuclear family is itself subordinated to the interests of the Great Family (should any conflict between the two arise, the family that is "greater" must take priority). The Great Family, unlike the nuclear family, contains in effect only two categories of kin, both generally masculine. There are "fathers", who are primarily represented as strong, determined leaders who are enlightened politically. Their worthy "sons" are exemplary citizens, or citizens of extraordinary potential, whose exploits mark them out from the others but who are as yet limited in their ability to assume leadership roles (to become "fathers") by an immaturity that is of course political, but is commonly represented in literature, film, and other status quo reinforcing cultural products as an almost boyish hotheadedness, an impulsivity or tendency to act on their own initiative and not be sufficiently guided by the Party.

The identification between developmental and political immaturity in the "sons" is facilitated by the fact that their impetuousness is represented as a form of *stikhiinost'*. *Stikhiinost'*, which would be translated literally as "elementalness" since its root *stikhiia* means "the elements", can be used for a wide range of arbitrary, wilful or headstrong behaviour but is at the same time a technical term in Marxism for "spontaneity". "Spontaneity", in one of the most abstract versions of the overall Marxist model for historical progress, is locked in dialectical conflict with political consciousness or *soznatel'nost'*.

In effect, the socialist realist novel is a kind of Bildungsroman with the Bildung, or formation of character, having more to do with public values than individual development. In the myth of the Great Family, the model "son's" spontaneity must be tempered under the guidance of an exemplary, highly conscious "father" before he can gain that status for himself. Each novel is structured as a story of how a particular model "son" (the positive hero) progresses over time as his spontaneity is tempered under the guidance of a highly conscious "father". Towards the end of the novel, in a highly charged moment, the hero's attainment of mastery is recognized in a sort of ritual of initiation that enables him to cross over to the status of a "father". Generally, what this initiation amounts to is a conversation, conducted with a particular aura, between the "son" and his moral/political mentor, his "father", who may, in addition to his homily, hand him a Party or Komsomol card as a form of passing on the baton. In some instances, this conversation is the last testament of a loyal communist before a heroic death (whether in revolutionary battle, or because he has ruined his own health in his tireless work for the cause).

This event (the initiation), or series of events (of encounters between the "son" and his "father") in the individual life of the hero represents the broader processes taking place in society at large. The general plot, with its emphasis on the succession by a more robust "son" to the status of his "father" who is most often shown as spent and in decline (or about to be posted elsewhere so that the son literally succeeds him in the local hierarchy), affirms that the country is progressing in a series of ever greater passages or revolutionary leaps to that end moment when the country will attain a state of fully achieved communism. This moment (the initiation) is also one when the dialectical conflict between the (politically) conscious and those whose political consciousness is as yet inchoate and undisciplined, will be resolved. Then, all will be conscious politically without sacrificing spontaneity completely, and all will have attained an extra-personal identity, having jettisoned their narrow, counterproductive, self-centred identities.

In a typical socialist realist novel this general process unfolds at a deep structural level and is manifested largely only in the encounters between "father" and "son" which, in the interests of maintaining an elevated tone for such moments, are infrequent but crucial. At the surface level, the hero is otherwise shown to progress, to mature, as he undergoes all sorts of trials and tackles insurmountable obstacles, thus enhancing his stature as a true hero. Most socialist realist novels are structured around the task the hero is to perform in the public sphere (such as raise the yield of grain in the collective farm, build a bridge or a power station, exceed the plan's figures for his factory's output, or drive the enemy out of a particular town), the obstacles confronting the hero are often from the natural world. For example, as he tries to build a power station in his district, he may find the project threatened by a flood. Even more frequently, the obstacles in fact come from within the world of the hero's bureaucratic administration, or from military life, but are represented *as if* from the natural world. This is particularly the case for representing the enemies (national or class) who may be described as beasts or vipers, or as advancing like a firestorm or a flow of molten lava.

In presenting the hero principally with natural or natural-like obstacles, writers were effectively realizing the metaphor that is at the base of *stikhiinost'*. As, in a given work, the hero learns to control the "elemental" that is without, as he shows his mastery over it, this signifies his mastery of *political* consciousness. Alternatively, he may have to learn to master the seething passions within, a process that is *de facto* conflated with political mastery.

When the positive hero crosses over to a higher order of consciousness, when he makes his "great leap forward", this affirms that the country under the present leadership is on its proper course towards communism. The novel is both a primer for the Soviet Everyman to follow and a repository of myths of maintenance for the Soviet status quo.

This parabolic structure of the socialist realist novel is enabled by a common convention followed by the majority of Stalinist novels: the novel is set not in Moscow or Leningrad, but in a provincial locale. This locale, the novel's microcosm, is generally depicted as a relatively hermetic unit situated a considerable distance from these major cities. The novels that *are* set in Moscow or Leningrad are generally set in a particular factory or city district. The isolated, provincial locale that is the setting of most socialist realist novels functions as a "typical" place, a microcosm in which one may see to scale the general processes taking place in society. But the microcosm is, as befits its location, more backward both politically and economically than Moscow, that higher point of orientation for all the novel's characters.

Thus the myth of Moscow was also an integral element in the socialist realist tradition. This myth was not, however, generated only within literature and film. At more or less the same time as the doctrine of socialist realism was established, a central preoccupation of the leadership was a project for the reconstruction of the city of Moscow to make it an exemplum of the socialist city. Moscow, as capital of a highly centralized society, was to be an enhanced space, ahead of its time physically as the leaders were politically. Hence, in socialist realism the provincial setting of a given work functioned as a periphery, contrasted as such with the "centre" that was Moscow.

Thus the positive hero progresses both through time (in a ritual of maturation) and through place. In so doing, he bridges the gap between "the periphery" and "Moscow", and he narrows the gap between ordinary citizens (those of the "periphery") and the country's elite.

Thus the "son" figure in a socialist realist novel, or in other words the protagonist, is both ordinary and extraordinary. For most of the novel, he appears as one of the most politically committed and inspiring representatives of the Soviet Everyman. Like most ordinary human beings, he is impulsive and subject to the passions. However, he is generally distinguished from the other characters by brimming with greater energy and initiative. Thus he can be more appealing as a model for the reader to emulate than the "father" figure who is much more perfect, disciplined, and austere than his "son" and generally appears in the novel much less (it is, after all, more difficult to organize a readable, or particularly suspenseful, novel around a model figure).

This dual identity in the positive hero (ordinary/extraordinary) is a characteristic of socialist realism. Zhdanov, in his speech to the First Writers' Congress, called for the new Soviet literature to combine "the most matter-of-fact, everyday reality and the most heroic prospects". As if in response, novels kept oscillating between "realistic" representation and a hyperbolically heroic world where heroes perform seemingly impossible feats. Moreover, the transition between ordinary and extraordinary is often quite unmotivated.

The lack of motivation for shifts in mode is not problematical within the system of socialist realism because each of the major characters in a given work is not really a character *per se*, so much as he (sometimes it is a she) is a sub-function of his moral/political role ("son" or "father"). Indeed, the positive heroes are marked as having that special status by a cluster of iconic traits and epithets that indicate symbolically their moral/political identity or, in other words, their function as a positive form of "consciousness" or "spontaneity" incarnate. "Consciousness", for example, is indicated by such epithets as "calm", "determined", "austere", and "stern". Another cluster of clichéd epithets and attributes indicate the position that each of the two positive characters occupies on the life cycle. Regardless of their respective ages, a character whose function is that of a "son" must be youthful and full of vigour, and a "father" figure decidedly older (possibly with a bent back or heavily lined face that reveals how much he has sacrificed himself for the cause). These small details effectively functioned as a code. Indeed, it was partly in these tiny details that, over time, one saw development in the socialist realist tradition.

Each novel was written in a context affected by change, controversy, and even the author's own position. All these factors bore upon how the code was deployed in an individual work and had the power to change its meanings. New meanings could come from within the system of signs by the slightest rearrangement, emphasis, or shading of the standard signs and sequences. Such changes may be scarcely perceptible to an outsider not schooled in the tradition, but they would be striking to most Soviet readers.

The patterns outlined here emerged in the 1930s. However, they remained generally applicable in the 1940s because of the cultural conservatism that characterized that decade. Even though the 1930s saw the worst purges of Soviet history, the 1940s enjoy the reputation of being the worst period of Soviet cultural history, known as the Zhdanov era. The era took its name from Andrei Zhdanov, who had delivered one of the keynote speeches to the First Writers' Congress and who, in 1946, delivered a lecture on the journals *Zvezda* and *Leningrad* (directed also against the writers Anna Akhmatova and Mikhail Zoshchenko). This barrage, together with other speeches and newspaper attacks that appeared in its wake, signalled the end of hopes of liberalization, and a return to rigid adherence to the socialist realist canon (which had been less strictly enforced during the war years). Consequently, there was less modification of the socialist realist code during that period than one might otherwise have expected. However, given the stress on adherence to the conventions of socialist realism, writers, in their anxiety to prove their dedication, tended to overdo their obeisance to the masterplot. Most of its standard functions do not just occur, but are proliferated throughout a given novel. For example, a typical novel of the 1940s has not just one mentor figure as its main character, but many. Functions lost their logic and their ideological purpose in the novel's overall design and became yet another pattern of whorls in some superabundant decoration.

The two functions used with greatest extravagance in 1940s novels were the mentor's "last testament" and the scene in which he symbolically "passes the baton" to the hero. Most novels do not rest with one such scene, but contrive to introduce at least two or three. Perhaps the novel that outdoes them all in this respect is the 1951 rewritten, canonical version of Valentin Kataev's *Za vlast' sovetov* [For the Power of the Soviets], whose protagonist, Pet'ia, receives so many "batons" from older, Party and partisan stalwarts (many of them entrusted as they are dying, or even posthumously) that one begins to suspect his primary function is to receive batons.

The effect of such superabundance in 1940s novels is not to reinforce the masterplot but rather to undermine it. The result is the main weakness of these novels – incongruity. Indeed, in novels published after Zhdanov's "signal" lecture the mode was tilted so far away from the "realistic" in favour of the "romantic" (the glossy or larger-than-life) that even before Stalin died (as early as 1951) critics began to complain that there was too much "varnishing of reality" (*lakirovka deistvitel'nosti*), a charge that was heard more loudly and insistently once Stalin had died in 1953.

After Stalin's death, there was a return to more realistic, less bombastic – or simply improbable – depiction of Soviet reality. Yet one should not assume that writers were merely "strait-jacketed" in the Stalin years, mere afflati of the official position. After all, many of them were serious intellectuals. Since the clichés of socialist realism effectively formed a code, they could be used not only to establish a given writer's political loyalty, but to hint at meanings that he might not be able to make explicit.

If a Soviet writer wanted to be sure his novel would be published, he had to use the proper language (epithets, catch phrases, stock images, and so on) and syntax (to order the events of the novel in accordance with the *de facto* masterplot). To do so was effectively a ritual act of affirmation of loyalty to the State. Once the writer had accomplished this, his novel could be called "party-minded". But he had room for *some* play in the ideas these standard features expressed because of the variety of potential meanings for each of the clichés. The system of signs was, simultaneously, the components of a ritual of affirmation and a surrogate for the Aesopian language to which writers resorted in tsarist times when they wanted to outwit censors. Thus, paradoxically, the very rigidity of socialist realism's formations permitted freer expression than would have been possible (given the watchful eye of the censor) if the novel had been less formulaic.

KATERINA CLARK

Thaws, Freezes, and Wakes: Russian Literature, 1953–1991

If the 1930s and 1940s saw the dominance of socialist realism in all areas of Soviet cultural endeavour, the years following Stalin's death saw its inexorable decline and eventual death. Indeed, it was no longer the "basic method" by as early as 1962, because a plurality of voices and styles had by then fatally subverted its monolithic hold on culture. Still, in the minds of Party ideologues socialist realism remained a valid cultural concept, and even as late as 1984 the Party General Secretary Konstantin Chernenko was calling for writers to return to the "positive hero" as an inspiration for society. By then, however, such appeals were too late.

After Stalin's death writers did not need long to voice doubts and concerns over the Party's control of literature, and in the 1950s and early 1960s there were several Thaws, with writers at the forefront of liberal enquiry, and Freezes as the Party and its advocates took fright at the increasing demands for intellectual freedom and tolerance being voiced in the media. Thus, the first Thaw of 1953–54 was marked by the publication of critical articles in leading literary "thick" journals. The period got its name from the title of a fortuitously published novel by Il'ia Erenburg, but it was criticism and publicism that then, just as 30 years later during Gorbachev's Thaw, were the quickest to react to changes in the political environment. Fedor Abramov's 1954 article "Liudi kolkhoznoi derevni v poslevoennoi proze" [People of the Collectivized Village in Post-War Soviet Literature] attacked the falsity of literary conventions in the depiction of rural Russia since the war, singling out for special criticism some of the most celebrated socialist realist novels (by Stalin Prize-winners Semen Babaevskii and Galina Nikolaeva, among others). Vladimir Pomerantsev's "Ob iskrennosti v literature" [On Sincerity in Literature] denied the ideological prerogative of literature, and insisted on the writer's own personal intuition as the true mark of authenticity in a given work. Both articles were mercilessly lambasted in the conservative and Party press. As a consequence of publishing these articles, Aleksandr Tvardovskii was removed as editor-in-chief of *Novyi mir*, replaced by the loyal conservative Konstantin Simonov.

Another Thaw occurred in 1956, marked this time with the appearance of literary works. The publication of Vladimir Dudintsev's novel *Ne khlebom edinym* (*Not by Bread Alone*) and several controversial shorter pieces (most notably by Aleksandr Iashin and Nikolai Zhdanov) in the second volume of the almanac *Literaturnaia Moskva* [Literary Moscow] caused some anxiety to diehard literary bureaucrats, and seemed again to signal an easing of the cultural control mechanisms. However, they were again followed by a Freeze in the wake of the suppression of the Hungarian uprising that year. In particular, the campaign of abuse and vilification waged against Boris Pasternak following the publication in Italy in 1957 of *Doctor Zhivago* was a clear sign that the Party still insisted on its control of literature, and would continue to persecute those who chose their own path. Seemingly paradoxically, though, Tvardovskii was reinstated at *Novyi mir* in 1958. Nothing in Soviet literary politics was ever quite what it seemed.

Following the 22nd Party Congress in 1961 came the third Thaw, marked by the removal of Stalin's body from Lenin's Mausoleum and culminating in the publication of works by Aleksandr Solzhenitsyn in 1962–63, especially *Odin den' Ivana Denisovicha* (*One Day in the Life of Ivan Denisovich*) and *Matrenin dvor* (*Matryona's House*). Even in 1962, however, there were signs that the Party was not happy with cultural pluralism. During Khrushchev's unexpected visit to an exhibition of modernist art in the Manezh gallery he verbally abused some artists as sexual deviants and criticized modernism generally as decadent and antithetical to socialist realism. His words came to be seen as Party policy. The trial of the young poet Iosif Brodskii in March 1964 reinforced the idea that the Party was not yet prepared to accept any art that was not subservient to its ideology. With the dismissal of Khrushchev as General Secretary of the Communist Party in October 1964 de-Stalinization was brought to an end, and a tougher, less tolerant cultural policy took hold. Writers, artists, and intellectuals generally were made abundantly aware of this when in 1966 the writers Andrei Siniavskii and Iulii Daniel' were sentenced to seven years' imprisonment for printing their fictional and critical works in the west. In 1968 the writers Aleksandr Ginzburg and Iurii Galanskov were sent to the Gulag for protesting publicly about the Siniavskii-Daniel' trial (Galanskov died there in 1972, at the age of 33).

Nevertheless, the death of Stalin had at least destroyed the monolithic sterility of Soviet literature. Even during the various Freezes, as the Party and its watchdogs struggled to contain new modernist trends, both "conservative" and "liberal" writers continued to coexist, albeit often uneasily, and both sides had their official supporters. Indeed, to a large extent culture as a whole became something of a political football, kicked about by both conservatives and liberals as part of a broader agenda. Throughout the 1950s and early 1960s there was debate and discussion, and the emergence of significant talents. Throughout the 1950s, for instance, there appeared a series of semi-fictional sketches (*ocherki*) and short prose pieces by Valentin Ovechkin, Gavriil Troepol'skii, Vladimir Tendriakov, Efim Dorosh, and others criticizing the calamitous state of agriculture and the pathetically low social level of the Russian village, and calling for reform and change. It was also in this period that writers such as Fedor Abramov, Vasilii Shukshin, Vasilii Belov, and Andrei Bitov, to name a few, began writing fiction that was heavily influenced by the spirit of the Thaw. Nevertheless, at the same time the arch-conservative Vsevolod Kochetov was publishing pro-Stalin pieces and anti-liberal tracts, such as *Brat'ia Ershovy* [The Brothers Ershov] (1958) and *Sekretar' obkoma* [The Party District Committee Secretary] (1961). The ideological battle-lines adopted by writers were reflected also in the stand-off between literary journals, most notably that of the liberal *Novyi mir* and the conservative *Oktiabr'*.

Even under the more ostentatious repression of the Brezhnev years, writers such as those associated with Village Prose continued to push back the borders of the permissible. Indeed, by the time Mikhail Gorbachev came to power in 1985 and embarked on his policy of cultural openness and ideological pluralism, many forbidden topics had, in fact, already been broached, if not fully explored. Moreover, if in 1953 Russian literature was divided into two ideologically opposed camps – that of the Soviet Union and that of the emigration – by 1991 that distinction had all but disappeared. Émigré writers and their works, both those from the first emigration and those still alive, and therefore still regarded as "hostile", became available in print to the Soviet reading public. After 1986 émigrés were invited to the Soviet Union, meetings between émigrés and Soviet writers and critics were officially encouraged, and public discussion of the culture of the emigration flourished. Even the greatest iconoclast of them all, Aleksandr Solzhenitsyn, was published, including that most damning indictment of the Soviet regime, *Arkhipelag GULag* (*The Gulag Archipelago*).

Let us return, however, to the 1950s, and attempt to penetrate the surface of significant events. To be sure, the death of Stalin seemed to change relatively little. Socialist realism remained the "basic artistic method", and the vast majority of works published in the 1950s and 1960s conformed to the established model of the "masterplot". Even those that strove to pose difficult questions and thereby push back the frontiers of censorship, such as Il'ia Erenburg's *Ottepel'* (*The Thaw*) 1954, Vladimir Dudintsev's *Not by Bread Alone*, and the controversial pieces in the second volume of *Literaturnaia Moskva*, did not question the legitimacy of Soviet power but merely raised questions of the excesses of Stalin's rule and the moral and spiritual consequences for society.

Indeed, the dominant motif of post-Stalin literature of the 1950s was the "rediscovery" of simple human values and emotions, and the longing for a new, more humane society. Works that criticized the Stalinist legacy could do little more than reject the heavy-handed ways of the recent past and call for more tolerance and human understanding. Nevertheless, there was a clear shift away from ideology, and a new-found celebration of the little man and the simple pleasures of life. Perhaps nowhere is this better exemplified than in Vladimir Soloukhin's *Vladimirskie proselki* (*A Walk in Rural Russia*) 1958, simultaneously an affirmation of the joys and beauty of the unspoilt Russian countryside well away from the metropolis, and at the same time a triumphant re-discovery of Russia's historical (i.e. pre-revolutionary) past.

The first work that explicitly questioned the rationale of Soviet power was Solzhenitsyn's *One Day in the Life of Ivan Denisovich*, a novella of blistering power that not only laid bare the raw facts of life within the Gulag, but also showed that the Gulag *was* the system. In the building of socialism, the Soviet people were constructing their own prison. The next year saw the publication of Solzhenitsyn's shorter *Matryona's House*, which is at the same time both a damning critique of rural devastation since the collectivization of agriculture in the late 1920s, and an affirmation of the durability of an age-old Russian spirituality and moral goodness. This latter work is generally seen as the inspiration for the Village Prose movement that began in earnest a few years later.

In the Soviet Union culture was, of course, always linked with politics, but whereas under Stalin politics suppressed and perverted the creative impulse, after Stalin culture became the stimulus for critical debate, however muted, that then reinvented itself as public opinion. The anti-Stalinist messages in the poetry of Evgenii Evtushenko in the 1950s and 1960s warned against the dangers of a return to the old totalitarian ways. The guitar poetry of Aleksandr Galich, Bulat Okudzhava, and Vladimir Vysotskii reached a vast audience and inspired a generation of young people with its sheer accessibility and simplicity. The extremely popular plays of Aleksei Arbuzov, Eduard Radzinskii, and Viktor Rozov touched on topical problems of youth alienation and moral and spiritual stagnation, but, because of the official sanction of the theatre, could go no further than slight social criticism.

Perhaps the most important aspect of the cultural regeneration of the 1960s was the rediscovery of the past. A major contribution to this was the publication in instalments in the first half of the decade of Il'ia Erenburg's memoirs under the title *Liudi. Gody. Zhizn'* (*Men, Years, Life*) 1961–66, which introduced to the younger generation of Soviet intellectuals important names of which they would have had but a faint inkling: Marina Tsvetaeva, Osip Mandel'shtam, Vsevolod Meierkhol'd, Roman Jakobson, Kazimir Malevich, and many others.

It was in this area, as elsewhere, however, that prose fiction led the way. Village Prose emerged as a distinct literary trend that followed on from the socially-minded criticism of agricultural practice and management in the 1950s, and Solzhenitsyn's picture of a holy Russia not yet tainted with materialism and urban culture. Works such as Sergei Zalygin's *Na Irtyshe* [On the Irtysh] (1964), and Vasilii Belov's *Plotnitskie rasskazy* (*Carpenters' Yarns*) 1968, discussed openly for the first time the excesses and injustices of the collectivization of agriculture, and also created a climate in which issues of historical relevance could no longer be ignored. Collectivization became a popular subject for Village Prose writers, and for Belov, Boris Mozhaev, and Vladimir Soloukhin it became the cornerstone of their work from the 1960s up to the late 1980s. Even establishment figures such as Mikhail Alekseev felt bound to touch on it in such works as *Drachuny* [The Brawlers] (1982).

Village Prose was significant not only for its opening up of an important area of historical enquiry, but also for its discussion of the present. If socialist realism had emphasized man's dominance and conquest of the natural world, Village Prose presented in lyrical, contemplative images man's humility before it. In the 1970s, delight in the natural world became replaced by a concern for it as, in Viktor Astaf'ev's *Tsar'-ryba* [King Fish] (1976) and Valentin Rasputin's *Proshchanie s Materoi* (*Farewell to Matyora*) 1976, the consequences of Soviet man's attempts to remake the world according to ideological criteria had increasingly alarming implications for his moral, spiritual, and even physical well-being.

The moral state of the nation and the individual was of concern to writers interested in other areas of Soviet life. By far the most popular theme throughout the 1960s and 1970s was World War II, and, although stalwarts such as Ivan Stadniuk and Aleksandr Chakovskii expressed pro-Stalinist sentiments and glorified the sacrifices made by the Russian people, others, such as Vasil' Bykov and Iurii Bondarev showed that the conflicts and losses of the past have far-reaching consequences for the present. Indeed, Bykov shows a murkier side to the Soviet war effort, depicting cowardice and treachery in *Sotkinov* (*The Ordeal*) 1970, and pointing to falsification and injustice in *Obelisk* [The Obelisk] (1972). One of his most powerful works, *Mertvym ne bol'no* [The Dead Feel No Pain] (1966), linked these negative features with the Stalinist legacy, and was severely criticized.

Another writer who courted politically-minded criticism was the leading exponent of so-called Urban Prose, Iurii Trifonov. He was concerned above all by the moral dilemmas of the post-war intelligentsia, especially that based in Moscow, revealing that the price for gaining material prosperity and status was moral compromise. In his Moscow stories of 1969–75 he shows weak, vacillating intellectuals who either capitulate to a cynical materialism, or are crushed. In his latter years he became increasingly outspoken, and in *Dom na naberezhnoi* (*The House on the Embankment*) 1976, he drew a bleak picture of the type of mediocrity who prospered under Stalin through the denunciation of others. It was a bitterly ironic portrait, and attracted criticism from the head of the Writers' Union, Georgii Markov. In subsequent works, such as *Starik* (*The Old Man*) 1978, he looked back as far as the Revolution and the Civil War in his search for the loss of contemporary idealism and values, and in the posthumously published *Ischeznovenie* (*Disappearance*) 1987, he showed the destruction of the Old Bolsheviks and their idealism during the Ezhov terror of 1937.

A new phenomenon in Soviet Russian literature was the emergence, from the mid-1960s onwards, of so-called "women's literature", that is, fiction written by women, about women, and largely for women. With the publication in 1969 of Natal'ia Baranskaia's "Nedelia kak nedelia" ("A Week Like Any Other"), and subsequent novels and novellas by I. Grekova in the 1970s and 1980s, the "double burden" of the working mother was brought home to the Russian reading public, as were the emotional and social difficulties faced by single mothers, widows, and pensioners. It was an acute social problem and, like the issue of collectivization, became the subject of heated public discussion through the medium of literature. Other important women writers who began to acquire a reputation in these years include Viktoriia Tokareva and Nina Katerli.

By the 1970s Russian literature was in dialogue with itself. Its soul had been profoundly affected by external events, such as the Hungarian uprising of 1956, the fall of Khrushchev in 1964 and the invasion of Czechoslovakia in 1968, and there was within the intelligentsia disillusion with the prospect of liberalization, often bordering on despair. Political repression was mirrored in the cultural arena. Of considerable interest to Sovietologists, but rather less to literary scholars or observers of the Soviet cultural scene, was the award of the prestigious Lenin Prize in 1979 to Leonid Brezhnev, General Secretary of the Communist Party, for his autobiographical trilogy *Malaia Zemlia* [Little Land], *Vozrozhdenie* [Rebirth] and *Tselina* [Virgin Lands], published in print-runs of several million in 1978. All three were near-perfect examples of socialist realism, with stereotyped characters and hidebound plots. Within the Soviet Union there was an escalating tension between writers who struggled against increasing odds to keep alive the spirit of de-Stalinization, and the diehard writers and literary bureaucrats trying to maintain ideological hegemony in the spirit of the Brezhnev trilogy.

Censorship and ideological vigilance became ever more stifling. In 1979 a group of writers, including Andrei Bitov, Evgenii Popov, Fazil' Iskander, and Vasilii Aksenov, attempted to publish an almanac entitled *Metropol'* without the permission of the Writers' Union. The almanac included pieces by Popov, Aksenov, Iuz Aleshkovskii, Vladimir Vysotskii, and Andrei Voznesenskii. For their involvement, Aksenov was forced into exile and Popov banned from further publication. However, the controversy surrounding the almanac, like that associated with *Literaturnaia Moskva* two decades earlier, ensured that the authors and editors achieved a degree of renown that would otherwise perhaps have eluded them. The almanac was immediately circulated among interested readers through that most Soviet of institutions, *samizdat*.

In the 1960s and 1970s phenomena that could only have come about in a totalitarian state emerged: *samizdat* and *tamizdat*. By no means confined to artistic literature, *samizdat* ("for the drawer") was the publication and distribution of works that had either been banned from official publication or written with the express intention of not being officially published. Such literary works that circulated across the land in the 1960s and 1970s included all of Solzhenitsyn's writings, Venedikt Erofeev's *Moskva-Petushki* (*Moscow Circles*), Vladimir Voinovich's *Zhizn' i neobychainye prikliucheniia soldata Ivana Chonkina* (*The Life and Extraordinary Adventures of Private Ivan Chonkin*), Georgii Vladimov's *Vernyi Ruslan* (*Faithful Ruslan*), and many others. As a result of appearing in *samizdat*, most works then appeared in editions published in the west, usually the United States or Germany. This was known as *tamizdat*, literally "books published over there" (i.e. the west). In the case of the guitar poets, another phenomenon emerged. *Magnitizdat* was the recording on a tape-recorder (*magnitofon*) of songs that were then re-recorded and circulated across the land, thus bringing about the vast nationwide popularity of Vysotskii and Okudzhava, from the Baltic to the Pacific ocean.

There was, moreover, a fundamental struggle going on, one that sought to claim the soul of Russian culture. Both the literature of the Soviet Union and the emigration had long vied for the right to be the true legacy of the classical Russian tradition. Certainly, by the mid-1970s, the undoubted greats of the 20th century were all living abroad: Nabokov, Iosif Brodskii, and Aleksandr Solzhenitsyn. Within a few years Nabokov, the last representative of a lost Russia, was dead, but the ranks of émigrés were being swollen with the "third wave", representing the flower of the post-war creative intelligentsia: Vasilii Aksenov, Vladimir Voinovich, Georgii Vladimov, Fridrikh Gorenshtein, Sergei Dovlatov, Aleksandr Zinov'ev, and many others. By the mid-1980s the Russian emigration boasted more genuinely reputable creative talents than the motherland.

One of the key works of Soviet Russian literature of the 1970s was Andrei Bitov's *Pushkinskii dom* (*Pushkin House*) 1978. Although published in Russia only in 1987, the novel explicitly places Nabokov within the Russian literary tradition, and denies that 1917 provided a break in the Russian literary process. The emphasis throughout is on continuity and evolution. Bitov's novel can be seen to have prepared the ground for the re-integration of Soviet and émigré cultures that began under Gorbachev.

The lifting of Party control of culture that accompanied Gorbachev's accession to power in 1985 was both exhilarating for the reading public and shattering for the hold of ideology on the minds, if not the hearts, of the population. Glasnost began rather cautiously, as was to be expected, with the publication in 1986–87 of poems by safely dead, though avowedly anti-Soviet, writers, such as Nikolai Gumilev and Vladislav Khodasevich, Vladimir Nabokov's novels *Zashchita Luzhina* (*The Defence*) and *Mashen'ka* (*Mary*), as well as some of his poetry and literary criticism. There were also major works by writers from the past who had at least been tolerated by the Soviet canon. Among these were the following major works: Mikhail Bulgakov's satirical and subversive *Sobach'e serdtse* (*The Heart of a Dog*), and many other plays and prose works; Andrei Platonov's anti-Utopian, and thus anti-Bolshevik, *Kotlovan* (*The Foundation Pit*) and *Chevengur*; Aleksandr Tvardovskii's childhood lament *Po pravu pamiati* [By Right of Memory], which discusses his kulak father's downfall during collectivization; Anna Akhmatova's *Rekviem* (*Requiem*), her great epic poem devoted to, and written on behalf of, all the women who suffered loneliness and loss during the Ezhov Terror of 1936–38; Nikolai Kliuev's epic poem *Pogorel'shchina* (*The Burned Ruins*), a highly original and linguistically-challenging account of the fate of the Russian village after the Revolution.

Another feature was the appearance of previously banned works by writers still living in the Soviet Union. These included Sergei Antonov's *Ovragi* [Ravines], an account of collectivization seen from the point of view of the activists who came to enforce it from the town; Bitov's *Pushkin House*; Vladimir Dudintsev's *Belye odezhdy* [White Robes], an account of the persecution of Soviet biologists in the late 1940s; and particularly Anatolii Rybakov's *Deti Arbata* (*Children of the Arbat*), concerning the beginnings of the purges and the individuals who took part in them or were affected by them. These works all raised hopes that the current Thaw would not stop at publishing merely a few selected authors and texts, as had been done on previous occasions. Moreover, this Thaw went much further than previous ones in the range of authors either discovered for the first time by Soviet readers, or authors whose work had only been partially known. Thus important writers, both from the emigration and from within the Soviet state, who became known to the Soviet reading public in these years include Leonid Dobychin, Mikhail Osorgin, Gaito Gazdanov, Boris Poplavskii, Georgii Obolduev, Evgenii Chirikov, and Konstantin Vaginov. It did seem that Russian culture would at last become whole.

In 1988–89, though, glasnost assumed a qualitatively different aspect with the publication of Pasternak's *Doctor Zhivago*, and in particular Vasilii Grossman's novels *Zhizn' i sud'ba* (*Life and Fate*) and *Vse techet* (*Forever Flowing*). Grossman's works threw up a fundamental challenge to the whole edifice of Marxism-Leninism. They had offered so devastating a critique that the Soviet Politburo in the early 1960s had declared *Life and Fate* unpublishable for several centuries. It was clear that Soviet literature, if it could adapt and survive at all, would never be the same. Furthermore, 1989 also saw the re-emergence of works by Solzhenitsyn in Soviet print, and, together with works by other former dissidents and exiles, it now seemed distinctly possible that a few years of cultural freedom had fatally undermined an already demoralized and weakened totalitarian system.

Yet alongside the exhilaration of cultural revival there were other emotions stirred up. Nationalism in its various guises had been rearing its head since the 1960s, especially in the works of some of the Village Prose writers, who found a platform in the journal *Nash sovremennik*. The Village Prose writers surviving into the 1980s were now able to indulge their nationalistic tastes to produce controversial works of varying xenophobic and anti-modernist hues in Valentin Rasputin's *Pozhar* (*The Fire*) in 1985, and in 1986 Viktor Astaf'ev's *Pechal'nyi detektiv* [The Sad Detective] and Vasilii Belov's *Vse vperedi* (*The Best is Yet to Come*). Belov continued his cycle of novels on collectivization under the general title *Kanuny* [The Eves] and *God velikogo pereloma* [The Crucial Year], begun in 1972, with further instalments in 1987 and 1989 that became ever more vitriolic and anti-Semitic. On the other hand, the late 1980s saw the publication of both fictional and private writings by the recently deceased Fedor Abramov, especially his short story "Poezdka v proshloe" [The Journey into the Past], and by Vladimir Tendriakov, in particular the novel *Pokushenie na mirazhi* [Shooting at Mirages]. Both had been respected, but hardly eminent, figures from the 1960s and 1970s, but now a thorough reappraisal of their reputations became necessary. They have emerged as free-thinking and courageous individuals whose best work, published only posthumously, exhibits great satirical power, a clear vision of the evils of their environment, but also anguish at being forced to live and work within an iniquitous system.

By the turn of the decade it was obvious that the Soviet state could not survive the monumental upheaval brought about by freedom of expression. Things were changing very quickly, not least the role of the writer and the importance of the written word. The role of the "thick" journals, for over 150 years the main outlet for cultural production, was also changing. In the early months glasnost was enacted largely by the "liberal" monthlies: *Novyi mir*, since 1986 edited by Sergei Zalygin; *Ogonek*, edited by Vitalii Korotich; *Druzhba narodov*, edited by Sergei Baruzdin; and *Znamia*, edited by Grigorii Baklanov. Soon, though, other journals not noted for their liberal leanings, such as *Moskva*, *Neva*, and *Oktiabr'* also got in on the act. Initially sales soared as people in their millions rushed to read the latest revelations or long-lost works, and journals competed to publish previously banned pieces by émigrés or other established Soviet figures. However, in a time of worsening economic crisis, amid paper shortages and ever-decreasing resource allocations, some journals found life difficult. Nevertheless, despite straitened circumstances, most survived in one form or another and continued to prosper into the 1990s.

The amazing transformations in Soviet cultural life in the late 1980s had many consequences, most of them positive, but some, as with the resurgent nationalism, giving cause for disquiet. In addition, many new voices also came to be heard, including those of younger writers such as Tat'iana Tolstaia, Sergei Kaledin, and Valeriia Narbikova. More significant were the "new" voices of older writers who were enabled to express publicly their true selves for the first time. These include Liudmila Petrushevskaia, who had published some short stories and plays in the "stagnation" years, but among whose major works are *Novye Robinzony* (*A Modern Family Robinson*) 1989, and *Svoi krug* ("Our Crowd") 1988. Others include Vladimir Makanin, whose first prose works appeared in 1967 but whose most powerful work was published only after glasnost, and Evgenii Popov, who had some short stories published in 1976 and, as a result of his involvement in the *Metropol'* affair, had been unable to publish for six years. He soon brought out two major novels, *Dusha patriota ili razlichnye poslaniia Ferfichkinu* (*The Soul of a Patriot or Various Epistles to Ferfichkin*) 1989 and *Prekrasnost' zhizni* [The Splendour of Life] (1990).

The year 1991 was a major turning-point in the history of Russia. Russian culture also underwent a profound and probably irreversible transformation. If we see the struggles of the post-Stalin period as a reflection of the creative desire, on the one hand, to gain freedom of expression and, on the other, the political need to subjugate the creative impulse to the demands of the State, we can also see that the resolution of this battle in favour of the former also brought to an end a particular feature of Russian culture: namely, its civic-mindedness. With the death of a totalitarian society and the birth of a democracy, no longer could the writer see himself as the moral guide or teacher of his people, bridging the vast gulf between the rulers and the ruled. Viktor Erofeev announced a "wake" for Soviet literature in a celebrated article in 1990. Moreover, in the post-industrial age, the Russian writer, just like his western counterpart, now had to compete with varying forms of popular entertainment and information technology for the attention of an increasingly selective and informed reading public. In short, with what is regarded in the west as the "normalization" of the creative process came the death of Soviet literature, and a severe challenge to the place and role of the writer in an increasingly diversified and pluralistic society.

In 1991 a world and a culture came to an end. Ideology had been defeated. Russian culture was united, the past had been overcome. The struggle, ongoing since 1953, for greater freedom had finally been resolved. The great themes of these decades – the return to nature, memory of the past and the correction of historical injustice, the call to human values – had been played out against a lively, occasionally tumultuous background of literary politics, but had made a great contribution to the overhauling of an oppressive and murderous regime. The last few years of this regime were vitally important but also bewildering, as works from the past appeared alongside works by new writers, as socialist realism vied with modernism and postmodernism, as competing political ideologies made themselves heard through works that purported to be fiction. The overiding motif was that one world was over, but there was not yet another to replace it.

Perhaps the best illustration of this is to be found in the work of the avant-garde writer Vladimir Sorokin (b. 1955), whose two major novels *Norma* [The Norm] and *Roman* [Novel] were written in the 1980s, though published in full in Russia only in 1994. Sorokin's prose is distinguished by its eagerness to shock, disgust, and appal the reader with its unashamed preoccupation with bodily functions, dismemberment, cannibalism, and all manner of physical and verbal abuse. Sorokin subverts and destroys all symbols of authority, and his satire is particularly ferocious when directed at Lenin, the father of the Soviet state. Even linguistic conventions become mangled beyond recognition, and the language of the totalitarian state tears itself apart so that ultimately it becomes gibberish. Sorokin's prose rips away the falsity and pretence of a society built on lies and violence; but it leaves the reader staring into the abyss with no indication of a way out.

The four decades between the death of Stalin and the death of the Soviet Union proved to be cataclysmic not only for society, but also for its culture. Literature bore the brunt of those upheavals, with arrests, imprisonment, and exile of some writers, and the stagnation of the cultural process in general. Russian literature abroad flourished and developed alongside the hidebound home-grown product, continually enriched by the exiled individuals filling its ranks. In Russia, writers were increasingly drawn into social and political debate on the future of the country. By the late 1980s the contradictions of a freely functioning literary process and the needs of a One-Party State had become irreconcilable. Whereas in 1953 an oppressive ideology had dominated literature, by 1991 literature had played a decisive part in its downfall.

DAVID GILLESPIE

Russian Literature in the Post-Soviet Period

The year 1990, often known as Solzhenitsyn Year, since several of the main literary journals were then rushing to get out his remaining prose works in case the literary "thaw" was succeeded by a new "freeze", marked the end of both glasnost and of the literary boom that had begun in 1986. The publication of most of the *Arkhipelag GULag* (*The Gulag Archipelago*) in *Novyi mir* in 1989 meant that the official censorship system had finally been overcome, but it simultaneously signified the beginning of a new literary situation, wherein literature would have to exist in conditions of freedom of speech and freedom of the press.

This is what all writers who were in one way or another opposed to the regime had apparently been dreaming of, but few people then realized that official support for socialist realism was the prerequisite not only for "approved" art and literature but also the precondition for the appearance of such diverse anti-totalitarian works as Vladimir Dudintsev's *Belye odezhdy* [White Robes], Anatolii Rybakov's *Deti Arbata* (*Children of the Arbat*), the novels by B. Iampol'skii, Iurii Dombrovskii, Vasilii Grossman, Aleksandr Bek, and others that had led to the literary boom at the beginning of the period of perestroika. All these works had been undermining the ideological walls surrounding the aesthetic field of the socialist realist novel, the validity of whose foundations these and other writers denied. When the walls finally collapsed, there was no need for other works of this type. Readers, who had been following the struggle of anti-establishment literature against the system of taboos and "disapproved-of" themes, language, and forms with the intensity of spectators at a top-rated sporting event, quickly lost interest after it became clear that there were no more officially forbidden subjects or styles of writing.

In 1991 the last remaining "bastions" were taken. Many people had felt that, because of the all-pervasive "modesty trope" inherent in Soviet socialist realism, it was more likely that *The Gulag Archipelago* would be printed in Russia than Nabokov's *Lolita*, not to speak of Iuz Aleshkovskii's *Nikolai Nikolaevich*, containing large chunks of "non-normative" language, and that, if some of the works by Vasilii Aksenov and by Eduard Limonov were passed for publication, then substantial cuts would be required. But in that year it was easy enough – at least in the largest cities of the USSR – to pick up a "Soviet" edition of Aleshkovskii's novella as well as Limonov's novel *Eto ia, Edichka!* (*It's Me, Eddie!*). It was now the writers (and not the Party or the State) who would have the final say as to the language, as well as the form and content, of their works. There were no longer any words that had to be censored out of all printed matter.

The dividing line between the previous literary period and the present one was drawn by the failed coup attempt in August 1991 and the subsequent economic reforms introduced at the beginning of 1992. There were now virtually no official restrictions on what could be published (other than limitations of the sort found in the most mature liberal democracies), but henceforth the writers had to cope on their own with the vagaries of the chaotic free-for-all of the unregulated post-Soviet market.

One of the key signs of this problem is the critical state of the traditional Russian "thick" literary monthlies. Subscription rates have not been able to keep up with galloping price rises in general, and the increasing costs of paper, printing, and postage in particular. Entire issues, completely ready to go to press, gather dust at the printers and reach subscribers and sales outlets several months late. The number of copies published and sold has been declining steeply. For instance, in 1990 the journal *Novyi mir* had a print run of 2,660,000, whereas the figure for 1991 (*before* the economic reform and concomitant price increases) was 958,000. This dropped in 1992 to 250,000, in 1993 to 74,000, in 1994 to 53,000 and in 1995 to 25,000 (most copies went to libraries, supported by a project of the Soros Open Society Foundation). Circulation is therefore considerably lower now than in the "years of stagnation", prior to glasnost, when *Novyi mir* was printed in an edition of some 250,000 to 300,000 copies. (The figure for January 1996 was 30,200, but it had sunk to 20,570 in July.) This trend is characteristic of all Russian literary magazines. Readers now cannot afford and/or do not want to buy and read "serious" writing.

There is also a general crisis in the publishing industry. State publishers have been starved of cash, and even contemporary writers who were popular in the perestroika period are experiencing difficulties in reprinting their earlier works and publishing their new ones. Most of the new private publishers, having successfully helped to weaken their state-owned competitors, are naturally driven mainly by the logic of commerce and the search for profits to give priority to bestsellers and pot-boilers, for which, as in all other countries, there is a ready market. At the same time, collections of works by authors such as Mikhail Bulgakov, Mikhail Zoshchenko, Andrei Platonov, and Boris Pasternak, émigré Russian writers (and philosophers) and, of course, the classics have proved to be commercially viable, so the more discerning reader has a wider choice than ever before. That, however, is of little comfort for contemporary Russian writers and literary critics unless they are capable of producing works that look as though they will immediately find a ready sale.

There is also a sense of a much more profound crisis than that manifested by the problems of the literary journals and the publishing industry – the widely perceived difficulty of the role and function of literature itself. Russian society no longer focuses on literature as a crucial orientating factor, and many writers, unable to adapt to a situation where they are no longer near the centre of public attention, feel that they are redundant and even that "high" culture itself is surplus to society's present requirements.

This has produced a new split in the world of the arts, not so much on political grounds (as, during perestroika, between supporters and opponents of reforms, between democrats and anti-democrats, monetarists and anti-monetarists), as on aesthetic and to some extent generational grounds. On 4 July 1990, *Literaturnaia gazeta* published an article by Viktor Erofeev called "Pominki po sovetskoi literature" ("A Wake for Soviet Literature"), which proved to be the start of, and provided the basis for, a long-running discussion. Erofeev declared that all the texts generated by the Soviet system, whether supportive of or hostile to it, were now out-dated and irrelevant; what was needed was a different sort of literature, which did however already exist (and which we are inclined to trace back to Venedikt Erofeev's *Moskva-Petushki* [*Moscow Circles*], dating from 1969). The main features and the demarcation lines of this "other" literature were extremely difficult to pin down, but it had to be politically uncommitted, devoid of moralizing and preaching, and to go beyond the boundaries of "ordinary" realism as well as those of socialist realism. A tighter definition of this "other" or "new" literature was provided by Mikhail Berg, a theoretician of the artistic "underground" and editor of the independent St Petersburg periodical *Vestnik novoi literatury*, founded in 1989 and setting its face against the traditional Russian and Soviet "thick" journals. From the outset the magazine gave priority to three literary movements: religious poetry by Elena Shvarts, Viktor Krivulin, Sergei Stratanovskii, L. Aronzon, A. Shel'vakh, V. Filippov and others (Berg prefers to call this the "Leningrad School of Poetry"); "Moscow Conceptualism", with three of its four main pillars (Vsevolod Nekrasov, Dmitrii Prigov, Lev Rubinshtein, but not, so far, Vladimir Sorokin) and their precursors E. Kropivnitskii, Ia. Satunovskii and M. Sokovnin; and the "new postmodernist prose" by B. Kudriakov, Viktor Erofeev, Evgenii Popov, N. Isaev, S. Korovin *et al.* (see Berg's article in *Znamia*, 1 [1995], 175–76). Berg defines this "other" or "new" literature as literature of the end (of the century, of an era, of a system) and as a "literature without illusions", meaning not only social and political but also "psychological and metaphysical illusions that result in a rigid attitude to human nature as such".

Another much-discussed article was Aleksandr Ageev's *Konspekt o krizise* [Notes on the Crisis] (*Literaturnoe obozrenie*, 3 [1991], 15–21), which insisted that the crisis in Russian literature was deeper and more comprehensive than it initially appeared, that this was linked to literature's claims to provide moral guidance, and that in the future the only books that could expect to gain the reader's attention were those that focused on the sphere of values of the private individual.

In the early 1990s another proposition was put forward, according to which the potential of all existing styles had been exhausted, a fact that would inevitably generate a literature that played with a variety of styles, as is typical of postmodernism. Considering the characteristics of postmodernism to be quotational and other meaningful references to other texts, a heightened degree of introspection, a propensity for commentating and self-documentation, a tendency towards syncretism, interweaving, and the fusion of a variety of art forms, V. Kuritsyn asserts – with perhaps more than a touch of irony – that the "postmodernist consciousness, continuing its decisive and derisive expansion, remains ... the only aesthetically vital factor in the literary process" (*Novyi mir*, 2 [1992], 225–32).

Despite such attempts to define the issues, the vagueness of concepts like "new literature", "other literature", Conceptualism and postmodernism enables proponents of each of them to lay claim to adjacent territories or simply to try to take them over. One of the most talented members of the generation in its forties, Vladimir Sorokin, is claimed as "one of them" both by the Conceptualists and by the postmodernists. His novels *Serdtsa chetyrekh* [The Hearts of the Four] (1994), *Norma* [The Norm] (1994), and *Roman* [Novel] (1994) have delighted those who like his virtuoso game-playing with other styles and his extraordinarily inventive examples of sadism, and disgusted those who are not inclined to think that literature requires detailed descriptions of the consumption of excrement and pus or of how best to dismember corpses. Although writers like Mark Kharitonov, Viacheslav P'etsukh, and the distinctive St Petersburg author A. Melikhov have spoken publicly about postmodernism in very cool terms, that has not prevented some critics from discovering postmodernist elements in their works.

In 1990 and 1991 many critics who until then had written sympathetically about politically-committed anti-Soviet *belles-lettres* switched their attention and preferences to the literary "underground", which was then confidently coming up to the surface and moving onto the stage of public artistic life. Viktor Erofeev, Evgenii Popov, and others were then continually reminding people of the 1979 *Metropol'* almanac that had caused such a scandal at the time, even though it was intended not as an act of political defiance but as an aesthetic statement indicating that the boundaries of Soviet literature and the official style were not too narrow for the adequate expression of artistic freedom. Yet when, in 1991, this legendary anthology was finally published in Moscow, Pavel Basinskii, a young critic who had been brought up on tales about the importance of the volume that had acquired mythological status, wrote angrily that "It would have been better if there hadn't been such a text ... *Metropol'* is of interest only as a myth or as a historical reference work" (*Literaturnaia gazeta*, 19, [1992], 4).

Another point became clear in 1991. This "new" or "other" literature had seemed to constitute a single entity, but only because it existed in defiance of an official veto. In conditions of freedom some of its practitioners were perfectly capable of wrangling and bickering with their colleagues in full view of the public. Not long after Viktor Erofeev's article on the end of Soviet literature, Ol'ga Sedakova, a sophisticated and highly cultured underground poet who enjoyed experimenting in a variety of styles, commented that the entire generation of self-proclaimed writers of a supposedly "new" literature, including Erofeev himself, belonged in actual fact to the "post-Soviet" school. "They have inherited the same old aesthetic irresponsibility ... It's simply disgusting. They are behaving like the generals of Soviet literature. For me they aren't anything new, they are the tail-end of Soviet literature. Its witches' sabbath" (*Gumanitarnyi fond*, 31 [1991], 3).

At about the same time, the practitioners of this "different" literature were having to answer questions like "Different from what?" From the aesthetics and content of socialist realism? But if there's *no* official literature at all any longer, doesn't that mean a change in the status of "different" literature?

The theoreticians of conceptual poetry and "sotsart" (straight-faced parodies of socialist art) commended themselves for "washing" words and concepts clean of the "greasy fingers of the state". The critic Aleksandr Arkhangel'skii said that these "washermen" had fallen into a trap laid for them by "official" art, since they could function only as long as it did. If it passed away, no one would understand or care what Igor' Irten'ev was making fun of in his verse (or what Melamid and Komar were sending up in their paintings). By the end of 1992 this was indeed largely the case, which for some members of the former "underground" was more traumatic and harder to bear than their recent confrontations with the political authorities. The public was no longer interested in the writer's stance *vis-à-vis* the State, and many writers found that they could not operate in conditions of political (but not usually economic) freedom.

In the 19th century the critic Vissarion Belinskii introduced the idea of annual surveys of the latest *belles-lettres*. Between 1986 and 1990 a number of journals tried to carry on this tradition, but in the 1990s, because of the general crisis, this gave way to newspaper questionnaires. At the end of 1991 and the beginning of 1992 several publications, including *Literaturnaia gazeta*, *Nezavisimaia gazeta*, *Moskovskie novosti* and *Ogonek*, attempted to sum up the recent and current literary situation. The prevailing feeling among professionals was one of disappointment, all the harder to bear because of what had proved to be unfounded hopes of a cultural boom once Party tutelage was removed. Moreover, the predominant tone of the experts' forecasts was pessimistic. Lovers of realistic prose complained that contemporary fiction had lost the ability to find any sense or meaning in the current period. Recent supporters of the avant-garde (for example, B. Kuz'minskii) admitted that it had not met their expectations and that it was the least gifted of its practitioners who had become the market leaders and completely adjusted to the new situation. Yesterday's *aficionados* of postmodernism cannot hide their disappointment. Many of them agreed that the squabbles and in-fighting between and within groups and grouplets is having a deleterious impact on literature.

If we take a look at the analogous questionnaires filled in a year later, at the end of 1992, we find that the tone has changed substantially. Apocalyptic prophecies have disappeared. No one writes about the impending demise of Russian literature as a whole, or even of the collapse of literary journals in particular. Instead of gloomy forecasts there is a matter-of-fact recognition of a protracted crisis and a catalogue of successes as well as failures. There is an awareness that the cultural sphere has collapsed into a multitude of subcultures, each of which is more or less self-sufficient. The expectations are guardedly optimistic. What had occurred in 1992 to impart this feeling of hope? Had the literary critics got used to a state of crisis, or had the nadir been passed? An important factor was that not one single well-known literary journal published in Russia had folded; moreover a host of new journals had appeared, ranging from the narrowly professional (*Novoe literaturnoe obozrenie*, *De visu*) to highbrow culturological (*Apokrif*, *Mirovoe drevo*, *Novyi krug*, *Logos*), and including ephemeral publications like *Chernyi zhurnal*, *Bezhin lug*, *Zlatoust*, *Bogema* and *Zolotoi vek*, the magazine of the Union of Graphomaniacs (and not to be confused with the splendid periodical with the same title published since 1991 by Vladimir Salimon and rather reminiscent of the aesthetic tastes of the Silver Age of Russian culture at the beginning of the 20th century). Another initiative was the creation of an elitist Moscow-St Petersburg illustrated journal called *Russkaia viza*, which began by publishing the memoirs of Natal'ia Krandievskaia and fiction by Sasha Sokolov and Venedikt Erofeev. Some of the contents of some of these periodicals, as well as of other journals or magazines not listed here, can be regarded as "the outcome of an epidemic of graphomania", but critics such as Alla Marchenko have a valid point when they state that it would be better to talk about "the emission of vital energy", regarding the efforts to start up new journals at a time of such difficulties as proof of the inexhaustible literary potency still to be found in the Russian Federation.

In 1992 and 1993 the situation in book publishing was also changing. Whereas in the preceding years contemporary Russian literature appeared almost exclusively in journals, with book publishers concentrating on established works and popular foreign literature, by 1993 there was an increasing interest on the part of book publishers in contemporary Russian literature. Moreover, many Russian "traditionalist" writers were recovering their self-assurance in the face of the failure of the avant-garde and postmodernism to attract the interest of the post-Soviet Russian readership. The "alternative" literature mentioned earlier was providing very few new texts worthy of serious discussion, despite all the attempts to stage literary happenings and scandals. In 1992 many critics and writers discussed the harm being done by the much publicized book launches and other noisy public literary events intended to raise the profile and create an image of "the writer", but in reality turning literature into a game, if not a farce. Equally characteristic of the time was the counter-attack mounted by, among others, Dmitrii Prigov, the maestro of Muscovite Conceptualism, who insisted that the image, gesture, and behaviour pattern of the writer mean no less than his *artistic* image. Disputing this, Ian Probshtein noted ironically that substituting the writer's image for his literary works must be very attractive for those who have few worthwhile texts of their own to offer, although it must be said that Prigov himself has a multitude of texts, individual lines of which have already turned into popular sayings, and one of whose characters, an ultra-loyal Soviet militiaman, has now become part of Russian folklore. Probshtein maintains that the present Russian avant-garde, for all its power of negation and attempts to shock, is derivative and imitative, adding nothing to what had already been done by the avant-garde in the early decades of the 20th century. In his view, the "new" avant-garde has failed to respond to the spiritual and creative requirements of the time and is unlikely to bequeath any texts of intrinsic significance to the future (*Literaturnaia gazeta*, 30 April 1993). There were similar assertions about (and occasional acknowledgements of) the low quality of most Russian postmodernist writing. As a result, it was obvious by 1993 that there had not been any aesthetic revolution. The "new" literature was being published in *Vestnik novoi literatury* and *Labirint* (St Petersburg), *Ekstsentr* (Ekaterinburg), later in the combined *Labirint-Ekstsentr*, and in the newspaper *Gumanitarnyi fond*, but all these publications came out in a small number of copies and seemed to arouse more interest among foreign literary specialists than in Russia (hence the ironic term "literature for Slavists"). S. Chuprinin also felt by 1993 that the avant-gardists, whether postmodernists, Conceptualists or whatever else, had become academically respectable and *passé*, a striking change in attitude, as he had earlier been one of those who had placed great hopes on the "new" literature. He named three authors currently working in the "artistic danger zone" near the front line dividing and linking high culture and mass culture (*Znamia*, 9 [1993], 181–88): Viktor Pelevin, Evgenii Popov, and Anatolii Kurchatkin.

Pelevin's novella *Omon Ra* (*Znamia*, 5 [1992]), a mixture of science fiction and thriller, gloomily and ironically demythologizing the Soviet space programme, was the most striking literary debut of the year. He followed this with another novella, *Zhizn' nasekomykh* (*The Life of Insects*) (*Znamia*, 4 [1993]), which, if less original, was no less powerful. Popov's remake of a Turgenev novel, *Nakanune nakanune* [On the Eve of on the Eve] (*Volga*, 4 [1993]), replacing the amiable landowners with squabbling dissidents who can think and talk of nothing but the KGB, shows that a writer associated with Russia's alternative literature from the time of *Metropol'* can still retain Chuprinin's sympathy (Pelevin too is regarded by many as a postmodernist, which shows how fluid are the dividing lines between one school and another). Kurchatkin's *Strazhnitsa* [The Guardian] (*Znamia*, 5 [1993]), about a woman obsessed by Gorbachev, was lambasted by some sophisticated critics as nothing but kitsch.

There can be no doubt that Chuprinin's attitude was well-founded and widely shared. Most highbrow Russian critics, for instance, were cool and sceptical from the outset towards a work such as Viktor Erofeev's *Russkaia krasavitsa* (*Russian Beauty*). They regarded it more as an illustration of views expressed in his article, "A Wake for Soviet Literature", and as a game with various artificial literary rules and regulations than as a new word in Russian literature. A number of foreign academic experts, however, were persuaded that Erofeev was a brave innovator who represented the beginning of a new wave in Russian literature.

Vladimir Sorokin is a more complex figure, who began to attract attention in the mid-1980s with his verbal virtuosity, sparkling originality, and bold detonations of ossified literary devices. Sorokin was better known abroad than in Russia until 1992–93, but after he was short-listed for the Booker Prize in 1992 (for *Serdtsa chetyrekh*) it stopped being politically incorrect to disparage his works, and young as well as older critics were not afraid to "come out" and state that they found his postmodernist rewriting of and attacks on the Russian classical novel somewhat tedious and dated, no matter that he was an undeniably gifted author.

In 1993 even a traditionalist journal like *Novyi mir* published a postmodernist novel, V. Sharov's *Do i vo vremia* [Before and During], in which the author plays with history and literature in an intellectually provocative game. The narrator, a patient in a hospital where experiments are being carried out on his memory, asserts that the ascetic thinker Nikolai Fedorov (1828–1903) – the author of *The Philosophy of the Common Cause* – had an affair with Madame de Staël (1766–1817), which resulted in the birth of their child – Joseph Stalin (1879–1953). This postmodernist phantasmagoria would not have had such an impact if the journal had not printed a letter by two members of its own editorial staff, I. Rodnianskaia and S. Kostyrko, "Sor iz izby" [Washing Our Dirty Linen in Public], containing an extremely strong attack on the novel, which the two editors viewed as a threat to the very existence of Russian literature.

In 1993 it also became apparent that it was no longer possible to use a term that had been very popular in Soviet times, "the literary process". Natal'ia Ivanova was one of the first to notice that in the minds of literary critics "it has been replaced by 'the literary situation' or, even more accurately, 'the literary landscape'" (*Znamia*, 9 [1993], 190). It is a landscape that is blurred and fuzzy, sadly lacking in harmony and charm.

The three major Soviet literary monthlies fiercely opposed to the introduction of liberal democracy to Russia, *Nash sovremennik*, *Moskva*, and *Molodaia gvardiia*, are still publishing today. *Nash sovremennik* supports the radical nationalists; *Moskva* favours the "back-to-the-soil" movement and is seriously interested in the Russian Orthodox Church and Russian religious thought and philosophy; *Molodaia gvardiia* is closer to the (neo)-communists and particularly close to the armed services and the "military-industrial complex". Many of the works published in these three journals (for example Aleksandr Prokhanov's *Poslednii soldat imperii* [The Last Soldier of the Empire] *Nash sovremennik*, 7–9 [1993] and Iu. Kozlov's *Geopoliticheskii romans* [A Geopolitical Romance] *Nash sovremennik*, 11 [1993]) collapse and disintegrate once they are subjected to aesthetic analysis, but it is a pity that most professional critics completely ignore everything published in these periodicals. At least one of the stories published by Valentin Rasputin in *Nash sovremennik*, 8 (1995), for example, is a masterpiece. *V tu zhe zemliu …* [Into that Selfsame Earth], about an elderly woman who has spent her whole life working on the "great building-sites of communism", who has only a minute pension and a wretched little flat to show for it, and who has to bury her aged mother secretly at night, shows that great literature can still be produced by people regarded by liberals and democrats as having completely unacceptable political views.

It cannot be excluded that, when the development of Russian literature in the early 1990s is seen in historical perspective, a significant place will be given to the prose of other "nationalist" writers such as Vladimir Lichutin (1993 saw the publication in *Nash sovremennik* [nos. 10–11] of the beginning of his historical novel *Krestnyi put'* [The Way of the Cross], which forms part of his trilogy *Raskol* [The Split]), Vladimir Krupin, and Leonid Borodin. It is characteristic of this period (1993–95) that works published in "right-wing" journals were simply not discussed by liberal and democratic critics and journalists. On the other hand, virtually no distinction was made by this time between émigré writers and works produced by authors living in Russia. Whereas the first years of perestroika saw the belated publication in Russia of older works by "third-wave" émigrés, which had already come out abroad, journals in Russia itself since 1991 have been the first publishers of new works by émigrés such as Vasilii Aksenov, Vladimir Voinovich, Iuz Aleshkovskii, Fridrikh Gorenshtein, Georgii Vladimov, and Iurii Miloslavskii. (One should note that Russian émigré publishing houses and periodicals have lost much of their importance in the 1990s. Even though the print-runs of "metropolitan" magazines and books are now much lower than in the Soviet period, the print-runs of émigré publishing-houses were and are lower still.) Critics based in the Russian Federation have until recently paid perhaps too much attention to, and been too indulgent of, émigré authors, even forgiving Eduard Limonov for his political eccentricity based on the dangerous combination of Bolshevism and Russian nationalism. The concept of "the émigré writer" has been gradually disappearing, especially as most émigré authors visit Russia regularly, and little attention is devoted to where a writer spends most of his time. Among the most significant works written abroad and (rather than "but") *first* published in Russia are Gorenshtein's novel *Mesto* [Place] (1991); Aksenov's *Moskovskaia saga* [Moscow Saga], chapters of which were published in *Iunost'* as early as 1991; Iuz Aleshkovskii's novella *Persten' v futliare* (*A Ring in a Case*), an ironic description of the literary world in the 1980s (*Zvezda*, 7 [1993]); and Sergei Iur'enen's *Zhelanie byt' ispantsem* [The Desire to Be a Spaniard], the story of the love of a Moscow student and a young Spanish girl (*Soglasie*, 7 and 8–12 [1993]). All these works were and are being read and analysed on a par with works written in Russia. It was therefore quite logical and no great surprise that the winner of the 1995 Booker Prize for the best piece of Russian prose fiction first published the previous year was a writer who happened to be living abroad, Georgii Vladimov. His novel *General i ego armiia* (*The General and His Army*) (*Znamia*, 4–5 [1994]), about a talented military leader who falls foul of the Stalinist system, was regarded as an outstanding text and a significant literary event by almost all Russian critics, who were not concerned with where the author was when he was writing the novel.

The Russian Booker Prize, established in 1992, has had a positive impact on post-Soviet literature and its readership, and even helped to structuralize the Russian literary world, not least because the prize is awarded to the most deserving text, regardless of the status of its author. The first shortlist of novels and novellas (by Vladimir Makanin, Liudmila Petrushevskaia, Gorenshtein, Sorokin, Aleksandr Ivanchenko, and Mark Kharitonov) was in itself enough to dispel gloom about the "crisis" of Russian literature in the early 1990s. Only the novel by Sorokin belonged clearly to the category of "new" or "other" literature. Ivanchenko's *Monogramma* [The Monogram] (*Ural*, 2–4 [1992]), despite its postmodernist devices (such as playing games with Buddhist texts), rests firmly on the realist tradition. So does the winning book, Kharitonov's *Linii sud'by, ili Sunduchok Miloshevicha* (*Lines of Fate*) published in *Druzhba narodov*, 1–2 (1992). This novel also contains postmodernist elements, but is written for the most part in the Russian realist tradition with more than a trace of the western intellectual novel; the influence of Hermann Hesse and Thomas Mann is especially apparent (the almost unknown Kharitonov had translated both these authors). Having beaten the favourites for the prize, the much better known Makanin, Petrushevskaia, and Gorenshtein, Kharitonov found it much easier to publish his earlier and new fiction, and has thus become an established figure on the Russian literary scene. His 1995 novel, *Vozvrashchenie niotkuda* [Return from Nowhere], modernist rather than postmodernist, and set in a mysterious, possibly non-existent, world recalling Nabokov rather than Orwell, has confirmed his reputation as a master.

The 1993 Booker Prize was widely expected to be awarded to Oleg Ermakov for his novel *Znak zveria* [Sign of the Beast] (*Znamia*, 6–7 [1992]), about Soviet soldiers serving in the war in Afghanistan in the 1980s, and questioning in the classical Russian tradition the purpose of the loss of life on both sides. However, instead of giving the award to the young writer from Smolensk, the judges chose the novella by Makanin, *Stol, pokrytyi suknom i s grafinom poseredine* (*Baize-Covered Table with Decanter*) (*Znamia*, 1 [1993]). This work – far from Makanin's best – well describes the Kafkaesque surrealism of Soviet life, where an application to go abroad requires a public confession under torture. Makanin is a key figure in contemporary Russian literature, having moved away from his earlier dispassionate, realistic manner to experiment with new forms, such as science fiction (*Laz* [*Escape Hatch*], *Dolog nash put'* [*The Long Road Ahead*], and "Kavkazskii plennyi" ["The Captive of the Caucasus"]). This last work, freshly and vividly written, graphically reveals the absurd metaphysics of war by turning the tables on classical Russian fiction set in the Caucasus, and focusing not on a Russian captured by locals but on a local man captured, loved, and murdered by a Russian.

The 1994 Booker Prize was awarded to Bulat Okudzhava for his autobiographical novel *Uprazdnennyi teatr* [The Closed Theatre] (*Znamia*, 9–10 [1993]). This unexpected choice (the focus of attention had been on two much younger writers, Petr Aleshkovskii and Aleksei Slapovskii) can perhaps be explained by the fact that both the style and the content of the work marked a new departure for the popular 70-year-old writer, known hitherto for his more sentimental and romantic songs and his historical novels set in the 19th century. The sympathetic portrayal of Okudzhava's relatives and their friends, communists who genuinely, if naively, wanted to "remake the world" and institute a system of social justice, was a real challenge to the "political correctness" of the last few years, which required such idealists to be depicted as absurd individuals and objects of mockery.

Apart from the main award, the "small" Booker Prize (financed by an anonymous British benefactor) is also awarded annually, but each year for a different kind of literary activity. In 1992 this prize, which was split, was awarded to two new journals that had done most, in the opinion of the judges, to promote the development of the new Russian literature. One of the winners, the St Petersburg *Vestnik novoi literatury*, edited by Mikhail Berg, is a journal for aesthetes that sets itself not only against politicized Soviet criteria, but also against realism as the traditionally dominant current in Russian art. The other winner *Solo*, edited by Aleksandr Mikhailov, is aesthetically omnivorous, with traditional prose and poetry intermingled with experimental texts that are intended to shock. *Solo* quickly became a journal for new names in literature, and although it is unprepossessing in appearance and has a very small circulation it makes an important contribution to contemporary literature. In 1993 the "small" Booker was awarded to the most promising short-story writer, deemed to be Viktor Pelevin, whose collection *Sinii fonar'* (*The Blue Lantern*) also included some of his novellas. Pelevin has perhaps received more critical attention than any other Russian writer of his generation, for he appeals equally to lovers of "sots-art" (parodies of socialist realism), of the egocentric "underground", and of Russian postmodernism. Pelevin's prose is dynamic, has a strong story-line, and is accessible to the reader at several levels. There is usually no clear dividing-line between fantasy and reality. In his novella *Prints Gosplana* [The Prince of the Planning State Organization] the world of computer games takes over from the real world; virtual reality replaces reality.

In 1994 the "small" Booker Prize was awarded to the journal published outside Moscow and St Petersburg that had made the greatest contribution to Russian literature in the preceding year. The two strongest contenders were *Ural* (Ekaterinburg) and *Volga* (Saratov), both of which had been, until recently, typical Soviet provincial literary periodicals, but which by the end of the 1980s had used the opportunities presented by glasnost to publish hitherto banned writers and "difficult" texts, sometimes ahead of their Moscow and Leningrad colleagues. *Ural*, which was showing strong postmodernist inclinations, published members of the "Ekaterinburg wave" like the aforementioned Aleksandr Ivanchenko (short-listed for the main Booker Prize in 1992 for his novel *Monogramma*). *Volga* regularly printed local authors, especially the extremely prolific Aleksei Slapovskii (short-listed in 1994 for his novel *Pervoe vtoroe prishestvie* [The First Second Coming]), but also "risqué" works by writers living in Moscow, such as Evgenii Popov's postmodernist *Nakanune nakanune*. *Volga*, which finally won out against *Ural*, demonstrates that not all Russian literary life is concentrated in the two major cities and shows that a magazine published in the provinces does not have to be, in the pejorative sense, provincial. In the following year the "small" Booker Prize was intended for the most deserving Russian-language literary periodical(s) still being published outside the Russian Federation. The winners were *Rodnik* (Riga, Latvia), which had played a very important role in the early years of perestroika, and *Idiot* (Vitebsk, Belarus), a new, small-circulation avant-garde journal, suggesting that Russian "émigré" literature still has a future.

The Russian Booker Prize has generated a number of other developments. In 1993 St Petersburg writers founded the Peterbooker Award, which required all entries to be submitted anonymously in the hope of avoiding favouritism. The first winner was a literary outsider, a professional mathematician called Aleksandr Melikhov, for his novel *Izgnanie iz Edema. Ispoved' evreia* [Out of Eden. The Confession of a Jew] (*Novyi mir*, 1 [1994]). Not only the subject-matter, the problems of national self-identification, but also Melikhov's mastery of language have made this writer an important figure in the literary landscape. This prize was later renamed "Severnaia Palmira" (The Palmyra of the North). The prize can now be awarded for any work of literature or literary criticism first published in St Petersburg (regardless of where the author lives) and/or for publishing activities in that city. The 1995 awards went to the St Petersburg poet Aleksandr Kushner (for his collection *Na sumrachnoi zvezde* [On a Gloomy Star]), the prose writer Feliks Roziner, resident in the United States (for his novel *Akhill begushchii* [Achilles on the Run], *Neva*, 7–8 [1994]), and to Feliks Lur'e for his documentary account of the life of the 19th-century revolutionary Sergei Nechaev.

Whereas this prize has only a symbolic value in financial terms, the "Anti-Booker Prize" established in 1995 by *Nezavisimaia gazeta* brings the winner one dollar more than does the original Russian Booker Prize. The newspaper felt that the Booker judges (five in all, in office for only one year, each panel being made up of Russians and foreigners) had proved to be unable to appreciate "new literature". The first winner of the Anti-Booker Prize (shortly to be renamed) was, however, Aleksei Varlamov, for his traditional realistic novella *Rozhdenie* [Birth] (*Novyi mir*, 7 [1995]), about the struggle of the parents of a seriously ill infant to save his life. This suggests that works deriving from the Russian realist tradition will set the tone for future developments. The answers to a questionnaire published in the last issue of *Literaturnaia gazeta* for 1995 are guardedly optimistic. No one prophesies "the end of literature", although all admit that the role of literature in Russia is on the wane. This is the main conclusion of a survey of the most recent years of Russian literature.

ALLA LATYNINA AND MARTIN DEWHIRST

WRITERS AND WORKS

A

Fedor Aleksandrovich Abramov 1920–1983

Novelist and short-story writer

Biography

Born in Verkola, 29 February 1920. Attended secondary school in Karpogora; studied philology at Leningrad State University, from 1938; completed degree at Leningrad State University after demobilization, 1945–48; postgraduate study and dissertation on Mikhail Sholokhov's *Podniataia tselina* (*Virgin Soil Upturned*) and the theme of collectivization, 1951. Enrolled in the artillery division of the Soviet Army: seriously wounded, 1941; after a long period of convalescence, worked as political instructor in Archangel and then senior investigator in the counter-espionage section of the army (SMERSH), 1942–45: decorated. Lecturer, then senior lecturer in the department of Soviet literature at Leningrad State University, 1951–55. Member of the Writers' Union, 1960; full-time writer from 1962. Married: Liudmila Vladimirovna Krutikova in 1976. Recipient: State Prize for Literature, 1975. Died in Leningrad, 14 May 1983.

Publications

Collected Editions

Sobranie sochinenii, 3 vols. Leningrad, 1980–82.
Swans Flew by and Other Stories. Moscow, Raduga, 1986.
Sobranie sochinenii. Leningrad, 1990 – (3 vols to date)

Fiction

"Brat'ia i sestry" [Brothers and Sisters], *Neva*, 9 (1958), 3–142.
"Vokrug da okolo" [Round and About], *Neva*, 1 (1963), 109–37.
"Dve zimy i tri leta", *Novyi mir*, 1 (1968), 3–67; translated as *Two Winters and Three Summers*, by D.B. and D.C. Powers, Ann Arbor, Ardis, 1984; also translated by Jacqueline Edwards and Mitchell Schneider, San Diego, Harcourt Brace Jovanovich, 1984.
"Pelageia", *Novyi mir*, 6 (1969), 31–70.
"Al'ka", *Nash sovremennik*, 1 (1972) 2–36.
"Dereviannie koni" [Wooden Horses], in *Povesti i rasskazy*, Leningrad, 1972.
"Puti-pereput'ia" [Roads and Crossroads], *Novyi mir*, 1–2 (1973), 3–114; 5–58.
"Dom" [The House], *Novyi mir*, 12 (1978), 3–164.
"Mamonikha", in *Babilei: Rasskazy. Povesti*, Leningrad, 1981.
"Poezdka v proshloe" [The Journey into the Past], *Novyi mir*, 5 (1989), 5–38.
"Kto on?" [Who is He?], *Znamia*, 3 (1993), 140–60.

Essay

"Liudi kolkhoznoi derevni v poslevoennoi proze" [People of the Collectivized Village in Post-War Soviet Literature], *Novyi mir*, 4 (1954), 210–31.

Critical Studies

A History of Post-War Soviet Writing: The Literature of Moral Opposition, by Grigori Svirski, edited and translated by Robert Dessaix and Michael Ulman, Ann Arbor, Ardis, 1981.
Scenes from Soviet Life: Soviet Life Through Official Literature, by Mary Seton-Watson, London, BBC Publications, 1986.
Fedor Abramov: Lichnost'. Knigi. Sud'ba, by I. Zolotusskii, Moscow, 1986.
Fedor Abramov, by A. Turkov, Moscow, 1987.
Dom v Verkole, by L. Krutikova, Leningrad, 1988.
Dom na Ugore: o Fedore Abramove i ego knigakh, by Iu. Oklianskii, Moscow, 1990.
The Life and Work of Fedor Abramov, edited by David Gillespie, Evanston, Illinois, Northwestern University Press, 1997.

Bibliography

Bibliograficheskii ukazatel', edited by V.V. Moshareva, A.N. Rychkova and Archangel, 1993.

Fedor Aleksandrovich Abramov was a respected writer associated with the movement of Russian Village Prose. The youngest son of a large peasant family, he was born in the village of Verkola in the north of Russia where he experienced the culture and life that forms the basis of his fiction. Before launching his literary career, he worked as an academic and a specialist in Soviet literature, but his name first became widely known in 1954 with the publication of a controversial article in the journal *Novyi mir*.

In "Liudi kolkhoznoi derevni v poslevoennoi proze" [People of the Collectivized Village in Post-War Soviet Literature], Abramov condemns the falsified depiction of rural life characteristic of Soviet novels, a criticism that earned him a reputation for outspokenness and caused the journal to be censured. Four years later, Abramov established himself as a writer with the publication of his first work of fiction, the novel *Brat'ia i sestry* [Brothers and Sisters], the first part of the tetralogy known under the collective name *Brat'ia i sestry* as well as *Priasliny* [The Priaslins]. This novel is Abramov's written testimony of his experience as a young soldier sent to the rear to recover from serious injuries, where he witnessed the heroic deeds of the peasants.

In the novel, the action is set in the fictional village of Pekashino, where a community hampered by the absence of able men is striving to live through the war years. In an unassuming manner and a language rich in local colour, a strategy sustained throughout his works, Abramov describes the daily life of many characters, including the Priaslin family.

The overall image that emerges is that of a tough existence dominated by hard work, periodically darkened by dramatic news received from the front, but counterbalanced by the great spirit of solidarity that unites the community, led by the supportive chair of the collective farm, Anfisa Minina.

Although characterization lacks a certain finesse, this novel constitutes an honest and bold account of life in a Soviet village in the 1940s. It was well received by critics and was followed by a sequel to the Pekashino chronicle in the early post-war years, *Dve zimy i tri leta* (*Two Winters and Three Summers*). The third novel of the cycle, *Puti-pereput'ia* [Roads and Crossroads] tells of the end of an era, and of the dawn of a new one. The thematic content is rich and controversial: the cult of personality, style of leadership and agricultural policy in the late 1940s and early 1950s are examined, alongside the gradual disintegration of family structure and community spirit. Access to publication was arduous and attacks against the work continued thereafter. The final novel in the cycle, *Dom* [The House], concludes the Pekashino chronicle and develops the theme of moral and social disintegration. It has more of a philosophical and historical dimension with the inclusion in the text of separate extracts about the life of local figures and heroes of the revolution.

The public success enjoyed by the tetralogy has been helped in recent years by a theatrical adaptation based on Abramov's novels. Lev Dodin of Leningrad's Malyi Theatre received a State Prize in 1986 for his version of Abramov's works.

Although Abramov's star rose with these novels, his talent is also shown in his novellas, short stories and articles. The semi-fictional essay "Vokrug da okolo" [Round and About] was a landmark in his career, as it caused him to be virtually barred from publication for five years. It describes in a forthright way the life of workers in a poorly administered collective farm, "The New Life". Branding it a "pessimistic account", critics launched an orchestrated campaign against the author, culminating in the appearance in the press of an open letter of protest addressed to Abramov, and signed by people from his native village. Besides the publication of *Two Winters and Three Summers* in 1968, Abramov's return to print was marked with the publication of three substantial novellas that demonstrate a maturing of his writing skills. In *Pelageia* the eponymous heroine is a village baker who has always worked relentlessly but is left with unfulfilled hopes at the end of her life. Milent'evna is a legendary figure and the heroine of *Dereviannie koni* [Wooden Horses]. She embodies all the qualities of the traditional Russian peasant type now dying out in contemporary Soviet society, just as wooden figureheads are now rarely seen adorning the roofs of northern houses. *Al'ka* the sequel to *Pelageia*, describes the return of the baker's daughter to her native village and how she eventually breaks away from that environment. Taken together, *Pelageia* and *Al'ka* show the sociological changes undergone in the rural world, a theme that is developed again in *Mamonikha*. Abramov's short stories, too numerous to be mentioned individually, span the whole of his career and constitute a rich assortment of anecdotal pieces about daily life in rural northern Russia, narrated in vivid terms in the local speech that conveys the author's empathy for his characters.

Since Abramov's death in 1983, his widow has continued to bring out new material hitherto unpublished. The novella *Poezdka v proshloe* [The Journey into the Past] (1989), is a post-glasnost publication that critics welcomed as a significant work that confirms Abramov's literary stature. Dating back from the late 1960s and written "for the drawer" it deals with the themes of collectivization and dekulakization in the 1930s. The journey of the central character into his own past is a pretext for a ruthless examination of the historical and political events that shaped contemporary Russia. The unfinished story "Kto on?" [Who is He?] (1993), also reflects on the recent past. It sheds some new light on Abramov's controversial role during the war as an investigator in SMERSH and, enriched by the author's own annotations alongside the main body of the text, it reads as a tentative analysis of the mechanism behind secret police practices and of the balance between individual and collective responsibility.

As yet unpublished is the last, unfinished novel that the author was in the process of writing at the time of his death. *Chistaia kniga* [The Pure Book] focuses on the question of national identity and its role in the historical process, and was destined to be a philosophical novel on the Civil War in the north of Russia, based on detailed research into local history.

GILDA BAÏKOVITCH

Two Winters and Three Summers

Dve zimy i tri leta

Novel, 1968

Two Winters and Three Summers, written between 1960 and 1966, first appeared in *Novyi mir* in 1968 and ended five years of silence imposed on the author for his controversial essay "Vokrug da okolo". Many obstacles had to be overcome prior to its publication, including a rejection by the journal *Zvezda* in 1966. But when it appeared, it was well received by most critics who recognized this depiction of life in rural Russia in the early post-war years as an honest account of the real state of affairs. The novel confirmed Abramov's reputation as a forthright and uncompromising writer.

It is the second volume in the tetralogy *Brat'ia i sestry* that tells the story of a northern peasant community from the War years until the 1970s. The setting, the main characters, and the basic themes of *Two Winters and Three Summers* are the same as those found in the first novel, *Brat'ia i sestry* (1958). In the village of Pekashino, the daily drudgery of the inhabitants continues. However, the few years that separate the two narratives show the changes in the life of the community and allow the reader to evaluate the impact of the war.

As the title indicates, the story is conducted in a chronicle form that follows the passing of seasons, which provide a framework for the action and contribute to the imagery of the novel. The novel starts with the return of Mikhail Priaslin to the village at the end of the timber-floating season in late spring. The main support of the Priaslin household since the death of the father in the war, Mikhail is established from the start as one of the central figures of the novel and embodies the traditional peasant type – hard-working with a strong sense of responsibility. His young sister Liza also plays a significant part in the novel as the selfless carer of the younger siblings. She, too, is portrayed positively, but plays a further role in the characterization by helping to define Mikhail's relationship with his best friend and opposite, Egor: a conflict arises between the two as they fight for her love and attention. The two young men have much in common as they share the same background and the same aspirations. But whereas Mikhail is tied to his family and the village because of his responsibilities, the carefree Egor can leave and fulfil his ambition to become a tractor driver. Such an opposition is the strategy most often employed by the author for characterization. The author does not over-simplify his characters, instead he maintains a good balance between their positive and negative traits, which gives them a certain complexity. Thus, Mikhail's sense of loyalty to his family is juxtaposed with a feeling of envy for his friend's lifestyle and, despite his defects, Egor is a popular, at times selfless character, bursting with energy and forever ready to seize any good opportunity. Such measured analysis takes the novel beyond its definition as a purely "peasant novel" that deals with rural life, and makes it into a work with a more philosophical dimension, centred on human nature and the human condition. From the collection of individual stories that overlap one another to form the substance of the narrative emerges the image of a tragic life often dictated by events out of the control of the characters.

The main theme of the novel is the continual suffering of the peasants, the victims of history and of high-handed policies. During the course of the novel, it is shown in an unequivocal way how life failed to improve in rural areas after the end of the war, and as the narrative proceeds, the situation seems to become worse still. Unreasonable demands are continually imposed from above on the Pekashino farm workers: plans still have to be overfulfilled, heavy taxes are collected. As the disillusionment grows, the former trust between the chair Anfisa Minina and the workers is destroyed; she is dismissed from her post and replaced by Lukashin, who eventually shares her fate. Women are portrayed as the forgotten victims of the war: they have aged prematurely through grief and hard work and now the lack of suitors leads them to form relationships that are doomed to fail. Thus, the relationship between the mature Varvara and the young Mikhail Priaslin throws the community in discord. The difficult question of the re-integration of ex-prisoners from German prisoner-of-war camps is also evoked with the return of Timofei Lobanov who is ostracized by his family and dies a lonely, sick man.

As regards the imagery of the novel, it draws from the natural world that forms the background to the action (weather, forests, river, and animals), and although lengthy lyrical descriptions of nature are absent from the narrative, nature is often used as a framework for human emotions.

The narrative is conducted for the most part in the local speech of the Archangel region where the action takes place, and this anchors the novel deep in the reality of life in northern rural Russia. The use of a localized dialect also increases the vividness of the depiction and renders the characters more authentic.

In the preface to the English translation, the translators highlight one of Abramov's main characteristics as a writer, namely: "his talent for conveying to the reader the real texture of peasant life, with very little distortion, propaganda, or sentimentalizing", a comment that befits this work.

GILDA BAÏKOVITCH

Gennadii Nikolaevich Aigi 1934–

Poet

Biography

Born Gennadii Lisin in Shaimurzino (Chuvash ASSR), 21 August 1934. Changed name to Aigi (a Chuvash tribal name) in 1969. Attended Batyrevo Pedagogical Institute, 1949–53; Gor'kii Literary Institute, Moscow, 1953–59. Married four times; five sons and one daughter. Expelled from Komsomol and threatened with expulsion from the Literary Institute, 1958. Began writing in Russian, c.1955. First Chuvash book published, 1959. Apart from 11 early poems published in journals (1961–64), no Russian work published in USSR until 1987. First poem published abroad, 1962. After brief stay in Cheboksary (Chuvashia) 1959–60, settled in Moscow; associated with the artistic avant-garde. Organized exhibitions, Maiakovskii Museum, Moscow, 1961–71. Worked as a translator and screenwriter. Recipient: Prix Desfeuilles of French Academy for his Chuvash anthology of French poetry, 1972. Reprimanded by Chuvash Writers' Union for the publication of poems in *Kontinent*, 1976. First of many foreign trips, 1988. First volume of Russian poems published in USSR, 1991.

Publications

Poetry

Stikhi 1954–71. Munich, Sagner, 1975.

Otmechennaia zima [Winter Marked by God]. Paris, Sintaksis, 1982.

Tetrad' Veroniki (bilingual edition), translated by L. Robel. Paris, Le Nouveau Commerce, 1984; reprinted Moscow, 1997; translated as *Veronica's Book*, by Peter France, Edinburgh, Polygon, 1989.

Vremia ovragov [Time of Ravines] (bilingual edition), translated by L. Robel. Paris, Le Nouveau Commerce, 1990.
Zdes' [Here]. Moscow, 1991.
An Anthology of Chuvash Poetry, translated by Peter France. London, Forest Books, 1991 (unpublished in Russian or Chuvash).
"Poslednii ot"ezd", *Literaturnaia gazeta* (6 March 1991); translated as "Final Departure", by Peter France, in *Index on Censorship*, 22/10 (1993).
Teper' vsegda snega [There is Always Snow Now]. Moscow, 1992.
Poklon peniiu [Salute to Singing] (bilingual edition), translated by F.P. Ingold. Berlin, Rainer, 1992.
Selected Poems (bilingual edition), translated by Peter France. London, Angel, 1997.

Critical Studies

Poets of Modern Russia, by Peter France, Cambridge, Cambridge University Press, 1982, 210–19.
Aigui, by L. Robel, Paris, Seghers, 1993.

Gennadii Aigi is an outstanding representative of the Russian poetic avant-garde. He has been writing in Russian since the mid-1950s, but he is a Chuvash, belonging to a Turkic people who live on the Volga close to Kazan. His father, a village teacher of Russian, translated the works of Pushkin into Chuvash; his mother was the descendant of a line of "pagan" priests. Aigi himself has translated a great deal of European poetry into his native tongue; he has celebrated his culture in an anthology of Chuvash poetry published in several European languages. While he has always avoided ornamental folklorism, Chuvash themes and images (field, forest, etc.) permeate his poetry, which is informed by the values (reverence for life, simple goodness) of his ancestral peasant culture.

His work combines three traditions: Chuvash culture; the Russian avant-garde of the early 20th century; and European modernism, in particular French poetry. At the Gor'kii Institute he learnt French and came to feel an affinity for such poets as Baudelaire and René Char. Other major points of reference include Nietzsche, Kafka, Kierkegaard, and the liturgy and theology of the Orthodox Church. Writing for many years for a very limited public, he owed a great deal to friendships: Pasternak, whom he knew at the end of the older poet's life, was a source of inspiration, but, above all, Aigi lived during the 1960s at the centre of a rich underground artistic culture.

He was an "underground" writer, attracting persecution through his critical independence, as well as through his links with Pasternak. From 1964 to 1987 his Russian work remained unpublished in the Soviet Union. He was officially classed as a Chuvash writer and translator and often had to suffer considerable material hardship. From 1962, however, he began to be published in the west, in Russian and in translation, and gradually gained a reputation throughout Europe as one of Russia's most significant poets. The publication of some poems in the émigré journal *Kontinent* in 1976 stirred up further trouble at home. Aigi is not a political writer – for him poetry is a spiritual activity – but many of his poems reflect the sufferings of those around him, in particular the sequence *Pora blagodarnosti* [Time of Gratitude] written during 1976–77 after the political assassination of his close friend, the translator Konstantin Bogatyrev. Only after 1985 was his importance recognized belatedly in Russia and Chuvashia: his works were published, and he began to travel widely abroad.

Aigi has written several aphoristic pieces explaining his conception of poetry, notably "Son-i-poeziia" [Sleep-and-Poetry]. He sees poetry as a sacred rite, attempting to restore a lost human community, to recreate life in the face of darkness and death, to reunite humanity with the rest of creation. His poetry is not concerned with the expression of pre-existing ideas, feelings, or impressions; more akin to whispering than to public speaking, it is a difficult, tentative approach to what cannot be said, and as such calls for the kind of innovative procedures pioneered in painting by Malevich, one of his constant masters. Silence is valued, like the frontier between sleep and waking, as a reservoir of creativity: "pauses are the places of worship: before Song".

His Russian poetry divides into two groups. There is the large collection of occasional verse originally titled *Zimnie kutezhi* [Winter Revels] and later changed to *Stikhi raznykh let* [Poems of Different Years]. Neither of these collections has been published in book form in Russian, and the same is true of the 16 "books" or cycles which make up his fundamental body of writing, from *Otmechennaia zima* [Winter Marked by God] (1960–61) to *Vse dal'she v snega* [Ever Further into the Snows] (1985–89). Two important recent publications are "Poslednii ot"ezd" (*Final Departure*), a sequence written in 1988 in memory of Raoul Wallenberg, and *Poklon peniiu* [Salute to Singing], written 1988–91, consisting of 36 four-line variations on Chuvash and Tartar themes.

This poetry is highly innovative and has proved disconcerting to many Russian readers. Unusually among his contemporaries, Aigi wrote from the start in free verse. Although often impelled by a strong rhythmic drive, his poems seem fragmented, both graphically and syntactically: normal sentence construction and punctuation are replaced by new systems – using spaces, dashes, parentheses, visual symbols and many other typographical devices – to break up the expected connections between words, introducing ambiguities and suggesting new connections. Aigi is very sensitive to the sound of words, coining new ones, or fusing existing words in new creations. Even so, this poetry is at the opposite pole to that of Brodskii; it is rarely witty, nor is it lexically rich. Concrete words and images are relatively rare, often figuring in the title, and carrying a great semantic weight. Starting from an object or place – a rose, a birch tree, a clearing, a queue for paraffin – Aigi characteristically seeks universal value in humble detail.

The poems are best read in groups, as part of a continuous whole. Starting with lower-case letters, as if in mid-sentence, they are linked to one another by their titles, and by the repeated words and images that echo one another throughout a book. Although the books differ from one another, they show a continuity of inspiration and aspiration from 1960 to 1990. Light and whiteness (as of snow) represent an ideal, ecstatically glimpsed in the petals of flowers, or in human faces. The spiritual freedom of the Chuvash field is set against the actual world of humiliation and violence, pain inflicted by one human being on another. The poor and suffering are carriers of the highest values – associated with the poet's mother and the Chuvash people. This extraordinary poetry of pain and luminosity reaches a summit in *Tishina-preduprezhdenie* [Quietness-Premonition] (1974–76), and *Pora blagodarnosti*.

The most accessible of Aigi's major writings, however, is *Tetrad' Veroniki* (*Veronica's Book*), a varied and deeply felt evocation of the first six months of his daughter's life. Old themes are fused here with a new subject-matter, making this the ideal starting-point for an exploration of his work.

PETER FRANCE

Chingiz Torekulovich Aitmatov 1928–

Prose writer

Biography

Born in Sheker, Kirgizstan, 12 December 1928. Attended Kirgiz Agricultural Institute, graduated in animal husbandry, 1953; Gor'kii Literary Institute, Moscow, 1956–58. Married: 1) Keres Aitmatova, two sons; 2) Maria Urmatova in 1974, one son and one daughter. Assistant to the secretary of Sheker Village Soviet from 1943. Editor of the magazine *Literaturnyi Kirghizstan*, late 1950s; worked for *Pravda* for five years. Member of the Communist Party, 1959–91. First secretary, 1964–69, and chair, 1969–86, Cinema Union of Kirgiz SSR. Deputy to Supreme Soviet, 1966–89. People's writer of Kirgiz Soviet Socialist Republic, 1968. Member of the Central Committee, Kirgiz SSR, 1971–90. Vice-chair, Committee of Solidarity with Peoples of Asian and African Countries, 1974–89; chair, Writers' Union of Kirgizstan, and Issyk-Kul Forum, since 1986. Member of the editorial board of *Novyi mir* and *Literaturnaia gazeta*; editor, *Druzhba narodov*; editor-in-chief, *Inostrannaia literatura*, 1988–90. Member of Congress of People's Deputies of USSR, 1989–91. Member of Mikhail Gorbachev's Presidential Council, 1990–91. Recipient: Lenin Prize, 1963; Order of the Red Banner of Labour (twice); State Prize, 1968, 1977, 1983; Hero of Socialist Labour, 1978. Member of Kirgiz Academy of Science, 1974; European Academy of Arts, Science, and Humanities, 1983; World Academy of Art and Science, 1987. Appointed Soviet and (subsequently) Russian Federation ambassador to Luxemburg, 1990; currently Kirgiz ambassador to Belgium, Holland, and Luxemburg.

Publications

Collected Editions

Tri povesti. Erevan, 1965; translated as *Short Novels: To Have and to Lose; Duishen; Mother-Earth* [no translator named], Moscow, Progress, 1964.

Posle skazki (Belyi parokhod); *Materinskoe pole*; *Proshchai, Gul'sary!*; *Pervyi uchitel'*; *Litsom k litsu*; *Dzhamilia*; *Topolek moi v krasnoi kosynke*; *Verbliuzhii glaz*; *Svidanie s synom*; *Soldatenok*. Frunze, 1974.

Izbrannye proizvedeniia, 2 vols. Tashkent, 1978.

Sobranie sochinenii, 3 vols. Moscow, 1982–84.

Rasskazy, ocherki, publitsistika [Stories, Essays, Articles]. Moscow, 1984.

Ekho mira: povesti, rasskazy, publitsistika [Echo of the World: Novellas, Stories, Articles]. Moscow, 1985.

Mother Earth and Other Stories, translated by James Riordan. London, Faber, 1989.

Fiction

"Litsom k litsu" [Face to Face], *Oktiabr'*, 3 (1958).

Rasskazy [Stories]. Moscow, 1958.

Dzhamilia. Moscow, 1959; translated as "Jamila", by Fainna Glagoleva and Olga Shartse, in *Tales of the Mountains and Steppes*, Moscow, Progress, 1969.

Melodiia [Melody]. Frunze, 1959.

Topolek moi v krasnoi kosynke [My Little Poplar in a Red Headscarf]. Moscow, 1961.

Verbliuzhii glaz [The Camel's Eye]. Moscow, 1962.

Pervyi uchitel' [The First Teacher]. *Novyi mir*, 7 (1962); translated as "Duishen", in *Short Novels*, 1965; and by Fainna Glagoleva and Olga Shartse, in *Tales of the Mountains and Steppes*, Moscow, Progress, 1969.

Povesti gor i stepei. Moscow, 1962; translated as *Tales of the Mountains and Steppes*, by Fainna Glagoleva and Olga Shartse, Moscow, Progress, 1969.

Materinskoe pole. Moscow, 1963; translated as "Mother-Earth", in *Short Novels*, 1965; also by James Riordan, in *Mother Earth and Other Stories*, 1989.

"Proshchai, Gul'sary!", *Novyi mir*, 3 (1966); Moscow, 1967; translated as "Farewell, Gul'sary!", by Fainna Glagoleva and Olga Shartse, in *Tales of the Mountains and Steppes*, Moscow, Progress, 1969; and by John French, London, Hodder and Stoughton, 1970.

"Belyi parokhod", *Novyi mir*, 1 (1970); translated as *The White Ship*, by Mirra Ginsburg, New York, Crown, 1972; also as *The White Steamship*, by Tatyana and George Feifer, London, Hodder and Stoughton, 1972.

Rannie zhuravli. Moscow, 1976; translated as *The Lament of a Migrating Bird*, by John French, Felixstowe, Premier Press, 1973; and as *The Cranes Fly Early*, by Eve Manning, Moscow, Raduga, 1983.

Lebedi nad Issyk-Kulem [Swans above Issyk-Kul]. Moscow, 1976.

Pegii pes, begushchii kraem moria. Moscow, 1977; translated as *The Piebald Dog Running Along the Shore and Other Stories* [no translator named], Moscow, Raduga, 1989.

Legenda o rogatoi materi-olenizhe [The Legend of the Horned Mother Deer]. Alma-Ata, 1979.

I dol'she veka dlitsia den'. Frunze, 1981; reprinted as *Burannyi*

polustanok (I dol'she veka dlitsia den') [The Snowstorm Halt]. Frunze, 1981; translated as *The Day Lasts More than a Hundred Years*, by John French, Bloomington, Indiana University Press, and London, Macdonald, 1983.
Plakha [The Block]. Moscow, 1987; translated as *The Place of the Skull*, by Natasha Ward, London, Faber, and New York, Grove Press, 1989.
Legenda o ptitse Donenbai: iz romana "I dol'she veka dlitsia den'" [The Legend of the Donenbay Bird: From the Novel *The Day Lasts More than a Hundred Years*]. Frunze, 1987.
Svidanie s synom [An Appointment with the Son]. Frunze, 1987.
Sineglazaia volchitsa: Otr. iz romana "Plakha" [Blue-Eyed She-Wolf: From the Novel *The Block*]. Frunze, 1987.
Shestevo i sed'moi: Otr. iz romana "Plakha" [Sixth and Seventh: From the Novel *The Block*]. Frunze, 1987.
"Beloe oblako Chingiskhana" [The White Cloud of Ghengis Khan], *Znamia*, 8 (1990).
Tavro Kassandry [The Mark of Cassandra]. Moscow, 1994.

Play
Voskhozhdenie na Fudzhiiamu, with Kaltai Mukhamedzhanov (produced Moscow, 1973); translated as *The Ascent of Mount Fuji*, by Nicholas Bethell (produced Washington, DC, 1975), New York, Farrar Straus and Giroux, 1975.

Essays, Articles, and Lectures
V soavtorstve s zemleiu i vodoiu. Stat'i, razgovory, interv'iu [In Co-Authorship with the Earth and Water. Articles, Conversations, Interviews]. Frunze, 1978.
My izmeniaem mir, mir izmeniaet nas [We Change the World, the World Changes Us]. Frunze, 1985.
On Craftsmanship, with Chinghiz Aitmatov, by V. Novikov. Moscow, Raduga, 1987.
Chas slova. Moscow, 1988; translated as *The Time to Speak Out*, by Paula Garb, Moscow, Progress, 1988.
Stat'i, vystupleniia, dialogi, interv'iu [Articles, Statements, Dialogues, Interviews]. Moscow, 1988.
Oda velichiiu dukha: dialogi [Ode to the Greatness of the Spirit. Dialogues], with Daisaku Ikeda. Moscow, Progress, 1994.

Critical Studies
Chingiz Aitmatov: Ocherk tvorchestva, by Vladimir Voronov, Moscow, 1976.
Soviet Literature in the 1970s, by N.N. Shneidman, Toronto, University of Toronto Press, 1979.
"Am I Not in My Own Home?", by Boris Pankin, *Soviet Studies in Literature*, 18/3 (1981).
"The Child Narrator in the Novels of Chingiz Aitmatov", by Nina Kolesnikoff, in *Russian Literature and Criticism*, edited by Evelyn Bristol, Berkeley, California, Berkeley Slavic Specialties, 1982, 101–10.
"A Poetic Vision in Conflict: Chingiz Aitmatov's Fiction", by Constantin V. Ponomareff, in *Russian Literature and Criticism*, edited by Evelyn Bristol, Berkeley, California, Berkeley Slavic Specialties, 1982, 158–66.
Chingiz Aitmatov i mirovaia literatura, by G. Gachev, Frunze, 1982.
"Chingiz Aitmatov: A Feeling for the Times", by Nikolai Khokhlov, *Soviet Literature*, 4/421 (1983).
Chingiz Aitmatov: Problemy poetiki, zhanra, stilia, by V. Levchenko, Moscow, 1983.
"Both Are Primary: An 'Author's Translation' is a Creative Re-Creation", by Munavvarkhon Dadazhanova, *Soviet Studies in Literature*, 20/4 (1984).
"Time to Speak Out" (interview) by Vladimir Korkin, *Soviet Literature*, 5/434 (1984).
"Chingiz Aitmatov's First Novel: A New Departure?", by Stewart Paton, *Slavonic and East European Review*, 62 (1984), 496–510.
"Prose Has Two Wings", by Keneshbek Asanliyev, *Soviet Literature*, 2/443 (1985).
"Chingiz Aitmatov's *Proshchai, Gul'sary*", by Sheelagh Duffin Graham, *Journal of Russian Studies*, 49 (1985).
"India Has Become Near", by Miriam Salganik, *Soviet Literature*, 12/453 (1985).
Chinghiz Aitmatov, by V. Novikov, Moscow, Raduga, 1987 [with *On Craftsmanship*].
"Chingiz Aitmatov's *The Execution Block*: Religion, Opium and the People", by Robert Porter, *Scottish Slavonic Review*, 8 (1987), 75–90.
"Chingiz Aytmatov's *Plakha*: A Novel in a Time of Change", by Riita H. Pittman, *Slavonic and East European Review*, 66 (1988), 357–79.
"On Chinghiz Aitmatov and His Characters: For the Author's 60th Birthday", by Evgenii Sidorov, *Soviet Literature*, 11/488 (1988).
Four Contemporary Russian Writers, by Robert Porter, Oxford, Berg, 1989.
"Chingiz Aitmatov's Second Novel", by J.B. Woodward, *Slavonic and East European Review*, 69 (1991), 201–20.
Parables from the Past: The Prose Fiction of Chingiz Aitmatov, by Joseph P. Mozur, Jr, Pittsburgh, University of Pittsburgh Press, 1995.
Spirit of the Totem: Religion and Myth in Soviet Fiction, 1964–1988, by Irena Maryniak, Leeds, W.S. Maney, 1995.

The fiction of popular Soviet writer Chingiz Aitmatov evolved under the influence of two powerful, yet highly different literary cultures – the polished moral and philosophical prose of 19th-century Russia, in particular the works of Dostoevskii and Tolstoi, and the oral tradition of his native Kirgizstan. What makes Aitmatov's fiction unique among contemporary Soviet writers is the way he integrates oral folklore into his prose both to "universalize" the contemporary events portrayed and to comment parabolically on their significance for society. Kirgiz folklore also served as an effective Aesopian "screen" to counter the numerous levels of Soviet censorship.

Aitmatov's literary debut came in 1952 with the publication of two short stories in the Russian language journal *Kirghizstan*. Other short stories soon appeared in both Kirgiz- and Russian-language journals, opening for Aitmatov the doors to the Writers' Union, and enabling him to enrol in the prestigious Gor'kii Literary Institute in Moscow. His years at the Gor'kii Literary Institute coincided with the post-Stalin cultural Thaw and proved to be a turning-point in the young author's life, contributing significantly to his liberation from literary schemata. His first major literary success, the novella *Dzhamilia* ("Jamila"), came during his final year at the Institute; it was translated into French by Louis Aragon, who thought it "the most beautiful love story in the world". *Dzhamilia* depicts a Kirgiz woman's betrayal of her soldier husband during World War II, while he is convalescing from his wounds in hospital. The spirit of the Thaw, with its focus on personal freedom, makes itself felt as the author violates the standard approach to wartime infidelity and celebrates the heroine's choice of personal happiness over her obligations to family and clan.

After graduating from the Literary Institute and his first taste of international fame, Aitmatov continued to refine his control of the genre of novella, experimenting with different forms and points of view. The heroes in Aitmatov's *Topolek moi v krasnoi kosynke* ("My Little Poplar in a Red Headscarf") 1961, *Verbliuzhii glaz* ("The Camel's Eye") 1962, and *Pervyi uchitel'* ("The First Teacher") 1962, break in a number of ways with the clichés of socialist realism and reveal the writer's efforts to create believable human characters. Together with *Dzhamilia*, the three novellas mentioned above make up the collection *Povesti gor i stepei* (*Tales of the Mountains and Steppes*), for which Aitmatov was awarded the Lenin Prize in 1963.

The culmination of Aitmatov's literary apprenticeship came with the publication of the novella *Materinskoe pole* (*Mother-Earth*) in 1963. This dialogue between a Kirgiz war widow and the Earth, is an abrupt formal departure from the tenets of "classical" socialist realism. A third voice, the narrator's, functions like a dramatist's voice and gives only the "stage directions" for the woman's confession. The widow laments the loss of her sons and husband in the war, and the Earth "responds" with compassion. In his deification of a barren field, Aitmatov falls back on the century-old Kirgiz view of the world and the cult of "Umai-ene", the Kirgiz goddess of human and earthly fertility. The widow's personal grief is thereby elevated to a condemnation of all wars and her personal sorrow represents that of all women who have lost their men to war. The concrete historical circumstances in which the widow's lament is embedded (World War II) are effaced by the epic form of her lament. Conservative critics found fault with the novella's lack of an unambiguous stance on the righteousness of Soviet sacrifices in the war.

Characterizing almost all of Aitmatov's works after *Mother-Earth* is a greater reliance on folklore structures in the depiction of Soviet contemporaneity, a penchant for the tragic, and a desire to expose the evil of the Stalinist mindset. *Proshchai Gul'sary*! ("Farewell, Gul'sary!") portrays the excesses of the "cult of personality" in Soviet Kirgizia. The story of Tanabai Bakasov, a rank-and-file Party member working as a shepherd at a small kolkhoz, reveals the author's conviction that a man must preserve the purity of his ideals, despite the lawlessness of Communist Party authorities. *Belyi parokhod* (*The White Steamship*) portrays the futile struggle of a young boy to escape the world of brute force created by his sadistic uncle, Orozkul, whose cynical tyranny evokes the image of Stalin. The work is a full-fledged mythological novel, with the Kirgiz totemistic myth of the Deer-mother providing the subtext for viewing the characters' actions and motives. The influence of Mikhail Bulgakov's *Master and Margarita* is clearly evident in Aitmatov's treatment of quasi-religious myth.

Aitmatov has continued to write in the spirit of *The White Steamship*. *Rannye zhuravli* (*The Cranes Fly Early*), *Pegii pes, begushchii kraem moria* (*The Piebald Dog Running Along the Shore*, *I dol'she veka dlitsia den'* (*The Day Lasts More than a Hundred Years*), and *Plakha* (*The Place of the Skull*) all emphasize the tragic side of man's existence. The author's use of myth, legend, and religious motifs in these works continued to call attention to the need for greater respect of the pre-revolutionary cultural heritage of the Soviet Union's peoples. In response to criticism in the Soviet press for experimenting with mythological forms and failing to write "straightforward" prose, Aitmatov persistently and successfully argued that Soviet literature should break with obsolete one-dimensionality by legitimizing non-realistic forms, thereby deepening the reader's experience of reality.

Aitmatov's glasnost novel, *The Place of the Skull*, written at the beginning of Gorbachev's campaign for more openness in Soviet society, seriously questions the materialistic ideology on which Soviet society was founded. Its positive treatment of religious beliefs made the work a sensation throughout the Soviet Union. The main character, Avdii Kallistratov, is a defrocked seminarian, seeking to save Soviet society from intolerance and hedonism. Avdii's message concerning man's need of repentance conveys Aitmatov's appeal to his countrymen to come to terms with the intolerance and inhumanity of the Stalinist legacy. While some Soviet critics pointed to structural and aesthetic deficiencies, Aitmatov's novel clearly signalled the beginning of unprecedented freedom for Soviet letters in the following years.

In the years following glasnost Aitmatov has "rewritten" or restored sections of his works cut or omitted because of censorship, publishing, for example, a new chapter, "The White Cloud of Ghengis Khan" (1990), for *The Day Lasts More than a Hundred Years*. This portrays the arrest, interrogation, and death of one of the novel's central characters, Abutalip Kuttybaev, contrasting Stalinist cruelty with the terror inflicted by the Mongol warlord. After the demise of the Soviet Union, Aitmatov co-authored a book with Japanese Buddhist leader Daisaku Ikeda, discussing the state of world ecology, culture, human rights, and other pressing issues. Aitmatov here takes the opportunity to state his views on the ideological intolerance of the former Soviet Union.

In 1994 Aitmatov published his first post-Soviet novel, *Tavro Kassandry* [The Mark of Cassandra], revealing its author's continuing fascination with ecological and societal failures. The philosophical narrative, set both in the US and outer space, portrays the inability of the world's leaders to cope with the new challenges of global impact. Imbued with a heavy dose of pessimism, it reveals Aitmatov's fears that humanity's noble causes are destined to fail when confronted by irrational evil, embodied in dishonest and shallow people, so easily seduced by fame and privilege. Critical response has been mixed, and Aitmatov's readers miss the familiar epic subtext that was the hallmark of his best works.

Aitmatov is a talented writer seeking new literary forms to express his deep-seated concern for the fate of humankind in the coming millennium. His Soviet experience of having to write for years under censorship has made him particularly sensitive to the dangers of unrestrained power, whether for the natural environment or for human civilization. While likening the literary freedom he enjoys today to that of a man "standing in confusion before a vast plain, not knowing where to turn", he continues to write in the post-Soviet era, unlike many former Soviet writers, and his fiction remains compelling reading.

JOSEPH P. MOZUR, JR

Tales of the Mountains and Steppes

Povesti gor i stepei

Short-story collection, 1962

In 1963 Aitmatov received the Lenin Prize for a collection of stories that appeared under the title *Povesti gor i stepei* (*Tales of the Mountains and Steppes*). The original collection figures in Soviet political/literary history as the book that received the Lenin Prize in that year instead of Aleksandr Solzhenitsyn's *Odin den' Ivana Denisovicha* (*One Day in the Life of Ivan Denisovich*).

Aitmatov's volume contains four novellas originally written in the author's native tongue, Kirgiz: *Dzhamilia* ("Jamila"), *Topolek moi v krasnoi kosynke* ("My Little Poplar in a Red Headscarf"), *Verbliuzhii glaz* ("The Camel's Eye") and *Pervyi uchitel'* ("The First Teacher"). The English-language version *Tales of the Mountains and Steppes* purports to be a translation of the Russian volume, but it contains only two of the four stories found in the Russian edition: "Jamila" and "The First Teacher" (here titled "Duishen" after the main character). Further complicating matters, the English-language version includes an additional story, "Farewell Gul'sary!", not found in the original collection and important, *inter alia*, as Aitmatov's first story not translated from Kirgiz, but written originally in Russian, and his first work to deal openly with the legacy of Stalinism.

The original four short works have much in common: themes, characters and images, and narrative features. Each story illustrates a personal spiritual triumph over social/physical adversity. They all share a love theme. All four sympathetically comment on the woman's lamentable position in traditional Kirgiz society, and all take place during times of radical social transformation. The heroes and heroines in all four pieces are young, and each story is told in the first person.

The first of the four novellas in the Russian *Tales of the Mountains and Steppes* is Aitmatov's most famous short work: "Jamila". It is the story of the eponymous protagonist and her lover, the wounded soldier Daniiar. The story takes place during World War II, and is set, as are almost all of Aitmatov's works, in the author's native Kirgizia. The whole story is related through the eyes of a 15-year-old narrator, Seit, an aspiring painter and stepbrother-in-law to Jamila. Seit relates the love of Daniiar and Jamila. Daniiar's songs prove a spark that fuels Jamila's love and she finally flees with him from the society that will not accept what she will not deny, her love for a man other than her husband. The narrative is framed, and the conclusion brings the story around full circle; "Jamila" begins and ends with a painting of the couple.

The second story, "Topolek moi v krasnoi kosynke" is narratively more complex. The story is related via three different first-person narratives and describes the life of a reckless hard-drinking truck-driver Il'ias, his love for and elopement with a local girl Asel', and then the collapse of his life. At first life is good for the trucker and his "little poplar". They have a son, Samat, the apple of his father's eye, and life is nearly ideal. But after a trucking mishap in which Il'ias abandons a trailer on the road, things take a turn for the worse. He begins to drink and takes up with another woman, Kadicha. When Asel' finds out she leaves with her child to be saved by the positive hero, Baitemir. There are some touching scenes, but the execution of the complex narrative structure (foreshadowing future, more successful efforts) is uneven, and this story is the least convincing of the collection.

Unlike the other tales here, the third piece, "The Camel's Eye" is an unframed first-person account of events during a young man's summer working in the virgin lands of Kirgizia. Though physically defeated by the brutish antagonist, Abakir (he will prove a model for future Aitmatov villains), the boy protagonist, Kemel, refuses to be defeated spiritually. At a spring that he christens the Camel's Eye, Kemel meets a pretty shepherdess only to have Abakir frighten her away with his crude advances. Finally, when Kemel, whose history teacher Aldiiarov had fired his interest in the region, finds a gold artefact under a plough, Abakir proves his irrevocable villainy and absconds with the valuable piece. This story is notable for its inversion of the expected character types in Soviet socialist realism. Instead of a positive hero-labourer and ignorant, spiritually deficient intellectual, it is the worker who is morally deformed and the curious young "academic" who is cast in a good light in "The Camel's Eye".

The fourth tale, "The First Teacher", is reported in the form of a letter, and tells of a semiliterate young Kirgiz communist, Duishen, who returns to his father's ancestral village to start a school in 1924. His educational efforts are earnest but his most important achievement is the gallant rescue of a bright young orphan, Altynai, from a life of misery as the second wife of a savage nomadic shepherd. She eventually becomes a Moscow academician. Like "Jamila" this last story is framed by a young artist whose musings over his artwork both prompt his prose and draw the story to a close. Thus the volume *Tales of the Mountains and Steppes* concludes in a curious but effective symmetry with its beginning.

"Farewell Gul'sary!", included in the Soviet English "translation" of *Tales of the Mountains and Steppes* but not in the original collection, is very different from the original four. It is more than twice the length of the other stories. Romance is of little importance. The hero is an old man, Tanabai, and his sad story (and the even sadder one of his horse Gul'sary) is told in the third person. The narrative is complex but polished and the work is full of ominous implications about the communist regime. Adding the story to the collection may have been an attempt by Progress publishers to answer some of the sharp criticism of the draconian Soviet literary policies of the mid-1960s (the trials of Brodskii, Siniavskii, and Daniel' and the refusal to print Solzhenitsyn's *Rakovyi korpus* [*Cancer Ward*]), but whatever the reasons, and despite its very real literary merits, its inclusion in the English redaction disrupts the compositional unity found in the original volume.

NATHAN LONGAN

The White Steamship

Belyi parokhod

Novella, 1970

Chingiz Aitmatov's *The White Steamship* appeared in the January 1970 issue of the literary journal *Novyi mir*, the last issue to be published under the stewardship of the liberal Aleksandr

Tvardovskii before he was forced to resign in that Soviet jubilee year – 100 years after Lenin's birth.

The novella is a painful tragedy about the triumph of evil over good and the life of a seven-year-old boy in an isolated outpost in the pristine mountains of Kirgizia. The boy is being raised by his maternal grandfather and his second wife who live at the post with another daughter and her brutally abusive husband. The grandfather, Momun (the name in Kirgiz evokes the idea of "good" or "kind"), is the boy's idol. The uncle, Orozkul (intentionally very close to the Kirgiz for "Russian slave") is the boy's nemesis. The boy's parents have abandoned him. The title of the story comes from the white steamship that the boy sees plying the waters of lake Isyk-Kul and on which he believes his father works. The lonely boy fantasizes of swimming downstream and out to the ship to meet his father. The boy seems to enjoy his private fairy tale of becoming a fish, but the reason for this fantasy is tragic – to escape the cruel tyranny of Orozkul in search of a father of dubious character. The boy is distracted from his bitter-sweet dream by his grandfather's tales. More than in Aitmatov's earlier work, myth, legend, and fairy tale form the compositional backbone of the novella. The favourite story of both the boy and his grandfather and the central tale of the novella is that of the Mother-Doe. This variation on the Kirgiz ethnogenetic myth, is the legend of how the Mother-Doe saved a boy and a girl and how their ancestors then revered the deer. According to the legend, the deer abandon the mountains when people begin to kill them.

The boy is profoundly impressed by his grandfather's story, and so believes that three deer recently seen in the forest are in fact the Mother-Doe and her family. The boy's fantasy of escape as a fish disappears from the story as he puts all his faith in the powers of salvation of the Mother-Doe whom he sees as his guardian. He is sure the deer will placate Orozkul (perhaps by giving him a child) and bring peace to the outpost. Instead, the doe is killed, though reluctantly, by none other than the boy's grandfather. Distraught at Momun's murder of his guardian, the boy returns to his tragic fantasy of escape as a fish and drowns when he slips into the fast-flowing, cold mountain river.

Aitmatov begins and ends his story with the boy's fantasy of becoming a fish, and thus, though more subtly than in his earlier works, ensures a symmetry of composition. Almost all the characters have literary relatives in Aitmatov's earlier work. The boy's predecessors include the parentless heroes of "The First Teacher", *Topolek moi v krasnoi kosynke* and "The Camel's Eye". His evil step-grandmother is a near twin to the wicked aunt in *Topolek*, and Orozkul can count Abakir from "The Camel's Eye" among his close cousins. As in all his work Aitmatov's language is simple and straightforward, apart from the use of some Kirgiz words, which provide local colour. The whole novella is told in the third person, but long sections of legend and myth are told from the grandfather's point of view. *The White Steamship* was subtitled, in parentheses, "Posle Skazki" [After a Fairy Tale], and traditional tales are essential to the message of the novella. In addition to the story of the Mother-Doe and the boy's own fantasy "tale" about becoming a fish, there are three other traditional Kirgiz stories woven into the text: a legend about the wind that protects the mountain Kirgiz from lowland invaders, a story of a Kirgiz prisoner who chooses death over slavery, and a fairy tale about a Kirgiz Tom Thumb swallowed by a wolf. All these stories play significant structural roles in the work and underscore the importance that Aitmatov placed and would continue to place on the role of myths for a people's identity.

Unlike most of his earlier works, *The White Steamship* offers readers no escape from tragedy. Even in stories in which the hero is physically beaten ("The First Teacher" and "The Camel's Eye", for instance), Aitmatov was always careful to show the triumph of morality. In *The White Steamship* only evil triumphs and good is vanquished completely. In the best traditions of classic Russian realist tragedy (strong parallels with A.N. Ostrovskii's *Groza* [*The Storm*] have been noted), Aitmatov only presents the problem. Any possible solution to the real-life problem described is left for the reader to discover or work towards.

The White Steamship sparked a highly polemical debate in the Soviet press about the role of tragedy in Soviet literature. As pure undiluted tragedy, the story was received coolly by conservative Soviet literary critics, who objected to its neglect of socialist realist didacticism in favour of classic Russian realist didacticism. There were other reasons for their antipathy toward the piece: the work can easily be read as thinly disguised commentary on Soviet society as a whole. For instance, in his servile acquiescence to the will of the Stalin-like Orozkul, Momun has been interpreted as a representation of Soviet society and its shared culpability in the crimes of the dictator. The conservative outcry apparently had some influence, for in its book form *The White Steamship* has an extra paragraph at the end. The narrator addresses the dead boy and tells him that he would have been saved by Kulubek (a positive but almost incidental character) if he had just waited. This addition is very minor, and the overall effect is still powerfully pessimistic. In its themes, images, characters, use of legend and overall tone *The White Steamship* presages almost all his later work including the novels *The Day Lasts More than a Hundred Years* and *The Place of the Skull*.

In 1977 Aitmatov received the Soviet Union's State Prize for *The White Steamship* and its screenplay.

NATHAN LONGAN

The Day Lasts More than a Hundred Years

I dol'she veka dlitsia den'

Novel, 1981

The Day Lasts More than a Hundred Years, Aitmatov's first full-length novel, appeared in the literary journal *Novyi mir* in November 1980 (and in book form the following year) to much acclaim and controversy. Aitmatov had established himself in the tightly controlled Soviet literary world with a succession of novellas that skirted the limits of the permissible, but never overstepped them. This first novel continued in that tradition (the fact of its publication alone speaks to its acceptability), but this work pushed the political limits as none of his earlier works had done. Not only are the sins of the Stalinist past examined, but the continuing damage of that legacy is illustrated and even implications for world peace are described darkly.

The "day" of the title delimits the central motivating device of the novel: a funeral procession through the steppes of the Central Asian republic of Kazakhstan organized and led by Edigei Zhangeldin to bury, in the Muslim tradition, his friend Kazangap

Asanbaev in an ancient cemetery. The long trek (30 kilometres on a camel's back) affords Edigei ample time to reflect on his own life, and these reflections, narrated in the third person – as is the whole novel – make up the bulk of the book. Edigei's thoughts include reminiscences of the high and low points in his life and long renditions of legends. The themes, events and characters of these recollections and legends coincide, intersect and overlap to flesh out the main thematic thrust of the novel: memory, personal and societal, is sacred and must be preserved if humans are to retain their humanity.

The central legend and the strongest single image is of the "mankurt". The legend tells of Zholaman who is captured and tortured by having a fresh camel-skin cap tied to his head until it dries. The process, if it does not kill, results in complete amnesia and produces for the captors an unflinchingly obedient and loyal slave, a "mankurt". So complete is the memory loss that Zholaman kills his own mother, Ana-Beiit, on command. At her death Ana-Beiit's scarf turns into the legendary white bird Donebai whose cry, "Donebai", evokes the name of Zholaman's father. The cemetery in which Edigei wishes to bury his friend is the cemetery of Ana-Beiit, and Karanar, Edigei's camel, is descended from Ana-Beiit's camel. The story of the "mankurt" is closely tied to the character Abutalip Kuttybaev. This geography teacher (modelled on one of Aitmatov's own teachers) is the character most consciously aware of the importance of heritage and history. In the last months of Stalin's regime Abutalip is arrested and accused of anti-Soviet sentiments in his extensive diaries and because of his efforts to preserve the folklore of the region. He dies at the hands of the secret police. The parallels between Abutalip and the "mankurt" legend are made clear, and the association is a powerful indictment of the Stalinist regime.

Thus Edigei's memories describe a complicated path of association that connects the universe of the myth to the universe of the steppe. The universe of the stars also figures in this novel and expands its message from the local to the global. Unbeknown to Edigei, the cemetery to which he is heading has been cordoned off as part of a secret space centre. From this centre (and one in Nevada in the United States) a joint Soviet-US mission has been launched. The mission has come into contact with a Utopian planet, but instead of welcoming this contact the superpowers launch a protective operation (dubbed "Ring") to keep the intelligent beings away. The metaphor of the "mankurt" is, in this way, extrapolated in the science-fiction sub-plot onto the whole planet. Finally, Edigei is forced to bury his friend outside the barbed-wire enclosure. As he returns to the whistle-stop railway station, which is his home, the first rockets of operation "Ring" take off.

The title of the work was originally to have been "Ring", but the word in Russian, *Obruch*, was deemed reminiscent of shackles. The present title is taken from a line of verse by Boris Pasternak, but even that was fraught with political complications when a book version was being prepared, since the poem had first been published outside the Soviet Union. This problem was solved by providing yet another title, *Burannyi polustanok* [The Snowstorm Halt, or Stormy Whistle Stop] to placate the conservative cultural constabularies, but that title has since been dropped. In 1990 Aitmatov published an additional chapter, "Beloe oblako Chingiskhana" [The White Cloud of Genghis Khan] (*Znamia*, August 1990). This chapter details the fate of Abutalip Kuttybaev and provides a legend about the brutality of Genghis Khan. It was withheld from the original publication as too strongly critical of Soviet history, but is included in new editions of the novel.

Although the introduction of a science-fiction plot was completely new for Aitmatov, *The Day Lasts More than a Hundred Years* shares much with earlier Aitmatov works. As in his previous works the characters of this novel are clearly divided into camps of positive and negative, and this sharp division underscores the didactic purpose of his prose. The use of nature and animal imagery, legend and folklore as metaphorical parallels to modern society is found in many of his earlier works. One departure from most of his earlier works is the setting. Many of Aitmatov's works were set in his native Kirgizia; *The Day Lasts More than a Hundred Years* is set in neighbouring Kazakhstan. This indicates Aitmatov's expanding vision of cultural unity among the Turkic peoples of the Soviet Union.

This attention to pre-Soviet native heritage notwithstanding, the influence of Russian letters is strongly felt in the novel. Solzhenitsyn's Ivan Denisovich provides a clear model for Edigei's sincerely positive attitude towards work. Pushkin's fairy tale in verse of the golden fish is adapted into one of Edigei's memories, and the refusal of the superpowers to free (with the help of the extraterrestrials) the people of the world from pain and suffering recalls the reaction of Dostoevskii's Grand Inquisitor to the appearance of Christ in *The Brothers Karamazov*. Though unlikely to be an eternal classic (the science-fiction ploy fails convincingly to give the novel's themes universal relevance) *The Day Lasts More than a Hundred Years* remains an important work of late Soviet literature.

NATHAN LONGAN

The Place of the Skull

Plakha

Novel, 1987

Aitmatov's novel *Plakha* [literally The Executioner's Block, translated as *The Place of the Skull*] was first published serially in 1986 and as a book in 1987. It is composed of three parts, loosely related through the story of the thinking, morally sensitive she-wolf Akbara. For the most part, the tale's setting is in rural Kazakhstan. Part 1, chronologically and allegorically the most complex, introduces the intrepid, independent Akbara and her powerful but subservient mate, Tashchainar. The wolves' behaviour appears humane in contrast to vicious and pervasive human evil.

Part 2 represents the decisive religio-philosophical core of the novel. Herein Avdii, a former seminarian, attempts to convince drug smugglers in Kazakhstan to cast aside their sins and turn to Christ. For his troubles, Avdii is mercilessly beaten and himself cast from a speeding train. While lying in a culvert, hovering between life and death, Avdii dreams of the meeting between Pontius Pilate and Christ. In Aitmatov's version, Christ informs Pilate of an array of essential Christian beliefs and values. Eventually Avdii again travels to Kazakhstan to marry. While awaiting his fiancée's return from an urgent trip, Avdii accepts temporary employment in order to obtain needed funds for his anticipated marriage. After Avdii boldly, if naively, urges another gang of rapacious misfits to repent and accept Christ, the drunken men administer a second beating and mockingly crucify Avdii on a tree.

Part 3, by far the most realistic and tragic, incorporates the story of two Kirgiz sheep rearers – the base, wily, and aggressive Bazarbai, and the energetic, ethical, and determined Boston (in Kirgiz his name means "grey fur coat," like a wolf's). While the she-wolf Akbara is away hunting, the covetous Bazarbai stumbles upon and hastily gathers up Akbara's cubs, potentially a source of profit at the market. Fleeing the irate Akbara, Bazarbai takes refuge in the home of his prosperous rival, Boston. Akbara and her mate track the cubs' scent to Boston's dwelling. Even though Bazarbai soon transfers the cubs to his own house, Akbara continues to believe that her offspring remain with Boston. Through unfortunate events, Boston reluctantly determines to kill the increasingly menacing wolves. He shoots Akbara's mate, Tashchainar, but Akbara escapes. Later, while Boston's two-year-old son Kendzhesh is playing in his yard, a distraught Akbara appears and – contrary to expectations – regards the child as she had her cubs, as vulnerable and innocent. Soon, apparently intending to care for the young boy in her den, she grasps Kendzhesh's shirt collar with her teeth and nimbly swings him onto her back. Boston sees the wolf and his son disappearing down the road. A fine marksman, the desperate Boston shoots and fatally wounds Akbara, but with the same bullet also accidentally kills his own much-loved son. Distraught and consumed with an obsession for revenge on he who appeared most responsible for his tormenting misfortunes, Boston shoots Bazarbai and, as the novel ebbs, Boston shuffles toward the district police station to confess his crime.

From Aitmatov's earliest writings in 1961, the problem of good and evil has engaged the author. His thought evolved from an optimism that good will eventually prevail over evil, to an increasing admission that unmotivated evil frequently emerges victorious in the mundane realm of particular events. Yet, Aitmatov's "defeated" idealists remain immortal on the strength of their quietly inspiring examples of loyalty to their rich cultural heritage, of courage, and of moral principle. However, only in *The Place of the Skull* is the question of good and evil's ontology the central issue. This novel relentlessly probes the being, reality, might, and most common contemporary expressions of good and evil. Now Akbara, Avdii, and Boston search largely in vain for meaning in suffering, and the narrator poses troubling questions about life's justice and heaven's power. Comforting legends and myths from the past have lost part of their explanatory and consoling powers. Formerly the reader felt sorrow at the tragic suffering of Aitmatov's positive heroes. In *The Place of the Skull* the narrator and his characters, to varying degrees, despair. Now the heroes have become existential in the familiar sense of the word: bereft of divine solicitude and perplexed in an absurd world of irrational adversity, they interrogate and embody their experience, illogical as all appears, with relentless tenacity.

In the course of the novel, Aitmatov's characters and narrator address several of life's deepest concerns: if there is a God, why does evil flourish and prevail? (Aitmatov does not formulate a theodicy – a defence of God's love and justice in a world arbitrarily scarred by evil. His Christian lessons are moral and ethical, not metaphysical or ideological.) Why does the world "most harshly punish her children for their purest ideas and impulses"? And how does one demarcate and appraise "success" in confronting good and evil? Since Dostoevskii, Platonov, and Pasternak, no Russian author has explored these vital questions with such candour, penetration, and anguish. Throughout the novel, external evil sits in judgment over the best this world knows: Akbara, Avdii, Christ, and Boston. Their examples teach that life's principal victory over evil, the only refutation of Aitmatov's despairing query – why does evil almost always conquer good? – is in the renunciation of violence and a concentration on self-purification.

Taking the novel as a whole, Aitmatov allows the world's might to seem irresistibly destructive, while metaphysical powers appear inaccessible or unreliable. Although Akbara, Avdii, and Christ lose their lives, they preserve their souls in existential solitude, perplexity, and valour through an inner allegiance to a call to eradicate evil from within themselves and to forsake force in relation to others. Neither society nor the heavens are able to perfect or protect the outer human being, but *The Place of the Skull* demonstrates that humankind can transform life's ideals into personal triumph through heeding the wisdom of ages, articulated here most fully by Christ. Akbara's, Avdii's, and Boston's solitary affirmations of personal good peal quietly but insistently from evil's vast darkness.

GARY BROWNING

Mikhail Natanovich Aizenberg 1948–

Poet

Biography

Born in Moscow, 23 June 1948. Attended the Moscow Institute of Architecture, graduated in 1972. Married; one daughter. Member of the Union of Architects since 1984. Employed as an architect specializing in restoration works until 1989. Contributing editor of the Moscow periodicals *Moskovskii nabliudatel'* and *Glas*, and "Russlit" Press, 1990–92.

Publications

Poetry

Untitled poems, *Kontinent*, 13 (1977).

"Kak shum perekrestnyi - vopros i otvet" [Like a Cross Noise - Question and Answer], *Vremia i my*, 62 (1981), 148–53.
"Net sledov ni dobra ni iada" [There Are No Traces of Good or Poison], *Vremia i my*, 63 (1981), 110–15.
Izbornik. Collected Poems 1968–82. Moscow, *samizdat* edition, undated.
"Iz novykh stikhov" [From the New Poems], *Sintaksis*, 23 (1988), 167–75.
Selected Poems, *Teatr*, 11 (1989).
Selected Poems, *Den' poezii 1989*, Moscow, 1989.
Selected Poems, *Molodaia poeziia 89*, Moscow, 1989.
Selected Poems, *Ponedel'nik*, Moscow, 1990.
Untitled Poems, translated by Alan Myers and J. Kates, *Glas*, 1 (1990).
Selected Poems, *Lichnoe delo*, Moscow, 1991.
"Stikhi iz shestogo rukopisnogo sbornika" [Verses from the Sixth Manuscript Collection], *Znamia*, 11 (1991), 167–75.
Selected poems, *Ogonek*, 6 (1992); 46–52 (1993).
"Siiaiushchim shelkom" [In Shining Silk], *Znamia*, 6 (1993), 118–22.
Ukazatel' imen [Index of Names]. Moscow, 1993.

Essays
"Nekotorye drugie" [Some Others], *Teatr*, 4 (1991).
"Vozmozhnost' vyskazaniia" [The Possibility of Expression], *Znamia*, 6 (1994).

The place of Mikhail Aizenberg in modern Russian poetry is not easily defined. During the Soviet period he was considered by leading literary critics neither as a young protégé of the establishment, nor as a particularly dissenting voice among the *samizdat* authors. At the same time his literary trajectory is the most exemplary manifestation of the ability of a poet to survive outside the strict confines of the Russian literary hierarchy. Paradoxically, this is the very theme of his poetic works and of his essays and public performances. He sees the task of the poet as creating a language capable of expressing those spiritual aspects of personal relationships, uncontaminated by partisan attitudes and the clichéd way of thinking endemic to any kind of officialdom in literature.

His initiation into Moscow literary life took place in the early 1960s, when he joined the company of poets that included Leonid Ioffe and Evgenii Saburov. This group of poets tried to circumvent the stale waters of Soviet literature by turning to the legacy of the Silver Age of Russian poetry and to the avant-garde of the 1920s (the OBERIU movement and Khlebnikov in particular) in order to remould the base, grim extremities of Soviet speech into a kind of new classicism. The early poems of Aizenberg in this period are manifestly influenced by Pasternak and Mandel'shtam; but their symbolism, and the metaphorical treatment of political dilemmas are superimposed on a network of highly personal, subjective references, while the logical development of the theme in a poem remains deliberately incomplete, so as to leave the ending open to interpretation. The main motif of Aizenberg's poetry, which clearly emerged during this period, is that of the impossibility of reconciling a loyalty to intimate personal bonds with the strictures of monolithic ideology. However, such ideology is only implicitly present in his poems.

Participation in a collective spiritual effort has always been a crucial element in Aizenberg's creative persona. This was again manifested in the late 1960s and early 1970s by his involvement, through Zinovii Zinik, in a circle of writers centred on such literary mavericks as the theatre critic Aleksandr Asarkan and *samizdat* author Pavel Ulitin. Earlier motifs in his poetry, concerning the chasm between the intimate and the ideological, then acquired a political dimension in the wake of mass departures from the Soviet intelligentsia to the west, which had resulted in the disintegration of many personal and literary associations. With Aizenberg's decision to remain in Russia, his style changed as he relied more and more on neutral conversational patterns of speech, colloquial in tone and lacking the ostentatious stylistic devices of his early works – as if in an attempt to present the reader with an example of survival on a meagre diet of solitary existence, evoking Khodasevich's late poems.

Paradoxically, this period of poetical austerity coincided with the formation of a most fateful literary association for Aizenberg's poetical development. In the mid-1980s he became closely affiliated with a group of poets loosely defined as "Conceptualists", Lev Rubinstein and Dmitrii Prigov among them. A meeting of friends had eventually evolved into a more formal poetical union, later named "The Almanac" group, which included such disparate voices as Sergei Gandlevskii and Viktor Koval, Denis Novikov and Timur Kibirov. With the collapse of censorship from the late 1980s, Aizenberg, together with other poets of the group, began a series of public readings in Russia and in Europe. These activities were crowned with the publication in Moscow of *Lichno delo* [Personal File] (1991) – a collection of poems and essays by the members of the Almanac Group.

In 1993 Aizenberg's poetic collection *Ukazatel' imen* [Index of Names] was officially published in Moscow. It reflects all three periods of his creative development over the two decades described above, incorporating selected poems written between 1972 and 1992. Although in Aizenberg's later poems one can discern the same ideological dilemmas that haunted him before, their former identity is manifested at times in the mode of expression, rather than in the theme of a poem. Aizenberg juxtaposes, in a striking fashion, the strictness of the classical quatrain with the baseness of street argot and the anarchy of a colloquial, sometimes folkloric, tone of delivery; sometimes the mundane, clichéd patterns of conversational speech are framed in his poems by the high rhetoric of philosophical propositions.

Aizenberg's essays on modern Russian poetry boosted his reputation among his fellow poets. The most controversial of his critical works was his detailed review of Russian unofficial poetry, ironically titled "Nekotorye drugie" [Some Others], in which Aizenberg described, in an encyclopedic fashion, the major trends and names, as well as the nature of the creative output of each of the poets who for the last three decades had been slotted into the general category of "unofficial". Aizenberg's attention turns particularly to those who were ignored both by the Soviet establishment and by the liberal or dissident elements of literary criticism. This lost tribe of Russian poets, as described by Aizenberg, are the victims of the highly centralized and incestuous character of the Russian literary process, in which even the literary underground becomes a mirror image of the establishment: those who do not belong to either category are eradicated from Russian history books. This critical essay provoked fury among established literary critics of the older generation (Stanislav Rassadin *et al.*). In the wake of this controversy, the merits of his poetry were recognized by such leading literary journals as *Znamia* and *Novyi mir*.

ZINOVII ZINIK

Bella Akhatovna Akhmadulina 1937–

Poet

Biography

Born Izabella Akhatovna Akhmadulina in Moscow, 10 April 1937, to a Tartar father and a Russian mother. Evacuated to Kazan during World War II. Graduated from high school in Moscow. Worked briefly for the newspaper *Metrostroevets*. Published first poem, "Rodina" [Homeland] 1955. Attended the Gor'kii Literary Institute, Moscow, 1955–60; expelled for "apolitical" verse, reinstated through the efforts of Pavel Antokol'skii. Entered the literary scene as one of the "New Wave" poets of the post-Stalin Thaw, 1953–63. Member of the Writers' Union. Married: 1) the poet Evgenii Evtushenko in 1954 (divorced); 2) Iurii Nagibin in 1962 (separated 1967); 3) Gennadii Mamlin; 4) Boris Messerer in 1974; two daughters. Member of the American Academy of Arts and Literature, 1977. Participated in unofficial almanac *Metropol'* with experimental prose story "Mnogo sobak i sobaka" ("Many Dogs and the Dog"). Recipient: State Prize for Literature, 1989. Resides in Moscow.

Publications

Collected Editions

Fever and Other New Poems, with a foreword by Evgenii Evtushenko, translated by Geoffrey Dutton and Igor Mezhakoff-Koriakin. Melbourne, Sun, 1968; New York, Morrow, 1969; London, Peter Owen, 1970.
The Garden: New and Selected Poetry and Prose, edited and translated by F.D. Reeve. New York, Holt, 1990; London, Marion Boyars, 1991.
"Odnazhdy v dekabre ...". Rasskazy, esse, vospominaniia ["Once in December ...". Stories, Essays, Memoirs]. St Petersburg, 1996.
Sochineniia, 3 vols. Moscow, 1997.

Poetry

Struna [String]. Moscow, 1962.
Stikhi. Tbilisi, 1962.
Skazka o dozhde [A Tale of Rain]. 1962.
Moia rodoslovnaia [My Genealogy]. 1964.
Prikliuchenie v antikvarnom magazine [Adventure in an Antique Store]. 1967.
Oznob [Chills]. Frankfurt, Posev, 1968.
Stikhi. Erevan, 1968.
"Snegopad" [Snowstorm], *Novyi mir*, 5 (1968).
Uroki muzyki [Music Lessons]. Moscow, 1969.
Stikhi. Moscow, 1975.
Metel' [Snowstorm]. Moscow, 1977.
Svecha [Candle]. Moscow, 1977.
Sny o Gruzii [Dreams of Georgia]. Tbilisi, 1977.
Three Russian Poets, with Margarite Aliger and Iunna Morits, translated by Elaine Feinstein. Manchester, Carcanet, 1979.
Three Russian Women Poets: Anna Akhmatova, Marina Tsvetaeva, Bella Akhmadulina, edited and translated by Mary Maddock. Trumansburg. New York, Crossing Press, 1983.
Taina: Novye stikhi [Secret: New Poems]. Moscow, 1983.
Sad: Novye stikhi [The Garden: New Poems]. Moscow, 1987.
Stikhotvoreniia. Moscow, 1988.
Izbrannoe. Stikhi [Selections]. Moscow, 1988.
Poberezh'e [Seashore]. Moscow, 1991.
Poems in *Contemporary Russian Poetry: A Bilingual Anthology*, translated by Gerald S. Smith. Bloomington, Indiana University Press, 1993, 124–37.
Larets i kliuch [The Chest and the Key]. St Petersburg, 1994.
Sozertsanie stekliannogo sharika: Novye stikhotvoreniia [Contemplating the Glass Sphere]. St Petersburg, 1997.

Fiction

"Mnogo sobak i sobaka", in *Metropol'*, Moscow, 1979, 21–47; translated as "The Many Dogs and the Dog", by H. William Tjalsma, in *Metropol*, New York and London, Norton, 1982.

Memoir

Mig bytiia [Moment of Being]. Moscow, 1997.

Critical Studies

"The Metapoetical World of Bella Akhmadulina", by Christine A. Rydel, *Russian Literature Triquarterly*, 1 (1971), 326–41.
"Poetic Creation in Bella Axmadulina", by Sonia I. Ketchian, *Slavic and East European Journal*, 28/1 (1984).
"'Taina' Belly Akhmaduliny", by Iu. Kublanovskii, *Grani*, 131 (1984), 291–93.
"Axmadulina's *Poemy*: Poems of Transformation and Origins", by Nancy Condee, *Slavic and East European Journal*, 29/2 (1985).
"Poeticheskii iazyk Belly Akhmaduliny", by S. Liubenskaia, *Russian Literature*, 17 (1985), 157–82.

"The Wonder of Nature and Art: Bella Axmadulina's *Secret*", by Sonia I. Ketchian, in *New Studies in Russian Language and Literature*, edited by Anna Lisa Crone and Catherine V. Chvany, Columbus, Ohio, Slavica, 1986.
"Have the Poets Yielded Their Former Position?" (interview), by Anatoli Ivanushkin, *Soviet Literature*, 6/483 (1988).
The Poetic Craft of Bella Akhmadulina, by Sonia I. Ketchian, University Park, Pennsylvania State University Press, 1993.

Bibliographies
Bibliography, by Christine A. Rydel, in *Russian Literature Triquarterly*, 1 (1971).
10 Bibliographies of 20th Century Russian Literature, edited by Fred Moody, Ann Arbor, Ardis, 1977.

Bella Akhmadulina entered the literary world wide-eyed with a variety of themes in her early period (until 1983): nature, friendship, modern technology, labour, Moscow topography, Georgia as a haven, Siberia, emotions, the months, poetry, the Russian cultural heritage. Soon her poetic vision, couched in luxuriant language and sparkling humour and lacking the classical Muse, crystallized into a slew of metapoetic poems. Her poetic speaker's early inspiration came from rainfall in summer and autumn, which Benedikt Sarnov terms the "living life" vital to creativity as seen in *Skazka o dozhde* [A Tale of Rain] (1962). Rain and cold bring on illness and isolation sufficient for concentration on sorting out summertime impressions in "Vstuplenie v prostudu" [Introduction to a Cold] and "Bolezn'" [Illness], that will ultimately be transferred into verse in winter when formlessness of water and conceits cede to sculpted hoarfrost, snow, and ice in "Dekabr'" [December]. Insulated within a snowbound house, she creates her poetry from summer impressions in "Zimniaia zamknutost'" [Winter Seclusion]; sound is reinvented as poetic words in "Snegopad" [Snowfall] that will reach the white paper in "Zimnii den'" [Winter Day]. Consolidation into winter white breaks down into the component seven colours in "My rasstaemsia – i odnovremenno" [We Part – and Simultaneously]. All these themes consolidate in the long narrative poems, *Skazka o dozhde*, *Oznob* [Chills], and even the autobiographical *Moia rodoslovnaia* [My Genealogy], which has a striking resonance with Pushkin's eponymous poem and bears civic overtones. The few lyrics treating love are gems: "Ne udeliai mne mnogo vremeni" [Do Not Spare Me Much Time] and "Prokhozhii, mal'chik" [Passerby, Boy]. All the poems, as F.D. Reeve suggests, "say little about her. The 'I' in them is a lyric persona kept at arm's length to project her emotional discoveries."

Some of the best and most original ideas of the early period consolidate in the mature, "garden period's" (1983–87) collection *Taina* [The Secret] (1983). Surrogate Muses – the moon, day, space, the bird cherry appear – and Akhmadulina emerges as a master of suggestive alliteration, wit, and verve. The speaker's mediumistic association with nature is, argues L. Shchemeleva, her sole haven and topic. In this brilliant poetry periphrasis, sound instrumentation, and visual imagery present the world anew. The tiresome fact of critics finding her verse senseless and abstruse has been turned into a humorous device here and in subsequent collections. This collection was mostly ignored in the Soviet Union.

Sad (*The Garden*) represents an extension of *Taina* and the post-bloom period of the bird cherry. One third of it takes place in Tarusa and the remainder finds the speaker in the North in Repino and other venues to catch the late bloom of the bird cherry where the theme of Blok emerges. The past is revered as in *Taina*. Humour graduates into irony and "fun and games". Nina Eremina finds that the collection "evokes in the reader the presentiment of a garden that exists beyond the limits of Soviet life about which one cannot speak because it is a secret". Expressed religiosity is of the folk variety, or better still noumenal. All its definitions inform the poetry of the garden period and the continuation of the mystery. In the "Godseeking" poems of prayer, Eremina perceives the theme of "Easter vigil" with its refusal to understand the mystery. The transformation of the speaker's nocturnal vigilance by the window to create verse under the guidance of surrogate Muses into an Easter vigil for prayer, evokes Akhmatova's speaker's prayers to her Muse as part of an early ritual for crafting verse. In *The Garden*, apart from the poetic speaker's own story, emotions and discoveries, Akhmadulina introduces the stories of other people that reveal malaise in society.

Early portrayal of illness as conducive to creation now advances to a portrayal of malady and hospital as a factor of life contiguous with death in proximity to the universe. Where Esenin idealized the village and unmasked Moscow of the taverns (*Moskva kabatskaia*), Akhmadulina depicts senseless cruelty and crime in the country that enhance society's ills parallel to individual illness in hospital. Rampant inebriation depicted in "Pashka" which leads to evil, evil as part of the village, evokes Bunin and civic topics of the 19th century. In the ballad "Lebedin moi" [My Lebedin], Lebedin's murder returns his soul to nature. Woven into the fabric of several poems is Keats's notion of the "guiding sound". Music serves as a symbol of creation and salvation from earlier muteness when the speaker again retreats to seek its inspiration. Ensconced like a mollusc in milky mother of pearl, she retains the whiteness for crafting that formerly derived from snow.

Akhmadulina's innovative poetry has been consistently misunderstood by the Soviet and Russian critics who recognize her talent but disparage her outlook and devices, particularly her alleged nonsensical verbosity, eliteness, reconditeness and modernist metapoetry. Among Akhmadulina's few prose pieces the autobiographical "Babushka" [Grandmother] represents an engagingly naturalistic portrayal that complements *Moia rodoslovnaia* and invites comparison with Gor'kii's grandmother in *Detstvo* (*Childhood*). As elsewhere, she artfully suppresses information about her parents.

Akhmadulina highlights the garden theme with further presentation of the key to the secret and an elaboration of the death theme touched on in *Taina*, and elaborated in *The Garden*, concurrently with the theme of malaise in the body, as in "Elka v bol'nichnom koridore" [A Christmas Tree in a Hospital Corridor], as well as that of evil and crime in members of society. This subject-matter may be seen to have a certain resonance with the post-Soviet Russian prose of monstrosity (or "alternative prose").

Akhmadulina grows increasingly masterful, compelling, and dense. In fact the ripples from *Taina* carry beyond *The Garden* to the compact collection *Larets i kliuch* [The Chest and the Key], a coda to the "garden" period and an elaboration of the third, religious and metaphysical period (from 1987). Of its 23 poems, the first part contains 11 poems from *The Garden* where the speaker's illness in hospital, presumably in St Petersburg, and the image of hovering death depict the human state. The hospital and its wall ostensibly symbolize the chest evocative of Annenskii's *Kiparisovyi larets* (*The Cypress Chest*) with its play on the cypress's funeral symbolism and a chest's closeness to a casket (*lar'* in Northern Russian dialects denotes a coffin) – hence enhancement of illness and death. Although the first poem, "Stena" [The Wall], opens with a view from her window onto the wall, the window loses the sense of vigils and primacy of *Taina*; now the interactive wall with its brick "letters" sprays the speaker's paper with thoughts. The speaker approaches death as an onlooker, before her time, in "Byl vkhod vozbranen" [There was no admission].

The second part's 12 new poems treat the key to the secret and an elaboration of the death theme, malaise of body (illness and hospital), and evil in society. If in *Taina* the speaker entered the past through bird-cherry delirium, her medium here is the white nights and the delirium of illness which send her to the Italy of her ancestors and the past of Pushkin's and Batiushkov's time. Pushkin, the focus of her literary universe, permeates the poems mainly through allusions to his praxis and his birthday, as in "Noch' na 6 iuniia" [The Eve of June 6]. All 12 poems reshuffle the notion of the key to the secret in *Taina*'s programmatic poem "Est' taina u menia ot chudnogo tsveteniia" [I have the key to wondrous blooming], and now entire flowers represent poems. The poem "Larets i kliuch" discloses the key's physical location "And the key lies at the bottom of the water". The poet returns to the themes of sickness, Christmas, and the past in the long poem "Nedug" [Malaise] (1995).

SONIA I. KETCHIAN

Skazka o dozhde

A Tale of Rain

Poem, 1962

Akhmadulina's long poems from her early period, *Skazka o dozhde* [A Tale of Rain], *Oznob*, and *Moia rodoslovnia*, share rich humour often covertly verging on satire. The latter and *Prikliuchenie v antikvarnom magazine* [Adventure in an Antique Store] derive impetus from Pushkin. *Skazka o dozhde* effectively coheres a number of salient early themes and devices and, as Christine Rydel notes, "solidifies the connections between symbols hinted at in other poems". In Akhmadulina's poetics unusual substitutes assume the Muse's role; in the early poetry rain serves as a conduit for artistic inspiration to be transformed into poetry in its ultimate instrument – the poetic speaker.

The plot is simple: inspiration in the guise of mischievous Rain follows the speaker thereby incurring severe drought in the land. When the speaker goes indoors, she manages to leave the Rain outside, sulking and suffering. During a visit to a fashionable home, the speaker finally invites Rain inside but the other guests eradicate the resulting flood. Without the Rain, the speaker goes out into a parched world where a water spot is all that remains of Rain and no end to the drought is forecast.

Pavel Antokol'skii discerns in the impetuous hilarity of a personified Rain an *alter ego* of the poetic speaker. The two are contrasted to the philistine house guests, who are routine admirers of great art without being truly inspired by it or among its creators. As Nancy Condee states: "the onset of inspiration ... isolates the poet entirely from her philistine admirers".

Dedicated to Evgenii Evtushenko, Akhmadulina's first husband, the poem's elaborate descriptive title underscores dialogue and the role of unnamed children viewed as a group: "A Tale of Rain in Several Episodes with a Dialogue and a Chorus of Children". Dialogue ensues between the speaker and the Rain, between her and the hosts and the guests. The children, who at first mention are shown dancing in glee about the speaker in appreciation of the Rain (as if she were a watering machine), sing in chorus. Indeed, the Rain's childish playfulness, use of pointing "with a child's finger", and other features align it with the children. The children are portrayed as resembling Rain: "a lacy silvery cloud of children were let in". The speaker's attempts to chase away the Rain to aid the weeping gardener remain futile, ostensibly because it senses her half-heartedness. Intrigued by its high spirits and unflagging devotion to her but pretending otherwise, the speaker resolves to attend to her business not understanding that when inspiration arrives, the ordinary must be put aside.

The location – a city resembling Moscow, the interiors of the café and the home bordering on kitsch – as L. Anninskii observes, is hardly traditional for a fairy tale. The people are uninspired and average as if the polished fashionable decor of the cosy dwelling magnifies the barrenness of their inner world and their fear of living in the forefront of art and thought. While comparable criticism of philistinism had currency at the time of writing, Akhmadulina differs from other poets of the period by infusing her poem with riotous merriment and the naivety of children who instinctively appreciate the Rain whose nature they mirror. Like Rain, Chills in the eponymous poem overthrow the speaker's authority and in the process free her from convention.

Some humour is directed against the speaker herself who idealizes the home's beauty and comfort – "lightness always created its own ballet in it". The speaker perceives it as a perfect home but its veneer and lustre translate as a hardening of liquid (always signalling a lack of creativity in Akhmadulina) and, hence a death of fluidity and of water: the polished parquet floor resembles a fossilized lake of amber, crystal (likened tacitly to ice) translates as a sleeping princess. Only the Rain can temporarily resurrect the crystal through its playfulness while the philistine world is gripped in drought. The Rain's puerile associations bring out the child in the speaker by loosening her tongue to voice rash thoughts to her hostess instead of polite platitudes ("in my fever I wallowed in the mud like a pig"). For her the Rain "was always alive like a beast or a child". In this same delirious state and fearful of losing her link to the Rain as the hosts are drying her by the fire, she invites the Rain into the apartment where its presence creates a flood in the orderly rooms. The furious mopping up of the Rain's wetness destroys it, and the fearful Weather Bureau no longer promises precipitation. Only the free artists and children can return Rain to the parched world for only they can appreciate and utilize the artistic and cerebral freedom invested through the agency of unfettered water.

Composed in iambic pentameter, this 13-part poem has an encircling rhyming pattern in its quatrains. Strategic lines in some quatrains are divided in two for emphasis but the rhyming pattern remains encircling with a couplet in the center: abCCba. The children's chorus in Part 9 contrasts lively iambic trimeter with alternate rhymes. Akhmadulina enriches her canvas with binding sound instrumentation, periphrasis, and a concentration of over two dozen similes. Through sophisticated repetition of images in ever new permutations she augments her plot and tacitly suggests connections to be developed more fully, such as fire equalling a brother, a dog, and finally Rain. The dog image is inaugurated in the minus mode for it "almost" figures in stanza one in lieu of "daughter". It functions as frustrated expectation: "[The Rain] again followed me like a little daughter". The dog image appears metonymically in stanza 5 when the Rain splatters the speaker's lips with "a puppy's smell" and is moreover hidden in the Rain's dogged pursuit of the speaker. And fire is linked to Rain and a dog through imagery – "my many-tongued dog", and its ability to "lick" her hands. Finally, Akhmadulina intertwines the Rain, the children, and her speaker by separately employing for each of them variations on the same image; for instance, first Rain is compared to a beggar, next she finds something "incurably beggarly" in herself. The result is a poem that functions well on the overt humorous level and even better on the symbolic level.

SONIA I. KETCHIAN

Taina

Secret

Poetry collection, 1983

Akhmadulina's most cohesive collection of verse *Taina* [Secret] appeared in 1983. Its overarching metapoetic leitmotif receives articulation and specificity in a succession of related clusters of poems. The coda of one poem anticipates the next one and then "spills over" to the subsequent, thematically related collection *The Garden* (1987). At least 15 poems appeared in previous collections but they fit into the intricate thematic and structural interweaving of poems, motifs, and imagery in *Taina* and also advance the artistic discourse. In Akhmadulina's early period, unfettered water germinated the art that she would formulate in a snowbound house with a candle and other means of inspiration. Now, on the one hand, the poetic speaker is inspired by the art and venue of her beloved masters, Pushkin and Tsvetaeva, and on the other, her inspiration comes from nature successively dominated by surrogates for the classical Muse – the Moon, day as deity, animated space, and the hallucinogenic bird cherry blossoms. To scrutinize nature on a grand scale she adopts surrogates from nature for ultimate transformation into verse to their dictation. Eventuating as nature's instrument only, the speaker has shed most of the early speaker's plurality. Actual biographical moments from Akhmadulina's life are kept to a minimum.

Given the need for a set of circumstances and rituals to create worthy verse, the speaker must withdraw to the country away from family and friends. Accordingly, she heads for the town of Tarusa on the Oka River where the Tsvetaeva family summered. For the first half of the collection Tsvetaeva represents the dominating force in the poems after which she relinquishes primacy to Pushkin.

The opening programmatic poem "Est' taina u menia ot chudnogo tsveteniia" [I have the secret of wondrous blooming] equates the beauty of nature with its ultimate refraction: speech, itself tantamount to verse. The collection proceeds to unravell this secret, at least in part. According to the speaker, the verdant grass and plants reflect the green of Tsvetaeva's eyes, while nature's flowering is grounded in her surname (the root *tsvet* denotes "flower" and "to bloom"). The key to learning, letters, and art is nature herself, and a poet's mission is to commune with nature and her agents as they create art and to record in human speech form the ultimate artistic product of fleeting moments.

The moon that serves the speaker as inspiration at night is at variance with the one permanent moon seen nightly by ordinary people, and each moon for which she hopes to craft a poem differs. Should a given moon fail to communicate to the persona a honed poem to recast in final verse form for humans by daybreak, it will vanish without a trace and will not be immortalized in a poem. The moon theme continues in *The Garden* and each day (as a 24-hour period) immortalized in its own poem has its own moon that helps nature create poetry. The moon is needed because the speaker's observations in these poems take place after midnight. In due course the moon cedes its verse-creating role to the concept of Day as Deity. A hint of elusive Perfect Beauty adds to its mystique. Akhmadulina looks to classical mythology, where the days were the children of Saturn, and to images of departing winter, laying one of her days "under the feathers of Mother-Warmth" (Spring), like a cuckoo egg. This alien day tries to undermine spring by blowing up a winter storm. Given the uniqueness of each day, the speaker tries to secure this moment in eternity by writing a poem about a number of them; however, not all days co-operate. She takes images from nature to weave a tale of departing winter slipping one of her severe days into March's nest, like a cuckoo egg. When this alien day (12 March) creates a fierce winter storm in spring's month of March, the speaker falls ill with the flu.

In her feverish state the speaker juggles two levels of time in "Vosled 27 dniu fevralia" [Following the 27th Day of February] – objective chronological time and the subjective retarded time of her inner creative world in which she can remain within the previous day while objective time passes by: "Again it's past three o'clock of the next / date, but I have not come out of yesterday". In poems on the bird cherry, this notion of two simultaneous temporal levels is manipulated to allow the speaker to experience two centuries simultaneously.

Space appears as frozen water in the form of snow in collusion with the day of 12 March – a day that attempts to return the seasonal clock to winter. Being hemmed in during zero visibility with spring trying to arrive, the speaker waxes philosophic, and Pushkin's presence grows stronger.

The bird cherry appears as the speaker places cut branches in her room. As elsewhere, periphrasis heightens the humour, such as the buds opening during forced blooming: "The constrained petals' knots are loosening". The device, impelling her to belittle those seeking sense in her verse, also obscures meaning for her detractors. For three days the heady scent of the bird-cherry blossoms effects a creative delirium and light-headedness and her mentor of the 20th-century, Tsvetaeva, re-emerges with the blooming. The bird-cherry delirium takes the speaker back to Tsvetaeva's girlhood in Tarusa while she simultaneously converses in the present. Try as she does, no meeting with the young Tsvetaeva occurs in this hallucinogenic state but Tsvetaeva's spirit reflects the greenness of her eyes in nature. The speaker gladly allows the bird-cherry fragrance to direct her writing:

What fantasy will you breathe into me?
Free to command,
What will you compose and what will you write
in my hand in my notebook?

In the course of a lively dialogue with the last surrogate Muse, the speaker extracts a promise to meet a second time under natural outdoor conditions where the bird cherry, enclosed in a ravine, will experience delirium. To prolong their communion, the speaker in *The Garden* heads North for the later bird-cherry blossoming. As her thoughts turn toward home in Moscow, the need for the surrogate Muses evoked in Tsvetaeva's territory of Tarusa diminishes and her sole inspiration becomes Pushkin in his favourite season of "golden autumn" in the concluding poem "My vse nachali vmeste" [We all began together]. But before the closure, the disputative speaker questions Pushkin, in "Progulka" [A Stroll], on notions of life, death (the abyss), and the universe. The choice of brief artistic fulfilment over a longer mundane life in "Sad vsadnik" [The Rider Garden] answers Tsvetaeva and Goethe. Moreover, fun and games coexist with thoughts on having experienced a full life with only old age still remaining unknown.

The poem "Peredelkino posle razluki" [Peredelkino after a Separation] pursues religious and philosophical deliberations already evident in Akhmadulina's concept of "uniqueness" (*edinstvennost'*) as a supreme higher being, if not God.

Taina concentrates the metapoetic theme in a dazzling presentation of Russia's nature, poetry, and poets through themes, imagery, symbols, syntax, semantics, and arresting sound instrumentation. The collection represents an unravelling of the secret mentioned in the opening poem and moves to the post-bloom period that is partly continued in *The Garden*.

SONIA I. KETCHIAN

Anna Andreevna Akhmatova 1889–1966

Poet

Biography

Born Anna Andreevna Gorenko in Bolshoi Fontan, near Odessa, Ukraine, 23 June 1889. Attended girls' gymnasium, Tsarskoe Selo; Smolnyi Institute, St Petersburg; Fundukleevskaia gymnasium, 1906, and law school, 1907, both Kiev; also studied literature in St Petersburg. Began writing poetry at the age of 11. Visited Paris, where she met Amedeo Modigliani, and northern Italy, 1910–12. Married: 1) Nikolai Gumilev in 1910 (divorced 1918), one son, the writer Lev Gumilev; 2) Vladimir Shileiko in 1918 (separated 1920, divorced 1928); 3) Nikolai N. Punin (died 1953). Associated with the Acmeist movement whose members included Gumilev, Mandel'shtam, Gorodetskii, Narbut, and Zenkevich. Librarian, Institute of Agronomy, Petrograd, 1920; banned from publishing her poetry, 1925–40. Lived in Leningrad, evacuated to Moscow, 1941; then to Tashkent, returned to Leningrad, 1945. Expelled from the Soviet Writers' Union, 1946. Recipient: Taormina Prize, 1964; D.Litt., Oxford University, 1965. Died at Domodedova, near Moscow, 5 March 1966.

Publications

Collected Editions

Sochineniia, edited by Gleb Struve and Boris Filippov. vols 1–2, Washington, DC, Inter-Language Literary Associates, 1967–68; vol. 3, Paris, YMCA-Press, 1983.

Selected Poems, translated by Richard McKane. London, Oxford University Press, 1969; revised edition, Newcastle upon Tyne, Bloodaxe, 1989.

Stikhotvoreniia i poemy. Leningrad, 1976.

Selected Poems, edited by Walter Arndt, translated by Robin Kemball and Carl R. Proffer. Ann Arbor, Ardis, 1976.

Stikhi i proza. Leningrad, 1977.

Stikhi, perepiska, vospominaniia, ikonografiia [Poems, Correspondence, Memoirs, Iconography], edited by Ellendea Proffer. Ann Arbor, Ardis, 1977.

Sochineniia, edited by V.A. Chernykh, 2 vols. Moscow, 1986.

Desiatye gody; Rekviem; Poema bez geroia; Foto biografiia; Posle vsego [Tenth Years; Requiem; Poem Without a Hero; Pictorial Biography; After Everything], edited by R.D. Timenchik *et al.*, 5 vols. Moscow, 1989.

Sochineniia, 2 vols. Moscow, 1990.

The Complete Poems, edited by Roberta Reeder, translated by Judith Hemschemeyer, 2 vols. Somerville, Massachusetts, Zephyr Press, 1990; revised 1 volume edition, Edinburgh, Canongate, 1992.

Poetry

Vecher [Evening]. St Petersburg, 1912.

Chetki [The Rosary]. St Petersburg, 1914; reprinted Ann Arbor, Ardis, 1972.

Belaia staia. Petrograd, 1917; translated as *White Flock* (bilingual edition), by Geoffrey Thurley, London, Oasis, 1978.

Podorozhnik [Plantain]. Petrograd, 1921.

Anno Domini MCMXXI. Petrograd, 1921; enlarged edition, 1923; reprinted Ann Arbor, Ardis, 1970.

Iz shesti knig [From Six Books]. Leningrad, 1940.

Izbrannoe. Tashkent, 1943.

Izbrannye stikhi. Moscow, 1946.

Stikhotvoreniia 1909–1945 [Poems 1909–1945]. Moscow and Leningrad, 1946.

"Poema bez geroia. Triptikh", *Vozdushnye puti. Al'manakh*, 1,

New York, 1960; Munich, 1963; Ann Arbor, Ardis, 1978; as "Poem Without a Hero", in *Requiem and Poem Without a Hero*, translated by D.M. Thomas, Athens, Ohio University Press, 1976; also as "Tale Without a Hero", by Jeanne van der Eng-Liedmeier and Kees Verheul, in *Tale Without a Hero and Twenty-Two Poems*, The Hague, Mouton, 1973; and as *A Poem Without a Hero*, by Carl R. Proffer and Assya Humesky, Ann Arbor, Ardis, 1973.

Stikhotvoreniia 1909–1960 [Poems 1909–1960]. Moscow, 1961.

Rekviem: Tsikl stikhotvorenii. Munich, Tovarishchestvo zarubezhnikh pisatelei, 1963; *Neva*, 6 (1987); edited by R.D. Timenchik, Moscow, 1989; translated as "Requiem", in *Requiem and Poem Without a Hero*, by D.M. Thomas, 1976; and as "Requiem 1935–1940", by Ross Barrand, *Irish Slavonic Studies*, 15 (1994) [1996], 65–73.

Beg vremeni [The Flight of Time]. Moscow and Leningrad, 1965.

Poems (bilingual edition), edited and translated by Stanley Kunitz and Max Hayward. Boston, Little Brown, 1973; London, Collins and Harvill, 1974.

Tale Without a Hero and Twenty-Two Poems, edited and translated by Jeanne van der Eng-Liedmeier and Kees Verheul. The Hague, Mouton, 1973.

Way of All the Earth, translated by D.M. Thomas. Athens, Ohio University Press, and London, Secker and Warburg, 1979.

Poems, translated by Lyn Coffin, with an introduction by Iosef Brodskii. New York, Norton, 1983.

Three Russian Women Poets: Anna Akhmatova, Marina Tsvetaeva, Bella Akhmadulina, edited and translated by Mary Maddock. Trumansburg, New York, Crossing Press, 1983.

Twenty Poems, translated by Jane Kenyon and Vera Sandomirsky Dunham. Saint Paul, Minnesota, Eighties Press and Ally Press, 1985.

You Will Hear Thunder, translated by D.M. Thomas. London, Secker and Warburg, 1985.

Selected Early Love Lyrics (bilingual edition), translated by Jessie Davies. Liverpool, Lincoln Davies, 1988.

Poem Without a Hero and Selected Poems, translated by Lenore Mayhew and William McNaughton. Oberlin, Ohio, Oberlin College Press, 1989.

Evening: Poems 1912 (bilingual edition), translated by Jessie Davies. Liverpool, Lincoln Davies, 1990.

Prose

O Pushkine: stat'i i zametki [On Pushkin: Articles and Comments]. Leningrad, 1977; 2nd edition, Gor'kii, 1984.

Anna Akhmatova: My Half Century: Selected Prose, translated by Ronald Meyer. Ann Arbor, Ardis, 1992.

Zapisnye knizhki Anny Akhmatovoi (1985–1966), edited by K.N. Suvorova. Moscow, RGALI, and Turin, Einaudi, 1996.

Translator

Koreiskaia klassicheskaia poeziia [Korean Classical Poetry]. Moscow, 1956; 2nd edition, 1958.

Lirika drevnevo Egipta [Ancient Egyptian Lyrics], with Vera Potapova. Moscow, 1965.

Golosa poetov [Voices of the Poets]. Moscow, 1965.

Leopardi, Dzhakomo. Lirika [Giacomo Leopardi. Lyrics], with Anatolii Naiman. Moscow, 1967.

Klassicheskaia poeziia vostoka [Classical Poetry of the East]. Moscow, 1969.

Iz armianskoi poezii [From Armenian Poetry]. Erevan, 1976.

Critical Studies

"O simvolike Anny Akhmatovoi", by Viktor Vinogradov, *Literaturnaia mysl'*, 1 (1922); reprinted Munich, Fink, 1970.

O poezii Anny Akhmatovoi (Stilisticheskie nabroski), by Viktor Vinogradov, Leningrad, 1925; reprinted The Hague, Mouton, 1969.

The Theme of Time in the Poetry of Anna Axmatova, by Kees Verheul, The Hague, Mouton, 1971.

Anna Akhmatova, by Sam Driver, New York, Twayne, 1972.

Tvorchestvo Anny Akhmatovoi, by V.M. Zhimunskii, Leningrad, 1973.

Zapiski ob Anne Akhmatovoi, by Lidiia Chukovskaia, 2 vols. Paris, YMCA-Press, 1975–80; revised and expanded edition, 3 vols, Moscow, 1997; volume 1 translated as *The Akhmatova Journals, Volume I, 1938–1941*, by Milena Michalski and Sylva Rubashova, London, Harvill Press, and New York, Farrar Straus and Giroux, 1994.

Anna Akhmatova: A Poetic Pilgrimage, by Amanda Haight, Oxford, Oxford University Press, 1976; reprinted 1990; translated into Russian as *Anna Akhmatova: Poeticheskoe stranstvie. Dnevniki, vospominaniia, pis'ma A. Akhmatovoi*, by A. Kheit, Moscow, 1991.

Akhmatova i Blok, by V.N. Toporov, Berkeley, Berkeley Slavic Specialties, 1981.

Nightingale Fever: Russian Poets in Revolution, by Ronald Hingley, New York, Knopf, 1981; London, Weidenfeld and Nicolson, 1982.

Akhmatova's Petersburg, by Sharon Leiter, Philadelphia, University of Pennsylvania Press, and Cambridge, Cambridge University Press, 1983.

The Prince, the Fool and the Nunnery: The Religious Theme in the Early Poetry of Anna Akhmatova, by Wendy Rosslyn, Aldershot, Hampshire, Gower, 1984.

The Poetry of Anna Akhmatova: A Conquest of Time and Space, by Sonia I. Ketchian, Munich, Sagner, 1986.

Anna of All the Russias: The Life of Anna Akhmatova, by Jessie Davies, Liverpool, Lincoln Davies, 1988.

Memoirs of Anna Akhmatova's Years, 1944–1950, by Sophie Kazimirovna Ostrovskaya, translated by Jessie Davies, Liverpool, Lincoln Davies, 1988.

Anna Akhmatova i muzyka: issledovatel'skie ocherki, by B. Kats and R.D. Timenchik, Leningrad, 1989.

Anna Achmatova and Russian Culture of the Beginning of the Twentieth Century: Papers of the Moscow Conference 1989, edited by V.N. Toporov, Moscow, 1989.

Soviet Literature (special Anna Akhmatova issue), 6 (1989).

Ob Anne Akhmatovoi: stikhi, esse, vospominaniia, pis'ma, edited by M. Kralin, Leningrad, 1990.

The Speech of Unknown Eyes: Akhmatova's Readers on Her Poetry, edited by Wendy Rosslyn, 2 vols. Nottingham, Astra Press, 1990.

Acumiana: Vstrechi s Annoi Akhmatovoi, I, Paris, 1991.

Vospominaniia ob Anne Akhmatove. Moscow, 1991.

Remembering Anna Akhmatova, by Anatoly Nayman,

translated by Wendy Rosslyn, London, Halban, and New York, Holt, 1991.
Kratkaia akhmatovskaia entsiklopediia: ot A do Ia, tysiacha slov - kratkikh spravok, by S.D. Umnikov, Leningrad, 1991.
Akhmatovskie chteniia, vols 1–3. Moscow, 1992.
In a Shattered Mirror: The Later Poetry of Anna Akhmatova, by Susan Amert, Stanford, Stanford University Press, 1992.
Anna Akhmatova, 1889–1989: Papers from the Akhmatova Centennial Conference, edited by Sonia I. Ketchian, Oakland, Berkeley Slavic Specialties, 1993.
Anna Akhmatova and Her Circle, edited by Konstantin Polivanov, translated by Patricia Beriozkina, Fayetteville, University of Arkansas Press, 1994.
Anna Akhmatova: Poet and Prophet, by Roberta Reeder, New York, St Martin's Press, 1994; London, Allison and Busby, 1995.
Akhmatova and Pushkin: The Pushkin Contexts of Akhmatova's Poetry, by David Wells, Birmingham, Birmingham Slavonic Monographs, 1994.
The Acmeist Movement in Russian Poetry: Culture and the Word, by Justin Doherty, Oxford, Clarendon Press, 1995.
Anna Akhmatova: Her Poetry, by David Wells, Oxford, Berg, 1996.
A Concordance to the Poetry of Anna Akhmatova, edited by Tatiana Patera, Dana Point, California, Ardis, 1996.

Bibliographies
Russkie sovetskie pisateli. Poety: Bibliograficheskii ukazatel', vol. 2, Moscow, 1978, 133–94.
Anna Akhmatova in English: A Bibliography 1889–1986–1989, by Garth M. Terry, Nottingham, Astra Press, 1989.

In one of her poems, Anna Akhmatova asks whether poetry is in fact one magnificent quotation; she considered her writing to be a dialogue, conducted through quotation, with her predecessors. Her poetry can be described as a creative engagement with Horace, Dante, Shakespeare, Byron, Dostoevskii, Annenskii, and above all Pushkin, and her contemporaries Gumilev, Mandel'shtam, and T.S. Eliot. Her expectation that her poetry would in turn receive a response has been realized in numerous poems, paintings, and sculptures by her contemporaries and latterly in, for example, a play by Hélène Cixous. Akhmatova's poems speak not only to successor poets and readers steeped in world literature, but also to the wide audience of general readers. She has been extensively translated, and is one of the few Russian poets whose entire *oeuvre* has been translated into English. Akhmatova rightly identified herself as one of the four great 20th-century Russian poets (with Mandel'shtam, Pasternak, and Tsvetaeva), and she and Tsvetaeva remain the outstanding women writers in Russian literature.

She began writing, self-taught, at the age of 11, and adopted a pseudonym to allay her father's fears that as a "decadent poetess" she would dishonour the family. Akhmatova shone in the brilliant culture of pre-revolutionary Russia, but soon fell victim to Marxist critics on sociological and ideological grounds, and her work was banned in 1924. Having been allowed to publish under relatively relaxed censorship during the war, she was again denounced in 1946. Excluded from public life, she lived on a meagre pension, augmented by her earnings as a translator, and created an oppositional way of life based on support for other suppressed writers, among whom were Osip Mandel'shtam and the young Brodskii, and on moral and practical sustenance from a network of devoted women friends (especially Nadezhda Mandel'shtam and Lidiia Chukovskaia). These friends, like Akhmatova, suffered the Terror through the incarceration and death of their loved ones and resisted it through literature: they were Akhmatova's ideal readers, their trustworthy memories ensured the survival of poems that could not be committed to paper, and they perpetuated their ethics and her spirit in their (only latterly publishable) biographical writings. In periods when she found writing poetry impossible Akhmatova researched the life and poetry of Pushkin, with the aim of putting to rights the record to be received by posterity. (Akhmatova was much concerned with her posthumous reputation, not having received in her lifetime the recognition she sought, and took care to indicate to her readers how her poems should be read, and her life understood.) When she was eventually allowed to publish again, she was no longer a poet of unhappy love, and had become a chronicler. Many of her poems, including *Rekviem* (*Requiem*), her memorial to Stalin's victims, could not be published in the USSR until glasnost. The great work of her maturity is the complex *Poema bez geroia* (*Poem Without a Hero*), on which she worked for over 20 years. The poem is a modernist analogy of Pushkin's *Evgenii Onegin*, which reflects on (in)authentic being and personal responsibility, interrogates cultural values, and is a dazzling display of metrical, narrative, and intertextual virtuosity.

With the exception of *Poem Without a Hero* Akhmatova's compass is usually the short lyric or fragment, though she paid considerable attention to the arrangement of individual cycles and collections of poems, which must be read as entities. She wrote with apparent simplicity and naturalness, but her work is laconic and highly elliptical, thus drawing the reader into the dialogue. When compared to such radical contemporaries as Tsvetaeva or Maiakovskii, she is metrically conservative and her rhyming is classical. She thus signals her inheritance from Pushkin. Her disciplined structures are sometimes the result of tranquility or resignation, but they often arise from powerful emotions that are ordered and controlled in retrospect.

The critical reception of Akhmatova's writing has, with the exception of the attacks by Soviet functionaries from Trotskii to Zhdanov, been relatively consistent. Among the early studies were classic Formalist analyses by Vinogradov and Eikhenbaum; later critics, the most distinguished of whom are V.N. Toporov and R.D. Timenchik, have elucidated the relationship between Akhmatova's poetry and other verbal and artistic texts. Akhmatova's work is rarely discussed in feminist terms, and in this respect it is overshadowed by Tsvetaeva's more gender-conscious and forceful writing. The interaction between Akhmatova's translations and her own poems has not yet been studied.

Although Tsvetaeva described Akhmatova as the Muse of Weeping, and her poetry often meditates on loss and death and expresses grief, it is also a monument of spiritual resilience. Through allusion, and beneath its surface simplicity, it presents a coded perpetuation of writers excluded from the record by the Soviet system, and an assertion of her own spiritual freedom, in spite of the controls exerted over her, to converse with kindred souls distant in time and space. Akhmatova sets herself the task of expressing elusive perceptions of self and other. The poetry is preoccupied with the representation and boundaries of the self. The early poems create a series of personae in various styles and genres; later Akhmatova creates doubles, analogies and substitutes for the self, and contemplates the self in history. The poems also present perceptions of the eternal and infinite, often through creative art, and a constant concern with conscience, guilt, and personal responsibility. Akhmatova developed a method of symbolizing the intangible through realia, often through domestic objects or evocative settings. Much of her poetry refers to Leningrad and Tsarskoe Selo, where she lived for most of her life alongside the shades of Pushkin, Dostoevskii, Annenskii, and Gumilev, and it represents an important continuation of their Petersburg myth, attributing the suffering of the city during the Terror and the siege to the moral chaos of its elite before the revolution.

WENDY ROSSLYN

Evening

Vecher

Poetry collection, 1912

Akhmatova's first collection of poetry, *Vecher* (*Evening*), was published under the imprint of The Poets' Guild with a foreword by Mikhail Kuzmin, in a print run of 300 copies. Nikolai Gumilev is believed to have helped in the selection from over 200 poems already written. Sergei Gorodetskii drew the lyre on the cover. The collection attracted favourable comments, soon sold out and was reprinted 13 times, often as a section within the collection *Chetki* [The Rosary]. In later volumes new poems were added and the order was changed.

Characterized by Akhmatova as "a small book of love lyrics", these are miniature honed poems of awakening – to life, love, grief, art, and the Muse. Early critics insisted on an elusive story-line for the entire collection, which the first edition indeed suggests and which later configurations of the poems obscure.

The collection divides into three sections. The first opens with the poem "Liubov'" ("Love"), defining the enamoured state through four images: a coiling snake, a cooing dove, sparkling hoarfrost, and a nodding gillyflower, all of which erode happiness and peace. Images of sweetly crying in prayer combine with the yearning plaintive violin. A wariness of recognizing first love in a stranger's smile connects metonymically with a person. In the triptych "V Tsarskom Sele" ("In Tsarskoe Selo"), the speaker's love for the location and for the man intertwine in the wound of the marble statue symbolizing love gone wrong and epitomizing the speaker's expectation of death and hope for fame. The image of the dusky lad – Pushkin – at Tsarskoe Selo prepares for Akhmatova's dusky Muse. The poems file by with variations on the essence of disappointment in love and both male and female suffering, anticipation of death, and nature addressing her. The wind in the trees whispers "die with me" in the famous "Pesnia poslednei vstrechi" ("Song of the Last Meeting"), where Akhmatova's attention to detail captures the distraught speaker racing out of the house at night slipping the left-hand glove on her right hand. Hints of a dead man and of another tormenting her, a marriage ring, and committing suicide follow.

Part 2 explores the opening poem's love definitions with several possibilities available to the speaker. The gillyflower and the snake reappear in new patterns. "Pesenka" ("Ditty") presents the Muse's first appearance as a "barefoot girl" weeping by a fence as the speaker weeds. The wandering blind friend prophesies hunger and inclement weather. Figurative use of the grape – intoxication with a voice – develops in several poems. Hints of the speaker's death project a biographical note because of Akhmatova's tuberculosis.

In Part 3 the previously unspecified Muse appears in the poem "Muza" ("Muse"). The notion of the Muse embodying Pushkin's legacy infuses the speaker's poetry and life, following experiences of love and grief for transformation into art. Complaints to the Muse on being unloved parallel the speaker finding herself shackled by marriage. The two poems of "Alisa" describe the situation of another woman stealing her beloved in an 18th-century scenario. "Maskarad v parke" ("Masquerade in the Park") follows as if to substantiate attendance of the masquerade. The surroundings could be western Europe, judging by the "southern" trees (elm and maple) and western titles – "prince", "marquess", and "count" – in "Alisa". Also relevant is proximity to the poem "Osen' ranniaia razvesila / Flagi zheltye na viaziakh" ("Early autumn has decorated / The elms with yellow flags"). "Vecherniaia komnata" ("Evening Room") depicts a woman returning to a castle with narrow windows to music of the masquerade. "Seroglazyi korol'" ("The Grey-Eyed King") juxtaposes the king and castle with 20th-century Tsarskoe Selo. The proliferation of royal personages reflects the town's name, meaning "The Tsar's Village". The scenery switches to the seashore and the engaging virile young plebeian fisherman who has caught every female eye.

Marital conflict takes centre stage in the seven-line poem "On tri veshchi liubil" ("He Loved Three Things"). The seemingly positive list, having minimal bearing on family life ("singing at vespers, white peacocks, worn maps of America"), veers toward the negative (crying children, tea with raspberry jam served during illness, female hysterics – probably as a result of being left alone during a long voyage). In revealing the speaker as the man's wife, the final line uncovers incompatibility and a floundering marriage – understated in this poem – that juxtaposes the positive list to negated family aspects followed by ellipsis of pause before postulating: "And I was his wife". The past tense in the first and last encircling lines hints at the marriage's breakdown. Some points in this poem, employing Akhmatova's method of showing with a paucity of explanation, refer to Gumilev and his voyages to Africa. The reader senses a reversal of the negative and positive parts in the wife's interpretation.

The poem "Segodnia mne pis'ma ne prinesli" ("Today No Letter Was Delivered to Me") shows that the separation from the beloved is killing the speaker: "And I am terrified that my heart will burst, / I will not finish writing these tender lines". Indeed, the last line is eloquently missing. Corroboration of near death comes in the following poem as the dying speaker's portrait will remain unfinished. The cause of death is abandonment: "He left, [and] is gazing into other eyes".

Later, in *Requiem*, the shifting focus and varied form are arguably an outgrowth of the faint plotline in *Evening* where each piece, complete in itself, comprises part of an overarching plot. The poem "Sladok zapakh sinikh vinogradin" ("Sweet is the Fragrance of the Purple Grapes") commences with a pleasant description of grapes growing in a garden. The speaker apparently hears his voice admonishing a rash action. So beautiful and gratifying is the intoxicating distance that the speaker emphatically asserts, "No one, no one do I pity", and yet the interlinking and transformation of images proves otherwise. The grape image's sweet fragrance graduates to "the intoxicating distance" and unnamed "berries" tangled in cobwebs, as if the relationship had long been terminated; the stems of the "agile clusters" are still "thin" – as if the girl's slender waist could thicken in unwed pregnancy. The speaker compares clouds to ice floes journeying down the river at a colder time, an image indicating death in Tiutchev and Annenskii. A voice, whether the beloved's, the sun's or her own inner one, suggests, "Go to the wave to whisper about your pain". The wave will "kiss" her since the beloved no longer does. In "Podrazhanie Annenskomu" ("Imitation of Annenskii") the rare masculine speaker resembles the estranged beloved, recalling the woman who either committed suicide in the water or attempted it.

"Tumanom legkim park napolnilsia" ("The Park Has Filled with a Light Mist") features a female speaker addressing a "sinful and idle" female dedicatee whom she alone will not reproach. "Kukushka" ("Cuckoo") finds the speaker comparing her life to a cuckoo clock wound up to sing. "Pokhorony" ("Funeral") illumines the male speaker's search for a burial place for his dead beloved, where he will remain. In "Sad" ("Garden") the unspecified speaker glimpses a "pale dull countenance" in the window, probably the suicide whose recent tracks are visible through the *thin* ice. In "Nad vodoi" ("Over the Water") the speaker's destination to the water "not out of grief but out of shame" resonates with the earlier hint of pregnancy. In "Tri raza" ("Three Times") the speaker dreams of a female who embodies death or the Muse. The now figurative spider web wrapping around her bed eventuates as an unforgiven lie. Effectively employing numerology, *Evening* divides into three parts, and its poems foreground the number three: "He loved three things" and "She came three times to torment me". It closes on an enigmatic note with unanswered questions.

SONIA I. KETCHIAN

Chetki

The Rosary

Poetry collection, 1914

Akhmatova's second collection *Chetki* [The Rosary], printed in 1000 copies in spring 1914, received tremendous acclaim. She recalls composing most poems in a horse-drawn cab to the patter of Petersburg rain and writing them at home. The epigraph from Baratynskii was added in 1940. Most of the poems are arranged in quatrains, which Nikolai Gumilev found rather long for Akhmatova's style. The poems reflect the dual meaning of the Russian "chetki" as religious prayer beads, where the collection represents a string of poems with religious overtones, and decorative beads adorning an alluring woman. Hence the coexistence of the speaker as *femme fatale* with the pious speaker. The latter prays to God and intones prayers to the Muse that will eventuate as poems. Six types of heroine have been identified in *Evening* and *Chetki*.

Each part of the collection underscores a specific period in the relationship between the speaker(s) and the male addressee(s) that is highlighted by certain motifs. In Part 1 eyes figure in every poem; as much a conduit of thoughts as words and voice, they are a window on unarticulated emotions, often the genuine underlayer of events, concealed from others but making the reader privy to the secrets. The speaker and the addressee are married to others and connect through their poems in "Ne budem pit' iz odnogo stakana" ("We Won't Drink from a Single Glass"). Eye imagery vanishes when the relationship ends in "V poslednii raz my vstretilis' togda" ("We Met Then for the Last Time"). In "Zdravstvui! Legkii shelest" ("Hello! A Faint Rustle"), the man who cannot see her eyes and hands does not comprehend her plight. His attention would prevent her from heading towards the water.

Part 2 substitutes images of "flowers and inanimate objects" for eye imagery as if the relationship were over. The pond with fish intimates that the speaker is not the suicide of Part One, or that the "narrative" is a flashback to prior events. The time is summer. The speaker as *femme fatale* causes the man to weep as the evening of parting draws near in "Kazhdyi den'" ("Every Day"). In the poem, "Mal'chik skazal mne: Kak eto bol'no" ("The Boy Said to Me: How Painful It Is"), he will perish. "Vysokie svody kostela" ("The High Vaults of the Church") reflect the boy's death and the speaker's guilt in undermining a mere boy's love for "a languidly-wanton" woman. Now she begs forgiveness in "Kak budto kopil primety" ("As if He Were Accumulating Signs"). Critics believe Vsevolod Kniazev's suicide, allegedly for love of Ol'ga Sudeikina, spurred these poems. Dedicated to Sudeikina, the poem "Golos pamiati" ("Memory's Voice") (June 1913), comprises four couplets of questions to her (Or do you see at your knees / The one who fled your captivity for white death?) and a final couplet of reply. The poem "Zdes' vse to zhe, chto i prezhde" ("Everything is the Same Here, the Same as Before") describes a house by the forest. With a detached air the poet speaks of someone hanging himself – his shade flashing in their parlour links him to her and leads into "Bessonnitsa" ("Insomnia"). Memorable descriptions of the Tver countryside, the location of the Gumilev estate, incur her displeasure in "Ty znaesh', ia tomlius' v nevole" ("You know, I Languish in Captivity").

The bird as singer of verse emerges in "Uglem nametil na levom boku" ("He Marked with Coal on My Left Side"), and all action moves to the future after the first sentence. The man's shot will release a bird representing her yearning. It will sing, inaugurating her song born of pain. The culprit of the pain, however, will pretend incomprehension.

In Part 3 the singing theme evolves as a life of crafting poems. The religious aspect of "chetki" unfolds through the thorny path evoking Princess Evdokiia as a trial when fate tempts the speaker with glory in "Dal ty mne molodost' trudnuiu" ("You Gave Me a Trying Youth"). Akhmatova's tuberculosis informs "Ty prishel menia uteshit'" ("You Came to Console Me") and "Umiraia, tomlius' o bessmert'i" ("Dying, I Yearn for Immortality"). Assuming a demanding posture, the speaker admonishes him against throwing away an unread letter: "Ty pis'mo moe, milyi, ne komkai" ("Don't Crumple My Letter, Dear"). Their illicit love ended, he ignores her in public meetings; her once-fiery embrace contrasts to the fear in her eyes. "V remeshkakh penal'" ("The Pencil-Box Was in Straps") treats both early meetings with the "cheerful" Gumilev who has transformed into a swan, symbolizing a poet, and the sadness in her life. "Ia s toboi ne stanu pit' vino" ("I Won't Drink Wine with You") continues the "mischievous boy" line but here her interest is evident. "Vechernie chasy pered stolom" ("Evening Hours in Front of the Table") shows writer's block caused by a man whose attractiveness saps her will.

In Part 4 "Kak vplelas' v moi temnye kosy" ("How a Silver Lock has Crept in My Dark Braids"), grief takes its toll on her youth. The "voiceless nightingale" comprehends the lock's appearance and this torment where earlier untold joy resonated in song. An "untold" comparison in "Ia prishla tebia smenit', sestra" ("I Have Come to Relieve You, Sister") shows a grey-haired, dull-eyed woman, no longer understanding the song of birds. Her reply is that the substitute with a flute wants to bury her whose voice was silenced long ago.

The diptych "Stikhi o Peterburge" ("Poems on Petersburg"), featuring Peter the Great, buttresses Akhmatova's reference to composing poems in a carriage during trips from Tsarskoe Selo. "Menia pokinul v novolun'e" ("He Left Me at the New Moon") portrays the speaker as an abandoned circus performer whose path leads to the river in "Znaiu, znaiu – snova lyzhi" ("I know, I know – once again skis"). The willow by the river is her last salvation, to hang on to for dear life.

"Venetsiia" ("Venice") switches the scene and the colouring, with blue and gold predominating. Due to the preceding death themes, the blackness of gondolas evokes a boat crossing the River Styx. "Protertyi kovrik pod ikonoi" ("The Worn Rug under the Icon") presents the speaker as a wife who dislikes her spouse (her "profile is delicate and cruel") observing the room, its icon and embroidery frame. She hides with revulsion her "much-kissed" hands, while the smell of tobacco lingers in her braids. "Gost'" ("The Guest") reveals an alienated lover, feigning jealousy, speaking with a married woman. Her survival lies in poetry. After visiting Blok with trepidation, attraction and respect, the speaker in "V to vremia ia gostila na zemle" ("At That Time I Was Visiting the Earth") swims in the sea with the Muse, a dusky "foreigner". To the fragrance of mint and the purple grapes, interlinking with *Evening*, the Muse enters wondrous words in her memory. In *Chetki* the once ingenue speaker has matured to incipient role reversal and to seek solace in religion and poetry.

SONIA I. KETCHIAN

White Flock

Belaia staia

Poetry collection, 1917

Belaia staia (*White Flock*), Akhmatova's third book of poetry, appeared at a particularly unpropitious moment in the history of Russian publishing, September 1917. Although as a result of the war and the revolution it received fewer reviews than her earlier collections, it was greeted with enthusiasm both in literary circles and by the general public. The first edition rapidly sold out and further editions (with minor variations) were published in 1918, 1922 and 1923.

In many ways, *White Flock* continues the work of *Evening* and *Chetki*. The dominant focus remains the emotional state of the lyric heroine in her search for a beloved worthy of her affections, the cycle of expectation and disappointment which this invariably entails, and the heroine's recourse to surrogates for fulfilment in love in her poetry and in religion. Akhmatova's language remains resolutely unmetaphorical and committed to the lucid explanation of everyday (if heightened) emotion.

However, as Akhmatova's early reviewers were quick to point out, *White Flock* also marks a new departure for her writing in several respects. It is not that the features outlined below are not present in Akhmatova's earlier work. They are certainly found in individual poems of *Chetki* and even to some extent *Evening*, but in *White Flock* they move to the centre stage. In a sense Akhmatova's third collection marks the beginning of her transformation from a poet of frustrated love to the philosophical and political poet she was to become by the late 1940s.

The emphasis on the present moment, which had been a defining element of Akhmatova's poetry before *White Flock*, gives way to a more reflective treatment of the heroine's state of mind. Gone are the urgent descriptions of specific episodes in the drama enacted between heroine and hero, the minutely registered details which offer a correlative of the intensity of their feelings. Instead we have an elegiac mode of discourse as the heroine remembers events that are clearly constructed as having taken place in the past. On occasion, the poems become entirely abstract, devoid of any realia from the heroine's biography. This is the case, for example, in the well-known "Est' v blizosti liudei zavetnaia cherta" ("In Closeness Between People There is a Hidden Border-Line"), which is addressed to Akhmatova's friend Nikolai Nedobrovo, and which justifies in rigorously theoretical terms her failure to respond to his declaration of love.

This concern for the universal is reflected in a heightened awareness of the potential for experience to be transformed into art. Many of the poems of *White Flock* examine the creative process, and poetry is seen both as a way of preserving the past and of overcoming it. The figure of the Muse, who is both the double of the heroine and her antagonist, appears with insistent regularity. Akhmatova continues too to deepen the resonances of her texts by allusion to folklore and to literary and cultural monuments of the past, notably the park at Tsarskoe Selo and the work of the 19th-century poets associated with it. Biblical and church imagery also occur with some frequency in *White Flock*, similarly evoking the authority of the cultural tradition.

One cause behind the broader seriousness of *White Flock* is doubtless World War I, the impact of which is discernible in many of the poems. As might be expected, there are references, for example, to the death of the hero in battle in the context of the heroine's reaction to the loss. There are also poems in which she pledges her allegiance to Russia in language as extreme as she had ever used for a lover. In other poems again, such as "Iiul' 1914" ("July 1914"), the war is seen in almost apocalyptic terms and a prophecy of ultimate victory combined with a profound sense of foreboding.

The weight of this thematic content is reflected in an increased formality in the linguistic and metrical structures of *White Flock* as compared to the earlier collections. The conversational vocabulary and syntax of *Chetki* is replaced by a diction which makes widespread use of Church Slavonicisms. The *dol'nik* tends to yield to the iamb, and the rhymes become more exact. These tendencies led early critics to link Akhmatova with the Pushkin school in Russian poetry and to proclaim her as a writer in the "classical" tradition.

An important part in the first, second and fourth editions of *White Flock* is played by the long poem "U samogo moria" ("By the Sea Shore"). In it Akhmatova demonstrates for the first time her command over a genre other than the short lyric poem, and its sustained narrative encapsulates the early phases of her poetry just as completely as *Poema bez geroia* (*Poem Without a Hero*) epitomizes her writing of the post-war period. The outline of the plot is closely reminiscent of "The Rosary". The young heroine waits expectantly at the sea's edge for her prince. Eventually the prince arrives, but his arrival is no consolation to the heroine: he is dead, washed up on the shore after a shipwreck. Many of the universalizing themes that have been mentioned in connection with the lyric poems of *White Flock* are woven into this framework. The power of art is emphasized through the figure of the Muse, dressed like a Russian peasant woman, who teaches the heroine a song by which the prince will recognize her. The action takes place against a background clearly shaped by the history and daily life of the Crimea with its old battle sites, its monasteries and its fishermen. The poem is moulded too by a stylized awareness of the folkloric tradition on which it draws for much of its imagery and its magical symbolism. It also relies heavily on Pushkin's verse *Skazka o rybake i rybke* (*Tale of the Fisherman and the Fish*). "By the Sea Shore" takes its title and also its metrical structure from this work, and relies on it to provide contextual depth for its powerful image of the sea as a source of fulfilment.

In Akhmatova's poetry after *White Flock* all these devices for expanding the "horizon of meaning" of her poems come increasingly to the fore. *White Flock* thus deserves particular attention as the first collection in which their use is widespread.

DAVID N. WELLS

Poem Without a Hero

Poema bez geroia

Poem, 1960–63 (written 1940–62)

Poem Without a Hero, Akhmatova's longest and most difficult work, was the main focus of her creative endeavour for a quarter of a century. It was begun in Leningrad in December 1940 (though its genesis might be traced to as early as 1917), and the first version was finished in Tashkent by August 1942. A later version, nearly twice as long, was declared finally complete in 1962; but similar assertions had been made in 1946 and 1960, and Akhmatova continued to revise her text until April 1965. In all, it passed through more than 30 redactions, involving several substantial accretions (e.g., the "Guest from the Future", following Akhmatova's encounter with Sir Isaiah Berlin in 1946). Her almost obsessive work on the *Poem* also motivated her to a substantial body of other writing: prose passages offering explanation (or pseudo-explanation) and commentary; "stanzas excluded from the *Poem*", and "accompanying" poetic works, long and short; even several cryptic versions of the libretto for a ballet into which she occasionally believed the poem would transmute. The result is, arguably, less an intractable textological dilemma than a deliberately open-ended text, consistent with the dissolution of fixed identities, and subversion of common-sense "logic", central to Akhmatova's method and meaning.

The *Poem* is in three parts, preceded, in its later version(s), by three verse dedications (the work is subtitled a "Triptych"), and a six-line "Introduction". A succession of complex allusive epigraphs of prose interpolations, overtly reminiscent of stage directions, and of mock-elucidatory authorial footnotes (one of the more evident signals of conscious affinity with the spirit of dazzling formal and conceptual innovation that distinguishes Pushkin's *Evgenii Onegin*), are other external characteristics of Akhmatova's multi-layered, *sui generis* text. The *Poem* lacks a consistent plot as well as a conventional "hero"; but generates extraordinary richness of meaning through an exceptionally dense mosaic of extra-textual reference – predominantly oblique or deeply concealed – to a multitude of poetic and, more broadly, "cultural" texts (opera, ballet, music, painting, architecture), frequently also to the individuals who created them (metonymy is common, and the boundaries of life and art are particularly fluid), and to events (and non- or potential events), public and intimately private, spanning a period of more than 30 years. The intentional effect is of a text that resembles a code ("a casket with a triple bottom", in Akhmatova's own formulation, composed in "mirror writing", with "secret ink"), enciphered less to circumvent censorship, than to encapsulate the enigma of the traumatic historical experience of the poet and her generation.

The first and longest part, "Deviat'sot trinadtsatyi god" ("1913"), opens with the poet alone by candle-light in the mirrored hall of the Sheremet'ev Palace on the eve of 1941. She awaits (or intends to summon by divination) a mysterious "guest from the future"; but instead, to her profound consternation, there appear before her the shades of December 1913, the masked figures of an earlier New Year celebration. The central event which ensues – shown more than once, from different perspectives, in uncertain chronological sequence – is the suicide from unrequited love of a young cornet of dragoons, an aspiring poet, who discovers his actress-beloved with a more illustrious and self-possessed rival. On one level, the participants in this sorry masquerade-drama may be identified, respectively, as Vsevolod Kniazev, Ol'ga Glebova-Sudeikina, and Aleksandr Blok; but the relationship of the *Poem*'s central figures to specific prototypes is never unambiguous or stable. "Kolombina desiatykh godov" ("Columbine of the 1910s") is also, among others, a double of the poet herself; while the death of the dragoon-Pierrot conceivably recapitulates an earlier tragedy (the suicide of Akhmatova's friend Mikhail Lindberg in 1911), and certainly foreshadows the deaths in very different circumstances of Nikolai Gumilev, Osip Mandel'shtam, and others who played out their allotted roles in a harsher era – "nastoiashchii dvadtsatyi vek" ("true twentieth century"), the advent of which, with the turning year, forms the doom-laden backdrop to the cornet's historically as well as emotionally naive demise. If, at the start of "1913", the past bars the way to the future, the future is nevertheless contained in the past, which is revisited by the conscience-stricken elder poet with mingled horror and pity, and a powerful sense of guilty complicity.

Part 2, "Reshka" ("The Reverse of the Coin"), begins as ostensible dialogue between author and hostile official editor, and constitutes a semi-ironic (though still densely allusive) commentary on the creative methods and sources of inspiration of Part 1. The poet recognizes in her anguished inability to resist the tenacious, seemingly demonic spell of her *Poem*'s music and themes a compelling burden of responsibility, and in its cryptogrammatic nature a means to transcend the shameful silence of years of political terror. Her initially inadvertent memories thus point to a moral duty of conscious recollection, of deliberate confrontation with and possible atonement for the past. The polyphonic work, which preserves the voices of those she has outlived nevertheless continues to lead an independent existence, the rejuvenated embodiment of a resilient cultural tradition.

The third part, "Epilogue", opens in the Leningrad of June 1942, now distanced – despite a fresh chronological shift – primarily in space rather than time: viewed in imagination from the painful exile-evacuation of Tashkent. In the indiscriminate cataclysm of the blockade, the retribution portended in 1913 seems to have been visited in full; but the near-apocalyptic sense of dislocation, dispossession, and destruction grows ever deeper as the focus gradually broadens, from the maple tree outside the window of the Sheremet'ev Palace, through the central image of the city of Leningrad, to fellow exiles, domestic and foreign, and finally to Russia itself, moving in horror eastward to Siberia. Prison and political exile, as well as the mass graves of war and the anguish of evacuation, define the essence of the "new" century, where tragedy is not private and individual, but all-engulfing. Yet Akhmatova's sombre mood is none the less tinged with ambivalence. The poet has survived. Through her, the spirit of her city (with which she can now identify as her narrower early self could not) might outlive destruction; and there is even a muted anticipation of renewal, in a future to which – with the ghosts of the past exculpated and appeased – the way is at least no longer closed.

Much valuable critical endeavour has gone a considerable way toward identifying and "decoding" the *Poem*'s many complex layers; while several additional textual fragments and emendations have appeared in Russia since the substantial variorum edition, produced by Elisabeth von Erdmann-Pandžić in Cologne in 1987.

MICHAEL BASKER

Requiem

Rekviem

Poetry cycle, 1963 (written 1935–40)

Akhmatova's poem-cycle *Requiem* (the Latin title has become the norm) is presented to posterity as a literary monument to the victims of Stalin's Terror, and in particular to the countless women whose husbands and sons were the victims of the Ezhov purges of 1936–38. It is Akhmatova's most sustained and powerful piece of writing in a predominantly public vein, and one of the most accomplished and intensely moving works of civic verse in 20th-century Russian literature.

The central core of *Requiem* consists of ten short, numbered poems, of varying length and metre. These are preceded by an epigraph, a brief prose passage "Vmesto predisloviia" ("Instead of a Foreword"), and two poems entitled "Posviashchenie" ("Dedication") and "Vstuplenie" ("Introduction"). The sequence is concluded by two numbered verse "Epilogues". The earliest poem chronologically (poem 1 of the central section) dates from November 1935, the remainder, apparently, from 1938–40. It is unclear when Akhmatova began to conceive of the constituent elements as a coherent cycle (their order of composition bears little relation to the final arrangement), but she evidently did so by March 1940, when the "Dedication" and second "Epilogue" were completed. The prose foreword was added in April 1957, and the four-line epigraph comes from a poem Akhmatova wrote in 1961. She apparently offered *Requiem* for publication in *Novyi mir* in 1962, but it was first published from a *samizdat* copy, without the author's knowledge, in Munich in 1963. Its first publication in Russia (although some of the individual items had appeared earlier) was in 1987 (*Oktiabr'*, 3 (1987); and, with slight variations: *Neva*, 6 (1987)). At the time the poems were originally composed, most were potentially too incriminating to preserve on paper, and they were instead committed to memory by Akhmatova and a close circle of friends. In consequence, reconstruction of an indisputably definitive text is no longer possible.

Requiem is autobiographically based, primarily on Akhmatova's experiences following the (re-)arrest of her son Lev Gumilev in 1938. Poem 1, however, originally reflected the arrest of her husband Nikolai Punin in 1935, and other close friends and victims of State Terror – including Osip Mandel'shtam, Nikolai Gumilev, and (in a different sense) Lidiia Chukovskaia – are obliquely invoked. The cycle's thematic development is in one respect straightforward. The central, numbered poems may be taken to trace the personal reactions of a lyric heroine, from her first howl of protest at the loved one's arrest (compared explicitly to a burial and implicitly to the Passion), through various stages of despair and spiritual atrophy during the 17-month period between arrest and the passing of sentence (poems 2–6), the finality of which prompts a resolve to "murder memory" in the fruitless endeavour to "learn once more to live" (poem 7). There follows an invocation of death – which even in its most terrible guise seems preferable to continued living (poem 8) – and the description of an incipient descent into the oblivion and moral abdication of madness (poem 9). The tenth poem, of a mere eight lines, switches from contemporary Russia to the scene of the Crucifixion, with an implicit identification of lyric heroine with Mary. This takes up religious imagery latent through all that precedes, with a generalizing force that also effects a transition to the framing poems. Thus the introductory pieces emphasize the widespread typicality of what poems 1–9 relate as private (and intensely solitary) experience, while the epilogues draw a powerful distinction between "ordinary" participant and the committed poet, who has transcended literally unutterable personal horror to achieve a detached confrontation and clear-sighted evaluation of the suffering shared with nameless millions. She determines to speak out on their behalf, to counteract mendacious State silence in producing a permanent testimony to their unchronicled historical ordeal.

It can also be argued, however, that *Requiem* consists of a discontinuous series of disparate fragments, which ultimately defy all critical endeavours to discern a conventionally unified, logical or symmetrical structure. Its settings shift bewilderingly from Moscow to Leningrad to the Don or the Ensisei, for poet and people are disorientingly bereft of place, and all is reduced to indifferent sameness in the ubiquitous shadow of the prison wall. Temporal progression is equally blurred, to convey a "non-time" or time suspended, in which the habitual values and order of life are systematically inverted or rendered senseless ("only the dead smile", and so forth). Above all, the central sequence of numbered poems lacks a consistently recognizable, single lyric persona; and this is in keeping with the harrowing and protracted process of self-dissociation, of loss of identity, moral integrity, and, finally, human aspect, which is the fundamental experience of both individual poems and the cycle as a whole. In this light, the spiritual and moral stature of the "poetic self" who emerges in the high solemnity of the cathartic closure might seem all the more imposing; but the personality which survives is nevertheless one circumscribed and disfigured by a suffering too extreme to ennoble, her formidable strength predicated on pitiless self-denial and inconsolable loss.

The numbing dislocation of inner self and outer world are consummately rendered by Akhmatova – in part, as implied above, by a series of poetic devices disconcertingly mimetic of disorientation or incoherence. By a further notable incongruity, the overt simplicity of a cycle avowedly constructed from the "poor words" of ordinary people also conceals a complex array of sophisticated intertextual reference: principally to the works of Pushkin, Mandel'shtam, and Blok; but also, for instance, to Shakespeare and Euripides; to Nekrasov, Maiakovskii, and Georgii Ivanov; even, perhaps, to Lebedev-Kumach and the Armenian poet Hovannes Tumanian. Consistently with the overall tenor of *Requiem*, of particular importance in this respect, is what may be termed the "disjunctive allusion", the function of which is to evoke unprecedented contemporary horror by emphasizing its remoteness from the familiar patterns of a more ordered past.

It is perhaps a reflection not just of *Requiem's* difficult literary-political history, but also of its combination of extreme directness and often densely encripted complexity, that while it was widely quoted in the west for the unrivalled force and authenticity of its testimony to political Terror, it received little detailed analysis before Akhamtova's centenary in 1989. In addition to a number of subsequent critical articles, of special note here is R.D. Timenchik's compilation of related poems and contemporary documents in his 320-page edition of *Requiem* (Moscow, 1989).

MICHAEL BASKER

Sergei Timofeevich Aksakov 1791–1859

Prose writer and Slavophile

Biography

Born in Ufa, 10 October 1791. Educated at home and later at gymnasium in Kazan; Kazan University, 1804–07: did not graduate. Worked in the civil service, St Petersburg, 1807–11; resigned, moved to Moscow, active as amateur in literary and theatrical life there from 1811; published first verse (anonymously), 1812. Enlisted in the militia, 1812. Married: Ol'ga Semenovna Zaplatina in 1816; six sons and eight daughters. Resident mainly at his estate (Aksakovo) in Orenburg province, 1816–26; thereafter in or near Moscow. Began to publish translations, theatre reviews, articles, early 1820s. Member of the Society of Lovers of the Russian Word. Appointed to Moscow Censorship Committee, 1827–29, 1830–32; dismissed for negligence in authorizing publication of "scurrilous" pamphlet on drunken policemen. Inspector, Grand Duke Constantine School of Surveying 1833; first director of the Geodetic Institute after its reorganization in 1835. Retired from civil service in 1838; managed family estates, to which he added Abramtsevo (near Sergiev Posad) in 1843; here he entertained, among many others, Gogol', Turgenev, and Tolstoi. Despite failing eyesight, worked throughout 1840s on his memoirs and on his "notes" on angling and hunting, published 1847–55; "autobiographical" trilogy published 1854–58. Through his sons, generally associated with Slavophiles, in whose publications many of his works first appeared. Died in Moscow, 12 May 1859.

Publications

Collected Editions

Polnoe sobranie sochinenii, 6 vols. St Petersburg, 1886.
Sobranie sochinenii, 4 vols. Moscow, 1955–56.
Sobranie sochinenii, 6 vols. Moscow, 1966.
Notes on Fishing and Selected Fishing Prose and Poetry, translated by Thomas P. Hodge. Evanston, Illinois, Northwestern University Press, 1997.

Fiction

Semeinaia khronika. Moscow, 1856; 2nd enlarged edition, Moscow, 1856; translated as *A Russian Gentleman*, by J.D. Duff, London, Edward Arnold, and New York, Longman Green, 1917; reprinted, Westport, Connecticut, Hyperion Press, 1977; Oxford, Oxford University Press, 1982; also translated as *The Family Chronicle*, by M.C. Beverley, London, Routledge, and New York, Dutton, 1924; reprinted Westport, Connecticut, Greenwood Press, 1985; also as *A Family Chronicle*, by Olga Shartse, Moscow, Raduga, 1984.
Detskie gody Bagrova-vnuka. Moscow, 1858; translated as *Years of Childhood*, by J.D. Duff, London, Edward Arnold, and New York, Longman Green, 1916; reprinted, Westport, Connecticut, Hyperion Press, 1977; Oxford, Oxford University Press, 1983; and as *Years of Childhood* by Alec Brown, New York, Random House, 1960; and in part in *The Family Chronicle* by M.C. Beverley, 1924; also as *Childhood Years of Bagrov Grandson*, by Olga Shartse, Moscow, Raduga, 1984.

Non-Fiction

Zapiski ob uzhen'e ryby [Notes on Angling]. Moscow, 1847; 2nd edition, 1854.

Zapiski ruzheinogo okhotinika Orenburgskoi gubernii [Notes of a Huntsman in the Province of Orenburg]. 2nd edition, Moscow, 1852.

Sobiranie babochek [Collecting Butterflies]. 1858.

Memoirs

Istoriia moego znakomstva s Gogolem [The History of My Acquaintance with Gogol']. 1855.

Vospominaniia. Moscow, 1856, published with *Semeinaia khronika*; translated as *A Russian Schoolboy*, by J.D. Duff, London, Edward Arnold, and New York, Longman Green, 1917; reprinted, Oxford, Oxford University Press, 1983.

Literaturnye i teatral'nye vospominaniia [Literary and Theatrical Reminiscences]. 1856–58.

Critical Studies

S.T. Aksakov: Zhizn' i tvorchestvo, by S.I. Mashinskii, Moscow, 1961; 2nd enlarged edition, Moscow, 1973.

The Great Confession: From Aksakov and De Quincey to Tolstoy and Proust, by Esther Salaman, London, Allen Lane, 1973.

Sergei Aksakov and Russian Pastoral, by Andrew R. Durkin, New Brunswick, New Jersey, Rutgers University Press, 1983.

When the Grass Was Taller: Autobiography and the Experience of Childhood, by Richard N. Coe, New Haven, Yale University Press, 1984.

"Mother Russia and the Russian Mother", in "Reminiscences of Childhood", by Richard N. Coe, *Proceedings of the Leeds Philosophical and Literary Society*, 19/6 (December 1984), 44–58.

The Battle for Childhood: Creation of a Russian Myth, by Andrew Baruch Wachtel, Stanford, Stanford University Press, 1990.

There was little in Sergei Aksakov's earlier literary career – verse epistles, translations, and theatre reviews – to prepare his contemporaries for the outburst of creative energy that marked his final decade and established him as a prose writer of major significance and enduring popularity. During his career as a censor he continued to publish reviews and translations, and for some months following his dismissal in 1832 became a regular contributor to Nadezhdin's *Molva*. By then, the Aksakovs' Saturday "at homes" were an established part of the literary life of the capital, frequented by (among many others) Belinskii and, on his visits to Moscow, Gogol', whom Belinskii met for the first time at the Aksakovs' in 1835. This tradition of hospitality was continued at Abramtsevo from 1843.

The publication in 1834 of a short sketch, "Buran" [The Snowstorm], is generally seen as a turning-point in Aksakov's development as a writer, although it was only after his retirement from the Civil Service in 1838 that he again began to write and publish. In 1840 he started work on his *Semeinaia khronika* (*The Family Chronicle*); he was soon absorbed in the project despite a painful eye disease that by 1845 made it necessary for him to dictate even private letters to an amanuensis. In that year he also began *Zapiski ob uzhen'e ryby* [Notes on Angling], a work combining practical hints with natural history and personal reminiscences of his favourite pastime. First published in 1847, reissued in an enlarged edition in 1854 and again in a third edition in 1856, it was followed by *Zapiski ruzheinogo okhotinika Orenburgskoi gubernii* [Notes of a Huntsman in the Province of Orenburg], which appeared in book form in 1852 and also went through two later editions (1854, 1857) in the author's lifetime. The acclaim which greeted these volumes was based on an almost universal response to the lyricism of Aksakov's descriptions of nature.

It was, however, the "autobiographical" works appearing between 1854 and 1857 that brought Aksakov recognition as a literary artist of the first rank. His "trilogy" – inevitably compared with those of Tolstoi and Gor'kii – can be so described only loosely, since the constituent parts belong to different genres. *The Family Chronicle*, following its earlier appearance in separate fragments, was published in two editions in 1856. The story of the Bagrov family is continued as Serezha's autobiography in *Detskie gody Bagrova-vnuka* (*Childhood Years of Bagrov Grandson*), begun in 1856 and published in part in 1857 and in full, as a separate volume, in 1858. The third volume, *Vospominaniia* (*A Russian Schoolboy*) – written between 1853 and 1855, and published with *The Family Chronicle* in both 1856 editions – is autobiography proper: here Aksakov abandons his Bagrov persona and tells the story of his own life at school and university in Kazan between the ages of eight and 16.

A Russian Schoolboy, though admired for the qualities that distinguish all of Aksakov's writing in this genre, is of less literary interest than the other volumes. *The Family Chronicle* is an evocation of patriarchal Russia which at the same time offers disturbing glimpses of its harsher realities. *Childhood Years of the Bagrov Grandson*, conceived partly as a book for children and partly as a book about childhood, traces the child's expanding consciousness as the family moves from town to country, from estate to estate; through its meticulous description of minutely observed detail and its constant focus on the child's response to his environment (and especially nature), it succeeds as few other literary "childhoods" do in recreating the child's world. Yet here too there is a subtext of tensions and anxieties arising from the child's observation of the life around him – the misery of the Bagrov peasants, the petty tyranny of the rich aunt, the horrors of the school in Ufa – and especially from his perception of the relationship between his parents. His mother, passionately devoted to nurturing in her son those finer qualities little regarded in the Bagrov milieu and dismayingly adept at emotional blackmail, and his ineffectual father, encouraging in his son a love of the countryside and its pleasures, become rivals for Serezha's love and loyalty; and his childhood becomes a painful education in adult treachery.

Warm in their praise of these works, Aksakov's contemporaries approached them from their own positions in the great debate of the times: the Slavophiles and conservatives praised his nostalgic picture of traditional Russian life, while the radicals discovered in it a condemnation (albeit unwitting) of serfdom and other injustices. The latter view, as elaborated by Chernyshevskii and Dobroliubov, became a commonplace of later Russian (and Soviet) criticism. Recent assessments in the English-speaking world have concentrated on questions of aesthetics and poetics (Durkin, 1983), on underlying patterns of myth and metaphor (Wachtel, 1990), and on the position of the trilogy within world literature of childhood (Coe, 1984).

In the years before his death, Aksakov published some further autobiographical pieces (*Sobiranie babochek* [Collecting Butterflies]) and a number of memoirs, including *Literaturnye i teatral'nye vospominaniia* [Literary and Theatrical Reminiscences] and, of special interest, *Istoriia moego znakomstva s Gogolem* [The History of My Acquaintance with Gogol'], where his characteristic gifts of honesty, linguistic precision and subtle psychological insight are brought to bear on the analysis of a tragic and enigmatic personality.

From the 1840s, Aksakov became part of a Slavophile circle, which included his sons Ivan and Konstantin. Yet, while his background and his innate conservatism made him sympathetic to the Slavophile ethos, he remained (in his own words) "alien to any exclusive tendency". Nevertheless, the Soviet critic S.I. Mashinskii, author of what remains the only full "life and work" study in Russian, felt constrained to stress the "healthy and progressive tendencies in the artist which succeeded in countervailing the backward, conservative aspects of his Weltanschauung" (Mashinskii, 1973). For the generations of readers who have recognized in him one of the masters of Russian realist prose, Aksakov has never required any justification.

JOHN MCNAIR

The Family Chronicle

Semeinaia khronika

Autobiography, 1856 (written 1840–56)

Begun in 1840, when Aksakov was in his 50th year, *The Family Chronicle* is the first volume in the autobiographical sequence on which his literary reputation rests: *Childhood Years of Bagrov Grandson* and *A Russian Schoolboy* complete the series. *The Family Chronicle* takes the form of five extracts (*otryvki*) from a memoir by Sergei Alekseevich Bagrov, presenting scenes and episodes in the life of his parents and grandparents between the family's move to the Ufa province in the 1780s and his own birth in 1791; of these, the first three were published in various periodicals between 1846 and the beginning of 1856, when they appeared in a separate volume; the remaining extracts were included in a second, enlarged edition published later that same year.

The first extract ("Stepan Mikhailovich Bagrov") is devoted to Bagrov's paternal grandfather, his success in creating a new estate from the virgin steppeland of Bashkiria and his rule as unchallenged autocrat over this demesne. The second takes the family history back some 20 years, and concerns Stepan Mikhailovich's ward, Praskov'ia Ivanovna, who marries against his wishes and whose treacherous and dissolute husband Kurolesov is eventually murdered by two of his own serfs. In the remaining three fragments, the attention shifts to the younger generation. "Zhenit'ba molodogo Bagrova" ("The Marriage of Young Bagrov") describes the courtship of Stepan Mikhailovich's only son Aleksei and Sof'ia Nikolaevna Zubina, the daughter of the vice-governor of the province, and the young man's struggle to overcome the opposition of his own family (based on the Zubins' non-gentry origins), the misgivings of his prospective father-in-law and the doubts of the young lady herself, who is only too aware of her superiority in intelligence, education, and sophistication. "Molodye v Bagrove" ("The Young Folk at Bagrovo") recounts the honeymoon visit of Aleksei Stepanovich and his bride to Bagrovo, the hostile reception she endures at the hands of her husband's sisters and her immediate success in winning the heart of Stepan Mikhailovich. "Zhizn' v Ufe" ("Life in Ufa") follows the young couple through the vicissitudes of their troubled early married life (the illness and death of Sof'ia's father, a difficult pregnancy, the death of an infant daughter) before the birth of a son brings general rejoicing.

Digressions within the loosely episodic structure extend the scope of the chronicle to include an account of Sof'ia Nikolaevna's early life and her persecution at the hands of her step-mother, the biography of her father's servant Kalmyk, the story of two serfs married to gratify the whim of Stepan Mikhailovich and other vignettes of relatives, neighbours, and retainers.

In substance, *The Family Chronicle* is the history of the Aksakov family as known to the author from the accounts of his parents and other relatives, although the names of the main characters have been changed in response to considerable family opposition: Aksakov to Bagrov, Zubin to Zubov, Kuroedov to Kurolesov. Other characters appear under their actual names, sometimes with supplementary information provided in footnotes. Editorial matter of this kind, as well as the reproduction in the text of actual letters and documents, contributes to the impression of straightforward family history; at the same time, however, Aksakov is careful always to conceal himself behind the fictional persona of the narrator, Bagrov the grandson, and complained to Turgenev of the "villains" rushing to identify his characters with their real-life prototypes. Defying any unambiguous categorization as "fact" or "fiction", *The Family Chronicle* belongs to that hybrid genre of creative autobiography in which Russian literature (as witness Herzen's *Byloe i dumy* (*My Past and Thoughts*), Korolenko's *Istoriia moego sovremennika* (*The History of My Contemporary*) or Gor'kii's trilogy *Detstvo* (*My Childhood*)) is particularly rich.

The authenticity of its recreation of a vanished way of life, together with the naturalness of its language (it was largely dictated by Aksakov, whose sight was deteriorating rapidly), the sureness of its characterizations, and the lyricism of its descriptions of nature account for the immediate success and enduring appeal of the work. For Turgenev, it comprised, together with Herzen's *My Past and Thoughts*, "a true picture of Russian life, only at its two extremes, and from two contrasting points of view"; and while readers of conservative and Slavophile sympathies rejoiced in its evocation of patriarchal Russia, there were others like Dobroliubov who read in its darker episodes (Grandfather's violent rages, Kurolesov's savagery) an indictment (however unwitting on the part of its author) of the evils of serfdom and the existing social order.

While later Russian and Soviet criticism has generally followed Dobroliubov, recent western studies have explored other approaches, relating *The Family Chronicle* to the tradition of the pastoral (Durkin, 1983) or drawing attention to the mythic patterns and folkloric structures which might underlie the narrative (Wachtel, 1990). Such readings enhance our appreciation of its significance as a work of imaginative literature (in Durkin's words) "with a structural complexity outweighing any potential political or social import". Similarly, whatever their origins in family history or their significance as social types, the characters of *The Family Chronicle* are literary creations as complex as the heroes of Tolstoi or any of the realist novelists whose work Aksakov's anticipates. Stepan Bagrov, as capable of kindness, shame and remorse as he is of physical brutality, is more than a "typical" serfowner or latter-day Old Testament patriarch; in his portrait, affectionate but unidealized, we find the fullest application of the philosophy of human nature made explicit in *The Family Chronicle*'s final paragraph ("May your memory never be slighted by any biassed judgement or any hasty word"). So too with Aleksei Stepanovich and Sof'ia Nikolaevna: transcending their function as representatives of different social castes or value-systems, they exist in their own right as individuals observed with intuitive sympathy and understanding; and in the story of their troubled and complex relationship, *The Family Chronicle* gives us what is surely one of the most percipient, compelling and uncomfortable analyses of a marriage in Russian literature.

JOHN MCNAIR

Childhood Years of Bagrov Grandson

Detskie gody Bagrova-vnuka

Prose, 1858

Childhood Years of Bagrov Grandson appeared in 1858, the last year of the life of its author, Aksakov. As a study of the developing mind, relationships and the inner world of a child, it is a work of great originality and artistry and is markedly different from anything that preceded it. Critics have been uncertain as to the genre to which it belongs: it has been included in studies of the novel, some refer to it as a "memoir", others more recently have dubbed it "pseudo-autobiography" on the grounds that real names have been changed and there is some ambiguity about the identity of author and narrator. The straightforward, "common-sense", view is that it is autobiography, "emotion recollected in tranquility", an immensely frank, sensitive, detailed, perceptive and unembarrassed account of the first ten years of a boy's life and of his relationship with his parents. It was certainly taken as autobiography by the public and by the Aksakov family, some of whom were reluctant for intimate facts to be published, while others revelled in reading of the incidents in which they had played a part. *Childhood Years of Bagrov Grandson* may be read both as imaginative literature and as a document of child development and of Russian social history.

The book is the second work of Aksakov's so-called "trilogy". The first recounts in the style of a novel the history of the family up to the author's birth, and the third, *A Russian Schoolboy*, continues the story of Aksakov's schooldays in Kazan, appearing as straight autobiography. The "trilogy", then, is linked by subject-matter, but the three components differ in style.

Childhood Years of Bagrov Grandson begins with some very early disconnected memories and passes quickly on to a chronological account of the narrator's childhood. There are evocative descriptions of long journeys and of people met *en route*; one such trip is to the remote family estate of Bagrovo, where Serezha and his sister are left with their mother's parents for a while. The separation is an unhappy experience for Serezha, since the grandparents show little fondness. Later the family returns home to Ufa, where they enjoy a varied social life. A two-month stay on a new country estate called Sergeevka follows, and when news arrives that Grandfather Bagrov is dying, the family sets out for Bagrovo again. The fears aroused in Serezha by his grandfather's illness and death are vividly described. The family takes up residence in Bagrovo. The consequent re-shuffling of the family hierarchy results in a change in the way Serezha and his parents are treated by his father's surviving relations. Serezha becomes very attached to Bagrovo. The reader learns of his informal education obtained through reading and experience of life on the estate. Serezha's strong attachment to his mother develops throughout the book; he is also fond of his father, and witnesses significant differences of temperament and character between the parents. A trip is undertaken to Churasovo to visit great-aunt Praskov'ia, whose wealth Serezha's father is hoping to inherit. Churasovo offers a new circle of inhabitants, which gives Serezha another chance to observe human nature and relationships. They then go back to Bagrovo, and the following summer to Churasovo again, from whence they have to return suddenly when Grandmother Bagrova falls mortally ill. The journey includes a terrifying crossing of the Volga in autumn spate. After Grandmother's death Serezha himself falls ill and is nursed by his devoted mother; after his recovery they return to Churasovo again, and from there make a trip to Kazan, a preparation for enrolling Serezha in the gymnasium or grammar school there. Here the book ends.

The events described are far less important than the way young Serezha assimilates and responds to his adventures and to the people he is with. The major theme of the work is the relationship with his mother. She is described as unusually able and well-educated and completely devoted to Serezha, while he reflects that he can scarcely love his mother enough. The thoughtful reader, however, using no more than the evidence the narrator supplies, realizes that she is a woman of great sophistication, but possessed of narrowness of mind, having little real intelligence, wisdom, moderation or ability, and that she sets out to dominate her son and shows jealousy when he is drawn to his father or to activities which she does not wish to share. The father, on the other hand, while presented as something of a bumpkin, inferior in intellect and personality, gives Serezha a lifetime's interest in the natural world and in country life and lore, and exerts a moderating influence on his upbringing. In one crucial incident the father upbraids his wife for her foolishness in rebuking Serezha for apparent lack of love towards her, as she says, "forgetting that he had a mother"; he thus provokes a storm of reproach; the narrator states that only many years later did he fully understand the justice of his father's words.

There are many other themes of great interest in this work: the portrayal of other family relationships, peasant life, the natural world, life in the godforsaken remote town of Ufa and on country estates in the last decade of the 18th century – all seen through the eyes of an old man recalling his feelings as a child. It is scarcely surprising that the work has been on the whole well received, but not always fully understood by the public and by fellow writers. Turgenev particularly admired the treatment of nature. Shchedrin described it as a priceless enrichment of Russian literature. Left-wing and Soviet writers have found it difficult to come to terms with the apparent lack of criticism of serfdom in the work, and have either disparaged it for this reason or produced contrived arguments to vindicate Aksakov. A recurrent theme in critical comment is the work's objectivity, dispassionateness, its lack of satirical intent and the sense of stillness and "being at peace with oneself". V.S. Pritchett expresses the comprehensive view: Aksakov is "simple, tender, comic, delicate and factual".

JAMES MUCKLE

Vasilii Pavlovich Aksenov 1932–

Prose writer and dramatist

Biography

Born in Kazan, 20 August 1932. Son of the writer Evgeniia Ginzburg. Attended Pavlov Medical Institute, Leningrad; graduated 1956. Married: 1) Kira Mendeleva in 1957 (divorced 1979), one son; 2) Maia Karmen in 1979. Medical doctor in the far north, 1956–60, then in Leningrad; worked in a tuberculosis clinic in Moscow for six months. Travelled to Poland, Japan, and India, 1962. Editor of the magazine *Iunost'*, from 1962. Regent lecturer and visiting professor, University of California, Los Angeles, 1975. Unsuccessful attempt, with a group of other writers, to publish work in the anthology *Metropol'*, without submitting it to the censor, 1979. As a result of the *Metropol'* affair banned from publishing and exiled in July 1980. Emigrated to the United States; writer-in-residence, University of Michigan, Ann Arbor, followed by various other academic appointments; Professor, George Mason University, Fairfax, Virginia, from 1988. Soviet citizenship restored, 1990.

Publications

Collected Editions

The Steel Bird and Other Stories [various translators]. Ann Arbor, Ardis, 1979.

Surplussed Barrelware, edited and translated by Joel Wilkinson and Slava Yastremski. Ann Arbor, Ardis, 1985.

Sobranie sochinenii. Ann Arbor, Ardis, 1987 –

Sobranie sochinenii, 5 vols. Moscow, 1994–95.

Fiction

Kollegi. Moscow, 1961; translated as *Colleagues*, by Margaret Wettlin, Moscow, Foreign Languages Publishing House, 1961; also by Alec Brown, New York and London, Putnam, 1962.

"Zvezdnyi bilet", *Iunost'*, 1961; translated as *A Starry Ticket*, by Alec Brown, New York and London, Putnam, 1962; also as *A Ticket to the Stars*, by Andrew R. MacAndrew, New York, New American Library, 1963.

"Na polputi k lune", *Novyi mir*, 7 (1962); translated as "Half Way to the Moon", by Andrew R. MacAndrew, in *Four Soviet Masterpieces*, Toronto, Bantam Books, 1963; also in *The New Writing in Russia*, edited by Thomas Whitney, 1964; also translated by Ronald Hingley, in *Half-Way to the Moon: New Writing from Russia*, edited by Patricia Blake and Max Hayward, New York, Anchor Books, 1965; and by Valentina G. Brougher and Helen C. Poot, in *The Steel Bird and Other Stories*, 1979.

"Apel'siny iz Marokko", *Iunost'*, 1963; translated as "Oranges from Morocco", by Susan Brownsberger, in *The Steel Bird and Other Stories*, 1979.

Katapul'ta [Catapult]. Moscow, 1964.

"Tovarishch Krasivyi Furazhkin", *Iunost'*, 12 (1964); translated as "Comrade Smart Hat", by Anthony Wood, in *Soviet Short Stories 2*, edited by Peter Reddaway, Harmondsworth, Penguin, 1968.

Pora, moi drug, pora. Moscow, 1965; translated as *It's Time, My Love, It's Time*, by Olive Stevens, London, Macmillan, 1969; as *It's Time, My Friend, It's Time*, Nashville, Tennessee, Aurora, 1969.

Malen'kii kit - lakirovshchik deistvitel'nosti. Tallin, 1965; translated as "Little Whale - Varnisher of Reality", by Susan Brownsberger, in *The Steel Bird and Other Stories*, 1979.

Mestnyi "khuligan" Abramashvili [The Local "Hooligan" Abramashvili]. Tbilisi, 1966.

"Zatovarennaia bochkotara", *Iunost'*, 3 (1968); published with *Randevu*, New York, Serebrianyi vek, 1980; translated as "Surplussed Barrelware", by Joel Wilkinson and Slava Yastremski, in *Surplussed Barrelware*, 1985.

Zhal', chto vas ne bylo s nami. Moscow, 1969; translated as "It's a Pity You Weren't With Us", by Paul Cubberly, in *The Steel Bird and Other Stories*, 1979.

"Liubov' k elektrichestvu" [Love for Electricity], *Iunost'*, 1971.

"Stal'naia ptitsa", *Glagol* (Michigan), 1 (1977); translated as "The Steel Bird", by Rae Slonek, in *The Steel Bird and Other Stories*, 1979.

"Poiski zhanra" [In Search of a Genre], *Novyi mir*, 1 (1978).

Zolotaia nasha Zhelezka. Ann Arbor, Ardis, 1980; translated as *Our Golden Ironburg*, by Ronald E. Peterson, Ann Arbor, Ardis, 1988.

Ozhog. Ann Arbor, Ardis, 1980; translated as *The Burn*, by Michael Glenny, Boston, Houghton Mifflin, and London, Hutchinson, 1984.

Ostrov Krym. Ann Arbor, Ardis, 1981; translated as *The Island of Crimea*, by Michael Henry Heim, New York, Random House, 1983; London, Hutchinson, 1985.

Pravo na ostrov: rasskazy. Ann Arbor, Hermitage, 1983; translated as *Quest for an Island* [various translators], New York, Performing Arts Journal Publishing, 1987.

Bumazhnyi peizazh [Paperscape]. Ann Arbor, Ardis, 1983.
Skazhi izium: roman v moskovskikh traditsiiakh. Ann Arbor, Ardis, 1985; translated as *Say Cheese!*, by Antonina W. Bouis, New York, Random House, 1989; London, Bodley Head, 1990.
"Kapital'noe peremeshchenie" [Capitalist Displacement], *Voprosy literatury*, 8 (1990).
"Zheltok iaitsa" [The Yolk of an Egg], *Znamia*, 7–8 (1991).
Moskovskaia saga [Moscow Saga]. 3 vols, Moscow, 1993–94; translated as *Generations of Winter*, by John Glad and Christopher Morris, New York, Random House, 1994.
Negativ polozhitel'nogo geroia. Rasskazy [The Negative of a Positive Hero]. Moscow, 1996.

Plays
Kollegi, from his novel of the same title (produced Paris, 1962).
Vsegda v prodazhe [Always on Sale] (produced Moscow, 1965).
"Vash ubiitsa", *Performing Arts Journal* (Spring 1977), 111–44; translated as "Your Murderer", by D.C. Gerould and J. Kosicha, in same issue.
"Chetyre temperamenta", in *Metropol'*, Moscow, 1979; translated as "The Four Temperaments", by Boris Jakim, in *Metropol*, New York and London, Norton, 1982; reprinted in *Quest for an Island*, 1987.
Aristofaniana s liagushkami [Aristophaniana and the Frogs]. Ann Arbor, Hermitage, 1981.
"Tsaplia" (produced Paris, 1984), in *Sovremennaia dramaturgiia*, 3 (1990); translated as "The Heron", by Edythe Haber, in *Quest for an Island*, 1987.

Stories for Children
Moi dedushka pamiatnik [My Grandfather is a Monument]. Moscow, 1969.
Sunduchok v kotorom chto-to stuchit [The Box in Which Something Thumps]. Moscow, 1976.

Film Script
Bliuz s russkim aksentom [The Blues with a Russian Accent], *Grani*, 139 (1986).

Travel Writing
"Kruglye sutki non-stop" [Around the Clock Non-Stop], *Novyi mir*, 8 (1976).

Memoirs
V poiskakh grustnogo bebi: knigi ob Amerike. New York, Liberty, 1987; translated as *In Search of Melancholy Baby*, by Michael Henry Heim and Antonina W. Bouis, New York, Random House, 1987.

Editor
Metropol': literaturnyi al'manakh, with Viktor Erofeev, Fazil' Iskander, Andrei Bitov, and Evgenii Popov. Ann Arbor, Ardis, 1979; translated as *Metropol: A Literary Almanac*, New York and London, Norton, 1982.

Translator
Buran, by T. Akhtanov. Alma-Ata, 1971.
Indiiskaia povest', by T. Akhtanov. Alma-Ata, 1972.
Ragtime, by E.L. Doctorow, *Inostrannaia literatura*, 9–10 (1978).

Critical Studies

"Aksenov and Soviet Literature of the 1960s", by Priscilla Meyer, *Russian Literature Triquarterly*, 6 (1973), 447–60.
The Function of the Grotesque in Vasilij Aksenov, by Peter Dalgård, Aarhus, Arkona, 1982.
"Pryzhok v storonu", by Iu. Zhediliagin, *Grani*, 124 (1982), 269–78.
"Glotok svobody", by E. Gessen, *Grani*, 140 (1986), 161–77.
"Aksenov and Stalinism: Political, Moral and Literary Power", by Priscilla Meyer, *Slavic and East European Journal*, 30 (1986).
Vasiliy Pavlovich Aksenov: A Writer in Quest of Himself, edited by Edward Mozejko, Boris Briker, and Peter Dalgård, Columbus, Ohio, Slavica, 1986.
"Vasilij Aksionov's Aviary: *The Heron* and *The Steel Bird*", by D. Barton Johnson, *Scando-Slavica*, 33 (1987).
"Aksenov Beyond 'Youth Prose': Subversion Through Popular Culture", by Greta N. Slobin, *Slavic and East European Journal*, 31/1 (1987).
"Vasilii Aksenov and the Literature of Convergence: *Ostrov Krym* as Self-Criticism", by Olga Matich, *Slavic Review*, 47/4 (1988).
"Vasilii Aksenov's Novels *Ozhog* and *Ostrov Krym*", by J. Dunlop, in *Aspects of Modern Russian and Czech Literature*, edited by Arnold McMillin, Columbus, Ohio, Slavica, 1989, 118–28.
"Vasilii Aksenov's Writing in the USSR and the USA", by Arnold McMillin, *Irish Slavonic Studies*, 10 (1989), 1–16.
"Western Life as Reflected in Aksenov's Work Before and After Exile", by Arnold McMillin, in his *Under Eastern Eyes: The West as Reflected in Recent Russian Émigré Writings*, London, Macmillan, 1991, 50–61; New York, St Martin's Press, 1992.
The Artist and the Tyrant: Vassily Aksenov's Works in the Brezhnev Era, by Konstantin Kustanovich, Columbus, Ohio, Slavica, 1992.
Their Father's Voice: Vassily Aksyonov, Venedikt Erofeev, Eduard Limonov and Sasha Sokolov, by Cynthia Simmons, New York, Peter Lang, 1993.
Vasili Aksenov: literaturnaia sud'ba. Samara, 1994.

Vasilii Aksenov is a productive prose writer and dramatist whose career flourished both in the Soviet Union and in America. His first novels, *Kollegi* (*Colleagues*), *Zvezdnyi bilet* (*A Ticket to the Stars*) and *Na polputi k lune* (*Half Way to the Moon*) brought in equal measure controversy and popular success: although basically optimistic, they presented an implicit challenge to socialist realism by their portrayal of free-thinking, sometimes disorientated young people whose speech was peppered with realistic (albeit expletive-free) slang. He became *de facto* leader of the so-called Youth Prose trend of the early 1960s. Aksenov's writing, however, continued to develop, and elements of the fantastic and grotesque soon became prominent in his fiction. A small early masterpiece was "Pobeda" [Victory], a densely textured story of a symbolic, albeit ambiguous, chess match between a grand master and an overbearing anti-Semitic vulgarian: the contrast and contest between tyrant and victim was to become a recurrent motif in much of his later writing.

Fantasy, humour, and grotesque parody are the hallmark of *Zatovarennaia bochkotara* (*Surplussed Barrelware*), but a particular landmark is the novella *Stal'naia ptitsa* (*The Steel Bird*), an anti-Stalinist allegory of a mysterious bird-like figure that comes to occupy and dominate a block of flats. This story looks forward to Aksenov's mature fiction in the use of multiple heroes and a distinct jazz rhythm in the narrative. The year as a visiting scholar in California provided the inspiration for his semi-fantastic travelogue, *Kruglye sutki non-stop* [Round the Clock Non-Stop]. Fantastic elements predominate in the hybrid novella *Zolotaia nasha Zhelezka* (*Our Golden Ironburg*), as they also do in his last work to be published in the Soviet Union, *Poiski zhanra* [In Search of a Genre], one of Aksenov's many depictions of quests, be they for personal identity, ideal women, spiritual values, or artistic freedom.

In 1979 the *Metropol'* episode was a watershed, whose events were later reassessed in a transparent *roman à clef*, *Skazhi izium* (*Say Cheese!*), about a group of photographers seeking to publish their work without censorship. This is a rich and wide-ranging novel, particularly remarkable for its portrayal of the workings of the Soviet security organs, and it shows Aksenov's writing at its most confident. Ultimately more significant, however, was the publication in America immediately after his expulsion of *Ozhog* (*The Burn*), a work that seems bound to be his *magnum opus*. This dense yet highly modernistic work is marked by constant spatial, temporal, stylistic, linguistic, and narrational twists. Its main male characters comprise what has been described as a polypersona consisting of representatives of various branches of the intelligentsia: a physicist, doctor, writer, sculptor, and saxophonist (jazz symbolizing freedom throughout Aksenov's writing) who share, *inter alia*, patronymics, fates and, to some extent, women; the latter also seem to transmogrify, but in a less patterned way. In the first part of this immense and brilliant novel, "Muzhskoi klub" ("In the Men's Room"), the heroes carouse, debate endlessly, and struggle, for the most part impotently, against repressive authority. The helter-skelter of Part 1 is followed by "Piatero v odinochke" ("Five in Solitary"), which describes in more sober, realistic terms the polypersona's adolescence as Tolia von Steinbock in the prison city of Magadan. Part 3, "PPP ili Poslednie prikliucheniia post-radavshego" ("The Victim's Last Adventure") reverts to semi-fantasy, ending on a note of mystery as Moscow life stops for a brief moment before returning to its normal bustle. *The Burn* may be regarded as a composite picture of Aksenov's own generation, rich in hilarious cameos, lists and repetitions, which go some way to preserving the reader's sense of orientation as the narrative crosses and recrosses between dream, reality, and hallucination.

If *The Burn* is a novel of deception and the suppression of truth, in his other major novel published in 1980, *Ostrov Krym* (*The Island of Crimea*), the main theme is self-deception. Far more formally conventional than *The Burn*, *The Island of Crimea* is based on the historical fantasy that Crimea is an island, rather than peninsula, which remained in White hands after the Civil War. This western-style democracy is, however, in a state of permanent decadent carnival and seemingly doomed to ingestion by its rapacious neighbour. In the struggle between East and West the values of each seem doomed; against this sinister pre-apocalyptic background a wide spectrum of characters play various political and sexual games, allowing Aksenov great scope for satire, irony, parody, language play, and the exuberant exercise of his powers as a storyteller.

Bumazhnyi peizazh [Paperscape] was the first example of Aksenov's "American" prose. In this short novel the Gogolian hero Velosipedov, oppressed by a flood of paper, finds himself championed and victimized as a supposed dissident, following an incautiously worded letter to Brezhnev. The best chapter is perhaps the last, set in America, where the hero again finds himself surrounded by paper and fellow-Russians on the banks of the Hudson. In 1987 Aksenov published *V poiskakh grustnogo bebi* (*In Search of Melancholy Baby*), a thoughtful quasi-memoir of his experiences in the United States. His most recent major work, however, returns to a Russian theme: *Moskovskaia saga* (*Generations of Winter*) is a largely realistic three-volume epic tracing the history of a doctor's family from the revolution to the present.

In all of Aksenov's five plays fantasy and the grotesque play a greater or lesser role. The most avant-garde of the four plays written in the 1960s, *Chetyre temperamenta* (*The Four Temperaments*), which is thematically linked to *The Steel Bird*, seems to show Aksenov's dissatisfaction with the limitations of the theatre. *Aristofaniana s liagushkami* [Aristophaniana and the Frogs] is an antique burlesque rich not only in classical reference but also in contemporary parody and satire. *Tsaplia* (*The Heron*), written a decade after the other plays, is perhaps the most dramatic of them. The spirit of a modernized, disillusioned Chekhov is felt throughout, not least in the bird symbolism.

Aksenov's drama has not enjoyed the success of his prose (many of the plays were kept off the stage by the censor), but it forms an integral part of the *oeuvre* of one of the most protean and popular of all modern Russian writers.

ARNOLD MCMILLIN

A Ticket to the Stars

Zvezdnyi bilet

Novel, 1961

The second of Vasilii Aksenov's novels (also translated as *A Starry Ticket*) was published in the journal *Iunost'* (Youth) in 1961, causing an immediate furore and was subsequently translated into some 30 western languages. The work is in four parts, the first, "Heads or Tails", mainly narrated by Viktor Denisov, a 28-year-old postgraduate preparing for his Candidate of Science degree. Through him we meet his rebellious 17-year-old brother Dimka who is in fact, the novel's main hero. We are also introduced to his friends: Iurii, a sportsman who is disappointed not to be picked for the basketball team to visit Hungary; Alik, an ambitious would-be film maker; and Galia, Dimka's girlfriend, who dreams of a career in the theatre. Part 2, entitled "The Argonauts", describes, through authorial narration, their impulsive escape from Moscow to perhaps the most European Soviet city, Tallin in Estonia. Once homesickness has been overcome, they at first enjoy casual beach life, but boredom soon sets in, and things really turn sour when Galia succumbs to the ageing charms of an unscrupulous actor (Chekhov's *The Seagull* (*Chaika*) was to be echoed and parodied more than once in Aksenov's later fiction). The third part, "System V.V.", is again narrated by Dimka's elder brother, and gives a glimpse of the corrupt world of Soviet pseudo-science, as Viktor is expected to distort his own work in order not to contradict the findings of a world-famous scientist in the same institute. The last part of the novel is narrated by Dimka and describes how the young men find partial fulfilment in an unidealized fishing collective that helps to put their possible future careers in some kind of perspective. Dimka's coming of age, however, is hastened by the news of Viktor's death in an air crash. His quest for meaning in life becomes associated with the starry ticket of the title, a patch of stars visible from Viktor's window, at which the young scientist had often gazed as he pondered his work. This is Dimka's inheritance, and the novel ends with his wondering, "But to what destination would that ticket take me?"

Written a decade after *The Catcher in the Rye*, but apparently a year before Aksenov read Salinger's story, *A Ticket to the Stars* is remarkable mainly for its frank and essentially sympathetic portrayal of young people's newly liberated attitudes and, particularly, their slang. The story aroused tremendous empathy among Soviet youth, brought up in the rigid moulds of Stalinism and, at the time the novel appeared, beginning to sense, through occasional western broadcasts, films and concerts, the possibility of a far freer form of life. The extensive use of, mostly Westernized, slang in the dialogues of this novel, as well as in parts of the narration, evoked a tremendous response from Aksenov's contemporaries, older and younger generations alike. Few works have brought such swift and widespread popularity to a Russian writer. Not surprisingly, however, many of the older generation, accustomed to order and Soviet conformity, were outraged by Aksenov's linguistic "excesses", and even such respected and serious figures as Kornei Chukovskii advised more restraint. The war novelist Iurii Bondarev is said to have declared the heroes fit only to be locked up. Some of the older people's reactions to the young are, in fact, portrayed early on in the novel, so that the teenage rebellion, depicted sympathetically by the author, is not without context.

Even more controversial than the slang was the young people's "immature" and "irresponsible" attitude to the Soviet Establishment, epitomized by the parodying of Party slogans and, indeed, an instinctive rejection of everything they sensed to be phoney, a casual, disrespectful approach to study and culture, and an almost complete absence of interest in the work ethic that had been so widely glorified in Soviet literature and official life of the previous generation. Critics attacked Aksenov and his heroes for such anti-social failings as neutralism, indifference, and ignorance of political, social, and historical reality. The novel signalled unmistakably and with striking originality the particularly deep rift between Soviet generations at this time, and provoked debates that went on in *Literaturnaia gazeta* and other publications for over a year. It is significant that, despite Aksenov's immense popularity at that time, the authorities showed their concern and displeasure by not reprinting the work in book form for over two decades.

Aksenov has come a long way since *A Ticket to the Stars*. Interviewed in 1989, he declared his early works to have been "somewhat naive" and even "hack work"; a fellow-exile, the novelist Vladimir Maksimov has referred to them, rather unfairly, as "Komsomol literature". None the less, Aksenov is a consistent as well as a constantly developing writer, and his second novel presages several features of his more mature and experimental fiction. The theme of a romantic quest for truth, reality, and freedom may be seen in the greater number of his later novels, stories, and plays, where elements of the grotesque and satire are developed and intensified. An inventive, liberational attitude to the Russian language is also a notable feature of his fiction as a whole, as is the use of shifting points of view. And his interest in sport, travel, bohemian freedom, and western values (symbolized particularly by jazz) remained with Aksenov up to and well beyond his expatriation from Russia in 1980.

A Ticket to the Stars made Aksenov immediately famous, and, despite his above-quoted reservations, he has approved it for re-publication in a forthcoming edition of Collected Works. It is also referred to in his *magnum opus*, *The Burn*. The novel marked a watershed in Russian literary and social attitudes at a turning-point in the post-Stalin period.

ARNOLD MCMILLIN

The Burn

Ozhog

Novel, 1980

Aksenov's major novel, *The Burn*, was written between 1969 and 1975, and published in the United States in October 1980 after Aksenov was forced to leave the USSR. It is at once an autobiography and a portrait of Aksenov's generation during the 1960s and 1970s in Russia. The title refers both to the "burn" of Stalinism as well as to the gift of creativity. The hero is represented by five members of the "creative intelligentsia" who share the patronymic Appolinarievich: the research biologist Aristarkh Kunitser, the saxophonist Samson Sabler, the doctor Gennadii Mal'kol'mov, the sculptor Radius Khvastishchev, and the writer Pantelei Pantelei. They also share a common past, represented by the young Tolia fon Shteinbok. Tolia's teenage years closely resemble Aksenov's. At the age of 17 he was reunited with his mother, Evgeniia Ginzburg, upon her release from a ten-year term in prison camp as an "enemy of the people". Her account of life in exile in Magadan with her second husband Anton Val'ter is given in her second volume of memoirs, *Krutoi marshrut* (*Within the Whirlwind*); Aksenov's modernistic fictionalization of this material focuses on the trauma of his mother's rearrest by the sadistic KGB man, Cheptsov. Tolia is torn between the desire to be a normal Soviet schoolboy and to be loyal to the ideals of his Jewish mother and Volga German Catholic stepfather Martin, and finds escape in basketball and John Wayne movies. This story is told in fragments in Book 2, entitled "Five in Solitary". It provides some explanation of the debauched state of the intelligentsia in the late 1960s portrayed in Book 1, "The Men's Club". Book 3, "The Victim's Last Adventure", dissolves into a phantasmagoria that merges historical periods and transfers the conflict between the oppressors and the intelligentsia to the imaginative plane, where it is left in suspension: Cheptsov is transformed into a "philosophical construct".

Aksenov presents the intelligentsia's problem as a failure to protect its muse. The literal basis of this central metaphor is established in a Magadan scene: Tolia is unable to rescue a Polish girl, Alisa, from a convoy of prisoners. The pathos of her situation is underscored by the prospect of her rape by prison guards. In the 1960s Alisa reappears in a variety of guises, among them a nurse, Arina Beliakova; a daughter of a KGB offficer, Nina Lyger; and the daughter of a White émigré officer, Marina Kurago, who is the lover of each of the five Appolinarieveches at some point. By Book 3 two of the women end up in emigration, another becomes a KGB spy.

The members of the intelligentsia are shown to be as depraved as their oppressors, and thus unwittingly in collusion with them; having stood by while the muse was raped during the Terror, the intelligentsia then takes advantage of her, and she finally betrays them. Political sticks and material carrots reduce them to a state of alcoholism, lazy provincialism, and impotent passivity.

In failing to nurture their muse, the five heroes lose their memory. Throughout Book 1 they keep trying to remember their collective past – the tragedy of fon Shteinbok as well as their literary heritage. To provide an image of freedom, the muse must inspire them with the culture of the Silver Age and of the west. Catalogues of western cities, artists, and goods and the character Patrick Thunderjet are emblematic of the spirit of the 1960s when Russia became more open to the west, but the sense of freedom they carry is proven illusory.

The moral problem of *The Burn* – revenge or forgiveness – revolves around Cheptsov, who is characterized by his sado-masochistic sexuality. The oppressors are all sexually perverse; interrogating prisoners brings Cheptsov to the verge of orgasm, but the victims are equally debauched. Outside the amphisbaena of victims and victimizers is an alternative, the "third model" propounded by its inventor, Sania Gurchenko. In the course of the novel, Sania evolves from Tolia's Magadan adventure hero into a universal ideal figure. The counterpart of the muse, Sania represents the Judaeo-Christian tradition. For Aksenov, he represents the ideals of Anton Val'ter as well as of the sportsman whom Aksenov continues to associate with "healthy" Soviet life. Twenty years after Magadan, Pantelei meets Sania in Rome where he is an athletic Jesuit priest. He explains the "third model":

> Sometimes man comes close to it in moments of creativity – in music, poetry, in mathematics ... The inexplicable – that is the third model ... Christianity is like a breakthrough into space, the most courageous and far-reaching spurt toward the third model. Christianity, being itself fantastic, relies on fantastic emotions and proves the existence of the fantastic.

Applying this to life, Gurchenko concludes:

> It is not so much our actions that are important ... as the spiritual meaning of our actions; in other words, the quality that belongs to the realm of the fantastic, that is what is capable of breaking through toward the "third model", into the truly real world.

Aksenov applies the "third model" within *The Burn* to determine how to respond to Stalin's crimes, how to forgive oneself for failing to protect one's loved ones, how to accept one's impotence. Tolia is unable to accept Martin's ideal of forgiveness, but later Dr Mal'kol'mov is unable to go against his profession and saves Cheptsov on the operating table though he knows he is resuscitating a criminal.

The "third model" resolves the struggle between revenge and forgiveness. Fiction itself is the realm of the inexplicable, a means to "break through to the truly real". Aksenov wreaks revenge on Cheptsov in the novel, showing him in all his depravity. At the same time, Mal'kol'mov the doctor (Martin is a doctor, Aksenov was a doctor) resuscitates Cheptsov with his brilliant discovery, "Lymph-D", an elixir of life. It is not for one man to judge another; Aksenov has Cheptsov pass judgment on himself. In *The Burn* Aksenov entertains a range of responses to Stalin's evil, and in the imaginative process, expiates his guilt at his inability to take action in life, while taking action in art according to Gurchenko's philosophy.

PRISCILLA MEYER

The Island of Crimea

Ostrov Krym

Novel, 1981

The Island of Crimea is one of the two major novels which, written in the Soviet Union, were published in America shortly after Aksenov's expatriation. But whereas *The Burn* is a post-modernist work with a strong element of fantasy, *The Island of Crimea* (written 1977–79, published 1981) is far more traditional in construction and realistic in style. A novel of self-deception, it is based on a piece of historical fantasy, namely that the Crimea (a place of mythical resonance for many Russian writers, including Aksenov) is here not a peninsula but an island, miraculously saved by the Whites in 1920 and supporting a Russian, yet western, democracy alongside the Soviet mainland. This republic is not, however, a model society, but reflects the west as a place of permanent half-crazy, decadent carnival comparable to Hong Kong, Singapore, Honolulu, an image no doubt partly formed during Aksenov's year as a visiting professor in southern California. Moreover, the west seems doomed to forcible ingestion, like a carefree rabbit, by the totalitarian colossus alongside. This "gigantic, sleek and senseless shark" towards the end of the book assumes the form of a giant Soviet aircraft carrier. Alongside the background of "octopus-like" ideological and political struggles in which not only the West and its civilization but also traditional Russian moral values are doomed, a wide spectrum of characters play various political and sexual games, allowing Aksenov tremendous scope for satire, irony, parody, language play, and to exercise his skill as an entertaining storyteller.

At the centre of the novel is Andrei Luchnikov, son of Arsenii, one of the original members of Wrangel's army, who becomes a professor of history and a millionaire. Andrei himself is something of a playboy and would-be poet, but also publisher-editor of Crimea's most influential newspaper ("Everyone knows the *Russian Courier* skyscraper", begins Aksenov, deliciously hinting at the novel's basic conceit). Luchnikov appears to have learnt few of the lessons of history: rejoicing in the rampant materialism of Crimea, he also hankers after the seedy mateyness he finds on his many visits to Moscow, and uses all his powers to influence public opinion in favour of his Idea of a Common Fate, in other words, the incorporation of Crimea as the 16th state of the Soviet Union. Marlen Kuzenkov, the other character drawn sympathetically by Aksenov, is a functionary reporting to the Soviet Central Committee on Crimean affairs. Ironically, he – enjoying the fleshpots and personal freedom of Crimea, and knowing full well what unification would mean – is totally (though of necessity secretly) opposed to the Idea, as is Andrei

Luchnikov's son Anton, who is both a hippy and a convinced Crimean nationalist.

The communist ideologists and representatives of the KGB are, predictably, treated with great wit and scorn, particularly odious being Oleg Stepanov, later to become head of an ideological institute in Moscow, who is portrayed as ridiculous and despicable, as well as potentially powerful. In Aksenov's work showers, steam baths and lavatories often form the setting for philosophical discussions: in *The Island of Crimea* Stepanov, in the steam baths, achieves an unwanted and humiliating erection while propounding a new trinity of Communism, Soviet Power, and Nationality to replace Count Uvarov's celebrated Orthodoxy, Autocracy, and Nationality. He is only one of the preachers of a semi-fascist ideology with strong elements of chauvinism, and anti-Semitism in particular. For all the novel's fast-moving and exciting plot, the humour and splendid set-pieces, many of the ideas in it are the bleakest yet found in his fiction. The "portraits" who control Soviet policy, for example, are masked and de-personalized as "The Important Personage", "The Rather Reserved Personage", and "The Extraordinarily Unpleasant Personage", underlining their brutality and cynicism.

The novel evidences many familiar aspects of Aksenov's writing. Luchnikov, on the eve of visiting his beloved Russia, makes a long list of unobtainable items that he must take with him, including something to eat. Sexual imagery and, indeed, acts of all kinds are rife, with the female characters mainly assessed for their potential as spies and lovers; for instance, Luchnikov's girlfriend Tania, sitting in his penthouse late at night, wonders, not unreasonably, whether she is just a convenient domestic appliance for sexual gymnastics. A partial exception is the no less sexy American Kristina, for she is (in one of the novel's many paradoxes) symbolically linked with Old Russia, and her death at the hands of a driver of a car with shark-like fins is, in Aksenov's highly referential world, significant. She is, indirectly, just one of Luchnikov's many sacrifices, for although he persuades the Crimean lotus-eaters to seek union with their Soviet neighbour, the latter, unused to voluntary alliances, mounts a full-scale bombardment and invasion – which the naive Crimeans take to be just another TV spectacular. At the end of the novel Aksenov introduces an unexpected note of optimism as Luchnikov's son and his family, helped by a clever Jew, flee the apocalyptic destruction by boat, and are miraculously spared by the Soviet helicopter sent to destroy them.

The Island of Crimea shows very clearly Aksenov's pre-exile fascination with western life and his attitude to the cultural and political gulf between East and West. He has often been asked whether the novel is a fable or a dystopia, but prefers to call it a "false real" book. The novel has also been described, with *The Burn*, as akin to Thomas Pynchon's novels of disintegration and paranoia, but Aksenov, who was previously quite unfamiliar with Pynchon, sees no particular resemblance. On the question of the so-called conventional form, it was used:

> because the main idea of the novel was the fantastic, the surrealist from its very beginning. It was based on the fantastic ground of unexisting territory, unexisting customs, unexisting culture, unexisting people, that's why I decided to avoid many of my favourite surrealist ways of writing. That's why it looks like a conventional, realistic novel although the whole novel is a huge hyperbole.

Conventional Aksenov's novel certainly is not, although it is his most approachable major work: a thriller that is also a great feat of imagination and, at the same time, an important and essentially sombre intellectual document of its time. It has been brilliantly translated into English by Michael Henry Heim.

ARNOLD MCMILLIN

Mark Aleksandrovich Aldanov 1886–1957

Novelist and journalist

Biography

Born Mark Aleksandrovich Landau in Kiev, 7 November 1886. Attended Kiev University, degrees in law and natural sciences, 1910; studied at the Collège des Sciences Politiques et Économiques, diploma from the École des Sciences Sociales, Paris, early 1920s. Industrial chemist in Petrograd, 1914–17 and in Paris, October 1917. Secretary to the delegation of anti-Bolshevik parties seeking to raise money in Turkey and England, 1918–19. Emigrated to Paris, 1919; full-time writer from 1919. Founder of the journal *Griadushchaia Rossiia*, Paris, 1920 (two issues). Associate of the Parisian daily newspaper *Poslednie novosti*, 1920–41. Editorial associate in various capacities of the émigré monthly *Sovremennye zapiski*, Paris, 921–41. Visited Berlin, 1922; literary critic for the newspaper *Dni*, Berlin then Paris, 1922–33. Married: his cousin, Tat'iana Markovna Zaitseva in 1924. Lived in the United States, 1941–47; many extracts from his later works published in the New York daily newspaper *Novoe russkoe slovo*, 1941–57; co-editor of the émigré monthly *Novyi zhurnal*, 1942–47. Lived in Nice, 1947–57. Died in Nice, 25 February 1957.

Publications

Collected Editions

A Night at the Airport: Stories by Mark Aldanov, translated by Joel Carmichael. New York, Scribner, 1949.

Sobranie sochinenii, 6 vols. Moscow, 1991–93.

Sochineniia, 6 vols. Moscow, 1994–96.

Fiction

Myslitel'. Tetralogiia [The Thinker. A Tetralogy]:

1. *Deviatoe termidora*. Berlin, Slovo, 1923; translated as *The Ninth Thermidor*, by A.E. Chamot, New York, Knopf, 1926.

2. *Sviataia Elena, malen'kii ostrov*. Berlin, Neva, 1923; translated as *Saint Helena, Little Island*, by A.E. Chamot, New York, Knopf, 1926.
3. *Chortov most*. Berlin, Slovo, 1925; translated as *The Devil's Bridge*, by A.E. Chamot, New York, Knopf, 1928.
4. *Zagovor* [The Conspiracy]. Berlin, Slovo, 1927.

Kliuch. Berlin, Slovo, 1930; translated as *The Key* [no translator named], London, Harrap, 1931.

Desiataia simfoniia. Paris, Sovremennye zapiski, 1931; translated as *The Tenth Symphony*, by Gregory Golubeff, New York, Scribner, 1948.

Begstvo. Berlin, Slovo, 1932; translated as *The Escape* (also includes *The Key*) [no translator named], New York, Scribner, 1950.

Peshchera [The Cave]. vol. 1, Berlin, Slovo, 1934; vol. 2, Berlin, Petropolis, 1936.

"Bel'vederskii tors", *Russkie zapiski* (Paris), 1938; includes play *Liniia Brungil'dy*.

"Nachalo kontsa", part 1, *Russkie zapiski*, 1939; with part 2, translated as *The Fifth Seal*, by Nicholas Wreden, New York, Scribner, 1943; complete text in *Oktiabr'*, 7, 8, 11, 12 (1993); also in *Sobranie sochinenii*, 1993 – .

Punshevaia vodka i Mogila voina. Paris, Dom knigi, 1940; "Mogila voina" translated as *For Thee the Best*, by Nicholas Wreden, New York, Scribner, 1945.

Istrebitel'. Rasskaz [Exterminator]. Frankfurt, Posev, 1948.

Istoki. Paris, YMCA-Press, 1950; translated as *Before the Deluge*, by Catherine Routsky, New York, Scribner, 1948.

Zhivi kak khochesh', 2 vols. New York, Izdatel'stvo imeni Chekhova, 1952; translated as *To Live as We Wish*, by Nicholas Wreden, New York, Dutton, 1952.

"Bred", *Novyi zhurnal*, 38–42 (1954–55) and 48 (1957); translated as *Nightmare and Dawn*, by Joel Carmichael, New York, Duell Sloane and Pearce, 1957; also translated as *The Scoundrel* [no translator named], London, Arthur Baker, 1960.

Samoubiistvo [Suicide]. New York, Izdatel'stvo literaturnogo fonda, 1958.

Povest' o smerti [The Tale of Death]. Frankfurt, Posev, 1969.

Essays

Ogon' i dym [Fire and Smoke]. Paris, Franko-russkaia pechat', 1922.

Sovremenniki [Contemporaries]. Berlin, Slovo, 1928.

Portrety [Portraits]. Berlin, Slovo, 1931.

Zemli, liudi [Land and People]. Berlin, Slovo, 1932.

Iunost' Pavla Stroganova i drugie kharakteristiki [The Youth of Pavel Stroganov and Other Characteristics]. Belgrade, Svetlost', 1935.

Portrety. vol. 2, Paris, 1936.

Political Journalism

Armageddon. Petrograd, 1918.

Lénine. Paris, J. Povolozky et Cie, 1919; translated as *Lenin* [no translator named], New York, Dutton, 1922.

Deux Révolutions, la Révolution Française et la Révolution Russe. Paris, Imprimerie Union, 1921.

La politica estera dei Soviets. Rome, Libreria russa Slovo, 1921.

L'Enjeu des Neutres. Paris, Oreste Zeluk, 1939.

Literary Criticism

Tolstoi i Rollan [Tolstoi and Rolland]. Petrograd, 1915.

Zagadka Tolstogo [The Mystery of Tolstoi]. Berlin, Ladyzhnikov, 1923; reprinted Providence, Rhode Island, Brown University, 1969.

Philosophical Writing

Ul'mskaia noch'. Filosofiia sluchaia [An Ulm Night. The Philosophy of Chance]. New York, Izdatel'stvo imeni Chekhova, 1953.

Critical Studies

"The Problems of Historical Destiny in the Works of M. Aldanov", by Yvonne Grabowska, PhD dissertation, University of Toronto, 1969.

The Novels of Mark Aleksandrovich Aldanov, by C. Nicholas Lee, The Hague, Mouton, 1969.

Die Philosophischen Aspekte von Mark Aldanovs Werk, by V. Setschkareff, Munich, Sagner, 1996.

Bibliography

Bibliographie des Oeuvres de Marc Aldanov, by D. and H. Cristesco, Paris, Institut d'Études Slaves, 1976.

Mark Aldanov's interest in and knowledge of the natural and social sciences, literature, and philosophy all contribute to his literary profile. One of his university specialties was organic chemistry, he worked as a chemist during World War I, and he published three monographs on subjects connected with chemistry. In the novel cycle devoted to the period of the October Revolution, *Kliuch* (*The Key*), *Begstvo* (*The Escape*), *Peshchera* [The Cave], one of the leading characters is a chemist who uses his talents to help anti-Bolshevik conspirators manufacture explosives. Less colourful chemists figure less prominently in novels set in the years just after World War II, *Zhivi kak khochesh'* (*To Live as We Wish*) and *Bred* (*Nightmare and Dawn*).

Aldanov took a university degree in law and spent most of his years between graduation and emigration in the intellectual ambiance of affluent St Petersburg professionals. The *dramatis personae* of the October Revolution novels include a retired chief of the tsarist police, a criminal investigator, a double agent, and a couple of clerks, who work for a Jewish lawyer who also plays a leading role in the story. Several lawyers also figure in *Istoki* (*Before the Deluge*), which culminates in the assassination of Alexander II, and in *Samoubiistvo* [Suicide], centred on the October Revolution. In the lower ranks of the justice system, there is a varied assortment of double agents and conspirators all playing some role in Aldanov's fiction.

Both Aldanov's cultural Europeanism and his passion for literature were already prominent in his second published monograph, which compares Tolstoi and Romain Rolland. All his novels feature at least one *raisonneur* with encyclopedic erudition and a love for aphoristic eloquence, and *Nachalo kontsa* (*The Fifth Seal*) foregrounds a professional French writer. On the Russian side, Aldanov once wrote that for him the divine nature of Tolstoi's literary talent was more than just a metaphor. It is the Tolstoi of *War and Peace*, as much as his own temperament and circumstances, that gives a historical and philosophical orientation even to Aldanov's contemporary novels. Genealogical links bind all the characters in his long fictional work and what he designated as "philosophical tales" – *Desiataia simfoniia* (*The Tenth Symphony*), *Punshevaia vodka* [Vodka Punch], *Mogila Voina* (*For Thee the Best*) – which cover a time frame stretching from the 13th to mid-20th century. In the preface to *The Tenth Symphony* he called "the stirring bond of time" the central theme of all his writing.

While sharing Tolstoi's interest in history, Aldanov challenged his conclusions. *Zagadka Tolstogo* [The Mystery of Tolstoi] explores the dichotomy between the optimistic philosophy of *War and Peace* and a misanthropic pessimism which Aldanov considers to be the master's true nature and which he shares himself. Aldanov has a more systematic education in philosophy than Tolstoi. He particularly admires the methodical doubt of Descartes, the inspiration for his philosophical treatise *Ul'mskaia noch'* [An Ulm Night], which recommends the cultivation of *kaloskagatos*. This ancient Greek concept, combining beauty and good, is also adopted as a rule of life by an aging philosopher in *To Live as We Wish*, who proposes it as the foundation for an ill-fated, short-lived philosophical society. A more prominent Aldanov fictional philosopher is the *raisonneur* of the novels devoted to the period of the French Revolution, a melancholy, acerbic Jew with the symbolic sobriquet Pierre Lamort and the conviction that all human history is summed up in the "vanity of vanities" verses from the Book of Ecclesiastes. Aldanov was a secularized intellectual Jew, like many of his fictional characters, and the prominent place of philosophical discussion in his novels bear witness that rabbi and *philosophe* both coexist in his nature.

In *Armageddon*, written in 1918, Aldanov's pessimism moves from the realm of philosophy to current events. Emigration was certainly the most traumatic event in his life, probably making him decide to be a belletrist rather than a scientist and motivating apocalyptic forebodings in all his major fiction. He was the only writer of the first-generation Russian diaspora to earn his living entirely from his literary output, much of it work as a political journalist for the periodical press. The five books of opinion pieces, travel notes, and biographical sketches published during his lifetime comprise only part of his prolific journalistic output. He was particularly esteemed for his portraits of historically noteworthy characters, which also add a dimension of factual authenticity and psychological complexity to his *belles-lettres*, sometimes as part of the fictional narration, sometimes interpolated as separate chapters. His experience as a newspaper columnist finds fictional expression in one of his most appealing characters, an enterprising Jewish journalist who appears in all the October Revolution novels and in *To Live as We Wish*.

The second book Aldanov published in France, a monograph comparing the French and Russian Revolutions, served as the point of departure for the fictional treatment of the same topic, the four novels grouped under the title *Myslitel'* [The Thinker]. This is the *diable-penseur* gargoyle leaning on the roof of the Parisian Cathedral of Notre Dame with its tongue sticking out, a gesture that symbolizes the author's attitude to the human drama in general and Bolshevik theories of history and historically significant individuals in particular. The prevailing ironical detachment of these novels gives way to a more elegiac mood in the October Revolution fictional cycle, a requiem for a noble civilization that need not have perished: Aldanov's art and thought are based on his conviction that history is shaped not by Marxist historical determinism, but by "His Majesty Chance". In the "philosophical tales" of the 1930s he ventures beyond the framework of the French and Russian Revolutions for his historical material: *The Tenth Symphony* treats "the stirring bond of time" in mid-19th-century Vienna and Paris; *Punshevaia vodka* is "a tale about all five happinesses" on the eve of Catherine the Great's accession; and *For Thee the Best*, subtitled "a tale about wisdom", focuses on Alexander I and Lord Byron. From the mid-1930s Aldanov gave more of his novels contemporary settings: France and Civil War Spain for *The Fifth Seal*, post-war Paris for *To Live as We Wish*, 1953 Berlin for *Nightmare and Dawn*. These works are, however, all inferior to those written at the same time but set in the more distant past: *Before the Deluge* in the 1870s, *Povest' o smerti* [The Tale of Death] in the 1840s, *Samoubiistvo* at the beginning of the 20th century.

Most of Aldanov's genius was captured by the critic who called him "intelligent, sober, and bitter". Intelligent in presenting the complexities of human nature, sober in assigning praise and blame, he made espionage a legitimate theme in serious literature, free from the superficialities of Marxist cant and journalistic sensationalism. Initially bitter at the triumph of irrational barbarism over rational civilization in the October Revolution, with time he began to temper his early misanthropic pessimism with what he called indulgence for human frailty, and to entertain the hope that love and fidelity to unselfish moral principles not only give meaning to individual lives, but make some difference in the fate of nations. His current popularity in Russia, where his works could not be published before the era of glasnost, can be attributed to his very considerable intrinsic literary merit as well as to his subject-matter. He belongs among the most important Russian writers of the 20th century.

C. NICHOLAS LEE

Iuz Aleshkovskii 1929–

Humourist

Biography

Born Iosif Efimovich Aleshkovskii, in Krasnoiarsk, 21 September 1929. Schooling in Moscow interrupted by World War II. Military service in navy terminated by a four-year prison sentence for breaking military discipline, 1950–53. Worked as a driver and on building sites. Literary career began in 1955. Combined writing children's stories, film and television scripts with singing underground songs and guitar poetry. First story in *samizdat*, 1970. Emigrated to Vienna, 1978, and to the United States, 1979, where he lives in Middletown, Connecticut.

Publications

Collected Edition

Sobranie sochinenii, 3 vols. Moscow, 1996.

Fiction

Nikolai Nikolaevich. Maskirovka [Nikolai Nikolaevich. Camouflage]. Ann Arbor, Ardis, 1980.

Ruka (Povestvovanie palacha). New York, Russica, 1980; translated as *The Hand, or The Confession of an Executioner*, by Susan Brownsberger, London, Halban, 1989; New York, Farrar Straus and Giroux, 1990.

Kenguru. Ann Arbor, Ardis, 1981; translated as *Kangaroo*, by Tamara Glenny, New York, Farrar Straus and Giroux, 1986.

Sinen'kii skromnyi platochek [The Humble Little Blue Kerchief]. New York, Chalidze, 1982.

Karusel' [Carousel]. New York, Chalidze, 1983.

Kniga poslednikh slov. 35 prestuplenii [The Book of Last Words. 35 Crimes]. New York, Chalidze, 1984; excerpt translated as "The Book of Final Statements", by Priscilla Meyer, *Partisan Review*, 3 (1984), 367–74.

Smert' v Moskve [Death in Moscow]. New York, Chalidze, 1985.

Bloshinoe tango [Fleas' Tango]. Middletown, Connecticut, Pisatel'-Izdatel', 1986.

"Persten' v Futliuve", *Zvezda*, 7 (1993); translated as *A Ring in a Case*, by Jane Ann Miller. Evanston, Illinois, Northwestern University Press, 1995.

Poetry

"Tri pesni" [Three songs], in *Metropol'*, Ann Arbor, Ardis, 1979.

"'Ne unyvai, zimoi dadut svidanie...'", *Novyi mir*, 12 (1988), 121–24.

Critical Studies

"Volk i zvezdy", by K. Sapgir, *Kontinent*, 28 (1981), 422–27.

"Dushevnye bolezni bezdushnogo mira", by Iurii Mal'tsev, *Kontinent*, 33 (1982), 390–93.

"*Skaz* in the Work of Juz Aleskovskij", by Priscilla Meyer, *Slavic and East European Journal*, 28/4 (1984), 455–61.

"'... Ottogo i diki slova moi!': O tvorchestve Iuza Aleshkovskogo", by Lev Loseff, *Russkaia mysl'* (28 October 1984), 3.

"Takaia karusel'...", by Dora Shturman, *Novoe russkoe slovo* (20 November 1984), 3.

"Skaz o sovetskom cheloveke", by Elena Tudorovskaia, *Strelets*, 2 (1986), 17–19.

"Povtorenie neproidennogo", by Andrei Bitov, *Znamia*, 6 (1991), 192–206.

Russia's Alternative Prose, by Robert Porter, Oxford, Berg, 1994, 31–38.

In the USSR Iuz Aleshkovskii published children's books and wrote orthodox film and television scripts, while at the same time singing subversive songs to private gatherings and writing wittily scabrous stories for *samizdat* and the drawer. In a country where doublethink was common, his literary schizophrenia is remarkable principally for the great contrast between the lighthearted children's works and the "adult" material and taboo-breaking vocabulary of the works for which he is best known. Aleshkovskii's writing, however, is far from the pornography and gratuitous vulgarity that has defaced some Third-Wave émigré writing: always inventive, he is a master of *skaz* (narration in the first person), using the raw material of coarse words less as a cudgel than as a rapier, weaving intricate, poetic, and refined comic patterns to reveal the contrast between official Soviet reality and the truth that can only come with freedom. He is one of the most talented and popular humorous Russian writers today, although his linguistically specific works do not translate well into foreign languages.

Aleshkovskii's best-known underground song was "Tovarishch Stalin, Vy bol'shoi uchenyi" [Comrade Stalin, You Are a Great Scholar], and its satirical irony is a hallmark of all his unofficial and émigré writing. *Nikolai Nikolaevich*, written in 1970 but published only in 1980, enjoyed extremely wide currency in *samizdat*. Like many of Aleshkovskii's other works, it is cast in the form of an ironical monologue, which gives full reign to the author's versatility with Russian, parodying and mocking the deceitful linguistic sterility of much official Soviet literature. Here, a young thief, released from the camps, works in a biological institute as a professional masturbator for the quasi-scientific purpose of creating energy; with myriad obscenities the story ridicules the absurdities of, among other things, Lysenkoism and, indeed, all Soviet science (the latter characterized by one professor as "a dry wank"), as well as many classics of Soviet literature.

Calculated bad taste is also a feature of the picaresque *Kenguru* (*Kangaroo*), written during 1974–75, published in 1981, in which an old thief, Fan Fanych, tells Kolia, his faithful but invisible friend, of his long struggles with a KGB operator who, having caught him and saving him for a special show trial, makes him devise his own heinous crime – which turns out to be raping Gemma, the oldest kangaroo in Moscow zoo. *Maskirovka* [Camouflage], written in 1978, published in 1980, is a wildly comic story about drunkenness, in which we learn from the hero's crazy alcohol-induced ravings that he has realized with horror, but can only express through garbled slogans and advertising jingles, that all Soviet society is a kind of camouflage.

Ruka (*The Hand*), written in 1977–80, published in 1980, is a rather longer and grimmer monologue, telling how a boy, orphaned and rendered impotent during the de-kulakization process, has worked his way up through the KGB to become one of Stalin's cruelist bodyguards, and now seeks, as a last task, revenge on Gurov, the man who as a boy had frozen his testicles, and whose father had killed his father. The book is a week-long rambling monologue of hate and rage addressed to the corrupt and bloated communist official, but some of the incantatory denunciations of the demonic Soviet regime are startling rather than amusing in their obsessive hyperbole. The language in this over-long story is, however, as rich as elsewhere, and Aleshkovskii makes a specific, though typically ironic statement of its purpose: "dirty words, the worst Russian oaths" offer personal salvation in "the foetid prison cell that is now the home of our mighty, free, great, etcetera, etcetera language".

Madness is given grotesquely comic treatment in *Sinen'kii skromnyi platochek* [The Humble Little Blue Kerchief] (1982), a monologue in letters by a crazy war veteran writing from a lunatic asylum. The hilarious reported conversations of the inmates produce a cumulative obscene lament on the woes of Russia, where the falsity and corruption of Leonid Brezhnev himself plays a natural part in the veteran's version of reality. As always with Aleshkovskii, the zany detail is striking: to give an example which also shows the author's distrust of people, rather than animals or even parts of the body, in this story the hero feels guilty that he has betrayed his own leg by allowing it to be interred in the tomb of the Unknown Soldier and by having disowned it for its undesirable associations with an enemy of the people. *Karusel'* [Carousel], written in 1979, published in 1983, comprises letters from a much-decorated Jewish labourer and war veteran who wishes to emigrate from the anti-Semitic USSR. Aleshkovskii's satirical pen pinpoints many negative aspects of Soviet life, drawing a bleak picture of oppression and disillusionment.

Kniga poslednikh slov [The Book of Last Words] (1984), perhaps Aleshkovskii's best work to date, comprises the final courtroom speeches of 35 plaintiffs, accused of crimes ranging from petty theft to murder. Each offence is briefly described before the accused take over the narration, protesting innocence and loyalty to the state in a linguistically virtuosic blend of subliterate vulgarity, meaningless, distorted officialese with numerous quirkily grotesque digressions and details that condemn equally the speakers and the state whose representatives they are trying to impress. Aleshkovskii's use of speech distortion and *skaz* often recalls Zoshchenko, although he is more lexically extreme than the earlier writer. In his way he is equally successful in using language to convey the extraordinary flavour of the Soviet regime as it affects the lives of its humbler victims.

Iuz Aleshkovskii is one of the most popular of all living Russian humorous writers. His mastery of first-person narration and his linguistic virtuosity, applauded by Joseph Brodskii, among others, enables him to present a very distinctive satirical picture of the Soviet Union past and present. It is greatly to be regretted that his skilful and imaginative use of coarse language has, apparently, been the cause of his complete omission from several recent western reference works. Without it his stories would lose much of the grotesque realism that gives their humour its edge. Without Aleshkovskii, on the other hand, contemporary Russian literature would be a much poorer phenomenon.

ARNOLD MCMILLIN

Leonid Nikolaevich Andreev 1871–1919

Prose writer and dramatist

Biography

Born in Orel, 21 August 1871. Attended local gymnasium, 1882–91; St Petersburg University, from 1891; sent down for failing to pay fees, 1893; enrolled at Moscow University in same year. Published first stories in *Orlovskii vestnik*, 1895. Graduated in law, 1897; practised briefly as a barrister. Began contributing court reports to *Moskovskii vestnik* and then *Kur'er*, from late 1897. Associated with the *Sreda* group of realists. First book of stories published by *Znanie*, 1901. Married: 1) Aleksandra Mikhailovna Veligorskaia in 1902 (died 1906), two sons; 2) Anna Il'inishna Denisevich in 1908, three children. Arrested and imprisoned for hosting an illegal political meeting, 1905. Editor of the modernist-leaning literary almanac *Shipovnik*, 1907–08. Moved to Vammelsuu, Finland, 1908. Adopted pro-war position during World War I; co-editor of the patriotic newspaper *Russkaia volia*, 1916–17. Issued famous SOS appeal for allied intervention from Finland in March 1919. Died suddenly on 12 September 1919, apparently of a heart attack.

Publications

Collected Editions

Sobranie sochinenii, 13 vols. St Petersburg and Moscow, 1911–13.

Polnoe sobranie sochinenii, 8 vols. St Petersburg, 1913.

The Little Angel and Other Stories, translated by W.H. Lowe. New York, Knopf, and London, Hodder and Stoughton, 1916; reprinted, Sawtry, Cambridgeshire, Dedalus, and New York, Hippocrene, 1989.

The Seven That Were Hanged and Other Stories [no translator named]. New York, Random House, 1958; reprinted 1962.

Povesti i rasskazy, 2 vols. Moscow, 1971.

Krasnyi smekh: Izbrannye rasskazy i povesti [The Red Laugh ...]. Minsk, 1984.

Visions: Stories and Photographs, edited by Olga Andreyeva-Carlisle. San Diego, Harcourt Brace Jovanovich, 1987.
Three Plays: The Black Maskers, The Life of Man, The Sabine Women, translated by C.I. Meader and F.N. Scott. New York, Fertig, 1989; reprint of *Plays*, New York, Scribner, 1915.
Sobranie sochinenii, 6 vols. Moscow, 1990 [Only 2 vols published].

Fiction
Zhizn' Vasiliia Fiveiskogo [The Life of Vasilii Fiveiskii]. 1904.
Krasnyi smekh. 1905; translated as *The Red Laugh*, by Alexandra Lindem, Sawtry, Cambridgeshire, Dedalus, 1989.
Rasskaz o semi poveshennykh. 1908; translated as "The Seven That Were Hanged", in *The Seven That Were Hanged and Other Stories*, 1958; also translated in *Great Russian Short Stories* , edited by Norris Houghton, New York, Dell, 1958, and in *Visions: Stories and Photographs*, edited by Olga Andreyeva-Carlisle, 1987.
Sashka Zhegulev. 1911.

Plays
K zvezdam. 1905; translated as *To the Stars*, by A. Goudiss, in *Poet Lore*, 18/4 (1907); also translated by Maurice Magnus, London, C.W. Daniel, 1921.
Zhizn' cheloveka. 1906–08; translated as *The Life of Man*, by C.J. Hogarth, London, Allen and Unwin, and New York, Macmillan, 1913; also translated by C.I. Meader and F.N. Scott, in *Three Plays*, 1989.
Chernye maski. 1908; translated as "The Black Maskers", by C.I. Meader and F.N. Scott, in *Three Plays*, 1989.
Prekrasnye sabinianki. 1911; translated as "The Sabine Women", by C.I. Meader and F.N. Scott, in *Three Plays*, 1989.
Tot kto poluchaet poshchechinu. 1915; translated as "He Who Gets Slapped", by F.D. Reeve, in *Twentieth Century Russian Plays*, New York, Norton, 1963; also translated by Gregory Zilboorg, Westport, Connecticut, Greenwood Press, 1975 (reprinted from *The Dial*, March 1921, 250–300).
P'esy. Moscow, 1959.
P'esy. Moscow, 1991.

Photography
Photographs by a Russian Writer, edited by Richard Davies. London, Thames and Hudson, 1989.

Letters and Diaries
Pis'ma Leonida Andreeva [The Letters of Leonid Andreev]. Leningrad, 1924.
S.O.S. - Dnevnik (1914–1919). Pis'ma. Stat'i i interv'iu. Vospominaniia sovremennikov. Moscow and St Petersburg, 1994.

Critical Studies
O smysle zhizni; F. Sologub, L. Andreev, L. Shestov, by R.V. Ivanov-Razumnik, 2nd edition, Moscow, 1910; reprinted Letchworth, Bradda, 1971.
O Leonide Andreeve, by Kornei Chukovskii, St Petersburg, 1911.
Leonid Andreyev: A Critical Study, by Alexander Kaun, New York, Huebsch, 1924; reprinted New York, Blom, 1969.
Leonid Andreyev: A Study, by James B. Woodward, Oxford, Clarendon Press, 1969.
Leonid Andreyev, by Josephine Newcombe, Letchworth, Bradda, 1972; New York, Ungar, 1973.
Tvorchestvo Leonida Andreeva 1892–1906, by L.I. Iezuitova, Leningrad, 1976.
Twentieth Century Russian Drama, by Harold B. Segel, New York, Columbia University Press, 1979; 2nd edition, Baltimore, Johns Hopkins University Press, 1993.
Leonid Andreev i traditsii russkogo realizma, by V.I. Bezzubov, Tallin, 1984.
A Semiotic Analysis of the Short Stories of Leonid Andreev 1900–09, by Stephen Hutchings, London, Modern Humanities Research Association, 1990.
"The Silence of Rebellion: Women in the Work of Leonid Andreev", by Eva Buchwald, in *Gender and Russian Literature: New Perspectives*, edited by Rosalind Marsh, Cambridge and New York, Cambridge University Press, 1996, 229–43.

Bibliography
Leonid Nikolaevich Andreev. Bibliografiia, vyp. 1 Sochineniia i teksty. Moscow, 1995.

Like several Russian writers before him, Leonid Andreev ended his career as a publicist. As is the case with his more illustrious predecessors, Andreev's polemical leanings are conspicuous, too, throughout his belletristic writing.

Andreev's earliest published work dates from the end of the 19th century. After an abortive start to his legal career, he began producing court reports for the Moscow newspaper *Kur'er*, sometimes writing under the pseudonym of "James Lynch". It was for this paper that he wrote his first important artistic piece: "Bargamot i Garas'ka" [Bargamot and Garas'ka] – an Easter story with a deceptively optimistic ending which caught the attention of Gor'kii. From here began a stormy relationship that first saw Andreev in close allegiance with Gor'kii's *Znanie* publishing house. But following Andreev's fatalistic attitude to the failure of the 1905 Revolution, their relationship progressively deteriorated. Andreev's spectacular rise to fame (which reached its peak around 1910) can be attributed in part to Gor'kii's patronage. However, from early on Andreev exhibited considerable independence. While his early prose reflects the influence of Chekhovian realism – his story "Prizraki" [Ghosts], for example, recapitulates many of the themes of "Palata No. 6" ("Ward Six") – Andreev had always been willing to experiment with modernist innovations and adapt them to his polemical needs. Thus, the hyperbolous imagery of Expressionism and the Symbolist notion of *dvoemirie* (double-worldedness) proved conducive to his penchant for existential despair and the personification of grand abstractions such as Death, Man, Reason and War. Andreev's mature technique attained its apotheosis in *Krasnyi smekh* (*The Red Laugh*) – a semi-allegorical diatribe against the insanity unleashed by war, *Zhizn' Vasiliia Fiveiskogo* [The Life of Vasilii Fiveiskii] – a fantastic rewriting of the Job story aimed at subverting religion's call to faith in the face of death, and *Rasskaz o semi poveshennykh* (*The Seven That Were Hanged*) – an emotive protest against capital punishment.

Andreev's increasing attraction to the somber tones of

Decadence, heightened in 1906 by the death of his first wife, finds its most characteristic form in a series of plays written between 1906 and 1909 and incorporating some of the most radical theatrical techniques of the time. The most successful of these was *Zhizn' cheloveka* (*The Life of Man*) – a stark allegory depicting the futility of human existence. The play was produced by both Meierkhol'd and Stanislavskii. Following Symbolism's decline, Andreev turned to a more conventional style of drama in which psychology was the main focus. It was only in 1915 that, in the much acclaimed *Tot kto poluchaet poshchechinu* (*He Who Gets Slapped*), Andreev readopted and perfected his unique blend of stylized ambiguity and realistic characterization. This is the only Andreev play that is still performed in Russia and the west.

During the last portion of his career, Andreev concentrated on drama, though he continued to write stories and in 1911 published a singularly unsuccessful novel, *Sashka Zhegulev*. By the beginning of World War I his political views had turned full circle and he adopted a fiercely patriotic stance. He was vigorously opposed to the October Revolution and in 1919 made an impassioned appeal for allied intervention. By the time of his death, Andreev's star had already waned. The years of Stalinism (to which his son, Daniil, fell victim) ensured that he remained *persona non grata* until the Thaw, when the slow process of rehabilitation began. Since then a number of scholarly articles and several monographs devoted to Andreev have appeared in Russia and the west, as well as a fine collection of his colour photographs (the ever-flamboyant Andreev was a prolific photographer and a competent painter). However, his brand of hysterical melodrama has not worn well with modern, ironic sensibilities. Judged according to current criteria of literary value, his fate is likely to be that of a longish footnote to Russian literary history.

In the challenge that he poses to literary and cultural typologists, Andreev perhaps offers more. The task of categorizing his work has confounded generations of critics. There is barely a single "-ism" that has not been applied to his work. But the very difficulties Andreev presents for those attempting to classify him according to superficial literary groupings mask his true position at the nexus of a deep structural shift affecting the literary-cultural process during the Silver Age. The shift is best explored at the heart of Andreev's Fantastic, whose overriding principle is that of the collapse of the hierarchies and the differences on which meaning-production is founded. Often this involves the espousal of oxymoron: martyrdom in treachery in *Iuda Iskariot* (*Judas Iscariot*) – Andreev's provocative attempt to turn the tables on Christian passivity; life within death in *The Seven That Were Hanged*; the insanity of reason in "Prizraki". The collapse is reflected narratologically in his consistent conflation of the levels of "discourse" and "story". In "Stena" [The Wall], the notion of an omnipresent wall as discursive figure for the forces imprisoning man is actualized as the bizarre story of a lepers' colony constrained for perpetuity behind an enormous, insurmountable barrier. These features recur across the full range of "-isms", confirming that, far from standing alone, Andreev was very much in tune with the deep loss of faith in language and stable meanings that beset the whole of early 20th-century culture.

The turn of the century was marked by a related trend at whose centre Andreev can likewise be placed. In Russia, amid the reaction against compartmentalizing, analytical thought generated a dramatic broadening of the aesthetic sphere across a range of phenomena previously considered sub-aesthetic: photography, music hall, etc. In this context Andreev's position on the borders of artistic taste appears in a new light; when art opens its doors, unfamiliar figures are bound to gather at its threshold. This explains why Andreev was, for a time, received with such enthusiasm by sophisticates like Blok and Belyi. (For Blok, the fact that Andreev's crude images were "invading the cosy living-rooms" of aesthetic puritans was cause for celebration). Theorists have long argued that it is a culture's marginal figures and genres which offer the most illuminating insights into its inner workings. Herein lies Leonid Andreev's claim to durability.

STEPHEN HUTCHINGS

The Seven That Were Hanged

Rasskaz o semi poveshennykh

Story, 1908

The Seven That Were Hanged is Andreev's most celebrated story. The *Shipovnik* almanac in which it was published in 1908 sold out within a few days and the story was reprinted in multiple editions between 1909 and 1911. The text was introduced to the English-speaking world by Herman Bernstein with great acclaim in 1909 and has since been included in almost every translated edition of Andreev's works.

The work's reception can be attributed in part to the enduring relevance of its subject, and in part to the power to move which, to this day, it undoubtedly possesses. It was conceived as a reaction to the mass executions that followed the 1905 Revolution, although Andreev was careful to stress the universality of his theme. Indeed, he dedicated the 1909 edition to Tolstoi whose own, religiously-inspired protest against the death penalty ("Ne mogu molchat'" ["I Cannot Be Silent"]) was written virtually simultaneously with *The Seven That Were Hanged*. The story's impact derives from Andreev's manipulation of the tension between the horror that accompanies certain knowledge of the hour and manner of one's death, and the human capacity to overcome that fear, and thus death itself. The work marked Andreev's own emergence from the pall of gloom that descended upon him after his first wife's death, and his new-found belief in the immortal spirit of life.

The Seven That Were Hanged depicts the final days shared by two common criminals, and five revolutionaries convicted of a terrorist bombing. It begins, however, with a chapter describing the inner turmoil suffered by a government minister informed of a plot to assassinate him. Though the conspiracy has been thwarted, the minister is beset with terror at the impossible burden of knowing that he was to die the following day. Thus Andreev lays the ground for the series of juxtapositions, parallels, and contrasts around which his text is structured.

The opening segment is rich in techniques which, despite the realistic context, link the writer with the slippages of meaning associated with modernism. Thus, in an inversion typical of Andreev, the minister imagines death standing over him in the form of the very sentinels whose task it is to shield him from his fate. The chapter culminates in a vivid rendition of the fragmentation of the minister's consciousness as he succumbs to a heart attack.

Next follows a chapter relating the sentencing of the terrorists. Here Andreev begins to exploit the temporal displacements that define his radically non-linear approach to plot. The age of one terrorist, we are told, is hard to define, "like that of a corpse about to decompose". The temporal plane beyond the story's end is thus projected into its beginning – a particularly effective device since it works in harmony with the story's theme: the unwarranted intrusion of death into the open-endedness of life.

Andreev's spatio-metaphoric approach to narrative is reflected in the main portion of *The Seven That Were Hanged* that consists of discrete chapters allotted to each of the condemned and intended to reveal contrasting attitudes to a single fate. Andreev begins, strategically, with the two criminals – Ianson and Tsyganok. The accumulation of sordid detail in Ianson's chapter is intermittently interrupted by the pathetic refrain, "I don't want to die" – to be read first against the hardened attitude of the defiant Tsyganok, then against the tragi-heroic dispositions of the five revolutionaries. The common thread is that of the fear of dying which each person, in his or her different way, must confront. The chapter devoted to Sergei Golovin – a colonel's son – tells in maudlin tones of the condemned's brave last encounter with his grieving parents. However, Golovin's dignified demeanour is itself later set in relief by the absurd devotion to physical fitness that he manifests in his last hours.

Characteristically, Andreev accords the greatest inner strength to his female characters. The section dealing with the young girl Musia's preparations for death emphasize her passionate belief that "when thousands kill one, this means that the one is victorious". The displacement strategy is then redeployed to new effect as Musia triumphantly asserts her claims to immortality, declaring that even if her coffin were brought to her she would deny that it is she who lies in it. The writer's greatest admiration is reserved for Tania Kovalchuk. Her grief stands out from that of the others in that it is directed purely outwards. It is no coincidence that she is the last to die and that her concern is, even at the scaffold, less with her imminent execution than with the fact that she is now alone, deprived of the fellow-beings who gave her life meaning.

Andreev insisted that he considered the weakest personalities most worthy of sympathy. Into this category falls Vasilii Kashirin – the fourth revolutionary. Andreev's portrayal of Kashirin's incipient mental collapse reveals the writer's gift for conveying the alienating effects of sheer existential terror. When visited by his mother, Kashirin is described as being so estranged from human companionship that he sees only a "mother doll". The last of the terrorists, Werner, represents Andreev's adaptation of a Russian literary type: the ratiocinating intellectual. Fittingly, he is shown occupying his final moments with chess problems: an attempt to counter the unknown with reason and will. But, in what is the text's key scene, Werner is subjected to a dramatic (and not altogether well motivated) transformation, suddenly experiencing a vision of Life and Death as two sides of a knife-edged ridge that blend into one joyous whole at the horizon. Like many Andreev stories, *The Seven That Were Hanged* thus accomplishes an erasure of the very distinctions around which it is constructed, subsuming its constituent components into a single, indeterminate sensation that saturates every level of its semantics.

The tale ends with a volley of Andreevan melodrama which intensifies the sense of absurdity surrounding the executions: Kashirin wrapping a handkerchief around his neck to keep himself warm on the way to the scaffold, Golovin looking frantically for a galosh. In the closing lines Andreev invokes Christ's crucifixion, as Musia requests to be hanged alongside the criminal, Tsyganok. The final images are of the distorted bodies, Golovin's lost galosh, and the rising sun.

The Seven That Were Hanged combines melodramatic cliché with bold imagery, "low" sub-literary polemics with "high" philosophical themes, traditional realistic thematics with innovatory modernistic technique. It thus furnishes a microcosm of the contradictions traversing Andreev's entire *oeuvre*.

STEPHEN HUTCHINGS

He Who Gets Slapped

Tot kto poluchaet poshchechinu

Play, 1915

He Who Gets Slapped is one of the more famous productions of the post-Symbolist theatre of the Russian Silver Age, probably because of its comparative accessibility and because of a number of successful, provocative productions in the west, as well as an opera, *Pantaloon*, by Robert Ward, premiered in 1956 on which it was based.

He Who Gets Slapped was first presented at the Moscow Dramatic Theatre on 27 October 1915, and then in a famous production at the Aleksandrinskii Theatre, Petrograd, on 2 February 1916. This production, which was acclaimed with great enthusiasm, was filmed, with a few changes of cast, later in the same year, by Aleksandr Ivanov-Gai, and premiered on 16 October 1916. The film, too, was a success, though perhaps less so than the play: after three acts of the production at the Aleksandrinskii, Andreev was called onto the stage and garlanded with laurel wreaths. The play is an almost unique combination of the exotic and the realistic, the romantic and the trivial, the melodramatic and the banal. It tells the story of HE, a philosopher whose "thought" has been stolen by another and published under the other's name. The fact that the "other" has also stolen HE's wife adds to the irony of his situation and the bitterness which engulfs his mind. In the play, all that is in the past and we only learn of it in the third act. We first encounter HE as he applies to join the circus of Papa Briquet, a lugubrious entrepreneur whose care of his troupe does not extend to protecting the young bareback rider, Consuelo, from the predatory Baron Regnart. Into what is in fact the rather venal atmosphere behind the scenes of the circus, HE introduces a kind of romantic idealism, symbolized by his onstage performance: he will enact with his partner the ritual wherein the buffoon clown is continually slapped, or slapped down, by his more worldly-wise partner. This symbolic echoing of HE's real-life tragedy in the sawdust ring is hugely successful with the spectators, but HE's career is halted when he falls in love with the beautiful but exploited Consuelo himself. But she has agreed to marry the Baron, and so the despairing HE gives her poison which she unknowingly drinks, and then he drinks the rest himself. Consuelo dies, the Baron shoots himself and HE, terrified that the Baron will reach Consuelo first, dies quickly himself.

The melodramatic climax betrays the weakness of the play, and Andreev's inability to resolve the issues he raises. The hopeless romanticism of HE's world-view makes him less, not more, interesting than he might otherwise seem, and the banality of the eternal triangle that Andreev conjures up is concealed under the exotic paraphenalia of the circus. Yet this exoticism is itself consciously undermined by the dramatist, who shows up the circus and its people in a thoroughly tawdry light. Most are mean-spirited and selfish, with hardly more imagination than those from beyond their enclosed world. In other words, here is a potentially challenging play which constantly finds promising dramatic material, but it is reduced by its author's unwillingness to find a single style or motif to clothe his various ideas in.

Probably the single most unexpected characteristic of *He Who Gets Slapped* is its basic naturalism. The title, the milieu, the central character's deliberately enigmatic name, and the play's apparent affinities with contemporary theatricalist works like *Balaganchik* (*The Puppet Show*) by Aleksandr Blok, suggest a less true-to-life style than is actually created. Rather, Andreev sets these theatricalist characteristics in a more realistic context, and perhaps shows them to be futile. This is most clearly seen in the way HE runs away to join the circus when his life becomes unbearable in the real world. But Andreev shows that this is no true escape, for the circus is populated by people who are just as self-centred and myopic as those in the "real world". This relationship between the world of the circus and the world beyond is in fact the most stimulating feature of the play. The eternal triangle whose workings in the real world have driven HE to flee are repeated even more contemptibly here: in the real world, HE's wife did not marry his rival until she thought HE was dead, but here the vapid Consuelo is content to marry the Baron for money.

So the themes of the play are interestingly laid out: imagination is set against real life, and shown to be disappointingly similar. The appearance of the fantastic or the exotic conceals merely the same depressing reality, and the circus performer's mask hides nothing more than a fairly ordinary face. This reading of the play has no need to seek the "mythic substructure" which H.B. Segel finds in the play (see Harold B. Segel, 1993), it merely appreciates Andreev's anger that the circus performer's make-up cannot disguise the depressing truth of life. The problem, however, may be with the author: the lonely intellectual he places behind the clown white may in fact be nothing more than a self-centred snob. What is most exciting about this play, despite it being judged by some a failure, is the dramatists's ambition. He creates a flawed piece, but one which is striving for the highest reaches of the drama. Perhaps the time and the place militated against him, perhaps he lacked the final modicum of talent; but his play repays the price of a theatre ticket because its many facets constantly stimulate the spectator's imagination.

ROBERT LEACH

Innokentii Fedorovich Annenskii 1855–1909

Poet, critic, and literary translator

Biography

Born in Omsk, 1 September 1855. Attended secondary schools in St Petersburg, 1865–72, with interruptions because of ill-health (serious heart condition) and family impecuniousness; St Petersburg University, 1875–79, graduated as candidate in historical philology (on basis of original dissertation). Held several school-teaching posts, 1879–1906; demoted to Inspector of Petersburg Educational District, 1906–09. Married: Nadezhda Valentinovna Khmara-Barshchevskaia; one son and two stepsons. Wrote articles and reviews on pedagogical issues, from 1881; translated Euripides' plays, with scholarly apparatus, from 1894. Wrote poetry at school, but little early work survives. Because of official position, published original verse under the pseudonym Nik. T-o until 1906; remained aloof from literary life until involvement with the literary journal *Apollon*, from March 1909. Died of heart failure outside Tsarskoe Selo (afterwards Vitebsk) Station in St Petersburg, 13 December 1909, having petitioned for retirement some weeks earlier.

Publications

Collected Editions

Stikhotvoreniia i tragedii. "Biblioteka poeta: Bol'shaia seriia". 2nd edition, Leningrad, 1959; 3rd edition, Leningrad, 1990.

Knigi otrazhenii [Books of Reflections] (includes miscellaneous critical articles, letters, and autobiography). Moscow, 1979.

Poetry

Tikhie pesni. S prilozheniem sbornika stikhotvornykh perevodov "Parnastsy i prokliatye" [Quiet Songs. With an Appended Volume of Verse Translations "Parnassians and Poètes Maudits"] (under the pseudonym Nik. T-o). St Petersburg, 1904.

Kiparisovyi larets: Vtoraia kniga stikhov. Posmertnaia. Moscow, 1910; translated in *The Cypress Chest* (bilingual edition), by R.H. Morrison, Ann Arbor, Ardis, 1982.

Posmertnye stikhi Innokentiia Annenskogo [Posthumous Poems of Innokentii Annenskii]. Petrograd, 1923.

Magdalina. Poema [Magdaline. A Narrative Poem]. Moscow, 1997.

Literary Criticism

Kniga otrazhenii [Book of Reflections]. St Petersburg, 1906.

"Antichnyi mif v sovremennoi frantsuzskoi poezii" [Antique Myth in Contemporary French Poetry], *Germes*, 7–10 (1908), 177–85; 209–13; 236–40; 270–88.

Vtoraia kniga otrazhenii [Second Book of Reflections]. St Petersburg, 1909.

"O sovremennom lirizme" [On Contemporary Lyricism], *Apollon*, 1–3 (1909); 12–42; 3–29; 5–29.

Plays

Melanippa-Filosof [Melanippa the Philosopher]. St Petersburg, 1901.

Tsar' Iksion. Tragediia v 5-i deistviiakh, s muzykal'nymi antraktami [Tsar' Iksion]. St Petersburg, 1902.

"Laodamiia. Liricheskaia tragediia v 4-x deistviiakh i s muzykal'nymi antraktami", *Severnaia rech'* (1906), 137–208; separate edition, St Petersburg, 1907.

Famira-Kifared: Vakkhicheskaia drama [Thamyras Cytharoede: A Bacchic Drama]. Moscow, 1913; 2nd edition, Petrograd, 1919.

Letters

"Pis'ma k S.K. Makovskomu" [Letters to S.K. Makovskii], published by A.V. Lavrov and R.D. Timenchik, in *Akademiia Nauk SSSR. Pushkinskii Dom. Ezhegodnik Rukopisnogo otdela na 1976 g.*, Leningrad, 1978, 222–41.

"Pis'ma k M.A. Voloshinu" [Letters to M.A. Voloshin], published by A.V. Lavrov and V.P. Kupchenko, in *Akademiia Nauk SSSR. Pushkinskii Dom. Ezhegodnik Rukopisnogo otdela na 1976 g.*, Leningrad, 1978, 242–52.

Translator

Teatr Evripida [Theatre of Euripides]. vol. 1, St Petersburg, 1906; vols 1–3, Moscow, 1916–21.

Poeziia frantsuzskogo simvolizma [French Symbolist Poetry]. Moscow, 1993.

Critical Studies

"Innokentii Annenskii po semeinym vospominaniiam i rukopisnym materialam", by Valentin Krivich, *Al'manakh literaturnaia mysl'*, 3 (1925), 208–55.

Studies in the Life and Work of Innokentij Annenskij, by Vsevolod Setchkarev, The Hague, Mouton, 1963.

La Poesia de Innokentij Annenskij, by E. Bazzarelli, Milan, Mursia, "Civilta letteraria del Novecento", sez. russa 1, 1965.

"Metricheskii repertuar I. Annenskogo (Materialy k metricheskomu spravochniku)", by Iu.M. Lotman, *Uchenye zapiski Tartuskogo gosudarstvennogo universiteta*, 385 (1975), 122–47.

I.F. Annenskijs poetische Reflexionen, by Barbara Conrad, Munich, Fink, 1976.

"Annenskij and Mallarmé: A Case of Subtext", by David Borker, *Slavic and East European Journal*, 21 (1977), 46–55.

"O sostave sbornika Innokentiia Annenskogo *Kiparisovii larets*", by Roman Timenchik, *Voprosy literatury*, 8 (1978), 307–16.

"Intrinsic and Extrinsic Aspects of Structure in Annenskij's 'Verbnaja nedelja'", by David Borker, *Slavic and East European Journal*, 23 (1979), 491–504.

"Innokentii Annenskii v neizdannykh vospominaniakh", edited by A.V. Lavrov and Roman Timenchik, *Pamiatniki kul'tury. Novye otkrytiia. Pis'mennost'. Iskusstvo. Arkheologiia. Ezhegodnik 1981*, Leningrad, 1983, 61–146.

Innokentii Annenskii: lichnost' i tvorchestvo, by A. Fedorov, Leningrad, 1984.

"Bacchic Revels: Annensky's *Famira-kifared* and the Satyrs", by Catriona Kelly, *Essays in Poetics*, 10/2 (1985), 76–93.

"Iunosheskaia avtobiografiia Innokentiia Annenskogo", by A.V. Orlov, *Russkaia literatura*, 2 (1985), 169–75.

"Poeziia I. Annenskogo v chitatel'skoi srede 1910-x gg.", by Roman Timenchik, *Uchenye zapiski Tartuskogo gosudarstvennogo universiteta*, 680 (1985), 101–16.

Innokentij Annenskij and the Acmeist Doctrine, by Janet G. Tucker, Columbus, Ohio, Slavica, 1986.

"'Zagadochnoe budnichnoe slovo' I. Annenskogo: Arkhaizmy i gallitsizmy", by Anna Ljunggren, in *Text and Context: Essays to Honour N.Å. Nilsson*, Stockholm, Almqvist & Wiksell, 1987, 76–85.

Akhmatova i Annenskii: Zametki k teme, by A.E. Anikin, Preprints, vols 1–7, Novosibirsk, 1988–90.

"The Poetic Universe and Thematic Unity of Innokentij Annenskij's 'Trefoils' in the Earliest and Final Variants", by Marina Tarlinskaja, *International Journal of Slavic Linguistics and Poetics*, 38 (1988–95), 119–41.

"Classical Tragedy and the 'Slavonic Rennaissance': The Plays of Vjačeslav Ivanov and Innokentij Annenskij Compared", by Catriona Kelly, *Slavic and East European Journal*, 33 (1989), 235–54.

"*Kiparisovyi larets* i ego avtor", by N.A. Bogomolov, in *Kiparisovii larets*, by I.F. Annenskii, Moscow, 1990, 10–50.

"Skvoznye motivy liriki I. Annenskogo", by M.V. Trostnikov, *Izvestiia Akademiia Nauk SSSR, Seriia literatury i iazyka*, 50 (1991), 328–37.

Pushkinskaia traditsiia v russkoi poezii pervoi poloviny XX veka: Ot Annenskogo do Pasternaka, by V.V. Musatov, Moscow, 1992.

"Annensky's 'Trefoil in the Park' (Witness to Whiteness)", by Nancy Pollack, in *A Sense of Place: Tsarskoe Selo and Its Poets*, edited by Lev Loseff and Barry Scherr, Columbus, Ohio, Slavica, 1993, 171–90.

"'Classical' and 'Tsarskoe Selo' in the Works of Annensky: Some Observations in Regard to Acmeism", by A.E. Anikin, in *A Sense of Place: Tsarskoe Selo and Its Poets*, edited by Lev Loseff and Barry Scherr, Columbus, Ohio, Slavica, 1993, 191–214.

"Gumilev, Annensky and Tsarskoe Selo: Gumilev's 'Tsarskosel'skii krug idei'", by Michael Basker, in *A Sense of Place: Tsarskoe Selo and Its Poets*, edited by Lev Loseff and Barry Scherr, Columbus, Ohio, Slavica, 1993, 215–41.

Humaniorum studiorum cultores: Die Gräkophilie in der russischen Literatur der Jahrhundertwende am Beispiel von Leben und Werk Innokentij Annenskijs und Vjačeslav Ivanovs, by Alexandra Ioannidou, Frankfurt, Peter Lang, 1996.

Bibliographies
Bibliografiia Innokentiia Annenskogo, by Evgenii Arkhipov, Moscow, 1914.
"A Bibliography of Works by and about Innokentii Fedorovich Annenskii", by Felix Philipp Ingold, *Russian Literature Triquarterly*, 11 (1975), 508–32; also in *10 Bibliographies of 20th Century Russian Literature*, edited by Fred Moody, Ann Arbor, Ardis, 1977, 11–36.

Innokentii Fedorovich Annenskii was born in Omsk in 1855. His father, a pupil of the Alexander Lyceum, was a prominent Siberian administrator: he lapsed into poverty in later years and was ostracized from polite society. His brother became one of the most influential propagandists of the radical-democratic movement, and organizer of a Populist party group. At St Petersburg University, Annenskii studied the history of the Russian language under the tutelage of several outstanding philologists. After graduating in 1879 he was appointed a secondary-school (gymnasium) teacher, and worked in the field of education until the end of his life. Having married a widow with two children while still a young man (they had a son in 1880, who was to publish poetry under the pseudonym of V. Krivich, and left memoirs of his father), he was always to remain dependent on his official salary. He was only intermittently able to pursue his philological research, to translate, and to write poetry, and suffered constantly from the resultant dichotomy. In the course of his official career he was Head of the P. Galagan College in Kiev (1891–93), which he left after irreconcilable conflict with activists of the Ukrainian nationalist intelligentsia, Head of the Eighth Gymnasium in St Petersburg (1893–96), and thereafter Head for ten years of the prestigious Nikolaevskii Boys' Gymnasium at Tsarskoe Selo, from which he was dismissed as a result of the leniency he displayed towards pupils during the unrest of 1905, and forced to serve out the remainder of his career as Educational District Inspector. During his lifetime he gained a certain recognition as translator of Euripides, though managing to publish only the first of the three volumes he had prepared (1906). His translations project the Greek dramatist as the ironical "demystifier" of a world in a state of crisis. Annenskii's two *Knigi otrazhenii* [Books of Reflections] (1906 and 1909) – collections of essays on the new literature, in a mode of free improvisation on the margins of others' texts quite unfamiliar in the Russian tradition – did not achieve significant popularity. And as the instiller of new life into the Russian lyric, his contemporary dialogue with a broad readership conspicuously failed to take place.

The main impetus towards Annenskii's creation of an individual poetic style had been his work on translations of French verse – by the Parnassians, the Symbolists, and the "poètes maudits". Annenskii's own poetry borrows from the French tradition the themes of the "torments of the ideal" amid the ever-inventive variety of universal ennui, and of a questioning unbelief and solitude as the ineluctable promise of death. But Annenskii's originality lay not so much in his declared themes and propositions, as in his virtuoso construction of multivalent poetic texts, which, in his own words, "one can understand in two or more ways, or simply feel without fully understanding, and then mentally complete oneself". Thus, Annenskii's lyric poetry actively moulds its reader, programming the specifics of reader behaviour, oriented toward the discovery of a hidden key. The demonstrative adogmaticism of the poetic utterance prompted a few readers of Annenskii's first collection, *Tikhie pesni* [Quiet Songs], to intuit the presence of a "secretive soul" (Blok) – all the more so because the volume was published under the pseudonym "Nik. T-o" (another rebus to be deciphered by the reader, the "answer" to which discloses the name by which Odysseus had identified himself to the cyclops Polyphemus). This combination of two unattractive unknowns ensured an almost complete dearth of attention.

Annenskii embarked on his next offering of verse to a wider public during 1909, when he became closely associated with S.K. Makovskii, editor of the projected journal *Apollon*, in connection with which it had also been planned to establish a publishing house. In the event, Annenskii's second collection, *Kiparisovyi larets* (*The Cypress Chest*) was published by Moscow publishers Grif four months after Annenskii's death. Coloured by the legend of the author's sudden demise on the steps of the Tsarskoe Selo station, it became a *sui generis* textbook for poets of the next generation (Anna Akhmatova, Osip Mandel'shtam, Boris Pasternak and many others). This time readers were struck by "astounding sincerity" (V. Briusov), "a drama enacted in poetry" (V. Khodasevich), "the energy of pity" (V. Ivanov), and insight into "the darkest and most inaccessible recesses of the human soul" (N. Gumilev). The combination of analytical psychologism with grotesque irony, unambiguous moralism with the microscopic dissection of aesthetic experience, and an interchangeability of stylistic masks with the indelible imprint of individuality, made Annenskii an authoritative model for several generations of 20th-century poets.

Annenskii was the author of four verse dramas on subjects from Greek mythology: *Melanippa-Filosof* [Melanippa the Philosopher], *Tsar' Iksion*, *Laodamiia*, and *Famira-Kifared* [Thamyras Cytharoede]. The last of these was memorably staged by A. Tairov in a production at the Moscow Kamernyi Theatre in 1916.

The 1990s have seen a growth of interest in the legacy of Annenskii and a steadily increasing recognition of his fundamental role in shaping the general complexion of 20th-century Russian poetry.

ROMAN TIMENCHIK

The Cypress Chest

Kiparisovyi larets

Poetry collection, 1910

Published in 1910, a few months after the poet's death, *The Cypress Chest*, together with Blok's "third book" sets the seal on Russian Symbolism: its hundred poems, carefully arranged in three cycles, not only represent the best of Annenskii's later lyrics (from 1904 to 1909), but the perfection of the urban, Verlainean and Mallarméan sensitivity and musicality that Annenskii brought to the Russian language. Many poems anticipate the cosmopolitan craftsmanship of the Acmeists and a few (such as "Trilistnik shutochnyi" ("The Joke Trefoil")) anticipate the Futurists' verbal experimentation.

The book is only Annenskii's second, and its form may not be exactly as he intended, for a day before his death he gave his son,

Valentin Krivich, a plan and instructions, according to which the poems were taken from the exercise books Annenskii kept in a cypress-wood box. But the choice from among Annenskii's many variants and the final order of the poems may have been decided by Krivich.

Poems are arranged thematically and formally, not chronologically; most of the book consists of 25 "trefoils" each of three poems based on a central motif – a location (a Verlainean park or railway station), a season (autumn), or an emotion (sentimental, doomed, mourning). The two other sections of *The Cypress Chest* are "Skladni", ("Hinged Icons", i.e. pairs, not triplets of poems, while single poems are gathered under the heading of "Razmetannye listy" ["Scattered Leaves"]). Anguish (*toska*) is a key word, in fact a genre, in Annenskii's mature work. These are poems in which the impossibility of union or happiness or communication is divined in a nocturnal or crepuscular static world of sounds and sights. The imagery of separation may be sexual or existential; it can be the bow and violin locked up apart in the black-lined violin case ("Smychok i struny" ("The Bow and the Strings")), or two sails on one boat. Annenskii's anguish is a tantalizing proximity, just short of contact, the beloved or the numinous. The force behind this suffering is often seen as a demonic musician, an organ-grinder or a violinist, producing music out of the agony of short-lived contact (whether of bow on strings or the organ's pipes and pins); in other poems the universal force is a watchmaker or clockwork mechanism driving a pendulum. The rich sensuality of Annenskii's imagery – autumnal parks, bejewelled starry nights – contrasts with an appalling starkness, which Annenskii evokes by a wholly new use of what the Chinese call "empty words", pronouns such as "that" and "this". These he raises to the level of title or rhyme words, creating a powerful sense of both anguish and meaninglessness, such as in the bow's call to the violin "Ty ta li, ta li" (Are you the same, the same?).

Apart from the influence of Verlaine in Annenskii's evocative phonetic line, the laconic dialogue between disillusioned spectral lovers, the "sentimental colloquia" in frozen parks, there is a strong streak of the St Petersburg novelists' dreamers and nightmares. Annenskii, appropriately in view of his sudden death on the steps of the Tsarskoe Selo station in St Petersburg, was, like Dostoevskii and Tolstoi, particularly sensitive to the horror of railway stations as places of disorientation, disappointment and dismay. The "trefoil of railway carriages" mingles the atmosphere of Baudelaire's *Les Fleurs du mal* (*The Flowers of Evil*) with that of Dostoevskii's *The Idiot*. Equally Dostoevskian (and Blokian) is the sense of the split personality: the poems "Drugomu" ("To Another") and "On i ia" ("He and I") develop the sense that we gain from *The Idiot* of the killer and the saviour (Rogozhin and Myshkin) being two aspects of one personality: in Annenskii it is the creature of fire and the creature of ice, the dreamer and the moralist locked in a fatal Jekyll-and-Hyde duality. The other influence dominant in Annenskii is that of German romanticism, particularly those minor poets whose work Schubert set to music: Wilhelm Müller's *The Organ Grinder*, the last song of *Die Winterreise*, is the key to the wintry mood as well as the imagery of *The Cypress Chest*.

Annenskii's achievement in this book as an innovator has still not been appreciated: he imported an enormous range of vocabulary hitherto outside the poetic language. Apart from the Decadents' flora of tuberoses and water-lilies and the Baudelairean and Laforguean street furniture, apart from the bald pronouns, he breaks down words into syllables, so that the full nonsense of a word like *nevozmozhno* (impossible) can be appreciated as a sequence of sounds, ve, ze, em. In the poem "Nevozmozhno" ("Impossible"), Annenskii writes: "There are words – their breath, their colour / Is just as tender and as white-alarming,", a statement of daring synaesthesia. The experimentations in "The Joke Trefoil" involve breaking words up at the end of the line to create new possibilities of rhyme, making monosyllables function outside the syntactic net so as to bring out the full absurdity of "Oh", "Yes", "No", "You", "Thou". Annenskii also uses "dog" language, the last vestige of French used in Russian to this day when addressing dogs – *tubo* (tout beau), *fil'* (file!).

Two poems in *The Cypress Chest* can be regarded as Annenskii's *art poètique*. One is "Ia liubliu" ["I love") that gives a list of his inspirations: some are Pushkinian, the echo of a furious troika in the forest; some are Decadent, "The period of languid exhaustion (*istoma*) after the flash of teasing laughter"; some are purely Symbolist: "I love everything that has neither harmony nor echo in this world." The last poem of the book, and the last that Annenskii ever wrote, defines his whole lyrical output: "Moia toska" ("My Anguish"). His *toska* is to a certain degree the eternal feminine that drew all the Russian Symbolists on and which outlives the poet. Like Blok's eternal feminine, she is tainted: "She is sexless, she has smiles for everyone / She is a liar, she has a depraved taste". But unlike Blok and Belyi, Annenskii sees her as wholly his invention, not part of any universal Christian myth: "I invented her – and still she is my vision, / I do not love her – And she is close to me, / Doubting, she is my doubt / Everywhere cheerful, she is my anguish." This Schopenhauerian subjectivity in *The Cypress Chest* combines with Annenskii's grimly Euripidean view of fate, and thus makes the poems so convincing a testimony of not just an individual poet, but of an era.

The influence of *The Cypress Chest* has yet to be explored: Osip Mandel'shtam in 1922 took one of Annenskii's titles "Posle kontserta" ("After the Concert") to write a commemorative elegy for the poet and for the whole of Russian poetry. Many of Annenskii's powerful images, e.g., starlight on water as salt on an axe, are also to be found in Mandel'shtam in a still grimmer poetic universe. The poetry of Khodasevich, Akhmatova, and Gumilev would have been far poorer were it not for the new precision and musicality that Annenskii's last poems taught them.

DONALD RAYFIELD

Mikhail Petrovich Artsybashev 1878–1927

Prose writer

Biography

Born in Dobroslavovka, Akhtyrka district of Kharkov Province, 6 November 1878. (Maternal great-grandfather was Polish statesman Tadeusz Kościuszko, 1746–1817). Attended school in Akhtyrka until the age of 16. Office work in town, 1895–97. Published earliest tales in provincial papers, 1895–98; Attended Kharkov School of Art, 1897–98. Attempted suicide, mid-1897. Married: 1) Anna Vasil'evna Kobushko in 1898 (separated 1900), one son, the émigré New York artist, Boris Artzybasheff; 2) Elena Ivanovna (surname unknown) in 1920s. Moved to St Petersburg, 1898, failed to enter Academy of Fine Art. Made living by writing humorous stories. Expelled from city for participation in demonstration, 1901. First important tale "Pasha Tumanov" (1901), accepted in St Petersburg, but banned by censor; published 1905. Contributed to the journals *Mir bozhii* and *Zhurnal dlia vsekh*, 1903–06. Literary editor of *Zhurnal dlia vsekh*, 1904. Visited Yalta for treatment for tuberculosis, 1906. Expelled from Yalta because of notorious reputation; seriously ill, but recovered, 1908. Editor of the Moscow review *Zemlia*, 1911; moved to Moscow, 1912. Published anti-Bolshevik *Zapiski pisatelia* [Notes of a Writer], 1917–18. Moved to Warsaw; became Polish citizen, 1923; active part in city's émigré community, co-editor of the anti-Bolshevik newspaper *Za svobodu!*. Financial problems and failing health from 1924. Died in Warsaw, 3 March, 1927.

Publications

Collected Editions

Sobranie sochinenii, 10 vols. St Petersburg and Moscow, 1905–17.
Rasskazy, 2 vols. St Petersburg, 1908–09.
Etiudy [Etudes]. St Petersburg, 1910.
Mstitel': sbornik rasskazov [The Avenger: A Collection of Short Stories]. Munich and Leipzig, Müller, 1913.
Sobranie sochinenii, 3 vols. Moscow, 1994.

Fiction

Smert' Ivana Lande [The Death of Ivan Lande]. 1904.
Milliony. 1908; translated as *The Millionaire*, by Percy Pinkerton, London, Martin Secker, and New York, B.W. Huebsch, 1915.
Sanin. Nice, 1909; reprinted Letchworth, Bradda, 1969; translated as *Sanine*, by Percy Pinkerton, London, Martin Secker, 1914; "Sanin" (excerpt), in *An Anthology of Russian Neo-Realism*, edited by Nicholas Luker, Ann Arbor, Ardis, 1982, 217–31.
U poslednei cherty. Munich and Leipzig, Müller, 1910–12; translated as *Breaking-Point*, by Percy Pinkerton, London, Martin Secker, and New York, B.W. Huebsch, 1915.
Tales of the Revolution, translated by Percy Pinkerton, London, Martin Secker, and New York, B.W. Huebsch, 1917.

Plays

Revnost', in *Zemlia*, 12 (1913); translated as "Jealousy", in *Jealousy, Enemies, The Law of the Savage* [no translator named], New York, Boni and Liveright, 1923.
Voina, in *Al'manakh "Voina"*, Moscow, 1914; translated as *War*, by Thomas Seltzer, New York, Knopf, 1916; also by Percy Pinkerton and Ivan Ohzol, London, Grant Richards, 1918.
Zakon dikaria. 1915; translated as "The Law of the Savage", in *Jealousy, Enemies, The Law of the Savage* [no translator named], New York, Boni and Liveright, 1923.
Vragi, in *Zemlia*, 19 (1917); translated as "Enemies", in *Jealousy, Enemies, The Law of the Savage* [no translator named], New York, Boni and Liveright, 1923.
D'iavol [The Devil]. Warsaw, Izdanie knizhnago sklada, 1925; Letchworth, Prideaux Press, 1977.

Critical Studies

"M. Artsybashev", by Kornei Chukovskii, in *Ot Chekhova do nashikh dnei: Literaturnye portrety, kharakteristiki*, 2nd edition, St Petersburg, 1908, 114–28.
Neugasimaia lampada: sbornik statei v pamiat' M.P. Artsybasheva. Warsaw, Edinenie, 1928.
"Izdaleka", by Maksim Gor'kii, in *Nesobrannye literaturno-kriticheskie stat'i*, Moscow, 1941, 427–35.
"Mikhail Artsybashev in the Criticism of Zinaida Gippius", by Temira Pachmuss, *Slavonic and East European Review*, 44 (1965–66), 76–87.
"M.P. Arcybašev's Roman 'Sanin'. Zur Aktualitat eines vergessenen Skandals", by Sigrid Nolda, *Zeitschrift fur Slavische Philologie*, 43 (1983), 387–99.
"A Vegetarian's Nightmare: Artsybashev's *Krov'*", by Nicholas Luker, *New Zealand Slavonic Journal* (1985), 89–104.
In Defence of a Reputation: Essays on the Early Prose of Mikhail Artsybashev, by Nicholas Luker, Nottingham, Astra Press, 1990.
"'Wild Justice': Mikhail Artsybashev's *Mstitel'* Collection (1913)", by Nicholas Luker, *New Zealand Slavonic Journal* (1993), 63–83.

Bibliography

Mikhail Artsybashev: A Comprehensive Bibliography, by Sally O'Dell and N.J.L. Luker, Nottingham, Astra Press, 1983.

Mikhail Artsybashev's short life began and ended in obscurity. But during it, thanks to his sensational novel *Sanin*, he achieved in his way a reputation unequalled by any writer of his time. Whether his readers agreed or disagreed with what his work advocated, all were impassioned by it, and the furore that it provoked echoed both within Russia and beyond her borders.

Before attending the Kharkov School of Art and while studying there, Artsybashev began to write, publishing stories in various provincial newspapers. Among them were "Iz rasskazov ofitsera" [From the Tales of an Officer] (1895), "Pod lunnym svetom" [By Moonlight] (1896), and "Dve smerti" [Two Deaths] (1898), pieces reflecting events of his youth. Moreover, at the age of 16 he had begun a novel entitled *Iurii Svarozhich*, the basis for *Sanin*.

Artsybashev's move to St Petersburg in 1898 proved decisive. He initially made a living by writing humorous pieces for cheap newspapers. In 1901 his important tale "Pasha Tumanov" was accepted by the prestigious *Russkoe bogatstvo* but then banned and not published until 1905. Its schoolboy hero, fearing expulsion, begs his headmaster for a reprieve, and when refused it, shoots him point-blank. Highly topical at the time, the story demonstrated the need for reform of the ultra-conservative education system that failed to equip its pupils for real life. It was followed by "Kupriian" (1902), the story of a village horse-thief, which portrays the poverty and violence endemic to Russian peasant life; and by the grim "Podpraporshchik Gololobov" [Sub-Ensign Gololobov] (1902), which examines the phenomenon of suicide, a motif common in Artsybashev's later work. "Smekh" [Laughter] (1903), set in an asylum, also features instability and emphasizes the inexorable nature of death. The finely-crafted "Krov'" [Blood] (1903), stands apart: a forceful vegetarian *pièce à thèse*, it condemns hunting and the slaughter of animals for meat. "Bunt" [The Revolt] (1904), examines the serious issue of prostitution, its heroine rebelling against her prostitute's existence and the class-ridden society that forced her onto the street. Apparently autobiographical, "Zhena" [The Wife] (1904), reveals the constraints of marriage and family responsibility. The pictorial quality of its nature descriptions recalls that painting was Artsybashev's first love. By contrast, "Uzhas" [Horror] (1905), tells of rape and murder, presenting a chilling picture of bestiality. These stories, published in Artsybashev's first collection in 1905 (further editions came in 1907–08), display diverse themes and treatments. Though dissimilar in subject-matter, several emphasize the gulf between aspiration and reality, stressing the disenchantment caused when hopes are dashed. Despite their focus on death, Artsybashev affirms the joy of life in a natural world filled with colour and beauty.

His first significant long work, *Smert' Ivana Lande* [The Death of Ivan Lande] (1904), shows the influence of both Dostoevskii and Tolstoi. Its saintly hero devotes himself to the love of others, only to die abandoned by all. Two later tales of the early 1900s, "Teni utra" [Morning Shadows] (1905), and "Krovavoe piatno" [The Bloodstain] (1906), portray revolutionary activity. While the first centres on a premeditated St Petersburg assassination attempt, the second shows spontaneous revolt by provincial folk in 1905. Both demonstrate Artsybashev's awareness of the need for fundamental social change.

When *Sanin* appeared in 1909, it enjoyed a *succés de scandale* like that surrounding D.H. Lawrence's *Lady Chatterley's Lover* 50 years later. Regarded in general terms as highly suggestive, the novel was considered unashamedly pornographic in places. Set in a provincial town (perhaps Artsybashev's Akhtyrka), it shows Vladimir Sanin's effect on his family and their acquaintances when he returns home after several years' absence. During his five-month stay, he acts as a catalyst on people around him: he saves his pregnant sister from suicide; publicly humiliates an officer who then shoots himself; virtually rapes an attractive schoolmistress; then, catching a train, disappears.

Unfortunately, the novel's appearance during the immense vogue enjoyed by erotic writing after the failure of the 1905 Revolution resulted in its automatic inclusion in that category, even though, as Artsybashev asserted, it had been submitted for publication in 1903. He thus fell victim to socio-political circumstance, for when the work appeared, it was seen as exemplifying a contemporary phenomenon.

Sanin's behaviour demonstrates Artsybashev's conviction that man is no longer true to his essential self because he is constrained by empty conventions and false priorities. Serving as the author's mouthpiece, he is a preceptive figure who considers it his duty to become involved in his fellow-men's lives and to demonstrate his *Weltanschauung* to them. The assumption that Sanin derives from Nietzsche's *Übermensch* (superman) uently in criticism of Artsybashev. But the author denied any influence, revealing instead his closeness to Max Stirner (1806–56), the German individualist anarchist philosopher and author of *Der Einzige und sein Eigentum* (1844). Believing that modern man should supplant Christianity with supreme love of his unique self, Stirner's self-willed egoist denies any being higher than himself, considering himself the God of all that lives in a world where God has given way to man. However great Sanin's desire to propagandize his fellow-men, they fail to emulate him, and finding their society constrictive, he quits it. Artsybashev's vigorous hero who leaps off the moving train into splendid isolation at the close is a descendant of Stirner's "king of the world", a defiantly egoistic God-man who acknowledges no authority save his own unique will.

While the years 1908 and 1909 found Artsybashev busy with editorial work, 1908 witnessed the appearance of *Chelovecheskaia volna* [The Human Wave], a reflection of the 1905 Potemkin mutiny, and *Milliony* (*The Millionaire*), a revelation of the loneliness of the rich. The year 1910 brought the publication of his rare collection *Etiudy* [Etudes], prose pieces including "Schast'e" [Happiness], "Na belom snegu" [On the White Snow] and "Doktor" [The Doctor]. Several again mirror the unrest of 1905, but others examine hallucination, a pogrom and, strangely, an execution by electric chair. *U poslednei cherty* (*Breaking-Point*), an unsuccessful novel that returns to the suicide motif and affirms death as the sole reality was published 1910–12. Most critics considered it merely a continuation of his earlier work.

Though 1913 brought the publication in Germany of Artsybashev's collection *Mstitel'* [The Avenger] – stories variously concerned with vengeance – the years 1913–16 were devoted chiefly to drama. While in many ways his plays restated themes of his prose, they did not pass unnoticed. His first, *Revnost'* (*Jealousy*) created a literary storm, while those that followed were sensations too: *Voina* (*War*), whose performance was banned; *Zakon dikaria* (*The Law of the Savage*) and *Vragi* (*Enemies*). Apart from *Voina*, which reflects Russia's involvement in World War I, these dramas examine the social roles of men and women, their psychological intensity and sexual explicitness recalling Wedekind, Strindberg, and Ibsen.

A ten-volume edition of Artsybashev's works was completed in 1917, while the following year brought the writing of his only purely philosophical piece, *Vechnyi mirazh* [The Eternal Mirage], published in Berlin in 1922. The "mirage" is man's quest for happiness, which to Artsybashev is futile, for the "better future" is an eternally receding mirage. Instead, he advocates love for the "suffering man of our today ... with all his weaknesses". Strangely, this affirmation of humanity is countered by one of his last works, the "tragic farce" verse play

D'iavol [The Devil], completed in 1921. Here the Devil triumphs, proclaiming at the close that "Evil is the ... only eternal master!"

Artsybashev's work displays a wide variety of approaches and treatments that indicates a versatility not generally associated with the author of *Sanin*. It contradicts his notorious reputation as an apolitical author preoccupied exclusively with hedonism and sexual gratification. Much of it demonstrates his concern for the well-being of Russian society and his indignation at the injustice that bedevils it. Though more persuasively expressed by his 19th-century predecessors, such humanitarian preoccupations set Artsybashev firmly in the mainstream of the Russian prose tradition.

NICHOLAS LUKER

Arzhak *see* Daniel'

Nikolai Nikolaevich Aseev 1889–1963

Poet and critic

Biography

Born in Lgov, Kurskaia guberniia, 10 July 1889. Attended Kursk technical school, until 1907; Moscow Institute of Commerce also attending lectures at philological faculty of Moscow University, 1908–10. With several young poets founded the group Lirika, 1914; left it (together with Sergei Bobrov and Boris Pasternak) for the Futurist Tsentrifuga group, 1914. Served in the army, 1915 and 1917. Married: Oksana Mikhailovna Siniakova in 1917. Lived in Vladivostok, then Chita where he joined the avant-garde group Tvorchestvo, 1917–22. Returned to Moscow and joined Maiakovskii in creating the Left Front in Literature (LEF). Member of the organizational committee of 1st Soviet Writers' Congress, 1934; secretary of the Soviet Writers' Union. Among first group of writers decorated with orders, 1939. Recipient: Stalin Prize for the narrative poem *Maiakovskii nachinaetsia* [Maiakovskii Begins], 1940. Died in Moscow, 16 July 1963.

Publications

Collected Editions

Sobranie stikhotvorenii, 2nd edition, 4 vols. Moscow and Leningrad, 1931–32.
Sobranie sochinenii, 5 vols. Moscow, 1963–64.
Stikhotvoreniia i poemy. Leningrad, 1967.
Izbrannoe, edited by Igor Shaitanov. Moscow, 1990.

Poetry

Nochnaia fleita [The Night Flute]. Moscow, 1914.
Zor. Khar'kov, 1914.
Letorei [Soaring of Years]. Khar'kov, 1915.
Oi konin dan okein [I Love Your Eyes]. 1916.
Oksana. Moscow, 1916.
Bomba [Bomb]. Vladivostok, 1921.
Stal'noi solovei [The Steel Nightingale], Moscow, 1922.
Liricheskoe otstuplenie [Lyrical Digression], in *Lef*, 2 (1924).
Nasha sila [Our Strength]. Moscow, 1939.
Maiakovskii nachinaetsia [Maiakovskii Begins]. Moscow, 1940.
Razdum'ia [Meditations]. Moscow, 1955.
Lad [Harmony]. Moscow, 1961.
Samye moi stikhi [My Own Verses]. 1962.

Literary Theory

Rabota nad stikhom [Work on a Verse]. Leningrad, 1929.
Zachem i komu nuzhna poeziia? [Who Needs Poetry and Why?]. Moscow, 1961.
Rodoslovnaia poezii [Genealogy of Poetry]. Moscow, 1990.

Diary

Dnevnik Poeta [A Poet's Diary]. Leningrad, 1929.

Critical Studies

Nikolai Aseev, by Dmitrii Moldavskii, Moscow and Leningrad, 1965.
Russian Futurism: A History, by Vladimir Markov, Berkeley, University of California Press, 1968.
Nikolai Aseev: Ocherk tvorchestva, by A.S. Karpov, Moscow, 1969.
Nikolai Aseev: Literaturnyi portret, by V. Mil'kov, Moscow, 1973.
Vospominaniia o Nikolae Aseeve, edited by K.M. Aseeva and O.G. Petrovskaia, Moscow, 1980.
Lirika Aseeva, by O. Smola, Moscow, 1980.
"K tvorcheskoi istorii poemi 'Maiakovskii nachinaetsia'", by A.M. Krukova, in *Literaturnoe nasledstvo*, 93, Moscow, 1983.
V sodruzhestve svetil: poeziia Nikolaia Aseeva, by Igor Shaitanov, Moscow, 1985.

"*Oksana*: stikhi 1912–16 godov", by Boris Pasternak, in his *Sobranie sochinenii*, vol. 4, Moscow, 1991.

Bibliography
Russkie sovetskie pisateli. Poeti: bibliograficheskii ukazatel', vol. 2 (Aseev-Bednyi), by N.G. Zakharenko, V.V. Serebriakova, and V.F. Sulimova, Moscow, 1978.

Nikolai Aseev's first publication was in *Vesna*, in 1909. It was at the editorial office of this cheap literary journal, publishing mainly young poets, that in 1907 or 1908 Aseev met Sergei Bobrov and Boris Pasternak whose friendship he enjoyed and whose literary views he shared for the next five years. They all moved from a Symbolist youth to a radical experiment announced by many groups, proliferating under the name of Russian Futurism. Its heyday fell in the last pre-war spring, in 1914. Aseev's evolution from early romantic mysticism to the "resurrection of the word", undertaken by the Futurists, is reflected in his first book-titles: *Nochnaia fleita* [The Night Flute]; *Zor*; *Letorei* [Soaring of Years] (co-authorship with G. Petnikov); *Oi konin dan okein* (in gypsy language: "I Love Your Eyes"). His next book of poems, *Bomba* [Bomb], was to come out only five years later in Vladivostok, and it assimilated the experience of war and revolution. Aseev returned to Moscow at Maiakovskii's invitation. The two poets first met in 1914 and became friends, united by their whole-hearted acceptance of the revolution and inspired by its Utopian ideas. From then on they worked together in *Lef* and *Novyi Lef* – journals of the revolutionary avant-garde. Aseev's role in literature, though, was never restricted to group activities; after his return to Moscow he wrote criticism for the most influential periodicals, *Pechat' i revolutsiia* and *Krasnaia nov'*, and he was a member of the writers' press, *Krug*. After Maiakovskii's death Aseev considered himself a successor to the former's line in literature, which he unswervingly defended in his speech at the First Congress of the Writers' Union. Aseev's poetic output was considerable: in the years after the revolution he published more than 70 books of verse, including three sets of Collected Works. Aseev was a professional critic and in his youth an ambitious theoretician of poetry.

Born in the very heart of Russia, where every local name was a reminder of a national past steeped in folk tradition, Aseev acknowledged in his later autobiography that his first lessons had been taken "from the old chronicles, from the archaic *orlovsko-kurskii* mode of speech, so superbly mastered by my grandfather". He later came to realize the poetic value of these early impressions. With the foundation of the Tsentrifuga group, the young rebels (Aseev among them) declared war on Symbolism. Around that time Aseev met Khlebnikov and subsequently developed a taste for rare words. When accused of excessive neologisms, he proudly claimed that his vocabulary was based on old Russian. To words artificially coined, he preferred those once forgotten and now resurrected with a new poetic identity.

The key-term of the poetic theory he endorsed was the "word-"or "sound-image" (*slovo-* or *zvuko-obraz*). In accordance with this, the poetic ear had to be tuned to rough consonant sounds intensely alliterated through the line. The intonation contour was to be modelled on speech-patterns, as opposed to the Symbolist musical tone with its semantic evanescence. This word-image technique allowed the poet to create a rough texture, thus revealing the primeval meaning in verbal roots. Similar in sound, these were held to possess semantic affiliations too. The second of Aseev's books bore a programmatic title – *Zor*. The word does not exist, but it is immediately provocative: it is as if an idea is just taking shape, freshly touched by sound. Semantic variety cannot be ruled out; the root "zor" might develop either into the word *zor'ka* (sunrise) or into *razzor* (devastation). Both (and certain other) possibilities suggest images of new life, clashing with the apprehension of war, which had recently broken out.

Zor was the first book devoted to the woman Aseev loved and later married and to whom each of his books would be dedicated ("Like all the rest – to Oksana Siniakova"). One of Aseev's finest early collections bore her name – *Oksana*. Among its 50 or so poems, most had been published before, and in 1916 were carefully selected to represent the mature poet. Aseev never cared for descriptive particulars; he did not write a lyric diary, and his emotions were not to be dissected into separate shades of feeling. His love, however, was in turn seized by autumnal grief, fear of death, and anguish at the loneliness in a world where only God's eyes watched from above. He wrote as if his was the primordial love, and described it in terms of mythic allusions and words freshly sounding. In later years, commenting on his earlier style, Aseev confessed that many of the images he used were vague, even to him, but he could do no better than to trust his sensations to the language.

Aseev's first reaction to war was an enthusiastic poetic exploration of national identity, but very soon this was replaced by grief and horror. He came to view war as waged against both humanity and nature. When the Russian front-line began to crumble in 1917, Aseev set out on a long journey from the western border of the Russian empire to its Far East. It was in Vladivostok that he began to write for newspapers in the genre that he was later to call "lyric satire" (*liricheskii fel'eton*), suggesting a counterpart to Maiakovskii's high rhetoric; both poets agreed, however, on the idea of "creating poetry" that should be socially useful. Poetry and nature had to be divested of their romantic images and put to use in industry – *Stal'noi solovei* [The Steel Nightingale] – or in political activity. Aseev was also himself susceptible to "reform"; in accordance with the *Lef* programme he had to abandon all "lyricism" as an individualistic left-over, but theoretical regulations were frequently violated by poets. Aseev too was subjected to attack when he wrote a longer poem, *Liricheskoe otstuplenie* [Lyrical Digression], the title of which can be interpreted both as a lyrical digression or a lyrical retreat. He was accused of politically retreating, especially on the grounds of the lines endlessly quoted by his opponents: "How can I become your bard, communist folk, when the time is not red-bannered but red-haired."

Seeking to establish his reputation as a true Soviet poet, Aseev made every effort to prove his sincere ideological loyalty, to repent and to atone for what his critics called "a bourgeois and Bohemian past". His concern was to voice national folk history in his poetry, to present its legendary heroic image. In response to what was "socially commissioned", he celebrated the tenth anniversary of the October Revolution with the revolutionary epic, *Semen Proskakov*, based on the authentic diary of a red partisan in the Civil War. Later Aseev pointed out that, in his epic poem, the large scale use of documentary evidence and montage as a compositional device anticipated Dos Passos's experiments in the novel. However, Aseev was always at his best when he allowed himself more lyrical freedom and was not apprehensive of critical attack on his "formalistic verse". Under these circumstances, he wrote such inspired works as "Sinie Gusary" [Blue Hussars], a poem for the centenary of the Decembrist revolt in 1825; or more personal ones, such as his verse recollections in *Maiakovskii nachinaetsia* [Maiakovskii Begins]. He continued to write about his late friend, publishing memoirs, articles, and poems.

In the 1930s, when Aseev took over Maiakovskii's mantle, his voice was too often overstrained by rhetoric and his lyrical vein was buried under the current of everyday issues. The "social commission" left no time for inspiration and thought. He wrote some fine poems during World War II in Chistopol', the town on the Kama to which he was evacuated; these were his verse letters to Oksana – about how he missed her, how distressed he was by the suffering of the people, and the squalor and dismay he witnessed on his way there. Too "pessimistic" from the official point of view, they were not to be published at that time, and only appeared much later in a small book, the last in Aseev's lifetime, and significantly titled *Samye moi stikhi* [My Own Verses]. This had been preceded by two more books of late lyrical verse, participating in the new poetic wave – *Razdum'ia* [Meditations] and *Lad* [Harmony]. Aseev's later poetry returned to the world of pure colours and nature to which it had once belonged, although his final simplicity of style and image presented a huge contrast to the Futurist vagueries of his early poems that had so memorably explored the world of Slavonic word and myth.

IGOR SHAITANOV

Viktor Petrovich Astaf'ev 1924–

Prose writer

Biography

Born near Krasnoiarsk, 1 May 1924. Son of a peasant. Orphaned as a child; later brought up by his grandmother. Started writing while in an orphanage. Worked, from the age of 17, at the local railway station, then volunteered for active service. Seriously wounded during World War II. Lived in Chusovo, Perm district, 1945. Worked at a variety of manual jobs before publishing first story in local newspaper, 1951. Continued publishing, largely in the newspaper *Chusovskoi rabochii*, 1951–55, also *Zvezda*, Perm, 1954–59. Published first book (collection of short stories), 1953; first novel 1958. Studied at the Gor'kii Literary Institute, Moscow, 1959–61. Lived in Vologda, 1969–79. Returned to Krasnoiarsk, 1980, where he currently resides. Recipient: Gor'kii Prize, 1975; USSR State Prize, 1978. Associated with Russian nationalism and anti-Semitism since glasnost.

Publications

Collected Edition

Sobranie sochinenii, 4 vols. Moscow, 1979–81.

Fiction

Do budushchei vesny [Until Next Spring]. Perm, 1953.
Taiut snega. Roman [The Snows Melt]. Perm, 1958; reprinted 1962.
"Pereval. Povest'" [The Pass], *Ural*, 5 (1959), 43–104; Sverdlovsk, 1959.
Starodub [Old Oak]. Perm, 1960.
"Zvezdopad" [Starfall], *Molodaia gvardiia*, 9 (1960), 119–43.
Vesennii ostrov. Rasskazy [Spring Island]. Perm, 1964.
Kon' s rozovoi grivoi. Rasskazy. Sverdlovsk, 1965; translated as *The Horse with the Pink Mane, and Other Siberian Stories*, by Robert Daglish, Moscow, Progress, 1970; reprinted 1978.
"Krazha" [The Theft], *Sibirskie ogni*, 8–9 (1966), 3–83, 21–85.
"Gde-to gremit voina" [Somewhere War is Raging], *Molodaia gvardiia*, 2 (1967), 3–67.
Poslednii poklon [The Last Bow]. Perm, 1968; further chapters in *Nash sovremennik*, 5–6 (1974), 15–58, 18–69; *Nash sovremennik*, 1 (1978), 3–105; *Novyi mir*, 4 (1987), 122–44; *Nash sovremennik*, 6 (1988), 3–26; published together in 2 vols, Moscow, 1989.
"Pastukh i pastushka. Sovremennaia pastoral'" [The Shepherd and Shepherdess], *Nash sovremennik*, 8 (1971), 2–70.
"Zatesi. Rasskazy", *Sever*, 11 (1971), 7–19; further stories in the cycle published in *Nash sovremennik*, 10 (1987), 49–60; *Nash sovremennik*, 6 (1993), 59–69.
"Oda russkomu ogorodu. Rasskaz" [Ode to the Russian Kitchen Garden], *Nash sovremennik*, 12 (1972), 47–72.
"Tsar'-ryba. Povestvovanie v rasskazakh" [King Fish], *Nash sovremennik*, 4–6 (1976), 3–81; 22–91; 6–78; further chapter published in *Nash sovremennik*, 8 (1990), 3–30.
"Pechal'nyi detektiv" [The Sad Detective], *Oktiabr'*, 1 (1986), 8–74.
"Liudochka", *Novyi mir*, 9 (1989), 3–27; translated by David Gillespie, in *Soviet Literature*, 8 (1990), 3–39; and by Andrew Reynolds, in *The Penguin Book of New Russian Writing: Russia's "Fleurs du mal"*, edited by Reynolds and Viktor Erofeev, Harmondsworth and New York, Penguin, 1995, 22–76.
"Prokliaty i ubity" [The Damned and the Dead], *Novyi mir*, 10–12 (1992), 60–106; 188–226; 168–246.

Plays

"Cheremukha. Drama v dvukh aktakh" [Bird Cherry], *Teatr*, 8 (1978), 127–47.

"Prosti menia. Drama v dvukh deistviiakh" [Excuse Me], *Nash sovremennik*, 5 (1980), 84–108.

Articles and Memoirs

Vsemu svoi chas [All in Good Time]. Moscow, 1985.

"Zriachii posokh" [The Sighted Staff], *Moskva*, 1–3 (1988), 3–67; 63–101; 42–106.

Critical Studies

"*Vo glubine Rossii ...*" *Kritiko-bibliograficheskii ocherk o Viktore Astaf'eve*, by A.N. Makarov, Perm, 1969.

"Povesti Viktora Astaf'eva", by Sergei Zalygin, *Znamia*, 7 (1976), 227–30.

"Viktor Astafiev: The Soviet Bard of Siberia", by N.N. Shneidman, *Russian Language Journal*, 33/114 (1979), 99–197.

Viktor Astaf'ev: Ocherk tvorchestva, by N.N. Ianovskii, Moscow, 1982.

Mig i vechnost': Razmyshleniia o tvorchestve V. Astaf'eva, by V. Kurbatov, Krasnoiarsk, 1983.

Soviet Literature in the 1980s: Decade of Transition, by N.N. Shneidman, Toronto, Toronto University Press, 1989, 108–13.

Proza V. Astaf'eva. K problemam masterstva, edited by A.F. Panteleeva, Krasnoiarsk, 1990.

Bibliography

Vitkor Petrovich Astaf'ev. Bibliograficheskii ukazatel', by I.B. Shakel', Krasnoiarsk, 1989.

As a writer Viktor Astaf'ev defies easy labelling. He has much in common with the Village Prose Writers, as he has written about the Russian village, the countryside, and the ecological dangers of industrialization, but he has also written much on World War II. His most controversial work, *Pechal'nyi detektiv* [The Sad Detective], belongs more to urban prose than to any other genre. A feature of all his writing is that it is based on his own experience, and the central character usually represents the author's own values or ideas.

Astaf'ev's first major work was his novel *Taiut snega* [The Snows Melt], and this was quickly followed by three novellas (*povesti*) that encapsulate his major concerns. "Pereval" [The Pass], is based on the author's childhood; "Zvezdopad" [Starfall] is set during World War II; *Starodub* [Old Oak] discusses man's relationship to the natural world. "Krazha" [The Theft] is also based on Astaf'ev's childhood as it is set in an orphanage in the 1930s. In 1968 he published, in book form, a series of stories, most of which had been published separately, under the collective title *Poslednii poklon* [The Last Bow], and continued to add to the cycle until 1987. This is perhaps Astaf'ev's most personal work, dedicated to his grandmother and imbued with the author's love, gratitude and, finally, guilt towards her. It also contains a panorama of village life in Siberia in the 1930s.

"Pastukh i pastushka" [The Shepherd and Shepherdess] is a doom-laden story of love during World War II, containing brutal and frank descriptions of battle (including atrocities committed by both German and Soviet troops), lyrical depiction of the relationship between Boris Kostiaev and Liusia, and a seemingly pacifist stance towards war. Kostiaev dies on his way back to Siberia, not only from physical wounds, but also from the weariness of his soul. Astaf'ev's short piece "Oda russkomu ogorodu" [Ode to the Russian Kitchen Garden] and the longer *Tsar'-ryba* [King Fish] are both devoted entirely to ecological themes. The latter, indeed, is one of the most important literary contributions to the awakening of a "green" consciousness in Russia, where man and the natural world – here the Siberian taiga – are seen as part of the same moral universe. Industrial pollution of waterways is viewed with the same moral condemnation as individual poaching. More importantly, like Valentin Rasputin's *Proshchanie s Materoi* (*Farewell to Matyora*), it shows the failure of the Soviet desire to tame nature, as the rationalist Goga Gertsev, certain that he can tame nature, is in fact drowned in the Enisei river. Gertsev is, in contrast to Akim, the man of the taiga who respects the natural world and its laws.

Astaf'ev has always been a highly individual writer who conforms to no movements or stereotypes. Nevertheless, the appearance in 1986 of *Pechal'nyi detektiv* alarmed many critics both in the Soviet Union and the west with its thoroughly negative stance. It attacks modern mores, young people, emancipated women, urban life, western ways, and offers a depressingly relentless catalogue of violence and crime against weak individuals. In the short story "Liudochka" the eponymous young girl is raped and driven to suicide not long after she has arrived in the town from the countryside. Astaf'ev seemed to be moving towards a reactionary and chauvinistic stance that sought to blame Russia's ills on outside and foreign (i.e. western) influences and their dehumanizing effect on the young. This impression was given further credence with the publication of his correspondence with the Jewish historian Natan Eidel'man, where Astaf'ev attacks the Jews as being responsible for Russia's woes (in particular the execution of Nicholas II). In the same year Astaf'ev had also published a short story depicting Georgians as corrupt, decadent and dirty, that caused the Georgian delegation at the Eighth Soviet Writers' Congress to walk out in protest. In contrast, Astaf'ev – surprisingly, in the view of many – did not sign collective letters by right-wing Russian writers deploring, among other things, Jewish and western influences in Russia, which were published in the nationalist press in 1990. As ever, his was an individual stance, and in 1993 he published in *Nash sovremennik*, a positive appraisal of the Catholic Church and Pope John Paul II, in the very same issue in which other writers lambasted them.

Moreover, unlike his other erstwhile nationalist comrade-in arms, Rasputin, Astaf'ev continues to write fiction and broaden his range of creative possibilities. He has always remained true to himself, and has retained a certain hard-edged integrity. His novel *Prokliaty i ubity* [The Damned and the Dead] is a gritty, typically uncompromising picture of war, with many naturalistic descriptions in a style the author has developed since the cathartic *Pechal'nyi detektiv*. Astaf'ev remains very much a writer who refuses to be easily categorized: he is neither a Village Prose Writer, nor a writer of "war prose", nor a writer who explores the mistakes of the recent Soviet past. At the same time, he is all of these. Capable of surprising and even shocking his reader, Astaf'ev maintains a deep lyrical sense that has produced what Eidel'man called "the best descriptions of nature for decades".

More than any other writer living in Russia today (with the possible exception of Solzhenitsyn), he is a writer who examines man as subjected to and moulded by the total Soviet experience.

DAVID GILLESPIE

Avvakum 1620–1682

Autobiographer and sermonist

Biography

Born in Grigorov, 25 November 1620. Married: Anastasia Markovna in 1638. Became deacon, Nizhnii-Novgorod, 1642; ordained priest in Lopatishchii, 1644. First trip to Moscow and acquaintance with Stefan Vonifatiev, 1647 or 1648. Archpriest in Iur'evets-Povol'zhskii; headed for Moscow at the invitation of the tsar, 1652. Arrested, 21 August 1653; first period of exile (with family) in Tobolsk. Left Tobolsk, exiled to Enisseisk in region of River Lena in Iakutsk, summer 1655. With family joined Pashkov's expedition in Dauriia. Began three years of wandering: from Enisseisk to Bratskii ostrog; moved through the Baikal region to Lake Irgen and to Lake Ingoda. Departure from the Nerchinsk Settlement, 1662. Returned to Moscow, 1664; wrote first supplication to the tsar. Family sent out of Moscow to Mezen for a year and a half while Avvakum was investigated; stripped of his rank and condemned by Church Council in Uspenskii Cathedral, 13 May 1666; interrogated for the last time before being exiled to Pustozersk in August 1666. Sent to Pafnut'ev Monastery until 30 April 1667; wrote fifth supplication to the tsar, 1669; final exile in Pustozersk, 1672/3. Composition of the *Zhitie* [Life]. Burnt at the stake after 14 years of incarceration, 1682.

Publications

Collected Editions

Pustozerskii sbornik. Avtografy sochinenii Avvakuma i Epifaniia [Pustozersk Collection ...], edited by N.S. Demkova. Leningrad, 1975.

Pamiatniki literatury drevnei Rusi: XVII vek. Kniga vtoraia [Monuments of Old Russian Literature: The 17th Century], edited by N.S. Demkova. Moscow, 1989, 351–97.

Editions

Zhitie protopopa Avvakuma, im samim napisannoe, i drugie ego sochineniia, with an introduction and commentary by N.K. Gudzii. Moscow, 1935; Moscow, 1997.

Zhitie protopopa Avvakuma, with an introduction by V.E. Gusev. Moscow, 1960.

Zhizneopisaniia Avvakuma i Epifaniia, edited by A.N. Robinson. Leningrad, 1963.

Zhitie protopopa Avvakuma. Ann Arbor, Ardis, 1982.

Translations

The Life of the Archpriest Avvakum by Himself, by Jane Harrison and Hope Mirrlees, with a preface by D.S. Mirsky. London, Hogarth Press, 1924; reprinted, 1963.

"The Life of Archpriest Avvakum by Himself", by Serge A. Zenkovsky, in his *Medieval Russia's Epics, Chronicles, and Tales*. New York, Dutton, 1963, 399–448.

Archpriest Avvakum: The Life Written by Himself, by Kenneth N. Brostrom. Ann Arbor, Michigan Slavic Publications, 1979.

Critical Studies

"K izucheniiu stilia protopopa Avvakuma, printsipov ego slovoupotrebleniia", by V.V. Vinogradov, *Trudy otdela drevnerusskoi literatury*, 14 (1958), 371–79.

Chelovek v literature drevnei Rusi, by D.S. Likhachev, Leningrad, 1970, chapter 10.

"The Archpriest Avvakum and Quirinus Kuhlmann: A Comparative Study in the Literary Baroque", by John M. Gogol, *Germano-Slavica*, 2 (1973), 35–48.

Zhitie protopopa Avvakuma (tvorcheskaia istoriia proizvedeniia), by N.S. Demkova, Leningrad, 1974.

Early Russian Literature, by John Fennell and Antony Stokes, Berkeley, University of California Press, and London, Faber, 1974, 231–49.

"The Autobiography of the Archpriest Avvakum. Structure and Function", by P. Hunt, *Ricerche slavistiche*, 22–23 (1975–76), 155–78.

"O Moskovskoi literature i protopope Avvakume", by D.S. Mirsky, in his *Uncollected Writings on Russian Literature*, edited by Gerald S. Smith, Berkeley, Berkeley Slavic Specialties, 1991, 145–55.

Bibliography

"Bibliografiia sochinenii Protopopa Avvakuma i literatura o nem 1917–1952", edited by V.I. Malyshev, in *Trudy otdela drevnerusskoi literatury*, 10 (1954), 435–48.

The son of a parish priest, Archpriest Avvakum began his career as deacon in Nizhnii-Novgorod, moving to the town of Lopatishchii in the Volga region where he was ordained priest in 1644. In 1647 he travelled to Moscow for the first time. There, in the group known as the "Zealots of Piety" who were led by Stefan Vonifat'ev and included the future Metropolitan Nikon, Avvakum found co-religionists who shared his determination to restore order to the customs, ritual and calendar of the Church.

As Archpriest, he became the outstanding leader and polemicist of the Old Believers who resisted the Church reforms of Metropolitan Nikon in 1653 and brought about the religious and social crisis known as the Schism. Avvakum gained literary greatness as the author of a remarkable autobiography, *Zhitie protopopa Avvakuma, im samim napisannoe* (*The Life of the Archpriest Avvakum by Himself*), and a series of polemical writings.

For Avvakum and his followers Nikon's reforms were unacceptable. The adoption of such features of the Greek rite as making the three-fingered sign of the cross, the introduction of a third Allelujah, and the correction of sacred texts had great significance. The reforms indicated a repudiation of the Stoglav Council of 1551, reversals for which Nikon and Tsar Alexis had no authority in the eyes of the Old Believers. Behind such revisions the Old Believers detected the presence of the Antichrist. In the framework of the theory of the Third Rome whereby Moscow, after the fall of Constantinople in 1454, became the final bastion of Orthodox Christianity before the Second Coming the reforms led to apocalyptic forebodings.

The suppression of the Old Believers by Nikon and Tsar Alexis was severe. Avvakum suffered two prolonged periods of exile in Siberia: the first period is split between an initial period in Tobolsk (1653–55), followed by a peripatetic exile with the expedition of General Pashkov in Dauriia that moved to Enisseisk and through the Baikal region to the lakes Irgen and Ingoda, all memorably described in the *Life*. In 1664 Avvakum returned to Moscow at the bidding of the Church Council where he sent the first of five petitions (*chelobitnye*) to Tsar Alexis. In 1666 the Church Council condemned the ever-defiant Avvakum. After a period of incarceration in the Pafnut'ev Monastery his exile continued in Pustozersk. It is this final period that sees the composition of the fifth and final petition to Tsar Alexis, a harrowing vision of the damnation that awaits the tsar for his betrayal of the true faith.

Apart from writing the *Life* in his exile at Pustozersk, Avvakum composed a series of homilies collected in a book as the *Kniga Besed* [Book of Conversations]. For Avvakum the sermons represent an opportunity to enter into conversation with the Apostle Paul by imitating the Saint Chrysostom. As Avvakum comments on passages from the Apostle his thoughts often return to his own plight. Whereas Avvakum's model devotes most effort to illuminating Christian precept, for Avvakum the homily is an opportunity to denounce the Nikonian Church. In the trials, abominations, and tortures of his own day Avvakum sees a direct parallel with the persecutions faced by the early Christians, affirming that his own age is as close to the Second Coming as the Age of the Apostles was to the Coming of Christ. Similarly in his work of exegesis *Kniga tolkovanii* [The Book of Interpretations] discussions often stray from their stated purpose of clarifying the Book of Isaiah. Following the traditional method of textual exegesis, Avvakum discerns foreshadowing of events of the New Testament in the Old Testament, and assserts their prophetic character. However, he is often moved to see a further third parallel extension in events of his own day. In his *Kniga oblichenii* [Book of Exposures] Avvakum enters the fray for the purity of his faith, but this time his tract is directed to his fellow prisoners in Pustozersk. The priest Fedor in discussion with his fellow exiles has uncovered certain inconsistencies in Avvakum's notions of dogma: the all-important questions of the essence of the Trinity, the conception of Christ and others are at issue. For Avvakum and his supporter Lazarus, the Trinity is tripartite, with Christ considered distinct from the Son of God. Avvakum's absolute insistence on the purity of his faith erupted in this book, disputed by Fodor in his Epistle to his son Maksim.

Completed in 1675 but banned from official publication until 1862, Avvakum's *Life* went through numerous revisions before being completed and copied by his followers in Pustozersk. The publication of the text by Fedor Bouslaev restored to Russian literature an outstanding personality, an important historical chronicler and a literary stylist of unique stature in the 17th century. The strength of his style, the amazing variety of his powers of description, the artfulness of his rhetoric, poised between thundering denunciation and a beguiling sweetness, the range of biblical quotation and the author's self-conscious creation of his own persona, make him unique in 17th-century Russian literature. If it is impossible to understand him outside the religious controversy of his time, his appeal as a personality and writer have a justifiable fascination of their own. As D.S. Mirsky pointed out, it is in his life that the fusion of rhetoric, religious conviction and personality results in something entirely new for Russian literature.

Two organizing principles clash in the structure of the *Life*: the old model of the saint's life with its emphasis on static episodes corroborating the sanctity of the hero; and the more realistic biographical approach. Oblivious to the arrogance of attesting to his own sanctity, Avvakum recounts miracles of healing which he performed; he recalls the vision of a figure that sets him on his course in life; he draws on the biblical parallels that are adduced to demonstrate the conformity of the subject with the saintly type. In his selection of materials for his *Life* Avvakum is guided by the image of the fighter that he draws of himself. Periods of relative calm, scenes of everyday life lacking conflict and moral weight are of little interest to Avvakum. The little dog that comes to him in prison and licks his wounds reminds Avvakum of the dogs who lick the wounds of Lazarus in the New Testament. What allies the *Life* to the New Testament and sets it apart from the more static Russian hagiographic tradition is the breadth of the canvas – the wide geographic range, the dynamic of detention and miraculous release, the number of figures including holy fools, widows, the sick, sympathizers, and martyrs. Avvakum regarded contemporary events as a great religious upheaval; his text is meant to bear witness to the concrete, historical catastrophe that was imminent. Even in a more secular age the urgency of his convictions is compelling.

ANDREW KAHN

B

Isaak Emmanuilovich Babel' 1894–1940

Prose writer and dramatist

Biography

Born in Odessa, Ukraine, 13 July 1894. Attended Nicholas I Commercial School, Odessa, 1905–11; Institute of Financial and Business Studies, Kiev, later in Saratov, 1911–15, graduated 1915. Served in the army, 1917–18. Married: Evgeniia Gronfein in 1919, one daughter; also one daughter by Antonina Pirozhkova. Lived in Petrograd from 1918: worked on Gor'kii's magazine *Novaia zhizn'*, 1918; editor, Ukrainian State Publishing House, 1919–20; news service correspondent with First Cavalry on the Polish campaign, 1920, and correspondent for Tiflis newspaper in Caucasus. Lived in Moscow from 1923; secretary of the village soviet at Molodenovo, 1930; out of favour in the 1930s; arrested, and manuscripts confiscated, 1939. It is now established that he was executed, 27 January 1940. Posthumously cleared of charges, 1954.

Publications

Collected Editions

Collected Stories, edited and translated by Walter Morison. New York, Criterion, 1955; Harmondsworth, Penguin, 1961; 1974.

Izbrannoe. 1957; reprinted Letchworth, Bradda, 1965.

Liubka the Cossack and Other Stories, edited and translated by Andrew R. MacAndrew. New York, Signet, 1963.

The Lonely Years 1925–29: Unpublished Stories and Private Correspondence, edited by Nathalie Babel, translated by Max Hayward and Andrew R. MacAndrew. New York, Farrar Straus and Giroux, 1964.

Zabytye rasskazy [Forgotten Stories]. Letchworth, Bradda, 1965.

Izbrannoe. Moscow, 1966.

You Must Know Everything: Stories 1915–1937, edited by Nathalie Babel, translated by Max Hayward. New York, Farrar Straus and Giroux, 1969.

Benya Krik, The Gangster, and Other Stories, edited by Avrahm Yarmolinsky. London, Vallentine Mitchell, 1971.

The Forgotten Prose, edited and translated by Nicholas Stroud. Ann Arbor, Ardis, 1978; as *Zabytyi Babel'*, Ann Arbor, Ardis, 1979.

Detstvo i drugie rasskazy [Childhood and Other Stories], edited by Efraim Sicher. Jerusalem, Biblioteka Aliia, 1979.

Chetyre rasskazy/Four Stories, edited by A.B. Murphy. Letchworth, Prideaux Press, 1981; revised edition, London, Bristol Classical Press, 1993.

Sochineniia, 2 vols. Moscow, 1991.

Collected Stories, translated by David McDuff. Harmondsworth. Penguin, 1994.

Sochineniia, 2 vols. Moscow, 1996.

Fiction

Na pole chesti [On the Field of Honour], *Lava*, 1 (1920), 10–13.

Rasskazy [Stories]. Moscow, 1924; reprinted Letchworth, Prideaux Press, 1976.

Konarmiia. Moscow and Leningrad, 1926; revised edition, 1928; *Konarmiia/Red Cavalry*, edited by Andrew Barratt, London, Bristol Classical Press, 1994; translated as *Red Cavalry*, by John Harland, London, Knopf, 1929; also translated by Walter Morison, in *Collected Stories*, 1955; by Andrew R. MacAndrew in *Liubka the Cossack and Other Stories*, 1963; and by David McDuff, in *Collected Stories*, 1994.

Bluzhdaiushchie zvezdy: rasskaz dlia kino [Wandering Stars: A Cine-Story]. Moscow, 1926; reprinted Ann Arbor, Ardis, 1972.

Istoriia moei golubiatni [The Story of My Dovecot]. Moscow and Leningrad, 1926.

Benia Krik: kinopovest', *Krasnaia nov'*, 6 (1926); translated as *Benia Krik: A Film-Novel*, by Ivor Montague and S.S. Nolbandov, London, Collets, 1935; reprinted 1984.

Korol' [The King]. Paris, 1926.

Evreiskie rasskazy [Jewish Tales]. Moscow, 1927.

Odesskie rasskazy. Moscow and Leningrad, 1931; translated as *Tales of Odessa*, by Walter Morison, in *Collected Stories*, 1955; and by David McDuff, in *Collected Stories*, 1994.

Rasskazy. Moscow, 1936.

Plays

Zakat (produced 1927). Moscow and Leningrad, 1928; reprinted Letchworth, Prideaux Press, 1976; translated as "Sunset", by Raymond Rosenthal and Mirra Ginsburg, in *Noonday*, 3 (1960).

Mariia (produced 1964). Moscow and Leningrad, 1935; reprinted Letchworth, Prideaux Press, 1976; translated as "Marya", by Michael Glenny and Harold Shukman, in *Three Soviet Plays*, edited by Glenny, Harmondsworth, Penguin,

1966; reprinted as *The Golden Age of Soviet Theatre*, Harmondsworth, Penguin, 1981.

Diaries

1920 Diary, edited by Carol J. Avins, translated by H.T. Willetts. New Haven, Yale University Press, 1995.

Critical Studies

Isaac Babel, by Richard W. Hallett, Letchworth, Bradda, 1972; New York, Ungar, 1973.

The Art of Isaac Babel, by Patricia Carden, Ithaca, Cornell University Press, 1972.

Isaac Babel, Russian Master of the Short Story, by James E. Falen, Knoxville, University of Tennessee Press, 1974.

An Investigation of Composition and Theme in Babel's Literary Cycle "Konarmija", by Ragna Grøngaard, Aarhus, Ankona, 1979.

Isaac Babel's Red Cavalry, by Carol Luplow, Ann Arbor, Ardis, 1982.

Metaphor in Babel's Short Stories, by Danuta Mendelsohn, Ann Arbor, Ardis, 1982.

"Art as Metaphor, Epiphany, and Aesthetic Statement: The Short Stories of Babel", by Efraim Sicher, *Modern Language Review*, 77/2 (1982), 387–96.

"The Road to a Red Cavalry: Myth and Mythology in the Works of Babel", by Efraim Sicher, *Slavonic and East European Review*, 60 (1982), 528–46.

The Place of Space in Narration: A Semiotic Approach to the Problem of Literary Space, with an Analysis of the Role of Space in Isaak Babel's Konarmija, by J.J. van Baak, Amsterdam, Rodopi, 1983.

"Isaac Babel and Violence", by Peter Stine, *Modern Fiction Studies*, 30 (1984), 237–55.

Style and Structure in the Prose of Isaak Babel, by Efraim Sicher, Columbus, Ohio, Slavica, 1986 (includes bibliography, 137–69).

Isaac Babel, by Milton Ehre, Boston, Twayne, 1986.

Isaac Babel, edited by Harold Bloom, New York, Chelsea House, 1987.

The Field of Honour, by Christopher Luck, Birmingham, Birmingham Slavonic Monographs, 1987.

Vospominaniia o Babele, Moscow, 1989.

Procedures of Montage in Isaak Babel's Red Cavalry, by Marc Schreurs, Amsterdam, Rodopi, 1989.

"Isaak Babel and His Film Work", by Jerry Heil, *Russian Literature*, 27 (1990), 289–416.

"A Poetic Inversion: The Non-Dialogic Aspect in Isaac Babel's *Red Cavalry*", by David K. Danow, *Modern Language Review*, 86/4 (1991), 939–53.

"Konarmiia" Isaaka Babelia, by G.A. Belaia *et al.*, Moscow, 1993.

"The Trials of Isaac: A Brief Life", by Efraim Sicher, *Canadian Slavonic Papers*, 36/1–2 (1994), 7–42 (part of Babel' centenary special issue).

Babel'/Babel, by A.K. Zholkovskii and M.B. Iampol'skii, Moscow, 1994.

Figures of War and Fields of Honour: Isaak Babel's Red Cavalry, by Christopher Luck, Keele, Keele University Press, 1995.

The KGB's Literary Archive, by Vitaly Shentalinsky, translated by John Crowfoot, London, Harvill Press, 1995.

Jews in Russian Literature after the October Revolution: Writers and Artists Between Hope and Apostasy, by Efraim Sicher, Cambridge, Cambridge University Press, 1995.

The Twentieth-Century Russian Novel: An Introduction, by David Gillespie, Oxford, Berg, 1996.

"Prichina smerti rasstrel". Khronika poslednikh dnei Isaaka Babelia, by S. Povartsov, Moscow, 1996.

Red Cavalry: A Critical Companion, edited by Charles Rougle, Evanston, Illinois, Northwestern University Press, 1996.

Like any artist Isaak Babel' means different things to different people, and even after many readings of his works it is still possible to gain new insights or see fresh perspectives. Who, for example, are the first-person narrators, who populate much of his work? Are they shades of the author himself? The "verbal masks" (Carden, 1972) that he creates and the fabric of *skaz* with which his work is interwoven, coupled with his predilection for ironic understatement, at times juxtaposed with the grotesque, the violent and the shocking, leave the reader not only stunned but groping for some sure sign of definitive authorial feeling.

Babel''s upbringing, his Jewish roots and changing environment, his service on various war fronts, his different post-revolutionary jobs and the trips to visit his family, who had settled in western Europe, all helped to influence and shape his work as did the turbulence of revolutionary Russia and the ensuing years of repression and fear. Yet Babel''s *modus operandi* was often to distort facts, places, and dates; even in his brief autobiography of 1926 he could not resist the false claim of a childhood spent entirely in Odessa, when in reality most of his early years between 1894 and 1905 were spent in the smaller Black Sea port of Nikolaev.

Babel''s Jewish roots and his proximity to Odessan life in his early youth engendered a short cycle of stories, known as *Odesskie rasskazy* (*Tales of Odessa*). Set in the Moldavanka, the Jewish part of Odessa, the four stories celebrate the colour and vitality of the underworld and its inhabitants through the creation of grotesque caricatures, imbued with propensities for violence and farce, whose appearance and behaviour are portrayed in lurid colours and rich imagery. The protagonist of three stories is Benia Krik (Benia the Yell), who represents the opposite of the archetypal face of oppressed Judaism. He is all-conquering and violent and encapsulates a celebration of the Jewish exercise of power: attributes that in the shape of Cossack soldiers of the First Cavalry Army both attracted the sickened Babel''s other most significant central persona, Liutov, in *Konarmiia* (*Red Cavalry*).

Many of the stories of this latter cycle, the most celebrated of Babel''s literary output, appeared concurrently with *Tales of Odessa*, but they contrast with them in many ways. The controlled, laconic narration of the ironically named Liutov, the "Fierce one", reflects a Babel' of a different mood, who places at the sentient centre of his war epic a Jew "with spectacles on his nose and autumn in his heart". Parallels between the two cycles can nevertheless be discerned, not least of which is the assault conducted in both on traditional moral and cultural values by respectively the Cossacks and Benia and his henchmen.

In 1911 with the "numerus clausus" preventing his entering the University of Odessa, Babel' was attracted, when he went to study in Kiev, to Tolstoism, with its message of non-resistance to evil and the brotherhood of man. Unsurprisingly, the violence and anti-Semitic hatred of the pogroms that he had witnessed as a child had bred in him feelings of repugnance for brutality and its perpetrators, yet his main narrators also express admiration for these same people and their ability to act with singularity of purpose, and it is this underlying tension, one of a number, which informs his work. Not long after graduating in 1915 from the Institute of Financial and Business Studies Babel' went to St Petersburg (then Petrograd) to seek literary advancement, unsuccessfully at first, until he met Gor'kii who became his literary mentor. Two of his stories were published in Gor'kii's *Letopis'* in November 1916.

Babel''s six-year sojourn "among the people" on Gor'kii's advice, from 1917 to 1923 coincided with the Revolution and its immediate aftermath. In 1917, as part of his quest for experience of life, he volunteered to serve at the Romanian front, where he fell ill with malaria and was sent back to Odessa. On recovering he is said to have returned to Petrograd to serve with the Cheka, the counter-revolutionary organ. Babel''s attitude to the revolution is indicated in "Dnevnik" [The Diary], six essays in which he expresses concern for the under-privileged and handicapped, suffering under a regime that prided itself on its humanity. His focus thus was an oblique one and his interests were seen to be the "little man" and social conditions, rather than the revolution's central issues or main protagonists.

From 1918 to 1919 Babel' worked for the People's Commissariat of Education (Narkompros), returning to Odessa in 1919 to marry Evgeniia Gronfein, an artistic girl whom he had met in his Kiev days. His earlier bout of military service had only served, however, to make him seek out fresh experience of war and he attached himself first to the Northern Army, opposing Iudenich's anti-Bolshevik forces, and then to the First Cavalry Army under Budennyi, whose mission was to drive the Poles from the Ukraine. While he was serving there in 1920 as a war correspondent, his first short cycle of war stories, *Na pole chesti* [On the Field of Honour], was published. After his military service, and in poor health, Babel' left for the Caucasus, where he worked as a correspondent for the journal *Zaria vostoka*; there he practised the different registers of his *skaz* writing and began his *Red Cavalry* stories.

While Babel' is best known for his short stories, he also wrote film scripts and two plays. The first play *Zakat* (*Sunset*) ran for only a few performances, yet its impact was undeniable. At a time when pressure was being exerted on writers by Stalin to look ahead to future hopes and achievements, Babel', in his play's treatment of the pre-revolutionary Moldavanka and the removal of a tyrannical patriarch in the person of Mendel Krik, was seen to distance himself from revolutionary aspirations and possibly to hint obliquely at anti-Stalinism. The setting of Babel''s second play *Mariia* might at least have gained him some approval, for it is post-revolutionary Petrograd; however, his work was readily condemned by the authorities. Their litany of complaints ranged from the play's lack of socialist realism and its preoccupation with sex and violence, to its ethos of fear and suffering and its portrayal of members of the old order grappling with the harsh climes of the new. Babel' did not persist with his writing for the stage. However, the political climate was also ill-suited to his prose-writing themes.

As Stalin's paranoia intensified in the 1930s, so Babel''s published literary output diminished. His celebrated 1934 speech to the First Congress of Soviet Writers, in which he asserted his mastery of the genre of silence and his regret at no longer having the right to write badly, masked, through ironic humour and self-deprecation, his cry of anguish. Sources speak nevertheless of Babel' working on two novels at this time. "Kolyvushka" (1930) and "Gapa Guzhva" (1931) may well be the surviving chapters of a portrayal of the effects of Soviet collectivization, as "Evreika" [The Jewess] also points to the planning of a saga of Jewish family life under communism. The few other published stories of this period continue Babel''s earlier themes – for example, the harking back to an Odessan childhood – or point up the tensions of the old world trying to come to terms with the new.

Babel''s fame was at its height in the late 1920s and early 1930s; he was regarded as a considerable literary talent, a superb stylist whose prose combined the grotesque and the poignant in new and shocking ways. But just as General Budennyi had voiced his displeasure at the contents of *Red Cavalry* in 1924, so in the 1930s did the Soviet establishment grow increasingly displeased with Babel'. His "bol' za cheloveka" ("suffering for his fellow man"), his family ties with the west, his Jewishness, his focus on the grotesque and the violent, his stance *vis-à-vis* things Soviet and his unwillingness to compromise by breaking his avowed literary silence, all brought him into disfavour.

Shklovskii's comment in 1937, when Babel' was working on some film scripts, is perhaps a fitting and poignant epitaph to a writer whose literary output, like that of so many of his contemporaries, was stunted by the regime in which he lived: "Babel' was walking quietly and dejectedly ... He appeared very tired, spoke softly and simply could not tie up and finish whatever it was he wanted to say." Babel''s own creative quest was, at least, in part unfulfilled, for he was arrested on 15 May 1939 and, we have learnt subsequently from a note with the KGB transcript of his interrogation, he was shot soon after his arrest.

CHRISTOPHER LUCK

Red Cavalry

Konarmiia

Short-story cycle, 1926

In 1916 Maksim Gor'kii adjured the young Babel' to go out and seek life among the people with the result that the author's best-known work *Red Cavalry* ensued some seven or more years later. Babel''s masterpiece portrays the testing of a Jewish intellectual, middle class persona, in the shape of his central narrator Liutov, within a milieu of war. Here life and death are starkly juxtaposed and social acceptability among larger-than-life Cossack men of machismo is scarcely to be won, without at least some compromising of values, self-belief and ensuing self-condemnation.

In 1920, while serving as a war correspondent for the journal *Krasnyi kavalerist* in Budennyi's First Cavalry regiment in southern Poland, Babel' wrote a diary that contains a series of explicit personal observations on a variety of events captured in a private shorthand of a few words. The welter of material that fell into his field of vision is recorded in incoherent fashion but it possesses a rawness and spontaneity that contrasts with the polish of his finished work, *Red Cavalry*. Of the cycle's 35 stories, however, only 13 have direct links with Babel''s diary, a substantial part of which has been lost. Moreover the filtering of this raw material into the final product reveals a process of authorial distortion that reflects a similar approach by Babel' in his fashioning of his central protagonist and narrator, Liutov. He tantalizes the reader, searching for a glimpse of the author himself through a portrayal of Liutov's traits and circumstances, which in turn both link and distance the work's sentient centre with and from its creator.

Babel''s *Red Cavalry* stories started to appear in 1923, yet they were not his first attempt at writing on the theme of war. In 1920 he had already published a short cycle entitled *Na pole chesti*, based on the German front in World War I. These early stories include themes that were to be developed in his second cycle, such as the blurring of the roles of hero and villain, of oppressor and victim, and the stark delineation of the personal dilemmas and suffering that war evokes. *Red Cavalry* was well received; as the bulk of the stories emerged in groups between 1923 and 1925, Babel''s fame grew, and by the late 1920s and early 1930s he was regarded as a considerable literary talent.

The establishment voiced its displeasure, however. Babel''s "anxiety for his fellow man", a theme that recurs throughout his works, brought him into disfavour with Soviet critics of the day, who complained of an author content to celebrate the negative aspects of life in the immediate post-revolutionary years. General Budennyi, too, condemned *Red Cavalry*, seeing it not as a celebration of the Cossack ethos but as a slur against his army, accusing Babel' of cultural corruption and political ignorance.

Babel''s portrayal of war in *Red Cavalry* is indeed a negative one. Unlike his first cycle of stories (three of the four were adaptations from a French source) Babel''s second cycle was written from firsthand experience of violence and death and it is these impressions that inform the brutalized perspective of his Cossack narrators and the angst-ridden perception of Liutov ("fierce one"). While Babel' transfers a sense of awe for Cossack heroes and a nostalgic affection for his Jewish roots to his primary narrator, he also imbues him with a revulsion for the brutality of the former and a palpable loathing for the degradation in which the Jews live. Babel' relentlessly pursues the psyche of the heroes and victims of war and, just as he blurs historical details and points to the timelessness of man's tyranny in inflicting violence upon his fellows, so do his heroes and victims merge, each forming part of the other.

A distinctive feature of *Red Cavalry* is the language that the author employs. Babel''s work embodies a richness of imagery, a proliferation of tropes, which link him with the ornamental trends of the 1920s. But these are never mere ornaments to some supposed non-metaphorical language; they lie at the very heart of his use of language and are central to depicting the respective psyches of each of his narrators and protagonists. The aspirations and fallibilities of his central persona, of Cossacks like Sidorov, Balmashov, Konkin or Pavlichenko, of characters like the aged, bemused, Jewish shopkeeper, Gedali, or the itinerant, heretical artist, Apolek, become apparent through the tropes formed about them or "by" them.

It is the sequential linking of the primary narrator's tropes, however, which distinguishes them from those of others in the cycle. One trope begets another and leads into a third. Such sequences not only arrest and shock, but also link one story to another in subtle ways, binding the cycle into a unified whole that is at first not apparent. Epithets depicting Liutov's changing moods recur; insight and ambivalence result from the interplay of metaphorical nuances, such as the use of "to creep" (*polzti*) in "Smert' Dolgushova" ("The Death of Dolgushov"), where the verb initially portrays the passage of the doomed Dolgushov's entrails over his knees, and subsequently the spread of the narrator's fear as he is threatened with death for not administering the *coup de grâce* to the hapless Dolgushov. The verb's recurrence links the circumstances of the two men and exemplifies the blurring of their respective roles; both are simultaneously oppressor and victim, persecutor and persecuted.

Babel''s portrayal of war is indeed largely visual, yet a relative lack of explicitly violent or militaristic imagery reflects his philosophy of "understatement", of forcing his reader to forge a network of interactions from the language employed and then to select appropriate associations and connotations. In his range of synaesthetic metaphors he embodies the fusion of unlike generic entities with startling results. While auditory imagery is used to create crescendos of suspense, there is only occasional recourse to the senses of smell, taste, and touch.

Babel''s primary narrator, moreover, is an agent of distortion; he more usually stamps his mood on nature, his perspective on the surroundings than vice-versa. The heavy lenses of his emblematic spectacles filter his inner moods to us as they focus on events and circumstances around him. Liutov indeed represents the sufferings of all victim-protagonists and he shares too in their fleeting, short-lived triumphs. A part of each subsidiary character resides in him. But it is the heroic stoicism of victims like Grishchuk, his driver, with which he most closely identifies. The eventual omission of Grishchuk's story from *Red Cavalry* renders him an enigmatic figure in the cycle. Yet the figures of Grishchuk and Liutov merge and interact in a revealing way when the diary entries and eponymous story are read in conjunction with "Uchenie o tachanke" ("Discourse on the Tachanka") and "The Death of Dolgushov".

Many of *Red Cavalry*'s protagonists manifest the desire to control or subjugate their environment for their own purposes or ends, since they are motivated by a sense of insecurity or uncertainty. Liutov, however, invests his tropes with defamiliarization, a device that exposes the disorientation and sense of isolation that he feels. Babel''s prime aim is thus to disconcert, to impart to his reader the primary narrator's anxiety and uncertainty as he confronts issues of life and death, friendship and enmity, bravery and cowardice amid an environment that for the most part is repugnant to him, but which fleetingly does at least permit him some sense of personal triumph. Liutov's killing of the goose in "Moi pervyi gus'" ("My First Goose") allows him an entrée into a Cossack world that had seemed inaccessible to him and in the cycle's last line his final act of triumph is celebrated: "My dream was fulfilled. The Cossacks stopped following me and my horse with their eyes" ("Argamak"). Liutov's earlier sense of ostracism by the Cossacks (for his inability to ride a horse like them) has been overcome, but his exultation reflects a greater triumph in fact: that of his own personal survival in a world that is alien to him.

CHRISTOPHER LUCK

Tales of Odessa

Odesskie rasskazy

Short stories, 1931 (written 1921–24)

The four stories known as *Tales of Odessa* were written in the years 1921–24 and represent Babel''s ornamental writing at its most playful and exuberant. They present in hyperbolic images and bright, often lurid, colours a highly entertaining caricature of life in the Moldavanka, the Jewish ghetto of Odessa, with its shopkeepers, brokers, whores and gangsters. The stories are entitled "Korol'" ("The King"), "Kak eto delalos' v Odesse" ("How It Was Done in Odessa"), "Otets" ("The Father"), and "Liubka Kazak" ("Liubka the Cossack"), and are linked together not only by the narrator's constant search for the picturesque and the picaresque, for colour and operatic comedy, but also by some of the characters. In these early stories Babel' was, in a sense, answering the call in his own 1916–17 essay "Odessa" for literature to emerge from the shadows of northern introspection into southern sunshine. Nowhere else in his work do we find such unremittingly bright comedy, though, as in all great comic writing, there is also an occasional serious element.

In "The King", the first of the stories, we are introduced to Benia Krik, gangster and king of gangsters, who sports a chocolate jacket, cream trousers and raspberry boots, as well as a red car whose horn plays "Ridi, Pagliaccio", underlining its owner's role as part clown, part operatic hero. In this mock epic the men of the ghetto are rich and poor, potent and weak, while the women are almost all sex-starved amazons with prodigious breasts and no time for inadequate partners. Like the other stories, "The King" presents stories within stories in the manner of a folk-tale. One such tells how poor but resourceful Benia became the son-in-law of rich Zender Eikhbaum, "a man who owned sixty milk cows minus one". Slaughtering Eikhbaum's cattle to extort protection money – an uncharacteristically violent act – Benia glimpses their owner's daughter clad only in a nightgown, "and the victory of the King became his defeat". In the main part of the story Benia, presiding at the wedding of his 40-year-old sexually rapacious sister Dvoira to a timid young man he has bribed to marry her, learns that the police are planning to raid the proceedings. Before long, however, the police station is in flames, and the story ends with the fearsome Dvoira dragging her terrified husband off to the marriage bed "like a cat who, holding a mouse in its jaws, tests it gingerly with its teeth".

"How It Was Done in Odessa" is related by the old story teller Ar'e Leib, who claims some credit for making the King who he is. His advice is simple, yet not for everyone:

> Forget for a while that you have spectacles on your nose and autumn in your heart. Stop making a commotion at your desk and stammering when you're with people. Imagine for a moment that you are making a commotion in the squares and stammering on paper. You are a tiger, you are a lion. You spend the night with a Russian woman and satisfy her.

Benia, we are told, "had his way, for he was passionate, and passion rules the universe"; his exploits, however, often verge on the farcical. In this tale a council of gangsters set Benia the task of robbing a giant "Jew-and-a-Half", famous for his daring and wealth – and for the frequency with which he is robbed. In the course of the hold-up Savka, one of Benia's accomplices, shoots a miserable clerk of whom we are told "his name was Muginshtein, but by first name Iosif, the unmarried son of Aunty Pesia, the chicken trader from Seredinka Square". Devastated, Benia arranges a magnificent funeral for Muginshtein and pronounces a memorably grotesque oration before announcing that he has despatched Savka in retribution, whereupon he in turn receives an elaborate funeral.

In "The Father" we read of an ageing gangster, Froim Grach, who wants to marry off his alarmingly statuesque daughter, Basia. One candidate, the son of a rich grocer's family, proves woefully inadequate:

> At the sight of the weedy Solomonchik Kaplun she began to shuffle with her fat legs encased in a man's lace-up boots, and said to her father: "Dad - she said in a voice of thunder, look at this feeble little gent, he's got legs like a doll's, I would smother legs like that ...".

Benia comes to the rescue by marrying the amorous amazon himself (two wives seem hardly out of the ordinary in this hyperbolic cartoon world); he extracts, moreover, two thousand roubles from the Kapluns as compensation for Basia's humiliating rejection. The fourth story, "Liubka the Cossack", contains some of the same elements, although Benia Krik is absent. It tells of how the small but resourceful salesman Tsudechkis becomes the manager of Liubka's combined grain store, contraband cache, and brothel. Despite her mountainous breasts, Liubka neglects to nurse her child, who is of even more epic proportions than his natural food supply. The bold Tsudechkis ingeniously weans the child, and ends up as Liubka's righthand man.

In Babel''s *Tales of Odessa* there is none of the pathos of his *Red Cavalry* cycle or his plays. Their literariness is decidedly self-conscious, recalling to some extent both Gogol' and Leskov, in their humorous discursiveness and in their suspension of the normal rules of logic. The narrator's role is interventionist, digressive and virtuosic, employing extraordinary and colourful imagery, personification, rhythmic prose, and parallels and repetitions to create hyperbolic, often bathetic pictures of Jewish bravadoes and their exploits. There is no room here for the more familiar introspective, religious, moral or even respectable sides of Jewish life in this ritualized celebration of derring-do and sensuality. The comedy derives in part from the over-writing of trivial events or unimportant (though certainly not humble) people, the latter's grandiose speech and behaviour bearing little relationship to their circumstances. There are occasional reflective moments, as when Benia reflects on God's "mistake" in settling Jews in Russia ("for them to be tormented worse than in Hell"), rather than in, for instance, Switzerland, but the author leaves his charmingly absurd hero on the level of comic whimsy. The puppet master or cartoonist is never far from Babel''s creations, and he constantly underlines their artificiality. Realistic *Tales of Odessa* are not, but as brightly coloured baubles these entertaining mock-epic stories of a half-imaginary and certainly long-departed world occupy a distinct and lasting place in Babel''s *oeuvre* and in Russian literature as a whole.

ARNOLD MCMILLIN

Eduard Georg'evich Bagritskii 1895–1934

Poet

Biography

Born Eduard Godelevich Dziubin, in Odessa, 3 November 1895. Attended the Odessa *Realschule*, but played truant and was an unwilling trainee surveyor. Began publishing under pseudonym, 1913. Episodic existence, sailing and fishing, until 1917. Worked briefly in the militia, then volunteered for the Persian front. Responsible for provisioning a medical detachment. Returned to Odessa, 1918. Joined the Red Army as an instructor in the political section of partisan detachment, 1919; worked for the Ukrainian Press Bureau and Iugrosta. Married: Lidiia Gustavovna Suok in 1920; one son. Regular contributor of poems to the Odessa newspapers *Moriak* and *Odesskie izvestiia*, 1921. Visited Moscow, 1924–25; moved to Kuntsevo, on the outskirts of the city, 1925. Briefly a member of the Pereval group. Member of the Literary Centre of Constructivists, 1926 or 1927 to 1930. First collection of poems, *Iugo-zapad*, published in 1928. Member of the editorial board of *Literaturnaia gazeta*, 1928. Headed the poetry section of *Novyi mir*, 1930. Joined MAPP (Moscow Association of Proletarian Writers), 1930. Moved to central Moscow, housebound by illness. Died in Moscow, from chronic asthma, 16 February 1934.

Publications

Collected Editions

Odnotomnik. Stikhi [Single Volume], edited by K. Zelinskii. Moscow, 1934.
Sobranie sochinenii, edited by I. Utkin. Moscow and Leningrad, 1938.
Stikhotvoreniia i poemy, edited by E. Liubareva and S. Kovalenko. Moscow and Leningrad, 1964.
Dnevniki. Pis'ma. Stikhi. Moscow, 1964.
Izbrannoe. Moscow, 1975.
Stikhi i poemy. Moscow, 1976.

Poetry

Iugo-zapad. Stikhi [South-West]. Moscow and Leningrad, 1928; 2nd edition, 1930.
Sobolinyi sled. Stikhi [Sable Trail]. Moscow and Leningrad, 1930; 2nd edition, Moscow, 1933; 3rd edition, Moscow, 1934.
Zvezda mordvina. Stikhi [The Star Mordvina]. Moscow, 1931.
Pobediteli. Stikhi [The Victors]. Moscow and Leningrad, 1932.
Posledniaia noch'. Stikhi [The Last Night]. Moscow, 1932.
Duma pro Opanasa. Stikhi [The Song of Opanas]. Moscow, 1932; reprinted Letchworth, Prideaux Press, 1976.
Izbrannye stikhi. Moscow, 1932.
Stikhi. Moscow, 1933.

Autobiography

Sovetskie pisateli. Avtobiografii. Moscow, 1966, vol. 3, 34–43.

Letters

Letters in *Literaturnoe nasledstvo*, vol. 74. Moscow, 1965, 436–66.

Critical Studies

"Tvorcheskii put' Eduarda Bagritskogo", by D.S. Mirsky, in Bagritskii's *Al'manakh*, Moscow, 1936, 5–23.
"Eduard Bagritskii", by Andrei Siniavskii, in *Istoriia russkoi sovetskoi literatury v 3-kh tomakh*, edited by A. Dement'ev, Moscow, 1958, vol. 1, 397–420.
"V serdtse obraza", by V. Gusev, in *Navstrechu budushchemu*, by B. Galanov and A. Makarov, Moscow, 1962, 109–39.
"O dol'nike sovremennoi russkoi poezii (Statisticheskaia kharakteristika dol'nika Maiakovskogo, Bagritskogo, Akhmatovoi)", by A. Kolmogorov and A. Prokhorov, *Voprosy iazykoznaniia*, 1 (1964), 75–94.
Eduard Bagritskii. Zhizn' i tvorchestvo, by E. Liubareva, Moscow, 1964.
Poeziia Eduarda Bagritskogo, by I. Rozhdestvenskaia, Leningrad, 1967.
"Stikhotvornoe masterstvo Bagritskogo (Na materiale sbornika *Iugo-zapad*)", by A. Karpov, *Voprosy sovetskoi i zarubezhnoi literatury*, Tula, 1969, 75–100.
Sovetskaia romanticheskaia poeziia. Tikhonov, Svetlov, Bagritskii, by E. Liubareva, Moscow, 1973.
Eduard Bagritskii. Vospominaniia sovremennikov, edited by L.G. Bagritskaia, Moscow, 1973.
"Eduard Bagritsky: a Biographical Sketch with Three Unpublished Letters", by Luba Halat Kowalski, *Russian Literature Triquarterly*, 8 (1974), 472–85.
"The Path to Paradise: Recurrent Images in the Poetry of Eduard Bagritsky", by Wendy Rosslyn, *Modern Language Review*, 71/1 (1976), 97–105.
"Bagritskii's 'Duma pro Opanasa': The Poem and Its Context", by Wendy Rosslyn, *Canadian-American Slavic Studies*, 11/3 (1977), 388–405.
Lot's Wife and the Venus of Milo. Conflicting Attitudes to the Cultural Heritage in Modern Russia, by Boris Thomson, Cambridge, Cambridge University Press, 1978, 83–97.
"The Unifying Principle of Bagritsky's 'Yugo-Zapad'", by Wendy Rosslyn, *Essays in Poetics*, 4/1 (1979), 20–34.

Bibliography

"Eduard Bagritsky: A Selected Bibliography", by Luba Halat Kowalski, *Russian Literature Triquarterly*, 8 (1974), 540–42.

Eduard Bagritskii was a Romantic poet who lived out a poeticized existence close to nature, at the same times as earning a living as a professional poet, translator and editor, mostly while suffering severely from chronic asthma. The attraction of his colourful personality is attested by numerous affectionate memoirs. After early rejection of his Jewish background and systematic education, he became a street urchin and then spent his time sailing, fishing and hunting, which he later combined successfully with routine, even bureaucratic, literary activity; when obliged to live in the city he still kept birds and rare fish. Much of his poetry celebrates escape from constraint and petty bourgeois values.

He began his writing career alongside Odessa contemporaries

such as V. Kataev, Narbut, Olesha, Il'f, Petrov, Babel' and Inber, experimenting with Futurism (after the visit of Maiakovskii) and Acmeism, and publishing in local anthologies. He soon became a lyric poet with a gift for concrete portrayal of a dynamic world with immense potential for both pleasure and pain. This world he perceived vividly and with unapologetic subjectivity, which frequently verged on fantasy or grotesque. (He was also a graphic artist of some talent, which he used subsequently for producing propaganda posters.) He greeted the 1917 Revolution naively as the conversion of reality into romantic adventure and as the definitive defeat of the petty bourgeoisie, and found it personally liberating. Moral sense, loyalty to the revolution and the need for income made him devote himself to various kinds of propaganda work, including the routine writing of topical poems, and (later) reviewing and translating, which was artistically unproductive and did not spare him from the posthumous effect of repression: the second volume of his collected works was banned in 1938 and his widow, L.G. Bagritskaia, spent many years in the camps.

His real *oeuvre*, however, is the small number of poems that he selected for his collections. The poems of 1917–24 are characteristically poems of liberation, in which the energetic wayfarer heroes celebrate their freedom, and revel in a fresh, bright, and vital world. Nature is the embodiment of growth, dynamism, creation, and spontaneity. These are the poems which, Babel' said, were as aromatic as fish soup cooked on the beach on an unbridled July day and as moist as one of the water-melons he and Bagritskii cracked open in their youth down in the port. The poems of 1924–27 reveal a fall from original harmony into confusion. Nature fades and disintegrates into grotesque forms, and the alienated heroes travel uncertainly, fall victim to hostile forces, and are unable to find meaning to their lives. Many of the poems are bitterly ironic, and the poet doubts the relevance of romanticism (though this is clearly the romanticism of the frustrated idealist). The collection *Iugo-zapad* [South-West] of 1928 combines nostalgia for the lost Golden Age with disillusion and apathy, and with dreams and aspirations for some better future. If romanticism could no longer be identified within the here and now, it had to be re-defined, and Bagritskii rejected escapism into fantasy or sheer physical enjoyment of the outdoors in favour of a search for a meaning to existence, which in the context of the time took the form of an attempt to integrate into Soviet society and to adopt a more politically orthodox ideology. One of his most successful poems was *Duma pro Opanasa* [The Song of Opanas], a narrative poem that combined fantasy and historical realia and located itself in the tradition of the *Slovo o polku Igoreve* (*The Lay of Igor's Campaign*) and Shevchenko. It relates the fate of a peasant who is recruited into the Red Army and deserts, only to be forced into a band of Makhnovite anarchists. The poem reflects on conflicting loyalties and dramatizes the precipitation of the hero from the uncommitted centre-ground towards equally repugnant extremes, at the cost of his integrity. The creative starting-point for the poem was experimentation with syncopated rhythm – Bagritskii was a metrically aware and sophisticated poet who developed particular rhythmic variations of the *dol'nik* and *taktovik*. His rhythmic readings of poetry, some of which survive on record, were much praised.

Few of the literary groupings to which Bagritskii belonged affected or reflected his writing. The important exception was his entry into MAPP in 1930. Many of Bagritskii's later poems provide the hero with a mentor, who guides him towards a meaning for his existence; these can be read as internalization of the growing pressures on writers in the late 1920s and early 1930s. MAPP, however, required that he abandon the theme of opposition of the personality of the *intelligent* to the collective, and the relationship between the poet and the group was not easy. Much ink was devoted (at the time and subsequently) to discussions of the appropriateness of romanticism, and to Bagritskii's politics as evinced by his poems. Bagritskii remained loyal to the idea of revolution, in spite of the distortions to which it was subjected, looked sincerely for romanticism in life's prose, and called for poets to integrate themselves into society among other workers and to function as barometers of social health. His cult of freedom turned into a search for companionship. His Romantic nightingale was caged, but continued to sing. *Pobediteli* [The Victors] expresses a sense of purpose and of life renewed. However, Bagritskii wrote very little between 1928 and 1932 and devoted himself, as did other poets, to translation and to literary administration. His health was also failing. His last poems postpone hopes for the realization of his ideals until the future; while some are didactic, others conduct a moral examination of his own life's path.

Bagritskii was, like Maiakovskii, sincerely committed to the cause of revolution, and unwisely put his art at the service of ideology. But he was a genuine Romantic who had experienced liberation, and could convey the pain of disillusion the more poignantly.

WENDY ROSSLYN

Grigorii Iakovlevich Baklanov 1923–

Prose writer

Biography

Born Grigorii Iakovlevich Fridman in Voronezh, 11 September 1923. Completed nine classes of secondary education, passing tenth class as external student; completed one course at aviation technical college. Employed briefly as metal worker in aviation factory before World War II. Volunteered for active service, December 1941. Member of the Communist Party, 1942. Attended Second Leningrad artillery academy, which had been evacuated to the Urals, late 1942. Fought at the Front with rank of junior lieutenant, August 1943. Severely wounded in battle; spent six months in various hospitals, declared unfit for active service. Despite wounds Baklanov returned to his unit, assuming former post. Took part in various military operations in Hungary and Austria. By the end of the war full lieutenant and recipient of four military wards. Attended Institute of Literature, studied under Konstantin Paustovskii, 1946–51. Married in 1953; one son and one daughter. Accused of Remarquism, along with Iurii Bondarev, Vasil' Bykov, Bulat Okudzhava, and Viktor Nekrasov. Member of the secretariat of the Writers' Union, 1986. Editor of the journal *Znamia*, 1986–93. Published interviews with *afgantsy* critical of the war in Afghanistan; outspoken supporter of perestroika and Gorbachev reforms. Turned down opportunity to be deputy of the Supreme Soviet. Recipient: State Prize for Literature. Lives in Moscow.

Publications

Collected Editions

Iul' 41 goda [July 1941]. Moscow, 1965; translated as *Juillet 41*, by Claude Ligny, Paris, R. Lafont, 1966.
Voennye povesti [War Stories]. Moscow, 1967.
Karpukhin. Povesti i rasskazy. Moscow, 1967.
Izbrannoe. Moscow, 1974.
Piad' zemli. Povesti. Rasskazy [The Foothold]. Moscow, 1978.
Izbrannye proizvedeniia. Moscow, 1979–80.
Sobranie sochinenii, 4 vols. Moscow, 1983–85.
Povesti i rasskazy. Moscow, 1987.

Fiction

"Iuzhnee glavnogo udara", *Znamia*, 1 (1958), 49–143; translated as *South of the Main Offensive* [no translator named], London, Chapman and Hall, 1963.
"Piad' zemli", *Novyi mir*, 5–6 (1959), 3–45, 62–111; translated as *The Foothold*, by R. Ainsztein, London, Chapman and Hall, 1962.
"Mertvye sramu ne imut" [The Dead Feel No Shame], *Znamia*, 6 (1961), 18–59.
Druz'ia [Friends]. Moscow, 1975.
Ekhali zemliaki [The Fellow-Countrymen Went]. Moscow, 1976.
Naveki - deviatnadtsatiletnie. Moscow, 1980; translated as *Forever Nineteen*, by Antonina W. Bouis, New York, Lippincott, 1989.
"Svoi chelovek" *Znamia*, 11 (1990), 7–120; translated as *The Moment Between the Past and the Future*, by Catherine Porter, London, Faber, 1994.
"Vkhodite uzkimi vratami" [Come in Through the Narrow Gates], *Znamia*, 9 (1992), 7–54.

Play

"Pristegnite remni!" [Tighten Your Belt!], (produced 1975).

Screenplay

Byl mesiats mai [It Was the Month of May]. Moscow, 1971.

Essays and Articles

O nashem prizvanii [About Our Vocation]. Moscow, 1972.
Den' nyneshnii i den' minuvshii [Days Present and Past]. Moscow, 1977.
Zagadka prostoty, sbornik statei [The Mystery of Simplicity, A Collection of Articles]. Moscow, 1984.
Vremia sobirat' kamni [A Time to Gather Stones]. Moscow, 1989.

Critical Studies

"Mera vsekh mer", by A. Kondratovich, *Novyi mir*, 4 (1966), 241–44.
Radi zhizni na zemle, by P. Toper, Moscow, 1971.
"Istselisiia sam ...", by B. Anashenkov, *Voprosy literatury*, 1 (1976), 54–57, 60–75.
Powie ci wojenne Grigorija Baklanowa, by Bronisław Kodzis, Wydawnictwa Uniwersytetu Wrocławskiego, Wrocław, 1977.
"The Problem of Remarquism in Soviet Russian War Prose", by Frank Ellis, *Scottish Slavonic Review*, 11 (1988), 91–108.

Although in recent years Grigorii Baklanov has written on current affairs, in particular assuming prominence as the editor of *Znamia*, he is best known as the author of a number of highly realistic prose works based on his wartime service.

Baklanov's four most important war stories – *Iuzhnee glavnogo udara* (*South of the Main Offensive*), *Piad' zemli* (*The Foothold*), *Mertvye sramu ne imut* [The Dead Feel No Shame], and *Iul' 41 goda* [July 1941] – are hard-hitting, unvarnished accounts of war with considerable psychological interest, and political relevance for the decade after 1956. They mark a definite shift away from officially supported portrayals of World War II with their over-simplified and crude assertions that the Soviet victory vindicated the principles of Marxism-Leninism. Baklanov was not alone in offering this personal revision of the war experience. Viktor Nekrasov, Vasil' Bykov, Bulat Okudzhava, Vasilii Grossman, and Iurii Bondarev all sought direct inspiration in their own personal experience and memory. In a system where artistic and intellectual conformity were considered *de rigueur*, diversion from aesthetic norms frequently incurred draconian penalties, even after 1953.

Much of the excitement and action in Baklanov's fiction is based on small military units and sub-units, often in desperate situations, led by young officers. The operational-strategic picture is generally, though not always, vague. Moral obligation under enormous pressure, fear, heroism, cowardice and duty are recurring themes in Baklanov's war prose. Not content to remain within the sanitized boundaries of ideology, and largely indifferent to strategy, Baklanov's small-unit scenarios posed a serious challenge to the more anodyne views about the war disseminated and upheld as the truth.

South of the Main Offensive, *The Foothold* and *Mertvye sramu ne imut* follow the closing campaigns of the war on the southern Soviet flank. Based on battles for the liberation of Hungary, *South of the Main Offensive* provides a foretaste of what was to come in the other two works. In both of these Baklanov gives a powerful portrayal of treachery and dereliction of duty, and it was this as much as anything else that led to accusations of Remarquism and writing in the style of "the truth of the trenches" (*okopnaia pravda*).

Dereliction of duty and incompetence are central themes in *Iul' 41 goda*, Baklanov's uncompromising account of the summer debacle that nearly cost the Soviet Union the war. An obvious weakness of the Soviet military is that far too much power rests in the hands of the political commissars who oversee the planning and execution of military operations. Explanations for the failures emerge in the many flashbacks to the purges of the military in 1937, and the neutered professionalism of the Soviet officer corps.

The schizophrenic nature of the Soviet command structure adds a dimension to the Soviet war novel that is absent from its western counterpart. Whether relying on the more conventional chronological narrative, or on flashbacks, Baklanov is able to exploit this pervasive tension to bring the events of the immediate pre-war years, specifically the purges, and the costly incompetence of the Soviet leadership into sharp convergence.

The ubiquitous Major Shalaev underscores Baklanov's point about crass political interference in military matters. Through various nuances and hints, we are given to understand that Shalaev is a member of the NKVD. Perversely, he is not shocked by Soviet military reversals, but by the scale of treachery on his own side. How else, he asks himself, is it possible to explain the "rout and retreat of our army"? Shalaev, and by analogy the entire Party apparatus, is trapped in the paranoid world of the purges where reality is what the Party says it is. Traitors, real or imagined, have, therefore, to be uncovered. The tireless zeal for uncovering the class enemy and traitors blinds Shalaev to the fundamental and practical explanations of the Red Army's failures: junior officers promoted beyond their abilities; a climate hostile to all forms of initiative; the crippling complacency of the Soviet leadership in the weeks before the invasion; and the confusion and uncertainty both among the civilian and military population resulting from such inaction.

Much of the blame for this disastrous state of affairs must, of course, rest with Stalin. The purges of the military were his device, aimed at strengthening his grip on Soviet society, even at the expense of weakening the Soviet Union's defences. As for the question as to why Stalin, despite the alarming evidence of Hitler's hostile intentions towards the Soviet Union, failed to act in time, Baklanov provides no real answer.

Baklanov's appointment as editor of *Znamia* in 1986 hinted that serious cultural change was in the offing. Hitherto, *Znamia* was generally regarded as a timid and conformist journal with a readership consisting largely of middle-ranking officials in the bureaucracy and KGB. Baklanov's avowed aim was to return those writers to the Soviet readership who had been suppressed and denigrated throughout the Soviet period.

Neither, however, did Baklanov ignore contemporary issues. Questions concerning Soviet military involvement in Afghanistan were aired in *Znamia* and undoubtedly helped to change public opinion. Interviews with Soviet soldiers highlighted the general disillusionment with the war, the lack of any real purpose and the shameful manner in which returning veterans – the *afgantsy* – unlike those of World War II, were being ignored, or even shunned. Oleg Ermakov's "Afganskie rasskazy" [Afghan Tales] depicted the grim drudgery and enervating frustration of war; there is more than a passing resemblance here to some of Baklanov's own fiction, published a generation earlier.

Baklanov's consistent and able support for the policy of glasnost, and the need to face up to the past, often condemned as "wholesale disparagement" by its opponents, brought him into open conflict with those who defended the status quo. Mutual hostility spilled out into the open at the 19th Party Conference, where Baklanov's stinging rebuke of Nina Andreevna and Iurii Bondarev was one of the highpoints.

Bureaucracy and "stagnation" came in for some harsh and unrelenting criticism during the glasnost period as the spotlight was turned on the Party elite. *Svoi chelovek* (*The Moment Between the Past and the Future*), Baklanov's satirical portrayal of Evgenii Stepanovich Usvatov, a senior party official, is thus very much in tune with the time. Usvatov's ability to climb the Party ladder depends on his unerring sensitivity to the latest Party line. He talks, thinks and behaves in clichés, which leads to a progressive loss of identity. Usvatov seems to have no perceptible life or interest beyond the securing of privileges and comforts. The unremitting lust for awards and the morbid consumption of food – one of Baklanov's main satirical devices – remind us of Gogol'. But the critical humour is finely balanced by the miserable conditions of Usvatov's childhood and the imperatives of survival in a grim Moscow tenement block of the 1930s. Just a hint of sympathy from Baklanov rescues Usvatov from total wretchedness. Retribution comes with Brezhnev's death – the moment between the past and the future – which leads to the unravelling of Usvatov's protective cocoon.

By the end of Baklanov's editorial tenure in November 1993 *Znamia* had been transformed into one of Russia's most famous and respected liberal-democratic publications with circulation figures reaching the million mark for a single issue. The political landscape had also changed: unwittingly, perhaps unavoidably, journals such as *Znamia* hastened that change, and in some ways this may turn out to be Baklanov's most important bequest to Russian letters. He helped Russia to confront its past and face the uncertainties of the future, reasserting the unique role of the Russian writer as social conscience and political commentator.

FRANK ELLIS

The Foothold

Piad' zemli

Novel, 1959

Separated from the main Soviet force, a small unit occupies a beachhead on the bank of the river Dniester overlooked by the Germans. The eventual plan is to force the river, but in the mean time, the locally stronger Germans must be held. Such is the tactical background to Baklanov's *The Foothold* that is set on the Soviet southern flank in the summer of 1944. Despite the overall strategic situation – the western allies have landed in France, the Soviet armies are preparing to strike into the heart of the Third Reich – the atmosphere on the precarious beachhead is bleak, its survival in doubt.

Contrasting the tactical and overall strategic situations in such a way, Baklanov isolates soldiers on the beachhead psychologically from those in relative safety across the river, and from the larger events in progress elsewhere. With the battle under way, the Lethean symbolism of the river becomes apparent: the soldiers feel forgotten, even abandoned by their own side, and the tension between duty and survival becomes all-important.

That the Germans cannot win the war only serves to heighten the tension. With victory in sight, is it still necessary to fight to the death? Final victory would have been impossible without the sacrifices made when the Germans seemed to be carrying all before them in 1941. Those fighting on the beachhead are not just bound by a code of military discipline and honour: they are morally indebted to the dead. To spare themselves now is to prolong the war and its suffering. Thus the victories of 1944 and 1945 are inextricably linked to the defeats of 1941 and 1942.

The two sides of this conflict are represented by a junior officer, Motovilov (almost certainly modelled on Baklanov himself), and a rather reluctant soldier in Motovilov's platoon, Mezentsev. Above all Mezentsev is a survivor. While he appears not to have blotted his copy-book during the German occupation of Odessa, he is never fully able to dispel the cloud of suspicion. One of Motovilov's fellow officers defends Mezentsev's record, pointing out that millions of Soviet citizens were forced to live under German occupation, and make the most of it. His intervention is unusual, and even risky for a Soviet officer, since the presumption of treachery automatically fell on those Soviet citizens who had lived in the German-occupied territories. For returning Soviet prisoners of war the penalties were even worse. Such arbitrary behaviour would have been well known to Baklanov's Soviet reader.

Arguments on behalf of Mezentsev are a ploy: they carry an implied rebuke for the often brutal manner in which the Soviet authorities treated their citizens. Before the German advance the arguments for and against Mezentsev's behaviour are reasonably balanced. Motovilov appears to be motivated by envy, or simply to be wrong. Once battle is joined the moral balance tilts decisively against Mezentsev. He fails to replace the damaged signalling line – though giving the impression that he has – and exploits the chaos of the ensuing battle to get back across the river. Mezentsev's negligence has unforeseen consequences. Artillery fire cannot be brought to bear on the German attack. Only a desperate Soviet counter-attack can save the situation, which, as it turns out, is not necessary. The Germans, under pressure from a large-scale Soviet advance to the north, withdraw their tanks, and the Soviet commander who led the counter-attack is killed by a random shell. Motovilov encounters Mezentsev after the battle, now resplendent in new uniform, serving in the divisional commander's orchestra, and beyond Motovilov's grasp. The war moves on, and the question of crime and punishment is left unresolved.

The Foothold revived arguments which had first come to the fore in the late 1920s and 1930s after the publication of Remarque's World War I novel, *All Quiet on the Western Front*. It was at this time that the term Remarquism was coined. With the appearance of works by Baklanov and others in the 1950s, terms such as *okopnaia pravda* (the truth of the trenches), *literatura rascheta* (literature of account i.e., coming to terms), *degeroizatsiia* (the demythologization of the hero) and *leitenantskaia proza* (lieutenant's prose) entered the lexicon alongside Remarquism. From the Soviet standpoint Remarquism contained a number of serious weaknesses. It signified a loss of faith in authority and progress, encouraging fatalism. War is seen as a permanent feature of human societies. The just war is thus an illusion. The Remarquist experience, Soviet critics argued, derived from the aggressive, imperialist, anti-socialist nature of World War I. Thus, Remarquism could have no relevance for the Soviet *Kriegserlebnis*, which could only be interpreted on the basis of Marxist-Leninist ideology.

In *The Foothold* Baklanov strives to portray the war as he experienced it, through the eyes of a young artillery officer. The flashbacks to life before the war, the love interest and the letters from home are standard and recognizable features of the war novel *per se*. So, too, are the unpalatable ones. Baklanov notes – and he is by no means alone in this – the misunderstanding, even mutual hostility that arises between those at the front and rear. Extreme situations will induce bravery and self-sacrifice, as well as indifference and selfishness. Far from being alien, as Soviet critics have suggested, the character of Mezentsev seems all too convincing. He is more than just a ruthless opportunist. His plausible rationale for abandoning the bridgehead mirrors the thinking put forward by a deserter to explain Germany's war of conquest, the sole criterion being that which is useful to the state, or in Mezentsev's case to him, the individual. Given this convergence of interest, it is quite outrageous that Mezentsev receives no comeuppance for his behaviour.

The absence of any obvious, condign retribution for Mezentsev is either Baklanov's masterstroke, or a deeply pessimistic view of human nature in war. But it does underline the danger posed by Remarquism, which highlighted the many absurdities, contradictions and inconsistencies that confronted the individual at war. These cannot be resolved by recourse to any ideology.

FRANK ELLIS

Konstantin Dmitrievich Bal'mont 1867–1942

Poet and translator

Biography

Born near Shuia, Vladimir province, on his father's estate, 15 June 1867. Attended school in Shuia and in Vladimir; entered Moscow University, 1886, excluded for participating in revolutionary activities, 1887; studied briefly in Moscow and Iaroslavl, 1888–89, abandoned courses after suffering nervous disorders; largely self-taught. Married: 1) Larisa Mikhailovna Garelina in 1889 (divorced 1894); 2) Ekaterina Alekseevna Andreeva in 1896; 3) Elena Konstantinovna Tsvetkovskaia (this marriage was never formalized and Bal'mont remained married to E.A. Andreeva); one son and two daughters. Settled in Moscow, 1889; established first as a translator and then as a leading poet of the Decadent branch of Symbolism; travelled widely in Russia and western Europe, 1896–1905, visited Mexico and California, 1905; left Russia after the authorities' hostile reception of political poems, 1905; based in Paris; travelled to the Pacific, 1912; returned to Russia following the amnesty of 1913; toured Siberia and Japan, 1916; unsympathetic to the Bolshevik government, left Russia on official business for the Ministry of Education, 1920, never returned; lived in straitened conditions in Paris, and from 1927 in Capbreton on French Atlantic coast; showed increasing signs of mental illness from 1932; and moved to Russian rest home at Noisy-le-Grand, 1936. Died 24 December 1942.

Publications

Collected Editions

Polnoe sobranie stikhov, 10 vols. Moscow, 1907–14.
Stikhotvoreniia. Leningrad, 1969.
Svetlyi chas: stikhotvoreniia i perevody [The Bright Hour]. Moscow, 1992.
Gde moi dom: stikhotvoreniia, khudozhestvennaia proza, stat'i, ocherki, pis'ma [Where is My House?]. Moscow, 1992.
Sobranie sochinenii, 2 vols. Mozhaisk, 1994.

Poetry

Pod severnym nebom [Under the Northern Sky]. St Petersburg, 1894.
V bezbrezhnosti [Boundless]. Moscow, 1895.
Tishina [Silence]. St Petersburg, 1898.
Goriashchie zdaniia [Buildings on Fire]. Moscow, 1900.
Budem kak solntse [Let Us Be Like the Sun]. Moscow, 1903.
Tol'ko liubov' [Only Love]. Moscow, 1903.
Liturgiia krasoty [Liturgy of Beauty]. Moscow, 1905.
Feinye skazki [Faerie Tales]. Moscow, 1905.
Zhar-ptitsa [The Fire-Bird]. Moscow, 1907.
Zelenyi vertograd [The Green Garden]. St Petersburg, 1909.
Zarevo zor' [The Glow of Twilights]. Moscow, 1912.
Belyi zodchii [The White Architect]. St Petersburg, 1914.
Iasen' [The Ash Tree]. Moscow, 1916.
Sonety solntsa, meda i luny [Sonnets of the Sun, Honey, and the Moon]. Moscow, 1917.
Sem' poem [Seven Poems]. Moscow, 1920.
Marevo [Mirage]. Paris, 1922.
V razdvinutoi dali [In Distances Drawn Apart]. Belgrade, 1929.
Severnoe siianie [Northern Lights]. Paris, 1931.

Essays and Articles

Poeziia kak volshebstvo [Poetry as Enchantment]. Moscow, 1915; reprinted Letchworth, Prideaux Press, 1973.
Pod novym serpom [Under a New Sickle]. Berlin, 1923.
Vozdushnyi put' [Air Path]. Berlin, 1923.
Visions solaires. Paris, 1923.
Gde moi dom? [Where is My House?]. Prague, 1924.

Critical Studies

"Balmont: A Reappraisal", by Vladimir Markov, *Slavic Review*, 2 (1969), 221–64.
"Bal'mont: zhizn' i poeziia", by V. Orlov, Introduction to Bal'mont's *Stikhotvoreniia*, Leningrad, 1969, 5–74.
"K. Bal'mont: Escapism as a Form of Revolt", by Tatyana Schmidt, *Slavonic and East European Review*, 47 (1969), 323–43.
"Balmont: In Search of Sun and Shadow", by Rodney L. Patterson, *Russian Literature Triquarterly*, 4 (1972), 241–64.
"Bal'mont – Poet of the Existential Void", by Ellen Chances, *Russian Language Journal*, 31/110 (1977), 65–75.
"Bal'mont", by Rodney L. Patterson, in *Modern Encyclopedia of Russian and Soviet Literature*, vol. 2, 1978, 75–85.
Kommentar zu den Dichtungen von K.D. Balmont, 1890–1909, by Vladimir Markov, Cologne, Böhlau, 1988.
"Shelley in the Mind of the Russian Symbolist Bal'mont: Six Kinds of Influence/ Appropriation", by Martin Bidney, *Comparative Literature Studies*, 25 (1988), 57–71.
"K. Bal'mont: A Champion of Russian Culture", by G. Cheron, in *American Contributions to the Tenth International Congress of Slavists*, edited by Jane Gary Harris, Columbus, Ohio, Slavica, 1988, 97–109.
Bal'mont v Iaponii, by K.M. Azadovskii and E.M. D'iakonova, Moscow, 1991.
Kommentar zu den Dichtungen von K.D. Balmont, 1910–1917, by Vladimir Markov, Cologne, Böhlau, 1992.
Serebrianyi gost': o liricheskom geroe Bal'monta, by Viktor Dmitriev, Tenafly, New Jersey, Hermitage, 1992.

Although he was first published as early as 1885, Konstantin Bal'mont's entry into the literary world was a difficult one, and he received little recognition until after the publication of his translations of Shelley in 1893. During the late 1890s, however, he very rapidly emerged as a leading poet of the new Decadent school. The poems of his early books express an existential unease that is assuaged in the contemplation of death and in a search for meaning through mystic and erotic exploration. The poet constructs himself as an outcast tormented by self-doubt and torn between carnality and spirituality. This preoccupation with self is seen in an opposite light in the best of Bal'mont's early books, *Budem kak solntse* [Let Us Be Like the Sun], as a celebration of vitality and individualism. At an early stage Bal'mont perfected a virtuoso technical style in which he employed a dazzling variety of metres (while generally remaining within the bounds of conventional versification) and made full (and sometimes excessive) use of the euphonic possibilities of alliteration, assonance, rhyme, and syntactic parallelism to increase the emotional impact of his verse.

To his contemporaries Bal'mont appeared for a while to be a major revitalizing force in Russian poetry. Indeed, his verbal experimentation exercised a profound (and understudied) influence on a whole generation of Symbolist and post-Symbolist poets. However, by 1905 his authority was already on the wane. The two collections that followed *Budem kak solntse* failed to develop its thematic and technical achievements. Moreover, Bal'mont gradually became a victim of his overwhelming urge to create: his seeming inability to edit his work critically led to the publication of much substandard material, and to an increasing unwillingness on the part of his reviewers to make the necessary effort to sort the wheat from the chaff.

In 1905 Bal'mont left Russia for Paris for a period of over seven years, fearing persecution as a result of the anti-monarchist poems he had written in response to the revolution of that year. He was to return only after the political amnesty of 1913. The poetry he wrote during this period of self-imposed exile is particularly uneven, and although, for example, his adaptations of Russian and world folklore were reasonably well accepted by the public, Bal'mont's critical reputation continued to fall. *Zelenyi vertograd* [The Green Garden], none the less, was praised by as astute a reviewer as Gumilev for its powerful evocation of the Russian religious sectarians.

By this time Bal'mont had left behind the worst excesses of his infatuation with sound patterning, and his poetry begins to show a new restraint. This is already noticeable in *Zarevo zor'* [The Glow of Twilights], but is particularly evident in *Iasen'* [The Ash Tree] and in *Sonety solntsa, meda i luny* [Sonnets of the Sun, Honey, and the Moon], where the discipline imposed by the sonnet form gives his writing a much clearer focus. The themes of Bal'mont's second period also show a greater philosophical maturity. His exultation in nature, art, love, and exotic experience of all kinds is still present, but is now tempered by a greater sense of realism and a deeper willingness to reflect.

With the revolutions of 1917 Bal'mont returned for a while to political poetry as he tried unsuccessfully to come to terms with the new order. After his removal to France in 1920 he went through a lengthy period of adjustment in which his civic anger was directed against the Bolshevik regime that he had been obliged to flee. A strong note of nostalgia for Russia enters his verse, partly no doubt in response to the material difficulties of his life in emigration, but this is compensated by an increasing acceptance of the tribulations of life as well as its rewards.

By the late 1920s, Bal'mont's poetry was almost entirely disregarded by readers both in the Soviet Union and among the émigré communities. The exception to this was perhaps Poland and other countries of east central Europe, where he still retained a following, and which he visited between 1927 and 1929. Yet in spite of this neglect, the poetry of Bal'mont's last period, before he succumbed to alcoholism and mental decline, contains work of genuine value. This is especially true of the 1929 collection, *V razdvinutoi dali* [In Distances Drawn Apart]. Here the search for the absolute that had informed his poetry from the outset is directed not so much towards external phenomena as internally within the poet's own spiritual world. The longing for Russia remains, but Bal'mont is able to find expansive consolation in examination of the beauty of nature, and in memory and the contemplation of the knowledge he has gained through his life. As with earlier collections, it is with the stricter poetic forms, particularly the sonnet, that Bal'mont is most successful.

Bal'mont was not only a prolific original poet. His numerous and accomplished translations did much to acquaint the Russian audience with authors as diverse as Tennyson, Poe, Rustaveli, Kalidasa, and Vrchlický. His insatiable appetite for travel and for absorbing the languages and cultures of other nations is reflected not only in the broad exoticism of much of his poetry, but also in numerous travel sketches and essays on literary themes. His short book *Poeziia kak volshebstvo* [Poetry as Enchantment] of 1915 lucidly expounds his belief in the ability of Symbolist poetry to create new and heightened realities through the magic and music of words. Bal'mont also turned his hand to drama, and with rather more success to prose fiction and autobiography.

Bal'mont's fluctuating reputation provides a case study in the vicissitudes of literary taste. Within the space of only a few years, from being heralded as epitomizing the spirit of the age, his name came to be synonymous with insubstantial showiness and vulgarity. Yet his early work was very widely studied and valued, and his writing continued to be appreciated by, for example, Marina Tsvetaeva. For all his prolixity and his indiscriminate virtuosity, Bal'mont's best writing has a very high measure of emotive power. In recent years his poetry, and especially that of his later period, has begun to be rescued from critical oblivion, and his significance for Russian literature is coming to be assessed at a more realistic level.

DAVID N. WELLS

Budem kak solntse

Let Us Be Like the Sun

Poetry collection, 1903

This collection of poems secured Bal'mont a leading role among Russian Symbolists. It was written in spring 1902 and was subtitled "The Book of Symbols". It was highly praised by Briusov, who considered it to be the best work published by the poet. Due to its popularity it has come through a further four editions since 1903. In Mirsky's view it contains Bal'mont's best poems. It embodies the main principles of Russian Symbolism: combining aesthetical ideals with mysticism, displaying the virtuosity of the author's craftsmanship, and most of all expressing the new philosophy of life, enriched with the Neoplatonic vision of the world, pointing to the existence of "des forêts de symboles" (Baudelaire). Perhaps the best achievement of the book is the fertility of its verbal and rhythmic expressiveness, although, in places, this is excessive; however, the brilliant spectacle of sound was something new in Russian poetry. In one of the poems Bal'mont stresses this point by proclaiming: "I am the refinement of Russian speech".

The collection creates a cosmogonic picture of the world, centred on the four elements: thus, the first cycle, "Gimn Ogniu" [Hymn to Fire], praises fire as the main force of life; it is followed by poems featuring water ("Vozzvan'e k okeanu" [Appeal to the Ocean] and the cycle "S morskogo dna" [From the Ocean Floor]); there are poems dedicated to the element air (such as "Veter" [Wind], "Zavet bytiia" [The Commandment of the

Universe]); and towards the end of the book the reader finds some poems praising landscapes and gardens (the earth element appears in the cycle "Trilistnik" [Trefoil] and in the final poem "Velikoe nechto" [The Great Nothing]). It is posssible to underline two important themes permeating this collection: the motif of the eternal cycle of life, and the beautiful distinctiveness of every single moment of life. In the last poem of the collection the Chinese philosophical concept of the Great Nothingness (empty space) from the period 960–1279 is contrasted to the passion and pleasure of various moments in the life of the lyric hero. All the elements in the book (discussed earlier) merge in a profound way. The poet concludes that "earth and sky form an arch of the mute cathedral".

Apart from the references to ancient Chinese culture, many poems allude to ancient Greek philosophy, to the paintings of the great Spanish and Italian masters, to Russian medieval history, and to the poetry of Tiutchev, Pushkin, and Goethe. The scope of topics is just as wide, but the main definition of love and the philosophical lyrics are impressionistic. In the poem "Skazat' mgnoven'iu: Stoi!" [To Say "Stop!" to the Moment], which brings to mind the opening scenes of Goethe's *Faust*, the lyric hero argues that the human mind cannot perceive everything in depth, only a moment can be captured, and dreams are more powerful than common sense: "There is only one opportunity to say 'Stop!' to the moment: / having broken the chain of thought, to be forged – like a dream".

One of the most exciting examples of rhythmical richness is the poem in which Bal'mont identifies himself with Russian speech; the musical arrangement of the text is unique. The language flows slowly and smoothly; there is an abundance of long words and the poet makes use of seductive sounds, such as "n" and "m". The lyric "I" abandons its own physical shape in order to imitate all the flexibility offered by the speech:

I am elegancy of Russian slow speech ...
I was the first to discover this speech's slants,
Its melodic, relentless and tender chimes ...
Its gentle splashes, torn and joined at the same time,
These uniquely-coloured stones of the unsurpassed land ...

The narrator invites readers to look at all the shades of meaning of the words as well as of the sound patterns.

The cycle "S morskogo dna" reflects on the poet's affair with the poet Mirra Lokhvitskaia, whose Romantic and Decadent style is mimicked in some of the passages. Her voice is distinctive in the second poem of the cycle: "Forgive me, pale sisters, / I am not like you / And I want someone different". The fourth poem depicts the place of their meetings by the sea. (The autobiographical elements of the book have been analysed in detail by Vladimir Markov, 1988.)

The egocentric nature of Bal'mont's poetry is especially evident in the opening poem of the collection, "Ia v etot mir prishel, chtob videt' solntse" [I Came to this World to See the Sun]. Eleven of the lines of this short five-stanza poem start with "I". The poem flows as follows: "I came to this world to see the Sun, I came to see the sea, I encompass all the worlds in my glance, I conquered the eternity". However, in the short cycle "Golos zakata" [The Voice of the Sunset], the theme of reflectiveness prevails: the lyric hero is happy to dissolve himself in the light of the sunset. The symbolism of these poems is shaped by the theosophical ideas fashionable in Russia at the time. To the Symbolist poets interested in theosophy, the sunset signified rebirth and awakening to another, divine, self. Similar imagery and themes can be found in the poetry of Belyi, Ivanov, and Voloshin. Therefore, taken in the context of the cultural and philosophical atmosphere of the period, Bal'mont's book can be understood as an awakening to the new light of the divinity.

Bal'mont's other collections of poetry develop the same themes, and often offer a replay of the ideas and experiences expressed in *Budem kak solntse*. By 1909 many critics started to talk about his fall from influential literary heights. In 1909 Blok despised his style, calling his poetry nothing but "a conglomeration of words, at times ugly, at times laughable". However, many of his poems are experimental, offering descriptions of the inner self without employing verbs, and achieving better results than for example can be observed in the poetry of Fet.

ALEXANDRA SMITH

Natal'ia Vladimirovna Baranskaia 1908–

Prose writer

Biography

Born Natal'ia Radchenko-Rozanova, in St Petersburg, 31 December 1908. Lived in Berlin, 1912–15; Moscow, 1915–17 and 1922–26; Kiev, 1918–21. Attended school in Moscow; student on Higher State Literary Courses, 1926–29. Married: 1) fellow-student in 1927 (divorced 1932); 2) Nikolai Nikolaevich Baranskii in 1936 (died 1943); one daughter and one son. First husband arrested and imprisoned; lived with exiled mother in Voronezh, 1929–30; joined husband in exile in Kazakhstan, then returned to Moscow and worked as a proofreader, 1932. Lived in Saratov, 1936–39, then Moscow, 1940–41. Evacuated first to Saratov, then to Altai in western Siberia, 1941–43. Returned to Moscow, 1943, after husband killed near Briansk. Postgraduate student of literature at Moscow University, 1944–45; worked as curator at State Literary Museum, 1944–57. Deputy director of State Pushkin Museum, 1958–66. Began writing short stories, 1966, when forced to retire; first literary publication, 1968. Full-time writer from 1969, but able to publish only intermittently. Joined the Soviet Writers' Union, 1979.

Publications

Fiction

"Dva rasskaza" [Two Stories], *Novyi mir*, 5 (1968), 77–89.

"Nedelia kak nedelia", *Novyi mir*, 11 (1969), 23–55; translated as "A Week Like Any Other Week", by E. Lehrman, *Massachusetts Review*, 15/4 (1974), 657–703; also translated as "A Week Like Any Other", by Pieta Monks, in *A Week Like Any Other: A Novella and Short Stories*, London, Virago, 1989.

"Otritsatel'naia Zhizel'" [Negative Giselle], *Iunost'*, 8 (1971), 78–81.

"Dva rasskaza", *Zvezda*, 11 (1973), 101–20.

"Chemu raven iks?" [What does "x" Equal?], *Iunost'*, 5 (1974), 43–51.

"Dva rasskaza", *Iunost'*, 7 (1976), 4–12.

"Tsvet temnogo meda" [The Colour of Dark Honey], *Sibir'*, 3 (1977).

Otritsatel'naia Zhizel': Rasskazy, malen'kie povesti [Negative Giselle]. Moscow, 1977.

Zhenshchina s zontikom: Povest' i rasskazy [The Woman with an Umbrella]. Moscow, 1981.

Portret, podarennyi drugu: Ocherki i rasskazy o Pushkine; Povest' [Portrait to a Friend: Sketches and Stories about Pushkin]. Leningrad, 1982.

"Udivitel'nye shariki" [The Marvellous Orbs], *Ural*, 4 (1983), 100–10.

Den' pominoveniia: Roman, povest' [Remembrance Day]. Moscow, 1989.

"Nasledstvo" [The Inheritance], *Sel'skaia nov'*, 12 (1990).

Avtobus s chernoi polosoi; Ptitsa [The Funeral Bus; The Bird], *Grani*, 166 (1992), 5–54; 54–64.

"Rasskazy", *Grani*, 168 (1993), 38–113.

Autobiography

"Avtobiografiia bez umolchanii" [A Frank Autobiography], *Grani*, 156 (1990), 122–48.

Critical Studies

"Vozmozhnosti 'kamernoi' povesti", by Iu. Surovtsev, *Zvezda*, 2 (1971), 191–201.

"Women in Soviet Society", by Mary Seton-Watson, in her *Scenes from Soviet Life: Soviet Life Through Official Literature*, London, BBC Publications, 1986, 13–23.

"A Woman's Work", by Susan Kay, *Irish Slavonic Studies*, 8 (1987), 115–26.

"Interview with Natalya Baranskaya", by Pieta Monks, in *Writing Lives: Conversations Between Women Writers*, edited by Mary Chamberlain, London, Virago, 1988, 26–36.

"*Zhenskaia Proza* and the New Generation of Women Writers", by K.A. Simmons, *Slovo: A Journal of Contemporary Soviet and East European Affairs*, 3/1 (1990), 66–78.

"I. Grekova and N. Baranskaya: Soviet Women's Writing and De-Stalinisation", by Catriona Kelly, *Rusistika*, 5–6 (1992), 39–43; 14–18.

"Introduction", by Peter Doyle, to Baranskaia's *Nedelia kak nedelia*, London, Bristol Classical Press, 1993, vii–xiii.

A History of Russian Women's Writing, 1820–1992, by Catriona Kelly, Oxford, Clarendon Press, 1994, 363–64, 397–409.

Natal'ia Baranskaia belongs to the older generation of Soviet women writers and came very late to literature, making her debut in *Novyi mir* in 1968, at the age of 60. Widowed with two children in 1943, Baranskaia never remarried, brought up her family single-handed, and was able to write fiction only after retirement from her full-time career as a museum-curator, her previous writings being confined to the co-authorship of specialist academic publications. With the controversial publication of "Nedelia kak nedelia" ("A Week Like Any Other") in 1969, her pioneering and candid account of a typically arduous week in the life of a young working mother, she achieved immediate national and international recognition, but subsequently had difficulty getting her work published and was therefore unable to sustain this early prominence. Some short stories appeared intermittently in the 1970s, but her first collection was not sanctioned until 1977. A second collection of stories came out in 1981, followed a year later by a volume of documentary essays and fiction relating to Pushkin and his wife. Publication of Baranskaia's most substantial work, the novel *Den' pominoveniia* [Remembrance Day], written in 1981–84, was delayed for censorship reasons until 1989. Since then her work has mainly been published in the émigré journal *Grani*. She is currently working on a history of her family, provisionally entitled "Poiski doma" [In Search of Home].

The principal themes of Baranskaia's earlier stories are love, marriage, motherhood, childlessness, loneliness, relationships at work, and the insecurities and moral problems of the young. Her ethical standpoints are clear and, perhaps reflecting the enforced disruptions in her own life, her social attitudes are not radical: she has little doubt that women most naturally achieve fulfilment through happy marriage and peaceful family life. Her debut stories are characteristic. In the semi-autobiographical "U Nikitskikh i na Pliushchikhe" [By the Nikitski Gates and on Pliushchikha Street], set in 1923, a small girl tries to understand why her parents live apart and her mother is always out at work. "Provody" [The Retirement Party] shows a lonely widow, forced to retire by an insensitive boss. The volume *Otritsatel'naia Zhizel'* [Negative Giselle] is mainly devoted to young people and their concerns, and does not always avoid triteness and didacticism. The title story contrasts a girl's enthusiastic response to her first ballet, with her mother's puritanical disapproval. Other stories are about coping with a first job ("Liushkina rabota" [Liushka's Job]), a poor boy's temptation to use stolen money he has found to buy a bike ("Borin velosiped" [Boria's Bicycle]), and a teenage girl's subjection to a trial by her neighbours for rowdy behaviour ("Liubka"). Most of Baranskaia's more subtle and effective stories are contained in *Zhenshchina s zontikom* [The Woman with an Umbrella]. These include the title story, in which a mysterious woman frequents a park and is dismissed as a mad old maid by other visitors – she turns out to be the wife of a victim of the Terror, who now lives only for her academic work; and "Dom Laine" [Laine's House], which depicts an Estonian woman, proud of the old guest-house she efficiently runs, but scarred by childhood memories of war and of her soldier brother buried in the garden.

The most imaginative and original work in the Pushkin volume is "Tsvet temnogo meda" [The Colour of Dark Honey], a long story about Natal'ia Goncharova, in the first year after her husband's death. The title refers to the material of one of her dresses, and Natal'ia is depicted from a variety of narrative viewpoints with sensitivity and sympathy, as she returns to her family home in the country and struggles to come to terms with her grief and sense of guilt, haunted by dreams of Pushkin and surrounded by hostile relatives, gossiping servants, and petty intrigues. Society's judgement of Natal'ia is unjust, Baranskaia suggests, for she took her marital and maternal duties seriously, and her flirtatiousness was the result of inexperience and insecurity rather than cynicism.

Baranskaia directly tackles the horrors of the Soviet past in "Avtobus s chernoi polosoi" [The Funeral Bus], an outspoken story written in 1975 but only published in 1992, and partly based on the fate of her first husband. The female narrator dreams of being on a funeral bus in which the innocent victims of an infamous *agent provocateur* and informer relate their terrible stories of injustice, suffering, and premature death in prison-camps. Their betrayer has typically enjoyed a comfortable career and a complimentary obituary, and the dead complain that they are the still forgotten casualties of the lawless and violent rule of a cruel maniac.

The Soviet past and the suffering and devastation caused by World War II feature prominently in Baranskaia's wide-ranging and ambitious, if not entirely successful novel, *Den' pominoveniia*. Set in 1970, the work follows a varied group of war-widows (one of whom, Mariia Nikolaevna, is a fictionalized portrait of Baranskaia) as they travel by train to visit their husbands' or sons' graves, and narrate their lives and wartime experiences. The novel, which frankly depicts collectivization, famine, Stalin's purges, Nazi atrocities, and the appalling conditions away from the front line, records and commemorates the common anguish, endurance, and maternal self-sacrifice of ordinary Soviet women, from unsophisticated peasants and workers to members of the intelligentsia. The narrative is occasionally cumbersome and sentimental – for example, when Baranskaia lauds motherhood, symbolized by the Madonna and child, as the moral bedrock of society, on which world peace depends – but *Den' pominoveniia* is unique in its comprehensive and compassionate portrayal of specifically female suffering.

Though none of her later works has made as strong an impact as "A Week Like Any Other", the range and diversity of Baranskaia's fiction has been insufficiently appreciated. While it is true that her attitudes generally reflect those of her generation, and that her work is linguistically and formally conservative, she nevertheless remains a talented and competent writer of mainly realist prose, whose achievements go well beyond the single story for which she is best known.

PETER DOYLE

A Week Like Any Other

Nedelia kak nedelia

Story, 1969

The delayed November 1969 edition of *Novyi mir* containing Baranskaia's "A Week Like Any Other" was quickly sold out, and the story became the talk of Moscow literary circles for many months, though it was little reviewed elsewhere in the Soviet press. It created, in the words of a later critic, an "explosion of reader interest". Baranskaia, virtually unknown at the time, received hundreds of letters from women expressing their deep gratitude for the publication of her story. It was soon widely translated and Baranskaia's international, as well as national, fame was assured.

In theory Soviet women enjoyed full political and legal equality with men, and a whole range of enlightened social facilities. In practice, the realities of their lives bore little resemblance to their supposedly liberated and equal status. Neither were these realities reflected in the stereotyped portrayals of women in much of official literature. "A Week Like Any Other" was instantly successful because it presented, for the first time in print, an honest and unvarnished picture of the stressful and difficult lot of the average, educated, Soviet working mother, a picture that readers recognized as truthful and realistic. The story helped to bring the true position of women to public attention and initiated a wider debate on women's issues.

"A Week Like Any Other" takes the form of a diary written by a 26-year-old scientist Ol'ga Voronkova, who is married with two young children and who is employed in a Moscow scientific institute as a research assistant, working on the development of a new type of fibreglass. Seven entries, one for each day, give a detailed account of how she spends her time, and graphically they convey the various pressures to which she is subjected both at home and at work. The motivation for telling her story is provided by a searching questionnaire that she and her colleagues have to fill in, giving details of how they spend a typical week.

The first-person narrative, with its tone of confiding intimacy, ensures that the reader sees everything from a female viewpoint and is sympathetic to Ol'ga, who is lively, resilient, sensitive, keenly observant, and endowed with an ironic sense of humour. On the surface, as she herself realizes, Ol'ga has every reason to be content. She is the envy of her friends, all of whose circumstances seem less favourable. She has a degree, an interesting job, supportive and confiding colleagues, a happy marriage, beautiful children, and a new and reasonably spacious flat. Yet it soon becomes apparent, as she rushes round trying to juggle her various tasks, that she can barely survive the demands made upon her, let alone adequately cope with them.

At work she feels under pressure to complete her project on time, and feels guilty about her enforced lack of punctuality and frequent absences caused by her children's ill-health. She also constantly worries about neglecting her children who attend kindergarten and nursery-school. Home provides little respite, for Ol'ga unquestioningly accepts that all the many domestic chores and the burden of child-care are primarily her responsibility. Her long days are frantically busy, and evenings and weekends are taken up with cleaning, washing, cooking, and mending. Her good-natured husband, Dima, is supportive after a fashion, but tacitly assumes that his needs should take priority and resents the little time he does spend on household chores at the expense of his career.

Ol'ga receives emotional support from her women friends at work; though her week contains brief periods of satisfaction and joy, these are not enough to relieve the stress and exhaustion she feels. The strain on her is apparent: she almost breaks down at work, she loses her temper with her children and cries uncontrollably, conversations with Dima descend into petty quarrels. Lack of money, sleep, and free time, and the constant fear of pregnancy (she had considered an abortion when expecting her second child) are all taking their toll on her marriage and health. She angrily rejects Dima's suggestion that she should abandon the career for which she is as well qualified as he is. Ol'ga seems to be trapped and almost overwhelmed by the competing pressures of work, home, marriage, and motherhood, and no obvious solution to her predicament is offered. The story implies that, despite the official propaganda to the contrary, Soviet women are hindered rather than helped by the State, which expects women to contribute both to the economy (by their labour) and to the labour force (by having two or more children), but provides a generally poor standard of such facilities as shops, transport, housing, and child-care. Similarly, the bureaucratic questionnaire and a compulsory political-education class are seen as time-wasting irrelevances.

"A Week Like Any Other" is a deceptively simple work, which is so well written and skilfully narrated that the reader is given both a remarkably full picture of Ol'ga, with all her vitality and emotional sensitivity, and a broad insight into the realities of Soviet life. The narrative is fresh and colloquial, and is enlivened by devices such as contrast, humour, and ironic understatement. A lyrical interlude, narrated in the third-person and describing Ol'ga's romance and Crimean honeymoon several years before, also adds perspective and variety. In addition, Ol'ga's limitations as a narrator are apparent, for she unwittingly reveals more than she herself realizes: many readers will be less tolerant of Dima's thoughtless assumptions about domestic responsibilities than she is, and will be critical of her rather passive acceptance of her lot. Notable for its lack of tendentiousness, "A Week Like Any Other" raises important questions about society and women's lives, but does not preach, draw conclusions or propound solutions. Its concentration on down-to-earth but true detail and avoidance of explicit comment in fact enhance its radical impact. To consider Baranskaia's story to be simply a factual, sociological document, rather than a technically-accomplished literary work of critical realism is to do it less than justice.

PETER DOYLE

Evgenii Baratynskii 1800–1844

Poet

Biography

Born in the village of Viazhlia, Kirsanov district, Tambov province, 2 March 1800. The family moved to Moscow, 1808 or 1809. Attended German boarding school, St Petersburg, 1812; the Corps of Pages, St Petersburg, 1813: expelled for theft, 1816. Moved to Podol'skoe, Smolensk province, Mara. Returned to St Petersburg, made friends with young littérateurs including Del'vig, Kiukhel'beker, and Pushkin, 1818. Served in the army, 1818–26, rising through the ranks to retire as ensign: served in south-eastern Finland. Published first book, 1826. Settled in Moscow. Married: Anastasiia L'vovna Engel'gardt in 1826; nine children (two died in infancy). Became an *habitué* of Zinaida Volkonskaia's salon and yet closer friends with Pushkin, 1826–29; published in Del'vig and Pushkin's journal *Severnye tsvety*. Worked in the government land surveying office, 1827–31. Close friendship with the philosopher Ivan Kireevskii, 1829 to mid-1830s; contributed to Kireevskii's *Evropeets*, 1832. Also contributed to *Moskovskii nabliudatel'*, 1835. Became estranged from Moscow circles, late 1830s; published only in St Petersburg journals from 1836. Travelled (with family) to western Europe: Germany, 1843, Paris, winter 1843–44; left for Italy and died suddenly in Naples, 11 July 1844.

Publications

Collected Editions

Polnoe sobranie sochinenii, 2 vols. St Petersburg/Petrograd, 1914–15.
Polnoe sobranie stikhotvorenii, 2 vols. Moscow, 1936.
Stikhotvoreniia. Poemy. Proza. Pis'ma. Moscow, 1951.
Polnoe sobranie stikhotvorenii. Moscow, 1957.
Stikhotvoreniia. Poemy. Moscow, 1982.
Polnoe sobranie stikhotvorenii. Moscow, 1989.

Poetry

Eda, finliandskaia povest', i Piry, opisatel'naia poema [Eda, A Tale of Finland, and Feasts, A Descriptive Poem]. St Petersburg, 1826.
Stikhotvoreniia. Moscow, 1827.
"Bal. Povest'" [The Ball: A Tale], in *Dve povesti v stikhakh* [Two Tales in Verse], St Petersburg, 1828.
Nalozhnitsa [The Concubine]. Moscow, 1831; reprinted as *Tsyganka* [The Gypsy Girl], Moscow, 1835.
Stikhotvoreniia, 2 vols. Moscow, 1835.
Sumerki [Twilight]. Moscow, 1842.

Prose
"Persten'" [The Ring], *Evropeets*, 1–2 (1832), 165–87.

Letters
Selected Letters of Evgenij Baratynskij, translated by Glynn Richard Barratt. The Hague, Mouton, 1973.

Critical Studies
E.A. Baratynsky, by Benjamin Dees, New York, Twayne, 1972.
Evgenii Baratynskii: zhizn' i tvorchestvo, by Geir Kjetsaa, Oslo, Bergen, and Tromsö, Universitetsforlaget, 1973.
Baratynskii: A Dictionary of the Rhymes and a Concordance to the Poetry, by Thomas Shaw, Madison, University of Wisconsin Press, 1975.
"Baratynsky's Elegiac Code", by Nils Åke Nilsson, in *Russian Romanticism: Studies in the Poetic Codes*, edited by Nilsson, Stockholm, Almqvist & Wiksell, 1979, 144–66.
Russian Metaphysical Romanticism: The Poetry of Tiutchev and Boratynskii, by Sarah Pratt, Stanford, Stanford University Press, 1984.
A History of Russian Literature of the Romantic Period, by William Edward Brown, Ann Arbor, Ardis, vol. 3, 1986.
"*Ia* i *ty* v lirike Baratynskogo: (Iz etiudov o russkom poeticheskom iazyke)", by G.O. Vinokur, in his *Filologicheskie issledovaniia*, edited by M.I. Shapir, Moscow, 1989, 241–249 and 357–362 (comments).
"On Baratynsky's 'French Trifle': *The Elysian Fields* and Its Context", by Igor Pilshchikov, *Essays in Poetics*, 19/2 (1994), 62–93.
"New Love or Old Flower? Kant and Schelling in Derzhavin's and Baratynskii's Poetry", by Paul M. Waszink, *Australian Slavonic and East European Studies*, 9/2 (1995), 1–26.
"Notes on the Semantics of *Otzyv* in Baratynsky", by Igor Pilshchikov, *Irish Slavonic Studies*, 15 (1994) [1996], 75–101.
Resetting the Margins: Russian Romantic Verse Tales and the Idealized Woman, by Luc J. Beaudoin, New York, Peter Lang, 1997.

Evgenii Baratynskii (also known as Boratynskii) is considered second only to Pushkin in the poetic hierarchy of the Golden Age. His principal accomplishment in the 1820s was the re-created love elegy in which the world of the psyche is depersonalized and is subject to "demolishing" intellectual analysis. In Baratynskii's work, the poetry of sentiment became the poetry of thought; his meditative lyrics of the 1830s abandoned genre divisions and acquired metaphysical depth. His narrative poems were a provocative attempt to develop a unique style.

French Neoclassicism was the literary background for all the poets of the "Pushkin Pleiad"; and among them, the young Baratynskii "le marquis" was the "most" French. He began precociously with epicurean *pièces fugitives*; a brief early period resulted in "Vospominaniia" [Recollections] (1819), a fragmented and elegized version of the meditative poem that combines extracts from Gabriel Legouvé and Delille, reworked following the stylistic principles of Batiushkov and Voeikov. Baratynskii did not include this poem in any of his collections, but used parts of it in other works. His later translations (1823–28, all from French), though comparatively few, are fairly diverse: an exemplary "dismal elegy" and elegiac pieces (Millevoye), erotic poems (Parny), "antique" fragments (Chénier), and a verse tale (Voltaire).

Baratynskii's transfer to Finland was regarded as exile (similar to Pushkin's southern exile). The image of the outcast in a northern wilderness provided a Romantic personal and (pseudo) biographical frame for his elegies: historical, as in "Finliandiia" [Finland] (1820), meditative, as in "Vodopad" [The Waterfall] (1821), or rustic, as in "Sel'skaia elegiia" [Country Elegy] or "Rodina" [Homeland] (1820–21). Perceived as a Romanticist, Baratynskii was foreign to the newly-born Byronism: his lyrics speak of pessimistic melancholy rather than rebelling despair, reasoning rather than passion. This is reflected in his love elegies: for example, "Razluka" [The Parting] and "Razuverenie" [Dissuasion]. They are, in fact, anti-erotic, with their sober registering of expiring affection and the negation of the very possibility of love communion. "Priznanie" [The Declaration] (1823), which was immediately accepted as the last word in the erotic elegy, is a declaration of non-love, and concludes with a moral philosophical aphorism. Baratynskii's attitude to the epistle is also characteristic of his ambiguous position. In his work of the 1820s "friendly" epistles (often hardly distinguishable from elegies) are not at variance with "didactic" ones. Characteristically, in the former, he speaks to his poet friends (Del'vig, Konshin etc.), whereas in the latter he addresses an older or a dead poet (Gnedich and Bogdanovich).

Baratynskii's first indisputably successful attempt at the narrative poem was *Piry* [Feasts] (1820). Plotless, with free thematic shifts, direct addresses to friends, and elegiaco-meditative digressions, this descriptive poem absorbed the elements of both the friendly epistle and the elegy. *Eda* (1824–25; published 1826) is a narrative poem in a strict sense. Baratynskii's intention was "to go his own, new way", to avoid any resemblances with Pushkin's Byronic "southern poems"; hence restrained northern colours, uninvolved narration, an abundance of precise details, and a "simple" story of a Finnish girl seduced by a Russian hussar. Fashionable tendencies of the power of passions and strong heroes are, however, obvious in Baratynskii's two "ultra-romantic" poems: *Bal* [The Ball] (1828) and *Tsyganka* [The Gypsy Girl], first published in 1831 as *Nalozhnitsa* [The Concubine]. With the publication of these poems, Baratynskii became both an ally and a rival of Pushkin who, incidentally, called the *femme fatale* Nina (of *Bal*) a "perfectly novel character" in Russian literature. Both poems provoked a scandal and accusations of amoralism. Baratynskii's popularity was on the wane.

His lyrics from the Moscow period bear witness to his growing philosophical involvement and, at the same time, reflect his disillusionment in the possibility of a mature poet's success. "Moi dar ubog, i golos moi negromok ..." [My gift is poor, and my voice is not loud ...] (1828), presents poetic communication as an appeal to the "other's" response, a response that one cannot hope to find in the modern world. For the poet himself, it is a spiritual healing: see "V dni bezgranichnykh uvlechenii ..." [In days of limitless transports ...] (1831), or "Boliashchii dukh vrachuet pesnopen'e ..." [Song healeth the afflicted spirit ...] (1835). In "Muza" ("The Muse") 1829), he declares his awareness of her "uncommon look". The genre composition of his poems evolved towards metaphysical meditation. The elegiaco-epistolary communicative structure ("I" to "Thou") disintegrated: the decrease in the number of poems with an addressee (1827–34) was followed by a sharp rise in the number of poems without "I" (1835–41), thus one can speak of impersonal lyrics, represented by Baratynskii's late verse, which was an unprecedented form in Russia literature.

Philosophical themes had appeared in Baratynskii's poetry from the early and mid-1820s, as in *Dve doli* [Two Lots] (1823), or *Cherep* [The Skull] (1824), but only now did they begin to predominate. In 1827 he created a mystic vision of "the fate of the living", "Posledniaia smert'" [The Last Death]; in 1828 a metaphysical apologia, "Smert'" ("Death"), was composed, in which Death, although hostile to humans, is treated as the regulating principle of Being. A commemorative poem, *Na smert' Gete* [On the Death of Goethe] (1832), presents the image of the "great elder" who lived in perfect harmony with nature. Its rhetorical form is typical of Baratynskii's poetic reasoning: the conclusion gives alternative versions of Goethe's existence/non-existence beyond the grave. Oppositions remaining unresolved, no final answer is given. This became the discursive strategy in *Sumerki* [Twilight] (1842), the collection that included poems composed in 1835–41.

In the poems written after *Sumerki*, such as *Na posev lesa* [On Sowing a Forest], *Piroskaf* [The Pyroscaphe] or *Diad'ke-ital'iantsu* [To the Italian Tutor], Baratynskii found new themes – the search for faith, acceptance of reality, personal reconcilement with death – and seemed to be outlining yet another new poetics. Thus, *Diad'ke-ital'iantsu* is a highly original synthesis of the epistle to the dead and the epistle to the inferior. His last poems are deserving of fuller appreciation: they attracted the attention of very few of his contemporaries and only a handful of later connoisseurs.

IGOR PILSHCHIKOV

Tsyganka

The Gypsy Girl

Narrative poem, 1835

Tsyganka [The Gypsy Girl] represents one of Baratynskii's few attempts at penning a long poem. Together with *Piry*, *Eda*, and *Bal*, *Tsyganka* forms a cycle of ventures on Baratynskii's part to break from his usual elegiac mode and engage in an extended poetic discourse. Although the poem did not enjoy much success when it appeared in 1831 under the title *Nalozhnitsa* [The Concubine], someone as discriminating as Aleksandr Pushkin praised it highly. Pushkin's view, however, was in the minority, and *Tsyganka* did not enjoy popularity until the turn of the century when it appealed to the Russian Symbolists.

Tsyganka focuses on the tale's three dramatis personae (the protagonist, Eletskoi; his concubine, the gypsy girl Sara; and Eletskoi's latest romantic fixation, the fashionable but as yet unspoiled Vera). The narrator, more often than not highly dramatized in the Romantic age, especially of the late 1820s and the 1830s, is almost completely masked behind an omniscient voice. All other figures in the tale are relegated to the same background as the poem's superfluous detail. Rather than thrust such detail to the foreground, and rather than focus reader attention on history or social mores (a common occurrence in long poems of the period), Baratynskii contracts the action into eight chapters of rhymed verse of inconstant pattern and unequal stanza length. Through brief mention of setting and historical moment, and through a representation of the character's thoughts, Baratynskii permits the reader into Eletskoi's condition. He is Byronic: an outsider, lost to the world and to himself, repugnant to many, even to himself, a wayfarer without direction, a thoroughly superfluous man, much on the pattern of Pushkin's Onegin and, later, Lermontov's Pechorin.

The poem begins as a party breaks up and Eletskoi surveys the damage done to the room where he and his friends have played the epicure. The condition of the room, bespattered and wrecked, is symbolic of Eletskoi's state. He peers from the window and surveys Moscow. It, too, is spiritually empty. The narrative shifts (chapter 2) to Eletskoi's past, his upbringing, the loss of his parents, his isolation, profligacy, debauchery, and eventual flight abroad, where his prodigal ways were only confirmed by the behavioural code of those, like him, in Europe who aped an idea of Byron and his dramatis personae. Surfeited by this emptiness, Eletskoi returns to Moscow with nothing more than the desire to continue his masquerade – he mocks society's conceits and unmasks its deceits by bringing the gypsy girl, Sara, into his home where they live in wanton abandon – their evenings spent in wine, song, dance, and illicit sex. From this relationship came the poems's original (and scandalous) title: *Nalozhnitsa* [The Concubine].

Tiring, à la Onegin, of the eternal round of balls, theatre, salons, men's clubs, and nights with Sara, Eletskoi begins to seek an Other whose sensibilities might match his own, whose "soul" might return his to him. Enter Vera (chapter 3), whom he pursues for most of a year. His reputation precedes him; she remains wary of his manoeuvres, at least until they dance at a masked ball – he mystifies her with his "secret" heart. Sara finds entry to the ball and threatens Vera, who apparently has read neither Byron nor Pushkin. Essentially weak as an individual and undifferentiated emotionally and intellectually, Eletskoi bows to Sara's wishes and remains with her (chapter 4), but Vera's silent call draws him ever toward her and away from Sara. On a fateful evening, again at a ball, Eletskoi assaults Vera with the extent of his longing and his desire, manipulates her callow mind, throws her into confusion, and demands a confession from her as he himself has confessed (chapter 5). Vera promises to elope with him (chapter 6). Eletskoi returns to Sara to break the news, but before his arrival (chapter 7), Sara procures from an old gypsy woman a potion she believes will deliver Eletskoi's heart back to her. It is poison – Eletskoi drinks it and dies. Sara goes mad, and the news of Eletskoi's death drives a now despondent Vera to Europe. She returns to Moscow a cold princess and lives amid society, but not as a part of it. No one reaches her pain, no one wins her heart.

Baratynskii's concise, fast-paced story is rich in psychologically telling gesture and in the multivalenced word, especially "dusha/soul" and the many references to sight ("vzgliad", "vzor", "glaza/ochi", and related verbs and adverbs) and to light ("luch", "blesk", "svecha", "zerkalo", "ogon'", "luna"). His rhymes are not hackneyed, and the iambic tetrameters move with force and balance. The poem is based on a series of structural, formal, emotional, and ideational opposites, which give the verse drive and a feeling of comprehensiveness.

The criticism the poem received was ill-deserved, as Pushkin noted, for the story line and its embodiment in the concise and restrained verse, typical of Baratynskii, bespeak a masterly skill. What is more the poem recreates the Byronic type familiar to an audience schooled on *Evgenii Onegin*, but in Baratynskii's

Russian embodiment it is superior as a psychological portrait. Where Tat'iana discovered the secret Byronic heart of her beloved through reading Evgenii's marginalia, the reader of *Tsyganka* is permitted more direct access through reference to lying and self-deceit (as well as their counterparts, gullibility and obliviousness).

The old woman who passes on the poison to Sara lies to her about its efficacy. Sara believes the potion will bring Eletskoi's love, not death. Sara entices Eletskoi to imbibe it, saying that it will bring him a peaceful sleep. Eletskoi believes Sara and in fact falls asleep, but forever. Every transaction is marked by deception. Eletskoi attempts to deceive Sara about his love for Vera, Sara does not believe him and plots with the old woman to work their respective lies. Vera, by consenting to elope with Eletskoi, deceives her guardian. Other than at the level of narrative, there is only one instance in which this pattern of deception is moot: when Eletskoi confesses his love to Vera, he believes what he says to her as much as she eventually does.

More central to the poem than Eletskoi's death is his self-delusion in thinking that he can remain constant to Vera by altering a pattern of life inseparable from his identity. His love of Vera represents his hope (hence her name meaning "faith") about himself and his future. She is mere projection. Since his words and actions are all a mask, there is no evidence presented in the poem that he can be trusted to alter himself in the least. In fact, he seeks change only through an Other, not through his own wellsprings, which are undeveloped, perhaps even non-existent. Consequently, Eletskoi's self-deception constitutes the ultimate lie of the text. It convinces Vera because it convinces Eletskoi. At the lexical, symbolic, psychological, and ideational centre of the poem, therefore, we find continual reference to "sight" or "vision"; these words capture metaphorically the epistemological theme (the pursuit of a knowledge adequate to reality) that structures the poem.

Vera pays for the consequences of Eletskoi's lie, Eletskoi pays for Sara's, and Sara pays for the old woman's. The central form of evil, then, is constituted of the one who remains unaffected by it, the old gypsy woman, who might be considered the authentic *tsyganka* (gypsy woman) of the poem's revised title. Unhappiness results inevitably, as presaged and thematized in a variety of forms of separation that are symbolized and literalized in the poem. In Baratynskii's concluding words to chapter 5, from identities to lives, all is "darkness", "destruction", "desiccation", and "emptiness".

LEWIS BAGBY

Sumerki

Twilight

Poetry collection, 1842

Sumerki [Twilight], a collection of 26 poems (27 in the manuscript), was Russia's first fully integrated poetic cycle that was not constructed in conformity with some generic principle and that formed a single titled book. "Twilight" is the time of decline, both personal and in spiritual culture itself. It is a Romantic work written after the "high-point" of Romanticism; moreover, its poetic language is archaized as compared with the language of the "Pushkin Pleiad". Anachronism and archaism become almost declarative; the exposition of "modern" topics is ornamented with classical allusions, themes of modernity interlace with those of antiquity. Ambivalence and duality govern the "twilight" discourse; everything is subordinated to the logic of transition and ambiguity. A series of leitmotifs binds the work into a "lyrical unity", but this unity is self-contradictory: recurrent motifs form semantic oppositions ("the old" and "the new", "life" and "death", "intuition" and "*ratio*", "meaning" and "senselessness", "communion" and "solitude") that are presented as unresolvable. The complicated structure conveys a philosophical doubt that undermines all values, both social and personal: it is the objectification of the alienated spirit, estranged from Others and Self. In *Sumerki*, Baratynskii's impersonal tone is developed to the full extent: 13 out of 26 poems have no lyrical "I", eight are not "addressed"; in seven of them, neither the speaker nor addressee are explicit.

The dedicatory poem, "Kniaziu Petru Andreevichu Viazemskomu" [To Prince Petr Andreevich Viazemskii], occupies a special place. Its title is printed in the book's half-title, serving as the dedication to the whole collection. Viazemskii's name itself is a symbol – he is a "star from the scattered Pleiad". The poet speaks either to "nobody" or to an audience from his past; contemporaneity is not supposed to understand him. The opening (actually second) piece, "Poslednii poet" ("The Last Poet"), describes the fate of a genuine singer; the offspring of Hellas/Nature, he is rejected by modernity and commits suicide. Two antiquities, classical and that of "natural" man, represent the lost ideal. In the modern world the truthful "language" of past cultures is forgotten, as in "Prejudice! it is a fragment (of the truth of old) ..." ; so is the "language of Nature", as in "Signs" ("Primety"). The "love" relationship between Nature and man has been broken; she (Nature) speaks to the heart rather than to the mind; rational man has become unable to understand the meaning of her signs.

The next poem, "Vsegda i v purpure i v zlate ..." [Always in both purple and gold ...], is a madrigal to an aging beauty (woman of "twilight"). The praise here is an oxymoron: "a shade", she is said to be more alive than those who live. In "Filida s kazhdoiu zimoiu ..." ("Phyllida") the same theme is treated with mockery that (as is normal in Baratynskii's epigrams) suddenly expands to the sublime ("the sepulchral Aphrodite"). Both the madrigal and the epigram develop a classical topos, both can be perceived as "epigrams imitated from the ancients". Motifs of transition (day to night, life to death) constitute the theme of "intermediacy" that becomes explicit in "Nedonosok" [The Stillborn], a soliloquy of a "poor spirit", "a winged sigh" that cannot find its place "between earth and heavens". Deprived of mythological identification, this personage is unique in the Russian lyrics of the time. Although this embodied oxymoron is a figure of fantasy, its situation is similar to that of a poet-prophet who speaks, in solitude, to a goblet of wine, as he is depicted (a self-portrait) in "Bokal" [The Goblet]; the poet hovers between extremes ("revelations of Hell or heavenly dreams"), like the strange spirit itself.

The theme of time (historical or individual) predominates in *Sumerki*. Unidirectional, time comes to an inevitable and senseless end (death); opposed to it is cyclic "timeless" time. In "Nedonosok", the two concepts collide in the concluding rhyme, "skorotechnost'-vechnost'" ("transience-eternity"), the latter being called "senseless" (uncensored manuscript). In the poem,

"Na chto vy, dni! Iudol'nyi mir iavlen'ia ..." [What use are you, days? The earthly world (will not change) its phenomena ...], with its unresolvable duality of soul and body, the soul "drowses", seeing "recurrent dreams", whereas the body "senselessly gazes" at the "fruitless" recurrence of days and nights. Both eternity and earthly life are meaningless and, in this sense, equal. They are contrasted, however, in "Tolpe trevozhnyi den' priveten, no strashna ..." [To the crowd the agitated day is welcome, but terrible ...] that describes, using both classical ("Pagan") and biblical ("Christian") allusions, the spiritual ascent (from illusive unreality through material reality to mystic suprareality) of which the artist is capable. "Osen'" [Autumn], the central poem of the collection, leads to a different conclusion.

The opening stanzas of "Osen'" expose a solemn picture of "the evening of the year" and describe activities of the ploughman who now represents "natural man". The life of nature is circular; and so too is the time in which the peasant lives. Autumn has given him its fruits, and the coming winter is a long awaited break before a new agricultural cycle. The further development of the poem is a metaphysical interiorization of natural scenes, exploiting the biblical symbolism of fruits/ harvest. Will "the worldly furrows" reward the poet thinker ("the ploughman of the field of life")? No, he will remain "alone with anguish", and his word "will find no response". For him, "there is no harvest"; winter becomes the metaphor of death.

The theme of the response to the poet "frames" the collection; it appears in "Poslednii poet", forms the nucleus of "Osen'", and occurs in the closing poem, "Rifma" [Rhyme], in which the position of the modern poet is contrasted to that of the ancient orator. Unlike the latter, the former meets with no understanding. It is only rhyme (poetry itself) that "consoles him by its response", a pessimistic finale to the concluding piece of Baratynskii's last book of poetry.

IGOR PILSHCHIKOV

Anna Aleksandrovna Barkova 1901–1976

Poet

Biography

Born in Ivanovo-Voznesensk, 29 July 1901. Daughter of school janitor. Educated to secondary level at M.I. Kramarevskaia's private gymnasium, Ivanovo-Voznesensk; joined "The Circle of Genuine Proletarian Poets", 1918; began working as journalist and writer for the Circle's newspaper *Rabochii krai*, 1919. Wrote under the pseudonym, Kalika perekhozhaia. Moved to Moscow, 1922; worked as Lunacharskii's secretary and published two books. Began working at *Pravda* newspaper, c.1924. Arrested and sentenced to five years in a labour camp for writing subversive poems, 1934; released into exile in Kaluga, 1939; arrested a second time, 1947; in camps until the Khrushchev amnesty of January 1956; arrested again in connection with a satirical poem about Molotov found in her private correspondence, and denunciations from neighbours, 1957; released, 1965; allowed to return to Moscow, 1967. Recipient: Prize of the Ivanovo Regional Administration in 1993, for her posthumous collection *Vozvrashchenie* [Return] (1990). Died of cancer in Moscow, 29 April 1976.

Publications

Collected Edition

Izbrannoe: iz gulagskogo arkhiva [A Selection: From the Gulag Archive]. Ivanovo, 1992.

Poetry

Zhenshchina [Woman]. Petrograd, 1922.

Poems in *Dodnes' tiagoteet*, Moscow, 1989, 335–55.

"Stikhi raznykh let" [Poems of Various Years], *Lazur'*, 1 (1989), 31–48.

"Rovesnitsa veka" [The Same Age as the Century], *Volga*, 5 (1989), 165–68.

Vozvrashchenie [Return]. Ivanovo, 1990.

"Plamia snegov" [Flame of Snows], *Literaturnoe obozrenie*, 8 (1991), 7–12.

Geroi nashego vremeni [A Hero of Our Time]. Moscow, 1992.

An Anthology of Russian Women's Writing 1777–1992, edited by Catriona Kelly. Oxford, Oxford University Press, 1994 (contains three of Barkova's poems in Russian and in English).

Russian Women's Prison Camp Memoirs, edited by John Crowfoot and Simeon Vilensky. London, Virago, and Bloomington, Indiana University Press, 1995 (contains six of Barkova's poems, translated by Catriona Kelly).

Play

Nastas'ia Koster [Nastas'ia Bonfire]. Moscow and Petrograd, 1923.

Fiction

"Kak delaetsia luna" [How the Moon Grows]; "Vosem' glav bezumiia" [Eight Chapters of Madness]; "Schast'e statistika Plaksiutkina" [The Happiness of the Statistician Plaksiutkin], in *Izbrannoe: iz gulagskogo arkhiva*, 1992, 89–222.

Essays and Reviews

"Sof'ia Parnok, *Rozy Pierii*. Stikhi", *Pechat' i revoliutsiia*, 3 (1923).

"Obretaemoe vremia" [Time Being Found Again], in *Izbrannoe: iz gulagskogo arkhiva*, 1992, 267–70.

Diaries and Notebooks

"Otryvki iz dnevnikov i zapisnykh knig" [Extracts from Diaries and Notebooks], in *Izbrannoe: iz gulagskogo arkhiva*, 1992, 225–66.

Critical Studies

"Predislovie", by L.N. Taganov, in *Vozvrashchenie*, 1990, 1–20.

"Krestnyi put' Anny Barkovoi", by Lev Anninskii, Introduction to "Plamia snegov", *Literaturnoe obozrenie*, 8 (1991).

"Anna Barkova – verhinderte Weiblichkeit", by Steffi Lunau, in *Russland aus der Feder seiner Frauen: zum femininen Diskurs in der russischen Literatur: Materialien des am 21/22 Mai 1992 im Fachbereich Slavistik der Universität Potsdam durchgeführten Kolloquims*, edited by Frank Göpfert, Munich, Sagner, 1992.

"Anna Barkova – Untergründe und Wandlungen", by Steffi Lunau, in *Beiträge zur Baltistik und Slawistik: Wissenschaftliche Beiträge der EMA-Universität*, Greifswald, 1992, 63–70.

Prosti moiu nochnuiu dushu, by L.N. Taganov, Ivanovo, 1993.

"Anna Barkova", by Catriona Kelly and Carol Ueland, in *Dictionary of Russian Women Writers*, edited by Marina Ledkovsky, Charlotte Rosenthal, and Mary Zirin, Westport, Connecticut, Greenwood Press, 1994, 57–60.

Anna Barkova is one of the most important poets to be rediscovered during the glasnost period. Like many women writers (and indeed writers generally), she had disappeared from Russian literature in the late 1920s; what was more, her mature work was so overtly anti-Soviet that publication would have been unthinkable before the late 1980s. Incarcerated in labour camps, or living in the harsh conditions of provincial exile, for the best part of 30 years, Barkova wrote with great frankness of her experiences in the camps, and also of her nauseated disillusion with the system that she, like many other young people from working-class backgrounds, had originally welcomed wholeheartedly. The protégée of Anatolii Lunacharskii, who had extravagantly described her birthplace as "a new poetic Athens", Barkova had been welcomed by Soviet critics as everything from a new Joan of Arc to a new Akhmatova, and had enthusiastically flung herself into Soviet literary life, writing work that she herself later described as representing the "abstract romanticism" of the early 1920s, and lambasting Sof'ia Parnok's Neoclassical collection *Loza* [The Vine] as "of no interest to young working people". But as early as 1927 Barkova had begun to regard Soviet literature, and Soviet life in general, with a high degree of cynicism, and her poems of the early 1930s pour scorn on the institutions and slogans of the day, from VAPP to compulsory optimism.

Barkova's poetry is remarkable not only for its bitterness, however, but for its honesty. She sees herself and her contemporaries not just as victims and martyrs, but as the responsible agents of their own fates. Her uncompromising standpoint towards herself and the rest of the world is communicated by means of uniquely harsh and acerbic intonation, diction, and imagery. In a poem of 1955, the camps are apostrophized as "pens for human cattle" (*Vozvrashchenie* [Return]); "Patrioticheskii tsikl'" [Patriotic Cycle] (1946), part of "Stikhi raznykh let" [Poems of Various Years], introduces the powerful and repellent image of human flesh trampled by muddy boots in a mass grave; in another poem, written a decade earlier, Barkova speaks less naturalistically, but with equal forcefulness, of a generation "trodden like plums till the juice oozes" ("Plamia snegov" [Flame of the Snows]). In her late poetry, she was equally critical of the post-Thaw Soviet Union of the 1960s; some of her last work, collected in *Izbrannoe*, apocalyptically anticipates the wholesale destruction that would be brought by a nuclear war.

The ferocity of Barkova's language defies conventional Russian views of what constitutes appropriate femininity – as she herself anticipated in her 1954 poem "Nechto avtobiograficheskoe" [A Few Autobiographical Facts]. It also offends against the customary codes of educated speech, a fact for which Lev Anninskii felt compelled to apologize in his introduction to a selection of Barkova's verse published in 1990, as Lunacharskii had in his laudatory, if slightly patronizing, preface to *Zhenshchina* [Woman] in 1922 – the only collection of Barkova's verse to be published in her lifetime. But if the violence of Barkova's poetic language, and the roughness of the balladic stanzas that she preferred, radiate a proletarian independence of literary culture and *kul'turnost'* more generally, her poetry is, for all that, far from sophisticated. Widely read from childhood, she had a broad selection of favourite authors, including Oscar Wilde (whose "Ballad of Reading Gaol" is likely to have influenced her own prison poems), Edgar Allan Poe, Sappho (whom several of her poems treat as an *alter ego*), and Osip Mandel'shtam, as well as the more predictable Dostoevskii, Nadezhda Mandel'shtam and Anatole France. Her poetry also displays a strong awareness of literary and historical parallels, and the masking that in her early work sometimes seemed mere posing and posturing became, in her later writing, the source of tragic irony. In some of the poems that she wrote in the camps, such as "V barake" [In the Camp Barracks] (1935) (in *Geroi nashego vremeni*), she juxtaposed the female Symbolist persona of the Tartar Princess as created by Elizaveta Kuz'mina-Karavaeva, and the squalid surroundings of her camp living-quarters, to powerfully sardonic effect. Elsewhere, in "Patrioticheskii tsikl'", for example, the degradation of traditional intellectual culture draws her bile; Pushkin and Shakespeare are just two of many victims of totalitarian terror. And in her fine poem "Robespierre" (1953) (part of "Plamia snegov"), she sees the revolutionary hero as an ice-eyed, but sentimentally enthusiastic psychopath, associated with Peter the Great on the one hand (he operates a "capstan wheel"), and with Stalin on the other (he prates of "speculation" as an evil to which he intends to put an end). Barkova was also gifted with a strong sense of humour, which varied, if it did not soften, the accusatory tone of many of her poems. In an epigrammatic 1970s piece, "Shutka" [Joke] (in *Izbrannoe*), for example, the sight of a tablet to the "grandfather of Soviet aviation" causes Barkova to name herself the "grandmother of proletarian poetry", before observing that this is one grandmother who has outlived her descendant. Above all, in her late love poetry (much of which is addressed to her friend Valentina Makotinskaia), she adopts an intimate, contemplative and often self-questioning manner that complements the harshly expostulatory character of her civic verse.

Besides poetry, Barkova was the author of *Nastas'ia Koster* [Nastas'ia Bonfire], a vivid and memorable study of the female leader of a 17th-century popular rebellion. Her occasional excursions into prose, most particularly her essay on memory "Obretaemoe vremia" [Time Being Found Again] (a play on the Russian title of Proust's *A la recherche du temps perdu*) and her diaries and notebooks, are also forceful and original expressions of her unique talent. Since her death, contacts of the poet, in particular L.N. Taganov and Z.Ia. Kholodova, have been working to collect Barkova's scattered archive, collecting materials from NKVD and KGB holdings as well as from Barkova's surviving friends; Taganov is also the author of an excellent biography of Barkova. But much bibliographical work still remains to be done; definitive texts need to be established and variants collated in order to facilitate the detailed critical study that this fine poet so richly deserves.

CATRIONA KELLY

Konstantin Nikolaevich Batiushkov 1787–1855

Poet and prose writer

Biography

Born in Vologda, 29 May 1787. Attended private boarding schools in St Petersburg: Pensionnat Jacquinot, 1797–1800; Pensionnat Tripoli, 1801–02; then under the tutelage of Mikhail Murav'ev. Served in the Ministry of Public Education, January 1803–04 and 1805–07. Began to publish poetry, 1805. Associated with Aleksei Olenin's group. Took part in Prussian campaign, 1807; Finnish campaign (as Jägers officer), 1808–09. Entered Moscow literary circles, started publishing in Karamzin's journal, *Vestnik Evropy*, 1809–10. Accepted into The Free Society, but soon left, 1812. Worked as Assistant Keeper of Manuscripts at Imperial Public Library (St Petersburg), 1812. Took part in "foreign" campaign against Napoleon, 1813–14, decorated. Returned to St Petersburg via England and Sweden, 1814. Routine military service, Kamenets-Podolskii (Bessarabia), 1815. Accepted into Arzamas society, 1815, and The Society of Lovers of Russian Letters at Moscow University, 1816. Transferred to Household Guards and retired, 1816. Diplomatic service in Italy, 1819–21. Granted indefinite leave because of increasing insanity, 1821–22; sent to St Petersburg, as a result of his persecution mania, 1823, the *Maison de santé* in Sonnenstein (Saxony), 1824–28; Moscow, 1828–33; Vologda (released from service, granted a life pension). Died in Vologda, 19 July 1855.

Publications

Collected Editions

Sochineniia, 3 vols. St Petersburg, 1885–87.
Sochineniia. Moscow and Leningrad, 1934; reprinted, The Hague, Europe Printing, 1967.
Polnoe sobranie stikhotvorenii. Moscow and Leningrad, 1964.
Sochineniia, 2 vols. Moscow, 1989.

Poetry and Essays

Opyty v stikhakh i proze [Essays in Verse and Prose], 2 vols. St Petersburg, 1817.
"Love in a Boat; The Prisoner; To the Rhine", translated by John Bowring, in *Specimens of the Russian Poets*, London, 1821–23.
"The Dying Tasso: The Friend's Shadow", in *Anthology of Russian Literature from the Earliest Period to the Present Time*, translated by Leo Wiener, vol. 2, New York and London, Putnam, 1902–03.
"To Bacchante; A Jovial Hour", in *Russian Poems*, translated by Charles Fillingham Coxwell, London, Daniel, 1929.
Opyty v stikhakh i proze. Moscow, 1977.
"My Penates; The Shade of My Friend", in *The Ardis Anthology of Russian Romanticism*, edited by Christine Rydel, Ann Arbor, Ardis, 1984.

Literary Criticism

O grecheskoi antologii [On the Greek Anthology], with S.S. Uvarov. St Petersburg, 1820; unsigned.

Critical Studies

Poeziia Batiushkova, by N.V. Fridman, Moscow, 1971.
"The Simile in Batyushkov and Zhukovsky", by Doris Johnson, *Russian Literature Triquarterly*, 7 (1973), 407–22.
Konstantin Batyushkov, by Ilya Z. Serman, New York, Twayne, 1974.
A History of Russian Literature in the Romantic Period, vol. 1, by William Edward Brown, Ann Arbor, Ardis, 1986.
Konstantin Batiushkov: stranstviia i strasti, by V.A. Koshelev, Moscow, 1987.

Konstantin Nikolaevich Batiushkov (along with Zhukovskii) is generally accepted to be the founder of a new (Romantic) school in Russian poetry of the early 19th century. He created exemplar models for several genres in the Golden Age: the erotic and "historical" elegy, the "friendly" epistle, and the anthological poem. Batiushkov's exquisite poetry assimilated the heritage of the late French and Russian classicism, at the same time anticipating the essentially Romantic tendency to blur genre boundaries. His metapoetic prose essays raised the level of literary criticism. His familiar letters (which began to appear in the press from the 1820s) are of great literary interest.

Batiushkov began his literary career under the patronage of Mikhail Murav'ev, the creator of Russian Sentimentalist "light verse", and under the influence of Olenin's Neoclassicist circle; hence his interest in both Latin and Scandinavian antiquity,

Italian Renaissance poetry, and the French *poésie légère* – a combination already found in one of his earliest pieces, "Mechta" [Dream]. Containing both original and translated fragments, it is Batiushkov's artistic "archetype" as well as the symbol of his poetic evolution, for he continuously reworked it and published its successive wordings. Batiushkov's attitude to contemporary Russian literary life revealed itself as early as the satirical "Poslanie k stikham moim" [Epistle to My Verses], his first published work, which mocks the stylistic extremes of both epigone Sentimentalism and "Slavo-Russian" archaism. The poems written in 1804–11 established Batiushkov's artistic image – that of a "voluptuary" Horatian hedonist.

The poet's military and erotic experiences in the year 1807 formed the background for two elegies: "Vospominaniia 1807 goda" [Recollections of 1807] or "Vospominanie" [Recollection], first published in 1809, and "Vyzdorovleniie" [Convalescence] (1817); they had a considerable influence on the development of the Romantic elegy. During 1807–08 Batiushkov undertook the verse translation of Torquato Tasso's *Jerusalem Delivered*. Only two extracts appeared (1808–09); however, the famous Italian became a personage in his poems: the epistle imitated from La Harpe, "K Tassu" ("To Tasso") 1808, was later eclipsed by the elegy, "Umiraiushchii Tass" ("The Dying Tasso") 1817, Batiushkov's best-known verse work. In 1809–11 Batiushkov composed numerous "imitations", including those from Tibullus (III,3; I,10; I,3) and "the French Tibullus" – Parny: "Prividenie" [Ghost], "Istochnik" [The Torrent] etc.; he called himself "a little Tibullus", and was known to his contemporaries as "the Russian Parny". Batiushkov's original works are filled with classical and Neoclassical allusions, while his translations are highly original; he contributed a great deal to the formation of the new poetic language.

"Videnie na beregakh Lety" [A Vision on the Shores of the Lethe] (1809), made Batiushkov famous as a satirist. This caustic and offensive poem – not intended for publication and appearing only in 1841 – describes a dream: all Russian poets have died, and their works sink into the Lethe. Attacking the same targets as before, Batiushkov "drowned" all his contemporaries except for Karamzin and Derzhavin (not mentioned), and Krylov ("saved"). Another satire (in a form of pastiche), "Pevets v Besede liubitelei russkogo slova" [The Bard in The Colloquy of the Lovers of the Russian Word], (written 1812, with Izmailov), confirmed his reputation as a fighting Karamzinist. In 1811–12 a masterpiece of a different kind was composed: "Moi Penaty" ("My Penates"), "an epistle to Zhukovskii and Viazemskii" (published 1814), extraordinary for the diversity of contrasting themes and its "light" metre (iambic trimeters). The poem's main device (the open mixing of antiquity and modernity) became fashionable; the 3-foot "friendly" epistle was recognized as a separate genre.

The "Patriotic War" against France (1812) marked a turning-point in Batiushkov's poetics. His interest in French poetry decreased and his hedonistic motifs disappeared. An epistle-elegy, "K Dashkovu" [To Dashkov], is an eloquent expression of this new attitude. In "Ten' druga" ("The Shade of My Friend") (1814–15), the evil of war becomes personal grief. Another crisis – an unhappy love relationship – produced, however, his finest love elegies: "Ia chuvstvuiu, moi dar v Poezii pogas ..." [I Feel My Gift of Poetry Has Died ...], "Moi Genii" [My Genius] and "Razluka" [The Parting]. In addition, he made his first attempt "to broaden the range of the elegy" as, for example, in "Na razvalinakh zamka v Shvetsii" [On the Ruins of a Castle in Sweden], where meditative "elegism" acquired a historical dimension. The verse tale, *Strannik i domosed* [The Wanderer and the Home-Lover], and prose essays on Russian and Italian poets were written, as well as two outstanding pre-Romantic "manifestos": a program article "Nechto o poete i poezii" [A Word on the Poet and Poetry] and "Rech' o vliianii legkoi poezii na iazyk" [A Discourse on the Influence of Light Verse on Language] (1816). In the latter, Batiushkov invents his poetic genealogy: a Pan-European light verse tradition, from the Ancient idyllists and elegists to the Russian Sentimentalists, whereas in the former, the unity of the poet's life and poetry is emphasized: "live as you write, and write as you live". This period includes brilliant translations (Millevoye, Parny), and is crowned by an epistle/elegy, "K drugu" [To a Friend] (Viazemskii), which synthesizes focal themes of Batiushkov's poetry, symbolically representing his life's path.

The success of Batiushkov's Collected Works (1817) was immense; he was proclaimed one of the two leading poets (along with Uvarov), who appeared as the immediate predecessors of Pushkin. Most of the poems, written especially for this edition, do not belong to the "light" genre. Three, epic-lyric in character, were later called "historical elegies": "Geziod i Omir - Soperniki" [Hesiod and Homer - Rivals] (from Millevoye), "Perekhod cherez Rein: 1814" [The Crossing of the Rhine: 1814], and "The Dying Tasso". Along with the anthological cycle (1821; under Herder's influence), 13 epigrams from the Greek Anthology (1817–18?; published 1820) were to make Batiushkov the founder of the Russian anthological verse tradition. Little is known about his works written abroad. Among his extant poems are two *chefs d'oeuvre*: an elegized version of a stanza from Byron's *Childe Harold* (published 1828, probably with Pushkin's editorial corrections) and a *huitain* devoted to Baia (published 1857). In 1834 Batiushkov's piece from the early 1820s, "Izrechenie Mel'khisedeka" [The Apophthegm of Melchizedek], appeared as if posthumously. After he became mentally ill, he wrote only a few incoherent texts, and was considered, in Belinskii's words, "as if dead".

IGOR PILSHCHIKOV

Battle Beyond the Don *see* Zadonshchina

Dem'ian Bednyi 1883–1945

Poet

Biography

Born Efim Alekseevich Pridvorov, near Kherson, 13 April 1883, into a peasant family. Attended school in Gubovka; Kiev Military School for Medical Assistance, 1896–1900. First publication, 1899. Studied history and philology at St Petersburg University, 1904–08. Literary career began in 1909 with publications in *Russkoe bogatstvo*. Adopted the pen name Dem'ian Bednyi in 1911. Joined Bolshevik section of the Socialist Democratic Party in 1912. Contributed regularly to *Pravda* and *Zvezda*. Served as a doctor in the Russian Army during World War I and served in the Red Army during the Civil War. Following controversial publications, expelled from the Communist Party, 1938. Died in May 1945.

Publications

Collected Editions

Polnoe sobranie sochinenii, 19 vols. Moscow and Leningrad, 1925–33.
Sobranie sochinenii, 5 vols. Moscow, 1953–54.
Izbrannye sochineniia, 2 vols. Moscow, 1959.
Stikhotvoreniia, 8 vols. Moscow, 1963–65.
Stikhi, basni [Poetry, Fables]. Moscow, 1973.

Critical Studies

Popular Poetry in Soviet Russia, by George Z. Patrick, Berkeley, University of California Press, 1929, 95–108; reprinted New York, Blom, 1971.
Dem'ian Bednyi, by I.S. Eventov, Moscow, 1953.
Dem'ian Bednyi, by V. Kurilenkov, Moscow, 1954.
Dem'ian Bednyi, Ocherk tvorchestva, by V.A. Tsybenko, Novosibirsk, 1958.
Dem'ian Bednyi, by A. Makarov, Moscow, 1964.
Vospominaniia o Dem'iane Bednom, edited by D.E. Pridvorov and A.V. Priamkov, Moscow, 1966.
Dem'ian Bednyi, by K. Brazul', Moscow, 1967.
Zhizn' i tvorchestvo Dem'iana Bednogo, by I. Eventov, Leningrad, 1967.
Poet krasnogo Pitera, by I. Eventov, Leningrad, 1968.
"Memoirs", by M. Kanivez, *Minuvshee*, 7 (1989), 58–111.

Dem'ian Bednyi adopted the style of Ivan Krylov, especially in his fables, which were mostly published in 1913. He also continued the tradition of civic poetry in the vein of Nekrasov and Kurochkin. One such poem appeared in *Zvezda* in 1911 – "O Dem'ian Bednom, muzhike vrednom" [About Dem'ian Bednyi, the Harmful Bloke] – and was the first time he used his pseudonym. From then on his satirical verse, fables and stories became the mouthpiece of socialist propaganda (see, for example, *Pro zemliu, pro voliu, pro rabochuiu doliu* [About Land, Freedom and the Worker's Lot] 1917, and "Kommunisticheskaia marcel'eza" [The Communist Marseillaise] 1918). Before the October Revolution, Bednyi produced sharp criticism of the shortcomings of the capitalist system in Russia. His fable "Dom" [House], for instance, refers to a newspaper article about a St Petersburg landlord who, because of his debts, was forced to build a new house out of old bricks; the six-storey building later collapsed. This episode is used by Bednyi as an allegory of Russia on the verge of collapse. "Dom" contains half-veiled allusions to the House of Romanov: the dynasty was preparing to celebrate its 300th anniversary. According to Bednyi's letter to a journalist, he would often use misleading epigraphs in his fables in order to "smuggle anti-monarchist verse into print".

During the Civil War Bednyi wrote political jingles, satirical verse and Red Army songs. By aiming at an uneducated audience his poems became hugely popular among the soldiers and peasants. In the early 1920s his verse was used in the crackdown on religion. (See for example his "Novyi zavet bez iz''iana evangelista Dem'iana" [The New Testament Without the Omission of the Evangelist Dem'ian]). The narrative poem *Nepgrad* provides a satirical picture of Russia during the period of New Economic Policy. In 1930 the publication of his poem "Slezai s pechi!" [Get off the Stove!] brought his career to a halt. It was seen by officials as a crude portrayal of the Russian populace as a lazy lot; even so, RAPP appreciated his work as the embodiment of truly socialist literature. Further criticism came from Bukharin, in 1934 at the First Writers' Congress. In 1936 Bednyi rewrote the libretto for Borodin's comic opera *Bogatyri* [Epic Heroes] but his attempt to create a new style of folk opera was sharply criticized by the authorities, who accused him of producing a satire on Russian history and Russia's conversion to Christianity; subsequently he was excluded from the Communist Party in 1938. Some accounts suggest that Bednyi's downfall in 1936 was provoked by his personal criticism of Stalin. According to M. Kanivez's memoirs, Bednyi was close to Stalin in the mid-1930s, but an informer – Professor Prezent – penetrated Bednyi's circle and recorded all his conversations with the poet in a diary. Bednyi's criticism of Stalin was reported to the NKVD, which led to official criticism of his work in press. (Prezent reported, for example, that Bednyi allegedly criticized a banquet where Stalin had eaten strawberries while the rest of the country starved.)

Bednyi's work was published again only during World War II when he wrote anti-fascist satirical verse. At the end of his life he never regained the position he had earlier enjoyed as a leading literary figure. He died following an illness in May 1945. A Party resolution issued on 24 February 1952 denounced the 1950 and 1951 editions of his work as a political distortion of Soviet history. However, after the death of Stalin his work was recognized and became essential reading at schools and universities as an example of revolutionary poetry. Soviet scholarship praised his work for its innovative democratic character. His civic verse and fables influenced the much celebrated Soviet poets M. Isakovskii and S. Mikhalkov as well as other avowed socialist realists of the 1960s and 1970s. According to Gor'kii, Lenin appreciated the propagandist efforts of Bednyi, but found his poetry too crude and too primitive. Bednyi wrote an epitaph on Lenin's death – "Snezninki" [Snowflakes] – which depicts the nation's mourning over the leader's death in a sentimental and lyrical mode. In spite of its limited range of themes, Bednyi's poetry is an interesting example of the literary imitation of spoken folk-verse, famous for its short lines, AABB rhymes, and flexibility of metre.

ALEXANDRA SMITH

Vissarion Grigor'evich Belinskii 1811–1848

Literary critic and social thinker

Biography

Born in Sveaborg, Finland, 11 June 1811. Attended local school in Chembar, Penza Province; gymnasium in Penza from 1825; Moscow University, 1829–32: expelled, mainly for writing a juvenile play, *Dmitrii Kalinin*, containing tirades against serfdom. Contributor to *Teleskop*, 1834–36: journal was closed down for publishing Chaadaev's first "Philosophical Letter", 1836. Editor of *Moskovskii nabliudatel'*, 1838–39. Moved to St Petersburg to write for *Otechestvennye zapiski*, 1839. Married: Mariia Vasil'evna Orlova in 1843; one son (died 1847) and one daughter. Travelled abroad for the first time, in the company of Annenkov, May–November 1847. On return began writing for *Sovremennik*. Died of consumption in St Petersburg, 7 June 1848.

Publications

Collected Editions

Polnoe sobranie sochinenii, 13 vols. Moscow, 1953–59.

Selected Philosophical Works [no translator named]. Moscow, Foreign Languages Publishing House, 1956.

Belinsky, Chernyshevsky, and Dobroliubov: Selected Criticism, edited by Ralph E. Matlaw [no translator named]. New York, Dutton, 1962; 2nd edition, Bloomington, Indiana University Press, 1976.

Critical Studies

Literaturnoe nasledstvo, 55–57, Moscow, 1948–51.

Vissarion Belinski 1811–1848: A Study in the Origins of Social Criticism in Russia, by Herbert E. Bowman, Cambridge, Massachusetts, Harvard University Press, 1954.

"Social and Aesthetic Values in Russian Nineteenth-Century Literary Criticism (Belinskii, Chernyshevskii, Dobroliubov, Pisarev)", by René Wellek, in *Continuity and Change in Russian and Soviet Thought*, edited by Ernest J. Simmons, New York, Russell and Russell, 1955, 382–97.

Studies in Rebellion: A Study of Aleksandr Ivanovich Hertzen, Vissarion Grigor'evich Belinskii and Mikhail Aleksandrovich Bakunin, by Evgeny Lampert, London, Routledge and Kegan Paul, 1957.

A History of Modern Criticism: 1750–1950, by René Wellek, New Haven, Yale University Press, 1965; London, Jonathan Cape, 1966, vol. 3, 243–64.

Dostoevskij and the Belinskij School of Literary Criticism, by Thelwall Proctor, The Hague, Mouton, 1969.

"Belinskii's Romantic Imagination", by C.V. Ponomareff, *Canadian-American Slavic Studies*, 7 (1973), 314–73.

Belinskij and Russian Literary Criticism: The Heritage of Organic Aesthetics, by Victor Terras, Madison, Wisconsin University Press, 1974.

"Vissarion Belinskii", by Isaiah Berlin, in *Russian Thinkers*, Harmondsworth, Penguin, 1978, 150–85.

"Vissarion Belinskii", by Joe Andrew, in his *Writers and Society During the Rise of Russian Realism*, London, Macmillan, and Atlantic Highlands, New Jersey, Humanities Press, 1980, 114–51.

"Belinskii and V.F. Odoyevsky", by Neil Cornwell, *Slavonic and East European Review*, 62 (1984), 6–24.

On Psychological Prose, by Lydia Ginzburg, edited and translated by Judson Rosengrant, Princeton, Princeton University Press, 1991.

Vissarion Grigor'evich Belinskii's career spans the period 1834–48 and thus coincides both with the middle of the repressive reign of Nicholas I, in which imaginative literature and literary criticism were the main outlets for the free spirit, and with the beginning of the Golden Age of Russian literature in which Pushkin, Gogol', and Lermontov were writing. Ultimately Belinskii significantly influenced the direction of that literature. Most importantly, he gave literature a lasting place of supreme importance in the national life and established a view of authorship as a sacred and patriotic vocation.

Belinskii's work as a whole is informed by integrity, moral intensity and a restless, passionate quest for truth, goodness and beauty, and by intolerant condemnation of falsehood, insincerity or triviality in literature and life. (He was known as "furious Vissarion".) He consistently admired Homer, Shakespeare, Goethe, Schiller, Scott, and in Russian literature, Pushkin and Gogol'. Peter the Great he revered as the ruler who had introduced western civilization to Russia and had thus made it possible to dislodge the oriental barbarism imposed on Russia as far back as the 13th century by the Tartars. Alongside these constants in Belinskii's writings, though, there were many variables, notably his view of the role of art and its relationship to reality, and his political persuasions, which changed as he was affected by new philosophical currents and works of literature.

In the early part of his career, under the influence of Schelling – notably in his first major work, "Literaturnye mechtaniia" ("Literary Reveries"), 1834 – Belinskii argued that literature in the true sense is a coherent body of works that express the consciousness of a people. He comes to the alarming conclusion that Russia, lacking an organic life of her own, does not yet have an autochthonous literature. The true artist he sees at this period (for instance in his next major essay "O russkoi povesti i o povestiakh g. Gogolia" ("About the Russian Novella and the Novellas of Mr Gogol'"), 1835, as creating unconsciously, through inspiration. In another article of 1835 Belinskii also unmade the reputation of the poet Benediktov, thus beginning a sustained attack on what he saw as the inflation and falsity of romanticism. There followed, in 1836–37, a brief flirtation with the ideas of Fichte. He also suffered from a serious illness and recuperated at friends' expense in the Caucasus. By the spring of 1838 Belinskii was under the spell of Hegel. He enthusiastically expounded German aesthetic theories, while denouncing the French 18th-century rationalist stream of thought. In this period he upheld art as an end in itself and in his article "Mentsel' – kritik Giote" ("Menzel, a Critic of Goethe") 1840, attacked the "little great men, like the minor German critic Menzel, who demanded topicality and partisanship of the artist. In a review of 1839 of a work on the Battle of Borodino he celebrated his "reconciliation with reality", exalting the authoritarian state as the ultimate reality, asserting with reference to Shakespeare's *Richard II* the divine right of kings, and allowing no sympathy for those rebels, like Aleko in Pushkin's poem "Tsygane" ("The Gypsies"), who are crushed by the "leaden weight of [society's] gigantic palm".

By 1841, Belinskii, by now writing for *Otechestvennye zapiski* in St Petersburg, fount of westernism and radical views, was veering away from Hegelian conservatism towards French rationalism and Utopian socialism and was expressing revolutionary leanings. This conversion, and Belinskii's revulsion with his former self, find clearest expression in his voluminous correspondence, particularly with Botkin, but they are also apparent in his published articles. In 1840–41 his two articles on Lermontov, and particularly his encomium to Lermontov's hero Pechorin, reflect a sympathy for the rebellious hero at odds with his environment. Articles on the poets Apollon Maikov, Polezhaev, and Baratynskii (all 1842) reflect Belinskii's view that poetry can no longer ignore current social concerns. His long essay apropos of a speech made by Nikitenko ("Rech' o kritike Nikitenko", 1824) most clearly expounds the view that the artist in the present age may no longer indulge in "bird-song" but is obliged to address the issues of the day. A review of a work by the French writer Eugène Sue (1844) gives a highly critical portrayal of the mores of the French bourgeoisie. At the same time Belinskii uses many opportunities, particularly his annual surveys of Russian literature for 1844 and 1846, to mount scathing attacks on Slavophilism, which he associates with obscurantism, servitude and oriental barbarism.

Over the period 1843–46 Belinskii published a monumental series of 11 essays on Pushkin in which he definitively established the place of the poet in Russian literature. The paramount importance of Pushkin in Russian literature is not threatened, Belinskii believes, by the fact that the critic writing about him a few years after his death, from the vantage point of an age in which a degree of topicality and utility were required in art, could clearly see that for Pushkin the end of poetry was beauty. Belinskii sets great store by Pushkin's lyric poetry, his major narrative poems (but not his light-hearted ones, such as "Graf Nulin" ("Count Nulin")), *Evgenii Onegin* (which he famously described as an "encyclopedia of Russian life"), and *Boris Godunov*. Belinskii holds Pushkin's prose in relatively low esteem, and only a few pages at the end of the last article of the cycle are devoted to it.

Much of Belinskii's energy in his final years was devoted to the promotion of the "Natural School" of writers, who sought to depict reality in a supposedly clinical, objective way and who concentrated sympathetic attention on the urban and rural poor. Belinskii himself contributed four pieces to two volumes of the almanac, *Fiziologiia Peterburga* [The Physiology of St Petersburg] (1845), edited by Nekrasov on behalf of this school, and he vigorously defended the school in his last annual survey of Russian literature, for the year of 1847. This piece provides perhaps Belinskii's most famous demand for commitment in the artist. And yet Belinskii is still conscious of the need for the artist to remain an artist rather than a mere copier of reality if his work is to have effect.

Contemporaries regarded Belinskii's famous "Letter to Gogol'", written in Silesia during his fruitless trip to the spa in 1847 in search of a cure, as his testament. The letter had a wide, illegal distribution throughout Russia in the years following Belinskii's death. It represents a furious response to the writer whom he had championed but who, in his reactionary tract *Izbrannye mesta iz perepiski s druz'iami* [Selected Passages from a Correspondence with Friends], seemed to have reneged on the obligation Belinskii had placed on the Russian writer to serve truth and civilization.

DEREK OFFORD

Vasilii Ivanovich Belov 1932–

Prose writer

Biography

Born in Timonikha in Vologda region, 23 October 1932. Attended seven-year village school and received industrial training in a factory school. Worked on the land and as a carpenter before military service, 1952–55. Journalist for the provincial press and studied at night school before admittance to the Gor'kii Literary Institute, Moscow, 1959–64. Member of the Communist Party, from 1956. Began to publish prose fiction, 1956. Since 1964, has lived mainly in Vologda and Timonikha. Recipient: State Prize for Literature, 1981. Member: Committee of Union of Russian Writers, from 1980; Soviet Writers' Union, from 1981. Secretary of the Union of Russian Writers, from 1990.

Publications

Collected Editions

Izbrannye proizvedeniia, 3 vols. Moscow, 1983–84.
Sobranie sochinenii, 5 vols. Moscow, 1993.

Fiction

Dereven'ka moia lesnaia [My Little Woodland Village]. Vologda, 1961.
Znoinoe leto [A Sultry Summer]. Vologda, 1963.
Rechnye izluki [Bends in the River]. Moscow, 1964.
Tisha da Grisha [Tisha and Grisha]. Moscow, 1966.
"Privychnoe delo", *Sever*, 1 (1966); translated as "That's How It Is", by Eve Manning, *Soviet Literature*, 1 (1969), 3–131.
Za tremia volokami [Over the Hills and Far Away]. Moscow, 1968.
Plotnitskie rasskazy. Arkhangel'sk, 1968; translated as "Carpenter's Yarns", by Eve Manning, in *Morning Rendezvous*, by V.B. Belov, Moscow, 1983.
"Bukhtiny vologodskie zaviral'nye v shesti temakh" [Nonsensical Vologda Whimsies in Six Themes], *Novyi mir*, 8 (1969), 158–84.
Sel'skie povesti [Village Tales]. Moscow, 1971.
Den' za dnem. Stranitsy derevenskogo iumora [Day after Day. Pages of Village Humour]. Moscow, 1972.
Dialog: iumoristicheskie rasskazy i povesti [Dialogue: Humorous Stories and Tales]. Petrozavodsk, 1972.
Kholmy [Hills]. Moscow, 1973.
Tseluiutsia zori ... [The Dawns Kiss ...]. Moscow, 1975.
Kanuny [The Eves]. Moscow, 1976.
Gudiat provoda [The Wires Hum]. Moscow, 1978.
Vospitanie po doktoru Spoku [Child-Rearing According to Dr Spock]. Moscow, 1978.
Vse vperedi. Moscow, 1986; translated as *The Best is Yet to Come*, by P.O. Gromm [*sic*], Moscow, Raduga, 1989.
"God velikogo pereloma: khronika deviati mesiatsev" [The Crucial Year: A Chronicle of Nine Months], *Novyi mir*, 3 (1989), 6–95.

Plays

"Raionnye stseny" [Regional Scenes], *Moskva*, 8 (1980).
Tri p'esy [Three Plays]. Moscow, 1983.

Essays

Lad: ocherki o narodnoi estetike [Harmony: Sketches on Popular Aesthetics]. Moscow, 1982.

Critical Studies

"Ivan Afrikanovich", by Efim Dorosh', *Novyi mir*, 8 (1966), 257–61.
"Tochka opory", by L. Anninskii, *Don*, 7 (1968), 175–87.
"The Contemporary Countryside in Soviet Literature: A Search for New Values", by Gleb Zhekulin, in *The Soviet Rural Community*, edited by J.R. Millar, Urbana, Illinois, University of Chicago Press, 1971, 376–403.
"Sovremennost' traditsii. Zametki o tvorchestve Vasiliia Belova", by Iu. Seleznev, *Nash sovremennik*, 11 (1974), 162–72.
"Vasilii Belov - Chronicler of the Soviet Village", by Geoffrey Hosking, *The Russian Review*, 34/2 (1975), 165–85; and in his *Beyond Socialist Realism: Soviet Fiction since "Ivan Denisovich"*, London, Granada, and New York, Holmes and Meier, 1980.
"Samim soboiu ostavaias'", by V. Oboturov, *Nash sovremennik*, 10 (1979), 158–66.
"Trud - nravstvennost' - literatura (O knige V. Belova 'Lad')", by P.S. Vykhodtsev, *Russkaia literatura*, 1 (1982), 32–46.
"Town and Country in the Work of Vasilii Belov", by Arnold McMillin, in *Selected Papers from the Second World Congress for Soviet and East European Studies: Russian Literature and Criticism*, edited by Evelyn Bristol, Berkeley, Berkeley Slavic Specialties, 1983, 130–43.
Scenes from Soviet Life: Soviet Life Through Official Literature, by Mary Seton-Watson, London, BBC Publications, 1986.
"O romane V. Belova 'Vse vperedi'", by Mikhail Nazarov, *Grani*, 146 (1987), 227–36.
Russian Village Prose: The Radiant Past, by Kathleen F. Parthé, Princeton, Princeton University Press, 1992.

Vasilii Belov is one of the most gifted of the so-called "Village Prose writers" (*derevenshchiki*) who came to prominence in the 1960s, but who seemed to have lost their audience by the early 1980s, adopting a strongly nationalist position by the end of that decade. Belov's best work, *Privychnoe delo* (*That's How It Is*) was written in 1966, but two decades later works like *Vse vperedi* (*The Best is Yet to Come*) showed a sharp decline in literary talent compounded by right-wing extremism and anti-Semitism. Influential in its time, Village Prose is now a phenomenon of the past, and its practitioners, not least Belov, are largely discredited as writers.

Belov was admitted to the Gor'kii Literary Institute as a poet, and he produced a narrative poem, *Sekretar' raikoma* [Secretary of the Regional Committee], while he was there, later also publishing an anthology of poems in Vologda. His early reputation, however, was made with prose. The first simple, sometimes plotless, sketches about country life in the Vologda region attracted readers by their rich and faithful reproduction of demotic rural rather than hackneyed urban speech. At first

Belov's sketches and stories were somewhat one-dimensional in their contrast of town and country, but his work soon acquired more universal significance.

That's How It Is was immediately recognized as the most integrated and artistically polished of his works, as, indeed, it is to this day. The story reveals the inner world of a gentle, feckless peasant, Ivan Afrikanovich Drynov, whose uncomplaining, essentially passive rural existence is ruined when he attempts to change it to help his wife and their many children. Ivan's trivial daily cares, his loving attitude to all living things, and his strong instinctive sense of tradition govern his life entirely, so that he is not a victim of the Soviet system, or even an exploited pawn, but simply an embodiment of a passing age. Belov's mastery of vivid narration using quasi-direct discourse brings the reader to the heart of a rural Russian Everyman. This rich and touching portrait elicited a massive response from commentators of all shades, no doubt partly because the hapless yet essentially decent and honest Ivan Afrikanovich embodied what was seen as either the salvation or the eternal backwardness of Russia.

The theme of loss and bitter separation from the past runs throughout much of Belov's writing of the 1960s, and the novella *Plotnitskie rasskazy* (*Carpenter's Yarns*) begins with the narrator making a nostalgic visit to his country roots, where he finds much of village life irrevocably destroyed. The story mainly consists of his account of the arguments of two old peasants, one who represents gentle, humane traditional values and the other an eager supporter of the "new era" and the inhuman commandments that had transformed the countryside. It is clear where Belov's sympathies lie, but he presents his elegiac message through dialogue rather than authorial statement.

The transformation of the Russian countryside, which began in earnest at the end of the 1920s, is the theme of Belov's major novel *Kanuny* [The Eves], set in 1928. The first two parts of this work were published in 1972 and present a perhaps idealized portrait of life in Shibanikha, a village in the Vologda region, depicting in rich social and ethnographical detail a stable and viable way of life, with its customs, games and holidays as well as work, and highlighting the peasants' respect for tradition and for each other. Into this peaceable environment comes a vindictive social outcast whose disruptive activities not only cause misery but are unmistakably linked with the Party policies that were soon to be furiously unleashed in the dekulakization and collectivization campaigns. The novel is continued in *God velikogo pereloma* [The Crucial Year], but the tenor of the work is completely different, foregrounding what Belov tendentiously chooses to regard as the leading role of Jews in the atrocities of 1929–30. The first part of this novel, however, is one of the strongest literary portrayals of collectivization in all Russian literature.

Belov's dislike of urban and modern life is well illustrated in *Vospitanie po doktoru Spoku* [Child-Rearing According to Dr Spock], which also gives a taste of his ever-growing chauvinism. Far more interesting are "Bukhtiny vologodskie zaviral'nye v shesti temakh" [Nonsensical Vologda Whimsies in Six Themes], a virtuoso display of *skaz* technique, which through a series of grotesque tall stories, and in a manner peculiar to the Vologda folk tradition, presents a comically absurdist picture of the Russian peasantry over half a century.

Belov's first attempt at drama was in 1973 with *Nad svetloi vodoi* [Above the Bright Water], which portrays the destruction of a northern village for ideological reasons; the hidebound, impersonal Party functionary is particularly well drawn. Despite the success of this play, however, he has not written a great deal for the theatre. An extraordinary piece of creative journalism, *Lad: ocherki o narodnoi estetike* [Harmony: Sketches on Popular Aesthetics], provoked huge interest and discussion at the time. In it Belov presents the social organism and culture of the northern Russian village in their totality, as a network of interrelated and intersecting processes. The tone is elegiac, and the paeon to tradition is made with restrained sorrow lightened by humour.

Belov has lost many readers by his support for extremist right-wing organizations, and this aspect of his writing is illustrated in the ironically titled novel *The Best is Yet to Come* where idealization of the countryside and the past still figures, but overshadowed by a virulent anti-urban tone, with an unmistakable anti-Semitic bent, Jews being castigated as responsible for all Russia's ills, along with Freemasons, lesbians, hypnotists, pure-bred dogs, computers, whisky and pop music – the list could be greatly extended. The shallow characterization and strident tone of the novel make it one of this writer's artistically least successful works.

Disappointing as Belov's development has been, he remains in his works of the 1960s and 1970s a leading exponent of Village Prose, writing sensitively and with an unusual mastery of style about a way of life that is gone forever.

Arnold McMillin

Andrei Belyi 1880–1934

Poet and prose writer

Biography

Born Boris Nikolaevich Bugaev in Moscow, 26 October 1880. Attended Polivanov gymnasium, 1891–99; studied science, and then philology and philosophy, at Moscow University, 1899–1906. Began using the pseudonym Andrei Belyi with the publication of his first prose work, 1902. Outstanding and prolific member of the Symbolist movement: as novelist, poet, theorist, critic, and memoirist. Married: 1) Asia Turgeneva (Anna Alekseevna) in 1914 (separated 1921); 2) Klavdiia Nikolaevna Vasil'eva in 1931. Associate editor, *Vesy*, 1907–09; worked for the publishing house Musagetes, 1909–10. Travelled to Europe, and studied anthroposophy 1912–16, settling eventually at the anthroposophical colony in Dornach, near Basel. Lecturer in Moscow and Petrograd, 1917–21; in Berlin, 1921–23. Returned to Russia in 1923. Published and re-published in Russia only sparingly throughout the Soviet period. Died in Moscow, 8 January 1934.

Publications

Collected Editions

Stikhotvoreniia. Berlin, 1923; reprinted Moscow, 1988.
Stikhotvoreniia. Leningrad, 1940.
Stikhotvoreniia i poemy. Moscow and Leningrad, 1966.
Rasskazy, edited by Ronald E. Peterson. Munich, Fink, 1979; translated as *Complete Short Stories*, by Ronald E. Peterson. Ann Arbor, Ardis, 1979.
Stikhotvoreniia, edited by John E. Malmstad, 3 vols. Munich, Fink, 1982–84.
Izbrannaia proza. Moscow, 1988.
Sochineniia, edited by V. Piskarev. 2 vols. Moscow, 1990.
Simfonii [Symphonies], edited A.V. Lavrov. Leningrad, 1991.
Simvolizm kak miroponimanie [Symbolism as a World-View]. Moscow, 1994.
Kritika. Estetika. Teoriia simvolizma [Criticism. Aesthetics. The Theory of Symbolism], 2 vols. Moscow, 1994.
Sobranie sochinenii: stikhotvoreniia i poemy. Moscow, 1994.
Sochineniia, 4 vols. Moscow, 1994–95.
Serebrianyi golub'. Rasskazy [The Silver Dove. Stories]. Moscow, 1995.

Poetry

Zoloto v lazuri [Gold in Azure]. Moscow, 1904.
Pepel [Ashes]. St Petersburg, 1909; revised edition, Moscow, 1929.
Urna [The Urn]. Moscow, 1909.
Khristos voskres [Christ is Arisen]. Petrograd, 1918.
Korolevna i rytsari [The Princess and the Knights]. Petrograd, 1919.
Pervoe svidanie. Petrograd, 1921; reprinted Munich, Fink, 1972; translated as *The First Encounter* (bilingual edition), by Gerald Janecek, Princeton, Princeton University Press, 1979.
Zvezda [The Star]. Petrograd and Moscow, 1922.
Posle razluki: Berlinskii pesennik [After the Parting: A Berlin Songbook]. Petrograd and Berlin, 1922.
Stikhi o Rossii [Verses about Russia]. Berlin, 1922.

Fiction

Simfoniia (2-aia, dramaticheskaia). Moscow, 1902; translated as *The Dramatic Symphony*, by Roger and Angela Keys, with *The Forms of Art*, translated by John D. Elsworth, Edinburgh, Polygon, 1986; New York, Grove Press, 1987.
Severnaia simfoniia (1-aia, geroicheskaia) [The Northern Symphony (First, Heroic)]. Moscow, 1904.
Vozvrat; III-'ia simfoniia [The Return: Third Symphony]. Moscow, 1905.
Kubok metelei: chetvertaia simfoniia [A Goblet of Blizzards: Fourth Symphony]. Moscow, 1908.
"Serebrianyi golub'", *Vesy*, 1909; as separate edition, Moscow, 1910; reprinted Munich, Fink, 1967; Ann Arbor, Ardis, [1979]; translated as *The Silver Dove*, by George Reavey, New York, Grove Press, 1974.
"Peterburg", *Sirin*, 1913–14; as separate edition, Petrograd, 1916; reprinted Letchworth, Bradda, 1967; revised and abridged edition, Berlin, 1922; reprinted Munich, Fink, 1967; "Literaturnye pamiatniki" edition, Moscow, 1981 [definitive 1916 text]; translated as *St Petersburg*, by John Cournos, New York, Doubleday, 1959; London, Weidenfeld and Nicolson, 1960; and as *Petersburg* [based on the 1922 edition], by Robert A. Maguire and John E. Malmstad, Bloomington, Indiana University Press, and Brighton, Harvester, 1978; also as *Petersburg* [1916 edition], by David McDuff, Harmondsworth, Penguin, 1995.
Chetyre simfonii [Four Symphonies]. Moscow, 1917; reprinted Munich, Fink, 1971.
"Kotik Letaev", *Skify*, 1–2, 1917–18; as separate edition, Petrograd, 1922; reprinted Munich, Fink, 1964; and Chicago, Russian Language Specialties, 1966; translated as *Kotik Letaev*, by Gerald Janecek, Ann Arbor, Ardis, 1971.
Kreshchennyi kitaets (as "Prestuplenie Nikolaia Letaeva"), 1921; as separate edition, Moscow, 1927; reprinted Munich, Fink, 1969; translated as *The Christened Chinaman*, by Thomas R. Beyer, Jr, Tenafly, New Jersey, Hermitage, 1991.
Zapiski chudaka [Notes of an Eccentric]. Moscow and Berlin, 1922.
Moskovskii chudak [The Moscow Eccentric]. Moscow, 1926; reprinted with *Moskva pod udarom*, as *Moskva*, Munich, Fink, 1968.
Moskva pod udarom [Moscow in Jeopardy]. Moscow, 1926; reprinted with *Moskovksii chudak*, as *Moskva*, Munich, Fink, 1968.
Maski [Masks]. Moscow, 1932; reprinted Munich, Fink, 1969.
Moskva [Moscow novels and *Maski*]. Moscow, 1989.

Plays

Gibel' senatora (Peterburg). Istoricheskaia drama [The Downfall of a Senator (Petersburg). A Historical Drama], edited by John E. Malmstad. Berkeley, Berkeley Slavic Specialties, 1986.

Moskva. Drama v piati deistviiakh [Moscow: A Play in Five Acts]. Moscow, 1997.

Essays and Literary Criticism

Lug zelenyi [The Green Meadow]. Moscow, 1910.

Simvolizm [Symbolism]. Moscow, 1910; reprinted Munich, Fink, 1969.

Arabeski [Arabesques]. Moscow, 1911; reprinted Munich, Fink, 1969.

Tragediia tvorchestva: Dostoevskii i Tolstoi [The Tragedy of Creation: Dostoevskii and Tolstoi]. Moscow, 1911; reprinted Letchworth, Prideaux Press, 1971.

Rudol'f Shteiner i Gete v mirovozzrenii sovremennosti [Rudolf Steiner and Goethe from a Contemporary Point of View]. Moscow, 1917.

Revoliutsiia i kul'tura [Revolution and Culture]. Moscow, 1917; reprinted Letchworth, Prideaux Press, 1971.

Na perevale [At the Divide], 3 vols. Petrograd, 1918–20; reprinted Petrograd and Berlin, 1922.

Sirin uchenogo varvarstva [The Siren-Bird of Scholastic Barbarism]. Journal publication, 1918; first book edition, Berlin, 1922.

Glossolaliia: poema o zvuke [Glossolalia: Poem about Sound]. Berlin, 1922.

O smysle poznaniia [On the Meaning of Cognition]. Petrograd, 1922.

Poeziia slova [Poetry of the Word]. Petrograd, 1922.

Ritm kak dialektika i "Mednyi vsadnik" [Rhythm as Dialectic and "The Bronze Horseman"]. Moscow, 1929.

Masterstvo Gogolia [The Art of Gogol']. Moscow and Leningrad, 1934; reprinted Munich, Fink, 1969; Ann Arbor, Ardis, 1982; as *Masterstvo Gogolia. Issledovanie*, Moscow, 1996.

Selected Essays, edited and translated by Steven Cassedy. Berkeley, University of California Press, 1985.

Memoirs

Vospominaniia ob A.A. Bloke [Reminiscences of A.A. Blok]. Journal edition, Berlin 1922–23; reprinted Letchworth, Bradda, 1964; Chicago, Russian Specialties, [c.1970]; Moscow, 1995.

Odna iz obitelei tsarstva tenei [One of the Dwelling-Places of the Kingdom of Shadows]. Leningrad, 1924; reprinted Letchworth, Prideaux Press, 1971.

Na rubezhe dvukh stoletii [On the Border of Two Centuries]. Moscow and Leningrad, 1930; reprinted Letchworth, Bradda, 1966; revised edition, edited by A.V. Lavrov, Moscow, 1989.

Nachalo veka [The Turn of the Century]. Moscow and Leningrad, 1933; reprinted Chicago, Russian Language Specialties, 1966; revised edition, edited by A.V. Lavrov, Moscow, 1990.

Mezhdu dvukh revoliutsii [Between Two Revolutions]. Leningrad, 1934; reprinted Chicago, Russian Language Specialties, 1966; revised edition, edited by A.V. Lavrov, Moscow, 1990.

Kak ia stal simvolistom ... [How I Became a Symbolist]. Ann Arbor, Ardis, 1982.

Vospominaniia o Shteinere [Memoirs of Steiner]. Paris, La Presse Libre, 1982.

Letters

A. Blok i A. Belyi: perepiska, edited by V. Orlov, Moscow, 1940; reprinted Munich, Fink, 1969.

"Andrej Belyj: Lettre autobiographique à Ivanov-Razumnik" [1–3 March 1927], *Cahiers du monde russe et soviétique*, 15 (1974), 45–82.

Critical Studies

Aleksandr Blok. Andrei Belyi, by R. Ivanov-Razumnik, Petrograd, 1919; reprinted Letchworth, Bradda, 1971.

Vershiny: A. Blok. A. Belyi, by R. Ivanov-Razumnik, Petrograd, 1923.

The Frenzied Poets: Andrey Bely and the Russian Symbolists, by Oleg Maslenikov, Berkeley, University of California Press, 1952.

Andrei Belyi, by Konstantin Mochul'skii, Paris, YMCA-Press, 1955; translated as *Andrei Bely: His Life and Works*, by Nora Szalavitz, Ann Arbor, Ardis, 1977.

The Poets of Russia, 1890–1930, by Renato Poggioli, Cambridge, Massachusetts, Harvard University Press, 1960.

Andrey Bely, by John D. Elsworth, Letchworth, Bradda, 1972.

The Apocalyptic Symbolism of Andrej Belyj, by Samuel D. Cioran, The Hague, Mouton, 1973.

"Anthroposophy in *Kotik Letaev*", by Gerald Janecek, *Orbis Litterarum*, 29 (1974), 245–67.

Andrej Belyj: The "Symphonies (1899–1908). A Re-Evaluation of the Aesthetic-Philosophical Heritage", by Anton Kovac, Bern, Peter Lang, 1976.

The Poetic World of Andrey Bely, by Boris Christa, Amsterdam, Hakkert, 1977.

Andrey Bely: A Critical Review, edited by Gerald Janecek, Lexington, University Press of Kentucky, 1978.

Andrey Bely: Centenary Papers, edited by Boris Christa, Amsterdam, Hakkert, 1980.

Andrej Belyj's Short Prose, by Ronald E. Peterson, Birmingham, Birmingham Slavonic Monographs, 1980.

Vospominaniia o Belom, by K.N. Bugaeva, edited by John E. Malmstad, Berkeley, Slavic Specialties, 1981.

Word and Music in the Novels of Andrey Bely, by Ada Steinberg, Cambridge, Cambridge University Press, 1982.

The Dream of Rebirth: A Study of Andrej Belyj's Novel "Peterburg", by Magnus Ljunggren, Stockholm, Almqvist & Wiksell, 1982.

Andrei Belyi's "Petersburg", James Joyce's "Ulysses" and the Symbolist Movement, by Alexander Woronzoff, Bern, Peter Lang, 1982.

Andrey Bely: A Critical Study of the Novels, by John D. Elsworth, Cambridge, Cambridge University Press, 1983.

"Andrey Bely and the Development of Russian Fiction", by Roger Keys, *Essays in Poetics*, 8/1 (1983), 29–52.

Andrei Bely: The Major Symbolist Fiction, by Vladimir E. Alexandrov, Cambridge, Massachusetts, Harvard University Press, 1985.

"O romane-poeme Andreia Belogo 'Peterburg': k voprosu o katarsise", by D.E. Maksimov, in his *Russkie poety nachala veka*, Leningrad, 1986, 240–348.

Andrey Bely: Spirit of Symbolism, edited by John E. Malmstad, Ithaca, Cornell University Press, 1987.

Body of Words: A Reading of Belyi's "Kotik Letaev", by

Michael Molnar, Birmingham, Birmingham Slavonic Monographs, 1987.
"The Grotesque Style of Belyi's *Moscow* Novels", by Olga Muller Cooke, *Slavic and East European Journal*, 32/3 (1988), 399–414.
Andrei Belyi i ego roman "Peterburg", by L.K. Dolgopolov, Leningrad, 1988.
Andrei Belyi: problemy tvorchestva, edited by S. Lesnevskii and A. Mikhailov, Moscow, 1988.
James Joyce and the Russians, by Neil Cornwell, London, Macmillan, 1992.
Iazyk Andreia Belogo, by N.A. Kozhevnikova, Moscow, 1992.
A History of Russian Symbolism, by Avril Pyman, Cambridge and New York, Cambridge University Press, 1994.
"Belyi's Symbolist Abyss", by Laura Goering, *Slavic and East European Journal*, 39/4 (1995), 568–84.
Andrei Belyi v 1900-e gody, by A.V. Lavrov, Moscow, 1995.
Andrei Belyi i teatr, by T. Nikolesku, Moscow, 1995.
Vospominaniia ob Andree Belom, edited by V.M. Piskunov, Moscow, 1995.
The Reluctant Modernist: Andrei Belyi and the Development of Russian Fiction, 1902–1914, by Roger Keys, Oxford, Clarendon Press, and New York, Oxford University Press, 1996.

Bibliographies
"Literaturnoe nasledstvo A. Belogo", by K.N. Bugaeva, A.S. Petrovskii [and D.M. Pines], in *Literaturnoe nasledstvo*, 27–28, Moscow (1937), 575–638.
"Bibliography", in *Andrej Belyjs Romane: Stil und Gestalt*, by A. Hönig, Munich, 1965, 117–24; supplemented by the bibliography compiled by Olga Muller Cooke and Ronald E. Peterson, in *The Andrej Belyj Society Newsletter*, 2 (1983), 15–60, further updated by J.J. Graffy in subsequent issues (from 1982: Texas A&M University).
"L'oeuvre polémique, critique et journalistique d'Andrej Belyj", by K.N. Bugaeva with additions by G. Nivat, *Cahiers du monde russe et soviétique*, 15 (1974), 21–39.
Russkie sovetskie pisateli: Poety: Biobibliograficheskii ukazatel', 3/1, Moscow (1979), 114–96.

Andrei Belyi, poet, mystic, thinker, literary analyst and theoretician of culture, is generally regarded as the greatest and most influential novelist to emerge from the Symbolist movement in Russia at the turn of the century, a key figure in what the philosopher Nikolai Berdiaev called Russia's "cultural renaissance", the period known more commonly today as the "Silver Age".

As with so many other writers of the so-called "second generation" of Russian Symbolists who began to publish their works in the 1900s, what was important to Belyi was not so much art as a self-sufficient realm of human activity, as the experience and insights of the artist prior to their concretization in artistic form. Like Aleksandr Blok, the greatest poet of the movement, Belyi was part mystic himself and had apocalyptic visions of "other worlds". His earliest view of art was influenced by his reading of Schopenhauer's *The World as Will and Representation* (1819), and was based on a belief that it is possible to acquire knowledge of the "world beyond" through the contemplation of artistic "symbols". Elsewhere he referred approvingly to Vladimir Solov'ev's "theurgic" view of art that regarded poetic symbols as "windows on eternity". This irrationalist view of artistic cognition underlay many of his early works, particularly his four "symphonies in prose" (1902–08), which were precisely attempts at glimpsing the infinite in the finite, by appropriating some of what Schopenhauer had argued to be music's metaphysical grandeur to verbal art.

Belyi's early works were also aesthetic "experiments", and critics have repeatedly emphasized the formal originality of the *Symphonies* and their importance in the development of literary modernism in Russia. The irrelevance of form as such to the writer's metaphysical purpose and the capacity of art in general to eschew tendentiousness, whether mystical or otherwise, were points well grasped by the critic Renato Poggioli when he wrote that:

> while some good Symbolist poetry was written in the illusion that the Holy Grail was within reach, far better poetry was written out of the fear that the quest would fail, or even the realization that it led to a dead end ... All the highest achievements of Symbolism were attained in a state of tension within its own system of belief, in a kind of antagonistic reaction against its very creed.

This, the recurrent dilemma of all modernist art concerned with metaphysical affirmation, is germane to the best work written by Belyi in what is generally regarded as the most fruitful period in his artistic output, particularly *Simfoniia (2-aia, dramaticheskaia)* (*The Dramatic Symphony*) and his first two novels, *Serebrianyi golub'* (*The Silver Dove*) and *Peterburg* (*Petersburg*).

The Silver Dove was the first part of a projected trilogy of novels entitled "East or West?" in which Belyi would seek to embody the spiritual dilemma of Russia as he saw it, impaled on the horns of unbridled instinct (the East) and excessive rationality (the West). Both here and in the novel's ostensible continuation, *Petersburg*, what might have been a routine sequel to the century-old cultural and philosophical dispute between Slavophiles and Westernizers turns into something different, as characters and events seem to be in thrall to malign influences from some other-worldly sphere. "A delusion called forth by terror and mortal anguish" was how Viacheslav Ivanov referred to one of the characters in *Petersburg*, a novel that he regarded as revealing "the innermost recesses of the subtlest consciousness of an epoch that has lost its faith in God". Belyi himself had promised in a letter to Blok that he would henceforth "refrain from any further depictions of the negative side of life", and the third part of his trilogy would instead be devoted to evoking the "sublime and healthy aspects of 'Life and the Spirit'." He had, he said, "had enough of burrowing around in the dirt".

The novels *Kotik Letaev* and *Kreshchennyi kitaets* (*The Christened Chinaman*) were the artistic result of Belyi's philosophical reorientation, rather than the projected third part of "East or West?". These are works in which the existential doubt so palpable in *Petersburg* is overtaken by anthroposophical certainty, where the "modernist" strain in his earlier fiction, with its refusal to endorse a unitary source of cognitive authority, gives way to what one might call a new "mythical realism". Belyi draws for the material of these novels on the experience of his own life. The theme of *Kotik Letaev* is broadly the adult narrator's recollection of his earliest childhood and his realization that the memories thus retrieved in fact encode a deeper memory reaching back to life in the spirit world before the child was born (referred to as the "memory of memory" in the novel).

Belyi became converted to anthroposophy in 1912 and remained a convinced adherent of the doctrine till the end of his life. After his final return to Russia from abroad in 1923 he began to feel increasingly isolated in Soviet society and felt at ease only in the company of a few, mainly anthroposophical friends. Despite the adverse ideological environment, he was able to publish novels, travel notes, memoirs and works of specialist literary criticism, though an even larger quantity of writing (chiefly works dealing with the history and theory of culture and with anthroposophical themes) remained unpublished. He began also to revise much of the poetry that he had produced earlier in his career although, as he had written in his *Vospominaniia ob A.A. Bloke* [Reminiscences of A.A. Blok], "I was already quite clearly aware ... how inferior a poet I was to the incomparable music of Aleksandr Aleksandrovich ... I have a greater command of prose, and have never managed to touch in verse what forms the central core of my inner aspirations." The novels that he published in his final years form the so-called "Moscow" cycle, *Moskovskii chudak* [The Moscow Eccentric] and *Moskva pod udarom* [Moscow in Jeopardy] and *Maski* [Masks]. These works, written in rhythmic prose and replete with neologism, depict characters involved in a process of anthroposophical spiritual self-transformation and have yet to find an appreciative audience beyond that of initiates.

R.J. KEYS

Zoloto v lazuri

Gold in Azure

Poetry collection, 1904

Andrei Belyi's first collection of verse, *Zoloto v lazuri* [Gold in Azure], was brought out in Moscow by the "Scorpion" publishing house, under the active encouragement of its director, Valerii Briusov, in March 1904. It contained 143 lyrics and seven prose poems from the years 1900–04, more than half the poems being composed in the six-month period from March to August 1903. The manuscript was with the publisher by late August 1903, but Belyi continued to make emendations and substantial additions until the book went to press the following spring. The prose poems and roughly half (73) of the lyrics appeared under individual titles, while the remainder were grouped into 22 titled cycles of between two and six poems each. In keeping with the established practice of Bal'mont and Briusov – the former, especially, a major influence on Belyi's early verse – the entire corpus was also arranged into titled sections: "Zoloto v lazuri", "Prezhde i teper'" [Before and Now], "Obrazy" [Images], "Liricheskie otryvki v proze" [Lyrical Fragments in Prose], and "Bagrianitsa v terniiakh" [Crimson in Thorns].

Zoloto v lazuri is immediately striking for the exuberantly imaginative scope of its imagery, its lexical and rhythmical inventiveness, a striving for what Belyi later termed "sonic expressiveness", and a dazzling impressionism that led Briusov, reviewing the collection in *Vesy*, to liken its sumptuous visual effects to "flashes of lightning, the sparkle of precious stones, scattered in handfuls, the majestical glow of crimson skies". Its title, according to Belyi, was inspired by the gold of ripened cornfields and the azure air of the Russian countryside. These are also, however, the iconic colours of the Divine Sophia (most crucially in the writings of Vladimir Solov'ev), and the title points accordingly not only to a dualistic world-view typical of mystical Symbolism, but also, specifically, to the apprehension of a potential unity of natural world (or manifest being) and its divine hypostasis that informs the poet's recurrent apocalyptic expectation, and occasional frustrated despair, of personal and universal transfiguration. Characteristic are the two poems under the heading "Zolotoe runo" [The Golden Fleece], ingenious variations on the themes, imagery, and moods that essentially account for the entire opening section where they appear. The first depicts a radiant sunset seemingly emblematic of the divorce of the material world from the ideal: its fading reflections linger tantalizingly amid gathering cold and despondency. The second describes the passionate clarion-call to a voyage of recovery, a soaring spiritual flight that culminates in intoxicating fusion with the rekindled sun – the "golden fleece" of a latter-day "Argonaut-elite" whose ecstatic transcendence of the world of suffering is somehow predicated on unwavering faith in an acute mystical intuition. Yet while the general contours of the mythical allegory are relatively plain, emotional tonality takes typical precedence over intellectual precision. The nature of the ideal, like the means to its realization, remains obscure.

The thematic coherence of subsequent sections is considerably more tenuous. "Prezhde i teper'" combines 18th-century stylizations, avowedly inspired by Somov, with scenes from faded provincial gentry and contemporary urban life, all seemingly evocative of the automatism of human behaviour and the paltriness of temporal aspirations. "Obrazy", the longest and most heterogeneous section, may be regarded as a series of objectivized projections of the poet's spiritual condition. Flamboyant meteorological "mythologizations" (e.g., the "Giant" cycle) or bizarre contaminations of the fantastic and the everyday (the "Centaur" poems) appear alongside mask-like projections of the poetic persona in elevated, Zarathustrian solitude, and introspective lyrics, punctuated by apprehensions of the Infinite, or abhorrence of eternal recurrence. The prose poems provide further cosmic visions, with disturbing glimpses, in improbable settings, of the chaos that threatens existence. The longest returns to the sunward voyage of the Argo, in a mock-realistic, despairingly ambivalent, futuristic account. "Bagranitsa v terniiakh", aptly martyrological in title, resumes in a new key the subject-matter of "Zoloto v lazuri". Loneliness now typically replaces identification with a mystical-artistic elect, and several poems evoke deceased mentors. Hopes of resurrection fluctuate; and the Messianic pretensions of the poet as prophet and redeemer are sometimes bitterly subverted by images of madness and falsehood that intensify previous self-irony. Again, too, there are some conventionally meditative lyrics, and the collection closes on a subdued, but relatively even note, more inclined towards hope than despair.

A quintessential embodiment of Russian Symbolism, *Zoloto v lazuri* exerted extensive influence on the immediately post-Symbolist generation: not only Maiakovskii, but also, for instance, Kuzmin, Khodasevich, and Severianin; Gumilev, Gorodetskii, and Akhmatova. Belyi himself, however, expressed persistent disaffection with his work, judging its alleged ineptitudes with unremitting harshness, while insisting that the spiritual experience to which he had endeavoured to give form was uniquely and enduringly significant. The result was a characteristic, seemingly obsessive series of reorganizations and revisions of the original volume, undertaken in earnest on at least five occasions: in 1914, 1916–17, 1923, 1925, and 1929–31. Belyi succeeded in publishing only the 1923 redaction – already utterly different in composition from the first, with many radical emendations of the texts retained. But only in January 1931, after two years of intense "moral effort" in (further) drastic revision of each item, frequently out of all recognition, did he pronounce himself relatively content he had finally captured the "potential" of the 1904 text. This he unequivocally renounced, commending to posthumous readers only his "second" *Zoloto v lazuri* – incorporated into the then unpublishable *Zovy vremen* [Summonses of the Times] (1931, 1932).

The formidable textological problems to which Belyi's revisions and authorial pronouncements give rise have evidently proved a disincentive to critical study, for *Zoloto v lazuri* has not received the attention that its intrinsic merits and place in literary history deserve. There is as yet no substantial account of the evolution of the various redactions, nor even a very satisfactory thematic or structural analysis of any single edition. The work's multifarious sources (in painting, philosophy, and occultism, as well as literature) require further elucidation; so do subsequent influence, and, particularly, the compositional principles that underlie individual sections, and the book(s!) as a whole. Aspects of Belyi's versification, including metrical repertoire, rhyme, and the intonational effect of the pioneering "columned" segmentation of metrical lines, have prompted valuable study, but here too, his experimental first volume offers considerable scope for further investigation.

MICHAEL BASKER

The Silver Dove

Serebrianyi golub'

Novel, 1909

The Silver Dove was to be the first volume in a projected trilogy entitled "Vostok ili zapad" [East or West?], a subject that fascinated Belyi throughout his literary career. Before *The Silver Dove* appeared as a separate book in 1910, it was serialized in *Vesy* in 1909. Virtually every crisis that preoccupied Belyi's mind between 1906 and 1909 was reflected in the novel. Among the themes treated were the fate of Russia, the role of consciousness, the conflicts between the intelligentsia and the folk, as well as the struggle between the forces of light and dark. The novel can also be read as a *roman à clef*, reflecting the debacle of his love affair with Aleksandr Blok's wife. Indeed, as his memoirs *Mezhdu dvukh revoliutsii* [Between Two Revolutions] attest, a "sense of impending destruction" characterized Belyi's first novel. Moreover, its publication coincided with the appearance of *Simvolizm* [Symbolism], wherein Belyi attempted to formulate his aesthetic credo.

The Silver Dove's main character is the philosopher-poet Petr Dar'ial'skii. Perpetuating the line of Dionysian, Faustian and Christ-like figures first encountered in Belyi's short stories and *Symphonies*, Dar'ial'skii rejects the decadent and rational west in favour of merging with the folk (*narod*), or better peasant sectarians. He abandons his sweetheart, Katia, symbol of pure and idealized love, for Matrena, a pock-marked wench, with whom he is chosen to create a Dove child. The Doves, headed by Kudeiarov, an impotent carpenter, select Dar'ial'skii as surrogate father, for they need a Dove-child to take Kudeiarov's place in maintaining the sect's secret mysteries. Although Kudeiarov keeps a voyeuristic eye on the couple, he discovers that the lovers' trysts involve more than merely coupling for the sake of a spiritual cause. Kudeiarov becomes jealous and plots to kill Dar'ial'skii. Indeed, what Dar'ial'skii learns too late is that money and eroticism are the driving powers in the Doves' lives. Before he is brutally murdered, the hero believes that he is involved in a struggle with an occult force. The novel suggests an atavistic return of long-buried forces that are mistakenly interpreted as spiritual in nature, but are materialistic in actuality. It is difficult to take the aspirations of the Doves seriously, as they are steeped in eroticism, murderous conspiracies and fake rituals. Indeed, among the many polemical subjects evoked in the novel are mystical anarchism and the dangers of uniting with the people in the hopes of creating a Utopia.

While *The Silver Dove* can easily be enjoyed on the level of plot interest, the novel's multi-faceted narrative structure forces the reader to plummet the depths of its meanings. Written using a *skaz* technique reminiscent of Gogol''s *Vechera na khutore bliz Dikanki* (*Evenings on a Farm Near Dikanka*), Belyi's novel depends on rich associations with narrative traditions of the past. Rhetorical flourishes, digressions, and musical leitmotifs give the novel its richly varied texture. Within the confines of this structure appear a series of mocking antitheses, for the novel cannot escape its ironic stance. Belyi's characters are not full-blooded figures in the Tolstoian sense; they are caught between reality and dreamscapes, rarely in control of their destiny. The richness of Belyi's novel lies in his ornamental style, in his ability to capture a haunting, mesmerizing sense of apocalyptic doom. This Belyi achieves by evoking mysticism and spiritualism in the scenes where the Doves partake of their "happenings" (*delan'ia*). Strewn throughout the novel are menacing images such as the "black figure" and "the invisible force", preparing the reader for the consummation of a violent act, namely Dar'ial'skii's "crucifixion". Even though Schmidt warns his friend of his impending doom, he cannot halt the spiritual disintegration and final downfall of Dar'ial'skii.

The personal cataclysm of Dar'ial'skii finds its mirror image in social unrest and nation-wide upheavals, all of which forecast the doom of Russia. In the background of the novel, labour strikes as well as peasant revolts and secret police activities spread all over the land, while in the foreground we witness the destruction of the hero. Virtually every class is represented, from peasants and carpenters, to merchants and the clergy, to aristrocrats and the landed gentry. The division between the East and West is represented not only stylistically and socially but also geographically. Gugolevo, site of western rationalism, provides the backdrop for decayed estates and baronial traditions not unlike Chekhov's *Vishnevyi sad* (*The Cherry Orchard*). Its diametrical opposite is Likhov, location of Eastern chaos and brute occult forces, as well as the headquarters of the Doves and the site of Dar'ial'skii's death. The centre of this world is Tselebeevo, standing for wholeness. Indeed, the geography of the novel resembles a map of Dar'ial'skii's's mind, described in a freer language and unencumbered by logic. While he inhabits all of these locations, he is at home in none of them. Rather than to describe a place, Belyi hints at a locale, constructing a pattern of intimations. Nothing is arbitrary – names are all symbolic. Probably the single most important feature of Belyi's thought is a constant striving for synthesis, cohesion, and integration. In this way, Dar'ial'skii represents a perfect embodiment of this deep-seated life-long striving, whether it is a marriage of flesh and spirit or of the intelligentsia and the folk. At the same time, Belyi reveals that spiritual regeneration is impossible.

In so far as one can discern aspects of Belyi in the depiction of Dar'ial'skii, Maria Carlson has observed that *The Silver Dove* represents a programmatic illustration of three fundamental concepts developed by Belyi, namely, theurgy, "the creation of life" (*zhiznetvorchetsvo*), and experience (*perezhivanie*). While Nikolai Berdiaev saw the novel as an "amazing book", representing the return to the traditions of great Russian literature "on the basis of the achievements of the new art", there is no question about the novel's remarkably original texture. Indeed, for John Elsworth "as an artistic monument to the second generation of Russian Symbolists *The Silver Dove* has no rivals".

OLGA COOKE

Petersburg

Peterburg

Novel (serialized 1913–14), 1916

Belyi's masterpiece is considered one of the finest and most original novels of the 20th century. It exerted the greatest influence on post-Symbolist writers by virtue of both its stylistic innovation and its treatment of Russian history. Written in 1911–13, it was originally conceived as the second part of a trilogy on the theme of East and West, following *The Silver Dove* (1909), as the first part; the third part, "Nevidimyi grad" [The Invisible City], was never written. The title was suggested by Viacheslav Ivanov. The novel was first published in installments in *Sirin* (1913–14), and in book form in 1916. Belyi published his own revised version in Berlin in 1922, abridged by one-third but preserving the macrostructure: eight chapters with prologue and epilogue. In 1924–25 the author adapted the novel for the stage, but it had only a few performances. The Berlin edition with the author's and censors' revisions was reprinted in 1928 and posthumously in 1935. Apart from some initial, unfavourable criticism of the manuscript, the novel was immediately recognized as a masterpiece on publication.

The novel arose from the general atmosphere of crisis at the turn of the 20th century in life, thought, culture and word, together with anticipation of cataclysmic events, as well as Belyi's own personal crises. Osip Mandel'shtam said that *Petersburg* is unmatched in its powerful evocation of pre-revolutionary *Angst* and turmoil. The novel is ingrained in the cultural context of the Silver Age, and reflects a blend of various influential trends, e.g., Steiner's antroposophy, occultism, etc. It is both a continuation and a radical departure from 19th-century Russian prose in ideas and form. It is saturated with 19th-century literary allusions, mainly to works set in Petersburg, starting with Pushkin's *Mednyi vsadnik* (*The Bronze Horseman*). Each chapter begins with an epigraph taken from various works of Pushkin. Belyi explores the Gogolian literary trend by creating a grotesque world of abstractions, fusing essentials and trivia, seriousness and laughter, objects and living beings. He also engages in unusual psychological analysis, partially influenced by Dostoevskii. The work can be interpreted on many levels. The plot is obscured by its peculiar stream of verbally-oriented consciousness; Belyi deliberately mixes reality and hallucinations, life and art, science and fantasy, thus creating a world of distorted perspectives. He aims to capture the unique revelation of truth in a given moment. His prophetic forebodings are expressed through "bubbling" a non-traditional verbal expression. The units of the different levels interact with each other, and symbolically evoke an unending chain of suggestive meanings.

The novel continues and marks the apogee of the 200-year-old St Petersburg myth, which has been closely linked to national identity ever since the controversial founding of the city, and polemicizes with it. The city is not merely the setting, but truly the main character of the novel, a living entity; the city symbolically expands into the entire cosmos or shrinks to a point. St Petersburg is represented by a series of geometrical images, lines and concentric circles, focused on the Bronze Horseman, the monument to Peter the Great located on Senate Square adjacent to the Senate, the political centre of the bureaucracy. The statue itself expands and contracts in tempo with the entire city. The Prologue to the novel already introduces the notion of total ambiguity by alluding to the focus of the novel as something elusive, "phantasmagoric veiled by green mist"; the novel itself is labelled as "cerebral play". Man and the city belong to different universes: physical, spiritual, mental, psychological, astral. On all these levels the city and each individual in it are torn between the opposing forces of East and West, building toward an apocalyptic explosion.

The composition on all levels is based on the coexistence and merger of the rational Apollonian and intuitive Dionysian elements, the fusion of mathematics and music, the circle and the line. Sounds mirror the underlying dichotomy of natural chaos and order brought by civilization. The system of antinomies permeate the novel and these engage in dialectical interplay, constantly turning into each other or other things. The narrative incorporates inextricably interwoven plot threads: family, politics, history, psychology, suspense, philosophy, astrology, all symbolizing a larger realm.

The most concrete level is the social-political plot line, which focuses on a terrorist act in the days of the 1905 Revolution. The novel spans nine days in October, but concentrates on the 24 hours from the setting of a bomb, concealed in a sardine tin, to its explosion, during which period the sense of anticipation builds to fever pitch. This concrete time span integrates past, future and mythical timelessness. The individual terrorist act enters into manifold relations; above all, it alludes to the terrorism of the state and connects the personal lives of the characters with all the other levels. The plot is set in motion by three forces, centring on three characters: the terrorist party (Dudkin), the state (Senator Apollon Apollonovich Ableukhov), and the intelligentsia (the Neo-Kantian Nikolai Apollonovich Ableukhov). On the level of the family saga, Belyi incorporates autobiographical elements in the figure of Nikolai Ableukhov; this character vows to participate in the assassination of a government official who turns out to be his father. Terrorism thus reflects the generational conflict and the love-hate relationship between father and son. Terrorism turns into patricide, power gives birth to revolt against itself, and creator turns into destroyer. The ultimate question remains open: will Petersburg transcend history or sink beneath it in the apocalyptic battle? The doomed atmosphere foreshadows the demise of the visible city, but the ultimate reality underlying the surface, the spirit of the city and the Russian soul, will have a new beginning. As Diana Festa-McCormick states, "the symbolic meaning of the novel ... is ... a forewarning of the collapse of Russia, condemned to die so that it may be born again".

The novel is born of sounds that pre-exist ideas, pointing beyond reality and violating the reader's expectations. Belyi's innovative disjointed prose is rhythmical and sound-oriented, leaning metrically toward the anapest. All levels of the composition are dominated by musical principles of leitmotif, repetition, and variation of devices (e.g., the colour and space attributes of the characters), ranging from pauses and sounds to allusions and periphrases of other texts, mirrored graphically as well. Due to the highly idiosyncratic and esoteric qualities of the novel, it never reached the broad public. However, with this novel Belyi helped establish modern rhythmic ornamental prose, and the work evokes unceasing critical attention.

MARIA PAVLOVSZKY

Kotik Letaev

Novel (serialized 1917–18), 1922

Kotik Letaev, Belyi's third novel, is one of the most original accounts of early childhood in literature. A thinly disguised autobiography, it describes the experiences of its hero, Nikolai Letaev, from the age of three to five, though its initial sections seem intended to convey memories of life in the womb and of birth.

By 1912, Belyi had become actively interested in Rudolf Steiner's anthroposophy, an offshoot of theosophy, spent several years travelling around Europe attending Steiner's lectures, and eventually in 1914 settled at Dornach, Switzerland, where the Goetheanum, an anthroposophical temple and centre, was being built under the direction of Steiner. Belyi himself worked on the construction and during this time *Kotik Letaev* was written. While anthroposophical elements are present in Belyi's preceding novel *Petersburg*, in *Kotik Letaev* they become one of the most important formative influences. Steiner's main principle is that each human being contains a subconscious cosmic memory, that is, a complete knowledge of the history of the universe, which by special spiritual training can be brought to consciousness. Spiritually gifted individuals of the past, such as Buddha and, especially, Christ, have had greater access to this "suprasensible" knowledge than others, but this greater access is within the power of everyone with Steiner's guidance and training. Belyi engaged in such training. One exercise involved the concentrated recollection of the past in which the student would recall in as much detail as possible first what happened the day before, then the week before, etc., back to birth and, for those adept enough, before birth, before conception, even before the existence of the human race. *Kotik Letaev*, written in 1915, was at least in part a result of such exercises. The novel opens with an epigraph from *War and Peace* in which Natasha expresses her feeling that it is possible to remember life before one was born. The novel, however, is arranged chronologically, with two chapters devoted approximately to each of the three years covered. Among the unique features of the novel is its dual narrative perspective, in which Belyi presents elaborate mental and physical impressions from the viewpoint of the child experiencing them but verbalized in the sophisticated language of an adult Symbolist poet. This produces a remarkably extended and rich example of defamiliarization in which, for example, a bout of scarlet fever is described in terms that suggest the birth of the universe, or a first visit to an Orthodox Church liturgy is made to seem a mysterious and mystical experience. A chicken is a strange clucking thing and a deacon is a magnificent sparkling old man holding up a ribbon.

The plot of the novel centres on the conflict between the boy's parents about how he should be raised. His mother, a society woman, wants to coddle him and keep him from turning into a big-headed intellectual like his father, who is a mathematician (Belyi's father was the renowned mathematician and dean of Moscow University, Nikolai Bugaev), while the father would like to educate the boy. Fights between the parents cause the boy to feel torn apart ("I am a sinner: with Mama I sin against Papa; with Papa against Mama. How can I exist and not sin?"). His refuge is the maid Raisa, who accepts him as he is and reads him fairytales. The conflict between parents eventually leads to the maid being let go, a catastrophe for the boy.

As in other Belyi novels, but most thoroughly and effectively implemented in *Kotik Letaev*, plot events are mirrored on all levels of verbal structure from the use of sounds to the overall arrangement of material. From Belyi's Preface, it is clear that this is not an ordinary prose work. The elaborate imagery, parallel constructions and sonic richness establish a poetic frame of reference. There is a marked ternary rhythm throughout the novel, though flexibly employed to avoid becoming monotonous. The repetition of key phrases, passages and even whole sections (sometimes verbatim but usually with developmental changes, a device first used by Belyi in his four *Symphonies*, 1902–08), gives the work a quasi-musical architecture. One must keep track of these recurrences and their developments, just as one would musical motifs in a symphony or opera. Another original feature of the novel is its unique layout, with many passages separated out by double dashes and indentation, thus giving visual embodiment to its poetic structures.

The basic conflict in the novel between parents is reflected in its title: "Kotik" (little cat) is the mother's pet name for the boy and with her he acts kittenish and cuddly, while his surname "Letaev" (based on the Russian root "to fly") connects him with his father's mental flights. The mother's side comes to represent the aesthetic/artistic realm as opposed to the father's intellectual/scientific realm. This "scissor"-like division was fundamental to Belyi's problematic and his attempts to resolve the conflict were a major preoccupation throughout his life. Thus Steiner's promise of knowledge of the spiritual realm with scientific accuracy was appealing. In the novel, the Son is seen as an intersection, in fact a battleground, between the worlds of Mother and Father. On the sonic level, words and names with the combination "kl" are especially prominent. On a more advanced level the mother's world of music, dance and ballrooms and the father's world of mathematics are joined in the concept of rhythm, and the artistic world of poetry is linked to the intellectual world of education in the key word *obrazovanie* (literally "education" but in the novel also directly linked to its root meaning of "forming images"), the specific issue about which the parents dispute. Images connected with the mother typically involve swirling or swarming (*roi*) (such as the feverish delirium of the first childhood memories or the dancers at a ball), while the father's world is one of structure and seeming order (*stroi*). The sound "st" thereby gives form to the swarm and the resulting image is a spiral, i.e. a structured swirl, another important image in the novel. The child's growth of consciousness in the course of the novel is presented finally as describing circles of greater diameter as he first encompasses the apartment he lives in, then the street and city outside and finally Russia and the whole world and the "stairway of my expansions". As he ascends this spiral staircase, he finds himself sacrificed on the Cross as the ultimate Son.

Parallel to this growth of self-consciousness in the boy as he goes from chaotic, whirling feverishness to a clearer sense of his place in the world are descriptions and references that retrace the formation of the cosmos itself as it moves from swirling matter through the dinosaur period to the advent and development of the human race. At the same time, Belyi covers the history of philosophy from the Pre-Socratics through Plato, Nietzsche, and Solov'ev to conclude, implicitly, with Steiner. Thus the boy retraces the collective unconscious of the human race as seen by Jung, Haeckel, and Steiner. Finally, the novel is a brilliant study in child psychology as Belyi intuitively evokes the process of a child's understanding of the world and his use of language to deal with it, predating Piaget in some of his insights.

Excerpts from the novel were published in the St Petersburg newspaper *Birzhevye vedomosti*, 2 May 1916, a complete version in the almanac, *Skify* 1 and 2 (1917–18) and finally in book form in Petrograd, 1922. A Soviet edition was planned for 1928 but did not materialize and a new edition did not appear there until 1989. Its first translation appeared in English in 1971.

Along with Sologub's *Melkii bes* (*The Petty Demon*) and Belyi's own *Petersburg*, *Kotik Letaev* is one of the greatest prose works of Russian Symbolism.

GERALD J. JANECEK

The First Encounter

Pervoe svidanie

Narrative poem, 1921

Belyi's narrative poem *The First Encounter* was written in 1921 in Moscow on the occasion of *Dukhov den'* (Whit Monday), 20 June. Like his *Kotik Letaev* and *The Christened Chinaman*, this is one of Belyi's many autobiographical works, recalling events in the poet's youth. Unlike the other works, this poem is written in a clear, light-hearted manner, inspired by Vladimir Solov'ev's poem *Tri svidaniia* [Three Meetings] (1898), where the philosopher discusses his three mystical encounters with the incarnation of "Eternal Feminine", or "Sophia". Belyi provides footnotes for the numerous names, places and images that he recalls throughout the work.

The poem consists of a foreword, four sections, and a brief conclusion. The foreword presents a mock invocation of the muses and the power of the word. Part 1 is a recollection of Belyi's student days, with his interests appearing somewhere between the pure sciences and mysticism ("fantomnyi bes/ atomnyi ves" [phantom demon/atomic weight]). The poet compares those days with the present ones (1921) that he is trying to reconcile ("teper' peremenilis' roli/ I bol'she net metamorfoz" [now the roles are changed/and there are no more metamorphoses]). Part 2 evokes the feelings of his warm friendship with Sergei Solov'ev and the Solov'ev family. He recalls the family's hospitality, and the visits of the patriarch of the family, Vladimir Solov'ev, the Symbolists' spiritual inspiration. Discussions with "Serezha" Solov'ev lead to the subject of Sophia, and the poet confesses to having seen her incarnation in a Liubov' Kirillovna Zarina (one of Belyi's and Symbolism's favourite images is *zaria* (the dawn) who has been identified as Margarita Kirillovna Morozova (1872–1958) the wife of millionaire-industrial-philanthropist M.A. Morozov, the owner of the Put' publishing house. Belyi likewise recollects meetings with other Symbolists: Kliuchevskii, Merezhkovskii and, of course, Aleksandr Blok. In Part 3 Belyi recounts a concert held at the Moscow Concert Hall, "Blagorodnoe sobranie" (House of Nobles). The concert was directed by Glavich and Safanov, the former a conductor and the latter the Director of the Moscow Conservatory. It is at this concert that Belyi encounters his "Sofia", "Zarina" Morozova seated in the audience. Part 4 takes place after the concert, and in a more contemplative mood the poet takes his thoughts and feelings into the cold night. The poem ends with a dramatic dialogue between a coachman and Vladimir Solov'ev who asks to be taken to Novodevichii Convent where he has since been buried. The Conclusion briefly describes the poet's current spiritual state at the writing of this work.

Critics and literary scholars almost universally regard *The First Encounter* as one of the great narrative poems of the Russian language and certainly of the 20th century. It is often compared to Pushkin's *Evgenii Onegin* in its evocation of the social life of Moscow, its various families, landscapes, and social events. As in *Onegin*, the narrator constantly interrupts himself with witty asides and various commentaries on life. As opposed to many of Belyi's other autobiographical narratives, the images in this poem are clear, although one may read into them oblique references to Belyi's former works, his relationships with other Symbolists, Symbolist clichés and his interest in theosophy.

The work is written in rhymed iambic tetrameter and is highly readable, lacking many of the more obscure images Belyi used in other works. It is highly melodic, containing numerous internal rhymes ("kak zybi, zyblemye v vetry" [like waves, waving in the wind]); ("god-devianostyi: zori, zori! / Voprosy, broshennye v zori" [The year-nineteen hundred: dawns, dawns! / Questions, thrown to the dawns]). The poem's playful nature is reflected in numerous entertaining rhymes; one of Belyi's favourite devices is rhyming the foreign names of teachers, philosophers and scientists with Russian words: "Gol'berg Gent / student" [Golber Gent / student]; "polonen/ 'poudre Simon'", [imprisoned / poudre Simon]; "kotil'iona / Atkinsona" [from the cotillion / from Atkinson]; "vostorg / Svedenborg" [joy / Swedenborg]. Present also are various references to favourite images of Belyi's lexicon. *Roi* (swarm) the image of chaotic formlessness presented in *Kotik Letaev* and other works is encountered four times. The first reference is also made to Belyi himself: "Bogov belogolovyi roi" [The gods' white-headed swarm]. He uses the word to rhyme with itself as well: "Monashek riasofornyi roi / Prokhodit v kel'i chernyi roi" [The nuns' cassocked swarm / The black swarm passes into the cells]. *Kotik Letaev* is likewise referred to through puns: "u nog ty - vot kak chernyi kot" [at my feet, you're just like a black cat], and the more directly, "I moi otets, dekan Letaev" [And my father, Dean Letaev]. The one reference to Belyi's real name is treated both with a line, "Bodaem zhalobnyi bugaem" [We butt like a mournful bull], as well as with a footnote, "Bugai - byk po malorosiiski" [a "bodai" is a bull in Ukrainian].

Because it appeared well after the Symbolist period, *The First Encounter* has not received the attention it deserves by scholars and critics. The poem was published by the publishing house Alkonost' in 1921 and reprinted by Prideaux Press, Letchworth, in 1974, with a bilingual edition appearing in 1979.

GEORGE KALBOUSS

Moscow

Moskva and Masks (Maski)

Novel cycle, 1926–32

The final period of Belyi's creativity, embracing approximately ten years (1924–34), was replete with disappointments and crushing defeats. On his return to Russia from Berlin in 1923, Belyi was prevented from publishing his *Vospominaniia ob A.A. Bloke* [Recollections of A.A. Blok]. This coincided with Leon Trotskii's blasphemous denunciation of Belyi in his famous *Literature and Revolution*. While Soviets were suspicious about Belyi's short stay abroad, not to mention his vague position *vis-à-vis* the Revolution, Russian émigrés questioned his political loyalties to the extent that he was later unjustly considered a communist and traitor, particularly after the publication of his memoirs. As the tenets of socialist realism were fast encroaching on the arts, Belyi's eclectic style was more and more out of touch with Russian readers, and especially with official literary circles. Belyi's correspondence with contemporaries, particularly with his closest ally in those years, Ivanov-Razumnik, testify to the difficulty of having to perform before the public.

The history of the composition of the Moscow novels goes a long way toward describing the fate of Russia's most famous living Symbolist, for Belyi wrote them over a period of six years and then it took a further two for the last volume to be published. Appearing in 1926, volume 1, *Moskva* (*Moscow*), is divided into two parts: *Moskovskii chudak* [The Moscow Eccentric] and *Moskva pod udarom* [Moscow in Jeopardy]. The second volume, *Maski* [Masks], was completed in 1930 and published in 1932. Like his earlier novels Belyi envisaged the final works to comprise a tetralogy, but parts three and four were never written. The Moscow novels not only represent a continuation of the dazzling linguistic architectonics found in *Petersburg* and *Kotik Letaev*; they express completely new themes couched in a new method of characterization. Whereas *The Silver Dove* and *Petersburg* present two-dimensional, cardboard cut-outs, rather than full-blooded personalities, the final novels depict complex, multi-faceted characters who experience a genuine transformation of personality. There is also a greater regard for plot construction.

The first volume focuses on the struggle of Professor Korobkin, a renowned mathematician, to keep his potentially dangerous invention out of reach of the freelance spy and arch-villain Mandro. Although the discovery is never revealed, it seems to deal with optical mechanics. If abused by the wrong party, the invention can obliterate the entire world. Mandro schemes to sell Korobkin's mathematical equations to a European firm. Thus, with the aid of his spies, Mandro entraps the professor. Once Korobkin refuses to part with his secret, Mandro culminates his evil purposes by burning Korobkin's eye with a candle and tearing his mouth with a hammer. A secondary plot involves another crime: Mandro rapes his daughter, Lizasha. The first volume ends with both Korobkin and Mandro going mad. *Maski* constitutes the antithesis of *Moscow*. On his release from the lunatic asylum, the half-blind Korobkin sees the errors of his devotion to science and gains insight into the nature of his guilt. This awareness brings about a complete metamorphosis, with Korobkin forgiving Mandro and reconciling Lizasha with her father.

The novels' inherent spatiality does not simply remove all traces of time-value, as past, present and future merge. These features were already present in *Petersburg*. What stands out as revolutionary in Belyi's final novels is colour. Colour represents independent fields of energy, much the way Wassily Kandinsky used paint on his canvases. Belyi had long considered, through the intermediary of Rudolph Steiner, that colours express a moral quality. The significance of Goethe's colour theories in his *Farbenlehre* (1810) find their reflection in the novels for, according to Goethe, all colour arises out of the reciprocal action of the forces of light and darkness. This same reciprocity operates in thematic polarities of darkness and light, murder and rebirth, hope and despair. Belyi not only offers new types of heroes, with the victim also the torturer, and vice versa, but also casts his doubles Korobkin/Mandro in twin roles on a journey entailing blindness, death and resurrection; he paves the way for the type of new man needed to embody the spiritual revolution he anticipated in virtually all his anthroposophical writings. It is an essential premise of Belyi's anthroposophy that the world as traditionally perceived is inadequate, and that new forms of perception have to be developed. Moreover, Belyi came to the conclusion that ordinary characterization was insufficient to depict the radical changes occurring under the surface level of consciousness. Just as the novels entail Korobkin's movement from a Newtonian world view to an Einsteinian one, so Belyi approximates the non-Euclidean space-time world of relativity with references to different worlds, different constellations, where men with higher states of consciousness reside. Korobkin evolves from a scientist whose discoveries can lead to the explosion of the world, to a Tolstoian with a commune of pacifists, to a clairvoyant mystic. For the first time, Belyi presents likeable characters. Korobkin is a bungling, delightful holy fool intent on reconciling all his past adversaries and changing the course of man's wrong thinking. Had Belyi written a third volume he would have located Korobkin in the Caucasus, surrounded by loyal followers, a type of anthroposophical collective of individuals, forming a Utopian commune and bringing about social change.

In *Pisatel'skie sud'by* [The Writer's Destiny] Ivanov-Razumnik called the Moscow novels "the highpoints not only in Russian but also in European literature". And Klavdiia Bugaeva argued that *Maski* was her husband's finest novel. However, most contemporaries considered the author's last novels the works of a failing master. Not only did Belyi's writings not adhere to the characteristics of mass culture desired by the Stalinist regime, but his "new man" was painfully out of touch with Soviet reality. After all, the majority of his fellow Symbolists had died or lived in exile. Moreover, his attempts, however feeble, to reach a rapprochement with the government, particularly during the year 1932, fell on deaf ears. Thus Belyi was relegated solely to the camp of pre-revolutionary literature.

OLGA COOKE

Nina Nikolaevna Berberova 1901–1993

Novelist and memoirist

Biography

Born in St Petersburg, 8 August 1901. Graduated from high school in Petrograd, 1918. Moved with family to Moscow, then Rostov-on-Don, 1918. Attended preparatory class, then School of Philology, Rostov University, 1919–20. Returned with family to Petrograd and attended lectures at Zubovskii Institute, 1921. Married: 1) (common-law) Vladislav Felitsianovich Khodasevich in 1922; 2) Nikolai Makeev in 1937; 3) George Kochevitskii in 1950. Emigrated to Berlin, 1922; with Khodasevich, lived in Maksim Gor'kii's household in Germany, Czechoslovakia, and Sorrento, Italy, for extended periods, 1923–25; settled in Paris, 1925. Affiliated with *Poslednie novosti*, *Dni*, and other Russian-language émigré periodicals, 1925–40. Editor, with David Knut, *Novyi dom*, 1926. First book published, 1930. Literary editor of *Russkaia mysl'*, 1947. Emigrated to the United States, 1950. Editor of *Mosty*. Professor of Russian literature, Princeton University, New Jersey, 1958–62; Yale University, New Haven, Connecticut, 1963–71. Began to be published in Russia, 1989. Died in Philadelphia, 26 September 1993.

Publications

Collected Editions

Oblegchenie uchasti: shest' povestei. Paris, YMCA-Press, 1949; reprinted as *Povesti*, Moscow, 1992.
Biiankurskie prazdniki [Biiankursk Festivals]. Paris, YMCA-Press, 1950.
Izbrannaia proza. New York, Russica, 1982.
Stikhi, 1921–1983. New York, Russica, 1984.
Three Novels: The Resurrection of Mozart; The Waiter and the Slut; Astashev in Paris, translated by Marian Schwartz. London, Chatto and Windus, 1990; and *Three Novels: Volume II: In Memory of Schliemann; The Black Death; The Tattered Cloak*, translated by Marian Schwartz, London, Chatto and Windus, 1991; reprinted as *The Tattered Cloak and Other Novels*, New York, Knopf, 1991.

Fiction

Poslednie i pervye [Last and First]. Paris, 1930.
Povelitel'nitsa [Mistress]. Berlin, Parabola, 1932.
Akkompaniatorsha, *Sovremennye zapiski*, 58 (1935); translated as *The Accompanist*, by Marian Schwartz, London, Collins, 1987; New York, Atheneum, 1988.
Bez zakata [No Sunset]. Paris, Dom Knigi, 1938.
Mys Bur' [Cape Bur]. Paris, YMCA-Press, 1950.
Mysliashchii trostnik. New York, 1958; translated as *The Revolt*, by Marian Schwartz, London, Collins, 1989.

Play

Madame. Paris, 1938.

Autobiography and Biography

Chaikovskii: istoriia odinokoi zhizni [Tchaikovskii: The Story of a Solitary Life]. Paris and Berlin, Petropolis, 1936; St Petersburg, 1993.
Borodin. Paris and Berlin, Petropolis, 1938.
Alexandre Blok et son temps. Paris, Editions du Chêne, 1947; translated as *Aleksandr Blok: A Life*, by Robyn Marsack, New York, Braziller, and Manchester, Carcanet, 1996.
Kursiv moi: avtobiografiia. Munich, Fink, 1972; revised edition New York, Russica, 1983; Moscow, 1996; translated as *The Italics Are Mine*, by Philippe Radley, New York, Harcourt Brace Jovanovich, and London, Longman, 1969; revised edition London, Chatto and Windus, 1991; New York, Knopf, 1992.
Zheleznaia zhenshchina: rasskaz o zhizni M.I. Zakrevskoi-Benkendorf-Budberg, o nei samoi i ee druz'iakh [The Iron Lady: A Story about the Life of M.I. Zakrevskaia-Benkendorf-Budberg, about Her and Her Friends]. New York, Russica, 1982.

Essays

"25 let posle smerti A. Bloka", *Orion*, 1947.
Delo Kravchenko [The Kravchenko Business]. Paris, Russkaia mysl', 1949.
"Vladislav Khodasevich, russkii poet 1886–1939", *Grani*, 12 (1951); as "Vladislav Khodasevich: A Russian Poet 1886–1939], *Russian Review*, 11/2 (1952), 78–85.
Liudi i lozhi: russkie masony II stoletiia [People and Lies: The Russian Freemasons in Their Second Century]. New York, Russica, 1986.

Memoirs
"Iz peterburgskikh vospominanii" [From the Petersburg Memoirs], *Opyty*, 1 (1953).

Critical Studies
Russkaia literatura v izgnanii, by Gleb Struve, New York, Izdatel'stvo imeni Chekhova, 1956, 292–94.
"Kursiv vremeni", by A. Chagin, *Literaturnaia gazeta*, (19 April 1989).
"V nikh tri ingredienta ...", by R. Gul', *Literaturnaia Rossiia*, (9 June 1989).
"Miss serebrianogo veka", by T. Khoroshilova, *Komsomol'skaia pravda*, (12 September 1989).
"Neobkhodimy utochneniia", by V. Baranov, *Druzhba narodov*, 12 (1990).

In her long and active career, Nina Nikolaevna Berberova wrote poetry, novels, short stories, plays, biography, criticism, history, and reviews. She contributed extensively to the Russian émigré press as a writer, journalist, and editor, particularly in Paris between the two world wars, and also in the United States after World War II, publishing frequently in *Poslednie novosti*, *Dni*, *Sovremennye zapiski*, *Novyi zhurnal*, *Vozrozhdenie*, *Opyty*, *Grani*, and *Zveno*, among others. Literary recognition came to her late in life, when her works were translated into English, French, and other European and non-European languages. After the proclamation of glasnost, several of her works were republished in Russian in the Soviet Union and Russia in *Druzhba narodov* and *Voprosy literatury* and in book form. She remains best known for her autobiography, *Kursiv moi* (*The Italics Are Mine*), which details her involvement with and observations of many outstanding Russian writers of the 20th century, including Belyi, Bunin, Pasternak, Gor'kii, and her long-time companion Vladislav Khodasevich. It has also become a standard source on the literary world of Petrograd and the Russian diaspora.

Berberova was introduced to literary Petrograd as a schoolgirl, when she attended "The Poets to the Warriors", a cultural evening held in the spring of 1915 that featured Sologub, Blok, Akhmatova, and Kuzmin. In 1916, her father, Nikolai Berberov, a civil servant of Armenian descent, took her to hear Valerii Briusov, who had come to Petrograd for a reading at the Tenishev School in connection with the publication of Poetry of Armenia. After the Revolution, Berberov took his family to Moscow, following the government. After her father's dismissal, the family moved to Rostov-on-Don, where Berberova continued her education.

The family returned to Petrograd in the spring of 1921. There, Berberova attended readings and other events at the House of Arts and the Poets' Union and was made a member of the latter on 30 July 1921. For one month, until his arrest, she attended Gumilev's poetry workshop at the House of Arts. Before her emigration, Berberova published a single poem, which appeared in the Serapion Brothers' miscellany *Ushkuiniki* in 1922.

Berberova left Petrograd with Khodasevich and arrived in Berlin on 30 June 1922. There, the Russian Club – Erenburg, Khodasevich, Shklovskii, Pasternak, Belyi, Zaitsev, Berberova, and others – met weekly to read poetry. For their first three years in exile, she and Khodasevich lived at various times in Germany and Czechoslovakia and also in the household of Maksim Gor'kii for extended periods, especially in Sorrento, Italy.

"Stateless", Berberova and Khodasevich moved to Paris in April 1925, where she began her long association with *Dni*, in which she published her first fiction, "Noch' poleta" [Night of Flight], and *Poslednie novosti*, for which she wrote her *Biiankurskie prazdniki* [Biiankursk Festivals] story cycle. In the 1920s she contributed to a chronicle of Soviet literature for *Vozrozhdenie*, under the pseudonym "Gulliver", and in 1926 she became co-editor with David Knut of the magazine *Novyi dom* in Paris. Although Berberova had written three novels by the mid-1930s, by far her most successful genre from both the artistic and publishing standpoints was the novella. Berberova's incisive style, acerbic, unsentimental and highly refined, often etched the sordid tales of Paris's White Russian community, the former generals and ladies of the court who inhabited certain working-class districts of Paris and now worked on the line at the Renault plant or were taxi-drivers and laundresses, if not worse.

By the time France fell to the Germans, Berberova had published three novels and two biographies. Her biography of Tchaikovskii was translated into French at the time and created a sensation by its frank discussion of the composer's homosexuality.

Berberova did not write at all during the war years, when she was living outside Paris with her second husband, the painter Nikolai Makeev, but in 1947 she became literary editor of the newly founded *Russkaia mysl'*. That year, she reported for the weekly on the Kravchenko case, which gave wide publicity to Stalin's Gulag for the first time; the magazine later published these articles as a book.

Berberova's career took a new turn after her emigration to the United States in 1950. By 1958 she had joined the Slavic Department of Yale University and later went on to teach Russian literature at Princeton University. In the early 1980s, the new Russian emigration began publishing her non-fiction and poetry, old and new. In the mid-1980s, the French "discovered" her, and by the late 1980s and early 1990s, Berberova's works were appearing regularly on the French best-seller lists. In 1989, the French government named Berberova a Chevalier of the Order of Arts and Letters, and in that same year she returned to Russia for the first time to give readings and lectures. In 1992 she received an honorary doctorate from Yale University, and in 1993 French director Claude Miller made a well-received film from her 1935 novella *Akkompaniatorsha* (*The Accompanist*).

In the course of her life, Berberova knew and corresponded with famous figures in literature, art, and politics, including Nobel Prize winner Ivan Bunin and Aleksander Kerenskii, once the head of the Provisional Government, whom she met in Berlin in 1922. Berberova's papers are deposited at Yale University.

MARIAN SCHWARTZ

Ol'ga Fedorovna Berggol'ts 1910–1975

Poet and prose writer

Biography

Born in St Petersburg, 16 May 1910. Attended school in Uglich, 1918–20, and Petrograd/Leningrad, 1921–26; Institute of Art History, Leningrad, 1926, Leningrad University philological faculty, journalism department, 1927–30. Married: 1) Boris Petrovich Kornilov in 1928 (divorced 1929); 2) Nikolai Stepanovich Molchanov in 1930 (died 1942); 3) Georgii Panteleimonovich Makogonenko in 1942 (divorced 1954); two daughters, both died in childhood; third child stillborn in prison in 1939. Began to publish, 1925. Member of the Leningrad literary group "Smena" in the 1920s. Journalist in Kazakhstan, 1930–31; editor of Komsomol section of factory newspaper, Leningrad, 1931–37. Joined the Soviet Writers' Union, 1934; Communist Party, 1936; expelled from the Writers' Union and Party, 1937; reinstated, 1938. Arrested December 1938; released from prison July 1939; expelled from the Party after arrest; reinstated, 1940. Full-time writer, except in 1937–38, teacher of Russian in Leningrad school. Broadcast on Leningrad Radio during the siege of 1941–44. Recipient: Stalin Prize, 1950. Died in Leningrad, 13 November 1975.

Publications

Collected Editions

Izbrannye proizvedeniia, 2 vols. Leningrad, 1967.
Sobranie sochinenii, 3 vols. Leningrad, 1972–73.
Izbrannye proizvedeniia. Leningrad, 1983.
Sobranie sochinenii, 3 vols. Leningrad, 1988–90 (volume 3 withdrawn).

Poetry

Stikhotvoreniia [Poems]. Leningrad, 1934.
Kniga pesen [A Book of Songs]. Leningrad, 1936.
Leningradskaia poema [Leningrad Poem]. Leningrad, 1942.
Leningradskaia tetrad' [Leningrad Notebook]. Moscow, 1942.
Leningradskii dnevnik [Leningrad Diary]. Leningrad, 1944.
Leningrad. Moscow, 1944.
Tvoi put': stikhi i poemy [Your Path]. Leningrad, 1945.
Izbrannoe. Moscow, 1948.
Stikhotvoreniia i poemy. Moscow and Leningrad, 1951.
Izbrannoe. Moscow, 1954.
Lirika [Lyric Poems]. Moscow, 1955.
Stikhi. Moscow, 1962.
Izbrannaia lirika. Moscow, 1964.
Uzel: novaia kniga stikhov [The Knot]. Moscow and Leningrad, 1965.
Stikhotvoreniia. Leningrad, 1966.
Vernost' [Loyalty]. Moscow, 1970.
Pamiat' [Memory]. Moscow, 1972.
Leningradskaia poema [Leningrad Poem]. Leningrad, 1976.

Fiction

Glubinka [The Provinces]. Moscow and Leningrad, 1932.
Uglich [The City]. Moscow and Leningrad, 1932.
Pimokaty s Altaiskikh [Felt-Boot Makers from the Altai Streets]. Leningrad, 1934.
Noch' v "Novom mire" [Night in "The New World"]. Leningrad, 1935.
Mechta [Dream]. Leningrad, 1939.
Dnevnye zvezdy: avtobiograficheskaia povest' [Daytime Stars: An Autobiographical Novella]. Leningrad, 1959.
"Dnevnye zvezdy: glavy iz vtoroi knigi" [Daytime Stars: Chapters from the Second Book], *Prostor*, 6 (1964), 43–44.
"Dnevnye zvezdy: vtoraia chast'" [Daytime Stars: The Second Part], *Ogonek*, 19 (1990), 15–16.

Plays

"U nas na zemle" [On Our Earth], with G.P. Makogonenko, *Zvezda*, 12 (1947), 120–61.
Vernost' [Loyalty]. Leningrad, 1954.
"Rozhdeny v Leningrade" [Born in Leningrad], in *P'esy i stsenarii*, Leningrad, 1988, 117–66.

Screenplays

"Oni zhili v Leningrade" [They Lived in Leningrad], with G.P. Makogonenko, *Znamia*, 1–2 (1944), 102–58.
"Leningradskaia simfoniia" [Leningrad Symphony], with G.P. Makogonenko, *Zvezda*, 3 (1945), 50–80.
"Pervorossiane", in *P'esy i stsenarii*, Leningrad, 1988, 248–311.
"Dnevnye zvezdy" [Daytime Stars], in *P'esy i stsenarii*, Leningrad, 1988, 328–56.

Autobiographical Writing and Diaries

Govorit Leningrad: glavy iz knigi [Leningrad Speaks: Chapters from the Book]. Moscow, 1964.
"Iz dnevnikov Ol'gi Berggol'ts" [From the Diaries of Ol'ga Berggol'ts], *Vremia i my*, 6/57 (1980), 276–302.
Dnevnye zvezdy; Govorit Leningrad [Daytime Stars; Leningrad Speaks]. Moscow, 1990.
"Tragediia moego pokoleniia" [The Tragedy of My Generation], *Literaturnaia gazeta*, (18 July 1990), 5.
"Iz dnevnikov" [Diary Extracts], *Zvezda*, 5–6 (1990), 182–91, 153–74.
"Iz dnevnikov: 1949 g." [Diary Extracts: 1949], *Znamia*, 3 (1991), 160–72.

Critical Studies

"Poeziia i proza Ol'gi Berggol'ts", by Andrei Siniavskii, *Novyi mir*, 5 (1960), 225–36.
Ol'ga Berggol'ts, by G. Tsurikova, Leningrad, 1961.
Ol'ga Berggol'ts: kritiko-biograficheskii ocherk, by Natal'ia Bank, Moscow and Leningrad, 1962.
Stikh i serdtse: ocherk tvorchestva Ol'gi Berggol'ts, by Aleksei Pavlovskii, Leningrad, 1962.
Ol'ga Berggol'c: Aspekte ihres lyrischen Werkes, by E.M. Fiedler-Stolz, Munich, Sagner, 1977.
Vspominaia Ol'gu Berggol'ts. Leningrad, 1979.
Ot serdtsa k serdtsu: o zhizni i tvorchestve Ol'gi Berggol'ts, by D. Khrenkov, 2nd edition, Leningrad, 1982.

"Ol'ga Berggol'ts", introduction to *Izbrannye proizvedeniia*, by Aleksei Pavlovskii, Leningrad, 1983, 5–48.
Die sowjetische Lyrik-Diskussion: Ol'ga Berggol'c Blockadedichtung als Paradigma, by Carin Tschöpl, Munich, Fink, 1988.
"Ol'ga Berggol'ts", by V. Lakshin, in *Otkrytaia dver'*, Moscow, 1989, 332–61.
"Put' vozvrata: k 80-letiiu so dnia rozhdeniia O.F.Berggol'ts", by L. Chashchina, *Iskusstvo Leningrada*, 5 (1990), 21–28.
"Na mnogo let vpered", by Lev Levin, in *Takie byli vremena*, Moscow, 1991, 160–72.
"The Other Veterans: Soviet Women's Poetry of World War Two", by Katharine Hodgson, in *World War Two and the Soviet People*, edited by John and Carol Garrard, London, Macmillan, 1993, 77–97.
Die Autobiographie einer sowjetischen Dichterin: Mythisierungen in Ol'ga Berggol'c Dnevnye zvezdy, by S. Schaffner Baumgartner, Bern, Slavica Helvetiva 43, 1993.
"Kitezh and the Commune: Recurrent Themes in the Work of Ol'ga Berrgol'ts", by Katharine Hodgson, *Slavonic and East European Review*, 74/1 (1996), 1–18.
Written with the Bayonet: Soviet Russian Poetry of World War Two, by Katharine Hodgson, Liverpool, Liverpool University Press, 1996.

The critical reception of O'lga Berggol'ts's work has focused almost entirely on poems written and broadcast during the siege of Leningrad. The belief that war suddenly transformed her from an unremarkable young poet to tragic witness of human endurance has proved persistent in Russia and the west, even though the publication in 1965 of poems concerning her imprisonment clearly showed this was not the case. Western scholars have tended either to celebrate Berggol'ts as a dissenting voice, or to dismiss her as a conformist Soviet writer. To assume that the two views are incompatible is, however, to ignore their complex interrelationship.

Berggol'ts's early poetry concentrates on rural themes, echoing the work of Esenin and her first husband Boris Kornilov. The relative complexity and variety of imagery and formal attributes are largely absent in later work. While in poetry of the early 1930s her style becomes simplified, sometimes to the level of slogans, Berggol'ts continues to focus on her emotional experiences, now viewed from the perspective of an enthusiastic young communist. The reconciliation of private concerns with those of state and society is a dominant theme that gradually assumes a tragic colouring. Initially Berggol'ts celebrates the integration of family life into the life of society, without ignoring inherent difficulties. Poems relating to her persecution and arrest unite personal and public concerns in the growing awareness that the state has abandoned the ideals it proclaims. Her prison poems record a sense of pained loyalty, moving through defiance to resigned disillusion.

These poems help to explain the emotional intensity of her war poetry, in which Berggol'ts saw her country, like herself, as a victim of arbitrary violence. Mutual support discovered among fellow-prisoners becomes a model for her role as war poet. Berggol'ts's war poetry shows a curious mixture of registers; the rhetoric of "official" war-time verse rubs shoulders with a pared-down conversational style, creating an unconventionally modest concept of the Leningraders' heroism. The literary establishment was ambivalent about her frankness, but this did not prevent Berggol'ts from becoming a prominent and a popular writer.

After World War II Berggol'ts made a number of attempts to unite conflicting elements of her life into a seamless whole. In works of the late Stalin period, however, the public and private spheres remain separate. In 1949, as she was composing her Stalin Prize-winning poem "Pervorossiisk", an epic tale of a workers' commune founded in 1918, elsewhere she spoke of political terror and hypocrisy. This period saw a number of excursions into drama. Although *Vernost'* [Loyalty] a verse tragedy of 1954, is too static to be successful in performance, associated poems are a fierce defence of tragedy as a genre, a retort to critics who attacked her preoccupation with "depressing" themes.

Lyric poetry provided some refuge from the "gigantomania" of the time. The poems Berggol'ts wrote in 1952 when she visited the Volga-Don canal are far from unambiguous. They combine themes of disappointed love with hints of the canal's labour-camp origins. Parallels with the victory at nearby Stalingrad suggest the human costs of grandiose achievements. Shortly after Stalin's death in 1953, then at the Writers' Union Congress the following year, Berggol'ts called for a return to lyric poetry that dealt with individual emotions rather than with uncontroversial generalizations. In 1956 she stated publicly that the 1946 Resolutions should be withdrawn immediately.

Her autobiography *Dnevnye zvezdy* [Daytime Stars] is a lyrical, non-chronological prose work that draws together episodes from the poet's Civil War childhood in Uglich, the Leningrad siege, the electrification of Russia, and reflections on Russian and Soviet literature. The resulting picture emphasizes wholeness and steady development. Conflicts, such as the events of the late 1930s, are only referred to obliquely. Berggol'ts saw *Dnevnye zvezdy* as her major work, around which other texts clustered. One of these, *Uzel* [The Knot], published six years later in 1965, contains many poems about her persecution and imprisonment. Later works make repeated use of the image of the legendary city Kitezh to link *Dnevnye zvezdy*, the screenplay based on "Pervorossiisk", and the poems about the Volga-Don canal. Recently published extracts from Berggol'ts's diaries reinforce these connections. A planned second volume of autobiography that, apparently, was to have dealt with the contradictions faced by her generation, once confident of socialism's imminent arrival, was never completed. Loneliness, drink problems, and chronic illness impeded major projects in the last decade of her life.

As stated earlier, it is Berggol'ts's war-time poetry and its relationship with her earlier work that has attracted most critical comment. Bank (1962) notes elegies to "missing" friends in the late 1930s; Pavlovskii (1983) argues the case for a steady development of a tragic awareness in the pre-war years, as does Chashchina (1990). However Levin (1991) feels that such an approach risks overshadowing Berggol'ts's war-time achievements. Some of the best Soviet writing on Berggol'ts can be found in Siniavskii's 1960 article. His description of *Dnevnye zvezdy*, "her whole life, concentrated into a single moment", is an apt description for her best work, with its network of interlinking themes and images.

Western scholars have until recently concentrated either on her war poetry or on her part in literary debates of 1953–54.

Tschöpl's study (1988) examines her blockade lyrics in the context of the debate on lyric poetry. Schaffner Baumgartner (1993) presents an interesting study of *Dnevnye zvezdy* as an attempt to resolve a fundamental crisis of identity. While attempts at synthesis in her war poetry tend to emphasize contradictions, later works do, to a certain extent, offer a model for the reconciliation of the public and private aspects of her life. In her diaries and poems Berggol'ts claims to speak for her generation. The unevenness of quality and style in her work, its preoccupation with conflict and reconciliation, bear witness to the problems faced by a writer attempting to reconcile artistic integrity with loyalty to a system that she felt had betrayed its original ideals.

KATHARINE HODGSON

Bestuzhev *see* Marlinskii

Andrei Georgievich Bitov 1937–

Prose writer

Biography

Born in Leningrad, 27 May 1937. Spent time in Leningrad, 1941–42; then evacuated to Urals and Uzbekistan. Attended schools in Leningrad; Leningrad Mining Institute (Geology Prospecting Department). Worked as lathe operator, stevedore; on construction brigades as a soldier 1957–58; medical discharge. Married: 1) Inga Petkevich in 1958 (divorced 1973), one daughter; 2) Ol'ga Shamborant in 1973 (divorced 1979), one son; 3) Natal'ia Gerasimova in 1988, one son. Returned to Leningrad Mining Institute in 1958, graduated in 1962. First publication, 1960. Full-time writer from 1963. Attended advanced courses in cinematography in Moscow, 1965–67. Has lived both in Moscow and Leningrad/St Petersburg since 1978. Because of his involvement with *Metropol'* anthology (1979) and the publication of *Pushkinskii dom* (*Pushkin House*) in the west (1978), had difficulties getting published, 1977–85. With the advent of the Gorbachev era, work again published. President of first chapter of Russia's PEN Club, 1991–94.

Publications

Collected Editions

Life in Windy Weather. Short Stories, edited by Priscilla Meyer, translated by Priscilla Meyer *et al.* Ann Arbor, Ardis, 1986.

Sobranie sochinenii, Povesti i rasskazy, vol. 1. Moscow, 1991.

Sochinenii, 4 vols. Moscow/Kharkov, 1996.

Sobranie sochinenii, 5 vols. Moscow, 1997.

Fiction

Bol'shoi shar [The Big Balloon]. Moscow, 1963.

Takoe dolgoe detstvo [Such a Long Childhood]. Leningrad, 1965.

Dachnaia mestnost'. Povesti [A Country Place]. Moscow, 1967; "Zhizn' v vetrenuiu pogodu", translated as "Life in Windy Weather", by Priscilla Meyer *et al.*, in *Life in Windy Weather*, 1986, 117–44.

Aptekarskii ostrov. Leningrad, 1967; translated as "Apothecary Island", by Priscilla Meyer *et al.*, in *Life in Windy Weather*, 1986, 21–92.

Obraz zhizni. Povesti [A Way of Life]. Moscow, 1972.

Sem' puteshestvii [Seven Journeys]. Leningrad, 1976.

Dni cheloveka. Povesti [Man's Days]. Moscow, 1976.

Pushkinskii dom. Ann Arbor, Michigan, 1978; translated as *Pushkin House*, by Susan Brownsberger, New York, Farrar Straus and Giroux, 1987; London, Collins Harvill, 1990.

Voskresnyi den'. Rasskazy, povesti, puteshestviia [Sunday]. Moscow, 1980.

Fotografiia Pushkina. Moscow, 1987; translated as "Pushkin's Photograph", by Priscilla Meyer, in *The New Soviet Fiction*, edited by Jacqueline Decter, New York, Abbeville Press, 1989.

Chelovek v peizazhe. Povesti i rasskazy [Man in a Landscape]. Moscow, 1988.

Uletaiushchii Monakhov. Roman-punktir [Vanishing Monakhov]. Moscow, 1990; translated as "The Lover", by Priscilla Meyer *et al.*, in *Life in Windy Weather*, 1986, 187–364.

"Ozhidanie obez'ian", *Novyi mir*, 10 (1993), 6–102; translated as *The Monkey Link*, by Susan Brownsberger, New York, Farrar Straus and Giroux, 1995.

Oglashennye: Roman - stranstvie [The Proclaimer: Novel - Wanderings]. St Petersburg, 1995.

Pervaia kniga avtora (Aptekarskii prospekt, 6) [The Author's First Book ...]. St Petersburg, 1996.

Travel Writing and Essays

Uroki Armenii. Erevan, 1978; translated as "Lessons of Armenia. Journey Out of Russia", by Susan Brownsberger, in

A Captive of the Caucasus: Journeys in Armenia and Georgia, New York, Farrar Straus and Giroux, 1992; London, Harvill Press, 1993, 3–147.
Gruzinskii al'bom. Tbilisi, 1985; translated as "Choosing a Location, Georgian Album", by Susan Brownsberger, in *A Captive of the Caucasus*, 1992, 153–318.
Kniga puteshestvii [A Book of Journeys]. Moscow, 1986.
Stat'i iz romana [Articles from a Novel]. Moscow, 1986.
My prosnulis' v neznakomoi strane. Publitsistika [We Woke Up in an Unfamiliar Country]. St Petersburg, 1991.

Critical Studies
"Verfremdung bei Andrej Bitov", by Wolf Schmid, *Wiener Slawistischer Almanach*, 5 (1980), 25–53.
"Strannyi strannik", by Lev Anninskii, *Literaturnaia Armeniia*, 10 (1985), 63–70.
"Afterword, Autobiography and Truth: Bitov's *A Country Place*", by Priscilla Meyer, in *Life in Windy Weather. Short Stories*, 1986, 365–71.
"Sud'ba i rol' (Andrei Bitov)", in *Tochka zreniia. O proze poslednikh let*, by Natal'ia Ivanova, Moscow, 1988, 167–201.
"*Literaturnost'* as a Key to Bitov's *Pushkin House*", by Henrietta Mondry, in *The Waking Sphinx: South African Essays on Russian Culture*, edited by Mondry, Johannesburg, University of Witwatersrand Library, 1989, 3–19.
"Looking Back at Paradise Lost: The Russian Nineteenth Century in Andrei Bitov's *Pushkin House*", by Alice Stone Nakhimovsky, *Russian Literature Triquarterly*, 22 (1989), 195–204.
The Last Years of Soviet Russian Literature: Prose Fiction, 1975–1991, by Deming Brown, Cambridge and New York, Cambridge University Press, 1993, 45–53.
Andrei Bitov. The Ecology of Inspiration, by Ellen Chances, Cambridge, Cambridge University Press, 1993.
"No Room to Swing a Cat: Aggression in Bitov's 'Fig'", by Kurt Shaw, *Russian Language Journal*, 49/162–64 (1995), 205–19.
Russian Literature 1988–1994: The End of an Era, by N.N. Shneidman, Toronto, University of Toronto Press, 1995.
"Psychotic Postmodernism in Soviet Prose: Pushkin and the Motif of the Unidentified Past in Andrei Bitov's Poetics", by Sven Spieker, *Wiener Slawistischer Almanach*, vol. 35, Vienna, 1995.
The Twentieth-Century Russian Novel: An Introduction, by David Gillespie, Oxford, Berg, 1996, 152–70.
Figures of Memory and Forgetting in Andrej Bitov's Prose, by Sven Spieker, Frankfurt, Peter Lang, 1996.
"Bitov Reading Proust Through the Windows of *Pushkin House*", by Harold D. Baker, *Slavic and East European Journal*, 41/4 (1997), 604–26.

Bibliographies
"Materialen zu einer Bitov-Bibliographie", by Wolf Schmid, *Weiner Slawistischer Almanach*, 4 (1979), 481–95.
"Nachtrag zur Bitov-Bibliographie", by Wolf Schmid, *Weiner Slawistischer Almanach*, 5 (1980), 327–34.

Andrei Bitov is one of contemporary Russia's best and most significant writers. He began writing after seeing, in 1956, Federico Fellini's film *La Strada* and realizing that it was possible to create art about contemporary life. His first travelogues and short stories were about a young Leningrad man of approximately his age. The travelogue, "Odna strana" [One Country], and nine stories comprise his first published collection, *Bol'shoi shar* [The Big Balloon]. He wrote travelogues – *Takoe dolgoe detstvo* [Such a Long Childhood], "Koleso" [The Wheel], *Uroki Armenii* ("Lessons of Armenia"), "Azart" [The Gamble], "Vybor natury" [Choice of Location] – novellas and short stories – "Sad" ("The Garden"), *Zhizn' v vetrenuiu pogodu* (*Life in Windy Weather*), "Penelopa" [Penelope], "Infant'ev" [Infantiev] – during the 1960s and 1970s.

His two major novels are *Uletaiushchii Monakhov* [Vanishing Monakhov] (first published in complete form in English as "The Lover" in *Life in Windy Weather. Short Stories*), which includes short stories about a man over a 20-year period of his life – "Dver'" ("The Door"), "The Garden", "Obraz" ("The Image"), "Les" ("The Forest"), and "Vkus" ("The Taste"), and *Pushkinskii dom* (*Pushkin House*), 1964–71. He also wrote a travelogue/story/philosophical essay, "Ptitsy" [Birds].

His publications since the advent of the Gorbachev era include stories (*Fotografiia Pushkina* ["Pushkin's Photograph"], "Chelovek v peizazhe" [Man in a Landscape], and "Prepodavatel' simmetrii" [Teacher of Symmetry]); literary essays (*Stat'i iz romana* [Articles from a Novel]); publicistic essays, (*My prosnulis' v neznakomoi strane* [We Woke Up in an Unfamiliar Country]); and a major new work, *Ozhidanie obez'ian* (*The Monkey Link*).

Early assessments of Bitov categorized him as one of a group of young Soviet writers of the post-Stalin Thaw era of the 1950s and early 1960s, the so-called Young Prose writers, whose emphasis on characters' subjective internal thoughts distinguished them from socialist realists. It was common, too, for these new writers to dissolve the boundary between first- and third-person narration. Bitov soon acquired his own distinctive voice. His literary roots are at once classical and experimental. His literary influences include Tolstoi, Dickens, and Nabokov.

Bitov belongs to the St Petersburg tradition that extends from Pushkin and Gogol', through Dostoevskii and Mandel'shtam, to Iosif Brodskii and Evgenii Rein. He was a "pupil" of literary critic Lidiia Ginzburg, herself a pupil of critic and writer Iurii Tynianov, whose "lessons" of a literary word and work's dynamic inter-connectedness with neighbouring words of a text and with other works by the same writer and of the same period were important to Bitov's thematics and methodology.

Bitov is a highly original writer whose innovative methodology has been called "ecological prose" (Ellen Chances, 1993), for in his writing he creates an "ecological system", an "ecology". He creates and publishes a short story as an individual, independent entity. He then includes it in a collection of short stories, where he sometimes changes a character's name so that the story becomes part of a larger whole about one character. He then includes that same short story in another collection where it takes on still new meanings because of the stories or essays that surround the story. Thus, in one way, Bitov's works represent one large ecosystem that continues to grow.

Bitov's themes are the creation of boundaries and the dissolution of boundaries: between individual human beings, between human beings and animals, between one culture and another, between past, present, and future. His themes are the positive life forces that create links between and among people, between life and art, between earthly reality and the transcendent realms of artistic and spiritual inspiration. His themes are the negative forces that destroy personal relationships, societies, people's creative gifts, and life on earth. His characters range from innocent children to corrupted young adults, from writers and critics to wise old artists, from birds to bears to monkeys, from lovers to liars, from Armenians and Russians to Georgians and Uzbeks. He delves into a human being's psyche, and he contemplates the meaning of the contemporary human being in post-Stalin Soviet society and the contemporary human being's place in the universe. Bitov uses images of circles and spirals, in both positive and negative connotations. Expanding circles and cycles are life-affirming. Vicious circles and downward spirals are destructive.

His writings address psychological and ethical issues, film and art, science and literature. The story "Life in Windy Weather" concerns a writer's struggle to attain literary and spiritual inspiration. The story "The Taste", about life and death on a personal, societal, and cultural level, is structured according to spirals, the components of the structure of DNA. His major novel *Pushkin House*, structured according to the principles of organic chemistry, the science that studies relationships, addresses, in Soviet society of the 1960s, the historical, family, peer, and literary relationships that were poisoned by Stalin. The story "The Forest" concerns the ecology of a forest and of father and son. "Lessons of Armenia" is a philosophical travelogue-meditation on culture and values. His recent works include a playful excursion into the future and past by the grandson of characters in *Pushkin House* ("Pushkin's Photograph"); and the completion of a cycle, *The Monkey Link*, that includes a work by that name as well as the earlier philosophical essay "Ptitsa" and the story "Chelovek v peizazhe", about the human being's relationship to the world, to nature, and to other species.

ELLEN CHANCES

Life in Windy Weather

Zhizn' v vetrenuiu pogodu

Story, 1967

The story "Life in Windy Weather" (first published in *Dachnaia mestnost'. Povesti*. Moscow, 1967) is among Bitov's finest. Bitov originally wished to call the book in which the story appeared *Life in Windy Weather*, but the Soviet censors would not let him. The story is part of a two-work cycle, *Dachnaia mestnost'*, whose other work is entitled "Zapiski iz-za ugla" [Notes from Around the Corner], first published only after the advent of glasnost, in 1990, in the literary journal *Novyi mir*. It appeared in 1986 in English translation as "Notes from the Corner" together with "Life in Windy Weather", under the rubric "A Country Place" (in *Life in Windy Weather. Short Stories*).

The plot of "Life in Windy Weather" revolves around a main character, Sergei. His name is changed to Aleksei in some editions of the story in order to fit into a series of Bitov's works about a character named Aleksei. Aleksei is also the first name of Bitov's protagonist in his novel, *Uletaiushchii Monakhov*.

The "Notes from Around the Corner" provide the alleged journal entries, that is, the raw material of a writer, covering the same time period and some of the same incidents as the fashioned-as-fiction story, "Life in Windy Weather".

Sergei, in "Life in Windy Weather", is a writer who, with his wife and son, is spending some time in the countryside at the dacha of his parents-in-law. The story plots Sergei's struggles to write. He first expects the ideal location of his second-floor study, away from all distractions of the city, to be an instant stimulus to creation. With no distraction, he still cannot write. Little by little, Sergei discovers – through the natural phenomena of wind and storm, through his own movements between city and country, through his discovery of closeness between him and his father, him and his son, and him and his wife – the essence of the creative process in life and literature.

In the story, Bitov explores the ways in which "all parameters of his existence changed". He emphasizes how Sergei's perceptions of time change. He explores the ways in which Sergei's consciousness merged with his surroundings. He takes up the issue of parents' dependence on their children. He discusses the relationship of art to reality: art is reality, but art never copied reality. He highlights the loneliness of missed communications among people, and he spotlights the creative connections that love can forge, between generations, between man and wife, between friends, between a human being and nature.

Critical appraisals of the story have been extremely favourable. Russians, Americans, and Europeans alike have praised Bitov's emphasis on the psychology of an introspective character, and have lauded his attention to the search for spiritual values. German scholar Wolf Schmid sees the story as a journey in which Sergei learns about himself and learns to see the world through the intensely alive eyes of his child. Priscilla Meyer describes the story as Sergei's steps along the way to literary creativity. Ronald Meyer's focus is on the intergenerational aspects of "Life in Windy Weather". He, too, believes that the primary focus of the story is on the nature of artistic creativity. In his dissertation, Stephen Hagen turns the reader's attention to parallels between concepts of Zen Buddhism and major ideas in Bitov's story.

In the section of my book, *Andrei Bitov. The Ecology of Inspiration* (Cambridge, 1993), devoted to this story, I explain that Schmid's, P. Meyer's, R. Meyer's, and Hagen's interpretations of "Life in Windy Weather" are all valid. What Bitov creates is a story in which he speaks literally of the wind, of breath, and of its capacity to inspire Sergei. Bitov enfolds many levels of reality into his story, to come to the conclusion that if one escapes from the ossified, mechanized forms of life and of literature, it is possible to attain inspiration in life, literature, and in one's spiritual life. Bitov's story describes the evolving process of creativity in one person's life and literature.

He does so by constantly showing ways in which Sergei sees the world anew. The expected perfect time and place for writing will not automatically result in a person's being able to write. Parents depend on their children, instead of the other way around. Time stops, although time has passed. Sounds change. A landscape is first described as a book. Art is life. People are connected, almost physically, to one another. Gazes are connected, almost physically, to nature. Sergei sees through his son's eyes. Bitov describes the interconnection between people as Sergei, his wife, and his parents-in-law, guests at the dacha, pour tea for one another. Usual categories fall away, as it becomes unclear who the real guests are, and who the real hosts are. As in other Bitov works, the dissolution of many different kinds of boundaries is the key to understanding the story. The point at which Sergei comes to a deep appreciation and a profound understanding of life is described by the image of "accidental symmetry", when disparate pieces of life become interconnected for an instant.

"Life in Windy Weather" was written just before Bitov began to work on *Pushkin House*. Certain features mark both the story and the novel. Discussions about the nature of reality and the conventions of realist fiction are present in both. The novel is comprised of fictional sections told by a third-person narrator. Woven into the novel are sections entitled "The Italics Are Mine – A.B.", the presumably non-fictional musings by a first-person narrator. This compositional technique of *Pushkin House* can be directly traced to the structure of fictional work and accompanying non-fictional raw material that is evident in Bitov's pairing of "Life in Windy Weather" and "Notes from Around the Corner".

Thematically, the protagonist Leva's struggle, in *Pushkin House*, to escape from the ossified forms of his existence, is a much fleshed-out version of a basic skeletal frame that Bitov used in "Life in Windy Weather".

ELLEN CHANCES

Pushkin House

Pushkinskii dom

Novel, 1978

The work was completed in 1971 and sections of the novel were published separately in the Soviet Union throughout the 1970s. It was published as a whole in the United States in 1978. *Pushkin House* focuses on life among the Leningrad intelligentsia during the 1950s and 1960s. Taking its cue from the murder mystery, the prologue ("written after the rest") shows the dead body of the main character, Leva Odoevtsev, in the middle of Pushkin House, the Institute of Russian Literature of the Soviet Academy of Sciences. Posing as a detective, the narrator sets out to reconstruct the hero's life and death without, however, having any genuine interest in solving the mystery. Time and again, he calls into question the veracity of his own narrative and offers different "versions and variants" of the same events. Having grown up in the "museum city" of Leningrad, Bitov's protagonist belongs to an old aristocratic family. Both Leva's father and grandfather are renowned philologists, and at the time of his apparent death, Leva himself is a graduate student of philology at Pushkin House.

Pushkin House is based on the topos of the "unfinishable novel", a novel that must remain unwritten as no authoritative version of the events leading to Leva's demise may be found. The sequence of chapters and episodes in the text is as variable as are the constellations of its characters. The narrator invites the reader to insert "even a scrap of newspaper" at any point in the narrative. The non-linear fashion in which he presents his material directs the reader's attention away from the novel's *siuzhet* (plotline) to its extensive metatext. Here, the narrative events become the subject of the author's general disquisitions on memory, writing, art, and history ("The Italics Are Mine").

Unable to supply either the authentic sequence of events nor their true meaning, the narrator (for whom Leva Odoevtsev is first and foremost a "research topic") approaches both from a pseudo-scientific, experimental point of view. In doing so, he takes his cue from structuralist and semiotic theories of the 1960s that assume that every element in a given system (such as, for example, the Soviet intelligentsia of the 1960s) is connected to every other element in that same system and that each element receives significance only by dint of that interrelation. Leva Odoevtsev, too, interprets his relations with other people from a "scientific" point of view. For example, in assessing his relationship with his three girlfriends, Leva has "a distinct revelation that they were all components in a kind of structure". At the same time, however, he is perennially searching for an authentic vantage point outside of any structural field, for what he calls "the middle of the contrast". Leva witnesses this kind of authenticity both in Uncle Dikkens (an old friend and neighbour of his parents) and in his grandfather, Modest Platonovich. Both men, however, have paid a high price for their independence as both return from the labour camps as broken men.

The lack of authenticity that characterizes Bitov's protagonist is particularly evident in his inability to establish proper relations with his own aristocratic background and the (pre-revolutionary) past in general. Bitov based his novel on Modest Platonovich's inference that Russian history came to an end with the Bolshevik Revolution. As a result, the subsequent Stalinist period represents the culmination of all history, a period in which the notion of history has in itself become historical. Under Stalin, the past is replaced by the school curriculum, a pantheon of canonical names and texts with Pushkin at its top. The Stalinist curriculum plays an important role in *Pushkin House* as Leva's education is entirely based on it. The school curriculum is also present in the many chapter headings and epigraphs taken from the canon of 19th-century Russian literature ("Fathers and Sons", "A Hero of Our Time", etc.). In its capacity as a museum devoted to Pushkin and Russian literature in general, Leva's institute, too, serves as an emblem of the "end of history" and its substitution by the Stalinist archive of high culture. The past, in *Pushkin House*, exists merely as a sign whose original referent (and meaning) have disappeared from view forever.

The central event in Leva's adolescence is the death of the Soviet Union's paterfamilias, Stalin. On the level of the Odoevtsev family, the dictator's demise spells the return of the past. As the Odoevtsevs once again "permitted themselves to remember", the Stalinist certainties of life dissolve without anything else taking their place. Thus, when Modest Platonovich turns out to be alive and returns from the camps after 30 years, Leva learns that he was denounced by his own (Leva's) father. The protagonist is increasingly unsure who his true father might be. The formerly transparent present turns out to be highly ambivalent. Unable to come to terms either with the past or with the present, Leva and his intellectual friends cultivate the kind of "alcoholic" lifestyle that is a hallmark of Russian prose in the 1960s and 1970s. Here, the past and the present, pre-revolutionary culture, Pushkin and Russian literature in general all become tokens in a social practice that assumes that education and knowledge equal freedom and independence from ideological constraint. In his descriptions of Leva's gatherings with his companions, Bitov demonstrates, however, that their supposed metaposition *vis-à-vis* official culture as well as their view of themselves as the guardians of Russian pre-revolutionary culture is based on a misunderstanding. That misunderstanding lies in their inability to realize that the pre-revolutionary past and its culture may not be continued. Leva and his friends, it is implied, deceive themselves by confusing the school curriculum with history, quotation with the real thing, and the sign with its referent. Nowhere is this better illustrated than in Leva's drunken argument with Mitishat'ev during which the hero is apparently killed. At one point, Mitishat'ev begins to dance around with Pushkin's death mask. When he tries it on, it turns out to be too small. In the ensuing brawl, the mask is accidentally broken. Both Mitishat'ev and Leva are bewildered. Shortly afterwards, however, the narrator informs the reader that "of course, the mask wasn't real! A copy."

SVEN SPIEKER

Pushkin's Photograph

Fotografiia Pushkina

Fiction, 1987

Like most of Bitov's post-*Pushkin House* prose, "Pushkin's Photograph" has been scarcely considered in criticism. The text opens with a frame story about a writer (Bitov's *alter ego*) who has left the city in order to continue writing. One of his many unfinished texts involves a young philologist being sent from the year 2099 into the Pushkinian era. The frame ends with the beginning of this fragment, in which the protagonist seeks to produce a photographic image of the live Pushkin. However, his mission ends in failure as the representatives of past high culture, most notably Pushkin himself, withdraw into obscurity whenever the hero (who shares his name with the main character from *Pushkin House*, Igor' Odoevtsev) activates his recording equipment. Igor' is left in a state of emotional confusion.

Like much of Bitov's shorter fiction, the plot of "Pushkin's Photograph" features a journey. In the author's early prose, travelling proceeds as a modernist quest for novelty. Here, the outside (the village, the writer's dacha, the countryside, etc.) is conceived as a niche-like refuge from the constraints of official (urban) culture and its ideology. By contrast, in "Pushkin's Photograph", the interpretation of travelling as a search for the new has become historical. Thus, the fictitious writer has to realize that an ecological disaster has rendered meaningless any attempt to escape from the centre (the city) to the periphery (the countryside). Furthermore, a stranger informs him that his own dacha may, in fact, not belong to him. The reason for the writer's bewilderment lies in his realization that inside and outside, city and countryside, the "official" world of the city and the unofficial anti-world of the village have become mutually exchangeable.

This equivalence between inside and outside or immanence and transcendence informs "Pushkin's Photograph" throughout. In the central narrative, present and the past, fiction and fact are similarly depicted as mutually exchangeable. Thus, for the time-travelling Igor', the difference between history and fiction is reduced to a "grey blur" where the one cannot be distinguished from the other. Thus the protagonist participates in fictional events as if they were historical ones, experiencing, for example, the St Petersburg flood of 1824 as if it were the one described in Pushkin's poem *Mednyi vsadnik* (*The Bronze Horseman*) nine years after the event. Similarly, Igor' interacts with fictional characters as if they were real ones, while treating historical facts and characters as fictional. On a psychopoetic level, the protagonist's inability to tell the past from the present results in bouts of schizophrenic delusion. His ambition to participate (mimetically) in history by taking a photograph of the live Pushkin remains unfulfilled. The past, it turns out, may not be visited and remains dark and inaccessible as Pushkin adroitly avoids any interception by the hero.

The motif of the invisible past in "Pushkin's Photograph" is linked to a postmodern concept of history in Bitov's text. The modernist (as, for example, the Russian avant-garde) interprets the past as unhistorical and irrelevant. By contrast, in "Pushkin's Photograph", the hero's dilemma is characterized by his inability to conceive of anything as *not* being historical. Both the motif of the invisible past and that of the "Pushkin photograph" are prefigured in Nabokov's 1937 essay "Pouchkine, ou le vrai et le vraisemblable" ("Pushkin, or the Real and the Plausible"). Nabokov interprets the fact that no photograph was taken of Pushkin during the poet's lifetime as a guarantee of the continued historicity ("darkness") of the past. By contrast, in "Pushkin's Photograph", the false images and fictitious representations acquire in themselves the status of historical facts.

The official culture that sends Igor' on his trip in order to recover a photograph of the live Pushkin represents a Soviet state of the future, a totalitarian post-Utopia where any difference between the present and the past has been abolished. Having conquered space, Bitov's future age now seeks to conquer history, as well. It has recreated the past *in toto* by surrounding both "our old Earth" and the ancient city of St Petersburg with transparent cupolas. In this way, Bitov reinterprets the museum motif that had already played a central role in *Pushkin House*. In "Pushkin's Photograph", the museum delimits itself as the whole world becomes a museum. Here, fiction and fact as well as present and history are fully equivalent with each other. For example, Igor' experiences St Petersburg as an amorphous *mélange* of ancient buildings and fake copies of monuments that cannot be told apart from their vanished originals. In its post-Utopian emphasis on the "end of history", "Pushkin's Photograph" polemically argues with the Russian Utopian tradition in general and, more specifically, with Vladimir F. Odoevskii (*4338-oi god: fantasticheskii roman* (*The Year 4338*)) and Nikolai Fedorov, both of whom emphasize the preservation and recovery of the past as one of the most pressing tasks of the Utopian future.

The idea that history came to an end with the Bolshevik Revolution is a recurrent theme in Bitov's writing. Igor''s search for Pushkin allegorizes the Soviet intellectual's attempt to re-establish historical continuity with the pre-revolutionary past. Pushkin, in this context, is conceived as Russian culture's true progenitor whose untimely death constitutes its central trauma. It is not by coincidence that Igor''s journey into history is explicitly devoted to the attempt to reverse Pushkin's death by either forestalling his fatal duel or, failing that, by providing him with (anachronistic) medical assistance (penicillin). Igor''s failure to intervene in the poet's demise spells both the irretrievable loss of the past and, more generally, the Soviet intellectual's inability to engage in the kind of Oedipal struggle with his predecessors, which, in the west, has been described as the "anxiety of influence".

SVEN SPIEKER

Aleksandr Aleksandrovich Blok 1880–1921

Poet, dramatist, and prose writer

Biography

Born in St Petersburg, 28 November 1880. Spent childhood with grandfather, rector of St Petersburg University. Attended Vvedenskii School, St Petersburg, 1891–99; studied law, 1899–1901, and philology, 1901–06, at St Petersburg University. Married: Liubov' Dmitrievna Mendeleeva in 1903. Associated with the St Petersburg Symbolists, Merezhkovskii and Hippius. First publication in *Novyi put'*, 1903; full-time writer from 1906. Served in the army as a record keeper with an engineering unit, stationed at the Front near Pskov, 1916–17. Held various government jobs: edited testimony of former ministers of the tsar for the provisional government's Extraordinary Investigative Commission, 1917–18; on various cultural committees after 1918: in theatrical department of People's Commissariat for Education (and chairman of Repertory Section), 1918–19. Worked for Gor'kii's publishing house Vsemirnaia Literatura [World Literature], 1918–21. Adviser, Union of Practitioners of Literature as an Art, 1919. Arrested briefly for supposed counter-revolutionary activities, 1919. Chairman, Directorate of the Bolshoi Theatre, 1919–21, and the Petrograd division of the All-Russian Union of Poets, 1920–21. Died in Petrograd, 7 August 1921.

Publications

Collected Editions

Sobranie sochinenii, 7 vols (of 10 planned). Berlin, 1923.
Sobranie sochinenii, 12 vols. Leningrad, 1932–36.
The Spirit of Music, translated by I. Freiman. London, Lindsay Drummond, 1946; reprinted Westport, Connecticut, Hyperion Press, 1973.
Sobranie sochinenii, 8 vols. Moscow and Leningrad, 1960–63 [plus *Zapisnye knizhki, 1901–1920*, 1965].
Selected Poems [in Russian], edited by James B. Woodward. Oxford, Oxford University Press, 1968; reprinted London, Bristol Classical Press, 1992.
The Twelve and Other Poems, translated by Jon Stallworthy and Peter France. Oxford, Oxford University Press, 1970; as *Selected Poems*, Harmondsworth, Penguin, 1974.
Sobranie sochinenii, 6 vols. Moscow, 1971.
Selected Poems [in Russian], edited by Avril Pyman. Oxford, Pergamon Press, 1972.
Selected Poems, translated by Alex Miller. Moscow, Progress, 1981.
Teatr, edited by P.P. Gromov. Moscow, 1981.
Polnoe sobranie sochinenii, 20 vols. Moscow, 1997–

Poetry

Stikhi o prekrasnoi dame [Verses on the Beautiful Lady]. Moscow, 1904.
Nechaiannaia radost' [Unexpected Joy]. Moscow, 1907.
Snezhnaia maska [The Snow Mask]. St Petersburg, 1907.
Zemlia v snegu [The Earth in Snow]. Moscow, 1908.
Na pole Kulikovom [On the Field of Kulikovo]. Moscow, 1908.
Nochnye chasy [The Night Watches]. Moscow, 1911.
Sobranie stikhotvorenii, 3 vols. Moscow, 1911–12.
Skazki: Stikhi dlia detei [Fairy Tales: Poems for Children]. Moscow, 1913.
Kruglyi god: Stikhotvoreniia dlia detei [All the Year Round: Poems for Children]. Moscow, 1913.
Stikhi o Rossii [Poems about Russia]. Petrograd, 1916.
Kniga pervaia, 1898–1904 [First Book]. Moscow, 1916.
Kniga vtoraia, 1904–1907 [Second Book]. 3rd edition, Moscow, 1916.
Solov'inyi sad [The Nightingale Garden]. Petrograd, 1918.
Dvenadtsat'; Skify. Petrograd, 1918; reprinted Moscow, 1982; translated as *The Twelve and The Scythians*, by Jack Lindsay, London, Journeyman, 1982; *Dvenadtsat'* also as *The Twelve*, by C.E. Bechhofer, London, Chatto and Windus, 1920; also by B. Deutsch and Avrahm Yarmolinsky, New York, W.B. Huebsch, 1920; reprinted New York, Rudge, 1931; and as *Blok's "Twelve"*, by Robin Fulton, Preston, Akros, 1968; also translated in *The Twelve and Other Poems*, by Peter France and Jon Stallworthy, 1970; and as *The Twelve* (bilingual edition), edited by Avril Pyman, Durham, Durham Modern Language Series, 1989.
Iamby: Sovremennye stikhi (1907–1914) [Iambs: Contemporary Poems]. Petrograd, 1919.
Za gran'iu proshlykh dnei [Beyond the Bounds of Days Gone By]. Petrograd, 1920.
Sedoe utro [The Grey Morning]. Petrograd, 1920.
Stikhotvoreniia [Poems]. Petrograd, 1921.
Kniga tret'ia, 1907–1916 [Third Book]. 3rd edition, Petrograd, 1921.
Vozmezdie [Retribution]. Petrograd, 1922.

Plays

Balaganchik (produced 1906); in *Fakely I*, March 1906; also in *Liricheskie dramy*, St Petersburg, 1908; translated as *The Puppet Show*, by M. Kriger and Gleb Struve, *Slavonic Review*, 28/71 (1949–50).
O liubvi, poezii i gosudarstvennoi sluzhbe [About Love, Poetry, and the Civil Service]. 1907; Berlin, Skify, 1920.
Pesnia sud'by [The Song of Fate]. 1907; revised edition, Petrograd, 1919.
Korol' na ploshchadi [The King in the Square], in *Liricheskie dramy*, 1908.
Liricheskie dramy [Lyrical Dramas]. St Petersburg, 1908.
Neznakomka [The Stranger] (produced 1914); in *Liricheskie dramy*, 1908.
Primater [The Ancestress], from a play by Grillparzer (produced 1908).
Roza i krest (produced 1921). St Petersburg, 1913; translated as "The Rose and the Cross", in *The Russian Symbolist Theatre*, edited and translated by Michael Green, Ann Arbor, Ardis, 1986.
Ramzes [Ramses]. Petrograd, 1921.

Essays, Memoirs, and Travel Notes

Rossiia i intelligentsiia (1907–1918) [Russia and the Intelligentsia]. Moscow, 1918; revised edition, 1919;

translated in part by I. Freiman, in *The Spirit of Music*, London, Lindsay Drummond, 1946; reprinted Westport, Connecticut, Hyperion Press, 1973.
Katilina. Petrograd, 1919.
Poslednie dni imperatorskoi vlasti [The Last Days of the Imperial Regime]. Petrograd, 1921; reprinted Paris, Librairie de Sialsky, 1978.
Otrocheskie stikhi; Avtobiografiia [Adolescent Poems; Autobiography]. Moscow, 1922.
An Anthology of Essays and Memoirs, edited by Lucy E. Vogel. Ann Arbor, Ardis, 1982.

Letters and Diaries
Dnevnik Aleksandra Bloka, 1911–1913 and *1917–1921* [The Diary of Aleksandr Blok], 2 vols. Leningrad, 1928.
Perepiska/ Aleksandr Blok - Andrei Belyi [A Correspondence/ Aleksandr Blok and Andrei Belyi]. Moscow, 1940; reprinted Munich, Fink, 1969.
Pis'ma k zhene [Letters to His Wife], in *Literaturnoe nasledstvo*, vol. 89, 1978.

Critical Studies
Blok i Geine, by Iurii Tynianov, Petrograd, 1921; reprinted Letchworth, Prideaux Press, 1979.
Aleksandr Blok, by Konstantin Mochul'skii, Paris, YMCA-Press, 1942; translated by Doris V. Johnson, Detroit, Wayne State University Press, 1983.
Alexander Blok: Prophet of Revolution, by Cecil H. Kisch, London, Weidenfeld and Nicolson, and New York, Roy, 1960.
Aleksandr Blok: Between Image and Idea, by F.D. Reeve, New York, Columbia University Press, 1962; reprinted New York, Octagon Books, 1980.
Drama Aleksandra Bloka "Roza i krest": literaturnye istochniki, by V.M. Zhirmunskii, Leningrad, 1964.
Alexander Blok: A Study in Rhythm and Metre, by Robin Kemball, The Hague, Mouton, 1965.
A. Blok's "The Snow Mask": An Interpretation, by Irene Masing, Stockholm, Almqvist & Wiksell, 1970.
Aleksandr Blok: The Journey to Italy, by Lucy Vogel, Ithaca, Cornell University Press, 1973.
The Poet and the Revolution: Aleksandr Blok's "The Twelve", by Sergei Hackel (includes translation), Oxford, Clarendon Press, 1975.
Listening to the Wind: An Introduction to Alexander Blok, by James Forsyth, Oxford, Meeuws, 1977.
Aleksandr Blok: lichnost' i tvorchestvo, by L. Dolgopolov, Leningrad, 1978.
Poema Aleksandra Bloka "Dvenadtsat'", by L. Dolgopolov, Leningrad, 1979.
The Life of Aleksandr Blok, by Avril Pyman, 2 vols, Oxford and New York, Oxford University Press, 1979–80.
Aleksandr Blok - dramaturg, by A.V. Fedorov, Leningrad, 1980.
Hamayun: The Life of Aleksandr Blok, by Vladimir N. Orlov, translated by Olga Shartse, Moscow, Progress, 1980.
Aleksandr Blok v vospominaniiakh sovremennikov, edited by Vladimir N. Orlov, 2 vols, Moscow, 1980.
Literaturnoe nasledstvo, vol. 92, Books 1–5, 1980–83.
Poeziia i proza Aleksandra Bloka, by D.E. Maksimov, Leningrad, 1981.
Akhmatova i Blok, by V.N. Toporov, Berkeley, Berkeley Slavic Specialties, 1981.
Alexander Blok as Man and Poet, by Kornei Chukovsky, translated and edited by Diana Burgin and Katherine O'Connor, Ann Arbor, Ardis, 1982.
Aleksandr Blok's Ital'ianskie stikhi: Confrontation and Disillusionment, by Gerald Pirog, Columbia, Ohio, Slavica, 1983.
Aleksandr Blok Centennial Conference, edited Walter N. Vickery, Columbus, Ohio, Slavica, 1984.
Aleksandr Blok: issledovaniia i materialy. Leningrad, 1987.
Aleksandr Blok and the Dynamics of the Lyric Cycle, by David A. Sloane, Columbus, Ohio, Slavica, 1988.
Vospominaniia ob Aleksandre Bloke, by M.A. Beketova, Moscow, 1990.
A Comparative Study of Pushkin's "The Bronze Horseman", Nekrasov's "Red-Nosed Frost", and Blok's "The Twelve": The Wild World, by A.D.P. Briggs, Lewiston, New York, and Lampeter, Wales, Edwin Mellen Press, 1990.
"Chernyi vecher, belyi sneg": tvorcheskaia istoriia i sud'ba poemy Aleksandra Bloka "Dvenadtsat'", by O.P. Smola, Moscow, 1993.
Form and Meaning: Essays on Russian Literature, by James B. Woodward, Columbus, Ohio, Slavica, 1993.
A History of Russian Symbolism, by Avril Pyman, Cambridge, Cambridge University Press, 1994.
Aleksandr Blok: A Life, by Nina Berberova, translated from the French by Robyn Marsack, New York, Braziller, and Manchester, Carcanet, 1996.

Bibliographies
Blok, by N. Ashukin, Moscow, 1923; reprinted 1973.
Bibliography, by Avril Pyman, in *Blokovskii sbornik 1*, 1964; also in *Selected Poems*, 1972.
Bibliography, by P.E. Pomirchyi, in *Blokovskii sbornik 2*, 1972.
Biblioteka A.A. Bloka: opisanie, by O.V. Miller *et al.*, 3 vols. Leningrad, 1984–86.

Aleksandr Blok was a Symbolist poet, dramatist, and author of lyrical prose. Blok's work is subjective, even solipsistic, yet he compared the function of an artist to that of a witness: a witness to "contemporaneity". His poetry is redolent of cultural reminiscences suggested by rhythmic and structural allusion, yet all this is passed through the poet's own immediate experience, "the fever of the heart, the cold of mind", even – as Blok added in one of his frequent moments of self-deflation – the liver; even – as he hints in the article "Katilina" – the libido.

"I don't really need Blok any more", Anna Akhmatova is recorded as saying in the 1960s, "but when you begin to read ... Blok's poetry is as compelling as music". Indeed, the Formalist critic Viktor Shklovskii explains its attraction by association with "the simplest forms of romance".

Blok started publishing his work in 1903 (in *Novyi put'* and *Severnye tsvety* among other journals) at a time when critical realism was discredited and modernism appeared the only way forward. His world-view was rooted in Plato and Solov'ev, but his face was set towards the bleakest existentialism. As a result, the most joyous poems are tinged with foreboding, the darkest shot through with brightness: everywhere contrast and oxymoron. His "world-view" was compounded by history. Apocalyptic *fin-de-siècle* forebodings that shadowed Blok's boyhood were replaced by sober, life-long awareness of cultural crisis confirmed by two wars, three revolutions and Civil War. To these he bore witness; but always on his own terms and in his own way, as reflections of events "which have already taken place in our own souls".

The poet's first mentor was his grandfather Andrei Beketov, who, at the time of the poet's birth, was rector of St Petersburg University. "Home" to Blok was the country estate of Shakhmatovo that he inherited on Beketov's death in 1902, a modest "nobleman's nest", a "corner of paradise", which provided the chronotope for the central cycle of his first book: "The Mystic Summer, Shakhmatovo, 1901". The "quiet white house" finally went with the Bolshevik Revolution, sacked in November 1917, but long before had become the paradigm of paradise lost for one destined "to remain, in life, an ordinary man". Blok called the three volumes into which he was to edit his work (first in 1911–12, then again in 1916) "a trilogy of humanization (*ochelovechen'ia*)".

Stikhi o prekrasnoi dame [Verses on the Beautiful Lady], Blok's first book, is "single-stringed" and records a state of being in love (Platonic or Solov'evian with more than a touch of medieval chivalry), which empowers the poet to receive and record a "true testament": "of the soul of the people and of our souls, together with theirs reduced to ashes, may it be said simply and courageously: 'may they rise again'". The imagery is positive: glowing skies, soaring birds, fields of clover – but is soon counterpointed by the prosaic realism (albeit "bordering on the fantastic") of St Petersburg, with its dark backwaters, street-lamps and smoke-filled taverns. Haunting, hesitant rhythms, subverting conventional metre, lend the flow of experience, salutary or demonic, a dream-like spontaneity. The source of inspiration, a Feminine Presence, is always elusive and "unsaid". Blok's first volume, in which he later arranged these and other poems of the pre-1905 period, ends with the renunciation of a theme unsustainable for one who has abandoned religion for art, "a monastery of historical formation".

The long poem *Noch'naia fialka* [The Night Violet] celebrates the break and, together with his next collection, *Nechaiannaia radost'* [Unexpected Joy] and the *Liricheskie dramy* [Lyrical Dramas], marks a transition through Romantic irony to the triumphant affirmation of the artist's power as magician in the Freudian sense: one who seeks not a religious understanding of the given world but power to create his own. Blok uses the devices of threefold repetition, assonance, alliteration, colour symbolism and subversion of liturgical language to invoke "The Stranger", an act that touches off the Dionysian inspiration of *Snezhnaia maska* [The Snow Mask] and *Zemlia v snegu* [The Earth in Snow]. Here, the imagery is chaotic (night, flames, blizzards, and comets) and the emphasis on theatrical make-believe (grease-paint, masks, shadow-play). The chronotope is clearly defined: the streets and island of St Petersburg and interiors connected with Komissarzhevskaia's theatre during the winter seasons 1906–07 and 1907–08. Such is the poetry of *Kniga vtoraia* [Second Volume], associated in the minds of the poet and his fellow-Symbolists with Dante's *Inferno*. From it he emerges with the unrhymed, mercilessly sunlit iambics of *Vol'nye mysli* [Free Thoughts] (1908), and a scattering of experiments in free verse.

The poetic cycle *Na pole Kulikovom* [On the Field of Kulikovo] together with several prose articles on the "People and the Intelligentsia" introduce the theme of Russia and the crisis of post-Petrine culture as central to the *Kniga tret'ia* [Third Volume]. Some poems, particularly in the "Rossiia" cycle, evoke Blok's "anamnesis" and signpost dereliction of spirit, a return to "the road ahead". This last volume, however, has no time-place limits. Blok treats various themes, including well-worn classics such as the Dance of Death, Tannhaüser, Faust, Don Juan and Carmen, and seems anxious not so much to experiment with new forms as to perfect his mastery over "architecture" and "music", structure and orchestration. He does, though, reach out, towards *grand genre*, for instance in the long narrative poem *Vozmezdie* [Retribution], which, although it contains magnificent passages, refused to cohere as an objective statement of the poet's place in history. Journeys abroad to Italy in 1909, Brittany in 1911 and Guethary near Biarritz in 1913 gave Blok perspective and the humility to place himself in art as witness rather than magician, a lesson he spelt out in the key speech "On the Present State of Russian Symbolism" during the so-called "crisis of Symbolism" in 1910. His travels also inspired superb poetry celebrating the great "culture" of Europe's past and inveigling against the "senseless merry-go-round" of her present "civilization". "European" in inspiration are the play *Roza i krest* ("The Rose and the Cross") and the long poem *Solov'inyi sad* [The Nightingale Garden], a last "mythologized" statement of the poet's calling to quit paradise. More and more, the poetry shows the "lyrical hero" pacing the nocturnal streets of St Petersburg, identifying with beggars and prostitutes. Blok, said Khodasevich, suffered from "insomnia of the heart". For long stretches after 1912 depression and sickness would leave him dry, and there was a particularly long period from 1916 to January 1918 coinciding with war and revolution: "I am all ears, no voice". Then came *Dvenadtsat'; Skify* (*The Twelve and The Scythians*), in which he found the voice to speak for "contemporaneity". After this there was no more poetry: "There are no more sounds". Blok's last public statement was written in 1921 for the opening of the Academy of Sciences' Pushkin House, a gentle reassertion of the cultural values that were being so severely tried and, as he hoped, *tempered* in the furnace of revolution.

AVRIL PYMAN

Stikhi o prekrasnoi dame

Verses on the Beautiful Lady

Poetry collection, 1904

Blok's first book was published in October 1904, and the 93 poems that it contained form the nucleus of the first of the definitive three volumes of the poet's work. *Stikhi o prekrasnoi dame* [Verses on the Beautiful Lady] thus represents the essence of the early phase of Blok's poetry and marks his establishment as a Symbolist writer.

The poems are the reflection of an unspecified mystical experience that Blok underwent early in 1901. The exact nature of his vision remains unclear, but it is evident that Blok was vouchsafed a glimpse of a reality beyond the sublunary world, which he afterwards strove for and expected to attain. The figure of the Beautiful Lady is a correlative of this mystical other world and the object of Blok's poetic yearning and adoration.

There are two other salient factors that influenced Blok's thinking in formulating the figure of the Beautiful Lady. The first is the idealist philosophy of Vladimir Solov'ev. This posited an Absolute Reality, independent of the trammels of sensual perception, which might be reached through the medium of the principle of the "eternal feminine". Solov'ev saw this construction primarily in religious terms, as reflecting a human desire to escape from the chaos of this world into unity with God through the mediation of Sophia, the Divine Wisdom. There has been much debate as to the extent to which Blok was actually aware of Solov'ev's writings at the time he wrote *Stikhi o prekrasnoi dame*. Nevertheless, Solov'ev's ideas were very much part of the intellectual atmosphere of Russia at the turn of the century, and Blok can hardly have failed to come across them in some form.

The second factor informing *Stikhi o prekrasnoi dame* is Blok's relationship with his future wife, Liubov' Dmitrievna Mendeleeva, and the book is on one level a poetic diary of their courtship during the years 1901 and 1902. For much of this period Liubov' Dmitrievna was unable to respond to Blok's advances with the emotional intensity he would have desired; indeed, at one point in early 1902 she decided to stop seeing him altogether. The cycle of tension, expectation and disappointment that Blok experienced as a result is reflected in his attitude to the Beautiful Lady of the poems. Liubov' Dmitrievna was not, of course, Sophia, but she came to represent her not only in Blok's imagination, but also more extravagantly in the subsequent cult of the Beautiful Lady fostered by Blok's friends, in particular by Andrei Belyi.

The language of the collection is itself a carefully constructed metaphor of Blok's mystical experience. It combines a precise rhetorical and melodic structure that echoes the undeniability of the Lady as manifested to the poet with a semantic vagueness that is a reflex of her evasiveness and intangibility, and of the unfocused nature of the poet's emotional drive. Like other Symbolists Blok selected words far more for their allusive rather than their referential meanings. A relatively narrow vocabulary is repeated extensively, giving words such as shadow, darkness, dawn, a heightened symbolic significance. The literal meaning of Blok's poems is often obscure, even when external evidence reveals them as responses to specific events, but they can still cause a powerful response through the emotional force of their allusiveness, and because of the close attention Blok gave to the organization of his verse.

One rhetorical device that Blok adopted with some regularity is the so-called *kol'tso*, or ring, in which the beginning of a poem is repeated at the end, either word for word or in a modified form. This often represents an organizational restatement of the common situation in which a brief moment of heightened perception is preceded and followed by a lengthy period of anticipation. Other forms of syntactical repetition are also common, and tend to increase the emotional impact of the verse by producing an incantatory effect. Blok makes much use, for example, of anaphora and of other forms of parallelism both within the line and at the level of stanza or entire poem. Lexical elements are also repeated, as when, for example, the same adjective recurs with a series of different nouns. Similar attention is paid to the repetition of individual sounds through alliteration and particularly through assonance.

A different form of structure is given by the repetitive use of certain metaphors. The Lady is, for example, normally associated with the semantic fields of distance, height, splendour, and light while the poet is linked with fixed points on the ground and with darkness and austerity. Experience of the Lady is often expressed in religious terminology: the poet is a monk, confident in his faith in the divine spirit, or he is transfigured by the solemnity of a liturgical space. Music, especially the ringing of church bells, is frequently seen as a token of the Lady's presence.

Metrically, *Stikhi o prekrasnoi dame* is significant in that Blok employs, alongside the traditional syllabo-accentual metres of Russian verse, a verse form (the *dol'nik*) that allows a variable number of unstressed syllables between each accent. Although the *dol'nik* had been used experimentally by earlier writers, it had not previously been used in a sustained manner. The greater flexibility in manipulating the relationship between metre and rhythm that the *dol'nik* allows provided Blok with a further tool for the expression of fine shades of emotion.

The collection was not received with particular enthusiasm by the literary community at the time of its first publication, though it did provide Blok with an entrée into the circle of Symbolist writers such as Briusov and Viacheslav Ivanov. As Blok's career as a poet developed, however, his early achievement as a metrical innovator and his mastery of poetic organization began to be more clearly recognized, and indeed influenced profoundly the succeeding generation of poets. Further, the thematic significance of the image of the Beautiful Lady as it developed in Blok's subsequent writing led quickly to detailed consideration and imitation of this most powerful symbol of his early verse.

DAVID N. WELLS

Na pole Kulikovom

On the Field of Kulikovo

Poetry cycle, 1908

This miniature cycle forms one part of the larger cycle *Rodina* [Native Land], which is considered the apex of Blok's poetry. He addresses the theme of Russia and her destiny with acute sensibility, expressing a sense of personal anxiety and responsibility for her fate, especially concerning the role and duty of the intelligentsia. Blok's idiosyncratic Symbolism is joined by a new system of images, and the impending cataclysmic events are paralleled with turning points in history, such as the battle on the field of Kulikovo, where Dmitrii Donskoi first defeated the Tartars on 8 September 1380. In creating this cycle, Blok prophesied from the music of the time, verbalizing the truth about Russia's future.

The cycle consists of five poems (the famous poem "Rossiia" ("Russia") can be considered an epilogue to the cycle). The first three were written in a few days: "Reka raskinulas'. Techet, grustit lenivo" ("The river spread. It flows, mourns lazily"), 7 June 1908; "My, sam-drug, nad step'iu v polnoch' stali" ("We halted above the steppe at midnight"), 8 June 1908; "V noch', kogda Mamai zaleg s ordoiu" ("At night, when Mamai lay in hiding with the horde"), 14 June 1908; "Opiat' s vekovoiu toskoiu" ("Again with age-old despair"), 31 July 1908; "Opiat' nad polem Kulikovym" ("Now on the field of Kulikovo"), 23 December 1908. These poems were included in volume 3 of Blok's Collected Poems, as the centre of the cycle *Rodina*, (1907–16).

The Kulikovo cycle represents a consolidation of Blok's poetic development after the mystical and exalted cycle *Stikhi o prekrasnoi dame* and the despairing nightmares and bitterness of the urbanist poems. Blok finds a way out of this vicious circle in his new poetic ideal, the ultimate transformation of the Eternal Feminine in the image of the fair and gentle motherland, Russia. Russia's destiny is suggested by the forward motion symbolized by the road. His perception of Russia is above all metaphysical, transcending the traditional view based on nature and history.

This image embraces his poetic ideal in a profoundly ambivalent way. Russia, as a feminine image, reflects the dialectics of opposing traits: the heavenly and divine versus the demonic and savage; humility and patience versus rebellion and disorder; soundness, simplicity, and purity versus confusion and chaos. Russia as a heavenly bride and mother watches over the sleep of the warriors and, as a lady clad in rays of light, fortifies them with strength and hope, but she shares in the sorrows and prophetic cries of the earthbound poet. In the first poem of the cycle, "The river spread. It flows, mourns lazily", the traditional association of the native land with "mother" is superseded by "wife", introducing new symbolic meanings, which sound a polyvalent echo of Solov'ev's Eternal Feminine and Bloks's own Beautiful Lady, as well as alluding to such eminent representatives of the intuitive Russian soul as Dostoevskii's Nastasia Filippovna or Grushen'ka.

Blok seeks a clue to Russia's future through historical perspective, adapting certain concepts and polemicizing with others (e.g., Chaadaev's notion of Russia's lack of historical memory). In search of historical analogies based on the cyclic motion of time, Blok turns to the battle on the field of Kulikovo, which had direct relevance to the events and spirit of the time (the Russo-Japanese War, the 1905 Revolution) and had mystical, prophetic meaning for Blok. He treats the same theme, albeit distanced via the lyric persona, in his play *Pesnia sud'by* [The Song of Fate] and his article "Narod i intelligentsiia" [The People and the Intelligentsia]; he traces a reprise of the hostility between the Russians and Tartars in the intelligentsia's attitude toward the people and the impending calamities of his time, foreseeing the imminent revolution. In 1912, in his notes to the third volume of his Collected Works, Blok made his famous statement that: "The battle of Kulikovo is one of the two symbolic events in Russian history. Such events are destined to return. The divination of their true significance is still in the future", which echoes Nietzsche's concept of eternal recurrence. Regardless of the historical details, the cycle is considered more lyric than epic; in Blok's later historical works he moves toward a more objective interpretation, from lyrics through the verse epic *Solov'inyi sad* [The Nightingale Garden], the narrative poem *Vozmezdie* to essays. The lyric hero is situated outside the subjective world, in history; he stands at the battlefield as a medieval warrior and a modern poet ready to fight for his beloved wife, Russia. He relates to Russia with mystical reverence, although he is filled with love mixed with anguish, guilt, anger, hatred, and disgust. His manifest love for his homeland in spite of, if not because of her failings continues the attitude toward Russia exhibited by great writers of the 19th century (Lermontov, Tiutchev, Gogol', Dostoevskii). The lyrical suggestivity of the poems is expressed by polyvalent nature imagery: haze, mist, nightfall, smoke on the steppe, yellow mud, storm clouds, an allusion to the river Styx hidden in an anagram, and other images are displayed through the richness of tropes. The synaesthesia that introduces life – the motion quickened by each verse, the battle noise, riverflow, landscape colours, blowing wind – into the previous stagnation draws the reader effectively into this poetic world. All of its components are permeated with a tragic outlook, filled with dark and ominous presentiments of the great catastrophes that can only be overcome by the radiance associated with the organic element, the orchestral undertone within Russia the wife.

Russia is viewed dialectically in an historical perspective from the fateful, poor, ignorant, sinful present. But Blok's foremost concern is to save Russia's soul and to answer her Messianic call in accordance with the Slavophile spirit. Russia personified symbolizes the journey of an individual, the poet himself, and his struggle to fulfil his divine destiny. Blok's negative picture counterbalances despair with hope: the lack of civilization – the elemental, uncorrupted force – contains the life-giving roots for a potentially glorious future. From the unanalysable substratum of nature and the music of the elements, the clairvoyant poet foresees that the historical journey will lead through a purifying storm, crisis, and suffering, eventually reaching some kind of renewal. The poem ends on an apprehensive, solemn, and prayerful mood on the eve of the great event; the closing word is "Pray" – the only way to prepare for the future.

The cycle weaves intertextual references on many levels, creating a unique idiosyncratic mythology reflecting Old Russian Literature – *Zadonshchina*, "Skazanie o Mamaevom poboishche" ("Legend of the Rout of Mamai"), "Slovo o polku Igoreve" (*The Lay of Igor's Campaign*), "Slovo o pogibeli russkoi zemli" ("Orison on the Downfall of Russia"); elements of 19th-century literature that address the nation's destiny, especially Gogol''s image of the road as upward flight, as well as Tiutchev, Pushkin, Zhukovskii, Nekrasov, Solov'ev, Tolstoi; general literary, mythological, folklore, and religious references (the knight-warrior and his lady, the Apocalypse, etc.); and Blok's own recurrent symbolic imagery in the form of self-reminiscences, self-quotations (river, road, whirlwind, sound patterns, etc.).

The concept of eternal recurrences is reinforced by the circular composition, theme, motifs, time and space concepts, style, meter, allusions, language, and so forth: all are expressed by a sophisticated system of repetition. This cycle vitally influenced Belyi's historical views in the novel *Peterburg* (*Petersburg*).

MARIA PAVLOVSZKY

The Puppet Show

Balaganchik

Play, 1906

Blok's first "lyrical drama" was written and staged in 1906. Variously translated as *The Puppet Show*, "The Fair-Ground Booth" and "The Penny-Gaff", the word in its diminutive form (as Blok uses it) does suggest something in the nature of a children's puppet-show in the style of Punch and Judy, but "Balagan" in fact stands metaphorically for a noisy, disorderly farce and literally for a fairground stage on which knock-about comedies were enacted by live actors (acrobats, mimes, mummers). It was in response to Symbolist interest in folk theatre that Blok was requested to expand the short lyrical poem "Balaganchik" written in the autumn of 1905 into a play. The request was made on 3 January 1906, at a meeting at Viacheslav Ivanov's Tower organized by Georgii Chulkov between the host, Maksim Gor'kii, Vsevolod Meierkhol'd and others to discuss the future of Russian theatre. Gor'kii was enthused by the success of street theatre in promoting Bolshevik ideas during the recent Revolution; Ivanov was interested in the Dionysian origins of theatre as cult. Interest in classical and medieval theatre and extremes of modernist refinement met here with a new urban populism. Meierkhol'd, with ambitions to found a theatre of his own in St Petersburg to be called Fakely (Torches), suggested that a palatable way of introducing his public to popular forms might be through the *commedia dell' arte*. The theatre did not materialize but Blok's play was published in March 1906 in Chulkov's Almanac *Fakely I*, and, thanks to Meierkhol'd's engagement with the Komissarzhevskii Theatre, it reached the stage, under his direction and with his participation in the role of Pierrot, on 29 December of the same year. For Meierkhol'd, as director, it was a turning-point in his development; for Blok a *succès de scandale* that brought fame and notoriety, whistles, and applause: "I acknowledged both".

The play makes use of the stock "triangle": Pierrot, Harlequin, Columbine. The story line is simple: Harlequin steals Columbine from Pierrot and takes her sleigh-riding, but she tumbles out into the snow like a broken doll; Harlequin goes off in search of fresh adventures and Pierrot is left to sing a bitter-sweet complaint to the audience that passes into a delicate lament on the flute (music by M.A. Kuzmin). This melodrama, however, is enacted against a background of St Petersburg literary life: mystics, in the first act, conjure up a female being (the World Soul? the Most Beautiful Lady? Death?) and will not heed Pierrot's explanation that it is his fiancée, Columbine, who has answered their call. Daunted, Pierrot makes as if to leave, but Columbine follows him. Their exit is prevented by Harlequin, who leads her away for the promised sleigh-ride. The scene shifts to a masked ball, where motifs from Blok's own mystic love poetry are acted out by the dancers. Harlequin leads them in torchlit, Bacchic procession, then dives out through the window; Columbine reappears and the Author, an intrusive character from a more realist tradition who is always trying to interfere in the action, is about to join her hand with Pierrot's in the classic happy ending when the scenery is whirled away and Pierrot is left prostrate on an empty stage. He gets up – alone – to share the joke with the audience and lament the sadness of the world. The whole is a theatrical *tour de force*, creating and exposing illusion in a constant shimmer: a stage within a stage; double meanings, punning words and masked doubles; music, clowning, magic tricks, all the fun of the fair ... but, just as the blood is shown up as cranberry juice, the sword and helm as wooden props, the distant view of the world in spring glimpsed through the window as a painting on the crackly paper of a circus hoop ... "the hour of the mystery strikes" – and we are enchanted by Pierrot's song and wrapped in a new dream; more pure, more sad, more disembodied and infinitely more beautiful than the "rough magic" of the stage.

The play, like the poem from which it sprung, is redolent of "mystic scepticism" and heralds Blok's plunge into the "monstrous, glittering Hell of Art" that he knew to be "necessary" but from which, in the 1910 article "O sovremennom sostoianii russkogo simvolizma" ("On the Present State of Russian Symbolism"), he sought to disassociate himself, quoting Vladimir Solov'ev:

> For ecstasy of soul he substituted calculated illusion
> And for the living language of the gods – the speech of slaves,
> For the temple of the Muses – a noisy fairground theatre,
> And so deceived the fools.

Indeed, the "fools", the wider public, only recognized Blok's artistry after he had effected these substitutions and it could be argued that only then did he truly become "an artist".

The play figures in Michael Greene's *Symbolist Theatre* and is treated in considerable detail in almost every monograph on Blok, both in relation to his other *Liricheskie dramy* and to *The Rose and the Cross* and more particularly to *The Twelve*, Columbine's tumble from the sleigh being perceived as prefiguring the death of Kat'ka. There is indeed a sense in which Blok was always writing the same drama ... from *The Puppet Show* to *The Twelve*: a drama of Romantic irony that disintegrates the "real world" of "coarse matter", takes it by surprise, turns it on its head, sends it up in smoke ... and leaves the reader with the consolation of "radost'-stradanie" (joy-suffering), an indissoluble residue of hope.

Avril Pyman

Vozmezdie

Retribution

Poetry, 1910–22

Blok used the title *Vozmezdie* [Retribution] twice, and simultaneously: once for a cycle of 17 lyrical poems in his *Kniga tret'ia* [Third Book], and again, as the title of an unfinished narrative poem inspired by the death of his father. In both cases "retribution" is understood primarily as the punishment visited on the older self for the sins of the young man, although the instrument by which fate exacts this retribution varies from supernatural avenging angel to the next generation. Blok's use of Ibsen's line, "Youth is retribution", as the epigraph to his narrative poem, suggests overtones of Ibsen's *The Master Builder* and of *Brand*.

The cycle of lyrics includes straightforward autobiographical effusions on the marital turmoil of 1908, the departure of Blok's wife ("About valour, glory and fame / I was forgetting on the wretched earth ... / Your face in its simple frame / With my own hand I removed from the desk."), her return with a baby that died shortly after ("Na smert' mladentsa" ("On the death of a baby")), and the bleak spring of 1909 that followed. To this diary in verse is appended an afterword in 1910–12 that raises these tribulations to the level of myth, notably in one of Blok's greatest poems, "Shagi komandora" ("The Commendatore's Footsteps"). The inspiration is not purely personal; the idealization of the beloved that marked Blok's early poetry remains. She is "Thou" with a capital "T", her garments are still raiments symbolic of the Symbolists' azure infinite: "You sadly wrapped yourself in your blue cloak", she is remembered in front of the iconostas. In the second poem of the cycle "Zabyvshie tebia" ("Those Who Have Forgotten You"), the desertion is reversed: it is the worshippers of the eternal feminine who have failed and left themselves unable to fight fate. Blok has hit upon the connection between a private disaster and the public moral depression that overcame Russian minds in 1908, an association of emotional and historic worlds that he makes explicit in his narrative poem *Vozmezdie*. In the lyrics the movement continues into existential anguish. Here Blok chooses different formal models. The disappearance of the beloved echoes Pushkin (compare Blok's "Days flew past, swirling in a cursed swarm" with Pushkin's poem to A.P. Kern, similarly about losing, dreaming of and forgetting the eternal feminine: "... in the dark of incarceration / My days quietly dragged"); but the universal depression is expressed in the bleak images and alternation of long and short lines that Sologub used to imitate a dog howling at the moon: "Night - is night, and the street is deserted / Always thus! ... / Day - is day; the problem's solved: / All will die." The harrowing lyrics of the cycle are overshadowed by the mythopoeic "The Commendatore's Footsteps": poet and beloved are transformed into Don Juan and Donna Anna, the latter plunged into timeless catalepsy while the *commendatore* comes to fetch the errant "Don Juan who has known fear" in a black car – a touch of genius that Blok felt unsure about, even though it links the retribution exacted on Juan to the arrests of political rebels by the police. This poem is the last word in the Russian reworking of the *Don Juan* myth: Donna Anna, the eternal feminine, involuntarily deserts the rebel, as Russia deserts her revolutionaries or the Muse her poets: we can see here the genesis of Blok's greatest play, *The Rose and the Cross*. The poem is remarkable for the diffusion of the phonemes of the key words throughout the verse. Blok's favourite (and un-Russian) vowel combination "ua" in Zhuan is spread through words like "bezumna", "glukha", "tuman", "pusta" (mad, deaf, mist, empty), while the double "n"'s of Donna Anna create an atmosphere of dead, nocturnal stillness.

One image connects this cycle of poems with the narrative *Vozmezdie*, that of the black motor car that is like an owl; Blok sees Russia as nests of fledglings preyed on by a hawk, and his demonic father likewise as a bird of prey visiting his mother and her family. The narrative poem must, however, be judged as a partial failure. Blok completed the third chapter first, in the same unhappy 1909, when he was summoned, too late, to his father's deathbed in a Warsaw hospital. This chapter is the finest part of the poem: the estranged son loves his father for the first and last time on seeing him in his coffin and reflects on the horrors of this brilliant but demonic man reduced from a Byronic seducer and poet to a miserly eccentric, a radical become an extremist, exiled among alien Poles, unspeakable to his son's family. Why this fate is a retribution is not immediately clear: the son's visit is an afterword, not a prelude to his death. Blok worked on the poem intermittently, right until his death in 1921; for its published form he wrote in 1919 a prose foreword in which he set out his plan:

> in the form of concentric circles, each becoming narrower ... how the maelstrom of the world sucks almost everyone into its funnel ... my *Rougon-Macquart* free themselves gradually of their *éducation sentimentale* ... The poem was to consist of a prologue, three bug chapters and an epilogue ... The first chapter develops in the 1870s against the background of the Russo-Turkish War ... in an enlightened liberal family. Into this family comes a "demon", the first swallow ... with the disease of the age, the oncoming *fin de siècle*. The second chapter, which has not been written except for the introduction, was to be devoted to this demon's son; ... of him nothing will remain, except the spark, the seed thrown in a passionate sinful night into the womb of some quiet female daughter of an alien people. The third chapter describes the end of the father's life ... in the epilogue was to be described the baby held and nursed on its simple mother's lap ... The leitmotif of *Vozmezdie* is a mazurka, a dance on whose wings came Marina [Mniszek], dreaming of a Russian throne, Kosciuszko thrusting his right hand to the heavens and Mickiewicz at Russian and Parisian balls.

Of the plan only the third chapter is fully realized and effective. The prologue does not live up to the Wagnerian image of Blok's iambic verse, like a *Notung* sword, striking jewels out of the ore of life. The first chapter takes Baratynskii's iambic metre and phrases to define the 19th century as an iron age. But Blok is clearly not at home with a chronological order (as opposed to the musical structure of *The Twelve*). The public element of the poem is often banal; the parallels of Blok's childhood and of his father's end with the assassination of Alexander II and the accession of Alexander III in 1881 are emphasized but never properly justified. *Vozmezdie* shows the failures of inspiration that afflicted Blok, together with the most retributive and Ibsenian of diseases, at the end of his life: brilliant evocations (the funeral of his father) and the occasional telling aphorism are lost in a stream of unoriginal and even crudely versified reflections.

DONALD RAYFIELD

The Twelve

Dvenadtsat'

Narrative poem, 1918

This poem was written by Blok in the wake of the disbandment of the Constituent Assembly by Bolshevik sailors on 7 January 1918 and published on 5 March within a week of the government's decision to remove to Moscow, signalling the end of the St Petersburg period. An expression of the historical moment when, as the poet said, "There was a storm in every sea", the poem owes its initial world-wide notoriety to the fact that it was regarded as a political statement. First translated into English as "A Bolshevick Poem" (*Times Literary Supplement*, 1920), it was in fact briefly banned from public reading in Bolshevik Petersburg. On the Vatican index, it was long banned in Fascist countries (including the Colonels' Greece). Excoriated or extravagantly praised, this violent poem with its scrape-up of street slang and popular rhythms shocked some and delighted others precisely because it came from the pen of the exquisite, decadent, Symbolist poet Aleksandr Blok. Abroad, translators and commentators alike, ignorant of or uninterested in the fact that Russian literature produced a chorus of astonishing poetry to celebrate the passing of the old order and to will harmony from chaos, made no attempt to discover why this particular poem had achieved such resonance. The score or more translations made over the years into some kind of English, including the Scots dialect of McGuthrie and the Beatnik slang of Anselm Hollo, together with the growth of knowledge about Russian literature and language, have gradually altered attitudes. Scholars throughout the world still seek to penetrate the meaning of a work that the author himself refused to interpret. Above all, it is the presence in the equation of Jesus Christ that has led to endless controversy.

Lenin's honest "I don't understand", Trotskii's impatient "Why climb our mountain to crown it with a medieval shrine?" gave way in the Soviet period to various attempts (on both sides of the curtain) to reduce the figure of Christ to "symbolic" status as a figure for the "new culture" that would arise from the ashes of the old, for "freedom" (Reeve), for "socialist altruism" (Dolgopolov), or to perceive it as an extension of Blok's mythologema of the Beautiful Lady (most cogently, Masing-Delic), as an alternative to the "serene" Sophianic apocalypse (Cioran). Others, notably Ivanov-Razumnik, first publisher and critic, Sergei Makovskii and, in English, Sergei Hackel, have concentrated on the Old-Believer spelling of the "Isus" that links this Christ – as, in a sense, the social revolution of 1917 was linked – to the pre-Petrine period. Christ has been seen by some as "leading" the Twelve and by others (following Max Voloshin) as fleeing before them; as a demonic apparition (S. Bulgakov and an anonymous Russian priest who may or may not have been Pavel Florenskii); as a proper subject for sermons by Vvedenskii's "Renewed" Church. The debate is now open more freely than before in Russia, but it seems unlikely that any interpreter will do better than D.E. Maksimov, who felt that Jesus Christ will inevitably mean different things to different readers and cannot therefore be a paradigm of anything other than Himself.

Blok did write, however, that it was his fate to "become a catacomb": an inherent danger for the atheist state? For faithful Orthodox as well as their Catholic brethren? Or a bearer of some lingering Bolshevik contagion? It is fear of this last possibility, surely, which has made it fashionable to belittle the artistic merit of the poem, for, unquestionably, *The Twelve* is an achievement in its own terms. It is Blok's first successful attempt and the first successful modernist attempt to revive the genre of the narrative poem (*poema*) in a literature that had all but destroyed conventional narrative in the course of the long modernist war on causality. The juxtaposed fragments, different in length, rhyme scheme, rhythm and lexical register were to serve as a model for the Acmeist Akhmatova, and the "sounds of the street" were to convince the Futurist Maiakovskii.

Blok had spent two months prior to his composition of *The Twelve* walking the streets, and the snatches of conversation written into the poem, the almost cinematic, angled glimpses of hurrying figures slipping and sliding over or behind drifts or standing rooted in indecision as the storm rages around them work as in a brilliantly cut documentary film. Yet, far from "throwing Pushkin from the steam-ship of modernity", Blok conjures his "Devils" in the description of the blizzard, and harks back to romantic Decembrist laments (presented in subverted snatches), to Nekrasov, to popular ballads, to the cruel romance and the "chastushka", and to old revolutionary songs. Orthodox prayers for the dead and the spelling of Isus imbue the present moment with the past. "'Russia is perishing', 'There is no Russia', 'Eternal Memory to Russia' – so I hear all about me", Blok noted as he was writing *The Twelve*. "Yet before me I see – Russia: the same Russia that our great writers saw in terrifying and prophetic dreams". In this poem, he encompasses this amalgam of past and present through the material of words and sounds, yet achieves classically precise structure. The poem is laconic, explaining nothing. A prologue sets and peoples the scene. The melodramatic *crime passionel* (the murder of Kat'ka by the circling patrol of twelve Red Guards) is conveyed almost entirely through rhythm and dialogue and reaches a climax precisely at the natural turning-point, in the sixth part. A build-up towards a second climax, delayed briefly by Petia's monologue, culminates in the appearance, through blinding blizzard and rattling gunfire, of the invulnerable Christ beneath a red flag. Although the Twelve patrol in circles, a linear substructure is established by the threefold repetition, first at the beginning, twice at the end of the poem, of the question "What's out ahead?". Visually, this is confirmed by the processional, marching "into the distance". Musically, the different rhythms are unified by the wind – "a terrible noise, growing within me and all around", "a great noise within me and all around me", "roaring, roaring" – stilled only in the last line.

AVRIL PYMAN

Dmitrii Vasil'evich Bobyshev 1936–

Poet

Biography

Born in Mariupol, 11 April 1936. Grew up in Leningrad. Graduated from Leningrad Technological Institute, 1959. Worked as chemical engineer and then in Leningrad television. Published in *samizdat*, émigré journals and sparsely in Leningrad almanacs. Emigrated to the United States, 1979; currently lives in Milwaukee, combining the professions of engineer, poet and teacher of Russian literature at the University of Illinois, Urbana.

Publications

Poetry

Ziianiia [Gapings]. Paris, YMCA-Press, 1979.

"Russkie tertsiny" [Russian Terza Rima], *Kontinent*, 31 (1982); separate edition, St Petersburg, 1992.
Zveri Sviatogo Antoniia. Bestiarii [St Anthony's Beasts. Beastiary]. New York, Apollon Foundation, 1989.
Polnota vsego [The Plenitude of Everything]. St Petersburg, 1992.
Poems in *Contemporary Russian Poetry: A Bilingual Anthology*, translated by Gerald S. Smith. Bloomington, Indiana University Press, 1993.
Bestiarii [Beastiary]. New York, Appollon Foundation, 1994.
Poems in *Zvezda*, 1 (1994); 11 (1995).

Critical Studies

"Poeziia Dmitriia Bobysheva", by Iurii Ivask, *Vestnik russkogo khristianskogo dvizheniia*, 134 (1981), 181–84.
"The Other Worlds of Dmitry Bobyshev", by Barbara Heldt, *World Literature Today*, Winter (1984), 27–30.
"Vezde chelovek", by Viktor Dmitriev, *Literaturnaia gazeta*, 20/5448, (19 May 1993), 4.

Dmitrii Bobyshev began writing poetry in the mid-1950s. These early works were first published in the *samizdat* journal *Sintaksis* and later reprinted in *Grani*, 58 (1965). In 1959 he met Anna Akhmatova, an event that had a strong impact on his whole life. Together with his poet-friends – Iosif Brodskii, Evgenii Rein, and Anatolii Naiman – Bobyshev was close to Akhmatova until her death in 1966. She dedicated the poem "Piataia roza" ("The Fifth Rose") to him, and he reciprocated with his "Traurnye oktavy" [Mournful Octaves] (1971), in which he calls himself and his friends "Akhmatova's orphans". For Bobyshev and his friends, who formed an opposition group to official Soviet ideology and culture, Akhmatova personified a genuine living culture and represented continuity in spiritual tradition.

Bobyshev's work is in direct descent from the moral and aesthetic experience of classical Russian literature and the Silver Age. One can detect the influence of Tiutchev and Baratynskii on the one hand, and of Viacheslav Ivanov, Mandel'shtam, and Akhmatova on the other. Bobyshev adheres to the traditions of the St Petersburg poetic school not only thematically but also in so far as he employs complex interlacings of historical-cultural associations, while striving to penetrate the secrets of nature and cultural evolution. He thus enriches the emotional and ideological content of his verse. The poet's belief in the higher mission of art and its power of transformation and inspiration protects him from any element of philosphical and aesthetic scepticism. His awareness of the continuity of time and poetry's inexhaustible creative energy is evident throughout much of his verse.

Bobyshev experiments with new possibilities and variations of classical poetic forms, broadening the stylistic and lexical range of his verse as he combines archaisms in language with modern intonations and meanings. His is the poetry of philosophical quest: a search for sense, beauty and for the divine in the earthly. His other lyrical themes include poetry itself and love. His poems stem from an initial lyrical impulse, and are subsequently grouped into cycles. His cycle *Russkie tertsiny* [Russian Terza Rima], for instance, written during 1977–81, in 90 stanzas depicts Bobyshev in spiritual conflict with Soviet society, with Russian history, and with emigration.

In 1972, Bobyshev converted to Orthodox Christianity, the ideas of which are naturally reflected in his writing, enriching it with spiritual insights, greater depth and a quality of perspective. Among the poets who most influenced his work, Bobyshev names Rilke and Iurii Ivask, a Russian émigré poet (1907–86). At the same time he remains a typical poet of the St Petersburg school with regard to his multi-faceted vision of the world, his readiness for renovation and a strong respect for basic traditions. Bobyshev is a rare example of an émigré poet who is guided by a deeply-rooted need for creative self-realization and the constancy of his poetic destiny, rather than superficial or external circumstances. At the same time, his poetry is rich in imagery, diction, verbal innovation, and sonic effect.

Bobyshev's literary and public stance soon left him ostracized by official Soviet literature, as was the case for many other talented Russian authors. In Russia his poems were only published in the 1960s in the journal *Iunost'* and in a range of Leningrad-based almanacs. From the 1970s he was published only in the west, in such Russian-language journals as *Grani* and *Kontinent*. The year of his emigration, 1979, saw the publication of his first book, *Ziianiia* [Gapings], in Paris. In 1989 his *Zveri Sviatogo Antoniia* [St Anthony's Beasts] was published, and in 1994 his *Bestiarii* [Bestiary], illustrated by Mikhail Shemiakin, came out in New York. Since the end of the 1980s, Bobyshev has been widely published in Russia, in the journals *Zvezda*, *Znamia*, and *Literaturnoe obozrenie*, to name but a few.

Mikhail Sheinker

Iurii Vasil'evich Bondarev 1924–

Novelist

Biography

Born in Orsk, 15 March 1924. Served in the army, 1942–45; artillery academy then to Stalingrad. Served as artillery officer, ending the war in Czechoslovakia. Member of the Communist Party from 1944. Studied writing at Gor'kii Literary Institute, Moscow, 1946–51, attending K. Paustovskii's seminar. Member of the Writers' Union and the Union of Cinematographers. First story published, 1949; first collection published, 1953. Made important contributions to literature of war and reconstruction. Member of the board of the Writers' Union from 1967; chairman, from 1971. Member of the Supreme Soviet RSFSR, 1975–89. Co-chairman of the International Union of Writers' Unions, 1995. Hero of Socialist Labour. Recipient: Lenin Prize, 1972; USSR State Prize, 1974 and 1983; RSFSR State Prize, 1975; Lev Tolstoi Prize, 1993. His later works indicate a definite shift towards a more conservative appraisal of Soviet society and its relationship with the west. Outspoken critic of perestroika.

Publications

Collected Editions

Na bol'shoi reke. Rasskazy [On the Large River]. Moscow, 1953.

Pozdnim vecherom. Rasskazy [Late in the Evening]. Moscow, 1962.

Batal'ony prosiat ognia. Poslednie zalpy. Povesti [The Battalions Request Fire Support. The Last Shots]. Moscow, 1966.

Sobranie sochinenii, 4 vols. Moscow, 1973–74.

Izbrannye proizvedeniia, 2 vols. Moscow, 1977.

Tri povesti. Moscow, 1980.

Sobranie sochinenii, 6 vols. Moscow, 1984–86.

Sobranie sochinenii, 8 vols. Moscow, 1993.

Fiction

"Inzhenery" [The Engineers], *Oktiabr'*, 3 (1953), 20–33.

Iunost' komandirov [The Youth of the Commanders]. Moscow, 1956.

"Poslednie zalpy". Moscow, 1959; translated as *The Last Shots*, by N. Lukoshkova, Moscow, Foreign Languages Publishing House, 1959.

"Tishina", *Novyi mir*, 3–5 (1962), 3–45; 64–135; 43–92; translated as *Silence: A Novel of Post War Russia*, by Elizaveta Fen, London, Chapman and Hall, 1965; retitled as *Silence: A Novel by Yurii Bondaryev*, Boston, Houghton Mifflin, 1966.

"Dvoe" [Two], *Novyi mir*, 4–5 (1964), 21–67; 5–51.

"Goriachii sneg", *Znamia*, 9–11 (1969), 3–51; 5–110; 7–90; translated as *The Hot Snow*, by Robert Daglish, Moscow, Progress, 1976.

"Rodstvenniki" [Relatives], *Oktiabr'*, 8 (1969), 85–175.

"Bereg", *Nash sovremennik*, 3–5 (1975); translated as *The Shore*, by Keith Hammond, Moscow, Raduga, 1984.

"Stranitsy iz zapisnoi knizhki" [Pages from a Notebook], *Novyi mir*, 1 (1976), 131–42.

"Stranitsy iz zapisnoi knizhki", *Znamia*, 7 (1976), 104–20.

"Mgnoveniia" [A Moment], *Novyi mir*, 8 (1977), 157–70; 3 (1984), 112–22.

"Vybor", *Nash sovremennik*, 10–11 (1980), 14–125; 17–108; translated as *The Choice*, by Monica Whyte, Moscow, Raduga, 1983.

"Igra" [The Game], *Novyi mir*, 1–2 (1985), 6–73; 80–155.

"Iskushenie" [Temptation], *Nash sovremennik*, 1–2 (1991), 28–119; 62–155.

Editor

Povesti i rasskazy o Velikoi Otechestvennoi Voine [Stories about the Great Patriotic War] (co-editor). Moscow, 1977.

Poeziia Velikoi Otechestvennoi Voiny i antifashistskogo Soprotivleniia: stikhi poetov NRB, VNR, GDR, MNR, PNR, SSSR, CHSSR [Poetry of the Great Patriotic War and the Anti-Fascist Opposition ...] (co-editor). Moscow, 1980.

Rasskazy sovetskikh pisatelei [Stories by Soviet Authors]. Moscow, 1982.

Critical Studies

Iurii Bondarev, by Oleg Mikhailov, Moscow, 1976.

Grani talanta, o tvorchestve Iuriia Bondareva, by Iurii Idashkin, Moscow, 1983.

"Ot voiny k miru. O tvorchestve Iuriia Bondareva", by Aleksandr Ovcharenko, *Nash sovremennik*, 5 (1983), 163–78.

Kontseptsiia geroicheskoi lichnosti v tvorchestve Iuriia Bondareva, by Viktor Polozhii, Kiev, 1983.

"Soviet Union", by Don Piper, in *The Second World War in Fiction*, edited by Holger Klein, London, Macmillan, 1984, 131–72.

Twórczość Jurija Bondariewa, by Bronisław Kodzis, Wrocław, Wydawnictwa Uniwersytetu Wrocławskiego, 1985.

Khudozhestvennye otkrytiia Bondareva, by Nikolai Fed', Moscow, 1988.

Iurii Bondarev, ocherk tvorchestva, by Ekaterina Gorbunova, Moscow, 1989.

Russian Literature 1988–1994: The End of an Era, by N.N. Shneidman, Toronto, Toronto University Press, 1995, 67–72.

Like Grigorii Baklanov, with whom he would cross swords in the glasnost period, Bondarev joined the army in the middle of World War II, serving as an artillery officer at Stalingrad. After the war both Baklanov and Bondarev embarked on literary careers that drew heavily on their war experiences. As their respective careers progressed, so clear political differences began to emerge. Whereas Baklanov during the mid-1980s proved to be a staunch supporter of the Gorbachev reforms, Bondarev became identified with forces alarmed at the speed and direction of reform. In 1988 at the 19th Party Congress the differences between these two famous writers appeared to be irreconcilable.

Two important prose works based on his wartime experience marked Bondarev's literary debut. *Batal'ony prosiat ognia* [The Battalions Request Fire Support] and *Poslednie zalpy* (*The Last

Shots) reflect the same interest in small military units, or the fate of a few individual soldiers, which can be found in the work of Vasil Bykov, Bulat Okudzhava, Viktor Nekrasov and the early *povesti* of Baklanov. Baklanov offers the obvious parallel, with both authors favouring the infantry company or artillery battery situated in highly vulnerable, tactical situations.

In *Batal'ony prosiat ognia*, Colonel Guliaev's two battalions are ordered to force the river Dnieper at night to support a unit that has already established a bridgehead. Artillery support, which was promised, is not delivered. Indeed, no sooner have the two battalions crossed the Dnieper than Iverzev, the divisional commander, has to deploy artillery to the north. German troops supported by members of Vlasov's Liberation Army attack the bridgehead, convinced that this is the main Soviet counter-offensive. Only later do a few survivors of Guliaev's battalions learn that the mission was intended as a diversion for a much larger operation. The two battalions were sacrificed to draw off German forces from the north. The central theme is the conflict between ends and means: between military expediency and the need to save lives. But the problem appears insoluble, as the author notes: "You can't fight a war without cruelty".

Recognized as a "war writer", Bondarev has, nevertheless, tried to qualify the term war novel, preferring instead to regard his works as novels about people caught up in war. War may represent an extreme state but the same moral and psychological problems are still present, exacerbated to be sure by the risk of violent and sudden death. *Batal'ony prosiat ognia* and *The Last Shots* can, in part, be seen as a commentary on contemporary Soviet society where individuals have to make moral choices, which are often at odds with the Soviet state.

Inevitably, any discussion of Bondarev's early prose on the subject of the Russo-German war cannot bypass the question of Remarquism and *okopnaia pravda* (truth of the trenches). Many Soviet critics resented the latter term, seeing it as an artificial distinction between the front-line soldier and the high command. Terms, such as "the soldier in the trench" or "the view of the soldier from the trench", argues Aleksandr Ovcharenko, one of Bondarev's admirers, imply a narrowness of vision, as if "our soldiers and officers were not the political and moral embodiment of the nation's strength". As a replacement term, Ovcharenko offers the curious hybrid, "optimistic tragedy", which fails to respect any definition of classical tragedy and somewhat stretches any understanding of optimism when measured against the circumstances of either *Batal'ony prosiat ognia* or *The Last Shots*.

The fact of the matter is that the term *okopnaia pravda* meets the critical purposes for which it was coined. It underscores the difference between those at the sharp end of war – that is, those doing the killing and being killed – and the senior officers and planners who, in the rear, are removed from the immediate threat of danger. This separation, with all the antagonism and resentment that stem from it, is a brute fact of military life. The problem for Soviet literary criticism was that it was duty-bound to portray all soldiers and officers as utterly united. Any hint of difference from whatever source threatens this unity, and must, therefore, be ignored or pilloried. Tough and brutal in their depiction of war, with the same hallmark of personal experience and honesty that we find in Bykov and Baklanov, *Batal'ony prosiat ognia* and *The Last Shots* are excellent examples of *okopnaia pravda*.

Bondarev returns to the theme of the Russo-German war in *Goriachii sneg* (*The Hot Snow*). The setting is Stalingrad. The novel's military action is driven by the Soviet determination to thwart German attempts, led by General Manstein, to break the ring encircling the German 6th Army. The narrow focus of the earlier *povesti* is replaced by a much broader range of characters and scenes – from individual soldiers at the front to the Soviet headquarters.

Since 1971 Bondarev has occupied a series of senior administrative posts in the Union of Writers. From 1980 to 1989 he was a deputy of the Supreme Soviet of the Russian Federation, a position that brought him to the very heart of Soviet political power. The question understandably arises as to whether he has been able to reconcile his calling as a writer – with his obvious and sincere admiration of Tolstoi and what Tolstoi means for Russian literature – with the demands and high profile of a senior functionary in the literary establishment. Suffice it to say, the precedents are not encouraging.

Certain aspects of glasnost and the systematic, ideological dismantling of the Soviet state clearly angered Bondarev. On the one hand, the fact that long-suppressed Russian authors were published was welcomed; on the other, the dangers (as seen by Bondarev) of Russia's being opened up to the onslaught of western fashions and consumer tastes was a source of great concern, and one that remains so. In this respect, mention should be made of Bondarev's membership of the editorial board of *Nash sovremennik*, a journal known for its scepticism of things western, and hostility towards what it regards as the creeping and damaging westernization of Russian culture and society.

FRANK ELLIS

Silence

Tishina

Novel, 1962

Silence was first published in *Novyi mir* in 1962, some six months before Solzhenitsyn broke his own silence about Stalin's camps in *Odin den' Ivana Denisovicha* (*One Day in the Life of Ivan Denisovich*). At face value *Silence* can be seen as a retrospective examination of the war experience, in some ways a standard returner or *Heimkehrer* novel, of which Remarque's *The Road Back* (1931) is one of the better known examples. The standard ingredients of the genre are all there: the problems of soldiers trying to adapt to civilian life after military service; the daily grind of survival in a war-ravaged economy; and the obvious gulf separating the returning soldiers from their civilian peers. Bondarev's veterans, Sergei and Konstantin, are no longer the callow youths who unquestioningly accepted the slogans and false optimism of the 1930s. As a minor character notes: "There is the generation which grew up in war, and the generation which grew up in the rear. You fought, we studied. There are two different generations, even though the gap in years is hardly anything".

From the Party's point of view the large numbers of demobilized soldiers posed an essentially ideological problem. Expectations of a better Russia had been raised during the war, but now in victory had to be stifled. This function, among others, fell to the orchestrators of the latest purge, the *Zhdanovshchina*.

The allusion to peace in the title is, therefore, deceptive, especially given the chronology of the novel's three parts. The guns have fallen silent but the ideological struggle, interrupted during the war, is now to be resumed in all its viciousness. *Silence* charts the growing Zhdanovite terror, whose tentacles spread throughout Eastern Europe in the late 1940s, culminating in the Stalinist-fabricated Doctors' Plot in the period 1952–53. The novel concludes with Stalin's death, a watershed in Soviet history, leaving the reader on the threshold of the Thaw.

Memory, guilt, duty, and loyalty are the main themes of *Silence*. They are the points of friction and conflict, played out against the ideological background of the *Zhdanovshchina*. These themes emerge from situations that are sometimes banal, and sometimes quite terrifying.

Sergei, the main character, feels bound by a code of duty that seems to have no place in the post-war Moscow. He encounters a certain Uvarov, a former soldier, whose failure to carry out orders in wartime led to the arrest and punishment of another officer. A key question, at least for Sergei, is whether he should draw a line under the past: should Uvarov's dereliction of duty be consigned to the memory of the war and left at that?

Uvarov epitomizes a negative type frequently found in Soviet war prose. Sometimes cowardly or incompetent, and always opportunistic, this type avoids punishment, and indeed, by manipulating the system, thrives when others are cut down. The same Uvarov, who, we learn later in the novel, burnt his Party card during the war, an act that carried the severest penalties in the Soviet state, now enjoys the trust of the Party. In Bondarev's moral universe Sergei's rejection of Uvarov's overtures of reconciliation is entirely justified.

The personal conflict between Uvarov and Sergei, which invokes the past and the theme of memory, has echoes of something much larger and uglier. It points us towards the purges of the 1930s, and especially the contemporary *Zhdanovshchina*, which is drawing Sergei into its net. The campaign against "rootless cosmopolitans" (Stalin's anti-Semitic campaign) singles out one of Sergei's neighbours, the artist Mukomolov, accusing him of "ideological sabotage" and "bowing down to the West". Sergei's father is also under suspicion because a safe in his charge, and containing party documents, went missing during a break-out of encirclement in the war. In fact, an atmosphere of doom hangs over him from the moment Bondarev mentions this blot on his copy-book.

Bondarev shows an acute sensitivity to the nuances of the investigative process. Above all it functions as a form of psychological intimidation and weakening of the designated victim, so that, when the blow of arrest finally falls, the victim co-operates willingly with his interrogators. This willingness on the part of the arrestee to accept arrest as something normal, to interpret his guilt as something infallibly predetermined by the very fact of arrest itself, and, therefore, beyond question, is one of the most disturbing aspects of the arrest theme in Soviet Russian literature. The challenge to this supposed infallibility is made with some irony, when Sergei, making enquiries about his arrested father, is told by an official that: "Nobody is arrested by mistake in the Soviet state". Bondarev describes the insidious process whereby the relatives of those arrested become outcasts. As a Party member Sergei is obliged to inform his Party committee of the arrest of a relative. Again, the real purpose is hidden by a mask of bureaucracy. The party cell is routinely informed of such matters. The real aim is to humiliate and to intimidate the victim's relatives. A consequence of this is that Sergei's notions of honour, duty and loyalty, so crucial to the military victory, are being undermined by the state he helped to save from destruction. This is a battlefield for which Sergei's military service has not prepared him. It makes the general point that physical courage on its own is insufficient when dealing with the devil.

Despite the many details of the *Zhdanovshchina* and its effects on the lives of his characters, Bondarev does not really offer a satisfactory explanation for what is going on. People are arrested and interrogated, careers are broken, families destroyed, children are brain-washed, but Bondarev provides no obvious answer as to why this is taking place. Mukomolov, a victim of the cultural witch hunt, seems to think that Beria (chief of secret police under Stalin) is solely to blame. The result is that the characters seem to move in two worlds, one which is recognizably domestic and personal, and another which is hostile, impersonal and intrudes upon the domestic world with a terrifying unpredictability (demonstrated by the death of Stalin and the scenes of crowd panic). The link between these two worlds, the private and public, is the Party and its ideology and it is Bondarev's own "silence" satisfactorily to explain the Party's motives that is the main flaw of this novel.

FRANK ELLIS

Leonid Ivanovich Borodin 1938–

Prose writer

Biography

Born in Irkutsk, 14 April 1938. Educated at school in Nizhneudinsk. Expelled from Irkutsk University for involvement in unofficial students' circle "Svobodnoe slovo" (The Free Word), 1956; also expelled from Komsomol, 1957. Worked as labourer in Noril'sk; enrolled on correspondence course in history at the D. Banzarov Pedagogical Institute, Ulan-ude; graduated 1962. Headmaster of secondary school in Serebrianka, near Leningrad, 1962–67. Formed the "Democratic Party", 1964. Joined underground organization VSKhSON (All-Russian Social Christian Alliance for the Liberation of People), 1965. Arrested with other members of VSKhSON; sentenced to six years' imprisonment in strict regime camp, 1968; transferred to Vladimir prison for campaigning for rights of political prisoners, 1970. Began writing in prison. Released from prison, 1973. Worked as labourer near Lake Baikal; wrote prose and co-edited *samizdat* journal *Veche*; started to publish *samizdat* magazine *Moskovskii sbornik*, 1974. Began to publish abroad, 1975; first collection of stories published, 1978. Sentenced to ten years in strict regime camp and five years internal exile for anti-Soviet agitation and propaganda, 1983. Released, 1987. Began to be published in Russia, 1988. Currently lives with his wife and daughter in Moscow. Editor of the journal *Moskva*.

Publications

Fiction

Povest' strannogo vremeni: Rasskazy. Frankfurt, Posev, 1978; translated as *The Story of a Strange Time*, by Frank Williams, London, Collins Harvill, 1990.

God chuda i pechali. Frankfurt, Posev, 1981; translated as *The Year of Miracle and Grief*, by Jennifer Bradshaw, London and New York, Quartet, 1984.

Tret'ia pravda. Frankfurt, Posev, 1981; translated as *The Third Truth*, by Catriona Kelly, London, Collins Harvill, 1989.

"Gologor", *Grani*, 124 (1982), 5–154.

Rasstavanie. Frankfurt, Posev, 1984; translated as *Partings*, by David Floyd, London, Collins Harvill, and San Diego, Harcourt Brace Jovanovich, 1987.

"Pravila igry" [The Rules of the Game], *Grani*, 140 (1986).

"Barguzin", *Literaturnaia Rossiia*, 19 (1988), 12–13.

"Zhenshchina v more" [The Woman in the Sea], *Iunost'*, 1 (1990), 6–32.

"Tainstvennyi vystrel" [The Mysterious Shot], *Slovo: v mire knig*, 1–4 (1991), 57–63; 14–20; 23–29; 56–63.

"Bozhepol'e" [God's Field], *Nash sovremennik*, 1–2 (1993), 11–56; 52–92.

Poetry

"Stikhi, napisannye v tiur'me, gde ikh pishut mnogie" [Poems, Written in Prison, Where Many People Write Them], *Grani*, 105 (1977), 163–67.

"Stikhi", *Grani*, 136 (1985), 83–85.

"Odnazhdy proch'" [Once Averse], *Literaturnaia Rossiia* (20 July 1990), 14.

Critical Studies

Voln'aia russkaia literatura 1955–75, by Iurii Mal'tsev, Frankfurt, Posev, 1976; as *Freie Russische Literatur 1955–80*, Frankfurt, Posev, 1981, 281–83.

"Leonid Borodin – chelovek i pisatel'", by R. Redlikh, *Posev*, 6 (1982), 2–4.

"Tvorchestvo i oblik Leonida Borodina", by R. Dudin, *Russkoe vozrozhdenie*, 29 (1985), 82–102.

"My Friend, Leonid Borodin", by G. Vladimov, *Index on Censorship*, 7 (1987), 14–15.

"Tri pravdy", by V. Verin, *Literaturnaia gazeta* (7 February 1990), 4.

"Vory i dissidenty", by P. Ul'iashov, *Knizhnoe obozrenie* (16 March 1990), 11.

"Poslednii iz dissidentov?", an interview by T. Khoroshilova, *Komsomol'skaia pravda* (24 April 1990).

"Pravdy i pravdezhki", by L. Anninskii, *Literaturnaia gazeta* (7 November 1990), 5.

"'Don Quixote' i 'Tret'ia pravda'", by S. Kuniaev, *Literatura v shkole*, 2 (1991), 56–62.

"Sila i bessilie soblazna", by A. Nemzer, *Novyi mir*, 9 (1991), 209–12.

"Interview" by L. Fomin, *Moskovskaia pravda* (29 June 1991), 3.

"Ne palachi, ne zhertvy (o proze Leonida Borodina)", by A. Varlamov, *Literaturnaia gazeta* (13 May 1992), 4.

Leonid Borodin is a historian and teacher who began writing in the late 1960s while he was serving a six-year prison term for his involvement in the activities of an underground organization, the All-Russian Social-Christian Alliance. While his first literary efforts consisted of cycles of poetry, and he is also the author of several publicistic works on religious and national themes, it is chiefly as a prose writer that he has established himself.

Borodin's first collection of stories entitled *Povest' strannogo vremeni* (*The Story of a Strange Time*) was published in the west in 1978 and led to his second term in a strict regime camp for "Anti-Soviet agitation and propaganda". This collection, which later earned the author the French PEN Club's Freedom Prize, highlights the ruinous effects of Soviet ideology on the lives of ordinary people. Borodin tests the spiritual integrity of his heroes by confronting them with difficult moral choices that have far-reaching and often tragic consequences. The notion of personal responsibility coupled with a feeling of national reconciliation and forgiveness runs throughout this collection and constituted an appeal for the resurrection of Russia's spiritual traditions lost after the October Revolution. Implicit in this sentiment is Borodin's fundamentally Christian attitude.

Three of Borodin's *povesti* or novellas were published abroad between prison sentences. In *God chuda i pechali* (*The Year of Miracle and Grief*), the author skilfully blends realistic and fairytale elements to provide a serious discussion on the nature of forgiveness and revenge. Borodin's vision of the wonders of nature, which is clearly apprehended as religious in quality, is movingly captured through the eyes of a child seeing the Siberian landscape for the first time. *Tret'ia pravda* (*The Third Truth*) is generally acknowledged, however, as Borodin's most important work of the period in terms of artistic merit and political maturity. It has been translated into many languages and has established the author's international reputation. The *povest'* focuses on the fates of two men of the taiga as they grapple with political nefariousness in the aftermath of the Civil War and attempt to live their lives according to their own "third truth". Riabinin, the game-warden, believes that he has found "truth", when he converts to Christianity during a 25-year term in the Gulag. However, for the poacher, Selivanov, truth lies in maintaining his freedom in the taiga and resisting all forms of imposed rule, be it White or Red. Both truths prove to be flawed, for in each case an ideological approach to life that leaves little room for human compassion or understanding leads to a despairing state of alienation. *Gologor*, the third of these Siberian tales, is the harrowing story of a young woman's experiences within a community of Siberian fur hunters in the beautiful but harsh conditions of the *taiga*.

Borodin's first novel *Rasstavanie* (*Partings*) and his novella, *Pravila igry* [The Rules of the Game], published in the west during the author's second term in prison, move away from the Siberian setting. *Partings* is set in Moscow and is a gently satirical novel that reveals Borodin's view of the inconsistencies and hypocrisy at large within the intellectual and political ferment of the dissident movement in the 1970s. It is distinctive in its humorous and subtly ironic treatment of theme and character, which reflect Borodin's growing maturity as a writer. *Pravila igry* is set in camp and centres on a political prisoner as he prepares himself psychologically for his impending release. An appeal to take part in a hunger-strike, which will undoubtedly lead to a further sentence, compels him to re-evaluate not only the black and white interpretations of the camp's code of conduct, which leave little room for spiritual independence, but his own moral probity.

Borodin gained an early release from prison in 1987. After 20 years of literary obscurity at home, his works subsequently began to be published in Russia to generally enthusiastic critical responses. Borodin has also published several new works, a short story entitled "Barguzin" and, of more significance, three *povesti*. The first of these, *Zhenshchina v more* [The Woman in the Sea], is a semi-autobiographical work set in the Crimea against the background of Gorbachev's policy of perestroika. A latterday "hero of our time" meets a young couple with mafia connections. Their blatant disdain for the protagonist's firm moral standards sets in sharp relief his attempt to gauge the cost of his lifetime of non-conformity and imprisonment. *Tainstvennyi vystrel* [The Mysterious Shot] is set in a Siberian village and reads as an absorbing detective story full of action, intrigue and suspense. When a robbery takes place at a despatch office in the *taiga*, the village plenipotentiary attempts to track down those responsible so that he may retire in triumph on a pension. Borodin's recent story, *Bozhepol'e* [God's Field] is unusual in that it depicts life from the other side of the political fence, from the view of privileged people. It is a reflective, psychologically probing work that traces, not without sympathy, the rise of a man from his lowly peasant origins to the heights of political intrigue and personal betrayal. The story not only demonstrates Borodin's capacity for capturing the subtle nuances and flavour of various historical periods, but also displays a deep compassion even for oppressors who suffer for their convictions.

The lyrical quality of Borodin's writing, his interest in the traditions of simple, country people and love of his native Siberia, initially led to comparison with the Village Prose writer, Valentin Rasputin. His publicistic works also display many of the stridently anti-Soviet and Slavophile views that we have come to associate with Aleksandr Solzhenitsyn. Yet the thematic breadth of Borodin's literary works and his generic versatility defy easy categorization. If there is a single, overarching message to be gleaned from Borodin's prose, it is that the complexities of the human soul render futile any attempt to contain it within the framework of any ideology or dogma.

JACQUELINE FRENCH

Valerii Iakovlevich Briusov 1873–1924

Poet, prose writer, and literary critic

Biography

Born in Moscow, 13 December 1873. Attended Kreiman gymnasium, 1884–90; Polivanov gymnasium in Moscow, 1890–93; studied classical philology and history, Moscow University, 1899. Married: Ioanna Matveevna Runt in 1897. Liaison with the writer Nina Petrovskaia, 1904–11. First literary publications, 1894; adopted various journalistic pseudonyms: Avrelii, Pentaur, Garmodii, V. Bakulin, and others. Editorial secretary of the monthly journal *Russkii arkhiv*, 1899–1902; co-founder of Skorpion, Russian Symbolism's leading publishing house, 1899; secretary and later staff writer of the monthly *Novyi put'*, 1902–04; active in Moscow spiritualist movement, early 1900s; editor of the Symbolist journal *Vesy*, 1904–09; president, Moscow Literary-Artistic Circle, 1908–18; joined the monthly *Russkaia mysl'*, 1910; editor of the literary section, 1911–12. War correspondent in Poland, 1914–15; director of translation and publication of Armenian poetry, 1915–16; lecturer in Erevan, Echmiadzin, Tbilisi, and Baku, 1916–17. Supported provisional government, February 1917; head of office for registration of printed works, 1917–19; entered People's Commissariat for Enlightenment (*Narkompros*) 1919, organizer, Literary Section, 1920; joined the Communist Party, 1920. Professor, First Moscow State University, 1921–24; head of Higher Institute of Literature and Art, 1921–24. Died in Moscow, 9 October 1924.

Publications

Collected Editions

Russkie simvolisty [Russian Symbolists], nos 1 and 2. Moscow, 1894; no. 3, 1895.
Puti i pereput'ia [Roads and Crossroads], 3 vols. Moscow, 1908–09.
Polnoe sobranie sochinenii i perevodov. 1–4, 12–13, 15, 21 (of 25 projected), St Petersburg, 1913–14.
Izbrannye proizvedeniia, 3 vols. Moscow and Leningrad, 1926.
Izbrannye stikhi. Moscow and Leningrad, 1933.
Neizdannaia proza. Moscow and Leningrad, 1934.
Izbrannye sochineniia, 2 vols. Moscow, 1955.
Stikhotvoreniia i poemy. Leningrad, 1961.
Sobranie sochinenii, 7 vols. Moscow, 1973–75.

Poetry

Chefs d'oeuvre. Moscow, 1895.
Me eum esse. 1897.
Tertia vigilia. 1900.
Urbi et orbi. 1903.
Stephanos. 1906.
Vse napevy [All Melodies]. 1909.
Stikhi Nelli. Moscow, 1913.
Poslednie mechty [Last Dreams]. Moscow, 1920.
Mig [A Moment]. Berlin, Grzhebin, 1922.
Dali [Distances]. Moscow, 1922.
Mea! Moscow, 1924.

Fiction

Zemnaia os'. Rasskazy i dramaticheskie stseny [Earth's Axis]. Moscow, 1907; 2nd enlarged edition, 1910; translated as *The Republic of the Southern Cross and Other Stories* [no translator named], London, Constable, 1918; New York, McBride, 1919; reprinted Westport, Connecticut, Hyperion Press, 1977.
Ognennyi angel. Moscow, 1908; translated as *The Fiery Angel: A Sixteenth Century Romance*, by Ivor Montagu and Sergei Nalbandov, London, Humphrey Toulmin, 1930; Westport, Connecticut, Hyperion Press, 1977.
Altar' pobedy. Roman [Victory's Altar]. Moscow, 1913.
Nochi i dni [Nights and Days]. Moscow, 1913.
"Gora Zvezdy (1895–1899)" [Star Mountain], *Fantastika* 73–74, Moscow, 1975.

Plays

Zemlia. Stseny iz budushchikh vremen [Earth. Scenes from the Future]. St Petersburg, 1914.
Putnik (Psikhodrama) [Traveller]. St Petersburg, 1914.
Protesilai umershii [Protesilai, the Deceased]. St Petersburg, 1914.
"Dachnye strasti" [Country Passions], *Zvezda*, 10 (1939), 223–35.
"Diktator" [The Dictator], *Sovremennaia dramaturgiia*, 4 (1986), 176–98.

Literary Criticism and Theory

"Kliuchi tain" [Keys to the Mysteries], *Vesy*, 1 (1904), 3–21.
"Strast'" [Passion], *Vesy*, 8 (1904).
"Sviashchennaia zhertva" [The Holy Sacrifice], *Vesy*, 1 (1905), 23–29.
"Ispepelennyi. K kharakteristike Gogolia" [Reduced to Ashes. A Description of Gogol'], *Vesy*, 4 (1909), 98–120.
Dalekie i blizkie [Distant and Close]. Moscow, 1912; reprinted Letchworth, Bradda, 1973.
Nauka o stikhe. Metrika i ritmika [The Study of Verse. Metrics and the Rhythm System], part I, Moscow, 1919.
Osnovy stikhovedeniia. Metrika i ritmika [The Fundamentals of Prosody], parts I–II, Moscow, 1924; reprinted Letchworth, Bradda, 1971.
Moi Pushkin [My Pushkin]. Moscow, 1929; reprinted, Munich, Fink, 1970.
Sredi stikhov: 1894–1924; Manifesty, stat'i, retsenzii [Among the Poems: 1894–1924; Manifestos, Articles, Reviews]. Moscow, 1990.

Memoirs, Letters, and Autobiography

Za moim oknom [Beyond My Window]. Moscow, 1913.
"Avtobiografiia", in *Russkaia literatura XX veka*, Moscow, 1914, 101–19.
Iz moei zhizni [From My Life]. Moscow, 1927.
Dnevniki. 1891–1910. Moscow, 1927; reprinted Letchworth, Bradda, 1973; translated as *The Diary of Valery Bryusov (1893–1905) with Reminiscences by V. F. Khodasevich and Marina Tsvetaeva*, by Joan Delaney Grossman, Berkeley, University of California Press, 1980.
Pis'ma V.Ia. Briusova k P.P. Pertsovu, 1894–1896. Moscow, 1927.

Translator

Romans bez slov [A Romance Without Words], by Paul Verlaine, Moscow, 1894.
Frantsuzskie liriki XIX veka [French Lyric Poetry of the 19th Century], St Petersburg, 1909.
Sobranie stikhov [A Collection of Verse], by Paul Verlaine, Moscow, 1911.
"Gertsoginia Paduanskaia" [The Duchess of Padua], by Oscar Wilde, in *Polnoe sobranie sochinenii*, vol. 4, St Petersburg, 1912.
Sobranie stikhov 1883–1915 [A Collection of Verse 1883–1915], by Emil Verhaeren, Moscow, 1915; 4th revised edition, Petrograd and Moscow, 1923.
Polnoe sobranie poem i stikhotvorenii, by Edgar Allan Poe, Moscow and Leningrad, 1924.
Faust, by J.W. Goethe, Part 1, Moscow and Leningrad, 1928.
Sobranie sochinenii, by J.W. Goethe, vol. 1, Moscow and Leningrad, 1932.
"Amfitrion", by Molière, in *Sobranie sochinenii*, vol. 3, Leningrad, 1939.

Editor

Poezii Armenii s drevneishikh vremen do nashikh dnei [The Poetry of Armenia from Ancient Times to Today], translated by Briusov, *et al.*, Moscow, 1916.

Critical Studies

Valerii Briusov i nasledie Pushkina, by Viktor Zhirmunskii, Petrograd, 1922; reprinted, The Hague, Mouton, 1970.

"Briusovskaia stikhologiia i nauka o stikhe", by Roman Jakobson, *Nauchnye izvestiia Akademicheskogo tsentra Narkomprosa*, 2 (1922), 222–40.

"Oderzhimii (o Briusove)", by Zinaida Hippius, in *Zhivye litsa*, Prague, Plamja, 1925; reprinted, Munich, Fink, 1971.

"Valerii Briusov", by Iurii Tynianov, in *Arkhaisty i novatory*, Leningrad, 1929; reprinted, Munich, Fink, 1967.

Valerii Briusov v avtobiograficheskikh zapiskakh, pis'makh, vospominaniiakh sovremennikov i otzyvakh kritiki, edited by N. Ashukin, Moscow, 1929.

"Briusov", by V. Khodasevich, in *Nekropol': Vospominaniia*, Brussels, Petropolis, 1939; reprinted, Paris, YMCA-Press, 1976.

"Geroi truda (zapisi o Valerii Briusove)", by Marina Tsvetaeva, in her *Proza*, New York, Izdatel'stvo imeni Chekhova, 1953.

"The Narrative Prose of Brjusov", by V. M. Setschkareff, *International Journal of Slavic Linguistics and Poetics*, 1/2 (1959), 237–65.

Valerii Briusov, by Konstantin Mochul'skii, Paris, YMCA-Press, 1962.

Briusovskie chteniia 1963, edited by K.V. Aivazian *et al.*, Erevan, 1964; *1966*, Erevan, 1968; *1971*, Erevan, 1973; *1973*, Erevan, 1976; *1980*, Erevan, 1983.

"The Maker and the Seer: Two Russian Symbolists", by Victor Erlich, in his *The Double Image: Concepts of the Poet in Slavic Literatures*, Baltimore, Johns Hopkins Press, 1964.

Briusov. Poeziia i pozitsiia, by D.E. Maksimov, Leningrad, 1969.

Briusovskii sbornik, edited by V.S. Dronov *et al.*, Stavropol', 1974; 1975; 1977.

Valery Briusov and the Rise of Russian Symbolism, by Martin P. Rice, Ann Arbor, Ardis, 1975.

Literaturnoe nasledstvo: Valerii Briusov, vol. 85, Moscow, 1976.

"Biograficheskie istochniki romana Briusova Ognennyi angel", by S.S. Grechishkin and A.V. Lavrov, *Wiener Slawistischer Almanach*, 1–2 (1978), 79–107, 73–96.

Valery Bryusov and the Riddle of Russian Decadence, by Joan Delaney Grossman, Berkeley, University of California Press, 1985.

"Zhizn' i smert' Niny Petrovskoi" (includes Petrovskaia's memoir of Valerii Briusov), by Nina Petrovskaia, *Minuvshee*, 8, Paris, Atheneum, 1989.

Literaturnoe nasledstvo: Valerii Briusov i ego korrespondenty, 98, 2 vols, part 1, Moscow, 1991.

"Valery Briusov and Nina Petrovskaia: Clashing Models of Life in Art", by Joan Delaney Grossman, in *Creating Life: The Aesthetic Utopia of Russian Modernism*, edited by Grossman and Irina Paperno, Stanford, Stanford University Press, 1994.

Bibliographies

Bibliografii Valeriia Briusova 1889–1912. Moscow, 1913.

Bibliografiia V. Ia. Briusova 1884–1973, edited by E.S. Danel'ian, Erevan, 1976.

The acknowledged organizing genius of the Russian Symbolist movement, Valerii Briusov ranks also as one of the leading literary figures in pre-revolutionary 20th-century Russia. Poet, novelist, dramatist, translator, critic, he also provided vigorous leadership in enterprises vital to the development and spread of the "new art". Among these were the publishing house Skorpion and the Symbolist monthly journal *Vesy*, which published both new Russian writing and a wide selection of translations. Briusov's critical writings in *Vesy* and elsewhere offered models of clarity and critical acumen. Moreover, his scholarly approach to the literary text had a major impact on early 20th-century Russian editorial practice. Convinced of the need for reliable critical editions, as editor (notably of Pushkin) he set a new standard, only later revised by the Formalists. After 1910, when Symbolism waned, Briusov's literary activity scarcely abated. While he no longer led a movement, his pace of writing, editing, translating, and other activities made him a force to be respected.

As fashions changed, Briusov's reputation suffered. After the 1917 Bolshevik Revolution, he accepted positions in the new power structure. Consequently, on the one hand he was regarded as an anachronism while simultaneously elevated into an official icon. On the other, he was viewed as a traitor by émigré writers, often former associates and even allies. Assessments of Briusov's significance for modern Russian literature have often reflected these various viewpoints. As a result of this fact and of the neglect of his work by Soviet authorities doubtful about a Decadent-Symbolist Communist, Briusov scholarship was scarce for decades after his death, both in Russia and in the west. The cost to understanding the Russian literary process in the first third of the 20th century arguably has been considerable.

The eldest of five children, Briusov was the grandson of a former serf who prospered as a Moscow cork merchant. His modestly educated parents held the free-thinking views of "people of the seventies". Briusov recalled reading Charles Darwin before learning the multiplication tables. In time, besides a man of letters, he became a classicist, a mathematician, a student of history and philosophy, and an authority on world literatures.

Briusov's early scientific ambitions gave way to a literary bent that found its focus in the new European movement known as Symbolism or Decadence. A diary passage from 1893, often cited to show his single-minded pursuit of fame, reveals ideas that helped shape his career:

> Say what you will, whether [Decadence] is false, or ridiculous, it is moving forward, developing, and the future will belong to it when it finds a worthy leader. And that leader will be I! Yes, I!

The notion that native poetry had lost its direction and needed to look abroad for help was just taking hold in Russia. The calculated brashness of this diary entry gave notice of the coming campaign and its central goal: to determine Russian poetry's future direction. At an early stage in his life, Briusov came to see history as dynamic flow and clash. The passion to be at the forefront, to sense the direction of change, marked him from the start. This passion resounds insistently in his poetry and presumably also influenced career decisions.

Concealed in Briusov's declaration was a central unanswered question: what is Symbolism, what is Decadence? After prolonged investigation of these concepts, he reached a position that soon clashed radically with the theurgic view of art formulated by Andrei Belyi and Viacheslav Ivanov. Standing on different philosophical ground, Briusov viewed Symbolism as the artistic method suited to expressing the Decadent world-view. This view premised human personality as capable of unbounded spiritual exploration and expansion. Art was its vision. Rejecting limits of any kind issued in extreme individualism was a stance that Briusov and many other Symbolists embraced eagerly.

Briusov's literary career began in 1894 with the first two anthologies of poetry and translations called *Russkie simvolisty* [Russian Symbolists], followed by a third in 1895. The work was mostly his, but he used pseudonyms to create the impression of a movement. The enterprise attracted notice, thanks especially to Vladimir Solov'ev's caustic and witty reviews in the prestigious *Vestnik Evropy*.

Between 1895 and 1900 Briusov published two volumes of poetry, *Chefs d'oeuvre* and *Me eum esse*. He also explored new attitudes towards art and reality and a new artistic language to express them. If *Tertia vigilia* announced preliminary sightings, *Urbi et orbi* marked the summit and his next two books, *Stephanos* and *Vse napevy* [All Melodies], the culmination of this phase of his creative history. A constant feature of his career was a passion for poetry sometimes confused with Parnassian "art for art". But with equal passion he asserted art's inseparability from life. Poetry was essentially life in all its guises refracted through the poet's soul. His insistence that art must not be the instrument of any cause whatsoever – social, religious, political – clashed with theurgic Symbolism and, later, with post-Revolutionary ideology.

While Briusov thought of himself primarily as a poet, his output in other genres was impressive. The two collections *Zemnaia os'* [Earth's Axis] and *Nochi i dni* [Nights and Days] contain only some of his shorter fiction and dramatic pieces. His work in these genres advances several themes important in his total *oeuvre*. The anti-Utopian theme, for example, posits a reality holding many truths, not merely one: Utopia limits personal freedom. This theme was often combined with futuristic science fiction. Two notable examples are the story "Respublika iuzhnogo kresta" ("The Republic of the Southern Cross"), with obvious ties to Dostoevskii and to Poe's "The Imp of the Perverse", and the play *Diktator* [The Dictator], published only in 1986.

His historical novel *Ognennyi angel* (*The Fiery Angel*) – on which Prokofiev's opera is based – achieved instant fame for its autobiographical subtext involving Briusov, Andrei Belyi, and Nina Petrovskaia. However, it had a long prehistory in its author's creative biography. The adventure plot woven around the witch Renata skilfully combines elements of the erotic, the occult, and Briusov's impressive imaginative grasp of medieval Germany. It obviously drew heavily on his research over many years in medieval occult sciences and his interest in modern spiritualism. Both pursuits, were, at least in part, ventures outside the limits of consciousness into the unexplored reaches of the human personality. This theme was also explored in the shorter fiction.

As Briusov's archive continues to yield unpublished work, the final word on his contribution to literature remains to be said.

JOAN DELANEY GROSSMAN

Urbi et orbi

Poetry collection, 1903

When *Urbi et orbi* appeared in 1903, Briusov was already a central figure on the literary scene. This fourth book of poetry established beyond any doubt both his reputation as a poet and his dominant role in the Symbolist movement. The book's provocative title inevitably recalled the youthfully audacious name of his first collection *Chefs d'oeuvre*. Now, by using a formula normally reserved for solemn papal pronouncements, Briusov underlined the crucial importance of his message, not only to the narrow "city" of Symbolism, but to the world at large. That message concerned art, the artist, and their relation to that world.

A companion piece to *Urbi et orbi*, Briusov's programmatic essay "Kliuchi tain" [Keys to the Mysteries] appeared in January 1904, in the first issue of the Symbolist monthly *Vesy*. Based on Schopenhauer's dictum that art comprehends the world by other than rational means, it claimed that Symbolism, alone among aesthetic theories, enabled the artist to undertake this task of exploration. In *Urbi et orbi* the poet followed this line, as he meditated on art's power and freedom and the challenges offered to the artist.

In his foreword to *Chefs d'oeuvre* Briusov located the essence of a work of art in the artist's personality. This notion evolved but did not change fundamentally as Briusov's familiarity with the "new art" deepened. Moreover, a period of intense if eclectic philosophical reading convinced him of the rightness of his intuition. The attuned individual might, in unrepeatable moments, catch deep glimpses into the ever-changing universe. Poetry recorded these glimpses, refracted through the poet's soul. From here it was one step to the lyric hero who, having emerged in Briusov's 1900 book *Tertia vigilia*, reached his full stature in *Urbi et orbi*.

For Briusov's lyric hero-poet the essence of poetry is discovery. Grown increasingly bold and confident in his explorations of life, he is enriched and strengthened by his experience. Now at the height of his powers, he stops to ponder, in the opening section "Dumy" [Meditations], what it means to be a poet. In poetic form and in range of themes *Urbi et orbi* marks a distinct advance over Briusov's previous books. This is seen in his free handling of genre and especially his bold erotica. The deceptively named cycle "Ballady" [Ballads], a set of lyrical monologues erotic in theme and imagery, led the Formalist Viktor Zhirmunskii to dub Briusov "poet of passion". These poems (seven in the original edition), along with certain lyrics found elsewhere that employ similar formal devices, Zhirmunskii judged to form a special genre containing the essence of Briusov's poetic achievement. Critical adherence to this argument has perpetuated a one-sided view of Briusov's total *oeuvre*. Overlooked is the fact that, in treating the body and passion as yet another mystery to be plumbed, this "genre" was part of Briusov's larger conception of poetry. His article "Strast'" [Passion] expressed his belief that the moment of sexual embrace is one of those great revelatory moments that constitute poetry's essence.

The charge of immorality levelled at Briusov's later poems, especially the ballads, confirmed him as Russia's leading Decadent. With some reason these "poems of passion" have been called cold, even cruel. The lyric hero's rejection of lasting human ties is part of a refusal to accept any limits to his ceaseless testing of reality. The extreme individualist, he allows no conventions – of morality or poetry – to block his path.

Some, like the poet Aleksandr Blok, quickly recognized in Briusov's "lyric hero" a valuable means of creating a unified poetic record of spiritual experience. *Urbi et orbi* became especially important for Blok as the structural model for his *Stikhi o prekrasnoi dame* [Verses on the Beautiful Lady], then in preparation. Particularly relevant was Briusov's use of cyclization to unite form and content in a single expression of the poet's persona. His conception of the book of poems as a coherent entity was in place as far back as *Chefs d'oeuvre*. The foreword to *Urbi et orbi* now stated it succinctly:

> A book of poems must be, not a random *collection* of poems of various types, but precisely a *book*, a closed whole, unified by a single thought. Like a novel, like a treatise, a book of poems reveals its content in successive steps from the first page to the last ... The sections in a book of poems are no more nor less than chapters, one illuminating the other, which cannot be interchanged arbitrarily.

In previous experiments with cyclization Briusov used chiefly thematic headings to mark the progression. Now he used genres, redefined and tailored to match the poet's tone, mood or thought, like an orator's or a singer's intonations.

Blok and also Andrei Belyi believed they had found another, highly meaningful element in *Urbi et orbi*. Briusov's life-oriented lyric hero seemed to them capable of overcoming what the newly forming theurgic stream of Symbolism saw as death-oriented Decadence. Mistaking his single-minded devotion to poetry for devotion to a different ideal, they hailed Briusov as the bearer of the new Symbolist message. His poem "Mladshim" [To the Young Ones] gently corrected this view. The later rift within Symbolism leading to its "crisis" in 1910 may be said to have had its origin in this misunderstanding and the distrust that grew out of it.

Despite the self-confidence displayed, Briusov in *Urbi et orbi* suffered uncertainties. Self-doubt and even self-disgust visited his lyric hero. "Ennui de vivre" was not only a lyric's title, but also a recurrent mood. The vocation of poet, like some others, carried with it the danger of finding the vision – or oneself – to be false. But "In Hac Lacrimarum Valle" takes the hero to a witches' sabbath, from which he returns confirmed: "I came into life a poet, I was chosen by fate, / And even against my will I shall remain."

The poem "V otvet" [In Answer] deals again with the problem of vocation, while looking at Briusov's conception of poetry from another angle. The poet's "dream" – not only inspiration, but that elusive faculty that captures, shapes, and holds it – appears in unexpected guise: "Forward, dream, my faithful ox!" Dreamers in Briusov's poems were hardy adventurers, and poetry was strenuous work. Turned into an emblem of pedestrian effort by Marina Tsvetaeva in her essay on Briusov "Geroi truda" [Hero of Labour] (1925), Briusov's ox, nevertheless, in his own context, bears a different image: that of unremitting devotion to a task and faith in an ultimate reward. For Briusov poetry was never merely "art for art's sake", but its moments of vision were reward enough and justification for its existence.

JOAN DELANEY GROSSMAN

The Fiery Angel

Ognennyi angel

Novel, 1908

This novel was greatly admired by Briusov's contemporaries. Voloshin and Tsvetaeva considered it to be his best work. Metner claimed that Briusov's novel can be matched only by Pushkin's prose. Belyi and Solov'ev wrote about the elegance of its style, claiming that the novel had no precedent in Russian literature because it was an imitation of German medieval literature. Furthermore, some German critics expressed their astonishment in 1910 that such knowledge of German culture could be displayed by a foreigner. It was primarily modernists who gave the book this warm reception, but its popularity secured for it immediate translation into many languages (although it appeared in English only in 1930). Prokofiev wrote an opera based on the book in 1927.

Briusov gave a detailed account of his preparation for the novel, claiming that he had studied all aspects of life in the 16th century, including alchemy, the occult, black magic, etc. His research extended even to tables of coins, common ointments, costumes and gestures. In the introduction to the Russian edition of the novel Briusov explains his pre-occupation with the occult in terms of rationalization of culture:

> ... the intensive development of the occult science started in the Renaissance and continued well into the 16th and 17th centuries. The irregular practice of fortune-telling and black magic in the medieval age was transformed in the 16th century into a science; there were more than twenty scholars specializing in it ... The prevailing spirit of this epoch was scholastic, and that is why it managed to turn occult into a discipline, it introduced some sense and logic into fortune-telling, it explained witchcraft ...

The main characters of the novel, Ruprekht and Renata, are involved in occult activities. Renata is denounced by the Inquisition as a witch baptized by the Devil (chapter 15). Her mystical hallucinations are treated as an admission of guilt: she confesses, for example, that she turned into a wolf and ate lambs, destroyed harvests, and sent an army of rats to villages. Her illness is overlooked, she herself wants to be burnt in order to be saved from her tormented conscience and agony. Briusov also introduces real historical figures into his narration. One of them is Hans Veyer, a doctor, who understands that Renata needs medical treatment. Doctor Faust also appears in the novel as a famous magician and follower of the occult. The narrator, Ruprekht, describes in chapters 11 and 12 his meeting and journey with Doctor Faust.

The plot of the novel is intriguing. It is based on the love story and travel adventures of the main character Ruprekht. Briusov's work is an imitation of Pushkin's *Povesti Belkina* (*Tales of Belkin*): the real author appears to be the editor of someone else's memoirs. In this novel, Briusov's strategy has double-edged implications. He creates a historical novel, pretending to reproduce a chronicle written in the 16th century, and manages carefully to conceal the autobiographical background of the work used by him as the main source of inspiration. The love-triangle between Ruprekht, Renata, and Count Henrik resembles the real love complications between Briusov, Nina Petrovskaia, and Belyi. Some references to their relationship can be found in the collections of poems *Stephanos*, *Vse napevy* [All Melodies], and in particular in his poem to Andrei Belyi. The affair was a source of inspiration for Briusov's novel. According to Belyi's memoirs *Nachalo veka* [The Turn of the Century], the affinity between Renata the fictional character and Petrovskaia is striking, as if "it is a dissertation about her nervous breakdown". The fictional and the biographical were so intertwined that Petrovskaia wrote to Briusov: "I want to die, so you can use my death to describe the death of Renata. I would love to be a model for the last and beautiful chapter of your book". In the love triangle Belyi symbolized light, Briusov wanted to be seen as a dark force, "the devil in love". Petrovskaia was torn between the two. The three of them were interested in the occult, and practised spiritualism. Briusov believed in a possible future marriage between science and the occult. One of the characters of the novel, Agrippa von Nettesheim (Nettesgeimskii), was based on a real figure, a soldier, physician, and an amateur alchemist. Briusov's narrator claims to have met him at the time he was renouncing his magical works; he is also portrayed surrounded by a pack of dogs (chapter 6). Yet it is known that Agrippa denounced his occult work only on his death, telling his black dog (who accompanied him everywhere): "Be gone, wretched animal, entire cause of my destruction!" There are chronological distortions and compressions. Briusov describes Agrippa's death in the last chapter in a mystical manner, focusing on the alleged suicide of the dog, and imagining Agrippa as a saint who is above the common tricks of the followers of black magic. Briusov's Agrippa displays more similarities to Briusov himself than to the historical figure. At times he talks like a preacher of Russian Symbolism. For example, he claims one would find Sybil among the best occultists, and also the three kings who brought gifts to the baby Christ; and that "the follower of black magic must be a theurgist, devoted to sacred knowledge, and a prophet".

The text is saturated with references to Latin poetry, Dante, and even Voltaire. In spite of Briusov's extensive research on the subject of medieval occult and anti-clerical writings, his novel tends to be more of a history of his own love affair and spiritual awakening than a historical account. The treatment of Christian imagery in the novel and the exalted style of the narration are similar to that found in other writings of the period. Some of the passages can be easily mistaken for the work of Guro or Merezhkovskii.

The title of the novel is symbolic, and signifies the extraordinary passion of the heroine who is visited by the Devil disguised as the Spirit of Light. The novel is dedicated to an anonymous woman with whom Briusov was in love: "... it is dedicated to you, angelic, mad, unhappy woman, who loved much and died from love ... from your loyal servant and faithful lover". The vision of love as a sweet and poisonous drink, as a mad passion leading to death and resurrection is often found in Briusov's poetry of this period. In the collection of poetry *Stephanos* the lyric hero refers to his "burnt soul" and to his experience of love as "a fiery and fatal drink". His novel is another attempt to immortalize his experience; yet it is felt throughout the work that Briusov's main sympathy lies with the pragmatically minded Agrippa von Nettesheim. In *Gody stranstvii* [Years of Wandering] (1930) Chulkov gave a profound account of the writer's interest in the occult: "Briusov thought that he could marry science with the occult. Highly sensible and business-like Briusov hoped to bring some order into the world of spirits".

ALEXANDRA SMITH

Iosif Aleksandrovich Brodskii 1940–1996

Poet and essayist

Biography

Born in Leningrad, 24 May 1940. Attended schools in Leningrad to the age of 15. Married; one son and one daughter. Arrested in January 1964 and convicted as a "social parasite"; sentenced to five years' hard labour in the far north; released in November 1965 and returned to Leningrad. Later exiled by the Soviet government. Emigrated to the United States in 1972, and became US citizen in 1977. Taught at the University of Michigan, Ann Arbor, 1972–73, 1974–80; and at various colleges in the states of New York and Massachusetts; later professor of literature, Mount Holyoke College, South Hadley, Massachusetts. He wrote some of his later prose and verse in English. Recipient: Nobel Prize for Literature, 1987; D.Litt.: Yale University, New Haven, Connecticut, 1978. Member, American Academy of Arts and Letters (resigned in protest over the honorary membership of Evgenii Evtushenko, 1987). Corresponding member, Bavarian Academy of Sciences. US Poet Laureate, 1991–92. Died in New York, 28 January 1996.

Publications

Collected Editions

Forma vremeni [The Form of Time], 2 vols. Minsk, 1992.
Sochineniia Iosifa Brodskogo, 4 vols. St Petersburg, 1992–95.
Izbrannye stikhotvoreniia, 1957–1992. Moscow, 1994.
Sochineniia, 6 vols. St Petersburg, 1997–.

Poetry

Stikhotvoreniia i poemy. Washington, DC, Inter-Language Literary Associates, 1965.
Elegy to John Donne and Other Poems, translated by Nicholas Bethell. London, Longman, 1967.
Ostanovka v pustyne [A Halt in the Wilderness]. New York, Izdatel'stvo imeni Chekhova, 1970; corrected edition, Ann Arbor, Ardis, 1988.
Selected Poems, translated by George L. Kline. New York, Harper and Row, and Penguin, Harmondsworth, 1973.
Debut, translated by Carl R. Proffer. Ann Arbor, Ardis, 1973.
Three Slavic Poets, with Tymoteusz Karpowicz and Djordje Nikolic, edited by John Rezek. Chicago, Elpenov, 1975.
Konets prekrasnoi epokhi: Stikhotvoreniia 1964–1971 [The End of the Belle Epoque: Poems 1964–1971]. Ann Arbor, Ardis, 1977.
Chast' rechi: Stikhotvoreniia 1972–1976. Ann Arbor, Ardis, 1977; translated as *A Part of Speech*, by Anthony Hecht *et al.*, New York, Farrar Straus and Giroux, and Oxford, Oxford University Press, 1980.
V Anglii [In England]. Ann Arbor, Ardis, 1977.
Verses on the Winter Campaign 1980, translated by Alan Myers. London, Anvil Press, 1981.
Rimskie elegii [Roman Elegies]. New York, Russica, 1982.
Novye stansy k Avguste: Stikhi k M.B. 1962–1982 [New Stanzas to Augusta: Poems to M.B. 1962–1982]. Ann Arbor, Ardis, 1983.
Uraniia [Urania]. Ann Arbor, Ardis, 1987.
To Urania (selected poems). New York, Farrar Straus and Giroux, and London, Viking, 1988.
Primechaniia paporotnika [A Fern's Commentary]. Bromma, Sweden, Hylaca, 1990.
Osennii krik iastreba [The Hawk's Cry in Autumn]. Leningrad, 1990.
Stikhotvoreniia [Poems]. Leningrad, 1990.
Chast' rechi: Izbrannye stikhi 1962–1989 [A Part of Speech: Selected Poems 1962–1989]. Moscow, 1990.
Bog sokhraniaet vse [God Preserves All Things]. Moscow, 1991.
Kholmy: bol'shie stikhotvoreniia i poemy [Hills: Longer Poems]. St Petersburg, 1991.
V okrestnostiakh Atlantilly: novye stikhotvoreniia [In the Environs of Atlantis]. St Petersburg, 1995.
So Forth (poems in English). New York, Farrar Straus and Giroux, and London, Hamish Hamilton, 1996.
Peizazh s navodneniem [Landscape with a Flood]. Dana Point, California, Ardis, 1996.

Plays

Mramor. Ann Arbor, Ardis, 1984; translated as *Marble: A Play in Three Acts*, by Alan Myers, New York, Farrar Straus and Giroux, and Harmondsworth, Penguin, 1989.
Demokratiia/Démocratie (bilingual edition in Russian and French). Paris, Éditions à Die, 1990; translated as "Democracy", by Alan Myers, *Granta*, 30 (1990), 199–233.

Essays

Less than One: Selected Essays. New York, Farrar Straus and Giroux, and London, Viking, 1986; Harmondsworth, Penguin, 1987.
The Nobel Lecture. New York, Farrar Straus and Giroux, 1988.
Razmerom podlinnike [In the Meter of the Original] (includes essays by others about Brodskii's work). Tallin, Estonia, 1990.
Watermark. New York, Farrar Straus and Giroux, and London, Hamish Hamilton, 1992; Moscow, 1992; Harmondsworth, Penguin, 1997.
On Grief and Reason. New York, Farrar Straus and Giroux, 1995; London, Hamish Hamilton, 1996.

Literary Criticism

"Tragicheskii elegik (o poezii Evgeniia Reina)" [A Tragic Elegist (on the Poetry of Evgenii Rein)], *Znamia*, 7 (1991), pp. 180–85.

Editor

Modern Russian Poets on Poetry: Blok, Mandelstam, Pasternak, Mayakovsky, Gumilev, Tsvetaeva, with Carl Proffer. Ann Arbor, Ardis, 1982.
An Age Ago: A Selection of Nineteenth-Century Russian Poetry, translated by Alan Myers. New York, Farrar Straus and Giroux, 1988.
The Essential Hardy. Hopewell, New Jersey, Ecco Press, 1995.

Critical Studies

"A Struggle Against Suffocation", by Czesław Miłosz, *New York Review* (14 August 1980).
Poets of Modern Russia, by Peter France, Cambridge, Cambridge University Press, 1982, 198–209.
O poezii Iosifa Brodskogo, by Mikhail Kreps, Ann Arbor, Ardis, 1984.
Poetika Iosifa Brodskogo, edited by Lev Losev, Tenafly, New Jersey, Hermitage, 1986.
"Delo Brodskogo", by Ia. Gordin, *Neva*, 2 (1989), 134–66.
Joseph Brodsky: A Poet for Our Time, by Valentina Polukhina, Cambridge, Cambridge University Press, 1989.
Iosif Brodskii razmerom podlinnika. Tallin, 1990.
Brodsky's Poetics and Aesthetics, edited by Lev Loseff and Valentina Polukhina, London, Macmillan, and New York, St Martin's Press, 1990.
"Prostranstvo Uranii", by Anatolii Naiman, *Oktiabr'*, 12 (1990), 193–98.
"V okrestnostiakh Brodskogo", by Petr Vail and Aleksandr Genis, *Literaturnoe obozrenie*, 8 (1990), 23–29.
"Poeziia novogo izmereniia", by Iurii Kublanovskii, *Novyi mir*, 2 (1991), 242–46.
"Home and Abroad in the Works of Brodskii", by Lev Loseff, in *Under Eastern Eyes: The West as Reflected in Recent Russian Émigré Writing*, edited by Arnold McMillin, London, Macmillan, 1991, 25–41; New York, St Martin's Press, 1992.
"England in Russian Émigré Poetry: Iosif Brodskii's 'V Anglii'", by Gerald S. Smith, in *Under Eastern Eyes: The West as Reflected in Recent Russian Émigré Writing*, edited by Arnold McMillin, London, Macmillan, 1991, 17–24; New York, St Martin's Press, 1992.
Brodsky Through the Eyes of His Contemporaries, by Valentina Polukhina, London, Macmillan, and New York, St Martin's Press, 1992.

Joseph Brodsky and the Creation of Exile, by David M. Bethea, Princeton, Princeton University Press, 1994.
"Brodsky's Genres": *Russian Literature* (special issue; guest editor, Valentina Polukhina), 37/2–3 (1995).
The Dictionary of Brodsky's Tropes, by Valentina Polukhina and Ülle Pärli, Tartu, Estonia, Tartu University Press, 1995.
"Joseph Brodsky: Recent Studies and Materials", by Gerald S. Smith, *The Harriman Review*, 8/2 (July 1995), 12–20.

Bibliographies
Bibliography by George L. Kline, in *10 Bibliographies of 20th Century Russian Literature*, edited by Fred Moody, Ann Arbor, Ardis, 1977.
Bibliography, in *Joseph Brodsky: A Poet for Our Time*, by Valentina Polukhina, Cambridge, Cambridge University Press, 1989.
Iosif Brodskii: Ukazatel' literatury na russkom iazyke za 1962–1995gg, St Petersburg, 1997.

By most accounts Iosif Brodskii is the greatest poet to have been born in Soviet times and, with the possible exceptions of Pasternak and Akhmatova, the most important poet writing in Russian in the second half of the 20th century. Brodskii's legendary erudition, largely self-taught, and his inspiring dialogue with the poetic "shades" of his own and other cultures were staggering in their energy, wit, prosodic and strophic inventiveness, stylistic brilliance, speculative intelligence, and generosity of spirit. Brodskii became, in the manner of his poetic "godmother" and early discoverer, Akhmatova, the cultural memory of his age and, to many of his generation, Russia's greatest gift to the west. Largely through him, Soviet poetry again learned to be "Russian", cosmopolitan, truly modern (and even potentially postmodern). Brodskii's interlocutors were always the most distinguished poets in the western tradition, his beloved "dead poets' society": Homer, Virgil, Ovid, Martial, Catullus, Horace, Dante, Donne, Hardy, Mandel'shtam, Akhmatova, Tsvetaeva, Auden, Frost, and Lowell. His ability to construct a lyric poem as a haunting medley or "round-table" of departed but still audible voices was unparalleled among his peers and became his special signature. It was not untypical of the mature Brodskii, for example, to have a favourite Russian precursor (say, Mandel'shtam) experience cultural anamnesis in the words of a favourite non-Russian precursor (say, Dante), thereby implicating the belated poet himself as a triangulated and disembodied residue of this exchange. The poet may exist on one plane as an infirm body or rejected lover or political outcast, but what really matters, wrote Brodskii repeatedly, are the "twists of his language", which enter into a discourse older than the State and synonymous with human freedom, dignity, spiritual beauty.

Brodskii's life was also the quintessential "life of the poet", although he himself, with characteristic irony and self-deprecation, often denied the reader's tendency to romantic myth-making. This life, which now looks eerily like the last in a "bardic" or "vatic" tradition going back to Pushkin and his "Prorok" ("Prophet") 1826, was marked on the one hand by fierce service to the Muse (and to "Culture" in general) and on the other by exile, loneliness, personal hardship, deteriorating health, and linguistic struggle with an adopted language. Brodskii's was the last biography of a major poet coming of age in a country where, to quote Nadezhda Mandel'shtam, "People can be killed for poetry", though Brodskii was not political, nor technically a dissident, except in the sense that his inabililty to "fit in" and his insistence at following his own "vector" (one of his favourite words) was an affront to the State and to the period of stodgy tyranny known as Brezhnevian *zastoi* ("stagnation"). No other Russian writer of modern times, forced to exit his homeland and native culture, more masterfully remade himself as western man of letters: the one brilliant exception of Vladimir Nabokov – essentially and formatively pre-Soviet and a prose writer – is telling in its difference. Brodskii's various honours, including the Nobel Prize in 1987 and a stint as US Poet Laureate (1991–92), as well as his access to the western literary press, gave him a visibility unmatched by any Russian of his generation. The poet's premature passing from long-standing heart problems on 28 January 1996 was indeed the end of an era.

Brodskii was banished from the former Soviet Union in May 1972: his two early books of verse, *Stikhotvoreniia i poemy* [Poems and Narrative Verse] (1965), and *Ostanovka v pustyne* [A Halt in the Wilderness] (1970; revised 1988), had been illegally published abroad and as a result had "produced a body the system found alien enough to reject". By the mid-1960s Brodskii had developed a distinctive voice; perhaps its most salient features are, on the one hand, a sublime elegiac lyricism whenever the poet addresses a great forebear (say, Donne in "Bol'shaia elegiia Dzhonu Donnu" ["The Great Elegy to John Donne"] 1963) and, on the other, a powerful "self-estranging" irony and semantic/rhetoric deflation whenever the poet addresses his own outcast status and love life. Moments of "plainspeaking" and intentional coarseness come to coexist in unlikely equipoise with a "scholasticism" virtually unique among Brodskii's contemporaries (an important exception being Aleksandr Kushner). The *difficilia quae pulchra* quality of Brodskii's verse, first learned from Donne, means that many poems appear "hermetic" (their primary addressees were Brodskii's immediate circle of cultivated friends) and unabashedly occasional – that is, tethered to a specific time, place, relationship, or event. Furthermore, Brodskii's tendency to deploy for the first time in Russia what can only be called a metaphysical conceit – that "hammering out" or "difficult joining" whereby an often bizarre analogy is made the axis of an extended poetic argument – is made possible both by the poet's exuberant, often "self-cancelling" word- and root-play (paronomasia) and especially by his syntax, some of the most daunting and convoluted in all Russian poetry.

Several of Brodskii's early love poems and elegies, including "Dlia shkol'nogo vozrasta" [For School Age] (1964), "Sem' let spustia" [Seven Years Later] (1969), "Pen'e bez muzyki" [A Song to No Music] (1970), "Pamiati T.B." [In Memory of T.B.] (1968), are Russified applications of Donne's famous compass conceit in "A Valediction: Forbidding Mourning", which Brodskii also translated. Themes from the Bible (the sacrifice of Isaac by Abraham) as well as from antiquity (Odysseus' farewell to Telemachus, Theseus' victory over the Minotaur made pyrrhic against a background of Ariadna's duplicity) begin increasingly to make their way into Brodskii's verse, often as subtle extensions of the poet's own mythically constructed biography. Eventually Brodskii's work will become fixated on the notion of antiquity as busts, torsos, Ovidian candelsticks metamorphosed by time – in short, ruins (a variation in space of the poet's favourite notion of time as erosion/petrification). The Greek theme (Hector,

Orpheus, Artemis, etc.) will gradually be replaced by the Roman theme (Martial, Tiberius, etc.), particularly in the latter's incarnation as "empire" – a trajectory, as Brodskii knew, that was deeply "Mandel'shtamian".

Once forced into emigration, Brodskii was helped initially by his hero W.H. Auden and by Carl Proffer, then professor at the University of Michigan, whose influence succeeded in securing a post for his friend as "poet-in-residence" in Ann Arbor and whose publishing house (Ardis) produced two of Brodskii's most celebrated volumes of verse – *Konets prekrasnoi epokhi* [The End of the Belle Epoque: Poems 1964–1971] and *Chast' rechi* (*A Part of Speech*). These two collections, perhaps more than any others, cemented Brodskii's reputation, especially after the death of Akhmatova in 1966, as the greatest living poet writing in Russian. Their principal themes are: travel in time and space to the far corners of "empire", both eastern and western (Lithuania, Yalta, Italy, England, United States, Mexico, etc.); an ancient world in decline that is hauntingly modern ("Pis'ma rimskomu drugu" [Letters to a Roman Friend], 1972); Christian existentialism amid thoughts of birth and death ("Natiurmort" [Nature morte], 1971, "Sreten'e" [Nunc Dimittis], 1972); language as the paper-thin shield (the conceit of the butterfly's wing) separating us from the non-being (*nichto*) of pure time ("Babochka" [The Butterfly], 1972); eulogies for departed friends, loved ones, and historical figures ("Pokhorony Bobo" [The Funeral of Bobo], 1972, "Na smert' Zhukova" [On the Death of Zhukov], 1974); and the tragic impossibility of keeping love alive in exile (the great cycle "A Part of Speech"). These books were followed in the 1980s by the Russian language *Uraniia* and the English language *To Urania* (this latter a partial translation of *Uraniia* together with selections from earlier collections), in which Brodskii's speculative fervor reached new heights in such mature *tours de force* as "Osenii krik iastreba" ("A Hawk's Cry in Autumn"), 1975; "Rimskie elegii" ("Roman Elegies"), 1981; and "Mukha" ("The Fly"), 1986.

Finally, with the help of glasnost and the opening of the former Soviet market, the 1990s saw the appearance of numerous editions and collections of Brodskii's verse. Two new books of poetry, one in Russian entitled *Peizazh s navodneniem* [Landscape with a Flood] and another in English entitled *So Forth*, were being prepared at the time of Brodskii's death: these collections are intended to present new poetry completed since *Uraniia* and *To Urania*, respectively. Despite Brodskii's status as US Poet Laureate, many feel that his greatest contribution to Anglophone culture is not his poetry, which normally either he or fellow poets translated (often ingeniously) from the Russian, but his essayistic and memoiristic prose, especially that collected in *Less than One* (1986), an undisputed masterpiece in the genre, and more recently in *On Grief and Reason* (1995). Brodskii's "signature" as a lyric poet, based as it was on a richly inflected language with virtually infinite rhyming possibilities and a more vivid collective memory for the subtle links between semantics and prosody, did not completely "translate" into contemporary English, while his genius as a thinker and advocate for "poetic" values did, fully and brilliantly, in his prose.

DAVID M. BETHEA

Ostanovka v pustyne

A Halt in the Wilderness

Poetry collection, 1970

Ostanovka v pustyne [A Halt in the Wilderness] is the second collection of Brodskii's verse. Like the first, it was published in the United States while he was still living in the Soviet Union. It contains poems written between 1961 and 1969, some of which are reprinted from the earlier *Stikhotvoreniia i poemy* [Poems and Narrative Verse] (1965), and represents the crystallization of Brodskii's early poetic thought.

From a very early stage Brodskii saw in his task as a poet the revalorization of a Russian literary language which had been debased by decades of ideological cliché. Like many other poets of the Thaw generation, he sought to reassemble the fragments of the literary past and to return to the literary tradition at the point where it was cut off by the imposition of socialist realism. In the poems of *Ostanovka v pustyne* Brodskii succeeds in doing this with consummate skill and, as has been very widely acknowledged by practising Russian poets, has at the same time opened up new vistas of possibility for poetry and poetic language.

In effecting this renewal Brodskii turned not so much to models in the Russian modernist tradition as to foreign writers. Certainly his elegiac style owes much to the example of his mentor Akhmatova, and the density of his metaphors may be compared to Mandel'shtam's, but in *Ostanovka v pustyne* the most salient affinities are with the English tradition of Donne, Eliot and Auden. Brodskii's admiration of these writers is expressed in central poems written to and about them: the "Bol'shaia elegiia Dzhonu Donnu" ("The Great Elegy to John Donne"), for example, or his *Stikhi na smert' T.S. Eliota* [Verses on the Death of T.S. Eliot]), itself written in imitation of Auden's valedictory poem to Yeats. The connection with Donne, especially, is underlined by the last section of *Ostanovka v pustyne*, which consists of Brodskii's translations from the 17th-century English poet. The influence of all three writers on both Brodskii's ideas and style is in fact quite profound. From Donne, in part, come the wide-ranging and lengthy discussions of philosophical themes and the use of the rhetorical device of the "conceit", a complex metaphor that dominates a poem and evolves as it progresses. Eliot and Auden provided the translocation of this metaphysical tradition into the present and showed how poetic language and poetic memory could be used as a defence against the passing of time. (This theme is prominent too in, for example, the late poetry of Akhmatova, but the expansion of horizons outside the native tradition constitutes an important focus for Brodskii's poetics of renewal).

In *Ostanovka v pustyne*, Brodskii makes frequent use of themes and motifs from the Christian tradition, alluding, for example, to the nativity of Christ or retelling the story of Abraham and Isaac. References to classical mythology – for example, to Orpheus or to Dido and Aeneas – are equally common. Brodskii uses these and other narratives as illustrations of his discussion of broad issues of human concern, just as relevant for the present as for the past. The dominant theme is that of separation, whether it is the parting of a man from a woman he loves, or the parting caused by exile or by death, or more abstractly that caused by separation from cultural roots, or indeed the disappointment caused by unfulfilled promises or expectations at either a personal or a national level. Very often several strands are combined in a single poem. "Enei i Didona" [Aeneas and Dido], for example, combines the narrative of Dido abandoned by her lover with the theme of Carthage eventually succumbing to the political might of the Roman empire. The poem "Ostanovka v pustyne", which gave its name to the whole collection, laments the destruction of the Greek church in Leningrad to make place for a modern concert hall, seeing this as a denial of Russia's Christian heritage. At the same time it obliquely protests at Stalin's persecution of minority peoples such as the Russian Greeks. The note of direct political opposition present here is repeated elsewhere, but it never becomes the overriding concern of Brodskii's poetry. His view of the society in which he lives is predominantly that of an ironic but engaged observer commenting on a world that has lost sight of its past.

Ostanovka v pustyne is particularly striking in its manipulation of language and verse structure. And while Brodskii, in the 1960s, turns to traditional metres after an early period of experimentation, his treatment of, for example, the iambic or anapaestic line is extremely diverse. In some poems, such as "The Great Elegy to John Donne", he aims at the maximum possible saturation of stresses and at rigorously end-stopped lines. In others he chooses to emphasize the meandering logic of his reflective discourses by employing a very large measure of enjambment. The length of Brodskii's poems is varied: he writes tightly constructed sonnets with the same facility as discursive elegies. Many poems are written in strict stanzaic forms and with regular rhyme patterns, but there is also blank verse. In "Pis'mo v butylke" [A Letter in a Bottle], as the narrator becomes increasingly detached from present reality, his disorientation is reflected in a series of textual interpolations indicating that parts of the poem have been washed away by sea water. In the complex "Gorbunov i Gorchakov" [Gorbunov and Gorchakov], on the other hand, the schizophrenic and fragmentary dialogue of two patients in a psychiatric hospital is set off by an extremely demanding and rigid poetic form. It consists of 14 sections each containing 100 lines of iambic pentameter. All but two of these are divided into ten stanzas and rhyme AbAbAbAbAb. Brodskii's poetry, moreover, uses a wide spectrum of linguistic registers, ranging from clear narrative exposition to the densely metaphorical language of the elegy to Donne, to the playful inclusion of German in "Dva chasa v rezervuare" [Two Hours in a Tank].

DAVID N. WELLS

A Part of Speech

Chast' rechi

Poetry collection, 1977

A Part of Speech (published in English translation in 1980) is one of the most perfect of all Brodskii's collections and it is also perhaps the most important. The very title indicates that Brodskii shares Beckett's belief that "the quality of language is more important than any system of ethics or aesthetics". The theme of the supremacy of language recurs throughout the core poems, which unite the Russian and the English collections. There is, however, a considerable difference between the two collections: the Russian book consists of 42 poems written after Brodskii's exile, only 34 of them are translated into English, the remaining 22 poems are taken from his other Russian collections – *Ostanovka v pustyne*, *Konets prekrasnoi epokhi* [The End of the Belle Epoque] and even from *Uraniia* (*To Urania*). The English version of *A Part of Speech* is therefore more representative, it stretches from 1965 to 1978 and gives a better idea of the poet's evolution. Brodskii took great care in choosing his translators: apart from his first American translator, George L. Kline, and his faithful English translator, Alan Myers, some of the best American poets such as Richard Wilbur, Anthony Hecht, and Derek Walcott helped him approximate the translations to the original poems so that "every poem in the book reads as if English had been its first home" (Henry Gifford). The poet himself took an active part in the process of narrowing the gap that always exists between the original and the translation: he had produced an interlinear version for the poets, corrected Daniel Weissbort's, David Rigsbee's and some of Alan Myers's versions and had composed one poem, "Elegy: for Robert Lowell", in English. As a result we have a book that has strengthened Brodskii's reputation as a major poet of considerable stature, "a poet of true nobility" (Harold Pinter), who "welds a late Romantic imagination to a forcing mind that shapes the world to its own mental patterns, patterns which are original, shocking, fresh and consistent" (George Szirtes).

Thematically both collections reveal considerable complexity and diversity: individual versus Empire; man versus time ("man is his own end / and just forth into Time"); time versus faith, love, memory and creativity, poet versus language and language versus time. According to his own admission, Brodskii writes "exclusively about one thing: about time and what time does to man, how it transforms him". It is identified now with dust, now with cold; things, too, can be regarded as masks for time. When observations are made "from the point of view of time", man's accepted hierarchy of things turns out to be defective and it is replaced by the principle of relativity, and this is stated in many of Brodskii's poems: "of any great faith, / as a rule, only holy relics remain"; "Great issues leave a trail of words behind". Exile also holds a prominent position in many poems. When the invitation to perpetual exile was issued, the horizon of the future looked like "a minus sign / on the spent life". The feeling of orphanhood and fear of silence are expressed in one of the first poems written in exile, "1972", although only indirectly, through triple dactylic rhymes: *otchaian'ia / odichaniia / molchaniia* (despair / isolation / silence). Written with power and beauty, the poem has been praised for its "formal inventiveness" (G.L. Kline) and for its almost Calvinistic spirit of dismissal of pain and loss (Czesław Miłosz). Brodskii has never allowed himself to dramatize the situation and to consider himself a martyr. Moreover, he was determined to turn his linguistic isolation to his own advantage, "by seeking out affinities and extensions" (H. Gifford). He seems to feel most at home in an alien culture by appropriating with equal ease Greek mythology ("Odysseus to Telemachus") and the Old and New Testament ("Nunc Dimittis"); the classical world of Latin poets ("Letters to a Roman Friend") and the Elizabethans ("A Song to No Music"). One can detect other voices in the collection. In one of his most "Dantesque" poems, "December in Florence", Brodskii clearly identifies himself with the great Italian by echoing Dante's "terza rima". One can also sense the presence of T.S. Eliot, W.H. Auden, and Samuel Beckett. The latter had a very specific impact on Brodskii's poetics and *Weltanschauung*. In one of the most technically accomplished poems in the collection, "Babochka", where the mastery of rhyme, enjambment and trope is especially striking, Brodskii exhibits an amplitude that no other Russian poets among his contemporaries can claim. His range is such that he combines the incompatible: a Pushkinian lightness and elegance of style and the Elizabethan "use of conceit with Beckett's way of looking at the world, which demands a dotting of all the i's" and then leaves only the dots: the butterfly is seen as merely "a frail and shifting buffer", dividing nothingness and man.

The shadow of exile falls over other poems: "Lagoon", "The Thames at Chelsea", "Plato Elaborated". Brodskii's profoundly tragic pathos is strongly felt in "Lullaby of Cape Cod", where he achieved a baroque sense of wonder and displayed his formal and linguistic virtuosity. There is a subtle interplay between the American and the Russian landscapes, whether through irony or meditation. His concern with the abandoned country would not go away. The change of Empire brings no change in the existential nature of being because "man brings his own dead-end no matter what / spot on the globe he is on". In his dazzling cycle "A Part of Speech", consisting of 20 poems (five of them are not translated into English), baroque imagery progresses "from the visual to the visionary". He moulded concrete and abstract into an exquisite form displaying a genuinely metaphysical quality. This sensuous cycle has rightly acquired a *sub rosa* reputation. His lyrical persona is depicted in a very impersonal manner with increasing anonymity of a Beckettian kind: "a nameless lodger, a nobody", "a passerby with a creased face". Brodskii continues to subtract "the greater from the lesser - Time from the man" in order to profess that "what remains of a man is a part / of speech". He also would like to remind us that poetry is "an instrument of self-betterment", "a form of sentimental education" as well as "the highest form of linguistic activity", therefore it is above any social order or institution.

Brodskii not only survived in exile, he triumphed, thanks to his belief that "a poet's biography is in his vowels and sibilants, in his meters, rhymes, and metaphors ... With poets, the choice of words is invariably more telling than the story line", that "life is hostage to his *metier*". Brodskii identifies language with Muse as the poet's voice. With the aid of the word (language) Brodskii reorganized the classical triangle (Spirit - Man - Thing) into a rectangle: Spirit - Word - Man - Thing. That rectangle stands as a sign for Brodskii's extended journey, not just into the realm of the Spirit, but also in the opposite direction, "into that *nowhere* of pure thought ... / beyond the naked eye". The poet, "a mumbling heap / of words", managed to transfer the Russian language, by means of its own resources, to the centre of world culture, finding "the protected source of energy" (Mandel'shtam) in the language itself, for a poem is "in itself an act of love, not so much of an author for his subject, as language for a piece of reality".

VALENTINA POLUKHINA

To Urania

Uraniia

Poetry collection, 1987

Brodskii's seventh Russian collection, *Uraniia*, consists of 74 poems written between 1975 and 1986; only 30 of them are included in his third English book, *To Urania: Selected Poems 1965–1985*; four poems are taken from Brodskii's early collections and 12 are written in English. The difference between the two volumes is not only in the contents but also in the principle of composition. The English collection is more various but less structured: it is difficult to detect either a chronological order (the first poem is dated 1980 and the last one 1968) or a thematic one. Unlike the English, the Russian book is divided into three thematic sections; the poems are arranged in chronological order: short poems are followed by long ones. "Osenii krik iastreba" ("The Hawks's Cry in Autumn") provides the subtitle for the first part. This poem has been perceived by the critics as a tribute to Baratynskii's famous poem "Osen'" [Autumn] and "stands as an equal to it" (A. Naiman). Vertically orientated, like Brodskii's "Bol'shaia elegiia Dzhonu Donnu" ("The Great Elegy to John Donne"), this majestic and magisterial poem expresses the "idea of the world as an endless ascending hierarchy" (Gordin). The ability of the poet to take "a step aside, away from his own body", to depict the world as if "from the point of view of time" is reinforced in such poems as "Polden' v komnate" ("Midday in the Room") and "Bagatelle". The title poem "Uraniia" provides the semantic centre for the second part and indicates, that Brodskii takes Tiutchev and Auden as his models. Like Tiutchev in his "Uraniia" and Auden in "Homage to Cleo", the poet meditates on man's relationship with time and space: "One cold resembles another / cold. Time looks like time. What sets them apart is only / a warm body. Mule-like, stubborn creature, / it stands firmly between them ... / preventing the wandering of the future / into the past". In Auden-like tone and stanzas Brodskii continues the dialogue with his favourite English poet in the cycle "V Anglii" ("In England"). The third section, "Zhizn' v rasseiannom svete" ("A Life in Diffused Light"), offers some means to overcome time: as long as man has language he is not defenceless against time and space, he is given the possibility of widening his horizons, of lengthening the radius of his purview by the word through the "all-seeing eyes of words". For Brodskii, language – like Spirit – exists outside Time. That is why "Time worships language", language worships God, the poet worships both. Brodskii's preoccupation with the idea of the poet as the voice of language manifests itself in his every collection. The world is also viewed by Brodskii through the prism of culture, and culture for him is "love plus memory". The many references to other cultures can be interpreted as the poet's attempt to establish "a link between times". Empire as one of Brodskii's principal themes also figures in this collection – "Biust Tiberiia" ("The Bust of Tiberius"), "Litovskii noktiurn" ("Lithuanian Nocturne") – and has been interpreted as a conceptual metaphor for "forced harmonization in the face of deep internal troubles" (Gordin).

The landscape in both collections varies. It ranges from Lithuania (Brodskii's mother's birthplace) to Afghanistan, from the native city that rejected him, to the city that honoured him by making him the fifth Poet Laureate of the United States. This reflects on the dimensions of his poems; some of them have a country-wide, or even continent-wide range, others measure up to some abstract notion ("Ekloga 4-ia (Zimnaia)" ("Eclogue IV: Winter")). He has changed the scale of lyric poetry dramatically by increasing a sense of distance and discovering his way into foreign poetic traditions. This "most latinate of lyric poets" (George Steiner) brought back to life the classical world of Virgil and Horace in two of his Eclogues and in *Rimskie elegii* [Roman Elegies]. As Virgil does in his Third and Fourth Eclogues, Brodskii alternates personal time and ontological, consciously placing side by side the physical and metaphysical. Brodskii's *Rimskie elegii*, written with wit and taste, breadth and lucidity, emphasize that questions of moral choice and moral values will not go away as long as man breathes.

Among his long poems there is his earlier masterpiece, "Gorbunov and Gorchakov", written in the style of his beloved Beckett. The 1400 iambic pentameters of poem-dialogue constitutes a brilliant work, both in its philosophical complexity and its verbal inventiveness. A dialogue between two patients (or a schizoid monologue) reflects two opposing points of view on the world, art and man; from it a long series of oppositions has been derived: genius and villainy, harmony and elemental force, love and treachery, individual and state, good and evil, and so on. A master of contrast and paradox, Brodskii fills the poem with aphorisms, self-irony and linguistic wit. An example of the latter is the alienation of the verb "said" in the mouth of a man whose "lips sing in two voices": "He said, then vanished". "On the platform see / he-said." "He said." "But if he-said's a dead / object, should not the same be true of he?" The view of human life as fundamentally absurd is expressed with Beckett-like daring, by means of the transformation of a simple verb into the image of a ring, boat, ripple on the water. It would be hard to find any display of pathos or melodrama by such "a stern metaphysical realist" (Miłosz). The motif of stoic resistance to all the terrible ordeals of life is characteristic of many of Brodskii's poems. "Absolute calm in the face of absolute tragedy" (Parshchikov) is Brodskii's ethical position.

In many ways Brodskii is an impersonal poet, his lyrical self is no longer a hero of his own drama. He does not believe that "our egos are the best material for poetry, even wounded egos". He has rejected "the use of what in the past has been most characteristic of Russian lyric poetry – that excitable, hot-blooded, hysterical note" (Rein). His tendency to place himself lower in the scheme of things than others, to see the worst in himself becomes increasingly evident in his love poems. Poetry, for Brodskii, is a "celebration of self-humiliation, not of self-indulgence". He has evoked a whole system of masks, of tropes of anonymity, of archetypes behind which he hides his self – see his impressive "Dvadtsat' sonetov k Marii Stiuart" ("Twenty Sonnets to Mary Queen of Scots"). From this collection the poet appears to us as a figure of intellectual sobriety with a sense of perspective. Two particular qualities characterize the book as a whole. First, Brodskii uses the full force of his intellectual power in order to offer new answers to old questions, thus providing an unforgettable intellectual education. Second, his remarkable power of observation is of a very specific kind, sometimes taking in whole continents, sometimes a fleeing cat. These qualities, prosaic in nature, in Rein's view, permit Brodskii to become the last great innovator in Russian poetry.

VALENTINA POLUKHINA

Mikhail Afanas'evich Bulgakov 1891–1940

Prose writer and dramatist

Biography

Born in Kiev, Ukraine, 14 May 1891. Attended First Kiev High School, 1900–09; studied medicine at Kiev University, 1909–16. Served as a doctor in front-line and district hospitals, 1916–18. Married: 1) Tat'iana Nikolaevna Lappa in 1913; 2) Liubov' Evgen'evna Belozerskaia in 1924; 3) Elena Sergeevna Shilovskaia in 1932. Worked as a doctor in Kiev, 1918–19: abandoned medicine in 1920. Organized a "sub-department of the arts", Vladikavkaz, 1920–21. Moved to Moscow, 1921; worked as journalist for various groups and papers. Associated with the Moscow Arts Theatre from 1925: assistant producer, 1930–36. Librettist and consultant, Bolshoi Theatre, Moscow, 1936–40. Much of his writing was published posthumously. Died in Moscow, 10 March 1940.

Publications

Collected Editions

P'esy. Moscow, 1962.

Dramy i komedii [Dramas and Comedies]. Moscow, 1965.

Izbrannaia proza. Moscow, 1966.

The Early Plays, edited by Ellendea Proffer, translated by Ellendea and Carl R. Proffer. Bloomington, Indiana University Press, 1972.

Romany. Moscow, 1973.

Neizdannyi Bulgakov: teksty i materialy [The Unpublished Bulgakov], edited by Ellendea Proffer. Ann Arbor, Ardis, 1977.

Sobranie sochinenii, edited by Ellendea Proffer. Ann Arbor, Ardis, 1982–90 [volumes 1–4 and 8 published].

P'esy 1920-kh godov [Plays of the 1920s]. Leningrad, 1989.

Izbrannye proizvedeniia, 2 vols. Kiev, 1989.

Sobranie sochinenii, 5 vols. Moscow, 1989–90.
Six Plays, edited by Lesley Milne, translated by Michael Glenny *et al.* London, Methuen, 1991.
P'esy 1930-kh godov [Plays of the 1930s]. Moscow, 1994.

Fiction
Zapiski na manzhetakh. 1922–23; also in *Zvezda vostoka*, 3 (1967); as separate edition, New York, Silver Age Publishing, 1981; translated as *Notes on the Cuff and Other Stories*, by Alison Rice, edited by Ellendea Proffer, Ann Arbor, Ardis, 1991.
Diavoliada: Rasskazy. Moscow, 1925; translated as *Diaboliad and Other Stories*, by Carl R. Proffer, edited by Ellendea and Carl R. Proffer, Bloomington, Indiana University Press, 1972.
"Belaia gvardiia", *Rossiia*, 4–5 (1925); as *Dni Turbinykh (Belaia gvardiia)*, 2 vols. Paris, Concorde, 1927–29; reprinted as *Belaia gvardiia*, Letchworth, Bradda, 1969; translated as *The White Guard*, by Michael Glenny, London, Collins Harvill, 1971.
"Rokovye iaitsa", in *Diavoliada: Rasskazy*, Moscow, 1925; translated as "The Fatal Eggs", by Carl R. Proffer, in *Diaboliad and Other Stories*, 1972.
Zapiski iunogo vracha. Moscow, 1963; enlarged edition translated as *A Country Doctor's Notebook*, by Michael Glenny, London, Collins Harvill, 1975.
"Zapiski pokoinika (Teatral'nyi roman)", in *Izbrannaia proza*, 1966; translated as *Black Snow: A Theatrical Novel*, by Michael Glenny, London, Collins Harvill, 1967.
Master i Margarita. Moscow, 1966–67; uncut version, Frankfurt, Posev, 1969; complete version, Moscow, 1973; revised edition, Moscow, 1989; translated as *The Master and Margarita*, by Mirra Ginsburg, New York, Grove Press, 1967; uncut version, translated by Michael Glenny, London, Harvill Press, 1967; reprinted London, Everyman, 1992; complete version translated by Diana Burgin and Katherine Tiernan O'Connor, edited by Ellendea Proffer, Dana Point, California, Ardis, 1995; London, Vintage, 1996; also translated by Richard Pevear and Larissa Volkhonsky, Harmondsworth, Penguin, 1997.
Sobach'e serdtse. 1969; edited by Avril Pyman, London, Bristol Classical Press, 1994; translated as *The Heart of a Dog*, by Michael Glenny, London, Collins Harvill, 1968; also translated by Mirra Ginsburg, Moscow, Raduga, 1990.

Plays
Dni Turbinykh, adapted from his novel (produced 1926); published with *Poslednie dni (Pushkin)*, Moscow, 1955; translated as "The Days of the Turbins", by Eugene Lyons, in *Six Soviet Plays*, London, Gollancz, 1935; also translated by Ellendea and Carl R. Proffer, in *The Early Plays*, 1972; and as *The White Guard*, by Michael Glenny, London, Methuen, 1979.
Zoikina kvartira (produced 1926); edited by Ellendea Proffer, Ann Arbor, Ardis, 1971; translated as "Zoya's Apartment", by Ellendea and Carl R. Proffer, in *The Early Plays*, 1972; also as "Madame Zoya", by Michael Glenny, in *Six Plays*, 1991.
Bagrovyi ostrov (produced 1928); in *P'esy*, 1971; translated as "The Crimson Island", by Ellendea and Carl R. Proffer, in *The Early Plays*, 1972.
Mertvye dushi [Dead Souls], from the novel by Gogol' (produced 1932); published with *Ivan Vasil'evich*, Munich, Tovarishchetsvo zarubezhnykh pisatelei, 1964.
Kabala sviatosh (as *Mol'er*, produced 1936); published in *P'esy*, 1962; translated as "A Cabal of Hypocrites", by Ellendea and Carl R. Proffer, in *The Early Plays*, 1972; also as "Molière", by Michael Glenny, in *Six Plays*, 1991.
Don Kikhot [Don Quixote], from the novel by Cervantes (produced 1940); published in *P'esy*, 1962.
Poslednie dni (Pushkin) (produced 1943); published with *Dni Turbinykh*, 1955; translated as "The Last Days (Pushkin)", by Carl R. Proffer, *Russian Literature Triquarterly*, 15 (1978), 49–97; and by William Powell and Michael Earley, in *Six Plays*, 1991.
Rashel', edited by Margarita Aliger, music by R.M. Glière (broadcast 1943; produced 1947); edited by A. Colin Wright, *Novyi zhurnal*, 108 (September 1972); Bulgakov's original text, Moscow, 1988.
Beg (produced 1957); in *P'esy*, 1962; edited by J.A.E. Curtis, London, Bristol Classical Press, 1997; translated as *Flight*, by Mirra Ginsburg, New York, Grove Press, 1969; and by Michael Glenny, in *Six Plays*, 1991; translated as *On the Run*, by Avril Pyman, London, Ginn, 1972.
Ivan Vasil'evich (produced 1966); published with *Mertvye dushi*, Munich, Tovarishchestvo zarubezhnykh pisatelei, 1964; translated as "Ivan Vasilievich", *Modern International Drama*, 7/2 (1974).
"Poloumnyi Zhurden", from *Le Bourgeois Gentilhomme* by Molière, in *Dramy i komedii*, 1965 (produced 1972).
"Blazhenstvo (Son inzhenera Reyna v 4-kh deistviakh)", *Zvezda vostoka*, 7 (1966); translated as *Bliss*, by Mirra Ginsburg, with *Flight*, New York, New Directions, 1985.
"Adam i Eva", in *P'esy*, 1971; translated as "Adam and Eve", by Ellendea Proffer, *Russian Literature Triquarterly*, 1 (Autumn 1971), 164–215; also translated by Michael Glenny, in *Six Plays*, 1991.
Minin i Pozharskii, edited by A. Colin Wright, *Russian Literature Triquarterly*, 15 (1976).
Batum, in *Neizdannyi Bulgakov*, 1977.
Voina i mir [War and Peace], from the novel by Tolstoi, edited by A. Colin Wright, *Canadian-American Slavic Studies*, 15 (Summer–Fall 1981), 382–439.
Chernoe more [The Black Sea]. Moscow, 1988.
Petr Velikii [Peter the Great], *Sovetskaia muzyka*, 2 (1988), 48–62.

Biography
Zhizn' gospodina de Mol'era. 1962; translated as *The Life of Monsieur de Molière*, by Mirra Ginsburg, New York, Funk and Wagnalls, 1970; reprinted New York, New Directions, 1986.

Letters and Diaries
Pod piatoi. Moi dnevnik [Under the Heel. My Diary]. Moscow, 1990.
Manuscripts Don't Burn: A Life in Letters and Diaries, edited by J.A.E. Curtis, London, Bloomsbury, 1991; reprinted London, Harvill Press, 1992.

Critical Studies

Bulgakov's "The Master and Margarita": The Text as a Cipher, by Elena N. Mahlow, New York, Vantage Press, 1975.

The Master and Margarita: A Comedy of Victory, by Lesley Milne, Birmingham, Birmingham Slavonic Monographs, 1977.

Russian Literature Triquarterly (special Bulgakov issue), 15 (1978).

Mikhail Bulgakov: Life and Interpretations, by A. Colin Wright, Toronto, University of Toronto Press, 1978.

Analiz iudeiskikh glav "Mastera i Maragarity" M. Bulgakova, by Genrikh El'baum, Ann Arbor, Ardis, 1981.

Canadian American Slavic Studies (special Bulgakov issue), edited by Nadine Natov, 15/2–3, (1981).

Untersuchung zu Bulgakovs Romanen "Belaia gvardiia" und "Master i Margarita", by M. Fiesler, Hildesheim, Georg Olms, 1982.

Tvorcheskii put' Mikhaila Bulgakova, by L. Ianovskaia, Moscow, 1983.

Bulgakov: Life and Work, by Ellendea Proffer, Ann Arbor, Ardis, 1984.

A Mind in Ferment: Mikhail Bulgakov's Prose, by Kalpana Sahni, New Delhi, Arnold-Heinemann, 1984; Atlantic Highlands, New Jersey, Humanities Press, 1996.

Evangelie Mikhaila Bulgakova, by A. Zerkalov, Ann Arbor, Ardis, 1984.

Mikhail Bulgakov, by Nadine Natov, Boston, Twayne, 1985.

Mikhail Bulgakov v Khudozhestvennom teatre, by Anatolii Smel'ianski, Moscow, 1986; 2nd edition, 1989.

Between Two Worlds: A Critical Introduction to "The Master and Margarita", by Andrew Barratt, Oxford, Clarendon Press, 1987.

Bulgakov's Last Decade: The Writer as Hero, by J.A.E. Curtis, Cambridge and New York, Cambridge University Press, 1987.

Problemy teatral'nogo naslediia M.A. Bulgakova, Leningrad, 1987.

Vospominaniia o Mikhaile Bulgakove, Moscow, 1988.

Zhizneopisanie Mikhaila Bulgakova, by M. Chudakova, Moscow, 1988.

Zhizn' i smert' Mikhaila Bulgakova, by Anatolii Shvartz, Moscow, 1988.

Soviet Literature (special Bulgakov issue), 7/484 (1988).

The Shape of Apocalypse in Modern Russian Fiction, by David M. Bethea, Princeton, Princeton University Press, 1989.

The Literary Fantastic: From Gothic to Postmodernism, by Neil Cornwell, New York and London, Harvester Wheatsheaf, 1990.

Mikhail Bulgakov: A Critical Biography, by Lesley Milne, Cambridge, Cambridge University Press, 1990.

The Apocalyptic Vision of Mikhail Bulgakov's "The Master and Margarita", by Edward E. Ericson, Jr, Lewiston, New York, and Lampeter, Wales, Edwin Mellen Press, 1991.

The Gnostic Novel of Mikhail Bulgakov: Sources and Exegesis, by George Krugovoy, Lanham, Maryland, University Press of America, 1991.

The Writer's Divided Self in Bulgakov's "The Master and Margarita", by Riitta H. Pittman, London, Macmillan, and New York, St Martin's Press, 1991.

Mikhail Bulgakov (1891–1940): Un maître et son destin, by Marianne Gourg, Paris, Robert Laffont, 1992.

Bulgakov: The Novelist-Playwright, edited by Lesley Milne, London, Harwood Academic, 1995.

The KGB's Literary Archive, by Vitaly Shentalinsky, translated by John Crowfoot, London, Harvill Press, 1995.

Bulgakov's Apocalyptic Critique of Literature: The Use of Dante's "Divine Comedy", Goethe's "Faust" and The Bible in "The Master and Margarita", by Derek J. Hunns, volume 1, *An Eventful History*, Lewiston, New York, and Lampeter, Wales, Edwin Mellen Press, 1996.

Mikhail Bulgakov - Khudozhnik, by V.V. Novikov, Moscow, 1996.

The Master and Margarita: A Critical Companion, edited by Laura Weeks, Evanston, Illinois, Northwestern University Press, 1996.

Entsiklopediia Bulgakovskaia, edited by Boris Sokolov, Moscow, 1996.

Bibliographies

An International Bibliography of Works by and about Bulgakov, by Ellendea Proffer, Ann Arbor, Ardis, 1976.

"A Bibliography of Works by and about Mikhail Bulgakov", by Nadine Natov, *Canadian-American Slavic Studies*, 15 (Summer–Fall 1981), 457–61.

Mikhail Bulgakov in English: A Bibliography 1891–1991, by Garth M. Terry, Nottingham, Astra Press, 1991.

Mikhail Bulgakov's current reputation as a major 20th-century European writer is posthumous. The story of Bulgakov's reception illustrates the tragedy of Russian culture in the post-revolutionary period. In the latter half of the 1920s he enjoyed brief fortune as a dramatist and when he died in 1940 he was remembered as the author of just one play, *Dni Turbinykh* (*The Days of the Turbins*), sometimes translated into English as *The White Guard*. Bulgakov was both a dramatist and a prose writer, but from 1927 until 1962 none of his prose was published or even reprinted in the Soviet Union. His great comic novel *Master i Margarita* (*The Master and Margarita*) was not published until 1966–67 and it took until the 1980s, the era of Gorbachev and glasnost, before all Bulgakov's works could finally be published in Russia. Bulgakov maintained a sceptical distance from the official Soviet ideology of his day, refusing to adopt its value-system. The price he paid was to lose his audience in his own time; the price paid by Russian culture was to lose for a quarter of a century the voice of this great literary "outsider". There were, of course, other "great outsiders" – Akhmatova, Mandel'shtam and Pasternak, to name but three. Bulgakov's case is, however, unique for the sheer volume of work that was found – unpublished, unsuspected, and unexpected – in his archive. This in part explains the shock and delight that greeted the publication of *The Master and Margarita*.

After training and practising as a doctor, Bulgakov in 1920 took the decision to become a writer and made his Moscow literary debut from 1922 onward as a writer of sketches and satirical prose. His stories "D'iavoliada" ("Diaboliad") and "Rokovye iaitsa" ("The Fatal Eggs") were well enough received, given the intensity of the ideological debates of the time. But *Sobach'e serdtse* (*The Heart of a Dog*), written in 1925, was declared unpublishable: a harbinger of things to come. What made Bulgakov famous overnight was his adaptation of his first novel, *Belaia gvardiia* (*The White Guard*), into the play, *The Days of the Turbins*. It inaugurated a "theatrical period" in Bulgakov's career, and there was a moment in 1928 when he had three plays running in three of Moscow's leading theatres, and a fourth in prospect: *Zoikina kvartira* (*Zoya's Apartment*) at the Vakhtangov Theatre, *Bagrovyi ostrov* (*The Crimson Island*) at the Kamernyi Theatre and *The Days of the Turbins* at the Moscow Arts Theatre, with *Beg* (*Flight*) in rehearsal there also. But what had made Bulgakov literally a household name was the concerted ideological campaign mounted against him and all his works after the première of *The Days of the Turbins* in October 1926. By mid-1929 this campaign had achieved its object: the removal of all Bulgakov's plays from the repertoire. Thus publicly declared an ideological pariah and therefore unable to find work, Bulgakov faced destitution. In March 1930 he wrote a letter to the Soviet government describing his plight, declaring his ideological profile, and requesting permission to emigrate. The response to this letter was dramatic: a personal telephone call from Stalin, as a result of which Bulgakov was found employment as assistant director with the Moscow Arts Theatre. Apart from having a hand in the restoration of the play *The Days of the Turbins* to the Moscow Arts Theatre repertoire in 1932, however, Stalin did not extend his protection to any other of Bulgakov's works, nor did he allow the writer to emigrate. None the less this "patronage" from the awesomely powerful leader of the Soviet Union probably served as a kind of "safe conduct" throughout the 1930s, protecting Bulgakov from the arrests and executions that became the common fate.

In his time he was regarded as a dramatist; nowadays his reputation may rest more with his prose works; but Bulgakov himself maintained that he needed both genres "as a pianist needs both hands". The interrelationship between prose and drama runs throughout his work. Having turned his first novel into a play in 1926 he ten years later wrote the novel *Zapiski pokoinika (Teatral'nyi roman)* (translated as *Black Snow*), as a thinly disguised satirical account of this process. In addition to a play about Molière, *Kabala sviatosh: Mol'er* (*A Cabal of Hypocrites*), written in 1929, he wrote a biography of the French playwright, *Zhizn' gospodina de Mol'era* (*The Life of Monsieur de Molière*), in 1933. The theme of crime and atonement can be traced in his work from the early story "Krasnaia korona" ("The Red Crown") (1922), through the play *Flight*, written between 1926 and 1928, to the novel *The Master and Margarita*, written during the period 1928 to 1940.

In the first part of his career Bulgakov's works reflected his experience: as a country doctor; as a participant in the Civil War; and later, in Moscow, as an ironic witness of the pressures and incongruities of the era of the New Economic Policy. From 1927 onward, however, a new theme became dominant in his work, reflecting his experience in his literary career: the theme of the artist in conflict with the official ideology of his day. Bulgakov turned his back on writing for fame in his own time and wrote instead for his writer's archive, for posterity, for immortality. In this "wager on immortality" the figures of Molière and Pushkin, about whom Bulgakov wrote a play *Poslednie dni (Pushkin)* (*The Last Days (Pushkin)*), written in 1935, were important as role models of the true artist.

The reintegration of Bulgakov into Soviet Russian culture took place from the mid-1950s onward, initially with revivals and first productions of his drama, then, from the early 1960s, with the discovery of his prose heritage. The official attitude to his works was toleration rather than enthusiasm. However they achieved cult status among the Russian reading and theatre-going public, a process accelerated by the publications and new opportunities for discussion during glasnost. Today, Bulgakov's characteristic combination of scepticism and faith, irony and lyricism is in tune with the mood of intellectual Russian society, undergoing yet another period of transition and upheaval.

LESLEY MILNE

The White Guard

Belaia gvardiia

Novel, 1927–29 (written 1922–28)

The White Guard was Bulgakov's first novel and, in its stage adaptation, became his first major play under the title *The Days of the Turbins*. The novel was written, in the main, between 1922 and 1924 and the first two-thirds were published in 1925 in Moscow in the journal *Rossiia*. It was not, however, until 1929 that the novel was published in full, in Paris. Between 1925 and 1929 Bulgakov rewrote the two final, hitherto unpublished, chapters. The period of composition must therefore be extended to 1927 or 1928 in order to include this revision of the novel's ending.

The novel is set during the winter of 1918–19, and describes the battle for an unnamed city. This city is Kiev, known in Russian history as "the mother of Russian cities" and "the cradle of Russian literature". The City in *The White Guard* is both a specific place at a given historical moment and also a symbol of European high culture and civilization. Its ordered existence is under threat from the disruptive forces of revolution and Civil War.

The action of *The White Guard* centres on the Turbin household. Aleksei Turbin is a doctor who has returned to the City after service in World War I. His younger brother Nikolka is barely more than a schoolboy. Their sister Elena maintains the domestic rhythms and rituals of the Turbin home, the peace of which is threatened by the war on its threshold. The Turbins' apartment, with its books and music and threadbare comfort, embodies the cultural heritage of the Russian intelligentsia. Aleksei and Nikolka Turbin and their friends join the White Guard and take up arms to defend the City. They are Russians, fighting for the concept of Russian empire against Ukrainian separatists, for whom Kiev is the capital city of an independent Ukraine, and against the Bolshevik regime, newly installed in Moscow. In this battle the White Guard suffers defeat at the hands of the Ukrainian Republicans, but, as the novel ends, the City is about to be entered by a new enemy – the Bolsheviks.

The battle for the City is presented from ground level, from partial perspectives and as separate incidents, thereby evoking the confusion in which history is enacted and human choices have to be made. The last words of *The White Guard*, however, look from the blood-soaked earth to the stars, introducing into human affairs the reducing perspective of eternity.

Given its controversial subject-matter – a sympathetic treatment of the White Guard – the novel caused relatively little stir, although one reason for its muted reception may have been the fact that the 1925 publication was incomplete. The novel had to wait until 1966 for its full publication inside Russia, as part of the discovery of Bulgakov's literary heritage. Then his first novel was recognized as displaying the distinctive combination of ironic humour, poignant lyricism, and satirical scorn that marks the Bulgakov prose voice.

In Bulgakov's lifetime, however, his prose was overshadowed by his drama, and his drama was dominated by one play: *The Days of the Turbins* (sometimes translated and performed in English under the title *The White Guard*). In 1925 the Moscow Arts Theatre was in search of a new, post-revolutionary repertoire, but its particular theatrical style of psychological nuance was ill-suited to sloganizing propaganda. Bulgakov's novel created an artistic world with which the Arts Theatre could identify; it therefore commissioned him to adapt his novel for its stage.

In order to concentrate the dramatic action, Bulgakov conflated several of the novel's characters into one, with the result that the central character of Aleksei Turbin in the play is a colonel in the White Guard who dies during the defence of the city. Once alterations dictated by the transition from prose to drama had been made, further modifications were necessary before the play could pass the theatrical censor. What had attracted little attention as part of a novel in a journal assumed a much higher profile on the stage of a world-renowned theatre. After a flurry of last-minute textual changes, the play opened in October 1926.

The critical reception was ideologically hostile, to the point of becoming a campaign of vituperation against Bulgakov. The play was, however, a huge box-office success. In 1929 the theatre bowed to pressures and removed the production from its repertoire, but was able to restore it in 1932. By this time it was known to enjoy the protection of Stalin, who regarded it as a piece of pro-Bolshevik propaganda no less effective for being unintentional: if even such people as the Turbins are forced to admit defeat, that must mean that the Bolsheviks truly are invincible. Thereafter *The Days of the Turbins* ran at the Arts Theatre until 1941, when its sets were destroyed in a fire. The production became one of the great theatrical legends of the Soviet period. When Bulgakov died in 1940 *The Days of the Turbins* was his only artistic work to have reached a wide audience in his own lifetime. It had, however, only ever been allowed for performance by one theatre, the Moscow Arts.

On the increasingly bleak Soviet stage of the 1930s, Bulgakov's Turbins maintained a link with the cultural past. The Moscow Arts Theatre was traditionally the theatre of the intelligentsia, and the Chekhovian ceremonies of domesticity, symbolized by the Christmas tree in the last act of Bulgakov's play, formed the background to a painful drama of adjustment that corresponded to the experience of its contemporary audience. When the play was revived in 1954 in a production by one of the original cast, it heralded the return of Bulgakov to the Russian stage and re-established the cultural continuity between generations of the intelligentsia. Russian productions post-glasnost, freed from the ideological certainties imposed in the 1920s but also liberated from the nostalgia of the theatrical legend, are turning to the pre-censor texts in order to re-create the play for today's audiences.

LESLEY MILNE

Flight

Beg

Play, 1957 (written 1926–27)

Bulgakov's play *Flight* dates from 1926–27: the period of the author's greatest public success, when his *The Days of the Turbins* and *Zoya's Apartment* were being performed at the Moscow Arts Theatre and the Vakhtangov Theatre respectively, and yet another play, *The Crimson Island*, was shortly to open at the Kamernyi Theatre. Accepted by the Moscow Arts Theatre in January 1928, *Flight* was, however, banned by the censors of the Main Repertory Committee shortly after the beginning of rehearsals in October. Arguments about its production continued until the following year, when all of Bulgakov's plays were taken off. It was rehearsed once more in 1933 in an ultimately unsuccessful attempt to stage a revised version; further revisions, again not resulting in a performance, were made in 1937. The play finally opened 17 years after Bulgakov's death, in Stalingrad in 1957. There was a Leningrad production the following year, but its Moscow premiere had to wait until 1968. Since that time it has been performed frequently both in Russia and abroad; a film version was made in 1970. It was first published in the collection of plays: Mikhail Bulgakov, *P'esy*, Moscow, 1962.

Like other of his works, *Flight* illustrates Bulgakov's basic attachment to the old order, with characters – largely drawn from his own class – who are unable or unwilling to adapt to communism. Indeed, there are no real communist heroes in the play, and the later attempt of a number of Soviet critics to find one in a Red officer, Baev, who appears only in the first scene, was hardly convincing. *Flight* is first of all a historical play, in effect continuing the fate of the "White Guard" – now at the point of collapse during the Civil War – which Bulgakov had portrayed in *The Days of the Turbins*.

Because of changes made each time a performance was envisaged there are a number of different versions of the text. As published today, the play consists of four acts (originally there were five), each divided into two scenes entitled "dreams". Act 1 is set in the Northern Tauride and the Crimea in 1920, during the White Army's withdrawal. The central character is General Roman Khludov, based on the real-life General Slashchov, generally considered unbalanced if not insane. Disgusted with the war and the army leadership, Khludov has become a "jackal" and hangman. Fleeing with him, "under his wing", are the comical Cossack General Charnota with his mistress Lius'ka and two civilians, Golubkov and Serafima. In Act 2, with the war lost, these characters are reduced to living in penury in Constantinople. Consequently, Golubkov and Charnota decide to get money from Serafima's husband Korzukhin, the former assistant minister of commerce, who abandoned her. They find him in Paris, where Lius'ka (who has left earlier) has moved in with him, and Charnota wins from Korzukhin at cards what he has refused to give Golubkov. In the meantime, Khludov, a sick man, is haunted by visions of an orderly that he had hanged. When Charnota and Golubkov return to Contantinople, Khludov finally decides to redeem himself by going back to the Soviet Union, where execution almost certainly awaits him. Serafima and Golubkov, with nothing to fear, decide to go as well, while Charnota prefers to seek his fortune in Paris.

This final version essentially combines improvements made over ten years with the original ending, despite major variants in which Golubkov and Serafima also go to live in Paris and, more importantly, Khludov shoots himself – a version that for Bulgakov had considerable appeal. But a main theme of the play is illness resulting from guilt, and Khludov's decision to face up to his past and expiate his crimes by returning to the Soviet Union is ultimately more satisfactory than the alternative of suicide.

Sympathetic to the White cause as Bulgakov may have been, the characters in *Flight* are far from idealized, and in particular the White Commander-in-Chief (based on Wrangel) and the Archbishop Afrikan, both of whom Khludov hates, are shown as self-serving and hypocritical. Korzukhin, abandoning his wife as a matter of convenience, is the typical avaricious capitalist: at one point he lectures Golubkov on the power of money by launching into a bombastic "ballad of the dollar". The hilarious scene where Charnota fleeces him at cards, all the time dressed in lemon-coloured underpants, is one of the highlights of the play. In fact, Charnota, with his free-wheeling style, his various disguises, and his fascination with cockroach races in Constantinople, provides a comic foil to Khludov. Yet ultimately his fate is tragic, as he is left wandering aimlessly through life. Golubkov (an anagram of Bulgakov's own name) and Serafima – the two honest but ordinary characters caught up in events they are powerless to control – may appear somewhat colourless in comparison.

The play's strength lies above all in its dreamlike atmosphere, emphasized in the titles for each scene as well as by their designation as dreams that dissolve into each other. Stage directions are impressionistic and, with details that are unrealizable on stage, are clearly intended to be read. At times *Flight* borders on the grotesque, as in the second scene: a station waiting-room in the Northern Crimea with its blue electric "moons", green signal lamps, reflections from passing trains and, outside, the bags covering the bodies of men who have been hanged. Constantinople is shown as a strange town with minarets and Turkish music, while its cockroach races dramatize the central metaphor of the play: the fleeing White armies who are like cockroaches scurrying away into a bucket of water.

Arguably his best play, *Flight* demonstrates Bulgakov's gradual development away from the realism of his earlier *The Days of the Turbins* towards a more original and expressive form of theatre.

A. Colin Wright

The Master and Margarita

Master i Margarita

Novel, 1966–67 (written 1928–40)

When *The Master and Margarita* was published in two issues of the journal *Moskva* in 1966 (No. 11) and 1967 (No. 1) it caused a literary sensation among the Russian intelligentsia.

That first publication of *The Master and Margarita* was in a censored form, with many cuts, which rendered the text puzzling in places. The censored sections, however, soon began to circulate in *samizdat*. Of the two English translations that appeared in 1967, the one by Mirra Ginsburg is of this censored version of the novel. The translation by Michael Glenny is of a much fuller text, which Glenny had obtained through personal contacts. Both these translations have been reprinted many times without revision, despite the fact that a full text was published in Moscow in 1973 and therefore has long since been available in Russian. Although the full text contains sections that are not in the Glenny translation of 1967 and it differs from the Glenny text in certain details, the discrepancies between the two do not significantly hamper comprehension. A revised full text was published in Kiev in 1989 and is the one used in the five-volume *Sobranie sochinenii*, published in Moscow in 1989–90. There is now a new American translation of the novel, by Diana Burgin and Katherine Tiernan O'Connor, which is the most complete translation to date. Edited by Ellendea Proffer, the text is a compilation of the Russian published texts of 1973 and 1989.

The problems of establishing a text arise because Bulgakov himself did not prepare the novel for publication, and because he died while still in the process of its revision. Bulgakov's long period of work on *The Master and Margarita* generated many variants, which have been preserved in his archive and that offer a fascinating study of the novel's development. One of the most striking aspects of this process is the constancy of certain elements in the composition: right from the start, in 1928, it contained the story of Jesus and Pontius Pilate as told by a mysterious stranger, who turns out to be the devil. The themes of "the writer" and the love story that gives the novel its title enter the variants in 1931, concurrent with events in Bulgakov's own life. He had by then become aware of himself as a writer definitively and stubbornly out of step with the official ideology of an increasingly totalitarian regime and, in this position of isolated vulnerability, supported by the love, fighting spirit, and artistic faith of the partner who became his third wife. In many ways, *The Master and Margarita* is a book that tells the tale of its own composition. The first manuscript of the novel was burnt by Bulgakov in a fit of despair in 1930 when he perceived himself as having no future as a writer in the Soviet Union. But, in the words of the novel itself, "Manuscripts do not burn." The novel was resurrected – and ultimately published, to become a triumphant vindication of the author's refusal to conform to the officially imposed literary orthodoxies of his day.

The story of *The Master and Margarita* takes place on three planes, each of which provides a commentary on the others. There is a historical narrative set in ancient Jerusalem, where a moral dilemma is dramatized as Pontius Pilate, to save his own career, condemns to death a man whom he knows to be entirely innocent. Pilate's moment of cowardice has been described as one of the "mass sins" of the epoch in which the novel was written. Then there is a contemporary narrative set in Moscow, where the Master and Margarita of the title live and where the Master has written a novel about Pontius Pilate. The third narrative plane is that of the fantastic, introduced by the figure of the devil, who appears in Moscow with a retinue that includes an enormous black cat. The fantastic operates on two levels: it offers an opportunity for satire of contemporary Moscow (in particular the greed and mendacity of its literary and theatrical society); and it creates the possibility of escape into a realm of freedom and poetic justice. The figure of the devil, Woland, is central to both these functions. In this novel, therefore, the devil is not the quintessence of evil but rather an agent for good, a matter of which the reader is warned at the outset by the epigraph. Nor should the reader approach the text with too many fixed ideas about the figure of Jesus, here called Yeshua precisely to avoid any such preconceptions. While the portrayal of Yeshua does not preclude Christian belief, it does not require it, and remains equally accessible to members of the world's other great religions as well as to agnostics of every faith.

Bulgakov's last great novel is a compendium of his characteristic themes and a dazzling display of his different styles, from the austerely laconic to the richly ornamented, and from the grotesquely retributive to the simply compassionate. When *The Master and Margarita* first burst upon the Russian literary scene it brought a sense of liberation akin to revelation. After half a century of official atheism, here was a retelling of one of religion's most haunting narratives. Here too was laughter, as the world of officially propagated values sustained by calculating, or cowardly, conformism was turned upside down. *The Master and Margarita* quickly became a cult novel among the intelligentsia, renewing its popularity with each succeeding generation of readers. By demonstrating the potential of myth and fantasy as narrative devices it had a liberating influence on Russian literature in a period when it was seeking models to renew or replace the officially imposed method of socialist realism. *The Master and Margarita* has now taken its deserved place in the European cultural tradition and has already received its first literary echo outside Russia, having been acknowledged by Salman Rushdie as one of the structural influences on *The Satanic Verses*.

LESLEY MILNE

The Heart of a Dog

Sobach'e serdtse

Short novel, 1969 (written 1925)

The Heart of a Dog is dated January–March 1925. It is a short novel written at the height of the NEP period, at a time when the violence and extremism of the Revolutionary period had receded, and Party ideologues were struggling with the partial re-embourgeoisement of society that had been licensed by Lenin in an attempt to revive the country's ruined economy. Writers of unequivocally middle-class origin, such as Bulgakov, may well have felt that the worst was over and that a reassertion of liberal values might prove acceptable in the new atmosphere of limited compromise. Encouraged, perhaps, by the permission granted in 1924 for the publication of his blatantly satirical "The Fatal Eggs", Bulgakov in *The Heart of a Dog* takes up once again the theme of a professor struggling to contain the consequences of a scientific (and in allegorical terms social) experiment, which goes badly wrong.

The plot relates how a street mongrel, Sharik, is taken in and cared for by a sleek professor. In the opening sections of the text, the dog-narrator marvels at the opulence of his seven-room flat, the ostentation of his table, and the gruesome patients who flock to his surgery to receive transplants of animal organs in the quest for rejuvenation and sexual vigour. Professor Preobrazhenskii, whose very name suggests "transformation" or "transfiguration", has more serious scientific goals in view, however; and he decides to perform an experiment in which he replaces Sharik's testicles and pituitary gland with those of a human corpse. His assistant Bormental's diary then charts the astonishing consequences, as the dog not only survives but rapidly grows, sheds his fur, acquires the power of speech, and turns into a human male with just a few residual dog-like traits, such as a hatred of cats. The new creature develops into a reincarnation of the repellent proletarian whose corpse was used in the operation: he has no manners, no morals, no education, and spends most of his time swearing at the professor. When he comes under the influence of the Housing Committee led by the resentful communist Shvonder, he joins in their class-based attacks on the professor. He also takes on the ludicrous name Poligraf Poligrafovich Sharikov and starts to demand papers. After he denounces the professor to the authorities and draws a revolver on him and Bormental, the incensed scientists perform a reverse operation, so that when the police come to investigate the disappearance of Sharikov, all they find is a dog with a large scar round his skull.

The text is brilliantly comic, with an ingenious plot and complex satire. The shift between narrators from Sharik the dog to Bormental and to an "omniscient" narrator allows for witty observations of people and society from different, sometimes humorously limited, standpoints. The professor's household presents a hyperbolic vision of the bourgeois dream: the servants and obsequious porter, the ceremonious eating of lavish meals, the insistence on good manners, and the all-powerful professor's constant humming of arias from *Aida* and Tchaikovskii's *Don Juan* seem an extension of that vision of the domestic haven Bulgakov describes in the Turbins' household in *The White Guard*. We can sympathize with the professor's distaste for Sharikov's behaviour and some of his outbursts about the irksome social consequences of Bolshevik rule. Bulgakov, who lived in the professor's street and must have shared his outlook in many respects, nevertheless distances himself to some extent. The satire remains ambiguous: the professor's income derives from dubious medical practices justified in the name of research; he has a complacent disregard for the problems of the workers' society around him, and is protected only by the highly-placed Bolsheviks he treats. The scientific operations he performs on Sharik are both described in terms of violence against the defenceless.

The work was offered for publication in 1925, but not accepted; no less a figure than L.B. Kamenev pronounced it entirely unsuitable for publication. Bulgakov signed a contract in March 1926 to adapt it for the stage for the Moscow Arts Theatre, but this had to be cancelled when the manuscript and two typed copies were confiscated in the course of a search of his flat by the OGPU in May of the same year. In the event, thanks to the intercession of Gor'kii and of his wife, the work was returned to him. It remained unpublished until long after Bulgakov's death: western editions came out for the first time in 1968 and 1969, and it was not until 1987 that it was at last published within the Soviet Union. It was an instant success, particularly as stage productions of adaptations of the work were immediately mounted within the USSR and abroad.

This novel must rank as one of Bulgakov's outstanding works: as ever sensitive to dialogue (hence its appealing theatricality), and to the details of everyday life delightfully refracted through the uncomprehending voice of Sharik/Sharikov, its sustained comedy raises serious questions as well. The numbing literalness of the communists is juxtaposed with the critical intelligence of the professor, and the whole is brought to life by the wry knowingness of the dog, who is as sceptical about the proletariat as is the professor. The text has been read as an allegory of the 1917 Revolution, with the great Marxist "scientific" experiment in transforming mankind unmasked as a costly delusion; instead, the author lodges a claim on behalf of natural evolutionary processes if progress is to be achieved (a distinction drawn by Bulgakov explicitly in his letter to the Soviet government of March 1930). But there is also a genuine concern here about medical ethics and the danger of the eugenic experiments that so fascinated the international scientific community during the 1920s. The professor learns that his cavalier interference with the processes of nature will be no more successful than the Bolsheviks' policy of terror in achieving a healthy transformation of Russian society.

J.A.E. CURTIS

Ivan Alekseevich Bunin 1870–1953

Prose writer and poet

Biography

Born in Voronezh, 22 October 1870. Completed four classes at high school; thereafter tutored privately by brother, Iulii. First poem published in 1887. Journalist in Orel, and librarian in Poltava, 1889–95. Liaison with Varvara Pashchenko, 1889–94. Married: 1) Anna Nikolaevna Tsakni in 1898 (separated 1900; divorced 1921), one son (died aged five); 2) Vera Nikolaevna Muromtseva in 1922 (his common-law wife from 1907 and author of invaluable memoirs). Was poor and homeless, living almost entirely in temporary accommodation in various towns and cities, including Kharkov, Moscow, St Petersburg, and Odessa, 1889–1920. Left Moscow for the Ukraine, 1918; worked in Odessa on Volunteer Army's newspaper. With Vera Nikolaevna boarded a French refugee ship, January 1920; ultimately reached Paris, March 1920. Lived in France, mostly in Grasse (Maritime Alps), with brief visits to Britain, Italy, and Estonia. Recipient: Pushkin Prize, 1903, and 1909 (jointly with Aleksandr Kuprin); Nobel Prize, 1933. Elected to the Academy of Sciences, 1909. Died in Paris, 8 November 1953. Rehabilitated in his homeland, 1955.

Publications

Collected Editions

Sobranie sochinenii, 6 vols. Petrograd, 1915.
The Gentleman from San Francisco and Other Stories, translated by D.H. Lawrence, S.S. Koteliansky, and Leonard Woolf. London, Hogarth Press, 1922; reprinted, with an introduction by William Sansom, London, Chatto and Windus, 1975.
The Dreams of Chang and Other Stories, translated by Bernard G. Guerney. New York, Knopf, 1923; reprinted as *Fifteen Tales*, London, Martin Secker, 1924; 2nd edition, 1935.
Sobranie sochinenii, 12 vols. Berlin, 1934–39.
The Elaghin Affair and Other Stories, translated by Bernard G. Guerney. New York, Knopf, 1935.
Dark Avenues and Other Stories, translated by Richard Hare. London, John Lehmann, 1949.
Sobranie sochinenii, 5 vols. Moscow, 1956.
Sobranie sochinenii, 9 vols. Moscow, 1965–67.
Stories and Poems, translated by Olga Shartse and Irina Zheleznova. Moscow, Progress, 1979; reprinted as *Light Breathing and Other Stories*, Moscow, Raduga, 1988.
Sochineniia, 3 vols. Moscow, 1982–84.
In a Far Distant Land: Selected Stories, translated by Robert Bowie. Ann Arbor, Hermitage, 1983.
Long Ago, translated by David Richards and Sophie Lund. London, Angel, 1984; reprinted as *The Gentleman from San Francisco and Other Stories*, Harmondsworth, Penguin, 1987.
Stikhotvoreniia i perevody [Poetry and Translations]. 1985.
Sobranie sochinenii, 6 vols. Moscow, 1987.
Sobranie sochinenii, 4 vols. Moscow, 1988.
Wolves and Other Love Stories, translated by Mark C. Scott. Santa Barbara, California, Capra Press, 1989.
Sobraine sochinenii, 6 vols. Moscow, 1997.

Fiction

Derevnia. Moscow, 1910; translated as *The Village*, by Isabel F. Hapgood, London, Martin Secker, 1923; reprinted 1933; also translated by Olga Shartse, in *Stories and Poems*, 1979.
Sukhodol [Dry Valley]. Moscow, 1912.
Chasha zhizni: rasskazy, 1913–1914gg. [The Cup of Life]. Moscow, 1915; Moscow, 1983.
"Grammatika liubvi" [A Grammar of Love]. Moscow, 1915; translated as "The Primer of Love", by David Richards and Sophie Lund, in *Long Ago*, 1984.
"Gospodin iz San-Frantsisko", in *Gospodin iz San-Frantsisko: proizvedeniia, 1915–1916gg.*, Moscow, 1916; translated as "The Gentleman from San Francisco", by D.H. Lawrence *et al.*, in *The Gentleman from San Francisco and Other Stories*, 1922; and in *The Gentleman from San Francisco and Other Stories*, by Bernard G. Guerney, New York, Knopf, 1923, and numerous subsequent reprints.
Mitina liubov' [Mitia's Love]. Paris, 1925; Leningrad, 1926.
Zhizn' Arsen'eva. Paris, 1930–39; complete edition, New York, Izdatel'stvo imeni Chekhova, 1952; translated in part as *The Well of Days*, by Gleb Struve and Hamish Miles, London,

Leonard and Virginia Woolf, 1933; New York, Knopf, 1934; reprinted as *The Life of Arsen'ev*, edited by Andrew Baruch Wachtel, Evanston, Illinois, Northwestern University Press, 1994.
Temnye allei. New York, 1943; Paris, La Presse Française et Etrangère, 1946; translated as "Dark Avenues", by Richard Hare, in *Dark Avenues and Other Stories*, 1949; and as *Shadowed Paths*, by Olga Shartse, Moscow, Progress, 1958.
Rasskazy/Selected Stories, edited by Peter Henry. Letchworth, Bradda, 1962; revised edition London, Bristol Classical Press, 1993.
Kholodnaia vesna [Cold Spring]. Moscow, 1986.
Povesti i rasskazy [Short Stories and Stories]. Moscow, 1990.
Solnechnyi udar [Sunstroke]. Moscow, 1992.

Poetry
Listopad [The Fall of the Leaves]. Moscow, 1901; reprinted Moscow, 1982.
Stikhotvoreniia. Leningrad, 1956.
Stikhotvoreniia. Rasskazy [Poetry. Stories]. Moscow, 1986.

Essays, Memoirs, and Letters
Okaiannye dni [The Cursed Days]. Berlin, 1935; reprinted as commemorative edition (20 years after Bunin's death), London, Izdatel'stvo Zaria, 1973.
Vospominaniia [Memoirs]. Paris, 1950.
Ustami Buninykh. Dnevniki Ivana Alekseevicha i Very Nikolaevny Buninykh [From the Lips of the Bunins], edited by M. Grin, 3 vols. Frankfurt, Posev, 1977–82.
Pis'ma Buninykh k khudozhnitse T. Loginovoi-Murav'evoi (1936–1961) [Letters from the Bunins to the Artist T. Loginovoi-Murav'evoi (1936–1961)]. Moscow, 1982.

Biography
O Chekhove [About Chekhov] (unfinished). New York, 1955.

Critical Studies
"The Art of Ivan Bunin", by Renato Poggioli, in his *The Phoenix and the Spider*, Cambridge, Massachusetts, Harvard University Press, 1957, 131–57.
Zhizn' Bunina. 1870–1906. Besedy s pamiat'iu, by V.N. Muromtseva-Bunina, Paris, n.p., 1958; reprinted Moscow, 1989.
"Ivan Bunin", by K.G. Paustovskii, in *Tarusskie stranitsy*, Kaluga, 1961, 28–34; translated in *Pages from Tarusa. New Voices in Russian Writing* [various translators], edited by Andrew Field, London, Chapman and Hall, 1964, 330–46.
The Works of Ivan Bunin, by Serge Kryzytski, The Hague, Mouton, 1971.
"The Evolution of Bunin's Narrative Technique", by James B. Woodward, *Scando-Slavica*, 16/4 (1971), 383–96.
"Memory and Time Past: A Theme in the Works of Ivan Bunin", by D.J. Richards, *Forum for Modern Language Studies*, 7/2 (1971), 158–69.
O Bunine. Stat'i i zametki o literature, by A. Tvardovskii, Moscow, 1972.
Buninskii sbornik, edited by A.I. Gavrilov *et al.*, Orel, 1974.
"Comprehending the Beauty of the World: Bunin's Philosophy of Travel", by D.J. Richards, *Slavonic and East European Review*, 52/129 (1974), 514–32.
"V mire liriko-filosofskoi prozy Bunina", by V.Ia. Grechnev, in his *Russkii rasskaz kontsa XIX–nachala XX veka (problematika i poetika zhanra)*, Leningrad, 1979, 44–100.
"Bunin, Ivan Alekseevich", by Serge Kryzytski, in *The Modern Encyclopedia of Russian and Soviet Literature*, edited by Harry B. Weber, Gulf Breeze, Florida, Academic International Press, 1979, 171–82.
Ivan Bunin: A Study of His Fiction, by James B. Woodward, Chapel Hill, University of North Carolina Press, 1980.
Ivan Bunin, by Julian W. Connolly, Boston, Twayne, 1982.
"Sud'ba Bunina", by L. Dolgopolov, in his *Na rubezhe vekov. O russkoi literature kontsa XIX–nachala XX veka*, Leningrad, 1985, 261–318.
I.A. Bunin: zhizn' i tvorchestvo, by O. Mikhailov, Tula, 1987.
Kholodnaia osen'. Ivan Bunin v emigratsii 1920–1953, by V. Lavrov, Moscow, 1989.
Mir i chelovek v tvorchestve L. Tolstogo i I. Bunina, by V. Linkov, Moscow, 1989.
Ivan Alekseevich Bunin. Zhizn' i tvorchestvo, by L. Smirnova, Moscow, 1991.
"Introduction", by Peter Henry, in *Rasskazy/Selected Stories*, London, Bristol Classical Press, 1993, vii–xx.
Ivan Bunin. Russian Requiem, 1885–1920. A Portrait from Letters, Diaries, and Fiction, edited by Thomas Gaiton Marullo, Chicago, Ivan R. Dee, 1993.
Ivan Bunin, by Iurii Mal'tsev, Moscow and Frankfurt, Posev, 1994.
Ivan Bunin: From the Other Shore, 1920–1933. A Portrait from Letters, Diaries, and Fiction, edited by Thomas Gaiton Marullo, Chicago, Ivan R. Dee, 1995.
"Writing the Road to the Russian Émigré Identity: Temporal Framing, Autobiography and Myth in Bunin's *The Life of Arsenev*", by Stephen C. Hutchings, *Essays in Poetics*, 22 (1997), 89–138.
The Narratology of the Autobiography: An Analysis of the Literary Devices Employed in Ivan Bunin's "The Life of Arsen'ev", by Alexander F. Zweers, New York, Peter Lang, 1997.

Bibliography
"Ivan Bunin in English, 1916–83: A Checklist", by Leland Fetzer, *Russian Literature Triquarterly*, 20 (1988), 223–32.

Ivan Alekseevich Bunin, prose writer and poet, was the first Russian to be awarded the Nobel Prize for literature. He was born into an impoverished gentry family of ancient lineage; his ancestors include the poets Anna Bunina and Vasilii Zhukovskii. His formative years were spent on the family's farmsteads in Orel Province, Central Russia, lovingly recreated in the autobiographical novel *Zhizn' Arsen'eva* (*The Life of Arsen'ev*); they provide the setting and themes of numerous poems and prose works. The Bunins' economic situation deteriorated rapidly, and he completed only four grades at high school, whereafter he was tutored by his eldest brother Iulii.

Aged 19, Bunin began an itinerant existence. He found employment in Orel, on the newpaper *Orlovskii vestnik* that published a collection of his poems in 1891. Between 1892 and 1894 stories and poems appeared in "thick" periodicals – *Russkoe bogatstvo*, *Severnyi vestnik* and *Vestnik Evropy* – and he became acknowledged in the literary worlds of St Petersburg and Moscow. In 1902 he joined the Znanie group of "democratic" writers, headed by Maksim Gor'kii; he and Gor'kii repeatedly declared their friendship and admiration for each other's writings. To the consternation of the democrats, Bunin accepted his election, in 1909, to the Imperial Academy of Sciences. Thereafter his friendship with Gor'kii cooled, ending in open hostility in the 1920s.

Bunin's first important collection of poems was *Listopad* [The Fall of the Leaves], which, with his excellent translation of Longfellow's *Song of Hiawatha* (1896), won him the Pushkin Prize in 1903. His poetry, sometimes described as Parnassian, is in the tradition of Maikov, Fet, and Polonskii. Blok rated his nature poetry highly; Briusov conceded that "although [Bunin] is not a Symbolist, he is a genuine poet" (1906).

His first major prose work, *Derevnia* (*The Village*), a grimly realistic portrayal of the deteriorating rural world, aroused much interest and controversy. The semi-autobiographical short novel *Sukhodol* [Dry Valley] is a nostalgic record of the decline and annihilation of the family home. Here and elsewhere in his rural prose Bunin portrays a richly varied, but gravely flawed world, with a lament for its passing. His rural stories include "Nochnoi razgovor" ("A Conversation at Night"), which echoes Turgenev's "Bezhin lug" ("Bezhin Meadow"), "Khoroshaia zhizn'" ("A Goodly Life"), about a ruthless and selfish peasant woman, and "Ioann Rydalets" ("Ioann the Weeper"), Ioann being a "Fool in Christ". The central characters in "Zakhar Vorob'ev" and "Kniaz' vo kniaz'iakh" ("A Prince Among Princes") are respectively a doomed peasant-*bogatyr'* and a prosperous, but repulsive kulak. Here Bunin demonstrated the virtual identity of the lives and mentality of the middle gentry and the peasants. He saw rural Russia as the real Russia, and the peasant as the soul of the Russian people.

Between 1900 and 1916 he made several trips abroad, visiting Europe, the Mediterranean countries, the Middle East, and the Far East. The places he visited, notably Constantinople, Egypt, Arabia and Ceylon, inspired a number of poems, stories and travel sketches. Stories like "Roza Ierikhona" ("The Rose of Jericho") and "Skarabei" ("Scarabs") reflect a growing interest in eastern thought and religions. Elsewhere he deals with Eurasian and colonial themes, not always successfully. While on Capri in 1915, Bunin began his internationally celebrated story "Gospodin iz San-Frantsisko" ("The Gentleman from San Francisco").

Bunin saw the revolutions of 1917 as the unleashing of monstrous forces that threatened to destroy his country. In 1920 he emigrated to France. He adopted an unswervingly anti-Bolshevik stand, expressed notably in his diary for 1918–20, *Okaiannye dni* [The Cursed Days]. In *Vospominaniia* (*Memoirs*), he wrote vitriolic denunciations of Bolshevism and the "traitors" of Russian literature.

A tragic, not pessimistic, perception underlies his writings, his major preoccupations being the drama of life and its tragic and mysterious core. The major motifs of his prose and poetry are nature in its infinite variety, the seasons, rural Russia, human destiny, love, passion, and death. Much of his poetry is contemplative, his lyrical hero being generally an adult or ageing person looking back on youth, a vanished golden age. He wrote on love and sex without sentimentalizing or sensationalizing them. "Grammatika liubvi" ("The Primer of Love"), an intriguing, potentially sentimental tale, is sharply deromanticized at its climax. In "Legkoe dykhanie" ("Light Breathing"), the seduction and murder of a beautiful, vivacious schoolgirl is told with remarkable artistic economy, arranged like a musical composition and ending in a pantheistic image. "Solnechnyi udar" ("Sunstroke"), an unsensational adulterous tale, has a harder edge than Chekhov's "Dama s sobachkoi" ("The Lady with the Dog"). "Temnye allei" ("Dark Avenues") relates the unexpected encounter of former lovers: it closes with neither of them regretting the end of the affair, relieved that it cannot be revived. The middle-aged lovers in "V Parizhe" ("In Paris") are a waitress and a former general in the White Army. The prosaic style of the narrative intensifies the pathos of their situation. These and other stories exemplify Bunin's distancing treatment of emotional and lyrical themes.

Bunin wrote some of his finest works in emigration, like the novels *Mitina liubov'* [Mitia's Love], a compelling study of an intense youthful love that culminates in suicide, and *Delo korneta Elagina* (*The Elaghin Affair*), based on a *crime passionnel*. In France he also wrote *The Life of Arsen'ev*, his technique of recall here being comparable to that of Marcel Proust.

Throughout his long life, Bunin was true to himself and stood by his artistic convictions, unaffected by current trends or events. An isolated figure by choice, he could claim that "I belonged to no literary school, calling myself neither a Decadent nor a Symbolist, neither a Romantic nor a Realist. I donned no false mask and waved no gaudily tinted banner" ("Avtobiograficheskii ocherk" [Autobiographical Sketch], 1934). He fostered a precise and loving treatment of language, tended to think in images, possessed phenomenal descriptive powers and conveyed atmosphere and the passage of time with remarkable verbal economy. Like Chekhov, Bunin made a unique contribution to the novella genre, both insisting that "brevity is the sister of talent". But his prose is more concentrated, "harder", than Chekhov's. Obsessed with achieving the irreducible verbal minimum, he revised his writings frequently, on each occasion shortening the text. Some of his stories are less than a page long; many of them are basically plotless, lyrical monologues.

While his themes, language, and style are firmly in the classical realist mode, with some modernist-decadent ingredients, Bunin created an evocative, richly textured, "pitiless" idiom. His language is a poet's prose, often emotionally charged, never extravagant, often lyrical, rarely sentimental. His poetics is "magical realism" (Edmond Jaloux). Marina Tsvetaeva described him as "the end of an epoch". He is the last of the Russian classics.

PETER HENRY

The Village

Derevnia

Novel, 1910

The Village is set in central Russia during the first Russian Revolution (1904–05). The related meanings of *derevnia* – village, country(side) – indicate the two levels of this work. For Bunin, peasant Russia is the real Russia. One of the characters says: "Russia, all Russia is just a village – and don't you ever forget that!". Bunin argues that the lives and mentality of the Russian gentry are the same as those of the peasants, and much simpler and more typically Russian than depicted by Tolstoi and Turgenev. Demolishing traditional notions of the stoic, God-bearing Russian peasant, Bunin portrays him "frankly, without adornment". Yet he is the embodiment of "the Russian soul ... its peculiar complexity, its depths, both bright and dark, though almost invariably tragic" (Foreword to the English translation, 1923).

Bunin subtitled his densely written, but effectively static novel a *poema* (epic, major work). It is "a large fresco, a diptych, picturing Russian village life during the first Revolution" (Gleb Struve). The two central characters are the brothers Tikhon and Kuz'ma Krasov, based distantly on Bunin's brother Evgenii and the author. Part One centres on Tikhon, a tough and prosperous kulak and inn-keeper, rich enough to buy the Durnovo estate. In Parts Two and Three the brothers are brought together and Kuz'ma's travels in southern Russia and the Ukraine are related. The novel ends inconclusively with a village wedding, suggesting that Bunin had difficulties in finishing his novel.

Bunin creates a grim cumulative record of an alienated rural community caught in a downward spiral of decay, spiritual, social, and economic. It goes well beyond Chekhov's in "V ovrage" ("In the Ravine") and "Muzhiki" ("Peasants"). Tales of squalor, brutality, superstition, depravity and ignorance abound, sometimes presented in stark naturalistic detail. Unlike his 19th-century predecessors, Bunin treats sex frankly and bluntly. Two major images dominate the narrative: grinding poverty that scars the whole of provincial Russia and, related to it, "the power of the soil". Bunin argues, through Kuz'ma, that the crux of the problem is the Russian peasant's inveterate inertia and incapacity for organized action. He saw no way out of the deepening crisis: Village Russia was poised to erupt in anarchy and bloodshed, followed by some unimaginable nightmarish future. The physical destruction of the Russian peasantry in the 1930s proved that his forebodings were prophetic.

The large cast of characters includes ramified family networks, local persons, and various travellers from beyond the stagnant world of Durnovka. Some characters are identified by name, others have impersonal names – Molodaia (The Young One), Odnodvorka (Smallholder), Chuchen' (Scarecrow), Slepoi (The Blind One), and Seryi (Grey). The rest are dispossessed peasants, wanderers, artisans, domestics and seasonal workers, night watchmen, saddle-makers, drovers, all of whom have a story to tell and are described in detail. In Gogolian style, there are journeys and visits to cemeteries and fairs. Thus a powerful record of the rapidly deteriorating rural situation is built up; it is deepened in Tikhon's and Kuz'ma's thoughts and soliloquies and in childhood memories. This endows *The Village* with its stupendous encyclopedic density and the status of an invaluable "human document" (V. Vorovskii).

Bunin's contempt for rebellion and revolution comes out in his satirical portrayals of the rural rebel Komar (Mosquito) and of Deniska Seryi (Grey), the migrant revolutionary. Deniska purveys cheap novelettes and revolutionary tracts and speaks about the "role of the protelariat" [*sic*]. The local gentry and their estates are barely mentioned, beyond reports of estates being burned down. The once-hallowed village commune (*mir*) is mentioned once. The religious dimension is marginal. There are passing references to the Russo-Japanese War and the Treaty of Portsmouth, the Constitution and land reform; names of leading politicians are bandied about. But political events are presented as largely irrelevant for peasant Russia, and in successive redactions Bunin systematically pared down the political dimension still further.

Kuz'ma differs markedly from Tikhon. He is a truth-seeker, drawn to Tolstoianism, a tramp and self-taught poet, writing short pieces for local newspapers, and is variously a huckster, drover, candle-vendor, saddler, and broker. In a somewhat contrived discussion on Russian literature, the peasant "free-thinker" Balashkin expounds to Kuz'ma the tragedy of Russia's writers. His pronouncement "Your Karataev has been eaten up by lice", referring to Tolstoi's stoic peasant-philosopher – is another reminder that Russia's rural world has fundamentally changed.

A major theme is sterility, symbolizing perhaps the eclipse of the Russian peasantry, and therefore of Russia. Tikhon is denied descendants – his first wife acccidentally suffocated their baby girl; his second gave birth to stillborn daughters, a pilgrimage to Zadonsk was to no avail. Molodaia, a married woman and distant model of the Feminine Ideal, whom he takes as his mistress, also fails to provide him with offspring. The matrimonial situation, revolving around Molodaia, is altogether dark, complex, and sordid. Having been Tikhon's mistress, she becomes his brother's cook. At the end of the novel she marries Deniska, an arrangement designed by Tikhon against Kuz'ma's wishes.

The outstanding feature of this, "one of the sternest, darkest, and bitterest books in Russian literature" (D.S. Mirsky), is its "pitiless" language, its immediacy and strong physicality. Much of the text is written in dialogue form – often this is oral narrative disguised as conversation – and the characters speak in the regional vernacular or in semi-literate Russian. Sometimes words and phrases are given in their phonetic dialect form, snatches of folk songs and occasional flashes of humour and folk etymology (e.g., "Vitia" is Count S. Witte). There are stark images of death and a wealth of descriptive detail, sometimes taken to excess. A group of *muzhiks* is described as: "red-haired, grey, dark, all equally ugly, gaunt, and dishevelled". Kuz'ma's driver is "a young man, enormous, stout, wearing bast shoes and white puttees, a short cloth jacket girded with some trimming, a peaked cap on his straight, yellow hair. He smelled of a chimneyless hut and hemp – a ploughman in days of yore! – his face was white, without a moustache, his throat swollen, his voice husky". Symbols and images are concrete and unsophisticated. The novel's pervasive colour is grey (*seryi*), Durnovka (from *durnoi*, evil, ugly) is "Eviltown". An express train passing at night, trailing loose braids of smoke, is seen as a flying witch; an old woman has the face of a lioness.

After the publication of *The Village* Bunin was hailed in democratic circles as the leading authority on the rural scene. Gor'kii wrote that "before it, nobody had dealt with the village so profoundly, so historically", but also commented on the novel's density: "... there's too much material ... Three or four objects crammed into every sentence, every page a museum!" E. Koltonovskaia described it in 1914 as a "terrifying" and "wonderful" book. Vorovskii regarded this portrayal of the old Russian village as "arch-real", but criticized the omission from it of new, energetic forces, the emergent rural bourgeoisie. Bunin saw it as his first major prose work; André Gide considered it his masterpiece.

The remarkable artistic power and unrelenting pressure, physical and emotional, of *The Village*, its numerous secondary characters, the rising ferment of a teeming subworld, strong images of nature and the premonitions of a tragic future make this the outstanding prose work of pre-war 20th-century Russian literature.

PETER HENRY

The Gentleman from San Francisco

Gospodin iz San-Frantsisko

Short story, 1916

"Gospodin iz San-Frantsisko" ("The Gentleman from San Francisco") is probably Bunin's best-known short story. Highly praised at the time of publication, it is paradoxically rather untypical of Bunin's prose as a whole, in that it is set in Italy with a non-Russian as its central character. In the years immediately preceding the outbreak of World War I, Bunin and his wife made several extended trips to Europe – and they were well acquainted with the Isle of Capri, where they visited Maksim Gor'kii. "The Gentleman from San Francisco" was written in 1915, in the shadow of war and a recollection of a vanished world. This may account for its particularly bleak, doom-laden atmosphere. It is also an extraordinarily dense work – historical and cultural allusions, together with rich and complex imagery are crammed into a mere 20 pages.

The story opens with the nameless Gentleman and his wife and daughter on a cruise-liner taking them from the New World for an extended and long-awaited trip to the Old. A wealthy factory-owner, the Gentleman has resolved to leave drudgery behind and start "living". The routine of work is exchanged for the routine of pleasure that the shipping company offers. Yet, the very name of the cruise-liner – "Atlantis" – hints at the prospect of disaster ahead. The liner's cocooned, meticulously-programmed luxury is set against the unpredictable primitive force of the surrounding elements. Despite the storm and the cold, nothing must interfere with the relentless pursuit of pleasure, which the author depicts in the finest detail. But the "Atlantis" is a hollow, ephemeral microcosm, typified by the dancing couple, paid to impersonate honeymooners and by the fateful roar of the engines in the hold ("the ninth circle of hell"). Through the eyes of the Gentleman, this whole edifice appears to exist for his gratification alone – his wife and daughter may find it intimidating, but foreigners and seasickness hold no terrors for him.

As the storm-tossed passengers disembark at the Isle of Capri, Bunin has a little in-joke, describing some scruffy, Russian intellectuals disembarking, presumably on their way to visit Gor'kii. But if the Russians are not worthy of notice, the Gentleman is greeted by a reception party and the whole town, it seems, is enlivened by his arrival.

However, even at the moment of his triumphant arrival, the sense of impending doom is never far away. The Gentleman is surprised to find the obsequious hotel-proprietor somehow familiar – has he not dreamt of him the night before? Yet when he tells this, jokingly, to his family, his timid, unattractive daughter suddenly experiences "grief and a terrible loneliness". There follows the long, ritualistic preparation for the evening meal. The gentleman dresses for dinner, as "though for his coronation", yet even as he prepares to go forth, like a high priest to a pagan ceremony, the shadow passes over again, and he says to himself twice, without knowing why, "This is awful ..." The reader might pick up these clues, and also the fact that the Gentleman is constricted and uncomfortable in his evening dress as evidence that all is not well, yet when the moment comes it is still profoundly shocking. In the reading-room, as he awaits his family, the Gentleman has a fatal seizure and collapses in front of a "grey-haired German, looking like Ibsen" – another curious and unexplained touch.

From this moment, the whole tone of the story changes. The death, as the author points out with bitter irony, is an embarrassment, an unpleasantness that must be got out of the way by the hotel staff as quickly as possible. And so, within a quarter of an hour, the dying Gentleman is lying on a plain bed in a bare room to where he has been moved to avoid upsetting the guests. His final humiliation comes when, in the absence of a coffin, his body is placed in a crate used for soda-water bottles. Thus Bunin demonstrates how death turns the tables. The Gentleman can no longer command respect, or demand service – even his grieving wife and daughter are denied the luxuries they have taken for granted. Yet there is a note of compassion and reconciliation to be heard. As the family from San Francisco board the boat to return home, we are reminded of the history of Capri and the tyrant Tiberius who can still strike fear in the heart. But that is not the whole story of the island, for it remains a place of beauty, of calm and ancient tradition, and the last glimpse of Capri shows two mountain-dwellers stopping to give thanks at a shrine to the Virgin Mary as they climb to a summit in the morning sunshine. And we wish this peace and reconciliation to reach the body of the Gentleman who in his life experienced "much humiliation and human indifference" – a strange epitaph, surely, to the once mighty magnate of the New World.

The first version of the story appears to have ended on this note. However, a few months later, Bunin added a conclusion that gives a rather different slant. We return to the "Atlantis", now sailing west to the Straits of Gibraltar in another terrible storm. More compressed and nightmarish are the same descriptions of the enclosed world of the ship, with its same tenuous opulence, presided over by the captain in the guise of a heathen god. The Devil sits on the Rock of Gibraltar, as the "Atlantis" approaches and the final scene develops into a titanic struggle between the mighty vessel and the raging elements. The passengers continue their *danse macabre*, oblivious to the storm outside and to the "thing" in the hold (a hint, perhaps of an "undead" lying in a soda-water box, not yet at peace). The outcome of the struggle is uncertain, but the final lines do seem to suggest that, unlike its namesake, the "Atlantis" will not go down. This symbol of the New World may yet be capable of "overcoming the gloom, the ocean and the storm."

MICHAEL FALCHIKOV

The Life of Arsen'ev

Zhizn' Arsen'eva

Novel, 1952 (written 1930–39)

The Life of Arsen'ev was the crowning achievement of Bunin's illustrious career, and it is one of the most significant explorations of the émigré experience in Russian literature. Although Bunin had completed all the pieces of the novel by 1933, he did not publish the final text until 1952. Formally, the work is a pseudo-autobiographical "portrait of the artist as a young man". Writing in France in the 1920s, the narrator Aleksei Arsen'ev, describes, in lyrical and evocative prose, his life in pre-revolutionary Russia from the doubly distanced position caused by unrecoverable time and unbridgeable space. Arsen'ev was the youngest son of a financially-ruined gentry family. Through his retrospective narration, we see him develop from his earliest days on the family estate, to his school years in a Russian provincial city, and into his early youth as a writer struggling to find his voice in the Russia of Alexander III.

Bunin's novel is the culminating work of a specific tradition of Russian writing: the pseudo-autobiographical novel devoted to childhood. Earlier examples include Tolstoi's *Detstvo* (*Childhood*), 1852; *Otrochestvo* (*Boyhood*), 1854; *Iunost'* (*Youth*), 1857; and Aksakov's *Detskie gody Bagrova-vnuka* (*Childhood Years of Bagrov Grandson*), 1858. All the traditional characteristics of the Russian pseudo-autobiography – idealization of life on a country estate, bittersweet nostalgia for lost time and space, an idealized mother figure, an eccentric father and the sensitive central figure of the experiencing child – are present and receive an unprecedentedly satisfying treatment in *The Life of Arsen'ev*.

Bunin built consciously on the work of those who had come before him. But the circumstances of post-revolutionary emigration lent Bunin's nostalgia a depth that was rarely possible for 19th-century writers. For Tolstoi, Aksakov and their gentry followers, nostalgia was primarily for lost time. The innocence of youth was gone, but the basic surroundings (even if threatened by change) remained. Bunin was fated to experience an irrevocable displacement in space as well; not only was youth spent, but the Russia he had known, along with its characteristic social structures, had been destroyed. What is more, the great line of Russian gentry culture had been severed by the social upheavals that accompanied the revolution. Bunin felt himself to be the last of his race, the end of a historical line, and this feeling is strongly expressed in his novel.

While, in many respects, Arsen'ev's life parallels Bunin's own, it would be a mistake to consider *The Life of Arsen'ev* an autobiography. The facts of Bunin's life make up only one of the novel's subtexts, just as Arsen'ev's personal story constitutes only one part of the narrative. Far more significant is Arsen'ev's/Bunin's quest to show the interplay of the personal with the literary and historical worlds of his youth and thereby to rescue them from oblivion.

The problem of origins is one of Arsen'ev's central concerns; the narrator wishes to pierce the veil of personal consciousness, to describe the world before he was born. Arsen'ev constitutes his "pre-natal" world through an exploration of his historical and cultural roots. He is always fascinated by things seemingly lost that have nevertheless left a trace in the present: frescoes depicting saints on a monastery gate, a barrow, oral legends. Anything that leaves a record has, in effect, cheated death and prolonged the forces of life in the world. The saints, for example, have done so both through their painted presence on the gates (which implies the work of an unknown human artist) and through the parchments they hold, through the written word: the very medium Arsen'ev himself has chosen to cheat death and decay, thereby imparting immortality both to himself, his former way of life, and to the whole human race.

Throughout the novel Arsen'ev strives to orientate himself in the flow of historical time. In addition to personal memory and to history, however, there is another, parallel, although not synchronized, process in which he must find a place. Arsen'ev is a professional writer who measures his perceptions and his writing against the achievements of Russian literature; his autobiography becomes an extended dialogue with the Russian literary past. Indeed, Arsen'ev creates entire chapters of his novel through a series of poetic quotations accompanied by short explanatory commentaries.

For Arsen'ev, both history and literature, important as they are in and of themselves, are particularly crucial because they represent the poeticization of loss, death, and destruction. Ultimately, the themes of death and decay and Arsen'ev's growing ability to come to terms with them, primarily through the act of writing, become the central concern of the novel.

In adapting the pseudo-autobiography to the new literary and social conditions prevailing in exile after the revolution, Bunin was an archaist and an innovator simultaneously. In matters of style he is unquestionably an archaist: many of his sentences could easily have come directly from Tolstoi or Turgenev. The family structures and childhood situation he depicts are similar to those that Aksakov and Tolstoi had described. Nevertheless, there is much that is new in Bunin's work. He makes his central character a professional writer. This fits with the general modernist trend to produce "a portrait of an artist", helps to motivate the existence of the text, and allows the narrator to weave large portions of his text around other works of literature. Equally importantly, Bunin weaves the historical situation of his narrator into the text in subtle and complicated ways. Arsen'ev feels his connection to real events in the real world very strongly. Bunin felt a need to explain not just himself, but the revolution, and this necessity (which directs the novel away from the more personal orientation of its precursors) is reflected in Arsen'ev's constant concern with the historical situation.

In the final analysis, Bunin's novel represents an extraordinary balancing act: although it speaks almost exclusively of death, destruction, and decay, the vitality of the prose, the vividness of the descriptions, and the narrator's fervent belief that his work can both preserve himself and his former world combine to form a novel that is simultaneously encomium and eulogy.

ANDREW BARUCH WACHTEL

Anna Petrovna Bunina 1774–1829

Poet and prose writer

Biography

Born in Urusovo, Riazan province, 18 January 1774. Mother died in childbirth. Brought up by various relatives; received only rudimentary education. Began writing at about the age of 13. First publication, 1799, under the pseudonym -a -a (also used pseudonyms -a -a -a and A. B-na). Moved to St Petersburg, 1802; set up independent home, employed private tutors to acquire advanced education. Unlike most writers of the period, devoted herself entirely to writing. Supported herself by combination of patronage, subscriptions, and sales. Awarded pensions by members of imperial family, 1809, 1810, 1813. Member of Derzhavin-Shishkov circle, 1807–10. Honorary member of Colloquium of Admirers of Russian Writing, 1811. Visited Britain 1815–17 for (unsuccessful) treatment of breast cancer. Honorary member of the Free Society of Lovers of Russian Literature, 1820. Left St Petersburg on account of illness, 1824; lived with relative but maintained financial independence. Died in Denisovka, Riazan province, 16 December 1829. Buried at Urusovo.

Publications

Collected Edition

Sobranie stikhotvorenii, 3 vols. St Petersburg, 1819–21.

Poetry

Neopytnaia muza Anny Buninoi [The Inexperienced Muse]. St Petersburg, 1809.

O schastii, didakticheskoe stikhotvorenie iz 4-kh pesen [On Happiness]. St Petersburg, 1810.

Neopytnaia muza [The Inexperienced Muse], part 2. St Petersburg, 1812.

Pesn' Aleksandru Velikomu, pobediteliu Napoleona i vosstanoviteliu tsarstva [Song to Aleksandr the Great, Conqueror of Napoleon and Saviour of the Kingdom]. St Petersburg, 1816.

Poems in *Russkie poetessy XIX veka*. Moscow, 1979.

Poems in *Tsaritsy muz*, edited by V. Uchenova. Moscow, 1989.

Poems translated by Sibelan Forrester, in *An Anthology of Russian Women's Writing, 1777–1992*, edited by Catriona Kelly. Oxford, Oxford University Press, 1994, 3–11.

Fiction

Sel'skie vechera [Country Evenings]. St Petersburg, 1811; reprinted in part as *Spasenie Fiv, geroicheskaia povest'* [The Salvation of Fiv, a Heroic Tale]. St Petersburg, 1811.

Essay

"Liubov'" [Love], *Ippokrena*, 86/4 (1799), 113–19 .

Autobiography

"Otryvki iz zaveshchaniia Anny Petrovny Buninoi" [Extracts from the Will of Anna Petrovna Bunina], *Damskii zhurnal*, 2 (1831), 23–24.

Literary Theory

Pravila poezii, sokrashchenno-perevedennye iz abbata Batte, s prisovokupleniem rossiiskogo stoposlozheniia [The Rules of Poetry, Abridged and Translated from Abbot Batte ...]. St Petersburg, 1808.

Translator

"Agar' v pustyne" [Agar in the Desert], *Syn otechestva*, 40 (1817), 170–85.

Nravstvennye i filosoficheskie besedy. Iz sochinenii Doktora Blera [Sermons of Hugh Blair]. Moscow, 1829.

Critical Studies

Iz istorii zhenskoi lichnosti v Rossii. Lektsii i stat'i, by E.N. Shchepkina, St Petersburg, 1914, 206–24.

A History of Russian Literature of the Romantic Period, by William Edward Brown, Ann Arbor, Ardis, 1986, vol. 1, 302–06.

Terrible Perfection: Women and Russian Literature, by Barbara Heldt, Bloomington, Indiana University Press, 1987, 108–10.

Il silenzio delle albe. Donne e Scrittura nell'Ottocento russo, by Giovanna Spendel, Turin, Tirennia Stampatori, 1993, 1–32.

"Anna Petrovna Bunina", in *Dictionary of Russian Women Writers*, edited by Marina Ledkovsky, Charlotte Rosenthal, and Mary Zirin, Westport, Connecticut, Greenwood Press, 1994, 107–11.

"Anna Bunina's 'Unchaste Relationship with the Muses': Patronage, the Market and the Woman Writer in Early Nineteenth-Century Russia", by Wendy Rosslyn, *Slavonic and East European Review*, 74/2 (1996), 223–42.

"Conflicts Over Gender and Status in Early Nineteenth-Century Russian Literature: The Case of Anna Bunina and Her Poem *Padenie Faetona*", by Wendy Rosslyn, in *Gender and Russian Literature: New Perspectives*, edited by Rosalind Marsh, Cambridge and New York, Cambridge University Press, 1996, 55–74.

Anna Bunina (1774–1829) and the Origins of Women's Poetry in Russia, by Wendy Rosslyn, Lampeter, Wales, Edwin Mellen Press, 1997.

Anna Bunina was one of the first Russian women to publish books of poems, and one of the first Russian writers of either sex to live by the pen. She was born into an affluent noble family, but became motherless at birth and lived in the families of various relatives, with the result that her education was almost entirely neglected. However, she displayed a talent for writing verse that was encouraged by another relative, B.K. Blank, and by P.I. Shalikov, both derivative Sentimentalist poets. Her first publication was an essay on love, calling on women to exercise reason to control passion, and implicitly disputing Rousseau's principle of the complementarity of the sexes. In 1802 at the age of 28 she came into a legacy that enabled her to move to St Petersburg, set up home independently of her family, and acquire a systematic higher education from private tutors. She went into debt on this account, and earned her living thereafter by a combination of patronage, sales, and subscriptions. Her first and most stalwart patron was A.S. Shishkov, whose literary circle she joined in about 1807.

Bunina's first book, published in 1808, is a manual of poetics for the use of young women that attracted the patronage of the Dowager Empress Maria Fedorovna. Her second was a collection of poems, *Neopytnaia muza* [The Inexperienced Muse], only the fourth book of poems to be published in Russia by a woman. In this work, Bunina rejects the Sentimentalist image of the woman as companion, mother, and moral exemplar, and writes in romantic vein of women's desires, passionate and literary. Several poems discuss allegorically the gender implications of writing, and the anxiety felt by the woman writer on entering the literary arena. In this collection Bunina creates a poetic persona that is as individual and specific as that of Derzhavin. The book was well received in some quarters, but success made Bunina the object of satirical attacks from Batiushkov, in the course of his polemics with Shishkov's circle, and from 1810 onwards Bunina was regularly targeted by Karamzin's sympathizers, and later by Arzamas, as a representative of archaism. This was not inappropriate inasmuch as some of her patriotic poems were in the tradition of the solemn ode and used complex syntax and abundant Slavonicisms. But her best poems were either the poetic equivalent of lively and witty conversation, or lyrics elegantly structured as variations on a verbal, syntactic and/or rhythmic theme (not unlike Tsvetaeva's), and these were conveniently ignored by her critics. Her next work, *O schastii* [On Happiness], is a long didactic poem, derivative, but appreciated for its conservative philosophy.

In 1811 Bunina became an honorary member of the Colloquium of Admirers of Russian Writing, of which Shishkov was President, along with Anna Volkova and the doyenne poet Ekaterina Urusova. To one of its readings she contributed under the name of Mr Anonymous (*Neizvestnyi*) a mock epic *Padenie Faetona* [The Fall of Phaethon], which at the time was probably interpreted as a critique of Alexander I's liberalism, though it can also be read as an allegory of the woman who has high aspirations but is cast down on account of the threat she poses to social stability. The poem was read successfully by Krylov and published in the society's journal with substantial cuts and alterations. Angered by this treatment, Bunina published the original version in her second book of poems, then going to press. She also recorded in her album her view that meekness was to the detriment of women, since male competitors took advantage of it. This caused a temporary rift with Shishkov.

Bunina's second collection of poems, entitled *Neopytnaia muza*, part 2, both articulates desires for freedom and self-realization and voices apprehension about becoming enslaved to these romantic strivings, commending the virtues of submissiveness and modesty. It also reflects on the situation of the woman writer in literary life, comparing her to a Chinese woman with bound feet who nevertheless competes in races. Bunina was also aware that in order to achieve recognition as a writer a woman must write for a male audience, and that on this account, and because of her aspirations and education, the woman writer was alienated from most of her own sex. However, the subscription list for her *Sobranie stikhotvorenii* [Collected Poems] suggests that as time passed her women readers became more numerous.

From about 1812 Bunina suffered from incurable breast cancer and wrote relatively few poems. The major work of her last years was a translation of 19 of Hugh Blair's sermons commissioned by Elisaveta Alekseevna, the consort of Alexander I. Bunina worked on it in spite of great pain, combated pettifogging censors, and saw it through the difficulties of production from her deathbed. Even in her last years she maintained her financial independence (though her medical needs left her in poverty) and refused to become a burden on her relatives: she was nursed by a niece who thus repaid a debt of gratitude for Bunina's earlier patronage.

Bunina's literary reputation went into decline as a result of criticism from Arzamas and Pushkin, who focused on her weakest poems and satirized her as a bluestocking and an archaist in the course of their attacks on Shishkov. Belinskii dismissed her work without having read it, and compared it unfavourably to Gan's, ignorant that the feminist awareness he approved of in the latter's work was to be found to a much greater degree in Bunina's writing. Bunina was largely forgotten, except by feminist historians and by various members of her family who were critics or writers, until the 1970s, when some of her poems were republished and translated into English. Her reassessment as an original poet who was one of the first in Russia to express a specifically feminine consciousness, long before the campaign for women's emancipation began in Russia, is now under way, principally in the west.

WENDY ROSSLYN

C

Anton Pavlovich Chekhov 1860–1904

Dramatist and short-story writer

Biography

Born in Taganrog, 29 January 1860. Attended a school for Greek boys, Taganrog, 1867–68; Taganrog grammar school, 1868–79; Moscow University Medical School, 1879–84. Practised medicine in Moscow, 1884–92; worked in Melikhovo, 1892–99, and in Yalta from 1899. Wrote for humorous magazines while still in medical school; began to publish in St Petersburg daily papers, *Peterburgskaia gazeta*, from 1885, and *Novoe vremia*, from 1886. Travelled across Siberia to Sakhalin Island, where he undertook a study of social and economic conditions, 1890; published the results of his research as *Ostrov Sakhalin* (*The Island: A Journey to Sakhalin*), 1895. Suffered from tuberculosis; forced to live as a semi-invalid after a severe haemorrhage of the lungs, 1897. Recipient: Pushkin Prize, 1888. Member of the Imperial Academy of Sciences, 1900 (resigned 1902). Married: the actress, Ol'ga Knipper in 1901. Died in Badenweiler, Germany, 15 July 1904.

Publications

Collected Editions

Tales, translated by Constance Garnett, 13 vols. London, Chatto and Windus, and New York, Macmillan, 1916–22.

Polnoe sobranie sochinenii i pisem [Complete Works and Letters], 20 vols. Moscow, 1944–51.

Plays, translated by Elisaveta Fen. Harmondsworth, Penguin, 1959.

Lady with Lapdog and Other Stories, translated by David Magarshack. Harmondsworth, Penguin, 1964.

The Oxford Chekhov, edited and translated by Ronald Hingley, 9 vols. London, Oxford University Press, 1964–80; excerpted in "The World's Classics", Oxford, Oxford University Press, as *Seven Stories*, 1974; *Eleven Stories*, 1975; *Five Major Plays*, 1977; *The Russian Master and Other Stories*, 1984; *Ward Number Six and Other Stories*, 1988; *A Woman's Kingdom and Other Stories*, 1989; *The Princess and Other Stories*, 1990; *The Steppe and Other Stories*, 1991; *Twelve Plays*, 1992.

Polnoe sobranie sochinenii i pisem, 30 vols. Moscow, 1974–83.

Plays, edited and translated by Eugene K. Bristow. New York, Norton, 1977.

The Kiss and Other Stories, translated by Ronald Wilks. Harmondsworth, Penguin, 1982.

Plays, translated by Michael Frayn. London and New York, Methuen, 1982; revised editions, 1988, 1993.

The Early Stories 1883–1888, edited and translated by Patrick Miles and Harvey Pitcher. London, John Murray, 1982; London, Abacus, 1984; Oxford, Oxford University Press, 1994.

The Duel and Other Stories, translated by Ronald Wilks. Harmondsworth, Penguin, 1984.

The Party and Other Stories, translated by Ronald Wilks. Harmondsworth, Penguin, 1985.

The Fiancée and Other Stories, translated by Ronald Wilks. Harmondsworth, Penguin, 1986.

The Chekhov Omnibus: Selected Stories, translated by Constance Garnett, revised and edited by Donald Rayfield. London, Everyman, 1994.

Chekhov's Major Plays: Ivanov, Uncle Vanya, and The Three Sisters, translated by Karl Kramer and Margaret Booker. Lanham, Maryland, University Press of America, 1996.

The Plays of Anton Chekhov, translated by Paul Schmidt. New York, HarperCollins, 1997.

Fiction (selected)

"Drama na okhote" [Drama on a Hunt]. 1884–85; translated as *The Shooting Party*, by A.E. Chamot, edited by Julian Symons, London, André Deutsch, 1986.

"Step'". 1888; translated as "The Steppe".

"Skuchnaia istoriia". 1889; translated as "A Dreary Story"; also as "A Boring Story"; and as "A Tedious Story".

"Duel'". 1891; translated as "The Duel".

"Poprygun'ia". 1892; translated as "The Grasshopper".

"Palata No. 6". 1892; translated as "Ward Six".

"Chernyi monakh". 1894; translated as "The Black Monk".

"Student". 1894; translated as "The Student".

"Moia zhizn'". 1896; translated as "My Life".

"Dom s mezonimom". 1896; translated as "The House with the Mezzanine".

"Muzhiki". 1897; translated as "Peasants".

"Kryzhovnik". 1898; translated as "Gooseberries".

"Ionych". 1898.

"Chelovek v futliare". 1898; translated as "Man in a Case"; also as "Man in a Suitcase"; and as "Man in a Box".

"Dama s sobachkoi". 1899; translated as "The Lady with a Lapdog"; also as "The Lady with a Dog"; "The Lady with a Little Dog"; "Lady with Lapdog" and as "The Lady with the Dog".

"Dushechka". 1899; translated as "The Darling".

"Arkhierei". 1902; translated as "The Bishop".
"Nevesta". 1903; translated as "The Fiancée"; also as "The Bride".

Plays
"O vrede tabaka", 1886; translated as "On the Harmfulness of Tobacco"; also as "Smoking is Bad for You"; and as "On the Injurious Effects of Tobacco".
Ivanov. 1887; revised edition, 1889; translated as "Ivanov".
"Lebedinaia pesnia". 1888; translated as "Swan Song".
"Medved'". 1888; translated as "The Bear"; also as "The Boor"; and as "The Brute".
"Predlozhenie". 1889; translated as "The Proposal"; also as "A Marriage Proposal".
"Svad'ba". 1889; translated as "The Wedding".
Leshii. 1889; translated as "The Wood Demon".
"Tragik ponevole". 1890; translated as "The Reluctant Tragedian"; also as "A Tragedian in Spite of Himself"; and as "A Tragic Role".
"Iubilei". 1892; translated as "The Anniversary"; also as "A Jubilee"; and as "The Celebration".
Chaika. 1896; translated as *The Seagull*.
Diadia Vania. 1897; translated as *Uncle Vanya* and *Uncle Vania*.
Tri sestry. 1901; translated as *Three Sisters*.
Vishnevyi sad. 1904; translated as *The Cherry Orchard*.
Neizdannaia p'esa, edited by N.F. Bel'chikov, 1923; translated as *That Worthless Fellow Platonov*; also as *Platonov*; *Don Juan (in the Russian Manner)*; and as *Wild Honey*.
"Tat'iana Repina", in *Polnoe sobranie sochinenii i pisem*, 1944–51; translated as *Tatyana Repin*.
"Na bol'shoi doroge", in *Polnoe sobranie sochinenii i pisem*, 1944–55; translated as "On the Highway"; also as "On the High Road".

Letters
The Selected Letters of Anton Chekhov, translated by Sidonie K. Lederer, edited by Lillian Hellman. New York, Farrar Straus, and London, Hamish Hamilton, 1955; reprinted London, Picador, 1984.
Letters of Anton Chekhov, edited by Avrahm Yarmolinsky. New York, Viking Press, 1973.
Letters of Anton Chekhov, translated by Michael Henry Heim, edited by Simon Karlinsky. New York, Harper and Row, and London, Bodley Head, 1973; as *Anton Chekhov's Life and Thought: Selected Letters and Commentary*, Berkeley, University of California Press, 1975; reprinted Evanston, Illinois, Northwestern University Press, 1997.
Anton Chekhov: A Life in Letters, translated and edited by Gordon McVay. London, Folio Society, 1994.
Dear Writer ... Dear Actress ...: The Love letters of Olga Knipper and Anton Chekhov, edited and translated by Jean Benedetti. London, Methuen, 1996.

Travel Writing
Ostrov Sakhalin. 1895; translated as *The Island: A Journey to Sakhalin*, by Luba and Michael Terpak, Washington, DC, Washington Square Press, 1967; reprinted London, Century, 1987; also translated as *A Journey to Sakhalin*, by Brian Reeve, Cambridge, Ian Faulkner, 1993.

Critical Studies
Anton Chehov: A Critical Study, by William Gerhardie, London, Duckworth, and New York, Duffield, 1923; revised edition, London, Macdonald, 1974.
Chekhov: A Life, by David Magarshack, London, Faber, 1952; Westport, Connecticut, Greenwood Press, 1970.
Anton Chekhov, by Walter Horace Bruford, New Haven, Yale University Press, and London, Bowes and Bowes, 1957.
Chekhov: A Biography, by Ernest J. Simmons, Boston, Little Brown, 1962; London, Jonathan Cape, 1963.
The Breaking String: The Plays of Anton Chekhov, by Maurice Valency, New York, Oxford University Press, 1966.
Chekhov and His Prose, by Thomas Winner, New York, Holt Rinehart and Winston, 1966.
Chekhov: A Collection of Critical Essays, edited by Robert Louis Jackson, Englewood Cliffs, New Jersey, Prentice-Hall, 1967.
Chekhov in Performance: A Commentary on the Major Plays, by J.L. Styan, Cambridge, Cambridge University Press, 1971.
The Real Chekhov: An Introduction to Chekhov's Last Plays, by David Magarshack, London, Allen and Unwin, 1972; New York, Barnes and Noble, 1973.
The Chekhov Play: A New Interpretation, by Harvey Pitcher, London, Chatto and Windus, 1973; Berkeley, University of California Press, 1985.
Chekhov: The Evolution of His Art, by Donald Rayfield, London, Paul Elek, and New York, Barnes and Noble, 1975.
A New Life of Anton Chekhov, by Ronald Hingley, London, Oxford University Press, and New York, Knopf, 1976.
Chekhov as a Master of Story-Writing: Essays in Modern Soviet Literary Criticism, edited by Leo Hulanicki and David Savignac, The Hague, Mouton, 1976.
Chekhov's Art of Writing: A Collection of Critical Essays, edited by Paul Debreczeny and Thomas Eekman, Columbus, Ohio, Slavica, 1977.
Chekhov: A Study of the Major Stories and Plays, by Beverly Hahn, Cambridge, Cambridge University Press, 1977.
On the Theory of Descriptive Poetics: Anton Chekhov as Story-Teller and Playwright, by Jan van der Eng *et al.*, New York, Humanities Press, 1978.
Chekhov: A Structuralist Study, by John Tulloch, London, Macmillan, and Totowa, New Jersey, Barnes and Noble, 1980.
Chekhov's Great Plays: A Critical Anthology, edited by Jean-Pierre Barricelli, New York, New York University Press, 1981.
Chekhov: The Critical Heritage, edited by Victor Emeljanow, London, Routledge and Kegan Paul, 1981.
Anton Chekhov, by Irina Kirk, Boston, Twayne, 1981.
Chekhov and the Vaudeville: A Study of Chekhov's One-Act Plays, by Vera Gottlieb, Cambridge, Cambridge University Press, 1982.
Chekhov's Art: A Stylistic Analysis, by Peter M. Bitsilli, translated by Toby W. Clyman and Edwina Jannie Cruise, Ann Arbor, Ardis, 1983.
Chekhov's Poetics, by Aleksandr Pavlovich Chudakov, translated by Edwina Jannie Cruise and Donald Dragt, Ann Arbor, Ardis, 1983.
Chekhov: A Study of the Four Major Plays, by Richard Peace, New Haven, Yale University Press, 1983.

Chekhov: New Perspectives, edited by René Wellek and Nonna D. Wellek, Englewood Cliffs, New Jersey, Prentice-Hall, 1984.

A Chekhov Companion, edited by Toby W. Clyman, Westport, Connecticut, Greenwood Press, 1985.

A Handbook to Eighty-Six of Chekhov's Stories in Russian, by Edgar H. Lehrman, Columbus, Ohio, Slavica, 1985.

Anton Chekhov, by Laurence Senelick, London, Macmillan, and New York, Grove Press, 1985.

Chekhov (biography) by Henri Troyat, translated by Michael Henry Heim, New York, Dutton, 1986; London, Macmillan, 1987.

File on Chekhov, by Nick Worrall, London and New York, Methuen, 1986.

Chekhov and Women: Women in the Life and Work of Chekhov, by Carolina de Maegd-Soëp, Columbus, Ohio, Slavica, 1987.

Chekhov on the British Stage, 1909–1987: An Essay in Cultural Exchange, by Patrick Miles, Cambridge, Sam and Sam, 1987.

Critical Essays on Anton Chekhov, edited by Thomas A. Eekman, Boston, G.K. Hall, 1989.

Reading Chekhov's Text, edited by Robert Louis Jackson, Evanston, Illinois, Northwestern University Press, 1993.

Chekhov on the British Stage, edited and translated by Patrick Miles, Cambridge and New York, Cambridge University Press, 1993.

"The Cherry Orchard": Catastrophe and Comedy, by Donald Rayfield, New York, Twayne, 1994.

Chekhov's "Three Sisters", by Gordon McVay, London, Bristol Classical Press, 1995.

Chekhov's "Uncle Vania" and "The Wood Demon", by Donald Rayfield, London, Bristol Classical Press, 1995.

Chekhov's Plays: An Opening into Eternity, by Richard Gilman, New Haven, Yale University Press, 1996.

Anton Chekhov: A Life, by Donald Rayfield, London, HarperCollins, 1997.

Chekhov Then and Now: The Reception of Chekhov in World Culture, edited by J. Douglas Clayton, New York, Peter Lang, 1997.

The Chekhov Theatre: A Century of the Plays in Performance, by Laurence Senelick, Cambridge, Cambridge University Press, 1997.

Chekhov and Russian Religious Culture: The Poetics of the Marian Paradigm, by Julie W. de Sherbinin, Evanston, Illinois, Northwestern University Press, 1997.

A Systems Approach to Literature: Mythopoetics of Chekhov's Four Major Plays, by Vera Zubarev, Westport, Connecticut, Greenwood Press, 1997.

Understanding Chekhov, by Donald Rayfield, London, Bristol Classical Press, 1998.

Bibliographies

Anton Chekhov: A Reference Guide to Literature, by K.A. Lantz, Boston, G.K. Hall, 1985.

Chekhov Bibliography: Works in English by and about Anton Chekhov, by Charles W. Meister, Jefferson, North Carolina and London, McFarland, 1985.

Anton Chekhov Rediscovered: A Collection of New Studies with a Comprehensive Bibliography, edited by Savely Senderovich and Munir Sendich, East Lansing, Michigan, Russian Language Journal, 1987.

Chekhov Criticism: 1880 Through 1986, by Charles W. Meister, Jefferson, North Carolina and London, McFarland, 1989.

Anton Chekhov's art reflects the man – elusive, subtle and understated, humane, modest, and undogmatic. In a land of preachers and partisans, he persistently refused to pontificate, with the result that he was often reviled for "lack of principles" and absence of philosophical or political purpose. Such charges worried him, although his life might serve as a model of positive practical endeavour. Despite his own ill-health, he supported his family, treated peasants for their everyday ailments and at times of famine and cholera, planted trees, built schools, donated books to the Taganrog library, and performed innumerable undemonstrative acts of kindness. Whereas other "great" Russian authors incline to excess, with elements of neurosis and *folie des grandeurs*, Chekhov presents a remarkably unified and balanced personality, devoid of rhetoric and megalomania.

As the son of a grocer and grandson of a serf, his origins were inconspicuous. After a grim childhood, marred by a father who was both petty tyrant and religious fanatic, young Anton early cultivated the qualities of moral self-discipline, emotional and intellectual independence, and responsibility towards his large family. Shortage of money compelled him, while studying medicine at Moscow University, to compose and publish hundreds of comic short stories, often under the pseudonym Antosha Chekhonte. For several years he combined twin professions, as doctor and writer, regarding medicine as his lawful wife and literature as his mistress.

Although Chekhov began his career as a purveyor of carefree bagatelles for the humorous, light-weight journals of Moscow and Petersburg, from late 1885 he found himself fêted by celebrated authors such as Dmitrii Grigorovich, and by the publisher Aleksei Suvorin. He attracted the attention of serious, "thick" journals, publishing his long stories "Step'" ("The Steppe") in 1888 and "Skuchnaia istoriia" ("A Boring Story") in 1889, as well as various collections. Several plays were performed, including popular one-acters such as "Medved'" ("The Bear") and "Predlozhenie" ("The Proposal"), and more complex full-length dramas such as *Ivanov* and *Leshii* (*The Wood Demon*). Chekhov was to nourish a lifelong love-hate feeling for the theatre, and an ardent enthusiasm for the farce-vaudeville.

As his fame increased towards the end of the 1880s, a number of critics (mainly journalists of a utilitarian, socially committed hue) began to assail him for his apparent failure to propound aims, ideals, opinions, and "solutions" in his works. In response to such attacks, between 1888 and 1890 Chekhov gradually formulated his own concept of the dispassionate, objective, non-judgemental author. As a point of principle, he not only disclaimed authorial omniscience and the right or duty to moralize, but actually professed the positive value of disclosing one's own ignorance. He emphasized that the writer's task was to pose a question correctly, but not to offer solutions.

Nevertheless, although Chekhov's scientific training and habitual scepticism inclined him towards non-didactic objectivity, he remained deeply aware of the value of "aims" for an author, and of the aimlessness that he deemed characteristic of himself and the writers of his generation. Furthermore, despite his dispassionate air, Chekhov was never a totally neutral and impartial observer. He selected his material carefully, inviting the readers to act as jury. He aspired to truthfulness, brevity, originality, and sincerity, cultivating "indifference" and "coldness" as a deliberate artistic method, to intensify the emotional effectiveness of his writing. For all his restraint and seeming inscrutability, Chekhov valued culture, civilization, charity, and sensitivity. He was never a proponent of "amoral" art.

In a letter of 4 October 1888 the singularly reticent Chekhov made his most famous pronouncement on truth and freedom:

> I'm not a liberal, or a conservative, or a gradualist, or a monk, or an indifferentist. I should like to be a free artist and that's all ... My holy of holies is the human body, health, intelligence, talent, inspiration, love, and the most absolute freedom imaginable, freedom from violence and lies, no matter what form these may take ...

It was perhaps his veneration of freedom that prompted him, in 1890, to undertake the unexpected and arduous journey across Siberia to Sakhalin, where he conducted a detailed census of some 10,000 convicts and settlers condemned to live out their lives on that Devil's Island.

Chekhov's own life-sentence, as decreed by his tubercle bacilli, was to be a further 14 uncertain years, largely spent with the family on his estate in Melikhovo or at his villa in Yalta. While professing a streak of south Russian indolence, he toiled unremittingly. Though ill-health and fastidiousness reduced the quantity of his output, he achieved after 1890 many of his finest stories, including "Palata No. 6" ("Ward Six"), "Student" ("The Student"), "Dom s mezoninom" ("The House with the Mezzanine"), "Muzhiki" ("Peasants"), "Chelovek v futliare" ("Man in a Case"), "Ionych", "Dama s sobachkoi" ("The Lady with a Dog"), and "Arkhierei" ("The Bishop"). In 1895 his scientific and humanitarian treatise *Ostrov Sakhalin* (*The Island: A Journey to Sakhalin*) eventually appeared in book form.

Painstakingly and unostentatiously, Chekhov illumined everyday, mundane material, to illustrate his perpetual themes – the elusiveness of love, the fragility of marriage, the near-impossibility and even undesirability of personal (and hence selfish) happiness, the pervasiveness of human waste, loneliness, and frustration, the ubiquity of *poshlost'* (vulgar, trite banality), the gulf between aspiration and achievement, the inexorable passage of time, and yet also mankind's indomitable longing for meaning, freedom, the ideal. Chekhov's mature short stories, like his plays, are distinguished by their subtlety of "mood", unobtrusive musicality, and inconclusive conclusions, and by episodes of "epiphany", when the present moment opens unexpectedly into eternity.

His final years were plagued by haemorrhoids, blood-spitting, loneliness, and depression (with a massive lung haemorrhage in 1897), and brightened by his meetings with Lev Tolstoi and Maksim Gor'kii, his association with the Moscow Arts Theatre, and his marriage, in 1901, to the actress Ol'ga Knipper. In his last decade, while increasingly ravaged by tuberculosis, Chekhov composed the great dramatic quartet – *Chaika* (*The Seagull*) – disastrously premiered in St Petersburg in 1896 – *Diadia Vania* (*Uncle Vania*), *Tri sestry* (*Three Sisters*), and *Vishnevyi sad* (*The Cherry Orchard*) – which was scrupulously, if at times over-fussily, staged by Stanislavskii and Nemirovich-Danchenko in 1898–1904 at the Moscow Arts Theatre. These plays, with their "subtext" and "undercurrents", their characteristic blend of triviality and profundity, relevance and irrelevance, laughter and tears, require for performance a selfless ensemble and the most delicate orchestration.

Chekhov's reputation during the past 100 years has fluctuated, but is now firmly established. The essential ambiguity of his tragi-comic art has led some to view him as a wistful, autumnal pessimist, a killer of human hopes, while others perceive him as fundamentally a humorist, ironic, absurdist, or detached. Chekhov combines compassion with irony, freedom from illusion with a yearning for faith, something close to despair with something akin to hope. He helps us to endure. It seems particularly apt that a man who loathed labels triumphantly escapes categorization.

GORDON MCVAY

The Steppe

Step'

Story, 1888

Ever since 1886, when major writers first noticed his talent, Chekhov had been tempted to write a serious, extensive piece. "The Steppe" was written in a little over two months in early 1888. It was inspired by Chekhov's first return to the south, where the idyllic landscapes of his childhood had been, where sheep and horses had grazed the prairie lands and great deciduous forests stood: it was, in the early 1880s, turned into an industrial wasteland by developers such as the Welsh mining engineer Hughes. After a number of short stories with lyrical or mournful evocations of this disappearing paradise, "The Steppe" is the concluding work in a cycle about the south and childhood revisited. The story describes a two-month journey of 700 miles across the Ukraine, a memorial to a wild countryside that was now despoiled. It is one of Chekhov's first "green" pieces, and equally the first work where he subordinates plot to atmospheric evocation. Already he begins to abandon the all-knowing authorial standpoint and lets the story unfold through the uncomprehending but responsive eyes of his main character, here a bewildered boy. In his loneliness, self-sufficiency and receptiveness, Egorushka has undoubtedly some autobiographical traits. Much of the scenery of the story was to haunt Chekhov in his very last works. The sets of encounters, with the rebellious brother of the Jewish landowner, with the drovers, the fractious peasant Dymov, the gruff businessman Varlamov – and, above all, the kindly, worldly priest Khristofor – create not just a gallery of characters who are to be transformed in Chekhov's later stories and plays, they are Chekhov's first composite picture of the Russian ethos, or rather its southern, restless nomadic element. Here he rivals Leskov, whose stories are also (intuitively) a picture of the national collective unconscious. Many of the narrator-author's conclusions have become accepted wisdom, for instance the notion, after the drovers' tales of richer days, that the Russian can only be happy in retrospect and cannot live in the present. Some of the psychological associations typical of Chekhov, e.g., of rebellion with disease, of female malleability and male hardness, are established in this work. The many magnificent set pieces, culminating in the storm in which Egorushka catches a chill, also develop the magical moments of Leskov in which nature reduces human beings to humble, marginal witnesses of incomprehensible processes. The plot abandons many elements – the search for the wool-merchant Varlamov, for instance, peters out. It is open-ended, which leaves the possibility for a sequel and denies the reader any moment of judgement or moralization. Although the narrator seems not to interfere with the child's perception of reality, in effect Chekhov is building up a model of life as a journey through an unknown landscape to a fearful destination that has myth-like implications: Egorushka is as much Everyman as a child, while father Khristofor and later the drover Pantelei are Virgils to his Dante. Although no major suffering is inflicted on the hero, the tales of murder he hears and the brawls and quarrels that flare up suggest the precariousness of human life, the vulnerability of human beings on an unforgiving landscape.

While writing, Chekhov was most preoccupied with "tone", "musicality", "poetry in prose"; for the first time he had set out to rival Pushkin and Gogol', "the king of steppe descriptions"; as a result, "The Steppe" is literally a masterpiece. It is the first work in which he takes no notice of his editors or their readers, and it was the first work he destined for a prestigious literary journal, *Severnyi vestnik*. It is one of the few stories about which Chekhov, despite bouts of dissatisfaction, admitted his own genius: "the material is poetic, and if I don't break off the tone I began in, some of it will come out quite exceptional." It was also the first work fully to satisfy such grand old men of literature as Pleshcheev and Grigorovich, who had lamented the waste of a talent writing for newspapers read one day and discarded the next. It won Chekhov the Pushkin prize and determined his future as a professional writer. Its success can be measured by the fact that the editor of the journal in which it was published asked Chekhov to name his fee; Chekhov even toyed with a sequel where Egorushka would become a 17-year-old suicide case. Even critics who missed a strongly delineated plot or ideology put the work on a level with the best of Dostoevskii and Tolstoi. Tolstoi himself singled it out for the author's success in seeing the world through a child's eyes. E.M. Forster admired it for its "beauty, sense of completeness, imaginative fullness". Professional literary scholars such as Peter Bitsilli regard it as a turning-point in the evolution of a new genre, half-story, half-prose poem, in which the author's lyrical digressions are inseparable from the protagonist's stream-of-consciousness.

The characters of the Jewish innkeeper's rebellious brother and the trouble-making Dymov were seen as the first seeds of radicalism in Chekhov. But more significant is the central role of the kindly, sensitive Father Khristofor, one of several priests in Chekhov's work who, as in the stories of Nikolai Leskov, symbolize the author and artist in their gift for communication, for inspiring trust and for responding to distress. "The Steppe" influenced Chekhov's later work: the combination of cherry blossom and a cemetery in the opening chapter lays the scene for *The Cherry Orchard*, which was to appear 16 years later. It is also instructive to compare "The Steppe" to Katherine Mansfield's masterpiece *Prelude*: they have the same disoriented child's intense impressionistic view of exotic nature and adult distress.

DONALD RAYFIELD

Uncle Vania / The Wood Demon

Diadia Vania / Leshii

Plays, 1889–97

In the summer of 1888 Chekhov planned to write with his publisher, patron and friend, Aleksei Suvorin, a comedy: characters were to be drawn from Suvorin's own family – himself, his young second wife, his children, and French governess – and they were to be mixed with characters based on the Lintvarev family and friends, the Chekhov family's hosts at Sumy in the Ukraine: the river Psiol and its water-mills were to be the setting. The play, *Leshii* (*The Wood Demon*), has as its central character a highly strung ecologist and medic, Khrushchev, with more than a passing resemblance to the author. Suvorin, however, rapidly backed out of the project, and during 1889 it took on darker hues. Its improbable plot, focusing on the suicide of an Uncle Georges, and weddings and reconciliations a few weeks later, reflects the death of Anton's brother Nikolai at Sumy in May 1889 followed by the wedding of his elder brother Aleksandr. The play is full of melodramatic musical references, to Tchaikovskii and Rubinstein; it is crowded (14 speaking parts), and three of the four acts centre on a family meal. The plot line and motivation are obscure. The enthusiasm of Pavel Svobodin, an actor-friend, overcame Chekhov's doubts and his other friends' frank criticism, and it had five disastrous performances in Moscow in December 1889. The faults are glaring: Uncle Georges' suicide – apparently because he is upset by rumours that Elena, the professor's new wife is his mistress – is badly motivated. The misunderstanding that leads to the rumour and the discovery of his diaries that refute it are theatrical clichés unworthy of any good dramatist, while the three conciliations at the picnic in Act 4 are embarrassingly syrupy.

The failure of *The Wood Demon* deterred Chekhov from writing another full-length play until 1895 (*The Seagull*). Why Chekhov retrieved this failure and rejigged it is a matter for conjecture. Periodic demand for *The Wood Demon* to be printed probably led Chekhov to re-write the play as *Diadia Vania* (*Uncle Vania*). When he rewrote it is more certain: it was during August and September 1896, after finishing *The Seagull*, but before its first performance in St Petersburg (17 October 1896) again made him forswear the theatre. Details added to *Uncle Vania* such as the professor wearing galoshes on a hot day, the nurse herding chicks, Astrov going out to a village called Malitskoe, all reflect realia of the summer of 1896 in Chekhov's own life. He drastically cut the number of characters down to eight; he merged the drinking, womanizing Orlovskii with the high-minded Khrushchev to make a very convincingly flawed Dr Astrov, he also got rid of those characters (Orlovskii senior, Zheltukhin etc.) who acted as confidants in *The Wood Demon*, thus leaving an assortment of individuals who have nobody they can communicate with. Chekhov added only the old nurse Marina, whose faith contrasts with the other characters' despair. Act 2 was kept almost intact; much of Act 1 was re-used, but very little of Act 3 and almost nothing of Act 4. Chekhov found in *Uncle Vania* the "new ending" he had been seeking for three years: there is no development, those who arrived in Act 1 depart, leaving the "resident" characters fully aware of their hopeless predicament. Action becomes inconsequential: Uncle Georges kills himself, but Uncle Vania, although he fires point-blank at his brother-in-law the professor, resolves nothing. The setting is moved from the prosperous Ukraine to a desolate central Russia, somewhere on the railway line from Moscow to Kharkov. Everything is concentrated. All the action takes place on the Voinitskii estate, to which the professor returns with his second wife, whereas the action of *The Wood Demon* was spread over three different settings. The imagery becomes grimmer: very little of the water-sprite imagery pervading *The Wood Demon* survives, only the reference to Elena as a *rusalka*, a water-nymph. The musical references are reduced from snatches of operatic arias to Telegin's aimless strumming of the guitar and a piano that the professor does not allow Elena to play. Imminent bankruptcy – the professor's need to dispossess the household – makes a more powerful plot motivation, whereas in *The Wood Demon*, the professor merely proposes to sell a portion of forest to finance his retirement and new marriage. A mass of telling and original detail, for instance Uncle Vania's "dandy" tie, the chirruping cricket, the famous irrelevant remark about the heat in Africa, ousts the clichés of *The Wood Demon*. Although now subtitled "scenes from country life", *Uncle Vania* is still a comedy, only more cruel, as it leads only to disillusion. A device typically used by Chekhov in later years is the inclusion of an act haunted by a character who has recently died, a skeleton in a cupboard that is never opened. This is brought out in relief in the more austere *Uncle Vania*: the professor's first wife, Vera Petrovna and her illness, agony and death cast a pall of guilt, there is also a contrast of lost harmony with present disharmony that is only latent in *The Wood Demon*. The Acts flow, as in *The Seagull*, with no sub-division into scenes. The ecological message, delivered by Dr Astrov to an astounded Elena, is strengthened, and takes *Uncle Vania* back to the original outline agreed with Suvorin.

Uncle Vania was first mentioned as existing in December 1896; it appeared in print as the last in a collection of plays in 1897, and passed unnoticed by critics. It was first performed in the provinces, and only two and a half years later it was produced in Moscow by Nemirovich-Danchenko and Stanislavskii's Moscow Arts Theatre. The Imperial Theatre's Committee had originally demanded changes before it could be performed at the state theatre; these changes were unacceptable to Chekhov. (Two censors, Professors Veselovskii and Storozhenko, were horrified at the disrespect to the professoriat in the treatment of Professor Serebriakov.) Given the modern sympathies of the theatre, Stanislavskii's carefully planned *mise-en-scène* and performance as Astrov, and Ol'ga Knipper's desire to please Chekhov with her Elena, the play had a success with the public as overwhelming as the failure of *The Wood Demon*. The play was not considered for any award, as it was regarded by critics to be merely a revision of *The Wood Demon*. Over subsequent years, however, it became Chekhov's most popular and profitable play, both in Russia and abroad. It has been adapted to Irish and American settings. This combined with the Konchalovskii film version (though void of comedy) and the André Gregory *Uncle Vanya on 42nd Street* (1993) prove its vitality. In Soviet and some other productions, attempts were made to make Sonia's last speeches about rest and diamonds in the sky a prediction of social justice, rather than a desperate improvisation to console the weeping Uncle Vania. Since the 1980s these positive interpretations have vanished. *The Wood Demon*, however, has, as Chekhov wished, almost entirely vanished from the repertoire. (Attempts to revive it, such as the production by Sergei Zhenovach, in Moscow in 1994, have invariably failed.)

DONALD RAYFIELD

A Boring Story

Skuchnaia istoriia

Story, 1889

Published in 1889 and subtitled "From an Old Man's Notebook", *Skuchnaia istoriia* ("A Boring Story") is one of Chekhov's longer short-story masterpieces. It provoked much discussion, due at least in part to the alleged affinities between its central character and narrator, Nikolai Stepanovich, and the author himself. Chekhov, however, scoffed at such claims, although it can be argued that he may have "protested too much". At the time that we are introduced to him, Nikolai Stepanovich is a highly esteemed world-renowned medical scientist and professor who knows at the age of 62 that he is incurably ill and has not long to live. Speaking to us in a voice that often evokes that of a personal journal, he alternately admits to being depressed, irritable, self-pitying, and terrified. Not surprisingly, his sense of imminent mortality also causes him to reassess his life and to engage in the kind of metaphysical self-questioning not uncommonly associated with end-of-life reflections. Although his wife Varia and daughter Liza and also his former ward Katia – a failed actress and "woman with a past" with whom he has a close but perfectly chaste friendship – are sensitive to his changed state, they have their own problems, and are therefore oblivious to the extremity of Nikolai's physical and mental state. Varia and Lisa are preoccupied with Lisa's possibly adventuristic suitor, unsuspiciously named Gnekker, whom Nikolai heartily dislikes and distrusts (with seeming justification), and Katia, who appears to be a more or less chronic depressive, feels abandoned when Nikolai, whom she reveres as a father, cannot provide her with answers to her virtually unanswerable questions (How am I to go on living? What am I to do?).

When the story ends, Nikolai is alone in a hotel in Kharkov (where he has gone to make inquiries about Gnekker, only to find that no one there recognizes his name!), having learned that his daughter and Gnekker have secretly married, and having just said farewell to a disappointed and dispirited Katia (who is upset over his failure to provide her with answers to her "burning questions"). Thus he is left with a feeling of futility and ineffectuality regarding his own efforts, however reluctant and inadequate, to help others, just as he himself is now beyond the help of others in his own dire state. Despite the stark poignancy of the ending, there is also the sense that the depression and loneliness that Nikolai experiences at the end of his life is *situational*: that is, it is related to his realization that his love of science and the scientific method may have given him immense gratification and served his needs during his lifetime, but that it is unable to provide him with much psychological or philosophical comfort *now* that he knows he is dying. It is, therefore, only at the end of his life that he is made aware of the lack of a unifying or guiding principle (namely, faith?) and of the psychic distress that lack has triggered.

There is, however, a kind of stubborn integrity to Nikolai's innate inability to rediscover himself and/or to "see the light" beyond the impinging darkness. He is not, in other words, to be given the kind of death-bed epiphany that is visited on Tolstoi's Ivan Il'ich in *Smert' Ivana Il'icha* (*The Death of Ivan Ilych*), 1986. Nor is he to experience the kind of spontaneous conversion that befalls the scientist-materialist who is the hero of Paul Bourget's popular novel *Le Disciple*, which was being serialized in Russia when Chekhov was writing "A Boring Story" and to which he responded with hostility in his letters to Suvorin (who had been lavish in his praise of the novel in *Novoe vremia*). When we take another look at *The Death of Ivan Ilych*, the work in Russian literature to which it is inevitably compared, what is most striking about the comparison is the consistency with which the Chekhov text seems to counter or oppose that of Tolstoi. To begin with, Nikolai Stepanovich is *not* an ordinary man; he is an acclaimed scientist with an eccentric personality. His consciousness of impending death does not lead him to renounce his former life or to regret his dedication to science. On the contrary, it is just that, as he faces death, he comes to realize that his "belief" in science and the scientific method is not of the kind that gives you strength and comfort in your hour of need. However, there is also the sense that he accepts this fact with dignity, because he is what he is. Moreover, he recognizes that the despondency, depression, and irritability that he experiences now as symptoms of his failing health, do not cause him to devalue the personal and professional gratifications that have been his good fortune during his lifetime.

Although no one would argue for any simple autobiographical link between Chekhov and his character, Nikolai Stepanovich – certainly, the facts of their separate biographies have little in common – they do share a number of *attitudinal* affinities, as any reader of Chekhov's correspondence would be quick to realize. In any event, the ties between the author and his character are clearly intricate and complex and probably account for the extreme touchiness of Chekhov's response to the allegations of kinship between himself and his character (seen particularly in his oft-quoted letter to Suvorin of 17 October 1889). The explanation for this might have partly derived from the specific circumstances of Chekhov's own life when he was writing "A Boring Story". It was written for the most part in the summer of 1889, not long after his brother Nikolai had died of tuberculosis, the disease from which Chekhov was already showing active symptoms and which would claim his life 15 years later. Needless to say, although Chekhov was hardly then facing imminent death himself, he had just experienced the loss of his similarly afflicted brother whose name, in fact, is given to the hero of "A Boring Story". In Chekhov's case he had been a doctor administering to a dying brother, but not actually present at the moment of his death; in the case of Nikolai, the doctor is his own patient, as it were, and the text also ends without witnessing his death. The letters that Chekhov wrote from Yalta, where he was composing the story, attest to the depression and despondency that infected his mood following his brother's death. His letters also suggest that the writing of "A Boring Story" may have served as a kind of cathartic purge, not only of the experiential realities of death and dying (both felt and observed) but also of the negative feelings and emotions that his depression over his brother's death engendered in himself. In his famous letter to Suvorin, Chekhov argued for the symptomatic nature of Nikolai's attitudes and ideas, that is, their organic connectedness to the illness that was killing him. By infecting his character Nikolai with some of the same philosophical and emotional "symptoms" that may have appeared in Chekhov himself after his brother's death, Chekhov seems to be attempting a transfer of effect to cause. Whether catharsis was truly achieved we cannot know, but that a writing act of self-exorcism was performed there can be no doubt. No wonder, then, that Chekhov was so seemingly over-sensitive to allegations of kinship between himself and his professor. The completion of the story was to have ended all that.

KATHERINE TIERNAN O'CONNOR

Ward Six

Palata No. 6

Story, 1892

Published in November 1892, after almost a year's labour, this was the first major story to win Chekhov wide and immediate acclaim. The abuse of psychiatry was a well-established theme in Russian history, with the declaration by Nicholas I in 1836 that the philosopher Chaadaev was mentally ill and must be detained for compulsory treatment. Such material was first developed in a documentary story by Leskov, "Inzhenery-bessrebreniki" [The Unmercenary Engineers], where an officer who refuses to take part in corruption is ostracized, depressed, declared insane and driven to suicide. Chekhov had already broached the theme in "Pripadok" ("An Attack") 1888, in which a student who denounces brothels is prescribed sedatives and those who condone prostitution declared to be normal.

The story is classically simple and symmetrical. The highly-strung Gromov's brushes with authority convince him that anyone can be imprisoned: he develops persecution mania and is incarcerated in a horrific asylum where the indolent Doctor Ragin, though convinced it is pointless to resist suffering, evil and death, is fascinated by Gromov's articulacy. Their relationship attracts attention and the doctor is tricked into becoming a patient in his own ward, where he collapses and dies after being beaten by his own charge-hand. The story can be read as a portrait of a typical provincial hospital, with a fictional symmetry in the revenge that fate exacts on one of the perpetrators of this cruelty. Certainly, Chekhov had been concerned for many years and had carefully read and annotated a monograph on Russia's mental hospitals. His sojourn in 1890 among the convicts and warders of the island of Sakhalin had created the mood and material framework for a study of a closed world in which the guards were as dehumanized as the inmates. But every reader saw the allegorical potential of the work. Leskov is said to have exclaimed: "In 'Ward Six' we have a miniature representation of all our system and characters. Everywhere is Ward Six. This is Russia. Chekhov wasn't thinking what he had written (he told me so), but it still is so. His ward is mother Russia." In his last years Leskov paid tribute to Chekhov's story and returned to the theme in his oddest work, "Zaiachii remiz" [The March Hare], in which a secret policeman finally finds security and death in a psychiatric asylum and is nursed by the radical he persecuted. Even Lenin declared he felt he had been locked in a Ward Six of his own (although his attitude to dissent was not softened).

"Ward Six" begins deceptively as a first-person guided tour of a provincial hospital, its nettles, ramshackle buildings, and its part in the usual Chekhovian town plan (where hospital, prison and bone-factory gather together on the outskirts). It then develops a classical peripeteia, and, in its plot, a unique example in Chekhov's work of a classical tragedy: Dr Ragin shows hubris, suffers the catastrophe of incarceration and undergoes a momentary catharsis (a vision of the deer) before merciful nemesis. No other major work by Chekhov has such a grim plot, otherwise "Ward Six" would be just another argument between a quietist (the inert doctor) and an activist (the manic patient). In Chekhov's preceding major work, "Duel'" ("The Duel"), the plot is also built around the arguments of a Darwinist activist and a Tolstoian quietist: both sides are proven wrong and a third force, intuitive, altruistic, appears to triumph, perhaps naturally, given the sunlit southern landscape of the story. But here, however, in the colder north there is no third force, no cause for hope, only a hideous grey town (the quintessential provincial setting for Chekhov's most pessimistic work), no love interest, virtually no female presence, and both philosophers are punished beyond their deserts for daring to dissent. Stoicism, Tolstoi and Schopenhauer's philosophy all prove hollow self-deception; the story represents Chekhov at his most depressed, and the political interpretation belongs to his readers. The depression evident in Chekhov's letters of the time in which he sees the earth and human life as mere accidents in a dead and meaningless cosmos accords with the mood of "Ward Six". V.S. Pritchett called it "a study of the nightmare of absolute solitude". If there is any consolation at all in the work (for it is hard to believe that Gromov's cries, that truth and justice will prevail, represent what the author feels), it is in the narrator's reflection that Ragin must have known what progress medicine was making abroad and in the references to the progressive treatment of the insane in Vienna's asylums. To this extent the work can be read as a longing for Europe, for an escape from the Asiatic in the Russian state and soul, a longing that Chekhov was to satisfy in the years to come, but which did not result in any imported European liberal humanist solution to the inhuman horror of "Ward Six". Undoubtedly, Schopenhauer provides not just an excuse for Ragin to put up with evil and suffering, but also an authorial framework in which scientific progress could be held to bring just minimal relief to human anguish. "Ward Six" marks the ultimate depth in Chekhov's despondency: never again was he to write a work in which the reader is so deprived of co-ordinates in time and space, of colour, of the female. The only light in the work is the hallucination at the moment of Ragin's death, and afterwards when a green light shines on his corpse.

DONALD RAYFIELD

The Seagull

Chaika

Play, 1896

Chekhov was a reluctant dramatist. Feeling more at ease with the short story than with drama, he once colourfully remarked: "The narrative form is a lawful wife, whereas the dramatic form is a gaudy, loud-mouthed, brazen and tiresome mistress ..." (letter of 15 January 1889).

Accordingly, by 1895, when he composed *The Seagull*, Chekhov was chiefly renowned as a writer of short stories who had occasionally dabbled with the dramatic form. His full-length play *Ivanov* (1887, revised 1889) had caused critical controversy through its non-judgemental depiction of an enigmatic, permanently perplexed hero. Chekhov came to hate his next major play, *The Wood Demon*, while fondly viewing his various one-act vaudevilles, such as "The Bear" and "The Proposal", as lucrative but trivial farces. His first straggling theatrical effort, commonly known as *Platonov* (1878–81?), was not discovered until after his death.

From the outset Chekhov evidently regarded *The Seagull* as an innovatory work. On 21 October 1895 he informed his confidant, Aleksei Suvorin: "I'm writing it not without a certain enjoyment, although I'm offending terribly against the conventions of the stage. It's a comedy, with three female roles, six male, four acts, a landscape (a view of a lake), much talk about literature, little action, and five tons of love ..." A month later, on 21 November 1895, he apprised Suvorin: "Well, I've finished the play. I began it *forte* and ended it *pianissimo* – contrary to all the rules of dramatic art. It's turned out like a story. I'm more dissatisfied with it than satisfied, and reading my new-born play convinces me yet again that I'll never be a dramatist ..."

Like Chekhov's other major plays, *The Seagull* is in many respects a family drama, set against a background of rural torpor. An ageing actress, Irina Arkadina (43), egoistic and mean, foolishly seeks to prolong her youth and her limited glory, while neglecting her son and striving to retain her lover, the well-known writer Boris Trigorin. Meanwhile, Trigorin (under 40) is obsessed with the compulsion to write. As he tires of their liaison, Trigorin transfers his amorous attention to the aspiring young actress, Nina Zarechnaia, who is besotted with his alleged "fame". The main loser is Arkadina's 25-year-old son, Konstantin Treplev, who loves Nina, craves his mother's affection, and dares to challenge the literary and theatrical establishment by advocating "new forms" in art.

These four central characters dominate each act in turn – Konstantin with his play-within-a-play (Act 1), Trigorin when expounding the torments of being a writer (Act 2), Arkadina with her hammy acting, as she manipulates her son and her lover (Act 3), Nina on her distracted return after an absence of two years (Act 4). Apart from these two writers and two actresses, however, the cast is extended by a gallery of non-artists – the blandly satiated Dr Dorn (aged 55); Arkadina's ailing brother Sorin (60), the man who never lived; the impecunious and hence money-obsessed schoolteacher Medvedenko; the vodka-swilling, snuff-sniffing, self-dramatizingly morose Masha (22); her surly, reminiscent father Shamraev; and his Dorn-doting wife Polina. Locked together in the house and garden of Sorin's estate, these ten figures dream and yearn, rage and pine, as the shadows lengthen.

For a supposed "comedy", the main plotline appears distinctly grim. By the end of Act 4 Nina, having lost her baby by Trigorin and been abandoned by him, walks out into the lonely night to face a hazardous future as a provincial actress. At the final curtain Konstantin's suicide is announced. Most of the cast are caught in a chain of unrequited love – Medvedenko pursues Masha who longs for Konstantin who adores Nina who worships Trigorin (who prefers fishing); Arkadina clings to

Trigorin, while Polina sighs for Dorn (who is fully sated). Yet, whereas the anguish of Nina and Konstantin is real, the multitudinous blunderings on love's merry-go-round are meant to be viewed with quizzical detachment.

The play affords considerable ambiguity. Its pervasive (and over-portentous) seagull-symbol may be applied to Nina, Konstantin, or something more abstract, while the artistic talent of both Trigorin and Konstantin is unclear. Nina in Act 4 may be doomed and destroyed, or perhaps she will survive, for she alone approaches the strength and wisdom to endure, when perceiving that one should "bear one's cross and have faith".

The Seagull seems a self-consciously literary work, containing numerous allusions to *Hamlet* and to Maupassant's fiction. Various characters and incidents have a real-life basis (thus, the Nina-Trigorin story echoes the relationship between Lika Mizinova and the writer Ignatii Potapenko; Arkadina may be modelled on an actress such as Lidiia Iavorskaia; a Talezh schoolteacher suggested Medvedenko; the shooting of the seagull parallels Levitan's shooting of a woodcock in 1892). Aspects of Chekhov himself may be reflected in Konstantin's artistic rebelliousness, Trigorin's obsessive note-taking and fishing, and the detachment of Dr Dorn.

Despite Chekhov's aspiration to dramatic innovation, *The Seagull* displays many of the features of more traditional theatre, such as set speeches and confrontations, a clear division between major and minor roles, obtrusive symbolism (the seagull itself), structural artifice (the awkward gap between Acts 3 and 4), and a closing suicide. With its incestuous concentration on two authors and two actresses, *The Seagull* appears more localized than Chekhov's later works (*Uncle Vania*, *Three Sisters*, *The Cherry Orchard*), and hence the weakest item in the great quartet.

Nevertheless, even after a century, *The Seagull* remains perennially alive, since it touches on such universal themes as youth and age, innocence and experience, frustration, love, loneliness, creativity, and misplaced goals. The young desire fame, the famous covet youth, and nearly everyone chases the phantom of love. The play is also enhanced by such typically "Chekhovian" elements as the blending of laughter and grief, a tendency towards ensemble orchestration, and the elusive subtlety of mood and meaning.

Chekhov had once declared: "... A dramatist's life is full of anxiety and doesn't suit my temperament. I'm not cut out for ovations, backstage alarums, successes and failures, for I have a lazy soul that can't stand sharp fluctuations in temperature ..." (letter of 21 February 1889). On 17 October 1896 this "lazy soul" witnessed the disastrous St Petersburg premiere of *The Seagull*. Despite the efforts of Vera Komissarzhevskaia as Nina, the piece was under-rehearsed and unwisely presented to an unsophisticated first-night audience. Although more warmly received on subsequent evenings, it was taken off after only five performances. Chekhov never forgot his humiliation at the Aleksandrinskii Theatre, after which he immediately vowed to abandon for ever the writing of plays. That his "pride was hurt" (letter of 22 October 1896) is hardly surprising, since he was offering the public his first new full-length play since *The Wood Demon* seven years earlier.

The creation of the Moscow Arts Theatre in 1898 was to stimulate a remarkable late flowering of Chekhov the dramatist. On 17 December 1898, in its inaugural season, Vladimir Nemirovich-Danchenko and Konstantin Stanislavskii staged a triumphant revival of *The Seagull*, thereby easing somewhat the pain of the 1896 fiasco. This legendary success became permanently enshrined in the seagull-logo adorning the Arts Theatre's curtains and programmes. Numerous productions throughout the world have confirmed the viability and pathos of the vulnerable, errant Seagull.

GORDON MCVAY

The Lady with the Dog

Dama s sobachkoi

Story, 1899

Written in autumn 1899 and published at the end of the year, "The Lady with the Dog" is Chekhov's only work to use Yalta as a main setting, even though Chekhov had already lived there for a year and was to spend most of the next five years there. Ladies parading along the promenade with a white dog in Yalta or Kislovodsk were not uncommon, however, none of the claimants to be the original needs to be taken seriously.

The initial material for the story stems from the winter of 1897–98, which Chekhov spent in Nice: here his notebooks show the story's fundamental idea – very heretical in a culture of Christian confession, as exemplified by Dostoevskii and Tolstoi – that a human being's real intimate life is a secret to be protected in a civilized society from others' eyes. Various details of the story, the hero's impression that women's underwear is made of fish scales, and the governor's daughter at the opera wearing a boa, also stem from 1897. While in Nice, Chekhov's French improved so much that he was able to read Maupassant in the original. The importance of seascape on the mood of the characters reminds one of Maupassant, particularly *Pierre et Jean*, while the plot outline of an adulterous love in the artificial world of a holiday resort has much in common with *Mont Oriol*. Nietzsche's influence is also clear in "The Lady with the Dog", not only in Gurov's initial contempt for women as "the lower race", but also in the distinctly anti-Christian bias of the morality (implicitly the narrator's as well as the hero's: Gurov's reflections as he watches dawn break with Anna on a mountain top have a Nietzschean setting and turn of phrase, for he reflects how beautiful the universe is except what human beings do and think when they forget higher ideals). In 1896 Chekhov was so infected by the Nietzschean enthusiasm of his colleague Dr Korobov that he asked the latter to translate a passage of Nietzsche for use in fiction.

Undoubtedly, much of the concentrated power of "The Lady with the Dog" comes from its autobiographical input: Chekhov in his first year in Yalta made similar excursions with a variety of pretty and impressionable young women, and yet by mid-1899 was seriously considering monogamy. (Gurov's reflections on his own unhappy marriage as an accumulation of petty irritations augur strangely for an author considering wedlock.) Chekhov, too, as a Muscovite, was as ambivalent as Gurov about the mild, un-Russian Crimean climate. Nevertheless, the story is unusual for Chekhov, in that it involves the conversion of the hero from his contemptuous arrogance to compassionate love. As critics pointed out, Gurov is nevertheless strangely passive: in the opening paragraphs we are told that he was "married off", and his subsequent actions, seducing Anna Sergeevna, then travelling to the provincial hell-hole where she lives to abduct her, are more actions under the influence of casual impressions and circumstances than a series of undertakings.

The story achieves its concentration by a number of devices more usual in Chekhov's plays: e.g., the use of absurd contrasts of mundane and ideal, for instance the remark of Gurov's colleague on hearing his confession, "The sturgeon was gamy", or Gurov's eating melon and ordering tea while Anna weeps. Much is conveyed without dialogue: Anna's Christian submissiveness is rendered by her pose as a Mary Magdalene, by candles and penitent weeping. As in *Three Sisters* so in "The Lady with the Dog" there are references to Sidney Jones's operetta *The Geisha*, a Russian version of which was performed in 1899 in both Moscow and Yalta. It is at a performance of *The Geisha* in a provincial town that Gurov recaptures Anna. Not only is there something geisha-like in Anna's passivity, vulnerability to her seducer and her bondage to the lien (von Diederichs) who is her husband, but phrases from the operetta about "two parrots kept in separate cages" are echoed in Chekhov's comparison of the lovers to parted "male and female migratory birds".

Many elements of Chekhov's earlier stories recur: the grey fence that imprisons Anna in her provincial town is to be found in the townscapes of many Chekhov stories; the very name of S. was used a year earlier in "Ionych" as code for a symbolic hell-hole, whether Serpukhov, Samara or Saratov does not matter. The symbolism of weather, in Gurov's attempt to explain to his daughter why there is no thunder in winter, is the finest of Chekhov's meteorological analogies to human emotional life. Critical reaction to the story was very lively: the abrupt ending left many puzzled, some furious. Unusually for a Chekhov story, the reader is tempted greatly to empathize with the hero's own hopes and to invent a happy outcome, even though we are left in doubt as to whether Gurov has really converted from a Don Juan to a true elective affinity, or whether catching sight of his first grey hairs in the mirror has led him to make the best of what may be his last opportunity. Certainly the story's most disconcerting feature is the narrator and hero talking of new beginnings at the moment when the reader spots the white paper of the end of the story. Readers demanded a continuation or an explanation. Some critics felt that the refusal to continue was the sign that the denouement would be too cruel and tragic to tolerate. Other critics, rightly seeing the story as a counterblast in morality and form to Tolstoi's *Anna Karenina*, condemned "The Lady with the Dog" for condoning adultery. Tolstoi himself felt it was about two Nietzschean animals who had decided they were beyond good and evil: after Chekhov's portrayal a year before of "Dushechka" ("The Darling") as an ideal of feminine loyalty he was horrified at the "amorality" of "The Lady with the Dog".

Many women claimed to be the original lady with the dog; certainly there were many copies. Tourism in Yalta and Oreanda, business at the Japanese shop and at the Moscow hotel, The Slavonic Bazaar, all benefited from the story's notoriety. Later "The Lady with the Dog" generated a fine film by Heifetz and a ballet.

DONALD RAYFIELD

Three Sisters

Tri sestry

Play, 1901

The first totally new play to be written by Chekhov for six years, *Three Sisters* was also the first to be written specifically for the Moscow Arts Theatre. Chekhov announced his intention to write it in November 1899. It was not completed until January 1901, in Nice, and performed, towards the end of the 1900–01 season, on 31 January 1901. When printed in February and April its appearance ended a three-year dearth of Chekhov's plays, removed from the market by the monopoly Chekhov had granted to the publisher Adolf Marx. Chekhov's longest and most complex mature play, *Three Sisters* incorporates material from Chekhov's notebooks, reading, and experiences since the early 1880s. The theme of three sisters is not only commonplace in Russian folklore, but also in literature: the three unfortunate Epanchin sisters of Dostoevskii's *The Idiot* are ancestors of Chekhov's Prozorov sisters. In Chekhov's own life at least five sets of "three sisters", the Goldens, Markovs, Ianovs, Lintvarevs, and Shavrovs, played an important part. The main prompt for the plot is very likely a reading in 1895 of Olga Peterson's biography of the Brontë sisters: the Brontës, three highly cultivated sisters with a talented brother whose failings wreck their hopes, stuck in a remote northern vicarage under the tutelage of a dominating father, bear a striking semblance to the Prozorovs. The plot and several details of Sidney Jones's *The Geisha*, very popular in Moscow in 1899, where three English officers flirt with and then desert three Geishas, very probably influenced *Three Sisters*. After "Potselui" ("The Kiss") and "The Duel", this is the third work of Chekhov's in which the military are contrasted with the civilians. The material stems from the artillery battalion stationed in Voskresensk who befriended the Chekhovs: a Lieutenant Egorov, who became a civilian in order to work, contributes certain traits to Tuzenbakh, while a Lieutenant Schmidt who travelled, in disgrace, with Chekhov across Siberia provided some characteristics for Solenyi. The setting, presumably the town of Perm in the foothills of the Urals, also recalls the inauspicious beginning of Chekhov's Siberian journey. Many minor details were accumulated over the years: the "Tra-ta-ta" code by which Masha and Vershinin conduct their love affair was overheard by Chekhov in 1896; Chebutykin singing "Tarara-boom-dee-ay" when Masha appears develops a motif from "Volodia bol'shoi i Volodia malen'kii" ("Big Volodia and Little Volodia") 1893: by 1900 "Tarara-boom-dee-ay" was not only a louche music-hall song, but a marching tune for an artillery regiment. The play was written not only for the resources and talents of the Moscow Arts Theatre, but with specific actors in view: Masha, the adulterous sister, and perhaps Chekhov's strongest characterization, was written for Ol'ga Knipper, already regarded as Chekhov's fiancée, as well as the theatre's most important actress. Kulygin, the conformist schoolteacher and complacent husband, was written for Vishnevskii, a naive actor who had shared Chekhov's schooldays and knew the teachers Chekhov wanted to caricature.

Three Sisters has features typical of mature Chekhovian drama: it opens in spring and ends in autumn, the main characters are under the sway of a character recently dead (here the father of whom they often speak and the mother whom they rarely mention); time in the form of anniversaries, hours, minutes, is constantly referred to; casual absurd remarks – "Balzac got married in Berdichev", "Smallpox rages in Syktyvkar" – are invested with ominous meaning; a family is dispossessed of its house; two male characters argue out two scenarios, one activist, one quietist, about the beautiful future that will replace the drab present; the new arrivals of Act 1 (the military), after awakening and turning upside down the lives of the residents, then depart, leaving them stranded and fully aware of their hopeless predicament; the action is observed and commented on by a doctor who refuses to treat, let alone sympathize. *Three Sisters*, however, stands apart: not only does it have far more human suffering, and a longer time span (three years), it is far darker (even though Stanislavskii remarked to his sister in 1903 that "Chekhov still thinks his *Three Sisters* is a very funny piece"). Masha's unhappy affair with Vershinin, Natasha's systematic dispossession of her sisters-in-law and enslavement of her husband, the persecution, ending in murder by duel, of Tuzenbakh by Solenyi, and Chebutykin heartlessly presiding over all this suffering precluded even Chekhov from subtitling the play a "comedy". The symbolism of the play, with the fire that rages through the town and the breaking of the clock (a common motif in Chekhov's life, full of ruined timepieces), is darkened by the elaborate musical counterpoint: in contrast to "Tarara-boom-dee-ay" and the artillery marches we have the maiden's prayer, as well as the ominous (for Chekhov) colour green that Natasha wears in Act 1. The literary allusions are darker than in previous plays: Natasha walking across the stage, snuffing out candles, or Solenyi trying to wash the smell from his hands, refer to Shakespeare's *Macbeth*, while the references to Pushkin and Lermontov both remind the audience of a duel with a fatal outcome. The rich casting gives the play far greater impact: as well as a girl in black and a girl in white, we have the garish Natasha and the grey Ol'ga. To contemporary audiences the play seemed to sum up the female condition in the Russian provinces.

The success of *Three Sisters* with the Moscow public and critics was followed in March 1901 by unprecedented success with the St Petersburg public, even though critical hostility to Chekhov was only partly abated; Viktor Burenin produced a vicious parody, *Nine Sisters and Not a Single Groom*, where sisters called Cretina, Idiota, and Hysteria acted with Stanislavskian trained cockroaches and mosquitoes. No Chekhov play, however, ever had such empathy from the audience, or produced such a flood of letters. The play was awarded the Griboedov Prize in 1902. A few reactions were negative: Tolstoi was indignant at Chekhov's condoning adultery and attacking marriage; others felt that the sisters' motivation in not leaving for Moscow was inexplicable (as Mandel'shtam put it in 1935, "Give the three sisters a railway ticket each at the end of Act 1 and the play would be over"). The play secured both Chekhov's and the Moscow Arts Theatre's finances and fortunes; after its Berlin production it brought Chekhov to the attention of world theatre. Some of the motifs of *Three Sisters* were re-used by Chekhov in his last story "The Bride" – three women (of three different generations) trapped in a northern provincial town and an Andrei who plays the violin. In "The Bride", however, the main heroine makes her escape to Moscow.

DONALD RAYFIELD

The Cherry Orchard

Vishnevyi sad

Play, 1904

> Everything on earth must come to an end ... And if one day you hear that my end has come, just remember this old ... horse and say: "Once on this earth there was a certain ... Simeonov-Pishchik ... God rest his soul" ... What marvellous weather ... Yes, indeed ...

These ordinary words, taken from Act 4 of *The Cherry Orchard*, typify its tragi-comic tone. "It has turned out to be not a drama, but a comedy, in places even a farce", declared Anton Chekhov in a letter of 15 September 1903. "It isn't a comedy or a farce, as you claim – it's a tragedy", retorted his director, Konstantin Stanislavskii, on 22 October, after perusing the dramatist's final offering. Between the twin poles of comedy and tragedy all productions of *The Cherry Orchard* must oscillate.

Stanislavskii recalls that Chekhov had plans for one further play, featuring two jealous lovers on a polar expedition, with the last-act scenery portraying a large ship crushed amid icebergs, and a white vision in the snow representing the shade or soul of the deceased woman they had both loved. A spectral aura also haunts *The Cherry Orchard*, this puzzling piece written by a dying consumptive. Its characters drift plaintively by, ships lost in the night, all unmoored and unmarried. Firs mutters impenetrably about forgotten harmony; Charlotta laments her unknown origins and destination; the hapless Epikhodov nurtures a pistol lest life's petty cruelties prove unbearable; Gaev comforts himself with fruit drops and aerial billiards. Others cling to a dream – of Paris or far-flung convents, of economic prosperity or the "bright future". Money and love are painfully scarce.

Chekhov leaves us free to bestow our sympathies on the young (Trofimov, Ania), the ageing (Ranevskaia, Gaev), or the ancient (Firs); or on the visionary (Trofimov, Ania), the improvident (Ranevskaia, Gaev), or the practical (Lopakhin). It is possible also to withhold our sympathy and to emphasize the ironic coolness of Chekhov's observation. At times, *The Cherry Orchard* may seem like a non-play – about non-love, non-shooting and non-catastrophe after the non-saving of the orchard. There is no suicide, and no religious solace. In the only play Chekhov wrote as a married man, people are lonelier than ever before. Adults frozen in the nursery, phantom revellers at a ball. Empty words, eerie thuds. And the elusive breaking string.

These reflections may sound too solemn for approaching a "comedy" or a "farce", yet *The Cherry Orchard* is plainly open to a multitude of interpretations, ranging from the revolutionary to the symbolic. The basic plot seems straightforward. Ranevskaia and Gaev are in debt, and their family house, together with the adjoining orchard, is likely to be auctioned on 22 August. The businessman Lopakhin, who is of serf origin, forewarns them in May (Act 1), but they are incapable of action. Lopakhin duly purchases the estate (off-stage, Act 3), and, when the former landowners leave in October, the orchard is already being demolished (off-stage, Act 4) to make way for profitable summer cottages. The theme of dispossession, usurpation, and change suggests autobiographical and historical parallels – Chekhov had experienced the loss of a childhood home in

Taganrog in 1876, while the fate of the fictional orchard might mirror, in 1904, the decline of the Russian aristocracy and the rise of capitalism.

On one level, the play seems unmistakably tragic, passing from animated arrival to shuttered desolation, from spring to autumn, from blossom to blight. The company that assembles in Act 1 disintegrates in Act 4. The happy ending of traditional comedy is conspicuously absent – there is no harmonious reconciliation. Lopakhin fails to propose to Varia, Ranevskaia returns to Paris, Firs is close to death, and the axe cuts into the tree. No matter how incompetent its erstwhile owners may be, the cherry orchard itself, as Mikhail Gromov has eloquently attested (in *Chekhov*, 1993), can be identified as a profound and complex symbol of Russia's past and of life itself, vulnerable, destructible, beautiful, moral, poetic, pure, and wholly positive.

Yet, equally, the play appears ineluctably comic, inhabited by a gallery of grotesque eccentrics. Can one really grieve over Ranevskaia, so fecklessly prodigal with money and love, or Gaev, vapidly apostrophizing a centenarian bookcase and Mother Nature? Does the quirkily antique Firs contain the stuff of tragedy? Can that strange man-woman Charlotta stir the heart, with her perpetual conjuring tricks, devouring a cucumber after bewailing her isolation? And what is one to make of that walking disaster zone, Epikhodov, or the apoplectic Simeonov-Pishchik (falling asleep in mid-sentence, yet ending triumphantly flush with money)? Duniasha (feverishly giddy) and Iasha (caddishly pretentious) merely ape their social betters, Ranevskaia and Gaev. Even the more "serious" characters, such as Lopakhin and Trofimov, have their absurd side – Lopakhin, industrious and decent, regards himself as a pig and a peasant; Trofimov, radical and prophetic, is priggishly afraid of love. At times, Trofimov's rhetoric uncannily echoes Gaev's loquaciousness. When seen from a comic perspective, all human effort appears fatuous.

Thus, everything perches on a knife-edge, meaningful and meaningless. Ranevskaia is vibrantly (if superficially) alive; Gaev's lozenges and billiard-fixation may mask his sense of inadequacy; Lopakhin plods the path of hard work; Trofimov points to socio-political progress; Varia's emotions are sadly untapped. Several characters are lovelorn and lonely; Ania offers untried hope. These fleeting figures can perplex, move, and amuse us, dwelling in tiny worlds of their own, and occasionally emerging to touch upon our little worlds. They are foolish, lost children, caught between life and death, glimpsed for one moment in a blinding light, before it is night once more. No wonder Chekhov felt able to call the play a comedy, while Stanislavskii beheld a tragedy.

Throughout 1903 Chekhov wrestled slowly and painfully with *The Cherry Orchard*, polishing and revising until, on 14 October, he dispatched the completed manuscript to Moscow. On 17 January 1904, his 44th birthday, he reluctantly attended the premiere of his farewell play, performed by a Moscow Arts Theatre cast that included his wife in the role of Ranevskaia. The stricken author was made to come on stage, to endure the ordeal of wordy speeches celebrating his 25 years of literary endeavour.

The Cherry Orchard lacks the emotional depth and yearning, the heart-rending suffering, manifest in *Uncle Vania* and *Three Sisters*. Chekhov's last piece is so elusive in tone that it may be impossible to achieve a "perfect" production. When the extremes of genteel, autumnal sentimentality and hard-nosed, revolutionary activism are (justifiably) discarded, there remains perhaps a hollow centre, cool and clear and evanescent – like cherry blossom.

GORDON MCVAY

Nikolai Gavrilovich Chernyshevskii 1828–1889

Critic and novelist

Biography

Born in Saratov, 24 July 1828. Attended seminary in Saratov, 1842–45; St Petersburg University, 1846–50; graduated from the department of history and philology, 1850. Taught at St Petersburg Cadet Corps, 1851; returned to Saratov to teach Russian language and literature at local gymnasium, 1851–53. Married: Ol'ga Sokratovna Vasil'eva in 1853; two sons. Returned to St Petersburg in 1853 and began to publish in *Otechestvennye zapiski* and, from January 1854, in *Sovremennik*. Unsuccessfully defended his Master's thesis, *Esteticheskie otnosheniia iskusstva k deistvitel'nosti* (*The Aesthetic Relation of Art to Reality*), 1855. Editor of literary criticism section of *Sovremennik*, 1856, then co-editor of the journal, 1859–62. Arrested, 7 July 1862, and imprisoned in Peter and Paul Fortress, for criticizing as insufficient the terms of Tsar Alexander II's Emancipation of the Serfs, 1862–64. Wrote *Chto delat'?* (*What is to Be Done?*), published in 1863. Convicted of attempting to overthrow the regime; seven years' hard labour and exile for life. Departed for Siberia, 1864; hard labour at Nerchinsk, 1864–66, then Irkutsk, 1866–71. Lived in exile in Viliuisk, 1871–83. Wrote semi-autobiographical novel *Prolog* [Prologue], partly published abroad, 1877. Permitted to join his family in Astrakhan, 1883; returned to Saratov, June 1889. Died in Saratov, 29 October 1889.

Publications

Collected Editions

Polnoe sobranie sochinenii. 16 vols, Moscow, 1939–53.
Selected Philosophical Essays [no translator named]. Moscow,

Foreign Languages Publishing House, 1953; reprinted Westport, Connecticut, Hyperion Press, 1981.

N.G. Chernyshevskii. Stat'i, issledovaniia, materialy [N.G. Chernyshevskii. Articles, Studies, Material], 7 vols. Saratov, 1958–75.

Delo Chernyshevskogo. Sbornik dokumentov [Chernyshevskii's Work. A Collection of Documents]. Saratov, 1968.

Fiction

"Chto delat'?", *Sovremennik*, 3–5 (1863); translated as *What is to Be Done?*, by Benjamin R. Tucker; revised by L.B. Turkevich with an introduction by E.H. Carr, London and New York, Vintage Russian Library, 1961; reprinted, expanded by Cathy Porter, London, Virago, 1982; also by N. Dole and S.S. Skidelsky, with an introduction by Kathryn Feuer, Ann Arbor, Ardis, 1986; also by Michael R. Katz, Ithaca, Cornell University Press, 1989.

Al'ferev. 1863.

Prolog. Petrograd, 1918; Moscow, 1988; translated as *Prologue: A Novel for the 1860s*, by Michael R. Katz, Evanston, Illinois, Northwestern University Press, 1995.

Essays

Esteticheskie otnosheniia iskusstva k deistvitel'nosti, St Petersburg, 1855; translated as "The Aesthetic Relation of Art to Reality", in *Selected Philosophical Essays*, Moscow, 1953; also in *Russian Philosophy*, edited by James M. Edie *et al.*, Chicago, Quadruple, 1965, vol. 2.

"Ocherki gogolevskogo perioda russkoi literatury", *Sovremennik*, 12 (1855), 1–2, 4, 7, 9–12 (1856); translated as "Essays on the Gogol Period of Russian Literature", nos 6–7, in *Selected Philosophical Essays*, Moscow, 1953.

"Antropologicheskii printsip v filosofii", *Sovremennik*, 4/5 (1860); translated as "The Anthropological Principle in Philosophy", in *Selected Philosophical Essays*, Moscow, 1953; also in *Russian Philosophy*, edited by James M. Edie, *et al.*vol. 2, 1965.

Belinsky, Chernyshevsky, Dobrolyubov: Selected Criticism, edited by Ralph E. Matlaw, New York, Dutton, 1962; Bloomington, Indiana University Press, 1976.

Critical Studies

N.G. Chernyshevskii: ego zhizn' i deiatel'nost', 1828–1889, 2 vols, by Iu. M. Steklov, Moscow and Leningrad, 1928.

N.G. Chernyshevskii, by Francis B. Randall, New York, Twayne, 1967.

Chernyshevskii: The Man and the Journalist, by William F. Woehrlin, Cambridge, Massachusetts, Harvard University Press, 1971.

The Thought and Teachings of N.G. Chernyshevsky, by Norman G.O. Pereira, The Hague, Mouton, 1975.

Chernyshevskii – romanist, by G.E. Tamarchenko, Leningrad, 1976.

"Estetika Chernyshevskogo i russkaia literatura", by G. M. Fridlender, *Russkaia literatura*, 2 (1978), 11–35.

"Dostoevsky and Chernyshevsky", by D.C. Offord, *Slavonic and East European Review*, 57 (1979), 509–30.

Nasledie N.G. Chernyshevskogo – pisatel' i sovetskoe literaturovedenie: Itogi, zadachi, perspektivy izucheniia, by U. Gural'nik, Moscow, 1980.

The Russian Revolutionary Novel: Turgenev to Pasternak, by Richard Freeborn, Cambridge and New York, Cambridge University Press, 1982.

Women in Russian Literature, 1780–1863, by Joe Andrew, London, Macmillan, and New York, St Martin's Press, 1988, 155–80.

Chernyshevsky and the Age of Realism, by Irina Paperno, Stanford, Stanford University Press, 1988.

Chernyshevsky – romanist i literaturnye traditsii, by Iu. K. Rudenko, Leningrad, 1989.

"Nikolay Chernyshevsky: A Russian Utopia", by Joseph Frank, in his *Through the Russian Prism: Essays on Literature and Culture*, Princeton, Princeton University Press, 1990 (first published in *Southern Review*, January 1967).

Bibliography

N.G. Chernyshevskii: Ukazatel' literatury, 1960–1970, Saratov, 1976.

Nikolai Chernyshevskii was born in Saratov to the local priest, and was himself intended for the priesthood. His seminary education, however, was cut short in 1845, but his publicistic writings, characterized by dogmatism, moral fervour, zeal and dedication, bear its stamp. In 1846, Chernyshevskii entered St Petersburg University. During his years in the capital, acquaintance with members of the Petrashevskii circle, and the works of many western thinkers, especially Ludwig Feuerbach, Louis Blanc, Pierre Joseph Proudhon, Charles Fourier, as well as witnessing the failed revolutions of 1848, persuaded him of the futility of liberalism and helped him to mould a radical world-view. After graduation, he taught in Saratov for several years, but returned to St Petersburg in 1853 to write his Master's thesis. His views also found a new outlet: that year, he began his journalistic career, publishing a few articles for the liberal journal, *Otechestvennye zapiski* before moving to *Sovremennik* early in 1854. Initially, he published mainly literary criticism. Like Belinskii before him, who deeply influenced him and whose post as leading critic of Russian literature he would later fill, Chernyshevskii demanded civic responsibility in art, believing that literature was one of the key forces of progress. In his work he maintained that the role of art was to portray real life, to make it understandable to the reader, and to pass judgment on it. However, the extreme materialist aesthetics ("beauty is life") that he formulated in his Master's thesis, *Esteticheskie otnosheniia iskusstva k deistvitel'nosti* ("The Aesthetic Relation of Art to Reality"), which he unsuccessfully defended in 1855, proved to be as offensive to many of his co-workers as they had been to his thesis supervisor, A.V. Nikitenko. He succeeded in alienating many of *Sovremennik*'s important writers, including Lev Tolstoi, Ivan Turgenev, and Aleksandr Druzhinin, who eventually left the journal. He continued to express and elaborate his views on the role of the writer and literature in a number of critical reviews, most importantly in "Ocherki gogolevskogo perioda russkoi literatury" ("Essays on the Gogol Period of Russian Literature"), in which he hailed Gogol', long revered for what was considered his faithful depiction of the corrupt aspects of Russia, as Russia's greatest writer. Supported by the editor, N.A. Nekrasov, Chernyshevskii was the leading critic of *Sovremennik*, and by 1859, exerted considerable influence on all editorial questions.

In 1857, Chernyshevskii devoted himself entirely to socio-economic questions, and left *Sovremennik*'s literary criticism section in the hands of his protégé, N.A. Dobroliubov. Hopeful about the possibility of reform under the new tsar, Alexander II, Chernyshevskii was pleased to deal more explicitly with socio-economic questions, although his literary criticism had always served as a forum for critique of the existing order. In 1858–59, he wrote numerous articles about serfdom and the potential value of the peasant commune, as well as proposals for land reform, which have since earned him the title "Utopian" socialist. For several years, he wrote monthly reviews of political and historical events relevant to Russia's development. In addition to his many articles of a political and economic nature, Chernyshevskii wrote the ethical treatise, "Antropologicheskii printsip v filosofii" ("The Anthropological Principle in Philosophy"), which was strongly influenced by the Utilitarian principles of John Stuart Mill. In "The Anthropological Principle in Philosophy", he maintained that as all human behaviour is motivated exclusively by self-interest, and that the interests of the individual are inextricably linked to the interests of society, man can be taught to serve the common good if he is made to understand that it will ultimately benefit his own interests.

By the close of the decade, however, Chernyshevskii had become doubtful about the prospect of reform from above and began to be recognized as the leader of a section of the intelligentsia that was becoming increasingly radical. Provoked by an alarming rash of peasant disturbances and student unrest, the authorities thought it prudent to remove the apparent leader of the radicals, who had been under surveillance by the Third Section for almost a year. Though they were not able to prove that Chernyshevskii was connected with the events, a letter from Herzen to N.A. Serno-Solov'evich, in which Herzen offered to print the prohibited *Sovremennik* in London, gave the authorities a sufficient pretext for his arrest. On 7 July 1862, Chernyshevskii was arrested and imprisoned in the Peter and Paul Fortress. While in prison, he wrote the novel *Chto delat'?* (*What is to Be Done?*), which the censors mistakenly permitted to be serially published in *Sovremennik*. It was Chernyshevskii's first and last noteworthy work of fiction. Though widely considered didactic and poorly-written, the novel was extremely popular and went on to influence a number of later revolutionaries, including Vera Zasulich and Lenin.

Despite an obvious lack of evidence, Chernyshevskii was found guilty of attempting to overthrow the regime, and was sentenced to seven years of hard labour and exile for life. His unreasonably harsh sentence helped further to alienate many from the regime, and assured Chernyshevskii's status as a martyr. While serving his sentence, he wrote a number of short stories and novellas, in addition to the autobiographical novel set during the last half of the tumultuous 1850s, *Prolog* (*Prologue*), part of which was published abroad in 1877. But these, as well as the novella *Al'ferev*, and several stories he wrote while still in the Fortress, have been largely forgotten. Chernyshevskii was finally permitted to return to his birthplace in 1889, where he died later that year at the age of 61.

JENNIFER LONERGAN

What is to Be Done?

Chto delat'?

Novel, 1863

What is to Be Done? was written by Chernyshevskii during his imprisonment in the Peter and Paul Fortress. Due to a blunder by the censors, the novel was allowed to be published serially in the radical journal *Sovremennik* early in 1863. Set in Russia in the 1860s, it is the story of the evolution of a young and intelligent woman, Vera Pavlovna Rozalskaia, who was stifled by her family and limited by her position in it. The story is told by an arrogant narrator who frequently interrupts his narrative to mock the reader and assist in the interpretation of the novel.

Vera's weak-willed father is the manager of the house of the former State counsellor, and an assistant in a government department. Her domineering and abusive mother is a pawnbroker who will stop at nothing to make money. To keep the peace in her house, Vera Pavlovna agrees to consider the marriage proposal of a wealthy but despicable man. However, she yearns for freedom and independence, and confesses her desire to be an actress to her brother's tutor, Lopukhov. Lopukhov, a medical student, sympathizes with her plight, and promises to help her. Soon, however, she is forced to abandon her dream, and Lopukhov's efforts to secure her a position as a governess are also in vain. Lopukhov offers to marry her to rescue her from her oppressive family life. He makes the arrangements, they are secretly married, and Vera is free of her former life.

Now married, they live a tranquil, if unconventional home life, occupying separate rooms, meeting for tea and meals in a common room, and entering each other's bedrooms only when invited to do so. Lopukhov finds work, and Vera Pavlovna gives piano lessons. Soon, wishing to do something more useful, she establishes a dressmaker's shop, in which the enterprise's profits are equally distributed among the workers. The steps Vera takes to establish the co-operative are described in intricate detail. Admittedly there are some initial difficulties, but her shop is soon a success. On Vera's suggestion, the co-operative establishes a bank, from which workers can borrow money interest-free, and a purchasing agency, which buys staple foods and other items in bulk, thus cutting costs for the workers. To make better use of the purchasing agency, the workers begin to live near each other, and eventually, most are living in one house.

A case of pneumonia forces Lopukhov to send for his former friend and colleague, the medical student Kirsanov. Kirsanov had ceased his visits to the Lopukhovs' some years before, but now resumes them to tend to his old friend. Despite their efforts and intentions, Vera and Kirsanov fall in love. Lopukhov soon perceives the nature of their feelings and, wishing to extricate himself from a burdensome situation and to give his wife the opportunity to marry Kirsanov, Lopukhov fakes his own suicide. Vera and Kirsanov are married and several years pass. They have a baby, Vera opens a second and a third shop, and finally decides to become a doctor herself. Lopukhov returns to the scene as Charles Beaumont from America and marries the daughter of a man with whom he is conducting some business. His return is joyfully greeted by Vera and Kirsanov, and the two couples move in together and share their happy lives.

What is to Be Done? was both a defence of the younger generation, and its guide to life in the 1860s. Chernyshevskii's depiction of "new people" who were honest, rational, and socially responsible, as well as warm, sincere, and human, constituted an answer to Turgenev's Bazarov (*Ottsy i deti* [*Fathers and Sons*] 1862), who, unlike the heroes of *What is to Be Done?*, was destroyed by his feelings and convictions. Chernyshevskii's novel was successful because it served as a manual to an enlightened, rational, different life in a setting that no longer held out the imminent promise of change. After the disappointing rule of the "tsar liberator" Alexander II, educated Russians could no longer hope for reform from above, but *What is to Be Done?* indicated that they could implement reform on a personal level, in their private lives.

The themes of the novel mirrored the ideas that characterized radicalism in the 1860s and lent it optimism: faith in science, in equality, of men and women, and of all social classes, and in the goodness of human nature. Chernyshevskii uses a variety of artless techniques (which he sometimes explains to the reader) to stress bluntly important messages. Vera's dreams reiterate the author's points: enlightenment and the love of humanity are the keys to liberty and progress; labour is cleansing and edifying; people are intrinsically good, but are corrupted by their environment; and it is both natural and rational for humans to live and to work communally. Rakhmetov, possibly the first professional revolutionary depicted in Russian literature, is introduced into the novel to stress the ordinary nature of the other characters, lest their behaviour and achievements should seem unattainable to the reader. Reasons for decisions made by the characters are painstakingly described by the author in order to demonstrate that, generous though they may appear, they are all motivated exclusively by self-interest, and that people can and must be enlightened as to their true interests, which naturally coincide with those of society. *What is to Be Done?* is a story of a woman's emancipation and evolution, and as such is a decisive assertion of the intellectual and moral equality of men and women. Indeed, the work was an important document in the debate of the 1850s and 1860s about the position of women, and was later considered a great feminist novel by figures such as Aleksandra Kollontai.

What is to Be Done? has been widely considered an extremely bad novel, and its artless style and didactic tone repelled many readers. "Chernyshevskii's manner", wrote Turgenev, "rouses physical revulsion in me"; Dostoevskii granted it a "punch in the nose". Yet it was an intelligent work that displayed wit and irony such as was rarely found in Chernyshevskii's voluminous publicistic writings. It was enthusiastically greeted by the younger generation, many of whom, according to contemporaries, were prompted by Vera's example to establish communes and co-operatives, and generally behave as the novel prescribed. Many notable revolutionary figures, including Rosa Luxembourg, Vera Zasulich, and Lenin, would later acknowledge the influence of the novel, which was continuously studied in Soviet schools and has been reprinted many times.

JENNIFER LONERGAN

Oleg Grior'evich Chukhontsev 1938–

Poet

Biography

Born in Pavlovskii Posad, Moscow Region, 8 March 1938. Father was an economist. Attended local school; studied humanities at Teachers' College of the Moscow Region, 1958–62; degree in philology in 1962. Teacher at various secondary schools; also a translator. Editor of the poetry section for *Novyi mir* since 1986. In recent years has travelled extensively to the United States and Germany; often featured in the broadcasts of *Radio Free Europe*. Married: the writer Irina Povolotskaiia.

Publications

Poetry

Iz trekh tetradei [From Three Notebooks]. Moscow, 1976.
Slukhovoe okno [Rooftop Window]. Moscow, 1983.
Vetrom i peplom [Like Wind and Ashes]. Moscow, 1989.
Stikhotvoreniia. Moscow, 1990.
"Poems", in *Contemporary Russian Poetry: A Bilingual Anthology*, edited by Gerald S. Smith, Bloomington, Indiana University Press, 1993, 176–89.
"Osazhdennyi" [The Blockaded], *Literaturnaia ucheba* (May–June 1994), 63–73.

Editor

Dissonant Voices: The New Russian Fiction, London, Harvill Press, 1991.

Critical Studies

"Dobro ne mozhet byt' staro", by Naum Korzhavin, *Kontinent*, 17 (1978), 315–30.
"Predchuvstviia i pamiat'", by I. Rodnianskaia, *Novyi mir*, 10 (1982), 227–37.
"Tesnina byta, vozdukh bytiia", by L. Anninskii, *Iunost'*, 3 (1985), 93–95.
"O prostom i vysokom", by Igor' Shaitanov, *Literaturnoe obozrenie*, 2 (1985), 47–51.

"Sharing the Damage", by Gerald S. Smith, *Times Literary Supplement* (20–26 April 1990), 429.

Oleg Chukhontsev's first poems appeared in 1958, in journals for young readers such as *Iunost'* and *Molodaiia gvardiia*. Some of these poems were included in the annual Moscow collection of poetry *Den' poezii*. In 1968 Chukhontsev's poem "Povestvovanie o Kurbskom" [Narration about Kurbskii] was published in *Iunost'* (1, 1969); it was sharply criticized by the official watchdogs because of its suggestive remarks that the treason committed by Kurbskii during the reign of Ivan the Terrible was merely a response to tyranny. The publication of this poem coincided with the spectacular escape to the United States (via Hungary and Yugoslavia) of the writer and critic A. Belinkov; he had spent more than 25 years in Soviet camps for writing an anti-Soviet novel, and works on Tynianov and Olesha. Thereafter Chukhontsev's work was banned until 1976, when his first collection of poems – *Iz trekh tetradei* [From Three Notebooks] – was published to favourable reviews. Chukhontsev's second and more substantial collection of poetry, *Slukhovoe okno* [Rooftop Window], appeared in 1983. Chukhontsev is now well-known in Russia as a literary critic and a translator. Since 1986 he has worked as an editor of the poetry section for one of the most influential literary journals, *Novyi mir*. *Vetrom i peplom* [Like Wind and Ashes], appeared in 1989. It was followed by a selected edition of his work, published in 1990. He lives in Moscow together with his wife, the prose writer, Irina Povolotskaiia. Today Chukhontsev is considered to be one of the leading poets of his generation. He edited an anthology of contemporary Russian fiction (*Dissonant Voices: The New Russian Fiction*, 1991), which includes stories by Makanin, Petrushevskaia, Popov, Erofeev, Bitov, and a story by his wife, "The Rosy-Fingered Dawn".

Chukhontsev's poetry is philosophical; he is concerned with expressing his inner self, rather than responding to the political pressures of the time. His imagery and style are original; his poetic vision is often akin to the Christian principles of love and active resistance to evil. He sympathizes with the persecuted and those who suffer. In his world universal aspects blend well with historical themes and imagery. Some critics label him a traditional poet. However, the atmosphere of sadness and loss (reinforced by Christian imagery, with meditations on death and loneliness) makes his poetry conflict with the official trends in Soviet literature in the 1970s and 1980s.

There have been very few publications of Chukhontsev's work in recent years. One of his most interesting works, the narrative poem *Osazhdennyi* [The Blockaded], was published for the first time in *Literaturnaia ucheba* in 1994, although it was written in January 1960. It is a historical poem, covering the period of the Tartar invasion of Russia in the 13th century. The poem narrates the story of Novgorod trying to retain its independence from Ghengis Khan's grandson, Khan Batu (1227–55), who was trying to overrun Russia. The narration, in the manner of epic folklore, is based on repetitive structures, and Batu is constantly referred to as "the son of a bitch, who has thousands of horses ... the son of a bitch, who has thousands of sabres ...". The depiction of events fits the traditional mode of thinking adopted by Soviet historiography. In comparison, Lev Gumilev's Eurasian account of the Tartar invasion offers a very different view of Batu. In Gumilev's opinion Batu saved Novgorod from becoming part of Poland and taught the Russian army to use cavalry in the steppes (see *Nashe Nasledie*, 3 (1991), 19–26). Chukhontsev discovered the poem in his desk after many years, and offered it for publication in a journal for young authors to show his own experimental techniques. Its innovative quality lies in the author's attempt to merge the style of Russian epic medieval literature with colloquial modern Russian. All Chukhontsev's poetry has a distinctly dissonant stamp; his quest for inner wisdom and moral strength clearly links him with the poetry of Bunin and Annenskii.

ALEXANDRA SMITH

Lidiia Korneevna Chukovskaia 1907–1996

Prose writer and memoirist

Biography

Born in St Petersburg, 24 March 1907. Pre-school education in the Finnish settlement of Kuokkala (now Repino). Impressions of childhood described in memoirs. Attended school in Leningrad; Leningrad Institute for the History of Art. Married: 1) the literary critic Tsezar' Vol'pe; 2) the astrophysicist Matvei Bronshtein (died 1937); one daughter. Editor in the children's literature department of State Publishing Organization (OGIZ) under Samuil Marshak. Editorial board was decimated: friends and colleagues were arrested; Marshak moved to Moscow; second husband arrested and killed in prison, 1937. Continued editorial work; member of the Writers' Union. In 1960s reacted strongly to waves of oppression against intelligentsia and took up a position of civic defiance, writing open letters in defence of Siniavskii and Daniel', Solzhenitsyn, and Sakharov. Close friendship with Solzhenitsyn; praised his work openly; expelled from the Writers' Union, 9 January 1974. Chukovskaia's position changed radically with the onset of perestroika; spontaneous proposal made to restore her membership of the Writers' Union. Literary group "Aprel'" awarded her special prize "for civic courage". Lived and wrote at Peredelkino. Died 7 February 1996.

Publications

Collected Editions

Protsess iskliucheniia [The Process of Exclusion]. Moscow, 1990.

Izbrannoe. Minsk, 1997.

Fiction

"Sof'ia Petrovna", *Novyi zhurnal*, 83 and 84 (1966), 5–45 and 5–46; edited by John Murray, London, Bristol Classical Press, 1998; translated as *Sofia Petrovna*, by David Floyd, London, Collins Harvill, 1989; corrupt version published as *Opustelyi dom*, Paris, Piat' kontinentov, 1965; translated as *The Deserted House* by Aline B. Werth, London, Barrie and Rockliff, and New York, Dutton, 1967; revised by Eliza Kellogg Klose as *Sofia Petrovna*, Evanston, Illinois, Northwestern University Press, 1988.

Spusk pod vodu. New York, Izdatel'stvo imeni Chekhova, 1972; translated as *Going Under*, by Peter M. Weston, London, Barrie and Jenkins, and New York, Quadrangle, 1972.

Povesti. Moscow, 1988.

Poetry

Po etu storonu smerti: Iz dnevnika 1936–1976 [On This Side of Death: From My Diary 1936–1976]. Paris, YMCA-Press, 1978.

Articles, Memoirs, and Literary Criticism

Povest' o Tarase Shevchenko [A Story about Taras Shevchenko]. 1930.

Na Volge [On the Volga]. 1931; later edition as "Istoriia odnogo vosstaniia" [The Story of One Rising]. 1940.

Slovo predostavliaetsia detiam [Children's Turn to Speak]. Tashkent, 1942.

N.N. Miklukho-Maklai. Moscow, 1950.

Dekabristy, issledovateli Sibiri [The Decembrists - Explorers of Siberia]. Moscow, 1951.

Boris Zhitkov, Kritiko-biograficheskii ocherk [Boris Zhitkov - A Critical Biographical Sketch]. Moscow, 1955.

S. Georgievskaia: Kritiko-biograficheskii ocherk. Moscow, 1955.

V laboratorii redaktora [In the Editor's Laboratory]. Moscow, 1960; 2nd edition, 1963.

"Byloe i dumy" Gertsena [Herzen's "My Past and Thoughts"]. Moscow, 1966.

Zapiski ob Anne Akhmatovoi, vol. 1, Paris, YMCA-Press, 1976; 2nd edition 1984; vol. 2, Paris, YMCA-Press, 1980; revised and expanded edition, 3 vols, Moscow, 1997; volume 1 translated as *The Akhmatova Journals Volume 1, 1938–1941*, by Milena Michalski and Sylva Rubashova, London, Harvill Press, and New York, Farrar Straus and Giroux, 1994.

Otkrytoe slovo [An Open Word]. New York, Khronika, 1976.

Protsess iskliucheniia: Ocherk literaturnykh nravov [The Process of Exclusion ...]. Paris, YMCA-Press, 1979.

Pamiati detstva. New York, Chalidze, 1983; translated as *To the Memory of Childhood*, by Eliza Kellogg Close, Evanston, Illinois, Northwestern University Press, 1988.

Critical Studies

"Zhivoi obraz pisatelia", by D. Bregova, *Novyi mir*, 10 (1955), 270–72.

"Khranitel'nitsa traditsii: Lidiia Korneevna Chukovskaia", by E. Breitbart, *Grani*, 104 (1977), 171–82.

"Otets i doch'", by E. Etkind, *Vremia i my*, 66 (1982), 168–83.

"Reading Loyalty in Chukovskaia's *Zapiski ob Anne Akhmatovoi*", by Stephanie Sandler, in *The Speech of Unknown Eyes: Akhmatova's Readers on Her Poetry*, edited by Wendy Rosslyn, 2 vols, Nottingham, Astra Press, 1990, vol. 2, 267–82.

Women's Works in Stalin's Time: On Lidiia Chukovskaia and Nadezhda Mandelstam, by Beth Holmgren, Bloomington, Indiana University Press, 1993.

Lidiia Chukovskaia's first literary story, "Leningrad-Odessa", was published in 1928 under the pen-name of Uglov. During the period of growing terror and Stalinism, she continued to work as an editor, devoting herself to critical studies and literary history. To this period belong works that have subsequently been partially published on Taras Shevchenko, the Decembrists, S. Georg'evskaia, and Boris Zhitkov. She also worked extensively on the writing of Herzen, whom she greatly admired. As her *Zapiski ob Anne Akhmatovoi* (*The Akhmatova Journals*) show, she also took a strong interest in the poetry of Adam Mickiewicz. In 1956 she published in the almanac *Literaturnaia Moskva* an article entitled "Rabochii razgovor" [A Working Conversation] on the significance of, the care needed for, and possible distortions produced by editorial work. This article anticipated a book, *V laboratorii redaktora* [In the Editor's Laboratory], which brought the author great popularity.

Parallel to her official editorial and scholarly work, Chukovskaia also engaged in secret writing. As early as 1939–40 she produced her first book-length prose fiction, *Sof'ia Petrovna*, which was published in the west in 1965 as *Opustelyi dom* (*The Deserted House*). This book, written at the same time as Akhmatova's *Rekviem* (*Requiem*), describes the terrible fate of the mother of a "model komsomol member". Incapable of grasping the sense of the absurdity and nightmare into which the life of her favourite son, and at the same time her own life, have been thrown, poor Sof'ia Petrovna refuses to believe the obvious and gradually loses her mind. Through the hopelessness and horror of the situation described, we feel the stifling atmosphere of growing terror and the tragic breakdown of normal life in the country, and realize the extent of the suffering of countless direct and indirect victims of the mass repressions.

A second book about this period, *Spusk pod vodu* (*Going Under*), undoubtedly (contains elements of autobiography. The action is set in 1949, as a woman writer goes to stay in a quiet rest-home where she expects to find inner peace amid nature, and hopes for the chance secretly and quietly to write a book about the first years of the Terror that had robbed her of her beloved husband. Soon, however, she discovers that the prison-camp system, like a tumour, covers the whole country, and that there is no escape from repression. Even those who at first sight seem to be favourites of fortune are destined for ruin and destruction. Like *Sof'ia Petrovna*, *Going Under* is a remarkable example of women's writing about the tragedy of Stalin's reign.

The poems collected in *Po etu storonu smerti: Iz dnevnika* [On This Side of Death: From My Diary] cover the four decades from

1936 to 1976. Their basic theme is the fate of the author and of her family and near ones: the poems are about her love for her murdered husband, about death, nature, partings, the emigration of friends, and, indeed, the entire spectrum of experiences encountered by the writer in the course of her difficult life.

The two volumes of *Zapiski ob Anne Akhmatovoi* contain invaluable documentary material concerning the years 1938–41 and 1952–62. They portray the complex, tragic personality of the great poet, giving a vivid impression of her everyday life, of the colossal nervous stress of the struggle to find her son Lev Gumilev in the camps, and they also provide much information on the views, habits, reading, personal life and moods of Akhmatova. At the same time, the work conveys the general atmosphere of life at a time of State lawlessness, the ruinous destruction of various strata of society, and particularly the intelligentsia. This work is and will always remain one of the most important sources for understanding the times and personality of the great poet.

The life and work of Lidiia Chukovskaia stands as a monument to a terrible and tragic age that crystallized, but did not break, the pure and strong personality of a most talented and courageous writer.

SVETLANA SHNITMAN-MCMILLIN

Sof'ia Petrovna

Novella, 1966

Chukovskaia's novella *Sof'ia Petrovna*, first published under the title *Opustelyi dom* (*The Deserted House*), took a long time to reach its readers. To this day it remains the greatest work of a woman writer about the contemporary events it describes. As Lidiia Chukovskaia herself says, "However imaginably great future novels and stories may be, they will still belong to another age, separated from 1937 by decades. My novella, on the other hand, was written on the fresh trail of recent events. In this I see its right to the reader's attention."

The book was written during the winter of 1939–40. Apart from the arrest and death of a large circle of friends and colleagues, Chukovskaia's husband, an astrophysicist and author of popular scientific books, fell victim to repression. The personal tragedy produced a wound that never healed, and turned Chukovskaia into one of the many women standing day and night in prison queues to whom Akhmatova dedicated her *Requiem*. Like Akhmatova, she never lost hope that the end of that inhuman age would sometime come, and she herself became a witness of it. Preserving the exercise book with the manuscript at great risk to herself, she "looked on it not so much as being a story as a piece of evidence which it would be dishonourable to destroy". On the eve of World War II the NKVD (People's Commissariat for Internal Affairs) began to hunt for the book and the threat of arrest hung over the writer, but, paradoxically, she was saved by the outbreak of war. During the blockade, when she and her daughter were evacuated, the exercise book remained in Leningrad, miraculously surviving, even though, tragically, the friends who looked after it did not. In the years of Khrushchev's Thaw Chukovskaia began to hope that the novella might be published, but the political climate changed quickly, and the book remained unpublished; accepted for publication, it was subsequently turned down. Chukovskaia then embarked on an unprecedented law-suit against the publishing house, demanding full payment of her fee – and won the case. None the less the book remained unpublished in the USSR until the beginning of perestroika.

The novella's heroine, Sof'ia Petrovna (in the 1965 Paris edition, *The Deserted House*, she bears the name Ol'ga Petrovna), is the widow of a well-known Leningrad doctor bringing up her only son Nikolai, to whom she has entirely devoted her life. He is turning out very well – handsome, successful at school and a model Komsomol member – well nigh perfect, in the eyes of his mother. To pay for his education Sof'ia Petrovna takes up work as a typist. Fresh impressions from her work and contact with others give new meaning and interest to the life of this pleasant but somewhat limited and naive woman. Her son finishes school and enters higher education, but suddenly leaves the nest, setting off for work in Sverdlovsk, in the far-off Urals. Sof'ia Petrovna misses him greatly, but her constant loving thoughts about him, as well as her work, occupy her life. Terrible things, however, begin to happen in the outside world. The newspapers start to carry colourful stories about cases of unthinkable sabotage, in all of which Sof'ia Petrovna believes implicitly. Then repression begins against colleagues of her dead husband in which it is far harder to believe. After that they arrest the director of the publishers where she works. And then a most terrible misfortune falls on the uncomprehending woman – her own son, Nikolai, is arrested.

Convinced of his innocence, Sof'ia Petrovna runs up against the complete impossibility of a normal human or professional conversation with the representatives of authority. She falls into a new and incredibly terrible world of prison, queues, deprived children and women: "It seemed to her that she was not in Leningrad but in some alien, unfamiliar city." With amazing speed more and more of her friends are drawn into this circle of misfortune. Her young friend Natasha commits suicide, her son's best friend is arrested. Sof'ia Petrovna increasingly loses her contact with reality and understanding of what is going on. Unable to reconcile herself with what has happened and to bear her personal spiritual hell, she begins to suffer schizophrenic delusions, dreaming up for herself a new reality in which justice triumphs and her son is released. However, she is torn out of this radiant but insane circle by ever more terrible events: she is sacked from her job, and her son is reported to have confessed his crimes and to have been given a ten-year sentence. Detecting any sense in this blackness is beyond the powers of Sof'ia Petrovna. Suddenly she experiences a miracle that makes everything plain: she receives a letter from her son in which he tells of his arrest after being denounced, and of his "confession of guilt" under torture. For his mother this truth is more terrible and unbearable than ignorance, as it gives a faint hope of a happy outcome. For this reason Sof'ia Petrovna, having discovered that she lives in a state where no one in power has any interest in the truth, follows the advice of a sister in misfortune, destroying the incriminating document and renouncing the struggle for the restoration of rights and liberty to her son. Now she is faced with living in that condition of fear, that civic paralysis and spiritual numbness, into which Stalin's regime had driven the entire country.

Sof'ia Petrovna conveys the atmosphere of ever-thickening terror that destroys more and more victims. At the same time, this novella is about the populations' betrayed trust in their cannibalistic state, about the crushing of people's spirits, the utter loneliness of everyone who came into contact with the terrible state mechanism of destruction. In the centre of the work is the figure of a mother – the symbol of total and selfless love. And it is precisely because we do not have before us a bright, thinking intellectual personality, but a trusting, cultured though limited woman, that her response to being made a victim is particularly affecting. An obedient and easy object of political manipulation, she falls into the merciless machine of Stalinist repression where her beloved son perishes and where she loses both her spirit and her mind.

The strength of Lidiia Chukovskaia as witness remains undiminished by the decades that separate us from the nightmare of Stalin's era. The moral power of her novella is particularly important at a time of great movement and change, as a lesson and as an inoculation against the repetition of bloody mistakes.

SVETLANA SHNITMAN-MCMILLIN

Going Under

Spusk pod vodu

Autobiographical novel, 1972

Women's literature from and about Stalin's era forms a separate branch of Russian prose. Its principal genre – memoir – is represented by two brilliant works, Evgeniia Ginzburg's *Krutoi marshrut* (*Journey into the Whirlwind*) and Nadezhda Mandel'shtam's *Vospominaniia* (*Hope Against Hope*), as well as other touching and remarkable testimonies. The main woman writer of fiction to turn to this bloody theme is, however, Lidiia Chukovskaia.

Going Under, written in 1949, is in the form of a memoir-like diary, and is clearly autobiographical in nature. The heroine, Nina Sergeevna, is the widow of a scientist who was arrested and died in the Gulag. The circumstances and time of his death are not known. Nina Sergeevna has a small daughter with whom she lives in a communal flat, after returning from evacuation. The murder of her husband has left an unhealing wound, but love for her daughter, her writing, poetry, and nature all help her to keep her head above water. Hoping for peace and the chance to get on with some secret writing, Nina Sergeevna arrives at a writers' rest-home. She is writing a book, dedicated to the memory of her beloved husband, about the time she is living in: the Terror, repression, death, and madness. By writing she hopes to lose her grief and to leave literary witness to the Stalinist nightmare. The writing of this book she calls "going under", a leaving of the surface of life with its domestic quarrels, boorishness, and the continuing Terror. Nina Sergeevna is receptive to the spiritually restorative effects of the natural world of which she has a strong and subtle awareness. Many pages of the book are devoted to the natural surroundings, and it may be said that since Bunin Russian prose has not known such masterful evocations of the beauties of nature. The descriptions recall Kuokkala (Repino) where the writer spent her childhood years.

Arriving at the rest-home, Nina Sergeevna at first tries to keep to herself, avoiding contacts, both with the ingratiating staff and with the representatives of the privileged intelligentsia, flirting, playing cards, walking lazily, and, between times, getting on with their writing. The only man she allows to come close is a former front-line soldier, the Jewish poet Wexler who reads to her verses in Yiddish. With unerring literary instinct she catches the poetic music of the unknown tongue. But in the newspapers there rages a "campaign against cosmopolitanism", and one night a black maria comes to take Wexler away.

Walking one day, Nina Sergeevna by chance meets the director of the rest-home whom she had previously thought a spoilt, sleek, and dry woman. It turns out, however, that she too is deeply unhappy: her favourite, younger sister has for more than a decade been in exile, moving from one camp to another, often beyond the reach even of the regular parcels that had been sent to her. Similarly by chance, Nina Sergeevna meets a little girl, the sister of a young woman working in the rest-home, and again she is faced with the story of a broken life. The retreating Soviet army did not evacuate the population, and the young woman, having experienced the nightmare of occupation, is no longer trusted by her own authorities: her civil rights are restricted, she is forbidden to study, and is thus fated to spend her whole life doing simple, unqualified work. Her younger sister faithfully helps her to maintain their meagre way of life; the girl's impoverished childhood is not even enlivened by the usual Russian fairy stories.

But these meetings are merely the overture to the main meeting of Nina Sergeevna's month's stay in the rest-home. The writer Bilibin, at first sight a jolly, healthy fellow, touching up his "production novel" for his editors and the censorship, turns out to have come from the terrible world where Nina Sergeevna's husband perished. Having experienced the camps and forced labour, surviving by a miracle and preserving at least the appearance of his previous magnificent health and strength, he is the first living witness of hell, and is perceived by Nina Sergeevna as a messenger from her dead husband. Their closeness rapidly develops, and their spiritual intimacy and mutual understanding gradually grows into love. But this feeling is soon destroyed by merciless reality: Bilibin finishes his novel and asks Nina Sergeevna to read it. And when she does, she realizes that he has made use of his experience of forced labour in exile to write an ordinary, conformist production novel, which passes over the Gulag in silence. She sees this adaptability as a betrayal of those who were tortured and perished, as well as those still suffering in camps and prisons. With the cruelty of a deeply suffering person she tells him to his face what she thinks of his writing and its falseness. Their relationship is broken off and their lives part, and it is only gradually that Nina Sergeevna realizes the harshness of her swift judgement. Before her was a physical invalid, permanently ill, incapable of earning his living by any other means, who had been forced to prostitute his only gift in order to survive. And although Nina Sergeevna cannot help feeling guilty, their paths separate for ever: each has their own individual existence, pain, and reality.

Going Under is a book about creative honesty, about a writer's duty to bear witness, and about the impossibility of judging victims. It is an attempt to describe and comprehend the Stalin epoch, its meaning, its cruel mechanisms: an epoch that separated people, destroying them physically or mentally; an epoch when the destruction of moral values and the power of pure fear made collaborators of people who had been morally crippled by the regime. In her book *Protsess iskliucheniia* [The Process of Exclusion] Chukovskaia wrote: "I want there to be studied screw by screw the machine which turned a man full of life, flourishing and active, into a cold corpse. What brought us to this fantastic misfortune? Here there is a huge amount of work for historians, philosophers, sociologists. And above all for writers." Chukovskaia remained true to this aim throughout her life. *Going Under* is one of the most merciless and honest books of post-war Russian literature, the living personal and social testimony of its courageous author.

SVETLANA SHNITMAN-MCMILLIN

Kornei Ivanovich Chukovskii 1882–1969

Critic, memoirist, literary translator, and children's writer

Biography

Born Nikolai Vasil'evich Korneichuk, in St Petersburg, 31 March 1882. Grew up in Odessa, expelled from fifth class in gymnasium, self-taught. Married: Mariia Borisovna (died 1955); four children. Started work for the newspaper *Odesskie novosti* in 1901: correspondent in London, 1903–04. Returned to Russia and moved to St Petersburg, 1905. Editor of the short-lived satirical journal, *Signal*. Moved to Kuokkala, Finland (now Repino), 1912. Wrote literary criticism and translated the works of American and English writers into Russian. Director of the children's section of *Parus* publishing house, 1916. Settled in Petrograd, 1917; wrote the majority of his children's poems, 1916–27. Moved to Moscow and to Peredelkino, 1930s. Recipient: Lenin Prize and Honorary D. Litt. from Oxford University, 1962. Died in Kuntsevo (near Moscow), 28 October 1969. Buried in Peredelkino.

Publications

Collected Edition

Sobranie sochinenii, 6 vols. Moscow, 1965–69.

Literary Criticism and Theory

Poeziia griadushchei demokratii [Poetry of the Coming Democracy]. Petrograd, 1918.

Printsipy khudozhestvennogo perevoda [Principles of Literary Translation]. 1919, (includes a chapter on poetry by Nikolai Gumilev); 2nd edition, expanded as *Iskusstvo perevoda*, Leningrad, 1930; 3rd edition as *Vysokoe iskusstvo*, Moscow, 1941; translated as *The Art of Translation: Kornei Chukovsky's "A High Art"*, by Lauren G. Leighton, Knoxville, University of Tennessee Press, 1984.

Kniga ob Aleksandre Bloke. Berlin and Petrograd, 1922; 2nd edition as *Aleksandr Blok kak chelovek i poet*, Petrograd, 1924; translated as *Aleksandr Blok as Man and Poet*, by Diana Burgin and Katherine Tiernan O'Connor, Ann Arbor, Ardis, 1982.

Poet i palach (Nekrasov i Murav'ev). Petrograd, 1922; translated as *The Poet and the Hangman (Nekrasov and Muravyov)*, by R.W. Rotsel, Ann Arbor, Ardis, 1977.

Malen'kie deti [Small Children]. 1928; later editions as *Ot dvukh do piati*; translated as *From Two to Five*, by Miriam Morton, Berkeley, University of California Press, 1963.

Liudi i knigi shestidesiatykh godov [People and Books of the 1960s]. Leningrad, 1934; later editions as *Liudi i knigi* [People and Books]. Moscow, 1958; 1960.

Masterstvo Nekrasova [The Craft of Nekrasov]. Moscow, 1952; 1959; 1962.

Chekhov. 1958; later edition as *O Chekhove*, 1967; translated as *Chekhov the Man*, by Pauline Rose, London, Hutchinson, 1945; New York, Haskell House, 1974.

Poetry for Children

Vania i Krokodil [Vania and the Crocodile]. 1917; later as *Prikliucheniia Krokodila Krokodilovicha* [The Adventures of Krokodil Krokodilovich]; translated as *Crocodile*, by Babette Deutsch, Philadelphia, Lippincott, 1931; also translated by Richard Coe, London, Faber, 1964.

Moidodyr. Petrograd, 1923; translated as *Wash 'Em Clean*, by E. Felgenhauer, Moscow, Progress, 1969.

Skazki. 1935; translated as *Wonder Tales*, by Dorian Rottenberg and E. Felgenhauer, Moscow, Progress, 1973.

Memoirs and Diaries

Gimnaziia. Vospominaniia detstva [The Gymnasium. Memoirs of Childhood]. Moscow, 1938; later edition as *Serebrianyi gerb*; translated as *The Silver Crest: My Russian Boyhood*, by Beatrice Stillman, New York, Holt Rinehart and Winston, 1976; Oxford, Oxford University Press, 1977.

Repin, Gor'kii, Maiakovskii, Briusov. Vospominaniia. Moscow, 1940.

Iz vospominanii [From My Memoirs]. Moscow, 1958; expanded edition, 1959.

Sovremenniki. Portrety i etiudy [Contemporaries. Portraits and Etudes]. Moscow, 1962.

Dnevnik 1901–1929, [Diary 1901–1929]. 2nd corrected edition, Moscow, 1992.

Dnevnik 1930–1969 [Diary 1930–1969]. Moscow, 1993.

Other Writing

Chukokkala. Rukopisnyi al'manakh [An Album of Manuscripts]. Moscow, 1979.

Critical Studies

"Kornei Chukovskii", by Iurii Tynianov, *Detskaia literatura*, 4 (1939), 24–26; translated as "Kornei Chukovskii", *Soviet Studies in Literature*, 24/2 (1988), 95–100.

Kniga o Kornee Chukovskom, by Miron Petrovskii, Moscow, 1966.
"Siuzhetnoe masterstvo kritika", by E. Dobin, *Novyi mir*, 3 (1970), 223–39.
"'Ia – dobryi lev'. Iz vospominanii o Kornee Chukovskom", by Veniamin Kaverin, *Iunost'*, 4 (1972), 70–76.
Vospominaniia o Kornee Chukovskom, edited by K.I. Lozovskaia, Z.S. Papernyi, and E.Ts. Chukovskaia, Moscow, 1977.
Zhizn' i tvorchestvo Korneia Chukovskogo, edited by Valentin Berestov, Moscow, 1978.
"Chukovskii, Kornei Ivanovich", by Lidiia Korneevna Chukovskaia, in *The Modern Encyclopedia of Russian and Soviet Literatures*, vol. 4, Gulf Breeze, Florida, Academic International Press, 1981, 126–37.
"Grandfather Kornei: On the Centenary of the Birth of Kornei Chukovsky", by Dmitrii Urnov, *Soviet Literature* 4/409 (1982), 123–27.
"Sobesednik klassikov", by Z. Papernyi, *Oktiabr'* 3 (1982), 179–83.
Russian Poetry for Children, by Elena Sokol, Knoxville, University of Tennessee Press, 1984, 3–24, 60–92 and *passim*.
"Kornei Chukofsky, Whitman's Russian Translator", by Gay Wilson Allen, *The Mickle Street Review*, 9/2 (1988), 35–41.
"Humor in the Lyrical Stories for Children of Samuel Marshak and Korney Chukovsky", by Andreas Bode and Martha Baker, *The Lion and the Unicorn: A Critical Journal of Children's Literature*, 13/2 (December 1989), 34–55.
Pamiati detstvo, by Lidiia Korneevna Chukovskaia, Moscow, 1989; translated as *To the Memory of Childhood*, by Eliza Kellogg Close, Evanston, Illinois, Northwestern University Press, 1988.
"La traduction selon Chukovsky", by Sylvie Clamogeran, *Revue Langues et Linguistique*, 5 (1989), 295–304.

Bibliography
Sovetskaia khudozhestvennaia literatura i kritika, 1938–1948. Bibliografiia, by N. Matsuev, Moscow, 1952, 362–64.

Kornei Ivanovich Chukovskii was born Nikolai Vasil'evich Korneichuk on 31 March 1882, in St Petersburg. His mother, Ekaterina Korneichukova, was a peasant from the Poltava *guberniia*; his father, a Petersburg student, abandoned her when Nikolai was three years old. Korneichukova moved with the two children to Odessa and supported them by doing laundry. The young Nikolai was expelled from the fifth class of the Gymnasium after an imperial edict banned lower-class, so-called "cooks' children", from higher education. He continued to teach himself and worked at a number of odd jobs; he recalled tracing and erasing English words he was memorizing with his trowel in roofing tar. Bitterly aware of his poverty and illegitimacy, he found Odessa full of deadening middle-class self-satisfaction.

In 1901 Chukovskii started writing for *Odesskie novosti*, signing all his work with the pseudonym formed from his last name, erasing both its "peasant" sound and all traces of his father. At about the same time he married and encouraged his wife, Mariia Borisovna, to teach herself English as well. In 1903–04 he was sent as a correspondent to London, where he read in libraries all day and "fell in love" with Anglo-American literature. The Odessa paper stopped printing his letters about books and writers, but they interested Valerii Briusov, who invited Chukovskii to contribute to the journal *Vesy*. Back in Russia in 1905, Chukovskii moved to St Petersburg and began publishing literary criticism that combined biography with impressionistic interpretation. He edited a weekly satirical journal, *Signal*, closed after the fourth issue for overly brave satire and cartoons; Chukovskii himself was arrested and briefly jailed. His first son Nikolai (1904–65), received the first name that Chukovskii himself had shed; he later became a novelist. Lidiia, born in 1907, became a prominent dissident, novelist and publicist. Chukovskii's first slim book of translations of Walt Whitman appeared in 1907, but in 1914 his *Poeziia griadushchei demokratii* [Poetry of the Coming Democracy] was "destroyed by the censor" and not reissued until 1918. In 1912 the Chukovskii family began to live all year-round at a dacha in the village Kuokkola on the Gulf of Finland, a place they had visited since 1906.

Regretting his imperfect education, Chukovskii positioned himself on the sidelines of creative literature as a critic, admirer, editor, recorder, and handmaid to artists. He visited and entertained important literary and artistic figures. Waking early every day, he worked constantly, revising his books for every new edition, even when not plagued by his lifelong insomnia – a problem that encouraged prolificity. No one was allowed to disturb him while he worked, but when he finished he would play with his children and their friends, rowing them on the Gulf, reciting poetry loudly to the waves and teaching them to worship literature and imagination as he did. He began observing children's language with his own children, but after describing this interest in an article he began to receive letters from other parents and educators. This initiated his work on children's language acquisition and his writing for children.

In 1917 the family moved to Petrograd, and from 1918 Chukovskii worked in the Anglo-American division of "Worldwide Literature" (*Vsemirnaia literatura*) until that publisher was closed in the 1920s. He changed his name legally as soon as possible after the Revolution. For several years the family shared the general poverty of war communism, sometimes having to take turns going outside since the family owned only one pair of galoshes. Chukovskii's background and political opinions inclined him to welcome the new system, but in the new Soviet regimentation of literary life he turned from the increasingly dangerous arena of literary criticism to many other interests. This change of emphasis, if not of profession, meant editing, translating, literary scholarship and writing for and about children. He devoted special attention to Nikolai Nekrasov, a favourite whose poetry had been distorted by tsarist censorship and fallen into obscurity; Chukovskii considered the annotated 1926 edition of Nekrasov's *Polnoe sobranie stikhotvorenii* [Complete Collected Verse] to be his major work. His children's poems, a new form based on English nursery rhymes and Russian folklore, won immediate and lasting popularity. To his chagrin, Chukovskii became famous not as a critic or scholar, but as the author of "Aibolit" and "Mukha-Tsokotukha". The poems were condemned in the 1920s as fantastic and irresponsible nonsense by such leading lights of pedagogy as Nadezhda Krupskaia, and Chukovskii prudently reduced production.

The Chukovskiis' youngest child Mariia died painfully of

tuberculosis at the age of 11 in 1931, and their second son, Boris, died fighting in the early part of World War II – personal tragedies in a time of societal convulsions. During and after the Stalinist terror, Chukovskii tried to help many people who were arrested or repressed, writing reams of letters to well-connected acquaintances, but he also kept himself out of trouble. His essential optimism, class background and work habits suited the Soviet model; it did not hurt that Lenin himself had praised his early work on Nekrasov. After moving to Moscow, Chukovskii continued literary life there. For decades he was a defining part of Peredelkino, setting up a children's library, building bonfires every winter and reciting poetry for the local children. In evacuation during World War II he wrote more poetry for children, fearing the effects of war and violence on children's psyche. Chukovskii's wife Mariia Borisovna died in 1955, leaving him even more plagued by insomnia.

In 1957 Chukovskii received an honorary doctorate in philology; in 1962 he won a Lenin Prize for his *Masterstvo Nekrasova* [The Craft of Nekrasov] and became the second Russian honorary doctor of letters at Oxford University. By the time he died on 28 October 1969, his many books had appeared in hundreds of separate editions and had sold several tens of millions of copies. His only surviving child, Lidiia Korneevna Chukovskaia, maintained his three rooms in the Peredelkino dacha as a museum of his library, archive, and tradition of literary and personal contacts.

SIBELAN FORRESTER

Mikhail (Mikhailo) Dmitrievich Chulkov c.1734–1792

Poet

Biography

Born in Moscow, probably in 1734, into an impoverished family of the merchant class. Actor with Volkov's Iaroslav troupe; performed in St Petersburg, 1752. Attended Moscow University gymnasium, 1756. Performed with the Court Theatre in St Petersburg, 1761. Appointed to service in Imperial household, 1765. Civil servant with rank of Collegiate Registrar; served in the Senate, 1772. Financial situation improved, acquired estate with peasants. Elevated to the service nobility, 1789. Died 4 November 1792.

Publications

Fiction

Peresmeshnik, ili slavenskie skazki [The Mocker, or Slavonic Fairytales], parts 1–4, St Petersburg, 1766–68; 3rd revised edition, parts 1–5, Moscow, 1789.

Prigozhaia povarikha, ili Pokhozhdenie razvratnoi zhenshchiny [The Comely Cook, or, A Dissolute Woman's Progress]. St Petersburg, 1770; in *Russkaia literatura XVIII veka*, Moscow, 1970; translated as *The Comely Cook* (excerpts), by Harold B. Segel, in *The Literature of 18th-Century Russia*, vol. 2, New York, Dutton, 1967.

Poetry

Plachevnoe padenie stikhotvortsev. Satiricheskaia poema. Stikhi na kacheli, Stikhi na semik, na maslenitsu [The Lamentable Fall of Poets. A Satirical Poem. Verses about a Swing, Verses on the Feast of the Seventh Thursday after Easter, on Shrove-Tide], St Petersburg, 1775; selections edited by B.V. Tomashevskii, in *Iroi-komicheskaia poema*, Leningrad, 1933; also in *Poety XVIII veka*, vol. 1, Leningrad, 1958.

Play

Kak khochesh' nazovi [Call It What You Like], edited by N. Khardzhiev, *Literaturnoe nasledstvo*, 9–10, 1933.

Historical Writing

Istoricheskoe opisanie rossiiskoi torgovli [Historical Description of Russian Trade], 21 vols. 1781–88.

Editor

Kratkoi mifologicheskoi leksikon [A Short Dictionary of Mythology]. St Petersburg, 1767.

Sobranie raznykh pesen [Collection of Diverse Songs] parts I–IV. St Petersburg, 1770–74; 2nd edition, vol. 1, 1776; 3rd expanded edition, parts I–IV, Moscow, 1780–81.

Slovar' russkikh sueverii [A Dictionary of Russian Superstitions]. St Petersburg, 1782; 2nd edition, Moscow, 1786.

Critical Studies

Chulkov, Levshin, by Viktor Shklovskii, Leningrad, 1933.

Mikhail Čulkov, by J. Garrard, The Hague, Mouton, 1970.

"Some Comments on Narrative Prose Fiction in 18th-Century Russian Literature, with Special Reference to Chulkov", by J. Goodliffe, *Melbourne Slavic Studies*, 5–6 (1970).

"Mikhail Chulkov's 'Double-Talk' Narrative (*Skazka o rozhdenii taftianoi mushki* – The Tale of the Origin of the Taffeta Beauty Patch)", by I.R. Titunik, *Canadian-American Slavic Studies*, 9 (1975), 30–42.

A History of 18th Century Russian Literature, by William Edward Brown, Ann Arbor, Ardis, 1980.

"Mikhail Chulkov's *The Comely Cook*", by Alexander Levitsky, *Russian Literature Triquarterly*, 21 (1988), 97–115.

The retrospective critical analyses of two centuries have presented Mikhail Chulkov to us finally as the consolidator of the picaresque tradition in 18th-century Russia. As an author whose role in the creation of the Russian novel is so central, however, Chulkov ought properly to be seen against the background of his numerous other literary guises, for he flourishes at just the moment that sees the emergence in Russia of the native man of letters, devoted to any number of belletristic pursuits through vocation.

This many-faceted engagement with literary legacies, styles of telling, and tones of voice illuminate Chulkov's first important publication. *Peresmeshnik, ili slavenskie skazki* [The Mocker, or Slavonic Fairytales], volumes of which appeared during the late 1760s. Behind the persona of the "mocker", which he came to believe fitted him well, Chulkov presents a variegated assemblage of anecdotes and adventure stories drawing on a fantastical folk-world of his own imagining, with details and echoes from actual traditions. Here is a kaleidoscopic amalgam of the "wandering themes" of medieval tale-telling, of chivalric deeds, classical mythology, the Russian oral inheritance, the crooked line of the picaro's progress through life. Magically conditioned by the several agencies of good and ill which they encounter, the heroes' adventures in a variety of half-recognizable, half-mythologized locations meander as one expects from 18th-century fiction towards a vaguely moral conclusion that alludes distantly to optimism, virtue and Providence. Chulkov the novelist, poet, journalist, economist, and folklorist was manifestly a "littérateur", but no moralist. Perhaps, in the French sense of an observer and delineator of traits, "mortaliste" would be closer; and this entertaining anthology can in that regard be held to adumbrate Chulkov's masterwork, the novel in which his eye for detail and ear for the demotic are most successfully brought to bear.

The novel on which Chulkov's reputation stands, *Prigozhaia povarikha, ili Pokhozhdenie razvratnoi zhenshchiny* [The Comely Cook, or, A Dissolute Woman's Progress], was published in 1770. The beautiful young widowed cook Martona is the opportunist's opportunist, lying, stealing, and cheating her way towards financial security in a readily recognizable "real-life" environment, conjured efficiently in image and dialogue. It is Chulkov's task to prevent the readers' sympathies with Martona from evaporating entirely – and she is not in fact incapable of disinterestedness and affection – and it is in the author's manipulation of the attractiveness of bad behaviour that his subtle ironies and imaginative deftness are worked through. The reader is presented with the facts of familiar, quotidian Russian life on each page of the novel. It is a novel replete with phrases, jokes, proverbs, the common coin of street wisdom. Characters are placeable: Martona's husband was killed at the Battle of Poltava, and the circumstances of her poverty – the spur of her self-advancement are unstintingly supplied. The interior of buildings, the sort of things that shop-assistants say, the lies that Martona tells her lovers, and they her, are "realia" that act as a fixative for readers. The comely cook is psychologically tangible and no mere archetype, though naturally she is that too. Her progress towards wealth concretizes a number of abiding concerns: poverty, ambition, deceit, and so on, not to mention the fact that the hero is a heroine, an amusing and deeply "literary" device, at once waving the flag for women and setting fire to it. Instead of the predictable sermonizing of the "edifying" novel we have evidence of Chulkov's immersion in the techniques of fiction-writing, deployed delightedly for their own sake, indulged in for the pleasure of a reading public that already knows right from wrong. To her lovers the cook is a "Venus" a "Helen of Troy", and to many readers a mere trollop. The author is at pains to intrude no censure or final word at all on the manner of her betterment.

Familiar himself with the class of the merchants, shopkeepers, clerks, the uncelebrated and hard-working broad sweep of literate but uneducated Russia, Chulkov's journalistic writing talks to these people in their own language, understanding their interests, diversions and wants. The journalistic field was very busily expanding in the 1760s and 1770s, with the progressivistic, "Enlightening" efforts of Nikolai Novikov, of Ruban, or Emin. Chulkov's own chief journalistic publication, *I to i se* [This and That] is smaller-scale: the importance of thrift, domestic economy, the weight of the rouble and the arshin.

Fascination with folklore shows here too, in re-tellings of old tales, explanations of spells and incantations. Interest in folklore and song impelled Chulkov to publish, from 1770 to 1774, his four-volume *Sobranie raznykh pesen* [Collection of Diverse Songs], the first Russian printed songbook and a compendium of historical and contemporaneous examples of ballads, sung tales, fragments of folk epics, and heroic-comic burlesques, of which Chulkov was an *amateur*, and samples of which he attempted at times. Implied throughout is a rejection of the generic canons of classicism (still prevalent) in favour of a rich eclecticism, a persistent theme in many of Chulkov's journalistic forays.

Anthologizing of folklore and songbooks aside, Chulkov also wrote a play, *Kak khochesh' nazovi* [Call It What You Like], unpublished in his lifetime, and the monumental and ground-breaking 21-volume *Istoricheskoe opisanie rossiiskoi torgovli* [Historical Description of Russian Trade] (1781–88).

NICHOLAS CROWE

D

Iulii Markovich Daniel' 1925–1988

Prose writer, poet, and literary translator

Biography

Born in Moscow, 15 November 1925. Served in the Soviet Army, 1943–44: severely wounded and discharged. Studied philology at Kharkov University and at Moscow District Pedagogical Institute, 1946–51. Married: Larisa Bogoraz in 1950. Teacher in Kaluga, 1951–54, and then in Moscow. His novella, *Begstvo* [Flight], printed by Children's State Publishing House, 1958, but prohibited from sale. Worked as a translator into Russian of Yiddish, Slavonic, and Caucasian poetry from 1957. Simultaneously with "legitimate" work, began to publish "subversive" stories abroad under the pseudonym of Nikolai Arzhak, 1956–63. Arrested with Andrei Siniavskii, September 1965; tried for anti-Soviet activities (*tamizdat* writing), February 1966, and sentenced to five years' hard labour. Released in 1970. Lived first in Kaluga, then Moscow. Died 30 December 1988.

Publications

Collected Edition

Govorit Moskva: Proza, poeziia, perevody [This is Moscow Speaking: Prose, Poetry, Translations]. Moscow, 1991.

Fiction

Govorit Moskva. Washington, DC, Inter-Language Literary Associates, 1962; translated as *This is Moscow Speaking and Other Stories*, by Stuart Hood, Harold Shukman, and John Richardson, London, Collins and Harvill Press, 1968; New York, Dutton, 1969.

Ruki i Chelovek iz MINAPa. Washington, DC, Inter-Language Literary Associates, 1963; translated as *The Man from M.I.S.P. and Hands*, by M.V. Nesterov, London, Flegon Press, 1966.

Iskuplenie [Atonement]. Washington, DC, Inter-Language Literary Associates, 1964.

Poetry

Stikhi iz nevoli. Biblioteka samizdata, 3, Amsterdam, Fond imeni Gertsena, 1971; translated as *Prison Poems*, by David Burg and Arthur Boyars, London, Calder and Boyars, 1971.

Critical Studies

"'Priroda i t'iurma': O tvorchestve Abrama Tertsa i Nikolaia Arzhaka", by B.A. Filippov, *Grani*, 60 (1966), 75–93.

On Trial: The Case of Sinyavsky (Tertz) and Daniel (Arzhak), edited by Leopold Labedz and Max Hayward, New York, Harper, and London, Harvill Press, 1966; revised edition, Westport, Connecticut, Greenwood Press, 1980.

Belaia kniga po delu A. Siniavskogo i Iu. Danielia, edited by A. Ginzburg, Frankfurt, Posev, 1967.

Andrei Siniavskii and Julii Daniel': Two Soviet "Heretical" Writers, by Margaret Dalton, Würzburg, Jal, 1973.

"The Theme of Atonement in Yulii Daniel's 'Atonement'", by R.L. Chapple, *South Atlantic Bulletin*, 40/4 (1975), 53–60.

Tsena metafory ili prestuplenie i nakazanie Siniavskogo i Danielia, edited by E.M. Velikanova and L.S. Eremina, Moscow, 1989.

"Vozvrashchenie s progulki (K urokam odnogo politicheskogo protsessa)", by Igor' Ivolgin, *Iunost'*, 12 (1990), 58–61.

As a writer Iulii Daniel', though talented in prose and verse, was always in the shadow of his more prolific and colourful co-defendant at their notorious trial, Andrei Siniavskii (Abram Terts). Apart from his translations, several of which were highly praised by the authors of the originals, Daniel''s published literary output consists only of four prose stories and a slim book of prison poems. The highly personal verses are formally conventional and deceptively simple; the stories are written in a realistic, albeit ironical manner and with a sharp satirical edge and strong psychological perception.

"Ruki" ("Hands") 1956–57, the earliest and shortest of the stories, is based on a real occurrence. Narrated by a factory worker who has been recruited into the Cheka in the 1920s, it tells, in the form of reminiscences to an unseen friend, of his recruitment, training, and work, culminating in an order to kill three priests, the third of whom traumatized him by miraculously refusing to die (the Chekist colleagues had put a blank in his pistol as a joke). Following this episode, chronically trembling hands led to his dismissal as unfit for service. The use of a simple worker as narrator affords Daniel' many possibilities. *Skaz* (narration in the first person) brings humour to the picture of life in the Cheka and grotesquely highlights moral problems of which the simple narrator is barely aware. The author shows himself a master of low colloquial Russian mixed with Soviet slogans of the time, using the comical naivety of his narrator to contrast with the cruel events described. The morality of killing for the sake of an idea, exemplified by the order to murder innocent priests, is raised in still more direct form in the next story, *Govorit Moskva* (*This is Moscow Speaking*) 1962.

Set in contemporary Moscow, Daniel''s second story, written

in a matter-of-fact ironic style, combines realism with grotesque fantasy. Moscow radio announces an official "Day of Public Murders", which permits any citizen to murder any other citizen. This situation affords opportunities for satire on many topics, including Soviet broadcasting, hack literature, political naivety and quietism, lax morality, anti-Semitism, and racism. Most striking, however, are the reactions of the Moscow intellectuals who, instead of challenging the monstrosity of such an ordinance, think mainly of how the government is trying to trick and compromise them, and of how to protect their own skins. Few murders are in fact committed, for most people hide, but the hero, Andrei Kartsev, gradually comes to understand the official intention behind the announcement, namely to intimidate the population. Of the many characters in the story who are quick to forget this day afterwards (implying, of course, the absurdity of much of official Soviet life), only Kartsev remembers the chastening implications of the Day: "You must not let [them] frighten you. You have to answer for yourself and through this you answer for others."

Chelovek iz MINAPa (*The Man from M.I.S.P.*) 1963, is in a lighter, more purely farcical vein of satire. It tells of how a student at the Moscow Institute of Scientific Profanation, Volodia Zaleskii, suddenly acquires miraculous erotic powers, namely that he can determine the sex of children at the climax of coitus by thinking of Karl Marx for a boy and Klara Zetkina for a girl. He becomes popular with Moscow housewives for a time, but is eventually caught in the act and tried for immorality by the Young Communist organization in a brilliant parody of a Stalin show trial. Soon, however, Zaleskii's talent is recognized as of benefit to the State, which claims him as a triumph of Soviet genetics, and, in a hilarious Party meeting, sets about his commercial and propagandistic exploitation. Again Daniel' displays a lively command of colloquial speech and humorous satirical observation.

Iskuplenie [Atonement] (1964) is the most serious and sombre as well as the longest of the stories. Its narrator, Viktor Vol'skii, like Kartsev in *This is Moscow Speaking*, is an easy-going, conformist Moscow intellectual who is suddenly faced by a moral crisis, this time one from within: he is accused of an earlier political denunciation by a former fellow student, Chernov, who has spent ten years in the camps for anti-Soviet propaganda and is now out for revenge. Vol'skii cannot prove his innocence, and as a result loses his friends and his beloved. Burdened by hostility and psychological pressure, he ends up in an asylum, aware that, although innocent of Chernov's charge, he is in fact guilty by silence and inaction for all the denunciations and repressions of the Stalin years. Like Kartsev, he has an acute sense of collective responsibility. The story is more ambitious than its predecessors, bringing to the foreground moral and ethical problems, and also introducing an interesting stratum of poetry, subtle fantasy, and symbolism, rising to a metaphysical level absent in his earlier works.

Daniel' wrote verse throughout the post-war years, although none was published. The prison poems reflect some of the main ideas of the stories, including punishment for sins of silence and omission, but they are also, naturally, concerned with lack of freedom, family loyalty, uncertainty, and the moral and physical squalor of the KGB and their prison. The poems are notably erudite and informed by a strong religious feeling, forceful and morally resilient. Anna Akhmatova described Daniel' as "a poet with a great and clear mind"; in technique he seems to have learned from, among others, Pasternak and Zabolotskii. Particularly important features are the poems' rich and original imagery, and Daniel''s combination of conventional Russian strophic forms with typically Jewish barbed humorous cadences.

If the poems are classical with a Jewish tinge, the stories with their vivid use of *skaz* and satirical bent recall something of Zoshchenko and Il'f and Petrov. The satire of Daniel'/Arzhak may well in turn have influenced later writers like Aksenov and Aleshkovskii. His greatest fame, however, is as defendant at a highly documented trial.

ARNOLD MCMILLIN

Ekaterina Romanovna Dashkova 1743–1810

Prose writer

Biography

Born in Moscow, 28 March 1743, into an influential diplomatic and political family. Educated privately, partially in Europe. Director of St Petersburg Academy of Sciences from 1783. President of the Russian Academy, 1783–96. Active in governmental and diplomatic circles. Retired from public life to family estate at Troitskii, near Moscow, 1801. Died in Troitskii, 16 January 1810.

Publications

Collected Edition

Dashkova, E.R. Literaturnye sochineniia [Literary Works]. Moscow, 1990.

Play

Toisiokov. Komediia v piati deistviiakh. St Petersburg, 1786.

Editor

Novye ezhemesiachnye sochineniia [New Monthly Compositions]. St Petersburg, 1786–96.

Memoirs

Zapiski, first published in English as *Memoirs of the Princess Daschkaw*, translated by Mrs W. Bradford, London, Henry Colburn, 1840; (in Russian) London, 1859; reprinted St Petersburg, 1907; Moscow, 1990; translated as *The Memoirs of Princess Dashkova*, by Kyril FitzLyon, with an introduction by Jehanne M. Gheith, Durham, North Carolina, Duke University Press, 1995.

Zapiski, 1743–1810 [Memoirs]. Leningrad, 1985.

Dashkova, E.R. Zapiski. Pis'ma sester M. i K. Vil'mot iz Rossii [Memoirs. Letters from the Sisters M. and C. Wilmot from Russia], edited by S.S. Dmitriev. Moscow, 1987.

Critical Studies

Vo glave dvukh akademii, by L. Ia. Lozinskaia, Moscow, 1983.

Russkaia memuaristika XVIII–pervoi poloviny XIX v. Ot rukopisi k knige, by A.G. Tartakovskii, Moscow, 1991.

Ekaterina Romanovna Dashkova: Issledovaniia i materialy. St Petersburg, 1996.

In an entire range of highly-polished memoirs, journals, reflections, and society correspondence, Princess Dashkova left a portrait of the manners and circumstances of the late 18th-century milieu with which she was familiar. Her multifarious observations are characteristically well-turned, elegant and witty, although her attachment to the *bon ton* is in all matters underlaid by an acute critical sharpness that at once sets her outside her genteel-born environment on which she comments. Her intelligence, her discrimination and judgements were keen and utterly her own; naturally her cast of mind, its relaxed responses, and her education were of the type that came to her by right of birth. These elementary components of her writing used regularly to be confounded in 19th-century scholarship of the older kind, but latterly their engaging interaction has been stimulating to criticism in such a way as to present the figure of the Princess in the round.

Dashkova was deeply involved in the journalistic culture of her time, and it was in this arena – taken to be a serious literary genre in the climate of the "new" Russian culture – that she properly cut her teeth. Working alongside her friend and confidante, Empress Catherine II, for instance as co-editor of *Sobesednik liubitelei Rossiisskogo slova* [Companion of Lovers of the Russian Word], the Princess shared the Empress's view of the philological investigations, literary criticism, literature in translation, and drama that the journal promulgated. That is, the frame of reference was largely conservative, or at the very least traditional in character, counterpointing a different school of journalistic writing, far more iconoclastic and challenging, which was then flexing its muscles under the "Enlightened" proprietorship of Nikolai Novikov. Something of the same can be said of Dashkova's *Novye ezhemesiachnye sochineniia* [New Monthly Compositions], but none of this is to imply that the Princess was implicated in the sparring – occasionally malicious – indulged in by the more fractious siblings of the so-called "family of journals" characterizing journalistic writing in the late 18th century. The breezy salon-style, light-conversational timbre of much of contemporary society literature (often written off as dilettantism, then as now) also accounts for Dashkova's foray into drama – *Toisiokov* (1786), an amusing and rather unambitious *comédie de moeurs* whose very title – deriving from a phrase meaning "this and that" – points up its episodic lightness of touch.

Dashkova's more substantial work, her journals and memoirs, began to be composed at a slightly later date, at the start of the 19th century. Written in French and posthumously published as (usually) *Zapiski* (*Memoirs*), they were highly prized by, among numerous others, Pushkin and, later, Herzen, who arranged publication in London of this treasure-trove of 18th-century social and political lore. In this latter respect they proved invaluable, for example, to the Free Russian Press in unravelling the political complexities of the period.

The memoirs range comprehensively, treating of foreign travel and the luminaries (including Voltaire and Diderot) encountered, the experience of Dashkova's presidency of two Russian academies (the St Petersburg Academy of Sciences and the Russian Academy), Russian mores under four tsars, from the Elizabethan period through Peter III, Catherine II and Paul I. The future Alexander I, then uncrowned, is also alluded to, most unflatteringly. The intrigue of the Catherinian court, the perpetual fog of plotting and hatching, is unhesitatingly evoked. The fate of the court favourites is there to read, together with the fate of those who signally failed to win imperatricial favour (Alexander Radishchev, for example), generally accompanied by Dashkova's own comment and observations.

After much persuasion, the elderly Princess was eventually prevailed upon to set down her memoirs by Martha Wilmot, the daughter of some English friends, who stayed at the Princess's estate at Troitskii, not far from Moscow, from 1803 to 1808, and to whom the *Memoirs* (1804–05) were cordially dedicated. As she makes clear at several points in the memoirs, and as is plentifully testified to in correspondence, Dashkova did not intend them to be published in her lifetime. This was largely a matter of due propriety, and it allowed her often censorious pen freer play, but there is no doubt that she did want her imaginatively conceived observations to appear sooner or later before a wider public than that for which an earlier generation of memoirists (including her elder brother, Prince A.R. Vorontsov) had written.

Owing to Dashkova's disinclination to oversee the banausic incidentals of publication and transmission, the *Memoirs* underwent tortuous journeys in manuscript before finally they appeared. Dashkova's autograph was copied by Martha Wilmot, and simultaneously by Catherine Wilmot, her sister, then also a guest at Troitskii. Catherine's copy went back with her to England, Martha's went into Dashkova's personal archive. In 1807 Martha, on her way home to England, decided with the Princess's blessing to take the original autograph with her, together with some letters to Dashkova by the late Empress. In the event, however, Anglo-Russian diplomatic awkwardness, and the suspicion that Martha might be trying to smuggle seditious or otherwise sensitive documents into England, meant that the papers were confiscated and destroyed before they left Russian soil. It was, then, the Wilmots' French copies, one in Russia, one in England, that came to provide the original texts for belated publication of the *Memoirs*, which only then came about (first in English translation, then in Russian) through the good agency of the Princess's vast network of friends and family. What immediately recommended their contents – largely by that time of purely antiquarian interest – was the freshness and fluency of

Dashkova's literary manner: historically accurate, cosmopolitan, patrician, and at all points thoroughly querulous.

NICHOLAS CROWE

Anton Antonovich Del'vig 1798–1831

Poet

Biography

Born in Moscow, 17 August 1798, into a Russified Baltic family of German origin. Attended Tsarskoe Selo *lycée*; became close friends with Pushkin. Began writing poetry in his teenage years. Connected with A.N. Olenin's literary circle, the Green Lamp literary group, and the Free Society of Lovers of Russian literature. Involved in publication of the journal *Poliarnaia zvezda*, 1823–24; editor of *Severnye tsvety*, 1825. Married: Sof'ia Mikhailovna Saltykova; one daughter. Entered the civil service, 1828. Published his only collection of verse, 1829. Editor of *Literaturnaia gazeta*, 1830. Died in St Petersburg, 26 January 1831.

Publications

Collected Editions

Polnoe sobranie stikhotvorenii. Leningrad, 1934; 2nd edition, 1959.

Sochineniia. Leningrad, 1986.

Critical Studies

"Literaturnaia gazeta" A.A. Del'viga i A.S. Pushkina, 1830–31, by E.M. Blinova, Moscow, 1966.

Baron Delvig's "Northern Flowers 1825–1832: Literary Almanac of the Pushkin Pleiad, by John Mersereau, Jr, Carbondale, Southern Illinois University Press, 1967.

Anton Antonovich Del'vig: A Classicist in the Time of Romanticism, by Ludmilla Koehler, The Hague, Mouton, 1970.

Severnye tsvety: istoriia al'manakha Del'viga-Pushkina, by V.E. Vatsuro, Moscow, 1978.

Poety Pushkinskoi pory, by V.I. Korovin, Moscow, 1980.

Iz istorii literaturnogo byta pushkinskoi pory, by V. Vatsuro, Moscow, 1989.

Anton Del'vig's family were russified Livlanders. The eldest of eight children, he was educated in the Tsarskoe Selo *lycée*, a hothouse of poetic genius. Here he became Pushkin's closest friend. A slow developer of phenomenal sloth, he nevertheless displayed a quirky individualism and was in his teens looked up to as a critic and as a poet in a Horatian vein. He was one of the first to declare Pushkin a genius. He played a leading part in the journal *Poliarnaia zvezda* in 1823–24, but shunned the radicalism of the Decembrists. As an editor and literary midwife, he takes the credit for the almanac *Severnye tsvety* in 1825. The disaster that struck him in 1825 was purely private: his marriage to Sof'ia Mikhailovna Saltykova was made in hell; her callous promiscuity broke up the classical dream world of his lyrics and turned him into a stark, tragic romantic. At the same time, by making herself the centre of a salon, Sof'ia Mikhailovna established Del'vig as the still point around which Pushkin's literary world revolved in the later 1820s. In 1828 Del'vig became a civil servant, and in 1829 published his sole collection of verse *Stikhotvoreniia barona Del'viga*, which was politely dismissed by most critics as an anachronism in a new age. For most of 1830 Del'vig published and edited *Literaturnaia gazeta*. His distaste for romantic effusion alienated many poets of his generation, and the frank articles he published about the French Revolution angered the authorities, in particular the chief of police, Count Benckendorff. Del'vig was too idle, or too despondent, to defend his journal effectively against scurrilous attacks, especially from the officially sponsored *Severnaia pchela*, and *Literaturnaia gazeta* was closed down after 64 issues. It revived briefly in 1831, but died with Del'vig. Despondency and a particularly bad chill are generally held responsible for the poet's sudden death at the age of 32. He left a one-year-old daughter who survived until 1913.

Del'vig's chief importance has been seen as an influence, especially posthumously, on Pushkin, who was deeply affected by the death of his closest friend ("The first death to make me weep ... Around him our poor handful gathered. Without him we are as good as orphaned," Pushkin wrote to Pletnev, January 1831). In his poetry, Pushkin felt Del'vig's death as an omen, even a summons to oblivion. In general, he was a poet's poet, forgotten by the Russian reader. At first reading, his vocabulary seems limited, his diction stylized, and his range of emotions narrow. But his vocabulary is no more limited than Verlaine's, and the repeated epithets acquire symbolic value. Del'vig's stylization deliberately creates an unsustainable private world, whose imminent death is the recurrently feared disaster, without which the poet would have lacked inspiration. The most important aspect of his poetry is to create a pastiche of classical idylls that contains a fearsome anticipation of the irruption of reality into an artificial dream world. The dream world is not so much one of erotic Arcadian delights as the sense of a band of noble brothers, and the reality is not just the prose of the daytime world, but treachery, official pressure, and loss of inspiration. Only poets such as Pushkin, who had experienced and retreated from Romantic freedoms, appreciated the emotional power that

Del'vig released so economically. To the ordinary reader, then as now, Del'vig merely seemed to be writing more chaste and less tortuous elegies for classicism than we find in his French masters, e.g., Evariste Parny. Del'vig's extended poems, however, such as "Kupal'nitsy" [The Bathers] (1824), and, in particular, "Konets zolotogo veka" [The End of the Golden Age] (1828), infiltrate modern awareness into myth. Beginning the latter poem with the declaration, "No, I am not in Arcadia ...", Del'vig's poetic persona is a time-traveller who flees the paradise he has imagined when he sees Shakespearean tragedy haunting it. Del'vig's nymph dies like Ophelia: "Singing her song, not sensing perdition nearing, / As if she was born to old father Ocean in liquid, / Before she had finished her sad song, she drowned". These idylls were more widely appreciated by Del'vig's contemporaries than his attempts at other genres, but not until the Neoclassicism of the 20th century do we find their influence in Russian poetry (very strongly, for instance, in Osip Mandel'shtam's *Tristia*).

Del'vig's tribute to romanticism lies in his pastiches of folk verse. Before Kol'tsov or Nekrasov, Del'vig caught the motifs and moods – and far better than later pasticheurs – the subtle displacements of rhythm: his "Russkaia pesnia" [Russian Song] (1820–21), rivals Goethe in its convincing evocation of a peasant girl's despair. Del'vig's widest influence was, however, in his romances, many of which are perpetuated by the music of Glinka; he is also one of the few Russian poets of the time to take sonnet form seriously. In 1822 he composed a number of very fine sonnets, which amount to an *art poétique*. The best known is "Vdokhnovenie" [Inspiration], which begins "Not often does inspiration fly down to us" and shows Del'vig's fundamentally moral stance in an amoral milieu with its conclusion:

And he [the darling of the muses], pursued by mankind
Wandering alone under the skies,
Speaks with ages yet to come;
He puts honour above all other parts,
His fame takes vengeance on slander
And he shares immortality with the gods.

Just before he died Del'vig's private hell inspired him to a few stark lyrics that are as powerful as Pushkin's last elegies. One is a poem to death: he invites "Death, calming of the soul" to come not to dinner but to his bleak solitary bed, where "In vain expectation / My night flows past". Del'vig's most memorable and hard-hitting poem, however, is his public vengeance on his widow: "Why, why have you poisoned / My life incurably?" Still more striking are Del'vig's unfinished ventures into other genres. Many of his idylls stray into drama and fragments such as "Otstavnoi soldat" [The Retired Soldier] (1829), or "Noch' na 24 iiunia" [The Eve of 24 June] show an original talent and a lack of momentum. An unwritten novel (or short story) that Del'vig had composed in his mind and which is based on the story of his unhappy marriage was narrated, apparently verbatim to friends. It may be the greatest work he never wrote.

DONALD RAYFIELD

Gavrila Romanovich Derzhavin 1743–1816

Poet

Biography

Born near Kazan, 14 July 1743, into a family of impoverished gentry. Received his early education at Kazan gymnasium; registered in the military, 1760. Served in Preobrazhenskii Regiment, 1762–73; first as private, then as a commissioned officer, 1772. Distinguished himself during the Pugachev Rebellion under General Bibikov, 1773–76. Resigned his commission, 1777. Married: 1) Ekaterina Bastidon in 1778; 2) Dar'ia D'iakova. Appointed as clerk in the Senate, 1778–84; Governor of Olonetsk Province, 1784; Governor of Tambov Province, 1785. Appointed personal secretary to Catherine II, 1791. Senator, 1793–94; while in the Senate became head of the Commerce Collegium, 1794. Minister of Justice of Russia, 1802–03. Retired to his estate Zvanka in the Novgorod region, 1803. Attended graduation at the Lyceum in Tsarskoe Selo and recognized the poetic genius of the young Pushkin, 1814. Died at Zvanka, 20 July 1816.

Publications

Poetry

Sochineniia Derzhavina s ob''iasnitel'nymi primechaniiami Ia. Grota, 9 vols. St Petersburg, 1864–83.
Stikhotvoreniia. Leningrad, 1933.
Stikhotvoreniia. Leningrad, 1957.
Stikhotvoreniia. Moscow, 1958.

Plays

Herod i Mariamna [Herod and Mariamna]. 1807.
Temnyi [The Dark One]. 1808.

Critical Studies

"Poetika Derzhavina", by B.M. Eikhenbaum, *Apollon*, 8 (1916), 23–45.
"Iz istorii odnoi ody 18-ogo veka", by G.A. Gukovskii, *Poetika*, 3 (1927), 129–47.
"Sochineniia Derzhavina," by V.G. Belinskii, in his *Polnoe sobranie sochinenii*, vol. 6, Moscow, 1955.
Masterstvo Derzhavina, by V.A. Zapadov, Moscow, 1958.
Rileggendo Derzhavin, by Angelo Maria Ripellino, Rome, Beniamino Carucci, 1961.

"Dans quelle mesure Derzhavin est-il un Baroque?", by Claude Backvis, in *Studies in Russian and Polish Literature*, edited by Zbigniew Foljewski *et al.*, The Hague, Mouton, 1962, 72–104.

Gavrila Romanovich Derzhavin, by V.A. Zapadov, Moscow, 1965.

Farbe, Licht und Klang in der malenden Poesie Derzhavins, by Helmut Kolle, Munich, Fink, 1966.

G.R. Derzhavin: A Political Biography, by Jesse V. Clardy, The Hague, Mouton, 1967.

Derzhavin, by I.Z. Serman, Leningrad, 1967.

"Literaturno-teoreticheskie vzgliady Derzhavina i 'Beseda liubitelei russkogo slova'", by M.G. Al'tshuller, *XVIII vek*, 8 (1969), 5–18.

"The Creative Imagination in Evolution: A Stylistic Analysis of G.R. Derzhavin's Panegyric and Meditative Odes, 1774–94", by Jane Gary Harris, Columbia University, PhD dissertation, 1969.

"Spornye voprosy v estetike Derzhavina", by A.N. Kulakova, *XVIII vek*, 8 (1969), 25–41.

"Derzhavin i Pushkin", by G.P. Makagonenko, *XVIII vek*, 8 (1969), 113–27.

"In Defence of Derzhavin's Plays", by J.A. Harvie, *New Zealand Slavonic Journal*, 2 (1975), 1–15.

G.R. Derzhavin: A Poet's Progress, by Pierre R. Hart, Columbus, Ohio, Slavica, 1978.

"The Chiasmatic Structure of Derzhavin's 'Bog'", by Anna Lisa Crone, *Slavic and East European Journal*, 38/3 (1994), 407–18.

Derjavine: Un poète russe dans L'Europe des Lumières [various authors], Paris, Institut d'Études Slaves, 1994.

"Doing Justice to Potemkin: Paradox, Oxymoron and Two Voices in Derzhavin's 'Waterfall'", by Anna Lisa Crone, *Russian History*, 21/3 (1994), 1–26.

Gavrila Derzhavin, edited by Efim Etkind and Svetlana El'nitskaia, Northfield, Vermont, Norwich University Press, 1995.

"New Love or Old Flower? Kant and Schelling in Derzhavin's and Baratynskii's Poetry", by Paul M. Wazzink, *Australian Slavonic and East European Studies*, 9/2 (1995), 1–26.

"Cheating Death: Derzhavin and Tsvetaeva on the Immortality of the Poet", by Anna Lisa Crone and Alexander Smith, *Slavic Almanach*, 3/3–4 (1995), 1–30.

Gavrila Derzhavin was the greatest Russian poet of the 18th century and remained the grey eminence of Russian poetry through Zhukovskii's literary debut to the youth of Pushkin and the poets of his Pleaide. With the writing of his famous ode to Catherine "Felitsa" (written 1782, published in 1783), Derzhavin began the most illustrious, if rocky, administrative career of any great Russian writer. Often accused of insubordination in administrative life, Derzhavin was likewise a maverick in his poetic career that spanned Neoclassicism, Sentimentalism, and pre-Romanticism.

After a brief period as a literary apprentice of Lomonosov (period of the Chitagalai odes, up to 1778) Derzhavin struck out on his own, writing a host of occasional, panegyric, and philosophical-spiritual odes. He elaborated his own odic form, at once panegyric and satiric – "Felitsa", "Videnie Murzy" ("The Murza's Vision"), "Reshemyslu" ("To 'Solution-Maker'"), "Vel'mozha" ("The Nobleman") – written in his "playful style" (*zabavnyi slog*). These works dealt a death blow to the classicist genre system. The language of most of Derzhavin's mature works and the hybrid ones in particular violates the classicist recommendations of Lomonosov in myriad ways. Words from Lomonosov's high and low styles coexist side by side, in a complete flaunting of the adjustment of style/lexicon and phraseology to genre and subject-matter. Russian and Church Slavic lexicon and grammar appear in every possible mixture. Derzhavin's inverted word orders and complex syntax have some affinities with the poetry of the baroque: excessive syntactic piling (ten subjects per verb, ten predicates for a single "supersubject"), as in "Na smert' kniazia Meshcherskogo" ("On the Death of Prince Meshcherskii") 1779, or intensive exploitation of verbs of motion with accusative directional complements, as in "Na vziatie Izmaila" ("On the Taking of Izmail"). The excessive inversions force the reader to wait for complements or even subjects of sentences. Such verbal and grammatical pyrotechnics are complemented by rich colour imagery and sound effects. The effect of this "aesthetics of excess" is to dazzle the reader/listener. It frequently results in a partial or delayed comprehension that for Derzhavin is part of the aesthetic experience. In his 1811 "Rassuzhdenie" ("Thoughts on Lyric Poetry or the Ode"), written when he was a member of Shishkov's archaizing Beseda, he describes the reader/hearer of an inspired ode or dithyramb as a man in a canoe being thrust by a wild river (the verbal torrent) through rough rapids or down a precipitous waterfall.

Perhaps the masterpiece of this literary type is "Vodopad" ("The Waterfall. On the Death of Potemkin") 1791–94, which encompasses elements of the Pindaric panegyric, with the funereal ode, the military ode, and philosophical meditation on human greatness, and heroism against the background of time-death's inexorable flow. Natural phenomena – the waterfall, the mountain – are described in their own right and yet stand as emblems for the human fates that are described. Potemkin, known as the "Prince of Darkness" for his mixed qualities, is not praised here without qualification but treated as "the bright darkness of a falling mountain", as the paradoxical complex of qualities that produce surpassing greatness. It is remarkable and indicative of Derzhavin's independent spirit that this ode was written at a time when many were trampling on the memory of Potemkin.

Of Derzhavin's several notable spiritual odes, the 1783 "Bog" ("God") is by far the most important. Drawing its lexicon and even imagery to a surprising degree from Lomonosov's two meditations on God's greatness, its verbal material is organized as a large chiasmus (11 stanzas) with numerous smaller chiasmata within, with man placed at the crux – the very middle of stanza 6. The ideas and the verbal material within "God" are Derzhavin's personal recasting of the theory of the Great Chain of Being. God, like the poet here, contains all the monads and connects the ends of the chain with its beginning. Thus the work becomes a verbal demonstration-in-action of the Deity described within it. An orgy of light imagery, like much of Derzhavin's verse, the ode treats God as Light and human enlightenment. It was one of the first Russian poetic works to be translated into a host of west European languages as well as into Japanese.

Though he initially became famous for his odes and was often rewarded by the Tsarina for them, Derzhavin always wrote lighter verse, and it became increasingly important in his *oeuvre* after 1794. Derzhavin's anacreontic poetry is adapted to Russian language and the realia of Russian life. He also wrote Russian songs with considerable folk flavour. He was an interesting early experimentor with sound textures and in versification. Derzhavin had a long-standing interest in classical music and in his later years, after 1804, he wrote operas and operettas on patriotic themes and for children. He authored one historical tragedy *Herod i Mariamna* [Herod and Mariamna] – the one serious theatrical work that was staged, based on a subject from Jospehus Flavius.

Derzhavin began his poetic and bureaucratic careers believing in enlightened absolutism as embodied in the rule of Catherine II. Unlike his contemporary Radishchev, he felt that Russia's ills lay not in the system itself but in corruption, abuses of privilege and the generally insufficient patriotism and vocation of the noble class, the constant brunt of his satirical odes, such as "The Nobleman". As his involvement in the administration, the Senate, and Catherine's court deepened, Derzhavin was unable to maintain his early faith in Russian absolutism and the general tenor of his odes moves sharply from praise to strong censure. He redefines the role of the true poet as standard-bearer of truth and justice, and evinces a stubborn adherence to his personal idea of the right, a trait that made him many enemies in the court and government service. Even his detractors begrudgingly granted that he was unusually devoted to patriotic service.

Much is written about Derzhavin's political savvy and his deft use of poetry to bail himself out of the many career problems to which his reformative zeal led. Yet it is unfair to label Derzhavin a careerist. Close reading of his civic poetry in the 1780s and 1790s shows that he valued his administrative career less and less. By the early 1790s it is clear that he had a strong sense of supreme importance in his own right as a poet and moral arbiter. Derzhavin's role in the evolving concept of the office of poet in Russia as a moral authority independent of the autocracy was important for the next generation and is generally underestimated.

Derzhavin had the same reformative, even revolutionary attitude towards the classicist aesthetic. In poetry, as in politics, he was a law unto himself, finally irreducible to any literary rubric or classification. For many years Derzhavin's independent achievement was overshadowed in scholarship by interest in Pushkin and the altogether different Pushkinian aesthetic that succeeded it. Idolized by his contemporaries, Derzhavin was appreciated by Belinskii and especially by Gogol'. His general stature in Russian letters, however, was most enhanced by the work of Iakov Grot. The latter's model multi-volume edition of Derzhavin remains the landmark in the field and played no small role in the renewed interest in Derzhavin in the Silver Age. In its wake Derzhavin was rediscovered by such poets as Mandel'shtam, Maiakovskii, Tsvetaeva, Khodasevich, and the émigré poet Nikolai Gronskii. Recent scholarship has moved towards evaluating Derzhavin's remarkable achievements in the context of the declining classicism of Catherinian Russia and in terms of Derzhavin's own sense of poetic beauty.

ANNA LISA CRONE

Iurii Osipovich Dombrovskii 1909–1978

Novelist

Biography

Born in Moscow, 12 May 1909. Attended school in Moscow; student on Higher State Literary Courses, 1926–29; studied at Moscow College of Music and Drama, 1930–32. Arrested in 1932, exiled to Alma-Ata for hooliganism and anti-Soviet agitation, 1933. Teacher, 1933–35. Arrested for embezzlement, 1935; declared innocent and released six months later. Resumed teaching; began to publish, 1937; worked as curator at Central Kazakhstan Museum, 1938–39. Arrested, 1939; sentenced to eight years' imprisonment for anti-Soviet agitation and propaganda, 1940; in Kolyma and other Siberian labour camps, 1940–43; released early on health grounds, returned to Alma-Ata, 1943. Worked as teacher and translator of Kazakh literature, 1944–49. Arrested, 1949, sentenced to ten years' imprisonment for anti-Soviet agitation and propaganda; in labour camps at Taishet, 1949–55; released, 1955, settled in Moscow. Rehabilitated and re-admitted to the Soviet Writers' Union, 1956; full-time writer and translator, 1956–78, but frequently unable to publish. Arrested for hooliganism and imprisoned briefly, 1966. Married: Klara Faizulaevna Turumova in 1969. Died in Moscow, 29 May 1978. Buried at Kuz'minki cemetery.

Publications

Collected Editions

Smuglaia ledi: Povest', roman i tri novelly o Shekspire [The Swarthy Lady: A Story, A Novel, and Three Novellas about Shakespeare]. Moscow, 1985.
Fakul'tet nenuzhnykh veshchei: Roman v dvukh knigakh [The Faculty of Unnecessary Things: A Novel in Two Volumes], (*Khranitel' drevnostei*; *Fakul'tet nenuzhnykh veshchei*). Moscow, 1989.
Sobranie sochinenii, 6 vols. Moscow, 1992–93.

Fiction

"Krushenie imperii" [The Collapse of the Empire], *Literaturnyi Kazakhstan*, 1–4 (1938), 10–43; 5–22; 34–47; 59–96; in separate edition as *Derzhavin*, Alma-Ata, 1939.
Obez'iana prikhodit za svoim cherepom [The Ape is Coming for Its Skull]. Moscow, 1959.

"Khranitel' drevnostei", *Novyi mir*, 7–8 (1964), 3–90; 10–67; translated as *The Keeper of Antiquities*, by Michael Glenny, London, Longman, and New York, McGraw-Hill, 1968; reprinted London, HarperCollins, 1991.
Smuglaia ledi: Tri novelly o Shekspire [The Swarthy Lady: Three Novellas about Shakespeare]. Moscow, 1969.
Fakel: Rasskazy [The Torch]. Alma-Ata, 1974.
"Iz zapisok Zybina" [From the Notes of Zybin], *Vestnik russkogo khristianskogo dvizheniia*, 122 (1977), 104–25.
Fakul'tet nenuzhnykh veshchei. Paris, YMCA-Press, 1978; also in *Novyi mir*, 8–11 (1988), 5–139; 40–97; 7–92; 92–132; translated as *The Faculty of Useless Knowledge*, by Alan Myers, London, Harvill Press, 1996.
"Istoriia nemetskogo konsula" [The Story of the German Consul], *Kontinent*, 72/4 (1992), 16–77.

Poetry
"Ia zhdu, chto zazhzhetsia iskusstvom moia nesterpimaia byl'..." [I Wait for My Unbearable Existence to Light Up with Art], *Iunost'*, 2 (1988), 56–59.
"Iurii Dombrovskii", in *Sred' drugikh imen*, edited by V.B. Murav'ev. Moscow, 1990, 217–33.

Essays
"Zapiski melkogo khuligana" [The Notes of a Petty Hooligan], *Znamia*, 4 (1990), 5–37.

Critical Studies
"Dombrovskij's 'The Keeper of Antiquities'", by O. Hassanoff, *Melbourne Slavonic Studies*, 5–6 (1971), 194–202.
"Iouri Dombrovski ou La leçon de ténèbres", by J. Cathala, in Dombrovskii's *La Faculté de l'Inutile*, translated by Dimitrii Sesemann and J. Cathala, Paris, Albin Michel, 1979, 433–46.
"Krugi zhizni i tvorchestva Iuriia Dombrovskogo", by I. Shenfel'd, *Grani*, 111–12 (1979), 351–77.
"Dombrovski et Dostoievski", by M. Guilleray, *Annales de la Faculté des Lettres et Sciences Humaines de Nice*, 41 (1981), *Lettres Grecques Modernes, Slaves et Hongroises*, 125–44.
"Etot khranitel' drevnostei (O pisatele Iurii Dombrovskom i ego knigakh)", by G. Anisimov and M. Emtsev, in *Fakul'tet nenuzhnykh veshchei: Roman v dvukh knigakh*, by Iu. Dombrovskii, Moscow, 1989, 694–716.
"Pis'ma druga, ili Shchedryi khranitel'", by P. Kosenko, *Prostor*, 5 (1989), 61–112.
"Strela v polete (Uroki biografii Iu. Dombrovskogo)", by I. Shtokman, *Voprosy literatury*, 3 (1989), 84–109.
"'Glubokii kolodets svobody ...' Nad stranitsami Iuriia Dombrovskogo", by A. Zverev, *Literaturnoe obozrenie*, 17/4 (1989), 14–20.
"Iouri Dombrovski (1909–1978)", by S. Markish, in *Histoire de la littérature russe*, edited by E.G. Etkind *et al.*, vol. 5 (*Le XXe siècle: Gels et dégels*), Paris, Fayard, 1990, 827–38.
"Homo Liber (Iurii Dombrovskii)", by V. Nepomniashchii, *Novyi mir*, 5 (1991), 234–40.
"A Russian Stoic? A Note on the Religious Faith of Jurij Dombrovskij", by J.B. Woodward, *Scando-Slavica*, 38 (1992), 33–45.
"The 'Cosmic Vision' of Iurii Dombrovskii: His Novel *Fakul'tet nenuzhnykh veshchei*", by J.B. Woodward, *Modern Language Review*, 87/4 (1992), 896–908.
"Iurii Dombrovskii's Exile in Alma-Ata", by Peter Doyle, *Slavonica*, 2/1 (1995–96), 71–90.

Iurii Dombrovskii was a Soviet writer of immense courage and integrity whose life and literary career were repeatedly disrupted by unjust arrests and long periods of imprisonment. First detained in 1932, while still a student, he spent a total of 23 years in exile in Alma-Ata and in Siberian labour camps, including Kolyma. Even after his return to Moscow and rehabilitation in 1956, he was never free of surveillance and harassment by the Soviet authorities. Only able to publish infrequently, and denied permission to travel or to receive royalties from foreign translations, Dombrovskii was forced to eke out a meagre existence by translating works of Kazakh authors, writing film-scenarios, and reviewing typescripts submitted to *Novyi mir* and other literary journals. Despite the arduous circumstances of his life, he produced original works of very high quality, and achieved wide international recognition following the publication of *Khranitel' drevnostei* (*The Keeper of Antiquities*) in 1964. He devoted the next 11 years to writing its sequel, *Fakul'tet nenuzhnykh veshchei* (*The Faculty of Useless Knowledge*). With no prospect of Soviet publication, he sent the manuscript abroad, and was overjoyed to receive a copy of the Paris edition shortly before his death in 1978, his physical decline doubtless hastened by several violent attacks to which he had been subjected.

Dombrovskii's principal works reflect his wide-ranging intellectual and cultural interests, profound erudition, and uncompromising independence of mind. He consistently defends reason, creativity, culture, truth, conscience, and freedom of thought against the authoritarian State that seeks to impose an appallingly narrow, dogmatic, and irrational ideology by brutality and terror. His first work *Derzhavin*, written in 1937–38 and influenced by the historical novels of Tynianov, is surprisingly frank in its depiction and condemnation of the poet's brief and ruthless service as an interrogator and torturer in 1773–74 during the Pugachev rebellion. Derzhavin's unthinking careerism proves futile, but his humanity and conscience are awoken by a debate with an idealistic renegade and particularly by his struggle to write genuine poetry. Though Dombrovskii's novel is well-documented and uses an appropriately archaic language, his portrayal of Derzhavin is idiosyncratic and there are implicit parallels between the authoritarian State of the 1770s and the totalitarian Stalinist State of the 1930s.

In *Obez'iana prikhodit za svoim cherepom* [The Ape is Coming for Its Skull], written from 1943 to 1958, and set in an unspecified west European country occupied by the Germans, Dombrovskii presents an ethical and philosophical analysis of the ideology of Nazism and explores the themes of cowardice, betrayal, and individual moral choice. The central character Professor Mezonier is an unworldly scholar of palaeoanthropology, whose academic work exposes the false premises of Nazi racial theories. Betrayed by his colleagues, Mezonier follows the example of his favourite author and luminary, the Roman Stoic philosopher Seneca, and commits suicide rather than renounce his integrity and collaborate with the Nazis. Though artistically flawed in places (the Prologue and Epilogue, added later and set in the cold-war period, are weaker), Dombrovskii's novel is unusually interesting for its examination of the clash between brute force and reason. As a study of totalitarian power that crushes intellect and cripples consciousness, the novel's allusions to Stalinism and the Soviet Union can hardly be doubted, and it was treated with considerable caution: few, albeit favourable reviews, appeared and no re-publication was allowed in Dombrovskii's lifetime.

Dombrovskii's finest works are undoubtedly *The Keeper of Antiquities* and *The Faculty of Useless Knowledge*. Though the second novel was originally intended to be a continuation of the first (and a case can certainly be made for treating both novels as a single entity as do some critics), Dombrovskii himself considered *The Faculty of Useless Knowledge* to be a separate and different work. Both novels are based on personal experience, are set in Alma-Ata in 1937, and ironically and subtly explore the absurdities and fantasies of Stalin's Terror. In *The Keeper of Antiquities* Dombrovskii succeeds in discrediting Stalinism by means of the often comic and disjointed recollections of an obscure and unnamed museum-curator. Narrated in the first person, the novel conveys most effectively both the threatening atmosphere of menace as the Terror begins to affect every aspect of the museum's work, and the spirited Keeper's gradual realization that official propaganda is totally untrue. By the end of the novel his arrest is imminent. *The Faculty of Useless Knowledge*, a much longer and more analytical work, is narrated in the third person and chronicles the arrest and interrogation of the Keeper (now named Zybin) by the NKVD (People's Commissariat for Internal Affairs). The combative and argumentative Zybin, made aware of the full extent and nature of the Terror by cell-mates, resists all pressures and refuses to compromise, but is surprisingly released as a result of purges within the NKVD. Dombrovskii's interest lies not so much in the details of prison life, as in the apparatus of terror, the NKVD personnel, and their surreal investigative processes.

Graphic scenes of Zybin's incarceration in labour camps years later are included in two long extracts from *The Keeper of Antiquities* that were cut in 1964 but subsequently published as *Iz zapisok Zybina* [From the Notes of Zybin] and *Istoriia nemetskogo konsula* [The Story of the German Consul]. Most of Dombrovskii's small but powerful body of poetry is also devoted to his prison-camp experiences and deserves to be better known.

Reflecting a lifelong interest and standing somewhat apart from the rest of Dombrovskii's works are the novellas on Shakespeare, written between 1946 and 1967. Imaginative, sympathetic, and well-researched reconstructions of gaps in Shakespeare's biography, they concentrate on difficulties in his life (such as his unhappy marriage and his last illness and death), rather than his creative career.

Dombrovskii's other publications include short stories, letters, and autobiographical documents; *Fakel* [The Torch], a book of essays on Kazakh artists; and articles on Pushkin and Shakespeare. A novel on Dobroliubov, commissioned in 1973, remained unfinished at his death. Since 1985 virtually all Dombrovskii's works have been published in the Soviet Union/Russia to critical acclaim and he has been justly recognized as an outstandingly talented writer of major importance.

PETER DOYLE

The Keeper of Antiquities

Khranitel' drevnostei

Novel, 1964

Dombrovskii wrote *The Keeper of Antiquities* in Moscow and Alma-Ata from 1961 to 1964. As the demands of censorship necessitated substantial revisions, Dombrovskii worked closely on the final text with Anna Berzer, an experienced editor at *Novyi mir*, prior to its publication in the journal by Tvardovskii in 1964 and shortly before the fall of Khrushchev. The novel was an immediate success, and was soon translated into many languages, bringing the then little known Dombrovskii national and international recognition. *Novyi mir* received hundreds of enthusiastic letters in praise of the novel that was considered to be its best publication of 1964. No reviews were allowed to appear in the Soviet Press, however, though Igor' Zolotusskii eventually succeeded in publishing a favourable assessment in Irkutsk (*Sibirskie ogni*, 10 (1965), 179–81). Until recently, the novel has received surprisingly little attention from western critics.

Set in Alma-Ata in 1937, *The Keeper of Antiquities* is a fictionalized account of Dombrovskii's own experiences while working in the Central Kazakhstan Museum in 1938–39. It addresses the theme of Soviet totalitarianism by chronicling the fortunes of an idealistic and knowledgeable young curator, as his local community is increasingly gripped by the fear, suspicion, and irrationality brought about by Stalin's Terror. Loosely structured and decidedly comic in parts, the novel is narrated in the first person with considerable irony, humour, and intelligence by the unnamed Keeper of the title, and it reveals how he is gradually made aware of the terrible forces that threaten not only his work, freedom, and very existence, but also the entire fabric of normal human society. The insidious horror of the Terror is emphasized all the more by the colourfully exotic background of Alma-Ata and the surrounding countryside. Much of the novel takes place in the museum, which is housed in a beautiful former cathedral. Other scenes are located on a nearby collective farm that the Keeper frequently visits as it is the site of an archaeological dig with which he is involved. One of the most effective of the novel's many evocative images is that of a mythical boa-constrictor, supposedly at large on the farm; in reality the whole country is clasped by the fantastic and unseen coils of the NKVD and is being slowly squeezed to death. As the novel makes clear, Stalinist despotism has little use for the world's past and culture, for truth, freedom of thought, and independent scholarship, and these "antiquities" are being ruthlessly suppressed in favour of an absurdly narrow and dogmatic ideology. In such circumstances the semi-autobiographical Keeper, a wryly outspoken guardian of both the museum's ancient objects and more generally of humanity's cultural past and age-old values, is inevitably doomed, and the novel ends when his arrest is imminent.

The intimate device of first-person narration gives the reader insight into the Keeper's interests, enthusiasms, and attitudes, as he provides lyrical descriptions of Alma-Ata and its natural environment, and digresses at length into such fields as architecture, art, archaeology, ancient history, and ethnography. The Keeper has great respect for creative people, who contribute beauty and knowledge to humanity, and he singles out a local architect, a painter, and an amateur archaeologist for particular praise. Though his own special field is Roman history and philosophy, he is deeply interested in every aspect of history and the culture of the past, which is as alive and real to him as the present. He naively hopes that his professional interest in the ancient world will allow him to remain aloof from the world of contemporary politics, but his honesty and frankness ensure that he incurs the hostility of more powerful functionaries. A series of events in the museum and elsewhere, apparently trivial and unconnected at first, but then progressively more serious and menacing, gradually brings home to him the fact that there is no escape; he eventually realizes that official propaganda about nationwide anti-Soviet conspiracies and sabotage is totally false and that the arrests and denunciations of 1937 are based on ludicrous fantasy. He has some allies in the museum, particularly the Director, a colleague and admirer called Klara, and a drunken carpenter and odd-job man. However, as the museum's exhibitions are purged and replaced by banal displays, dictated by political expediency and aimed at so-called mass-education, his struggles to preserve genuine scholarship and knowledge become increasingly futile.

Yet the novel is, as Dombrovskii insisted, essentially optimistic. The Keeper's familiarity with Roman history enables him to put Stalinism in a broad historical context, and, implicitly at least, to draw striking parallels between Roman and Soviet tyranny. The novel implies that Stalinism is neither revolutionary nor new, but is merely a retrogressive modern-dress version of ancient despotisms, all of which came to an end sooner or later. The Keeper remains free in spirit and, unlike some, uncorrupted by the madness and fear around him. For all its physical (but ephemeral) power, Stalinism can only suppress rather than destroy the culture, knowledge, ideals, and values that he defends. Compared to what it rejects, Stalinism represents a terrible impoverishment of the human spirit, which subordinates everything to the political aims of the moment; these are themselves based on irrationality and fantasy, engender fanaticism and betrayal, and depend on fear, imprisonment, and execution for their implementation.

The removal from the novel of long sections, considered unpublishable in 1964, and later published separately as *Iz zapisok Zybina* and *Istoriia nemetskogo konsula* probably enhanced rather than harmed the novel. They broadened the scope of the narrative by the introduction of the prison-camps, Nazi Germany, the similarities between Nazism and Stalinism, and the Keeper's eventual release in the 1950s, but these themes were not fully developed or integrated into the main narrative whose focus is so effectively the year 1937. The text as published, with which Dombrovskii ultimately remained very satisfied, is a most original and perceptive work, which utterly discredits Stalinism by deceptively indirect methods.

PETER DOYLE

The Faculty of Useless Knowledge

Fakul'tet nenuzhnykh veshchei

Novel, 1978

Following the success of *The Keeper of Antiquities*, Dombrovskii was commissioned by *Novyi mir* to write a sequel and he began work on *The Faculty of Useless Knowledge* on 10 December 1964. The novel was to be his major work, a constant preoccupation for the next 11 years until its completion on 5 March 1975 (pointedly the anniversary of Stalin's death). Early hopes of fairly rapid publication soon faded, as the work grew in complexity and the changed political climate ensured that it would not pass the censor. Though extracts were published in Alma-Ata in 1967 and 1970, Dombrovskii arranged for the novel to be brought out in Paris, there being by then no prospect of Soviet publication. He received a copy of the Paris edition shortly before his death in 1978. The first Soviet publication was in *Novyi mir* in 1988.

The novel, written without regard to possible censorship, follows on from *The Keeper of Antiquities*, covers the last months of 1937, and records in detail the Keeper Zybin's direct confrontation with the system of terror. Zybin is arrested in the countryside while trying to track down an ancient burial site and missing gold; the principal setting is the grey NKVD headquarters in Alma-Ata where Zybin is imprisoned and interrogated, while the NKVD tries to fabricate a large-scale conspiracy in order to hold a local show trial on the Moscow model. Zybin learns of the full extent and horrific nature of the Terror and prison-camp system from cell-mates, but refuses the suggestion that he should collaborate or plead guilty to a lesser charge, however untrue, and thereby save himself. A consistent opponent of coercion and injustice from childhood, Zybin finds the inner strength to resist the NKVD's methods of continual interrogations, physical pain, and solitary confinement. Sustained by vivid memories and dreams of a past sea-side romance (with Lina, with whom he was reunited shortly before his arrest, and who scornfully refuses to betray him when questioned), he becomes fearlessly defiant and argumentative, treats his various interrogators with humorous contempt, declares a hunger strike, and awaits execution. He is instead unexpectedly freed, for sudden changes at the top of the NKVD result in a purge of local personnel and the token release of a few prisoners.

In *The Faculty of Useless Knowledge* Dombrovskii switches to third-person narration, both to give a sense of objectivity and to allow him to range far beyond Zybin's personal experiences. The novel contains a uniquely detailed portrayal of the secret world of the NKVD, and the attitudes and motivation of its agents, ranging from novice and brutal interrogators to the specialist prosecutor from Moscow, Shtern. He is a suave but depraved intellectual, who revels in the manipulative "creativity" of his virtuoso role and writes socialist realist dramas, falsely depicting the moral regeneration of prisoners. In reality, the brutal Stalinist system is characterized by the complete absence of legality, justice, individual rights, freedom, reason, truth, conscience, ethical norms, or humane values: the "unnecessary things" of the novel's title. The fact of arrest is equated with guilt, expediency determines the charge, informers provide false evidence, and the object of the "investigation" is to extort a written confession from the hapless prisoner. Yet the privileged elitist existence of those who serve the NKVD is precarious for they too are potential victims, at the mercy of political caprice. Zybin therefore pities rather than hates his oppressors, especially the young and inexperienced Tamara Dolidze, who has no answers to Zybin's reproaches and is eventually sickened by her insights into the horrific realities of the camps.

For the most part, Dombrovskii portrays the NKVD staff as alarmingly ordinary and banal. Similarly, his portrait of the all-powerful Stalin, who explains his philosophy of terror to Zybin in a dream, and later authorizes the astounding release of a former fellow-revolutionary, is less that of a super-monster than of a vengeful, limited human being, deeply affected by childhood experiences, and only capable of ruling by violent means.

Zybin remains unbroken by the power of the totalitarian state, morally free, spiritually strong, concerned above all to preserve his inner peace and self-esteem. Others are destroyed. An archaeologist colleague, Kornilov (also given semi-autobiographical attributes by Dombrovskii), attempts to outwit the NKVD and defend his drinking companion, a lascivious former priest and ex-prisoner, Father Andrei, only to find that Andrei has already betrayed him. Kornilov is tricked into becoming an informer, denounces Zybin, and takes refuge in drink. Through such unpromising characters, Dombrovskii introduces an important religious dimension into the novel. Father Andrei is the author of an erudite work on the trial of Christ, which indicates breaches of judicial procedures and subtly exculpates Pilate, Judas, and a second secret betrayer. An implicit parallel is suggested between Christ's inspiring self-sacrifice on the cross for his beliefs, and Zybin's exemplary willingness to face execution rather than renounce his conscience and values. The parallel is reinforced by the novel's ending, in which the artist Kalmykov, a self-styled universal genius and totally free spirit, immortalizes in a painting the newly-released Zybin as he sits on a bench flanked by the informer Kornilov and the sacked interrogator Neiman. Shortly before, Neiman, who now despairingly realizes his "emptiness", located the missing gold and witnessed a quasi-religious ceremony over the body of a drowned girl (one of the novel's many images of death and beauty) at which ideas of forgiveness, redemption, and immortality were enunciated.

Dombrovskii considered the writing of *The Faculty of Useless Knowledge* to be his civic duty as one of the surviving witnesses of what he termed "the greatest tragedy of our Christian era". His remarkable novel, a sophisticated, optimistic, and profound analysis of the evils of Stalinism, is a worthy monument to the sufferings of his generation and to the indomitability of the human spirit, and is, in the words of its French translator Cathala, "perhaps the masterpiece which will best resist the erosion of time".

PETER DOYLE

Domostroi

Anonymous 16th-century prose work

Editions

Domostroi, edited by I. Zabelin. Moscow, 1882; edited by W.F. Ryan, Letchworth, Bradda, 1971.

Pamiatniki literatury drevnei Rusi: Seredina XVI veka. Moscow, 1985, 70–172.

Domostroi. Moscow, 1990.

Translation

The Domostroi: Rules for Russian Households in the Time of Ivan the Terrible, edited and translated by Carolyn Johnston Pouncy. Ithaca, Cornell University Press, 1994.

Critical Studies

Istoriia Rossii s drevneishikh vremen, by S.M. Solov'ev, edited by L.V. Cherepnin, Moscow, 1960, Book 4, vol. 7–8, 155–89.

"Chelovek v uchitel'noi literature Drevnei Rusi", by V.P. Adrianova-Peretts, *Trudy otdela drevnerusskoi literatury*, 27, Leningrad, 1972.

Slovar' knizhnikov i knizhnosti Drevnei Rusi: Vtoraia polovina XIV–XVII, Part 2, Leningrad, 1972, 323–33.

"K voprosu o kruge chteniia drevnerusskogo pisatelia", by V.P. Andrianova-Peretts, *Trudy otdela drevnerusskoi literatury*, 28, Leningrad, 1974, 24–29.

Pamiatniki literatury drevnei Rusi: Seredina XVI veka, Moscow, 1985, 580–86.

"Domostroi bez domostroevshchiny", by V.V. Kolesov, in *Domostroi*, Moscow, 1990, 5–23.

Of several works in 16th-century Russian literature, *Domostroi* is the one that is most worthy of our attention. Critics have used various adjectives such as "narrow", "petty" and "obscurantist" with which to describe *Domostroi*, but these are inadequate. There are two reasons why *Domostroi* has received such rough handling from its critics. First, its failure to disguise its unashamed use of Christianity for social ends and, second, its revelation of a world of petty bourgeois standards, which have not lost their potency even today, and which many would rather forget, both now and in the past. Aksakov wrote in 1850:

> there is so much in it which is contrary to the character of a Russian ... that it reminds one completely of the modern mercantile way of life and manners, in particular where

civilization is imperceptible ... where everything is done for one's guests, everything is done for show. If, however, *Domostroi* is regarded not from any religious or aesthetic point of view, but as a work of sociology, where it seems more appropriately to belong, then it deserves more serious attention than critics and researchers have been prepared to give it.

It is a book on how to behave. In the established form of the redaction usually quoted it is divided into three parts dealing with religious observances (chapters 1–15), moral behaviour (chapters 16–29) and housekeeping (chapters 30–63), and also contains the concluding letter from Sil'vestr to his son, which is largely the reason for the assumption that he was its author or at least its compiler. It makes no real difference to the value of the work as a source whether or not it was Sil'vestr who was one of Ivan IV's advisers. That is a question more important to our understanding of the character of Sil'vestr.

Written in the 1550s (the earliest manuscript was written in 1560), *Domostroi* gives us an outline of the positive religious, moral and everyday style of life by which the family should guide itself. It sets down a picture of an ideal family situation, a picture of a family that is economically self-supporting – or nearly so – which keeps itself to itself and does not involve itself in tittle-tattle and gossip, and tries its best not to cause any scandal. At the same time it sets out the delegation of the household functions and gives advice on carrying them out. The picture it presents is basically one of a patriarchal society in which allegiance is to the Tsar and the Church, not to those around one, nor to one's social peers. It relies heavily on the social, moral and religious attitudes of the time, and through a study of it we can determine the viewpoint of the 16th-century Russian. Its author lived in Moscow, the "third Rome", which was acknowledged to be unquestionable and unshakeable. The function of the work was not to present a critical view of different aspects of 16th-century Muscovite society and its basis, but to raise up and present the bases of that society as an ideal.

Good service is rewarded by good treatment. Common allegiance to the tsar and to the teaching of the Russian Orthodox Church would lead to the elimination of social conflict. However, wealth and Christianity are not seen as incompatible, indeed much advice is given on how to increase one's wealth. What is criticized as unchristian is the abuse of wealth. The mentality of *Domostroi* can almost be seen as approving the "business deal", as "making a deal with God". Good actions are not prescribed by the author for their own sake; they are seen as leading to a better life.

The social scheme described in the work could actually have dispensed with the Church altogether. Christianity is incorporated first and foremost as an incentive (the choice is between Heaven and Hell) and second, in order to produce social conformity through religious observances. The author was quite right, however, to see that social ridicule in the present was a far more cogent argument for good behaviour than divine wrath. Children should be kept down when they are young so that they grow up respectful. An unruly son is the worst threat to social stability and a daughter in trouble brings a shame that the family simply cannot bear.

Further, owners of estates and property should act in a way that enables them to justify their position. It is the wife who should wake up the servants, not the other way round. Neither is it precluded that the owners of the property should look after it and do their own gardening, or keep the house safe from intruders. Everywhere we see the author's love of neat, tidy patterns and of organization.

He also preaches non-resistance to evil and the avoidance of hostility to one's neighbours, which was more important in his view than an internal quarrel between mother and servant. The themes of non-resistance to evil, the ground on which pre-revolutionary critics also attacked *Domostroi* most violently, was due perhaps to the embarrassment that Lev Tolstoi's doctrines caused the Russian government.

The type of reader for whom *Domostroi* was intended can be broadly defined as any head of a family below the rank of boyar. This would include the landlord with a large estate, the merchant and small tradesman with his shop (there are numerous references to markets and the buying of household supplies), or the civil servant with a family and home to care for. Primarily, it was aimed at those who were assuming positions of authority or responsibility for the first time, and who were in need of detailed and literal instructions on how to conduct oneself. Delays in government offices could cause oppression to others and lay heavy exactions on the peasants and others.

Ever since the middle of the 15th century the numbers of such people in Russia had been increasing steadily as the position of the boyars weakened and this opened up opportunities for people of other social strata. The reforms of the early part of the reign of Ivan IV were intended to swell their numbers still further. *Domostroi* likewise is not to be seen simply as the product of the 1550s. It is a synthesis of useful precepts and information that has been built up over a period extending as far back as the late 15th century.

A reader of *Domostroi* would probably deduce that Russian society consisted of a number of families, of closed family units, but this would not, of course, be the actual picture, but simply a description of the family unit that the author and his supporters would like to have seen established throughout the country. In each household there would be a strict delegation of authority and functions, with the head of the family as final arbiter, and each member of the family and household knowing exactly his or her position in the household hierarchy. The head of the family should swear allegiance, not to a particular group in society but directly to the two supreme authorities – the tsar and the Church. The author envisaged an entirely new society. Far from being obscurantist, the author was Utopian in his belief that goodwill, as he understood it, could move mountains.

John Sullivan

Fedor Mikhailovich Dostoevskii 1821–1881
Novelist

Biography
Born in Moscow, 11 November 1821. Educated at home to the age of 12. Attended Chermak's School in Moscow; Military Engineering Academy, St Petersburg, 1838–43: commissioned as ensign, 1839, as 2nd lieutenant, 1842; graduated 1843 as War Ministry draftsman; resigned 1844. Following his translation of Balzac's *Eugénie Grandet* in 1844, published first novel, *Bednye liudi* (*Poor Folk*), 1846. Associated with the Petrashevskii circle; entire group arrested for political conspiracy, 1849. Sentenced to death: after a mock execution, reprieved at the last moment, and sentenced to penal servitude, imprisonment in Omsk, Siberia, 1850–54; then exiled as a soldier at Semipalatinsk, 1854: corporal, 1855, ensign, 1856. Married: 1) Mar'ia Dmitrievna Isaeva in 1857 (died 1864), one stepson; 2) his stenographer, Anna Grigor'evna Snitkina in 1867, two daughters and two sons. Resigned commission when exile ended, 1859. Co-founder, with his brother, *Vremia*, 1861–63; editor of *Epokha* on his brother's death, 1864–65. Lived in western Europe, 1867–71. Editor of *Grazhdanin*, 1873–74 and *Dnevnik pisatelia*, 1876–77. Died in St Petersburg, 9 February 1881 following a haemorrhage in his throat. Buried in the Aleksandr Nevskii monastery, St Petersburg.

Publications
Collected Editions
The Novels, translated by Constance Garnett, 12 vols. London, Heinemann, 1912–20.
Polnoe sobranie khudozhestvennykh proizvedenii, 13 vols. Moscow and Leningrad, 1926–30.
Sobranie sochinenii, 10 vols. Moscow, 1956–58.
The Gambler; Bobok; A Nasty Story, translated by Jessie Coulson. Harmondsworth, Penguin, 1966.
Great Short Works of Fyodor Dostoevsky, translated by David Magarshack. New York, Harper and Row, 1968.
Notes from Underground. The Double, translated by Jessie Coulson. Harmondsworth, Penguin, 1972.
Polnoe sobranie sochinenii, 30 vols. Moscow, 1972–90.
Poor Folk and Other Stories, translated by David McDuff. Harmondsworth, Penguin, 1988.
Uncle's Dream and Other Stories, translated by David McDuff. Harmondsworth, Penguin, 1989.
Notes from the Underground and The Gambler, translated by Jane Kentish. Oxford, Oxford University Press, 1991.
A Gentle Creature and Other Stories, translated by Alan Myers. Oxford, Oxford University Press, 1995.
Dostoevsky's Occasional Writings, translated by David Magarshack. Evanston, Illinios, Northwestern Unversity Press, 1997.

Fiction
Bednye liudi. St Petersburg, 1846; translated as *Poor Folk* with *The Gambler*, by C.J. Hogarth, London, Everyman, 1916; revised by W.J. Leatherbarrow, London, Everyman, 1994; also by Constance Garnett, in *The Novels*, 1917; by Robert Dessaix, Ann Arbor, Ardis, 1982; and by David McDuff, in *Poor Folk and Other Stories*, 1988.
Dvoinik, in *Otechestvennye zapiski*, 2 (1846); translated as "The Double", by Constance Garnett, in *The Novels*, 1917; also by Jessie Coulson, in *Notes from Underground. The Double*, 1972; as *The Double: Two Versions*, by Evelyn Harden, Ann Arbor, Ardis, 1985.
Belye nochi, in *Otechestvennye zapiski*, 12 (1848); translated as "White Nights", by Constance Garnett, in *The Novels*, 1918; also by David Magarshack, in *Great Short Works of Fyodor Dostoevsky*, 1968; by David McDuff, in *Uncle's Dream and Other Stories*, 1989; and by Alan Myers, in *A Gentle Creature and Other Stories*, 1995.
Netochka Nezvanova, in *Otechestvennye zapiski*, 1–2/5 (1849); translated as "Netochka Nezvanova", by Constance Garnett, in *The Novels*, 1920; also by Jane Kentish, Harmondsworth, Penguin, 1985.
Selo Stepanchikovo i ego obitateli. St Petersburg, 1859; translated as *The Village of Stepanchikovo and Its Inhabitants*, by Ignat Avsey, London, Angel, 1983; revised edition, Harmondsworth, Penguin, 1995.
Diadushkin son, in *Russkoe slovo*, 3 (1859); translated as "Uncle's Dream", by Constance Garnett, in *The Novels*, 1919; and by David McDuff, in *Uncle's Dream and Other Stories*, 1989.
Unizhennye i oskorblennye, in *Vremia*, 1–7 (1861); translated as *The Insulted and the Injured*, by Constance Garnett, in *The Novels*, 1915; also by Olga Shartse, Moscow, Progress, 1977.
Zapiski iz mertvogo doma, in *Vremia*, 4, 9–11 (1861), 1–3, 5, 12 (1862); translated as *The House of the Dead*, by Constance Garnett, in *The Novels*, 1915; and by David McDuff, Harmondsworth, Penguin, 1985; also as *Memoirs from the House of the Dead*, by Jessie Coulson, Oxford, Oxford University Press, 1965.
Zimnie zametki na letnikh vpechatleniiakh, *Vremia*, 2–3 (1863); translated as *Summer Impressions*, by Kyril FitzLyon, London, John Calder, 1954; retitled as *Winter Notes on Summer Impressions*, London, Quartet, 1985; also translated by Richard Lee Renfield, New York, Criterion, 1955; and by David Patterson, Evanston, Illinois, Northwestern University Press, 1988.
Zapiski iz podpol'ia, in *Epokha*, 1–2, 4 (1864); edited by Gordon Humphreys, London, Bristol Classical Press, 1994; translated as "Notes from Underground", by Constance Garnett, in *The Novels*, 1918; also by Jessie Coulson, in *Notes from Underground. The Double*, 1972; by Michael R. Katz, New York, Norton, 1989; by Jane Kentish, in *Notes from the Underground and The Gambler*, 1991; and by Richard Pevear and Larissa Volokhonsky, London, Vintage, 1993.
Igrok. St Petersburg, 1866; translated as *The Gambler* with *Poor Folk*, by C.J. Hogarth, 1916; revised edition, 1994; by Jessie Coulson, in *The Gambler; Bobok; A Nasty Story*, 1966; by Victor Terras, with *Diary*, by Polina Suslova, Chicago, University of Chicago Press, 1973; and by Jane Kentish, in *Notes from the Underground and The Gambler*, 1991.
Prestuplenie i nakazanie, in *Russkii vestnik*, 1–2, 4, 6–8, 11–12

(1866); separate edition, St Petersburg, 1867; translated as *Crime and Punishment*, by Constance Garnett, in *The Novels*, 1912–20; and by David Magarshack, Harmondsworth, Penguin, 1951; by Jessie Coulson, London, Oxford University Press, 1953; this translation edited by George Gibian, New York, Norton, 1964; and edited by Richard Peace, Oxford, Oxford University Press, 1995; also translated by David McDuff, Harmondsworth, Penguin, 1991; and by Richard Pevear and Larissa Volokhonsky, London, Vintage, 1993.

Idiot, in *Russkii vestnik*, 1–2, 4–12 (1868); separate edition, St Petersburg, 1869; translated as *The Idiot*, by Constance Garnett, in *The Novels*, 1913; by David Magarshack, Harmondsworth, Penguin, 1954; by Alan Myers, Oxford, Oxford University Press, 1992; and by Richard Pevear and Larissa Volokhonsky, London, Vintage, 1993.

Vechnyi muzh, in *Zaria*, 1–2 (1870); translated as "The Eternal Husband", by Constance Garnett, in *The Novels*, 1917; and by David Magarshack, in *Great Short Works of Fyodor Dostoevsky*, 1968.

Besy, in *Russkii vestnik*, 1–2, 4, 7, 9–11 (1871), 11–12 (1872); translated as *The Possessed*, by Constance Garnett, in *The Novels*, 1913; also as *The Devils*, by David Magarshack, Harmondsworth, Penguin, 1954; also as *Devils*, by Michael R. Katz, Oxford, Oxford University Press, 1992; and as *The Possessed*, by Richard Pevear and Larissa Volokhonsky, London, Vintage, 1994.

"Bobok", in *Dnevnik pisatelia*, in *Grazhdanin*, 1–50 (1873); translated by Jessie Coulson, in *The Gambler; Bobok; A Nasty Story*, 1966.

Podrostok, in *Otechestvennye zapiski*, 1–2, 4–5, 9, 11–12 (1875); translated as *A Raw Youth*, by Constance Garnett, in *The Novels*, 1916; also as *An Accidental Family*, by Richard Freeborn, Oxford, Oxford University Press, 1994.

"Krotkaia", in *Dnevnik pisatelia*, St Petersburg, 1876; translated as "A Gentle Spirit", by Constance Garnett, in *The Novels*, 1917; and by David Magarshack, in *Great Short Works of Fyodor Dostoevsky*, 1968; and as "A Gentle Creature", by Alan Myers, in *A Gentle Creature and Other Stories*, 1995; also as *The Gentle Spirit*, by David McDuff, Harmondsworth, Penguin, 1996.

"Son smeshnogo cheloveka", in *Dnevnik pisatelia*, St Petersburg, 1877; edited by W.J. Leatherbarrow, London, Bristol Classical Press, 1994; translated as "Dreams of a Ridiculous Man", by Constance Garnett, in *The Novels*, 1912–20; also by David Magarshack, in *Great Short Works of Fyodor Dostoevsky*, 1968; and by Alan Myers, in *A Gentle Creature and Other Stories*, 1995.

Brat'ia Karamazovy, in *Russkii vestnik*, 1–2, 4–6, 8–11 (1879), 1, 4, 7–11 (1880); translated as *The Brothers Karamazov*, by Constance Garnett, in *The Novels*, 1912; revised edition by Ralph Matlaw, New York, Norton, 1975; also by David Magarshack, Harmondsworth, Penguin, 1958; and by Richard Pevear and Larissa Volokhonsky, London, Vintage, 1990; David McDuff, Harmondsworth, Penguin, 1993; and as *The Karamazov Brothers*, by Ignat Avsey, Oxford, Oxford University Press, 1994.

Letters

Selected Letters, edited by Joseph Frank and David I. Goldstein, translated by Andrew R. MacAndrew. New Brunswick, Rutgers University Press, 1987.

Complete Letters (vol. 1, 1832–59; vol. 2, 1860–67; vol. 3, 1868–71; vol. 4 1872–77; vol. 5, 1878–81), edited and translated by David Lowe and Ronald Meyer. Ann Arbor, Ardis, 1988–91.

Memoirs, Diaries, and Notebooks

Dnevnik pisatelia. St Petersburg, 1876–81; translated as *The Diary of a Writer*, by Boris Leo Brasol, 2 vols. New York, Braziller, 1954; reprinted Santa Barbara, California, Peregrine Smith, 1979; Salt Lake City, Gibbs M. Smith, 1985; also translated as *A Writer's Diary*, by Kenneth Lantz, 2 vols. Evanston, Illinois, Northwestern University Press, 1994; London, Quartet, 1995.

The Notebooks for The Idiot; Crime and Punishment; The Possessed; A Raw Youth; The Brothers Karamazov, edited by Edward Wasiolek, translated by Wasiolek, Katharine Strelsky, and Victor Terras, 5 vols. Chicago, University of Chicago Press, 1967–71.

Neizdannyi Dostoevskii. Zapisnye knizhki i tetradi 1860–1881. Moscow, 1971; translated as *The Unpublished Dostoevsky: Diaries and Notebooks, 1860–81*, edited by Carl R. Proffer, 3 vols. Ann Arbor, Ardis, 1973–76.

Critical Studies

Dostoevsky, by André Gide, translated by Arnold Bennett, London, Dent, 1925; New York, New Directions, 1961.

Dostoevsky in Russian Literary Criticism 1846–1954, by Vladimir Seduro, New York, Columbia University Press, 1957.

Dostoevsky: His Life and Art, by Avrahm Yarmolinsky, New York, Criterion, and London, Arco, 1957; 2nd edition New York, Criterion, 1959.

Dostoevsky's Underground Man in Russian Literature, by Robert Louis Jackson, The Hague, Mouton, 1958.

Tolstoy or Dostoevsky: An Essay in the Old Criticism, by George Steiner, New York, Knopf, 1959; London, Faber, 1960.

The Undiscovered Dostoyevsky, by Ronald Hingley, London, Hamish Hamilton, 1962.

Dostoevsky: A Collection of Critical Essays, edited by René Wellek, Englewood Cliffs, New Jersey, Prentice-Hall, 1962.

Dostoevsky: The Major Fiction, by Edward Wasiolek, Cambridge, Massachusetts, MIT Press, 1964.

Dostoevsky and Romantic Realism: A Study of Dostoevsky in Relation to Balzac, Dickens and Gogol, by Donald Fanger, Cambridge, Massachusetts, Harvard University Press, 1965.

Dostoevsky's Quest for Form: A Study of His Philosophy of Art, by Robert Louis Jackson, New Haven, Yale University Press, 1966; reprinted Bloomington, Physsardt, 1978.

The Structure of "The Brothers Karamazov", by Robert L. Belknap, The Hague, Mouton, 1967.

Dostoevsky: His Life and Work, by Konstantin Mochulsky, translated by M. Minihan, Princeton, Princeton University Press, 1967.

The Young Dostoevsky (1846–1849): A Critical Study, by Victor Terras, The Hague, Mouton, 1969.

Dostoyevsky: An Examination of the Major Novels, by Richard

Peace, Cambridge, Cambridge University Press, 1971; reprinted London, Bristol Classical Press, 1992.
Political Apocalypse: A Study of Dostoevsky's Grand Inquisitor, by Ellis Sandoz, Baton Rouge, Louisiana University Press, 1971.
Twentieth-Century Interpretations of "Crime and Punishment": A Collection of Critical Essays, edited by Robert Louis Jackson, Englewood Cliffs, New Jersey, Prentice-Hall, 1974.
Dostoevsky and the Age of Intensity, by Alex de Jonge, London, Secker and Warburg, and New York, St Martin's Press, 1975.
Dostoevskii's Image in Russia Today, by Vladimir Seduro, Belmont, Massachusetts, Nordland, 1975.
Dostoyevsky: The Novel of Discord, by Malcolm V. Jones, London, Paul Elek, and New York, Barnes and Noble, 1976.
Dostoevsky: The Seeds of Revolt 1821–1849, by Joseph Frank, Princeton, Princeton University Press, and London, Robson, 1977.
Dostoevsky and the Novel, by Michael Holquist, Princeton, Princeton University Press, 1977; reprinted Evanston, Illinois, Northwestern University Press, 1986.
Dostoevskii in Russian and World Theatre, by Vladimir Seduro, North Quincey, Massachusetts, Christopher, 1977.
Ideology and Imagination: The Image of Society in Dostoevsky, by Geoffrey C. Kabat, New York, Columbia University Press, 1978.
Crime and Punishment: Murder as Philosophic Experiment, by A.D. Nuttall, Falmer, Sussex, Sussex University Press, 1978.
Crime and Punishment: The Techniques of the Omniscient Author, by Gary Rosenshield, Lisse, Peter de Ridder Press, 1978.
Unconscious Structure in "The Idiot": A Study in Literature and Psychoanalysis, by Elizabeth Dalton, Princeton, Princeton University Press, 1979.
F.M. Dostoevsky (1821–1881): A Centenary Collection, edited by Leon Burnett, Colchester, University of Essex Press, 1981.
The Art of Dostoevsky: Deliriums and Nocturnes, by Robert Louis Jackson, Princeton, Princeton University Press, 1981.
Fedor Dostoevsky, by W.J. Leatherbarrow, Boston, Twayne, 1981.
Dostoevsky's Dickens, by Lorelei MacPike, Totowa, New Jersey, Barnes and Noble, and London, Prior, 1981.
Dostoevsky and "The Idiot": Author, Narrator and Reader, by Robin Feuer Miller, Cambridge, Massachusetts, Harvard University Press, 1981.
The Boundaries of Genre: Dostoevsky's "Diary of a Writer" and the Traditions of Literary Utopia, by Gary Saul Morson, Austin, University of Texas Press, 1981.
A Karamazov Companion: Commentary on the Genesis, Language and Style of Dostoevsky's Novel, by Victor Terras, Madison, University of Wisconsin Press, 1981.
Character Names in Dostoevsky's Fiction, by Charles E. Passage, Ann Arbor, Ardis, 1982.
New Essays on Dostoyevsky, edited by Malcolm V. Jones and Garth M. Terry, Cambridge and New York, Cambridge University Press, 1983.
A Dostoevsky Dictionary, by Richard Chapple, Ann Arbor, Ardis, 1983.
Dostoevsky: The Years of Ordeal, 1850–1859, by Joseph Frank, Princeton, Princeton University Press, 1983; London, Robson, 1984.
Dostoevsky, by John Jones, Oxford, Clarendon Press, and New York, Oxford University Press, 1983.
Problems of Dostoevsky's Poetics, by Mikhail M. Bakhtin, edited and translated by Caryl Emerson, Minneapolis, University of Minnesota Press, and Manchester, Manchester University Press, 1984.
Tyrant and Victim in Dostoevsky, by Gary Cox, Columbus, Ohio, Slavica, 1984.
Dostoevsky: New Perspectives, edited by Robert Louis Jackson, Englewood Cliffs, New Jersey, Prentice-Hall, 1984.
The Experience of Time in "Crime and Punishment", by Leslie A. Johnson, Columbus, Ohio, Slavica, 1985.
Varieties of Poetic Utterance: Quotation in "The Brothers Karamazov", by Nina Perlina, Lanham, Maryland, University Press of America, 1985.
Dostoevsky: Myths of Duality, by Roger B. Anderson, Gainesville, University of Florida Press, 1986.
Dostoevsky: The Stir of Liberation, 1860–1865, by Joseph Frank, Princeton, Princeton University Press, 1986; London, Robson, 1987.
Dostoevsky and the Human Condition after a Century, edited by Alexej Ugrinsky, Frank S. Lambasa, and Valija K. Ozolins, New York, Greenwood Press, 1986.
Fyodor Dostoevsky: A Writer's Life, by Geir Kjetsaa, translated by Siri Hustvedt and David McDuff, New York, Viking, 1987; London, Macmillan, 1988.
Fyodor Dostoevsky, by Peter Conradi, London, Macmillan, and New York, St Martin's Press, 1988.
Dostoevsky and the Process of Literary Creation, by Jacques Catteau, translated by A. Littlewood, Cambridge, Cambridge University Press, 1989.
The Genesis of "The Brothers Karamazov": The Aesthetics, Ideology and Psychology of Text Making, by Robert L. Belknap, Evanston, Illinois, Northwestern University Press, 1990.
Dostoyevsky after Bakhtin: Readings in Dostoyevsky's Fantastic Realism, by Malcolm V. Jones, Cambridge, Cambridge University Press, 1990.
The Brothers Karamazov and the Poetics of Memory, by Diana Oenning Thompson, Cambridge, Cambridge University Press, 1991.
Fyodor Dostoevsky: "The Brothers Karamazov", by W.J. Leatherbarrow, Cambridge, Cambridge University Press, 1992.
Dostoevsky's "Notes from Underground", by Richard Peace, London, Bristol Classical Press, 1993.
Dostoevsky and the Woman Question: Rereadings at the End of a Century, by Nina Pelikan Straus, London, Macmillan, and New York, St Martin's Press, 1994.
Dostoevsky: The Miraculous Years, 1866–1871, by Joseph Frank, Princeton, Princeton University Press, and London, Robson, 1995.
Dostoevskii and Britain, edited by W.J. Leatherbarrow, Oxford, Berg, 1995.
Dostoevsky's "Crime and Punishment": An Aesthetic Interpretation, by Henry Buchanan, Nottingham, Astra Press, 1996.
An Annihilation of Inertia: Dostoevsky and Metaphysics, by

Liza Knapp, Evanston, Illinois, Northwestern University Press, 1996.
Dostoevsky and Soloviev: The Art of Integral Vision, by Marina Kostalevsky, New Haven, Yale University Press, 1997.

Bibliographies
F.M. Dostoevskii, Bibliografiia proizvedenii F.M. Dostoevskogo i literatury o nem 1917–65, edited by A.A. Belkin, A.S. Dolinin, and V.V. Kozhinov. Moscow, 1968.
"Dostoevsky Studies in Great Britain: A Bibliographical Survey", by Garth M. Terry, in *New Essays on Dostoevsky*, edited by Terry and Malcolm V. Jones, Cambridge, Cambridge University Press, 1983.
Fedor Dostoevsky: A Reference Guide, by W.J. Leatherbarrow, Boston, G.K. Hall, 1990.
For bibliographical and further critical material, see *The Bulletin of the International Dostoevskii Society*, later *Dostoevskii Studies* (1970 –).

Fedor Dostoevskii's literary career began in January 1846 with the publication of his first novel *Bednye liudi* (*Poor Folk*) to widespread critical acclaim. The young author and his novel had been enthusiastically sponsored by Vissarion Belinskii, the leading literary critic of the time, who saw in this exchange of letters between a poor civil servant and a seamstress an eloquent and humane defence of the underdog and a model that progressive Russian literature should follow. Belinskii, along with Dostoevskii's other readers, was less impressed by his second novel *Dvoinik* (*The Double*), which appeared the following month. While retaining the St Petersburg setting and civil servant hero, this work skirts the irrational in its depiction of a man haunted by a look-alike who eventually usurps his position and leads him to insanity. Belinskii dismissed it as fantasy and an abrogation of the writer's social responsibilities, but he failed to recognize that, even in *Poor Folk*, the focus of Dostoevskii's art was psychological rather than social and that in both of these early novels Dostoevskii was experimenting with narrative forms that would allow direct, unmediated access to the consciousness of a hero disintegrating under conflicting perceptions of his identity. In his other works of the 1840s Dostoevskii was to experiment further with narrative structures that recreated the fluid and subjective nature of experience itself, and he continued to people his works with figures who enacted complex, irrational responses to their dual existences as both social and private beings. In these works Dostoevskii was conducting a sustained polemic with Nikolai Gogol', whose works eschewed psychological depth in favour of grotesque caricature, as well as working out the narrative and thematic ingredients of his own later novels.

In April 1849 Dostoevskii was arrested when the Petrashevskii discussion circle was broken up by the police and its members charged with plotting against the tsarist regime. Along with the other ringleaders, he was sentenced to death, a sentence that was commuted to penal servitude and Siberian exile only after the grotesque enactment of a mock execution designed to teach the young conspirators a lesson. The effect on the writer was traumatic. He spent four years in the Omsk penal settlement, among the dregs of humanity, and a further five years in the ranks in Semipalatinsk. The whole Siberian experience wrought a profound change in Dostoevskii's convictions. His firsthand experience of the criminal mind disclosed to him the profound irrationality of human nature and its capacity for evil. It also disabused him of any belief that political solutions could ever redeem a corrupt soul. From the copy of the New Testament that was his constant companion in Siberia he learned that salvation was to be found not in political or institutional change, but in the complete religious transformation of human nature. Disabused of naive humanism, he returned from Siberia in December 1859 as a writer with a religious mission. This period also revealed to him the profound spiritual resources of the ordinary people; from then on religious populism and a deep faith in the superiority of native Russian cultural and moral values over those of the west dominated his thought and informed the ideological content of his major writings. Dostoevskii returned to literary prominence with three works that derive in different ways from his Siberian experiences: *Zapiski iz mertvogo doma* (*The House of the Dead*) offers a fictional account of prison life; *Unizhennye i oskorblennye* (*The Insulted and the Injured*) reflects the author's refutation of naive Utopianism in the face of evil; and *Zimnie zametki o letnikh vpechatleniiakh* (*Winter Notes on Summer Impressions*), an account of Dostoevskii's trip to western Europe in 1862, discloses his xenophobia and Russian chauvinism.

But it was not only Dostoevskii who had evolved during his Siberian exile. The Russia he returned to in 1859 had also changed and was now poised on the brink of modernization and reform. Intellectual life had been reinvigorated following the death of Tsar Nicholas I, and it witnessed furious polemics among conservatives, liberals, and the new radical intelligentsia that had sprung up under the mentorship of Nikolai Chernyshevskii. Dostoevskii threw himself into this polemical fray, launching the journals *Vremia* and, subsequently, *Epokha* with his brother Mikhail. In the pages of these publications he first advocated a course of national reconciliation, but gradually he evolved a stance that was hostile to the radicals. The novel *Zapiski iz podpol'ia* (*Notes from Underground*), which appeared in *Epokha* in 1864, offers both a vigorous refutation of Chernyshevskii's ideas and a striking new hero, whose razor-sharp consciousness, perverse irrationality, and capacity for self-contradiction mark a fresh stage in Dostoevskii's development as a writer. *Notes from Underground* also contains a philosophical toughness and tenacity that is new in Dostoevskii's fiction, and it stands as a forerunner of the great philosophical, psychological, and religious novels that were to follow.

The first of these, *Prestuplenie i nakazanie* (*Crime and Punishment*), also started as a refutation of Chernyshevskii and of those who would enact his ideas; but it transcends the polemical to become a powerful account of an individual's fall and redemption, successfully blending social and psychological truth with elements of religious mythography centred on the theme of the raising of Lazarus. *Idiot* (*The Idiot*) also combines the mimetic and the mythic, as the moral and spiritual downfall of Russia's Europeanized upper classes is revealed dramatically through the catalyst of Prince Myshkin, a Christ-like figure whose compassion and humility expose both the bankruptcy of the society through which he moves and the frailty of his own humanist ideals. A similarly apocalyptic note is struck by *Besy* (*The Devils*) as political lampoon gives way to exploration of the spiritual nihilism of the age.

The last decade of Dostoevskii's life produced two novels: *Podrostok* (*A Raw Youth*), generally regarded as inferior to his other mature novels, and *Brat'ia Karamazovy* (*The Brothers*

Karamazov), the crowning achievement of his career as a novelist. The same decade also saw the serial publication of his *Dnevnik pisatelia* (*The Diary of a Writer*), a generically innovative work, and his acclaimed Pushkin Speech, delivered at the unveiling of a statue to the poet in 1880. When he died in 1881 Dostoevskii was at the peak of his powers, his reputation as novelist, psychologist, philosopher, and prophet firmly established in his own land. In the 20th century this reputation has been further enhanced and has spread throughout the world. The works of Dostoevskii are now regarded as the culmination of the 19th-century novel and the forerunner of the forms taken by narrative fiction in the 20th.

W.J. LEATHERBARROW

Poor Folk

Bednye liudi

Novel, 1846

Poor Folk is a novel made up entirely of an exchange of letters between a poor, middle-aged copying-clerk, Makar Devushkin, and a young seamstress, Varvara Dobroselova, who live on opposite sides of the same courtyard. Through correspondence they maintain a supportive father/daughter relationship in the face of extreme poverty. In order to provide Varvara with necessities, Makar Devushkin exchanges the room he rents in a lodging house for a corner of another, deprives himself of food and warm clothing, including an overcoat. Self-denial threatens his frail physical being. He has written so many letters to her by candlelight that his eyesight is failing. She genuinely appreciates his devotion, for it helps her cope with the depression she experiences when thinking of past abuse and her hopeless future.

For Makar this relationship, incomplete though it is, offers rare consolation in a dreadful life. The only other pleasure he gains is from self-styled "literary" evenings in the room of another of the lodgers. He shares this interest in literature with Varvara and enjoys relating to her romantic stories written by his acquaintance. She in turn introduces him to Pushkin's *Povesti Belkina* (*The Tales of Belkin*), and sends him her first attempts at poetry for approval.

Literature provides only a brief escape from the hardship of everyday life, however. Varvara recounts her past to Makar to explain how her situation has deteriorated. Her descent into despair had begun with the death of the breadwinner, her father. She and her mother had then gone to live with a distant relative, Anna Fedorovna, who claimed to be their saviour, but constantly humiliated and exploited them. It was here that Varvara fell in love with the tutor Pokrovskii, but both he and her mother were soon to die. Anna Fedorovna then introduced her to the aptly named landowner, Bykov (the bull), at whose hands, it is implied, she suffered physical abuse. It is to his advances that she finally succumbs, agreeing to marry him because she can no longer cope with her desperate poverty. Her departure leaves Makar devastated.

When it was first published, *Poor Folk* created a tremendous stir. The writers Nekrasov and Grigorovich were so impressed by Dostoevskii's first work that they woke him up in the middle of the night to applaud his genius. Nekrasov proceeded to inform the influential critic Vissarion Belinskii that Dostoevskii was "the new Gogol'". On meeting Dostoevskii, Belinskii exclaimed "Do you yourself understand *what* you have written?"

Modern critics, however, have tended to regard *Poor Folk* as an interesting social document, "the acme of the 'philanthropic' literature of the forties" (Mirsky, 1949), but a mediocre novel. Ronald Hingley (1962), by contrast, doubts whether Dostoevskii intended showing any compassion for these miserable creatures, claiming that its characters and incidents would reduce the modern reader to laughing. Victor Terras (1969), on the other hand, regards this implausibility as deliberate, as part of Dostoevskii's "travesty of the sentimental novel, and anti-parody of Gogol''s ... *Overcoat*". It is precisely the wealth of literary echoes noted by Terras that holds the key to *Poor Folk*'s significance.

Dostoevskii's Makar suffered a similar plight to Gogol''s Akakii Akakievich, both "little men", both minor civil servants living on the bread line, the one consoled by a possession, his coat, the other by a woman. Certainly Akakii, Makar and Varvara were from a vulnerable underclass, exploited by those with the power and money to abuse their position. Dostoevskii's primary concern was not, however, their social problems, but their psychological dilemmas. With this in mind, he adopted two archaic, 18th-century conventions – an epistolary form, and a sentimental tone. These features provide a limited viewpoint deliberately chosen to restrict the reader's perception of events to that of the two characters. In this way their trapped existence and deprived mental life, with all the psychological problems this entails, can be conveyed. The characters express themselves in a mawkish fashion partly because their communication pattern has been affected by the sentimental literature they read, partly because it allows them to communicate feelings for which there is no other outlet. If they do so awkwardly it is because they are unused to articulating their emotions. They avoid contact with others because they feel threatened. Living as they do by letter means they exist primarily in the past. Varvara, precursor of so many of Dostoevskii's exploited, tormented heroines, attempts to rise above her awful circumstances by taking an interest in literature. When she tries to write poetry, however, it is as much to reassure both herself and Makar that she has not succumbed to despair, as it is for pleasure.

The depth of their psychological plight is highlighted even further by the use of the *skaz* form, in the story within a story, as the two characters recount their past lives to one another. The effect is that their present and past lives are conveyed once removed, a way of expressing what might be termed "dialogue at a distance". The technique also underlines Makar's inability to face personal contact. Better for him a vicarious relationship by letter, one that is unconsummated (hence "the maiden" element in his surname). To support her, he denies himself the overcoat that had been Akakii Akakievich's substitute for the love of a real person. Self-denial, then, characterizes both his physical and spiritual life. Subconsciously he may be hoping that while he can avoid meeting her, he will not have to face involvement, or endure hurt. But whenever human emotions are involved, complexity and pain are not far away. Intense suffering is inflicted on the powerless Makar when he, "the meek, little man" (in his own words), loses Varvara to the predator. Evil, the sexually rampant bull, Bykov, enjoys a twofold victory, vanquishing Good in the form of two virginal creatures, Varvara (her surname suggests goodness) and Makar. The power of the exploiter has rendered the powerless "little" people quite incapable of controlling either their own destinies, or even their own small corner of the world.

In *Poor Folk* Dostoevskii explored the complexity and pathos of the individual psyche in the psychological intercourse of poor people on the verge of going under in a threatening urban environment, thereby foreshadowing the direction of his later work.

MARILYN MINTO

The Double

Dvoinik

Novel, 1846

Dostoevskii's second novel was published only a few weeks after his first in February 1846 when the author was 25 years old and living in St Petersburg. After the heady success of the ostensibly philanthropic *Poor Folk*, which had led to influential critics like Belinskii proclaiming its author as "a second Gogol'", *The Double* was greeted by humiliating incomprehension and hostility, causing Dostoevskii, who thought it "ten times higher", great shock and disappointment. Eventually acknowledging the work's execution to have been imperfect, he nevertheless continued to believe in the importance of its idea. A planned revision of it was prevented by his arrest and exile in 1849, but Dostoevskii continued to believe in the intrinsic importance of the idea, and made a partially revised version of it in 1866 for the third edition of his collected works. The work's main significance, however, is to be seen in the various doubles that occur in his major post-exile fiction.

The story begins with a minor civil servant, Iakov Petrovich Goliadkin, waking up in St Petersburg after a long sleep. After an excruciatingly neurotic toilet, he sets off in a carriage, not for the office but to visit his unnervingly imposing doctor, Krest'ian Ivanovich Rutenshpits; the consultation reveals the ambitious Goliadkin to be not only socially inept and volubly inarticulate, but afflicted by a series of neuroses, relating to, among other things, sex and authority. He leaves the doctor and sets off on an extraordinary shopping expedition followed by a visit to a restaurant where he is embarrassed by the surroundings and, especially, by meeting two rather familiar colleagues before whom he makes a series of social and psychological gaffes. He has already anticipated the double motif by wondering whether to pretend to be someone else identical to himself to avoid an unwanted social encounter. Goliadkin aspires to social success and, in particular, the affection of Klara Olsuf'evna, daughter of Civil Counsellor Berendeev, his sometime benefactor. His unwelcome intrusion into the young lady's birthday party is one of Dostoevskii's most excruciating scenes of embarrassment, tempered only by the sub-Gogolian mock-heroic description of the magnificence of the setting in which the debacle occurs.

It is after this that Mr Goliadkin Junior begins to make his presence felt. He appears to be everything that Goliadkin Senior is not: bold, socially adroit, popular, and with an unerring sense of where his best interests lie. Neither Goliadkin has any real moral sense, but Junior's more ruthless ambitiousness is met with success, whereas Senior's attempts at sophistication and social advancement are only risible; even authority over his servant Petrushka is lost ("decent people don't have doubles"), and Senior's life is made a complete misery in a dramatically escalating series of scenes leading to the final scandal. The circular nature of the story becomes apparent when Goliadkin Senior again finds himself in the reception room of Olsufii Berendeev, scene of his earlier humiliation. Once more he is forced to leave the room in precipitate disgrace, this time not in the direction of his double, but into an asylum.

The literary antecedents of *The Double* are many. The "double" theme itself goes back to E.T.A. Hoffmann and his German contemporaries, whose black romanticism is perhaps reflected in the somewhat Gothic first meeting of the two Goliadkins. The influence of Gogol' is also evident, both in thematic echoes from "Nos" ("The Nose") and "Zapiski sumasshedshego" ("Diary of a Madman"), among other works, but also in some of the convoluted, hyperbolic, loquacious descriptions, notably in set scenes like Klara Olsuf'evna's party. A contemporary writer, Konstantin Aksakov, reviewing the book under a pen-name, described it as a "pitiful parody of Gogol'", and it is certainly true that the latter's masterly and highly individual use of whimsical alogicality, grotesque contrasts, and byzantine syntax are painfully wooden in Dostoevskii's hands. The feeling of unsuccessful imitation is reinforced by specific reminiscences of detail in the description of paranoid symptoms, and the tragic feeling of growing paranoia in *The Double* is considerably lessened by over-elaborate comparisons, prolix descriptions and Dostoevskii's often cruel sense of humour. The link between the cold and windswept landscape of St Petersburg and Goliadkin's miserable mental state is overplayed and too reminiscent of Gogol'. Aksakov was right that Gogol''s style was, literally, inimitable, and the Hoffmannesque confusion of dreams, letters and jumbled events undoubtedly lack the charm and, indeed, often the purpose of the *Märchen*.

It must be remembered, however, that this was Dostoevskii's first attempt at third-person narration, and that his aim was more ambitious than that of Hoffmann, Gogol', or, indeed, late romantics like R.L. Stevenson with his tale of Jekyll and Hyde. While Stevenson is clearly in control from beginning to end, and while Gogol' makes no bones about the supernatural nature of "The Nose" or the fantastic nature of the grotesque in "Diary of a Madman", Dostoevskii aims to maintain ambiguity from the start, with the description of a half-waking state, and in this way to present spontaneously a more realistic, almost medical, psychological portrait of the onset and development of paranoid schizophrenia. This is the first of many pathological states to be described in Dostoevskii's fiction, and the concept of split personality was to be richly mined in such characters of his later fiction as Raskol'nikov, Svidrigailov, Myshkin and Rogozhin, Versilov, Stavrogin, and Ivan Karamazov, to name but the principal ones. In his notebooks of 1872–75 the writer expressed pride at having created in Goliadkin his "most important type of underground man", and, indeed, the hero of *The Double* in many ways prefigures the far more complex but no less alienated Underground Man himself in his mixture of pride, conflicting instincts and social inadequacy, though he has none of the later character's defiance and spite.

The Double is an ambitious early work, which in the context of Dostoevskii's *oeuvre* must count as a failure, but is important for presaging the sophisticated polyphony and psychological realism of his great fiction.

ARNOLD MCMILLIN

Notes from Underground

Zapiski iz podpol'ia

Novel, 1864

Notes from Underground was first published in Dostoevskii's own journal *Epokha*. It aroused little critical comment at the time, but has since been acclaimed as a key work in Dostoevskii's *oeuvre* – a prelude to his major novels, adumbrating in condensed form ideas, techniques and psychological insights, which are regarded as typically Dostoevskian.

In form the work is a confession (a title that Dostoevskii originally thought of giving the "Notes"). It is in two parts. The first is the "philosophy" of the Underground Man, presented, not as a coherent rational treatise, but through arguments conducted with imaginary readers often in a jeering manner, challenging common sense and received wisdom, yet with a strong element of humour. This first part is set in the 1860s and addresses the fashionable philosophical theories of the day. By contrast, Part 2 is largely narrative and is set in the 1840s. The discrepancy in chronology and genre between the two parts is striking, yet the psychology of the central figure is recognizably the same: Part 2 is the "philosophy" of Part 1 in action.

Notes from Underground begins with an authorial footnote suggesting the hero as an inevitable product of Russian cultural development. The "underground" is not a real place but a psychological state of extreme introspection – a refuge from the outer world, which brings its own self-laceration as well as its perverse compensations. A central concept for the "underground" is "consciousness", perhaps better understood as "acute self-awareness".

Part 1 is divided into 11 sections, each of which has a central idea, but is permeated by ideas and themes from other sections, reworked, subverted and even inverted. Thus there is a constant flux of ideas, which not only typifies the thought processes of the Underground Man, but provides a key to the techniques of Dostoevskii's major novels. The polemical thrust of Part 1 is against the socialist materialists of the 1860s, in particular Chernyshevskii whose novel, *Chto delat'?* (*What is to Be Done?*), was presented as a textbook of behaviour for the younger generation. Everything for Chernyshevskii could be reduced to reason and his chief doctrine of "rational egoism" maintained that man always acts in his own self-interest, which, rationally understood, embraces the self-interest of others, and makes possible the perfect society of the future. The Underground Man mocks such naivety: the rational part of man, he argues, constitutes a mere 20th part of his make-up. How then can man live for one 20th part of himself? He is against anything that constrains man – scientific attempts to codify his behaviour and even laws of nature. Man's greatest self-interest is to do exactly as he wants: it is the freedom to act against his own self-interest if he so chooses. His most capricious whim is dearer to him than any rationally prescribed "self-interest". Limited, practical men stop short when confronted with a "wall" of impossibility, but the Underground Man will never be reconciled to a "wall" just because it is a "wall". The rationalists believe in the formula 2 x 2 = 4, but such a formula is a challenge to man's freedom, and the Underground Man can see the attraction of 2 x 2 = 5. Perfection itself is constraining: it is not the beginning of life but death; for as an ultimately achieved state it is static and dead. Therefore the "perfection" of the rationally achieved, model society (symbolized in the image of the crystal palace) marks the end of man's freedom. In the crystal palace all man's actions will be transparent; his desires and needs will be codified and foreseen, but this will destroy what is essentially human; for "who wants to want according to a table?"; like a game of chess the real point of life is the play itself, not the final dead formula of checkmate.

In his image of the crystal palace, Dostoevskii is polemicizing with Chernyshevskii's image for the perfect society in *What is to Be Done?*, but he also has in mind the Crystal Palace in London, an edifice built to celebrate the western concept of progress. *Notes from Underground* bears traces of Dostoevskii's visit to western Europe in 1862 and his record of this experience in *Winter Notes on Summer Impressions* in which he records his negative reaction to the Great Exhibition. In rejecting Chernyshevskii's facile rationalistic optimism, Dostoevskii is also rejecting the scientific and materialistic values of western society.

Chernyshevskii's theories derived from the English Utilitarians, in particular J.S. Mill with his principle of "enlightened self-interest" and Jeremy Bentham, whose "Felicific Calculus" posited a balance sheet, codifying pleasure and pain. Darwin and Malthus are also in the Underground Man's sights and Henry Buckle, whose *History of Civilization* suggested that civilization had made man less bloodthirsty. The Underground Man, however, points to the terrible blood-letting that has already marked the 19th century, and concludes that civilization has not diminished man's barbarity, merely given him means to refine and develop it.

The construction of Part 1 is like a web of criss-crossing threads and looping warps with the spinner of fictions himself at its centre. Yet its development of themes may also be seen in musical terms, and it is a musical analogy that links the two parts. A memory, like some "annoying musical motif" at the end of Part 1, is recounted in Part 2. Part 2 takes to task the sentimental humanism of the 1840s. Its epigraph is a poem by Nekrasov on the redemption of a prostitute: the hero's own attempt to save Liza from prostitution ends up as a travesty of this romantic, noble deed. The transition to Part 2 is also effected through a "philosophical" opening section, but now the Underground Man vents his bile on romantics, in particular Russian romantics. This soon passes into an account of how he harboured resentment against an officer, whom he considered had insulted him. His need to acquire respectable clothes in order not to yield ground to him on the street reads like a parody of Gogol''s "Shinel'" ("The Overcoat"), a story that profoundly influenced the sentimental humanism of the 1840s (including Dostoevskii's own early work). The sub-title of Part 2, "On Account of Sleet", is an oblique reference to a dominant motif in such writing. The central episodes of Part 2 continue this attack on the values of the 1840s with an "underground" reappraisal of the lofty themes of friendship and humanitarianism. The Underground Man insists on joining former school "friends", whom he has never liked, in honouring a colleague whom he particularly loathes. His behaviour poisons the sense of conviviality, and when they leave to go to a brothel, he too rushes to join them. There he meets Liza, whom he lectures and offers to help. Yet when she later visits him, he insults and humiliates her, and she realizes that he is more to be pitied than her.

The behaviour of the Underground Man is strongly influenced by reading. Throughout Part 2 he is aware that his actions are "literary", and Liza herself comments that he speaks "as though from a book". But the Underground Man turns this on his readers: it is their vice too, without a book they do not know what to do or what to think.

Notes from Underground is more than a parable on Russian intellectual development, it points to the dark recesses of the human psyche and the limits of reason. It raises the philosophical problems of freedom and has been seen as a precursor to Existentialism.

RICHARD PEACE

Crime and Punishment

Prestuplenie i nakazanie

Novel, 1866

The first recognizable draft of what was to become *Crime and Punishment* appeared in a letter Dostoevskii wrote in September 1865 to M.N. Katkov, the editor of *Russkii vestnik*, in which he outlined a plan for a novel that was to be the "psychological account of a crime". The action was to be contemporary, and the crime, the murder of a pawnbroker, was to be carried out by a young student acting under the influence of "strange, half-baked ideas that are floating about in the air". In this letter Dostoevskii thus signalled the twin concerns of *Crime and Punishment*: first, its focus is inward, towards the psychological landscape of the hero's mind, rather than outward, towards the topographical and social phenomena of the world he inhabits; second, the novel's primary thrust is polemical; it is to engage and challenge the dominant ideologies of the age, of which the hero Raskol'nikov is a product. The work was serialized in Katkov's journal during 1866, enjoying considerable popular acclaim, and published in book form the following year.

Raskol'nikov's crime and its aftermath are designed to take issue with the views on human nature and morality advanced by N.G. Chernyshevskii, editor of the journal *Sovremennik* and an inspiration for the younger generation of radical intelligentsia of the 1860s. Chernyshevskii had insisted in his works that human behaviour was reducible to rational and materialist principles, and that empirical science yielded no evidence of a spiritual side to man. From this basis he had developed an ethical theory rooted in the principles of rational egoism and utilitarianism, which denied the concept of an absolute morality derived from spiritual sources. In *Crime and Punishment* Raskol'nikov enacts these ideas, attempting to justify the murder of the pawnbroker in terms of its advantageous social consequences, the greater good of the greater number. For Dostoevskii, by now convinced of the powerlessness of reason to redeem a corrupt soul and anxious to demonstrate that salvation lay in man's spiritual resources, such ideas were anathema. The events of the novel disclose to Raskol'nikov the inadequacy of a Utilitarian morality, as under the influence of the meek, Christian prostitute Sonia he confronts "unsuspected and unanticipated feelings" deriving from the depths of a soul he is reluctant to acknowledge and leading him ultimately to confession and redemption. The psychological details of Raskol'nikov's suffering and uncertainty are drawn with great insight, but the reader is possibly less convinced by Dostoevskii's rather conventional attempt to nudge his hero into spiritual resurrection in the novel's epilogue.

The psychological intensity of the main body of the novel is achieved by Dostoevskii's use of an unstable and subjective narrative viewpoint. Eschewing a conventional, omniscient point of view, Dostoevskii employs a third-person narrator whose omniscience is selective and whose authority is open to doubt by virtue of his proximity to Raskol'nikov. The reader is drawn immediately into a world that is displaced and warped by the consciousness of the hero dominating it. An intense and disorientating complicity is established between the reader and Raskol'nikov, whose point of view he shares for much of the novel's duration. No dominant authorial figure shapes this confusion or offers the reader a sign-posted path through it. The experience is, as Robert Louis Stevenson observed, akin to that of illness. All certainty disappears, dissolved in the confusion that overtakes Raskol'nikov as his beliefs yield to despair and delirium. Even the basic parameters of the novel, those of time and space, are rendered uncertain by this narrative device. The reader experiences time as Raskol'nikov experiences it: infinitely drawn out in places, precipitate in others. Space, too, becomes a function of consciousness as we lose, along with Raskol'nikov, all sense of the relationship between things. The hero's room, crushingly claustrophobic with its yellow, peeling wallpaper, seems to expand and open out during his periods of lucidity and optimism. The stiflingly narrow back streets of the capital seem like an extension of Raskol'nikov's state of mind, a psychic, rather than topographic labyrinth through which he moves. Indeed, at times it is difficult to tell where Raskol'nikov ends and St Petersburg begins.

The same narrative uncertainty corrodes our understanding of Raskol'nikov's psychology and of his motive for the crime. As his initial rational certainties are compromised by the discovery of irrational depths to his nature, so the original motive, based on rational and Utilitarian considerations, gives way to ever darker and more irrational possibilities. Is the crime an affirmation of Raskol'nikov's egoism and Napoleonic will to power? Is it an attempt at self-definition on the part of a hero who does not know whether he is a superman or a louse? Or is it the proud, irrational protest of a young man who cannot accept his ordinariness? We share Raskol'nikov's continual re-thinking of himself as he becomes the criminal in search of his motive.

The reader's perception of the secondary characters in *Crime and Punishment* is similarly subjective. These figures offer no refuge from the commanding consciousness of the hero, no world of alternatives that would allow us to measure Raskol'nikov's experiences against those of others. Instead they lose all qualities of objective "otherness" as they are drawn into his gravitational field and endowed with the burden of his expectations. The libertine Svidrigailov becomes an embodiment of the amoral will to power; the timid Sonia stands as an emblem of the submissive multitude; the drunken Marmeladov travesties Raskol'nikov's capacity for self-hurt and self-abasement; and the strange detective Porfirii Petrovich seems to satisfy his desire for pursuit and capture.

With its urban setting and themes of poverty, prostitution,

drunkenness, etc., *Crime and Punishment* is furnished with many of the traditional ingredients of the 19th-century social novel. However, its inward focus and psychological complexity render it much more than this, and in its use of a destabilizing, participating narrator it anticipates many of the paths taken by narrative fiction in the 20th century and thus strikes today's reader as startlingly contemporary, a tribute to the modernity of Dostoevskii's artistic vision.

W.J. LEATHERBARROW

The Idiot

Idiot

Novel, 1868

Some critics cannot bring themselves to write about *The Idiot* at all. Others are so fascinated that they return to it again and again. It was Dostoevskii's second major novel, first serialized in 1868 in the journal *Russkii vestnik*, during a period of his life when he was undergoing great crises. He had fled abroad on Good Friday 1867 with his new, young wife to escape relatives and creditors. The intention was to be away for three months. In the event, without any clear aim, Dostoevskii and Anna Grigor'evna remained in exile for four years and three months. During this period he was a constant prey to extreme xenophobia, a ruinous gambling obsession, recurrent marital stress caused in large measure by his own irritability and irresponsibility at the gaming tables, and an increasing tendency to violent epileptic attacks. These were aggravated, no doubt, by the death of their three-month-old daughter Sonia in Geneva. The consciousness of the novel's remarkable hero, Prince Lev Nikolaevich Myshkin, reflects much of this anguish and permeates the whole narrative. Myshkin, who evolved through a series of plans from a Dostoevskian sinner to emerge in the published version as a Dostoevskian saint, is inspired by the highest ideals of Christian purity, but fascinated by the chaos and disorder around him in contemporary St Petersburg: by the money-grubbing, the passions, the ambitions, the pretensions, the suicidal tendencies, the apocalyptic atmosphere. He has nostalgic memories composed of blissful moments in the mountains of Switzerland – a flawed idyll in which the beastliness of human nature asserts itself and human alienation from Nature haunts him – and obsessive thoughts about the experience of a condemned man on the way to his own execution – memories that he feels compelled to share with others. He is himself an epileptic and the description of his epileptic fits – the moment of supreme beatitude in which beauty and prayer coalesce, followed by descent into an abyss of spiritual darkness – portends the apocalyptic tenor of the whole narrative, a narrative that in one way or another enfolds all the other characters. It is not for nothing that some critics have spoken of the novel as the product of an "epileptic consciousness", a novel whose structure, like the human society it depicts, teeters uneasily on the brink of collapse and self-destruction but somehow manages to retain some sort of elusive coherence and to assert a haunting ideal of human perfectibility.

The key to this structural coherence has been the subject of endless discussion. The plot itself, if reduced to its bare bones, is obviously a key factor. The hero, an innocent and saintly young man, seen by some as a Christ figure, by others as an embodiment of the Russian "holy fool", returns to St Petersburg by train from a lengthy period of convalescence in a Swiss clinic. He has no money and only the most tenuous contacts, though he is of a princely family and has some (possibly exaggerated) expectations. On the train he falls in with a man of dark passions (Rogozhin) who is in a stormy relationship with a beautiful, high-spirited St Petersburg woman of questionable reputation and unpredictable mood. Myshkin's interest is awakened and he is subsequently drawn both to this Romantic *femme fatale* (Nastas'ia Filippovna Barashkova) and no less to the very beautiful, neurotic, and spoilt youngest daughter of his nearest Petersburg relativės (Aglaia Epanchina) to whom he eventually becomes engaged. After many unpredictable twists to the plot, in which Myshkin acquires and gives away an inheritance, he ends up by marrying neither. Nastas'ia Filippovna is murdered by Rogozhin, and Aglaia is so desperate to escape into her fantasy world that she marries a bogus Polish count. The prince is reduced by these experiences to a state of idiocy and is returned to Switzerland. The prognosis is not promising.

However such a summary is too neat. In a traditional novel the triangle suggested above would dominate the plot. In fact at times we are almost allowed to forget Nastas'ia Filippovna, and the narrative is hijacked by other characters whose role in the plot development cannot justify the space they occupy. Such are the tragi-comic figures of the gossip and fixer Lebedev with his far-fetched apocalyptic theories, the down-at-heel General Ivolgin who can no longer distinguish between reality and his own tall stories, and the boxer Keller; or the group of unprincipled, young nihilists out to cheat Myshkin of his inheritance; or Ippolit Terentev, whose "confession" dominates Part 3 of the novel. Dostoevskii has been accused of losing control of his plot and this has been accounted by some to his own sick state of mind at the time of writing. But this is not an ordinary novel and the "state of mind" reflected in the text, whether it be attributed to the author or the dominant characters or the society they inhabit, is one in which the threshhold between dream and waking experience, fantasy and reality, sanity and madness, normality and deviation, paranoia and dispassionate judgement, coherence and incoherence is constantly blurred and where readers, like the characters, stray imperceptibly from one realm to the other, uncertain whether they are experiencing reality in a state of mental disorientation or an anxiety-dream based on a reconstruction of real events. The text raises the question of the reliability of experience and of the capacity of language to express the deepest truths.

The narrative structure, which has also been the subject of critical censure, reinforces such questions. The narrative voice, whether that of an omniscient narrator, of a chronicler ignorant of vital matters, or of the novelist appealing for his reader's understanding, is at times clearly demarcated and at times subject to slippage. Moreover, we are not dealing merely with shifts in narrative point of view, but also with accompanying changes in genre conventions. The effect of this constant shifting is to awaken expectations and then to subvert and relativize them, and to force the attentive reader to question the adequacy of language and narrative in rendering experience. Looked at from this point of view *The Idiot* is clearly not a failure, and moreover it is a true forerunner of modernism and post-modernism and

Dostoevskii's sickness, as he would have argued himself, a gateway to higher awareness.

MALCOLM V. JONES

The Devils / The Possessed

Besy

Novel, 1871–72

The Devils is sometimes translated as *The Possessed*. Either title can be justified. The Russian actually means "devils": the epigraphs are from Pushkin's poem by the same name and the story of the Gadarene swine in St Luke 8: 32–35. The novel is about a provincial town whose citizens are seemingly possessed by the spirit of nihilism and intent on self-destruction. *The Devils* was Dostoevskii's third major novel, written after *The Idiot*, and first published in *Russkii vestnik* in 1871–72, towards the close of the fraught four years and three months (1867–71) that he spent in Europe following his marriage to his second wife, Anna Grigor'evna. Dostoevskii did not feel at home in Europe and was subject to a destructive gambling obsession, xenophobia, homesickness, frequent epileptic attacks, depression, and irritability. His young wife somehow put up with all this, even pawning her wedding ring, and helped him through it. His mood was not improved, however, by news of political events, particularly those arriving from home in 1869, about the murder of a young revolutionary called Ivanov in a park near the Moscow Agricultural College where he was a student. It turned out that the murder had been carried out by a group of five fellow-revolutionaries under the leadership of Sergei Nechaev, a self-styled disciple of Bakunin who had composed *The Catechism of a Revolutionary* with him. Among many other nihilistic tactics the *Catechism* advocated confusing, exploiting, ensnaring, and compromising empty-headed persons, especially women, occupying high positions in society, in order to create a situation propitious to revolution. This episode instantly awakened all Dostoevskii's apocalyptic forebodings and his dread of the revolutionary movement as a vehicle for the Antichrist. It also gave an overtly political thrust to his creative thinking and this now occupied his attention.

He immediately seized on the idea for the core of a new novel in which the Nechaev-figure is played by the young Petr Verkhovenskii, whose sinister, calculated mischief-making ensnares the governor of the province and his wife, and other leading figures in the town, and leads to riots, arson, nervous breakdowns, sacrilege, suicides, murders and widespread social and psychological disorder. The centre-piece of this underlying plot is the murder of the Ivanov-figure (Shatov) by the group of five led by Verkhovenskii, ostensibly because of doubts about Shatov's loyalty, but actually to cement the loyalty of the remaining members of the group through common guilt for Shatov's murder. There are other memorable set-piece scenes, of which the most accomplished is the build-up to and realization of the "fête", a great public occasion in which exaggerated hopes are placed by all the participants, high and low, and which, thanks to Verkhovenskii's machinations, is foredoomed to disaster. It is one of the great "scandal scenes" for which Dostoevskii is famous, but on a broader social scale than ever before or after. In writing the novel, however, Dostoevskii incorporated ideas from his never-to-be-written "Life of a Great Sinner" on which he had also been working, about a middle-aged man who has lost his faith. This theme is represented by Stepan Verkhovenskii, a "liberal of the forties", father of the young nihilist and intimate friend of the widowed Varvara Petrovna Stavrogina, a leading figure in provincial society. Stavrogina is the mother of Nikolai Stavrogin, a shadowy, enigmatic figure, hero-worshipped at some time or other by all the major figures. It becomes evident that, although he is not a revolutionary himself, Stavrogin is in some measure responsible for the various forms of spiritual nihilism in the novel. He himself is haunted by devils and at various times he has entertained a variety of ideological positions, making converts at each stage. It is evident that this titanic hero believes in none of them and that he is spiritually empty, to the point where he descends to the trivial (biting the governor's ear), the perverse (marrying the simple-minded cripple Maria Timofeevna) and the sadistic (allowing an innocent young girl to be punished for a theft he has committed himself and standing by as she subsequently commits suicide). Eventually he commits suicide himself, but meanwhile his disciples Petr Verkhovenskii (with his pseudo-revolutionary creed), Shatov (a fledgling Slavophile who believes in Christ and that the Second Coming will take place in Russia, but does not yet believe in God) and Kirillov (with his eccentric, Messianiac belief that he can save humanity by taking his own life, but who is nevertheless persuaded to confuse the issue by falsely confessing to the murder of Shatov) all come to grief, as does Stavrogin's mistress Liza Tushina. At the close the stage is strewn with corpses. Readers have often felt that Stavrogin is insufficiently strongly characterized in view of the influence he is supposed to exercise on events. One reason for this impression is the "missing chapter" "At Tikhon's". Two variants survive, but neither were published in Dostoevskii's lifetime, either in the serialized version (since the editor, Katkov, thought it unsuitable for a family journal) or in the first edition of the complete novel in 1873. In this chapter Stavrogin reads his prepared confession to Bishop Tikhon. It demonstrates the roots of his spiritual torment and self-laceration. But the fact that Dostoevskii chose never to restore the chapter demonstrates that he felt its absence (and the consequent mystification) did no serious harm to the novel. After all it is fitting that a novel about spiritual emptiness has a void at its centre.

The Devils is not regarded by many as Dostoevskii's best novel. Although many critics rate it above *A Raw Youth*, they also find it flawed by its overt political thrust. For some, too, its lack of a positive spiritual counterpoint to the nihilists is a serious shortcoming. And others point to structural flaws. Like *The Idiot*, its narrative point-of-view shifts dramatically from the limited chronicler to the omniscient narrator, though here it is the chronicler who dominates, in the guise of one of the irresponsible young people fascinated by the unfolding disaster and not reluctant to play a minor role in it. It does however have some notable set-pieces and its political impact, as an analysis of the peculiar character of the Russian revolutionary movement, was considerable. "Shigalevism", named after a minor member of Verkhovenskii's group, was the doctrine that the idea of unlimited freedom somehow leads to unlimited despotism. The writers of the collection of articles known as *Vekhi* [Landmarks], which appeared in 1909, repeatedly appealed to it in their critique. The French Existentialist Albert Camus featured it in his study of rebellion *L'Homme révolté* (*The Rebel*), 1951, and dramatized Dostoevskii's novel in his own last major work, *Les Possédés* (*The Possessed*), 1959.

MALCOLM V. JONES

The Brothers Karamazov

Brat'ia Karamazovy

Novel, 1879–80

Dostoevskii worked on *The Brothers Karamazov*, his final novel, throughout 1879 and 1880, finishing it only two months before his death from emphysema in January 1881. The novel was serialized in the journal *Russkii vestnik*. It marks the crowning achievement of Dostoevskii's career, deepening and synthesizing many of the ideas and projects that had occupied the author for much of his life. It reflects in particular his deepest preoccupations during the final decade of his life, a period when he had found some financial and emotional stability and when his reputation as a novelist and thinker was firmly established. Despite its psychological, philosophical, and religious profundity, *The Brothers Karamazov* is constructed around an extremely simple plot, dealing with the murder of the father of the Karamazov family by his illegitimate son, Smerdiakov, and the subsequent wrongful arrest and imprisonment of Dmitrii, one of three legitimate Karamazov sons. The theme of family disorder and disintegration was one that had occupied Dostoevskii throughout the 1870s, and it had found earlier expression in his novel *A Raw Youth*. The metaphor of the "accidental family", in which the concepts of brotherhood and filial responsibility had been lost, served as a powerful expression of the loss of unity and moral purpose that Dostoevskii found in contemporary society at large.

The central event of *The Brothers Karamazov*, the crime of parricide, provided Dostoevskii with a richly suggestive symbol of the pathological condition not only of the Karamazov family, but also of the age that had spawned such a family. The atheism of the younger generation of Russian radicals, embodied in the novel in the figure of Ivan Karamazov, who pits his own human logic against divine reason in a breathtaking act of revolt, was also for Dostoevskii an act of parricide, the turning of "sons" away from their heavenly father. The passing of a death sentence on Alexander II by a political terrorist group in 1879 was a further symptom of contemporary disorder, the breakdown of healthy relations between the tsar, the "little father" in folk parlance, and his "children". But moral disorder and breakdown were for Dostoevskii not confined to contemporary familial, social, political, or religious structures and institutions. They also affected the very psyche of modern man, whose integrality and well-being were compromised by the egoism, narrow rationalism, materialism and loss of true faith characteristic of the 19th century. In *The Brothers Karamazov* Dostoevskii gives expression to this idea through the device of a collective hero, the three legitimate Karamazov brothers, each representing in isolation one of the three aspects of man's being: reason (Ivan), emotion (Dmitrii), and faith (Alesha). The failure of the three brothers to achieve fraternal unity of purpose is thus deeply symbolic.

It is clear that if the plot of *The Brothers Karamazov* is simple, its thematic preoccupations, and indeed its artistic innovations, are startlingly ambitious. The novel addresses with unprecedented profundity such major themes as atheism and belief, the nature of man, socialism and individualism, freedom and justice, and the state of European civilization. And it does all this in an artistic form that both draws upon existing novelistic traditions and transcends them, preparing the way for many of the directions taken by practitioners of the genre in the 20th century. Essentially, it is a novel concerned with confrontations between order and disorder, justice and injustice, harmony and chaos, unity and fragmentation, and it evolves a distinctive artistic form and apt narrative strategies to convey its thematic concerns. It explores these confrontations in a variety of settings, including the psychological, the familial, the social, the moral, and the metaphysical. In all these manifestations it seeks to show man the way forward from what Dostoevskii saw as the underlying disorder and emptiness of his age into a new state of moral and spiritual certainty rooted in the author's own convictions as an Orthodox Christian. In this respect *The Brothers Karamazov* is an overtly didactic work, a great achievement of Christian literature. Dostoevskii himself described his work on the novel as a "civic feat", designed to show people "the way to the church". It is therefore a measure of Dostoevskii's greatness as an imaginative artist that such a morally purposive work should manage to avoid the dogmatic and the stridently evangelical. Although a novel of ideas, *The Brothers Karamazov* relies on dramatic confrontations of great force and narrative techniques of great subtlety in order to establish its moral priorities. The section entitled "Pro and Contra", which Dostoevskii regarded as the "culminating point" of the novel, offers perhaps the best illustration of this. Ivan's "humanist" rebellion against divine justice, as he regales his brother Alesha with harrowing examples of senseless cruelty to children, is implicitly negated by his own inability to love his fellow man except in the abstract. His emphatic affirmation in his poem "The Grand Inquisitor" of an earthly paradise based on human, rather than divine law is subtly undercut by the overblown rhetoric and pretentiousness of his narrative, and then exposed to comparison with the monk Zosima's humble and inspired account of his life and beliefs. In such ways *The Brothers Karamazov* achieves artistic as well as philosophical greatness. It is not to be read simply as a religious tract: it is, in the end, the result of a lifetime's reflection on the most burning issues of the age by a novelist celebrated even in his own time for his penetrating psychological and moral insights, prophetic vision, and revolutionary approach to the art of fiction.

W.J. LEATHERBARROW

Sergei Donatovich Dovlatov 1941–1990

Prose writer

Biography

Born in Ufa, 3 September 1941, of Armenian and Jewish parentage. Brought up in Leningrad from 1945. Studied Finnish philology at Leningrad University 1959–62, did not graduate. Served in the Soviet Army as a Gulag guard in the Komi ASSR 1962–65. Journalist for various Leningrad publications 1965–74; member of the "Gorozhane" group of writers, which included Gubin, Maramzin, Vakhtin, and Efimov; short stories began circulating in *samizdat*. Moved to Tallin to find journalistic work, 1974–76. Short stories published in western journals from 1977; official displeasure resulted in arrest and expulsion from the Union of Journalists before permission was given to emigrate, 1978. Brief spell in Vienna, then moved to New York, where his works began to be published. Co-founder of the newspaper *Novyi Amerikanets*, 1980; chief editor for two years. Recipient: Pen Club Prize. Began to be published in Russia, 1989. Died in New York, 24 August 1990.

Publications

Collected Editions

Sobranie prozy, 3 vols. St Petersburg, 1993.

Maloizvestnyi Dovlatov [The Lesser-Known Dovlatov]. Moscow, 1995.

Fiction

Nevidimaia kniga. Ann Arbor, Ardis, 1978; translated as *The Invisible Book*, by Katherine O'Connor and Diana L. Burgin, Ann Arbor, Ardis, 1979.

Solo na undervude [Solo on an Underwood]. Paris, Tret'ia volna, 1980; expanded edition Holyoke, New England Publishing, 1983.

Kompromiss. New York, Serebriany vek, 1981; translated as *The Compromise*, by Anne Frydman, London, Chatto and Windus, and New York, Knopf, 1983.

Zona. Ann Arbor, Hermitage, 1982; translated as *The Zone: A Prison Camp Guard's Story*, by Anne Frydman, New York, Knopf, 1985.

Zapovednik [The Preserve]. Ann Arbor, Hermitage, 1983.

Nashi. Ann Arbor, Ardis, 1983; translated as *Ours: A Russian Family Album*, by Ann Frydman, London, Weidenfeld and Nicolson, 1989.

Marsh odinokikh [The March of the Lonely]. Holyoke, New England Publishing, 1983.

Remeslo [Craft]. Ann Arbor, Ardis, 1985.

Inostranka. New York, Russica, 1986; edited by Vigail Rashkovsky and Donald Fiene, Dana Point, California, Ardis, 1995; translated as *A Foreign Woman*, by Antonina W. Bouis, New York, Grove Weidenfeld, 1991.

Chemodan. Tenafly, New Jersey, Hermitage, 1986; translated as *The Suitcase*, by Antonina Bouis, New York, Grove Weidenfeld, 1990.

Predstavlenie i drugie rasskazy [The Performance and Other Stories]. New York, Russica, 1987.

"Filial" [The Branch], *Zvezda*, 10 (1989).

Zapisnye knizhki [Notebooks]. New York, Slovo-Word, 1990.

Critical Studies

"S.D. Dovlatov", by L. Loseff, in *Modern Encyclopedia of Russian and Soviet Literature*, 5 (1981).

"Po techeniiu", by A. Karpov, *Literaturnaia gazeta* (20 December 1989).

"Vesti iz filiala, ili Duratskaia retsenziia na prozu Sergeia Dovlatova", by V. Kuritsyn, *Literaturnoe obozrenie*, 1 (1990).

"Obzor", by A. Ar'ev, *Neva*, 1 (1990).

Interview in *Besedy v isgnanii: russkoe literaturnoe zarubezh'e*, edited by John Glad, Moscow, 1991.

"Zapiski sluchainogo postoial'tsa", by A. Zverev, *Literaturnoe obozrenie*, 4 (1991).

"Iskusstvo avtoportreta", by P. Vail' and A. Genis, *Literaturnaia gazeta* (4 September 1991).

"O Serezhe Dovlatove", by Iosif Brodskii, *Zvezda*, 2 (1992).

Zvezda (special Dovlatov issue), 3 (1994).

Contemporary Russian Satire: A Genre Study, by Karen L. Ryan-Hayes, Cambridge and New York, Cambridge University Press, 1995.

Sergei Dovlatov: vremia. mestro, sud'ba, by I.G. Sukhikh, St Petersburg, 1996.

After over a decade of attempts to publish his short stories in the Soviet Union (two were in fact published in the early 1970s but were renounced by their author as "hack-work"), Sergei Dovlatov's debut *Nevidimaia kniga* (*The Invisible Book*) took as its very subject the impossibility of publishing literature of any merit in his homeland. The narrator Dovlatov, with the help of various documents, chronicles the endless refusals of editors to publish his stories about a prison-camp guard, despite almost unanimous approval of them; when he finally seems near to success the KGB prevents the book's appearance. As a result the narrator remains a frustrated, embittered journalist who ends up treating prospective authors in much the same way he himself had been treated.

The Invisible Book has close links with many of Dovlatov's other works; *Solo na undervude* [Solo on an Underwood] was the name given to a selection of jottings that he expanded throughout his career and later combined with an "American" section "Solo on an IBM" to make up *Zapisnye knizhki* [Notebooks]; *Remeslo* [Craft] is similarly divided into Soviet and American halves, comprising "The Invisible Book" stripped of some of its more pretentious or apparently irrelevant moments, followed by "The Invisible Newspaper", in which an account of the rise and fall of an émigré newspaper is once again interspersed with excerpts from "Solo on an Underwood". Most importantly, perhaps, the reminiscences of a camp guard described in *The Invisible Book* were eventually published after almost 17 years' delay as *Zona* (*The Zone*).

The final form of *The Zone* is very different to its original inception, as Dovlatov tells us in an introductory "letter to the publisher"; the manuscript had been smuggled out of the USSR in separate parts and some of it had been lost. These details are certainly corroborated by the disparity of the 14 stories, although they hardly explain why some are written in the first person by

"Boris Alikhanov", others in the third person about him, and still others, which concern completely different characters. The events depicted vary from self-mutilation and attempted murder to the beginning of a love affair or a typical prisoner conversation; between the stories, further letters to the publisher provide a retrospective commentary on the text, with additional anecdotes and glimpses of émigré realia combining with explanations of prison slang and discussions of more traditional camp literature (which, it is pointed out, is written mostly by political prisoners rather than guards of criminal camps). Dovlatov's main theme posits that there is little difference between the inmates and their guards, and between the zone and "freedom" outside – all around is a "single soulless world". This realization is the basis of his subsequently constant theme that life, whether in the Soviet Union or America, is absurd.

Dovlatov's predilection for short forms is often reflected in his books' structure – *Kompromiss* (*The Compromise*), for example, consists of 11 stories outlining the origins of 11 of Dovlatov's journalistic articles and the truth that lay behind them. Despite the unifying factor of the Tallin setting in the mid-1970s, the stories often differ in tone (some of them do not seem to be compromises at all), and it is noticeable that many appeared separately prior to their publication in one volume. This disregard for unity was unfortunately reflected in the addition of a story from the collection *Predstavlenie i drugie rasskazy* [The Performance and Other Stories] to subsequent Russian editions of *The Compromise*; less incongruously, *The Zone* has also been expanded to include the masterful short story "The Performance". Dovlatov found a much tidier method to combine shorter narratives in *Chemodan* (*The Suitcase*), where each of the objects in the narrator's suitcase, taken out of the USSR into emigration, prompts a humorous story from his varied past; the result is one of Dovlatov's most artistically successful books.

Zapovednik [The Preserve], a more extended narrative, is another example of fictionalized memoirs, Dovlatov's favoured genre (he himself used the term "pseudo-documentalism" and compared his approach to that of Voinovich in *Ivan'kiada* (*The Ivankiad*)). The plot is almost entirely autobiographical, recounting a summer spent as a tour guide at the Pushkin Museum near Pskov; the narrator is once again called Alikhanov, but echoes Dovlatov's views on provincial life, Village Prose and the extravagances of the Pushkin cult, and becomes increasingly anxious about the prospect of emigration. *Nashi* (*Ours: A Russian Family Album*) is perhaps Dovlatov's most overtly autobiographical book, but nevertheless frequently appears fictional (his grandfather's three sons seem closely related to the "bylina" tradition). Such reliance on personal experience led to an increased preoccupation with émigré and American themes, but Dovlatov remained primarily concerned with his motherland – the American settings of *Inostranka* (*A Foreign Woman*) and "Filial" [The Branch] are for the most part merely frameworks for evocations of Russia.

Dovlatov's style is almost always conversational (with occasional lyrical touches). He claims to have conceived and refined many of his stories orally, and this has resulted in an apparently effortless tone, with many digressions and asides, which belies a rare linguistic meticulousness; he shows particular skill in reproduction of slang and makes sparing but effective use of vulgar language. Unfortunately this oral approach is also responsible for a great deal of repetition in different books, ranging from entire anecdotes to individual similes.

Dovlatov's most important influences are usually cited as the American prose writers so popular in the USSR in his youth (in particular Hemingway), and certainly this is suggested by his use of concise dialogue and understatement. However, Russian literary influences were just as important for him, especially the laconicism of Pushkin and Chekhov, the notebooks of Il'f and Olesha, the absurd tradition centred on Kharms, and the pessimistic humour and brilliant *skaz* technique of Zoshchenko. His unusual modesty and readability have contributed towards a lack of serious critical assessment, but have helped him achieve the huge popularity in Russia which, unfortunately, he himself did not live to see.

THOMAS PEDRICK

Arkadii Trofimovich Dragomoshchenko 1946–

Poet

Biography

Born in Potsdam, Germany, 3 February 1946. Father served in the Soviet Army. Brought up in Vinnitsa, Ukraine. Studied Russian language and literature at the Vinnitsa Pedagogical Institute. Attended courses at the Leningrad Theatre Institute, 1968–73. Married: Zina Smakous in 1969; one son. Worked for APN (Novosti News Agency), Kiev, 1967–69. Worked for Smolensk State Theatre, 1973–74. Watchman and boilerman in Leningrad, late 1970s and 1980s. Associated with the *samizdat* journal *Chasy*, 1974–83. Member of Club-81, independent association of Leningrad writers and artists, from 1983. Co-editor of the *samizdat* journal *Mitin Zhurnal*, 1984–87. Member of the Writers' Union, 1991.

Publications

Poetry

Krug [Circle] (anthology by members of Club-81). Leningrad, 1985.

Dvoinaia raduga [The Double Rainbow]. Moscow, 1988.

Poems in *Rodnik*, 9 (1988) and 12 (1990).

Nebo sootvetstviia [A Sky of Conformity]. Leningrad, 1990.
Description, translated by Lyn Hejinian and Elena Balashova, with an introduction by Michael Molnar. Los Angeles, Sun and Moon Press, 1990.
Selected poems translated by Michael Molnar, in *Child of Europe*, edited by Michael March. Harmondsworth, Penguin, 1990, 205–11.
Antologiia russkogo verlibra. Moscow, 1991.
Xenia, translated by Lyn Hejinian and Elena Balashova. Los Angeles, Sun and Moon Press, 1994.

Essays
Kitaiskoe solntse [Chinese Sun]. St Petersburg, 1997.

Critical Studies
"Afterword", by Michael Molnar, *PN Review*, 47 (1985), 49–51.
"The Vagaries of Description", by Michael Molnar, *Essays in Poetics*, 14/1 (1989), 76–98.

In the 1970s and early 1980s Arkadii Dragomoshchenko made his name in the only way open to him at the time, through private distribution of his work in typescript and "publication" in Leningrad *samizdat* journals such as *Chasy*. He was an active member of Club-81, a group of unofficial Leningrad writers formed in 1981, and took part in many of their readings. For him and most of the other contributors, their group anthology, *Krug* (1985) was their first Soviet publication. His contribution, "Velikoe odnoobrazie liubvi" [The Great Monotony of Love] (1973), is subtitled "Opyt priamoi rechi" [An Experiment in Direct Speech] like many of his titles, it displays a linguistic self-consciousness that is part of his explicit poetic strategy, e.g., "Summa opisanii" [The Sum of Descriptions], "Smutnye osnovy povestvovaniia" [Obscure Bases of Narration], "Primechaniia" [Footnotes], "Nabliudenie padaiushchego lista, vziatoe v kachestve poslednego obosnovaniia peizazha (chtenie)" [Observation of a Fallen Leaf as the "Ultimate Basis" of Landscape (a Reading)].

Leningrad's literary counter-culture was more conservative than that of Moscow and his work was often criticized for being mannered or obscure, or summarily dismissed as "un-Russian" simply because he worked in free verse. Although, even from the prevailing traditionalist viewpoint, this particular judgment was unjustified, since one can find antecedents for both his form and themes in Khlebnikov and the OBERIU poets among others. His "Sentimental'naia elegiia" [A Sentimental Elegy] quotes Aleksandr Vvedenskii as its epigraph. In this poem, that plays with time and memory, Dragomoshchenko demonstrates his ability to transform abstract speculation into poetic imagery: "Some word like the mould of a rule reveals the world reversed/ mirrored down the axis of matter" ("Sentimental'naia elegiia").

Although his later work has been increasingly discursive and concerned with the transmutation of perceptions as they are channelled through language, he also possesses a vein of lyricism and a meditative feeling for sceneries, both country and city. Above all he has an Archimboldesque faculty for translating states of mind or mental activity into aspects of landscape, as in "Vozvrashchenie Grigoriia Skovoroda" [The Return of Grigorii Skovoroda], his affectionate homage to his fellow countryman, the eccentric theologian:

> He hadn't forgotten there were such things as dreams. And
> in each body
> Weave nests, as in black poplars birds rear fledglings that
> shrill plaintive cries –
> Such was recall. Or rather was erased:
> Light sand of the glimmering body blissfully flowing round
> an island of memory ...

Dragmoshchenko's work explores the way our perceived and conceptual worlds are constructed through language. Self-consciousness, mannerism and a degree of abstraction are inevitable hazards in this territory, they are also concomitants of an individual voice obstinately pursuing its own themes. The fundamental characteristics of his work remain constant and may be summarized in the title of his first American translations: *Description*.

In his version of description, commentary and primary object are not strictly segregated: the second-level description (describing the act of describing) is woven into the actual description itself. In this respect Dragomoshchenko can even be considered a nature poet. Although he has spent his entire adult life in Leningrad/St Petersburg, he continues to mine a vein of natural imagery that reverts, in part, to his youth in the Ukraine. The natural objects or landscapes in his work are, at the same time, both themselves and units of meaning in a superimposed conceptual schema, a hybrid language/world: "And not a building site, a pilgrimage the page / stretched beyond the ripples of the alphabet" ("Smutnye osnovy povestvovaniia" [Obscure Bases of Narration]).

By the late 1980s Dragomoshchenko began to find an audience among promising younger writers, such as the poet Aleksei Parshchikov, and the prose writer Andrei Levkin, who was to publish Dragomoshchenko's verse in his influential journal, *Rodnik*. But it is in the United States that he has attracted most attention through the translations of Lyn Hejinian and Elena Balashova, which have given him an audience there, specifically among those writers associated with the so-called Language School of poetry whose ideology welds together such influences as Black Mountain College and Russian Formalism. These connections have also led to visiting professorships at universities in Buffalo and San Diego.

Dragomoshchenko's syntax is less disjunctive than that of his American counterparts but, like them, he regards the subject of discourse as a construct rather than a natural object. For him, as for them, the ideas of "self-expression" or the poet's "character" always require inverted commas, and he views language itself as part of a sphere of shifting potentiality from which the apparent self and its worlds emerge: "Have I enough meanings for myself to be able to stop / What is being written reducing itself to what has been written ..." ("Elegiia vtoraia po schetu" [Elegy the Second]).

MICHAEL MOLNAR

Aleksandr Valsil'evich Druzhinin 1824–1864
Prose writer, critic, and translator

Biography

Born in St Petersburg, 20 October 1824. Educated at home. Trained in the Corps of Pages, 1841–43; graduated August, 1843. Ensign in Finland regiment, 1843–46; head of regiment library: resigned, January 1846. Collegiate assessor in War Ministry Office, 1846–51. Began to publish, 1847; chief literary critic for *Sovremennik*, 1851–55. Moved to the rival journal *Biblioteka dlia chteniia*, 1856; became its editor and chief literary critic, 1856–58; co-editor with A.F. Pisemskii, 1858–60. Initiated establishment of a fund for needy writers, 1859. Published occasionally in *Russkii vestnik*, *Sovremennik*, and other journals, 1861–64. Died of consumption in St Petersburg, 31 January 1864.

Publications

Collected Editions

Sobranie sochinenii, 8 vols. St Petersburg, 1865–67.
Povesti. Dnevnik, edited by B.F. Egorov, "Literaturnye pamiatniki", Moscow, 1986.

Fiction

"Polin'ka Saks", *Sovremennik*, 12 (1847), 155–228; translated as "Polinka Saks", in *Polinka Saks and The Story of Aleksei Dmitrich*, by Michael R. Katz, Evanston, Illinois, Northwestern University Press, 1992.
"Zhiuli", *Sovremennik*, 1 (1848) 5–164.
"Rasskaz Alekseia Dmitricha", *Sovremennik*, 2 (1848), 209–304; translated as "The Story of Aleksei Dmitrich", by Michael R. Katz, in *Polinka Saks and The Story of Aleksei Dmitrich*, Evanston, Illinois, Northwestern University Press, 1992.
"Doktor i patsienty" [Doctor and Patients], *Sovremennik*, 6 (1848), 103–58.
"Khudozhnik" [The Artist], *Sovremennik*, 7 (1848), 5–20.
"Samoubiistvo" [Suicide], *Sovremennik*, 12 (1848), 85–108.
"Malen'kii bratets" [The Little Boy], *Sovremennik*, 8 (1849), 153–82.
"Sharlotta Sh-ts", *Sovremennik*, 12 (1849), 287–312.
"Pevitsa" [The Singer], *Sovremennik*, 12 (1851), 131–70.
"Lola Montes", in *Zhivye kartiny. Povesti i rasskazy pisatelei natural'noi shkoly*, Moscow, 1988.

Literary Criticism

"Pis'ma inogorodnego podpischika o russkoi zhurnalistike" [Letters from an Out-of-Town Subscriber about Russian Journalism], *Sovremennik*, 1 (1849), almost monthly until 3 (1854).
"Galereia zamechatel'neishikh romanov" [A Gallery of the Most Outstanding Novels], *Sovremennik*, 1–5, 9–10 (1850).
"Grecheskie stikhotvoreniia N. Shebriny" [The Greek Verse of N. Shebrina], *Sovremennik*, 6 (1850).
"O sovremennoi kritike vo Frantsii" [About Contemporary Criticism in France], *Sovremennik*, 11 (1850).
"Dzhonson i Bosvell'" [[Samuel] Johnson and Boswell], *Biblioteka dlia chteniia*, 110 (1851), 111–12, 115–16 (1852).
"Pis'ma inogorodnego podpischika ob angliskoi literature i zhurnalistike" [Letters from an Out-of-Town Subscriber about English Literature and Journalism], *Sovremennik*, 12 (1852); 3, 4, 10 (1853); 4 (1856).
"Zhizn' i dramaticheskoe proizvedenie R. Sheridana" [The Life and Dramatic Works of Richard Sheridan], *Sovremennik*, 1, 9, 10 (1854).
"V. Skott i ego sovremenniki" [Sir Walter Scott and His Contemporaries], *Otechestvennye zapiski*, 3, 4, 6, 9, 10 (1854).
"A.S. Pushkin i poslednee izdanie ego sochinenii" [A.S. Pushkin and the Last Publication of His Works], *Biblioteka dlia chteniia*, 130 (1855).
"G. Krabb i ego proizvedenie" [George Crabbe and His Works], *Sovremennik*, 11, 12 (1855), 1–3, 5 (1856).
"Stikhotvoreniia A.A. Feta" [A.A. Fet's Poetry], *Biblioteka dlia chteniia*, 137 (1856).
"Kritika Gogolevskogo perioda russkoi literatury i nashi k nei otnosheniia" [The Criticism of the Gogol' Period of Russian Literature and Our Attitude Towards It], *Biblioteka dlia chteniia*, 140 (1856).
"Ocherki iz krest'ianskogo byta A.F. Pisemskogo" [Sketches from the Peasant Life of A.F. Pisemskii], *Biblioteka dlia chteniia*, 141 (1857).
"Stikhotvoreniia A.N. Maikova" [A.N. Maikov's Poetry], *Biblioteka dlia chteniia*, 153 (1859).

Critical Studies

"A. V. Druzhinin", by S.A. Vengerov, *Vestnik Evropy*, 1–2 (1895).
"Esteticheskaia kritika", by N.I. Prutskov, in *Istoriia russkoi kritiki*, vol. 1, Moscow and Leningrad, 1958.
"Druzhinin's View of American Life and Literature", by A. Brojde, *Canadian American Slavic Studies*, 10 (1976), 382–99.
"The Crisis in Russian Literary Criticism: 1856 – The Decisive Year", by George Genereux, *Russian Literature Triquarterly*, 17 (1982), 117–40.
Early Russian Liberals, by Derek Offord, Cambridge, Cambridge University Press, 1985.
"Proza A.V. Druzhinina", by B.F. Egorov, in *Povesti. Dnevnik*, by A.V. Druzhinin, Moscow, 1986, 429–58.

Bibliography

Russkie pisateli, 1800–1917. Biograficheskii slovar', vol. 2, Moscow, 1992.

Aleksandr Druzhinin was born into a wealthy gentry family in St Petersburg. He was educated at home, where he was taught French, English, and German, before entering the Corps of Pages and later the Finland regiment. Druzhinin showed signs of an inclination toward literature early in life, composing witty stories for his friends in school, and later becoming regimental librarian. He began his publishing career with the short epistolary novel, *Polin'ka Saks*. Inspired in part by George Sand's *Jacques* (1834), the work was well received, winning the praise of V.G. Belinskii and other *littérateurs*. The novel marked the beginning of Druzhinin's long association with *Sovremennik*, where he soon published *Rasskaz Alekseia Dmitricha* (*The Story of Aleksei Dmitrich*), which was greeted by Belinskii with even more enthusiasm. It is a man's story about his adolescent friendship with an unusual and captivating boy, and his deep love for the boy's sister who refuses his hand in marriage, choosing instead to spend her life protecting her ungrateful father from her hateful stepmother. Druzhinin's early works, including the banned *Lola Montes*, a story of a young woman made to marry an older man for his money, have been compared to those of Dostoevskii. Nevertheless, the bulk of Druzhinin's prose, including the light and entertaining short stories "Freilein Vil'gemina" [Miss Wilhemina] (1848), and "Khudozhnik" [The Artist], the novel *Zhiuli*, and the comedy *Sharlotta Sh-ts*, has been largely forgotten. A variety of popular, frivolous *feuilletons* about St Petersburg life that appeared periodically from 1850 until 1862, including the "Sentimental'noe puteshestvie Ivana Chernoknizhnikova po peterburgskim dacham" [Sentimental Journey of Ivan Chernoknizhnikov Round the Petersburg Dachas] and the series, "Zametki peterburgskogo turista" [Notes of a Petersburg Tourist], have met a similar fate.

Early in 1849, Druzhinin began to turn his attention toward literary criticism. In January, 1851, he left his position in the government service to devote himself to a literary career. Despite differences of approach and opinion, he soon occupied Belinskii's former position as chief critic of Russian literature. His light review series, "Pis'ma inogorodnego podpischika o russkoi zhurnalistike" [Letters from an Out-of-Town Subscriber about Russian Journalism], appeared in *Sovremennik* on a near-monthly basis for almost five years. He also wrote similar reviews of literature and criticism in France and in England for the same journal: "O sovremennoi kritike vo Frantsii" [About Contemporary Criticism in France], and "Pis'ma inogorodnego podpischika ob angliskoi literature i zhurnalistike" [Letters from an Out-of-Town Subscriber about English Literature and Journalism]. In 1850, Druzhinin began to publish a series of critical reviews of "outstanding novels", including Samuel Richardson's *Clarissa; or, The History of a Young Lady*, Oliver Goldsmith's *The Vicar of Wakefield*, Ann Radcliffe's *The Romance of the Forest*, the Comte de Tressan's *Histoire du Petit Jehan de Saintre*, and Honoré de Balzac's *Histoire des treize* (*History of the Thirteen*), which included much biographical and historical information. He soon added to these a series of lengthy essays on the life and works of Samuel Johnson, Sir Walter Scott and his contemporaries, Richard Sheridan, George Crabbe, as well as works about Dickens and Thackeray. Druzhinin was instrumental in acquainting the Russian reader with English and French literatures, and was well respected for his contribution in this area (Turgenev called him "the expert").

In 1856, Druzhinin accepted an invitation to head the journal *Biblioteka dlia chteniia*, where he had also published several works in recent years. As chief critic, he now engaged in a polemic regarding aesthetics with N.G. Chernyshevskii, *Sovremennik*'s new leading critic whose increasing authority Druzhinin had tried unsuccessfully to oppose while still at that journal. Prompted by a new 1855 edition of Pushkin's works and subsequently by Chernyshevskii's "Ocherki gogolevskogo perioda russkoi literatury" ("Essays on the Gogol' Period of Russian Literature"), Druzhinin wrote "Kritika Gogolevskogo perioda russkoi literatury i nashi k nei otnosheniia" [The Criticism of the Gogol' Period of Russian Literature and Our Attitude Towards It]. In this and several other review articles of this period, Druzhinin established his aesthetic views and emerged as the leading advocate of the theory of "pure" art, as opposed to the "didactic" art espoused by his opponents. The role of literature, he argued, was not to concern itself with topical issues of fleeting importance, to expose the negative aspects of life, or to instruct the reader on these or other questions, but to rise above current issues and present themes of eternal and universal human significance, to depict life in all its truth and wholeness. Druzhinin maintained that Pushkin, who was aristocratically detached from the concerns of his day, was Russia's ideal writer, not Gogol', whose *Mertvye dushi* (*Dead Souls*) had long been celebrated by Belinskii and his followers for its satirical critique of the corrupt aspects of contemporary Russia. But, to an intelligentsia preoccupied with reform, Druzhinin's views seemed to reflect a lack of concern for the plight of the oppressed, and Druzhinin's popularity diminished in favour of those who called for civic responsibility in art. *Biblioteka dlia chteniia* was not as successful with Druzhinin at its helm as its publisher had hoped it would be, and in 1858, A.F. Pisemskii was made co-editor until Druzhinin left the editorial board of the journal in 1860. Because of illness, he wrote considerably less in the last few years of his life. Having previously published translations of *King Lear* (1856) and *Coriolanus* (1858), he now returned to Shakespeare to make the most significant contribution of this period with translations of *King Richard III* (1860) and *King John* (posthumously, 1865).

Druzhinin was a significant literary figure in the first half of the 1850s when he was the chief voice of Russian literary criticism and leader of the "pure" art school. He was well respected by his contemporaries, including Tolstoi, Turgenev, and others, and his translations and studies of English literature, particularly his works on Crabbe and Thackeray, were highly respected by his colleagues; several of his articles on English writers continue to be important Russian sources. But when the "seven gloomy years" came to an end, neither his light, often frivolous writings, nor his studied detachment were suited to the spirit of the times. Almost immediately after his death, Druzhinin was forgotten, and has only recently begun to receive attention for his contributions to Russian literature.

JENNIFER LONERGAN

Polinka Saks

Polin'ka Saks

Story, 1847

Polinka Saks appeared in the journal *Sovremennik* in 1847. The story had been written three years previously, partly in response to George Sand's *Jacques*, which was translated into Russian in 1844. In Sand's epistolary novel, Jacques's young wife Fernande falls in love with another man, who returns her feelings. Convinced of their true love, Jacques commits suicide to allow his beloved wife to be free to follow her heart. With considerably different consequences, a similar plot unfolds in a series of letters between four people in *Polinka Saks*: Konstantin Saks, his young wife Polin'ka and two of their old friends, Pavel Zaleshin and Annette Krasinskaia. In the first letter, from Saks to Zaleshin, Saks discusses different aspects of his life during the year since he married Polin'ka. Though he loves her deeply, Polin'ka was a naive young child when she married, and Saks has spent a frustrating year trying to educate her, to develop in her a taste for art, music and literature – in short, he has been "trying to mould a nice, sensible helpmate for my tortured soul". He blames her parents for her worthless upbringing, but concedes that "her parents were not so much to blame as society, which, with all its demands, forces women to become like little children". In the second letter, from Polin'ka to her old school friend Annette, we discover that Polin'ka had formerly been set to marry Annette's brother, but, having finally married Saks, she had no regrets and is genuinely fond of him. She admits that people find him eccentric, but she has met with some success in her efforts to make him more like other people. The tone and details of her letter confirm that she is indeed naive, uninformed, and childish. The third letter, from Zaleshin, informs Saks about a certain Prince Galitskii, who, on his way to the capital, offered to deliver Zaleshin's letter. It is now clear to the reader that Prince Galitskii is the man Polin'ka was going to marry. He had been courting Polin'ka, and was so sure of his success that he neglected to ask her parents for her hand before setting off on a trip abroad. He was astounded and depressed when he learned of Polin'ka's marriage. As for Polin'ka's re-education, Zaleshin cannot advise Saks, since Saks seems not to know what he expects of his wife. The fourth letter is from Annette to Polin'ka and is also delivered by Galitskii. Her brother, Annette reports, was traumatized by her marriage and ill upon his return to Russia. Now he wants to see her, and Annette begs Polin'ka to indulge him. The inevitable soon occurs. Saks is called away on business. Still in love with Polin'ka, Galitskii arranges for a lengthy delay in the resolution of Saks's business, allowing him time to pursue Polin'ka. When Saks returns, Polin'ka and the prince are in love. Saks banishes Galitskii for a month while he thinks things over. At the end of the month, Saks summons Galitskii to a secret location outside St Petersburg. Convinced of the sincerity of their feelings for each other, Saks announces that he has procured a divorce, leaving Polin'ka free to join Galitskii. He advises them to go abroad, and ominously urges Galitskii to endeavour to make Polin'ka happy. Some time after their departure, Polin'ka falls ill. As she nears death, she recognizes the profound nobility of Saks's action, and realizes that she truly loved him all along. Anxious that he should know that his efforts to educate her ultimately met with success, she confesses her feelings in a letter, which is delivered to him upon her death.

Polinka Saks is entertaining, often witty, and was very well received. Belinskii greeted it with enthusiasm in his personal correspondence, as well as in an article, outlining his view of Russian literature, published in 1847. Though he admitted that much in the story echoed "immature thought", in it there was "so much truth, so much sincere warmth and a true, conscious understanding of reality, so much talent, and so much originality in that talent, that the story immediately attracted general attention". The work's "civilizing influence" on the generation of readers at that time was noted by the narrator in Dostoevskii's *Podrostok* (*A Raw Youth*), 1875. Tolstoi's correspondence reveals that he, too, was influenced by the novella.

The enthusiasm of its reception, despite its shortcomings, emphasizes its significance as a revealing document of its era. It addressed the burgeoning issue of women's limited position in the family and in society, and its unfortunate consequences: Polin'ka's typical but lamentable upbringing and education ultimately destroyed the happiness of three people. Many other issues of contemporary significance are also broached by the author, especially in the character of Saks. Saks is a civil servant, but a diligent, incorruptible one who works long hours to expose corruption. He is a landowner, but a progressive one, who has lowered the peasants' *obrok* (quit-rent) and takes some other measures to alleviate their burden, without real financial injury to himself. He has house-serfs, but at least once laid out his own clothes while his valet was eating, eccentric behaviour that shocked and dismayed his young wife. He is irreligious, but has an abiding faith in science, to which the skeletons, books, and serpents in his study attest. Saks represents the aspirations of a rising generation in Russia, and his predicament represents their frustration. Though the morally and intellectually developed Saks rejects convention, opting for a more reasonable solution, the consequences are nevertheless fatal. Indeed, though the problem of the love triangle that was developed by Sand in *Jacques*, and treated more realistically by Druzhinin in *Polinka Saks*, was addressed repeatedly in Russian literature, most notably by Aleksandr Herzen in *Kto vinovat?* (*Who is to Blame?*), 1845–46, but was only solved by the eminently rational trio in Nikolai Chernyshevskii's *Chto delat'?* (*What is to Be Done?*), 1863.

JENNIFER LONERGAN

Vladimir Dmitrievich Dudintsev 1918–

Prose writer and journalist

Biography

Born in Dupiansk, in the Kharkov region of Ukraine, 29 July 1918. First work published 1933. Attended Moscow University, graduated in law 1940. Served in World War II; wounded in action, 1942. Worked for a military tribunal in Siberia until 1945. Correspondent, *Komsomol'skaia pravda* 1946–51. Achieved literary prominence during the Thaw period; little was heard of him thereafter, until the Gorbachev years.

Publications

Fiction

U semi bogatyrei [With Seven Knights]. Moscow, 1952.

Ne khlebom edinym. Moscow, 1957; reprinted 1979; translated as *Not by Bread Alone*, by Edith Bone, London, Hutchinson, and New York, Dutton, 1957.

Rasskazy. Moscow, 1963; includes "Vstrecha s berezoi", translated as "The Birch-Tree", by Roger Cockrell, in *Russian Writing Today*, edited by Robin Milner-Gulland and Martin Dewhirst. Harmondsworth, Penguin, 1977.

Novogodnaia skazka. Moscow, 1965; translated as *A New Year's Tale*, by Max Hayward, London, Hutchinson, and New York, Dutton, 1960.

Belye odezhdy [White Robes]. Moscow, 1988.

Critical Studies

Beyond Socialist Realism: Soviet Fiction since "Ivan Denisovich", by Geoffrey Hosking, London, Granada, and New York, Holmes and Meier, 1980.

A History of Post-War Soviet Writing: The Literature of Moral Opposition, by Grigori Svirski, edited and translated by Robert Dessaix and Michael Ulman, Ann Arbor, Ardis, 1981.

Soviet Fiction since Stalin: Science, Politics and Literature, by Rosalind J. Marsh, London, Croom Helm, and Totowa, New Jersey, Barnes and Noble, 1986.

Although a collection of Vladimir Dudintsev's stories *U semi bogatyrei* [With Seven Knights] was published in 1952, Dudintsev's fame rests almost entirely on the novel *Ne khlebom edinym* (*Not by Bread Alone*). Published in the journal *Novyi mir* in 1956 and in book form in 1957, it is regarded as one of the seminal documents of the Thaw.

His second novel *Belye odezhdy* [White Robes], first published in *Neva* in 1987, deals with Lysenko's campaign against those geneticists who refused to accept that acquired characteristics could be passed on genetically. Originally titled "Neizvestnyi soldat" [The Unknown Soldier], the novel was begun as early as 1964. It is set in 1949 in the All-Union Institute of Agriculture and deals with the period, which followed the adoption, in August of that year, of Lysenko's theories on genetics. Like *Not by Bread Alone*, the novel has a biblical title. In *Belye odezhdy* the reference is to Revelation 7:13, the beginning of a passage that says those arrayed in white robes "came out of great tribulation". Their suffering, however, is at an end, for "God shall wipe away all tears from their eyes". As in the earlier novel, the conflict is between honest selflessness and fraudulent self-interest and, specifically, between Ivan Strigalev, who has bred a new hybrid potato, and Kasian Demianovich Riadno. Riadno is a fraud who has built up a spurious plant-breeding empire with the personal backing of Stalin. This empire is sustained by repressive measures that drive true scientists underground. The conflict between Strigalev and Riadno mirrors the struggle between Lysenko and Nikolai Vavilov, which led to the arrest and imprisonment of the latter in 1940. The novel clearly has more than documentary interest and is intended as an exposure of the moral corruption of a whole society. Unfortunately, it suffers from many of the faults of *Not by Bread Alone*, not least that of schematic characterization. The villain (Riadno), the doubter (Fedor Dezhkin, whose task it is to whip dissidents into line), the cowardly professor (Porai), the security agent (Sveshnikov), the upright communist (Tsviakh), and the persecuted visionary (Strigalev) are all two-dimensional, poorly differentiated characters. The novel is peppered with historical references, particularly to the Spanish Inquisition, and is a difficult read.

Dudintsev's short stories are, for the most part, no more distinguished. Most date from the late 1940s and early 1950s although one of them, "Beshennyi mal'chishka" [The Mad Boy], dates from 1958. This story of a stray dog adopted by the inhabitants of a Moscow apartment block is unusual, too, in not being set in the frozen wastes of Siberia. Such is the setting for a group of stories dealing with explosives experts building a railway: "Stantsiia Nina" [Station Nina], "Izbushka Snarskogo" [Snarskii's Hut], "U semi bogatyrei", "Lyzhnyi sled" [Ski Tracks], and the longest of them "Na svoem meste" [In His Place]. This story, typically, focuses on a single central character, Fedia Gusarov, and his ultimately successful efforts to have a proper library and "House of Culture" built for the workers of a Siberian mining project. The industrial setting and the battle between an idealist and his unsympathetic superiors make "Na svoem meste" an important forerunner of *Not by Bread Alone*. In both works the minor characters are little more than ciphers, and the love interest is as unconvincing as that in "Lyzhnyi sled" and "Stantsiia Nina". The best of the short stories are the war stories "Ruka druzei" [The Hand of Friends] (1947), and "Vstrecha s berezoi" ("The Birch-Tree"), 1946. In both stories the hero is an 18-year old soldier, and both are wistful tales of young love lost. In the first Misha Nogotov falls in love with his married nurse but is dissuaded by his friends from embarking on a disastrous affair with her. The second is the tale of a young man returning from the war to find that the girl he loved and her two friends have left Moscow with their factory colleagues during the war. Only a message carved on a birch tree in Sokol'niki park remains. Both stories are saved from sentimentality by their conciseness. In "The Birch-Tree", for instance, Dudintsev describes the boy's six years of service in the army in just over a single page.

Novogodniaia skazka (*A New Year's Tale*) is noticeably different in tone from Dudintsev's other works. Somewhat reminiscent of Olesha's work, this short piece of surrealistic science fiction has been interpreted by some as a political allegory alluding to the events of 1956 and, in the person of the "reformed bandit", to Khrushchev himself. Indeed, the rather pretentious obscurity of the fable allows many interpretations; all that can be said for certain is that the main theme of *Not by Bread Alone* – selfless dedication to the truth – is repeated here rather more concisely. Once again the hero, who is the first-person narrator, is an inventor opposed and persecuted by hide-bound conformists, led by his arch-rival S. The hero is engaged in studying the condensation of the sun's rays in order to provide a permanent source of energy for the inhabitants of the eternally dark half of the universe. A new theme, however, is that of time, symbolized by a mysterious giant owl, a lotus flower grown from 2000-year-old seed and a watch that will run for a year without being rewound. Dudintsev appears to be saying that the content of time, rather than its duration, is what matters. The hero believes he has only a year to live but in that time he finds success in both his personal life and his professional life.

Dudintsev's name was conspicuously omitted from many Soviet surveys of the Thaw period. For example, the chronology given in the fourth volume of the *Istoriia sovetskoi literatury* [History of Soviet Literature] (1967–71) makes no mention of him. For a number of years after 1960 Dudintsev was forced to work as a translator into Russian of works in Armenian, Bashkir, Kazakh, Koriak, Uzbek, Ukrainian, and Iakut. In 1976, rather surprisingly, Dudintsev attacked Trifonov's *Dom na naberezhnoi* (*The House on the Embankment*). In 1979 *Not by Bread Alone* was republished after a delay caused, so Rosalind Marsh suggests, by Dudintsev's refusal to alter the novel.

MICHAEL PURSGLOVE

Not by Bread Alone

Ne khlebom edinym

Novel, 1957

The artistic shortcomings of this novel are many: weak characterization of all but a few central characters, clumsy transitions, unlikely coincidences, heavy-handed symbolism and a surfeit of static, wordy scenes, full of technical jargon. However, the importance of this book lies not so much in its artistic merits as in the fact that its author became, in the words of Mihajlo Mihajlov, "a symbol of 1956". In other words, the book is a symbol of the de-Stalinization programme announced by Khrushchev at the 20th Party Congress in February 1956. Set in the late 1940s in the fictional Siberian industrial town of Muzga, home of a huge and secret industrial combine, the novel deals with the struggle of a schoolteacher-turned-inventor, Lopatkin, to have his revolutionary pipe-casting machine accepted. He is supported at first and then opposed by the plant director, Leonid Ivanovich Drozdov, a dynamic, forceful, manipulative, philistine workaholic. Drozdov, who is content to be feared and to have no friends, is at least psychologically convincing. The other villains in the novel are more or less indistinguishable; chief among them is Vasilii Zakharovich Avdiev, the inventor of a much inferior machine who nevertheless enjoys ministerial support. Lopatkin, who has been tricked out of his job by Avdiev, is, however, supported by the ordinary workers and by Drozdov's estranged wife Nadia, who is shocked by the contrast between Lopatkin's poverty and her own privileged existence. She, like Lopatkin, works in the local school, itself a microcosm of the town and of Soviet society in general. The workers' and Nadia's support is of no avail and Lopatkin's enemies succeed in getting him sentenced to eight years in a prison camp on trumped up charges. Lopatkin's defiant words became famous in the Soviet Union: "The words 'deprivation of freedom' are incorrect. A man who has learned to think cannot be completely deprived of freedom". Although Lopatkin's conviction is eventually overturned, his enemies change jobs and survive. The clash between the idealist Lopatkin and the materialist Drozdov is the crux of the novel; while apologists for the regime claimed that such clashes were atypical, Dudintsev himself clearly intends the opposite. In the 1950s the word "Drozdovism" became current to denote the most negative features of the bureaucracy in general.

As the critic Geoffrey Hosking has pointed out, *Not by Bread Alone* is "a socialist realist novel in the grand manner", from its biblical title to its clash between good and evil and the positive role assigned to those members of the "people" (*narod*) who share Lopatkin's faith. What is new is the fact that evil is represented by the Soviet *nomenklatura*, or privileged elite. However, this is no anti-Party novel. Indeed the role of the Party is minimal, a fact which, in itself, caused difficulties for the author. In one of the few references to the Party, Dudintsev is very careful to show that Lopatkin owes his eventual triumph to "true Party men", such as the prosecutor who has his conviction overturned. Indeed Lopatkin himself is a "true communist", selfless and dedicated, with a long literary ancestry. In a postscript to the English translation Dudintsev somewhat disingenuously berates foreign critics who focused exclusively on those passages of the novel that criticize the regime. Elsewhere he claimed to have been motivated to write the novel by a patriotic desire to make Soviet technology equal or superior to that of the west. Nevertheless, the novel was attacked by the Party orthodox such as V. Ozerov, who saw in it the implication that the attitudes of Lopatkin's enemies were typical of Soviet society rather than the exception. Although liberals like Paustovskii came to Dudintsev's defence, notably in an unpublished speech of 1956, he was forced, in December 1957 to acknowledge the "validity" of the criticism. In 1958 the arch-conservative novelist Vsevolod Kochetov published a novel, *Brat'ia Ershovy* [The Ershov Brothers], which attempts to link dissident scientists with Nazi collaborators. Only in 1959, at the instigation of Khrushchev, who, in May 1957, had denounced the author as a "calumniator", did the attacks on Dudintsev subside. At the Third Congress of Soviet Writers in that year Khrushchev claimed that he had read the novel with interest and that, although the author had exaggerated negative features of Soviet society he "was never our enemy and was not an opponent of the Soviet system".

The novel caused a furore both in the Soviet Union and in the west and has been translated into at least 18 languages. In the Soviet Union it was read avidly by young people for its devastating portrayal of members of a corrupt academic and political elite who, while proclaiming the virtues of "collectivism" and denouncing Lopatkin as an "individualist", feathered their individual nests. The novel was reissued in the Soviet Union in 1979 with a prefatory note stressing that the events described had taken place 30 years previously, while in the US two film versions have been made. *Not by Bread Alone* transcends the merely topical. For instance, the statement by Drozdov that a lone genius is no longer necessary and that the "worker ants" will always win is chillingly reminiscent of

Shigalev's nightmarish Utopia in Dostoevskii's *The Devils*. There are a number of references to Dostoevskii in the novel that suggest a link between Drozdov and the Ivan Karamazov type to whom "everything is permitted" and between Lopatkin and the Dostoevskian "dreamer" figure. Dudintsev expands the concept of "inventor" beyond those scientific inventors who had rallied to Dudintsev's support at their Congress in 1956. The concept includes the pioneering creative artist. It is significant that the figure of the 18th-century *homo universalis*, Mikhail Lomonosov, who was both poet and scientist, is repeatedly evoked. Equally Dudintsev's thesis that the Soviet system will protect the Drozdovs and Avdievs while being incapable of protecting the Lopatkins from the most crass abuse has, in post-Soviet times, struck a prophetic cord.

MICHAEL PURSGLOVE

Nadezhda Andreevna Durova 1783–1866

Prose writer

Biography

Born in Ukraine, September 1783. Raised in a military environment as the family travelled on manoeuvres until 1788. Sent to live with relatives in Ukraine, later summoned home. Married: Vasilii Chernov in 1801; one son. Soon abandoned both husband and son, she then ran away from parent's home, joining Cossack regiment under the name of Aleksandr Vasil'evich Sokolov, September 1806. Enlisted as cavalry soldier in Konnopolsk Uhlan Regiment, March 1807. Mother died, and father wrote to the tsar requesting that his daughter be found and returned; Durova was summoned to St Petersburg to see the tsar. Alexander I was sympathetic to her desire to serve in the military as a man and allowed her to use the name Aleksandr Andreevich Aleksandrov. Recipient: St George's Cross for heroism – the only woman to receive it until World War I. Fought in the war of 1812, wounded at Borodino. Retired with rank of captain, 1816; lived in St Petersburg, returning to Sarapul, 1822. Moved to provincial town of Elabuga, 1830 or 1831. Encouraged by Pushkin to publish her memoirs under the name of Durova. Remaining literary output appeared under versions of the name Aleksandrov, 1837–40. Died in Elabuga, 10 April 1866. Buried with military honours.

Publications

Collected Editions

Povesti i rasskazy, 4 vols. St Petersburg, 1839.

Zapisky kavalerist-devitsy [Notes of a Cavalry Maiden]. Kazan, 1960.

Izbrannye sochineniia kavalerist-devitsy. Moscow, 1983.

Izbrannoe. Moscow, 1984.

Izbrannye sochineniia kavalerist-devitsy N. A. Durovoi, Moscow, 1988.

Memoirs

Kavalerist-devitsa. Proisshestvie v Rossii. [The Cavalry-Maiden: A Happening in Russia]. St Petersburg, 1836; reprinted in single volume with *Dnevnik Partizanskikh deistvii 1812 g.* [Diary of Partisan Activities of 1812], by Denis Davydov, Leningrad, 1985; translated as *The Cavalry Maiden: Journals of a Female Russian Officer in the Napoleonic Wars*, by Mary Fleming Zirin, Bloomington, Indiana University Press, and London, Angel, 1988; also as *The Cavalry Maid: The Memoirs of a Woman Soldier of 1812*, with an introduction by John Mersereau and David Lapeza, Ann Arbor, Ardis, 1988.

God zhizni v Peterburge, ili Nevygody tret'ego poseshcheniia [A Year of Life in St Petersburg, or the Disadvantages of a Third Visit]. St Petersburg, 1838.

Zapiski Aleksandrova (Durovoi). Dobavlenie k Devitse-kavalerist [Notes by Alexandrov (Durova). An Addition to the Maiden-Cavalry Officer]. Moscow, 1839.

Fiction

"Pavil'ion" [The Pavilion], *Otechestvennye zapiski*, 2/3 (1839), 2–138.

"Sernyi kliuch", in *Sto russkikh literatov*, St Petersburg, 1839; translated as "The Sulphur Spring", in *Russian Women's Shorter Fiction: An Anthology, 1835–1860*, by Joe Andrew, Oxford, Clarendon Press, 1996.

Gudishki [Hooters]. St Petersburg, 1839.

Klad [The Treasure]. St Petersburg, 1840.

Ugol [The Corner]. St Petersburg, 1840.

Iarchuk: Sobaka-dukhovidets [Iarchuk: The Dog Who Saw Ghosts]. St Petersburg, 1840.

Critical Studies

"Nadezhda Andreevna Durova (Kavalerist-devitsa)", by D. Mordovtsev, in *Russkie zhenshchiny novogo vremeni: Zhenshchiny deviatnadsatogo veka*, St Petersburg, 1874, 97–150.

"Nadezhda Durova: Russia's Cavalry Maid", by Barbara Heldt, in *History Today*, (February 1983), 24–27.

Terrible Perfection: Women and Russian Literature, by Barbara Heldt, Bloomington, Indiana University Press, 1987.

Introduction by Mary Fleming Zirin to *The Cavalry Maiden: Journals of a Russian Officer in the Napoleonic Wars*, translated by Zirin, Bloomington, Indiana University Press, 1988, ix–xxxvii; bibliography, 233–38.

Nadezhda Durova's relatively small literary opus is enough to secure her place as a unique and dashing figure both in Russian history and in Russian letters. She is best remembered for her memoirs, entitled *Kavalerist-devitsa* (*The Cavalry Maiden*), in which she relates some of her extraordinary adventures disguised as a man in the Russian military during the Napoleonic years. Rumours had been circulating about her already during the war, and the story of her rejection of life as a woman and successful embrace of a military life created a sensation when she published her memoirs 20 years later. *The Cavalry Maiden* is marked by a vital, sincere, energetic narrative voice that reveals much about the appealing psychology of the author/heroine as she confronts the strict social order of her family and then of the different branches of the military. The several other tales Durova published between 1836 and 1840 also deal with the ramifications of rigid social structures on the fate of the individual.

As she poignantly describes, Durova's early life was a struggle to survive in her family without submitting to her mother's version of a woman's life, which amounted to a bleak existence of unbearable (for Durova) physical confinement and emotional isolation. Durova's close relationship with her father, who taught her to ride and encouraged her "masculine" tendencies – he apparently told her frequently that she would have made a good son, and he himself gave her as a gift the Cossack clothing that she eventually used as a disguise – eventually led her to consider seriously the possibility that she might renounce her female identity altogether and live as a man.

The single act of running away from her parents' home to join the army under a male alias was not, however, a psychological anomaly in Durova's life, nor was it based solely on her rejection of her sex. In fact, accounts of her adventures and exploits reveal an impulsive and even reckless personality. Not only did she not avoid danger, but many of the episodes she describes involve a thoughtless action on her part that leads to unforseen consequences.

Durova's story is remarkable, and it is told in a remarkable way, which reflects all the tension and peculiarity of the author's situation. She explains in matter-of-fact terms how she achieved her deception; she admits, but does not belabour, the obvious physical difficulties she faced as a woman performing on the field and in camp as a man. She takes full responsibility for all of her failures, mistakes, and weaknesses, never once resorting to the cliché of calling upon her feminine delicacy to explain a failing. Nevertheless, she writes in an emphatically female voice (with feminine grammatical endings, even though she had to speak with masculine endings to maintain her disguise), and explicitly for a female audience. She was extremely sympathetic to the women she met during her travels with the army, showing an attentiveness to their lives that was uncharacteristic for male memoirists and travel writers. Yet she stops short of criticizing the patriarchal order she herself took such desperate measures to escape. Indeed, Durova frequently expresses an enthusiastic patriotism and adoration of the tsar that may in part explain why she was scrupulously ignored during the first decades of the Soviet regime.

Returning to civilian life after the Russian victory over Napoleon, Durova continued to maintain her assumed identity. She dressed in male clothing, pursued activities that were considered masculine (e.g., riding, smoking a pipe), and generally continued to flout social expectations.

The story of Durova's short career as a writer – rare enough in itself for a woman in the first half of the 19th century – also reflects her eccentricity. Durova's brother had a passing acquaintanceship with Pushkin, and, knowing that his sister had "a suitcase full" of notes from her army days, he arranged for her to send them to Pushkin. Her original intent, at least as she represented it in her correspondence, was to offer the great writer material for his own pen. Instead, Pushkin encouraged her to publish them in her own version, and he even placed a first fragment in the journal *Sovremennik* in 1836. Their correspondence shows that Durova became impatient with Pushkin's cautious schedule and suggestions for revisions (she eventually acquiesced to his urging to publish them as "notes" [*zapiski*] under her own name rather than as the story of "the Russian Amazon"). She forged ahead and published the entire work herself, with the help of a cousin, but then had trouble at first in selling the books. When she did achieve a certain amount of interest and esteem among the reading public, she immediately capitalized on her success by publishing extremely prolifically for the next four years. Yet when she felt that she had exhausted her material (much of her fiction is also drawn from her life) and realized that her Romantic style was becoming obsolete, she suddenly cut short her literary career, retired to live with her brother in the provinces, and never published again.

By 1840, Durova's reputation had declined; the social sensation she had caused subsided, and some of her later tales are of only mediocre quality. But *The Cavalry Maiden* has much to recommend it as an enduring piece of literature. It displays an organic structure, in which the protagonist gradually matures in the army, though without losing her naive curiosity and enthusiasm. Her observations dwell on the routine functions of everyday army life, rather than on the battle tactics that interest many other military memoirists. She frankly appraises her own behavior in both complimentary and uncomplimentary terms. The prose is clear and unadorned, so modern for its time that Belinskii compared it to that of Pushkin. Commenting on the fragment that appeared in *Sovremennik*, Belinskii suggested that it might be Pushkin's own mystification and wondered how the author, especially if she were a woman, could have commanded such wonderful language as early as 1812.

After her initial success, Durova and her memoirs fell into almost complete obscurity. Interest in her story revived around the turn of the century, but she remained a mysterious figure, as much a myth as a real woman. Her life was the subject of so many rumours that many articles on her contained inaccuracies (see bibliography in Zirin). Durova has in fact been portrayed as a fictional heroine numerous times, especially at the turn of the century and duing World War II, when her patriotism was held up as an example of heroism.

The Cavalry Maiden and Durova's other works remain readable and interesting today, both for their early role in the Russian autobiographical tradition – their demonstration of the psychological bases for the heroine's behaviour was an innovation – and for what they tell us about gender roles in Russian society of their time.

CAROLYN JURSA AYERS

E

Fedor Aleksandrovich Emin 1735–1770

Prose writer and translator

Biography

Born Mahomet-Ali Emin, probably in Constantinople, 1735, son of Russian parents (possibly Islamic converts). Details of early life and education unknown. Claimed to have served in Turkey as a janissary. Travelled widely in the Middle East and throughout Europe. Applied to the Russian Embassy in London for Russian citizenship, granted on condition of conversion to Orthodoxy, 1758. Moved to St Petersburg and became Russian citizen, 1761. Studied, then taught, at the Cadet Corps in St Petersburg. Worked as a translator. Titular Counsellor and member of Imperial Cabinet. Died in St Petersburg, 29 April 1770.

Publications

Fiction

Nepostoiannaia fortuna, ili Pokhozhdenie Miramonda [Inconstant Fortune, or Miramond's Peregrinations], parts 1–3. St Petersburg, 1763; 3rd edition, St Petersburg, 1792 (includes a brief, unreliable description of the author's life).

Prikliucheniia Femistokla, i raznye politicheskie, grazhdanskie, filosoficheskie, fizicheskie i voennye ego s synom svoim razgovory; postoiannaia zhizn' i zhestokost' fortuny ego goniashchei [The Adventures of Themistocles ...]. St Petersburg, 1763; 2nd edition, Moscow, 1781.

Nagrazhdennaia postoiannost', ili Prikliucheniia Lizarka i Sarmandy [Rewarded Constancy or the Adventures of Lizark and Sarmanda]. St Petersburg, 1764; 2nd edition, St Petersburg, 1788.

Pis'ma Ernesta i Doravry [The Letters of Ernest and Doravra], parts 1–4. St Petersburg, 1766; 2nd edition, St Petersburg, 1792; extracts reprinted in *Khrestomatiia po russkoi literature XVIII veka*, compiled by A.V. Kokorev, 2nd edition, Moscow, 1956, 574–79.

Poetry

Nravouchitel'nye basni [Edifying Fables]. St Petersburg, 1764; 3rd edition, St Petersburg, 1793.

Translator

[Italian, author unknown], *Besschastnyi Floridor. Istoriia o printse rakalmutskom*. St Petersburg, 1763.

[Portuguese, author uncertain, possibly Emin himself], *Liubovnyi vertograd, ili Nepreoborimoe postoianstvo Kambera i Ariseny*. St Petersburg, 1763.

[Spanish, author unknown], *Gorestnaia liubov' markiza de Toledo*. St Petersburg, 1764.

Critical Studies

"Emin i Sumarokov", by G.A. Gukovskii, *XVIII Vek*, 2, Moscow and Leningrad, 1940.

"Iz istorii literaturnoi bor'by 60-kh godov XVIII veka. (Neizdannaia komediia Fedora Emina *Uchenaia shaika*)", by I.Z. Serman, *XVIII Vek*, 3, Moscow and Leningrad, 1958.

"F. Emin i sud'ba rukopisnogo nslediia M.V. Lomonosova", by D.D. Shamrai, *XVIII Vek*, 3, Moscow and Leningrad, 1958.

"Novoe o F. Emine", by M.A. Arzumanova, *Russkaia literatura*, 1 (1961).

"Fedor Emin and the Beginnings of the Russian Novel", by David E. Budgen, in *Russian Literature in the Age of Catherine the Great. A Collection of Essays*, edited by A.G. Cross, Oxford, Meeuws, 1976, 67–94.

A History of 18th Century Russian Literature, by William Edward Brown, Ann Arbor, Ardis, 1980.

What remains of Fedor Aleksandrovich Emin is his books. No other aspect of his life as a novelist in 18th-century Russia can be spoken about with any confidence. The circumstances of his life are obscure to the point of opaqueness. No satisfactory memoir has ever been written, and the various autobiographical accounts are inconsistent. It may be that the elusiveness was a deliberate decision, or at any rate an exorcism of a personal history that is best described as turbulent – an unnecessary complication for one who, from a Turkish Muslim background, chose to throw in his lot with ordinary middle-class Russian life as a civil servant and novelist, whose writings were largely protective of the bourgeois value-system, which he was pleased to embrace and which was happy to welcome him. None of this is to decry – in the infelicitous manner of much Soviet scholarship on Emin – his assured place in the early days of the Russian novel. If not quite the only begetter, he was at least one of the originators of the form in Russia and in that regard alone is worthy of serious scrutiny.

Emin's life was short, and his writing career lasted for little more than nine years, but in that fertile period he produced more than 25 books. His erudition and uncommonly wide-ranging linguistic prowess are discernable chiefly in his translations, but a more general sympathy with western-European modes, acquired during his early peripatetic years, is spread across the entire corpus. His journalistic work leans primarily on French exemplars, as his own periodical, *Adskaia pochta* [Hell's Post], 1769 (reissued 1788), illustrates, with its cue taken from Lesage, and reliance on translated material. Emin's intention in this publication, and in its companion journal *Smes'* – to reach the widest readership possible – informs the novels to no less a degree.

Emin shared with Chulkov (their relationship was otherwise mutually caustic) the view that, in the grand plan of the novel, enlightening didacticism and classically approved edification should play second fiddle to incident, adventure, and colour. In an Emin novel the moral is upheld to the extent that the virtuous finish happy and the vicious are confounded, but it is useless to look for much beyond this. Far more engaging is the panoply of quests undergone by the characters as their destiny catapults them into any number of exotic mettle-testing environments. Incident is the bread and butter of Emin's fiction. Storms, shipwrecks, pirates, fights, love-scenes, reversals of fortune, long-lost relatives and an omnipresent *deus ex machina* are the stuff of the heroes' experiences. One can, of course, read the facts of Emin's own deracination into all this at will, and it is true that the style, the mode, is thoroughly European in conception. The plot of *Nepostoiannaia fortuna, ili Pokhozhdenie Miramonda* [Inconstant Fortune, or Miramond's Peregrinations] subsumes the European and the fashionably Oriental into a kaleidoscopic whistle-stop tour of romantically charged locations: Turkey, England, Morocco, Egypt, Venice, Germany, France, and so on. All this excitement is distantly supported by the recurring implication that travel broadens the mind and provides its own education, and although it is never the purpose of the novels, the business of acquisition of wisdom comes regularly to the surface. Broadly speaking, Emin toes the line of the enlightened rationalists of the day, the advocates of the golden mean and the *homme moyen sensuel*, who attain temperate sagacity through exposure to the ways of the world: the viewpoint is adopted in Derzhavin's moderate epicureanism or the maxims of Fonvizin's famous fictional agony-uncle Starodum. A good example among Emin's novels is *Prikliucheniia Femistokla* [The Adventures of Themistocles]. The adventures are there all right but they are threaded together by sententious advice sessions between the eponymous Themistocles and his naïve son Neocles, after the manner of Fénelon's *Télémaque*. Emin genuinely believed that his action-packed chronicles could be as intellectually enriching as they were manifestly entertaining, and likely to replace "philosophical and physical works which people are rarely inclined to read".

A different, equally important facet of the European inheritance informs Emin's epistolary novel *Pis'ma Ernesta i Doravry* [The Letters of Ernest and Doravra]. This Sentimentalist four-parter was published in 1766, three years before the first Russian translation of its demonstrable progenitor, Rousseau's *Julie, ou la Nouvelle Héloïse*, and was a very early introduction to the literature of the tender heart. It adumbrates many of the Sentimentalist motifs of the Karamzinian literature of the 1780s and 1790s, and its appearance in the year of Karamzin's birth was much relished by a Russian readership to whom its introspective, highly-strung emotionalism was as novel as its epistolary form. Ernest is a vacillating melancholic, not well off, who is in romantic thrall to well-heeled Doravra (he is already married), whose honour he is terrified of besmirching. When Doravra duly confesses her reciprocal feelings the letters become flooded with emotion as the lovers bare their souls for the reader's delectation – the syntax itself often threatening to crumble under pressure. The Sentimentalist apparatus becomes clear: the beauty of nature and the necessity of "empathy" with it, saturated emotions, the primacy of love, super-sensitivity as a badge of moral worth, the whole package constituting a use to which Russian prose had not so far been put. Social disparity is less important as a sticking point here than in Rousseau, and Ernest already has a wife who is imminently to return from her travels anyway, but it is unattainability that counts, not the manner of its contrivance. Emin tries his hardest to make Ernest three-dimensional, and gives him opinions (the French are frivolous, the English make fine shop-keepers) but, like the Sentimentalists whom he anticipates, the novelist feels compelled to play down psychology in favour of the intensity of the intrigue, whether picaresque or amorous.

NICHOLAS CROWE

Epifanii Premudryi c.1360–1419

Hagiographer

Biography

Born in the third quarter of the 14th century. A monk, whose career began either in the Monastery of Gregory the Theologian in Rostov, well known as a centre of learning in the first half of the 14th century, or in St Sergii's Trinity Monastery at what is now Zagorsk. From 1380 in residence at the latter monastery, though he probably spent some time in Moscow, 1390–1415, and may have visited Constantinople, Jerusalem, and Mount Athos. Developed skills of copying, icon-painting and writing in the Trinity Monastery. Spiritual adviser to the monks. Probably died in 1419, but certainly before 1422.

Publications

Hagiographic Writing

Zhitie Stefana Permskogo [The Life of St Stefan of Perm].
Zhitie sv. Stefana, episkopa permskogo, napisannoe Epifaniem Premudrym [The Life of St Stefan, Bishop of Perm, Written by Epifanii Premudryi], reprinted from V. Druzhinin's edition of 1897 with an introduction by Dmitrij Čiževskij, The Hague, Mouton, 1959; excerpt translated as "Panegyric to Stefan of Perm", in *Medieval Russia's Epics, Chronicles, and Tales*, by Serge A. Zenkovsky, New York, Dutton, 1963.
Pokhval'noe slovo/ Zhitie Sergiia Radonezhskogo [The Life of Sergii of Radonezh].
Die Legenden des heiligen Sergij von Radonez. Nachdruck der Ausgabe von Tichonravov, edited by Ludolf Müller, Slavische Propylaen, Munich, Fink, 1967.
"Zhitie prepodognago i bogonosnago ottsa nashego, igumena Sergia chudotvortsa. Spisano byst' ot Premudreishago Epifania", edited by D.M. Bulanin with a modern Russian translation by M.F. Antonova and D.M. Bulanin, in *Pamiatniki literatury drevnei Rusi, XIV–ser. XV v.*, edited by D.S. Likhachev and O.V. Tvorogov, Moscow, 1981; translated as "The Life, Acts and Miracles of Our Reverend and Holy Father Abbot Sergius, by Epiphanius", an abridged version in *A Treasury of Russian Spirituality*, edited by G.P. Fedotov, London, Sheed and Ward, 1950.

Epistle
"Poslanie ieromonakha Epifaniia k nekoemu drugu svoemu Kirillu" [Epistle from Father Epifanii to a Friend of His, Kirill], edited by O.A. Belobrova with a modern Russian translation, in *Pamiatniki literatury drevnei Rusi, XIV–ser. XV v.*, edited by D.S. Likhachev and O.V. Tvorogov, Moscow, 1981.

Critical Studies
The Literary Style of Epifanij Premudryj: "pletenie sloves", by Faith C.M. Kitch, Munich, Sagner, 1976.
Medieval Slavic and Patristic Eulogies, by J. Alissandratos, Florence, La Lettere, 1982.
Visions of Glory: Studies in Early Russian Hagiography, by Jostein Børtnes, Atlantic Highlands, New Jersey, Humanities Press, 1988.

Bibliography
Slovar' knizhnikov i knizhnosti, edited by D.M. Bulanin and G.M. Prokhorov, vol. II, part 1, Leningrad, 1988.

The reputation of Epifanii Premudryi (the name means "The Most Wise"), rests on his two hagiographical works, *Zhitie Stefana Permskogo* [The Life of St Stefan of Perm] (late 1390s), and the life of the founder of the famous monastery at Zagorsk, St Sergii of Radonezh (1417–18) (*Zhitie Sergiia Radonezhskogo*). He was also the author of at least one epistle, an icon-painter and may have written *Slovo o zhit'i i o prestavleniia velikogo kniazia, Dmitriia Ivanovicha* [The Tale of the Life and Death of the Grand Prince, Dmitrii Ivanovich], as well as being, perhaps, one of the contributors to the Moscow chronicle.

Zhitie Stefana Permskogo takes as its subject Epifanii's friend, the first bishop to the Permians, a people living to the east of Muscovy, and now known as Zyrians. Stefan had picked up a similar Finnic language during his childhood in Velikii Ustiug in north-east Russia. After training in the monastery of Gregory the Theologian in Rostov, where he prepared Permian translations of essential liturgical and biblical texts, Stefan set off on a mission to convert the Permians. The main part of the "Life", which is divided into narrative segments akin to chapters, depicts Stefan's encounters with hostile pagans, and his gradual success, threatened briefly by a dangerous shaman, whom Stefan defeats in a trial of faith. Conversion of the bulk of the Permians is followed by Stefan's consecration as bishop and, shortly after, by his death. The work is unusual for a number of reasons. First, instead of the usual accounts of posthumous miracles (there were none in this case), Epifanii inserts three long sections, the lament of the Permian people, then of the Permian Church (this in the form of a widow's lament), and finally of the author, who expresses both his deep personal sense of loss and admiration for Stefan through a poetic eulogy. Second, rather than presenting Stefan's life as an *imitatio Christi* as was commonly done in earlier Russian hagiography, Epifanii stresses the parallels between Stefan's life and events in the Bible and Church history, thereby presenting Stefan as the most recent contributor to the great history of Christianity. Third, he provides a mass of detail about the land of Perm and its people. Some of this is purely factual, but the accounts of the Permian religion and social attitudes are often presented in scenes, which, despite the inclusion of prayers and abstract meditations, do not lack drama. Last, the work is the supreme example of Epifanii's highly rhythmical, ornate rhetorical style, usually known as *pletenie sloves* (or word-weaving). His prose tends to group words in pairs, or in clauses of similar length or construction, often given rhythmical effect by chiming verbal and nominal endings, semantic parallelisms, and repetition of various kinds. In the final laments, his style achieves lyrical heights that suggest Epifanii's aim was the elevation of his subject as an object of veneration.

There is nothing essentially new here; all the elements can be found in Byzantine and Kievan rhetorical writing, though Old Testament poetry (particularly the Psalms, from which Epifanii quotes extensively), liturgical poetry and the ornate Lives of 13th-century Serbian saints seem to have been particular influences. Epifanii's originality stems from the poetic concentration of these devices and their sustained if varied use in and throughout *Zhitie Stefana Permskogo*.

Whereas Epifanii knew Stefan personally and was writing shortly after his death, *Zhitie Sergiia Radonezhskogo* was composed well after Sergii died in 1391/92. Epifanii relied therefore on collected records, notes, and oral testimony (sometimes folklorized) of monks and others who had known the leader of the spiritual monastic revival of the second half of the 14th century. Unfortunately the "Life" was rewritten a number of times by Pakhomii Serb in the 1440s and 1450s, probably mainly with the aim of reducing its excessive length. Though Epifanii's version does not survive intact, it is generally agreed that there is one manuscript close to the original. Like *Zhitie Stefana Permskogo* it divides the narrative into "chapters", employs, by the standards of the time, dynamic narrative, also ending originally with Sergii's death (ie. without all the miracle accounts that were subsequently appended). It is structured in paired episodes round a compositional centre, rather like an icon with scenes from the life of the subject round the edge. Such structure is more evident because it appears Epifanii avoided the excessive ornamentation of *Zhitie Stefana Permskogo*, reserving it for a concluding encomium, a masterpiece of "word weaving". This has sometimes been regarded as a quite separate work, and/or ascribed to Pakhomii, but it bears little in common with Pakhomii's much more measured and less emotive rhetoric in his other writings, and, despite a certain amount of repetition, serves as a fitting end to the life of the most revered Church figure of the early Muscovite period.

Apart from the two major Lives, Epifanii has often been credited with the composition of *Slovo o zhit'i i o prestavleniia velikogo kniazia, Dmitriia Ivanovicha*. This work is composed in an ornate language, reminiscent of Epifanii's "word-weaving". The arguments for the attribution to Epifanii rest primarily on style, with scholars who suppport this view dating the work to the late 14th or early 15th century. Noting similarities with other writings of the period, they propose that Epifanii's period in Moscow was spent in a writing workshop attached to the metropolitanate, where he was involved *inter alia* in the compilation of the Moscow chronicle. Such conjectures remain pure hypothesis. Those opposed to this view argue that the work was composed around 1448, and thus could only be by an imitator of Epifanii. Their arguments are given weight by the style of the tale, which is much more turgid and obscure than Epifanii's "word-weaving".

FAITH WIGZELL

Nikolai Robertovich Erdman 1900–1970

Dramatist and screenwriter

Biography

Born in Moscow, 16 November 1900. Attended the School of Peter and Paul, Moscow. Brief military service with the Red Army during the Civil War. Associated with the Imaginist group, 1919–24. Started writing operetta librettos and satirical sketches for small-form theatre, early 1920s. First full-length play, *Mandat* (*The Mandate*), performed, 1925. Married: 1) the actress Nadezhda Iashke (stage name Vorontsova) in 1926; 2) Natalia Chidson in 1950; 3) Valentina Kirpichnikova in 1965. His second play, *Samoubiitsa* (*The Suicide*), was banned in 1932. Author of interludes, music hall revues, and film scenarios. Arrested for anti-Soviet writing, 10 October 1933. Exiled to Siberia (Eniseisk and Tomsk). Returned to Kalinin, 1936. Worked in NKVD Ensemble of Song and Dance, 1940–48. Official permission to return to Moscow, 1949. Continued writing film scenarios, animation scripts, and a few stage adaptations. Member of the Writers' Union from 1954. Literary consultant at the Taganka Theatre in the 1960s. Recipient: Stalin Prize for the scenarios of *Volga Volga*, 1941, and *Smelye liudi* [Courageous People], 1951. Died in Moscow, 10 August 1970. Buried in cemetery of Donskoi Monastery. Official rehabilitation in 1990.

Publications

Collected Editions

"The Mandate" and "The Suicide", translated by George Genereux, Jr, Marjorie Hoover, and Jacob Volkov. Ann Arbor, Ardis, 1975.

P'esy, intermedii, pis'ma, dokumenty, vospominaniia sovremennikov [Plays, Interludes, Letters, Documents, Memoirs], edited by Aleksandr Svobodin. Moscow, 1990.

Moskva s tochki zreniia [Moscow from a Point of View], edited by Elizaveta Uvarova. Moscow, 1991.

The Major Plays of Nikolai Erdman: "The Warrant" and "The Suicide", edited and translated by John Freedman. New York and London, Harwood Academic, 1995.

A Meeting about Laughter: Sketches, Interludes and Theatrical Parodies by Nikolai Erdman with Vladimir Mass and Others, edited and translated by John Freedman. New York and London, Harwood Academic, 1995.

Plays

"Gibel' Evropy na Strastnoi ploshchadi" [The Destruction of Europe on Holy Square]. 1924; *Sovremennaia dramaturgiia*, 4 (1994), 214–22.

"Kvalifikatsiia" [The Qualification], 1924; *Teatr*, 5 (1989), 114–18.

"Mandat" (produced Moscow, 1925), *Teatr*, 10 (1987); *Mandat*, edited and with an introduction by Wolfgang Kasack, Munich, Sagner, 1976; translated as "The Mandate", in *"The Mandate" and "The Suicide"*, by George Genereux Jr, *et al.*, 1975; and by John Freedman, in *The Major Plays of Nikolai Erdman*, 1995.

"Zasedanie o smekhe", with Vladimir Mass, 1932; in *God XVI*, Moscow, 1933; edited by Anna Mass, *Voprosy literatury*, 1 (1988), 261–66; *Teatral'naia zhizn'*, 19 (1989); translated as *A Meeting about Laughter*, by John Freedman, in *A Meeting about Laughter: Sketches, Interludes and Theatrical Parodies* ..., 1995.

"Samoubiitsa" (produced in Swedish, 1969; in Russian, 1982), *Novyi zhurnal*, New York, 112–14 (1973–74); *Sovremennaia dramaturgiia*, 2 (1987); translated as "The Suicide", *Russian Literature Triquarterly*, 7 (1973); by George Genereux Jr *et al.*, in *"The Mandate" and "The Suicide"*, 1975; and by John Freedman, in *The Major Plays of Nikolai Erdman*, 1995.

Interludes

"Lev Gurych Sinichkin" (Lenskii), directed by Ruben Simonov, 1924; in *P'esy, intermedii* ..., 1990.

"Hamlet", directed by Nikolai Akimov, 1932; in *P'esy, intermedii ...*, 1990.
"Princess Turandot" (Gozzi), directed by Evgenii Vakhtangov, 1932; in *P'esy, intermedii ...*, 1990.
"Mademoiselle Nitouche" (Hervé), directed by Ruben Simonov, 1944; in *P'esy, intermedii ...*, 1990.
"The Two Gentlemen of Verona", directed by Evgenii Simonov, 1952; in *P'esy, intermedii ...*, 1990.
"Pugachev" (Esenin), directed by Iurii Liubimov, 1967; in *Teatr*, 5 (1989); *P'esy, intermedii ...*, 1990.

Film scenarios (selected)
Mitia, directed by Nikolai Okhlopkov, 1927.
Veselye rebiata [Jolly Fellows], with Vladimir Mass and Grigorii Aleksandrov, directed by Aleksandrov, 1934.
Volga Volga, directed by Grigorii Aleksandrov, 1938.
Smelye liudi [Courageous People], with Mikhail Vol'pin, directed by Konstantin Iudin, 1950.
V nekotorom tsarstve [In a Certain Kingdom], animation, directed by I. Ivanov-Vano, 1958.

Critical Studies
"Nikolai Erdman: A Soviet Dramatist Rediscovered", by Marjorie Hoover, *Russian Literature Triquarterly*, 2 (1972), 413–34.
"Nikolai Erdman: An Overview", by John Freedman, *Slavic and East European Journal*, 28/4 (1984), 462–76.
"The Plays of Nikolay Erdman", by Robert Russell, in his *Russian Drama of the Revolutionary Period*, London, Macmillan, and Totowa, New Jersey, Barnes and Noble, 1988, 102–14.
"Nikolai Erdman na stsene i v pechati Ameriki i Anglii" [Erdman on Stage and in Press in America and England], by John Freedman, *Sovremennaia dramaturgiia*, 5 (1989), 238–44.
Silence's Roar: The Life and Drama of Nikolai Erdman, by John Freedman, Oakville, Ontario, Mosaic Press, 1992.

Bibliographies
"Osnovnye daty zhizni i tvorchestva Nikolaia Robertovicha Erdmana", compiled by A. Guterts and J. Freedman, in Erdman, *P'esy, intermedii ...*, 1990, 513–23.
"Selected Bibliography", in *Silence's Roar: The Life and Drama of Nikolai Erdman*, by John Freedman, Oakville, Ontario, Mosaic Press, 1992, 212–24.

Nikolai Erdman's work can be divided according to his associations with different literary groups: the poet-Imaginist; the satirical dramatist; the film scenarist. His literary career began when he was introduced by his brother Boris to the circle of the Imaginists led by Sergei Esenin. In the early 1920s he started writing lyrics, operetta librettos and revue sketches. Together with Vladimir Mass, Viktor Tipot, and David Gutman, he composed the opening revue for the Theatre of Satire, *Moskva s tochki zreniia* [Moscow from a Point of View], which established him among the writers for the small-form theatre ("miniatiury"). He continued writing sketches for the revues staged at the newly established Satire Theatres in Moscow and Leningrad, and the Music Hall in Leningrad, often in conjunction with Vladimir Mass. At the same time, he became a highly valued literary consultant for the Vakhtangov Theatre, writing interludes of a topical and parodic nature for the classic repertoire. Erdman's first one-act play, *Gibel' Evropy na Strastnoi ploshchadi* [The Destruction of Europe on Holy Square], builds on the principle of a word understood on an abstract level by one character, and on a concrete level by another, which would become the characteristic feature of his writing.

His first full-length play, *Mandat* (*The Mandate*), was first performed at the Meierkhol'd Theatre in 1925. It is a satire on the petty bourgeoisie of the NEP period where the identity of a character is defined by objects (documents, dress, appearance). The Guliachkins try to maintain their bourgeois way of life, pretending only superficially to accept Soviet values. For the sake of securing the marriage of his sister to the former aristocrat Smetanich, Pavel Guliachkin agrees to join the Party, and soon realizes the power that comes with Party membership. He uses the mandate to tyrannize everybody around him and assert his authority; however, the warrant is forged, and thus Pavel remains uncommitted to the new order. In the mean time, through a series of coincidences, the Guliachkins' cook Nastia is mistaken for the princess Anastasia Romanova. Smetanich, who is hoping for the return of the monarchy, decides that such a time has now come, and – through a misunderstanding – proposes to Nastia. The satire is directed at the false belief of the petty bourgeoisie that a return to the old order is possible. At the same time, the abuse of power that comes with Party membership is satirized; however, no representative of the new Soviet order was portrayed in the play, so that the satirical element did not arouse the suspicion of the censors. The play is based on slapstick as well as verbal humour; language as a means of communication is satirized: words command people, rather than people mastering language. *The Mandate* was very popular and generally well received, even by high ranking writers and officials, such as Gor'kii and Lunacharskii; it was staged by more than 40 Soviet theatres in the period 1926–27. By 1928, however, the cultural climate had changed substantially and venomous attacks against the play began to emerge in the press alongside those against Bulgakov's comedies; in 1934 the production was dropped from the repertoire of the Meierkhol'd Theatre. It was revived briefly, but unsuccessfully, in the climate of the Thaw by Erast Garin who had played the part of Pavel Guliachkin in the original production. Erdman even satirized the bureaucratic apparatus responsible for the fate of his plays in the short piece *Zasedanie o smekhe* (*A Meeting about Laughter*) where a meeting has to decide what kind of laughter is allowed, since one of the members present will only laugh at a joke once an official decision has been taken.

The Meierkhol'd Theatre commissioned a second play from Erdman that was completed in 1931. *Samoubiitsa* (*The Suicide*) was rehearsed both by Meierkhol'd and by Stanislavskii at the Moscow Arts Theatre. However, the censorship board Glavrepertkom stopped rehearsals in 1932. Erdman was arrested on 10 October 1933 for writing anti-Soviet fables, possibly recited at a reception at the Japanese Embassy earlier that year, and exiled to Eniseisk and later Tomsk in Siberia. The Meierkhol'd Theatre was closed in 1938, Meierkhol'd's wife Zinaida Raikh was murdered by the security police in 1939, and Meierkhol'd himself, arrested in the same year, was shot in 1940. Between 1940 and 1948 Erdman was drafted to the NKVD

Ensemble of Song and Dance, where he served in the same unit as the artistic elite represented by Iurii Liubimov, Mikhail Vol'pin, Ruben Simonov, Nikolai Okhlopkov, Sergei Iutkevich, Boris Messerer, Dmitrii Shostakovich, and Isaak Dunaevskii. Erdman was in charge of writing the sketches for revues that were to provide entertainment for the Internal Affairs sector.

After his return to Moscow he worked mainly in film, a medium in which he had been successful before: *Veselye rebiata* [Jolly Fellows], the first Soviet film comedy about a peasant becoming a successful musician, fitted in with the concept of socialist realism in showing the potential contribution of the proletariat and peasantry to art; however, as in *Volga Volga* with its similar plot, Erdman and Mass's names did not appear on the cast-list. Erdman wrote film scenarios and animation scripts, often jointly with Mikhail Vol'pin; adaptations of prose works, such as Dostoevskii's *Selo Stepanchikovo i ego obitateli* (*The Village Stepanchikovo and Its Inhabitants*), or Lermontov's *Geroi nashego vremeni* (*A Hero of Our Time*), for the theatre; and scenarios for circus performances. When Iurii Liubimov became artistic director of the Taganka Theatre in 1964, Erdman became his literary consultant, although he was never officially designated as such. However, Erdman had by then withdrawn from active writing for the theatre and had almost entirely devoted himself to the cinema. He wrote over 30 scenarios and more than a dozen animation scripts, many of which received awards.

Until the publication of a substantial amount of archival material in 1990, little was known about Erdman. His date of birth was given as 1902 instead of 1900 after an erroneous entry in the Soviet Encyclopedia of 1934. He was thought by some critics never to have returned from exile; others believed that there was a third full-length play, *Zasedanie o smekhe*, which turned out to be a sketch. It emerged, though, that between 1933 and 1945 Erdman had been working on the play *Gipnotizer* [The Hypnotist] for which he even signed contracts with two Moscow theatres, but the play was abandoned, and only fragments of it have survived.

After half a century in oblivion, Erdman is now recognized as the finest Russian satirist among 20th-century playwrights. Although Erdman's contribution to dramatic literature has thus been rectified, his work in film and his satirical revues have not so far been fully appreciated.

BIRGIT BEUMERS

The Suicide

Samoubiitsa

Play, 1969 (written 1928)

The theme of suicide was prominent in literature after Esenin's suicide in 1925 had provoked a debate about social (rather than personal) causes. Erdman himself dealt with the theme in his scenario *Mitia*, where a suicide sits up unexpectedly in his coffin. Kataev wrote a story in 1926 ("Samoubiitsa ponevole" [Suicide against One's Will]), in which a citizen fails to commit suicide because all the devices he employs are defective; he decides to live, and dies from eating sausage of poor quality. In Erdman's play the sausage does not kill, it only triggers off a chain of events that lead to a suicide, but not that of the (non-) hero Podsekal'nikov, but of the non-character Petunin.

The unemployed Semen Podsekal'nikov asks his wife Masha for some sausage in the middle of the night. Following a series of misunderstandings, he is suspected of being about to commit suicide because of his hopeless situation (he has to rely on his wife to make a living). However, the thought of suicide had not occurred to him at all, since the solution to his dilemma was obvious: he would learn to play the tuba and then earn a living as a musician. Unfortunately, the manual "Teach Yourself to Play the Tuba" requires the use of a piano to learn the scales. Meanwhile, the news about Podsekal'nikov's "suicidal" tendencies has spread, and the neighbour Kalabushkin has set up a business: he takes money from those who need publicity, promising them that Podsekal'nikov will leave a farewell note claiming to have killed himself for the relevant cause. Thus, Aristarkh Dominikovich Goloshchapov (Grand-Skubik) wants Podsekal'nikov to die for the Russian intelligentsia, while Kleopatra Maksimovna needs him to kill himself out of love for her, hoping thereby to outdo her rival Raisa Filippovna and to draw their common lover's attention to herself (they represent spiritual and physical love respectively). Egor expects Podsekal'nikov to commit suicide for the Marxist cause; the butcher Pugachev for the cause of tradesmen; the priest Elpidii for the church; finally, the writer Viktor Viktorovich for the concerns of the artistic world. Flattered by all this attention, Podsekal'nikov agrees to die for any of their ideas, even though originally he had no intention whatsoever of killing himself. But it is too late: a farewell banquet takes place, Podsekal'nikov gets drunk and, on returning home, climbs into the coffin, which has been delivered together with the wreaths. He is found there by the mourning sponsors who arrive for the funeral the next day. During the funeral speeches he is so moved that he rises, only to be blamed for being alive. After he has affirmed his desire to live, a message comes with the news that a certain Petunin has committed suicide and left a note saying that Podsekal'nikov was right: it is indeed not worth living.

The characters who ask Podsekal'nikov to die for their cause in protest against the maltreatment of their respective social group are satirized: Aristarkh is a caricature of the selfish intellectual, too weak to speak out himself: "In times like ours ... only a dead man can say what a live man thinks"; and Egor perverts Marxism to the extent that when he peeps through the keyhole he claims to look at women only "from a Marxist point of view".

There are a number of misunderstandings where language confuses rather than clarifies: Maria in the first scene needs Kalabushkin as a man (to open the bathroom door); Kalabushkin, himself having an affair with a married woman, sends Maria away to rub herself down with cold water. Kalabushkin is subsequently called on to stop Podsekal'nikov from committing suicide, but effectively he provides him with both the means and the motive for suicide. Similarly, Aristarkh arrives to ask Podsekal'nikov to die for the cause of the intelligentsia exactly at the moment when he is about to shoot himself, thereby diverting him from the act he has come to ask him to perform. In these instances actions work counter to the intention of the characters who carry them out. Podsekal'nikov is a hero only ironically – the man who does not commit suicide. Petunin commits the deed in the end, and he is, therefore, really the hero who tragically transforms the word into a deed.

Podsekal'nikov is a mere object of everybody's plans, without the right to make his choices, until he expresses his individuality by choosing to stay alive. The play is "the study of a man who is forced to discover for himself reasons to live, rather than reasons to die" (Freedman). Erdman also employs elements of slapstick, which seem to be taken straight from music-hall entertainment: the tuba only produces obscene sounds; the liver sausage is mistaken for a revolver; the dead Semen suddenly turns out to be alive; Semen is so drunk that he believes he is in heaven.

The play also contains a number of parodic comments on the state: Podsekal'nikov calls the Kremlin, but nobody is there to lead the country. The paper *Izvestiia* is said to promulgate one thing today and another tomorrow, alluding to the rapid changes of policy after 1928. The satire of Soviet life appears to have been the reason for the prohibition at a time when the exposure of the system to criticism was becoming incompatible with the dogma of socialist realism, which would be formulated in 1934.

The play attracted the interest of three Moscow Theatres: the Vakhtangov, the Moscow Arts Theatre and the Meierkhol'd Theatre. The Vakhtangov Theatre dropped the idea after an artistic council in 1930. Stanislavskii wrote a pleading letter to Stalin in 1931 and was granted permission to rehearse the play. Both he and Meierkhol'd conducted rehearsals during 1931 and 1932. In December 1931 the playwright V. Vishnevskii attacked the play in *Literaturnaia gazeta*, because the production of his own *Germaniia* had been postponed by Meierkhol'd to give priority to *The Suicide*. In October 1932 the Glavrepertkom censor, Lazar Kaganovich, attended a rehearsal at the Meierkhol'd Theatre and banned the play. In 1965 Iurii Liubimov attempted in vain to include *The Suicide* in the Taganka Theatre's repertoire; Erdman's hope for publication of the play in *Teatr* in 1968 ended when the journal's editor was dismissed for ideological reasons. *The Suicide* was first staged in Gothenburg, Sweden in 1969. The play remained banned in the Soviet Union until the abolition of theatre control in 1987, although the Theatre of Satire had been granted special permission to stage a version edited by Sergei Mikhalkov in 1982; however, this production was banned by the Ministry of Culture after six performances. The Soviet premiere was at the Satire Theatre in 1987, where the play had been directed by Meierkhol'd's pupil Valentin Pluchek.

The Suicide was first published in the Soviet Union in 1987 in *Teatr*; the text of this publication was based on a self-censored version prepared by Erdman for possible publication in 1968. This was followed in 1990 by a book publication of Erdman's writings which contains the most reliable version, based on the five-act text used by Meierkhol'd.

BIRGIT BEUMERS

Il'ia Grigor'evich Erenburg 1891–1967

Prose writer, poet, and essayist

Biography

Born in Kiev, 27 January 1891, into the family of an engineer. Moved to Moscow, 1896. Attended First Moscow gymnasium; excluded from 6th grade for revolutionary activities. Arrested in 1908; emigrated to France in December 1908, settled in Paris until 1917; war correspondent for Russian newspapers, 1915–17. First poem published in 1910, when first poetry collection appeared in Paris. After his return to Russia, lived in Kiev, Kharkov, Kerch, Feodossiia, and Moscow; travelled to Georgia with Osip Mandel'shtam. Married: Liubov' Kozintseva in 1919; one daughter. Lived in Berlin, 1921–24. Settled in Paris, 1925–41. Extensive visits to the USSR in 1924, 1926, and 1931. Travelled to Spain, 1931. Delegate to the First Congress of Soviet Writers in Moscow, 1934. Correspondent for Soviet newspaper *Izvestiia* in the Spanish Civil War, 1936–38. Settled in Moscow in 1941. World War II correspondent, 1941–45. Visited Canada and the United States, 1946. Vice President, World Peace Council, 1950–67; Deputy of the Supreme Soviet of the USSR, 1950–67. Recipient: Stalin Prize, 1942 and 1948; International Lenin Peace Prize, 1952; Order of Lenin (twice); Order of the Red Star; Knight of the Legion of Honour. Died in Moscow, 31 August 1967.

Publications

Collected Editions

Polnoe sobranie sochinenii, 8 vols. Moscow and Leningrad, 1927–28.

Sobranie sochinenii, 9 vols. Moscow, 1962–66.

Fiction

Neobychainye pokhozhdeniia Khulio Khurenito i ego uchenikov, Moscow and Berlin, Gelikone, 1922; translated as *The Extraordinary Adventures of Julio Jurenito and His Disciples*, by Usick Vanzler, New York, Covici-Friede, 1930; and as *Julio Jurenito*, by Anna Bostock and Yvonne Kapp, London, MacGibbon and Kee, 1958; Chester Springs, Pennsylvania, Du Four, 1963; reprinted Westport, Connecticut, Greenwood Press, 1976.

Trest D.E. [Trust D.E.]. Berlin, 1923; Moscow, 1994.

Liubov' Zhanny Nei. Moscow, 1924; translated as *The Love of Jeanne Ney*, by Helen Chrouschoff Matheson, London, Peter Davies, 1929; New York, Doubleday Doran, 1930; reprinted New York, Greenwood Press, 1968.

Burnaia zhizn' Lazika Roitshvanetsa. Paris, 1928; reprinted Munich, Fink, 1974; translated as *The Stormy Life of Laz Roitshvantz*, by Alec Brown, London, Elek, 1965.

Desiat' loshadinykh sil. Berlin, Petropolis, 1929; translated as *The Life of the Automobile*, by Joachim Neugroschel, New York, Urizen, 1976.
Den' vtoroi. Moscow, 1934; translated as *Out of Chaos*, by Aleksandr Bakshy, New York, Holt, 1934; reprinted New York, Octagon, 1976; also as *The Second Day*, by Liv Tudge, Moscow, Raduga, 1984.
"Padenie Parizha", *Roman-gazeta*, 3–5 (1942); Moscow, 1942; translated as *The Fall of Paris*, by Gerard Shelley, London, Hutchinson, 1942; New York, Knopf, 1943.
Buria. Moscow, 1948; translated as *The Storm*, by Eric Hartley and Tatiana Shebunina, London, Hutchinson, 1949; and by J. Fineberg, New York, Gaer, 1949.
Deviatyi val. Moscow, 1953; translated as *The Ninth Wave*, by Tatiana Shebunina and Joseph Castle, London, Lawrence and Wishart, 1955; Westport, Connecticut, Greenwood Press, 1974.
Ottepel' [Part I]. Moscow, 1954; complete edition, Moscow, 1956; reprinted Letchworth, Prideaux Press, 1978; translated as *The Thaw*, by Manya Harari, London, Harvill Press, and Chicago, Regnery, 1955.

Poetry
Stikhi. Paris, 1910.
Ia zhivu. Stikhi [I Live]. St Petersburg, 1911.
Opustoshaiushchaia liubov' [A Devastating Love]. Berlin, Ogon'ki, 1922.
Vernost' [Loyalty]. Moscow, 1941.
Stikhi o voine [War Poems]. Moscow, 1943.
Derevo [Wood]. Moscow, 1946.
Stikhi 1938–58. Moscow, 1959.

Play
Zolotoe serdtse. Veter [Golden Heart. Wind]. Moscow and Berlin, Gelikon, 1922.

Essays and Memoirs
Portrety russkikh poetov [Portraits of Russian Poets]. Berlin, Argonavty, 1922; reprinted Munich, Fink, 1972.
Perechityvaia Chekhova. Moscow, 1960; translated in part as *Chekhov, Stendhal, and Other Essays*, by Anna Bostock, Yvonne Kapp and Tatiana Shebunina, London, MacGibbon and Kee, 1962; New York, Knopf, 1963.
Liudi. Gody. Zhizn', 2 vols. Moscow, 1961–66; translated as *Men, Years, Life*, 6 vols, London, MacGibbon and Kee, 1962–66; as *Memoirs*, Cleveland, Ohio, World, 1964.
1. *Childhood and Youth, 1891–1917*, translated by Anna Bostock and Yvonne Kapp, 1962.
2. *First Years of Revolution, 1918–21*, translated by Anna Bostock and Yvonne Kapp, 1962.
3. *Truce, 1921–33*, translated by Tatiana Shebunina, 1963.
4. *Eve of War, 1933–41*, translated by Tatiana Shebunina, 1963.
5. *The War, 1941–45*,translated by Tatiana Shebunina, 1964.
6. *Post-War Years, 1945–54*, translated by Tatiana Shebunina and Yvonne Kapp, 1966.

Chernaia kniga. Jerusalem, Tarburt, 1980; translated as *The Black Book*, by John Glad and James S. Levine, New York, Holocaust Publications, 1981.
V smertnyi chas (Stat'i 1918–1919gg) [At the Hour of Death (Articles, 1918–1919)]. St Petersburg, 1996.

Critical Studies
Il'ia Erenburg, by T. Trifonova, Moscow, 1952; 2nd edition, 1954.
"Motives of Pessimism in Erenburg's Early Works", by H. Oulanoff, *Slavic and East European Journal*, 11 (1967), 266–77.
Ilya Ehrenburg. Writing, Politics and the Art of Survival, by Anatol Goldberg, London, Weidenfeld and Nicolson, 1984; as *Ilya Ehrenburg: Revolutionary, Novelist, Poet, War Correspondent, Propagandist: The Extraordinary Epic of a Russian Survivor*, New York, Viking, 1984.
Ehrenburg: An Attempt at a Literary Portrait, by Michael Klimenko, New York, Peter Lang, 1990.
Il'ia Erenburg: Put' pisatelia, by Aleksandr Rubashkin, Leningrad, 1990.
Ilya Ehrenburg: An Idealist in an Age of Realism, by Julian L. Laychuk, New York, Peter Lang, 1991.
Il'ia Erenburg. Khronika zhizni i tvorchestva, by Viacheslav Popov, St Petersburg, 1993.
Jews in Russian Literature after the October Revolution: Writers and Artists between Hope and Apostasy, by Ephraim Sicher, Cambridge, Cambridge University Press, 1995.
Tangled Loyalties: The Life and Times of Ilya Ehrenburg, by Joshua Rubenstein, New York, Basic Books, 1996.

Bibliography
Russkie sovetskie pisateli. Prozaiki, vol. 6, Part II, Moscow, 1969, 217–337.

The degree to which Il'ia Erenburg has descended into oblivion in recent decades paradoxically matches the degree to which he was in the centre of world-wide attention during his lifetime. Erenburg's books were translated into dozens of languages, and his fame reached far beyond the realm of literature: numerous passionate Erenburg articles written during World War II informed international audiences of Nazi atrocities and Soviet soldiers' heroism, his speeches attacking the arms race were cherished as powerful tools for the peace movement, and his anti-Stalinist memoirs in the 1960s made headlines in many western countries. The sole fact that it was Erenburg's novel *Ottepel'* (*The Thaw*) that provided the term for an entire epoch in Soviet history is telling of Erenburg's prominence during the Cold War.

From the 1930s to the 1960s, Erenburg was one of the most visible Soviet figures, presented as living proof of the Russian intelligentsia's loyalty toward the communist system. Without being a member of the Communist Party, he was honoured in every possible way and appointed to the most influential political functions. A literary bureaucrat with an overbooked schedule, hastening from conference to conference, from meeting to meeting, Erenburg spent the second half of his life as a respected messenger of the Soviet state and a "fighter for peace in the name of the Soviet people". The more his political commitments grew in number and importance, the more his fictional work became a marginal endeavour, written in airplanes, hotels and in pauses between official assignments. This could not but have an effect on the quality of his writing: Erenburg's later novels are voluminous, dull, fictionalized political statements of inexhaustible wordiness, obviously authored by a semi-official representative of his country, and populated with grey, impersonal mouth-piece characters.

However, Erenburg's outlook at the beginning of his long and complex career was quite different. The offspring of an upper-middle-class Jewish family, he joined the revolutionary struggle under the influence of Nikolai Bukharin, who became one of his closest personal friends. Then, Erenburg's emigration to France in 1908 at the age of 17 introduced him to a seductive bohemian milieu: in the famous café "Rotonde" the exotic Russian radical made friends with Modigliani, Picasso and other legendary figures, who in turn inspired him to try his hand at poetry. But Erenburg also showed a characteristic down-to-earthness when he decided to make a living by writing political articles and sending them to the very bourgeois Russian newspapers that he otherwise despised. His early poetry, more personal and less pragmatic than the political writings, was informed by apocalyptic presentiments. Like many intellectuals, he shared the feeling that European cultural tradition was on the verge of a breakdown and that something entirely new was about to emerge.

Erenburg's ambivalence regarding the anticipated universal apocalypse determined his initial scepticism toward the Bolshevik Revolution, whose bloody vigour he none the less welcomed as inevitable to cleanse the "rotten old world" (in this radical, yet somewhat resigned approval of Bolshevism Erenburg's position resembled that of his friend Osip Mandel'shtam). His first and arguably most authentic prose work, the grotesque novel *Neobychainye pokhozhdeniia Khulio Khurenito i ego uchenikov* (*Julio Jurenito*) reflects the author's meandering between the horror of societal chaos and the attempt to defend some individual sanctuary for the creative individual. This fundamental dichotomy between society as a profoundly destructive entity, and the single person as a refuge of creative potentials, was a basic theme throughout Erenburg's works.

Another feature of Erenburg's early prose that he retained throughout his evolution as a writer was the broad international scope of his plots – his narratives are often set in a number of countries; see, for example, *Trest D.E.* [Trust D.E.] – and the explicit dismissal of everything he secretly loved – from western art, culture and lifestyle to intellectual diversity and tolerance. Yet, what makes his prose works of the 1920s more enjoyable than the later socialist realist books, is their stylistic daring and experimental, albeit eclectic character. But faced with the awesome consolidation of communist society in the late 1920s and early 1930s, Erenburg increasingly viewed his enjoyment of western values as an embarrassing weakness that he had to purge. His search for a legitimate position in the Soviet system made him recant his avant-garde beginnings. Erenburg toured the construction sites of central industrial enterprises (Donbass, Kuznetsk), which provided him with the kind of superficial knowledge he needed to fictionalize the newly adopted communist dogma. His novel *Den' vtoroi* (*The Second Day*) may be viewed as an indirect novelistic confession in which Erenburg has the main character, an engineer named Safonov, experience his own painful separation from the "working masses", a dilemma that results in the suicide of this isolated intellectual. The fictional suicide was an act of symbolic relevance for Erenburg: he himself wilfully ceased his growth as an individual artist and began a phase of social functionalism that would ultimately alienate him from his artistic vocation.

Erenburg's involvement in the political turmoils of the Spanish Civil War, the observation of fascism's rise in Germany and Italy, and of French society's defeatism, were reflected in his ever-growing literary output, both fictional and journalistic, most importantly in the novel *Padenie Parizha* (*The Fall of Paris*), which described Nazi Germany's occupation of France. By then, the apocalyptic undertones of the early Erenburg had been transformed and made to fit neatly in the patterns of Soviet ideological officialdom. *The Fall of Paris*, as well as the subsequent parts of Erenburg's epic trilogy about global class struggle, *Buria* (*The Storm*) and *Deviatyi val* (*The Ninth Wave*), were meant to prove the communist view that bourgeois societies were unable, if not unwilling, to defend themselves against fascism's barbaric challenge. Particularly the last novel represents a shameful apogee in Erenburg's denunciation of west European and United States administrations as war-mongerers and quasi-allies of international fascist forces.

Erenburg was certainly aware of how profoundly he had betrayed ethical standards in *The Ninth Wave* and numerous other works, published against the backdrop of infamous anti-Semitic campaigns that took the lives of some of Erenburg's best friends. Likely, it was remorse about his all-too deep involvement in the Stalinist network that caused Erenburg's astoundingly fast turn toward liberalization and modest de-Stalinization announced in his novel *The Thaw* and the multi-volume memoirs *Liudi. Gody. Zhizn'* (*Men, Years, Life*), which paved the way for other authors' more coherently sincere, truly artistic works to come. Here, as in general, it was the controversial reception of Erenburg's works rather than their innate literary value that constituted their relative importance as cultural and political signals, shaping four decades of Soviet literary discourse.

PETER ROLLBERG

Julio Jurenito

Neobychainye pokhozhdeniia Khulio Khurenito i ego uchenikov

Novel, 1922

Hardly known for lasting loyalty, Il'ia Erenburg still admitted at the end of his life to have maintained a strong affection for his debut novel. And indeed, *Julio Jurenito*, written during June and July 1921 in Belgium and published soon afterwards in Germany and then Russia, has proved worthy of such faithfulness. Even today it irradiates a considerable originality lost in Erenburg's later works. In part, the author's almost sentimental attitude toward his early creation may have come from its very personal character. After all, the novel's principle settings – the café "Rotonde" on the Montparnasse, Russia after the Bolshevik coup, as well as many European metropoles – were Erenburg's environment for more than a decade; moreover, his own fearful expectations of what the new century harboured permeates the narrative.

Hidden behind the provocatively long title is a narrative outrageous in several respects: It is blasphemous toward Christianity, contemptuous of Russian spirituality, obsessed with negative national stereotypes, disapproving of the old world order and ambiguous about the newly emerging Soviet system.

The title character, Julio Jurenito, supposedly born in 1888 as the son of a Mexican sugar businessman, dies at the age of 33 in a provincial Russian town. Considering the main character's age and many other allusions, the author's intent to parody the Gospels becomes quite clear. However, sometimes he seems to enjoy deviations from the sacred model, for example, by limiting the number of Jurenito's disciples to seven. Yet, the way this motley crowd worships Julio Jurenito makes his role as a Christ – or rather an Antichrist – figure unequivocal. Resembling stereotypical images of the devil (whose very existence he explicitly denies), Julio Jurenito, or "the Teacher", as Erenburg typically refers to him in quasi-biblical fashion, obviously possesses an enormous charisma, but is entirely stripped of other worldliness. All his teachings are solely based on hatred for the present and lofty aspirations regarding the future; he worships biological vitality in its crudest form and abhors sensitivity and sensuality; he favours rationality and fights viciously against any belief system; he promotes the advance of technology and the destruction of beauty and all arts unless there is a Utilitarian purpose for their products. Julio Jurenito, in spite of the mystery surrounding him, is intended to represent the godless God of Modernity, the cynical prophet of total matter-of-factness. His ideas, conscientiously written down by his self-proclaimed disciple – the author, narrator and character Erenburg – represent a confusing blend of Hegel, Marx, Feuerbach, Nietzsche, Bakunin, Lenin, and avant-garde radicals. A master manipulator and diabolical visionary, Jurenito seems to be involved in behind-the-scene plotting somehow connected with the progression toward World War I and the Russian Revolution, although the actual nature of his involvement never becomes entirely clear and retains a certain occult flavour.

Each of Jurenito's seven disciples appeals to the reader's own preconceptions of national stereotypes. They include Mr Kuh, the American industrial entrepreneur and bigot; Monsieur Delé, the epicurean and libertarian Frenchman; Signor Bambucci, the easy-going Italian; Herr Schmidt, the cold-hearted and militaristic German; Aleksei Spiridonovich, the verbose Russian spiritual seeker; and Aisha, the noble and naive African. The first disciple, Erenburg himself, expresses varying degrees of sympathy for the other six; Aisha he likes the most, for his purity and honesty, and Schmidt the least, for his completely void soul and frightening rationality. Thrown into the global turmoil of war and revolution, the disciples follow their guru through German and Russian prison camps, engage in bogus-diplomatic activities for the fictitious state of Labardan, disrupt political meetings in Bolshevik Petrograd, do profitable business, buy prostitutes, and starve or gorge on delicacies.

It is the narrator who finds himself most strongly drawn to Julio Jurenito, because the Teacher helps him to discard the idealistic elements in his thinking. As a matter of fact, he assists him in replacing all of his ideals with one idol, namely the Teacher himself.

In *Julio Jurenito*, a number of discourses are closely intertwined. Erenburg relentlessly attacks the Church, the print-media, all governmental institutions, the pacifists, the socialists, and sometimes, albeit cautiously, the communists. The latter criticism must have instilled great fears in him during the 1930s and 1940s. Yet, the chapters devoted to Jurenito's and his disciples' sojourn to communist Russia are among the most successful, whereas the central plot constructs, the parody of the Gospels, nowadays appears rather bookish and dry, probably because it remains a series of pronouncements and rarely transgresses into the sphere of situations and images. Concerning the ethnic stereotypes that Erenburg employs so heavily, they may strike a contemporary reader as outmoded and even embarrassing. Likewise, the overabundance of contemporary, literary and cultural allusions, and the inclusion of authentic characters such as Picasso, Maiakovskii, Riviera, Tatlin or Chaplin can do little to prevent the novel's visible ageing. However, *Julio Jurenito* does contain a good dosage of sarcastic humour that has in part kept its freshness until today. And, above all, what renders this novel interesting still, is its focus on the European cultural crisis and the eschatological feelings it evokes.

Julio Jurenito is also an act of blatant self-stylization and self-mythologization. The author-narrator, appearing under his real name, reasons like a political philosopher, journalist, activist, preacher. But he also reveals sides of himself that challenge his image as an icon of liberal humanism, an image that mainly determines the novel's point of view. Yet this very image is contradicted by his dependency on bohemian Paris lifestyle and the riches of western bourgeois culture that he enjoys and decries at the same time. This Il'ia Erenburg, in his assumed role of an actively involved narrator, never bothers to work and indulges in begging, borrowing, promising, and serving "the Teacher". The latter's depiction inevitably leads to the conclusion that the author was unconsciously portraying his own super-ego, the internalized authority that ultimately furnishes Erenburg's transformation into a loyal servant of the totalitarian State.

The book's virtues, although unevenly distributed in the text, justify the pride that Erenburg took in *Julio Jurenito*. Still, it is hardly the political predictions contained in the novel that grant it longevity; rather, it is the expression of Erenburg's sincere pain over Europe's foolish self-destruction and his fear over the gradual disappearance of western civilization that informed his first novel with a lasting atmosphere of melancholic gloom.

PETER ROLLBERG

The Thaw

Ottepel'

Novel, 1954–56

Ever since eager audiences both inside and outside the Soviet Union read Erenburg's *The Thaw*, it has been commonplace to declare that this novel is "far from being a masterpiece", "not an enduring work of art", "poorly written", and that it derives its importance from extra-literary factors. All of these general and somewhat trivial references to the book's overall artistic quality ring true, yet the convenient derogatory and apologetic epithets attached to *The Thaw* may have prevented literary historians from deeper analysis in the context of Soviet literature of the 1950s and Erenburg's own *oeuvre*. On the one hand, the novel is much less exceptional than some critics would have us believe: its avoidance of real conflicts, its flatness of psychological characterization, its many declamatory passages clearly link it to the Soviet mainstream. On the other hand, *The Thaw* is also recognizable as a typical Erenburg text: its overabundance of abstract reasoning and lack of imagery, its reliance on newspaper rather than life experiences, and its tendency to wishful thinking make identification easy. The characters' endless discussions of foreign policy issues ("Eisenhower's latest speech", "the strikes in France", and the like), and the author's indulgence in stark, dichotomic contrasts between the groups of people populating his world, are remnants of Erenburg's avant-gardist heritage, albeit stripped of freshness and artistic daring.

The novel's main character, Dmitrii Koroteev, is the "positive hero" required by the standards of socialist realism; yet, his status is somewhat modified – Koroteev is not just a gifted engineer who works in a provincial town, he is also unhappily in love. It takes him some time to realize this, and the confusion it causes is deeply frustrating. Lena, the object of his desire, is married to Ivan Zhuravlev, the influential director of the local factory and a stereotypical bureaucrat. Dmitrii's instinct tells him that Zhuravlev is not the right person for the new epoch dawning on the horizon; cold-hearted and uncaring, the director always puts the needs of the enterprise before the needs of the workers. Also, Zhuravlev surrounds himself with yes-men, who support his budget manipulations, for example, using the money designated for workers' dwellings for a new foundry.

While Dmitrii and Lena develop their subtle relationship behind the back of an unsuspecting Zhuravlev, the author introduces a whole gallery of characters whose lives are in one way or other intertwined with those of the central triangle. There is Volodia Pukhov, a painter and cynical go-getter whose career flourishes as a result of his ideological corruption. His counterpart Saburov stubbornly insists on painting the way his inner calling tells him and pays the price – a shabby life on the outskirts of town. Furthermore, we encounter Andrei Pukhov, a retired schoolmaster and old-guard communist, who is horrified by his son Volodia's moral rottenness, but whose vital energies still suffice to fight his approaching death and whose belief in the bright future of communism is unfailing. Finally, there is Vera Sherer, a Jewish doctor, who consoles Lena in her marital problems and is herself in love with Sokolovskii, the factory's chief designer.

It is telling that all these characters have feelings and shyly communicate them, but do not initiate any serious action. Moscow is the magic place from which the impetus for change comes: Zhuravlev is called to the capital never to return again, obviously ousted because of his inadequate style of leadership. Consequently, Volodia Pukhov's portrait of Zhuravlev becomes worthless overnight, whereas Saburov's still-lifes gain appreciation. Slowly, the characters take charge of their personal lives, acknowledge their own emotions and admit them to each other, often in public, at meetings or "readers' conferences".

Indeed, little happens externally in *The Thaw*. The various chapters consist mainly of lengthy inner monologues with straightforward authorial explanations of what is right and wrong. However, Erenburg, whose narrative may seem monotonous to us but likely made for breathtaking reading for his contemporaries, spiced up the text with a number of taboo violations. Thus, he mentions that Koroteev's stepfather was arrested in 1936; Vera Sherer recalls the anti-Semitic hysteria following the doctors' trial in 1952; Sokolovskii's wife went to the west, their daughter lives in Belgium. But, given the moderate risk that it took to touch on minor unspeakable truths of Soviet society, *The Thaw* is far from a lucid societal analysis – a claim that was often made as an excuse for its artistic dullness. Erenburg was writing about moods, slight atmospheric transformations, and little else.

The first part of the novel came out in the May 1954 issue of *Znamia*, a second, revised and expanded version was published in April 1956. By that time, the book's title had already provided the west with a label for the new period of Soviet history, or rather the new strategy of mild de-Stalinization (and implied self-whitewashing) of Khrushchev's gang. Doubtless, the sensation that it caused was strategically calculated. Intended as a call to the Soviet intelligentsia for renewed loyalty to the system, *The Thaw*, also offered an easy explanatory pattern for the Stalinist past, the dilemmas of the present, and the promises for the future. Moreover, it supplied Erenburg, who had been among the most enthusiastic public worshippers of the Stalinist regime, with a place among the reformers. The harsh criticism of Erenburg's opus expressed mostly by literary hacks, could only authenticate his claims to belong to the forefront of liberalization.

The real explosiveness of the novel lies in its title, probably going beyond what Erenburg ever intended to convey. At first sight, "thaw" signified quite simply the unfreezing of Soviet internal politics. But why did the Soviet establishment not adopt this term? After all, in the USSR the word *ottepel'* never made it into official documents or history books, remaining an insider's code, reserved for reformist intellectuals in their kitchen discussions. It is possible that the wide use of the term by western politicians and journalists rendered it suspicious to the watchdogs of dogma. Also, they must have sensed the metaphor's dangerous ambiguity: the implication alone that there ever was a Stalinist "winter" was unacceptable. Moreover, "thaw" does not really connote progress but a circular development, which eventually leads back to fall and winter. Finally, the change of seasons does not depend on human will or reason; it occurs as part of a different order. But, despite the title's dangerous ambiguity, it is easy to share Russell Kirk's view that "the most bigoted functionary of the Old Regime, in either France or Russia, never would have thought of suppressing or even denouncing so timorous and ineffectual a work of fiction".

PETER ROLLBERG

Venedikt Vasil'evich Erofeev 1938–1990

Novelist, dramatist, and essayist

Biography

Born in Zapoliar'e, Murmansk region, 24 October 1938. Father repressed in 1939 and spent 16 years in Gulag. Spent three school years in a children's home. Left secondary school with gold medal, 1955; expelled from Faculty of Classical Languages at Moscow University for not attending military training courses, 1958. Made two more attempts to obtain higher education: expelled from Department of Language and Literature at Orekhovo-Zuevo Pedagogical Institute for "moral degeneracy", 1959; expelled on the same grounds from a similar department at Vladimir Pedagogical Institute, 1961. Apprentice bricklayer on Moscow suburban sites, 1958–59; worked on (unfinished) Moscow–Peking highway, 1960–61; worked at a biological research station in the Ukraine, 1962–64; telephone cable layer in Vladimir and in districts of Tambov, Lipetsk, Mogilev, Gomel, and Tula, also in Lithuania. Married twice; one son. Repaired telephone cable lines in the Moscow region, 1969–74. Participated in parasitological expedition, 1974–76, and a geophysical expedition to northern Karelia, 1976. Later declared unfit for work because of alcoholism. Spent his last years in Moscow and at Abramtsevo. Died of cancer of the throat, 11 May 1990.

Publications

Collected Edition

Ostav'te moiu dushu v pokoe: Pochti vse [Leave My Soul in Peace: Almost the End], edited by Aleksei Konstanian. Moscow, 1995; 1997.

Fiction

"Moskva-Petushki, Poema", *AMI* (Israel), 3 (1973); as separate edition, Paris, YMCA-Press, 1977; 2nd edition, 1981; [in Russia], *Trezvost' i kul'tura*, 1–3 (1988); and in *Vest': Proza. Poeziia. Dramaturgiia* (almanac). Moscow, 1989, 418–506; translated as *Moscow to the End of the Line*, by W. Tjalsma, New York, Taplinger, 1980; reprinted Evanston, Illinois, Northwestern University Press, 1992; translated as *Moscow Circles*, by J.R. Dorrell, London, Writers and Readers Publishing Co-operative, 1981; also translated as *Moscow Stations*, by Stephen Mulrine, London, Faber, 1996.

Plays

"Val'purgieva noch' ili 'Shagi komandora'" [Walpurgis Night; or, The Commander's Footsteps], *Kontinent*, 45 (1985), 96–185.

"Dissidenty ili Fanni Kaplan (Tragediia v 5-i aktakh)" [Dissidents; or, Fanny Kaplan], *Kontinent*, 67 (1991), 285–317.

Essays, Memoirs, and Criticism

"Vasilii Rozanov glazami ekstsentrika", in *Neue Russische Literatur*, Salzburg, 1978; separate edition as *Glazami ekstsentrika*, New York, Serebrianyi vek, 1982; translated as "Through the Eyes of an Eccentric", by Stephen Mulrine, in *The Penguin Book of New Russian Writing*, edited by Viktor Erofeev and Andrew Reynolds, Harmondsworth and New York, Penguin, 1995, 126–45.

"Moia malen'kaia Leniniana" [My Little Leniniana], *Kontinent*, 55 (1988), 187–202.

"Iz zapisnykh knizhek", *Strelets*, 67/3 (1991), 7–13.

"Poslednii dnevnik. Oktiabr' 1989g.–mart 1990g." [Last Diary. October 1989–March 1990), edited by I. Avdiev, *Novoe literaturnoe obozrenie*, 18 (1996), 169–98.

Critical Studies

"Ispoved' rossiianina tret'ei chetverti XX veka", by M. Muravnik, *Tret'ia volna*, 6 (1979), 27–34.

"Literaturnye mechtaniia", by P. Vail' and A. Genis, *Chast' rechi*, 1 (1980), 204–32.

"Vstan' i idi", by B. Gasparov and I. Paperno, *Slavica Hierosolymitana*, 5–6 (1981), 387–400.

"*Moskva-Petushki* Venedikta Erofeeva i traditsii klassicheskoi poezii", by M. Al'tshuller, *Novyi zhurnal*, 146 (1982), 75–85.

"Strasti po Erofeevu", by P. Vail' and A. Genis, in their *Sovremennaia russkaia proza*, Ann Arbor, Hermitage, 1982, 41–50.

"Shutovskoi khorovod", by M. Kaganskaia, *Sintaksis*, 13 (1984), 45–89.

"Venedikt Erofeev, *Val'purgeva noch'*", by P. Vail' and A. Genis, *Grani*, 139 (1986), 138–50.

Venedikt Erofeev, "Moskva-Petushki" ili "The Rest is Silence", by S. Geisser-Schnittmann, Bern and New York, Peter Lang, 1989.

"Venedikt Erofeev glazami gogoleveda", by E.A. Smirnova, *Russkaia literatura*, 3 (1990), 58–66.

"Nekrolog, sotkannyi iz pylkikh i blestiashchikh natiazhek", by Chernousyi (I. Avdiev), *Kontinent*, 67 (1991), 285–317.

"Neskol'ko nekrologov o Venedikte Erofeeve", *Teatr*, 9 (1991), 80–86.

"Apofeoz chastits, ili dialogi s khasom. Zametki o klassike, Venedikte Erofeeve, poeme 'Moskva-Petushki', i russkom postmodernizme", by M. Lipovetskaia, *Znamia*, 8 (1992), 214–24.

"Klassicheskie traditsii v 'drugoi' literature: Venedikt Erofeev i Fedor Dostoevskii", by Iu. Levin, *Literaturnoe obozrenie*, 2 (1992), 45–50.

"Palata No. 3, ili v chuzhom piru", by M. Rudenko, *Strelets*, 68 (1992), 159–76.

"Vremeni net ...", by I. Shmel'kova, *Literaturnoe obozrenie*, 2 (1992), 39–45.

Their Fathers' Voice: Vassily Aksyonov, Venedikt Erofeev, Eduard Limonov and Sasha Sokolov, by Cynthia Simmons, Bern and New York, Peter Lang, 1993, 57–90.

Russia's Alternative Prose, by Robert Porter, Oxford, Berg, 1994, 72–87.

Contemporary Russian Satire: A Genre Study, by Karen L. Ryan-Hayes, Cambridge, Cambridge University Press, 1995.

"The End in V. Erofeev's *Moskva-Petushki*", by Vladimir Tumanov, *Russian Literature*, 39/1 (1996).

Komentarii k poeme "Moskva-Petushki", by Iu. Levin, Graz, Grazer Gesellschaft, 1996.
Venedikt Erofeev's "Moscow-Petushki": Critical Perspectives, edited by Karen L. Ryan-Hayes, New York, Peter Lang, 1997.

Bibliographies
"Samovozrastaiushchii logos" (Venedikt Erofeev): Bibliograficheskii ocherk, by Sergei Bavin, Moscow, 1995.
"Bibliograficheskii spisok proizvedenii pisatelia i rabot o nem", by I. Avdiev, *Novoe literaturnoe obozrenie*, 18 (1996), 199–209.

Venedikt Erofeev's creative career began very early. Unfortunately the great majority of his first works have been lost, and no large items were found in his archive after his death. One work, written in the form of a diary in 1956–58, "Zapiski veselogo nevrastenika" [Notes of a Merry Neurasthenic], remained unpublished. In 1964 he wrote a book, "Dobrye vesti" [Good Tidings], of which the manuscript is lost. In the years 1968–69 he produced many verses for his son, calling them "anthologies of my own poems", imitating Greek and Alexandrine modes of writing, canzonas, sonnets, *vers libre*, ballads, and so on. Later, Erofeev wrote for his son a history of the world "with all the usual ideas overturned". But, as he told the author of this article, "the greater part of what was for me a joyous piece of work was used by my mother-in-law to light the stove". The novel *Moskva-Petushki* (*Moscow Circles*) was written between 18 January and 7 March 1970. "Dmitrii Shostakovich" was written from 3 February to the beginning of April 1972; the manuscript of the latter is lost, as is that of his "Zapiski psikhopata" [Notes of a Psychopath].

Moscow Circles is Erofeev's most important work, often reprinted, and translated into many languages, which brought the author worldwide fame. The "poem" (as the author calls it) is the description of a day in the life of alcoholic Venichka Erofeev, setting out from Moscow to the small provincial town of Petushki to meet his sweetheart. Drinking more and more in the course of the journey, the hero finally falls into an alcoholic delirium, in which he has visions of terrible murders and he experiences his own metaphysical murder. The book is full of deep and biting social and political satire. The hero conducts an anecdotal monologue in the course of which countless clichés of speech and thought are mocked. At the same time the book is the story of a soul irreversibly perishing in the heartless atmosphere of a totalitarian state. The contrast of the humorous element with the hero's tragic end creates one of the book's most striking effects. It circulated widely in *samizdat*, and was published in Israel and later France, but until the beginning of perestroika remained banned in the Soviet Union. Publication of the book in Russia confirmed Venedikt Erofeev as one of the greatest and most popular Russian writers of the post-war period. In recent years *Moscow Circles* has increasingly been performed on the stages of theatres in Russia and elsewhere: Moscow, St Petersburg, Warsaw, Berlin, Lausanne, Paris, and London (as well as the airways of the BBC's Radio Three).

Erofeev's second published book was the essay on Vasilii Rozanov, *Glazami ekstsentrika* ("Through the Eyes of an Eccentric"), devoted to Erofeev's favourite philosopher. The extraordinary and contradictory nature of Rozanov's personality, the depth, vividness and paradoxicality of his thinking, as well as his creative energy were for Erofeev the source of great admiration: "This vile, poisonous fanatic, this toxic old man – no, he did not provide me with a complete drug against moral feebleness, but he saved for me *honour and air to breathe*".

Moia malen'kaia Leniniana [My Little Leniniana] is a collection of quotations, mainly from the works and letters of Lenin, but also from the published letters of those close to him like Krupskaia and Inessa Armand. This collection of excerpts "from first sources" creates an unusual image of the leaders and founders of the "new type of state", destroying the familiar clichéd images of the humanity, self-sacrifice, fairness and so on of the most important figures in the Soviet myth.

The last work published in Erofeev's lifetime is the play *Val'purgieva noch' ili "Shagi komandora"* [Walpurgis Night; or, The Commander's Footsteps]. The action takes place in a lunatic asylum to which an alcoholic member of the intelligentsia, Lev Gurevich, has been committed. The inhumanity of relations between patients and staff, the hopelessness, the lack of normal treatment, the beatings, and anti-Semitism are all an intensified projection of the abnormal relations of the entire Soviet state. Having decided to use an anaesthetizing dose of alcohol, Gurevich steals a bucket of spirit that turns out to be methyl alcohol. As a result, all his crazy drinking partners die one by one, and he himself goes blind. The staff, infuriated by the thought of bearing the responsibility for what has happened, beat Gurevich viciously. This play is one of a series of five dramatic works by Erofeev, but so far only two have been published; the other one, *Dissidenty ili Fanni Kaplan* [Dissidents; or, Fanny Kaplan], came out in 1991.

Erofeev died as the author of one work of genius, *Moscow Circles*. His coruscating talent and exceptional personality have given an immense creative impetus to Russian literary satire and to the tragic spirit of Russian literature.

SVETLANA SHNITMAN-MCMILLIN

Moscow Circles

Moskva-Petushki

Novel, 1973

Venedikt Erofeev's prose poem *Moscow Circles* (also translated as *Moscow to the End of the Line* and *Moscow Stations*) was written in 1970. It spread like wildfire in *samizdat*, bringing its author great fame among a wide readership, but the book was banned in the USSR until well into perestroika. First published in Israel in 1973, it was translated into most of the European and some oriental languages. It was also given stage performances in many European countries. After publication in Russia in 1988 *Moscow Circles* was quickly recognized there as a masterpiece of Russian literature; soon dramatized, it was put on in several Moscow and provincial theatres. Thanks to this work, Erofeev enjoyed great celebrity, albeit in the last years of his life.

The famous sculptor Ernst Neizvestnyi has written that all life in the USSR revolved around two things: power and vodka. Power was held in the hands of a small, closed circle of people. Vodka, on the other hand, was and remains the property of all the population. Venedikt Erofeev, an alcoholic himself, was the first Russian writer to reproduce in his book what the critic Mikhail Bakhtin had called "the mystical and metaphysical atmosphere of Russian alcoholism". The hero of the book confesses that for him alcohol is the means to achieve mystic inspiration, with the help of which he passes "from contemplation to abstraction", from the external perception of reality to the solution of metaphysical and existential problems.

The hero of *Moscow Circles* is a Muscovite bearing the name of the author, Venedikt Erofeev, usually called Venichka in the book. Every Friday he sets off from Kursk station in Moscow to see his sweetheart who lives in the small provincial town of Petushki. Sometimes he goes beyond Petushki to where his son lives. The book describes the hero's 13th such journey. The entire duration of the "poem" amounts to one day. The book begins with Venichka waking up on the stairway of the entrance to some unknown building where he crashed out the day before in a state of complete intoxication and oblivion. The hero emerges into the street with the idea of possibly visiting the Kremlin, and with the firm conviction that, if he does not see this citadel of the state, he will reach Kursk station. Having got there, his supply of spirits filled, he gets into the train and begins his day of drunkenness and the monologue that forms the major part of the book. *Moscow Circles* is full of powerful social and political satire, but the tragic tinge to the laughter anticipates the hero's ruin. As the journey proceeds and alcoholic delirium draws nearer, Venichka begins to experience nightmares and hallucinations. He loses all sense of time and space. Having arrived, as he thinks, at Petushki, he discovers that he is in Moscow by the Kremlin wall that "he had never seen before". There suddenly appear from the shadows four murderous criminals who start to follow him – a symbiosis of the leaders of the world proletariat and of the four horsemen of the apocalypse. The last vision of Venichka's fading consciousness is of his own crucifixion and murder, committed on the hall stairway where he began his morning journey. Thus, the composition of the book is circular.

A striking feature of this text is the huge quantity of direct and indirect quotations and allusions it contains. It is possible to speak of four thematic areas of quotation and their basic functions. The first group is of biblical quotations. On the very first page we meet a paraphrase of Christ's words in the Garden of Gethsemane: "the spirit indeed is willing, but the flesh is weak" (Matthew 26:41). In *Moscow Circles* the hero, intoxicated by coriander vodka, announces that with him it "turned out the other way round": "the spirit had very greatly strengthened, but [my] limbs had grown weak". The end of the book is a scene of the crucifixion. The fate of the Moscow alcoholic is juxtaposed with the fate of Jesus Christ, lending the narrative the character of an oxymoron. In Erofeev's narration the Gospel plays an oxymoronic role.

The second group is of literary and philosophical quotations and quotations connected with the theatre and music. Three writers, Dostoevskii, Gogol', and Bulgakov, figure particularly frequently. In the text as a whole there are more than 40 Russian, European, Oriental and classical writers and poets. The broadening and deepening of the thematic range of the text, its range of contrasts, its pathos, irony, and satire, are the main functions of the literary "glass bead game" in the text of *Moscow Circles*. The theatrical quotations envelop the whole work in a dramatic atmosphere: the world is a theatre, man is an actor on its stage. Musical quotations provide the background that this needs. The collection of dramatic and operatic works included in the text is very broad: Pushkin's *Mozart and Salieri* and *Boris Godunov*, Shakespeare's *Hamlet* and *Othello*, Wagner's *Lohengrin*, *Faust* (both in Goethe's text and the music of Gounod), as well as many others. But the "theatre of the world" in *Moscow Circles* becomes the "theatre of the antiworld". And in its tragic farce the hero of the book plays the main part.

The third group comprises historical and political quotations that have three main functions in the text. They deepen the temporal perspective of the narration, linking various historical epochs. At the same time they make the narration real by bringing the story into the framework of a concrete historical situation: for instance, the "glorious century" and the "socialist obligations" associated with it, by which is meant the centenary of Lenin's birth celebrated in 1970. The third main role of this group of quotations is decorative, the filling of the grotesque space of the narration; an example in the text is the story of the murder of Hypatia.

The fourth group comprises folklore, pithy sayings, catchphrases, colloquial clichés, and the clichés of official Sovietese. These quotations have a strong carnival function, giving to the "poem" a merry topical tone and a sharply satirical element. The free handling of routine words and thought patterns lends the narrative a sense of frivolity in contrast to the official seriousness of Soviet life.

This game with quotations lends a multi-layered quality to the symbolism and chronotope of the narration, sweeping away the boundaries of three-dimensional space and time. In the voice of the narrator can be heard a multi-voiced, sick, tragic and mocking choir: Erofeev's prose poem is a polyphonic monologue.

The genre of *Moscow Circles* is complex. By using quotations the author brings into the narration a variety of genre elements: 1) the poem in prose, recalling Gogol'; 2) the epic journey with travel notes, reminiscent of Radishchev; 3) lyric poetry: rhythmic prose, ballad form, the inclusion in the text of "poems in prose"; 4) drama: elements of stage tragedy and comedy; 5) satire: eccentric farce, a symposium, menippea. The style of Erofeev's poem is equally varied, vivid and dependent on the different kinds of quotations.

The capricious, non-canonic combination of heterogeneous stylistic and generic elements, the surrealism, scorn for familiar concepts of time and space, and the ubiquitous irony allow the genre of Erofeev's book to be broadly defined as tragic grotesque. However it is defined, it stands as one of the greatest works of 20th-century Russian prose.

SVETLANA SHNITMAN-MCMILLIN

Viktor Vladimirovich Erofeev 1947–

Novelist and critic

Biography

Born in Moscow, 1947. His father, a high-ranking Soviet diplomat, was special assistant to Molotov and worked as an interpreter for Stalin. Part of childhood spent in Paris. Graduated from the Philological Faculty of Moscow State University in 1970; completed postgraduate work at the Institute of World Literature, Moscow, 1973. Candidate's degree for thesis on Dostoevskii and French Existentialism, 1975. Began organizing, with co-operation of Vasilii Aksenov and other writers, literary almanac, *Metropol'*, which aimed to "provide a roof" for "homeless", outcast literature, 1978; *samizdat* publication in 1979; this outraged the authorities, who subjected contributors to varying degrees of harassment. Dismissed from his post and expelled from the Writers' Union. Prose not published until 1988, although it circulated widely through the literary underground. Married with one son.

Publications

Collected Editions

Sobranie sochinenii, 3 vols. Moscow, 1994–96.

1. *Russkaia krasavitsa: Roman. Rasskazy*. 1994.
2. *V labirinte prokliatykh voprosov: Esse*. 1996.
3. *Strashnyi sud: Roman. Rasskazy. Malen'kie esse*. 1996.

Fiction

"Iadrena Fenia", "Prispushchennyi orgazm stolet'ia", "Trekhglavoe detishche", in *Metropol': Literaturnyi al'manakh*, edited by Vasilii Aksenov, Viktor Erofeev, *et al.*, (*samizdat* publication), Moscow, 1979; in book form, Ann Arbor, Ardis, 1979, 89–102; translated as "Two Stories and a Novella" ("A Fin de Siècle Orgasm", "Humping Hannah", and "A Creation in Three Chapters"), by Martin Horwitz, in *Metropol: Literary Almanac*, edited by Vasily Aksyonov *et al.*, New York, Norton, 1982, 457–526.

"Popugaichik", *Ogonek*, 49 (December 1988), 22–24; full version in *Telo Anny, ili konets russkogo avangarda*, Moscow, 1989, 48–60; translated as "The Parakeet", by Leonard J. Stanton, in *Glasnost: An Anthology of Russian Literature Under Gorbachev*, edited by Helena Goscilo and Byron Lindsay, Ann Arbor, Ardis, 1990, 367–77.

Telo Anny, ili konets russkogo avangarda. Moscow, 1989.

"Telo Anny, ili konets russkogo avangarda", in *Telo Anny, ili konets russkogo avangarda*, 1989, 43–47; translated as "Anna's Body, or The End of the Russian Avant-garde", by Leonard J. Stanton, in *Glasnost: An Anthology of Russian Literature Under Gorbachev*, edited by Helena Goscilo and Byron Lindsay, Ann Arbor, Ardis, 1990, 379–82.

"Govnososka", in *Telo Anny, ili Konets russkogo avangarda*, 1989, 18–25; also in *Karmannyi apokalipsis, ili izbrannoe*, Moscow, Paris and New York, Tret'ia volna, 1993, 23–28, translated as "Sludge-Sucker", by Cathy Porter, in *Dissonant Voices: The New Russian Fiction*, edited by Oleg Chukhontsev, London, Harvill Press, 1991, 268–74.

Russkaia krasavitsa. Moscow, 1990; reprinted 1992; translated as *Russian Beauty*, by Andrew Reynolds, London, Hamish Hamilton, 1992; New York, Viking, 1993; Harmondsworth, Penguin, 1994.

Zhizn' s idiotom. Rasskazy. Povest'. Moscow, 1991.

"De profundis", in *Karmannyi apokalipsis, ili izbrannoe*, 1993, 43–49; translated as "De profundis", by Andrew Bromfield, in *Glas: New Russian Writing, Soviet Grotesque*, edited by Natasha Perova *et al.*, Moscow, 1991, 97–105.

"Skuly i nos, i ovrag", in *Karmannyi apokalipsis, ili izbrannoe*, 1993, 69–79; translated as "Cheekbones, a Nose and a Gully", by Andrew Bromfield, in *Glas: New Russian Writing, Soviet Grotesque*, edited by Natasha Perova *et al.*, Moscow, 1991, 105–19.

"Zhen'kin tezaurus", in *Karmannyi apokalipsis, ili izbrannoe*, 1993, 29–42; translated as "Zhenka's *A to Z*", by Andrew Reynolds, in *The Penguin Book of New Russian Writing: Russia's "Fleurs du mal"*, edited by Reynolds and Viktor Erofeev, Harmondsworth and New York, Penguin, 1995, 349–68.

Libretto

Life with an Idiot. Opera in two acts by Alfred Schnittke, CD recording with Russian text and English, French and German translations, New York, Sony Classical, 1992; English version, translated by Andrew Reynolds and Anthony Legge, published as part of the programme of *Life with an Idiot*, London, English National Opera, 1995.

Literary Criticism

"Ostaetsia odno: Proizvol" [One Thing is Left: Arbitrary Rule] (on Lev Shestov), *Voprosy literatury*, 10 (1975), 153–88.

"Russkii metaroman V. Nabokova, ili v poiskakh poteriannogo raia" [The Russian Meta-Novel of V. Nabokov, or In Search of Paradise Lost], *Voprosy literatury*, 10 (1988), 125–60.

V labirinte prokliatykh voprosov [In the Labyrinth of Accursed Questions]. Moscow, 1990.

"Pominki po sovetskoi literature", *Literaturnaia gazeta*, 27 (1990), 8; reprinted in Russian language edition of *Glas*, 1 (1991), 221–32; translated as "Soviet Literature: In Memoriam", by Andrew Meier, *Glas*, 1 (1991), 226–34.

"Desiat' let spustia" [Ten Years Later], *Ogonek*, 37 (1990), 16–18.

Naiti v cheloveke cheloveka (*Dostoevskii i ekzistentsializm*) [To Find the Person Within the Person (Dostoevskii and Existentialism)]. Benson, Vermont, Chalidze, 1991.

"Mesto kritiki" [The Critic's Place], *Moskovskie novosti*, 45–46, (15 November 1991), 11.

"*The Little Demon*: Harsh Lessons", introduction to *The Little Demon*, by Fyodor Sologub, translated by Ronald Wilks, Harmondsworth, Penguin, 1994, vii–xxx.

"Russkie tsvety zla" (full version unpublished in Russia), translated as "Russia's *Fleurs du Mal*", by Andrew Reynolds, Introduction to *The Penguin Book of New Russian Writing: Russia's "Fleurs du mal"*, edited by Reynolds and Viktor Erofeev, Harmondsworth and New York, Penguin, 1995, ix–xxx.

Essays
Muzhchiny [Men]. Moscow, 1997.

Editor
Sobranie sochinenii, 4 vols, by V.V. Nabokov, Moscow, 1990; supplementary volume, Moscow, 1992.
Nesovmestimye kontrasty zhitiia: literaturno-esteticheskie raboty raznykh let, by V.V. Rozanov, Moscow, 1990.
The Penguin Book of New Russian Writing: Russia's "Fleurs du mal", with Andrew Reynolds, Harmondsworth and New York, Penguin, 1995.

Critical Studies
"Mir kak tekst", by Mark Lipovetskii, *Literaturnoe obozrenie*, 6 (1990), 63–65.
"Zhizn' prekrasna?", by Natal'ia Ivanova, *Iunost'*, 1 (1991), 60–63.
"Chernovoe pis'mo", by Oleg Dark, *Strelets*, 1/68 (1992), 177–87.
"Lolita Grows Up", by Elisabeth Rich, *The Nation*, 21 June 1993, 875–78.
The Last Years of Soviet Russian Literature: Prose Fiction, 1975–1991, by Deming Brown, Cambridge and New York, Cambridge University Press, 1993.
Russia's Alternative Prose, by Robert Porter, Oxford, Berg, 1994, 1–30, 138–62.
After the Future: The Paradoxes of Postmodernism in Contemporary Russian Culture, by Mikhail N. Epstein, translated by Anesa Miller-Pogacar, Amherst, University of Massachusetts Press, 1995.
Russian Literature 1988–1994: The End of an Era, by N.N. Shneidman, Toronto, University of Toronto Press, 1995.
"'Russkaia krasavitsa' pered 'Strashnym sudom'", by Igor' Iarkevich, *Moskovskie novosti*, 26/778, (16–23 April 1995), 19.
"One Bright Page of Evil", by Mark Frankland, *The Observer* (Review), (30 July 1995), 12.
"Izzhivanie smerti. Spetsifika russkogo postmodernizma", by Mark Lipovetskii, *Znamia*, 8 (1995), 194–205.
"Re-Surfacing: The Shades of Violence in Viktor Yerofeyev's Short Stories", by Serafima Roll, *Australian Slavonic and East European Studies*, 9/2 (1995), 27–46.

Viktor Erofeev, "one of the most interesting and controversial figures of the contemporary Russian literary scene" (N.N. Shneidman), has enjoyed considerable commercial and critical success in the west. Although Erofeev's work is valued by many leading writers and the wider reading public in Russia, the reaction of Russian literary critics and western Slavists has been mixed. Erofeev is an acknowledged legislator of Russia's "alternative prose", but viewing him merely as an exemplary Russian postmodernist (whether this be a good or a bad thing), paying close attention to surface features in his work, may lead to undervaluation. Erofeev's exaggerated revolt against his literary precursors is a necessary overcoming, transformation, and synthesis of his cultural heritage; as Elizabeth Rich has noted, his writing "represents a natural link ... in the unnatural evolution of Russian literature".

Erofeev first gained attention as a literary critic, his articles indicating the future directions of his own fiction. His polemical article "Pominki po sovetskoi literature" ("Soviet Literature: In Memoriam") provoked widespread replies, virtually all violently opposed to his argument that official Soviet literature and dissident literature alike no longer served any useful purpose. This was further developed in "Russkie tsvety zla" ("Russia's *Fleurs du mal*"), and, more importantly, in the compilation of texts representative of the "literature of evil" (*The Penguin Book of New Russian Writing*, 1995).

Erofeev's fiction is characterized by what some call an obsessive interest in sex, violence, horror, absurdity, evil, and death. Once the reader recovers from the initial "ethical and aesthetic provocations" (Lipovetskii), he is meant to realize that the excesses lay bare the conventional nature of all literary devices. Laughter at the horrors depicted is encouraged: after all, it is only a literary game, a highly intertextual, "polystylistic" mockery of cherished themes, works and genres, centred on parodies of Russian classics and socialist realist works alike (the latter are the Soviet equivalent of "pulp" fiction). Unlike in western postmodernism, however, the deconstruction of cherished ideas is not allowed to conceal the serious questions, even if some find the means (the violently pornographic depiction of sexual violence against women and men) not always justified by the moral and aesthetic ends. One such deconstruction of the "Russian ideology" is "Zhizn' s idiotom" [Life with an Idiot]. Readings of this story and stagings of the opera have tended to be one-dimensional, seeing it as an allegory of Soviet society under communism. The work's wider message, however, is that every individual and nation has his or her idiot(s), describable in political, existential, or psychological terms. It parodies the Russian idealization of the holy fool, both as embodied in particular texts (especially Dostoevskii's *The Idiot*) and in the culture as a whole. This leads into an examination of the wider belief of the (alleged and actual) benefits of Russian moral maximalism: the phenomenon D.H. Lawrence termed "sinning one's way to Jesus". The story also investigates the similar idealization of culture implicated in the failure of 20th-century civilization to resist barbarism and tyranny. Another story, "Popugaichik" ("The Parakeet"), blends vocabulary and syntax from four distinct stages of the Russian language to emphasize that scenes of senseless torture, delight in violence, fear of other cultures, and pressure to conform, are a constant of Russian history.

Occasionally, Erofeev the critic manipulates story and reader rather too visibly, but in his best works, especially the novels, the "two Erofeevs" work hand in hand. *Russkaia krasavitsa* (*Russian Beauty*), Erofeev's best-known work, attracted attention by its "erotic" content (for many Russian critics it is "pornographic"), but it is Irina's existential drama (mirroring that of Russia) that has interested western reviewers, leading some to hail it a masterpiece. The sexually-liberated heroine and narrator functions as a complex symbol and is a literary manifesto in herself; but Irina is also successful as a character. One of the book's major themes is a polemic against Messianic versions of Russian history: Russia can only be Russia if she is not saved. The work satirizes the various ways in which one could save Russia (communist, dissident, nationalist, and western blueprints). Irina comes to see herself as a new Joan of Arc (and a parody of the Virgin Mary), believing that, if she is raped by some evil spirit on an ancient Russian battlefield, she will save Russia (and perhaps mankind). On one level, this is all silly, and deliberate; but because Irina's behaviour is seen as madness, and because the metafictional element of literary challenge and parody allows a suspension of disbelief in the work's more hyperbolic elements, one realizes that Erofeev's Irina, as a symbol of Russia, may offer some salvation after all. Sexual beauty, the implication seems, may save the world; more significantly, for all the apparent mockery of Russian Messianism, the descriptions of Russian life, nature, and mentality in the book reveal Erofeev to be "an acute and subtle writer who knows his country painfully and tenderly" (Sally Laird).

A superficial reading of Erofeev's second novel, *Strashnyi sud* [The Last Judgement] might argue that it simply reverses *Russian Beauty*: its (anti-?) hero Sisin is merely a male Irina, the story his sexual Odyssey, and the metaphysical drama his attempt not to save humanity but to destroy it for taking the wrong turn (Sisin believes himself the son of Christ). However, this work is far wider in scope and takes greater risks; the satire (particularly of western civilization and its contents) hits harder; the sex is both erotic and pornographic; the ideas more interesting. As in *Russian Beauty*, the plot is complex and non-linear, but its stylistic innovations surpass the earlier work. The narrative mixes multiple streams of consciousness within a section, paragraph, or even sentence, setting them within an associative "outer" narration (with ever-changing narrative voices) to create unexpected and productive juxtapositions and ambiguities. The result is a new type of multi-choice narrative, in which the reader is really less free than might be supposed, as the simultaneous investigation and parody of literary themes fuses modernist and postmodernist versions of intertextuality. *Strashnyi sud* is that perfect postmodern paradox: a work that displays the benefits of the postmodern approach, in particular the important "interactive" role given to the reader, and the pleasures – some questionable – obtainable from a text full of *jouissance* in both senses of the word. Yet this parody of trendy shibboleths suggests that Erofeev finds a certain anti-humanism here, leading to a moral and aesthetic dead-end. In his "Russia's *Fleurs du mal*", he points out that the new Russian literature has swung away from "lifeless humanism ... a bright page of evil has been entered into the annals of Russian literature". Yet despite this obsession in the novel, the partial triumph of plot-levels and characterization of "the human", of a controversial fusion of love and sexual beauty as something capable of saving individuals, or even the world, could make *Strashnyi sud* the most significant text yet of Russian "post-realism". Not just an epilogue to Soviet literature and Russian postmodernism, it is also a harbinger of whatever is to come.

Erofeev's is undoubtedly a cruel talent; but in having the courage to work in dangerous areas of metaphysical *pro* and *contra*, and in staying with his own version of the truth, he is being cruel to be kind. It is difficult to predict the next issue of Erofeev's marriage of Heaven and Hell, but his work deserves more serious critical attention – not excluding stringent analysis of his alleged faults and excesses – than it has received thus far.

ANDREW REYNOLDS

Sergei Aleksandrovich Esenin 1895–1925

Poet

Biography

Born in the village of Konstantinovo, Riazan province, 3 October 1895. Attended Konstantinovo primary school, 1904–09; Spas-Klepiki church boarding school, 1909–12. Moved to Moscow in 1912; worked at Sytin's printing house, occasionally attending lectures at Shaniavskii University. Lived with Anna Izriadnova, 1913–15; one son. Married: 1) Zinaida Raikh in 1917 (divorced 1921), one daughter and one son; 2) Isadora Duncan in 1922 (separated, but not divorced 1924); 3) Sof'ia Tolstaia in 1925; also had a son in 1924 from a relationship with Nadezhda Vol'pin. First verse published in Moscow journals by 1914. Began to achieve national fame from March 1915 in Petrograd; there he met Blok, Sergei Gorodetskii, and the peasant poet Nikolai Kliuev, with whom he formed close friendship and literary alliance. Military service in Tsarskoe Selo 1916–17, deserted from the army after the 1917 February Revolution. Returned to Moscow, 1918; close friendship with the poet Anatolii Mariengof. Founding member of the Imaginist movement, early 1919; issued several volumes of his own verse, critical theory, and a play (often under the imprint "Imazhinisty"); contributed to numerous Imaginist collections, 1919–22. Travelled to western Europe and the United States with his wife, the dancer Isadora Duncan, 1922–23. Returned to Russia, 1923; wrote prolifically, including pro-Soviet verse; became increasingly depressed, homeless, and alcoholic. Broke with the Imaginists in 1924; travelled in the Caucasus 1924–25. Died, evidently from suicide by hanging, in a Leningrad hotel, 28 December 1925.

Publications

Collected Editions

Sobranie stikhotvorenii, vols 1–3. Moscow and Leningrad, 1926.

Stikhi i proza, vol. 4. Moscow and Leningrad, 1927; vols 1–4 reprinted, Leningrad, 1927–28.

Sobranie sochinenii, 5 vols. Moscow, 1961–62.

Sobranie sochinenii, 5 vols. Moscow, 1966–68.

Poems by Esenin, translated by Charles Brasch and Peter Soskice. Wellington, Wai-te-ata Press, 1970.

Confessions of a Hooligan: Fifty Poems by Sergei Esenin,

translated by Geoffrey Thurley. Cheadle Hulme, Cheshire, Carcanet Press, 1973.
Sobranie sochinenii, 6 vols. Moscow, 1977–80.
Selected Poems, translated by Jessie Davies. Youlgrave, Bakewell, Hub, 1979.
Izbrannye stikhotvoreniia i poemy/Selected Poetry (bilingual edition), translated by Peter Tempest. Moscow, Progress, 1982.
Gesammelte Werke, edited by Leonhard Kossuth. 3 vols, Berlin, Volk und Welt, 1995.
Polnoe sobranie sochinenii, 7 vols. Moscow, 1995 – .
Sergei Esenin v stikhakh i zhizni [Sergei Esenin in Poetry and Life], 4 vols. Moscow, 1995.

Poetry
Radunitsa. Petrograd, 1916; revised edition, Moscow, 1918; revised edition, Moscow, 1921; reprinted Liverpool, Lincoln Davies, 1972; Moscow, 1990; translated as *All Souls' Day*, by Jessie Davies, Liverpool, Lincoln Davies, 1991.
Isus Mladenets [The Infant Jesus]. Petrograd, 1918; revised edition, Chita, 1921.
Goluben'. Petrograd, 1918; revised edition, Moscow, 1920; translated as *Azure*, by Jessie Davies, Liverpool, Lincoln Davies, 1991.
Preobrazhenie: Stikhotvoreniia [Transfiguration: Poems]. Moscow, 1918; revised edition, Moscow, 1921.
Sel'skii chasoslov: Poemy [A Village Book of Hours: Longer Poems]. Moscow, 1918.
Treriadnitsa. Moscow, 1920; revised edition, Moscow, 1921.
Triptikh: Poemy [Triptych: Longer Poems]. Berlin, Skify, 1920.
Ispoved' khuligana [The Hooligan's Confession]. Moscow, 1921.
Izbrannoe. Moscow, 1922.
Sobranie stikhov i poem: tom pervyi [A Collection of Short and Long Poems: Volume One]. Berlin, Petrograd and Moscow, Izdatel'stvo Z.I. Grzhebina, 1922.
Stikhi skandalista [A Brawler's Poems]. Berlin, Izdatel'stvo I.T. Blagova, 1923.
Moskva kabatskaia [Moscow of the Taverns]. Leningrad, 1924; reprinted Moscow, 1990.
Stikhi (1920–24). Moscow and Leningrad, 1924.
Rus' Sovetskaia: Stikhi [Soviet Rus': Poems]. Baku, 1925.
Strana Sovetskaia [The Soviet Land]. Tiflis, 1925.
Pesn' o velikom pokhode [Song of the Great Campaign]. Moscow, 1925.
O Rossii i revoliutsii: Stikhotvoreniia i poemy [About Russia and the Revolution: Poems]. Moscow, 1925.
Persidskie motivy [Persian Motifs]. Moscow, 1925.
Berezovyi sitets [The Cotton Print of Birch Trees]. Moscow, 1925.
Izbrannye stikhi [Selected Verse]. Moscow, 1925.

Treatise on Poetry
Kliuchi Marii [The Keys of Mary]. Moscow, 1920.

Play
Pugachov. Moscow and Petrograd, 1922; Berlin, Russkoe universal'noe izdatel'stvo, 1922.

Critical Studies
Serge Ésénine (1895–1925): Sa vie et son oeuvre, by Francisca de Graaff, Leiden, E.J. Brill, 1933.
Sergej Esenin: Bilder- und Symbolwelt, by Christiane Auras, Munich, Sagner, 1965.
Sergej Esenin: A Biographical Sketch, by Frances de Graaff, The Hague, Mouton, 1966.
La forme poétique de Serge Esenin: Les rythmes, by Jacques Veyrenc, The Hague, Mouton, 1968.
Sergei Esenin: Ideino-tvorcheskaia evoliutsiia, by P.F. Iushin, Moscow, 1969.
Sergei Esenin: Literaturnaia khronika, by V. Belousov, part 1, Moscow, 1969; part 2, Moscow, 1970.
Poeticheskii mir Esenina, by Alla Marchenko, Moscow, 1972; 2nd revised edition, Moscow, 1989.
Sergei Esenin: Lichnost', tvorchestvo, epokha, by E. Naumov, Leningrad, 1973.
Sergei Esenin: Obraz, stikhi, epokha, by Iurii Prokushev, Moscow, 1975; translated as *Sergei Yesenin: The Man, the Verse, the Age*, by Kathleen Cook, Moscow, Progress, 1979.
Esenin: A Life, by Gordon McVay, Ann Arbor, Ardis, and London, Hodder and Stoughton, 1976; reprinted, New York, Paragon, 1988.
Sergey Esenin, by Constantin V. Ponomareff, Boston, Twayne, 1978.
Sergei Esenin: Zhizn' i tvorchestvo, by A.V. Kulinich, Kiev, 1980.
Isadora and Esenin: The Story of Isadora Duncan and Sergei Esenin, by Gordon McVay, Ann Arbor, Ardis, and London, Macmillan, 1980.
Sergei Esenin: Poet of the Crossroads, by Lynn Visson, Würzburg, Jal, 1980.
Esenin: A Biography in Memoirs, Letters, and Documents, edited and translated by Jessie Davies, Ann Arbor, Ardis, 1982.
Vesennei gulkoi ran'iu ... : Etiudy-razdum'ia o Sergee Esenine, by S. Koshechkin, Moscow, 1984; reprinted, Minsk, 1989.
S.A. Esenin: Materialy k biografii, edited by N.I. Guseva, S.I. Subbotin, and S.V. Shumikhin, Moscow, 1992 [issued 1993].
Esenin bez tainy: Poiski i issledovaniia, by Anatolii Panfilov, Moscow, 1994.
The Poetic Soul of Russia: Sergei Esenin (1895–1925), by Jessie Davies, Liverpool, Lincoln Davies, 1995.
Sergei Esenin, by Stanislav Kuniaev and Sergei Kuniaev (in the series "Zhizn' zamechatel'nykh liudei", No. 727), Moscow, 1995.
Sergei Esenin: A Centenary Tribute, by Gordon McVay, Oxford, Meeuws, 1998.

Bibliographies
"S.A. Esenin in England and North America: A Review Article", by Gordon McVay, *Russian Literature Triquarterly*, 8 (1974), 518–39.
"S.A. Esenin v kul'turnoi zhizni angloiazychnykh stran: Obzor", by Gordon McVay, *Russian Language Journal*, 128 (1983), 103–29; reprinted in *O, Rus', vzmakhni krylami: Eseninskii sbornik*, vol. 1, Moscow, 1994, 193–217.
Russkie sovetskie pisateli: Poety: Biobibliograficheskii ukazatel', vol. 8: *S.A. Esenin*, Moscow, 1985.

Prizhiznennye izdaniia S.A. Esenina: Bibliograficheskii spravochnik, by N.G. Iusov, Moscow, 1994.

Sergei Esenin led a short and turbulent life, which quickly passed into legend and myth. From his meteoric literary debut in Petrograd in 1915 until his suicide in a Leningrad hotel in 1925, Esenin assumed in rapid succession a number of literary "masks" – pastoral angel (1915–16), peasant prophet (1917–18), last poet of the village, tender hooligan (1919–21), tavern rake (1922–23), ex-hooligan (late 1923), would-be bard of the new Soviet Russia (mid-1924 until March 1925), and, finally, elegiac foreteller of his own imminent death (1925).

Although Esenin's poetry is highly autobiographical and even "confessional", the connection between the private man and his poetic persona is not entirely straightforward. By single-mindedly dedicating himself to the writing of poetry and the achievement of fame, Esenin blurred the boundaries between his "mask" and his "real face", sacrificing the possibility of ordinary human happiness.

A peasant from Riazan province, Esenin enjoyed conspicuous success in the pre-revolutionary literary salons of Petrograd. His first volume of poetry, *Radunitsa* (*All Souls' Day*), reflected the decorative, traditional aspects of village life. Rus', his ancient Russian motherland, was already the beloved heroine of his verse, a motherland that may be sad and impoverished, yet is also calm and imbued with a simple peasant religiousness. The poet knelt in pantheistic prayer before the temple of Nature.

Esenin's life was drastically affected by the February and October Revolutions of 1917. He welcomed these upheavals enthusiastically but vaguely in a series of longish "Scythian" poems, couched in abstruse religious and animal symbolism. These poems, which alternate between optimism and anxiety, prayerfulness and blasphemy, maintain a lofty cosmic tone far removed from the grim reality of earth-born Bolshevism.

By 1919, Esenin appeared a promising peasant poet, whose natural gifts displayed the influence of folk poetry, Kliuev, and Blok. Thenceforth, however, pursuing national fame, he sought creative independence within Moscow's anarchic literary bohemia. The last six years of Esenin's life witnessed the blossoming of his poetic talent and the disintegration of his inner peace.

As a founding-member of the enterprisingly avant-garde "Imaginist" group, Esenin achieved instant notoriety by emphasizing the unresolved dissonances in his personality and plight. Voicing his deep-rooted romantic attachment to old-fashioned, non-industrialized Rus' he lamented the imminent encroachment of the "iron guest" (urban industrialization) in "Ia poslednii poet derevni" ("I'm the Last Poet of the Village"), 1920, and cursed the "vile guest" (the train which defeats the living horse) in "Sorokoust", (1920). In "Ispoved' khuligana" ("Confessions of a Hooligan"), 1920, his lyrical hero is coarse and tender, desperate and kind; full of provocative vulgarity, and yet also "gently sick with childhood recollections".

After his marriage to Isadora Duncan in 1922, and an ill-starred, 15-month tour of western Europe and the United States, Esenin composed the controversial cycle *Moskva kabatskaia* [Moscow of the Taverns]. The setting is the tavern, the inhabitants are prostitutes and bandits, syphilitic accordionists, down-and-outs seeking to drown their misery in alcohol and dreams. Written in a universally understandable, non-Imaginistic language, these poems immediately appealed to thousands of Russians who saw in them a reflection of their own anguish.

The poetry of Esenin's last two years, after his return to Russia in 1923, combines a new-found, "Pushkinian" simplicity of style with a mood of ever-deepening tragic isolation. In the cycle "Liubov' khuligana" [A Hooligan's Love] (1923), his lyrical hero sought to break with hooliganism, passing into autumnal resignation. A profoundly elegiac note permeates the outstanding lyrics of 1924, "My teper' ukhodim ponemnogu" ("We Are Now Gradually Departing") and "Otgovorila roshcha zolotaia" ("The Golden Grove has Ceased to Speak").

Esenin had never been openly "counter-revolutionary" and, after his disillusioning travels in the west, he strove at times to compose pro-Soviet verse, praising Lenin and endeavouring to accept the changed face of Russia. Such attempts often proved poetically lifeless, however, with many critics doubting his sincerity and aptness for such topics. Esenin appeared more plausible in the role of "prodigal son" than as Soviet Russia's "most ardent fellow-traveller".

Toward the end of 1925 Esenin's poetry entered its most tragic phase. Isolated, alcoholic, uprooted, he created a sequence of short poems set in a frozen landscape. His deepening mental instability was now echoed by wintry iciness. On 12–13 November 1925 he wrote down the only extant version of his poem "Chernyi chelovek" ("The Black Man"), revealing his desperate struggle against alcoholic hallucinations and a tormented conscience. On 27 December Esenin wrote his last poem, "Do svidan'ia, drug moi, do svidan'ia" ("Goodbye, My Friend, Goodbye"), in his own blood, and the next day he was found hanging in a Leningrad hotel-room.

As a literary phenomenon, Esenin has been compared with Robert Burns and Arthur Rimbaud, with Dylan Thomas and, above all, François Villon; yet such is his complexity that he has also been characterized as the "Don Quixote of the village and the birch-tree" (V. Shershenevich, in *Trud*, Klintsy, 19 January 1926), and even likened to St Francis of Assisi. He has been called a poet of death, and a poet of eternal youth.

Throughout the Stalin era Esenin suffered official disfavour, being branded as a chauvinist, decadent, anti-Semite, drunkard, hooligan, anarchist, reactionary, and kulak. From 1955 to 1989 he was increasingly restored as a Soviet patriot and "great Russian national poet"; since 1989 he has sometimes unconvincingly been presented as an innocent victim and martyr, murdered by the Bolsheviks and/or the Jews, an anti-Soviet patriot, virtually worthy of canonization.

Despite all such vagaries of his posthumous fame, Esenin remains the most popular and most widely-read Russian poet of the 20th century. He is exceptionally "Russian", a temperamental peasant embodying tragic pathos and the forlorn dream of a rural idyll. Esenin is an individual, vulnerable, fragile, sinful, all-too-human. He is conscious of the beauty of the earth and the sorrow of transience, lost youth, human imperfection and unreliability, the elusiveness of happiness, the loss of faith. The romantic in Esenin is resolutely opposed to the 20th century with its mechanization and over-rationalization.

Scholars in the west (mainly non-Russian urban intellectuals) often disparage the simplicity, emotionality, melodiousness, and technical deficiencies of Esenin's verse, preferring the sophisticated subtlety of Pasternak, Mandel'shtam, Akhmatova, and Tsvetaeva. It is perhaps time to challenge this elitist judgement. A Russian critic perceptively observed during Esenin's lifetime (Andrei Shipov [Ivan Rozanov], in *Narodnyi uchitel'*, 2 (1925)): "In certain respects Esenin should without doubt seem inferior to some of his contemporaries: he lacks the sweep and crude strength of Maiakovskii, the cultural saturation of Mandel'shtam, or the dazzling lyrical intensity of Boris Pasternak, but he has a quality which is perhaps the most valuable of all for a lyric poet – the ability to reach the reader's heart and even – a thing to which we are now especially unaccustomed – the ability at times to move and touch us ..."

GORDON MCVAY

All Souls' Day

Radunitsa

Poetry collection, 1916

Esenin's first collection of poetry bears a virtually untranslatable title: the name of a folk funeral ritual, the "Commemoration of the Dead" held on Tuesday of the second week after Easter, when the dead are summoned from their tombs to the joy of the resurrection. This feast day evokes a mixed mood: the mourners grieve for their beloved deceased while rejoicing over Christ's resurrection. This atmosphere of mixed joy and grief permeates the book, marking Esenin's Slavophile identification with the ancient Slavonic customs of his people. Esenin signed the contract for *All Souls' Day* in Averianov's publishing house on 16 November 1915, just after Kliuev contracted for his volume *Mirskie dumy* [Worldly Thoughts].

The book is divided into two parts: "Rus'" (15 poems) and "Makovye pobaski" [Poppy Tales] (18 poems), most of them written no earlier than autumn 1914, the beginning of Esenin's mature period. Esenin selected meticulously from his previously published poetry (about 120 poems) and added 15 new poems. As soon as he received his author's copies, he took a highly critical view of the volume and regretted the inclusion of certain poems; two subsequent post-revolutionary editions reflect significant changes. The 1918 edition (in typical Imaginist style, the volume was dated "2nd year, 1st century") contains 28 poems, replacing 14 from the 1916 edition; the 1921 Imaginist edition contains 20 poems, 16 from the original, two from 1918, and two new works.

Contemporary critics unanimously greeted Esenin as a true national talent, likening his fresh style to icon painting. The critic P.N. Sakulin remarked:

> Poetry is everywhere. One must only be able to sense it ... In Esenin there speaks the spontaneous feeling of the peasant. Nature and the countryside have enriched his language with wondrous colours ... Nothing is more precious for Esenin than his native land.

His world consists above all of profoundly spiritualized and anthropomorphized Russian nature. Nature, as the poet's "cathedral", reflects the primordial, elemental unity of man and nature. He prays before the haystacks and blue skies; willows are envisioned as humble nuns clicking their rosaries; a black wood-grouse issues a summons to an evening vigil. Against the background of nature, Esenin offers a vivid picture of village life through everyday objects, costumes, traditions, and the spiritual realm. He reprises the Russian peasant's world-view as it is preserved in the folk culture of the Russian village. Certain poems evoke such folk rituals as wakes, the chanting of blind wandering musicians, the market, courtship, the *devichnik* (a bachelor's party for girls), the sowing and the harvest, Trinity Day, and St John's Eve (the midsummer night when Esenin was born). Christianity, patriarchal peasant ethics, and folk religious practices, both archaic and modern, are reflected in the artistic form of these poems as a peculiar blend of folk poetics and the modernistic literary trends of the Russian Silver Age: the elemental earthiness of the peasantry contrasts with the more refined atmosphere of the 20th century and the poet's acute perceptions.

These poems have a song-like natural musicality and conversational poetic quality. The style and imagery are pure, delicate, and simple at first glance. Some poems can be reduced to a single, predominant image. Nature becomes humanized; movement is introduced into the landscape and captures the mood evoked by the landscape in the soul of the lyric persona. The first nine poems are predominantly religious. The lyric persona is a transient in this world, identifying in turn with a pilgrim, a wanderer, a monk, and a shepherd, constantly connecting the earthly with the heavenly: "To this land I've come, intending / Very soon to go away". The narrative poem "Mikola" tells the story of Russia's favourite saint (St Nicholas), who is sent by God on a mission to man (i.e., the peasants). His movements match the daily ascent and descent of the sun, as well as other agricultural, seasonal, and daily cycles. Two main points reappear constantly in Esenin's religiosity: Esenin's Christ stands up for the poor, the beggars, the outcasts, and those at the margins of society; and Esenin instantiates the special Russian attitude toward the Virgin Mary. She brings her risen Son down again for a second crucifixion among the poor in the poem "Ne s burnym vetrom tuchi taiut" [The clouds melt not with stormy wind] and sends him to live without shelter in the bushes, in the bosom of nature. The narrator passes by the hungry Saviour under a stump, and in the poem "Shel Gospod' pytat' liudei v liubovi" [The Lord came to try people's love] the Lord appears as a beggar and shares dry bread with an old man. The poet concludes the book by reiterating his faith in the protection of the Virgin Mary ingrained in him since birth. As the imagery of the entire collection is oriented around the juxtaposition of the Church and the details of peasant life, Church-Slavonic and dialectal vocabulary are thoroughly mixed on the lexical level, e.g., in the image "cottages in the guise of icons".

MARIA PAVLOVSZKY

Moskva kabatskaia

Moscow of the Taverns

Poetry collection, 1924

This collection includes poems from the Berlin collection *Stikhi skandalista* [A Brawler's Poems] (1923) and three poems from the Imaginist journal *Gostinitsa dlia puteshestvuiushchikh v prekrasnom* [An Inn for Travellers in the Beautiful] (1924). Esenin prepared many versions under the title *Moskva kabatskaia*; and on six occasions he planned to publish the cycle.

Some of these poems he recited during his trip to the west. The title refers both to the individual book of poems as well as to poems included in other editions of his poetry which are thematically tied to this cycle, but were published in various editions during Esenin's lifetime, thus engendering confusion as to whether *Moskva kabatskaia* should be called a book or a cycle.

The cycle can be properly understood only against the background of Esenin's preceding poetical development. This cycle closely conveys Esenin's internal descent to the deepest, darkest phase, with which he was to struggle until his suicide in 1925. These poems comprise an intimate and utterly sincere lyrical expression of his inner life in the form of a confession. In his poetic development the book *Moskva kabatskaia* appears as a counterpoint after the emotional upheaval caused by the false hopes raised by the Bolshevik Revolution. It conveys his psychological experiences: revulsion, disillusionment, and lyrical sadness, which gain outward expression in alcoholism and debauchery as a subconscious protest against events. Esenin's life was falling apart on every level simultaneously: political, personal, and artistic: his alienation from the Imaginists, disagreements with Kliuev; bohemian life in the Imaginist literary café "Pegasus' Stall"; the increasing effects of alcoholism on his body and mind; and disruptions in his personal life, such as the divorce from Zinaida Raikh in 1921, his unsuccessful trip to the west and subsequent split with Isadora Duncan, and his constantly unsettled and often homeless life. His tragic striving for a way out of his dilemmas is temporarily resolved by reaching a new spiritual and artistic pinnacle. The lines lamenting his previous simple faith mirror the poet's crumbling world: "I'm ashamed that I once had faith, / Yet that faith I bitterly miss".

Following the tradition of the Russian classics, this book is a poetic record of Esenin's inner journey through his fall into the lower depths of Dante's Inferno and his step-by-step return to the light through suffering, repentance, and death – a spiritual purification through love, providing a renewed and more profound metaphysical view of life. The work signifies Esenin's search for and discovery of a new poetic voice, the highpoint of his *oeuvre*. All the poems written in this new diction during 1924–25 display equal artistic merits and are unquestionably first-rate. The thematic orientation shifts from the more tangible to a more philosophical look at life. The essential poetic topics – the ultimate problems of existence, good and evil, life and death, eternity and immortality, and the like – become the focal points of these verses.

The opening poem, "Vse zhivoe osoboi metoi ..." [The lives of us all are moulded], reveals the organizing pattern: the temporal juxtaposition of past and present, the antithesis of the poet's village past versus his current city life; the high and heavenly versus the low, the hellish, and the earthly: the self and the hostile environment developed in the first four poems. The poet identifies with a wolf hounded from all sides. He feels a tremendous affinity toward the poor, the outcasts, those at the margins of society, i.e., the beasts (prostitutes, crooks, brawlers, scoundrels, etc.). The second section, "Moskva kabatskaia", focuses on the attempt to break away from the "din's infernal den". The third section, "Liubov' khuligana" [A Hooligan's Love], was written in the second half of 1923, after his return to Russia, and is dedicated to the actress Avgusta Miklashevskaia. This cycle retains the antithetical composition featuring the dialectics of past and present, adding the dichotomy of *you* and *I*. It introduces hope through healing love: at first, love of a woman reflects a cynical view of life and self-destructive tendencies ("Our life is sheets and bed / Our life is a kiss, and then into the whirlpool"), then it develops into an all-embracing and all-reconciling universal love expressed through the union of antithetical concepts (e.g., the black toad marries a white rose, devils in the narrator's heart turn into angels, etc.).

The concluding poem, "Ne zhaleiu, ne zovu, ne plachu ..." [I will not weep, regret or scold ...], is one of the greatest ever written in Russian. When recited, it evoked feelings of shock in audiences by expressing a vast range of contradictory emotions common to every human being; on the level of the sound texture, its pure, transparent images and perfect musical flow captivate even the non-Russian speaker. Several poems from this cycle have lent themselves to splendid musical settings.

The book's final note is a seed of hope that the lost human soul can overcome the confusion following the Revolution by returning to traditional moral, ethical, and aesthetic values. The images take on highly complex form, sometimes evading comprehension. The ornate Church-Slavonic lexicon and the ecclesiastic imagery is replaced by deliberately vulgar, substandard diction and base imagery, sometimes describing repulsive bodily functions.

After Esenin's death, the prohibition of his poetry, and its subsequent underground circulation, popular culture associated the title of the book with the first cycles (the latter parts often were considered separately by scholars), and it came to be viewed as an unhealthy turn in his personal and poetic development, reflecting a moral fall of the lyrical persona under the influence of his bohemian life, a mood of pessimism as a result of the difficult circumstances brought about by the New Economic Policy, and decadence in general.

MARIA PAVLOVSZKY

Evgenii Aleksandrovich Evtushenko 1933–

Poet and prose writer

Biography

Born in Stantsiia Zima, Irkutsk region, Siberia, 18 July 1933. Accompanied his father on geological expeditions to Kazakhstan, 1948, and the Altai, 1950. Attended the Gork'ii Literary Institute, Moscow, early 1950s. Famous as precocious Thaw-period poet. Controversial at home, travelled abroad widely throughout the Khrushchev and the Brezhnev periods. Married: 1) Bella Akhmadulina in 1954 (divorced); 2) Galina Semenova; 3) Jan Butler in 1978; 4) Maria Novika in 1986; five sons. Member of Congress of People's Deputies of USSR, from 1989; vice president, Russian PEN, since 1990. Recipient: USSR Committee for Defence of Peace Award, 1965; Order of Red Banner of Labour (twice); State Prize, 1984. Honorary member, American Academy of Arts and Sciences, 1987.

Publications

Collected Editions

Stikhi raznykh let [Poems of Several Years]. Moscow, 1959.
Selected Poems, translated by Peter Levi and R.R. Milner-Gulland. Harmondsworth, Penguin, and New York, Dutton, 1962.
Selected Poetry, edited by R.R. Milner-Gulland. Oxford, Pergamon Press, 1963.
The Poetry of Yevgeny Yevtushenko (bilingual edition), edited and translated by George Reavey. New York, October House, 1964; London, Calder and Boyars, 1966; revised edition, London, Marion Boyars, 1981; as *Early Poems*, London, Marion Boyars, 1989.
Yevtushenko's Reader: The Spirit of Elbe, A Precocious Autobiography, Poems. New York, Dutton, 1966.
Yevtushenko Poems (bilingual edition), translated by Herbert Marshall. Oxford, Pergamon Press, 1966.
New Works: The Bratsk Station, translated by Tina Tupikina-Glaessner and Geoffrey Dutton. Melbourne, Sun, 1966; as *Bratsk Station and Other New Poems*, New York, Praeger, and London, Hart-Davis, 1967.
Poems, translated by Herbert Marshall. New York, Dutton, 1966; Oxford, Pergamon Press, 1967.
Stolen Apples, translated by James Dickey *et al.* New York, Doubleday, 1971; London, W.H. Allen, 1972.
Izbrannye proizvedeniia, 2 vols. Moscow, 1975.
The Face Behind the Face, translated by Arthur Boyars and Simon Franklin. London, Marion Boyars, and New York, Marek, 1979.
Invisible Threads, translated by Paul Falla *et al.* London, Secker and Warburg, and New York, Macmillan, 1981.
Sobranie sochinenii, 3 vols. Moscow, 1983–84.
Stikhotvoreniia i poemy 1951–1986, 3 vols. Moscow, 1987.
The Collected Poems 1952–1990, edited by Albert C. Todd. Edinburgh, Mainstream, and New York, Holt, 1991.
Moe samoe-samoe [The Same Old Things of Mine]. Moscow, 1995.

Poetry

Razvedchiki griadushchego [The Prospectors of the Future]. Moscow, 1952; reprinted Ann Arbor, University Microfilms, 1976.
Tretii sneg [Third Snow]. Moscow, 1955.
Shosse entuziastov [Highway of the Enthusiasts]. Moscow, 1956; reprinted Ann Arbor, University Microfilms, 1976.
"Stantsiia Zima", *Oktiabr'*, 10 (1956); Frankfurt, Posev, 1964; translated as *Winter Station*, by Oliver J. Frederiksen, Munich, Gerber, 1964.
Obeshchanie [Promise]. Moscow, 1957.
Luk i lira [The Bow and the Lyre]. Tbilisi, 1959.
Iabloko [The Apple]. Moscow, 1960.
Vzmakh ruki [A Wave of the Hand]. Moscow, 1962.
Nezhnost': novye stikhi [Tenderness: New Poems]. Moscow, 1962.
Posle Stalina [After Stalin]. Chicago, Russian Language Specialties, 1962.
"The Heirs of Stalin", *Current Digest of the Soviet Press*, 14/40 (1962); as *Nasledniki Stalina*, London, Flegon Press, 1963.
Bratskaia GES. Chicago, Russian Language Specialties, 1965; Moscow, 1967; translated as "Bratsk Station", by Tina Tupikina-Glaessner and Geoffrey Dutton, in *Bratsk Station and Other New Poems*, 1967.
Khotiat li russkie voiny? [Do The Russians Want Wars?]. Moscow, 1965 (music by Eduard Kolmanovskii).
Kater sviazi [Torpedo Boat Signalling]. Moscow, 1966.
Kachka [Swing-Boat]. London, Flegon Press, 1966.
The Execution of Stepan Razin, op.119, score by Dmitri Shostakovich; text by Evtushenko, Moscow, 1966.
Poems Chosen by the Author (bilingual edition), translated by Peter Levi and R.R. Milner-Gulland. London, Collins and Harvill, 1966; New York, Hill and Wang, 1967.
Idut belye snegi [The White Snows Are Falling]. Moscow, 1969.
Ia-sibirskoi porody [I Am Siberian]. 1971.
Doroga nomer odin [Highway Number One]. Moscow, 1972.
Poiushchaia damba [The Singing Dam]. Moscow, 1972.
Poet v Rossii - bol'she, chem poet [A Poet in Russia is More than a Poet]. Moscow, 1973.
Intimnaia lirika [Intimate Lyrics]. Moscow, 1973.
Ottsovskii slukh [Father's Hearing]. Moscow, 1975.
V polnyi rost: novaia kniga stikhov i poem [At Full Growth: New Book of Verse and Poetry]. Moscow, 1977.
Utrennyi narod: novaia kniga stikhov [The Morning Crowds: New Book of Poetry]. Moscow, 1978.
Ivan the Terrible and Ivan the Fool, translated by Daniel Weissbort. London, Gollancz, and New York, Marek, 1979.
Svarka vzryvom: stikhotvoreniia i poemy [Explosion Welding]. Moscow, 1980.
Tochka opory [Fulcrum] (includes *Pirl-kharbor* [Pearl Harbour]). Moscow, 1981.
A Dove in Santiago (novella in verse), translated by D.M. Thomas. London, Secker and Warburg, 1982; New York, Viking, 1983.
Mama i neitronaiia bomba i drugie poemy [Mother and Neutron Bomb and Other Poems]. Moscow, 1983.
Pochti naposledok: novaia kniga. Moscow, 1985; translated as

Almost at the End, by Antonina W. Bouis and Albert C. Todd, London, Marion Boyars, and New York, Holt, 1987.
Posledniaia popytka: stikhotvoreniia iz starykh i novykh tetradei [Last Attempt: Poetry from Old and New Books]. Petrozavodsk, 1988.
Pochti v poslednii mig [Almost at the Last Moment]. Uzhgorod, 1988.
Nezhnost' [Tenderness]. Kiev, 1988.
Poemy o mire [Poems about Peace]. Alma-Ata, 1989.
Stikhi. Dushanbe, 1989.
Grazhdane, poslushaite menia... [Citizens, Listen to Me...]. Moscow, 1989.
Liubimaia, spi... [Loved One, Sleep ...]. Moscow, 1989.
"Pomozhem svobode!" [We Will Help Freedom!], *Znamia*, 4 (1990).
Pre-Morning. Predutro (bilingual edition). Moscow, 1995.

Fiction
"Chetvertaia meshchanskaia" [The Fourth Vulgar Woman], *Iunost'*, 2 (1959).
Ardabiola. Moscow, 1981; London, Granada, and New York, St Martin's Press, 1984.
Iagodnye mesta. Moscow, 1982; translated as *Wild Berries*, by Antonina W. Bouis, New York, Morrow, and London, Macmillan, 1984.
Ne umirai prezhde smerti. Moscow, 1993; translated as *Don't Die Before You're Dead*, by Antonina W. Bouis, London, Robson, and New York, Random House, 1995.

Plays
Bratskaia GES (produced Moscow, 1968). Moscow, 1967.
Under the Skin of the Statue of Liberty (produced Moscow, 1972).

Screenplay
Detskii sad [Kindergarten]. Moscow, 1989.

Autobiography
Avtobiografiia. London, Flegon Press, 1964; translated as *A Precocious Autobiography*, by Andrew R. MacAndrew, New York, Dutton, and London, Collins and Harvill, 1963.

Essays
Talant est' chudo nesluchainoe [Talent is a Miracle That Comes Not by Chance]. Moscow, 1980.
Voina – eto antikultura [War is Anti-Culture]. Moscow, 1983.
Politika privilegiia vsekh [Everybody's Privilege]. Moscow, 1990.
Propast' – v dva pryzhka? [The Precipice – in Two Leaps?]. Kharkov, 1990.
Fatal Half Measures: The Culture of Democracy in the Soviet Union, edited and translated by Antonina W. Bouis. Boston, Little Brown, 1991.

Translator
Mlechnyi put' [The Milky Way], by D. Ulzytuev, Moscow, 1961.
Seti zvezd [A Network of Stars], by T. Chiladze, Tbilisi, 1961.
Na koleni ne padat'! [Don't Fall to Your Knees!], by G. Dzhagarov, Moscow, 1961.
Tiazhelee zemli: stikhi o Gruzii, poety Gruzii [Heavy Earth: Poems about Georgia, the Poets of Georgia]. Tbilisi, 1979.

Photography
Divided Twins - Razdel'ennye bliznetsy: Alaska and Siberia, photographs by the author and Boyd Norton. London, Viking Studio, 1988; New York, Viking, 1989.

Critical Studies

"Herbert and Yevtushenko: On Whose Side is History?", by George Gömöri, *Mosaic*, (Winnipeg, Manitoba), 3/1 (1969).
"The Politics of Poetry: The Sad Case of Yevgeny Yevtushenko", by Robert Conquest, *New York Times Magazine* (30 September 1973).
"An Interview with Evgeniy Evtushenko", by Gordon McVay, *Journal of Russian Studies*, 33 (1977).
"Women in Evtushenko's Poetry", by Vickie A. Rebenko, *Russian Review*, 36 (1977).
Soviet Russian Literature since Stalin, by Deming Brown, Cambridge, Cambridge University Press, 1978.
"Yevtushenko as a Critic", by Vladimir Ognev, *Soviet Studies in Literature*, 18/3 (1981).
"Yevgeni Yevtushenko's Solo: On His 50th Birthday", by Yevgeni Sidorov, *Soviet Literature*, 7/424 (1983).
"Two Opinions about Evgenii Evtushenko's Narrative Poem: 'Man and the Neutron Bomb': And What if This is Prose? And What if It is Not?", by Adol'f Urban and Gennadii Krasnikov, *Soviet Studies in Literature*, 20/1 (1983–84).
"The Poetry of Yevgeny Yevtushenko in the 1970s", by Irma Mercedes Kaszuba, *USF Language Quarterly*, (San Francisco), 25/1–2 (1986).
"Evtushenko's *Jagodnye mesta*: The Poet as Prose Writer", by Richard N. Porter, *Russian Language Journal*, 40/135 (1986).
"'Queuing for Hope': About Yevgeni Yevtushenko's Poem 'Fuku!'", by Pavel Ulyashov, *Soviet Literature*, 9/462 (1986).
Evgenii Evtushenko: lichnost' i tvorchestvo, by E. Sidorov, Moscow, 1987.
"Yevtushenko's *Stantsiya Zima*: A Reassessment", by Michael Pursglove, *New Zealand Slavonic Journal*, 2 (1988).
"The Transformation of *Babi Yar*", by Richard Sheldon, in *Soviet Society and Culture*, by Sheldon and Terry L. Thompson, Boulder, Colorado, Westview Press, 1988, 124–61.
Soviet Literature in the 1980s, by N.N. Shneidman, Toronto, University of Toronto Press, 1989, 159–66.
"Russia's Muse on the Barricades: Yevtushenko's *August 19*", by A.D.P. Briggs, *Rusistika*, (4 December (1991), 26–29.

Bibliographies

Evgenii Evtushenko. Bibliograficheskii ukazatel', by Iu. Nekhoroshev and A. Shitov, Cheliabinsk, 1981.
Russkie sovetskie pisateli - poety, 7, Moscow, 1984.

Although Evgenii Evtushenko published his first poem in *Sovetskii sport* as early as 1949, it was in 1956 that he became famous with the long autobiographical poem *Stantsiia Zima* (*Winter Station*). Here, as in a number of subsequent poems such as "Otkuda vy?" [Where Are You From?] (1959), and

"Ziminskaia ballada" [Zima Ballad] (1975), the hero returns to his Siberian birthplace in order to discover "the truth", an elusive concept for a young man born in 1933, the first 20 years of whose life had been lived in the deep shadow cast by Stalinism. In his *Avtobiografiia* (*A Precocious Autobiography*) the poet records how he wept on learning of the death of Stalin. This text, in which Evtushenko displays considerable formal subtlety, became one of the key documents of the Thaw and the poet one of its most distinguished, even glamorous products. This reputation was subsequently enhanced by two equally famous poems, "Babii Iar'" (1961), and *Nasledniki Stalina* ("The Heirs of Stalin"), 1962. "Babii Iar'", published in *Literaturnaia gazeta* on 19 September 1961, in time for the 20th anniversary of the massacre, is one of a number of literary treatments of a notorious massacre of Jews in occupied Kiev on 29 September 1941. The poet's unequivocal identification with the Jewish victims of this and other anti-Semitic outrages led to accusations that Evtushenko was overlooking the sacrifices made by millions of Russians in the struggle against fascism. Indeed, when Shostakovich set the words to music as part of his Thirteenth Symphony, additional lines were added to rectify this "omission". However, the subject of anti-Semitism in Russia remained so touchy that the poem was not republished there until 1984, although the poet frequently recited it both in Russia and abroad. "The Heirs of Stalin", published presumably with Party approval in *Pravda* (21 October 1962) and warning that Stalinism had long outlived its creator, was not republished until 1987, when its publication was a notable event in Gorbachev's policy of glasnost.

A "performance poet" *par excellence*, Evtushenko is firmly in a tradition begun by Vladimir Maiakovskii, one of the major influences on his work, both as a writer and as a man (in Maiakovskii he claims that the bullet with which Maiakovskii killed himself in 1930 merely anticipated the executioner's bullet that would surely have been his in 1937, had he lived). Like Maiakovskii, an exuberant self-publicist, Evtushenko is also, like Maiakovskii, capable of a tender lyricism, which is in marked contrast with his frequent use of brash verbal pyrotechnics involving oxymorons, word-play, alliteration, assonance, startling juxtapositions and an overall oratorical tone. Among the best of his lyrics is "So mnoi vot chto proiskhodit" ("This is What's Happening to Me"), one of the poet's strongest pleas for an end to *razobshchenie*, that which separates or "disconnects" people. Many of these poems are known by heart even by Russians who have come to view Evtushenko with a degree of scepticism and even hostility. The charge is that he was a licensed Soviet liberal, too ready to acquiesce to political demands, as, for example, when he published anti-Chinese poems in 1969 at a time of a border dispute between the USSR and China. The charge is unfair, since, over 40 years, Evtushenko's record as a defender of unpopular causes has been a good one.

After the accession of Gorbachev to power, Evtushenko turned increasingly to other spheres of activity apart from poetry. In the 1980s he introduced Soviet readers to many poets repressed by Stalin in a series of articles in the flagship journal of glasnost, *Ogonek*; as a parliamentarian he highlighted the intolerable burden endured by many Soviet women. He has espoused ecological causes, particularly raising public awareness of the pollution of Lake Baikal in his native Siberia. Most famously, on 20 August 1991 he read his poem "August 19 1991" to those assembled in the Russian Parliament, the "White House". The poem was printed in Russian the following day and in English the day after that. After the collapse of communism he was instrumental in getting a monument to the victims of Stalinist repression placed opposite the Lubianka, headquarters of the KGB.

He has acted in films, and has written several pieces of prose fiction: *Ardabiola* (1981), a fantasy, and the novel *Iagodnye mesta* (*Wild Berries*), 1982. The novel, once again set largely in Zima Station, is typically ambitious, so much so that N.N. Shneidman describes it as "oversaturated". Despite critical failure both at home and abroad, the novel, like much of Evtushenko's work, was a huge commercial success. This may account for the relative dearth of critical material on both his life and his work. There is general agreement that he is highly gifted and that, on occasions this superabundance of talent is his undoing, in that his work can appear showy and facile and his lexicon overloaded with modish foreign words. The Soviet critic Lev Ozerov dismissed him as a mere stylistic eclectic who had borrowed from at least 14 poets. Formally speaking, Evtushenko is fairly conservative and, indeed, in 1964 he wrote a poem, "Khochu ia stat' nemnozhko staromodnym" ("I Want to Be a Little Old-Fashioned") in favour of the "good old iambic". In his best poetry, such as "Svad'by" [Weddings] (1955), his handling of rhythm is brilliant. The poem describes how Evtushenko, as a child, danced at wedding feasts in 1941 for young men about to go off to almost certain death in the disastrous Soviet campaign of that year. Evtushenko is at his best in such narrative or descriptive poems. In philosophical mode, on the other hand, he is often trite, portentous, and unconvincing. "Tret'ia pamiat'" [The Third Memory] (1966), illustrates the best and worst of Evtushenko's enormous output. The third memory, the "memory of the body", by which he means physical sensations, is the stuff of Evtushenko's best poetry but a philosphical poem based on this fact is among his weakest.

Michael Pursglove

Winter Station

Stantsiia Zima

Narrative poem, 1956

Evtushenko's narrative poem, *Winter Station* was first published in the journal *Oktiabr'* in 1956. Zima is a town on the Trans-Siberian railway and the River Oka, north-west of Irkutsk. It is the poet's birthplace and the place to which he was evacuated between 1941 and 1944. The poem, which is set in late 1953, just after Stalin's death, is heavily autobiographical and tells how the poet returns to his birthplace from Moscow in order to rediscover his roots and the truth about Russia. The poem catapulted its then unknown author to fame mainly because of its thematic content. Here was the testimony of a young man, born in 1933, who had lived all his life under Stalinism, had been led to believe many of its precepts and who was now accepting nothing on trust. The poem may be tentatively divided into 12 unequal sections: 1) an introduction, in which the author speaks of his rebellious Ukrainian ancestor who was exiled to Siberia; 2) a description of the author's mother and father; 3) an evocation of the author's childhood in Zima; a dialogue between

"Childhood" and "Youth"; a description of the author's return to Zima; 4) the River Oka and an old man's argument with his nephew; 5) a berry-picking episode and a second dialogue, this time between the author and the Wheat; 6) Pankratov, the Stalinist bureaucrat who heads the local kolkhoz; 7) the head of the household; 8) the author communes with Nature, his uncles, a tea shop, a tipsy journalist; 9) the local club; musings on love; 10) more musings on love; 11) the railway, the rebellious Vovka; and 12) the answer given by Zima to the author's question "What is Truth?". This summary makes it clear that the poem, like all of Evtushenko's work, has two registers: the narrative and the philosophical. What it does not show is that, while the narrative passages show Evtushenko at his best, the philosophical passages are banal and pedestrian. Six concepts dominate the poem: youth; truth; growth; discovery; thought; and simplicity. The Russian roots that equate to these (*molod-*; *pravda*; *rasti*; *otkryt'*; *dumat'*, and *prost-*) recur as leitmotifs throughout the poem in a bewildering variety of guises. One of the best examples combines chiasmus, alliteration, assonance and word-play to produce a witty aphorism that defies translation into English: "Est' molodezh', a molodosti net". This generalization, as so often in Evtushenko, is followed by a specific example, as an old man laments the lack of youthful zest in his nephew. The verb *dumat'* (to think) is almost as important as the concept of youth and takes on a significance beyond its dictionary meaning. While the author admires the lack of thought, the carefreeness, the *nezadumchivost'* of the woman picking berries, it is his painful duty to give himself over to meditation (*razdumiia*). This must involve real thought, not the conditioned reflexes of the typical Soviet hack writer. If he does think genuinely and profoundly, the poet will discover the Truth both about himself and about the society in which he lives. This theme is announced in the very first line of the poem, "My chem vzroslei, tem bol'she otkrovenny" [the more grown-up we become, the more candid we are], where the etymological link between *otkrovennyi* and *otkryt'* is fully exploited. There are minor themes in the poem, too, which are related to the six key concepts: as the poet grows up he changes and becomes aware of the changes around him. Hence the Russian root *-men-* ("change") is repeated, with different prefixes. As the poet strives for "simplicity", that is to say "straightforwardness" in political, social and personal dealings, he also focuses on its corollary "complexity" (*slozhnost'*). In Soviet times "complexity" was often a euphemism for "shortcoming" and a line including the word was excised from the journal version of the poem. On this score alone, a strong case can be made for the formal brilliance of this poem, an aspect that has been overshadowed by the documentary significance of the work. That a case has to be made at all is unusual in a work by Evtushenko, whose verbal pyrotechnics are often alleged to mask a paucity of thought. The majority of the 975 lines are written in iambic pentameters arranged in alternating rhyme. There are significant deviations from this scheme, particularly when the poet imitates folk-song. The poem provides many examples, too, of inventive rhyme, a forte of Evtushenko. A particular device used in this poem is the "false" couplet, in which two successive lines end with cognate words that do not in themselves constitute the actual rhyme, which comes a line later.

The town of Zima has provided inspiration for three other narrative poems by Evtushenko: "Soiti na tikhoi stantsii Zima" [To Get Out at Quiet Zima Station] (1953), "Otkuda vy?" [Where Are You From?] (1959), and "Ziminskaia ballada" [Zima Ballad] (1975). All three have thematic and formal similarities with *Winter Station*, with "Otkuda vy?" being a sequel, 680 lines long, to *Zima Junction*. Other works with a Siberian theme include *Ia - sibirskoi porody* [I Am Siberian], *Po Pechore* (*On the Pechora River*), *Bratskaia GES* (*Bratsk Station*), and the novel *Wild Berries*.

Despite, or, possibly, because of its importance, the poem has only appeared three times, once in journal form and twice in collections of Evtushenko's poetry. It is not among the works that Evtushenko recites. Nevertheless it is, together with Dudintsev's *Ne khlebom edinym* (*Not by Bread Alone*), a key document of the period following Khrushchev's "secret" speech to the 20th Party Congress. As a result of its publication Evtushenko was expelled from the Komsomol.

MICHAEL PURSGLOVE

F

Aleksandr Aleksandrovich Fadeev 1901–1956
Novelist and literary functionary

Biography

Born in Kimry, Tver Province, 24 December 1901. Attended commercial school in Vladivostok, 1910–19, and at the Mining Academy in Moscow, 1921–24. Joined the Communist Party, 1918; Party name: Bulyga. Served in Red partisan detachments and the People's Revolutionary Army, 1919–21. Began to publish in 1923. Engaged in political Party work in the Kuban region and Rostov-on-Don, 1924–26. Elected to the presidium of the North Caucasus Association of Proletarian Writers, 1925. Married: 1) Valeria Anatol'evna Gerasimova in 1925 (divorced 1932); 2) Angelina Iosifovna (Osipovna) Stepanova in 1936 or 1937, two sons. Returned to Moscow; full-time writer from 1926. Elected to the governing boards of the All-Union Association of Proletarian Writers, 1926–28, and Russian Association of Proletarian Writers, 1928–32. Elected to the presidium of the Organizing Committee of the Soviet Writers' Union, 1932–34. Member of the presidium of the board of the Soviet Writers' Union, 1934–39; and secretary thereof, 1939–43. Reporter for *Pravda* during World War II. Member of the Central Committee of the Soviet Communist Party, 1939–56; delegate to the USSR Supreme Soviet, 1946–56. Recipient: Stalin Prize for Literature, first class, 1946. Secretary general of Soviet Writers' Union, 1946–53, and chairman of the board, 1953–54. Secretary of the Union's board, 1954–56. Played a prominent role in the Soviet-orchestrated peace movement at home and abroad, 1948–55. Committed suicide, 13 May 1956.

Publications

Collected Edition

Sobranie sochinenii, 7 vols. Moscow, 1969–71.

Fiction

Protiv techeniia [Against the Current]. Moscow, 1924; as *Amgun'skii polk* [The Amgun'sk Regiment], Moscow, 1934; and as *Rozhdenie Amgun'skogo polka* [The Birth of the Amgun'sk Regiment], Moscow, 1934.

Razliv [The Flood]. Moscow, 1924.

Razgrom. Moscow, 1927; as *Razgrom/The Rout*, edited by Roger Cockrell, London, Bristol Classical Press, 1995; translated as *The Nineteen*, by R.D. Charques, London, Martin Lawrence, 1929; reprinted Westport, Connecticut, Hyperion Press, 1973; also translated as *The Rout*, by O. Gorchakov, Moscow, Foreign Languages Publishing House, c.1957.

Poslednii iz Udege [The Last of the Udege]. Moscow, 1941.

Molodaia gvardiia. Moscow, 1946; translated as *The Young Guard*, by Violet Dutt, Moscow, Progress, 1958; reprinted Moscow, Raduga, 1987.

Chernaia metallurgiia [Ferrous Metallurgy]. Moscow, 1951–56.

Memoirs, Letters, and Literary Criticism

Leningrad v dni blokady: Iz dnevnika. Moscow, 1944; translated as *Leningrad in the Days of the Blockade*, by R.D. Charques, London, Hutchinson, 1946; Westport, Connecticut, Greenwood Press, 1971.

Za tridtsat' let: Izbrannye stat'i, rechi i pis'ma o literature i iskusstve [Over Thirty Years: Selected Articles, Speeches and Letters on Literature and Art], edited by S. Preobrazhenskii, 2nd edition, Moscow, 1959.

Pis'ma 1917–1956 [Letters]. 2nd edition, Moscow, 1959.

Critical Studies

Russian Literature since the Revolution, by Edward J. Brown, Cambridge, Massachusetts, Harvard University Press, 1963; 2nd edition, 1982, 134–40.

Russian Literature under Lenin and Stalin, 1917–1953, by Gleb Struve, Norman, University of Oklahoma Press, 1971, 134–37.

Aleksandr Fadeev, by V. Ozerov, 4th edition, Moscow, 1976.

Russian Literature and Ideology: Herzen, Dostoevsky, Leontiev, Tolstoy, Fadeyev, by Nicholas Rzhevsky, Urbana, University of Illinois Press, 1983, 133–48.

Aleksandr Fadeev: Pisatel'skaia sud'ba, by V. Boborykin, Moscow, 1989.

"Introduction", by Roger Cockrell, in *Razgrom/ The Rout*, London, Bristol Classical Press, 1995, v–xviii.

Bibliographies

A. A. Fadeev: Seminarii, by N.I. Nikulina, Leningrad, 1958.

"Aleksandr Aleksandrovich Fadeev", in *Russkie sovetskie pisateli prozaiki: Biobibliograficheskii ukazatel'*, vol. 5, Moscow, 1968, 245–321.

Aleksandr Aleksandrovich Fadeev, Soviet novelist, literary theorist, and admininstrator, was a communist by upbringing and persuasion. His parents (a schoolteacher and a nurse) and his step-father were revolutionaries. Fadeev joined the Communist Party at the age of 16 and in 1919 he left the Vladivostok commercial school to fight with the Red partisans against the Whites and the Japanese. In March 1921 as a delegate to the 10th Party Congress he took part in the suppression of the Kronshtadt rebellion. In 1924, while a student at the Moscow Mining Academy, he was sent to southern Russia to do political Party work.

Fadeev began his literary career with the stories *Protiv techeniia* [Against the Current] and *Razliv* [The Flood], both dealing with the revolution and war in the Far East. *Razliv*, written before *Protiv techeniia*, is concerned with a social and political feud in a remote village in 1917. Fadeev openly sympathizes with the Bolsheviks, portraying them as vigorous and courageous people. The story's central event is a successful operation organized by a village Bolshevik to rescue the peasants threatened with drowning by a sudden flood. The story suffers from a superficial delineation of its characters, a fragmented narrative, and a copious use of figurative language. Most of the contemporary critics acclaimed *Razliv* for the political significance of its theme.

The title of *Protiv techeniia* symbolizes the struggle of individual communist commissars against a mutinous regiment of the People's Revolutionary Army. The mutineers' attempt to seize a steamer is thwarted by its resourceful commissar who lures the unruly soldiers into a trap and orders his platoon to open fire on them. *Protiv techeniia* is superior to *Razliv* in terms of composition and style, but its characters are still schematic, lacking psychological complexity. The critics applauded the story's vivid representation of the clash between the "elemental" forces of the revolt and the conscious class will of the proletariat.

In 1926 Fadeev returned to Moscow. The publication of his novel *Razgrom* (*The Rout*) made him a major proletarian writer and enhanced his authority in the field of literary theory. As a leader of the Russian Association of Proletarian Writers he advocated the "dialectical-materialist creative method", which required the description of life from a Marxist viewpoint. He equated materialism with realism and rejected romanticism as a manifestation of idealism, an embellishment of reality, and a defence of the exploiting classes. After the dissolution of proletarian literary organizations in 1932, Fadeev held high posts in the newly created Soviet Writers' Union.

Fadeev's second novel, *Poslednii iz Udege* [The Last of the Udege], remains incomplete. Conceived as a vast epic, it presents a multitude of characters from various social strata before and during the revolution. The story of the Udege, a far-eastern tribe, illustrates the idea that the salvation from the evils of capitalism lies not in the return to a primitive way of life, but in the transition to socialism. The novel's four published parts reveal a poorly developed plot and loose construction.

A collection of sketches entitled *Leningrad v dni blokady* (*Leningrad in the Days of the Blockade*) and the novel *Molodaia gvardiia* (*The Young Guard*) are Fadeev's principal contributions to the literature of World War II. Blending fact and fiction, *The Young Guard* is a dramatic story of an underground Komsomol organization of the same name operating in a Ukrainian town under Nazi occupation. The author highlights the political maturity of the young men and women, who managed to organize effective resistance without direct guidance by the local Party functionaries. The Komsomol fighters are highly idealized and romanticized, reflecting Fadeev's new belief that romanticism is vital for the representation of the ideals and dreams of the Soviet people. The novel's lyrical and heroic passages call to mind Nikolai Gogol''s *Taras Bulba*, while Tolstoi's influence is felt in the psychological probings.

The Young Guard was received with unanimous critical acclaim. But late in 1947 two articles inspired by Stalin accused Fadeev of failing to show the Party's leadership over the Komsomol underground and of describing the retreat of the Soviet troops and the evacuation of population as disorderly. Fadeev had to revise his novel radically. After slow, tortuous labour a new version of *The Young Guard* appeared in 1951. The author eliminated or softened episodes of panic and chaos during the 1942 retreat and added several chapters and scenes depicting the underground exploits of adult communists and their wise guidance over the Young Guards. Other insertions glorified Stalin and the Red Army. Except for a few political corrections prompted by de-Stalinization, the 1951 version was continually reprinted as the definitive text until 1990.

In September 1946 Fadeev was elected – in fact appointed – secretary general of the Soviet Writers' Union to carry out the Party directives for a total subordination of literature to political interests of the State. He did his duty by calling for a stiff rebuff to all alien ideologies and by attacking individual writers found guilty of ideological transgressions.

The heavy administrative burden virtually prevented Fadeev from writing fiction. In the early 1950s he managed to do some work on the industrial novel *Chernaia metallurgiia* [Ferrous Metallurgy], which focuses on the struggle around a technological discovery. After Stalin's death it transpired that the prototypes of Fadeev's daring innovators were indeed unscrupulous careerists while the prototypes of the "enemies of the people" turned out to be loyal Soviet citizens.

Due to de-Stalinization Fadeev lost his top post in the Writers' Union. His health was undermined by alcoholism. He was troubled by memories of the persecution of writers under Stalin and of his own role in this process. He was deeply disturbed by the growing bureaucratic oppression of literature and other arts and wrote about it to Nikita Khrushchev and Georgii Malenkov. His letter to the Party Central Committee concerning the ruination of literature was written on the day of his suicide.

HERMAN ERMOLAEV

The Rout

Razgrom

Novel (serialized 1925–26), 1927

The Rout originally appeared chapter by chapter in various journals during 1925 and 1926, and was first published as a separate edition in 1927. It immediately achieved enormous popularity and was subsequently reprinted many times. Fadeev continued to work on the text for more than 20 years, introducing a number of stylistic changes, amending chapter headings and eliminating material that might have been considered offensive. Its theme, like that of so many other works of fiction written in Soviet Russia during the 1920s, is the Civil War between the Bolsheviks and the Whites. Although the ideological content of the stories and novels dealing with this topic was constrained within fairly narrow and predictable bounds, the overall impression of such literature is one of variety rather than of grey uniformity. This arises not simply from the wide range of narrative method and form; there are also considerable differences in the extent to which historical events and the author's own experiences are used as the basis for the fictional story. In this respect *The Rout*, like so much else in Fadeev's life and career, takes a middle course, lying somewhere between the "factographical" approach of Furmanov's *Chapaev* and the almost nightmarish detachment from reality of Vsevolod Ivanov's *Bronepoezd 14-69* (*Armoured Train 14-69*). Set in the far east of Russia, it recounts the story of a detachment of Red partisans who, in the course of three months in 1919, are driven from their quarters by enemy forces, are forced to flee across unfamiliar terrain, succeed in extricating themselves from a seemingly impossible position, only to be ambushed and totally destroyed as a unit; only 19 of them survive.

The Rout differs in a number of significant respects from other stories and novels which were published roughly at the same time, and which are ostensibly of the same type – works such as *Chapaev*, Libedinskii's *Nedelia* (*A Week*), and Serafimovich's *Zheleznyi potok* (*The Iron Flood*). It is rare to have a story written by a committed Bolshevik that culminates in a catastrophe for his own side. The detachment's leader Levinson, who is at least partly responsible for the final debacle, is generally portrayed as someone who is far removed from the iron-jawed, infallible and legendary heroes of other contemporary fiction of this type. Levinson is seen not only from the outside, as a leader who commands the respect of his men, but also from the inside, beset by doubts, hesitations, and anxieties. Ostensibly he is in total control both of himself and of the situation; in actual fact, when crucial decisions concerning the detachment's future have to be made, he is as uncertain about the course of action to be taken as anyone else. Furthermore, although Levinson himself is clearly a Bolshevik (in his physical appearance he is not unlike Lenin) the story as a whole seems apolitical, lacking slogans, overt propaganda, or any direct references to Marxism-Leninism, the Revolution, Moscow, Petrograd, or the wider political struggle. For the greater part of the novel the majority of the characters are, like Levinson, portrayed in a non-stereotyped way, and Fadeev seemingly allows his readers to come to their own conclusions about them.

This, however, is sleight-of-hand. Fadeev's primary aim is to "tell" rather than "show", and indeed he drops all pretence of objectivity with the novel's two concluding paragraphs, immediately after the description of the ambush and the rout. The first shows the survivors riding out of the forest into a sunlit valley, with fields being harvested by happy, industrious workers and stretching as far as the eye can see. It is an extraordinary millennial scene deriving from Fadeev's romanticized notion of socialism and precisely anticipating the content and spirit of socialist realist paintings of the following decade. The second, and final, paragraph represents an equally abrupt change of tone, with its sober statement that it is necessary to fulfil one's duty. It is this banal platitude that contains the moral of the story: that people should be judged according to their sense of duty and their ability to respond to it. This can be seen, at least with hindsight, in the relationship and contrast between Mechik, the city intellectual whose cowardly act of treachery is the immediate cause of the detachment's destruction, and Morozka, the hotheaded and impulsive miner who acts foolishly and inconsiderately at first, but who comes to understand the need to behave responsibly. In so far as Levinson, and other characters such as Baklanov, Varia, and Goncharenko are concerned, it might be claimed that Fadeev is not so much criticizing them for their faults, as praising them for continuing to fight on in the face of extremely adverse circumstances; it is not by chance that the original title of Fadeev's second published story was *Protiv techeniia* [Against the Current], nor that such heroic achievement against the odds was precisely the theme of his later novel *The Young Guard*.

Taking the novel as a whole it is not immediately obvious that the socialist paradise glimpsed in the penultimate paragraph is worth all the struggle and the sacrifice, for Fadeev fails to show a believable link between the two. Even the person who embodies the qualities that Levinson lacks, the impulsive platoon leader Metelitsa, is unable to point the way ahead, and his death, for all his courage and *élan*, becomes merely an absurd irrelevance. Certainly Fadeev was taken to task by many on the left wing of the Bolshevik Party for producing in *The Rout* a work that was not suited to the new socialist era; instead of poor imitations of Tolstoi and psychological posturings they wanted a "literature of fact" that would inspire the work-force to greater productivity. Such criticism, however, consigns *The Rout* to a limbo, in which it is neither a proper work of art nor an effective political tract. In Fadeev's defence, it would be fairer to acknowledge that, in an age dominated by ideology and dogma, the qualities of moderation and balance assume a particular significance and value.

ROGER COCKRELL

Konstantin Aleksandrovich Fedin 1892–1977

Novelist and literary functionary

Biography

Born in Saratov, 24 February 1892, into a merchant family. Attended school in Saratov; Institute of Commerce (Moscow), 1911–14; degree in commerce in 1914. Moved to Germany 1913; arrested and interned as hostile alien until 1918; worked as interpreter and reporter, 1918–20. Married: Dora Sergeevna in early 1920s (died 1953); one daughter. Member of the Serapion Brothers. Worked as a correspondent during World War II. Recipient: Stalin Prize, 1948, 1950. President of the Soviet Writers' Union, 1971. Member of the editorial board, *Novyi mir*. Died 15 July 1977.

Publications

Collected Editions

Sobranie sochinenii, 6 vols. Moscow, 1952–54.
Sobranie sochinenii, 10 vols. Moscow, 1969–73.
Sobranie sochinenii, 12 vols. Moscow, 1984 – .

Fiction

Bakunin v Drezdene [Bakunin in Dresden]. Petrograd, 1922.
Pustyr' [The Wasteland]. Moscow, 1923.
Goroda i gody. Leningrad, 1924; translated as *Cities and Years*, by Michael Scammell, Westport, Connecticut, Greenwood Press, 1975; reprinted Evanston, Illinois, Northwestern University Press, 1993.
Muzhiki. Povest'. Leningrad, 1926.
Transvaal'. Leningrad, 1927; translated as *Transition Stories*, edited by Eugene Jolas and Robert Sarge, New York, Walter McVee, 1929.
Brat'ia [Brothers]. Leningrad, 1928.
Pokhishchenie Evropy [The Rape of Europe]. Leningrad, 1933–35.
Sanatorii Arktur. Moscow, 1940; translated as *Sanatorium Arktur*, by Olga Shartse, Moscow, Foreign Languages Publishing House, 1957.
Novye rasskazy [New Stories]. Moscow, 1940.
Pervye radosti. Moscow, 1946; translated as *Early Joys*, by Hilda Kazanina, Moscow, Foreign Languages Publishing House, 1948.
Davno i nedavno. Rasskazy [A Long Time Ago and Recently]. Moscow, 1947.
Neobyknovennoe leto. Saratov, 1948; translated as *No Ordinary Summer: A Novel in Two Parts*, by Margaret Wettlin, Moscow, Foreign Languages Publishing House, 1950.
Koster. Moscow, 1961–67; translated as *The Conflagration*, by Olga Shartse, Moscow, Progress, 1968.

Play

Ispytanie chuvstv [A Test of Feelings]. Moscow, 1942.

Memoirs

Gor'kii sredi nas [Gor'kii Among Us]. 1943.

Articles

Pisatel', iskusstvo, vremia. Stat'i [The Writer, Art, Time. Articles]. Moscow, 1957; 2nd edition, 1961.

Critical Studies

Konstantin Fedin, by Berta Brainina, Moscow, 1951; revised editions 1962, 1980.
Russian Fiction and Soviet Ideology: Introduction to Fedin, Leonov and Sholokhov, by Ernest Simmons, New York, Columbia University Press, 1958.
Konstantin Fedin: A Descriptive and Analytic Study, by Julius Blum, The Hague, Mouton, 1967.
Konstantin Fedin: Ocherk tvorchestva, by Nikolai Kuznetsov, Moscow, 1969.
"Some Problems of Construction in Fedin's *Cities and Years*", by Elizabeth K. Beaujour, *Slavic and East European Journal*, 16 (1972), 1–18.
Fedin i zapad, by Berta Brainina, Moscow, 1979.
K.A. Fedin - khudozhnik. Problemy metoda i stilia, by Nikolai Kuznetsov, Tomsk, 1980.
Stupeni masterstva: Ocherk tvorchestva Konstantina Fedina, Anatolii Starkov, Moscow, 1985.
Vospominaniia o Konstantine Fedine, compiled by N.K. Fedina, Moscow, 1988.
"Two Pioneers of the Soviet Novel: Konstantin Fedin and Boris Pil'niak", by Victor Erlich, in *Modernism and Revolution, Russian Literature in Transition*, Cambridge, Massachusetts, Harvard University Press, 1994, 121–44.

Konstantin Fedin's first published work "Melochi" [Trifles] appeared in *Novyi satirikon* in 1913. Just before the outbreak of World War I Fedin went to Germany to improve his German. He was caught up in the war and detained in Silesia, then in Saxony until 1918. He worked as an interpreter at the first Soviet Embassy in Germany. On his return to Russia he worked in various institutions, and during 1919 and 1920 he was employed by a number of frontline newspapers as a reporter. He worked in Leningrad as a journalist and as an editor of *Kniga i revoliutsiia* (1921–24); there he met his wife Dora Sergeevna. In 1920 he became a friend of Gor'kii, who liked Fedin's stories and introduced him to the Serapion Brotherhood; his contributions were included in their almanac in 1922.

Fedin's first collection of stories was *Pustyr'* [The Wasteland]. Despite some elements of ornamental prose, his works display the influence of more traditional authors such as Chekhov and Bunin. His story "Sad" ("The Orchard"), set in the revolutionary period, tells of a frustrated gardener who sets his master's estate on fire; the work won first prize at the House of Writers. His novel *Goroda i gody* (*Cities and Years*), published in 1924, is one of the first Soviet novels about the October Revolution and the Civil War. It reflects on the fate and destiny of the Russian intelligentsia in their new circumstances. Andrei Startsov, the main character, is another "superfluous man" produced by Russian literature. He studies in Germany before the outbreak of World War I, where he befriends an artist, Kurt Wahn, as well as a certain Marie Urbach; both of them help him to escape to Russia. Startsov meets Kurt again in Semidol, where he gets involved in revolutionary activities. The novel ends tragically with Andrei's execution at Kurt's hands, but Fedin includes Kurt's explanation of why he killed Andrei at the beginning of the novel. The disruption of the chronology reveals Fedin's attempt to break with the narrative modes of 19th-century literature; he focuses instead on the psychology of the characters, and the atmosphere, allowing some documentary details to permeate the story line. The novel proved a great success.

Fedin's second novel *Brat'ia* [The Brothers] was published in 1928. It features another intellectual, Nikita Karev, a composer who would like to find his place in the new life. His attempts to bow to political demands of the time are ambiguous. The novel is written in the modernist manner, containing also temporal displacements. Fedin then went on to spend several years in Europe (1928–34), where he underwent treatment for tuberculosis and met many European writers. His next novel, *Pokhishchenie Evropy* [The Rape of Europe], published between 1933 and 1935, was inspired by his stay in Switzerland. It is a critical depiction of Europe, seen through the eyes of the Soviet journalist Ivan Rogov, who defends socialist ideals. It was sharply criticized for its poor characterization and weak plot.

In spite of the fact that Fedin was labelled a fellow-traveller in the 1920s, he was elected to the board of the newly created Writers' Union in 1934. His novels became very conformist and uninspiring. Another portrayal of the west in decline appeared in his 1940 novel *Sanatorii Arktur* (*Sanatorium Arktur*). Fedin was a war correspondent during World War II; his patriotic play *Ispytanie chuvstv* [A Test of Feelings] depicts the heroine Aglaia, involved with the anti-German resistance. His memoirs about Gor'kii and other literary figures of the 1920s, *Gor'kii sredi nas* [Gor'kii Among Us], was criticized in the official press and was withdrawn from circulation. Fedin responded to this criticism by producing a trilogy, featuring positive heroes: *Pervye radosti* (*Early Joys*), *Neobyknovennoe leto* (*No Ordinary Summer*), and the unfinished third part, *Koster* (*The Conflagration*). The main characters of this trilogy, Kirill Izvekov and Petr Ragozin, are professional revolutionaries. Once again the questions of new art and revolutionary humanism are central in these novels. Some critics noted the influence of Tolstoi on Fedin's style; especially in relation to the portrayal of Pastukhov, a writer who grows to accept the demands of his times. Fedin received the Stalin Prize in 1948 and 1950. In 1959 he became the First Secretary of the Writers' Union, then in 1971 he was elected chairman; from then until his death in 1977 Fedin was on the editorial board of *Novyi mir*. Having failed to support Pasternak over *Doctor Zhivago*, he was also responsible for the ban on Solzhenitsyn's *Rakovyi korpus* (*Cancer Ward*) in 1968, thus confirming, against original expectations, his hardline attitude towards reformists and dissidents.

ALEXANDRA SMITH

Cities and Years

Goroda i gody

Novel, 1924

A novel of considerable interest in its time, acclaimed both for its novelty in structural, stylistic terms and for its latter-day "superfluous man" theme, *Cities and Years* has not survived changes of taste and government as well as most early works of Soviet literature. This must be due partly to Fedin's own reputation. Although he contributed to Soviet literature in the 1920s by displaying elegance and stylishness in his writing, this could not hide a certain lack of substance which, in the post-World War II period, led him to write a trilogy of almost sycophantically orthodox socialist realist novels (*Early Joys*; *No Ordinary Summer*; *The Conflagration*) covering Russian history in the first half of the century. His official role as First Secretary of the Soviet Writers' Union also tarnished his reputation by turning him into a Party spokesman on literature which meant, among other things, that he was responsible for preventing the publication of Solzhenitsyn's *Cancer Ward*.

Yet his reputation as a writer can now be seen to be diminished in other ways. Superficially Fedin seemed to promise much – an elegance of expression reminiscent of 19th-century writing, a concern with intellectual issues, a capacity for a Tolstoian broad sweep in his treatment of subjects, a certain "western" or "European" tone – but the superficial promise, for all its surface brightness and interest, did not sustain close scrutiny and tended in the end to suggest a tentativeness in the writer bordering on cowardice, especially in dealing with questions of individual moral choice and conscience.

Cities and Years illustrates some of these weaknesses, but it also has redeeming strengths. In so far as Andrei Startsov is the novel's hero, then it is the story of his imprisonment in Germany during World War I where he meets and falls in love with a girl from a wealthy German family, Marie Urbach. He has a rival for her affections in a local aristocrat, Markgraf von zur Mühlen-Schönau, who aids him when he is captured after escaping from internment. Such help invokes a debt of honour which for Andrei is to prove lethal. After returning to Russia he and his close friend Kurt Wahn, a German artist who has committed himself to the communist cause, are sent to an area of the Volga where they set about working to introduce new Soviet institutions. A bloodthirsty uprising among the Mordov people, somewhat improbably engineered by the Markgraf who had been Andrei's rival, is put down; he seeks Andrei's help and Andrei, still deeply in love with Marie Urbach, arranges for him to be supplied with false documents so that he can escape back to Germany. There he is able to resume his aristocratic life oblivious of what has happened, whereas Andrei Startsov, his saviour, is exposed as a class enemy and summarily executed by Kurt Wahn, his erstwhile best friend.

The contrivances of the story are evident from this brief synopsis. They are more obvious still in the way the novel is structured. It opens with Kurt Wahn justifying his role as executioner and only later supplies the background – Andrei's German experience, the relationship with Marie and so on – which can be said to turn Andrei into the supposed class enemy who deserves such a fate. There is a token circularity to the way the novel is composed that provides a degree of novelty to the otherwise improbable story, but this cannot disguise the fact that the characters themselves, especially the German "hero" Kurt Wahn and his German counterpart, the "villain", the Markgraf, appear implausibly thin, ideological constructs rather than figures with blood in their veins.

Yet this is a novel that recounts events involving terrible bloodshed and violence in vivid and horrifying detail. The autobiographical element in the novel supplied by Fedin's imprisonment in Germany during World War I provides a deeply atmospheric picture of German provincial life. Similarly, scenes of incidents during the Civil War in Russia involving brief pen portraits of communists, peasants, citizens of Petrograd and so on are testimony to Fedin's descriptive powers as a writer and give his work an undoubted strength and authority. There is a similar authority about the novel's principal portrait, that of the "superfluous man", Andrei Startsov. A pacifist, characterized by the vaguely humanitarian idealism of the pre-revolutionary intelligentsia, attracted to Tolstoianism after a fashion, a man of words on the whole rather than a man of action, Andrei Startsov has the makings of a tragic hero. He is tragic in the sense that he finds himself "superfluous" in Soviet Russia, to which he cannot ideologically or emotionally commit himself; and in the inevitable conflict between his individualism and the new social and political conformity imposed by communism he chooses personal happiness and so becomes a class enemy and social pariah. His portrayal is sympathetic enough for his dilemma to seem real despite the fact that his love for Marie Urbach or the girl Rita, who becomes his mistress, is scarcely credible as overpowering passion. As a portrait of an intellectual faced by difficult choices, he is memorable largely because he was honest enough to doubt the fashionable nostrums of the time.

Fedin was remorseless towards his hero, but his novel's message was sufficiently ambiguous and original in a political sense for it to require a certain amount of reworking for editions published in 1932 and 1959. Nevertheless, it retained its intrinsic freshness. Although manifestly silly in some aspects of its story-line, the novel can still claim a reader's attention and admiration for its literary quality and its power to evoke the revolutionary atmosphere of the Soviet period. In the end one must pay due respect to Fedin himself for having given his novel such a catchy title, even though "cities and years" explains very little about it.

RICHARD FREEBORN

Afanasii Afanas'evich Fet 1820–1892

Poet and memoirist

Biography

Born in Novoselki, Mtsensk on the estate of Afanasii Neofitovich Shenshin, a Russian landowner, in October or November 1820 (three different dates given for his birth). Mother, Charlotte Fet (Foeth), was German. The child was baptized as Shenshin's son but probably fathered by Charlotte's legal husband, Johann Foeth; latter did not recognize child as his son. Shenshin and Charlotte Fet married, 1822; but church authorities forbade poet to use name Shenshin, or claim inheritance. Attempts to attain necessary army rank to entitle him to status of nobleman thwarted when threshold was twice raised. Achieved the right to call himself Shenshin and rank and privileges of a nobleman only in 1873. Attended a German boarding-school in Lithuania; studied in the faculty of history and philology, Moscow University, 1838–44. Joined cavalry regiment, 1844. First collection *Liricheskii panteon* [Lyrical Pantheon] published, 1840. Collected Works published, 1850. Love affair with Mariia Lazich, 1848–50. Poverty prevented their marrying; Mariia died in a fire, 1850. Married: Mariia Petrovna Botkina in 1857. Left the army 1858. Withdrew from literature and retired to Stepanovka, his estate in Mtsensk province, 1860. Abandoned farming and moved to Vorob'evka in Kursk province, 1877. Resumed literary career, 1881. Died in Moscow, 3 December 1892.

Publications

Collected Editions

Polnoe sobranie stikhotvorenii. Leningrad, 1959.
Sochineniia, 2 vols. Moscow, 1982.
I Have Come to Greet You: Selected Poems, translated by James Greene. London, Angel, 1982.

Poetry

Liricheskii panteon [Lyrical Pantheon]. 1840.
Vechernie ogni [Evening Fires]. 1883; reprinted Moscow, 1971.

Memoirs

Vospominaniia. Moscow, 1983.

Critical Studies

The Imagination of Spring: The Poetry of Afanasii Fet, by R.F. Gustafson, New Haven, Yale University Press, 1966.
"Dynamic Elements in the Lyrics of Fet", by Rimvydas Silbajoris, *Slavic Review*, 26 (1967), 217–26.
"Annualarity as a Melodic Principle in Fet's Verse", by A.D.P. Briggs, *Slavic Review*, 28 (1969), 591–603.
"Lermontov, Tyutchev and Fet", by T.J. Binyon, in *Nineteenth-Century Russian Literature: Studies of Ten Russian Writers*, edited by John Fennell, London, Faber, and Berkeley, University of California Press, 1973, 168–224.

"The Metrical Virtuosity of Afanasy Fet", by A.D.P. Briggs, *Slavonic and East European Review*, 52 (1974), 355–65.
Afanasy Fet, by Lydia Lotman, translated by Margaret Wettlin, Boston, Twayne, 1976.
"Metamorphoses of the Will: Schopenhauer and Fet", by H. Stammler, in *Western Philosophical Systems in Russian Literature: A Collection of Critical Studies*, edited by Anthony M. Mlikotin, Los Angeles, University of Southern California Press, 1979, 35–58.
"A.A. Fet", by Vasily Botkin, translated by G. Genereux, *Russian Literature Triquarterly*, 17 (1982), 23–63.
"On the Sources of Fet's Aesthetics of Music: Wackenroder, Schopenhauer and Ševyrev", by Emily Klenin, *Die Welt der Slaven*, 30 (1985), 319–44.
"On Groups of Poems in Books by Fet", by Emily Klenin, *Elementa*, 2/3–4 (1996), 295–310.

Afanasii Fet was the leading Russian representative of the movement known variously as "Art for Art's sake", "Pure Art" or "Parnassianism". It is easier to define by what it is *not*, than by what it *is*. Fet's poetry is not, for example, concerned with any of the dominant political or social issues of the day. Thus there is no mention of serfdom, autocracy, the future of Russia, urban squalor or the woman question. When Belinskii, reinterpreting Hegel, was calling in 1840 for engaged, committed literature, Fet was publishing his first poems. Soon he was to publish his famous poem "Ia prishel k tebe s privetom" ("I Have Come to Greet You"). This 16-line lyric celebrates, in a single sentence, the coming of spring which, for Fet, was always a symbol not only of creativity and poetic inspiration, but also of eternity and it occurs in many of his most celebrated poems, such as "Eshche maiskaia noch'" [Again a May Night] (1857), and "Pchely" [Bees] (1854). The "you" of "I Have Come to Greet You" is the beloved who, here, as in many of Fet's poems, such as "Alter ego" (1878), is a barely glimpsed presence. It is, perhaps, not too far-fetched to regard the "you" as the Russian reader to whom the young poet will narrate (the word recurs four times in the poem) his new vision of poetry. The last two lines – "I don't know what I will / Sing, but only that a song is maturing" – underline the fact that Fet was a true lyricist. He regarded poetry as song and valued musicality above any other poetic virtue. In reponse to laudatory words from Tchaikovskii, Fet wrote: "Tchaikovskii is a thousand times right, since I've always been drawn from the definite sphere of words into the indefinite sphere of music, into which I retreated as far as my strength would allow". He claimed that music was necessary for the expression of poetic feeling because it alone "can convey both thought and feelings not separately, not consecutively, but together like, as it were, a cascade". Elsewhere he wrote: "Poetry and music are not only related; they are inseparable. All poetic works through the centuries, from the prophets to Goethe and Pushkin are, in essence, musical works – songs". Such statements, reminiscent of Verlaine's "De la musique avant toute chose", were particularly attractive to the Russian Symbolists who embraced Fet, as they had Tiutchev, as an indigenous precursor of their movement. Equally such statements were anathema to left-wing figures such as Chernyshevskii and Saltykov-Shchedrin, who were scathing in their denunciation of Fet. The former, while acknowledging that Fet had talent, wrote that the poems could as well have been written by a horse as a human, while the latter described Fet's poetic world as "narrow, monotonous and limited". Even Nekrasov, whose *Sovremennik* journal had made Fet the best-known poet of the 1850s, turned against him in the 1860s. The point is not that Fet's verse is any more musical than, say, that of Pushkin, but that musicality predominates over content. The most extreme form of this can be seen in the celebrated verbless poems "Buria na nebe vechernem" [Storm in the Evening Sky] and "Shepot. Robkoe dykhanie" [A Whisper. Timid Breathing]. Both poems are impressionistic in form, consisting mainly of a series of nouns. The focus is not on the storm or the whisper but on the effect of these on the poet. Indeed, the emotions of the poet lie at the centre of Fet's work – the word "heart" (*serdtse*) is omnipresent in his poems. The emotions may be pleasurable but there is a dark side to Fet's work. In, for instance, "Na stoge sena iuzhnoi noch'iu" [On a Hayrick, on a Southern Night] (1857), the poet feels at one with the night sky. The last line, however, is ominous: "I drown ever more irrevocably". By nature given to pessimism, a state doubtless exacerbated by his disrupted childhood and protracted struggle to claim his birthright, Fet was much influenced by the philosophy of Schopenhauer, a debt which he acknowledged explicitly in "Izmuchen zhizn'iu ..." [Exhausted by Life] (1864). There is very little development in Fet's poetry. A work such as "Sentiabr'skaia roza" ("The September Rose") (1890), which, in three quatrains moves from the blooming of the last rose of summer, to its queen-like beauty and its being worn on the bosom of a young woman, could as well have been written at the height of his fame in the 1850s as in his old age. Roses appear in many of his poems, most notably in the programmatic "Solovei i roza" [The Nightingale and the Rose] (1847). The garden, too, is a frequent image in Fet's poetry and there are over 70 references to nightingales in his work. He remained a poet of the countryside, of the Russian estates that meant so much to him during his lifetime: the family estate at Novoselki; Berezovka, the estate of his fellow-officer and lifelong friend Aleksei Brzheskii and Fedorovka, in Kherson province, the estate of the Lazich family. The poem "Staryi park" [The Old Park] (1853) is the poetic equivalent of such wistful evocations of the rural idyll as Turgenev's *Dvorianskoe gnezdo* (*A Nest of the Gentry*).

Fet's other verse is relatively unimportant. It consists of three narrative poems and a large number of translations from, among others, Goethe, Schiller, Byron, Chenier, Musset, and Mickiewicz. His prose output consists of seven short stories, the most interesting of which is "Kaktus" [Cactus] (1881) where the "gypsy" theme evident in such poems as "Iarkim solntsem v lesu plameneet koster" [Like a Bright Sun in the Forest the Bonfire Flares] (1859) is also clearly to be seen. He also wrote articles on both agriculture and literature, notably on his fellow poet Fedor Tiutchev, and conducted a rich correspondence, most importantly with his fellow Parnassian Iakov Polonskii and with Lev Tolstoi. However, apart from his lyrics, it is his memoirs, running to more than 1500 pages, which will ensure Fet's place as one of the leading literary figures of the 19th century.

MICHAEL PURSGLOVE

Denis Ivanovich Fonvizin 1745–1792

Dramatist and translator

Biography

Born in Moscow, 14 April 1745. Attended Moscow University gymnasium, 1755–60; Moscow University, 1760–62. Moved to St Petersburg and entered civil service: secretary to Ivan Elagin in Foreign Ministry, 1763–69; secretary to the statesman Count Nikita Ivanovich Panin, from 1769. Granted an estate, 1773. Married: Ekaterina Khlopova in 1774. Travelled to France and Germany, 1777–78; achieved dramatic success with the St Petersburg production of *Nedorosl'* (*The Minor*); retired from public life following the death of Panin (1783) and after incurring the displeasure of Catherine the Great. Founding member of Russian Academy, 1783. Works temporarily banned, early 1780s. Travelled to Germany and Italy, 1784–85; suffered a severe stroke, 1785. Planned to launch a periodical, *Starodum*, which never appeared on account of censorship. Travelled to Austria for health reasons, 1786–87. Died in St Petersburg, 12 December 1792.

Publications

Collected Editions

Polnoe sobranie sochinenii, 4 vols. 1830.

Pervoe polnoe sobranie sochinenii. St Petersburg and Moscow, 1888.

Sobranie sochinenii, 2 vols. Moscow and Leningrad, 1959.

The Dramatic Works (includes *The Minor*, *The Brigadier*, *The Selection of a Tutor*, and excerpt of *A Good Mentor*), translated by Marvin Kantor. Bern and Frankfurt, Lang, 1974.

Sochineniia, edited by A.I. Vredinskii. Moscow, 1983.

Plays

Korion [Korion], from a play by Jean-Baptiste Gresset (produced St Petersburg, 1764).

Brigadir (produced St Petersburg, 1780); translated as "The Brigadier", in *The Literature of Eighteenth-Century Russia* 2, edited and translated by Harold B. Segel, New York, Dutton, 1968; also by Marvin Kantor, in *The Dramatic Works*, 1974.

Nedorosl' (produced St Petersburg, 1782), 1783; translated as "The Young Hopeful", by George R. Noyes, in *Masterpieces of the Russian Drama*, edited by Noyes, New York and London, Appleton, 1933; also as "The Minor", by F.D. Reeve, in *Anthology of Russian Plays 1*, New York, Vintage, 1961; also by Marvin Kantor, in *The Dramatic Works*, 1974; and as "The Infant", by Joshua Cooper, in *Four Russian Plays*, Harmondsworth, Penguin, 1972.

Vybor guverneva (produced 1790), in *Polnoe sobranie sochinenii*, 1830; translated as "The Choice of a Tutor", in *Five Russian Plays with One from the Ukrainian*, edited by C.E.B. Roberts, London, Paul Trench Trubner, 1916; also as *The Selection of a Tutor*, by Marvin Kantor, in *The Dramatic Works*, 1974.

Alzir; ili, Amerikantsy [Alzire; or, The Americans], from a play by Voltaire, in *Pervoe polnoe sobranie sochinenii*, 1888.

Letters, Biography, and Essays

Lettres de France de D.I. von Vizine à sa soeur à Moscou, edited by E.M. de Vogüé. 1888.

Zhizn' grafa N.I. Panina [The Life of Count N.I. Panin], 1784 (in French); 1786 (in Russian).

The Political and Legal Writings of Denis Fonvizin, translated by Walter Gleason. Ann Arbor, Ardis, 1985.

Translator

Basni nravouchitel'nye s iziasneniami [Moralistic Fables with Explanations], from Holberg's fables, 1761; augmented edition, 1765.

Geroiskaia dobrodetel'; ili, zhizn' Sifa [Heroic Virtue or the Life of Sif], by Jean Terrasson, 4 vols, 1762–68.

Liubov' Karity i Polidora [The Love of Carita and Polydore], by Jean-Jacques Barthélémy, 1763.

Torguiushchee dvorianstvo [The Commercial Nobility], by Gabriel-François Coyer, 1766.

Sidny i Silly [Sidney and Silly], by François-Thomas Baculard d'Arnaud, 1769.

Joseph, by Paul-Jérémie Bitaube, 1769.

Rassuzhdenie o natsional'nom liubochesti [An Essay on National Patriotism], by Johann Zimmermann, 1785.

Critical Studies

Tvorchestvo Fonvizina, by K.V. Pigarev, Moscow, 1954.

Fonvizin v russkoi kritike, Moscow, 1958.

Denis Fonvizin, by G.P. Makogonenko, Moscow and Leningrad, 1961.

Russian Comedy 1765–1823, by David J. Welsh, The Hague, Mouton, 1966.

"Fonvizin and Holberg: A Comparison of 'The Brigadier' and 'Jean de France'", by Marvin Kantor, *Canadian Slavic Studies*, 7 (1973), 475–84.

Denis Fonvizine. La Russia des lumières, by Alexis Strycek, Paris, Librairie de cinq continents, 1976.

"Brigadir" i "Nedorosl'" D.I. Fonvizina, by I.V. Isakovich, Leningrad, 1979.

Denis Fonvizin, by Charles A. Moser, Boston, Twayne, 1979.

A History of 18th Century Russian Literature, by William Edward Brown, Ann Arbor, Ardis, 1980.

Fonvizin, by Stanislav Rassadin, Moscow, 1980.

Russian Drama from Its Beginnings to the Age of Pushkin, by Simon Karlinsky, Berkeley, University of California Press, 1985.

Bibliography

Saggio di una bibliografia del Fonvizin, by L. Savoj, Rome, 1935.

Denis Fonvizin, a late-18th-century satirical dramatist, whose name derives from German ancestry (Von Wiesen), occupies a special place in the Russian theatre. His early work may be disregarded by all but the specialist. A poor verse translation of Voltaire's *Alzire* in 1762 was followed two years later by something only slightly more original, an adaptation of Gresset's sentimental verse drama *Sidnei*, given the Russian title *Korion*. Stilted and clumsy though it was, this play possessed some modest quality and knew a certain success. It is best remembered for historical rather than artistic reasons: it was confident enough to give a substantial part to a serf character, Andrei, and it was an early promoter of French-style sentimental drama, which was soon to enjoy great popularity in Russia. Fonvizin had no natural poetic instinct, however, and it was only when he turned to prose, unconventionally for a leading dramatist of that time, that his work broke new ground and showed real quality. His reputation rests on a small body of work, only two comedies, one of which (*Nedorosl'* (*The Minor*)) remains popular to this day.

Fonvizin's first real success was *Brigadir* (*The Brigadier*). Long considered an imitation, this play is now established as an original work. An amusing comedy, it depends for its quality less upon the story or even its characters than its one big idea, the satirizing of Francomania, which had infected the Russian nation. Since the worst manifestation of this absurdity occurred in modern speech the piece is full of linguistic jokes. It is therefore as effective when read as it would be on the stage, and perhaps for this reason it has not survived as a serious contender for performance nowadays. The story concerns two fathers who are supposedly arranging a marriage between their offspring, but each of them woos the other man's wife; a sequence of rather farcical embarrassments is ultimately resolved so that the good are rewarded and the scoundrels shamefully exposed. The play is written in Russian prose, except that some of the characters begin almost every speech with "Hélas!", "Madame", "Mon dieu!" or some similar French exclamation and interlard snippets of French into every other sentence. This affectation is amusing enough in itself, but what is even more entertaining is the constant coining of pseudo-Russian words from French originals when perfectly good Russian equivalents already exist. *Diskiutirovat'* (to discuss), *ekskiuzovat'* (to excuse) and even *ekzistirovat'* (to exist) are preferred to such common expressions as *razgovarivat'*, *izvinit'* and *sushchestvovat'*. Patriotic Russian audiences took to this healthy repudiation of an unwanted national habit and much enjoyed the verbal fun. Beyond that the play has little meaning or achievement.

More successful in every way was Fonvizin's masterpiece, *The Minor* (also translated as *The Infant*, *The Young Hopeful*, etc) (1782), which has no close rival for the title of Russia's finest pre-19th-century play. It carries forward the credit balance of overt humour in *The Brigadier* (some of it on similar themes) and adds to that sum both a more serious purpose and an artful method. *The Minor* goes beyond its predecessor, holding up to ridicule several different, and more significant, aspects of contemporary life. The nobility in general, their corruption, conservatism, philistinism, and barbaric treatment of the lower orders, their tedious process of raising successive generations schooled in the same detestable defects of character and quality – all of this is castigated in the play.

Despite the conventional plot, many coincidences and sermonizing passages, not to mention the prissiness of the virtuous characters, *The Minor* has much to offer, especially in the depiction of negative types, who manage to seem almost like real people with only slight exaggeration of their human failings. The author was proud of his uninteresting "inspirational" characters, but time has played a friendly trick on him. Their otherworldliness now disqualifies them from serious attention, whereas their repulsive adversaries still enjoy a humorous negative charm akin to that of Molière's familiar archetypes. The same applies to a number of uplifting rhetorical passages filled with noble sentiments. Necessary and exemplary in their day, they are now required for other reasons, partly as historical curiosities but mainly to serve as a foil for the comedy, decisive breaks in the flow of entertainment.

Humorous dialogue nicely distracts from the satirical intent throughout *The Minor*. In the first scene Prostakova sets the tone by pampering her brutish boy, henpecking her miserable spouse and treating her serf-tailor like an animal, the satirical message being well-wrapped in funny business. This is how the play will proceed, skilfully diverting the audience and sometimes skipping through quite risky moments, as in the last act when Starodum holds forth on the qualities of the ideal monarch, possibly implying that Russia does not possess one. Nowadays the play's success on the stage will depend substantially on its unsubtle humour, as in the fawning of Prostakova on Sof'ia's uncle in Act II, her egging-on of her son to be equally obsequious in Act III, and a series of absurd tutors hired for Mitrofan, these last on loan, it might seem, from Molière's *Le Bourgeois Gentilhomme*. *The Minor* can still be watched with unfeigned pleasure; it is a genuinely funny play.

Fonvizin was never to equal this achievement. His last writings are either incomplete or predominantly concerned with civic duty and politics. It is for his two plays that he is remembered with pride in Russia.

A.D.P. Briggs

The Minor

Nedorosl'

Play, 1782

Fonvizin's play *The Minor*, a five-act comedy of manners completed and first performed in 1782, is usually considered the outstanding achievement of Russian drama before Griboedov's *Gore ot uma* (*Woe from Wit*). Although the play has a moralizing tone and a number of stilted characters its effective comic scenes, its lively portrayal of the philistine elements in the provincial nobility in the age of Catherine II (ruled 1762–96), and its vigorous language raise it artistically above the rhetorical set pieces written in the Neoclassical mode by Fonvizin's near contemporary Sumarokov. At the same time the play's discourse on the actual and ideal mores of the contemporary nobility lend it interest for the intellectual historian.

Set on a provincial estate the play begins with a number of scenes showing an ignorant, selfish family of nobles in which Madame Prostakova tyrannizes her husband, Prostakov, and her brother Skotinin (whose dominant trait is his love of pigs), not to mention her ill-treated serfs. She also dotes on her lazy, obtuse and gluttonous son, Mitrofan, the "minor" of the play's title. Living with the Prostakovs is Sof'ia, an orphaned relation on the husband's side of the family, whom it is planned to marry off, without her consent, to Skotinin. Sof'ia, however, unexpectedly receives a letter (which the Prostakovs, being illiterate, are unable to read) from her uncle, Starodum, who has been away for many years in Siberia (a symbol of uncorrupted territory where it is still possible to prosper by honest means). Starodum has amassed a fortune to which Sof'ia is to be the heir. On hearing news of Sof'ia's undreamt-of potential wealth Prostakova conceives the idea of marrying her off to Mitrofan instead. It emerges, however, that Sof'ia herself is in love with Milon, a worthy young officer stationed with his regiment in the neighbourhood. In Act III Starodum himself appears and with the help of Pravdin (who is a sort of plenipotentiary of the enlightened local governor, with instructions to ensure the good conduct of the local gentry) and of Milon (whom Starodum interviews and approves) he eventually succeeds in rescuing his niece from the clutches of Prostakova, though not before an attempt has been made, in Act V, to abduct her. The play ends with Pravdin dispensing justice: the estate is sequestered, so that the wrongs done by Prostakova to her serfs may cease, and the brat Mitrofan is sent away to serve the state.

The characters are crudely divided into two camps, their merit or lack of it clearly indicated by their names. On the one side we have Starodum (suggesting an old way of thinking; Fonvizin has in mind the supposedly good morals of the Petrine gentry); Pravdin (the name implies *pravda*, "truth" or "justice"); Sof'ia (the name is derived from the Greek word for "wisdom"); and Milon (the name carries associations of goodness and kindness, even charity and mercy). On the other side we have the Prostakovs (i.e. "simpletons") and Prostakova's coarse brother, Skotinin (the name relates to *skot*, "cattle"). The plight of the serfs is represented by the sufferings of the faithful old house-servant, Mitrofan's maid Eremeevna. There are also three tutors engaged in the thankless task of trying to instruct Mitrofan in grammar, scripture, arithmetic, geography and other disciplines: Kuteikin (the word suggests *kuteinik*, a derogatory term for a member of the priesthood); Tsyfirkin (derived from *tsifra*, "figure" or "number") and the foreigner Vral'man (a Germanized derivation from *vral'*, "liar"). These tutors are figures of fun, although Tsyfirkin is finally presented as having some integrity inasmuch as he refuses the fees due to him for his lessons on the grounds that he has failed to teach Mitrofan anything. Vral'man – who has inveigled himself into the gullible Prostakov household and who, with his atrocious Russian, is the butt of some xenophobic comedy – is eventually humbled when he is revealed as Starodum's former coachman and is taken back into Starodum's employ as the latter sets off for Moscow at the end of the play.

The play should be seen against the background of the consolidation of the nobility's privileged position in the second half of the 18th century, following their exemption from service to the state in 1762 by Peter III (their rights were confirmed in the Charter issued by Catherine in 1785). It represents Fonvizin's contribution to the debate among the better educated and more enlightened members of that class as to the responsibilities that such privilege might entail. Fonvizin is concerned to cultivate ideals of good character and morality that owe much both to classical Roman and 18th-century French examples. To that end his virtuous characters set a tone at the beginning of each act after Act I by expatiating on such subjects as honour, glory, self-seeking, cupidity, and corruption at court. Thus Fonvizin implicitly points to an ideal state of affairs in which an enlightened monarch ensures that in the well-ordered polity noblemen act virtuously and mete out condign punishment for immoral conduct (*zlonravie*), a moral pointed up by Starodum in the closing line of the play. The key to the development of the good morals is education, conceived in a broad sense and embracing moral upbringing as well as acquisition of practical knowledge. It is lack of education, on the other hand, which in the last analysis explains the brutishness of the Prostakovs who, with their contempt for knowledge that does not obviously serve their selfish material interest, represent the bulk of the provincial nobility of Fonvizin's day.

DEREK OFFORD

Frol Skobeev, the Rogue

Anonymous late 17th-century tale

Edition

"Povest' o Frole Skobeeve", in *Pamiatniki literatury Drevnei Rusi. XVII vek. Kniga pervaia*, edited by L.A. Dmitriev and D.S. Likhachev. Moscow, 1988, 55–64.

Translation

Frol Skobeev, the Rogue, by Serge A. Zenkovsky, in his *Medieval Russia's Epics, Chronicles, and Tales*. New York, Dutton, 1963, 397–409.

Critical Study

A History of Seventeenth-Century Russian Literature, by William Edward Brown, Ann Arbor, Ardis, 1980.

Povest' o Frole Skobeeve (*Frol Skobeev, the Rogue*) is an excellent illustration of the late 17th-century appearance in Russia of a truly secular literature, composed primarily as entertainment and in clear contrast to earlier medieval moralistic didacticism. The reforms of Peter the Great encouraged widespread secularization of society and increased literacy, resulting in the Church authorities losing their long-held monopoly over literary activity. This tale is often considered the first native Russian picaresque novella and was obviously extremely popular judging by the numerous extant manuscript copies. One version mentions the year 1680 as the time of the action, although it is most probable that the tale was not actually written until the very end of the 17th century. Taking into account the language, the apparent similarity of some of the names in the tale to well-known contemporary figures, and detailed topographical knowledge of the city, it is most likely that the author was a Muscovite.

The tale recounts how Frol Skobeev, an impecunious nobleman and infamous local rogue from the district of Novgorod, devises a scheme to enable him to marry Annushka, daughter of the wealthy Nardin-Nashchokin who served at the tsar's court in Moscow. Disguised in female attire, Frol tricks his way into a party held by Annushka and orchestrates a chance to be alone with Annushka in her bedchamber, where he forcibly seduces her. Annushka adopts a stoic attitude towards her lost innocence, admitting that what is gone cannot be regained, and proceeds to detain Frol at her home for a further three days and nights of carnal abandonment. Annushka is soon, however, called to Moscow where potential suitors await her. Frol's lower social status automatically excludes him from the list, although he follows Annushka to Moscow anyhow. Annushka rapidly and cunningly arranges her own elopement with Frol and they are married immediately. They remain in hiding until the tsar himself becomes involved in the search and Frol fears dire punishment. When he finally informs Nardin-Nashchokin of the marriage, Annushka's parents are enraged and curse their daughter's rash and disobedient actions. They send a servant to Frol's home to discover how Annushka is faring, but once again they are outwitted by Frol, who instructs his wife to feign serious illness. Citing parental anger as the cause of Annushka's grave condition, he hints that, should they send her their blessing, her suffering would be eased. Not only is their blessing sent, but also icons, gold, gems and money. With time Nardin-Nashchokin forgives Annushka and appears begrudingly to accept Frol into his family, although remaining anxious to keep secret the fact that such a rogue has wed his daughter, even sending the couple off to a large and distant country estate, where he essentially pays them to remain. A life of luxury and comfort is seemingly guaranteed, as, on Nardin-Nashchokin's death, Frol inherits all his father-in-law's wealth and property.

Structurally the tale divides easily into two halves: the first half comprises a chain of rapid action and intrigue, the reader being carried along on a compulsive wave of suspense and unexpected turns in the plot, which serve only to increase the amusing and erotic nature of the eventual seduction. The narrator frequently labels Frol a rogue, but further characterization is minimal. Indeed, no character is sufficiently developed to resist the intentions of another, and so the flow of action is never interrupted – a rather primitive form of narration which has more to do with authorial convenience and control than creative composition. This first section, full of action and entertainment, ends with Frol and Annushka's marriage.

In the second half of the tale, however, the emphasis is clearly different: psychological reasoning, desire, the emotive reactions between the characters and their suffering are all elaborated on to bring the character portraits alive. Frol remains a rogue, up to his habitual tricks of manipulation and deceit, yet he is no longer the central character: Annushka now appears as a strong determined figure, equally competent in arranging matters to suit herself. This is a very important development in literary characterization: formerly, capable female characters had only been found in folklore or other works incorporating folkloric motifs. Annushka, however, is of a totally different mould: she copes admirably with Frol's original seduction; it is *she* who detains Frol after her party, for her enjoyment as much as his; the elopement is organized by Annushka, with Frol only realizing what is happening when it is almost all over! The secondary characters are similarly developed in the second half of the tale to an unusual degree.

This work is stylistically typical of the Petrine period. Little if any effort is made to disguise a basic bureaucratic style of writing, which is almost totally unconcerned with traditional literary etiquette. The language is unadorned vernacular and often lacking in poetic fluency. Frequent passages of dialogue emphasize the seeming reality of the tale, as well as increasing considerably the possibilities for more in-depth characterization. It is quite possible that the author composed the tale in this manner to match the rather bawdy contents, for which traditional high style literary rhetoric would have been wholly unsuitable; or perhaps the author intended some cynical comment on the effects of moral and social decline brought about by Peter's secularizing reforms.

In terms of overall Russian literary evolution, this work is very advanced – a thoroughly secular and entertaining tale, with no trace of divine retribution striking down the irredeemable and remorseless Frol. Blackmail, bribery, manipulation and deceit in the selfish pursuit of wealth and the good life, however, are all ingredients of real life as well as of the tale, and doubtless the audience would have found, for almost the first time, a very concrete element of self-identification, all too often elusive in earlier didactic literature. The tale was clearly intended to portray a lightly satirical sense of reality, marking an important stage in the secularization of Russian literature.

Rosalind McKenzie

Dmitrii Andreevich Furmanov 1891–1926

Prose writer

Biography

Born in Sereda, Kostroma Province, 7 November 1891. Attended school in Ivanovo-Voznesensk, 1899–1908; technical high school in Kineshma, 1909–12; Moscow University, 1912–14. Served as a medical orderly on hospital trains in the Urals and the Caucasus, 1914–15; Western Front, 1915–16. Returned to Ivanovo-Voznesensk as teacher in workers' faculty, 1916; elected as delegate to All-Russian Democratic Conference, Petrograd, September 1917. Member of executive committee Ivanovo-Voznesensk Provisional Soviet, deputy commissar of culture for Ivanovo Province, 1918. Joined the Bolshevik Party, July 1918: appointed secretary of Ivanovo-Voznesensk district party committee, 1918. Married: Anna Nikitichna Steshenko in 1918, one daughter. Political commissar of 25th Division, 4th Army, Eastern Front (served under General Chapaev), 1919; appointed head of political section, Turkestan Front, 1919. Delegate, 7th All-Russian Congress of Soviets and 8th All-Russian Conference of Bolsheviks, 1919. Head of special Party delegation to Semirech'e to investigate insurrection in Vernyi (Alma-Ata), 1920. Editor of the Red Army newspaper *Krasnyi voin*, 1921. Full-time writer, 1921–26; secretary, Moscow Proletarian Writers' Association, 1923–24. Died in Moscow, 15 March 1926.

Publications

Collected Edition

Sobranie sochinenii. 4 vols, Moscow, 1960–61.

Fiction

Chapaev. Moscow, 1923; translated as *Chapaev* [no translator named], London, Martin Lawrence, and New York, International Publishers, 1935; reprinted Westport, Connecticut, Hyperion Press, 1973; also as *Chapayev* [no translator named], Moscow, Foreign Languages Publishing House, 1955.

"Krasnyi desant" [Red Attack], *Tkach*, 1–2 (1923).

"Epifan Kovtiukh", *Krasnoarmeets*, 54 (1923).

V vosemnadtsatom godu [In 1918]. Krasnodar, 1923.

"Frunze", *Krasnaia nov'*, 10 (1925).

Miatezh [The Rebellion]. Moscow, 1925.

"Marusia Riabinina", *Pravda* (7 March 1926).

"Letchik Tikhon Zharov" [Airman Tikhon Zharov], *Oktiabr'*, 7–8 (1926).

Autobiography

"Avtobiografiia", *Izvestiia* (16 March 1926).

Critical Studies

Russian Literature since the Revolution, by Edward J. Brown, Cambridge, Massachusetts, Harvard University Press, 1963; 2nd edition 1982, 150–61.

"Chapaev" D.A. Furmanova, by A.F. Berezhnoi, Moscow and Leningrad, 1965.

Furmanov, by Aleksandr Isbakh, Moscow, 1968.

Iskaniia, bor'ba, tvorchestvo. (Put' D.A. Furmanova), by P. Kuprianovskii, Iaroslavl, 1968.

Bibliographies

D.A. Furmanov. Letopis' zhizni i deiatel'nosti, bibliografiia, materialy, by B.A. Bartenev, Ivanovo, 1963.

Russkie sovetskie pisateli. Prozaiki. Bibliograficheskii ukazatel', vol. 5, Moscow, 1968, 491–568.

Dmitrii Andreevich Furmanov was a member of that group of Russian writers who came of age, creatively speaking, with the Bolshevik Revolution of 1917. From early childhood he had shown a passionate interest in literature of all kinds, particularly the Russian classics of the 19th century. As a student at Moscow University he spent much of his time studying and writing on Dostoevskii. Like so many of his contemporaries, however, his studies and youthful aspirations were interrupted first by the war with Germany and then the Civil War within Russia. His decision to give up his university studies shortly after the outbreak of war in 1914 to become a medical orderly testifies to his sense of civic duty and social commitment. Four years later he was in the first group of volunteers to leave Ivanovo-Voznesensk to join the Red Army fighting on the Eastern Front against the forces of Admiral Kolchak. Although he devoted much of his adult life in this way to socially or politically responsible tasks, it would be misleading to see him as in any sense divided between literature and politics. Furmanov considered that these two areas were not mutually exclusive and could be combined in order to educate people in the spirit of socialism. This in turn demanded of the writer a sense of discipline and political awareness; his decision to join the Bolshevik Party in 1918 after a brief flirtation with the anarchists reflected his belief in such Leninist virtues.

With these qualities and background Furmanov was ideally suited for the position of political commissar within the Red Army, and it was his experiences in such a post during the summer of 1919 that led directly to the creation of his most famous work, *Chapaev*. In this and in his succeeding novel, *Miatezh* [The Rebellion], Furmanov interweaves documentary detail, personal reminiscences and psychological analysis (not, it must be admitted, of a particularly profound kind) to create a work that inhabits the shadowy borderland between fact and fiction. Both novels suffer from an inconsistency of tone that betrays Furmanov's relative immaturity as a writer, but they have rather more to offer than the term "factographical", which is usually applied to them, would seem to suggest. As well as being of documentary and educative value, each work – *Chapaev* more successfully than *Miatezh* – reflects the author's purely literary and aesthetic interests. As his comments on his own work reveal, he is concerned not just with telling the story, but with how the story is to be told. There are constant reminders furthermore of his abiding interest in the classics of 19th-century literature; in both works, for example, we find echoes of the Tolstoian theme of the relationship between individual action and the broad sweep of historical events. In *Miatezh* we sense the influence of Dostoevskii, with Furmanov's depiction of the mutineers as men *in extremis* who no longer possess the ability to judge and behave rationally; they are not therefore unequivocally condemned, despite the fact that they are rebels against the Soviet cause. For although Furmanov's readers are never left in any doubt about the author's political sympathies, and although much of the characterization is black-and-white, there is less ideological bias in his portrayal of characters than is apparent in many other committed writers of that era. It is one of Furmanov's strengths, and arguably also one of his weaknesses, that he occupies the middle ground between ambiguity and fanaticism.

This quality of moderation is evident in the dozen or so other works that Furmanov produced between 1920 and his untimely death six years later. Just as with the two novels, all these works – variously described as longer stories (*povesti*), short stories (*rasskazy*), or sketches (*ocherki*) – derive from Furmanov's own experiences during the Civil War. Some of these earlier works are little more than preliminary sketches for *Chapaev* (written and published in 1923). Others recount various engagements against the Whites in which Furmanov was involved. The most interesting story of this group is "Krasnyi desant" [Red Attack], in which the author focuses not so much on the details of the fighting as on the thoughts, fears, and reactions of the people involved. Again, the calm heroism displayed by many of the characters in the face of danger and the admiration that Furmanov clearly feels for them bring Tolstoi to mind. Yet a third group of stories, written towards the end of this period, consists of discursive portraits of individuals who distinguished themselves in one way or another during the Civil War and who, in Furmanov's eyes, embodied precisely those heroic and charismatic qualities that were essential not just for the defeat of the Whites but for the eventual triumph of socialism. Three of these sketches – "Frunze", "Letchik Tikhon Zharov" [Airman Tikhon Zharov], and "Marusia Riabinina" – are in effect obituaries, whose hagiographical tone is tempered by an elegiac wistfulness. The mood of the fourth sketch, "Epifan Kovtiukh" (the model for Kozhukh in Serafimovich's novel *Zheleznyi potok* [*The Iron Flood*]), is more uplifting and optimistic.

In addition to work on these stories and sketches, Furmanov turned with renewed vigour to plans for rewriting *Chapaev*, a stage version of *Miatezh*, and, towards the end of 1925, a new novel with the provisional title of *Pisateli* [The Writers]. Throughout this period of intense creative activity, however, he had become more and more involved in the fierce debates taking place within the Association of Proletarian Writers. Some wished to turn the union into a militant force with the power to expel, and effectively to silence, any member who did not unambiguously support Bolshevik ideals. Others, including Furmanov, who in 1924 had been elected as secretary of the Moscow branch of the association and who even after the Civil War continued to regard himself as "a fighter in the front line", advocated a more liberal approach; characteristically, this struggle was to have been the central theme of *Pisateli*. He had, however, become physically weakened by many years of intense activity; in early 1926 he caught influenza, which became rapidly and progressively worse, ending in his death on 15 March. He was never to complete his novel or learn the outcome of the events it was to have depicted. With him in his grave were buried, symbolically, a copy of *Chapaev* together with the sword that he had worn during the Civil War.

ROGER COCKRELL

Chapaev

Novel, 1923

When *Chapaev* was first published in 1923 it was very soon being hailed within Russia as a classic of the Civil War. The novel, which in its first edition bore the subtitle "Sketches of the Civil War in the Ural Steppes", recounts the actions of a Red Army division during the summer of 1919, its heroic achievements against the White forces of Admiral Kolchak, and its eventual rout together with the death of its commander, Vasilii Ivanovich Chapaev. Although *Chapaev* is ostensibly a work of fiction, the novel is in fact largely autobiographical; its third-person narrator, the division's political commissar, Fedor Klychkov, is based to a considerable extent on the author himself. An examination of Furmanov's own meticulously kept diary entries for the period reveals the close association between the flow of events as he perceived them and the fictional narrative. His main object in writing the novel was to educate and enlighten, not only in the sense of using fiction as a device to tell "the truth" about historically important events, but also to inculcate in his readers particular qualities and attitudes that were the prerequisites for the establishment of a new socialist society: discipline, a sense of duty, political awareness, and ethical responsibility.

There is, however, another side to the novel. The contention of many critics, particularly from the west, that it possesses no aesthetic merit at all, and that Furmanov sacrificed all notions of artistic storytelling for ideological purposes is unfair. *Chapaev* is hardly a masterpiece of world literature, but, within definite limitations, Furmanov offers more than simply propaganda and exhortation. Whatever the author's intention might have been, the novel has a sense of immediacy and authenticity that helps to explain its popularity with a reading public for whom the Civil War was a source of apparently endless fascination. Through reading works such as these – and *Chapaev* was one of the very first of its kind to be published – Russians were able to re-create in their own imaginations significant and stirring events that for the most part had appeared hitherto only in the form of terse and dry communiqués from the front. For many, therefore, it was above all an exciting story with at least a fair measure of human interest.

Chapaev represents therefore something of a balancing act between two possibly irreconcilable principles, the aesthetic and the political. The point of intersection of the novel's narrative and ideological lines is naturally enough the figure of Chapaev himself, who even by this relatively early stage of the Civil War had gained a formidable reputation as a succesful commander and charismatic leader. When in chapter 3 Klychkov first hears of his appoinment as Chapaev's commissar he can scarcely believe that he will be working side by side with such a legendary figure. When, however, the two of them actually meet and their relationship begins to develop, it becomes clear that Furmanov intends more than a simple hagiography: without in any way undermining the qualities which he, through Klychkov, so obviously admires, he is setting out to portray Chapaev from a socialist perspective. Klychkov becomes not so much Chapaev's adoring disciple, as might have been expected, as his teacher. His primary duty is to harness Chapaev's undoubted strengths, together with those of the apolitical peasants whom he leads, to the Bolshevik cause. Herein lies one of the main political concerns of the novel. In the view of Lenin, and others, the greatest impediment to Bolshevik success in the Civil War lay in the naturally anarchic tendencies of the Russian people; it was therefore essential to instil in Chapaev the qualities that were dearest to Furmanov's own heart: political awareness and a sense of discipline. The learning process, however, is by no means all one way. If Furmanov is showing that Chapaev's "fault" is his spontaneity, then equally he is saying, with perhaps more than a hint of self-criticism, that Klychkov's is his excessive intellectualism. In the event each learns from the other, with Klychkov coming to acknowledge that rational abstraction is an insufficient basis for a full human relationship.

Despite this deliberate attempt on Furmanov's part to "humanize" his hero, Chapaev none the less never really escapes from the legendary, heroic mode into which he has been placed from the beginning. His death and the manner in which it is transformed into victory in the closing paragraphs of the novel merely serve to emphasize this. In the final analysis his fascination derives less from his character than from his achievement. Politically, this might answer Furmanov's purpose. Artistically, it is a portrait which, together with the "dense masses of workers" roaring their approval at the beginning of the novel and the "bestial" behaviour of the White troops at the end, belongs to an earlier age, unclouded by irony and modernist uncertainties. Even those scenes that are portrayed with some subtlety and complexity, such as the poignant description of the peasant soldiers asleep around the camp fire on the eve of the battle of Slomikhinskii, or Klychkov's disgust at his own "cowardly" behaviour in the same engagement, do little more than underline Furmanov's debt to Tolstoi and the gulf between them.

After the publication of the first edition of *Chapaev*, Furmanov continued to work on the novel. A second edition, with minor amendments, appeared in the same year (1923) and two years later a more substantially revised version was published. Furmanov's primary concern in this new edition was to simplify the language, and to free it from clichés and ornate phraseology. Shortly before his death he embarked on a radical rewriting of the novel but he succeeded in completing less than half. Its popularity within Russia, however, was assured. In the quarter century after Furmanov's death it was reprinted 125 times, with an overall circulation figure of nearly three million. It has been translated into 34 languages, appearing in English for the first time in 1935. A year earlier a film version had appeared, highlighting Chapaev's heroic and romantic qualities.

ROGER COCKRELL

G

Aleksandr Arkad'evich Galich 1919–1977

Poet, *chansonnier*, and dramatist

Biography

Born Aleksandr Arkad'evich Ginzburg in Dnepropetrovsk (Ekaterinoslav), 19 October 1919. Studied at the Gor'kii Literary Institute, Moscow, 1935–36; the Stanislavskii Studio, 1935–38. Actor in the Moscow Theatrical Studio of Valentin Pluchek and Aleksei Arbuzov, 1938–41; and in the theatre of the Northern Navy during World War II. Married: 1) the actress, Valentina Arkhangel'skaia, one daughter; 2) Angelina Prokhorova. Wrote scenarios, plays, prose, poems, and songs. Expelled from the Writers' Union and Litfond in December 1971. Emigrated in 1974; lived in Oslo, 1974; Munich, 1975; and Paris, 1976. Died in Paris, from accidental electrocution, 15 December 1977. Buried in the Russian cemetery of Sainte-Geneviève-des-Bois, Paris.

Publications

Collected Editions

Pesni [Songs]. Frankfurt, Posev, 1969.
Pokolenie obrechennykh [The Generation of the Doomed]. Frankfurt, Posev, 1972.
General'naia repetitsiia [The Dress Rehearsal]. Frankfurt, Posev, 1974.
Kogda ia vernus' [When I Return]. Frankfurt, Posev, 1977; reprinted 1986.
Polnoe sobranie stikhov i pesen. Frankfurt, Posev, 1981.
Alexander Galich: Songs and Poems, edited and translated by Gerald S. Smith. Ann Arbor, Ardis, 1983.
Izbrannye stikhotvoreniia, edited by A. Shatalov. Moscow, 1989.
Peterburgskii romans [A Petersburg Romance], edited by A. Shatalov. Leningrad, 1989.
Vozvrashchenie [The Return], edited by G. Solov'eva. Leningrad, 1990.
Ia veril v chudo [I Believed in a Miracle], edited by Leonid Vilenskii. Moscow, 1991.
Ia vybiraiu svobodu. Aleksandr Galich [My Choice is Freedom], edited by A. Shatalov. Kostroma, 1991.
General'naia repetitsiia [The Dress Rehearsal], edited by A. Shatalov. Moscow, 1991.
... ia vernus' ... [I Shall Return], edited by Alena Arkhangel'skaia-Galich. Moscow, 1993.

Plays

"Gorod na zare" [City of the Dawn] with Aleksei Arbuzov (published under Arbuzov's name), 1940; *Teatr*, 11 (1957).
"Duel'" [The Duel], with Isai Kuznetsov and Vsevolod Bagritskii, 1941.
"Vas vyzyvaet Taimyr" [Taimyr Calling], with Konstantin Isaev. *Ogonek*, 22 (1948).
"Polozhenie obiazyvaet", ("Moskva slezam ne verit") [Moscow Does Not Believe in Tears], with Georgii Munblit. 1949.
"Puti, kotorye my vybiraem" [The Paths We Choose]. 1953; in *General'naia repetitsiia*, Moscow, 1991.
"Pod schastlivoi zvezdoi" [Under a Lucky Star]. 1954.
"Matrosskaia tishina" [Seaman's Silence]. 1955–56; in *General'naia repetitsiia*, 1991.
"Pokhodnyi marsh, ili Za chas do rassveta" [Campaign March], *Teatr*, 3 (1957).
"Parokhod zovut 'Orlenok'" [The Name of the Ship is "Eagle"], *Sovremennaia dramaturgiia*, 6 (1958).
"Avgust" [August], 1958; in *General'naia repetitsiia*, 1991.
"Mnogo li cheloveku nado" [Does a Man Need Much], 1959.

Fiction

"General'naia repetitsiia" [The Dress Rehearsal], in *General'naia repetitsiia*, 1974.
"Bloshinyi rynok" [Flea Market], *Vremia i my*, 24 (1977), 25 (1978).

Critical Studies

"Teatr Galicha", by Andrei Siniavskii, *Vremia i my*, 14 (1977), 142–50.
"Horace's Heirs: Beyond Censorship in the Soviet Songs of the Magnitizdat", by Rosette C. Lamont, *World Literature Today*, 53 (1979), 220–27.
"Silence is Connivance", by Gerald S. Smith, in *Alexander Galich: Songs and Poems*, Ann Arbor, Ardis, 1983.
"Galich in Emigration", by Gerald S. Smith, in *The Third Wave: Russian Literature in Emigration*, edited by Olga Matich and Michael Henry Heim, Ann Arbor, Ardis, 1984, 118–23.
Songs to Seven Strings: Russian Guitar Poetry and Soviet "Mass Song", by Gerald S. Smith, Bloomington, Indiana University Press, 1984.
Das sowjetrussische Autorenlied: eine Untersuchung am Beispiel des Schaffens von Aleksandr Galič, Bulat Okudžava

und Vladimir Vysockij, by Dagmar Boss, Munich, Sagner, 1985.
"Erika beret chetyre kopii: vozvrashchenie Galicha", by S. Pedenko, *Voprosy literatury*, 4 (1989), 80–112.
"Ne tol'ko slovo: vslushivaias' v Galicha", by V. Frumkin, *Muzykal'naia zhizn'*, 14/15 (1989).
Zaklinanie dobra i zla, edited by Nina Kreitner, Moscow, 1991.

Bibliography
"A. Galich: bibliografiia, diskografiia", compiled by R. Shipov, *Sovetskaia bibliografiia*, 1 (1993), 60–68.

Aleksandr Galich had two vocations: writing and acting. He first studied at the Gor'kii Literary Institute in Moscow, but soon changed to an acting course at the Moscow Arts Theatre run by Konstantin Stanislavskii. After Stanislavskii's death he joined the studio theatre, which had been set up by Aleksei Arbuzov in order to encourage young writers. This collective of young actors and future playwrights jointly researched the construction of the city of Komsomolsk and turned the material into the play *Gorod na zare* [City of the Dawn], which Arbuzov subsequently published, taking sole credit for its composition. The studio's activities came to a halt with the war, during which Galich (who was rejected for service on medical grounds) worked as an entertainer.

After the war Galich continued writing plays about "the problems of Soviet youth". These plays were successful, and could be found in the repertoires of Moscow and Leningrad theatres. At a time when drama was under severe constraints (the "no conflict" policy set out by Nikolai Virta had deprived drama of its most essential ingredient), Galich managed to write the satirical but nevertheless ideologically correct *Vas vyzyvaet Taimyr* [Taimyr Calling], a vaudeville based on mix-ups and misunderstandings. Galich's reputation during the 1950s was that of a leading younger dramatist; he also wrote numerous scenarios for films.

In 1957 the Sovremennik Theatre was founded by Oleg Efremov, who intended to open the first season with Viktor Rozov's *Vechno zhivye* [Alive Forever] and Galich's *Matrosskaia tishina* [Seaman's Silence]. Galich's play deals with a Jewish family before, during and after World War II. As a young boy, David is set to become a violinist, but is then drafted in the war and dies for his country. His father is shot during the deportation of Jews from the ghetto. After the war, David's son and his mother, the Russian Tania, wonder about their future. The play had been rehearsed at several theatres, but was dropped from the planned repertoire when "rumours" concerning its ideological flaws were spread. Efremov's production was banned in 1957 although it had been passed by the literary censorship board, *Glavlit*. The final dress rehearsal, recounted by Galich in his autobiographical sketch *General'naia repetitsiia* [The Dress Rehearsal], took place in the presence of Solov'eva, "a lady in brick red" from the Ministry of Culture, and Sokolova, "a lady in bottle green" from the Central Committee. At the Central Committee offices she told Galich that the play was by no means banned, but that it was not recommended for the stage. The official reason was the treatment of Jews: their contribution to winning the war and fighting fascism, and their integration with the Russian population were not deemed suitable for representation on stage at a time when ideology was being tightened in preparation for the 40th anniversary of the Revolution (1957). In the opinion of the Central Committee officials there were "enough Jews" in artistic and intellectual circles, a remark that must have transported Galich back into the late 1940s with its campaign against "cosmopolitans". *General'naia repetitsiia* is Galich's only autobiographical work, in which he renders this dress rehearsal in lively detail embedded in childhood memoirs. He offers a profound insight into the cultural policies of the period of the Thaw.

Until 1958 Galich had been a figure of the Soviet cultural establishment. He even composed the texts for official mass songs. After the banning of *Matrosskaia tishina* Galich deliberately began to distance himself from officialdom and to write poems, which he sang to the guitar (guitar poetry), following the path first adopted by Bulat Okudzhava in 1960. Galich created characters whose lives he portrayed in his songs. He satirized the system, its victors as much as its victims: in "Kolomiitsev v polnyi rost" ("Kolomiitsev at Full Height") both the worker Klim and the Party official are ridiculed: Klim for reading the wrong speech, the Party official for not realizing the mistake. Galich investigated the grind of everyday Soviet reality, such as sexual exploitation for social advancement ("Tonechka"), or adultery and subsequent denunciation ("Krasnyi treugol'nik" ("The Red Triangle")).

In his longer poem "Stalin" he juxtaposed the figures of Christ and Stalin while taking the reader through the history of the Soviet Union from Stalin to Khrushchev. Stalin recognizes Christ as a potential usurper and enemy in the struggle for power, certain, however, that Stalin will emerge as superior: he will impose his will by force, and therefore his kingdom will last forever. Towards the end of his life, Stalin seeks forgiveness in his solitude. After his death, he is recognized as a traitor, and the final segment "Ave Maria" looks at the aftermath: the traitors, the victors, and the victims of the lives of Stalin in the Soviet Union, and Christ in the Roman province.

Galich also composed a series of songs in memory of the victims of literary politics, such as Pasternak, Akhmatova, Kharms, and Mandel'shtam. The public performance in 1968 of "Pamiati B.L. Pasternaka" ("Pasternak in Memoriam") is thought to have contributed to Galich's expulsion from the Writers' Union in 1971. In this song, he acclaimed Pasternak's civic courage to insist on staying and dying in Russia, despite possible arrest or exile. Galich regarded himself as belonging to the "generation of the doomed" – survivors of the Purges and of campaigns against "cosmopolitanism", who preferred, however, to immerse the memory of those days in oblivion. He acknowledged a collective guilt, which to him lay in silence about the past. "Peterburgskii romans" ("Petersburg Romance") and "Staratel'skii val'sek" ("Goldminers' Waltz") are full of self-reproach for his own lack of outspokenness at the right time. His song "Kogda ia vernus" [When I Return] reflects both the desire and hope to return, and the need for the Russian soil, culture, and audience.

After his expulsion from the Writers' Union and Litfond he stayed in Russia for another three years before finally and reluctantly emigrating ("Zaklinanie dobra i zla" [Conjuration of Good and Evil]). Around 1972 he adopted the Orthodox faith and was christened by Father Aleksandr Men'. In 1974 he was confronted with the choice of emigrating or facing trial; he left for Oslo, where he spent a year, followed by a year in Munich with Radio Liberty; this job finally took him to Paris. His second prose work "Bloshinyi rynok" [Flea Market] remained unfinished. Galich died in December 1977 from electrocution as he tried to connect a radio recorder. He is buried in Paris. His works were published in the Soviet Union only after 1990, but he has not been paid the full attention he deserves, either as a guitar poet (ranking with Okudzhava and Vysotskii) or as a dramatist.

BIRGIT BEUMERS

Elena Andreevna Gan 1814–1842

Prose writer

Biography

Born Elena Andreevna Fadeeva, at Rzhishchev, near Kiev, 23 January 1814. Also wrote as Zeneida R-va. Daughter of Princess Elena Pavlovna Dolgorukaia. Educated at home, principally by her mother. Visited Crimea 1827; began writing. Married: Petr Alekseevich Gan (Hahn) in 1830; four children. Began writing seriously mid-1830s. In St Petersburg, 1836–37. Met Senkovskii in 1836. First story, "Ideal", published in *Biblioteka dlia chteniia*, 1837, as Zeneida R-va. Left St Petersburg in 1837; spent remaining five years of life in southern Russia, travelling frequently. Travelled to Odessa and the Caucasus; met some of the exiled Decembrists. Health deteriorated rapidly in late 1830s. Began publishing in *Otechestvennye zapiski*, 1841. Died in Odessa, 6 July 1842.

Publications

Collected Editions

Sochineniia Zeneidy R-voi, 4 vols. St Petersburg, 1843.

Polnoe sobranie sochinenii Zeneidy R-voi, 6 vols. St Petersburg, 1905; 2nd edition 1909.

Fiction

"Ideal", *Biblioteka dlia chteniia*, 1837; reprinted in *Russkaia romanticheskaia povest'*, edited by V.I. Sakharov, Moscow, 1980, 435–80; translated as *The Ideal*, by Joe Andrew, in his *Short Fiction by Russian Women Writers, 1835–1860*, Oxford, Oxford University Press, 1996.

Medal'on [The Locket]. 1839.

Sud sveta. 1840; reprinted in *Dacha na Petergovskoi doroge: proza russkikh pisatel'nits pervoi poloviny XIX veka*, edited by V.V. Uchenova, Moscow, 1986, 148–212; translated as *Society's Judgement*, by Joe Andrew, in his *Short Fiction by Russian Women Writers, 1835–1860*, Oxford, Oxford University Press, 1996.

Naprasnyi dar [A Futile Gift]. 1842; reprinted in *Serdtsa chutkogo prozren'em...: Povesti i rasskazy russkikh pisatel'nits XIX v.*, edited by N.I. Iakushin, Moscow, 1991, 109–71.

Critical Studies

"The Concept of Love and the Conflict of the Individual versus Society in Elena A. Gan's *Sud sveta*", by Marit B. Nielsen, *Scando-Slavica*, 24 (1978), 125–38.

Mothers and Daughters: Women of the Intelligentsia in Nineteenth Century Russia, by Barbara Alpern Engel, Cambridge, Cambridge University Press, 1983.

Narrative and Desire in Russian Literature, 1822–49: The Feminine and the Masculine, by Joe Andrew, London, Macmillan, and New York, St Martin's Press, 1993, 85–138.

"A Futile Gift: Elena Andreevna Gan and Writing", by Joe Andrew, in *Gender Restructuring in Russian Studies: Conference Papers - Helsinki, August 1992*, edited by Marianne Liljeström *et al.*, *Slavica Tamperensia II*, Tampere, 1993, 1–14.

A History of Russian Women's Writing, 1820–1992, by Catriona Kelly, Oxford and New York, Oxford University Press, 1994.

Elena Gan was one of the cohort of women writers who, along with Durova, Pavlova, Zhukova, and others, entered the male bastion of the Russian literary world in the 1830s and offered not only the first, however tentative, answers to the "woman question" but also played an important part, hitherto "hidden from history", in the generic experimentation and other developments that were to lead to the Great Tradition of the realist novel in the middle of the century. Gan was probably the most radical of this group, both as a writer and as an exponent of women's issues.

Gan began writing at the age of 13, and launched a serious literary career in the mid-1830s, especially after her military husband was posted to St Petersburg in 1837. From then and for most of the rest of her short life, Gan published regularly in Senkovskii's journal *Biblioteka dlia chteniia*. Writing became a central part of her life: it was an outlet for stifled mental and spiritual energies, and emotional satisfaction that seems to have been lacking in her marriage. She was a deeply conscientious author who suffered intensely because of the hostility shown to her as a woman writer. She observed that "I am regarded as a fairground fright, a snake in flannel"; in Russia, she noted, "women writers are still on the same footing as rare beasts". The hardships and sufferings of the woman writer in Russia in the 1830s are dramatized in *Naprasnyi dar* [A Futile Gift].

Many of Gan's works fuse genres, especially *Medal'on* [The Locket] and *Sud sveta* (*Society's Judgement*). These two also use the common devices of the period, the "discovered document" or the tale within the tale. Typically for the 1830s Gan's work is a mixture of high romanticism with a core of realism. This is seen both in the deployment of "ethnic" material (*Utballa* and *Dzhellaledin* for example), and in the use of the key genre of the period, the "society tale". One of Gan's main concerns was to depict the contemporary morals and psychology of her society, usually from a critical, if not openly satirical angle as in *Ideal* (*The Ideal*) or *Society's Judgement*. She is especially venomous about the superficiality and love of appearances of society, and the tedium of provincial life, particularly for women who, like the writer herself, were "military wives". In these stories, as well as others (*Naprasnyi dar*), we see the conflict between a venal society and the woman of unusual gifts, who is often in search of the "Ideal". This may be found in nature, or in an actual spiritual life: often the disappointed heroine will find fulfilment in Christian belief, and the religious element in Gan's work and *Weltanschauung* is strong.

The central theme, throughout Gan's work, is the "woman question". She was "one of a number of cultivated women ... who passed the ordinary limits of women's consciousness of their age to look at the larger world around them" (Richard Stites). Often women, through gossip, were their own worst enemy. Nearly all of Gan's tales have love and marriage as their main plot, notable exceptions are *Naprasnyi dar* and the "literary joke", "Vospominaniia o Zheleznovodske" [Memories of Zheleznovodsk]. Rarely is marriage based on love, and the arranged marriage is a common plot and theme. In part, as a consequence of this, the sexual fidelity of the heroine becomes an issue. Whether as (usually older) husbands, or as rakes, most male characters in Gan are unsympathetic. The heroines are usually treated positively, although by no means simplistically. The most valued female type in Gan's fiction, however, is the mother or maternal type. Examples of the quasi-reverential approach to motherhood are found in *The Ideal*, *Society's Judgement* and *Medal'on*; *Naprasnyi dar* and *Liubin'ka* are notable exceptions. From the "good" mother the heroine usually receives an excellent education, although this theme is treated ambivalently by Gan. In most of her stories the "ideal" upbringing provided by the mother is almost counter-productive as it raises expectations that could never be fulfilled in contemporary social conditions. Quite apart from the demands of realism, Gan was not a simplistic proto-feminist. Although her works sympathetically decry the narrowness of traditional roles, she could also write: "Woman is a domestic animal; her life, feelings, opinions should never cross the threshold of her doors; the whole world should consist for her of her family."

Because all her works were published originally in journals, little critical attention was paid to Gan's writing until her Collected Works were published posthumously in 1843. They created something of a sensation, and were acclaimed by Belinskii, but also by more conservative critics. Gan was generally thought to have been the leading woman writer of the period. Little attention was paid to her after this, however, and although her complete works were republished in 1905, it is only in the last ten years that literary critics have turned to her once more. Gan remains an important figure as an illuminator of women's issues and as a significant writer in the late romantic, early realist period.

JOE ANDREW

Naprasnyi dar

A Futile Gift

Novella, 1842

Naprasnyi dar was first published in *Otechestvennye zapiski* (3, 1842). The work was unfinished on Gan's death earlier that year. It should be seen as the writer's testament and summation of several of her predominant themes and concerns, in particular the difficulties encountered by the talented woman, especially the woman writer, in a patriarchal society. It is among the first prose works in Russian that deal with the pain, suffering and above all the anxiety of a woman who becomes a writer. It is largely autobiographical but also based on the life and premature death, at the age of 18, of the poet Elizaveta Kulman.

The tale of Aniuta the poet is told by a doctor, who tries to treat her for galloping consumption, to two educated, travelling noblewomen. Aniuta had grown up in a family of modest means, in which she seemed, like Pushkin's Tat'iana, to be a foundling. Despite her family's circumstances, a tutor is hired for her brother, and with him Aniuta develops her great intelligence and talents, learning French and German. She reads widely, and learns much, both about literature and the natural sciences. At the age of 15 she discovers the world of poetry and soon begins writing herself. Attempts are made to have her work published in St Petersburg, but Aniuta's hopes are dashed. Even worse she is obliged to give up writing as a condition of becoming a governess (her mother is deeply opposed to Aniuta's literary aspirations). Under these various stresses her health deteriorates rapidly, and she dies a premature death, but not before she has been persuaded that her "gift" had not been "futile". (There is a very brief beginning to a further section of the story, but this bears no obvious connection with the seemingly self-contained Aniuta story.)

Naprasnyi dar mainly addresses issues concerning women and writing, but sets these issues in the broader context of gender roles and expectations. The travelling (female) narrator opens the story by ruminating on the inequalities that exist between men and women, and wonders whether the many manifest injustices are: "a mistake of nature, or the finger of a higher plan?" More generally, the work continues Gan's previous discussions of the nature and value of education for women, and poses the question that such education might actually be counterproductive, in that it raises expectations that cannot be fulfilled in a world where only traditional roles for women are permissible. Gan concentrates on such philosophical and gender issues by, almost uniquely in her *oeuvre*, not making love the central plot mechanism.

Instead, presumably knowing this would be her valedictory work, she focuses on the underlying issues of the previous five years of her career – the conflict between the woman of talent and a venal society; the valorization of woman as writer; the essential differences between male and female writing. In this tale, however, the initial image of the female writer must be construed as negative: Aniuta appears in the story (because of the temporal dislocation employed in its telling) as already well on the way to an early grave and, seemingly, as somewhat deranged. She is a ghostly figure who haunts the garden and runs away when approached. As the story unfolds it becomes clear that it is exceptionally difficult for a woman to enter the predominantly male world of writing. Indeed, the tutor (and her main support and mentor) Heilfreund ("saviour" and "friend"), while recognizing her talent, tries to dissuade her at first from developing a "gift" that he is sure is doomed to remain "futile".

Once Aniuta discovers writing she also discovers ecstasy. The implication of Gan's treatment of this theme is that for a woman to become a writer is to discover the ideal, a concept Gan had been investigating since her first published work (1837), which bears the title: "Oh, so this is it, this is the heaven of which, in anguish, her soul had dreamed". Just before her death Aniuta reflects: "Yes, I have happiness, peace, fame, friends ... and my poetry ... my wonderful, celestial gift." Yet the story retains a profound ambiguity on the issues of women's writing, at least in the social conditions that Gan herself experienced. Creativity may bring the woman to a kind of "heaven", but it also leads to despair or even a form of madness. The title may be said to speak for itself. Heilfreund suggests as much when he argues that a woman writer is doomed to "freeze in the wilderness, in obscurity, far from the world ... from all resources for learning for which her soul thirsts, simply because she is a woman! ... and futile is her gift!" And although Aniuta does find religious peace and consolation at her death, her writing must be said to have brought her more suffering than joy.

Naprasnyi dar is a rather abstract work, with perfunctory plotting and characterization. It is not an altogether successful *mélange* of styles, switching between high romanticism and realism, with a sentimental ending. But it is written with great passion and conviction. Its interrogation of the central issues of gender and writing give it a resonance and significance ahead of its time that remain relevant and timely.

Joe Andrew

Vsevolod Mikhailovich Garshin 1855–1888

Prose writer

Biography

Born at Priiatnaia Dolina, near Bakhmut (Artemovsk), Ukraine, 14 February 1855. Attended St Petersburg high school 1863–74; Institute of Mining, 1874–77. First mental breakdown, 1872–73. Volunteer-private in Russo-Turkish War; wounded, 1877. Suffered a major breakdown, 1880; in mental institutions, then convalescence, 1880–82. Married: Nadezhda Zolotilova, a young medical student in 1883. Employed by Associated Russian Railways, St Petersburg, 1883–87. Member of the Executive Committee of Litfond, 1885–87. Committed suicide (threw himself down a stairwell) in St Petersburg, 5 April 1888.

Publications

Collected Editions

Rasskazy. St Petersburg, 1882; reprinted as *Pervaia knizhka rasskazov* [First Book of Short Stories].
Vtoraia knizhka rasskazov [Second Book of Short Stories]. St Petersburg, 1885.
Tret'ia knizhka rasskazov [Third Book of Short Stories]. St Petersburg, 1888–91.
Stories from Garshin, translated by E.L. Voynich. London, Unwin, 1893.
Polnoe sobranie sochinenii. St Petersburg, 1910.
"The Signal" and Other Stories, translated by Rowland Smith. London, Duckworth, 1912; New York, Knopf, 1915; reprinted, Freeport, New York, Books for Libraries Press, 1970.
Polnoe sobranie sochinenii, edited by Iu. G. Oksman. Moscow and Leningrad, 1934.
Stories, translated by Bernard Isaacs. Moscow, Foreign Languages Publishing House, 1959; reprinted, Moscow, Progress, 1982.
Sochineniia. Moscow and Leningrad, 1963.
Sochineniia. Moscow, 1983.
From the Reminiscences of Private Ivanov and Other Stories, translated by Peter Henry, Liv Tudge, and Donald Rayfield. London, Angel, 1988.

Fiction

"Krasnyi tsvetok", *Otechestvennye zapiski*, October, 1883; translated as "The Red Flower", by E.L. Voynich, in *Stories from Garshin*, 1893; also translated by Rowland Smith, in *"The Signal" and Other Stories*, 1912; by Bernard Isaacs as "The Scarlet Flower", in *Stories*, 1959; by Peter Henry *et al.*, in *From the Reminiscences of Private Ivanov and Other Stories*, 1988; and by Isadora Levin, San Diego, Harcourt Brace, 1989.

Critical Studies

Pamiati V.M. Garshina. Khudozhestvenno-literaturnyi sbornik, St Petersburg, 1889.
Vsevolod Garshin. A Study of a Russian Conscience, by Fan Parker, New York, King's Crown Press, 1946.
"Vsevolod Garshin als Vorläufer des russischen Symbolismus", by Hans Jürgen Gerigk, *Die Welt der Slaven*, 8 (1962), 246–92.
V.M. Garshin, by Grigorii A. Bialyi, Leningrad, 1973.
"Impressionist Tendencies in the Work of Vsevolod Garšin", by Karl D. Kramer, in *American Contributions to the Seventh International Congress of Slavists*, vol. 2, edited by Victor Terras, The Hague, Mouton, 1973, 339–65.

Sovremenniki o V. M. Garshine. Vospominaniia, edited by G.F. Samosiuk, Saratov, 1977.
Vsevolod Garshin, by Edmund Yarwood, Boston, Twayne, 1981.
A Hamlet of His Time. Vsevolod Garshin: The Man, His Works, and His Milieu, by Peter Henry, Oxford, Meeuws, 1983.
"'The Red Flower' of V.M. Garshin and 'The Black Monk' of A.P. Chechov - A Survey of One Hundred Years of Literary Criticism", by Martine Artz, *Russian Literature*, 20/3 (1986), 267–95.
Grustnyi soldat, ili zhizn' Vsevoloda Garshina, by Vladimir I. Porudominskii, Moscow, 1986.
Vsevolod Garshin. Tvorchestvo i sud'ba, by Alla Latynina, Moscow, 1986.
"Mithra and St George: Sources of 'Krasnyj tsvetok'", by Harry Weber, *The Slavic Review*, 46 (1987), 281–91.

Bibliography
"A Bibliography of Works by and about Vsevolod M. Garshin (1855–1888)", by Edmund Yarwood, *Russian Literature Triquarterly*, 17 (1982), 227–41.

Vsevolod Mikhailovich Garshin completed and published 21 short stories, *ocherki* (sketches) and fairy-tales, some verse and poems in prose, essays on art, and translations. Two major works, *Liudi i voina* [People and War] and an epic set in Petrine Russia, were unfinished; archival publications include numerous drafts and fragments. His father was an army officer, a gentle and eccentric man; his mother was active in the women's emancipation movement. His was a disturbed and lonely childhood and adolescence. The family split in 1860, when his mother eloped to St Petersburg with her son's tutor P.V. Zavadskii, a member of a terrorist movement in Kharkov. In 1863 she took Vsevolod to the capital, where he entered the Institute of Mining in 1874 and was in contact with St Petersburg artists, which yielded four substantial and perceptive reviews of art exhibitions (all 1877); four more were to follow.

In 1877 he volunteered for service in the Russo-Turkish War ("in order to share in the suffering of the people") and was wounded in action. His short story "Chetyre dnia" ("Four Days"), 1877, brought him instant fame. It was published in the St Petersburg periodical *Otechestvennye zapiski*, where, until 1883, most of his stories were published. An intense stream-of-consciousness record of the anguish and pangs of guilt of a wounded soldier left on the battlefield beside the corpse of an enemy soldier whom he has killed, it is an impassioned denunciation of war.

Between 1878 and 1880 he wrote a great deal, much of which he destroyed, and published several other stories on military themes, including the mock-ironic "Ochen' koroten'kii roman" ("A Very Brief Romance"). "Denshchik i ofitser" ("Orderly and Officer") is based on the formula of hero and foil, a simple-minded peasant soldier and his vain and self-indulgent master. Here he began writing on a broader canvas, and with great verbal economy successfully conveyed the tedium of army routine. In "Proisshestvie" ("An Incident") he wrote on prostitution, a theme to which he reverted in a longer, melodramatic story, "Nadezhda Nikolaevna" (1885). In "Vstrecha" ("An Encounter") an apparently dedicated young teacher is progressively revealed as a humbug and philistine. In "Khudozhniki" ("Artists") Garshin refined the hero-and-foil format; it is written in alternating diary entries by two artists, Riabinin, a socially committed artist, and a cynic for whom painting is a lucrative occupation. Riabinin paints the portrait of a furnace-man working in dehumanizing conditions. His obsession results in a nightmare as powerful as Raskol'nikov's in *Crime and Punishment*. "Attalea princeps" is an ambiguous allegory with a political subtext. A palm-tree makes a bid for freedom from its captivity in a conservatory by breaking through the glass dome, but is instantly disenchanted. The story was viewed as a prophetic parable on the fanatical heroism and failure of The People's Will. "Noch'" ("Night") is a powerful Dostoevskian psychological study of a young intellectual on the brink of suicide.

The year 1880, when the confrontation of Reaction and Revolution was at its height, was a critical one for Garshin. His abortive bid by personal intervention to save a revolutionary terrorist from execution initiated a major mental collapse. Before being committed to a lunatic asylum, he visited Tolstoi, and the two writers discussed at length the roots of violence and injustice and how to eradicate them.

After a two-year absence from literature, he wrote "Iz vospominanii riadovogo Ivanova" ("From the Reminiscences of Private Ivanov") 1883, his most sustained and balanced work, presenting a broad perspective on army life and well-drawn character portraits. That year he wrote his best-known work, "Krasnyi tsvetok" ("The Red Flower") and "Medvedi" ("The Bears"), creating evocative pictures of provincial life with a Gogolian touch of the bizarre. "Skazanie o gordom Aggee" ("The Legend of Haggai the Proud") 1886, is written in the simple idiom of a Russian legend. "Signal" ("The Signal") 1887, portrays two railway workers, one meek and pious, the other tough and rebellious, and reflects his equivocal response to Tolstoianism.

His fairy-tales include "To, chego ne bylo" ("What Never Was"), 1882, a learned debate by a dung-beetle, snail, lizard, etc., on the meaning of life, "Skazka o zhabe i roze" ("The Tale of the Toad and the Rose") 1884), an imaginative restatement of the Beauty and the Beast theme, and the humorous cautionary tale "Liagushka-puteshestvennitsa" ("Travelling Frog") 1887.

As his extensive correspondence and reminiscences by contemporaries show, Garshin was a central figure in the St Petersburg intelligentsia. His numerous friends included poets, writers and artists: Nadson, Polonskii, Gleb Uspenskii, Iliia Repin (for whom he posed as the model of the dying Tsarevich in his monumental painting "Ivan the Terrible and His Son"), Iaroshenko and Malyshev. Turgenev saw Garshin as one of his "heirs" and the most important writer of the rising generation. Tolstoi invited him to write for *Posrednik* and preferred his stories to those of Chekhov. Garshin was among the few who appreciated the originality of the latter's story "Step'" ("The Steppe") (1888); Chekhov wrote a story about "a man of the Garshinian cast", "Pripadok" ("The Breakdown") 1889. Leonid Andreev, among others, acknowledged his debt to Garshin. Merezhkovskii recognized him as "a bold innovator" and a master of the concentrated miniature.

He had a superb command of the linguistic and stylistic registers of Russian and excelled at creating atmosphere. He showed originality in the use of light and colour, image and symbol, and the selection of detail. He avoided lengthy descriptions, his sentences are controlled and balanced. Garshin led the way out of the vacuum left by the eclipse of the realist novel. The pioneer of literary impressionism, he was a precursor of Chekhov and Bunin.

PETER HENRY

The Red Flower

Krasnyi tsvetok

Story, 1883

"The Red Flower" was first published in the October issue of the St Petersburg journal *Otechestvennye zapiski* in 1883. Garshin wrote the story three years after his mental breakdown and a four-month stay in a lunatic asylum. It thus relates to his own experience of insanity, but is not an autobiographical record; Garshin described his story as "something fantastic, but in fact strictly real". It is dedicated to the memory of Turgenev, who had died earlier that year and had been Garshin's mentor, encouraging and supporting him in many ways.

Set in a lunatic asylum, it is a succinct and densely written third-person narrative about a madman who perceives three poppies in the hospital grounds as the embodiment of Evil and sees his mission in destroying them, thereby averting cosmic disaster. The Russian psychiatrist I. Sikkorskii wrote a detailed analysis of the story, and it was republished in medical textbooks; Havelock Ellis described it as "the most perfect study of madness". But it is more than a psychiatric document – it is an allegory with mythic overtones and affinities with the magic folk-tale and Promethean legend, an artistic expression of man's quest to go beyond his mortality into the world of the spirit and eternity.

The story is compressed into six short chapters, covering the period from his admission to the hospital to his death. The hero is anonymous throughout, being either "the Patient", or simply "he". Nothing is provided about his identity or his past; he exists only in the present. The writing has a hallucinatory clarity and although some areas of the hospital and its grounds are described in credible visual detail, a model of time and place cannot be established. The poppies are at various times located in different places, and random references like "three days later" merely emphasize the deceptive nature of the "realistic" setting.

The narrative has the intensity of a confessional statement. It is structured on a series of crucial episodes and rhythmic patterns. The action is propelled by a powerful dynamic that intensifies and magnifies the story's bizarre theme, concepts and images and elevates the lonely, anonymous Patient to the status of hero-martyr and saviour. In his consciousness, the bathroom episode in chapter 1 is a parody of baptism, an inquisition and ordeal that qualify him, like a medieval saint, for a mission, as yet uncomprehended. In chapter 3 in a conversation with the hospital doctor, the Patient states his cosmology in a cryptic formula – "Alkalis at one end, acids at the other, such is the equilibrium of the world, in which opposing forces are neutralized" – and voices his conviction that he lives in all ages, and that time and space are mere fictions. Later he expands the hospital into a metaphysical prison, inhabited by the living and the dead, people from all times and all lands. He experiences an apocalyptic vision of the liberation of mankind and cosmic rebirth, in which he will play a leading role. But gradually his altruistic mission fades from his mind and is replaced by a solipsistic compulsion to engage in single combat with Evil, which only he knows is contained in the flowers in the hospital grounds. The focus is narrowed and intensified as the task becomes a private quest, and qualifying phrases like "it seemed to him" are replaced by absolute statements.

The underlying mythologies are Zoroastrianism and the Mithraic doctrine. In chapter 5 the "frightful, bizarre spectre" is identified as "Ahriman, the antithesis of God, in humble and innocent guise". Ahriman is the Lord of Darkness, master of demonic forces wreaking disaster and disease, creator of poisonous plants and wild beasts. He is the eternal antithesis of Ormuzd, the God of Light. Echoes of these mythologies can be traced in the story's inner structure and imagery. At the same time, many of the Patient's thoughts and utterances bear a marked similarity with those of Christ in the Garden of Gethsemane, and the Patient's farewell to the world in the final chapter is a re-enactment of the Last Supper. The Christian dimension is further reflected in his appeals to "Saint George, thou holy martyr, into thy hands I commend my body" and to "all those martyred before me". But acceptance of martyrdom also generates an overweening pride, that of the Nietzschean *Übermensch*, he consciously associates himself with the demonic figure of Peter the Great and dies not a victor, but an undefeated hero, "the first fighter of mankind".

Initially, night is the time of calm, respite and lucidity, while in the morning "he is insane again" and engages in constant manic activity, mental and physical. But as his obsession becomes more intense and exclusive, the action occurs at night. The innocuous poppy becomes a writhing, serpentine monster, "ramifying and assuming monstrous forms", exuding electric charges and poison into the Patient's body. He associates that poison with opium, while in one of several ironic asides we learn that, in order to calm him, the medical staff inject morphine into him and that it is not effective.

Seen by some as a tribute to the "madness of the brave" of the dedicated revolutionary, Garshin's ironic tale is in effect an inversion both of the Russian folk-tale of the benign Little Scarlet Flower and Edgar Allan Poe's "Masque of the Red Death". Chekhov deals with insanity in his stories "Palata No. 6" ("Ward Six"), 1892, and "Chernyi monakh" ("The Black Monk"), 1894, in which there are a number of analogies and parallels with Garshin's story. "The Red Flower" echoes Dostoevskii's "Son smeshnogo cheloveka" ("Dreams of a Ridiculous Man"), Baudelaire's *Les Fleurs du mal*, Flaubert's *La Tentation de Saint Antoine*, and has a surrealist dimension akin to that of Rimbaud, Apollinaire, and Nerval. Such is the power of Garshin's integrity and artistic mastery that, for all its strangeness and incongruities, the story does not lose credibility. An established favourite with Russian readers, "The Red Flower" has been translated into most European languages.

PETER HENRY

Gaito Ivanovich Gazdanov 1903–1971

Prose writer

Biography

Born in St Petersburg, 6 December 1903. Attended various schools in Russia, then in Constantinople (Turkey), Shumen (Bulgaria), and at the Sorbonne, Paris. As a teenager, participated in the Civil War. Evacuated with Vrangel's army in 1920. Reached France in 1923 and spent most of his life there. Married: Faina Dmitrievna Lamzaki. Began to publish, 1926. First important short stories published in the journal *Volia Rossii* (Prague and Paris), 1927–31.Taxi driver in Paris 1928–52. Participated in French Resistance during World War II. Freemason, 1932–71. Literary editor at Radio Liberty, Munich and Paris, 1953–71. Most major works (novels and short stories) published in émigré journals, 1947–72. Published in the Soviet Union from 1988; several major collections appeared in 1990. The novel *Polet* [The Flight], incompletely published in 1939, had its first full edition in Russian in the west in 1992, to be reprinted in Russia in 1993. Died in Munich, 5 December 1971. Buried in the Russian cemetery of Sainte Geneviève-des-Bois, near Paris.

Publications

Collected Editions

Vecher u Kler. Nochnye dorogi. Prizrak Aleksandra Vol'fa. Vozvrashchenie Buddy. Romany [An Evening with Claire. Night Roads. The Spectre of Alexander Wolf. Buddha's Return. Novels], edited by R.Kh. Totrova. Vladikavkaz, 1990.

Vecher u Kler. Romany i rasskazy [An Evening with Claire. Novels and Short Stories], edited by S. Nikonenko. Moscow, 1990.

Prizrak Aleksandra Vol'fa. Romany [The Spectre of Alexander Wolf. Novels], edited by S. Nikonenko. Moscow, 1990.

Sobranie sochinenii, 3 vols, edited by Laszlo Dienes *et al.* Moscow, 1996.

Fiction

Vecher u Kler. Paris, Povolotskii, 1930; reprinted Ann Arbor, Ardis, 1979; translated as *An Evening with Claire*, by Jodi Daynard, Ann Arbor, Ardis, 1988.

Istoriia odnogo puteshestviia [The History of a Journey]. Paris, Dom knigi, 1938.

"Polet" [The Flight], *Russkie zapiski*, 18–20/21 (1939) (incomplete); first complete edition edited by Laszlo Dienes, The Hague, Leuxenhoff, 1992; also published in full in *Druzhba narodov*, 8–9 (1993), 97–159; 95–130.

"Nochnaia doroga" [Night Road], *Sovremennye zapiski*, 69–70 (1939–40); reprinted in separate edition as *Nochnye dorogi* [Night Roads], New York, Izdatel'stvo imeni Chekhova, 1952; Moscow, 1992.

"Prizrak Aleksandra Vol'fa", *Novyi zhurnal*, 16–18 (1947–48); translated as *The Spectre of Alexander Wolf*, by Nicholas Wreden, London, Jonathan Cape, and New York, Dutton, 1950.

"Vozvrashchenie Buddy", *Novyi zhurnal*, 22–23 (1949–50); translated as *Buddha's Return*, by Nicholas Wreden, New York, Dutton, 1951.

"Piligrimy" [Pilgrims], *Novyi zhurnal*, 33–36 (1953–54); edited by Galina and Asia Gusevykh, *Drugie berega*, 1 (1992), 80–112, 114–40, 143; 2–3 (1993), 64–106; 23–54.

"Probuzhdenie" [The Awakening], *Novyi zhurnal*, 78–82 (1965–66).

"Evelina i ee druz'ia" [Evelina and Her Friends], *Novyi zhurnal*, 92, 94–105 (1968–71).

"Perevorot" [The coup d'état], *Novyi zhurnal*, 107–09 (1972) (posthumous edition of unfinished novel).

Critical Studies

Russian Literature in Exile: The Life and Work of Gajto Gazdanov, by Laszlo Dienes, Munich, Sagner, 1982.

S togo berega: pisateli russkogo zarubezh'ia o Rossii: proizvedeniia 20–30-kh gg., edited by I.A. Kuramzhina, Moscow, 1992.

Bibliography

Bibliographie des oeuvres de Gaito Gazdanov, by Laszlo Dienes, Paris, Institut d'Études Slaves, 1982.

Gaito Gazdanov's literary career began in 1927 with the publication of his first story in Marc Slonim's journal *Volia Rossii* (Prague and Paris) where he published eight more stories until 1931. It was the year 1930, however, that marked the beginning of Gazdanov's fame in emigration. In January his first (and according to many of his contemporaries, his best) novel *Vecher u Kler* (*An Evening with Claire*) came out in Paris and was met with great critical acclaim, soon to be followed by another success, the short story "Vodianaia tiur'ma" [Water Prison], widely considered the best piece of fiction in the first issue of the new, and controversial, journal *Chisla*. As a result, Gazdanov was seen as the second most talented and promising young writer in emigration, after Nabokov. Even Gor'kii had a high opinion of *An Evening with Claire* and proposed to publish it in "the land of Soviets". This success opened for Gazdanov the doors to the leading émigré journal *Sovremennye zapiski*, where two of his novels, *Istoriia odnogo puteshestviia* [The History of a Journey] and *Nochnye dorogi* [Night Roads], and eight of his short stories were published in the 1930s. In the pre-war years Gazdanov was an active member of the Parisian Russian literary and intellectual world; he gave several readings of his prose, participated in the meetings of literary groups, especially those of "Kochev'e", published a few essays and reviews and provoked a heated discussion in 1936 when he wrote a very pessimistic appraisal of Russian literature abroad, claiming, modestly, that it did not produce any significant talent except for Nabokov. After World War II most of Gazdanov's work was published in the New York journal *Novyi zhurnal*. The first two post-war novels, *Prizrak Aleksandra Vol'fa* (*The Spectre of Alexander Wolf*) and *Vozvrashchenie Buddy* (*Buddha's Return*), were translated into English (as well as some other European languages) and published in London and New York. Although they were fashioned somewhat in the mould of psychological and metaphysical thrillers, they did not lead to recognition by the non-Russian western reader. From 1953 Gazdanov worked as literary editor at Radio Liberty, which initially meant a drop in his productivity as a writer. The 1960s, however, saw a resurgence of his creative energy resulting in several novels and short stories. Yet, of all the remaining six novels written since 1938 only one, *Nochnye dorogi*, was ever published in Russia in book form during the writer's lifetime.

Gazdanov did not live long enough to witness the revival of interest in émigré literature which brought about first a reprint, then a translation into English of his *An Evening with Claire*; a series of reprints of other works in the émigré press; a monograph in Germany; a bibliography in France; a first complete edition in Russian of one of his best novels, *Polet* [The Flight], in the Netherlands; and at least ten book-form editions of his works (three of which were collections) and more than 30 publications in periodicals in Russia itself between 1988 and 1994. The time has come, as predicted by Iu. Ivask, when: "a complete collected works will be published ... not in Paris or New York, but in Moscow and Leningrad. His prose will undoubtedly reach the Russian reader just as Nabokov's did ..."

Gazdanov's fiction is mostly (although seldom openly) autobiographical: we are given the lyrical recollections of the narrator-hero (often himself a writer) who describes the psychological, inner journeys of his characters, the subtle "movements of the soul", as he likes to call them. These heroes undergo transformations, "metamorphoses" while searching for their true identity, happiness, or the answers to life's great questions. The latter allows Gazdanov to introduce philosophical meditations, as well as to "thicken" the plot by introducing an element of suspense (often a murder). Gazdanov was a Russian writer who went through the shattering experiences of world and civil wars, the total collapse of a civilization. More importantly, he had that special modern experience that can be called – following Tolstoi and Shestov – "the terror of Arzamas": the loss of self, of identity, the anguish and anxiety that besets man when he contemplates the ultimate questions of human existence in a world reduced to exclusively human dimensions. Gazdanov managed to communicate this existential experience and this makes him a truly contemporary, 20th-century writer in the western sense of the word. Most of his novels are both an illustration of, and perhaps an attempt to overcome, the terror of seeing meaningless chance rule over all human life. Towards the end of his life the sceptical Gazdanov "mellowed" somewhat, and in some of his late novels, in particular *Piligrimy* [Pilgrims] and *Probuzhdenie* [The Awakening], he seemed to rejoin the great tradition of classical Russian literature in affirming that love, compassion and helping others can give meaning to our otherwise apparently meaningless human existence. There are a number of themes that recur throughout his *oeuvre*: of fate, chance, and death; the theme of the unpredictability and meaninglessness of human life, illustrated by the most unexpected and unbelievable human metamorphoses; the theme of art and literature as a desperate attempt to make sense of it all; and the theme of love and our emotional life as the foundation from which all rational thoughts, logical systems and moral and social ideologies spring.

The style of Gazdanov's prose is characterized by a strict economy, a careful selection of suggestive detail, a reliance on sound, an impeccably sustained rhythm and a fine sense of language. The high emotional intensity is subdued and restrained by the firmly controlled, lucid, and well-balanced classical style that does not allow turmoil of the heart to disrupt the orderliness of the prose. Ultimately, Gazdanov's works operate through language and style: the separation of "content" becomes impossible, for what he says lies in how he says it. The way he articulates his knowledge contains his knowledge. Commentary is often expressed in the angle of vision and objective description is never given other than for psychological reasons. The suggestiveness of his prose comes from its extraordinarily graphic and sensuous quality: we are made to experience physically, to feel, see, smell, and touch. It is a biological, physiological kind of art where insight, intuition, and intellectual contemplation are effected through and by the sensuous and visual dimensions of existence. The critics' praise for this aspect of his writing was unanimous. The deceptive simplicity of Gazdanov's style comes from the apparent ease with which the writer can manipulate his material and the seeming lack of means with which he creates his authentic landscapes of mood and atmosphere.

Another unusual combination in much of Gazdanov's fiction is the simultaneous presence of a story-telling talent that makes his writings very "interesting" and "readable" and a propensity for meditative, intellectual prose. This latter feature becomes particularly highly developed in his late short stories, such as "Nishchii" [The Beggar] or "Pis'ma Ivanova" [Ivanov's Letters], and suggests an attempt to create a new kind of contemplative prose in the classicistic mould, perhaps in the style of Camus, to whom the French critics compared Gazdanov. The most striking feature of Gazdanov's style, however, is the resolved tension (or, in other words, the hard-earned harmony and balance) between the emotional intensity of the lives he depicts and the reserve and simplicity of his easy-flowing language. This may well be another French influence. Gazdanov's prose has been called "a distillation of literary Russian", a prose of great clarity and purity which, when combined with its modern, existential themes, makes for a truly original style.

LASZLO DIENES

Gertsen *see* Herzen

Evgeniia Semenovna Ginzburg 1904–1977
Memoirist

Biography
Born in Moscow, 20 December 1904. Educated in Kazan. Teacher, journalist, college instructor and Party activist. Married: 1) Dmitrii Fedorov, one son; 2) Pavel Aksenov, one son, the writer Vasilii Aksenov; 3) Anton Walter, one adopted daughter. Arrested, 1937: solitary confinement in Iaroslavl, labour camp in Kolyma. Released, 1947. Lived in exile in Magadan, while Anton Walter was finishing sentence, 1947–49, during which time Vasilii Aksenov lived with Ginzburg. Rearrested, 1949. Released, rehabilitated, and allowed to return to Moscow, 1955–56. Moved to L'vov with Walter. Lived in Moscow after Walter's death in 1959. Began publishing short stories, reviews, and essays in *Iunost'* and other journals. Died in Moscow, 25 May 1977.

Publications
Fiction
Tak nachinalos' [This is the Way It Began]. Kazan, 1963.
"Edinaia trudovaia" [The Sole Labouress], *Iunost'*, 11 (1965).
"Studenty dvadtsatykh godov" [Students of the 20s], *Iunost'*, 8 (1966).
"Iunosha" [The Youth], *Iunost'*, 9 (1967).

Memoirs
Krutoi marshrut I. Milan, 1967; Frankfurt, Posev, 1967; Riga, 1989; Moscow, 1990; translated as *Journey into the Whirlwind*, by Paul Stevenson and Max Hayward, New York, Harcourt Brace, and London, Collins and Harvill, 1967; reprinted as *Into the Whirlwind*, Harmondsworth, Penguin, 1968.
Krutoi marshrut II. Milan, 1979; translated as *Within the Whirlwind*, by Ian Boland, New York, Harcourt Brace, 1981.

Critical Studies
Vol'naia russkaia literatura 1955–1975, by Iu. Mal'tsev, Frankfurt, Posev, 1976, 235–42.
"Evgeniia Ginzburg", by Barbara Heldt, in *Modern Encyclopedia of Russian and Soviet History*, edited by Harry B. Weber, Gulf Breeze, Florida, Academic International Press, 1977, 165–68.
Kolyma: The Arctic Death Camps, by Robert Conquest, London, Macmillan, and New York, Viking Press, 1978.
Na lobnom meste. Literatura nravstvennogo soprotivleniia (1946–1976), by Grigori Svirski, London, Overseas Publications Interchange, 1979; translated as *A History of Post-War Soviet Writing: The Literature of Moral Opposition*, by Robert Dessaix and Michael Ulman, Ann Arbor, Ardis, 1981.
Ozhog, by Vasilii Aksenov, Ann Arbor, Ardis, 1980; translated as *The Burn*, by Michael Glenny, Boston, Houghton Mifflin, and London, Hutchinson, 1984 (fictional impressions by her son).
"Kniga-zhizn'", by V. Iverni, *Kontinent*, 23 (1980), 286–92.
Tri portreta, by Lev Kopelev and Raisa Orlova, Ann Arbor, Ardis, 1983.
"E. Ginzburg's *Krutoi marshrut* and A. Aksenov's *Ozhog*: The Magadan Connection", by David Lowe, *Slavic and East European Journal*, 27/2 (1983), 200–10.
Vasily Pavlovich Aksenov: A Writer in Quest of Himself, edited by Edward Mozejko, Columbus, Ohio, Slavica, 1984.
Put' otrecheniia, by Mark Al'tshuller and Elena Dryzhakova, Tenafly, New Jersey, Hermitage, 1985, 277–82.
Terrible Perfection: Women and Russian Literature, by Barbara Heldt, Bloomington, Indiana University Press, 1987.
Russian Writing since 1953: A Critical Survey, by David Lowe, New York, Ungar, 1987.
"Evgeniia Ginzburg v kontse krutogo marshruta", in *My zhili v Moskve 1956–1980*, by Raisa Orlova and Lev Kopelev, Ann Arbor, Ardis, 1988, 311–44.
"Meetings and Conversations with Aleksandr Tvardovskii", by Roy Medvedev, *Michigan Quarterly Review*, edited by Jane Burbank and William Rosenberg, 28/4 (1989), 604–38.
"Evgeniia S. Ginzburg", by Adele Barker, in *Dictionary of Russian Women Writers*, edited by Marina Ledkovsky, Charlotte Rosenthal, and Mary Zirin, Westport, Connecticut, Greenwood Press, 1994, 205–06.
"For the Good of the Cause: Russian Women's Autobiography in the Twentieth Century", by Beth Holmgren, in *Women Writers in Russian Literature*, edited by Toby W. Clyman and Diana Greene, Westport, Connecticut, Greenwood Press, 1994, 127–48.
Dva sledstvennykh dela Evgenii Ginzburg, edited by A.L. Litvin, Kazan, 1994.

Evgeniia Ginzburg received international recognition with her two-volume masterpiece, *Krutoi marshrut I* (*Journey into the Whirlwind*) and *Krutoi marshrut II* (*Within the Whirlwind*). This autobiographical work places her in the company of two other great talents who survived Stalin's Gulag, namely Solzhenitsyn and Shalamov, "writers able to transform the rude facts of history into artistic structures". When asked how she could remember hundreds of names, places and facts over an 18-year period through the vast Siberian archipelago of labour camps, Evgeniia Ginzburg answered: "Very simply: because just remembering it all to record it later had been the main object of my life throughout those 18 years". Thus, Ginzburg was motivated by the responsibilities of a survivor to bear witness. It was also to Ginzburg's credit that her "whirlwind" memoirs helped inaugurate the dissident movement.

Ginzburg's literary career began shortly after her rehabilitation. Before her celebrated memoirs became the most widely circulated *samizdat* publication of the 1960s, Ginzburg wrote and published stories, sketches and reviews, based on her experience as a teacher, journalist and party activist. *Tak nachinalos'* [This is the Way It Began], a novella published in 1963, describes her life as a teacher in Kazan. The autobiographical approach continues in her subsequent stories, published in *Iunost'* between 1965 and 1967. "Edinaia trudovaia" [The Sole Labouress] covers the period of the 1920s and what it was like to be a child of the Revolution undergoing a new Soviet education. "Studenty dvadtsatykh godov" [Students of the 20s] chronicles the post-revolutionary "sky is the limit" thinking, while depicting the human pitfalls of an ideology based on class warfare. In her novella, "Iunosha" [The Youth], about Aleksandr Ginzburg (no relation to the author), the commissar who was executed during the Purges, there is already a hint of the type of documentary narrative present in her memoirs.

Inspired by the 22nd Party Conference and the publication of Solzhenitsyn's *One Day in the Life of Ivan Denisovich*, Ginzburg submitted her manuscript to the two most popular "thick" journals, *Iunost'* and *Novyi mir*. Although the majority of *Novyi mir*'s editors approved it, Aleksandr Tvardovskii, editor-in-chief, rejected the manuscript on the grounds that Ginzburg had focused on the arrests of privileged communists, and had failed to write about the peasants. Ginzburg's memoirs then embarked on a five-year odyssey of their own through *samizdat*. Roi Medvedev admits to circulating the manuscript himself around Moscow and Leningrad. Applauding her testimony were Erenburg, Paustovskii, Kaverin, Chukovskii, Solzhenitsyn, Evtushenko, Voznesenskii, Panova, to mention but a few. While her first volume was serialized in the émigré journal *Grani*, it appeared concurrently in Italy in 1967, and was quickly translated into many languages. The author admitted that her internal censor, her impulse to curb the urge to indict, was motivated by the desire to publish in her native land. Thus, while indicting Stalin, Ginzburg ends her first volume calling herself a "rank and file Communist" ever grateful that "the great Leninist truths have prevailed". It took another 12 years for the sequel to appear posthumously. Volume 2 bears no traces of self-censorship, for not only does she indict her Party, but she holds every Russian guilty, including herself.

Journey into the Whirlwind begins with a now famous first line: "The year 1937 really began on 1 December 1934", underscoring the pivotal historical moment which anticipated the Terror, Sergei Kirov's assassination. The two volumes span more than two decades, from 1934 to 1955. Before her arrest in 1937 there was no greater cause in her life than the Party. When the threat of arrest became imminent her husband, Pavel Aksenov, a high-ranking member of the Kazan Regional Party Committee (who, too, would soon be imprisoned) consoled her by implying that the Party would have to put everybody in jail if it were to arrest a loyal communist like Ginzburg. While she could have escaped into the country as her mother-in-law suggested, or produced a false confession in order to avoid arrest, the idealistic author accepted her fate along with thousands of other loyal Party members, and was thus charged with "Trotskyist terrorist activity". Thus, volume 1 traces the chaos of mass arrests, mock trials, solitary confinement and interrogations, consisting of the dreaded "conveyor" (a form of assembly-line torture in which the prisoner is forced to stand for days and days of gruelling interrogations without sleep and food), followed by the train journey through Siberia, transit camps, and ends in Kolyma.

It was her misfortune to end up in the deadliest of all the labour camps, Kolyma, particularly in the women's camp, Elgen. This is where the second volume begins in 1940 and covers the remaining years of her sentence. Ginzburg refrains, however, from dwelling on misfortune; instead, she sees small miracles throughout her ordeal mysteriously conspiring to keep her alive, like her transfer to a hospital for children, or her love affair with Anton Walter (whom she would later marry), or the mysterious way in which she was able to convince the powers-that-be to permit her son, the writer, Vasilii Aksenov, to join her in Magadan, after she was rehabilitated. Throughout strategies of survival are created with the affirmation: "You can survive anything!" One such strategy of survival is poetry. The author's own poetry permeates the first volume and is juxtaposed with memorized lines from Blok, Akhmatova, and Pasternak. On the first night that Ginzburg and her son are alone together in Magadan, poetry serves to heal their 12-year separation as they realize their favourite poets constituted their spiritual family. Indeed, one discerns that memorizing poetry is as therapeutic as nursing fellow patients back to health.

One of the extraordinary features of Ginzburg's artistry is her ability to convey brutality and unbearable suffering with irony and humour. Ginzburg counterbalances the incongruity of certain situations with understatement in a unique generic blend of documentary, autobiographical, and fictional modes. The lines "penal servitude, what bliss", from Pasternak's narrative poem *Leitenant Shmidt* [Lieutenant Schmidt], ironize the author's privileged perspective, which can find profound spiritual sustenance in confined quarters: "Sitting in a cell, you don't chase after the phantoms of worldly success ... You can be wholly concerned with the highest problems of existence, and you approach them with a mind purified by suffering". Just as Solzhenitsyn revealed that a union of brotherhood in the camps made imprisoned life bearable, almost preferable to being outside, so Ginzburg describes the rare sisterhood that develops among women in the Gulag. Ginzburg's accounts are replete with epiphanies, such as the time she discovers that one of the many casualties of prison life for women is the prospect of becoming sexless. After spending two years in solitary confinement, the heroine is led out of her cell and encounters the shapes of other women, but shapes who have lost their feminine contours: "So, this is what Elgen had in store for us. We had already lost our professional and Party status, our citizenship, our families; we were now to lose our sex as well". Volume 2 is much more sombre than the first volume. While there are noticeably fewer poetic allusions, and the author faces what clearly seems like an improvement in her case, Ginzburg was aware that the volume would not see the light of day in Soviet Russia in her lifetime.

Ginzburg, unlike the author with whom she is most often compared, Solzhenitsyn, does not permit her co-prisoners the luxury of philosophizing about life; rather her persona is too busy in maintaining a sense of continuity. In general, the women prisoners refrain from calling attention to themselves, but rather exemplify perseverance and steadfastness, underscored by the ties forged between the women of the camps. Ginzburg remains true throughout to an age-old ideal in Russian literature of woman as a long-suffering creature, who must endure without lapsing into self-pity.

OLGA COOKE

Lidiia Iakovlevna Ginzburg 1902–1990

Memoirist, prose writer, and literary theorist

Biography

Born in Odessa, 18 March 1902. Attended a young women's gymnasium in Odessa; Petrograd State Institute for the History of the Arts (GIII), 1922–26; Leningrad State University, Candidate's degree, 1938; Doctoral degree, 1958. Studied under Iurii Tynianov and Boris Eikhenbaum, associated with the "Young Formalists". Taught seminars in 19th-century Russian poetry at GIII, 1926–30. Worked for the publishing house *Detgiz*, and wrote a detective novel for adolescents in 1932; taught language and elementary courses in literature in *Rabfak* (workers' school) and adult education programmes. Banned from institutions of higher education until 1947. Taught at Petrozavodsk University, 1947–50. Connected with two important court cases: the "Zhirmunskii case" in 1933 and the case against Eikhenbaum and the Faculty of Russian literature at Leningrad State University in 1952. Editor for State Radio in Leningrad during World War II and the Blockade. Major publications appeared after the Thaw, 1964–90. Recipient: State Prize for Literature, 1988. Died in Leningrad, 15 July 1990.

Publications

Fiction

Agentstvo Pinkertona [The Pinkerton Agency]. 1932.

Memoirs

O starom i novom [On the Old and the New]. Leningrad, 1982.

"Tynianov-uchenyi" [Tynianov the Scholar], in *Vospominaniia o Tynianove. Portrety i vstrechi*, Moscow, 1983, 147–72.

"Zabolotskii kontsa dvadtsatykh godov" [Zabolotskii at the End of the 1920s], in *Vospominaniia o N. Zabolotskom*, 2nd edition, Moscow, 1983, 145–56.

"Zapiski blokadnogo cheloveka", *Neva*, 1 (1984), 84–104; translated as *Blockade Diary*, by Alan Myers, London, Harvill Press, 1995.

"Eshche raz o starom i novom (Pokolenie na povorote)" [Once Again on the Old and the New (Turning Point of a Generation)], in *Tynianovskii sbornik. Vtorye Tynianovskie chteniia*, Riga, 1986, 132–40; translated as "Tsvetayeva et Pougatchev", *Lettre Internationale*, 22 (1989), 69.

Literatura v poiskakh real'nosti [Literature in Search of Reality]. Leningrad, 1987.

Chelovek za pismennym stolom [The Person Behind the Desk]. Leningrad, 1989; excerpt translated as "Tolstoj e Proust", *La Nuova Rivista Europea*, October–December (1978), 39–44.

"Vspominaia Institut Istorii Iskusstv" [Remembering the Institute of the History of the Arts], in *Tynianovskii sbornik. Chetvertye Tynianovskie chteniia*, Riga, 1990, 278–88.

"Dve vstrechi" [Two Encounters], *Russkaia mysl'*, 3852, (2 November 1990).

Pretvorenie opyta [Recreation of Experience], edited by Nikolai Kononov. Leningrad, 1991.

"Zapisi 20–30-x godov (Iz neopublikovannogo)" [Entries of the 1920s and 1930s (previously unpublished)], *Novyi mir*, 6 (1992), 1–41.

"Iz dnevnikov Lidii Ginzburg" [From the Diaries of Lidiia Ginzburg], *Literaturnaia gazeta*, 41/5469 (13 October 1993), 6.

Literary Criticism

"Viazemskii – literator", in *Russkaia proza*, edited by B.M. Eikhenbaum and Iu.N. Tynianov, Leningrad, 1926, 102–34; translated as "Vyazemsky – Man of Letters", in *Russian Prose*, edited and translated by Ray Parrott, Ann Arbor, Ardis, 1985, 87–108.

O lirike [The Lyric]. Leningrad, 1964; last chapter translated as "The Poetics of Osip Mandelstam", by Sona Hoisington, in *Twentieth Century Russian Literary Criticism*, edited by Victor Erlich, New Haven, Yale University Press, 1975, 284–312.

O psikhologicheskoi proze. Leningrad, 1971; translated as *On Psychological Prose*, by Judson Rosengrant, Princeton, Princeton University Press, 1991.

O literaturnom geroe [On the Literary Hero]. Leningrad, 1979.

Critical Studies

"Lidiia Ginzburg. O lirike", by I. Podol'skaia, *Izvestiia Akademii Nauk SSSR: Seriia literatury i iazyka*, 34/1 (January–February 1975), 81–83.

"Mashtabnost' issledovaniia", by Iakov Gordin, *Voprosy literatury*, 1 (1981), 273–81.

"Lidiia Ginzburg's Contribution to Literary Criticism", edited by Sarah Pratt, *Canadian-American Slavic Studies* (special issue), 19/2 (1985), 119–99.
"Tvorcheskii portret L.Ia. Ginzburg", by Boris Gasparov *et al.*, *Literaturnoe obozrenie*, (1989), 78–86.
"Lidiia Ginzburg and the Fluidity of Genre", by Sarah Pratt, in *Autobiographical Statements in Twentieth Century Russian Literature*, edited by Jane Gary Harris, Princeton, Princeton University Press, 1990, 207–16.
"Lidiia Iakovlevna Ginzburg", by Jane Gary Harris, in *Dictionary of Russian Women Writers*, edited by Marina Ledkovsky, Charlotte Rosenthal, and Mary Zirin, Westport, Connecticut, Greenwood Press, 1994, 206–10.
"In Memoriam: Lidiia Ginzburg", edited by Jane Gary Harris, *Canadian-American Slavic Studies* (special issue), 28/2 (1994), 125–285.
"The Crafting of a Self: Lidiia Ginzburg's Early Journal", by Jane Gary Harris, in *Gender and Russian Literature: New Perspectives*, edited by Rosalind Marsh, Cambridge and New York, Cambridge University Press, 1996, 263–82.

Bibliography
"L.Ia. Ginzburg: An International Chronological Bibliography of Primary and Secondary Works", by Judson Rosengrant, *The Russian Review*, 54/4 (October 1995), 587–600.

Lidiia Iakovlevna Ginzburg, distinguished literary theorist and writer, known primarily outside Russia for *O lirike* [The Lyric], *O psikhologicheskoi proze* (*On Psychological Prose*), and *O literaturnom geroe* [On the Literary Hero], gained prominence at the end of her life as a major thinker, writer, witness, and public spokesperson. Only in the last decade of her life, did Ginzburg reveal herself as a master of the art of the journal, the essay, and recorded conversation, which she practised as new forms of contemporary prose. In 1988, at the age of 86, on being awarded the prestigious State Prize for Literature, she defined her writing in an interview:

> A sense of the author's presence is developing apace in contemporary prose ... One takes up one's pen for a conversation about life – not to write an autobiography, but to express one's life experience, one's views on reality directly ... This is the path of future literary developments ... which I prefer myself. (*Smena*, 1988)

While Ginzburg's scholarship ranges from lyric poetry to narrative prose, her theory of the "intermediary genres" is closely associated with her literary practice. She theorized the nature of materials not previously considered "aesthetic" as she mastered the art of genres not previously considered "literary". Indeed, Ginzburg's life-long contemplation of the correlations between reality or "lived experience" and literary creation provides the key to all her writing, but above all, to her own art of the *zapis'* (journal entry), the philosophical or memoiristic essay, and the "recorded conversation". Titles of such later collections as *Literatura v poiskakh real'nosti* [Literature in Search of Reality], or her last authorized publication, *Pretvorenie opyta* [Recreation of Experience], afford entry into Ginzburg's primary intellectual and literary themes, namely, how "lived experience" is creatively transformed into literature, how narrative and dialogue influence "reality", and how social and cultural behaviour interact with their aesthetic representation to give meaning to human life at different times and under different guises. Major literary influences included Rousseau, Tolstoi, Viazemskii, Mandel'shtam, and Proust, practitioners of self-reflexive, but not self-indulgent, analytical prose.

Born in Odessa into a family of liberal Jewish intelligentsia, Ginzburg left home in 1922 for Leningrad (then Petrograd) and GIII (the State Institute of the History of the Arts), where her teachers included Eikhenbaum, Tynianov, Tomashevskii, Zhirmunskii and Vinogradov. Her student years (1922–26) coincided with a revolution in the study of the verbal arts initiated by OPOIAZ, the Formalist movement she later described in *Pokolenie na povorote* [Turning Point of a Generation] as a "source of ferment" and integral part of the broader intellectual and cultural currents of the epoch. She viewed her circle, the "Young Formalists", in terms of the epoch's literary alignments, as part of the "innocent opposition" of the independent-minded Formalists.

After graduating from GIII in 1926, Ginzburg was appointed a *nauchnyi sotrudnik* (research scholar). She broadly defined herself at that time as a "littérateur", and initiated her private journal modelled at first on that of the 19th-century poet and "littérateur" Prince Viazemskii, the subject of her earliest scholarly publication, "Viazemskii – literator" ["Viazemskii – Man of Letters"]. Thus began her double life as literary scholar and writer. With the closing of GIII in 1930, Ginzburg was forced to find new employment. She worked at the Childrens Publishing House (*Detgiz*), producing a detective novel for adolescents, *Agentstvo Pinkertona* [The Pinkerton Agency], and obtained teaching assignments in workers' schools (*Rabfak*) and adult education classes. She was effectively banned from institutions of higher education except when she taught at Petrozavodsk University.

Ginzburg remained in Leningrad throughout World War II, living at the State Radio station where she worked as an editor. She used her blockade journal to create the highly acclaimed *Zapiski blokadnogo cheloveka* (*Blockade Diary*), a quasi-fictional existential narrative concerning the experience and behaviour of a human being living under conditions of war. It was not accepted for publication until 1984; its sequel, "Conversations from the Leningrad Blockade", appeared only posthumously.

The first of Ginzburg's two "direct encounters with the organs" took place in 1933. She was "so psychologically unprepared" that she burst out laughing when asked if she "knew Zhirmunskii to be a spy" ("Dve vstrechi" [Two Encounters]). However, for Ginzburg the immediate post-war years of vicious anti-intellectual and anti-Semitic attacks (1946–53) were "the most terrifying" because the "moral and psychological variant" used by the "creative intelligentsia" in the 1930s "no longer worked"; people finally woke up to their own naivety to confront the horrors of their social environment. She came to repudiate as repulsive her work of the later Stalinist years – her Doctoral dissertation on Herzen, which she was only permitted to defend in 1958. Her Candidate's dissertation on Lermontov was defended in 1938.

Ginzburg's second KGB "encounter" occurred at the close of 1952, when she was unsuccessfully recruited to develop a case against her former teacher, Boris Eikhenbaum. Saved by Stalin's death, she experienced her first feelings of renewal and hope, combined with a new sensation of being part of the "older generation" ("O starosti i ob infantilizme" [Old Age and Infantilism]). Though energized by the Thaw, she recognized its precariousness.

While Ginzburg's major theoretical works began to appear in print in the 1960s, it was not until 1982 that her prose began to come to light. Encouraged by sympathetic editors at the Sovetskii pisatel' publishing house and the magazine *Novyi mir*, her first "memoirs of contemporaries" were printed along with her first *zapisi* (journal entries).

The publications of the 1980s frequently reflect their genesis in conversations with younger colleagues – the result of Ginzburg's cult-like status in post-Stalinist Leningrad as mentor and support for writers and scholars unrecognized by the official Soviet hierarchy. Her unique role as an intellectual conduit between the pre- and post-Stalininst generations of the Russian intelligentsia was instrumental in establishing a viable sense of cultural continuity and in reviving intellectual life in the 1960s–80s. Theoretical supposition, literary analogues, and semiotic analysis supplement Ginzburg's personal recollections, providing a judicious assessment of the behaviour of the Soviet intelligentsia. Even during the worst of times, she claimed, ordinary life never ceased, for everyone was equally involved, no one's life was an exception, "as in wartime". But, "no one escaped unscathed".

By the end of the 1980s, Ginzburg had become a publicly powerful spokesperson. Having lived long enough to voice her opinion freely, she took moral satisfaction in the principle of glasnost: "People have been stirred up to talk. That's the most important thing ... The principle itself – that I can say what I think – is an event of enormous moral consequence ..." (*Literaturnaia Rossiia*, 1988).

JANE GARY HARRIS

Gippius *see* Hippius

Anatolii Tikhonovich Gladilin 1935–

Prose writer

Biography

Born in Moscow, 21 August 1935. Completed secondary education. Worked as an electrician. Studied at Military Academy; later at Gor'kii Literary Institute, Moscow. Worked as a manual labourer; journalist for the newspaper, *Moskovskii komsomolets*. First publication, "Khronika vremen Viktora Podgurskogo" [Chronicle of the Times of Victor Podgurskii], in *Iunost'*, 1956. Associated with the "Youth Prose" movement. Extensive travel through USSR. Member of the Writers' Union, 1960, but never accepted by official critics; supported by Valentin Kataev. Signed protest against trial of Siniavskii and Daniel', 1966; therafter denied publication in USSR. Emigrated to Paris, April 1976; worked as broadcaster for Radio Liberty.

Publications

Fiction

"Khronika vremen Viktora Podgurskogo" [Chronicle of the Times of Victor Podgurskii], *Iunost'*, 9 (1956).
Idushchii vperedi [The One in Front]. Moscow, 1958.
Brigantina podnimaet parusa [The Brigantine Hoists Its Sails]. Moscow, 1959.
Dym v glaza [Smokescreen]. Moscow, 1959.
Pesni zolotogo priiska [Songs of the Gold Mine]. Moscow, 1960.
Vechnaia komandirovka [The Never-Ending Business Trip]. Moscow, 1962.
Pervyi den' novogo goda [The First Day of the New Year]. Moscow, 1963.
Istoriia nashei kompanii [The History of Our Crowd]. Moscow, 1965.
Tigr perekhodit ulitsu [There's a Tiger Crossing the Street]. Moscow, 1965.
Evangelie ot Robesp'era [The Gospel According to Robespierre]. Moscow, 1970.
Prognoz na zavtra [Tomorrow's Weather]. Frankfurt, Posev, 1972.
Sny Shlissel'burgskoi kreposti [Dreams of the Schlusselburg Fortress]. Moscow, 1974.
Repetitsiia v piatnitsu [Rehearsal on Friday]. Paris, Effect, 1978.
Parizhskaia iarmarka [The Paris Fair]. Paris, Effect, 1980.
Bol'shoi begovoi den' [Derby Day]. Ann Arbor, Ardis, 1983; translated as *The Moscow Racetrack*, translated by R.P. Schoenberg and Janet G. Tucker, Ann Arbor, Ardis, 1992.
FSSR Frantsuzskaia Sovetskaia Sotsialisticheskaia Respublika [The Soviet Socialist Republic of France]. New York, Effect, 1985.
Kakim ia byl togda [How I Was Then]. Ann Arbor, Ardis, 1986.

"Kontsert dlia truby s orkestrom" [Concerto for Trumpet and Orchestra], *Ogonek*, 30 (1989).
Menia ubil skotina Pell [I Was Killed by that Bastard Pell]. 1989; reprinted Moscow, 1991.

Memoirs
The Making and Unmaking of a Soviet Writer: My Story of the "Young Prose" of the Sixties and After, translated by David Lapeza, Ann Arbor, Ardis, 1979.
"The West and in Particular France, Through the Eyes of a Distracted Russian", in *Under Eastern Eyes: The West as Reflected in Recent Russian Émigré Writing*, edited by Arnold McMillin, London, Macmillan, 1991, 76–83; New York, St Martin's Press, 1992.

Critical Studies
"Urok zhizni i prosto urok", by V. Shitova, *Iunost'*, 5 (1960).
"V krivom zerkale paradoksov", by E. Gromov, *Smena*, 22 (1960).
"Material i priem", by I. Solov'eva, *Novyi mir*, 4 (1963).
Russian Literature since the Revolution, by Edward J. Brown, Cambridge, Massachusetts, Harvard University Press, 1963; 2nd edition, 1982.
Soviet Russian Literature since Stalin, by Deming Brown, Cambridge, Cambridge University Press, 1978.
"Chto nasha zhizn'?", by Irina Basova, *Grani*, 135 (1985).
"Gladilin", by Priscilla Meyer, in *The Modern Encyclopedia of Russian and Soviet Literatures*, vol. 8, edited by Harry B. Weber, Gulf Breeze, Florida, Academic International Press, 1987.
"Can You Win at Chess with a Marked Deck of Cards?", by Nora Buhks, in *Under Eastern Eyes: The West as Reflected in Recent Russian Émigré Writing*, edited by Arnold McMillin, London, Macmillan, 1991, 84–90; New York: St Martin's Press, 1992.
"'Svoboda' luchshe nevoli", an interview by T. Kulikova, *Kuranty*, Moscow, (20 November 1991).

The main theme of Anatolii Gladilin's early works is the lives of young people who, for whatever reason, do not behave in accordance with the expectations of "public opinion". His characters are trying to find and live by their own values. Priscilla Meyer considers Gladilin to be the real founder of Youth Prose, a number of his works having been published before those of Aksenov began appearing from 1959.

In Magadan he wrote the novella *Pesni zolotogo priiska* [Songs of the Gold Mine]. In 1960 Gladilin was accepted into the Writers' Union, becoming its youngest member at that time, but never winning acceptance as a member of the writers' establishment. He was never elected even as a delegate to congresses of the Writers' Union itself. In interviews Gladilin has said that the principal problem for his characters is how to continue the work of their fathers without repeating their mistakes. "I aim to write only the truth, without varnishing or prettifying reality. Some other writers have already fed our readers quite enough crudely rosy writing."

Gladilin's formal originality is mainly in the area of narrative, using different narrators in a single work, and imitation of diary-based narrative. In the introduction to *Prognoz na zavtra* [Tomorrow's Weather], Posev publishers compare him to Vasilii Aksenov, Anatolii Kuznetsov, Vladimir Voinovich, Georgii Vladimov, and others. Youth Prose writers introduced heroes re-evaluating the world about them, who needed to be allowed to find their own way. There is a suggestion that the current order is in need of radical change, and there is a heartfelt confessional tone from characters who are "extremely sensitive, if outwardly tough, with no faith in the conventional wisdom, and wary of grand pronouncements".

Prior to his emigration, Gladilin's writing was squeezed between the Scylla of Youth Prose and the Charybdis of socialist realism. When, in 1966, he signed a petition against the trial of Siniavskii and Daniel' he found himself denied further publication. Although he continued to work vigorously, he was only able (as was also the case with Vladimir Voinovich) to see himself in print again by contributing to the series *Plamennye revoliutsionery* [Fervent Revolutionaries], for which he wrote the volumes *Evangelie ot Robesp'era* [The Gospel According to Robespierre] and *Sny Shlissel'burgskoi kreposti* [Dreams of the Schlusselburg Fortress], 1974. Gladilin's reminiscences of the saga of Soviet publication and non-publication of his works are to be found in his memoir *The Making and Unmaking of a Soviet Writer*.

Gladilin emigrated to Paris in April 1976, together with his wife and daughter, and very soon became a leading broadcaster with Radio Liberty/Radio Free Europe. His major works in emigration are the novels *FSSR Frantsuzskaia Sovetskaia Sotsialisticheskaia Respublika* [The Soviet Socialist Republic of France], and *Menia ubil skotina Pell* [I Was Killed by that Bastard Pell].

Not many anti-Utopian detective novels can lay claim to serious literary merit, but this is undoubtedly the case with *Frantsuzskaia Sovetskaia Sotsialisticheskaia Respublika*. Strictly speaking, the novel is a simple joining of two fragments belonging to different genres. It begins as a detective story, with an attractive superman anti-hero telling the tale of how he met his Waterloo by establishing – as a spy free of all constraints – the Soviet socialist system in France. The substance of the novel is very much the story of the unseen struggle between intelligence agencies in Paris and the pulling of secret political levers. The work is characterized by quick-fire changes of scene, and an enumerative tone as if a video sequence were being described. The narrator keeps strictly to chronological order in his description of the unfolding of the military events accompanying the seizure of France by Soviet troops, but the view from military headquarters is invariably qualified by the eyewitness impressions of a typically French man in the street.

All Gladilin's narrative subtleties would, however, be insufficient were they not mediated through the author's irony and the narrator's constant wryly humorous attitude towards himself. The narrator of the story has himself established Soviet power in France, and now from his position as head of a provincial steam-ship operation he watches the television news and sees the workers of France queueing for fresh cabbage, almost like "our own Soviet people". He has been sent off into honourable exile by a caprice of fate, his part in establishing Soviet power in the country having proved no defence. He does at least manage to come to one conclusion that is very important to him personally. At the end of the anti-Utopia he explains to a French communist serving a sentence in a Soviet camp that serving a totalitarian regime is not the path to happiness.

Everything in the novel is straightforward and banal, but is brought to life by the fundamental incongruity of the notion that it might be possible to build a Soviet socialist Republic in France.

Menia ubil skotina Pell, is a frank and honest account of the life of an émigré journalist Andrei Govorov, for whom Gladilin himself is evidently the prototype. The hero, having lost his job and with no prospect of finding another, wanders round Paris with a pistol in his hand looking for a suitable spot to shoot himself. The novel consists of Govorov's unsystematic reminiscences during his final walk-about, with constant flashbacks to a past in which the participants, under their own names, are the émigré writers Aleksandr Galich, Viktor Nekrasov, and Vasilii Aksenov. Such titles as *Vselennaia* [Universe] and *Zapiataia* [Comma] transparently mask the leading émigré journals *Kontinent* and *Sintaksis*. Gladilin has also published a number of works for children.

BORIS LANIN

Fedor Vasil'evich Gladkov 1883–1958

Prose writer

Biography

Born in Chernavka, Saratov Province, 21 June 1883. Attended school in Chernavka, 1893–94, and Ekaterinodar, 1897–1900. Teacher at various primary schools in Transcaucasus, 1902–05. Studied at Pedagogical Institute, Tbilisi, 1905–06. Arrested for revolutionary activities, 1906; in labour camps and exile in Siberia, 1906–10. Settled in Novorossiisk, 1910. School Inspector, village of Pavlovskaia in Kuban, 1914–18. First meeting with Maksim Gor'kii, 1917. Married: Tat'iana Nilovna Zaitseva. Political instructor in 9th Army in Novorossiisk, 1920; elected member of Novorossiisk Soviet, 1921. Moved to Moscow, 1921; joined literary group "Kuznitsa" (The Smithy) and became full-time writer, 1923; joined editorial board of *Rabochii zhurnal*, 1924, *Novyi mir*, 1925, and *Zemlia i fabrika*, 1926. Lived part of the year in Dneprostroi in the Ukraine, on the site of the Dnepr hydroelectric power station, 1928–31. Member of the Soviet Writers' Union from 1934. Worked as *Izvestiia* correspondent in Sverdlovsk, 1941–44. Director of the Gor'kii Literary Institute, Moscow, 1945. Visited Bulgaria and Yugoslavia; editor-in-chief, *Sovetskii Soiuz*, 1948. Recipient: Order of Lenin, 1939; Order of the Red Banner, 1943; Stalin Prize, second class, 1950; State Literary Prize and Stalin Prize, first class, 1951; second Order of Lenin, 1953. Elected Deputy of RSFSR Supreme Soviet, 1955. Died in Moscow, 20 December 1958. Buried in Novodevichii Cemetery, Moscow.

Publications

Collected Edition

Sobranie sochinenii, 8 vols. Moscow, 1958–59.

Fiction

"Edinorodnyi syn" [The Only Son], *Letopis'*, 5–6 (1917); as "Puchina" [The Gulf], in *Sobranie sochinenii*, vol. 1, 1958.
"V izgnanii" [In Exile], *Nashi dni*, 2 (1922); as "Izgoi", in *Sobranie sochinenii*, vol. 1, 1958.
"Tsement", *Krasnaia nov'*, 1–6 (1925); revised editions, 1932, 1947, 1950; translated as *Cement*, by A.S. Arthur and C. Ashleigh, London, Martin Lawrence, and New York, International Publishers, 1929; reprinted Evanston, Illinois, Northwestern University Press, 1994; also translated by Liv Tadge, Moscow, Progress, 1981.
"Energiia" [Energy], *Novyi mir*, 1–10 (1932); 6–8, 10, 12 (1937); 10–12 (1938); first separate edition Moscow, 1939.
Malen'kaia trilogiia [Little Trilogy]. Moscow, 1933.
"Berezovaia roshcha" [The Birch Wood], *Novyi mir*, 3 (1941).
"Serdtse materi" [A Mother's Heart], *Novyi mir*, 11–12 (1942); as "Mat'" [Mother] in *Sobranie sochinenii*, vol. 5, 1959.
"Boets Nazar Suslov", *Oktiabr'*, 11 (1942).
"Malkino schast'e" [Malkin's Happiness], in *Govorit Ural*, Sverdlovsk, 1942; as "Malashino schast'e" [Malashin's Happiness], in *Sobranie sochinenii*, vol. 5, 1959.
"Opalennaia dusha" [The Singed Heart], *Izvestiia*, 165, (16 July 1942).
"Masha iz Zapol'ia" [Masha from Zapol], in *Kliatva*, Moscow, 1944.
"Kliatva" [The Oath], *Oktiabr'*, 1–4 (1944).
"Povest' o detstve" [Story of a Childhood], *Novyi mir*, 2–4 (1949).
"Vol'nitsa" [The Outlaws], *Novyi mir*, 7–9 (1950).
"Likhaia godina" [Hard Times], *Novyi mir*, 1–4 (1954).

Plays

Burelom [Wind-Fallen Trees]. Novorossiisk, 1921.
Vataga [The Gang]. Moscow, 1923.
Tsement [Cement]. Moscow, 1928.
Gordost' [Pride]. Moscow, 1935.

Literary Criticism

O literature [On Literature]. Moscow, 1955.
"Moia rabota nad *Tsementom*" [My Work on *Cement*], in *Sobranie sochinenii*, vol. 2, 1958, 410–26.

Critical Studies

"Pochemu ponravilsia Tsement", by Osip Brik, *Na literaturnom postu*, 2 (1926), 30–32.

"Tsement i ego kritiki", by Valer'ian Polianskii, *Na literaturnom postu*, 5–6 (1926), 50–53.
Tvorcheskii put' F. Gladkova, by I.P. Ukhanov, Moscow, 1953.
"New Editions of Soviet Belles-Lettres, A Study in Politics and Palimpsests", by Maurice Friedberg, *American Slavic and East European Review*, 13 (1954), 72–88.
Fedor Gladkov. Ocherk zhizni i tvorchestva, by Berta Brainina, Moscow, 1957.
"Tsement" F. Gladkova, by Berta Brainina, Moscow, 1965.
"Kak sozdavalsia Tsement", by L.N. Smirnova, *Tekstologiia proizvedenii sovetskoi literatury: Voprosy tekstologii*, 4 (1967), 140–227.
Fedor Gladkov: Zhizn' i tvorchestvo, by A.P. Volozhenin, Moscow, 1969.
"Gladkov's *Cement*: The Making of a Soviet Classic", by Robert Busch, *Slavic and East European Journal*, 3 (1978), 348–61.
The Soviet Novel: History as Ritual, by Katerina Clark, Chicago, University of Chicago Press, 1981.
F.V. Gladkov: Seminarii, by G.D. Sinenko, Minsk, 1982.

Bibliographies
Russkie sovetskie pisateli. Prozaiki. Bibliograficheskii ukazatel', vol. 1, Leningrad, 1959, 464–99.
Bibliografiia tekstov F.V. Gladkova, 1900–1964. Moscow, 1965.

Fedor Vasil'evich Gladkov's childhood was exceptionally harsh, even by the standards of late 19th-century provincial Russia. Born into a strict Old Believer family, his earliest memories were of fasts and other religious rituals in which he was an unwilling participant. Far worse, however, were the strained relations between his parents and the regular beatings that his mother had to endure at the hands of his father. He records how, as a 12-year-old, he: "dreamt all the time how he could avenge his mother", and that his father only stopped when Fedor ran at him one day with a knife and threatened to cut his throat. More importantly for his future development, these childhood experiences instilled in him a desire to fight to change the social and political circumstances that engendered such backwardness and violence. There were significant compensations, however. His mother, and especially his grandmother, introduced him as a young boy to the magical world of Russian folklore, and he would spend the long winter evenings listening to them reciting poems, legends, and fairy tales. At primary school, encouraged by his teacher, he started to read the Russian classics, together with French and German authors, developing a particular love for the work of Victor Hugo. At the same time, against his father's wishes, he started to keep a diary and to write poetry himself.

Hatred of the existing system, a desire for a better world, and love of literature – these were the three passions that arose from Gladkov's childhood experiences and which were to play the dominant role in his life and career. There is much here that is reminiscent of another romantic revolutionary, Maksim Gor'kii, and it was indeed Gor'kii who served as the inspiration for Gladkov's early stories. Almost all these stories concern the fate of people from the "lower depths", without any ray of light in their broken and impoverished lives. Gladkov oscillates between sympathy for such characters and condemnation of them for so meekly resigning themselves to their fate. This latter attitude is especially evident in his articles and stories set in Siberian prisons, which he knew at first hand from living and working in Siberia where he had gone to be close to his parents, who were wrongfully accused of forgery. As a result of his involvement in the 1905 Revolution he was sent to Siberia where he spent four years in prison and exile. Although he continued to write prolifically, largely on prison themes, very few of his articles and stories, published for the most part in provincial journals, were reprinted after 1917.

Gladkov achieved almost instant fame with the publication of his novel *Tsement* (*Cement*) in 1925. He was never to repeat this success with his later works, although many of them became part of the staple diet of Soviet literature. His post-revolutionary creative work can be most conveniently divided into four phases: the 1920s, the 1930s, the war years and a final "autobiographical" period, each of these dominated by one particular work (*Cement*, *Energiia* [Energy], *Kliatva* [The Oath], and *Vol'nitsa* [The Outlaws] respectively). Although the artistic merits of the first three of these works are debatable, each of them depicts different stages in the development of Soviet Russia and is therefore of at least sociological (perhaps now one might even say historical) interest. If *Cement* is very much the child of the 1920s, *Energiia* is the archetypal construction novel, reflecting the high noon of Stalinism with its combination of euphoria, grandiose achievement, and paranoiac suspicion. This vast, sprawling work recreates the heady days of the first Five-Year Plan and the building of a hydroelectric power station. Some of the themes familiar from *Cement* are here: the role of the intelligentsia, the problems of the socialist family, and the constant fight to overcome the enemies of socialism, but these are all set within the new conditions of the 1930s. The Party has become unquestionably the infallible guide and source of all virtue; the enemies are now "Trotskyites" and "saboteurs", and every achievement is measured against that of the US; we are told repeatedly that Soviet workers and workmanship are at least the equal of American. Most importantly, the fate of the various individual relationships is shown to be inextricably bound up with the collective.

Gladkov spent most of the war against Germany (1941–45) as a correspondent for *Izvestiia* in the Urals, writing reports and articles on the aircraft and tank factories that were located there. He also wrote a number of works whose general theme was the heroism of the Soviet people, and the vital contribution being made to the war effort by those who were not actually fighting the enemy. In *Kliatva*, the best-known of these works, he shows how two groups of workers, one local, the other recently evacuated from Leningrad, merge to form an effective and co-operative unit. Along the way, they have to overcome resistance from narrow-minded individuals wedded to bureaucratic ideas (a favourite target of Gladkov's), but they triumph in the end, thanks partly to a wise and benevolent Stalin. As they sit making the oath to their leader, their faces "adopt a solemn expression, illumined by an inner light". "Let this oath shine constantly in our hearts", one of them intones. The story "Serdtse materi" [A Mother's Heart] depicts a mother's heroic exploits as a factory worker; like Gor'kii's *Mat'* (*Mother*) from which it clearly derives, it suffers from sentimental and idealized characterization.

Almost all the stories and novels published before 1945 are on contemporary (i.e. Soviet) themes. In his last years Gladkov returns to his own childhood, with the publication of his autobiographical trilogy, *Povest' o detstve* [Story of a Childhood], *Vol'nitsa*, and *Likhaia godina* [Hard Times]. He depicts a Russia of poverty, ignorance, and exploitation; the hypocrisy and cruelty of those in authority are unmasked in a manner reminiscent of Saltykov-Shchedrin. This sombre picture is offset by the many lyrical passages reflecting Gladkov's love for Russia and its simple working people. Artistically these are Gladkov's most successful works, combining sharpness of observation with genuine passion. They bear witness to what might have been, had their author not sacrificed his talent and his best years to Stalinism.

ROGER COCKRELL

Cement

Tsement

Novel, 1925

In *Cement* Red Army soldier Gleb Chumalov returns from the war to find a changed world. His wife Dasha now works and has placed their child in a home. His former workplace, the cement factory, lies in ruins. Its workers are physically and morally debilitated; they need work to revitalize them. It falls to Gleb, a warrior of epic proportions, to reopen the factory and to re-establish a family life. A man of action and energy, he immediately acts. But Dasha is one "enemy" he cannot defeat through force and action. Dasha has become strong and independent, Gleb's equal. He must instead tame his feelings of jealousy and his desire for dominance over her. Although he wins the battle to reopen the factory, Gleb loses the battle with Dasha; in the last chapter they are living apart. Dasha represents the transformation of the family in the new State; she becomes mother, wife, and homemaker to all. She is attentive and demanding when dealing with the orphanages, while her own house is in a shambles. She saves many children, although her own dies. She refuses to have sexual intercourse with her husband, but willingly sleeps with many soldiers going off to battle. She asserts her right to choose her partners, and refuses to limit herself to one.

Cement was first published in the journal *Krasnaia nov'* in 1925. The novel was chosen as one of the prototypes for socialist realism in the early 1930s. But Katerina Clark contends that it is only an "embryonic example of such novels". With almost every new edition of the book Gladkov made changes that bring it closer to the model of socialist realism. Robert Busch writes that the changes "transformed a novel with organic ties to the experimental context of the 1920s into one reflective of socialist realism". Major revisions in the text were made in 1932, 1947, and 1950. The translation that is possibly most commonly read in the west is from the 1920s. Therefore, a reader of the novel in English will have a radically different impression from someone reading a more recent Soviet edition.

Gladkov felt it necessary to defend depicting his characters as all good or all bad. Even so, Clark asserts that Gleb is not "typical" enough for a socialist realist work; Gleb and other characters act spontaneously, not needing to understand Party theory in order to act in accordance with it. But in later versions criticism of Party apparatus is toned down or removed altogether, and Gleb begins spouting party ideology. The "man-as-machine" imagery, which reflects Gladkov's membership in the "Kuznitsa" ("The Smithy") organization, is also removed. The new literary metaphor for society shifted away from the machine; this image was too impersonal and did not allow for guidance from the Party.

Another change stems from Soviet attitudes toward the family unit. In the 1920s decrees granted complete freedom of divorce, gave legal equality for legitimate and illegitimate children, legalized abortion, and decriminalized incest, bigamy, and adultery. These policies were reversed in the 1930s and support for the individual family unit was reinstated. In later editions Gladkov replaced the image of society as one large family with one that emphasized the importance of the nuclear family.

In keeping with this change, Dasha becomes less independent in later versions. Her work is now less important. Instead of being elected chair of the presidium, she is only elected a member, along with Gleb and Gromada, one of the men she originally defeats. She still chairs a meeting but is no longer as authoritative, for example, she no longer makes a proposal. She is especially changed in her relationship with Gleb; she becomes less defiant, hostile, and physically threatening. Instead of "comrade" she now calls him "dear" ("rodnoi", "milyi"). In the original she refuses to have sex because she does not want to be subjugated. She wants to choose when and with whom to have relations. But in later versions she wants only Gleb. Now it is not explicitly stated that Dasha has had sex with others. Nor does she push Gleb into a relationship with Polia.

Dasha becomes a better housekeeper; their room is cleaner, and references to mice, mould, and insects disappear. Conditions in the children's home are also better, so her decision to put Niurka there becomes less negative. In the original Dasha does nothing for Gleb, but in later versions she runs home to feed him with provisions she herself has obtained. In the original she makes up a bed for herself. In later versions, she makes up a bed for him too.

As Dasha changes, so too does Gleb. He is no longer confused by her, reduced to begging and pleading, and he is less jealous and violent. They still part, but only so that Dasha can care for a sick comrade. Gleb must master his sexual jealousy, which is now totally unfounded. Therefore his fate is no longer in Dasha's hands; he himself can change and thereby regain his wife and home. This reshapes Gleb into a character with control, more suitable to the image of the positive hero.

In "Moia rabota nad *Tsementom*" [My Work on *Cement*], Gladkov echoes the official definition of socialist realism: "The task of art is to depict not only that which is, but also that which ought to be, that is, art ought to depict reality in its aggressive movement and evolution." It follows that if "that which ought to be" changes, so too must the work of literature. Hence *Cement*'s many transformations. The original leaves two conflicts unresolved: that between the masses and the Party and that between Dasha and Gleb. Through revisions these conflicts are removed, resulting in a work that is a much truer example of socialist realism. Ironically, according to Maurice Friedberg, the revised *Cement* was "used by the Soviet critics as an historical document, truthfully depicting the conditions of Russia on the eve of the NEP".

ERIC LAURSEN

Nikolai Vasil'evich Gogol' 1809–1852

Prose writer and dramatist

Biography

Born in Sorochintsii, Poltava, Ukraine, 1 April 1809. Attended Poltava boarding school, 1819–21, and Nezhin high school, 1821–28. Moved to St Petersburg, December 1828. Worked as civil servant, 1829–31; taught history at the Patriotic Institute, St Petersburg, and worked as a private tutor, 1831–34. Short-lived academic career as assistant lecturer in history, St Petersburg University, 1834–35. Formed acquaintance with Pushkin, Zhukovskii, and other leading literary figures. Visited Germany, Switzerland, and France, 1836; lived in Rome, 1837–39. Travelled in western Europe and throughout Russia, 1839–48. Began association with the fanatical spiritual leader, Father Konstantinovskii, 1847; visited the Holy Land, 1848; re-settled in Russia, 1849. Died in Moscow, 4 March 1852.

Publications

Collected Editions

Sochineniia, 4 vols. St Petersburg, 1842.

Collected Works, translated by Constance Garnett, 6 vols. London, Chatto and Windus, 1922–27.

Polnoe sobranie sochinenii, 14 vols. Moscow and Leningrad, 1937–52.

The Collected Tales and Plays (Constance Garnett's translations revised by the editor), edited by Leonard J. Kent. New York, Pantheon, 1964; New York, Modern Library, 1969.

Diary of a Madman and Other Stories, translated by Ronald Wilks. Harmondsworth, Penguin, 1972.

Sobranie sochinenii, 7 vols. Moscow, 1977.

The Theatre of Nikolay Gogol: Plays and Selected Writings, edited by Milton Ehre, translated by Milton Ehre and Fruma Gottschalk. Chicago, University of Chicago Press, 1980; as *Plays and Selected Writings*, Evanston, Illinois, Northwestern University Press, 1994.

Sobranie sochinenii, 8 vols. Moscow, 1984–86.

The Complete Tales, edited by Leonard J. Kent. 2 vols. Chicago, University of Chicago Press, 1985.

Hanz Kuechelgarten, Leaving the Theater and Other Works, edited and translated by Ronald Meyer. Ann Arbor, Ardis, 1990.

Village Evenings Near Dikanka and Mirgorod, translated by Christopher English. Oxford, Oxford University Press, 1994.

Plays and Petersburg Tales, translated by Christopher English. Oxford, Oxford University Press, 1995.

Fiction

Vechera na khutore bliz Dikan'ki, 2 vols. St Petersburg, 1831–32; translated as "Evenings on a Farm Near Dikanka", by Constance Garnett, in *Collected Works*, 1926; and by Leonard J. Kent, in *The Complete Tales*, 1985; also as "Village Evenings Near Dikanka", by Christopher English, in *Village Evenings Near Dikanka and Mirgorod*, 1994.

Mirgorod. St Petersburg, 1835; translated as "Mirgorod", by Constance Garnett, in *Collected Works*, 1928; and by Leonard J. Kent, in *The Complete Tales*, 1985; and by Christopher English, in *Village Evenings Near Dikanka and Mirgorod*, 1994.

Arabeski. St Petersburg, 1835; translated as *Arabesques*, by Alexander Tulloch, Ann Arbor, Ardis, 1982.

"Nos", *Sovremennik*, 3 (1836); translated as "The Nose", by Constance Garnett, in *Collected Works*, 1922–27; and by Leonard J. Kent, in *The Complete Tales*, 1985; by Ronald Wilks, in *Diary of a Madman and Other Stories*, 1972; also by Christopher English, in *Plays and Petersburg Tales*, 1995.

"Koliaska", *Sovremennik*, 1 (1836); translated as "The Coach", by Constance Garnett, in *Collected Works*, 1922–27; and by Leonard J. Kent, in *The Complete Tales*, 1985; also translated as "The Carriage", by Christopher English, in *Plays and Petersburg Tales*, 1995.

Mertvye dushi. Moscow, 1842; translated as "Dead Souls", by Constance Garnett, in *Collected Works*, 1922–27; and by David Magarshack, Harmondsworth, Penguin, 1961; by George Reavey, edited by George Gibian, New York, Norton, 1985; by Christopher English, Moscow, Raduga, 1987; and by B.G. Guerney, New Haven, Yale University Press, 1996.

"Portret", *Sovremennik*, 27/3/4 (1842); revised edition [from *Arabeski*, 1835]; translated as "The Portrait", by Constance Garnett, in *Collected Works*, 1922–27; and by Leonard J. Kent, in *The Complete Tales*, 1985; also by Christopher English, in *Plays and Petersburg Tales*, 1995.

"Rim", *Moskvitianin*, 3 (1842); translated as "Rome", by Constance Garnett, in *Collected Works*, 1922–27; and by Leonard J. Kent, in *The Complete Tales*, 1985.

Shinel', in *Sochineniia*, 1842; translated as "The Overcoat", by Constance Garnett, in *Collected Works*, 1923; and by Leonard J. Kent, in *The Complete Tales*, 1985; by Ronald Wilks, in *Diary of a Madman and Other Stories*, 1972; and by Christopher English, in *Plays and Petersburg Tales*, 1995 [other translations as "The Cloak"; and "The Greatcoat"].

"Taras Bul'ba", in *Sochineniia*, 1842; revised edition [from *Mirgorod*, 1835]; translated as "Taras Bulba" by Constance Garnett, in *Collected Works*, 1922–27; and by Leonard J. Kent, in *The Complete Tales*, 1985; also by Christopher English, in *Plays and Petersburg Tales*, 1995.

Plays

Revizor. St Petersburg, 1836; *"Revizor" (The Government Inspector: A Comedy in Five Acts)*, edited by M. Beresford, Lewiston, New York, and Lampeter, Wales, Edwin Mellen Press, 1996; translated as "The Government Inspector", by Constance Garnett, in *Collected Works*, 1927; and by Milton Ehre, in *The Theatre of Nikolay Gogol*, 1980; also as "The Inspector General", by Leonard J. Kent, in *The Collected Tales and Plays*, 1964; and by Christopher English, in *Plays and Petersburg Tales*, 1995; and as "The Inspector", by Joshua Cooper, in *Four Russian Plays*, translated by Joshua Cooper, Harmondsworth, Penguin, 1972 [there have been many other translations].

Zhenit'ba. St Petersburg, 1842; translated as "The Marriage", by Constance Garnett, in *Complete Works*, 1927; and by Leonard J. Kent, in *The Collected Tales and Plays*, 1964; also as "Marriage", by Milton Ehre, in *The Theatre of Nikolay Gogol*, 1980; and by Christopher English, in *Plays and Petersburg Tales*, 1995.

Igroki. St Petersburg, 1843; translated as "The Gamblers", by Constance Garnett, in *Collected Works*, 1927; and by Leonard J. Kent, in *The Collected Tales and Plays*, 1964; also by Milton Ehre, in *The Theatre of Nikolay Gogol*, 1980.

Letters

Vybrannye mesta iz perepiski s druz'iami. St Petersburg, 1847; translated as *Selected Passages from Correspondence with Friends*, by Jesse Zeldin, Nashville, Vanderbilt University Press, 1969.

Letters of Nikolai Gogol, edited by Carl R. Proffer, translated by Carl R. Proffer and Vera Krivoshein. Ann Arbor, University of Michigan Press, 1967.

Non-Fiction

Razmyshleniia o bozhestvennoi liturgii; translated as *Meditations on the Divine Liturgy*, by L. Alexieff, London, Mowbray, 1913; and as *The Divine Liturgy of the Eastern Orthodox Church*, by Rosemary Edmonds, London, Darton Longman and Todd, 1960.

Avtorskaia ispoved'; translated as "An Author's Confession", by David Lapeza, *Russian Literature Triquarterly*, 10 (1974), 101–28.

Critical Studies

Gogol', by V.V. Gippius, Leningrad, 1924; translated by Robert Maguire, Ann Arbor, Ardis, 1981; reprinted Durham, North Carolina, Duke University Press, 1989.

Masterstvo Gogolia, by Andrei Belyi, Moscow and Leningrad, 1934; reprinted Ann Arbor, Ardis, 1982; Moscow, 1996.

Nikolai Gogol, by Vladimir Nabokov, Norfolk, Connecticut, New Directions, 1944; revised edition New York, New Directions, 1961; London, Weidenfeld and Nicolson, 1973; Oxford, Oxford University Press, 1985.

Nikolai Gogol (1809–1852): A Centenary Survey, by Janko Lavrin, London, Sylvan Press, 1951; New York, Russell and Russell, 1968.

Gogol: A Life, by David Magarshack, New York, Grove Press, and London, Faber, 1957.

Gogol as a Short Story Writer: A Study of His Technique of Composition, by F.C. Driessen, The Hague, Mouton, 1965.

Gogol: His Life and Works, by Vsevolod Setchkarev, translated by Robert Kramer, New York, New York University Press, 1965; London, Peter Owen, 1966.

The Simile and Gogol's Dead Souls, by Carl. R. Proffer, The Hague, Mouton, 1967.

Gogol, by Victor Erlich, New Haven, Yale University Press, 1969.

The Subconscious in Gogol' and Dostoevskij and Its Antecedents, by Leonard J. Kent, The Hague, Mouton, 1969.

Gogol: The Biography of a Divided Soul, by Henri Troyat, translated by Nancy Amphoux, New York, Doubleday, 1973; London, Allen and Unwin, 1974.

Nikolay Gogol, by Thaïs Lindstrom, New York, Twayne, 1974.

Gogol from the Twentieth Century: Eleven Essays, edited by Robert A. Maguire, Princeton, Princeton University Press, 1974; revised edition, 1976.

V teni Gogolia, by Abram Terts [Andrei Siniavskii], London, Overseas Publications Interchange, 1975; reprinted Paris, Sintaksis, 1981; Moscow, 1992.

The Sexual Labyrinth of Nikolai Gogol, by Simon Karlinsky, Cambridge, Massachusetts, Harvard University Press, 1976.

Through Gogol's Looking Glass: Reverse Vision, False Focus, and Precarious Logic, by William Woodin Rowe, New York, New York University Press, 1976.

Poetika Gogolia, by Iurii Mann, Moscow, 1978.

Gogol's Dead Souls, by James B. Woodward, Princeton, Princeton University Press, 1978.

Nikolai Gogol's Quest for Beauty: An Exploration into His Works, by Jesse Zeldin, Lawrence, Kansas, Regents' Press of Kansas, 1978.

Dostoevsky and Gogol: Texts and Criticism, edited by Priscilla Meyer and Stephen Rudy, Ann Arbor, Ardis, 1979.

The Creation of Nikolai Gogol, by Donald Fanger, Cambridge, Massachusetts, Harvard University Press, 1979.

The Enigma of Gogol: An Examination of the Writings of N.V. Gogol and Their Place in the Russian Literary Tradition, by Richard Peace, Cambridge, Cambridge University Press, 1981.

Gogol's Forgotten Book: "Selected Passages" and Its Contemporary Readers, by Ruth Sobel, Washington, DC, University Press of America, 1981.

Out from under Gogol's Overcoat: A Psychoanalytic Study, by Daniel Rancour-Laferrière, Ann Arbor, Ardis, 1982.

Gogol's Overcoat: An Anthology of Critical Essays, edited by Elizabeth Trahan, Ann Arbor, Ardis, 1982.

The Symbolic Art of Gogol: Essays on His Short Fiction, by James B. Woodward, Columbus, Ohio, Slavica, 1982.

Nikolai Gogol and Ivan Turgenev, by Nick Worrall, London, Macmillan, 1982; New York, Grove Press, 1983.

Gogol and the Natural School, by Victor V. Vinogradov, translated by Debra K. Erickson and Ray Parrott, Ann Arbor, Ardis, 1987.

"Such Things Happen in the World": Deixis in Three Short Stories by N.V. Gogol, by P.M. Waszink, Amsterdam, Rodopi, 1988.

Nikolay Gogol: Text and Context, edited by Jane Grayson and Faith Wigzell, London, Macmillan, 1989.

Novel Epics: Gogol, Dostoevsky and National Narrative, by Frederick T. Griffiths and Stanley J. Rabinowitz, Evanston, Illinois, Northwestern University Press, 1990.

Essays on Gogol: Logos and the Russian Word, edited by Susanne Fusso and Priscilla Meyer, Evanston, Illinois, Northwestern University Press, 1992.

Designing Dead Souls: An Anatomy of Disorder in Gogol, by Susanne Fusso, Stanford, Stanford University Press, 1993.

The Pragmatics of Insignificance: Chekhov, Zoshchenko, Gogol, by Cathy Popkin, Stanford, Stanford University Press, 1993.

Nikolai Gogol and the Baroque Cultural Heritage, by Gavriel Shapiro, University Park, Pennsylvania State University Press, 1993.

Exploring Gogol, by Robert A. Maguire, Stanford, Stanford University Press, 1994.

Gogol's "The Government Inspector", by Michael Beresford, London, Bristol Classical Press, 1997.

Bibliography
Gogol: A Bibliography, by Philip E. Frantz, Ann Arbor, Ardis, 1989.

Nikolai Vasil'evich Gogol' was born in 1809 in the Ukrainian town of Sorochintsii into a family of minor land-owning gentry. His real surname was, in fact, Ianovskii, but in an attempt to claim more noble Cossack ancestry, the writer's grandfather had tacked on the name *Gogol'* (which means "golden eye duck"). Gogol' himself had a long and "beaky" nose, and it is as though the future comic writer was born under the sign of a joke. Bogus social status proclaimed through the bathos of a comic bird (Gogol' himself would later drop the Ianovskii element of his own name) noses, overweening pretensions, comic names, the motif of birds, the Ukraine – all these would figure prominently in his later writing. After an undistinguished school career he left the Ukraine for St Petersburg in December 1828, convinced he would achieve eminence as a civil servant, a writer, or even as an actor. He did not take to the civil service life of the capital city, and his undoubted skills as an actor were rejected, yet his ultimate triumph as a writer allowed him to exploit his failure in the other two fields, providing him not only with material but also with a demanding view of stagecraft. Yet success was not immediate. He began as a poet with the anonymous publication of a poem entitled "Italiia" ("Italy"), then a longer poem written under a pseudonym and printed at his own expense "Gants Kiukhel'garten" (the strange form of the German forename, Hans, avoids too close an identification with a comic bird: *gans* is the German for "goose"). After personally distributing the work to St Petersburg booksellers, Gogol' fully expected acclaim as a genius. When this was not forthcoming he took back all the copies of his poem and burned them – the burning of his works was to be a feature of his writing career.

Almost immediately he undertook a mysterious trip to Germany, appropriating money entrusted to him by his mother for mortgage repayments. The "scam" would again be another of his major comic themes, and his intense but difficult relationship with his mother goes a long way to explaining the strange role occupied by women in his writing.

His first literary success "Vecher nakanune Ivana Kupala" ("St John's Eve") was published anonymously. It is a fairy tale influenced by German romanticism but based on Ukrainian folklore. He went on to develop this vein in the collection of stories entitled *Vechera na khutore bliz Dikan'ki* (*Evenings on a Farm Near Dikanka*). The pestering of his mother to provide details of Ukrainian life and folklore reveals a constant feature of his artistic personality: the reliance on others to provide him with material (later he would claim that Pushkin had given him the plots for two major works – *Revizor* (*The Government Inspector*) and *Mertvye dushi* (*Dead Souls*)).

The rumbustious naivety of *Evenings on a Farm Near Dikanka* is deceptive, and at times the prose achieves a poetic quality denied to Gogol''s earlier attempts in verse. There is also a darker side, particularly in "Strashnaia mest'" ("A Terrible Revenge") and the ending of "Sorochinskaia iarmarka" ("Sorochintsy Fair"). Moral responsibility is shifted from the protagonists, not only by the intervention of supernatural powers, but also by a narrative filtered through a complicated hierarchy of narrators. "Ivan Fedorovich Shpon'ka i ego tetushka" ("Ivan Fedorovich Shponka and his Aunt"), the only purportedly "written" story, looks forward to the mature Gogol'. Here the fantastic is glimpsed not in the supernatural, but in the banality of reality itself.

Gogol' continued the Ukrainian theme in the four apparently disparate, but interconnected, stories of *Mirgorod* (1835). Thus "Taras Bulba" is an heroic evocation of the Ukrainian past (graced at its end by the appearance of the golden eye duck) whereas "Povest' o tom kak possorilsia Ivan Ivanovich s Ivanom Nikiforovichem" ("The Story of How Ivan Ivanovich Quarrelled with Ivan Nikiforovich") (in which discord arises from appending "gander" (*gusak*) to a noble name) is a commentary on the present state of Cossackdom. Yet through the motif of birds both stories hint at deeper personal statements.

With the publication in 1835 of the collection *Arabeski* (*Arabesques*) Gogol' launched a second theme – St Petersburg as the fantastic city. "Portret" ("The Portrait") and "Nevskii Prospekt" focus on the artist and on the gulf between reality and ideal, between surface and content. In "Zapiski sumasshedshego" ("Diary of a Madman") it is a minor civil servant who is caught up in such tensions and finally goes mad.

In 1834 Gogol', with no academic qualifications, was appointed a lecturer in history at St Petersburg University (he had wanted the chair of history at Kiev University). Gogol' could not measure up to his own aspirations, and his appointment was a disaster. The absurdity of overweening pretensions is the covert theme of the totally bizarre story "Nos" ("The Nose") and it is significant that this period of personal setback is artistically the most productive of his whole life, yet one with a price to pay: frustrated ambitions as a teacher would later resurface as a desire to turn art itself into a vehicle for lecture and instruction. The chief fruit of his bogus university career was the play *The Government Inspector*. The theme of the nonentity Khlestakov mistaken for someone of importance (a government inspector) not only hints at personal neurosis (Gogol' would later compare himself to Khlestakov) but also suggests social criticism that Gogol' himself would later seek to deny. After the first night, given in the presence of the tsar, Gogol' fled Russia for western Europe, basing himself principally in Rome. Here he wrote his *magnum opus Dead Souls* – a novel which Gogol' insisted on calling an epic poem (*poema*). Its rogue hero Chichikov travels Russia buying up the documents of dead peasants in a swindle exploiting Russia's bizarre poll tax. The theme is comic and socially pointed, yet in chapter 6 of Part 1 the reader senses a change of direction. Gogol', the teacher, begins to take over. His new plan for his *poema* is to be Dantesque: it will show Russia itself the path to moral regeneration. Although three parts were envisaged, only the first was completed. Part 2 was burned twice and only fragments from the two versions remain.

The year 1842, which saw the publication of Part 1 of *Dead Souls*, also revealed that, for a collection of his works, Gogol' had been rewriting earlier stories: "Taras Bulba" – in the spirit of Great Russian nationalism and "The Portrait" – to stress that art must contain a spiritual message. A new story "Shinel'" ("The Overcoat"), which also appeared in 1842, had an enormous impact on later writers who saw it as a depiction of the "little man" in a hostile society, yet its subtext is obsession with writing reduced to mere form and the old gulf between surface and content. It was content above all else that Gogol' now strove to communicate through his writing, and in 1847 he published *Vybrannye mesta iz perepiski s druz'iami* (*Selected Passages from Correspondence with Friends*) in an attempt to "lecture" Russian society on morality. Its tone and *jejeune* commonplaces merely succeeded in alienating friends both on the left and the right of the political spectrum. His staunchest champion, the critic Belinskii, on the eve of his death violently denounced Gogol' in a notorious letter. Gogol' in despair again sought flight. He undertook a spiritual journey to the Holy Land, which brought him no consolation and only increased his malaise. It was his failure to impart true moral content to *Dead Souls* that led to the burning of Part 2. Immediately after the second conflagration, he recognized what he had done, yet his explanation is worthy of the evasion of responsibility associated with the naive narrators of *Evenings on a Farm Near Dikanka* – it was all the work of the devil. During Lent of 1852 he refused to take any food. Various bizarre remedies were employed to make him eat – spirits were poured over his head, hot loaves applied to his person, leeches attached to his nose – all in vain. He died on the 4th of March 1852.

RICHARD PEACE

Evenings on a Farm Near Dikanka

Vechera na khutore bliz Dikan'ki

Short stories, 1831–32

With the publication of a slender volume of short stories entitled *Evenings on a Farm Near Dikanka* in 1831, Nikolai Gogol' came to the attention of the Russian reading public. This success was especially welcome to Gogol' after the failure of his first attempt at literary fame, the narrative poem *Gants Kiukhel'garten* (*Hanz Küchelgarten*), printed in 1829. The reception of *Evenings on a Farm Near Dikanka* was so positive that Gogol' published a second volume of stories with this title in 1832. Although Gogol' is better known for such later works as *Dead Souls* and *The Government Inspector*, the two volumes of *Evenings on a Farm Near Dikanka* provide a stimulating introduction into the peculiar world of Gogol''s imagination.

Scholars have identified in *Evenings on a Farm Near Dikanka* an amalgam of two distinct literary traditions and styles. On the one hand, readers can see the influence of the comic tradition of the Ukrainian puppet theatre (with its use of stereotypical characters, a confined space for action, and the succession of brief scenes featuring the interaction of two characters at a time). On the other hand, one can also find evidence of the influence of the lyrical tradition of German romanticism, with the incorporation of supernatural elements from the artistic fairy tale (*Kunstmärchen*). Each volume of the collection contains four stories with a introduction prepared by a folksy narrator named Rudyi Pan'ko. The stories that follow are in turn the product of other narrators, primarily a local deacon and a more haughty, urbane figure who wears a pea-green jacket. This set of fictional narrators provides Gogol' with a series of masks behind which to hide his own face and it offers him opportunity to create a stylistically rich verbal narrative.

The stories themselves range in tone from the farcical to the horrific. In the words of the Russian scholar Vasilii Gippius, most of the stories are linked by a recurrent theme, "the invasion of people's lives by the demonic and their battle against it". Nearly all the stories reflect this theme, although its treatment varies from the satirical to the serious. The stories in each part of the collection fall into a roughly symmetrical pattern. The first story in each part is comical. The tale that opens the collection, "Sorochinskaia iarmarka" ("The Fair at Sorochintsy") tells how a young man manipulates popular fear of the devil to convince a reluctant father to allow his daughter to marry him. Corresponding to this in the second part is "Noch' pered rozhdestvom" ("Christmas Eve"), which also features the efforts of a young man to overcome parental opposition and to marry a young woman. In this instance, however, the devil actually makes an appearance: the valiant lad forces the devil to fly him to St Petersburg where he can obtain slippers worn by the Empress and give them to the woman he loves.

The second story in each part presents a more sinister vision of experience. "St John's Eve" depicts the fate of a man who makes a pact with demonic forces to obtain wealth so he can marry his beloved. To win this wealth, however, he must kill the brother of the woman he loves. The memory of this murder lies repressed in his mind for a year, but the ultimate recollection of his deed results in his own incineration. The second story of the second part, "A Terrible Revenge" offers an even more horrifying portrait: a wicked sorcerer is driven by a family curse to destroy his son-in-law, his daughter, and his grandchild, only to be destroyed himself by the spirit of a man treacherously murdered by the sorcerer's ancestor.

Contrasting to these horror tales are the third stories in each section. Returning to the optimistic formula of the opening tales, "Maiskaia noch', ili Utoplennitsa" ("A May Night, or The Drowned Maiden") depicts a Cossack lad winning the permission of a village mayor to marry his daughter, this time with the help of a woman who appears to the hero in a dream. The third story of the second part, however, is anomalous. "Ivan Fiodorovich Shponka and His Aunt" deals with neither demons nor ghosts, but rather provides a strange look into the sheltered life of a man terrified by the thought of getting married. Concluding with a surrealistic dream in which Shponka imagines his wife appearing first with the face of a goose, and later as a piece of woollen cloth, this story looks forward to Gogol''s later work, with its characteristic depiction of people who have lost all sense of proportion, overvaluing the insignificant, and minimizing what might be of genuine importance. Gogol' concludes each section of the cycle with a comic tale featuring the encounter of the narrator's grandfather with demonic forces. Though primarily farcical in tone, these final stories leave one with the impression that the demonic is not to be taken lightly, even by brave Cossacks.

Although the mythical, enclosed world of the Ukrainian countryside would ultimately be left behind by Gogol' in his literary fiction, *Evenings on a Farm Near Dikanka* displays several features that recur in Gogol''s later work. For example, one notes his tendency to depict female characters either as idealized beauties or as domineering shrews (or even witches). On the other hand, the bold contrasts evident in the Dikanka tales tend to become more muted in the later work. Thus, the sharp distinctions between the everyday world and the supernatural world gradually erode, and in his most celebrated works, such as *Dead Souls* or "The Overcoat", one notes that the demonic has become more subtle; the forces that drive his characters to ruin have their seat within their very souls.

Evenings on a Farm Near Dikanka reveals some unevenness in Gogol''s artistry, but the collection establishes the broad contours of the great fiction to come.

JULIAN W. CONNOLLY

Mirgorod

Short stories, 1835

The cycle *Mirgorod* was published in March 1835, subtitled: "Tales Serving as a Continuation of 'Evenings on a Farm Near Dikanka'", Gogol''s first prose work that appeared in 1832 and brought him instant fame. During the three years that passed between those publications Gogol' tried his hand at other genres, comedy in particular; this period in his career was a time of quest for new themes, new settings, new characters, and its result was *Mirgorod* and *Arabesques*.

Mirgorod consists of four stories: "Starosvetskie pomeshchiki" ("The Old-Fashioned Landowners"), "Taras Bulba", "Vii" and "The Story of How Ivan Ivanovich Quarreled with Ivan Nikiforovich". All four stories retain the Ukrainian setting of the first cycle, but the garrulous narrator of *Evenings on a Farm Near Dikanka* is dispensed with.

The first story depicts the quiet life of an old couple: Afanasii Ivanovich and Pul'kheria Ivanovna, their death and the subsequent decline of their estate. The story is told in the third person by an outside narrator, a man from the big city, who, as he puts it, "sometimes likes to descend for a minute into the domain of this unusually isolated life". The narrator's opening sentences establish the remoteness both in time and in place of the life he portrays, thus setting the story's "musical key" – one of quiet melancholy and regret over the disappearance of a way of life. Gogol' creates in this story a near idyll, interspersed with gentle criticism from a more sophisticated observer. The life of the old couple revolves chiefly around food: eating, preparation and conversation about various dishes; their passion becomes the object of the narrator's good-natured ridicule, invariably mixed with tenderness. The overall feeling pervading the story is one of sadness and melancholy. This story is undoubtedly one of Gogol''s masterpieces, with every word and every image conveying a richness of meaning, subtlety and ambivalence, attained probably for the first time in his writing.

"Taras Bulba" (first version, 1835; second, 1842, and it is the second version that is discussed here) stands in stark contrast to the first story. Contrast (one could almost say counterpoint) is the key compositional device of the whole cycle that endows it with unity and lends it additional depth. In "The Old-Fashioned Landowners" Gogol' re-creates a life of torpor and stagnation, a narrow and closed world hidden behind fences and doors. "Taras Bulba", on the contrary, is all movement and action; it is set in the wide, almost infinite, spaces of the Ukrainian steppes, as well as other countries: Poland, Turkey and beyond, providing the perfect backdrop for this heroic tale. In "Taras Bulba" life is full of deeds of derring-do; it is exuberant and vibrant. Generically, the story may be defined as a historical narrative with epic overtones, although many critics pointed out numerous anachronisms and general inaccuracy of detail. Walter Scott's influence is felt throughout the story. In "Taras Bulba" Gogol' again depicts a vanished way of life; evocation of the past is one of the motifs running through *Mirgorod* and enhancing its unity.

While the key elements in "The Old-Fashioned Landowners" are inaction and an almost complete absence of events, "Taras Bulba" is brimming with wars, sieges, battles, public executions and so on. It seems that Gogol''s aim was to present a positive, national Ukrainian (or Russian, as he equates the two) hero, a leader of his men, primeval, cruel and fierce, who did not hesitate to kill his own son, Andrii, when he learned about the latter's treason. In Gogol''s own words Taras represents: "... an unusual phenomenon of Russian strength". This story is a glorification of Russian might, of the Russian people. Its tenor is almost Slavophile, and that before Slavophilism had fully developed.

In "Vii", the third story of the cycle, Gogol' continues his exploration of some earlier motifs, notably the fantastic, but the similarity with the Dikanka cycle is largely misleading. *Mirgorod* was written during Gogol''s experimental phase and it demonstrates a new direction in his writing. "Vii" is the story of a young seminary student, Khoma Brut, his encounter with the demonic forces represented by a witch and his death resulting from his nocturnal adventure. On the surface, it reads like a folk-tale, but a closer examination reveals the parody at the heart of the story. "Vii" is a parody of a folk-tale, where nothing is what it seems, in the same way as "The Old-Fashioned Landowners" parodies an idyll. In "Vii" Gogol' parodies and thereby undermines the genre of the folk-tale. "Taras Bulba" also contains elements of parody, though there it is probably unintentional.

The story of the quarrel of the two Ivans, the last in the cycle, marks a clear departure from the three previous ones in its temporal setting. The story is set in the present (i.e., early 19th century), moreover precise dates are given by the author, a rare thing for Gogol'. The time span of the story from the date of the initial quarrel (7 July 1810) covers 15 years. In 1825 the narrator, who is used as a device only in the first and last story, visits Mirgorod 15 years after the start of the quarrel, and learns of its imminent conclusion in the court from both Ivans. Yet the reader knows that this is an illusion, the case will not be resolved in the near future, and the law-suit will continue. The drab reality depicted in this story, the petty quarrel of the two Ivans, in a way parodies the world of action in "Taras Bulba". This quarrel is a very distant and dim echo of the glorious warlike past of the Cossacks; one pointer to it is that it flares up because of a weapon (useless to both) and not because of money, possessions or a woman.

Thus the vein of parody that Gogol' exploited in this cycle not only leads outwards, to other genres, but inwards, with one story parodying another, thus creating interesting motifs of counterpoint. The cycle ends on a very sad note: "It's boring in this world, Gentlemen!" are the narrator's parting words before moving on to new and perhaps more exciting places.

Mirgorod and *Arabesques* mark the end of Gogol''s youthful quest as a writer and the start of a period of maturity that was to bring forth *The Government Inspector*, *Dead Souls*, and "The Overcoat".

RUTH SOBEL

Diary of a Madman

Zapiski sumasshedshego

Short story, 1835

The short story, "Diary of a Madman" was first published in 1835 as part of the collection of stories and other writings, *Arabesques*. It is now considered one of Gogol''s "St Petersburg Tales", a critical convention used to refer to five stories set in the Russian capital. These stories are among the first in European literature to explore the theme of alienation in the modern metropolis, to present the debased and trivial world of individuals who live in an urban wilderness that is bereft of any sense of community. All five stories that comprise the "collection" have at the centre a lonely, friendless and kinless man who struggles to retain his dignity, his sanity, and, ultimately, his life. (Indeed, several of the "heroes" of these tales lose their sanity and/or their life.)

Like the most famous of these tales, the later "The Overcoat", "Diary of a Madman" has as its central male character an obscure, middle-aged clerk who is oppressed by the impersonal bureaucratic apparatus of the Petersburg civil service. The "hero", Poprishchin is a minor civil servant of scruffy attire and appearance. Although a lowly "pen-pusher" he has bizarrely formed a fixation on Sophie, the daughter of his boss. From the outset, indeed, his diary entries reveal signs of inappropriate thoughts and behaviour, and his nascent insanity rapidly develops. Rebuffed on all sides he starts hallucinating, reproducing in his own writings the letters "written" by two dogs. Eventually, his grasp on reality slips completely. The entries to his diary become increasingly chaotic and disordered, and he is ultimately carted off to a lunatic asylum, where he interprets the sadistic treatment he receives as his initiation as the King of Spain.

Like many of Gogol''s works, "Diary of a Madman" had a paradoxical reception. The conservative traditionalist writer found himself vilified by conservative critics for his alleged concentration on the "dirty" aspects of Russian life, while the liberals and radicals hailed him as the champion of the downtrodden "little man", and as a social critic. The exact nature of Gogol''s social orientation has occupied readers and critics ever since, and many other interpretations have been added to this original pairing.

Central to any interpretation of this and the other "St Petersburg Tales" is the recognition of their innovative qualities as specifically urban works. Within the Russian context, this theme has more particular resonances in terms of the reinterpretation of the image of St Petersburg itself. This "artificial" city, the creation of Peter the Great at the beginning of modern Russian history at the start of the 18th century, had been seen for the first 100 years of its existence as the symbol of Russia's imperial might and glory. This tradition reached its culmination in Pushkin's *Mednyi vsadnik* (*The Bronze Horseman*). This work also, however, began to explore the darker backstreets of the city, as well as the miserable lives of their oppressed inhabitants. Gogol' was the first Russian writer to develop this new orientation into a major theme, and his St Petersburg, which forms the backdrop to "Diary of a Madman", is an almost imaginary city, where ghosts walk the streets, where dogs write letters to each other, and where, as he put it in "Nevskii Prospekt", "the Devil himself lights the lamps for the sole purpose of showing everything in a false aspect". Gogol' also followed Pushkin here, as in the other tales, by concentrating on the lower ranks of society, and was thereby central to the establishment in Russian literature of the theme of the "little man". Poprishchin is an impoverished, pathetic nonentity who bewails his lot, and struggles vainly to escape his preordained destiny. As is often the case in such works, he ends up even worse than he started.

This raises again the whole question of whether "Diary of a Madman", and other works by Gogol', should indeed be read as works of social criticism. Without question, and whether he wished to or not, he does reveal the inequalities and miseries of life in the backstreets of the modern city. Poprishchin's life is circumscribed not by an impersonal destiny, but by the more immediate forces of the rigid rank system, introduced by the same tsar who had built the city, and by the seemingly immutable bureaucratic pecking order of the office in which he copies documents. Going beyond these seemingly sociological concerns, Gogol' sought to address the human and moral aspects of benighted modern living. Madness is obviously a central theme in this work as it was in at least two other of the tales of the cycle, and the story of Poprishchin's collapse is indeed a moving, and frightening account of mental and spiritual anguish. At the same time, he explores the inhumanity and indifference to one's neighbour (in the Christian sense) that seemed to him so much part of modern life. We see this both in the mockery with which Poprishchin is treated throughout, and, especially, in the cruelty meted out to him in the asylum.

More recent critics have taken the debate on apace. Gogol' is now seen as the precursor of modern writing, and the basic theme of this story could be seen as man's terror and aloneness in a hostile and indifferent universe. Another productive approach to his writing has been feminist readings. Many of his stories recount the downfall of the hero, and, more often than not, a woman is at the centre of his tragedy. Poprishchin, in his increasingly vindictive ravings, sums up the motif that runs through all the "St Petersburg Tales". He denounces not only Sophie (who "betrays" him by not even noticing him), but all women: "O this is a perfidious creature – women! ... Up to now no-one has found out who she is in love with: I discovered it first. Woman is in love with the Devil."

The question remains: where does Gogol' stand in all this? My own view is that he was not at all a social critic, but a highly idiosyncratic Christian moralist who condemns Poprishchin, along with the rest of the denizens of St Petersburg, for the pathetic, restricted lives they lead. Women especially are in thrall to the Devil, and men are too weak to resist his, and their wiles.

JOE ANDREW

The Nose

Nos

Short story, 1836

Gogol''s first prose work, the cycle *Evenings on a Farm Near Dikanka*, gained immediate popularity and made him a celebrity overnight. The success of his juvenile stories, which was both instant and enormous, probably gave him the confidence to adopt the vocation of a writer. The decade that followed (1832–42) saw Gogol''s great talent grow and develop. The years he spent in St Petersburg (until 1836) witnessed a burst of creativity not matched at any other period of his literary career. "The Nose" was conceived and written during that period; most probably the idea for the story had begun to evolve sometime in 1833. Its literary background is of some interest. V. Vinogradov devoted a study to the antecedents of Gogol''s "nosology" and showed that in the 1820s–30s it was a popular subject; it seems that the adventures of the nose in the guise of a state-counsellor must have been much less puzzling for Gogol''s contemporary readers than for the 20th-century ones.

As is well known, at first Gogol' intended the adventures of the nose to take place in Major Kovalev's dream, and he even called the story "Son" (a dream and also *nos* in reverse), thus providing a logical explanation for the unusual events narrated in the story. However, at some stage he dispensed with this conventional device and in a moment of inspiration created one of the most enduringly enigmatic and least "explainable" stories in Russian and probably in all literature.

The story may be divided into three parts or plots: the plot of Ivan Iakovlevich, the barber, which also provides the framework for the story; the plot of Major Kovalev's nose transformed into a civil servant and back into nose; and the central plot of Major Kovalev's quest to recapture his runaway nose.

Gogol' had at first planned to publish the story in *Moskovskii nabliudatel'* but its editors rejected it for being "filthy and vulgar". Pushkin, who had at that period begun to publish his own journal, *Sovremennik*, showed much greater discernment and taste accepting it for publication and prefacing it with a brief note in which he called the work "an inspired joke".

"The Nose", like many other works by Gogol', contains motifs borrowed from other writers, both Russian and foreign, but Gogol''s story is a profoundly original work and has baffled critics and readers from the moment of publication until today. The key problem posed by the story is that of interpretation. The complete lack of motive behind all that happens in the story, especially the disappearance of the nose, its transformation and subsequent return, are enhanced by Gogol''s playful narrative stance, using phrases such as: "... and afterwards everything became enveloped in mist ...", all of which makes any attempt to unravel the mystery even more futile. At the end of the story, the narrator with ever increasing playfulness concludes: "No matter what anyone says, such occurrences do happen in this world, rarely, but they do happen", thus emphasizing the reality of what he has just narrated, tongue-in-cheek, no doubt. Such a serious assertion of the improbable is the author's final "turn of the screw", for, in spite of this assertion, he has succeeded in creating a story for which no key (i.e. no overall interpretation that accounts for all the unusual occurrences) has, as yet, been found.

Once the story's basic absurdity and illogicality at the level of the plot, at least, is accepted, once the reader "suspends his disbelief", other aspects may be examined, and most importantly, the picture of the world the story presents. In *Evenings on a Farm Near Dikanka*, Gogol' paints a gay and lively picture, with an occasional sombre touch. The horrors he depicts, for example in "A Terrible Revenge", are too remote to really frighten the sophisticated urban reader. *Mirgorod* and *Arabesques*, which contain several stories from the so-called St Petersburg cycle, are a different matter. "The Nose", which is part of the latter cycle, conveys a picture of the world very different from that of the Ukraine of long-ago. The loss of his nose undermines Major Kovalev's whole being and forces him to question his identity: "Were I without an arm or a leg, even that would have been better, were I without ears – a bad thing, yet it is not so unbearable, but without a nose a man is, the devil knows what ..." It is significant that mention of the devil (this occurs several times in the story) comes at crucial moments when poor Kovalev tries falteringly to put into words the essence of human identity, and fails.

For Major Kovalev the loss of his nose is equated with the loss of his humanity while assenting that no other corporal loss would have had an equal effect. Of course, on one level this statement is comic, bringing out the character's dim-wittedness, but on another this is just as piercing a *cri de coeur* as that of Poprishchin in "The Diary of Madman": "Mother, save your poor son! Drop a tear on his sick head! look how they torture him ...", or the pathetic questions of Akakii Akakevich in "The Overcoat".

The problem of identity that interested Gogol' throughout his career, the problem of the "real man", is most prominent in the Petersburg cycle. Another theme which is present in "The Nose" is that of rank (*chin*) or rather what Gogol' so aptly described as the "electricity of rank". Gogol' often portrays the desperate longing of a man at the bottom of the social ladder. Major Kovalev's arrival in the capital is the direct result of his burning ambition to move up in the world and he is actively trying to fulfil this ambition by two most common methods: obtaining a good job and marrying a rich bride.

"The Nose" is a fascinating example of Gogol''s attempt to portray an ordinary man (a "poshlyi chelovek") with average ambitions and desires, placed in the most extreme, nightmarish situation, in which he is faced with great loss and even betrayal (the nose is, in a sense, betraying its master). The effect of all these hardships on Major Kovalev, once his nose returns to his rightful place, is nil. If a similar experience were described in realistic prose, the hero would have undergone a profound change. Kovalev, however, remains essentially the same. The metamorphosis affects only the nose, and not its "bearer". Herein lies yet another mystery of this story.

RUTH SOBEL

The Government Inspector

Revizor

Play, 1836

The Government Inspector is the centrepiece of Russian classical drama. Its plot is simple and unoriginal. Khlestakov, a vain feather-brained young civil servant is travelling from St Petersburg to his father's country estate when he loses all his money gambling on cards and is stranded in a small provincial town. He is taken by the local officials to be a government inspector who they believe is visiting their province incognito. Finding himself fawned upon and treated as an important personage, Khlestakov readily takes to the part and after being wined and dined he indulges in shameless boasting and extravagant lies, making himself out to be a St Petersburg celebrity who is both a highly respected official and a prolific man of letters. He exploits the situation with relish, accepting gifts and money offered to him as bribes. In rapid succession he woos the Governor's daughter and wife, becomes engaged to the former, then abruptly departs. Shortly afterwards, the townspeople discover his true identity from a letter opened by the local postmaster, in which Khlestakov makes most unflattering remarks about all the officials. Before they have time to recover from their shocked sense of outrage they are plunged into consternation by the announcement that the real inspector has arrived.

It is an irony that *The Government Inspector*, which unfolds the tragicomic consequences of mistaken identity, has itself been a constant victim of mistaken identity. From the time when it first appeared it has been misinterpreted by actors, audiences and critics alike. Some have dismissed it as a trivial farce bearing no relation to Russian realities and presenting characters who are grotesquely implausible. Many have seen it as a scandalous attack on the tsarist bureaucracy and, by implication, on the whole tsarist system. Hardly anyone has recognized it for what it is, a serious comedy about many forms of human corruption, not just bribery.

There is no political motive behind the play. Gogol''s purpose was to expose dishonest people to ridicule and censure, in the Utopian hope that this would induce such people to mend their ways. He was a conservative who would never have dreamt of attacking the tsar or any tsarist institution; he was even a defender of serfdom. Radicals like Belinskii and liberals like Turgenev were aghast when Gogol' revealed his true political colours in his *Selected Passages from Correspondence with Friends*, published in 1847, by which time the play had become public property and was generally treated as a political satire rather than a moral one. Gogol' had been deeply shaken by the reception of his play and he sought to correct the many misunderstandings about it, but with little success, either in Russia or anywhere else. He wrote several detailed commentaries on the play and how it should be acted, but his guidance has mostly been ignored by actors and directors who think they know better than the writer of genius who created it. Above all his plea for restraint in the acting has gone unheeded to a large extent, for the comedy is often burlesqued as the actors play for laughs and overdo it, disregarding the subtleties and intricacies of the text.

Owing to its enormous comic vitality, *The Government Inspector* is popular with the theatres of the English-speaking world, but its serious aspect is almost entirely overlooked by them. Moreover, it has been woefully mutilated in many of its English translations, even the best of which fail to match the stylistic variety and eccentricity of Gogol''s Russian. Some translators have taken the liberty of modifying and adapting the play, altering its structure, adding new characters and inserting material of their own, so much so that many acting versions are sheer travesties of the original, degenerating into knockabout farce. And the late 20th-century colloquialisms used in some versions clash with the candles, carriages and furbelows of the early 19th century.

In *The Government Inspector* Gogol' departed from the tradition of comedy that had grown up in Russia from the 18th century. He retained the structure and many of the technical devices of conventional comedy but purged it of much of its artificiality and extended its range, freeing it from the limitations of the love-plot with a happy ending. There is no trace in Gogol''s play of the didacticism that characterizes earlier Russian comedies. There are no champions of virtue, no knights in shining moral armour. His characters, unlike those of his predecessors, are not neatly divided into good and bad, but recognizable human beings, though not as fully rounded as those of Chekhov or Tolstoi. There is an element of caricature in the portrayal of most people in his play, but this is not taken to the point of being grotesque and it does not destroy their essential humanity. Gogol''s caricature is mild, just as his satire is gentle, nothing like that of a Swift or a Voltaire. His town officials are rogues, but good-natured rogues. Like the other characters in the play, they are unmistakably human types who belong to their own period and class, but their kind can be found in many other times and places.

The Government Inspector is remarkable as a drama in uniting very different, seemingly incongruous elements in one harmonious whole. It combines surface gaiety with hidden horror, and farce with tragedy. It mingles laughter with tears, the literal with the symbolical, and the trivial with the profound. It is at once absurdly frivolous and deeply serious. Its style ranges from the highly formal to the lowly informal and this unique blend of qualities makes it difficult to classify the play within any of the recognized dramatic genres. It is a work of impressive scale, at one extreme an entertaining comedy of errors, at the other an illuminating drama of corruption. No single interpretation encompasses all its meaning; it may be understood and appreciated at several different levels – the anecdotal, the satirical, and the metaphysical. It is a play of great originality, which contains the inexhaustible riches of all great art. Its theme is universal and it speaks to the eternal human condition. It transcends its own time and people, belonging to all times and all peoples.

MICHAEL BERESFORD

The Overcoat

Shinel'

Story, 1842

"The Overcoat", Gogol''s best known "Petersburg story", was written at the height of his productive years and published in 1842, the same year as the first part of *Dead Souls*. It is an important work, as its influence can be detected in Russian prose fiction writings all through the second half of the 19th century and into the 20th century.

The apparently free-flowing, discursive narration, with its admixture of humour, irony, satire, and at times of the absurd, conceals the submerged tight structure of the story that leads the reader in a straight line from the hero's birth – a farcical description of how Akakii Akakievich was christened (in Gogol''s words, how he "occurred") – to a complex threefold ending.

The plot is simple. Akakii Akakievich is a lowly government clerk capable of performing only one simple task, that of copying, in a lovely hand, official documents and letters. At the beginning of the winter he notices that his old overcoat has reached the state where it cannot be repaired or patched. The price demanded by Petrovich the tailor for a new overcoat is beyond Akakii Akakievich's means, but by drastically economizing on food, clothing, and even on lighting, he finally manages to save enough money to have a warm overcoat made with a luxurious fur collar. The new overcoat is noticed by others in the office, and a colleague offers to organize a party to mark the acquisition. Akakii Akakievich, who has long given up on parties and other kinds of entertainment, is persuaded to join in the celebration. But finding that no one is paying attention to him or to his new overcoat, he leaves the party. On the way home he is attacked in a dark square by thieves who steal his overcoat. Unable to find help in recovering his overcoat from the local authorities, he follows the suggestion given to him to request an audience with an Important Personage – a director of a department with the rank of a general. The Important Personage refuses even to listen to his request for help and, to show his power, treats Akakii Akakievich so harshly that the latter manages with difficulty to reach his lodgings, goes to bed, and dies of fright within three days. Soon rumours begin to circulate in the city that a dead civil servant roams the streets in the night and steals the overcoats of passers-by. The Important Personage, returning one night in a sleigh from a very pleasant party, has his comfortable, warm overcoat pulled from his back by a ghost, whom he recognizes to his horror to be the late Akakii Akakievich. But that does not seem to satisfy the vengeful ghost: the stealing of coats continues, even though now the ghost is not that of a feeble clerk but of a big man with a moustache and enormous fists.

It is, then, a story about an "insignificant clerk" who has been subjected to ridicule and sniggering – as Gogol' remarks at the beginning of his narration – by innumerable scribblers. In this case, however, it is more than a story with a message about an underprivileged and oppressed person. By the peculiarity of his talent, Gogol' manages to make the protagonist into a function of the language, where "how it is said" becomes more important than "what is being said", and this "how" gives depth and breadth to the narrative. The result is that the story is more than the tale of the sad fate of Akakii Akakievich, it encompasses the life of bureaucratic St Petersburg and, by extension, of the whole country.

Gogol''s language has been extensively studied. Its important feature is the idiosyncratic use of mainly service words in unexpected places and with a transposed meaning. In the case of "The Overcoat", this peculiarity of style has been given an additional twist by ascribing it to the hero of the story: "Akakii Akakievich expressed himself mainly by means of prepositions, adverbs and, finally, by those kinds of particles that have decisively no meaning at all" (my translation). But even more important is Gogol''s use of syntax. The sentences are complex, with a great number of subordinate clauses that are not always governed by the finite verb of the main clause. For example, while everyone in the city was relaxing after a day's work – says the narrator – Akakii Akakievich was not, and rather preferred to make a copy of an official letter brought home especially for this purpose. To say this, Gogol' needs a six-words-long main clause, preceded by 14 co-ordinate and 16 subordinate clauses made up of 212 words. In this monstrous sentence he describes how governmental clerks spend their free time after they have dined: some go to the theatre, others for a stroll in the street, some go to a party, others just to visit a colleague and play cards. We are also told how they inspect women's hats or flirt with pretty young things, how they drink tea, smoke pipes, and gossip in shabbily furnished lodgings. This accumulation of at times loosely connected details, however, adds vitality and colour to the narrative and creates a feeling of dynamism that the rather thin plot would not otherwise have done.

Gogol''s idiosyncratic use of language, which appeared to approximate the spoken language of the time, in fact helped – as the musical critic V.V. Stasov says in his memoirs – to create the contemporary spoken Russian. Here, the influence of Ukrainian, which surrounded Gogol' in his childhood, can be detected in the use of robust and colourful images and in the creation of narrative dynamics by means of stringed associations. This stylistic manner, defined by the Formalists as *skaz*, showed that it was permissible to use the language freely, outside the existing norms of the existing standards. The important role "The Overcoat" played in this modernization of the Russian literary language should not be overlooked.

GLEB ŽEKULIN

Dead Souls

Mertvye dushi

Novel, 1842 (written 1835–52)

Dead Souls was Gogol''s most ambitious achievement. It was also his most devastating failure. Work on the novel (or "poem", as he termed it) occupied – and increasingly preoccupied – Gogol' from as early as 1835 right through to his death in 1852. One volume appeared in 1842. For most readers this first and only complete volume *is* Gogol''s great novel. For Gogol' himself it came to represent a flawed prelude to the true masterpiece that was always just beyond his grasp.

At its barest the plot is little more than a somewhat macabre anecdote. The (anti-) hero, Pavel Ivanovich Chichikov, arrives in the provincial town of NN seeking to buy "dead souls": that is, to acquire the notional ownership of serfs ("souls") who had in fact already died but whose names had not yet been removed from their masters' inventories. The purpose was financial fraud: a paper transaction whereby he could relocate these cheaply-bought possessions onto cheaply-bought lands, mortgage the lot at close to full value and make a nice profit. Gogol' claimed that Pushkin had suggested the theme to him in a conversation in 1835.

The anecdote lends itself to episodic repetition. In the first half of the book Chichikov does the rounds of the local landowners: the unctuous and uxorious Manilov; the wary old woman Korobochka; the boisterous and bellicose Nozdrev; the ponderous and stolid Sobakevich; the decrepit and miserly Pliushkin. Back in NN to formalize the transactions the chameleonic Chichikov meets and intrigues the town's equally idiosyncratic inhabitants, before departing in a flurry of rumour and suspicion.

Chichikov's wheeling is as prominent thematically as his dealing. Indeed, the wheel on his coach elicits the first dialogue on the first page of the book: it will get as far as Moscow, opines one studiously idle *muzhik* to another, but not as far as Kazan. Thenceforth and throughout the story the carriage and the road serve not only to link the various episodes in sequence but also to generate reflections – digressions, as they can appear – on anything from the weather to the fate of nations. By the final page of this parodic pilgrim's pseudo-progress Chichikov's carriage with its dodgy wheel has been transmuted into the troika of Rus itself, stirring the air into wind, speeding into the distance, leaving all others straggling in its wake.

This is one manifestation of a pervasive paradox both in *Dead Souls* itself and, perhaps more acutely, in critical responses to the novel. On the one hand Gogolian depiction is essentially static. Characters are assemblages of fixed and often incongruously exaggerated attributes. They are created from and fixated on the superficial: gloriously, unselfconsciously and irredeemably (as it seems) trivial and vulgar. The inner life is fully expressed in the outer mannerisms and obsessions. The book's title is of course ironic, or even – as the censors spotted – potentially blasphemous: it is the living whose souls are dead. In the Dantesque trilogy that *Dead Souls* was to become in Gogol''s plans, this was the equivalent to Inferno. Here was the living hell: soullessness, spiritually barren, an absence of substance.

On the other hand, as the text progresses Gogol' implies ever more strongly, and not always with irony, that significance and substance *can* be found or acquired; that a potential for spiritual motion and metamorphosis is as much an attribute of his oddball characters as of the wheel on Chichikov's carriage. There is an ever-widening gap between Gogol''s depicted world of stagnant, self-contained triviality and Gogol''s implied world of significance and value.

How can or should the gap be bridged? This question, or variants of it, has generated much of the critical discussion surrounding *Dead Souls* from Gogol''s time to the present. Gogol' became convinced that his own mission was to show the way, through the projected second and third volumes. The story of his failure to do so is pathetic to the point of tragedy. His audience colluded in his delusion. Through the 1840s readers who took the published volume to be a bitter satire on the ills of Russia looked to Gogol' to bestow on them a literary solution to the moral and social impasse. Volume two of *Dead Souls* was the answer that never came. The didactic *Selected Passages from Correspondence with Friends* was a disappointing substitute. Gogol' barely hid even his own frustration: his preface to the second edition of volume one is a pained plea for help. Twice he burnt his drafts, the second time just a few days before his death. Versions of a few insipid chapters were later discovered in some mislaid notebooks. The problem was obvious. Gogol' the moralist set tasks that simply did not match the highly specific creative talent of Gogol' the writer. The world of volume one of *Dead Souls* was as it was, not because Gogol' prescribed it thus, but because that was the way the unfettered Gogol' wrote. To change the substance of that world meant – to borrow a phrase from Maiakovskii – stepping on the throat of his own song.

The paradoxes of volume one could not be vanquished in a didactic sequel, but that does not mean that Gogol''s "poem" is necessarily marred by contradiction. Its cohesiveness is artistic rather than logical. Why should one seek consistency from a writer whose trademark was incongruity? In this respect the digressive, lyrical narratorial voice is not odd, and not at odds with the narration. The specific features of artistic coherence in *Dead Souls* have of course been elucidated in various ways. Some stress the sheer fertility of Gogol''s imagination, and the sheer energy of his prose, seeing both the structural and the apparently anti-structural shapes as, in effect, rhythmic devices regulating the flow of images. Others take the ostensible meanings more seriously, emphasizing that Gogol''s extended similes and digressions stretched the range of the book to encompass – by association and generalization – "all of Russia". Some see the novel as celebrating the potency of invention itself, where the characters join the author in making their fictions live. Others have found the key concealed below the surface, in patterns of interconnected symbols that form a kind of cryptic code. However, the range of critical readings perhaps reveals less about *Dead Souls* specifically than about variant approaches to Gogol''s art as a whole.

SIMON FRANKLIN

Ivan Aleksandrovich Goncharov 1812–1891

Novelist

Biography

Born in Simbirsk, 18 June 1812. Attended local boarding school, 1820–22; Moscow Commercial School, 1822–31; Moscow University, 1831–34. Civil servant in St Petersburg from 1834: secretary to Admiral Pitiatin on trip to Far East, 1852–55. Worked as official censor, St Petersburg, 1856–60; member of the committee of review of Russian censorship groups, 1863–67; retired from civil service as Actual Councillor of State, 1867. Died 27 September 1891.

Publications

Collected Editions

Sobranie sochinenii, 8 vols. Moscow, 1952–55.

Sobranie sochinenii, 8 vols. Moscow, 1977–80.

Polnoe sobranie sochinenii i pisem, 20 vols. Moscow, 1996– .

Fiction

Obyknovennaia istoriia, *Sovremennik*, 3–4 (1847); as a separate edition, St Petersburg, 1848; translated as *A Common Story*, by Constance Garnett, New York, Collier, 1894; also translated as *The Same Old Story*, by Ivy

Litvinova, Moscow, Foreign Languages Publishing House, 1957; and as *An Ordinary Story* with *Viktor Rovoz*, edited and translated by Marjorie L. Hoover, Ann Arbor, Ardis, 1993.

Oblomov, Otechestvennye zapiski, 1858–59; 2 vols, St Petersburg, 1859; "Literaturnye pamiatniki", Leningrad, 1987; translated as *Oblomov*, by C.J. Hogarth, London, 1915; also by Natalie Duddington, New York, Macmillan, 1929; David Magarshack, Harmondsworth, Penguin, 1959; Ann Dunnigan, New York, Signet, 1963.

Obryv, Vestnik Evropy, 1–4 (1869); separate edition, 2 vols, St Petersburg, 1870; translated as *The Precipice*, by M. Bryant, London, Hodder and Stoughton, 1915; also by Laury Magnus and Boris Jakim, Ann Arbor, Ardis, 1993.

Literary Criticism, Letters, and Memoirs

Literaturno-kriticheskie stat'i i pis'ma [Literary Critical Articles and Letters], edited by A.P. Rybasova. Moscow, 1938.

"Ivan Turgenev", in *The Complection of Russian Literature*, by Andrew Field, New York, Atheneum, and London, Allen Lane, 1971, 131–47; reprinted Harmondsworth, Penguin, 1973.

I.A. Goncharov-kritik (selection), edited by V.I. Korobov. Moscow, 1981.

Ocherki. Stat'i. Pis'ma. Vospominaniia sovremennikov [Essays. Articles. Letters. Reminiscences of Contemporaries]. Moscow, 1986.

Travel Writing

Russkie v Iaponii v kontse 1853 i v nachale 1854 godov [Russians in Japan at the End of 1853 and the Beginning of 1854]. St Petersburg, 1855; revised edition, as *Fregat Pallada*, 2 vols, St Petersburg, 1858; edited by D.V. Oznobishin, 1986; translated as *The Voyage of the Frigate Pallada: Notes on a Journey*, by N.W. Wilson, London, Folio Society, 1965.

Critical Studies

"Chto takoe Oblomovshchina?", by N.A. Dobroliubov, 1859; in his *Sobranie sochinenii*, 9 vols, Moscow, 1961–64, vol. 4, 307–44; translated as "What is Oblomovism?" [no translator named], in *Belinsky, Chernyshevsky and Dobrolyubov: Selected Criticism*, edited by Ralph E. Matlaw, New York, Dutton, 1962; reprinted Bloomington, Indiana University Press, 1976.

Ivan Gontcharov: un maître du roman russe, by André Mazon, Paris, 1914.

"Oblomovka Revisited", by Leon Stilman, *American Slavic and East European Review*, 7 (1948), 45–77.

Goncharov, by Janko Lavrin, New Haven, Yale University Press, 1954.

I.A. Goncharov v russkoi kritike. Moscow, 1958.

Roman I.A. Goncharova "Oblomov", by A.F. Zakharkin, Moscow, 1963.

Ivan Goncharov, by Alexandra Lyngstad and Sverre Lyngstad, New York, Twayne, 1971.

Oblomov and His Creator: The Life and Art of Ivan Goncharov, by Milton Ehre, Princeton, Princeton University Press, 1973.

The Rise of the Russian Novel: Studies in the Russian Novel from "Eugene Onegin" to "War and Peace", by Richard Freeborn, Cambridge, Cambridge University Press, 1973.

Ivan Goncharov: His Life and His Works, by Vsevolod Setchkarev, Würzburg, Jal, 1974.

Realizm I.A. Goncharova, by V.I. Mel'nik, Vladivostok, 1985.

Ivan Gontcharoff ou le Réalisme Impossible, by Jean Blot, Saint-Amand, Cher, 1986.

Oblomov: A Jungian Approach: A Literary Image of the Mother Complex, by Natalie Baratoff, Bern, Peter Lang, 1990.

Oblomov: A Critical Examination of Goncharov's Novel, by Richard Peace, Birmingham, Birmingham Slavonic Monographs, 1991.

The Autobiographical Novel of Co-Consciousness: Goncharov, Woolf, and Joyce, by Galya Diment, Gainesville, University of Florida Press, 1994.

Bibliographies

Bibliografiia Goncharova 1832–1964, by A.D. Alekseev, Moscow, 1968.

Ivan Goncharov: A Bibliography, edited by Garth M. Terry, Nottingham, Astra Press, 1986.

Ivan Goncharov was the son of a prosperous grain merchant in the provincial town of Simbirsk. Technically members of the gentry class, his family was more similar to the merchant class that was later to provide such rich material for Aleksandr Ostrovskii's plays in its conservatism and belief in the virtues of hard work and making one's own way in the world. In 1819 Goncharov's father died and the children were handed into the care of their godfather, Nikolai Tregubov, a liberal-minded aristocrat, more in tune with the ideals of late 18th-century France, and whose personality, and those of people like him, was later to be depicted by Goncharov in his most famous novel (*Oblomov*). Educated at boarding school and the Moscow Commercial School, he entered Moscow University in 1831 where he failed conspicuously to join in any of the student circles with their faith in the ideals of German Romantic philosophy. Although it is clear from his novels that he believed in the value of lofty aspirations, he was always too sceptical, materialistic, even prosaic to overstress their importance. After graduating he entered government service in 1835 where he remained until he retired in 1867. For 12 of those years he was a senior official in the state censorship, coinciding with a period of intended liberalization. Showing signs of some mental instability from his teens, Goncharov was later to develop a form of paranoia, highlighted by his much publicized accusation that Turgenev stole the plots of his novels from conversations the two had held. Even Flaubert was accused of writing *L'Éducation sentimentale* (*Sentimental Education*) on the advice of Turgenev who had got the idea from Goncharov. He wrote an amazing account of the events entitled *Neobyknovennaia istoriia* [An Uncommon Story]. Published only in 1924, it verges on the psychopathic and reveals a side to his character that contrasts sharply with the air of respectability he tried to portray to most of his contemporaries. After the publication of his last novel in 1869 and the negative response it drew from nearly everyone, he spent the rest of his days in lonely and bitter recriminations. He wrote little: a few reminiscences of his childhood, an interesting essay on

Griboedov and a series of short sketches about Old Servants. He never married.

Goncharov's first novel, *Obyknovennaia istoriia* (*A Common Story*), appeared in 1847. It was used by Belinskii as, (after Dostoevskii's *Bednye liudi* [*Poor Folk*]), the best example of the emerging realistic, or critical, school of literature. Indeed, it has frequently been seen as the first realistic novel in all Russian literature, and was welcomed whole-heartedly by both critics and readers. It may contain some autobiographical elements, for it deals with a young man, Aleksandr Aduev, who leaves the provinces for St Petersburg with the hope of gaining fame and fortune. He does not take kindly to having to work for a living, preferring to compose sentimental verses and indulge in daydreams. By contrast his uncle Petr is a very successful bureaucrat and businessman. In opposition to the romantic meanderings of his nephew, he is a man of action. What Russia needs is knowledge, hard work, and the entrepreneurial spirit. He has long arguments with his nephew about the practicalities of life. He would do far better, affirms his uncle, to give up poetry for translating books on agriculture. Slowly Aleksandr is convinced, enters government service and in a dozen years is a changed man. Unfortunately Goncharov does not see fit to show the reader how his hero managed it. At the end he is a reliable, successful, if rather dull, bureaucrat. For Goncharov this is a sign of progress.

Goncharov was always more at home with types rather than individuals and looked for what he thought were representative characters in Russian society; this can be seen from "Son Oblomova" ("Oblomov's Dream"), 1849, the germ for his best novel. Events, however, took him away from Russia. He was sent on a diplomatic mission to Japan and did not take well to the long sea voyage and even less to having to return overland across Siberia. The result was *Fregat Pallada* (*The Voyage of the Frigate Pallas*), an unusual collection of "travel notes". Goncharov did not find the Orient as exotic as most of his contemporaries, rather a curiosity. Romanticism is almost parodied by the contrast of lush nature descriptions, savage and interesting people, and stormy seas with scruffy towns, and dull natives; and the oceans he finds generally boring. Yet the tales are full of humour where ideals collapse in the face of an unprepossessing reality.

In 1858 Goncharov's greatest novel, *Oblomov*, which is his main, some would say only, claim to a Russian classic, was serialized and published in book form the following year. Once again he contrasts dreams with reality through the character of his hero, a representative of the declining landowning gentry who have sunk into lethargy and apathy, something that was classified as "Oblomovism". The novel is clearly portraying Russia's need for "new men", as seen in the bustling, energetic Shtolts, yet the passing of the old order is also a matter of regret. Oblomov has many virtues that are lacking in Shtolts: love of art, tenderness, compassion. That Goncharov has made him a sympathetic, although by no means tragic, character whereas the active Shtolts remains largely one-dimensional and consequently unconvincing, obviously shows where the author's sympathies lay.

Obryv (*The Precipice*) was a long time in the writing and is usually lumped together with a large number of "Anti-nihilist" novels of the 1860s and 1870s. It relates, rather ploddingly, the rivalry between three men for the love of a mysterious woman. A weak-willed artist, Raiskii, the energetic, if unexciting, and practically minded Tushin, (both of whom might be compared with Aleksandr and Petr in *A Common Story*), and the evil nihilist Volokhov are the three rivals. Politically speaking, the novel is not as anti-nihilist as has often been suggested. Goncharov seems to want to strike a balance between the reactionary traditions of the past and the new radicalism. Although most of the characters appear destined to live out their lives happily enough, it is through Tushin that Goncharov propounds the virtues of progress, education, art, and the family. As a piece of literature, however, the work is a complete failure. Its style is melodramatic and its dialogues long and bombastic. Critics have often pointed out that Goncharov was as incapable as Gogol' of seeing inside his creations, and their psychology is often equally contentious and unsatisfactory. This helps explain how *The Precipice* fails to charm. It also shows Goncharov's faults: little imagination, poor plotting, little narrative interest, subjectivity in characterization, no "poetry". If it were not for *Oblomov*, Goncharov would no doubt be as forgotten today as he was by his contemporaries at his death.

A.V. KNOWLES

A Common Story

Obyknovennaia istoriia

Novel, 1847

According to Goncharov's account, *A Common Story* was conceived in 1844, written mostly in 1845, and completed in 1846. It was published in *Sovremennik* in 1847. The novel was popular and especially welcomed by Belinskii and the critics of the left as a blow for the new realism in art, or, as it was called then, "the natural school".

A Common Story describes the education in modern city life of a young man from the provinces, a topic to be found in Dickens, Balzac, and many 19th-century novels. Aleksandr Aduev receives his training from his uncle Petr, an urbane and practical business man. Much of the novel is a dialogue between the two, though Petr's wife plays an important role toward the end. By sympathizing with the beleaguered Aleksandr, she compels the reader to readjust his or her own sympathies.

Petr's instructional method, as he tries to wean his nephew from bucolic innocence, approximates the traditional procedures of writers struggling to break from atrophied literary traditions – parody. Indeed parody was at the heart of realism, which saw itself as a corrective to romanticism. The parody proceeds in a number of ways.

Goncharov simply parallels their speech. After their first meeting they simultaneously report their impressions to friends:

Aleksandr My Uncle is very prosaic ... It is as if his spirit is chained to the earth and never rises to a pure reflection, isolated from earthly squabbles, of the phenomena of the spiritual nature of man.

Petr He's a quiet fellow. He has his odd points – he throws himself upon me to kiss me, speaks like a seminary student – well, he'll get over that ...

Petr completes Aleksandr's sentences or repeats his stock romantic phrases in a coarse and colloquial context:

Aleksandr Life is like a lake ... it is full of something mysterious, alluring, concealing in itself so much –

Petr Slime, my good fellow ...

At times Petr's commentaries are less oblique. He assumes the role of literary critic and comments directly on Aleksandr's overblown rhetoric:

Aleksandr And I thought you were bidding farewell before your wedding to your true friends, whom you sincerely love, with whom you would recall for the last time your gay youth, and, perhaps on parting, would press fast to your heart.

Petr Come now! In those several words of yours there is everything that does not and should not exist in life ...Really! you say *true friends* when there are simply friends and *goblet* when people drink out of wine glasses or ordinary glasses and embraces *on parting* when there is no question of parting. Oh, Aleksandr!

Through the collision of two speech styles the exceptional is reduced to the common, the extraordinary to the ordinary. Aleksandr fancies himself a writer and his efforts are filled with the trappings of romantic fiction: "the furnishings were luxurious: American nature, mountains, and in the midst of all this an exile who has abducted his beloved". Petr, in his critique, downgrades the exotic to the banal: Petersburg is not the Kirgiz steppes, he points out, and a duel in "our age" is not conducted with weapons but with wit and cunning whose purpose is "to present the rival in a common aspect, to show that the modern hero is 'so-so'".

A Common Story is then, to a significant degree, a programmatic novel, a fictional manifesto of the new realism. Aleksandr's conversion, his move from an abstract, inflated rhetoric to a language of common things is a turn from romanticism to the realism that was being born at the time. Aleksandr finally discovers a language of concrete things: "the poetry *of a great sky, a broken fence, wicket gate and a muddy pond*" – he is paraphrasing Pushkin (from *Otryvki iz puteshestviia Onegina* [Excerpts from Onegin's Journey]). The novel also marks the personal development of the writer – the poems he ascribes to Aleksandr and ruthlessly parodies are his own youthful efforts: he had indulged a romantic style in several of his early stories.

Action follows the same deflationary course as Aleksandr's dialogues with his uncle. As the parody lowers his inflated rhetoric to common usage, experience moves downward from his dreams of an extraordinary fate to acceptance of the common lot. Infatuated by a young girl, he takes a boat across the Neva for a rendezvous anticipating "a promised land" – Goncharov's fiction is filled with dreams of an idyllic state. His enthusiasm is such that he wishes to hasten the journey by walking on the water, and promptly falls in. A stolen kiss is followed by Naden'ka's threat to tell mama, and "Aleksandr falls from the clouds".

After a number of such ups and downs Aleksandr, exhausted, gives in and becomes like his uncle – a practical man of the world. The comic reversal is marked by the appearance of a number of phrases and gestures repeated through the novel, but not with their evaluations reversed. (Goncharov was again to employ leitmotifs in *Oblomov*, but there for lyrical as well as comic effects.) "Career and fortune", "filthy lucre" are now good; "colossal passion" and "sincere effusions" are bad.

The most important of these returning images is yellow flowers. They are associated by Aleksandr with home, the countryside, love and friendship, the powers of poetry. At the denouement we discover that the uncle also had a history of yellow flowers. *A Common Story* is only ostensibly about two diametrically opposed characters. The uncle's "common story" of idealistic hopes and subsequent disillusion took place before the novel began.

As one strand of the novel extends into the past, another hints at the future. A nagging backache is a sign that all is not well with Petr's calculated life. As Aleksandr gives up his youthful dreams, Petr exclaims, "You resemble me completely. Only the backache is lacking!" "I have a stitch there sometimes ...", Aleksandr concedes.

The novel ends in ironic deadlock. Both romantic enthusiasm and prudent practicality are seen as inadequate to the problems of life. *A Common Story* is a comedy of coming of age, the loss of illusions, and the compromises of maturity as repeated in the lives of the two central characters, not as an object lesson, but as comedy's perception of the way of the world.

A slight work, often charming and amusing, but too meticulous in its symmetries, *A Common Story* points, in its opposition of the practical life and the life of dream, to Goncharov's great masterpiece, *Oblomov*.

MILTON EHRE

Oblomov

Novel, 1858–59

Goncharov's novel *Oblomov* (stress on the second syllable) was written in two distinct stages. What is now the ninth chapter of the novel's first section, "Son Oblomova" ("Oblomov's Dream"), was published in 1849 under the title "An Episode from an Unfinished Novel" and treated as a work in itself. After several years of literary quietude in 1857 Goncharov suddenly completed all the rest of the novel in a burst of feverish activity lasting less than two months. Published the following year in the journal *Otechestvennye zapiski*, it was seized on by radical polemicists, who saw it as a devastating critique of contemporary society, and the novel became the subject of much controversy. It was the subject of a famous article by Dobroliubov, "Chto takoe Oblomovshchina?" ("What is Oblomovism?") (1859). ("Oblomovism" seems inadequate to translate the Russian word *Oblomovshchina*, with its strongly pejorative suffix.)

The plot of the novel is insubstantial and, in the first and last (of four) parts, almost non-existent. Frustration of the reader's expectations of excitement and incident is deliberate, even inevitable, since the eponymous hero, Il'ia Il'ich Oblomov, is the epitome of mental, physical, and spiritual lethargy. He lies on his couch in St Petersburg choosing to do nothing more demanding than dream dreams, put off decisions of all kinds and argue wearily with his morose manservant, Zakhar. His country estate, Oblomovka, is meanwhile sliding into ruin through mismanagement and failure to modernize. A stream of self-interested visitors, some of them out to defraud him, cannot rouse Oblomov, but eventually he does stir into incipient activity. The agent of his would-be self-reform is a childhood friend, Andrei Shtolts, his very antithesis, a man of decisive action and efficiency, half-German by birth. Shtolts coaxes him out into the real world where, after a week of distasteful involvement in society and business, Oblomov is saved from immediate recidivism by falling in love with a young woman, Ol'ga Ilinskaia. For a time it seems almost possible that she will complete what Shtolts has begun – the pair manage repeatedly to surmount their own doubts and even become engaged – but the challenge is beyond Oblomov's capabilities. Relapsing into his old, longed-for inertia, he marries not Ol'ga, but a buxom, undemanding widow, Agafia Pshenitsina, who bears him a son. All that remains is for him to decline into effortless contentment before fading peacefully away in the gentlest death in all of Russian literature. By this time, although he has suffered financial ruin, his enemies' worst machinations have been frustrated by Shtolts who, now married to Ol'ga, adopts the son of his dead friend.

The radical critics took this novel at face value; it was so obviously a savage indictment of the existing class system. Dobroliubov linked the "hero" to several preceding male protagonists in Russian literature, seeing them as "Superfluous Men", all afflicted by the same disease of inactivity. Oblomov had brought their inadequacies to a refined art and in doing so had indicated clearly where the source of Russia's troubles lay – in the feudal system of masters and peasants. He was a true symbol of a landowning class that had had its day. By contrast, Shtolts and Ol'ga were near to being positive heroes, shining examples of the people needed to modernize the country. Conservative voices accepted little of this. They pointed to the endearing qualities of the lovable hero, a man accepted by everyone as having a heart of gold, a repository of truly Russian spiritual qualities. Against him Shtolts looked like a wooden puppet in literary terms and a tedious businessman in the putative real world. The inconclusiveness of this debate was due to the open-endedness of Goncharov's novel. Oblomovka is built on ambiguity; it is a rundown settlement of outrageous privilege on the very brink of collapse and, at the same time, a rural enclave making no demands on anyone, protective, timeless and as enchanting as a fairy-tale kingdom of rich food and happiness ever after. Most readers, contemplating its inhabitants and their way of life, will find their annoyance tempered by sympathy, envy, and amusement.

Oblomov himself is one of the greatest of Russian literary creations, a true archetype. On the surface he is all scruffiness, sloth and ruinous procrastination, but he also personifies an escapist attitude to life that everyone must at some time be tempted towards. He speaks to that part of us which would dearly like not to get up in the morning, to stay in bed all day, to give up the petty and futile struggle of everyday life, to stand and stare or do even less. Who could withhold sympathy from his view that he was created "in order to demonstrate the ideally restful aspect of human experience"? He is also wonderfully funny, providing unforgettable set-pieces: Oblomov trying to get out of bed and managing in 150 pages no more than to insert his toes into a slipper, Oblomov at the opera yawning fit to swallow the stage, Oblomov wriggling in prevarication when asked whether he reads the papers or takes any exercise. He is convincing in psychological terms, Goncharov tracing his malady, if that is what it is, back to childhood, infancy, and even early babyhood. Not only was the tiny Il'ia Il'ich surrounded on every side by examples of seductive laziness, he was actively stifled in his every feeble attempt to break out beyond them. Found snowballing with the other boys he was quickly swaddled and brought back into the warmth.

In all its tranquillity this is also a deeply philosophical novel from which much can be learned. Oblomovka is so silent and static, especially in its regular state of massive postprandial relaxation, that it sinks into a state bordering on catalepsy. Death and life are almost indistinguishable. Old men pass away there imperceptibly, drifting into non-existence without a tremor. This is no trivial point. In "Oblomov's Dream", death is mentioned a dozen times. It is a major preoccupation, yet there is nothing morbid or frightening about it. No other Russian novel, perhaps no other novel, treats the subject with such sweet acceptability; death is presented to us as it appeared to the lucky denizens of Oblomovka – it is perfectly natural, universal and at the right time warmly welcome. Without disturbing us it should also inform our attitude to living by reminding us of the triviality of much that we do in our lives. This is one of the greatest of all the Russian realist novels, thin in storyline, but rich in every other way. Its language rises on occasions to poetic heights. In characterization, socio-political interest, psychological accuracy and humour it is imaginative and highly original. Its oriental wisdom, gently and amusingly purveyed, is enough to dispel the deepest worries. Anyone suffering from an excess of 20th-century Angst should go back and live with Oblomov.

A.D.P. Briggs

The Precipice

Obryv

Novel, 1869

While Goncharov's two earlier novels treat universal themes or "common stories" – the conflict between thought and feeling, poetry and action, practical activity and the passive imagination – *The Precipice* is overtly political. Conceived as early as 1849 but written mostly from 1858 to 1868 (published in 1869 in *Vestnik Evropy*), it was part of a flood of "anti-nihilist" (or anti-revolutionary) novels of the period (Dostoevskii's novels are the most outstanding examples of the trend). *A Common Story* told of Aleksandr Aduev's journey to make his way in the city; Oblomov, failing to adjust to impersonal urban life, dreams of returning to his country estate; Boris Raiskii, the dreamy hero of *The Precipice*, comes home. Malinovka, his ancestral estate, has been invaded by an intruder, the pernicious nihilist Mark Volokhov. Espousing the "new morality" of the "new men" he seduces Boris's cousin, the mysterious Vera, at the bottom of the precipice from which the novel takes its name. Boris also loves Vera but she falls for the man of action. Tat'iana Markovna, the crusty matriarch of Malinovka, upholds traditional values. So does Ivan Tushin, the positive hero, who is yet a third rival for Vera. Goncharov was not alone among Russians in collapsing political issues into questions of moral (and sexual) behaviour.

The resolution is marked by a general moving day at Malinovka. Vera confesses her sin to grandmother, is forgiven, and taken back into the bosom of the family; Tushin comes in from the great Russian forest (one of many allusions to his Russianness) to assume the management of Malinovka and presumably marry a redeemed Vera: his sister Marfen'ka returns with her fiancé, and several lost souls find a nest in the ancestral estate. Actually only one character, the reactionary Nil Andreich, who resides in the stagnating town (as opposed to the thriving estate), is excluded from this comic harmony. Mark Volokhov repents of his misdeed and joins the Russian army as penitence. Tushin's economic theories are quite progressive (Robert Owen, also an influence on the radicals, is his model!), and will keep the estate, which in this allegorical novel is identified with Russia, on a firm footing. Traditional Russia has been saved (by accommodation, not repression), but more importantly for Goncharov sexual intrigue has been banished. The real aim of this book is to affirm the family.

Melodrama has been defined as comedy without laughs. The wicked are condemned, the virtuous are saved but there is little fun in the process. Except for a few genre scenes of daily life on the estate, of which Goncharov was a master, and some fine character drawing, *The Precipice* is a hard read. Whether Vera will do it or not is worried about over so many pages that the reader ceases to care. The overblown prose strains to keep us interested:

> She fell to her knees at the threshold to the chapel, covered her face with her hands and froze into immobility. Raiskii silently approached her from behind. "Don't go, Vera", he whispered ...
>
> "What if he is returning – if my 'truth' has triumphed: Why else would he call? – O God!"
>
> Raiskii froze on the spot. "What is this, a fateful mystery or passion? Or one and the other?"

However, there is an interesting if unrealized theme lurking in the shadows of this potboiler. The original title was "Raiskii, the Artist", or simply "The Artist" and only in the late 1850s or early 1860s did Goncharov decide to turn it into a dramatic political novel. His earlier novels had been quite undramatic: *A Common Story* is a parodic comedy built around the fumblings of the hero in his attempts to grow up: *Oblomov* shares some of its parodic turns, but is also a psychological study of life, drawn with extraordinary depth and compassion. In departing from his true talent – the biographical novel – Goncharov may have been trying to accommodate to the fashion of the time, but he was also stuck on his original project, another biography of a soul: "It seems I took upon myself an impossible task: to portray the insides, the heart of an artist and the backstages of art."

Also the original project promised to treat the particular kind of life that interested Goncharov, one in which the illusions of a solitary individual collide with refractory reality, where art becomes confused with life. He wanted, he said, to trace the curious psychological process whereby "the power of imagination in artistic natures, when it is not applied to vital work, plunges into life itself ... producing those eccentricities and deformities that frequently abound in the lives of artists".

Raiskii is writing a novel which turns out to be the same novel that we are reading. A novel-within-a-novel may be used to achieve the kind of irony that characterizes Goncharov's other fiction – the characters' misapprehensions about life are set against "actual" experience. Here Raiskii's novel would be opposed to the actual novel that would be given the authority of true life. There are moments when this seems to be Goncharov's intention, but the ironic scheme never develops. Instead Raiskii fades out of view and the drama of the precipice takes over, resulting in a book that is split in two.

It is a pity, since there are interesting ideas in Raiskii's story. Like Aleksandr Aduev of *A Common Story* and Oblomov, Raiskii is a dreamer who tries to realize his dream in reality. But where Aduev and Oblomov sought their ideal in a "poetic moment" of love that would transcend ordinary human experience, Raiskii seeks his "paradise" (*rai* means "paradise") in ordinary sexual passion: "'Sacred, profound elevated love' is a lie! I want ordinary vital, animal passion. Passion is constant intoxication, eternal flowers beneath your feet, an idol." Since Freud, the relationship of sexual desire to creative activity has been a powerful interest. Perhaps Goncharov was too early, or perhaps the subject was too close for him to handle.

The critics never much cared for *The Precipice*, though for a while it was popular with the general reading public. Overly melodramatic as a tale of sexual intrigue, unrealized as a biography of a troubled artist, it still holds interest for its portraits of Russian people and life in the latter part of the 19th century.

MILTON EHRE

Natal'ia Evgen'evna Gorbanevskaia 1936–

Poet and editor

Biography

Born in Moscow, 26 May 1936. Attended Moscow University, expelled twice; Leningrad University, external degree 1964. Two sons. Librarian at All-Union Book Centre, 1958–64. Suffered from fear of heights; subsequently stayed in Kashchenko psychiatric hospital, 1959. Translator and editor at the State Institute of Experimental Pattern Design and Technical Research, 1964–68. Co-founder and editor of *Khronika tekushchikh sobytii*, *samizdat* journal, 1968–75. Involved in civil rights activities: arrested in 1969; stayed in prison hospital, 1970–72. Emigrated to France, 1975; editor of journals *Kontinent*, *Pamiat'*, and *La Pensée Russe*, in Paris.

Publications

Collected Editions

Selected Poems of Natalya Gorbanevskaya, translated by Daniel Weissbort. Oxford, Carcanet, 1972.
Ne spi na zakate: *Pochti polnoe izbrannoe. Stikhi* [Don't Sleep at Sunset: Almost a full selection. Poems]. St Petersburg, 1996.

Poetry
"V sumasshedshem dome" [In the Mad House], *Grani*, 67 (1968).
"Piat' stikhotvorenii" [Five Poems], *Grani*, 69 (1968).
Stikhi. Frankfurt, Posev, 1969.
"Sharmanka, poi, sharmanka voi" [Street-Organ Sing, Street-Organ Howl], *Grani*, 70 (1969).
"Stikhi, ne sobrannye v knigi" [Poems, Not Collected in Books], *Grani*, 76 (1971).
Poberezh'e [The Seaboard]. Ann Arbor, Ardis, 1973.
"Ne spi na zakate" [Don't Sleep in the Sunset], *Grani* (August–December 1974).
Tri tetradi stikhotvoreniia [Three Books of Poetry]. Bremen, K Presse, 1975.
"Chetyre stikhtvoreniia" [Four Poems], *Grani*, 100 (1976).
Pereletia snezhnuiu granitsu: stikhi 1974–1978 [Flying over the Snowy Border]. Paris, YMCA-Press, 1979.
Angel dereviannyi [Wooden Angel]. Ann Arbor, Ardis, 1982.
Poeticheskii traktat [Poetical Treatise]. Ann Arbor, Ardis, 1982.
Chuzhie kamni: stikhi 1979–1982 [The Stones of Others: Poems 1979–1982]. New York, Russica, 1983.
Peremennaia oblachnost': stikhi osen' 1982–vesna 1983 [Variable Cloudiness]. Paris, Kontakt, 1985.
Gde i kogda: stikhi iiun' 1983–mart 1985 [Where and When]. Paris, Kontakt, 1985.
"I vremia zhit', i vremia povtoriat'" [Both a Time to Live, and a Time to Repeat], *Oktiabr'*, 7 (1990), 102–08.
"Iz raznykh sbornikov" [From Various Collections], *Znamia*, 8 (1990).
"Iz stikhov poslednikh let" [From Poetry of Recent Years], *Novyi mir*, 11 (1992).
"Stikhi poslednikh let" [Poems of Recent Years], *Oktiabr'*, 11 (1992).
Poems in *Contemporary Russian Poetry. A Bilingual Anthology*, edited and translated by Gerald S. Smith. Bloomington, Indiana University Press, 1993, 100–11.
Nabor: Novaia kniga stikhov (mart 1994–fevral' 1996) [Set: New Book of Verse, March 1994–February 1996]. Moscow, 1996.

Essays
Polden': Delo o demonstratsii 25 avgusta 1968 goda na krasnoi ploshchadi, Samizdat, 1969; Frankfurt, Posev, 1970; translated as *Red Square at Noon*, by Alexander Lieven, London, Deutsch, and New York, Holt, 1972; Harmondsworth, Penguin, 1973.

Memoirs
Bezplatnaia meditsinskaia pomoshch', as appendix to *Stikhi*, 1969; translated as *Free Health Service*, by Daniel Weissbort, in *Selected Poems of Natalya Gorbanevskaya*, 1972.
Brodsky Through the Eyes of His Contemporaries, by Valentina Polukhina, London, Macmillan, and New York, St Martin's Press, 1992.

Critical Study
"The Early Poems of Natalja Gorbanevskaja", by Christine Rydel, *Russian Language Journal*, 123–24 (1982), 236–52.

Natal'ia Gorbanevskaia was born in Moscow in 1936. Expelled from Moscow University on two occasions, she received an external degree from the philological faculty of Leningrad University in 1963. From 1958 to 1964 she worked as a librarian in the All-Union Book Centre. In October 1959 she spent two weeks in the Kashchenko psychiatric hospital "as a result of extreme fatigue ... (at the time I was working and studying)". Gorbanevskaia refers to this experience and describes her subsequent harrowing stay in a maternity hospital and her return to Kashchenko in the series of notes entitled *Bezplatnaia meditsinskaia pomoshch'* (*Free Health Service*) (written in Moscow, March 1968). From 1964 to 1968 she worked in the State Institute of Experimental Pattern Design and Technical Research as a translator and editor. During the 1960s Gorbanevskaia was very active in the civil rights movement in Russia; she was, for example, one of the group of seven demonstrators who protested on Red Square on 25 August 1968 against the Soviet invasion of Czechoslovakia. On 24 December 1969 she was arrested and on 7 July 1970 she was declared to have contravened articles 190 and 191 of the Russian Criminal Code; it was also stated on that same occasion that she was suffering from "schizophrenia". As a direct result of such a "verdict" Gorbanevskaia was sent to the hospital section of Butyrka prison, Moscow and in January 1971 she was transferred to a "special" psychiatric hospital in Kazan where she remained until 24 February 1972. She emigrated to the west in late 1975 and has lived since then in Paris, where she continues to write and involve herself in literary activities, having editorial duties on the émigré journals *Kontinent*, *Pamiat'*, and *Russkaia mysl'*. Friends who knew her in Russia and those who have met her during the exile years refer to her sincerity, honesty, simplicity and profound religious faith. Her intimate love poetry has frequently been compared to that of Marina Tsvetaeva.

Gorbanevskaia's name gradually became known in the USSR in the 1960s through her close association with *Khronika tekushchikh sobytii*, the *samizdat* journal of dissident activities which she had helped to found and edit. At that time, too, some of her early poems were published in the influential *samizdat* journal *Feniks 1961*, including works written between 1956 and 1961. Several other *samizdat* editions of her poetry also circulated privately. Gorbanevskaia's striking and memorable imagery and her philosophical preoccupations can be noted in these early pieces, and critical attention was soon drawn to her. The untitled short poem (of ten lines) published in *Feniks 1961* with the first line "O drug moi!" [Oh, my friend!] touches on universal themes of friendship, fear and alienation, despite its brevity and seeming simplicity. *Moskovskii komsomolets* published nine of her poems on 16 May 1965 and *Znamia* (6, 1966) carried several poems by her. *Feniks 1966* published a short collection of her works, including the moving poem dedicated to Iurii Galanskov, "V sumashedshem dome" [In the Asylum]. Some of her poems also appeared in the journal *Zvezda vostoka* in 1968. Gorbanevskaia has also translated many foreign poets (especially from the Polish) and has published translations of poems by Federico García Lorca. After her release from prison, Gorbanevskaia prepared the collection *Tri tetradi stikhotvorenii* [Three Books of Poetry] during January and December 1973 and July 1974 in Moscow; this was subsequently published in Bremen in 1975. The second of these notebooks was dedicated to the literary scholar G. Superfin, who had been arrested on 3 July 1973 and sentenced to five years in a labour camp and two years in exile. This slim volume contains verses composed by Gorbanevskaia between 14 April 1972 and 21 July 1974. Gorbanevskaia's poetry began to be published again in Russia in 1990 when *Oktiabr'* presented a short collection of her works; there was no introduction to the poems.

Apart from the editions of her poetry published in English translation, three short collections of her poems had, in fact, appeared in western journals before her departure from Russia in 1975. *Index on Censorship* published 14 of her poems in English translation; the same periodical published an essay by Daniel Weissbort entitled "The Ordeal of Natalya Gorbanevskaya". Two separate editions of *Russian Literature Triquarterly* featured new English translations of her poems; in 1973 six poems were published, including "In My Native Twentieth Century", one of her most moving poems. In 1974 Gorbanevskaia's verse was included in the section entitled "Women in Russian Literature".

The settings for many of Gorbanevskaia's later poems are simple. She frequently portrays the world of daily life in cities, set against the background of the changing seasons. The language used is often concise and restrained, but extremely effective. The poem "Voskresen'e" [Sunday], for example, begins in the following way: "A day of verse and laundry..." ("Den' stirki i stikhov ..."). Her poems often tend to be allegorical and they frequently contain obvious religious motifs – allusions to the sufferings of Christ, for instance. Her love poems frequently depict the acute pain of separation and loss. There are also many references to other artists, such as Goya, Shakespeare, and Mozart.

Her verse written in exile has appeared in many small volumes, published from 1979 onwards. *Pereletaia snezhnuiu granitsu* [Flying over the Snowy Border] bears witness to the difficulty of "crossing over" to the west, one section of the collection bearing the title "Dolgoe proshchan'e" [The Long Farewell]. The "new world" is often associated with greyness, rain and mist. *Chuzhie kamni* [The Stones of Others] contains a selection of her verse written between 1979 and 1982, and includes her poem "Odna, odna v sovsem pustoi Parizhe ..." [Alone, quite alone in a deserted Paris ...].

Gorbanevskaia's poetic world is a very personal one. References to her previous political activity are rarely present; she tends instead to concentrate on giving an intense expression to her innermost feelings and, by doing so, her vulnerability clearly emerges.

MARGARET TEJERIZO

Maksim Gor'kii 1868–1936

Dramatist and prose writer

Biography

Born Aleksei Maksimovich Peshkov in Nizhnii Novgorod, 28 March 1868. Lived with grandparents as a child. Attended a parish school, Nizhnii Novgorod; Kumavino elementary school, 1877–78. Apprenticed to a shoemaker at the age of 11 and subsequently worked in a variety of odd jobs. Associated with revolutionary politics, from 1888: first arrest, 1889. Walked through much of Russia, 1888–89, 1891–92. First story published in the newspaper *Kavkaz*, 1892. Married: Ekaterina Pavlovna Volzhina in 1896 (separated); one son and one daughter. Literary editor of *Zhizn'*, St Petersburg, from 1899; worked for the publishing house Znanie from 1900; subsequently its leading editor. Exiled to central Russia, for illicit involvement with a secret printing press, 1901. Elected to the Russian Academy, 1902, but election declared invalid by the government: several members of the Academy resigned in protest. Joined the Bolshevik Party, 1905. Travelled to the United States, 1906; lived on the island of Capri, 1906–13; set up revolutionary propaganda school, 1909. Returned to Russia after general amnesty, 1913. Founding editor of *Letopis'* magazine, 1915–17, and the newspaper *Novaia zhizn'*, 1917–18. Established Vsemirnaia literatura publishing house; involved in Petrograd Workers and Soldiers Soviet, and in improving conditions of writers and scholars. Left Russia in 1921; editor of *Dialogue*, Berlin, 1923–25; lived in Sorrento, 1924–32. Visited Soviet Russia from 1928, returning permanently in 1933. Set up the Biblioteka poeta publishing project; associated with the implementation of socialist realism and founding of the Soviet Writers' Union; took leading role at first Congress of Soviet Writers, 1934. Recipient: Order of Lenin, 1932. Gor'kii Literary Institute established in his honour. Died (in suspicous circumstances) near Moscow, 18 June 1936.

Publications

Collected Editions

Through Russia, translated by C.J. Hogarth. London, Everyman, 1921.
Seven Plays, translated by Alexander Bakshy and Paul Nathan. New Haven, Yale University Press, 1945.
Sobranie sochinenii, 30 vols. Moscow, 1949–55.
Plays, translated by Margaret Wettlin *et al.* Moscow, Progress, 1968.
Polnoe sobranie sochinenii, 25 vols. Moscow, 1968–76.
Collected Works [in English translation], 10 vols. Moscow, Progress, 1978–83.

Five Plays, translated by Kitty Hunter Blair and Jeremy Brooks. London, Methuen, 1988.

Plays

Meshchane. St Petersburg, 1902; translated as *The Lower Middle Class*, by Edwin Hopkins, in *Poet Lore* 17/4 (1906); also translated as *The Petit-Bourgeois*, by Margaret Wettlin, in *Five Plays*, Moscow, 1956; and as *The Philistines*, by Dusty Hughes, Oxford, Oxford University Press, 1985.

Na dne (produced 1902). Moscow, 1903; edited by Kurt Klein and Ira Goetz, London, Bristol Classical Press, 1993; translated as "The Lower Depths", by Margaret Wettlin, in *Plays*, 1968; and by Kitty Hunter Blair and Jeremy Brooks, in *Five Plays*, 1988.

Dachniki. St Petersburg, 1905; translated as "Summer Folk", by Kitty Hunter Blair and Jeremy Brooks, in *Five Plays*, 1988.

Deti solntsa. St Petersburg, 1905; translated as "Children of the Sun", by Kitty Hunter Blair and Jeremy Brooks, in *Five Plays*, 1988.

Varvary. Stuttgart, J.H.W. Dietz Nachfolger, 1906; translated as "Barbarians", by Kitty Hunter Blair and Jeremy Brooks, in *Five Plays*, 1988.

Vragi. St Petersburg, 1906; translated as "Enemies", by Margaret Wettlin, in *Plays*, 1968; and by Kitty Hunter Blair and Jeremy Brooks, in *Five Plays*, 1988.

Poslednie [The Last Ones]. St Petersburg, 1908.

Vassa Zheleznova. St Petersburg, 1910; revised edition, 1935; 1968; translated by Tania Alexander and Tim Suter, Oxford, Amber Lane Press, 1988.

Vstrecha [The Meeting]. St Petersburg, 1910.

Chudaki. St Petersburg, 1910; translated as "Queer People", by Alexander Bakshy and Paul Nathan, in *Seven Plays*, 1945.

Zykovy. Berlin, 1914; translated as "The Zykovs", by Alexander Bakshy and Paul Nathan, in *Seven Plays*, 1945.

Starik. Berlin, I.P. Ladyzhnikov, 1921; translated as "The Judge", 1924; "The Old Man", 1956.

Egor Bulychov i drugie. Berlin, Kniga, 1932; translated as "Yegor Bulychov and Others", by Margaret Wettlin, in *Plays*, 1968.

Dostigaev i drugie. Moscow, 1934; translated as "Dostigaev and Others", in *The Last Plays of Maxim Gorki*, adapted by Gibson-Cowan, London, Lawrence and Wishart, 1937.

Somov i drugie [Somov and Others]. Moscow, 1941.

Fiction

"Makar Chudra", *Kavkaz*, (12 September 1892).

"Starukha Izergil'" [Old Woman Izergil'], *Samarskaia gazeta*, (16–27 April 1895).

"Konovalov", *Novoe slovo*, 6 (March 1896).

"Dvadtsat' shest' i odna", *Zhizn'*, 12 (1899); translated as "Twenty-Six Men and a Girl".

Foma Gordeev. 1900; revised edition, 1923; translated by Margaret Wettlin, London, Lawrence and Wishart, 1956; Westport Connecticut, Greenwood Press, 1974.

Troe [Three of Us], in *Rasskazy*, vol. 5, St Petersburg, 1901; translated as "Three of Them"; "Three Men"; "The Three".

"Pesnia o Burevestnike" [Song of the Stormy Petrol], *Zhizn'*, 4 (1901).

Mat'. Berlin, I.P. Ladyzhnikov, 1907; translated as *Comrades*, London, Hodder and Stoughton, 1907; and as *Mother*, by Margaret Wettlin, Moscow, Progress, 1949; also as *The Mother*, by Isidor Schneider, New York, Citadel Press, 1992.

Ispoved'. St Petersburg, 1908; translated as *The Confession*, by William Frederick Harvey, London, Everett, 1910.

Zhizn' nenuzhnogo cheloveka. Berlin, I.P. Ladyzhnikov, 1908; translated as *The Life of a Useless Man*, by Moura Budberg, New York, Doubleday, 1971; Harmondsworth, Penguin, 1972.

Gorodok Okurov [Okurov Town]. St Petersburg, 1910.

Zhizn' Matveia Kozhemiakina. St Petersburg, 1911; translated as *The Life of Matvei Kozhemyakin*, by Margaret Wettlin, Moscow, Foreign Languages Publishing House, 1960.

Detstvo, *Russkoe slovo*, 1913–14; *V liudiakh*, *Letopis'*, 1–12 (1916); *Moi universitety*, *Krasnaia nov'*, 2–4 (1923); translated as *My Childhood. My Apprenticeship. My Universities*, by Ronald Wilks, Harmondsworth, Penguin, 1966–79.

Delo Artamonovykh. Berlin, Kniga, 1925; translated as *Decadence*, by Veronica Dewey, New York, McBride, and London, Cassell, 1927; and as *The Artamonov Business*, by Alec Brown, London, Hamish Hamilton, and New York, Pantheon, 1948; also as *The Artamonovs*.

Zhizn' Klima Samgina (unfinished, written 1925–36); Berlin, Kniga, 1927–31 (vols 1–3); translated as *The Bystander* (4 vols), by B.G. Guerney, New York, Cape and Smith, and London, Jonathan Cape, 1930; as *The Magnet*, by Alexander Bakshy, New York, Cape and Smith, and London, Jonathan Cape, 1931; as *Other Fires*, by Alexander Bakshy, New York and London, Appleton, 1933; and as *The Spectre*, by Alexander Bakshy, New York and London, Appleton-Century, 1938.

Memoirs, Diaries, and Biography

Vospominaniia o Tolstom. Petrograd, 1919; translated in *Reminiscences of Tolstoy, Chekhov and Andreyev*, by Katherine Mansfield, S.S. Koteliansky, Virginia Woolf, and Leonard Woolf, London, Hogarth Press, 1934.

Zametki iz dnevnika. Berlin, Kniga, 1924; translated as *Fragments from My Diary*, by Moura Budberg, Harmondsworth, Penguin, 1940; revised edition, London, Allen Lane, 1972; Harmondsworth, Penguin, 1975.

Literaturnye portrety. 2nd edition, Moscow, 1967; translated as *Literary Portraits*, by Ivy Litvinov, Moscow, Foreign Languages Publishing House, 1982.

Essays and Historical Writing

Nesvoevremennye mysli, *Novaia zhizn'*, May 1917–July 1918; edited by Herman Ermolaev, Paris, Editions de la Seine, 1971; translated as *Untimely Thoughts*, by Herman Ermolaev, New York, Eriksson, 1968; reprinted New Haven, Yale University Press, 1995.

The City of the Yellow Devil: Pamphlets, Articles and Letters about America [no translator named], Moscow, Progress, 1972.

Letters

"Letters of Maxim Gor'kij to V.F. Xodasevič, 1922–1925", edited and translated by Hugh McLean, *Harvard Slavonic Studies*, 1 (1953).

Letters of Gorky and Andreev 1899–1912, edited by Peter Yershov, London, Routledge and Kegan Paul, 1958.
Perepiska M. Gor'kogo [Correspondence of M. Gor'kii], 2 vols. Moscow, 1986.
Correspondance: Romain Rolland, Maxime Gorki, edited by Jean Pirus. Paris, Michel, 1991.
Selected Letters, edited and translated by Andrew Barratt and Barry P. Scherr. Oxford, Clarendon Press, 1997.

Editor
Belomor. An Account of the Construction of the New Canal Between the White Sea and the Baltic Sea. New York, Smith and Haas, 1935; reprinted Westport, Connecticut, Hyperion Press, 1977.

Critical Studies
Maxim Gorky and His Russia, by Alexander Kaun, London, Jonathan Cape, 1932.
The Young Maxim Gorky 1868–1902, by Filia Holtzman, New York, Columbia University Press, 1948.
Gorki par lui-même, by Nina Gourfinkel, Paris, Editions du Seuil, 1954; as *Gorky*, translated by Ann Feshbach, New York, Grove Press, 1960; reprinted Westport, Connecticut, Greenwood Press, 1975.
Letopis' zhizni i tvorchestva A.M. Gor'kogo, 3 vols, Moscow, 1958–59.
Maxim Gorky: Romantic Realist and Conservative Revolutionary, by Richard Hare, London, Oxford University Press, 1962.
Stormy Petrel: The Life and Work of Maxim Gorky, by Dan Levin, New York, Appleton-Century, 1965; London, Frederick Muller, 1967.
Gorky: His Literary Development and Influence on Soviet Intellectual Life, by Irwin Weil, New York, Random House, 1966.
Maxim Gorky, The Writer: An Interpretation, by F.M. Borras, Oxford Clarendon Press, 1967.
The Bridge and the Abyss: The Troubled Friendship of Maxim Gorky and V.I. Lenin, by Bertram D. Wolfe, New York, Hoover Institution, and London, Pall Mall Press, 1967.
Maksim Gorki, by Gerhard E. Habermann, translated by Ernestine Schlant, New York, Ungar, 1971.
"Zhizn' Klima Samgina" M. Gor'kogo, by I. Vainberg, Moscow, 1971.
Slovar' avtobiograficheskoi trilogii M. Gor'kogo, by B.A. Larin, 3 vols, Leningrad, 1974–77.
Three Russians Consider America: America in the Works of Maksim Gor'kij, Aleksandr Blok, and Vladimir Mayakovskij, by Charles Rougle, Stockholm, Almqvist & Wiksell, 1976.
M. Gor'kii - dramaturg, by B.A. Bialik, 2nd edition, Moscow, 1977.
Maksim Gor'kii v vospominaniiakh sovremennikov, 2 vols, Moscow, 1981.
The Russian Revolutionary Novel: Turgenev to Pasternak, by Richard Freeborn, Cambridge and New York, Cambridge University Press, 1982.
Maxim Gorky and the Literary Quests of the Twentieth Century, by Alexander Ovcharenko, translated by Joy Jennings, Moscow, Raduga, 1985.
Fifty Years On: Gorky and His Time, edited by Nicholas Luker, Nottingham, Astra Press, 1987.
Gor'kii i russkaia zhurnalistika nachala XX veka, Literaturnoe nasledstvo, 95, Moscow, 1988.
Maxim Gorky, by Barry P. Scherr, Boston, Twayne, 1988.
Gorky, by Henri Troyat, translated by Lowell Bair, New York, Crown, 1989; London, Allison and Busby, 1991.
Gor'kii i ego epokha: issledovaniia i materialy, vypusk 1–3, Moscow, 1989–94.
The Battle for Childhood: Creation of a Russian Myth, by Andrew Baruch Wachtel, Stanford, Stanford University Press, 1990.
The Early Fiction of Maksim Gorky: Six Essays in Interpretation, by Andrew Barratt, Nottingham, Astra Press, 1993.
File on Gorky, edited by Cynthia Marsh, London, Methuen, 1993.
M. Gor'kii i dialog s istoriei, by L. Spiridonova, Moscow, 1994.
The KGB's Literary Archive, by Vitaly Shentalinsky, translated by John Crowfoot, London, Harvill Press, 1995.

Bibliographies
Literatura o M. Gor'kom: bibliografiia, 1955–1960, 1961–65, 2 vols, Moscow, 1965–70.
Literatura o M. Gor'kom: bibliograficheskii ukazatel', 1966–70, 2 vols, Leningrad, 1985; *1971–75*, Leningrad, 1987.
Maxim Gorky in English: A Bibliography, 1868–1986, by Garth M. Terry, Nottingham, Astra Press, 1986.
Maxim Gorky: A Reference Guide, by Edith Clowes, Boston, G.K. Hall, 1987.

Born Aleksei Maksimovich Peshkov in 1868 in Nizhnii Novgorod (renamed Gor'kii during the Soviet period), he adopted Maksim Gor'kii (i.e. "Maksim the Bitter") as his pen-name largely out of respect for his father, a man reputedly of skill and sensibility, who died when Aleksei was only four years old. The father's death meant that the boy was brought up in the harsh, petit-bourgeois world of his grandfather Kashirin who owned a small dye works in Nizhnii, which eventually failed and reduced the family to poverty. The world of his boyhood is memorably recreated in the first part of his autobiographical trilogy, *Detstvo* (*My Childhood*), 1913–14. The vicious squabbling over their patrimony between the boy's uncles, the harsh beatings meted out by his grandfather and the gradual degeneration of his own mother were elements in a brutalizing environment that might have destroyed the boy's spirit had it not been for the countervailing influence of his grandmother. Her unstinting charity and compassion for all the "unfortunates" surrounding her, as well as her fondness for folk-tales and literature generally, were to provide Gor'kii with a lifelong conviction as a writer that the real and ideal should coexist, that the heroic individual might rise above the most squalid circumstances.

In a formal sense Gor'kii received little education. He was mostly self-taught through a love of books. When, at about 11 years of age, he was turned out of the Kashirin household (as he describes it in *V liudiakh* (*My Apprenticeship*) 1916), his young life became an untidy saga of incomplete apprenticeships, lengthy trips on the Volga and journeyings over southern Russia and the

Ukraine (all described in the bitterly entitled *Moi universitety* [*My Universities*] 1923). "I came into the world in order to disagree" became the motto of his life and work.

Success followed quickly after the publication of his first short story "Makar Chudra" in Tbilisi in 1892. Combining brilliant nature description and internal narrative, it treated the issue of human dignity and freedom in a folkloric, ultra-Romantic manner. The same could be said of "Starukha Izergil'" [Old Woman Izergil'], 1895, containing the story of Danko who, in romantic fashion, tears out his fiery heart to light the way for his tribe. More effective as an attack on prevailing bourgeois standards was the harsh evocation of the dockside world in "Chelkash" (1895). A succession of short allegorical pieces and short stories offered studies emphasizing the protest, often ineffectual, often stupidly brave, of the "barefoot" ones, the migrant workers and assorted maverick types against the capitalist ethos in Russian society. Of these particularly striking are "Pesnia o sokole" ("The Song of the Falcon"), 1895, "Konovalov", 1896, "Suprugi Orlovy" ("The Orlov Couple"), 1897, and "Dvadtsat' shest' i odna" ("Twenty-Six Men and a Girl"), 1899.

By the turn of the century Gor'kii was examining the predicament of dissident types in the world of commerce (*Foma Gordeev*, 1900; *Troe* [Three of Us], 1901) in colourful, powerful, if rather shapeless novels. His first play *Meshchane* (*The Petit-Bourgeois*) 1902, explores the issue of rebellion against society in a bourgeois milieu and for the first time introduced a militantly proletarian hero. But his second play, *Na dne* (*The Lower Depths*) 1903, enjoyed far greater success. The message of the comforting lie preached to the doss-house dwellers by the quasi-religious figure of Luka was contradicted, if not effaced, by the vision of man as proud and free evoked in the play's final act. Sermonizing rhetoric became a feature of all Gor'kii's overtly political works.

Of these the most famous is his novel *Mat'* (*Mother*), 1907. Written for the greater part during a visit to America to raise funds for the Bolshevik cause, it depicted in the heroine, a mother who adopted the cause of socialism in a religious spirit after her son's arrest as a political activist. Approved by Lenin, the novel acquired unjustifiable fame during the Soviet period for its apparent championing of the proletarian cause. In fact, Gor'kii was less interested in this cause (although it dominated his play *Vragi* [*Enemies*]), than in exploring the lives of provincials, their essential futility despite their occasional protests, in a post-Chekhovian spirit. His plays *Dachniki* (*Summer Folk*) 1905, and *Deti solntsa* (*Children of the Sun*) 1905, and his prose works *Gorodok Okurov* [Okurov Town] 1910, and *Zhizn' Matveia Kozhemiakina* (*The Life of Matvei Kozhemiakin*) 1911, were indications of a readiness to detach himself, to a certain degree, from the pressing topics of the day, just as he was forced to detach himself physically from Russia by the tsarist authorities and lived mostly on Capri. His most characteristic work of this period was the short, first-person novel *Ispoved'* (*The Confession*) 1908, which demonstrated his interest in "God-building" as a substitute for socialism among the masses of the people.

Permitted to return to Russia in 1913, he was appalled at the excesses that occurred during the October Revolution and the Civil War and quarrelled bitterly with Lenin over his policies. Though these disagreements were suppressed during the Soviet period, his dislike of the draconian measures taken by the new regime, as well as his overt support for many cultural figures who fell victim to it, undoubtedly contributed as much to his decision to return to Capri as did the official explanation of ill health.

On Capri in the 1920s he wrote his best novel, *Delo Artamonovykh* (*The Artamonov Business*) 1925, dealing with three generations of a pre-revolutionary merchant family. He also embarked on an enormous epic work, *Zhizn' Klima Samgina* [The Life of Klim Samgin], unfinished at his death. These works, like his last plays *Egor Bulychov i drugie* (*Yegor Bulychov and Others*) 1932, and *Dostigaev i drugie* (*Dostigaev and Others*) 1934, clearly showed that he found it impossible to devote his creative gifts to Soviet reality even though, in 1928, he returned to Soviet Russia and became, towards the end of his life, an official spokesman for the government and an advocate of socialist realism.

His reputation suffered accordingly. Nowadays his achievement as the creator of many vivid portraits, as a brilliant memoirist and autobiographer and successor to Chekhov as a dramatist is undeniable. The circumstances surrounding his death in 1936 remain obscure. It may have been due to ill health or because he had allegedly incurred Stalin's mistrust and was poisoned on his orders.

RICHARD FREEBORN

Twenty-Six Men and a Girl

Dvadtsat' shest' i odna

Story, 1899

As the culmination of Gor'kii's work in the 1890s and his best and most representative short story, "Twenty-Six Men and a Girl" has a classical simplicity of theme and form. It has the subtitle "A Poem" and employs a poetic prose manner that is not significantly removed from realistic prose, but has a lilt reminiscent of oral literature to it. It is also endowed with a richly evocative, often metaphorical, vocabulary of the kind Gor'kii frequently used in his overtly autobiographical work; and this short story is autobiographical in the sense that it is based on his experiences in Kazan and evokes anew the world he portrayed in the most important of his stories devoted to the rootless "barefoot ones", his "Konovalov" (1896).

The story is simple. Twenty-Six jobbing bakers employed in the harsh, ill-lit conditions of a semi-basement workshop where they knead dough all day discover only one bright spot in their lives: an adolescent girl Tania, an embroidery seamstress who works on the floor above them in the same building. She makes regular visits to their dismal bakery world and enlivens their day with her beauty and vitality. They idolize her as their ideal. A handsome ex-soldier, one of the master bakers, appears on the scene and boasts of his success with women. A bet is made that he will not succeed in seducing Tania. The girl, in fact, succumbs and the 26 men, deprived of their ideal, sink back into their squalid working lives while she walks away from them "straight-backed, beautiful and proud".

A certain fairly obvious symbolism highlights the moral issues in what is an otherwise "realistic" descriptive manner. The first paragraph illustrates the point well:

> There were twenty-six of us – twenty-six living machines locked in a damp basement where, from dawn to dusk, we

> kneaded dough for making into biscuits and pretzels. The windows of our basement looked out onto a ditch dug in front of them and lined with brick that was green from damp; the windows were covered outside in fine wire netting and sunlight could not reach us through the flour-covered panes. Our boss had put the wire netting there so we could not give hand-outs of his bread to beggars or those comrades of ours who were without work and starving. Our boss used to call us scoundrels and fed us on rotten offal rather than any of his own bread … .

The narrator and his narration presuppose a solidarity with the "twenty-six" who are reified into "living machines" and scarcely individuated at all at any stage in the narrative. Exploited as machines in this primitive form of capitalism, the workers are represented as creatures forever immured within a prison presided over not only by a tyrannical, anonymous employer, but also by the giant oven that breathes fire and glowers at them with the two deep eyes of its air-vents – "pitiless and passionless eyes of a monster which always stared with the same dark stare, as if, tired of seeing such slaves and expecting nothing human from them, despised them with the cold loathing of its own wisdom". To alleviate the oppressive boredom of their workaday routines and allay the sense of being crushed in such a basement world by the whole weight of the three-storey building above them, they sing; and the dense, broad wave of sounds they create could seem like a wide, sunlit road along which they might escape.

Such escapism is only momentary. What brings an enriching sunlight into the lives of the 26 is the 16-year-old Tania. The daily visits by this girl with the small rosy face, laughing blue eyes and clear soft voice are the occasion of such complimentary talk it borders on idolatry. Indeed, they feed their idol with hot, newly-baked pretzels as if engaged in a form of religious worship. The narrator sums up their worshipful attitude by saying:

> We loved her – nothing more need be said. A man always wants to have someone to love although he sometimes oppresses that person with his love, sometimes pollutes and can even poison the other's life with his love because, in loving as he does, he has no respect for his beloved. We had to love Tania because we had no one else to love.

Their love, in short, has an idolatrous, sick, obsessive character. The dandified, self-confident lady-killer in the shape of the ex-soldier offers a clear contrast to them and yet, despite his macho style and evident attractiveness to women, he is repesented as similarly sick and limited in his humanity by his very power as a seducer. He is challenged to seduce Tania and the 26 know that they are engaged in a game with the devil in which Tania is their stake. At the appointed time the "prisoners", as Tania herself calls them, assemble by a fence and peer through its cracks to watch her enter a cellar doorway, followed shortly afterwards by the ex-soldier. When she emerges and it is clear she has succumbed, she is mocked and reviled by those who had previously idolized her. Turning on them, she curses them and walks proudly away, never again to visit their basement world.

The morality of the narrative is harsh. The men lose their ideal but, as is typical of Gor'kii, it is the female figure who outshines, morally speaking, the squalid, surrounding, predominantly male world. Although Tania is too thinly drawn to have more than a token reality, she illustrates Gor'kii's generally idealistic belief in humanity's moral resilience. The admiration of Chekhov and Tolstoi for this story gives it a special place in Gor'kii's work and highlights the fact that, so long as he spared the reader too much political axe-grinding, he could produce works of enduring art.

RICHARD FREEBORN

The Lower Depths

Na dne

Play, 1902

The Lower Depths, Gor'kii's second play, was written in 1902 and first performed at the Moscow Arts Theatre the same year. Despite the huge popularity Gor'kii was to enjoy subsequently, no other play, possibly no other work from his vast output, has exceeded its international reputation. It was produced in Berlin and London in 1903, and other European cities in the following years. It was seen in America in the early 1920s and was featured by the Moscow Arts Theatre company in their major tour to New York in 1923. The Royal Shakespeare Company in London gave it a major revival in 1972. It has been filmed, adapted and used as a source of inspiration by modern dramatists such as O'Neill and Ikole. In Russia it was awarded the Griboedov prize in 1904, though still banned outside the capital cities. A staple item in the Moscow Arts Theatre repertoire, it was subject to countless revivals all over the Soviet Union. In the new Russia Gor'kii is understandably neglected but *The Lower Depths* should resurface. Politics, religion and social problems mark modern Russia as much as they do Gor'kii's play.

The badinage and hopeless routine of the unemployed, ex-criminals and misfits in an urban doss-house are interrupted by the arrival of Luka, a semi-religious vagrant without passport or money. He offers compassion to those among them who suffer, almost unnoticed, in the squalor: a woman dying of consumption, an alcoholic actor, a young thief being lured to commit murder and a prostitute given to dreaming of romantic love. Luka's comfort brings temporary relief but fosters false hopes: the woman dies unsure of a promised heaven, the actor hangs himself unable to find the promised cure, the thief does not listen and the prostitute has to accept the reality of her fate. Condemned by some for not speaking the truth, Luka departs as quickly as he arrived when a domestic melodrama taking place in the family of the doss-house owner brings in the police. The owner is killed in a brawl by the young thief, urged on by the owner's wife, eager to be rid of her husband and jealous of the thief's affection for her sister. The murderer finds himself in prison and the sister disappears. This sordid tale drives the action forward but leaves most of the dossers untouched in their careless continuum. Their function is to comment on the actions of Luka. Satin, the murderer and ex-convict, engages with Luka's ideas and elaborates on them. He is sympathetic to the need to succour the suffering, albeit with the odd lie, but argues that far greater lies are the cause of the dossers' present misfortune. The exploitation by the rich of the poor leads to inequality, to the impossibility of true community and to the lack of appreciation of individual human worth.

Russia had a commercial theatre for only 20 years. The Imperial monopoly had been annulled in 1882 but theatre was unrepresentative, in Gor'kii's view, of a fast-changing Russia. The choice of setting for this play was both politically and artistically motivated. The "lower depths" are exposed as the refuge not of shirkers and idlers but of the exploited and unfortunate. Politically, Gor'kii wished to confront and challenge bourgeois complacency. He asserted the right of all to claim membership of the human race. Such a setting and such characters, he also knew, would challenge creative attitudes to theatre and expose its middle-class bias. In this way, the play and its production by the Moscow Arts Theatre brought politics openly to the theatrical medium, dynamite to a culture still controlled by a severe censorship. The choice of this milieu reflected for some critics Gor'kii's allegiance to the Left and particularly to Marxism. Even here, in this setting, regarded as outside or beneath society, the class struggle is evident. The owner's exploitation of the dossers is clear, but even among the down-and-outs, a pimp's exploitation of his prostitute exemplified the need for the class struggle to reach its resolution.

Philosophically, the play is enigmatic in posing enticing alternatives. The audience is asked to choose between the attractions of the compassionate, succouring untruth and hard-hitting, destructive truth. It is difficult not to sympathize with both extremes: with Luka, the gentle but lying comfort-giver, and with Satin, the inveterate dosser whose bar-room rhetoric calls for the truth, however unpalatable, to be exposed.

Both Vladimir Nemirovich-Danchenko and Konstantin Stanislavskii, literary and artistic directors of the Moscow Arts Theatre, felt the company was politically challenged by Gor'kii's play. Nevertheless, the production marked a high point in the search for authenticity and reality in playing style and stage design. Research was conducted in the notorious night shelters of Moscow. Gor'kii wrote copious notes on the vagrants, criminals, and unfortunates encountered during his travels of the previous decade. The relegation of the action to the domestic melodrama in the background, the use of the dossers' daily routine to structure the play, the colloquial and coarse language breaking stage convention, all reflected the aspirations to naturalism in the theatre, and, laced with the ever present jocularity of the dossers, made a potent challenge to the artistic expectations of the middle-class audience.

Often neglected in the voluminous criticism that accompanied the deification of Gor'kii and his writing in the Soviet period are the beauty of the metaphor Gor'kii created and his appropriation of Christian ideas. Leonid Andreev in 1902 and Innokentii Annenskii in 1906 were among the first to remark on Gor'kii's creative skills. They wrote of the beauty of Gor'kii's idea. The squalid atmosphere of the setting is shot through with the strength, the laughter and honesty of the human spirit: it shines through the metaphorical and actual absence of light in the lower depths. As for religion, Gor'kii perceived that it is the comforter not only to the poor in spirit but sometimes the only comforter to the materially deprived. Figures such as Luka should be admired for dealing with the suffering of the down-and-outs. It was a gospel of self-reliance, of seeing God in the everyday, of survival in the worst conditions, and implied the elevation of the individual to almost god-like status. This quasi-religious view was emphasized in Max Rheinhardt's 1903 production at the Kleines Theater in Berlin. Gor'kii made a number of statements at different points in his career about the play. He attempted to focus on its political rather than its spiritual impact as religious views became progressively inappropriate to a writer of his political stature.

The Lower Depths, despite, or in some senses because of, this uneasy mix of politics and religion, is a remarkable play for a relatively inexperienced dramatist. It entertained but confronted, challenged and divided the auditorium. The Moscow Arts Theatre and arguably Russian theatre were never to be the same again.

CYNTHIA MARSH

Enemies

Vragi

Play, 1906

Enemies focuses on industrial unrest. The Bardin Family in partnership with the Skrobotovs owns and runs a textile factory. The reinstatement of an unpopular foreman by Skrobotov has led to a confrontation and a threatened strike. Skrobotov is shot and killed. The factory is closed and the police are brought in. Bardin family loyalty is put to the test and begins to give way as various members find themselves in conflict. The workers try to protect the assassin under the leadership of a professional agitator. He is recognized by the police, and he and the workers' ringleaders are arrested.

Completed in 1906, *Enemies* has been considered Gor'kii's most overtly Marxist play (for example, by Plekhanov [1907] and Lunacharskii [1931]). The industrial disturbances and expectation of revolution of 1905 provided the contemporary historical context; the plot provided the class struggle. The play was conceived by Gor'kii when imprisoned in the Peter and Paul Fortress in 1905 and completed during his period in exile in America in 1906. Incarceration and exile may be responsible for the bitterness of the play's conflict and the sharpness of its focus. It has not often been remembered that by far the greater part of Gor'kii's work was created in exile or emigration. The Soviet literary critic chose not to consider the negative aspects of Gor'kii's isolation from the revolutionary movement and from Russia but to regard his early exile as a period of preparation for the great social change to come in 1917 and after (when Gor'kii was still living mostly in Italy). The habit of neglecting some of the works written in the early years in Italy because they are ideologically difficult (for example, *Poslednie* [The Last Ones] (1908), *Zhizn' nenuzhnogo cheloveka* (*The Life of a Useless Man*) 1908, *Ispoved'* (*The Confession*) 1908, has led to the removal of *Enemies* from its context within the running order of Gor'kii's creative works and of his plays in particular. Comparisons are often drawn with the novel *Mat'* (*Mother*), written concurrently, but there are also substantial differences. The works are linked by their heroic description of the hitherto unacceptable working class, and the role that might be played among the workers by a politically conscious (read Marxist) intelligentsia. But the individual focal points are completely different. *Enemies* concentrates on a fragmenting bourgeoisie for its character interest and on class struggle for its dramatic impact, whereas *Mother* relies on the growth to political awareness of a simple peasant woman for its focus.

What is important are the striking differences from, and similarities to, the plays that precede and follow *Enemies* at close intervals, *Varvary* (*Barbarians*) in 1906 and *Poslednie* in 1908. The former is set in rural Russia in a semi-Chekhovian backwater that is disrupted by the arrival of the railway and the engineers to construct it. Provincial merchantdom provides the moral tapestry and timeless dimension that are so rudely ripped apart. Police corruption, patriarchal hypocrisy, and family dissension inform the middle-class melodrama of *Poslednie*. Marxist characteristics of class conflict and heroic proletarians are markedly absent. Gor'kii's brush with an overtly publicistic theatre was short-lived.

In *Enemies* the characters are squarely divided into two class-driven camps: the workers, firm in their solidarity, and the factory owners and their dependents, interesting in their disintegration, and unequal to the class struggle that drives the play forward. Identification of class solidarity as the winning streak ensures lack of individualism among the workers. Individual acts of heroism are cited but are important only as contributions to the positive depiction of the proletariat. On the other hand, every weakness, every aspiration among the middle-class owners is dramatized and explored, in this respect liking *Enemies* to its neighbouring plays in Gor'kii's *oeuvre*. Thus Tat'iana, a successful actress but a flawed wife, can sing a hymn to the efficacy of art in moving people's hearts and minds, but cannot save her husband from alcoholism and suicide; and Nadia, the Bardins' young daughter, in a naively heroic gesture abandons her family for the workers' cause. The play is tightly constructed, tension builds palpably towards an unavoidable conflict of interests, and a proletarian moral victory. Sensitivity to the accompanying middle-class tragedy, however, prevents the work from being only Marxist propaganda.

The play has been vulnerable to the vicissitudes of 20th-century history. The elements that ensured disqualification by the censorship in 1907, sympathetic workers, the middle class in disarray, became the hallmarks of the work's acceptance in 1930s Russia. In the excited search for new forms in the 1920s Gor'kii's theatre works seemed old-fashioned. However, by 1933 under the new impositions on all culture *Enemies* offered a perfect model of orthodox conflict. True the workers' role was strengthened by Gor'kii and focus withdrawn from Nadia's histrionic defence of them with which the play had formerly ended. The play became a pillar of achievement for the Moscow Arts Theatre and was taken to Paris in 1937, and Gor'kii rather than Chekhov was claimed as the company's mentor.

Enemies had its premiere at Reinhardt's Kleines Theatre in Berlin in 1907 where it added to Gor'kii's international acclaim as an oppositionist writer. It only surfaced in the UK two generations later against a background of industrial unrest and curiosity about Russian political theatre. It was staged by the Royal Shakespeare Company in 1971. Once more, the ending was vulnerable: state oppression was intensified by the suggestion that the workers were to be executed: bags were placed over their heads and the play closed to a pistol shot.

Gor'kii is now (in the 1990s) unfashionable. His former political correctness and elevation to literary sainthood almost guarantee oblivion in the new Russia. And that is a great pity. Gor'kii's historical importance is enormous to Russian theatrical development: not only did he rouse theatre from its social narrowness but by so doing he also strengthened the notion of theatre as dialogue. Through his plays he conducted a vociferous debate with his audiences (rarely were performances of his plays quiet affairs), but even more, he provided a dialogic counterpart to Chekhov. Not only letters and meetings bear witness to their interaction: the intertextuality of their plays is the richest source of all. *Enemies*, redolent of Chekhov in its setting, which moves from garden to house, gives strident voice to the family and class tensions at which Chekhov chose only to hint. A sense of Gor'kii's energy, conviction and sheer dramatic skill needs to be rescued not only from threatening oblivion, but also from decades of unquestioning adulation.

CYNTHIA MARSH

Mother

Mat'

Novel, 1907

Mother begins with the picture of an ugly, monstrous factory from which exhausted lifeless workmen can be seen emerging. One of these is the husband of Pelageia Nilovna, the mother of the title. He is a brutish drunkard; their son Pavel is not much better. Abused by her husband and ignored by her son, the mother's only consolation is her religious faith. After she is widowed, both mother and son begin slowly to change. When Pelageia sees a picture of Christ on the road to Emmaus in Pavel's room, she assumes that he now shares her faith. She then notices him bringing forbidden books into the house. When he explains to her that he is engaged in forbidden revolutionary activity, she is terrified. Gradually however, she comes to accept his commitment, to admire the friends he brings to the house, and eventually to become involved herself. She has found a new family to look after, a cause to serve, without abandoning her faith in God. She becomes aware of the abuses perpetrated by those in positions of power. Shocked by the police and their disregard for person or property when they come to arrest her son, she is even more incensed by the judiciary, decrepit old judges who at Pavel's trial resemble hyenas lusting after Pavel's blood. After his imprisonment, the mother's protective instinct influences her decision to distribute leaflets so that the authorities will not guess Pavel's original involvement.

Of the other revolutionaries the mother becomes particularly fond of the Ukrainian, Andrei, who once killed a police informer, feels able to justify his action politically, but suffers morally. She is in awe of the middle-class intellectual Nikolai Ivanovich, who invites her to live with him, teaches her to read, and impresses her with his selfless devotion to improving the lot of the peasants and workers. She feels close to, if a little frightened of, the God-builder figure, the peasant Rybin. He believes that the people must create a type of socialist God, one with a merciful image who will both encourage the people to fight, rather than accept, evil, and strive for justice. She becomes even more convinced of the need for action, not resignation, after Egor dies from illness contracted in exile. At his funeral she senses a symbolic burial of God. While continuing to believe in Christ's words, her concerns about the traditional church deepen. The final straw comes after a dream in which she sees a priest colluding with the police in arresting the revolutionaries.

It is on May day that her son is arrested carrying a forbidden banner and is then sent for trial. In court Pavel uses the occasion to evangelize on behalf of the revolutionary party, to give a speech on the iniquity of the tsarist system that has caused so much wretchedness for the peasants and workers. The novel ends with Pavel's imprisonment, the mother's active involvement in the cause while her son is away, and her eventual betrayal by a police spy.

After publication in 1907 *Mother* was translated into the major languages and became immensely popular. Like Chernyshevskii's *Chto delat'?* (*What is to Be Done?*), it became a bible for young revolutionaries. Lenin regarded it as both timely and useful. By contrast Gor'kii said it had been written "in a state of excitable irritation".

His self-judgement is largely accurate, since only the portrait of the mother, Pelageia, was a success. Gor'kii based her character on Anna Zalomova, who had travelled the country distributing revolutionary pamphlets after her son had been arrested during the 1902 May Day demonstration in Sormovo. Gor'kii was able to show the way in which a simple woman was converted from religious to revolutionary faith as a result of maternal feeling. In joining the revolutionary cause, Pelageia continued her former life of sacrifice and self-denial, but in a way intended to effect God's kingdom on earth. For the first time in her life she felt needed. She could give and receive affection within a group of revolutionaries she regarded as her children, and who replaced in her mind the Christian martyrs she had been brought up to admire. Her support of their activity gave her life a meaning it had previously lacked. Her conversion is psychologically acceptable because it is based on love and devotion to those around her; it is also the result of her childlike joy at anything new. Emotional involvement with this group gradually brings her to a better understanding both of herself and others. She realizes, for example, how alienated she has become from her insensitive son. She recognizes that the inner strength that had helped her cope in the past, has helped bring out the rebel in her.

Pavel's characterization is, by contrast, a failure. He changes from a thug to a revolutionary, committed to the cause, single-minded, virtuous, intended as a role model for the young of the day, apparently a perfect hero of socialist realism. We do not empathize with him because he lacks credibility. He is cold, overbearingly prissy and surrounded by an aura of infallibility, a man who does everything "with resolution", around whom everything shines "brightly". Gor'kii presents him as white and wooden. At one point, for example, contrasting Pavel with the figure of his father, "a dark cloud", he refers to him as "a beautiful white birch tree".

Such blatant contrast is typical of the novel. The police and judges have faces described alternately as yellow, grey or the colour of hairy, over-ripe plums, their behaviour likened to that of aggressive animals ready to swallow their prey. Their victim, Pavel, on the other hand, is surrounded by a halo, bathed in white and gold. Evil, greed, and self-indulgence do battle with good and virtuous selflessness. Realism has given way to "the heroic". Bolshevik heroes are intended to stimulate in the reader a vision of life as it should be. Didacticism prevails. No conflict is dramatized. The workers and peasants who should have responded to the revolutionaries' zeal, fail to do so. The moral of this openly partisan novel, that the future lies with the revolutionaries' cause, has to be taken on trust.

MARILYN MINTO

My Childhood; My Apprenticeship; My Universities

Detstvo; V liudiakh; Moi universitety

Autobiography, 1913–23

The best-known product of Gor'kii's artistic maturity, the autobiographical trilogy is generally acknowledged to be a classic of the genre. Its constituent volumes – *My Childhood*, *My Apprenticeship* and *My Universities* – were published, respectively, in 1913–14, 1916 and 1923. A fourth volume, provisionally entitled *Sredi intelligentsii* [Among the Intelligentsia] was planned, but never completed. The sketches "Storozh" ("The Watchman"), "Vremia Korolenko" ("The Time of Korolenko"), "V.G. Korolenko", "O vrede filosofii" ("On the Harmfulness of Philosophy") and "O pervoi liubvi" ("On First Love") belong to this unfinished project.

Gor'kii's trilogy covers the years 1871–88 and it represents the most valuable single source of information about the writer's early life; it also provides a fascinating documentary record of late-19th-century Russian provincial life. A horrifying catalogue of the violence, ignorance and vice that prevailed in this milieu, it belongs to a contemporary tradition of writing that comprises such celebrated fictional works as Sologub's *Melkii bes* (*The Petty Demon*), Kuprin's *Poedinok* (*The Duel*), Belyi's *Serebrianyi golub'* (*The Silver Dove*) and Zamiatin's "Uezdnoe" ("A Provincial Tale").

Although the trilogy is a sequential chronological narrative, each of its volumes has its own distinctive focus. *My Childhood* tells the story of the young Aleksei Peshkov's life in the home of his maternal grandparents, the Kashirins, to whose care he was entrusted following the early death of his father. *My Apprenticeship* deals with the boy's adventures on being sent out into the world by his grandfather at the age of 11, while *My Universities* covers the years of his youth, concentrating in particular on his experiences as a participant in various underground political groups seeking to spread revolutionary ideas among the Russian peasantry.

Loosely constructed on the principle of the Bildungsroman, the trilogy contains many memorable (and often harrowing) scenes. Equally memorable are many of the characters the young hero encounters on his journey through life, such as his grandfather and grandmother (*My Childhood*), the cook Smuryi and "Queen Margot" (*My Apprenticeship*), Nikolai Evreinov and the populist agitator Romas' (*My Universities*).

The trilogy attracted wide critical attention on its first publication. The appearance of *My Childhood* was immediately recognized as a major literary event, even by those critics of the Symbolist camp who had so loudly proclaimed the "death" of Gor'kii as a literary artist in the years following the Revolution of 1905. While socialist critics were quick to seize on its significance as a piece of social criticism, most of the discussion focussed on the opposition within *My Childhood* between the figures of the child's grandmother and grandfather and their "two gods", the grandmother's god of mercy and the grandfather's god of punishment. The appearance in 1915 of Gor'kii's notorious article "Dve dushi russkogo naroda" ("The Two Souls of the Russian People"), in which he distinguished between the spirit of "Asiatic" obscurantism and the "European" pursuit of enlightenment, supplied another important dimension to the contemporary debate. After the Revolution, the publication of *My Universities* received equally wide acclaim. Again, the critics were unanimous in their praise for its technical achievement, especially Viktor Shklovskii, who championed Gor'kii's method of "plotless" narration as a model for the new Soviet literature. Nevertheless, the third volume also attracted some significant criticism, most notably from A.K. Voronskii, the editor of *Krasnaia nov'*, who complained of Gor'kii's unremittingly negative portrayal of life among the Russian peasants.

Following Gor'kii's canonization as the "father of Soviet literature", the autobiographical trilogy became the subject of immense critical attention. Emphasizing its importance as an indictment of the evils of life under the old regime, the new generation of critics also drew attention to the story of the boy-hero as an encouraging example of the emergence of the proletarian revolutionary from the "lower depths" of Russian society. Typical in this respect is the work of V.A. Desnitskii, who describes the trilogy as a "novel of education" that culminates in the young Peshkov's achievement of "culture" and "liberating knowledge".

In western criticism, by contrast, Gor'kii's autobiography has suffered from relative neglect, although essays by Scherr (1979), Wachtel (1990), and Barratt (1993) speak for a modest revival of interest. Wachtel's contribution is especially noteworthy, as his is a historical discussion that deals with the trilogy as part of a Russian tradition beginning with Aksakov and Tolstoi and concluding with Belyi and Bunin.

When Gor'kii's trilogy is viewed as a whole, it is the discontinuity between the three volumes that is perhaps the most striking feature of the project. This may be best described in terms of a progressive falling away from the heroic paradigm so magnificently invoked in *My Childhood*. As Erik Erikson has shown, the story of the boy-hero's rise to independence against the background of the decline – both financial and spiritual – of the Kashirin household represents one of the finest examples of autobiography as inspiring parable. But with the boy's release into the larger world at the beginning of *My Apprenticeship* this encouraging myth is both complicated and undermined. Like most of Gor'kii's novels, the trilogy begins to lose shape in its middle part, devolving at times into a series of apparently disconnected episodes which contribute in no obvious way to the boy's development as a "revolutionary hero". All too often, the young protagonist emerges in the latter volumes as a character who is simply overburdened by the dreadful impressions of a life that he finds profoundly alien and which lies beyond his powers of comprehension. This existential theme is particularly strong in *My Universities*, especially in its final scene, where the hero simply makes his escape from the site of his most recent painful experiences and heads off in the direction of the Caspian Sea. It is the tension between the protagonist's role as an active man of protest (and prototypical "positive hero"), on the one hand, and existential man, on the other, which creates the ambiguity that is the hallmark of all Gor'kii's greatest works.

ANDREW BARRATT

The Life of Klim Samgin

Zhizn' Klima Samgina

Novel, 1927–31 (written 1925–36): unfinished

Gor'kii's novel is longer than *War and Peace*, stretching to four volumes. The first two were published in Berlin (1927–28), followed by the third book published in 1931; the fourth volume was unfinished. It is an ambitious work; as Gor'kii wrote in 1926 to A. Voronskii, the leading Soviet critic, he intended to depict "all the classes, all the trends, all the tendencies, all the hell-like commotion of the end of the last century, and all the storms of the 20th century". It is a philosophical novel, centred on the life of Klim Samgin and his response to the different socio-political circumstances and ideologies of the period of the four decades preceding the October Revolution of 1917. Samgin, a petit-bourgeois Russian intellectual, is reluctant to be an active participant in the historical upheavals, unlike the Bolsheviks. The novel is not only a chronicle, it also reflects on different literary styles and cultural traditions. Its own style is eclectic and experimental, combining the satirical with the monumental and heroic.

The book starts with a description of the 1870s and 1880s: Gor'kii contrasted the liberals of the 1880s with the revolutionaries of the 1870s. In Gor'kii's view Decadent culture was rooted in the lifestyle and outlook of liberals similar to Ivan Akimovich Samgin and Dr Somov, whose struggle towards political compromise is condemned in the novel. One of the representatives of the 1890s, the writer Katenin, is also portrayed in a satirical vein; his understanding of the peasantry is superficial, and he is reduced to wearing peasant clothes, reciting folk-sayings, etc. The essence of the liberalism of the end of the 19th century lies, according to Gor'kii, in a self-centred reflectiveness. This outlook is especially featured in the character Tomilin, who after years of flirting with liberal ideas turned into a Decadent. This character has several prototypes: among them V. Rozanov, D. Merezhkovskii, and L. Shestov. Some of Tomilin's phrases are quotations from the writings of these three philosophers. He is depicted by Gor'kii as an influential figure, a source of inspiration for the younger generation. His impact on the outlook of Klim Samgin, Lidiia Varavka, Makarov, and Ivan Dronov is astonishing. Klim Samgin, for example, often mumbles Tomilin's ideas to himself; and Makarov applies the philosopher's scepticism to relationships between the sexes, suggesting that "masturbation and love between men is, perhaps, a desired freedom from women?". Another decadent character, Serafima Nekhaeva, propounds, that "in Russia people discuss issues of no importance, read books of no interest, and do things of no use". Varvara Samgina hosts a fashionable salon, where Decadent views are particularly welcome. Diomidov, one of the regulars at this salon, refers to the ideas of N. Fedorov, whom Gor'kii admired in private as a philosopher but criticized for his views on women and his hankering after Byzantine Christianity. The description of the 1890s is marked by the growing popularity of western writers: Klim Samgin, fascinated by Maeterlink's plays, introduces this fashionable author to his provincial circle of friends. Another character, Alina Telepneva, is also a great enthusiast of Symbolism, ardently reciting

Briusov's poetry. However, Gor'kii labels this fashion as anti-democratic and syrupy. His condemnation of the Decadent culture is strongly felt in the depiction of the 1905 Revolution, contrasting the salon discussions about the mystical meaning of the historical events with frenzied revolutionary activities. Gor'kii incorporated one of his essays, "9-ogo ianvaria" [9th January], into the book, editing it in such a way as to give the impression that the events are witnessed by Samgin, who is both horrified and confused. The style of the narrative is laconic and suggestive; we learn, for example, that Samgin "saw the soldier's trembling face, red from frost or anger".

Gor'kii chooses an epic style to depict the populace in various socio-historical situations that include: the Industrial Fair of 1896, the events of the 1905 Revolution in Moscow and St Petersburg, the funeral of Baumann, the great Russian persecution of Poles, Jews and Finns, World War I, the February Revolution, etc. The geographical area embraced by the events is vast: the location varies from St Petersburg, Moscow, and the Volga region, to Berlin and Paris. Gor'kii was concerned about the decay of the individual during the modern historical process, and in the novel his emphasis is on the masses. Although Kutuzov and his fellow Bolsheviks are not the main characters of the novel, the author sympathizes with their attempt to influence the course of history. Lunacharskii defined the novel as "a moving panorama of the decades", and the dynamism of historical development is felt throughout the book. The first volume consists of very lengthy chapters, but the rest of the book is narrated without any break, as if history itself flowed into its pages without intervention by the author. The evolution of the characters is unconventional: it is achieved through their changing oulook, which reflects different political moods and ideologies. Tomilin changes from sceptical individualist to ardent propagator of Orthodox Christianity, Nekhaeva from decadent lady to flagellant, Dronov from intellectual to cynical businessman. Due to Gor'kii's preoccupation with creating an ideological portrait of the period, the dialogues do not add drama to the narrative, but expand the characterization of different groups of people, enriching the polyphonic structure based on the recurrence of various motifs.

Gor'kii's portrayal of Samgin, a St Petersburg lawyer, is both realistic and symbolic. The account of his affairs, political speeches, travel, reading and constant pondering is realistic and convincing; yet Gor'kii tries to create a synthetic image of this representative of the doomed Russian middle class by adding symbolic remarks about the non-existence of such a type. Images of dust, greyishness, and dullness accompany his description. His spectacles look dusty, his appearance is very ordinary, and he is always doubting his commitments. A typical description of Samgin is, for example, "Samgin started thinking about his life over the last decade: he had been caught up in a dusty whirlwind at the crossing of two paths, not wishing to take either of them ..." He appears to be especially despised by Gor'kii in the arrest scene, where the police hunt for the revolutionaries: in spite of his inner doubts, he eventually confesses to seeing Kutuzov, Inokov, and other Bolsheviks. According to Romain Rolland, Samgin is capable of treachery, or semi-treacherous acts, but these actions could arise from respectable motives or be provoked by his doubts.

The image of the Russian intellectual as portrayed by Gor'kii has recently been revived in contemporary prose. Bitov's *Pushkinskii dom* (*Pushkin House*), for example, features a narrator of the same breed (Lev Odoevtsev) whose half-hearted commitments secure his survival at the expense of moral weakness.

ALEXANDRA SMITH

Daniil Aleksandrovich Granin 1919–

Prose writer

Biography

Born in Volyn, Kursk region, 1 January 1919. Attended the Leningrad Polytechnical Institute, graduated in electro-mechanics, 1940. Worked in Kirov factory; volunteered for service at the front, 1941, and fought until end of World War II in tank regiment. Joined the Communist Party, 1942. Until 1950, worked as engineer in industry and research. Published first story, 1949; became professional writer, 1950. Rose to prominence in post-Stalin Thaw period; severely criticized for story "Sobstvennoe mnenie" ("A Personal Opinion") (1956). Since 1954, member of the board of Soviet Writers' Union; member of the Board of Writers' Union of RSFSR, 1956; appointed secretary, 1965. Secretary of Leningrad branch of the Writers' Union, 1954–69; member of editorial staff of journal *Neva* since 1967. Since glasnost, best known as liberal publicist and political figure; member of Supreme Soviet in Gorbachev era; member of Yeltsin's Presidential Council, 1994. Recipient: USSR State Prize, 1971, for documentary prose work, *Klavdiia Vilor*.

Publications

Collected Editions

Izbrannye proizvedeniia, 2 vols. Leningrad, 1969.
Sobranie sochinenii, 4 vols. Moscow, 1978–80.
Sobranie sochinenii, 5 vols. Leningrad, 1989–90.

Fiction

"Spor cherez okean" [Dispute Over the Ocean], *Zvezda*, 8

(1949); as *Pobeda inzhenera Korsakova* [The Victory of Engineer Korsakov]. Leningrad, 1950.
Variant vtoroi [The Second Variant]. Leningrad, 1950.
Iaroslav Dombrovskii. Moscow, 1951.
"Iskateli", *Zvezda*, 7–8 (1954); Moscow and Leningrad, 1955; translated as *Those Who Seek*, by Robert Daglish, Moscow, Foreign Languages Publishing House, 1955.
"Sobstvennoe mnenie", *Novyi mir*, 8 (1956); translated as "A Personal Opinion", in *Bitter Harvest: The Intellectual Revolt Behind the Iron Curtain*, edited by Edmund O. Stillman, New York, Praeger, 1959.
"Posle svad'by" [After the Wedding], *Oktiabr'*, *Novyi mir*, 7–9 (1958); Moscow, 1959.
"Idu na grozu", *Znamia*, 8–10 (1962); Moscow, 1962 and 1963; translated as *Into the Storm*, by Robert Daglish, Moscow, Progress, 1965.
"Dom na fontanke". 1967; translated as "The House on the Fontanka", by Margarete Orga, in *The House on the Fontanka: Modern Soviet Short Stories*, edited by Orga, London, Kimber, 1970.
"Nash kombat" [Our Battalion Commander], *Sever*, 4 (1968).
"Kto-to dolzhen" [Somebody Must], *Zvezda*, 1 (1970); as *Kto-to dolzhen: povesti i rasskazy*. 1970.
"Eta strannaia zhizn'" [This Strange Life], *Avrora*, 1–2 (1974).
Dozhd' v chuzhom gorode: povesti [Rain in a Strange City]. Leningrad, 1977.
Kartina: roman [The Picture]. Leningrad, 1980.
Dva kryla [Two Wings]. Moscow, 1983.
Odnofamilets: povesti [Namesake]. Leningrad, 1984.
Trinadtsat' stupenek [Thirteen Steps]. Leningrad, 1985.
Eshche zameten sled: povesti i rasskazy [There is Still a Trace]. Leningrad, 1985.
Chuzhoi dnevnik: povesti i rasskazy [Someone Else's Diary]. Moscow, 1988.
Nash dorogoi Roman Avdeevich [Our Dear Roman Andreevich]. Leningrad, 1990.

Essays and Documentary Prose
Neozhidannoe utro: ocherki o zarubezhnykh stranakh [An Unexpected Morning: Essays on Foreign Countries]. Moscow and Leningrad, 1962; Leningrad, 1971 (includes "Prekrasnaia Uta" [Beautiful Uta]).
Mesiats vverkh nogami (Ocherki ob Avstralii) [A Month Down Under (Essays on Australia)]. Leningrad, 1966.
Primechaniia k putevoditeliu: ocherki ob Avstralii, GDR i Anglii [Notes for a Guide: Essays on Australia, the GDR and England]. Leningrad, 1967.
Sad kamnei [The Rock Garden]. Moscow, 1972.
Klavdiia Vilor. Moscow, 1977.
"Glavy iz Blokadnoi knigi" [Chapters from the Book of the Blockade], with Ales Adamovich, *Novyi mir*, 12 (1977); 11 (1981); as *Blokadnaia kniga* [Book of the Blockade], Moscow, 1982.
"O miloserdii" [On Charity], *Literaturnaia gazeta* (18 March 1987).
"Zubr" [The Buffalo], *Novyi mir*, 1–2 (1987); as *Zubr: povest'*. Leningrad, 1987.
Interview with D. Granin by I. Rishina, *Literaturnaia gazeta* (27 May 1987), 4.
Miloserdie [Charity]. Moscow, 1988.
O nabolevshem [On a Sore Point]. Leningrad, 1988.
Tochka opory. Stat'i, besedy, portrety [Point of Rest]. Moscow, 1989.
"Zubr v kholodilnike" [A Buffalo in the Fridge], *Literaturnaia gazeta* (21 July 1993), 3.

Critical Studies
"Novatorstvo - eto bor'ba", by Iu. Surovtsev and M. Shcheglov, *Novyi mir*, 11 (1954).
"Rasskaz, vyzyvaiushchii nedoumenie (pis'mo chitatelia)", by P. Starodubtsev, *Partiinaia zhizn'*, 17 (1956).
"O smelosti podlinnoi i mnimoi", by V. Baskakov, *Oktiabr'*, 1 (1957).
Daniil Granin: Ocherk tvorchestva, by O.S. Voitinskaia, Moscow, 1966.
"Daniil Granin and the World of Soviet Science", by Keith Armes, *Survey*, 90 (1974), 47–59.
"Novye povesti Daniila Granina", by L. Plotkin, *Neva*, 5 (1977), 183–87.
"Science, Love and the Establishment in the Novels of D.A. Granin and C.P. Snow", by A.G. Waring, *Forum for Modern Language Studies*, 14 (1978), 1–15.
Nravstvennye poiski geroev Daniila Granina, by A. Starkov, Moscow, 1981.
Neobkhodimost' Don Kikhota: kniga o Daniile Granine, by L. Fink, Moscow, 1988.
The Last Years of Soviet Russian Literature: Prose Fiction, 1975–1991, by Deming Brown, Cambridge and New York, Cambridge University Press, 1993, 36–38.
History and Literature in Contemporary Russia, by Rosalind Marsh, New York, New York University Press, and London, Macmillan, 1995.
Spirit of the Totem: Religion and Myth in Soviet Fiction, 1964–1988, by Irena Maryniak, Leeds, W.S. Maney, 1995.

Daniil Granin's first fictional works were based on his own experience of work in industrial research; his main theme was the impact of science and technology on Soviet society and human relations. His first story, "Spor cherez okean" [Dispute Over the Ocean] conformed to a theme common during the anti-cosmopolitan campaign of the late Stalin era: the USSR's superiority over the US.

During the high points of Khrushchev's Thaw, Granin became known as a "liberal" writer who tried to extend the limits permitted in Soviet fiction. His first major success was *Iskateli* (*Those Who Seek*), which treats the familiar theme of an idealistic inventor's struggle against bureaucrats and careerists preoccupied with petty aims such as money, fame or power. Although the character of the hero, Andrei Lobanov, who combines talent with integrity and party discipline, was quite conventional, Granin went further than other writers of 1954, implying that Soviet science was permeated by a corrupt network of scientists under their prominent chief, Professor Tonkov. Inevitably, comparisons with the dominance of the charlatan T.D. Lysenko over Soviet biology came to mind. Thus Granin's work is at the same time a critique of Stalinist practices and an endorsement of the official Soviet advocacy of science and technology.

Granin's sympathy for de-Stalinization became even more evident in his story "Sobstvennoe mnenie" ("A Personal

Opinion"), one of the most controversial works of the Thaw of 1956. Official critics considered that its portrait of Minaev, a technocrat and party official who had risen to a high position through a series of dishonest compromises with his conscience, cast too pessimistic a light on Soviet science and the party bureaucracy as a whole. Granin, a party member, felt chastened by the reprimand he received in 1957, and did not treat social problems as frankly again until the inception of glasnost.

Nevertheless, Granin's next two novels also discussed some delicate issues. *Posle svad'by* [After the Wedding] depicts a backward Soviet collective farm, and the improvement in management style caused by the rehabilitation of purge victims. *Idu na grozu* (*Into the Storm*) again treats the theme of scientific and moral integrity, in the light of the further de-Stalinization at the 22nd Party Congress (1961). It contains one of the first allusions to Beria's malign role as head of the Soviet atomic research programme, and treats other topical subjects such as anti-Semitism in science, the need for exploratory research, the fashions for jazz and abstract art, and the return of previously forbidden literature. Granin's first three novels were adapted for both the stage and screen.

In the Brezhnev era, Granin continued to write about the ethical and psychological problems of scientists, albeit without his former political sharpness. *Kto-to dolzhen* [Somebody Must] examines the conflict between assured success and a difficult, risky venture, between the performance of duty and self-sacrifice for the cause, and refers obliquely to the enduring power of Lysenko's disciples in Soviet science. *Eta strannaia zhizn'* [This Strange Life] contains documentary material about a botanist who was totally devoted to science, and displays some formal experimentation, combining various narrative genres, such as autobiographical lyricism.

As an official of the Soviet Writers' Union, Granin made numerous trips abroad, which were reflected in his lively collections of essays and travel writings, such as *Sad kamnei* [The Rock Garden] and *Primechaniia k putevoditeliu* [Notes for a Guide]. In the 1970s and 1980s, Granin also turned to documentary writing about the war. "Prekrasnaia Uta" [Beautiful Uta] evokes meetings between Germans and Russians 20 years after the war through a free association of reflection and autobiographical commentary. His *Blokadnaia kniga* [Book of the Blockade], compiled with the Belorussian writer Ales Adamovich, contains interviews with survivors of the siege of Leningrad, enhanced by contemporary commentaries.

Another of Granin's interests is conservation, especially a sympathetic approach to the preservation of old buildings, a preoccupation reflected in "Dom na Fontanke" ("The House on the Fontanka"), a nostalgic recollection of pre-war Russia. Similarly, *Kartina* [The Picture], Granin's best-known work of the Brezhnev era, depicts a provincial party official's bitter struggle to conserve a picturesque inlet and a timber merchant's house portrayed on an old painting of his town, an area of outstanding natural beauty designated as the site of a new computer factory.

In the Gorbachev era Granin created a sensation with his article "O miloserdii" [On Charity], which criticized the materialism and soullessness of contemporary Soviet society, advocating kindness and compassion to others and a return to universal human values independent of ideological categories.

Granin contributed to the glasnost of 1987 with *Zubr* [The Buffalo], a semi-fictionalized biography of the famous geneticist Nikolai Timofeev-Resovskii, who went to Berlin in 1925 and escaped the destruction of his science in the USSR by continuing to work in Germany throughout the war. There was bitter hostility from Lysenkoites towards the publication of *Zubr* in Russia; and it could not be published in the GDR until 1989, as Gorbachev's KGB was involved in an exchange of information with the Stasi on whether Timofeev had collaborated with the Nazis. Despite its frankness, *Zubr* did not exceed the level of pessimism about Soviet science officially permitted in 1987; Granin concealed Timofeev's incarceration in a "special prison" after 1947 and the extent of his persecution in the post-Stalin period. Granin became active in politics in the Gorbachev era, but by the end of the 1980s he came to be disparaged by writers and critics of the younger generation as a "liberal" and "member of the 1960s generation" (*shestidesiatnik*), who had been prepared to compromise with his conscience in order to publish his work. His story of 1990, *Nash dorogoi Roman Avdeevich* [Our Dear Roman Avdeevich], a satire on the former Leningrad boss Grigorii Romanov, received a critical reception; but he continues to publish articles and reviews in the post-communist period.

ROSALIND MARSH

Irina Nikolaevna Grekova 1907–

Prose writer and mathematician

Biography

Born Elena Sergeevna Ventsel' in Revel (Tallin), 21 March 1907. Attended Moscow University, graduated in mathematics, 1929; PhD in mathematics, 1954; Professor of cybernetics, Moscow Air Force Academy, 1955–67. First publication, 1957. Adopted the pseudonym I. Grekova, a play on words from the Russian word *igrek*, the mathematical term for "y", the unknown quantity in an equation. Professor, Zhukovskii Military Academy, forced to resign, 1970. Married (widow); three children. Member of the Soviet Writers' Union since 1967.

Has also published mathematical writings under her original name.

Publications

Collected Editions

Kafedra: povesti [The Faculty]. Moscow, 1980; reprinted 1983; "Kafedra", translated as "The Faculty", by Melinda Maclean, Jr, *Soviet Literature*, 9–10 (1979), 3–107; 16–128.

Porogi [The Rapids]. Moscow, 1986.

Na ispytaniiakh: Povesti i rasskazy [At the Testing Station]. Moscow, 1990.

Fiction

"Za prokhodnoi", *Novyi mir*, 7 (1962), 110–31; translated as "Beyond the Gates", in *The Young Russians*, edited by Thomas P. Whitney, New York, Macmillan, 1972.

"Damskii master", *Novyi mir*, 11 (1963), 89–120; translated as "The Ladies' Hairdresser", by L. Gregg, *Russian Literature Triquarterly*, 5 (1973), 223–64; and by Michael Petrov, in *Russian Women: Two Stories*, San Diego, Harcourt Brace Jovanovich, 1983.

"Letom v gorode", *Novyi mir*, 4 (1965); translated as "One Summer in the City", by Lauren G. Leighton, in *The Barsukov Triangle, The Two-Toned Blond and Other Stories*, edited by Carl and Ellendea Proffer, Ann Arbor, Ardis, 1984, 245–72; also as "A Summer in the City", in *The Image of Women in Contemporary Soviet Fiction: Selected Short Stories*, edited and translated by Sigrid McLaughlin, London, Macmillan, and New York, St Martin's Press, 1989, 20–52.

"Pervyi nalet" [First Raid], *Zvezda*, 11 (1965), 103–09.

Pod fonarem [Under the Streetlight]. Moscow, 1966.

"Na ispytaniiakh" [At the Testing Station], *Novyi mir*, 7 (1967).

"Malen'kii Garusov" [Little Garusov], *Zvezda*, 9 (1970).

"Khoziaika gostinitsy", *Zvezda*, 9 (1976); 7–123, translated as "The Hotel Manager", by Michael Petrov, in *Russian Women: Two Stories*, San Diego, Harcourt Brace Jovanovich, 1983.

Serezha u okna [Serezha at the Window]. Moscow, 1976.

Ania i Mania. Moscow, 1978.

"Vdovii parakhod", *Novyi mir*, 5 (1981), 66–147; translated as *The Ship of Widows*, by Cathy Porter, London, Virago, 1985; Evanston, Illinois, Northwestern University Press, 1994.

"Skripka Rotshil'da" [The Rothschild Violin], *Literaturnaia Rossiia* (5 July 1981), 12–13.

"Porogi" [The Rapids], *Oktiabr'*, 10 (1984), 72–149.

"Fazan" [The Pheasant], *Oktiabr'*, 9 (1985), 6–58.

"Bez ulybok", *Oktiabr'*, 11 (1986); translated as "World Without Smiles", by Alex Miller, *Soviet Literature*, 3 (1988), 19–48; and as "Without Smiles", by D. Dyraz-Freeman, in *The New Soviet Fiction*, edited by Sergei Zalygin, New York, Abbeville Press, 1989.

"Perelom" [The Break], *Oktiabr'*, 8 (1987), 72–149.

"Khoziaeva zhizni" [The Masters of Fate], *Oktiabr'*, 9 (1988), 3–13; translated as "Masters of Their Own Lives", by D. Dyrcz-Freeman, in *Soviet Women Writing*, New York, Abbeville Press, and London, John Murray, 1990, 85–105.

Svezho predanie. Roman [Fresh Legend]. Tenafly, New Jersey, Hermitage, 1994; Moscow, 1997.

Critical Studies

"Faust i fiziki", by I. Zolotusskii, *Voprosy literatury*, 11 (1965), 50–68.

"Real'nost' geroia", by A. Ninov, *Zvezda*, 7 (1967), 192–202.

"V zhanre damskoi povesti (o iazyke i stile povesti I. Grekovoi *Na ispytaniiakh*", by L.I. Skvortsov, *Russkaia rech'*, 1 (1968), 26–35.

"Kak khoroshi, kak svezhi byli rozy ...", by V. Oskotskii, *Druzhba narodov*, 4 (1977), 272–75.

"Cherty sovremennoi geroini", by N. Naumova, *Neva*, 10 (1978), 175–82.

"Svet i teni bytopisaniia", by Alla Latynina, *Literaturnoe obozrenie*, 1 (1979), 47–49.

Die Kultur der Weiblichkeit in der Prosa Irina Grekovas, by Elisabeth Menke, Munich, Sagner, 1988.

"Women Without Men in the Writings of Contemporary Soviet Women Writers", by Adele Barker, in *Russian Literature and Psychoanalysis*, edited by Daniel Rancour-Laferrière, Amsterdam, John Benjamins, 1989.

"Irina Grekova's *Na ispytaniiakh*: The History of One Story", by Adele Barker, *Slavic Review*, 43/3 (1989), 399–412.

"I. Grekova", by Sigrid McLaughlin, in *The Image of Women in Contemporary Soviet Fiction*, edited by McLaughlin, London, Macmillan, and New York, St Martin's Press, 1989, 18–20.

"Sto let zhenskogo odinochestva", by N. Startseva, *Don*, 3 (1989) ,158–65.

"Zhenskaia Proza and the New Generation of Women Writers", by K.A. Simmons, *Slovo*, 3/1 (May 1990), 66–78.

"Grekova's *Vdovii parakhod*: The Stalinist Heroine Revisited", by Catriona Kelly, *Rusistika*, 6 (1992), 14–18.

The Last Years of Soviet Russian Literature: Prose Fiction, 1975–1991, by Deming Brown, Cambridge and New York, Cambridge University Press, 1993, 38–42.

A History of Russian Women's Writing, 1820–1992, by Catriona Kelly, Oxford and New York, Clarendon Press, 1994, 358–62 *passim*.

The two names most clearly associated with the rise in the 1960s of women's writing, and of *byt* prose (prose of everyday life), are those of I. Grekova and Natal'ia Baranskaia. Irina Grekova first appeared in print in 1962 with the story "Za prokhodnoi" ("Beyond the Gates") and has published many short stories, *povesti* and novels since, her "Damskii master" ("The Ladies' Hairdresser") and *Vdovii parakhod* (*The Ship of Widows*) being the most widely known. Despite being often categorized in the west as rather "socialist realist", Grekova is capable of wit and sharp, if oblique, political criticism, as well as of a complex interweaving of sub-themes. She is best when writing in a light, ironic vein; certain of her texts, such as the story, *Fazan* [The Pheasant], containing the reminiscences of one Fedia (nicknamed "Fazan") about his not altogether successful life and death, are written in a pedestrian style that slips occasionally into sentimentality, a characteristic also of her *The Ship of Widows*, a tale of suffering motherhood, and of her story "Znakomye liudi" [Familiar People], a parable of human generosity.

Grekova's most notorious novel, for which she was forced to resign her professorial position at the Zhukovskii Military Academy, was *Na ispytaniiakh* [At the Testing Station], which appeared in *Novyi mir* in 1967, during that journal's liberal phase under the editorship of Aleksandr Tvardovskii (which was to come to an end in 1969). The novel, which describes the Red Army on military manoeuvres, (war is a theme common to many of Grekova's texts), was attacked by the press and Party, and, on the orders of General Epishev, army chief political administrator, banned from military libraries. The depiction of the non-communist background of her hero, the intelligent, General Sivers (who in fact does make a few broad comments about life during the Stalinist purges), and its selection of a Jew, General Gindin, as another central character, ensured that the work did not fit standard parameters stipulating high levels of *ideinost'*, *narodnost'* and *partiinost'*. Nor did her story "Khoziaeva zhizni" ("Masters of Their Own Lives") written in 1960, but only published in 1988, in which the protagonist, having suffered the purges, the madness and death of his wife, and 13 years in the Gulag, feels himself to be no "master of his fate", to parody the well-known socialist slogan that proclaimed communist man's ability to take the reins of destiny into his own hands.

In the story "V vagone" [In the Carriage] Grekova weaves a story around the idea of a scientist's ridicule at the hands of other scientists; in "Bez ulybok" ("World Without Smiles"), probably referring to her own fall from grace, Grekova describes what it is like to be out of political favour, in a world "without smiles". The heroine of "World Without Smiles", M.M., is a scientist accused of unorthodox work, and hauled before a committee for reprimand. Grekova describes what she calls the Treatment, i.e., the persecution campaign waged against those who have for some reason (often personal rather than political) become targets of those with enough authority to create scandal. She describes, with chilling humour, the howling and clamour of those appointed to debate her "case" and administer the preordained rebuke, in language that parodies the bombastic yet chilling slogans of the Stalinist years. Despite her feeling of being in the right, the heroine, like Bulgakov's Master in *Master i Margarita* (*The Master and Margarita*) feels the tremendous pressure of public opinion; and when such public opinion turns against one, that person "finds it hard to feel in the right".

It is in this story that Grekova points to one of her favourite themes, stating that "the hardest thing of all is to hang on within oneself to one's truth. Whatever they force you to do – you must stand up for your truth". Grekova constantly describes situations in which characters are forced to consider their "inner truth" and to defend it; this is the theme of "The Ladies' Hairdresser", about one Vitalii, a hairdresser, whose individualistic talent is eventually crushed by Soviet bureaucracy. It is a theme also of "Perelom" [The Break], in which doctor Kira ponders the ethics of informing critically ill patients of the truth, i.e. the likelihood of their imminent demise.

Although Grekova does describe male characters, such as Vitalii, or the "neudachnik", Neshatov, attempting to restructure his life after an accident in a scientific laboratory in *Porogi*, her protagonists are usually female. In *The Ship of Widows* there are four women, all widows; a former pianist, a former operetta singer, a peasant, and an artisan; in her novel *Kafedra* [The Faculty] the heroine is the scientist Nina Astashova, in "Perelom" it is Kira, a middle-aged doctor with two grown sons; even "The Ladies' Hairdresser" is as much about the typical Grekova woman – a strong-minded scientist, attempting to combine single parenthood with the demands of a career – as about the hairdresser himself. Grekova is no feminist writer, and has stated (in an interview in 1986) that equality of the sexes is questionable; but her female characters, by virtue of their ability to cope with demanding schedules, illness, tragedy and wartime, demonstrate their superiority. While Grekova's older, paternal figures, such as the scientist Gan in *Porogi* or the taciturn yet generous doctor Chagin in "Perelom", as well as her adolescent male characters (usually the sons of the heroine) tend to be portrayed as very "good" (a major exception being Vadim, the son of one of the widows in *The Ship of Widows*), husbands are most usually described as useless wastrels, idle cynics or even as wife-beaters.

Her work is distinguished by a stoical acceptance of life's problems; at times there is even a sense of optimism, a feeling that with the passing of time all will be well. Repentance is possible; even the reprobate Vadim in *The Ship of Widows* can at the novel's end realize the extent to which he has sinned against his suffering mother, can weep, and begin a "new life".

Grekova's style is plain and conventional, but leavened by masterful dialogue; reproducing linguistic idiosyncrasies, Grekova succeeds in creating extraordinarily alive characters with whom the reader feels an instant rapport. She is best at reproducing the simple, domestic lives of women coping with everyday life in the then Soviet Union; this, touched with gentle irony and, at times, with pathos, is *byt* prose of high quality.

S. Dalton-Brown

The Ladies' Hairdresser

Damskii master

Story, 1963

"The Ladies' Hairdresser", Grekova's second published story, and one of her best, synthesizes several characteristic Grekovian preoccupations: professional and personal integrity, creativity, gender identity, and generational differences. These themes are articulated through a bold twinning of two superficially contrasting characters: Mariia Vladimirovna Kovaleva, a successful middle-aged female mathematician, and Vitalii Plavnikov, the struggling young hairdresser of the story's title. Their relationship charts an unusual intersection of the mainstream with the marginalized within Soviet society, revealing sameness within differences.

Kovaleva is the quintessential divided Grekova protagonist. Torn between her role of single mother to two shiftless but charming college-age sons and her administrative duties as director of a computer institute, she neglects household duties and grooming regimens, yet functions as surrogate parent both to the talented, ambitious Vitalii and to her secretary Galia. In Kovaleva, Grekova dramatizes the familiar gendered dilemma of the double-duty syndrome, embedded in a social context that Grekova vividly captures with fluency and concision (the institute, the youth centre, the hair salon). While susceptible to the asymmetrical gender traditions that have accorded women's physical appearance extraordinary importance, Kovaleva finds "the greatest happiness on earth" in those rare moments of self-oblivious intellectual excitement vouchsafed by her research. In that respect she mirrors Vitalii, whose fanatical self-discipline and creativity raise hairdressing to a science and an art.

Although on first glance Kovaleva and Vitalii ostensibly

personify contrasting types (the established, educated head of a scientific institution versus the uneducated youth from an orphanage who cuts and perms women's hair), they gradually emerge as modified doubles: both find supreme self-fulfilment in their vocations; Vitalii disavows his biological parents, yet seeks parental guidance from Kovaleva, while she, similarly, plays surrogate mother and mentor to Vitalii and Galia, yet cannot find time for her own sons and housework; just as Kovaleva's "unfeminine" profession places her in virtually an all-male environment, Vitalii's "unmasculine" job likewise locates him in an almost exclusively female milieu; both benefit from and seem fascinated by each other's "Otherness".

Through situations, character types, and a series of comments emanating principally from Kovaleva as first-person narrator, the story explores Otherness as gender identity. Whatever the gender-bending implications of the text, it fundamentally subscribes to an essentialist polarization of the sexes. Kovaleva's bifurcated sense of selfhood reflects her gender ambiguity, her inarticulate ambivalence about the "rightness" of equating sex with gender, manifested in her confessed discomfort around women. The sharp exchange between Kovaleva and her assistant, Viacheslav Nikolaevich Lebedev, distils the unresolved conflict in eloquent terms: as his *female boss*, she strikes him as "unladylike" because she smokes; she finds him, a *male subordinate*, "too ladylike", largely because he dyes his hair. The scene exposes the story's symbolic identification of hair with identity in general, while inscribing traditional assumptions about the nature of inherent masculine and feminine traits. Those assumptions include equating femininity with physical appearance and casting women as "objects" of male enjoyment ("A man would probably like to pick up a little thing like that [Galia, wearing 'needle-sharp heels'] by the waist with two fingers and move it around from place to place"). As a category, men are generalized as unfaithful husbands, absent fathers, and hard drinkers. Women, despite their competitiveness and collusion in surface values so as to attract males, are depicted as more trustworthy ("I like girls who dance with each other. You can rely on them"), emotionally generous, and therefore apt to be disappointed or betrayed ("Female grief. It's always the same, and there's nothing you can do to ease it"). Part of this inequality may be attributed to the impersonal "mathematical" or "market" element of demographics: the disproportion of women to men in Soviet society that both Kovaleva and her author acknowledge ("My poor, poor girls. The war's long over, a new generation's grown up, and still there are too many of you"). Yet the story's imagery and plot denouement reinforce rather conventional gender binarism that seems to cut across historical specificity.

In a replay of the Pygmalion/Galatea myth, Vitalii is a "magician" and "sorcerer" who effects stunning metamorphoses, whereas Kovaleva, Galia, and the women on whose hair he practices and refines his skills merely constitute the "clay" awaiting transformation. Both Kovaleva and Galia prove steadfast in their "devotion" to Vitalii, who, at narrative's end, acquires the features of an overly pragmatic egotist (i.e., proves to be "masculine," in terms of the work's implicit value system). Deromanticizing his involvement with Galia as merely a professional opportunity to experiment with her hair, he unproblematically abandons the "art" of hairdressing for the materially more rewarding career of a factory metalworker. Grekova deftly prepares readers for the apparently abrupt change in Vitalii's persona by implicating him in the web of animal imagery associated only with males in the narrative – specifically, Kovaleva's "uncivilized" sons, with their request for her "paw", their clever, ingratiating note, which metaphorizes the mother/son relationship in terms of pigs and piglets, and their refusal to abandon the "male disease" of chess long enough to tidy up the "pigsty" of a house they inhabit and "soil". As a "cross between a fawn and a wolf cub", Vitalii may belong to a higher order of animal, but ultimately lacks the emotional human warmth that would elevate him to another species.

Generational differences reinforce gender distinctions. In contrast to Kovaleva, who strives to combine social responsibility, professional excellence, and personal loyalty, the younger, post-war generation – her sons, Vitalii, and Galia – tend to narrowness, frivolity, and self-centredness. Vitalii's chequered childhood, including his years at an orphanage, his drinking father and his terminally religious stepmother, may partly mitigate his self-absorption, but do not justify his cold-blooded treatment of Galia.

Like all of Grekova's fiction, "The Ladies' Hairdresser" exposes the crippling effects of a collective mentality inimical to any symptom of individualism, the Soviet system of privilege and hierarchy, the shoddiness of its service sector and its network of quid pro quos, its black market activities, and the society's comprehensive schizophrenia. But the most memorable and aesthetically realized aspect of the story is its investigation of identity via gender and its slippery signifiers.

HELENA GOSCILO

The Ship of Widows

Vdovii parokhod

Story, 1981

The Ship of Widows presents a woman's world, but extends its compass through figuring that world as a microcosm of the national devastation wrought by World War II. Anfisa Gromova as the battered icon of Motherhood betokens the incalculable horrors endured by Mother Russia throughout the years of heroic resistance against the German invader. Personal and national are inseparable: the ship of widows weathers the losses that orphaned young Soviet Russia for decades and left an indelible imprint on those survivors who lived to enshroud future generations in the tragedy of the past.

Grekova condenses the colossal scale of destruction visited upon Russia into the harrowing biographies of five widows in a Moscow communal apartment during and after the war. The ebb and flow of their turbulent relations provide the backdrop for the central drama of an accelerated Soviet Bildungsroman: the birth of Vadim Gromov – illegitimate son of the youngest widow, Anfisa – and his development into a spoiled, callous egotist who only becomes humanized after precipitating his long-suffering mother's premature death.

While documenting Russian women's prolonged material and psychological dispossession by the war, *The Ship of Widows* manages to touch myriad other weighty topics and to recast a number of traditional Russian literary concerns in a contemporary vein. Vadim, whose name, physical appearance, demonic pride, and supercilious manner evoke the 19th-century genres of the society tale and romantic novel, replays the drama of Dostoevskii's *Crime and Punishment*; his untested delusions of isolated superiority lead to the unwitting "murder" of his mother and his eventual, supremely Raskol'nikovian conversion to remorseful Christian humility. While paying homage to a rich cultural heritage of unaccommodating loners, Grekova freights her closed-form novella with an astounding wealth of social and psychological realia that coalesce into a palpably felt background. She accumulates eloquent details about housing conditions, food shortages, orphanages, factories, military medical units, Soviet hospitals, higher education, officialdom, the post-war enlistment of youth to work the virgin lands, sexual mores among Soviet teenagers, adolescent disillusionment, the entrenched network of bribery and mutual favours that ultimately throttled Soviet productivity, and more. Furthermore, Grekova's gallery of primary and secondary characters represent a broad cross-section of Russian society. Diversity in social origins and worldview, however, is most colourfully projected by the five widows whom circumstances force into unremitting proximity.

The imposed spatial constraints of a communal dwelling intensify not only the women's personal conflicts but also the reader's awareness of the class differences that partly account for each widow's distinct values and group persona: the religious peasant Kapitolina Gushchina, or Kapa, a niggardly retired night-watch blindly devoted to church ritual; the "mannish" fitter Pavla Zykova, or Panka, who passionately advocates Utopian-proletarian equality and justice, preferring universal wretchedness to the most innocuous hint of individual privilege; Ada Zaiats, the arch-romantic former operetta singer whose ludicrous fantasies and coquettish effusions overshadow her genuine kindness; Ol'ga Flerova, a member of the intelligentsia physically and psychologically shattered by the heavy bombardment that transforms her into an invalid, curtailing her envisaged career of concert pianist; and the simple but talented worker from the poverty-stricken countryside, Anfisa Gromova, ultimately doomed by her obsessive maternal love.

Involuntarily linked by kindred bereavements, the widows comprise a surrogate family, elaborated into a presiding image that intimates consolation on the edge of despair. Grekova replaces the psychologically coercive trope of the state as family – popularized by Stalin, the self-proclaimed Father – with an alternate family model anchored in empirical reality. Within this unit, reconstituted by the exigencies of war and post-war conditions, survivors/substitutes play out conventional familial roles.

The novella's symmetrical structure in a quasi-religious key deftly buttresses the image of surrogate families. Although *The Ship of Widows* opens with multiple deaths as definitive losses, it ends with death as cathectic triumph, actuating two resurrections. Anfisa's funeral prompts Vadim's tearful spiritual rebirth into a new life and liberates Flerova's repressed emotions through similarly healing tears. The "communal family's" farewell to Anfisa affirms the widows' capacity to draw sustenance from a shared life enriched by Anfisa's participation in it.

Whatever the differences in women's individual biographies, their common experience as daughters, wives, mistresses, and mothers is one of bleak deprivation. Their plots unfold in a rhythm of loneliness and physically exhausting work, marriages arranged in defiance of their needs and inclinations, affairs with drunken or brutal lovers that terminate in abandonment, and children who reward sacrifice with sarcasm. Grekova makes no attempt to idealize these woman or to minimize the part their weaknesses play in their circumstances. Yet unattributed comments scattered throughout the novella suggest that the miseries endured by women as a group are exacerbated by the indurate misogyny – especially the exploitation of female labour and the neglect of female needs – institutionalized by Soviet society along essentialist lines. Moreover, social indifference to women's welfare dovetails neatly with male attitudes; virtually all of the men in the novella express dismissive contempt for women in some form. Yet such remarks, far from betraying specifically *masculine* wrongheadedness, merely reflect the code-affirming gender binarism diffused throughout the novella. No dissenting voice posits alternative gender arrangements that differentiate between biology and socialization, between given and constructed, and in so doing entertain possibilities for change.

Ultimately, *The Ship of Widows* dramatizes the impossibility of forging genuine values and sustaining decent human relations – what one might call leading a normal life – in a place and time ruled by abnormalcy. Neither Anfisa's love nor Vadim's early development can escape the prevalent taint of aberrancy. The terrifying destruction of the wartime years finally differs little from the nightmare of Soviet post-war "peace" under Stalin. Both violate human life and leave their survivors maimed. If forced to assign responsibility, Grekova most probably would point a finger, then, not at female hysteria or filial heartlessness, but at the incalculable forces of history.

Whatever the degree of her incipient gender-consciousness, in one respect at least Grekova embraces her culture's mainstream tradition: the trope of womanhood for nation. As experiential yields to iconographic, Mother, the "supreme hypostasis" of woman, becomes Mother Russia.

HELENA GOSCILO

Aleksandr Sergeevich Griboedov 1795–1829

Dramatist, poet, and diplomat

Biography

Born in Moscow, 15 January 1795. Attended Moscow University, 1806–08, studying humanities, law, and natural sciences: graduated in law; education interrupted by Napoleon's invasion of Russia, 1812. Joined the Moscow hussars (General Kologryvov's reserve), but saw no military action. Married: daughter of the poet, Prince Aleksandr Chavchavadze in 1828. Joined Ministry of Foreign Affairs in St Petersburg, 1816; diplomat in Teheran, 1819–21; diplomatic secretary to General A.P. Ermolov, in Tiflis, 1821–23. Returned to Georgia, 1825. Arrested and held for four months on suspicion of involvement in Decembrist uprising, 1825. Returned to Caucasus after release, 1826. Prepared the text of the Treaty of Turkmanchai, concluding the Russian-Persian War. Promoted to Resident Russian Minister in Persia. Killed during the storming of the Russian embassy in Teheran, by a mob of insurgents, 11 February 1829.

Publications

Collected Editions

Polnoe sobranie sochinenii. Moscow, 1911–17; reprinted Hildesheim, Georg Olms, 1977.
Sochineniia. Moscow, 1953.
Sochineniia v stikhakh, Leningrad, 1967; reprinted Leningrad, 1987.
Polnoe sobranie sochinenii, 3 vols. St Petersburg, 1995.
Gore ot uma i drugie siuzhety. Moscow, 1996.
Litso i genii: Sbornik. Moscow. 1997.

Plays

Molodye suprugi [The Young Married Couple], from a play by Creuzé de Lesser (produced St Petersburg, 1815). 1815.
Student [The Student], with Pavel A. Katenin (produced St Petersburg, 1904). 1817.
Pritvornaia nevernost' [False Infidelity], with A.A. Zhandr [Gendre], from a play by Nicholas Barthe (produced St Petersburg, 1818). 1818.
Svoia sem'ia; ili, Zamuzhniaia nevesta [All in the Family; or, The Married Fiancée], with A.A. Shakhovskoi and Nikolai Khmel'nitskii (produced St Petersburg, 1818).
Proba intermedy [Test of an Interlude] (produced St Petersburg, 1819); in *Polnoe sobranie sochinenii*, 1911–17.
Kto brat, kto sestra; ili, Obman za obmanom [Who's the Brother, Who's the Sister; or, Deception for Deception], with Prince Petr Viazemskii and others (libretto; produced St Petersburg, 1824).
Gore ot uma (produced St Petersburg, 1825; complete version produced Kiev, 1831). 1825 (partial version); 1833 (censored version); 1861 (uncensored version); reprinted in many editions including: that edited by D.P. Costello, Oxford, Oxford University Press, 1951; "Literaturnye pamiatniki" series, Moscow, 1969; "Russkaia klassika s kommentariami" series, St Petersburg, 1994; and that edited by Richard Peace, Bristol Classical Press, London, 1995; translated as *The Misfortune of Being Clever*, by S.W. Pring, London, Nutt, 1914; also as "Wit Works Woe", by Bernard Pares, in *Masterpieces of Russian Drama, 1*, edited by G.R. Noyes, New York, Appleton, 1933; as "Chatsky", by Joshua Cooper, in *Four Russian Plays*, Harmondsworth, Penguin, 1972; as "The Folly to Be Wise", by A.G. Waring, *Russian Literature Triquarterly*, 23 (1990), 39–112; and as *The Woe of Wit*, by Alan Shaw, Tenafly, Hermitage, 1992; also translated as *Woe from Wit*.

Critical Studies

A.S. Griboedov: Ego zhizn' i sochineniia, compiled by V. Sokrovskii, 1911; reprinted Oxford, Meeuws, 1985.
"The Murder of Griboedov", by D.P. Costello, *Oxford Slavonic Papers*, 8 (1958), 66–89.
Griboedov et la vie littéraire de son temps, by J. Bonamour, Paris, Presses universitaires de France, 1965.
Griboedov: ocherk zhizni i tvorchestva, by Vladimir Orlov, Leningrad, 1967.
Tvorcheskaia istoriia "Goria ot uma", by N.K. Piksanov, Moscow, 1971.
A.S. Griboedov: Tvorchestvo. Biografiia. Traditsiia, Leningrad, 1977.
The Murder of Griboedov: New Materials, by Evelyn J. Harden, Birmingham, Birmingham Slavonic Monographs, 1979.
"A Defense of Sof'ja in *Woe from Wit*", by Gerald Janecek, *Slavic and East European Journal*, 21 (1979), 318–31.
Griboedov v vospominaniiakh sovremennikov, Moscow, 1980.
Meyerhold the Director, by Konstantin Rudnitsky, translated by George Petrov, Ann Arbor, Ardis, 1981, 421–35.
Russian Drama from Its Beginnings to the Age of Pushkin, by Simon Karlinsky, Berkeley, University of California Press, 1985.
A History of Russian Literature of the Romantic Period, by William Edward Brown, vol. 2, Ann Arbor, Ardis, 1986.
Griboedov: materialy k biografii. Sbornik nauchykh trudov, Leningrad, 1989.
Zhizn' i deianiia Aleksandra Griboedova, by V. Meshcheriakov, Moscow, 1989.
A.S. Griboedov: zhizn' i tvorchestvo, by P.S. Krasnov *et al.*, Moscow, 1995.
"Introduction", by Richard Peace to *Gore ot uma*, London, Bristol Classical Press, 1995, v–xxi.

After abandoning his intended postgraduate studies at Moscow University following Napoleon's invasion of Russia in 1812, Aleksandr Griboedov enlisted in the hussars, but did not see active service. Discharged from the army in 1816, he joined the College of Foreign Affairs and began his career as a diplomat. In the summer of 1818 he was posted as secretary to the Russian legation in Persia, but was delayed in Georgia and arrived in Teheran in February 1819 where he spent nearly two years. In early 1821 he returned to Georgia as secretary to General A.P. Ermolov who was commanding the Russian army in the Caucasus. Two years later he went back to Moscow on extended leave, returning to the Caucasus in May 1825. Arrested following the Decembrist uprising of 1825 because of his friendship with two of the leading conspirators, he was taken to St Petersburg and imprisoned for four months. After his release he was sent again to the Caucasus where Russia and Persia were at war. After the signing of the Peace of Turkmanchai in February 1828 he personally presented the treaty to Tsar Nicholas I. In recognition of his diplomatic service he was appointed minister to Persia. He left for Teheran and after a stay of some months in Tbilisi, during which time he married the daughter of the Georgian poet Aleksandr Chavchavadze, he reached the Persian capital early in January 1829. He was met by popular unrest caused largely by local resentment at the terms of the Peace. On 11 February a fanatical mob stormed the legation and slaughtered the staff. Griboedov's mutilated body was later recovered and he was buried in Tbilisi.

Throughout his short life and despite his diplomatic duties, Griboedov always took a keen interest in the theatre. As early as 1815 he had adapted de Lesser's *Le secret du ménage* as a one-act comedy in verse. It was staged in St Petersburg as *Molodye suprugi* [The Young Married Couple]. In 1817 he collaborated with P.A. Katenin on *Student* [The Student], a three-act prose comedy, a parody on the poets Zhukovskii, Batiushkov, and the Arzamas Circle. It also contained a scarcely disguised attack on M.N. Zagoskin who had dared to criticize some of Griboedov's verse in *Molodye suprugi*. The play was not produced in Russia until 1904. Neither of these plays has much to recommend it, but a third, *Svoia sem'ia* [All in the Family], a verse comedy written with A.A. Shakhovskoi and N.I. Khmel'nitskii in 1818, is usually considered the next best Russian Neoclassical comedy after Fonvizin's *Nedorosl'* (*The Minor*). It was extremely popular in its own time, mainly because it gave a challenging role for its heroine, Natasha. In a revival in 1896 she was played by the leading actress of the time, Mariia Savina. When a performance was staged by an émigré company in Paris during World War II, the fact that Natasha's role was taken by the celebrated Lila Kedrova, and that the director N.N. Evreinov wrote in the publicity that it was "a little-known play by Alexander Griboedov" shows how much the standing of two of the collaborators had changed from the time of its first production. Also in 1818 Griboedov and his friend Andrei Zhandr (or Gendre) produced a poor version of Nicolas Barthe's *Les fausses infidelités* which they entitled *Pritvornaia nevernost'* [False Infidelity].

The most popular theatrical genre in Russia throughout the first half of the 19th century was undoubtedly the vaudeville, which had grown out of the French comic opera, and was often based on French originals. Many leading Russian playwrights of the period tried their hands at the libretto, and Griboedov was no exception. Together with Prince P.A. Viazemskii he wrote *Kto brat, kto sestra; ili, Obman za obmanom* [Who's the Brother, Who's the Sister, or, Deception for Deception], which was staged in St Petersburg in 1824. More particularly it is a rather a *vaudeville en travesti* that always presented the leading actress with the chance to dress in male clothing and parade her shapely legs. Some contemporary critics, and more notably, actors, thought productions such as these had a rather less than artistic intention. This vaudeville, was, however, a complete failure and stayed in the repertoire for a mere four performances. Reasons for the debacle would include the inability of the leading actress to sing in tune, and its rather pro-Polish sentiments and pleas against chauvinistic opinions would have scarcely struck a sympathetic chord with contemporary audiences. The music, however, with its polonaises and mazurkas composed by Aleksei Verstovskii, has much to recommend it.

None of these plays gave any hint of what was to follow, his masterpiece *Gore ot uma* (*Woe from Wit*), which, with the exception of Gogol's *Revizor* (*The Government Inspector*), is by far the best Russian 19th-century comedy. Probably finished in 1823, it was produced, with cuts, in St Petersburg two years later. It was published, also censored, in 1833 and the full text appeared only in 1861. It is written in rhymed iambics, with lines of varying length, the verse being lively and innovative. Pushkin's prophecy that many of its lines would become proverbial and part of everyday speech has proved correct. The play retains many of the conventions of Russian Neoclassicism: the versification; the unities of time (24 hours), place (the Famusov household), and action (a picture of Moscow society); symbolic names for many of the characters; the love interest. It presents a bitingly satirical portrait of the contemporary society, culturally backward, politically conservative, and resistant to any change. Returning to Moscow, a young man, Chatskii, who is the earliest embodiment of the "superfluous man" in Russian literature, rails against all he sees there, finds himself out of place, and feels no possibility of any reconciliation. He finally runs from the home, Moscow and perhaps even Russia itself. The characters are convincingly and wonderfully created and they all retain their individuality. The dialogue is superb, the humour engaging. Despite its Neoclassical form it has often been presented as the first great work of Russian romanticism.

A.V. KNOWLES

Woe from Wit

Gore ot uma

Play, 1825

Griboedov first conceived the idea of writing a satirical drama in his late teens, the plan and earliest drafts going back to 1812. Over the period 1822–24 he wrote *Woe from Wit*; (also known in English as *Wit Works Woe*, *The Misfortune of Being Clever*, *The Disadvantages of Being Clever*, *Chatsky*, etc). Aleksandr Pushkin was one of the first to read it, in January 1825, and on doing so he issued a famous and accurate prediction that half of its lines would soon become Russian proverbs. The play could not be staged, because of difficulties with the censor's office, until 1831, at the St Petersburg Bolshoi Theatre, by which time the young author was two years dead. The uncensored version was kept out of print until 1864.

In regard to its form *Woe from Wit*, the last serious play in Russian to use verse, looks back to the 18th century. It is written in free iambic lines (from one to 13 syllables, almost half of them being hexameters); it contains characters with funny names (Famusov (Mr Famous), Skalozub (Mr Grinning), etc.); it obeys the three unities; its plot is unoriginal. The story concerns a young nobleman, Aleksandr Chatskii, who returns to Moscow after a three-year absence in order to pick up the threads of a relationship with a young lady, Sof'ia, and also to speak out against the corruption of contemporary life in Russia. After a number of caustic denunciations and furious clashes he is taken for a revolutionary and then, worse still, for a madman, and rejected by Sof'ia. She also ends badly, her relationship with the odious careerist, Molchalin, having been exposed as an attempt on his part to ingratiate himself with her father while at the same time trying his luck with her maid, Liza. Chatskii departs, presumably to continue his travels and take his complaints elsewhere. Moscow settles back into its familiar complacency, unruffled and unaffected by Chatskii's censures. After all that has been said and observed, Famusov's only concern in the closing words of the play are, "What will Princess Maria Alekseevna have to say about this?" – a clear and dispiriting measure of the hero's failure.

The story and characters of the play make little lasting impact on the imagination; they lack verisimilitude, meaningful interaction and any real sense of resolution. Chatskii stands quite alone ("twenty-five fools and one sensible man", as the author put it), mainly because he has been complaining to the wrong listeners, immovable old conservatives. In dramatic terms these people, however amusing as they parade before him in all their nauseating smugness and mediocrity, are two-dimensional figures borrowed from Fonvizin and others. Another 18th-century tendency is for the characters to prefer to address the audience rather than speak to each other. For these reasons, and also because of the play's extreme topicality, *Woe from Wit* has made little impression outside Russia. A bold attempt was made in 1993 when a new English translation, from the pen of a gifted, Russian-speaking writer, Anthony Burgess, was staged in London with a first-rate director and cast, but it made little impact beyond a few moments of linguistic cleverness. This is truly a play for which knowledge of the original language and the historical background appear to be essential.

For all its inability to impress foreign audiences, this work has attained remarkable heights of popularity and significance at home. There are good reasons for its success. Among all the stereotypes there is some outstanding characterization, Chatskii and Famusov (Sof'ia's father) presenting wonderful opportunities for the accomplished actor, and Sof'ia requiring a good deal of subtlety from an actress, since her character is unusually positioned halfway between foolishness and innocence. The humour, which covers a broad range, is shot through with venomous ironies producing a memorably acidic tone. Above all, satire worthy of Juvenal at his sourest and the bitterest sarcasm known to Russian letters pour out together in dialogue and monologue as the socio-political rhetoric of *Woe from Wit* strikes with vituperative directness. Chatskii's set-piece denunciations are among the most potent examples of declamatory vindictiveness in Russian verse or prose. The actual language of the play, the element that most stubbornly defies transposition on to the foreign stage, amounts to a unique achievement in Russian culture. *Woe from Wit* is, in proportion to its size, the most frequently quoted work in all Russian literature, from Pushkin to Nabokov and beyond. Dozens of lines, half-lines and happy phrases have entered the language and buried themselves deep in modern Russian speech, many of them no longer recognized in terms of their origin. For all the constraints imposed by the verse medium Griboedov's polished expressions shine with aptness, intelligence, epigrammatic incisiveness, and sardonic humour. The nearest parallel in western literature would be found in Oscar Wilde's prose, though without the self-advertising flamboyancy, whereas Griboedov's impact on the modern idiom of his compatriots can only be compared, on a smaller scale, to that of Shakespeare on modern English.

On the evidence of Griboedov's irrepressible fascination for literature and the unusual qualities of his one well-known work, there is every reason to believe that this man's premature death at the hands of Islamic fanatics in Teheran deprived Russian culture of untold works of genius which would surely have come from his pen.

A.D.P. Briggs

Dmitrii Vasil'evich Grigorovich 1822–1900

Prose writer

Biography

Born in Simbirsk, 31 March 1822. Attended Moscow gymnasium and private *pensions* from 1833; School of Engineers, St Petersburg, 1836–40. Lived in St Petersburg and shared an apartment with Dostoevskii, 1844. Visited Europe aboard the *Retvizan*, 1858 and recorded his experience in a series of sketches. Abandoned literature and became Secretary of the Society for the Encouragement of the Arts (*Obshchestvo pooshchreniia iskusstv*), 1864. Married in 1881. Began to publish again, 1883. "Discovered" Chekhov, 1886. Died in Vienna, 3 January 1900.

Publications

Collected Editions

Polnoe sobranie sochinenii, 12 vols. St Petersburg, 1896.
Izbrannye proizvedeniia. Moscow, 1959.
Izbrannoe (povesti i rasskazy). Moscow, 1984.

Fiction

Derevnia [The Village], *Otechestvennye zapiski*, 1846.
Anton-Goremyka, *Sovremennik*, 11 (1847); translated as "Anton", in *Anton; The Peasant. Two Stories of Serfdom*, by Michael Pursglove and N. Allan, Reading, Whiteknights Press, 1991.

Proselochnye dorogi [The By-Ways], *Otechestvennye zapiski*, 1–7 (1852).
Rybaki, *Sovremennik*, 1853; translated as *The Fishermen*, by A.S. Rappaport, Philadelphia, McKay, and London, Stanley Paul, 1916; reprinted 1920; 1925.
Pereselentsy [The Settlers], *Otechestvennye zapiski*, 1855–56.
Shkola gostepriimstva [The School of Hospitality], *Biblioteka dlia chteniia*, 1855.
Korabl' Retvizan [The Retvizan]. 1859–63.
Dva generala [Two Generals], *Russkii vestnik*, 1864.

Memoirs
Literaturnye vospominaniia [Literary Reminiscences], *Russkaia mysl'*, 1892–93; Moscow, 1961.

Play
Zamshevye liudi [The People of Chamois]. St Petersburg, 1891.

Critical Studies
"Grigorovich's 'The Village': An Etude in Sentimental Naturalism", by Robert L. Strong, Jr, *Slavic and East European Journal*, 12 (1968), 169–75.
"Peterburgskie povesti D.V. Grigorovicha: problema geroia", by M.V. Otradin, *Filologicheskie nauki*, 19/2 (1977), 21–31.
"A Landlord's Sketches?: D.V. Grigorovich and Peasant Genre Fiction", by J. Woodhouse, *Journal of European Studies*, 16 (1986), 271–94.
D.V. Grigorovich: The Man Who Discovered Chekhov, by Michael Pursglove, Aldershot, Avebury, 1987.

Bibliography
"Rukopisi i perepiska D.V. Grigorovicha", edited by B.N. Kapeliush, in *Ezhegodnik rukopisnogo otdela Pushkinskogo doma*, Leningrad, 1969.

That Dmitrii Grigorovich should have become a writer is extraordinary. Both his mother and maternal grandmother were French and Grigorovich did not set eyes on a Russian book until the age of eight. The only occasion he had to use Russian was to speak to the serfs at Dulebino, the estate in Tula Province that his father had bought in 1825 and which is described in such stories as "Smedovskaia dolina" [Smedva Valley] (1852). Originally destined for a military career, Grigorovich was influenced to take up literature by Fedor Dostoevskii, who entered the School of Engineers in 1838 and was Grigorovich's flat-mate from 1844 to 1846. Indeed Grigorovich played a leading role in the celebrated events that led to the publication of Dostoevskii's first major work *Bednye liudi* (*Poor Folk*) in 1846. By that time Grigorovich had already published his first short stories, "Teatral'naia kareta" [The Theatre Coach] (1844), "Sosedka" [The Lady Neighbour] (1844), and "Sobachka" [The Lap Dog] (1845). In the same year he contributed to Nekrasov's almanac *Fiziologiia Peterburga* [The Physiology of Petersburg] a short story and a "physiological sketch", "Peterburgskie sharmanshchiki" [Petersburg Organ-Grinders], which, with its ponderously humorous style and preoccupation with the lower strata of society, anticipates much of Grigorovich's later work. Grigorovich's first major work, *Derevnia* [The Village], was also published in 1846. This book, like *Anton-Goremyka*, describes a peasant whose life is ruined by serfdom. Akulina is an orphan brought up by uncaring foster parents and married off to a brutal husband by a landlord who merely wishes to witness a "rustic" wedding. Both *Derevnia* and *Anton-Goremyka* had an enormous effect on contemporary opinion. Among those who hailed the stories as a new departure in the depiction of the Russian peasant were Belinskii, Turgenev and, later, Lev Tolstoi. Turgenev's more famous *Zapiski okhotnika* (*Sketches from a Hunter's Album*), the first of which appeared in the interval between the publication of Grigorovich's two stories, were strongly influenced by them. It is largely on the strength of *Derevnia* and *Anton-Goremyka* that Grigorovich is conventionally assigned to the post-Gogolian "Natural School". Many of his subsequent stories, such as "Svetloe khristovo voskresen'e" [Easter Sunday] (1850), and "Chetyre vremeni goda" [The Four Seasons] (1851), have a rural setting but, with the exception of "Bobyl'" [The Labourer] (1848), they are idyllic rather than acerbic in tone. He also wrote stories with a St Petersburg setting, the best of which are "Kapellmeister Suslikov" (1848), and the semi-autobiographical "Neudavshaiasia zhizn'" [An Unsuccessful Life] (1849). Sometimes he combines urban and rural themes, as, for example in "Pakhatnik i barkhatnik" [The Ploughman and the Dandy] (1860), and "Gorod i derevnia" [Town and Country] (1892).

In the 1850s Grigorovich produced three novels, which met with varying degrees of success. The first, *Proselochnye dorogi* [The By-Ways], has a rambling plot and a mass of episodic characters. It was seen as a poor imitation of Gogol''s *Mertvye dushi* (*Dead Souls*) and was a critical failure. Critical reaction to the second novel *Rybaki* (*The Fishermen*) was more favourable and a German translation soon appeared. Set among the fishing communities of the River Oka, its "homespun" heroes are epitomized by the stern patriarchal figure of Gleb Savinov. His defence of traditional rural values clearly reflects the author's own views. *Pereselentsy* [The Settlers] also has a rural setting. Grigorovich was criticized for his portrayal of a liberal-minded aristocratic family, the Belitsyns, which, to some, marked a departure from his earlier radicalism. Nevertheless the author claimed that this novel "finally established" his reputation. It may be an indication of this enhanced reputation that in 1856, together with Turgenev, Lev Tolstoi and Aleksandr Ostrovskii, he concluded a deal with *Sovremennik* whereby he would write exclusively for that journal. The agreement was shortlived and produced from Grigorovich four unremarkable stories: "Ocherk sovremennykh nravov" [A Sketch of Contemporary Mores], "V ozhidanii paroma" [Waiting for the Steamer], "Skuchnye liudi" [Tedious People], and "Koshka i myshka" [Cat and Mouse].

In 1857 Grigorovich visited Denmark, France, Spain and Italy by boat, recording his experiences in *Korabl' Retvizan* [The Retvizan]. The work illustrates Grigorovich's love of fine art, an interest he was to develop further when he abandoned literature in 1864. He felt out of sympathy with the prevailing climate of radicalism and his last novel, the neo-Gogolian *Dva generala* [Two Generals], was a failure. Furthermore, he had offended the radical left with his lampooning of Chernyshevskii in *Shkola gostepriimstva* [The School of Hospitality]. It was not until 1883 that he returned to literature with the famous and much reprinted "Guttaperchevyi mal'chik" [Gutta-percha Boy], a melodramatic story of circus life. During the 1880s he returned to the manner of "Petersburgskie sharmanshchiki" with two further "physiological sketches", "Kar'erist" [The Careerist] (1884), and "Son Karelina" [Karelin's Dream] (1887). The latter may have influenced Chekhov's "Spat' khochetsia" [Sleepy] and some critics have detected the influence of *Pereselentsy* on "Step'" ("The Steppe"), the work Chekhov produced in response to Grigorovich's famous letter of 25 March 1886, urging him to try something more ambitious in literature than the humorous anecdotes to which he had hitherto confined himself. In 1891 Grigorovich, who had always taken a close interest in the theatre and had, as a young man, contemplated a career as an actor, wrote a five-act play, *Zamshevye liudi* [The People of Chamois]. The title refers to hypocritical philanthropists. In 1892 Grigorovich published his *Literaturnye vospominaniia* [Literary Reminiscences], which chronicled his career up to 1864 in a highly readable but factually inaccurate manner and gave ample written evidence of Grigorovich's notoriously caustic tongue, if not of his equally notorious philandering.

Although dwarfed by the great giants of 19th-century Russian literature, Grigorovich is a far from insignificant figure. A writer of considerable talent, he was an influential figure in Russian cultural life for more than 50 years. One of his obituarists summed up his career thus: "His talent was not of the greatest but he did have a virtue which is often undervalued in a writer: a pure, undeviating quest for Truth."

MICHAEL PURSGLOVE

Anton-Goremyka

Story, 1847

Together with the earlier novella *Derevnia*, this work constitutes Grigorovich's main contribution to the "Natural School" of writers who specialized in scenes of low-life, both urban and rural and who wrote sympathetically of the unhappy lot of the downtrodden poor. The word "goremyka" is difficult to translate. It derives from two roots: the noun "gore", meaning "grief", "woe", "wretchedness", which recurs frequently throughout the work, combined with the verb "mykat'", which has connotations of "dragging along" or "bearing a burden". A literal translation might be "The Wretch Anton". The eponymous hero of the story is a literate peasant who is forced by a bullying steward to pay off his debts by selling off his only horse at the local fair. Two gypsies pretend that they will get Anton a good price for the animal, but instead they steal his money. In desperation he turns to an old woman, who is supposed to have money, for help. He then falls in with her accomplices, one of whom is his long-lost brother Ermolai. They are all arrested for robbing a merchant and sent off to Siberia. Apollon Grigor'ev summarized it more succinctly: "A horribly long elegy about a stolen horse", but his negative reaction is not typical. Left-wing and liberal critics were unanimous in their praise. Belinskii, for example, the main Russian inspiration for the "Natural School", speaks highly of the work on several occasions, in both his published work and his private correspondence. A typical comment comes from a letter to Botkin: "Not a single Russian novella has produced on me such a terrible, oppressive, tormenting, stifling impression". Herzen, Turgenev, and Saltykov-Shchedrin write in similar vein, as do the Slavophiles I.S. Aksakov, S.P. Shevyrev, and M.P. Pogodin. The far right, in the persons of such critics as N.V. Berg and L.V. Brand, was unequivocally hostile to the work.

Anton-Goremyka is an angry denunciation of the harshness of rural life under serfdom. Its source is a real-life episode recounted in the memoirs of V.A. Sollogub, in which a notorious landlord was burned alive by rebellious peasants. In Grigorovich's original manuscript the same fate befell Nikita Fedorych but this was toned down by A.V. Nikitenko, who was a member of the censorship committee considering the story. Even in this toned-down version Grigorovich makes it plain that Anton's plight derives unequivocally from the evils inherent in the system, personified by his chief persecutor Nikita Fedorych. This mealy-mouthed, swindling steward is a close literary relative of Turgenev's Sofron in "Burmistr" ("The Bailiff"). We learn that, four years before the story opens, Anton, as the only literate man in the village, had acted as scribe for his fellow-villagers when they wanted to send a letter of complaint about Sofron's behaviour to their absentee landlord in St Petersburg. The letter was intercepted and with its interception the persecution of Anton had begun. His brother was sent off to the army and Anton was forcibly switched from paying quit-rent (*obrok*) to doing unpaid work on his landlord's land (*barshchina*), was given poor land to work and was refused permission to sell his goods in the town. Yet the steward's treatment of Anton is only a link in a long chain. Nikolai Fedorych himself has been foisted with his former landlord's discarded mistress and with Fatimka, who, it is broadly hinted, is the landlord's illegitimate daughter. Similarly, the two men who steal Anton's horse are depicted as victims of the harshness of rural life. *Anton-Goremyka* also has considerable literary merits. Belinskii comments on this in the letter to Botkin cited above: "Good Heavens, what knowledge of the ordinary Russian people in the minutely detailed description of the fair". Belinskii had in mind the fourth chapter of the work that exemplifies a number of features of Grigorovich's style: exclamations, inventories, carefully recorded local dialectisms. The set-piece description of the fair is matched in chapter 5 by a description of a posting-station and is typical of Grigorovich's work as a whole. In many instances these digressions tend to interrupt the narrative flow and appear to be indulged in for their own sake but in *Anton-Goremyka* they are fully integrated into the plot and serve to emphasize, for example, the helpless bafflement of the central character.

There is no doubting the impact of *Anton-Goremyka* on Grigorovich's contemporaries. Dostoevskii, for instance, who has the hero of *Podrostok* (*A Raw Youth*), 1875, retire to the country to read *Anton-Goremyka* and Druzhinin's *Polinka Saks*, describes them as "two literary works which had a huge civilizing influence on the younger generation of the time". In 1891 Lev Tolstoi, in one of his many lists, rated the story as having produced a "very big" impression on him, bigger even than that produced by Gogol''s "Shinel'" ("The Overcoat"). In 1893, on the 50th anniversary of Grigorovich's literary debut, Tolstoi again harked back to the story:

> I remember the emotion and rapture produced by ... *Anton*, which was a joyful revelation that one could and should describe the Russian peasant – our provider and, I would like to say, our teacher – without mockery, and not merely as a means of enlivening the landscape.

The radical Stepniak-Kravchinskii, also writing in the 1890s, bears out Tolstoi's comment, saying that, in its day, the work was as influential as Harriet Beecher Stowe's *Uncle Tom's Cabin*, while Vengerov, writing in 1900 talks of the "historical significance" of the story and, like many others, links it with Turgenev's *Sketches from a Hunter's Album*. In 1907 Kropotkin commented: "Not a single educated man of that time – or later, during my youth – could read of the miseries of Anton without weeping and being outraged at the horrors of serfdom". In Soviet times, as a "politically correct" work, the story was reprinted on numerous occasions. In post-Soviet times, however, the work appears to have been almost entirely forgotten.

MICHAEL PURSGLOVE

Aleksandr Stepanovich Grin 1880–1932

Prose writer

Biography

Born Aleksandr Stepanovich Grinevskii in Slobodskoi near Viatka, 23 August 1880. Educated at home and at schools in Viatka. Left Viatka for Odessa, 1896, served on Crimean ships. Travelled to Alexandria, 1897. Worked as clerk in Viatka, 1897; left for Baku, 1898; various casual jobs in south and in Urals, 1898–1900. Served in the army at Penza, March, 1902: deserted with help of local Socialist Revolutionaries, November 1902. Propaganda work for Socialist Revolutionary Party in Nizhnii Novgorod, Ekaterinoslav, Kiev, and Odessa, 1903. Arrested and jailed in Sebastopol, late 1903. Released under political amnesty before confirmation of ten-year sentence to Siberian exile, late 1905. Arrested again in St Petersburg, early 1906; exiled to Tobolsk Province; escaped *en route* and returned to Moscow. First story written in 1906. First legal work "V Italiiu" [To Italy] published December, 1906. Adopted the pseudonym A.S. Grin in 1907. Arrested as escaped exile and exiled again, to Archangel Province for two years, 1910. Married: 1) Vera Pavlovna Abramova in 1910 (separated 1913); 2) Nina Nikolaevna Koroshkova (née Mironova) in 1918. Exempted as unfit from tsarist army service, 1914. Banished from Petrograd to Finland for making derogatory remarks about the tsar, 1916; returned to Petrograd, February, 1917. Served in the Red Army, 1919–20. Lived in House of Arts in Petrograd, 1920–21. Moved from Petrograd to Feodosia, Crimea, 1924. Moved from Feodosia to Stary Krym, late 1930. Died in Stary Krym, 8 July 1932.

Publications

Collected Editions

Sobranie sochinenii, 3 vols. 1913.
Sobranie sochinenii, 15 vols (of which vols 2, 5, 6, 8, 11–14 appeared). 1927–29.
Sobranie sochinenii, 6 vols. Moscow, 1965; reprinted 1980.
"Alexander Grin (Four Stories)", translated by Nicholas Luker and R. Rotsel, *Russian Literature Triquarterly*, 8 (1974), 177–91.
The Seeker of Adventure: Selected Stories [no translator named], Moscow, Progress, 1978.
Selected Short Stories, translated by Nicholas Luker. Ann Arbor, Michigan, Ardis, 1987.
Sobranie sochinenii, 5 vols. Moscow, 1991.

Fiction

Shapka-nevidimka [The Magic Cap]. St Petersburg, 1908.
Alye parusa. Moscow and Petrograd, 1923; translated as *Scarlet Sails*, by Thomas P. Whitney, New York, Scribner, 1967.
Blistaiushchii mir [The Shining World], *Krasnaia niva*, 20–30 (1923).
Zolotaia tsep' [The Golden Chain], *Novyi mir*, 8–11 (1925).
Begushchaia po volnam [She Who Runs on the Waves]. 1928.
Dzhessi i Morgiana. Leningrad, 1929; reprinted Leningrad, 1966.
Doroga nikuda [The Road to Nowhere]. Moscow, 1930.
Ogon' i voda [Fire and Water]. Moscow, 1930.

Critical Studies

"Iz neizdannogo i zabytogo", by V. Rossel's, in *Literaturnoe nasledstvo*, Moscow, 1965, 629–68.
Romanticheskii mir Aleksandra Grina, by V. Kovskii, Moscow, 1969.
Aleksandr Grin, by E.P. Prokhorov, Moscow, 1970.
Vospominaniia ob Aleksandre Grine, edited by V. Sandler, Leningrad, 1972.
Alexander Grin, by Nicholas Luker, Letchworth, Bradda, 1973.
"Alexander Grin: A Survey", by Nicholas Luker, *Russian Literature Triquarterly*, 8 (1974), 341–61.
Poeziia i proza Aleksandra Grina, by V.V. Kharchev, Gorkii, 1975.
"Aleksandr Grin's 'Scarlet Sails' and the Fairy Tale", by Barry Scherr, *Slavic and East European Journal*, 20/4 (1976), 387–99.
"Alexander Grin's *Grinlandia*", by Nicholas Luker, in *Russian and Slavic Literature*, edited by Richard Freeborn *et al.*, Cambridge, Massachusetts, Slavica, 1976, 190–212.
Aleksandr Grin: The Forgotten Visionary, by Nicholas Luker, Newtonville, Massachusetts, Oriental Research Partners, 1980.
Aleksandr Grin, by L. Mikhailova, Moscow, 2nd edition, 1980.
"Flight of Fancy: Aleksandr Grin's novel *The Shining World* (*Blistaiushchii mir*, 1923)", by Nicholas Luker, in *Russian*

Literature and Criticism, edited by Evelyn Bristol, Berkeley, Berkeley Slavic Specialties, 1982, 111–29.
Roman Aleksandra Grina, by N.A. Kobzev, Kishinev, 1983.
"The Triumph of Conviction: Aleksandr Grin's *Alyye parusa* (*Scarlet Sails*)" by Nicholas Luker, *New Zealand Slavonic Journal*, (1987), 93–105.
Etiko-esteticheskaia kontseptsiia cheloveka i prirody v tvorchestve A. Grina, by I.K. Dunaevskaia, Riga, 1988.

Bibliographies
"A Selected Bibliography of Works by and about Alexander Grin (1880–1932)", in *10 Bibliographies of 20th Century Russian Literature*, edited by Fred Moody, Ann Arbor, Ardis, 1977, 103–18.
Aleksandr Grin: Bibliograficheskii ukazatel', by Iu.V. Kirkin, Moscow, 1980.

An utter exotic among his fellow-writers, Aleksandr Grin is one of Russian literature's most fascinating oddities. The bizarre legends that surrounded his name – notably that he was a ruthless desperado who systematically plagiarized the writings of an English sea captain whom he had robbed and killed in the Indian Ocean – were reinforced by both his chequered youth and the curiously foreign flavour of his work.

Stifled by his youth in philistine Viatka, the contemplative boy read voraciously. He was enthralled by romantic adventure writers such as Fenimore Cooper, Mayne Reid, and Bret Harte, compensating in impassioned dreams for the inadequacies of his unstimulating environment. It was in these early years filled with dissatisfaction and loneliness that his imaginary country, Grinlandiia had its beginnings. At school he composed satirical verse and occasionally offered pieces to the weekly journals *Rodina* and *Niva*, but without success. Much later, in 1902, his desertion from the army marked a watershed in his life, for it was while attached to the Socialist Revolutionary Party that he began to write. 1906 saw the appearance of his first two tales: "Zasluga riadovogo Panteleeva" [Private Panteleev's Service] and "Slon i mos'ka" [The Elephant and the Pug-dog], both illegal Socialist Revolutionary propaganda pamphlets. They were followed by "V Italiiu" [To Italy] (1906), his first legal story. In March 1907 he first used the pseudonym that would become customary for him, A.S. Grin. The following year brought the publication in St Petersburg of his first collection of stories, *Shapka-nevidimka* [The Magic Cap], subtitled *Rasskazy o revoliutsionerakh* [Tales of Revolutionaries], its ten varied items deriving from his Socialist Revolutionary experiences both in propaganda work and in prison. The year 1909 saw the appearance of his exotic story "Ostrov Reno" [Reno Island], which he would always consider his first work of genuine artistic merit and the turning-point in his career. Like "Koloniia Lanfier" [The Lanfier Colony] (1910), it has an imaginary setting and so anticipates the elaborate environment of his mature Grinlandiia.

Amazingly, Grin's continued disorderly way of life in St Petersburg after the outbreak of World War I did not prevent him from contributing scores of stories, fables, and poems to various cheaper periodicals, notably *Novyi satirikon*, *Sinii zhurnal*, and the popular *Dvadtsatyi vek*. The war prompted him to write many brief but effective tales on military themes, and though most are highly chauvinistic in tone, several are talented pieces that display great sensitivity to the feelings of ordinary people about war. As far as is known, however, he wrote very little that directly reflects the political and social crises suffered by Russia in 1917. Only the stories "Krasnye bryzgi" [Red Splashes of Blood] and "Trupy" [The Corpses], probably written shortly before the Bolshevik *coup d'état* in October 1917, convey some impression of the upheavals of that time.

The most significant year of Grin's career was 1920, for it saw the completion of his first novella, *Alye parusa* (*Scarlet Sails*), the work now traditionally associated with his name. He had been working intermittently on it since 1916 – after being struck by the sight of a beautiful yacht with scarlet sails in a Petrograd toyshop – and had carried the manuscript in his kit-bag throughout his months of war service. Vividly illustrating the power of conviction, the work was published in 1923.

Scarlet Sails was followed by five novels and dozens of varied tales, the vast majority set in Grinlandiia. While 1922 saw the appearance of the moving story "Korabli v Lisse" [Ships in Liss], one of Grin's finest pieces, the following year brought the publication of his novel *Blistaiushchii mir* [The Shining World], an unusual work whose hero possesses the miraculous gift of unaided flight and is persecuted for it by a repressive state. It was followed by *Zolotaia tsep'* [The Golden Chain], a novel of mystery and intrigue in the standard adventure style that emphasizes the illusory nature of wealth. The mid-1920s also saw the appearance of several successful stories, among them "Brak Avgusta Esborna" [Augustus Esborn's Marriage] and "Zmeia" [The Snake], while 1925 and 1926 brought the publication of no fewer than six collections of Grin's tales.

The intricate and haunting *Begushchaia po volnam* [She Who Runs on the Waves], arguably Grin's finest novel, appeared in 1928. It centres on a beautiful legendary sea wraith who runs forever across the ocean, generously helping those in distress. In persuasively lyrical terms, the work asserts through its many symbols every individual's right to his personal dream.

By contrast, 1928 also brought the completion of the little-known *Dzhessi i Morgiana*, a dark novel of jealousy and attempted murder that would prove the least successful of Grin's major pieces when published in 1929. Totally different was his last completed novel, *Doroga nikuda* [The Road to Nowhere], a powerful condemnation of passivity. It gave Grin the idea for *Nedotroga* [Touch-Me-Not], a novel begun in late 1930 but left unfinished at Grin's death. Sadly, the early 1930s showed the growing effects of RAPP's hard line Stalinist literary domination: Grin had fewer than ten items published in 1930 (among them the collection *Ogon' i voda* [Fire and Water]), and just five in 1931. Three new tales appeared only posthumously, in 1933, after RAPP was disbanded.

Throughout his life Grin went unrecognized by both the majority of critics and most contemporary writers, who failed to perceive the moral and spiritual values central to his *Weltanschauung*. Attacked as a rootless cosmopolitan and bourgeois reactionary in the late Stalin period, he began to enjoy proper critical evaluation only after 1956. His Grinlandiia is much more than an exotic setting where strenuous adventure and romantic love await those who escape from the real world. It is an environment geographically and politically independent of actuality where the forces of good may fearlessly engage those of evil. Since they are not political but moral and spiritual, the problems Grin poses and the solutions he offers are of universal significance. He believes that by spiritual strength and conviction man can turn his romantic ideal into living fact. In acquiring the dimensions and authenticity of an additional sub-continent, his Grinlandia became the setting where romantic visions could be miraculously transformed into reality.

NICHOLAS LUKER

Scarlet Sails

Alye parusa

Novella, 1923

The novella *Scarlet Sails* is Grin's best-known work, its title a symbol of the value of aspiration and purity of heart. Critics' reactions to it, though, were unkind: they saw its avoidance of contemporary issues as proof of Grin's lack of enthusiasm for the revolutionary cause and its romantic theme as irrelevant beside pressing contemporary concerns.

Anticipated by Grin's poem *Melodiia* [Melody], the work tells how, after her mother's death, the young Assol is brought up by her loving father, Longren, in the village of Kaperna near Liss in Grin's imaginary country of Grinlandiia. Grey, the only son of aristocratic parents, spends his childhood in a feudal castle, being groomed to take his place in the distinguished family line. While Assol lives in poverty, Grey is surrounded by plenty. One day Assol meets Egl, a wandering collector of folk-songs and fairy-tales, who predicts that when she is older, a handsome prince will come on a ship rigged with scarlet sails and carry her off to happiness in a shining land. Despite the villagers' derision, the girl believes stubbornly in this fantasy. Seven years later, finding Assol by chance asleep on the shore and learning of her faith in Egl's prophecy, Grey, now master of his own ship, fulfils her dream by equipping his vessel with scarlet sails and taking her away from Kaperna forever.

The eventual special destiny of hero and heroine is foreshadowed by their solitariness in childhood. Assol is lonely because she is rejected by other children who are influenced by their parents' antipathy towards her father. Grey, though, is isolated not socially but spiritually, because his unusual temperament makes him the black sheep of the family. He has no desire to comply with his parents' wishes for his future. Like Assol, he is introspective and solitary, living in a world of his own. Both hero and heroine break with their environments. Assol is forced to do so by external circumstances: scorned by the villagers for her faith in Egl's prophecy, she is obliged to join her father in his withdrawn way of life. The hostile environment of Kaperna thus predisposes her to believe in a dream that promises happiness, and Egl's prediction supplies that dream. By contrast, Grey's break with his milieu is wholly voluntary, the logical outcome of his compulsive need to go to sea. The picture of a sailing ship amid stormy seas, which he sees as a boy in his father's library, convinces him that the life of a sailor is the only one for him. What Egl's prediction does for Assol, the picture does for Grey, serving as "that necessary word in the dialogue between the soul and life, a word without which it is difficult to understand oneself".

Grin subtitled *Scarlet Sails* a "fairy-tale" (*feeriia*), and, in keeping with the conventions of that genre, the work's secondary characters are divided into "good" and "bad". Inspired by Egl's prophecy, Assol's dream is the agent of this division, and characters' attitudes to that dream determine into which category they fall. The small minority, who neither mock the girl for her faith nor attempt to disillusion her, constitute the "good" group. Longren, for instance, does not disenchant his daughter, while treating the prediction as only a kindly joke. The great majority, however, who ridicule Assol, constitute the "bad" group. The shopkeeper Menners, notably, describes Assol to Grey as a "half-wit obsessed with an absurd fantasy". But sympathy or scorn for Assol's dream becomes widened by Grin into an ethical contrast between the two groupings that is far more subtle than the white/black stereotypes found in the traditional fairy tale. The people of Kaperna are wholly devoid of the poetic sensitivity and spiritual beauty that distinguish both Assol and Grey. Limited and bigoted, they are unable to appreciate anything beyond their restricted ideas and pedestrian interests. They are instinctively hostile towards the unusual, hence their enmity for the girl who can believe wholeheartedly in the prophetic words spoken by a gentle old man.

That Grey is brought up in a castle and surrounded by abundance, while Assol, a poor sailor's daughter, knows only a humble village dwelling, is not important. The social differences between his hero and heroine do not primarily concern Grin. Though socially dissimilar, they are alike spiritually: each lives for the beautiful and unexpected. Moreover, both possess the ability to see beyond the immediately apparent, "beyond the visible". Assol can perceive the hidden essence of things ("everything around her became a gossamer web of mystery with the outward appearance of everyday life"). Furthermore, she dreams not at isolated moments but for most of the time, and lives altogether naturally in constant expectation of the fabulous. Grey shares her ability to feel over and above the apparent, in a second dimension of experience. And both see the unusual and mysterious as an accepted part of their lives. Just as she lives quite normally within the domain of fantasy, so he sees nothing strange in the splendid finale he engineers to realize her dream according to Egl's prophecy. Thus the ultimate happiness together of Assol and Grey emerges as the logical result of an organized process in which each plays an essentially passive role.

Scarlet Sails develops two themes central to Grin's romantic work. First, that given a powerfully creative imagination, one can fulfil not only one's own dreams but also those of others; and second, that beauty and fantasy constitute a formidable weapon against the insensitivity and malice of philistines like the people of Kaperna. The story demonstrates that unflinching faith in an ideal renders the believer immune to evil. For Grin the attitudes epitomized by Kaperna were prevalent among mankind and posed a grave threat to the precious aspirations of the small minority represented by Assol and Grey. But the glorious departure of Grey's vessel at the close is an escape from the problem, not its solution.

However inconclusive its denouement in wider terms, *Scarlet Sails* remains a work of unbridled optimism. Steadfast conviction and indomitable fantasy win the day over the forces of darkness and malice, and the visionary who was so cruelly scorned stands vindicated amid a blaze of triumphant happiness.

NICHOLAS LUKER

Vasilii Semenovich Grossman 1905–1964

Prose writer

Biography

Born in Berdichev, Ukraine, 12 December 1905. Attended secondary school in Kiev, 1914–19; Institute of Higher Education, Kiev, 1921; studied chemistry, Moscow University, 1924–29. Chemical analyst in the Donbass until tuberculosis diagnosed, 1932. Worked in Moscow pencil factory. Married twice. Published *Glück auf!*, 1934. Joined the Writers' Union, 1937. Second wife, Ol'ga Mikhailovna, arrested in 1937; Grossman wrote to Ezhov requesting her release; released, 1938. *Stepan Kol'chugin* published 1937–40. Nominated for Stalin Prize: denounced as "Menshevist" by Stalin, deleted from nominees. Joined military newspaper, *Krasnaia zvezda*, August 1941. Served on Briansk and Central Fronts. Reported Battle of Stalingrad, his sketches widely read. Detailed account of Nazi atrocities published as *Treblinskii ad* [The Hell of Treblinka], 1944. Grossman's only play published in 1946; attacked for non-materialist interpretation of history. *Za pravoe delo* [For a Just Cause] nominated by Aleksandr Fadeev for Stalin Prize; during campaign against so-called Doctors' Plot, Grossman again attacked. Sequel, *Zhizn' i sud'ba* (*Life and Fate*), finished 1960, published in the west, 1980. Recipient: medal "For Valour"; Red Banner of Labour for services to Soviet literature. 1955. Died in Moscow, 14 September 1964.

Publications

Collected Editions

Rasskazy. Moscow, 1937.
Stalingrad Hits Back, translated by A. Fineberg and D. Fromberg. Moscow, Foreign Languages Publishing House, 1942.
Stalingradskaia bitva [The Battle of Stalingrad]. Moscow, 1943.
Gody voiny. Moscow, 1946; translated as *The Years of War*, by Elizabeth Donnelly and Rose Prokofiev, Moscow, Foreign Languages Publishing House, 1946.
Zhizn', Rasskazy [Life, Short Stories]. Moscow, 1947.
Povesti i rasskazy. Moscow, 1950.
Povesti, Rasskazy, Ocherki. Moscow, 1958.
Staryi uchitel'. Povesti i rasskazy [The Old Teacher]. Moscow, 1962.
Dobro vam! [Peace Be to You!]. Moscow, 1967.
Neskol'ko pechal'nykh dnei [Several Sad Days]. Moscow, 1989.
Gody voiny [The Years of the War]. Moscow, 1989.
Vse techet: pozdnaia proza [Everything Flows: Late Prose]. Moscow, 1994.

Fiction

"Glück auf!", *God XVII, Al'manakh*, 4 (1934).
Schast'e [Happiness]. Moscow, 1935.
Chetyre dnia [Four Days]. Moscow, 1936.
Stepan Kol'chugin. 1937–40; as separate edition, Moscow, 1947; 1951; translated as *Kol'chugin's Youth, A Novel*, by Rosemary Edmonds, London and New York, Hutchinson, 1946.
Narod bessmerten. Moscow, 1943; translated as *No Beautiful Nights*, by Elizabeth Donnelly, New York, Soviet Russia Today, 1943; as *The People Are Immortal*, London, Hutchinson, n.d.
"Za pravoe delo" [For a Just Cause], *Novyi mir*, 7–10 (1952); as separate edition Moscow, 1956; 1964; 1989.
Vse techet, Frankfurt, Posev, 1970; 1974; *Oktiabr'*, 6 (1989), 30–108; translated as *Forever Flowing*, by Thomas P. Whitney, New York, Harper and Row, 1972; London, André Deutsch, 1973; London, Collins and Harvill, 1988.
Zhizn' i sud'ba. Lausanne, L'Âge d'Homme, 1980; *Oktiabr'*, 1–4 (1988); Moscow, 1989; 1990; translated as *Life and Fate*, by Robert Chandler, London, Collins and Harvill, 1985; London, Harvill Press, 1995.

Play

"Esli verit' pifagoreitsam" [If You Believe the Pythagoreans], *Znamia*, 7 (1946), 68–107.

Essays and Travel Writing

Treblinskii ad [The Hell of Treblinka]. Moscow, 1945.
"Poezdka v Kirgiziiu" [Trip to Kirgizia], *God XXXI, Al'manakh Pervyi*, Moscow, 1948, 207–37.
"V znakomykh mestakh" [In Familiar Places], *Ogonek*, 45 (1953), 9–16.
"Vasilii Grossman, iz zapisnykh knizhek voennykh let" [Vasilii Grossman, From His Wartime Notebooks], *Voprosy literatury*, 6 (1987), 157–77.

Editor

Chernaia kniga, with Il'ia Erenburg, Jerusalem, Tarbut, 1980.

Critical Studies

Nezabyvaemye vstrechi, by Lidiia Bat', Moscow, 1970.
Vasilii Grossman. Kritiko-biograficheskii ocherk, by Anatolii Bocharov, Moscow, 1970.
Na evreiskie temy. Vasilii Grossman, by Shimon Markish, Jerusalem and New York, Biblioteka Aliia, Sifrit-Aliia, 1985.
Stalingrad Vasiliia Grossmana, by Semen Lipkin, Ann Arbor, Ardis, 1986.
Vasilii Grossman. Zhizn', Sud'ba, Tvorchestvo, by Anatolii Bocharov, Moscow, 1990.
Zhizn' i sud'ba Vasiliia Grossmana/Proshchanie, by Anna Berzer and Semen Lipkin, Moscow, 1990.
"Vasiliy Grossman: The Challenge to Ideology", by Frank Ellis, in *Perestrojka und Literatur*, edited by Eberhard Reißner, Berlin, Arno Spitz, 1990, 25–43.
"Vasilii Grossman: The Genesis of Heresy 1937–41", by Frank Ellis, *Modern Language Review*, 85/3 (1990), 653–66.
"A Conflict of Visions. Vasilii Grossman and the Russian Idea", by John Garrard, in *The Search for Self-Definition in Russian Literature*, edited by Ewa M. Thompson, Amsterdam, John Benjamins, 1991, 57–75.

"Stepsons in the Motherland. The Architectonics of Vasilii Grossman's *Zhizn' i sud'ba*", by John Garrard, *Slavic Review*, 50/2 (1991), 336–46.
Zhizn' i sud'ba V. Grossmana: S raznykh tochek zreniia, edited by V.D. Oskotskii, Moscow, 1991.
Vasiliy Grossman: The Genesis and Evolution of a Russian Heretic, by Frank Ellis, Oxford, Berg, 1994.
"The Original Manuscript of *Forever Flowing*: Grossman's Autopsy of the New Soviet Man", by John Garrard, *Slavic and East European Journal*, 38/2 (1994), 271–89.
"Jewish Experience and Identity in Vasilii Grossman's Novels *Za pravoe delo* and *Zhizn' i sud'ba*", by Rita Geuzeleva, *Jews in Eastern Europe*, Spring (1994), 46–63.
The Bones of Berdichev: The Life and Fate of Vasily Grossman, by John Garrard and Carol Garrard, New York, Free Press, and London, Simon and Schuster, 1996.

The Soviet publication of *Zhizn' i sud'ba* (*Life and Fate*), 1988, and *Vse techet* (*Forever Flowing*), 1989, lifted the official anathema on Vasilii Grossman – in place since 1961 – and returned a writer to the public whose importance for Russian literature undoubtedly rivals that of Solzhenitsyn, Pasternak, Bulgakov, and Sholokhov.

Grossman made his literary debut in 1934 with the publication of "V gorode Berdicheve" [In the Town of Berdichev]. The story, part of Grossman's cycle set in the Russo-Polish war, depicts the fate of a female commissar, Vavilova, who falls pregnant and is left in the safe keeping of a Jewish family to give birth. Abandoning the child, she chooses the revolution. The quietism of her Jewish hosts and the dignity with which they persevere to hold their family together in the face of successive waves of Russian and Polish occupation are tacitly approved by Grossman and held up as a contrast to the heady romanticism of the revolutionaries. The work was favourably received, among others by Isaak Babel' ("Our Jewish capital has been seen through new eyes"). In 1962 the Soviet director A. Askol'dov adapted "V gorode Berdicheve" for the cinema. Entitled "The Commissar", the screen version narrowly escaped destruction, despite there being only a brief reference to Grossman, who in 1962 was in official disgrace. The film survived and was finally shown at the Berlin Film Festival in 1988.

Between 1929 and 1933 Grossman worked as a chemical analyst in the Donbass mines. This experience provided the basis for the novel *Glück auf!*, which Grossman submitted to Maksim Gor'kii in 1933. Gor'kii rejected the manuscript. Grossman rewrote the piece and *Glück auf!* was eventually published in 1934. This was followed by two separate collections of stories, *Schast'e* [Happiness] and *Chetyre dnia* [Four Days]. In 1937 Grossman joined the Writers' Union, devoting the next three years to the long novel *Stepan Kol'chugin* (*Kol'chugin's Youth*) described by one Soviet critic as "an epic of the socialist revolution".

These literary successes took place under the ever widening penumbra of Stalin's Terror and the deliberate fragmentation of Soviet society. In 1937 Grossman's second wife, Ol'ga Mikhailovna, was arrested. The most likely cause for her arrest was her first marriage to Boris Andreevich Guber, a member of the writers' group "Pereval" (The Pass). Whatever the reason, Grossman wrote to Ezhov requesting her release. She survived incarceration and was released in 1938.

Grossman's war service took him from the Briansk and Central fronts of 1941 to Stalingrad and thence to final victory in the ruins of Berlin in 1945. The summer retreat of 1941 served as the basis for his first successful *povest'*, *Narod bessmerten* (*The People Are Immortal*), but it was his reporting from Stalingrad that established Grossman's reputation as one of the Soviet Union's leading journalists alongside Simonov and Erenburg. In all Grossman wrote 13 sketches or *ocherki* for *Krasnaia zvezda*, many of which were reprinted in *Pravda*. They cover the full range of fighting at Stalingrad, reflecting the unremitting ferocity of the battle and the special nature of the fighting in an urban environment.

From 1946 until his death in 1964 Grossman became embroiled in a series of exhausting and bitter struggles with the Soviet literary establishment. The first took place in 1946, the year in which Stalin's Commissar of Culture, Andrei Zhdanov, initiated the *Zhdanovshchina*, an extensive purge of Soviet intellectual life. Grossman drew the fire of the Party after the publication of his play, *Esli verit' pifagoreitsam* [If You Believe the Pythagoreans] in *Znamia*. Written before the war, the play offers an interpretation of historical progress that owes very little to the dialectical materialism of the Party. Allusions to Heraclitus and Tacitus, as well as Pythagoras, complete the picture of an author who is at best highly sceptical towards the Party's claims that a society populated by the new Soviet man is being realized. The play was denounced by both Ermilov and Fadeev.

Worse was to come. Towards the end of 1952 Grossman was a target of sustained vilification that continued until after Stalin's death in 1953. The immediate cause of this latest attempt to break Grossman was the publication of *Za pravoe delo* [For a Just Cause], the first part of a long novel dedicated to the battle of Stalingrad. There is, however, no doubt that the attacks on Grossman were inextricably linked to the growing and virulent atmosphere of anti-Semitism characterized by the campaigns against "rootless cosmopolitans" and the frenzied exposure of the so-called Doctors' Plot. Stalin's timely death was probably the crucial factor in Grossman's survival.

The campaign to crush Grossman in the winter of 1952–53 marked the beginning of the final stages of his reckoning with Nazi and Soviet totalitarianism, a tortuous apostasy whose metamorphosis began in the 1930s. During the last decade of his life Grossman wrote *Life and Fate*, the chronological sequel to *Za pravoe delo*, and *Forever Flowing*, the devastating analysis of Lenin and Leninism.

Khrushchev's partial denunciation of Stalin in 1956 may well have encouraged Grossman to believe that publication of *Life and Fate* would be possible in the Soviet Union. In any case Grossman submitted the manuscript to the journal *Znamia* in October 1960. The editorial board denounced the novel as "anti-Soviet". A bizarre sequence of events ensued. In February 1961 the KGB "arrested" the novel. Even among the countless tales of betrayal and dreadful personal suffering, so familiar to the student of Russian letters, the arrest of Grossman's novel has its own special agony.

Grossman made strenuous efforts to secure the release of the manuscript. He wrote to Khrushchev, which led to a summons from Suslov, the Party's chief ideologist. There could, Suslov said, be no question of publication, at least not for some 250 to 300 years. Nor would the manuscript be returned. Still smarting from the adverse publicity surrounding the appearance of

Pasternak's *Doctor Zhivago* in the west, the Party was determined to close off all possible avenues of publication. Fortunately, the best efforts of the KGB were in vain. Copies of *Forever Flowing* and *Life and Fate* were smuggled out of the Soviet Union. *Forever Flowing* was published in West Germany in 1970, *Life and Fate* in Switzerland in 1980.

Grossman was little known to Soviet readers before publication of his main works under glasnost. *Life and Fate* and *Forever Flowing* constituted significant revelations, ensuring a place for their creator among the great names of Russian literature.

FRANK ELLIS

Forever Flowing

Vse techet

Novel, 1970

Even by the standards of the rehabilitation and publishing frenzy of the 1980s, the appearance of *Forever Flowing* in print in the Soviet Union was a remarkable political and literary event. Stark and totally uncompromising, *Forever Flowing* is Grossman's final reckoning with the Soviet state. Overwhelmingly, the targets of glasnost were Stalinism and the consolidation of the bureaucratic stratum during the Brezhnev years. In *Forever Flowing* Grossman goes to the roots of Stalinism, breaking the ultimate taboos of Soviet society: Lenin, the founder of the Soviet state and his political thought are pitilessly taken apart. Nothing like it had ever been written before. Such iconoclasm helps to explain, first the opposition to publication of *Forever Flowing*, and second, the determined attempts to limit the damage after publication.

Grossman employs a rich variety of styles and narrative techniques in the work. Logical analysis stripped of superfluous detail, irony, and understatement are the favoured weapons. Flashbacks to collectivization and the Terror remind the present of unpunished crimes. Conventional narrative is interspersed with digressions on Lenin's role in Russian history. Betrayal and envy, so essential to Stalin's consolidation of power, are examined in a mini-play. The long-suffering Ivan Grigor'evich is the hero of *Forever Flowing*. Released after many years in the camps, he returns to a Moscow that is trying to adjust itself to Stalin's death. He encounters those who denounced him, now well established in the Soviet intelligentsia, and desperate to justify themselves.

The systematic dismantling of the Leninist experiment, the theory and practice of which, Grossman argues, led ineluctably to Stalin, forms the deeply subversive core of *Forever Flowing*. Lenin, asserts Grossman, belongs to a long line of Russian autocrats. A vital difference, perhaps the single most important one, can be found in the articles of faith embodied in Marxism-Leninism. The absence of an analogous, all-embracing epistemology in the intellectual armoury of earlier Russian autocrats imposed limitations on their personal and imperial ambitions. However autocratic, the tsars were receptive to various liberal overtures to ameliorate the lot of their subjects: the abolition of serfdom was an obvious example.

Grossman identifies a number of reasons for the failure of the proletarian Utopia. First among them was the ethos of the party that was to rule the new Soviet society. Designed and tempered as an instrument for the prosecution of revolution and class war, Lenin's party was totally unsuited to the frustrations of democracy. Indeed, from the assumptions of the class struggle it followed that the class enemy had to be destroyed. Democracy and tolerance were politically incorrect. When a terrorist organization seizes power in the name of democracy or the proletariat, the result is terror on a grand scale. Again, this is quite consistent with a long and arduous underground struggle. No terrorist organization with a blueprint for a new order will voluntarily concede power – the whole point of the struggle – to a democratically elected body. The crushing of the Constituent Assembly on Lenin's orders was not unexpected. Grossman's dissection of Marxist-Leninist ideology builds on conclusions outlined in *Life and Fate*. Being an inclusive model of socio-economic reality based on class war, Marxism-Leninism can offer a ready-made tool for undermining most cultures and civilizations in a way in which Nazi race theory cannot. Perhaps most striking of all is Grossman's argument that the Leninist "synthesis of unfreedom with socialism" laid the foundations of Hitler's "new order".

When *Forever Flowing* was finally printed in *Oktiabr'* in June 1989, it was accompanied by a long article that bore the unmistakable stamp of the CPSU's Central Committee. The article, a discursive and tortuous apologia, was a desperate attempt to dissociate Lenin from Stalin, and thus preserve Leninist hagiography intact. Soviet officialdom's response to the publication of *Forever Flowing* comes as no surprise.

Western responses on the other hand have not been quite as straightforward. They range from conspicuous silence and anger to admiration. True, *Life and Fate* and *Forever Flowing* are now receiving the attention they deserve. Yet the fact remains that *Forever Flowing* was first published in the west as early as 1970. Apart from various reviews of Thomas Whitney's English translation, *Forever Flowing* was largely ignored by Anglophone scholarship until well into the 1980s. One possible explanation for this unusual neglect is ideological. In the early 1970s there was still considerable residual sympathy, even affection, for the Soviet Union among many western intellectuals. *Forever Flowing* would have forced them to confront the heart of a system that claimed to act in the name of human freedom yet raised the banner of totalitarianism ever higher. Moreover, in writing *Forever Flowing* Grossman discarded his earlier revolutionary convictions, breaking irrevocably with Soviet ideology. Such an intellectual and moral feat would have posed insuperable obstacles and challenges to western fellow-travellers devoted to the success of the Soviet enterprise. Shamed by their sympathy, the collectivist 1970s turned away in embarrassment from Grossman.

Then there is the question of Grossman's analysis of Russian history. Ideological opponents of Lenin could applaud the attacks on the Lenin cult and the Soviet state, but they were enraged by the notion of Russia's *rabskaia dusha* ("slave-like soul"). For them, Grossman adds insult to injury by challenging whether the Russian soul, venerated by Gogol' and Dostoevskii, has anything to offer Russia and the world. Russian émigrés in the 1970s bitterly resented what they regarded as Grossman's blatant Russophobia. (In the 1990s their ranks have been swollen by various coalitions of Russian nationalists.) Solzhenitsyn was a far more acceptable icon in the struggle against the Soviet Union than a Russian Jewish writer with heretical ideas. Taken together, these two factors, western intellectual fashion and wounded Russian national pride, offer some clues as to why *Forever Flowing* languished in obscurity for so long.

Both gloom and optimism can be found in the conclusion of *Forever Flowing*. The knowledge that the rudiments of the system, which had enslaved Russia were, even as Grossman was preparing his last great work for posterity, being exported wholesale beyond the borders of the Soviet Union, is deeply pessimistic. Hope, however, is implicit in Ivan Grigor'evich's stubborn refusal, like his creator, Vasilii Semenovich, to yield to the forces that generated the wretched hybrid, *homo sovieticus*.

FRANK ELLIS

Life and Fate

Zhizn' i sud'ba

Novel, 1980

Among the many testimonies written by those who have witnessed and survived the horrors of totalitarianism, *Life and Fate*, Grossman's *magnum opus*, occupies its own special niche. *Life and Fate* unravels the ideological web that bound Stalin's Russia and Hitler's Germany together. Far from dividing the two systems, eschatologies of race and class made them inseparable partners in a diabolical pact.

Life and Fate begins at a moment when the final outcome of the battle of Stalingrad remains undecided, although it is reaching its critical phase. Unable to break through the Russian defences, clinging precariously to the banks of the river Volga, the German offensive falters and loses momentum. Encircled as a result of a successful Soviet counter-offensive, the German 6th Army surrendered in February 1943.

As a purely firsthand account of the Battle of Stalingrad, one of the crucial battles on the Eastern front, *Life and Fate* has no obvious rivals in modern Russian literature. Grossman's diaries, meticulously maintained throughout the course of the battle, provide the basis for the detailed, graphic and at times eerily disjointed scenes of close quarter battle amid the ruins of the city. Scrupulous attention is paid to the skills of Russian snipers, who played a deadly game of cat and mouse with their German foes. The other master killers of the battlefield, the scouts or *razvedchiki*, carry out their execution at close range, and here, too, Grossman spares no details. Whether peering through the telescopic sight of the sniper's rifle, considering the tactical course of the battle from Chuikov's dugout, or expounding ideas on the nature of military strategy from Alexander the Great to the German General Staff, Grossman invites comparison with Tolstoi. Indeed, with its panoramic and epic treatment of the war, combined with the author's expert knowledge of front life, and the many digressions on the fate of man in the totalitarian state, *Life and Fate* is the most important war novel in Russian literature since *War and Peace*.

Russian victory at Stalingrad amounted to more than just the end of Hitler's dreams of Aryan conquest in the east. Hitler's defeat ensured Stalin's survival. Stalin was able to disavow various hints and tacit promises given to the Russian people that after the war there would be no return to the Terror of the 1930s. Victory at Stalingrad in effect prolonged the agony of the Russian people. That the consequences of a German victory would have been worse offers scant comfort.

The irreconcilable clash of interests between ordinary, non-party-affiliated Russians with hopes for something better after the war, and the party *apparatchiks* determined to reassert control as the threat of German victory recedes, is evident in virtually all the major and minor plot lines of *Life and Fate*. Russian soldiers occupying the forward observation post, house 6/1, openly discuss their hopes for post-war Russia: the removal of the collective farms; an end to coercion; and greater personal freedom. Alarmed by this spirit of independence, the Party tries to incriminate Captain Grekov, the observation post's unrepentant commander, as an "anti-Soviet element". Even in German captivity when one would expect hostility towards the Germans to be encouraged, similar manifestations of independence from Party rule are dealt with in the same ruthless manner. A plot to instigate an uprising among Soviet prisoners of war is foiled not by the Gestapo, but by commissars fearful that the Party's authority will be undermined if it succeeds. Among Russian intellectuals and scientists there is the same desperate longing for the Party to retreat from its claims of omniscience. The physicist, Viktor Shtrum, whose fictional biography would seem to owe much to Grossman's, must defend a major scientific breakthrough from party zealots who regard the conclusions as "Talmudic abstractions" because they clash with Lenin's views on the nature of matter. The witch hunt ceases only when it is obvious that Shtrum's discovery is a major step forward in the race to acquire the atomic bomb. Resistance to the Germans on the battlefield or the ubiquitous party machine are part and parcel of the same struggle for personal dignity and intellectual autonomy. It is conceivable that Grossman's novel might just have been spared its unusual fate, had his criticisms of Soviet society gone no further.

The essence of *Life and Fate*, however, is to be found in Grossman's thoughts and deeply speculative enquiry into the nature of totalitarianism. Grossman argues a compelling case for the fundamental congruency of the Nazi and Soviet regimes. It is these bold – and from the point of view of Soviet officialdom, utterly terrifying – conjectures, that led to the seizure of the manuscript in 1961.

Soviet ideology has interpreted the Nazi state as something uniquely aberrant and regressive, the very antithesis of the progressive Soviet state. One of Grossman's most percipient commentators in *Life and Fate* is the SS officer, Obersturmbannführer Liss. Hitler's Germany and Stalin's Russia are, he says, "a form of a single essence – the party state". Collectivization of the Russian peasantry, Hitler's Night of the Long Knives, Stalin's Terror, and the extermination of Europe's Jews are not only manifestations of pre-war and wartime rivalry between two tyrants vying for the totalitarian domination of Europe, but also lay the foundations for the super totalitarian state that will emerge with the victory of one of them. Liss's paradox, the belief that the Nazi essence will survive with the Soviet victory, is vindicated by Soviet post-war campaigns aimed at "rootless cosmopolitans". Such campaigns represented unfinished business: they were Stalin's back-handed compliment to his vanquished rival.

The impact that *Life and Fate* would have had on Soviet society had the novel been published in the early 1960s, as Grossman intended, poses one of the great unanswered questions of 20th-century Russian literature. Publication in 1962 of Solzhenitsyn's *One Day in the Life of Ivan Denisovich* was both a literary and political landmark in Soviet history, inspiring many others to write about their own personal experiences of the camps. Hopes for a more liberal Soviet Union were raised only to be dashed by Khrushchev's ousting. Yet the Soviet Union survived the publication of *One Day in the Life of Ivan Denisovich*. It is doubtful whether Stalin's heirs – and the ideological structures that supported them – could have so easily survived publication then of *Life and Fate*.

FRANK ELLIS

Nikolai Stepanovich Gumilev 1886–1921

Poet

Biography

Born in Kronshtadt, 15 April 1886. Attended schools in St Petersburg, Tbilisi, and Tsarskoe Selo; studied at the Sorbonne, Paris, 1906–08; St Petersburg University, 1908–10, 1912–14: did not graduate. Married: 1) the poet Anna Andreevna Gorenko (Akhmatova) in 1910 (divorced 1918), one son, the writer Lev Gumilev; 2) Anna Nikolaevna Engel'gardt in 1918, one son (illegitimate) and one daughter. Protracted expeditions to Africa (principally Abyssinia) in 1909–10, 1910–11, 1913. Volunteer during World War I: Uhlan and Hussar Regiments, 1914–17; on staff of Military Commissariat of Provisional Government in Paris, 1917; Russian Governmental Committee, London, 1918: ensign, decorated three times. Founder-member of "Academy of Verse" ("Akademiia stikha"), 1909, subsequently "Society of Zealots of the Artistic Word" ("Obshchestvo revnitelei khudozhestvennogo slova"), 1909–16; and of break-away "Guild of Poets" ("Tsekh poetov"), October 1911–14. Leading member of Acmeist movement, emergent from "Guild of Poets", 1912; published manifestos, January 1913. Poetry critic and occasional poetry editor of *Apollon*, 1909–17. In Petrograd, 1918–21; prominent member of several committees and editorial boards, lecturer at literary studios. Chairman of Petrograd branch of All Russian Union of Poets, from October 1920. Arrested on ill-founded charges of complicity in "Tagantsev conspiracy", 3 August 1921; executed 25(?) August 1921, probably at Berngardovka, near Petrograd. Rehabilitated in Russia, 1986.

Publications

Collected Editions

The Abinger Garland. Nicolai Gumilev. Poems Translated from the Russian, by Yakov Horstein. Dorking, Abinger Chronicle, 1945.

Sobranie sochinenii, 4 vols. Washington, DC, Kamkin, 1962–68.

Selected Works of Nikolai Gumilev, translated by Burton Raffel and Alla Burago. Albany, State University of New York Press, 1972.

Nikolai Gumilev on Russian Poetry, edited and translated by David Lapeza. Ann Arbor, Ardis, 1977.

Neizdannye stikhi i pis'ma [Unpublished Poems and Letters]. Paris, YMCA-Press, 1980.

Neizdannoe i nesobrannoe [Unpublished and Uncollected]. Paris, YMCA-Press, 1986.

Stikhotvoreniia i poemy. "Biblioteka poeta: Bol'shaia seriia", Leningrad, 1988.

Dramaticheskie proizvedeniia, perevody, stat'i [Dramatic Works, Translations, Articles]. St Petersburg, 1990.

Pis'ma o russkoi poezii [Letters on Russian Poetry]. Moscow, 1990.

Sochineniia, 3 vols. Moscow, 1991.

Poetry

Put' konkvistadorov [Path of Conquistadors]. St Petersburg, 1905.

Romanticheskie tsvety [Romantic Flowers]. Paris, published by the author, 1908; 3rd edition, Petrograd, 1918.

Zhemchuga [Pearls]. Moscow, 1910; 2nd edition, Petrograd, 1918.

Chuzhoe nebo [Alien Sky]. St Petersburg, 1912.

Kolchan [The Quiver]. Moscow and Petrograd, 1916.

Koster [The Pyre]. Petrograd, 1918.

Mik: Afrikanskaia poema [Mik: An African Poem]. Petrograd, 1918.

Shater: Stikhi 1918 g. [The Tent: Poems of 1918]. Sebastopol, 1921; augmented edition, Revel, 1922.

Ognennyi stolp [The Pillar of Fire]. Petrograd, 1921.

Stikhotvoreniia: Posmertnyi sbornik [Poetry: A Posthumous Collection]. Petrograd, 1922; augmented edition, Petrograd, 1923.

K sinei zvezde: Neizdannye stikhi 1918 g. [To the Blue Star: Unpublished Poems of 1918]. Berlin, Petropolis, 1923.

Plays

"Akteon", *Giperborei*, 7 (1913), 3–21.

"Gondla", *Russkaia mysl'*, 1 (1917), 67–97; separate edition, Berlin, Petropolis, 1923.

"Otravlennaia tunika" [The Poisoned Tunic], in *Otravlennaia tunika i drugie neizdannye proizvedeniia*, New York, Izdatel'stvo imeni Chekhova, 1952.

Fiction
Ten' ot pal'my: Rasskazy [The Shade of the Palm: Stories]. Petrograd, 1922.

Literary Criticism
Pis'ma o russkoi poezii [Letters on Russian Poetry]. Petrograd, 1923.

Translator
Emali i kamei [Emaux et Camées], by T. Got'e, St Petersburg, 1914.
Farforovyi pavil'on: Kitaiskie stikhi [The China Pavilion: Chinese Poems]. Petrograd, 1918; 2nd edition, Petrograd, 1922.
Gil'gamesh. Vavilonskii epos [The Epic of Gilgamesh]. Petrograd, 1919.
Poema o starom moriake [Ballad of the Ancient Mariner]. S.T. Kol'ridzh [Coleridge], Petrograd, 1919.
Frantsuzskie narodnye pesni [French Folk Songs]. Petrograd and Berlin, 1923.

Critical Studies
"Some Structural Patterns in the Poetry of Nikolaj Gumilev", by Ewa M. Thompson, *Die Welt der Slaven*, 19–20 (1974–75), 337–48.
Nikolay Gumilev, by Earl D. Sampson, Boston, Twayne, 1979.
"Lost in Space and Time: Gumilev's 'Zabludivšijsja tramvaj'", by Elaine Rusinko, *Slavic and East European Journal*, 26 (1982), 383–402.
"Gumilyov's 'Akteon': A Forgotten Manifesto of Acmeism", by Michael Basker, *Slavonic and East European Review*, 63 (1985), 498–517.
Nikolaj Gumilev: Papers from the Gumilev Centenary Symposium held at Ross Priory, University of Strathclyde, 1986, edited by Sheelagh Duffin Graham, Oakland, California, Berkeley Slavic Specialties, 1987.
Nikolai Gumilev v vospominaniiakh sovremennikov, edited by Vadim Kreid, Paris and New York, Tret'ia volna and Dusseldorf, Goluboi vsadnik, 1989; Moscow, 1990.
Nikolai Gumilev: Zhizn' poeta po materialam domashnego arkhiva sem'i Luknitskikh, by V. Luknitskaia, Leningrad, 1990.
Zhizn' Nikolaia Gumileva: Vospominaniia sovremennikov, St Petersburg, 1991.
"Nikolai Gumilev: Khronika", by E.E. Stepanov, in Gumilev's *Sochineniia*, vol. 3, Moscow, 1991, 344–429.
Muza stranstvii Nikolaia Gumileva, by Apollon Davidson, Moscow, 1992.
N. Gumilev i Russkii Parnas: Materialy nauchnoi konferentsii, 17–19 sentiabria 1991 g., St Petersburg, 1992.
N.S. Gumilev: Problemy mirovozzreniia i poetiki, by S.L. Slobodniuk, Dushanbe, 1992.
"An Acmeist in the Theatre: Gumilev's Tragedy *The Poisoned Tunic*", by Elaine Rusinko, *Russian Literature*, 31 (1992), 393–414.
Nikolaj Gumilev and Neoclassical Modernism: The Metaphysics of Style, by Raoul Eshelman, Frankfurt, Peter Lang, 1993.
"Gumilev, Annensky and Tsarskoe Selo: Gumilev's 'Tsarskosel'skii krug idei'", by Michael Basker, in *A Sense of Place: Tsarskoe Selo and Its Poets*, edited by Lev Loseff and Barry Scherr, Columbus, Ohio, Slavica, 1993, 215–41.
Nikolai Gumilev: Issledovaniia i materialy. Bibliografiia, St Petersburg, 1994.
N.S. Gumilev: Pro et contra. Lichnost' i tvorchestvo Nikolaia Gumileva v otsenke russkikh myslitelei i issledovatelei: Antologiia, edited by Iu.V. Zobnin, St Petersburg, 1995.
Posredine stranstviia zemnogo: Dokumental'naia povest' o zhizni i tvorchestve Nikolaia Gumileva. Gody 1886–1913, by V.V. Bronguleev, Moscow, 1995.
The Acmeist Movement in Russian Poetry: Culture and the Word, by Justin Doherty, Oxford, Clarendon Press, 1995.
Gumilevskie chteniia: Materialy mezhdunarodnoi konferentsii filologov-slavistov, 15–17 aprelia 1996 goda, St Petersburg, 1996.
"Three Poetic Responses to the Death of Nikolai Gumilev", by Justin Doherty, *Slavonica*, 3/2 (1996–97), 27–48.

Bibliographies
"Spisok perevodov, vypolnennykh N.S. Gumilevym dlia izdatel'stv 'Vsemirnaia literatura' i Z.I. Grzhebina", by I.F. Martynov, in *Gumilevskie chteniia, Wiener Slawistischer Almanach*, 15 (1984), 87–95.
N.S. Gumilev. Bibliografiia, by Vadim Kreid, Orange, Connecticut, Antiquary, 1988.
"Otechestvennaia literatura o N.S. Gumileve (1905–1988 gg.) (Materialy k bibliografii)", by V.N. Voronovich, in *Nikolai Gumilev: Issledovaniia i materialy. Bibliografiia*, St Petersburg, 1994, 632–60.

The reputation of Nikolai Gumilev rests primarily on his achievements as poet and literary critic, and as instigator and leading spirit of Russian Acmeism. His literary activities were broad-ranging, however. In addition to poetry (by no means limited to the eight books of lyric verse and one narrative poem published during his lifetime), frequent reviews, and occasional critical-theoretical articles, his output also included more than a dozen exotic short stories (a burgeoning career as author of short fiction being inexplicably abandoned in 1908–09); eight surviving plays, all with non-Russian settings, of which the full-length verse-dramas *Gondla* (based in 9th-century Iceland) and *Otravlennaia tunika* [The Poisoned Tunic] (based in 6th-century Byzantium), are of outstanding merit; autobiographical prose, documenting experiences in Africa and on active service in World War I; the opening chapters of a novel apparently concerning Russian sectarians; a film scenario after *The Thousand and One Nights*; the intriguing outlines of a "Theory of Integral Poetics"; and numerous verse translations, principally, but by no means exclusively, from English and French.

After largely unpublished juvenilia, derivative of Lermontov and Nadson, Gumilev's career began in earnest with his family's move to Tsarskoe Selo in 1903. There he "discovered" Nietzsche and the Russian Symbolists, and first encountered Anna Gorenko-Akhmatova, who provided major creative stimulus throughout his life. (It should be noted, however, that Gumilev was habitually inclined to encoded concealment of intimate biographical material.) His first collection of poems, *Put' konkvistadorov* [Path of Conquistadors], was immoderately imitative of Bal'mont and Belyi, with additional, indiscriminate echoes of the fashionable writings of other prominent Symbolists, and of 19th-century romanticism. A personal thematic core was in consequence virtually indiscernible. Under the tutelage of Briusov, with whom Gumilev initiated a crucially important correspondence following publication of *Put' konkvistadorov*, he nevertheless soon became acutely conscious of the deficiencies of his premature debut. He left Russia, determined to transform himself into an accomplished and original poet, not by resolute eschewal of further influence, but by an intense period of dedicated apprenticeship to more judiciously selected and congenial models. Foremost among these was Briusov himself, whose imprint is most strongly apparent in *Romanticheskie tsvety* [Romantic Flowers], and thereafter in *Zhemchuga* [Pearls]. Yet Gumilev also persisted with isolated experiments in the manner of other elder contemporaries; and as he progressed, with remarkable facility, from imitation to creative assimilation and occasional parody of Symbolist sources, his range of literary and cultural reference broadened immensely. This is initially manifest, in *Zhemchuga* and *Chuzhoe nebo* [Alien Sky], in the emergence of an enduring penchant for fresh exploitation of archetypal literary themes (Don Juan, Adam, Cain, the sea-voyage of discovery, etc.), and for comparable "conservative innovation" in the handling of formal traditions.

Around 1910, the powerful, practical impact of Briusov was effectively superseded, largely on a more abstract level of aesthetic premises, by the disparate examples of Viacheslav Ivanov and Innokentii Annenskii. The gradual evolution of Gumilev's Acmeism during 1910–12 is partly a result of his endeavour to counter the theoretical and biographical influence of Ivanov, to some extent through assimilation (or partial reinterpretation) of the precepts of Annenskii. Yet it was also an assertion of more definitive progression beyond a confidently mastered "Symbolist Heritage" (as his manifesto termed it); and the consciously comparative procedures by which Gumilev had achieved creative self-definition found their natural extension in a complex semantic exploitation of intertextual resonances, now generally considered fundamental to Acmeist poetics. A strong intertextual orientation consequently characterized his more mature poetry of *Kolchan* [The Quiver] and *Koster* [The Pyre], and reached sophisticated culmination, alongside a growing meta-literary element, in *Ognennyi stolp* [The Pillar of Fire].

Gumilev's intensive pursuit of artistic self-realization, and allied preoccupation with textual sources, has its thematic counterpart in a persistent fascination with the origins and nature of human personality, and the often dour and difficult path of the individual to self-fulfilment: something akin to that "flowering of all spiritual and physical forces" by which he was prone to define Acmeism. Beneath his celebrated "geographical" depictions of distant travel and heroic exploit, his exotic and literary-traditional subjects, the central focus of his work is in other words internal and psychological, typically adumbrating a form of psychical quest through imagery of dream and the occult, or speculative exploration of personal and cultural (or pre-cultural) collective memory. There is hence a clear continuity between, say, the experience of Caracalla, the poet-aesthete and dreamer of occult dreams pivotal to *Romanticheskie tsvety*; the "secret wisdom" and physiological exuberance by which Gumilev's Rabelais is able to transcend the curse of the fallen Adam in *Zhemchuga*; the image of Cadmus, the royal architect, magus, and "rational-mystic" hero of the Acmeist drama *Akteon*; the esoteric aspirations of the war poetry; and a series of "mythologized" artist-figures who crucially punctuate the later works: Annenskii and d'Annunzio in *Kolchan*; Gondla; Imr in *Otravlennaia tunika*; Moradita in *Poema nachala* [Poem of the Beginning]; the "Drunken Dervish" and aspects of the autobiographical persona in *Ognennyi stolp*. Yet the spiritual-psychic achievement of such individuals constitutes a hard-won and elusive ideal; and much of the poetry deals instead with the predicament of alienation in the civilized world, with modern man's sense of displacement and incompleteness. In Gumilev's later work, where his psychological emphasis acquires increasingly ontological coloration, the consequent sense of non-fulfilment assumes more tragic proportions. As before, however, it is almost invariably tempered by a sober acceptance of the limitations of this life.

Gumilev's execution by the Bolsheviks long precluded serious study of his work in the Soviet Union, and, together with simplistic notions of Acmeist style and thematics, strongly coloured his appraisal abroad. The fine émigré Collected Works of the 1960s, eventually followed by two substantial, complementary editions of his correspondence in the 1980s, paved the way for more balanced assessment; and additional texts, well-annotated editions, valuable biographical material and (to a lesser extent) searching critical examination have appeared in Russia since his rehabilitation at the outset of glasnost in 1986. This has led to increasing recognition of the sophistication of Gumilev's writing, an attendant rejection of the invidious critical stereotype of the "poet-warrior", and gradual redress of the long-accepted model of his creative path as a development from Symbolism to Acmeism and back to Symbolism. Yet with the exception of Eshelman's stimulating conception of Gumilev's *oeuvre* in terms of a "neo-rhetorical poetics", constituting an "alternative", "Neoclassical" modernism, the most fruitful interpretations to date have concentrated almost exclusively on individual works. Substantial, synthesizing critical and critical-biographical examination is now due.

MICHAEL BASKER

Gondla

Play, 1917

Gumilev is still thought of as a poet first, a critic second, and his dramas lie unperformed. *Gondla* is the only play to be performed in his own lifetime (in Rostov on Don in 1920, between January and July, at least once in Gumilev's presence) and, even after his judicial murder by the Cheka, in Petrograd in January 1922 by the Rostov Theatre Studio for whose transfer to Petrograd Gumilev had fought. Among the actors was the future dramatist Evgenii Shvarts. The play, despite its crowd scenes being enacted on a tiny stage, was a major success. Yet when the Petrograd audience called for the author, who was now officially an executed counter-revolutionary traitor, the play was removed from the repertoire and the theatre disbanded.

Gondla had evidently been important to Gumilev, for, when the lights once failed at a reading of the play, he was able to recite it word-for-word. Written and published in 1917, *Gondla* very inventively exploits material from the Old Norse Edda epic and other Icelandic sagas, although the hero Gondla is entirely

Gumilev's invention. The play is a historical (and fantastical) verse tragedy set in Iceland in the ninth century. Gondla is Irish (and Christian), and is supposed both by himself and by the chieftain of Iceland to be a prince, sent to Iceland to be brought up as a token of the future union of pagan Iceland and Christian Ireland. The play opens with Gondla being married to Lera (a half-Irish, half-Icelandic princess) and declared king. But jealous Icelandic earls rape his bride. In Act 2 Gondla seeks justice from the Icelandic chieftain, who tells him to fight a duel with his enemies. Gondla, a pacifist and a hunchback, refuses. He is, however, a poet and lyre-player, but his lyre has been cursed and this source of power is denied him. In Act 3 the earls stage a humiliating orgy with his bride; Gondla is about to be killed. Act 4 brings an Irish army to save him, but the Icelandic nobles reveal the truth: Gondla is just a minstrel's boy substituted for the prince who was murdered on the journey to Iceland; peripeteia follows peripeteia. The Irish visitors reveal that this minstrel is now King of Ireland so that Gondla is indeed a legitimate prince. The Icelandic earls surrender and Gondla demands they convert to Christianity. This they refuse until he kills himself with his sword, whereupon the earls abandon Valhalla for a Christian heaven; Iceland and Ireland are united, and Lera, now Gondla's loving bride again, insists on sailing away into the ocean with the body of the martyr.

The Symbolist dramatic tradition is evident in the Blokian feminine who vacillates between brutal force and poetic genius, and in the Mallarmean opposition of Germanic military brutality and Celtic magic gentleness. (It is noteworthy that Gnesin, who wrote the music for Blok's *Roza i krest* ("The Rose and the Cross") worked also on the Rostov production of *Gondla*.) But Gumilev steels the Symbolist scenario with a positive ideal of heroism: despite its "love-death", the ending of the play is triumphant. Moreover, there is a clear delineation of the roles of the "lupine" Icelandic pagans and the "swan-like" Christians who are their prey, which suggests a coexistence, if not peaceful, then at least symbiotic. In Acmeist spirit, Gumilev accepts the world as it is given, seeking only to clarify its nature, not to reject it because it is a nightmare. As in Gumilev's other tragedies (*Akteon*, *Otravlennaia tunika*) a sensitive hero, obsessed by love, is hounded to death: *Gondla* contains much that is typical of Gumilev's exoticism and personal sado-masochism in the humiliating trials that his protagonist undergoes before a heroic suicide. But the play's impact depends on two other factors: first, it is an appeal for an end to constant warfare and brutalization, an appeal which an audience that had endured World War I, the Revolution and Civil War found powerful. Second, it is a highly personal confession, for in Gumilev the Icelandic conqueror and the Irish poet coexisted, while the half-sister, half-bride, the wild Icelandic Valkyrie Lera (also known as Laik with her nocturnal, loyal Irish nature) more than hints at the relationship between Gumilev and Akhmatova. A typical critical response ran:

> The action of the poem develops in leaps and bounds, not always justified, but in places shows the enormous dramatic potential of the author. Here the second act is a particular case in point, where the Icelandic knights, children of the forests and of freedom, sense their ancient wolf-like ferment, become beasts, lose human form and stop speaking and start howling, stop walking and start creeping, and virtually before the spectators' eyes grow claws and wolf skins. Here you sense something elemental, the breadth and manner of Jack London. This part of the poem, which has no peer in the other acts for strength and expressiveness, is written so vividly, with such inspiration and dynamism that it leaves no doubt: in Gumilev we have lost not just a poet, but a dramatist.
>
> (Z.D. L'vovskii, *Vestnik teatra i iskusstva*, 4 [1922])

Gumilev's verse, however declamatory, is powerful and innovative: three-foot lines of anapaests with alternate rhymes, whose formality stresses the allegorical nature of the play. Critical reaction to the play as a printed text was favourable. Even Gor'kii (who failed to save Gumilev from the firing squad in 1921) is said to have exclaimed, after Gumilev read the play aloud, "What a giant talent has come out of you". *Gondla* was ideally suited (and possibly intended) to figure in a great cycle of imaginative historical plays that Gor'kii envisaged as part of a campaign to raise the proletariat to the intelligentsia. It was published in a joint Soviet-émigré edition in Berlin in 1923, but never referred to again under Soviet rule.

DONALD RAYFIELD

Ognennyi stolp

The Pillar of Fire

Poetry collection, 1921

Ognennyi stolp was the last collection of poetry compiled by Nikolai Gumilev. It contains a mere 20 poems, including one narrative piece of 195 lines, all composed between summer 1919 and July 1921. (A substantially different manuscript version of 1920 had incorporated some earlier items.) The collection was published by Ia.N. Blokh's "Petropolis", and appeared in Petrograd, in an edition of 1,000 copies, during the three weeks between the author's arrest and execution in August 1921. The same publisher brought out a reprint edition of 3,000 copies in Berlin the following year.

Despite the turbulent times and the circumstances of the poet's death, *Ognennyi stolp* was quite widely reviewed, in a dozen or more periodicals throughout Russia and in emigration. There was unanimous praise for Gumilev's outstanding technical mastery, but opinions were predictably more divided concerning topical "relevance", profundity of content, and the effectiveness of individual poems. For V. Piast, however, this was a work of "classical significance", of which "every page, line and word" was of the finest order (*Al'manakh Tsekha Poetov*, 3 [1922], 74); and subsequent commentators have routinely concurred that *Ognennyi stolp* is Gumilev's best and most important work. No major critical analysis yet exists, however. The most valuable studies to date have concentrated on individual poems: "Slovo" [The Word], "Dusha i telo" [Soul and Body], "Zabludivshiisia tramvai" [The Lost Tramcar], and "P'ianyi dervish" [The Drunken Dervish].

The title of the collection most obviously derives from the Old Testament image of divine guidance and protection (Exodus, Nehemiah), but might in addition be construed as an allusion to the seventh angel of the Apocalypse, and, with comparably pointed contemporary resonance, to the cataclysmic destruction of the city that was to precede Nietzsche's "Great Noontide" (*Thus Spoke Zarathustra*). In the context of poems by Lozinskii, Bal'mont, and Gumilev himself, the title also acquires more private, emotional, and artistic connotations. Like the implicit proclivity for high rhetoric, this wide range of partially conflicting association proves typical of *Ognennyi stolp*, in which Gumilev makes complex use of an extraordinary variety of literary sources, both Russian and non-Russian. The former include works by Lomonosov and Karamzin, Pushkin, Lermontov, Gogol', Tiutchev, and, among the author's contemporaries, Blok, Belyi, Briusov, Bal'mont, Kuzmin, Akhmatova, and the theoreticians of Futurism. The most prominent foreign sources are the writings of Baudelaire and Nietzsche, while a more extensive list would provisionally include Blake and Tennyson, Poe, Longfellow, Rimbaud, Mallarmé, Hauff, possibly Villon and Dante, Virgil, Homer, and, in one protracted instance, the 11th-century Persian poet Nasir-i-Khusraw. Fuller analysis might entail a distinction between sources with which Gumilev engages in intertextual dialogue or polemic, and those generally more obscure, and intentionally obscured, texts from which he adopts or freely adapts imagery, subject-matter or conceptual framework for the formulation of personal preoccupations. This latter strategy – consistent with Gumilev's explicit awareness that poetic images can rarely be created without significant precedent – has a close counterpart, too, in the poet's clear endeavour to explore and innovate within the limits of different generic traditions (the literary ballad, the *canzone*, the dispute of body and soul, the Classical Persian love lyric).

In addition to such purely literary inspiration, several of the poems are more or less identifiably grounded in everyday reality or incident: the route of a Petrograd tram, chance encounters with the "warrior-poet" S.A. Kolbas'ev and the political assassin Ia.G. Bliumkin, recent adverse criticism of Akhmatova's verse or Gumilev's own creative path, or particular moments in the relationship with several female addressees. At the same time, Gumilev's range of reference is greatly augmented by recourse to a formidable and characteristically eclectic array of spiritual doctrines and speculative thought: elements drawn from the Old and New Testaments and Russian Orthodoxy coexist alongside borrowings from Gnosticism, Neo-Platonism, Stoicism, Theosophy, Anthroposophy, Esoteric Freemasonry, Buddhism, Sufi mysticism, African, Celtic, Nordic, and Russian folklore, as well as modern Bergsonian philosophy, and the imaginative reconstruction of the contours of primitive cosmogonic myth.

The particular achievement of *Ognennyi stolp* is the synthesis of this disparate material into a series of highly original, internally cohesive, intellectually and emotionally demanding poems, the strikingly thorough differentiation of which one from another constitutes a further quite distinctive feature of the whole. An underlying connection is established by recurrent, if typically multivalent, archetypal imagery, such as that of wind and fire, wine and the body, light and dark, while the fundamental concern of the poems might tentatively be stated as an exploration of the complex nature and evolution of human personality, projected against the agonizing limitations and exhilarating potential of physical existence. In some poems this involves the objectification of personal biography, in a universalizing assessment not just of specific sensual, emotional and spiritual experience, but also, on occasion, of the discontinuities of identity over the course of a lifetime, or even (perhaps) past and future incarnations. Other poems entail supra-individual consideration of the national and racial formants of personality, man's primitive instincts, archetypal dreams, and visceral connections with the natural world; or turn instead, or as well, to the lessons of esoteric wisdom and mystical intuition. Frequent preoccupations in this latter respect are the loss of numinous contact with the Godhead, human relationships that are treated in differing historical (and prehistoric) contexts; and the consolatory, transformatory, or sacral and revelatory potential of art, poetry and the poet. The overt didacticism of several poems is invariably offset by underlying enigma, while the shifting perspectives of the collection as a whole constitute a maximally variegated, open-ended response to the intractable questions it confronts. The resultant sense of incessant search is reflected, moreover, on the formal level of versification: the technical virtuosity commended by Gumilev's early reviewers stems in part from his considerable metrical and rhythmical experimentation.

Understandably enough, *Ognennyi stolp* has generally been held to represent Gumilev's final "return to Symbolism". It is arguably distinguished from that, however, by his abiding anthropocentrism.

MICHAEL BASKER

Aleksandr Ivanovich Herzen 1812–1870

Prose writer, essayist, memoirist, and political theorist

Biography

Born in Moscow, 6 April 1812. Also wrote under the pseudonyms Iskander and I. Nionskii. Educated at home; studied physics and mathematics at Moscow University, 1829–33; completed dissertation, "Analytical Exposition of Copernicus' Solar System", 1833 (silver medal). Joined a group of students to debate progressive ideas: arrested and charged with "dangerous free-thinking", 1834; exiled to clerical service in Perm, 1835, then to Viatka, 1835–37; transferred to Vladimir to serve in governor's office, 1837–39. Married: 1) Natal'ia Aleksandrovna Zakhar'ina in 1838 (died 1852), eight children; (only eldest son and two daughters survived past infancy); 2) Natal'ia Alekseevna Tuchkova-Ogareva (unofficial). Returned to Moscow to serve in clerical office of Ministry of Internal Affairs, 1839. Moved to St Petersburg to serve in same department, 1840. Exiled to Novgorod for "the spreading of baseless rumours", 1841. Served in Novgorod as councillor to governing body, 1841–42. Resigned and lived and wrote in Moscow, 1842–46. First critical essay published, 1836 (in *Teleskop*); subsequent works in *Otechestvennye zapiski*, 1839–46. Emigrated with his family in 1847; lived in Paris 1847–49, visited Italy, 1848. After participating in anti-government demonstrations in Paris, fled to Switzerland in 1849. Refused to obey Tsar Nicholas I's order to return in 1850 to Russia and became an exile. Naturalized in Switzerland, 1851. Took part in revolutionary propaganda, edited *Poliarnaia zvezda* and *Kolokol*. Lived in London, 1852–64; returned to Switzerland and continued literary and political activities, 1865–69. Died in Paris, 21 January 1870. Buried in Nice.

Publications

Collected Editions

Sochineniia, 10 vols. Geneva, Basle, Lyon, 1875–79.
Polnoe sobranie sochinenii i pisem, 22 vols. Petrograd/Leningrad, 1915–25.
Sobranie sochinenii, 30 vols. Moscow, 1954–66.
Sochineniia, 4 vols. Moscow, 1988.

Fiction

"Kto vinovat?", *Otechestvennye zapiski*, 12 (1845); 4 (1846); as separate edition, St Petersburg, 1847; translated as *Who is to Blame? A Novel in Two Parts*, by Margaret Wettlin, Moscow, Progress, 1978; also translated by Michael R. Katz, Ithaca, Cornell University Press, 1984.
"Doktor Krupov", *Sovremennik*, 9 (1847); also in *Prervannye rasskazy Iskandera* [Interrupted Stories by Iskander], London, 1854.
"Soroka-vorovka", *Sovremennik*, 2 (1848); translated as *The Thieving Magpie. A Story*, by Avril Pyman, Moscow, Raduga, 1986.
"Povrezhdennyi" [Deranged Person], in *Prervannye rasskazy Iskandera*, London, 1854.
"Doktor, umiraiushchii i mertvye" [Doctor, the Dying, and the Dead], in *Sbornik posmertnykh statei A.I. Gertsena*. Geneva, 1870.

Articles and Essays

Vom Anderen Ufer. Hamburg, Hoffman and Kampe, 1850; *S togo berega*, London, 1855; translated as *From the Other Shore*, by Moura Budberg, London, Weidenfield and Nicolson, 1956; reprinted Oxford, Oxford University Press, 1979.
Le peuple russe et le socialisme. Lettre à Monsieur J. Michelet, Jercey, 1855; translated as *The Russian People and Their Socialism. A Letter to M.J. Michelet*, by V. Linton, London, 1855; in Russian as *Russkii narod i sotsializm*, London, 1858; also translated as *Open Letter to Jules Michelet*, by Richard Wollheim, London, Weidenfeld and Nicolson, 1956.
Pis'ma iz Frantsii i Italii. London, 1855; translated as *Letters from France and Italy, 1847–1851*, by Judith Zimmerman, Pittsburgh, Pennsylvania, University of Pittsburgh Press, 1995.
"Kontsy i nachala" [Ends and Beginnings], *Kolokol*, 138, 140, 142, 144, 145, 148, 149 (1862); 154, 156 (1863); also in *Esche raz. Sbornik statei Iskandera* [Once Again]. Geneva, 1866.
Pis'ma k staromu tovarishchu. Sbornik posmertnykh statei Aleksandra Ivanovicha Gertsena [Letters to the Old Comrade]. 1867–69; Geneva, 1870; 2nd edition, 1874.
Eshche raz Bazarov [Bazarov Once More]. 1869.

Philosophical Writing

Diletantizm v nauke [Dilettantism in Science]. 1842–43.
Pis'ma ob izuchenii prirody [Letters on the Study of Nature]. 1845–46.

Selected Philosophical Works, translated by Leo Navrozov. Moscow, Foreign Languages Publishing House, 1956.

Memoirs

"Byloe i dumy", *Poliarnaia zvezda*, 1 (1855), 2 (1856), 3 (1857), 4 (1858), 5 (1859), 6 (1861), 7 (1862), 8 (1869); also in *Kolokol*, 1857–67 (fragments).

Byloe i dumy Iskandera, vols 1–2, London, Vol'naia russkaia tipografia, 1861; vol. 4, Geneva, Vol'naia russkaia tipografia, 1867; also in *Sbornik posmertnykh statei Aleksandra Ivanovicha Gertsena*. 1870; Moscow, 1987; translated as *My Exile in Siberia*, by M. Meizenbug, 2 vols, London, Hurst and Blackett, 1855; also translated as *The Memoirs of Alexander Herzen*, parts 1 and 2, by J.D. Duff, New Haven, Yale University Press, 1923; 2nd edition, 1967; also as *My Past and Thoughts: The Memoirs of Alexander Herzen*, by Constance Garnett, 6 vols, London, 1924–27; abridged 1 vol. edition, New York, Knopf, 1968; 2nd edition, 1973; revised edition by Humphrey Higgins, Berkeley, University of California Press, 1982; also as *Ends and Beginnings* (parts 3 and 4), edited by Alice Kelly, Oxford, Oxford University Press, 1985; as *Childhood, Youth and Exile* (parts 1 and 2), by J.D. Duff, Oxford, Oxford University Press, 1979, reprinted 1994.

Critical Studies

Gertsen-pisatel'. Ocherk, by A.N. Veselovskii, Moscow, 1909.

The Romantic Exiles: A Nineteenth-Century Portrait Gallery, by Edward Hallett Carr, London, Gollancz, and New York, Frederick A. Stokes, 1933; Boston, Beacon Press, 1961; Harmondsworth, Penguin, 1968.

A.I. Gertsen. Literaturno-khudozhestvennoe nasledie, by N.S. Derzhavin, Moscow, 1947.

"Byloe i dumy" Gertsena, by Lydia Ginzburg, Leningrad, 1957.

Alexander Herzen and the Birth of Russian Socialism, 1812–1855, by Martin Malia, Cambridge, Massachusetts, Harvard University Press, and London, Oxford University Press, 1961; 2nd edition, New York, Grosset and Dunlap, 1965.

Problemy izucheniia Gertsena, edited by Iu.G. Oksman, Moscow, 1963.

"Byloe i dumy" Gertsena, by L.K. Chukovskaia, Moscow, 1966.

Letopis' zhizni i tvorchestva A.I. Gertsena. 1812–1870, vols 1–5, Moscow, 1974–92.

Alexander Herzen and the Role of the Intellectual Revolutionary, by Edward Acton, Cambridge, Cambridge University Press, 1979.

A.I. Gertsen, by L.E. Tatarinova, Moscow, 1980.

Russian Literature and Ideology, by Nicholas Rzhevsky, Urbana, University of Illinois Press, 1983.

Iz istorii russkogo romana XIX veka, Pushkin, Gertsen, Tolstoi, by E.G. Babaev, Moscow, 1984.

Gertsen protiv samoderzhaviia, by N.Ia. Eidel'man, Moscow, 1984.

"Byloe i dumy" A.I. Gertsena, by G. Elizavetina, Moscow, 1984.

Alexander Herzen 1812–1870, by Monica Partridge, Paris, UNESCO, 1984.

Alexander Herzen and European Culture, Proceedings of an International Symposium, Nottingham and London, 6–12 September 1982, edited by Monica Partridge, Nottingham, Astra Press, 1984.

Gertsen-myslitel', pisatel', borets. Moscow, 1985.

Gertsen i zapad. Literaturnoe nasledstvo, vol. 96, Moscow, 1985.

Aleksandr Gertsen, by V. Semenov, Moscow, 1989.

Midpassage: Alexander Herzen and European Revolution, 1847–1852, by Judith Zimmerman, Pittsburgh, Pittsburgh University Press, 1989.

On Psychological Prose, by Lydia Ginzburg, edited and translated by Judson Rosengrant, Princeton, Princeton University Press, 1991.

"Hertzen's Past and Thoughts: Dichtung und Wahreit", by Elena Dryzhakova, in *The Golden Age of Russian Literature and Thought*, edited by Derek Offord, London, Macmillan, and New York, St Martin's Press, 1992.

Tvorchestvo Gertsena v razvitii russkogo realizma, serediny XI veka, by S. Gurvich-Lishchiner, Moscow, 1994.

Bibliographies

A.I. Gertsen Seminarii, by M.I. Gillel'son, E.N. Dryzhakova, and M.K. Perkal', Moscow, 1965.

A.I. Gertzen. Materialy k bibliografii, vols 1–2, Leningrad, 1970.

Aleksandr Herzen from youth was interested most of all in political, social, and philosophical questions, in particular the theories of Utopian socialism of Saint-Simon, and the ideas of Fourier, Considerant, and Cabet. He and his closest friend, Nikolai Ogarev, considered themselves revolutionaries and "most of all advocated hatred toward any force, toward any arbitrary despotism". Herzen had particularly political and personal hostility toward Tsar Nicholas I, considering him a "tyrant" and a champion of slavery (serfdom). In the young Herzen's literary efforts of 1833–38 (unpublished during his lifetime), there was much rebellious romanticism à la Schiller, and in his first published works there is the poeticization of a free-thinking individual in conflict with vulgar Russian reality ("Zapiski odnogo molodogo cheloveka" [The Notes of a Certain Young Man], 1839–41).

Herzen's philosophical articles exerted a colossal influence on young people of the 1840s. Even Dostoevskii, no friend of abstract natural philosophy, later recalled these articles, maintaining that Herzen's was the "best philosophy not only in Russia, but in Europe".

In 1846, Herzen finished his only novel, *Kto vinovat?* (*Who is to Blame?*). Belinskii correctly noted in his critical review that it was "strictly speaking, not a novel, but a series of biographies, masterfully written and deftly combined". The fates of various people in complex confrontations within the Russian system of serfdom (land-owners, peasants, illegitimate children, intellectuals) are analysed in detail by Herzen, reconstructing a general, dysfunctional portrait of social existence. The denunciatory spirit, however, decreases towards the end of the novel. In the second part, the very question posed in the novel's title becomes the main problem: "who is to blame" for the uselessly spent life and tragic fate of the Russian intellectual personality: external reality or we ourselves? *Who is to Blame?* was the first Russian ideological novel that introduced into this genre the fate of the "superfluous man" (Bel'tov). Although it seems as if the dramatic conflict is focused on the sphere of personal problems (the love of Bel'tov for a married woman), in actuality Herzen is trying to show the general ethical crisis of an unreasonably and unfairly constructed society. By no means does he elevate Bel'tov, who did not find for himself a place or a task in life and, sympathizing with his bitter and lonely fate, Herzen proposes that the reader decide for himself who is to blame for this unhappiness. The novel had great success and provoked numerous responses. Encouraged by this success, Herzen wrote and published two stories in the journal *Sovremennik*, "Doktor Krupov" and "Soroka-vorovka" (*The Thieving Magpie*). Both were considered as belonging to the "natural school", which was then successfully developing in Russian literature.

After his departure from Europe, Herzen's first impressions abroad were reflected in various publicistic cycles, later comprising a book, *Pis'ma iz Frantsii i Italii* (*Letters from France and Italy*), 1855. Created in the years of the French Revolution of 1848–51, Herzen's letters persuade the reader that the European revolutionary movement could not have had success, because its political figures did not take into account the real arrangement of social forces. Simultaneously with these cycles was created Herzen's sharpest and most pessimistic book, *S togo berega* (*From the Other Shore*) (first published in German as *Vom Anderen Ufer*, 1850). This cycle of articles traces the stages of development of revolutionary ideology in Europe in the years 1847–51: "before the storm", "after the storm", "LVII year of the republic", etc. Herzen concludes that the European political movement has come to a dead end, and has uttered its final word in an unsuccessful attempt at social renewal. What is needed is to break with this "dying world", leave for the "other shore" and look for new soil for social renewal. For Herzen, Russia becomes that "other shore". In a series of articles from 1849 to 1853, he advocates the ideas of "Russian Socialism", i.e., the possibility of a new social structure on the basis of a Russian peasant commune (*obshchina*). These ideas coincide in part with Slavophilism, but they met with little sympathy among European political figures.

Having resettled in London in 1852, Herzen began work on the major labour of his life, the memoirs *Byloe i dumy* (*My Past and Thoughts*). At the same time he organized the Free Russian Press for the publication of articles, materials, and works forbidden by the Russian censor, for anti-serfdom and anti-despotism. In 1855 Herzen began to publish the almanac *Poliarnaia zvezda* in which were printed his own memoirs, articles, verse, and materials received from Russia. Nine issues appeared in all (1855–68). In 1856 Ogarev came to London and on his initiative the journal *Kolokol* (1857–67) began to be published. Here were printed sharp publicistic articles by Herzen, Ogarev, and Bakunin, offering responses to all the fundamental political events in Russia of the time.

Herzen published in *Kolokol* several epistolary-publicistic cycles. All of these, and many other cycles, together with *Pis'ma k staromu tovarishchu* [Letters to the Old Comrade] (1867–69), which was left unpublished during Herzen's lifetime, comprise the foundation of his publicistic legacy and testify to his evolution from radical socialism to a parliamentary, "conciliary" solution to political problems. Sharply refuting the Bakunin-Ogarev doctrine of violent, bloody revolutions, Herzen seeks compromises, now confirming the native soil-populist idea of listening to "what the *sovereign-people* say", now opposing the "false dogmatists" of "convict equality" "à la Babeuf" and the "communist corvée" à la Cabet with "learning", "advocacy", analysis and searches for "new forms" of just social organization (*Pis'ma k staromu tovarishchu*). Herzen sharply parted from the radical figures of the Russian revolutionary movement of the 1860s (from Chernyshevskii to Nechaev). In his last publicistic cycle *Eshche raz Bazarov* [Bazarov Once More], Herzen judged the political and social nihilism of the young generation, and, in personal letters to Ogarev and Bakunin, bitterly repented of the fact that his propaganda had enabled the proflagation of "the syphilis of our revolutionary promiscuity".

In his final years, Herzen tried to return to the genre of the dialogic sketch, which had been born in *Who is to Blame?* and in the tales of the late 1840s. A more successful example of this genre is the 1851 story "Povrezhdennyi" [Deranged Person], in which the author, whose personality is strongly marked, polemicizes with the representatives of two sharply opposed views: an optimist materialist doctor and his irritable patient (the "deranged person"), a paradoxical pessimist. Herzen successfully used similar devices "on two fronts" in *From the Other Shore* (see the chapter "Consolatio"). In 1868 he began a further series of sketches, "Skuki radi" [From Boredom], published in Russia under the pseudonym Nionskii (*Nedelia*, 1868–69). The protagonist of these sketches, a French doctor – a sceptic and materialist – re-emerges in Herzen's next cycle, *Doktor, umiraiushchii i mertvye* [Doctor, the Dying, and the Dead] (1870), which approaches fictional genres featuring a dying old man, "the Don Quixote of the revolution" of 1789, and his prosperous children: French bourgeoisie frightened by the events of 1848. This last tale of Herzen's was published posthumously.

ELENA DRYZHAKOVA

Who is to Blame?

Kto vinovat?

Novel, 1845–46

Who is to Blame? was Herzen's first fictional work to be published. He began writing it in 1841, in Novgorod, during his second period of internal exile. It was not finished at this time, and Herzen was inspired to rework and complete the novel by Belinskii's enthusiastic evaluation of it in 1845. It acquired its present title only in that year and was first published in 1845–46 in the journal *Otechestvennye zapiski*. In 1847 it was published in separate book form as a supplement to *Sovremennik*, and republished by Herzen with a Preface in London in 1859. Deeply flawed as an artistic whole, it is an important "problem novel" that summarizes the themes of the 1820s and 1830s (the individual and society and the "superfluous man"), while anticipating some of the ideas of later decades, especially the "woman question".

The novel opens on the estate of the minor noble, Negrov, where we are introduced to two major characters: Krutsiferskii, tutor to the household, and Negrov's illegitimate daughter, Liubov'. After comic and romantic interludes the young couple fall in love and are married. The "hero" Bel'tov is introduced and the rest of Part I details his background, which reveals him completely unprepared for Russian life: his doting mother and the lack of seriousness in his education had "prepared their own kind of moral Kaspar Hauser: Bel'tov at the age of 30, like a 16-year-old boy was still preparing to begin his life". In Part II he meets the Krutsiferskii family; he and Liubov' fall in love, but their love cannot develop. The trio disintegrates: Krutsiferskii resorts to drink, Liubov' dies (in the arms of Bel'tov's mother), while the superfluous hero, unable to achieve anything in love or in life, resumes his aimless wanderings.

Almost all the action of the novel takes place in the Russian provinces, on minor estates or in dull, anonymous towns. The picture is almost entirely negative, following the Gogol' of *Mertvye dushi* (*Dead Souls*) and anticipating Ostrovskii's "kingdom of darkness". At best the provinces are depressing and stultifying; more commonly they reflect brutality, cruelty, and exploitation. As Martin Malia has noted, "it is noteworthy that all the principal characters are victims of the gentry's inhumanity". The novel offers variations on patriarchal power, in the traditional sense of the term as well as the feminist.

The main plot thus concerns love, marriage and adultery, and the view taken is generally a pessimistic one. In the *ancien régime*, as represented by the Negrov household and their generation, there is either abuse of serf women, or sheer boredom and lovelessness. Krutsiferskii and Liubov' represent a new hope, one of greater equality and mutual respect, but their relationship is doomed to failure by lack of passion. When, however, passion is aroused (between Liubov' and Bel'tov) it is shown, in a manner that anticipates Turgenev's pessimism, to be an entirely destructive force. All three principals may be said to be stranded very definitely "on the eve". Female desire, as in earlier novels, leads not to fulfilment but to guilt, anguish and death.

With one important exception, the male characters are seen as unfit for the harsh realities of Russian life. Negrov is an unredeemed (and irredeemable) part of the status quo; Krutsiferskii is weak and Bel'tov a "superfluous man" *sans pareil*. Only the Voltairean *raisonneur* figure, Dr Krupov, receives approval and suggests the need for hard-headed practicality. Women fare little better. The novel again anticipates Turgenev in that the heroine is largely valorized, but virtually every other female character is denigrated: they are all either suffering, feminine victims or vicious tyrants. Frequently, it is the tyrannical harridans who oppress the other women. Sophie, mother of Bel'tov, is the only maternal figure in the novel given extended treatment, but again the picture is almost entirely negative. She starts as a persecuted virgin, emasculates her son, and ends by leading a half-life, living only for him. Liubov', thought to be a "strong" heroine, is certainly spoken of in these terms. In reality, she crumples at the first challenge, and dies a traditional death: that of a broken heart. The overall view of Russia, both the old and the new, is decidedly gloomy: lacking is the cautious hope of Turgenev's *Nakanune* (*On the Eve*), still less the Utopian optimism of Chernyshevskii's *Chto delat'?* (*What is to Be Done?*), the two novels that were the immediate successors of *Who is to Blame?*.

The critical reputation of the novel is decidedly mixed. By Herzen's contemporaries (Belinskii and Dobroliubov, for example) it was seen as very important, and it is now usually discussed for its ideas, not its artistic worth. Malia notes: "As literature it is only partly successful; Herzen was an excellent reporter of the Russian social scene, but he could not construct a plot or draw a character." This seems about right. The novel is a very important "staging-post" between *Evgenii Onegin* and the novels of Turgenev; it tackles the "woman question", although in a much more equivocal way than his female contemporaries (Gan and Zhukova), or his successor in this field, Chernyshevskii. Yet as a work of literature it is very poorly structured, with too many *longeurs*. Even so, it is a novel that repays attention, and is now deservedly receiving critical interest once again.

JOE ANDREW

My Past and Thoughts

Byloe i dumy

Memoirs, 1855–69

My Past and Thoughts is Aleksandr Herzen's best-known and unquestionably his most outstanding work. He began writing it at the end of 1852 in London, where he had settled after a series of political and personal "storms and losses". At first he conceived the memoirs as a confession of family drama. (His wife, partly under the influence of "new ideas" à la George Sand, had fallen in love with the German poet G. Gerverg, and was ready to leave her family, but ultimately, disillusioned in the object of her passion, died in complete emotional prostration.)

After starting his "confession", however, Herzen was transported "so far back" that he began *My Past and Thoughts* with a description of his youth, and decided to write his autobiography in the manner of Goethe's *Aus meinem Leben: Dichtung and Wahrheit* (*From My Life*), which he knew intimately. Indeed, his title borrows from Goethe's, merely reversing its components. Herzen continued *My Past and Thoughts* for the remainder of his life, printing many of its chapters in *Poliarnaia zvezda* and *Kolokol*, and publishing the first and second volumes as a separate edition in London (1861). The fourth and last volume came out in Geneva in 1867. Since the third volume consists of his old writings, it does not properly belong to the text of the autobiography.

From the outset Herzen viewed his "strange work" as a *sui generis* frame for a free narrative. In one of the ten prefaces to the memoirs that appeared in various editions, he characterized it as "A tombstone and a confession, *past and thoughts*, biography and speculation, events and ideas, things heard and seen, pain and suffering, recollections and more recollections". Thus *My Past and Thoughts* is an unfinished work on principle, its composition never fully defined by the author. Its defining feature as a work of art consists above all in the heterogeneous nature of the genre and style of its eight parts and all its chapters (42, plus another 40 that have no unified enumeration). Separate units within textual divisions (chapters and parts) are likewise heterogeneous.

The first two parts, comprising chapters 1–18, consist of *Detskaia i universitet* (*Nursery and University*) and *Tiur'ma i ssylka* (*Prison and Exile*). The sole principle of composition in these autobiographical notes, where descriptions, portraits, and details predominate, is the chronological presentation of successive events. The third part, *Vladimir na Kliaz'me* (*Vladimir-on-Kliazma*) (chapters 19–24), tells the story of Herzen's marriage to Natal'ia Aleksandrovna Zakhar'ina. Resembling the genre of a romance, it organizes its plot elements around the two principal characters – Aleksandr and Natasha.

Only in the last two chapters does it mesh with the chronology of the preceding two parts. The fourth part, *Moskva, Peterburg, i Novgorod* (*Moscow, Petersburg, and Novgorod*) (chapters 25–33), combines the genres of memoiristic notes, the philosophical sketch, and the belletristic diary. With the chronological relegated to the background, Herzen focuses primarily on his ideological concerns and those of his generation. Here we find brilliant portraits of Belinskii, Granovskii, Chaadaev, and "those who are with us" (*Nashi*), i.e. the Westernizers (Botkin, Korsch, etc.), as well as "those who are against us" (*Ne-nashi*), i.e. the Moscow Slavophiles (Khomiakov, Aksakov, and the Kireevskiis).

These first four parts made up the first and second volumes of the London edition of *My Past and Thoughts* (1861), which in overall composition and contents may be considered the definitive authorial version. Starting with the fifth part, *Parizh – Italiia – Parizh* (*Paris – Italy – Paris*) (chapters 34–43), the composition cannot be considered complete, for Herzen excluded from it the most important chapters (the story of his family drama), published posthumously in the Collected Works. Constructed according to fundamentally different principles from those that loosely united the earlier parts, the fifth separates public from private and privileges political journalism over narrative. Episodes and character sketches have a tendentious cast, and the selection of situations, the portraits, and the style are all subordinated to Herzen's basic political notions on the Revolution of 1848.

The last three parts of *My Past and Thoughts*, on which Herzen worked from 1852 until his death, remained unfinished, and only a part of them was published in *Poliarnaia zvezda* and *Kolokol*. The sixth part, *Angliia 1852–1864* (*England 1852–1864*) (ten unnumbered chapters and appendices), does not begin to encompass even the major events of Herzen's life during this period. He abandons chronological narration in favour of ideological allegiance: from the "mountain peaks" of European post-revolutionary emigration (Mazzini, Kossuth, Ledru-Rollin) to the "low-lying swamps" of *Schwefelbande* (Ruge, Blind, and Marx) and the "London mob" of spies and informers. Historical background is totally lacking, as is virtually anything personal. Furthermore, apologetic portraits compositionally unrelated to this part of the memoirs are none the less tacked onto them separately: *Robert Owen* and *Camicia rossa* (on Garibaldi).

The seventh part (seven unnumbered chapters and appendices) lacks a specific title and is devoted to events connected with the activities of the Free Russian Press. What the author intended regarding its composition and contents is unclear. Herzen apparently wanted to structure this part on the principle of *Apogee and Perigee* – recounting the rise and the decline of the Russian revolutionary movement of 1862–64. Concerned to protect the people involved, however, Herzen could neither provide psychological portraits of the movement's leaders nor discuss his connections with them. As a result, the effect is one of eclecticism, and his system of hints and allusions here deprives the narrative of the major Herzenian principle: that of *past and thoughts*, inasmuch as here the past has become the present. Only a few extracts from the seventh part were published in Herzen's lifetime.

The eighth part (13 fragments joined under the general title of *Bez sviazi* (*Without Links*)) consists of Herzen's travel diary during his last peregrinations through Europe in the period 1865–68. Short miniatures, feuilletons, and journalistic pieces here predominate. The author, seemingly now abandoning past and thoughts, concentrates emphatically on the incidental, the fleeting, the immediate – no longer his, nor subject to his unifying thoughts. Imbued now with merciless realism, Herzen saw himself as leaving the stage, aware of many political and personal mistakes.

While Herzen was still alive, extracts from *My Past and Thoughts* were published in English, German, and French translation. Reactions in the European press were basically sympathetic. As for Russian critics, since it was forbidden to mention Herzen's name in print until the very end of the century, comment on *My Past and Thoughts* was confined to the personal letters, diaries, and notebooks of such contemporaries as Turgenev, Dostoevskii, and Tolstoi.

ELENA DRYZHAKOVA

Zinaida Nikolaevna Hippius 1869–1945

Poet, prose writer, and dramatist

Biography

Born in Belev, Tula Province, 20 November 1869. Attended Kiev Institute for Girls, 1877–78; Fisher Private Classic School in Moscow, 1882; also educated at home. Married: D.S. Merezhkovskii in Tbilisi in 1888; moved to St Petersburg in same year. Published poetry and fiction in *Severnyi vestnik*; also wrote under the pseudonyms Anton Krainii, Roman Arenskii, Lev Pushchin, Comrade Herman, Anton Kirsha, and Vitovt. Widely acquainted with cultural personalities of the time. Contributed to *Mir isskustva* and other leading literary journals of St Petersburg and Moscow. Travelled to Germany, Greece, Italy and Sicily, 1894–1900. Organized the Merezhkovskiis' religious circle, 1900. Further travel in Europe, 1905–08. Returned to St Petersburg, 1908; joined Berdiaev's Religious-Philosophical Society. In charge of the literary section of P.B. Struve's *Russkaia mysl'* in Moscow. Several trips to France, 1909–14. Following October Revolution, escaped to Poland, December 1919; anti-Bolshevik activities in Poland. Left

Warsaw for Paris, October 1920; organized the Union of Irreconcilability against the Bolsheviks; initiated a literary journal, *Novyi korabl'*, and the literary and philosophical society "The Green Lamp". Participated in First Congress of Writers in Exile under auspices of the Yugoslav government, 1928. Visited Switzerland and Italy, 1934–38; friendship with Viacheslav Ivanov. Died in Paris, 9 September 1945.

Publications

Collected Editions

Stikhotvoreniia i poemy, 2 vols (vol. 1: 1899–1918; vol. 2: 1918–45), edited and with an introduction by Temira Pachmuss. Munich, Fink, 1972.
P'esy, edited and with an introduction by Temira Pachmuss. Munich, Fink, 1972.
Selected Works of Zinaida Hippius, edited and translated by Temira Pachmuss. Urbana, University of Illinois Press, 1972.
Peterburgskie dnevniki, 2nd edition, edited by S. Serebriannikov with an introduction by N.N. Berberova. New York, Telex, 1990.
Opyt svobody. Moscow, 1996.
Tikhoe plamia. Moscow, 1996.
Izbrannoe: Chertova kukla: Roman, Povesti i rasskazy, Moscow, 1997.

Poetry

Sobranie stikhov, 2 vols. Moscow, 1904–10.
Poslednie stikhi [Last Poems]. 1918.
Stikhi. Berlin, 1922.
Siianiia [Radiances]. Paris, 1938.
"Poslednii krug" [The Last Circle], edited by Temira Pachmuss, *Vozrozhdenie*, 198–99 (1968).
Stikhotvoreniia, edited by Temira Pachmuss. Paris, YMCA-Press, 1984.

Fiction

Novye liudi: rasskazy [New People]. St Petersburg, 1896; reprinted, Munich, Fink, 1973.
Alyi mech: rasskazy [The Scarlet Sword]. 1896; reprinted, Newtonville, Massachusetts, Oriental Research Partners, 1977.
Pobediteli [The Conquerors]. St Petersburg, 1898; reprinted, Munich, Fink, 1973.
Zerkala [The Mirrors]. St Petersburg, 1898; reprinted, Munich, Fink, 1977.
Tret'ia kniga rasskazov [The Third Book of Stories]. St Petersburg, 1902; reprinted, Munich, Fink, 1977.
Der Zar und die Revolution, with Dmitrii Merezhkovskii and Dmitri Filosofov. Munich, Piper, 1908 (from the French, *Le Tsar et la Révolution*, Paris, 1907).
Chernoe po belomu [In Black and White]. 1908; reprinted, Newtonville, Massachusetts, Oriental Research Partners, 1977.
Ivan Ivanovich i chert [Ivan Ivanovich and the Devil], in *Chernoe po belomu*, 1908; reprinted, Letchworth, Prideaux Press, 1979.
Vliublennye [In Love], in *Chernoe po belomu*, 1908; reprinted, Letchworth, Prideaux Press, 1979.
Chertova kukla [The Devil's Doll]. Moscow, 1911; reprinted with *Roman-Tsarevich*, Munich, Fink, 1972.
Lunnye murav'i: Book VI of Stories [The Moon Ants]. 1912; reprinted, Newtonville, Massachusetts, 1977.
Roman-Tsarevich. Moscow, 1913; reprinted with *Chertova kukla*, Munich, Fink, 1972.
Nebesnye slova i drugie rasskazy [Heavenly Words and Other Stories]. Paris, Zemgor, 1921.
Tsarstvo Antikhrista [The Kingdom of the Anti-Christ], with D.S. Merezhkovskii, D. V. Filosofov, and V.A. Zlobine. Munich, 1921.
Chto delat' russkoi emigratsii [What Russian Émigrés Should Do]. Paris, Rodnik, 1930.

Plays

Sviataia krov' [Holy Blood]. St Petersburg, 1901.
Net i da: grubye stseny [No and Yes: Crude Scenes], *Zolotoe runo*, 7/9 (1906).
Makov tsvet [The Red Poppy]. St Petersburg, 1908.
Zelenoe kol'tso. Petrograd, 1914; translated as *The Green Ring: A Play in Four Acts*, by S.S. Kotelianskii, London, C.W. Daniel, 1920.

Letters

Intellect and Ideas in Action: Selected Correspondence of Zinaida Hippius, edited by Temira Pachmuss. Munich, Fink, 1972.
Pis'ma k Berberovoi i Khodasevichu, edited by Erika Freiberger Sheikholeslami. Ann Arbor, Ardis, 1978.
"Zinaida Hippius and S.P. Remizova-Dovgello", edited by Horst Lampl, in *Wiener Slawistischer Almanach*, 1978.
"Letters to E.M. Lopatina and O.L. Eremeeva", edited by Temira Pachmuss, *Vestnik russkogo khristianskogo dvizheniia*, 132 (1980).
"Letters to I. Bunin", edited by Temira Pachmuss, *Cahiers du monde russe et soviétique*, Paris, 1981.
"Letters to Vera Nikolaevna Bunina", edited by Temira Pachmuss, *Russian Language Journal*, 35/121–22 (1981).
"Letters to M. Vishniak", edited by Temira Pachmuss, *Cahiers du monde russe et soviétique*, Paris, 1982.

Diaries and Memoirs

Literaturnyi dnevnik: 1899–1907 [Literary Diary: 1899–1907]. St Petersburg, 1908; reprinted Munich, Fink, 1970.
Zhivye litsa [Living Portraits]. Prague, Plamia, 1925; reprinted Munich, Fink, 1971.
Siniaia kniga. Peterburgskii dnevnik: 1914–1918 [The Blue Book. Petersburg Diary: 1914–1918], with V. P. Kocharovskii. Belgrade, Russkaia biblioteka, 1929; reprinted Tel-Aviv, 1980.
Dmitrii Merezhkovskii. Paris, YMCA-Press, 1951.
Between Paris and St. Petersburg: Selected Diaries of Zinaida Hippius, edited and translated by Temira Pachmuss. Urbana, University of Illinois Press, 1974.

Critical Studies

Bor'ba za idealizm, by A. Volynskii, St Petersburg, 1900.
Kniga velikogo gneva, by A. Volynskii, St Petersburg, 1904.
O blazhenstve imushchego: poeziia Z. N. Gippius, by M. Shaginian, Moscow, 1912.
Vstrechi, by Yuri Terapiano, New York, Izdatel'stvo imeni Chekhova, 1953.

Na Parnase serebrianogo veka, by S. Makovskii, Munich, Ob'edinenie politicheskikh emigrantov, 1962.
"The Spectre of Nothingness: The Privative Element in the Poetry of Zinaida Hippius", by Oleg Maslenikov, *Slavic and East European Journal*, 4 (1966).
"Disruption of Canonical Verse Norms in the Poetry of Zinaida Hippius", by Oleg Maslenikov, in *Studies in Slavic Linguistics and Poetics in Honor of Boris O. Unbegaun*, New York, New York University Press, 1968.
Zinaida Hippius: An Intellectual Profile, by Temira Pachmuss, Carbondale, Illinois, Southern Illinois Press, 1971.
The Religious Poetry of Zinaida Gippius, by Olga Matich, Munich, Fink, 1972.
"Gender as a Poetic Feature in the Verse of Zinaida Gippius", by Antonina Filonov Gove, in *American Contributions to the Eighth International Congress of Slavists (Zagreb, 1978)*, edited by Victor Terras, Columbus, Ohio, Slavica, 1978.
A Difficult Soul: Zinaida Hippius, by Vladimir Zlobine, edited by Simon Karlinsky, Berkeley, University of California Press, 1980.
"Aleksandr Blok and the Merezkovskijs", by Avril Pyman, in *Aleksandr Blok: Centennial Conference*, edited by Walter N. Vickery, Columbus, Ohio, Slavica, 1982.
Na beregakh Seny, by Irina Odoevtseva, Paris, Press Libre, 1983.
Malen'kaia Tereza, by Dmitrii Merezhkovskii, edited by Temira Pachmuss, Ann Arbor, Hermitage, 1984.
D.S. Merezhkovsky in Exile: The Master of the Genre of Biographie Romancée, by Temira Pachmuss, Bern, Peter Lang, 1990.
"A 'Fairy Tale of Love': The Relationship of Zinaida Gippius and Akim Volynsky (Unpublished Materials)", by Stanley J. Rabinowitz, *Oxford Slavonic Papers*, 24 (1991).
"The Silver Age: Highpoint for Women", by Charlotte Rosenthal, in *Women and Society in Russia and the Soviet Union*, edited by Linda Edmondson, Cambridge, Cambridge University Press, 1992.

Bibliographies
Bibliographie des oeuvres de Zenaïde Hippius, by A. Barta, Paris, Institut d'Études Slaves, 1975.
Zinaida Nikolaevna Gippius (1869–1945): Bibliograficheskie materialy. Moscow, 1995.

Zinaida Nikolaevna Hippius, one of the most influential figures of her time, distinguished herself as a poet, dramatist, prose writer, and critic. Her activities in the religious and philosophical societies in St Petersburg and the fashionable literary *soirées*, which she organized, first in St Petersburg and later in Paris, added to her fame in Russian literary circles. Her verse marked the beginning of modern Russian poetry. For her, the eternal properties of art were love of God, Christian ethics, spiritual elation, and religious transports. Her own law of art was formulated in the aphorism: "Art should reveal only the spiritual". Hippius's poetry and prose render her spiritual experiences in strikingly concrete imagery. Sounds, colours, smells, and moods blend in her poetic universe, instilling mystery and a passionate faith in God. She was esteemed as a brilliant innovative poet of the Symbolist period, with her "daring lyricism" and her "virtuosity of the word", by her contemporaries in literature, such as Innokentii Annenskii, Valerii Briusov, Andrei Belyi, and D.S. Mirsky. The latter wrote in 1933 that she was a "poet's poet", highly original and unlike any other writer in Russian literature. Her beautiful poems on love inspired Rainer Maria Rilke to translate some of them into German. Her metaphysical poetry and the poetry of political invective, combined with her anti-Bolshevik activity in Poland in 1919–20, made her unpopular in the Soviet Union, where her works were virtually prohibited. Her open criticism of the Bolsheviks for their betrayal of spiritual freedom and Russian historical and cultural traditions remained unpalatable.

As a poet, Hippius revised the syllabotonic canons of Russian versification by using *dol'niki*, writing allometric verse and availing herself of assonantal rhyme. With her versification, she influenced the poetry of other Symbolists, such as Aleksandr Blok, and the Acmeists and Futurists, among them, Anna Akhmatova, Osip Mandel'shtam, and Elena Guro. "Hippius led the way. Without her pioneering example, neither Aleksandr Blok nor Vladimir Maiakovskii could have been what they later became" (Karlinsky). Hippius's influence on subsequent Russian women writers of modernism – for example, Vera Bulich – was substantial.

Hippius and Merezhkovskii were closely associated with several leading literary journals of the time, such as *Severnyi vestnik*, Diagilev's influential *Mir iskusstva*, Briusov's *Vesy*, and Struve's *Russkaia mysl'*. She initiated the Religious-Philosophical Meetings in St Petersburg (1901–03) and the publication of a new literary journal, *Novyi put'* (1903–04), which printed the works of Symbolist writers and published the reports of the Religious-Philosophical Meetings.

At the turn of the century, Hippius was intensely preoccupied with religious and socio-ethical matters and advocated apocalyptic Christianity, based on a belief in the Second Coming. Her narratives reflect her views on various spiritual matters. Some of her stories treat the theme of transcendental sex, the psychological complexities of characters, and the entanglements in their intense personal relationships. Her stories, resembling medieval novelettes in their mysticism, verbal refinement, sophistication and humour, promote the Humanity of the Third Testament and treat psychological problems by way of introspective analysis.

Hippius's early novels, *Chertova kukla* [The Devil's Doll] and *Roman-Tsarevich*, deal with the question of revolution, which the author identifies with the movement into the future, into the Humanity of the Third Testament. At the same time, she reveals the psychology of man, whose heart harbours simultaneously both idealism and base treachery. Hippius was also the author of four plays: *Sviataia krov'* [Holy Blood], *Net i dat: grubye stseny* [No and Yes: Crude Scenes], *Makov tsvet* [The Red Poppy], and *Zelenoe kol'tso* (*The Green Ring*). Her first play, *Sviataia krov'*, reveals the peculiarities of her dramatic art and its proximity to experimental theatre in the west, particularly her dramatic method in distancing the recipient through special theatrical technique, such as deixis, the context of utterance, and estrangement. In all her plays, Hippius uses this dramatic technique to remove the audience from the imaginary worlds presented in the plays, making an emotional reaction to them more difficult, thus drawing attention to the artistic qualities and the spiritual emphasis of the play. *The Green Ring* was performed in 1915 at the Aleksandrovskii Theatre in St

Petersburg, under the direction of Vsevolod Meierkhol'd and it was a major event of the 1915 theatrical season in the capital. In Moscow, it was performed in 1916 at the studio of the Moscow Arts Theatre; Vakhtang Mchedelov was the director. Hippius's solution to the eternal conflict between "fathers and sons" and the play's uplifting spirit against the background of colourless "real life" fascinated Meierkhol'd and Mchedelov.

As a critic, Hippius wrote unconventional essays on literature, religion, and socio-political issues. They were published in leading Moscow and St Petersburg journals and newspapers under various pseudonyms. Her essays were widely read because they were brilliantly written and because in them she engaged in spirited exchanges of opinion on literary and current ideas with her prominent contemporaries. Hippius's style of criticism, like her poetry, was innovative in her time, and inspired much imitation. In 1925, she published her memoirs, *Zhivye litsa* [Living Portraits], about the leading writers of the day, which were highly praised by Vladislav Khodasevich and, later, by Simon Karlinsky. In 1928, at the First Congress of Writers in Exile in Belgrade, she received from King Alexander of Yugoslavia the Order of St Sava for her contribution to Russian literature and culture. In 1926, the Merezhkovskiis organized in Paris a new literary and philosophical society, "The Green Lamp", an offshoot of their Sunday *soirées*, which again fostered decades of Russian cultural dialogue. After Merezhkovskii's death, in 1941, Hippius began her memoir *Dmitrii Merezhkovskii*, published posthumously. Her Dantesque narrative poem, *Poslednii krug* [The Last Circle], treating her metaphysical views and expressing her ideas of love, faith, loyalty, and eternity, was published after her death.

Hippius's central themes – freedom, problems of good and evil, the search for God-Love, her interest in psychology, her idiosyncratic treatment of marriage, sexual ambivalence, and her sense of responsibility toward her fellow man – retain their validity in the light of modern existentialism. In her work, four chief aspects of the Russian cultural tradition – art, religion, metaphysical philosophy, and socio-political thought – receive their harmonious embodiment. As Karlinsky pertinently states, Hippius's works:

> are basic documents for the study of the momentous literary epoch during which Gippius lived and worked and to which she so prominently contributed. Together with her poetry, her plays, and her diaries, *Living Portraits* and *Dmitry Merezhkovsky* add up to one of the most valuable literary treasure troves of our century.

TEMIRA A. PACHMUSS

Chertova kukla and Roman-Tsarevich

Novels, 1911–13

Hippius, as a typical Russian Symbolist poet, regarded philosophy, religion, and ethics as the basis of literature. The central theme of her creative work is the spirit and the spiritual effort to attain the ultimate restoration of a harmonious relationship between love and eternity, life and death, and the real and the miraculous. The immediate objective of art was, in her opinion, the spiritual reorganization of life. In her journal, *Novyi put'*, she advocated a future religious culture, which would be true and universal, and attempted to reveal to her readers the aesthetic nature of the word and of poetic form. She always regarded beauty and culture as essential to human life.

In her works, Hippius portrayed the world as a chaotic interaction of spirit and matter. She regarded all physical phenomena in life as infused with the Deity, and often placed moral and intellectual ambiguities in the centre of her poetic universe: a fluctuation between strength and weakness, spirituality and sensuality, love for and contempt of man, nihilism and a personal desire for faith in God. A salient feature of Hippius's poetic temperament was her belief in service to humanity; she felt impelled by the will of God in all her deeds and actions, firmly believing that a "new religious consciousness" must replace the "lifeless dogmas" of the historical Church.

In her works, Hippius always associated revolution with universal movement into the future. Revolution, she insisted, must be universal and religious in nature. Only in the religion of the Third Testament would there be an end to the external power of the state; this end would signify an era of religious universality. Revolution opens a path to universal humanity. In *belles-lettres*, Hippius expressed these ideas in her two novels *Chertova kukla* and *Roman-Tsarevich*, which were much discussed at the time.

These two novels were intended to be the first and third parts of a trilogy. The second part, "Ocharovanie istiny" [The Charm of Truth], was never written, but Hippius used much of this material in *Roman-Tsarevich*, which then became the continuation of *Chertova kukla*. In the latter, she wished to reveal the "eternal and deep roots of revolution", whereas "Ocharovanie istiny" was supposed to depict the new "hero of non-existence". Hippius did not discuss her plans for the third part of the trilogy, but in all probability it was to portray the perfect merging of love, faith, truth, revolution, and ecumenity among the Russian revolutionaries who act in the name of God and Jesus Christ. Litta, the heroine, in *Chertova kukla* and in *Roman-Tsarevich*, states: "Love is always right. One must always take great pains to illuminate it with truth." In Litta's opinion, man must never lose the image and the idea of Christ in each of his actions.

Hippius firmly believed that it was her task to oppose the regressive forces that threatened to assert themselves after the failure of the revolutionary movement in 1905. She hoped to stimulate a transformation of man into a conscious being who would be able to affirm and to justify his new philosophy. Everything else in *Chertova kukla* serves to intensify the portrayal of the main character of the novel, Iurii Dvoekurov. He is a confirmed individualist, guided in all his actions by the selfish dictates of his ego. Even the title of this part of the trilogy suggests a deadly vacuum in his soul. He pleads the cause of rationality in human deeds, feelings and desires. Since he does not believe in God, he is destined to become monstrous. Hippius attempted to prove her case *ad contrarium* by criticizing Dvoekurov's "godless deeds": Dvoekurov, Hippius's "enemy", inadvertently makes the revolutionaries realize that a sublimation of practice and theory to lofty religious ideas is, in fact, necessary. Viktor Chernov, a Russian critic, maintained that in this work Hippius desired to blend religion with life, to make life holy, and to interpret the holiness of religions in life.

In *Roman-Tsarevich*, Hippius presents life as a solipsistic melodrama of a single person, who ruins many people on a whim. The basic idea of the novel affirms the author's belief that a simple Russian's faith in God is sacred and that no one should use it for his own purposes, even for an elevated goal, namely, the freedom of the people. Any abuse of this intuitive faith in God will inevitably lead to punishment. This is the solemn message of the second part of Hippius's trilogy.

The theme of pseudo-religious revolution links *Chertova kukla* and *Roman-Tsarevich* with Dostoevskii's novel *Besy* (*The Possessed* or *The Devils*), 1872. Both writers present in their respective novels revolution and reaction, Russian émigrés and their provocations, and the prostration and tedium that follow. Like Dostoevskii, Hippius dreamed about a "golden age" when the earth would merge with Heaven into one blissful Kingdom – when the Word would become the embodiment of Truth.

The critics R.V. Ivanov-Razumnik, V. Golikov, V. L'vov-Rogachevskii, and A. Zakrevskii accused Hippius of an "anti-social attitude", and pointed to her "tragic inability to answer the questions of the day". Among the favourable reviews, the most perceptive were written by V. Chudovskii, A. Izmailov, and E.A. Koltanovskaia. Chudovskii had a high esteem for the artistic quality of Hippius's novels: their beautiful descriptions of nature, their rhythmical patterns in the organization of phrases, their "narrative-impulse", and "musical appearance". Chudovskii stated that Hippius's "technique suited perfectly the characterization of the protagonist". V. Izmailov commended the refinement of the artistic form characteristic of *Roman-Tsarevich* and the treatment of the revolutionary theme, a topic of "the most indubitable and supreme significance". Koltanovskaia lauded Hippius's skill in developing psychological portrayals of contemporary educated men. Golikov endeavoured to establish the similarity between Hippius's Dvoekurov and Dostoevskii's Stavrogin and to describe their respective roles in the romantic, religious, and revolutionary uprisings.

In reality, the connection between Russian activities as portrayed by Hippius in her trilogy and "life as it is" was more profound than claimed by her contemporaries. For example, she described in an ironical light the meetings of the Religious-Philosophical Society organized by N. Berdiaev. There is a humorous description of Viacheslav Ivanov's famous *soirées* in his "Tower" in St Petersburg, later ridiculed by Hippius in her *Zhivye litsa*. Another sensational event, mentioned by Hippius in her trilogy, is the so-called Beilis Affair (1911–13). Among other matters of interest for the Russian reader of those distant days were Hippius's references to: insufficient understanding between Russian works and governmental officials; the acts of terrorism performed by some Russian revolutionaries; their innocent victims; several agent-provocateurs. The life of the Russian émigrés in France is also pictured in great detail. It rather seems that, as always, in her plays, short stories, novels, and other works, she reflects problems of both external and temporal significance.

In her works, Hippius did not simply continue the themes and ideas that she had inherited from the philosophical systems of Plato, Zoroaster, Mani, Nietzsche, Dostoevskii, Vladimir Solov'ev, Henri Bergson, and Otto Weininger; she transformed and enriched them to fit her own metaphysical and religious system of thought, with its own code of internal laws.

TEMIRA A. PACHMUSS

I

Nikolai Mikhailovich Iazykov 1803–1847
Poet

Biography

Born in Simbirsk province, 16 March 1803. Attended cadet school in St Petersburg, did not complete schooling; European University of Dorpat (Tartu), 1822–29; met Del'vig, Pushkin, and Zhukovskii; wrote poetry that was well-received; did not graduate. Moved to Moscow, worked as official in Surveyor's Office, 1829. Began to associate with Slavophile circles and figures such as Khomiakov, Aksakov, Pogodin, and Shevyrev. First collection published, 1833. Ill health forced a return to Simbirsk estate, 1833–38. Visited various spas in Europe in search of cure, 1838–43. Met Gogol' in Italy. Died in Moscow, 7 January 1847.

Publications

Collected Editions

Stikhotvoreniia. St Petersburg, 1833.
Stikhotvorenii. Moscow, 1844.
Novye stikhotvoreniia. Moscow, 1845.
Polnoe sobranie stikhotvorenii. Moscow and Leningrad, 1934; 2nd edition Moscow and Leningrad, 1964.
Stikhotvoreniia i poemy. Leningrad, 1988.

Critical Studies

"Sud'ba literaturnogo nasledstva N.M. Iazykova", by M. Azadovskii, *Literaturnoe nasledstvo*, 19–21 (1935), 341–70.
"N.M. Yazykov as a Slavophile Poet", by Ian K. Lilly, *Slavic Review*, 31 (1972), 797–804.
"Yazykov: His Lyric, Narrative and Dramatic Verse", by E.I. Bristol, *California Slavic Studies*, 7 (1973), 41–64.
"Yazykov's Lyrical Poetry", by Benjamin Dees, *Russian Literature Triquarterly*, 10 (1975), 316–29.
"Yazykov's Unpublished Erotica", by Benjamin Dees, *Russian Literature Triquarterly*, 10 (1975), 408–13.
"Grammatical Rhymes in N. Yazykov's Poetry", by Assya Humesky, in *Papers in Slavic Philology*, vol. 1, edited by B. Stolz, Ann Arbor, Michigan Slavic Publications, 1977, 121–41.
Poety Pushkinskoi pory, by V.I. Korovin, Moscow, 1980.
"The Stanzaic Forms of N.M. Jazykov", by Ian K. Lilly, in *Russian Poetics*, edited by Thomas Eekman and Dean S. Worth, Columbus, Ohio, Slavica, 1983, 227–34.

The son of a rich landowner and the youngest of three brothers, Nikolai Iazykov soon abandoned cadet school, gave in to his burning urge to become a poet and, after a year in St Petersburg, settled as a student in the relatively free and cosmopolitan atmosphere of the German-language University of Dorpat (Tartu), where he fused the grandeur of Russian 18th-century rhetoric and political ode with the life-asserting romanticism of Schiller and the Bacchic spirit of student songs. His stance was often that of a bard singing of past victories of freedom over Asiatic tyranny; in the context of the early 1820s he was widely admired as a hedonist poet in whom Schiller and Byron were subordinate to Russian patriotism, and appreciated as a peripheral supporter of Decembrist aspirations. More remarkable and highly praised was his revitalizing of fossilized poetic stances with rhythmic vitality and everyday imagery. In Dorpat he mixed with friends and relatives of Pushkin and Zhukovskii; not until 1826 did he meet Pushkin at Trigorskoe (an estate next to Mikhailovskoe): a short period of mutual admiration inspired both poets, especially Iazykov. In 1826 he mourned the execution of the Decembrist poet Ryleev: "Are you not the glory of our days, / The fiery sparks of freedom, / Ryleev died, like a criminal! / O, remember him, Russia / When you rise up from chains / And move your thunderous forces / Against the tyranny of Tsars!" But Iazykov's radical sympathies quickly faded. His attitude to Pushkin was contradictory: although a fellow-admirer of Byron, he deplored Pushkin's free-thinking discursiveness, fondness for telling detail and fecund narrative invention.

In 1829 Iazykov left Dorpat (without a degree) and moved to Moscow, where he followed Viazemskii's and Baratynskii's path as an official in the Surveyor's Office (a nominal job not for the salary, but merely to achieve civil rank). Here he fell into Slavophile circles and became more and more hostile to any western, prosaic, realistic or even late Romantic elements in the work of his contemporaries. The disease he had contracted in Dorpat recurred in Moscow and, from 1838 to 1843, forced him vainly to roam from one German and Italian resort to another. He died without issue and almost unmourned within three years of returning to Russia. Despite the publication of much of his best verse in 1833, his reputation had already waned, and he was bitterly attacked by the representatives of the new literature – Belinskii and Herzen – whom he deprecated from his new stance of orthodox passivity. In 1841 Iazykov admitted his own decline: "I feel that I am far from what I was before – and even further from what I should be at my present age." Nevertheless, in his last years he managed at last to achieve the extended forms that had eluded him in his youth – especially the fairy-tale "Zhar-ptitsa"

[The Fire Bird] (1836–38); but late recognition came to him only in the music to which Dargomyzhskii set his boisterous early lyrics.

Iazykov's reputation rests on one major achievement: he could write patriotic verse with neither doggerel nor cliché. It openly celebrates historic crises and covertly hints at imminent revolt:

The hand of the free man is stronger
Than the hand worn out by the yoke,
Thus thunder falling from heaven
Is more resonant than underground rumblings;
Thus a song of victory is louder
Than the muffled clanking of chains!

Iazykov's verses skip beats and avoid full stops, they use alliteration as dynamically as the folk epos (*bylina*), so that real bardic enthusiasm (which also owes a little to Macpherson's *Ossian*) infuses the formulae of patriotic exhortation. Like Pushkin, Iazykov could slip in the most telling, even bathetic prosaicism that suddenly infuses a whole series of conventional images with life. For instance, his farewells to student hedonism begin with the usual formulas: "In me the thirst for bliss has gone to sleep. / An inexorable ideal / Kept me alive and enchanted me" – but they end with unforgettable displacements: "And the stupidity of fateful passion / Has vanished in the youthful soul ... Thus, hearing a shot, the snipe/ Hurl themselves from the river into the air." Much of Iazykov's inspiration comes from his addressees: whether fellow poets or the women he was in love with, they infect him with a sense of common vivacity, shared joys and aims. Once in Moscow, this confederacy abandons Iazykov and his poetry. The last example of Iazykov's responsive dithyrambs is perhaps his best, "Trigorskoe", celebrating the summer of 1826 spent in Pushkin's company: the enjoyment of nature and company has the same vitality as the first chapters of *Evgenii Onegin*. Iazykov, unlike Pushkin, is however further excited by the sense of historic battles fought over the land he roams. In "Trigorskoe" Iazykov expresses an ecstasy beyond the Pushkinian bounds: "Darkness has drowned the skies; / Rain is released; the storm disturbs, / Rips up waters and forests, / Thunders, flashes and rages. / Wonderful moments!"

When Iazykov's talent soured, he occasionally achieved poetry despite himself. His "Zhar-ptitsa" was meant to satirize the excessive simplicity and frivolity of Pushkin's fairy tales, but unintentionally became a classic of naivety that anticipates Velimir Khlebnikov's pastorales. Iazykov's abuse of Westernizers such as Chaadaev is bilious enough to be enthralling: "You despised and betrayed all that is your own / But you are not yet wrecked; / But you stand, balding idol / Of petulant souls and weak women!"

DONALD RAYFIELD

Igor Tale *see* Lay of Igor's Campaign

Metropolitan Ilarion of Kiev fl. 11th century

Religious writer

Biography

The facts of Ilarion's life, works, and activities are mostly uncertain and hypothetical. Date and place of birth, as well as lay name, unknown. Must have obtained a thorough theological training in Greece, in the monasteries of Constantinople or Mount Athos; may also have visited Europe (France) as member of the Prince's embassy. Monk; priest of the church of the St Apostles, Kiev, in residence of Prince Iaroslav the Wise, until 1051; all his known works are dated around this period. Installed as Kievan Metropolitan by Prince Iaroslav in St Sophia's Cathedral, 1051. Co-author with Iaroslav the Wise in compiling the first Russian Nomocanon (The Statutes of Church Law), up to 1054. Presumed to be involved with first Russian chronographs. Replaced by Greek metropolitan Ephrem, 1055. Supposedly, in his last years, a monk of the Caves (*Pechory*) of Kiev. Date and place of death unknown.

Publications

Works

Slovo o zakone i blagodati, excerpted in *Khrestomatiia po drevnei literature XI–XVIII vekov*, edited by N.G. Gudzii, Moscow, 1962, 30–32; full text in "'Slovo o zakone i blagodati' mitropolitana Ilariona", by N.N. Rozov, *Slavia* 32/2 (1963), 141–75; and in *A Historical Russian Reader: A Selection of Texts from the Eleventh to the Sixteenth Centuries*, edited by John Fennell and Dimitri Obolensky, Oxford, Clarendon Press, 1969, 1–20; edited by A.M. Moldovan, Kiev, 1984; translated as "Sermon on Law and Grace", by Serge A. Zenkovsky, in his *Medieval Russia's Epics, Chronicles and Tales*, New York, Dutton, 1963, 78–83.

Molitva Ilariona Mitropolita Rossiiskogo v nashestvie inoplemennykh i za bezdozhdie i v smertonosie i za vsiako proshenie [Prayer for the Russian Land].

Ispovedanie very [Exposition of the Creed of Faith].
Pouchenie sviashchennikom [Exortation to the Priests].
Slovo k bratu stolpiku [Sermon to a Brother Stylite].

Critical Studies

"Slovo o zakone i blagodati i pokhvala kaganu Vladimira", by I.N. Zhdanov, in *Sochineniia I.N. Zhdanova*, St Petersburg, 1904, 1–80.
"Slovo mitropolita Kievskogo Ilariona v pozdneishei literaturnoi traditsii", by A.B. Nikol'skaia, *Slavia*, 7/3–4 (1928), 549–63.
The Russian Religious Mind: Kievan Christianity: The 10th to the 13th Centuries, by George P. Fedotov, Cambridge, Massachusetts, Harvard University Press, 1946; New York, Harper and Row, 1965.
"Gimn v 'Slove' Ilariona 'o zakone i blagodati'", by Roman Jakobson, in *The Religious World of Russian Culture*, II, The Hague, Mouton, 1975, 9–21.
Christentum und Theologische Literatur in der Kiever Rus', by Gerhard Podskalsky, Munich, Beck, 1982, 988–1237.

Bibliographies

Materialy dlia povremennogo spiska russkikh pisatelei i ikh sochinenii (X–XI veka), by N.K. Nikol'skii, St Petersburg, 1906, 122–26.
Des Metropolitan Ilarion Lobrede auf Vladimir den Heiligen und Glaubensbekenntnis nach der Erstausgabe von 1844 neu herausgegeben, by Ludolf Müller, Wiesbaden, (Slavistische Studienbücher, 2), 1962.
"Sinodal'nyi spisok sochinenii Ilariona, russkogo pisatelia XI veka", by N.N. Rozov, *Slavia*, 32/2 (1963).
Early Russian Literature, by John Fennell and Antony Stokes, Berkeley, University of California Press, and London, Faber, 1974, 41–60.

Metropolitan Ilarion, "a prudent and learned man and a faster", as a chronicle portrayed him, was one of the protagonists of the first age of Kievan Christianity; he can be regarded as the initiator of the original Russian (more correctly, East-Slavonic) literature in Old Church Slavonic, the *lingua docta* of Orthodox Slavdom. The fourth Metropolitan of Kiev (since the Baptism of Rus'), and the first Russian by origin among them, Ilarion participated in the ambitious educational projects of the Great Prince Iaroslav the Wise. He also happened to be the forerunner of the first monastic community in Rus', the Caves (*Pechory*) of Kiev, which became the heart of old Russian spiritual, cultural, and even political life. St Theodosii founded his brotherhood on the hills above the Dnieper, where Ilarion, not yet the Metropolitan, used to pray, and "dug a small cave for this purpose", as the chronicle reports.

A dazzlingly gifted pupil of his Greek teachers, Ilarion initiated one of the most successful genres of medieval Russian literature, the solemn Sermon (*Slovo*). He was followed by a number of distinguished preachers of the age: Kirill of Turov, Clement Smoliatich, Serapion of Vladimir and Luka Zhydiata, Bishop of Novgorod. Ilarion's patterns are to be found in the homilies of St John the Chrisostom, St Ephrem the Syrian, St Cyrill of Jerusalem and St Gregory the Theologian. However, the main source of his conceptual and stylistic inspiration must have been the Byzantine liturgical hymnography.

In Ilarion's homiletics one can grasp "The spirit not of Ilarion alone, but of a new Russian Christianity as a whole" (Fedotov). The main field of interest in his homileticas was not purely theological, contemplative or metaphysical and it barely dealt with ethics: its dogmatic and hermeneutic thought was not strong enough. Its concern was in fact the "holy history", from the creation of the world to its final transfiguration into the "new heaven and new earth". This attitude had a very pronounced eschatological accent. Ilarion's theology of history which was, for him, the triumphant process of salvation, had in its centre the thought of the providential destiny of the "Russian land" and the people of Rus', "the workers of the 11th hour". Closer to the Old Testament prophets than to his Greek teachers, Ilarion was concerned not with the individual souls of believers, but with the nation as a whole. He praises Rus', "not a humble land" in his "Sermon"; he grieves and prays for it in his "Prayer". In this perspective we can appreciate the peculiar, sacramental role that he prescribed for the Prince – the spiritual leader, educator, and protector of his people.

Presumably the purpose of Ilarion's *Slovo o zakone i blagodati* (*Sermon on Law and Grace*) was, as L. Müller supposed, to prepare the canonization of Prince Vladimir, the Baptizer of Rus': i.e., to prove his holiness and apostolic dignity. But the content of the sermon is much wider. The three-part structure of its text (masterly in organization) includes three themes and three genres.

The first, theological part follows the Pauline antinomy of Grace and Law, personified in the images of Hagar, the slave, and free beloved Sarah. The superiority of Grace is illustrated with symbolic comparisons: sun and candle, milk and water, cleansing and feeding, etc. The antinomy is complicated with the idea of dynamic nature of both the stages of salvation: Law led the chosen people to Grace – and Grace, in her turn, makes all the world enter the Life of the Future Age. The consequence is not linear or simply chronological: Grace was *before* Law, as Sarah was before Hagar, and it was Sarah who advised Abraham to have a child with her slave-girl. As for the Future Life, it seems to precede everything, for the "remembrance of Future Life" was the cause of Vladimir's conversion. This part of the "Sermon" is a mighty intellectual hymn, penetrated with the joy of Easter (Ilarion is supposed to have given his "Sermon" on the first day of Easter – 26 March 1049, in Rozov's opinion).

The second, historical part deals with the triumph of Grace, i.e., Christian Faith, among the new pagan peoples and the superiority of the new races, "fresh skins for new wine" in the face of the Jews, the former chosen and now rejected people. To illustrate the re-distribution of God's benevolence, Ilarion recalls the image of the fleece of Gideon (Judges, 6, 36–40): the fleece means the Jews: the dew was only on the fleece, when all the ground (i.e., the Pagan world) was dry; now, after the incarnation of the Word, everything is vice versa. The invectives of the Jews follow this statement.

The sharp anti-Jewish polemics of Ilarion requires explanation. Why did he contrast the young Christian Rus' not with its pagan past, but with Judaism? There is a wide range of answers. Some scholars (Müller, Podskalsky) find it but a conventional rhetorical theme of Byzantine heredity; others see in Ilarion's Israel the allegory of Byzance and even Bulgury (thus, Ilarion – and, with him, Prince Iaroslav, his patron who installed the first Russian Metropolitan before the agreement of Constantinople – would claim for the canonical independence of the Kievan Church). Finally, some of Ilarion's readers (from

Filaret the Metroplitan of Moscow, to Lev Gumilev and the "patriots" of our days) take his anti-Judaism literally as a testimony of the everlasting Jewish danger to Russia; the historical background of Ilarion's attitude would be the hostage of Khasars to young Kievan State. All explanations for this Anti-Jewish thrust (and, incidentally, of a mystical fear of the Old Testament, well-known in Rus') are far from being exhausted.

The third part of the "Sermon", the eulogical one, praises Prince Vladimir, the new Apostle of Rus'. Some arguments for Vladimir's holiness are quite peculiar: for example, Ilarion glorifies the military expansion of the pagan Prince: the fact that Vladimir was distant from the apostolic *paideia* is for his biographer a sign of some special grace ("nobody taught you, but God himself"). Significant also is the lack of the names of Cyrill and Methodius, the Apostles of the Slavs. The martyrs Boris and Gleb also receive no mention.

This part, which includes Vladimir's *vita*, was (over the centuries) the most influential on Russian (and Serbian) literature. It provided a pattern for the laudatory type of *vita*, which dominated Russian hagiography. The main concern of Ilarion's praise of Vladimir was, it seems, to establish the Christian identity and historical dignity of Rus' by linking her state power and Church, and thus pre-Christian and Christian eras.

It was not only the rich content that gave the "Sermon" the reputation of "a real masterpiece created dazzlingly early" (Podskalsky); nor less was it its rare poetical beauty. Its refined and elevated style (word-weaving) represents a kind of analogue to the monumental icon-painting. The text is saturated with biblical quotations, allegories and symbolic metaphors. Its rhythm is dominated by dual structures and triads. Ilarion demonstrates great skill in inventing symmetrical patterns, inversions, and juxtapositions. The effect of this verbal economy is the transfiguration of the concrete subject into an uncorporeal and mighty "angelic hymn".

Ilarion's works, both the "Sermon" and his "Prayer" for the Russian land (known in two versions, the full and the shortened) were included in the official prayer-books of the Russian Orthodox Church. They are known in numerous editions, copies, and replicas. The story of the texts is fairly well studied (see N. Rozov and A. Moldovan). The philological discovery of Ilarion's works and their first annotated edition was undertaken in 1844 by A. Gorskii.

OLGA SEDAKOVA

Il'ia Il'f and Evgenii Petrov

Satirical writers

Il'ia Il'f 1897–1937

Biography

Born Il'ia Arnol'dovich Fainzil'berg, in Odessa, 15 October 1897. Son of a bank clerk. Graduated from technical college, 1913. Worked successively in architect's office, telephone exchange, aeroplane works, and hand grenade factory, 1913–22. Moved to Moscow, 1923. Obtained post of librarian, then journalist for magazines *Gudok* and *Moriak*, 1923. Married in 1924. Toured Central Asia, 1925–26. Literary collaboration with Petrov began in 1927. Visited western Europe with Petrov, 1933–34. Travelled across the United States, 1935. Died of tuberculosis, 13 April 1937.

Evgenii Petrov 1903–1942

Biography

Born Evgenii Petrovich Kataev, in Odessa, 13 December 1903. Son of a schoolteacher and younger brother of the writer V.P. Kataev. Finished secondary education at classical high school, 1920. Worked for the Ukrainian Telegraph Company, 1921; Odessa Criminal Investigation Department, 1922. Appointed treasurer of the Praesidium of Odessa Union of Poets, 1923. Moved to Moscow, 1923. Appointed sub-editor of satirical journal *Krasnyi perets*, 1923. Joined staff of *Gudok*, first meeting with Il'f, 1925. Literary collaboration began, 1927. Married in 1929. Contributed to *Pravda* and *Krokodil*, from 1932. Travelled to western Europe, 1933–34. First play, *Pod kupolom tsirka* [Under the Circus Dome], written with Kataev, staged, 1934. Visited the United States, 1935. Joined Communist Party, 1940. Sent to the front as war correspondent, 1941. Died in a plane crash, 2 July 1942.

Publications

Collected Editions

Sobranie sochinenii, 4 vols. Moscow and Leningrad, 1938.
Sobranie sochinenii, 5 vols. Moscow, 1961.
Izbrannye rasskazy/ Selected Stories, edited by A.V. Knowles. London, Bristol Classical Press, 1994.

Fiction

Dvenadtsat' stul'ev. Moscow, 1928; revised edition with commentary by Iu.K. Shcheglov, Moscow, 1995; translated as *Diamonds to Sit On*, by Elizabeth Hill and Doris Mudie, London, Methuen, 1930; reprinted London, Labour Book Club, 1940; also as *The Twelve Chairs*, by John Richardson, London, Muller, 1965; reprinted London, Sphere, 1971.
Svetlaia lichnost' [A Pure Soul]. Moscow, 1928.
1001 den', ili Novaia Shakherezada [1001 Days, or a New Scheherazade]. Moscow, 1928.
Zolotoi telenok. Moscow, 1931; revised edition with commentary by Iu.K. Shcheglov, Moscow, 1995; translated

as *The Little Golden Calf*, by Charles Malamuth, New York, Farrar and Rinehart, 1932; reprinted London, Grayson, 1932; also *The Golden Calf*, by John C.H. Richardson, London, Muller, 1953; New York, Random House, 1962.
Odnoetazhnaia Amerika. Moscow, 1936; translated as *Little Golden America*, by Charles Malamuth, London, Routledge, 1944.

Critical Studies

I. Il'f i E. Petrov. Materialy dlia biografii, by T.N. Tsintsova, Moscow, 1959.
I. Il'f. E. Petrov. Ocherk tvoreniia, by A.Z. Vulis, Moscow 1960.
Il'ia Il'f: Evgenii Petrov, by B.E. Galanov, Moscow, 1961.
"Iskusstvo smeshnogo i nasmeshlivogo slova", by A.A. Shcherbina, *Russkaia literatura*, 17/1 (1974), 200–09.
"Ostap Bender as a Picaroon", by John L. Wright, in *Proceedings: Pacific Northwest Conference on Foreign Languages*, 25 (1974), 265–68.
Romany I. Il'fa i E. Petrova. Sputnik chitatelia, 2 vols, by Iurii Shcheglov, Vienna, Wiener Slawistischer Almanach, 1990–91.
Text Counter Text: Rereadings in Russian Literary History, by Alexander Zholkovsky, Stanford, Stanford University Press, 1994.

Il'ia Il'f and Evgenii Petrov, a team of writers and journalists, first met in Moscow in 1925 while both were working on *Gudok*, a magazine for railway workers. Individually they were both reasonably successful at journalism and writing feuilletons, mostly satirical, but at that time neither was known to more than a few readers. Il'f's early stories were normally short, amusing anecdotes or elaborations on news items that struck him as comic or incongruous and their humour is based on exaggeration or conversations at cross purposes. Sent by the editor of *Gudok* to Central Asia to report on how the area was coping with life under communism, Il'f was particularly struck by the clash between the old-fashioned customs and way of life of the inhabitants and the rather alien practices being forced on them. The humour he none the less found in the situation, while on occasions a little sharp, was tinged with a certain regret at what he saw as the inevitable passing of the old.

While Il'f always hankered after a literary career, Petrov, by contrast, had no ambitions to be a writer, but encouraged by his elder brother, Valentin Kataev, he began to compose short stories, based largely on comedy of situation, and a small collection was published in book form in 1924.

In 1921, with the Civil War virtually at an end, Lenin abandoned the policies, known as War Communism, as no longer workable and introduced the New Economic Policy. This restored some limited private trade and allowed the peasants to sell any surplus produce on the open market. Small businesses, including a number of publishing houses, were permitted to operate under private ownership. This period, until it was ended by the introduction of the first Five-Year Plan in 1928, was one of comparative freedom for writers and Il'f and Petrov made the most of their opportunities. They appreciated especially the satirical possibilities to be derived from the appearance of the so-called "NEP-man" or small businessman with his acquisitive nature and lack of scruples. It led to their writing jointly their best-remembered novel, *Dvenadtsat' stul'ev* (*The Twelve Chairs*). It was completed by January 1928 and was a huge success. Its plot, concerning the search for jewellery hidden in one of 12 chairs each sold to a different person, gave the writers the chance to present an extremely satirical picture of life in the Soviet Union under NEP. In so doing they also created one of the most popular heroes in Soviet literature, Ostap Bender, a clever, cynical, cunning, witty, and unscrupulous rogue who makes his way hilariously through a world of bankrupt NEP-men, poor clergymen, unimaginative time-servers, boring bureaucrats and philistine, materialist self-seekers.

The successful collaboration continued with a series of innocuous feuilletons, a novella, *Svetlaia lichnost'* [A Pure Soul], which has a complicated and fantastical plot and is generally considered to be of a lower quality. Commissioned by the journal *Ogonek*, it was completed in under a week and the haste in its composition is apparent in the rather disjointed style. This was followed by the much better collection of satirical novellas published with the overall title of *1001 den', ili Novaia Shakherezada* [1001 Days, or a New Scheherazade] in the literary magazine *Chudak* and written under the pseudonym of F. Tolstoevskii.

In 1931 the hero of *The Twelve Chairs* was resurrected (he had been killed at the end of the novel by a fellow treasure-seeker) in *Zolotoi telenok* (*The Golden Calf*). Ostap Bender, still determined to become a millionaire decides that the best way would be to find someone even richer and to relieve him of his wealth. If anything the satire is sharper but as it concerns the period of the first Five-Year Plan, introduced by Stalin in 1928 to replace NEP, it was met with disfavour by party critics, although it was as successful with its readers as its forerunner.

During 1933–34 the inseparable pair made a trip across the United States and their experiences are reproduced in *Odnoetazhnaia Amerika* (*Little Golden America*) of 1936, which is a sort of travelogue with perceptive and amusing comments on "Little America". Generally, though, they found the atmosphere in the Soviet Union in the 1930s to be less and less conducive to their brand of satire and what they published was less entertaining than before. After Il'f's death in 1937, Petrov wrote nothing of any importance and limited himself mainly to film scripts.

Although much of their subject-matter dealt with then contemporary phenomena and has lost its significance today, their work contains those deeper observations of human nature and its weaknesses, which, coupled with their skill at amusing their readers, make them still entertaining. While the 1949 reprint of their shorter works was found to be "ideologically pernicious" by the editor of *Literaturnaia gazeta*, the authors' value and importance was fully recognized in 1951 with a five-volume compilation. This established them as satirical and humorous writers second only (arguably) to M.M. Zoshchenko. Indeed, when the same *Literaturnaia gazeta* published the results of a poll in 1968 as to which Soviet writers of the period 1920–50 had best stood the test of time, Il'f and Petrov were placed third, behind only Sholokhov and Aleksei Tolstoi.

A.V. Knowles

The Twelve Chairs

Dvenadtsat' stul'ev

Novel, 1928

The Golden Calf

Zolotoi telenok

Novel, 1931

The Twelve Chairs was originally published in the first seven numbers of the journal *30 dnei* and then in book form in 1928. It was an immediate success. In his memoirs of Il'f, Petrov relates the novel's somewhat bizarre beginnings. One day Valentin Kataev, Petrov's brother, walked into the offices of the magazine *Gudok* where all three were employed and announced that he wanted to become the new Dumas *père*. He pointed at Il'f and Petrov, saying he would suggest a theme, they would each write a novel and he would judge whose was the better. His initial subject was that of some jewellery hidden in one of 12 chairs, each bought by a different person, and the subsequent search for it. The idea had its attractions, but Il'f and Petrov decided not to write different stories but just the one, which they would compose jointly. Thus began their fruitful literary collaboration.

The year 1928 marked the end of the NEP period that had been introduced at the end of the Russian Civil War in 1921 as a means of returning the economy to a more productive condition. It permitted a limited return to private trade and commerce and gave rise to the so-called "NEP-man", a small entrepreneur, often with less than honest practices. This was to provide the two authors with fertile ground on which their satirical talents would flourish. It also enabled them to create one of the most memorable characters in Soviet literature.

In essence *The Twelve Chairs* is a picaresque novel about a treasure hunt in which two rival groups seek the jewellery hidden in one of 12 chairs by a rich old lady during the upheavals of the Russian Revolution. Each chair must be found and searched, so the novel is a series of episodes criss-crossing the country. The plot is straightforward, but it provides the authors with the opportunity to describe all the contradictions of the NEP period. Thus they present a picture of the customs and practices of the 1920s, constructed in a series of scenes reminiscent of pantomime and humorous dialogue.

On her deathbed in 1919 the old landowner, Madame Petukhova, reveals to her nephew Vorob'ianinov, a former marshal of the nobility and now a modest functionary, that she has hidden her diamonds in a set of chairs that has been confiscated by the new regime. Unfortunately for Vorob'ianinov, the opportunistic priest who gave the last rites is also aware of the facts and the chase is on. Vorob'ianinov has befriended the happy-go-lucky businessman Ostap Bender, a cynical and clever scoundrel, and they both set off on a succession of adventures taking them all over the country. In the end they meet with failure in their search when they discover that the diamonds have been found and the proceeds spent on building a workers' club.

The novel owes its success almost entirely to the creation of Ostap Bender, who, according to Petrov, was originally conceived as a minor character. However, both the authors found he was hilariously taking over all the episodes in which he participated. While many of the other characters lament the past, Ostap lives entirely in the present, taking advantage of whatever opportunities present themselves. As he knows "four hundred ways to get money without working for it", he blithely and unscrupulously turns himself into a master crook. Yet he is no hard-headed swindler; he has the ability to see things, and himself, in an ironic light, and to appreciate the funny side of the many incongruous situations he finds himself in. It is this aspect of his personality that has ensured his, and the novel's, lasting popularity. While Russian readers were delighted with the novel, the official critical view was at best mistrustful. It failed to appreciate that Il'f and Petrov, while certainly pointing up many of the faults of the time, clearly did not wish to return to the past. Through Ostap they only mocked those who yearned for a return to the customs of pre-revolutionary Russia or a restoration of the monarchy. NEP might well be seen as a prelude to the establishment of a new form of social and political life so long as thieves, swindlers and especially bureaucrats could be eliminated.

Although Ostap had been killed at the end of *The Twelve Chairs*, Il'f and Petrov returned to him three years later in *The Golden Calf*. Times had, however, changed. NEP had been replaced by Stalin's first Five-Year Plan with its concentration on rapid industrialization of the Soviet Union and the establishment of "socialism in one country"; Ostap has changed too. Finding that conditions have changed so much and that any dreams of becoming a capitalist and millionaire have evaporated, he decides that the only way to obtain the wealth he seeks is to find someone who has managed to retain his millions, relieve him of them and then flee abroad. He understands that the government wants to build socialism, but he does not. He wants to leave the country, but not with empty hands. The provider of the wherewithal to guarantee his financial future is the wealthy and shady Aleksandr Ivanovich Kureiko. But while Ostap still wants to become rich, he now "respects the penal code" and turns against the very people he formerly epitomized, the crooks and swindlers of the NEP period. It is not the state monopoly of ownership that he opposes but those who purport to support but actually illegally thwart it. He turns from criminal to detective. He discovers that a large government department, called Hercules, serves only, in secret, to line the pockets of Kureiko. The satire is still present, more pointed even than in *The Twelve Chairs*, but the humour is rather less marked, despite, for example, the hilarity engendered by Kureiko having continuously to hide and deny his wealth. Yet the activities of Hercules, with its army of bureaucrats, dishonest employees and hypocritical humbugs, are severely attacked. To the authors, socialism will not be built if the state itself permits such atrocities in one of its largest governmental institutions. Ostap, however, succeeds in his quest at first. He relieves Kureiko of his millions, but in turn himself suffers a final defeat when his plans to cross the frontier come to nothing. He has converted all his money into gold and valuables. But he loses it all. The only thing he retains is the Order of the Golden Fleece (or Golden Calf), a medal symbolizing that money is no longer the moving force of the Soviet Union in the 1930s.

Although the plot is more fantastical than in *The Twelve Chairs*, it still takes the reader satirically through many levels of

Soviet society. The questions it also poses – how can one secretly become a millionaire under the Soviet regime? and what are the consequences of so doing? – found official disfavour and it took the personal intervention of Maksim Gor'kii to get the novel published.

A.V. Knowles

Leonid Moisseevich Ioffe 1943–

Poet

Biography

Born in Samarkand, 1943. A child of evacuees, grew up and was educated in Moscow. Graduated in mathematics from Moscow State University. Worked as a researcher in different scientific institutions in Moscow. Studied Hebrew, end of 1960s; subsequently became one of the leading teachers of Hebrew in Moscow, in association with the unofficial Zionist movement in Russia. Drafted into army during Soviet government's campaign to prevent mass emigration of Jewish intelligentsia to Israel, early 1970s. Emigrated and settled in Jerusalem, 1972. Lecturer in mathematics, Hebrew University, Jerusalem. Recipient: R.N. Ettinger Prize, 1985, awarded to Israeli writers for literary achievement in their native Russian language.

Publications

Poetry

Kosye padezhi [Oblique Declensions]. Jerusalem, 1977.
Put' zari [The Way of Dawn]. Jerusalem, 1977.
Tretii gorod [Third City]. Jerusalem, 1980; revised edition Riga, 1990.
Selected poems in *Znamia*, 3 (1994).
Trekhtomnik stikhotvorenii [Three Volumes of Verses]. Moscow, 1996.

Fiction

"Sportivnaia povest'"[A Sporty Story], *Menora*, (Jerusalem), 1979.
"Drevnevavilonskii" [Of Old Babylon], *Kultura*, literary supplement to *Nedelia*, (Tel Aviv), 13, 24 November 1993.

Essays

(Untitled), *Menora*, 23 (1980); also in 22, 49 (1986).

Leonid Ioffe's formative years as a poet coincide with the end of the Khrushchev Thaw. In the atmosphere of prevailing pessimism among the Soviet intelligentsia, there emerged a new generation of young nihilists, sceptical about the merit of any kind of political reform. Literary groupings, circles and semi-official associations proliferated at the beginning of the 1960s and Leonid Ioffe joined with Evgenii Saburov, Anatolii Makovskii, Valerii Shlenov and, later, Mikhail Aizenberg to form a group loosely united by their suspicion and distaste for the establishment, as well as a dissident political ideology. They perceived both official and unofficial camps and their literary representatives as distorted mirror images of each other, as social rather than literary phenomena, as the death of poetry. Instead, they began to seek salvation in a religious perception of world affairs or in the ecstatic notion of beauty.

Ioffe turns for poetical inspiration to the rediscovered poets of the Silver Age, Annenskii and Belyi in particular, and then to the 1920s, especially to the legacy of Khlebnikov and the OBERIU poets, as well as Mandel'shtam. Ioffe adopted an aesthetic according to which different levels of speech, highly charged with striking metaphorical patterns, are amalgamated into a self-supporting poetical entity in which logical connections are sometimes replaced by euphonics. References and allusions to this poetical tradition provided a firm moral background, rooting the poet in high culture, as opposed to the mundane deadliness of a vulgar Soviet life of misery and alienation. In Ioffe's first *samizdat* collections, the notion of beauty, understood as poetical integrity of style, is the redeeming factor amidst the muddy political waters.

Gradually, the central motif of Ioffe's poetry emerges as that of the outcast, incapacitated by the futility of joining any political or spiritual unity of people; at the same time, the poet craves a higher order of life and is crippled by a lack of belonging, a lack of identity. In the late 1960s these contradictory trends in the poet's psyche – romantic in essence – had acquired a political and moral dimension and Ioffe began a search for his religious identity and biblical roots, eventually joining the Zionist movement. His studies of Hebrew at that time could be seen as a rather idiosyncratic continuation of the same search, as in the early 1960s, for a new language or expression. This process finally led to his emigration to Israel in 1972.

Ioffe settled in Jerusalem and became one of the first Russian-language poets who managed to incorporate into his works both the metaphysical and visual landscape of his newly adopted country. An entirely new vocabulary had to be invented to describe an experience in which national wars and fear for survival clashed in his poems with a nostalgic view of his previous unjust, but heart-warming existence among friends in Soviet Moscow. The country of Israel only implicitly appears in his poetry. It is re-created by Ioffe not as a traditional Christian image of the Holy Land, but as a pinnacle of moral rectitude that numbs the profane lyre of an alien newcomer. The painful paradox here is reinforced by the fact that the newcomer is a rightful inheritor, at the same time incapable of giving up the memory of his Russian past which, in turn, prevents him from accepting whole-heartedly the beneficence of the legacy of his ancestors.

Since 1990 Ioffe's poems, which have appeared in all the major émigré periodicals, have also been published in the former Soviet Union. Publication of his selected poems in *Znamia* (1994) provoked a venomous attack from Aleksandr Kushner on the pages of *Literaturnaia gazeta* over Ioffe's idiosyncratic usage of Russian syntax and vocabulary. Three collections of his poems, published in Jerusalem, present the reader with an imperceptible metamorphosis by which a Russian poet, longing for spiritual salvation and seeking it in the notion of beauty, is transformed into a Jerusalemite who laments his Russian past. Characteristically for Ioffe, moral rigour is juxtaposed here with the aesthetic longing of a poet who has to use a language alien to his geographical location. Ioffe's idiosyncratic interpretation of the classic émigré predicament in an Israeli context was rewarded for its originality and power in 1985 with the Ettinger Prize.

ZINOVII ZINIK

Fazil' Abdulovich Iskander 1929–

Prose writer and poet

Biography

Born in Sukhumi, Abkhazia, 6 March 1929. Attended Sukhumi Secondary School No. 3, until 1948; student at State Library Institute, Moscow, 1948–51; Gor'kii Literary Institute, Moscow, 1951–54. Worked as a journalist in Briansk, 1954–55 and in Kursk, 1955–56. Editor, Abkhazian State Publishing House, 1956–62. Member of the Soviet Writers' Union, 1957. Moved to Moscow in 1962. Married; one daughter and one son. Elected member of the Congress of People's Deputies of the USSR, 1989.

Publications

Collected Editions

Forbidden Fruit and Other Stories, translated by Robert Daglish. Moscow, Progress, 1972; reprinted as *The Thirteenth Labour of Hercules*, Moscow, Progress, 1978.
Izbrannoe. Moscow, 1988.
Kroliki i udavy: proza poslednikh let [Rabbits and Boa Constrictors]. Moscow, 1988.
Sobranie sochinenii, 6 vols. Moscow, 1991–97.
Izbrannoe. Sandro iz Chegema, 2 vols. Moscow, 1996.

Fiction

"Sozvezdie kozlotury", *Novyi mir*, 8 (1966), 3–75; translated as *The Goatibex Constellation*, by Helen Burlingame, Ann Arbor, Ardis, 1975.
Zapretnyi plod. Moscow, 1966; title story translated as "Forbidden Fruit", by Robert Daglish, in *Forbidden Fruit and Other Stories*, 1972.
Trinadtsatyi podvig Gerakla. Moscow, 1966; translated as "The Thirteenth Labour of Hercules", by Robert Daglish, in *Forbidden Fruit and Other Stories*, 1972.
Derevo detstva [The Tree of Childhood]. Moscow, 1970; 1974.
Pervoe delo [The First Thing]. Moscow, 1972.
Vremia schastlivykh nakhodok [The Time of Lucky Finds]. Moscow, 1973.
"Sandro iz Chegema", *Novyi mir*, 8–11 (1973), 152–88; 70–104; 100–32; 71-125); uncut version, *Sandro iz Chegema*, Ann Arbor, Ardis, 1979; *Sandro iz Chegema: novye glavy*, Ann Arbor, Ardis 1981; complete version to date *Sandro iz Chegema*, 3 vols, Moscow, 1989; 2 vols, Moscow, 1991; translated as *Sandro of Chegem*, by Susan Brownsberger, London, Jonathan Cape, and New York, Vintage, 1983; and as *The Gospel According to Chegem*, by Susan Brownsberger, New York, Vintage, 1984.
Pervoe delo [The First Thing]. Moscow, 1974.
"Morskoi skorpion" [Sea Scorpion], *Nash sovremennik*, 7–8 (1976), 3–56 and 71–131.
Nachalo [The Beginning]. Sukhumi, 1978.
Pod sen'iu gretskogo orekha [Under the Shade of the Walnut]. Moscow, 1979.
Kroliki i udavy. Ann Arbor, Ardis, 1982; translated as *Rabbits and Boa Constrictors*, by Ronald E. Peterson, Ann Arbor, Ardis, 1989.
Zashchita Chika [The Defence of Chik]. Moscow, 1983.
Chik and His Friends, translated by Jan Butler. Moscow, Raduga, 1984.
Prazdnik ozhidaniia prazdnika [A Holiday in Waiting for a Holiday]. Moscow, 1986.
"Staryi dom pod kiparisom", *Znamia*, 7 (1987), 3–85; subsequent publications under the title "Shkol'nyi val's ili energiia styda" [The School Waltz or The Energy of Shame]; translated as *The Old House under the Cypress Tree*, by Jan Butler, London, Faber, 1996.
Stoianka cheloveka [A Man's Moorings]. Moscow, 1991; 1995.
Chelovek i ego okrestnosti [Man and His Surroundings]. Moscow, 1993; Moscow, 1995.
"Pshada", *Znamia*, 8 (1993), 3–36.
Detstvo Chika [The Childhood of Chik]. Moscow, 1994.

Poetry

Gornye tropy [Mountain Paths]. Sukhumi, 1957.
Dobrota zemli [The Goodness of the Earth]. Sukhumi, 1959.

Zelenyi dozhd' [Green Rain]. Moscow, 1960.
Deti Chernomor'ia [Children of the Black Sea]. Sukhumi, 1961.
Molodost' moria [Youthfulness of the Sea]. Moscow, 1964.
Zori zemli [The Earth's Dawns]. Moscow, 1966.
Letnii les [Summer Forest]. Moscow, 1969.
Put' [The Way]. Moscow, 1987.

Critical Studies
"Fazil' Iskander: An Examination of his Satire", by V. Babenko, *Russian Language Journal*, 106 (1976), 131–41.
"The Prose of Fazil Iskander", by Helen P. Burlingame, *Russian Literature Triquarterly*, 14 (1976), 123–65.
"Chem glubzhe zacherpnut'", by B. Sarnov, *Voprosy literatury*, 7 (1978), 126–51.
"*Sandro iz Chegema* i magicheskii realizm Iskandera", by Boris Briker and Per Dalgard, *Scando-Slavica*, 30 (1984), 103–15.
"Korotko, no ne koroche istiny" [Interview], *Literaturnoe obozrenie*, 11 (1985), 35–40.
"Fazil' Iskander's *Rabbits and Boa Constrictors*: A Soviet Version of George Orwell's *Animal Farm*", by Richard L. Chapple, *Germano-Slavica*, 5 (1985), 33–47.
"Fazil Iskander's View of Muslim Caucasia", by Margot Frank, *World Literature Today*, 60 (1986), 261–66.
"Potrebnost' ochishcheniia" [Interview], *Literaturnoe obozrenie*, 8 (1987), 32–34.
"The Unknown *Sandro*" [Interview], *Moscow News*, 28 (1988), 11.
"Usloviia igry", by M. Lipovetskii, *Literaturnoe obozrenie*, 7 (1988), 44–49.
"Iskander and Tolstoi: The Parodical Implications of the Beast Narrator", by Karen Ryan-Hayes, *Soviet and East European Journal*, 32/2 (1988), 225–36.
"O 'maloi proze' Iskandera", by S. Ivanov, *Novyi mir*, 1 (1989), 252–56.
"Vozvrashchenie k zdravomu smyslu", by V. Novikov, *Znamia*, 7 (1989), 214–20.
"Poslednii chegemets", by S. Rassadin, *Novyi mir*, 9 (1989), 232–47.
"Compilation in the Art of Fazil Iskander and as a Key to *Sandro iz Chegema*", by Laura Beraha, PhD Dissertation, McGill University, 1990.
Smekh protiv strakha, ili Fazil' Iskander, by Natal'ia Ivanova, Moscow, 1990.
"Fazil' Iskander v okruzhenii svoikh geroev", by V. Solov'ev, *Literaturnaia ucheba*, 5 (1990), 109–14.
"The Oral Illusion in Fazil Iskander's *Sandro iz Čegema*", by Laura Beraha, *Russian Language Journal*, 162–64/49 (1995), 177–91.
Contemporary Russian Satire: A Genre Study, by Karen L. Ryan-Hayes, Cambridge, Cambridge University Press, 1995, 445–63.
"Fazil' Iskander: From 'Petukh' to 'Pshada'", by Lesley Milne, *Slavonic and East European Review*, 74/3 (1996), 445–63.

Bibliography
Fazil' Iskander: biobibliograficheskii ukazatel', by Z.B. Mikhailova, Ulianovsk, 1982.

Fazil' Abdulovich Iskander was born in 1929 in Sukhumi, the capital of Abkhazia. He lived in Abkhazia until 1948, when he moved to Moscow as a student. After graduating from the Gor'kii Literary Institute in 1954, he worked as a journalist in Briansk, then as an editor in the state publishing house in his native Abkhazia. In 1962 he moved to Moscow, which has been his base ever since. Although Abkhazia provides the background to his work, Iskander writes in Russian.

Iskander started his literary career as a poet. His first volume of poetry was published in Sukhumi in 1957, and in that year he became a member of the Soviet Writers' Union. He has always continued to write poetry, but it is as a prose writer that he has made his distinctive contribution to Russian literature. His characteristic genre in prose is the story, either short (*rasskaz*), or long (*povest'*). From 1962 onwards short stories by Iskander began to appear regularly in periodicals. His first volume of collected stories, *Zapretnyi plod* (*Forbidden Fruit*), was published in 1966.

Also in 1966 the journal *Novyi mir* published his first *povest'*, *Sozvezdie kozlotury* (*The Goatibex Constellation*), a work that attracted widespread attention and established his reputation. The story is told in a conversational style, with many digressions. The dominant tone of the work is humorous, but there is satirical edge to this tale of the hybrid goatibex and the campaign for the "goatibexation of animal rearing", which functions as a comic metaphor for ideologically-driven campaigns of all sorts. *The Goatibex Constellation* was well received by both the critics and the reading public, who appreciated Iskander's characteristic mixture of "smiling satire", witty metaphors and aphorisms, and meandering digressions that might take a humorous, a lyrical, or a philosophical turn.

In the same year Iskander published the first story in what was to become the novel *Sandro iz Chegema* (*Sandro of Chegem*). This is a "novel" in an unusual form: a collection of stories around a main theme, which is the fictional Abkhazian village of Chegem and the adventures of the central character Sandro. The stories combine to give an epic account of Abkhazia before, during, and after the revolution, in the Stalinist period, and beyond. Sandro himself is an ambiguous figure: in part a rogue, ready to turn every situation to his advantage; in part an ideal hero, embodying traditional Abkhazian virtues. The mountain village of Chegem represents the bedrock of traditional Abkhazian values, and this offers a perspective from which to assess the political and historical progress made by the Soviet Union in the 20th century. The novel was first published in the journal *Novyi mir* in 1973, but in incomplete form because of censorship; *Sandro of Chegem* made its first appearance with the full complement of stories in America, in 1979 and 1981. The complete novel was first published in the Soviet Union in 1989, by which time it had acquired new stories and ran to three volumes. This process of adding to an existing text is characteristic of Iskander and has been described as "compilation"; it allows for continual extension to such works as *Sandro of Chegem*.

The dual publication of the *Sandro* epos, partly in the Soviet Union and partly in the US, illustrates Iskander's position in Soviet literature in the decade preceding glasnost, when he could be classified as both an "official" and an "unofficial" writer: as humorist and satirist he operated on the borderline between the permissible and the prohibited, constantly and deliberately overstepping the mark. In 1979 he was one of the participants in the almanac *Metropol'*, which issued a challenge to the Soviet system of censorship; in 1982 he published in the United States his satirical allegory *Kroliki i udavy* (*Rabbits and Boa Constrictors*), which was only published in the Soviet Union in the post-glasnost era, in 1988. This is an animal fable full of comic invention, with inspired parodies of Soviet slogans and official myths. Although the underlying message is a sombre one, and reflects a mood of despair, it is presented with an abundance of brilliant comic detail.

The relaxation of censorship during the period of glasnost allowed Iskander not only to publish previously banned works, but also to furnish previously published stories with a newly explicit political and historical context. Iskander had since his debut as a prose writer in the 1960s been noted for his stories of childhood, sometimes narrated in the third person about a boy named Chik, sometimes told by a first-person narrator. These stories now emerged as a body of work evoking the period of Stalinism as seen through the eyes of a child living, as Iskander had done, on the coast and in the mountains of Abkhazia. Some of these stories were brought together into a *povest'* under the title *Staryi dom pod kiparisom* (*The Old House under the Cypress Tree*), published in 1987; subsequent editions have been titled *Shkol'nyi val's ili energiia styda* [The School Waltz or The Energy of Shame]. Here the autobiographical context is open and poignant.

In the post-glasnost period Iskander has published two new titles structured according to his process of compiling stories into "novels". *Stoianka cheloveka* [A Man's Moorings] appeared in the journal *Znamia* in 1989 and as a separate publication in 1991. *Chelovek i ego okrestnosti* [Man and His Surroundings] was published in 1993. The disintegration of the structures of society after the collapse of the Soviet Union and, of course, the war fought between Abkhazia and Georgia have been a cause of distress to Iskander. He is conscious of his place in a Russian literary tradition where the writer is expected to offer moral guidance. This didactic impulse is marked in his recent work. He also turns frequently to the medium of newspaper articles as the swiftest way of reaching the Russian reading public, with whom he has always been one of the most popular writers.

LESLEY MILNE

Sandro of Chegem

Sandro iz Chegema

Novel (serialized 1973), 1979

When the uncut version of *Sandro of Chegem* was published in America in 1979, it established Fazil' Iskander's reputation on several planes: first, as a new type of post-imperial writer to be found in Britain and France as well as Russia, using the language of the conquerors to express the material of the colonized; second, as an exponent of a comic, even idyllic genre, in which epic and tragic material was dealt with; third, as the first living Russian-language writer to find a way of perpetuating the moral romanticism of Tolstoi. *Sandro of Chegem* has since grown: the repatriated Russian version of the 1990s is double the length of the underground *tamizdat* version, but the work remains essentially the same loosely-structured, semi-autobiographical fictional string of anecdotes, fairy-stories and reflections centring on an invented village and the author's uncle Sandro, the most cunning, ingenious and long-lived member of the village's most respected family. In its final version, the time scale stretches from the 1890s to the 1980s, from Prince Oldenburg to Eduard Shevardnadze, but the location never moves further than a day's journey by mule from Chegem. Chegem has a real location on the upper reaches of the river Kodori, in the mountains above Sukhum, and is remarkable not only as a community that best incarnates the age-old tribal values and economy of the Abkhaz, but as a village that borders on the lands of the Mingrelians, Svans and Circassians (not to mention the Greeks, Armenians, Jews and Russians), so that Chegem is also a microcosm.

Allowing for its panegyric tendencies, *Sandro of Chegem* is an ethnological study: the logic of blood feud and hospitality, the patriarchal clan structure, the conciliatory attitudes of tribal society to the state structures (whether Russian, Georgian or, earlier, Turkish) that envelop them, are all explained with anthropological objectivity as well as personal affection. The violence of the abductions, pillage and murders by which life is regulated is seen (as in Tolstoi's *Hadzhi-Murad*) as necessary to maintain a viable social structure that demonstrates its strength by surviving revolution, Stalinism and modern technology relatively intact. Iskander emphasizes the irrelevance of Christianity or Islam to a society that worships custom and propitiates nature, rather than doctrine or Gods. In the episodes that discuss the possible African origin of the Abkhaz or the provenance of the two negro villages near Novyi Afon, there is more than a hint of praise for a pantheist, totemistic culture whose religion depends not on the written word, but on oral tradition. Likewise, the phonetic and morphological complexity of the untranslatable Abkhaz language is seen as a model of the Chegem villagers' self-sustainable, impenetrable code of life.

The rest of Abkhazia outside Chegem is disturbingly half-real, half-invented. Certain places, such as Gudauta and Eshery, exist in the novel as they do on the map; others are lightly disguised. The capital Sukhum appears as a palindrome, Mukhus. But a parallel fictional city, Kengursk, also emerges. Iskander's chief addition to the bewildering ethnic richness of Abkhazia is an invented tribal entity, the Endurtsy. The Endurtsy (to whom Uncle Sandro's wife belongs) appear to be Abkhaz who have lost their innate moral values, and who ignore the taboos: myth proclaims them to be a people whom the Turks deported to the shores of Abkhazia. They are more vulnerable than anyone else to be turned into *homo sovieticus*. The etymology of the name could be "fools to the *n*th degree", but the meaning of this shadowy tribe, which haunts the whole novel, seems to be that they embody all our prejudices about alien ethnic entities. The *Endurtsy* are necessary as scapegoats to enable us to maintain our self-respect. Uncle Sandro is the reader's guide to the ethnic nature of conscience. He adds this quality of "life-teacher" to other mythical roles that the author gives him: sometimes (like his relative Kiazym) he is a Sherlock Holmes, sometimes he is a Brer Rabbit. His sharp vision and long life make him a witness to history.

Like Solzhenitsyn's *V kruge pervom* (*The First Circle*), the novel was sensational for the cameo appearances made by Stalin and his circle. Stalin is both enhanced in horror and diminished in significance three times by Uncle Sandro – once Sandro the boy sees Stalin the bandit, driving his loot on pack-horses after murdering his accomplices; then, in the 1930s, at a banquet with the Abkhaz leader Nestor Lakoba, Sandro dances for Stalin;

finally, after the war, Sandro dynamites fish for Stalin and is rewarded with a pair of Stalin's underpants. Iskander adds to the picture of an insecure psychopath, fatally manipulating his entourage by the surreal acrobatics of Sandro's dancing and Lakoba's marksmanship. However, in the entourage, Iskander takes details from Georgian and Abkhaz oral history: the narrative, although it deplores Bolshevik terror, elevates the deaf Nestor Lakoba to the status of fictional Abkhaz heroes, and the murder of Lakoba's family, when Nestor incurs Stalin's suspicions and is thrown to Beria's wolves, is portrayed as the tragedy of an entire culture. The gruesome picture Iskander paints of Beria, seizing power in the Caucasus, has been confirmed by the archival releases of the 1990s.

This mixture of real historical characters with the fictional, demands the genius of a Tolstoi if the seams in the narrative are to be invisible. Episodes that are included in the recent version of *Sandro of Chegem* are less successful: Iskander's friends appear transparently, for instance the archaeologist Iurii Voronov as Andrei, and are given fictional associates such as "The Carmen of Chegem", the nymphomaniac Zeinab who has to be shot like a dog by her father to prevent further disgrace to the family name. The reader is uncomfortably switched from the real to the fictional worlds. In the later episodes of the novel Sandro yields his place as a central figure to the author, a Moscow-based writer putting his roots down into soil that is unreceptive. Much of the material is that of Soviet anecdote, for instance the eternal battle of the Black Sea motorist with the corrupt auto-inspectorate, and the specific Abkhaz coloration fades. It is these later episodes ("O Marat", about the photographer, the Napoleon of love, who meets his Waterloo when he finds he is courting one of Beria's mistresses, or "The Carmen of Chegem") that have made successful films, because of their tenuous place in the novel's structure. Although the novel has been used by its author as a vehicle for episodic material, it can still claim to be the most enthralling prose in Russian since the 1970s; in the conversations between the hero and his author we hear the most persuasive arguments in Russian literature (since Tolstoi's Pierre talked to Platon Karataev) for a peasant against an intellectual culture.

DONALD RAYFIELD

Ivan IV 1530–1584

Autocrat and littérateur

Biography

Born in Moscow, 25 August 1530. Occasionally wrote under the pseudonym Parfenii Urodivyi. The elder son of Vasilii III by his second marriage to Elena Glinskaia (died 1538). Vasilii died in 1533 and Ivan became Grand Prince at the age of three. Ivan and his brother Iurii grew up under the tutelage of varying groups of boyars. Crowned tsar in 1547. His reign has been described as "one of the most spectacular, controversial and cruel in all Russian history" (Zenkovsky, 1980). Married: 1) Anastasiia Zakhar'ina; 2) Mariia Temriukovna; 3) Marfa Sobakina; 4) Anna Koltovskaia; 5) Anna Vasil'chikova; 6) Vasilisa Melent'eva; 7) Mariia Nagaia; five sons and three daughters, all of whom died in infancy – except Ivan (1554–81), whom he killed in a fit of rage; Fedor (1557–98), who succeeded him; and Dmitrii (1582–91), under whose name a number of impostors subsequently claimed the throne. Writings are very numerous, and no complete edition has been published. Died in Moscow, 8 March 1584.

Publications

Collected Editions

Poslaniia Ivana Groznogo [Epistles of Ivan Groznyi], text prepared by D.S. Likhachev and Ia.S. Lur'e, translation and commentary by Ia.S. Lur'e, edited by P. Adrianovoi-Peretts. Moscow and Leningrad, 1951.

Correspondence with Kurbskii (1564–79)

Sochineniia kniazia Kurbskago [Works of Prince Kurbskii]. vol. 1, *Sochineniia original'naia, Russkaia istoricheskaia biblioteka*, 31 (1914), 9–112, 121–24.

The Correspondence between Prince A.M. Kurbsky and Tsar Ivan IV of Russia, 1564–1579, edited with a translation and notes by John Fennell. Cambridge, Cambridge University Press, 1955; reprinted 1963.

Perepiska Ivana Groznogo s Andreem Kurbskim [Correspondence of Ivan Groznyi and Andrei Kurbskii], edited by D.S. Likhachev. Leningrad, 1979.

Reply to Jan Rokyta (1570)

Drevne-russkiia polemicheskiia sochineniia protiv protestantov, 1. Otvet tsaria Ioanna Vasil'evicha Groznago Ianu Rokite, with an introduction by Andrei Popov, *Chteniia v Imperatorskom Obshchestve istorii i drevnostei rossiiskikh pri Moskovskom universitete*, 2 (April–June 1878).

Poslanie k neizvestnomu protiv liutorov. Tvorenie Parfeniia Urodivago, pisatelia XVI veka (po rukopisi no. 423 b-ki A.S. Uvarova, byvshei I.N. Tsarskago) [Epistle to an Unknown Against the Protestants ...], *Pamiatniki drevnei pis'mennosti*, 60 (1886).

Tsar Ivan IV's Reply to Jan Rokyta, translated by Valerie A. Tumins. The Hague, Mouton, 1971 [the Harvard Russian manuscript in facsimile, transcription, and with an English translation].

Other Religious Writing
Stikhiry polozhenniia na kriukoviia noty. Tvorenie tsaria Ioanna despota Rossiiskago [Chants Set to Kriuk Notes ...], *Pamiatniki drevnei pis'mennosti*, 63 (1886).
"Dukhovnaia gramota Ivana IV, iiun'–avgust 1572 g." [Spiritual Document of Ivan IV ...], in *Dukhovnye i dogovornye gramoty velikikh i udel'nykh kniazei XIV–XVI vv.*, edited by L.V. Cherepnin. Moscow and Leningrad, 1950, 426–44.
"Kanon i molitva Angelu Groznomu voevode Parfeniia Urodivogo (Ivana Groznogo)" [Canon and Prayer to the Terrible Angel ...], by D.S. Likhachev, in *Rukopisnoe nasledie drevnei Rusi: Po materialam Pushkinskogo doma*, edited by A.M. Panchenko. Leningrad, 1972, 10–27.
"Tropar' i kondak na prenesenie chestnykh moshchei kniaziu Mikhailu Chenigovskomu, '... tvorenie Ivana, bogomudrago tsaria, samoderzhtsa rossiiskago' (k probleme atributsii)" [Troparion and Kontakion on the Bringing of the Saintly Relics of Prince Mikhail of Chernigov], by N.V. Ramazanova, in *Literatura drevnei Rusi: Istochnikovedenie: Sbornik nauchnykh trudov*, edited by D.S. Likhachev, Leningrad, 1988, 107–16.
"Stikhiry mitropolitu Petru 'tvoreniia' Ivana Groznogo" [Chants to the Metropolitan Peter: Works of Ivan Groznyi], by N.S. Seregina, in *Drevnerusskaia pevcheskaia kul'tura i knizhnost': Sbornik nauchnykh trudov*, edited by N.S. Seregina, *Problemy muzykoznaniia*, 4 (1990), 69–80.

Critical Studies
"Introduction", by Karl Stählin, in *Der Briefwechsel Iwans des Schrecklichen mit dem Fursten Kurbskij (1564–1579)*, edited and translated by Karl H. Meyer and Karl Stählin, Leipzig, Paul Schraepler, 1921, 5–21.
The Kurbskii-Groznyi Apocrypha: The Seventeenth-Century Genesis of the "Correspondence" Attributed to Prince A.M. Kurbsky and Tsar Ivan IV, by Edward L. Keenan, with an appendix by Daniel C. Waugh, Cambridge, Massachusetts, Harvard University Press, 1971.
Perepiska Groznogo i Kurbskogo: Paradoksy Edvarda Kinana, by R.G. Skrynnikov, Leningrad, 1973.
"Prince A.M. Kurbsky and Tsar Ivan IV", by John Fennell, in *Early Russian Literature*, by John Fennell and Antony Stokes, Berkeley, University of California Press, and London, Faber, 1974, 173–90.
"R.G. Skrynnikov: Perepiska Groznogo i Kurbskogo", review by John Fennell, *Russia Medievalis*, 2 (1975), 188–98.
Apocryphal - not Apocrypal: A Critical Analysis of the Discussion Concerning the Correspondence between Tsar Ivan IV Groznyj and Prince Andrej Kurbskij, by Niels Rossing and Birgit Ronne, Copenhagen, Rosenkilde and Bagger, 1980.
"Ivan Groznyi i Petr Velikii: Kontseptsii pervogo monakha", by A.M. Panchenko and B.A. Uspenskii, *Trudy Otdela drevnerusskoi literatury*, 37 (1983), 54–78.
The Image of Ivan the Terrible in Russian Folklore, by Maureen Perry, Cambridge, Cambridge University Press, 1987.
Ivan the Terrible: A Quarcentenary Celebration of his Death, edited by Richard Hellie, Irvine, California, Charles Schlacks, 1987 (special issue *Russian History*, vol. 14, nos. 1–4).
"Pervoe poslanie Kurbskogo Ivanu Groznomu v sbornike kontsa XVI–nachala XVII veka", by B.N. Morozov, *Arkheograficheskii ezhegodnik za 1986 g.* (1987), 277–89.
"Did Muscovite Literary Ideology Place Limits on the Power of the Tsar (1540s–1660s)?", by Daniel Rowland, *Russian Review*, 49 (1990), 125–55.
Mertvye knigi v moskovskom tainike: Dokumental'naia istoriia biblioteki Groznogo, by I.Ia. Stelletskii, Moscow, 1993.
"Tsar' Ivan Vasil'evich Groznyi kak pisatel'", by V. Kalugin, *Literaturnaia ucheba*, 3 (1993), 211–26.
"Ivan Groznyi - pisatel'?!", in *Ot Nestora do Fonvizina: Novye metody opredeleniia avtorstva*, edited by L.V. Milova, Moscow, Progress, 1994, 225–47.
"'Psy' i 'zaitsy' (Ivan Groznyi i protopop Avvakum)", by V.V. Kalugin, in *Staroobriadchestvo v Rossii (XVII–XVIII vv.): Sbornik nauchnykh trudov*, edited by E.M. Iukhimenko, Moscow, 1994, 44–63.
"Tsar' Ivan Groznyi: Stili khudozhestvennogo myshleniia", by V.V. Kalugin, in *Kul'tura srednevekovoi Moskvy XIV–XVII vv.*, edited by B.A. Rybakov, Moscow, 1995, 183–210.

Bibliographies
"Ivan IV (Ivan Vasil'evich)", by Serge A. Zenkovsky, in *Modern Encyclopedia of Russian and Soviet History*, edited by Joseph L. Wieczynski, vol. 15, Gulf Breeze, Florida, Academic International Press, 1980, 51–60 (historical bibliography).
Biblioteka Ivana Groznogo: Rekonstruktsiia i bibliograficheskoe opisanie, by N.N. Zarubin, supplemented by A.A. Amosova, Leningrad, 1982.
"Ivan IV Vasil'evich Groznyi", by O.Ia. Romenskaia, in *Slovar' knizhnikov i knizhnosti drevnei Rusi*, edited by D.S. Likhachev, issue 2, part 1, Leningrad, 1988, 376–86 [Ivan's writings and secondary literature].

Ivan IV Groznyi (Ivan the Terrible) was Grand Prince (from 1533) and tsar of all Russia (from 1547), a writer and publicist, whose works are preserved in manuscripts of the 16th, 17th, and 18th centuries. Ivan's writings consist principally of his *poslaniia* (epistles), official or semi-official letters addressed to named individuals, but often aimed at a wider audience. His correspondence with Prince A.M. Kurbskii (c. 1528–83) is made up of two letters from Ivan (1564 and 1577) and five from Kurbskii (1564, 1566, 1577, 1578, 1579). In them, and especially in his first epistle, Ivan reveals many of the distinctive features of his style: the fractured syntax of his Church Slavonic, the many instances of ellipsis due no doubt, at least in part, to the speed at which he dictated to his scribes, his lack of stylistic unity, consisting in abrupt changes in register from high-flown Church Slavonic to colloquial Russian; his deliberately vulgar abuse, evil sarcasm, and grim humour.

Kurbskii, one of Ivan's generals in the Livonian War and governor of Derpt (Dorpat, now Tartu) had defected to Polish-Lithuanian forces on 30th April 1564, and had sent a letter to Ivan accusing him of apostasy from the Orthodox faith: "To the Tsar, exalted above all by God, who appeared ... most illustrious, especially in the Orthodox Faith, but who has now ... been found to be the contrary" (Fennell, 1955). Ivan's apostasy, according to Kurbskii, consisted in destroying "the strong in Israel" (i.e., members of the old aristocratic and princely families) and killing the "voevodas given to you by God" (Fennell, 1955). In other words, Kurbskii considers the aristocracy as much a part of the God-given, natural order as the tsar himself and entitled by their birth to a share in the governance of the state.

The correspondence thus encapsulates the continuing crisis in the Muscovite state that had begun in the 15th century with the unification of the previously autonomous Russian principalities by Moscow in the reign of Ivan's grandfather, Ivan III, and the growing need for a more centralized and more effective system of administration to replace the old independent appanage principalities (Kurbskii's own ancestors had been independent princes of Iaroslavl, annexed by Moscow by 1473). Beginning with Ivan III, the grand princes of Muscovy had begun, through mass confiscations, to replace inherited patrimonies by service estates, possession of which was conditional on service to the state. The conflict between the autocratic pretensions of Ivan and the opposition of the conservative boyars was one of the critical issues of 16th-century Russian history.

This political argument was given a religious dimension by the medieval belief, fully shared by Ivan and Kurbskii, in the active intervention of God in human affairs. Political or military success was regarded as the result of divine intervention, to be secured through religious orthodoxy. The Byzantine Empire had fallen (in 1453), but "sviataia Rus'" had survived and prospered, not only securing the downfall of the Golden Horde (1480), but conquering two of its successor-states, the khanates of Kazan (1552), and Astrakhan (1556). Moscow's rulers had inherited the mantle of Constantine the Great. According to the Pskov monk Filofei, writing in the 1520s, two Romes had fallen, a third (i.e. Moscow) stood, and there would not be a fourth. The burning issue for Ivan and Kurbskii was: who was the guardian of the true Orthodox tradition (in its political application), and who the heretic?

Kurbskii proved the perfect foil for Ivan: whereas his first letter observes all the rules of 15th- and 16th-century epistolary correctness, in its brevity, stylistic unity, carefully contrived rhetorical devices and careful avoidance of any mention of specific persons or events, Ivan's reply is 20 times as long, has no stylistic unity, is careless and haphazard in its construction and contains a detailed account of intimate details of Ivan's early childhood. To Kurbskii's charge of apostasy, he replies that it is Kurbskii himself who has apostasized by breaking his oath of allegiance, given by kissing the cross. If power is God-given, then, by opposing it, he is opposing the will of God. Ivan himself is "free to reward our servants, and we are also free to punish them". He denounces the rule of the boyars during his minority as well as the government of the 1550s for tyrannizing over him. Kurbskii's reply, undated, but thought to have been composed not earlier than 1565 (but not despatched until 1578), is the earliest written example of literary criticism in Russian.

Kurbskii criticizes the length of Ivan's letter, calling it "beyond measure profusely in whole books", his extravagant language: "big-sounding ... belched forth", and inappropriate subject-matter: "about beds, about body-warmers, and other things ... as it were the tales of crazy women". Kurbskii recommends "measured lines or verse ... enclosing much wisdom in short words". Ivan's second letter, sent in 1577 from Wolmar, the town from which Kurbskii had first written, has a fine triumphant ring. The Russians were now at the western limits of their military expansion, and Ivan was clearly convinced of divine support for his actions. He lists all his titles and foreign conquests in his first sentence, which comprises 122 words, and continues "God grants power to whom He will", later repeated. Kurbskii's reply to this letter (probably written after the battle of Wenden, 1578) is interesting for the details it gives of Kurbskii's attitude to the Muscovite princes from Iurii Danilovich (1303–25) on.

Ivan's other writings include his letters to the rulers of Poland, Sweden, and England, the Hetman of Lithuania, to his *oprichnik* Vasilii Griaznyi, his extraordinary "petition" to Simeon Bekbulatovich, his theological dispute with the Czech Protestant Jan Rokyta, and his Epistle to the Kirillo-Belozersk monastery; D.S. Mirsky considered this last to be the most outstanding of Ivan's epistles. Other works attributed to him include a canon and prayer addressed to the Archangel Michael, written under the pseudonym Parfenii Urodivyi, chants (*stikhiry*) in honour of the 14th-century metropolitan Petr, and a troparion and kontakion in honour of the 13th-century prince Mikhail of Chernigov.

The authenticity of Ivan's letters to Kurbskii has been challenged by E.L. Keenan on account of the absence of 16th-century manuscripts of the *Correspondence* (the earliest manuscript dates from not later than 1621, see Morozov, 1987). Keenan's challenge comes down to the dating of Kurbskii's first letter. He claims that the author of Kurbskii' s first letter used a text by the monk Isai dated 1566. If this is the case, then the whole correspondence must be a forgery. From the textual evidence it has also been argued that it was Isai who borrowed from Kurbskii, although it is hard to explain how Isai, in prison, would have got hold of a copy of Kurbskii's text. The ultimate argument in favour of Ivan's participation (at least) in the compilation of the writings attributed to him from the 1550s to the 1580s is the constant presence of the same cruel mocking tone and grim humour – the same authorial style. We know that not one of Ivan's close collaborators – not a Viskovatyi nor a Basmanov – survived his entire reign. The only survivor – who must therefore be the author – is Ivan himself.

D.L.L. Howells

Georgii Vladimirovich Ivanov 1894–1958

Poet and prose writer

Biography

Born in Kovno, Lithuania, 10 November 1894. Educated in St Petersburg Cadet Corps; graduated 1912. Attended lectures at St Petersburg University, 1912–13. Married: 1) Gabrielle Evdovna Ternisien, French actress and dancer in Meierkhol'd's theatre (divorced before 1917 Revolution); 2) the poet Irina Odoevtseva in 1921. Began to publish in 1910. Briefly a member of the Ego-Futurists. Joined the Poets' Guild, Spring, 1912. Secretary, St Petersburg Writers' Union, 1920. Emigrated to Berlin, autumn 1922. Settled in Paris, 1923. Member of Russian émigré Green Lamp Society. Model for émigré poets of the "Parisian Note". Died in Hyères, France, 26 August 1958.

Publications

Collected Editions

Sobranie stikhotvorenii. Würzburg, Jal, 1975.
Izbrannye stikhi. Paris, Lev, 1980 (Contains "Biograficheskaia spravka", by Irina Odoevtseva).
Stikhotvoreniia. Paris, YMCA-Press, 1987.
Nesobrannoe, edited by Vadim Kreid. Orange, Connecticut, Antiquary, 1987.
Tretii Rim: Khudozhestvennaia proza. Stat'i [The Third Rome: Fiction. Articles], edited by Vadim Kreid. Tenafly, New Jersey, Hermitage, 1987.
Memuary i rasskazy [Memoirs and Short Stories]. Moscow, Progress, 1992.
Sobranie sochinenii, 3 vols. Moscow, 1994.

Poetry

Otplyt'e na o. Tsiteru. Poezy. Kniga pervaia [Embarkation for Cythera. Poetry. Book One]. St Petersburg, 1912.
Gornitsa. Kniga stikhov [The Chamber. A Book of Poetry]. St Petersburg, 1914.
"Ispytanie ognem. Voennye stikhi" [Trial by Fire. War Poems], *Apollon*, 8 (October 1914), 52–58.
"Voennye Stikhi" [War Poetry], *Apollon*, 1 (1915), 58–62.
Pamiatnik slavy. Stikhotvoreniia [Monument of Glory. Poetry]. Petrograd, 1915.
Veresk. Vtoraia kniga stikhov [Heather. The Second Book of Poems]. Moscow and Petrograd, 1916; 2nd edition, Berlin, Petrograd, and Moscow, 1923.
Sady. Tret'ia kniga stikhov [Gardens. The Third Book of Poems]. Petrograd, 1921; 2nd edition Berlin, 1922.
Lampada. Sobranie stikhotvorenii. Kniga pervaia [The Icon Lamp. Collected Poems. Book One]. Petrograd, 1922; 2nd edition Berlin, 1923.
Rozy [Roses]. Paris, Rodnik, 1931.
Otplytie na ostrov Tsiteru. Izbrannye stikhi 1916–1936 [Embarkation for Cythera. Selected Poems]. Berlin, Petropolis, 1937.
Portret bez skhodstva. Stikhi [Portrait Without a Likeness. Poems]. Paris, Rifma, 1950.
"Stikhi 1950 goda" [Poems of 1950], *Novyi zhurnal*, 25 (1951), 130–38.
"1943–1958. Stikhi", *Novyi zhurnal* (1958).
"Stikhotvoreniia", *Znamia*, 3 (1987), 140–41.
"Stikhi raznykh let" [Poems from Various Years], *Novyi mir*, 6 (1989), 238–40.
"Dnevnik (1955)" [Diary], *Druzhba narodov*, 7 (1989), 108–11.

Fiction

"Dama s Bel'vera" [The Lady from Belvedere], *Illiustrirovannaia Rossiia*, 222 (1929).
"Vasilisa", *Illiustrirovannaia Rossiia*, 225 (1929).
Raspad atoma. Paris, La Maison du Livre Etranger, 1938; reprinted by Dom knigi; translated as *The Breakup (Disintegration of an Atom)*, by Peter Rossbacher, *Russian Literature Triquarterly*, 11 (1975), 7–27.

Translator

Kristabel' [Christabel], by Samuel Taylor Coleridge, Berlin, Petropolis, 1923.
Orleanskaia devstvennitsa [La Pucelle d'Orléans], by Voltaire, with Georgii Adamovich and Nikolai Gumilev, 2 vols, Petrograd, 1924.
Anabazis [Anabase], by Saint-John Perse, with Georgii Adamovich, Paris, Povlotskii, 1926.

Memoirs and Letters

Peterburgskie zimy [Petersburg Winters]. Paris, La Source, 1928; 2nd edition, New York, Izdatel'stvo imeni Chekhova, 1952.
"Privetstviia A.M. Remizovu" [Greetings to A.M. Remizov], *Opyty*, 8 (1957), 127–29.
"Iz moei perepiski s pisatel'iami: Pis'ma G.V. Ivanova, M.I. Tsvetaevoi i M.A. Aldanova" [From My Correspondence with Writers], by Gleb Struve, *Mosty*, 13–14 (1967–68), 393–406.
"Perepiska cherez okean Georgiia Ivanova i Romana Gulia" [The Correspondence Across the Ocean of Georgii Ivanov and Roman Gul'], *Novyi zhurnal*, 140 (1980), 182–210.
"Riga Glazami Georgiia Ivanova" [Riga Through the Eyes of Georgii Ivanov], edited by Iurii Abyzov, in *Daugava: Literaturno-khudozhestvennyi i obshchestvenno-politicheskii ezhemesiachnyi zhurnal soiuza sovetskikh pisatelei Latvii*, 8/122 (August 1987), 110–19.
"Lunatik" [Lunatic], *Literaturnaia gazeta*, 11 (14 March 1990), 5 [on the poet Vladimir Piast].

Critical Studies

"O poezii Georgiia Ivanova", by Iurii Terapiano, in *Literaturnyi sovremennik*, 1954; reprinted in *Literaturnaia zhizn' russkogo Parizha za polveka (1924–1974): Esse, vospominaniia, stat'i*, Paris and New York, Al'batros-Tret'ia volna, 1987, 147–56.
"O poezii Georgiia Ivanova", by Vladimir Markov, *Opyty*, 8 (1957), 83–92.
"Nashi poety. I. Georgii Ivanov", by Georgii Adamovich, *Novyi zhurnal*, 52 (1958), 55–62.
"Russkie tsitatnye poety: zametki o poezii P.A. Viazemskogo i

Georgiia Ivanova", by Vladimir Markov, in *To Honor Roman Jakobson*, vol. 2, The Hague, Mouton, 1967, 1273–87.
"The Poetry of Georgii Ivanov", by Irina Agushi, *Harvard Slavic Studies*, 5 (1970), 109–58.
"Georgii Ivanov: Nihilist as Light Bearer", by Vladimir Markov, in *The Bitter Air of Exile: Russian Writers in the West 1922–1972*, edited by Simon Karlinsky and Alfred Appel, Jr, Berkeley, University of California Press, 1977, 139–63.
"Prokliatyi poet Peterburga", by Valerii Blinov, *Novyi zhurnal*, 142 (1981), 66–87.
Na beregakh Seny, by Irina Odoevtseva, Paris, La Presse Libre, 1983.
"Filosofiia v poezii Georgiia Ivanova", by Kirill Pomerantsev, *Novyi zhurnal*, 158 (March 1985), 123–29.
"O neudachnom izdanii stikhotvorenii Georgiia Ivanova", by Vadim Kreid, *Novyi zhurnal*, 167 (1987), 294–99.
"Talant dvoinogo zren'ia", by N. Bogomolov, *Voprosy literatury*, 2 (1989), 116–42.
Peterburgskii period Georgiia Ivanova, by Vadim Kreid, Tenafly, New Jersey, Hermitage, 1989.
"Exile and the Pastoral in the Poetry of Georgii Ivanov", by Eric Laursen, PhD Dissertation, Madison, University of Wisconsin, 1991.
"Paradise Overturned: Georgii Ivanov and the Antipastoral", by Eric Laursen, *Russian Language Journal*, 49/162–64 (1995), 161–76.

Bibliography
"K bibliografii Georgiia Ivanova", by Vadim Kreid, *Russian Language Journal*, 41/138–39 (Winter–Spring 1987), 205–17.

At the age of 16 Georgii Ivanov joined the Ego-Futurists and helped to formulate their manifesto. He soon became disenchanted with them and joined the Poets' Guild. After its demise, he took part in subsequent attempts to revive it. Ivanov was active in St Petersburg literary life and published six volumes of poetry before emigrating: *Otplyt'e na o. Tsiteru* [Embarkation for Cythera], *Gornitsa* [The Chamber], *Pamiatnik slavy* [Monument of Glory], *Veresk* [Heather], *Sady* [Gardens], and *Lampada* [The Icon Lamp].

In these collections Ivanov depicts a pastoral place of love, creativity and unity, most often the island of Cythera, an image drawn from the French artist Antoine Watteau. Ivanov frequently lyricized works of art (e.g., paintings, statues, and porcelain) that depict pastoral scenes. The pastoral realm is set in opposition to the real world, in which the persona exists in exile. Even *Pamiatnik slavy*, a book of war verse, depicts lovers exiled from a pastoral peacetime.

Reviewers perceived Ivanov's lyrics as technically perfect but lacking a message. This attitude became especially pronounced after the Revolution, when critics reviewed his collections as remnants of a best-forgotten literary past. In the politically charged atmosphere of the 1920s lyrics about shepherds and gardens were viewed as counter-revolutionary. This hostility, coupled with the execution of fellow Acmeist Nikolai Gumilev (August 1921) prompted Ivanov to emigrate in 1922 with his wife. After a year in Berlin, they settled in Paris.

In Paris Ivanov, Georgii Adamovich, and Nikolai Otsup formed a nucleus around which young Russian poets clustered. Adamovich instructed them to put their innermost thoughts and feelings into poems as they would a diary. Paying little attention to form, poets were to compose "human documents" of their experience in exile. This poetry was marked by nostalgia and despair, a quality that came to be called the "Parisian Note". Ivanov's first émigré collection, *Rozy* [Roses], is often said to have originated the Note.

In *Rozy* and the 1937 edition of *Otplytie na ostrov Tsiteru*, Ivanov's persona becomes a corpse existing in a snowy primordial darkness in which meaning has vanished. He is caught in a continual backward glance toward his beloved golden age, now transformed from Cythera into Russia. In this image the persona attempts to escape from the erosive effects of linear history. Yet, like Icarus – an image from one of Ivanov's early lyrics – the poet must always fall back to earth. Ivanov's persona is always in exile, whether from the stylized shores of Cythera and Scotland or the frozen banks of the Neva. In the 1930s this exile becomes more desperate, and images of frustrated travel and confinement recur. Memory becomes a predominant theme of Ivanov's émigré verse, for Russia now exists only in the exile's mind, and its image fades as the years pass.

Ivanov's émigré persona is split into competing voices. One half proclaims irrevocable exile. The other believes in a return home and dreams about the gardens of Paradise. These two halves face one another as in Ivanov's distorting mirrors of the 1950s. This "distorting reflection" is expressed in structure, imagery and rhyme. Opposites are juxtaposed, and almost identical syntactical constructions enclose antitheses, e.g., "Everything is unchanged and everything has changed".

During World War II Ivanov and his wife lived in relative luxury due to an inheritance. Ironically, their good fortune contributed to rumours of Nazi collaboration. Odoevtseva has vehemently denied this, and accusers have never provided proof or even detailed their accusations. Although Odoevtseva and Ivanov continued to publish, they became outcasts for several years. It was easy for contemporaries to suspect Ivanov of such a crime. He was a contradictory and enigmatic man, who, according to Odoevtseva, encouraged the notoriety that surrounded him. His biting wit and dark and seemingly nihilistic poetry added to his reputation. In addition, Ivanov was haunted by two controversial prose works. *Peterburgskie zimy* [Petersburg Winters] is an impressionistic account of St Petersburg literary life, concerned more with the essence of the times than historical facts. Many saw in this work only lies and betrayal. It was followed by *Raspad atoma (The Breakup (Disintegration of the Atom))*, an extremely negative and bitter expression of loss. This work, seen as pornographic, scandalized the émigré community.

In spite of his notoriety, Ivanov gained a new following after the war with *Portret bez skhodstva* [Portrait Without a Likeness]. For many émigrés in the 1950s, Ivanov became a spokesperson for their spiritual isolation and confusion about the future. In his final years Ivanov composed poems discussing his fate both as man and as poet; many of these were published under the title *Dnevnik* [Diary] in the New York émigré journal *Novyi zhurnal*. They were collected in 1958 and entitled *1943–1958. Stikhi* [1943–1958. Poetry].

Ivanov and Odoevtseva lost their inheritance and were forced to move to a home for the elderly in Hyères. Ironically, the Mediterranean, the object of longing in Ivanov's early poetry, proved detrimental to his health and is depicted as a private hell in his last poems. These poems inconsolably long for a return home, if not physically, then through publication of his poetry. His health deteriorated, and the Union of Russian Writers tried unsuccessfully to relocate Ivanov to a more suitable home closer to Paris. After three years in this, his final exile, Ivanov died on 26 August, 1958.

Soviet study on Ivanov came to a halt when he emigrated. In the west, scholarship consists primarily of short articles in émigré journals. Only two large-scale works have been published. One (Agushi, 1970) pays little attention to Ivanov's pre-emigration poetry, which comprises half of his lifework. The other (Kreid, 1989) covers only the pre-emigration poetry. In the late 1980s Odoevtseva returned to the Soviet Union, taking Ivanov's archive with her. This event, coupled with the new-found freedom of Soviet publishers, initiated a series of publications of Ivanov's work in his homeland. Georgii Ivanov was finally allowed to come home.

ERIC LAURSEN

Viacheslav Ivanovich Ivanov 1866–1949

Poet and literary theorist

Biography

Born in Moscow, 28 February 1866. Also wrote under the pseudonym Zaklès. Graduated from First Moscow gymnasium with gold medal, 1884; Moscow University, faculty of history and philology, 1884–86; University of Berlin, 1886–91; dissertation on Roman system of taxation, submitted to University of Berlin, 1895, but not defended (published, 1910). Married: 1) Dar'ia Mikhailovna Dmitrievskaia in 1886 (divorced in 1896), one daughter; 2) Lidiia Dmitrievna Zinov'eva (pseudonym: Zinov'eva-Annibal) in 1899 (died 1907), one daughter and three stepchildren; 3) Vera Shvarsalon in 1913 (daughter of Zinov'eva-Annibal from her first marriage, died 1920), one son. Lived in Europe, from 1886. Met Vladimir Solov'ev on visits to Russia, and Valerii Briusov in Paris, 1903. Began to publish unsigned journalistic articles in the late 1880s and poetry from the late 1890s. Introduced to Moscow and St Petersburg literary circles, 1904. Returned to Russia, 1905; lived in St Petersburg and hosted literary salon at the "Tower". Founder of "Ory" publishing-house and Poetic Academy in St Petersburg. Lived in Switzerland, France, and Italy, 1912–13; Moscow, 1913–20. Took an active part in Religious-Philosophical Society. Director of poetry circle in Moscow, 1920. Professor of classical philology, University of Baku, 1920–24. Emigrated to Rome, 1924. Converted to Catholicism, 1926. Lived in Rome, 1924–26, 1934–49; Pavia, 1926–34. Lectured at University of Pavia, and at Collegium Russicum and Ponteficio Institutum Orientale, Rome. Died in Rome, 16 July 1949.

Publications

Collected Editions

Sobranie sochinenii, edited by D.V. Ivanov and O. Deschartes, 4 vols. Brussels, Foyer Oriental Chrétien, 1971–87 (vols 5–6 forthcoming).

Stikhotvoreniia i poemy. Leningrad, 1976; reprinted, 1978.

Stikhotvoreniia. Poemy. Tragediia. St Petersburg, 1995.

Lik i lichiny Rossii [The Face and Masks of Russia]. Moscow, 1995.

Poetry

Kormchie zvezdy: Kniga liriki [Lodestars]. St Petersburg, 1903.

Prozrachnost': Vtoraia kniga liriki [Transparency]. Moscow, 1904; reprinted, Munich, Fink, 1967.

Eros. St Petersburg, 1907; reprinted, Moscow, 1991.

Cor Ardens. Chast' pervaia: Cor Ardens - Speculum Speculorum - Eros - Zolotye zavesy [Cor Ardens. First Part: ... Golden Veils]. Moscow, 1911.

Cor Ardens. Chast' vtoraia: Liubov' i smert' - Rosarium [Cor Ardens. Second Part: Love and Death ...]. Moscow, 1912.

Nezhnaia taina. Lepta [Tender Secret. Mite]. St Petersburg, 1912.

Mladenchestvo [Infancy]. Petrograd, 1918.

Zimnie sonety [Winter Sonnets], *Khudozhestvennoe slovo* (1920); translated as "Winter Sonnets", by Mary Jane White, in *Russian Poetry: The Modern Period,* edited by John Glad and Daniel Weissbort, Iowa City, University of Iowa Press, 1978; reprinted in *Twentieth-Century Russian Poetry*, edited by John Glad and Daniel Weissbort, Iowa City, University of Iowa Press, 1992.

Rimskie sonety [Roman Sonnets], in *Sovremennye zapiski*, 62 (1936).

Chelovek [Man]. Paris, Dom knigi, 1939.

De profundis amavi, in *Oxford Slavonic Papers*, 5 (1954).

Rimskii dnevnik 1944 goda [Roman Diary of 1944], in *Svet vechernii* (1962).

Svet vechernii [Vespertine Light], with an introduction by Sir Maurice Bowra and commentary by O. Deschartes, edited by Dimitri Ivanov (includes *De profundis amavi*, *Rimskie sonety* [Roman Sonnets], and *Rimskii dnevnik 1944 goda* [Roman Diary of 1944]). Oxford, Clarendon Press, 1962.

Plays

"Tantal" [Tantalus], in *Severnye tsvety assiriiskie: Al'manakh IV*, Moscow, 1905, 197–245; reprinted, Munich, Fink, 1972.

Prometei: Tragediia [Prometheus: A Tragedy]. Petrograd, 1919.

"Neokonchennaia tragediia Viacheslava Ivanova 'Niobeia'" [Viacheslav Ivanov's Unfinished Tragedy "Niobium"], edited with an introduction by Iu.K. Gerasimov, in *Ezhegodnik rukopisnogo otdela Pushkinskogo doma na 1980 god*, Leningrad, 1984, 178–203.

Essays

Po zvezdam: Stat'i i aforizmy [Following the Stars]. St Petersburg, 1909; reprinted, Letchworth, Bradda, 1971.

Borozdy i mezhi: Opyty esteticheskie i kriticheskie [Furrows and Landmarks]. Moscow, 1916; reprinted, Letchworth, Bradda, 1971.

Rodnoe i vselenskoe: Stat'i (1914–1916) [Familiar and Universal]. Moscow, 1917.

Perepiska iz dvukh uglov, by Viacheslav Ivanov and M.O. Gershenzon, St Petersburg, 1921; Moscow and Berlin, 1922; reprinted, Ann Arbor, Ardis, 1980; translated as "A Corner-to-Corner Correspondence", by Gertrude Vakar, in *Russian Intellectual History: An Anthology*, edited by Marc Raeff with an introduction by Isaiah Berlin, New York, Harcourt Brace, 1966, 372–401; also translated as *Correspondence Across a Room*, by Lisa Sergio, Marlboro, Vermont, Marlboro Press, 1984.

Dostojewskij: Tragödie - Mythos - Mystik, translated by Alexander Kresling, Tübingen, J.C.B. Mohr (Paul Siebeck), 1932; translated as *Freedom and the Tragic Life: A Study in Dostoevsky*, by Norman Cameron, with a foreword by Sir Maurice Bowra, edited by S. Konovalov, New York, Noonday Press, and London, Harvill Press, 1952.

Das alte Wahre: Essays, with an afterword by Victor Wittkowski, Berlin and Frankfurt, Suhrkamp, [1955].

Esse, stat'i, perevody [Essays, Articles, Translations]. Brussels, Foyer Oriental Chrétien, 1985.

Predchuvstviia i predvestiia: Sbornik [Premonitions and Portents: A Collection], edited by S.V. Stakhorskii. Moscow, 1991.

Classical Studies

"Ellinskaia religiia stradaiushchego boga: Opyt religiozno-istoricheskoi kharakteristiki" [Hellenic Religion of the Suffering god], *Novyi put'*, 1–3 (1904), 110–34; 48–78; 38–61; 5 (1904), 28–40; 8–9 (1904), 17–26, 47–70.

"Religiia Dionisa: Ee proiskhozhdenie i vliianiia" [The Religion of Dionysos: Its Origin and Influence], *Voprosy zhizni*, 6–7 (1905), 185–220; 122–48.

De societatibus vectigalium publicorum populi romani. Zapiski Klassicheskogo Otdeleniia Imperatorskogo Arkheologicheskogo Obshchestva, vol. 6, Prilozhenie. St Petersburg, 1910; reprinted, Rome, "L'Erma" di Bretschneider, 1971.

Dionis i pradionisiistvo [Dionysos and Pre-Dionysianism]. Baku, 1923; reprinted, St Petersburg, 1994.

Translator

Sobranie pesen i liricheskikh otryvkov v perevode razmerami podlinnikov Viacheslava Ivanova so vstupitel'nom ocherkom ego-zhe [Collected Songs and Lyrical Passages ...], by Alcaeus and Sappho. Moscow, 1914; 2nd augmented edition, 1915.

Avtobiografiia. Ispoved'. Sonety [Autobiography. Confession. Sonnets], by Petrarch, translated by M. Gershenzon and V. Ivanov. Moscow, 1915.

Tragedii [Tragedies], by Aeschylus. Moscow, 1989.

Other

Razgovory s Viacheslavom Ivanovym [Conversations with Viacheslav Ivanov], by M. Al'tman. Moscow, 1995.

Critical Studies

Sirin uchenogo varvarstva: Po povodu knigi V. Ivanova "Rodnoe i vselenskoe", by Andrei Belyi, Berlin, 1922.

Vstrechi, by V. Piast, Moscow, 1929.

Gody stranstvii: Iz knigi vospominanii, by Georgii Chulkov, Moscow, 1930.

Nachalo veka, by Andrei Belyi, Moscow and Leningrad, 1933; edited by A.V. Lavrov, Moscow, 1990.

Il Convegno (special issue), 8–12 (1933)

Die grüne Schlange: Lebenserinnerungen, by Margarita Woloschin, Stuttgart, Deutsche Verlags-Anstalt, 1954.

Vjačeslav Ivanov: Dichtung und Dichtungstheorie, by Carin Tschöpl, Munich, Sagner, 1968.

Russian Symbolism: A Study of Vyacheslav Ivanov and the Russian Symbolist Aesthetic, by James West, London, Methuen, 1970.

"The 'Zimnie Sonety' of Vjacheslav Ivanov", by Albert Leong, *Pacific Coast Philology*, 6 (April 1971), 43–49.

Vjačeslav Ivanovs Tragödie 'Tantal': Eine literarhistorische Interpretation, by Armin Hetzer, Munich, Sagner, 1972.

"Perepiska s Viacheslavom Ivanovym (1903–1923)", by S.S. Grechishkin, N.V. Kotrelev, and A.V. Lavrov, in *Literaturnoe nasledstvo*, vol. 85, *Valerii Briusov*, Moscow, 1976, 428–545.

Vjačeslav Ivanov: Estetica i filosofia, by Fausto Malcovati, Florence, La Nuova Italia Editrice, 1983.

Vyacheslav Ivanov: Poet, Critic and Philosopher, edited by Robert Louis Jackson and Lowry Nelson, Jr, New Haven, Yale Center for International and Area Studies, 1986.

Cultura e memoria: Atti del terzo Simposio Internazionale dedicato a Vjačeslav Ivanov, edited by Fausto Malcovati, 2 vols, Florence, La Nuova Italia Editrice, 1988.

The Poetic Imagination of Vyacheslav Ivanov: A Russian Symbolist's Perception of Dante, by Pamela Davidson, Cambridge, Cambridge University Press, 1989.

Vospominaniia: Kniga ob ottse, by Lidiia Ivanova, edited by John E. Malmstad, Paris, Atheneum, 1990; reprinted, Moscow, 1992.

Vjačeslav Ivanov: Russischer Dichter - europäischer Kulturphilosoph, edited by Wilfried Potthoff, Heidelberg, Universitätsverlag C. Winter, 1993.

A History of Russian Symbolism, by Avril Pyman, Cambridge, Cambridge University Press, 1994.

"Un maître de sagesse au XXe siècle: Vjačeslav Ivanov et son temps", *Cahiers du Monde russe*, 35/1–2 (1994).

"Viacheslav Ivanov: Materialy i publikatsii", edited by N.V. Kotrelev, *Novoe literaturnoe obozrenie*, 10 (1994).

Russian Symbolism and Literary Tradition: Goethe, Novalis,

and the Poetics of Vyacheslav Ivanov, by Michael Wachtel, Madison, University of Wisconsin Press, 1995.
Dichtung und Briefwechsel aus dem deutschsprachigen Nachlass, edited by Michael Wachtel, Mainz, Liber, 1995.

Bibliography
Viacheslav Ivanov: A Reference Guide, by Pamela Davidson, New York, G.K. Hall, 1996.

Viacheslav Ivanov's legacy as a major poet, critic, philosopher of culture, and translator far transcends his role in literary history as the leader of the movement of religious Symbolism that flourished in the first decade of this century.

When considered in terms of its external biographical contours, his life shows much evidence of change and discontinuity. Born in Moscow in 1866, he lost his father at an early age, and received a profound religious and cultural upbringing from his mother, interrupted by a brief spell of atheist rebellion during adolescence. Two years after embarking on the study of classical antiquity at Moscow University, he married and left for Europe where he pursued his studies under Theodore Mommsen and Otto Hirschfeld at the University of Berlin, living for extended stretches of time in Paris and Rome. Although he finally submitted his dissertation in 1895, he failed to defend it. During this period, under the influence of Nietzsche, his academic interests changed from Roman antiquity to an investigation of the religion of ancient Greece, and his personal life also underwent an upheaval, leading to the discovery of his poetic vocation. In 1893 in Italy he met the main inspiration and love of his life, the singer and future writer Lidiia Zinov'eva-Annibal. After an extended period of travel in Europe and the birth of their daughter, Lidiia, in 1896, they were married in 1899 and set up house in Geneva. In 1905 they finally returned to Russia permanently and settled in St Petersburg. The regular Wednesday gatherings at their home, known as the "Tower", became the central focus of cultural life in the capital. After the sudden death of Zinov'eva-Annibal in October 1907, the meetings still continued, although in a more sober vein. In 1910, prompted by an inner voice that he associated with the wishes of his dead spouse, Ivanov joined his life with Vera Shvarsalon, Zinov'eva-Annibal's daughter from her first marriage. Their son, Dimitrii, was born in 1912, a year before the solemnization of their marriage in 1913. When Vera died in 1920, the poet was left widowed for the second time in 13 years.

Although Ivanov never abandoned his scholarly research on classical antiquity, the main emphasis of his work from the time of his meeting with Zinov'eva-Annibal was literary rather than academic. By 1924, he had already published six books of verse, three collections of essays, two tragedies, numerous reviews and uncollected essays on literature, aesthetics, and the destiny of Russia, an exchange of letters with Gershenzon debating the metaphysical roots of culture, two volumes of scholarly studies in the field of classical philology, and translations from several languages, including Greek, Italian, French, German, and English.

In the summer of 1924, after spending nearly four years at the University of Baku as professor of classical philology, Ivanov left Russia with his two children and moved to Italy where he lived in Pavia and Rome until his death in 1949. This last quarter of a century of his life differed substantially from the previous 20 years spent in Russia. Following his conversion to Catholicism in 1926, his interests turned more in the direction of religion and culture viewed in the context of Christian humanism. During this period he played a much less public role in literary life and wrote relatively little new poetry. His long poem *Chelovek* [Man] was made up of sections written in Russia, and his last volume of collected verse, *Svet vechernii* [Vespertine Light], also comprised works mainly composed before emigration, with the exception of a handful of poems dating from the late 1920s and of the *Rimskii dnevnik 1944 goda* [Roman Diary of 1944]. Many of his publications during this period were either essays on aspects of Russian and European culture, or related to revisions of his earlier works and to the supervision of their translation into various languages. Up until the end of his life he worked on a unique, syncretic work of rhythmic prose, *Povest' o Svetomire tsareviche* [The Tale of Tsarevich Svetomir], a philosophical meditation on Russian history, written in the manner of a Byzantine romance and couched in the language of religious allegory.

To an outsider, such manifestations of change and discontinuity in the poet's outer life would seem to suggest paradox and contradiction in the inner life. How was it possible to reconcile within one person the Russian and the European, the scholar and the poet, the man of culture and the religious mystic, the follower of Dionysus and the Christian humanist, the Russian Orthodox believer and the Catholic convert, the leading theoretician of an avant-garde literary movement and the recluse of later years? And yet Ivanov's literary output conveys a remarkable continuity of vision and wholeness of spirit. Few of his contemporaries and critics were able to match his range of interests and depth of thought, and few of them shared the intensity of his drive towards integration and synthesis.

Ivanov's poetry represents an important but often neglected strand of Russian literature: poetry of thought, rich in religious and philosophical content. It invariably presents a stimulating challenge; as early as 1904, Briusov noted that "Ivanov requires a serious, inquiring reader, ready to bore into the hard rock of his verse in order to release its silver springs". Khodasevich compared the collection *Cor Ardens* to the cathedral of San Marco in Venice: a repository of past treasures, rich in history but difficult to imitate. Other critics have found his verse Alexandrian in its syncretism, Byzantine in its ornateness, and Latinate in its syntax.

Ivanov's early verse was indeed heavily saturated with references to classical mythology, further complicated by convoluted syntax, archaic language, and rich compound adjectives. The later verse, collected in *Svet vechernii*, achieves a more lucid balance of depth of thought and imagery, and comprises many outstanding lyrics. Ivanov's widely acknowledged mastery of the sonnet reached a peak in the three cycles composed between 1919 and 1924, *Zimnie sonety* (*Winter Sonnets*), *De profundis amavi*, and *Rimskie sonety* [Roman Sonnets].

In his critical and philosophical essays Ivanov developed the metaphysical school of criticism initiated by Vladimir Solov'ev, enriching it with a densely saturated, highly suggestive form of polyphonic prose. The depth and range of these essays, together with Ivanov's role as the chief ideologue of religious Symbolism and as an influential teacher of poetry, acted as a catalyst on the formation of the world-view and poetics of the post-Symbolist poets of the next generation, particularly on the Acmeist poets Gumilev and Mandel'shtam, and on the Futurist poet Khlebnikov.

Ivanov's critical reputation has undergone many fluctuations in the course of the 20th century, due partly to changes of political circumstance, and partly to the inability or unwillingness of his critics to recognize the underlying premise of his distinctive poetic voice, his view of culture as memory. Since the mid-1980s, however, his legacy has attracted a very marked resurgence of critical interest, both in the west and in Russia.

PAMELA DAVIDSON

Cor Ardens

Poetry collection, 1911–12

Ivanov's fourth major collection of poetry, written between 1904 and 1911, was published in two volumes (some of the poems appeared first in periodicals), divided into five books and further organized symmetrically into cycles and groups of poems. The book was issued by the Symbolists' publishing house Skorpion under Briusov's close supervision, although its publication was delayed by the doctrinal debates between Ivanov and other Symbolists grouped around the journal *Vesy*. The appearance of the book strengthened Ivanov's position as the leader and high priest of the religious Symbolists. The poems fit into the general atmosphere of the poetic life of the Symbolists; many of the poems are dedicated to Ivanov's contemporaries and reveal his relations at the time, as evidenced by the manifold intertextualities of the work. The Latin title signifies many levels: biblical, literary, Greek mythological, and medieval: from Dante's *La vita nuova*, it refers to the author's "burning heart" after losing Beatrice; from Catholic devotion, it suggests the sacred hearts of Jesus and the Virgin Mary as well as the burning hearts of the apostles on their way to Emmaus; and from Greek mythology, it refers to a Maenad. All of these connotations closely parallel Ivanov's personal life.

The poems of *Cor Ardens* are the product of seven years of the poet's life, and reflect essential formative changes in his poetic self. This time encompassed his final year in Switzerland and the famous period in St Petersburg, where he spent his legendary Wednesdays in the "Tower" (his Petersburg flat). The works reflect his relations with the representatives of intellectual life, especially Sergei Gorodetskii, Margarita Sabashnikova, and Anna Mintslova in 1906. There are also echoes of the death of his beloved wife Lidiia Dmitrievna in 1907, which exerted a paralysing effect on Ivanov; and his eventual emergence from this despair through his growing attachment to Lidiia Dmitrievna's daughter Vera, whom he married in 1913. The division of the poems into two volumes marks Lidiia Dmitrievna's death: part 1 was almost entirely completed before her death, while part 2 includes poems written after 1907 and not originally planned for this collection. After her death Ivanov switched the dedication of the collection from Valerii Briusov, who as a friend and fellow artist played an essential role in the creation of the book, to Lidiia Dmitrievna: "To the immortal light of Lidiia Dmitrievna Zinov'eva-Annibal, who, after being consumed on earth by my flaming heart, from flame became light in the house of the guest of the earth."

Part 1 consists of "Cor Ardens", "Speculum Speculorum", "Eros", and "Zolotye zavesy" [Golden Veils]; Part 2 contains "Liubov' i smert'" [Love and Death] and "Rosarium". The unifying message of the collection is the poet's quest for a synthesis of lower and higher reality, earthly love and celestial love, and is reflected in all levels of Ivanov's poetic world. This central idea is expressed through the combination and union of the Dionysiac and Christian views linking the concepts of suffering, sin, death, resurrection, and redemption.

In genre and form *Cor Ardens* ranges from the familiar to rare or exotic forms taken from western, eastern, and Russian folk traditions: sonnets (sometimes woven together, as in the famous "Venok sonetov" [Wreath of Sonnets]), ghazels, triolets, lais, canzones, rondeaux, rondels, huitains, ballads, and spiritual songs (*dukhovnyi stikh*), from short distichs to long narrative epics, such as the Russian folk-inspired "Solntsev persten'" [The Sun's Ring] or "Feofil i Mariia" [Feofil and Maria], a tale written in terzina. Ivanov practises closed forms with flawless perfection, not for its own sake, but as a means of communicating his own spiritual and creative experience – for Ivanov, artistic perfection and formal strictness were indivisible from inner growth. The imagery of the book builds on Ivanov's traditional recurring use of repeated antithetical concepts (fire-water, macrocosm-microcosm, light ray-reflection, dark of the abyss-light of redemption, agony/torment-joy, love-death, etc.), centred on the semantic field of the flaming heart in the title: blood, martyrdom, sacrifice, crown of thorns, loss, resurrection. The images are constantly developed and extended to new semantic fields, eventually taking on an all-encompassing character. In this contrapuntal world two realms are established – the earth and the heavens – divided by veils; all the earthly, primal images lack concreteness or tangibility; they are important because they point to the higher realm, with limitless allusions that blend various historical stages of mankind, representing diverse, seemingly unrelated cultures, such as the Bible, Byzantine literature, medieval European literatures, the European folklore tradition, and the Christian tradition: popular works, the Marian cult, Catholic and Byzantian hagiography, and some remote sources such as Armenian or Abyssinian. The poetic diction can be characterized, according to Poggioli, as "grand style", dignified and elegant, echoing the solemn odes of Russian Neoclassicism, featuring references to the classics of world literature, especially antiquity. The language is saturated with archaisms, Church-Slavonicisms, mythological terms, and words coined by Ivanov that match the spirit of the poems. The heavy style and philological elaborateness is alleviated by musical grace, and the combination of the two directs the reader towards intuitive perception.

The introductory book "Liubov' i smert'" reflects the poet's inner transformation within the first month after the tragedy of Lidiia Dmitrievna's premature death, close to the present for the poet, and then the subsequent books represent a flashback to earlier stages in the poet's spiritual journey, returning to the present in the fifth book "Rosarium". Placed as the opening book, "Liubov' i smert'" is a compressed expression of the whole *Cor Ardens*, conveying Ivanov's victorious trampling of death through his renewed faith and preservation and elevation of earthly love to a higher spiritual dimension. The high point of the book is "Venok sonetov", an ancient Italian genre in which sonnets are woven like flowers, into a wreath or garland. The sonnets are built on the unity of the antithetical two through the constant presence of the third, higher power, expressed in a circular structure that turns into a rising spiral. The subsequent books lead us through previous spiritual stages, describing an upward path from refined and ecstatic sensuality in Dionysiac terms toward higher stages of initiation, passing through several veils, or trials, and ending with Christian illumination, a new, qualitatively different form of love, imbued with Divine Light and ignited by Divine Love. "Rosarium" is the fifth and culminating book; it sums up both *Cor Ardens* and, indeed, his entire *oeuvre*. The cycle includes poems in which the symbol of the rose is illuminated from various sides, as if the technique of amplification were being employed on the scale of entire poems, making up the book.

Ivanov's creative development can be represented as a journey toward ever greater integration of life and art; *Cor Ardens* presents a deeper level of harmony and correspondence between the two. According to D.S. Mirsky, it is a high-water mark of the ornate style in Russian poetry. Ivanov's attempts to unify the heritage of various cultures with the Russian national element engendered a spiritual essence that unifies without dividing, includes without excluding, and ultimately leads to a higher reality. In this respect Ivanov achieved the kind of synthesis identified by Pushkin, which Dostoevskii had previously most closely approximated.

MARIA PAVLOVSZKY

Winter Sonnets and De profundis amavi

Zimnie sonety

Sonnet cycles (written 1919–20)

Winter Sonnets and *De profundis amavi* constitute two superb cycles of sonnets, each of which brings together a unified set of poems: with one exception, all were conceived in 1919 and 1920, during the years of turmoil and suffering after the Revolution. The cycles are acknowledged as the pinnacle of Ivanov's art: deeply spiritual masterpieces, a cry from his soul. These works testify that Ivanov was in tune with contemporary reality, both physical and spiritual. While re-evaluating his own inner development, he captured the essence of the time in a way reminiscent of his contemporaries. Although Ivanov continues to employ the set form of the sonnet with his usual virtuosity, they transcend his previous poems in simplicity of expression, greater artistic refinement, and the closer approximation of his ideal of perfection. This advance can be explained in terms of his poetic and personal development, which pointed in a new direction, incorporating more than ever the influence of objective reality outside of the poetic self. These two cycles were followed by some years of silence, until in 1924 Ivanov wrote the cycle *Rimskie sonety*, which joins them as the final phase of a triad, signifying a movement from darkness to light, from earthly, physical reality to the celestial and spiritual.

Winter Sonnets is a cycle of 12 sonnets, written between Christmas of 1919 and February 1920. It reflects the dark night of Ivanov's soul while his ill wife and children were in a sanatorium, and the exhausted poet would visit them on an open sled in the harsh winter. This cycle is regarded as a masterpiece of religious poetry. Ivanov's poetic diction moves from ornate solemnity to defined clarity, and his characteristic esoteric metaphysics gives way to a direct, intense and personal voice. This poetry is not aimed exclusively at the elite; it embodies the collective form of art, uniting each and every individual. Akhmatova praised the cycle: "To endure ... is not enough – but what he was able to do in 1919, when we were all silent, to turn his feelings into art, that is what has some meaning". The major poetic device is allegory; the sonnets are built on the natural parallel of the literature of the time: the revolution is viewed as the action of elemental forces, nature's winter reflects the winter of the exterior world (historical reality) and his own soul. The cycle likens man's moral and physical struggle with primordial reality to the trials and horrors of the revolution. The poet takes to the road, both physically and spiritually (like Dante's inner journey through the deepest circles of Purgatory), guided by the Radiant Lady (*Presvetlaia zhena*), his Muse, and the Unseen Heavenly Power. The poetic persona is split into internal and external halves, moving between dream and reality. The journey is a trial of the soul, leading to purification through all-embracing forgiveness. At this time faith must endure the greatest trial, but eventually emerges victorious; negativity, despair, and self-doubt are never overwhelming; distant hope and affirmation are constant elements and the cycle ends on a joyful Easter tonality. The allegorical allusions rest on dichotomous images: all the hardship, horror, and negativity of privation (lack of nourishment, shelter, memory, information, motion, human companionship), together with archetypical images of winter (cold, snow, ice, wolves howling), are set against warmth, both from the sun and inside the human soul. On a more universal level, this counterpoint reflects Ivanov's conception of the unity of opposites: natural and spiritual, earthly and heavenly. The semantic fields of the two ancient elements, water and fire, develop a full associative range: the metamorphosis of the winter state of water, ice and snow takes place under the life-giving energy of fire and sun (cf. the compact oxymoron "liquid fire"). Ice and snow turn into a river; the frozen, motionless state of nature starts to move; winter is followed by spring; death is conquered by life. This imagery alludes to the symbolic code of Ivanov's poetry, with semantic links that are never explored fully. We also encounter references to earlier poems, such as Sonnet V and his autobiographical narrative poem *Mladenchestvo*.

De profundis amavi includes nine sonnets, eight composed during June and August, 1920; the first four were written in a health spa, simultanously with *Perepiska iz dvukh uglov* (*Correspondence Across a Room*), the rest in his Moscow flat. The last sonnet was interrupted on 5 August after the words "So do not be jealous!", addressed to the Creator, referring to his wife Vera, who died unexpectedly three days later. Her death was the immediate impulse that wrenched the cycle from the depths of the poet's soul with the intensity of a prayer. The last sonnet was written 29 years later, in February, 1949. Ivanov entered his final corrections affecting the entire cycle on 14 July 1949. The last line of the sonnet is a clairvoyant vision of his own life, which ended two days later: "Death has cleft [me] with its merciless pole-axe". In the author's final edition this sonnet stands third; thus, the editions of the cycle testify to Ivanov's personal and poetic development up to his last day at the age of 83. The Latin title *De profundis amavi* [Love from the Depths] is a paraphrase of the opening line of Psalm 129 *De profundis clamavi* [Cry from the Depth], placing love at the focal point. The underlying theme of the cycle is the central concern of Ivanov's entire previous poetic *oeuvre*: the reconciliation and synthesis of earthly and spiritual love through the transforming force of Eros. The earlier cycles *Cor Ardens* and *Nezhnaia taina* [Tender Secret] end with the affirmation of this possibility, while this cycle extends this subject to physical love. The harmony of unity is replaced by anguish at revealing the contradictions, ambiguities, and even threatening aspects of sensuality. The sequence of the sonnets mirrors the poet's own spiritual development as he strove to conquer his stagnation, indecision, and conflict in order to take a new path of constant upward flight (at times interrupted by regressions) to pure spirituality, finally transcending sin and escaping from its stronghold, rising to everlasting union with God. The cycle ends by entering the realm beyond verbal expression: words are reduced to silence.

Winter sonnets was first published in Soviet Russia soon after its completion and then in a 1922 Berlin anthology of "revolutionary poetry" edited by Il'ia Erenburg. The first version of *De profundis amavi*, including eight sonnets, appeared in *Sovremennye zapiski*, (Paris, 1937). The final versions of both cycles, *De profundis amavi* including the ninth sonnet, with the author's corrections, appeared in *Oxford Slavonic Papers*, 5 (1954).

MARIA PAVLOVSZKY

Vsevolod Viacheslavovich Ivanov 1895–1963

Prose writer and dramatist

Biography

Born in Lebiazh'e, Pavlodar District, Semipalatinsk Province, 24 February 1895. Attended school in Lebiazh'e and agricultural college in Pavlodar. Typesetter in Pavlodar. Travelled around Siberia, Central Asia, and the Urals, 1913–15. Settled in Kurgan, western Siberia, 1915. First poem and story published, 1915. Also wrote under the pseudonyms Vs. Savitskii, Vs. Shatun, Vs.-ov, Vs. Tarakanov. Moved to Omsk, worked as a typesetter for an Omsk newspaper, 1917; went "underground" at start of Civil War in Omsk, 1918; joined partisan group in Novosibirsk, 1919. Moved to Petrograd, became full-time writer, 1921; joined the Serapion Brothers, expelled from Association of Proletarian Writers, 1922. Moved to Moscow, 1923. Married: Tamara Vladimirovna Kashirina in 1927; two sons and one daughter. Stayed with Gor'kii on the island of Capri, 1933. Evacuated to Kuibyshev, 1941; moved to Tashkent, returned to Moscow, 1942. Visited front line in Belorussia and Kursk, 1943. Correspondent for *Izvestiia* attached to First Belorussian Front, 1945; present at the capture of Berlin and the Nuremburg Trial, 1945. Visited Central Asia and Siberia, 1948. Professor of Literature at the Gor'kii Institute of World Literature, Moscow, 1954. Visited Buriat-Mongolian ASSR, 1956; in Belgrade for first performance of *Bronepoezd 14-69* (*Armoured Train 14-69*) in Serbo-Croat, 1957. Died 15 August 1963.

Publications

Collected Editions

Sobranie sochinenii, 8 vols. Moscow, 1958–60.
Selected Stories, translated by Keith Hammond *et al.* Moscow, Raduga, 1983.

Fiction

"Po Irtyshu" [Along the Irtysh], *Stepnaia rech'*, 37, 2 (1917).
"Partizany" [The Partisans], *Krasnaia nov'*, 1 (1921).
Tsvetnye vetra [Coloured Winds]. Petrograd, 1922.
"Bronepoezd 14-69", *Krasnaia nov'*, 1 (1922); translated as *Armoured Train 14-69*, by G. Cowan and A.T.K. Grant, New York, International Press, 1933; also translated as "Armoured Train 14-69", by Frank Miller, in Zamyatin/Ivanov, *The Islanders/Armoured Train*, Ann Arbor, Trilogy Publishers, 1978.
"Golubye peski" [Blue Sands], *Krasnaia nov'*, 3–6 (1922); 1, 3 (1923).
"Vozvrashchenie Buddy" [The Buddha's Return], *Nashi dni*, 3 (1923).
"Khabu", *Krasnaia nov'*, 2 (1925).
Tainoe tainykh [The Secret of Secrets]. Moscow, 1927.
"Gibel' Zheleznoi" [The Destruction of the Iron Division], *Krasnaia nov'*, 1 (1928).
Pokhozhdeniia fakira. Moscow, 1935; translated anonymously as *The Adventures of a Fakir*, New York, Vanguard Press, 1935; also translated as *I Live a Queer Life: An Extraordinary Autobiography*, London, Lovat Dickson, 1936.
Parkhomenko. Moscow, 1939.
"Na Borodinskom pole" [On Borodinskii Field], *Ogonek*, 30–38 (1943).
Pri vziatii Berlina [At the Capture of Berlin]. Moscow, 1946.
"My idem v Indiiu" [We're Going to India], *Sovetskii Kazakhstan*, 8–12 (1956).
Uzhginskii Kreml' [The Uzhga Kremlin]. Moscow, 1981; as *Kreml'*, Moscow, 1990.
Kreml'; U. Moscow, 1990.

Plays

Bronepoezd 14-69. Moscow, 1927; translated as *Armoured*

Train 14-69, by Gibson-Cowan and A.T.K. Grant, London, Martin Lawrence, 1933.
Golubi mira [Doves of Peace]. Moscow, 1939.
Parkhomenko. Moscow and Leningrad, 1941.
Diadia Kostia [Uncle Kostia]. Moscow, 1944.
P'esy [Plays]. Moscow, 1954.

Memoirs and Essays
"Vstrechi s Maksimom Gor'kim" [Meetings with Maksim Gor'kii], *Sibirskie ogni*, 3 (1946).
"Rasskaz o MKhAT" [A Short Story about the Moscow Arts Theatre], in *Povesti, rasskazy, vospominaniia*, Moscow, 1952.
"Istoriia moikh knig" [The Story of My Books], *Nash sovremennik*, 3 (1957); 1 (1958).

Critical Studies
"Vsevolod Ivanov", by A. Voronskii, *Krasnaia nov'*, 5 (1922).
Dramaturgiia Vs. Ivanova, by N. Zaitsev, Moscow and Leningrad, 1962.
"The Pioneers: Pil'nyak and Ivanov", by Robert A. Maguire, in *Major Soviet Writers: Essays in Criticism*, edited by Edward J. Brown, London, Oxford University Press, 1973, 221–53.
Vs. V. Ivanov v zarubezhnoi literature, by G.V. Anikin, Krasnoiarsk, 1978.
Khudozhestvennyi mir Vsevoloda Ivanova, by E.A. Krasnoshchekova, Moscow, 1980.
Zhizneliubivyi talant: Tvorcheskii put' Vsevoloda Ivanova, by L. Gladkovskaia, Leningrad, 1988.
"Myth in Vsevolod Ivanov's *The Kremlin*", by Valentina G. Brougher, *Canadian Slavonic Papers*, 25/3–4 (1993), 221–34.
"Vsevolod Ivanov's Satirical Novel *Y* and the Rooster Metaphor", by Valentina G. Brougher, *Slavic Review*, 53/1 (1994), 159–72.

Bibliography
Russkie sovetskie pisateli. Prozaiki. Bibliograficheskii ukazatel', vol. 2, Leningrad, 1964, 118–74.

In a number of respects Vsevolod Viacheslavovich Ivanov's biography seems to follow a path traced by many of his contemporary fellow-writers. Born at the end of the 19th century of humble background, he left school early and straight away entered the "university of life"; by the age of 20 his stories were being published in provincial journals, but it was the 1917 Revolution that marked the turning-point in his literary career. He leapt to fame in the mid-1920s with his Civil War stories, but he soon fell out of favour, and although he wrote much else besides, he was known right up to his death in 1963 largely as the author of one particular story, *Bronepoezd 14-69* (*Armoured Train 14-69*). Such a summary, however, does less than justice to an extraordinary, not to say unique, figure. Originally from what is now eastern Kazakhstan, Ivanov spent much of his early life on the move, rarely staying in any one place for long, and traversing, often on foot, huge areas of Siberia, the Urals, and Central Asia. Along the way he tried his hand at a number of jobs, including clown, wrestler, juggler, and acrobat. Once he had arrived in European Russia in 1921 he began to lead a rather more settled existence, but these early experiences lived on, directly or indirectly, in his fiction, giving it a distinguishing resonance and tonality. It seems, furthermore, as if he channelled the restless energy, which had inspired and sustained his wanderlust, into his creative activity, for he became one of the most prolific authors of his era; the eight volumes of the so-called "collected works" published during his lifetime represent but a fraction of his total output of stories, novels, plays, and articles.

Ivanov, therefore, was a free spirit; at the same time he supported the ideals of the Revolution and the Bolshevik Party. (For a brief period in 1922 he was simultaneously a member of both the Association of Proletarian Writers and of the Serapion Brothers.) The striking variety of form, content, and style of his fiction can be attributed to the tension between these contrary impulses of freedom and ideology. The experimental, intuitive, exotic, and fantastic often intertwined in the same work with the rational, realistic, sober, and topical. This can be seen, to varying degrees, in each of the four Civil War stories which first made his name – *Partizany* [The Partisans], *Tsvetnye vetra* [Coloured Winds], *Golubye peski* [Blue Sands], and *Armoured Train 14-69*. These stories reveal an author who is fascinated with language and style, but who is also preoccupied with the relationship between past and present, and with the way individuals respond to traumatic events, such as Revolution or Civil War, which they do not comprehend and over which they have no control. This question is explored further in two later stories, "Khabu" and "Vozvrashchenie Buddy" [The Buddha's Return]. The latter, in particular, relating the adventures of an elderly professor of history who has been commissioned to escort a bronze statuette of the Buddha from Petrograd to its home, a monastery on the borders of Mongolia, is a little-known masterpiece. Through the clash between old and new, the familiar and the exotic, the Russian and the Siberian, Ivanov shows the vulnerability of the European rational mind, when confronted by the "eyeless and savage darkness" of Asia. His portrait of the professor himself is curiously ambivalent, oscillating between the satirical and the sympathetic.

In *Gibel' Zheleznoi* [The Destruction of the Iron Division] the tone is more neutral, with an almost Tolstoian analysis of the hero's fears and reactions to catastrophic events. Ivanov's interest in the human psyche is further underscored in a whole cluster of stories written in the mid-1920s and collectively entitled *Tainoe tainykh* [The Secret of Secrets]. The emphasis here is on the irrational and subconscious aspects of human behaviour, with individuals from a wide range of backgrounds acting in mysterious ways and subject to seemingly uncontrollable impulses, sometimes of a violent or sexual nature. As might have been expected, this was hardly the kind of material likely to appeal to those intent on building socialism. Ivanov was accused of an unhealthy preoccupation with the "unscientific" theories of Bergson and Freud (although he claimed that he had never read either); by the end of the 1920s he was in official disfavour.

Although Ivanov continued to write prolifically, most of his work from the early 1930s onwards was considered unsuitable for publication; some of the rest he himself discarded. Three large-scale novels, however, did appear in print during his lifetime: *Parkhomenko* and *Pokhozhdeniia fakira* (*The Adventures of a Fakir*) in the 1930s, and *My idem v Indiiu* [We're Going to India] in the 1950s. The first is the most straightforwardly Soviet of all Ivanov's works. Its eponymous hero, a legendary Civil War hero in the Chapaev mould, possesses most of the qualities expected of such figures, but the portrait as a whole lacks conviction. Supporting roles are played by Lenin, Stalin, Budennyi, and Voroshilov. The other two novels – the second being in effect a continuation of the first, although separated by many years – are based on Ivanov's own experiences and adventures in Siberia and Central Asia. *The Adventures of a Fakir*, with its idiosyncratic language and colourful evocation of a vanished era, is far superior to its more conventional sequel.

Of the works Ivanov published posthumously, two are worthy of mention, both originally written in the 1930s. *Uzhginskii Kreml'* [The Uzhga Kremlin] focuses once again on the opposition between history and modernity, represented by the Orthodox Church and industry respectively. This is a work of power and subtlety, marred by a somewhat idealized conclusion. *U*, however, defies categorization. The pun embodied in its title – the Cyrillic "Y", as the epigraph makes clear, is the sound uttered by Tolstoi's dying Ivan Il'ich and also the universal symbol for any unknown or variable factor – sets the tone for a parodic, mocking, and at times self-referential work. Much of the irony is anti-Utopian in nature, threatening to subvert not only the novel itself, but the whole concept of socialist realism. Ivanov once said that "there are truths that are more trustworthy than our recantations"; more than any other work, *U* reveals its author's fundamentally anarchic, perhaps even heretical, spirit.

ROGER COCKRELL

Armoured Train 14-69

Bronepoezd 14-69

Novel, 1922

Armoured Train 14-69 was one of the first stories to portray the Russian Civil War in fictional terms. Written in 1921, it was first published in Aleksandr Voronskii's journal *Krasnaia nov'* in 1922, appearing as a separate edition in the same year. Like many other novels dealing with this topic it quickly achieved huge popularity; for 70 years it was one of the major works in the Soviet literary canon, being reprinted more than 50 times. Within ten years of publication, it had been translated into several western European languages, Chinese, and nine languages within the USSR; it first appeared in English in 1933. Ivanov wrote a stage version of the novel that received its premiere at the Moscow Arts Theatre in the same year.

Ivanov wrote the story after reading a newspaper account of an episode involving an armoured train in western Siberia. One such train belonging to the Whites had been ambushed by a group of Red partisans. In order to force the train to stop, a Chinese member of the group had lain down in front of it and had been crushed to death. The driver had looked out of the window to see what had happened and had been shot; as a result, the train, together with its guns, ammunition, and crew had been captured. Ivanov placed this incident at the centre of his story, but transferred the scene of the action to the Pacific coast region around Vladivostok. This was unfamiliar territory to him, but he considered that, whatever the story might lose in accuracy of observation, it would gain in breadth and scale. It would also have the advantage of topicality, since, at the time of writing, the Whites had been defeated in western Siberia and the focus of the Civil War conflict had moved to the Far East. *Armoured Train 14-69* ends with the surrender of Vladivostok to the Reds and the triumphant parade of the partisans through the city, led by their peasant commander, Nikolai Vershinin.

This relatively uncomplicated plot would seem to indicate a rather predictable adventure story with a cast of heroes and villains, set against an exotic background, and culminating with the victory of good over evil. In fact, in its original version of 1922, *Armoured Train 14-69* possesses many of the features of a nightmare, with curiously undelineated characters, no obvious heroes (apart perhaps from the train itself), and set in a bleak, monotonous landscape, somewhere on the Pacific coast. We are left with an overwhelming impression not merely of confusion and pointlessness, but also of the helplessness of individuals – whether White or Red – caught up in circumstances and a web of events that they are unable to control.

Over the course of the next 30 years the text underwent numerous revisions. The final version of 1957, on which a generation of Soviet schoolchildren was brought up and with which most Russians are familiar, retains the basic plot, but the changes since 1922 are substantial. New characters have been added, figures such as Vershinin and Nezelasov (the White commander of the armoured train) possess greater willpower and a sense of responsibility for their actions, and Ivanov attempts to show, without much conviction, that the Reds' ultimate triumph is not just another random episode, but one that is partly dependent on the guidance of politically aware Bolsheviks. The various focal points of the narrative remain the same – the White officers, the partisans, the train – but the switches from one to the other are less abrupt than in the earlier editions. Indeed in the opening scene of this version Ivanov portrays the White officers and their families in a surprisingly leisurely manner. The laughter, idle gossip, dancing, guitar-playing and singing are reminiscent of Chekhov, as indeed is the ironic contrast between the soothingly decadent atmosphere and the extreme vulnerability of their situation: events are taking place – Peklevanov's escape and the mobilization of the peasants, for example – which will lead to disaster not just for them personally but for their whole way of life. Outside there is no cherry orchard, simply a landscape made unrecognizable by fog, a natural phenomenon that pervades much of the work (in all its versions), shrouding the deliberations and actions of Reds and Whites alike. Visibility generally seems to be poor, with the fog disappearing, if at all, only at the approach of dusk. At one point, while the partisans are setting up their ambush, visibility appears to be normal, but the smoke from their bonfires soon throws a pall over events. The metaphor seems clear: despite the author's belated attempts to invest his characters with some sense of purpose, the fog has entered people's minds to affect their behaviour and clarity of vision. Only at the very end, with the fog symbolically lifted, do they march together in unison, moving as if on rails towards their destiny.

The fact that Ivanov adopted, almost certainly not of his own volition, a more orthodox political style and language in his later years should not cloud our judgment concerning the work's undoubted qualities. The language, although not as bold and as idiosyncratic as Pil'niak's, is frequently arresting with its counterpoint of broad-brush strokes: "Fog. Sea. Boats." and ornamentalist figures of speech: a dim-witted ensign has thoughts that are as "blunt as the toe of an American's boot"; hearts become as dry as a "broken twig"; the railway station, crammed with people, "sweats like a jar of worms". However one views the climactic scene of the ambush – and it has been variously described as "sombrely powerful" and "comically absurd" – few would question Ivanov's ability to create and sustain tension, or his skill in marshalling his forces so that they all come together at this critical juncture. Perhaps the story's greatest attraction lies in its intriguing ambiguity of tone, and in the refusal of the author, even in the final version, to lay all his cards on the table.

ROGER COCKRELL

K

Antiokh Dmitr'evich Kantemir 1708–1744

Satirist and translator

Biography

Born in Constantinople, 21 September 1708, the youngest son of a Moldavian aristocrat who became viceroy of Moldavia, 1710. The family moved to Russia in 1711; lived in Moscow, 1713–19 and then moved to the new capital, St Petersburg, 1719. Kantemir spoke Greek and Italian at home and was taught Russian and Latin by tutors. As a result of his father's service to Peter the Great, he became acquainted with court life at an early age. Accompanied his father on Peter's Persian campaign, 1722–23. Studied mathematics, physics, history, and moral philosophy under foreign professors brought to St Petersburg by Peter, 1724–25; subsequently served in Preobrazhenskii regiment. Started to produce literary works, from 1726 (including translations of first four satires of Boileau and a work by Fontenelle on Copernican heliocentric system). During the struggle that took place on accession of Anna to the throne, Kantemir took the side of the men of learning (prominent among them, Prokopovich), 1730; they represented the new Petrine gentry and opposed old aristocratic families seeking restoration of their privileges. Served as Russia's diplomatic representative in London, 1732–38; became ambassador to France, 1738–44. Died in Paris, 11 April 1744.

Publications

Collected Editions

Sochineniia, pis'ma i izbrannye perevody [Works, Letters and Selected Translations], edited by V.Ia. Stoiunin and P.A. Efremov. 2 vols. 1867–68.

Sobranie sochinenii, edited by F.Ia. Priima and Z.I. Gershkovich, "Biblioteka poeta", Leningrad, 1956.

Translation

"Satire I: To My Mind", in *The Literature of Eighteenth-Century Russia*, edited and translated by Harold B. Segel, 2 vols, New York, Dutton, 1967, vol. 1, 151–65.

Critical Studies

"Istoriia russkoi obshchestvennoi mysli", by G.V. Plekhanov, in his *Sobranie sochinenii*, 24 vols, Moscow and Leningrad, 1924–27, vol. 21, 78–102.

"Kantemir", by V.G. Belinskii, in his *Polnoe sobranie sochinenii*, 13 vols, Moscow, 1953–59, vol. 3, 613–34.

Russian Versification: The Theories of Trediakovskij, Lomonosov and Kantemir, by R. Silbajoris, New York, Columbia University Press, 1968.

A History of 18th Century Russian Literature, by William Edward Brown, Ann Arbor, Ardis, 1980, 31–53.

"The Eighteenth Century: Neoclassicism and the Enlightenment", by Ilya Serman, in *The Cambridge History of Russian Literature*, edited by Charles A. Moser, Cambridge and New York, Cambridge University Press, 1989, 45–53; revised edition, 1992.

A History of Russian Literature, by Victor Terras, New Haven and London, Yale University Press, 1991, 122–24.

Through his translations of such authors as Boileau, Horace and Anacreon, Antiokh Kantemir helped to introduce classical and western literature to a country, which before Peter the Great was ignorant of western learning. He also wrote a number of odes, fables, epistles and epigrammes, an unfinished epic poem on Peter the Great (whose reforms he lauded), and a treatise on versification, "Pis'mo Kharitona Makentina k priiateliu o slozhenii stikhov russkikh" [A Letter from Khariton Makentin (a near anagram of Antiokh Kantemir) to a Friend about the Composition of Russian Verses]; it was first published posthumously as an appendix to Kantemir's translation of some of Horace's epistles in St Petersburg in 1744. Kantemir's importance in Russian literature, however, rests on his nine satires. The first five satires were written in Russia between 1729 and 1731 and subsequently reworked; the last four were written later in London or Paris. The first eight satires were first published in a French prose translation in London in 1749, and then in a German verse translation in Berlin in 1752. The first Russian edition was published in St Petersburg in 1762, although the satires circulated in Russia in manuscript form before this.

Kantemir's first – and perhaps most famous and notable – satire, directed at "the detractors of learning" ("na khuliashchikh ucheniia"), is a scathing denunciation of those who for one reason or another resisted the western sciences and enlightenment introduced into Russia by Peter. By means of a series of colourful portraits of types, Kantemir identifies a number of opponents: first, the Church, which looks on learning as a source of heresy and a threat to ecclesiastical wealth and authority; second, those who see cultivation of the new sciences, which range from philosophy to physics, chemistry, medicine, astronomy, and mathematics, as unnecessary for the management of one's estates and unbecoming in an aristocrat; and third, those who object to scholarly occupations on purely hedonistic grounds. In the second half of the satire he goes on to condemn what he sees as the mores of the age, as reflected particularly in the agents of the Church and the law, who pursue wealth and rank in preference to knowledge and virtue. The second satire, which takes the form of a dialogue between Filaret (lover of virtue) and Evgenii (well-being), is directed against the "envy and pride of noblemen of bad morals" ("na zavist' i gordost' dvorian zlonravnykh"). It represents a defence of Petrine meritocracy (Peter's reforms are explicitly praised): nobility is not a right conferred by the antiquity of one's line, as Evgenii would wish, but a privilege to be earned by the virtuous who selflessly serve their country. The third satire, which is dedicated to Prokopovich and ends with an encomium to him, discusses the "diversity of human passions". Unlike the first two satires it is a rather tedious gallery of generalized embodiments of vices, such as the miser, the man whose pursuit of luxury drives him into debt, the gossip, the garrulous bore, the sanctimonious hypocrite, and the sycophantic social climber. In the fourth satire, "about the danger of satirical works" ("o opasnosti satiricheskikh sochinenii"), Kantemir regrets the unpopularity that the satirist courts from those he ridicules, but acknowledges that his own muse is a satirical one, insists on the integrity of the artist (who laughs in his verse but weeps in his heart), and emphasizes the morally reformative potential of the genre. The fifth satire, which at 748 lines is almost twice as long as any other, is a further generalized discussion in dialogic form of bad morals, and has little interest or vigour. The sixth satire, "about true bliss" ("o istinnom blazhenstve"), presents the Horatian ideal. The poet aspires to a life of serenity on a plot of land of his own, is content with modest material means, cultivates his mind and seeks virtue. In this way he frees himself from the desires and envy that are aroused by striving for rank and wealth and avoids the tedium and anxiety of life at court and in society. In the seventh satire, "on education", or perhaps more accurately "upbringing" ("o vospitanii"), Kantemir posits the primacy of environmental factors rather than innate qualities in the determination of character and – following Juvenal – emphasizes the importance of providing the child from the earliest age with good parental example as well as instruction. The purpose of education Kantemir sees as not merely the development of practical knowledge and skills but also the inculcation of good morals. The last two satires, which are of limited interest, are directed at "shameless impudence" ("besstydnuiu nakhal'chivost'") and the parlous state of the world respectively.

Taken as a whole Kantemir's satires raise many questions that were to prove of lasting importance in 18th-century (and 19th-century) Russia, such as the necessity for enlightenment in a backward country, the need to replace ecclesiastical superstition and obscurantism with secular knowledge and morality, the attributes of nobility and the role of the noble class in the post-Petrine state, the functions of art, and the nature, scope and importance of education. Thus at the very conception in Russia of a literature of a western kind the satires establish a connection between art and topical issues, set a tone that is critical of reality, define for literature a role in the improvement of the country's morals and impose on the writer a patriotic obligation. Their frequently contorted syntax, archaic diction, and primitive syllabic verse made them already very dated by the late 18th century. However, the best of them (particularly the first) are not without vividness and vigour, and, with their derisive exposure of folly and vice, their fast-moving, kaleidoscopic quality and their employment of a variety of devices and tones (monologue, dialogue, parody, frivolity, and high seriousness), they meet the timeless requirements of the genre.

Derek Offord

Vasilii Vasilievich Kapnist 1758–1823

Poet and dramatist

Biography

Born in the village of Obukhovka, Poltava province, Ukraine, 23 February 1758. His father, Vasilii Petrovich, was of Greek descent. Educated at home; sent to St Petersburg to begin military career, 1770. Promoted to sergeant, 1771. Transferred to Life Guards, Preobrazhenskii regiment; met G.R. Derzhavin, 1773. Composed first short poems. Resigned from army, 1775. Joined literary circle of Derzhavin, I.I. Khemnitser and N.N. L'vov, late 1770s. Returned to Obukhovka, with Khemnitser, 1780. Moved back to St Petersburg. Married: A.A. D'iakova in 1781. Inspector with the Directorate of Posts, 1782. In protest against Catherine the Great's treatment of the serfs, resigned and returned to the Ukraine. Elected to represent the nobility in province of Kiev. Staging and publication of *Iabeda* [Chicanery]; threatened with exile to Siberia, but order rescinded by Tsar Paul, 1798. Member of Directorate of Imperial Theatres, 1799; magistrate in province of Poltava, 1802; Director of Schools, 1812; Marshal of the Nobility, 1817. Died from tuberculosis, 9 November 1823, buried in Obukhovka on the banks of the river Psel.

Publications

Collected Editions

Sochineniia. St Petersburg, 1849.

Sobranie sochinenii, 2 vols. Moscow and Leningrad, 1960.

Izbrannye proizvedeniia. 2nd edition "Biblioteka poeta", Leningrad, 1973.

Poetry

Satira I [Satire I]. 1780; revised edition as *Satira pervaia i posledniaia* [Satire – My First and Last], 1783.

Plays

Iabeda [Chicanery]. St Petersburg, 1798.
Antigona [Antigone]. St Petersburg, 1809–11.

Critical Studies

"Kapnist", by V.G. Bitner, in *Istoriia russkoi literatury*, Moscow and Leningrad, 1947, vol. 2, part 2.
V.V. Kapnist, by P.N. Berkov, Leningrad and Moscow, 1950.
"Iabeda" V.V. Kapnista, by A.I. Matsai, Kiev, 1958.
XVIII vek, vol. 4, Moscow and Leningrad, 1959 [includes essays by P.N. Berkov, D.S. Babkin, and I.Z. Serman].
"V.V. Kapnist: kritiko-biograficheskii ocherk", by D.S. Babkin, in *Sobranie sochinenii*, Moscow and Leningrad, 1960.
Russian Comedy 1765–1823, by David J. Welsh, The Hague, Mouton, 1966.
A History of 18th Century Russian Literature, by William Edward Brown, Ann Arbor, Ardis, 1980.
Russian Drama from Its Beginnings to the Age of Pushkin, by Simon Karlinsky, Berkeley, University of California Press, 1985.
"Prophetic Stammering in V.V. Kapnist's *Iabeda* (1798)", by Charles Byrd, *Slavic and East European Journal*, 41/4 (1997), 541–53.

Vasilii Kapnist, the brother-in-law of G.R. Derzhavin, has claims to be considered the most elegant and skilled poet of his time, as well as the writer of one of the best plays in the 18th-century repertoire.

After a brief military career he took up residence in St Petersburg and joined the influential literary circle of Derzhavin, Khemnitser and L'vov. His first published poem, an ode celebrating the end of the war with Turkey in 1774, and written in French, appeared the following year. The members of the circle, each in their individual way, were critical of Russian life under Catherine the Great and many of their poetic works were satires on the malpractices of landowners and the bureaucracy. Kapnist's *Satira I* was one of the most abrasive. It is an outspoken attack on the stupidity which, despite the contemporary spread of education and the flowering of the arts, ruled supreme at all levels of Russian society and which was the main source of its corruption and vice. Although this aspect of the satire was not entirely unacceptable, controversy was created by a few lines criticizing some of his compatriots under rather too transparent pseudonyms: Obvesimov is clearly A.O. Ablesimov, Khrastov is D.I. Khvostov, Kotolskii is F.Ia. Kozelskii, and Rubov is Vasilii Ruban, who receives the most cutting of Kapnist's comments. The personal affront felt by many of Kapnist's acquaintances, the real butt of his satire, is epitomized by the reaction of the mother of his fiancée who accused him of keeping bad company and briefly forbade him ever again to cross her threshhold or see her daughter. Kapnist, though, took heed of the adverse reception, even though the poem established his name: he published no more satires and when he revised this, his first, in 1783, he changed the offending parts and entitled the work *Satira pervaia i posledniaia* [Satire – My First and Last].

When the pre-Romantic Ossianic movement reached Russia towards the end of the 1780s, elements began to appear in Russian poetry and it was soon to be as influential as it had been throughout western Europe. In 1791 Karamzin published in hisown *Moskovskii zhurnal* his translation of *Carthon* (*Karton, poema Ossiana*) and Kapnist attempted a version soon afterwards. Fearing criticism, Kapnist held on to it for 20 years before asking Derzhavin to arrange a public reading, which never took place. It was not published in full until 1941 under the title of *Karton, tvorenie drevnego Kaledonskogo barda Ossiana, syna tsaria Fingala* [Carthon. A Poem, the Work of the Ancient Caledonian Bard Ossian, Son of King Fingal]. The translation is 671 lines long and is a rather unsuccessful mixture of metres combining syllabo-tonic iambic lines and imitations of the rhythms of folk poetry.

While translating various psalms and composing generally competent, elegantly constructed "occasional" poetry, Kapnist continued his association with Derzhavin's circle, which was devoting itself to the study of Horace and the Anacreontica. One result was a series of admirable translations from Horace and a number of even more impressive versions and imitations, which arguably form the highpoint of Kapnist's poetic output. A second was his adoption of the original intentions of Anacreontics in a captivating collection of original compositions, almost more lyric than odic. Along with Derzhavin's rather more erotic and vinous versions, they are the best of Russian 18th-century *poésie légère* and are a worthy predecessor to K.N. Batiushkov in what Pushkin called the school of "harmonious precision".

If Kapnist was well regarded as a poet in his day and is still considered one of the finest products of Russian Neoclassicism, his fame then ultimately rested on his activities as a dramatist and provides the single most convincing reason why he is still remembered today, if only for *Iabeda* [Chicanery]. Although, having abandoned poetic satires, he exhibited his satirical talents to the full in this five-act verse comedy, completed in 1798. It is a savage onslaught on judicial corruption in a provincial town. The legal practitioners are depicted as an unredeemed band of thieves and extortioners. It also introduces some notable advances in the general competence of Russian dramatists: the verse and the dialogue are very well integrated, the use of stage properties is successfully exploited and the interplay of the serious and the farcical add to the audience's appreciation of the play's general import. Although it might justly be said that Kapnist's use of alexandrines is a little harsh and there are numerous outrages against the Russian language, the play produces its effect by its striking sarcasm. In the history of 18th-century Russian dramaturgy it is second only to Fonvizin's *Nedorosl'* (*The Minor*) and *Brigadir* (*The Brigadier*), representing a tradition of social satire that culminated in Griboedov's *Gore ot uma* (*Woe from Wit*). One critic remarked that Griboedov's play owes a lot to Kapnist's "crude and primitive" but none the less memorable contribution. Although it was banned for publication, legend has it that when Tsar Paul, hardly noted as a patron of the arts, demanded to see it, he was so impressed that he recalled Kapnist from the Siberian exile he had just imposed on him.

Kapnist's surviving correspondence, written in stylish Russian or French, shows him to be a sympathetic and concerned individual, not only on the personal level but also regarding the problems and manifest shortcomings of Russian life. According to his great-granddaughter, the family withheld a large number of his letters, and some of his poems, fearing some of his opinions and comments would meet with official disfavour.

Kapnist's present reputation tends to be framed in terms of his being impressive for his times but, in the end, he is regarded only as a worthy precursor of later and better poets and playwrights. Furthermore, he had the misfortune to outlive most of his friends and acquaintances, and he died a lonely and sad man. In one of his last poems, addressed to a young man, Kapnist expresses the touching hope that the former might find in his declining years so trusting and faithful an admirer as Kapnist has found in him.

A.V. KNOWLES

Iabeda

Chicanery

Play, 1798

It is this five-act comedy in verse that has secured Kapnist's reputation as a virtuoso in the art of stagecraft, earning as it did a just contemporary celebrity for its author, and continuing to be much anthologized, if rather less frequently staged, in the present time. Already known as a versatile and linguistically dexterous poet, Kapnist composed his play from 1794 to 1796, but it was not until two years later that he had it printed, and its first performance, at the Kamennyi (Bol'shoi) Theatre in St Petersburg, had to wait until 22 August 1798. The premiere was a benefit performance for the much-admired comic actor A.M. Krutitskii, playing the central part of the corrupt judge Krivosudov. Kapnist and Krutitskii were said by all accounts to have scored a remarkable success, but the combustibly satirical subject-matter of the piece – the double-dealing, hypocrisy, dissoluteness and overall corruption of the judiciary – led automatically to its almost immediate suppression by the new tsar, Paul I. After two months and four performances it was taken off. *Iabeda* returned to the stage in 1805 and remained as something of a standard in the repertoire until the mid-19th century, by which time many of its finely-turned *bons mots* and one-liners had passed into common parlance, attaining the status almost of proverbs. As a compendium of off-the-peg witticisms it stands in the Russian estimation alongside Griboedov's 1825 comic masterpiece *Woe from Wit*, but there is a conviction, even urgency, to the play which cuts much deeper than its lapidary carapace of cleverness.

The theme of *Iabeda* – the ingrained arbitrariness and injustice of the bureaucratic apparatus – came from personal experience. Kapnist had been embroiled in litigation with a Mrs Tarnovskaia, who had appropriated part of his brother's estate. *Iabeda* was already established as a subject for satirists (Sumarokov, Novikov, Fonvizin, Khemnitser and others), as too for dramatists (Verevkin, Sumarokov and, further afield, Beaumarchais). What chiefly distinguishes Kapnist's play from its imitators, such as, say, Sudovshchikov's *Neslykhannoe delo, ili chestnyi sekretar'* [An Unheard-of Matter, or, the Honourable Secretary] is the salient absence of heroic, or even usefully good, characters. Morally (not indeed linguistically), Kapnist's officials are all much of a muchness: all bad. There is little to leaven this but verbal humour, brittle as it may sometimes appear. To this extent the play is not a comedy of manners, it is not individuals, quirks and idiosyncrasies that are sent up, but the very institution of legal bureaucracy, condemned in the round through the persons of its sundry grubby representatives. Chicanery is, then, not merely the subject and object of the satirical broadside, but its central character or spirit.

With an assured mastery of his materials Kapnist sees to it that the verbal ingenuity is at its most lambent when the comedy is at its blackest. In fact it is rarely anything but black, although there are *tour de force* set pieces that stand out. In the third act a card-game held by a selection of increasingly intoxicated officials degenerates horribly into a punch-sodden binge, and, as more drink is hauled onto the stage (following a kind of Bacchanalian choric sub-structure all its own), into a rout of pillaging and grasping thievery. A refrain is set up by Khvataiko, the procurator, which hinges on the word "take" ("beri"), and soon all the rest are infected. There is practised art in the depiction of this descent from the conventional 18th-century stage-tableau of the card-table into a slough of debauched greed. Here, as elsewhere, the playwright is unobtrusively framing the explosive tension at the work's core: the external, civic destructiveness of the jurists and their lackeys set dramatically against the internal cohesiveness of their claque. Corruption, here, is social glue. It is what sustains them that destroys society. The banter, the repartee and quick-fire exchanges, frothy verbal stage-dressing in many another dramatist, were intended by Kapnist to set these evils off memorably: no mean feat.

In its superficial lineaments *Iabeda* fits fairly comfortably into the classical comedic canon: the five acts, the iambic hexameters (put on occasion to remarkable, stuttering, use), the "main" and "secondary" personages, the "meaning names" given to characters, and so on, but Kapnist marshals none of these formal hand-me-downs to any edifying end. If anything, it all leaves rather a bitter taste behind. This is because at a more important level the departures from classicism weigh more than the similarities. The audience, for example, is party not to an abstract fable of come-uppance enacted by a stable of well-worn archetypes, but to a devastatingly relevant condemnation of institutionalized sharp-practice. The knockabout oafs and suave cynics on stage may at any moment assume a horrible importance in the lives of the spectators, as witness Kapnist's brother. The intentional proximity of the play's contents to the daily experience of lived life reveals an origin in the *drames bourgeois* of mid-century France, popular in Russia in the 1770s. Unsettlingly recognizable too are the accurate allusions to legal procedures, couched in contemporary legal language. The judge, the procurator, the assessor, the usher, all are there. Codes and statutes – checkable – are there. Recreational activities guy it down further: drinking (that is, drunkenness), the social round (Krivosudov's "at-homes"), card-playing (then the ubiquitous pharaoh). Playing cards is the same as practising the law. You are deft, cheat efficiently, fix the cards: you win. Kapnist's technical gift is always visible, from the verse and the verbal pyrotechnics to the use of the stage-props, alternatively the instruments of slapstick violence or obstacles for reeling drunkards to fall onto, and much has been made in Kapnist scholarship of the gear-changes in dramatic register, as when verse modulates into a prose aside, or a physical joke is juxtaposed with a verbal one. The play pulls no punches, and is of a single-mindedness rarely encountered. It is highly charged, and these techniques are there, necessarily, to conduct Kapnist's lightning.

NICHOLAS CROWE

Nikolai Mikhailovich Karamzin 1766–1826

Prose writer, poet, and historian

Biography

Born in Mikhailovka, Simbirsk province, 12 December 1766. Attended a private boarding school in Simbirsk, then Professor J. Schaden's boarding school, Moscow, 1775–81. Enlisted in Preobrazhenskii Guards from birth, but served only 1782–83 in St Petersburg; resigned in 1784. First literary work published, 1783. Admitted to masonic lodge in Simbirsk c.1784. Moved to Moscow to join literary circle of N.I. Novikov and engage in journalistic activity, 1785. Travelled to Germany, France, Switzerland, and England, 1789–90. Independent career as writer and editor in Moscow, 1791–1803. Married: 1) Elizaveta Ivanovna Protasova in 1801, one daughter; 2) Ekaterina Andreevna Kolyvanova, the illegitimate daughter of Prince A.I. Viazemskii, in 1804, three sons and two daughters. Appointed Imperial Historiographer, 1803; undertook historical research and writing in Moscow, 1804–16. Composed *Zapiska o drevnei i novoi Rossii* [Memoir on Ancient and Modern Russia] and presented it to Tsar Alexander I in March 1811. Following Napoleon's occupation of Moscow, evacuated to Nizhnii Novgorod, 1813. Moved to St Petersburg 1816. Lived remaining years in St Petersburg and at Tsarskoe Selo. Elected to the Russian Academy, 1818. Died in St Petersburg, 2 June 1826. Buried in the Tikhvin Cemetery of the Alexander Nevskii Monastery.

Publications

Collected Editions

Sochineniia Karamzina, 8 vols. Moscow, 1803–04; 9 vols, 1814.

Izbrannye sochineniia, 2 vols. Moscow and Leningrad, 1964.

Polnoe sobranie stikhotvorenii. Moscow and Leningrad, 1966.

Selected Prose of N.M. Karamzin, translated with an introduction by Henry M. Nebel, Jr. Evanston, Illinois, Northwestern University Press, 1969.

Sochineniia, 2 vols. Leningrad, 1984.

Fiction

Bednaia Liza, in *Moskorskii zhurnal* (1792); translated as *Poor Lisa*, *German Museum*, January–February 1801; and as "Poor Liza", by J. Whittaker, in *The Literature of Eighteenth-Century Russia*, by Harold B. Segel, vol. 1, New York, Dutton, 1967; also as "Poor Liza", by Henry M. Nebel Jr, in his *Selected Prose of N.M. Karamzin*, 1969.

Iuliia. Moscow, 1796; translated as *Karamzin's Julia*, by Ann P. Hawkins, St Petersburg, 1803.

Pis'ma russkogo puteshestvennika, 6 vols. Moscow, 1797–1801; edited by Iu. M. Lotman, N.A. Marchenko, and B.A. Uspenskii, Leningrad, 1984; translated as *Travels from Moscow through Prussia, Germany, Switzerland, France and England*, by A.A. Feldborg, 3 vols, London, Braddock, 1803; *Letters of a Russian Traveler, 1789–1790*, by Florence Jonas, New York, Columbia University Press, 1957.

Russian Tales, translated by J.B. Elrington. London, G. Sidney, 1803.

Editor

Aonidy, 3 vols. 1796–99.

Panteon inostrannoi literatury [Pantheon of Foreign Literature], 3 vols. 1798.

Historical Writing

Istoriia gosudarstva rossiiskogo [History of the Russian State], 12 vols. St Petersburg, 1818–29; reprinted Moscow, 1988–89.

Critical Studies

N.M. Karamzin: A Russian Sentimentalist, by Henry M. Nebel, Jr, The Hague, Mouton, 1967.

N.M. Karamzins europäische Reise: Der Beginn des russischen Romans, by Hans Rothe, Berlin and Zurich, Bad Homburg v.d.H., 1968.

N.M. Karamzin: A Study of His Literary Career (1783–1803), by A.G. Cross, Carbondale, Southern Illinois University Press, and London, Feffer and Simons, 1971.

N.M. Karamzin's Prose: The Teller in the Tale, by Roger B. Anderson, Houston, Cordovan Press, 1974.

Essays on Karamzin: Russian Man-of-Letters, Political Thinker, Historian, 1766–1826, edited by J.L. Black, The Hague, Mouton, 1975.

Nikolay Karamzin, by Natalya Kochetkova, Boston, Twayne, 1975.

"The Peasant and the Station-Master: A Question of Realism", by E. Little, *Journal of Russian Studies*, 38 (1979), 23–32.

A History of 18th Century Russian Literature, by William Edward Brown, Ann Arbor, Ardis, 1980.

Russian Prose, edited by B.M. Eikhenbaum and Iu. Tynianov, Ann Arbor, Ardis, 1985, 21–44.

"Poor Liza, Poor Erast, Lucky Narrator", by Gitta Hammarberg, *Slavic and East European Journal*, 31 (1987).

Sotvorenie Karamzina, by Iu. M. Lotman, Moscow, 1987.

Women in Russian Literature, 1780–1863, by Joe Andrew, London, Macmillan, and New York, St Martin's Press, 1988.

From the Idyll to the Novel: Karamzin's Sentimentalist Prose, by Gitta Hammarberg, Cambridge, Cambridge University Press, 1991.

"Bednaia Liza" Karamzina. Opyt prochteniia, by V.N. Toporov, Moscow, 1995.

Karamzin: Sotvorenie Karamzina: Stat'i i issledovaniia 1957–1990. Zametki i retsenzii, St Petersburg, 1997.

Bibliographies

Materialy dlia bibliografii literatury o N.M. Karamzine, by S. Ponomarev, St Petersburg, 1883.

"Karamzin Studies", by A.G. Cross, *Slavonic and East European Review*, 45 (1967), 1–12.

Istoriia russkoi literatury XVIII veka: bibliograficheskii ukazatel', by V.P. Stepanov and Iu.V. Stennik, Leningrad, 1968.

Prose writer, poet, translator, literary critic, journalist, editor, creator of a new literary style, historian, Nikolai Mikhailovich Karamzin occupies a position of undoubted, if not always unchallenged significance in the history of Russian literature and culture from the final decades of the 18th century to the very end of the reign of Alexander I. For the Russian critic Belinskii, Karamzin gave his name to a whole period of Russian literature, following one dominated by Lomonosov and preceding that of Pushkin, and the very notion of "creating an epoch" was elaborated during his lifetime not only by his supporters but also by his opponents. The graph of Karamzin's posthumous reputation shows steep rises and falls: the object of a virtual official cult during the late 19th century, he was subjected to much arbitrary censure and neglect after the October Revolution. Moral and political considerations have often outweighed due appreciation of his literary talent and achievement. The youthful Pushkin might quip that Karamzin had written the best Russian but that was not saying much; the mature Pushkin knew better. Karamzin was Russia's first consummate prose artist.

Karamzin served his literary apprenticeship in the Moscow circle of the publisher and dedicated freemason Nikolai Novikov. Over the period 1785–89 Karamzin produced translations from English, French, and German, which were published separately (*Julius Caesar*, 1787, *Emilia Galotti*, 1788) and within the pages of *Detskoe chtenie dlia serdtsa i razuma*, the first Russian journal specifically aimed at children, which he edited from 1787. It was in this journal that his own first prose compositions and poems appeared, if anonymously. His emergence as a publicly acclaimed and independent author came only after his return from extensive travels through Europe and his decision to publish *Moskovskii zhurnal*, 1791–92.

Karamzin dominated the Russian literary scene over a relatively short period of 13 years (1791–1803), prior to his appointment as Imperial Historiographer. It is a career enclosed by two remarkable journals and embracing other innovative publishing initiatives – his poetic almanac *Aonidy*, 3 vols 1796–99 and his *Panteon inostrannoi literatury* [Pantheon of Foreign Literature], 3 vols, 1798 – by a writer, whose distinction as editor and journalist is often overlooked.

Moskovskii zhurnal was by general European standards an accomplished literary journal, in which the dominant and controlling voice was Karamzin's. Apart from poems by such as Derzhavin and Kheraskov, it was prose, and overwhelmingly Karamzin's prose, that gave the journal its particular stature. Karamzin provided book and theatre reviews (a controversial innovation), carefully chosen translations from contemporary European authors, and the original works that brought him instant and continuing fame: *Pis'ma russkogo puteshestvennika* (*Letters of a Russian Traveler*), running virtually from issue to issue and unifying to a marked degree the journal's component parts, and a series of tales, including pre-eminently *Bednaia Liza* (*Poor Liza*) and "Natal'ia, boiarskaia doch'" [Natalia, the Boyar's Daughter]. *Moskovskii zhurnal* established in Russia the credentials of a new trend, the literature of feeling, which is usually considered in west European criticism within the framework of Pre-romanticism but which in Russia, if only from the late 19th century, has been termed Sentimentalism. No less significantly, the journal heralded a stylistic revolution. Without the carefully wrought embroidery of what became known as "the new style" (*novyi slog*), the emotional finesse and nuance on which Sentimentalism relied could not have been realized.

Letters of a Russian Traveler, half of which appeared in the journal (the work was published in full only in 1801), became virtually the bible of the new literature of feeling to which enthusiasts could turn for the "correct" response to sentimental situations and set pieces. Only with caution can it be regarded as "the mirror of the soul" of its author as he travelled through Europe, but it was for all that a mine of information about the countries he visited. Karamzin saw himself both as a "young Scythian" in search of western enlightenment and as a Sternian "Sentimental Traveller", full of infinite jest and overbrimming sensibility. The epistolary form is manipulated with considerable skill, sustaining the illusion of a real correspondence with friends.

Karamzin was essentially a miniaturist, skilfully using the minor forms of prose, such as the letter, the sketch, the idyll, the fragment, the essay, and the short story. His stories appeared in his two journals, his literary almanac *Aglaia* (2 vols, 1794–95), and in the unique case of *Iuliia* (*Karamzin's Julia*), separately. In very few pages Karamzin constructs often deceptively simple plots and creates plausible if thin characters. In the early stories (1791–96) the crucial device is the use of the first-person narrator, who acts as intermediary between readers and the events, inviting their participation, directing their sympathies, creating a sense of authenticity and a feeling of intimacy. He is the protean "man of feeling", dictating the mood of elegiac sadness in *Poor Liza*, of bantering humour in "Natal'ia, boiarskaia doch'" of autumnal melancholy in "Liodor" (1792). In this last story, the narrator is identified with the writer of *Letters*, as he is in "Ostrov Borngol'm" [The Island of Bornholm] (1794), Karamzin's essay in the genre of the popular Gothic fragment. Karamzin very consciously provided Russian examples of stories popular in European literature. In *Iuliia*, he writes a *conte moral*, inspired by his much-admired Marmontel (whose tales he translated for *Moskovskii zhurnal*).

Karamzin's last journal, *Vestnik Evropy* (1802–03), gave Russia a new standard in journalism and was the worthy initiator of the tradition of the *tolstye zhurnaly* (fat journals). Like *Moskovskii zhurnal*, it was dominated by the personality and tastes of one man. Its strong literature section brought to a close Karamzin's endeavours as poet, translator and author of some remarkable fiction, revealing changes in approach to narrative and characterization ("Moia ispoved'" [My Confession] and "Rytsar' nashego vremeni" [A Knight of Our Time]), but it was also by design a political journal with extensive commentaries on European affairs and contained a series of essays expounding Karamzin's views on historical, social, and political questions. As writer and thinker, he was ready to "enter the temple of history" and devote himself to the *Istoriia gosudarstva rossiiskogo* [History of the Russian State].

ANTHONY CROSS

Poor Liza

Bednaia Liza

Story, 1792

On the plan of Moscow in the 1914 edition of Baedeker's *Russia* the "Lizin Pond", not far from the Simonov Monastery, is clearly marked and the accompanying commentary suggests that it is "well known through Karamzin's story of 'Poor Lizzie'". The pond was central to the tale's immediate and lasting impact and appeal. Visiting the spot 25 years after the tale's first publication (1792), Karamzin commented that it was "a simple tale, but so favourable for the young author that thousands of curious people went there to seek traces of Liza". Indeed, in an age when sentimental-literary pilgrimages were in vogue throughout Europe and Karamzin himself had visited Vevey "with Rousseau's *Héloise* in my hands", he had consciously provided a local habitation and name for his tale, published appropriately in *Moskovskii zhurnal*. Its appearance in a separate edition in 1796, now subtitled *Rossiiskaia povest'* [A Russian tale] and complete with an engraving of the pond, made it more generally available and brought visitors from far and wide, including young aspiring writers, who commented on the accuracy of Karamzin's descriptions and noted the overwhelmingly indecent inscriptions cut into the bark of the surrounding trees.

The tale Karamzin told was, as he himself suggested, a simple one, at least in its plot line: a peasant girl, innocent and loving, is seduced, and then abandoned by a nobleman, and seeks in death release from her despair. It was an oft-told tale, but not in Russian literature. Karamzin had an outstanding talent for assimilating what he had read in the work of western authors and fusing it – content, form, and style – into a "Russianness" that the reading public he addressed, and was partly responsible for creating, was prepared to accept. His heroine Liza and his hero Erast are skin-deep Russians, who speak and act on a stage well-trod by European characters. Liza conforms more to the European stereotype of the peasant heroine than to any woman observed in the environs of Moscow, and Erast, too, in name and in actions, exemplifies the European noble wastrel, not corrupt and evil, merely irresponsible and inconstant: "quite a rich gentleman, with reasonable intelligence and a good heart, good by nature, but weak and fickle". One has to look no further than the stories of Marmontel that Karamzin was concurrently translating for *Moskovskii zhurnal* to discover numerous parallels and precedents for Liza and Erast, and indeed, for Liza's old widowed mother. It is she who utters perhaps the most famous line Karamzin ever wrote: "for even peasant women know how to love" ("ibo i krest'ianki liubit' umeiut"), which is a felicitously phrased version of a sentiment long since trite in European literature and already enunciated in Russia in Pavel L'vov's novel *Rossiiskaia Pamela* [The Russian Pamela] (1789), but new enough for it to be endlessly echoed by Karamzinian imitators.

The discovery of the lower classes, and of the peasantry in particular, as subjects deserving of admiration and sympathetic literary portrayal belonged to the Enlightenment and the Age of Feeling. In Karamzin's story, there is scant regard for Russian realities, in the sense that Liza and her parents are not seen as the serfs they would have been but merely as contented dwellers of the fields, come upon hard times, but social differences are recognized in order to underpin the relationships between characters and, indeed, to hasten Liza's fall. Confiding to Erast that her mother wishes her to marry a rich peasant suitor and adding that she could not be Erast's wife because "I am a peasant", Erast assures her that it is her "sensitive, innocent soul" he prizes, only for them immediately to surrender to their passion.

All his life Karamzin was drawn to the idea of the Golden Age, mirrored in the idylls of Salomon Gessner (one of which provided his first published translation), but life's experience taught him also to regard it as a beguiling myth. Nevertheless, he was able to exploit creatively his ambivalent attitude, demonstrating through Erast the myth's attractions and dangers and providing through his narrator the often ironic and cautionary commentary. It is the narrator who interposes the following characterization of an Erast who:

> used to read novels, idylls; he had a lively imagination and often took himself mentally to those times (which might or might not have existed), when, if we are to believe the poets, all people wandered carefree through the meadows …

This suggests that Erast was conscious of playing a role. Not so Liza, whose reality comprised the very shepherds and shepherdesses, who were essentially figments of a bookish imagination for Erast. Karamzin highlights the rift between books and reality, the ideal and the human, and, at the same time, brings to bear some of the other common antitheses of the age, between poverty and wealth, innocence and corruption, the countryside and the town. By his denouement, in which the conventions of pastoral are undermined, he effects the transition of the traditional idyll into the sentimental short story. By adding the potent motif of the heroine's suicide by drowning and by locating that act – and her grave – at the pond near the Simonov Monastery he gave the tale its comparative notoriety and its reality.

Karamzin successfully blurs the boundaries of the real and the imagined, not least by explicitly contrasting through the narrators of his early fictions fact and truth (*byl'*, *istina*) on the one hand and fiction and lies (*vydumka*, *nebylitsa*) on the other, and in terms of genres, between the tale (*povest'*) and the novel/romance (*roman*). The narrator in "Poor Liza" regrets that he is relating "not a romance, but a sad true story". It is the narrator who in the famous overture to the story sets both the scene and the tone, who depicts himself as a connoisseur of the Moscow countryside at all seasons (but particularly in its autumnal melancholy), and also as an amateur of sad tales. It is the narrator who himself seeks traces of Liza and who, indeed, as we learn in the epilogue, had heard of the events from a repentant Erast. The narrator vies for attention with the characters, it is he who allows them to speak (but in the cases of Liza and her mother, not in "peasant language"), it is he who imposes the syntax and vocabulary of the "new style" and welds the story into "the harmonious whole" that Karamzin sought.

ANTHONY CROSS

Valentin Petrovich Kataev 1897–1986

Prose writer

Biography

Born in Odessa, 28 January 1897; son of a schoolteacher. Attended a school in Odessa. Began writing in childhood; first poems published in Odessa newspapers in 1910. Served as artillery officer in World War I, 1915–17. Fought for Volunteer White Army in Odessa, 1918–19; mobilized into the Red Army in 1919. Worked for ROSTA and YugROSTA in Odessa and Kharkov, 1920–22. Moved to Moscow, 1922; worked as journalist for *Gudok*, then as full-time writer. Also wrote under the pseudonyms Starik Sabbakin, Oliver Tvist, Mitrofan Gorchitsa, Tovarishch Rashpil'. Married: 1) Anna Sergeevna Kovalenko in 1923 (divorced); 2) Ester [Esther] Davydovna Brenner in 1935; one son and one daughter. War correspondent, 1941–45. Recipient: Stalin Prize (second class) for *Syn polka* [Son of the Regiment], 1945. Founding editor of *Iunost'*, 1955–62. Joined the Communist Party of the Soviet Union in 1958. Died in Moscow, 12 April 1986.

Publications

Collected Editions

Sobranie sochinenii, 5 vols. Moscow, 1956–57.
Sobranie sochinenii, 9 vols. Moscow, 1968–72.
Sobranie sochinenii, 10 vols. Moscow, 1983–86.

Fiction

Ser Genri i chert [Sir Henry and the Devil]. Berlin, 1923.
"Rastratchiki", *Krasnaia nov'*, 10–12 (1926); translated as *The Embezzlers*, by L. Zarine, London, Benn, and New York, Dial Press, 1929; and as *Embezzlers*, by Charles Rougle, Ann Arbor, Ardis, 1975 (in 1 volume with Iurii Olesha's *Envy*).
"Vremia, vpered!", *Krasnaia nov'*, 1–9 (1932); translated as *Forward, O Time!*, by Charles Malamuth, London, Gollancz, 1934; retitled as *Time, Forward!*, Bloomington, Indiana University Press, 1976; reprinted New York, Farrar and Rinehart, 1993; Evanston, Illinois, Northwestern University Press, 1995.
"Beleet parus odinokii", *Krasnaia nov'*, 5 (1936); translated as *Lonely White Sail; or Peace is Where the Tempests Blow*, by Charles Malamuth, London, Allen and Unwin, and New York, Farrar and Rinehart, 1937; and as *A White Sail Gleams*, by Leonard Stoklitsky, Moscow, Progress, 1954; 1973.
Ia - syn trudovogo naroda [I - Son of the Working People]. Moscow, 1937.
Syn polka [Son of the Regiment]. Moscow, 1945.
Za vlast' sovetov [For the Power of the Soviets]. Moscow, 1949; revised edition, 1951; further revised as *Katakomby* [The Catacombs], 1961.
Volny chernogo moria. Tetralogiia [Black Sea Waves. A Tetralogy]. Moscow, 1961 (contains *Beleet parus odinokii*, 1936; *Khutorok v stepi* [The Farm in the Steppe], 1956; *Zimnii veter* [Winter Wind], 1960; *Katakomby*, 1961).
"Sviatoi kolodets", *Novyi mir*, 5 (1966); translated as *The Holy Well*, by Max Hayward and Harold Shukman, London, Harvill Press, 1967.
"Trava zabven'ia", *Novyi mir*, 3 (1967); translated as *The Grass of Oblivion*, by Robert Daglish, London, Macmillan, 1969.
"Almaznyi moi venets" [My Diamond Crown], *Novyi mir*, 6 (1977).
"Uzhe napisan Verter" [Werther Has Already Been Written], *Novyi mir*, 6 (1980).
Iunosheskii roman [A Youthful Novel]. Moscow, 1983.

Play

"Kvadratura kruga", *Krasnaia nov'*, 5 (1928); translated as *Squaring the Circle*, by Eugene Lyons and Charles Malamuth, in *Six Soviet Plays*, edited by Eugene Lyons, London, Gollancz, 1935.

Memoirs and Essays

Pochti dnevnik [Almost a Diary]. Moscow, 1962; augmented edition, 1978.
Raznoe [Miscellany]. Moscow, 1970.
"Razbitaia zhizn' ili Volshebnyi rog Oberona", *Novyi mir*, 7–8 (1972); translated as *A Mosaic of Life or The Magic Horn of Oberon: Memoirs of a Russian Childhood*, by Moura Budberg and Gordon Latta, London, Angus and Robertson, 1976.

Critical Studies

Valentin Kataev: Ocherk tvorchestva, by B. Brainina, Moscow, 1960.
Pisatel' i ego vremia: Zhizn' i tvorchestvo V.P. Kataeva, by L. Skorino, Moscow, 1965.
Valentin Kataev, by Robert Russell, Boston, G.K. Hall, 1981.
Valentin Kataev: Ocherk tvorchestva, by Boris Galanov, Moscow, 1982.
"Oberon's Magic Horn: The Later Works of Valentin Kataev", by Robert Russell, in *Russian Literature and Criticism. Selected Papers from the Second World Congress for Soviet and East European Studies*, edited by Evelyn Bristol, Berkeley, Berkeley Slavic Specialties, 1982, 176–92.
Das Frühwerk Valentin P. Kataevs, by Josef Vogl, Munich, Sagner, 1984.
"Four Demons of Valentin Kataev", by Dodona Kiziria, *Slavic Review*, 44 (1985), 647–66.
"Valentin Kataev in His Eighties", by N.N. Shneidman, *Slavic and East European Journal*, 29 (1985), 52–63.
"Time, Backward!: Sasha Sokolov and Valentin Kataev", by Richard C. Borden, *Canadian-American Slavic Studies*, 21 (1987), 247–63.
Valentin Kataev: Razmyshleniia o Mastere i dialogi s nim, by B. Galanov, Moscow, 1989.
Poetics of Valentin Kataev's Prose of the 1960s and 1970s, by Ireneusz Szarycz, New York and Bern, Peter Lang, 1989.

Valentin Kataev was one of the most accomplished prose writers of the Soviet era, a writer whose reputation may have been seriously compromised by innate political conformism, yet whose talent and achievement are beyond dispute. Kataev's earliest works were patriotic verses published in Odessa and St Petersburg newspapers while the author was in his teens. In 1914 he met Ivan Bunin and became – in Kataev's own words – "his conscientious pupil". Bunin's mastery was to remain Kataev's ideal for the rest of his life, most obviously in the 1920s and again from 1965 until his death in 1986.

Kataev's early works generally fall into one of two categories: they are either romantic and lyrical or else they are satirical and imbued with warm humour. One of the recurrent features of his work of the 1920s is an interest in the nature of perception and the effect of illness, delirium, alcohol, drugs, madness, or passion. *Ser Genri i chert* [Sir Henry and the Devil] (1923), consists of the delirious dreams of a man dying from typhus. The protagonist's fever is the pretext for Kataev's experimentation with perception, for the intermingling of realism and fantasy, and for the creation of that dreamlike fluidity that marks much of his best prose. The stylistic experimentation of the early period, characterized by associative leaps and altered states of perception, was to recur in much of Kataev's late prose, beginning in 1966 with *The Holy Well*.

Kataev's major work of the 1920s is undoubtedly *Rastratchiki* (*The Embezzlers*), a warmly humorous, Gogolian, picaresque novel that recounts the adventures of two office workers who get drunk one day and discover that they have embezzled a large sum of money. On their travels they encounter a large number of scoundrels who appear to be flourishing in the Russia of the NEP period, and who attempt to part the gullible and essentially innocent embezzlers from their money. The embezzlers themselves are drunk most of the time, and some of the best satirical effects are achieved by juxtaposing drunken and sober views of the same thing.

Apart from *The Embezzlers*, Kataev's most famous work of the 1920s was the play *Kvadratura kruga* (*Squaring the Circle*), a lighthearted farcical comedy about a group of young people forced by the housing shortage to share a single room. Kataev continued to write plays for some years but he never recaptured the success of *Squaring the Circle*.

During the years of the first Five-Year Plan (1928–32), Kataev visited factories and collective farms in response to the "social command", the pressure to write literary sketches and fictional works about the achievements of the Plan. His major work of the period is *Vremia, vpered!* (*Time, Forward!*), one of the most interesting and inventive "production novels" of the early 1930s. Set in Magnitogorsk, *Time, Forward!* describes an attempt by a brigade of construction workers to beat the world record for the number of mixes of concrete that can be laid in a single shift. This apparently unpromising material is skilfully and energetically handled, with the black-and-white characterization proving less significant than the novel's pace and verve, which are cinematic in origin. *Time, Forward!* owes much more to the cinema than to literary antecedents. As Kataev remarked in an essay of 1936: "*Time, Forward!* is a work constructed literally on cinematic principles".

The major work of the second half of the 1930s was *Beleet parus odinokii* (*A White Sail Gleams*), a children's novel set in Odessa during the 1905 Revolution. Its success is due to the sensuous, Buninesque evocation of a childhood that Kataev knew from his own experience. Over the next two and a half decades he returned again and again to the characters of *A White Sail Gleams*, eventually producing a tetralogy to which he gave the name *Volny Chernogo moria* [Black Sea Waves]. The three sequels are all significantly less successful than *A White Sail Gleams*, especially *Za vlast' sovetov* [For the Power of the Soviets], written then re-written to order during the Zhdanovist period following World War II. The tetralogy represents many years of largely wasted effort on Kataev's part. Much more significant than his own writings in the 1950s was his editorship of *Iunost'* through which he encouraged many young writers such as Anatolii Gladilin and Vasilii Aksenov.

By the mid-1960s Valentin Kataev's position in Soviet literature appeared to have been determined: a talented fellow traveller of the 1920s who had responded to the demand for socialist realist novels and whose work had, as a result, eventually declined into mediocrity; a writer whose literary ambitions seemed to be more readily realizable through his patronage of younger talents than through any direct efforts of his own. But in 1966, to the astonishment of the reading public, Kataev published *The Holy Well*, the first of the series of modernistic, semi-autobiographical prose works that continued to appear until the year before his death and which, taken together, are at least as important in his *oeuvre* as the prose of the 1920s.

The narrator of *The Holy Well* experiences strange and disturbing dreams while anaesthetized during an operation. The dream logic allows the text to range freely in time and space, from America in the Khrushchev era to Russia and Georgia during the Stalinist period. The operation itself becomes symbolic, with the narrator dreaming that, as in Pushkin's "Prorok" ("Prophet"), his sinful and untruthful tongue has been ripped out and replaced by one that will tell the truth.

Trava zabven'ia (*The Grass of Oblivion*) is a key work for the understanding of Kataev's career. Superficially a memoir about Bunin and Maiakovskii, it is actually an apologia for the author himself, whose natural talent inclines towards that of Bunin but much of whose career has been spent serving the Revolution, as Maiakovskii did. Among the remaining works of the late period, all of which reveal Kataev's mature mastery, mention should be made of *Almaznyi moi venets* [My Diamond Crown] and *Uzhe napisan Verter* [Werther Has Already Been Written]. The former is a fictionalized memoir about Kataev's contemporaries, including Bulgakov, Mandel'shtam, Olesha, and many others, all of whom are given pseudonyms rather than their names because of the author's insistence that his work is not a straightforward literary memoir that purports to be factual. The latter is a reworking of a theme that had been present in several stories of the 1920s and in *The Grass of Oblivion*: the Red Terror during the Civil War.

Kataev's place in the history of Russian modernism has not yet been adequately investigated. A detailed study of his later work in conjunction with the prose of the 1920s is likely to reveal him as a figure of considerable significance in 20th-century Russian literature.

ROBERT RUSSELL

A White Sail Gleams

Beleet parus odinokii

Novel, 1936

Immediately after Kataev's novel appeared in print in 1936, it became one of the model works of Soviet literature, popular with young and old readers alike. The critical and public success was primarily due to Kataev's smooth turn from moderate experimentation in the 1920s to the type of Neoclassical socialist realism that the Stalinist establishment had been calling for in the 1930s. A writer of high professional standards and few moral qualms, Kataev was one of the first to satisfy the need for readable, conventionally narrated fiction with adventurous stories, permeated by a lofty romantic spirit.

The novel's plot is structured according to a pattern of expansion: the reader is initially provided with an introspection into the thoughts and feelings of the main character, nine-year-old Petia Bachei. Then, as outside forces intrude into the young protagonist's life, the point of view is steadily widened, to end in a panorama of tumultuous Russian society at the turn of the 20th century. This structure gave Kataev the opportunity to demonstrate his considerable skills as a psychological writer, while also enabling him to fulfil his obligations as an official Soviet author portraying class struggle as the foundation of social changes.

The story begins in the summer of 1905, with the Odessa gymnasium teacher Bachei and his two sons Petia and Pavlik returning home from a resort in Akkerman at the Black Sea (the boy's mother having died some years ago). As they are preparing for departure, Petia enjoys one last time the grandeur of the sea, its picturesque beauty and enigmatic depth. Suddenly, in the carriage to the port, the three travellers encounter a mysterious sailor who is said to have escaped from the rebellious battleship *Potemkin* after its staff was forced to surrender to Romanian authorities. Later in the day, on the steamship *Turgenev*, which is taking the family back to Odessa, Petia observes the vain efforts of a tsarist secret agent to capture the sailor, who finally jumps overboard and swims shorewards.

While the *Turgenev* is approaching Odessa, Petia's best friend Gavrik and his grandfather, a poor fisherman, pick up the sailor and hide him in their hut. Later, at a shooting gallery, the same secret agent whom Petia had seen before, interrogates Gavrik about the sailor, whose name is Rodion Zhukov. Gavrik turns for help to his older brother Terentii, a class-conscious proletarian and member of a revolutionary committee. When Terentii and other workers visit the sailor, police raid the hut. Although Terentii and the sailor manage to escape through the Odessa catacombs, the policemen arrest Gavrik's grandfather after beating him mercilessly. Gavrik is now on his own. He involves Petia, who has just enrolled in the gymnasium, in the preparations for a militant proletarian upheaval. Meanwhile Petia is discovering his dangerous passion for gambling. He loses all his possessions to his proletarian friend and ends up stealing money from his father and little brother to cover his gambling debts. He becomes increasingly alienated from his liberal bourgeois family and feels closer to the workers and their cause. The events in Odessa gain momentum – the police chief is killed by a bomb, then, Petia's father is attacked by the mob in a pogrom, and finally Cossacks kill the owner of the shooting gallery, one of the instigators of the upheaval. Gavrik's grandfather returns home, but soon dies, physically and mentally broken in prison, and Petia takes part in the funeral as well as in the celebration of "workers' Easter", on 1 May. Together with Gavrik, he assists in the arrested sailor's escape from prison. The novel ends with the image of a lonely white sail on the Black Sea – Rodion Zhukov is on his way to freedom.

The title *A White Sail Gleams* is related to Lermontov's famed romantic poem, "Parus" ("The Sail"), 1832, which Petia loves dearly and which he is not allowed to recite in full at the entrance examination to the gymnasium. Moreover, the sail acquires symbolic potential signifying the dynamic developments in Russia. At the end, the same symbol reappears with a different purpose, when Gavrik's boat, finally equipped with a sail he and his grandfather could never afford, serves the *Potemkin* sailor for his escape.

The novel covers approximately one year, from late summer 1905 to May 1906, in Soviet terminology the period of the "first Russian Revolution". Having drawn a conceptual frame precisely adjusted to the official historical dogma, Kataev could allow himself some stylistic leeway: like his literary father-figure Bunin, he indulges in catching the *mot juste* for colours, smells and all physical sensations, in finding the most precise similes, and in creating the most stunning metaphors both for images of nature and human moods. In great detail, he recalls the realia of an epoch gone for ever, including the names of clothes, drinks, and means of transportation. Thus Kataev verbally recreates the flair of a time that, although over for merely 30 years, already was lost to Soviet readers. This aesthetically conservative thoroughness contrasts strangely to the critical, anti-tsarist fervour displayed in the book's political messages.

A White Sail Gleams is situated at the crossroads between a novel of education and an adventure story. Petia's increasing comprehension of the class differences in tsarist Russia, his involvement with revolutionary workers, and the painful moral dilemma caused by his gambling, are all part of a rite of passage that ends in his initiation, "worker's Easter". Arguably, Kataev's characterization of Petia is his highest accomplishment in the art of psychological portraiture. Emulating Lev Tolstoi's depictions of children, he reveals the complexity of Petia's emotions, the sweet torture of the boy's early infatuations, his fears, joys and superstitions, his utter devotion to the pleasure of games, and the underlying motives for his interaction with adults and with infants. Much less depth is given to the novel's other characters, in particular Gavrik, who is more of a socialist realist "positive hero" intended to lead Petia on the path of communist virtue.

By superimposing an adolescent's revolt against the adult world onto the experience of societal destabilization, and depicting both as necessary processes of maturation, Kataev presents revolution and puberty as personally enriching, liberating romantic adventures. Likely, this very strategy granted *A White Sail Gleams* its lasting, albeit politically deceptive, charm for generations of Soviet readers.

PETER ROLLBERG

Almaznyi moi venets

My Diamond Crown

Novel, 1977

Although Kataev had worn the laurels of a "living classic of Soviet literature" since the 1930s, the critical response to his publication *Almaznyi moi venets*, in the June 1977 issue of *Novyi mir*, was noticeably mixed. Indeed, the novel-memoir can be regarded as the most controversial book of the "later Kataev", a term that encompasses the period from the early 1960s to the writers's death in 1986. The work irritated critics for a variety of reasons, among them the author's vain self-presentation, the text's provocative transgression of genre borders, the inclusion of unsubstantiated claims about famous Soviet literati, and the open elitism permeating it.

Most prominently, it is the author's awareness of himself as the last survivor of the Russian avant-garde that impregnates the narrative. Written with a high degree of aesthetic playfulness and with few qualms about the status he assigned to literary celebrities, Kataev approaches his topic in the refreshingly anti-traditional manner that is characteristic of his later years. After a long and successful career, it seems he felt completely free to concentrate entirely on his favourite game of verbalizing poeto-mnemonic associations and writing them down in a loosely organized fashion that resembles the way in which his mind produced them. Thus, although *Almaznyi moi venets* is not free of explicitly pro-Soviet exclamations, the political dimension never dominates the other parts of the narrative and, more importantly, does not determine or structure them. For Kataev, doubtless one of the great compromisers of Soviet literature, that meant a significant reversal of priorities, a step which he obviously dared only with posterity in mind.

In his role of author-narrator Kataev takes up several personae. First, he represents the ageing artist who remembers his famous friends and their tragic lot, his experiences in the turmoil of the 1920s and 1930s, and himself as an immature, bold, radical avant-gardist. Second, he narrates as the cosmopolitan traveller from "Soviet Moscow", who intensely enjoys sojourns to France, Italy, England, and the United States. Third, he talks as a connoisseur of literature sharing his expertise in poetic mastership. Connected with the latter persona is a continual narrative self-reflection, through which Kataev discusses the principles behind the creation of *Almaznyi moi venets* – truly a modernistic device. Also, he is occupied with the mysterious origin of literary fame, a theme that obviously disturbed him greatly.

The narrative structure of *Almaznyi moi venets* is deliberately erratic and scattered, consisting of pieces ranging from a few words to stories of several pages. One can discern a number of motif chains that are taken up time and time again, in a spiral-like fashion. At the very beginning, the first-person narrator encounters the extravagant Parisian sculptor Brunswick in his studio on the Montparnasse. Brunswick – one of the few completely fictitious characters in the text – is searching for a sculpting material that is light, transparent, and firm, in order to create perfect portraits. At the book's very end, Brunswick succeeds, and Kataev is invited to amble in a park populated with sculptures of his immortal poet-friends, a triumphant Olympus of the Soviet avant-garde, with his own bust completing the line. This magic image of a memorial garden embraces the entire narrative and informs it with a moving atmosphere of melancholy, evoked by Kataev's desire to create his unique poetic otherworld, and to conserve and legitimize it.

A second motif is that of an ongoing dialogue with curious literary scholars, predominantly in western countries where the author lectures in Slavonic departments. At times, where certain controversial questions of Russian letters are dealt with, the text itself acquires a lecture-like tone, something on which Kataev ironically comments.

A third strain of motifs is centred on Moscow, Kataev's beloved city and also the "capital of the World Revolution", a cause which the narrator romantically salutes on several occasions (the Revolution, he claims, was his and his friends' beloved). Kataev is somewhat ambiguous about the "miracle of Moscow's destruction", as he calls it. On the one hand, it pains him to see the *loci* of his memory disappear one by one, and he is overjoyed to discover that some of the houses, streets, parks, and squares associated with his past are still existent. On the other hand, the narrator repeatedly lauds the city's modernization, and there is no reason to doubt his sincere enthusiasm over Moscow's reconstruction. In turn, it is the reconstruction in Kataev's memory of the former names of those places, which often stands at the beginning of associative lines: layer after layer of the past is removed, and what appears are micro-portraits of poets who had lived in those places, anecdotes, and literary quotations in which the city's changing map is mirrored.

But, of course, the central motif cluster in *Almaznyi moi venets* is that of Moscow's literary society in the 1920s and 1930s, of its groups and circles and the fights between them. That motley crowd called avant-garde, their grandiose ambitions and abominable living conditions, their unhappy loves and first literary successes in the Soviet cauldron are the main focus of Kataev's homage. He cannot emphasize enough – and this may have been the main motivation to write *Almaznyi moi venets* – that he, who survived them all, really was once a participant in their literary gatherings, drinking parties, and glorious propaganda projects. Therefore, his portraits of Olesha, Maiakovskii, Esenin, Khlebnikov, Pasternak, Zoshchenko, Bulgakov and other immortals are coloured by an intimate familiarity; be they admiring or caustic, tender or mean, satirical or gossipy – they are always drawn "from the inside". Moreover, the fact that Kataev never lets any of the mentioned poets appear under their real name but gives each of them a code name such as Blue Eye, Little Key, Nutcracker etc., signifies that only the knowing few have full access to his story (in fact, after the text was published, lists decoding those names were circulating in Moscow).

Most appealing and truly artistic in *Almaznyi moi venets* is Kataev's insistence on his right to be as subjective as he pleased. Several times in the narrative he warns that he did not check the facts, that *Almaznyi moi venets* is a literary imprint of his personal memories, not a historically exact treatise. Also, Kataev takes pride in the fact that his work defies all genre definitions, being neither novel nor memoir. Maybe, this peculiar text should be called a poetic self-portrait, rather than a poetic memoir. For it is the self-portrait of a significant author, one who was gifted with an exceptional aesthetic sensitivity, and struck with a questionable moral indifference. In his last significant prose work, this author demonstrates how much profound sensual pleasure he still derives from creating verbal art; slowly, knowingly approaching his own death, he is still searching for eternal springtime and beauty. At the end of this requiem to his life and times Kataev succeeds in synthesizing all these drives into a harmonious one: a work of art called *Almaznyi moi venets*.

PETER ROLLBERG

Nina Semenovna Katerli 1934–

Prose writer

Biography

Born in Leningrad, 30 June 1934. Daughter of the writer Elena Katerli. Attended Lensoviet Technical Institute; degree in engineering. Worked as an engineer. Married, with two children. Made her literary debut in 1973. Editor of the paper *Bar'er*, since 1992. Currently resides in St Petersburg.

Publications

Collected Edition

Sennaia ploshchad'. Povesti i rasskazy [Haymarket Square]. St Petersburg, 1992.

Fiction

Okno [Window]. Leningrad, 1981.

"Treugol'nik Barsukova", *Glagol*, 3 (1981); published as "Sennaia ploshchad'", in *Sennaia ploshchad'*, 1992; title story translated as "The Barsukov Triangle", by David Lapeza, in *The Barsukov Triangle, the Two-Toned Blond and Other Stories*, Ann Arbor, Ardis, 1984, 3–71.

"Proshchalnyi svet", 1981; translated as "The Farewell Light", by Valeria Sajez, in *Balancing Acts*, edited by Helena Goscilo, Bloomington, Indiana University Press, 1989, 143–63.

"Mezhdu vesnoi i letom", 1983; translated as "Between Spring and Summer", by John Fred Beebe and Regina Snyder, in *Balancing Acts*, edited by Helena Goscilo, 1989, 229–55.

"Chudovishche", 1983; translated as "The Monster", by Bernard Meares, in *Soviet Women Writing*, New York, Abbeville Press, and London, John Murray, 1990, 107–15.

"Polina", *Neva*, 1 (1984).

Tsvetnye otkrytki: povesti i rasskazy [Coloured Postcards]. Leningrad, 1986.

"Zhara na severe: povest'" [Heat in the North: A Tale], *Zvezda*, 4 (1988), 3–73.

Kurzal. Povesti [Kursaal]. Leningrad, 1990.

"The Old Woman Slowly", translated by John Fred Beebe, in *Lives in Transit*, edited by Helena Goscilo. Dana Point, California, Ardis, 1995.

Critical Studies

"Ostorozhno: intelligent", by A. Mikhailov, *Literaturnoe obozrenie*, 9 (1987).

"N. Katerli. *Tsvetnye otkrytki*", by Andrei Ar'ev, *Literaturnoe obozrenie*, 1 (1988).

"Introduction", by Helena Goscilo, in *Balancing Acts*, 1989.

"Introduction", by Helena Goscilo, in *Lives in Transit*, 1995.

During her early years as a writer Nina Katerli moved between experimental fantastic prose ("Chudovishche" ["The Monster"]) and gritty realism. "The Monster" is a brief tale in the magical realism mould, almost a children's story one might say, featuring: "a shaggy creature with a single crimson eye in the middle of its forehead and a long scaly tail ... But why go in for description?"; this creature, among other pranks, can turn one resident of the apartment block "into an aluminium saucepan for a whole month". With the years, she wisely abandoned the "monster" mode, which had deployed inexplicable shifts in locale and viewpoint, radical temporal leaps, unexpected juxtapositions, the presence of "otherworldly emanations", and modified stream of consciousness in a rather coy and unconvincing blend. By contrast, her more realistic texts, which recreate modern urban settings in concrete detail, absorb grotesque elements with considerable skill and focus rather more effectively on what genuinely preoccupies Katerli: family problems, romantic liaisons, communal living, and the irrational, destructive impulses that drive human behaviour.

The novella "Treugol'nik Barsukova" ("The Barsukov Triangle") superbly realizes her fantasy-infused realistic manner. It vividly conveys the mundane horrors to which tenants in a communal apartment daily subject each other and themselves through their passions, prejudices, and insecurities. Few, if any, texts of this period (of the later Brezhnev years) match Katerli's skill at creating a complex microcosm of a neurotic, ailing society that approaches most aspects of life as bitter, ceaseless warfare. Written in 1977 and published abroad four years later (thereby causing Katerli difficulties with the Soviet authorities), "The Barsukov Triangle" appeared in Russia only in 1991, retitled "Sennaia ploshchad'" [Haymarket Square]. A locus forever associated with Dostoevskii, Haymarket Square suggests that the pattern of crime and punishment continued throughout the Soviet era, if in a less philosophical and "romantic" key. Katerli has claimed repeatedly that the mentality of the typical "Soviet citizen" (the *sovok*) constitutes the mystery her works attempt to fathom.

The main point of departure for Katerli's fiction is human relations – people's failure to identify and realize their dreams, to make meaningful contact, and to understand one another –

within the context of everyday Soviet life. Families, neighbours, and co-workers form the nexus of relationships that is anatomized in her fiction. Katerli's cast of characters covers the full spectrum of the old, the middle-aged, the young, and the adolescent of both sexes. Perhaps her most successful character portraits, however, are of older Russian Jews: good examples are the unendurable yet pathetic protagonist of "The Old Woman Slowly ..." and the two querulous old timers in "The Profitted Land".

From a feminist standpoint, Katerli's novella *Polina* offers particularly rich rewards, for it envisions an unorthodox alternative to the paradigmatic Soviet ideal of domesticated womanhood. Its eponymous heroine finds fulfilment in her profession – a job requiring technical skills and efficient supervision of male workers – even as she negotiates an anomalous intimacy with an impotent, unrecognized poet on the fringes of bohemia. Criticism of her protagonist's drinking, freewheeling style of life, and unconventional pronouncements bombarded Katerli when the novella appeared.

Unlike the majority of Russian women prose writers, Katerli surveys the world most frequently from a male centre of consciousness. The hallmarks of her fiction include irony, parallel plot lines, an elliptical style complicated by animal imagery, as well as literary allusions, marked by jagged sentence fragments and rich in colloquialisms.

Her most substantial recent work – written in 1991, as yet unpublished – straddles the genres of reportage and novel. Titled *Isk* [The Lawsuit], it documents the legal and political experiences she underwent in a case of anti-Semitism. Combating anti-Semitism, in fact, is the cause that increasingly absorbs Katerli's time; it now provides the heartbeat of her journalism, and has drawn her into serious political activity in St Petersburg.

HELENA GOSCILO

Veniamin Aleksandrovich Kaverin 1902–1989

Prose writer and dramatist

Biography

Born Veniamin Aleksandrovich Zil'ber in Pskov, 19 April 1902. Attended grammar school in Pskov, 1912–17; secondary school in Moscow, 1917–19; Moscow University 1919–20; transferred to Petrograd University, enrolled at the Institute of Oriental Languages, 1920. Married: the sister of his first literature teacher and mentor, Iurii Tynianov. Member of the Serapion Brothers, 1921. Graduated in Oriental languages, 1923, and from the faculty of history and philology, 1924. Visited the Salsk steppes in the south of Russia to see the famous sovkhoz "Gigant", 1930. War correspondent, visiting several fronts including Murmansk, 1941–45. Recipient: State Prize for Literature for his novel *Dva kapitana* (*Two Captains*), 1946. Member of the editorial board of the two-volume anthology *Literaturnaia Moskva*, 1956. Prominent liberal during both Thaw and glasnost periods. A signatory to the letter to the Presidium of the CPSU requesting that the writers Siniavskii and Daniel' be freed, 29 March–8 April 1966; wrote open letter in support of Aleksandr Solzhenitsyn, January 1968. Died in Moscow, 2 May 1989.

Publications

Collected Editions

Sobranie sochinenii, 3 vols. Leningrad, 1930.
Sobranie sochinenii, 6 vols. Moscow, 1963–66.
Izbrannye proizvedeniia, 2 vols. Moscow, 1977.
Sobranie sochinenii, 8 vols. Moscow, 1980–83.
Khudozhnik neizvesten i drugie proizvedeniia [The Unknown Artist and Other Works]. Jerusalem, Pamiat', 1982.
Letiashchii pocherk: romany i rasskazy [Flying Handwriting]. Moscow, 1986.
Samoe neobkhodimoe: povesti, rasskazy [The Most Essential Thing]. Moscow, 1987.

Fiction

Mastera i podmaster'ia [Masters and Apprentices]. Moscow and Petrograd, 1923.
"Bochka" [The Barrel], *Russkii sovremennik*, 2 (1924), 100–26.
"Deviat' desiatykh sud'by" [Nine Tenths Fate], *Kovsh*, 3 (1925), 73–120; 4 (1926), 139–205.
"Konets Khazy" [The End of the Gang], *Kovsh*, 1 (1925), 161–236.
Rasskazy. Moscow, 1925.
"Skandalist, ili Vechera na Vasil'evskom ostrove" [The Troublemaker, or Evenings on Vasilevskii Island], *Zvezda*, 2–7 (1928).
Prolog [Prologue]. Moscow, 1930–31.
Chernovik cheloveka [Rough Copy of a Man]. Leningrad, 1931.
Khudozhnik neizvesten. Leningrad, 1931; translated as *The Unknown Artist* (with Iurii Olesha's *Envy*), by P. Ross, London, Westhouse, 1947; Westport, Connecticut, Hyperion Press, 1973.
Ispolnenie zhelanii [The Fulfilment of Desires]. Moscow, 1937; translated as *The Larger View*, by E. Leda Swan, London, Cassell, and New York, Stackpole Sons, 1938.
Dva kapitana. Moscow, 1940; translated as *Two Captains*, by E. Leda Swan, New York, Modern Age Books, 1942; by

Brian Pearce, London, Lawrence and Wishart, 1957; also by Bernard Isaacs, Moscow, Progress, 1972.
Rasskazy. Moscow, 1942.
Otkrytaia kniga. Moscow, 1956; translated as *Open Book*, by Brian Pearce, London, Lawrence and Wishart; Moscow, Foreign Languages Publishing House, 1955; 2nd edition, 1990.
Poiski i nadezhdy [Searches and Hopes]. Moscow, 1956.
Neizvestnyi drug [The Unknown Friend]. Moscow, 1960.
"Kusok stekla" [A Piece of Glass], *Novyi mir*, 8 (1960).
Dvoinoi portret [Double Portrait]. Moscow, 1967.
Pered zerkalom. Roman v pis'makh [Before the Mirror]. Moscow, 1972.
Osveshchennye okna: trilogiia [Open Windows: Trilogy]. Moscow, 1978.
"Verlioka", *Novyi mir*, 1 (1982).

Plays
Ukroshchenie Mistera Robinzona ili Poteriannyi rai [The Taming of Mr Robinson or Paradise Lost]. Moscow, 1933.
"Lichnye schety" [Private Accounts], *Literaturnyi sovremennik*, 12 (1936), 127–59.
"Aktery" [Actors], *Literaturnyi sovremennik*, 12 (1937), 100–40.
Bol'shie nadezhdy [Great Hopes]. Moscow, 1942.
P'esy. Moscow, 1959.

Literary Criticism and Memoirs
Baron Brambeus. Leningrad, 1929; 2nd edition Moscow, 1966.
"Ocherk raboty" [A Sketch of Work], in *Sobranie sochinenii v shesti tomakh*, vol. 1, Moscow, 1963.
Sobesednik: vospominaniia i portrety [Interlocutor: Memoirs and Portraits]. Moscow, 1973.
Literator: dnevniki i pis'ma [Man of Letters: Diaries and Letters]. Moscow, 1988.
Epilog: memuary [Epilogue: Memoirs]. Moscow, 1989.
Schast'e talanta: vospominaniia i vstrechi, portrety i razmyshleniia [The Joy of Talent: Memoirs and Meetings, Portraits and Meditations]. Moscow, 1989.

Critical Studies

"Veniamin Kaverin", by N. Maslin, *Novyi mir*, 4 (1948), 272–90.
"Avtobiograficheskaia proza Kaverina", by T. Khmel'nitskaia, *Novyi mir*, 1 (1967), 253–56.
V.A. Kaverin: A Soviet Writer's Response to the Problem of Commitment: The Relationship of "Skandalist" and "Khudozhnik neizvesten" to the Development of Soviet Literature in the Late Nineteen-Twenties, by D.G.B. Piper, Pittsburgh, Duquesne University Press, 1970.
The Serapion Brothers: A Critical Anthology, edited by Gary Kern and Christopher Collins, Ann Arbor, Ardis, 1975.
The Prose Fiction of Veniamin A. Kaverin, by Hongor Oulanoff, Cambridge, Massachusetts, Slavica, 1976.
"A Long Fidelity: The Career of Veniamin Kaverin", by Rosemarie Kieffer, *World Literature Today*, 52/4 (1978), 577–80.
"Kaverin's *Before the Mirror*", by Elizabeth Klosty Beaujour, *Slavic and East European Journal*, 24/3 (1980), 233–44.
"Prototipy odnogo romana", by M. Chudakova and E. Toddes, *Al'manakh bibliofila*, 10 (1981), 172–90.
V. Kaverin: kriticheskii ocherk, by O.I. Novikova and V.I. Novikov, Moscow, 1986.
"The Last Serapion", by Gary Kern, *Russian Literature Triquarterly*, 24 (1991), 439–63.
"The Metafictional Turn in 'Russian Hoffmannism': Veniamin Kaverin and E.T.A. Hoffmann", by Erika Greber, *Essays in Poetics*, 17/1 (1992).
"Knowing the Artist: Veniamin Kaverin", in *Beyond Metafiction: Self-Consciousness in Soviet Literature*, by David Shepherd, Oxford, Clarendon Press, 1992.

Veniamin Aleksandrovich Kaverin was born into the family of a musician. At first he showed signs that he would be following in his father's footsteps, but his interests soon turned to literature for which, as a schoolboy, he was to acquire a passion that stayed with him all his life. At the age of 16 he left his native city of Pskov for Moscow where, having completed secondary school, he enrolled as a student of literature at Moscow University. In 1920 he transferred to Petrograd University, studying under teachers who were to become formative influences in his own work and career; these included Iurii Tynianov, Boris Eikhenbaum and Viktor Shklovskii. It was the latter who, in 1920 was responsible for introducing Kaverin to the Serapion Brothers, who, with their commitment to artistic freedom and their dislike for the use of propaganda in art, most suited Kaverin's temperament and literary tastes. Early experiments in various literary forms led to the publication in 1923 of *Mastera i podmaster'ia* [Masters and Apprentices], a collection of fantastic adventure stories in the manner of E.T.A. Hoffmann and Edgar Allan Poe.

Two years later he wrote *Konets Khazy* [The End of the Gang], a short novel depicting the underground world of the criminals and robbers of Leningrad at the height of the New Economic Policy (NEP), and introducing a more realistic element based on contemporary reality to his writing. Many other stories of the 1920s, however, continued the theme of the fantastic, until the appearance of *Skandalist, ili Vechera na Vasil'evskom ostrove* [The Troublemaker, or Evenings on Vasilevskii Island], Kaverin's first truly realistic novel set in the academic and literary milieu of Leningrad. In 1930 Kaverin travelled to the Salsk steppes in the south of Russia to visit state farms. A cycle of travel stories and documentary sketches, *Prolog*, based on this journey and portraying the contradictions and contrasts of the lives of state farm workers, had a mixed critical reception. His novel *Khudozhnik neizvesten* (*The Unknown Artist*) was subjected to even more hostile criticism and not republished until 1964.

During the mid-1930s Kaverin worked on his novel *Ispolnenie zhelanii* [The Fulfilment of Desires] dealing with the conflict between conservative and "progressive" elements in Leningrad academic circles at the end of the 1920s. This continues in the realistic manner, focusing on young people and their attempts to respond to the particular challenges of the Soviet era. Perhaps the most successful character is the largely autobiographical figure of Trubachevskii, the science student whose efforts to conquer "anti-social" elements within himself, such as individualism, ambition and excessive introversion, only meet with success after considerable struggle. *Ispolnenie zhelanii* was closely followed by Kaverin's best-known novel *Dva kapitana* (*Two Captains*). Based on the real-life story of a fellow-patient Kaverin met while convalescing in a Leningrad sanatorium, this colourful and eventful novel centres on the fulfilment of a young boy's dreams. *Two Captains* ranges widely in both time and space, covering the period from immediately before the 1917 Revolution to the end of World War II, with the action moving from the town of Ensk (in reality Kaverin's native town of Pskov) to Moscow and Leningrad, and from there to the towns and settlements of the far North. As in all classic adventure stories, there is a conflict between good and evil characters, ending inevitably in the triumph of the latter. The novel was very favourably received by readers of all ages in the Soviet Union where it was to be republished 42 times.

Shortly after the war, during which Kaverin had served as a correspondent producing a number of articles and documentary stories reflecting his experiences, he embarked on the writing of what was to eventually become a major trilogy, *Otkrytaia kniga* (*Open Book*). As in earlier works, the author takes as his main theme the problems and struggles that are entailed in scientific achievement. The trilogy covers 35 years in the life of a microbiologist, Tania Vlasenkova, who tells her own story, first as a girl, then as a young unmarried woman, and then finally as a completely formed person. As Kaverin himself relates, the writing of *Open Book* did not come easily to him; not only did the mastering of the scientific background entail much painstaking work, but he also had to contend with many critics who censured him for occupying himself "too much with the theme of love". Even more provocative for conservative critics was the third part of the trilogy, published during the post-Stalinist Thaw and entitled *Poiski i nadezhdy* [Searches and Hopes], which exposed the aura of corruption and treachery pervading Soviet science in the late 1940s. The novel was one of the first to speak openly about such matters as political denunciation, arrest, and imprisonment in a Soviet labour camp.

Kaverin continued to attack Stalinism, both in its historical form as well as in its later manifestations, in other works such as *Kusok stekla* [A Piece of Glass] and *Pered zerkalom* [Before the Mirror], but his feelings were most directly made manifest in his open and courageous defence of the dissident writers Siniavskii and Daniel', and later his actions in support of Solzhenitsyn and the scientist Zhores Medvedev. In the final years of his life he concentrated increasingly on literary memoirs and essays. Much of this material, some of it going back to the 1970s, appeared posthumously in *Epilog* [Epilogue]. This anthology combines personal reminiscences with portraits of many contemporaries over the years, including Gor'kii, Viktor Shklovskii, Kornei Chukovskii, Pasternak, Aleksandr Tvardovskii, and Solzhenitsyn. The pieces contained in this collection, sometimes sharp, often sympathetic, and always full of interest and insight, mark in their own way a fitting tribute to someone whose originality, ability to entertain, artistic talent, and personal integrity remained unscathed even during the worst excesses of an era that seemingly went out of its way to destroy precisely such qualities.

ROGER COCKRELL

The Unknown Artist

Khudozhnik neizvesten

Novel, 1931

The youngest of the Serapion Brothers, Kaverin rose swiftly to prominence in the Leningrad of the 1920s, displaying from the outset a penchant for intricate plots and stylistic experimentation. He was also very much involved in the literary debates of the time and this too finds expression in his work of the 1920s and early 1930s.

Published in 1931, *The Unknown Artist* depicts a crucial point in the relationship between the Soviet regime and the artistic community. The story of Arkhimedov poignantly reflects the problem that confronted the creative intelligentsia during the highly-charged period of collectivization and the first Five-Year Plan: Is there a future for an autonomous, apolitical art and is there a place for the old cultural values in the new materialist society? This theme was not in itself unusual for the period, but Kaverin's treatment of it is certainly unorthodox. For instance, it is widely accepted that the figure of the artist Arkhimedov is based on the poet Khlebnikov. While the novel appears to be set in 1929 and Khlebnikov had died in 1922, nevertheless, in resurrecting the unworldly genius for his hero, Kaverin is implying that he still believes in a literature whose intrinsic dynamics and devices render it qualitatively different from "real life". This was not an easy view to hold by the end of the 1920s, in the face of officially-inspired assaults on Formalism, fellow-travellers and the like.

The novel is divided into eight parts ("Encounters") with an epilogue. Except for the opening Encounter, a first-person narrator plays an important role throughout, often digressing to comment, or discuss his own preoccupations with the reader. The novel opens on a Leningrad street scene, peopled by various examples of low life. Arkhimedov and his neighbour Shpektorov meet and go to Arkhimedov's run-down studio where he lives with his wife Esfir and baby son Ferdinand (named after the German socialist Lassalle). Shpektorov knows that Arkhimedov has failed to adapt to "real life" – Arkhimedov wants to carry on living his own internal life. The narrator/novelist enters the second Encounter, explaining that Shpektorov is an old school-friend, who was an ardent revolutionary at the age of 17, but has since settled into a productive existence as a road engineer.

A chance meeting at Lassalle's statue between the narrator and Arkhimedov with Ferdinand leads to a night of conversation, after which the narrator resolves to write a book about Arkhimedov at some future date. He is impressed by Arkhimedov's unworldliness and his determination to uphold the values of "truth and honesty", but is diverted by the need to finish a book on Senkovskii (Kaverin published such a work – but in 1926). Meantime, Arkhimedov has drifted away from Esfir and now spends his time in a children's theatre, with two disciples, Zhaba and Vizel'. Zhaba is the more intellectual of the two and his role in the novel suggests an individual constantly changing tack to keep in step with the times. Thus, in response to Zhaba's call to "repaint the whole world", Arkhimedov only wants to grasp the wonderful colours of the world as it is. The children's theatre plays an important role in uniting two themes – the world of illusion and the idea that the future of art belongs to the next generation. In the next section, Zhaba, now married to Esfir's friend Tania, has himself turned to painting. He is no good, however, but appreciates Arkhimedov's genius and acknowledges that Arkhimedov only lives so that his own particular vision will eventually be recognized. Meanwhile Zhaba and Tania are looking after Ferdinand and the author suddenly suggests that Arkhimedov is not the father.

The next Encounter takes the author away from Leningrad to a state farm in the steppes where Shpektorov is working. This episode appears at first sight to have little connection with the rest of the novel, but it does introduce a virtually compulsory theme for the period, that of socialist construction. There is an important moment, however, when the author sees a signed photograph of Esfir in Shpektorov's room and realizes the truth of his comment to Zhaba about Ferdinand's parentage. However the significance of the state farm episode becomes clearer in the next section, when the author, after two months "in the real world", returns to Leningrad to find that he cannot any longer understand the notes he has made on Arkhimedov and informs us that the book was only completed because others helped and it "wrote itself to a conclusion". A Dr Veselago now enters the story and tells a touching tale of encountering Arkhimedov in the street, defending a group of homeless people, who are being cleared out of the city as undesirables. Arkhimedov takes up their plea for trust and is himself arrested. The author goes looking for him and finds Esfir working in the theatre as a costumier. However, Shpektorov is already there and the author and Vizel overhear a conversation in which he begs her to give up Arkhimedov and acknowledge Ferdinand as their child. But she refuses and, shockingly, a short while after, throws herself to her death from the fifth floor. Thus, Esfir is seen as a source of inspiration, destroyed by both romanticism and materialism.

It is another three months before the author finds Arkhimedov again. A half-crazed drunk, he wanders the city, disrupts a church wedding, and delivers a speech about a brave new world. A further six months passes, by which time the author has once again abandoned the subject of Arkhimedov, only finishing the book because of a chance encounter with Zhaba, now turned linguist, who delivers a lecture on the "Bureaucratization of Language", and then proceeds to account for his "conversion" with a long confused tale of smashing up the theatre. So Zhaba has "adapted" and Arkhimedov is about to lose his final illusion as he agrees to hand over Ferdinand for adoption by Shpektorov. The enigmatic epilogue describes a painting depicting the scene of Esfir's death, with the final cryptic designation – "Artist Unknown".

MICHAEL FALCHIKOV

Dvoinoi portret

Double Portrait

Novel, 1967

Dvoinoi portret is one of the best novels written by Veniamin Kaverin, formerly a member of the Serapion Brothers, a post-revolutionary group of writers whose aim was to preserve the aesthetic quality of literature. After the group had been disbanded at the end of the 1920s, its members made their individual, often successful careers. Kaverin remained one of the most prominent writers not to betray his art, even under strong political pressure. The key to his post-war literary creations is to be found in his early prose in which he, in common with the other Serapions, protested against the petrified nature of Russian literature in the second half of the 19th century. Kaverin's early writing, including his studies in history and philosophy (especially in oriental studies) and his dissertation "Baron Brambeus. Istoriia Osipa Senkovskogo" [Baron Brambeus - the History of Osip Senkovskii] (1929), inclined him towards complicated, psychologically constructed plots in which he often used the poetics of the adventure novel or the detective story.

Dvoinoi portret features a biologist involved in research in the Caspian Sea: the fauna is gradually losing its marine character and fresh-water organisms are beginning to prevail. A strengthening of the marine character of the region is necessary. Ostrogradskii, the hero, suggests bringing in a special kind of worm, but his opponent, Snegirev, attempts to compromise him by organizing an expedition which is to prove that the worm will be a dangerous predator and persuading his student Cherkashin to falsify the experiments. Ostrogradskii loses out, and Cherkashin, newly wed and the father of a baby, commits suicide.

This story serves as material for an article that is to be written by a journalist named Kuzin and published in a scientific journal. Cherkashin's widow leaves the university to earn money to support her family; she is also helped by her dead husband's friend Lepestkov. Ostrogradskii is charged with political crimes and sent to a concentration camp in the Far East. The main action takes place in 1954, after Stalin's death, when the first political prisoners began to return from the numerous camps in Siberia. Ostrogradskii is allowed back to Central Russia, but he has many problems over permission to stay permanently in Moscow. Kuzin organizes a meeting of all the participants, including Snegirev and Ostrogradskii. Snegirev tries to find a compromise, offering to help Ostrogradskii with accommmodation and a job, but the latter refuses. Meanwhile, Ostrogradskii falls in love with Cherkasina, is awaiting rehabilitation, but then suddenly dies of a heart attack.

The novel consists of 61 chapters and an epilogue. The story of Ostrogradskii and Snegirev ("the double portrait") is not narrated directly: Kaverin employs a specific narrative strategy; the plot is revealed gradually and elaborated in the form of a detective story and of investigative journalism. The numeral "two" or "double" is extremely important. There are not only the two men ("a double portrait"), but also the two documents informing us about the mysterious events, about the two enemies, about the crime and the suicide. A newspaper article is to be written by Kuzin; other documentary material is written by Lepestkov. Reality is observed from different angles and interpreted from contradictory points of view. Kuzin is very moderate, careful, and precise; Lepestkov is more radical and critical in his interpretation of events. A further viewpoint comes from Cherkashina, who had been unsatisfied in her marriage, and tired of endless scientific and political discussions with her husband.

Kaverin is a master of psychological prose. His depictions of Moscow in the early 1950s are colourful and atmospheric. His characters reflect the horrors of the epoch and, at the same time, all the great expectations connected with the coming Thaw period. Yet, Kaverin is also objective: his Snegirev is a complicated character, and the positive heroes, such as Ostrogradskii and Lepestkov, are not flawless. There is a certain touch of irony and relativism in all events and human deeds: in the epilogue, Lepestkov has published his book, which has turned out to be much more moderate (there are no crimes and the book seems to be mainly scientific as it is called "Sketches of the History of Biological Discussion"). Time flies and people forget all the injustices. The "double" character of Kaverin's novel is also supported by the parallel existence of the text (the story) and the metatext (the interpretation of the story in Kuzin's newspaper article and in Lepestkov's "Sketches"). Moreover, the opposition between the story (*fabula*) and the plot (*siuzhet*), as conceived by the Russian Formalists, is demonstrated by a further artistic layer: the whole novel can be seen as a superstructure of its author's preceeding novels, based on previous depictions of the lives of scientists and scholars including the Formalists themselves: i.e., *Skandalist, ili Vechera na Vasil'evskom ostrove* [The Troublemaker], *The Unknown Artist*, *Ispolnenie zhelanii* [The Fulfilment of Desires], and *Open Book*. Kaverin now ironizes his method of "double portraiture", used in the earlier novels, in which the plot is developed in terms of conflict between parallel characters.

In this sense, Kaverin was more artistically subtle than some of his successors, who also utilized the themes of Stalin's camps and freedom in scientific work, connected in particular with genetics and cybernetics, which had been banned under Stalin. Back in the 1950s Vladimir Dudintsev wrote his novel *Ne khlebom edinym* (*Not by Bread Alone*), 1957; later, in the perestroika period, his long novel *Belye odezhdy* [White Robes] (1988), appeared. The former dealt with the sad fate of an inventor, fighting against Soviet bureaucracy, the latter with the survival of the banned field of cybernetics. In 1987 Daniil Granin published the novel *Zubr* [The Buffalo], depicting the fate of the legendary figure of world genetics Nikolai Timefeev-Resovskii (1900–81).

The narrative strategy of Kaverin's *Dvoinoi portret* is based on the switching of narrative point of view and on the metamorphoses of spatio-temporal relations; its poetics go back also to the 19th-century psychological novel with its sense of the atmosphere of the time.

IVO POSPÍŠIL

Iurii Pavlovich Kazakov 1927–1982

Short-story writer

Biography

Born in Moscow, 8 August 1927. Enrolled at Moscow School of Architecture, 1944; studied cello at Gnesin Music School, 1946–51; Gor'kii Literary Institute, Moscow, 1953–58. Instructor at Moscow Conservatory; musician 1952–54. Writer, from 1952. Member of the Writers' Union. Recipient: Dante Prize for Literature, 1971. Married; one son. Died 29 November 1982.

Publications

Collected Editions

Selected Short Stories (in Russian), with an introduction by George Gibian. New York, Macmillan, 1963; Oxford, Pergamon Press, 1964.

The Smell of Bread and Other Stories, translated by Manya Harari and Andrew Thomson. London, Harvill Press, 1965.

Zapakh khleba. Nekrasivaia. O muzhestve pisatelia [The Smell of Bread. The Plain Girl. The Courage of a Writer]. Letchworth, Bradda, 1975.

Izbrannoe. Moscow, 1985.

Selected Stories/ Izbrannye rasskazy, edited by A. Pavlov. London, Bristol Classical Press, 1993.

Plachu i rydaiu ... [I Cry and Sob ...]. Moscow, 1996.

Fiction

Na polustanke [At the Halt]. Moscow, 1959.

Po doroge [Along the Road]. Moscow, 1961.

Goluboe i zelenoe [Blue and Green]. Moscow, 1963.

Dvoe v dekabre [Two in December]. Moscow, 1966.

Osen' v dubovykh lesakh. Alma-Ata, 1969; translated as *Autumn in the Oak Woods*, by Bernard Isaacs, Moscow, Progress, 1970.

Severnyi dnevnik [Northern Diary]. Moscow, 1973.

Vo sne ty gor'ko plakal [You Wept Bitterly in Your Dreams]. Moscow, 1977.

Olen'i roga [Deer's Antlers]. Moscow, 1980.

Dve nochi [Two Nights]. Moscow, 1986.

Critical Studies

"Svoe i chuzhoe", by Iu. Nagibin, *Druzhba narodov*, 7 (1959).

Russian Literature since the Revolution, by Edward J. Brown, Cambridge, Massachusetts, Harvard University Press, 1963; 2nd edition, 1982.

"Jurij Kazakov: The Pleasures of Isolation", by Karl D. Kramer, *Slavic and East European Journal*, 10 (1966), 22–31.

"Yurii Kazakov", by George Gibian, in *Major Soviet Writers: Essays in Criticism*, edited by Edward J. Brown, London, Oxford University Press, 1973, 321–32.

A History of Post-War Soviet Writing: The Literature of Moral Opposition, by Grigori Svirski, translated by Robert Dessaix and Michael Ulman, Ann Arbor, Ardis, 1981.

Iurii Kazakov, by I.S. Kuz'michev, Moscow, 1986.

"The Voice of Iurii Kazakov", by Gareth Williams, *Essays in Poetics*, 19/1 (1994), 47–57.

Iurii Kazakov's first published work was a one-act play dating from 1952. After that he concentrated almost exclusively on short stories, of which, in the course of his lifetime, he published relatively few, some 35 in all, spread over nine short volumes. They are typical products of the Thaw – allusive, open-ended, and ambiguous. His heroes and heroines are indecisive, unsure, vulnerable and isolated, both physically and emotionally. They include a buoy-keeper on a Northern river (Egor in "Trali-vali" [Fiddle Faddle]), a post girl on the White Sea ("Man'ka"), a blind dog in "Arktur - gonchii pes" ("Arcturus the Hunting Hound") and the ailing Chekhov, compelled to live apart from his wife in Yalta in "Prokliatyi sever" [The Accursed North]. Like Chekhov, who together with Ivan Turgenev, Mikhail Prishvin, Ivan Bunin and Konstantin Paustovskii, is a major influence on his work, Kazakov offers no easy solutions. For example, Sonia in "Nekrasivaia" [The Plain Girl] is, like Chekhov's heroine of the same name in Uncle Vania, painfully aware of her lack of physical attractiveness. No one asks her to dance at the party with which this story, like a number of Kazakov's stories, opens. Her subsequent encounter with a drunken – and equally lonely – young man ends in tears. Although the experience gives her a new realization of her worth as a human being, she will still be lonely and plain.

This story, like many of Kazakov's stories, is set in provincial Russia. Kazakov, whose parents were provincials, had a particular love of the *pomor'e* area along the White Sea coast and reproduced the local dialect in a number of stories. A visit to the Far North in 1956 was seen by Kazakov as a turning-point in his creative life. He claimed to have been "born again" and said that ever afterwards he metaphorically pointed north, like the needle of a compass. His *Severnyi dnevnik* [Northern Diary] is a mixture of stories and sketches set in the area. The contrast between the provinces and Moscow, between town and country, a recurrent theme in Russian literature, is seen to best effect in "Zapakh khleba" ("The Smell of Bread"), one of three stories he contributed to the famous almanac *Tarusskie stranitsy* [Pages from Tarusa] (1961). The sophisticated Muscovite Dusia returns, somewhat reluctantly, to the village where her mother has just died. Only then does she realize the extent of her loss and the degree of her estrangement from her roots. This story, itself heavily influenced by Konstantin Paustovskii's "Telegramma" [The Telegram], prefigures much of the work of the Village Prose writers of the 1970s, particularly in its emphasis on the adjective *rodnoi* (native, or, in this context, Russian) and similar cognate words. It demonstrates, too, that Kazakov is essentially a transitional writer between the classics of the 19th and early 20th century and the modern period.

It might be alleged that Kazakov's scope is limited, that he ploughs a very narrow furrow. What is indisputable, however, is that his handling of language is masterly. One of the last journalists to interview him highlighted this aspect of his work: "... his language startles you not only by its faithfulness to the classical tradition but also by something uniquely Kazakovian". He exploits all the resources of the Russian language, particularly its prefixes, suffixes and diminutives in a way that is almost impossible to convey in translation. For instance, every Kazakov story is saturated in sounds, which are rendered either through standard literary words or through neologisms of his own invention, based on standard roots. On occasions he resorts to onomatopoeic transcription, most notably in "Nochleg" [A Place for the Night] where a mysterious sound emanating from a lake is rendered by multiple repetition of a single vowel. Striking though these transcriptions are, they are perhaps the least successful of the stylistic devices employed by Kazakov, tending too often to resemble the attempts made in ornithological textbooks to transcribe birdsong.

Smells also dominate Kazakov's stories, the smells of nature, people, places, and products. Kazakov regarded smell as the most evocative of the senses and the eponymous hero of "Arcturus the Hunting Hound" is blind and therefore particularly dependent on his sense of smell in order to survive. The changes rung by Kazakov on the root *-pakh-* (smell) testify once again to his stylistic versatility.

In Kazakov's stories the unspoken is frequently more important than the spoken. The unspoken is conveyed by facial gesture, such as the raising or lowering of eyes, and by body language, frequently the offering, refusing, lighting, or smoking of a cigarette. This is particularly marked in the exchanges between Sonia and Nikolai in "Nekrasivaia" and between the unnamed boy and girl in "Na polustanke" [At the Halt].

Attacked for his "pessimism" and "morbidity" by the Brezhnevite literary bureaucracy, Kazakov fell prey to drink and depression. In poor health and beset by persistent hostle criticism of his work, he lived an almost hermit-like existence in the house he had bought in 1968 in the writers' colony of Abramtsevo, near Moscow, and published no new stories in the last five years of his life. Indeed his output had begun to fall away as early as 1969, a phenomenon he ascribed to the inordinate amount of time he devoted to a translation of a novel trilogy, *Krov' i pot* [Blood and Sweat], by his friend, the Kazakh writer Abidzhamil Nurpeisov. His collection *Osen' v dubovykh lesakh* (*Autumn in the Oak Woods*) was published not in Moscow but in Alma-Ata, as was a memoir on Paustovskii in 1971. The isolation and the uniqueness of the writer are the subject of "O muzhestve pisatelia" [The Courage of a Writer]. Part autobiographical sketch, part literary credo, this is one of Kazakov's few excursions outside the short story genre. In January 1981 Kazakov acknowledged the meagreness of his output: "So much was planned; there were such grandiose projects – but nothing materialized". When Kazakov died, the obituary in *Literaturnaia gazeta* was almost perfunctory. Since his death, however, he has attracted increasing literary attention, both in Russia and in the west.

MICHAEL PURSGLOVE

Mark Sergeevich Kharitonov 1937–

Prose writer and translator

Biography

Born in Zhitomir, Ukraine, 31 August 1937. Attended Moscow Pedagogical Institute. Secondary schoolteacher; executive secretary for a newspaper. Married: Galina Edelman; one son and two daughters. Editor in a publishing house, 1960–69; freelance writer and editor since 1969: translated the works of Franz Kafka, Stefan Zweig, Elias Canetti, Herman Hesse, Thomas Mann and others. Novella *Den' v fevrale* [A Day in February], published in *Novyi mir*, 1976. No further publication followed until 1988 with a collection of prose under the title *Den' v fevrale*. Recipient: Russian Booker Prize, 1992 (the first time the prize was awarded) for *Linii sud'by* [Lines of Fate, or Milashevich's Trunk].

Publications

Collected Editions

Den' v fevrale [A Day in February]. Moscow, 1988.
Izbrannaia proza, 2 vols. Moscow, 1994.

Fiction

Prokhor Men'shutin. 1971.
Etiud o maskakh [Etude on Masks]. 1971.
Den' v fevrale [A Day in February]. 1974.
Dva Ivana [Two Ivans]. 1980.
Storozh [The Guard]. 1988.
Golosa [Voices]. 1990.
"Linii sud'by, ili Sunduchok Milashevicha" [Lines of Fate, or Milashevich's Trunk], *Druzhba narodov*, 1–2 (1992); translated as *Lines of Fate*, by Helena Goscilo, New York, The New Press, 1996.
"Provintsial'naia filosofiia" [A Provincial Philosophy], *Novyi mir*, 11 (1993).
"Vozvrashchenie niotkuda" [Return from Nowhere], *Znamia*, 1–2 (1995), 56–91; 65–119.
Agasfer. 1975; translated as "Ahasuerus", by Arch Tait, in *Booker Winners and Others, II, Glas New Russian Writing*, 10 (1996).

Essays

Sposob sushchestvovaniia [A Means of Survival]. 1994.

Critical Studies

Russian Literature 1988–1994: The End of an Era, by N.N. Shneidman, Toronto, University of Toronto Press, 1995.
"Mark Xaritonov: un symboliste ironiqe", by Marc Weinstein, *Revue des Études Slaves*, 68/1 (1996), 37–54.

Mark Kharitonov is one of a generation of writers whose works were all but unpublishable until the glasnost period. After his first publication of any significance, *Den' v fevrale* [A Day in February] of 1974, he was ignored by Soviet editors until 1988. However, his philosophical novel *Linii sud'by* (*Lines of Fate*), written during 1981–85, brought him to international attention when it won the first Russian Booker Prize in 1992. *Lines of Fate*, a fragmentary and highly intertextual novel, represents Kharitonov's ambitious attempt, through a complex artistic edifice, to supply some sort of a unitary worldview. Accordingly, the present entry concentrates on this, his major work to date.

The plot of *Lines of Fate* is expounded by an ironical narrator who follows the efforts of a literary researcher, Anton Andreevich Lizavin, to understand the allusive and fragmented writings of Simeon Kondrat'evich Milashevich. Lizavin has written his candidate's dissertation in the early Brezhnev period on writers of the 1920s who were connected with his home town of Nechaisk. He stumbles on Milashevich, who was exiled to Nechaisk in 1909, but the novel's shifting plot is as confusing as the jumbled heap of sweet wrappers that were the only writing paper available to Milashevich after the 1917 revolutions. On these he has written what appear to be random insights, from which Lizavin tries to piece together the outlines of a novel, and an understanding of Milashevich's biography and philosophy.

Other information about Milashevich and the circumstances of his life comes either through Lizavin's various incomplete archival discoveries, or speculatively from the narrator on the basis of what may be autobiographically-based detail in Milashevich's stories. As new information comes to light, earlier interpretations of particular wrappers have to be revised.

A comparison of extant versions of Milashevich's stories, an incomplete police file dating from 1912, and an autobiographical fragment and interview dating from 1926, suggest the following story. After the 1905 Revolution a student known as Ahasuerus had turned the head of a girl from Nechaisk, taken her back with him to Moscow, but had then disappeared, leaving Milashevich, a student at Moscow University, to marry her. Ahasuerus turns up again in 1909 but is ill, and Milashevich is apparently obliged to leave his young wife with him while he goes off to deliver a suitcase containing items for an assassination to an address that proves to be under police surveillance. He is arrested and exiled to Nechaisk. Although we are not told as much, it would seem that Ahasuerus and Aleksandra emigrate together. Milashevich moves to the nearby town of Stolbenets in 1912, and later to St Petersburg, where he is accused of having plagiarized a story previously published under his real name of Bogdanov. He chooses not to refute the libel and, like one of the heroes in another of his stories, apparently prefers to adjust his life to the fiction and to live in St Petersburg as a literary pariah.

Milashevich is, Lizavin speculates, possibly a natural provincial, and returns to Stolbenets to take up residence with the local owner of a toffee factory (whence the sweet wrappers). It is here that he next meets his wife after the revolutions of 1917, when she is sent back by the Bolsheviks to arrest the local bourgeois authorities. He is released and resumes his married life with her.

Nothing definite can be discovered about the circumstances of Milashevich's life after 1926, partly because the local history collections have suffered from periodic fires or been subject to periodical purging. "A wooden country", Lizavin reflects ruefully, "has an unreliable memory." He encounters a final nonsensical reference in the local newspaper to Milashevich-Bogdanov's being among "those who have tried to use the opium of religion to sabotage the great struggle for the liquidation of the rich kulak peasants as a class", and decides against further investigation. Aleksandra apparently also perished in the purges.

Milashevich's experience of solitary confinement seems to have developed in him a peculiarly alienated way of seeing the world. He is more interested in isolated phenomena than in the rationally connected world. His "provincial philosophy" is an appreciation of humdrum minutiae, in which logic is merely an irksome distraction. A character in one of his stories remarks that provincial taste should not be disregarded:

> It would be very unwise to look down on it if we want to understand the intellect of the new class of waifs and strays which is increasingly replacing the old peasantry. We shall be unable to understand the new nation which will emerge if there is any abrupt fracture in our history. And finally, we shall be unable to understand something crucial within ourselves.

Kharitonov's novel is about the very nature of meaning and literary form, and the affinity of concepts related at a sub-verbal and sub-rational level. Immersing himself in Milashevich's hypnotic writings:

> Lizavin immersed himself in this saturated solution as if into a semi-hypnotic state: something was stirring and shifting, some diffuse, unrecognizable voice rumbled. *Just one tiny effort more ... all our life we have been involuntarily resisting this lightness and freedom ... we need to find the words to pull alongside it, if only for a moment ...* immaterial particles, free from gravity, free from rational explanation were waiting to test each other freely, as is possible in those moments of genius in a dream. All that was missing was a thread for the tiny crystals to begin to form.

As Lizavin looks at the wrappers scattered on his desk they remind him of random iron filings. By chance the next paper he picks contains the words, "charged particles". "He smiled wryly at something, took up the pen again and continued, further defining his insight, 'the force field of time, lines of destiny'".

ARCH TAIT

Daniil Kharms 1905–1942

Prose writer, poet, and dramatist

Biography

Born Daniil Ivanovich Iuvachev in St Petersburg, 30 December 1905. Attended school in Tsarskoe Selo, Peterschule, 1915–22; Second Soviet Labour School, 1922–24; Leningrad Electro-Technical College, 1924–25; did not graduate. Enrolled on film course, Leningrad Institute of the History of the Arts, 1926; did not graduate. Married: 1) Ester Aleksandrovna Rusakova in 1925 (divorced 1932); 2) Marina Vladimirovna Malich in 1934. Member of Aleksandr Tufanov's group, Orden Zaumnikov DSO [The Order of Trans-rationals], 1925–26; member of the philosophical circle known as the "chinari" in 1925 (group lasted until 1941); co-founder, with Aleksandr Vvedenskii, of the School of Chinari (*Shkola chinarei*), 1926; joined the Leningrad branch of the All-Russian Union of Poets, 1926 (excluded 1929); two poems published in Union anthologies, 1926–27. Collaborated with the experimental theatre group Radiks, 1926; founder-member of OBERIU (The Association of Real Art). Published literature for children in the journals *Ezh*, 1928–35, and *Chizh*, 1930–41; and 12 books of children's stories, 1928–40. Short-term service in the Red Army, 1928. Arrested in 1931, along with other children's writers. Imprisoned, then exiled to Kursk, July–November 1932. Accepted into the newly-organized Soviet Writers' Union, 1934; banned from publishing, 1937–38; second arrest, 1941. Died in captivity, probably 2 February 1942. Rehabilitated 1956. Children's works began to be republished in 1962. First posthumous and isolated publication of "adult" writing in USSR, 1965; first Soviet book publication, 1988.

Publications

Collected Editions

Russia's Lost Literature of the Absurd: A Literary Discovery. Selected Works of Daniil Kharms and Alexander Vvedensky, edited and translated by George Gibian. Ithaca, Cornell University Press, 1971; revised edition as *The Man with the Black Coat – Russia's Literature of the Absurd: Selected Works of Daniil Kharms and Alexander Vvedensky*, Evanston, Illinois, Northwestern University Press, 1987.

Izbrannoe, edited by George Gibian. Würzburg, Jal, 1974.

Sobranie proizvedenii, edited by Mikhail Meilakh and Vladimir Erl. Bremen, K-Presse, 1978 – (only 4 vols published).

Polet v nebesa: Stikhi. Proza. Dramy. Pis'ma, edited by A.A. Aleksandrov. Moscow, 1988; 2nd edition, 1991.

The Plummeting Old Women, edited and translated by Neil Cornwell. Dublin, Lilliput Press, 1989; revised and expanded edition as *Incidences*, London, Serpent's Tail, 1993.

Sobranie sochinenii, 2 vols. Moscow, 1994–95.

Polnoe sobranie sochinenii, 4 vols. St Petersburg, 1997 –

Fiction

Sluchai (written 1933–39), first published as integral cycle in *Polet v nebesa*, Moscow, 1988; translated as "Incidents", by Neil Cornwell, in *Incidences*, 1993, 49–85.

Starukha (written 1939), first published in *Izbrannoe*, 1974; edited by Robin Aizlewood, London, Bristol Classical Press, 1995; translated as "The Old Woman", by Neil Cornwell, in *Incidences*, 1993, 17–46.

Iz domu vyshel chelovek. Stikhi dlia detei, i ne tol'ko [A Man Came Out of a House]. New York, Rego Park, 1982.

Plays

Komediia goroda Peterburga [The Comedy of the City of Petersburg] (produced 1927), first published in *Sobranie proizvedenii*, 1978, vol. 1.

Elizaveta Bam (produced 1928), first published in *Izbrannoe*, 1974; translated as "Yelizaveta Bam: A Dramatic Work", by Neil Cornwell, in *Incidences*, 1993, 155–84.

Notebooks, Letters, and Diaries

"'Bozhe, kakaia uzhasnaia zhizn' i kakoe uzhasnoe u menia sostoianie': Zapisnye knizhki. Pis'ma. Dnevniki", ["God, What an Awful Life and What an Awful Position I'm In": Notebooks. Letters. Diaries], compiled by Vladimir Glotser, *Novyi mir*, 2 (1992), 192–224.

Critical Studies

"'Left Art' in Leningrad: the OBERIU Declaration", by Robin Milner-Gulland, *Oxford Slavonic Papers*, (new series) 3 (1970), 65–74.

"Materialy D.I. Kharmsa v rukopisnom otdele Pushkinskogo Doma", by Anatolii Aleksandrov, in *Ezhegodnik rukopisnogo otdela Pushkinskogo Doma 1978*, Leningrad, 1980, 64–79.

Laughter in the Void: An Introduction to the Writings of Daniil Kharms and Aleksandr Vvedenskii, by Alice Stone Nakhimovsky, Vienna, Wiener Slawistischer Almanach, 5, 1982.

"Čexov and Xarms: Story/Anti-Story", by Ellen Chances, *Russian Language Journal*, 36/123–24 (1982), 181–92.

"'Kovarnye stikhi': Notes on Daniil Kharms and Aleksandr Vvedensky", by Robin Milner-Gulland, *Essays in Poetics*, 9/1 (1984), 16–37.

"De la réalité au texte: L'absurde chez Daniil Harms", by Jean-Philippe Jaccard, *Cahiers du monde russe et soviétique*, 26/3–4 (1985), 269–312.

"Tradition in the Topsy-Turvey World of Parody: Analysis of two Oberiu plays", by Anatoly Vishevsky, *Slavic and East European Journal*, 30/3 (1986), 355–66.

"Oberiu (problema smeshnogo)", by Anna Gerasimova, *Voprosy literatury*, 4 (1988), 48–79.

"Towards a Poetics of the Absurd: The Prose Writings of Daniil Kharms", by Ann Shukman, in *Discontinuous Discourses in Modern Russian Literature*, edited by Catriona Kelly, Michael Makin, and David Shepherd, London, Macmillan, and New York, St Martin's Press, 1989, 60–72.

"'Guilt Without Guilt' in Kharms's Story 'The Old Woman'", by Robin Aizlewood, *Scottish Slavonic Studies*, 14 (1990), 199–217.

Daniil Kharms and the Poetics of the Absurd: Essays and Materials, edited by Neil Cornwell, London, Macmillan, and New York, St Martin's Press, 1991.

Daniil Harms et la fin de l'avant-garde russe, by Jean-Philippe Jaccard, Bern, Peter Lang, 1991; translated into Russian as *Daniil Kharms i konets russkogo avangarda*, St Petersburg, 1995.

"Zaumnik Daniil Kharms: Nachalo puti", by Jean-Philippe Jaccard and Andrey Ustinov, *Wiener Slawistischer Almanach*, 27 (1991), 159–228.

Teatr (special OBERIU issue), 11 (1991)

"A Matter of (Dis)course: Metafiction in the Works of Daniil Kharms", by Graham Roberts, in *New Directions in Soviet Literature: Selected Papers from the Fourth World Congress for Soviet and East European Studies, Harrogate, 1990*, edited by Sheelagh Duffin Graham, London, Macmillan, 1992, 138–63.

Aspects of Dramatic Communication: Action, Non-Action, Interaction (A. P. Čechov, A. Blok, D. Charms), by Jenny Stelleman, Amsterdam, Rodopi, 1992.

"Of Words and Worlds: Language Games in *Elizaveta Bam* by Daniil Kharms", by G.H.J. Roberts, *Slavonic and East European Review*, 72/1 (1994), 38–59.

"Daniil Kharms and the Act of Negation", by Neil Carrick, *Slavonic and East European Review*, 72/4 (1994), 707–21.

"A Familiar Story: Insurgent Narratives and Generic Refugees in Daniil Kharms's *The Old Woman*", by Neil Carrick, *Modern Language Review*, 90/3 (1995).

"Daniil Kharms: filosofiia i tvorchestvo", by D.V. Tokarev, *Russkaia literatura*, 4 (1995), 68–93.

Kharmsizdat predstavliaet: issledovaniia, esse, vospominaniia, katalog vystavki, bibliografiia, St Petersburg, 1995.

"Poor Liza: The Sexual Politics of *Elizaveta Bam*", by Graham Roberts, in *Gender and Russian Literature: New Perspectives*, edited by Rosalind Marsh, Cambridge and New York, Cambridge University Press, 1996, 244–62.

The Last Soviet Avant-Garde: OBERIU – Fact, Fiction, Metafiction, by Graham Roberts, Cambridge, Cambridge University Press, 1997.

"The Rudiments of Daniil Kharms: In Further Pursuit of the Red-Headed Man", by Neil Cornwell, *Modern Language Review*, 93/1 (1998), 133–45.

Bibliographies

"Daniil Harms: Bibliographie", by Jean-Philippe Jaccard, *Cahiers du monde russe et soviétique*, 26/3–4 (1985), 493–522.

"Selected Bibliography", by Neil Cornwell and Julian Graffy, in *Daniil Kharms and the Poetics of the Absurd*, edited by Neil Cornwell, London, Macmillan, 1991, 268–77.

"Bibliografiia", by Galina Nosova, in *Kharmsizdat predstavliaet*, St Petersburg, 1995, 122–30.

The literary career of Daniil Kharms (the most frequently-used pseudonym of Daniil Ivanovich Iuvachev, which may have been inspired by the English words harms/charms) began in 1925 and ended with his untimely death in captivity in 1942. Over that decade and a half he produced poetry, drama, and prose, as well as a great number of pieces (mostly in verse) for children. Works such as *Ivan Ivanych Samovar* (1928) and *Million* (1930) quickly became classics of Soviet children's literature. Apart from his writing for children, however, Kharms published only two poems in his entire lifetime (these were contained in anthologies produced by the Leningrad branch of the All-Russian Union of Poets, in 1926 and 1927).

Kharms collaborated with a number of experimental literary groups in the 1920s, including, in 1926, the Radiks theatre group, alongside Igor' Bakhterev and Aleksandr Vvedenskii. He is perhaps best known as one of the founder members of the Leningrad literary avant-garde group generally referred to as OBERIU (a distorted acronym for *Ob"edinenie real'nogo iskusstva* or The Association of Real Art), which lasted in a number of guises (and with various names) from 1926 to 1930, and which numbered among its members Bakhterev (b. 1908) and Vvedenskii (1904–41), as well as Nikolai Zabolotskii (1903–58), Konstantin Vaginov (1899–1934), Boris-Doivber Levin (1904–42), and Sergei Tsimbal (1907–78). There are those, however, who accord greater importance to another circle to which Kharms belonged, namely the self-styled "chinari". This group, which Kharms joined in 1925, met for regular discussions of philosophical topics between 1922 and 1941, and consisted essentially of Kharms and Vvedenskii, the poet Nikolai Oleinikov (1898–1942), the children's writer Leonid Lipavskii (1904–41), his wife Tamara Lipavskaia (née Meier, 1903–82), and the mathematician, musicologist, and philosopher Iakov Druskin (1902–80). Much of Kharms's writing may reflect aesthetic and ethical issues discussed by the chinari.

Although critics have tended to focus on Kharms's short (and very short) stories, Kharms spent a number of years as a poet and dramatist before turning to prose in the early 1930s. Between 1925 and 1926, Kharms (along with Vvedenskii) was a member of the group of "trans-rational" poets, which was called Orden Zaumnikov DSO and headed by Aleksandr Tufanov. Kharms's verse, with its emphasis on rhythm and its often bewildering semantic shifts, has little in common with the "pure", phonetically-based *zaum'* of Tufanov. Instead, Kharms attempts to transcend the limits of established cognitive systems by placing generally recognizable words or objects (and, less frequently, syllables) in unfamiliar contexts, in order to achieve a fuller understanding of the meaning of the world, and the meaning of "meaning". Whether the sense of fragmentation and dislocation that this produces in his work brings us any closer to a real understanding of phenomena (what Kharms termed their "fifth meaning") is, however, a much-debated question.

In *Odinnadtsat' utverzhdenii Daniila Kharmsa* [Eleven Assertions of Daniil Kharms], written in 1930, Kharms claimed to think "fluidly" (*tekuche*), rather than logically. Such a notion is echoed in many of his dramatic dialogues written at around the same time. In *Mest'* [Vengeance] (1930) and *Voda i Khniu* [Water and Khniu] (1931), for example, modes of thought or discourse that are either figuratively or literally aquatic are privileged. The desire for (cognitive) transcendence in "fluid" thinking is also evident in some of the other leitmotifs that appear in Kharms's writing. These include images of escape, such as "window" or "sky", of perfection (particularly the sphere) and of flight (see in particular *Polet v nebesa* [Flight into the Heavens] 1929). Against these, however, are balanced images of confinement, such as "house", "trunk" or "guard", and of falling (see, for example, the poem "Padenie s mosta" [A Fall from a Bridge] (1928)).

Kharms numbered Khlebnikov among his mentors, and a number of his poetic and dramatic works contain allusions to Khlebnikov and his work. *Lapa* [The Paw] (1930), for example, features Khlebnikov himself, riding the sky on various animals before symbolically flying off on a pencil and snatching a piece of the sky. As Milner-Gulland observes (in Cornwell, 1991), there are a number of similarities between Kharms's and Khlebnikov's poetic systems. Khlebnikov's influence is apparent in Kharms's most famous dramatic work, *Elizaveta Bam*, premiered at the "Three Left Hours" evening given by OBERIU at the Leningrad Press Club on 24 January 1928. This play erases the distinction between verbal play and reality, a common feature of Khlebnikov's drama and beyond that of the Russian folk-theatre in general.

Works such as *Elizaveta Bam* and the play *Komediia goroda Peterburga* [The Comedy of the City of Petersburg] (1927), in which Kharms parodies the St Petersburg tradition of Russian literature, contain much that is illogical, even "nonsensical". These plays have contributed to Kharms's reputation as a writer of the "Absurd", as has much of his prose, a genre to which he increasingly turned throughout the 1930s. Kharms's prose works can be divided into two groups: his (very) short pieces, which include the 30 numbered texts that make up the cycle known in Russian as *Sluchai* (translatable as "Incidents", "Cases" or "Happenings"), and his novella *Starukha* (*The Old Woman*), written in 1939. Many of Kharms's prose miniatures seem to bear out his comment, made in a diary entry in 1937, that he was interested only in the nonsensical and meaningless (*chush'*). Kharms fills his stories with apparently insignificant, irrelevant details, which frequently leave the reader wondering what the real "point" is. In his prose as in his poetry, we find the same epistemological and ontological doubt, but this time it is given a more metafictional turn, since it appears as the impossibility of telling stories, or a lack of faith in the reality of a story once it is told. A tendency to blur the distinction between the horrifying and the humorous is another feature of Kharms's poetry that also appears in his prose.

Kharms's work has been described variously as "surreal", "absurdist", "metafictional", "carnivalesque", "parodic", "fantastic", and "postmodern" (the above list is by no means exhaustive). Kharms's primitivist, minimalist style has justifiably earned him comparisons with the Futurist poets Khlebnikov and Khruchenykh, and with the artist Kazimir Malevich (Kharms felt a strong sense of admiration for Malevich, as witnessed in his poem "Na smert' Kazimira Malevicha" [On the Death of Kazimir Malevich] 1935). Parodying a host of literary conventions, and a number of canonical authors and texts, Kharms looks back to writers like Gogol' and Koz'ma Prutkov (both of whom he cited among his favourite authors). In some respects Kharms anticipates western "Absurdist" writers, although this is a far more complex question than most Kharms scholars suggest. More recently, Kharms has been mentioned in discussions of the Russian "Conceptualist" poets of the 1980s, and of the "Cruel Prose" of Evgenii Popov and Venedikt Erofeev.

GRAHAM ROBERTS

Elizaveta Bam

Play, 1928

Kharms's celebrated absurdist drama was first performed at the Leningrad Press Club on 24 January 1928. Kharms wrote it in only 12 days in December, 1927. It formed part of the OBERIU evening entitled *Tri levykh chasa* [Three Left Hours], which also included music and film. The evening might be best described as a mixture of vaudeville and performance art. The memoirs of Igor Bakhterev (a member of OBERIU and someone closely involved with the staging of the performance) give a good account of the preparations for the evening and of the performance itself. The OBERIU antics were greeted with some incredulity and disgust by a reviewer in the Soviet press the following day who deliberately garbled OBERIU into "Ytuerebo" (*Krasnaia gazeta*, 24 [1694], 25 January 1928). Subsequent public performances were rare and indeed another hostile review in 1930 accusing OBERIU of "reactionary sleight-of-hand" seems to have signalled the end of its existence. The play itself was not performed again in Russia until the 1980s, although productions were staged in Poland in 1966 and in West Berlin in 1983. The most complete English translation is published in Neil Cornwell's *Incidences* (1993). Since the early 1980s, the Ermitage (formerly the Miniatur) Theatre in Moscow has staged OBERIU-type spectacles directed by Mikhail Levitin.

Elizaveta Bam can be seen in part as a successful dramatization of the OBERIU view of theatre outlined in its "Declaration". Kharms himself wrote the section on theatre that explains that *Elizaveta Bam* was "commissioned" by OBERIU. Kharms warns his potential audience to forget notions of theatre acquired elsewhere. The *Oberiuty* (members of OBERIU) took to the extreme the blurring of the division between on and off stage. In practice, their view of drama was so broad as to consider theatrical virtually anything that occurred on a stage. One might draw parallels with modern notions of performance art.

Elizaveta Bam defies ready plot summary, for it features a number of outlandish and illogical "events". The play is divided into 19 "bits" (*kuski*) rather than acts, which follow one another in apparently arbitrary manner. A certain cyclical pattern is, however, established with the last "bit" recalling the first almost word for word. The lack of lateral progression underlines Kharms's insistence in "The OBERIU Declaration" that art has a logic of its own quite separate from the logic of life.

The opening scene introduces two characters, Petr Nikolaevich and Ivan Ivanovich, who have come to arrest one Elizaveta Bam for a crime she has yet to commit. That crime, of which she is accused, Elizaveta and the audience learn more later, is the murder of Petr Nikolaevich, one of the same characters who has come to arrest her. Defenceless against the powerfully articulated, but false logic of her accusers, Elizaveta Bam is branded a criminal because she has no voice. Thus the animating event of the play is arbitrary arrest. Such manifest absurdity and injustice are perfectly acceptable within the peculiar world of the play, which allows for persistent inversion of the normal course of cause and effect, leading to random association of disparate events.

An audience familiar with the repressive policies of Soviet governments would have no difficulty drawing political implications from this confused state of affairs. However, the play need not be seen entirely as a satire on the dangers of arbitrary Soviet rule. One should remember that it pre-dates Stalinist excesses.

From a literary-historical perspective, one finds numerous points of interaction between Kharms's verbal experimentation and the nonsensical word-play of *zaum'* (literally, trans-sense) verse of Futurists, such as Khlebnikov and Kruchenykh. The play's language recalls some of the playful experimentation of Kharms's own "neo-Futurist" poetry of the 1920s. Although in their Declaration the *Oberiuty* explicitly claim *zaum'* is inimical to them, both Kharms and his fellow *Oberiut* Vvedenskii were earlier closely associated with Tufanov and *zaum'*. By giving the play's various "bits" mock titles indicating the play's presumed generic antecedents, Kharms signals his conscious parodying of theatrical practice and literary genre. Moreover, Kharms's stage directions indicate his awareness of Formalist critical methods and give further weight to the idea of *Elizaveta Bam* as a literary-polemical work.

The play can indeed be seen in the wider context of the history of Russian theatre. It is worth noting that the first performance made use of the backdrop created initially for Terentiev's modern production of *Revizor* (*The Government Inspector*). The motif of false and mistaken identity and the flat and fluid characterization in *Elizaveta Bam* owe much to Gogol''s play. The emphasis on emotion and reaction to extraneous (off-stage) events is in the mould of turn-of-the-century European naturalist drama and of Chekhov in particular. Associations with the plays of Blok and Evreinov are equally discernible. One contemporary account of the *Oberiuty* in general referred to them perceptively, though pejoratively as "dadaists". More favourable comparisons with modern European drama have credited Kharms with prefiguring the plays of the post-war Theatre of the Absurd. Detailed textual comparisons have been made between *Elizaveta Bam* and the drama of Beckett and Ionesco. Aleksandr Vvedenskii's *Elka u Ivanovykh* [Christmas at the Ivanov's], written after *Elizaveta Bam* in 1938, remains perhaps the single truly comparable Russian drama.

Elizaveta Bam in some respects marks a consolidation of Kharms's earlier poetic work and indeed Kharms's eccentric public performance of that work. Much of it may be regarded as pure nonsense, associations of pure sound. Yet at the same time the play introduces some of the darker themes that were to preoccupy Kharms in his work of the 1930s, which changes in political and personal circumstances consigned to the desk drawer. The actual events of the play (false accusations, battle, psychological oppression) such as they are lend it an altogether sinister character. Violence and discord are never far away. Along with the semantic instability of the characters' lines comes the ethical instability of their actions. The play lacks direction both structurally and morally. It is almost prescriptively anarchic: anything can happen and almost certainly will. The moral vacuum of *Elizaveta Bam* resurfaces later in Kharms's banal, but brutal short stories.

NEIL CARRICK

The Old Woman

Starukha

Novella, 1974 (written 1939)

Kharms's prose mostly comprises minimalist short stories, so *The Old Woman*, easily the longest of his prose works, with its explicit sub-title *povest'*, marked something of a new departure. Yet despite the generic distinction, *The Old Woman* represents a culmination rather than an abandonment of the thematic pre-occupations of Kharms's mature prose.

Like most of Kharms's work, this text remained unpublished until well after his death. Indeed the definitive Russian text appeared only in 1988 (*Novyi mir*, 4 (1988)). An earlier version published by George Gibian in *Daniil Kharms: Izbrannoe* (1974) is incomplete, as is Gibian's translation into English in *The Man with the Black Coat* (1987). A new English translation from the complete text by Neil Cornwell is contained in *Incidences* (1993). The original manuscript remains in private possession.

Kharms's *The Old Woman* is set in Leningrad/St Petersburg. The tale is told in the first person by a narrator figure who is also a writer. In many of his beliefs and statements (his violent aversion to children and his inability to write), the narrator resembles the persona of Kharms one encounters in his own diaries and notebooks. This identification of Kharms in the text encourages psycho-analytical readings of the work.

The plot of *The Old Woman* works as much by random association as by obvious authorial direction. The constant switch from present to past tense and back makes it difficult to determine to what extent the narrator has command of his own tale. He lives in a state of perpetual delirium and cannot himself readily distinguish what he has dreamt from what he has consciously witnessed. The questionable credibility of the narrator's perspective allows for other interpretations of events to vie with his own. The narrator's reaction to finding the old woman's corpse in his apartment is conditioned by his own awareness of the likely literary interpretation of events: that the police will see it as a classic St Petersburg scenario, in which a young man murders an old woman. He readily admits that his plan to dispose of the evidence, the old woman's dead body, comes to him from his reading (from novels and newspapers) about how murderers act. Pre-formed and potent narrative sequences restrict the freedom of action one generally associates with authorship.

The narrator's impotence is in contrast to the mysterious, even miraculous power of the old woman. Her unwelcome intrusion into the narrator's life and her untimely and inexplicable death in his flat provide the real motivation for a bizarre sequence of events. She seems even to possess supernatural powers. She is able to tell the time from a watch with no hands and apparently overcomes death itself. To the narrator's mind she is a *bespokoinik* (literally, one without rest), similar perhaps to the mythical Wandering Jew. In all respects the old woman can be said not to belong to the narrator's world. She hails from another realm and possibly another text.

A dead old woman in a tale set in St Petersburg encourages not only the narrator, but also the reader to think of other stories, most obviously Dostoevskii's *Prestuplenie i nakazanie* (*Crime and Punishment*) or Pushkin's *Pikovaia dama* (*The Queen of Spades*). Consequently much of the critical reaction to the text has focused on Kharms's apparent willingness to rely on well-known themes and narratives, apparently appropriated from classic St Petersburg tales. Furthermore, critics have noted affinities with other works by Dostoevskii, especially *Zapiski iz podpol'ia* (*Notes from Underground*), Gogol''s St Petersburg stories, the novels of Knut Hamsun and Meyrink's novel *Der Golem* (a favourite text of Kharms). Moreover *The Old Woman*'s modernist thematics suggest parallels with Andrei Belyi's *Petersburg*. The text also contains many elements common to Kharms's shorter prose and in particular the *Incidents* cycle of stories, where old women, violence, and death are commonplace and where Kharms continually plays with accepted notions of story-telling. The theme of an indolent writer who bears a remarkable resemblance to Kharms himself features in the story "Utro" ("Morning") (1931–32).

Although *The Old Woman* could be regarded primarily as parodic, there is surely something rather peculiar in the extent to which Kharms employs other literary texts and incorporates them wholesale into his own work. Even the narrator's own story of the miracle worker, who chooses to work no miracles, draws parallels with the desires and designs of Akardii Dolgorukii in Dostoevskii's *Podrostok* (*A Raw Youth*). The presence of so many dominant and preformed narratives impinges on the ability of the narrator to make his tale his own. The influence of such narratives calls into question the effectiveness of human agency. The narrator's actions and attempts to record them are seriously curtailed by the presence of other complete hermeneutics – better-known stories and even ready-made characters – in the text. The impression is created that details of the narrator's story and his life have already been scripted elsewhere.

The result for the reader is to give the text an extraordinary sense of claustrophobia and familiarity. Although the reader cannot predict the next event, there is little sense of shock or surprise when it happens: it is as though it were meant to be. That sense of foreknowledge is remarkable in the anarchic world of Kharms's prose and may perhaps explain the curious and unusual references to God and faith in the text.

As his final act, the narrator turns to God with a prayer. Although the act appears unmotivated, one can see this final event as part of an investigation into the nature of authorship that runs through the entire story. In his religious debate with his friend and confidant, Sakerdon Mikhailovich, the narrator speaks of human desire and will. The narrator's ambition is of course thwarted by factors beyond his control, but the final prayer may indicate the ultimate source of power to whom even the old woman is beholden. In a work relying on so many authors, God stands alone as supreme author and originator of events, for whom literary authorship is a convenient metaphor. Thus *The Old Woman* becomes an exercise not only in metafiction, but also in metaphysics.

NEIL CARRICK

Incidents

Sluchai

Collection of texts, 1988 (written 1933–39)

Incidents occupies a unique position in Kharms's *oeuvre*. His work is generally marked, even defined, by fragmentation and incompletion, by isolation and destruction; but *Incidents* is a cycle, which brings together individual pieces in a larger whole, and which is almost musical in its composition.

Incidents comprises 30 texts in all, dating from 1933 to 1939 (the same year as Kharms's only other longer work of the 1930s, the story *The Old Woman*). Kharms wrote out the cycle in a special notebook, with a dedication to his second wife Marina Malich. Many of his best and most famous pieces, such as "Golubaia tetrad' No. 10" ("Blue Notebook No. 10"), "Vyvalivaiushchie starukhi" ("The Plummeting Old Women"), and "Anekdoty iz zhizni Pushkina" ("Anecdotes from the Life of Pushkin") are included.

The Russian title *Sluchai* can be translated in a number of ways: it can mean "chances", reflecting the randomness of Kharms's world; it can mean "happenings" or "incidents", reflecting the typical orientation towards action and events; or it can mean "cases" or "incidences", reflecting the fact that the random happenings of the Kharmsian world may be related to a higher order. Indeed he once defined the essence of art as a "purity of order" which, while incomprehensible in rationalist terms, is simultaneously reflection and creation of the world. The title also carries with it a definition of genre derived from any small forms, literary or non-literary, which typically recount "what happened" (the anecdote, children's story, folk-tale, fable, even the police or judicial record). The texts that make up *Incidents* form a string, or montage, of heterogeneous pieces. The heterogeneity is of medium as well as of genre: 22 are prose stories of some sort, seven are dramatic sketches or dialogues, and one piece starts as a story and then switches into dramatic dialogue; moreover, although prose dominates, there are two instances of verse. Such fluidity is a typical feature of Kharms's poetics in general.

Incidents explores the characteristic themes of Kharms's prose, and displays his characteristic orientation towards a humour that is unsettling in its absurdity and blackness, even to the point where things no longer remain funny but move into the realm of the horrific. Many of the stories include random death, violence, evil and manifestations of what Iakov Druskin, the philosopher and Kharms's friend, called the type of the "subhuman man". There is also the typical Kharmsian concern with the erosion of boundaries, between sleep or dream and reality, for example, or between life and death.

Incidents can be read against the context of the times: the theme of evil, the motifs of random death and disappearance, all bear an obvious relation to Stalinism, and the individual's moral and human reaction to this situation are invoked. The cycle also has both a parodic and a non-parodic relation to Russian literature, with overt and hidden references to Gogol', Pushkin, and Chekhov among others: Pushkin and Gogol' even figure in a dramatic sketch in which they keep on falling over each other.

A key to the understanding of the absurd in Kharms lies in his breaking of conditions of communication, and yet communication also has a vital significance as the way to assert identity and even existence. The opening story "Blue Notebook No. 10" illustrates this perfectly. It is the classic model of a Kharmsian text that self-destructs, since it proceeds forward by denying the existence of its subject, a red-headed man, feature by feature:

> There was a red-haired man who had no eyes or ears. Neither did he have any hair, so he was called red-haired theoretically. He couldn't speak, since he didn't have a mouth. Neither did he have a nose. He didn't even have any arms or legs. He had no stomach and he had no back and he had no spine and he had no innards whatsoever. He had nothing at all! Therefore there's no knowing whom we are even talking about. In fact it's better that we don't say any more about him.

This text not only parodies narration as such, but also questions communication and signification. Paradoxically, however, the final line suggests a continuing presence, and can be read as an invitation to restore identity through communication (communication between author and reader – "we" – is only just beginning). But through the suggestion of a continuing presence, the ending also raises fundamental questions concerning cognition and being: man's essential being and the way to understanding lie beyond reason and the categories of the world of phenomena (Kharms wrote "against Kant" alongside this story).

After "Blue Notebook No. 10" the introductory part of the cycle proceeds with three more pieces that move from the general to the specific while at the same time broadening the reference. The fourth piece "Sonet" ("A Sonnet") – not a poem – ends with the motif of dispersal, and the cycle now shifts into diverse variations. Towards the middle of the cycle the themes of breakdown in communication and violence reach their most concentrated form, after which the cycle continues with renewed variation as the texts become longer and more diverse, before the final two stories round off the cycle in circularity (interestingly, there are striking similarities in this composition with the principles that Kharms identified in Chopin's music). *Incidents* presents an unsettling picture of the world, but it provides an eloquent expression of art's "purity of order".

ROBIN AIZLEWOOD

Velimir Khlebnikov 1885–1922

Poet and prose writer

Biography

Born Viktor Vladimirovich Khlebnikov in Malye Derbety, near Tundutovo, Astrakhan province, 9 November 1885. Attended Kazan Third gymnasium, 1898–1903; studied mathematics and natural sciences at Kazan University, 1903–08; studied biology and Slavonic languages, St Petersburg University, 1909–11: did not graduate. Associated with Futurist and other literary groups, especially "Hyleia". Lived in Moscow, 1912–15. Served in the tsarist army, 1916–17. Travelled across Russia; arrested by the Whites in Kharkov, then by the Reds, 1919. Worked in Caucasus propaganda bureau (Rosta) in Baku, 1920; lecturer in revolutionary army headquarters in Persia, 1921. Night watchman in Rosta office in Piatigorsk, 1921. Died of malnutrition in Santalovo, Novgorod province, 28 June 1922.

Publications

Collected Editions

Sobranie proizvedenii, 5 vols. Moscow, 1928–33.

Neizdannye proizvedeniia. Moscow, 1940; reprinted with above as *Sobranie sochinenii*, 4 vols. Munich, Fink, 1968–71.
Stikhotvoreniia i poemy. Leningrad, 1960.
Snake Train: Poetry and Prose, edited by Gary Kern, translated by Gary Kern *et al.* Ann Arbor, Ardis, 1976.
The King of Time: Selected Writings of the Russian Futurian, edited by Charlotte Douglas, translated by Paul Schmidt. Cambridge, Massachusetts, Harvard University Press, 1985.
Stikhotvoreniia. Poemy. Dramy. Proza. Moscow, 1986.
Tvoreniia [Creations]. Moscow, 1986.
Collected Works:
Volume 1: *Letters and Theoretical Writings*, edited by Charlotte Douglas, translated by Paul Schmidt. Cambridge, Massachusetts, Harvard University Press, 1987.
Volume 2: *Prose, Plays and Supersagas*, edited by Ronald Vroon. Cambridge, Massachusetts, Harvard University Press, 1989.

Poetry
Uchitel' i uchenik [Teacher and Pupil]. Kherson, 1912.
Igra v adu [A Game in Hell], in collaboration with Kruchenykh. Moscow, 1912.
Tvoreniia (1906–1908) [Creations]. Moscow, 1914.
Izbornik stikhov 1907–1914 [Selected Poems]. Petrograd, 1914.
Riav! Perchatki 1908–1914 [Roar! The Gauntlets]. Petrograd, 1914.
Bitvy 1915–1917: Novoe uchenie o voine [Battles: The New Teaching about War]. Petrograd, 1914.
Vremia mera mira [Time the Measure of the World]. Petrograd, 1916.
Truba marsian [The Martian Pipe]. Kharkov, 1916.
Ladomir [Goodworld]. Kharkov, 1920; reprinted 1985.
Noch' v okope [A Night in the Trench]. Moscow, 1921.
Nochnoi obysk. Moscow, 1921; translated as "Night Search", by Neil Cornwell, in *Snake Train*, 1976; and by Paul Schmidt, in *The King of Time*, 1985.
Zangezi. Moscow, 1922; reprinted Ann Arbor, Ardis, 1978.
Vestnik Velimira Khlebnikova [Velimir Khlebnikov's Herald]. 1–2, Moscow, 1922.
Otryvok iz dosok sud'by [Fragment from the Boards of Destiny]. 1–3, Moscow, 1922–23.
Stikhi. Moscow, 1923.
Nastoiashchee [The Present Day]. Moscow, 1926.
Vsem: Nochnoi bal [For Everyone: The Night Ball]. Moscow, 1927.
Zverinets [Menagerie]. Moscow, 1930.

Play
Oshibka smerti [Death's Mistake] (produced 1920). 1916.

Fiction
Ka, in *Moskovskie mastera*, Moscow, 1916; translated as *Ka*, by Paul Schmidt, in *Collected Works*, vol. 2, Cambridge, Massachusetts, Harvard University Press, 1989, 56–74.
Proza [Prose]. Moscow, 1990.

Critical Studies
Noveishaia russkaia poeziia, by Roman Iakobson [Jakobson], Prague, 1921; excerpts translated by Judson Rosengrant, in *Major Soviet Writers: Essays in Criticism*, edited by Edward J. Brown, London, Oxford University Press, 1973, 58–88.
The Longer Poems of Velimir Khlebnikov, by Vladimir Markov, Berkeley, University of California Press, 1961.
Russian Futurism: A History, by Vladimir Markov, Berkeley, University of California Press, 1968.
"Image and Symbol in Khlebnikov's 'Night Search'", by R.F. Cooke, *Russian Literature Triquarterly*, 12 (1975), 279–94.
Der Orient im Werk Velimir Chlebnikovs, by Saloman Mirsky, Munich, Sagner, 1975.
Velimir Klebnikov: Zhizn' i tvorchestvo, by N. Stepanov, Moscow, 1975.
"On the Poetics of Chlebnikov: Problems of Composition", by B.A. Uspensky, *Russian Literature*, 9 (1975), 81–85.
"Khlebnikov and $3^6 + 3^6$", by R.D.B. Thompson, in *Russian and Slavic Literature*, edited by R. Freeborn *et al.*, Cambridge, Massachusetts, Slavica, 1976, 297–312.
Xlebnikov and Carnival: An Analysis of the Poem "Poet", by Barbara Lonnqvist, Stockholm, Almqvist & Wiksell, 1979.
"On the Poetics of a Xlebnikov Tale: Problems and Patterns in 'Ka'", by Henryk Baran, in *The Structural Analysis of Narrative Texts. Conference Papers*, edited by A. Kodjak *et al.*, Columbus, Ohio, Slavica, 1980, 112–31.
"Velimir Khlebnikov's 'Razin: Two Trinities': A Reconstruction", by Ronald Vroon, *Slavic Review*, 39 (1980), 70–84.
Utopisches Denken bei Velimir Chlebnikov, by Peter Stobbe, Munich, Sagner, 1982.
Velimir Khlebnikov, poète futurien, by Jean-Claude Lanne, 2 vols, Paris, Institut d'Études Slaves, 1983.
Grammatika idiostilia: V. Khlebnikov, by V.P. Grigor'ev, Moscow, 1983.
Velimir Xlebnikov's Shorter Poems: A Key to the Coinages, by Ronald Vroon, Ann Arbor, Ardis, 1983.
Velimir Chlebnikov and the Development of Poetical Language in Russian Symbolism and Futurism, by W.G. Weststeijn, Amsterdam, Rodopi, 1983.
Velimir Chlebnikov: A Stockholm Symposium, edited by Nils Åke Nilsson, Stockholm, Almqvist & Wiksell, 1985.
Slovotvorchestvo i smeshnye problemy iazyka poeta, by V.P. Grigor'ev, Moscow, 1986.
Velimir Khlebnikov (1885–1922). Myth and Reality: Amsterdam Symposium on the Centenary of Velimir Khlebnikov, edited by Willem G. Weststeijn, Amsterdam, Rodopi, 1986.
Velimir Khlebnikov: A Critical Study, by Raymond Cooke, Cambridge, Cambridge University Press, 1987.
Language in Literature, by Roman Jakobson, edited by Krystyna Pomorska and Stephen Rudy, Cambridge, Massachusetts, Harvard University Press, 1987.
"Determining Textual Incoherence in Khlebnikov's 'Ka'", by C. Simmons, *Slavic and East European Journal*, 31/3 (1987), 334–55.
Russian Futurism Through Its Manifestoes, 1912–1928, edited by Anna Lawton, Ithaca, Cornell University Press, 1988.
Velimir Khlebnikov: priroda tvorchestva, by R.V. Duganov, Moscow, 1990.
Khlebnikovskie chteniia: materialy konferentsii, 27–29 noiabria 1990, St Petersburg, 1991.

"Two Images of Africa in Russian Literature of the Beginning of the Twentieth Century: 'Ka' by Chlebnikov and Gumilev's African Poems", by V.V. Ivanov, *Russian Literature*, 29/4 (1991), 409–26.
Poetika russkoi literatury nachala XX veka, by Henryk Baran, Moscow, 1993.
Slovar' neologizmov Velimira Khlebnikova, by Natal'ia Pertsova, Vienna and Moscow, Wiener Slawistischer Almanach, 1995.
Russian Literature (special issue), 38/4 (1995).

Shortly after his literary debut in 1908, Velimir Khlebnikov, rejected by the more respectable schools of literature, found himself at the centre of the newly formed Cubo-Futurist movement. In 1912 he was a signatory with Maiakovskii, Kruchenykh, and David Burliuk to the manifesto "Poshchechina obshchestvennomu vkusu" ("A Slap in the Face of Public Taste"), which provocatively condemned all existing literature and proposed a radical re-evaluation of poetic language. In the years that followed, Khlebnikov's work was printed in numerous Futurist collections and promoted by his colleagues in the movement, though Khlebnikov himself played little part in their outrageous self-publicity campaigns or in public readings.

Partly because of a natural reticence, partly because of the practical difficulties of publication between the outbreak of war and Khlebnikov's death in 1922, and partly again because of Khlebnikov's nomadic existence during his final years, relatively little of what he wrote was in fact published during his lifetime. Much of his work has been lost without trace and what remains presents considerable textual problems in that Khlebnikov, in a manner reminiscent of pre-literate oral composition, often wrote multiple versions of what is essentially the same piece and was happier to rewrite his work from scratch than to edit it. Moreover, he often left the final form of those works that he did publish to his Futurist colleagues, and many early poems were written jointly, most often with Kruchenykh.

One result of this method of composition is the characteristic Khlebnikov genre of the "supertale" (*sverkhpovest'*), of which *Zangezi* is a salient example. The supertale consists of a loose collection of texts in a mixture of forms, embracing, for example, verse, prose and dialogue, which maintain their individual identity but which together achieve a multifaceted conceptual unity. On other occasions Khlebnikov cultivated the genre of the poetic fragment.

Khlebnikov's main contribution to the Futurist aesthetic was in the area of language. One of his earliest published works was the notorious poem "Zaklinanie smekhom" [Incantation by Laughter], which consists entirely of a string of invented words derived from the root *sme-* (laugh). Khlebnikov invented elaborate theories about the semantic values of word-roots and of individual phonetic elements and regularly used the *zaum'* or "transrational language" thus created as the medium for his creative work. On occasion this takes the form of pure sound painting, but more often *zaum'* is combined with normally referential language in which sound play, neologisms, puns and complex strings of metaphorical and etymological associations create an evocative discourse that appeals as much to the senses as to reason. At the same time, he was capable of a more orthodox type of writing, as in *Nochnoi obysk* (*Night Search*), which, however, still retains an essential impressionism.

It was Khlebnikov's use of *zaum'* that was particularly valued by the other Futurists, who, in what they published of his work, tended to underplay other aspects of his writing. Khlebnikov did not embrace the urban and industrial themes of, for example, Maiakovskii, and based his art firmly on vernacular traditions. His vocabulary and the sources of his neologisms are thus Slavonic rather than western in their inspiration. He preferred the coinage *Budetlianin* (man of the future) over the clearly imported *Futurist*. He drew much inspiration from Russian folklore, history, and peasant life. His work is, however, by no means confined to these areas and Khlebnikov uses images and themes taken from a very wide range of sources, particularly from the various world-wide traditions of magic, mythology, and ritual.

Notwithstanding Khlebnikov's reluctance to promote himself publicly, he saw the poet as a prophet with a duty to teach, enlighten, and to bring happiness to the people. The status of the poet with regard to his audience is an important theme, particularly in his later work. As a prophet, Khlebnikov was deeply concerned to discover a set of laws ruling the universe, and in particular to identify the laws governing time. This preoccupation with the absolute is a corollary of Khlebnikov's attempts to create a universal language in his *zaum'* and is reflected too in his insistent numerological researches. For a long period, for example, Khlebnikov's calculations were dominated by the number 317, which represented the interval in years at which significant events in world history supposedly occurred. Later, Khlebnikov came to see time as based on units of two and three. The purpose of Khlebnikov's research was essentially Utopian – to study destiny in order to be able to control it. The assault on time is often seen in openly military terms, reflecting Khlebnikov's view of world history as a series of military conquests. Particularly after 1915, however, by which time he had actually come into firsthand contact with the effects of war, Khlebnikov's aim is to use his knowledge of the laws of fate to abolish conflict altogether.

Although Khlebnikov's poetry and prose is conceptually esoteric and linguistically challenging, collections of his work continued to be published in Russia at infrequent intervals throughout the Soviet period. It is only relatively recently, however, that the painstaking bibliographical and editorial work needed for a full picture of his achievement has begun. Khlebnikov may never gain a mass audience, but he has been valued by authors as diverse as Maiakovskii, Mandel'shtam, and Olesha. His work is in many ways the archetype of the Russian avant-garde and will continue to exercise the imagination of anyone keen to explore the possibilities of Russian poetic language.

DAVID N. WELLS

Ka

Novella, 1916

A note jotted down by Khlebnikov indicates that he worked on *Ka* over a period of about two weeks, from late February to early March (Old Style) 1915; in the essay "Svoiasi" [Self-Statement], where he comments on *Ka* several times, he speaks of it having taken a week. As is the case with a number of Khlebnikov's works, the original manuscript has not survived; all we have left is the text (possibly incomplete) of the first publication (1916), a set of proofs, and the many riddles of one of his most fascinating ventures into prose.

Ka, which in its most recent English rendition runs to less than 20 pages, has a dual protagonist, an unnamed yet autobiographical first-person narrator and his *ka* – according to the ancient Egyptians, one of several elements of the human personality, a man's active double, his personal genius. Written in a language that resembles Pushkin's in its precision and flexibility, the tale belongs to the category of fantastic fiction in its contemporary, postmodern variant. It is crammed full of characters and events, brought together with playful disregard for distinctions between the real, the imaginary, and the fictive, the actual and the potential, the objective and the subjective. "There are no barriers for the Ka in time", claims the narrator, "he moves from dream to dream, breaks through time, and reaches the goalposts of bronze (the bronze of time)." Thanks to the Ka's powers, he and his "owner" shift with ease between different loci in time and space and meet personages drawn from myth, legend, history, the present day, and the future. They appear in such places as a provincial Russian city (probably Astrakhan), St Petersburg in 1915, the year 2222, paradise as imagined by Muslims, a jungle in present-day Africa, and Egypt during the reign of the monotheistic Pharaoh Akhnaten (Amenhotpe IV). These encounters constitute distinct episodes ranging anywhere from a brief sentence to a whole section in size; transitions between them are swift and minimal, which forces the reader to assimilate a constantly changing frame of reference. The tale is a mosaic of exotic names, literary quotations and allusions, verbal puns and riddles. Many passages require annotation; some remaining lacunae still defy commentators' efforts.

An even greater challenge is establishing the basic meaning of *Ka*: separating the primary elements of the narrative from the secondary, and determining which among the many motifs and scenes define the principal theme of the text, and which are there for "local" effect. The main thrust of the novella may be sought on one of several levels. For one, *Ka* may be regarded as an illustration of Khlebnikov's theory of temporal cycles: at a minimum, it played a role in who he included among his tale's cast of characters. Second, there are allusions, partly clarified, to Khlebnikov's fellow-Futurists (such as Maiakovskii) and other literary figures; it is possible to view *Ka* as a polemical reaction to the literary-artistic bohemia of St Petersburg (several earlier of his works, such as the short play "Chertik" [The Little Devil], belong to this category). There is also the novella's role as an "echo to [Pushkin's – H.B.] 'Egyptian Nights', the attraction of northern snowstorms to the heat of the Nile" ("Svoiasi"): is *Ka*, therefore, an instance of characteristic avant-garde play with the heritage of Russia's Golden Age, whereby literary biographies and texts are reworked in the light of a new poetics and aesthetics? Finally, the most important issue: given the autobiographical narrative "I", is it possible to link the text in a deeper way with Khlebnikov himself? Breaking with earlier views regarding Futurism, current scholarship has shown that the key to many of Khlebnikov's works is found in the realm of his responses to specific people and events in his life. To what degree has Khlebnikov projected his own persona and experiences into *Ka*, and to what extent do they fuse into a component of his private symbolic system, his poetic mythology?

Notwithstanding the authorial play with narrative conventions, a personal, tragic theme is clearly present in the novella. The principal figure encountered by the hero and his double is the Pharaoh Akhnaten, whose murder – which occurs twice, since Khlebnikov reincarnates him into the body of an ape, only to be killed again – is the dramatic and emotional highpoint in the convoluted narrative. The choice of Akhnaten for the role of victim reflects Khlebnikov's broader interest in the Egyptian reformer. In "Svoiasi", he calls the Pharaoh "Egypt's Mohammed", during whose reign "Egypt smashed its religious beliefs like a handful of rotten sticks and individual deities were replaced by the hand-rayed Sun, shining with multitudes. The Unclothed Sun, the Naked Sun-Disk, became for a while ... the sole divinity of the ancient shrines". Elsewhere, Khlebnikov includes Akhnaten among those figures of the past whose activity is analogous to his own daring attempt to change human society by uncovering the "laws" of time, and whose biography is linked with his own by recurrent temporal cycles. Akhnaten's tragedy in *Ka* may therefore also in some measure be regarded Khlebnikov's own, as a dramatization of his fears for his Utopian ideas and doubts about his role as poet-visionary (ever more anguished expressions of such doubts regularly appear in his last period). In this connection, another passage in "Svoiasi", concerning the pain Akhnaten's final utterance – the "transrational" (*zaum'*) exclamation "Manch! Manch!" – had caused his creator, is particularly revealing.

Yet Akhnaten in *Ka* is not only a religious reformer but also a lover longing for his beloved (in both his human and simian incarnation), a role that involves him in the other principal narrative line in the novella. Khlebnikov borrows and transforms the celebrated tale of the star-crossed lovers Layla and Majnun (best known through a 12th-century poem by Nizami, and found as well in other literary and folk traditions of the Orient), turning it into a sequence of encounters across time and space that end only when the heroine recognizes her original beloved in the novella's narrator. Such a happy resolution belies the reiterated emphasis on loss and separation (references to several other pairs of lovers are woven into the narrative). It appears that Khlebnikov simultaneously hides within the text details of a troubled personal relationship and engages in literary wish-fulfilment; this aspect of the novella requires further analysis and clarification.

There are drafts from 1916 of a later prose work involving a Ka, where the poet again fused autobiographical allusions with cultural and literary borrowings. Regrettably, this text, which he termed a "mystery play", was not completed.

The novella played a considerable role in establishing Khlebnikov's reputation as an innovator in prose, one whose achievements in this area were assessed very highly by such notable figures as Osip Mandel'shtam, Iurii Olesha, and Vsevolod Ivanov.

HENRYK BARAN

Night Search

Nochnoi obysk

Poem, 1921

The long poem *Night Search*, one of Khlebnikov's finest and most accessible works, was written in early November 1921, while he was living and working in Piatigorsk. Together with two other long poems from this period, "Noch' pered sovetami" [Night Before the Soviets] and "Nastoiashchee" [The Present Day], it is part of the so-called "triptych of revolution" – a set of poetic responses to the October Revolution and the subsequent Civil War, each of which explores the theme of retribution for historical wrongs. It was first published from an autograph in the *Sobranie proizvedenii* edited by Stepanov; subsequently, after a hiatus of nearly six decades, it was included by Grigor'ev and Parnis in their 1986 *Tvoreniia* volume of Khlebnikov's works.

The action of *Night Search* takes place in an unnamed city (probably Petrograd). A group of Red sailors, a revolutionary patrol similar to the one featured in Blok's *Dvenadtsat'* (*The Twelve*), bursts into the apartment of a family suspected of siding with the Whites and demands money and jewels. When a young man, Vladimir, fires at them, the sailors execute him on the spot; subsequently they discover and shoot another White officer. Vladimir's elderly mother is spared, as is a young woman, his wife or sister, but the sailors require them to prepare food for a feast they wish to hold in the apartment. The sailors then engage in a wild bout of drinking, during which their leader, an older man, becomes introspective. With admiration and pity he recalls Vladimir's courage in facing death; he feels tormented and challenged by an icon of Christ, grows maudlin and conducts an imaginary conversation with Christ. These ramblings are abruptly interrupted when the sailors realize that the apartment is on fire, set deliberately by the old woman, and that she has locked the door. At this point, the sailors' leader emulates Vladimir's stance towards death, while his companions are unsure whether to let themselves asphyxiate or to commit suicide. The old woman utters the poem's final line: "Whatever you wish!".

Khlebnikov's conception of temporal cycles – specifically, his notion that a period of 2^m days separates analogous historical events, while a span of 3^n days separates an event from its antithesis or "counter-event" – provides the overall rationale for the plot of *Night Search*: the killings of the White soldiers at the start of the poem may be seen as leading to the death of their executioners at its end. In addition, critics have suggested that the poem refers to another, supplementary level of historical action and reaction, although they have disagreed about its nature. Such ideas stem largely from a two-line jotting found in the manuscript next to the title: "7 XI 1921 / $3^6 + 3^6$". Stepanov incorporated the mathematical expression in his publication of the poem, making it the epigraph. The artist Petr Miturich (cited by Stepanov) saw the expression as indicating the number of minutes it takes to read the poem, presented in terms of total number of heartbeats (assuming an average rate), and hence as marking the span of time between Vladimir's death and the final conflagration. Although Miturich was close to Khlebnikov at the end of his life, a fact which gives his views special weight, his interpretation has been seriously questioned. More recent studies of the poem have linked the epigraph to events of the Civil War, be it the Bolsheviks' recognition in November 1921 of the tsarist government's foreign debts, an action which would indicate a political shift opposed to the original impulse of the October Revolution (Thompson), or to the Soviet government's suppression of the mutinous Kronstadt sailors in March 1921 (Poulin), an event that could certainly be treated as a prime case of historical reversal. The editors of *Tvoreniia* took a wholly different approach to this issue: they left out the epigraph altogether, viewing the jotting simply as evidence that the poem was written in connection with the fourth anniversary of October, and the expression $3^6 + 3^6$ as a calculation of the four-year span in terms of number of days. The entire issue of the jotting and the poem's possible subtext is still unresolved.

While Blok's *The Twelve* undoubtedly affected Khlebnikov's choice of subject-matter and use of language, there are significant differences between the two works. Although he links the current merciless struggle to earlier popular risings in Russian history (such as the Pugachev rebellion), Khlebnikov, unlike the Symbolist poet, is far more ambivalent about the Revolution, and especially about its relationship to the moral order of Christianity. Blok ultimately places Jesus Christ at the head of the marching Red sailors, thus sanctifying the Revolution despite the brutality it has unleashed; Khlebnikov, who several times terms his sailors "holy killers", distances Christ from the elemental force of Bolshevism. The old sailor refers to the "accusing" eyes of the icon; counterposes himself, a "dark divinity of the night" (*temnoe nochnoe bozhestvo*) that has visited unexpected death on Vladimir, to the God of Christianity; and declares that he wishes to "conquer God". At the same time, the sailor is drawn to the figure of Christ (imagined as a girl he might woo), while his death, like that of Vladimir, is presented in terms analogous to the self-sacrifice of Jesus.

This picture of a complex personality, torn between revolutionary ideals, Nietzschean-style rebellion, and traditional Christian morality, did not fit the expectations of official Soviet iconography (especially in its late Stalinist variant) of a proletarian revolutionary. Similarly, the sailors' actions, set off by a raid in search of loot as well as hidden Whites, could not be easily subsumed under the label of a historically justified, merciless, yet morally pure class warfare. Not surprisingly, in 1948, during the Zhdanov period, the critic Boris Iakovlev found in the poem "patently anti-Soviet and anti-Bolshevik sentiments".

Much of the considerable artistic effect of *Night Search* derives from the way in which other levels of the text reinforce its compact, dramatic plot. The poem consists of nearly 700 lines, only a small portion of which involve descriptions of actions; instead, Khlebnikov extensively uses the characters' own discourse, in a manner characteristic of his long poems in general, and especially of works written in his last years. The sailors' highly idiomatic, often elliptical speech, which mixes coarseness with folk ditties, reflects their proletarian background and revolutionary attitudes, while their leader's extended soliloquy is conveyed with full regard for the unpredictability, repetitiveness, and whimsicality of internalized discourse. The poem's rhythmical patterns are similarly dynamic (most of the lines are quite short) and variable: this feature correlates with the rapid development of the action and the quick flow of spoken language. At the same time, several recurrent images (especially *more*, "the sea", and *belyi*, "white") constitute a set of semantically charged symbols that help bind the poem's quickly moving, constantly shifting verbal mass into a powerful artistic whole.

In 1922, while planning to rework *Zangezi*, Khlebnikov considered adding *Night Search* to this complex montage of quasi-autonomous works. His plan was realized during the 1990s by an avant-garde Moscow theatrical company: its highly successful staging of *Night Search* as part of the "supertale" attested to the dramatic and poetic power of Khlebnikov's creation.

HENRYK BARAN

Zangezi

Supertale, 1922

The last work that Khlebnikov prepared for print and his first posthumous publication, *Zangezi* preoccupied the poet in 1920–21, and was "collated and decided" in January 1922. It is a summary of Khlebnikov's *oeuvre*, being composed of fragments, many already written, representing not just each of Khlebnikov's genres – lyrical, narrative, theoretical – but every plane of his language, from conventional contemporary poetic register to the "phonography" (*zvukopis'*) of "bird" and "god" language. Named a "supertale" (*sverkhpovest'*), it has no plot and little action: first the narrator states his constructional principles and sets the mountainous, almost perpendicular scene for his protagonist, the seer-poet Zangezi, to appear. Then follows a series of 19 "planes" (*ploskosti*). The first is a dawn song in a form of "phonograhy", a phonetic recreation of the song of a number of forest birds, including a warbler, a bunting, a brambling and a jay – a musical composition that Khlebnikov's ornithological expertise justifies. The second plane introduces a heterogeneous group of gods, from the Mongol-Chinese Tien to the Zulu Ulunkulunkulu, including just one Slavonic god, Veles. Their language is a sequence of syllables with no dictionary meaning, but often linked by internal declension – pattern of consonants, varied only by changing the vowel – so that sense appears imminent in, say, Veles' "Pench, panch, pench" and Eros' "Emch, Amch, Umch! / *Du*mchi, *da*mchi, *do*mchi ... Ol'ga, El'ga, Al'ga". Here the phonography also recalls the early lyrics of Khlebnikov, such as "Beobobi", where the sequence of sounds recreates for the listener or reader the actual movement of a human face contorted by the effort of articulation. Plane III introduces human beings ("from a pack of very various verbal planes"), discussing the "forest fool" (i.e. Zangezi) who is about to preach. In Plane IV one of these passers-by picks up a fragment of manuscript that has fallen from Zangezi's hands into a mouse hole and reads aloud the "Tables of Fate", the mathematical formulae that Khlebnikov had elaborated 15 years earlier for calculating the rise and fall of empires on the basis of the number of human heartbeats per minute and infantry steps per hour. For a moment the power of these calculations deadens the audience's contempt and they declare themselves to be the floor over which Zangezi's unknown strides must take place.

Zangezi opens Plane VI with Khlebnikov's finest lyric:

I, a butterfly, which has flown
Into the room of human life,
Am to leave the handwriting of my dust
On the harsh windows, in the signature of a prisoner,
On the strict panes of fate ...
Eternal numbers knock from the other side
Calling me to my homeland, calling a number to return to numbers.

(This lyric left its mark, the association of the fragile butterfly poet and the other, harshly numeric world of mathematics, on Mandel'shtam's poetry, notably the eight-line lyrics of 1932–34.)

The audience are unresponsive, however. Just one disciple demands that Zangezi then sing of his metalogical (*zaumnaia*) language, of the inherent meaning in each consonant, regardless of language. Here the reader is taken to Khlebnikov's best known poem-treatise, such as "The Word of El", and in Plane VII Zangezi again gives the names of the generals in the White Army to prove that "K" is a consonant of evil, and deals with the "flying" sonants "L" and "R" by showing their combination in the word for "eagle", *oReL*: this plane is a poem in itself, in which "K", the consonant of death, is defeated by "L" through "M" (*L* makes a *m*ole for *m*arine *m*ortality) and the force of "R" (in the words for Russia, destruction, horn, the thunder god Perun) is saved from its innate destructiveness. What Rimbaud did for vowels, Khlebnikov does here for consonants – the poem's argument given post-Chomskian linguistics seems less ridiculous scientifically than it did then, but Zangezi's listeners are even less impressed. Khlebnikov's hero develops the poem on consonantal meaning – astral language – in Plane VIII to deal with "KH" and labial sounds. The listeners now echo Zangezi antiphonically, like respondents in a catechism, and the main point of this supertale emerges. Poetic speech frees us from the fetters of conventional language; words do not exist, only their components in free association. *Zangezi* here helps us see the link between Khlebnikov's linguistics and his revolutionary politics. People are likewise to be liberated from old structures and re-combine freely. Language and society are physical worlds to be atomized before re-associating.

We move from logic to mysticism in Plane IX. Khlebnikov takes the Sanskrit mystical syllable "Om" and associates it with the Russian syllable "Um" (mind), prefixing it with every permutation of consonant and vowel; this level of metalogy, where a known root conveys meaning to new combinations, can be annotated, and Khlebnikov gives glosses, more or less fantastical, that infuse the percussive string of "-um" sounds with the sense of some ritual of human brotherhood, as well as creating a pseudo-Slavonic, but not Indo-European, language of prefixes. After exhausting the possibilities of "-um", Zangezi produces a poem on the syllable "mog-" (able, could), a virtuous improvisation which links "could" to "thought" and "Mohicans" in an aggressive exhortation to human power. Zangezi has now roused the rabble: thousands of voices shout out "Mogu" (I can).

Now, in Plane XI, the gods fly off in panic at the victorious approach of the alphabet that Zangezi has freed from its verbal confines. The name Zangezi seems to justify its superficial resemblance to Zarathustra. Not just the mountain from which the prophet speaks, but his usurpation of godhood and his sense of total freedom align Khlebnikov with Nietzsche.

After this climax, Zangezi becomes an anthologizer of Khlebnikov: we have a sample of the purely Slavonic recombination of known root morphemes and archaic affixes into new, semi-intelligible words. Despite the crowd's ever increasing impatience, Zangezi gives new "phonographic" miniatures – "*Veo-veia* is the green of a tree, / *Nizheoty* is the dark trunk ...", and two long poems follow. Plane XVII is a political philosophical poem in standard (if naive) register, while Plane XX sets Zangezi aside for a verse dialogue between Sorrow and Laughter. Sorrow has many of Khlebnikov's (and Zangezi's) images, notably the frail butterfly; laughter, so important in early Khlebnikov, who stresses the identity of the roots "to laugh" and "to dare" (*sme-*), offers itself up to death. Khlebnikov and his protagonist appear to have resolved a conflict between the lyrical and the experimental in the poet: the death of laughter is the death of the free poet. The crowd, in "a merry place", reads a report that Zangezi has cut his throat, because of the destruction of his manuscripts. The rumour is scotched by Zangezi's final word: "Zangezi lives". To this, in an emendation to his fair copy, Khlebnikov added "This was a stupid joke". No poet made a "stupid joke" so comprehensive and testamental: the ideas and the pathos of *Zangezi* have had to wait until today for Russian poets to exploit their unrealized possibilities.

DONALD RAYFIELD

Vladislav Felitsianovich Khodasevich 1886–1939

Poet and critic

Biography

Born in Moscow, 28 May 1886. Attended gymnasium in Moscow and studied at Moscow University. First book published, 1908. Continued writing poetry, and earned living as literary critic and translator. Taught at *Proletkult* in Moscow, 1918–19. Lived in Petrograd, 1920–22. Published collection *Tiazhelaia lira* [The Heavy Lyre], 1922; emigrated to Berlin with Nina Berberova (his common-law wife), 1922. Travelled around Europe, eventually settled in Paris, 1925. Became leading critic for journal *Vozrozhdenie*, 1927. Thereafter wrote little poetry, turned to writing memoirs and biographies. Suffered chronic ill health. Died in Paris, 14 June 1939.

Publications

Collected Editions

Sobranie stikhov. Paris, Vozrozhdenie, 1927; reprinted New York, Russica, 1978; Paris, La Presse Libre, 1982.
Literaturnye stat'i i vospominaniia [Literary Articles and Memoirs]. New York, Izdatel'stvo imeni Chekhova, 1954.
Izbrannaia proza, 2 vols. New York, Rego Park, 1982–83.
Sobranie stikhov, 2 vols. Paris, La Presse Libre, 1982–83.
Sobranie sochinenii, edited by John Malmstad and Robert Hughes, 5 vols. Ann Arbor, Ardis, 1983–90.
Stikhotvoreniia. 3rd edition, Leningrad, 1989.
Sobranie stikhov (Serebrianyi vek). Moscow, 1992.
Sobranie sochinenii, 4 vols. Moscow, 1996–97.

Poetry

Molodost' [Youth]. Moscow, 1908.
Schastlivyi domik [The Happy House]. Moscow, 1914; 2nd edition, Petrograd, 1921; 3rd edition Berlin, Petrograd, and Moscow, 1922.
Putem zerna [By Means of the Grain]. Moscow, 1920; 2nd edition Petrograd, 1921; reprinted Berkeley, University of California Press, 1977.
Tiazhelaia lira [The Heavy Lyre]. Moscow and Petrograd, 1922; 2nd edition, Berlin, 1923; reprinted Ann Arbor, Ardis, 1983; Moscow, 1990.
Evropeiskaia noch' [European Night]. Paris, Vozrozhdenie, 1927 [as part of *Sobranie stikhov*].

Memoirs

Nekropol'. Vospominaniia. Brussels, Petropolis, 1939; reprinted Paris, YMCA-Press, 1976.

Literary Criticism

Stat'i o russkoi poezii [Articles on Russian Poetry]. 1922; reprinted Letchworth, Prideaux Press, 1971.

Biography

Derzhavin. Paris, Sovremennye zapiski, 1931; reprinted Paris, YMCA-Press, 1986; Moscow, 1988.

Critical Studies

"Vladislav Khodasevich: A Russian Poet", by Nina Berberova, *Russian Review*, 11/2 (1952), 78–85.
"Pis'ma M. Tsvetaevoi k V. Khodasevichu", edited by Simon Karlinsky, *Novyi zhurnal*, 89 (1967), 102–14.
The Italics Are Mine, by Nina Berberova, translated by Philippe Radley, London, Longman, and New York, Harcourt Brace Jovanovich, 1969; revised edition London, Chatto and Windus, 1991; New York, Knopf, 1992.
"A Double-Edged *Ars Poetica* (Vladislav Khodasevich)", by V. Veidle, *Russian Literature Triquarterly*, 2 (1972), 339–47.
"Khodasevich: Irony and Dislocation: A Poet in Exile", by R.P. Hughes, *Triquarterly*, 27 (1973), 5–66; reprinted in *The Bitter Air of Exile: Russian Writers in the West 1922–72*, edited by Simon Karlinsky and Alfred Appel, Jr, Berkeley, University of California Press, 1977.
"The Adamovič – Xodasevič Polemics", by Roger M. Hagglund, *Slavonic and East European Journal*, 20 (1976), 239–52.

Pereput'ia, by Vladimir Orlov, Moscow, 1976.
"Stanza Rhythm and Stress Load in the Iambic Tetrameter of V.F. Xodasevič", by Gerald S. Smith, *Slavonic and East European Journal*, 24 (1980), 25–36.
Khodasevich: His Life and Art, by David M. Bethea, Princeton, Princeton University Press, 1983.
"The Versification of V.F. Khodasevich: 1915–1939", in *Russian Poetics*, edited by Thomas Eekman and Dean S. Worth, Columbus, Ohio, Slavica, 1983, 373–90.
V.F. Chodasevič. Dualität und Distanz als Grundzüge seiner Lyrik, by F. Gübler, Munich, Sagner, 1988.
V. Khodasevich. Portrety slovami. Ocherki. Zhizn' khudozhnika. Memuary. Moscow, 1995.

Vladislav Khodasevich's status as Russia's greatest poet of the 1920s is the only topic on which Maksim Gor'kii and Vladimir Nabokov ever agreed. His background – Polish nobleman father, Jewish mother, converted to Catholicism, and Russian peasant wet-nurse ("Not by my mother, but by a Tula peasant woman/ By Elena Kuzina I was weaned") – accounts for his extraordinarily diverse sensibility and universality. His education in a Moscow gymnasium brought him into close contact with Symbolists such as Valerii Briusov and Viktor Gofman and made him a precocious poet. His first book, *Molodost'* [Youth], was published in 1908 to condescending approval. He abandoned his university law course and began to make a precarious living as a conscientious poet, translator, critic and hack, while experiencing marital entanglements typical of Moscow's decadents. His second book, *Schastlivyi domik* [The Happy House], showed a reversion to the Pushkinian heritage that is his fundamental tone. Rarely commenting on reality, Khodasevich ignored World War I, but greeted the February Revolution and the Provisional Government with his one burst of optimism. He recorded the horrors of the October Revolution dispassionately, concurring, like Mandel'shtam, in their necessity, but recognizing that his world had now collapsed: "For the first time in my life / Neither 'Mozart and Salieri' nor 'The Gypsies' [by Pushkin] / Quenched my thirst that day". In 1920 Khodasevich moved to Petrograd, to the House of Arts, where he collaborated with Gor'kii in a massive project to bring creative writing and the great texts of world literature to the proletarians. In the same year he published *Putem zerna* [By Means of the Grain], a work still more saturated in Pushkinian classicism, despite its themes of regeneration. Khodasevich managed in his very short Petrograd period to produce fine translations, mainly from Polish and Yiddish. In 1922 his first undeniably great collection – a mere 45 poems, *Tiazhelaia lira* [The Heavy Lyre], appeared. On the wave of this achievement (but depressed by the deaths of Blok and Gumilev) he left Russia for Berlin with Nina Berberova (who stayed with him until 1938). After peregrinating all over western Europe he settled in Paris, where his lyrical inspiration rapidly dried up and his talents were devoted to memoirs – for instance, *Nekropol'* [Necropolis] – fine studies of Derzhavin (1931) and of Pushkin (1924 and 1937). Most of his last poems, arguably his greatest, were collected in *Evropeiskaia noch'* [European Night], which was published as part of his collected work in 1927. In the late 1920s his attitude to Bolshevik Russia hardened to total rejection, but he harboured no illusions whatsoever on any political or personal theme. Only few among the émigré community appreciated Khodasevich's greatness. His death (childless), after chronic ill health, spared him from the Nazi extermination camps. His immediate heritage was a mere 200 published poems and a number of critical studies. Since his death another 200 poems or drafts have slowly surfaced from archives; a full collection of his critical writings awaits a complete trawl of émigré journals.

Khodasevich's achievement was to free himself from contemporary schools. He had the Symbolists' appreciation of the apocalypse, the Acmeists' obsession with formal perfection and clarity, the Futurists' quest for renovating the Russian language as 18th-century poets had done – but (despite his admiration for Blok) he lacked the religious pretensions of Symbolism, the self-conscious pastiche of the Acmeists or Futurist charlatanism. Like Mandel'shtam, Khodasevich could adapt Derzhavin, Baratynskii, Pushkin, and Tiutchev without imitation. No Russian poet had a better understanding of the rhythms and metres of his language. His imagery is classical, but deeply original – for example his recurrent image of mice as underground forces (to be propitiated by offerings of biscuits), and as forces sacred to Apollo. A decade before W.H. Auden, by taking the essential from Baudelaire's Parisian poems, Khodasevich added to Russian poetry an ability to make without condescension horrific ballads out of the misery of obscure lives.

Khodasevich's poetry of the 1920s is unbearably, but modestly stark: he addresses Lady Macbeth: "For three hundred years you haven't been able to sleep, / I haven't been able to either for six". The bleakness is often murderous:

> I keep waiting for somebody to be crushed / By a rabid motor car ... / And that will start it and begin: / A shaking apart, a turning inside out, disaster, / A star will fall upon the earth / And water turn bitter. / Dreams that stifle the soul will stop, / Everything I want will begin, / And angels will put out the sun / Like an unwanted candle. (1921)

Khodasevich's humour and language could be transcendental: "Transgress, trans- what you like, / But burst out, like a stone from a sling ... / God knows, what you mumble to yourself / Looking for your pince-nez or keys". But transcendental language, as practised by Futurists, repelled him: "God lives! Logical, not metalogical, / I walk through my verses / Like an uncompromising abbot among his humble friars ... / O, if my dying groan / Could be clad in a precise ode!" The virtual lyrical silence he imposed on himself for the last ten years of his life is puzzling, in the light of new, narrative ventures such as the ballad "John Bottom" (1926), which deals lightly with the horrific plight of the ghost of the unknown soldier.

DONALD RAYFIELD

Tiazhelaia lira

The Heavy Lyre

Poetry collection, 1922

This collection was written in 1920–22, and was published just before Khodasevich's departure for Berlin in 1922; the second edition appeared in Berlin and in Moscow in 1923. Most of the poems were written in Petrograd, when Khodasevich was living in the House of Arts (which Forsh described satirically in her novel *Sumasshedshii korabl'* [The Mad Ship]). Some of the poems (for example, "Iz okna" [From the Window], and

"Smotriu v okno – i preziraiu ..." [I look through the window – and feel contempt ...]) form part of the urban landscape that Khodasevich observed from the window of his flat. As Nina Berberova recollected in *Kursiv moi* (*The Italics Are Mine*), Khodasevich was in a reflective mood while working on his verse of this period:

> His window in the House of Arts looked out onto the bridge, and through it you could see all of the Nevsky. His semicircular room and the window were a part of Khodasevich's life: for hours he would sit and look through it – the greater part of the verse in *The Heavy Lyre* was essentially born at this window, out of this view ... In the conversations we had with one another all of January and February [1922] it was not a matter of "you" and "I", of facts and events, of recollections and hopes, but a matter of chains of thoughts, of linking our minds with the awareness of our limits.

Khodasevich's collection of poems was published during the renaissance of Russian poetry (this period was marked by the appearance of Pasternak's *Sestra moia zhizn'* (*My Sister – Life*), Tsvetaeva's *Versty* [Mileposts], and Mandel'shtam's *Tristia*). The book conveys the inner world and emotional experience of a poet whose artistic and creative background (Khodasevich's father was an artist) prevented his reconciliation with the social and political changes that were transforming Russia into a land of hunger, humilation, and poverty. *Tiazhelaia lira* is a diary in verse, which can be fully appreciated when put into the socio-political context; it tells of what it was like to be at odds with the propagators of mass culture who were destroying the roots of cultural identity.

Khodasevich's immediate reaction to the consequences of the October Revolution is expresed explicitly and implicitly throughout the collection of verse. The opening poem "Muzyka" [Music], for example, does not rhyme, giving the impression of distortion of the world's harmony. It tells the story of a man who is cutting wood with his neighbour one cold winter morning in Advent. Their perception of the world is strikingly different: the lyric hero keeps hearing divine music, which is out of tune with the earthbound music; the poem can be seen both as a philosophical sketch, and a socio-political satire with contrasting images of axes and a sky full of flying angels. The poem "Iskushenie" [Temptation] openly condemns the social changes leading to the triumph of the philistine and pragmatic outlook. In the lofty style of the civic poetry of Pushkin's epoch, Khodasevich proclaims: "Light off, Tacitus' lamp! ... There is no need for beauty! / The treacherous world isn't worth a song!"

The title of the collection suggests the author's yearning for the past, his shouldering the burden of being a Russian poet, the preservation of identity. There are many references to the free spirit inherited by the poet from his predecessors; it is compared to Psyche tormented by reality. In "Liubliu liudei, luibliu prirodu" [I love people, I love nature], the poet proclaims that he knows for sure the populace would not understand his writings. Indeed his work relies on the poetic tradition and holds greatest appeal for other poets. The variety of stanzas and metres enrich the thematic structure of the collection, reminding the readers that poetry is a craft not a tool of mass production. The recurrence of iambic structures in the collection appears like a concealed homage to Pushkin. The variety of stanzas is particularly striking: the poem "Gostiu" [To the Visitor] consists of nine lines, while "Sumerki" [Twilight] contains 13 lines, and "Porok i smert'" [Vice and Death] is a six-line poem. Most of the poems of the collection are in Pushkinian style: the poet strives to achieve simplicity of expression, focusing on the meaning of the words rather than sound effects, a feature of the poetics of Symbolists and Futurists. (Perhaps, it was not a coincidence that at the beginning of the 1920s Khodasevich was extensively researching Pushkin's writings.) In "Na tuskneiushchie shpili ..." [On the darkening spires ...], the poem dedicated to Ol'ga Forsh, the urban landscape is very laconic: the first snow is covering automobiles and the spires of cathedrals; this scene had been witnessed by the narrator many times. However, the psychological twist, introduced in the middle of this lyric poem, suggests that the hero has changed over the last year. He has become a Christian and his perception of the world has changed dramatically; this time his vision of the snow is different from before:

> And in this new world,
> Tense and hostile,
> The first snow fell today...
> For me it's not like everyone else's.

The appraisal of the individualistic vision of the world permeates the whole collection. Some of the poems can be defined as dramatic sketches, in which inner tension and emotional conflicts clash with the well-balanced, almost detached description of the surrounding reality.

In his book *On Poets and On Poetry*, Vladimir Veidle wrote about the "cruel piercingness" of Khodasevich's verse. This sharpness and unexpectedness of psychological motivation carefully introduced in the narrative structure is especially striking in such poems of the collection as "Sumerki", "Ne mater'iu, no tul'skoiu krest'iankoi ..." [Not by mother, but by a peasant from Tula ...], and "Avtomobil'" [Automobile]. It is suggested in "Sumerki", for example, that the hero is tempted to commit murder on a cold winter evening. The hero imagines the death of his would-be victim and the crowds of people attracted to the scene of the murder, "like a swarm of ants", who would all be asking each other why and how this man was killed. The concluding line carries a psychological twist: the lyric hero confesses that nobody would guess that he could have loved the person he murdered.

The important feature of the collection is the blend of modernity with Neoclassical imagery and themes. Some of the genres used in the collection, such as elegies and ballads, signify the resurrection of the romantic tradition; yet the mythic quality of the collection predominates. The poetic tradition followed by Khodasevich encompasses not only Russian cultural heritage but also ancient Greek and Latin poetry. In the final poem of the book, "Ballada" [Ballad], the lyric hero describes his experience of the fantastic as something metaphysical: in a whirlwind of music he sees himself being transformed into a mystical beast to whom Orpheus presented the heavy lyre. Khodasevich subverts the contemporary use of the genre, which had become popular in Soviet poetry to describe stories featuring revolutionary activity. He turns instead to phantasmagoria and fantasy, undermining modern history and seeking a reconciliation with the past. Perhaps due to its intimacy and old-fashioned sophistication the book was nearly overlooked by contemporaries. It awaits its reassessment; in the Soviet period Khodasevich's name was resurrected only in 1963 when a few poems appeared in the popular periodical *Moskva*. Khodasevich was constantly attacked by Soviet scholars for creating a lyric hero bored to death by the revolutionary events that were shaking the world.

ALEXANDRA SMITH

Aleksei Stepanovich Khomiakov 1804–1860

Poet, dramatist, and essayist

Biography

Born in Moscow, 14 May 1804. Religious upbringing; educated privately. Studied mathematics at Moscow University: graduated, 1821. Associated with the society of "Wisdom Lovers", early 1820s. Published poetry in *Moskovskii vestnik*. Brief military career; ran away to help Greeks, 1821; fought in the Russo-Turkish war 1828–30. Travelled to Europe, visited France, Italy, and Austria, 1825. Married: Ekaterina Mikhailovna (sister of the poet Nikolai Iazykov) in 1836; one son. First collection of poems published, 1844. Visited England, 1847; set up link with Anglican church; also sent his inventions ("Silent Motor" steam engine) to be exhibited in England. Became increasingly depressed following his wife's death and the Crimean War. Died from cholera in Lipetsk province, 5 October 1860.

Publications

Collected Editions

Sochineniia, 4 vols. 1861–73; 2nd edition, 1879–82.

Polnoe sobranie sochinenii A.S. Khomiakova, edited by D.A. Khomiakov, 8 vols. Moscow, 1900–07.

Sochineniia, 6 vols. 1915.

Izbrannye sochineniia. New York, Izdatel'stvo imeni Chekhova, 1955.

Stikhotvoreniia i dramy, with an introduction and notes by B.F. Egorov, Leningrad, 1969.

Sochineniia, 2 vols. Moscow, 1994.

Sochineniia bogoslovskie. St Petersburg, 1995.

Poetry

13 poems translated by Larry Andrews, *Russian Literature Triquarterly*, 8 (1974), 72–82.

Letters

Correspondence Between Mr William Palmer and M. Khomiakoff, 1844–1854. London, Rivington Percival, 1895.

Critical Studies

"The Life and Works of Alexei Khomiakov", by F.P. Marchant, *Anglo-Russian Literary Society Proceedings*, 17 (1914), 36–52.

A.S. Khomiakov et le mouvement slavophile, 2 vols, by A. Gratieux, Paris, Editions du Cerf, 1939.

Holy Moscow: Chapters on the Religious and Spiritual Life in Russia in the 19th Century, by N.S. Arseniev, London, SPCK, 1940.

"Khomiakov and the Orthodox Church", by C. Manning, *Review of Religion*, 6 (1942), 169–78.

Three Russian Prophets: Khomiakov, Dostoevsky, Soloviev, by Nicolas Zernov, London, S.C.M. Press, 1944; translated into Russian by Iu.M. Tabak, Moscow, 1995.

An Introduction to Nineteenth-Century Russian Slavophilism: A Study in Ideas, vol. 1, A.S. Xomjakov, by Peter K. Christoff, The Hague, Mouton, 1961.

"Khomiakov and the Slavs", by Janko Lavrin, *Russian Review*, 23 (1964), 36–48.

"Khomiakov kak poet", by E.A. Maimin, in *Pushkinskii sbornik*, Pskov, 1968, 69–114.

Khomiakov filosof slavianofil'stva, by A.D. Sukhov, Moscow, 1993.

Although an amateur philosopher, poet, inventor, and social activist, Aleksei Khomiakov is the most important and most admirable of all the Slavophiles. Brought up with his brother by their mother (a Kireevskii) to be an ascetic Christian, he had no crises of faith. Educated privately, he was fluent in classical and modern languages, notably English; he graduated in mathematics from Moscow University at the age of 17 and very soon had a fine command of German philosophy (notably Schelling and Hegel) as well as theology. He had a brief military career – from running away to help the Greeks in 1821 to action in the Russo-Turkish War 1828–30 – but was unable to kill. He sympathized with Decembrists officers but rejected violence as a political tactic. His first journey to western Europe in 1825 gave him respect for the Catholic cultures of France and Italy, but real love for the Slavs of the Austrian empire. In 1836 he married Ekaterina Mikhailovna, the sister of the poet Iazykov, a marriage made in heaven, by which he had a son Dmitrii (who survived until the 1920s). His only collection of poems (1844) met with a devastating critique from the Westernizer Vissarion Belinskii. In 1847 Khomiakov made a journey to England: passionate Anglophilia radically altered his thinking. Not only did he send his inventions, such as the "Silent Motor" steam engine, to be exhibited in England: he began a dialogue (which continues to this day) with Anglican churchmen such as William Palmer; Khomiakov became convinced that the English were a lost Slav tribe, the Uglichi. His euphoria was destroyed by his wife's death from a misdiagnosed illness, a blow he regarded as a signal from heaven. By day he functioned, but his nights were sleepless penitence. The Crimean War he saw as a similar signal to Russia, and he responded with poetry that many regarded as defeatist, but which has the pathos of an Old Testament prophet's reproaches to Israel. His death from cholera was a horrible irony considering all he did to combat the epidemic in Russia, and it deprived Russia of its greatest moral authority at the very time when the new freedom of the press would have spread his influence. Khomiakov's thoughts were propagated in censured articles of the 1830s and 1840s, in translation abroad, and in his voluminous private correspondence.

His most influential articles are "Mnenie inostrantsev o Rossii" [The Opinion of Foreigners about Russia] (1845), and "Mnenie russkikh ob inostrantsakh" [The Opinion of Russians about Foreigners] (1846), witty, tolerant and informed works that undo the damage caused by the Marquis de Custine in 1839 and by the chauvinism of official and early Slavophile publicists. The improvement of both opinions, removing foreigners' hatred and contempt, and Russians' ignorance and suspicion, Khomiakov argues, could only come about by the spread of learning and science. Although he shared Chaadaev's admiration for the harmony of church and state in the west, Khomiakov condemned the formalism and *ad hoc*, unprincipled nature of political developments in Europe, making an exception for England, where he sensed a Russian priority of intuition over logic in Disraeli's dictum "English manners save England from English laws". Even the Crimean War did not dampen Khomiakov's Anglophilia: Palmerston was an English weakness, he asserted in his foreword to the biography of Lord Metcalfe (written c.1857), but its strengths were in the natural Christian and civic sense of every individual and the high morality that resulted, like the elimination of plague and drought, from English technology. Khomiakov was an active supporter of western freedoms, he practised as well as preached the emancipation of the peasantry and industrial development. Nevertheless, like Leont'ev, Khomiakov used a biological metaphor to express the impossibility of importing western solutions into Russia: a culture, he said, is an organic body that reacts with fever and illness to the injection of alien bodies. Khomiakov's one militant call was the movement to liberate the Serbs from the Turkish yoke (he also offered the army an improved rifle of his own invention). His objective, more pacific, historical writings were not published until ten years after his death, but had no effect in civilizing the chauvinism of the next generation of Slavophiles.

Khomiakov's theological writings are the most important Orthodox documents of the 19th century; in his lifetime his "Neskol'ko slov pravoslavnogo khristianina o zapadnykh veroispovedaniiakh" [A Few Words by an Orthodox Christian about Western Confessions] (1853–55) could only be published in Paris and Leipzig in French. He proclaims (like Solov'ev 30 years later) the schism to be Christianity's greatest disaster, but sees a return to Orthodoxy as the sole outcome for western Christians. Khomiakov had a telling image of the Catholic Christian as a brick in an edifice, the Protestant as a grain of sand in a dune, but the Orthodox as a living part of an organic body: qualities that Khomiakov called *sobornost'* (congregationality) and *tsel'nost'* (integrality) are essentials of the Orthodox Church, lost to the west. His "Neskol'ko slov ..." ends:

> Three voices are loudest in Europe: "Submit and believe my decrees," says Rome. "Be free and try to make yourself a faith," says Protestantism. But the Church calls to its own: "Let us love one another and in unanimity confess the Father, Son and Holy Ghost."

Khomiakov's patriotic plays are no longer performed, but his verse during the Crimean War was the finest political poetry between Pushkin and Blok. His "Rossii" [To Russia] (1854) is sublime and created the moral framework for Alexander II's reforms:

> Black with black injustice in courts / And branded with the yoke of slavery; / Full of godless flattery, rotting lies, / Dead and disgraceful sloth, / And every kind of foulness, / O, unworthy of election, / You have been chosen! Quickly wash / Yourself with the water of penitence / Lest the thunder of double punishment / Resound over your head.

DONALD RAYFIELD

Nadezhda Dmitrievna Khvoshchinskaia 1824–1889

Prose writer, poet, and critic

Biography

Born in Riazan province, 1 June 1824. Educated largely at home. (Her sisters, Sof'ia and Praskov'ia, were also writers; the three have sometimes been compared to the Brontë sisters). Lived most of her life in Riazan; this strongly affected her fictional and critical writing. Began to publish poetry in 1847, prose in 1850; also wrote under the pseudonyms V. Krestovskii-psevdonim, V. Porechnikov, Nikolai Kuratov, and N. Vozdvizhenskii. Critical works include a series of articles in *Otechestvennye zapiski* entitled "Provintsial'nye pis'ma o nashei literature" [Provincial Letters about Our Literature]. Father died in 1856; Khvoshchinskaia supported her family (sisters, mother, nephews) by her writings. Close ties with Shchedrin and Kraevskii and published most of her works in their *Otechestvennye zapiski*. Married: Ivan Zaionchkovskii in 1865. Moved to St Petersburg after her mother's death, 1884. Died in Staryi Petergof, 20 June 1889.

Publications

Collected Editions

Romany i povesti, 8 vols. St Petersburg, 1859–1866.
Sobranie sochinenii, 5 vols. St Petersburg, 1892–1898.
Polnoe sobranie sochinenii V. Krestovskogo, edited by A.A. Kaspari, 6 vols. St Petersburg, n.d.
Povesti i rasskazy, edited by M.S. Goriachkina. Moscow, 1984.

Fiction

"Anna Mikhailovna", *Otechestvennye zapiski*, 6 (1850).
"Dnevnik sel'skogo uchitelia" [Diary of a Village Teacher], *Otechestvennye zapiski*, 12 (1850).
"Kto zhe ostalsia dovolen?" [Who Remains Content?], *Otechestvennye zapiski*, 4–5 (1853).
"Na doroge. Ocherk". 1854; translated as "On the Way: A Sketch", in *Russian Women's Shorter Fiction: An Anthology, 1835–1860*, translated by Joe Andrew, Oxford: Clarendon Press, 1996, 301–18.
"Svobodnoe vremia" [Free Time], *Otechestvennye zapiski*, 11–12 (1856).
"Poslednee deistvie komedii" [The Last Act of the Comedy], *Otechestvennye zapiski* (1856).
"Bariton" [Baritone], *Otechestvennye zapiski*, 10–11 (1857); separate edition, St Petersburg, 1879.
"Bratets" [Old Chap], *Otechestvennye zapiski*, 10 (1858).
"V ozhidanii luchshego" [In Hope of Something Better], *Russkii vestnik* 14–17 (1860); separate edition, Moscow, 1861; St Petersburg, 1880.
"Pansionerka" [The Schoolgirl], *Otechestvennye zapiski*, 3 (1861).
"Za stenoiu" [Behind the Wall], *Otechestvennye zapiski*, 10 (1862).
"Pervaia bor'ba" [First Battle], *Otechestvennye zapiski*, 8–9 (1869); separate edition, St Petersburg, 1879.
"Bol'shaia medveditsa" [Ursa Major], *Vestnik Evropy*, 3–4; 7–9 (1870) and 4–6, 11 (1871); separate editions St Petersburg, 1872, 1875 and 1883; translated into French, *Journal de S. Petersbourg*, 1871.
"Al'bom, gruppy i portrety" [Album, Groups and Portraits], *Vestnik Evropy*, 1874–75, 1877; separate edition, St Petersburg, 1879.
"Svidanie" [A Meeting], *Otechestvennye zapiski*, 2 (1879); reprinted in *Svidanie*, edited by V. Uchenova, Moscow, 1987, 363–416.

Poetry

Poems in *Poety 1840–1850-kh godov*, Leningrad, "Biblioteka poeta, bol'shaia seriia", 2nd edition, 1972, 259–70.
Poems in *Russkie poetessy XIX veka*, Moscow, 1979.
Poems in *Tsaritsy muz*, edited by V. Uchenova, Moscow, 1989.

Play

"Utrennii vizit" [Morning Visit]. 1852.

Literary Criticism

"Provintsial'nye pis'ma o nashei literature" [Provincial Letters about Our Literature], *Otechestvennye zapiski* (a regular column), 1862–63.

Critical Studies

"Zhenskoe bezdushie. (Po povodu sochinenii V. Krestovskogo-psevdonim)", by N.V. Shelgunov, *Delo*, 9 (1870), 1–34.
"V. Krestovskii (psevdonim)", by K.K. Arsen'ev, in *Kriticheskie etiudy po russkoi literature*, by M.M. Stasiulevich, St Petersburg, 1888, 255–350.
"Nadezhda Dmitrievna Khvoshchinskaia (Iz vospominaniia starogo zhurnalista)", by Vl. Zotov, *Istoricheskii vestnik*, 10 (1889), 93–108.
"Vospominaniia o N.D. Khvoshchinskoi", by A. Vinitskaia, *Istoricheskii vestnik*, 1 (1890), 146–55.
"N. D. Khvoshchinskaia-Zaionchkovskaia (V. Krestovskii-psevdonim)", by V. Semevskii, *Russkaia mysl'*, 10–12 (1890).
"Ocherk zhizni N.D. Khvoshinskoi-Zaionchkovskoi (V. Krestovskogo psevdonima)", by M. Tsebrikova, *Mir Bozhii*, 12 (1897), 1–40.
"Iz vospominanii o N. D. Khvoshchinskoi-Zaionchkovskoi. (V. Krestovskii-psevdonim)", by A. Karrik (Markelova), *Zhenskoe delo*, 9, 11–12 (1899).
"Khudozhnik-psikholog. Romany i povesti V. Krestovskogo-psevdonim)", by M. Tsebrikova, *Obrazovanie*, 1–2 (1900).
"Russkaia pisatel'nitsa-pioner'ka", by A. Nalimov, *Ezhemesiachnye sochineniia*, 5–6 (1901), 29–39; 125–36.
"Volny russkogo progressa", by A. Skabichevskii, in *Sochineniia A. Skabicheskogo*, 3rd edition, St Petersburg, 1903, vol. 1, 649–86.
"Nasha sovremennaia bezzavetnost'", by A. Skabichevskii, *Sochineniia A. Skabicheskogo*, 3rd edition, St Petersburg, 1903, 817–50.
Ideals and Realities in Russian Literature, by P. Kropotkin, London, Duckworth, 1905, 179–82.
M. M. Stasiulevich i ego sovremenniki v ikh perepiske, edited by M.K. Lemke, vol. 5, St Petersburg, 1913, 92–130.
Polnoe sobranie sochinenii, by N. Shchedrin, edited by V.Ia. Kirpotin *et al.*, Moscow, 1939, vol. 19 (*Pis'ma*, book 2).
"Auf den Spuren des Vergessens. Zur Rezeptionsgeschichte der russischen Schriftstellerin N. D. Chvoscinskaja", by Arja Rosenholm, *Studia Slavica Finlandensis*, 4 (1989), 63–91.
"Writing the Self: Creativity and the Female Author", by Arja Rosenholm, in *Gender Restructuring in Russian Studies*, Tampere, Finland, University of Tampere Press, 1993, 193–208.

Bibliographies

Bibliograficheskii slovar' russkikh pisatel'nits; Nashi pisatel'nitsy, by N.I. Golitsyn and S.I. Ponomarev, 1889–1891; reprinted, Leipzig, 1974.
Bibliography by D.D. Iazykov, *Russkaia mysl'*, 7 (1890), 191–95.
Bibliography by D.D. Iazykov, in *Obzor zhizni i trudov pokoinykh russkikh pisatelei i pisatel'nits*, 9, Moscow, 1905, 25–30.
Nadezhda Dmitrievna Khvoshchinskaia-Zaionchkovskaia (V. Krestovskii-psevdonim). Bibliograficheskie o nei materialy, by L.A. Chizhikov, Odessa, 1914.

Nadezhda Khvoshchinskaia was a poet, prose writer, translator, literary and art critic; she wrote prose fiction under the pseudonym V. Krestovskii, and used other (male) pseudonyms for her literary criticism.

Khvoshchinskaia, known by contemporary critics for her irony and her commitment to changing society, was a brilliant writer of the provinces. She portrayed provincial manners, mores and *poshlost'* (vulgar banality) in psychologically subtle and often hysterically funny detail. Although she was an influential and prominent author in her own day, Khvoshchinskaia is little known in Russia or the English-speaking world today; few English translations of her works exist, though one is in preparation (*The Schoolgirl* [*Pansionerka*] by Karen Rosneck). This lack of attention is unfortunate because Khvoshchinskaia's works are intriguing both historically and aesthetically, and they call into question traditional conceptions of the history of Russian literature.

The reasons for her obscurity include the following: Khvoshchinskaia was a self-proclaimed writer of the 1850s, a period overshadowed by the generations of the 1840s and 1860s. Also, as a female prose writer, a group that has only recently begun to be studied, she faced societal disapproval, for, as her sister Praskov'ia noted, it was considered "improper and unfeminine" for women to write. In addition, while many noblemen could take certain life experiences for granted – like education or access to literary circles, these were often great obstacles for women; it was also quite difficult for women to find support, both financial and moral, for their writing. Financial need was particularly significant in Khvoshchinskaia's case, for, as an adult, she supported her family by writing. Recovering Khvoshchinskaia's works is part of rediscovering an important period in Russian literary history (the 1850s), and a way to explore the politics of gender and writing as they were configured in Russia.

Khvoshchinskaia lived in Riazan for most of her life. Her two sisters were also writers, Sof'ia as Iv. Vesen'ev and Praskov'ia as S. Zimarev; their brother Kesar' served as an officer in the Caucasus. Their mother, Iuliia Vikent'evna, née Drobysheva, was well educated and passed this along to her children; their father, Dmitrii Kesarevich, lost his position in the Civil Service when he was accused of embezzling funds; more than ten years later, he was reinstated.

Like many women of the 19th century, Khvoshchinskaia had an irregular formal education, but made up for this by avid reading of literary works by, among others, Polevoi, Dante, and Milton). She was briefly at a girls' school, but left, probably for financial reasons; she learned Latin from her brothers' tutor and French, music, and Italian when she lived in Moscow with her uncle's family for a year.

Female friendship, collaboration, and support was important to Khvoshchinskaia as a motivation for writing from a very early age. Khvoshchinskaia was particularly close to her sister Sof'ia who was the first reader and critic of nearly all of Khvoshchinskaia's works. (Also, as a girl, with a (female) friend, N.E. fon Vinkler, Khvoshchinskaia wrote novels at night, and then hid them under the mattress; when fon Vinkler got sick and had to stay at home, Khvoshchinskaia stopped writing temporarily (until they spent time together again).) Khvoshchinskaia again stopped writing (for about two years) after Sof'ia died in 1865.

With her sisters' encouragement, Khvoshchinskaia began publishing poetry in 1847; her first poems appeared in Vladimir Zotov's *Literaturnaia gazeta*. Zotov encouraged Khvoshchinskaia to turn to prose, which she did, after some hesitation. In 1850 she published her first prose work (*Anna Mikhailovna*) in *Otechestvennye zapiski*, using the pseudonym V. Krestovskii, which she later changed to V. Krestovskii-psevdonim when a male author, Vsevolod Krestovskii, began publishing as V. Krestovskii.

Her best-known series of critical articles (written under the pseudonym V. Porechnikov) is "Provintsial'nye pis'ma o nashei literature" [Provincial Letters about Our Literature], published in *Otechestvennye zapiski* in the early 1860s. She also wrote other critical articles under various pseudonyms.

Living in Riazan, it was difficult for Khvoshchinskaia to make connections in the literary world. Beginning in the 1850s, Khvoshchinskaia and Sof'ia regularly visited St Petersburg for months at a time. There they met many leading literary and intellectual figures, such as Andrei Kraevskii, Nikolai Shcherbina, and the Shelgunovs. Khvoshchinskaia also knew Saltykov-Shchedrin, for he was vice-governor of Riazan (1858–60); their relationship continued into the 1880s.

In her writings, Khvoshchinskaia sensitively examines social issues ranging from gender relations of the aristocracy to serfdom and other classes (*soslovie*): she explores the lives of an actress, of hangers-on (*prizhivalki*), of a schoolteacher, and of seminarians in, respectively, *Ridneva*, *V ozhidanii luchshego* [In Hope of Something Better], *Svidanie* [A Meeting], *Bariton* [Baritone] (a work often compared to Pomialovskii's *Ocherki bursy* [*Seminary Sketches*] 1862–63). The range of class in Khvoshchinskaia's works is unusual as is the depth and multi-faceted nature of her portrayals.

Khvoshchinskaia raises questions about the norms for women in Russian society in many of her works (for example, *Za stenoiu* [Behind the Wall], *Pansionerka* [The Schoolgirl], *V ozhidanii luchshego*, *Bol'shaia medveditsa* [Ursa Major], *Ridneva*, *Svidanie*). Her female characters are not idealized; most evince some form of independence and also reveal the limitations of society's expectations of women. In *Za stenoiu*, a tale based on eavesdropping, conventional marriage is radically questioned; in *Pansionerka*, the heroine, Lelen'ka, has the option of either love or creative work, she cannot have both. In *Svidanie*, Khvoshchinskaia explores the limits of liberal politics in the relationship between an aristocratic woman and her sister-in-law of a much lower class (*odnodvorka*).

Khvoshchinskaia's works provide new perspectives on many of the canonical works of Russian literature: *Bol'shaia medveditsa* gives new insight into the "superfluous man" by making the heroine a fuller character and presenting her view of the relationship between herself and Verkhovskoi, a "superfluous man". *Pervaia bor'ba* [First Battle] is a kind of reverse *Ottsy i deti* (*Fathers and Sons*): here, in the battle between the generations, the father is a progressive and the son a determined aristocrat. *Pervaia bor'ba* is a complicated first-person narrative that brilliantly depicts conflicting systems of belief in 1860s Russia.

On account of her dialogue with traditional themes and because her works do not fit the usual categories of society tale, romantic fiction, philosophical novel, physiological sketch, or even realist fiction, examining Khvoshchinskaia's works and her trajectory as a writer invites, or rather, demands reconceptualizing the history of Russian letters.

JEHANNE M. GHEITH

Timur Kibirov 1955–

Poet

Biography

Born in 1955, son of an army officer. Career as poet began in late 1970s; member of Moscow underground movement. Associated with the Conceptualists: Sorokin, Prigov, and Aizenberg. First publications in *samizdat*. Published officially only from the time of perestroika.

Publications

Poetry

Poems in *Ponedel'nik. Sem' poetov samizdata*. Moscow, 1990, 111–25.

Poems in *Golodnaia russkaia zima/The Hungry Russian Winter* (bilingual edition), edited by Victor Kulle. Moscow, 1991, 48–59 (contains "When Lenin was Little" – extracts; "A Song to Servelat [Salami]").

Stikhi o liubvi [Verses on Love]. Moscow, 1993.

Santimenty [Sentiments]. Belgorod, 1994.

"My prosto gibnem i zhivem. Stikhi" [We Simply Perish and Live. Poems], *Znamia*, 10 (1994), 3–6.

"Dvadtsat' sonetov k Sashe Zapoevoi. Stikhi [Twenty Sonnets to Sasha Zapoevyi], *Znamia*, 9 (1995), 3–5.

Kogda byl Lenin malen'kim: Stikhi [When Lenin was Little]. St Petersburg, 1995.

Parafrazis: Kniga stikhov. St Petersburg, 1997.

Critical Studies

"'I zamysel moi dik - igrat' noktiurn na pionerskom dome!'", by Marina Kulakova, *Novyi mir*, 9 (1991), 235–38.

"Sochineniia Timura Kibirova", by Sergei Gandlevskii, in *Santimenty*, Belgorod, 1994, 5–10.

"Glagol vremen. G. Derzhavin i T. Kibirov: opyt parallel'nogo prochteniia", by Il'ia Falikov, *Literaturnaia gazeta*, 42 (1994), 4.

"Antologiia muzhestva i zdravogo smysla", by Aleksandr Panov, *Nezavisimaia gazeta*, (17 September 1994), 7.

"Ch'i teksty chtit vsiak sushchii zdes' slavist?", by Viacheslav Kuritsyn, *Literaturnaia gazeta*, 45 (1995), 4.

"Timur Kibirov: Tol'ko i delaiu, chto potakaiu svoim slabostiam", by Tat'iana Rasskazova, *Segodnia*, (14 January 1995), 12.

Timur Kibirov, born in 1955, the son of a Russian army officer, started his poetic career in the late 1970s as a member of the Moscow "underground" movement. Official literature and art had almost come to a standstill during the reign of Brezhnev (the period of "stagnation"), but unofficially there was considerable activity, especially in the capital. The best-known group to emerge from the underground movement was that of the so-called Conceptualists, young writers, poets and artists who did not want to have anything to do with socialist realism and sought an alliance with international postmodernism. The artists of the group turned out to be particularly successful. Il'ia Kabakov, with his "installations" of Soviet life, and Vitalii Komar and Aleksandr Melamid, with their ironic paintings of Stalin, are now world-famous. The writers and poets, among whom, apart from Kibirov, are Vladimir Sorokin, Dimitrii Prigov, Lev Rubinstein and Mikhail Aizenberg, are considered to be the foremost avant-gardists of contemporary Russian literature.

Kibirov's first publications, like those of the other Conceptualists, appeared in *samizdat*, the official channels being closed to them. Only during Gorbachev's perestroika did the Conceptualists succeed in publishing their books and in finding their way into the literary journals. Kibirov's work is now generally accessible. His poems regularly appear in even the respectable "thick" literary journals and are read on radio and television. In 1994, his poetry was published in a 400-page edition of 10,000 copies, an impressive print-run for post-Soviet times.

Like many other Conceptualists, Kibirov is still very much involved with Soviet life. This daily life (*byt* in Russian) can be considered the main theme of his poetry. His attitude to *byt* is ambivalent. On the one hand he hates it and thinks back on it with feelings of disgust and revulsion; on the other hand he seems attracted to it. In many of his poems there is an undertone of nostalgia for the time of his youth that has irrevocably disappeared. His love-hate attitude towards the stable, but utterly tedious, Soviet life during the Brezhnev era is undoubtedly one of the reasons for his present popularity in Russia.

Kibirov, being the bard of Soviet life (one of his critics characterized his work as a "physiological sketch in verse"), uses language from all levels, from the idealized, petrified jargon of the party officials to the language of the street and the extremely rich Russian *mat* (swearwords). The latter category of words, with such expressions as *govno* (shit), *pizdets* (bullshit) and *khue-moe* (I'll be fucked!), was until recently strictly taboo in literary texts and did not even officially exist, even the lexicographers were obliged to omit all references to vulgar and obscene language. One of the most typical aspects of Kibirov's poetry is the mixture, within one and the same poem, of coarse language and all kinds of other registers, thus creating a veritable stylistic pot-pourri. The result is a predominantly ironic mood. Official language and traditional poetic language are stripped of their seriousness, communist pomposity is debunked and highflown language brought back to "normal".

Ironic effects are also created by the introduction of quotations from other Russian poets. Many of Kibirov's poems contain a direct quotation from, or at least an explicit allusion to, well-known Russian poems, from the Old-Russian masterpiece *Slovo o polku Igoreve* (*The Lay of Igor's Campaign*) to the Zhivago poems by Pasternak. Often the first line of a poem is quoted, as for instance in the fifth part of *Poema "Zhizn' K.I. Chernenko"* [The Poem "The Life of K.I. Chernenko"], which opens with the Pasternak quotation (from *Hamlet*): "The noise abated. He stepped onto the stage" ("Vot gul zatikh. On vyshel na podmostki"). Chernenko's behaviour on the stage – he addresses the Writers' Union with a speech consisting only of worn-out phrases – is in flat contradiction to the suggestive, expectant beginning of the first line.

There are particularly frequent references to the Golden Age of

Russian poetry; Pushkin and his contemporaries, Batiushkov, Viazemskii, Lermontov, and Davydov. Apart from direct quotations from such poetry, Kibirov adopts the typical genres (ballad, romance, eclogue, elegy, epistle) with their concomitant stanza-forms, rhyme schemes and metre. The long poem *Sortiri* [Water Closets] (1991), which, as regards content, is obviously inspired by Pushkin's *Evgenii Onegin*, consists of 106 stanzas of eight lines, each with the same rhyme scheme (abbababc) and the same metric structure (an iambic pentameter with feminine rhyme in the second, fourth and sixth lines and masculine rhyme in the first, third, fifth, seventh and eighth lines), as in Pushkin's "Domik v Kolomne" ("The Little House in Kolomna") and Byron's *Don Juan*. Employing a different verse for each individual poem, Kibirov demonstrates great technical skill, particularly in his mastery of metre and rhyme. Very few contemporary poets can be considered his equal in this respect. Sometimes his skill threatens to get the better of him, resulting in poems in which the poetical fireworks dominate the content. With his free use of poetic aspects of the past, his constant wavering between satire and seriousness, his ironic attitude, which often leads to bathetic and mock-heroic effects, Kibirov can be considered a typical postmodern poet. His work is not really difficult, but presupposes a good knowledge of Soviet life, Russian poetry, and Russian slang.

WILLEM G. WESTSTEIJN

Kirill of Turov c.1130–1182

Religious writer

Biography

Biographical details are scant, and since none come from sources contemporary with Kirill, many may be spurious. Born in the thriving town of Turov, the son of wealthy parents, c.1130. Entered a monastery at an early age where he was noted for his asceticism, while his works of biblical exegesis brought him fame. Consecrated bishop of Turov, probably late 1160s. Involved in an attempt to unmask the heresy of Fedor, who had occupied the bishopric of Rostov with permission of the Metropolitan, 1169. Usually thought to have died in 1182. However, he might have become bishop only after 1182, remaining a monk through the 1160s and 1170s.

Publications

Collected Allegories and Sermons

"Tvoreniia Kirilla, episkopa Turovskogo, rossiiskogo vitii XII veka" [The Works of Kirill, Bishop of Turov, Russian Orator of the 12th Century], edited by Konstantin F. Kalaidovich, in *Pamiatniki rossiiskoi slovesnosti XII veka*, Moscow, 1821.

"Literaturnoe nasledie Kirilla Turovskogo" [The Literary Legacy of Kirill of Turov], *Trudy otdela drevnerusskoi literatury*, 11 (1955); 12 (1956); 13 (1957); 15 (1958); translated in *Sermons and Rhetoric of Kievan Rus'*, by Simon Franklin, Cambridge, Massachusetts, Harvard University Press, 1991.

Prayers

Kirill von Turov. Gebete, Slavische Propylaen 6, Munich, Fink, 1965.

Canons

Istoriia russkoi tserkvi [A History of the Russian Church], by Metropolitan Makarii, vol. 3, 3rd edition, St Petersburg, 1888.

Materialy dlia istorii drevnerusskoi pis'mennosti [Material Towards a History of Old Russian Literature], edited by N.K. Nikol'skii, St Petersburg, 1907.

Critical Studies

"Oratorskoe iskusstvo Kirilla Turovskogo", by I.P. Eremin, in *Literatura drevnei Rusi*, Moscow and Leningrad, 1967.

Sermons and Rhetoric of Kievan Rus', translated with an introduction by Simon Franklin, Cambridge, Massachusetts, Harvard University Press, 1991.

Bibliography

Slovar' knizhnikov i knizhnosti, edited by D.M. Bulanin and O.V. Tovorgov, vol. I, Leningrad, 1987.

Any discussion of the literary career and writings of Kirill of Turov, the 12th-century monk and bishop, runs up against serious problems. No work exists in manuscript from that period, nor do any extant sources actually refer to him. The Life dedicated to him is of much later composition, but contains, beyond generalities, some facts to indicate that there was a real Kirill. Certainly he enjoyed considerable prestige as a writer through the centuries, such that large numbers of works were ascribed to him, often spuriously, and both dubia and genuine writings were constantly copied. It is generally agreed that he is the author of eight homilies (on which his fame primarily rests), three allegorical commentaries, a cycle of prayers, and two canons.

In manuscript sources, there are 23 prayers attributed to "Kirill the Monk", with a further nine that are unattributed but regularly copied in the same group. The prayers form a seven-day liturgical cycle and are extremely well constructed and tightly structured. Kirill makes use of the rhetorical devices traditional in liturgical poetry; words appear in threes with rhyming endings, whole phrases are repeated or constructed to give a strongly rhythmical effect. The poetic effect underscores the predominant mood in the prayers, which is one of abject humility. Repeatedly Kirill expresses a deep sense of his own sinfulness, abasing himself before God, whom he perceives not, as might be expected from someone with so strong a sense of his own failings, as the vengeful God of the Old Testament but a loving God, who forgives the transgressions of the penitent. Such sentiments are consistent with Kirill's experience as a monk of an ascetic inclination.

Like the prayers, the homilies form a cycle based on the ecclesiastical calendar from Palm Sunday to the Sunday before Pentecost. Most take a New Testament story as the basis, but elaborate and embellish it for emotional effect. The aim is to make the events depicted in the homily seem immediate to the audience. Two structural devices are employed to this end: first, Kirill brings the past and the present closer together by constantly reminding the audience that "on this day" such and such happened, "on the day before yesterday our Lord Jesus Christ was crucified" or appealing to the audience to step back in their imagination into the past ("let us now travel in our minds to the Mount of Olives"). Where this device is not used, Kirill dramatizes the original story by the addition of elaborate dialogues. Both methods are reinforced with flights of rhetoric. Kirill is particularly fond of elaborating a sub-theme with additional details and the use of repetition. Thus, in what is perhaps his most famous composition, *Slovo na antipaskhu (faminu nedeliu)* [Sermon for Low Sunday, also known as Sermon on the First Sunday after Easter], Kirill evokes the meaning of the Resurrection as the renewal of Creation and deliverance of the world. Much of the sermon is devoted to a triumphant poetic description of spring as a symbol of the Resurrection ("On this day spring in its finery brings life to earthly nature; the stormy winds blow gently and generate the fruits, and the warmth gives nurture to the seeds and brings forth green grass: for this fine spring is the faith that delights in Christ, which in baptism brings rebirth to mankind ...").

Like the homilies, the allegorical commentaries (such as *Pritcha o sleptse i khromtse* [On the Lame and the Blind]) are primarily directed at a monastic audience. They have attracted less critical attention than the sermons, because the weaving of rhetorical patterns typical of the sermons has of necessity been sacrificed to the demands of form. The aim is to reveal the deeper significance of biblical stories, each point of which is explained and its contribution to a cohesive argument underlined. In this context the emotive use of elegant literary formulations and images have little part to play. The longest of the three commentaries has often been regarded as a diatribe against Fedor, who had usurped the bishopric of Rostov, but the alllusions in the text are so sparse that this cannot be considered more than one aspect of a more general argument. The story is that of the lame man and the blind man, set to guard their lord's garden, but who enter the garden, steal the fruit and are punished. Each segment of the story receives a detailed exegesis: the two men represent the soul and the body who are commanded by the Lord to watch over the garden of Eden (or the monastery, or the sanctuary of a church). The taking of fruit is compared to sin in general and, more particularly, to usurpation of Church office, and the punishment is that of the Last Judgement. Though somewhat abrupt in the way they pass from explication of one detail to the next, the commentaries as a whole are well structured and coherent in their argument.

Kirill of Turov has often been deemed original, but such judgements are anachronistic, since the aim of the medieval Russian writer was to follow tradition, composing in a manner appropriate to the literary form chosen. Thus his sermons rely on the homiletic traditions of the Fathers of the Church, which were available in Slavonic translation. They do not, however, copy verbatim, preferring instead to use themes and images from a variety of sources. The value placed on traditionalism helps explain the wide variations in style between the homilies and the allegorical commentaries: the first celebrates and the second elucidates the truths of Christianity. Kirill should be regarded as a writer who understood the demands of traditional form and rhetorical style and was able to work within these constraints to produce tightly structured works whose impact is carefully calculated. A master of Kievan rhetoric is not an unjustified title.

FAITH WIGZELL

Vil'gel'm Karlovich Kiukhel'beker 1797–1846

Poet and critic

Biography

Born in St Petersburg, 21 June 1797 of German parents. Brought up in Livonia, Estonia, and Smolensk province. Attended the Lycée in Tsarskoe Selo, 1811–17, where he met Pushkin and Del'vig. Published first poem, 1815. Civil servant at the Central Archive of the Foreign College; taught Russian literature at St Petersburg Gentry Pension; associated with the major St Petersburg literary circles; member of Masonic Lodge of Michael the Chosen, 1817–20. Editor of the journal *Nevskii zritel'*, 1820. Secretary to A.L. Naryshkin on travels throughout Europe, 1820–21; gave politically overt lectures at Paris "Athénée" society and as a result was sent back to St Petersburg, August 1821. Served in the Caucasus under General Ermolov until spring 1822. Moved to Moscow in 1823; editor of the literary almanac *Mnemozina*, 1824–25. Returned to St Petersburg, involved in Decembrist conspiracy and revolt, 1825;

fled to Warsaw, but captured. Sentenced to death, 1826; sentence commuted. Spent ten years in solitary confinement, 1826–36. Lived in exile in Siberia; married illiterate girl; four children. Died of tuberculosis in Tobolsk, 23 August 1846.

Publications

Collected Editions

Izbrannye proizvedeniia, 2 vols. Moscow and Leningrad, 1967.
Puteshestvie. Dnevnik. Stat'i [Travel. Diary. Articles]. Leningrad, 1979.

Poetry

Kassandra. (written 1822–23).
David. (written 1826–29).
Agasver [Ahasuerus]. (written 1832–46).

Plays

Argiviane [Men of Argos]. 1824–25 (published in part); 1939 (complete edition).
Izhorskii. (written 1826–41).
Prokofii Liapunov. (written 1834).

Literary Criticism

"On the Trend of Our Poetry, Particularly, Lyric, in the Past Decade", in *Russian Romantic Criticism: An Anthology*, edited and translated by Lauren G. Leighton, New York, Greenwood Press, 1987, 55–68.

Editor

Mnemozina, 1–4, St Petersburg, 1824–25; reprinted Hildesheim, Georg Olms, 1986.

Critical Studies

Kiukhlia, by Iurii Tynianov, Moscow, 1925 [historical novel].
Arkhaisty i novatory, by Iu. Tynianov, Leningrad, 1929.
"Kyukhel'beker and Crabbe", by Y.D. Levin, *Oxford Slavonic Papers*, 1965, 99–113.
Pushkin i ego sovremenniki, by Iu. Tynianov, Moscow, 1969.
"Lichnost': literaturnaia pozitsiia Kiukhel'bekera", by N.V. Koroleva and V.D. Rak, in *Puteshestvie. Dnevnik. Stat'i*, Leningrad, 1979, 571–645.
Russian Drama from Its Beginnings to the Age of Pushkin, by Simon Karlinsky, Berkeley, University of California Press, 1985.
A History of Russian Literature of the Romantic Period, by William Edward Brown, vol. 2, Ann Arbor, Ardis, 1986.
V.F. Odoevsky: His Life, Times and Milieu, by Neil Cornwell, London, Athlone Press, and Athens, Ohio University Press, 1986, 237–41, 354–56.
"A Russian Romantic Abroad: Vil'gel'm Kjuchel'beker's Trip to Europe (1820–21)", by Ruth Sobel, *Russian Literature*, 23 (1988), 295–318.

The son of German nobility, Vil'gel'm Kiukhel'beker was perfectly bilingual: he learnt Russian first from his nurse before he learnt German from his parents. His childhood was spent in Livonia and Estonia, as well as Smolensk province. Although mocked for his high-flown sentiments and love of classical genres, he was ranked as a young poet at the Tsarskoe Selo school, second only to Pushkin. Classical Greek, the German baroque (Klopstock) and Goethe inclined him to write odes of "civic romanticism", glorifying heroes who sacrifice themselves in the fight against tyranny; Kiukhel'beker compensated by an exaggerated striving to avoid all non-Slavonic elements in his language and thus bridged the language of the "archaicists" and the sentiments of the "innovators". His didactic tendencies made him an effective schoolteacher in his late teens, as well as a fine editor and critic of his contemporaries: he was the main force (with Vladimir Odoevskii) in the almanac *Mnemozina* of 1824–25 that presented the poetry, prose and literary views of the younger generation, as well as a substantial body of his own youthful work. The example of the ancient Greeks and the struggle of the modern Greeks for independence made Kiukhel'beker a radical antiquarian. He admired Byron and at the same time imitated Shakespeare's historical plays and prepared the basic principals for translating them. His quixotic nature soon cost him his post in that haven for young poets, the archives of the Ministry of Foreign Affairs: his public defence in verse of Pushkin, after the latter was exiled in 1820, made him a marked man for the authorities. He became sufficiently well known to be considered for a chair of Slavonic languages at Edinburgh. When he accompanied Prince Naryshkin in a tour of Europe, he not only had an interview with Goethe, but delivered a number of lectures to the "Athénée" society in Paris on Russian literature and language, so full of libertarian sentiments that the French authorities and Naryshkin sent him back to St Petersburg (August 1821): the many revolts and demands for constitutions all over Europe in 1820 and 1821 made Kiukhel'beker an overtly political poet, prepared to sanction the murder of the tsar if it would bring about constitutional, representative government.

He served in the Caucasus under General Ermolov until spring 1822, when he was wounded in a duel and force to retire. At this time, during the composition of the first acts of *Gore ot uma* (*Woe from Wit*), he became a close friend of Griboedov, and some of his characteristics are portrayed in Chatskii (Kiukhel'beker is also Pushkin's Lenskii in *Evgenii Onegin*). As a poet he influenced his contemporaries: Pushkin's "Prorok" ("Prophet") has several phrases that echoes Kiukhel'beker's "Prorochestvo" [Prophecy] of 1822. Kiukhel'beker attached great importance to his first major work, a narrative poem *Kassandra*, whose main role, consciously or not, he adopted for himself: "I see black destiny / But shall not deflect it: / Far off into the storm blasts I shall fly / To meet an early end!" Kiukhel'beker had poetic ambitions beyond his talent: plays such as *Argiviane* [Men of Argos] (begun 1822, published in part, 1824–25, complete edition, 1939) have a vast cast and rhetorical, posturing speeches portraying the quandaries of justifiable regicide. Kiukhel'beker spent the years 1823 to 1825 in Moscow teaching, editing and writing critical and lyrical work. Travelling to St Petersburg in search of paid work, he settled in with the Decembrists, A.I. Odoevskii and K.F. Ryleev: inevitably, by October 1825 he was drawn into the "Northern Society" and the Decembrist conspiracy. In the revolt of December 1825 Kiukhel'beker twice tried to fire a pistol, at Grand Duke Mikhail and a general; alone of the Decembrists he fled, but was arrested in Warsaw and in the spring of 1826 sentenced to be beheaded. Kiukhel'beker's friends deliberately encouraged the opinion that he was a demented, impractical fool. Grand Duke Mikhail generously had his sentence commuted. The naive victim who pays the price for a sophisticate's crimes in much of Pushkin's post-Decembrist work has its basis in this condescending view of Kiukhel'beker.

He spent the next ten years in solitary confinement, but humane guards allowed correspondence and writing materials: the bulk of Kiukhel'beker's work, including a "mystery" play, *Izhorskii*, a play on Russian resistance in the Time of Troubles, *Prokofii Liapunov*, two enormous epic poems (one based on the Bible, entitled *David*), and a survey of Europe's heroes by the eternal Jew, *Agasver* [Ahasuerus], was begun, and first drafted, in his prison cell. Kiukhel'beker's work could not be published, although in the 1830s Tsar Nicholas I permitted Pushkin to print some fragments anonymously.

Kiukhel'beker was widely known as a quixotic martyr. In 1836 he was released to live in exile in Siberia. Although he married a young, illiterate girl who bore him four children, he was unable to settle; looking after cattle, drying moss and other tasks vital to life as a Siberian exile were beyond him, especially after the crippling effects of prison. Unhappy in his love affairs, moving from one remote Siberian outpost to another, he did not develop as a poet; his style and subject-matter were frozen in his Lycée days. Although he wrote comic work (*Shekspirovy dukhi* [Shakespeare's Spirits]), his wit is heavy-handed. Despite his inclination for a heavy Slavonic rhetoric he could produce convincing speeches for his peasant characters, but he lacked interest in motivation and character. Likewise, his lyrical poetry suffers from a disinclination for introspection. He did however read and learn from his contemporaries in European Russia, being impressed primarily by their theme of the "superfluous man" and of a gratuitously tragic fate.

Kiukhel'beker's achievement however is as great as it is obscure: his diary, which he began in prison in 1831, is a critical gold mine; constantly revised, his mystery play *Izhorskii* takes the Onegin and Pechorin heroes of Pushkin and Lermontov as a model and finds a way of redeeming the outcast: *Izhorskii* is, in its most successful episodes, the first true Russian Faust, seeking freedom, and finding, despite a pact with the devil, redemption at the hands of the woman he has destroyed. Tuberculosis and blindness destroyed Kiukhel'beker, generating a handful of very fine bitter lyrics: "Uchast' russkikh poetov" [The Fate of Russian Poets] – "Bitter is the fate of poets of all tribes, Worst of all fate punishes Russia" – commemorates the deaths of Ryleev, Griboedov, Pushkin and Lermontov, as well as his own. Kiukhel'beker's collected work was first published in Weimar in 1880. Only after the Revolution, when Iurii Tynianov began several decades' work on his archive, and fictionalized his life (*Kiukhlia*), did Kiukhel'beker's importance become apparent. New works from the archive are still surfacing. His reputation would benefit from stringent selection: episodes from *Izhorskii* and *David*, a few critical paragraphs from his diaries and letters and a handful of late lyrics entitle him to equal status with others, such as Del'vig, in the Pushkin pleiad.

DONALD RAYFIELD

Nikolai Alekseevich Kliuev 1884–1937

Poet

Biography

Born in the Koshtug (Volgograd region), Olonets province, Siberia, 10 October 1884. Attended school in Vytegra for two years, one year in medical assistant school, Petrozavodsk. Entered Solovetskii Monastery, 1898; joined wandering sect in Riazan province, 1898. Twice imprisoned for religious and political views, 1906. Began to publish, 1904. Sectarian secret mission to Baku; may have travelled to Iran, India, and Central Asia, 1906–08. Returned to St Petersburg, 1911; participated in literary life. Acquainted with Ivanov, Remizov, Voloshin, Blok, and Esenin. First collection published, 1912. Informally associated with peasant poets (Klychkov, Esenin, and others); later sympathized with the Scythians. Expelled from Communist Party, 1920. Arrested for anti-Soviet and kulak propaganda, 2 February 1934; sentenced to five years' hard labour, commuted to exile in the Narym district, western Siberia. Wrote narrative poem *Kreml'* [Kremlin], glorifying the communist leaders, 1935; transferred to Tomsk; rearrested. Remainder of life spent in exile. Two versions of his death exist: either he died of a heart attack on his return to Moscow for reexamination of his case, or, more probably, was shot by the authorities, August 1937. Posthumously rehabilitated, 1957; republished in USSR, 1977.

Publications

Collected Editions

Polnoe sobranie sochinenii, 2 vols. New York, Izdatel'stvo imeni Chekhova, 1954.
Sochineniia, 2 vols. Munich, A. Neimanis, 1969.
Poems, translated by John Glad. Ann Arbor, Ardis, 1977.
Stikhotvoreniia i poemy. 3rd edition, "Biblioteka poeta, Malaia seria", Leningrad, 1977.
Izbrannoe: Stikhotvoreniia i poemy. Moscow, 1981.

Poetry

Sosen perezvon [Chimes of Firs], Moscow, 1911; 2nd edition, 1913.
Bratskie pesni [Brotherly Songs], 1–2. Moscow, 1912.
Lesnye byli [Forest Tales]. Moscow, 1912.
Lesnye byli. Kniga tret'ia [Forest Tales. Book 3]. Moscow, 1913.
Mirskie dumy [Worldly Thoughts]. Petrograd, 1916.

Mednyi kit [Bronze Whale]. Petrograd, 1919; reprinted Moscow, 1990.
Pesnoslov [Hymnologue], I–II. Petrograd, 1919; reprinted Petrozavodsk, 1990.
Pesn' solntsenostsa. Zemlia i zhelezo [The Song of the Sunbearer. Earth and Iron]. Berlin, Skify, 1920.
Izbianye pesni [Songs of a Peasant Hut]. Berlin, Skify, 1920; 2nd edition Berlin, 1922.
L'vinyi khleb [Lion's Bread]. Moscow and Berlin, 1922.
Chetvertyi Rim. Petrograd, 1922; reprinted Letchworth, Prideaux Press, 1974; translated as "The Fourth Rome", by John Glad, in *Poems*, 1977.
Mat'-Subbota. Petrograd, 1922; translated as "Mother Sabbath", by John Glad, in *Poems*, 1977.
Lenin. Moscow, 1924; excerpts translated by Bernard Meares, in *Twentieth Century Russian Poetry: Silver and Steel: An Anthology*, with an introduction by Yevgeny Yevtushenko, edited by Albert C. Todd, and Max Hayward. New York, Doubleday, and London, Fourth Estate, 1993, 118–19.
"Derevnia" [The Village], *Zvezda*, 1927.
Izba i pole [Hut and the Field]. Leningrad, 1928.
Pogorel'shchina. 1928; translated as "The Burned Ruins", by John Glad, in *Poems*, 1977.
Plach o Esenine. New York, Most, 1954; translated as "Lament for Esenin", by John Glad, in *Poems*, 1977.
"Pesn' o velikoi materi" [Song of the Great Mother], *Znamia*, 11 (1991), 3–44.
"Kain. Poema", *Nash sovremennik*, 1 (1993), 94–99.

Critical Studies

"Nikolai Kliuev: Materialy dlia biografii", by Boris Filippov, in Kliuev's *Sochineniia*, 1969, vol. 1, 5–183.
"Pogorel'shchina", by Boris Filippov, in Kliuev's *Sochineniia*, 1969, vol. 2, 113–41.
"Nikolai Klyuev: Some Biographical Materials", by Gordon McVay, in Kliuev's *Sochineniia*, 1969, vol. 1, 185–209.
"Nikolay Kluev", by Emmanuil Raikh, in Kliuev's *Sochineniia*, 1969, vol. 2, 51–112.
"Nikolaj Kljujew", by Heinrich A. Stammler, in Kliuev's *Sochineniia*, 1969, vol. 2, 7–50.
"N.A. Kluev: Unpublished Letters and Photographs", by Gordon McVay, *Russian Literature Triquarterly*, 4 (1972), 377–95.
"The Life and Works of Nikolay Klyuyev (1887–1937)", by Jessie Davies, *New Zealand Slavonic Journal*, 2 (1974), 65–75.
"Rannee tvorchestvo N.A. Klilueva", by Konstantin M. Azadovskii, *Russkaia literatura*, 3 (1975), 191–212.
"Poeziia N. Klilueva", by V.G. Bazanov, in *Stikhotvoreniia i poemy*, 3rd edition, Leningrad, 1977, 5–84.
"K simvolike krasnogo konia", by V.G. Bazanov, *Russkaia literatura*, 4 (1980), 21–33.
"Poema o drevnem Vyge", by V.G. Bazanov, *Russkaia literatura*, 4 (1980), 77–96.
"Olonetskii vedun. N. Kliuev", by Valerii Dement'ev, in *Slovo v russkoi poezii*, Moscow, 1980, 37–85.
"Nikolay Klyuev and Sergei Klychkov: Unpublished Texts", by Gordon McVay, *Oxford Slavonic Papers* (new series), 17 (1984), 90–108.
"Proza Nikolaia Klieva v gazetakh 'Zvezda Vytegry' i 'Trudovoe slovo' (1919–1921 gody). Voprosy stiliia i atributsii", by S.I. Subbotin, *Russkaia literatura*, 4 (1984), 136–50.
"Unpublished Texts of Nikolay Klyuyev", by Gordon McVay, *Slavonic and East European Review*, 63/4 (1985), 560–66.
"'Plach v roditel'skuiu subbotu' Nikolaia Klieva", by Konstantin M. Azadovskii, *Russkaia rech'*, 4 (1986), 17–24.
"Lichnost' i sud'ba Nikolaia Klieva", by Konstantin M. Azadovskii, *Neva*, 12 (1988), 177–88.
"Liricheskie novelly Klieva", by N.I. Nezhenets, in *Poeziia narodnykh traditsii*, Moscow, 1988, 7–48.
"Nikolai Kliuev v poslednie gody zhizni: pis'ma i dokumenty", by S. Subbotin, *Novyi mir*, 8 (1988), 165–201.
"Krov' moia ... sviazuet dve epokhi", by Iurii Khardikov, *Nash sovremennik*, 12 (1989), 179–89.
Nikolai Kliuev: Put' poeta, by Konstantin M. Azadovskii, Leningrad, 1990.
S rodnogo berega: O poezii Klieva, by V.G. Bazanov, Leningrad, 1990.
"Ot poezii 'izbianogo kosmosa' k pis'mam iz Sibiri", by A.M. Mikhailov, *Nash sovremennik*, 5 (1992), 141–52.
"Esenin i Kliuev (K istorii tvorcheskikh vzaimootnoshenii)", by S. Subbotin, in *O, Rus', vzmakhni kryliami: Eseninskii sbornik*, vyp. 1, Moscow, 1994, 104–20.
The KGB's Literary Archive, by Vitaly Shentalinsky, translated by John Crowfoot, London, Harvill Press, 1995.

Bibliography

Russkie sovetskie pisateli. Poety, vol. 11, Moscow, 1979.

Nikolai Kliuev's poetry made an impression on his contemporaries not only because of his enigmatic magnetism (there are two contrary views: "angel on earth" or "cunning peasant"), but also through his poetics. His poetry has its roots in Kol'tsov's folk orientation toward the word and stylization, but with greater sophistication. During the hot disputes of the Silver Age, he appeared as a messenger from the peasant Russia of the North, representing the ideal union between the people and the Russian land.

Despite his lack of formal education, he acquired enormous erudition and scholarly knowledge in folk culture: the poetry, religion, and art of the Russian people. He was born to educated, well-to-do peasant parents, both of whom were artistically gifted: his father was a great reader and a songwriter, and his mother was a professional mourner. She formally belonged to the Orthodox Church, but was oriented toward the spirituality and practices of the flagellant Khlyst sect of Old Believers. Kliuev's poetry reflects the folk traditions of the Russian North, especially the religious sectarians (the Khlysty, Skoptsy, and Beguny), saturated with biblical references. After joining the literary life of the Silver Age, his poetry underwent the influence of Symbolist poetics, but soon he regained his identity as a distinctive peasant poet, fusing both trends and thus constructing an enigmatic and highly stylized poetic world, a deliberate juxtaposition of the pure and the elaborate.

In 1907 he began to correspond with Blok, who helped him publish in the leading journals. True recognition came to him after the 1911 publication of his collection *Sosen perezvon* [Chimes of Firs], dedicated to Blok. This book already indicates his orientation to folk-poetry he collected. This tendency deepened in the subsequent collections *Bratskie pesni* [Brotherly Songs] and *Lesnye byli* [Forest Tales]. *Bratskie pesni* was conceived as a collection of sectant folk-poetry, but eventually turned into an artistic and prophetic recreation of the originals, evoking the spirituality of Golgotha and the Second Coming. Similarly, *Lesnye byli* are Kliuev's stylization of folk-songs, ballads, epic tales, laments, spiritual songs, ritual incantations, etc. The collection was met with hostility from the Left, and became emblematic for the SRs and Scythians. The following collection, *Mirskie dumy* [Worldly Thoughts], is written in the style of popular laments praising the Russian national identity during World War I. Kliuev's cosmology centres on the peasant hut as a natural continuation of the universe, uniting the folk motifs and traditions of past times with the present; the realia of peasant life, in harmony with nature, are zoomorphized and/or anthropomorphized.

At first Kliuev, like many other poets, greeted the Revolution ecstatically, but from the point of view of agrarian Messianism, seeing a parallel with the myth of Kitezh town (said to have been founded in 1168 during the invasion of Batu Khan and vanished under water, preserving the true faith to which only the elect could find their way); he even wrote some abominable poetry (the cycle *Lenin*) glorifying it.

Soon Kliuev was disillusioned by the Revolution, which betrayed and all but destroyed the peasantry, religion, and art; he developed an even stronger antagonism toward the city as a manifestation of the new order. He published in the journal *Skify* some of his masterpieces: *Izbianye pesni* [Songs of a Peasant Hut], *Pesn' solntsenostsa* [The Song of the Sunbearer], *Fevral'* [February]. These poems reflect his changing attitude toward the Revolution, accepting a Scythian outlook and marking his growing disagreements with Esenin.

Two polemical works appeared in 1922: *Chetvertyi Rim* (*The Fourth Rome*), with an epigraph from Esenin, and *L'vinyi khleb* [Lion's Bread]. *The Fourth Rome* is a neo-Slavophile manifesto, a reply to Ivanov-Razumnik's view that the Third International was the embodiment of the third Rome, and that there will be no fourth. Kliuev pours out his hope for a fourth Rome that will belong to the peasants. He also attacked Esenin for betraying the village and him by becoming a *citoyen*. In the latter work he turns to exotic topics. His collection *Mat'-Subbota* (*Mother Sabbath*) is a high-water mark in Russian poetry, a return to the symbolic old Russian word, centred on the earth-mystery and the hope of the resurrection after Golgotha, and glorifying the mother image.

His attitude toward the ongoing political upheavals became more and more hostile, bringing down upon him the wrath of the state. He was pronounced a kulak writer and criticized for his reactionary, anti-Soviet, and anti-revolutionary writings. He experienced increasing difficulties with censorship, which eventually resulted in all but his complete disappearance from print. During the 1920s he managed to publish a few volumes of new poetry, a two-volume edition of *Pesnoslov* [Hymnologue], and in 1926 his Collected Works. In 1927 his most expressedly anti-Soviet narrative poem *Derevnia* [The Village] appeared in the literary journal *Zvezda*; it resulted in more accusations of anti-Soviet views and, subsequently, the author's arrest, and the editorial staff's dismissal. Without publications or income, he recited his poetry at friends' homes, first in Leningrad, later in Moscow and in the provinces, where he would pass round the hat for donations. Despite the persecution and paucity of publications from the late 1920s, Kliuev's poetry reached a new plateau of artistic mastery.

In 1926 he appeared at a Esenin memorial, and a year later his *Plach o Esenine* (*Lament for Esenin*) appeared, but was quickly banned. It was written in one of his favourite folk genres, the lament. Laments for beloved relatives and friends build into a great all-embracing cry for the fading of poetic culture and the Russian spirit. The crowning work of this genre is the large narrative poem *Pogorel'shchina* (*The Burned Ruins*), which focuses on the idea that nature is higher than civilization, conveyed by the death of a mythical village, an ideal community in harmony with nature, as a result of the evil of the Revolution. Kliuev often read this poem in friendly circles, and word of it eventually reached the authorities, contributing to his arrest. His last collection published during his lifetime, *Izba i pole* [Hut and the Field], evoked hostile reactions.

Despite the hardship of everyday survival and his increasing health problems, Kliuev worked through this period with renewed spiritual strength and reached the summit of his *oeuvre*. At the time of his death, he was working on what was destined to become his most important poem, *Pesn' o velikoi materi* [Song of the Great Mother], but much of it has been lost forever.

Kliuev's poetry represents a miraculous combination of various stylistic elements, from the archaic to the modernistic. The most intriguing part of Kliuev's poetics is the correlation of literary and folk elements, the treatment of folk sources, the modification of his attempt to be the voice of the people by his refined literary culture. On the one hand, he stylized some of his own songs and tales in the spirit of original folk works, while on the other hand he made the original folk works more literary; often the two processes coexist within the same work. His highly ornate style utilizes a broad spectrum of poetic devices and metres. His poetry seems complicated because of the coded character of his imagery, which is unapproachable for those uninitiated in the sectarian and Orthodox traditions. His complex imagery and allusions, combining Christian and pagan traits, and his rich intertextuality, arising from quotations and paraphrases of folklore, biblical, religious, and literary texts, are expressed in language that dwells on the margins of Russian: dialectisms, archaisms, and his own nonce coinages based on these models. Thus, his poetry preserves from oblivion a significant layer of the vocabulary reflecting ancient Slavonic spirituality.

Kliuev is unquestionably one of the most intriguing and under-appreciated 20th-century poets, with a great talent for uniting ancient religious and folk traditions combined with a unique poetic voice veiled by manifold layers of cultural contexts and mannerisms.

MARIA PAVLOVSZKY

Iakov Borisovich Kniazhnin 1740–1791

Dramatist, poet, and translator

Biography

Born in Pskov, 14 October 1740. Son of the vice-governor of Pskov. Educated at home, until the age of 16; thereafter privately tutored in St Petersburg and at the Academy of Sciences gymnasium. Entered Ministry of Foreign Affairs, 1764. Noble status and rank (of captain) subsequently withdrawn through non-payment of debts and misappropriation of government funds. Re-appointed to civil service as secretary to Main Curator of Institutions of Education and Enlightenment, 1778. Elected to the Russian Academy, 1783. Died in St Petersburg, 25 January 1791.

Publications

Collected Editions

Sobranie sochinenii, 4 vols. St Petersburg, 1787; 3rd edition, 5 vols, St Petersburg, 1817–18.
Sochineniia, 2 vols. St Petersburg, 1847.
Izbrannye proizvedeniia. Leningrad, 1961.

Plays

Didona [Dido]. 1769.
Vladimir i Iaropolk. 1772.
Titovo miloserdie [The Clemency of Titus]. 1778.
"Neschast'e ot karety". 1779; also in *Russkaia komediia i komicheskaia opera XVIII veka*, Moscow and Leningrad, 1950; translated as "The Ill-Fated Coach", by J. Eyre, *Slavonic Review*, 22, 58 (1944); also as "Misfortune from a Coach", by Harold B. Segel, in *The Literature of 18th-Century Russia*, vol. 2, New York, Dutton, 1967.
Sbitenshchik [The Sbiten'-Seller]. 1783.
Rosslav. 1784.
Khvastun [The Boaster] (produced St Petersburg, 1785). 1786.
Sofonisba. c.1787.
Vadim Novgorodskii, tragediia v stikhakh [Vadim of Novogorod]. St Petersburg, 1793; reprinted with a foreword by P.A. Efremov, Moscow, 1871; with a foreword and full restoration of text by V. Sadovnik, Moscow, 1914.
Chudaki [The Eccentrics]. St Petersburg, 1793.

Translator

Genriada, geroicheskaia poema v desiati pesniakh [Henriade], by Voltaire, St Petersburg, 1777.
Smert' Pompeeva. Tsinna, ili Avgustovo miloserdie [The Death of Pompei. Tsinna or the Clemency of Augustus], by Pierre Corneille, St Petersburg, 1779.
Izbienie mladentsev, poema v chetyrekh pesniakh [Massacre of the Innocents], by D. Marino, Moscow, 1779.
Rodoguna, tragediia v 5-i deistviiakh, by Pierre Corneille, Moscow, 1778.

Critical Studies

"Kniazhnin – pisatel'", by V.Ia. Stoiunin, *Istoricheskii vestnik*, 7–8 (1881).
"Ia.B. Kniazhnin (1740–91]", by L.I. Kulakova, *Russkie dramaturgi XVIII–XIX vv.*, vol. 1, Moscow and Leningrad, 1959.
Introduction to *Kniazhnin, Ia.B. Izbrannye proizvedeniia*, by L.I. Kulakova, Leningrad, 1961.
The Literature of Eighteenth Century Russia, by Harold B. Segel, New York, Dutton, 1967.
A History of 18th Century Russian Literature, by William Edward Brown, Ann Arbor, Ardis, 1980.
Russian Drama from Its Beginnings to the Age of Pushkin, by Simon Karlinsky, Berkeley, University of California Press, 1985.

Iakov Kniazhnin has come down to us primarily as the author of monumental classical tragedies and as the translator of Voltaire's epic *Henriade*, upon which project he devoted most of his time from 1773 to 1778. At the same time he delighted theatre-goers and readers with lighter pieces, of a different genre, but as scrupulously observant of their canonical proprieties – comic play-writing, and sentimental verse after the manner, say, of the Swiss pastoralist Salomon Gessner, or his Russian *amateur* Nikolai Karamzin. In such lyrics one finds none of the tendentious didacticism of the day, but an agreeable, mild epicureanism that celebrates the individual's comfortable place among his fellows. Similarly, in his fables, Kniazhnin's attachment to the "moral" at the end is more a formal than a thematic point. Throughout the entirety of this verse (and the only form that seemed not to interest him was the odic), Kniazhnin's voice remains unassertive, accurate in point of detail and image. Chief among his models here would be Gresset.

France is also the inspiration for Kniazhnin's two famous comedies, *Khvastun* [The Boaster], and *Chudaki* [The Eccentrics], in which latter piece is detectable the background influence of Destouches's *L'Homme singulier*. The comedies are galleries of wanton types: gallomanes, fops, cunning servants, and so on. There is the occasional nod to Russian mores, but in essence these plays are comic intrigues à la Marivaux. Slightly greater concessions are found in Kniazhnin's comic-operatic output, of which the two most interesting examples are *Sbitenshchik* [The Sbiten'-Seller] and the highly successful *Neschast'e ot karety* (*Misfortune from a Coach*), the latter utilizing the Russian type of the "odnodvorets", or independent freeholder, to resolve the tension of the plot.

More impressively substantial is Kniazhnin's series of tragedies, which began in 1769 with *Didona* [Dido], the Virgilian theme already having been popularly reworked by French and Italian dramatists: Metastasio was uppermost in Kniazhnin's mind at the time. The native model for this and later tragedies was Sumarokov, presiding deity – as he saw it – of Russian classicism (and incidentally Kniazhnin's father-in-law), but Kniazhnin appeared more adept at creating psychologically flexible characters. Just as familiar on stage was the figure of the Roman emperor Titus: Kniazhnin's own *Titovo miloserdie* [The Clemency of Titus] was commissioned by Catherine II, and the result is duly panegyric, a hugely extravagant piece of Roman flummery, with a chorus, a ballet, a swarming cast of highlife and lowlife respectively to populate Senate and Forum – but through all this spectacular theatricality one descries genuinely new features of Russian stagecraft, in terms of detailed and descriptive stage directions and dressings, tight coherence of plot, and so forth. These and other tragedies from antique classical subjects may emphasize spectacle at the expense of proper classical civic-mindedness, but this will change strikingly as Kniazhnin's tragic style evolves, and his subjects become increasingly "Slavonic". In 1772, for example, Kniazhnin manages to work motifs from Racine's *Andromaque* into the Old Russian manuscript story of the murder by Prince Vladimir Sviatoslavich of his brother Iaropolk (*Vladimir i Iaropolk*). Henceforth in the plays the *raisonneur* comes into his own, the theme of absolutism looms even larger, and audiences are encouraged to understand that a nation's true heroes are its enlightened courtiers and grandees, advocating the national cause, putting checks on the monarchy, whose own paraded integrity, valiance, and patriotism may need to be called into question. Kniazhnin went on further to show what a writer of his time he was, investigating the relation of ruler with ruled, the definition of national identity, the wellsprings of historical change, of revolution; and the "narod" (the people) come to the fore as the earlier focus on the grandees diminishes. A tighter control of dramatic technique goes hand in hand with a more assured treatment of content and theme.

Kniazhnin's principal tragic work, *Vadim Novgorodskii* [Vadim of Novgorod], written in the months immediately prior to the French Revolution, exemplifies this type of inspiration. Here the ideological conflict between the republican (Vadim) and the monarchical (Rurik) is tricked out in an arena shorn of the spectacular indulgences of Kniazhnin's earlier work. Vadim, returning to Novgorod, is the archetypal "Roman-Russian" (the Gracchi, Cato, Brutus and the rest are all subsumed in him), and Rurik, a just father of the people, is no two-dimensional tyrant, but simply of necessity a hate-figure for the heroic Vadim because of the iniquitous role that he occupies. In the battle that is started by Vadim's crusading republicanism, Rurik is to emerge as victor, but at the expense of the moral high-ground that had meant so much to him as a "thinking" monarch. The kneeling populace of Novgorod implores Prince Rurik not to eschew the crown, and Vadim – the moral if not actual victor – is constrained to fall on his sword, having forced Rurik to justify himself and seek comradeship – rejected of course – with the unbowed and scornful republican.

In 1793, two years after Kniazhnin's death, the manuscript of the play was discovered among his papers and sold to a bookseller who printed and distributed it, a copy falling inevitably into the hands of Catherine II, who was appalled and terrified at the message that it intended, mindful as she was of the turbulence in France. The Empress commanded the piece to be burnt and immediately sought out for punishment Kniazhnin's offspring, the bookseller-printer (one Glazunov), and others who had had access to the piece. It was published in its full original form only in 1914, it was either omitted from earlier collections or altered.

NICHOLAS CROWE

Khvastun

The Boaster

Play, 1785

Traditionally, *Khvastun* has been set alongside Kniazhnin's two other important works of stage comedy – *Chudaki* and *Misfortune from a Coach* – to represent the author's "lighter" side, a breath of fresh air across the severe monumentality of his succession of verse-tragedies, with the implication that they were somehow less interesting than the tragic corpus. Since the first performance of *Khvastun*, however, in St Petersburg in 1785, and its publication as a text the following year, it has steadily accrued a fascination of its own. With some claim to being the first Russian five-act verse comedy, it has been revived more often than any other of Kniazhnin's plays, and decades of scholarly examination and popular delectation alike have re-presented it to the modern period as a witty and satirically engaging piece in its own right, more or less conventional in the forms of its expression in point of characters and plot, but thoroughly inseparable none the less from the French exemplars (in particular, Destouches's *Le Glorieux*), whose influence on Kniazhnin literary historians have long been at pains rather otiosely to demonstrate.

The psycho-social back-cloth to the piece would be quite familiar to the 18th-century theatre-going public. The verse-comedy is a satire, and that genre required certain criteria, ranged according to convention. We are in the familiar St Petersburg bourgeois town-house. We have a central character, the boaster Verkholet, in the grip of a ludicrous delusion, and a supporting cast of characters (whose plans are severely skewed by his obsession) that divides into the witty colluders and dupes, and the colourless moralists. (This latter group will of course win the war despite having lost all the battles). Cunning and verbally ingenious servants are on hand to provide a running commentary on the tightening and unravelling of the plot. Here the valet Polist has been helping his master Verkholet put it about that he is a man of substance, a *favorit* at court, who has been elevated to the rank of count with an estate "at Torzhok or Tver". Instantly intimations of toadying and base flattery switch us into satirical mode. This Verkholet swaggers about amusingly with a nemesis-inviting braggadocio that none will be slow to associate with the Gogolian Government Inspector. Although the agency of the comedy is farce, and a possibly slightly over-egged satire, it was perfectly possible for real-life Verkholets to exist and flourish under Catherine II's dispensation, and many a nobody did find himself fantastically ennobled in actual fact: for reasons of stagecraft Kniazhnin is careful at all points to narrow down the traditional type of the vacuous braggart, to make it weigh with the audience. Verkholet's imposture is believed in by his uncle Prostodum, who is expecting some financial "indulgence" from him, and by Mrs Chvankina, a wholesome but rather dim landowner who wants to make her daughter a countess by arranging a match with the *soi-disant* aristocrat. Plenty of the others want a slice of the cake too. In due course Verkholet is undone, but somewhat unusually for an 18th-century unmasking there is no real *deus ex machina*. Generally speaking a long-rusticated or newly wealthy uncle could be found to clear the obstacles and help love find a way, and the ideal candidate here would be Cheston, the father of love-lorn Zamir, and a feeble reflection of Fonvizin's wise old owl, Starodum. Verkholet, however, turns out to be the agent of his own undoing. He has been running up huge debts – the tangible analogue to the moral bankruptcy to which he has succumbed – and, lacking the wherewithal, he is carried off to prison. The comedy, as such, finishes here but if Kniazhnin intends us to take his fawning braggart as representative to any degree, then his serious point has been made.

In common with plays of its type *Khvastun* operates along lines of characterization that often conform rather predictably to type, in respect particularly of the "positive" characters, with their textbook platitudes about rational virtue. Yet the comedy is allowed to crackle away, and Verkholet, in thrall to an infelicitous humour, conforms splendidly to the Molièresque archetype of the obsessive monomaniac, whose fixed idea has led him into a type of stiff inhumanity. On a closer level of audience response, Kniazhnin makes Verkholet a toady at court in ways that they would understand. At a third level the play is roped directly into the circumstances of the time, the mid-1780s, with Catherine II as ruler. A specifically appreciable sort of ambition, calibrated by the "Table of Ranks", plays an important role. There is a reference (Act II, scene 4), cryptic and ill-intentioned, to the writer Nikolev, then claiming for himself primacy among poets. Allusions are made to players and skirmishes in the Turkish conflict, in which Verkholet lays bogus claim to having fought. Mention of the popular diversions of the day – card games, Polish minuets – knits the drama memorably together for the spectator.

Throughout it is important to be aware that in spite of these devices, and the concomitantly intentional involvement of audience with characters, Kniazhnin's purpose is more general than specific. Cheston, the civil servant of integrity, speaks of the attributes of the notional "ideal nobleman" (in speeches whose interest is gravely qualified by their length) but, indicating the lack of these people in the world, he draws attention to a fault in mankind, in life, rather than to the failings of this or that political or social system. The frame of reference is a deeply flawed Catherinian Russia but the playwright has it in mind to satirize the frailty of mankind rather than those temptations to the frailty of mankind which are held to be specifically Catherinian. The circumstances of the piece will lend it an assured piquancy, provoking as appropriate laughter, applause, and reflection, but what impels the comedy is human weakness: vanity, stupidity, cupidity.

A successfully Russianized comedy-drama of the "bourgeois" type, *Khvastun* enjoyed a great success, consolidated in the 19th century by, especially, the celebrated actors M.S. Shchepkin and I.I. Sosnitskii, who were able, by all accounts, to bring out the snappy and proverb-like quality of the play's best exchanges.

NICHOLAS CROWE

Aleksandra Mikhailovna Kollontai 1872–1952

Prose writer and politician

Biography

Born Aleksandra Mikhailovna Domontovich in St Petersburg, 31 March 1872. Studied literature; and for teaching certificate, tutored in literature by Viktor Ostrogorskii. Married: 1) Vladimir Ludvigovich Kollontai in 1893 (separated 1898), one son; 2) Pavel Dybenko in 1918 (separated 1922). Studied economics in Zurich, 1898; English workers' movement in London, 1899. Published first book and began propaganda work, 1903. Joined workers' procession to Winter Palace; met Lenin, 1905. Attended First All-Russia Women's Congress; accused of being member of Social-Democratic Party, fled to Germany to avoid arrest, 1908. Propaganda work in various western countries, 1909–12. Joined the Bolshevik Party, 1914. Anti-war tours to the US, 1915–16. Returned to Russia, organized workers' strikes in Petrograd, arrested by the Kerenskii government; elected member of Bolshevik Central Committee; People's Commissar for State Welfare, 1917. Director of Women's Department (Zhenotdel) of Central Committee, 1920; vice-president of International Women's Secretariat of Communist International, 1921. Threatened with expulsion from Party. Diplomatic service in Norway and Mexico, 1922–30. Recipient: Order of Lenin for organizational work with women, 1933. Negotiated peace with Finland, 1940. Nominated for the Nobel Peace Prize, 1945. Died in Moscow, 9 March 1952.

Publications

Collected Editions

Izbrannye stat'i i rechi. Moscow, 1972; translated as *Alexandra Kollontai: Marxisme et Révolution Sexuelle*, edited and translated by Judith Stora-Sandor, Paris, F. Maspero, 1973.

Selected Writings of Alexandra Kollontai, edited and translated by Alix Holt. London, Allison and Busby, and Westport, Connecticut, Hill, 1977.

Alexandra Kollontai: Selected Articles and Speeches, edited by Cynthia Carlile. New York, Progress, 1984.

Fiction

Liubov' pchel trudovykh (three narratives: *Liubov' trekh pokolenii* [The Love of Three Generations], *Sestry* [Sisters], *Vasilisa Malygina*). Petrograd, 1923; various Russian reprints; *Vasilisa Malygina* translated as *Red Love*, New

York, Seven Arts, 1927; also as *Free Love*, by C.J. Hogarth, London, Dent, 1932; *Sestry* and *Liubov' trekh pokolenii* (with *Bol'shaia liubov'*) translated as *A Great Love*, by Lily Lore, New York, Vanguard Press, 1929; reprinted Freeport, New York, Books for Libraries Press, 1971; three narratives translated in full as *Love of Worker Bees*, by Cathy Porter, London, Virago, 1977; Chicago, Academy Press, 1978.

Zhenshchina na perelome: psikhologicheskie etiudy [Woman at the Threshold: Some Psychological Studies] (three narratives: *Tridtsat'-dve stranitsy* [Thirty-Two Pages], *Podslushannyi razgovor* [Conversation Piece], *Bol'shaia liubov'* [A Great Love]). Moscow and Petrograd, 1923 (published as A.M. Domontovich); various Russian reprints; three narratives translated in full as *A Great Love*, by Cathy Porter, New York, Norton, and London, Virago, 1981.

Political Writing

Zhizn' finliandskikh rabochikh [The Life of Finland's Workers]. St Petersburg, 1903.

Finliandiia i sotsializm: sbornik statei [Finland and Socialism: A Collection of Articles]. St Petersburg, 1906.

Sotsial'nye osnovy zhenskogo voprosa. St Petersburg, 1909; excerpt translated as "The Social Basis of the Women's Question", by Alix Holt, in *Selected Writings of Alexandra Kollontai*, 1977).

Po rabochei evrope: siluety i eskizy [On Worker's Europe: Silhouettes and Studies]. St Petersburg, 1912.

Obshchestvo i materinstvo [Society and Motherhood]. Petrograd, 1916.

Novaia moral' i rabochii klass. Moscow, 1918 (contains: "Liubov' i novaia moral'", translated as "Love and the New Morality", by Alix Holt, in *Selected Writings of Alexandra Kollontai*, 1977; "Novaia zhenshchina", translated as "The New Woman", by Alix Holt, in *Selected Writings of Alexandra Kollontai*, 1977.

Sem'ia i kommunisticheskoe gosudarstvo. Moscow and Petrograd, 1918; translated as *Communism and the Family*, London, Workers' Socialist Federation, 1918; New York, Workers' Party, 1920.

"O 'Drakone' i 'Beloi ptitse'" *Molodaia gvardiia*, 1923; translated as "Of 'Dragon' and 'The White Bird'", by Alix Holt, in *Selected Writings of Alexandra Kollontai*, 1977.

"Dorogu krylatomu Erosu!", *Molodaia gvardiia*, 1923; translated as "Make Way for the Winged Eros!", by Alix Holt, in *Selected Writings of Alexandra Kollontai*, 1977.

Polozhenie zhenshchiny v evoliutsii khoziaistva [The Position of Women in the Evolution of the Economy]. Moscow, 1923; reprinted as *Trud zhenshchiny v evoliutsii khoziaistva* [Women's Labour in the Evolution of the Economy]. Moscow, 1926.

Memoirs

Iz moei zhizni i raboty: vospominaniia i dnevniki [From My Life and Work: Memoirs and Diaries]. Odessa, 1921; Moscow, 1974.

Otryvki iz dnevnika 1914 g. [Extracts from My 1914 Diary]. Leningrad, 1924.

"Ziel und Wert Meines Lebens", in *Fuhrende Frauen Europas*, edited by Elsa Kern, Munich, 1927; translated as *Autobiography of a Sexually Emancipated Woman*, by Salvator Attanasio, New York, Herder and Herder, 1971; reprinted, London, Orbach and Chambers, 1972.

Vospominaniia ob Il'iche [Memoirs of Il'ich]. Moscow, 1959.

Critical Studies

Revoliutsioner, tribun, diplomat: stranitsy zhizni Aleksandry Mikhailovny Kollontai, by Anna M. Itkina, Moscow, 1964; expanded edition, Moscow, 1970.

Bolshevik Feminist: The Life of Aleksandra Kollontai, by Barbara Evans Clements, Bloomington, Indiana University Press, 1979.

Aleksandra Kollontai: Socialism, Feminism, and the Bolshevik Revolution, by Beatrice Farnsworth, Stanford, Stanford University Press, 1980.

Alexandra Kollontai: The Lonely Struggle of the Woman who Defied Lenin, by Cathy Porter, London, Virago, and New York, Dial Press, 1980.

"The Political Function of Domestic Objects in the Fiction of Alexandra Kollontai", by Birgitta Ingemanson, *Slavic Review*, 48 (1989), 71–82.

Bibliography

"Alexandra Kollontai. Essai bibliographique", by Henryk Lenczyc, *Cahiers du monde russe et soviètique*, 14 (1973), 205–41.

Aleksandra Kollontai – the only woman member of Lenin's Central Committee, a career diplomat throughout Europe and the Americas, and a tireless political organizer and polemicist for the emancipation of both women and the working class – wrote, in mid-life, six works of fiction that allowed her to address issues she also explored in her lectures, political activism, and non-fictional works. These issues were the view that marriage must be separate from economics; the vision of lovers united by shared ideals and shared political work; the conflict many women experience between their craving for love and their passion for work; the danger of sexual possessiveness; and the intimate connection between psychological and political freedom.

She first experimented with fiction in her twenties; as a young mother feeling trapped at home, she wrote a story about a woman who left her husband (as she herself was later to do, to study Marxist economics in Zurich). When the story was rejected as propaganda, and when even a supportive friend implied that the story was in fact an article masquerading as literature, she vowed never to write fiction again. In her subsequent voluminous writing, she continued to deal with women's issues, which she integrated into her treatment of class issues. She was opposed to middle-class women's movements that attempted to deal with women's emancipation without regard for the context of class; she was equally opposed to political allies (whether among the Mensheviks, the Bolsheviks, or the Workers' Opposition) who considered women's oppression a minor question to be dealt with, if at all, only later. In various works and speeches she advocated freedom, honesty, and justice in economic and family life. At times, she used literature as a point of reference and cultural barometer. In *Novaia zhenshchina* (*The New Woman*), for example, she presented a galaxy of fictional characters (drawn from contemporary Russian, French, German, British, and American novels) who exemplified the self-sufficient woman. In O *"Drakone" i "Beloi Ptitse"* (*Of "Dragon" and "The White*

Bird"), she praised the poetry of Anna Akhmatova for the seriousness with which the poet approaches women's self-consciousness and the need for work; Kollontai invites her readers to create a society in which the conflicts Akhmatova evokes would be less wrenching.

Kollontai's six fictional works were published in 1923, and were designed to make her ideas accessible to working women (her target audience). As she explained in *The New Woman*, she saw realism, not romanticism, as the appropriate mode for this material. Varying in length from four pages to about 100, the stories deal with women's suffering in their love relationships as they try to pursue professional goals, while loving men whose affection and understanding are at best sporadic.

The first collection – *Liubov' pchel trudovykh* (*Love of Worker Bees*) – consists of the novella *Vasilisa Malygina* and two stories, "Liubov' trekh pokolenii" ("Three Generations") and "Sestry" ("Sisters"). The heroine of *Vasilisa Malygina*, who met her husband during the invigorating turmoil of 1905, finds that she enjoys her independent political work and her efforts to set up a communal home much more than a pampered existence as the wife of an attractive man who is politically inconsistent, emotionally deceptive, and sexually unfaithful. After tolerating, reinterpreting, and excusing numerous acts of political recklessness and marital infidelity, she ultimately leaves him, gives her blessing to him and his young mistress, and returns to her work. Learning that she is pregnant, she looks forward to raising a thoroughly communist baby, and faces the future with energy and hope.

In "Three Generations" and "Sisters", women in crisis tell their stories to an unnamed first-person narrator (apparently a woman); they and the narrator see the dilemmas here as characteristic of the age. "Three Generations" deals with women's difficulties not only in negotiating their relationships with men, but with comprehending and assessing the choices other women make. Maria, who left her husband and bore a daughter to a man she passionately loves, was herself not a slave to convention, and chose love over custom and law; none the less, she is puzzled by her daughter Ol'ga's wish to maintain simultaneously (or, at any rate, antiphonally) relationships with both the husband who offers her intellectual comradeship and political compatibility and the lover who inspires her passion. And Ol'ga, in turn, is bewildered by her daughter Zhenia's sexual relationships, which are not only multiple, but apparently loveless. The central character, Ol'ga, is curious and troubled; the story offers no resolution. In "Sisters", a woman has left her husband – formerly a political comrade, now corrupted by his life as a NEP-man – not only because she has contempt for his shallow avarice, and because he brought home a prostitute, but because she resents his callous treatment of that prostitute, a woman whom she sees as a sister – worthy of sympathy and respect – and as a portent of her own fate.

The second collection – *Zhenshchina na perelome: psikhologicheskie etiudy* [Woman at the Threshold: Some Psychological Studies] – includes the novella *Bol'shaia liubov'* (*A Great Love*) and two sketches, "Tridtsat'-dve stranitsy" ("Thirty-Two Pages") and "Podslushannyi Razgovor" ("Conversation Piece"). In *A Great Love*, the heroine reflects – after what turns out to be her penultimate parting from her married lover, a leading political activist – on his insensitivity to her feelings, his lack of consideration for her ideas and work, and the abiding affection that had led her to disregard his flaws. The novella then presents a reunion of the lovers, which provides abundant examples of his limitations; at the end, she parts from him again, and this time with serenity, self-confidence, and self-possession. In "Thirty-Two Pages" the heroine prepares to tell her husband that she cannot continue leaving her library and her scientific thesis in order to visit him in the factory town; at the end, as he tries to convince her to move in with him, she is unable to refuse. Although the story has shown her love for her work and her belief that she cannot have both her work and her love, the ending is elliptical. "Conversation Piece" echoes a situation from "Three Generations"; the heroine, at a train station, is ending a relationship with her lover in order to rejoin her husband, an intellectual comrade. At the end, although the two figures "disappear in the crowd", the heroine has explicitly resolved to leave her lover for ever.

Contemporary Russian responses to Kollontai's fiction typically condemned what was seen as an unwholesome preoccupation with sexual matters. Reviewers assumed that Kollontai intended to endorse the sexual promiscuity of Zhenia in "Three Generations" – although the story itself dwells more on the mother's pain than on the daughter's policies, and Zhenia herself attributes the lack of love and passion in her sexual encounters to a lack of time. *A Great Love* was seen as primarily a *roman à clef* regarding Lenin, his wife Nadezhda Krupskaia, and Inessa Armand; *Vasilisa Malygina* was read as a semi-autobiographical account of Kollontai's marriage with Pavel Dybenko. In the 1970s and 1980s, however, Kollontai's fiction and non-fiction have been republished, in Russian and in translation. Recent readers, in Russia and abroad, have valued Kollontai's fiction as matching her own prescription, in *The New Woman*, for a "spiritual image" of the modern woman, "with all her migraines, her struggles, her problems, her contradictions, her complexity, and her aspirations ... ".

SHOSHANA MILGRAM KNAPP

Aleksei Vasil'evich Kol'tsov 1809–1842

Poet

Biography

Born in Voronezh, 15 October 1809, one of 18 children of a cattle dealer. Educated at home; later attended a local school, 1820. Frequently accompanied father on business trips; Kol'tsov only completed one class at school. Wrote his first poem "Tri videniia" [Three Visions] (now lost) in 1825, but followed father into cattle-dealing trade. Love affair with Duniasha, one of his father's serfs, 1827–28; to obviate an "unequal" marriage, Duniasha and her mother were sold. First poems published anonymously, 1830. Met N.V. Stankevich, 1830. Visited Moscow for first time, 1831; met Belinskii. Only collection of verse published in Kol'tsov's lifetime appeared with help of Stankevich and Belinskii. Visited both Moscow and St Petersburg; met many leading literary figures, including Pushkin, 1836. Further visits, 1838 and 1840. During last years of his life, affair with V.G. Lebedeva alienated him from his family. Died of consumption in Voronezh, 10 November 1842.

Publications

Collected Editions

The Complete Poems of Aleksey Vasil'evich Kol'tsov, translated by C.P.L. Dennis. London, 1922.
Polnoe sobranie stikhotvorenii. Moscow, 1958.
Sochineniia, 2 vols. Moscow, 1961.

Critical Studies

"Aleksei Kol'tsov. A Peasant Poet", by C. Manning, *Slavonic and East European Review*, 18 (1939), 175–83.
A.V. Kol'tsov: Zhizn' i tvorchestvo, by V.A. Tonkov, Voronezh, 1953.
"O zhizni i sochineniiakh Kol'tsova", by V.G. Belinskii, in his *Polnoe sobranie sochinenii*, vol. 9, Moscow, 1955, 497–542.
A.V. Kol'tsov: Kritiko-biograficheskii ocherk, by A.A. Moiseeva, Moscow, 1956.
"The Trochaic Song Metres of Kol'tsov and Kashin", by J. Bailey, *Russian Literature*, 12 (1975), 5–28.
Poeziia Alekseia Kol'tsova, by N. Skatov, Leningrad, 1977.
"Aleksei Kol'tsov", by William Edward Brown, in his *A History of Russian Literature of the Romantic Period*, Ann Arbor, Ardis, 1986, vol. 4, 82–96.

It has become customary to follow Vissarion Belinskii and to divide Aleksei Kol'tsov's work into three groups. The first, written in traditional syllabo-accentual metres, mostly iambic and trochaic, consists of sentimental, mostly derivative poetry, much influenced by, among many others, Bogdanovich, Lomonosov, Derzhavin, and Zhukovskii. The second group consists of his celebrated "songs" (*pesni*) and the third of his philosophical "meditations" (*dumy*). The three groups coincide partially, though not entirely, with the three main periods of Kol'tsov's life: 1825–30; 1831–36, and 1837–42. The first and last of these groups can be dealt with fairly briefly. To the first group belong such poems as "Razuverenie" [Dissuasion] (1828), "Sirota" [The Orphan] (1827), and "Zemnoe schast'e" [Earthly Happiness] (1830). The "songs" of his second period are much more distinctive and ensure for Kol'tsov a unique place in the history of Russian literature to the extent that some have even referred to him as the "Russian Robert Burns". The "songs" are, in reality, artificial folk-songs, a genre that has its origin in the 18th century and whose talented exponents hitherto had been Nikolai Tsyganov, Ivan Kozlov and, especially, Anton Del'vig. The work of this period is written in folkloric accentual metres, where the number of syllables between stresses is variable. Most genuine folk poetry employs a two-stress line. So, on frequent occasions, does Kol'tsov. On other occasions, however, he uses a three-stress accentual line that has no counterpart in genuine folk poetry.

Kol'tsov makes use of archaic expressions and folksy vocabulary. Some early poems, notably "Povest' moei zhizni" [Story of My Life] (1829–30), are full of regionalisms not found beyond the Voronezh area. Kol'tsov had begun to develop his distinctive voice as early as 1828 as can be shown by a comparison of the first draft and the final version of his poem "Putnik" [The Wayfarer] (1828). Whereas the draft is in conventional literary language, with the wayfarer riding on a "steed" (*kon'*), the final version has a more prosaic ring to it, with the wayfarer now seated on "his thin, tired old nag" ("na svoei / Kliachonke toshchei i ustaloi").

By 1830 Kol'tsov had found his own distinctive voice in such "songs" as "Kol'tso" [The Ring] and "Krest'ianskaia pirushka" [A Peasants' Carouse]. The latter poem is, like many of the songs, unrhymed. Apart from its metre, it has other features typical of the literary folk-song: repeated prepositions and truncated adjectival forms, repeated lines, diminutives (*starinushka*), alliteration and assonance, and a judicious scattering of colourful regionalisms such as *gorenka* (room) and *gutorit'* (to resound). This poem was described by D.S. Mirsky as "almost Homeric in the simple, unsentimentalized stateliness with which he endows simple life". His vocabulary draws heavily on the speech of those whom Kol'tsov encountered in his travels as a cattle-dealer in the steppe region. He omitted, however, the large number of obscenities he discovered in a study of folklore made at the suggestion of Kraevskii and Zhukovskii and remained ambiguous in his attitude to non-literary folk-songs. Nevertheless there is a hard-edged concreteness to his vocabulary and his songs, which lack the sentimentality and stylization of earlier attempts at the genre, mark a sharp break with the 18th-century pastoral idyll. Among the best are "Pesnia pakharia" [The Song of the Ploughman] (1831), which became so popular that it inspired popular woodcuts (*lubochnye kartiny*), "Urozhai" [Harvest] (1835), and "Kosar'" [The Reaper] (1836). In these poems the harshness of peasant life is accepted with a stoicism rooted in the simple Christian beliefs of the peasant. Its manifestations include the forced separation of couples, arranged marriages, poverty, indeed everything that can be subsumed in the expressive Russian word *gore* (woe). This, in fact, is the title of one song written in 1839. Kol'tsov places women at the centre of several of his poems. In one, the song beginning "Akh, zachem menia ..." [Why did they marry me against my will to an old man I did not love?] (1839), the theme is stated at the outset and the song is sung by the girl herself. In another, "Molodaia zhnitsa" [The Young Girl Reaping] (1832), the story of the girl toiling in the fields and pining for her unfaithful lover is told in the third person. His meditations, on the other hand, are written in conventional syllabo-accentual metre. Thematically some reflect Schellingian ideas that Kol'tsov had absorbed through his contacts with the Stankevich circle, while others show the influence of Belinskii and V.F. Odoevskii. "Les" [The Forest] (1837), was inspired by Pushkin's death while "Poslanie" [Epistle] (1839), and "Raschet s zhizn'iu" [Reckoning with Life] (1840) were dedicated to Belinskii, who had become a personal friend. Kol'tsov's letters to Belinskii are remarkably frank and shed much light on the spiritual suffering of a man unable to escape from the dominating influence of his father. "My world is narrow and filthy", he wrote in 1840. "It's a bitter thing to have to live in it". Equally, Belinskii's article "O zhizni i sochineniiakh Kol'tsova" [On the Life and Works of Kol'tsov] (1846), remains the most important account of the poet.

Kol'tsov's influence was considerable. Grigorovich was influenced by him in writing his seminal "peasant" story *Derevnia* [The Village] (1846), as was N.A. Nekrasov in his long poem *Komu na Rusi zhit' khorosho?* (*Who Can Be Happy and Free in Russia?*). In the 20th century both Maiakovskii and Esenin wrote poems in the manner of Kol'tsov's songs. He remains, however, virtually ignored by western critics.

MICHAEL PURSGLOVE

Ivan Konevskoi 1877–1901
Poet

Biography

Born Ivan Ivanovich Oreus in St Petersburg, 1 October 1877, the only child of military gentry family. Began to write between the age of ten and 12. Attended the First St Petersburg gymnasium, until 1896; studied at the faculty of history and philology, St Petersburg University, 1896–1901. First publication, 1896. Died by accidental drowning in the Baltic region, 21 July 1901.

Publications

Collected Editions

Mechty i dumy [Dreams and Meditations]. St Petersburg, 1900; reprinted, Berkeley, Berkeley Slavic Specialties, 1989.
Stikhi i proza, edited by Valerii Briusov. Moscow, 1904; reprinted as *Sobranie sochinenii*, edited by Dmitrij Tschizewskij, Munich, Fink, 1971.

Poetry

"Ot solntsa k solntsu" [From Sun to Sun] (16 lyrics), in *Kniga razdumii*, by K.D. Bal'mont, Valerii Briusov, Modest Durnov, Iv. Konevskoi, St Petersburg, 1899, 55–82.

Literary Criticism

"Ob otpevanii novoi russkoi poezii" [On the Burial of New Russian Poetry], in *Severnye tsvety na 1901*, 180–88; reprinted in *Mechty i dumy*, 1989.
"Mirovozzrenie poezii N.F. Shcherbiny" [World Outlook in the Poetry of N.F. Shcherbina], in *Severnye tsvety na 1902*, 194–214; reprinted in *Mechty i dumy*, 1989.

Letters

"Ivan Konevskoi: Pis'ma k Vl.V. Gippiusu", published by I.G. Iampol'skii, *Ezhegodnik rukopis'nogo otdela pushkinskogo doma n 1977 god*, 79–98.
"Perepiska s Iv. Konevskim (1898–1901)", edited by A.V. Lavrov, V.Ia. Morderer, A.E. Parnis, in *Literaturnoe nasledstvo*, "Valerii Briusov i ego korrespondenty", 98, 2 vols, part 1, Moscow, 1991, 424–554.

Critical Studies

"Mudroe ditia", (1901, with addendum 1910) by Valerii Briusov, in his *Sobranie sochinenii*, 7 vols, Moscow 1973–75, vol. 6.
"Iv. Konevskoi", by N.O. Lerner, in *Poety simvolizma*, edited by Modest Gofman, St Petersburg, 1908; reprinted, Munich, Fink, 1970.
"Ivan Konevskoi", by N.O. Lerner, in *Russkaia literatura XX veka*, edited by S.A. Vengerov, III, Moscow, 1916, 150–63.
"Ivan Konevskoi (Oreus) 1877–1901", by Sergei Makovskii, in *Na parnasse "serebrianogo veka"*, Munich, Fink, 1962, 177–94.
"Blok i Ivan Konevskoi", by V.Ia. Morderer, in *Literaturnoe nasledstvo*, "Aleksandr Blok: Novye materialy i issledovaniia", 92, 5 vols, Moscow, 1987, vol. 4, 151–78.
"A Forerunner of Russian Modernism: Ivan Konevskoy", by Avril Pyman, *Scottish Slavonic Review*, 14 (Spring 1990), 5–19.
"Ivan Konevskoi: *Bogatyr* of Russian Symbolism", by Joan Delaney Grossman, in *The Silver Age in Russian Literature*, edited by John Elsworth, London, Macmillan, and New York, St Martin's Press, 1992, 1–10.

Ivan Konevskoi's poetry, largely forgotten for much of the 20th century, is now recognized as a significant addition to the poetic corpus of Symbolism. Moreover, his extremely brief literary career offers valuable insights into the first formative years of that movement, as well as the cultural ethos from which it sprang. Initially mythologized as the young genius who perished in the birth-struggle of a new era, Konevskoi was indeed one of the very first Russian poets to be deeply acquainted with French Symbolism, English Pre-Raphaelite poetry and painting, Scandinavian drama, and modern German thought. Pantheist, mystic, philosophical individualist, he and his work do not fit perfectly into later conceptions of either Symbolism or Decadence. Perhaps partly for this reason, his poetry resonated beyond Symbolism in the writings of Gumilev, Mandel'shtam, Pasternak, and other modernists.

Konevskoi belonged to the philosophical – he would have said "mystical" – current in Russian poetry, with strong links to Tiutchev, Fet, Solov'ev, A.K. Tolstoi, Kol'tsov (less to Baratynskii). His committed belief in pantheism found nourishment in these, as well as in Goethe and in the English Romantic poets, most of all Shelley. He also enthusiastically imbibed the dynamic, eclectic philosophical ethos of the 1890s, where renewed interest in Spinoza and certain trends within neo-Kantianism made pantheism and panpsychism widely held views. For Ivan Konevskoi and for some others of his generation, pantheism appeared an essential means to penetrating secrets of the universe to which science could give only limited access. This was the goal of his poetry and, in his view, of all contemporary and future art.

Like other Symbolists-to-be, Konevskoi encountered the "new art" and the "new ideas" in the early 1890s through journals like *Severnyi vestnik* and *Vestnik Evropy*. The extensive reading, of which he kept careful notebook records from 1894 to 1901, took him much further. By social position and education Konevskoi was close to St Petersburg cultural life and the beginnings of St Petersburg Symbolism, but youth, personal awkwardness, and a relatively isolated existence set him apart. His life's epochal events were solitary journeys in the summers of 1897 and 1898 to western Europe – Austria, Germany, Switzerland and the Italian Alps. Sailing up the Rhine, viewing the Swiss artist Arnold Boecklin's paintings in Munich and Basel, hearing Wagner at Bayreuth: it was the typical tour for young Russians at that time (compare the artist Aleksandr Benois's memoirs), enhanced by a profound mystical experience in the mountains of Thuringia. He returned a Decadent poet. *Mechty i dumy* [Dreams and Meditations] (1900), was the record of this journey.

At Fedor Sologub's "evening" in St Petersburg in December 1898 Valerii Briusov and Konstantin Bal'mont heard Konevskoi read his poetry. Their enthusiastic reaction led to a small collection *Kniga razdumii* [Book of Reflections], to which those three and the artist Modest Durnov contributed. (Briusov observed that Sologub and Zinaida Hippius withdrew rather than appear with him and Konevskoi). The link between the two poets was important to both. In his autobiography Briusov credited Konevskoi with showing him the genuinely Symbolist, philosophical meaning of a poetic work.

Konevskoi's debt to Briusov took a different form. Shortly after his death, Briusov set out to publish Konevskoi's original writings and translations in full. The 1904 "Scorpio" edition of *Stikhi i proza* [Poems and Prose] was the result, though the translations (ranging from Swinburne and Verhaeren to Nietzsche) were ultimately omitted. In addition, Briusov made great efforts to insure that Konevskoi's poems were given the serious attention he believed they deserved, particularly from other Symbolists. Viacheslav Ivanov and Aleksandr Blok both undertook to review *Stikhi i proza*, though only Blok wrote about Konevskoi, and that was in a review of another work. Konevskoi's poetry did not blend with the dominant mood of Symbolism at that time, when its theurgic wing, led by Andrei Belyi, Blok, and Ivanov was on the rise.

In the rapidly developing world view of Symbolism, Konevskoi, it must be noted, remained a Decadent. Briusov wrote in his memorial essay "Mudroe ditia" [Wise Child], that, like all his fellow practitioners of the new art, Konevskoi sought two things: "freedom and power (*sily*)". However, where others sought these in transgressing all limits, "Konevskoi took the matter deeper", questioning the essence of human nature. Like Briusov, he believed in the supreme freedom of the human personality – a belief that came, not from Nietzsche, but perhaps from similar ground.

It was surely his attitude toward language that most drew later poetic innovators to Konevskoi. Rejecting aestheticization of poetic language and form, he turned to the earlier, classical tradition, at the same time revising it and forcing it to bear the weight of his thought.

Konevskoi left considerable critical and philosophical prose in manuscript, some fragmentary or incomplete, most of it found in the Russian State Archive of Literature and Art. In the 1930s N.L. Stepanov prepared a two-volume complete edition of his work for the series "Biblioteka poeta". That manuscript perished with the series' archive in the Leningrad blockade. Recent efforts to republish Konevskoi have so far not succeeded.

Most of Konevskoi's published writings are found in the two volumes of poetry and prose *Mechty i dumy* and *Stikhi i proza*. Despite considerable overlap, the two books function differently in their author's literary heritage. *Mechty i dumy*, poetry and essays of 1896–99, was Konevskoi's personal diary of discovery of self and the world. The arrangement is loosely thematic, not chronological. In Briusov's skilled hands the idiosyncratic personal record became part of a scholarly edition, with two forewords: a biographical sketch by Konevskoi's father (unsigned) and Briusov's essay "Mudroe ditia", revised from its first appearance in *Mir iskusstva*. Poems and prose are separated, dated, chronologically arranged, and annotated (oddly, the prose selections are omitted from the table of contents). In Briusov's edition, the emphasis has shifted from youthful explorer to mature poet. *Mechty i dumy* remains a revealing document, but the posthumous edition remains so far the main text for reading and studying Konevskoi the poet and the man.

JOAN DELANEY GROSSMAN

Vladimir Galaktionovich Korolenko 1853–1921

Prose writer

Biography

Born in Zhitomir, 27 August 1853. Attended gymnasium, until 1871; St Petersburg Technological Institute; did not graduate because of family commitments. Moved to Moscow to study at Petrov Academy of Agriculture and Forestry, 1874. Arrested for association with Populists and exiled to Kronstadt, 1876. Because of Populist militancy Korolenko and his elder brother were exiled to Glazov in Viatka province, 1879. Began his writing career in 1879. After refusing to sign an oath of allegiance to Alexander III, was exiled to East Siberia, 1881. Spent next three years in Amga region, 1881–84. After exile chose to live in Nizhnii Novgorod and became active as a journalist. Married: Evdokiia Semenovna in 1886; three daughters. Preoccupied with the famine in Lukianov district, Nizhnii Novgorod, 1892. As correspondent for *Russkie vedomosti*, visited Chicago World's Fair, via Europe, 1893. Involvement with *Russkoe bogatstvo* took him to St Petersburg in 1896; moved to Poltava, 1900. Elected to the Academy of Writers, from which he resigned in protest. Began writing his autobiography in 1905. Continued to write about social injustices. Died on 25 December 1921. Given a civic funeral.

Publications

Collected Editions

Polnoe sobranie sochinenii, 11 vols. St Petersburg/ Petrograd, 1914.

Makar's Dream and Other Stories, translated by Marian Fell. New York, Duffield, 1916.

Birds of Heaven and Other Stories, translated by Clarence A. Manning. New York, Duffield, 1919.

Sobranie sochinenii, 10 vols. Moscow, 1956.

Selected Stories [no translator named]. Moscow, Progress, 1978.

Autobiography

Istoriia moego sovremennika. St Petersburg, 1906–22; translated as *The History of My Contemporary*, by Neil Parsons, London, Oxford University Press, 1972.

Critical Studies

V.G. Korolenko kak chelovek i pisatel', by F.D. Batushkov, Moscow, 1922.

"V.G. Korolenko i ego khudozhestvennyi metod", by S.M. Gorodetskii, *Nashi dni*, 11 (1922), 335–49.

V.G. Korolenko: zhizn' i tvorchestvo, edited by A.B. Petrishchev, Petrograd, 1922.

"V.G. Korolenko", by A.B. Derman, *Russkaia mysl'*, 12 (1925), 1–24.

V.G. Korolenko, by G.A. Bialyi, Moscow, 1949.

"V.G. Korolenko (1853–1921): A Centennial Appreciation", by R.F. Christian, *Slavonic and East European Review*, 22, (1953–54), 449–63.

Sibirskie rasskazy V.G. Korolenko, by L.S. Kulik, Kiev, 1961.

Korolenko, by G. Mironov, Moscow, 1962.

"Korolenko's Stories of Siberia", by Lauren G. Leighton, *Slavonic and East European Review*, 49 (1971), 200–13.

"Elements of Light in the Fiction of Korolenko", by Natalia M. Kolb-Seletski, *Slavic and East European Journal*, 16 (1972), 173–83.

"Nature Descriptions and Their Function in Korolenko's Stories", by Victoria Babenko, *Canadian Slavonic Papers*, 16 (1974), 424–35.

Vladimir G. Korolenko: 1853–1921. L'homme et l'oeuvre, 2 vols, by Maurice Comtet, Lille, Université Lille III, 1975.

"Harmonious Composition: Korolenko's Siberian Stories", by R. Balasubramanian, *Rocky Mountain Review*, 44/4 (1990), 201–10.

The Poetics of Korolenko's Fiction, by Radha Balasubramanian, New York, Peter Lang, 1997.

Bibliographies

V.G. Korolenko, Opyt biograficheskoi kharakteristiki, by N. Shakhovskaia, Moscow, 1912, 167–85.

"Bibliograficheskii ukazatel' proizvedenii V.G. Korolenko i literatury o nem", in *Zhizn' i tvorchestvo V.G. Korolenko, Sbornik stat'ei i rechei k 65-emu iubeleiu*, by V.S. Vengerov, Petrograd, 1918, 98–140.

Istoriia russkoi literatury kontsa XIX–XX veka. Bibliograficheskii ukazatel', edited by K.D. Muratov, Moscow and Leningrad, 1963, 261–71.

Vladimir Galaktionovich Korolenko is well known not only as a publicist and a humanitarian, but also as a writer. His voluminous publicistic writing, based on his service to the people, championed truth and justice. It ranges from exposing activities of the local gentry in their manipulation of the city's bank, court, and local *zemstvo*, to condemning the revolutionaries openly, after they took over power, for not complying with the law and for forcing changes too rapidly. The help he rendered to the people in Lukianov province, Nizhnii Novgorod, during the famine of 1892, and their pathetic plight were described in articles and later compiled in book form and reprinted several times as, *V golodnyi god* [In the Year of Famine]. In 1896, along with Mikhailovskii, he was designated the "publisher" of *Russkoe bogatstvo*. At the same time Korolenko became involved in the "Udmurts case" and took over the defence of the Udmurts who were sentenced for a ritual murder. His triumphant ordeal was later published in the report "Multanskoe zhertvoprinoshenie" [Multan's Sacrifice]. Korolenko condemns the persecution of the Jews in works like "Pavlovskie ocherki" [The Essays about Pavlovo], "Dom No. 13" [House No. 13], and others. The ineffectiveness of the first Duma in carrying out legislation is bitterly described by Korolenko in his article "Bytovoe iavlenie" [An Everyday Occurrence]. Against doctor's advice Korolenko participated in Beilis's trial and saved Beilis's life after a guilty verdict. The ordeal is published as "Delo Beilisa" [The Case of Beilis]. Just before his death Korolenko wrote six letters to Lunacharskii, Minister of Education, about economic, social, and political problems. But they were not published in Russia until the policy of glasnost was adopted in the 1980s.

As a writer of fiction, Korolenko's contribution to Russian narrative prose is in the form of short stories. Korolenko has three different types of stories: (1) stories from actual memories and facts that can be easily discerned as fiction by their subtle artistic devices; (2) imaginative, artistic stories (legends and fairy-tales) that are unmistakably fiction; and (3) travelogues and essay-type sketches.

Korolenko's popularity as a writer of fiction is based on the first group (stories from actual memories and facts), which includes the Siberian stories. "Son Makara" ("Makar's Dream") 1885, which is the most famous of them, portrays an inarticulate hero, Makar, who is perceived as representing a typical Russian peasant reduced to a primitive state of hardship, exploitation, and oppression. "Sokolinets" [The Falconer] (1885), Chekhov's favourite story, is taken from a tale about escaped prisoners from Amga. The symbolic use of light and darkness corresponds to the mental state of the characters and adds to the poetic quality of this story.

The relationship between the people and the intelligentsia becomes a very important problem in such stories as "Chudnaia" [The Strange One] (1905), "Moroz" [The Frost] (1901), and "Fedor Bespriiutnyi" [Fedor the Homeless] (1885). The interaction between the first-person narrator and the people of different strata creates an opportunity to understand them and decide about their aspirations, motives, and dreams. Thus the narrator's relationship (or a character's who is similar to the narrator) to another person in the story becomes itself a theme of Korolenko's Siberian stories. His main concern is to reveal the totality of human beings – their strengths and weaknesses. He achieves mastery by combining nature and time to suit the characters' moods, actions, and thoughts. His short stories unravel spatially rather than temporally – that is, juxtaposition of episodes in a moment of time takes precedence over sequential presentation. It is as though the very volatility of the characters' present situation helps disclose a moment of decision from their past.

Korolenko wrote *Bez iazyka* [Speechless] (1895), a novella based on his impressions and observations when he visited the Chicago World's Fair, with a light refreshing humour. Instead of a travelogue, he presents a fictitious hero, Matvei Dyshlo, who travels to America in search of his sister's husband. The conflict between this natural man and the civilized world becomes an important theme in the work. Besides this, through the adventures of the illiterate hero, the narrator paints an unflattering picture of political, labour, and industrial institutions in America. The author also delves into the minds of immigrants, to search for their motives, the goals that led to their immigration and the changes that have taken place in them since their move.

Among the imaginative, artistic stories of the second group, "Noch'iu" [At Night] (1888) is a treat to read, conveying light humour through the technique of "making strange", as it was called by the Formalists. The birth of a child and the activity connected with this in the household is viewed from a young boy's point of view. The story ends with the child's innocence and outlook preserved and, maybe, that is one of the reasons for this story's success. The popular story "V durnom obshchestve" [In Bad Company] (1885) tests childhood logic and, fortunately, the adults comply with it, so reaffirming the qualities of compassion, sharing and friendship in the young mind and condoning thievery (the boy stealing his sister's doll), if done in a good cause. These stories leave the reader believing in universal goodness. Korolenko's famous, but controversial novella, *Slepoi muzykant* [The Blind Musician] (1886), does not so much strive to depict a blind person's struggle, as to show the natural attraction for a human being to the mysterious and unattainable. The story lacks psychological depth, but has a plot structured around the boy's reaction to light and darkness. It is a keen sense of hearing that replaces the boy's inability to see.

"Les shumit" [The Murmuring Forest] (1886), a tale of oppression, rape, and revenge, is presented through a framed setting that removes the horror and gives a feeling of melancholy and tragedy. The romantic aura in the frame encloses the reality of the human situation. Korolenko's "Skazanie o Flore, Agrippe i Menakheme, syne Iegudy" [The Legend of Flor, Agrippa, and Menakhem, Son of Yehudah] (1886) is not just a historic account of the Judean war, but also an answer to Tolstoi's motto of "non-resistance to evil". According to Korolenko, force cannot be judged as good or bad without knowing the purpose for which it has been used. Truth – the ultimate goal in Korolenko's life – is reworked in "Teni" [The Shadows] (1891) from the Socratic dialogues and is shown to be symbolized by light.

"V pustynnikh mestakh" [In Uninhabited Places] (1914) is a travelogue which, belonging to the third group, traces Korolenko's tours undertaken when he lived in Nizhnii Novgorod. Like his other sketches, it comprises descriptions full of his romantic and sentimental attachments to places and their pasts, with some historical facts. These works range from idyllic descriptions of nature to fantastic legends.

Korolenko spent his last 15 years writing the work *Istoriia moego sovremennika* (*A History of My Contemporary*) which he did not complete. In both fiction and autobiography, he wrote about that which was most familiar to him – namely, his own life.

RADHA BALASUBRAMANIAN

Viktor Borisovich Krivulin 1944–
Poet

Biography

Born in Krasnodon, Ukraine, 1944. Lived from an early age in Leningrad where he went to school and university. Graduated in Russian Literature, 1967. Involved in the "second culture" from early 1970s. Together with ex-wife Tat'iana Goricheva, edited first *samizdat* journal devoted to literature, art, religious, and cultural commentary – *37*, 1975–81. Co-editor, with Sergei Dediulin, *Severnaia pochta*, 1979–80; collaborated in unofficial seminars on religious and cultural problems. Work appeared in *samizdat* and in émigré journals in the west during the 1970s and 1980s. Also participated in semi-official activities of "Klub-81", early and mid-1980s; first Soviet publication was in the group's anthology *Krug* (Leningrad, 1986). Latterly his poetry and journalism has appeared in Russian newspapers and journals; has also written for *Frankfurter Allgemeine Zeitung*. Member of editorial committee, *Vestnik novoi literatury*; vice-president of St Petersburg PEN club.

Publications

Poetry

Poems in *Blue Lagoon Anthology*, edited by K.K. Kuz'minskii, 5 vols. Newtonville, Massachusetts, Oriental Research Partners, 1980–86, vol. 3.

Stikhi. Paris, Ritm, 1981.

Poems in *Krug*, edited by B.I. Ivanov and Iu.V. Novikov, Leningrad, 1985, 72–77.

Poems translated by Michael Molnar, in *Poetry World*, No. 1, edited by Daniel Weissbort. London, Anvil Press, 1986, 37–40.

Poems translated by Michael Molnar, *Bomb*, 17 (Fall 1986), 74–75.

Stikhi, 2 vols. Paris, Beseda, 1988.

Poems in *Vestnik novoi literatury*, 1 (1990), 98–107; 2 (1990) 5–64; 4 (1992) 203–23.

Poems in *Oktiabr'*, 7 (1990), 49–55.

Poems translated by Richard McKane, in *The Poetry of Perestroika*, edited by Peter Mortimer and S.J. Litherland. Newcastle upon Tyne, Iron Press, 1990.

Poems translated by Michael Molnar, in *Child of Europe*, edited by Michael March. Harmondsworth, Penguin, 1990, 219–23.

Poems translated by Michael Molnar, in *Third Wave: The New Russian Poetry*, edited by Kent Johnson and Stephen M. Ashby. Ann Arbor, University of Michigan Press, 1992, 235–42.

Kontsert po zaiavkam [Concert by Demand]. St Petersburg, 1993.

Predgranich'e [Borderland]. St Petersburg, 1994.

Posledniaia kniga. Viimane raamat [Last Book]. Tallin, 1996 (in Russian and Estonian).

Critical Studies

"Novaia literatura 70–80-kh", by V. Severin, in *Vestnik novoi literatury*, Leningrad, No. 1, 1990, 222–39.

"Ocherk drugoi poezii. Ocherk pervyi. Viktor Krivulin", *Volga*, 10 (1991), 258–66.

Viktor Krivulin's work is characterized by impending judgement and the necessity of commentary. His topic is cultural phenomena rather than the data of the senses; the poetry emerges from a moral view of the world, the poems themselves being instances of judgement. Though his critique of society is based on spiritual criteria, he works (like Nekrasov or Maiakovskii) in the tradition of civic verse. The "idea of Russia" has always played a key role in his poetry, and it is one that has now acquired enormous political and social significance. But the Russia that concerns him is a state of mind, and the political reality is only one of its manifestations.

As a spiritual cartographer Krivulin knows that all states are defined by their borders. One of his most recent collections is entitled *Predgranich'e* [Borderland] and the afterword opens with the statement: "It is strange to live and write poetry in a land without borders". Krivulin goes on to speak of the new post-Soviet Russia as an archipelago of Russian enclaves. Though this description of the new commonwealth is not surprising, it indicates the cultural-political matrix of his work, which is the friction between disparate concepts of state and society. In *Galereia* [Gallery] (1983) he contrasts the status of the word in Nicolaevan Russia with that in post-Brezhnev Sovdepiia:

however heartfelt Herzen, however right –
a language reigned there over natural forces
and the word was a bond – and there was a heliograph
now one reads Kushner through a magnifying glass
the Russian-speaking world has such short sight
who can make out – a metaphor? an act?
tiredness? courage? fright?

Krivulin's earlier poems were short preludes, often reminiscent of subliminal cogitation, with minimal or no punctuation and no capital letters, as visual equivalents of this open-ended structure. Here too there is a play around the borders of communication, though not in the modernist or avant-garde sense. As Severin pointed out, Krivulin's poetry deploys the signs of experimental verse within a conventional syntactic context as a mode of beguiling the reader. The overall rationale of Krivulin's work is that any single poem is by definition unfinished and must be read in conjunction with the entire opus. This poetic strategy has the advantage of giving space to fleeting and inconclusive observations: its negative aspect, most evident in his prolific 1970s period, has been an excess of works with too slight a perceptual or conceptual impact.

However in the early 1980s Krivulin entered a more disciplined phase and produced some memorable poetical sequences, such as poems on maps that chart spiritual terrain in geographical metaphors. Here the "maps" that plot our existence are both physiological ("into the fluting of the spinal cord / A map of the world is rolled") and transcendental ("a radiant map behind our shoulders"). He followed this cycle with *Galereia*, a series of tableaux that presents an idiosyncratic critique of Soviet art and culture through grotesque juxtapositions. For example, the Pasternak of "Second Birth" metamorphoses into a locomotive – "highcheeked the Hero and lowbrowed / but iron nodules pass across / his face" – or a cheap magazine reproduction of a Fragonard pinned to a wall fills a workers' dormitory "with clouds of aphrodisiac steam".

The talent for mockery and social critique shown in these poems and in the afterwords to recent collections has also found an outlet in journalism: during the last few years Krivulin has had a regular column in the *Frankfurter Allgemeine Zeitung*. However, his role as commentator is in no way new, for, as his biography shows, he was involved in the *samizdat* scene from its inception. As with many other unofficial writers of his generation and background, particularly those in Leningrad, he enjoyed the advantage of an elite audience, but this was linked to the disadvantage of an ingrown and isolated cultural base.

An important participant in the "second culture" – or alternative culture – of the 1970s and 1980s, Krivulin has now also become one of its best interpreters and literary historians. As he noted in a recent review ("Belyi svet nad chernoi rechkoi" in *Vestnik novoi literatury*, 4), for the participants in that culture, reading *samizdat* journals such as *37* or *Chasy* served as "an intellectual imitation of a journey to the west to those for whom the way there was categorically blocked". Underground culture was an imaginary and ersatz home in the west for writers deprived of roots.

One of Krivulin's recurrent themes has been his awareness of the lost Russian heritage. The notion of cultural authority as the antidote to Soviet ideology may carry a cargo of implicit self-righteousness, a danger Krivulin's poetry does not always evade, but one that becomes a virtue when harnessed to parody or journalism. In *Galereia* the two combine successfully and develop an anecdotic analysis of cultural malaise. The end of the Soviet Union has not meant the end of that particular malaise, on the contrary it has acquired further complications. In recent years Krivulin has entered seamlessly into the role of a semi-official cultural critic, while remaining true to his origins in the second culture and to liberal political values rooted in individual spirituality.

MICHAEL MOLNAR

Aleksei Eliseevich Kruchenykh 1886–1968

Poet and literary theorist

Biography

Born in Olivskii, Kherson region, 21 February 1886. Attended three-grade school, Kherson, and Odessa Art School; graduated with diploma to teach art in high school, 1906. Failed to gain admission to Moscow School of Painting, Sculpture and Architecture, 1907, but moved to Moscow as independent artist. Published series of caricatures. Became acquainted with the Burliuk family and involved in development of Cubo-Futurism in about 1907. First literary activities, 1912. Lived in the Caucasus area, 1914–21: worked as drawing teacher at women's high school, Batalpashinsk, 1915; military service as draftsman for Erzerum railway Sarykamysh beg, April 1916. Engaged in avant-garde literary and publishing activities in Tiflis, 1917–19; moved to Baku where he worked for BakROSTA and wrote for several local newspapers. Finally returned to Moscow, August 1921. Active in literary life of Moscow until 1930. For the remainder of his life he collected and sold rare avant-garde books and manuscripts in obscurity except for the brief recognition of his 80th birthday by the Writers' Union, 1966. Died of pneumonia in Moscow, 17 June 1968.

Publications

Collected Editions

Izbrannoe, edited by Vladimir Markov. Munich, Fink, 1973.
Kukish proshliakam [Cocking a Snook at Things of the Past], edited by S.V. Kudriavtsev. Moscow, 1992.

Poetry

Starinnaia liubov' [Old-Fashioned Love]. Moscow, 1912.
Igra v adu [A Game in Hell], in collaboration with Khlebnikov. Moscow, 1912.
Pomada [Pomade]. Moscow, 1913.
Golodniak [Feeling Hungry]. Moscow, 1922.
Chetyre foneticheskikh romana [Four Phonetic Novels]. Moscow, 1927.
Ironiada. Moscow, 1930.
Rubiniada. Moscow, 1930.

Opera

Pobeda nad solntsem [Victory Over the Sun]. St Petersburg, 1913; edited by G. Erbslöh, Munich, Fink, 1976.

Literary Theory

Slovo kak takovoe [The Word as Such], in collaboration with Khlebnikov. Moscow, 1913.
Chert i rechetvortsy [The Devil and the Speech-Makers]. St Petersburg, 1913.
Faktura slova [Texture of the Word]. Moscow, 1922.
Sdvigologiia russkogo stikha [Shiftology of Russian Verse]. Moscow, 1923.
Fonetika teatra [Phonetics of the Theatre]. Moscow, 1923.

Editor

Neizdannyi Khlebnikov. Moscow, 1928–33.

Critical Studies

Russian Futurism: A History, by Vladimir Markov, Berkeley, University of California Press, 1968.

"Sud'ba Alekseia Kruchenykh", by N.I. Khardzhiev, *Svantevit* (Denmark), Arg I, 1 (1975), 34–42.

"Alexei Kruchenykh: The Bogeyman of Russian Literature", by Gordon McVay, *Russian Literature Triquarterly*, 13 (1975), 571–90.

"Pobeda nad solntsem". Ein futuristisches Drama von A. Kručenych, by Gisela Erbsloh, Munich, Sagner, 1976.

"Aleksej Krucenych als Sprachkritiker", by Rosemarie Ziegler, *Wiener Slavistisches Jahrbuch*, 24 (1978), 286–310.

"Kručenych's Poem 'Dyr bul scyl'", by Nils Åke Nilsson, *Scando-Slavica*, 24 (1979), 139–48.

"Poetika A.E. Kruchenykh pory '41°'. Uroven' zvuka", by Rosemarie Ziegler, in *L'avanguardia a Tiflis*, edited by Luigi Magarotto, Marzio Marzaduri, and Giovanni Pagani Cesa, Venice, Quaderni del Seminario di Iranistica, Uralo-Altaistica e Caucasologia dell'Universita degli Studi di Venezia, 1982, 231–58.

The Look of Russian Literature: Avant-Garde Visual Experiments 1900–1930, by Gerald Janecek, Princeton, Princeton University Press, 1984.

"Aleksei E. Kruchenykh", by Rosemarie Ziegler, *Russian Literature*, 19 (1986), 79–104.

"Kruchenykhovskii stikhotvornyi triptikh 'Dyr bul shchyl'", by Gerald Janecek, *Chernovik*, 6 (1992), 146–51.

Aleksei Kruchenykh. Sud'ba budetlianina, by Sergei Sukhoparov, edited by Wolfgang Kasack, Munich, Sagner, 1992.

Aleksei Kruchenykh v svidetel'stvakh sovremennikov, edited by Sergei Sukhoparov, Munich, Sagner, 1994.

"Aleksej Kručenych's Literary Theories", by Gerald Janecek, *Russian Literature*, 39/1 (1996), 1–12.

Aleksei Kruchenykh's literary reputation has been based primarily on his role as the most radical and consistent of the Russian Cubo-Futurists. His most famous poem, "Dyr bul shchyl", written in December 1912 and published March 1913 in the lithographed book *Pomada* [Pomade], was the first work in so-called transrational language (*zaumnyi iazyk*), which Kruchenykh championed. It remains one of the most extreme examples of verbal experimentation in Russian poetry.

Kruchenykh's acquaintance with his Kherson neighbours, the Burliuk brothers, led to the formation of the Hylaea branch of Russian Futurism, also known as Cubo-Futurism, which included Khlebnikov and Maiakovskii. In 1912 Kruchenykh decisively abandoned the career in art for which he had been trained and began to publish poetry. His first books of 1912, *Starinnaia liubov'* [Old-Fashioned Love] and *Igra v adu* [A Game in Hell] (co-authored by Khlebnikov), are relatively traditional though parodistic in their content and versification, but notable for their primitive manuscript lithography of text and illustration. Kruchenykh actively participated in the drafting of the group's first literary manifesto, "Poshchechina obshchestvennomu vkusu" ("A Slap in the Face of Public Taste"), 1912, which gained for the group its initial public notoriety. In addition to its most famous phrase about throwing Pushkin and other famous writers "from the Ship of Modernity", it advocated word creation and made vague reference to the "self-centred" (*samovitoe*) word. Reportedly at this time David Burliuk suggested to Kruchenykh that he try writing a poem made up of "unknown words" and "Dyr bul shchyl" was the result. The poem in three parts is in fact a carefully designed abstract structure based on triplicity and comparison-contrast. One or more root meanings can be identified in most of the words, though their precise meaning and grammatical form remain elusive. Nevertheless, even at its most abstract the poem retains a sonic and semantic suggestiveness and can be interpreted erotically.

In the summer of 1913, Kruchenykh joined forces with K. Malevich and M. Matiushin to create the most important large work of Cubo-Futurism, the opera *Pobeda nad solntsem* [Victory Over the Sun], staged in St Petersburg that December. Kruchenykh's elaborate, absurdist libretto, which purports to describe the capture of the sun in some future time and place, is saturated with transrationality on all levels ranging from pure sound to plot structure. Matiushin's score used sharp dissonance and microtones, while Malevich's stage designs and costumes laid the foundation for the subsequent development of Suprematist art. The performances were a scandalous success.

In 1913 Kruchenykh also began to publish a series of theoretical works that argued for the significance and need for transrational language. In his interpretation, it was not meant to be either meaningless (as in the usual public opinion of it) or more iconic than standard language (Khlebnikov's aim), but rather *indefinite* (*neopredelennyi*), open to multiple interpretations that might in fact be mutually exclusive. This indefiniteness was produced by various kinds of dislocations (*sdvigi*) from the norms of standard language ranging from unorthodox letter or sound combinations to incorrect syntax and illogical thought patterns. His works of these years demonstrate in practice a full spectrum of such possibilities. At the same time, his numerous booklet publications of 1912–21 in very limited editions, ranging from crudely scrawled lithography to elaborate typesetting, show a visual inventiveness unparalleled in Russian literature.

Circumstances forced him to move to the Caucasus, where he joined forces in Tbilisi with Il'ia Zdanevich and Igor' Terent'ev to form "41°", the most avant-garde literary group in the period 1917–19. Zdanevich's influence led Kruchenykh to publish works more florid in their typography than had been the case, but at the same time, perhaps because his military obligations caused him to be away from Tbilisi, he produced a long series of handmade booklets approaching minimalism in their restricted verbal and polygraphic means. Some of these, done with pencil and carbon paper, consist of pages with only a few scattered letters or curves.

Upon his return to Moscow in 1921, he immediately became active in literary life, giving frequent public readings with his Futurist colleagues and publishing new works. By this time he had ceased writing in his most radical transrational style, but elements of his former practice continued to spice his poetry throughout the 1920s. At the same time he produced a series of theoretical works, *Faktura slova* [Texture of the Word], *Sdvigologiia russkogo stikha* [Shiftology of Russian Verse], *Fonetika teatra* [Phonetics of the Theatre], which deserve attention and show him to be a significant and original theoretician of the avant-garde. Subsequent theoretical writings, however, show him attempting unsuccessfully and unconvincingly to accommodate his radical theories to the increasingly conservative political climate and are less interesting, though rarely without a dose of idiosyncracy. For instance, he produced a long set of booklets that tried to deflate the reputation of the immensely popular lyric poet Esenin, and several unremarkable plays with village themes. By the end of the 1920s, his access to print became restricted and he once again resorted to handmade productions using *steklografiia*, a form of mimeography. In this medium he produced several of his own poems, *Ironiada* and *Rubiniada* (both 1930), several poetry anthologies, and an extensive series called *Neizdannyi Khlebnikov* [Unpublished Khlebnikov], a valuable contribution on his Futurist colleague.

Kruchenykh then sank into obscurity, perhaps saved from liquidation by his reputation as a harmless eccentric. He survived by gathering and selling literary artefacts, such as autographs and rare editions. In some cases he assembled materials into albums devoted to an author, such as Pasternak and Aseev, which have a historical value. In the late 1950s and 1960s he occasionally served as a mentor to young poets with an innovative bent, such as Gennadii Aigi and Vladimir Kazakov. While many still consider him to be of secondary importance compared to his Futurist colleagues Khlebnikov and Maiakovskii, and he has received notably less attention than they, his legacy is now being actively studied and, as a result, his reputation continues to grow. Eventually he is likely to assume a place of primary importance as one of the most original and innovative figures in 20th-century Russian poetry.

GERALD J. JANECEK

Ivan Andreevich Krylov 1769–1844

Fabulist and dramatist

Biography

Born in a provincial town near St Petersburg, 13 February 1769. His father, an army captain (in the bureaucracy), died when Krylov was ten. Composed poetry and played the violin at early age; wrote first opera at the age 14. Wrote five comic operas, 1783–93. Completed Francophile education and was centre of small intellectual circle in St Petersburg. Published satirical journal, *Pochva dukhov* in 1789. Composed Orientalist tales. Faced political persecution from repressive government of Catherine the Great. Left St Petersburg c.1797. Tutored at country estate of a patron. Served as governor's secretary 1801–02. Lived in Moscow 1801–06. Returned to St Petersburg, 1806. Devoted himself to writing fables from 1809. Worked in public library 1812; organized Russian section until 1843. Died in St Petersburg, 21 November 1844.

Publications

Collected Editions

Polnoe sobranie sochinenie, 3 vols. St Petersburg, 1847; 2nd edition, 1859.
Krilof and His Fables, translated by W.R.S. Ralston. London, Strahan, 1869.
Polnoe sobranie: Basni. Moscow, 1900; reprinted, Moscow, 1997.
Kriloff's Fables, translated by C. Fillingham Coxwell. London, Paul-Trench-Trubner, and New York, Dutton, 1920.
Krylov's Fables, translated by Bernard Pares. London, Jonathan Cape, 1926; New York, Harcourt Brace, 1927; as *The Russian Fables of Ivan Krylov*. Harmondsworth, Penguin, 1942.
Sochineniia, 2 vols. Moscow, 1955; reprinted 1969.
Basni [Fables]. 5th edition Moscow, 1962.
Krylov's Birds and Beasts: A Selection of the Fables, translated by E.E. Ralphs. London, Howard Baker, 1990.

Plays

Prokazniki [The Mischief Makers]. 1788.
Trumf/Podshchipa. 1799.
Modnaia lavka [The Fashion Shop]. 1807.
Urok dochkam [The Daughters' Lesson]. 1807.

Critical Studies

Russkaia muzykal'naia kul'tura XVIII veka v ego sviaziakh s literaturoi, teatrom, i bytom, by Tamara Livanova, Leningrad, 1952–53.
Krylov, by N.L. Stepanov, Moscow, 1963; translated as *Ivan Krylov*, edited by Nicholas P. Vaslef, New York, Twayne, 1973.
"I.A. Krylov i ego znachenie v istorii russkoi literatury i russkogo literaturnogo iazyka", by V.V. Vinogradov, *Russkaia rech'*, 4 (1970), 3–15.
"Ivan Krylov and the Mock Eulogy", by Pierre R. Hart, *Satire Newsletter*, 9/1 (1971), 1–5.
I.A. Krylov: Poeziia narodnoi mudrosti, by V. Arkhipov, Moscow, 1974.
Krylov fabuliste: étude littéraire et historique, by Maurice Colin, Paris, 1975.
Ivan Andreevich Krylov: Ses oeuvres de jeunesse et les courants littéraires de son temps, by François de Labriollé, 2 vols, Paris, 1975.
"The Function of Concessive Construction in Some of Krylov's Fables", by H. Hamburger, in *Dutch Contributions to the Eighth International Congress of Slavists*, edited by Jan M. Meijer, Amsterdam, Benjamins, 1979, 249–78.

"The English and Krylov", by A.G. Cross, *Oxford Slavonic Papers*, 16 (1983), 91–140.

Zhizn' Ivana Krylova, by A. Gordin, Moscow, 1985.

Russian Drama from Its Beginnings to the Age of Pushkin, by Simon Karlinsky, Berkeley, University of California Press, 1985.

A History of Russian Literature of the Romantic Period, by William Edward Brown, Ann Arbor, Ardis, 1986, vol. 1, 124–35.

Poet i mudrets. Kniga ob Ivane Krylove, by V.I. Korovin, Moscow, 1996.

During his earlier years, Ivan Krylov constantly experimented with literary forms, notably the fable. After some of his translations of La Fontaine were warmly praised in 1805 by the then-leading poet Ivan Dmitriev, he began focusing on the genre. The first collection, containing 23 fables, appeared in 1809 and was an immediate and unprecedented success. He eventually produced 203 fables (in nine books), many of them – or at least many lines of them – destined to become essential (and essentializing) parts of the consciousness not only of poets, poetry devotees, and other *littérateurs*, but of persons from all walks of life. This consciousness ranges from the strictly literary repertoire of fellow writers, to helpful guides through the perennial disarray of Russian life, to *materia prima* for apt repartee at any social gathering. His fables remain integral to Russian primary and secondary education to this day and probably will remain so for the foreseeable future, if only because of the perennial relevance of their political satire.

Krylov's role in St Petersburg salon culture was many-sided. His success with the poetry of the fable was conjoined throughout his long life with his evolving music. He played the violin in innumerable family concerts, in quartets with the best virtuosi of the day, and, as a soloist. Among his many friends, the closest was Ivan Gnedich, translator of the still standard Russian *Iliad* (remarkable among *Iliads* for its ethnographic precision and realism). Another notable friend was Aleksandr Pushkin, whose first line in *Evgenii Onegin* is a reworking of a line from Krylov. In the last decades before his death, Krylov was a loved, respected, and even revered member of St Petersburg artistic culture, particularly the circle of A.N. Olenin. The public and still perduring image of a wise and kindly "Grandpapa Krylov" gradually crystallized, an image which, given his often bitter realism and political messages, is no more accurate than the similar image of Robert Frost.

Krylov's fables stand out in the grand Euro-American tradition that runs from Aesop to La Fontaine to Marianne Moore's poems and translations; they also figure prominently in the international spectrum that saliently includes India, Africa, and Native America (for example, the Coyote stories) – "fable" here meaning "a fictitious narrative intended to teach some truth or precept in which animals or objects are often the actors". In these contexts, Krylov stands out because of at least four features that, while not unique to him, are at least exemplified and interdigitated with unsurpassed brilliance.

First, there is the critical cliché that the fables are miniature satires or dramas (comedies and, often, tragedies): with acuity and narrative tension, they evoke and capture the gist of dilemmas, problems, and problematic situations common to all people – such as relations between persons of different categories (for example, gender), or the results of the differential power between caste and class. Krylov's representations include a gallery of human stereotypes such as peasant, phenomena such as death, objects such as river or bush, and, most often, animals: wolf, bear, sheep, crow, lion, and, above all, fox – a projection of the author's own "cheerful cunning of the mind" (the phrase is Pushkin's). His animals, as foremost Krylov scholar N.L. Stepanov astutely noted, blend a naturalistic characterization of the animal with an allegorical stereotypification of the human.

Second, the language of Krylov's fables is animated by a tension between colloquial, often peasant-associated, speech (notably in the vocabulary and the use of diminutives) and, on the other hand, great formal elegance in metrics (iambic lines of varying length), in the tempo of the syllable ("a syncopy of intonation"), and an overall musical effect of a solo, duet or chamber ensemble. More specifically, a pithy line of his may draw equally from peasant proverb as from epigrams of the salon in order to achieve a condensed characterization of the human condition. In this almost systematic exploitation of the proverb for high art, Krylov may be compared to an otherwise very different poet, Sergei Esenin.

Third, Krylov draws and improves on the tradition of mordant social criticism à la Fonvizin, Novikov, and Radishchev (a social criticism that was couched in fables, to judge by the prolific fable-writing of major 18th-century Russian poets). An underground writer to a degree, Krylov's unpublished manuscripts, such as "Podshchipa" (1797), were widely read. His two satirical comedies, *Modnaia lavka* [Fashion Shop] and *Urok dochkam* [The Daughters' Lesson] (both 1807), were great hits in their day and were produced until the 1840s. But, his fables, such as "Kvartet" [Quartet], while apparently or ostensibly conservative and supportive of the status quo – that every man should know and accept his place ("No matter how you sit / As music-makers you'll not fit") – are often criticisms of the establishment, the more brutal mores of his own aristocratic class, the patterns of corruption and incompetence in the government, and the tyrannical rule of the tsars, particularly of Paul I.

Krylov believed that reform could be aided through perspicacious social criticism. Thus, the social content of his fables and their signal musicality amount to a maximization and harmonic integration of the two poles which, until recently, have been fundamental throughout the history of Russian poetry: the commitment to music, even mellifluousness, by the more aesthetic camps, and the commitment to social and political relevance by the civic or utilitarian critics and writers. Krylov's synthesis of music and politics is literally classical (for instance, Horace *dulce et utile*), but he was an anti-classicist in some ways, such as in his disparagement of the ode.

Fourth and last, Krylov was the architect of a version of literary realism that has a very audible and Russian feeling to it. This was partly linguistic: he "determined the course of the realist movement, above all through his language ... language became the real hero of his literary work, giving life to the characters of fable and making them vivid and real" (Stepanov). Pushkin's role as one founder of "Russian realism" owes an enormous debt to Krylov's language. But Krylov's realism is also a matter of the nonlinguistic world: a sympathizing but unsentimental, usually playful, but often bitter view of the human condition. In both the social and linguistic senses, he deeply influenced Griboedov,

Gogol', and Nekrasov, among others. More concretely, the Russianness of his realism entails a conscious recourse to Russian oral poetry, notably the proverb, a recourse so consistently successful that Gogol' and many others classified him memorably as a folk or popular poet *par excellence*. Among the many fables known to most literate Russians, one might single out the following originals and translations: "Kvartet", "Gusy" [The Geese], "Dva golubia" [Two Doves], "Krest'iane i reka" [Peasant and River], "Orel i pauk" [Eagle and Spider], "Ruchei" [Stream], "Prud i reka" [Pond and River], "Orel i krot" [Eagle and Mole], "Vorona i lisitsa" [Crow and Fox], "Vasilek" [Cornflower], "Larchik" [The Box], "Osel i solovei" [Donkey and Nightingale], and "Lev i mysh" [Lion and Fly].

In sum, building on Russian antecedents such as Ivan Dmitriev and Konstantin Sumarokov (author of more than 300 fables), Krylov went on to equal or to surpass all of his models by synthesizing many potentials of the genre, notably: the wit and economy of La Fontaine, the gnomic truthfulness of fable and proverb in Russian folk culture, social and political criticism through satire and tropes of indirection, and, finally, the verve of a language that is both conversational and musical and that, whether monologic meditation or brisk dialogue, asks to be read and recited aloud. "Dmitriev writes his fables, Krylov tells them".

PAUL FRIEDRICH

Aleksandr Ivanovich Kuprin 1870–1938

Prose writer

Biography

Born in Narovchat, Penza Province, southern Russia, 7 September 1870. Attended Razumovskii boarding school, Cadet Corps and Alexander Military Academy, Moscow, 1876–90. First story published in Moscow paper, 1889. Joined infantry regiment in south-western Ukraine, 1890. Left the army in 1894; worked as a correspondent for Kiev newspapers. Travelled widely in southern Russia, taking various casual jobs, 1896–1900, and met Bunin, Chekhov, and Gor'kii. Associated with *Znanie* literary group. Editorial work in St Petersburg, 1901–04. Married: 1) Mariia Karlovna Davydovna in 1902 (divorced 1907); 2) Elizaveta Moritsevna Geinrikh in 1909, three daughters (third died in infancy, 1909). Travelled extensively to the Crimea, St Petersburg, and to Helsinki, 1906. Settled in Gatchina near St Petersburg, 1911. Visited southern Europe, 1912. Served in Russian army in Finland, 1914–15. Visited Lenin in the Kremlin to discuss projected newspaper for the peasantry, December, 1918. Left Russia with family for Helsinki, 1919, where he took up editorial activity. Reached Paris mid-1920; worked on Russian émigré journals, 1921–31. Began publication of autobiographical novel *Iunkera* [The Junkers], 1928. Published the story "Koleso vremeni" [The Wheel of Time] in 1929, and the Parisian tale "Zhaneta" in 1933. Returned to Russia in May 1937, already suffering from ill health. Recipient: Pushkin Prize (jointly with Ivan Bunin), 1909. Died in Leningrad, 25 August 1938.

Publications

Collected Editions

Sobranie sochinenii, 9 vols. Moscow, 1964.
Sobranie sochinenii, 9 vols. Moscow, 1970–73.
Gambrinus and Other Stories, translated by B.G. Guerney. Freeport, New York, Books for Libraries Press, 1970.
A Slav Soul and Other Stories, translated by B.G. Guerney. Freeport, New York, Books for Libraries Press, 1971.
"At the Circus", "Emerald", "The Bracelet of Garnets", translated by Nicholas Luker, in *An Anthology of Russian Neo-Realism*, edited and translated by Nicholas Luker. Ann Arbor, Ardis, 1982, 138–210.
Izbrannye proizvedeniia. Moscow, 1984.
Sobranie sochinenii, 6 vols. Moscow, 1991.

Fiction

Molokh [Moloch]. 1896.
Poedinok. 1905; translated as "The Duel", by Andrew R. MacAndrew, in *The Duel and Selected Stories*, New York, New American Library, 1961.
Iama. 1908–15; translated as *The Pit*, by B.G. Guerney, London, John Hamilton, 1930; New York, Modern Library, 1932.
Iunkera [The Junkers]. 1928–32.

Critical Studies

"A.I. Kuprin", by I.V. Koretskaia, in *Sochineniia v trekh tomakh*, Moscow, 1953, iii–xxxix.
"A.I. Kuprin's *River of Life*", by Robert Louis Jackson, in his *Dostoevsky's Underground Man in Russian Literature*, The Hague, Mouton, 1958, 108–12.
"A.I. Kuprin", by L. Plotkin, in his *Literaturnye ocherki i stat'i*, Leningrad, 1958, 413–45.
Aleksandr Ivanovich Kuprin, Kritiko-biograficheskii ocherk, by Vladislav Afanas'ev, Moscow, 1960.
Tvorchestvo A.I. Kuprina, by Anatolii Volkov, Moscow, 1962.
Tvorcheskii put' A.I. Kuprina, by F. Kuleshov, Minsk, 1963.
"A.I. Kuprin", by Anatolii Volkov, in *Russkaia Literatura XX veka*, Moscow, 1966, 277–303.

"Povest' A.I. Kuprina *Poedinok*", by I. Gura, in *Voprosy zhanra i stilia*, edited by V.V. Gura, Vologda, 1967, 84–116.
"Romashov and Nazansky: Enemies of the People", by G. Williams, *Canadian Slavonic Papers*, 9/2 (1967), 194–200.
A.I. Kuprin, by L. Krutikova, Leningrad, 1971.
Alexander Kuprin, by Nicholas Luker, Boston, Twayne, 1978.

Bibliography
"A Selected Bibliography of Works by and about Alexander Kuprin (1870–1938)", by Nicholas Luker, in *10 Bibliographies of 20th Century Russian Literature*, edited by Fred Moody, Ann Arbor, Ardis, 1977, 3–10.

Aleksandr Kuprin flung himself into life with unparalleled zest, displaying a voracious appetite for astonishingly varied experiences. Driven by boundless curiosity, he had diversity as his lifelong watchword. No wonder, then, that autobiographical elements abound in his writing, based as it so often is on events of his life. Moreover, in his fiction he was always reluctant to use situations and characters with which he himself was not familiar.

From his early verse (some 30 poems – patriotic, satirical, and political) written chiefly between 1883 and 1887, Kuprin moved on to prose, publishing his first story "Poslednii debiut" [The Last Debut] in 1889. Based on the suicide by poisoning on stage of the singer E.P. Kadmina in 1881, it was followed by several tales that examined abnormal states of mind, and then by the very different piece "Doznanie" [The Enquiry] (1894), his first army story. The most important work of his years as a soldier, it was also the first in a series of tales about the military that would culminate ten years later in his novel *Poedinok* (*The Duel*). The story is an indictment of conditions in the Russian army and its brutal punishments for trivial offences. Central to Kuprin's literary development, it presents the first in a succession of sensitive young officers painfully aware of the injustice prevalent in the army, later exemplified by Romashov in *The Duel*.

Kuprin's varied journalistic work for several newspapers in Kiev in the 1890s launched him on his literary career. Later he asserted that the experience of journalism was the finest apprenticeship for a writer. Among his more important pieces for Kiev papers were topical accounts of contemporary city life, 16 satirical portraits of types of people observed in the city, "Kievskie tipy" [Kiev Types] (1896), weekly chronicles of Kievan events, and four documentary industrial sketches (1896–99). Set in the iron and steel region of the Donbass north of Rostov-on-Don, the latter foreshadow the *povest'*, *Molokh* [Moloch] (1896), his most significant early work.

Thematically *Molokh* belongs firmly in the 1890s and reflects many of the social and economic issues of that decade. It focuses on the damaging aspects of Russian capitalism as seen by its sensitive hero, Bobrov, who is caught in the industrial maelstrom of the late 1800s. But it also raises other topical issues: the social effects of technological progress, the underprivileged position of the working class, and the relations between the bourgeoisie and the intelligentsia. Through the experience of his partly autobiographical hero as a reluctant servant of capitalism in the Donbass, Kuprin points to the social injustice and economic tyranny endemic to newly-industrialized Russia.

His unfinished *Poles'e* [Woodlands] cycle of stories (1898–1901), set in southern Belorussia, contrasts starkly in its timeless rural beauty with the industrial environment that he found so repugnant in *Molokh*. Its most notable piece is the finely-crafted novelette "Olesiia" (1898), the poetic story of the love between an urban intellectual and a beautiful country girl, a tale drawn from Kuprin's own biography.

Kuprin's move to St Petersburg in the early 1900s proved the watershed in his career: in 1902 the co-operative publishing house *Znanie*, founded by Gor'kii, issued a collection of Kuprin's tales and he swiftly achieved both literary and social success. Important stories of these years focus on circus folk, "V tsirke" ("At the Circus") 1902; the rural peasant, "Boloto" [The Swamp] (1902); and the underprivileged and dispossessed in a society that measured success by wealth – notably "Trus" [The Coward] (1903), "Zhidovka" [The Jewess] (1904), and "Chernyi tuman" [Black Fog] (1905). In other pieces of the early 1900s, particularly "Mirnoe zhitie" [A Quiet Life] (1904), "Kor'" [Measles] (1904), and "Zhrets" [The High Priest] (1905), Kuprin exposed the hypocrisy, bigotry, and degeneracy that underlay "respectable" Russian society of his time.

But it was his novel *The Duel* that brought him lasting fame. Highly critical of brutal conditions and philistine attitudes prevailing in the tsarist army, it appeared just when the disastrous war with Japan was drawing to its ignominious close. Arising from Kuprin's army days, the work tells of its hero's growing distaste for military life and his gradual realization that he is a uniquely individual human being. But before he can leave the service to act on that realization, he is killed in a duel by the husband of the woman he loves.

The decade after *The Duel* saw the publication of many of Kuprin's finest works. Among them are "Shtabs-Kapitan Rybnikov" [Staff-Captain Rybnikov] (1906), which, though set in St Petersburg, has a close bearing on the Russo-Japanese War in the Pacific; "Reka zhizni" [The River of Life] (1906), which is an indictment of the social conditions in Russia that cripple the capacity of the young for effective revolutionary action; "Gambrinus" (1907), which presents a paradigm of events in Russia from the turn of the century to after the 1905 Revolution; "Izumrud" ("Emerald") 1907, the tale of a successful racehorse that is poisoned; "Sulamif" (1908), a moving love story based closely on *The Song of Songs*; and his famous "Granatovyi braslet" ("The Bracelet of Garnets") 1911, where hopeless love finds its quietly tragic apotheosis. Importantly, 1915 saw the appearance of the third and final part of *Iama* (*The Pit*) begun in 1908, Kuprin's last major work – a lengthy, semi-documentary study of prostitution inspired by his time in Kiev.

Kuprin's work written in emigration – most notably his documentary autobiographical novel *Iunkera* [The Junkers] (1928–32) and his elegiac tales "Koleso vremeni" [The Wheel of Time] (1929) and "Zhaneta" (1933) – is generally inferior in quality, pervaded both by nostalgia for the Russia of his youth and sadness at the long separation from his native land. In the early 1930s his sight deteriorated, and his handwriting became so impaired that after "Zhaneta" he wrote only four short tales. Back in Moscow he produced just two brief newspaper pieces: his fragmentary reminiscences of Gor'kii and a sketch expressing his gladness at returning to the Soviet capital.

For all the wistful retrospection of his declining years, Kuprin's position in the history of Russian literature is highly significant. Born into an age overshadowed by the great Russian novel, he turned to the short story as the genre best suited both to his own restless temperament and to the manifold preoccupations of his troubled generation. With his contemporaries Chekhov, Gor'kii, and Bunin, he was to bring the genre of the short story to an efflorescence without parallel in Russian letters.

NICHOLAS LUKER

The Duel

Poedinok

Novel, 1905

The Duel is the best-known and probably most important of Kuprin's works. *The Duel*, which first brought Kuprin to the forefront of Russian literature, paints a bleak picture of stultifying existence in a provincial army garrison in the mid-1890s. The book was, however, published in 1905, and as a result acquired particularly strong resonance from the recent defeat of Russia in the war with Japan – many thought that the low morale so graphically depicted in the novel explained what lay behind the shock and humiliation of Port Arthur and other battles. Kuprin himself had undergone a long military training followed by service in the army from 1900 to 1904. In the novel he was – as so often – writing from personal experience, and presents a grim picture of the life of junior officers in an army dominated by meaningless routine, cruelty, immorality, boredom, and despair. The book was enthusiastically praised by many contemporary writers and by the liberal intelligentsia, but attracted violent criticism from the dismayed military establishment, although it seems that some of the army reforms that took place between 1905 and 1917 may have been prompted by this powerful work.

The novel consists of a series of scenes from regimental life, featuring a wide range of officers and a few soldiers. The latter seem to be uniformly miserable and oppressed; the officers, bound by the harsh conditions and traditions of their work, are, none the less, very varied. Vetkin is feckless and carefree, hidebound Commander Sliva simply stupid, and Bek-Agamalov hot-tempered and bloodthirsty; Osadchii eulogizes his concept of "an unbridled and merciless war", while widower Zegrzht constantly worries about money; Lieutenant-Colonel Rafal'skii finds solace in his menagerie, Bobetsinskii in dressing foppishly and pretending to be a guards officer, and Arakchovskii exists by cheating at cards. The range of portraits is enormous, but almost all the characters are united by cynical egotism and moral crudity, engaging in loveless affairs or unprovoked violence simply to avoid the prevailing demoralization and boredom.

Three characters stand out: Second Lieutenant Romashov, his friend Nazanskii, and the woman they both love, Shura, the wife of fellow-officer Nikolaev. At the start of the novel Romashov is arrested for going to the aid of a soldier who is being tormented during training, and this action says much about his impulsive, idealistic nature. Seemingly, a strongly autobiographical character (many of his details correspond to those of the author) he expresses some of Kuprin's Utopian ideas, a longing to escape from the army, and dreams of a peaceful and more just world. Nazanskii is a less impulsive thinker, but he also seems to give voice to some of the author's thoughts at this time. He is endowed with Kuprin's own love of life, but as a fictional character not made particularly life-like, he acts more as a channel for ideas. He is a natural rebel, but not in a political or social sense; in fact, his views are heavily tinged with Nietzschean dreams of a strong individual personality able to overstep the moral boundaries that restrict others. Romashov is not only better drawn, but more humane as a character, and his tragedy affects the reader more deeply than the other events in what is in part almost a piece of documentary fiction. Shura, trapped in a loveless marriage, is depicted as a woman of exceptional beauty and charm. As the novel progresses, however, we see that she is entertaining the genuinely passionate Romashov as a lover mainly as part of a devious plan to help her husband gain entry to a better, more prestigious world. For all the junior officers not wishing to leave the army or to fester until retirement, the principal escape is through the General Staff Academy to the higher ranks where life appears to be more pleasant and easier in all respects. Shura's deception operates at several levels: she lives with a husband whose advances she finds physically repulsive, believing him to be her only key to escape and social advancement; she exploits the youthful innocence of her idealistic lover, Romashov, and, eventually, when it is expedient in terms of her ambitions, betrays him to her husband, thus precipitating the duel of the title.

It is, however, institutional life in the army, rather than individual ambitions and passions that forms the main subject of the novel. In the second chapter Kuprin underlines the dire situation by describing a regimental inspection in which all are found severely wanting: the soldiers abused and demoralized, and the officers cruel and incompetent. The officers' entertainments are also unedifying, notably picnics and heavy-drinking parties, after one of which the participants decamp to the local brothel, the scene of the quarrel between Romashov and Nikolaev. Be it at work or play, the officers in *The Duel*, including the main characters, are depicted as almost uniformly unattractive. Nazanskii is a heavy drinker, and Romashov himself, always prone to self-analysis and dreaming, when driven to despair takes to alcohol and other stimulants to deaden the pain. The vivid descriptions of their hangovers and disillusionment adds to the overall negative colouring of the novel.

Duelling had been made legal in May 1894 after decades of being banned. Cuckolded Nikolaev challenges Romashov and kills him, thus snuffing out the last vestige of idealism in the book. Kuprin had wanted to describe the duel in the same detail as the rest of the events, but in the end left it, probably more effectively, as a curt second-hand report, somewhat as Chekhov did in *Tri sestry* (*Three Sisters*).

The novelist Konstantin Paustovskii described *The Duel* as "one of the most remarkable and merciless works in Russian literature". Reprinted many times and translated into numerous languages, this novel's condemnation of a tedious, backward, cruel society is no less powerful now than it was in 1905 when its publication first shocked a rapidly changing Russia.

ARNOLD MCMILLIN

Mikhail Nikolaevich Kuraev 1939–

Prose writer

Biography

Born in Leningrad, 18 June 1939, into a family of pre-revolutionary intelligentsia. Attended the Leningrad Institute of the Arts, from 1958. Simultaneously enrolled as a correspondence student at Institute of Philosophy, Moscow; graduated with diploma in cinematography, 1961. Scriptwriter and editor at Lenfilm Studios, 1961–88. Author of seven screenplays. Wrote script for a two-part film for television about the life of Socrates, 1991. First prose work *Kapitan Dikshtein* published in *Novyi mir*, 1987. Works have been widely translated. Full-time writer.

Publications

Collected Editions

Malen'kaia semeinaia taina [A Small Family Secret]. Moscow, 1992.

Night Patrol and Other Stories, translated by Margareta O. Thompson. Durham, North Carolina, Duke University Press, 1994.

Fiction

"Kapitan Dikshtein", *Novyi mir*, 9 (1987), 5–80; translated as "Captain Dikshtein", by Margareta O. Thompson, in *Glasnost: An Anthology of Russian Literature under Gorbachev*, edited by Helena Goscilo and Byron Lindsey, Ann Arbor, Ardis, 1990; also in *Night Patrol and Other Stories*, 1994.

"Nochnoi dozor", *Novyi mir*, 12 (1988), 80–114; translated as "Night Patrol", by Margareta O. Thompson, in *Night Patrol and Other Stories*, 1994.

"Malen'kaia domashniaia taina" [A Small Family Secret], *Novyi mir*, 3 (1990), 9–30.

"Petia po doroge v tsarstvie nebesnoe", *Znamia*, 2 (1991), 9–58; translated as "Petya on His Way to the Heavenly Kingdom", by Margareta O. Thompson, in *Night Patrol and Other Stories*, 1994.

"Druzhby nezhnoe volnen'e" [The Tender Excitement of Friendship], *Novyi mir*, 8 (1992), 6–40.

"Kuranty b'iut" [The Bells Ring], *Znamia*, 11 (1992), 24–37.

"Zerkalo Montachki" [Montachka's Mirror], *Novyi mir*, 5–6 (1993), 3–68 and 67–132; as *Roman "Zerkalo Montachki" s podzagolovkom "Kriminal'naia siuita v 23-kh s introduktsiei i teoremoi o prizrakakh"*. Moscow, 1994.

"Blok-ada" [Block-ade], *Znamia*, 7 (1994), 74–112.

"Vstrechaite Lenina" [Meet Lenin], *Novyi mir*, 9 (1995), 5–27.

Articles

"Chekhov s nami" [Chekhov With Us], *Znamia*, 6 (1990), 206–12.

"Kapitan Dikshtein, Rembrandt van Reine i bezdomnaia dama" [Captain Dikshtein, Rembrandt van Reine and the Homeless Woman], *Literaturnaia gazeta*, (27 February 1991).

"O Rembrandte i o sebe" [On Rembrandt and Myself], *Druzhba narodov*, 8 (1992).

"Kto voidet v dom Chekhova?" [Who Enters Chekhov's House?], *Druzhba narodov*, 1 (1993), 198–208.

"Kak ia staralsia ne stat' pisatelem" [How I Tried Not to Become a Writer], *Zvezda*, 8 (1994), 131–44.

"Za kogo oni nas prinimaiut?" [Who Do They Take Us For?], *Sintaksis*, 34 (1994), 164–96.

Critical Studies

"Gosudarstvennyi sumasshedshii", by A. Ageev, *Literaturnoe obozrenie*, 8 (1989), 48–52.

"Kak uderzhat' litso", by Lev Anninskii, *Znamia*, 9 (1989), 218–21.

"The Space of Prose", by Andrei Sinyavsky, in *The Louisiana Conference on Literature and Perestroika*, Esbjerg, South Jutland University Press, 1989, 73–80.

"Rewriting History and Reviving Modernism", by Colin F. Dowsett, *Canadian Slavonic Papers*, 2 (1991), 113–22.

"Zapiski zhivogo, ili Petia-durachok na karnavale besov", by E. Kanchukov, *Literaturnoe obozrenie*, 10 (1991), 61–63.

"Ten' 'Amarcorda'", by N. Eliseev, *Novyi mir*, 4 (1995), 215–26.

Russian Literature 1988–94: The End of an Era, by N.N. Shneidman, Toronto, University of Toronto Press, 1995.

Mikhail Kuraev's first novella *Kapitan Dikshtein* (*Captain Dikshtein*) was published in 1987. The publication of two further works, *Nochnoi dozor* (*Night Patrol*) and *Malen'kaia domashniaia taina* [A Small Family Secret], established the author as one of the most promising writers to have emerged during the period of glasnost. The particular success of these works during the late 1980s can in part be attributed to the author's abiding interest in historical themes. Only in *Druzhby nezhnoe volnen'e* [The Tender Excitement of Friendship], which drew little critical attention, has Kuraev diverged from this area of concern.

Kuraev distinguished himself by his highly individualistic and artistic approach to historical excavation and documentation. In the first instance, Kuraev's works may be seen as a counter-history to "monumental" histories, that is a history devoted to people and subjects not usually entertained as significant within the grand historical canvas. *Captain Dikshtein*, for example, is ostensibly a work about a factual historical event, the Kronstadt Rebellion of 1921. The greater part of his novella, however, describes a pensioner's trip to exchange his bottles for cash so he can celebrate the visit of his nephew with some beer. Implicit in this passion for the seemingly trivial details of everyday existence is a retreat from Soviet abstractions about society, which in the author's view have nurtured a special indifference to man and life's immanence.

Beyond Kuraev's revisionism on specific topics, his prose is also unorthodox in terms of style. The high priority he placed on literary form, on structure and language earned him the unfettered praise of Andrei Siniavskii in 1989. Indeed, his preference for the experimental, playful, anti-dogmatic traditions associated with modernism extend the Gogolian line in

Russian fiction forcibly interrupted in the 1920s. Kuraev's works are concerned ultimately with exposing the uniformity of Russian historical fantasies and the sorrowful consequences for ordinary people whose fate it has been to mirror these fantasies. Hence, while the majority of Kuraev's works are set in the 1960s, he makes frequent forays deep into the Russian past in search of "patterns and coincidences" that may help to illumine the present. The consistency with which the author returns to the reign of Peter the Great suggests that he draws a direct link between Petrine reforms and the Soviet descent into totalitarianism. Kuraev frequently explores this link through his ironic recourse to the demonic Petersburg urban tradition. The city in the Soviet period becomes even more insubstantial, its citizens even more phantom-like, in a world of constantly shifting realities where people, words, streets, and buildings disappear often only to re-emerge under a different name. The question of identity, a major concern of the "Petersburg myth", also dominates Kuraev's works. Here the Russian sense of living in a schizophrenic world celebrated in the works of writers like Dostoevskii and Gogol' persists as a characteristic of Soviet life. In *Captain Dikshtein*, a man develops a split personality when he is compelled to assume the name of an executed officer to avoid retribution from the authorities for his part in the Kronstadt Rebellion of 1921. The inner tension caused by a lifetime spent struggling to subdue his natural personality leads symbolically to his death from a heart attack at the end of the story. In *Night Patrol*, Kuraev's compelling psychological portrait of an agent of Stalinist repression, this mental dissonance assumes the proportions of state psychosis. The impossibility of coherence between the hero's actions and emotions becomes manifest as he proudly recalls how he used to dig holes for the bodies of victims of state terror while waxing lyrical about the song of the nightingale.

Like *Night Patrol*, Kuraev's next two works, *Petia po doroge v tsarstvie nebesnoe* (*Petya on His Way to the Heavenly Kingdom*) and *Kurantyi b'iut* [The Bells Ring], demonstrate the sorrowful consequences of an all-consuming attachment to life as blind faith. The most important of these in terms of artistic achievement is Kuraev's tragi-comic portrayal of the wretched life and senseless death of a retarded young man called Petia. Petia labours under the illusion that he is grooming himself for power. He is accidentally killed when, in his anxiety to be recognized by the secret police, he sets off in pursuit of a runaway convict. The suggestion of spiritual odyssey contained in the title is clearly intended to parody Petia's unstinting belief that Soviet power as the embodiment of all that is true, good and just will lead him to his earthly paradise.

In spite of its undoubted literary merit, "Petia" garnered little critical praise. The author returned to prominence, however, with his much-celebrated novel *Zerkalo Montachki* [Montachka's Mirror] in which the problem of identity is dramatically reiterated. Here the author uses an element of the pure fantastic in the form of disappearing reflections to underscore how the mental and spiritual invasion of man in the Soviet era contributed to the systematic loss of a true sense of self. The implication that his heroes have been transformed into ghosts (only ghosts have no reflection), following contact with a retired KGB agent, allows the author to examine the close links that exist in the Russian mind between political, religious, and supernatural power. That the city of St Petersburg and its chaotic history should haunt Kuraev's consciousness is unsurprising, for the roots of the author's life are deeply in the city. Indeed, Kuraev's 1994 work *Blok-ada* [Block-ade] describes the vicissitudes of his own family's fate during the siege of Leningrad of 1941–42. Kuraev does not close his eyes in the midst of horror and tragedy – he describes in poignant detail the death of his own baby brother – and neither does he yield to them. As this story of human courage vividly demonstrates, Kuraev retains an idealistic faith in the independence of man from his external environment. In the face of imminent death, the lives of his heroes are not barren of what is good, true, and beautiful in human experience.

JACQUELINE FRENCH

Anatolii Nikolaevich Kurchatkin 1944–

Prose writer

Biography

Born in the Urals, 1944. Educated in Sverdlovsk (now Ekaterinburg). Worked as a milling-machine operative; then as design engineer at Urals Machinery Factory. Completed national service; then worked at local youth newspaper. Graduated from the Gor'kii Literary Institute. Experienced problems with censors; completed *Vechernii svet* [Light of Evening] in 1981; refused to re-write it and subsequently none of his work was published for five years. Currently resides in Moscow.

Publications

Collected Editions

Sem' dnei nedeli [Seven Days of the Week]. Moscow, 1977.

Perekhod v seredine sezona [Transition in Mid-Season]. Moscow, 1978.

Cherez Moskvu proezdom [In Transit Across Moscow]. Moscow, 1981.

Zvezda begushchaia [Running Star]. Moscow, 1986.

Istorii raznykh mest [A History of Various Places]. Moscow, 1986.

Povesti i rasskazy. Moscow, 1988.

Polosa dozhdei [A Belt of Rain]. Moscow, 1989.
Portret romanticheskogo molodogo cheloveka [Portrait of a Romantic Young Man]. Moscow, 1991.

Fiction
Vechernii svet. Roman [Light of Evening]. (written in 1981), Moscow, 1989.
"Vesnianka" [Spring-Song] (written in 1986), *Oktiabr'*, 9 (1989), 3–90.
"Gil'otina", "Labirint" and "Son v letniuiu noch'" (written in 1989); translated as "The Guillotine", "The Maze", "A Midsummer Night's Dream", by Rachel Polonsky, Rosamund Shreeves, Graham Pover, *Soviet Literature*, 12 (1990), 3–40.
"Zapiski exstremista" [Diary of an Extremist], *Znamia*, 1 (1990), 8–63.
"Nachalo dachnogo sezona" [The Start of the Dacha Season], *Ural*, 1–2 (1991), 4–48; 22–72.
"Rekviem" [Requiem], *Znamia*, 9 (1991), 62–105.
"The Quest for a Letterbox" [V poiskakh pochtovogo iashchika], translated by Arch Tait, *Confrontation*, 50 (1992), 49–56.
"The Crickets" [Sverchki], translated by Michael Pursglove, *Staple*, 23 (1992), 28–40.
"Home" [Dom], translated by Arch Tait, *Glimmer Train*, 8 (1993), 108–23.
"Strazhnitsa" [The Watchwoman], *Znamia*, 5–6, (1993).

Critical Studies
"The Courage to Live Without a Destiny", by Vladimir Bondarenko, *Soviet Literature*, 10 (1989), 5–9.
"Situatsiia", by Sergei Chuprinin, *Znamia*, 1 (1990).
The Last Years of Soviet Russian Literature: Prose Fiction, 1975–1991, by Deming Brown, Cambridge and New York, Cambridge University Press, 1993.
"The Russian Disease: Kurchatkin's Diagnosis", by Arch Tait, *Slavonic and East European Review*, 71/1 (1993), 14–34.
Russian Literature 1988–1994: The End of an Era, by N.N. Shneidman, Toronto, University of Toronto Press, 1995.

Anatolii Kurchatkin is a meticulous chronicler of Russian society from the outbreak of World War II until the present. On another level, however, he is an author whose characters transcend their dismaying local circumstances to achieve universal interest, and whose technical mastery of his craft and ear for dialogue make almost any of his works a delight to read.

Kurchatkin was classified in the late 1970s as one of the "40-Year-Old Writers" (although he was still in his 30s at this time), and placed in a canon that includes Vladimir Makanin, Andrei Bitov, Anatolii Kim, Ruslan Kireev, Vladimir Krupin, and Sergei Esin. His first story was written in 1966, the year of the trial of Daniel' and Siniavskii, and was promptly banned.

Kurchatkin has the sceptical view of human nature of a natural conservative. He represents the Soviet Union as a country where experiments on society and human nature led to a disastrous break with traditional standards, causing many to indulge the dark forces that a cultured society should keep reined in. The legacy of the 1917 coup was a catastrophic decline in personal and social morality, in individual and communal integrity and initiative, and in the family. The Bolshevik cult of dynamic state power deprived the intelligentsia of its role and left society rudderless. The price Soviet society paid for its cult of economic dynamism was a curiously sterile sense of façade and unreality. People had nothing inside them. In a fantastic vein, which owes something to Leonid Andreev, the end result is portrayed in Kurchatkin's novella *Zapiski ekstremista* [Diary of an Extremist], where an underground colony of dissidents replicates the history of the Soviet Union, passing from initial rebellious euphoria to disappointment, to galvanization by social terror, to stagnation.

Many stories show the corrupting of professional morality, a necessary corollary of the cloud-cuckoo-land of the political ideology and the divergence of the ideal from reality in economic relations. Those with common sense are politically dangerous. They are too aware that the emperor has no clothes, and preference is accordingly given to the venal, the incompetent, and the bullying. As a writer from the Urals, Kurchatkin often uses Moscow as a code for the whole ramshackle edifice of tricky mechanisms that govern the society, comparing it unfavourably with more straightforward dealings in Sverdlovsk, or the Urals or the Siberian countryside.

The sheer nastiness of the amoral Soviet administrative apparatus attracts into positions of authority those with less than admirable personal attributes. Their general bestiality is fantastically portrayed in "Novyi lednikovyi period" [The New Ice Age], where people are actually turning into hairy monsters who hunt together as a pack within the Soviet administrative apparatus, with a sexual hierarchy reminiscent of animal collectives. Indeed, it is the collectivism of the thrusting mediocrities that enables them to conquer.

Kurchatkin does have a number of heroines, but many of his female characters are evil, well equipped with grasping materialism for survival in such a system. The absurd property relations of "developed socialism" are, however, manipulated by aggressive, hard, corrupt men, as well as women, to their own advantage. The officiousness that permeates every level of this society, where everybody is brazenly asserting their right to work badly, is something Kurchatkin is good at communicating in dialogue. Echoes of the "dictatorship of the proletariat" still reverberate in a type of militant plebeian he identifies, an obsessive handyman full of animosity. The Stalinist Chapai in the novella *Nachalo dachnogo sezona* [The Start of the Dacha Season] remains the scourge of the intelligentsia. His connection with revolutionary terror was as an agent of Smersh, and he retains the smell of bloody deeds to the present day.

In a nanny state full of matriarchal attitudes, Kurchatkin's most masculine character is Khvatkov in *Vechernii svet* [Light of Evening], who literally can find no application for his physical strength and intellectual energy. The Soviet Union is a country where the strong and straightforward are broken, and only the devious prosper.

The Soviet Union in the aftermath of Stalinism is a culturally dead society. Kurchatkin wields a mean switchblade when describing the resulting culture substitute with which the attempt is made to dupe its population. There is, however, a special niche in hell reserved for those who have collaborated with the security organs. Evlampiev is summoned to the deathbed of a fairly nondescript acquaintance, who confesses he denounced the first love of Evlampiev's wife to the NKVD, with fatal consequences. "All I need now is a hole six foot deep ... Nothing more ... "

The victory of the system is not, however, by any means complete. Many are immune, from the young who adopt an attitude of total cynicism, which sometimes combines paradoxically with a sterling personal integrity, to the old who still, after all the Stalin period and its aftermath have thrown at them, retain the attitudes of an earlier age. It is in bringing together the young and the old that Kurchatkin sees the road to recovery. His second novel, *Strazhnitsa* [The Watchwoman], deals with the rise and fall of Gorbachev as seen through the eyes of a schizophrenic woman, hypnotized by his television appearances.

Kurchatkin is not a practising Christian, but he has a strongly rooted belief in the continuing applicability of the Ten Commandments. No facile optimist, he nevertheless sees at the end of *Vechernii svet* a spiritual reward for strenuously living life as a moral human being rather than as an animal. If the NKVD informer Korostylev longed only for the oblivion of the grave, Evlampiev, not in the best of health, senses the approach of his own death. Life was something to be lived and at the end, for all the infirmities of old age, the tricks of memory, the weariness of his body, come the spring his soul was young again and could live forever. "... his soul was drawn impetuously towards life, and exulted and sang".

ARCH TAIT

Aleksandr Semenovich Kushner 1936–

Poet

Biography

Born in Leningrad, 14 September 1936. Attended Gertsen Leningrad Pedagogical Institute, 1954–59. Married: Elena Vsevolodovna Nevzgliadova in 1982; one son. Teacher of Russian literature for senior schools, 1959–70. Full-time writer, since 1970. Member of the Soviet Writers' Union since 1965, and the PEN club since 1987. Recipient: Severnaia Palmira Prize, 1995.

Publications

Collected Editions

Izbrannoe. Moscow, 1992.
Izbrannoe: Stikhotvoreniia. St Petersburg, 1997.

Poetry

Pervoe vpechatlenie [First Impression]. Leningrad, 1962.
Nochnoi dozor [Night Patrol]. Leningrad, 1966.
Primety [Signs]. Leningrad, 1969.
Zavetnoe zhelanie [Cherished Desires]. Leningrad, 1973.
Pis'mo [Letter]. Leningrad, 1974.
Priamaia rech' [Direct Speech]. Leningrad, 1975.
Bol'shaia novost' [Big News]. Leningrad, 1975.
Gorod v podarok [A City as a Present]. Leningrad, 1976.
Golos [Voice]. Leningrad, 1978.
Velosiped [The Bicycle]. Leningrad, 1979.
Kanva [Canvas]. Leningrad, 1981.
Tavricheskii sad [Tauride Garden]. Leningrad, 1984.
Stikhotvoreniia. Leningrad, 1986.
Dnevnie sny [Daytime Dreams]. Leningrad, 1986.
"Srok liubvi" [Time of Love], *Novyi mir*, 8 (1987).
Kak zhivete? [How Are You?]. Leningrad, 1988.
Zhivaia izgorod' [Hedge]. Leningrad, 1988.
Pamiat' [Memory], with I. Auzin'. Riga, 1989.
Fleitist. Stikhi [Tha Flautist. Poems]. Moscow, 1990.
"Chetyre stikhotvoreniia" [Four Poems], *Novyi mir*, 6 (1990).
"Novye stikhi" [New Poems], *Oktiabr'*, 1 (1990).
"Iz liriki" [From Poems], *Druzhba narodov*, 7 (1990).
"Novyi Orfei" [New Orfei], *Znamia*, 1 (1990).
Nochnaia muzyka [Night Music]. Leningrad, 1991.
Poems in *Contemporary Russian Poetry: A Bilingual Anthology*, translated by Gerald S. Smith. Bloomington, Indiana University Press, 1993, 112–23.
Na sumrachnoi zvezde [On a Gloomy Star]. St Petersburg, 1995.

Essays

"Zametki na poliakh" [Notes in the Margin], *Voprosy literatury*, 10 (1981).
"Vtoraia real'nost" [Second Reality], *Literaturnaia gazeta*, (29 August 1984).
"Inye, luchshie mne dorogi prava ..." [I Would Prefer the Other Ways ...], *Novyi mir*, 1 (1987).
Apollon v snegu: zametki na poliakh. Leningrad, 1991; translated as *Apollo in the Snow: Selected Poems*, by Paul Graves and Carol Ueland, New York, Farrar Straus and Giroux, 1991; London, Collins Harvill, 1992.

Critical Studies

Khudozhnik v poiskakh istiny, by Irina Rodnianskaia, Moscow, 1989.
"The Poetic Vision of Aleksandr Kushner", by John Elsworth, in *Symbolism and After: Essays on Russian Poetry in Honour of Georgette Donchin*, edited by Arnold McMillin, London, Bristol Classical Press, 1992.

Bibliography

Russkie sovetskie pisateli. Poety, vol. 12. Moscow, 1989, 4–34.

Born in 1936, Aleksandr Semenovich Kushner effectively made his poetic debut in 1962 with the volume *Pervoe vpechatlenie* [First Impression]. Overshadowed at the time by poets who gained a mass following from the topicality of their themes, he has since established himself as one of the leading poets of his generation. He has published many separate collections of poetry and a substantial quantity of prose, devoted entirely to reflections on the nature and history of Russian poetry. During the Soviet period he avoided confrontation with the authorities, and never lost the possibility of publishing his work, although its uncommitted and non-ideological nature nevertheless gave rise to official condemnation on occasion. Since the collapse of the Soviet regime he has introduced political themes, about which it was formerly impossible to speak with honesty. Denying the possibility of such a thing as "Soviet" poetry, he has always been deeply conscious of tradition: the prosodic traditions of Russian poetry, with their limitless opportunities for intertextual echoes; the poetic tradition of his city, Leningrad/St Petersburg; and the longer traditions of Russian and European culture, the continuity of human experience.

Kushner's poetry is not confessional and there is little attempt in it to project the image of a particular personality. It has been said that his poetry lacks any clearly identified lyrical hero. In an article on Pushkin, Kushner himself noted that lyrical poetry is in principle not concerned with establishing the character of the author, and that this most subjective of literary genres is at the same time the most universal. The poetic persona in Kushner's work is not set apart from the world he inhabits and observes; he does not judge or admonish or pretend to any special wisdom, he assumes that his experience is very similar to that of his readers, and thus, without claiming any privileged status, he becomes something like the mouthpiece of his generation. Above all he lacks that voluntarism in his attitude to the world and to history that marked the era in which he grew up and the poetry of the older contemporaries whose popularity overshadowed his debut.

Kushner's sense of history leads him to seek its recurrent patterns. The city in which much of his poetry is set embodies in its geography and architecture models of experience that extend beyond history to myth. He writes of his country's vastness with an increasing concern that its lack of human scale can lead to the devaluing of human life, and sets against it a southern courtyard with a well and a fig tree. In an introductory note to his essay collection *Apollon v snegu* (*Apollo in the Snow*) 1991, he develops the image of a statue of Apollo, snow-covered in the park of Pavlovsk, into a metaphor for a central paradox of Russian culture, its inner warmth contrasting with the cold of the country's climate, both meteorological and political, and its sense of form and proportion belied by the obliterating snow. Several poems reflect on the particular task of the Russian poet to confer order and form on such recalcitrant material. But Kushner also maintains a sharp awareness of the individual's dependence on the time of his birth – "time is our skin, not our clothing" – and in his work of the post-glasnost period expresses sympathy for those who raised their hands in support of Stalin's villanies. He challenges the view that Mandel'shtam was always a clear-sighted critic of the regime, seeing a greater ambiguity in his attitudes and thus a greater affinity with the tragedy of his time.

A move towards more topical themes is visible in his work of the past decade. His sense of history's patterns instils a wary scepticism about the future of Russia's democracy. Increased freedom of movement engenders a broader dialogue about cultural comparisons and affinities, while renewed acquaintance with compatriots who emigrated in the 1970s provides a fresh perspective on both these issues.

Kushner's perception of the world is marked by a sense of its transparency. Both artefacts and natural things can afford glimpses of a deeper and more mysterious reality that defies exact formulation. He reflects upon such things in a manner not unlike Tiutchev's, but reaches no metaphysical conclusions. His more recent poetry seems to incline to a more religious stance, but his general view remains agnostic. The world is even more miraculous if there is no creator determining its patterns. Life appears to him as an island of light between two darknesses, but death is not threatening if the awareness is retained that death makes you the contemporary of everyone except those who are still alive. Kushner's sense of wonder is focused mainly on the quotidian. His love of poetry, an important aspect of his work, concentrates on the simple mystery of closeness, although the pain of love lost is a strong theme in some poems of the mid-1970s.

Kushner's awareness of the traditions of Russian poetry, coupled with his preference for the canonical metres of 19th-century poetry, confers on the metres of his poems a generative energy of their own. The poetic reminiscences, in which his work abounds, appear often to arise involuntarily out of the poetic metre, and frequently Kushner turns this aspect of the workings of tradition into a thematic element. There is hardly a major poet since the 18th century who is not intertextually present in Kushner's poetry, as he conducts an unceasing debate with those who will, in due course, become his contemporaries. But it is the Apollonian tradition of Petersburg, of Annenskii and Kuzmin, or of Mandel'shtam (less, perhaps, of Akhmatova, by whom he admits to being over-awed), that is most faithfully maintained in Kushner's poetry. His work is marked by a clear inner consistency. The lyrical persona, lacking self-assertion but characterized by an intense receptivity to all that surrounds him in space and time, eschewing tragedy and heroism, even the heroism of resistance, reflects with humility and humour on everyday joys and griefs, their transience, and their transformation into poetry.

JOHN ELSWORTH

Mikhail Alekseevich Kuzmin 1872–1936

Poet and man of letters

Biography

Born in Iaroslavl, 18 October 1872 (other dates frequently cited in error). Attended schools in Saratov and St Petersburg, 1884–91; studied at St Petersburg Conservatory, under N.A. Rimskii-Korsakov and others, for three years of a seven-year course; spent two further years studying music at private school of V.V. Kiuner (Kühner). Travelled to Egypt via Greece and the Near East, 1895, and to Italy, 1897. Retreated to Old-Believer settlements of Volga and northern Russia, late 1898 or early 1899; returned permanently to St Petersburg in early 1900s. Entered wholeheartedly into elite circles of musicians, artists, and writers in the capital, 1903–04; effective literary debut, 1904. Fame (or notoriety), 1906–07. Thenceforth full-time writer, composer, and librettist; prolific critic, and translator. Efforts to establish literary journals under the banner of "Emotionalism" (*Emotsionalizm*) met with official hostility in early 1920s. Rarely able to publish after 1924, with the remarkable exception of last book of verse in 1929. No original work appeared thereafter; but continued writing and translating, in desperate poverty and failing health. Openly homosexual, Kuzmin never married: many brief affairs, but lived almost uninterruptedly with Iurii Ivanovich Iurkun from 1913. Died of pneumonia in a Leningrad hospital, 1 March 1936.

Publications

Collected Editions

Sobranie sochinenii, 9 vols. Petrograd, 1914–18.
Wings: Prose and Poetry, edited and translated by Neil Granoien and Michael Green. Ann Arbor, Ardis, 1972.
Sobranie stikhov, edited by John E. Malmstad and Vladimir Markov, 3 vols. Munich, Fink, 1977–78.
Selected Prose and Poetry, edited and translated by Michael Green. Ann Arbor, Ardis, 1980.
Proza, edited by Vladimir Markov with Fridrikh Shol'ts, 9 vols. Berkeley, Berkeley Slavic Specialties, 1984–90.
Izbrannye proizvedeniia, edited by A.V. Lavrov and R.D. Timenchik. Leningrad, 1990.
Arena: Izbrannye stikhotvoreniia, edited with an introduction by A.G. Timofeev. St Petersburg, 1994.
Teatr, 4 vols, in 2 books, compiled by A. Timofeev, edited by V. Markov and G. Cheron. Oakland, Berkeley Slavic Specialties, 1994–
Stikhotvoreniia. "Novaia biblioteka poeta", St Petersburg, 1996.

Poetry

Seti. Pervaia kniga stikhov [Nets: First Book of Verse]. Moscow, 1908; reprinted Petrograd and Berlin, Petropolis, 1923; New York, Russica, 1979.
Kuranty liubvi. Slova i muzyka [The Chimes of Love: Words and Music]. Moscow, 1910.
Osennie ozera. Vtoraia kniga stikhov [Autumn Lakes: Second Book of Verse]. Moscow, 1912.
Glinianye golubki. Tret'ia kniga stikhov [Clay Doves: Third Book of Verse]. St Petersburg, 1914.
Vozhatyi. Stikhi [The Guide: Poems]. Petrograd, 1918.
Dvum [To Two]. Petrograd, 1918.
Zanaveshennye kartinki [Pictures under Wraps]. Amsterdam [i.e. Petrograd], 1920; reprinted Ann Arbor, Ardis, 1972.
Ekho. Stikhi [Echo: Poems]. Petrograd, 1921.
Nezdeshnie vechera. Stikhi, 1914–1920 [Otherworldly Evenings: Poems 1914–1920]. Petrograd, 1921; reprinted New York, Russica, n.d.
Paraboly. Stikhotvoreniia 1921–22 [Parabolas: Poems 1921–22]. Petrograd and Berlin, Petropolis, 1923; reprinted Letchworth, Prideaux Press, 1978.
Novyi Gul' [The New Hull]. Leningrad, 1924.
Forel' razbivaet led. Stikhi 1925–1928 [The Trout Breaks the Ice: Poems 1925–1928]. Leningrad, 1929; reprinted Ann Arbor, Ardis, 1978.

Fiction

Kryl'ia. Moscow, 1907; translated in *Wings: Prose and Poetry*, 1972.
Prikliucheniia Eme Lebefa [The Adventures of Aimé Leboeuf]. St Petersburg, 1907.
Pervaia kniga rasskazov [First Book of Stories]. St Petersburg, 1910.
Vtoraia kniga rasskazov [Second Book of Stories]. St Petersburg, 1910.
Tret'ia kniga rasskazov [Third Book of Stories]. Petersburg, 1913.
Pokoinitsa v dome. Skazki [A Dead Woman in the House. Fairy Tales]. St Petersburg, 1914.
Zelenyi solovei [The Green Nightingale]. Petrograd, 1915.
Voennye rasskazy [War Stories]. Petrograd, 1915.
Plavaiushchie-puteshestvuiushchie [Travellers by Sea and by Land]. Petrograd, 1915.
Antrakt v ovrage [Interlude in the Ravine]. Petrograd, 1916.
Babushkina shkatulka. Rasskazy [Grandmother's Casket. Stories]. Petrograd, 1918 (as *Sobranie sochinenii*, 1914–18, vol. 2).
Devstvennyi Viktor i drugie rasskazy [Virginal Victor and Other Stories]. Petrograd, 1918 (as *Sobranie sochinenii*, 1914–18, vol. 9).
Chudesnaia zhizn' Iosifa Bal'zamo, grafa Kaliostro [The Miraculous Life of Joseph Balsamo, Count Cagliostro]. Petrograd, 1919; reprinted, with an introduction by Gennadii Shmakov, New York, Russica, 1982.

Plays

Tri p'esy [Three Plays]. St Petersburg, 1907.
Komedii [Comedies]. St Petersburg, 1908; contents reprinted separately as *Komediia o Aleksee, cheloveke bozh'em, ili: Poteriannyi i obrashchennyi syn* [The Comedy of St Alexis, or: The Lost and Converted Son]; *Komediia o Evdokii iz Geliopolia ili: Obrashchennaia kurtizanka* [The Comedy of Eudoxia of Heliopolis, or: The Converted Courtesan]; and *Komediia o Martiniane* [Martinian: A Comedy], Letchworth, Prideaux Press, 1970.

Venetsianskie bezumtsy. Komediia [Venetian Madcaps: A Comedy]. Moscow, 1915.
Vtornik Meri. Predstavlenie v 3-kh chastiakh dlia kukol zhivykh ili dereviannykh [Mary's Tuesday: A Spectacle in Three Parts for Live or Wooden Dolls]. Petrograd, 1921.
Lesok. Liricheskaia poema dlia muzyki. S ob'iasnitel'noi prozoi, v 3-kh chastiakh [The Grove: A Lyric Poem for Music, with Elucidatory Prose, in Three Parts]. Petrograd, 1922.

Literary Criticism
"O prekrasnoi iasnosti" [On Beautiful Clarity], *Apollon*, 4 (1910), 5–10.
Uslovnosti. Stat'i ob iskusstve [Conventions: Articles about Art]. Petrograd, 1923.

Translator
Apulei. Apologiia, Metamorfozy, Floridy [Apuleius. Apologia, Metamorphoses, Florida], translated by M.A. Kuzmin and S.P. Markish. Moscow, 1956.
Skekspir v perevodakh Mikhaila Kuzmina [Shakespeare in the Translations of Mikhail Kuzmin]. Moscow, 1990.

Diaries
"Pis'ma M.A. Kuzmina k Bloku i otryvki iz dnevnika M.A. Kuzmina" [Letters from M.A. Kuzmin to Blok and Extracts from M.A. Kuzmin's Diary], edited by K.N. Suvorova, in *Aleksandr Blok: Novye materialy i issledovaniia*, *Literaturnoe nasledstvo*, vol. 92, book 2, Moscow, 1981, 143–74.
"The Diary of Mikhail Kuzmin, 1905–1906", edited by G. Cheron, *Wiener Slawistischer Almanach*, 17 (1986), 391–438.
"Mikhail Kuzmin. Dnevnik 1921 goda" [1921 Diary], edited by N.A. Bogomolov and S.V. Shumikhin, *Minuvshee. Istoricheskii al'manakh*, 12 (1991), 423–94; 13 (1991).
"Mikhail Kuzmin. Dnevnik 1931 goda" [1931 Diary], edited by S.V. Shumikhin, *Novoe literaturnoe obozrenie*, 1994, 7.

Critical Studies
"Blok i Kuzmin (Novye materialy)", by G.G. Shmakov, *Blokovskii sbornik*, 2 (1972), 341–64.
"Mikhail Kuzmin and the Theater", by Michael Green, *Russian Literature Triquarterly*, 7 (1973), 246–66.
"'Wings' and 'The World of Art'", by Neil Granoien, *Russian Literature Triquarterly*, 11 (1975), 393–405.
"The Mystery of Iniquity: Kuzmin's 'Temnye ulitsy rozhdaiut temnye mysli'", by John E. Malmstad, *Slavic Review*, 34 (1975), 44–64.
"Kuzmin's 'The Trout Breaking Through the Ice'", by John Malmstad and Gennadii Shmakov, in *Russian Modernism: Culture and the Avant-Garde, 1900–1930*, edited by George Gibian and H.W. Tjalsma, Ithaca, Cornell University Press, 1976, 132–64.
"Mixail Kuzmin: A Chronicle of His Life and Times", by John E. Malmstad, in Kuzmin's *Sobranie stikhov*, Munich, Fink, 1977, vol. 3, 7–319.
"Poeziia Mikhaila Kuzmina", by V.F. Markov, in Kuzmin's *Sobranie stikhov*, Munich, Fink, 1977, vol. 3, 321–426; reprinted in *O svobode v poezii*, by V.F. Markov, St Petersburg, 1994.
"The Platonic Theme in Kuzmin's *Wings*", by Donald S. Gillis, *Slavic and East European Journal*, 22 (1978), 336–47.
"Akhmatova i Kuzmin", by R.D. Timenchik, V.N. Toporov, and T.V. Tsiv'ian, *Russian Literature*, 6 (1978), 213–305.
"Mixail Kuzmin's 'On Beautiful Clarity' and Vyacheslav Ivanov: A Reconsideration", by John F. Barnstead, *Canadian Slavonic Papers*, 34 (1982), 1–10.
"Kuzmin and the Oberiuty: An Overview", by G. Cheron, *Wiener Slawistischer Almanach*, 12 (1983), 87–101.
"Mikhail Kuzmin's *The Miraculous Life of Joseph Balsamo Count Cagliostro*: Artfulness and Metaphysics", by Joachim T. Baer, in *Studies in Russian Literature in Honor of Vsevolod Setchkarev*, edited by Julian W. Connolly and Sonia I. Ketchian, Columbus, Ohio, Slavica, 1986, 34–49.
Studies in the Life and Work of Mixail Kuzmin, edited by John E. Malmstad, Vienna, *Wiener Slawistischer Almanach*, 24, 1989.
"Mikhail Kuzmin i Vladimir Maiakovskii", by L. Seleznev, *Voprosy literatury*, 11 (1989), 66–87.
Mikhail Kuzmin i russkaia kul'tura XX veka: Tezisy i materialy konferentsii 15–17 maia 1990 g., edited by G.A. Morev, Leningrad, 1990.
"M.A. Kuzmin", by O.N. Gil'debrandt, *Litsa: Biograficheskii al'manakh*, St Petersburg and Moscow, 1992, 1, 262–90.
Michail Kuzmin: Studien zur Poetik der frühen und mittleren Schaffensperiode, by Klaus Harer, Munich, Sagner, 1993.
"Simvolika Mikhaila Kuzmina v sviazi s ego kontseptsiei knigi zhizni", by Omry Ronen, in *Readings in Russian Modernism*, edited by Ronald Vroon and John E. Malmstad, Moscow, 1993, 291–98.
"Materialy M.A. Kuzmina v Rukopisnom otdele Pushkinskogo Doma", by A.G. Timofeev (with appended unpublished poetry, drama, correspondence), in *Ezhegodnik Rukopisnogo otdela Pushkinskogo Doma na 1990 g.*, St Petersburg, 1993, 17–71.
"'Ital'ianskoe puteshestvie' M.A. Kuzmina", by A.G. Timofeev, in *Pamiatniki kul'tury: Novye otkrytiia. Ezhegodnik 1992*. Moscow, 1993.
"Meshes and Mirrors: Two Meta-Poems by Mixail Kuzmin", by John A. Barnstead, in *Alexander Lipson: In Memoriam*, edited by Charles Gribble *et al.*, Columbus, Ohio, Slavica, 1994, 11–23.
"Les thèmes italiens dans la poésie de Mikhail Kuzmin: L'Italie comme théâtre de la mémoire", by Anastasia Pasquinelli, *Cahiers du Monde russe et soviétique*, 35 (1994), 803–20.
"Khudozhestvennyi mir M. Kuzmina: Tezaurus formal'nyi i tezaurus funktsional'nyi", in *Izbrannye stat'i*, by M.L. Gasparov, St Petersburg, 1995, 275–85.
Mikhail Kuzmin: Stat'i i materialy, by N.A. Bogomolov, Moscow, 1995.
Mikhail Kuzmin: Iskusstvo, zhizn', epokha, by N.A. Bogomolov and John E. Malmstad, Moscow, 1996.

Bibliography
"M.A. Kuzmin", by A. Tishkov, *Al'manakh bibliofila*, 25 (1989), 188–207.

In the course of a remarkably varied artistic career, Mikhail

Kuzmin produced 12 volumes of poetry (including one vocal-instrumental cycle); more than 100 short stories and fables; several short novels; some 40 dramatic works, including fully scored ballet and operetta in addition to "mysteries", comedies, pastorals, masquerades, pantomime, and plays for children's and puppet theatres; numerous critical articles and reviews, covering literature, theatre, music, and painting; copious translations, of opera librettos as well as *belles-lettres*; and abundant vocal settings and music for theatre. Kuzmin's most outstanding achievements, however, are his fiction and, above all, his poetry. Though his literary work is uneven in quality, his modern editor, Vladimir Markov, is not alone in equating his best prose with the finest of the 20th century. The same can confidently be claimed of his magnificent later verse.

Kuzmin turned to literature relatively late. He had previously read voraciously in the major European and classical languages, and had surmounted a protracted spiritual crisis, which took him from attempted suicide and differing forms of worldly renunciation, to a clear-sighted acceptance of self, fate, and world, broadly characteristic of his writing. His purely literary debut was preceded by lyrics to accompany his own music (his *Kuranty liubvi* [The Chimes of Love] enjoyed considerable vogue from 1906); and music, his original pursuit and "parallel" career, always remained a fecund source of literary reference and inspiration: thematically, structurally, and arguably, too, in a virtuoso inventivenss of stanzaic form and intricacy of verbal texture (internal rhyme, paronomasia), scarcely equalled by his many form-conscious contemporaries.

The reception of *Kryl'ia* (*Wings*) and *Seti* [Nets] – Kuzmin's strikingly mature first books of prose and verse – firmly established the still enduring perception of their author as a mannered aesthete and amoralist (or immoralist), whose (homo-) erotic themes, and essentially insouciant, hedonistic delight in "everything bright, simple, and dear" (*Wings*), are conveyed with gracefully stylized elegance and lightness of touch. The concept of "beautiful clarity" (1910), routinely abstracted from the context of polemic with Viacheslav Ivanov in which it was formulated, seemingly both consolidated the literary-critical cliché and further deflected attention from Kuzmin's underlying seriousness. Love, predominantly homosexual and occasionally misogynistic, is indeed the main theme of his first books – but together with art, which is guided by love and lends it consummate expression (the metaliterary theme is announced in the second poem of *Seti*), it provides unique access to an ideal world of beauty and truth. The structure of *Seti* unfolds accordingly, from the irresistible snares and disappointments of physical passion (a strong awareness of transience lending piquancy to sensation), to a firm conviction in the immanent reality of higher, spiritual love: envisaged – through the afterwards recurrent image of enigmatic masculine "guide" (*vozhatyi*) – with a mystical intensity reminiscent of Blok, but the stuff, none the less, of spontaneous human experience, and an incessant source of personal and creative renewal, rather than immutable otherworldly stasis. For Kuzmin (who drew upon the Franciscans as well as Plotinus and Plato), love and world are equally God's gift; and his frequently maligned "poetry of objects" also consequently reflects the importance and particularity of all things. This accounts in turn for the disconcerting collocation of "high" and "low", "profound" and "trivial", which persistently typifies both individual manifestations of his art, and the broad compass of his variegated career. It might also be related to an abiding distrust of dogmatic fixity, moral absolutes and teleological purpose, variously manifest in, say, the plurality of discourses fundamental to *Wings*, or Kuzmin's ideological independence from Symbolism, Acmeism, and Futurist primitivism, despite close personal or creative ties with leading representatives of each.

The following period, to 1917–18, was Kuzmin's most prolific (particularly in prose, with 70 stories and four novels during 1913–17 alone); but saw a corresponding reduction in artistic intensity. Much in his immense thematic repertoire, from sectarian mysticism and foreign adventure tale to fictional portrayal of the contemporary literary milieu, naturally continues to intrigue; but the conceptual framework and structural procedures of his best work are essentially familiar: so, for example, in the short novel *Chudesnaia zhizn' Iosifa Bal'zamo, grafa Kaliostro* [The Miraculous Life of Joseph Balsamo, Count Cagliostro] completed 1916), characteristic disdain of "psychologism" and the undifferentiatedly rapid, externalized narrative of events of differing magnitude typically tend to conceal the metaphysical reflection on the precariousness of the individual's spiritual journey toward truth and imponderable relationship to the Divine plan. Subsequently, too, though Kuzmin's essentially religious, even pious, view of life becomes troubled by recurrent apprehensions of violence and latent chaos, his central concerns with the possibility of transformation through love and art, with incessant self-perfection and deepening understanding, are not fundamentally altered. From roughly 1918, however, there are significant shifts in means of expression – now primarily in poetry – toward startling intertextual complexity and increasingly avant-garde innovation. An initial stage, fully exemplified in *Nezdeshnie vechera* [Otherworldly Evenings], is an essentially "hermetic" (and occasionally transrational) art, deeply informed by Gnosticism (reflecting Kuzmin's enduring fascination with cultural syncretism), alchemy (with its emphasis on metamorphosis of matter) and occultism. By the time of *Forel' razbivaet led* [The Trout Breaks the Ice] (1929), a more densely metaphorical poetry is instead structured primarily on an ostensible flux of emotional and intellectual association. This draws on a bewildering array of sources – from *Dracula*, Expressionist cinema, and journalistic gossip, to Wagnerian opera, Renaissance poetry and the Lives of the Saints – which ultimately serve to "double", shape, and transform autobiographical experience (alternately personal-tragic or trivial and second-hand, but frequently defying critical reconstruction) into powerful symbol and myth. In prose, too, there is clear evidence of new departures, if nothing of comparable scope: a combination of grotesque anecdote, travesty, and linguistic play in the recently published short piece *Pechka v bane* [Stove in the Bathhouse] (written in 1926), unexpectedly reveals Kuzmin as a direct precursor of the *Oberiuty*. It is thus particularly regrettable that his unpublished manuscripts of the 1930s were entirely destroyed.

For reasons that doubtless include unenviable early reputation, formidable later difficulty, and unspectacular fate, Kuzmin has generally been less widely appreciated than many of his contemporaries. Thanks to a small number of scholars, he is nevertheless well served by academic editions – soon also to include his critical prose, archival materials and, most importantly, the diary he kept for more than 25 years. This may have radical consequences for the interpretation of Silver Age literary history in its entirety, while the exceptional richness and depth of Kuzmin's best work is bound to attract much further study in its own right.

MICHAEL BASKER

Wings

Kryl'ia

Novella, 1907

Wings first appeared in the journal *Vesy* in the November issue of 1906 and immediately achieved scandalous notoriety for its treatment of the theme of male homosexuality. A separate edition of 1907 quickly sold out, followed by equally popular subsequent editions, including a post-revolutionary one published in Berlin in 1923.

The novella was evidently the work of a poet who constructed his prose almost on the model of stanzas and exhibited unusual sensitivity to the aesthetic qualities of words and patterns of speech. Episodic though the effect might be when each section appeared as a brief encounter, an exchange of words or a small cameo lightly sketched without undue in-filling, the work may have seemed *faux naif* at first acquaintance because the subtext, the true emotional meaning, was not always clear. The literary quality was never in any doubt. Being of the age of E.M. Forster, it had – and retains – something of that writer's clarity of expression and ear for nuances of dialogue, just as, in its intimate, first-person study of adolescence, it bears comparison with Joyce's *A Portrait of the Artist as a Young Man*.

Thematically it was clearly autobiographical. The issue of homosexuality, however understated, involved unusual candour and boldness for its time. The novella, divided into three parts, described its young hero's gradual sexual awakening and ultimate readiness to become the lover of a glamorous older man.

Vania Smurov, despatched to St Petersburg after his mother's death to live with relatives, finds himself in a louche, untidy household. He is a vaguely narcissistic adolescent of student age who, studying himself dispassionately in a mirror, sees "a slightly insignificant round face with red cheeks, large grey eyes, a beautiful but still childishly full mouth and fair hair which, since it was not cut short, tended to curl. He neither liked nor disliked this tall, slender boy in a black blouse with delicate eyebrows". His supposed indifference towards himself does not deter others. He has soon attracted the interest of a wealthy aesthete, half-Russian, half-English, with the odd name of Stroop (the spelling suggests a Germanic provenance as well as echoes of Oscar Wilde), who is allegedly engaged to the daughter of the household but this, and other relationships with women, turns out to be a cover for a homosexual lifestyle. Vania's Greek teacher is also part of Stroop's circle of "Hellenists" into which Vania himself is gradually initiated, urged on to become "a new man", to become fully "contemporary", as Stroop puts it, to grow wings because in antiquity "human beings saw that all beauty, all love was divine, and they became free and bold, and they grew wings".

The combined effect of his Greek teacher's elegant, if oblique, initiation into classical and Renaissance treatments of the theme and Stroop's opulently cultured world clearly seduces Vania into a more physical awareness of male beauty. Stroop's claim, in asserting his Hellenism, that "miracles are around us at every turn: there are muscles and sinews in the human body which cannot be looked at without an excited trembling" has an obvious erotic appeal, except that the aestheticism is suddenly exposed for what it is when Vania finds himself involved in a young woman's suicide in Stroop's apartment and realizes the nature of the latter's relationship with his servant Fedor.

The locale of Part 2 is the Volga where Vania is a guest of his friend Sasha who has an aunt, a 30-year-old widow. She seems anxious from the start to seduce the boy and begins by candidly expounding the joys of such seduction:

> Think, Vania, how marvellous it would be having another person right there, a complete stranger, someone else's legs and skin and eyes – and he's all yours, all of him, all of him, you can see every part of him and kiss and touch him, every little mark on his body, no matter where it was, even the little golden hairs growing on his arms and every little fold and furrow of his fondly doting skin.

Vania's sentimental education is conducted against the background of the Old Believer world with which Sasha is associated. The spiritual answers to eternal questions offered by the Old Believers merely serve to set in relief Vania's delight in his own body. A scene on the Volga, when he narcissistically admires his naked body reflected in the water, ironically highlights the perishability of such beauty after the corpse of a drowned boy is found. Late that night he somewhat hysterically laments the contrast between his own healthy body and that of the corpse to Sasha's aunt who, naturally enough, takes this for an overture but is at once crudely rebuffed. There can be no doubt now about Vania's sexual preferences. His Greek teacher has meanwhile taken him under his wing and proposed that they go off to Italy together.

His sentimental and aesthetic education reaches its climax in Part 3 against Roman and Florentine backgrounds. Classicism in various forms, both musical and mythological, has the effect of emphasizing the cult of male beauty. The Greek teacher allays Vania's apprehensions about the perishability of such beauty by proclaiming that, as an idea, it cannot perish "and this is perhaps the sole valuable thing in the changing and transient diversity of life".

In Florence Vania meets Stroop again, is challenged to choose between him and his former life and in the end opts for "the path to the beautiful in life" in Stroop's company. As with the novella as a whole, its ending is as unemphatic in its coyness as are all the relationships in Vania's story. If he himself emerges as scarcely more than an emotional outline, the thumbnail sketches of incidental characters and events are usually brilliantly achieved and the dialogue, for all its self-conscious aestheticism in parts, can often be remarkably true to life in its humour and archness.

RICHARD FREEBORN

L

The Lay of Igor's Campaign

Anonymous heroic poem c.1185–86

Editions

Slovo o polku Igoreve, Igora syna Sviatoslavlia, vnuka Ol'gova. 1800; facsimile edition, Moscow, 1988.

Slovo o polku Igoreve po spisku naidennomu mezhdu bumagami imperatristy Ekateriny II, edited by P. Pekarskii. 1864.

Slovo o polku Igoreve, edited by A.S. Orlove. 1923; with modern Russian translation, 1950.

Slovo o polku Igoreve, edited by D.S. Likhachev. "Biblioteka poeta", Leningrad, 1967; 3rd edition, Leningrad, 1985.

Translations

La geste du Prince Igor, edited and translated by Henri Grégoire, Roman Jakobson *et al.* New York, Annuaire de l'Institut de philologie et histoire orientales et slaves, 1948.

"The Igor Tale", in *Anthology of Old Russian Literature*, edited by A. Stender-Petersen and Stefan Congrat-Butlar. New York, Columbia University Press, 1954.

The Song of Igor's Campaign, translated by Vladimir Nabokov. New York, Vintage, 1960; London, Weidenfeld and Nicolson, 1961; reprinted Ann Arbor, Ardis, 1988.

Selections translated as "The Lay of Igor's Campaign", by Dimitri Obolensky, in *The Penguin Book of Russian Verse*, Harmondsworth, Penguin, 1962, revised edition, 1965; reprinted as *The Heritage of Russian Verse*, Bloomington, Indiana University Press, 1976, 1–22.

The Tale of the Campaign of Igor, translated by Robert C. Howes. New York, Norton, 1973.

The Lay of the Warfare Waged by Igor (parallel English and modern Russian translations), translated by Irina Petrova. Moscow, Progress, 1981.

Critical Studies

History of Early Russian Literature, by N.K. Gudzii, translated by Susan Wilbur Jones, New York, Macmillan, 1949.

The Oriental Elements in the Vocabulary of the Oldest Russian Epos, the Igor' Tale, by Karl Heinrich Menges, New York, Linguistic Circle of New York, 1951.

Imagery of the Igor' Tale in the Light of Byzantino-Slavic Poetic Theory, by Justinia Besharov, Leiden, E.J. Brill, 1956.

History of Russian Literature from the Eleventh Century to the End of the Baroque, by Dmitrij Čiževskij, The Hague, Mouton, 1960.

Selected Writings, by Roman Jakobson, 7 vols, The Hague, Mouton, 1962–85.

Glossary of the Igor' Tale, by Tatjana Čiževska, The Hague, Mouton, 1966.

"The Authenticity of the 'Slovo o polku Igoreve'", by D.S. Likhachev, *Oxford Slavonic Papers*, 23 (1967).

"Slovo o polku Igoreve" i pamiatniki russkoi literatury XI–XIII vekov, by V.P. Adrianova-Peretts, Leningrad, 1968.

Slovo o polku Igoreve i ego sovremenniki, by B.A. Rybakov, Moscow, 1971.

Early Russian Literature, by John Fennell and Antony Stokes, Berkeley, University of California Press, and London, Faber, 1974.

Slovo o polku Igoreve i kul'tura ego vremeni, by D.S. Likhachev, Leningrad, 1978.

Poetika "Slovo o polku Igoreve", by Boris Gasparov, Vienna, *Wiener Slawistischer Almanach*, 1984.

Lances Sing: A Study of the Igor Tale, by Robert Mann, Columbus, Ohio, Slavica, 1990.

"Toward a New Critical Edition of the *Igor Tale*", by Harvey Goldblatt and Riccardo Picchio, *Russica Romana*, 2 (1995), 25–64.

Entsiklopediia "Slovo o polku Igoreve", 5 vols, St Petersburg, 1995.

"Slovo o polku Igoreve". Poetika i lingvistika teksta. "Slovo... i pushkinskie teksty, by T.M. Nikolaeva, Moscow, 1997.

Slovo o polku Igoreve (*The Lay of Igor's Campaign*) is the most densely poetic, the most intensely studied, the most celebrated and the most cryptic work of early East Slavonic literature. Though the text itself is brief, filling no more than about a dozen pages, its impact has been huge. It is one of a very small group of surviving non-ecclesiastical, non-monastic works which may be attributable to the period before the Mongol conquest. That alone would guarantee scholarly interest, but the qualities and puzzles of *The Lay of Igor's Campaign* set it in a class of its own as a source of inspiration, influence and intrigue far beyond academic debate. Its dazzling metaphorical agility is obvious, but almost everything else is obscure or controversial: its original text, its meanings, its form and genre, its date, its author, even its authenticity as a medieval work.

The Lay of Igor's Campaign takes a rather minor, local historical event and uses it as the basis for a series of lyrical and rhetorical meditations on the land and the rulers of Rus'. The ideology is nostalgic, the ethos is heroic, and the scope of the imagery is cosmic.

The historical core is an unsuccessful campaign undertaken in 1185 by a minor prince of the Chernigovan branch of the dynasty, Igor' Sviatoslavich of Novgorod-Seversk, deep into the steppes to confront the Polovtsy. Contrary to widespread myth, relations between the southern Rus' and the steppe nomads were fairly stable and peaceable for much of the pre-Mongol period. From time to time, however, one or more of the nomadic groups attempted to shift the balance of influence in the forest-steppe borderlands. In the 1180s and 1190s a robust Polovtsian alliance was formed under the leadership of Konchak, and Igor''s campaign of 1185 was one of several Rus' attempts to defeat and deter him. A successful venture into the steppes required the co-operation of several princes who could combine their forces. Igor' marched virtually unaided. Defeat should have been predictable. *The Lay of Igor's Campaign* celebrates his boldness, censures his rashness, and laments the lack of support from his kin.

The tale is not, however, primarily a sequential account of military events, it begins with a show of literary self-awareness, a homage to the 11th-century bard Boian. Igor''s defeat is complete barely a third of the way through the text, although a final section tells of his escape from captivity and of his joyous return to Kiev. The rest of the text consists of a series of excursuses: on the dark omens which foreshadowed the expedition; on strife among the princes; a lament by the women of Rus'; a symbolic dream of Prince Sviatoslav Vsevolodovich of Kiev (Igor''s senior kinsman) along with its interpretation by his boyars; Sviatoslav's own "golden word" of regret for Igor''s valiant foolhardiness; individual appeals to an array of princes who failed to come to Igor''s aid; recollections of past bickering among the princes; a lament by Igor''s wife.

The linkages are thematic rather than linear, lyrical rather than narrative, and the main integrating device is the imagery. Through metaphor, simile and symbol the events of the campaign fuse with the motions of the natural and supernatural world. Falcons descending on a flock of swans turn out to be Boian's fingers descending on the strings. Armies swoop as black ravens, princes prowl as grey wolves. Personified Disgrace arises as a maiden and splashes the sea by the Don with swan wings. A battle is a wedding feast with wine of blood; the battlefield – a harvest of bones. Wind, sun and river are invoked as participants. Trees bend to the ground in sorrow. Rivers speak, lances sing, the earth groans.

The tale is easier to describe than to categorize. It has affinities with many forms and genres, but is not comfortably subsumed to any single generic label. It has elements of heroic narrative, elements of lyrical lament and of rhetorical eulogy, besides containing smaller set-piece laments and eulogies within it. In its vocabulary, imagery, phraseology and syntactic formulae it has uniquely strong affinities with a number of Ukrainian and Russian folk genres, but as a complex whole it has no close folkloric equivalent. It is in many respects "poetic", but is it also an actual poem? Editors and (especially) translators often arrange it in "lines", but rarely agree on how best to do so. There is certainly no syllabic regularity (in this respect the tale is a very long way indeed from the work most often cited as its closest west European equivalent, the *Chanson de Roland*). There are perhaps certain recurrent patterns of stress, and some of the most productive recent research has aimed to recover early East Slavonic accentual and intonational features. Yet there is no consensus as to whether the surviving text of the *Tale* derives from an authentic oral poem, from a literary poem which echoed a range of oral genres, or from a prose work saturated with poetic devices.

Behind all such discussion lies a more fundamental uncertainty about the text and status of *The Lay of Igor's Campaign*. The known text apparently derives from a single manuscript, which was discovered in the early 1790s, copied out for Catherine II, published in 1800, and destroyed in the fire of Moscow in 1812. There is therefore no extant medieval manuscript of the work.

This raises serious problems on two levels. First, how close is the received text to its original? Several passages in the 1800 edition are plainly corrupt, and some are notoriously incomprehensible. Any detailed reading of *The Lay of Igor's Campaign* must be hypothetical. Conjectures and emendations abound at all points on a scale stretching from scrupulous caution to extravagant fantasy. Second, is there sufficient evidence to show that the hypothetical original was truly composed in the late 12th or early 13th century, in the immediate aftermath of the events on which it is based? Of all known works of early Russian literature, only the *Zadonshchina* appears to have significant textual links with *The Lay of Igor's Campaign*. Did the *Zadonshchina* borrow from *The Lay of Igor's Campaign* or vice versa? The latter has been dated to all centuries from the 12th to the 18th.

Scepticism has been an effective catalyst for research into the textual, linguistic and literary properties of the work, and in the process the arguments for its essential antiquity have been strengthened rather than undermined.

SIMON FRANKLIN

The Legend of Boris and Gleb

Anonymous 11th–12th-century prose narrative

Editions

"Skazanie o Borise i Glebe", in *Pamiatniki literatury Drevnei Rusi. Nachalo russkoi literatury. XI - nachalo XII veka*, edited by D.S. Likhachev and L.A. Dmitriev. Moscow, 1978, 279–304.

Translation

"The Narrative, Passion, and Encomium of Boris and Gleb", translated by Marvin Kantor, in *Medieval Slavic Lives of Saints and Princes*. Ann Arbor, Michigan Slavic Publications, 1983, 163–253.

Critical Study

The Martyred Princes Boris and Gleb: A Socio-Cultural Study of the Cult and the Texts, by Gail Lenhoff, Columbus, Ohio, Slavica, 1989.

The first native Russian saints to be officially recognized by the Orthodox Church were the two martyred princely brothers Boris and Gleb, sons of Vladimir I, responsible for the baptism of Rus' into the Orthodox Church. Boris and Gleb were victims of the bitter fratricidal struggle for the Kievan throne which arose on the death of Vladimir in 1015. They too died in 1015, killed by their elder half-brother Sviatopolk, and were eventually canonized in 1072, after the translation of their relics and reports of many miraculous events.

Saints Boris and Gleb to this day enjoy great and enduring popularity in Russia, their local cult of veneration originating as early as a few decades after their murder and rapidly spreading to embrace most parts of Rus'. Such widespread fame and glory has spawned numerous literary accounts of the martyrs' deaths and of posthumous miracles: for example, the learned monk Nestor composed a traditional and elegant hagiographical *zhitie* (biography) to honour them, *Chtenie o zhitii i o pogublenii blazhennuiu strastoterptsu Borisa i Gleba* [Reading on the Life and Slayings of the Blessed Martyrs Boris and Gleb]; the *Povest' vremennykh let* (*Primary Chronicle*) tells their story and many prayers and other devotional works are devoted to them. Nothing, however, has succeeded in capturing the imagination as much as the inspiring and anonymous *Skazanie o Borise i Glebe* [Legend of Boris and Gleb].

The legend opens with a brief ancestral history and news of Vladimir's death. Boris is returning from a military campaign when he learns of his father's death and that Sviatopolk has tried to conceal this information. Boris's lament is emotive and heartfelt, especially as he realizes that he himself – as a possible rival successor to the throne – may now be in grave danger from Sviatopolk. He vows to follow God's commandments and not resist any violence, preferring to die a martyr than use violence against his own brother. Boris muses on the futility of worldly vanity and power, and the approaching certainty of his own death. In stark contrast to these pious meditations and prayers, the legend then turns to Sviatopolk who is indeed hatching the deadly plot, gathering together his own villainous supporters. Several days later Sviatopolk's men catch up with Boris, and, amid scenes of great suspense and pathos, Boris is cut down, all the time praying that God accept him as a martyr. Sviatopolk fears that if he is found out in this crime he will be shown no mercy, and so decides to eliminate as many of his enemies as possible. Meanwhile, Gleb has heard of his father's illness and is making haste back to Kiev, when he learns of Vladimir's death and the murder of Boris. He falls weeping to the ground; his lament tells of his unbearable grief and loneliness, his readiness also to die a martyr. When the murderers find him, he pleads with them to spare him, reasoning that he is still a child and has never harmed them. At the end, though, he too offers no resistance to the butcher's sword and is slain. The brothers are buried hastily in open country and many people see pillars of fire and light rising from their graves. The legend then recounts how Iaroslav, another half-brother, seeks revenge for the murders and battles with Sviatopolk, finally driving him into the wilderness where he loses his senses and dies. Iaroslav finds the bodies of the martyrs and they are accorded suitable burial rites. A long eulogy and prayer contemplate the importance of protecting the holy land of Rus' and ridding it of internecine strife. Accounts of the posthumous miracles worked by Boris and Gleb complete the legend.

One of the principal themes of the work emerges as opposition to the long-familiar inter-princely feuding. This threatened to destroy any harmonious relations the principalities of Rus' had managed to build with one another, as well as to weaken the country in the eyes of foreign enemies. In this light Boris and Gleb appear to have gone to their deaths in the name of both the Christian faith and their native land, thus indicating they were eventually crowned as martyrs of political, just as much as religious, assassination. Indeed, Saints Boris and Gleb are renowned still for their divine protection, being awarded only to the rightful and true ruling dynasty.

Much of their popularity, however, appears to stem from another important theme; total humility and passivity in the face of evil. The Princes are portrayed as echoing the Passion of Christ, rendering their lives unquestioningly up to God: for a land still fresh from the baptismal font this was a powerful image. And the narrator of the legend never misses an opportunity to stress the Princes' youth, filial obedience, piety and innocence: the language is highly emotive, vigorous and dramatic, obviously designed to enduce sympathy for the Princes; they both reveal very real human fear at the approach of death, but, despite this, determine not to return the fight; passages telling of their prayers are followed directly by reference to Sviatopolk's evil intentions; historical reality is often conveniently swept aside in order to re-emphasize the apparent innocence and youth of these two already battle-hardened young men.

The exact date of composition of the legend has provoked endless debate. Some claim that it was written as early as the end of the 11th century, while others counter that it was put together as a compilatory work far later, long after the *Primary Chronicle* account (under the year 1015), and after Nestor had composed his *Chtenie o zhitii i o pogublenii blazhennuiu strastoterptsu Borisa i Gleba*. The most likely hypothesis is that the *Primary Chronicle* account was the first, although itself based on a written source of some kind which has not survived; this would have been followed by Nestor's *zhitie*; and the legend probably used at least both of these texts as a basic source.

Whatever the historical truth behind the composition of the legend, it stands as testimony to a fierce and proud cult of the Saints in the Russian Orthodox Church. It was also the inspiration for many future Russian "princely *zhitiia*", although few as powerfully and emotively narrated as the story of Boris and Gleb.

ROSALIND MCKENZIE

Leonid Maksimovich Leonov 1899–1994

Novelist and dramatist

Biography

Born in Moscow, 31 May 1899. Attended Moscow Third gymnasium, 1910–18. Brought up in Moscow and Archangel, where his father edited the local newspaper, *Severnoe utro*. First publications, poems, reviews, and news reports appeared in *Severnoe utro*, 1915. Intended to study medicine at Moscow University, but trapped in Archangel by outbreak of the Civil War until 1920. Served briefly with the Red Army in the south, contributed to Red Army newspapers. Demobilized in 1921 and settled in Moscow. First mature publications appeared in 1922. Married: Tat'iana Mikhailovna Sabashnikova in 1926; two daughters. Visited Gor'kii in Sorrento, July 1927. Elected President of the temporary governing body of the All-Russian Union of Soviet Writers, 1929. Evacuated to Chistopol, 1942. *Pravda* correspondent at the Nuremburg trials, 1945. Elected Deputy of Supreme Soviet of USSR, 1950. Recipient: Stalin Prize, March 1943 for *Nashestvie* (*The Invasion*); Lenin Prize, April 1957 for *Russkii les* (*The Russian Forest*). Visited by Mikhail Gorbachev on 90th birthday, 1989. Died 8 August 1994.

Publications

Collected Editions

Sobranie sochinenii, 5 vols. Moscow, 1928–30.

Rannie rasskazy [Early Stories]. Munich, Fink, 1972 (reprint of 1923 and 1926 story collections).

Sobranie sochinenii, 10 vols. Moscow, 1981–84.

Fiction

Barsuki. Moscow, 1924; translated as *The Badgers*, by Hila Kazanina, London, Hutchinson, 1947; Westport, Connecticut, Hyperion Press, 1973.

Vor. Moscow, 1927; revised edition, 1959; 1927 edition reprinted Munich, Fink, 1974; translated as *The Thief*, by Hubert Butler, London, Martin Secker, and New York, Dial Press, 1931.

Sot'. Moscow, 1930; translated as *The Sot*, by Ivor Montagu and S.S. Nalbandov, London and New York, Putnam, 1931.

Skutarevskii. Moscow, 1932; translated as *Skutarevsky*, by Alec Brown, London, Lovat Dickson and Thompson, and New York, Harcourt Brace, 1936.

Doroga na okean. Moscow, 1935; translated as *Road to the Ocean*, by Norbert Guterman, New York, Fischer, 1944.

Russkii les. Moscow, 1953; translated as *The Russian Forest*, by Bernard Isaacs, 2 vols, Moscow, Progress, 1962.

Evgeniia Ivanovna. Moscow, 1963; translated as "Eugenia Ivanovna", *Soviet Literature*, 5 (1964).

Piramida [Pyramid], 2 vols. Moscow, 1994.

Plays

Polovchanskie sady. 1938; translated as "The Orchards of Polovchansk" [no translator named], in *Seven Soviet Plays*, New York, Macmillan, 1946; reprinted Westport, Connecticut, Greenwood Press, 1979.

Volk [The Wolf]. 1938.

Metel' [The Blizzard]. 1939.

Nashestvie. Moscow, 1942; translated as "The Invasion", by Gerard Shelley, in *Four Soviet War Plays*, London, Hutchinson, 1944.

Zolotaia kareta [The Golden Carriage]. Moscow, 1946; revised edition 1957.

Critical Studies

"Leonid Leonov", by Helen Muchnic, in her *From Gorky to Pasternak: Six Writers in Soviet Russia*, New York, Random House, 1961, 276–303.

Dramaturgiia Leonida Leonova, by L. Fink, Moscow, 1962.

The Premature Revolution: Russian Literature and Society 1917–1946, by Boris Thomson, London, Weidenfeld and Nicolson, 1972.

Uroki Leonida Leonova: Tvorcheskaia evoliutsiia, Moscow, 1973.

Lot's Wife and the Venus of Milo: Conflicting Attitudes to the Cultural Heritage in Modern Russia, by Boris Thomson, Cambridge and New York, Cambridge University Press, 1978.

Leonid Leonov: A Critical Study, by George Harjan, Toronto, Arowhena, 1979.

Leonid Leonov: Tvorcheskaia individual'nost' i literaturnyi protsess, edited by V.A. Kovalev and N.A. Groznova, Leningrad, 1987.

Poetika romanov L. Leonova, by V.V. Khimich, Sverdlovsk, 1989.

V otvete za budushchee: Leonid Leonov: Issledovaniia i materialy, by V. Kovalev, Moscow, 1989.
Beyond Metafiction: Self-Consciousness in Soviet Literature, by David Shepherd, Oxford, Clarendon Press, and New York, Oxford University Press, 1992 (includes bibliography, 227–40).

Bibliographies
Leonid Leonov: Seminarii, by V.A. Kovalev, Moscow and Leningrad, 1964.
"Bibliography of the Works of Leonid Leonov", by R.D.B. Thomson, *Oxford Slavonic Papers*, 11 (1964), 137–50 (covers the years 1915–61).

Leonid Maksimovich Leonov was the son of a peasant-poet close to Surikov and Drozhzhin. After a brief period of service during the Civil War, spent mostly on army newspapers, he moved to Moscow, where he was to be based for the rest of his life.

His first stories appeared in 1922. They are characterized by a brilliant use of *skaz* (first-person narration). There are imitations of peasant narratives, for example "Buryga", stylizations of biblical and Oriental narratives, such as "Ukhod Khama" [Ham's Departure] and "Tuatamur", and imitations of E.T.A. Hoffmann: "Dereviannaia koroleva" [The Wooden Queen] and Dostoevskii: "Konets melkogo cheloveka" [The End of a Petty Man].

Leonov became famous with his first novel, *Barsuki* (*The Badgers*). The book falls into two parts. The first depicts the pre-revolutionary period in which two peasant-lads, Pavel and Semen Rakhleev, are taken from the village to work in Moscow. It ends with the outbreak of the Revolution. The second part jumps ahead four years with Semen returning to his village at the end of the Civil War. Here he sympathizes with the peasants' resistance to the forced grain requisitions by the Bolshevik government, and eventually becomes the leader of a peasant rising. At the end of the book his brother Pavel reappears as the leader of a Bolshevik force and the rising collapses. Despite the drama of the story Leonov's narrative is fairly humorous and light-hearted; the reasons why one village joins the Bolsheviks and another opposes them are shown to be local and far from ideological or political. His second novel *Vor* [*The Thief*] is a much more complex and ambitious work. It reveals a shift in the direction of Dostoevskii, whom Leonov regarded at this time as the most appropriate model for Soviet literature.

Leonov's works of the 1920s are concerned with heroes who are outsiders, outcasts or rebels. With the increase in political controls on literature at the end of the decade and the growing reputation of Leonov himself, his heroes become more respectable figures, usually intellectuals, engineers or scientists. On the face of it, these are Leonov's most conformist works. The first work in this new direction is the novel *Sot'* (*The Sot*) (the title refers to the name of a river). It reflects the imperatives of the literature devoted to the first Five-Year Plan (1928–32), and is concerned with the construction of a paper-mill in the north of Russia. Here Leonov depicts the brutal changes being forced on the natural environment and the people of the north. The second, *Skutarevskii* (*Skutarevsky*), depicts an ageing physicist coming to understand that scientific objectivity is inapplicable and even harmful in political matters. The finest of these novels is *Doroga na okean* (*Road to the Ocean*), which deals ostensibly with sabotage on the railways. The hero, commissar Aleksei Kurilov, however, plays little part in the action. He falls terminally ill with cancer early on. Leonov here raises the taboo question of death, and asks how a materialist and utilitarian communism can enable its followers to cope with extinction. By means of lengthy excursions into the past and future Leonov tries to show the value of Kurilov's life as a link between the generations.

The most interesting feature of these books is the nature of the opposition. Vissarion Bulanin (in *The Sot*) and Gleb Protoklitov (in *Road to the Ocean*) are trying to survive in Soviet Russia despite having served in the White armies during the Civil War. They are both ultimately destroyed even though they have constituted no threat to the Soviet order of things. Their hopeless situation makes them surprisingly sympathetic figures, and this gives these works rather greater tension than is usual in Soviet literature of the 1930s. *Road to the Ocean* came in for severe criticism, however, when it came out, and in the paranoid atmosphere of the later 1930s Leonov's position became increasingly insecure. His protector Gor'kii had died in 1936 and Leonov was left almost defenceless. The plays that he wrote after this novel, *Polovchanskie sady* (*The Orchards of Polovchansk*), *Volk* [The Wolf], and *Metel'* [The Blizzard] came in for harsh and even vicious criticism, and Leonov lived in fear of imminent arrest. He was probably saved by the outbreak of World War II. He wrote a large number of wartime propaganda articles, and regained his reputation with the most successful of all his plays, *Nashestvie* (*The Invasion*), which was awarded a Stalin Prize.

Soon after the war Leonov produced one of his most interesting works, the play *Zolotaia kareta* [The Golden Carriage]. It is set in the immediate aftermath of the war, and it frankly admits that besides the heroes there were profiteers and cowards in the Soviet population. The conflict in the play is built around the heroine Mar'ka who has to choose between the blinded tank-driver, Timosha, and the wealthy son of a successful geologist, who has managed to avoid military service. Contrary to all expectations Mar'ka chooses wealth and comfort, and this shocked Soviet critics. The play was denounced and quickly withdrawn. Leonov produced no more artistic works until after the death of Stalin.

During these years he composed a good deal of Cold War propaganda, and began to develop a keen interest in ecological matters, which eventually found expression in his last complete novel, *Russkii les* (*The Russian Forest*). The Thaw, surprisingly, did not inspire Leonov to a new period of productivity. Instead he embarked on a series of substantial revisions of his earlier and more controversial works, *The Thief*, "Konets melkogo cheloveka", *Metel'*, *The Invasion*, and *Zolotaia kareta*. Even the one apparently new work of these years, the novella *Evgeniia Ivanovna*, proved to be a revised version of a story that he had been working on since 1938. The story deals with a Russian woman who emigrates after the Revolution and eventually marries an English archaeologist. She continues to suffer from an intense feeling of guilt, however, at leaving her country, and, it is implied, eventually dies of it.

The last 30 years of Leonov's life were spent mainly on his ecological interests, in which he has become a national figure, and an unfinished novel, of which only fragments have appeared. A new novel, *Piramida* [Pyramid], was published in 1994. In the years 1924–60 Leonov was officially one of the leading Soviet writers, but in fact little read, partly because of the difficulties of his style. He could have been a leading figure during the Thaw, but spent those crucial years in revising his earlier works. Recently, however, there have been signs of growing interest in his work, and in particular in *The Thief*.

R.D.B. THOMSON

The Thief

Vor

Novel, 1927

Leonov's second novel, *The Thief*, is set in the peculiar atmosphere of the NEP period. In an attempt to accelerate the recovery of the economy devastated by seven years of war, in 1921 the communists had decided to permit the reintroduction of private enterprise, though on a strictly limited basis. By the middle of the 1920s this had led to the rise of a class of profiteers and careerists, which seemed to threaten the survival of the communist ideal. It is this strange overlap of historical periods, a capitalist interlude in a socialist revolution, that the novel attempts to re-create.

The hero of the novel, Dmitrii Vekshin, had been a commissar in the Red Army during the Civil War, but was expelled from the Party for killing a White prisoner. In spite of this disgrace he continued to serve loyally until the end. Yet with the coming of peace the traditional difficulties of a demobilized serviceman were compounded by the realities of the NEP period. He is publicly humiliated by the wife of a profiteer and his faith in communism is further shaken when he is confronted by two typical products of the age: Zavarikhin, the grasping peasant turned black-marketeer, and Chikilev, the parasite who has learnt how to exploit communist slogans to his own advantage. In protest Vekshin becomes a thief and, like a second Robin Hood, soon wins a formidable reputation as one of the most brilliant and daring leaders of the underworld. But he still remains loyal to the ideal of the Revolution, and never ceases to be aware that he is an outcast, "a planet that has broken out of its orbit", and makes strenuous efforts to reintegrate himself into Soviet society. *The Thief* is divided into four parts, each of which ends with the word "sun". Even if Vekshin has "broken out of orbit" he is still subject to its inexorable but life-giving pull. At the end of the novel he sets off towards Siberia and Leonov holds out the possibility of eventual redemption through physical labour and education.

Although the novel ends apparently optimistically, it contains many pessimistic reflections on the destiny of the Revolution, and the threat presented by such figures as Zavarikhin and Chikilev. Many of the characters ask whether human nature is able to live up to the ideals of the Revolution. The image of the "thief" in itself seems to epitomize the unreliability of the Russian character. In retrospect Soviet critics generally considered that Leonov had overestimated the power and threat presented by such "NEP-men" as Zavarikhin, but it could be argued that in the long run it was the Chikilev type that presented the greater danger. Certainly it is this type that is developed in Leonov's later works.

The structure of the novel is complicated by the presence of a novelist, Firsov, who is also writing about this milieu. As a character in Leonov's novel, Firsov is actively engaged in the action, but simultaneously stands outside it, observing the other characters and contriving dramatic situations for them in order to collect material for his own book. Leonov frequently mocks these falsifications of reality, while Firsov's style is a parody of Leonov's already high-flown language. Whereas Leonov, at the end of the novel, looks forward to redeeming and educating Vekshin, Firsov kills off his central hero. But in spite of all these reservations Firsov serves Leonov as an important mouthpiece for reflections that he was unwilling to express in his own name.

Leonov believed at this time that Dostoevskii was the most suitable model for Soviet literature to follow and the novel is strongly influenced by the style and psychological techniques of the older master (such as the use of doubles). If the overall design of the book is based on *Prestuplenie i nakazanie* (*Crime and Punishment*), the "infernal" heroine, Man'ka Dolomanova, recalls Nastas'ia Filippovna (*Idiot* (*The Idiot*)), while Chikilev clearly recalls Shigalev from *Besy* (*The Possessed* or *The Devils*). Vekshin himself bears traces of Raskol'nikov and Stavrogin.

Even before the last instalment of *The Thief* had appeared in the journal *Krasnaia nov'* the novel had aroused widespread interest; the completed novel, however, puzzled and disappointed the critics for its failure to provide a more definite conclusion. Its sceptical attitude to the events and values of the NEP period and the apparent glorification of a "thief" brought the book into increasing disfavour over the next few years. Some six editions were published in the years up to 1936, but since then it has never been re-issued in Russia in its original form. In 1959 Leonov brought out a heavily revised edition, but this reflects developments in Leonov himself rather than any concessions to political correctness. The plot, while remaining substantially unaltered, has been re-interpreted, and the second half of the novel, in particular, has been fundamentally rewritten. The main change concerns the hero, Vekshin. He is stripped of his romantic aura and doubts are cast even on his exploits during the Civil War. In 1927 he had been inspired by a hatred of the NEP period; now he is taken for a NEP profiteer himself. The romanticization of Vekshin in the earlier version is now blamed on Firsov who is identified with the young Leonov. Finally, even the optimistic original ending is reprinted only to be dismissed with the words: "all this is a matter for the conscience of the omniscient Firsov". Technically and formally the new version is an improvement; the plot is better organized, the vast cast of characters is handled more skilfully, and there are many fascinating digressions and reflections; but it lacks the urgency of the original. The 1927 edition had been built on the paradox of a rebel against Soviet power still somehow representing the ideals of the revolution. In 1959 Vekshin is seen as a thief without any redeeming features, and the demolition of this paradox has largely removed the novel's original *raison d'être*.

R.D.B. THOMSON

The Russian Forest

Russkii les

Novel, 1953

The Russian Forest, Leonov's sixth and last complete novel, was published in the last months of 1953, and so can be considered one of the first works of the Thaw. It brings together many of his most characteristic themes, the unity of Russian culture and history, the fate of the Russian intelligentsia, and the worthiness of the younger generation to inherit and to appreciate the hardships endured by their elders. The immediate inspiration for the novel lies in Leonov's growing interest in environmental questions. As early as 1947 he had written an article about the destruction of the forests of Russia, "V zashchitu druga" [In Defence of Our Friend]. Hundreds of letters containing information about the continuance of indiscriminate felling flowed in to Leonov, and he helped to found several societies for the protection of the natural environment. It is these concerns that provide the narrative framework. The novel is built round the rivalry of two men, Ivan Vikhrov, who represents Leonov's position, and Aleksandr Gratsianskii, who advocates a more exploitative approach. At the end of the book Gratsianskii is finally revealed to be in the pay of the Australian Secret Service (this detail reflects the fact that the book was written during the Korean War).

The novel opens in June 1941 on the eve of the German invasion. Polia, Vikhrov's daughter by his estranged wife, arrives in Moscow with the intention of unmasking her father. She has read the articles of his enemy Gratsianskii and has come to believe that he is the prime enemy of the Russian forest. Only after a long and painful process does she learn that she has been deceived. The war gives her a chance to redeem herself by acts of conventional but implausible heroism, and she is finally the one who executes judgment on Gratsianskii. The most interesting chapters are devoted to the earlier history of Gratsianskii. As a youth on the fringes of the revolutionary movement he had conceived the idea of "mimetism" – a scheme for penetrating the tsarist secret police, the *Okhrana*, and then carrying its methods to absurd lengths, so as to "blow it up from within". The police, however, outwit him and turn him into one of their own agents. Since the Revolution Gratsianskii's whole life has been devoted to concealing this secret from the Soviet authorities. Driven by a combination of fear and ambition he poses as a Marxist and has managed to enter the Communist Party, where it is implied that he has continued to practise mimetism. Far from rejecting such creatures, however, the Soviet system is shown to have encouraged and promoted them. It is this unscrupulous abuse of power that Leonov blames for the traumatic childhood of Polia and the cultural illiteracy of the younger generation. Even when, at the end of the book, Gratsianskii commits suicide, there is a hint that this may be only a charade. The death of Stalin was no guarantee of the end of the Gratsianskii type.

Leonov's novel is thus more than an environmentalist tract. It is not only about the Russian forest, but about the Russian people, and the two nouns are frequently bracketed, as, for example in Vikhrov's lecture on the Russian forest, which serves as an allegory of the history of Russia. The apparently innocuous theme of the forest acquires a specifically political charge when it is remembered that the export of timber was one of Soviet Russia's main sources of foreign currency during the Stalin period; the policies that Leonov and Vikhrov advocate had been denounced in the 1930s as unpatriotic, and the historical figures on whom Vikhrov was modelled had been disgraced and exiled. Furthermore the lumber was mostly produced in the appalling conditions of Stalin's labour camps. For thoughtful readers *The Russian Forest* was the boldest revelation of the recent past to appear until the first works of Solzhenitsyn almost a decade later.

The novel's combination of scientific debate and veiled historical comment helps to explain the controversy surrounding it from the time of its first appearance. Early in 1954 it was denounced by the Institute of Forestry in Leningrad and the Academy of Sciences in Moscow, who demanded that certain passages be cut. Leonov was vindicated, however, when one of his allies in the Institute produced figures to show that his predictions were substantially correct. At this his opponents changed their tune, and begged not to be identified as Gratsianskiis. The controversies ended only in 1957, when the novel was awarded a Lenin Prize and so placed beyond political attacks. Since then *The Russian Forest* has been unanimously hailed by Soviet critics as Leonov's masterpiece and it has been adapted for the stage and the radio. Certainly it draws together many of Leonov's lifelong concerns, his deep love and understanding of nature, and his elaboration of the interdependence of the eco-system into a metaphysical philosophy; his justification of the Russian intelligentsia, long vilified under Stalin, and his recurrent fear that the younger generation may have been morally and culturally stunted by the decades of Stalinism. The book will remain essential reading, but artistically it is inferior to Leonov's other novels. Apart from the brilliant chapters devoted to the young Gratsianskii, the style is often self-indulgent, and the cost of camouflaging the profoundly dissident nature of the content has involved too many concessions to the formulae of socialist realism.

R.D.B. THOMSON

Mikhail Iur'evich Lermontov 1814–1841

Prose writer, poet, and dramatist

Biography

Born in Moscow, 14/15 October 1814. Raised mainly by his grandmother on her estate in Central Russia. Received extensive education at home. Moved to Moscow, 1827; attended the School for the Nobility, Moscow, 1828–30; studied ethics and politics, and later, literature, Moscow University, 1830–32; enrolled in Junker School, St Petersburg, 1832–34: Cavalry cornet in Regiment of Life Guard Hussars. Exiled to the Caucasus for his poems commemorating Pushkin's death, 1837. Pardoned by the authorities; returned to St Petersburg. Publication of *Geroi nashego vremeni* (*A Hero of Our Time*) as separate edition, 1840. Because of a duel with French ambassador's son, again exiled, to Tenginskii Infantry Regiment on the Black Sea, 1840–41. While socializing in Piatigorsk spa, killed in a duel, 27 July 1841.

Publications

Collected Editions

Polnoe sobranie sochinenii, 5 vols. Moscow and Leningrad, 1936–37.

Sochineniia, 6 vols. Moscow and Leningrad, 1954–57.

The Demon and Other Poems, translated by Eugene M. Kayden. Yellow Springs, Ohio, Antioch Press, 1965.

A Lermontov Reader, translated by Guy Daniels. New York, Macmillan, 1965.

Sobranie sochinenii, edited by V. Arkhipov, 4 vols. Moscow, 1969.

Sobranie sochinenii, edited by I.M. Andronikov, 4 vols. Moscow, 1975.

Selected Works, translated by Avril Pyman, Irina Zheleznova, and Martin Parker. Moscow, Progress, 1976.

Narrative Poems by Pushkin and Lermontov, translated by Charles Johnston. New York, Vintage, 1983.

Sobranie sochinenii, 4 vols. Moscow, 1983–84.

Major Poetical Works, translated by Anatoly Liberman. Minneapolis, University of Minneapolis Press, and London, Croom Helm, 1984.

Sobranie sochinenii, edited by G.P. Makogonenko, 4 vols. Moscow, 1989.

Polnoe sobranie stikhotvorenii, edited by Iu.A. Andreev, 2 vols. Moscow, 1989.

Fiction

Kniaginia Ligovskaia. 1836; in *Russkii vestnik*, 1882; translated as "Princess Ligovskaya", by Guy Daniels, in *A Lermontov Reader*, 1965.

Geroi nashego vremeni. St Petersburg, 1840; translated as *Sketches of Russian Life in the Caucasus*, 1853; also translated as *A Hero of Our Time*, by Martin Parker, Moscow, Foreign Languages Publishing House, 1947; revised edition, edited by Neil Cornwell, London, Everyman, 1995; also translated by Vladimir and Dmitri Nabokov, New York, Anchor, 1958; reprinted Oxford, Oxford University Press, 1984; Ann Arbor, Ardis, 1988; by Paul Foote, Harmondsworth, Penguin, 1966; and by Philip Longworth, London, New English Library, 1975.

Vadim, in *Vestnik Evropy*, 1873; translated as *Vadim*, by Helena Goscilo, Ann Arbor, Ardis, 1984.

Poetry

Khadzhi Abrek, 1833; in *Biblioteka dlia chteniia*, 1835.

Sashka. 1835–39; in *Russkaia mysl'*, 1882.

Tambovskaia kaznacheisha. 1837–38; translated as "The Tambov Treasurer's Wife", by Guy Daniels, in *A Lermontov Reader*, 1965; also as "The Tambov Lady", by Charles Johnston, in *Narrative Poems by Pushkin and Lermontov*, 1983.

Mtsyri. St Petersburg, 1840; translated as *The Circassian Boy*, 1875; also translated as "The Novice", by Eugene M. Kayden, in *The Demon and Other Poems*, 1965; also as "Mtsyri", by Avril Pyman and Irina Zheleznova, in *Selected Works*, 1976.

Demon, fragmentary publication in *Otechestvennye zapiski*, 1842; in full, Karlsruhe, 1856; translated as *The Demon*, 1875; also translated by Eugene M. Kayden, in *The Demon and Other Poems*, 1965; and by Avril Pyman and Irina Zheleznova, in *Selected Works*, 1976; and by Charles Johnston, in *Narrative Poems by Pushkin and Lermontov*, 1983.

Play

Maskarad. 1836; St Petersburg, 1842; translated as "Masquerade", by Roger W. Phillips, *Russian Literature Triquarterly*, 7 (1973), 67–116.

Critical Studies

Geroi nashego vremeni M.Iu. Lermontova, by S. Durylin, Moscow, 1940; reprinted Ann Arbor, Ardis, 1986.

Lermontov, by Janko Lavrin, London, Bowes and Bowes, and New York, Hillary House, 1959.

Stat'i o Lermontove, by B.M. Eikhenbaum, Moscow and Leningrad, 1961.

Mikhail Lermontov, by John Mersereau, Jr, Carbondale, Southern Illinois University Press, 1962.

"The Similes of Pushkin and Lermontov", by Carl R. Proffer, *Russian Literature Triquarterly*, 3 (1972), 148–94.

The Rise of the Russian Novel: Studies in the Russian Novel from "Eugene Onegin" to "War and Peace", by Richard Freeborn, Cambridge, Cambridge University Press, 1973, 38–73.

Lermontov: Tragedy in the Caucasus, by Laurence Kelly, London, Constable, and New York, Braziller, 1977; reprinted London, Robin Clark, 1983.

Pechorin: An Essay on Lermontov's "A Hero of Our Time", by C.J.G. Turner, Birmingham, Birmingham Slavonic Monographs, 1978.

M.Iu. Lermontov: Issledovaniia i materialy. Leningrad, 1979.

Lermontov: A Study in Literary-Historical Evaluation, by B.M.

Eikhenbaum, translated by Ray Parrott and Harry Weber, Ann Arbor, Ardis, 1981.
Lermontov, by John Garrard, Boston, Twayne, 1982.
"The First Pečorin En Route to *A Hero of Our Time*: Lermontov's *Princess Ligovskaja*", by Helena Goscilo, *Russian Literature*, 11–12 (1982), 129–62.
"Lermontov's *Demon*: A Question of Identity", by Robert Reid, *Slavonic and East European Review*, 60 (1982), 189–210.
"Hero, Plot and Myth: Some Aspects of Lermontov's Caucasian *Poemy*", by Robert Reid, *Essays in Poetics*, 7/2 (1982).
Lermontovskii sbornik. Leningrad, 1985.
A History of Russian Literature of the Romantic Period, by William Edward Brown, Ann Arbor, Ardis, 1986, vol. 4, 140–261.
Sud'ba Lermontova, by Emma Gershtein, 2nd edition, Moscow, 1986.
"Lermontov's *Mtsyri*: Themes and Structure", by Robert Reid, in *Problems of Russian Romanticism*, edited by Reid, Brookfield, Vermont, Gower, 1986, 127–68.
Fiction and Society in the Age of Pushkin: Ideology, Institutions, and Narrative, by William Mills Todd III, Cambridge, Massachusetts, Harvard University Press, 1986.
Mikhail Iur'evich Lermontov: Zhizn' i tvorchestvo, edited by A.A. Karpova, Moscow, 1987.
A Wicked Irony: The Rhetoric of "A Hero of Our Time", by Andrew Barratt and A.D.P. Briggs, Bristol, Bristol Classical Press, 1989.
The Fey Hussar: The Life of the Russian Poet, Michael Yur'evich Lermontov, 1814–41, edited by Jessie Davies, Liverpool, Lincoln Davies, 1989.
M.Iu. Lermontov v vospominaniiakh sovremennikov, edited by M.I. Gillel'sona and O.V. Miller, Moscow, 1989.
Lermontov's Ironic Vision, by Marie Gilroy, Birmingham, Birmingham Slavonic Monographs, 1989.
Mikhail Lermontov: Commemorative Essays (1991), edited by A.D.P. Briggs, Birmingham, Birmingham Modern Languages Publications, 1992.
Mikhail Lermontov, 1814–1989, edited by Efim Etkind, Northfield, Vermont, Russian School of Norwich University, 1992.
"Ethnotope in Lermontov's Caucasian *Poemy*", by Robert Reid, *Russian Literature*, 31 (1992), 555–73.
Russian Literature and Empire: Conquest of the Caucasus from Pushkin to Tolstoy, by Susan Layton, Cambridge and New York, Cambridge University Press, 1994.
Lermontov's "A Hero of Our Time", by Robert Reid, London, Bristol Classical Press, 1997.

Bibliographies
Lermontov in English: A List of Works by and about the Poet, by Anna Heifetz, New York, New York Public Library, 1942.
Bibliografiia literatury o M.Iu. Lermontova 1917–77 gg., by O.V. Miller, Leningrad, 1980.
Lermontovskaia entsiklopediia. Moscow, 1981.

Mikhail Lermontov was a poet, dramatist, and novelist of the Romantic school. He maintained his poetic output throughout his creative life. His dramatic works, however, which were strongly influenced by the plays of Shakespeare and the early tragedies of Schiller, were all written before his creative maturity, which developed throughout the second half of the 1830s, during which time he devoted himself increasingly to works of prose.

As a composer of lyric verse Lermontov based his technique of composition on antithesis and opposition, his early poems being characterized by the presence of metaphysical extremes that provide the philosophical framework for many of his mature works, including those not given lyric form. Thus the contempt for pure love felt by the demon in "Moi demon" [My Demon] (1829), finds full expression in his long narrative poem *Demon* (*The Demon*), a work written and rewritten over the entire course of his creative life. While the image of heaven presented in the sacred song of praise that the eponymous angel ("The Angel"), sings as he brings a new soul into the "world of sorrow and tears" is reflected in a number of poems in which the poet or his persona laments the unattainability of a lost ideal, culminating in turn in the narrative poem *Mtsyri*. In the long lyric composition "1831-go iiunia 11 dnia" [On 11 June 1831], the human condition, in which "life is hateful, but death terrible", is seen as poised between the extremes of evil and good and is expressible in "neither demonic nor angelic language". This work comprises 32 octaves after the manner of Byron, whom the young poet read extensively and whose poetic inspiration is discernible in the personal philosophic reflections of which the work consists. Again, the poet's admission, "I despise the lives of others", reaches fruition in a mature work of a different genre, *Geroi nashego vremeni* (*A Hero of Our Time*), in which the cynicism of the late Romantic hero is fully revealed.

The first five years of Lermontov's military career, beginning in November 1832, saw a marked diminution of lyric output, although during this period he produced a number of narrative poems, of which *Khadzhi Abrek* (1833) became his first published work. Lermontov's return to regular lyric composition in 1837 led to the appearance of poetical works of great technical accomplishment and mellifluence, in which earlier Romantic themes are given more concrete form. The contrast between the divine ideal and the trials of human existence is embodied in the natural imagery of meditative works such as "Kogda volnuetsia zhelteiushchaia niva" [When the Yellowing Cornfield Waves] (1837) and the romance "Vykhozhu odin ia na dorogu" [I Step Out onto the Road Alone] (1841). The poet's earlier assertion, in "Net, ia ne Bairon, ia drugoi" [No I Am Not Byron, I Am Another] (1832) that he was, like Byron, also a pilgrim persecuted by the world, except that his soul was Russian, prefigured the appearance not only of a number of narrative poems on Russian historical subjects, but also of such poetic masterpieces as "Borodino" (1837) and "Rodina" [Motherland] (1841). It should be added, however, that alongside these he also wrote poems on foreign themes, such as "Vetka Palestiny" [The Branch from Palestine] (1837) and "Tri pal'my" [Three Palms] (1839), although the latter frequently remain essentially lyric and personal in tone.

Similarly, the sense of rebellious isolation characteristic of the Byronic hero, which had been given expression in "Parus" ("The Sail") 1832, one of Lermontov's best-known lyric works, acquires specific contours in the depiction of Pushkin in "Smert' poeta" ("Death of a Poet") 1837, where Pushkin is seen as standing "alone in the face of social opinion", only to be "slain". This important poem, which contributed more than any other to Lermontov's fame, well exemplifies the declamatory, oratorical style also found elsewhere in Lermontov's later works, for example, "Poslednee novosel'e" [The Last Change of Dwelling] (1841), while at the same time it illustrates a feature of his compositional technique long recognized in criticism and commented on by, among others, Boris Eikhenbaum. This may be called "creative borrowing", whereby Lermontov incorporates quotations from other poets, both foreign and Russian (sometimes from his own earlier works), into compositions in a manner that gives them new life and meaning. Thus the word "slain" (*ubit*) used of Pushkin in the seventh line of "Death of a Poet" and repeated before a caesura at the beginning of the eighth, echoes Pushkin's own double use of the same word in chapter 6, stanza 35 of *Evgenii Onegin*, first in the fourth line and then, again before a caesura, at the start of the fifth, even though the effect of the technique in each case is different: Lermontov employs it to denounce Pushkin's murderers, Pushkin – to express Onegin's distress on killing Lenskii in the duel.

The final 16 lines of "Death of a Poet", in which Lermontov denounces the "executioners of Freedom, Genius and Fame" who surround the tsar, incurred the particular wrath of the authorities and by way of punishment he was sentenced to exile in the Caucasus, where he remained until December 1837. By the end of this period he had gathered many ideas for his novel, *A Hero of Our Time*.

Lermontov's lyric poems are conceived and executed with the freedom of form and spirit characteristic of the Romantic movement. In place of the strict adherence to generic patterns of the previous age, his work, even within individual poems, creatively integrates a wide variety of styles, structural devices, figures, and metres in an innovative manner that did not always meet with the critical approval of contemporaries. In the poem "I skuchno i grustno" [I Am Vexed and Sad] (1840), the poet admits to essentially the same emotional atrophy with which he had invested the hero of his novel, Pechorin. It is a blend of questions, exclamations, dramatic contrasts, emotionally charged pauses and conversational turns of phrase and was, according to Belinskii, particularly disliked by the older generation of critics. Belinskii himself accepted the work, describing it as "a requiem for all human hopes and feelings"; on reading it "human nature trembles and the blood runs cold in one's veins". Belinskii's view may seem a little overstated in reference to a poem that begins with the prosaic remark, "I am bored"; however, it should be remembered that the word *skuchno* has undergone semantic narrowing since Lermontov's day, when it also included notions of vexation and melancholy.

When in April 1840 Lermontov was once again sentenced to exile in the Caucasus, on this occasion as punishment for his duel with Ernest de Barante, the son of the French ambassador, he commemorated the event in the poem "Tuchi" [Clouds] (1840), in which he contrasts himself to the clouds that have no native land and do not know exile. The driving dactylic tetrameter of the verse assured its immediate success as a fine example of the integration of form and content.

The philosopher Vladimir Solov'ev drew attention to a controversial aspect of Lermontov's creative work when he commented that the poet was preoccupied neither with the fate of his country nor with that of the people about him, but with his own fate as a prophet. In this respect the philosopher praised highly the poem "Son" [The Dream] (1841) seeing in it a manifestation of that "second sight" which, he believed, Lermontov had inherited from his Scottish ancestors. Certainly, Lermontov's poem describes in some detail the circumstances of his own death when, in July 1841, he quarrelled with Major N.S. Martynov, an old acquaintance of the family, and was killed outright in the ensuing duel.

David W. Martin

Masquerade

Maskarad

Play, 1836

Masquerade is the play on which the poet Lermontov's reputation as a dramatist rests. Written during 1835 and 1836, he was desperate to have it staged in a major theatre. The earliest version seems to have been in three acts, and completed in 1835, but he rewrote it with a fourth act before submitting it to the censor. Unfortunately, in January 1836 its theme and expression were pronounced too offensive for performance, though this is the version which is best known today. Lermontov however set to work and created another version, this time in five acts and renamed *Arbenin*, but this too was rejected, and the play was never staged in its author's lifetime. In 1852 selected scenes were presented at the Aleksandrinskii Theatre, St Petersburg, but the whole play was not staged until 1862, when it was presented to little acclaim at the Malyi Theatre, Moscow. There were a very few other provincial productions of the play before Vsevolod Meierkhol'd completely revolutionized opinions of its dramatic potential with a magnificent and lavish production at the Aleksandrinskii Theatre in February 1917. Still probably the most expensive dramatic production ever staged in Russia, Meierkhol'd and his designer, Aleksandr Golovin, created a world that scintillated and challenged conventions, fascinating and repelling audiences for more than 20 years. Indeed it was only the destruction of the extraordinary costumes, sets and accessories by German bombers during World War II that brought the production to an end, it having continued even after its director had perished in a Stalinist gaol. This production was probably responsible for the fact that *Masquerade* became an accepted part of the Russian and Soviet repertoire, and at least one film proved its popularity beyond the usual play-going or poetry-reading audiences. This was Sergei Gerasimov's 1941 version, its lush design was obviously echoing the dead and disgraced Meierkhol'd's creation.

The plot tells of a young, impetuous and gloomy nobleman, Evgenii Arbenin, whose spirit has been lifted by his marriage to the beautiful and innocent Nina. We first see him in a gambling hall, where the naive Prince Zvezdich has just lost a fortune. Arbenin, not without contempt, rescues him. They go to a fashionable masquerade, where Nina by misfortune loses one of a pair of bracelets that Arbenin gave her. It is recovered by Baroness Shtrahl, an apparently decorous but actually amorous young widow. She gives it, under cover of her mask, to Zvezdich as an earnest sign of her desire. Zvezdich is unsure who she is, but discovers the bracelet belongs to Nina. He therefore assumes it is Nina who has made the advance to him.

When Arbenin discovers this, he is furious and plots to make a fool of Zvezdich by the peculiar code of honour prevailing among the Russian aristocracy of the time: he accuses him of cheating at cards, slaps his face, and then refuses to accept his challenge to a duel. Meanwhile, Arbenin spies Nina speaking to Zvezdich at a society ball, and this finally convinces him of her guilt. Despite her protestations of innocence, he cold-bloodedly poisons her ice-cream, and takes her home to watch her die. Too late he learns of his dreadful mistake, and, in a final scene of genuine power, he is gradually driven horribly mad with remorse.

Despite this *Othello*-like plot, the play is perhaps primarily a vehicle for Lermontov's mordant social satire. It paints in stark tones a society where greed, selfishness and deceit reign, and are opposed only by boredom and indifference. Arbenin exists in a context of complete spiritual impoverishment, but he condemns not just this, but also those who are spiritual paupers. Like the author's more famous novel hero, Pechorin, Arbenin is a hero "of our time", aware of the brilliance of the time, and equally aware of its utter insignificance:

You are characterless, immoral, godless,
A vain, malicious, but weak man,
In you alone the whole age is reflected,
The present age, which is brilliant, but insignificant.

The masquerade itself is the quintessence of this: here the falsity of society finds its ultimate expression, truth is hidden under the masks, and men and women behave wantonly yet with impunity.

The point is reinforced by the other characters. The guiltless Nina, beautiful but pathetic, is too innocent to live in such a society. Baroness Strahl, lustful and scheming, is actually conscience-struck when she sees the results of her machinations, but she is powerless to stop the consequences. Prince Zvezdich is a classic gull, out of his depth and made stupid by the passions that swirl past him. The other gamblers, gossips, and schemers are also interesting, and well imagined: it is worth noting that there are a surprising number of excellent parts for actors.

Arbenin himself, Byronic and morose, is yet more than a Romantic stereotype. His social criticism, though stern, is just, and though he perverts it horribly, his striving for goodness and beauty lends him a wanly admirable air. How far he is a self-portrait by Lermontov, as has been suggested, is difficult to determine. His quest for a meaning in life beyond the vapid posturings of society makes him compelling, and he is set against the enigmatic Stranger, whose significance Meierkhol'd discovered when he made him Arbenin's antagonist, a kind of supernatural revenger acting on behalf of society.

Masquerade is written in flexible free verse iambics, (extremely difficult to translate effectively), and this more than anything enables the play to rise above mere melodrama. But the pervasive pessimism, the mood of brooding gloom, make it still a piece of its time and heavily romantic. One would have thought *Masquerade* was quite out of tune with Soviet Russia, where it became surprisingly popular. Whether this fact tells us more about the Soviet Union or the play itself may be a matter for debate.

ROBERT LEACH

Mtsyri

Narrative poem, 1840

Mtsyri is, after *The Demon*, Lermontov's second great narrative poem. Indeed it complements the better-known work thematically so that taken together these two works may legitimately be regarded as narratively constituting Lermontov's romantic aesthetic. The principal thematic difference between the two works is that, whereas *The Demon* operates at the rarefied level of the metaphysics of good and evil viewed *sub specie aeternitatis*, *Mtsyri* confines itself to a single human tragedy worked out in a specific ethno-historical context.

The work is based on a true story that Lermontov heard while serving in the Caucasus. According to this, a Russian general, probably Ermolov, captured a six-year-old Circassian boy, a Muslim, and left him to be brought up by monks in a Georgian monastery where he subsequently died of homesickness. This simple *fabula*, romantically congenial, was elaborated by Lermontov using techniques already well tried in his earlier narratives and lyrics. The final version of the poem, completed in 1839, and published the following year, tells of the child's difficult acclimatization to monastic life and exile. Refusing food he falls gravely ill but does not die and, after this crisis, appears outwardly to reconcile himself to his new life. He becomes a novice and appears destined for full participation in the monastic life. Secretly however he has never abandoned hope of seeing his family again. From his monk's cell he can see the distant mountains of his home and this feeds his longing. One night, taking advantage of a thunder storm, he flees from the monastery and spends three days wandering in the valley below unable to find his way home. Finally, weakened by hunger and thirst, and by wounds received fighting a mountain leopard, he is found near the monastery (having wandered in a circle), is brought back, and dies.

The plot and setting of *Mtsyri* allow Lermontov scope to develop and combine some key romantic themes. The affinity between the monk's cell and that of the prisoner was a staple romantic image that complemented the neo-platonic symbolism of the body as prison of the soul, and the earth itself as a place of imprisonment or exile. Freedom and slavery were of course cognate politico-philosophical preoccupations of Lermontov's. In this, *Mtsyri*, like *The Demon*, betrays Lermontov's neo-gnosticism: culture is repressive, and churches and monasteries, as the focal points of culture, are peculiarly repressive. Nature, by contrast, is the focus of freedom: it is self-evidently beautiful and elicits a positive reaction from the hero. Unlike *The Demon*, however, *Mtsyri* subjects this romantic premise to critical scrutiny. The novice monk, who has fled from culture into nature, finds that nature itself is inimicable to him. The thick woodland and undergrowth conspire to disorient him, the sun makes him delirious. At the same time he shows his typically human hostility to nature by attacking a mountain leopard that he turns into a test of strength. There is a profound ambiguity here: being close to nature simultaneously underlines the archetypally anthropological qualities of the hunter. He conquers the leopard by means of a weapon, a forked stick.

Of course Mtsyri's three days of freedom "in nature" are only a second best. The means has literally become the end. The hero's aim was not to test his survival skills but to get back to his native village. By not permitting him to return, Lermontov preserves the notion of homeland as a romantic separation, a figure of the ideal Other of integration and happiness to which unhappy mortals aspire. However, in setting up the opposition of home and exile, Lermontov problematizes nature. It cannot be for him, as for other romantic poets, a figure of our true spiritual home. It is rather a way of defining and circumscribing the vulnerability of man's cultural position and it stresses a double exile: the individual as a stranger in his culture, the cultural as an alien presence in nature. Moreover, according to what we may term the imperialist romantic paradigm in which Lermontov operated, the Circassian as "savage" should be more "natural" than the Georgian monk. The natural environment in which Mtsyri finds himself thus becomes a device for testing his identity: is he monk (culturally oriented) or Circassian (naturally oriented)? Mtsyri's three days at large seem to give a fairly explicit answer to this question. His behaviour is such as we might expect of a novice monk who has spent his youth in the shelter of the cloister. Of particular significance is his reaction to a Georgian girl whom he spies while she draws water from the river. He wishes, but cannot bring himself, to follow her and make himself known. We might also infer his physical weakness, notwithstanding his claim to have conquered the mountain lion, from the fact that a short period of enforced natural survival is sufficient to bring about his death. The fugitive Mtsyri proves himself to be precisely what the title of the work suggests – a *Mtsyri*: novice monk, and not Circassian. Nurture (culture) has prevailed in this instance over nature in its hereditary sense.

Yet it is nature in the wider sense with its manifold tactile experiences, and its plethora of sensations and ability to inflict mortal suffering that reveals Mtsyri's true identity. Before imminent death he is now trebly exiled, from his true home that he will never see, from his adopted home, and from nature that has destroyed him. Yet Mtsyri, as a true tragic hero, realizes that his experience has enlightened and individuated him, even though his initial aim remains unrealized and he is shortly to die. The poem conveys the message of the supreme importance of individual identity even at the expense of loss of human contact and of life itself and reflects Lermontov's interest in the workings of the human will. The description of Mtsyri's emotional turmoil, for all its romantic packaging, reflects that constant striving towards psychological realism that reaches its peak in Lermontov's novel *A Hero of Our Time* and is his great legacy to the later masters of this tradition in Russia, notably Dostoevskii.

Structurally too, *Mtsyri*, more complex than *The Demon*, shows some affinity with *A Hero of Our Time* in its use of that paradoxical medium of objectivity: first-person narrative. Mtsyri's story is first recounted briefly and omnisciently and then in reprise, and in greater detail, by the novice himself as he confesses to a monk on his deathbed. Thus the confessional narrative, a hallowed romantic device, is here subject to an objective check or balance and justified by strong contextual motivation. It is this same corroborated subjectivity that in more complex and polyphonic form imparts to *A Hero of Our Time* the strong impression of an encounter with a real personality. It is interesting to note such realist tendencies *in ovo* in a work so uncompromisingly romantic in genre and theme as *Mtsyri*.

ROBERT REID

A Hero of Our Time

Geroi nashego vremeni

Novel, 1840

A Hero of Our Time is Lermontov's only novel and ranks as one of the great classics of 19th-century Russian literature. Although a novel it is of unorthodox structure, consisting of five separate stories linked by a common hero, Grigorii Pechorin. Three of these stories, "Bela", "Fatalist" ("The Fatalist") and "Taman", were published as separate entites in 1839 and 1840 in a contemporary Russian literary journal. The other two, "Maksim Maksimych" and "Kniazhna Meri" ("Princess Mary"), were published as part of the complete novel in 1840. The work is autobiographical inasmuch as Pechorin's adventures in the Caucasus reflect the writer's own experiences during his military posting to the region. Most remarkably, Piatigorsk, the scene of Pechorin's duel with Grushnitskii in "Princess Mary", was also to be the place where Lermontov himself perished in a duel with an old sparring partner of his, Major Martynov.

The novel's structure is complex and unique and involves three narrative levels. The first constituent story, "Bela", introduces an unnamed "narrator" who is travelling through the Caucasus writing travel notes. He is befriended by Maksim Maksimych, an army staff captain, who helps the traveller to solve his transport difficulties and, to while away the time, regales him with a story about Grigorii Pechorin, a young Russian officer with whom he once shared a posting. This story forms the substance of "Bela": it is a romantic tale of abduction in which Pechorin steals a Circassian princess, Bela, keeps her at the Russian fort, and eventually tires of her; she is finally murdered by a vengeful Circassian. This story, which both wins our sympathy for Maksim Maksimych and whets our curiosity about Pechorin, is followed by "Maksim Maksimych", in which Pechorin himself makes an appearance. Maksim Maksimych and the narrator have gone their separate ways but meet up again two days later in a hotel in Vladikavkaz. Maksim soon ascertains that Pechorin is also staying in the town at the house of a colonel. Maksim sends a message to Pechorin in the expectation that the latter will immediately hasten to renew their friendship. However Pechorin appears to snub his old comrade by not turning up and Maksim eventually manages only the most cursory of meetings with him as he prepares to leave. Maksim Maksimych is both hurt and embarrassed by Pechorin's indifference to him and, after Pechorin's departure, he lets the narrator have Pechorin's "Journal" personal papers that he has been keeping for Pechorin until the latter tells him, on leaving Vladikavkaz, to do "whatever you like" with them. The end of "Maksim Maksimych" therefore marks an important turning-point in both the narrative and psychological development of the novel. The narrator acquires the material that is to constitute the rest of the novel, for the subsequent stories, "Taman", "Princess Mary" and "The Fatalist", are all extracts from this journal. Maksim Maksimych, having served his purpose as narrator of "Bela", drops out of the action (except for a brief appearance at the end of "The Fatalist"), permanently embittered by Pechorin's coldness towards him (an indifference which further augments the enigma of Pechorin's character and the reader's desire to solve it). The narrator too, after writing a short foreword to Pechorin's journal (in which we discover that Pechorin himself is now dead), passes the narrative baton to Pechorin who dominates the remaining stories both as narrator and protagonist.

The three stories from Pechorin's Journal illustrate different aspects of his character and together with the "Bela" story complete his portrait as a "superfluous man", a member of the post-Decembrist generation, unable to realize its hopes and ideals under the repressive regime of Nicholas I. The genealogy of the "superfluous man" as a literary type can be seen to run from the prototypical Chatskii in Griboedov's *Gore ot uma* (*Woe from Wit*), through Pushkin's Evgenii Onegin and Pechorin himself to the heroes of Turgenev and ultimately Dostoevskii. Importantly Pechorin contributes a degree of demonic cynicism to this tradition: he is more active and unscrupulous in his pursuit of excitement than his literary predecessors and displays a good deal more introversion, this precedent of psychological self-analysis being an influential factor in the development of the psychological realism of Dostoevskii, Tolstoi, and Chekhov.

The story, "Taman" finds Pechorin in a small provincial town where he pries into the activities of the local smugglers, one of whom, a girl, nearly succeeds in drowning him after luring him into a boat. The gender/power relation in this story neatly inverts that of the earlier "Bela". "Princess Mary", by contrast, is a society tale set in the spa town of Piatigorsk. Here Pechorin sets out to seduce the eponymous heroine, again in a more cynical and artificial repetition of the "Bela" theme (though chronologically the latter takes place after "Princess Mary"). In "Princess Mary", too, Pechorin clashes fatally with the dandy Grushnitskii, who is in many ways an unflattering parody of Pechorin. The last journal story, "The Fatalist", is, appropriately for its position, more broadly metaphysical in content and summatory in function. Here Pechorin speculates on whether fate or chance rules human existence, a question that in different guises recurs throughout the novel.

A Hero of Our Time represents a crucial moment in the development of the Russian novel and of the realist technique with which it becomes identified in the course of the 19th century. Paradoxically the first-person narrative, with its romantic-confessional overtones, which is used in all the constituent parts of the novel, yields in its plurality a realistic, since unprivileged, point of view. Moreover the experimental structure of the work – a novel that is a congeries of autonomous stories rather than organically subordinate chapters – forms an important bridge between the tentative short prose works of the earlier part of the century and the mature novels that began to appear towards the middle of the 19th century. These structural features, coupled with the three-dimensional portrait of the novel's hero, combine to make *A Hero of Our Time* one of the single most important Russian prose works of the 19th century.

ROBERT REID

The Demon

Demon

Narrative poem, 1856 (written 1829–39)

The Demon is Lermontov's most important narrative poem. It is remarkable for having been first drafted by the poet at the age of 14 and subsequently redrafted a total of seven times throughout his creative life. However, because of its ideologically controversial content, it did not appear in print during Lermontov's lifetime, being first published in its entirety abroad in 1856.

Its hero, a demon (it is not clear whether we are to identify him with Satan, though the evidence for such identity is strong) exiled from heaven after the fall of the angels, has wandered the universe for countless aeons unenthusiastically fulfilling his commission to "sow evil" on earth. Unreconciled to his situation, bored by the ease with which mortals succumb to his temptations, he constantly recalls his glorious former existence as an angel. Thus far the plot of the poem operates *sub specie aeternitatis*. However a specific chronotope emerges when the Demon, on his wanderings, flies over the Caucasus and catches sight of Tamara, a young Georgian woman who, on the eve of her wedding, is dancing with her attendants on the flat roof of her house. Smitten by her beauty, the Demon at once begins to hope that, by gaining her love and reciprocating it, he may be able to expiate his former sin and be restored to his angelic status.

However, if he is to bring this situation about, he must first eliminate the bridegroom who, at that very moment, is travelling through the mountains to reach his bride, accompanied by a rich caravan. The Demon fills the bridegroom's mind with passionate anticipations of Tamara so that he forgets to make a habitual prayer for protection at a wayside shrine and is soon after attacked and killed by robbers. His horse carries his corpse onwards to Tamara's house where its gruesome apparition is interpreted as a divine curse on the family.

The Demon now begins to visit and woo Tamara. Disturbed by his visitations Tamara persuades her father to send her to a convent where she will be safe from them. Here, however, the demonic apparitions continue and intensify emotionally, the Demon declaring his love to Tamara and promising to make her his queen. At length she succumbs to the Demon's approaches but his first fiery embrace kills her and the Demon, still hoping to recover her soul, finds his path to it blocked by a guardian cherub, who informs him that Tamara's suffering has made her worthy of salvation and that the Demon will henceforth have no contact with her. The Demon is effectively returned to the *status quo ante*, but his state is more hopeless than before, his one chance of salvation having proved illusory.

The Demon brings together two distinct aspects of Lermontov's romantic axiology. Its religio-philosophical confrontation explores the problem of evil from the typically romantic standpoint of neo-gnosticism: the Earth is regarded as a prison, presided over by an indifferent or negligent deity; under these conditions, a rebellious demon, though formally evil, can be seen as a tragic and sympathetic figure struggling for freedom, one which, for Lermontov's contemporary reader, would have had subversive political overtones. Yet this is only one aspect of the demonic identity. Lermontov's interest in the theme seems to have been influenced by a short poem by Pushkin ("Demon", 1823). In this the eponymous demon is not so much a spiritual being as a sceptical familiar of the poet, a sort of Socratic daemon, which tempts the idealistic poet towards cynical doubt and scepticism. This is the inevitable contrary of romantic individuation and self-confidence empowered by the epistemologies of Descartes and Hume. Romantic impatience with prescriptiveness and tradition is here taken to its nihilistic conclusion in a rejection of the *auctoritas* of all knowledge and morality. Lermontov's Demon shares sceptical features with Pushkin's, but, given more narrative scope, is able to display them in the arena of passionate human interaction. This demonic formula, purged of romantic figurativeness, also dictates the characteristics of Pechorin in *A Hero of Our Time*.

The somewhat rarefied and allegorical representation of human motivation inherent in the demonic hero gains considerably in concretization when combined with Lermontov's other great romantic preoccupation: the exotic landscape and peoples of the Caucasus. A significant turning-point in the draft evolution of *The Demon* occurs when in draft six (1838) Lermontov locates the scene of the Demon's drama in the specific setting of the Caucasus that he knew well, painted and wrote about in much of his creative work. Lermontov's use of the Caucasus is highly ambiguous in the romantic context. On one level he uses setting in the well-established Byronic tradition of oriental exotic romanticism, with strong undertones of Rousseau, an approach to the region that he inherited from Pushkin: a wild landscape populated by noble savages. On the other hand he shows his late romantic and proto-realist credentials in sometimes privileging his personal experience of this exotic setting over the aesthetic stereotype: the Demon's disdain for the beauty of the Caucasus does not prevent Lermontov polemicizing with him through authoritative descriptive passages that make such beauty self-evident.

Because of the psychological and philosophical affinities between the characters of the Demon and Pechorin, Lermontov critics have often preferred to regard *The Demon* as a romanticized instance of what is represented more fully and realistically in the character of Pechorin. This, however, is too reductive; the demonic identity of the poem's protagonist is precisely what is lacking in the prose work, however metaphorically demonic the character of Pechorin may be thought to be. By broaching questions of good and evil *sub specie aeternitatis*, *The Demon* addresses questions about the moral nature of the universe that can only be digressively dealt with in the socially determined context of a novel; the fusion of extravagant characterization with serious philosophical problematics is typically romantic (the ethics and aesthetics of *The Demon* owe a good deal to Schelling) and allows *The Demon* to approach important philosophical questions, less easily accessible in the empirical world of prose realism.

ROBERT REID

Nikolai Semenovich Leskov 1831–1895

Prose writer

Biography

Born in Gorokhovo, Orel province, 16 February 1831. Educated privately and at the Orel gymnasium, 1841–46. Served as a clerk in Orel criminal court, 1847–49. Transferred to Kiev as assistant clerk in the army recruiting bureau, 1847; there received two promotions and medal before leaving in 1857. Married: Ol'ga Smirnova in 1853 (separated 1861), one son and one daughter. Worked for firm of Scott (his British uncle by marriage) and Wilkins in estate management, 1857–60. Moved to Moscow, 1860; first articles published. Settled in St Petersburg to work as journalist and writer, 1861. Also wrote under the pseudonym M. Stebnitskii. First visit abroad to Eastern Europe and Paris, 1862–63. Lived with Katerina Bubnova, 1865–77; four step-children and one son (Andrei Leskov, 1866–1953, later to become the writer's biographer). Served on Scholarly Committee of the Ministry of Education until his dismissal, 1874–83. Further trips abroad, 1875 and 1884. Publication of Collected Works began, 1889. Volume 6, though all contents had previously been published, was banned by the censor. Died 5 March 1895.

Publications

Collected Editions

Polnoe sobranie sochinenii, 36 vols. St Petersburg, 1902–03.
The Amazon and Other Stories, translated by David Magarshack. London, Allen and Unwin, 1949; reprinted Westport, Connecticut, Hyperion Press, 1977.
Sobranie sochinenii, 11 vols. Moscow, 1956–58.
Selected Tales by N. Leskov, translated by David Magarshack. London, Secker and Warburg, 1961.
Satirical Stories, translated and edited by William B. Edgerton. New York, Pegasus, 1969.
Five Tales, translated by Michael Shotton. London, Angel, 1984.
Lady Macbeth of Mtsensk District and Other Stories, translated by David McDuff. Harmondsworth, Penguin, 1987.
Sobranie sochinenii (annotated edition), 12 vols. Moscow, 1989–
Sobranie sochinenii, 6 vols. Moscow, 1993.
Polnoe sobranie sochinenii, 30 vols. Moscow, 1996–

Fiction

Ovtsebyk, in *Otechestvennye zapiski*, 4 (1863); translated as "The Musk-Ox", by R. Norman, in *The Musk-Ox and Other Tales*, London, Routledge, 1944; Westport, Connecticut, Hyperion Press, 1977.
Nekuda [No Way Out], in *Biblioteka dlia chteniia*, 1–5, 7–8, 10, 12 (1864).
Ledi Makbet mtsenskogo uezda, in *Epokha*, 1 (1865); translated as "Lady Macbeth of Mtsensk", by David McDuff,

in *Lady Macbeth of Mtsensk District and Other Stories*, Harmondsworth, Penguin, 1987.
Na nozhakh [At Daggers Drawn], in *Russkii vestnik*, 10–12 (1870), 1–8 (1871).
Soboriane, in *Russkii vestnik*, 4–7 (1872); translated as *The Cathedral Folk*, by Isabel F. Hapgood, London, Allen Lane, 1924; reprinted Westport, Connecticut, Hyperion Press, 1971.
Zapechatlennyi angel, in *Russkii vestnik*, 1 (1873); translated as "The Sealed Angel", by K.A. Lantz, in *The Sealed Angel and Other Stories*, Knoxville, University of Tennessee Press, 1984.
Ocharovannyi strannik, in *Russkii mir*, 272–311 (1873); translated as "The Enchanted Pilgrim", by David Magarshack, in *The Enchanted Pilgrim and Other Stories*, London and New York, Hutchinson, 1946; also as "The Enchanted Wanderer", by G. Hanna, in *The Enchanted Wanderer and Other Stories*, Moscow, Foreign Languages Publishing House, 1958.
Vale of Tears and "On Quakeresses", translated by James Muckle, Nottingham, Bramcote Press, 1991.

Play
Rastochitel' [The Spendthrift], in *Literaturnaia biblioteka*, 7 (1867).

Critical Studies

N.S. Leskov v tvorcheskoi laboratorii, by V. Gebel', Moscow, 1945.
N. S. Leskov: Zhizn', tvorchestvo, poetika, by L. Grossman, Moscow, 1945.
Zhizn' Nikolaia Leskova, by Andrei Leskov, Moscow, 1954; Tula, 1981.
"The Storyteller: Reflections on the Works of Nikolai Leskov" by Walter Benjamin, *Chicago Review*, 16/1 (1963), 80–101; and in his *Illuminations*, translated by Harry Zohn, New York, Harcourt Brace, 1968; London, Collins/Fontana, 1973 (first published in German, 1936).
Nikolai Leskov: The Man and His Art, by Hugh McLean, Cambridge, Massachusetts, Harvard University Press, 1977.
Nikolai Leskov and the "Spirit of Protestantism", by James Y. Muckle, Birmingham, Birmingham Slavonic Monographs, 1978.
V poiskakh ideala (tvorchestvo N.S. Leskova), by I.V. Stoliarova, Leningrad, 1978.
Nikolay Leskov, by K.A. Lantz, Boston, Twayne, 1979.
"The *staraya skazka* of Leskov's *Soboryane*: Archpriest Tuberozov and Avvakum", by Faith Wigzell, *Slavonic and East European Review*, 63 (1985), 321–36.
"Le Problème féminin" et les portraits de femmes dans l'oeuvre de Nikolaj Leskov, by Inès Muller de Morogues, Bern and New York, Peter Lang, 1991.
"*The Enchanted Wanderer*: A Parable of National Identity", by R.A. Peace, *Russian Literature*, 29 (1991), 439–54.

Bibliographies

"Bibliografiia sochinenii N.S. Leskova", by P.V. Bykov, in *Sobranie sochinenii*, by N.S. Leskov, vol. 10, St Petersburg, 1890, i–xxv.
"K bibliografii N.S. Leskova", by S.P. Shesterikov, in *Izvestiia otdeleniia russkogo iazyka i slovesnosti Rossiiskoi akademii nauk*, 30 (1925), 268–310.
"Leskov's Fiction", in Hugh McLean, *Nikolai Lesko: The Man and His Art*, Cambridge, Massachusetts, Harvard University Press, 1977, 753–60.
L'oeuvre journalistique et littéraire de N. S. Leskov. Bibliographie, by Inès Muller de Morogues, Bern, Peter Lang, 1984.

Nikolai Semenovich Leskov was an outstandingly original writer of prose fiction. He published novels, short stories, novellas, and biographical studies, as well as numerous factual journalistic articles, many of which bear witness to his considerable literary talent. Some of the fictional works purport to be "memoirs", some are called "chronicles", "sketches", "studies", even in one case a "rhapsody", as if modestly to suggest that they do not belong to the established categories of "novel" or *povest'* (novella). Leskov is, however, principally remembered for his short stories and *povesti*. There is no poetry to speak of and only one stage play, *Rastochitel'* [The Spendthrift]. His writing is marked by a great variety of subject-matter as well as forms, a very original and entertaining use of the Russian language, of colloquial and peasant speech, pun, deliberate malapropism and folk etymology, a wide knowledge of far-away Russian provinces and of peasant and merchant life, a fondness for portraying religious believers of all sorts and for exploring the essence of the Christian religion, a talent for comic perception and a striking ability to impress and often to shock by bringing comedy and tragedy face to face in his stories. Leskov's portraits of Russian peasants and the lower classes are remarkable for their unsentimentality and realism, and his picture gallery of characters, taken across the whole range of his writing, is extraordinarily rich and vivid.

Leskov is, for a variety of non-literary reasons, probably the least well known of all the great Russian 19th-century prose writers. His political views were liberal and un-doctrinaire, which did not endear him to radical socialists who represented the dominant fashionable ideology of the 1860s. He was a Christian when agnosticism was common, and yet he opposed the rigidity of traditional Russian Orthodox clerics and laymen, thus antagonizing the religious conservatives. An early biography of him was aptly entitled *Against the Current*, and a contemporary critic devoted a rather grudging article to Leskov in 1891 under the heading "A Morbid Talent". The intellectual elite of the time, left and right, did not know what to make of Leskov, and he suffered in consequence, finding it hard to make a comfortable living from his writing until the last few years of his life. His reputation did not really revive under the Soviet regime, when his interest in religion was seen as an obstacle: Leskov was not studied in schools, and only a few scholarly monographs were devoted to his work. Many of his major works have been translated into English, French, and German without being very widely read abroad. Yet through all this Leskov remained popular with the public in Russia, and even in the Soviet years six-figure print runs of collections of his stories were usual.

Leskov came from the very minor gentry in the province of Orel and he received an informal education by tutors, followed by a few years of perfunctory study at the gymnasium in Orel, which he left at the age of 15 with a certificate appropriate to a 12-year-old. Civil service work in Kiev acquainted him with the "cradle of Russian civilization", and it gave him the opportunity to mix with university teachers. A few years working in estate management gave Leskov the wide experience of provincial village life on which he drew extensively in his stories.

He began his writing career in Moscow in 1860, soon moving to St Petersburg. His first major works were *Ovtsebyk* (*The Musk-Ox*), a portrait of an eccentric radical misfit and his search for truth, and *Ledi Makbet mtsenskogo uezda* (*Lady Macbeth of Mtsensk*), discussed elsewhere. Other shorter works of the 1860s were "Voitel'nitsa" ("The Amazon") 1866, another character-portrait of an eccentric, and "Zhitie odnoi baby" [Life of a Peasant Woman] (1863), a tragic exploration of peasant hardship. At this time Leskov made his first attempt at a novel, *Nekuda* [No Way Out]. In this Leskov painted a picture of his circle of acquaintances, which they found far from flattering; together with the reputation he had already earned from an unfortunate article written by him in 1861, this made him something of an outcast. (Most of these early works were published under the *nom de plume* of M. Stebnitskii). However, the next ten years saw more successful extended works, particularly one of his masterpieces, *Soboriane* (*The Cathedral Folk*), remarkable for the creation of Deacon Akhilla, once described as the most vivid character portrayal in Russian literature. Orthodox piety and spirituality were also notably explored in two more of Leskov's greatest achievements, *Zapechatlennyi angel* (*The Sealed Angel*) and *Ocharovannyi strannik* (*The Enchanted Wanderer*).

It is generally agreed that Leskov suffered an intellectual and religious crisis in 1875, after which he betrayed more scepticism towards Orthodox Christianity. The 1870s and 1880s brought many articles and stories on radical non-Orthodox believers, including his study of the English evangelist Lord Radstock, "Velikosvetskii raskol" [Schism in High Society] (1876). Numerous stories about "just persons" (*pravedniki*) included "Odnodum" [One Track Mind] (1879), and "Nesmertel'nyi Golovan" [Deathless Golovan] (1880). Stories questioning ecclesiastical assumptions and suggesting a more spiritual and less formalistic religious approach included "Na kraiu sveta" [On the Edge of the World] (1875), "Melochi arkhiereiskoi zhizni" [Trivia from Archiepiscopal Life] (1878–80), and "Nekreshchenyi pop" [The Unbaptized Priest] (1877). While Leskov's spiritual concerns were never far away, he continued to publish stories in great variety, on themes which were often historical, biographical, comic, satirical or curious. His best-known short story is "Levsha" ("Lefty") 1881, about the left-handed blacksmith who capped the work of some English experts by shoeing a tiny steel flea they had given the tsar; "Chelovek na chasakh" ("The Sentry") 1887, has made a successful stage and television play in English translation. By the late 1880s Leskov was having difficulties with the censor in view of his growing dissent. His later works included many treatments of ancient church legends, as well as "Polunoshchniki" [Night Owls] 1891, "Iudol'" ("Vale of Tears") 1892, "Zagon" [The Cattle Pen] 1893, "Zimnii den'" [A Winter's Day] 1894, and "Zaiachii remiz" [The March Hare] (1894, but not published until 1917).

JAMES MUCKLE

Lady Macbeth of Mtsensk

Ledi Makbet mtsenskogo uezda

Novella, 1865

Lady Macbeth of Mtsensk more accurately translated: "A Lady Macbeth of the Mtsensk District", a *long* short story described by its author as an *ocherk* (a sketch or study), was first published in 1865. It is one of Leskov's earliest and best works. The text available today is that of the Collected Works of 1889, which differs only very slightly from that of the book version of 1867. However, these two publications differ significantly from the original journal edition: at least 10 per cent of the 1867 text was added at that time.

The plot concerns Katerina L'vovna Izmailova, who has been married for reasons of convenience to a childless widowed merchant, Zinovii. Her life in a remote village is boring, the marriage loveless and childless. She finds no pleasure in her existence and is totally submissive to her husband and her father-in-law, Boris. During Zinovii's temporary absence she encounters Sergei, a new employee. A passionate relationship ensues. Boris spots Sergei climbing from her room. He has him flogged and locked up. Katerina discovers the will to oppose Boris; having unsuccessfully sought Sergei's release, she adds rat-poison to her father-in-law's dish of mushrooms, and he dies. Sergei now occupies her bedroom; Zinovii's absence, it is ascertained, is likely to be further prolonged. A mysterious cat appears in two dreams, filling her with foreboding and speaking to her in the person of the murdered Boris. At dead of night Zinovii returns, full of suspicion about his father's death. Katerina prepares more rat-poison for him, but in fact she overpowers him by her physical strength and she and Sergei murder him. To the world, Zinovii's disappearance is a mystery. Sergei is now firmly established as Katerina's surrogate husband. She attempts to obtain the right to conduct the business herself in view of Zinovii's "disappearance". However, it appears that the Izmailov family business was using capital from another source, and that any inheritance must be shared. Zinovii's young nephew and the joint heir to the property comes to live with Katerina. She and Sergei decide to dispose of him too. The suffocation of Fedia is, however, witnessed by some peeping Toms from the village, who had been hoping for a salacious view of Katerina and Sergei enjoying each other's company. The body of Zinovii is next discovered; Katerina and Sergei are arrested and condemned to exile. Her passion for Sergei unabated, Katerina longs to see him as they trudge into exile. He, however, is disillusioned with her; he bestows his sexual favours on other prisoners, particularly the malicious Sonetka. Katerina soon believes herself to be reconciled with Sergei; they spend a blissful half-hour together. But when he begs her last pair of woollen stockings from her, ostensibly to ease the discomfort caused by the shackles on his leg, and then next day she sees Sonetka wearing them, she spits in his face. He gains entrance to her barrack that night and beats her cruelly. Next day, as the prisoners embark on a Volga steamboat, she hurls herself on Sonetka and drags her into the river, where they both drown.

Several themes suggested by this material repay examination. There is Leskov's exploration of the criminal mentality: at the time he composed this work he had visited prisons and written articles about his experiences. Indeed, he wrote the story in a cell provided at Kiev University (as was customary in the 19th century) for unruly students. A difficult issue concerns the motivation for the actions of the dramatis personae: can the murders be made convincing, but can the reader be made to feel sympathy for the murderers? Do they become tragic figures in the Shakespearean sense? The excellent title of the story (changed from "Lady Macbeth of Our District" for the second version) suggests a tale of unscrupulous ambition in a remote and backward part of Russia, but it does not quite fulfil all its promise: despite superficial similarities, the only significant Shakespearean element is the presence of a strong female character determined to achieve her ambition at all costs for the man she loves. There is no exploration of conscience: Katerina's unscrupulousness and sexual obsessiveness are dominant. The eroticism and passion in the story are more reminiscent of *Antony and Cleopatra* than of *Macbeth*. The story was intended also partly as a contrasting response to Ostrovskii's play *Groza* (*The Storm*) 1860, another portrayal of family despotism among the merchant classes (and with a central character named Katerina).

Leskov vividly conveys the intense boredom of life in the Izmailov household, and later the wretched condition of the prisoners. Erotic scenes are hinted at with immense understatement; the reader's attention is drawn to a dark corner, the silence, a mouse gnawing at a feather or – most tellingly! – crickets calling to each other beneath the stove. One is reminded of the artist Boris Kustodiev's illustration showing nothing more than Sergei's belt lying on the bed. Other striking features of the story include the total lack of moralizing – the reader is left to draw any ethical conclusion – which goes alongside the automatic observance by most of the characters of the habits of religious observance, such as crossing themselves, attending to the icon lamps, giving Boris "a Christian burial" after murdering him, and the like.

Russian critics have praised the story for its tight construction, economy of expression and language, dramatic tension, and characterization – even of the minor characters. Dostoevskii, who had good reason to know, was well satisfied with the portrayal of prison. There has been criticism of the "melodrama": but if the events described are sensational, the treatment is remarkably restrained. Perhaps the finest tribute to the story is Dmitrii Shostakovich's opera of the same title (opus 29, 1934) and its later revision, "Katerina Izmailova" (opus 114, 1963), almost certainly the finest Russian opera of the 20th century. Though the plot is changed in certain important ways and the work is transposed into a very different medium, the composer re-creates the central characters, the stultifying merchant milieu, the criminality, passion, eroticism, greed and jealousy with great faithfulness to Leskov's original.

JAMES MUCKLE

The Cathedral Folk

Soboriane

Novel, 1872

The Cathedral Folk was originally planned as a much longer work, spanning a couple of centuries and embracing all social strata of a small provincial town, symbolically entitled Stargorod (Old Town). Ultimately Leskov settled for an endearing portrait of the clergy of Stargorod, something of a novelty in the Russian literary tradition. The hero is Archpriest Father Savelii Tuberozov, a man whose life has been a struggle against apostasy, atheism, and apathy. He is supported, if that is the word, by the other two contrasting members of the Stargorod clerical trinity, the meek and mild Father Zakhariia Benefaktov, and the unruly deacon, Akhilla Desnitsyn (the name ironically means "right-hand man"). The past history of Tuberozov's life is seen through his diary (his "demicoton book"), where he records his hopes, aspirations, and failures. As a young man, he came to Stargorod to combat the Old Belief (Schismatics), but, finding that he was merely meant to denounce them to the authorities or take bribes, gave up this fight. At the time the novel opens, Tuberozov is already an old man, depressed by his own inability to put his moral convictions into practice and turn the Orthodoxy of the townspeople into an active faith. His task is made no easier by the buffoonery and brawling of the irresponsible, if well-meaning, Akhilla, as well as the mischief caused by an atheist from within the clerical group of Stargorod, the son of the wafer-baker, now a teacher. His own downfall follows the arrival in the town of an amoral ex-nihilist, Termosesov. Inspired by a vision experienced in a forest storm, Tuberozov delivers a fiery sermon indicting the town dignitaries for religious hypocrisy. Denounced by Termosesov as a dangerous revolutionary, he is removed from his post and dies soon after, defeated. Left alone, Akhilla undergoes a maturing process, belatedly becoming his teacher's right-hand man, struggling in his own still somewhat comic way to defend Orthodoxy and the memory of Father Savelii. The book ends with his death, followed shortly after by that of Father Zakhariia. A new clerical staff, more to the taste of the ecclesiastical and secular authorities, takes charge at the Stargorod Cathedral.

The comic tone of much of the novel has caused critics, who judge the Russian novel by the criteria of the Dostoevskian or Tolstoian novel of ideas, to complain of the trivialization of issues such as the struggle between materialism and religion. Others dislike the overdrawn portraits of the "evil" characters, Termosesov in particular, and the replacement of a real plot by a series of anecdotes. The last two criticisms rest on assumptions derived from the classic "realist" novel of the 19th century, which preferred a well-structured plot and balanced portraiture. Leskov, however, attempting to develop a native Russian approach to long narrative, deliberately termed his work a chronicle (*khronika*) rather than a novel. By this he intended to indicate that it should be seen as history of a kind (no matter that it was fictional in character). Stargorod was to be a microcosm of old Rus', its symbolic significance evoked through a series of parallels with early Russian literature and folklore. Tuberozov himself is modelled on Archpriest Avvakum, the 17th-century leader of the Old Believers, Father Zakhariia is in the tradition of Russian saints who believed in non-resistance to evil, while Akhilla, who loves to gallop the steppe on his horse, is presented as one of the heroes of Russian folk epic. Episodes as well as characters may be folklorized; thus the incident where Akhilla struggles with a man dresssed up as the devil in goat skin with horns is a reworking of a folk-tale. Many of the characters have names that suggest their allegiance in the battle between good and evil: for example, Tuberozov's name suggests sweet-smelling roses, while Prepotenskii, the town atheist, has a name that suggests power – the power of man to control his own world and the power to do harm to old Russian values and beliefs.

The struggle between doubt and belief in *The Cathedral Folk* is less crudely one-sided than some critics perceive. All the positive characters have clear failings, though these are certainly treated indulgently, and there is no doubt that Termosesov and Prince Bornovolokov, his employer, are too unrelievedly black. More importantly, criticism is not extended only to radicals and to foreigners who do not have Russia's welfare at heart, but also to the Russian institution that should be at the heart of Russian Christianity, the Church. Through Tuberozov, Leskov indicts the bureaucratic consistory system of the Orthodox Church, accusing it of failing to lead a moral and spiritual crusade and condemning its far too cosy relations with the State. When he wrote *The Cathedral Folk*, Leskov still thought there was a chance that the Church could be revitalized: "I am no enemy of the Church, but her friend ...", he wrote, "I wish her honourable progress out of the stagnation into which she has fallen, crushed by her links with the state". Despite this, the end of *The Cathedral Folk* is deeply pessimistic, and, within a few years, Leskov had ceased to hold out any hope for the Russian Orthodox Church. Indeed, the positive virtues in the novel, termed by Tuberozov "staraia skazka" (literally, "old fairy-tale"), are national rather than religious. Through the complex subtext of allusions Leskov suggests they are made up of the best of traditional values, both religious and secular. "The ordinary people", remarked Leskov in an earlier draft, "are not wise ... but foolish and badly in need of guidance". Leskov is more a national romantic than a supporter of Orthodoxy.

If criticisms can be made of some aspects of *The Cathedral Folk*, few can resist the charms of its clerical heroes or fail to admire the linguistic virtuosity of Tuberozov's diary, composed in a vigorous and distinctive style, with bookish turns of phrase, Slavonicisms and biblical quotations. Even though some of this is lost in translation, the novel as a whole deserves to be better known.

FAITH WIGZELL

The Enchanted Wanderer

Ocharovannyi strannik

Story, 1873

The Enchanted Wanderer was written by Leskov after a voyage to Lake Ladoga in Karelia in the summer of 1872, and completed by early 1873. The story (termed by Leskov a tale (*rasskaz*), though it runs to well over a hundred pages) is one of the best examples of the author's skill in constructing narrative through a series of seemingly unconnected anecdotes. However, it was not well received at the time, the radical critic N.K. Mikhailovskii complaining that it had no plot, but was just "a whole series of stories strung togther like beads on a string". In the 20th century the tale has been re-evaluated as a brilliantly colourful small epic, where the episodes are linked not merely through the person of the hero, but also thematically and structurally.

The story opens with a frame situation. A group of educated Russians sailing across Lake Ladoga are joined by a novice monk of giant stature; two intriguing stories he tells lead them to press him for the story of his life. With the exception of the occasional interjection from the other passengers, the story from then on is narrated by the monk, Ivan Sever'ianovich Fliagin, a man of amazing vitality and spiritual depth, but incapable of analysis other than the attribution of events to divine causes. The first-person narrative is a typically Leskovian *tour de force* of *skaz*, the development of a highly idiosyncratic personal language, reflecting the status, life experience, and character of the narrator.

Ivan Fliagin's life is crammed with colour and dramatic incident. Born the son of a serf, as a young boy he is made to ride postilion on his aristocratic masters' coach. In a moment of arrogant exuberance, he whips a monk asleep on a haycart. The horses bolt and the monk is killed, reappearing in a dream, where he prophesies that Ivan will be near to death many times, but finally, remembering that his mother had promised him to God, will enter a monastery. This prophecy, which he sees as determining the course of his life, is his "enchantment". Shortly after, Fliagin risks his own life to save his master and mistress from death, but loses their good favour when he cruelly tortures a cat beloved of the countess. Forced to work on his knees hammering stones into the ground, he runs away and is employed to look after a baby whose mother has run off with an army officer. The mother returns for her baby, but Ivan refuses to betray his employer's trust until forced to choose between the caring mother and the child's irate father. Visiting a horse fair on the steppe, he becomes involved in a flogging match with a Tartar (actually a Kirgiz), in which he whips his stubborn opponent to death and is forced to flee to the steppe. He returns only ten years later, because the Tartars, who want him to stay, cripple him by sewing horsehair into the soles of his feet, bringing him literally to his knees. Using his childhood knowledge and love of horses, he becomes a "connoisseur", buying remounts for the army (the Russian variant *koneser* is an untranslatable pun on the word for horse *kon'*). He also becomes prone to serious drinking bouts, from which he is cured by a drunk who calls himself a magnetizer. The cure consists in replacing love of drink with a love of beauty; he falls for the gypsy girl Grusha on his last drinking spree. After being bought by Fliagin's infatuated master, and then abandoned, Grusha turns to Fliagin to save her from the sin of suicide by killing her. Out of love he agrees. His role as scapegoat continues when he takes the place in the army of the only son of an elderly couple, and later, playing the role of the Devil in pre-Lenten theatrical spectacles, is regularly beaten by all the actors. He then decides to enter a monastery, but peace does not come. Tormented by demons, and prophesying the imminent destruction of his country, Ivan is sent by his abbot out into the world as a holy pilgrim or *strannik*, to traverse the length and breadth of Russia travelling from one holy place to another.

In this story Leskov investigates the contradictory impulses in the Russian nature, epitomized by Ivan Fliagin, whose Christian name is the Russian equivalent of Jack and whose surname implies a toper (*fliaga* means flask). Thus scenes of mindless cruelty and violence alternate with moments of kindness, and self-sacrifice, while periods of sobriety and honesty contrast with those of abandon. The varied social and geographical settings reflect the huge expanses of Russia that Leskov knew so well. Generically the work follows the pattern of the epic and its light-hearted west European variant, the picaresque novel, in depicting the journey of a hero through Russia and through life, though Fliagin's peasant fatalism renders the concept of the quest inappropriate. Though *The Enchanted Wanderer* owes something to Gogol''s *Mertvye dushi* (*Dead Souls*), which combines a journey with a broader theme of the current state and future of Russia, it owes much more to earlier Russian literary and folk traditions. Fliagin himself has the capacity for drink, the strength, decency, and casual attitude to violence of the folk epic hero, the *bogatyr'*, while much in his biography is reminiscent of saints' lives (he was promised to God by his mother, has prophetic dreams, is tormented by demons and so on). There are links with other works of early Russian literature: the final image of Fliagin as a patriotic warrior monk finds a reflection in the figure of the monk Peresvet who participated in the famous battle of Kulikovo Pole against the Tartars in 1380, while the image of the hero battling against a predetermined fate, journeying and falling into temptation before finally entering a monastery owes much to the 17th-century *Povest' o Gore-Zlochastii* [Tale of Woe-Misfortune].

The repetition of motifs such as prophecy and suicide, and themes such as the established Church's failure to show true Christian charity (missionaries refuse to help Fliagin, the Church utterly condemns suicides) give the work its coherence. With its extraordinary vitality and colour, *The Enchanted Wanderer* is one of Leskov's masterpieces.

FAITH WIGZELL

Ekaterina Pavlovna Letkova 1856–1937

Prose writer

Biography

Born in St Petersburg, 2 December 1856. Educated at Mariinskaia gymnasium in Vologda, from 1872; Ger'e Courses of Higher Education for Women in Moscow, from 1879. While studying in Moscow became involved in literary and political circles, and met Turgenev, Goncharov, and others. First translation (of Legouvier) published in 1879; first story, "Rzhavchina" [Rust], 1881. Married: the architect Nikolai Vladimirovich Sultanov in 1884; one son. Moved to St Petersburg, 1884. Active in women's educational charities; with her friend, Baroness Ikskul', campaigned to raise money for Higher Women's Courses, 1899–1917. Member of Litfond from late 1880s. After the Revolution, worked in Vsemirnaia literatura and then Gosizdat, living first in The House of Arts (*Dom iskusstv*), and then in The House of Scholars (*Dom uchenykh*). Died in Leningrad, 7 January 1937.

Publications

Collected Editions

Povesti i rasskazy, 2 vols. St Petersburg, 1899.
Povesti i rasskazy, 3 vols. St Petersburg, 1900–03.
Ocherki i rasskazy. Petrograd, 1915.

Fiction

"Rzhavchina" [Rust], *Russkaia mysl'*, 10 (1881).
"Lishniaia" [The Superfluous Woman], *Russkaia mysl'*, 7 (1893).
"Lushka", *Severnyi vestnik*, 3 (1894).
"Otdykh" [The Holiday], *Russkaia mysl'*, 10 (1896).
"Mertvaia zyb'" [Ground Swell], *Russkaia mysl'*, 10–11 (1897); as separate edition, St Petersburg, 1900.
"Bab'i slezy" [Peasant Women's Tears], *Mir bozhii*, 5 (1898).
"Oborvannaia perepiska" [An Interrupted Correspondence], *Russkoe bogatstvo*, 3–4 (1902).
"Bez familii" [Without a Surname], *Russkoe bogatstvo*, 10 (1902).
"Mukhi" [Flies], *Russkoe bogatstvo*, 10 (1903).
"Kolodniki" [Shackled], *Russkoe bogatstvo*, 5 (1905).

Memoirs and Essays

"Krepostnaia intelligentsiia" [The Serf Intelligentsia], *Otechestvennye zapiski*, 11 (1883).
I.S. Turgenev: Zhizn' i tvorchestvo [I.S. Turgenev: Life and Works]. Petrograd, 1918.
"Pro Gleba Ivanovicha [Uspenskogo]" [On Gleb Ivanovich Uspenskii], *Zven'ia*, 5, Moscow and Leningrad, 1935.

Critical Studies

"Literatura i zhizn'", by N.M. Mikhailovskii, *Russkoe bogatstvo*, 8 (1899), 161–82.
"Letkova", by E.A. Koltonovskaia, in *Zhenskie siluety*, St Petersburg, 1912, 126–44.
"E. Letkova, *Rasskazy*", by A.G. Gornfel'd, *Russkoe bogatstvo*, 8 (1913).
"Letkova Ekaterina Pavlovna", by A.V. Alekseev and V.N. Baskakov, in *Russkie pisateli 1800–1917 gg.: biograficheskii slovar'*, Moscow, 1994, vol. 3, 350–51.
"Letkova, Ekaterina Pavlovna", by Irina Kazakova, in *Dictionary of Russian Women Writers*, edited by Marina Ledkovsky, Charlotte Rosenthal, and Mary Zirin, Westport, Connecticut, Greenwood Press, 1994, 371–73.

Ekaterina Letkova was perhaps the most talented of a number of interesting and neglected women realists working in the late 19th and early 20th centuries (her colleagues included Ol'ga Shapir, Valentina Dmitrieva, and Sof'ia Smirnova). Never a member of an explicitly feminist grouping, she might be described as a "fellow traveller" of the women's liberation movement, in that a number of her narratives explore aspects of the "woman question" that also came under scrutiny among liberal feminists.

The first of these was the discovery (distinguishing 1890s feminists from their predecessors in the 1860s and 1870s) that women's new access to employment did not necessarily accord them personal satisfaction or even economic independence. For Mar'ia Nilovna, heroine of "Otdykh" [The Holiday], work has been a source of exhaustion and frustration, yet has not gained her the resources to escape from her bullying mother; her state is closer to indentured slavery than to the ideal of self-fulfilment represented by Nadezhda Khvoshchinskaia's Lelia in the 1860 story *Pansionerka* [The Schoolgirl]. Letkova was also an important contributor to the long history of Russian women's disaffection with heterosexual relationships. Her representations of marriage were uniformally pessimistic. The heroine of the long *povest'* or short novel "Oborvannaia perepiska" [An Interrupted Correspondence] seems almost to revel in her decision not to leave her unfaithful husband, with whom she shares no common interests, even when his illegitimate son is imported to the household. A still grimmer evocation of the conjugal nightmare is "Kolodniki" [Shackled] (the title is a reference to an image used in Tolstoi's "Kreutzer Sonata"), which depicts a middle-aged couple whose daughter's wedding has crystallized their own mutual disillusion; the effect is exacerbated by flashbacks to the earlier days of their relationship. A destructive and apparently final quarrel is unexpectedly resolved by the assertion of custom, Pavlovian-reflex style: the wife's donning of her dressing-gown reminds her husband that he would like something to eat. But as for earlier writers, such as Gan, Zhukova, Panaeva, Tur, and Khvoshchinskaia, extra-marital relations do not necessarily offer greater opportunities of freedom than marriage. In "Oborvannaia perepiska", for instance, the heroine's attempt at an affair proves more sordid even than her marriage, and her failure to respond positively to the hero's hints of emotional involvement in his letters does not seem wholly unjustified, since he emerges as a distinctly self-absorbed individual.

"The woman question" was only one of Letkova's concerns in her fiction, however. The heroine of "Oborvannaia perepiska", at this point evidently the mouthpiece of her creator, makes clear that women's liberation was, for Letkova, exemplified above all by their involvement in mainstream social and political debate. Letkova's own preferred form of "forward thinking" (as for many women writers) was Populism. Populist views are expressed, for example, in an early essay on serf artists, "Krepostnaia intelligentsiia" [The Serf Intelligentsia] (written at the encouragement of the famous Populist ideologue N.M. Mikhailovskii), and also by several of her stories, some of which explore the lives of women radicals, and others the lives of peasant women. In "Lishniaia" [The Superfluous Woman], a selfless woman radical returns home after a gap of many years (her husband forced her to leave on account of her views), to find her daughters utterly unconcerned with social issues, uninterested in her, and self-centred; the title is blatantly and bitterly ironic. *Mertvaia zyb'* [Ground Swell], Letkova's most popular work (it went into three separate editions after appearing in the journal *Russkaia mysl'*), deals with a Populist mother torn between political and personal impulses. Still more pessimistic are Letkova's stories of peasant life: "Bab'i slezy" [Peasant Women's Tears] is, as the title suggests, an unremittingly bleak study of social and sexual exploitation in a village, while "Lushka" is a striking treatment of infanticide: a small girl inadvertently kills the baby brother to whom she plays nurse while her mother (a conscript's wife, and hence a *de facto* single mother) is away from home. Chillingly, the story suggests that child-murder through neglect may be systemic: the baby Lushka looks after is the only survivor of a long series of siblings, and when the child complains about nursing him, her mother suggests that she might well be liberated from the task before too long.

Letkova's visions of Russian society were uncongenial to some of her readers, who held a more idealistic view of "the people"; the critic Gornfel'd, for example, suggested in 1913 that their character might be less the product of observation than of Letkova's temperament (paradoxically, Gornfel'd also levelled the charge of lack of inventiveness at Letkova). On the whole, though, Letkova's fiction was well received in its own day, not only by Mikhailovskii (who had been emotionally, as well as intellectually, involved with Letkova before her marriage, a fact that may have affected his judgement), but also by other influential critics, such as E.A. Koltonovskaia. And deservedly so: her fiction is well observed, well structured and (unlike some of the work of, say, Ol'ga Shapir or Valentina Dmitrieva) crisply written. But, while sharing Chekhov's flair for concision, Letkova did not, however, share his preference for a *dégagé* perspective. Her stories are impassionedly didactic, both in their inclination to melodramatically intense endings and often too in their use of direct authorial commentary: the concluding line of "Kolodniki", for instance, reads: "The clock impartially and insistently counted out the seconds of departing life." But in no sense is her work straightforward agitprop. Admittedly "Lushka", for instance, is less aesthetically rich than a story with similar thematics by Chekhov, "Spat' khochetsia" ("Sleepy"). Letkova's story is narrated omnisciently rather than in internal monologue; the description of the protagonist's village milieu is workmanlike rather than symbolic, with nothing to resemble Chekhov's extraordinary recurring image of a lamp's moving reflection on the ceiling. But for all that, the morality of Letkova's story is in some ways more problematic. Chekhov's Var'ka is patently the victim of her appalling employers (who predictably come from the petit bourgeoisie): Lushka's mother is as downtrodden as she is, and there is a touching reference to how the mother, despite her less than ideal parenting and indigent existence, always remembers to bring presents back for the children when she has been away. Another interesting touch in the story is the harsh language that Lushka uses about and to her mother, upbraiding her for instance, "Where the hell've you skulked off to now?" Letkova was well aware that exploited children are not always easy subjects of pity, and she creates a remarkable portrait of a child isolated not only by her nanny role but even by her name (when some visitors on horses amuse themselves by giving sweets to the children, calling out each likely peasant name in turn, Lushka gets left out because her name, Luker'ia, is so peculiar). Quite different, but equally interesting, textual strategies are used in "Oborvannaia perepiska", which not only revives the epistolary genre, but also interweaves into the narrative the diary of Sergei L'vovich's grandmother, a montage of jottings, whose meaning must be pieced together laboriously by the characters and by the reader.

In some respects, then, Letkova could be seen as a predecessor of Liudmila Petrushevskaia: thought by some of her contemporaries to be a specialist in *chernukha* (studies of social decay), she was, in fact, also preoccupied by linguistic questions, not only in the sense of ventriloquism (the reconstruction of her characters' own language), but also in the sense of representation, *literaturnost'*.

Like some other established women writers (for instance, Tat'iana Shchepkina-Kupernik), Letkova gave up producing fiction after the Russian Revolution (this handsome, autocratic *grande dame* could have applied herself to proletarian subjects only with difficulty, one suspects). But she continued to be involved in literary activity, not only working in publishing, but also writing in various non-fiction genres – sketches, popular biography, memoirs – and working on translations of fiction and drama from the French (including Zola's *Germinal*, among others).

CATRIONA KELLY

Iurii Nikolaevich Libedinskii 1898–1959

Novelist

Biography

Born in Odessa, 10 December 1898. Attended high school in Cheliabinsk. Joined the Communist Party in 1920; became political commissar in the Red Army during the Civil War. Began writing *Nedelia* (*A Week*) in Ekaterinburg, 1920, and completed it after moving to Moscow in 1921. Very active in literary life throughout 1920s, became a leader of RAPP. Married twice. Attacked for his *Rozhdenie geroia* [The Birth of a Hero] (1930), and disgraced after the dissolution of RAPP, excluded from the Soviet Writers' Union and temporarily expelled from the Party, 1936. Seriously ill during World War II, remarried and gradually recovered. Devoted post-war years to writing lengthy historical novels centred on the Caucasus region. Died 24 November 1959.

Publications

Collected Editions

Sobranie sochinenii, vol. 1, Moscow, 1927; vol. 2, Leningrad, 1931.

Izbrannye proizvedeniia, 2 vols. Moscow, 1958; reprinted 1972.

Fiction

Nedelia. 1922; translated as *A Week*, by Arthur Ransome, London, Allen and Unwin, and New York, B.W. Huebsch, 1923.

Zavtra [Tomorrow]. 1923.

Komissary [Commissars]. 1925.

Rozhdenie geroia [The Birth of a Hero]. Leningrad, 1930.

Gory i liudi [Mountains and Men]. 1947.

Zarevo [Dawn]. 1952.

Utro sovetov [The Morning of Soviet Power], 3 vols. 1957.

Memoirs

Sovremenniki [Contemporaries]. Moscow, 1958; revised edition, 1961.

Critical Studies

The Proletarian Episode in Russian Literature 1928–32, by Edward J. Brown, New York, Columbia University Press, 1953; New York, Octagon, 1971 (chapter 7).

Iurii Libedinskii i ego povest' "Nedelia", by G.N. Medvedeva, Dushanbe, 1963.

Zelenaia lampa. Vospominaniia, by Lidiia Libedinskaia, Moscow, 1966.

Despite his readiness to devote his considerable writer's talents to lengthy works of historical fiction celebrating such issues as the rise of capitalism in the northern Caucasus (*Gory i liudi* [Mountains and Men]; or the famous strike of Baku workers in 1914 that figured in his *Zarevo* [Dawn]), Iurii Libedinskii is best known for his first work, the short novel *Nedelia* (*A Week*) 1922. It attracted instant attention for the freshness and clarity of the writing and for the fact that it was the first work of Soviet prose to depict communists as human beings with ordinary emotions faced by terrible fates at the hands of counter-revolutionary peasants during the Civil War. So candid was Libedinskii's study of these embattled Party workers that his novel fell into disfavour and was only later republished (in 1949) in a rewritten, far more innocuous form.

He was born in Odessa into the family of a doctor who soon moved his young family to the Urals where he had been appointed head of a hospital in a gold-mining community. For young Libedinskii's education, though, the family moved to Cheliabinsk. His education as a writer had already begun through avid reading of Tolstoi, Blok, Leonid Andreev, Gor'kii and especially Bunin and Belyi. The family's left-wing sympathies soon orientated him towards Marxism and he became active in the Cheliabinsk soviet. He joined the Bolshevik Party in 1920. Libedinskii intended *A Week* to be an answer to Pil'niak's *Golyi god* (*The Naked Year*), which, if outstanding as an early example of innovative Soviet prose, reduced the communists to mere "leather jacket" symbols of the new regime. Though propagandist in its aim, *A Week* contained portraits of a great variety of Party members, including the diligent, committed leader-type Klimin, the educated, sensitive, ex-bourgeois Martynov (modelled, one feels, on Libedinskii himself) and the time-serving bureaucrat, Matusenko, who would clearly fawn his way through the ensuing decades of Stalinist purges just as successfully as he survived the annihilating fury of the blood-thirsty peasantry. Passages of interior monologue in a stream-of-consciousness manner, or lovers' exchanges cast in suitably intimate, often sentimental, terms, help to highlight the private nature of lives and relationships in the embattled community of communists, but the total impression in literary terms is spoiled by an undue straining after prose-poetic effect.

Although manifestly and self-consciously a literary work, *A Week* has a documentary veracity to it. Its honesty about the lives of communists is to be seen at its most obvious in what appears to be a document inserted into the text in the shape of a letter to Klimin from a former Cheka, or secret police, associate. The letter (omitted from the rewritten version) tells graphically how a particularly brutal "liquidation" of members of the bourgeoisie so outraged the conscience of the writer that he lost faith in the communist cause.

It is testimony to the novel's power that Arthur Ransome chose to translate it and thus made it one of the first works of Soviet prose to appear in English. Libedinskii was never to have such good fortune again. His later works of the 1920s, such as *Komissary* [Commissars], were either boring in their treatment of communist officialdom and the need for army retraining, officially "correct" though such a theme might be, or they were politically "incorrect" in their lip-service to Trotskiite views, as in *Zavtra* [Tomorrow]. During the period of the Five-Year Plans his reputation suffered an eclipse after the appearance of his novel *Rozhdenie geroia* [The Birth of a Hero]. The self-questioning of the Old Bolshevik, Shorokhov, leads him to cast doubt on the aims of the Revolution. His return to the fold led him into more serious ideological error through his failure to take account of the Leninist-Stalinist re-interpretation of Marxism.

Being one of the leaders of RAPP, Libedinskii found himself in disfavour in the 1930s when the organization was disbanded. He published a volume of short stories in 1933, but was virtually silent for the rest of the decade. Exclusion from the Soviet Writers' Union in 1936 was followed by temporary expulsion from the Party. In spite of his long-standing commitment to communism, the tide seemed to have turned against him. This was reflected most obviously in his private life. Though not a victim of the purges in a strict sense, his disgrace caused the break-up of his marriage to Marianna, the beautiful wife with whom he had shared much of his Party life (and to whom he had dedicated *A Week*). She lectured him in approved fashion on his ideological "mistakes" and married someone else. Shortly afterwards she was herself arrested. Libedinskii petitioned Stalin for her release, to no immediate effect, although in 1944 she was freed and allowed to return to Moscow, but her mental condition was so disturbed that she hanged herself shortly after her return.

Libedinskii had meanwhile remarried (his second wife Lidiia has left an extraordinarily illuminating memoir of their marriage) and began to rehabilitate himself, despite bouts of serious ill-health, through composing lengthy, well-written but boringly orthodox historical novels dealing with revolutionary developments in the Caucasus. Of considerable complexity, they culminated in 1957 with the publication of the trilogy *Utro sovetov* [The Morning of Soviet Power].

A close friend of many Soviet writers and poets of the early period, about whom he published a book of extremely interesting reminiscences, Libedinskii was particularly close to Fadeev and Zabolotskii towards the end of his life. He had a reputation for selflessly encouraging younger writers, though few of his contemporaries matched his own steadfast dedication to the craft of writing. His efforts may not have produced outstanding results so far as his own later work was concerned, but they served in a modest way to demonstrate a welcome integrity and independence under conditions of extreme Stalinist repression.

RICHARD FREEBORN

Life of Iuliania Lazarevskaia *see* Tale of Ul'ianiia Osor'ina

---

Eduard Veniaminovich Limonov 1943–

Prose writer, poet, and essayist

Biography

Born Eduard Veniaminovich Savenko in Dzerzhinsk, Gor'kii region, 1943. Attended secondary school in Kharkov. Had a variety of jobs including as a fitter, builder, steel foundryman, and bookseller. Moved to Moscow to pursue literary career, 1967. Married: the poet Elena Shchapova. Emigrated to America, 1974; divorced soon after arrival. Lived in New York; held a variety of menial jobs, while trying to find a publisher for his works. Moved to Paris, 1979, where the majority of his novels have been published. Renewed Russian citizenship, 1991. "Shadow" minister of security in Vladimir Zhirinovskii's right-wing Liberal Democratic Party, 1992. Split with

Zhirinovskii's party and formed his own National Radical Party, November 1992. Continues to participate in Russian politics.

Publications

Fiction

Eto ia, Edichka!. New York, Index, 1979; translated as *It's Me, Eddie!*, by S.L. Campbell, London, Picador, and New York, Random House, 1983.

Dnevnik neudachnika [Diary of a Failure]. New York, Index, 1982.

Podrostok Savenko. Paris, Sintaksis, 1983; translated as *Adolescent Savenko*, by Judson Rosengrant, New York, Grove Press, 1989.

Histoire de son serviteur. Paris, Ramsay, 1984; translated as *His Butler's Story*, [no translator named], New York, Grove Press, 1987; London, Abacus, 1989.

Molodoi negodiai [The Young Rascal]. Paris, Sintaksis, 1986.

Palach [The Torturer]. Jerusalem, Chameleon, 1986.

Des incidents ordinaires. Paris, Ramsay, 1988.

Cognac Napoleon. Paris, Ramsay, 1990; in Russian as *Kon'iak "Napoleon"*. Moscow, 1995.

Memoir of a Russian Punk, translated by Judson Rosengrant. New York, Grove Weidenfeld, 1990.

Chuzhoi v neznakomom gorode [Stranger in an Unfamiliar City]. Moscow, 1995.

Poetry

"My - natsionalnyi geroi" [We Are the National Hero], in *Apollon*, edited by M. Shemiakin, Paris, 1977, 57–62.

Russkoe [Russian]. Ann Arbor, Ardis, 1979.

Troe [Three]. Los Angeles, Almanac-Press, 1981.

Political Writing, Articles, and Essays

"K spaseniiu strany" [Towards the Salvation of the Country], *Sovetskaia Rossiia*, 12 March 1992.

"Manifest rossiiskogo natsionalizma" [A Manifesto of Russian Nationalism], *Sovetskaia Rossiia*, 16 June 1992.

"Ia - rossiskii natsionalist" [I Am a Russian Nationalist], *Sovetskaia Rossiia*, 12 June 1992.

Ischeznovenie varvarov [Disappearance of the Barbarians]. Moscow, 1993.

Limonov protiv Zhirinovskogo [Limonov Against Zhirinovskii]. Moscow, 1994.

Interviews

"Eto on - Edichka", interview by D. Iakushkin, *Moskovskie novosti*, 32 (1988).

"Dialog s 'normalnym pisatelem'", interview by Viktor Erofeev, *Ogonek*, 7 (1990).

"Tri chashki kofe s Limonovym", interviews by Gallina Leont'eva, *Smena*, 4–6 (March 1992).

Conversations in Exile: Russian Writers Abroad, edited by John Glad, Durham, North Carolina, Duke University Press, 1993 (interview with Limonov by John Glad).

Critical Studies

"Taboos, Splits and Signifiers: Limonov's *Eto ya - Edichka*", by Ann Shukman, *Essays in Poetics*, 8/2 (1983), 1–18.

"Limonov's Coming Out", by Patricia Carden, in *The Third Wave: Russian Literature in Emigration*, edited by Olga Matich and Michael Heim, Ann Arbor, Ardis, 1984, 221–29.

"Vasily Trediakovski and Eduard Limonov: Erotic Reverberations in the History of Russian Literature", by I.R. Titunik, in *Russian Literature and American Critics: In Honor of Deming B. Brown*, edited by Kenneth N. Brostrom, Ann Arbor, Papers in Slavic Philology, University of Michigan, 1984, 393–404.

"The Moral Immoralist: Eduard Limonov's *Eto ja - Edička*", by Olga Matich, *Slavic and East European Journal*, 30/4 (1986), 526–40.

"Limonov's *Eti ia - Edichka* as the Failure of an American Dream", by Karen L. Ryan-Hayes, *Canadian Slavonic Papers*, 30/4 (1988), 438–59.

"And the Rest is Silence", by Paul Bailey, *Sunday Times* (28 August 1989).

"The Beauty Mark and the 'I's' of the Beholder: Limonov's Narcissistic Poem 'Ja v mysljax poderzu drugogo celoveka ...", by Alexander Zholkovsky, in *Russian Literature and Psychoanalysis*, edited by Daniel Rancour-Laferrière, Amsterdam, Benjamins, 1989.

"In Search of the Right Milieu: Eduard Limonov's Kharkov Cycle", by Patricia Carden, in *Autobiographical Statements in Twentieth Century Russian Literature*, edited by Jane Gary Harris, Princeton, Princeton University Press, 1990, 227–37.

"Eduard Limonov and the Benefit of the Doubt", by Robert Porter, in *Under Eastern Eyes: The West as Reflected in Recent Russian Émigré Writing*, edited by Arnold McMillin, London, Macmillan, 1991, 62–75; New York, St Martin's Press, 1992.

"Butchness and Butchery", by Paul Bailey, *The Guardian* (21 December 1992).

Their Fathers' Voice: Vassily Aksyonov, Venedikt Erofeev, Eduard Limonov and Sasha Sokolov, by Cynthia Simmons, Bern and New York, Peter Lang, 1993, 57–90.

"Eddie's Right Wing Chapter Shocks Russian Readers", by Helen Womack, *Independent on Sunday* (24 January 1993).

Russia's Alternative Prose, by Robert Porter, Oxford, Berg, 1994, 163–88.

Text Counter Text: Rereadings in Russian Literary History, by Alexander Zholkovsky, Stanford, Stanford University Press, 1994.

Contemporary Russian Satire: A Genre Study, by Karen L. Ryan-Hayes, Cambridge and New York, Cambridge University Press, 1995.

"The Doppelgänger or the Quest for Love: Eduard Limonov as Vladimir Maiakovskii", by Andrei Rogachevskii, *Canadian-American Slavic Studies*, 30/1 (1996), 1–44.

Eduard Limonov, notorious member of the third wave of Russian literary emigration, grew up in the industrial suburbs of Kharkov and it was there, in his mid-teens, that he began to write poetry. In 1967, he moved to Moscow intent on pursuing a literary career. Receiving no official acceptance, Limonov became part of Moscow's literary underground. The years 1967–74 represented the height of Limonov's success in Russia. During this time, as part of the Concrete Poetry Group, he became well known in unofficial literary circles and he married the Moscow poet Elena Shchapova. Despite this relative success, there are clear indications that he was already planning to emigrate and, indeed, Limonov's most famous work of this period is the prose-poem *My - natsionalnyi geroi* [We Are the National Hero], in which he imagines the rapturous reception that he and Elena will receive on their arrival in the west. He arrived in the United States in 1974 and quickly realized life would not be all that western propaganda and Russian dissident hearsay had promised. Limonov claimed that all he wanted from the west was the freedom to write, but this freedom was denied him, because he was the first Russian writer to criticize America "from within". The validity of this claim is disputable, but for various reasons Limonov had great difficulty in finding a publisher for his works in America. One possible explanation may lie in the sexually explicit nature of his works, his frequent use of obscene language, as well as his politically extreme ideas and opinions.

Following his arrival in America, Limonov turned from poetry to prose as his principal means of expression. He has written several novels about his adolescence in Russia, including *Podrostok Savenko* (*Adolescent Savenko*) and *Molodoi negodiai* [The Young Rascal], but the bulk of his work is set in the west: initially New York and later Paris, where he moved to in 1979. *Eto ia, Edichka!* (*It's Me, Eddie!*), *Dnevnik neudachnika* [Diary of a Failure], *Palach* [The Torturer] and *His Butler's Story* are the earliest of these New York stories. With the exception of *Palach*, these novels are autobiographical. There is a discernible development in the protagonist, from Eddie, the angry hero of *It's Me, Eddie!* and *Dnevnik neudachnika* to Eduard in *His Butler's Story*, who has a comfortable job as butler to a New York millionaire and is about to have his first novel published. Although he is still critical of American society, particularly its glorification of businessmen and capitalists, Eduard is calmer, more self-assured and feels at home in his adopted society. Of the New York novels, *Palach* differs slightly with a fictional hero, Oskar Khudzinskii, who is a Polish immigrant, but in keeping with the sexually explicit nature of the autobiographical novels, the hero makes his living as a sado-masochist in the superficial world of New York high society.

Critical opinions of Limonov are varied, ranging from outrage through to sympathy and admiration. Whether one regards Limonov's work as erotic and of literary value, or pornographic and of no literary worth, one cannot deny that his writing is indeed sexually explicit. Russian critics have tended to point to the shocking nature of Limonov's prose, perhaps because Russian literature has traditionally avoided the sexually explicit. Western critics, however, emphasize Limonov's search for love and identity as central themes of his work. The controversial nature of his works is reinforced by his use of obscene language. Critics and readers alike have been shocked by Limonov's use of *mat*. Although he is not the first Russian writer to do so, he is perhaps the first to use this register so prolifically. Limonov's prose is littered with obscenities that are used both literally and as expletives. Equally appalling to many is Limonov's corruption of the Russian language, which has been greatly influenced by American English. English words and phrases, transliterated into Russian, are found frequently in his work. Occasionally, he even adds Russian grammatical suffixes to English words.

When examining Limonov's desire to shock, one should not ignore his political extremism. In his early New York novels, he identifies with left-wing revolutionaries, but more recently he has taken an interest in "real" politics. Following the collapse of the Soviet Union, he returned to Russia and became involved with Vladimir Zhirinovskii's deceptively named Liberal Democratic Party. In November 1992 Limonov left the Liberal Democratic Party following considerable differences with its leader. Opinions vary as to the precise nature of the split with Zhirinovskii, but it resulted in the formation of Limonov's own National Radical Party, which has a set of policies that are alarming to say the least. In March 1992, in an interview with Galina Leont'eva, he stated that only a nationalist revolution could save Russia. Contradiction would seem to characterize Limonov's thinking in the sphere of politics. At the Wheatland Conference on Literature in Budapest in 1989, Limonov announced to a large group of writers that Salman Rushdie should be publicly executed "... for insulting the Muslim people and their noble religion ..." Only three years later, Limonov publicly expressed his support for the Serbs, for whom he has fought in Bosnia and whose policy of ethnic cleansing he advocates for Russia.

The collapse of the Soviet Union and its ensuing ramifications for the literary world, namely the disappearance of censorship, have meant Limonov's work ceases to have its former impact. The publication of previously censored alternative prose writers and the now widespread availability of pornography in Russia has considerably reduced the shock value of his work. One could argue that Limonov's move into politics has been brought about by his continuing desire to "shock". Indeed, the National Radical Party and his recent trips to Bosnia have earned him the same notoriety that his novels once had. Returning to Limonov's literary works, a useful conclusion is provided by another émigré writer, Vasilii Aksenov, who, in an interview with John Glad published in 1993, said: "Edward Limonov is back again, shrill, outrageous, dirty, vexing and dissonant, but mix all those things together and you end up with a pretty good bouquet."

HELEN L. TILLY

It's Me, Eddie!

Eto ia, Edichka!

Novel, 1979

Eduard Limonov's first novel, *It's Me, Eddie!* received much attention when it was first published in 1979. The work is, broadly speaking, "autobiographical" and depicts the difficulties faced by Limonov during his first few months as an émigré in New York. Through a picaresque series of incidents and experiences, we see the harsh realities of life in emigration: Eddie is deserted by his wife Elena shortly after their arrival in America; he is unable to work as a writer and is forced to take on a variety of menial jobs. All the men and women who Limonov befriends are themselves on the fringes of society – victims, loners and outsiders.

Eddie's search for identity in a strange country is one of the central themes of the work. Natalia Gross has described Limonov's novel as "... a tragic account of the hero's identity crisis". Eddie's reputation in Moscow's literary underground cannot sustain him as a writer in the west. Consequently, as a recipient of welfare who lives in a cheap and seedy New York hotel, he associates with other immigrants and drop-outs from

American society. *It's Me, Eddie!* illustrates the effects on an individual when all sense of cultural belonging is lost. Separated from his native land and language, it is hardly surprising that Eddie should feel isolated. Limonov is openly critical of American society and its values and the bitterness with which he regards them is obvious. Indeed, the novel begins with Eddie sitting naked on his balcony, eating *shchi* (cabbage soup) and criticizing the society in which he now lives. However, his anger is not directed solely at America. He also blames Russia's dissident heros, such as Solzhenitsyn and Sakharov, for seducing people like himself with western propaganda.

On publication, the novel met with outrage from critics and readers alike, partly because of Limonov's attitude towards America (the novel was published in New York), but primarily because of its sexually explicit content and Limonov's use of "vulgar" and linguistically corrupted Russian. In trying to come to terms with his new life, without his wife or a career, we see Eddie embarking on numerous affairs, both hetero- and homosexual. Indeed, the proliferation of sexual encounters has concerned, and in some cases, disgusted critics. To a great extent this criticism results from a decontextualization of these elements in Limonov's writing. One of the most "notorious" episodes in the novel is the explicit description of Eddie's first homosexual experience. Eddie meets Chris, a young black tramp, and the two have sex on a piece of wasteground in New York. This episode may be regarded as sordid, but it is symptomatic of Eddie's intense loneliness. Desperate for affection, he seizes the opportunity for some human contact and comfort, and the setting and nature of this encounter only add to its poignancy. Eddie's promiscuity is linked both to his fight for survival in America, and to his search for love, which is a major motivation in his life. Despite all the difficulties that he faces, he never ceases to believe in, and to seek, love. The link between promiscuity and the search for love is a complicated matter in Limonov's writing. His promiscuity is both a manifestation of his unhappiness and of his attempts to find love. When he fails to find love, he seeks solace in further casual sex, and thus a vicious circle emerges.

Although *It's Me, Eddie!* has both modern setting and subject-matter, the work has significant precedents in Russian literature. Like Dostoevskii's Underground Man, Eddie blames society for his problems. He too indulges in the negative emotions of envy, resentment, and self-pity. Eddie, like the Underground Man, seems to revel in his squalor and sordidness. He has a variety of menial jobs, and in this respect he can be likened to Gor'kii's proletarian heroes of the early 20th century. Eddie's negative Dostoevskian traits are often over-emphasized, while the honesty and resilience that make him an immensely likeable character are sometimes ignored.

The title of the work is significant. Edichka is the diminutive form of Limonov's name and its use in the novel is entirely appropriate. In New York Eddie behaves like a child, constantly making discoveries, both about himself and society around him, and having new experiences. The reader also observes a certain child-like development in Eddie during the course of the novel. His initial suspicion and hatred slowly turn into fascination and love for his adopted home. By the end of the novel, he refers to the city as "my New York" and considers himself to be one of the natives.

Given Limonov's frank depiction of life in emigration, Patricia Carden's description of *It's Me, Eddie!* would seem highly appropriate: "... the quintessential novel of the Third Wave emigration ... the book that any writer aspiring to immortalize the experience of his generation, will have to beat if he wants to lay claim to being its chronicler ...".

HELEN L. TILLY

Semen Izrailevich Lipkin 1911–

Poet, novelist, and translator

Biography

Born in Odessa, 19 September 1911. Attended the Fifth Odessa Secondary School; tutored by Eduard Bagritskii. Moved to Moscow and met Osip Mandel'shtam, 1929. Under the patronage of Bagritskii and Georgii Shengeli, published in "thick" journals. Group of young poets, including Lipkin, fell foul of RAPP and unable to publish. Married: 1) Nina Sergeevna Kulikova in 1933, two sons and two daughters; 2) the poet Inna L'vovna Lisnianskaia in 1968. Graduated from Institute of Economic Engineering, Moscow, in 1937. Full-time translator for Goslitizdat. First volume of poetry published only in 1967. Involved in *Metropol'* affair, 1979; resigned from the Writers' Union in protest at the expulsion of Evgenii Popov and Viktor Erofeev; thereafter published works abroad. Member of the Writers' Union again in October 1986. Currently lives in Moscow.

Publications

Poetry

Ochevidets. Stikhotvoreniia raznykh let [Eye-Witness. Poems of Various Years]. Moscow, 1967.
Vechnyi den'. Stikhotvoreniia [The Eternal Day]. Moscow, 1975.
Volia [Freedom], compiled by Iosif Brodskii. Ann Arbor, Ardis, 1981.
Kochevoi ogon' [Nomadic Fire]. Ann Arbor, Ardis, 1984.
Das Volk der Adler, translated by Wolfgang Kasack. Hamburg, Gerold and Appel, 1984.

Kartina i golosa [Picture and Voices]. London, Overseas Publications Interchange, 1986.
Lira. Stikhotvoreniia raznykh let [The Lyre. Poems of Various Years]. Moscow, 1989.
Dekada. Povesti. Poema [The Festival of Culture]. Moscow, 1990.
Lunnyi svet. Stikhi [Moonlight]. 1990.
Pis'mena. Stikhotvoreniia. Poema [Characters]. Moscow, 1991.

Fiction
Dekada [The Festival of Culture]. New York, Chalidze, 1983.
"Zapiski zhil'tsa", *Novyi mir*, 9–10, 1992; excerpt translated as "A Resident Remembers", by Arch Tait, in *Booker Winners and Others, Glas New Russian Writing*, 7 (1994), 43–55.

Memoir
Stalingrad Vasiliia Grossmana [Vasilii Grossman's Stalingrad]. Ann Arbor, Ardis, 1986.

Translator
Dzhangar. (Kalmyk), Moscow, 1940.
Manas. (Kirgiz), Moscow, 1946.
Girdousi. Poemy iz Shakh-name. (Farsi), Stalinabad, 1959.
O bogatyriakh, umel'tsakh i volshebnikakh. Tri povesti [On Bogatyrs, Skilled Craftsmen and Wizards]. Moscow, 1963.
Geser. Buriatskii geroicheskii epos [Geser. A Buryat Heroic Epos]. Moscow, 1973.
Idigei. (Tartar), Kazan, 1990 (banned by the Politburo in 1940 as "bourgeois nationalist").

Critical Studies
Dictionary of Russian Literature since 1917, by Wolfgang Kasack, New York, Columbia University Press, 1988.
"Ochevidets", by Stanislav Rassadin, in *Dekada*, 1990, 274–85.
Conversations in Exile: Russian Writers Abroad, edited by John Glad, Durham, North Carolina, Duke University Press, 1993.

Semen Lipkin was born in Odessa in 1911. He was schooled at the Fifth Odessa Secondary School where he developed a love of literature, and began his first faltering attempts at writing his own poetry. He was encouraged and tutored by Eduard Bagritskii, who was a literary consultant on the local *Odesskie novosti*. After moving to Moscow in 1929, Lipkin began to be published in "thick" literary journals: *Novyi mir*, *Oktiabr'*, *Molodaia gvardiia*, and *Zemlia i fabrika*. A group of young poets, which included Lipkin, Arkadii Shteinberg, Mariia Petrovykh, and Arsenii Tarkovskii, fell foul of RAPP, and found themselves unable to publish because their poetry was "not in harmony with the times". Tarkovskii was to be 55 and Lipkin 56 before seeing publication of their first volumes of poetry. Shengeli assisted them in finding employment with Goslitizdat translating classical and modern poetry of the peoples of the USSR, and they soon ceased to regard this as mere pot-boiling, becoming immersed in the study of the history and culture of the peoples whose literature they were translating. Iosif Brodskii has said, "Aside from Pasternak and Akhmatova, there were some remarkable people, Semen Lipkin, for instance. But no one knew anything about them. Even Lipkin's closest relatives, if he had any, must have been totally in the dark. People wrote only for 'the desk drawer'. Tarkovskii was writing, but no one could read any of it. He didn't come out into the open until the late 1960s, and Lipkin is even more recent". (John Glad, 1993)

Lipkin recalls:

> When it was decided in the period of Stalinist genocide to liquidate the nations of the Kalmyks, Chechens, Ingushetians, Balkars, Karachais, and the Crimean Tartars
> I was driven to my wits' end by the unbearable pain of it all.
> I would weep in the nights remembering my exiled friends.
> It is a pain which torments me to this day.

A number of poems appeared in *Novyi mir* in 1956. Despite vicious criticism, *Novyi mir* continued to publish Lipkin's work. An absurd campaign was launched against him in 1968, alleging that a poem which mentioned the Chinese tribe of I was actually a coded anti-Soviet defence of Israel.

A first collection of Lipkin's poetry, *Ochevidets* [Eye-Witness], appeared only in 1967, and was again damned for its non-Soviet perspective. Lipkin contributed to the uncensored anthology *Metropol'* in 1979 and, when Evgenii Popov and Viktor Erofeev were selectively expelled from the Writers' Union for their involvement, he, Inna Lisnianskaia, and Vasilii Aksenov themselves unprecedentedly resigned from the Union. They were subjected to a manic campaign of small-minded harassment, which even extended beyond removing Lipkin's translations from libraries, to commissioning hurried, inferior replacements in a lunatic attempt to "write him out" of Russian literary history.

Lipkin remarks that, thanks to the Writers' Union's preventing him from continuing to work as a translator, he wrote more than ever before. Two collections of his poetry were published in the west by Ardis, *Volia* [Freedom] and *Kochevoi ogon'* [Nomadic Fire], along with his memoirs *Stalingrad Vasiliia Grossmana* [Vasilii Grossman's Stalingrad]. He was able to begin a new career as a novelist, and produced *Dekada* [The Festival of Culture], about the persecution of the Chechens under Stalin, in 1979–80. He was successfully saved from cancer and has lived to see his books at last published freely.

Lipkin was restored to membership of the Writers' Union in 1986. *Dekada* was first published by the journal *Druzhba narodov*. His novel *Zapiski zhil'tsa* (*A Resident Remembers*) was published in *Novyi mir* and was shortlisted for the Russian Booker Prize in 1993. He has been awarded the state prizes of Tadzhikistan, Kalmykia, and Tartaria, as well as the Andrei Sakharov Prize, and was declared a People's Poet of Kalmykia.

The subject-matter of *Dekada* is the deportation of the Chechens (called the Tavlars in the novel) in 1942 at the whim of Stalin, and the immoderate fêting of their neighbours the Gushans (the Ingushetians). This is autobiographically-based fiction. Lipkin is uniquely qualified to examine the psychology of translators, poets, party and government officials of the Caucasus, and the moral quandaries in which they found themselves. He paints a vivid picture of the corrupting of the morality of these mountain peoples by the Stalinist police state. Those who do not sell their conscience are liable to end up in a concentration camp. By the end of the novel Khrushchev has returned the Tavlars to their native land, and a second folk festival, this time of Gushan and Tavlar literature and art, is planned. It will be no less corrupt than the earlier one.

Lipkin's *A Resident Remembers*, written in 1962–76, largely during the Brezhnev period, but published only in 1992 in *Novyi mir*, is comparable to Pasternak's *Doctor Zhivago* in the totally new perspective it gives to the events with which it is concerned. It is a historical and philosophical novel set in Odessa from the late 19th century until just before the death of Stalin, which acknowledges the importance of national self-esteem (the ignoring of which made Soviet Marxism so soulless), while warning against the siren of nationalistic superiority complexes that lead only to endless conflict. Stalinist Russia's problem was that there was no such thing as society, only the State. The loss of religious faith leaves the silent majority an easy prey to totalitarian ideologies.

Lipkin maintains a strong narrative presence in his novels. Also strikingly worked into the narrative are the set-piece discussions of large historical questions, as well as portentous philosophical generalization.

ARCH TAIT

Benedikt Konstantinovich Livshits 1887–1938/39

Poet and translator

Biography

Born in Odessa, 6 January 1887. Attended Richelieu Grammar School, Odessa; enrolled at the University of Novorossiisk, 1905: expelled for taking part in student protest movement; studied law at St Vladimir University, Kiev, 1907–12. Moved to St Petersburg, 1913, and became leading bohemian light; closely involved in Futurist groupings, especially Hylaea. Fought in World War I; wounded, shell-shocked, and awarded the Cross of St George. Lived in Kiev, 1916–22; then returned to St Petersburg. Arrested and sentenced to ten years' imprisonment without the right of correspondence (a euphemism for the death sentence) on 16 October 1937. He was apparently executed, 21 October 1938 (though according to official papers, he died of a heart attack on 15 May 1939).

Publications

Collected Editions

Kartvel'skie ody: Stikhi. Perevody [Georgian Odes: Poems. Translations]. Tbilisi, 1964.

Polutoroglazyi strelets: Stikhotvoreniia, perevody, vospominaniia [The One-and-a-Half Eyed Archer. Poetry, Translations, Memoirs]. Leningrad, 1989.

Poetry

Fleita Marsiia [The Flute of Marsyas]. Kiev, 1911.

Vol'che solntse [Wolves' Sun]. 2nd edition, Moscow, 1914.

Iz topi blat [Out of the Swamp]. Kiev, 1922.

Stikhi o Petrograde [Poems on Petrograd]. Kiev, 1922.

Patmos. Moscow, 1926.

Krotonskii polden' [Crotonian Noon]. Moscow, 1928.

Poems in *Modern Russian Poetry, 1910–1960*, edited by Vladimir Markov and Merrill Sparks. London, MacGibbon and Kee, 1966, 348–55.

Memoirs

Polutoroglazyi strelets. Leningrad, 1933; New York, Izdatel'stvo imeni Chekhova, 1978; translated as *The One and a Half-Eyed Archer*, by John E. Bowlt, Newtonville, Massachusetts, Oriental Research Partners, 1977.

Translator

Ot romantikov do siurrealistov [From Romanticism to the Surrealism]. Leningrad, 1934.

Frantsuzskie liriki XIX i XX vekov [French Lyric Poetry of the 19th and 20th Centuries]. Leningrad, 1937.

Critical Studies

Russian Futurism: A History, by Vladimir Markov, Berkeley, University of California, 1968; London, MacGibbon and Kee, 1969.

Russian Futurism Through Its Manifestoes, 1912–1928, edited by Anna Lawton, Ithaca, Cornell University Press, 1988.

"The Citadel of the Revolutionary Word: Notes on the Poetics of Benedikt Livšic", by Ronald Vroon, *Russian Literature*, 27 (1990), 533–55.

"Benedikt Livshits' *Patmos*: The Cycle and Its Subtexts", by Ronald Vroon, in *The Silver Age in Russian Literature*, edited by John Elsworth, London, Macmillan, and New York, St Martin's Press, 1992, 104–35.

"Benedikt Konstantinovich Livshits, 1887–1938", by Adol'f Urban, in *Raspiatye: Pisateli-zhertvy politicheskikh repressii*, 2nd edition, St Petersburg, 1994, 173–79.

Izbrannye stat'i, by M.L. Gasparov, St Petersburg, 1995.

Benedikt Livshits's first poetic efforts, as well as his first translations from French poetry, go back to 1907–08. He began publishing in 1909 (in an "Anthology of Modern Poetry", Kiev, 1909). On Nikolai Gumilev's recommendation, his poems were published in the St Petersburg-based journal *Apollon* 11 (1910).

His first book of poetry, *Fleita Marsiia* [The Flute of Marsyas], appeared in 1911 in Kiev, and included, in addition to his early poetry, a number of his translations. The book was favourably reviewed by Valerii Briusov. This collection was already stamped with the features typical of Livshits's later poetry: a combination of the historical and the cultural, lyrical and philosophical elements, and a clash between classical harmony and the modernist bent for the destruction of form. The influence of Russian Symbolism can be traced here, just as clearly as the influence of the "accursed" poets, such as Baudelaire, Rimbaud, and Verlaine, whom Livshits had admired from childhood. His friendship with the founders of Russian Futurism – the Burliuk brothers, Vladimir Maiakovskii, Velemir Khlebnikov, and Aleksei Kruchenykh, was an important influence on his life and work and he became a prominent member of the Hylaea group of Cubo-Futurists. Inspired by the energy of poetic experimentation and artistic avant-gardism, and having participated in the writing of Futurist manifestos and publishing ventures, Livshits strove to find an original means of expression in the middle ground between the avant-garde and traditionalism. This approach was evident in his book *Volch'e solntse* [Wolves' Sun], first published in Kherson and then reprinted in Moscow in 1914, in which verbal imagery is arranged according to the laws of painting, forming a mosaic of meaningful elements united by cross-associations. Analogously with Cubism in painting, Livshits employs the principle of split reality. He did not, however, aim at further disintegration of traditional forms, because his work was rooted too deeply in world culture and he attached great importance to the philosophical and historical problems of being. He eventually broke with the aesthetic of early Futurism, and in particular with its aggressive energy of destruction and eccentricity.

His poetic cycle of 1914–16, dedicated to St Petersburg and entitled "Bolotnaia Meduza" [The Marsh Medusa], treats the theme of the eternal struggle of chaos and order, civilization and the elemental, east and west. This internal struggle is intensified by various external forces, pushing the great city, the historic centre of Russian life, to the sidelines. In "Bolotnaia Meduza", Livshits tries to find new means of poetic expression, so as to convey the greatness of St Petersburg and its tragic downfall. He here gives up formal experimentation and goes back to a rich, meaningful verse form and metaphysical lyricism. This trend is found too in his next book, *Patmos*, which focuses on a Hellenic culture where chaos gives birth to harmony and where modern principles of spiritual and artistic consciousness had been shaped. Drawing on this material, the poet found that nourishing ground which helped him reach the particular unity of form and content that he had been searching for all his life. The collection *Krotonskii polden'* [Crotonian Noon] therefore may be said to represent the culmination of his poetic evolution.

In the 1920s and 1930s, Livshits was mainly engaged in translating poetry, and he succeeded in reaching great heights in this art. The anthologies of French poetry containing his translations reveal his fine understanding and the poetic skill of a virtuoso. These include *Ot romantikov do siurrealistov* [From Romanticism to Surrealism], and *Frantsuzskie liriki XIX i XX vekov* [French Lyric Poetry of the 19th and 20th Centuries]. He had already translated many other French authors. In his later years, Livshits fell in love with Georgian poetry and made a number of translations from the Georgian.

In 1933 he published what is now seen by many as his most famous book, *Polutoroglazyi strelets* (*The One and a Half-Eyed Archer*). This is an important book of reminiscences, covering the years 1911–14 and featuring leading members of the poetic and artistic avant-garde, such as the Burliuks, Vladimir Maiakovskii, Velemir Khlebnikov, Igor' Severianin, Elena Guro, Natal'ia Goncharova, and others. Their psychological portraits come across as true to life, while Livshits's thoughts on the events and aesthetic principles underlying the artistic life of those days have a double value: as an eye-witness account of what were momentous times, and as an analysis of Leftist art in the context of Russia's historical development, her cultural crisis, and thought. Livshits also wrote a number of essays on early 20th-century poetry and art. His legacy is of great historical and cultural interest, and he himself is one of the brightest and most significant figures in Russian culture of the first half of the century. After many years of total neglect, scholarly interest in Livshits is now being firmly re-established.

MIKHAIL SHEINKER

Mirra Aleksandrovna Lokhvitskaia 1869–1905

Poet

Biography

Born Mariia Aleksandrovna Lokhvitskaia in St Petersburg, 1 December 1869 (or, as she claimed, 1871). Educated at home; graduated from Moscow Aleksandrovskii Institute, 1888. Published first poetry, 1888; poetry published in "thick" journals, 1889. Married: Evgenii Zhiber in 1892; five children. First collection published, 1895. Recipient: Pushkin Prize for poetry, 1896; second Pushkin Prize announced in 1904, conferred posthumously in 1905. Died of tuberculosis in St Petersburg, 9 September 1905.

Publications

Poetry

Stikhotvoreniia. Moscow, 1895.
Stikhotvoreniia. 1896–1898. Moscow, 1898.
Stikhotvoreniia, vols 1–3. Moscow and St Petersburg, 1900.

Stikhotvoreniia, vol. 4. St Petersburg, 1903.
Stikhotvoreniia, vol. 5. St Petersburg, 1905.
Pered zakatom [Before Sunset]. St Petersburg, 1908.
Poems in *Poetry 1880–1890 -kh godov*. "Biblioteka poeta", 2nd edition, Leningrad, 1972, 601–34.

Critical Studies

"O sovremennom lirizme 3: 'One'", by Innokentii Annenskii, *Apollon*, 3 (1909), 5–29.
"Zhenshchiny-poety (Mirra Lokhvitskaia)", by Valerii Briusov, in *Dalekie i blizkie*, Moscow, 1912.
Kriticheskie otzyvy, by K.R. [Konstantin Romanov], Petrograd, 1915, 1–45 and 203–06.
"The Russian Sappho: Mirra Lokhvitskaia", by Samuel D. Cioran, *Russian Literature Triquarterly*, 9 (1974), 317–35.
"Mirra Lokhvitskaia", by Temira Pachmuss, in *Women Writers in Russian Modernism: An Anthology*, Urbana, University of Illinois Press, 1978, 85–92; translated poems 93–113.
"Mirra Lokhvitskaia's 'Duality' as a 'Romantic Conflict' and Its Reflection in Her Poetry", by R.C. Greedan, PhD dissertation, University of Pittsburgh, 1982.
"Russian Crepuscolari: Minskij, Merezhkovskij, Loxvickaja", by Vladimir Markov, in *Russian Literature and History: In Honor of Professor Ilya Serman*, edited by Wolf Moskovich *et al.*, Jerusalem, Soviet Jewry Foundation, 1989, 78–81.
"Mirra Aleksandrovna Lokhvitskaia", by Christine Tomei, in *An Encyclopedia of Continental Women Writers*, edited by Katharina M. Wilson, New York, Garland, and London, St James Press, 1991, vol. 2, 737–38.
Igor' Severianin: His Life and Work – The Formal Aspects of His Poetry, by Lenie Lauwers, Leuwen, Uitgevern Peeters en Departement Orientalistiek, 1993, 27–34.
"Mirra Lokhvitskaia", by N.V. Banikov, *Russkaia rech'*, 5 (September–October 1993), 20–24.
"Lokhvitskaia, Mirra Aleksandrovna", by Christi A. Groberg, in *Dictionary of Russian Women Writers*, edited by Marina Ledkovsky, Charlotte Rosenthal, and Mary Zirin, Westport, Connecticut, Greenwood Press, 1994, 381–84.

Mirra Lokhvitskaia was born in St Petersburg. Her father was a prominent lawyer and scholar; her three sisters were also writers, one of whom was the popular humorist Teffi. By the age of 15 Lokhvitskaia had decided to become a poet and began to visit older writers in St Petersburg to show them her work.

Lokhvitskaia published her first brochure of poems in 1888 and began publishing in journals in 1889. At first the prestigious "thick" journals were reluctant to publish her strikingly frank and passionate poetry, but before long her writing found many admirers. Her first book of poetry, *Stikhotvoreniia*, came out in 1895, and in 1896 it was awarded the Pushkin Prize for poetry. Over the next decade she was one of the most famous young Russian poets, known and advertised primarily as a "songstress of passion" (*pevitsa sladostrastiia*) because of her dominant themes of desire and physical love. She reputedly had an affair with Konstantin Bal'mont, the most flamboyant of the (then) young and scandalous Symbolist poets, in 1896–98. Bal'mont's profuse dedication to his 1903 volume *Budem kak solntse* [Let Us Be Like the Sun] describes her, among other writers, in provocative terms: "to the woman-artist of Bacchic visions, the Russian Sappho, M.A. Lokhvitskaia, who knows the secrets of sorcery". The label "Russian Sappho" has been applied to many female poets over the years, suggesting that only one woman at a time can incarnate the ideal of female genius – and be imagined in the Russian literary pantheon. (Clearly, Russians of Lokhvitskaia's time read Sappho as a passionate lover of men.) However, the timeless quality of an archetype does resonate with Lokhvitskaia's poetic exploitation of the "eastern". Her dark-haired elegance and expansive character fit that image as well as her passionate verses and made her very popular at poetry readings. A second book of poetry appeared in 1898 with the same title as all the volumes she published in her lifetime: *Stikhotvoreniia*. In 1900 her first two volumes came out in second editions, along with a new third volume.

With her unusually frank expressions of female desire and increasingly gloomy poetry, Lokhvitskaia was considered an ally of the so-called Decadent group. Her use of such oppositions as life and death, heaven and earth, and her ambivalence towards these oppositions relate her to other Symbolist writers. Her despotic or insubstantial lovers, too, parallel the Eternal Feminine with a kind of "Ideal Masculine". However, among the first generation of Symbolists only Bal'mont would recognize Lokhvitskaia as a poetic relative. The utilitarian critics of the time, as one would expect, condemned her "decadence", limited range of topics, and lack of "social content", calling her writingpornographic and egoistic. In her second volume, Lokhvitskaia replied with an assertive poetic statement of her preference for "burning and feminine" verse – pointing to passion and gender as the two defining elements of her writing, even as they troubled her critics and poetic contemporaries. Many readers saw the growing darkness of her later poetry, which may well have shown her awareness of declining health, as fashionable decadent pessimism. By ignoring abstract, intellectual or spiritual content when it appeared in her work, and by neglecting or oversimplifying her marked change of mood over time, critics seemed anxious to judge and dismiss her on the basis of her earliest writing.

Lokhvitskaia's poetic artistry is largely in sound, making a musical and sensual rather than an intellectual appeal to the reader or listener, especially in her early work. Taking inspiration from "eastern" and biblical texts such as the Song of Songs, she was the first Russian woman to claim Lilith as an active and superior female presence. Her use of the heterosexual romance, stressing a male beloved, borrowed an orientalist exoticism to cover the expression of female desire and certainly contributed to her success with readers. Her long verse dramas treat medieval, inquisitorial, and heretical or semi-pagan topics. The five-act drama that makes up half of her fifth volume of poetry depicts a witchcraft trial. Besides these links with Decadent poets of her own day, Lokhvitskaia powerfully influenced the early work of the next generation of women poets, from the briefly scandalous Cherubina de Gabriak to the now canonical Akhmatova and Tsvetaeva. Following her own contemporaries, many of Lokhvitskaia's "students" neglected to mention her when recalling their literary beginnings.

Lokhvitskaia died of tuberculosis on 9 September 1905, after her second (shared) Pushkin Prize for poetry was announced, but before she received it. Her family published a final posthumous volume of her work in 1908. Her fame lasted through the pre-revolutionary period: vocal "romansy" were written to her lyrics, some of her verse plays were successfully produced, and one branch of Futurists claimed her as an inspiration and ancestor. She was even well-represented in early Soviet anthologies of poetry. After the 1920s, damned by earlier Marxist critiques of her work, she vanished from scholarship into footnotes and neglect. Interest in other poets has drawn scholars and readers back to Lokhvitskaia, who was the standard of comparison for all the women who wrote and published poetry during the Silver Age.

SIBELAN FORRESTER

Mikhail Vasil'evich Lomonosov 1711–1765

Poet and scientist

Biography

Born in Kholmogory near the White Sea, 19 November 1711. Moved to Moscow, enrolled in Slavo-Greco-Latin Academy, 1731; attended the Imperial Academy of Sciences, St Petersburg, 1735; studied in Marburg, Germany, 1736; travelled to Freiburg to train in mining, 1739. Married: Elizabeth Christina Zilch in 1739; one daughter. Returned to Marburg, 1740–41. Moved back to St Petersburg, submitted dissertations to Academic Assembly on phsyico-chemical topics, 1741; appointed adjunct to the Academy, 1742. Under arrest, May 1743–January 1744. Professor of chemistry, 1745; established first chemistry laboratory at the Academy, 1748. Under the patronage of Count I.I. Shuvalov from 1750. Involved in building a factory to manufacture coloured glass, 1752. Founded Moscow University, 1755; member of Chancellery of the Academy, 1757. Moscow University began publishing the first volume of Lomonosov's Collected Works. In charge of the university and lyceum of the St Petersburg Academy, elected honorary member of Swedish Academy of Sciences; elected member of Academy of Arts in St Petersburg, promoted to State Councillor, 1763; member of the Bologna Academy of Sciences, 1764. Attended session of Academy's Assembly for the last time, 28 January 1765. Died in St Petersburg, 15 April 1765.

Publications

Collected Editions

Sochineniia M.V. Lomonosova, 4 vols. 1891–98.
Stikhotvoreniia. Moscow, 1935.
Izbrannye filosofskie proizvedeniia [Selected Philosophical Works]. Moscow, 1950.
Polnoe sobranie sochinenii, 11 vols. Leningrad, 1950–83.
Sochineniia. Moscow and Leningrad, 1961.
Izbrannye proizvedeniia. "Biblioteka poeta", Moscow and Leningrad, 1965.

Literary Theory

Ritorika [Rhetoric]. 1748.

Plays

Tamira i Selim [Tamira and Selim]. 1750.
Demofont. 1752.

Critical Studies

Znachenie M.V. Lomonosova v istorii razvitiia russkogo literaturnogo iazyka, by F. Buslaev, Moscow, 1861.
Materialy dlia biografii Lomonosova, by P. Biliarskii, St Petersburg, 1865.
K voprosu o russkom klassitsizme, by G. Gukovskii, Leningrad, 1928.
Michel Lomonosov et la langue littéraire russe, by Antoine Martel, Paris, Champion, 1933.
Lomonosov i literaturnaia polemika ego vremeni, 1750–1765, by P.N. Berkov, Leningrad, 1936.
The Life and Work of Mikhail Vasilyevich Lomonosov, by B.B. Kudriavtsev, Moscow, 1954.
Tvorcheskii put' Lomonosova, by B.G. Kuznetsov, Moscow, 1956.
"Michael Lomonosov and Benjamin Franklin: Two Self-Made Men of the Eighteenth Century", by W.C. Huntington, *Russian Review*, 18 (1959), 295–306.
M.V. Lomonosov i russkii iazyk, by A.I. Efimov, Moscow, 1961.
Otets russkoi poezii: O tvorchestsve Lomonosova, by A. Zapadov, Moscow, 1961.
M.V. Lomonosov i uchebnaia deiatel'nost' Petersburgskoi Akademii nauk, by E. Kuliabko, Leningrad, 1962.
"Poeziia Lomonosova v 1740-gody", by L.V. Pumpianskii, *XVIII vek*, 5 (1962), 33–70.
Poeticheskii stil' Lomonosova, by I.Z. Serman, Leningrad, 1966.
Russian Versification: The Theories of Trediakovskij, Lomonosov, and Kantemir, by Rimvydas Silbajoris, New York, Columbia University Press, 1968.
Stilisticheskoe uchenie M.V. Lomonosova i teoriia trekh stilei, by V.P. Vomperskii, Moscow, 1970.
Sud'ba biblioteki i arkhiva M.V. Lomonosova, by E. Kuliabko, Leningrad, 1975.
Peterburgskaia akademiia nauk i M.V. Lomonosov, by M.D. Kurmacheva, Moscow, 1975.
A History of 18th Century Russian Literature, by William Edward Brown, Ann Arbor, Ardis, 1980, 74–110.
"K istorii russkogo klassitsizma (Poetika Lomonosova)", by L.V. Pumpianskii, *Kontekst*, 2 (1982), 303–34.

"Iazyk M.V. Lomonosova i russkii literaturnyi iazyk", by G.N. Akimova, in *Lomonosov: Sbornik statei i materialov*, 8, Leningrad, 1983, 27–41.

Mikhail Lomonosov: Life and Poetry, by Il'ia Z. Serman, translated by Stephany Hoffman, Jerusalem, Centre of Slavic and Russian Studies, Hebrew University of Jerusalem, 1988.

Knigoizdatel'skaia deiatel'nost' Peterburgskoi Akademii Nauk i M.V. Lomonosov, by D.V. Tiulichev, Leningrad, 1988.

"More about the Early Iambic Tetrameter in M.V. Lomonosov's Poetry", by M.A. Krasnoperova, *Elementa*, 2/3–4 (1996), 233–56.

Mikhail Lomonsov's important contributions to Russian literature lie in his writings on language and literary style and in his poetry. Following the example of French Neoclassicism, he stabilized Russian literary decorum by establishing a correspondence between diction and a hierarchy of genres. In the second third of the 18th century the Russian literary language was in a state of flux as a Slavonic-based vocabulary came to be enriched by new coinages and calques from foreign words, and as secular literature grew and admitted new genres to Russian literature. In his imitations of Horace's *Satires* Antiokh Kantemir had attempted to employ a flexible style free from the bookish church language but was only partly successful. Vasilii Trediakovskii investigated the question of literary register and diction with relation to the prominence of the Slavonic element in the literary language. But it was left to Lomonosov to make the most definitive, coherent and in the end influential prescriptions on the literary idiom.

He established his rules in the *Ritorika* [Rhetoric] of 1748; the work went through numerous reprintings, becoming a standard textbook at Moscow University. The chief contribution is his adaptation of the doctrine of the three styles of diction. The high, middle, and low styles are each classified according to their use of the archaic Church Slavonic idiom. Where there were two words, Slavonic and vernacular, to denote the same thing, the Slavonic was to be preferred in the high style, while none but strictly colloquial expressions were to be used in the low style. Diction and literary genres are matched: high-style genres like the ode and the epic for grandeur and majesty require a more elevated lexicon and syntax; middle genres like the epistle require the polite diction of the middle style where there is neither pretence to sublimity nor easy informality; and finally works in the low style, like comedy and satire, may approximate speech by employing colloquial language.

Lomonosov also made a seminal contribution to the reform of Russian versification. In 1735 Trediakovskii published his *Novyi i kratkii sposob k slozheniiu rossiiskikh stikhov* (*A New and Brief Method for Composing Russian Verse*) in which he banned the iamb and advocated the troche as the basic foot of Russian verse. Like Trediakovskii, Lomonosov espoused the syllabo-tonic system as the rhythmic base of the verse line. However, in "Pis'mo o pravilakh rossiiskogo stikhotvorstva" [A Letter on Russian Versification] (1739) he refuted a number of features in Trediakovskii's strictures on prosody and syntax, and most importantly made the iamb rather than the troche the metrical norm. This work on versification ended with his poem, "Oda ... na vziatie Khotina" [Ode on the Capture of Khotin], a work he wrote while a student in Germany. The poem demonstrated the viability of iambic metre and was a literary sensation.

Lomonosov went on to write a series of 17 odes in praise of whichever Russian monarch happened to be on the throne and employing him, from Elizabeth I to Catherine II. In his hands the Solemn Ode, as it was called, became the definitive high genre of 18th-century Russian poetry, a showcase for linguistic experimentation as well as panegyric of the monarch. His odes take up topics of internal and foreign affairs, celebrate victory in warfare as in the "Khotin" ode, and champion peace as in his early poem in celebration of the Empress Elizabeth. Subjects are usually drawn from this well-defined inventory; it is not through variety of topic that the ode seeks to impress, although it would be wrong to underestimate the message that the poet felt himself chosen to convey. Lomonosov believed that reason should be united with passion, and that the task of eloquence and rhetoric was to arouse or pacify such passion.

In Lomonosov's odes the richness of each individual stanza detracts from the coherent progression of the whole; for him it is the principle of maximal activity and effect at every possible moment partly because in Lomonosov's conception the ode is a spoken, declaimed genre: the stronger the rhetorical basis of the verse, the more weight given to declamation and performance, the greater the significance of the individual moment or an individual thought or image. In structural terms then the ode became an open genre, liable to seemingly endless accretion of strophes and limited only by the stamina of the individual speaker. In the case of Lomonsov the average ode contains 23 or 24 stanzas of ten lines. In the odes the poetic persona can be repetitive and often seems to be in a state of ecstasy; his image has sweep, noise, and fire and all the hallmarks of the baroque style with violent contrasts in images and tone. Lomonosov loved to enhance emotional effect by amassing synonyms. The extent to which one or the other principle predominated in a writer's conception of the ode helped to define at least two separate schools of ode-writers – those who give priority to the logical unit and successive develpment of an argument from stanza to stanza, known as the "dry ode"; and others for whom the artistic dominant was the individual emotional impression conveyed from moment to moment and a cumulative effect made by association in what came to be called the "illogical ode". His rival Aleksandr Sumarokov emphatically favoured a clear style, and mocked Lomonosov's style in two of his own parodic poems.

Apart from the Solemn Ode Lomonsov wrote distinguished verse on scientific and theological topics. His "Vechernee razmyshlenie o bozh'em velichestve" [Evening Meditation Upon the Greatness of God] (1743) conveys a sense of wonder on the occasion of the northern lights, and expresses the scientist's amazement at the mystery of nature. He composed paraphrases of the Psalms, engaging in a famous competition with Sumarokov and Trediakovskii in a translation of "Psalm 143". Verse could also be put to the service of science, as in "Pis'mo o pol'ze stekla" ("Epistle on the Usefulness of Glass") 1752, written in the style of Lucretius, in which Lomonosov celebrates progress while denouncing the obscurantism of the Church who denied Copernicus' discoveries. Among his other writings there is an unfinished long poem, "Petr Velikii" [Peter the Great], written in six-foot iambics and paying thunderous tribute to Peter's combination of vision and practical skill; two plays in the Neoclassical mode, *Tamira i Selim* [Tamira and Selim], about a love conflict set in the context of the battle of Kulikovo in 1380, and *Demofont*. The scope of his literary *oeuvre*, all the more impressive given his activities as a scientist, and its spirit of linguistic and poetic reform, had an enormous influence on Russian literature of the 18th century and beyond.

ANDREW KAHN

Lev Vladimirovich Loseff 1937–

Poet and critic

Biography

Born Aleksei Vladimirovich Lifschuts [Lifshits] in Leningrad, 15 June 1937. Briefly wrote under pen name Aleksei Losev; officially changed his name to Lev Loseff. Attended Leningrad University, graduated 1959; University of Michigan, Ann Arbor, PhD, 1981. Freelance writer from 1959. Reporter for Sakhalin newspaper, 1959–60. Married: Nina Mokhova in 1962; one daughter and one son. Editor of journal, *Koster*, Leningrad, 1962–75. Emigrated to the United States in 1976. Editor, Ardis Publishing House, 1976–78; various teaching positions in American universities; Professor of Russian, Dartmouth College, from 1992. Member of American Association for the Advancement of Slavic Studies; American Association of Teachers of Slavic and East-European Languages, 1977. Recipient: University of Michigan Rackham Fellowship, 1977; Andrew B. Mellon Assistant Professorship, 1981–82; Die Deutsche Forschungsgemeinschaft Award, 1984; Dartmouth Senior Faculty Grant, 1988; *Ogonek* magazine Poetry Prize, 1993.

Publications

Poetry for Children

Zoosad [Zoo]. Leningrad, 1963.
Smelyi professor Bulavochkin [The Brave Professor Bulavochkin]. Leningrad, 1969.

Poetry

Chudesnyi desant [A Miraculous Raid]. Tenafly, New Jersey, Hermitage, 1985.
Tainyi sovetnik [A Privy Councillor]. Tenafly, New Jersey, Hermitage, 1988.
Poems in *Twentieth-Century Russian Poetry*, edited by John Glad and Daniel Weissbort. Iowa City, Iowa University Press, 1992.
Poems in *Contemporary Russian Poetry: A Bilingual Anthology*, edited by Gerald S. Smith. Bloomington, Indiana University Press, 1993, 156–75.
Novye svedeniia o Karle i Klare [New Information on Karl and Klara]. St Petersburg, 1996.

Plays

Neizvestnye podvigi Gerakla [The Unknown Deeds of Heracles]. Moscow, 1972; as *Malyi Herakles*, Prague, Ustav pro kulturné činnost, 1973.
Ved'ma na kanikulakh [A Witch on Vacation]. Moscow, 1973.
Goluboi i v polosku [He Who is Blue and Striped]. Moscow, 1974.
Vernis', Pantagriuel! [Come Back, Pantagruel!]. Moscow, 1974.
Slon priletel [The Elephant Has Landed], with Nina Mokhova. Moscow, 1975.
Medvozaitsy [Bearrabbits], with Leonid Vinogradov and Mikhail Eremin. Moscow, 1981.
Igraem v printsa i nishchego! [Let's Play Prince and Pauper!], with Iurii Mikhailov. Moscow, 1982.

Essays

Zhratva [Eats]. Ann Arbor, Hermitage, 1984.

Literary Criticism

On the Beneficence of Censorship: Aesopian Language in Modern Russian Literature. Munich, Sagner, 1984.
"Home and Abroad in the Works of Brodskii", in *Under Eastern Eyes: The West as Reflected in Recent Russian Émigré Writing*, edited by Arnold McMillin, London, Macmillan, 1991, 25–41; New York, St Martin's Press, 1992.
"A New Conception of Poetry", in *Brodsky Through the Eyes of His Contemporaries*, by Valentina Polukhina, London, Macmillan, and New York, St Martin's Press, 1992, 113–39.

Editor

Poetika Brodskogo. Sbornik statei [Brodskii's Poetics]. Tenafly, New Jersey, Hermitage, 1986.
Brodsky's Poetics and Aesthetics, with Valentina Polukhina. London, Macmillan, and New York, St Martin's Press, 1990.
Norwich Symposia on Russian Literature and Culture. Vol. I. Boris Pasternak (1890–1990). Northfield, Vermont, Russian School of Norwich University, 1991.
A Sense of Place: Tsarskoe Selo and Its Poets: Papers from the 1989 Dartmouth Conference Dedicated to the Centennial of Anna Akhmatova, with Barry Scherr. Columbus, Ohio, Slavica, 1993.

Translator

"Before the Dawn", by Aleksandr Borshchagolovsky, with Dennis Whelan, performed in American Stage Theatre, New York, 1985.

Critical Studies

"On Loseff's Poetry", by Joseph Brodsky, *Ekho*, 4 (1979), 66–67.
"Loseff's Theorem", by Boris Paramonov, *Panorama*, 232 (1987), 23.
"Flight of the Angels: The Poetry of Lev Loseff", by Gerald S. Smith, *Slavic Review*, 47/1 (1988), 76–88.
"Lev Loseff: 'Text is Life ...'", by Vladimir Ufliand, *Zvezda*, 1 (1990), 181–83.

For 20 years Aleksei Lifschuts wrote poetry and plays for children (the latter were staged by many puppet theatres throughout the Soviet Union) and nobody could have predicted that he would become the highly original poet Lev Loseff. Brought up in a family of writers and surrounded all his life by such brilliant poets as Sergei Kulle, Gleb Gorbovskii, Evgenii Rein, Mikhail Eremin, Leonid Vinogradov, Vladimir Ufliand, and Iosif Brodskii (all of them were and some still are his close friends), Loseff had no desire to become a poet. As Loseff admitted, Brodskii played a decisive role in his starting to write poetry at the age of 37. While Brodskii was in Russia, Loseff felt that he "didn't need any other poetry apart from Joseph's ... Everything I wanted to see expressed, he was expressing, and all so much more quickly, powerfully, strikingly, interestingly than I was capable of". But soon after Brodskii's departure in 1972, Loseff, to his own astonishment, realized that he had composed a poem, then 20 more poems followed, none of them like Brodskii's. Since his emigration to the United States in 1976, he has been widely published in the émigré press: *Ekho*, *Kontinent*, *Chast' rechi*, *Russica 81*, *Tret'ia volna*, *Strelets*.

It is not easy to establish his poetic genealogy. In his youth he was interested in the *oberiuty* (his parents personally knew Kharms, Zabolotskii, Vvedenskii, and Oleinikov) and he was responsible for introducing the poets of his generation to the poetics of the *oberiuty*, but later he lost interest in poetry of the absurd. He greatly admired Pasternak and met the poet in January 1956. The influence of Khlebnikov, who is, for Loseff, the master-poet, reveals itself through numerous palindromes, neologisms, and rich phonetic texture. Brodskii links Loseff's poetry to that of Prince Viazemskii's: "the same moderation, the same restrained tone, the same integrity". Others see links with Fet, Khodasevich, Georgii Ivanov, and Slutskii. This "unexpected sideshoot" of Russian poetry, "its razor-sharp branch" (Kushner), is philosophical, ironical, anti-lyrical, and anti-heroic: Loseff's poetry possesses neither lyrical hero nor lyrical addressee. He detests exhibitionism of any kind and either hides himself in the depth of his own texts or paints a self-deprecating portrait ("Levlosev"). Even the landscape in his poetry is deliberately null and dull. He cultivates a poetics of belittlement – belittlement of theme, imagery and vocabulary. His train of thought is not apparent, it is hidden under various masks (he often speaks with different voices). His associations are very diverse. His acrobatic rhymes and sophisticated rhythm discipline the extreme prosaicism of his poetry, which is dominated by speculative wit and paradox. He was writing "Conceptual" poetry well before the appearance of such Russian "Conceptualist" poets as Dmitrii Prigov and Lev Rubenshtein: the latter were dancing on the ruins of the Empire; Loseff was one of the very few who actually predicted its collapse as early as the beginning of the 1980s. Some of his poems are deliberately written in the style of "bad taste", precisely because bad taste and banality are his greatest enemy.

Apart from typically Russian public concern, many other no less interesting themes recur in Loseff's poetry, including art, literature, language, and faith. This "semiotic wizard" writes about the nature of sign and tends to assimilate linguistic concepts and grammatical categories into the poetic weave of his verse ("13"). He seems to think that the waste of literary analyses, as well as literature itself, are as good a material for poetry as any other. He is the master of the "cross-over" genre: high literature and satire ("I, who have travelled half my earthly road / was delivered into a long corridor"), the sacred and the profane ("And the earth / was without form and void. / In the aforementioned landscape / I recognized my homeland"), the profound and the banal are mixed in such a witty way that he creates a carnival of Russian literature, or rather a parody on it ("soiuz ts/ch/z-eka, byka i muzhika"). Russia, where "they've forgotten God" and where "the Devil is in every corner", is the theme that runs throughout his poems. Breathtaking simplicity is combined with an enormous toughness and depth of compassion. He has succeeded in synthesizing playful aesthetics with a rational approach to the topic, puritanism with subtle eroticism, realism with absurdity. But his heterogeneous poetics creates a unique harmony suggestive of chaos behind the text. "He has done for Russian poetry what Chekhov did for Russian prose, turned it from a collection of ingenious absurdities into a well-organized text" (B. Paramonov). The intertextual field of his poetry is so comprehensive and so compact that in the space of 100 pages one finds the whole of Russian literature from *Slovo o polku Igorove* (*The Lay of Igor's Campaign*) to the most recent work of the Russian Nobel Laureate. Being phenomenally well-educated, Loseff tends to view the world through the prism of culture: "that is a prism I've opted for in full consciousness of the choice". Culture, for Loseff, is not just a historical concept; it is an event and the centre of human activity. "Born in the Library", as one critic put it, "Loseff is an ideal reader and an ideal interpreter of literature" (Ivan Tolstoi). He was one of the first scholars to have subjected Brodskii's poetry to a serious, academic study (he has also edited two of the best Brodskii collections, *Chast' rechi* (*A Part of Speech*) and *Konets prekrasnoi epokhi* [The End of the Belle Epoque]) and still remains the best authority on the poet. He is the author of many oustanding articles on other Russian poets and writers. In his essays, as in his poetry, what interests him most is finding explanations for life's various manifestations.

VALENTINA POLUKHINA

Lev Natanovich Lunts 1901–1924

Prose writer and dramatist

Biography

Born in St Petersburg, 2 May 1901. Attended the First gymnasium, Petrograd, until 1918; studied history and philology, Petrograd University, 1918–22. Began literary career, 1919. Assistant lecturer in West European Literatures. Lived in the House of Arts under harsh conditions. Founder member of Serapion Brothers, Petrograd, 1921. Travelled to Hamburg, where parents lived, 1923. Treated for cardiac and nervous disorders; confined to bed for a year. Died of meningitis in Hamburg-Eppendorf, 9 May 1924.

Publications

Collected Editions

Rodina i drugie proizvedeniia [Native Land and Other Works]. [s.n.] Jerusalem, Pamiat', c.1981.

Zaveshchanie tsaria [The Tsar's Will], edited by W. Schrieck. Munich, Sagner, 1983.

Fiction

"V pustyne", *Serapionovy brat'ia*, 1 (1922); translated as "In the Wilderness", by Grigorii Gerenstein, in *The Terrible News*, London, Black Spring Press, 1991.

Iskhodiashchaia No. 37 [Circular No. 37], *Rossiia* (1922); translated as "The Outgoing Letter N.37", by Grigorii Gerenstein, in *The Terrible News*, 1991.

V vagone [In the Carriage]. 1922.

"Rodina", *Evreiskii al'manakh*, Petrograd and Moscow, 1923; translated as "Native Land", by Gary Kern, in *The Serapion Brothers: A Critical Anthology*, edited by Kern and Christopher Collins, Ann Arbor, Ardis, 1975.

Plays and Scenarios

"Vne zakona" [Outside the Law], *Beseda*, 1 (1921); reprinted Würzburg, Jal, 1972.

"Obez'iany idut!" [Here Come the Monkeys!], *Veselyi al'manakh* (1921).

V pristupe [In a Fit]. 1922; reprinted Munich, Sagner, 1973.

"Bertran de Born. P'esa", Gorod, 1 (1923).

Patriot. P'esa [The Patriot]. 1923.

Vosstanie veshchei. Kinostsenarii [Uprising of Things]. 1923; reprinted *Novyi zhurnal*, 79 (1965).

"Gorod pravdy", *Beseda*, 5 (1924); translated as *The City of Truth*, by John Silver, London, Fitzpatrick O'Dempsey, 1929.

Literary Criticism and Theory

"Pochemu my Serapionovy Brat'ia", *Literaturnye zapiski*, 3 (1922); translated as "Why We Are Serapion Brothers", by Gary Kern, in *The Serapion Brothers: A Critical Anthology*, edited by Kern and Christopher Collins, Ann Arbor, Ardis, 1975.

"Na zapad!", *Beseda*, 2 (1923); translated as "Go West!", by Gary Kern, in *The Serapion Brothers: A Critical Anthology*, edited by Kern and Christopher Collins, Ann Arbor, Ardis, 1975.

"Ob ideologii i publitsistika", *Novosti* (1923); in *Sovremennaia russkaia kritika 1918–1924*, Leningrad, 1925; translated as "Ideology and Publicistic Literature", by Gary Kern, in *The Serapion Brothers: A Critical Anthology*, edited by Kern and Christopher Collins, Ann Arbor, Ardis, 1975.

Letters

"Lev Lunts i Serapionovy Brat'ia" [Lev Lunts and the Serapion Brothers], *Novyi zhurnal*, 83 (1966), 132–84.

Critical Studies

The Serapion Brothers: Theory and Practice, by Hongor Oulanoff, The Hague, Mouton, 1966.

"Lev Lunc: Serapion Brother", by Gary Kern, PhD dissertation, Princeton University, 1969.

"The Serapion Brothers: A Dialectics of Fellow-Travelling", by Gary Kern, *Russian Literature Triquarterly*, 2 (1972), 223–47.

The Serapion Brothers: A Critical Anthology, edited by Gary Kern and Christopher Collins, Ann Arbor, Ardis, 1975 [with an introduction by Gary Kern, ix–xxxviii].

"The Dramatic Works of Lev Lunts", by Robert Russell, *Slavonic and East European Review*, 66/2 (1988), 210–23.

Lev Lunts is still today an under-rated Russian writer of Jewish origin (his father, Natan Iakovlevich was a pharmacist). A career as a university lecturer awaited this talented expert in western (French and Spanish) literatures. After acquiring Lithuanian citizenship in 1921, Lunts's parents moved to the west and settled in Hamburg. On account of his university studies Lunts had stayed in Petrograd and, when his parents left, he lived in the House of Arts, which during the period 1919–21 became the centre of intellectual life in Russia (among its residents were Mandel'shtam, Khodasevich, Zoshchenko and others). The beginning of Lunts's creative work dates from 1919, when he attracted the attention of Gor'kii and Zamiatin. Lunts was one of the founder members of the Serapion Brothers literary group, which was formed on 1 February 1921; these young writers, who had become acquainted in the House of Arts (the prose writers V. Kaverin, Vs. Ivanov, V. Shklovskii, K. Fedin, M. Zoshchenko, N. Nikitin, M. Slonimskii; the poets E. Polonskaia, N. Tikhonov, V. Pozner, and the literary critic I. Gruzdev), belonged to the literary avant-garde of the 1920s. In the House of Arts Lunts lived under extremely difficult conditions, and frequently went hungry, all of which left its mark on his health. With the help of Gor'kii, he received a grant to visit Spain and, by now a sick man, on 1 June 1923, he set off via Berlin for Hamburg, where his parents lived, and here began treatment for his cardiac and nervous disorders. His illness confined him to bed for a year, although he still continued with his literary work. He died of meningitis on 9 May 1924 in the clinic at Hamburg-Eppendorf.

Talented and extraordinarily erudite for his age, Lunts inspired and shaped the broad concepts of the Serapion Brothers, from whom sprang, in the words of V. Pozner, "the rebirth of Russian literature". If, in his article "Pochemu my Serapionovy Brat'ia" ("Why We Are Serapion Brothers") 1921 – an idiosyncratic manifesto "of a free association" of writers (with "no constitutions, no representatives, no elections, no voting") – Lunts inherited the bequest of the romantic E.T.A. Hoffmann and in the name of artistic freedom rejected utilitarianism and society's tutelage in art ("society has ruled Russian literature for too long and too painfully"), then in his article "Na zapad!" ("Go West!") 1923, he postulates for Russian literature, burdened as it was with social content, the narrational diversity characteristic of western literatures. Therefore he set his literary fellow-believers the task of mastering the art of plot-invention in the style of Stendhal, Hugo, and Dickens, and he declared himself in favour of the art of the heroic gesture, of heightened passions and conflicts. Lunts countered a certain limitedness in his basic creative theories by a search for truth and a prophetic gift that enabled him to view the state of the world and to predict its future development. A timeless view and the search for analogies between the past and the present were to be glimpsed in the early stories ("V pustyne" ["In the Wilderness"] and "Rodina" ["Nativeland"] both 1922). Especially in the story "In the Wilderness" one sees a "biblical" incident concerning the exodus of the Jews from slavery in Egypt and their search for the "promised land" parallelling the historic martyrdom of the Russian Revolution.

The timeless aspect is also present in a series of four plays by Lunts which, as it were, form four acts in one historical tragedy: the melodrama *Vne zakona* [Outside the Law] (1920, published 1921), written in the style of the romantic dramas of Victor Hugo, encapsulates the paradoxical rotation of revolutionary upheavals (the action takes place in Spain) – the transformation of one-time freedom-fighters into new tyrants once they gain power. *Bertran de Born* (1923) is likewise a romantic melodrama set in Medieval France during the reign of Henry II. The fate of the troubador Bertran de Born depicts the tragedy of the struggle of the descendants of a formerly noble family to regain their privileges, estates and freedom, which have been taken from them by the king. The new regime has reduced them to vassals. Having lost his petition with his fate, Bertrand will humbly praise the new monarchs – Richard the Lionheart and his wife Matilda – in verse and song. The one-act play *Obez'iany idut!* [Here Come the Monkeys!] (1920, published 1921) is a tragi-comedy employing the device of a play-within-a-play and containing elements of clowning and vaudeville, executed in the manner of the theatre of the absurd and suggesting a link with the pieces for stage written by Khlebnikov and the work of the *oberiuty*, especially Vvedenskii and Kharms. The play is in fact similar in manner to Samuel Beckett's *Waiting for Godot* – the characters are awaiting the arrival of the "barbarous monkeys" whose attack on the city portends the death of the inhabitants; this is connected with a prophetic moment in the depiction of the march of history: people, tyrannized by commissars, rise up in moments of mortal danger and fight for their very survival against an even worse evil. Lunts's last dramatic piece, *Gorod pravdy* (*The City of Truth*) (1923–24, published 1924), a tragedy bearing features of "mass anti-Utopian dramas", contains an accurate prophetic vision setting out the future paths – involving revolution – that mankind will take. The play exposes the myth of the search for a "just world": a detachment of soldiers, seeking "truth, happiness and work", are on their way back to Russia after five years' captivity in China. On the way, in the City of Truth and Equality, they clash with a uniform and stultified mass of humanity (the people "look like one another, dress the same, walk the same", they "work and keep quiet") – the play thus anticipates the historical tragedy of Russia. The armed soldiers murder the inhabitants of the City of Truth and continue their search for a world of "happiness and justice". The road to "happiness" is however paved with the "death" of those near to them and in fact leads to hell.

Just like Zamiatin, Lunts, in his sceptical and tragic visions of a morally deformed future, warned humanity of the ethical consequences of arbitrary interference with the natural ways of the world, interference that devastates man not only morally, but also, not infrequently, leads inexorably to the restoration of tyranny and totalitarianism. The range of genres in Lunts's work includes satirical short stories, feuilletons, and the film script *Vosstanie veshchei* [Uprising of Things] (1923). Satirical science fiction, *Iskhodiashchaia No. 37* [Circular No. 37] (1922), a tale with the fantastic motif of a Soviet bureaucrat "metamorphosing" into a "piece of office paper", and the satirical feuilletons, *V vagone* [In the Carriage] and *Patriot*, expose the absurdity and anomalies of life in the post-revolutionary period and suggest the wider scope of Lunts's talent. His literary fictions, as an expression of the combination of a metaphor-saturated poetics of neo-realism and neo-romanticism, opened up a new phase in the evolution of Russian avant-garde literature in the 20th century.

Miroslav Míkulašek

M

Vladimir Vladimirovich Maiakovskii 1893–1930

Poet and dramatist

Biography

Born in Bagdadi, Kutais region, subsequently Maiakovskii, Georgia (then part of the Russian Empire), 19 July 1893. Attended the gymnasium at Kutais, 1902–06; school in Moscow, 1906–08; Stroganov School of Industrial Arts, Moscow, 1908–09; Moscow Institute of Painting and Sculpture and Architecture, 1911–14. Member of the Moscow committee of the Russian Social Democratic Party (Bolshevik faction), 1908; arrested for political agitation and imprisoned for six months, 1909. Associated with Futurist circles (especially the Hyleans or Cubo-Futurists), from 1912. Editor of *Vzial* and *Novyi satirikon*, Petrograd. Served in the army, 1917. Reader at Poets Café, Moscow, 1918. Editor of *Gazeta futuristov*, 1918. Involved in the magazine *Iskusstvo kommuna*, 1918–19, and *Iskusstvo*, Petrograd. Designed posters and wrote short propaganda plays and texts for Russian Telegraph Agency (Rosta), Moscow, 1919–21. Travelled in Europe and America from 1922. Co-founder, with Osip Brik, *LEF* [Left Front of Art], 1923–25, and *Novyi LEF* [New Left Front], 1927–28. Committed suicide, 14 April 1930.

Publications

Collected Editions

Sobranie sochinenii, 4 vols. 1925.
Polnoe sobranie sochinenii, 13 vols . Moscow, 1934–38.
Polnoe sobranie sochinenii, 12 vols. Moscow, 1939–49.
Polnoe sobranie sochinenii, 13 vols. Moscow, 1955–61.
The Bedbug and Selected Poetry, edited by Patricia Blake, translated by Max Hayward and George Reavey. New York, Meridian, 1960; reprinted Bloomington, Indiana University Press, 1975.
The Complete Plays of Vladimir Mayakovsky, translated by Guy Daniels. New York, Washington Square Press, 1968; as *Mayakovsky: Plays*, Evanston, Illinois, Northwestern University Press, 1995.
Sobranie sochinenii, 12 vols. Moscow, 1978–79.
Selected Works, 3 vols. Moscow, Raduga, 1985–87.
Stikhi, poemy, materialy o zhizni i tvorchestve [Poetry, Poems, Material about Life and Work]. Moscow, 1988.

Poetry

Oblako v shtanakh. Petrograd, 1915; revised edition, 1918; translated as "The Cloud in Trousers", by Max Hayward and George Reavey, in *The Bedbug and Selected Poetry*, 1960; also as "Cloud in Trousers", by Herbert Marshall, in *Mayakovsky*, New York, Hill and Wang, and London, Dobson, 1965; as *Cloud in Pants*, by Dorian Rottenberg, in *Selected Works*, vol. 2, 1986; also translated in *How Are Verses Made?*, by G.M. Hyde, London, Jonathan Cape, 1970; expanded edition, London, Bristol Classical Press, 1990.
Fleita pozvonochnik. Petrograd, 1916; translated as "The Backbone Flute", by Max Hayward and George Reavey, in *The Bedbug and Selected Poetry*, 1960.
Prostoe kak mychanie [Simple as Mooing]. Petrograd, 1916.
Voina i mir. 1916; translated as "War and the World", by Dorian Rottenberg, in *Selected Works*, vol. 2, 1986.
Chelovek. Moscow, 1918; translated as "Man", by Dorian Rottenberg, in *Selected Works*, vol. 2, 1986.
150,000,000. 1921.
Liubliu [I Love]. Moscow, 1922.
Pro eto. Moscow and Petrograd, 1923; translated as "It", by Dorian Rottenberg, in *Selected Works*, vol. 2, 1986; also as "About This", by Herbert Marshall, in *Mayakovsky*, 1965.
Lirika [Lyrics]. 1923.
Vladimir Il'ich Lenin. 1924; translated as "Vladimir Ilyich Lenin", by Dorian Rottenberg, in *Selected Works*, vol. 2, 1986; also by Herbert Marshall, in *Mayakovsky*, 1965.
Khorosho! 1927; translated as "Fine", by Dorian Rottenberg, in *Selected Works*, vol. 2, 1986.
Mayakovsky and His Poetry, edited and translated by Herbert Marshall. London, Pilot, 1942; revised editions, 1945, 1955; new edition as *Mayakovsky*, New York, Hill and Wang, and London, Dobson, 1965.
Wi the Haill Voice [in Scots], translated by Edwin Morgan. Oxford, Carcanet, 1972.
Poems, translated by Dorian Rottenberg. Moscow, Progress, 1972.
Stihkotvoreniia: Poemy [Poetry: Poems]. Moscow, 1986.
Listen!: Early Poems 1913–1918, translated by Maria Enzensberger. London, Redstone Press, 1987; San Francisco, City Lights Books, 1991.
Poemy. Stikhotvoreniia [Poems. Poetry]. Moscow, 1989.

Plays

Vladimir Maiakovskii: tragediia (produced 1913). Moscow, 1914; translated as "Vladimir Mayakovsky: A Tragedy", by

Guy Daniels, in *The Complete Plays of Vladimir Mayakovsky*, 1968.
Misteriia-Buff (produced 1918; revised version, produced 1921). 1919; translated as "Mystery-Bouffe", by G.R. Noyes and A. Kaun, in *Masterpieces of the Russian Drama*, volume 2, New York and London, Appleton, 1933; also translated by Guy Daniels, in *The Complete Plays*, 1968.
Klop (produced 1929). Moscow and Leningrad, 1929; *Klop/The Bedbug*, edited by Robert Russell, Durham, University of Durham Press, 1985; translated as "The Bedbug", by Max Hayward, in *The Bedbug and Selected Poetry*, 1960; also by Guy Daniels, in *The Complete Plays*, 1968.
Bania (produced 1930). 1930; as "The Bathhouse", by Guy Daniels, in *The Complete Plays*, 1968.

Essays and Memoirs
Moe otkrytie Ameriki [My Discovery of America]. Moscow and Leningrad, 1926.
Kak delat' stikhi? 1926; translated as *How Are Verses Made?*, by G.M. Hyde, London, Jonathan Cape, 1970; expanded edition Bristol, Bristol Classical Press, 1990.

Letters
Pis'ma [Letters], edited by Lili Brik, Moscow, 1956.
V.V. Maiakovskii i L.Iu. Brik. Perepiska 1915–1930, edited by Bengt Jangfeldt. Stockholm, Almqvist & Wiksell, 1982; translated as *Love is the Heart of Everything: Correspondence Between Vladimir Mayakovsky and Lili Brik, 1915–1930*, by Julian Graffy, Edinburgh, Polygon, 1986.
Dorogoi diadia Volodia ... Perepiska Maiakovskogo i El'zy Triole [Dear Uncle Volodia ... Correspondence of Maiakovskii and El'za Triole], edited by Bengt Jangfeldt, Stockholm, Almqvist & Wiksell, 1990.

Critical Studies
Maiakovskii – dramaturg, by A.B. Fevral'skii, Moscow and Leningrad, 1940.
Maiakovskii novator iazyka, by V. Vinokur, Moscow, 1943.
Majakovskij e il teatro russo d'avanguardia, by Angelo Maria Ripellino, Turin, 1959; translated into French as *Maiakovskii et le théâtre russe d'avant-garde*, by Mario Rossi, Paris, L'Arche, 1965.
Satirik i vremia: O masterstve Maiakovskogo-dramaturga, by B. Miliavskii, Moscow, 1963.
Majakovskij and His Neologisms, by Assya Humesky, New York, Rausen, 1964.
The Symbolic System of Majakovskij, by Lawrence Leo Stahlberger, The Hague, Mouton, 1964.
Russian Futurism: A History, by Vladimir Markov, Berkeley, University of California Press, 1968; London, MacGibbon and Kee, 1969.
The Life of Mayakovsky, by Wiktor Woroszylski, translated by Boleslaw Taborski, New York, Orion Press, 1970; London, Gollancz, 1972.
Mayakovsky and His Circle, by Viktor Shklovsky, edited and translated by Lily Feiler, New York, Dodd Mead, 1972; London, Pluto Press, 1974.
Mayakovsky: A Poet in the Revolution, by Edward J. Brown, Princeton, Princeton University Press, 1973.
"On a Generation that Squandered Its Poets", by Roman Jakobson, in *Major Soviet Writers: Essays in Criticism*, edited by Edward J. Brown, London and New York, Oxford University Press, 1973.
Smert' Vladimira Maiakovskogo, by Roman Jakobson and D. Sviatopolk-Mirskii, The Hague, Mouton, 1975.
Vladimir Majakovskij: Memoirs and Essays, edited by Bengt Jangfeldt and Nils Åke Nilsson, Stockholm, Almqvist & Wiksell, 1975.
Zrelishche neobychaineishee: Maiakovskii i teatr, by Iu. Smirnov-Nesvitskii, Leningrad, 1975.
Maiakovskij and Futurism 1917–1921, by Bengt Jangfeldt, Stockholm, Almqvist & Wiksell, 1976.
Three Russians Consider America: America in the Works of Maksim Gor'kij, Aleksandr Blok, and Vladimir Majakovskij, by Charles Rougle, Stockholm, Almqvist & Wiksell, 1976.
Brik and Mayakovsky, by Vahan D. Barooshian, The Hague, Mouton, 1978.
Vladimir Mayakovsky: A Tragedy, by A.D.P. Briggs, Oxford, Meeuws, 1979.
I Love: The Story of Vladimir Mayakovsky and Lili Brik, by Ann and Samuel Charters, New York, Farrar Straus and Giroux, and London, André Deutsch, 1979.
Poets of Modern Russia, by Peter France, Cambridge and New York, Cambridge University Press, 1982.
Posledniaia liubov' Maiakovskogo, by Semen Chertok, Ann Arbor, Hermitage, 1983.
Vladimir Mayakovsky, by Victor Terras, Boston, Twayne, 1983.
Voskresenie Maiakovskogo, by Iurii Karabchievskii, 5th edition, Munich, Strana i mir, 1985.
Maiakovskii: Khronika zhizni i deiatel'nosti, by Vasilii Katanian, Moscow, 1985.
Mayakovsky's Cubo-Futurist Vision, by Juliette R. Stapanian, Houston, Texas, Rice University Press, 1986.
Russian Futurism Through Its Manifestoes, 1912–1928, edited by Anna Lawton, Ithaca, Cornell University Press, 1988.
Verse Form and Meaning in the Poetry of Vladimir Maiakovskii, by Robin Aizlewood, London, Modern Humanities Research Association, 1989.
Imia etoi temy liubov': sovremennitsy o Maiakovskom, edited by V.V. Katanian, Moscow, 1993.
Tochka puli v kontse: zhizn' Maiakovskogo, by A. Mikhailov, Moscow, 1993.
Vo ves' logos: religiia Maiakovskogo, by Mikhail Vaiskopf, Moscow, 1997.

Bibliography
"Mayakovsky: A Bibliography of Criticism (1912–1930)", by Gerald Darring, *Russian Literature Triquarterly*, 2 (1972).

Vladimir Maiakovskii is one of the most overtly gifted, but also controversial, poets of the early 20th century in Russia. His imagery, hyperbole, and emotional intensity, his innovative rhymes and rhythms can all be extraordinary. The early Maiakovskii made a very powerful impression, for example, on Pasternak. But the awe in which Pasternak initially held him gave way later to an estrangement from the Maiakovskii who became known, propagandized by his own rhetoric and public posture, as the poet of the Revolution. As recently as 1993, the anniversary of Maiakovskii's birth, Andrei Siniavskii prefaced a reading in Paris of the revolutionary poem "Levyi marsh" ("Left March") 1918, by noting that it would still be unthinkable for him to read it in Russia.

Maiakovskii committed suicide in 1930. Life and art cannot be separated in Maiakovskii, and his suicide provides the final perspective from which to view his life and work: it is the final exposure of the geological fault running through Maiakovskii's volcanic persona (his own image). But his suicide can also be seen as a highly significant cultural moment that highlights a rupture in the whole project of Left Art in the 1920s.

Maiakovskii's suicide note, echoing *Romeo and Juliet*, speaks of the wreck of "love's bark". Beneath his loud and often offensive rhetoric and behaviour, Maiakovskii's credo is expressed in his words that "love is the heart of everything". Here lies the most fundamental level of the tragic interaction between the poet's persona and the world. Maiakovskii's persona strives to encompass everything, a feature that Trotskii acutely termed "Maiakomorphosis". Mythologically, the poet creates a Promethean culture hero, a man-God in opposition to Christ, a rebel against God, the world and death-dealing time. But he is rejected by the world, and in a recurrent motif that echoes Dostoevskii, he feels that he has "no way out". Equally, while his poetry is based on sound and rhythm, and hence on an audience – one of his collections is called *Dlia golosa* [For the Voice] (1923) – another recurrent motif is the lack of response, or silence.

Maiakovskii's arrival on the poetic scene was marked by his participation in the scandalous Futurist manifesto "Poshchechina obshchestvennomu vkusu" ("A Slap in the Face of Public Taste") 1912. His training at the time was as an artist, and his earliest work brilliantly translates a painterly vision into poetry, such that Malevich called "Iz ulitsy v ulitsu" ("From Street into Street") 1913, "versified Cubism". The poems reveal an ambivalent urbanism, a fraught combination of Futurist championing of the new and martyrdom in an urban hell. At the same time the disjointed viewpoint of Cubism, allied to the emotional intensity of Expressionism, is embodied in the poet's persona itself, most notably in the cycle "Ia" ("I") 1913, and *Vladimir Maiakovskii. Tragediia* (*Vladimir Maiakovskii: A Tragedy*). Maiakovskii's first great longer poem, *Oblako v shtanakh* (*Cloud in Trousers*), was retrospectively presented by him as a series of attacks on "your" love, art, society, and religion. But when viewed as a whole, it becomes one of the most remarkable explorations in 20th-century literature of a persona on the edge of breakdown, a breakdown whose source is rejection in love.

In 1915 Maiakovskii met the love of his life, Lili Brik, and all his lyric work is dedicated to her. Though at the core of his life and art, his love poetry does not dominate in terms of volume. It principally takes the form of a central trilogy of long poems, *Cloud in Trousers*, *Chelovek* (*Man*), and *Pro eto* (*About This*); in addition there is the magnificent expression of love as pain, *Fleita pozvonochnik* (*The Backbone Flute*), and the more limited *Liubliu* [I Love]. Although *Man* has not generally received as much attention as other works, it is Maiakovskii's greatest poem, as he himself recognizes in *About This* when he makes its hero stand for his true persona. *Man* presents a quasi-Christian myth which sees human love as the only creative, and eternal force that opposes a mechanistic universal order. The poem's conclusion is deeply pessimistic, a pessimism only alleviated by the tragic faith in love, ironic honesty, and humour. *About This* is the last great manifestation of Maiakovskii's poetic gift, in its way a final confession and testament. In the poem his diminished and compromised post-revolutionary persona is offered an insecure vision of resurrection in a distant future, but the only way out in the present is through suicide. After *About This* the lyric poet fell almost completely silent.

Maiakovskii the poet of the Revolution is faced after 1917 with the task of how to locate himself in socialist society and art. In the play *Misteriia-Buff* (*Mystery-Bouffe*) and the long poem *150,000,000* Utopianism is combined with elements drawn from popular tradition and satire. One of his most successful ventures was the poster work for the ROSTA telegraph agency (1919–22). After 1923, although he achieved status as a Soviet poet and Soviet art's ambassador in Europe and America, Maiakovskii's work increased in volume, but the heart and even the Utopianism were gone, and the great talent had lost most of its brightness. The predicament of a persona at an impasse is encapsulated both in the late play *Klop* (*The Bedbug*), which places a worthless bourgeois as the sole defender of love in a future mechanized Utopia, and in the last unfinished poem, "Vo ves' golos" [At the Top of My Voice], which seemingly accepts that the poet has "stepped on the throat of his own song".

ROBIN AIZLEWOOD

Cloud in Trousers

Oblako v shtanakh

Narrative poem, 1915

Maiakovskii called *Cloud in Trousers* his "second tragedy", a reference to his first major work *Vladimir Maiakovskii: A Tragedy* (1913). The Tragedy, however, is still to some extent an experimental work in which Maiakovskii is searching for his own distinctive voice, but in *Cloud in Trousers* he senses "mastery". He has found his voice and style, and he has also found his most important theme, love. The poem, completed when Maiakovskii was still only 22, is the first of his five major love poems, the others being *The Backbone-Flute*, *Man*, *Liubliu*, and *About This*. The three longest, *Cloud in Trousers*, *Man*, and *About This*, form the central trilogy at the heart of Maiakovskii's work: in these poems his experience of love leads to a wide-ranging exploration of the human condition, yet still in the tragic mode defined by his first major work.

Cloud in Trousers was originally published in 1915, although with great holes in it due to censorship (the censor took particular exception to the blasphemous and flippant handling of religion, including the original title "The Thirteenth Apostle"). The poem only appeared in full in 1918, after the Bolshevik Revolution. It is over 400 lines long, although this is amplified on the page due to the "column" lay-out in which one metrical line may be split into two or more graphical lines down the page. The poem has a prologue and four parts. In the preface to the second edition in 1918, Maiakovskii described the poem in terms of "four cries": "Down with your love, down with your art, down with your order [i.e. socio-political system], down with your religion". Such a definition certainly catches the rhetorical force of much of the poem, but it ignores both the hierarchy of the themes and the way in which the rhetoric is balanced by lyricism.

In fact the crucial theme in the poem is love. The first part locates the hero in Odessa, waiting for his beloved, who is given the name Mariia, but when she arrives it is to announce that she is getting married. This rejection triggers a breakdown, and the second half of Part I is dominated by images of volcanic explosion, burning, drowning, and death. The rest of the poem is moved by the poet hero's need to reassert himself, to find fulfilment and a role in the world, but his underlying uncertainty makes for a composition of sudden shifts. In Parts II and III he turns first to art and then to revolution, but in each case the rhetoric breaks down. Part II, however, is more up-beat and aggressive, and seems to ride over the occasional puncturing of the rhetoric, such as the image of a dog licking the hand that beats it which is unexpectedly interposed between the proclamation of Futurist public performances as a Golgotha and the vision of impending revolution. Part III is much darker: it opens with the image of madness, art is invoked more as a defence, and the poet hero's rebellious posturing is much more unstable. In the ultimate image of sexual gratification he envisages the whole earth as his woman. But madness arrives, rather than a positive response to his art or his call for social revolution. The only recourse is to return once more to Mariia, which the poet hero does in the great emotional climax of the poem in the first half of Part IV. This passage is marked by a whole series of cries straight from the heart, for example: "Mariia, do you want someone like me? Let me in, Mariia!" Sexual fulfilment is not sufficient, however, and his need for love meets rejection. In the finale the poet builds himself up once more to take on the possible source of human unhappiness in love at its first cause, God, but the poem ends in a last, silent rejection as the sleeping universe fails to respond.

The extraordinary force of *Cloud in Trousers* derives from the tension between the poles that move it: between the poet hero and the world, and between the poet's divergent personae and voices. He is heroic, iconoclastic, loud, and vulgar on the one hand, and ironic, unsure, tender, and lyrical on the other. Tension and ambivalence are expressed in both the original title, "The Thirteenth Apostle", and the actual title "Cloud" (soft) "in Trousers" (coarse). Most strikingly, *Cloud in Trousers* is a work that conveys the experience of impending and real breakdown, while doing so through the poet's mastery of his art.

Maiakovskii's formal mastery is evident on every level of the poem. The innovative richness of his rhyming technique is on display, as is his mastery of a tonic verse that is free of traditional syllabo-tonic metres and rests on individual word stresses. The rhythms of the poem carry a range of voice, from rhetoric to lyricism to conversational informality. In accordance with the poetics of Futurism, Maiakovskii neologizes brilliantly. The word "love" itself is the subject of a linguistic exploration: it appears as a concrete noun, in two alternative genitive plural forms, and with two diminutive suffixes. Finally, in the imagery employed in the poem Maiakovskii displays his penchant for the combination of high and low, for hyperbole, for Futurist realized metaphor. One of the most famous passages is the extended realized metaphor of a heart on fire towards the end of Part I, in which the poet hero's heart is metamorphosed into a burning building:

> People sniff –
> there's a smell of burnt flesh!
> Here come some men.
> All shining!
> In helmets!
> No heavy boots please!
> Tell the firemen
> to go gently when the heart's on fire.
> Let me.
> I'll roll barrels of tears from my eyes.
> Let me – I'll brace against my ribs.
> I'll jump out! I'll jump out! I'll jump out! I'll jump out!
> They've collapsed.
> You can't jump out of your heart!

Maiakovskii could never escape his heart, and the lines of his tragic confrontation with life are already drawn in *Cloud in Trousers*.

ROBIN AIZLEWOOD

About This

Pro eto

Narrative poem, 1923

The idea for this poem came to Maiakovskii in 1922. It appears to be linked to Lili Brik's love affair with a prominent Soviet official, A.M. Krasnoshchekov (1880–1937). The poem acquired its final shape in late 1922 and early 1923, when Maiakovskii spent two months (28 December 1922–28 February 1923) in voluntary seclusion in the aftermath of the crisis in his relationship with Lili Brik. Three manuscripts of the poem have survived: a rough draft, a clean copy with corrections and additions, and a revised clean copy with only a few amendments. The two clean copies carry the same date for the end of the work, 11 February 1923. *About This* was first published in the magazine *Lef* (no. 1, 1923), with the dedication "to her and to me". A separate edition came out later that year with a photograph of Lili Brik on the front cover.

Maiakovskii himself said the poem was his "most and best polished". Its cryptic title (which provokes the inevitable question: "about *what*?") is uncoded in the introduction. The main subject is the phenomenon of love, which is treated by Maiakovskii with such awe that he even refuses to name it. The reader, however, is provided with a rhyming sequence of sounds that makes it easier to guess the key word (*liubov'*), which is hidden behind the ellipsis. In his autobiography the poet wrote more on the theme of *About This* which, as he put it, rested upon "my personal reasons [for condemnation] of the ordinary way of life [*byt*]". According to Maiakovskii, this *byt* "is currently our worst enemy. It has not changed [since the Revolution], and it is making philistines out of us" (Maiakovskii's speech at the Proletkul't, 3 April 1923).

The explanatory inscriptions, printed on the sidelines of the main text (e.g., "Fantastic Reality", "The Unbelievable", "Friends", etc.), serve as signposts in discovering the plot of the poem within the deliberately chaotic farrago of far-fetched hyperboles and idiosyncratic associations, symbolizing the hysterical state of the poet's soul. The autobiographical lyrical hero (in *About This* Maiakovskii incorporated some extracts from his diary, as well as from his correspondence and private conversations with Lili Brik) visits his close relatives and friends in Moscow and Paris, begging them to save another autobiographical character, a man who for seven years remained on a bridge in St Petersburg (a reference to Maiakovskii's earlier long love poem *Man*, on the imagery of which *About This* depends rather heavily). Only limitless love at its purest can release the poet's *alter ego*. Alas, the lyrical hero's kith and kin "have exchanged their love for tea-drinking" (tea-drinking symbolized for Maiakovskii the quintessence of *byt*; cf. Lili Brik's words quoted in Maiakovskii's letter to her of 1–27 February 1923: "I am not a saint myself, I like 'to drink tea'") and cannot help him much. In a desperate quest for love the poet splits the personality of his protagonist and crowds *About This* with his numerous doubles, from Jesus Christ to a young Komsomol member who commits suicide. Here Maiakovskii follows the rule that "the greater the versatility of the character you display, the more attention you are able to attract" (one of these doubles is a bear – perhaps because Lili Brik "loved animals" and enjoyed going to the zoo). Nevertheless, the lyrical hero perishes from the lack of love, and the only solution Maiakovskii can suggest is to revive him in the 30th century, when the contradictions between passion and *byt* are said to be happily resolved (despite his supposed atheism, the poet, influenced by the ideas of the Russian philosopher N.F. Fedorov (1828–1903), literally believed in the resurrection of the dead).

The skilfully prepared mixture of mutually incompatible ingredients recurs on the generic level, as well as in the verse and in the literary allusions. Iu. Tynianov noted that in *About This*, Maiakovskii "tried, as if groping about, all the systems of versification, all the hardened genres, as though he was looking for a way out of himself". The range of allusions included, among others, Blok, Lermontov, Dostoevskii, Oscar Wilde's *The Ballad of Reading Gaol* and Gogol''s "Noch' pered rozhdestvom" ("Christmas Eve") (the motif of Christmas emerges because Maiakovskii, speaking of himself, promised Lili Brik in a letter of early January 1923: "on 28 [February 1923] you will meet someone absolutely new to you"; in another letter to her, of 19 January, he calls his room the "Reading gaol"). To crown the well-organized spontaneity that reigns on the pages of the poem, Maiakovskii features all four main elements of the world: fire (the volcanic eruption of the telephone), water (a flat flooded by a sea of tears), air (the flying poet), and earth (represented by its geographical attributes, such as certain cities, mountains, etc.).

The critical reception of *About This* at the time was almost unanimously negative. Even Maiakovskii's colleague, N. Chuzhak, maintained that the poem suggested "not a way out, but a deadlock", and that Maiakovskii "allegedly unmasks the unpleasant *byt*, while being entirely overwhelmed by it". The only immediately appreciative response seemed to be by Lunacharskii, who called the poem "a search for a new ethics through the torments of a shuddering heart".

ANDREI ROGACHEVSKII

The Bedbug

Klop

Play, 1929

The Bedbug was written in 1928 in response to a request for a play from the theatre director Vsevolod Meierkhol'd, whose production opened in 1929. Described by Maiakovskii as "a magical [*feericheskaia*] comedy in nine scenes", the play is set both in contemporary Russia of the late NEP period (scenes 1–4) and in the Utopian future-world of 1979 (scenes 5–9). The central character, Prisypkin, is a worker who decides to abandon his pregnant girlfriend Zoia in favour of the daughter of a rich NEP-man because he wants some elegance and luxury in his life. In a number of amusing scenes Maiakovskii pokes fun at the uncouth, ignorant and pretentious Prisypkin, who changes his name to the more mellifluous Pierre Skripkin, and at Rozaliia Pavlovna, his future mother-in-law. The first half of the play concludes with a farcical "Red Wedding" scene, in the course of which the drunken guests set fire to the building. Everyone perishes except Prisypkin, who is preserved in a block of ice when the water from the firemen's hoses freezes.

Fifty years later, when the world has been transformed, Prisypkin is discovered and de-frosted, together with a bedbug that had been on his body and had been frozen with him. The world into which, like Rip Van Winkle, he awakens is one in which all the vices of the 1920s that he embodies have been eradicated. Alcohol and tobacco are banned substances, sentimental music is a thing of the past, love is now a rational and useful rather than destructive force. The world is politically united and technologically advanced, and the decision to revive Prisypkin is taken by the global population through an instant referendum. At first, he thinks he has been arrested for being drunk and has awoken in the police sobering-up cells, and is horrified to discover that 50 years have elapsed: what about all those unpaid trade union dues? Finding the world of the future unpleasantly sterile, he longs for the company of someone capable of understanding his old way of life. There is no one, though, and his sole companion is the bedbug who came with him from the past. Zoia, who survived a suicide attempt after Prisypkin rejected her and is now an old woman, tries to warn of the dangers to society represented by a philistine like Prisypkin. Her younger colleagues fail to comprehend, however, and he is allowed to resume his former way of life, complete with vodka, cigarettes, and a guitar on which to strum his "heart-rending romances". Soon he begins to infect others with the germs of philistinism and parasitism, and couples can be seen engaged in that most bourgeois of pastimes – dancing the fox-trot. The authorities are at first perplexed, but then realize that their mistake lay in wrongly classifying Prisypkin: they had been misled by the calluses on his hands into thinking that he was human and a member of the working class, whereas in reality he is a giant bedbug that differs from the ordinary variety in that it sucks the blood of the whole of humanity rather than that of an individual. Thus re-classified, Prisypkin is transferred to a cage in the zoo and is triumphantly presented to an excited crowd of spectators, including a party of schoolchildren. When the cage is uncovered, Prisypkin looks out into the theatre audience and recognizes there some people like himself, philistines sharing all his vices. Excited, he calls out to them: "Citizens! Brothers! My own ones! Where did you come from? How many of you are there? When were you de-frosted? Why am I the only one in a cage?" The crowd at the zoo are frightened, but the director manages to regain control of the situation, and the play ends with the band playing a march.

Similarities between *The Bedbug* and newspaper articles and satirical poems of 1927–28, as well as Maiakovskii's explicit comments, make it clear that the play was first conceived purely as a satire on the re-appearance of bourgeois habits and tastes among members of the working class. The first half is a typically vigorous and amusing NEP satire, similar in theme and treatment to works by Kataev, Il'f and Petrov, and others. Matters are complicated, however, by the Utopian second half, for the sterile, emotionless world of the future seems to attract Maiakovskii's satire no less forcefully than does the boorishness of Prisypkin. With its outlawing of vices and its purely rational, constructive approach to love, the society of 1979 resembles Zamiatin's satirical vision of the future in *We*. It seems unlikely that Maiakovskii consciously intended to warn against the future socialist world. Indeed, he explicitly remarked that the world portrayed was not socialist. In several of his long poems and all of his plays Maiakovskii contrasts the imperfect present with a Utopian future in which the sources of his personal pain, such as sexual jealousy, will have been eradicated by the transformation of society. *The Bedbug* continues this tradition in the poet's work, although the vision of the future is rendered ambivalent both by the need to preserve the comic tone of the play and by the dominant Constructivist aesthetic, which is evident in such details as the use of glass and the prominence of white. This latter feature of the play was further underlined in the Meierkhol'd production by the director's invitation to the Constructivist artist Aleksandr Rodchenko to design the sets and costumes for scenes 5–9.

A further factor that complicates the straightforward satirical intent of the play is Maiakovskii's identification with the caged Prisypkin. The character may be a boor, but his vices are all-too-human, and, whatever may have been Maiakovskii's intentions, his own sympathy and that of the audience switches to Prisypkin as he awakens in an alien environment and is categorized as an animal. Prisypkin's cry of recognition to members of the audience reminds us that there is a touch of Prisypkin in all of us and that the character's human fallibility is preferable to the dry, rational perfection of the future. What started out as a straightforward satire on backsliding in the NEP period becomes a more profound work on the complexity of human nature and the dangers inherent in attempting to alter it.

ROBERT RUSSELL

The Bathhouse

Bania

Play, 1930

Vladimir Maiakovskii's two last, and best-known plays, *The Bedbug* and *The Bathhouse*, encapsulate the major concepts of his aesthetic creed; deeply iconoclastic, politically astute, and filled with verbal satire and buffoonery, they stand as his final blow at the hated targets of smug philistinism and ignorant power-mongering. Both staged by Meierkhol'd, *The Bathhouse* was the less successful theatrical event, partly because of the increasing government and RAPP concern with the freedom permitted to satirists, and which ensured that the play received a particularly bad press (the play, completed by Maiakovskii and read to the Meierkhol'd assembly on 23 September 1926, had to be cut before it could be passed for performance). Vakhtangov's set constructions were also not well received, while Maiakovskii himself was displeased with the casting of Maksim Straukh for the main part of Pobedonosikov. Both plays are of equal quality, however, and if *The Bedbug* offered one of the most enduring figures of the chameleon bourgeoisie in the figure of Prisypkin, in *The Bathhouse* Maiakovskii created the equally famous Pobedonosikov, "Victoryman", the "new" Soviet man exposed in every humorous detail.

The plot of the six-act play *The Bathhouse* follows a series of typically Maiakovskiian incredible incidents. A time machine has been invented; although rather jocular suggestions are made as to how the machine can be used (for speeding up boring political speeches, for example), the invention is finally utilized as a means of contacting the future. The "Phosphorescent Woman", as she is called (played by Zinaida Raikh in the original production), a delegate from the year 2030, duly arrives, and, in Act 4, announces that her mission is to take people back with her, 100 years into the future. The Phosphorescent Woman, despite her belief that Soviet society is filled with individuals who will both approve of, and fit into, her future society in which discipline, efficiency, community spirit, creative inventiveness, pride in serving mankind, and hard work are cultivated, is to be somewhat disappointed. The wonderful opportunity to travel through time is turned by one Pobedonosikov, a Soviet party official, into a means for self-promotion.

Pobedonosikov is a man of astounding ignorance (who believes that Michelangelo was an Armenian and that the opera of *Evgenii Onegin* was written before it appeared as a text) and of hilarious pomposity. Maiakovskii shows us the bourgeois lurking beneath the camouflage coat of a socialist; Pobedonosikov is an arrant philistine. His self-righteous pronouncements are shown to be arrant hypocrisy when it is revealed that he is conducting an affair with the appropriately-named Messal'iansova; he intends to take the latter, and not his wife, on the journey through time. He arrives at the appointed departure time not only with his mistress, but with a vast amount of luggage, his own portrait painter, and sufficient paper to fuel the bureaucracy he confidently expects to control in the future.

Maiakovskii's final dig at this travesty of a good socialist occurs when the time machine operates, and Pobedonosikov is "thrown off", rejected utterly by the future. Pobedonosikov is left bemusedly questioning the author: "Do you mean by any chance that communism does not need the likes of me?"

Pobedonosikov's address to the author at the play's end reminds the spectator that Maiakovskii has been concerned with another theme in *The Bathhouse*, namely, that of literature. A hint at the author's interest in the debasement of language is evident early on; in Act 2 in particular, bureaucratese and political jargon applied to trivial situations are Maiakovskii's concerns. In Act 3 of *The Bathhouse* a metafictional moment occurs when the curtain rises to show spectators a stage and an audience; artifice is emphasized again when Pobedonosikov is shown talking to a theatrical director about the latter's plans to portray, in ridiculous manner, a certain character – one Pobedonosikov. The director retorts that he has special permission from the State Literary Committee to portray a negative literary character, but Pobedonosikov offers the standard governmental line, that writers should show only the "positive, the brighter aspects" of Soviet life.

Maiakovskii's concern with state interference in literature, and socialist realist demands for a rosy and unrealistic depiction of reality is demonstrated by the entire play, which highlights the dangers that Soviet society must overcome before it can attain the "radiant future". In Act 2 Maiakovskii also takes the opportunity of parodying a typical piece of *agitprop* theatre. The Director finally gives in and puts on a "symbolic" piece in which oppressed masses, comrade "capital", and women representing freedom, equality and brotherhood are paraded across the stage. To cap this triumph of didactic dullness, the actors form themselves into a human pyramid, symbolizing aspiring communism. The *Bathhouse* has its political points to make. But, ultimately, it is best viewed against the background of the quickly approaching tragedy of Maiakovskii's own decision that his life as a writer was over, and that the future, peopled by Prisypkins and Pobedonosikovs, and filled with ridiculously "optimistic" art, was one he would prefer not to see.

S. Dalton-Brown

Vladimir Semenovich Makanin 1937–

Prose writer

Biography

Born in the Urals (Orsk), 13 March 1937. Left the region in 1954. Studied mathematics at Moscow State University (MGU), graduated in 1960. Worked at MGU until 1970. Concurrently attended screenwriting courses at the Film Institute; a screenplay (filmed), became the basis for his first novel, *Priamaia liniia* [The Straight Line], 1965. Married; one daughter. Lives in Moscow. Recipient: Russian Booker Prize, 1993.

Publications

Collected Editions

Bezottsovshchina, soldat i soldatka. Povesti [Fatherless, Soldier and Female Soldier]. Moscow, 1971.
Povest' o Starom Poselke [Story about the Old Settlement]. Moscow, 1974.
Starye knigi [Old Books]. Moscow, 1976.
Kliucharev i Alimushkin. Moscow, 1979.
V bol'shom gorode [In a Large City]. Moscow, 1980.
Na zimnei doroge [On the Winter Road]. Moscow, 1980.
Predtecha [The Precursor]. Moscow, 1983.
Mesto pod solntsem [A Place Under the Sun]. Moscow, 1984.
Izbrannoe. Moscow, 1987.
Povesti. Moscow, 1988.
Odin i odna [All Alone]. Moscow, 1988.
Otstavshii. Povest' i rasskazy [Left Behind]. Moscow, 1988.
Utrata [Loss]. Moscow, 1989.
Escape Hatch and The Long Road Ahead: Two Novellas, translated by Mary Ann Szporluk. Dana Point, California, Ardis, 1996.

Fiction and Articles

"Priamaia liniia" [The Straight Line], *Moskva*, 8 (1965).
"Bezottsovshchina" [Fatherless], *Moskva*, 12 (1971).
"Kliucharev i Alimushkin", *Nash sovremennik*, 4 (1977); translated as "Klyucharev and Alimushkin", by Arch Tait, *Glas*, 4 (1993), 88–112.
Portret i vokrug [A Portrait and Its Surroundings]. Moscow, 1978.
Golosa [Voices]. Moscow, 1980.
"Chelovek svity" [One of the Retinue], *Oktiabr'*, 3 (1982).
"Predtecha" [The Precursor], *Sever*, 3–4 (1982).
"Antilider", *Ural*, 6 (1983); translated as "Antileader", by Jamey Gambrell, in *The New Soviet Fiction: Sixteen Short Stories*, edited by Sergei Zalygin, New York, Abbeville Press, 1989.
Goluboe i krasnoe [Blue and Red]. 1983.
"Grazhdanin ubegaiushchii" [The Fleeing Citizen], *Ural*, 9 (1984).
"Gde nebo skhodilos' s kholmami" [Where the Sky Meets the Hills], *Novyi mir*, 1 (1984), 68–102.
"Utrata" [Loss], *Novyi mir*, 2 (1987), 96–134.
"Odin i odna" [All Alone], *Oktiabr'*, 2 (1987).
"Otstavshii", *Znamia*, 9 (1987), 6–59; translated as "Left Behind", by Nadezhda Peterson, in *Glasnost': An Anthology of Literature under Gorbachev*, edited by Helena Goscilo and Byron Lindsey, Ann Arbor, Ardis, 1990, 195–270.
"Dolog nash put'", *Znamia*, 4 (1991), 3–47; translated as *The Long Road Ahead*, by Mary Ann Szporluk, in *Escape Hatch and The Long Road Ahead: Two Novellas*, Dana Point, California, Ardis, 1996.
"Tam byla para" [There was a Couple There], *Novyi mir*, 5 (1991), 83–133.
"Laz", *Novyi mir*, 5 (1991), 92–133; translated as *Escape Hatch*, by Mary Ann Szporluk, in *Escape Hatch and The Long Road Ahead: Two Novellas*, Dana Point, California, Ardis, 1996.
"Stol, pokrytyi suknom i s grafinom posredine", *Znamia*, 1 (1993), 9–53; translated as *Baize-Covered Table with*

Decanter, by Arch Tait, Columbia, Louisiana, Readers International, 1995.
"Kvazi" [Quasi], *Novyi mir*, 7 (1993), 124–47.
"Kavkazskii plennyi", *Novyi mir*, 4 (1995), 3–19; translated as "The Captive of the Caucasus", by Arch Tait, *Glas: New Russian Writing*, 11 (1996), 5–37.

Critical Studies
"Ochen' predvaritel'nye itogi: Vladimir Makanin", by N. Ivanova, *Literaturnaia ucheba*, 1 (1980), 118–27.
"Protiv techeniia: Avtorskaia pozitsiia v proze Vladimira Makanina", by M. Lipovetskii, *Ural*, 12 (1985), 148–58.
"Neznakomye neznakomtsy. K sporam o geroiakh Vladimira Makanina", by I. Rodianskaia, *Novyi mir*, 8 (1986), 230–48.
"Struktura labirinta", by Lev Anninskii, in Makanin's *Izbrannoe*, Moscow, 1987, 3–18 (reprint of an article in *Znamia*, 12 (1986); also in *Lokti i kryl'ia*, Moscow, 1989, 238–58).
"Vladimir Makanin's Solutions to the Loss of the Past", by N.L. Peterson, *Studies in Comparative Communism*, 21/3–4 (Autumn–Winter 1988), 349–56.
"Istina i svoboda. Vladimir Makanin: vzgliad iz 1990 goda", by A. Ageev, *Literaturnoe obozrenie*, 9 (1990), 25–33.
"Postmodernist Allegory in Contemporary Soviet Literature", by C. Dowsett, *Australian Slavonic and East European Studies*, 4/1–2 (1990), 21–35.
"Vokrug Makanina, ili Shtrikha k portretu", by E. Gessen, *Grani*, 161 (1991), 144–59.
"Ineffectual Ideas, Violent Consequences: Vladimir Makanin's Portrait of the Intelligentsia", by S. Dalton-Brown, *Slavonic and East European Review*, 70/2 (1994), 220–32.
"Signposting the Way to the City of Night: Recent Russian Dystopian Fiction", by S. Dalton-Brown, *Modern Language Review*, 90/1 (1995), 103–19.
"Lucrative Literature: The Russian Booker Prize", by S. Dalton-Brown, *Europa*, (1995), 23–34.
"The 'Urals Voice' in the Work of Vladimir Makanin", by S. Dalton-Brown, *Rusistika*, 12 (1995), 4–11.
Russian Literature 1988–1994: The End of an Era, by N.N. Shneidman, Toronto, University of Toronto Press, 1995.

Vladimir Makanin first came to prominence as a member of the so-called "sorokaletnie" group of writers, who were hailed as a new group in the 1980s (when most of these authors had reached their forties). Critics have included writers as varied as Andrei Bitov and Anatolii Kim, Anatolii Kurchatkin, Ruslan Kireev and Vladimir Krupin under this label, and have been as divided on the question of the central concerns of the group as they have been on the name by which it may be known. Sometimes called the followers of Trifonov, or the Moscow school, these authors are however noted for producing texts from the mid-1960s onwards in which urban *byt* (everyday life), failed marriages, and the moral compromises and mid-life crises of male *neudachniki* (failures) – all familiar Trifonovian themes – are the central issues. Certain of Makanin's early texts, such as "Polosa obmenov" [Period of Change] (1976) and "Chelovek svity" [One of the Retinue] (1982) demonstrate these Trifonovian concerns.

Makanin has been translated in both Germany and France since the late 1970s, but is far less well known in England. The English translation of *Otstavshii* (*Left Behind*) which appeared in a 1990 anthology of major glasnost writing first promoted his name; the shortlisting of *Laz* (*Escape Hatch*) for the 1992 Russian Booker Prize undoubtedly helped to bring his work to the attention of the west, attention later concentrated by the award of the 1993 Booker for his *Stol, pokrytyi suknom i s grafinom posredine* (*Baize-Covered Table with Decanter*).

Makanin's early period spans the years 1965–86; during the mid-1980s he discovered a more original voice. The theme of violence began to assume a greater prominence in his text, as his style, labelled "strogaia" (severe) and "bednaia" (poor) for its disciplined matter-of-factness, began to diversify from *byt* prose to works infused with mythic and religious motifs, to dystopian texts (*Escape Hatch* and *Dolog nash put'* [*The Long Road Ahead*]), to social commentary (*Kvazi* [Quasi]). His *Baize-Covered Table with Decanter* is a surreal, Kafkaesque depiction of the trial of the protagonist for an unnamed crime. In some of his shorter stories, for instance, Makanin depicts violence and blood as inevitable, even natural elements of his characters' grotesque existence. These may include descriptions of a giant hand that squeezes its victim to death, as well as other murders, and a scene of necrophilia. The theme of violence reached its apotheosis in his recent work, which appeared, prophetically, shortly before the outbreak of the war in Chechnia – the subject with which the story "Kavkazskii plennyi" ("The Captive of the Caucasus") deals.

Makanin's view of man's nature is a pessimistic one, and his depictions of love and harmonious interrelationships lack the power of his descriptions of man's inhumanity to man (or to beast). He is most at ease describing love linked to violence as in *Goluboe i krasnoe* [Blue and Red], which describes how two grandmothers battle for the love of their young grandson, Kliucharev. The love that Makanin's heroes advocate is a tough, universal and unselfish love, as typified by the healer Iakushkin with his philosophy of brotherly love in *Predtecha* [The Precursor]. It is love for one's family and kin, love for one's people, birthplace, for Russia, love that has a basis in conscience, which interests Makanin.

Makanin's texts are powerful analyses of man's innate capacity for violence, as well as of his ability to accept evil passively. His major theme is the guilt of the intelligentsia, who failed to support the suffering people during the Stalinist years. Plumbing the not so moral depths of man, Makanin analyses the guilt of the *intelligent*, dating it from the 1950s and 1960s, when the liberal intelligentsia had the opportunity to take a stand during the Khrushchev years, but did not. In his 1978 *Portret i vokrug* [A Portrait and Its Surroundings], Makanin pinpointed a major problem for the *intelligenty*; namely, his inability to recognize his guilt. *Portret i vokrug* revolves around a "man of the 60s", Starokhatov, a man who abuses his position as a well-known scriptwriter and producer to sign his name on scripts written by novice authors. In his 1987 text *Odin i odna* [All Alone], Makanin turned again to a depiction of the guilt of the *shestidesiatniki* (men of the 1960s). Gennadii Goloshchekov and Ninel' are two idealistic people who were involved in student politics during the 1950s, and who could never bring themselves to submit to the regime; they are innately honourable, but also pathetic, farcically inept characters. In Makanin's view, ineffectuality is ultimately as destructive as brutality; between the savage and the intellectual there is only a fine line, and both will find themselves inhabiting a world of darkness and chaos, of the type depicted by Makanin in his futuristic *The Long Road Ahead* and *Escape Hatch*. However strongly they tried to convince themselves that they were ignorant of Stalinist atrocities, as the narrator of *Baize-Covered Table with Decanter* bleakly remarks, the *intelligenty* "knew"; no one is immune from guilt – or judgement.

There are in Makanin's texts moments, digressions, interludes in which he is concerned not so much with the guilt of middle-aged men, as with the lives of legendary figures. These texts – *Golosa* [Voices], *Utrata* [Loss] and *Left Behind* – share a setting, that of the Urals. From his early years spent among the "yellow mountains" of the Urals come violent and vibrant stories in which Makanin attempts to formulate his own concept of the significance of legend. It is linked to several other key ideas in his work, namely, to his rather *derevenshchik* (Village Prose writer) belief in landscape as a morally invigorating force. In *Left Behind*, Makanin focuses on a mountain which, like a stern judge, "rejects" men, "not accepting their assurances or repentant words". In *Left Behind*, the story of the *iurodivyi* (holy fool) Lesha, the "otstavshii" of the title, becomes a Urals legend of a boy with a peculiar talent for finding gold, while in *Utrata*, the bizarre actions of Pekalov, whose obsessive aim in life is to complete a tunnel under the Urals, also becomes the base material of legend. The chapel erected in the "saintly" Pekalov's honour has long since crumbled away, but Pekalov remains in legend; he has achieved his small measure of eternity. The digging motif which dominates *Utrata* takes on a new significance; Pekalov is symbolically attempting, one may argue, to discover his roots, to dig back through the centuries. His digging can also be interpreted psychologically; as he digs backwards in time and his mania strengthens, he confronts the deeper, primeval layers of his own mind.

The idea of the violence "underneath" is a major feature of *Baize-Covered Table with Decanter*. The table featured in the title is a metaphor for the deceptive face of Soviet "justice" during the Stalinist years and later; underneath the table lie the Lubianka cellars in which "justice" is meted out with whips, torture, and rape. Makanin agreed (during an interview in 1995) that the text dealt with the idea that "one should not confuse earthly justice with heavenly". Soviet justice is shown to be completely corrupted; yet for those who are "guilty", those who did not speak out during the Stalinist years and after, there is a higher justice; the protagonist of the text, Kliucharev (who has appeared in four other texts (*Goluboe i krasnoe*, *Povest' o Starom Poselke* [Story about the Old Settlement], *Kliucharev i Alimushkin*, and *Escape Hatch*), is eventually struck down by a heart attack. This is a compelling text, written in stark, uncompromising prose, indicative of Makanin's deserved status as one of the finest of Russia's contemporary writers, one dealing with the essential theme of Russian literature (and, indeed, of Russian society) today – the residue of guilt from the past.

S. Dalton-Brown

Maksim Grek *see* Maxim the Greek

Vladimir Emel'ianovich Maksimov 1930–1995

Novelist, dissident, and publicist

Biography

Born Lev Alekseevich Samsonov in Moscow, 27 November 1930, into a peasant family [other sources: 9 December 1932]. Father was arrested in 1933 and spent subsequent years in prison. Raised in orphanages and detained in institutions for juvenile delinquents, 1945–50. Received professional education as construction worker and mason. Worked in factories and on collective farms throughout the USSR; participated in diamond expeditions in the Taimyr mountains. Began to write in 1952. Collection of early poetry ordered to be destroyed, 1954. First official poetry collection appeared, 1956. Prominence came with inclusion of novella in Paustovskii's almanac *Tarusskie stranitsy*, 1961. Member of Soviet Writers' Union, 1963; member of editorial board of *Oktiabr'*, 1967–68. Protested the Soviet-led invasion of Czechoslovakia in 1968. Several incarcerations in psychiatric hospitals. *Samizdat* publications, early 1970s. Excluded from the Writers' Union, 26 June 1973. Permitted to travel to France, 1974; lost Soviet citizenship, 1975. Lived in Brussels and Paris. Married, two daughters. Founder of the quarterly *Kontinent*, 1974: editor-in-chief until 1992. Active in émigré life and politics. Co-founder, with Vladimir Bukovskii and Eduard Kuznetsov, of the organization Resistance International. Transferred *Kontinent* to Moscow, 1990. Reinstatement of Soviet citizenship, 1991. Joined Union of Russian Writers. Died of cancer in Paris, 26 March 1995.

Publications

Collected Editions

Sobranie sochinenii, 6 vols. Frankfurt, Posev, 1975–79.

Sobranie sochinenii, 9 vols. Moscow, 1993.
Izbrannoe. Moscow, 1994.

Fiction
"My obzhivaem zemliu" [We Make the Earth Habitable], in *Tarusskie stranitsy*, Moscow, 1961.
Zhiv chelovek. Moscow, 1964; translated as *A Man Survives*, by Anselm Hollo, New York, Grove Press, 1963; reprinted Westport, Connecticut, Greenwood Press, 1975.
Shagi k gorizontu. Povesti [Strides to the Horizon. Tales]. Moscow, 1967.
My obzhivaem zemliu. Povesti [We Make the Earth Habitable. Tales]. Moscow, 1970.
Sem' dnei tvoreniia. Frankfurt, Posev, 1971; translated as *The Seven Days of Creation* [no translator named], London, Weidenfeld and Nicolson, 1974; New York, Knopf, 1975; Harmondsworth, Penguin, 1977.
Karantin [Quarantine]. Frankfurt, Posev, 1973.
Proshchanie iz niotkuda. Frankfurt, Posev, 1974; translated as *Farewell from Nowhere*, by Michael Glenny, London, Collins and Harvill Press, 1978; New York, Doubleday, 1979.
Kovcheg dlia nezvanykh. Frankfurt, Posev, 1979; translated as *Ark for the Uncalled*, by Julian Graffy, London and New York, Quartet, 1984.
Saga o nosorogakh [Legend of the Rhinoceroses]. Frankfurt, Posev, 1981.
Chasha iarosti [Proshchanie iz niotkuda, kniga 2] [Cup of Rage]. Frankfurt, Posev, 1982.
Zaglianut' v bezdnu [Looking into the Abyss]. Paris and New York, Tret'ia volna, 1986.
Kochevanie do smerti [Nomadism until Death], in *Izbrannoe*, Moscow, 1994.

Plays
"Stan' za chertu. Drama v trekh deistviiakh" [Stand Behind the Line], *Oktiabr'*, 2 (1967); revised *Novyi zhurnal*, 116–17 (1974), 5–25, 19–44.
P'esy. Frankfurt, Posev, 1979.
"Tam vdali za rekoi. Stseny iz emigrantskoi zhizni" [Far Over the River. Scenes from Émigré Life], *Kontinent*, 68 (1991), 123–66.
"Gde tebia zhdut, angel? Vstrechi v dvukh aktakh, shesti kartinakh" [Where Are They Waiting for You, Angel?], *Kontinent*, 75 (1993), 23–59.

Poetry
Pokolenie na chasakh. Stikhi [A Generation on Guard. Poems]. 1956.

Anthology
Russia's Other Writers. Selections from "Samizdat" Literature, edited by Michael Scammell, New York, Praeger, 1971.

Critical Studies

"Nravstvennyi konflikt v sovremennoi povesti", by Elena Krasnoshchekova, in *Zhanrovo-stilevye iskaniia sovremennoi sovetskoi prozy*, Moscow, 1971, 175–99.
"Krest i kamen'. O romane V. Maksimova *Karantin*", by N. Antonov, *Grani*, 92–93 (1974), 295–310.
"The Search for an Image of Man in Contemporary Soviet Fiction", by Geoffrey Hosking, in *Studies in Twentieth Century Russian Literature: Five Essays*, edited by Christopher J. Barnes, Edinburgh, Scottish Academic Press, and New York, Barnes and Noble, 1976, 61–77.
"The Significance of 'Stan' za chertu' in Vladimir Maksimov's Literary Development", by Anne Hughes, *Journal of Russian Studies*, 36 (1978), 19–29.
"Triptikh V.E. Maksimova: Algebra i garmoniia", by Leonid Rzhevskij, *Grani*, 109 (1978), 229–66.
Beyond Socialist Realism: Soviet Fiction since "Ivan Denisovich", by Geoffrey Hosking, London, Granada, and New York, Holmes and Meier, 1980, 123–35.
A History of Post-War Soviet Writing: The Literature of Moral Opposition, by Grigori Svirski, translated by Robert Dessaix and Michael Ulman, Ann Arbor, Ardis, 1981, 387–97.
Dva pisatelia (Aleksandr Solshenitsyn. Vladimir Maksimov), by A. Krasnov-Levitin, Paris, Poiski, 1983.
V literaturnom zerkale. O tvorchestve Vladimira Maksimova, edited by Dzhemma Kvachevskaia, Paris and New York, Tret'ia volna, 1986.
"Death as a Counterpoint to Life in Maksimov's *The Seven Days of Creation*", by Helen Prochazka, *Modern Language Review*, 84/4 (1989), 885–93.
"Present Imperfect: An Analysis of Time in Maksimov's *Sem' dnei tvoreniia*", by Helen Prochazka, *Modern Language Review*, 87/3 (1992), 652–63.

In histories of Russian literature Vladimir Maksimov's name usually is listed among Russian émigré writers who left the Soviet Union during the Brezhnev period. Yet, this author's world-view and aesthetic profile were distinctly different from the mainstream Third Wave, and his decision demonstratively to abandon communist Russia may well have been a continuation of what was a life of restless wanderings from its very inception. Deprived of family comfort at the age of three and an object of state-enforced care thereafter, young Maksimov reacted with exceptional sensitivity to any threat to his freedom and independence, regardless of whether these threats were Soviet or, later, western. In short stories such as "Zhiv chelovek" ("A Man Survives"), or "Saga o Savve" [The Legend of Savva], Maksimov's hero is the social outsider, ostracized by his environment, and frequently playing the role of the author's *alter ego*. At the end of his life, Maksimov pessimistically summarized his experiences of universal alienation in the novel *Kochevanie do smerti* [Nomadism Until Death], in which the lack of a father and a homeland are the main reasons for sadness and despair.

Born and raised in the Soviet lower depths, Maksimov knew the dark sides of communist reality like few of his literary peers. Not surprisingly, to him the promises of Marxist-Leninist Utopia held hardly any appeal – indeed, his rough and unintellectual background may have rendered Maksimov immune to the verbal manipulation that kept so many of his contemporaries in ideological chains. Rather, the discovery of literature as a medium of self-expression and Christianity as a spiritual guide proved crucial for the shaping of Maksimov's profile as artist and man: in his eyes, writing and religion were inseparably linked. To view literature as a means of truth-seeking and confessing surely was in accordance with 19th-century classics, and Maksimov insisted on continuing that tradition and living up to its high moral criteria. Faith and literature provided him with the stability that he otherwise missed throughout his life. For

Maksimov, as with Dostoevskii and Tolstoi whose example he consciously emulated, both the principles of writing and the principles of life were subject to the strict rules of Christian morality.

A direct outcome of Maksimov's confessional and sermonic philosophy of literature was the focus he put on his own personal experiences. Apart from explicitly autobiographical works such as *Proshchanie iz niotkuda* (*Farewell from Nowhere*), most of Maksimov's major prose works incorporate memories from the author's childhood and youth as well as scenes of contemporary literary life in the Soviet Union and abroad – as if only what the author had gone through himself was regarded worthy of being included in his literary texts. Literary work as personal testimony, but of a higher, socio-spiritual sort, came to fruition in passages of powerful artistic persuasiveness as well as in lamentable lapses of literary taste and verbose self-pity.

Maksimov was rarely successful in creating a coherent overall structure for his works. Not without justification, critics have accused him of "aesthetic unevenness" and an "irregular treatment of time and space". Most of his novels and short stories are composed of diverse text particles, or splinters – intermingled voices of different tonalities, criminal jargon, bureaucratese. Another characteristic feature is the mixture of genres such as legend, biography, play, memoir, letter, diary, proceedings of interrogations and historical article, all under the roof of the vague designation "novel". At best, his narratives resemble mosaics; all too often, however – especially in the 1980s – they give the impression of somewhat amorphous textual montages. For an otherwise traditional writer, this deviation from the classical rules of chronology and spatio-temporal logic seems surprising. However, the "shattered" appearance of Maksimov's prose can be understood as psychologically rooted in his lack of integration – both internal and external – which he lamented on various occasions. (His inability to maintain friendships and the extreme mood swings for which he was known could be explained in similar ways). With the exception of his best works, such as *Sem' dnei tvoreniia* (*The Seven Days of Creation*) and *Karantin* [Quarantine], Maksimov only partially achieved aesthetic syntheses of his visions and intensions. This notwithstanding, the very same inability informed his narratives with an atmosphere of painful disintegration and psychological authenticity, values that geniuses such as Dostoevskii always considered higher than aesthetic elegance. Moreover, Maksimov's gift for imitating speech manners and parodying different styles – in *Karantin*, for example, those of Evtushenko and Akhmadulina – made the satirical parts of his works brilliant.

The farther Maksimov could distance himself from his subject-matter and the more he could avoid an overly personal tone, the more cohesive was the artistic result. In *The Seven Days of Creation*, which is generally considered Maksimov's major achievement, the author balances the montage-like looseness of his material with a rigorous structure based on the title's biblical meaning. Probably the most aesthetically pleasing synthesis of Maksimov's personal vision and his artistic gifts is in *Karantin*. As in *The Seven Days of Creation*, the concise narrative structure is legitimized by a plot idea – an entire train with all its passengers is confined in quarantine because of a cholera epidemic; in other words, all episodes evolve around a central, tightly-knit plot core. The general sardonic tone of narration does not interfere with the historical pathos expressed through the main character, Boris Khramov, whose name and kin Maksimov traces back across one millennium, i.e. to the Christianization of Russia.

By diagnosing Russia's current moral state and attempting to lay bare the origins of that state, Maksimov explored vital questions of Russian history and mentality, especially during those "times of troubles" (*smuta*) of which incredible brutality and anarchism were typical. Statehood was one of the fundamental values of Maksimov's world view, for in Russia more than anywhere else the stability of the state has always been fragile. Maksimov's interpretation of Russian history – a task that he pursued urgently during his emigration – continued in novels such as *Zaglianut' v bezdnu* [Looking into the Abyss], which is devoted to Admiral Kolchak and his futile attempts to create an anti-Bolshevik republic.

In the end, however, Maksimov's original dichotomy of communism versus Christianity was replaced by the hypothesis of a universal plot against Russia; the west was described as a "civilization of rats", while the narrating persona himself was alien everywhere. Shocking to many, Maksimov expressed his disappointment with the west exactly in those newspapers that he had formerly attacked for their atheistic campaigns. After all, it was *Pravda* – turned patriotic and religiously tolerant – that wrote in its positive eulogy that Maksimov "cannot be imagined as an outsider to Russia, Russian literature and the Russian people".

PETER ROLLBERG

The Seven Days of Creation

Sem' dnei tvoreniia

Novel, 1971

Maksimov's first *tamizdat* novel – that is, one to be published by a Russian émigré press – *The Seven Days of Creation* made headlines in the west, served as the pretext for the author's expulsion from the USSR, and to this day has remained the best known of all of Maksimov's works.

The novel consists of six parts, each entitled after a day of the week centred on a different character; only the seventh part, "Sunday", is a one-sentence announcement. Although *The Seven Days of Creation* contains a cluster of characters and biographies, the one to which all other characters are linked in one way or another is Petr Vasil'evich Lashkov, a retired communist functionary in his seventies living in the provincial town of Uzlovsk. His younger daughter, Antonina, is an unhappy alcoholic. Lashkov's other five children left him long ago. Likewise, the connection with his two estranged brothers has been cut almost completely. Yet, the steady deterioration of his family never worried Lashkov since he lost his beloved wife Mariia 20 years ago. Only now, confronted with his daughter's despair, he attempts to analyse his own life and find causes for the family's decay. Major sections of the narrative consist of introspections into Lashkov's thoughts and dreams. The last part, "Sunday", makes it clear that Lashkov's visions are of divine inspiration and lead him toward spiritual cleansing.

In the first part, "Monday", Antonina falls in love with Lashkov's godson Nikolai who was just released from prison where he served a sentence for having beaten a Soviet official.

Lashkov, for the sake of his daughter's happiness, agrees to their marriage and even uses his connections to provide Nikolai with personal documents. Otherwise, Lashkov represents the typical "decent", ascetic communist who would never exploit his position to gain privileges and was unshakably firm in his loyalty to the Party, with one exception, however. In Mariia's lifetime Lashkov tolerated her Christian faith. After public criticism over icons displayed in his home forced him to discuss the matter with his wife, he decided simply to accept the presence of religion in his immediate family.

"Tuesday" describes the fate of Lashkov's brother, Andrei, whose wartime experiences turned him into a recluse, spending his days in Russia's remotest forests. His urban counterpart is Lashkov's second brother, Vasilii, who works as a janitor among quarrelling, scheming, and drinking tenants of a communal apartment in Moscow and whose life is described in "Wednesday". The fourth part, "Thursday", tells about one of Petr Lashkov's grandchildren, Vadim, a talented actor caught up in a tempestuous marriage and ultimately confined to a mental institution. In "Friday", Maksimov follows Antonina and her husband Nikolai to a construction site in the steppes of Central Asia. Nikolai's disgust over a corrupt boss and the suicide of a decent brigadier result in a fight and another prison term, ending Antonina's brief family happiness. In "Saturday", Petr Lashkov succeeds in gaining a passport for his newly released grandson, Vadim, who then decides to join his uncle, Andrei, in seclusion. Lashkov provides shelter to Antonina after her return from Central Asia, and for her new-born. Summing up his life, Petr Lashkov reunites with former foes, among them devoted Christian believers, and finds a new, albeit vague faith beyond his former, communist convictions.

Each of the novel's parts has its own tonality and rhythm. Andrei Lashkov's evacuation of a cattle herd during the war in Part two is saturated with adventuresome action, whereas Vasilii's conflicts in Moscow unfold in the brooding atmosphere of spatial restriction. Antonina and Nikolai's encounters at the construction site are full of dramatic tension, while the chapters devoted to Petr Lashkov's inner growth are filled with philosophical reflection. In the majority of episodes, Maksimov prefers direct one-to-one confrontation between characters; rarely are there more than two people acting in a scene. This structure supports the didactic purpose of the novel and unequivocally expresses its concepts.

Maksimov's forte lies in dramatic dialogues with short, sharp utterances. Also, he impressively depicts apocalyptic landscapes, abandoned villages, and cold dilapidated apartments. Yet whenever Maksimov deals directly with religious subjects, his narrative manner becomes ritualistic and the text itself seems to turn into a sermon. At times, Maksimov's style shows an unfortunate tendency toward wordiness and sentimentality, especially when dealing with love. The flashback technique, which he routinely uses to legitimize a character's inner change, becomes repetitive long before the end of the novel.

Although the autobiographical nature of Vadim's experiences in a mental institution is obvious, Maksimov avoids presenting *The Seven Days of Creation* as a self-aggrandizing martyrology. Primarily, he strives to show the dark side of Soviet reality with which few other authors were even vaguely familiar – provincial tristesse, habitual poverty, dirt, prostitution, cynicism, and mercilessness. He successfully captures the denigration within common morality, diagnosing how Soviet life hardens almost everyone until they reach a breaking-point of either physical self-destruction, passive resignation or madness.

Similar to other works of Soviet dissidents, *The Seven Days of Creation* is an openly didactic novel. But in a number of aesthetic and philosophical aspects it differs from political dissident fiction. Beginning with the explicit biblical references in both title and structure, the novel does not aim as much at exposing the evils of the totalitarian state machine as at presenting modes of spiritual transformation – resembling Tolstoi both in style and message. Decisive turning-points in people's lives are marked by the revelation of absolute truths to rank-and-file Soviet citizens with limited intellectual claim. It seems that, from the author's point of view, the Stalinist bureaucracy and its vices are the result of spiritual impoverishment, and not vice versa.

The Seven Days of Creation can itself be viewed as an act of faith. It is a novel about the Russian people and their chances to rectify their lives in a country in which even the slightest attempts at being happy are destroyed. Also, it is a novel about a doomed society whose ills are irreparable within its own framework. But, above all, *The Seven Days of Creation* is a passionate indictment of the communist Utopia with its promise of "universal idleness and gluttony". True, today Maksimov's belief in the inevitable unity of reason and goodness may seen naive, but his anticipation of a spiritual, rather than economic or political, implosion of Soviet society has proven accurate.

PETER ROLLBERG

Nadezhda Iakovlevna Mandel'shtam 1899–1980

Memoirist

Biography

Born Nadezhda Iakovlevna Khazin in Saratov, 31 October 1899. Daughter of well-educated Jewish lawyer. Educated in Kiev; well-read, spoke several European languages; studied art in the studio of Aleksandra Ekster. Met Osip Mandel'shtam at Kiev cabaret, 1 May 1919; went to Moscow with him, March 1921; married in 1922. Returned to Moscow with husband, lived in Herzen House. Close friendship with Anna Akhmatova, from 1925. Lived "in exile" with husband, 1934–38; then as widow, 1938–64: taught English at the University of Central Asia, Tashkent, during World War II; taught English in provincial towns until she was permitted to return to Moscow. Worked at preservation of husband's works and towards his rehabilitation (1956). Smuggled his archive to Princeton University, 1970s. Died in Moscow, 29 December 1980.

Publications

Memoirs

Vospominaniia. New York, Izdatel'stvo imeni Chekhova, 1970; translated as *Hope Against Hope*, by Max Hayward, New York, Atheneum, 1970; London, Collins and Harvill Press, 1971; Harmondsworth, Penguin, 1975; London, Collins Harvill, 1989.

Vtoraia kniga. Paris, YMCA-Press, 1972; Moscow, 1990; translated as *Hope Abandoned*, by Max Hayward, New York, Atheneum, and London, Harvill Press, 1974; Harmondsworth, Penguin, 1976; London, Collins Harvill, 1989.

Moe zaveshchanie i drugie esse [My Testament and Other Essays]. New York, Serebrianyi vek, 1982.

Tret'ia kniga [The Third Book]. Paris, YMCA-Press, 1987.

Literary Criticism

Mozart and Salieri, translated by Robert A. McLean, Ann Arbor, Ardis, 1973.

Critical Studies

Review of *Hope Abandoned*, by Simon Karlinsky, *New York Times Book Review* (20 January 1974), 1–16.

"The Rhetoric of Nadezhda Mandelshtam's *Hope Against Hope*", by Charles Isenberg, in *New Studies in Russian Language and Literature*, edited by Anna Lisa Crone and Catherine V. Chvany, Columbus, Ohio, Slavica, 1987, 168–82.

The Widows of Russia and Other Writings, by Carl R. Proffer, Ann Arbor, Ardis, 1987.

"The Rhetoric of *Hope Against Hope*", by Charles Isenberg, in *Autobiographical Statements in Twentieth-Century Russian Literature*, edited by Jane Gary Harris, Princeton, Princeton University Press, 1990, 193–206.

Women's Works in Stalin's Time: On Lidiia Chukovskaia and Nadezhda Mandelstam, by Beth Holmgren, Bloomington, Indiana University Press, 1993.

The daughter of a highly educated Jewish lawyer in Kiev, brought up with great indulgence with her two brothers and a sister, Nadezhda Iakovlevna Khazin could hardly have expected the decades of hardship and terror that awaited her. To have been wife and widow to Osip Mandel'shtam was not comparable to being a literary spouse to any other Russian writer. There were no children: it was by nurturing his poetry that she perpetuated her husband's existence. Nadezhda Mandel'shtam's greatest achievement was to memorize, copy, and distribute the later poetry of her husband and the drafts of many earlier works, from his first arrest in 1934 until in the 1970s she finally had his archive smuggled to Princeton University. She thus preserved some 200 poems and half a dozen major pieces of prose that would otherwise have been burnt in the cellars of the Lubianka. The fact of her personal survival, an outcast subject to harassment and arrest, if not extermination, until after the death of Stalin, is another miracle due not just to luck, but to intelligence, perseverance and the high regard that she inspired in the survivors of Stalin's holocaust among the intelligentsia and among ordinary people. It was a mission that saved her from suicide and enabled her to write her memoirs: the first volume is perhaps the finest testament written of life in the Great Terror between Mandel'shtam's first and last arrest, while the second expands in time from her marriage to Mandel'shtam in 1919 to her wanderings after his death. The first volume of memoirs (*Vospominaniia*) was published in English in 1970 as *Hope Against Hope*, the second (*Vtoraia kniga*) as *Hope Abandoned* in 1974. Neither was available in Russia until the 1990s. Their merits are convincingly total recall (largely corroborated by other memoirs, especially fragments from those of Anna Akhmatova) of incidents and conversations, by an acute judgement of character that can be coruscating or charitable, by a highly perceptive understanding of the mechanics of totalitarianism, both within the state and inside the minds of those who are forced to surrender to it. Central to Nadezhda Mandel'shtam's argument is a philosophy of survival not by a dignified surrender to the firing-squad, but by the victims' undignified screams of protest at the monstrous crimes and violence against them. Solzhenitsyn's *Arkipelag GULag* (*Gulag Archipelago*) or Robert Conquest's *The Great Terror* are statistical, representative contrasts to this highly personal, concrete and subjective view of the processes of Stalinism. Nadezhda gives a uniquely lucid account of the interdependence of the Bolsheviks, whether Bukharin or Ezhov, and the intellectuals, whether Mandel'shtam or Babel', both as privileged citizens and as victims of the extermination process.

The memoirs are valuable as adjuncts to literary biography, particularly in their portrait of the highly strung, witty and infinitely bereaved Anna Akhmatova, who emerges, together with the critic Viktor Shklovskii, as a latter-day saint in her moral courage. A composite picture emerges of the Russian class system, from the intelligentsia and the peasantry to the new version of the bureaucrat and secret policeman created by the Revolution, giving the memoirs considerable historical and sociological value. Nadezhda Mandel'shtam insists, despite the horrors and betrayals, that she is an optimist. The vignettes of the last months of her marriage, begging money from terrified friends, do in fact show unsuspected sparks of generosity and courage and make the chapters of nemesis surprisingly bright.

For the reader of Mandel'shtam's Voronezh poems, the memoirs are an indispensable tool; not only do they explain the original structure of the *Voronezhskie tetradi* (*The Voronezh Notebooks*), but the role of the variants, the "twins" and "triplets" among the poems, and the realia and allusions on which a comprehension of these often hermeneutic poems depend. Nadezhda Mandel'shtam's role was not only to listen to and commit to memory her husband's poems, she often observed, even before the poet himself, their gradual birth from a jumble of words or the trigger of an experience. Moreover, her complete lack of embarrassment or false pride enabled her to give a frank, even humorous account of the other loves (notably Ol'ga Vaksel') in Mandel'shtam's life, solving a number of riddles behind his finest love poems. A similar lack of inhibition is applied to members of the family, some of whom preferred to forget the connection once the secret police had chosen their victim.

Nadezhda Mandel'shtam in some ways was more widely educated than her husband; she became an expert in English language and literature and many of her comparisons of Russian poetry, for instance to Keats or John Donne, shed new light on the metaphysical and Neoclassical aspects of Mandel'shtam's poetry.

Nadezhda Mandel'shtam composed her memoirs in the late 1950s and 1960s, intending to publish them only when the approach of death guaranteed her against reprisals. In the event, they won so much international acclaim that the Brezhnev regime was unable to take action against her, and the mutilated selection of her husband's poetry that had been set up in type as early as 1959 was finally allowed into print in 1973. The result was ironic, for the full, properly annotated four-volume edition that had been compiled and edited by Gleb Struve with active, but covert, assistance from Nadezhda put the belated, censored Soviet edition to shame.

After her death, *Tret'ia kniga* [The Third Book] (1987) was assembled from Nadezhda Iakovlevna's unpublished writings. It includes some prose sketches that the author had printed under the pseudonym of Iakovleva in the 1961 collection *Tarusskie stranitsy* [Pages from Tarusa], and an essay called *Mozart and Salieri* that echoes Anna Akhmatova's opinion that Pushkin saw himself not as a carefree Mozart but as a struggling Salieri, but develops into a fine study of Pushkin as Akhmatova and Mandel'shtam understood him. Apart from Nadezhda Iakovlevna's letters to Nikita Struve and others in the west, the other value of this compilation is a series of notes on the origins and allusions of many of the more cryptic poems composed by Osip Mandel'shtam in the 1920s and 1930s. Few poets would choose to be commemorated by the memoirs of their widow; Mandel'shtam, however, is a poet for an understanding of whom a reading of his widow's works is an essential aid.

DONALD RAYFIELD

Osip Emil'evich Mandel'shtam 1891–1938

Poet, prose writer, literary critic, and translator

Biography

Born in Warsaw, Poland, 15 January 1891; moved to St Petersburg as an infant. Attended Tenishev School, St Petersburg, 1900–07. Travelled to Paris, 1907–08, and to Germany, 1908–10; studied Old French literature at the University of Heidelberg, 1909–10; studied philosophy at St Petersburg University, 1911–17: did not graduate. First poems published in the journal *Apollon*, August 1910. Member of "The Poets' Guild", 1911; close personal ties with Anna Akhmatova and Nikolai Gumilev. Welcomed February 1917 Revolution; hostile at first to October 1917 Revolution. Worked for Lunacharskii's Education Ministry, 1918. Married: Nadezhda Iakovlevna Khazin in 1922. Translated works by Upton Sinclair, Jules Romains, Charles de Coster, and others in the 1920s. Wrote a poem critical of Stalin in 1933; arrested 1934; intercession of Akhmatova, Bukharin, and Pasternak led to light sentence of three years' exile in Cherdyn; after suicide attempt, sentence commuted to exile in Voronezh, ending in 1937. Arrested again in May 1938, sentenced to five years in a labour camp for "counter-revolutionary activity". Died in a transit camp at Vtoraia rechka, near Vladivostok, 27 December 1938.

Publications

Collected Editions

Sobranie sochinenii, edited by Gleb Struve. New York, Izdatel'stvo imeni Chekhova, 1955.

The Prose of Osip Mandelstam, edited and translated by Clarence Brown. Princeton, Princeton University Press, 1965; corrected edition, 1967; revised as *The Noise of Time of Osip Mandelstam*, San Francisco, North Point Press, 1986; as *The Noise of Time and Other Prose Pieces*, London, Quartet, 1988.

Sobranie sochinenii, edited by Gleb Struve and Boris Filippov, 4 vols. 1967–81; vol. 1 revised, Washington DC, 1967; vol. 2 revised, New York, 1971; vol. 3, New York, 1969 [all] Inter-Language Literary Associates; vol. 4, edited by Nikita Struve *et al.*, Paris, YMCA-Press, 1981.

Complete Poetry, translated by Burton Raffel and Alla Burago.

Albany, New York, State University of New York Press, 1973.

Stikhotvoreniia. Leningrad, 1973; reprinted 1974, 1978, 1979.

The Complete Critical Prose and Letters, edited by Jane Gary Harris, translated by Harris and Constance Link. Ann Arbor, Ardis, 1979; as *The Collected Critical Prose and Letters*, London, Collins Harvill, 1991; revised and shortened as *The Complete Critical Prose*, Ann Arbor, Ardis, 1997.

Sochineniia, 2 vols. Moscow, 1990.

Sobranie proizvedenii. Moscow, 1992.

Sobranie sochinenii, 4 vols. Moscow, 1993–94.

Polnoe sobranie stikhotvorenii. "Novaia Biblioteka poeta", St Petersburg, 1995.

Poetry

Kamen'. St Petersburg, 1913; revised and augmented edition, Petrograd, 1916; as *Pervaia kniga stikhov*, Moscow and Petrograd, 1923; translated as *Stone* (bilingual edition), by Robert Tracy, Princeton, Princeton University Press, 1981; reprinted London, Collins Harvill, 1991.

Tristia. Petrograd and Berlin, 1922; as *Vtoraia kniga*, Moscow and Petrograd, 1923; translated as *Tristia*, by Bruce McClelland, Barrytown, New York, Station Hill Press, 1986.

Stikhotvoreniia. Moscow and Leningrad, 1928.

Moskovskie tetradi. (written 1930–34); translated as *The Moscow Notebooks*, by Richard and Elizabeth McKane, Newcastle upon Tyne, Bloodaxe, 1991.

Selected Poems, translated by Clarence Brown and W.S. Merwin. London, Oxford University Press, 1973; reprinted Harmondsworth, Penguin, 1977.

Selected Poems (bilingual edition), translated by David McDuff. Cambridge, Rivers Press, 1973; reprinted London, Writers and Readers, 1983.

"Chapter 42" by Nadezhda Mandel'shtam and "The Goldfinch" and Other Poems by Osip Mandel'shtam, translated by Donald Rayfield. London, Menard Press, 1973.

Octets, translated by John Riley. Lumb Bank, Yorkshire, Grosseteste Press, 1976.

50 Poems, translated by Bernard Meares. New York, Persea, 1977.

Poems, translated by James Greene. London, Elek, 1977; revised edition, London, Granada, 1980; expanded edition as *The Eyesight of Wasps*, London, Angel, 1989; revised edition, as *Selected Poems*, Harmondsworth, Penguin, 1991.

Voronezhskie tetradi, edited by V. Shveitser. Ann Arbor, Ardis, 1980; translated as "The Voronezh Notebooks", by Donald Rayfield, *Russian Literature Triquarterly*, 11 (1975), 323–62; also as *The Voronezh Notebooks: Poems 1935–1937*, by Richard and Elizabeth McKane, Newcastle upon Tyne, Bloodaxe, 1996.

Poems from Mandelstam, translated by R.H. Morrison. Rutherford, New Jersey, Fairleigh Dickinson University Press, and London, Associated University Presses, 1990.

Sokhrani moiu rech': mandel'shtamovskii sbornik [Preserve My Speech: A Mandel'shtam Collection]. Moscow, 1991; No. 2, Moscow, 1993.

A Necklace of Bees: Selected Poems, translated by Maria Enzensberger. London, Menard Press, and Berkeley, SPD, 1992.

Fiction

Shum vremeni. Leningrad, 1925; translated as "The Noise of Time", by Clarence Brown, in *The Prose of Osip Mandelstam*, 1965.

"Egipetskaia marka", *Zvezda*, 5 (1928), 51–76; translated as "The Egyptian Stamp", by Clarence Brown, in *The Prose of Osip Mandelstam*, 1965.

Egipetskaia marka. Leningrad, 1928 [includes "Shum vremeni", "Feodisiia"].

Chetvertaia proza. 1930; translated as "Fourth Prose", by Clarence Brown, in *The Prose of Osip Mandelstam*, 1965; and by Jane Gary Harris and Constance Link, in *The Complete Critical Prose and Letters*, 1979.

Literary Criticism

O poezii [On Poetry]. Leningrad, 1928.

Razgovor o Dante. Moscow, 1967; translated as "Conversation about Dante", by Jane Gary Harris, in *The Complete Critical Prose and Letters*, 1979.

Essays and Travel Writing

"Puteshestvie v Armeniiu", *Zvezda*, 5 (1933), 103–25; translated as "Journey to Armenia", by Clarence Brown, *Quarterly Review of Literature*, 17/3–4 (1973); revised edition, London, Faber, 1980; reprinted London, Redstone Press, 1989; also translated by Sidney Monas, San Francisco, G.F. Ritchie, 1979.

Selected Essays, edited and translated by Sidney Monas. Austin, University of Texas Press, 1977.

Proza [Prose]. Ann Arbor, Ardis, 1983.

Slovo i kul'tura [The Word and Culture]. Moscow, 1987.

Chetvertaia proza. Ocherki, sbornik [Fourth Prose. Essays, Collection]. Moscow, 1991.

Critical Studies

Vospominaniia, by Nadezhda Mandel'shtam, New York, Izdatel'stvo imeni Chekhova, 1970; translated as *Hope Against Hope: A Memoir*, by Max Hayward, New York, Atheneum, 1970; London, Harvill Press, 1971; Harmondsworth, Penguin, 1975; London, Collins Harvill, 1989.

Vtoraia kniga, by Nadezhda Mandel'shtam, Paris, YMCA-Press, 1972; Moscow, 1990; translated as *Hope Abandoned*, by Max Hayward, New York, Atheneum, and London, Harvill Press, 1974; Harmondsworth, Penguin, 1976; London, Collins Harvill, 1989.

Osip Mandelstam, by Clarence Brown, Cambridge, Cambridge University Press, 1973.

Osip Emilievich Mandelstam: An Essay in Antiphon, by Arthur A. Cohen, Ann Arbor, Ardis, 1974.

A Concordance to the Poems of Osip Mandelstam, by Demetrius J. Koubourlis, Ithaca, Cornell University Press, 1974.

Osip Mandel'stam: Five Poems, by Nils Åke Nilsson, Stockholm, Almqvist & Wiksell, 1974.

Osip Mandelstam and His Age: A Commentary on the Themes of War and Revolution in the Poetry 1913–1923, by Steven Broyde, Cambridge, Massachusetts, Harvard University Press, 1975.

"The Poetics of Osip Mandelstam", by Lidiia Ginzburg,

translated by Sona Hoisington, in *Twentieth-Century Russian Literary Criticism*, edited by Victor Erlich, New Haven, Yale University Press, 1975, 284–312.
"Mandelstam's Voronezh Poetry", by Donald Rayfield, *Russian Literature Triquarterly*, 11 (1975), 323–62.
"Fragment semanticheskoi poetiki O.E. Mandel'shtama", by D.M. Segal, *Russian Literature*, 10–11 (1975), 59–146.
Mandelstam: The Later Poetry, by Jennifer Baines, Cambridge, Cambridge University Press, 1976.
Essays on Mandelstam, by Kiril Taranovsky, Cambridge, Massachusetts, Harvard University Press, 1976.
"Zametki o poezii O. Mandel'shtama tridtsatykh godov. I", and "Zametki o poezii O. Mandel'shtama tridtsatykh godov. II ('Stikhi o neizvestnom soldate')", by Yu.I. Levin, *Slavica Hierosolymitana*, 3 (1978), 110–73; 4 (1979), 185–213.
Mandelstam: The Egyptian Stamp, by Daphne M. West, Birmingham, Birmingham Slavonic Monographs, 1980.
Nightingale Fever: Russian Poets in Revolution, by Ronald Hingley, New York, Knopf, 1981; London, Weidenfeld and Nicolson, 1982.
Poets of Modern Russia, by Peter France, Cambridge and New York, Cambridge University Press, 1982, 99–131.
Osip Mandelstam, by Nikita Struve, Paris, Institut d'Études Slaves, 1982; Russian edition as *Osip Mandel'shtam*, London, Overseas Publications Interchange, 1988; revised edition, 1990.
An Approach to Mandelstam, by Omry Ronen, Jerusalem, Magnes Press, 1983.
Osip Mandelstam. "Als rife man mich bei meinem Namen". Dialog mit Frankreich, by Ralph Dutli, Zurich, Ammann, 1985.
"The Child of Civilization", by Joseph Brodsky, in his *Less than One: Selected Essays*, New York, Farrar Straus and Giroux, and London, Viking, 1986; Harmondsworth, Penguin, 1987, 123–44.
Novoe o Mandel'shtame. Glavy iz vospominanii. O.E. Mandel'shtam v voronezhskoi ssylke (po pis'mam S.B. Rudakova), by Emma G. Gershtein, Paris, Atheneum, 1986.
Poetry in a Divided World, by Henry Gifford, Cambridge and New York, Cambridge University Press, 1986.
Substantial Proofs of Being: Osip Mandelstam's Literary Prose, by Charles Isenberg, Columbus, Ohio, Slavica, 1986.
A Coat of Many Colors: Osip Mandelstam and His Mythologies of Self-Presentation, by Gregory Freidin, Berkeley, University of California Press, 1987.
God's Grateful Guest: An Essay on the Poetry of Osip Mandelstam, by Ryszard Przybylski, translated by Madeline G. Levine, Ann Arbor, Ardis, 1987.
Tret'ia Kniga [The Third Book], by Nadezhda Mandel'shtam, Paris, YMCA-Press, 1987.
Osip Mandelstam, by Jane Gary Harris, Boston, Twayne, 1988.
"Osip and Nadezhda Mandelstam", by Seamus Heaney, in his *The Government of the Tongue*, London, Faber, and New York, Farrar Straus and Giroux, 1988.
The Later Poetry of Osip Mandelstam: Text and Context, by Peter Zeeman, Amsterdam, Rodopi, 1988.
Mirovozzrenie Osipa Mandel'shtama, by Sof'ia F. Margolina, Marburg, Blaue Hörner, 1989.
Zhizn' i tvorchestvo O.E. Mandel'shtama, edited by O.G. Lasunskii *et al.*, Voronezh, Izdatel'stvo voronezhskogo universiteta, 1990.
Slovo i sud'ba: Osip Mandel'shtam. Issledovaniia i materialy, edited by Z.S. Papernyi *et al.*, Moscow, 1991.
"Poet i kul'tura: Tri poetiki Osipa Mandel'shtama", by M.L. Gasparov, *De visu*, 10, 11 (1993), 39–70; reprinted in *Izbrannye stat'i*, Moscow, 1995, 327–70.
Stoletie Mandel'shtama: Materialy simpoziuma / Mandelstam Centenary Conference (Materials from the Mandelstam Centenary Conference, London 1991), edited by Robin Aizlewood and Diana Myers, Tenafly, New Jersey, Hermitage, 1994.
"En Masse: A Chronicle of the Last Days of Osip Mandelshtam", by Pavel Markovich Nerler, translated by Linda Tapp, in *Manoa: A Pacific Journal of International Writing* (Hawaii), 6/2 (Winter 1994), 182–205.
Osip Mandelstam and the Modernist Creation of Tradition, by Clare Cavanagh, Princeton, Princeton University Press, 1995.
The Acmeist Movement in Russian Poetry: Culture and the Word, by Justin Doherty, Oxford, Clarendon Press, and New York, Oxford University Press, 1995.
Mandel'shtam i antichnost', edited by O. Lekmanov, Moscow, 1995.
Mandelstam the Reader, by Nancy Pollak, Baltimore, Johns Hopkins University Press, 1995.
The KGB's Literary Archive, by Vitaly Shentalinsky, translated by John Crowfoot, London, Harvill Press, 1995.

Osip Mandel'shtam is probably the greatest Russian poet of the 20th century. He has "come to define the fullest complement of features making up Russia's symbolic authorial figure" (Gregory Freidin). However, the view of "our century's literary martyr" (Bruce Chatwin) propagated by the "Mandel'shtam myth", although not incorrect in its most important details, does not tell the whole story. Many accounts of Mandel'shtam's poetry place undue emphasis on the works published during his lifetime, even though many of his greatest poems are contained in the two *Moskovskie tetradi* (*The Moscow Notebooks*) (1930–31 and 1932–34) and in the *Voronezhskie tetradi* (*The Voronezh Notebooks*) (April 1935–May 1937), poems that differ in significant respects from the poems of *Kamen'* (*Stone*) and *Tristia*. The widely-held view of Mandel'shtam as a consistent opponent of the Soviet system is also an over-simplification: the problem facing critics is not only to trace Mandel'shtam's ever-changing attitudes to the Revolution, but to decide what significance should be attached to certain "pro-Soviet" poems, in particular his epigram to Stalin (1937).

Mandel'shtam's poetry is often viewed as "a poetry of poetry"; as pure, other-worldly lyricism far removed from politics and history; as classically controlled and coldly impersonal. Such characterizations can be applied to the earlier poetry only with major reservations, and hardly at all to the later poetry, which formally and thematically is open-ended, unconventional, subversive. In the later poetry the "poetic impulse" may be embodied in "twin" or "triplet" poems, poems that are linked but distinct; these poems may in turn form cycles, and the collections as a whole form a "lyric diary". Iosif Brodskii rightly noted that "the immense intensity of lyricism in Mandel'shtam's poetry ... set him apart"; yet history, politics, and the poet's personal experience all fuse in the complex intertextual constructs of the later poems, resulting in "an extension ... for the lyrical mode, through being constantly aware of private experience in the light of history" (Henry Gifford).

Conflict, ambiguity, paradox lie at the heart of both Mandel'shtam's life and his "poetics of contradiction" (Sergei Averintsev). For Mandel'shtam, the lyric poet "is a hermaphrodite by nature, capable of limitless fissions in the name of his inner dialogue". Mandel'shtam conducts this dialogue by intertextual means: like the Dante of his *Razgovor o Dante* (*Conversation about Dante*) 1933, a supreme act of literary criticism that is even more valuable as Mandel'shtam's own *ars poetica* and as a guide to the later poetry, he is a master of the "keyboard of references". In his autobiographical prose work *Shum vremeni* (*The Noise of Time*) 1925, Mandel'shtam describes how he fled the "Judaic chaos" of his origins. Socially and culturally an outsider, Mandel'shtam followed Chaadaev in having a "profound, ineradicable demand for unity, for higher historical synthesis" ("Petr Chaadaev", 1915). He sought to satisfy his need for unity (the Acmeist "longing for world culture") first in Rome, then in Orthodoxy. Yet even the Acmeist "manifesto-poem" "Notre Dame" (1912), does not try to conceal that chaotic, Dionysian forces are present even in Mandel'shtam's most Apollonian verse.

Tristia depicts a dying age, but the articles Mandel'shtam wrote during the first years of Soviet power are an attempt to reconcile his "Hellenized" version of Christianity with Soviet "humanism". The "Poems of 1921–25" (the final section of the 1928 volume *Stikhotvoreniia*), however, reveal fears that the articles, optimistically, try to ignore. These poems are a profound investigation of "the pervasive historical theme of Mandel'shtam's poetry and prose, the enigmatic relationship between Time, Society (State), and the Word" (Omry Ronen). "Grifel'naia oda" ("The Slate Ode") (1923) and the elegy "1 ianvaria 1924" ("1 January 1924") express the hope that the poetic word can still be a talisman and the need to accept the path of martyrdom that is the destiny of the greatest Russian writers.

Unable to resolve his ideological and poetic crisis in verse, Mandel'shtam turned to prose: no poems were written from 1925 to 1930. This may indicate that Mandel'shtam had lost the "consciousness of being right" that he saw as an essential for the poet; or that he needed to feel his way towards a new poetry via prose. His *Egipetskaia marka* (*The Egyptian Stamp*) is "a quasi-surrealistic ... shoring of fragments against the ruins of a vanishing St Petersburg" (Donald Fanger). A highly original reworking of the Gogolian/Dostoevskian theme of the "little man", it is ambiguously poised between self-mockery and self-affirmation.

In 1928 Mandel'shtam was unfairly accused of plagiarism, but the ensuing scandals set in motion a sequence of events – a trip to Armenia (described in *Puteshestvie v Armeniiu* [*Journey to Armenia*]), a positive re-evaluation of his Jewishness (Mandel'shtam describes the pride he now takes in "the honourable title Jew" in *Chetvertaia proza* [Fourth Prose]), and an increased, almost mystical identification with Pushkin's fate – which together seem to have caused his poetry to return in late 1930. Mandel'shtam now sees the outsider and his "unauthorized works" (which are "stolen air") as the only source of true culture. Yet although many of his poems reveal a new defiant independence, some of his doubts still persist: as Gregory Freidin notes, "many of Mandel'shtam's poems of 1931–32 display an ambiguous attitude to the Stalin revolution". The variety and quality of the poems in *The Moscow Notebooks* astound: they include poems about Armenia; grotesque allegories; Mandel'shtam's meditations on his role in the new society. Mandel'shtam writes about his favourite poets ("Batiushkov", "Ariosto") and about the German, Italian, and Russian languages. The complex "Octets" explore poetic cognition; a number of poems form an intertextual dialogue with Pasternak on the role of the poet, with Pushkin the ultimate point of reference.

The poems in memory of Andrei Belyi that conclude *The Moscow Notebooks* betray Mandel'shtam's certainty that the Stalin epigram, already recited to a few friends, would lead to his own death too. No doubt the shock of arrest and interrogation, and gratitude that his life had been spared, account in part for some of the "loyalist" poems of the Voronezh years; but one should see the vacillations in Mandel'shtam's views as a continuation of the quarrel with himself that was the source of his poetry. The greater quantity and quality of the poems critical of the regime suggests, however, that Mandel'shtam's dialogic search for the truth does not represent a significant threat to the "Mandel'shtam myth".

Through his identification with Dante and other writers and with the kenotic tradition of self-sacrifice of the Russian intelligentsia, and above all through his imitation of Pushkin and Christ, Mandel'shtam achieved the aim he had set himself in his article "Pushkin i Skriabin" (1917?). The image he constructed in life and art (reinforced by Nadezhda Mandel'shtam's memoirs) enabled him to become in death, like Skriabin, "a national symbol", and his death to become "the supreme act" of "his creative activity", in that "the death of an artist should not be excluded from the chain of his creative achievements, but should be viewed as its final, closing link". Eloquent testimony to Mandel'shtam's achievement is his influence on so many major writers, most crucially on Iosif Brodskii and Paul Celan, and, more importantly, on the spiritual and cultural life of the Soviet Union: in Brodskii's words, the Mandel'shtams' exemplary fusion of life and art shows that poetry can make something happen. "Only when one reads, for example, how the friends of Mandel'shtam and Akhmatova risked their own lives to take custody of a few scraps of verse, is it possible to realise fully what poetry can mean" (Henry Gifford).

ANDREW REYNOLDS

Stone

Kamen'

Poetry collection, 1913

Stone appeared in four different versions during Mandel'shtam's lifetime, three times in separate editions (1913, 1916 and 1923), and once as a section of his Collected Poems (1928). The slim volume that was published in 1913 was augmented considerably in the second edition, and Mandel'shtam subsequently continued both to add and to remove poems. Even as late as 1937 he was still reconsidering the content of the book. Nevertheless, the essential character of *Stone* was preserved through each of the revisions and it is reasonable to see it as an adequate reflection of the themes and manner of the first phase of Mandel'shtam's poetry.

The publication of the first edition of *Stone* in 1913 coincided with the formal establishment of the Acmeist group of writers and the appearance of the manifestos of the new movement in the journal *Apollon*. Mandel'shtam's book was thus widely seen as an illustration of the tenets and possibilities of Acmeism. As such it earned considerable critical recognition and established its author as a major figure in post-Symbolist Russian literature.

In actual fact, *Stone* marks a passage from the Symbolist-influenced poems of Mandel'shtam's literary apprenticeship towards a new humanist aesthetic. This stands out particularly clearly in the 1913 edition where roughly half of the poems were conceived before the elaboration of Acmeism. The development is highlighted by Mandel'shtam's general practice of arranging poems within a book in chronological order of composition. In his review, indeed, Gumilev even went so far as to locate the transition from Symbolism to Acmeism in a single poem of 1912, in which Mandel'shtam denies that the luminous clock-face on a public building has any connection with the moon, or indeed with anything at all outside itself: "No, it is not the moon, but a bright clock-face" ("Net, ne luna, a svetlyi tsiferblat").

Mandel'shtam's "Symbolist" writing eschews the religious framework generally espoused by the movement, but nevertheless focuses on an unknowable absolute in poems such as "Rakovina" ("Sea Shell") or "Silentium", which see poetry as a reflection of a universal force, whether primeval chaos or universal silence. Abstractions of this sort are regularly couched in characteristically Symbolist images of light and the abyss and through the acoustic patterning (particularly assonance) also associated with Symbolism. Patterns of all types are a major stylistic and thematic motif and regularly stand as a metaphor for poetic creativity.

The transition to Acmeism was not, of course, a clean break. Cultural activity and the role of literature and art continue to be Mandel'shtam's principal area of concern. However, the Symbolist rhetoric drops away and the source of the order imposed on the world by the creation of literary and artistic patterns is no longer a vague mystical space, but human ingenuity and endeavour. As Mandel'shtam puts it, the poets of the new movement would only ascend such towers as they could build themselves. Mandel'shtam's early abstraction is replaced, again according to the tenets of his manifesto, by a greater concentration on the concrete, by attention to both sound and meaning in poetic vocabulary.

The clearest verse statement of the Acmeist aesthetic is found in the famous series of "architectural" poems, in which the tangibility of stone replaces the fleeting impressionism of music that so fascinated the Symbolists. Mandel'shtam examines great monuments of European civilization such as the Byzantine cathedral of Hagia Sophia in Constantinople or Notre Dame in Paris or, closer to home, the Admiralty building in St Petersburg, and sees these complex aesthetic units as expressions of the triumph of the human will. Yet although they are seen as autonomous structures and without analogues in any mystical world, these buildings nevertheless possess considerable emotional power. Not only do they represent human achievement in a political sense, there exists too a "fifth element" that supersedes and encompasses the traditional categories of earth, water, air, and fire. This fifth element is to be found in the implicit assertion of the continuity of the cultural heritage that they represent, and this demonstrable power of art to transform provides a permanent confirmation of the validity of Mandel'shtam's own calling as a poet.

Mandel'shtam once defined Acmeism as "a nostalgia for world culture". Certainly his poetic practice in his early verse was to refer very widely to earlier writers and cultural figures. In *Stone* he commemorates the aesthetic power exercised not only by the great artists of the past, but also by an array of thinkers as diverse as Ossian, Wagner, Dickens and Luther, through whom he likewise asserts his own faith in the transcendency of art. Many poems in *Stone* evoke the classical world, and particularly that of ancient Rome. What attracts Mandel'shtam above all is the triumphant grandeur of Roman classical architecture, and also its reflection in the Neoclassicism of 18th-century Russia.

There is a sense too in which the poems follow a classical rhetorical model. Occasionally, Mandel'shtam will imitate, for example, the hexameters of Russian Neoclassical verse, but more significantly his emphasis on patterns and description leads him into a clarity of exposition that reflects the confidence of his vision. As a result, notwithstanding the importance of metaphor in the poems of *Stone*, they sometimes appear overly schematic, particularly when compared to Mandel'shtam's more mature work.

DAVID N. WELLS

Tristia

Poetry collection, 1922

Tristia first appeared in 1922, and was widely acknowledged as marking a new stage in Mandel'shtam's poetry and as a major achievement for Russian poetry. Its title was apparently not chosen by Mandel'shtam himself but by his editor, and when a second edition was published in 1923 it bore the prosaic name *Vtoraia kniga* [Second Book]. *Tristia* however, was restored for the collection's third (abbreviated) appearance during the poet's lifetime in the 1928 Collected Poems.

The poems of *Tristia* were written between 1916 and 1920 (a single poem of 1921 appeared in the first edition only), a time when Russian society was undergoing a rapid process of transformation. *Tristia* is thus on one level a reflection of Mandel'shtam's response to the events of World War I, to the Revolutions of 1917 and to the Civil War that followed them. At the same time it represents a continuation and a development of the philosophical and aesthetic concerns of *Stone* and an expansion of its reliance on the trope of metaphor.

Mandel'shtam had paid little attention to current events in *Stone*, but in *Tristia* there are several prominent poems that analyse revolutionary events more or less explicitly. Mandel'shtam's attitude to these events is deeply ambivalent: while in poems such as "Sumerki svobody" [The Twilight of Freedom] he recognizes a major historical turning-point has been reached, he remains fearful that more will be lost than will be gained. Above all he is concerned for the loss of cultural continuity that the upheaval implies.

Although, as in *Stone*, creativity itself remains the most prominent theme, in *Tristia* the sharpness of Mandel'shtam's vision is less definite, and doubt is cast on his ability to capture the poetic image. This hesitation is most succinctly expressed in the first line of the poem "I have forgotten the word that I wanted to say", but recurs in a wide variety of forms. There is never any question, however, that the patterns of art have disappeared: the poet is still able to discern them even if they escape from his grasp. The role of memory and recognition in preserving the cultural tradition become accordingly of paramount importance as Mandel'shtam attempts to escape from the "burden of time".

Perhaps because of this the number of classical references in *Tristia* is even greater than in *Stone*, though it is predominantly Greece to which Mandel'shtam now refers. The connection between the classical world and contemporary Russia is rendered all the more apparent by the juxtaposition of elements from the two semantic spheres. In making this connection Mandel'shtam draws on the historical presence of ancient Greek civilization in the Crimea. Yet the identification between Russia and ancient Greece is often uncomfortable. One link that is repeatedly stressed, and is implicit in the phonetic similarity of the words, is that between St Petersburg (or in the Neoclassical form also used by Mandel'shtam, Petropol') and the figure of Persephone/Proserpine. In mythology, Persephone is an ambivalent figure, being associated both with death and the underworld and with the coming of spring in the world above. She thus simultaneously represents both decay and renewal. It is the deathly aspect of Persephone that dominates in *Tristia*, and even when she is not mentioned directly her presence can be felt through reference to her traditional attributes, and notably in the phonetically related word *prozrachnyi* (transparent), which itself comes to represent death.

Another dominant motif in *Tristia* is the notion of exile. The banishment of Persephone to the realm of Hades for six months of the year is, of course, itself a form of exile, but Mandel'shtam's fear of being cut off from the cultural tradition is reflected in numerous other examples of the topos as well. Thus his excursions into the history of Russia focus on the expulsion from Moscow in the late 16th century of the tsarevich Dmitrii, or the Siberian fate of the Decembrist conspirators of 1825. The title *Tristia*, which is also the title of one of the central poems of the collection, alludes to the book of elegies of the same name written by Ovid in lament at his exile from Rome to what was for him the cultural wilderness of the Black Sea. The repeated motif of the black or buried sun, apart from its negative significance in terms of the mythology of regeneration, also has literary associations. Not only does it evoke Gérard de Nerval's famous image of despair in his sonnet "El Desdichado", but it also refers to the figure of Aleksandr Pushkin. Pushkin was widely known as the "sun" of Russian poetry, but his genius was not universally appreciated by his contemporaries. In his essay "Pushkin i Skriabin" [Pushkin and Skriabin], Mandel'shtam refers explicitly to Pushkin's furtive interment by the authorities to avoid drawing public attention to his death as the burial of the sun. In the poetry of *Tristia* the Pushkinian tradition is seen as similarly obscured by the political process.

However, for all this negative imagery, the promise of regeneration contained in the Persephone myth is not altogether forgotten. In several poems the Greek goddess is specifically associated with the creation of poetry. The poet is still able to envisage the resurrection of the sun in the "black velvet of the Soviet night". And indeed the structure of Mandel'shtam's own verse itself constitutes an affirmation of cultural continuity. Its complex mythopoeic constructions and its insistent reference to other literary works are matched by an equally sophisticated exploitation of the possibilities of syntactic and phonetic organization. The chiselled expository style of *Stone* comes to be replaced by a discourse based on the logic of association as one image merges into another. While remaining within the thematic realm of contemporary actuality and in his metaphors preferring the concrete over the abstract, Mandel'shtam in *Tristia* returns to many of the stylistic devices championed by the Symbolists. In particular he pays close attention to the appropriateness of sound patterning in conveying specific images and often relies on the repetition of key sounds, phrases or images for the propagation of his ideas.

DAVID N. WELLS

The Voronezh Notebooks

Voronezhskie tetradi

Poetry cycles, written 1935–37

The poetry that Mandel'shtam wrote from 1935 to 1937 while in exile in Voronezh was written in three cycles: Mandel'shtam was unpublished in Russia between his first arrest in 1934 and his posthumous rehabilitation, and these 80 or so poems were known only to a handful of people closest to him. Their appearance in the west and (fragmentarily) in Russia in the early 1960s caused amazement and shock, so different – often harsh, heterogeneous, elliptic, even obscure – do they seem in manner from the earlier Mandel'shtam. They are now recognized as equal to his greatest work and may be regarded as the most important poetry of the terrified silence of the 1930s in Russia and, arguably, the most important work inspired by a 20th-century holocaust.

The first "notebook" is the product of the spring and summer of 1935: after a year's silence the poet recovered from the psychological illness brought on by his arrest and he incorporates the certainty of his imminent extinction and the alien black-earth landscape of central Russia into his poetics. These lyrics are far from being mere landscape poems to map his journey to the forests of the Urals and the steppe that borders Voronezh, yet they do function as an autobiographical record. Inspired by music (a violinist playing Paganini, a singer of Schubert Lieder) or by private and public tragedies (the death of Ol'ga Vaksel' or the murder of Kirov), these 19 poems build up, in a new nervous, punning rhythm, with an ominously sonorous phonetic line, a precarious esteem for a self that can create without a reader for an indefinitely distant public: "I shall return my borrowed ash / Not like a floury white butterfly, / I want the thinking body / To turn into a street, a country."

The second notebook (42 poems) starts in December 1936, after the first wave of show trials and Mandel'shtam's longest silence. Every other poet in Russia was terrified into mediocrity or silence: Mandel'shtam ventured into virgin territory. New symbols and myths appear, some linked with Mandel'shtam's reading of Dante, some inspired by Voronezh – the art gallery's Rembrandt or the local birds, notably the Judaically-coloured goldfinch. The Mandel'shtamian love of twins and opposites dominates. Given the apparent necessity of capitulating with an epigram to Stalin, the victim now identifies himself with his oppressor: the syllable "os" links Osip Mandel'shtam and Joseph Stalin, in fateful antithesis. Poems such as ("Inside an idol lies, inert, an idol") – ending: "He thinks in bone and feels with his brow / And tries to recall his human form." – simultaneously apply to Stalin and to the poet, both cut off from their childhood and humanity, so that the victim's protest turns into empathy. In addition to Judaic Old Testament images of tortured prophets (Daniel in the lion's den), an apocalyptic Christian symbolism begins to dominate Mandel'shtam's imagery, whether Raphael's "wrathful lamb" or "He who makes us scream in sleep, the Judas of future nations." The second notebook is less nervous, more declamatory and questioning than the first. Its last poem, however, partly inspired by the grief of an actress for her arrested husband, could be an epitaph for the author: "My time is still unlimited: / I too have accompanied the universal delight, / As a *sotte voce* organ / Accompaniment to a woman's voice."

There was no gap in time before the appearance of the third, and greatest, of the notebooks (21 poems), which opens with the longest of Mandel'shtam's poems, *Stikhi o neizvestnom soldate* [Verses about the Unknown Soldier] (March 1937). The title and surface theme might conceivably have made the poem publishable, but the unknown soldier is only too obviously the poet, facing like millions of others, a violent death and unmarked grave. The greatness of the poem lies in its use of modern physics, optics and astronomy to suggest a new cosmos, in which light is matter, stars die and truth is relative – Stalin and Einstein have ended the era of absolute values. No suffering is commemorated for ever to be avenged or expiated – even the light of the battle of Waterloo is to be swallowed up in a black hole – the oyster of the universe, so that Stalin's massacre, "The battle of the Nations", has cosmic impunity. In a senseless universe poetry is just the human skull dreaming of itself, no longer a meaningful replica of the starry firmament, and the poet can offer only a quixotic defiance of the death of culture and the star-world – which had always symbolized truth and justice in Mandel'shtam's world. After this ultimate pessimism, the third notebook becomes, with the coming of warm weather, an unexpected celebration of the "sticky oath of the greenery". The last poems of spring 1937 are as musically rich as the poetry of the early 1920s, with a Keatsian sensuousness in their natural and their Hellenic imagery. Particularly important is the poem known as "Fleity grecheskoi teta i iota" ("The Greek Flute"). Inspired by the arrest of the Voronezh orchestra's flautist, the flute symbolizes the Orphic poetic spirit that cannot be recreated and which is now declining: Mandel'shtam continues an older visual understanding (see Maiakovskii's *Fleita pozvonochnik* [*The Backbone Flute*] of 1915 and Mandel'shtam's own image in "Vek" (1923) [The Age of 1923]) of the flute as a replica of the human spine and now associates it with the human lips (the actual source of all Mandel'shtam's poetry being his own moving lips). The poem is built on Hellenic associations of "sea" and "death" (*thalassa*, *thanatos*) and similar puns in Russian (*more*, *mor*). It has a musical as well as a thematic structure, the syllable "ub" being the basis for all its key words (lips, to kill, decline – *guby*, *ubit'*, *ubyl'*).

One consolation for the Mandel'shtams in Voronezh was the brave friendship of Natasha Shtempel'; a poem written for her closes the third Voronezh notebook (as we reconstruct the poet's intended arrangement of the poems). As in the other notebooks (and in Mandel'shtam's early poetry), woman is given the role of mourning and preserving. A nature goddess – "The ancestral mother of the tomb" – inseparable from this penultimate spring in Mandel'shtam's life, she now transcends sensuality "To accompany the resurrected and to be the first / To welcome the dead is their vocation. / And to demand caresses from them is criminal." Thus predicting the role of Natasha Shtempel' and of his widow, Mandel'shtam looks, in his last finished poem, ambiguously at futurity: "And all that will be is only a promise."

The Voronezh poems were first arranged in America by Struve and Filippov in the 1960s, following what hints they could gain from Mandel'shtam's widow. A long-delayed Soviet edition (1973) by Khardzhiev falsified the cycle for ideological reasons: the Averintsev edition (Moscow 1990) is probably the closest approximation to what Mandel'shtam might have done had he survived. The poems are so rich and wide-ranging in cultural and personal allusion, however, that critical apparatus is still in its infancy. Many clues to the poet's references can be gleaned from Nadezhda Mandel'shtam's memoirs; others are to be found in Mandel'shtam's reading of the time, notably Dante's *Divine Comedy* and Goethe's *Faust*.

DONALD RAYFIELD

Anatolii Borisovich Mariengof 1897–1962

Poet, prose writer, and dramatist

Biography

Born in Nizhnii-Novgorod, 6 July 1897. Attended the Nizhnii Novgorod Nobles' Institute; Penza high-school from 1913. Moved to Moscow, 1918; formed close friendship with the peasant poet Sergei Esenin. Founding member of the Imaginist movement, early 1919; issued several volumes of his own verse, critical theory, and plays (usually under the imprint "Imazhinisty") and contributed to numerous Imaginist collections, 1919–25. Married: the actress Anna Nikritina in late 1921; one son. Moved to Leningrad, 1928. Turned increasingly to prose and plays from 1926; published relatively little in the Stalin era. Died in Komarovo, near Leningrad, 24 June 1962.

Publications

Poetry

Vitrina serdtsa: Stikhi [The Heart's Shop-Window: Poems]. n.p., 1918.

Poems in the volume *Iav'* [Reality]. Moscow, 1919, 5–21.

Konditerskaia solnts: Poema [Pastry-Shop of the Suns: A Poem]. Moscow, 1919.

Magdalina. Moscow, 1919.

Ruki galstukom [Arms like a Necktie]. [Moscow], 1920.

Stikhami chvanstvuiu: Liricheskie poemy [I Show Off My Poetry: Lyrical Poems]. Moscow, 1920.

Razvratnichaiu s vdokhnoven'em: Poema [I Indulge in Lust with Inspiration: A Poem]. Moscow, 1921.

Tuchelet: Kniga poem [Cloud-Flight: A Book of Poems]. Moscow, 1921.

Razocharovanie [Disillusionment]. [Moscow], 1922.

Stikhi i poemy 1922–1926 [Poems 1922–1926] (on the front cover *Novyi Mariengof* [The New Mariengof]). Moscow, 1926.

Taksa Kliaksa [Smudge the Dachshund]. [Leningrad], 1927.

Miach prokaznik [The Mischievous Ball]. [Leningrad], 1928.

Bobka fizkul'turnik: Stikhi dlia detei [Bobka the Athlete: Poems for Children]. Moscow, 1930.

Poemy voiny [War Poems]. Kirov, 1942.

Piat' ballad [Five Ballads]. Kirov, 1942.

Treatise on Poetry

Buian-ostrov: Imazhinizm [Buian Island: Imaginism]. Moscow, 1920.

Plays

Zagovor durakov: Tragediia [The Conspiracy of Fools: A Tragedy]. Moscow, 1922.

Dvunogie: Ironicheskaia tragediia [The Bipeds: An Ironic Tragedy]. Moscow, 1925.

Shut Balakirev: Komediia v 4 d. [The Buffoon Balakirev: A Comedy in Four Acts]. Moscow and Leningrad, 1940.

Taras Bul'ba: P'esa v dvukh deistviiakh po odnoimennoi povesti N.V. Gogolia [Taras Bulba: A Play in Two Acts Based on the Story by N.V. Gogol']. Moscow and Leningrad, 1940.

Rozhdenie poeta [Birth of a Poet]. Moscow and Leningrad, 1951.

Strannyi kharakter [A Strange Character]. Moscow, 1955.

Malen'kie komedii [Little Comedies]. Moscow and Leningrad, 1957.

Rozhdenie poeta: Shut Balakirev: P'esy [Birth of a Poet: The Buffoon Balakirev: Plays]. Leningrad, 1959.

Fiction and Memoirs

Vospominaniia o Esenine [Memoirs about Esenin]. Moscow, 1926.

Roman bez vran'ia [A Novel Without Lies]. Leningrad, 1927; 2nd edition, Leningrad, 1928; 3rd edition, Leningrad, 1929; also Berlin, Petropolis, 1929; many subsequent reprints, including New York, N'iu Iork, 1978; Oxford, Meeuws, 1979; Tel Aviv, Elshits, 1979; Tel Aviv, Uvlekatel'naia kniga, n.d.; Kiev, 1990; Vladikavkaz, 1993; Moscow, 1995.

Tsiniki: Roman. Berlin, Petropolis, 1928; reprinted Tel Aviv, Elshits, 1978; Moscow, 1990, reissued 1991; and in *Glas: Daidzhest novoi russkoi literatury*, 1 (1991), 6–114; translated as *Cynics: A Novel*, by Valdemar D. Bell and Louis Coleman, New York, Boni, 1930; reprinted Westport, Connecticut, Hyperion Press, 1973; also translated as "Cynics", by Andrew Bromfield, in *Glas: New Russian Writing*, 1 (1991), 6–114.

Brityi chelovek: Roman [Shaven Man: A Novel]. Berlin, Petropolis, [1929 or 1930]; serialized in *Strelets*, 2–5 (1984).

"Ekaterina: Fragmenty iz romana" [Catherine: Fragments from a Novel], *Literaturnyi sovremennik*, 9–10 (1936), 57–83, 86–107.

"Iz vospominanii Anatoliia Mariengofa" [From the Memoirs of Anatolii Mariengof], *Russkaia literatura*, 4 (1964), 149–65.

"Roman s druz'iami" [A Novel with Friends], *Oktiabr'*, 10–11 (1965), 83–126; 79–98.

Roman bez vran'ia: Tsiniki: Moi vek, moia molodost', moi druz'ia i podrugi [A Novel Without Lies: Cynics: My Lifetime, My Youth, My Friends Male and Female]. Leningrad, 1988; reprinted 1991.

Moi vek, moi druz'ia i podrugi: Vospominaniia Mariengofa, Shershenevicha, Gruzinova [My Lifetime, My Friends Male and Female: The Memoirs of Mariengof, Shershenevich, and Gruzinov]. Moscow, 1990.

Eto vam, potomki!: Zapiski sorokaletnego muzhchiny: Ekaterina. Roman [For You, My Descendants!: Notes of a Forty-Year-Old Man: Catherine. A Novel]. St Petersburg, 1994.

Critical Studies

Voploshchenie: Esenin – Mariengof, by Arsenii Avraamov, Moscow, 1921.

Proroki i predtechi poslednego zaveta: Imazhinisty: Esenin, Kusikov, Mariengof, by Sergei Grigor'ev, n.p., [1921].

Imazhinizma osnovnoe, by Ivan Gruzinov, Moscow, 1921.

Chetyre vystrela v Esenina, Kusikova, Mariengofa, Shershenevicha, by Riurik Ivnev, Moscow, 1921.

Imazhinizm i ego obrazonostsy: Esenin, Kusikov, Mariengof, Shershenevich, by V. L'vov-Rogachevskii, [Moscow], 1921.

Komu ia zhmu ruku (on the front cover *Shershenevich zhmet ruku komu*), by Vadim Shershenevich, [Moscow], [1921].

The Russian Imaginists, by Nils Åke Nilsson, Stockholm, Almqvist & Wiksell, 1970.

Esenin: A Life, by Gordon McVay, Ann Arbor, Ardis, and London, Hodder and Stoughton, 1976.

"Anatoly Mariengof and Sergei Esenin", by Gordon McVay, in Mariengof's *Roman bez vran'ia*, Oxford, Meeuws, 1979, vii–xxx (reprint of the 1928 Leningrad edition).

Russian Imagism 1919–1924, 2 vols, by Vladimir Markov, Giessen, Schmitz, 1980.

"The Prose of Anatolii Mariengof", by Gordon McVay, in *From Pushkin to "Palisandriia": Essays on the Russian Novel in Honour of Richard Freeborn*, edited by Arnold McMillin, London, Macmillan, and New York, St Martin's Press, 1990, 149–67.

"Introduction", by Gordon McVay, in *Iav'*, Oxford, Meeuws, 1993, i–xxi (reprint of the 1919 Moscow edition).

"'Tsinicheskaia' proza Mariengofa", by Boris Averin, in

Mariengof's *Eto vam, potomki!: Zapiski sorokaletnego muzhchiny: Ekaterina. Roman*, St Petersburg, 1994, 5–17.

Bibliography
In *Russian Imagism 1919–1924*, by Vladimir Markov, vol. 1, Giessen, Schmitz, 1980, 116–20.

Few scholars in Russia or the west have devoted serious critical attention to the life and works of Anatolii Mariengof. Were it not for his intimate friendship with the phenomenally popular Sergei Esenin (chronicled in Mariengof's memoir, *Roman bez vran'ia* [A Novel Without Lies]), Mariengof might have been marginalized to a mere footnote in literary history. Yet such relegation would be unjust, and his "rediscovery" may be at hand.

This process of reassessment covers three main areas – Mariengof the man, the poet, and the prose writer. During the heyday of his notoriety, from 1919 to 1927, Mariengof revelled in literary-bohemian "scandals" as a founding father of Russian Imaginism. Under the group's own imprint, "Imazhinisty", he issued controversial verse, drama, and theory, baiting the Moscow public and provoking outrage to the gamut of aesthetic sensibilities (from aristocratic to proletarian) by a show of cynicism and amoralism.

For this he was predictably rewarded by almost universal abuse. Some bloodthirsty poems in the volume *Iav'* [Reality] (1919) drew a sharp rebuke from the newspaper *Pravda*, which branded Mariengof's "deafening yelping" as alien to the proletariat. Two years later in *Izvestiia* Anatolii Lunacharskii, the People's Commissar of Enlightenment, denounced the Imaginist volume *Zolotoi kipiatok* [Golden Boiling Water] (1921) – a joint effort by Esenin, Mariengof, and Vadim Shershenevich – as a "prostitution of talent, soiled B in stinking filth".

Posing in anachronistic top-hat as an Oscar Wilde from Penza, the youthful Mariengof relished such brick-bats. Dmitrii Furmanov fulminated: "Mariengof himself is a typical glossy dandy. He creates the most repulsive impression, that is, by his openly bourgeois essence ...". Ivan Bunin dubbed him "the greatest scoundrel" – a view shared by numerous critics in the 1920s and since, who saw nothing in Mariengof's verse and character but vulgar *épatage*, sadistic sickness, nightmarish anarchy, and urban decadence.

In vain, fellow-Imaginist Riurik Ivnev protested that Mariengof was essentially calm, stagnant, and harmless – a *poseur*. The harm had been done, and the cynical pose, which had paved the way to notoriety, earned Mariengof increasing opprobrium as the 1920s advanced. For most of the Stalin era he licked his wounds, a man made sadder and wiser by the awfulness of the times and the accumulation of personal tragedy – the death of his father in Penza in 1918, killed by a stray bullet; the suicide of Sergei Esenin in 1925; and the suicide of his only son, Kirill, in 1940 (by hanging, like Esenin). The belated testimony of friends, and his marriage of 40 years to Anna Nikritina, suggest that the youthful *poseur* developed into a man of sensitivity and principle.

Yet the fact remains that, judged by conventional moral standards, the content of much of Mariengof's poetry from 1919 to 1925 is profoundly offensive. In his "revolutionary" contributions to the volume *Iav'* he systematically plays with dissonances, constantly verging on blasphemy by juxtaposing the sacred and the profane. Thus, mention of a human blood-bath is immediately followed by the exclamation "Christ is risen!". Christ's "puny body" is tortured on the rack in a Bolshevik political police cell, while His blood is splashed out "like water from a wash-stand". This typically heady mixture of blood and blasphemy, couched in compressed "chains" of images, was intended to shock and impress. In his theoretical tract *Buian-ostrov* [Buian Island] (1920), the poet attempted a philosophical justification for the Imaginistic precept of combining high and low, the "clean" and the "unclean", while claiming that Imaginism was a movement that embraced both realism and mysticism, and extolling the importance of strict formal mastery.

The calculatedly "shocking" *content* of Mariengof's early verse has tended to divert critical attention from the merits of his poetic *form*. Mariengof tirelessly experimented with rhythm, rhyme, and imagery, ranging freely across various lexical registers, from archaic Slavonicisms to contemporary jargon. Vladimir Markov (1980) investigated Mariengof's religious and sexual imagery, elaborate stanzas, and heteroaccentual rhyme. Markov maintains:

> Perhaps the most original of all the Russian Imagist poets, though not precisely to everyone's taste, Mariengof stops just short of the first rank. He is nevertheless a poet of remarkable craftsmanship and frequently of great strength ...

As Imaginism ran its course, gradually disintegrating in the mid-1920s, so Mariengof became less active as a poet. He published a reflective volume of verse in 1926 before turning to the creation of provocative prose. (His achievement as a dramatist is of lesser importance.) In 1927 he gained further notoriety with *Roman bez vran'ia* [A Novel Without Lies]. This unretouched portrait of Esenin and his fellow-Imaginists may be cynical and condescending, but it is also amusing, vivid, and valuable in catching much of the atmosphere of the Imaginists' bohemian life. Understandably, those seeking an idealized picture of Esenin were outraged by Mariengof's candour, and the book was widely vilified before being consigned to protracted oblivion.

By October 1928 Mariengof's first fictional novel, *Tsiniki* (*Cynics*), was issued in Berlin. Personal baseness and amorality are depicted against a background of general social, economic, and political disorder. The author deploys a terse, telegraphic, image-packed style, starkly juxtaposing disparate fragments of fiction and fact in a memorable display of harrowing anti-aestheticism. This abidingly "topical" novel, far removed from the tenets of socialist realism, has been reissued several times in post-communist Russia. In contrast, Mariengof's second novel, *Brityi chelovek* [Shaven Man], appears little more than a whimsical and rather wearisome anecdote.

During the 1930s, Mariengof was sharply criticized in the Soviet press, but was never arrested. He managed to publish "Ekaterina: Fragmenty iz romana" [Catherine: Fragments from a Novel] in two issues of a Leningrad journal in 1936. (A much fuller version appeared in 1994.) In his final years he worked on a lengthy memoir, which has been posthumously published.

Although he will undoubtedly remain a controversial figure, Mariengof's reputation is rising as prose writer and memoirist. In 1979 Nina Berberova described his novels as "remarkable", "he was gifted and intelligent, especially in the literary context of that time", while Boris Averin (1988) has asserted that "Mariengof ranks with such writers as Platonov, Pil'niak, and Zamiatin".

GORDON MCVAY

Aleksandr Marlinskii 1797–1837

Poet and prose writer

Biography

Born Aleksandr Aleksandrovich Bestuzhev in St Petersburg, 3 November 1797. Attended the Cadet Corps of Engineers, 1806–17. Began to publish, 1817; member of the Free Society of Lovers of Russian Letters, 1820; first book and prose tales published, 1821. Served in Light Dragoon Regiment, 1817–22; appointed adjutant to court adviser, General Augustin A. Betancourt, 1822. Co-editor, with Kondratii Ryleev, of the literary almanac *Poliarnaia zvezda*, 1823–25. Joined conspiratorial Northern Society, 1823. Stripped of rank and noble status for involvement in Decembrist Revolt, 14 December 1825; exiled to Siberia, 1827–29; transferred to the Caucasus as common soldier, 1829–37. Wrote in exile under the pseudonym Marlinskii, 1829–36. Died in battle (in mysterious circumstances), 19 June 1837.

Publications

Collected Editions

Sobranie stikhotvorenii. Leningrad, 1948.
Sochineniia, 2 vols. Moscow, 1958.
Polnoe sobranie stikhotvorenii. Leningrad, 1961.
Povesti i rasskazy. Moscow, 1976.
Sochineniia, 2 vols. Moscow, 1981.
Kavkazskie povesti [Stories of the Caucasus]. "Literaturnye pamiatniki", St Petersburg, 1995.

Poetry

Poezdka v Revel' [A Journey to Revel]. 1821.

Fiction

"Vecher na bivuake", *Poliarnaia zvezda* (1823); translated as "An Evening on Bivouac", by Lauren G. Leighton, in *Russian Romantic Prose: An Anthology*, edited by Carl R. Proffer, Ann Arbor, Translation Press, 1979, 138–44; also in *The Ardis Anthology of Russian Romanticism*, edited by Christine Rydel, Ann Arbor, Ardis, 1984, 206–11.
"Ispytanie", *Syn otechestvo i Severnyi arkhiv* (1830), 29–32; translated as "The Test", by Lewis Bagby, in *Russian Romantic Prose: An Anthology*, edited by Carl R. Proffer, Ann Arbor, Translation Press, 1979, 145–95.
"Latnik: Rasskaz partizanskogo ofitsera" [The Cuirassier: A Partisan Officer's Story], *Syn otechestvo i Severnyi arkhiv* (1832), 1–4.
"Ammalat-bek", *Moskovskii telegraf*, 1–4 (1832); excerpts translated by Lewis Bagby, in *The Ardis Anthology of Russian Romanticism*, edited by Christine Rydel, Ann Arbor, Ardis, 1984, 212–41.
"Fregat Nadezhda" [The Frigate *Hope*], *Syn otechestvo i Severnyi arkhiv* (1833), 9–17.
"Morekhod Nikitin" [The Sailor Nikitin], *Biblioteka dlia chteniia*, 4 (1834).
"Mulla Nur", *Biblioteka dlia chteniia* (1836), 17.

Critical Studies

Romantizm Aleksandra Bestuzheva, by A.P. Sharupich, Minsk, 1964.
Aleksandr Bestužev-Marlinskij, by Horst von Chmielewski, Munich, 1966.
Estetika russkoi romanticheskoi povesti (A.A. Bestuzhev-Marlinskii i romantiki-belletristy 20–30kh godov XIX veka), by F.Z. Kanunova, Tomsk, 1973.
Alexander Bestuzhev-Marlinsky, by Lauren G. Leighton, Boston, Twayne, 1976.
"Bestuzhev-Marlinskii's "The Frigate Hope": A Decembrist Puzzle", by Lauren G. Leighton, *Canadian Slavonic Papers*, 22 (1980), 173–86; revised in his *The Esoteric Tradition in Russian Romantic Literature: Decembrism and Freemasonry*, University Park, Pennsylvania State University Press, 1994.
Russian Romantic Fiction, by John Mersereau, Jr, Ann Arbor, Ardis, 1983.
A History of Russian Literature of the Romantic Period, by William Edward Brown, vol. 2, Ann Arbor, Ardis, 1986.
"Decembrist Romanticism: A.A. Bestuzhev-Marlinsky", by Neil B. Landsman, in *Problems of Russian Romanticism*, edited by Robert Reid, Brookfield, Vermont, Gower, 1986, 64–95.
Alexander Bestuzhev-Marlinsky and Russian Byronism, by Lewis Bagby, University Park, Pennsylvania State University Press, 1995.

Aleksandr Bestuzhev, who wrote under the pseudonym Marlinskii, was born in 1797, the fifth child of eight in a family that joined the ancient aristocracy on the father's side with the Russian merchant class on the mother's. Bestuzhev senior was a writer, educator, publisher, and military officer whose family had once enjoyed the favours of the crown, but they had fallen on hard times and been discredited in the tsar's court during the 18th century. Aleksandr and his brothers laboured to restore the family name, but in a most unusual manner. They conspired to overthrow the government of Alexander I in a movement that even contemplated regicide. With the sudden and unexpected death of Alexander I, the brothers worked actively on behalf of their rebellious cause to supplant the Romanov dynasty with a constitutional form of government. Marlinskii was the first of the underground society (later called the Decembrists) to lead insurgent troops out onto Senate Square on 14 December (Old Style) 1825. His brothers and many others soon followed, but not in sufficient numbers to secure victory. Nicholas I took charge on this, the first day of his reign, and dispersed the Decembrists and their supporters with grapeshot and cannon fire. The remainder of Marlinskii's life (as well as that of his older brothers) was spent in exile, where in 1837 he died, it seems, during a skirmish against the local Cherkes, natives on Adler Promontory on the Black Sea. His body was never recovered, a fact that engendered wild rumours about his escape into the Caucasian mountains where he lived the remainder of his days with the "primitives". These heroic dreams represent another form of conspiracy in Marlinskii's life, a conspiracy between his idea of himself, which he projected in his fiction, criticism, and letters, and the audience he had at his feet. The point of contact between Marlinskii's self idea and its reception among a growing Russian plebeian readership was an aesthetics that combined both his art and the artfulness of his daily life.

At the age of 20 Marlinskii entered the literary arena as a critic. He originally represented the Karamzin camp, particularly in the debates against those who held a more conservative aesthetic line. But Marlinskii challenged Karamzinian francophilia for its linguistic and emotional narrowness. Marlinskii found a more adequate (in his opinion) model in British writers, particularly Sir Walter Scott, Ann Radcliffe, and eventually Lord Byron. In time, however, Marlinskii's art too was influenced by *l'Ecole Frénétique*, and traces of Balzac, Hugo, and Zola made their way into his mature fiction. If Marlinskii's entry into the literary arena was callow, it nevertheless made a major impact on literary society.

Together with his friend and political conspirator, the poet Kondratii Ryleev, Marlinskii published *Poliarnaia zvezda*, a literary almanac that enjoyed enormous success, to such an extent, in fact, that it became the model of similar, rival publications that eventually overshadowed it. Three issues of *Poliarnaia zvezda*, (1823–25) appeared prior to the Decembrist revolt; they contained some of the finest verbal art of the early 1820s and included contributions from all the major figures of the Golden Age of Russian Verse: Pushkin, Viazemskii, Baratynskii, Del'vig, Venevitinov, and others. Marlinskii's own fiction appeared here alongside his literary criticism. In 1821 *Poezdka v Revel'* [A Journey to Revel] was published. It enjoyed limited success as a generic hold-over from the early part of the century. Marlinskii's forte was not poetry, which he freely admitted, and he turned to prose fiction. The same year also witnessed the publication of his first prose, "Gedeon" and "Zamok Venden" [The Castle Wenden], both works indicate the degree to which his call for a native prose was beyond his reach. They were highly derivative of Scott and Radcliffe. But by 1823 "Roman i Ol'ga" [Roman and Olga] appeared, a story from the Russian tradition, certainly influenced by Scott, but fitted with distinct Russian characters, landscapes, history, and language. It established his name as a premier writer of fiction in an era noted for its meagre contribution to the genre.

By 1824 Marlinskii's journal, his tales, his criticism, his success in military service, and his persona at court, in men's clubs, and at balls, secured for him what many swore was a promising future. He joined at that time, and under Ryleev's influence, the Northern Society, the conspiratorial organization that staged the Decembrist revolt. "Zamok Neigauzen" [The Castle Neuhausen], "Revel'skii turnir" [The Tournament at Revel], and "Izmennik" [The Traitor] came out in rapid succession – all tales mitigating violence against feudal governmental structures. The revolutionary note was pronounced. Within a short time Marlinskii had the opportunity to test in real life on Senate Square the literary, heroic persona he had projected of himself through his narrators and fictional characters. On that fateful day he played the hero until dusk. The following day Marlinskii turned himself in at the Winter Palace and confessed everything, even the Society's plans of regicide.

Marlinskii did not hold up to interrogation well, was dutiful in his assistance to the crown, for which he was rewarded with a commuted sentence (20 years' exile) and the right to continue publishing under the pseudonym he had occasionally used in the debates of the early 1820s, Marlinskii. His brothers, who were less involved than he in the revolt, received more severe punishments, presumably for greater recalcitrance during interrogation. Ryleev and four other leaders were hanged. Marlinskii had much to reconcile in his heroic persona from this moment on.

Marlinskii was first exiled in 1826 to Finland, then in 1827 to Siberia, and finally, upon indirect entreaty to the tsar, to the Caucasus in 1829 where he was enlisted as a common soldier in the imperialist cause against the Turks and the peoples of the Caucasus. During this time he deepened his commitment to his self ideal through appealing to Byronic categories. This was relatively easy to accomplish for the simple reason that his life, from his perspective, conformed to that literary model: outsider with a secret crime in his past; carelessness of life and limb; literariness in speech, pose, and gesture; eternal wanderer in vain search of fulfilment.

From "Ispytanie" ("The Test") 1830, in which he questioned the Decembrist behavioral code, to "Mulla-Nur" (1836), wherein Marlinskii rallies himself against personal doubts about the legitimacy of heroism in real life, his prose and letters of the 1830s encapsulated these Byronic traits. Most representative of his Caucasian tales was "Ammalat-bek" (1832), which enjoyed great popularity in society, the poems of which were set to music and performed in salons in Moscow and St Petersburg, not to mention Saratov and Rylsk, and was even recreated on stage. These tales, and those treating Russian subjects, "Leitenant Belozor" [Lieutenant Belozor] (1831), "Fregata 'Nadezhda'" [The Frigate *Hope*] (1832), and "Morekhod Nikitin" [The Sailor Nikitin] (1834), as well as the many travelogues to which Marlinskii turned (as his life became more troubled and dangerous, as his belief in his ability to contribute to Russian prose fiction was challenged, and as his place in Russian literature was assaulted in the press), contributed to the popular reader's perception of Marlinskii as the hero he sought to be all his life.

By 1837 Marlinskii's place in Russian letters had declined among the literati. His physical health became more and more precarious. His hopes of finding an early release from exile had been dashed repeatedly. Military assignments took him to Russian fortresses with the highest mortality rates in the Caucasus. He was terribly shocked by the deaths of both Griboedov and Pushkin. His youngest brother's exile and eventual madness disturbed him deeply. Marlinskii wrote a last will and testament on 18 June 1837 and on the following day concluded his fifth act. It was reported by some that he was slashed to pieces by Cherkes natives; by others, that he had escaped.

LEWIS BAGBY

Samuil Iakovlevich Marshak 1887–1964

Poet

Biography

Born in Voronezh, 3 November 1887. Attended the Ostrogozhsk gymnasium, 1899–1902; gymnasium in St Petersburg, 1902–04; for health reasons continued school in Yalta, under Maksim Gor'kii, 1904–06. Began to publish from 1907. Not allowed to enter university. Extended trip to Near East. Married: Sofiia Mikhailovna Milvidskaia in 1911; one daughter and two sons. Travelled to England as a freelance journalist; studied at the University of London; lived at Simple Life School, Wales, and visited Ireland, 1912–14. Returned to Russia on the eve of World War I. Exempt from army service on account of his poor eyesight. Worked in children's social services in Voronezh and Finland, 1915–17; at a children's colony, Petrozavodsk, 1918; worked for a local paper and was head of children's homes, Krasnodar, 1919–22. Head of the literary section of a new Theatre for Young Spectators (TIuZ), Petrograd, 1922–24. Published poetry for children, from 1923; editor of a children's magazine, 1923–25; head of the children's section of the State Publishing House (Gosizdat); literary consultant to Children's Publishing House (Detizdat), 1924–37. Visited Gor'kii in Italy, 1933; moved to Moscow, 1938. Recipient: Stalin Prize, for children's poetry (1942), war poetry (1946), translations of Shakespeare's sonnets (1949), and children's play *Dvenadtsat' mesiatsev* [The Twelve Months], (1951); Lenin Prize, 1963. Chair of commission on children's literature, Writers' Union. Died in Moscow, 4 July 1964.

Publications

Collected Editions

Skazki, pesni, zagadki [Fairytales, Songs, Riddles]. 1935.
Sochineniia, 4 vols. Moscow, 1958–60.
Sobranie sochinenii, 8 vols. Moscow, 1968–72.

Poetry

Detki v kletki [Children in a Cage]. Petrograd and Moscow, 1923.
Bagazh [Baggage]. Leningrad, 1926.
Izbrannoe lirika. Moscow, 1962.
Liricheskie epigrammy. Moscow, 1965.
Stikhotvoreniia i poemy. Leningrad, 1973.

Plays

Dvenadtsat' mesiatsev [The Twelve Months]. Moscow, 1943.
Umnye veshchi [Clever Things]. Moscow, 1964.

Literary Criticism

"Za bol'shuiu detskuiu literaturu", *Detskaia literatura*, 1 (1936), 18–23; translated as "For a Great Children's Literature", by Jean Laves Hellie, *Soviet Studies in Literature*, Spring (1988), 42–54.

Autobiography

V nachale zhizni. Stranitsy vospominanii. Moscow, 1962; translated as *At Life's Beginning: Some Pages of Reminiscence*, by Katherine Hunter Blair, London, Gollancz, and New York, Dutton, 1964.

Critical Studies

"Marshak – redaktor", by Lidiia Chukovskaia, in her *V laboratorii redaktora*, 2nd edition, Moscow, 1963, 219–334.
S. Ia. Marshak. Zhizn' i tvorchestvo. 4th edition, by Boris Galanov, Moscow, 1965.
"Marshak", by Kornei Chukovskii, in his *Vysokoe iskusstvo*, in *Sobranie sochinenii*, vol. 3, Moscow, 1966, 455–66; translated as *The Art of Translation: Kornei Chukovsky's "A High Art"*, by Lauren G. Leighton, Knoxville, University of Tennessee Press, 1984, 183–94.
Samuil Marshak: Ocherk poezii, by Benedikt Sarnov, Moscow, 1968.
"Sonety Shekspira – perevody Marshaka", by N. Avtonomova and M. Gasparov, *Voprosy literatury*, 13/2 (1969), 100–12.
Ia dumal, chustvoval, ia zhil. Vospominaniia o Marshake. Moscow, 1971.
Zhizn' i tvorchestvo Marshaka. Marshak i detskaia literatura. Moscow, 1975.
"Samuel Marshak and his 'Children's Town' Theater", by Anna Bogdanova, in *Through the Magic Curtain: Theater for Children, Adolescents and Youth in the U.S.S.R.*, edited and translated by Miriam Morton, New Orleans, Anchorage Press, 1979, 11–17.
"Samuil Marshak", in *Russian Poetry for Children*, by Elena Sokol, Knoxville, University of Tennessee Press, 1984, 93–121.
"Strannyi geroi s Basseinoi ulitsy", in *Knigi nashego detstva*, by Miron Petrovskii, Moscow, 1986, 99–146.
"Liricheskie epigrammy Marshaka", by Valentin Berestov, *Novyi mir*, 9 (1987), 242–50.
"On Marshak's Russian Translation of Robert Burns", by De You Yang, *Studies in Scottish Literature*, 22 (1987), 10–29.
"O S. Marshake", by Iurii Karabchievskii, in "Filologicheskaia proza", *Novyi mir*, 10 (1993), 234–40.

Known above all as a prominent children's poet and important organizer of children's literature in the early Soviet period, Samuil Marshak was also an eminent translator and accomplished lyric and satirical poet. He displayed poetic talent early in childhood, composing his first verses at the age of four and, seven years later, translating an ode by Horace. When he was 15, through a fortuitous meeting with a wealthy art patron in St Petersburg, where he was visiting his family during his summer holiday from school, Marshak made the acquaintance of Stasov and, later, Gor'kii, each of whom played a role in his secondary education. Gor'kii would remain an influential friend until his death in 1936.

The development of Marshak's literary career is often compared with that of his older colleague Kornei Chukovskii (1882–1969). Both came to St Petersburg as young writers from the provinces and began contributing to literary and satirical periodicals. Perhaps the most striking coincidence in their lives was that each, in his twenties, lived for an extended time in England. Prevented from entering a Russian university, Marshak pursued his education at the University of London. The time he spent in Britain significantly shaped his subsequent development as a writer, giving him the opportunity to become fluent in English and to immerse himself in English poetry, including the folk tradition. Among the first tangible results of Marshak's English experience was his translation of poems by Blake. Then as his attention turned to children, a focus he specifically chose after the tragic death of his little daughter in 1915, his acquaintance with English nursery rhymes, together with his knowledge of Russian children's folklore, came to inspire his own lifelong writing of plays and poems for children.

After an initial encounter with children's theatre in post-revolutionary Krasnodar, Marshak returned to Petrograd in 1922, where he became the head of the literary section of the new Theatre for Young Spectators [Teatr iunykh zritelei, or TIuZ]. Soon he became involved in a workshop for children's writers, making his debut as a children's poet in 1923. Along with original poetry, he published the first edition of his renditions of English nursery rhymes, on which he had begun working in Britain ten years earlier. After a brief interlude at a short-lived children's magazine, Marshak moved with his fellow staff writers to the Leningrad State Publishing House (Gosizdat) in 1925, where he ran the children's section. At a time when imaginative literature for children was heavily attacked by proletarian critics and educators (the so-called "pedologists"), Marshak none the less managed to convince many talented young writers to turn their creative energy to children's literature. Outstanding among these were Evgenii Shvarts, Nikolai Oleinikov, and two poets from the avant-garde group OBERIU, Daniil Kharms and Aleksandr Vvedenskii. From the late 1920s into the 1930s he served as editor-in-chief of two memorable children's magazines – *Ezh* and *Chizh*. On Gor'kii's instigation, a separate children's publishing house (Detgiz) was established, where Marshak continued his editorial work until his staff fell victim to Stalin's purges in 1937. Along with many of Leningrad's persecuted intelligentsia, Marshak soon moved to Moscow.

Not untypically, Marshak's literary creativity was strongly affected by the political demands of Stalinism. A close study of his work for children, therefore, would reveal just how he adapted his style to suit the times. Such fanciful works of the mid-1920s as "Morozhenoe" [Ice Cream], "Bagazh" [Baggage], and "Vot kakoi rasseiannyi" [That's How Absent-Minded] gave way first to a paean to the First Five-Year Plan, "Voina s Dneprom" [War with the Dnieper] (1931), and then to heroic socialist realism, "Rasskaz o neizvestnom geroe" [Story of an Unknown Hero] (1938). With the outbreak of war against Hitler, Marshak became fully engaged as a publicist and writer of satirical verse. Especially well remembered are his captions to the political cartoons drawn by three artists known collectively as Kupryniksy. During the war he also pursued his earlier literary interests – lyric poetry and poetic translation. Already in 1938 he had begun to publish his renditions of poems by Robert Burns, continuing to work on them until the end of his life. During World War II he turned to Shakespeare's sonnets, publishing them as a book in 1948. Some of his own lyric poems appeared in a slim volume in 1946.

In the post-Stalin period, which coincided with the last decade of this life, Marshak devoted special energy to his lyric poetry. At the same time he maintained his role as a prominent public cultural figure and a specialist on children's literature, who, along with Chukovskii, was continually in demand for "official" events. Unofficially, he was an important mentor to a new generation of young poets in Moscow, who in the 1960s and 1970s renewed the modern tradition of Russian poetry for children, to which Marshak had made such a notable seminal contribution decades earlier.

If one disregards the clearly irrational, politically-motivated criticism of the antagonistic proletarian critics and the somewhat later caprices of Stalinism, the reception of Marshak's work during the Soviet period, on the whole, was highly positive. That so much of the poetry and plays in verse he wrote for children have become part of the canon of Russian children's literature is sufficient proof of his achievement. During his lifetime he was certainly well received as a translator of British poetry, especially that of Burns, and gained solid praise from Chukovskii in *Iskusstvo perevoda* (*The Art of Translation*). The clear, uncomplicated themes and style of his own lyric poetry no doubt helped make it popular with Soviet readers and critics alike. In contrast, those same qualities tended to irritate critics who maintained a rather sceptical stance toward officially accepted writers. Thus, Tomas Venclova in his short entry on Marshak in the *Handbook of Russian Literature* (1985) refers to the adult poetry as "epigonic". Iurii Karabchievskii, in a posthumously published article (1993), is most damning of Marshak as a translator, referring to his achievement as "faceless, indifferent, pointless; empty, formal versification". Tendentious views of his work notwithstanding, Marshak made notable contributions to several areas of Russian literary culture in the Soviet period: as a creator and organizer of children's literature; as a poetic translator, especially from English; and as an original lyric and satirical poet.

ELENA SOKOL

Maxim the Greek c.1470–1555

Translator and tractarian

Biography

Born Michael Tribolès (or Trivolis) in Arta, Greece, c.1470, into aristocratic family. Moved to Corfu to study, c.1480; then to Florence to study under John Lascaris, c.1492. Visited Bologna, Padua, Milan, 1495–96. Lived in Venice, 1496–98, 1501. In the service of Gianfrancesco Pico della Mirandola until June 1502; there learnt of execution of Savonarola and underwent religious conversion. Entered Dominican house of San Marco at Florence, 14 June 1502. Returned to Greece and entered the monastery of Vatopedi on Mount Athos, 1505/06. Sent to Moscow to assist in translation of works from Greek into Slavonic, under Basil [Vasilii] III of Muscovy, June 1516. Became involved in religious debates and displeased ecclesiastical authorities. Arrested November 1524: found guilty of heresy and treason, 1525; incarcerated in Volokolamsk; further trial, 1531; imprisoned in Dormition Monastery, Tver. Continued literary work in confinement. Released c.1548; settled at Trinity Monastery of St Sergius, near Moscow, where he died probably in December 1555. Officially canonized in 1988.

Publications

Collected Editions

Sochineniia prepodobnogo Maksima Greka, 3 vols. Kazan, 1860–62; vols 1 and 3, Kazan, 1895–97; the first edition originally appeared in fascicules appended to the periodical *Pravoslavny sobesednik*, February 1859–December 1862.

Sochineniia prepodobnogo Maksima Greka v russkom perevode, 3 vols, by the monk Morsei, Sergiev Posad, 1910–11; reprinted Moscow, 1996.

Critical Studies

Maksim Grek i ego vremia. Istoricheskoe issledovanie, by Vladimir Ikonnikov, Kiev, 1915 (Sobranie istoricheskikh trudov, vol. 1).

Prepodobnyi Maksim Grek i grecheskaia ideia na Rusi v XVI veke. Istoricheskoe issledovanie s prilozheniem tekstov diplomaticheskikh snoshenii Rossii s Turtsiei v nachale XVI stoletiia po dokumentam Moskovskogo arkhiva Ministerstva inostrannykh del, by V. Dunaev, Moscow, 1916.

"Opyty po istorii russkoi publitsistiki XVI veka. Maksim Grek kak publitsist", by Viacheslav Rzhiga, *Trudy otdela drevnerusskoi literatury*, 1 (1934), 5–120.

Maxime le Grec et l'Occident. Contribution à l'histoire de la pensée religieuse et philosophique de Michel Trivolis, by Élie Denissoff, Louvain, 1943 (Université de Louvain, Recueil de travaux d'histoire et de philologie, 3rd series, vol. 14).

"Les éditions de Maxime le Grec", by Élie Denissoff, *Revue des Études Slaves*, 21 (1944), 112–20.

Maximos ho Graikos, ho prôtos phôtistès tôn Rhôssôn, by Gregorios Papamichael, Athens, 1950.

Maksim Grek als Theologe, by Bernhard Schultze, Rome, 1963 (Orientalia Christiana Analecta, vol. 167).

Ho Hèpeirôtès Maximos hôs promachos tès Orthodoxias, by Philaretos Bitalès, Athens, 1965.

"Ricerche sull'opera di Maksim Grek", by Mietta Baracchi, *Acme*, 21 (1968), 217–56, 261–325.

From Italy to Muscovy. The Life and Works of Maxim the Greek, by Jack Haney, Munich, Fink, 1971 (Humanistische Bibliothek, 1st series, vol. 19).

Sudnye spiski Maksima Greka i Isaka Sobaki, by Nikolai Pokrovskii, Moscow, 1971.

"La lingua di Maksim Grek", by Mietta Baracchi, *Rendiconti dell'Istituto Lombardo. Accademia di Scienze e Lettere. Classe di lettere e scienzi morali e storiche*, 105 (1971), 253–80; 106 (1972), 243–67.

"Maksim Grek i ital'ianskoe vozrozhdenie", by Aleksei Ivanov, *Vizantiiskii vremennik*, 33 (1972), 140–57; 34–35 (1973), 112–36.

"Maksim Grek kak uchenyi na fone sovremennoi emu russkoi obrazovannosti", by Aleksei Ivanov, *Bogoslovskie trudy*, 16 (1976), 142–87.

Maksim Grek v Rossii, by Nina Sinitsyna, Moscow, 1977.

"Italy, Mount Athos and Muscovy: The Three Worlds of Maximos the Greek (c.1470–1556)", by Dimitri Obolensky, *Proceedings of the British Academy*, 67 (1981), 143–61; reprinted as "Maximos the Greek", in *Six Byzantine Portraits*, by Dimitri Obolensky, Oxford, Clarendon Press, and New York, Oxford University Press, 1988, 201–19.

Perevody i poslaniia Maksima Greka. Neizdannye teksty, by Dmitrii Bulanin, Leningrad, 1984.

Maksim Grek, Byzantijn en humanist in Rusland. Een onderzoek naar enkele van zijn bronnen en denkbeelden, by Arno Langeler, Amsterdam, Jan Mets, 1986.

"A Learned Greek Monk in Muscovite Exile: Maksim Greek and the Old Testament Prophets", by Hugh Olmsted, *Modern Greek Studies Yearbook*, 3 (1987), 1–73.

"Knizhnaia sprava i perevody Maksima Greka kak opyt normalizatsii tserkovnoslavianskogo iazyka XVI veka", by Elena Kravets, *Russian Linguistics*, 15 (1991), 247–79.

"Proekt izdaniia sochinenii Maksima Greka", by Nina Sinitsyna, *Cyrillomethodianum*, 17–18 (1993–94, published 1995), 93–141.

Bibliographies

Literaturnoe nasledie Maksima Greka. Kharakteristika, atributsii, bibliografiia, by Aleksei Ivanov, Leningrad, 1969 (see the review by Hugh Olmsted in *Kritika*, 7 (1971), 1–27).

"Maksim Grek", by Dmitrii Bulanin, in *Slovar' knizhnikov i knizhnosti Drevnei Rusi*, 2/2, Leningrad, 1989, 89–98.

Michael Tribolès, born c.1470, underwent a thorough Renaissance education in late 15th-century Greece and Italy, meeting many leading intellectual figures of the time, before entering the service of Pico della Mirandola. Following a religious conversion, he entered a monastery in Florence where Savonarola had been prior. Returning to Greece, to a monastery on Mount Athos in 1505/06, he was tonsured with the name Maximos.

In a letter dated 15 March 1515 to the protos of Athos, Basil III of Muscovy requested that the monk Sabas of Vatopedi be sent to Moscow to assist in the translation of works from Greek into Slavonic. When Sabas declined the invitation on the grounds of old age, Maxim, now aged over 40, agreed to go in his stead and in June 1516 left for Constantinople. There can be no doubt that during his stay in Constantinople Maxim was given instructions by Patriarch Theoleptus I. Although their precise nature is unknown, at least two aspects are clear from Maxim's writings: the encouragement of an anti-Ottoman Muscovite policy to free the Greeks from Turkish rule (*Sochineniia* 2, 318) and the restoration of patriarchal authority over the Russian Church (*Sochineniia* 3, 154–56), which had lapsed *de facto* when on 15 December 1448 Jonah was elected metropolitan at Moscow to succeed Isidore, who had fled to the west in 1441 after his failure to impose the Union of Florence of 1439 on his flock.

At first, since Maxim knew little or no Slavonic, he translated from Greek into Latin, which was then translated by others into Slavonic. Inevitably mistakes were made that Maxim had no means of correcting but which nevertheless were later cited to support a charge of heresy against him. In addition to his translation work Maxim also took part in the controversy over the true nature of the monastic vocation that was raging in Moscow. One party held that a monk should withdraw from the world and live by his own toil; the leading advocate of this view had been Nil Maikov, and, since his death in 1503, Bassian Patrikeev. The other party held that a monk should serve the world by acts of charity, for which purpose a monastery should possess estates with peasants to work them; the leading advocate of this view had been Joseph Sanin, who had founded the Monastery of the Dormition at Volokolamsk, where his successor as abbot was Daniel. Maxim befriended Bassian and wrote several works against the possession of large estates by monasteries. Maxim's most powerful attack on monastic estates, the exploitation of peasants and usury takes the form of a dialogue – a platonic form that Maxim frequently used – between Aktemon (literally Non-Possessor) and Philoktemon (Lover of possessions) (*Sochineniia* 2, 89–118). Maxim also displeased the ecclesiastical authorities by rejecting the theory that the Russian Church had the right to elect its own metropolitan because the patriarchs of Constantinople were under the authority of infidels (*Sochineniia* 3, 154–56).

On 27 February 1522 Daniel was appointed metropolitan to replace Barlaam, who had been sympathetic to the non-possessor party. Maxim's position from then on became increasingly fragile. In November 1524 he was arrested and during April and May 1525 he was tried before Basil III and Daniel, and found guilty on various charges, including heresy, an accusation based mainly on his actual and alleged mistranslations, and treason, because of his contacts with Skinder, the Ottoman ambassador in Moscow. Maxim was incarcerated at the possessor stronghold at Volokolamsk.

The question of ecclesiastical estates had not been brought up at the trial since Bassian Patrikeev was still in favour with Basil III. Later, however, Patrikeev fell from favour and, since Maxim stubbornly refused to repent of his heresies, it was decided to link the two and in 1531, as a prelude to Patrikeev's trial later that year, Maxim was once again put on trial. Once more condemned, he was incarcerated in the Dormition Monastery at Tver. The local bishop, Acacius, befriended him and after a time allowed him to continue his literary work in his confinement, although all appeals for his release fell on deaf ears. It was probably in 1548, but not before, that Maxim was at last released and allowed to settle at the Trinity Monastery of St Sergius near Moscow, where he died in the odour of sanctity probably in December 1555. Although revered as a saint from soon after his death, he was only officially canonized in 1988.

Maxim's literary output was enormous. Besides his hundred or so translations he wrote some 250 works dealing with theology, monasticism, statecraft, social ills and injustices, philology and astrology, which latter superstition he attacked as contrary to free will. His theological works include polemics against Catholics, Muslims, Armenians and Lutherans, as well as attacks on the "neopaganism" of the Renaissance. In his writings on statecraft he advocated a harmony of the spiritual and temporal authorities but insisted on the primacy of the former over the latter. He launched many attacks on social ills, one of the most remarkable being his allegorical depiction of Muscovy as a widow named Basileia, namely Empire, sitting weeping beside the road and surrounded by lions, bears, wolves, and foxes. In a dialogue with Maxim she explains that she is crying as she is subject to those who love fame and power and abandon themselves to the lower passions, rob the defenceless and condemn the innocent. Maxim also attacked the lax morality of the clergy, as in his reply to Acacius' question why God had allowed the conflagration of 1537 in which the cathedral and many of Tver's churches had been consumed: Christ tells the bishop that He wants a righteous life, not splendid icons and sumptuous services in churches built at the expense of the poor, while the clergy live a life of ease.

During his lifetime Maxim compiled two collections of his works, both of which begin with a confession of faith in which he defends himself against all charges of heresy and of hostility towards the state. Until a critical edition of his works has been prepared a definitive assessment of his thought will remain impossible since it is uncertain whether all the works ascribed to Maxim are actually his. Similarly, some works hitherto considered original may turn out to be translations.

Although his approach to questions of philology, grammar, and textual criticism reveal an acquaintance with the humanist traditions of the Renaissance, Maxim's thought was basically medieval in outlook and his purely theological works are neither original nor profound. He has not earned his place in history as an original thinker but as a critic, preacher, and moralist whose reforming zeal, inspired by Savonarola's example, never dimmed and whose powerful writings reveal an uncompromising attitude towards social ills.

FRANCIS J. THOMSON

Dmitrii Sergeevich Merezhkovskii 1865–1941

Poet and prose writer

Biography

Born in St Petersburg, 14 August 1865. Attended the Third Classical gymnasium, St Petersburg; studied history at the universities of Moscow and St Petersburg, 1884–89. Married: the poet Zinaida Hippius in 1888. Prolific writer. One of the founders of Religio-Philosophical Society in St Petersburg. Major figure of Symbolist movement; lectured extensively on religion and culture. Lived in Paris and in Italy, 1905–12; returned to Russia from time to time; lived in St Petersburg, 1912–19. Following the October Revolution escaped to Poland, December 1919; settled in Paris in 1920. Lived in Switzerland and Italy, 1934–38. Sympathized with Mussolini and Hitler. Died in Paris, 9 December 1941.

Publications

Collected Editions

Sobranie stikhov 1883–1910. St Petersburg, 1910; reprinted Letchworth, Bradda, 1971.
Polnoe sobranie sochinenii, 17 vols. St Petersburg, 1911–13.
Polnoe sobranie sochinenii, 24 vols. St Petersburg, 1914; reprinted Hildesheim, Georg Olms, 1973.
Malen'kaia Tereza [Novel, Letters], edited by Temira Pachmuss. Ann Arbor, Hermitage, 1984.
Pavel 1. Aleksandr 1. Bol'naia Rossiia: Drama dlia chteniia. Roman. Esse [Pavel 1. Alexander 1. Sick Russia: Drama to be Read. Novel. Essay], compiled with an introduction by O.N. Mikhailova, Moscow, 1989.
Sobranie sochinenii, 4 vols. Moscow, 1990.

Fiction

Khristos i Antikhrist (novel trilogy):
Otverzhennyi [Outcast]. St Petersburg, 1896; 2nd edition as *Smert' bogov. Iulian Otstupnik*; translated as *The Death of the Gods*, by Herbert Trench, London, Constable, and New York, Putnam, 1901; also translated by Bernard Guilbert Guerney, New York, Modern Library, 1929.
Voskresshie bogi. Leonardo da Vinchi. St Petersburg, 1902; translated as *The Forerunner: The Romance of Leonardo da Vinci*, by Herbert Trench, London, Constable, 1902; retitled as *The Romance of Leonardo da Vinci*, New York, Putnam, 1902; also translated by Bernard Guilbert Guerney, New York, Modern Library, 1928.
Antikhrist. Petr i Aleksei. St Petersburg, 1905; complete Russian edition published Moscow, 1990; translated as *Peter and Alexis*, by Herbert Trench, London, Constable, and New York, Putnam, 1905; also translated by Bernard Guilbert Guerney, New York, Modern Library, 1931.
Der Zar und Die Revolution, with Zinaida Hippius and D. Filosofov. Munich and Leipzig, Piper, 1908.
Aleksandr 1. St Petersburg, 1913.
14 Dekabria. Petrograd, 1918; Paris, 1921; translated as *December the Fourteenth*, by Natalie Duddington, London, Jonathan Cape, 1923; New York, International Publishers, 1925.
Rozhdenie bogov: Tutankhamon na Krite [Birth of the Gods: Tutenkamun on Crete]. Prague, 1925.
Napoleon. Paris, 1928; reprinted with an afterword by A.N. Nikoliukin, Moscow, 1993; translated as *Napoleon the Man*, by Catherine Zvegintsov, New York, Dutton, 1928.
Iisus neizvestnyi. Belgrade, 1931; Moscow, 1996; translated as *Jesus the Unknown*, by H. Chroushoff Matheson, London, Jonathan Cape, 1933.
Jesus der Kommende (published in German only). Frauenfeld, 1934.
Tod und Auferstehung (published in German only). Frauenfeld, 1935.
Dante. Brussels, Petropolis, 1939; reprinted Tomsk, 1997.

Poetry

Stikhotvoreniia. St Petersburg, 1888.
Simvoly. Stikhi [Symbols]. St Petersburg, 1892.
Novye Stikhotvoreniia [New Poems]. St Petersburg, 1896.

Essays and Articles

Vechnye sputniki [Eternal Companions]. St Petersburg, 1897; reprinted Letchworth, Bradda, 1971; reprinted with *Tolstoi i Dostoevskii*, Moscow, 1995.
Tolstoi i Dostoevskii. St Petersburg, 1901–02; reprinted with *Vechnye sputniki*, Moscow, 1995.
Gogol' i chert [Gogol' and the Devil]. St Petersburg, 1906.
Taina Zapada. Atlantida – Evropa. Belgrade, 1930; translated as *The Secret of the West*, by John Cournos, New York, Brewer Warren and Putnam, and London, Jonathan Cape, 1933.
Izbrannye stat'i [Selected Articles]. Munich, Fink, 1972.
V tikhom omute: Stat'i i issledovaniia raznykh let [In Still Waters: Articles and Studies from Various Years]. Moscow, 1991.

Play

Pavel 1. St Petersburg, 1908.

Critical Studies

Dmitri Mérejkowsky: esquisse de littérature russe, by Jean Chuzeville, Paris, Bossard, 1922.
Dmitrii Merezhkovskii, by Zinaida Hippius, Paris, YMCA-Press, 1951.
Vstrechi, by Iu. Terapiano, New York, Izdatel'stvo imeni Chekhova, 1953.
Merezhkovskij als Literaturkritiker: Versuch einer religiösen Begründung der Kunst, by Ute Spengler, Lucerne, Frankfurt, 1972.
The Seeker: D.S. Merezhkovskiy, by Harold C. Bedford, Lawrence, University of Kansas Press, 1975.
D.S. Merezhkovsky and the Silver Age: The Development of a Revolutionary Mentality, by B.G. Rosenthal, The Hague, Martinus Nijnhoff, 1975.
"Russian Metapolitics: Merezhkovsky's Religious Understanding of the Historical Process", by Heinrich Stammler, *California Slavic Studies*, 9 (1976), 123–39.
"Stages of Nietzscheanism: Merezhkovsky's Intellectual

Evolution", by B.G. Rosenthal, in *Nietzsche in Russia*, Princeton, Princeton University Press, 1986, 69–94.

D.S. Merezhkovsky in Exile: The Master of the Centre of Biographie Romancée, by Temira Pachmuss, New York and Bern, Peter Lang, "Slavic Languages and Series", vol. 12, 1990.

Dmitrii Merezhkovskii was born in St Petersburg, in 1865, into the family of a court official. He began his career as a Symbolist poet in 1881, and later wrote novels and essays on religio-philosophical issues as well as historical novels. By 1904 he had published a number of collections of his verse. In 1889 he married another Symbolist poet, Zinaida Hippius. Both of them were to become the most prominent figures in Russian pre-revolutionary literary life. From 1901 until 1920 they lived with D.V. Filosofov, symbolizing the new sexual liberty and a mystical union to their contemporaries. The three of them opened their own church in 1901, and in November the same year they organized a religio-philosophical society, attracting some of the most prominent figures of Russian culture. His first philosophical novel, *Khristos i Antikhrist* [Christ and Anti-Christ], was published between 1896 and 1905 as a trilogy. His books on Pushkin, Lermontov, Tolstoi, and Dostoevskii (published between 1896 and 1901) were considered masterpieces by his contemporaries. The views conveyed in them shaped the aesthetic and philosophical identity of Russian culture for many years to come. These works have been rediscovered in Russia today, and are receiving considerable attention. The second part of Merezhkovskii's trilogy was devoted to Leonardo da Vinci, and was translated the same year (1902) into English. From 1905 until 1912 Merezhkovskii lived in Paris; he became a wealthy man and a very popular writer both in Russia and in the west. The 17 volumes of his collected writings were published between 1911 and 1913, followed by a further 24 volumes in 1914. Merezhkovskii and Hippius were both openly opposed to the October Revolution; after living for a while in Warsaw they fled to Paris in 1920, where they spent the rest of their lives being active opponents of the communist regime. Merezhkovskii continued to publish historical novels up to 1925, thereafter he switched to philosophical writings, the most significant of which are *Iisus neizvestnyi* (*Jesus the Unknown*) published in 1931, and *Tod und Auferstehung* [Death and Resurrection], published in Germany in 1935. He and his wife lived in Italy from 1936 until 1938 and met Mussolini on several occasions. At this time Merezhkovskii was writing a novel about Dante and working on the life of the Spanish Saints. His final novel, *Malen'kaia Tereza* [Little Theresa], completed just before his death in 1941, was inspired by Hippius's poems and essays on St Thérèse whom the couple saw as the embodiment of eternal femininity. In spite of Merezhkovskii's profound curiosity about the history of Christianity, he was also interested in the exceptional qualities of the saints. This is reflected in the total fascination for Nietzsche that never left him. In 1939 he welcomed the beginning of Hitler's invasion of Europe, seeing Hitler as the personification of mystical force born to destroy the evil roots of pragmatism that was permeating western civilization. As Iurii Terapiano has recollected, Merezhkovskii spoke on French radio in 1939 and compared Hitler to a Jeanne d'Arc with knights, reinforcing new spiritual values. Because of his mystical statements and anti-Soviet pronouncements Merezhkovskii was never published in the Soviet Union before perestroika.

His work has found its way to Russian readers only since 1986 and has been studied relatively little. His poems, legends, and narrative poems about saints and historical figures (such as Francis of Assisi, Job, and Avvakum) merit further investigation, especially in conjunction with the ideas expressed in his novels. Some of his poems, such as "Titany" [Titans], can be compared to the monumental and heroic style of Briusov's poetry, although Merezhkovskii's artistic outlook was more influenced by Nietzsche than the authors of Ancient Greece and Rome. Belyi characterized Merezhkovskii as a better writer than philosopher:

> He was not a bad person, and his book on Tolstoi and Dostoevskii is a work of a genius; he dreamt of being a Russian Luther, but did not have the guts for it. In his other books he stands out as ... a little, narrow-minded, self-centred and silly person, juggling with great, unlimited, social and highly original issues.

His impact on early 20th-century Russian culture was enormous; he was also admired by contemporaries as a remarkable lecturer. Blok, for example, admits feeling so ecstatic after Merezhkovskii's lectures that he wanted to kiss his hand.

ALEXANDRA SMITH

Mikhail Larionovich Mikhailov 1829–1865

Prose writer, poet, and essayist

Biography

Born in Ufa, 15 January 1829. Educated at home by French and German tutors, then at Ufa gymnasium, 1845. Began to publish, 1845; attended St Petersburg University, 1846–48. Moved to Nizhnii Novgorod and took a job in the civil service, 1848–52, continued to write and translate; returned to St Petersburg, 1852; full-time writer and translator. Met Liudmila Shelgunova, the wife of Nikolai Shelgunov, 1855, with whom he had a life-long affair. Participated in literary expedition organized by Naval Ministry, 1856–57; travelled abroad with Shelgunovs, 1858–59; while abroad, began to write publicistic works; visited Herzen, 1859, and returned to St Petersburg. Travelled to western Europe and printed 600 copies of a revolutionary pamphlet in London, 1861. On his return, arrested for his role in the smuggling and distribution of the pamphlet, imprisoned in Peter and Paul Fortress, September 1861; sentenced to six years' hard labour, exile for life. In prisons in Tobolsk, Irkutsk, hard labour in Nerchinsk, 1862–65; moved to Kadai. Died 14/15 August 1865.

Publications

Collected Editions

Polnoe sobranie sochinenii, 4 vols. St Petersburg, 1914.
Sochineniia, 3 vols. Moscow, 1958.
Sobranie stikhotvorenii. Leningrad, 1969.

Fiction

"Adam Adamych", *Moskvitianin*, 18, 19–20 (1851), 186–264; 389–449.
"Kruzhevnitsa" [The Lace-Maker], *Sovremennik*, 5 (1852), 5–38.
"Sviatki" [Christmas-Tide], *Otechestvennye zapiski*, 3 (1853), 1–31.
"Pereletnye ptitsy" [Birds of Passage], *Otechestvennye zapiski*, 9–12 (1854), 1–96; 191–240; 133–92; 341–410.
Sibirskie ocherki [Siberian Essays]. 1867.
Vmeste [Together]. Published in part, 1870.

Poetry

"Ee on bezmolvno, no strastno liubil" [He Loved Her Silently, but Passionately], *Illiustratsiia* (July 1845).
"Nadia", *Literaturnaia gazeta*, 18 (1847), 278.
"Pomeshchik" [The Landowner] (originally published as "Okhotnik" [The Hunter]), *Literaturnaia gazeta*, 19 (1847), 294–95.
"Grunia", *Illiustratsiia*, 27 (1847), 35.

Play

"Tetushka" [Aunty], *Russkoe slovo*, 1 (1860), 354–91.

Memoirs

Vospominaniia, 2 vols, by M.L. Mikhailov, N.V. Shelgunov, and L.P. Shelgunova, Moscow, 1967.

Essays

"Zhenshchiny, ikh vospitanie i znachenie v sem'e i obshchestve" [Women and Their Significance in Society and in the Family], *Sovremennik*, 4, 5, 8 (1860), 473–500; 89–106; 335–50.
"Zhenshchiny v universitete" [Women in University], *Sovremennik*, 4 (1861), 499–507.
"Uvazhenie k zhenshchinam" [Respect for Women]. 1866.

Travel Writing

Parizhskie pis'ma [Paris Letters]. 1858–59.
Londonskie zametki [London Notes]. 1859.
Uralskie ocherki [Essays from the Urals]. 1859.

Translator

Pesni Geine v perevode M.L. Mikhailova [Songs of Heine]. St Petersburg, 1858.

Critical Studies

M.L. Mikhailov – revolutsioner, pisatel', publitsist, by P.S. Fateev, Moscow, 1969.
"M.L. Mikhailov and the Emergence of the Woman Question in Russia", by Richard Stites, *Canadian Slavic Studies*, 3 (1969), 178–99.
"M.L. Mikhailov and Russian Radical Ideas about Women, 1844–1865", by Jennifer Lonergan, PhD dissertation, University of Bristol, 1996.

Bibliographies

"Bibliografiia sochinenii M.I. Mikhailova", by P.V. Bykov in *Polnoe sobranie sochinenii*, by M.L. Mikhailov, 4 vols, St Petersburg, 1914.
"M.L. Mikhailov – kritik", *Trudy po russkoi i slavianskoi filologii IV*, Tartu, 1961.

Mikhail Mikhailov began his literary career writing and translating poetry. His first published works were a translation from Heinrich Heine, and an original poem, "Ee on bezmolvno, no strastno liubil" [He Loved Her Silently, but Passionately], which appeared in July 1845, when Mikhailov was only 16. In 1846 he moved to St Petersburg where he attended lectures at the University. He continued to publish poetry and short stories in *Illiustratsiia* and soon after in *Literaturnaia gazeta* whose editor, V.R. Zotov, strongly encouraged the young Mikhailov, and welcomed his contributions; in 1847 alone, Zotov's journal published more than 60 poems and short stories by Mikhailov. Mikhailov continued to translate poetry throughout his career, but in 1847 began to write more original poetry, and the occasional short story. In 1848, financial circumstances forced Mikhailov to leave the capital to take a civil service job in Nizhnii Novgorod. In 1851, *Moskvitianin* published "Adam Adamych", a short story based on the sad life of his childhood German tutor, which brought Mikhailov recognition, and enabled him to leave his job the following year and attempt a full-time writing career in the capital. In 1852, in addition to translated and original poetry, he published a number of short stories, including the favourably-received "Kruzhevnitsa" [The Lace-Maker]. He also produced a weekly review of happenings in the capital, *Peterburgskaia letopis'*. As of 1852, Mikhailov largely abandoned poetry and began to devote his energy primarily to prose. The short stories and plays that Mikhailov published during these years were typical of the "natural" school, demonstrating sympathy for downtrodden sections of society. Like other writers during the "seven gloomy years", Mikhailov did not deal directly with social and political issues. Nevertheless, stories such as "Skromnaia dolia" [A Modest Fate] (1852), "Kumushki" [Gossips] (1852), "Nash dom" [Our House] (1855), and "Golubye glazki" [Blue Eyes] (1855), were sympathetic portrayals of the difficult and tedious lives of the simple people, and show signs of a growing awareness of social issues. Almost half of Mikhailov's early fiction reflected a growing interest in, and sympathy for, the plight of women. Such stories as "Duniasha" (1847), "Nianiushka" [Nanny] (1851), "Poet" [The Poet] (1852), "Mar'ia Ivanovna" (1853), "Pereletnye ptitsy" [Birds of Passage] (1854), and "Napraslina" [The Wrongful Accusation] (1856), were sensitive depictions of intelligent, kind-hearted women corrupted or ruined as a result of their restricted positions.

During 1856–57, Mikhailov's literary endeavours were suspended while he was sent on a fact-finding mission organized and financed by the Naval Ministry. This opened Mikhailov's eyes to the backwardness and squalor of conditions in rural Russia. The expedition gave rise to the highly critical *Ural'skie ocherki* [Essays from the Urals]. After his return and a prolonged battle with typhus, Mikhailov went to Europe with Nikolai and Liudmila Shelgunov, whom he had met in 1855 and officially "took up residence" with in the spring of 1858. He now began to turn toward publicistic writing, composing a series of lively and informative travel notes, *Parizhskie pis'ma* [Paris Letters], and later *Londonskie zametki* [London Notes], in which he recorded his impressions of French and English plays, books, morality, and manners. While in France, he became involved in the debate raging there about the "woman question", provoked by P.J. Proudhon's recently-published *De la Justice dans la Révolution et dans l'Église*. Henceforth, his publicistic writings were almost exclusively devoted to the woman question, which had also begun to be discussed in Russia. His most significant article, "Zhenshchiny, ikh vospitanie i znachenie v sem'e i obshchestve" [Women and Their Significance in Society and in the Family], was pioneering in its length, comprehensiveness, and variety of its sources of evidence. Mikhailov denied that women were the intellectual and moral inferiors of men and called for their equality in the family and in society, arguing that, without it, progress was impossible. Unlike most of his contemporaries, including his progressive colleagues, Mikhailov stressed woman's intrinsic right to equality as a human being, rather than the potential advantages of an educated, emancipated woman to the family or society. This article was followed by "Zhenshchiny v universitete" [Women in University], and other articles, which provoked considerable debate in the press. By 1861, Mikhailov was considered the defender of women, and the champion of the woman question.

The disappointing Emancipation Edict sealed Mikhailov's radicalization. In September 1861, he was arrested for his role in the writing and distribution of the revolutionary pamphlet "K molodomu pokoleniiu" [To the Younger Generation]. Mikhailov's role in the writing of the pamphlet remains unknown, but he undoubtedly approved of it, had it printed by Herzen in London, and smuggled it into Russia. The Shelgunovs were also involved, but in an effort to spare them, Mikhailov accepted full responsibility for the pamphlet. He was sentenced to six years of hard labour in Siberia and lifelong exile. Once again, Mikhailov turned his attention to poetry, both original and translated, and to prose. He translated works by Goethe, George Eliot, Thomas Hood, and Robert Burns, wrote several short stories, including *Sibirskie ocherki* [Siberian Essays], a novella, *Vmeste* [Together], the essay "Uvazhenie k zhenshchinam" [Respect for Women], and many other works. Because of the ban on his name, they were published anonymously, or pseudonymously, and many did not appear until after his death. He also wrote his memoirs while in exile, where he died in 1865 at the age of 36.

As the first victim of political repression during the reign of the "tsar liberator", Alexander II, Mikhailov was assured martyr status. Although he is now remembered for his brief involvement in the burgeoning revolutionary situation of the 1860s, he was well-liked and well-respected by his contemporaries for his lively, witty personality, his diligence as a co-worker, his involvement in the woman question, and his literary endeavours, particularly his translations. He was very well-read and his professional opinion was widely valued by his peers. Mikhailov's translations were highly praised; in a review of his *Pesni Geine v perevode M.L. Mikhailova* [Songs of Heine], N.A. Dobroliubov declared that Mikhailov was the best translator of Heine. In addition to German, Mikhailov published translations of works from French, English, ancient and modern Greek, Latin, Serbian, Spanish, and other languages. Although much of his fiction has been forgotten, many of his tales and short stories, including "Sviatki" [Christmas-Tide], "Adam Adamych", "Kruzhevnitsa", and others, continue to be published in Russia today.

JENNIFER LONERGAN

Misery-Luckless-Plight *see* Tale of Woe-Misfortune

Vladimir Vsevolodovich Monomakh 1053–1125

Statesman and writer

Biography

Born in 1053. Excelled as politician, warrior, and writer. Successively prince of Smolensk, Chernigov, Pereiaslavl; finally prince of Kiev, from 1113. Died in 1125.

Publications

Works

Polnoe sobranie russkikh letopisei. Lavrent'evskaia letopis', Povest' vremennykh let [Complete Collected Russian Annals. The Laurentian redaction, Primary Chronicle]. 2nd edition, Leningrad, 1926, vol. 1, cols. 240–56.

The Russian Primary Chronicle, edited and translated by Samuel Hazzard Cross and Olgerd P. Sherbowitz-Wetzor. Cambridge, Massachusetts (Mediaeval Academy of America Publication 60), 1953, 301–13 (appendices I and II give a translation of the *Instruction*, the letter to Oleg and the prayer attributed to Monomakh).

"Pouchenie Vladimira Monomakha" [Instruction of Vladimir Monomakh], in *Khrestomatiia po drevnei russkoi literature XI–XVII vekov*, edited by N.K. Gudzii, Moscow, 1962, 35–40; also in *A Historical Russian Reader: A Selection of Texts from the Eleventh to the Sixteenth Centuries*, edited by John Fennell and Dimitri Obolensky, Oxford, Clarendon Press, 1969, 52–62.

Epistoliarnoe nasledie drevnei Rusi XI-XIII [The Epistolary Heritage of Ancient Russia, from the 11th to the 13th centuries], by N.B. Ponyrko, St Petersburg, 1992, 41–48 (annotated text of the letter with a Russian translation).

Critical Studies

Kniaz' Vladimir Monomakh i ego "Pouchenie", by I. Ivakin, Moscow, 1901.

Vladimir Monomakh, by Aleksandr Orlov, Moscow, 1946.

History of Russian Literature from the Eleventh Century to the End of the Baroque, by Dmitrij Čiževskij, The Hague, Mouton, 1960, 64–67.

"O vremeni i meste vkliucheniia v letopis' sochinenii Vladimira Monomakha", by N.N. Voronin, in *Istoriko-arkheologicheskii sbornik k 60-letiiu A.V. Artsekhovskogo*, Moscow, 1962, 265–71.

Early Russian Literature, by John Fennell and Antony Stokes, Berkeley, University of California Press, and London, Faber, 1974, 64–79.

"The Writings of Prince Vladimir Monomakh", by D.S. Likhachev, in *The Great Heritage: The Classical Literature of Old Rus'*, translated by Doris Bradbury, Moscow, Progress, 1981, 136–54.

Six Byzantine Portraits, by Dimitri Obolensky, Oxford, Clarendon Press, and New York, Oxford University Press, 1988, 83–114.

Vladimir, named Monomakh after his mother, the daughter of a Byzantine emperor, excelled as a politician, warrior, and writer. He employed all three abilities in his efforts to promote peace within the borders of the increasingly fragmented and troubled territory of Rus'. During his career he was successively prince of Smolensk, Chernigov, Pereiaslavl and finally prince of Kiev from 1113 to 1125.

Since the days of Monomakh's paternal grandfather, Iaroslav the Wise, when Rus' was divided into principalities and city-states, quarrelling had broken out over the patrimonies allotted to the princes. After the descendants of Prince Sviatoslav were dispossessed of Chernigov, their patrimony, their attempts to reclaim it resulted in ceaseless interprincely feuding, thereby exposing Rus' to attacks from nomadic tribes. Monomakh energetically strove to reconcile the princes by arranging conciliatory talks, as well as uniting them against their enemies.

Monomakh's extant literary works relate directly to his concerns as a prince of Rus'. These comprise his *Pouchenie* (*Instruction*) and a letter to his cousin Oleg. Both works occur in the Laurentian redaction of the *Povest' vremennykh let* (*Primary Chronicle*) *s.a.*1096. A prayer consisting chiefly of quotations from the Lenten Liturgy (which follows the *Instruction* and letter), previously attributed to Monomakh, has since been shown to be of later origin. These writings are found in only one manuscript, which suggests that they were added by a later scribe. Judging by the lacuna of four and a half lines at the beginning of the text and the absence of a clear division between the *Instruction* and letter, it is probable that these works were copied from a separate, well-thumbed notebook.

Monomakh's *Instruction* was written foremost for his children as rulers in Rus' but also aimed at a wider audience. It falls into three sections: an introduction and extracts from the "divine writings"; Monomakh's own advice on the duties of a prince at home and abroad; and thirdly a résumé of his "puti" – travels, battles, and hunting expeditions with his concluding remarks. When exactly Monomakh wrote his *Instruction* is not clear, although the text contains several hints. The introduction relates an incident that probably took place in 1099. The last skirmish recorded in Monomakh's "puti" can be dated 1117. Monomakh may have composed his work over a number of years and only produced a complete edition in his old age. This is borne out by his remark describing himself as "on a distant journey and sitting on a sleigh", which, if taken metaphorically, signifies approaching death.

The *Instruction*, his main work, can be linked in a general sense to the tradition of a father's instructions to his children, a literary form that has existed from time immemorial. Attempts to relate it more specifically to particular works by Anglo-Saxon or Byzantine writers have been less successful. The first section of the work begins with a moral dilemma embodied in the veiled threat of the messengers to join in the conspiracy against his kinsmen or else ... Should Monomakh sacrifice his personal interests and security for the wider concern for Rus', and so respect his oath guaranteeing the integrity of each principality? Monomakh answers with a resounding "no": first in his initial refusal to join the conspiracy, and second in his selection of quotations from the Psalter that follows. Using the words of the Psalter, Monomakh affirms that there is a God who will judge the wicked and vindicate the righteous. Then he quotes from patristic literature, laying down guidelines for behaviour at mealtimes, and towards elders, equals and juniors, and women. If insulted, the writer urges restraint in action and thought, bearing in mind God's great mercy and fatherly love. Monomakh insists that the three virtues of repentance, tears, and almsgiving are sufficient to gain salvation. He concludes the section of "divine writings" with praise to God, echoing lines from John the Exarch's work *Six Days of Creation* (Shestodnev). In the second section of the *Instruction*, composed from "my poor mind", Monomakh gives advice for the daily routine of a prince's life. He advocates rising for matins, with prayer and genuflection before sleep. During the day on horseback he recommends the silent recitation of the prayer "Lord, have mercy". He urges the princes to support the orphan and widow, showing respect and love to the clergy. Under no circumstance should one take the life of a Christian or swear an oath that cannot be honoured. At home and at war Monomakh emphasizes the need to be diligent, attending to arrangements oneself. While travelling, he counsels respect for the rights of local inhabitants and generosity to beggars and strangers. He commands his reader to visit the sick, accompany the procession for the dead and when at home to love his wife but grant her no power over him. In both spheres of life, sacred and secular, Monomakh drives home an uncompromising message of hard work. Monomakh's unrelenting pace is felt in his "puti" – from c.1068 to c.1117. Strings of active verbs, "I went", "I attacked", "I set out" convey the intense activity of those years. Stamped on, gored and wounded on different hunting expeditions, Vladimir survives to urge his reader to be diligent and to fear God. Despite inattention to stylistic niceties or to an obvious structure, Monomakh's work is united by a conviction that Christianity is a layman's religion, joyful and practical, providing a moral basis to meet all life's circumstances.

Monomakh's letter to Oleg played a part in the tragic events of 1096. Oleg, attempting to regain his patrimony by force and treachery, attacked the town of Murom and killed Monomakh's son, Iziaslav. It was Mstislav, Iziaslav's brother, Monomakh admits in the letter, who urged him to write to Oleg as a gesture of peace, forestalling further bloodshed. He confesses his surprise that Oleg, having seen Iziaslav "as he lay like a withered flower or a slaughtered lamb", did not take the initiative. For his own part, he remembers his duty before God, and the prospect future judgement. If Christ submitted himself to scourging, who is he, he asks, to withhold forgiveness. Beside which, he considers death as judgement from the hand of God and a common fate of princes in battle. Monomakh's letter illustrates a fine command of language, conveying with refreshing honesty his practical faith.

Although Monomakh's main literary work, his *Instruction*, was neither much imitated or even commonly available (judging by the one manuscript), it indelibly impresses the ethics and activity of one lay writer, princely ruler, and determined warrior.

JOY H. BACHE

Boris Andreevich Mozhaev 1923–1996

Prose writer

Biography

Born in Pitelino (Riazanskaia oblast'), 1 June 1923. Attended local village school in Potap'evo; worked as village teacher for six months. Failed to gain admittance to Leningrad military engineering and technical college (on account of his father who had been branded an "enemy of the people" for refusal to join collective farm in early 1930s). Army service in the Soviet Far East. Admitted to engineering college and studied at Leningrad University (philological faculty) at same time, 1943–48. Attended meetings and workshops at the Leningrad House of Writers. Followed courses in scriptwriting in Moscow. Returned to the Soviet Far East as naval engineer; lived and served in China, 1949–51. Left the army to pursue a career in journalism, 1954; then became a professional writer. Excluded from the Writers' Union, 1959 (but reinstated six months later) for the critical content of his works. Married: Milda Emil'evna Shnorna in 1962; one daughter and two sons. Recipient: USSR State Prize for Literature for Book II of *Muzhiki i baby* [Peasant Folk], 1989. Died 2 March 1996.

Publications

Collected Editions

Izbrannye proizvedeniia, 2 vols. Moscow, 1982.
Sobranie sochinenii, 4 vols. Moscow, 1989–90.

Fiction

"Zemlia zovet. Ocherk" [The Earth Calls. A Sketch], *Dal'nii vostok*, 4 (1955), 118–42.
Udegeiskie skazki [Udeheskian Tales]. Vladivostok, 1955.
"V taezhnom sele. Rasskaz" [In a Taiga Village], *Dal'nii vostok*, 3 (1956), 96–112.
"Vlast' taigi. Rasskaz" [The Power of the Taiga], *Oktiabr'*, 8 (1957), 110–29.
Zheleznyi kliuv. Udegeiskie narodnye skazki [The Iron Beak. Udeheskian Folk Tales]. Blagoveshchensk, 1959.
Vlast' taigi. Povest' i rasskazy [The Power of the Taiga]. Vladivostok, 1959.
Sania. Naled'. Tonkomer. Povesti [Sania. Coating of Ice. Thin Gauge]. Blagoveshchensk, 1961.
V amurskoi dal'nei storone [In the Distant Land by the Amur River]. Moscow, 1963.

Poliushko-pole. Povest' [Field, My Field]. Moscow, 1965.
"Iz zhizni Fedora Kuz'kina" [From the Life of Fedor Kuz'kin], *Novyi mir*, 7 (1966), 42-118; as "Zhivoi" [Lively], in *Lesnaia doroga*, 1973; translated as *Dans la vie de Fédor Kouzkine*, by Jean Cathala, Paris, Gallimard, 1972.
Istoriia sela Brekhova, pisannaia Petrom Afanas'evichem Bulkinym [A History of Brekhovo Village Written by Petr Afanas'evich Bulkin]. Moscow, 1968.
"Lesnaia doroga. Ocherk" [The Forest Path], *Novyi mir*, 9 (1969), 132–50.
Propazha svidetelia [The Witness Disappears]. Moscow, 1969.
Dal'nevostochnye povesti [Far Eastern Stories]. Moscow, 1970.
Dal'nie dorogi [Distant Paths]. Moscow, 1970.
Lesnaia doroga. Povesti i rasskazy [The Forest Path]. Moscow, 1973.
Padenie lesnogo korolia [The Fall of the Forest King]. Moscow, 1974.
Muzhiki i baby. Roman [Peasant Folk]. Moscow, 1976; reprinted 1979.
Starye istorii. Povesti i rasskazy [Old Stories]. Moscow, 1978.
Zhivoi. Povest' i rasskazy [Lively]. Moscow, 1979.
Minuvshie gody. Roman, povesti [Past Years]. Moscow, 1981.
"Poltora kvadratnykh metra" [One and a Half Square Metres], *Druzhba narodov*, 4 (1982), 105–57.
Tonkomer. Povesti [Thin Gauge]. Moscow, 1984; reprinted 1985.
Dozhd' budet. Roman, povesti, rasskazy [There Will Be Rain]. Moscow, 1985.
"Muzhiki i baby. Roman-khronika. Kniga vtoraia" [Peasant Folk. Book Two], *Don*, 1–3 (1987), 18–136; 5–129; 62–106.
Muzhiki i baby. Roman [Peasant Folk]. Moscow, 1987; reprinted Moscow, 1988.
"Izgoi. Roman" [The Outcast], *Nash sovremennik*, 2–3 (1993), 5–49; 19–70.
"Sviaz' vremen. Ulichnye razgovory. Ispoved' chistoserdechnogo cheloveka" [The Connection of Times. Street Conversations. Confession of a Sincere Person], *Don*, 3–4 (1993), 3–24.

Poetry
"Zabiaki" Kniga dlia malyshei ["Zabiaki" A Book for Children]. Vladivostok, 1954, contains some poems by Mozhaev.
Zori nad okeanom: Stikhi, pesni, poema [Dawn Over the Ocean]. Vladivostok, 1955.

Plays
"Kak zemlia vertitsia. Komedia v dvukh deistviakh" [That's How the World Goes Round], *Teatr*, 1 (1986), 3–33.
"Edinozhdy solgavshi. Tragikomedia" [Cry Wolf], *Iunost'*, 4 (1988), 18–39.

Screenplays
"Den' bez kontsa i bez kraia. Kinopovest'" [A Day Without End], *Novyi mir*, 9 (1973), 19–66.
Uvazhenie k zemle. Ocherki, kinopovest' [Respect for the Land]. Moscow, 1979.

Essays
Samostoiatel'nost'. Ocherki [Independence]. Moscow, 1972.
Zapakh miaty i khleb nasushnyi. Esse, polemicheskie zametki [The Smell of Mint and Daily Bread]. Moscow, 1982.

Critical Studies
Pereklichka epokh: Ocherki, portrety, stat'i, by F.F. Kuznetsov, Moscow, 1976, 300–07; 2nd editon, 1980, 271–77.
"Promezhutochnaia literatura", by Iu. Mal'tsev, *Kontinent*, 25 (1980), 285–321.
A History of Post-War Soviet Writing: The Literature of Moral Opposition, by Grigori Svirski, translated by Robert Dessaix and Michael Ulman, Ann Arbor, Ardis, 1981.
"Gor'kovskie traditsii v tvorchestve Borisa Mozhaeva (Na materiale povesti "Zhivoi")', by A.V. Koshkin, in *Gor'kovskie traditsii v sovetskoi literature*, edited by V.V. Agenosov, Moscow, 1983, 110–16.
"'Kvadratnaia kaplia': o povesti Borisa Mozhaeva 'Poltora kvadratnykh metra'", by K. Sapgir, *Grani*, 131 (1984), 294–98.
"Vniz po techeniiu derevenskoi prozy", by L. Vil'chek, *Voprosy literatury*, 6 (1985), 34–72.
"Chitateli o romane B.A. Mozhaeva 'Muzhiki i baby'", *Don*, 12 (1987), 161–69.
"Pamiat'", by G. Murikov, *Zvezda*, 12 (1987), 166–76.
"'Vykhodia iz bezgranichnoi svobody ...'. Model' 'Besov' v romane B. Mozhaeva 'Muzhiki i baby'", by L. Saraskina, *Oktiabr'*, 7 (1988), 181–99.
"History, Politics, and the Russian Peasant: Boris Mozhaev and the Collectivization of Agriculture", by David Gillespie, *Slavonic and East European Review*, 67/2 (1989), 183–210.
"Roman 'Muzhiki i baby' v vypusknom klasse", by I.I. Chernova, *Vecherniaia sredniaia shkola*, 4–6 (1992), 35–39.
"Collectivization and the Utopian Ideal in the Works of Boris Mozhaev", by D.M. Holohan, PhD dissertation, University of Bath, 1994.

Even while he was still in the navy, Boris Mozhaev wrote poetry and stories; some of his early poems were made into songs in 1952 and enjoyed considerable popularity. However, Mozhaev has never taken his poetry seriously and he is principally a writer of prose. His interest in film has resulted in the successful production of more than ten film scripts, some adapted by him from his own prose works. He has also shown an interest in the theatre: his stage version of *Zhivoi* [Lively] or *Iz zhizni Fedora Kuz'kina* [From the Life of Fedor Kuz'kin] (1966), was banned at the Taganka Theatre and the director Liubimov was stripped of his Party membership (later reinstated). He has also written two plays, one of which, *Edinozhdy solgavshi* [Cry Wolf], was completed in 1966 but not published until 1988. Both *Edinozhdy solgavshi* and his other play, *Kak zemlia vertitsia* [That's How the World Goes Round], were banned during rehearsals at the Moscow Arts Theatre and Mozhaev had to tolerate delays virtually throughout his writing career; from 1974, for almost ten years, none of the "thick" journals would publish his work. He complained about being ignored as a writer in June 1986 at the 8th Writers' Congress in Moscow.

Mozhaev's early works were criticized for focusing on what critics called "the negative aspects of life": in "Tonkomer" [Thin Gauge], "Naled'" [Coating of Ice], and "Sania", he portrays communities living in squalid conditions, slavishly adhering to an unrealistic plan handed down from higher authorities who know little of the reality of working conditions. Characters in positions of authority who show initiative and take a personal interest in those in their charge have to battle constantly with officials of a mechanistic, Stalinist mentality. Mozhaev often ends his stories on a note of ambiguity: the "hero" or "heroine" is not victorious and has to pay a high price, both physically and spiritually, for the stand taken. These works also show a strong concern for ecological issues. It was for these works that he was excluded from the Writers' Union.

The publication of his story *Zhivoi* caused a stir in Soviet society, similar to that provoked by Solzhenitsyn's *One Day in the Life of Ivan Denisovich*. Mozhaev had to agree to the suggestion (made by Tvardovskii) that the title be toned down to sound less provocative: Grigorii Svirskii has noted that the title "seemed like a clarion call to the dead and lifeless who were coming into their own in 1966, the year before the 50th anniversary of the Revolution". The beginning of the story is startling in that it is set within a religious context, St Florov's Day, a device that Mozhaev repeats in Book II of his novel *Muzhiki i baby* [Peasant Folk]. Kuz'kin (modelled on Mozhaev's own father) is no longer able to stay within the kolkhoz (collective farm) system because of the poor remuneration offered to the workers after other organizations with a higher priority have been paid: debts to the state and the Machine and Tractor Station (MTS) workers had to be settled first, often leaving little for the kolkhoz workers themselves. In his struggle to escape the spite of officials and to provide his family with the bare necessities to survive, Kuz'kin almost loses his life and Mozhaev implies that the kolkhoz worker lives and works in a state of near feudalism. Kuz'kin is one of Mozhaev's most memorable characters: he has an endearing wit, vivacity and tenacity, and can be seen as a prototype for similar rural characters in his novel *Muzhiki i baby*; he adds a note of humour to an otherwise very bleak situation.

Mozhaev differs markedly from other Village Prose writers with whom he is most often associated (though he rejected the label Village Prose writer or *derevenshchik*). His work has a strong publicistic quality, he uses a variety of genres, and he often addresses issues of agricultural practice and organization current at the time of writing. Hence in *Zhivoi*, issues such as the link system and the *trudoden'* (workday-unit) means of payment are addressed. In his detective novel trilogy, *Vlast' taigi* [The Power of the Taiga], *Propazha svidetelia* [The Witness Disappears] and *Padenie lesnogo korolia* [The Fall of the Forest King], he combines his interest in Udegei folklore (evident in the latter two works) with a keen concern for ecological issues and law breaking, which is officially ignored.

Although the picture Mozhaev paints of rural life is generally bleak, he did write about it in a comic vein and he can be seen at his most humorous in *Istoriia sela Brekhova, pisannaia Petrom Afanas'evichem Bulkinym* [A History of Brekhovo Village Written by Petr Afanas'evich Bulkin]. The very title is reminiscent of Gogol''s *Mirgorod* story of the two Ivans, and of Saltykov-Shchedrin's *Istoriia odnogo goroda* (*The History of a Town*), and the humour reflects both writers: Saltykov-Shchedrin's satire on history and the Russian monarchy is paralleled in Mozhaev's ridiculing of official Soviet historiography, politics, and associated Soviet rhetoric, and the story includes scenes of near slapstick comedy reminiscent of Gogol', but set in the context of major events in Soviet history, such as collectivization and dekulakization.

In his screenplay *Den' bez kontsa i bez kraia* [A Day Without End], Mozhaev questions the scientific-materialistic basis of Marxism-Leninism. The controversy over Lysenko's ideas is re-enacted in this work between the biologist Mariia Tverdokhlebova and a senior researcher Liasota (clearly a parody of Lysenko himself). However, the work goes much deeper than this: the Marxist insistence on the influence of the social environment on the character of man is challenged. Liasota's attempt to adapt a strain of wheat to the inimical northern climate is juxtaposed with discussions about the attempt to change man, to create a new Soviet man by manipulating the social environment. There is also a scene in which a productive peasant is dispossessed on the thin pretext that he is a kulak, a theme developed subsequently in Mozhaev's novels.

One of Mozhaev's works that does not have a rural setting is his *Poltora kvadratnykh metra* [One and a Half Square Metres], set in a small provincial town. Mozhaev brings to bear his keen sense of humour to a ludicrous situation, but he makes a serious point. It is the epic story of an inhabitant of a communal block of flats, Poluboiarinov, who tries to solve the problem of a neighbour who habitually lies in a drunken stupor outside his door that opens out into the corridor: thus the man stops the door from opening and prevents the tenants from using the communal bathroom. The solution requires taking one and a half square metres of communal corridor to move the door and allow it to open into the flat. It is a story of bureaucracy and petty-mindedness gone mad, as officials in the town victimize Poluboiarinov for what they interpret as "pre-revolutionary acquisitiveness", the chief accusation levelled at so-called kulak families in the early 1930s. As with so many of Mozhaev's other works, the story ends on a depressing note: Poluboiarinov becomes a broken man after years of desperately seeking justice and a rational outcome to his problem through legal channels.

Many of the themes and preoccupations mentioned above are explored in greater depth in his novel *Muzhiki i baby*. The fates of some of the characters of this novel were developed further in his late novel *Izgoi* [The Outcast]. Mozhaev frequently has characters make a second (and even a third) appearance in subsequent works. Besides his novellas and numerous short stories, Mozhaev produced a large number of publicistic works that appeared regularly in newspapers and magazines and the subjects are typically: the regeneration of rural communities; the reorganization of kolkhoz management and greater freedom for farmers to act independently of the state; bureaucracy in all its forms; the need for greater investment in the rural infrastructure, particularly in roads, hospitals and education; ecological issues; literature and the changing role of the writer in post-glasnost Russian society.

DAVID M. HOLOHAN

Muzhiki i baby

Peasant Folk

Novel, 1976–87

Mozhaev remarked that the campaign for the full collectivization of agriculture (1929–30), the subject of the novel *Muzhiki i baby*, is a topic that interested him all his life. Many characters in Mozhaev's works that pre-date *Muzhiki i baby* can be seen as prototypes he develops more fully in the novel: the indomitable Fedor Kuz'kin of his *povest'* (novella) *Zhivoi* has much in common with the peasant Andrei Borodin of the novel; the demagogic official Sudeikin of his *Den' bez kontsa i bez kraia*, who seeks out and dispossesses some of the most productive peasants, is transformed into the far more vicious officials Zenin, Vozvyshaev, and Ashikhmin of *Muzhiki i baby*.

Mozhaev's interest in folklore and rural crafts, seen most notably in his early stories of the Udegei people and in *Propazha svidetelia* and *Padenie lesnogo korolia*, forms an interesting backdrop to the turmoil created by the officials, as they destroy the rural community in their eagerness to outdo one another's efforts in fulfilling what they perceive as their duties.

The detective novel genre of *Propazha svidetelia* and *Padenie lesnogo korolia* also finds its way into *Muzhiki i baby* and lends the novel its basic structure: the narrative line of Book 1 of the novel focuses on Andrei Borodin's searching for his stolen horse, but in Book 2 the hunter becomes the hunted, as officials try to corner him and force him to join the kolkhoz. In Mozhaev's second novel, *Izgoi*, the fate of Borodin is revealed; he is dispossessed and dies in a labour camp in the Soviet Far East.

Muzhiki i baby comprises a series of tableaux, often powerfully narrated (but sometimes amusing), and they attest to the fact that Mozhaev is principally a writer of shorter genres. As with many of his works, Mozhaev's *Muzhiki i baby* was subjected to a long delay before it was published. Book 1 was finished in 1973, but the numerous rejections by editors forced him to seek a less orthodox route; unusually, it was published in book form without having appeared in a journal. Book 2 (the more outspoken of the two) was subjected to even longer delay: completed in 1980, it was not published until 1987, in the provincial journal *Don*.

Book 1 sets the scene before the actual onset of the campaign for full collectivization of agriculture and follows the "middle peasant", Andrei Borodin, as he tries to find his stolen horse. He strongly suspects the notorious local thief Zhadov and his gang. Borodin's searching brings him into contact with a number of peasants and local craftsmen, all of whom are becoming increasingly concerned about the campaign for full collectivization. Book 1 also introduces the local teacher and former co-operative bookkeeper, Uspenskii, and a group of other intellectuals and activists who discuss their work of collecting grain and persuading reluctant peasants to relinquish their private holdings and join the kolkhoz movement. Some activists and intellectuals question the wisdom of the policy and discuss alternative stratagems. Mozhaev portrays the peasantry as a fiercely independent and hard-working people, who enjoy the freedom of the NEP era. There is a memorable market scene and descriptions of local crafts and traditions, such as horse-racing on market day. He describes a generally united and prosperous community that shows great initiative in trading, but is clearly nervous of the radical changes made in recent history, and yet to come.

Book 2 is set within the religious context of Christmas: Andrei Borodin has sensed the danger of his position as a "middle peasant" and has witnessed the arbitrary way in which farmers are being classified as kulaks by officials: he decides to leave while he can, but eventually thinks better of this and returns to his family. Violence and bitterness escalate as the activists, Zenin, Vozvyshaev and Ashikhmin, set about their work, forcing unwilling peasants to join the collective movement. Some abandon their property and flee; others destroy it in an act of defiant self-dispossession. Uspenskii, as the son of a priest, engages in bitter arguments with the activists, incurring their enmity. The intellectuals engage in philosophical discussions on Russian history, thought and the intelligentsia, in an attempt to understand the source and nature of Russian radicalism. Uspenskii and Mariia (an activist who hands back her party card) become lovers, but their relationship is cut short when Uspenskii (an ex-Red Army soldier) dies in an attempt to save a village lad from the bullet of one of a group of soldiers sent to quell the riot at the end of the novel. The communist Ozimov is also shot while attempting to arbitrate between local peasants and the more extreme officials who control the campaign in the area. Thus both Christian *intelligent* and thinking communist die at the hands of extremists. Mozhaev's vivid scenes of dispossession, the splitting up of families, the desecration of local churches and the seeking out of "class enemies" are narrated with great passion and drama. By the end, the whole community has been destroyed: the vibrant market scene of Book 1 is reduced to a mere parody of its former hustle and bustle.

Despite their separate publication, Books 1 and 2 are intended to be taken as one cohesive work. The novel is an important sociological and historical work: over many years of study and talking to peasant eye-witnesses, Mozhaev went to great pains to portray an accurate and unromanticized picture of rural life in the pre- and post-collectivization era. There has been much critical acclaim for the accuracy of his portrayal on this level. His aim was to set the historical record straight, since these events had been greatly sanitized by official Soviet historians.

On the political level, however, Mozhaev offers a much less objective assessment of events: by citing their more militant statements from the Civil War period until the end of the 1920s, he attributes blame to Trotskii, Zinov'ev, Preobrazhenskii, Kamenev, and Kaganovich. Mozhaev implies that the NEP period should have been extended, that communes should have been allowed to flourish and that the delicate union between rural folk and urban workers should have been nurtured as Lenin had advocated. These ideas were all vigorously supported by Bukharin at the end of the 1920s, yet Mozhaev quotes only his more militant statements from the early 1920s and does not credit him with any of his radical policy changes. Over half the politicians quoted and blamed are Jewish, as is Zenin, the most spiteful of all the activists in the novel. Lenin is praised for his wisdom, and Stalin also emerges unscathed. In short, Mozhaev's political views appear authoritarian and anti-Semitic, in common with several other Village Prose writers.

Past leaders such as Peter the Great, radicals such as Stenka Razin, and the *intelligenty* of the 1830s onwards are all blamed for wanting to overturn the status quo in an effort to find quick solutions to Russia's long-standing problems. Mozhaev sees a similar influence at work in the 20th century in the radical left wing of the Bolshevik Party, and particularly in Bukharin and others mentioned above.

Early western socialist thinkers are allotted a considerable share of the blame too, for infecting Russia with radicalism, principally through the Petrashevskii circle in St Petersburg from the mid-1840s. The Utopian visions of early socialist thinkers such as Cabet, Fourier, Blanqui, Sismondi, Babeuf, and Buonarotti are discussed, and the intellectuals refer to Plato's *The Republic* and Tommaso Campanella's *La città del sole* (*The City of the Sun*). As far as Mozhaev's right-wing intellectuals are concerned, all such thinkers are guilty of demagogy, of stifling individualism and reducing life to a mechanistic level, where people respond in a predictable, logical way to social stimuli and edicts. The depiction of the drive for full collectivization is associated with building a western Utopian model of society, at the end of the novel called a "great experiment", for which Russia paid dearly in human life and damage to the economy. This philosophical aspect of *Muzhiki i baby* makes the novel unique among works dealing with collectivization.

Mozhaev completed his *roman-khronika* with *Izgoi*, in which he continued the themes and described the fate of some of the characters featured in *Muzhiki i baby*, extending its scope through the era of Stalinism to the late 1960s.

DAVID M. HOLOHAN

N

Vladimir Vladimirovich Nabokov 1899–1977

Prose writer, translator, and lepidopterist

Biography

Born in St Petersburg, 22 April 1899. Attended Tenishev school, St Petersburg; fluent English and French speaker. Wrote under the pseudonym Vladimir Sirin until 1940. Published two collections of poetry, 1916 and 1918. Family emigrated in 1919; studied Romance and Slavonic Languages at Cambridge University, England. Moved to Berlin; worked as translator and writer, 1922–37. Father assassinated by monarchist extremists, 1922. Married: Vera Evseevna Slonim in 1924; one son. Moved to Paris, 1937; worked as translator, language teacher, and tennis instructor. As Europe fell to the Nazis, sailed to the United States, 1940. Thereafter wrote in English and translated important works of Russian literature. Taught at Wellesley College; also held a Harvard Research Fellowship in lepidoptera. Professor of Russian Literature, Cornell University, Ithaca, New York, 1948–59. Retired after the success of *Lolita*; moved to Montreux, Switzerland, 1960, where he continued to write and set about finalising his literary affairs. Died in Lausanne, 2 July 1977. Began to be published in Russia only in 1986.

Publications

Collected Editions

Nine Stories. Norfolk, Connecticut, New Directions, 1947.

Nabokov's Dozen: A Collection of Thirteen Stories. New York, Doubleday, 1958; London, Heinemann, 1959; Harmondsworth, Penguin, 1960.

Nabokov's Quartet, translated by Dmitri Nabokov. New York, Phaedra, 1966; London, Weidenfeld and Nicolson, 1967.

Poems and Problems (bilingual edition). New York, McGraw-Hill, 1970; London, Weidenfeld and Nicolson, 1972.

A Russian Beauty and Other Stories, translated by Dmitri Nabokov and Simon Karlinsky. New York, McGraw-Hill, and London, Weidenfeld and Nicolson, 1973; Harmondsworth, Penguin, 1975.

Tyrants Destroyed and Other Stories, translated by Dmitri Nabokov. New York, McGraw-Hill, and London, Weidenfeld and Nicolson, 1975; Harmondsworth, Penguin, 1981.

Details of a Sunset and Other Stories, translated by Dmitri Nabokov with the author. New York, McGraw-Hill, 1976.

Five Novels. London, Collins, 1979.

The Man from the USSR and Other Plays, translated by Dmitri Nabokov. New York, Harcourt Brace Jovanovich, 1984; London, Weidenfeld and Nicolson, 1985.

Sobranie sochinenii, 10 vols. Ann Arbor, Ardis, 1987 – [vols 1, 3, 6, 9, 10 published].

Rasskazy. Moscow, 1989.

Istreblenie tiranov: Izbrannaia proza [Tyrants Destroyed]. Minsk, 1989.

Krug [Circle]. Leningrad, 1990.

P'esy [Plays]. Moscow, 1990.

Sobranie sochinenii, edited by Viktor Erofeev, 4 vols. Moscow, 1990; supplementary volumes, 1992, 1995.

The Stories of Vladimir Nabokov. New York, Knopf, 1995; London, Weidenfeld and Nicolson, 1996; as *The Collected Stories of Vladimir Nabokov*, Harmondsworth, Penguin, 1997.

Fiction

Mashen'ka. Berlin, 1926; reprinted Ann Arbor, Ardis, 1974; translated as *Mary*, by Michael Glenny with the author, New York, McGraw-Hill, 1970; London, Weidenfeld and Nicolson, 1971; Harmondsworth, Penguin, 1973.

Korol', dama, valet. Berlin, 1928; reprinted Ann Arbor, Ardis, 1979; translated as *King, Queen, Knave*, by Dmitri Nabokov with the author, New York, McGraw-Hill, and London, Weidenfeld and Nicolson, 1968.

Zashchita Luzhina. Berlin, 1930; reprinted Ann Arbor, Ardis, 1979; translated as *The Defence*, by Michael Scammell with the author, New York, Putnam, and London, Weidenfeld and Nicolson, 1964; Oxford, Oxford University Press, 1986; as *The Luzhin Defense*, Harmondsworth, Penguin, 1994.

Vozvrashchenie Chorba. Berlin, 1930; reprinted Ann Arbor, Ardis, 1976; title story translated as "The Return of Chorb", by Dmitri Nabokov, in *Details of a Sunset and Other Stories*, 1976.

"Sogliadatai", *Sovremennye zapiski*, 44 (1930). *Sogliadatai* [as collection] 1938; reprinted Ann Arbor, Ardis, 1978; translated as *The Eye*, by Dmitri Nabokov with the author, London, Weidenfeld and Nicolson, 1966; Harmondsworth, Penguin, 1992.

Kamera obskura. Paris, 1932; reprinted Ann Arbor, Ardis, 1978; translated as *Camera Obscura*, by Winifred Roy, London, John Long, 1936; also as *Laughter in the Dark*, by the author, New York, 1938; revised edition New York, New Directions, 1960; London, Weidenfeld and Nicolson, 1961; Harmondsworth, Penguin, 1963.

Podvig. Berlin, 1932; reprinted Ann Arbor, Ardis, 1974; translated as *Glory*, by Dmitri Nabokov with the author, New York, McGraw-Hill, 1971; London, Weidenfeld and Nicolson, 1972; Harmondsworth, Penguin, 1974.
"Otchaianie", *Sovremennye zapiski*, 54 (1934); Berlin, Petropolis, 1936; reprinted Ann Arbor, Ardis, 1978; translated as *Despair*, by the author, London, John Long, 1937; revised edition, New York, Putnam, 1966; Harmondsworth, Penguin, 1981.
Priglashenie na kazn'. 1935–36; Paris, 1938; reprinted Ann Arbor, Ardis, 1979 and 1984; translated as *Invitation to a Beheading*, by Dmitri Nabokov with the author, New York, Putnam, 1959; London, Weidenfeld and Nicolson, 1960.
"Dar", *Sovremennye zapiski*, 63 (1937); first integral edition, New York, Izdatel'stvo imeni Chekhova, 1952; 2nd edition Ann Arbor, Ardis, 1975; translated as *The Gift*, by Dmitri Nabokov and Michael Scammell with the author, London, Weidenfeld and Nicolson, 1963; Harmondsworth, Penguin, 1981.
"Solus Rex" (fragment of novel), *Sovremennye zapiski*, 70 (1940); translated as "Solus Rex", by Dmitri Nabokov and Simon Karlinsky, in *A Russian Beauty and Other Stories*, 1973.
The Real Life of Sebastian Knight. Norfolk, Connecticut, New Directions, 1941; 1959; London, Weidenfeld and Nicolson, 1960; Harmondsworth, Penguin, 1964; reprinted, 1995.
"Ultima Thule", *Novyi zhurnal*, 1 (1942); translated by Dmitri Nabokov and Simon Karlinsky, in *A Russian Beauty and Other Stories*, 1973.
Bend Sinister. New York, Holt, 1947; London, Weidenfeld and Nicolson, 1960; Harmondsworth, Penguin, 1974.
Lolita. Paris, Olympia, 1955; London, Weidenfeld and Nicolson, 1959; (Russian edition New York, Phaedra, 1967; reprinted Ann Arbor, Ardis, 1976); Harmondsworth, Penguin, 1980; reprinted 1995; *The Annotated Lolita*, edited by Alfred J. Appel, Jr, New York, McGraw-Hill, 1971; reprinted New York, Vintage, 1991; London, Weidenfeld and Nicolson, 1993; Harmondsworth, Penguin, 1995.
Vesna v Fial'te [Spring in Fialta]. New York, 1956; reprinted Ann Arbor, Ardis, 1978; title story translated in *Nabokov's Dozen*, 1958.
Pnin. New York, Doubleday, and London, Heinemann, 1957; Harmondsworth, Penguin, 1960; translated into Russian by Gennadii Barabtarlo, Ann Arbor, Ardis, 1983.
Pale Fire. New York, Putnam, 1962; Harmondsworth, Penguin, 1973; reprinted with an introduction by Mary McCarthy, 1991; translated into Russian as *Blednyi ogon'*, by Vera Nabokova, Ann Arbor, Ardis, 1984.
Ada or Ardor: A Family Chronicle. New York, McGraw-Hill, and London, Weidenfeld and Nicolson, 1969; Harmondsworth, Penguin, 1970 [includes "Notes to *Ada* by Vivian Darkbloom"].
Transparent Things. New York, McGraw-Hill, 1972; London, Weidenfeld and Nicolson,1973; Harmondsworth, Penguin, 1975.
Look at the Harlequins. New York, McGraw-Hill, 1974; London, Weidenfeld and Nicolson, 1975; Harmondsworth, Penguin, 1980.
The Enchanter, translated by Dmitri Nabokov. New York, Putnam, 1986; London, Picador, 1987; original Russian as "Volshebnik", *Russian Literature Triquarterly*, 24 (1991), 9–41; in *Sobranie sochinenii*, vol. 3, Ann Arbor, Ardis, 1991.
"La veneziana", translated by Dmitri Nabokov, in *The Stories of Vladimir Nobokov*, 1995.

Poetry
Stikhi. Petrograd, 1916.
Grozd' [The Bunch]. Berlin, Gamayun, 1922; reprinted Jerusalem, n.p., 1981.
Gornyi put' [The Mountain Path]. Berlin, Grani, 1923.
Stikhotvoreniia 1929–51. Paris, Rifma, 1952.
Poems. New York, Doubleday, 1959; London, Weidenfeld and Nicolson, 1961.
Stikhi. Ann Arbor, Ardis, 1979.

Plays and Screenplays
"Sobytie", *Russkie zapiski*, April (1938); translated as "The Event", by Dmitri Nabokov, in *The Man from the USSR and Other Plays*, London, Weidenfeld and Nicolson, 1985.
"Izobretenie val'sa", *Russkie zapiski*, November (1938); translated as *The Waltz Invention*, by Dmitri Nabokov, New York, Phaedra, 1966.
Lolita: A Screenplay. New York, McGraw-Hill, 1974.

Memoirs and Letters
Conclusive Evidence: A Memoir. London, Gollancz, and New York, Harper, 1951; revised edition as *Speak Memory: An Autobiography Revisited*, New York, Putnam, 1966; London, Weidenfeld and Nicolson, 1967; in Russian as *Drugie berega*, New York, Izdatel'stvo imeni Chekhova, 1954; 2nd edition, Ann Arbor, Ardis, 1978.
Strong Opinions. New York, McGraw-Hill, 1973; London, Weidenfeld and Nicolson, 1974.
The Nabokov-Wilson Letters: Correspondence Between Vladimir Nabokov and Edmund Wilson 1940–71, edited by Simon Karlinsky. New York, Harper and Row, 1979.
Perepiska s sestroi [Correspondence with Sister]. Ann Arbor, Ardis, 1985.
Selected Letters 1940–1977, edited by Dmitri Nabokov and Matthew J. Bruccoli. San Diego, Harcourt Brace, 1989; London, Weidenfeld and Nicolson, 1990.

Literary Criticism
"Pouchkine, ou le vrai et le vraisemblable". 1937; translated as "Pushkin, or the Real and the Plausible", by Dmitri Nabokov, *New York Review of Books* (31 March 1988), 38–42.
Nikolay Gogol. Norfolk, Connecticut, New Directions, 1944; reprinted 1961; London, Weidenfeld and Nicolson, 1973; Oxford, Oxford University Press, 1985.
Notes on Prosody from the Commentary to His Translation of Pushkin's Eugene Onegin. Princeton, Bollingen Foundation, 1963; London, Routledge and Kegan Paul, 1965.
Lectures on Ulysses. Bloomfield Hills, Michigan, Bruccoli Clark, 1980.
Lectures on Literature, edited by Fredson Bowers. New York, Harcourt Brace Jovanovich, and London, Weidenfeld and Nicolson, 1980.
Lectures on Russian Literature, edited by Fredson Bowers. New York, Harcourt Brace Jovanovich, 1981; London,

Weidenfeld and Nicolson, 1982; as *Lektsii po russkoi literature*, Moscow, 1996.
Lectures on Don Quixote, edited by Fredson Bowers. San Diego, Harcourt Brace Jovanovich, and London, Weidenfeld and Nicolson, 1983.

Translator
Ania v strane chudes [*Alice in Wonderland*]. Berlin, Gamayun, 1923; reprinted New York, Dover, 1976; Ann Arbor, Ardis, 1982.
Three Russian Poets: Selections from Pushkin, Lermontov and Tyutchev in New Translations. Norfolk, Connecticut, New Directions, 1944; as *Pushkin, Lermontov, Tyutchev: Poems*, London, Lindsay Drummond, 1947.
A Hero of Our Time, by Mikhail Lermontov (with Dmitri Nabokov), New York, Doubleday, 1958; Oxford, Oxford University Press, 1984.
The Song of Igor's Campaign: An Epic of the Twelfth Century. New York, Random, House, 1960; London, Weidenfeld and Nicolson, 1961; reprinted Ann Arbor, Ardis, 1988.
Eugene Onegin, by Alexander Pushkin, 4 vols. New York, Bollingen Foundation, and London, Routledge, 1964; revised edition Princeton, Princeton, University Press, 1975.

Critical Studies
Escape into Aesthetics: The Art of Vladimir Nabokov, by Page Stegner, New York, Dial Press, 1966.
Nabokov: His Life in Art, by Andrew Field, London, Hodder and Stoughton, and Boston, Little Brown, 1967.
Keys to Lolita, by Carl R. Proffer, Bloomington, Indiana University Press, 1968.
Nabokov: Criticisms, Reminiscences, Translations and Tributes, edited by Alfred J. Appel, Jr, and Charles Newman, *Triquarterly*, 17 (Winter 1970); Evanston, Illinois, Northwestern University Press, 1970.
Nabokov's Dark Cinema, by Alfred J. Appel, Jr, Oxford and New York, Oxford University Press, 1974.
Nabokov: His Life in Part, by Andrew Field, London, Hamish Hamilton, and New York, Viking Press, 1977.
Nabokov Translated: A Comparison of Nabokov's Russian and English Prose, by Jane Grayson, Oxford, Oxford University Press, 1977.
Vladimir Nabokov: America's Russian Novelist, by G.M. Hyde, London, Marion Boyars, 1978.
Vladimir Nabokov, His Life, His Work, His World: A Tribute, edited by Peter Quennell, London, Weidenfeld and Nicolson, 1979; New York, Morrow, 1980.
Nabokov and the Novel, by Ellen Pifer, Cambridge, Massachusetts, Harvard University Press, 1980.
"Teksty-Matreshki" Vladimira Nabokova, by Sergei Davydov, Munich, Sagner, 1982.
An English-Russian Dictionary of Nabokov's "Lolita", edited by A. Nakhimovsky and S. Paperno, Ann Arbor, Ardis, 1982.
Nabokov: The Critical Heritage, edited by Norman Page, London, Routledge and Kegan Paul, 1982.
Nabokov's Fifth Arc: Nabokov and Others on His Life's Work, edited by J.E. Rivers and Charles Nicol, Austin, University of Texas Press, 1982.
Nabokov's Novels in English, by Lucy Maddox, Athens, University of Georgia Press, and London, Croom Helm, 1983.
Vladimir Nabokov: A Critical Study of the Novels, by David Rampton, Cambridge and New York, Cambridge University Press, 1984.
Nabokov's "Ada": The Place of Consciousness, by Brian Boyd, Ann Arbor, Ardis, 1985.
Worlds in Regression: Some Novels of Vladimir Nabokov, by D. Barton Johnson, Ann Arbor, Ardis, 1985.
Vladimir Nabokov: The Life and Art of Vladimir Nabokov, by Andrew Field, New York, Crown, 1986; London, Queen Anne Press, 1987.
Freud and Nabokov, by Geoffrey Green, Lincoln, University of Nebraska Press, 1988.
Find What the Sailor Has Hidden: Vladimir Nabokov's "Pale Fire", by Priscilla Meyer, Middletown, Connecticut, Wesleyan University Press, 1988.
Phantom of Fact: A Guide to Nabokov's "Pnin", by Gennady Barabtarlo, Ann Arbor, Ardis, 1989.
Contingency, Irony and Solidarity, by Richard Rorty, Cambridge, Cambridge University Press, 1989.
Nabokov: The Mystery of Literary Structures, by Leona Toker, Ithaca, Cornell University Press, 1989.
Vladimir Nabokov: The Russian Years, by Brian Boyd, Princeton, Princeton University Press, and London, Chatto and Windus, 1990.
Russian Literature Triquarterly (special issue), 24 (1991)
Nabokov's Otherworld, by Vladimir E. Alexandrov, Princeton, Princeton University Press, 1991.
Vladimir Nabokov: A Pictorial Biography, edited by Ellendea Proffer, Ann Arbor, Ardis, 1991.
Vladimir Nabokov: The American Years, by Brian Boyd, Princeton, Princeton University Press, and London, Chatto and Windus, 1992.
Nabokov's Early Fiction: Patterns of Self and Other, by Julian W. Connolly, Cambridge and New York, Cambridge University Press, 1992.
Aerial View: Essays on Nabokov's Art and Metaphysics, by Gennady Barabtarlo, New York, Peter Lang, 1993.
Nabokov's Art of Memory and European Modernism, by John Burt Foster, Princeton, Princeton University Press, 1993.
A Small Alpine Form: Studies in Nabokov's Short Fiction, edited by Charles Nicol and Gennady Barabtarlo, New York, Garland, 1993.
Nabokov Studies [Journal]. Los Angeles, Charles Schlacks, 1994–
Lolita, by Richard Corliss, London, British Film Institute, 1994.
The Magician's Doubts: Nabokov and the Risks of Fiction, by Michael Wood, London, Chatto and Windus, 1994; Princeton, Princeton University Press, 1995.
The Garland Companion to Vladimir Nabokov, edited by Vladimir E. Alexandrov, New York, Garland, 1995.
Lolita: A Janus Text, by Lance Olsen, New York, Twayne, 1995.
Pniniad: Vladimir Nabokov and Marc Szeftel, by Galya Diment, Seattle, Washington University Press, 1997.

Bibliographies
Nabokov: A Bibliographv, by Andrew Field, New York, McGraw-Hill, 1973.

The Vladimir Nabokov Research Newsletter/The Nabokovian, Lawrence, University of Kansas Press, 1978 –

Vladimir Nabokov: A Reference Guide, by Samuel Schuman, Boston, G.K. Hall, 1979.

Vladimir Nabokov: A Descriptive Bibliography, by Michael Juliar, New York, Garland, 1986.

The scion of a rich and well-connected family, two generations of which had played a crucial role in governing Russia, Vladimir Nabokov learnt English and French virtually as well as he learnt Russian, and received his education at St Petersburg's most innovative school, the Tenishev. Almost his entire family escaped Russia during the Revolution via the Crimea, before scattering in the diaspora. Nabokov took a degree in Cambridge, before being reunited with other Nabokovs in Berlin. Here his bland conventional poems and his increasingly subtle short stories, but always highly polished and inventive language, won him acceptance as the leading young writer in the Berlin Russian community (then 200,000-strong, with a major publishing house and two profitable literary journals). For the period 1922 to 1925 Berlin was a meeting place for Soviet and émigré writers: even though Nabokov had little contact with figures such as Belyi or Gor'kii, the feelings of exile were muted. The shock of his father's assassination by monarchist extremists in 1922 opened up new depths in Nabokov's work and gave a tragic undercurrent to his sophistication. By 1925, under the pseudonym Sirin, he was able to make literature, and not just the teaching of languages and tennis, his main source of income: stories such as *Vozvrashchenie Chorba* (*The Return of Chorb*) showed his capacity for expressive anguish, perfect symmetry and classical tragedy; while his first novel, *Mashen'ka* (*Mary*), established the pattern for all his novels of the tragic failure of the adult exile to reconstruct the lost homeland and its idyll. A horrific anguish that splits the personality apart is the key-note to all the early work, a remarkable strand considering Nabokov's hostility to modern schools of psychology. In 1924 he married Vera Evseevna Slonim (by whom he had one son, Dmitri in 1934), a lifelong partnership that enabled him to make an impenetrable front to both enemies and sympathizers. The surrealist novel *Korol', dama, valet* (*King, Queen, Knave*), the more straightforward, realistic study of a chess player's madness, *Zashchita Luzhina* (*The Defence*), and the moving *Otchaianie* (*Despair*) won even more acclaim, despite their hint of German expressionism (German being a language that Nabokov claimed never to have read). Nabokov, significantly, worked both as a scenario writer and as an extra for silent films at the time. His early novels were unique among Russian émigré work for finding translation and sales among the host community. Although Paris émigrés greeted this success with an envy and denigration symptomatic of the degeneration of Russian culture abroad, Nabokov was in demand for readings and lectures in France. His work took on a more political implication with *Podvig* (*Glory*) and *Priglashenie na kazn'* (*Invitation to a Beheading*), where a principled hero perishes at the hands of unprincipled forces; but the essence of both novels is more the battle of art against philistinism, spirit against flesh, than merely the exiled Russia of Pushkin against Bolshevism. The latter novel invites comparison with Kafka, although it is possible to read it as a defiant assertion of the immortality of the spirit. In 1937 Nabokov began his finest (and last complete) Russian novel, *Dar* (*The Gift*). After the release that year by Hitler of his father's killer, Nabokov fled the Nazis to Paris – quite apart from principle, Vera Evseevna was Jewish. Finding no substantial recognition in France and no university post in England, the Nabokovs then accepted a loan from Rachmaninov and sailed to America. At Cornell University he became not only a respected, if wayward, professor of Russian and Comparative Literature and entomologist, but a great English-language novelist, nurtured by Edmund Wilson (whom Nabokov repaid with scorpion-like ingratitude), until he achieved universal acclaim with *Lolita* and *Pale Fire*. His English-language novels, however, have their roots in his Russian work, both thematically and technically, while the late works, such as *Ada*, can probably only be fully appreciated by a reader as bilingual as their author. In America, apart from collating his shorter prose of the 1930s into one book, *Vesna v Fial'te* (*Spring in Fialta*), Nabokov wrote only memoirs and verse in Russian. His memoirs, *Drugie berega* [Other Shores] (translated into English as *Speak Memory*), are a poeticized recall of childhood and adolescence, as evocative as Osip Mandel'shtam's *Shum vremeni* (*The Noise of Time*). It is curious that the earlier and later English variants, *Conclusive Evidence* and *Speak Memory*, differ substantially, even in points of fact, from the Russian version. (Many of Nabokov's English versions of his Russian texts are not just translations, but variants, commissioned or carried out by himself.) Like his earlier plays, Nabokov's verse does not bear comparison with his prose, except when it is attributed to a character of a novel; Nabokov's lyrical poetry is as ingenuous as his prose. Presumably, his elusive, God-like persona is containable only within the shifting framework of the novel. Nabokov's American period was devoted to studies of Russian literature, of which the most controversial is his translation of, and commentary to, Pushkin's *Evgenii Onegin*. The translation is a covert attempt to prove the work untranslatable, while the commentary, apart from its stress on Pushkin's saturation in French literature, is largely a series of amusing provocations, The wealth brought by *Lolita* enabled Nabokov to reconstruct the luxury of his St Petersburg childhood in a Montreux hotel: his relationships with the new Russian literature in exile (Solzhenitsyn, Siniavskii) were almost nil.

Nabokov's novels function as psychological, tragic dramas in the tradition of Flaubert or Bunin; but they are also mythopoeic and often cryptic puzzles that involve the reader and critic in frustrating games. In his analysis of human motivation and his pursuit of lost time Nabokov appears to distil the essence of Proust. His Pushkinian clarity goes with the mystification of Gogol' – the reader is often teased by the author's ambiguities. Nabokov has much in common with James Joyce in his awareness of language and of sexuality. Much of his symbolism – squirrels, butterflies, for instance – suggests a disturbing belief in other worlds, even though the word God disappears from his work after his father's death. His own adoration of his father and fascination with sexual love is clearly fundamental to his work. For all the critical puzzlement he has engendered, Nabokov is probably the greatest Russian novelist since the Revolution, within or without Russia.

DONALD RAYFIELD

The Return of Chorb

Vozvrashchenie Chorba

Story, 1925

The Return of Chorb was written shortly after Nabokov completed his first novel, *Mary*, and was published in two consecutive issues of the Berlin émigré journal *Rul'* in 1925. It appeared again in 1930 as the title story of a collection of 15 stories dating from 1924 that includes "Bachman", "Groza" ("The Thunderstorm"), "Kartofel'nyi el'f" ("The Potato Elf"), "Passazhir" ("The Passenger"), "Pis'mo v Rossiiu" ("A Letter that Never Reached Russia"), "Podlets" ("An Affair of Honour"), "Putevoditel' po Berlinu" ("A Guide to Berlin"), "Rozhdestvo" ("Christmas"), "Skazka" ("A Nursery Tale"), "Uzhas" ("Terror"), and "Zvonok" ("The Doorbell").

Nabokov described *The Return of Chorb* as "a good example of my early constructions". The term "construction" has a specific significance, indicating that the work is more than an unconventional story about grief. Chorb, an impoverished Russian émigré, marries a middle-class provincial German girl. On their honeymoon in the south of France she is electrocuted when she inadvertently touches a live telegraph wire. She is buried in France and Chorb returns to Germany to break the news to his in-laws. When he arrives at the Kellers' house on a rainy night, the maid informs him that they are out. Unable to utter the truth, he asks her to tell them that their daughter is "ill". This message causes the Kellers to panic. Their suspicions are fuelled by an innate distrust of Chorb. In the meantime, Chorb, deeply disturbed and disorientated, decides to stay at the cheap hotel where he and his wife spent their wedding night. Afraid of sleeping there alone, he pays a prostitute to share his bed. At midnight he wakes up, sees the girl lying next to him, and starts to scream in terror, thinking she is his wife returned from the dead. Meanwhile, the Kellers have come in search of Chorb and, just as the prostitute is escaping from the room, they appear at the door.

Chorb's experience is distinctive in that it is both traumatic and enlightening. His wife's death leaves him in a state of extreme shock, but the experience is also strangely positive. It has offered him a brief glimpse of the purity and beauty of the spirit world and his memories are inspired by the bright light of the electric current that transported her there. Her spirit is omnipresent, contained in the delicate, ephemeral lights and shadows of the smallest objects: the shape or colour of a pebble on a beach, the "silvery-gray" slates on a roof, the "white torrent" of a stream or a spider's web "beaded with droplets of mist". Set against the sordid dinginess of the city these images have a vivid and potent impact.

Apart from the subliminal implications of Chorb's "return" – from France to Germany, from past to present, from autumn to spring, from the dead to the living – the story has a complex metaphorical subtext. Integral to the story's "construction" are the references to Parsifal and Orpheus that both infuse and parody Chorb's behaviour. Related to the Orpheus myth is the possible inference of the ancient Greek mystic religion, Orphism, which emphasized the coexistence of good and evil in the human spirit and the necessity of purging evil through reincarnation. Chorb sets himself the task of painstakingly reliving every moment spent with his wife in a retrograde process from the moment of her death back to their wedding night. His intention is to "immortalize" his wife's image; memory enables him to preserve a set of associations that are controllable and inviolable. He does not want to bring her back from the dead, for his sense of her spiritual presence terrifies him.

The Parsifal connection serves to enhance the sense of mystic ritualism surrounding Chorb's "ordeal", but at the same time undermines Chorb's heroic potential. Parsifal is set the task of retrieving a "sacred spear", but Parsifal, like Chorb, is ignorant of the meaning of the ritual in which he participates. Nabokov exposes Chorb's lack of awareness by comically undermining his moment of "awakening". The ritual's denouement occurs when Chorb is literally half-asleep. When he realizes the girl is not his wife, he uncovers his eyes and heaves a sigh of relief. This inadvertent and misplaced reincarnation, which has resulted in an exorcism rather than a recovery, combined with the explicit contrast to Orpheus' tragedy, is comically underscored by the very unheroic image of Chorb staring vacantly at the girl, clutching his "hairy shins" and smiling.

The story's precisely calculated structure and its subtle shifts in narrative focus have a specific dramatic purpose. When Chorb falls asleep in the hotel the reader's intimate involvement with him is finally suspended. The prostitute's perspective replaces his and through her eyes, Chorb's behaviour is exposed as abnormal and inexplicable. Not only does this anticipate and reinforce the Kellers' reaction in the final scene but it also gives these characters a new credence. Up until this point, circumstances have prevented a confrontation. By delaying the inevitable, Nabokov generates tension, but also a sense of distance, so that when the characters converge the result is farcical rather than tragic.

The concluding story of the later collection, "Terror", mirrors *The Return of Chorb* in its exploration of themes of mortality, but Nabokov focuses on an existential perspective that emphasizes the terrifying absurdity, rather than the comforting banality of reality. Themes of death, and of the power of memory to reanimate the past as a means of spiritual release, were to feature in later works such as *Ultima Thule* and *Ada*. As an early "construction" *The Return of Chorb* displays Nabokov's ability to exploit the concise and concentrated form of the short story to produce a highly structured, elaborate drama, a comic parody and a profoundly sensitive evocation of the experience of loss.

BARBARA WYLLIE

Mary

Mashen'ka

Novel, 1926

Mary, Nabokov's first novel, was written in 1925 and published by Slovo in 1926, under the pen-name Nabokov used during his years in Berlin, Vladimir Sirin. The topical subject of the novel, combined with Nabokov's unusual, evocative yet concise descriptive style, made an immediate impact, establishing him as a highly original and gifted writer of considerable potential. Of all his works, *Mary* was one of the last to be translated. On returning to it after 45 years, Nabokov made no major changes to the original text. Although Nabokov may have been reluctant to reconsider *Mary*, particularly following the achievements of works such as *Lolita*, *Pale Fire* and *Ada*, its significance as a first novel should not be underestimated.

Set in Berlin in 1924, *Mary* vividly and eloquently portrays the lives of seven Russian émigrés who share the confined space of a dilapidated boarding house. Nabokov squeezes his disparate characters into cramped, cluttered rooms, creating an invasive, claustrophobic atmosphere. The émigrés' identity is encapsulated in a few random belongings that are as vulnerable and as carefully preserved as the nostalgia they share for their lost home. The beginning of the novel comprises a series of staged scenes; gentle, comic parodies of Russian and French theatre that augment the chaos of the émigrés' lives and their meagre attempts to establish order and stability in an alien, hostile environment.

The action takes place within a specific frame of real time, between Sunday 1 and Saturday 7 April. Nabokov's disenchanted hero, Lev Ganin, a former White Guard officer, is the son of a wealthy upper-class family. He discovers that the middle-aged Alferov's estranged young wife is his own former lover, Mary, whom he left behind when he escaped Russia at the outbreak of the Civil War in 1917. She is due to arrive on the following Saturday, the day when Ganin plans to leave Berlin, and she is to have his room. Ganin decides that he must meet her again and that she must be prevented from joining Alferov. At his farewell party on Friday evening Ganin plies Alferov with drink until he is unconscious and resets his alarm clock so that he will arrive too late to meet Mary. As he leaves for the station early on Saturday morning, Ganin suddenly changes his mind, abandons his plan altogether and instead boards a train for France.

Ganin's extreme sense of alienation sets him apart from the rest of the group. He exists in a ghostly world of shadows where time has been reversed, where the only reality for him is his past. Rather than taking any positive action, he indulges in temporary, futile acts of escapism. Ironically, his most evocative escapist dream has the force ultimately to liberate him. Ganin's victory over entropy is inspiring but it is also scarred by his solipsistic immorality. Ganin's arrogant indifference is a characteristic that many of Nabokov's heroes, or rather anti-heroes, possess; a flamboyant, romantic disenchantment reminiscent of Lermontov's "superfluous" hero, Pechorin. Ganin's departure is similar to Martin Edelweiss's disappearance at the end of *Glory*, in that neither acknowledge any responsibility for the suffering they may be causing others. Ganin leaves in his wake two broken-hearted women, a dead poet, a betrayed husband, and an abandoned lover.

The dramatic pace of the novel is amplified by the precise limits of time and space and the expectation of Ganin's cathartic reunion with Mary. By frustrating this expectation Nabokov at first seems to distort the entire focus of the novel. There is more to this than shallow trickery, however. There is an element of "splendid insincerity" contained in the fabric of *Mary*, so crucial in the composition of Nabokov's notorious chess problems, which indicates the underlying motivations of the novel. Its theatrical quality allows the potential for fantasy to be exploited and for the dimensions of "actuality" to be extended. Much of the novel's energy is generated by the tension of paradox. For example, the three things that shock Ganin into action are not radical, dramatic events, but insubstantial and ephemeral visions; a fleeting celluloid image, a hazy photograph, and the airy frame of a half-built house. Ganin's perceptions are suddenly dislocated by these images, they force him to see beyond his subjective view of the present, offering him a glimpse of a vital reality. The delicate skeleton of the yellow beams reflects the obscure subtlety of the novel's design that acts on the reader in the same way that the frame's airy brightness acts on Ganin. Within this complex frame, Nabokov infuses the text with casual, seemingly inconsequential motifs, such as Podtiagin's visa or Klara's bag of oranges, which, when repeated in a different, seemingly arbitrary context, take on a new significance. The delayed release of meaning magnifies their implications, like echoes reverberating endlessly around a room, or ripples caused by a stone thrown into water.

Although Ganin and Mary are not reunited, the novel contains a structural catharsis, which provides an alternative resolution. The discrepancy between the old calendar dates used to number the émigrés' rooms and the novel's time-span – seven rather than six days – corresponds metaphorically with Ganin's liberation. The repeating cycle of April 1st to April 6th is broken, as Ganin breaks away from his past and leaves Berlin on April 7th. The neat symmetry of this solution is a distinctively Nabokovian device.

Nabokov's particular preoccupation with the notion of time as a regressive cycle, as exemplified by Ganin's predicament, has its genesis here. Nabokov's later solution to this problem was contained in the image of the spiral. As the spiral revolves it encompasses past, present and future, but unlike the circle, it does not repeat, it moves forward. *Mary* displays the beginnings of a method that Nabokov was to continue to develop and refine; an intricate patterning of imagery and form that enabled him to access the most remote and intangible of concepts in his subsequent fiction.

BARBARA WYLLIE

The Defence

Zashchita Luzhina

Novel, 1930

Students of Nabokov's work generally regard *The Defence* as the writer's first masterpiece. Written in 1929 and published the next year, the novel leads the reader into that special terrain of the imagination that would become characteristic of Nabokov's mature art. "Great literature skirts the irrational", Nabokov declared in his monograph on the work of Nikolai Gogol'. *The Defence* represents his own first attempt to offer a sustained exploration of the rapture and the terror that arise when one becomes immersed in a world of visions, delusions, and obsession. The protagonist of *The Defence* is a sensitive chess master named Aleksandr Luzhin. A shy and lonely child, the young Luzhin looks to mathematics and to the stories of Sherlock Holmes to find intimations of order and control that he feels are lacking in his own personal life. One day, he hears that chess is a fabulous game with infinite possibilities, and he asks his aunt to teach him the game. This aunt happens to be his father's mistress, and thus Nabokov provides a subtle hint that, for the young Luzhin, obsession with chess can be as dangerous as his father's obsession with an illicit romance. Nothing deters Luzhin from his preoccupation with chess, however. He becomes a chess phenomenon, entering and winning international chess competitions while still an adolescent. Yet Luzhin's constant mental exertions take an ominous toll. Participating in a chess tournament in Berlin, Luzhin finds it increasingly difficult to make the transition from the cerebral kingdom of chess manoeuvres back to the quotidian world of everyday reality. During the final match Luzhin suffers a mental breakdown, which necessitates a slow recuperation under the watchful eye of a young woman who has come to love him.

Even as he recuperates, however, Luzhin falls prey to a new obsession. Observing the world around him, Luzhin begins to notice that certain episodes and events from earlier stages in his life seem to recur in the present. Gradually he becomes convinced that an infinitely cunning opponent is attempting to anticipate and manipulate the events of Luzhin's life. Desperate to find a "defence" against this powerful opponent, Luzhin decides to "drop out of the game", which he literally does by falling from his apartment window. As he prepares to drop to his death, though, he notes that the pattern of light and shadow in the courtyard below seems to arrange itself into the form of a giant chessboard. Thus it is an open question whether death will bring Luzhin the release that he so fervently desires.

Nabokov's handling of Luzhin's obsession provides an intriguing introduction into what D. Barton Johnson has called the "two-world theme" in his study of Nabokov's fiction (*Worlds in Regression)*. Luzhin may be deluded in believing that events in his life are being manipulated by a chess opponent, but his suspicion that some kind of intelligent force affects his life is, in essence, correct. The problem is that he has misinterpreted the nature of this force. While Luzhin does notice a few elements of recurrence in his life, the careful reader of the novel will realize that Nabokov has created a highly resonant network of repetition, recurrence, and allusion around his protagonist. For example, near the outset of the book (and of his life) Luzhin observes a small girl eating an apple near a provincial railroad station. Later, the narrator describes a painting that hangs in the apartment of Luzhin's future in-laws: the painting depicts a country girl eating an apple. The higher consciousness that Luzhin detects at work in his environment is not a chess opponent, but rather the creator of the fictional world in which Luzhin has been placed, and this creator has planted many clues giving evidence of his control over the fictional world. Indeed, Nabokov's transformation of a "live" girl into a painted depiction serves as an ironic reminder that all the "living" creatures in the novel are artistic creations.

Nabokov incorporates these markers of the fictionality of his created world not simply to indulge in metafictional play. They point to the writer's serious concern with metaphysics as well as metafiction. The type of patterning that the observant reader discerns in *The Defence* is meant to illustrate Nabokov's view that our own lives may be subject to the designs of some kind of higher consciousness or force. Although Nabokov was remarkably reticent about articulating his metaphysical beliefs, his fiction hints at their general outlines. In fact, as Brian Boyd argues in his critical biography of Nabokov (*Vladimir Nabokov: The Russian Years*), one can detect in Luzhin's life the influence of more than one supernatural being. In Boyd's opinion, the spirits of Luzhin's father and grandfather work behind the scenes to mould Luzhin's destiny. The existence of such forces gives hope that one's death does not mark the end of life as such: on the contrary, after death one may attain the freedom to roam through time and space unfettered by the constraints of mortal being.

Luzhin, of course, is not comforted by signs that his life is ordered by a higher consciousness, and his distress is representative of a tragically fearful attitude toward existence itself. Awkward and introverted in his childhood, he rebuffs the efforts of his well-meaning but ineffectual father to establish close relations with him. Although he has the good fortune later in life to meet a kind woman who loves him, he is not willing to share with her the nature of the obsessions that torment him (strangely, the reader never learns the woman's name, and this perhaps serves to indicate the lack of intimacy between Luzhin and his wife). As a result, Luzhin is doomed to live in a kind of self-imposed cocoon. Though gifted with rare powers of intellect, he lacks the attentiveness to the external world that is required not only of artists, but of all who wish to derive the fullest pleasure from human life. In *The Defence* Nabokov provides a haunting portrait of the joys and limitations of human consciousness.

JULIAN W. CONNOLLY

Despair

Otchaianie

Novel, 1934

Written in 1932 (and originally published in 1934), *Despair* is one of the most fascinating novels that Nabokov wrote during the early part of his career. The novel offers Nabokov's first extensive use of an "unreliable" first-person narrator, the failed businessman and wild dreamer Hermann Karlovich. Hermann tells his readers that he is an accomplished artist. His medium, though, is not something so conventional as painting, or sculpture, or music. He chooses to prove his artistic genius in the realm of crime! Meeting a man whom he believes to be his identical double, Hermann arranges to kill the man and to fool the world into thinking that it was he, Hermann, who was murdered. The reader learns, however, that according to the police, the murdered man does not bear any resemblance to Hermann. Hermann's deception is exposed, and the novel concludes with the imminent capture of the deluded criminal.

Nabokov lays bare in *Despair* the pernicious consequences of a solipsistic approach to the surrounding world. Hermann is a consummate narcissist (and there are multiple allusions to the myth of Narcissus in the novel). He tells the reader that his wife Lydia is devoted to him, but the reader discerns through many clues provided by Hermann that Lydia is having an affair with an artist named Ardalion. It is not entirely clear whether Hermann is consciously aware of the affair, or whether he is so short-sighted that he remains oblivious to all evidence of it. The very unreliability of Hermann's narration makes it difficult to ascertain just what Hermann perceives and what he does not. In some cases, one suspects that Hermann has a greater awareness of an underlying reality than he wishes to admit. He seems to shy away from acknowledging unpalatable truths.

Hermann expresses nothing but disdain for Ardalion, but Nabokov allows this artist figure to articulate some of the most important concepts in the novel. For example, Ardalion declares that every human face is unique, and that what the artist perceives is primarily the *difference* between things, not their resemblance. In addition to literature, Nabokov's other great love was lepidoptery, and he believed that an artist should apply the same degree of careful observation to the world's phenomena as the scientist. Hermann fails miserably at the task of observing the minute details that render every living thing unique. Yet this is just one of his significant failings as a would-be artist.

Hermann's other major failing is his desire to control everything in his environment. This desire for control covers the spectrum from metaphysics to art. Hermann declares that he does not wish to believe in God because he perceives this notion as someone else's myth, not something that he created himself. Second, he rejects the notion of the existence of God because he does not wish to be anyone's slave. He turns to art as the realm in which he will demonstrate his supreme control. Yet it is here, in Hermann's fundamental misconception about the nature of art, that one finds Hermann's greatest error. While it is true that Nabokovian artists can be the supreme masters of the artificial worlds they create in their art, this sense of mastery or control cannot be extended to the world in which they live. Hermann attempts to control and manipulate everyone he meets; he believes that he can even kill a man to demonstrate his artistic genius. Nabokov's aesthetics, however, carry clear ethical implications. Hermann's crime does not prove his artistic genius. On the contrary, it underscores his limitations as an artist on several planes.

Perhaps the most ironic way in which Nabokov exposes Hermann's limitations as an artist is to use art itself as the medium through which Hermann's shortcomings are revealed. Hermann tells the reader that he began writing his chronicle in an effort to make clear to an ignorant world the true genius of his work. Unsatisfied with the reception of his work of art on the physical plane (the police found no resemblance between the murdered man and Hermann), Hermann takes up his pen to justify and explain his work. Little does he suspect, however, that Nabokov – the authentic artist – uses Hermann's very own words to highlight the would-be artist's failings. Hermann's narrative represents one of the finest examples of a "dual-voiced" discourse in Nabokov's works. That is, while the ostensible author of the narrative intends his words to say one thing, the actual author of the work speaks through these words to present quite a different message.

Hermann's failings as a writer are evident everywhere in his narrative. For example, he cannot control the tone or style of his writing, and he fails to follow the structural design he had laid out for his narrative. Most striking, though, is his apparent blindness to his relationship to the literary tradition in which he writes. Hermann seeks to demonstrate that he is an original artist, a creator of genius. Nabokov, however, utilizes a whole series of literary allusions and subtexts, some overt and some subtle, to indicate that far from being an original *creator*, Hermann is merely one more in a long line of fictional *creations*. Among the writers whose work shines through Hermann's dark narrative are Pushkin, Gogol', and Dostoevskii. At one point Hermann detects a faint similarity between himself and Raskol'nikov, the tormented murderer of *Prestuplenie i nakazanie* (*Crime and Punishment*), which Nabokov viewed as a "badly written book" (see Nabokov's *Lectures on Russian Literature)*. In typical fashion, however, he dismisses the comparison, and thus remains oblivious to the rich design that his creator, Nabokov, has stamped onto his life.

The imprint of Nabokov's sovereignty over Hermann and the created world of the novel may be discerned on several levels in *Despair*. In the original Russian version of the text, Nabokov even embedded coded references to his own name into the sentences of Hermann's discourse. *Despair* is an extremely resonant work, and in it Nabokov provides intimations of such later achievements as *Lolita* and *Pale Fire*.

JULIAN W. CONNOLLY

Invitation to a Beheading

Priglashenie na kazn'

Novel, 1935–36

The first draft of *Invitation to a Beheading* was completed in June 1934 in what Nabokov described as a "fortnight of wonderful excitement and sustained inspiration". The novel was a considerable departure for Nabokov, both in content and style. Its political focus prefigured *Bend Sinister* (1947), and stories such as "Oblako, ozero, bashnia" [Cloud, Castle, Lake] (1937), and "Istreblenie tiranov" [Tyrants Destroyed] (1938). Critics have commented on its similarity to Kafka's *The Trial*, but it is also reminiscent of Zamiatin's grim science-fiction fantasy, *My* (*We*), in theme and form. Inspired by events in the Soviet Union and the rise of fascism in Germany in the 1930s and by Nabokov's research into the life of Chernyshevskii for *The Gift*, *Invitation to a Beheading* presents a lurid vision of the "dull beastly farce" of institutionalized repression.

Invitation to a Beheading opens as the death sentence is pronounced on Cincinnatus C, condemned for the crime of "gnostic turpitude". A "lone, dark obstacle" in a world of "transparent souls", his inherent complexity is intolerable in a society concerned only with superficialities. For 19 days Cincinnatus occupies one small cell in a vast, empty prison, awaiting his execution. He is presided over by his gaoler, Rodion, the prison director, Rodrig Ivanovich, his lawyer, Roman Vissarionovich, the director's daughter, Emmie, and a spider. During this time he is visited by his wife, Marthe, her lover, her family, her two illegitimate children, and his estranged mother. On the fifth day, he is introduced to a new inmate, Monsieur Pierre, whom he later discovers is his executioner. On the 20th day he is paraded through town to the guillotine, cheered by excited crowds. As the axe is about to fall, Cincinnatus suddenly splits into two; one half remains prone on the block, while the other walks away, causing the scene to collapse around him like a stage set.

Cincinnatus's experience is nightmarish and *Invitation to a Beheading* incorporates all the elements of dreams: fantasy, illusion, surrealism, burlesque, horror, and surprise. Everything in Cincinnatus's world is a sham and a deception, and his increasing sense of this serves to augment the intensity of his isolation and persecution. Artifice pervades the novel at every level, from dead-ends and trap doors, collapsing rooms and vanishing objects to the constantly shifting roles played by Monsieur Pierre, the prison director and Emmie. At the same time, the atmosphere's comic potential is fully exploited. The three figures of authority, Rodion, Roman and Rodrig, behave like vaudeville clowns, unashamedly stupid and inept. The conspiratorial complicity implied by their similar sounding names suggests that they are devoid of any personality or individuality, making them ideal puppets in Monsieur Pierre's grotesque games. This element of farce does not detract from the evil of the situation, but, as in "Istreblenie tiranov", laughter serves a double function, as an effective antidote to pain and as a powerful expression of dissent. *Invitation to a Beheading* dramatically illustrates Nabokov's belief that "tyrants and torturers will never manage to hide their comic stumbles behind their cosmic acrobatics".

The extent of Cincinnatus's torment is evoked both by the objective commentary of the third-person author-narrator and by the excerpts from Cincinnatus's diary and letters. Cincinnatus's humiliation and despair is augmented by the foolish, inconsequential preoccupations of the other characters. The despotic Monsieur Pierre is the epitome of banality: unimaginative, insensitive, crude, self-righteous, conceited, obsessed with petty trivia and phoney superstitions, sentimental, irrational, egocentric, and highly manipulative; the ultimate tyrant. He runs the prison like a circus with Rodrig Ivanovich as circus master and himself as clown, magician, strongman, and acrobat rolled into one. Cincinnatus is the freak show.

According to Nabokov, the fools of this world are those who believe they are mortal. Cincinnatus is mortal for as long as he allows others to hold his life in their hands, but his predicament is so extreme that his only means of escape is imaginary. The chaos of the execution scene is amplified by images combining vivid realism and extraordinary fantasy that disrupt the conclusion of the novel. The vision of the vomiting librarian and the axeman's "still swinging hips" imply that Cincinnatus has been executed, overtly conflicting with the image of another Cincinnatus, grown to giant proportions, striding away from the scaffold. Rather than suddenly shifting to stark realism at this crucial moment to convey the full horror of the situation, as Kafka does in *The Trial*, Nabokov takes the opportunity to extend the boundaries of surrealism. This not only denies tyranny its inevitable victory, but also suggests that there does exist an alternative form of freedom within the scope of the imagination that defies physical mortality.

The novel's structure is simple, one chapter corresponding to each day Cincinnatus spends in prison. The passage of time is dramatized by Cincinnatus's pencil that gradually decreases in size until it is worn down to a stub by the 19th chapter, the last day of Cincinnatus's incarceration, emphasizing the irrevocability of Cincinnatus's impending demise. Action is also demarcated by the activities of the spider, which is fed daily by Rodion. Every time the spider receives a treat, Cincinnatus endures a fresh torture, usually in the form of a frustrated hope. This cycle is broken on the final day, when a moth manages to avoid capture by Rodion. As Cincinnatus is led away his cell disintegrates, the spider shatters and the moth flies away. The moth in Nabokov's fiction symbolizes both physical and imaginative freedom, and its presence in Cincinnatus's cell signals the existence of a world beyond the novel's nightmare reality, inspiring Cincinnatus's belief in the power of the imagination to transform and liberate.

Nabokov's use of fantasy and surrealism in earlier works such as *Katastrofa* (translated as *Details of a Sunset*) and *Sogliadatai* (*The Eye*) prefigured *Invitation to a Beheading*'s unusual and explicit display of conspicuous artifice. Such works also indicated the extent of Nabokov's artistic preoccupation with the tension between subjective and objective experiences of reality and the dilemma of mortality, which was to continue to be a dominant theme in his fiction.

BARBARA WYLLIE

The Gift

Dar

Novel, 1937–38

"What a pity that nobody overheard the brilliant conversation which I meant to have with you." "It doesn't matter, it hasn't been a waste of time. I'm even glad it happened that way. Who cares if we parted at the first corner and that I am carrying on an invented dialogue with myself, using inspiration as my primer." This interchange between two poets, the Nabokovian protagonist of *The Gift*, Godunov-Cherdyntsev, and the Khodasevich-like Koncheev, tells us what the "gift" is: apart from poetic genius, it is the ability to invent dialogues better than reality. The gift is to invent a past, a Russia, friendship and love that surpass and bypass the defective reality and make exile among strangers and mediocrities bearable. Nabokov's greatest Russian-language novel is not only about, but also the embodiment of, that gift. Its elaborate composition, in which the author's text interacts with the hero's text, anticipates his finest English-language work, notably *Pale Fire*. It is Nabokov's first narrative that develops its plot unhurriedly, confidently. None of Nabokov's works took so long to come to fruition. He conceived it in 1932, and began writing in 1935. Serial publication in 1937 was interrupted by flight from Germany and then from France. Not until the 1950s did the book appear in New York: as a major Russian novel, it deserves to be ranked with Belyi's *Petersburg* and Bulgakov's *Master i Margarita* (*Master and Margarita*) for its daring formal counterpoint and its thematic richness, and perhaps above either for its linguistic virtuosity and perfect match of satire, lyricism, authorial wisdom, and psychology.

The Gift can be read at several levels. Like Lermontov's *Geroi nashego vremeni* (*A Hero of Our Time*) it can be seen as a string of narratives whose total impact is more than the sum of its parts. Superficially, the novel is an almost Dostoevskian story of the impoverished poet Godunov-Cherdyntsev, forced to seek new lodgings and finding true love with his landlady's daughter, a happy ending only slightly shadowed by the loss of the hero's clothes, money, and keys. On a level typical of later Nabokov, it is the story of a writer's two books, their genesis, their relationship to his life, and their fate among the critics. It opens with Godunov-Cherdynstev's first book of verse, breathtakingly unadorned, on the verge of banality, which gives him recognition; it ends with his Lytton Strachey-style biography of Chernyshevskii, which infuriates both the Right and the Left wings of the émigré community and ostracizes him. On this level the Nabokovian theme of the double creeps in, for Chernyshevskii, as Godunov-Cherdyntsev sees him, is an *alter ego* to his biographer: the likeness is signalled by the fact that they share the initial syllable of a surname. Both in exile, both self-motivated and indifferent to their environment, both in love with one woman only, they are polar opposites. The biographer is an agile, tanned sportsman, who knows his trees and butterflies and revels in the forests and lakes of his Berlin exile; Chernyshevskii is a clumsy, ink-stained clown, completely ignorant of the natural world and indifferent to the Siberian taiga. Cherdyntsev is loved by his fiancée, Chernyshevskii is betrayed by his wife. Godunov-Cherdyntsev sustains himself by an imaginary friendship with the poet Koncheev; Chernyshevskii sees in Dobroliubov a friend and fellow-martyr. Cherdynstev lives to reconstruct a dream-like past, Chernyshevskii tries to map a phantasmagoric future. Chernyshevskii is obsessed by learning foreign languages, but cannot express himself lucidly in his own; Cherdyntsev appears to speak no German, and is concerned only for the richness and precision of his Russian. The biography of Chernyshevskii is thus the core of the novel, a brilliant attempt to write not as the author, but as the character would. Nabokov thus anticipates *Pale Fire*, where the problem of the novelist is to produce a specimen of work by a writer greater than himself. Here, he produces a biography that is factually correct, but full of mystification in its selectivity and in its disguise of sources, not to mention its merciless mockery.

There are many other levels on which *The Gift* operates. With its imaginary debates and inner monologues about Pushkin and Russian poetry, the novel is a self-obsessed, narcissistic work of literature: Godunov-Cherdynstev is clearly authorial in his passion for Pushkin and Gogol' and his scorn for Dostoevskii. The deepest level of *The Gift*, however, is not satirical but lyrical – the evocation of the hero's father and of his Russia. Here the novel is tied to Nabokov's later memoirs: Godunov-Cherdyntsev, like Nabokov, is an ancient surname with Tartar overtones. *The Gift* also embodies a Nabokovian constant – his novels from *Mary* to *Ada* are about attempts, tragic or happy, to reconstruct in adulthood the lost paradise of childhood. Godunov-Cherdyntsev dreams of his father's return and minutely recollects a Russia that he does not for a moment believe to have any prospect of resurrecting. Nabokov's own cult of his father is transferred to Godunov-Cherdyntsev's fictional father, who incorporates sanitized elements of the heroic explorer Nikolai Przhevalskii, in his single-mindedness and his contempt for the central Asia that he explores, and where he vanishes.

In its day, *The Gift* made its impact as a satire on the Russians in Berlin. To many readers it was a *roman-à-clef*: Koncheev was obviously the fastidious poet Khodasevich, the touchingly devoted couple of living Chernyshevskiis (Aleksandr Ivanovich and Aleksandra Ivanovna), who patronize Godunov-Cherdyntsev, were recognizable as Dmitri Merezhkovskii and Zinaida Hippius. Each faction of the emigration, their journals and publishing houses is subjected to caricature, sometimes vicious, sometimes affectionate: there are few comparable evocations of a community in exile (although here, and in other respects, *The Gift* recalls Turgenev's *Dym* (*Smoke*)). To a large extent, like Turgenev, Nabokov was using the novel as an instrument of vengeance on those who had dismissed his talent: not only Hippius, but also Georgii Adamovich, Georgii Ivanov, and their journals, are lampooned.

The Gift is also important for sowing the seeds of *Lolita*. Shchegolev, the odious and anti-Semitic stepfather of Zina Merts, the hero's beloved, speculates what a tragic story could be written about a paedophile who marries a woman for the sake of access to her daughter and how the pervert would suffer from the girl's closeness and indifference to him. The salutary character of the "uncle in America" plays a minor part in *The Gift*, but also signals elements of *Lolita*.

DONALD RAYFIELD

Semen Iakovlevich Nadson 1862–1887

Poet

Biography

Born in St Petersburg, 26 December 1862. Father, an official of Jewish extraction, died in an asylum, 1864. Mother died of consumption, 1873. Attended the Second Military gymnasium (later the Second Cadet Corps) in St Petersburg (expenses borne by the state), 1872–79. First poem published, 1878. Attended Pavlovsk Military Academy, St Petersburg, 1879–82. Became sub-lieutenant in 148th Caspian Regiment stationed in Kronstadt, 1882. Suffered from chronic consumption. Retired prematurely on health grounds, July 1884. Secretary in the editorial office of *Nedelia*. Went abroad for health reasons; stayed in Menton, October 1884–August 1885. Lived with Garshin's cousin and her husband in Novskovtsy, Podolsk province, September 1885–April 1886. Moved to Kiev, April 1886. Contributed literary reviews to *Zaria*, May–September 1886. Forced by his health to move to Crimea, September 1886. Died in Yalta, 31 January 1887. Buried next to Dobroliubov in Volkov Cemetery, St Petersburg.

Publications

Collected Editions

Proza. Dnevniki. Pis'ma [Prose. Diary. Letters]. St Petersburg, 1913.

Polnoe sobranie sochinenii, edited by M.V. Vatson, 2 vols. Petrograd, 1917.

Polnoe sobranie stikhotvorenii. Moscow and Leningrad, 1962.

Izbrannoe. Moscow, 1994.

Poetry

Na mogile A.I. Gertsena [At the Grave of A.I. Herzen]. 1885–86.

Critical Studies

"Poety perekhodnogo vremeni", by M. Protopopov, *Russkaia mysl'*, 1/2 (1899), 179–93.

"Pevets 'trevogi iunykh sil'", by P.F. Iakubovich (L. Mel'shin), in his *Ocherki russkoi literatury*, St Petersburg, 1911, 237–76.

"Nadson", by L.N. Nazarova, in *Istoriia russkoi literatury XIX veka*, vol. 9, Moscow and Leningrad, 1956, 446–60.

"S.Ia. Nadson", by G.A. Bialyi, in Nadson's *Polnoe sobranie stikhotvorenii*, Moscow and Leningrad, 1962, 5–46.

"Semen Iakovlevich Nadson", by V.I. Kuleshov, in his *Istoriia russkoi literatury XIX veka. 70–90-e gody*, Moscow, 1983, 193–97.

"A Son of His Days. On the Centenary of the Death of S.Ya. Nadson", by N.S. Parsons, *Scottish Slavonic Review*, 9 (1987), 49–66.

Bibliographies

"Bibliograficheskie materialy o Nadsone", by N.K. Piksanov, in *Proza. Dnevniki. Pis'ma*, St Petersburg, 1913, iii–xii.

"Bibliograficheskii ukazatel'", in *Istoriia russkoi literatury XIX veka*, Moscow and Leningrad, 1962.

Semen Nadson was the last civic poet of note in 19th-century Russian literature. In his poetry he was concerned almost exclusively with the plight of the intellectual in what he called "the deep and cheerless darkness of these latter days". His poetry thus provides a portrait of the "superfluous man" of the 1880s.

The declamatory eloquence of his poetry, its highly personal accents, and that melodiousness which led to many poems being set to music are features reminiscent of Lermontov, whom Nadson greatly admired. Unlike Lermontov, however, Nadson does not stand above and apart from his contemporaries. This "hero of his time" is beset by a sense of inadequacy and weakness, which reflects the confusion of the age. Nadson soon gained a large and receptive audience, which heard in his verse the expressions of sentiments with which it readily identified. As the critic Protopopov observed in 1899: "Nadson was our equal, our faults and weaknesses were his faults and weaknesses, his interests – our interests." At the heart of his poetry is a conflict between a despairing pessimism, and a yearning for positive belief and self-commitment.

Nadson repeatedly stressed his bonds with his generation. Many poems are addressed to "my friend", "my brother", or simply begin with the word "we" or "you". They include several prison-poems, expressing his admiration for political prisoners, and there are frequent expressions of his admiration for and envy of the man of action, the revolutionary (*boets*). However, like Garshin, Nadson's attitude to revolutionary violence was ambivalent, he was naturally drawn towards non-violent positions. Nevertheless, the vision of an enslaved, unhappy Russia is central to his poetry. Particularly effective expressions of this view of Russia are given in such poems as *Na mogile A.I. Gertsena* [At the Grave of A.I. Herzen] (1885–86), and the two contrasting pictures of Russia in "Khudozhniki ee liubili voploshchat'" [Artists Liked to Represent Her] (1885).

When Nadson described his times as "morbid", "oppressive", he was thinking not only of the crushing of the revolutionary movement and the reactionary absolutism of Alexander III, but just as much of what he saw as the materialism, hypocrisy, and vulgarity of contemporary society. Thus many of his most pessimistic poems contain a strong element of social, as distinct from political, criticism. The poem "Zavesa sbroshena: ni novykh uvlechenii" [The veil is thrown off ...] (1881), is a typical expression of the deep disillusionment in men and life that became in the 1880s the dominant feature of Nadson's outlook. These were "post-heroic" times of mediocrity and *poshlost'* (vulgarity), which fostered within him a corrosive scepticism, a sense of isolation and futility:

> How little has been lived – yet how much experienced!
> Bright hopes, and youth, and love...
> And all has been mourned... mocked... forgotten...
> Buried – and will not rise again!

He strove to settle with what he called his "demon of anguish and doubt". In his later poetry the ideal of forgiveness and reconciliation comes increasingly to the fore. "I have chosen as a deity love and all-forgiveness", he proclaims, hoping that this creed of the heart will provide an avenue of escape from the scepticism and disillusionment that has prevented the emergence of anything positive in his life.

In his last years Nadson turned with interest to Buddha. He planned a long poem about the life of Buddha, to which he ascribed considerable importance. Though it is not possible to glean his intentions from the three mainly descriptive fragments that he wrote, it is likely that he would have suggested the relevance of aspects of Buddhist teaching to the Russia in which he lived. The frail Nadson did not live long enough for any coherent philosophy to crystallize. His poetry nevertheless reflects the searchings of his generation for something that would confer a new sense of dignity and purpose, and suggests that the road led away from revolutionary activity in the direction of charity and service to others.

Nadson also wrote a number of poems that were of a purely private nature or excursions into the realm of "pure art". The language is sometimes insipid and conventionally sentimental. Some of his love-poems and nature-lyrics contain rather too many "roses", "nightingales" and "weeping willows" for modern taste. Such flaws, however, are much more apparent in his earlier work. The later poems reveal a poet of considerable gifts.

But it was not these poems that won him fame, nor does he himself appear to have attached any importance to them. He was acclaimed and remembered as a poet who reflected to the fullest the anguish and searchings of his generation. He was also, and this was part of his secret, a poet of the purity and virginal idealism of youth. His high-minded pessimism and misty idealism found favour with an unusually broad section of society.

In the period up to 1917 Nadson remained the most popular poet in Russia. Collections of his poems were published almost every year, and his influence can be seen in the early verse of Bunin, A.N. Tolstoi, Kuprin, and Merezhkovskii. After 1917 his reputation suffered an abrupt, almost total decline. In the new world of the Soviets the "moaning" Nadson, as Briusov had termed him, seemed hopelessly out of place. In time, his significance as a cultural-historical phenomenon came to be appreciated anew and in 1962, to mark the centenary of his birth, his *Polnoe sobranie stikhotvorenii* [Complete Poems] were published. Nadson is certainly not forgotten – the trouble is that his name has become a by-word for triteness, tedium, and lamentation. It is inconceivable that he will ever regain the favour he once enjoyed. His poetry is too intimately linked with a particular historical epoch, the reactionary stagnation of the 1880s and beyond. However, those who are prepared to ignore the caustically dismissive judgements of his always numerous detractors, and are ready to make his acquaintance for themselves, will find a poet of rare musical and rhetorical power whose art can still impress today.

NEIL PARSONS

Iurii Markovich Nagibin 1920–1994

Prose writer

Biography

Born in Moscow, 3 April 1920. Educated briefly at medical school; then attended the Institute of Cinematography. Began to write under the influence of his stepfather, Ia. S. Rokachev; published his first story "Dvoinaia oshibka" [Double Mistake] in journal, *Ogonek*, 1940. Served in the army during World War II; invalided out with a wound that ultimately cost him his hearing; later served as war correspondent for the newspaper, *Trud*. Member of the Writers' Union, 1942. Worked as journalist on *Sotsialisticheskoe zemledelie*. Member of the editorial board of *Znamia*, 1955–65; also worked for *Nash sovremennik*. Married five times, including to Bella Akhmadulina, 1962–67. Died 17 June 1994.

Publications

Collected Editions

Selected Short Stories (in Russian), edited by D.J. Richards. Oxford, Pergamon Press, and New York, Macmillan, 1963.
Izbrannye proizvedeniia, 2 vols. Moscow, 1973.
Sobranie sochinenii, 4 vols. Moscow, 1980–81.
The Peak of Success and Other Stories (in Russian), edited by Helena Goscilo. Ann Arbor, Ardis, 1986.
Buntashnyi ostrov: Povesti i rasskazy [Buntashny Island ...]. Moscow, 1994.
Liubov' vozhdei: Povesti i rasskazy [Love of Leaders]. Moscow, 1994.
Izbrannoe, 3 vols. Moscow, 1996.

Fiction

Chelovek s fronta. Rasskazy [The Man from the Front]. Moscow, 1943.
Zerno zhizni [The Seed of Life]. Moscow, 1948.
The Pipe: Stories, translated by V. Shneerson, Moscow, Foreign Languages Publishing House, 1955.
Zimnii dub. Moscow, 1956; "Zimnii dub" translated as "The Winter Oak", by V. Shneerson, in *The Pipe*, 1955.
Trudnoe schast'e. Moscow, 1956; "Trudnoe schast'e" translated as "Happiness Hard-Won", *Soviet Literature*, 4 (1957).
Dreams: Stories [no translator named]. Moscow, Foreign Languages Publishing House, 1958.
Skalistyi porog [A Rocky Threshold]. Moscow, 1958.
Chistye prudy [Clear Ponds]. Moscow, 1961.
Na tikhom ozere [On a Quiet Lake]. Moscow, 1966.
Kniga detstva [Book of Childhood]. Moscow, 1967–71.
Pereulki moego detstva [Lanes of My Childhood]. Moscow, 1971.
V aprel'skom lesu [In an April Forest]. Moscow, 1974.
Pik udachi [The Peak of Success]. Moscow, 1975.
Berendeev les. Rasskazy. Ocherki. Moscow, 1978; "Berendeev les" translated as "Berendey's Forest", *Soviet Literature*, 2 (1980).
Island of Love, translated by Olga Shartse. Moscow, Progress, 1982.
Nauka dal'nikh stranstvii [The Study of Distant Travel]. Moscow, 1982.
Ne chuzhoe remeslo [A Familiar Craft]. Moscow, 1983.
"Blestiashchaia i gorestnaia zhizn' Imre Kal'mana" [The Brilliant and Pitiful Life of Imra Kal'man], *Oktiabr'*, 4 (1984).
"Sil'nee vsekh inykh velenii" [Stronger than All Other Orders], *Nash sovremennik*, 12 (1984).
"Poezdka na ostrova" [Trip to the Islands], *Neva*, 1 (1986).
Vstan' i idi. Moscow, 1987; translated as *Arise and Walk*, by Catherine Porter, London, Faber, 1990.
"Buntashnyi ostrov" [Buntashny Island], *Iunost'*, 4 (1994).
Dafnis i Khloia epokhi kul'ta lichnosti, voliuntarizma i zastoia [A Daphnis and Chloe of the Era of the Cult of Personality, Voluntarism and Stagnation]. Moscow, 1995.

Play and Screenplay

"Zastupnitsa: P'esa" [The Patroness], *Teatr*, 6 (1980).
Kinotsenarii. Moscow, 1980.

Travel Writing

"Letaiushchie tarelochki. Puteshestviia po Amerike" [Flying Saucers. Travels Round America], *Nash sovremennik*, 2 (1980).

Literary Criticism

Literaturnye razdum'ia [Literary Meditations]. Moscow, 1977.

Other Writing

Vsploshnyi zvon. O Moskve [Unbroken Sound. On Moscow]. Moscow, 1997.

Critical Studies

"Vetvi zimnego duba", by E. Vorob'ev, *Novyi mir*, 11 (1955), 247–50.

"Frontovye povesti Iuriia Nagibina", by I. Aizenshtok, *Zvezda*, 6 (1961), 208–10.

Russkii sovetskii rasskaz, edited by V.A. Kovalev, Moscow, 1970, chapter 8.

"Jurij Nagibin's Short Stories: Themes and Literary Criticism", by Ellen Joan Cochrum, PhD dissertation, Michigan State University, 1977.

Iurii Nagibin, by Irina Bogatko, Moscow, 1980.

"The Poacher and the Polluter: The Environmental Theme in Nagibin", by Earl D. Sampson, in *Studies in Russian Literature in Honor of Vsevolod Setchkarev*, edited by Julian W. Connolly and Sonia I. Ketchian, Columbus, Ohio, Slavica, 1986, 222–32.

"The Genre of Silence: Iurii Nagibin's *Zamolchavshaia vesna*", by Michael Pursglove, in *The Short Story: Structure and Statement*, edited by William J. Hunter, Exeter, Elm Books, 1996, pp. 159–71.

Bibliography

By Ellen Joan Cochrum in *Russian Language Journal*, 115 (1979).

Iurii Nagibin was a prolific author who, in a career of more than 50 years, covered a wide range of themes. He once said: "I do not regret writing about a lot. My only regret is that there is a lot I haven't written about." Throughout his long career Nagibin concentrated largely on the short-story form and became famous with the stories "Zimnii dub" ("The Winter Oak") and "Komarov" (both 1953), and with his collection *Trudnoe schast'e* [Happiness Hard-Won]. Before 1960, on his own admission, he found it impossible to create fictional characters and was much troubled by this. However he then discovered that one of his role models, Nikolai Leskov, was afflicted by the same problem. His first story containing entirely fictional characters was "Ekho" [The Echo] (1960), which began life as a film script. Nagibin had a lifelong interest in films and wrote many screenplays, most notably for *Predsedatel'* [The Chairman] (1965), based on his story "Stranitsy zhizni Trubnikova" [Pages from the Life of Trubnikov] (1962), and for the award-winning Russo-Japanese film *Dersu Uzala* (1975), directed by Akira Kurosawa. Equally successful was "Pogonia" [The Chase] (1962), one of over 20 stories written between 1954 and 1964 and describing life in the Meshchera region, south-east of Moscow, particularly the region of Lake Pleshcheevo. Its main character, the stolid, self-contained hunter Anatolii Ivanovich, appears in a number of the stories, which feature not only hunters but others making their living from Nature. Nature is a major theme in Nagibin's stories, instilled in him by his nanny Veronia. His detailed and sensitive descriptions of it reflect both the influence of Ivan Bunin and Nagibin's own practical experience as a hunter. He took an early interest in environmental matters, reflecting the influence of Andrei Platonov. His view of the Russian village has been described as "Westernist" in that he regards the primitive Russian village as badly in need of modernization. The traditional tension between town and country is to be seen in "Slezai, priekhali" [Get Down, We've Arrived] (1954). Asked to specify the major themes in his work, Nagibin named war; children; sports; hunting and fishing; village life; life abroad; love; historical personalities. Of these, the theme of war belongs mainly to Nagibin's early work, such as his first collection *Chelovek s fronta* [The Man from the Front], although it is also present in such later works as "Pavlik" (1958), "Gibel' pilota" [Death of a Pilot] (1964), and "Gde-to vozle konservatorii" [Somewhere Near the Conservatory] (1972). Of the stories that might be termed "love stories", the best-known is "Srochno trebuiutsia sedye chelovecheskie volosy" [Grey Human Hair Urgently Required]. The theme of children is to be seen in one of Nagibin's earliest stories, "Knut" [The Knout] (1941), the title of which refers to the whip given to a ten-year-old boy to control a flock of sheep. With it he unintentionally kills a cockerel and realizes Man's potential for destroying Nature. Children are the heroes of the cycle *Chistye prudy* [Clear Ponds], set in the eponymous region of Moscow where the author lived as a child in the 1930s. The stories of this cycle and two other cycles, *Leto moego detstva* [Summer of My Childhood] and *Pereulki moego detstva* [Lanes of My Childhood], were later included in the collection *Kniga detstva* [Book of Childhood] (1967–71). "Zamolchavshaia vesna" [The Spring that Fell Silent] (1982) is in similar vein. This story, which refers to the author's struggle with deafness, is, in many ways, an exemplar of a Nagibin short story. Overtly autobiographical, it has the slightest of plots and lacks both a conventional beginning and a traditional "twist" at the end. In this, Nagibin is following his mentor Anton Chekhov who recommended that, immediately on finishing a story, a writer should eliminate both its beginning and its end, for authorial lies proliferate in these two areas. The story lacks any overt "message" and is free of the facile optimism typical of the Stalinist era. Yet here, and throughout Nagibin's work, there is an unmistakable "Sovietness" (which might be defined as a mixture of sentimentality and truism) about the writing. This is allied to a rather forced literariness, with contrived literary references and unnecessary neologisms. The story is related to the earlier "Nemota" [Dumbness] (1972), in which Nagibin uses the twin themes of deafness and dumbness in a more metaphorical way to refer to a writer's ability or inability to write. The wartime incident that resulted in his deafness ironically enabled him to overcome "writer's block" and, on a second occasion, a visit to Pushkin's house in Kishinev and a fishing trip had a similar effect.

There are other themes in Nagibin's work, besides the ones he listed. For instance "Khazarskii ornament" ("The Khazar Ornament"), published in the second volume of the famous anthology *Literaturnaia Moskva* [Literary Moscow] (1956), deals with the intellectual community in Stalin's time. From the mid-1970s Nagibin turned increasingly to historical themes as, for example, in "Beglets" [The Runaway] (1978), in which the main character is the 18th-century poet Trediakovskii. Other stories deal with poets (Pushkin, Del'vig, Grigor'ev, Tiutchev, Fet, Annenskii, and Bunin), and composers (Rakhmaninov, Tchaikovskii, Bach, Verdi, and Wagner). He also wrote a number of stories with a strong fantastic element, such as "Pik udachi" ("The Peak of Success"), "Chuzhoe serdtse" [Alien Heart] and "Sredi professionalov" [Among the Professionals].

Nagibin has only rarely essayed longer prose forms and firmly rejects any notion that the short story is an inferior literary genre, writing that "the short story writer must feel the same generous empathy with life and have the same deep knowledge of it as the novelist ... The short-story writer's task of compressing the material that he has collected and interpreted into the most concise possible form is in no way easier than the novelist's". One of his rare longer works is the novel *Vstan' i idi* (*Arise and Walk*), a poignant evocation of the Gulag. This work, once again strongly autobiographical, focuses on the changing attitude of a son towards his wrongly imprisoned father.

MICHAEL PURSGLOVE

Vasilii Trofimovich Narezhnyi 1780–1825

Prose writer

Biography

Born in the Poltava district of the Ukraine in 1780. Attended the Moscow University, 1799–1801: left without degree. Entered the civil service, 1801. Posted briefly to Caucasus, returning subsequently to St Petersburg. Died in penury, St Petersburg, 3 July 1825.

Publications

Collected Editions

Izbrannye romany [Selected Novels]. Moscow, 1933.
Izbrannye sochineniia, 2 vols. Moscow, 1956.
Bursak: malorossiiskaia povest'; Dva Ivana, ili strast' k tiazhbam; Garkusha, malorossiiskii razboinik; romany [The Seminarist: A Little-Russian Tale; The Two Ivans, or a Passion for Litigation; Garkusha, the Little-Russian Brigand; Novels]. Kiev, 1988.

Fiction

Slavenskie vechera [Slavic Nights]. St Petersburg, 1809.
Rossiiskii Zhil'blaz [A Russian Gil Blas]. St Petersburg, 1814; Petrozavodsk, 1983.
Aristion, ili perevospitanie [Aristion, or Re-Education]. St Petersburg, 1822.
Zaporozhets [The Zaporozhian Cossack]. St Petersburg, 1824.
Bursak [The Seminarist]. St Petersburg, 1824.
Dva Ivana, ili strast' k tiazhbam [The Two Ivans, or a Passion for Litigation]. St Petersburg, 1825.
Chernyi god, ili gorskie kniaz'ia [A Black Year, or the Mountain Princess]. St Petersburg, 1829.
Garkusha, malorossiiskii razboinik [Garkusha, the Little-Russian Brigand]. St Petersburg, 1950 (fragments).

Play

Dmitrii Samozvanets [Dmitrii the Pretender]. St Petersburg, 1804.

Critical Studies

V.T. Narezhnyi. Istoriko-literaturnyi ocherk, by N. Belozerskaia, St Petersburg, 1896.
Stanovlenie realizma v russkoi proze kontsa XVIII–pervoi chetverti XIX vv. (Tvorchestvo V.T. Narezhnogo), by F.I. Kondratskaia, Leningrad, 1952.
"Russkii roman pervoi chetverti XIX veka. Ot sentimental'noi povesti k romanu", by L.N. Nazarova, in *Istoriia russkogo romana v dvukh tomakh*, edited by G.M. Fridlender, vol. 1, Moscow and Leningrad, 1962.
Russian Romantic Fiction, by John Mersereau, Jr, Ann Arbor, Ardis, 1983.
A History of Russian Literature of the Romantic Period, by William Edward Brown, Ann Arbor, Ardis, 1986, vol. 2, 175–202.
The Russianization of Gil Blas: A Study in Literary Appreciation, by Ronald D. LeBlanc, Columbus, Ohio, Slavica, 1986.

That Vasilii Narezhnyi should have fallen into a sort of literary oblivion so soon after his death in 1825 is anomalous – given his talents – but explicable. An accomplished writer of novels and short stories alike, he represented the high point of the 18th-century fictional legacy rather than the modes of the rapidly evolving literary environment of the early 19th century in which he happened to find himself working. For imaginative sweep, wit, satirical acuity, and consummate gifts in the art of story-telling one could, during that period, do worse than turn to Narezhnyi, but his blend of high-minded civic satire and frankly nostalgic Ukrainian whimsy was no longer piquant to the palate of a newly sophisticated Russian readership that was already beginning to savour Pushkin, and which was presently to experience Gogol'. Narezhnyi, to them, was redolent of earlier attitudes, narrower, westward-looking and imbued with the worthy but now fusty virtues of enlightened rationalism. Compositionally and perhaps thematically dated, Narezhnyi's influence, when it did declare itself, seemed thoroughly parochial: the clear parallels between Narezhnyi's Ukrainian scenarios and those of Gogol', for instance (the Dikan'ka tales and *Mirgorod*), were generally worked out critically to Narezhnyi's discredit. To portray his writing merely as a sourcebook for droll provincial anecdotes is assuredly to ignore his attainments as the inheritor and fine-tuner of that solid 18th-century novel-writing tradition in Russia that established prose as a workable and valid medium.

Narezhnyi's earliest and most important novel, *Rossiiskii Zhil'blaz* [A Russian Gil Blas], employs the winning formula of a picaresque structure, of the sort propagated slightly earlier by Chulkov and Levshin, supported by an overtly satirical intention. Prior to lighting upon this, Narezhnyi had dabbled with some success in other genres: his 1804 play *Dmitrii Samozvanets*

[Dmitrii the Pretender] had tapped a particularly acceptable historical seam, and a collection of Ossianic tales of Old Russia, *Slavenskie vechera* [Slavic Nights], had been a sounding-board for creation, and so on. *Histoire de Gil Blas de Santillane* by Alain-René Lesage (1715–35) had consolidated the Spanish picaresque mode in France (joining the home-grown corpus of Scarron, Sorel and Furetière, among others), and Narezhnyi's novel, claiming an immediate spiritual kinship from the title onwards, attempted definitively to do the same for Russia, capitalizing on the Chulkov-Levshin exemplars. Lesage's sprawling novel had been translated into Russian in 1745 and been through seven editions by the time Narezhnyi set pen to paper in order to bring immediately home to a native readership what he took to be a universally admired form.

In the novel the part of the roaming picaro is played by Chistiakov. He is destined ultimately and as a result of his multifarious adventures to arrive at a serene, "Enlightened" plateau or wisdom, at which point he is able to narrate the novel of which he is hero, but when he started his peregrinations the school of hard knocks had already made him a cynical and corrupt opportunist. A free-floating observer of contemporary Russian manners, Chistiakov moves among the highest of the land and the lowest, scaling the heights and plumbing the depths, permitting Narezhnyi serially to wield his scalpel on whichever social or institutional iniquity, folly or foible seems to deserve it in a colourfully degenerate Russia. There is little psychology applied to Chistiakov or to the rogues and grotesques whom he encounters (this is one strand of authorial observation, developed earlier in Karamzin, which is lacking in Narezhnyi), but there is plenty of indignation on the author's part. We are witness to an old tradition brightly re-polished: *castigat ridendo mores* and, as scholarship reiterates, the way is set fair for Gogol' and Saltykov-Shchedrin. Unlike his fellow Ukrainian Gogol', however, Narezhnyi writes not from a paternalistic position of theocratic foreboding, so much as from an old 18th-century feeling for ratio, for enlightened virtue and civilized propriety, which held that vice was wrong because it was ugly, and remediable best through satire (in this he stretches the line, then anachronistic, which had included Kantemir, Novikov and Fonvizin). In the articulation of this world-view, Narezhnyi makes free with a more recent literary licence: the dialogic register is appropriately base when required, which is not rarely, and the general crudities of daily living are outlined with a gusto to which "classical" writers would never have consented to condescend. Narezhnyi's satire is not political, and for the most part the tone is mild and rather world-weary, but satire it indubitably is, and this sufficed to earn the last three parts of the novel an official prohibition by the censor, while the first three parts were suppressed on publication. The novel in its entirety had to wait until 1938 to see the light of day.

Like many another writer whose celebrity is established by a successful first work, Narezhnyi suffered something of a falling-off in later novels. *Chernyi god, ili gorskie kniaz'ia* [A Black Year, or the Mountain Princes], published posthumously in 1829 after extensive run-ins with the censor, dissects officially sanctioned corruption in the Caucasus, of which region Narezhnyi had had first-hand experience. The episodic and intrigue-riven structure of the plot recalls *Rossiiskii Zhil'blaz* but the language and scenarios are more allegorical, "Aesopic" in the Krylovian sense, attacking the injustices of provincial governmental policy on the ostensible pretext of ridiculing Asiatic or Eastern malpractice. In *Aristion, ili perevospitanie* [Aristion, or Re-Education] Narezhnyi's satire is concentrated didactically against Russian systems of education, with "democratizing" alternatives suggested, taking their cue largely from Rousseau's *Emile*. More muted variations on the theme of picaresque satire are to be found in Narezhnyi's somewhat pastoralized Ukrainian novels *Zaporozhets* [The Zaporozhian Cossack] and *Bursak* [The Seminarist], which counterpoise a rosily recollected noble Ukrainian history, devotedly conjured via description of mores and social organization, with the implied vicissitudes of modern times. Much of the descriptive detail here is heart-felt and sharply evoked, and the same might be said of *Dva Ivana, ili strast' k tiazhbam* [The Two Ivans, or a Passion for Litigation], which lends itself effortlessly to the Gogolian treatment of the story, and an unfinished novel about a sort of Ukrainian Robin Hood, *Garkusha*. As time passed Narezhnyi by, he became acutely aware that his time had come and gone, and he looked back increasingly to the past, in terms of his own career (Garkusha the kind-hearted bandit appeared as a character in *Rossiiskii Zhil'blaz*, Narezhnyi's finest moment) and more generally, with wistful resignation.

NICHOLAS CROWE

Nikolai Alekseevich Nekrasov 1821–1878

Poet and journalist

Biography

Born in Nemirov, Ukraine, 10 December 1821, where father's regiment was garrisoned. Moved to father's estate in Greshnevo, near Iaroslavl. Attended Iaroslavl gymnasium, 1832–37; military academy in St Petersburg, went to university classes, 1838–40. Began writing verses, reviews, plays, and stories for journals. First collection of verses published, 1840; collection criticized by Belinskii and copies were subsequently bought up by Nekrasov and destroyed. Worked for the journal *Zapiski otechestva*, early 1840s. Purchased *Sovremennik*, with

I.I. Panaev, 1847, and turned it into leading progressive journal. Worked with Chernyshevskii and Dobroliubov. First major illness in mid-1850s, cured by a stay in Italy. After the publication of a poem depicting the misery of railway workers *Sovremennik* was closed down by the government, 1866. Acquired *Zapiski otechestva* with Saltykov-Shchedrin, 1868, and became editor-in-chief. Diagnosed as fatally ill, early 1875. Died in St Petersburg, 8 January 1878 after a long and painful illness.

Publications

Collected Editions

Stikhotvoreniia. Pervoe posmertnoe izdanie [Poems. The First Posthumous Edition]. St Petersburg, 1879.

Poems by Nicholas Nekrassov, translated by Juliet M. Soskice (includes "Russian Women", "Red-Nosed Frost", "The Pedlars"). London, Oxford University Press, 1929; reprinted Wilmington, Delaware, Scholarly Resources, 1974.

Polnoe sobranie sochinenii i pisem, 15 vols. Leningrad, 1981–85.

Poetry

Mechty i zvuki [Dreams and Sounds]. St Petersburg, 1840.

Stikhotvoreniia. Moscow, 1856; St Petersburg, 1861, 1864, 1869, 1873.

Korobeiniki [The Pedlars], *Sovremennik*, 10 (1861).

Moroz, krasnyi nos [Red-Nosed Frost], *Sovremennik*, 1 (1864); Letchworth, Bradda, 1963.

Dedushka [The Grandfather], *Otechestvennye zapiskii* (1870), 9.

Nedavnee vremia [Recent Times], *Otechestvennye zapiski* (1871), 10.

Russkie zhenshchiny [Russian Women], *Otechestvennye zapiski* (1872–73).

Sovremenniki [Contemporaries], *Otechestvennye zapiski* (1875), 8.

Poslednie pesni [The Last Songs]. St Petersburg, 1877.

Komu na Rusi zhit' khorosho? 1881; translated as *Who Can Be Happy and Free in Russia?*, by Juliet M. Soskice, London, Oxford University Press, 1917; Westport, Connecticut, Hyperion Press, 1977.

Critical Studies

Zhizn' i deiatel'nost' N.A. Nekrasova, by V.E. Evgen'ev-Maksimov, 3 vols, Moscow and Leningrad, 1947–52.

Nekrasov, l'homme et le poète, by Charles Corbet, Paris, Institut d'Études Slaves de l'Université de Paris, 1948.

Masterstvo Nekrasova, by K.I. Chukovskii, Moscow, 1952.

Nikolai Nekrasov, by M.B. Peppard, New York, Twayne, 1967.

Nikolaj Nekrasov: His Life and Poetic Art, by S.S. Birkenmayer, The Hague, Mouton, 1968.

N.A. Nekrasov. Zhizn' i tvorchestvo, by N.L. Stepanov, 2nd edition, Moscow, 1971.

"The Pessimism of N.A. Nekrasov's *Moroz, krasnyi nos*", by Michael Ransome, *Journal of Russian Studies*, 45 (1983), 9–18.

"Dar'ia's Secret, or What Happens in *Moroz, krasnyi nos*", by Richard Gregg, *Slavic Review*, 45/1 (1986), 38–48.

"The Textual Misrepresentation of N.A. Nekrasov's *Komu na Rusi zhit' khorosho?*", by Michael Ransome, *Slavonic and East European Review*, 65/2 (1987), 169–82.

A Comparative Study of Pushkin's "The Bronze Horseman", Nekrasov's "Red-Nosed Frost" and Blok's "The Twelve" – The Wild World, by A.D.P. Briggs, Lewiston, New York, and Lampeter, Wales, Edwin Mellen Press, 1990.

Bibliographies

Nekrasov, by A.N. Pypin, St Petersburg, 1905.

Istoriia russkoi literatury XIX veka. Bibliograficheskii ukazatel', by K.D. Muratova, Moscow and Leningrad, 1962.

"Bibliografiia literatury o Nekrasove 1970–74", by N.N. Mostovskaia, in *Nekrasovskii sbornik*, VI, Leningrad, 1978.

Nikolai Alekseevich Nekrasov's contribution to 19th-century Russian literature was uniquely varied. Born in 1821, he became both one of the leading publishers of his day and one of its foremost writers. For some three decades he was responsible for editing two journals – *Sovremennik* (1847–66) and *Zapiski otechestva* (1868–77) – and he succeeded in turning both into tsarist Russia's most progressive monthly publications. His work on the journals brought him into contact with virtually every major figure in the literary world and he persuaded most of them to allow him to be the first to publish at least some of their works. At the same time, he earned for himself the reputation of arguably the most widely-read and ardently discussed poet of the mid-century period.

Nekrasov's literary output covered many genres. In the early years of his career he wrote reviews and articles for various journals, a large number of minor dramatic works and several pieces of prose fiction. However, these compositions are of interest only to the specialist scholar, since none of them was sufficient to set him apart from the many other popular writers of the time. It was on his lyric and narrative poetry that Nekrasov's substantial and enduring reputation was established. His first publication, a collection of imitative romantic verse entitled *Mechty i zvuki* [Dreams and Sounds], was an abject failure, but the young Nekrasov quickly progressed to find his mature artistic identity as a critical realist. Having earned the approval of the great critic Belinskii, Nekrasov soon became acknowledged as the leading Russian exponent of civic poetry. By the time his first volume of collected verse appeared in 1856, his renown was so great that the entire edition was sold out within weeks and all subsequent publications bearing his name enjoyed a similar fate. Final confirmation of his popularity was provided by the huge number of people who attended his funeral. Dostoevskii was among those who gave addresses at the grave, causing uproar when he suggested that Nekrasov was as great a poet as Pushkin. Many of the assembled crowd responded to this by shouting their belief that Nikolai Alekseevich was greater even than his illustrious predecessor.

Although Nekrasov has attracted relatively little critical attention in the west, in Russia the opposite has always been the case. During his lifetime and after his death his stature as the leading civic poet meant that scholars could not afford to neglect him, while after the Revolution his popularity became even greater since he was identified as a progressive thinker whose ideals were broadly in keeping with those of the new Soviet state. Nekrasov's fate in literary criticism has been to be viewed merely as a poet whose aim was to use his verse to convey social comment and to encourage a spirit of optimism in his readers. While this may be accepted to have been his intention in the majority of his poems, in the case of his greatest works the author's purpose must be acknowledged to have incorporated a further dimension.

Throughout his mature career as a writer Nekrasov found inspiration in the theme of the Russian peasantry, repeatedly returning to it in order to present his reader with characters from the broad masses of the people in a way previously never encountered in Russian literature. This theme produced his foremost creations: the narrative poems *Korobeiniki* ("The Pedlars"), *Moroz, krasnyi nos* ("Red-Nosed Frost"), and *Komu na Rusi khit' khorosho?* (*Who Can Be Happy and Free in Russia?*). Many of Nekrasov's works were destined to be of interest only to the reading public of his age. This was the fate, for example, of his compositions that took as their subject famous people from recent history or contemporary reality. Such works as *Dedushka* [The Grandfather] (1870) and *Russkie zhenshchiny* ("Russian Women") 1872–73, whose heroes were figures linked with the Decembrist uprising, or *Nedavnee vremia* [Recent Times] (1871) and *Sovremenniki* [Contemporaries] (1875), which satirized the privileged classes, were greatly enjoyed when they were published. Well-executed examples of their type, the attraction of such pieces is, however, reduced for the modern reader now that their allusions have lost their immediacy. This is not the case for his three main narrative poems, whose pre-eminence is secured by the fact that they alone among Nekrasov's works combine a high standard of artistic achievement with weighty philosophical content that is of universal and eternal relevance.

The artistic success of the three major works stems from a masterly combination of various elements. They all show to differing degrees Nekrasov's skill at its most accomplished in the depiction of landscape and character, in the succinct and engaging narration of an interesting story and in the assimilation of the Russian folk-style and lexicon for the enrichment of the literary language. In addition, they bear witness to the poet's lightness of touch in the metrical composition of his verse, with "Red-Nosed Frost" in particular showing remarkable prosodic dexterity.

Other creations of the poet's Muse might, of course, be argued to rival the artistry of these three narrative poems. Such works as "Vlas" (1855), or "Zheleznaia doroga" [The Railway] (1864), shorter, slighter pieces on the peasant theme, are only two examples that could be described as outstanding poetic creations. However, neither they nor any of his other compositions possess the depth and broadness of scope to rank them among Nekrasov's best works. These three narrative poems can be argued to offer at their most profound the same bleak message of a hostile universe in which the individual stands alone, with no hope of protection from any quarter, human or divine. "The Pedlars" was the first to suggest this, with its depiction of the travels and fate of two peasant hawkers. While illustrating social ills, Nekrasov also drew for this work, as he often did, on the folk tradition. He used allusions to the figure of "Woe-Misfortune" (*Gore-zloschastie*) to suggest the pessimistic belief that suffering can often be determined by the maleficent influence of Nature and Chance, free from any concern for justice. This cheerlessness was again in evidence in "Red-Nosed Frost" and *Who Can Be Happy and Free in Russia?* and can be taken to represent the essence of Nekrasov's considered view of the human condition.

MICHAEL RANSOME

Red-Nosed Frost

Moroz, krasnyi nos

Narrative poem, 1864

Just over a thousand lines long, the narrative poem "Red-Nosed Frost" tells the tragic story of a Russian peasant family whose troubles begin when its breadwinner, Prokl, catches a chill and dies in the prime of life. His family bury him and on the same day his wife, Dar'ia, freezes to death while chopping wood to heat the family hut after Prokl's funeral. Simple in terms of narrative content, the poem was the product of a creative process that continued intermittently over a period of more than two years. Nekrasov first had the idea for it in 1861, though it was 1863 before an extract appeared in print and 1864 before the final version of the text was produced. It is undoubtedly Nekrasov's most accomplished work and can also be argued to offer the essence of his philosophical views, as his true perception of the human condition receives untrammelled expression in the same way that his technical skill as a poet was shown at its unforced best.

The high standard of the poem's poetic achievement has received almost unanimous recognition from the time of its publication. Critics have gone as far as suggesting that "Red-Nosed Frost" ranks Nekrasov on a par with Pushkin at his best and earns a place in the front rank of world literature. The reasons for such extravagant claims are easily understood. From its dramatic opening the poem engages its reader and proceeds at a breathless pace to recount what led up to the death of the peasant husband and wife and to offer a full description both of the family's grief at bereavement and also the many joyous aspects of their life together. The pitfall of sentimentality is successfully avoided throughout by deliberate emotional understatement and by reordering the story's chronology. Character and landscape are evoked with laconic skill and memorable imagery, while rhythmic and metrical modulation of the verse suggest a poet at the height of his powers. There can be no question that the praise universally accorded this poem for its artistic excellence is deserved.

Less easily accepted is the view generally advanced by literary criticism of its content. Western scholars have devoted little attention to the mood or meaning of the poem, though this is surely to ignore one of its most important facets, on which Russian critics have always focused. Influenced by the social tendentiousness of Nekrasov's earlier works, they often greeted the publication of this poem with reference to its considerable importance for contemporary Russian society. The positive portrayal of its peasant heroes was seen as presenting an optimistic view of the historical fate awaiting the Russian *narod*, a theme that became the leitmotif of Soviet Nekrasov scholarship.

The subject-matter of "Red-Nosed Frost" is the age-old and world-wide problems of death, grief, and the relationship of humankind to nature. Nekrasov chooses as his heroes representatives of the Russian peasantry not to score easy points at the expense of the 19th-century tsarist regime. Rather he uses the fate of Prokl and Dar'ia as extreme examples of the lot of Everyman, directly exposed as they are to the influence of Fate without the cocoon of privilege or affluence that can blur the truth about the human condition. The poet can be seen to imply a cheerless assessment of the mortal predicament, showing the individual to be at the mercy of non-social forces that he is powerless to combat and to be unable to depend on help from any source, human or preterhuman, Christian or pagan, to ensure that justice determines his destiny.

A great love of the peasantry and respect for its virtue and fortitude undoubtedly pervade the whole poem. Tangential reference is made to some of the social burdens placed on Russian peasants in the 19th century, such as the need to pay taxes (XIV) and conscription to the army (XXIV), but the overall impression is overwhelmingly of the happiness enjoyed by Dar'ia's family. Her joy as she imagines the onset of spring (XIX), her son's wedding (XXIII) or harvesting (XXXIII–IV) impresses on the reader that Russian village life can often be cheerful and rewarding. However, the brighter mood of such scenes, together with the admiring depiction of the physical and moral strengths of Prokl and Dar'ia, serves ultimately only to point up more sharply the injustice of their fate.

When Prokl has by chance caught his fatal chill, his mother unsuccessfully tries a variety of folk remedies (XII), leaving Dar'ia to lament the passing of the human protector in whom she had put her faith (IX, XX–IV, XXXIII–IV). Divine intervention proves no more trustworthy than human help when Dar'ia turns to God to save Prokl with a miracle-working icon (XII and XXV–VIII). In the poem's depiction Nature joins God and man in failing the individual. Winter is shown throughout as unremittingly harsh, while summer is equally merciless (XXI) and the rest of creation looks on indifferently as Dar'ia pours out her grief (XI, XVII). The main embodiment of Nature is the figure of *Morozko*, or Frost, familiar to Russians from a popular fairy tale whose reassuring moral is that mortal goodness will be rewarded by natural forces. Immediately conjuring up associations with this comforting notion by choosing the title he does, Nekrasov finally reworks the tale to make Frost a depressingly arbitrary malevolent figure, emphatically removing any last hope of intervention by natural forces to ensure that justice is done.

"Red-Nosed Frost" is a skilfully constructed work, the laconic style of which successfully conveys memorable depictions both of landscapes and characters. Social conditions assume a role of secondary importance as it is able to exhibit universal and timeless relevance. The message, which the poem conveys with a lightness of touch often lacking in Nekrasov's other works, is indeed a cheerless one, for above all else it suggests that it is man's lot to stand alone and defenceless against an unbridledly hostile universe.

MICHAEL RANSOME

Who Can Be Happy and Free in Russia?

Komu na Rusi zhit' khorosho?

Narrative poem, 1881 (published in parts 1866–76: unfinished)

Who Can Be Happy and Free in Russia? was Nekrasov's "favourite child" and by far his longest creation (over eight and a half thousand lines). It occupied his attention for the major part of the last two decades of his life, though he was eventually unable to complete it before he died in early 1878. It tells the story of seven peasants who set off on an odyssey around Russia asking everyone they meet the question that gives the work its title. Nekrasov had time to write a general prologue and four major parts, each of which splits into smaller sections or "chapters". These parts are largely independent in the stories they recount and receive only the loosest general unity from the peasants' repeated question.

Central to critical consideration of *Who Can Be Happy and Free in Russia?* has been the fact that it remained unfinished and largely unrevised when the poet died. Over-ambitious in intention and weak in cohesion, the work has been subject to much debate about the shape and message it might eventually have had. The text emerged gradually: the "Prolog" ("Prologue") in 1866; the five chapters making up "Chast' pervaia" ("Part One") in 1869 and 1870; "Posledysh" ("The Die-Hard") in 1873; "Krest'ianka" ("The Peasant Woman") in 1874; "Pir – na ves' mir" ("A Feast – for All") was largely completed by 1876, but appeared only in 1881 with cuts made by the censor. Nekrasov intended to compose at least three more parts, though writing for these sections never progressed beyond a few preliminary extracts. It was a great disappointment to him that work on the poem was not finished, but he left no explanation of the message he ultimately wished it to convey.

Its piecemeal publication made it difficult for Nekrasov's contemporaries to comment in this respect. Reviews at the time often split along partisan lines, praising or criticizing artistic achievement according to political sympathies and concentrating on a civic moral. The poem lends itself to preoccupation with its social implications. There is much satire at the expense of exploiters of the masses and the peasantry is highlighted as the exclusive source of good national traits. While the language used by the poet is authentically that of the *narod*, the artistic achievement of the work is, however, uneven. At its weakest it is predictable, banal, and prolix; at its best it offers depictions of character and landscape that rival the heights of "Red-Nosed Frost".

With its many examples of the inequity of Russian society, *Who Can Be Happy and Free in Russia?* was predictably a favourite of Soviet critics and literally hundreds of articles and monographs have been dedicated to it. Their unanimous approach, echoed by western scholars, has been to stress the poet's desire to criticize the Emancipation and post-Reform reality, to reaffirm faith in the invincible moral and physical strengths of the *narod*, and to propagandize the optimistic idea that a peasant revolution could achieve individual and collective happiness. This interpretation is supported by an ordering of the poem's extant parts that follows the chronology of their creation, even though this ignores the description of the parts given by

Nekrasov himself. The poet clearly designated "The Die-Hard" as "from the second part", "A Feast – for All" as "Part II. Second Chapter", and "The Peasant Woman" as "from the third part". Although frequently debated, the sequencing issue has not been resolved, the literary establishment preferring to ignore Nekrasov's documented intentions for ideological reasons. Critics identifying an overall mood of optimism in the work feel happiest with "A Feast – for All" at the end because its tone is apparently brighter than that of the alternative concluding part, "The Peasant Woman". However, close examination of the poem overall can suggest that an optimistic interpretation is no more appropriate to *Who Can Be Happy and Free in Russia?* than it is to "Red-Nosed Frost".

As early as the "Prologue" the logic of the poem is that the difficulties endured by the *narod* can only partially be blamed on the social regime. The wanderers come from villages with allegorical names: "Patched", "Holey", "Barefoot", "Shivering", "Burned", "Hungry" and "Harvestless". Unworthy aspects of society can certainly be detected here, though by also suggesting natural calamities like fire, famine, and crop failure, the poet immediately hints too at the malevolence of a higher authority. The rest of the work continues to propose this idea, with repeated depiction alongside social injustice of tragedies that become inevitable only because of the vagaries of Nature and Chance.

The five chapters of "Part One" recount the peasants' meetings with a priest and a landowner and their experience at a village fair. "The Die-Hard" offers a more intense denunciation of the landowning class, while "A Feast – for All" further depicts the suffering endured by the *narod*. It also briefly presents a young seminarist, Grisha Dobrosklonov, who seems to be the personification of a positive hero to lead the people to happiness. Critics have laid great emphasis on his song of hope at the end of this part, though this optimism must surely be flawed when the poet tells us that Grisha's health is poor and his fate will be to die young of consumption. "The Peasant Woman" again illustrates the worthiness of the *narod* and the suffering unjustly inflicted upon it. Its unremitting tragedy, in which everything seems to be against its innocent victims, makes it hard to feel sanguine about Russia's future.

Criticism of contemporary society is obviously present throughout *Who Can Be Happy and Free in Russia?*, though beyond this Nekrasov may be seen to remind his audience that the causes of human suffering are not exclusively socio-political in character. His "favourite child" joins "Red-Nosed Frost" in repeatedly highlighting man's inability to be master of his own fate, his impotent dependence on the caprice of Nature and Chance, and the bitter reality that no superior force is at work in the universe to ensure that justice is done. Not even the possibility of revolutionary change is able to temper this pessimistic message.

MICHAEL RANSOME

Viktor Platonovich Nekrasov 1911–1987

Prose writer

Biography

Born in Kiev, 17 June 1911. Lived in Paris as a young child, returning to Kiev, 1915. Attended school in Kiev, subsequently trained as an architect, but did not enter the profession. Became actor and stage-designer in small theatre companies touring Ukraine and Russian provinces, late 1930s. Served in the Red Army, 1941–45; commander of sapper battalion at the defence of Stalingrad. Subsequently wounded and invalided out with rank of Captain, January 1945. Joined the Communist Party and the Writers' Union, 1944. First work ("Stalingrad") published, 1946. Became full-time writer. Visited Italy, 1957 and 1962; United States, 1960; France, 1964. Attacked for travel sketches and threatened by Khrushchev with expulsion from the Party, 1963. Became associated with campaigns in support of Solzhenitsyn and others, against anti-Semitism and the invasion of Czechoslovakia, late 1960s. Married: Galina Viktorovna; one stepson. Subjected to harassment by KGB, expelled from the Party and forced to emigrate, September 1974. Settled in Paris, where he continued to publish. Travelled extensively (including Britain, the United States, and Australia). Recipient: Stalin Prize, 1947. Died in Paris, 3 September 1987.

Publications

Collected Editions

Vtoraia noch' [The Second Night]. Moscow, 1965.
Vasia Konakov. Kiev, 1965.
Puteshestviia v raznykh izmereniiakh [Journeys of Various Dimensions]. Moscow, 1967.
Viktor Nekrasov v zhizni i pis'makh [Viktor Nekrasov in Life and Letters]. Moscow, 1971.
Po obe storony steny – povesti i rasskazy [On Both Sides of the Wall]. New York, Effect, 1984.
Malen'kaia pechal'naia povest' – proza raznykh let [A Sad Little Story – Prose of Various Years]. Moscow, 1990.
V okopakh Stalingrada [In the Trenches of Stalingrad]. Moscow, 1990; reprinted Leningrad, 1991.
Postscripts: Short Stories, translated by Michael Falchikov and Dennis Ward. London, Quartet, 1991.

Fiction

"Stalingrad", *Znamia*, 8/9–10 (1946), 3–82, and 38–145; republished as *V okopakh Stalingrada*, Moscow, 1947;

translated as *Front-Line Stalingrad*, by David Floyd, London, Harvill Press, 1962; reprinted London, Fontana, 1975.
"V rodnom gorode" [In His Home Town], *Novyi mir*, 10–11 (1954), 2–65, and 97–178.
"Kira Georg'evna", *Novyi mir*, 6 (1961), 70–126; separate edition, Moscow, 1962; edited by Militsa Greene and Hector Blair, Cambridge, Cambridge University Press, 1967; revised London, Bristol Classical Press, 1992; translated as *Kira*, by Moura Budberg, London, Cresset Press, 1960; also translated as *Kira Georgievna*, by Walter N. Vickery, New York, Pantheon, 1962.
"Sluchai na Mamaevom kurgane" [Incident on Mamai Tumulus], *Novyi mir*, 12 (1965), 35–54.
Malen'kaia pechal'naia povest' [A Sad Little Story]. London, Overseas Publications Interchange, 1986.

Essays and Travel Notes
"Pervoe znakomstvo" [First Meeting], *Novyi mir*, 7–8 (1958) 142–81, and 123–59.
"Po obe storony okeana", *Novyi mir*, 11–12 (1962), 110–48; translated as *Both Sides of the Ocean: A Russian Writer's Travels in Italy and the United States*, by Elias Kulukundis, London, Jonathan Cape, and New York, Holt Rinehart and Winston, 1964.
"Mesiats vo Frantsii" [A Month in France], *Novyi mir*, 4 (1965), 102–63.
Zapiski zevaki [Notes of a Bystander]. Frankfurt, Posev, 1976.
"Vzgliad i nechto" [A Look and Something], *Kontinent*, 10 (1976), 13–85; 12–13 (1977), 90–119, 7–82.
"Dolgaia i schastlivaia zhizn'" [A Long and Happy Life], *Kontinent*, 25 (1980), 355–57 (review of poetry of Gennadii Shpalikov).
Saperlipopet (esli by da kaby...) [And Pigs Might Fly]. London, Overseas Publications Interchange, 1983.

Critical Studies

"Molodost' chuvstv", by Iurii Bondarev, *Literaturnaia gazeta*, 17 June 1961.
"Byt' dostoinym nashego chitatel'ia", by V. Bykov, *Novyi mir*, 11 (1963).
Literatura o voine, by L. Plotkin, 1967.
"Reconstructions of Realities in Art – Viktor Nekrasov's 'Incident on Mamaj Tumulus'", by Dennis Ward, *Poetics and Theory of Literature*, 4 (1979), 285–98.
"Art, Life and Truth in Viktor Nekrasov's 'Kira Georgievna'", by Michael Falchikov, *Forum for Modern Language Studies*, 1 (1981), 26–38.
A History of Post-War Soviet Writing: The Literature of Moral Opposition, by Grigori Svirski, translated by Robert Dessaix and Michael Ulman, Ann Arbor, Ardis, 1981.

Viktor Nekrasov's background reflects the best of the pre-1917 Russian intelligentsia – radical, humanitarian, and European in outlook. His mother, a medical graduate of Lausanne University, worked in a Paris military hospital in the early months of World War I, his aunt, Sof'ia Motovilova, was a friend of Krupskaia. The family returned to Russia in 1915 and settled in Kiev, which was to remain Nekrasov's home base for the next 60 years. After the death of his father, and the shooting of his elder brother during the Civil War, Nekrasov was brought up by his grandmother, mother and aunt, strong-minded, resourceful women who coped determinedly with the privations and uncertainties of life during the NEP years. In later years, Nekrasov wrote affectionately about 1920s Kiev, his childhood, and his family. Despite an early interest in writing, on leaving school he trained as an architect and, though he never practised, he retained a lifelong interest in buildings and cityscapes. He turned to the theatre instead and toured with a repertory company, as actor and stage-designer – at one point even auditioning, unsuccessfully, for Stanislavskii. These were the years of the Stalin Purges and, years later Nekrasov expressed surprise that, despite its intelligentsia/émigré antecedents, his immediate family remained untouched.

The Great Patriotic War, however, was the turning-point in Nekrasov's life and the formative experience that started him on his literary career. As an officer in a sapper battalion, he participated in the retreat towards Stalingrad, in its successful defence and the ensuing advance, before being wounded in Poland and invalided out in January 1945. The following year, his novel *Stalingrad* (later *V okopakh Stalingrada*, translated as *Front-Line Stalingrad*) was published in the journal *Znamia*. Nekrasov was awarded the Stalin Prize, and began a successful career as a Soviet writer. The theme of war and its aftermath occupies much of his writing of the 1950s and 1960s. His second major work, *V rodnom gorode* [In His Home Town], dealt with the problems of a demobbed soldier and many of his most successful short works, such as "Vtoraia noch'" [The Second Night] and "Tri vstrechi" [Three Meetings] focus on comradeship, survival, and the memories of a shared experience. During the Thaw, and particularly after Khrushchev's speech at the 20th Party Congress, Nekrasov became an influential figure among writers, strongly associated with the "liberals" and the journal *Novyi mir*, which published most of his work. Though memory of the war is still a significant theme, the more general question of the past and how to come to terms with it, especially in the light of the revelations about Stalin, is reflected in the novella *Kira Georg'evna*. In this work, a middle-aged sculptress is forced to re-examine both her own personal life and her attitude to her art, through a combination of a love-affair with her young model and the unexpected reappearance of her first husband, a purge victim who has survived a long period of imprisonment and has returned, eager to catch up on the life he has missed. The Kira of the title is forced to recognize that her art is false because her life has been false. *Kira Georg'evna* not only confronted the corrosive effect of Stalinism in general, but also posed uncomfortable questions about the role of the artist in Soviet society. Memory and coping with one's past are at the heart of the remarkable *Sluchai na Mamaevom kurgane* [Incident on Mamai Tumulus]. In this engaging fantasy, Nekrasov revisits his wartime haunts in Stalingrad and goes back in time, metamorphosing into Lieutenant Kerzhentsev from *Front-Line Stalingrad*, except that he has forgotten how to defuse a mine but knows how the war ended!

Nekrasov's other major interest was travel literature. Able to travel abroad at last, starting in 1957, Nekrasov visited Italy, France, and the United States. He developed the genre with his own particular mixture of fact, anecdote, and digression, with works such as *Po obe storony okeana* (*Both Sides of the Ocean*) and "Mesiats vo Frantsii" [A Month in France]. He did his utmost to see the sights and meet the people as he wanted, not as his Party mentors wished, and to write spontaneously without the officially prescribed "balance of pluses and minuses". *Both Sides of the Ocean* was heavily criticized; even Khrushchev, himself under pressure from Politburo hardliners, called for his expulsion from the Party. This particular row blew over, but times were to become harder for people like Nekrasov.

Nekrasov's last Soviet volume, *Viktor Nekrasov v zhizni i pis'makh* [Viktor Nekrasov in Life and Letters] and in particular the "Rasskazy s postskriptum" [Stories with a PS] show increasing preoccupation with memories and the compulsion to re-create and sometimes re-invent the past – about Kiev, the war, old friendships. The present was certainly not treating him kindly. His call for a monument to mark the site of Babii Iar in 1966 led to accusations of "Zionism" and his opposition to the invasion of Czechoslovakia and contacts with Solzhenitsyn and other dissidents led to harassment and police searches. On 12 September 1974 he and his wife emigrated, settling in Paris. In emigration, Nekrasov continued to write, to travel a great deal and, as always, to make friends. As well as republishing *Stalingrad* and some lesser "Soviet" works, he produced four new volumes. The first, *Zapiski zevaki* [Notes of a Bystander], is a delightful mixture of reminiscences, sketches, and comments on life, literature, and the architecture of Kiev. The other three works, however, are more rooted in his émigré existence. *Saperlipopet (esli by da kaby...)* [And Pigs Might Fly] confronts his relationship with the Soviet Union. *Po obe storony steny* [On Both Sides of the Wall] begins with divided Berlin, and goes on to family remniscences. His last work, *Malen'kaia pechal'naia povest'* [A Sad Little Story], is one of his best, and also the nearest thing since *Kira Georg'evna* to a full-scale novel. It is a story of three friends from 1960s Leningrad, whose friendship is put to the test over many years by emigration, fame, and distance. It is the vivid and touching farewell of a writer to whom friendship and the ordinary pleasures of life were so vital.

Viktor Nekrasov's life and writing was a bridge between Russia and the west. He lived just long enough to see the beginning of change in Russia, though sadly not long enough to participate as he would have wished. However, he was one of the first émigré writers to be "reclaimed" during glasnost.

MICHAEL FALCHIKOV

Front-Line Stalingrad

V okopakh Stalingrada

Novel, 1947

Stalingrad, or as it later came to be known, *V okopakh Stalingrada* (*Front-Line Stalingrad*), was Nekrasov's first published work and the one by which he is best known, with translations into most European languages. Many years later, Nekrasov explained that the 1946 *Znamia* edition turned into *V okopakh Stalingrada* [In the Trenches of Stalingrad] because the latter description was felt to be more appropriate to a work that did not concentrate on grand themes and great men but on the everyday lives of ordinary soldiers. Indeed, Nekrasov used to recall that he had initial difficulty with the publishers because of the paucity of references in the work to Stalin at a time when adulation of the *vozhd'* [leader] seemed a prerequisite of any work of art. By the same token, some suspicion was expressed post-1956 because of a reference to a Stalin broadcast and mention of his photograph hanging in a trench. (Ironically, when a German trench is captured, a photograph of Hitler is discovered.)

In the work, the action is seen almost entirely through the eyes of Lieutenant Kerzhentsev, in peacetime an architect from Kiev. Kerzhentsev is obviously autobiographical, as are, apparently, most of the hero's experiences; the main part of the novel centres on the seige of Stalingrad in the autumn of 1942. The characters are almost all ordinary soldiers or junior officers (fictional, of course, but based on Nekrasov's real-life comrades).

The work begins, however, rather strikingly, with the order to retreat. Thus, initially, Nekrasov stresses the confusion and uncertainty of the preceding months, when Russian forces retreated towards the Volga and the Caucasus, the fronts collapsed, nobody seemed to be in charge and units and battalions fragmented and lost touch with each other. In the orginal Russian, a sense of immediacy, of events unfolding before the reader's eyes, is emphasized by the use throughout of the "historic present", as though Lieutenant Kerzhentsev were writing as he went along. Friendships are made – and lost, as the groups get split up. Nobody knows where the front is, rumour is rife, but when our hero finally reaches Stalingrad, the determination to retreat no further begins to take hold. Before the German attack begins, there is a brief, almost peaceful interlude, when life in the city, bathed in early autumn sunshine, seems normal, Kerzhentsev is billeted with an ordinary family and just briefly resumes something resembling peacetime life, bathing in the river, reading old journals in the library and going for walks with a girl named Lusia. This interlude is brutally cut short by an air-raid and the siege of the city begins in earnest. During the weeks of trench warfare that follow, Nekrasov conveys very well the mixture of boredom and danger – often nothing happens for long periods, or a game of cat-and-mouse is played with an enemy almost close enough for hand-to-hand combat. Sometimes, even, a trench becomes almost homely, with time and space to read and sleep. But these periods of relative calm are punctuated by sudden fierce bursts of fighting that leave many of Kerzhentsev's comrades wounded or dead, often in grotesque fashion, though, if anything, the horror and violence is somewhat understated.

The fact that this is a story of ordinary soldiers, fighting to defend each little piece of territory, is underlined by the absence of any sense of a "master plan". There are no insights into the world of the High Command – even the HQ of General Chuikov, the field commander at Stalingrad, is only mentioned in passing. Only rarely is there any discussion of the war in a wider context, as when, on Revolution Day the papers arrive with Stalin's speech, and news of the war on other fronts. Then briefly, the heroic defence of Stalingrad is seen as part of the great turning of the tide in the war as a whole, with allied operations in North Africa approaching a successful conclusion and renewed talk of a second front. But mostly, the defenders of Stalingrad live in their own enclosed world, where pre-war is a distant memory and where their shared experience of fighting increasingly sets them apart from civilian life. This latter point emerges with particular force at the end of the book when Kerzhentsev returns to the front after two months in hospital, following a wound, and experiences excitement as though returning home after long absence.

There is little in *Front-Line Stalingrad* about larger philosophical issues. There is one interesting moral dilemma, when an unpopular officer is court-martialled for having exceeded his authority and wasted lives, but otherwise what motivates Kerzhentsev and his comrades is not so much a crusade against fascism, as a simple need to defend one's homeland, at whatever cost. The thread of comradeship also runs strongly through the work, with some memorable characters portrayed – Farber, the earnest intellectual, Chumak, the chancer who comes good, and above all, Valega, the orderly, Kerzhentsev's favourite, who of course features more than once in Nekrasov's work.

Front-Line Stalingrad has been compared to Erich Maria Remarque's *All Quiet on the Western Front* and certainly there are parallels – the trench warfare of Stalingrad resembled that of World War I and the sense of an exclusive world in the trenches is not dissimilar. Indeed, a link is made when the author recalls an old British magazine of 1914 that carried pictures of the first battles of that war. But a closer parallel is probably that of Tolstoi's *Sevastopol'skie rasskazy* (*The Sebastopol Sketches*), which was similarly a work drawn from experience (interestingly, Kerzhentsev has retreated from Sebastopol). But whereas in that work Tolstoi went from patriotism to a growing sense of the futility of war and of the haphazardness and disorganization of life at the front, in *Front-Line Stalingrad* the reverse seems to be the case, as the work ends on an upbeat note. The Germans are in retreat and, with intimations of peace, an officer is leading his men, like tourists "to have a look at the Volga."

MICHAEL FALCHIKOV

Nestor c.1056–after 1113

Monk, hagiographer, and chronicler

Biography

Born c.1056. One of the few known writers in Old Russian literature; entered the Caves Monastery, monastic centre of Kievan Rus', shortly after the Abbot Theodosius' death in 1074. He never knew Saint Theodosius personally, and no evidence that he himself was canonized. Apart from what can be extracted from his works, biographical information is sparse (further details about his life and literary activity have been reconstructed by M.D. Priselkov from Nestor's works). Compiled comprehensive edition of *Povest' vremennykh let* (*The Russian Primary Chronicle*), 1113. Died after 1113.

Publications

Texts

"Nestorovo chtenie o zhitii i o pogublenii blazhennuiu strastoterptsu Borisa i Gleba" [Nestor's Reading on the Life and Slaying of the Blessed Martyrs Boris and Gleb], in *Anthology of Old Russian Literature*, edited by Ad. Stender-Petersen, New York, Columbia University Press, 1954; reprinted 1966, 92–99 (excerpts); "Chtenie o zhitii i o pogublenii blazhennuiu strastoterptsu Borisa i Gleba", in *Die altrussischen hagiographischen Erzählungen und liturgischen Dichtungen über die Heiligen Boris und Gleb*, edited by D. Abramovich, *Slavische Propyläen* (Munich), 14 (1967).

"Zhitie prepodobnogo ottsa nashego Feodosiia, igumena pecher'skogo monastyria", in *Uspenskii sbornik XII–XIII vv.*, edited by O.A. Kniazevskaia *et al.*, Moscow, 1971, 71–135; translated as "The Life of Saint Theodosius", in *The Paterik of the Kievan Caves Monastery*, by Muriel Heppell, Cambridge, Massachusetts, Ukrainian Research Institute of Harvard University, 1989, 24–88.

Editor

Povest' vremennykh let po lavrent'evskoi letopisi 1377 g., with modern Russian translation by D.S. Likhachev, Moscow and Leningrad, 1950; translated as *The Russian Primary Chronicle*, by Samuel Hazzard Cross and Olgerd P. Sherbowitz-Wetzor, Cambridge, Massachusetts, Mediaeval Academy of America, 1953; 3rd edition, 1973.

Critical Studies

"Neskol'ko slov o Nestorovom zhitii Feodosiia", by A.A. Shakhmatov, *Izvestiia otdeleniia russkogo iazyka i slovestnosti Akademii nauk*, vol. 1, St Petersburg, 1896, 46–65.

"K voprosu o kharaktere i ob"eme literaturnoi deiatel'nosti prepodobnogo Nestora", by S.A. Bugoslavskii, *Izvestiia otdeleniia russkogo iazyka i slovesnosti imp. Akademii nauk* (St Petersburg), 19/1 (1914), 131–86.

Nestor-Letopisets. Opyt istoriko-literaturnoi kharakteristiki, by M.D. Priselkov, Petrograd, 1923.

"Studien zur altrussischen Legende der Heiligen Boris und Gleb", by L. Müller, in *Zeitschrift für slavische Philologie* (Heidelberg), 23 (1952), 60–77; 25 (1956), 329–63; 27 (1959), 272–322; 30 (1962), 14–44.

History of Russian Literature from the Eleventh Century to the End of the Baroque, by Dmitrij Čiževskij, The Hague, Mouton, 1960, 40–60.

"K kharakteristike Nestora kak pisatelia", by I.P. Eremin, in *Trudy otdela drevnerusskoi literatury*, vol. 17, Moscow, 1961, 54–64.

"Chronologia utworów Nestora hagiografa", by A. Poppe, *Slavia Orientalis*, (Warsaw), 14 (1965), 287–305.

"Frame Technique in Nestor's Life of St. Theodosius", by Jostein Børtnes, *Scando-Slavica*, 13 (1967), 5–16.
"Literature of the Kievan Period. 11th-12th Centuries", by John Fennell and Antony Stokes, in *Early Russian Literature*, Berkeley, University of California Press, and London, Faber, 1974, 11–64.
"Nestor's *Life of Saint Theodosius*: Imitation of Christ and Mystagogia", by Jostein Børtnes, in her *Visions of Glory: Studies in Early Russian Hagiography*, Atlantic Highlands, New Jersey, Humanities Press International, 1988, 48–87.
The Martyred Princes Boris and Gleb: A Socio-Cultural Study of the Cult and the Text, by Gail Lenhoff, Columbus, Ohio, Slavica, 1989.

Bibliographies
"Nestor", *Slovar' knizhnikov i knizhnosti drevnei Rusi. XI – pervaia polovina XIV v.*, Leningrad, 1987, 274–78.
"Select Bibliography", *The Hagiography of Kievan Rus'*, translated with an introduction by Paul Hollingsworth, Cambridge, Massachusetts, Harvard University Press, 1992, 233–48.

As a prototypical hagiographer, Nestor's task was to transform the biographical material of his characters into the representation of a sanctification process, the paradoxical correlation of the incarnation of the Logos and the deification of man, being at the base of his work. Setting off to illuminate for his initiated audience in newly converted Rus' the points of similarity between the character's *imitatio Christi* and Christ, Nestor himself participated in the verbal aspect of the Orthodox Holy Tradition, the apostolic idea of the "handing down" of the Divine Logos.

Composed as a *vita-martyrium*, Nestor's *Chtenie o zhitii i o pogublenii blazhennuiu strastoterptsu Borisa i Gleba* [Reading on the Life and Slaying of the Blessed Martyrs Boris and Gleb] is one of three different, but textually interrelated, versions of the same account of how the Kievan Princes Boris and Gleb were killed by their stepbrother Sviatopolk in the power struggle that ensued after Vladimir's death in 1015. The oldest known record of the work is that of the 14th-century *Sil'vestrovskii sbornik*. In terms of rhetorical treatment, Nestor's style differs from that of the chronicle account and the anonymous *Skazanie i strast' i pokhvala sviatuiu mucheniku Borisa i Gleba* [Narrative and Passion and Eulogy of the Blessed Martyrs Boris and Gleb], by being more restrained. Keeping with the structure and style of a Byzantine saint's life, Nestor employs a dual mode of expression: he is simple and artless when relating historical facts, but uses all the devices of panegyrical oratory when amplifying and interpreting the historical narrative. At the base of the work lies the principle of antithesis, so that after an extensive historical introduction (including the fall of Adam and Eve, the struggle of the prophets with idolatry, and the incarnation and crucifixion of Christ), the saintly princes are compared to Joseph and Benjamin, and represented as active champions of the Christian ideals of fraternal love and humility, whereas Sviatopolk is compared to Cain, and appears as a tool for the devil's machinations. Viewing the misdeeds committed within the context of universal history in this manner, Nestor represents the two brothers' acceptance of a violent death without resistance as an *imitatio Christi*. Furthermore, with a light symbolism characteristic of his hagiographical art, he brings out the anagogical dimension of the saints as images of the divine figure of Christ, and a complementarity is established between the terrestrial and the celestial aspects of the saint's imitation process. Comparing the fate of Boris and Gleb to that of Saint Eustace, Romanus the Melode, Julian the Apostate, and others, Nestor thus contributes to the legend of the two Russian martyr princes which pursued a political as well as a religious end, and creates a *zhitie* (life story) that was to serve as a model for subsequent hagiographical writing.

As pointed out by Nestor himself in the foreword to his *Zhitie prepodobnogo ottsa nashego Feodosiia, igumena pecher'skogo monastyria* (translated as *The Life of Saint Theodosius*), he began writing this only after the completion of the *Chtenie o zhitii pogublenii blazhennuiu strastoterptsu Borisa i Gleba*, probably in the 1080s. The oldest extant manuscript being that of the 12th-century *Uspenskii sbornik*, Nestor's *Life of Saint Theodosius* belongs to a major genre of hagiography, the *vitae sanctorum* (the confessor-lives), and is a story of a saint's apotheosis with strong eschatological tendencies, relating both to the personal and cosmological dimensions. The significant antithesis human/divine determines its structure, providing Nestor with a pattern that underlies his rhetorical transformation of Theodosius into a dual image of Christ.

Following the canons of Byzantine hagiography, it starts with an *exordium* (invocation to God, introduction of the hagiographer himself, justification of his task, and an apostrophe to his fellow monks), which already contains the leading idea of the work. Through a dual allegory, the saint and the monastery are likened to the historical, kenotic Christ and his "sphere of activity", but simultaneously, the saint is also elevated to the presence of Christ the Pantocrator, and the monastery to the position of the Divine Kingdom. An equivalence is thus established between the two figures and the two locations, and in each of these cases between the mundane and the supramundane, the profane and the sacred.

Replete with such hagiographical commonplaces as the saint's being born by good Christian parents, preferring holy books to childish games and beggarly rags to fine clothes, the first part of Nestor's *narratio* also contains a more untraditional element. Objecting to her son becoming a monk by repeatedly beating and tormenting him, Theodosius' mother is the main cause of his childhood abasement and suffering. However, this "realistic" effect of Nestor's representation is subordinate to the primary function of the saint's humiliation, which is to show his imitation of Christ. The process of battle between earthly and celestial powers in the figure of the saint is developed further in the second part of the narrative: the saint as a monk excels in both monastic and ascetic virtues, overcomes diabolical visitations, performs both excruciating penitential exercises (*pokaianie*) with true humility, and, in the role of shepherd and provider, a series of (mostly mundane) miracles. The narrative is then amplified with several mystical light visions, by which the life of the saint as abbot is transformed into a prefiguration of his celestial glory. Through figural interpretation, and linking the past with the present in the work's *conclusio*, Nestor has invested a factual event with special spiritual meaning by allegorically interpreting it in terms of eschatology, thus achieving an anagogical dimension in his work. On a different level, depicting the growth of a community of cave-dwelling hermits into a stately monastery of economical and political importance in Kievan Rus', Nestor's *Life of Saint Theodosius* is a significant historico-cultural source.

Nestor's name is also associated with the authorship of the *Povest' vremennykh let* (*The Russian Primary Chronicle*). Based mainly on a reference to "Nestor, the monk of Theodosius' Caves Monastery" in a 16th-century copy of the work, and another to Nestor "who wrote the chronicle" in the oldest part of the *Kievo-pecher'skii paterik* (*The Paterik of the Kievan Caves Monastery*), arguments have been raised for this attribution. However, challenging this view, current scholarship commonly considers Nestor as the compiler-reviser of the first, comprehensive edition of the work (1113), which has not been preserved.

Nestor the monk is the first notable Russian hagiographer, and, as such, a remarkable writer in control over his medium. The eminent use of literate Slavonic, Greek syntax, and scriptural quotations, the poetic use of motifs and themes together with the incorporation of political episodes, is all subordinated to the edificatory-theological goal of his work. The merits of his art are perhaps best seen in *The Life of Saint Theosophius*, "one of the most influential, most popular, and aesthetically most valuable monuments of early Russian literature" (Dmitrij Čiževskij).

KNUT GRIMSTAD

Afanasii Nikitin early 15th century–1472

Travel writer

Biography

Born early 15th century. Merchant in Tver. Travelled to the East with merchants and diplomats, 1466–72. Wrote an account of his journey: *Khozhenie za tri moria* [Journey Beyond the Three Seas]. Travelled to Derbent, Baku, stayed in Persia for ten months; spent some years in India, returned to Russia via Ethiopia, Arabia, Persia, Armenia. Died before reaching Smolensk, 1472.

Publications

Editions

First publication in *Istoriia gosudarstva Rossiiskogo* [History of the Russian State], by N.M. Karamzin, 12 vols. St Petersburg, 1818–29; reprinted Moscow, 1988–89.

Khozhenie za tri moria Afanasiia Nikitina v 1466–1472 gg. Moscow and Leningrad, 1948; 2nd revised edition, 1958.

Afanasii Nikitin. Khozhenie za tri moria. Moscow, 1950.

Khozhenie za tri moria Afanasiia Nikitina. Moscow, 1960.

Kniga khozhenii. Zapiski russkikh puteshestvennikov XI–XV vekov, edited by N.I. Prokofieva, Moscow, 1980.

Khozhenie za tri moria Afanasiia Nikitina, edited by N.I. Prokofieva, Moscow, 1980.

Pamiatniki literatury drevnei Rusi: Vtoraia polovina XV veka, edited by L.A. Dmitriev and D.S. Likhachev, Moscow, 1982, 444–77.

Khozhenie za tri moria Afanasiia Nikitina, Literaturnye pamiatniki, Leningrad, 1986.

India in the 15th Century, translated by Conur Wielhovsky. New York, Hakluyt Society, vol. 22, n.d.

Critical Studies

"Khozhenie za tri moria Afanasiia Nikitina v 1466–1472 gg", by I.I. Sreznevskii, in *Uchenie zapiski vtorogo otdeleniia AN*, vol. 2, St Petersburg, 1856, 225–307.

Puteshestvie Afanasiia Nikitina, by K. Kunin, Moscow, 1947.

Afanasii Nikitin i ego vremia, by A.M. Osipov, V.A. Aleksandrov, and N.M. Gol'dberg, Moscow, 1952; 1956.

Afanasii Nikitin – pervyi russkii puteshestvennik v Indiiu, by M.A. Il'in, Kalinin, 1955.

Zapiski Afanasiia Nikitina ob Indii XV veka, by N.V. Vodovozov, Moscow, 1955.

"'The Journey Beyond the Three Seas' by Afanasij Nikitin as a Literary Monument", by N.S. Trubetskoi, in *Three Philological Studies* (Michigan Slavic Studies, 3 (1963), 23–51); reprinted from *Versty*, 1 (1926); English translation by Kenneth N. Brostrom, in *Readings in Russian Poetics: Formalist and Structuralist Views*, edited by Ladislav Matejka and Krystyna Pomorska, Cambridge, Massachusetts, MIT Press, 1971, 199–219; reprinted Ann Arbor, Michigan Slavic Publications, 1978.

Stranstvie Afanasiia Nikitina, by M.N. Vitashevskaia, Moscow, 1972.

"Between Formalism and Structuralism: N.S. Trubetzkoy's 'The Journey Beyond the Three Seas' by Afonasij Nikitin as a Literary Monument", by I.R. Titunik, in *"Sound, Sign and Meaning", Quinguagenary of the Prague Linguistic Circle*, edited by Ladislav Matejka, Ann Arbor, Michigan Slavic Publications, 1976, 303–19.

"Beyond Three Seas: Afanasij Nikitin's Journey from Orthodoxy to Apostasy", by Gail Lenhoff, *East European Quarterly*, 13 (1979), 431–47.

"Dualisticheskii kharakter russkoi srednevekovoi kul'tury (na materiale 'Khozheniia za tri moria' Afanasiia Nikitina", by B.A. Uspenskii, in *Vtorichnye modeliruiushchie sistemy*, Tartu, 1979, 59–63.

Puteshestvie Afanasiia Nikitina, by L.S. Semenov, Moscow, 1980.

"Ob odnom 'temnom' meste v 'Khozhenii' Afanasiia Nikitina", by R.Kh. Azhalieva, *Russkaia rech'*, 3 (1990), 117–21.

Afanasii Nikitin is known for his travelogue *Khozhenie za tri moria* [Journey Beyond the Three Seas], which transcended its genre to become a classic of Russian literature.

Afanasii, son of Nikita, was a merchant in the city Tver, and undertook a business trip to the East with other merchants and diplomats lasting from 1466 to 1472. His journey followed the Volga to the Caspian Sea; after a Tartar attack and a heavy storm he arrived in Persia, where he spent ten months. He travelled to India across the Indian Ocean, reaching India before Vasco da Gama (1487) and remaining there for three or four years. Without major trade successes he set off for home, and his return journey took him via the Indian Ocean, Ethiopia, Arabia, Persia, Armenia, and the Black Sea. He was not destined to return to his native Tver; he died near Smolensk in 1472. During his travels he became an interested observer of life in foreign lands, and on returning to Russia he probably wrote the beginning and end of his travelogue, because in these places he mentions the three seas that he had crossed (the Caspian and Black Seas and the Indian Ocean). It is most probable that some other merchant brought his notes to Deacon Vasilii Mamyrev, Ivan III's chief clerk, and they were subsequently incorporated into chronicles. The original is lost, but seven copies survive.

Nikitin's travelogue has particular significance in the development of genres in Old Russian literature. It puts a new twist on pilgrimage literature during a time when world-wide exploration and travel virtually exploded; earlier travel accounts detailed the hardship of pilgrimages to the Holy Land motivated by religious zeal. Not only was Nikitin's destination a pagan land, but his motivation was business: to find new, trading partners, and even personal profit. Eventually, as his focus shifted toward exploration, he became a curious observer of other cultures and peoples, exhibiting enterprise and initiative. The ecclesiastic literary genre of the pilgrimage is secularized and enriched with stories from everyday life, not only for the sake of information, but also for entertainment. The work focuses on the spiritual isolation of Nikitin – an unfortunate Christian – among people of other faiths. Structurally, the work is split into three sections: the journey to India, the years Nikitin spent there, and the return journey; the narrative is sandwiched between prayers – in Church Slavonic at the beginning and Arabic at the end. From a literary standpoint, most noteworthy is the description of India. As a practical merchant Nikitin takes a sober look at the widespread exotic images of "the riches of India". His detailed description incorporates from time to time fantastical elements and legends.

The composition is well balanced: even-handed descriptions alternate with religious-lyrical digressions. The narrative discourse moves between subjectivity and objectivity, between the lyrical and the epic. The most objective layer consists of strictly informative, factual, static descriptions containing abundant and accurate factual information about the nature, traditions, and everyday life of India for the benefit of future travellers. In another layer he depicts these lands from his own subjective point of view, including personal remarks and retelling stories that caught his attention. These vivid descriptions and stories transport the reader to an exotic, fairy-tale-like milieu that was new in the first-hand Russian literary tradition. The most intimate layer arises when Nikitin, as if writing a diary, reveals his personal feelings in lyrical, confession-style, emotional digressions, especially his grief at being torn away from his native land and Orthodox faith. This is the most compelling aspect of the work in both style and narrative.

During his lengthy journey Nikitin experienced a profound change in his own personality. Leaving the familiar Orthodox way of life, faced with numerous unfamiliar impressions, and isolated from his countrymen, his perspective undergoes extraordinary broadening for his time. He experiences inner confusion, torn between the excitement of the new discoveries and torment over losing touch with his traditional value system. He does not notice how his personality blends the old and new within him. From the very beginning of the account he considers himself a sinner not by will, but by circumstances. The feeling of guilt for this sinful journey, which distances him from Christianity, evokes a desire for self-expression and self-understanding. Striving to preserve his Orthodox faith, he succeeds in maintaining its spirit, but cannot keep up the traditions (e.g., losing his books prevents him from observing the Orthodox fast days). His prayers, the ultimate outcries of his heart, are permeated with formulas from the Koran, and the language shifts from Russian to Turkish, Arabic, and Persian merchant dialect. As the language shifts, his view changes involuntarily, and he wants to express it solely for himself in language not accessible to others. As a result of his long-term exposure to people of differing religions, he pronounces in the spirit of ecumenism that the same God is found in both Christianity and Islam, an unusual expression of religious tolerance for the Middle Ages. Suggestions that he may have actually converted to Islam require further substantiation. Nevertheless, Nikitin concluded that he must return to Russia in order to regain his spiritual balance.

Judging by his intelligent and multifaceted observations, Nikitin must have been well-educated and widely read, although he was not style-conscious. He uses Church-Slavonicisms in a very limited way; his language is a peculiar mixture of Russian vernacular and phrases from the jargon of the merchants of the lower Volga region, based on Turkish, Arabic, and Persian vocabulary. Curiously, his description includes very few Hindi words. He creates a certain local colour by using terminology denoting exotic realia; as these terms are often lacking from Russian, he introduces borrowings from foreign languages. He uses very few stylistic figures; the most characteristic are repetitions and long periodic sentences with inner rhythm. The first part is stylistically well-constructed and precise, but the second part was never revised because of Nikitin's unexpected death.

MARIA PAVLOVSZKY

O

Aleksandr Ivanovich Odoevskii 1802–1839

Poet

Biography

Born in St Petersburg, 8 December 1802. First cousin of Prince V.F. Odoevskii. Educated privately. Entered civil service, February 1815. Commissioned into Guards, 1821. Joined Decembrist Northern Society, December 1824. Participant in Decembrist Uprising, December, 1825; detained pending sentence in the Peter and Paul Fortress, St Petersburg. Sentenced to 15 years' hard labour, commuted to 12 years. Surviving poetry written in exile. Transferred to active service. Died of a fever in the Caucasus, 27 August 1839.

Publications

Collected Editions

Polnoe sobranie stikhotvorenii i pisem. Moscow and Leningrad, 1934; reprinted The Hague, Europe Printing, 1967.

Polnoe sobranie stikhotvorenii. Moscow and Leningrad, 1958.

Stikhotvoreniia. Moscow, 1982.

Critical Studies

"Aleksandr Odoevskii", by V.G. Bazanov, in *Ocherki dekabristskoi literatury. Poeziia*, Moscow and Leningrad, 1961, 334–96.

"Aleksandr Ivanovich Odoevskii (1802–39)", by S.M. Kliuev, *Russkaia rech'*, 6 (1977), 30–38.

A. Odoevskii, by V.P. Iagunin, Moscow, 1980.

"No v nas poryvy est' sviatye", by V.P. Iagunin, introductory article to *A. Odoevskii. Stikhotvoreniia*, Moscow, 1982, 5–26.

A History of Russian Literature of the Romantic Period, by William Edward Brown, Ann Arbor, Ardis, 1986, vol. 2, 111–19.

The Life, Times and Milieu of V.F. Odoyevsky, 1804–1869, by Neil Cornwell, London, Athlone Press, and Athens, Ohio University Press, 1986, 228–31 and *passim*.

The corpus of verse bequeathed to posterity by the Decembrist poet Prince Aleksandr Odoevskii is small: 57 poems only are extant, amounting to slightly over 3,000 lines of verse. Taken alongside an amount of literary correspondence with important writers of the time, however, his poetry does make an interesting contribution not only to Decembrist literature but also to the general aristocratic cultural milieu of the first third of the 19th century. It is known that Odoevskii wrote substantially more poetry than has survived. His attitude towards his poems as artefacts was perhaps a little careless, and he seemed unconcerned about their publication during his lifetime. Much of what has survived was transcribed by Odoevskii's fellow exiles P.A. Mukhanov, N.I. Lorer, M.A. Nazimov, and A.E. Rozen, his first publisher. A few pieces were published from 1830–31 in the journals *Literaturnaia gazeta* and *Severnye tsvety* through the anonymous agency of Mukhanov, Del'vig and Viazemskii, but it was only after Odoevskii's premature death that anything like a representative selection came to see the light of day.

The tenor of Odoevskii's verse – nature poetry, ballads, the hero-rebel, the glories of Russian history, exile and imprisonment – was distilled from the cosmopolitan and cultured literary education that the poet received as appropriate to his station. There was an early affinity with literature and languages, and with Russian history. In particular his cousins Aleksandr Griboedov and Vladimir Odoevskii opened his eyes to the broad sweep of Russian literature, to music, to western literature and philosophy. A passion for free-thinking liberalism was transmitted to Odoevskii, via the confraternities and circles to which he found himself increasingly drawn, from readings of Voltaire, Diderot, Rousseau, Schiller, and the economists Sismondi and Adam Smith. The romanticism of the Schlegels and Schelling, much in vogue, offered immediate attractions. Literary acquaintances, notably Griboedov, Bestuzhev, Ryleev, and Kiukhel'beker, encouraged the idealistic Odoevskii to associate his soaring, expansive, and enthusiastic literary sentiments with political agitation. In St Petersburg Odoevskii produced a body of committed, polemical verse, almost all of it now lost, and he tried his hand at literary criticism of a general type. He was taken effortlessly and as it were inevitably into the conspiratorial cenacle that was to hatch the failed uprising of December 1825. It could be said that Decembrism, as an intellectual and emotional focus, awoke the poet dormant in Odoevskii. For his part in that seditious plot Odoevskii was sentenced to a long term of hard labour, a sentence whose gravity was progressively mitigated over the years through the intercession of the poet's well-connected family and friends. It was during his initial detention in the Peter and Paul Fortress in St Petersburg that the weight of his recent personal trauma first coalesced poetically with the literary ambience of his upbringing: here, and later, more convincingly, in Siberian exile, Odoevskii's muse came of age.

Odoevskii's own brand of romanticism, now emerging clearly, moved away from the metaphysical imponderabilities of Schelling and the mysticism of Zhukovskii towards the naive, civic high-mindedness of such as Raevskii, Ryleev, and Fedor

Glinka. The depressive spiritual crisis occasioned by Odoevskii's imprisonment was made manifest in the poet's retreat into a sense of his noble inner self, in such poems as *Son poeta* [The Poet's Dream], *Utro* [Morning], and *Bal* [The Ball], in which last piece the spiritually dead denizens of high society are figured as corpses. A sort of comradely literary culture subsisted in captivity, and it was Odoevskii as the spokesman of a community of poetic souls, rather than as an individual, who composed the celebrated poem "Strun veshchikh plamennye zvuki" [The Ardent Sounds of Prophetic Strings] as a response to a sympathetic epistle in verse from Aleksandr Pushkin.

A buoyant optimism in the teeth of personal adversity was often contrived by Odoevskii's recourse to the glorious national past. In a piece entitled *Deva 1610 goda* [A Maiden of the Year 1610], part of a projected narrative poem about Vasilii Shuiskii, Odoevskii returns to the Time of Troubles to conjure an allegorical "Freedom-Maiden" who laments the sorry state of a fallen nation and urges Russians to remember their freedom-loving forebears. A whole series of poems, including, for instance, *Staritsa-prorochitsa* [Zosima, The Old Prophetess], and *Otryvok* [A Fragment] recall with pride the dearly-won independence from Moscow of the old free towns of Novgorod and Pskov, with the concomitant implication, common in historical Decembrist poetry, of an up-to-date political relevance. Quasi-Utopian expressions of an essential "Russianness" recur frequently, drawing now from martial history, now from the folklore pool, where the heart of the immemorial Holy Rus' was supposed still to beat. Such is the inspiration of Odoevskii's most substantial extant (but corrupt and unfinished) poem, the narrative piece *Vasil'ko* (1829–30), which remembers the internecine conflicts of the 11th century, and specifically the manuscript tale of the blinding of Prince Vasil'ko Rotislavich by Prince David Igorevich, at which atrocity Vasil'ko's adoring subjects are compelled to take up arms. In another poem devoted to the inspirational clangour of a common cause, *Slavianskie devy* [Slavonic Maidens], Odoevskii imagines the spiritual unification of all the Slav peoples as a huge, irresistible tidal wave.

When, in 1837, Odoevskii was transferred to active service in the Caucasus, he contracted a brief but intense friendship with Mikhail Lermontov, who (together to a lesser extent with Nikolai Ogarev) proved to be the final important poetic influence on him. In a few of his lyrics Lermontov recalls this association, valuing highly as he did the "human" qualities which he perceived in Odoevskii – the probity and commitment – as well as the literary gifts. Both poets found the experience of eastern exile to be imaginatively transmutable into verse, but whereas in Lermontov the fact of exile was a *point de départ*, provoking wider meditations, in Odoevskii it became the be-all and end-all, perpetually the inspiration or the content of his stirring and patriotic verse.

NICHOLAS CROWE

Vladimir Fedorovich Odoevskii 1804–1869

Prose writer and cultural dignitary

Biography

Born [probably] 12 August 1804 [or 1803]. A "prince" (*kniaz'*), with lineage back to Rurik. Subsequently Russia's premier nobleman. His father, a director of Moscow Assignation Bank, died in 1808. Brought up by relatives; first cousin of the poet A.I. Odoevskii. Attended the Pension for Nobility of Moscow University; graduated with gold medal, 1822. Member of S.E. Raich's circle and founder of the Society of Wisdom Lovers [*Liubomudry*], 1823; co-editor, with Vil'gel'm Kiukhel'beker, of *Mnemozina*, 1824–25: activities ceased following the Decembrist revolt. Married: Ol'ga Stepanovna Lanskaia. Entered government service, and moved to St Petersburg, 1826. Leading role in cultural life: co-founder, with Pushkin, of *Sovremennik*; principal backer in the relaunch of *Otechestvennye zapiski*; organizer of charity concerts and a founder of St Petersburg and Moscow Conservatories. Many offices held, 1826–69, including: Censorship Committee; Economic Department; educational consultant (Ministry of State Domains); Second Department; deputy-director of the Imperial Public Library, and director of the Rumiantsev Museum. Administrator, Society for Visiting the Poor of St Petersburg, 1846–55. Returned to Moscow as Senator, 1862. Died in Moscow, 11 March 1869.

Publications

Collected Editions

Sochineniia kniazia V.F. Odoevskogo, 3 vols. St Petersburg, 1844.

Povesti, 3 vols. St Petersburg, 1890.

Romanticheskie povesti [Romantic Tales]. Leningrad, 1929; reprinted, with an introduction by Neil Cornwell, Oxford, Meeuws, 1975.

Povesti i rasskazy. Moscow, 1959.

Povesti. Moscow, 1977.

Sochineniia, 2 vols. Moscow, 1981.

Poslednii kvartet Betkhovena: Povesti, rasskazy, ocherki. Odoevskii v zhizni [Beethoven's Last Quartet: Tales, Stories, Essays. Odoevskii in Life]. Moscow, 1982; and subsequent reprints.

Povesti i rasskazy. Moscow, 1985.

Povesti i rasskazy. Moscow, 1988.

The Salamander and Other Gothic Tales, edited and translated

by Neil Cornwell. London, Bristol Classical Press, and Evanston, Illinois, Northwestern University Press, 1992.
Pestrye skazki/Skazki Dedushki Irineia. Moscow, 1993.

Fiction
"Dni dosad (pis'mo k luzhnitskomu startsu)" [Days of Vexation ...], *Vestnik Evropy*, 9, 11, 15–18 (1823).
Chetyre apologa [Four Apologues]. Moscow, 1824.
"Elladii (kartina iz svetskoi zhizni)" [Elladii (A Scene from Society)], *Mnemozina*, 2, 1824.
Pestrye skazki s krasnym slovtsom, sobrannye Irineem Modestovichem, Gomozeikoiu, magistrom filosofii i chlenom raznykh uchenykh obshchestv, izdannye V. Bezglasnym [Variegated Tales ...]. St Petersburg, 1833; revised and much abridged in *Sochineniia* (1844); revised as *Pyostryye skazki*, edited by Neil Cornwell, Durham, University of Durham, 1988; facsimile reprint of 1833 edition, Moscow, 1991.
"Kniazhna Mimi", *Biblioteka dlia chteniia*, 7 (1834); separate edition as *Kniazhna Mimi; domashnye razgovory*. St Petersburg, n.d.; translated as "Princess Mimi", by David Lowe, in *Russian Literature Triquarterly*, 9 (1974); reprinted in *Russian Romantic Prose*, edited by Carl R. Proffer, Ann Arbor, Translation Press, 1979.
"Segeliel'. Don Kikhot XIX stoletiia. Skazka dlia starykh detei (otryvok iz 1-i chasti)" [Segeliel: A Don Quixote of the 19th Century ...], in *Sbornik na 1838 A.F. Voieikova i V.A. Vladislavleva*, St Petersburg, 1838; reprinted *Russkii arkhiv*, 19/2 (1881).
"Sil'fida", *Sovremennik*, 5 (1837); translated as "The Sylph", by Neil Cornwell, in *The Salamander*, 1992.
"Kniazhna Zizi" [Princess Zizi], *Otechestvennye zapiski* (1839).
"Kosmorama", *Otechestvennye zapiski* (1840); translated as "The Cosmorama", by Neil Cornwell, in *The Salamander*, 1992.
"Iuzhnii bereg Finliandii". 1841; "Salamandra". 1841 [subsequently "El'sa"]; reprinted together as "Salamandra", in *Sochineniia*, 1844; translated as "The Salamander", by Neil Cornwell, in *The Salamander*, 1992.
"Zhivoi mertvets", *Otechestvennye zapiski* (1844); translated as "The Live Corpse", by Neil Cornwell, in *The Salamander*, 1992.
Russkie nochi. St Petersburg, 1844; revised edition, Moscow, 1913; reprinted Munich, Fink, 1967; Literaturnye pamiatniki, Leningrad, 1975; translated as *Russian Nights*, by O. Koshansky-Olienikov and Ralph E. Matlaw, New York, Dutton, 1965; reprinted with an Afterword by Neil Cornwell, Evanston, Illinois, Northwestern University Press, 1997.
4338-oi god: fantasticheskii roman. Moscow, 1926; translated as "The Year 4338. Letters from Petersburg", in *Pre-Revolutionary Russian Science Fiction: An Anthology*, edited and translated by Leland Fetzer, Ann Arbor, Ardis, 1982; and as "4338 A.D.", by Alex Miller, in *Russian 19th-Century Gothic Tales*, Moscow, Raduga, 1984.

Children's Literature
Detskaia knizhka dlia voskresnykh dnei [A Child's Book for Sundays]. St Petersburg, 1833; reprinted 1835.
Gorodok v tabakerke. Detskaia skazka Dedushki Irineia [The Town in a Tobacco Tin ...]. St Petersburg, 1834; reprinted 1847.
Skazki i povesti dlia detei Dedushki Irineia [Fairy Stories and Tales for Grandad Irinei]. St Petersburg, 1841.
Sbornik detskikh pesen Dedushki Irineia [A Collection of the Children's Songs of Grandad Irinei]. St Petersburg, 1847.

Essays, Criticism, Memoirs, and Diaries
"Iz bumag kniazia V.F. Odoevskogo" [From V.F. Odoevskii's Papers], *Russkii arkhiv*, 7–8 (1864), 804–49; and 2nd edition, 994–1041.
Nedovol'no [Not Good Enough]. Moscow, 1867.
"Iz bumag kniazia V.F. Odoevskogo", *Russkii arkhiv*, 1 (1874), 278–360.
"Iz bumag kniazia V.F. Odoevskogo", *Russkii arkhiv*, 2 (1874), 11–54.
"'Tekushchaia khronika i osobye proisshestviia'. Dnevnik V.F. Odoevskogo 1859–1868gg". ["A Current Chronicle and Particular Happenings". V.F. Odoevskii's Diary, 1859–1868], *Literaturnoe nasledstvo*, 22–24, Moscow, 1935, 79–308.
Izbrannye pedagogicheskie sochineniia [Selected Pedagogical Works]. Moscow, 1955.
Muzykal'no-literaturnoe nasledie [Musical-Literary Legacy]. Moscow, 1956.
[Various philosophical pieces] in *Russkie esteticheskie traktaty pervoi treti XIX veka v dvukh tomakh*, vol. 2, Moscow, 1974, 156–92.
O literature i iskusstve [On Literature and Art]. Moscow, 1982.

Editor
Mnemozina [Mnemosyne], with V.K. Kiukhel'beker. Nos 1–4, Moscow, 1824–25; reprinted Hildesheim, Olms, 1986.
Sel'skoe chtenie [Rural Reading], with A.P. Zablotskii. St Petersburg, 4 books, 1844–47; collected edition, 1863; and subsequent editions.
Rasskazy o boge, prirode i cheloveke: kniga dlia chteniia [Stories of God, Nature and Man: A Reader], with A.P. Zablotskii. St Petersburg, 1849.

Critical Studies
"Sochineniia kniazia V.F. Odoevskogo", by V.G. Belinskii, 1844; collected in his *Polnoe sobranie sochinenii*, vol. 8, Moscow, 1955; reprinted (abridged) in *Poslednii kvartet Betkhovena*, 1982.
Iz istorii russkogo idealizma. Kniaz' V.F. Odoevskil. Myslitel'-pisatel', vol. 1, parts 1–2, by P.N. Sakulin, Moscow, 1913 [vol. 2 was never completed].
"'Uzkii put". Kniaz' V.F. Odoevskii i romantizm", by V.V. Gippius, *Russkaia mysl'*, 12 (1914), 1–26.
"Predislovie" and "Siluet, vstupitel'naia stat'ia", by Orest Tsekhnovitser, *Romanticheskie povesti*, 1929; reprinted Oxford, Meeuws, 1975, 5–99.
The Russian Hoffmannists, by Charles E. Passage, The Hague, Mouton, 1963.
"'A Hollow Shape': The Philosophical Tales of Prince Vladimir Odoevsky", by Simon Karlinsky, *Studies in Romanticism*, 5/3 (1966), 169–82.
"Trois notes sur l'oeuvre littéraire du prince Vladimir Odoevski", by Claude Backvis, *AIPS*, 19 (1968), 517–97.

Russkaia filosofskaia estetika (1820–30ye gody), by Iu.V. Mann, Moscow, 1969.
E.T.A. Hoffmann's Reception in Russia, by Norman W. Ingham, Würzburg, Jal, 1974.
Die Zukunftsperspektiven des Fürsten V.F. Odoevskij: Literatur, Futurologie und Utopie, by Winfried Baumann, Frankfurt, Peter Lang, 1980.
Moskovskii kruzhok liubomudrov, by Z.A. Kamenskii, Moscow, 1980.
Russian Romantic Fiction, by John Mersereau, Jr, Ann Arbor, Ardis, 1983.
"V F. Odoevskij's 'Knjažna Zizi'", by Lewis Bagby, *Russian Literature*, 17–18 (1985), 221–42.
A History of Russian Literature of the Romantic Period, by William Edward Brown, 4 vols, Ann Arbor, Ardis, 1986.
The Life, Times and Milieu of V.F. Odoyevsky, by Neil Cornwell, London, Athlone Press, and Athens, Ohio University Press, 1986.
Problems of Russian Romanticism, edited by Robert Reid, Brookfield, Vermont, Gower, 1986.
Stranitsy russkogo romantizma: kniga statei, by V.I. Sakharov, Moscow, 1988.
V.F. Odoyevsky and the Formation of Russian Musical Taste in the Nineteenth Century, by James Stuart Campbell, New York, Garland, 1989.
Skazki Irineia Modestovicha Gomozeiki, by M.A. Tur'ian, supplement to *Pestrye skazki*, Moscow, 1991.
"Strannaia moia sud'ba ...". O zhizni V.F. Odoevskogo, by M.A. Tur'ian, Moscow, 1991.
Narrative and Desire in Russian Literature, 1822–49: The Feminine and the Masculine, by Joe Andrew, London, Macmillan, and New York, St Martin's Press, 1993.
Vladimir Odoevsky and Romantic Poetics: Collected Essays, by Neil Cornwell, Oxford, and Providence, Rhode Island, Berghahn Books, 1998.
The Society Tale in Russian Literature: From Odoevskii to Tolstoi, edited by Neil Cornwell, Amsterdam, Rodopi, 1998.

Prince Vladimir Fedorovich Odoevskii was a central figure in Russian culture over a period of nearly half a century. From an "angry young man" of Russian literature in the early 1820s, when he edited the thrusting almanac *Mnemozina* (together with the future Decembrist Vil'gel'm Kiukhel'beker), he went through a flourishing period as a leading romantic writer of mystical and Gothic leanings, before maturing into an over-conscientious public servant and an indefatigable philanthropist. At the end of his life he was a Moscow senator, a leading musicologist, a keen amateur scientist and would-be court historian. Earlier, he had also been an enthusiastic theorist of romantic aesthetics, a cultural thinker, Russia's first important music critic (and a minor composer), a prominent popular educator (the predecessor, in certain respects, of Lev Tolstoi), and even a culinary columnist (under the pen-name "Doctor Puff"). Despite his aristocratic lineage, he depended throughout on his government salary and publishing royalties for a living. A range of commentators, at various times, have dubbed him "the philosopher-prince", "the Russian Hoffmann", "a Russian Faust" and even "the Russian Goethe".

Odoevskii was close to the major historical events of his time, from the Decembrist uprising of 1825 to the reforms of the 1860s, and was well acquainted with virtually all the leading Russian cultural personalities, from Griboedov, Pushkin and Glinka to Turgenev, Tolstoi and the young Tchaikovskii, as well as playing host to Berlioz, Liszt, and Wagner on their visits to Russia. His salon thrived for some 30 years in St Petersburg and again in the 1860s in Moscow, as a centre for literary and musical discussion and cultural exchange. According to his friend, the critic Shevyrev, on Odoevskii's divan could be found seated "the whole of Russian literature". Odoevskii was influenced by, and moreover himself duly influenced, most of the major Russian writers from Pushkin to Tolstoi, while being clearly one of the most extraordinarily versatile figures of 19th-century Russia. However, a reputation for eccentricity, "encyclopedism" and dilettantism caused him to be taken less seriously during his lifetime than was his due. Neglected for many years thereafter, he underwent a minor revival of interest in the early part of the 20th century; this was repeated in the 1950s, when important collections of his educational, musical, and literary writings were published. By the late Soviet period, his star was once again firmly in the ascendant.

Throughout his intellectual career, Odoevskii never ceased to conceive grandiose philosophical, literary, cultural, encyclopedic, and educational projects. Few of these achieved more than a fragmentary existence. The two literary projects that he did complete, *Pestrye skazki* [Variegated Tales] and *Russkie nochi* (*Russian Nights*), were both conceived in the 1820s, yet contrive to mark the onset and the climax, respectively, of Odoevskii's mature period as a writer. His fiction of the 1820s can be broadly described as didactic – whether social satire in the manner of Griboedov (but in prose, in such proto-society tales as "Dni dosad" [Days of Vexation] or "Elladii") or the terse allegory of a series of apologues; by the end of the decade, Odoevskii had versed himself thoroughly in the poetics, as well as the philosophy, of romanticism – both the "high" German romanticism of Schelling, Novalis, Hoffmann, Wackenroder, and Jean Paul [J.P.F. Richter], and the "lower" varieties of the French *école frénétique*.

This experimentation led to uneven artistic success. Nevertheless, the range of stories written in the decade or so from the late 1820s is remarkable. *Pestrye skazki*, as a cycle, provides an early demonstration of this, along with the "artistic biographies", "Poslednii kvartet Betkhovena" [Beethoven's Last Quartet] (1830) and "Sebastian Bach" (1835); these two stories, along with "Opere del Cavaliere Giambattista Piranesi" (1831) and "Improvizator" [The Improvisor] (1833), which were all originally intended for a cycle to be called "House of Madmen", may be numbered among Odoevskii's best, and were eventually incorporated into *Russian Nights* – which itself stands as one of the more fascinating formal curiosities of Russian literature. Caustic satirical tales, such as "Brigadir" [The Brigadier] (1833) and "Nasmeshka mertvetsa" [The Mockery of a Corpse] (1834), frequently with supernatural or fantastic elements attached, led their author in at least two directions: towards the fully-blown society tales, "Kniazhna Mimi" ("Princess Mimi") 1834, and "Kniazhna Zizi" [Princess Zizi] (1839), in which the social portraiture of female characters is to the fore; and to stories of mixed genre, such as "Zhivoi mertvets" ("The Live Corpse"), dated 1838, a pot-pourri of didactic satire and romantic philosophy in fantastic trappings (which, along with "Brigadir", can be seen as a precursor to Tolstoi's "Smert' Ivana Il'icha"

["The Death of Ivan Ilych"]). Odoevskii's mystical and alchemical studies contributed to his most interesting, yet long neglected, trio of romantic-Gothic stories: "Sil'fida" ("The Sylph") 1837, "Kosmorama" ("The Cosmorama") 1840, and the substantial double-story (or "dilogy") "Salamandra" ("The Salamander") 1841. Other genres in which Odoevskii operated over these, his most fertile years, include Gogolian whimsy, anti-Utopian satire (one of the most striking features of *Russian Nights*) and proto science-fiction, notably the futuristic *4338-oi god* (*The Year 4338*).

After 1844, when he published his Collected Works in three volumes (with *Russian Nights* appearing for the first time as Part 1), Odoevskii wrote and published very little fiction, becoming more and more occupied with his multifarious other activities. He resurfaced in the 1860s with a few publicistic pieces, but a projected second edition of his Collected Works never came to fruition and a late dabbling in the genre of the realist novel, to have been called "Samarianin" [The Samaritan], remained at his death largely unwritten.

His prominence in other fields not withstanding, Odoevskii is now remembered mainly as a writer of fiction (both romantic and children's). His reputation lies somewhere around the borderline that would purport to separate the more minor major writers from the more major of their minor counterparts. More telling, though, may be the observation that more editions of his fiction have appeared since 1975 than in the whole of the previous century.

NEIL CORNWELL

Pestrye skazki

Variegated Tales

Short-story cycle, 1833

Published in St Petersburg in 1833, *Pestrye skazki* was one of only two major literary projects that Odoevskii actually completed. This collection of stories is a transitional work between Odoevskii's fictional output of the 1820s and the 1830s, marking the beginning of the most successful and productive period in his literary career. It is a work that has never produced much critical consensus; this seems to be shared equally by the author as critic, given that, when appropriating "Excerpts from Variegated Tales" for his Collected Works (1844), Odoevskii omitted much of the original cycle and rearranged what remained. Writing in *Moskovskii telegraf*, N.A. Polevoi concurred with the author's apparent dissatisfaction, criticizing the collection as cold imitations of Hoffmann, containing too much allegory and too little thought. However, Odoevskii's friends and associates (including Gogol', who claimed to have had a hand in the book's design) responded more enthusiastically: Odoevskii's old school-teacher and one of the first Russian Schellingists, I.I. Davydov, praised *Pestrye skazki* as the first attempt in Russian literature at the philosophical tale; however, a little later, A.I. Koshelev wrote to Odoevskii of his stories: "In general they have not made any great impression: there are very few people who understand them and still fewer who would genuinely appreciate their quality."

Framed between two prefaces – one from the stories' "publisher" and the other from their "collector" – and an epilogue, we are presented with stories numbered one to eight; however, there are really seven in total. The prefaces establish a whimsical tone, while introducing the reader to the figure of the collector. The publisher's remark that, in addition to gathering stories, the collector is working on his autobiography and "historical researches", reveals Gomozeiko to be more than just another pen-name for Odoevskii; the author undoubtedly had further plans for him. The choice of hero-narrator for this cycle provides clear evidence of the influence of Gogol' and Pushkin: the honest but socially awkward Gomozeiko recalls Gogol''s Rudiy Panko and can be seen as a civic and educated version of Ivan Petrovich Belkin. Furthermore, as a middle-aged eccentric and impoverished encyclopedist, Gomozeiko is obviously a light-hearted *alter ego* or future projection of the author himself.

The opening tale, "Retorta" [The Retort], is an intriguing mixture of social satire and fantastic adventure that provides the motivation for the subsequent stories. While attending a society ball the narrator discovers the house and all its occupants to be enclosed in a glass retort; "an accursed Chemist had placed a lamp under us and without mercy was distilling the estimable public". However, the tormentor of St Petersburg society is no exalted diabolic entity but simply a demonic five-year old with barely-sprouted horns, who promptly casts the narrator into a Latin dictionary. Within its pages he encounters a spider, a dead body, a night-cap, Igosha, and others who have become so seeped in words that they have begun to turn into fairy tales (*skazki*); the narrator himself soon begins to undergo this transformation: "... my eyes turned into an epigraph, from my head a few chapters sprouted, my torso became a text, and my nails and hair took up the space for linguistic mistakes, an unavoidable appurtenance to any book ..."

As the ball ends, the exodus of guests breaks the retort; the young devil makes off with the dictionary, dropping some pages and fictional captives in his haste. The narrator reassumes human form and gathers some of his ex-companions from the abandoned pages, in order to present them to his "esteemed reader". This opening gambit neatly allows Odoevskii to present, at various removes, the succession of unlikely and "motley" stories featuring these unusual characters.

"Skazka o mertvom tele neizvestno komu prinadlezhashchem" ("The Tale of a Dead Body Belonging to Nobody Knows Whom") (II) is an exercise in satirical grotesque with the provincial bureaucracy as its target. Particularly worthy of note in this story is the attention to background detail and the description of the protagonist's mental progress as he awaits the claimant of the unidentified body. The presence of such elements has led critics to compare the story with Gogolian techniques. The incongruous dialogue between the clerk and the invisible owner ranks as a humorous highlight of the collection, while the multi-ending denouement, which provides no rational explanation for events, is classical fare for many later fantastical narratives.

Written not later than the first half of 1830, "Zhizn' i pokhozhdenie odnogo iz zdeshnikh obyvatelei v steklianoi banke" [The Life and Adventures of One of Our Local Inhabitants in a Glass Jar] was probably intended to appear as an independent work before its inclusion in this cycle. With its presentation of a spider's narrative about his hostile environment in captivity, and his exhausting efforts to protect his wife from the ravages of his cannibalistic father, it is one of the most unusual of Odoevskii's stories. The subtitle is purely ironic, as the story is primarily a burlesque of "frenetic" French romantic forms, particularly that, popular in Russia, featuring the noble animal as a leading protagonist.

"Igosha" (V) comprises a child's narrative of visitations from a supposedly mythical, limbless prankster, put into his mind by the utterances of his nanny and an anecdote of his father's. The first example of the "psychological fantastic" in Odoevskii's work, it is the only story in the collection to have provoked an individual critical study. The interest lies largely in the reader's uncertainty as to the existence of Igosha, created by the single, non-corroborated perspective of the child. However, in a reworking for the 1844 collection, Odoevskii effectively removes any doubt as to the figure's "actual" existence by the addition of a final paragraph clarifying it as a "play of the imagination", thus transforming, and impoverishing, the story into the retrospective narrative of an adult, rather than a child's eye view.

"Skazka o tom, kak opasno devushkam khodit' tolpoiu po Nevskomu prospektu" ("The Tale of How it is Dangerous for Girls to Walk in a Crowd along Nevskii Prospekt") (VII) is an allegorical cautionary tale of the adulteration of Russian beauty that fully displays Odoevskii's satirical powers. The heart of an unfortunate Slav girl is extracted and mixed with the novels of de Genlis, Chesterfield's "Letters", and various other western frivolities – a treatment that turns her into a doll able only to parrot others' words. Thrown out of the window by her frustrated purchaser, in "Ta zhe skazka, tol'ko na izvorot" [The Same Tale, Only in Reverse] (VIII), the girl is bewitched and worn down by a monstrous, wooden-hearted man who "again" throws her onto the street. Despite Odoevskii's undisguised didactism, the story still manages effectively to expose the unimaginative, inartistic upbringing of Russian girls.

While these tales may be individually slight, Odoevskii enriches them with a diversity of satire, the grotesque, and a sparkling imagination. Not for the only time in this author's work one has a sense that the whole may exceed the sum of the parts. Although attempts at presenting the fantastic may be less sophisticated than we expect from later writers, and the social satire is less polished than that of Gogol', this cycle represents an undeniably important stage in 19th-century stylistic development.

CLAIRE WHITEHEAD

Russian Nights

Russkie nochi

Frame-tale novel, 1844

Russian Nights may perhaps best be described as a "philosophical frame-tale"; it has sometimes been termed a "philosophical novel". It comprises a series of short stories of an assorted romantic nature (most of which had earlier been published separately), collected and embedded in a philosophical discussion on romantic aesthetics and the prospects for Russia as a force for the reinvigoration of the "dying west". As such it is a formal curiosity, unique in Russian literature and perhaps even in European literature.

Generic comparisons have been made with *The Decameron*, the Platonic dialogues, Hoffmann's *Die Serapions-Brüder* (*The Serapion Brothers*) and various other works from the German romantic period, and Joseph de Maistre's *Les soirées de Saint-Pétersbourg*. None of these is valid in isolation, though all may have been contributory influences. What can be said is that it is an illustration *par excellence* of the romantic principle, inspired by Schelling, Novalis and others, of the mixing of genres. It derives from romanticism and from the antecedents of romanticism, including the Gothic, alchemical, and esoteric traditions. *Russian Nights* has been aptly called, in the Soviet 1981 *Istoriia russkoi literatury* [History of Russian Literature], "an encyclopedia of romanticism".

What sets it apart from other models is the almost equal treatment accorded the philosophical and the "fictional" elements. Whereas in most instances of comparable cycles or frame-tales the "frame" is very perfunctory, in *Russian Nights* it occupies almost as much space as the fiction, it introduces the apparently authorial protagonist named Faust, and it constitutes the forum for many of the main ideas of the work. This is especially the case in its lengthy epilogue, which provides an ample coverage of the main strands of Russian thought of the 1820s and 1830s: a kind of proto-Westernizer/Slavophile debate in itself.

The stories comprising the fictional element had been written over a period of about 15 years, nearly all being published along the way, and the entire project grew out of a grandiose abandoned scheme, to have been called "Dom sumasshedshikh" [The House of Madmen]. Many of these stories enjoyed individual success during the 1830s; several, including those centering on such "sublime eccentrics" as Piranesi, Beethoven, and J.S. Bach, stand comparison with Odoevskii's best stories, and indeed with most of the romantic and society tales produced in the 1830s in Russia (only obvious works of genius, such as Pushkin's *Pikovaia dama* (*The Queen of Spades*) and Gogol''s "Shinel'" ("The Overcoat") can claim a clear superiority). "Sebastian Bach", in particular, is a minor masterpiece in its own right; an alternative "inner biography", it ironically depicts its arch-classical subject in ultra-romantic terms. Cycles within the main cycle, elaborate narrative distancing devices, social satire, and explorations of the ideas of such thinkers as Jeremy Bentham and Thomas Malthus are further features of what is now generally seen as Odoevskii's *magnum opus*. Taken together, the links and themes connecting these stories with their surrounding frame (the power of music, the quest for truth and communication, social responsibility, touches of the supernatural and anti-Utopian fantasy) only struck their author with their full significance, or so it would seem, with hindsight; the whole, one continues to suspect, exceeds the sum of the parts. Only since the pathbreaking work of Iurii Mann (1969) and the 1975 edition in the "Literaturnye pamiatniki" series, edited by B.F. Egorov and Evgenii Maimin, has the hidden poetic scheme underlying *Russian Nights* as an integral work even begun to be fully appreciated.

Russian Nights, then, is an unusual work, even in Russian literature, and a key source-book, both for Russian romanticism and for Russian social and aesthetic thought of its epoch. Published as an entity only in 1844, it represents the culmination of Russian romanticism and proved to be, to all intents and purposes, the valedictory work of Odoevskii's literary career: a fond retrospective over Russian – and indeed European – romanticism, which appeared slightly late, at the dawn of the new age of psychological realism (as a comparison with the major prose of Lermontov and the early Dostoevskii will soon reveal). Already perceived as somewhat out of date on its appearance, it made less of a critical impact than would have been the case had it appeared a decade earlier (as the constantly overworked Odoevskii – a man of many parts and careers – had originally intended). *Russian Nights* has taken well over a century to recover from this, despite occasional minor flurries of interest in Odoevskii (at the turn of the century; in the 1920s; and again in the Thaw period of the 1950s). *Russian Nights* achieved a new printing only in 1913, Odoevskii himself having failed to complete a second edition of his works in the 1860s, and then again not before 1975; the English translation published in 1965 – out of print for many years – is now happily available again. And yet, even within Odoevskii's lifetime, it has recently been revealed, the stories of *Russian Nights* did not remain totally unnoticed in the world at large: one of the most striking of them, "Improvizator" ("The Improvisor"), was plagiarized almost word for word, via its French translation, by the Irish-American writer Fitz-James O'Brien (who renamed it "Seeing the World" in 1859).

NEIL CORNWELL

Nikolai Platonovich Ogarev 1813–1877

Poet and prose writer

Biography

Born in St Petersburg, 6 December 1813. Family moved to Moscow, 1820. Educated at home; studied mathematics, philology, and political science at Moscow University, 1830–33. Clerk in Moscow Archive of Foreign Affairs, 1832. Arrested for singing anti-government songs, 1834; sent to Penza province, 1835–38. Wrote under the pseudonyms Anton Postegaikin and R.C. Married: 1) Mariia L'vovna Rosslavleva in 1836 (separated 1844); 2) Natal'ia Alekseevna Tuchkova in 1853 (separated 1857); relationship with Mary Seatherland, from 1858 until his death. Unsuccessful attempt to organize socialist-based peasant commune in Riazan province, 1838–40. Returned to Moscow. Published verses in *Otechestvennye zapiski*, 1840. Moved to St Petersburg, 1841. Travelled abroad, 1841–46. Unsuccessful organization of factories based on peasant labour at Penza estate resulted in financial ruin, 1846–55. Arrested for suspected connection with "communist sect"; under police surveillance, 1850. Emigrated to London and joined Herzen's political propaganda efforts, 1856; publisher of the journal *Kolokol*, 1857–67. Tried to create revolutionary organization, "Zemlia i volia", 1861–63. Close to M.A. Bakunin; advocated peasant revolution, 1861–71. Moved to Geneva as active revolutionary propagandist, 1865–74. After Herzen's death, without financial support, abandoned political agitation; returned to London, 1874. Died in London, 12 June 1877.

Publications

Collected Editions

Izbrannye sotsial'no-politicheskie i filosofskie proizvedeniia, 2 vols. Moscow, 1952–56.

Izbrannye proizvedeniia, 2 vols. Moscow, 1956.

Poetry

Stikhotvoreniia. Moscow, 1856.

Stikhotvoreniia. London, Trubner and K, 1858.

Stikhotvoreniia i poemy. Leningrad, 1956.

Stikhotvoreniia i poemy. Moscow, 1980.

Fiction

"Kavkazskie vody (Otryvok iz moei ispovedi)" [Waters of the Caucasus (Extract from My Confession], *Poliarnaia zvezda*, 6 (1861).

"Zapiski russkogo pomeshchika" [Notes of a Russian Landowner], *Byloe*, 27–28 (1924).

Letters and Literary Criticism

Za piat' let (1855–1860). Politicheskie i sotsial'nye stat'i [Over Five Years]. London, Trubner and K, 1861.

Lettres inedites à Alexander Herzen fils, edited by Michel Mervaud. Mont-Saint-Aignan, Université de Haute Normandie, 1978.

N.P. Ogarev o literature i iskusstve [N.P. Ogarev on Literature and Art]. Moscow, 1988.

Critical Studies

Ogarev, Nekrasov, Gertsen, Chernyshevskii v spore ob ogarevskom nasledstve. Delo Ogareva – Panaevoi. Po arkhivnym materialam, by Ia.Z. Cherniak, Moscow, 1933.

The Romantic Exiles: A Nineteenth-Century Portrait Gallery, by Edward Hallett Carr, London, Gollancz, and New York, Stokes, 1933; Harmondsworth, Penguin, 1968; reprinted Cambridge, Massachusetts, MIT Press, 1981.

N.P. Ogarev. Zhizn', mirovozzrenie, tvorchestvo, by V.A. Putintsev, Moscow, 1963.

Revoliutsionnaia bor'ba A.I. Gertsena i N.P. Ogareva i tainoe obshchestvo "Zemlia i volia" 1860, by Ia.I. Linkov, Moscow, 1964.

Pervye ogarevskie chteniia. Materialy nauchnoi konferentsii (Obshchestvennye i gumanitarnye nauki). Saransk, 1974.

N.P. Ogarev. Evoliutsiia filosofskikh vzgliadov, by N.G. Tarakanov, Moscow, 1974.

Problemy tvorchestva Ogareva (Mezhvuzovskii tematicheskii sbornik nauchnykh trudov). Saransk, 1980.

V Sviatoi tishi vospominanii. Po materialam liriki i pisem Nikolaia Ogareva, by I. Reshetilova, Moscow, 1990.

Bibliography
"Materialy dlia bibliografii opublikovannykh pisem Ogareva", by I. and R. Mandel'shtam, *Literaturnoe nasledstvo*, 61 (1953).

From their youth Nikolai Ogarev and his friend Aleksandr Herzen regarded themselves as free-thinkers and continuers of the freedom-loving traditions of the Decembrist movement. Ogarev was very hostile to Russian serfdom, and ideas of a social reorganization of the world attracted him. Ogarev started writing verse in 1825 and already in 1835 considered his poetic calling the main thing in life. Ogarev's legacy consists of several hundred poems, written up until his final days.

In the early poems from 1833–39, the melancholic motifs of the German romantics predominate, supplanted gradually by Byron's bilious irony. Grief, anxiety, depression, longing, anger towards the world, gloomy presentiments – these were the fundamental themes of Ogarev's lyrics, and out of this came corresponding genres: monologues, confessions, and friendly epistles. Almost all these verses were either unfinished or unpolished, and were not published during the author's lifetime. Only in 1840, for the first time moving away from romantic exaltation, did Ogarev create several poems in the spirit of the "natural school" – little pictures from the life of simple folk: "Derevenskii storozh" [The Village Watchman], "Kabak" [The Pigsty], "Izba" [The Hut], and others. Together with a poem printed in *Otechestvennye zapiski*, "Staryi dom" [The Old House], they won Belinskii's praise. Later, however, when the more reflective "Hamlet-like" trend once again seized Ogarev ("Monologi" [Monologues], 1844–47), Belinskii sharply condemned him and did not even want to publish his work in *Sovremennik*. Already in their first publications, however, Ogarev's gloomy "demonic" meditations had their admirers (A.I. Herzen, V.P. Botkin, A.A. Grigor'ev, and others). Later, his name was lauded to the skies by N.G. Chernyshevskii (1856), but this was already motivated by political considerations. The poem "Iumor" [Humour] met with particular success, and excerpts from it circulated in manuscripts from 1840 to 1841; separate parts were printed later in *Poliarnaia zvezda*, but the author never finished the poem. In the poem "Iumor", the reader will find the ideas of political maximalism, hatred towards slavery and despotism, sympathy towards new socialist studies, irony and even sarcasm toward Russian reality – and all this in the form of a free confession, without a plan and without extensive rewriting of verses. One finds reminiscences from Pushkin, Lermontov, Byron, and Goethe, but the poet feels disgust and hatred for everything that is portrayed and admits that "in his heart" boiled "the wrath of Robespierre".

Starting in the mid-1840s, Ogarev worked on several poems or, as he himself often called them, "novellas" in verse: "Derevnia" [The Village], "Gospodin" [The Squirrel] and "Zimnii put'" [The Winter Path]. They included considerable autobiographical material, in particular an attempt to talk about his unsuccessful economical and business affairs. The main idea, though, was the condemnation of the landowners' way of life and accusatory hatred for all gentry. Russian censorship being as it was, Ogarev did not even try to publish these poems.

In the middle of the 1850s, Ogarev prepared a separate publication of his selected poems; it came out in 1856 and included 83 texts, parts of which were included in a book (without Ogarev's knowledge) by his friend N.M. Satin. This volume was highly valued by N.G. Chernyshevskii in a special article in *Sovremennik* (1856). Chernyshevskii saw in Ogarev a poet whose irreconcilable position in relation to the existing regime was close to his own.

In March 1856, Ogarev left Russia, clearly not planning to return. Arriving in London, he immediately joined the activities of the Russian Free Press, organized by Herzen. He started with a cycle of articles under the general heading "Russkie voprosy" [Russian Issues] (*Poliarnaia zvezda*, 1856–57; *Kolokol*, 1858). In these four articles, Ogarev analysed the economic and legislative situation in Russia before the reforms, which had been declared in the manifestos of Alexander II. The third article was entirely devoted to the *obshchina* (peasant community); in it, Ogarev tried to see the way to the "original harmonic development" of the Russian economy after the abolition of serfdom.

From 1857 to 1867, at Ogarev's instigation, Herzen and Ogarev's journal *Kolokol* began publication; here Ogarev printed his political and economic articles, in particular an analysis of the Manifesto of 19 February 1861 on the abolition of serfdom. Dissatisfied with Alexander II's reforms, Ogarev proposed that the people "join forces against the Tsar and magnate" and snatch up all the land for themselves without waiting for the laws. At this point, Ogarev, together with other Russian revolutionaries, organized the secret society "Zemlia i volia", which issued a series of proclamations urging the people not to obey the authorities. In 1861 he published a collection of political articles (*Za piat' let* [Over Five Years]). In *Poliarnaia zvezda* and separate publications he printed various works that had been banned in Russia, in particular works on the Decembrist movement, and the collection *Russkaia potaennaia literatura* [Russian Secret Literature] (1861). In the prefaces to these two books, Ogarev proved himself a sharp and radical critic.

During the London years of active revolutionary propaganda, Ogarev continued to write verses and poems. Some of these were lyrical in his former style of confession and monologue: "Noch'" [The Night], "Sny" [Dreams], "Nocturno", and "Isopoved' lishnego cheloveka" [The Confession of a Superfluous Man]. Others had a political subtext: "Matvei Radaev", "S togo berega" [From the Other Shore]; some from the point of view of a hero of the common people: "Rasskaz etapnogo ofitsera" [The Story of a Deport Officer]; others markedly like memoirs: "Tiur'ma. Otryvok iz moikh vospominanii" [Prison. A Fragment from My Memories]. Many of these poems were printed only fragmentarily in *Poliarnaia zvezda* and in *Kolokol*, and much, left unfinished by the author, was never printed during his lifetime. It is interesting to note that Dostoevskii, who held Ogarev's poetry in high esteem, praised in print his poem "Rasskaz etapnogo ofitsera". A.G. Dostoevskaia herself testifies that her husband was on friendly terms with Ogarev during their life as neighbours in Geneva (1867) and, according to V.V. Timofeeva, Dostoevskii loved to recite lines from Ogarev's poem "Arestant" [The Prisoner].

In 1858 Ogarev's *Stikhotvoreniia* was published, which included 106 items. Some were repetitions of the 1856 Moscow edition. Many of Ogarev's verses, especially from the later period of his life (1867–77), remained unpublished.

Worthy of note are Ogarev's proclamations in verse: "Goi, rebiata, liudi russkie" [Hail, Russian Fellows!], "Student" [The Student], "Muzhichkam" [To the Muzhiks], "Vstrecha" [The Encounter], and others. They were all written between 1868 and 1869, when Ogarev had sharply migrated to the left and preached about a "massacre of the people" together with Bakunin and Nechaev. Dostoevskii used the poem "Student" in his novel *Besy* (*The Possessed* or *The Devils*).

From what Ogarev himself called his "senile sketches", very little deserves attention. Even the piece written before his grief had left him – "Mertvomu drugu" [To a Dead Friend] (1875) on the death of Herzen – testifies to his complete poetic helplessness. The Muse had clearly turned away from the poet, who was by then suffering from severe illness.

ELENA DRYZHAKOVA

Bulat Shalvovich Okudzhava 1924–1997

Guitar-poet and novelist

Biography

Born in Moscow, 9 May 1924, to Armenian mother (Ashkhen Stepanovna Nalbandian) and Georgian father (Shalva Stepanovich Okudzhava). Both parents arrested as "enemies of the people" in 1937; father executed, mother held in camps until 1955. Educated in schools in Tbilisi, Moscow, Nizhnii Tagil, and in the Urals. Volunteered for military service; served at the front, 1942: wounded and served in reserves. Attended Tbilisi State University, 1945–50. Married: 1) Galina Vasil'evna Smolianinova in 1947 (separated 1962); 2) Ol'ga Vladimirovna Archimovich in 1965; two sons. Taught Russian language and literature in village school, Kaluga district, 1950–54. Worked in Kaluga local youth newspaper, 1954–56. Moved to Moscow in late 1956. Worked for the publishing house Molodaia gvardiia, 1957–59. Journalist for *Literaturnaia gazeta*, 1959–62. Member of the Writers' Union from 1961. Professional writer from 1962. Recipient: Russian Booker Prize for *Uprazdnennyi teatr* [The Closed Theatre], 1994. Died 12 June 1997.

Publications

Collected Editions

Bud' zdorov, shkoliar. Stikhi (opublikovannye i neopublikovannye) [Goodbye Schoolboy. Verses Published and Unpublished]. Frankfurt, Posev, 1964.

Proza i poeziia [Prose and Poetry]. 3rd edition, Frankfurt, Posev, 1968; 7th edition, 1984.

Izbrannaia proza. Moscow, 1979.

Izbrannaia proizvedeniia, 2 vols. Moscow, 1989.

Izbrannoe. Stikhotvoreniia. Moscow, 1989.

Chaepitie na Arbate. Stikhi raznykh let [Tea Drinking on the Arbat. Poems of Various Years]. Moscow, 1996.

Fiction

"Bud' zdorov, shkoliar. Povest'", in *Tarusskie stranitsy*, edited by K. Paustovskii, Moscow, 1961; translated as "Goodbye, Schoolboy", by Robert Szulkin, in *Fifty Years of Russian Prose: From Pasternak to Solzhenitsyn*, edited by Krystyna Pomorska, Cambridge, Massachusetts, MIT Press, 1971, vol. 2, 171–227; retitled as "Lots of Luck, Kid", in *The Barsukov Triangle*, edited by Carl and Ellendea Proffer, Ann Arbor, Ardis, 1984, 305–70.

"Promoxys", *Iunost'* (1965); translated by Helen Colaclides, in *Fifty Years of Russian Prose: From Pasternak to Solzhenitsyn*, edited by Krystyna Pomorska, Cambridge, Massachusetts, MIT Press, 1971, 228–44.

"Bednyi Avrosimov", *Druzhba narodov* (April–June 1969); reprinted as *Glotok svobody*, Moscow, 1971; translated as *A Taste of Liberty*, by Leo Gruliow, Ann Arbor, Ardis, 1986.

"Fotograf Zhora" [Zhora the Photographer], in *Grani*, 73 (1969), 99–170; also published in *Dva romana*, Frankfurt, Posev, 1970.

Dva romana [Two Novels: "Bednyi Avrosimov" and "Fotograf Zhora"]. Frankfurt, Posev, 1970.

"Mersi, ili Pokhozhdeniia Shipova. Starinnyi vodevil'", *Druzhba narodov*, 12 (1971), 88–199; reprinted as *Pokhozhdeniia Shipova. Starinnyi vodevil'. Istinnoe proisshestvie*. Moscow, 1975; translated as *The Extraordinary Adventures of Secret Agent Shipov in Pursuit of Count Leo Tolstoy, in the Year 1862*, by Heather Maisner, London, Abelard-Schuman, 1973.

"Puteshestvie diletantov, iz zapisok otstavnogo poruchika Amiran Amilakhvari" [Dilettantes' Travels, from the Notes of Lieutenant Amiran Amilakhvari, Retired], *Druzhba narodov*, 8–9(1976); 9–1978); as separate edition, Moscow, 1979; translated as *Nocturne: (From the Notes of Lieutenant Amiran Amilakhvari, Retired)*, by Antonina W. Bouis, New York, Harper and Row, 1978.

Iskusstvo kroiki i zhit'ia, Moscow, 1979; translated as "The Art of Needles and Sins", by Michele A. Berdy, in *The New Soviet Fiction: Sixteen Short Stories*, edited by Sergei Zalygin, New York, Abbeville Press, 1989.

"Svidanie s Bonapartom" [A Meeting with Bonaparte], *Druzhba narodov*, 1983; Moscow, 1985.

Devushka moei mechty. Moscow, 1988; translated as "Girl of My Dreams", by Alex Miller, *Soviet Literature*, 3 (1988), 88–97; and by Leo Gruliow, in *The Human Experience:*

Contemporary American and Soviet Fiction and Poetry, New York, Knopf, and Moscow, 1989, 91–101.
Zaezzhii muzykant, proza [Travelling Musician, Prose]. Moscow, 1993.
"Uprazdnennyi teatr" [The Closed Theatre], *Znamia*, 9–10 (1993), 4–55, 77–112.

Poetry
Lirika. Kaluga, 1956.
Ostrova. Lirika [Islands]. Moscow, 1959.
Po doroge k Tinatin. Stikhi Gruzii i perevody. [On the Road to Tinatin, Georgian Verses and Translations]. Tbilisi, 1964.
Veselyi barabanshchik. Kniga stikhov [The Merry Drummer]. Moscow, 1964; London, Flegon, 1966.
Mart velikodushnyi [Magnanimous Month of March]. Moscow, 1967.
Arbat moi Arbat [Arbat, My Arbat]. Moscow, 1976.
65 Pesen. 65 Songs (bilingual edition), edited by Vladimir Frumkin, translated by Eve Shapiro. Ann Arbor, Ardis, 1980; *Songs; Volume II*, Ann Arbor, Ardis, 1986.
Stikhotvoreniia. Moscow, 1984.
Posviashchaetsia vam. Stikhi [Dedicated to You]. Moscow, 1988.
Pesni Bulata Okudzhavy. Melodii i teksty pesen [Songs of Bulat Okudzhava. Melodies and Texts]. Moscow, 1989.
Poems in *Contemporary Russian Poetry: A Bilingual Anthology*, translated and edited by Gerald S. Smith. Bloomington, Indiana University Press, 1993, 26–39.
Poems in *Twentieth Century Russian Poetry: Silver and Steel: An Anthology*, with an introduction by Yevgeny Yevtushenko, edited by Albert C. Todd and Max Hayward, New York, Doubleday, and London, Fourth Estate, 1993, 739–50.
Zal ozhidaniia: Stikhi [Waiting Room: Poems]. Nizhnii Novgorod, 1996.

Play
Mersi, ili starinnyi vodevil'. P'esa [Merci, or An Old Fashioned Vaudeville. A Play]. Leningrad, 1975.

Screenplays
Vernost'. Kinopovest' [Fidelity], with P. Todorovskii. Odessa, 1965.
"Zhenia, Zhenechka i 'katiusha' ili Neobyknovennye dostopouchitel'nye frontovye pokhozhdeniia gvardii riadovogo Evgeniia Kolyshkina, vcherashnego shkoliara. Kinopovest'" [Zhenia, Zhenechka and "katiusha" or the Unusual Instructive Adventures at the Front of Private Eugene Kolyshkina, Formerly Schoolboy], with V. Motyl. Moscow, 1968.

Stories for Children
Front prikhodit k nam: povest' [The Front Comes to Us]. Moscow, 1967.
Prelestnye prikliucheniia (dlia detei) [Wonderful Adventures (for children)]. Tbilisi, 1971.
Prelestnye prikliucheniia [Wonderful Adventures]. Tel-Aviv, 1975.

Critical Studies
"To grusten on, to vesel on ...", by G. Krasukhin, *Voprosy literatury*, 9 (1968), 40–54.
Der Hoffnung kleines Orchester – Bulat Okudzhava-Lieder und Lyrik, by Hildburg Heider, Frankfurt, Peter Lang, 1983.
Songs to Seven Strings: Russian Guitar Poetry and Soviet "Mass Song", by Gerald S. Smith, Bloomington, Indiana University Press, 1984, 111–44.
"Okudzhava Marches On", by Gerald S. Smith, *Slavonic and East European Review*, 66 (1988), 553–63.
"Uprazdnennyi teatr. S Bulatom Okudzhavoi beseduet zhurnalist Il'ia Mil'shtein", *Ogonek*, 19 (1991), 4–6.
Die Poetik der Prosawerke Bulat Okudžavas, by Renate Hansen-Kokoruš, Munich, Sagner, 1992.
The Last Years of Soviet Russian Literature: Prose Fiction, 1975–1991, by Deming Brown, Cambridge and New York, Cambridge University Press, 1993.

Though Bulat Okudzhava earned his place in the history of 20th-century Russian popular culture principally as a result of the enormous popularity and influence of his songs, he is highly esteemed for his purely literary accomplishments in both verse and prose as well.

Okudzhava's songs number some 200, and they are unquestionably his best-known genre. He began singing for friends in the mid-1950s, and in the decades since, many of his songs have become virtual anthems. One would be hard-pressed to find an educated Russian unfamiliar with such of his songs as "Poslednii trolleibus" [The Last Trolley-Bus], "Arbat, moi Arbat" [Arbat, My Arbat], or "Bumazhnyi soldat" [The Paper Soldier]. Okudzhava's performances were among the very first to be distributed through *magnitizdat*, the magnetic tape equivalent of *samizdat*, and he is invariably mentioned in the same breath with the other two pillars of Russian/Soviet "guitar poetry" – Vladimir Vysotskii and Aleksandr Galich. Even into the 1990s Okudzhava was still touring and performing.

Interestingly, the first verses designated as songs came out (minus music) only in 1964, three years after his first prose and eight years after his first collection of poetry. In part this reflects the discomfort the Soviet culture police had dealing with Okudzhava's themes in a genre not explicitly authorized by precedent or Party decree. But it also speaks of the central role of the poetry in his songs. His songs without the music can be and are still appreciated as poetry. The reverse does not hold.

Whether set to music or not, all Okudzhava's poetry is unpretentious. He favoured a simple vocabulary, and his rhyme schemes are not particularly complex or sophisticated. This is not to say that his poetry is artless in any sense of the word. Subtlety and irony are universally recognized hallmarks of Okudzhava's best poetry, and with the simplest of forms he can combine the lyric and the self-conscious to humorous effect. The oxymoron is one of his favourite devices, and he was fond of coupling the everyday and the exalted. His characters are unassuming. Women hold a place of special reverence in Okudzhava's poetic cast of characters ("Pesen'ka o golubom sharike" [Song of the Blue Balloon], "Vashe velichestvo, zhenshchina" [Your Majesty, Woman]), but all his heroes are of the lowly not the epic: anonymous soldiers and musicians, a nurse, the lonely and the lovelorn. Moscow and especially his childhood neighbourhood, the Arbat region, figure prominently in much of his poetry, and most of his settings are both urban and mundane: a street, an alley, a courtyard, the metro.

Okudzhava's themes cover a broad spectrum, but the majority of his verses deal with the eternal questions, the old stalwarts – love and longing, art and the artist, friendship and faith, the fragility of humanity and the ferocity of war. Love is often painful ("Dezhurnyi po Apreliu" [On April Duty]); faith and hope, though rarely quashed completely, are often disappointed ("Staryi pidzhak" [The Old Jacket]); war is always senseless ("Voinskii parad" [The Military Parade]). Though a major part of his life and poetry, Okudzhava consistently refuses to glorify World War II, or any war, and, while never vociferously anti-Soviet, his steady concentration on the travails of the individual and neglect of the State often put him at odds with the spirit, if not the letter, of the sanctioned Soviet cultural order.

The first conflict with this order, however, was not in reaction to Okudzhava's poetry, but to his prose. In 1961, during Khrushchev's Thaw, the story "Bud' zdorov, shkoliar!" ("Lots of Luck, Kid!") was published under the auspices of the liberal writer Konstantin Paustovskii in the collection *Tarusskie stranitsy* [Pages from Tarusa]. The story is a first-person narrative about the life of a young soldier at the front. There are no heroics, no victories, no proclamations of pro-Soviet enthusiasm. This sort of war story did not sit well with the watchdogs of Soviet art, and, though Okudzhava was accepted into the Writers' Union and recognized as a major author, he was never to be a Soviet darling.

Okudzhava's prose is weaker than his poetry, and it has not enjoyed the popularity of his songs, but it is not without its merits. There are works (like the short novel *Fotograf Zhora* [Zhora the Photographer]) that do not fit the pattern, but his prose falls roughly into two groups: autobiographical shorter works and "historical" novels. The former are more successful. Like "Lots of Luck, Kid!", several of the autobiographical pieces deal with Okudzhava's wartime experience, others relate his experiences as a village schoolmaster ("Noven'kii kak s igolochki" [Brand-New], "Iskusstvo kroiki i zhit'ia" ("The Art of Needles and Sins")). Most of the stories are structurally straightforward, light in tone and entertaining, though almost always with a hint of something more sombre.

The autobiographical works contain one longer piece, the family chronicle *Uprazdnennyi teatr* [The Closed Theatre], but Okudzhava has dedicated most of his efforts in this genre to more famous historical events. The major historical novels form a sort of continuum from Napoleon's invasion of Russia through the Decembrists to the late 19th century and Lev Tolstoi's life and social activity. *Svidanie s Bonapartom* [A Meeting with Bonaparte] relates a Russian's chance encounter with the French emperor from a variety of perspectives. *Glotok svobody* (*A Taste of Liberty*) are "notes" by a country bumpkin taken during the trial of the Decembrist Pavel Pestel, and *Pokhozhdeniia Shipova...* (*The Extraordinary Adventures of Secret Agent Shipov...*) relates the antics of a tsarist secret agent sent to spy on Count Tolstoi. The books have been objected to by Russian critics who find a poet's right to "self expression" (i.e. his liberty to invent events) out of place in prose that purports to be "historical", and they lack the narrative focus that his autobiographical pieces have. Nevertheless, the theme of individual freedom in these novels helped ameliorate the Soviet cultural suffocation of the Brezhnev years.

In addition to poetry and prose, Okudzhava wrote a play and two screenplays. His poetry in the 1980s became more sombre, and more outspokenly political, but the essence of Okudzhava's best art is constant. It conveys a message of universality, of truth, of sympathy and hope. In 1994 Okudzhava was controversially honoured with the Russian Booker Prize, for his novel *Uprazdnennyi teatr*.

NATHAN LONGAN

Uprazdnennyi teatr

The Closed Theatre

Novel, 1993

This novel, which won the 1994 Booker Russian Prize, is a family history. Okudzhava describes his fictionalized approach as "a crude pocket torch" with which he is trying to track the goldfish of history. His Georgian father and Armenian mother were both senior figures in the Communist Party in the 1920s and 1930s, and he tells the story of the times through their lives and those of their parents and many brothers and sisters. The story ends in 1937 with the arrest and execution of this father ("Ten years exile without correspondence rights"), and the subsequent arrest of his mother.

The narrator is Ivan Ivanovich, looking back from 1990 at his own childhood, at what he understood of the events unfolding around him, and of what he was ignorant. Three of his Georgian uncles are exiled, two of them Bolsheviks accused of being unrepentant Trotskiites, and one a cranky old anarchist revered for having thrown a bomb at the governor of Kutaisi. Even his sick, apolitical aunt is exiled, while her husband, a tormented alcoholic poet, is awarded a Lenin Prize for literature.

The unifying theme of the novel is the deep-seated but concealed jealousy and animosity of Lavrentii Beria, who was to become Stalin's Chief of the Secret Police, towards Shalva Okudzhava, the hero's father. This can be seen as the unknown force behind the disasters that systematically befall the family. After a visit to Beria to intercede for her husband, Ashkhen, the hero's mother, is arrested at the end of the novel. Another cohesive factor is the settings, to which the young 'Vanvanych is very sensitive. The first of these is a squalid communal flat in Moscow, to which the Caucasian communists come when their marriage is first registered. Here neighbouring rooms are shared by a Polish factory-owner, his wife and daughter, the former owners of the whole flat, who are constantly visited in the night by NKVD officers on confiscatory raids, their former nanny (who teaches five-year-old 'Vanvanych about God and is sent back to the country by his outraged mother), and a terrified peasant accused of being a "kulak" (hence destined for extermination as a class enemy). 'Vanvanych's father is no longer there, having been sent back to work in Georgia.

'Vanvanych returns on holiday to Tiflis, a fragrant, warm, bustling city, and becomes aware of another thread, the growing disparity between the living standards of high-up Party workers, like his father and uncles, and those of the rest of the population. There are whispers about famine in the Ukraine, which nobody is allowed to acknowledge; this is dramatized by an encounter with a starving woman and her daughter on the beach at Evpatoriia, where the young 'Vanvanych is enjoying being treated like a lord on account of the important position held by his parents and an Armenian aunt's ability to charm the chief consultant of the local sanatorium.

He returns to Moscow, newly aware of the squalor in which the neighbouring children live while Russia is waiting for socialism to be built. In Tiflis the venomous Beria, still at an early stage in his career, is making life impossible for his father, who succeeds in gaining an audience with Stalin's right-hand man (shortly to commit suicide), Sergo Ordzhonikidze. Ordzhonikidze enables him to move as first secretary of the Party committee to a dismal site in the Urals, where a huge railway carriage-building works is being constructed. At last the family is reunited, travelling from Moscow in the opulence of an "international" railway compartment by courtesy of the Party's Central Committee to a two-bedroomed flat that contrasts starkly with the workers' stinking barracks. This is as nothing compared to the palatial villa enjoyed by the director of the construction site. The delusion that the dreadfulness of the Soviet system is merely a temporary price to be paid for future happiness becomes increasingly difficult to sustain. A young woman whom Shalva helps improve her position later proves an adept blackmailer. The increasingly mad years between the murder of Kirov and the Party Purges of 1937 coincide with the difficult adolescence of the hero. His father is promoted to first secretary of the municipal party committee in nearby Nizhnii Tagil. His parents' faith in the Party begins to be tested to breaking point as Shalva leads the attack on supposed enemies of the people, even as his own brothers are picked off by Beria back in Tiflis. The family now live in a mansion, although his father has insisted on regulation furniture.

'Vanvanych begins to regard these privileges (which his parents despise and reject) as no more than his due. He has a sleigh sent from Party headquarters to collect him from school, and steals his father's Party card to enable him and his girlfriend to watch an evening of wrestling from the Party box at the local circus. One day he suddenly finds himself surrounded at school by unprivileged schoolmates chanting "Trotskiite" at him. His father has been dismissed from his post "for negligent work, political blindness, patronage of alien elements, and for being related to enemies of the people now unmasked". The next day 'Vanvanych encounters the exotic "international" wrestlers leaving the circus, and finds that in daylight the "German world champion" Benno Schaaf and the mighty Black American Frank Good are Russian impostors, concerned only with going for a beer with the local prostitute. He and his mother return third class to Moscow. Despite her sister-in-law's warning on keeping a low profile, she obtains an audience with Beria to plead her husband's cause. He is charm itself and promises to deal with the matter the very next day. In the night she is arrested.

The strength of Okudzhava's novel is the directness that comes from a major writer describing the fate he saw befall his immediate family. He speaks of "a tragic and relentless tune as one person after another was taken away from him, one thing after another, more and more frequently, faster and faster ... This tune would accompany him throughout his life. Its slurred half-tones, drowned out by daily events, were written in his memory, or perhaps in his soul."

This pseudo-autobiographical style can create technical difficulties for the narration, as "Ivan Ivanovich" talks directly to the reader: "I find it difficult, almost impossible, to imagine now, in 1990, the objects impressing themselves on 'Vanvanych's consciousness then, at the end of the 1920s." When he is trying to re-imagine his own childhood, this produces a number of technical problems where neither the young 'Vanvanych nor the older Ivan Ivanovich writing in 1990 can convincingly have the necessary knowledge and the only way out seems to use apologetically fictional dialogue. However, this too occasionally lapses into straight autobiography. His father rejects an appeal for clemency from a school-friend whose father was an anti-Bolshevik lawyer:

> 'Vanvanych of course had no inkling of any of this, gazing into his daddy's eyes, avidly seeking out every new wave of love for himself. He certainly could never have guessed that in 1982, 60 years later, this episode would produce an echo in his own life.

For all that, this is important testimony on the psychology of Stalinism by a talented and uniquely placed "insider".

ARCH TAIT

Nikolai Makarovich Oleinikov 1898–1937

Poet

Biography

Born in Kamenskaia on the Don, August 1898, into a White-sympathizing Cossack family. Broke with family beliefs and fought for Bolsheviks in Civil War. Member of Communist Party, 1920. Set up two journals, *Kochegarka* and *Zaboi*, in the Donbass region, early 1920s. Persuaded by Evgenii Shvarts to go to Leningrad; worked as writer and editor in children's literature section of State Publishing House, from 1925. Associated with OBERIU. Ordered to take part in grain-requisitioning in native land, but feigned illness, 1933. Wrote many poems for children; three poems published in the journal, *Tridtsat' dnei*, October 1934. Wrote film-scripts with Evgenii Shvarts, 1935–36. Arrested in 1937. Shot in prison, 24 November 1937.

Publications
Poetry
Poems in *Tridtsat' dnei*, 10 (1934).
Stikhotvoreniia, edited by L. Fleyshman. Bremen, K-Presse, 1975.
Ironicheskie stikhi [Ironic Poems], edited by Lev Losev, New York, Serebrianyi vek, 1982.
Puchina strastei [Gulf of Passions]. Leningrad, 1991.

Critical Studies
My znali Evgeniia Shvartsa. Moscow and Leningrad, 1966.
"Grandsons of Kozma Prutkov", by Robin Milner-Gulland, in *Russian and Slavic Literature*, edited by Richard Freeborn *et al.*, Cambridge, Massachusetts, Slavica, 1976.
Vospominaniia o Zabolotskom. Moscow, 1977.
"Zabolotsky's *Vremya*", by Robin Milner-Gulland, *Essays in Poetics*, 6/1 (1981).
"Tvorchestvo Oleinikova", by S. Poliakova, *Russian Literature Triquarterly*, 23 (1990), 327–55.
Vanna Arkhimeda, edited by A. Aleksandrov. Leningrad, 1991.
"Beyond the Turning-Point", by Robin Milner-Gulland, in *Daniil Kharms and the Poetics of the Absurd: Essays and Materials*, edited by Neil Cornwell. London, Macmillan, and New York, St Martin's Press, 1991.
The Life of Zabolotsky, by Nikita Zabolotsky, edited by Robin Milner-Gulland. Cardiff, University of Wales Press, 1994.
Oleinikov i ob Oleinikove i drugie raboty po russkoi literature, edited by S. Poliakova, St Petersburg, 1997.
The Last Soviet Avant-Garde: OBERIU — Fact, Fiction, Metafiction, by Graham Roberts, Cambridge, Cambridge University Press, 1997.

> I am interested in the following: nourishment, numbers, insects, journals, poems, light, flowers, optics, entertaining reading, women, "Pythagorism-Leibnitzism", pictures, arrangement of living-quarters, rules for life, experiments without instruments, tasks, recipes, scales, global dispositions, signs, matches, wineglasses, forks, keys etc., ink, pencil and paper, ways of writing, the art of making conversation, interactions with other people, hypnotism, homespun philosophizing, 20th-century people, boredom, prose, cinema and photography, ballet, daily notes, nature, "Aleksandr-Grinery", the history of our times, experiments on oneself, mathematical operations, magnets, the purposes of various instruments and animals, illumination, forms of infinity, the abolition of fastidiousness, tolerance, pity, cleanliness and dirt, aspects of boastfulness, the internal structure of the earth, conservatism, certain conversations with women.

Virtually every item in this heterogeneous list has its place in the few dozen poems for which Nikolai Oleinikov, one of the strangest and most intriguing figures in 20th-century literature, is remembered. The existence of the list itself points to the fundamental context of Oleinikov's work: he was a "companionable" poet, writing for friends and acquaintances without thought of publication. Similar eccentric yet revealing lists were made by his close associates Daniil Kharms and Nikolai Zabolotskii – both also major but then little-known writers – when with a few others they embarked on a long series of intimate discussions (as the "Club of Semi-Literate Scholars") in the early 1930s (records of these were kept by the host, Leonid Savel'ev). Their bantering, witty, fantastical yet also quasi-philosophical and personally revealing tone is to a large extent that of Oleinikov's verse.

Oleinikov seems to have been an arresting personality: Cossack warrior, writer, mathematician, fervent womanizer, practical joker, wit. Born in the Donbass, the tempestuously energetic future writer broke with his prosperous, White-sympathizing family, fought in the Civil War, became a Bolshevik party member and (without any experience) set up a couple of journals in his native region (*Kochegarka* and *Zaboi*). He was "discovered" there in 1923 by the dramatist Evgenii Shvarts, who persuaded him to come to Petrograd/Leningrad to work as writer and editor in the children's literature section of the State Publishing House. He arrived in 1925 equipped with a document from his village council testifying that "citizen Oleinikov is authentically beautiful: issued to gain admission to the Academy of Arts" (he had persuaded the council chairmen that only beautiful people were admitted). Once installed in the State Publishing House, he sharpened his wits with and against his "best friend and bosom enemy" Shvarts, while together they constructed mystifications and practical jokes for the benefit of their own circle and for impressionable visitors; Samuil Marshak, poet and director of the Children's Literature sector, was a frequent target of his barbs. Apart from editorial work he wrote much fiction and poetry for children, usually under the pseudonym "Makar Svirepii" (the fierce).

The surviving "non-children's" poems by Oleinikov are dated from the mid-1920s to 1937, but are chiefly concentrated in the early 1930s. Only three were published in his lifetime (in the journal *Tridtsat' dnei*, October 1934), and drew a predictable critical volley from A. Tarasenkov. He is usually characterized as a parodist, the "modern Kozma Prutkov": indeed he claimed to be "grandson of Prutkov in the direct line". He is certainly on occasion capable of wickedly sharp parodies of individual writers and works (for example, of the lofty sentimentality of Bagritskii's "Smert' pionerki" [Death of a Girl Pioneer] in "Karas", on a dead fish). But as is also often the case with Prutkov, Oleinikov goes far beyond the bounds of normal parody: from specific parody he moves into a general parody or pastiche, of poetic forms, attitudes and sentiments, thence into realms of imaginativeness and fantasticality where his targets are difficult to determine and perhaps not really "targets" at all. At first it may seem that ridicule of the sententious, sentimental, petty-bourgeois outlook of the poetic "hero" is the chief intention; but soon laughter dies on the lips as we realize that neither reader nor poet himself are free from involvement in the object of attack – which is language itself as much as the attitudes it expresses. Any residual humour is very black, with disturbing feeling for the reality of violence and the dissolution of the flesh, as well as for the high-flown euphemisms used to describe them (see, for example, *Smert' geroia* [Death of a Hero], on a beetle, and *Tarakan*, where a cockroach awaits dissection by zoologists – here Oleinikov picks up and continues, in ever-more harrowing episodes, an incomplete fable by Captain Lebiadkin, the crazy poet created by Dostoevskii in *Besy* [*The Devils* or *The Possessed*]).

As with Lebiadkin, and before him Gogol', Oleinikov taps the copious wells of *poshlost'* (pretentious vulgarity), particularly in the erotic sphere, with disconcerting comprehensiveness. Love and lust appear as a series of postures, some grotesque, some alarming, some conventionally sentimental, some ludicrous. A more generalized *poshlost'* characterizes the poems that Oleinikov attributes to an invented Soviet Prutkov-equivalent, "Tekhnoruk N.", particularly the poetic cycle *V kartinoi galeree (Mysli ob iskusstve)* [In a Picture Gallery (Thoughts about Art)]. Here brief, deadpan descriptions of well-known paintings make no overtly humorous point, but leave us with a sense of the absurdity of our aesthetic responses as we try to define art in everyday terminology. But the most memorable persona in Oleinikov's work is that of the "philosophizing domestic poet", with his pervasive technological-scientific interest in everyday technical triumphs ("Praise to inventors, / who have dreamt up small and funny devices – / sugar-tongs and cigarette-holders / ... who thought to fit a spout and lid to a teapot, / who constructed the first dummy out of rubber ..."), just as he applies his mental microscope to the lowlier denizens of nature: beetles, fish, fleas, flies etc. There are serious subtexts here, and by 1937 he is able to compose a comparatively long "philosophical poem", *Puchina strastei* [Gulf of Passions], probably related to, though not directly parodying, the natural-philosophical concerns of Zabolotskii in the 1930s, where the "geometry" and meaningfulness of the natural world are explored ("As a schoolboy reads an alphabet / so I read in the forest / ... I see how into ideas / all objects are transformed").

The sharp-minded and uncompromising Oleinikov saw earlier than most intellectuals where the Soviet Union was heading in the 1930s. A Party member, he was ordered in 1933 to take part in a grain-requisitioning detachment to his native steppe country, and confided in Zabolotskii how he feigned illness to avoid this horrific task. He was arrested in 1937 and later shot. Naturally, his name was suppressed thereafter in Russia till the 1960s, when it began to resurface tentatively in memoir literature. But his impact was far from negligible. His personality, lightly fictionalized or metamorphosed, can be detected in Zabolotskii's strange poem "Lodeinikov" (a jocular distortion of his surname). He features too in many of Kharms's works – whether more or less intricately encoded or more directly: he seems to have been the prototype of the character "Sakerdon Mikhailovich" in Kharms's prose masterpiece *Starukha* (*The Old Woman*) 1939, and was the addressee of a pseudo-classical, pseudo-hostile poetic missive of 1935 ("Conductor of numbers, wicked mocker of friendship ... Your verse sometimes amuses, sometimes disturbs one's feeling ... and it hastens to sink itself in a chasm of trivial thoughts"). Even more significantly, Oleinikov – a lone figure who did not even join his close friends' group OBERIU (1928–30), and scarcely thought of his poems as "literature" – became a name to be conjured with, circulating in *samizdat* among a wide public in the later years of the Soviet Union, and a significant influence on Russian "post-modern" writing.

ROBIN MILNER-GULLAND

Iurii Karlovich Olesha 1899–1960

Prose writer, poet, and dramatist

Biography

Born in Elizavetgrad, Ukraine, 3 March 1899, into a middle-class Polish family. Family moved to Odessa, 1902. Educated at home; Rishelevskii gymnasium, Odessa, 1908–17; studied law for two years at Novorossiiskii University, Odessa. Red Army volunteer, 1919: served as a telephonist in a Black Sea naval artillery battery. Married: Ol'ga Gustavovna Suok. Propagandist, Bureau of Ukrainian Publications, Kharkov, 1921; published first story, "Angel", 1922. Moved to Moscow, 1922; staff member of the railway journal *Gudok*. In a speech to the First Congress of Soviet Writers, 1934, defended the need for independent literature. Evacuated with the Odessa Film Studio to Ashkhabad in Turkmenistan, 1941; returned to Moscow, 1946. Died 10 May 1960.

Publications

Collected Editions

Izbrannye sochineniia. Moscow, 1956.

Povesti i rasskazy. Moscow, 1965.

Envy and Other Works, translated by Andrew R. MacAndrew. New York, Anchor Books, 1967; reprinted New York, Norton, 1981.

P'esy [Plays]. Moscow, 1968.

Izbrannoe. Moscow, 1974.

Complete Short Stories and Three Fat Men, translated by Aimée Anderson. Ann Arbor, Ardis, 1979.

The Complete Plays, edited and translated by Michael Green and Jerome Katsell. Ann Arbor, Ardis, 1983.

Fiction

Zavist'. Moscow, 1927; Ann Arbor, Ardis, 1977; translated as *Envy*, by P. Ross, with Veniamin Kaverin's *The Unknown Artist*, London, Westhouse, 1947; also translated by Andrew R. MacAndrew, in *Envy and Other Works*, New York, Anchor Books, 1967; by T.S. Berczynski, in *Envy*, with V. Kataev's *Embezzlers*, Ann Arbor, Ardis, 1975; by Clarence Brown, in *The Portable Twentieth-Century*, edited by Brown, Harmondsworth, Penguin, 1985; and by J.C. Butler, Moscow, Raduga, 1988.

Tri tolstiaka. Moscow, 1928; translated as *The Three Fat Men*, by Fainna Glagoleva, Moscow, Progress, 1963; reprinted 1982; and by Aimée Anderson, in *Complete Short Stories and Three Fat Men*, 1979.

Vishnevaia kostochka [The Cherry Stone]. Moscow, 1930.

Zapiski pisatelia [Notes of a Writer]. Moscow, 1931.

Rasskazy. Selected Stories. Letchworth, Prideaux Press, 1971.

Poetry
Zubilo. Stikhi [Chisel. Verses]. Moscow, 1924.
O Lise [About Lisa] (for children). Moscow, 1948.

Plays
Zagovor chuvstv. (produced 1929); translated as "The Conspiracy of Feelings", by Michael Green and Jerome Katsell, in *The Complete Plays*, 1983.
Spisok blagodeianii. Moscow, 1931; translated as "A List of Assets", by Andrew R. MacAndrew, in *Envy and Other Works*, New York, Anchor Books, 1967; also as "A List of Blessings", by Michael Green and Jerome Katsell, in *The Complete Plays*, 1983.

Autobiographical Writing
Ni dnia bez strochki: iz zapisnykh knizhek. Moscow, 1965; translated as *No Day Without a Line*, by Judson Rosengrant, Ann Arbor, Ardis, 1979.

Critical Studies

Dostoevsky's Underground Man in Russian Literature, by Robert Louis Jackson, The Hague, Mouton, 1958; reprinted Westport, Connecticut, Greenwood Press, 1981.
The Invisible Land: A Study of the Artistic Imagination of Jurij Olesha, by Elizabeth Klosty Beaujour, New York, Columbia University Press, 1970.
"Yury Olesha's 'Zavist": An Interpretation", by D.G.B. Piper, *Slavonic and East European Review*, 48 (1970), 27–43.
Masterstvo Iuriia Oleshi, by M.O. Chudakova, Moscow, 1972.
"The Theme of Sterility in Olesha's *Envy*", by William E. Harkins, in *Major Soviet Writers: Essays in Criticism*, edited by Edward J. Brown, New York, Oxford University Press, 1973, 280–94.
"Through the Wrong End of Binoculars: An Introduction to Jurij Olesha", by Nils Åke Nilsson, in *Major Soviet Writers: Essays in Criticism*, edited by Edward J. Brown, New York and Oxford, Oxford University Press, 1973, 254–79.
Sdacha; gibel' sovetskogo intelligenta. Iurii Olesha, by Arkadii Belinkov, Madrid, Castilla, 1976; Moscow, 1997.
"My zhivem vpervye": o tvorchestve Iuriia Oleshi, by V. Pertsov, Moscow, 1976.
"Yury Olesha's Three Ages of Man: A Close Reading of 'Liompa'", by Andrew Barratt, *Modern Language Review*, 75/3 (1980), 597–614.
"The Principle of Distortion in Olesha's *Envy*", by Neil Cornwell, *Essays in Poetics*, 5/1 (1980), 15–35; reprinted as "Olesha's 'Envy'", in *The Structural Analysis of Russian Narrative Fiction*, edited by Joe Andrew, Keele, Essays in Poetics Publications, 1984, 115–36
Yurii Olesha's "Envy", by Andrew Barratt, Birmingham, Birmingham Slavonic Monographs, 1981.
"The Life/Death Dichotomy in Jiurij Oleša's Short Story 'Liompa'", by Kazimiera Ingdahl, in *Studies in 20th Century Russian Prose*, edited by Nils Åke Nilsson, Stockholm, Almqvist & Wiksell, 1982, 155–85.
The Artist and the Creative Act: A Study of Jurij Oleša's Novel Zavist, by Kazimiera Ingdahl, Stockholm, Almqvist & Wiksell, 1984.
"Olesha's 'The Cherry Stone'", by Robert Russell, in *The Structural Analysis of Russian Narrative Fiction*, edited by Joe Andrew, Keele, Essays in Poetics Publications, [1984], 82–95 (first published in *Essays in Poetics*, 1/2 (1976), 66–81).
The Poetics of Yury Olesha, by Victor Peppard, Gainesville, University of Florida Press, 1989.
"The Imagination of Failure: Fiction and Autobiography in the Work of Yury Olesha", by Elizabeth Klosty Beaujour, in *Autobiographical Statements in Twentieth-Century Russian Literature*, edited by Jane Gary Harris, Princeton, Princeton University Press, 1990, 123–32.
"Olesha's *Zavist'*: Utopia and Dystopia", by Milton Ehre, *Slavic Review*, 50 (1991), 601–11.
"At the Circus with Olesha and Siniavskii", by Neil Cornwell, *Slavonic and East European Review*, 71/1 (1993), 1–13.
A Graveyard of Themes: The Genesis of Three Key Works by Iurii Olesha, by Kazimiera Ingdahl, Stockholm, Almqvist & Wiksell, 1995.
Revolution Betrayed: Yurij Oleša's "Envy", by Janet G. Tucker, Columbus, Ohio, Slavica, 1996.

Iurii Olesha could well be described as the archetypical fellow-traveller novelist. A distinguished student and a keen footballer (his interest in the game would inspire one of the first literary accounts of a football match in the novel *Zavist'* (*Envy*)), Olesha spent two years studying law at Novorossiisk University. On leaving university, and already writing poetry, Olesha participated in Odessa's literary discussion groups and developed his talents among young writers, including Valentin Kataev, Eduard Bagritskii, and Il'ia Il'f. He emphatically rejected the monarchist sympathies of his parents by volunteering for the Red Army in 1919. After the Civil War he worked as a journalist-propagandist and moved to Moscow where, in 1922, he joined Il'f and Petrov, Kataev, Isaak Babel' and Mikhail Bulgakov on the railway journal *Gudok*, writing satirical verse. In 1927 his famous novel *Envy* was published to considerable critical acclaim amid the literary conflicts of the 1920s; this was followed by the publication of the novella *Tri tolstiaka* (*The Three Fat Men*) in 1928, four years after its original composition. In 1929 and 1930 he adapted his novels for the stage (*Envy* was retitled *Zagovor chuvstv* [*The Conspiracy of Feelings*]). From this time, until 1932, he wrote several highly regarded short stories and, in 1931, a play called *Spisok blagodeianii* (*A List of Assets*). Following this, until the posthumous publication of his autobiographical *Ni dnia bez strochki* (*No Day Without a Line*) Olesha published little of note except a few translations and film scenarios.

After Gogol', with whom he shared an immersion in Ukrainian holiday culture, Olesha may be regarded as the most thoroughly carnivalesque of Russian writers. In *The Three Fat Men* the Revolution is transformed into a joyful, carnivalesque overthrow of the gluttonous and repressive authorities by "the people" under the leadership of the circus stars Tibul and Suok. Almost every episode involving the central characters of the story is presented as a game played out on a public square before a public who interact with the proceedings. Having adopted the forms and stock characters of the fairy-story, Olesha undermined unity of narrative point of view by placing the narrator in the position of being a participant in an ever-changing carnival crowd. Like Maiakovskii's *Misteriia-Buff* (*Mystery-Bouffe*), Olesha's story polarizes the world into a pre-salvation time marked by slapstick humour, a layered grotesque and a world of harmony that is ushered in with the collapse of the old regime. Olesha thus replaces the magical transformations typical of the fairy-story with a social transformation in which revolutionary struggle is transformed into play.

By 1927, however, the writer's celebration of the new society was much more ambivalent, and the images of popular festival were to be reworked so as to cast a critical light on the bureaucratic trajectory of the developing Soviet state. Olesha's *Envy* continues to receive much critical attention both in Russia and the west, and its pivotal place in the literary history of the period has begun to be acknowledged. The NEP society is seen as a polarized arena in which officialdom threatens to stifle creative independence but where those who cling to the romantic notions of the past are the sterile products of a world that has exhausted itself. The story is structured around a series of doubles: Andrei and Ivan Babichev represent the epitomes of the old and new worlds, the former a celebrated director of a sausage-making factory who aims to develop a universal communal catering facility, the latter an unproductive buffoon whose scandalous antics and feverish imagination are directed against the utilitarian values Andrei represents. Between these two "kings", the dissolute and failed music-hall writer Kavalerov searches for a place in society that will be both functional and recognized. The new world demands complete adaptation to utilitarian values, while the old leaves the artist with only the option of nihilistic opposition and notoriety. As Kavalerov comes to learn, the writer is forced to act as the fool of one "king" or another. The perfectly adapted artist of the new age is the footballer and ideologist Volodia, Andrei's chosen heir, who hides his individuality among the team and works for its victory.

While both of Olesha's prose texts were adapted for the stage incorporating the talents of Meierkhol'd and proving very popular, and although Olesha wrote another play, *A List of Assets* in 1931, his forte was undoubtedly prose writing. After *Envy* he produced an acclaimed collection of short stories called *Vishnevaia kostochka* [The Cherry Stone] in which the split between the inner world of the artistic consciousness and the outer world of everyday concerns is shown to be widening. Nevertheless, Olesha struggled to keep his faith in the regime, and the title story of the collection presents an apparent reconciliation of historical progress and aesthetic values. However, Olesha's subsequent struggle for orthodoxy stifled his celebrated ability to produce some of the most striking imagery in contemporary prose. In a speech to the Writers' Union in 1934 he noted how recent criticism of the hero of *Envy*, Kavalerov, who looked at the world through his creator's eyes, was destroying his dignity as an artist. The posthumously published *No Day Without a Line* shows the writer struggling to regain his productivity but unable to maintain a unity of conception.

Olesha's carnivalesque, self-reflexive, and highly ambivalent approach to Soviet society was to become a model for more oppositional work in the 1930s when he himself was silent. Exploring the principles of composition and the struggle of the writer to find a place in the new society, Olesha's work powerfully dramatized the dilemma of the literary intelligentsia in a society that increasingly regarded creative independence with suspicion. If his work represents the epitome of fellow-traveller poetics, then his critical reception in Russia also reveals the attitude of officialdom towards those writers. In 1928 *Envy* was praised for its original form and skilfully dramatized theme in the pages of *Zvezda*, while the proletarian writers' organ *Na liternaturnom postu* saw the novel as the drama of an individualist who resists assimilation into the collective while unreservedly accepting the new order. The following year Olesha's "dualism and vacillation" in his attitude towards his heroes was deemed an "inadequacy". In 1934, however, the novel was unambiguously condemned for its "reactionary" stylistic tendencies and, by 1937, for "antihumanism". Fellow-travellers were, by degrees, presented with the choice of either Olesha's silence or Bulgakov's secret dissidence.

CRAIG BRANDIST

Envy

Zavist'

Novel, 1927

First published in 1927, *Envy* is now aknowledged as an outstanding example of Russian modernist fiction and one of the most controversial literary products of its age. Dealing with the crucial theme of the clash of old and new values in Soviet Russia, the novel proved immensely topical and even somewhat prophetic of the shape of things to come.

Envy tells the story of Nikolai Kavalerov, a gifted 28-year-old itinerant, and his relations with the two Babichev brothers, Andrei and Ivan. The first of the novel's two parts concentrates on Kavalerov's involvement with Andrei, a hero of the Revolution who now holds an important position in the food industry. Although Andrei has treated him kindly, offering him both temporary shelter and employment, Kavalerov resents the older man and envies him his power and success. When his growing hostility finally finds expression in an angry letter, Kavalerov is evicted from Andrei's apartment. Now swearing vengeance against his erstwhile benefactor, Kavalerov encounters Andrei's brother, Ivan, on the street.

If Andrei represents the spirit of Soviet society as it entered the first phase of construction, Ivan is the self-confessed opponent of the new age. Part 2 of the novel describes his ill-starred alliance with Kavalerov. But despite Ivan's efforts to harness the younger man's anger to his own cause, which he calls the "conspiracy of feelings", and to incite him to a murderous act against his brother, the outcome is a monumental anti-climax. In the end, Kavalerov proves incapable of this (or any) action, while Ivan himself simply withdraws from the scene, effectively conceding victory to Andrei and the rising generation, in the form of Ivan's estranged daughter Valia and her football-playing fiancé, Volodia Makarov.

If the plot of *Envy* translates quite readily into a simple allegory about the new Russia and its inevitable victory over those who represent the pre-revolutionary world, it nevertheless represents a profoundly ambiguous statement about the condition of contemporary Soviet society. This ambiguity is guaranteed, above all, by Olesha's decision to render the first part of the novel through a first-person monologue by the envious Kavalerov himself. A masterpiece of sustained invective, it consistently undermines Andrei's image, emphasizing his gluttony and ridiculing his work as a "great salami-maker". At the same time, Kavalerov presents himself as a man of immense artistic gifts who has been pushed to the margins of a society that can find no place for the sensitive dreamer.

Olesha's contemporaries were quick to seize on the political implications of this ambiguous vision. Although most were prepared to accept that, in the figures of Kavalerov and Ivan Babichev, Olesha had successfully depicted the "envy of little people, of the petty bourgeois, washed out of their lairs by the Revolution" (as the *Pravda* reviewer put it), many readers and critics were dismayed by what they felt to be a scurrilous satire against the new Russia as represented by Andrei and Volodia. And despite the efforts of such influential figures as Lunacharskii and Polonskii to argue for tolerance of the novel's ambiguous vision, *Envy* soon fell victim to the growing militance of the Stalin age and was republished only with the coming of the Khrushchev Thaw.

Envy began to attract wide scholarly interest from the late 1950s onwards. Soviet critics generally promoted a very cautious reading of the novel, both by stressing the negative features of the "bourgeois individualists" Kavalerov and Ivan Babichev and, presenting Andrei and Volodia as the positive heroes of the piece. Western scholars, by contrast, have often displayed a preference for an autobiographical approach, emphasizing the kinship between Kavalerov and his creator. Thus *Envy* is converted into a classic statement about the tragic fate of the creative artist in the crude utilitarian society promoted by the Bolsheviks and represented by the grotesque figures of the new industrialist Andrei and the young enthusiast Volodia.

Olesha's aesthetics have also been a major source of interest to *Envy* scholars, who have established the writer's links both with such European movements as impressionism and expressionism, and with the post-Symbolist aesthetics of the Russian Futurists and Formalists. Like the Formalist critic Viktor Shklovskii (see his early articles "The Resurrection of the Word" and "Art as Device"), Olesha felt that the main purpose of art was to break the spell of "automatized" language that hinders a "pure" perception of the physical world. Olesha achieves this aim by means of the many memorable metaphors and similes that have an enduring charm of their own. Unlike the images employed by such writers as Zamiatin and Babel', these are not primarily intellectual in nature; instead, they have a specifically visual quality about them. As Olesha himself explained it: "the point of the metaphor is that the artist prompts the reader to define a resemblance that already crossed the reader's mind but he had never formulated".

Envy is also an intensely literary novel. Robert Louis Jackson has explored the connection between Olesha's novel and Dostoevskii's *Zapiski iz podpol'ia* (*Notes from Underground*), arguing that Kavalerov is a latter-day version of the alienated Underground Man, and a character who, just like his celebrated prototype, serves both to expose the failings of his society while himself embodying an individualism that is ultimately pernicious. The attentive reader will also find echoes of many other works on the pages of *Envy* – from the New Testament and *King Lear* to Edmond Rostand's *Cyrano de Bergerac* and Mark Twain's *The Prince and the Pauper*, from Gogol''s "Shinel'" ("The Overcoat") and Goncharov's *Oblomov* to the science-fiction novels of H.G. Wells, Karel Čapek's *R.U.R.* and the films of Charlie Chaplin.

Several of Olesha's short stories offer an interesting gloss on the themes, characters and situations of *Envy*. Equally interesting is the play *Zagovor chuvstv* (*The Conspiracy of Feelings*), Olesha's own dramatization of the novel, written in 1928 and viewed by most scholars as a sign of the author's determination to meet the charges levelled against the novel by the more militant of the party-line critics.

ANDREW BARRATT

No Day Without a Line

Ni dnia bez strochki

Autobiography, 1965

No Day Without a Line, first published in 1965 and reprinted many times in editions exceeding 100,000 copies, belongs to the genre of the autobiography and personal memoir, although its form is unusual. Instead of a sustained narrative with a discernible beginning, middle, and end examining the author's experience and the formation of his identity, the book is a series of discrete, almost random entries ranging from vivid evocations of Olesha's pre-revolutionary childhood, to recollections of notable cultural figures, to detached, often original ruminations on literature, especially Russian literature in the 20th century. With a few exceptions, those entries have been taken from the notebooks Olesha began to keep in the 1920s, material much less thematically and chronologically motivated than it has been made to seem by the posthumous editors of the text. Perhaps it would be better to say merely that *No Day Without a Line* has strong autobiographical affinities, since it is chary of conventional biographical details and relationships, evidently preferring the texture of the author's life and times to their psychological, social, or historical meaning. Olesha's reluctance to investigate and interpret his experience systematically or to incorporate it in overarching narrative structures may frustrate some readers, at least those in search of comfortable generalization, but the others who are able to appreciate intensity of vision and exactness of expression unencumbered by *a priori* conceptual schemes will find his brand of literary pointillism not only attractive but rich in significance.

No Day Without a Line was perhaps Olesha's favourite project of the last period of his life, and, despite the demands of his other literary activities, he worked on it constantly – indeed, as the title from Pliny the Elder suggests, almost daily – eventually accumulating a very large manuscript of both revised and new material. But because he died without completing the book, without even indicating what its ultimate shape might be, the published version is necessarily something of an editorial curiosity. For *No Day Without a Line* is Olesha's only in the sense that he wrote its parts; the disposition of those parts is the work of the editors. And that work involved some element of discretion, since it was rarely possible to know just what Olesha intended. His manuscript consisted of a disordered collection of unpaged and mostly undated fragments, sometimes thematically linked and sometimes complete in themselves. Because the fragments could not simply be published in the order they had been written (there was, after all, no way of telling that), it was necessary to derive their interconnection from evidence in the texts themselves, organizing them by the chronology of the events mentioned, or according to the themes and topics discussed, or by some other principle, but in any case one implicit in the manuscript and not imposed by the editors.

This effort was begun by the author's widow, Ol'ga Suok-Olesha, and by her brother-in-law, the writer and scholar Viktor Shklovskii (and, for a time, by the critic Arkadii Belinkov), whose approach was first to sort the fragments into rough working categories, such as "controlling images" ("botanical", for example), "family", "school", "the circus", "literary figures", "critical comments", and so on. Since Olesha sometimes repeated himself, evidently seeking more precise or expressive formulations, it was necessary to select the best of those fragments dealing with the same subject, and since he sometimes left whole sections unfinished, either in the sense that they were not completely polished or had simply been abandoned, it was necessary to omit material. Fragments were also excluded as a matter of policy if they touched on living people or were otherwise sensitive. For the most part, however, the writings in the manuscript were complete and suitable for publication. After Suok-Olesha and Shklovskii had finished their labours, the textual critic Mikhail Gromov of Moscow University proceeded with the editing, quickly putting the book into its present form. His procedure was largely one of intuition; he worked not according to a deliberate plan but sought instead to arrange the book in a way that would reflect what he saw as its internal logic. Although the result is not necessarily what Olesha intended, and not without its questionable decisions, it remains a cogent alternative.

In book form, then, *No Day Without a Line* is an assemblage of texts usually no longer than a few paragraphs. The texts are artfully composed self-contained units, in which an image is developed, a memory delineated, or an idea entertained. Occasionally, the units coalesce into a chain of reflections on a common autobiographical, biographical, or critical theme (for example, Olesha's memories of the *Potemkin* mutiny in 1905, his recollections of the poet Maiakovskii, or his discussion of Lev Tolstoi). This variegated material has been divided by the editors into five chapters: "Childhood" and "Odessa", dealing primarily with Olesha's childhood and school years and the period immmediately after his graduation in 1917; "Moscow", memoirs of his arrival in Moscow in the early 1920s and his apprenticeship as a writer at the railroad journal *Gudok*, including portraits and sketches of many principal literary figures of the day and related reflections on literature and the arts; "The Golden Shelf", devoted to impressionistic, though acute criticism and reminiscence; and last, "The Wonderful Intersection", an evocation of the city of Moscow and an occasion for remarks and observations on contemporary life and literature.

Their more or less chronological arrangement notwithstanding, these chapters are essentially thematic groupings. Of course, they are sufficiently comprehensive that much in them might easily be rearranged without substantially altering the effect. Yet whatever their presentation, the fragments of *No Day Without a Line* do convey in highly arresting fashion Olesha's vital engagement with his time and place. The book must therefore be regarded as a fundamental part of the enduring legacy of a major 20th-century Russian writer.

JUDSON ROSENGRANT

Aleksandr Nikolaevich Ostrovskii 1823–1886

Dramatist

Biography

Born in Moscow, 12 April 1823. Attended the First Moscow gymnasium, 1835–40; studied law at Moscow University, 1840–43: did not graduate. Clerk in commercial court, Moscow, 1843–51. First play *Bankrot* [The Bankrupt] published, 1847; revised version of the play was not passed by the censor and Ostrovskii was placed under surveillance: as a result lost his civil service post. Married: 1) Agaf'ia Ivanovna (surname unknown) in 1849 (died 1865); 2) the actress Mariia Vasil'eva in 1869. Editor of *Moskvitianin*, 1850–51: several of his early plays published in this journal. Dependent on income from writing plays and from editorial work. *Ne v svoi sani ne sadis'!* [Keep to Your Own Sledge!], produced 1853; many of his plays published in *Sovremennik*, 1856–66, and *Otechestvennye zapiski*, 1868–84. Commissioned by the Marine ministry to travel to the source of the Volga and record his observations, 1856–57. Travelled in western Europe, 1862. Co-founder of the Moscow Arts Circle, 1865; founder and director of the Association of Russian Playwrights and Composers, 1870, and worked for the Imperial Commission on the Theatre. Finally granted state pension by Alexander III, 1884; director of the Moscow Imperial theatres, 1886. Recipient: Uvarov Prize, 1860 and 1863. Died in Shchelykov [now Ostrovskoe Raion], Kostroma region, 14 June 1886.

Publications

Collected Editions

Sobranie sochinenii, 10 vols. Moscow, 1874–84.

Polnoe sobranie sochinenii. Moscow, 1904–05.

Plays (includes *It's a Family Affair – We'll Settle It Ourselves*; *Poverty is No Crime*; *The Storm*; *Even the Wise Can Err*; *More Sinned Against than Sinning*), translated by G.R. Noyes. New York, Scribner, 1917.

"Easy Money" and Two Other Plays (includes *Even a Wise Man Stumbles*, *Wolves and Sheep*), translated by David

Magarshack. London, Allen and Unwin, 1944; Westport, Connecticut, Greenwood Press, 1970.
Polnoe sobranie sochinenii, 16 vols. Moscow, 1949–53.
Stikhotvornye dramy (verse plays). 2nd edition, Moscow, 1961.
Five Plays (includes *The Scoundrel*; *It's a Family Affair – We'll Settle It Ourselves*; *The Forest*; *The Poor Bride*; *The Storm*), translated by Eugene K. Bristow. New York, Pegasus, 1969.
Polnoe sobranie sochinenii, 12 vols. Moscow, 1973–80.
Plays (includes *Poverty is No Crime*; *The Storm*; *Even the Wise Can Err*; *More Sinned Against than Sinning*), edited by Margaret Wettlin. Moscow, Progress, 1974.
Without a Dowry & Other Plays, translated by Norman Henley. Dana Point, California, Ardis, 1995.
Sobranie sochinenii, 3 vols. Moscow, 1996.

Plays (selected)
Bankrot [The Bankrupt]. 1847; revised version, as *Svoi liudi-sochtemsia!* (produced 1860), 1850; translated as *It's a Family Affair – We'll Settle It Ourselves*, by G.R. Noyes, in *Plays*, 1917; and by Eugene K. Bristow in *Five Plays*, 1969.
Semeinaia kartina (produced 1855). 1847; translated as "A Domestic Picture", in *A Treasury of Classic Russian Literature*, edited by John Cournos, 1961.
Ne v svoi sani ne sadis'! [Keep to Your Own Sledge!] (produced 1853). 1853.
Bednaia nevesta (produced 1853). 1854; translated as "The Poor Bride", in *Masterpieces of the Russian Drama 1*, edited by G.R. Noyes, New York, Appleton, 1933; also by Eugene K. Bristow, in *Five Plays*, 1969.
Bednost' ne porok (produced 1854). 1854; translated as "Poverty's No Vice", by G.R. Noyes, in *Plays*, 1917; also as "Poverty is No Crime", by Margaret Wettlin, in *Plays*, 1974.
V chuzhom piru pokhmel'e [Hangover from Someone Else's Party] (produced 1863). 1857.
Dokhodnoe mesto [A Profitable Position] (produced 1863). 1857.
Vospitannitsa (produced 1859). 1860; translated as "A Protegée of the Mistress", by G.R. Noyes, in *Plays*, 1917.
Groza (produced 1859). 1860; edited by A.V. Knowles, Oxford, Blackwell, 1988; translated as *The Thunderstorm*, 1927; and in *World Drama 2*, edited by G.R. Noyes and B.H. Clarke, 1956; also as *The Storm*, by David Magarshack, 1960; reprinted Ann Arbor, Ardis, 1988; also as "Thunder", by Joshua Cooper, in *Four Russian Plays*, Harmondsworth, Penguin, 1972.
Grekh da beda na kogo ne zhivet (produced 1863). 1863; translated as "Sin and Sorrow Are Common To All", by G.R. Noyes, in *Plays*, 1917.
Voevoda: Son na Volge [Dream on the Volga] (produced 1865). 1865; revised version (produced 1886), 1890.
Na vsiakogo dovol'no prostoty (produced 1868). 1868; translated as "Enough Stupidity in Every Wise Man", in *Moscow Art Theatre Series of Russian Plays 2*, edited by O.M. Sayler, 1923; also as "Even a Wise Man Stumbles", by David Magarshack, in *"Easy Money" and Two Other Plays*, 1944; as "The Scoundrel", by Eugene K. Bristow, in *Five Plays*, 1969; as "Even the Wise Can Err", by Margaret Wettlin, in *Plays*, 1974; and as *Diary of a Scoundrel, or, Too Clever by Half*, by Rodney Ackland, New York and London, Applause Theatre Book, 1988.
Beshenye den'gi (produced 1870). 1870; translated as "Fairy Gold", *Poet Lore*, 40 (1929); also as "Easy Money", by David Magarshack, in *"Easy Money" and Two Other Plays*, 1944.
Les (produced 1871). 1871; translated as *The Forest: Comedy in Five Acts*, by Clara Vostrovsky and G.R. Noyes, London, Samuel French, 1926; and by Eugene K. Bristow, in *Five Plays*, 1969; subsequent translations under same title.
Snegurochka [The Snow Maiden] (produced 1873). 1873.
Volki i ovtsy (produced 1875). 1875; translated as "Wolves and Sheep", in *Poet Lore*, 37 (1926); also by David Magarshack, in *"Easy Money" and Two Other Plays*, 1944.
Bespridannitsa (produced 1878). 1879; translated as "Without a Dowry", by Norman Henley, in *Without a Dowry and Other Plays*, 1995.
Talanty i poklonniki (produced 1881). 1882; translated as *Artistes and Admirers*, by Elisabeth Hanson, Manchester, Manchester University Press, and New York, Barnes and Noble, 1970.
Bez viny vinovatye (produced 1884). 1884; translated as "More Sinned Against than Sinning", by Margaret Wettlin, in *Plays*, 1974.

Diary
Vsia zhizn' – teatru, edited by N.S. Grodskaia, Moscow, 1989.

Critical Studies

"Luch sveta v temnom tsarstve", by N.A. Dobroliubov, 1860; in his *Izbrannoe*, Moscow, 1970, 226–302.
Ostrovsky et son théâtre des moeurs russes, by J. Patouillet, Paris, 1912.
A.N. Ostrovskii i russkaia dramaturgiia ego vremeni, by L.M. Lotman, Leningrad, 1961.
Masterstvo Ostrovskogo, by E. Kholodov, Moscow, 1963.
Artists and Admirers, by L. Hanson, Manchester, Manchester University Press, 1970.
Literaturnoe nasledstvo, vol. 88, Moscow, 1974.
Iskusstvo dramaturgii A.N. Ostrovskogo, by A.I. Reviakin, 2nd edition, Moscow, 1974.
A.N. Ostrovskii, by V.Ia. Lakshin, Moscow, 1976.
"Problems of Style in the Plays of Ostrovsky", by Irene Zohrab, *Melbourne Slavonic Studies*, 12 (1977), 35–46.
"Thematic Analysis of Ostrovsky's *Poverty is No Crime*", by André van Holk, *Essays in Poetics*, 3/2 (1978), 41–76.
Alexander Ostrovsky, Marjorie L. Hoover, Boston, Twayne, 1981.
Ostrovskii, by A. Lakshin, Moscow, 1982.
"Problems of Translation. The Works of A.N. Ostrovsky in English", by Irene Zohrab, *Melbourne Slavic Studies*, 16 (1982), 43–88.
Frazeologiia v tvorcheskoi laboratorii A.N. Ostrovskogo, by A.G. Lomov, Tashkent, 1987.
"A.N. Ostrovsky's *The Thunderstorm*: The Dramatization of Conceptual Ambivalence", by R.A. Peace, *Modern Language Review*, 84/1 (1989), 99–110.
Drama A.N. Ostrovskogo "Groza" v russkoi kritike, edited by I.N. Sukikh, Leningrad, 1990.

Bibliography
Bibliografiia literatury ob Aleksandre Nikolaevichem Ostrovskom 1847–1917, by K. Muratova, Leningrad, 1974.

It is hardly an exaggeration to suggest that Aleksandr Ostrovskii was the founder of Russian national drama. He was also the instigator of many reforms in the organization and management of Russia's theatres. While other, and arguably better, dramatists preceded him, their output was comparatively small and their subject-matter diverse. Ostrovskii, however, left an extensive repertory dealing largely with Russian themes and national problems and preoccupations. Many of them retain their interest and popularity and are still performed regularly. This might be explained by their "Russianness", by his competence as a dramatist, and by the many excellent roles they provide for actors and actresses. From the time of the first staging of *Ne v svoi sani ne sadis'!* [Keep to Your Own Sledge!] in 1853, hardly a year passed without his writing a new play. It was in these that he established a tradition of social realism on the Russian stage.

Ostrovskii was born and brought up in Moscow, on the south side of the river. It was an area inhabited by merchants, minor civil servants and (mainly unqualified) lawyers. In many respects their way of life resembled more the pre-Petrine era than the 19th century. Although many of them liked to think they were civilized, they behaved more like the petty tyrants they so professed to despise; they terrorized their families and employees alike. The object of the good life was to make money, whether legally or not, and they would spend it on ostentatious living, presenting to the outside world an air of importance and even of grandeur. Many of them possessed a remarkable strength of character and they had no respect for the opinions or feeling of others. Consequently this was the world Ostrovskii knew best; never before had it been represented on the Russian stage and he felt that it would provide rich material. His success can be seen from the early *Svoi liudi-sochtemsia!* (*It's a Family Affair – We'll Settle It Ourselves*), which the influential critic Apollon Grigor'ev praised highly for its effective portrayal of business people and especially for its convincing description of an old merchant who claims bankruptcy for personal financial gain and is then relieved of his ill-gotten gains by his son-in-law and left to the debtor's prison. The play contains no positive characters and presents an entirely negative view of the world. Ostrovskii stresses that such people are only too common and audiences must accept that they behave in such a way; his was a realistic portrayal. Nor, in the first part of his career, was he moralistic in his judgements; he felt no compunction to make good triumph over evil. Only very rarely did he allow himself to be swayed by external considerations, tradition, the contemporary moral climate, or even the censor. He saw his duty to put certain characters on the stage, faithfully to represent their personalities and concerns, and make them speak as they would in life. The language he uses is vivid, colloquial, and down-to-earth. This might go some way towards explaining why his plays are rarely, let alone successfully, produced outside Russia.

Ostrovskii's reputation grew throughout the 1850s, especially with *Bednaia nevesta* (*The Poor Bride*), which depicts the unhappy lives of women in Russian society whose only hope is to find a rich husband, and *Dokhodnoe mesto* [A Profitable Position], with its poor civil servant and his wife whose scruples condemn them to poverty and moral collapse, while all around them prosper from bribery and corruption. His position as Russia's leading playwright was finally established by the publication of *Groza* (*The Storm*) in 1860. While his other plays of the 1850s depict petty government clerks subjugated by their dishonest employers or domineering wives, spendthrifts and talentless, mercenary egoists, or the victims of poverty and serfdom, the reception of *The Storm* was coloured by an article reviewing the first decade of Ostrovskii's career by the radical critic Dobroliubov, entitled "Temnoe tsarstvo" [The Kingdom of Darkness]. He argued that the most characteristic setting for an Ostrovskii play was usually the business world of Moscow, with its concentration on the acquisition of wealth, its lack of education and culture, and the widespread abuse of authority. To characterize those who personified the domestic and commercial despotism of this "dark kingdom" he used the word *samodur* (petty tyrant) that Ostrovskii himself had coined in *V chuzhom piru pokhmel'e* [Hangover from Someone Else's Party]. The *samodur*'s home is without happiness; he is violent, authoritarian, and heartless. All must bow to his will or accept the consequences. Very rarely does he face retribution or let rational argument or finer feelings get in his way. According to Dobroliubov, Ostrovskii had done his country great service by depicting on the stage these old-fashioned, conservative representatives of the aspiring middle-class, bred on superstition, ignorance, and cruelty. Nor, one might add, is the *samodur* necessarily male. Two of the most frightening examples are indeed women: the cruel, aristocratic guardian in *Vospitannitsa* (*A Protegée of the Mistress*) and of course the most monstrous of them all, Kabanova in *The Storm*. The dramatic possibilities of such a character are also amply displayed in Janáček's opera *Katia Kabanova*, based on the play.

After the 1861 Emancipation of the Serfs Ostrovskii attempted to reflect the changing social conditions and his plays take on a rather more moralistic tone. For example, *Na vsiakogo dovol'no prostoty* (*Even the Wise Can Err*) finally brings retribution to a young man who has risen in society by flattering and knowing "the right people"; *Beshenye den'gi* (*Easy Money*) contrasts an impoverished nobleman with the self-made entrepreneur; and others depict former landowners, now deprived of their cheap serf workforce, trying to make their way in the new industries and occupations. The best of these are *Volki i ovtsy* (*Wolves and Sheep*), *Bespridannitsa* (*Without a Dowry*) and *Bez viny vinovatye* (*More Sinned Against than Sinning*). In *Les* (*The Forest*) Ostrovskii examines the effect of a domineering, selfish noblewoman on the lives of a young couple and her eventual downfall. The days of the *samodur* are numbered. He also tried his hand at historical dramas, *Voevoda: Son na Volge* [Dream on the Volga] being the most convincing and best constructed, and at plays depicting actors and their professional difficulties, whose conditions he tried so much to improve.

A.V. KNOWLES

The Storm

Groza

Play, 1859

The Storm is probably Ostrovskii's most powerful play, yet it is possibly better known in the west in the operatic version by Leos Janáček, *Katia Kabanova*. This may be regretted, since the play, first performed at the Malyi Theatre, Moscow, on 16 November 1859, is Russian drama at its most intense.

The play begins ordinarily enough, with a series of rather unremarkable characters chatting idly; but gradually the intensity increases as we understand that Katia (Katerina), who clearly is not so ordinary, is married to Tikhon, but in love with Boris. Katia is guilt-ridden and fearful, and does not know that Varvara is aware of her secret. In the Kabanov's claustrophobic house, ruled by Katia's tyrannical mother-in-law, she cannot trust herself, and wants to accompany Tikhon on a business trip. When he rejects her and leaves, Varvara gives her the key that will enable her to escape to Boris. She does so, and enjoys forbidden moments with him, while Varvara herself is being courted by Kudriash. Tikhon returns home earlier than expected, and Katia is confused and despairing. As the thunderstorm draws closer, Varvara elopes with Kudriash, and Boris is packed off to the Far East. Katia pleads to go with him, but he rejects her. Distraught, she confesses her "sin" to her husband and, finding no alternative to suicide, throws herself into the Volga, leaving Tikhon to face a grim future under his mother's thumb.

In this play, Ostrovskii forges a naturalistic style perhaps more extreme than any other play written at that time. The famous actor Shchepkin is reported to have walked out of the dress rehearsal because he could smell the sheepskin coats, and many wondered how Ostrovskii had achieved such truth to life. But this naturalism is somewhat deceptive. The diction, for instance, has a timbre that is like reality, but heightened, and the names of the characters – Dikoi, evoking both savagery and the preposterous, Kabanov, a wild boar, Tikhon, the quiet man, and so on – indicate that all is not quite governed by the chance of life.

The play's construction is deceptively simple, swelling to a tragic climax, and leaving the impotent Tikhon's whining despair hanging at the end. The central confrontation is magnified and refracted through the amusing or despicable minor characters who Ostrovskii creates to provide Katia's tragedy with a context. The appearance of the mad lady, for instance, clearly intensifies Katia's guilt. And the formal balancing of Katia's plea to Tikhon to take her with him in Act 2 with her similar plea to Boris in Act 5 indicates the playwright's control of his material.

Set on the banks of the Volga, the play depicts a traditionally oppressive society where hatred, love, and fear bubble menacingly beneath the outwardly calm surface of life, and may remind playgoers of Lorca's Spain. The struggle focuses on a series of classic confrontations – conformity to tradition is opposed by youth, growth and new ideas; reason is against spontaneity; authority against freedom; duty against love. Ostrovskii gives concreteness to his opposites, for instance setting the stuffy interior of the Kabanovs' dwelling against the expansiveness of the Volga valley. But most obviously the antagonism is located in the characters, with Marfa Kabanova, the mother-in-law, dominating her house, and controlling the lives of her son and his wife, contrasted with Katerina herself, the dreamy, "difficult", hopeful girl, religious yet focused on future happiness in this world. Katia desires to rise above her mother-in-law's narrow-mindedness, but does not know how. She imagines she could flee: "I feel so stifled at home ... I want to run, run, run! And then the thought occurs to me that if I were free to do as I liked, I'd go sailing on the Volga, singing songs ... ". Ironically, of course, when she does flee to the Volga at the end of the play, it is to drown herself.

The character of Katia Kabanova is at base realistic in Zola's sense. She has been brought up in an oppressive religion, which conditions all her perceptions. It has made her naive and consequently open to experience, yet it also brings the feeling of overwhelming guilt that kills her. She cannot cope intellectually with what is happening to her, and hence her despair. Simultaneously, her religion also seems to explain her almost other-worldly qualities. She clashes with the environment in which she lives, and her near-mystical defiance seems to provoke the thunder. Certainly her relationship with the forces of nature is provocative: highly imaginative, unable to balance the complexities of her life, she is a poetic soul, trying to repel repressive reality, and she symbolizes on one level womankind's constant struggle for personal freedom and the right to self-expression.

The earthbound characters who make her life a misery, especially her mother-in-law and her husband, but also Boris's uncle, Savel Dikoi, and others, stand in stark contrast to the richly sympathetic Katia. The mother-in-law is bound to a code of conduct which, paradoxically, is as stultifying to herself as it is to others. She rules by fear and bullies those around her mercilessly. Yet committing suicide or whining about her is no solution to the problem such a tyrant poses. Dikoi is a similar sort of despot over Boris, his nephew. Vindictive and selfish, he is nevertheless terrified of the threat Katia and Boris pose to him, and ruling by fear, he is himself fearful – of change and of the processes of natural justice. Boris, the only educated character in the play, objects to being victimized by Dikoi, but finds no escape, while Tikhon is similarly weak-willed and submissive. Varvara, on the other hand, is a foil to Katia. Not highly educated, she nevertheless manages to cope with the repressions of society through a mixture of low cunning and high spirits, and her attempts to lure Katia into a similar dash for freedom are well meaning if obviously doomed.

Katia's dilemma may be seen as Russia's own in the 19th century. The dreariness of stultifying family life matches the backward provincialism of the locality, and is contrasted with the River Volga as a symbol of hope and freedom. But Katia can only find freedom in death. The pessimism of the play is pervasive. At the end, Katia is dead, Tikhon subdued, and Boris packed off to China. Only the harsh Dikoi and the cruel Marfa Kabanova remain untouched in Kalinov.

ROBERT LEACH

The Forest

Les

Play, 1871

Ostrovskii began *The Forest* probably in August of 1870 and completed it in December. The premiere was at the Imperial Aleksandrinskii Theatre in St Petersburg on 1 November 1871. Shortly after, it opened in the theatre that has been called "Ostrovskii's House," the Malyi of Moscow. The play was published in the same year. It was at first coolly received. Ostrovskii had departed from his favourite milieu, the merchant class; critics complained of a paucity of action – the appeal of his plays is their verbal energy and richness of characters. Some also deplored the eccentricity of the characters, though this was nothing new either for Ostrovskii or Russian comedy. Nevertheless, the play soon became a standard of the Russian repertoire and has remained so to the present day.

In the west Ostrovskii has not won the reputation he deserves. Difficulty of translation may be the reason – the extraordinary vigour and colour of his language are local, as is his subject-matter. He is the most rooted in place and custom of Russian playwrights. This Russian Dickens, uninhibitedly given to melodramatic heightening and comic extravagance, is without the soul-searching we have come to expect from Russian writers. He has his eye firmly fixed on the implications of class and wealth. The unquenchable vitality of ordinary people impresses him. Using traditional forms, he injects them, after the realist manner, with the illusion of "real life". Intelligently observant, he is also intensely humane. Chekhov, though a daring innovator, admired him enormously.

The Forest is one of the masterpieces of comic theatre, Russian or otherwise. In the 1870s Ostrovskii widened his interest from the semi-feudal Russian merchant class to developing Russian society – capitalist entrepreneurs, men on the make, women struggling for independence, the declining gentry. The theatre itself becomes a subject, as he seeks in art alternative values to those of a hopelessly degraded society.

The Forest confronts ordinary society and the bohemian culture of actors. The widow Gurmyzhskaia, who has been called a female Tartuffe, is the landowner of the play. Much of her estate is forest land, which she is selling off. The "forest" is a metaphor for Old Russia, isolated and brutish. The serfs have been emancipated but serfdom's oppressive habits remain. Gurmyzhskaia mouths the platitudes of conventional morality while seducing her young protégé, the dimwitted Aleksei Bulanov. Profligate in rewarding her own lovers, she is too stingy to furnish a dowry for her impoverished ward, Aksinia, who crosses class lines by falling in love with the son of a foxy merchant, Vosmibratov. The syrupy Milonov and boorish Bodaev round out the portrait of the gentry; the cynical Karp and the servile Ulita, that of the servants.

The critic Nikolai Dobroliubov was perhaps the first to remark that Ostrovskii's realm (he dubbed it a "dark kingdom") is a battleground of the rich and the poor, the young and the old, parents and children. The old order has lost its confidence, the new has not yet taken shape. Freedom (*volia*) is a central word in Ostrovskii's plays. His young people proudly assert it, especially his women. Aksinia is no shrinking violet: "I am my own woman", she declares, and when nothing else seems to be working she threatens to drown herself in a lake like Katerina of *The Storm*, an act as much of desperate rebellion as of hopelessness.

An actor saves the day. Two down-and-out performers, one a tragedian, the other a comedian (Neschastlivets and Schastlivets or "Mr Unhappy" and "Mr Happy"), drop in to sponge on Gurmyzhskaia until things pick up (Neschastlivets is a distant relation). In a hilarious scene of bluff melodrama Neschastlivets compels Gurmyzhskaia to come up with 1000 roubles for Aksinia's dowry (Gurmyzhskaia had owed him the money, so it is really his sacrifice). The lovers unite, the two actors hit the road.

Neschastlivets is one of the great comic creations of the Russian stage. He plays his role in life as well as art, and one of the many charms of *The Forest* is the balletic verbal dance (after Molière and Gogol') between Neschastlivets and Schastlivets, as one takes an elevated or tragic view of life, and the other provides comedy's pragmatic antidote: "Oh, these tragedians! Loads of nobility and not a drop of common sense." To hide the fact that they are mere actors they disguise themselves as master (*barin*) and lackey, which gives Neschastlivets an opportunity to exhibit the aristocratic virtues of honour, loyalty, and chivalry. These shine through the humorous hyperbole.

The community Neschastlivets represents, in opposition to the hypocritical pretensions of the greedy Gurmyzhskaias and the mushy sentimentality of the Milonovs, is based neither on birth nor on class. It is instead bound together by art. The tragic actor offers Aksinia escape into the theatre: "Here there is no response to your sobs and moans, but there for your one tear a thousand eyes will weep." She refuses, choosing love, but for Neschastlivets (and Ostrovskii) the creative life and the life of love are both expressions of the passionate nature of men and women. Passion is life's answer to petty calculation: "Clowns? No, we are artists, noble artists, and you are the clowns. If we love, we love; if we quarrel, then we quarrel; if we help each other, then it's with our last kopeck." When Neschastlivets launches into a characteristic tirade at the end of the play, denouncing the society of the forest as a "brood of crocodiles", he is still moving in the realm of art; challenged for his subversive language, he informs the local tyrants that he is quoting Schiller.

MILTON EHRE

Without a Dowry

Bespridannitsa

Play, 1878

Ostrovskii began work on *Without a Dowry* in November 1874 and completed it in October 1878. The first performance took place in Moscow at the Malyi Theatre on 10 November 1878 and in St Petersburg at the Alexandrinskii Theatre on 22 November 1878. The play was first published in *Otechestvennye zapiski* in January 1879 and included in Ostrovskii's *Polnoe sobranie sochinenii*, vol. 10, St Petersburg, 1884.

Of Ostrovskii's 48 original plays *Without a Dowry* is the 40th and one of only four dramas with a violent and tragic ending, though few of its characters possess any of the heroic attributes of tragedy. "With this play begins a new type of my works", Ostrovskii wrote. It is representative of the third and last period of his creative activity from 1875 to 1886. Certain aspects of its form and content anticipate the plays of Ibsen and Chekhov, especially *Et dukkehjem* (*A Doll's House*) 1879, *Chaika* (*The Seagull*) 1896, and *Tri sestry* (*Three Sisters*) 1901.

On the surface or social level the drama depicts the position of women, namely that of the heroine Larisa, the dowerless girl of the title, in the changing and increasingly acquisitional Russian society of the late 1870s. It features an almost "thriller"-type plot, revolving around the "ownership" of the beautiful and talented Larisa, unnaturally objectified by society, and the four men who seek to possess her.

On the underlying level it is an exploration of the human condition, wherein the poetic and self-aware Larisa, preoccupied with the problem of identity of self, feels a deep existential anguish. Nothing can deliver her from the pain of living, which is expressed in her desire to escape beyond her hollow socio-domestic environment into the wide expanses of the River Volga and its tranquil, leafy landscape on the other shore.

The drama illustrates the extent to which Ostrovskii expanded the framework of the realistic theatre and transcended the limitations of its conventions, achieving a consistent "poetry of the theatre" within its confines. While arousing a high level of suspense and anticipation, the underlying dramatic form of the play expresses the tragic rhythm of the action and constitutes the "soul of tragedy": the strivings of the heroine Larisa to express her deep yearnings for the ideal and her inability to reconcile it with reality. This is played out against a setting reflecting the timeless beauty of nature, as well as sham middle-class interiors, both replete with symbolic overtones. The action takes place in a large provincial town, Briakhimov, situated on the high bank of the River Volga. It begins one sleepy afternoon in the town's boulevard and ends catastrophically that night in the same setting. Thus the first and last act are set in public, outside a coffee-house with a look-out enclosed by an iron railing overlooking the Volga. The river stretches out below into the distance, with the dim outlines of forests and villages visible on the horizon.

The socio-economic forces that determine the mode of life of this community are established in the exposition with the appearance of two representatives of the new sophisticated moneyed class: Knurov, a millionaire industrialist, and young Vozhevatov, a merchant-agent for a large import-export company. In the course of their conversation the relationships between all the main characters in the drama are revealed, as well as their own attitudes and competition for Larisa, the dowerless girl.

The audience learns that Larisa has agreed to marry Karandyshev, a minor civil servant with pathetic aspirations for recognition. Larisa was abandoned a year earlier by the dashing "barin" Paratov, a member of the gentry and now a shipowner, who is returning to sell his ship "Lastochka" to Vozhevatov. Karandyshev, being morbidly touchy and poor, is not, according to Knurov, a suitable match for Larisa because she has been created for a life of brilliance and splendour: "An expensive diamond requires an expensive setting" – "And a good jeweller" adds Vozhevatov. Larisa finds her life of pretense and humiliation harsh and distressing. She wants Karandyshev to take her away into the countryside, into what she envisages as idyllic domesticity akin to "Paradise". Thus all the main themes are established and all the personages introduced and characterized, including "Lord" or "Sir" Robinson, who is the actor Schastlivtsev and whose function is not only to provide comic relief, but also to mirror the treatment of Larisa. In Act 2, memorable for Larisa's singing and set in her mother's house, the "complication" sets in, as Karandyshev invites everyone to his dinner-party that evening. The tempo rises dramatically in Act 3 as Karandyshev is ridiculed and duped by his guests, who leave for an evening party on the Volga. Larisa, with abandon, agrees to accompany Paratov, for she is still in love with him. Karandyshev is lacerated with pain and humiliation and rushes out after them with a gun, while swearing vengeance. In Act 4 Larisa recognizes that she has misinterpreted Paratov's true intentions; he is, after all, to forfeit his "freedom" and marry a rich bride. As Knurov and Vozhevatov toss a coin to see who will approach Larisa, the winner, Knurov, offers to take her to Paris with him as his mistress. She wishes to die, but is provoked by Karandyshev into agreeing that she is an "object" and therefore deserves the best owner. Karandyshev fires at her and she dies, thanking him and repeating that no one is to blame, as a gypsy chorus is heard singing in the background.

The Christian belief that we must love those who suffer, because in them we must find Christ, is a sentiment that is employed by Ostrovskii in a secular setting, thus endowing the ending with almost sacrilegious overtones. The larger meanings inferred from the text are embedded in its web of literary and theatrical devices, such as allusions, image clusters, motifs, foreshadowing, sound effects, mirroring, and analogical patterning. The conflicts often depicted in Ostrovskii's "plays of life", including this one, reflect the fundamental polarity of Russian culture as expressed in the dual character of its structure.

Without a Dowry was not a success when it first appeared, but was much admired around the turn of the century, being revived in 1896 with Vera Komissarzhevskaia playing the part of Larisa. It remained in her repertoire until 1905.

IRENE ZOHRAB

Nikolai Alekseevich Ostrovskii 1904–1936

Prose writer

Biography

Born in Viliia, Ukraine, 29 September 1904, son of a labourer. Joined the Komsomol, 1919, fought with the Red Army against Poles, 1920; seriously wounded. Electrician, 1921–22; became Komsomol official, 1923. Member of the Communist Party, 1924. Debilitated by illness and wounds, bed-ridden from 1927, and afflicted by progressive blindness. Wrote autobiographical novel *Kak zakalialas' stal'* (*How the Steel Was Tempered*) in order to further the Bolshevik cause, 1928. Hugely popular, and highly acclaimed by communist ideologues. Died in Moscow, 22 December 1936, and subsequently claimed by Soviet ideologues as a martyr to the cause.

Publications

Collected Editions

Sobranie sochinenii, 3 vols. Moscow, 1955–56.
Sobranie sochinenii, 3 vols. Moscow, 1967–68.
Sobranie sochinenii, 3 vols. Moscow, 1974.
Sobranie sochinenii, 3 vols. Moscow, 1989.

Fiction

"Kak zakalialas' stal'", *Molodaia gvardiia*, 4–9 (1932); Part II, *Molodaia gvardiia*, 1–5 (1934); Moscow, 1934; revised edition 1935; translated as *The Making of a Hero*, by Alec Brown, New York, International Publishers, 1937; also as *How the Steel Was Tempered*, by R. Prokofieva, Moscow, Foreign Languages Publishing House, 1952.

"Rozhdennye burei", *Molodaia gvardiia*, 7–10 (1935), 5–6 (1936); translated as *Born of the Storm*, by Louise Luke Hiler, New York, Critics Group Press, 1939; reprinted Westport, Connecticut, Hyperion Press, 1975.

Critical Studies

Nikolai Ostrovskii, by N. Vengrov, Moscow, 1952.
Nikolai Ostrovskii: Kritiko-biograficheskii ocherk, by S. Tregub, Moscow, 1954.
Zhizn' i tvorchestvo Nikolaia Ostrovskogo, by S. Tregub, 2nd edition, Moscow, 1975.
The Positive Hero in Russian Literature, by Rufus Mathewson, 2nd edition, Stanford, Stanford University Press, 1975, 247–53.
Nikolai Ostrovskii, by R. Ostrovskaia, Moscow, 1984.
The Soviet Novel: History as Ritual, by Katerina Clark, 2nd edition, Chicago, University of Chicago Press, 1985.
"Kak zakalialas' stal'" Nikolaia Ostrovskogo, by Lev Anninskii, 3rd corrected edition, Moscow, 1988.
"Education and Conversion: The Road to the New Man in the Totalitarian *Bildungsroman*", by Hans Günther, in *The Culture of the Stalin Period*, edited by Hans Günther, London, Macmillan, 1990, 193–209.
The Twentieth-Century Russian Novel, by David Gillespie, Oxford, Berg, 1996, 62–80.

Nikolai Ostrovskii is known primarily for his novel *Kak zakalialas' stal'* (*How the Steel Was Tempered*), regarded as a classic of socialist realism and an essential part of the Soviet secondary-school literature syllabus until the mid-1980s. Its central character, Pavel Korchagin, is the ideal "positive hero", and seen as a figure of emulation for subsequent generations of Soviet schoolchildren.

The novel was composed in 1928, partly written by Ostrovskii himself and partly dictated by him as he suffered from increasing paralysis. The first version was lost in the post on its way to a publisher, and Ostrovskii rewrote it. It was at first rejected by the journal *Molodaia gvardiia*, then accepted after a second review. Its original publication, and the book edition, both in 1932, went largely unnoticed. Part 2 was published in 1934, and attention was focused on it only after 1935, after a favourable review in the Communist Party newspaper *Pravda*. From that moment on, Ostrovskii became famous throughout the country.

How the Steel Was Tempered concerns the development of Pavel Korchagin from a strong-willed 12-year-old, both victim of and witness to the injustices of tsarist society. Through his exposure to the Bolshevik ideas of Zhukhrai, a radical sailor on the run from the authorities, and whom Pavel helps escape when captured, Pavel becomes committed to the Bolshevik cause. Having endured various injuries and diseases, Pavel is transformed into an embodiment of sheer political will. Pavel consciously tries to subdue his human weaknesses, such as smoking and swearing, in order to hone the "steel" of his rational personality. Thus the "steel" of the title. Ostrovskii shows Pavel playing the accordion; this is not a frivolous entertainment, but, moreover, an indicator that Pavel has an intuitive feeling for folk-music, and thus has strong links with the people. However, like the early Christian saints in Russian and western hagiography, Pavel's faith and commitment to the cause increases the more physical torments he endures. Even suffering blindness and paralysis, Pavel wishes to return to the ranks by writing about his life. In Katerina Clark's formulation, Pavel Korchagin passes through several stages of development, progressing from innocent and elemental "spontaneity" to a state of hardened political "consciousness".

Pavel's love of the Party prevents him from indulging in any emotional relationships. His early love is Tonia, a middle-class girl from whom he later distances himself because of his love for the Party and the cause of the working class. Even when he eventually does get married, to Taia, his decision is a purely rational one, not based on any emotional attachment. Rather, he wishes to teach her about the cause, and he wants her to become his amanuensis.

The novel contains the standard motifs and much of the symbolism of other Stalinist novels of socialist realism. Pavel and his young comrades fight not only against human enemies, but struggle with and finally conquer nature in laying down a railway track in the wilderness as winter approaches. Shepetovka, Pavel's home town, where much of the action of the Civil War takes place in Part 1 of the novel, serves as a microcosm of the greater struggle taking place in the country. First, Shepetovka is a railway junction, and therefore inhabited by a large contingent of the industrial proletariat. Second, it is close to the Ukraine-Polish border, and is taken and occupied, variously, by Germans, Red Guards, White forces, Ukrainian nationalists, Poles and, finally, the smiling and victorious Red Army. Shepetovka serves therefore not only as a metonymic symbol for the whole of Ukraine, but also as an indicator of the magnitude of the struggle throughout what was to become the USSR.

Although the novel's focus is on Pavel as a "typical", in socialist realist terminology, representative of his generation, other ideologically charged and committed characters include Valia and Serezha Bruzzhak, who both die fighting for the cause, and Ivan Zharkii, who in some ways inherits Pavel's mantle. Older Bolsheviks, such as Zhukhrai and Tokarev, look fondly on the younger generation as carrying on the fight. The trouble-free link of one generation with another is therefore ensured.

The novel has a clear and simple chronological progression, its narrative style is straightforward, as most events and characters are portrayed by the all-seeing and all-judging third-person narrator. It repeats the stock Stalinist condemnation of Trotskii as an enemy, and has no kind words on the New Economic Policy, which Stalin brought to an end in 1928 (there is a particularly negative and distasteful depiction of a thriving market-place, for example). Towards the end of the novel, the scene of a Komsomol congress held in the Bolshoi Theatre is dominated by impersonal, constructivist imagery, where the thousands of individual delegates merge into a "single, mighty transformer of never-fading energy". The novel does, indeed, burn with the fire of belief that "the future belongs to us".

Ostrovskii's second novel, *Rozhdennye burei* (*Born of the Storm*), was meant to portray the years 1918–19 in the western Ukraine, but remained unfinished at the time of the writer's death. Departing from the author's own experience, it is regarded as poorly written and clichéd.

DAVID GILLESPIE

Vladislav Aleksandrovich Ozerov 1769–1816

Dramatist and poet

Biography

Born in Kazansk (or possibly Borki) near Tver, 11 October 1769. Attended boarding school from an early age; Infantry Corps of Nobles, 1776–89: graduated with gold medal. Entered Southern Army as lieutenant; aide first to General de Balmen and then, from 1790 to 1794, General Angalt: engaged in work of a civilian nature, including teaching. Worked in civil service forestry department, 1794–1808. Left Civil Service, September 1808, expecting generous pension following good work in department and much acclaim after *Dmitrii Donskoi* (1806); pension refused for no good reason, 1809. Last play, *Poliksena*, failed; money promised from the performances did not materialize. Acutely depressed, burned all his manuscripts and drafts; wrote only embittered poetry, 1809–10. Bed-ridden and suffered from fits, paralysis, and mental disorder, taken into care by his father. Died 17 September 1816.

Publications

Collected Edition

Tragedii. Stikhotvoreniia, edited by I.N. Medvedeva. Leningrad, 1960.

Plays

Iaropolk i Oleg [Iaropolk and Oleg]. 1798.
Edip v Afinakh [Oedipus in Athens]. 1804.
Fingal. 1805.
Dmitrii Donskoi. 1806.
Poliksena. 1809.

Critical Studies

"Vladislav Ozerov", by I.N. Medvedeva, in *Tragedii. Stikhotvoreniia*, 1960, 5–71.
Russian Drama from Its Beginnings to the Age of Pushkin, by Simon Karlinsky, Berkeley, University of California Press, 1985, 195–216.
A History of Russian Literature of the Romantic Period, by William Edward Brown, 4 vols, Ann Arbor, Ardis, 1986.

A mediocre poet but serious dramatist, Vladislav Ozerov enjoyed a career that resembled a remarkably steep parabola. Rising rapidly from insignificance to national fame, he became for a short time one of the most illustrious men in all of Russia, only to relapse, via the painful experience of seeing himself cruelly parodied, into obscurity a mere decade after his death. His role in the Russian theatre was as transient as it was transitional. He stands at the very turning-point between ancient and modern; to the detriment of his lasting reputation he looked more clearly back into the 18th century than forward into the 19th.

His forte was classical tragedy, of which (disregarding a modest early attempt, *Iaropolk i Oleg* [Iaropolk and Oleg]) he wrote four good examples: *Edip v Afinakh* [Oedipus in Athens]; *Fingal*; *Dmitrii Donskoi*; and *Poliksena*. All of these plays are written in imported Alexandrines, in which all the niceties (caesurae, end-stopping, regular rhyming, etc.) are strictly observed. So are the unities and the distancing of action, which is always reported by messenger. Ozerov has thus not strayed far, in formal terms, from his French masters, Corneille and Racine, or indeed from his Russian predecessor, Sumarokov. When Pushkin castigated Ozerov a few years after his death for having produced tragedies that were mannered, imprecise, and stale he had in mind precisely this continuing enslavement to the rules and unities laid down outside Russia, at the expense of spontaneous and warm-blooded inspiration.

Ozerov fared little better in relation to the themes that he attempted to explore. Lacking any knowledge of Greek and with no special expertise in early Russian history, he did not pretend to anything approaching historical accuracy or to any real sense of classical tragedy. Instead, he used his ancient or historical material to explore once more concepts already examined by the French with some thoroughness: fate, duty and honour (Corneille) as well as feeling and passion (Racine). His leading characters, especially the women, are predominantly creatures of feeling; tender and reflective, they show great sensitivity on all occasions. In this one respect Ozerov does show attunement to the spirit of the new age, following in the footsteps of Karamzin by espousing the cause of Sentimentalism; human feeling, itself guided by reason, is seen as something that liberates and ennobles our species.

All in all, the deficiencies of Ozerov's theatre – old-fashioned artificiality and the lack of any real human or narrative interest – stand out with some clarity. It is easier to see why he fell so rapidly into oblivion than to understand why he rose in the first place to acclaim. He was helped, to some extent, by circumstances. His first play having failed, *Edip v Afinakh* was taken up by Shakhovskoi and given the full treatment: nothing but the best as far as sets, cast and music were concerned. The opening chorus, ostensibly addressed to Theseus, King (tsar) of Athens, rang out with royalist patriotism that appealed to both the public and the authorities of state. The play's success gave a new impetus to an obsolescent genre and set Ozerov well on his way towards enthusiastic acceptance at both popular and official levels. The coup was repeated on a massive scale in 1807 with *Dmitrii Donskoi*, a drama (taken from a moment of triumph in Russian history, the great military victory of 1380) that amounted to a transparent allegory of actual and hoped-for contemporary political events. The crowds that packed the St Petersburg Bolshoi Theatre well beyond the limits of safety, cheering and thundering their applause, were not celebrating a triumph in Russian dramaturgy; they were shouting for Russia and the tsar at a time when the nation felt itself under threat, and thus re-invoking the spirit that had once delivered their ancestors from tyrannical rule. The action of the play may have treated Dmitrii's defeat of Mamai, leader of the oppressing Mongol forces, but the audience had no difficulty in equating the hero with Alexander I, Mamai with Napoleon and the Russian princes with Alexander's foreign and military staff. Patriotic fervour was the real reason behind this play's success. The tsar rewarded the author with a jewelled snuff-box, an accolade that marked the high point of his career.

The glory did not last for long. Ozerov prospered for some years, to the extent of having as many as three of his plays on the boards simultaneously, but neither *Fingal*, (an Ossianic tragedy), which preceded *Dmitrii Donskoi*, nor *Poliksena*, which followed it, was to achieve lasting popularity. The last play was as out of touch with public taste as its predecessor had been in with it; a dismal tale from antiquity depicted a heroine whose only wish was to die in order to be reunited with her lover, Achilles. From now on the playwright's troubles multiplied and his descent was swift. No one can be certain of what really happened during this catastrophic decline. For many subsequent decades it was held that a conspiracy to discredit Ozerov had been orchestrated by Shakhovskoi; 20th-century research appears to have exculpated the latter and perhaps pointed the finger at no less a personage than Gavriil Derzhavin. Whatever the truth of it, Ozerov was savaged by the anti-Karamzin school of modernists, parodied without mercy by Griboedov and others, deprived of a deserved and expected pension by an ambivalent tsar, and so utterly discouraged that he destroyed all his current work and future schemes. If he had once succeeded somewhat beyond his virtues, he now suffered in excess of any shortcomings in character or ability. His work, which has been gaining in critical approval in recent years, remains as a valuable monument to Russian dramaturgy in a turbulent age of transition.

A.D.P. BRIGGS

P

Avdot'ia Iakovlevna Panaeva 1819–1893

Prose writer

Biography

Born Avdot'ia Iakovlevna Brianskaia in St Petersburg, 31 July 1819 (or 1820). Attended a theatrical school in St Petersburg: family wanted her to have career on stage. Married: 1) Ivan Panaev in 1837 (died 1862), several children (died in infancy); 2) common-law wife of Nikolai Nekrasov, two children (died in infancy); 3) Apollon Golovachev in 1864, one daughter, the writer Evdokia Apollonovna Nagrodskaia (1866–1930). Ran a literary salon, St Petersburg, 1840s–60s. Wrote under the pseudonym N. Stanitskii. Closely associated with the journal *Sovremennik*. Involved in women's emancipation movement; wrote *Zhenskaia dolia* [A Woman's Lot], 1862. Memoirs published, 1889–90; provided important information on the literary scene of the 1840s and 1850s. Died in St Petersburg, 30 March 1893.

Publications

Fiction

Tri strany sveta [The Three Countries of the World], with Nikolai Nekrasov. 1848; reprinted in *Polnoe sobranie sochinenii*, by Nikolai Nekrasov, Moscow, 1948, vol. 7.

Mertvoe ozero [The Dead Lake], with Nikolai Nekrasov. 1848; in *Polnoe sobranie sochinenii*, by N.A. Nekrasov, Moscow, 1948, vol. 8.

"Neostorozhnoe slovo" [A Careless Word], *Sovremennik*, 3 (1848), 65–67.

"Zhena chasovogo mastera" [The Wife of the Watch Expert], *Sovremennik*, 2 (1849), 168–81.

"Paseka" [The Beehive], *Sovremennik*, 18/11 (1849).

"Neobdumannyi shag" [A Hasty Step], *Sovremennik*, 19/1 (1850).

"Kapriznaia zhenshchina" [The Capricious Woman], *Sovremennik*, 24/12 (1850).

"Melochi zhizni" [The Trivialities of Life], *Sovremennik*, 1–4 (1854); separate edition St Petersburg, 1854.

"Stepnaia baryshnia" [Lady of the Steppe]. 1855; in *Dacha na Petergofskoi doroge: Proza russkikh pisatel'nits pervoi poloviny XIXv.*, Moscow, 1986; translated as "The Young Lady of the Steppes", by Joe Andrew, in *Russian Women's Shorter Fiction: An Anthology, 1855–1860*, Oxford, Clarendon Press, 1996, 319–97.

"Roman v peterburgskom polusvete" [Romance in St Petersburg's Half-Light], *Sovremennik*, 3–4 (1860); separate edition St Petersburg, 1863.

"Zhenskaia dolia" [A Woman's Lot], *Sovremennik*, 3–5 (1862).

"Fantazerka" [The Fantasist], *Sovremennik*, 104 (1864).

Semeistvo Tal'nikovykh [The Tal'nikov Family], published under the pseudonym N. Stanitskii, written in 1848 (banned until 1866); reprinted in *Russkie povesti XIX veka: 40–50 godov*, Moscow, 1952, vol. 2.

Istoriia odnogo talanta [Story of One Talented Person]. *Niva*, 1888.

Memoirs

"Vospominaniia", as A.Ia. Golovacheva, *Istoricheskii vestnik*, 1889; separate edition, 1890; reprinted Moscow, 1948, 1956, 1972.

Critical Studies

Zhena poeta, by K. Chukovskii, Petrograd, 1922.

"Avdot'ya Panaeva: Her Salon and Her Life", by Marina Ledkovsky, *Russian Literature Triquarterly*, 9 (1974), 423–32.

"A Brackish Hippocrene: Nekrasov, Panaeva and the 'Prose in Love'", by Richard Gregg, *Slavic Review*, 34 (1975), 731–51.

Dichterinen und Schriftstellerinen in Russland von Mitte des 18. bis zum Beginn des 20. Jahrhunderts, eine Problemskizze, by Frank Gopfert, Munich, 1992 (chapter on Panaeva).

Avdot'ia Iakovlevna Panaeva was born in 1819 (or 1820) in St Petersburg into a family of well-known actors. Her childhood was unhappy, she was probably a neglected or unloved child. The education she received at the Theatrical School was fairly superficial. Her parents wanted her to train for the ballet, but at the age of 18 she married Ivan Panaev, a budding author, in order to escape going on the stage. Panaev came from a wealthy land owning family and their marriage was, at first, frowned upon by his relatives. Panaeva's married life was not happy. The Panaevs had several children, all of whom died young. After several years the marriage became a sham, though they never separated.

Panaeva was a beautiful woman, intelligent and kind; among the many men who frequented her literary salon some fell in love with her, notably Dostoevskii and Nikolai Nekrasov. Most probably in 1847 Panaeva became Nekrasov's mistress. They stayed together for about 16 years. The Panaevs and Nekrasov lived in a curious *ménage à trois* in the same flat. Panaeva collaborated with Nekrasov on two novels, while with her husband she contributed a regular column on fashion to

Sovremennik, which Panaev and Nekrasov bought from Pletnev in 1846 and edited jointly.

Her life with Nekrasov was also far from idyllic. They had two children, both of whom died in infancy. Nekrasov was a difficult person to live with: moody, with a tendency to depression, ill-humour and dejection; he was also a compulsive gambler and a womanizer. Towards the end of their life together he found a new mistress, whom he married on his deathbed. His relationship with Panaeva went through several crises in the second half of the 1850s.

Panaev died after a short illness in 1862 and Nekrasov could marry his mistress, but their relationship, strained for many years, finally ended in 1863. In April of that year Panaeva left their flat at Liteinyi and in 1865 she sold her share in *Sovremennik* to Nekrasov. She married Apollon Golovachev, a journalist on the staff of *Sovremennik* in 1864; however, her ties with the journal were not severed and she continued to publish her stories there. Panaeva had a daughter by her second husband, the only one among all her children to survive beyond infancy. Both Golovachev and Nekrasov died in 1877. Her husband's death left Panaeva in a desperate financial situation: in order to earn her living and support her daughter she went back to writing, though without much success. Not long before her death, in 1893, she started to work on her memoirs, the most enduring part of her work, and undoubtedly one of the most important memoiristic works covering the period from the 1840s to the 1860s.

Panaeva's first work was the novel *Semeistvo Tal'nikovykh* [The Tal'nikov Family], written probably in 1848, banned by the censor for "undermining morality and parental authority". The issue of the magazine where it was due to appear was destroyed. Panaeva's first novel is undoubtedly largely autobiographical; it presents a repulsive picture of family life where love is virtually non-existent. It is probably the first Russian "childhood" novel and, unlike those that followed, it has a female narrator.

Her next forays into fiction came with the two novels written in collaboration with Nekrasov, largely to fill the pages of the journal with material the censor would not find objectionable. The first of these novels *Tri strany sveta* [The Three Countries of the World], published in 1848, has a highly melodramatic plot, which was, in the main, Panaeva's contribution. The second novel, entitled *Mertvoe ozero* [The Dead Lake], was written with the same purpose in mind and is also very melodramatic. The chapters depicting the life and loves of provincial actors were probably written by Panaeva who knew that milieu well; they present some interest. Both novels abound in major and minor characters, and numerous sub-plots and are not very well constructed.

In her stories and novels written independently Panaeva often deals with the so-called women's issues, which were also among the main preoccupations in European literature of that period. In her fiction she portrays female characters and various aspects of the female situation in the family and in society. Women's inferior position is a recurrent theme in her work. She shared the fairly widespread conviction of that period that, if women could have access to education, they would be able to improve their status in society, be financially independent, and thus more in control of their fate. Her stories often deal with the fate of the Russian peasant woman (usually a serf) whose lot is the hardest of all.

Panaeva's most valuable contribution to Russian literature are her memoirs. She embarked upon them towards the end of her life when she herself was a forgotten literary figure. Factual mistakes and inaccuracies, especially as far as dates are concerned, lessen their value somewhat. Panaeva, thanks to her association with *Sovremennik*, was acquainted with most of the writers and critics of that period, among them Belinskii, Dostoevskii, Dobroliubov, Turgenev, Herzen, and many others. She was on very friendly terms with many of them, notably Belinskii and Dobroliubov, and this lends to her narrative a degree of compassion lacking perhaps in those of her male contemporaries. Her memoirs remain until today a rich source of information on the literary life of that most important period in Russian literature. Her other works remain virtually unknown to contemporary readers.

Panaeva died in St Petersburg in 1893, forgotten by her contemporaries and the new generation of Russian readers.

RUTH SOBEL

Vera Fedorovna Panova 1905–1973

Prose writer and dramatist

Biography

Born in Rostov-on-Don, 20 March 1905. Did not complete gymnasium schooling; largely self-educated. Started work for *Trudovoi Don* newspaper, 1922; also worked for other local newspapers and on publications for children. Married: 1) Arsenii Starosel'skii in 1925 (divorced 1927); 2) Boris Vakhtin (separated); 3) David Iakovlevich in 1945; three children. Wrote first drama, 1933. Moved to the Ukraine, 1937; then to Leningrad, 1940. Lived in various places during the war years; worked on a newspaper and for radio in Perm, 1944–45. Travelled on military train with medical workers; this experience led to first major work of fiction, *Sputniki* (translated as *The Train*), 1946. Returned to Leningrad, 1946. Contributed to *Novyi mir*, from early 1950s. Member of the board of the Soviet Writers' Union, from 1954; RSFSR Writers' Union, from 1958. Travelled to the United States, 1960. Recipient: Stalin

Prize, 1947, 1948, 1950. Suffered a stroke, 1967. Died in Leningrad, 3 March 1973. Buried in Komarovo, near St Petersburg.

Publications

Collected Editions

Izbrannye proizvedeniia, 2 vols. 1980.

Sobranie sochinenii, 5 vols. Leningrad, 1987–89.

Fiction

"Sputniki" [The Travelling Companions], *Znamia*, 1946; translated as *The Train*, by Eve Manning and Marie Budberg, London, Putnam, 1948; New York, Knopf, 1949.

"Kruzhilikha", *Znamia*, 1947; translated as *The Factory*, by Marie Budberg, Putnam, London, 1949; reprinted Westport, Connecticut, Hyperion Press, 1977; also translated as *Looking Ahead*, by David Skvirsky, Moscow, Foreign Languages Publishing House, 1955.

Iasnyi bereg [The Clear Shore]. Leningrad, 1949.

"Vremena goda", *Leningradskii al'manakh*, 1953; revised 1956; translated as *Span of the Year*, by Vera Traill, London, Harvill Press, 1957; reprinted Westport, Connecticut, Hyperion Press, 1977.

"Serezha", *Novyi mir*, 1955; translated as *Time Walked* [no translator named], Cambridge, Massachusetts, Arlington Books, 1959; reprinted as *A Summer to Remember*, New York, Barnes, 1962; also reprinted as "Seryozha", in *Fifty Years of Russian Prose: From Pasternak to Solzhenitsyn*, edited by Krystyna Pomorska, Cambridge, Massachusetts, MIT Press, 1971, vol. 2, 245–326.

"Sentimental'nyi roman" [Sentimental Novel], *Novyi mir*, 1958.

"Evdokia", *Leningradskii al'manakh*, 1959.

"Valia", *Oktiabr'*, 1959.

"Volodia", *Oktiabr'*, 1959.

"Rabochyi poselok" [The Workers' Settlement], *Novyi mir*, 1964.

"Rano utrom" [Early in the Morning], *Novyi mir*, 1964.

"Sasha", *Novyi mir*, 1964.

Liki na zare [Images at Daybreak]. Moscow and Leningrad, 1966.

"Kotoryi chas?" [What Time is It?], *Novyi mir*, 9 (1981).

Plays

"V Staroi Moskve" [In Old Moscow], *Neva*, 1957.

"Metelitsa" [The Blizzard], *Priboi*, 1957.

"Provody belykh nochei" [Farewell to White Nights], *Novyi mir*, 1961.

"Skol'ko let, skol'ko zim" [How Many Summers, How Many Winters], *Novyi mir*, 1961; translated as "It's Been Ages", in *Contemporary Russian Drama*, translated by F.D. Reeve, New York, Pegasus, 1968.

"Kak pozhivaesh, paren'?" [How Are You, Lad?], *Teatr*, 1962.

"Eshche ne vecher" [It's Not Evening Yet], *Zvezda vostoka*, 1967.

"Nadezhda Milovanova", *Zvezda*, 1967.

"Trediakovskii i Volynskii", *Neva*, 6 (1968).

"Svad'ba kak svad'ba" [Wedding Like a Wedding], *Teatr*, 1 (1973).

P'esy [Plays]. Leningrad, 1985.

Memoirs

"Iz zapasnikov pamiati" [From the Stores of Memory], *Neva*, 1971.

O moei zhizni, knigakh i chitateliakh [About My Life, Books and Readers]. Leningrad, 1987.

Critical Studies

V mire geroev Very Panovoi, by S. Fradkina, Perm, 1961.

Tvorchestvo Very Panovoi, by L.A. Plotkin, Moscow, 1962.

Women in Soviet Fiction, 1917–64, by Xenia Gasiorowska, Madison, University of Wisconsin Press, 1968.

Soviet Russian Literature since Stalin, by Deming Brown, Cambridge, Cambridge University Press, 1978.

Vera Panova: zhizn', tvorchestvo, sovremenniki, by A. Ninov, Leningrad, 1980.

Vospominaniia o Vere Panovoi, Moscow, 1988.

Vera Panova: stranitsy zhizni: k biografii pisatel'nitsy, by Serafima Iur'eva, Tenafly, New Jersey, Hermitage, 1993.

Vera Panova was born in Rostov-on-Don in southern Russia. Her father, a bank clerk, drowned when she was only six years old and, consequently, her mother went to work as a book-keeper. Panova did not complete her education, for financial reasons, and went to work as a journalist for various local newspapers. In 1937 she left Rostov-on-Don with her family and settled in the Ukraine, in a village called Shishaki. From there she travelled to Moscow and Leningrad. By the beginning of World War II, however, she was living in the town of Pushkin (formerly Tsarskoe Selo). Pushkin then fell to the Nazis in 1941 and Panova was due to be deported to a German concentration camp. On the way to Estonia she managed to escape and made her way back to the Ukraine. Following the liberation of the Ukraine in 1943, she moved to the city of Perm in the Urals where she worked for a local newspaper and radio station. In December 1944 she was invited to travel from Perm on board a military train in the company of a group of medical workers. This led to the writing and publication in the magazine *Znamia* in 1946 of what is considered Panova's fictional debut – the hugely popular novel *Sputniki* (*The Train*). The novel, a vivid and truthful description of human suffering during World War II, was awarded a Stalin Prize. In 1964 it was turned into a film called *The Charity Train* and then in 1975 into a four-part television series.

Panova wrote regularly for the journal *Novyi mir* from the early 1950s. During this period she became friendly with its liberal editor, Aleksandr Tvardovskii. In 1960 she travelled to the United States as part of a delegation of Soviet authors. This was the first time, after a long interval, that Soviet writers had been able to make such a visit to the west. Panova later described her impressions in a collection of essays entitled "Iz Amerikanskikh vstrech" ("From My American Encounters"). In the summer of 1967, having taken part in the 4th Congress of Soviet Writers, Panova suffered a severe stroke, from which she never completely recovered. She died on 3 March 1973.

Panova was essentially a Party writer, whose books were considered (on the whole) ideologically sound. Against a generally mediocre socialist realist background, however, she was noted for her vivid descriptions of real-life situations. Furthermore, the reader could identify with her characters who were not portrayed in purely black-and-white terms as either heroes or villains. She wrote about everyday life, love and the need for affection and sympathy, about family life and people's problems and emotions. Her style was warm and vivid and, for an ordinary Soviet reader brought up on stodgy ideologically-sound prose, her books represented in comparative terms a "good read".

Higher literary authorities, with their concern for moral judgement and propaganda, never quite accepted the human touch in Panova's writing and accused her of "naturalism". Her novel *Vremena goda* (*Span of the Year*), for example, an objective attempt to depict Party bosses, was criticized for alleged lack of ideological emphasis, for simply portraying life without passing a judgement. Panova, indeed, showed a sympathetic understanding even for those of her characters who did not quite fit into the ideal socialist society. She showed them to be victims of society, an idea that went somewhat against the authoritative grain of the times.

Among her other writings, mention should also be made of her novella "Serezha" (*Time Walked*), which was widely praised for its description of family life as seen through the eyes of a five-year-old boy. One of the most popular Russian children's writers, Kornei Chukovskii, pointed out that this was the first book written by a Soviet writer that dealt with the psychology of a small child and his attempts to understand and to come to terms with his environment. This novella was turned into a film in 1960, which received the main prize at the 12th International Film Festival in Karlovy Vary. Her *Sentimental'nyi roman* [Sentimental Novel] was largely autobiographical, employing the double narrative perspective customary in such works, and aroused controversy over its depiction of the 1920s. In her later works, Panova introduced themes from Russian history: *Liki na zare* [Images at Daybreak] provoked criticism by its positive treatment of Christianity, while the play *Trediakovskii i Volynskii* presents an allegorical treatment of the relationship between the artist and the state.

Panova was a prolific writer of novels and stories. From the 1930s she also composed a number of plays. Although favoured by the Party, she rose above the mediocrity of socialist realism to produce fiction that revealed both sympathy for the individual and a considerable degree of psychological insight.

ANNA PILKINGTON

Sofiia Iakovlevna Parnok 1885–1933

Poet

Biography

Born Sofiia Iakovlevna Parnokh in Taganrog, 11 August 1885. Educated at home and at gymnasium in Taganrog; studied at the Conservatory of Music in Geneva, 1905–06. Began to publish, 1906. Enrolled in Faculty of Jurisprudence, St Petersburg University, 1908–09. Married: Vladimir Mikhailovish Volkenshtein in 1907 (divorced 1909). Committed long-term relationships: 1) Nadezhda Pavlovna Poliakova, 1902–07; 2) Liudmila Vladimirovna Erarskaia, from 1916; 3) Ol'ga Nikolaevna Tsuberbiller, from 1924; creatively significant love affairs with Marina Ivanovna Tsvetaeva, 1914–16; Nina Evgen'evna Vedeneeva, 1932–33. Full-time (self-supporting) writer and literary critic, from 1910. Professional translator from French and German; librettist (major libretto: *Almast*, 1918). Permanent critic (using the pseudonym Andrei Polianin) for *Severnye zapiski*, 1913–17, and *Russkaia molva*. Visited Switzerland, Italy, and England, 1914. Lived in Crimea (Sudak), 1917–21. Arrested in Sudak, January 1921, released by mid-March. Active participant in Moscow poetry circles, 1922–25; founding member and officer of Uzel (The Knot) poets' publishing co-operative, 1926–28. Unable to publish after 1928. Died in Karinskoe (outside Moscow), 26 August 1933.

Publications

Collected Edition

Sobranie stikhotvorenii. Ann Arbor, Ardis, 1979.

Poetry

Stikhotvoreniia. Petrograd, 1916.
Rozy Pierii [Roses of Pieria]. Moscow and Petrograd, 1922.
Loza [The Vine]. Moscow, 1923.
Muzyka [Music]. Moscow, 1926.
Vpolgolosa [Half-Voiced]. Moscow, 1928.
Bol'shaia medvetitsa [Ursa Major]. 1932.
Nenuzhnoe dobro [Useless Good]. 1932–33.
"Almast", in *Sobranie stikhotvorenii*, 1979.
92 lyric poems, translated by Diana Lewis Burgin, in her *Sophia Parnok: The Life and Work of Russia's Sappho*, New York, New York University Press, 1994.

Critical Studies

"Vstupitel'naia stat'ia", by Sofiia Poliakova, in Parnok's *Sobranie stikhotvorenii*, Ann Arbor, Ardis, 1979.
Zakatnye oni dni: Tsvetaeva i Parnok, by Sofiia Poliakova, Ann Arbor, Ardis, 1983.
"After the Ball is Over: Sophia Parnok's Creative Relationship with Marina Tsvetaeva", by Diana Lewis Burgin, *Russian Review*, 4 (1988).
"Sophia Parnok and the Writing of a Lesbian Poet's Life", by Diana Lewis Burgin, *Slavic Review*, 51/2 (1992), 214–31.
"Laid Out in Lavender: Perceptions of Lesbian Love in Russian Literature and Culture of the Silver Age 1893–1917", by Diana Lewis Burgin, in *Sexuality and the Body in Russian*

Culture, edited by Jane T. Costlow *et al.*, Stanford, Stanford University Press, 1993.

Sophia Parnok: The Life and Work of Russia's Sappho, by Diana Lewis Burgin, New York, New York University Press, 1994.

A History of Russian Women's Writing, 1820–1992, by Catriona Kelly, Oxford and New York, Clarendon Press, 1994, 285–300.

Throughout her creative life Sofiia Parnok took pride in her idiosyncrasy and non-indebtedness to other poets, noting in one of her poems that she and her "touchy muse" went their own way, glad not to be the travelling companions of any "venerable master". Today Parnok continues to stand alone, a veritable "stranger" in Russian poetry, as Sofiia Poliakova (1979) calls her. In addition to composing a body of lyrics that cannot rightly be said to exemplify or belong to any of the poetic styles or movements of her day, Parnok defied the aesthetic and moral norms (what she would call the "patriarchal virtues") of Russian poetry by writing openly as a lesbian about lesbian experience and sexuality.

As a young poet Parnok wished for the courage "to shout" what she wanted to shout. Her poetic speaker returned frequently to the creative issue of "how to relate" in words what was most important to her. At times she felt the need to silence herself for want of the ability to find her words, real words, as she thought of them, that could express the inner life of her soul and accomplish her lifelong creative goal of direct soul-to-soul communication with her readers.

Entirely self-nurtured, discouraged, and sometimes hampered by her tacitly hostile, homophobic poetic culture, Parnok's search for her own words was long and torturous, and she did not come into her own as a poet until about a decade before her early death. Ironically, she discovered her own voice at precisely the time when lyric voices of all stripes were becoming increasingly suspect and prone to being silenced in Soviet literature. Because of the lesbian content of her lyrics, however, Parnok ultimately suffered a double poetic isolation, as she herself implied in her 1928 poem "Prolog" [Prologue]. In a dramatic dialogue with the voices of her contemporaries who ignore her pleas for communication, the poet in "Prolog" realizes that not only Soviet literary officialdom, but more painfully, her Soviet poet-brethren have turned a deaf ear to her "bewitching" voice, condemning her for non-conformity, hubris, and for "daring to speak out loud what people hide, even from themselves".

Apart from her belated first book, *Stikhotvoreniia*, none of Parnok's collections were reviewed in a serious way, and for most of her life she was known and remembered by her peers more as a lesbian than as a poet. By 1927, she acknowledged in one of her poems that she had become an "invisible woman" in Russian poetry, and her last book, *Vpolgolosa* [Half-Voiced], was issued in a mere 200 author's copies. As often happens with lesbian writers, Parnok's *oeuvre* has not survived in its entirety. Several verse fairy tales and all the prose fiction she wrote have been lost, including a 1913 novella, "Anton Ivanovich", that she considered her "first big work". Her critical writings and reviews from both before and after the 1917 Revolution have not as yet been collected and republished. Her 1922 essay on Khodasevich remains unpublished, and articles she wrote in the early 1920s on Akhmatova and Efros have apparently been lost. The fullest collection of Parnok's poems, *Sobranie stikhotvorenii* (1979), does not contain her juvenilia (1900–03) and early verse (1905–06), or any of the uncollected poems she published in journals from 1906 to 1914 – a total of more than 100 lyrics.

With the exception of her abstract, ponderously allegorical poems of 1905–06, written under the questionable guidance of her friend (and later, husband) Vladimir Volkenshtein, and with the equal exception of some of her "too aesthetic" (Parnok's own description) and emotionally inauthentic anthological poems (*Rozy Pierii* [Roses of Pieria] 1922), written under the artistically unsuccessful mediation of her ancient Lesbian poet-mentor, Sappho, Parnok's lyrics are profoundly rooted in her life experience. Her poetry illustrates to perfection a comment of Virgina Woolf's, that "Every secret of a writer's soul, every experience of his life ... is written large in his work". The life Parnok "writes large" in her lyrics, if one looks on them rightly, as links in a continuous lyrico-narrative chain, seems to be a consciously created life, specifically of a lesbian poet. Her adolescent juvenilia tell us artlessly and delightfully about her burgeoning sexuality, first love affairs, and quarrels with her father over her "tastes". The love lyrics of the years 1908–15, which, together with often erotically suggestive nature lyrics, constitute the majority of her poems in that period, describe the poet-speaker's lesbian adventures and lovers in Moscow's high-society salons and bohemian demi-monde. Many of the love lyrics in *Stikhotvoreniia* were inspired by Parnok's tempestuous love affair with Marina Tsvetaeva. The 23 closely interrelated poems of *Loza* [The Vine] chart Parnok's life journey as a poet and lover of women from her birth in Taganrog through her spiritual and creative rebirth in Sudak, where she spent the Civil War years. In *Muzyka* [Music], a retrospective collection, Parnok expresses the strikingly ambivalent music that reasonated in her long, passionate relationship with Liudmila Erarskaia. The spiritual dynamism and ecstatic quiet of *Vpolgolosa* inform the "seraphic eros" (Poliakova 1979) of Parnok's love for her "ultimate blessed friend" and "angel", Ol'ga Tsuberbiller, who gave the formerly homeless poet a home and soothed the anguish she suffered in her poetic isolation. Finally, Parnok's *magnum opus*, the cycles *Bol'shaia medvetitsa* [Ursa Major] (1932) and *Nenuzhnoe dobro* [Useless Good] (1932–33), are an intimate diary of her last, creatively sublime, and tragic love affair with the physicist Nina Vedeneeva.

Parnok's lyricism, with its emphasis on yearning (*toska*), empathetic nature, creativity, the soul, and love, comes out of the 19th-century Russian romantic tradition exemplified by her favourite poets, Baratynskii, and especially, Tiutchev. Thematically all of a piece from beginning to end, her poetry underwent a profound stylistic change, which begins to be observable in the poems she wrote during her stay in Sudak, and which radically transformed the expressive means of her late and best verse. From 1922, gone is the high-flown, heavy romantic diction that had weighed down so many of Parnok's pre-revolutionary poems with excessively long lines, a superfluity of epithets, and vague, timeworn metaphors. Her mature verse, by contrast, is remarkable for its simplicity, lack of metaphor, rhythmic surprises, inventive rhymes, and its combined intensity and lightness. Ultimately, Parnok enabled herself to find her own words, and through them, a way of expressing her traditional romantic spirit in the modernist cadences of authentically colloquial Russian speech. It is precisely this idiosyncratic blend of high-romantic lyricism and a scaled-down, at times even prosaic, poetic diction that represents Parnok's most original and lasting contribution to Russian poetry.

DIANA LEWIS BURGIN

Aleksei Parshchikov 1954–

Poet

Biography

Born in the town of Olga, north of Vladivostok, 1954. Grew up in Belarus and Ukraine. Attended the Gor'kii Literary Institute in Moscow, where he attended Mikhailov's poetry seminar. Married: 1) the psychologist and filmmaker Ol'ga Sviblova, one son; 2) Martina Huegli. Lived in Bern, early 1990s; studied for a time at Stanford University, California. Returned to Moscow.

Publications

Collected Edition

Vybrannoe [A Selection]. Moscow, 1996.

Poetry

Poems in *Vremia i my*, 81 (1984), 85–93.

Dneprovskii avgust [August on the Dnepr]. Moscow, 1986.

"Shkol'nyi portret; Stekliannye bashni" [School Portrait; Glass Towers], *Literaturnaia gazeta*, 11 (11 March 1987).

Figury intuitsii [Figures of Intuition]. Moscow, 1989.

Poems in *Zerkala: Al'manakh* [Mirrors: An Almanac]. Moscow, 1989, 163–76.

Poems translated by Michael Molnar, in *Child of Europe*, edited by Michael March, Harmondsworth, Penguin, 1990, 213–17.

Poems translated by John High, Michael Molnar, and Michael Palmer, and Andrew Wachtel, in *Third Wave: The New Russian Poetry*, edited by Kent Johnson and Stephen M. Ashby, Ann Arbor, University of Michigan Press, 1992, 23–35.

Poems translated by Gerald S. Smith, in *Contemporary Russian Poetry*, edited by Smith, Bloomington, Indiana University Press, 1993, 306–15.

Poems translated by John High, Michael Molnar, and Michael Palmer, in *Blue Vitriol*, Penngrove, California, Avec, 1994.

Cyrillic Light. Moscow, 1995.

Critical Studies

"Metametafor Alekseia Parshchikova", by K. Kedrov, *Literaturnaia ucheba*, 1 (1984).

"Metamorfoza", by Mikhail Epshtein, in his *Paradoksy novizny*, Moscow, 1988, 139–76.

"An Interview with Aleksei Parshchikov", by John High, *Five Fingers Review*, 8/9 (1990), 39–46.

"Introduction", by Marjorie Perloff, in *Blue Vitriol*, Penngrove, California, Avec, 1994.

Aleksei Parshchikov began writing in the mid-1970s but first attained a certain fame and brief notoriety in the mid-1980s. This was partly as a result of a poetic controversy around his long poem "Novogodnie stikhi" ("New Years Verse") that was discussed not only in *Literaturnaia gazeta* but even on television, for this was in the last years before perestroika, when poetry was still taken seriously enough to play a civic role. Critics were baffled, some by the extravagant imagery, others by the ideological or religious implications of such lines as: "a toy sees the other side of the moon, but not ours, one not yet risen, circling the sandpit the toy chatters with Krishna". Since the poem is about creation and re-creation it was fitting that it should have served as a polemical focus in the familiar-versus-experimentalism conflict. Its final lines light-heartedly hand over the poetic task of making order out of the world's vertiginous confusion to a new generation: "And what's sand? – it's clothing without buttons, it's the limits of the chance of being chosen from similar milliards elements of a desert. There's sand for the kids, let them build their walled cities!"

Parshchikov's earlier work had affinities with the young Pasternak of *Sestra moia zhizn'* (*My Sister-Life*), at least in terms of the verve of its imagery. In the early collection, *Dneprovskii avgust* [August on the Dnepr], we encounter the same sensual saturation, the astonishment of experience registered through accumulating metaphors, a literal and metaphorical journey into the unknown: "Curled shavings of whinnying disturb your dreams / From fields of stubble shorn like conscripts, out among the halberd reeds / the moon is moored with hawsers". However, the metaphorical superstructure of Parshchikov's work bears a particular relation to its source that differentiates it from that of his predecessors. Like a microscope or telescope image, differences in scale create a new level of comprehension. Parshchikov is fascinated by the fantastic realities that modern physics postulates: he projects his poetic personae into hallucinatory dimensions that might exist if those hypotheses were perceived fact. This was one reason why the poet and critic Konstantin Kedrov saddled him with the title of "meta-metaphorist" early on in his career. Mikhail Epshtein subsequently devised the term "metarealist" and pressganged a motley collection of writers into that "school", at whose fringes he located Parshchikov, halfway to Conceptualism. However, Parshchikov himself has justifiably disputed this concentration on the metaphor as the primary device, pointing out that it is fragmentation and metonymy that underlie his poetics. In

Parshchikov's poetry the base line is the disparity between language and the multiple worlds it is required to represent. Science, economics, and history extrapolate our experience into transhuman spheres of knowledge; these are some of the areas that Parshchikov's baroque imagery attempts to actualize. It does not, however, express the essential quiddity of the object (as seen in its extreme form in the work of Francis Ponge). Instead Parshchikov works outward from multifaceted subjective perception. "Novogodnie stikhi" grafts a Bildungsroman view of the recent past onto a creation myth. In "Ia zhil na pole Poltavskoi bitvy" [I Lived on the Battlefield of Poltava] the poetic persona is a reporter roving through multifarious perspectives on vast historical events. In "Liman" [Mudflats] experience is reduced to a tangle of tracks across a cosmic mudflat in which footprints – or time and space – may be turned backwards or inside out: "Draw a blank here, a joke, a ridiculous sackrace. Littering funnels of slime behind us like smokestacks. ... Just the wrench of a vista heavy as a punctured ball, Just a hole in the ground or simply the lack of a hole."

Like Dragomoshchenko, Parshchikov has been in close contact with American avant-garde poetry and with the leading edge of poetic theory. During his period at Stanford University he studied under Marjorie Perloff and he has translated the work of Michael Palmer, who has, in turn, been one of his translators.

MICHAEL MOLNAR

Boris Leonidovich Pasternak 1890–1960

Poet, prose writer, essayist, and translator

Biography

Born in Moscow, 10 February 1890. Son of the artist, Leonid Pasternak and the concert pianist, Rosa Kaufman. Attended Moscow Fifth gymnasium, 1901–08; Moscow University, 1909–13; also studied at the University of Marburg, 1912. Studied music and philosophy, before turning to poetry. Active member of the Futurist Tsentrifuga group. Worked as private tutor and in chemical factory in the Urals, 1915–17; librarian, Soviet Ministry of Education, 1918. Married: 1) Evgeniia Vladimirovna Lourie [Lur'e] in 1922 (marriage dissolved 1931), one son; 2) Zinaida Nikolaevna Neigauz in 1934, one son. Member of the Writers' Union, from 1932; expelled over the "Zhivago affair", 1958. Recipient: Medal for Valiant Labour, 1946; Nobel Prize for Literature (refused), 1958. Died at Peredelkino, 30 May 1960.

Publications

Collected Editions

The Collected Prose Works, edited by Stefan Schimanski, translated by Beatrice Scott and Robert Payne. London, Lindsay Drummond, 1945; revised edition as *Prose and Poems*, edited by Stefan Schimanski, with an introduction by J.M. Cohen. London, Ernest Benn, 1959.

Safe Conduct, An Early Autobiography and Other Works, translated by Alec Brown. New York, New Directions, 1958; London, Elek, 1959.

Sochineniia, edited by Gleb Struve and Boris Filippov, 3 vols. Ann Arbor, University of Michigan Press, 1961.

Stikhotvoreniia i poemy, with an introduction by A.D. Siniavskii. Moscow and Leningrad, 1965.

Collected Short Prose, edited by Christopher Barnes. New York, Praeger, 1977.

Vozdushnye puti: Proza raznykh let [Aerial Ways: Prose of Various Years]. Moscow, 1982.

Zhenia's Childhood and Other Stories, translated by Alec Brown. London, Allison and Busby, 1982.

Selected Poems, translated by Jon Stallworthy and Peter France. London, Allen Lane, 1983; Harmondsworth, Penguin, 1984.

Izbrannoe, 2 vols. Moscow, 1985.

The Voice of Prose, edited and translated by Christopher Barnes, 2 vols. Edinburgh, Polygon, and New York, Grove Press, 1986–90.

Sobranie sochinenii, 5 vols. Moscow, 1989–92.

Selected Writings and Letters, translated by Catherine Judelson. Moscow, Progress, 1990.

Izbrannye proizvedeniia, edited by E.B. Pasternak. Moscow, 1991.

Fiction

Detstvo Liuvers, *Nashi dni* 1(1922); translated as "The Childhood of Luvers", by Beatrice Scott and Robert Payne, in *The Collected Prose Works*, 1945; as "Zhenia's Childhood", by Alec Brown, in *Safe Conduct, An Early Autobiography and Other Works*, 1959; and in *Zhenia's Childhood and Other Stories*, 1982; also as "Zhenya Luvers' Childhood", by Christopher Barnes, in *The Voice of Prose*, 1986.

Rasskazy. Moscow, 1925; as *Vozdushnye puti* [Aerial Ways], 1933.

Povest' [A Tale]. Leningrad, 1934; translated as *The Last Summer*, by George Reavey, London, Peter Owen, 1959; Harmondsworth, Penguin, 1960; and as "Seryozha's Story", by Christopher Barnes, in *The Voice of Prose*, 1990.

Doktor Zhivago. Milan, Feltrinelli, 1957; Ann Arbor, University of Michigan Press, 1958; Moscow, 1988; translated as *Doctor Zhivago*, by Max Hayward and Manya Harari, London, Collins Harvill, 1958; London, Fontana, 1961; numerous subsequent reprints.

Juvenilia B. Pasternaka: 6 fragmentov o Relikvimini [B.

Pasternak's Juvenilia ...], edited by Anna Ljunggren. Stockholm, Almqvist & Wiksell, 1984.

Poetry

Bliznets v tuchakh [Twin in the Clouds]. Moscow, 1914.

Poverkh bar'erov [Over the Barriers]. Moscow, 1917; revised edition, Moscow and Leningrad, 1929; reprinted Moscow, 1931.

Sestra moia zhizn': Leto 1917 goda. Berlin, Petrograd and Moscow, Grzhebin, 1922; reprinted Ann Arbor, Ardis, 1976; translated as *My Sister-Life*, by Mark Rudman and Bohdan Boychuk, with *A Sublime Malady*, Ann Arbor, Ardis, 1983; Leek, Staffordshire, Aquila, 1989; reprinted Evanston, Illinois, Northwestern University Press, 1992.

Temy i variatsii [Themes and Variations]. Berlin, Helikon, 1923; reprinted Ann Arbor, Ardis, 1972.

"Leitenant Shmidt", *Novyi mir*, 8–9 (1926); 2–5 (1927).

Deviat'sot piatyi god. Stikhi. Moscow, 1927; title poem translated as *The Year Nineteen Five* (bilingual edition), by Richard Chappell, London, Spencer, 1989.

"Vysokaia bolezn'", *Novyi mir*, 11 (1928); translated as *A Sublime Malady*, by Mark Rudman and Bohdan Boychuk, with *My Sister-Life*, Ann Arbor, Ardis, 1983; Leek, Staffordshire, Aquila, 1989.

Spektorskii. Poema. Moscow, 1931.

Vtoroe rozhdenie [Second Birth]. Moscow, 1932.

Stikhotvoreniia v odom tome. Leningrad, 1933; 2nd edition, 1935; 3rd edition, 1936.

Na rannikh poezdakh [On Early Trains]. Moscow, 1943.

Zemnoi prostor [Earth's Vastness]. Moscow, 1945.

Poems, translated by Eugene M. Kayden. Ann Arbor, University of Michigan Press, 1959.

The Poetry of Boris Pasternak 1917–1959, edited and translated by George Reavey. New York, Putnam, 1959.

Kogda razguliaetsia: Poems 1955–1959 (bilingual edition), translated by Michael Harari. London, Collins Harvill, 1960; reprinted with *An Essay in Autobiography*, translated by Manya Harari, London, Collins Harvill, 1990.

In the Interlude: Poems 1945–1960, translated by Henry Kamen. London and New York, Oxford University Press, 1962.

Fifty Poems, translated by Lydia Pasternak Slater. London, Allen and Unwin, and New York, Barnes and Noble, 1963; reprinted as *The Poems of Boris Pasternak*, London, Allen and Unwin, 1984.

The Poems of Doctor Zhivago, translated by Eugene M. Kayden. Kansas City, Hallmark, 1971.

Poems/Stikhotvoreniia (bilingual edition) compiled by Evgeny Pasternak. Moscow, Raduga, 1990.

Second Nature: Forty-Six Poems, translated by Andrei Navrozov. London, Peter Owen, 1990.

Play

Slepaia krasavitsa, edited by Christopher Barnes and Nicholas J. Anning. London, Flegon Press, 1969; translated as *The Blind Beauty*, by Max Hayward and Manya Harari, London, Collins and Harvill, and New York, Harcourt Brace, 1969.

Essays and Autobiography

Okhrannaia gramota. Leningrad, 1931; as "The Safe Conduct", by Beatrice Scott and Robert Payne, in *The Collected Prose Works*, 1945; also translated in *Safe Conduct: An Early Autobiography and Other Works*, by Alec Brown, 1959; and by Angela Livingstone, in *Pasternak on Art and Creativity*, Cambridge, Cambridge University Press, 1985; also by Christopher Barnes, in *The Voice of Prose*, 1986.

An Essay in Autobiography, translated by Manya Harari. London, Collins and Harvill Press, 1959; as *I Remember: Sketch for an Autobiography*, edited and translated by David Magarshack, New York, Pantheon, and London, Harvill Press, 1959; partial Russian text, as "Avtobiograficheskii ocherk", in *Sochineniia*, 1961; and as "Liudi i polozheniia", in *Novyi mir*, January 1967; in *Vozdushnye puti*, 1982.

Pasternak on Art and Creativity, edited by Angela Livingstone. Cambridge and New York, Cambridge University Press, 1985.

Boris Pasternak ob iskusstve [Boris Pasternak on Art], edited by E.B. and E.V. Pasternak. Moscow, 1990.

Letters

Letters to Georgian Friends, edited and translated by David Magarshack. London, Secker and Warburg, and New York, Harcourt Brace, 1968; Harmondsworth, Penguin, 1971.

Perepiska s Ol'goi Freidenberg, edited by Elliott Mossman. New York, Harcourt Brace Jovanovich, 1981; Moscow, 1990; translated as *The Correspondence of Boris Pasternak and Olga Freidenberg*, by Elliott Mossman and Margaret Wettlin, New York, Harcourt Brace Jovanovich, and London, Secker and Warburg, 1982.

Rainer Maria Rilke, Marina Zwetajewa, Boris Pasternak: Briefwechsel, edited by Yevgeny Pasternak, Yelena Pasternak, and Konstantin M. Azadovsky. Frankfurt, Insel, 1983; translated as *Boris Pasternak, Marine Tsevtaeva, Rainer Maria Rilke: Letters, Summer 1926*, by Margaret Wettlin and Walter Arndt, San Diego, Harcourt Brace Jovanovich 1985; London, Jonathan Cape, 1986; Oxford, Oxford University Press, 1988.

Perepiska Borisa Pasternaka [Correspondence of Boris Pasternak]. Moscow, 1990.

Pis'ma B.L. Pasternaka k zhene Z.N. Neigauz-Pasternak [Letters of B.L. Pasternak to His Wife, Z.N. Neigauz-Pasternak]. Moscow, 1993.

"Boris Pasternak i Sergei Bobrov: pis'ma chetyrekh desiatiletii", *Stanford Slavic Studies*, 10 (1996).

Translator

Izbrannie perevody [Selected Translations]. Moscow, 1940.

Gamlet prints datskii [Hamlet], by William Shakespeare, Moscow, 1941; Moscow, 1975; Novosibirsk, 1980.

Romeo i Dzhul'etta [Romeo and Juliet], by William Shakespeare, 1943.

Antonii i Kleopatra [Antony and Cleopatra], by William Shakespeare, 1944.

Otello, venetsianskii mavr [Othello], by William Shakespeare, Moscow, 1945.

Gruzinskie poety [Georgian poets] (collection of translations). Moscow, 1946.

Genrikh chetvertyi [Henry IV, parts 1 and 2], by William Shakespeare, 1948.

Stikhotvoreniia, by N.M. Baratashvili, 1948.
Korol' Lir [King Lear], by William Shakespeare, 1949.
Vil'iam Shekspir v perevode Borisa Pasternaka [William Shakespeare in Translation by Boris Pasternak]. 1949.
Faust (part 1), by Goethe, 1950; complete version, 1953.
Vitiaz ianoshch, by Sándor Petöfi, 1950.
"Makbet" [Macbeth], in *Tragedii*, by William Shakespeare, 1951.
Mariia Stiuart, by Schiller, 1958.
Stikhi o Gruzii. Gruzinskie poety. Izbrannye perevody [Poems about Georgia. Georgian Poets. Selected Translations]. Tbilisi, 1958.
Zvezdnoe nebo. Stikhi zarubezhnykh poetov [The Starry Sky. Poems by Foreign Poets]. Moscow, 1966.
Zarubezhnaia poeziia v perevodakh B.L. Pasternaka [Foreign Poetry Translated by B.L. Pasternak]. 1990.

Critical Studies
Courage of Genius: The Pasternak Affair, by Robert Conquest, London, Collins and Harvill Press, 1961.
The Three Worlds of Boris Pasternak, by Robert Payne, New York, Coward-McCann, 1961; London, Robert Hale, 1962.
The Poems of Dr Zhivago, by Donald Davie, Manchester, Manchester University Press, 1965; reprinted Westport, Connecticut, Greenwood Press, 1977.
Pasternak's Lyric: A Study of Sound and Imagery, by Dale L. Plank, The Hague, Mouton, 1966.
Pasternak, edited by Donald Davie and Angela Livingstone, London, Macmillan, 1969; Nashville, Aurora, 1970.
Boris Pasternak, by J.W. Dyck, New York, Twayne, 1972.
The Poetic World of Boris Pasternak, by Olga R. Hughes, Princeton, Princeton University Press, 1974.
Themes and Variations in Pasternak's Poetics, by Krystyna Pomorska, Lisse, Peter de Ridder Press, 1975.
Nine Poems from Doktor Zhivago: A Study of Christian Motifs in Boris Pasternak's Poetry, by Per Arne Bodin, Stockholm, Almqvist & Wiksell, 1976.
Boris Pasternak: Essays, edited by Nils Åke Nilsson, Stockholm, Almqvist & Wiksell, 1976.
Boris Pasternak: A Critical Study, by Henry Gifford, Cambridge, Cambridge University Press, 1977; reprinted Bristol, Bristol Classical Press, 1991.
Meetings with Pasternak: A Memoir, by Aleksandr Gladkov, translated by Max Hayward, London, Collins Harvill, 1977.
Pasternak: A Collection of Critical Essays, edited by Victor Erlich, Englewood Cliffs, New Jersey, Prentice-Hall, 1978.
Boris Pasternak's Translations of Shakespeare, by Anna Kay France, Berkeley, University of California Press, 1978.
A Captive of Time: My Years with Pasternak, by Olga Ivinskaya, translated by Max Hayward, London, Collins Harvill, 1978.
Boris Pasternak, 1890–1960: colloque de Cérisy-la-Salle (11–14 septembre, 1975), Paris, Institut d'Études Slaves, 1979.
Boris Pasternak v dvadtsatye gody, by Lazar' Fleishman, Munich, Fink, 1980.
Boris Pasternak: His Life and Art, by Guy de Mallac, Norman, University of Oklahoma Press, 1981.
Writers in Russia, 1917–1978, by Max Hayward, San Diego, Harcourt Brace Jovanovich, and London, Harvill Press, 1983.
Pasternak: A Biography, by Ronald Hingley, London, Weidenfeld and Nicolson, and New York, Knopf, 1983.
Boris Pasternak v tridtsatye gody, by Lazar' Fleishman, Jerusalem, Magnes Press, 1984.
Porozhdenie interteksta (elementy intertekstual'nogo analiza s primerami iz tvorchestva B.L. Pasternaka), by I.P. Smirnov, Vienna, Wiener Slawistischer Almanach, 1985.
Pasternak's Novel: Perspectives on Doctor Zhivago, by Neil Cornwell, Keele, Essays in Poetics Publications, 1986.
Boris Pasternak's "My Sister-Life": The Illusion of Narrative, by Katherine Tiernan O'Connor, Ann Arbor, Ardis, 1988.
Boris Pasternak: A Literary Biography, Vol. I: 1890–1928, by Christopher Barnes, Cambridge and New York, Cambridge University Press, 1989.
Poetika Pasternaka ("Putevye zapiski" and "Okhrannaia gramota"), by Jerzy Faryno, Vienna, Wiener Slawistischer Almanach, 1989.
Boris Pasternak and His Times: Selected Papers from the Second International Symposium on Pasternak, edited by Lazar' Fleishman, Berkeley, Berkeley Slavic Specialties, 1989.
Boris Pasternak: Doctor Zhivago, by Angela Livingstone, Cambridge and New York, Cambridge University Press, 1989.
Boris Pasternak: materialy dlia biografii, by Evgenii Pasternak, Moscow, 1989.
Poeziia Borisa Pasternaka, by V. Al'fonsov, Leningrad, 1990.
Doktor Zhivago Borisa Pasternaka, compiled by L.V. Bakhov and L.B. Voronin, Moscow, 1990.
Boris Pasternak: The Poet and His Politics, by Lazar' Fleishman, Cambridge, Massachusetts, Harvard University Press, 1990.
Boris Pasternak: A Biography, by Peter Levi, London, Hutchinson, 1990.
Boris Pasternak: The Tragic Years, 1930–1960, by Evgeny Pasternak, translated by Michael Duncan, London, Collins Harvill, 1990.
Vospominaniia o Borise Pasternake, Moscow, 1993.
Pasternak's Short Fiction and the Cultural Vanguard, by Larissa Rudova, New York, Peter Lang, 1994.
Doctor Zhivago: A Critical Companion, edited by Edith W. Clowes, Evanston, Illinois, Northwestern University Press, 1995.
Boris Pasternak and the Tradition of German Romanticism, by Karen Evans-Romaine, Munich, Otto Sagner, 1997.
Understanding Boris Pasternak, by Larissa Rudova, Columbia, University of South Carolina Press, 1997.

Bibliographies
Boris Leonidovich Pasternak: Bibliografiia, by N.A. Troitskii, New York, All-Slavic Publishing House, 1969.
Pasternak's "Doctor Zhivago": An International Bibliography of Criticism (1957–1985), by Munir Sendich and Erika Greber, East Lansing, Michigan, Russian Language Journal, 1990.
Boris Pasternak: A Reference Guide, by Munir Sendich, New York, G.K. Hall, 1994.
Russkie pisateli i poety: bibliograficheskii ukazatel', 18. B. Pasternak, St Petersburg, 1995.

After a brief flirtation with Symbolism in his earliest poetry, Boris

Pasternak soon came under the influence of the newly formed Futurist movement, joining the Tsentrifuga group in 1914; his mature poetry, however, falls outside the orbit of any particular school. In his autobiographical work of 1931, *Okhrannaia gramota* (*Safe Conduct*), Pasternak writes that "focused upon a reality that is dislocated by feeling, art is the record of that dislocation". His poetry of the 1910s and 1920s makes full use, in the Futurist manner, of a wide range of linguistic and metrical devices to achieve a discursive reflection of this dislocation and to show the world in an unaccustomed light. It is characterized by the dense accumulation of metaphor, by the widespread use of personification, by unusual rhymes and metres, by highly developed patterns of alliteration and assonance, and by semantic linkages that grow from the phonetic associations of words. Pasternak avoids for the most part the urban and industrial concerns of some Futurists, preferring to explore the borders between one psychological state and another, as highlighted by such dislocatory experiences as illness, travel, and love. The world of nature provides another primary source of dislocation in that the poetic "I" of Pasternak's lyrics is regularly subsumed into it and indeed identified with it. Nature is effectively equated with life, and poetry too is subsumed into a holistic view of the universe, glimpsed in a series of revelatory moments. *Sestra moia zhizn'* (*My Sister-Life*), which appeared in 1922 and epitomizes both the thematic and stylistic concerns of Pasternak's early verse, immediately secured him recognition as a major poet.

In the mid-1920s, Pasternak moved away from purely personal themes and began to reflect on historical and moral concerns flowing from the Bolshevik consolidation of power. The prose piece *Vozdushnye puti* [Aerial Ways] shows revolution as an abstract force on a par with nature, and Pasternak, following the fashion of the times for works of epic stature, also wrote the long poems *Deviat'sot piatyi god* (*The Year Nineteen Five*) and *Leitenant Shmidt* [Lieutenant Schmidt], which capture the fervour of revolution and see in it transcendent qualities. In his collection *Vtoroe rozhdenie* [Second Birth], which was published in 1932, Pasternak attempted to reconcile the public and lyrical elements of his writing within a consciously simpler poetic language, but after this, as the newly formed Writers' Union increasingly imposed the doctrine of socialist realism, he gradually ceased to produce original work. Instead, like many others at this time, he turned to translation, an art in which he showed an unrivalled talent. His translations include a volume of Georgian lyrics, published in 1935, and notably many of the plays of Shakespeare, which occupied him through the 1940s, and Goethe's *Faust* and Schiller's *Maria Stuart*, both of which appeared in the 1950s.

The poems that Pasternak was able to publish during the cultural Thaw of the war years – *Na rannikh poezdakh* [On Early Trains], *Zemnoi prostor* [Earth's Vastness] – continue to combine civic and personal themes in their patriotic examination of people's lives at a time of crisis. After the war the direct civic content disappears, while an interest in historical and moral problems remains. The principal focus of Pasternak's creativity (apart from his translations) became the ill-fated novel *Doctor Zhivago*, which considers the crises of its hero's personal life against a background dominated by the Revolution and the autonomy of the natural world and in the context of Zhivago's vocation as a poet.

The "Poems of Yurii Zhivago" and Pasternak's other verse of the 1950s which was published in *Kogda razguliaetsia (When the Weather Clears)* share a simplicity which is quite different from his style of the 1920s. The rhymes and metres are more conventional; the word-play continues, but in an attenuated form; the emphasis on verbs and action is replaced by a focus on nouns and contemplation. Pasternak's perennial theme of the essential unity of human existence is stated more simply and broadened to include a cyclical view of art, nature, and history. Religious motifs, particularly in the Zhivago poems, add a further, metaphysical, dimension.

Pasternak is a rare example of a Russian writer who was established before the Revolution and who continued to function in literature throughout Stalin's rule without seriously compromising his professional integrity. His broad sympathy with socialist goals and his early association with Maiakovskii and the Left Front of Art no doubt counted for something with the Soviet authorities, but even during the 1920s he was attacked for his subjectivity and complexity. Yet for a while in the 1930s he was allowed to participate in literary officialdom through the Writers' Union and even to travel abroad. Though he was not always able to publish his poetry, unlike many of his contemporaries he was able to maintain his material situation and reputation. The most serious threat to Pasternak's position came not under Stalin, but under Khrushchev, when he was expelled from the Writers' Union in 1958 in the scandal that followed the publication of *Doctor Zhivago* in the west, and obliged to renounce the Nobel Prize. The campaign of vilification that was launched against him at that time may well have contributed to his death in 1960. Unofficially Pasternak's poetry and prose remained extremely popular, and a gradual official rehabilitation took place after his death, though it was not until the very end of the Soviet period that *Doctor Zhivago* could be made available to a Russian audience.

DAVID N. WELLS

My Sister-Life

Sestra moia zhizn'

Poetry collection, 1922 (written 1917)

Published only in 1922, *My Sister-Life* is arguably Pasternak's greatest book of poetry. Its sense of unity and cohesiveness can be attributed to its focus on a love affair (or affairs), which emerges as conterminous with the spring and summer that spans the February and October Revolutions of 1917: a dominant presence, although many references can be missed on a first reading. Equally omnipresent is the theme of poetic creation – not only the poet's own but also that of his poet-mentors (such as Lenau who provides the epilogue and Lermontov to whom the book is dedicated). To borrow the camera imagery of one of its most spectacular poems, "Groza momental'naia navek" ("A Thunderstorm Instantaneous Forever"), *My Sister-Life* is a blinding illumination or flash-photo of the poet's simultaneous experience of love, poetic creation, and revolution.

Its 50 poems are organized into ten chapters, each carrying its own title and exhibiting a certain thematic or discursive consistency and sometimes a shared setting. Moreover, poems interconnect with each other in a variety of intricate ways. *My*

Sister-Life has a highly premeditated structure. Beginning with a dedicatory poem to the Demon, underscoring Lermontov's privileged position, chapter 1 ("Ne vremia l' ptitsam pet'?" ("Isn't it Time for the Birds to Sing?")) goes on to add Byron, Edgar Allan Poe, and Rudyard Kipling. The book's famous title poem (a *train*-poem, itself significant for the structural thematics of the book) then shifts focus to the poet himself, whose idiosyncratic delight in nature distinguishes him from ordinary mortals and makes him the equal of life itself: in effect the *brother* of the *sister*. This peer relationship with nature is further explored in the poems of the *garden*-cycle, enframed within which is the *mirror*-cycle: a brilliant meditation on the poet's reflection of nature, through the medium of the mirror's reflection of the garden. The beloved, heretofore an elusive *fata Morgana*, finally appears in the concluding poem, where the poet announces "she is with me". This paves the way for "Kniga stepi" ("Book of the Steppe"), presenting a broad overview of the affair itself: its various locales and settings and the contrasting "scenes" and moods enframed. The chapter concludes with a nostalgic evocation, framed by allusions to the historical present (1917), thereby executing a subtle transition to the succeeding chapter, which focuses on the beloved's "diversions" – two of which are, respectively, romantic love and the revolution-in-progress. Here the famous "Slozha vesla" ("With Oars Crossed") appears: an ecstatic yet ironically self-aware meditation on the delights of conventional romantic bliss. The beloved's "diversions" conclude with "Uroki angliiskogo" ("English Lessons"), a bravura demonstration of Pasternak's own inventive familiarity with Shakespeare, thus paving the way for *his* "pursuit of philosophy" and the *definition*-cycle that demonstrates his perception of poetry, creativity, and the soul in purely poetic terms, relating to the world of nature and feeling. His "pursuit" also embraces a thunderstorm, a vehicle for both love affair and revolution. "Zamestitel'nitsa" ("The Replacement"), the chapter's concluding poem, is the live-action "photo" of the beloved that the poet carries in her absence. Its elaborate Lermontov-intertext completes (together with "Pamiati Demona" ("In Memory of the Demon")) another frame in the poetic sequence.

"Pesni v pis'makh, chtoby ne skuchala" ("Songs in Letters, so She Won't Get Bored") is a kind of synthesis of the preceding two chapters. The reference to letters evokes the lovers' physical separation and signals a shift in setting and locale, to the wooded environs of Moscow. A whole gamut of emotions accompanies the affair: from mutual exhilaration with the moment (Trinity Sunday in "Vorob'evy gory" ["Sparrow Hills"]) to a lovers' "scene" and the sense of vulnerability (hers) engendered by time's too quick passing (in "Mein Liebchen ..."). The final poem, "Raspad" ("Collapse") offers another perspective on time and again shifts the poetic narrative away from Moscow. Another *train*-poem, it shows the poet again *en route* (as in the book's title poem), impatient lest time pass too slowly. The familiar area around Balashov recurs, transformed by the turmoil and *collapse* of revolution. Thus the "romantic" impatience seen in the title poem is contrasted with another kind of impatience – lest the historical present last too long. "Romanovka" has the area around Balashov as its setting. The opening "Step'" ("The Steppe") immortalizes the steppe in words and images that are both solemn and sensuous, for here the lovers enact their own restaging of the Fall. As befits "after the fall", the setting becomes more confined and constricted (in the two *sultry*-poems) as we move inside the heat-prostrated town of Romanovka. Martial imagery recalls the revolutionary summer of 1917 and the mood is one of anxiousness, even paranoia. We progress along the Balashov Tambov railway line, from Romanovka to Muchkap, in the next chapter ("Popytka dushu rasluchit'" ("The Attempt to Separate My Soul")), which is one of transition: the poet's imminent departure from the area coinciding with his implied separation from his beloved. The heat, prostration, and sense of confinement from the preceding chapter are carried over, but now with a sense of the poet progressively distancing himself from all this. The concluding title poem, which follows an emotionally charged encounter between poet and beloved, records his actual disengagement from her and from the settings so indelibly associated with their affair. "Vozvrashchenie" ("The Return") translates imminence into actuality and shows the poet *en route*. The shortest chapter, it begins with the book's longest poem, "Kak usypitel'na zhizn'" ("How Soporific Life Is!") – another *train*-poem. Here the insomnia and soul-searching characteristic of long trips, coupled with apocalyptic evocations of the journey itself, blend with fleeting recollections of other times and places. The attempted separation from the beloved translates into her literal absence from the text, ending with the poet back in Moscow, thus completing the frame of *Moscow*-poems. Having returned, he now seeks release from the revelations of his journey and from *all that* through the oblivion of sleep.

Only in the penultimate epilogic chapter ("Elene" ["To Elena"]), is the beloved given a name. Recaptured in its experiential immediacy, the affair is also imbued with an irrevocable sense of *pastness*. The focus gradually shifts from the lovers to the seasonal and historical setting. The penultimate poem, "Leto" ("Summer") is a sensual evocation of fading summer, interspersed with fleeting references to the politics of Kerenskii's Provisional Government. The casualness of these references suggests that history has contributed a special colouring and tone to the summer, without overshadowing it. The brilliant "A Thunderstorm Instantaneous Forever" takes a final keepsake photo (by means of the storm itself) of the locale and railroad stop (*polustanok*) immortalized by the affair. The proliferation of textual echoes suggests the replacement of the book's narrative linearity by a circularity, marking completion and end, which continues into the final chapter, "Posleslov'e" ("Afterword"), containing numerous textual links with the opening chapter. "Liubimaia – zhut'!" ("Darling – It's an Awesome Sight!") celebrates the epic passions of the poet in love (echoing the book's title poem) and the majestic "Davai roniat' slova" ("Let's Scatter Words ...") (echoing "Balashov") compares the poet's craftmanship as a "sower of words" with that of nature's creator. Associated settings reappear, but the sublime transcendence of earlier poems is absent and there are disquieting allusions to the historical present. The final poem, fittingly named "Konets" ("The End"), conveys a combined incredulity and fatigue, seeking again the soothing oblivion of dreamless sleep.

KATHERINE TIERNAN O'CONNOR

The Childhood of Luvers

Detstvo Liuvers

Story, 1922

The Childhood of Luvers, first published in the almanac *Nashi dni* (1 [1922]), and later included in Pasternak's 1925 volume of *Rasskazy* [Stories] established the author's reputation as a prose writer. This not so short story, originally planned as the beginning of a novel, and destined to become "central" in Pasternak's *oeuvre*, was in fact never completed.

As early as his book of verse *My Sister-Life* (written in 1917), Pasternak was bidding "goodbye to verse", and granting the reader "a *rendez-vous* ... in a novel" (*Osen'* [*Autumn*]). He then told Marina Tsvetaeva about his intention of writing a long novel "with love and a heroine, like Balzac". By 1918 much of the work, with the supposed title "Three Names", had been completed. The unifying element referred, in Pasternak's words, to "the moment of shaping in human consciousness an abstract idea, and the consequences this had on a character". Thus the novel with an ethical undertone appears to be present in Pasternak's creative intentions almost from the beginning.

Pasternak worked on prose concurrently with verse and, as the poems of *Doctor Zhivago* testify, the two sides of his creative expression were considered complementary. Roman Jakobson pointed out the natural affinity between the poet's preference for metonymy and his inclination towards prose. A semantic analysis of Pasternak's early attempts by Iurii Lotman also revealed an approach typical of the prose writer, primarily concerned with *meaning*. Verse represented a shorthand account of a momentary impression and, as Pasternak stated in a letter to an English correspondent, this was to be further developed in prose, a medium more fitted to deal with "ambient reality".

However, Pasternak's longing to complete a novel had to wait for decades, before reaching fruition with *Doctor Zhivago*. Like Iurii Zhivago, who had been dreaming of "a big prose work" from his school years, Pasternak was too young to paint a broad biographical canvas, and at the beginning of the 1930s he destroyed the continuation of the manuscript. We can only guess at the type of novel *The Childhood of Luvers* might have become, had it been completed.

Pasternak's most characteristic ethical-philosophical concerns are already present, revealing a certain continuity from the early prose to *Doctor Zhivago*. The Christian idea of concern for another human being substantiates Zhenia Liuvers's relationship to "a third person". Tsvetkov, the man previously noticed by Zhenia, is killed in an accident caused by her parents' horse carriage, and Zhenia feels responsible for this death. The proximity between art and death was to become a recurrent motif in Pasternak's work.

The aspiration to express philosophical ideas in *The Childhood of Luvers* is complicated by a certain stylistic obscurity, or an over literal application of "biographical realism", that lay at the core of Pasternak's personal aesthethics. Unlike in his mature novel, Pasternak here makes no attempt to impose his own voice. Indeed, Zhenia has been called a *patiens* to whom everything is notified. She is endowed with the highly sensitive "organs of perception" of which art itself is composed. Apart from certain biographical coincidences (the foreign surname and the childhood spent in the Urals), she is not to be identified with Zhivago's Lara. Zhenia embodies poetry itself, opening to absorb reality like a "sponge", to use Pasternak's favourite term in defining art (*Neskol'ko polozhenii* [*Some Propositions*]).

The story explores the realm in which poetry is born. The dazzling showers of Pasternak's impressionistic imagery are ordered into a somewhat more consequential sequence than usual, as Zhenia contemplates the world. The affinity between her and the poet, made explicit in the parallel between "a woman of beauty" and "a man of genius", which Pasternak established in his first autobiography *Safe Conduct*, stems from the "penchant for suffering" that a creative nature shares with the feminine. Zhenia's encounter with the outside world and her discovery of womanhood act as a pretext to display Pasternak's vision of the world. He too is a non-participant, apprehending life spontaneously, constantly worried about the deeper pattern of interlocking destinies. What in *Doctor Zhivago* is solved through fortuitous coincidences, in *The Childhood of Luvers* is left to an elliptical structure of narration, made up of the girl's circumscribed shifts from her room to the backyard, and from there to the street behind. While there is little plot, the prosaic details encountered on this everyday journey stimulate the girl's imagination into an endless process of recreating reality. The only logical chain linking the digressions, *omissis* and unrelated switches from which the story is woven lies in Zhenia's life experience. Her role has been defined as that of a "travelling observer". Scenes replace each other as the heroine moves in the limited spaces of everyday existence and new images encroach on her horizon, only to be freely recomposed in her mind into a sort of Cubist painting made of random bits and pieces. The resulting whole gives a uniquely unedited, though still down-to-earth, picture.

The biographical definition of realism practised in *The Childhood of Luvers* renders Pasternak's prose consanguineous with such innovations of European literature as J.P. Jacobsen's *Niels Lyhne* or Rainer Maria Rilke's *Die Aufzeichnungen Malte Laurids Brigge* (*The Notebook of Malte Laurids Brigge*). Zhenia and Malte, joined in a common effort to destroy the habitual surface of inanimate things, and to belong to the restricted category of children predisposed to act as intermediaries between the universe and its need for renewal. Linguistic defamiliarization plays an important role: the search for words typical of a child, to which Zhenia repeatedly resorts, communicates a tangible immediacy of being. Time and again Zhenia finds herself at the very beginning of the creative process as described by Pasternak in *Safe Conduct*:

> We cease to recognize reality. It manifests itself in some new category. And this category appears to be its own inherent condition and not our own. Apart from this condition everything in the world has a name. Only it is new and is not yet named. We try to name it – and the result is art.

When first published, *The Childhood of Luvers* was welcomed as the "freshest Russian prose of the past three or four years", clearly distinguishable from evocations of childhood by Aleksei Tolstoi, Andrei Belyi or Vsevolod Ivanov. Gor'kii gave it enthusiastic backing in a foreword to an unrealized English translation, even though his appraisal of the story, as the work of a rebellious romantic, quite missed the subdued quality of the poetic images that disperse, rather than concentrate on, the poet's *ego*. As its latest English translator Christopher Barnes maintains (*The Voice of Prose*, 1986), if there are romantic traits to be found in Pasternak's prose, they participate in a Keatsian empathy with all creation, where the poet is a medium rather than an active agent. *The Childhood of Luvers* flows in the mainstream of European modernism; this still much-admired work of Pasternak's prose is the moulding force of life from which poetry is born. *The Childhood of Luvers* is a *Künstlerroman* in its infancy.

DAŠA ŠILHÁNKOVÁ DI SIMPLICIO

Safe Conduct

Okhrannaia gramota

Autobiographical essay, 1931

Pasternak described *Safe Conduct* as a series of recollections, not particularly interesting in themselves, apart from the fact that they contained an honest and frank effort to understand culture and art, if not in general, at least in the life of a single man.

Safe Conduct, the most complex and intriguing of Pasternak's short prose, and essential for an understanding of his poetics, was first published as a volume in 1931. Extracts had appeared previously in the periodicals *Zvezda*, 8 (1929) and *Krasnaia nov'*, 4/5–6 (1931). It was not included in the 1933 edition of Pasternak's prose, *Vozdushnye puti*. The next Moscow edition of Pasternak's prose writings, under the same title (*Safe Conduct* included), had to wait until 1982. *Safe Conduct* has appeared in all editions of his Collected Works, and is usually referred to as Pasternak's "first autobiography".

In his second autobiographical essay, "Liudi i polozheniia" [People and Circumstances] (1956), Pasternak rejected his early biographical narrative as pretentious and overloaded with unnecessary mannerism. Christopher Barnes, whose translation of the work appeared in 1986 (*The Voice of Prose*), does not try to equal Pasternak's mannered rendering, yet the essential message is still there, conveying to the English reader some of the most original views on art ever expressed by a Russian poet. Mature artists are not always the best judges of their creative work; "Liudi i polozheniia", although providing a more complete account of the poet's life, is certainly a lesser work of art in itself.

The genre of *Safe Conduct* is not easily defined. The belief that the poet should not choose his genre, but the genre should choose its poet can be applied to *Safe Conduct*, and to Pasternak's work as a whole. In an effort to embrace varying features of a multifarious existence, Pasternak blurs boundaries. Half essay and half autobiography, *Safe Conduct* can be viewed from an informative or from a creative perspective. It echoes circumstances of cultural history and of the author's personal creative development.

When analysed against its historical background, the title *Safe Conduct* acquires a significance that stretches beyond Pasternak's creative intention, assuming the role of a defence of the lyrical poet's right of existence. This becomes particularly evident when one reads the passages omitted for ideological reasons from the original 1931 publication, and restored in the 1986 English translation. Aesopic images of lions' muzzles, nosing into everyone's privacy, were quite easy to decipher in Soviet times. More cryptic is the leonine roar of an imaginary immortality (part 2, 17) that threatens the artist's reputation and therefore provokes his passionate reaction.

The shy attempts made to attune his verses to the age, as represented by the epic poems of the 1920s, were sufficient to gain for Pasternak the position almost of an "acknowledged" poet, which was utterly at odds with his intentions. An acute awareness of the falsehood of this situation required clarification. Thus *Safe Conduct* became Pasternak's personal manifesto at a moment when such things were no longer popular. The more obsolete the content, the more Pasternak clung to it as to a sort of cherished talisman of his creative journey.

The fact that *Safe Conduct* was originally intended as an essay about a congenial fellow-poet is perfectly consonant with Pasternak's poetics. In 1926, at a moment of personal and creative crisis, Pasternak received a letter from his father, informing him that Rilke, to whom *Safe Conduct* is dedicated, knew and admired his verse. Under the spell of happiness aroused by this discovery, Pasternak started a brief and intense correspondence between himself, Rilke, and Marina Tsvetaeva. Within this triangle Tsvetaeva would act as Pasternak's *alter ego*, and he in return would receive news about Rilke from her. Tsvetaeva repeatedly attempted to organize a personal meeting of the three, but Pasternak (as well as Rilke) was reluctant. His ideal corresponded to just this type of contingent relationship, soon to be cut short by Rilke's death. To fill this vacancy, Pasternak decided to write an essay on Rilke. As on other occasions, he soon lost the thread of his discourse, distracted as usual by side references. Inevitably, he ended up writing about his own poetic world. Since he considered himself Rilke's creation (letter to R.M. Rilke of 12 April 1926), he could only end by rediscovering his own poetic origins. Hence the statement: "I am not presenting my recollections in memory of Rilke. On the contrary, I myself received them as a gift from him."

This indirect way of depicting life's events remained characteristic of Pasternak's creative approach to reality. When writing about Rilke's verse, Skriabin's music, Symbolist and Futurist poetry, Marburg philosophy, Venetian painting and Maiakovskii, Pasternak actually gives a metonymical self-portrait, made up of meaningful encounters. Each one contains a parting, clearing the way for the next infatuation. The emotional energy required for this process is transformed into a creative outburst; therefore, "any love is a crossing over into some new faith".

Only two "protagonists" of this "collective story" of Pasternak's genealogy remain as lasting revelations: Rilke, whom Pasternak had encountered twice by chance before he could even realize his link with the author of *Mir zu Feier*; and the world's *marginalia*, which he is eager to make speak. Poetry stems from the real world that has refused a symbolic transfer into higher spheres, and it stands out tangibly, preserving the plastic quality of the visual arts on which both Rilke and Pasternak were brought up. It is among the models for still life that the hidden soul of apparently common things, and with it the poet's vocation, is discovered. However, Pasternak had a long time to wait before he could give free expression to his words.

The few biographical data contained in *Safe Conduct* are usually described in terms of metonymical jumps: from music to philosophy, from philosophy to poetry. Yet his real choice lay only between the two truly creative types of occupation. Piano improvisation could only be replaced by the verse sketch, and not by philosophy, which would have required a serious professional attitude. The heaps of open books scattered in his Marburg room exemplify Pasternak's unbounded way of thinking, which was capable of combining the town's medieval history and its present-day philosophy into a "manuscript": inspiring for a poet, but not too fruitful for a would-be philosopher.

Safe Conduct might have continued with chapters on Georgia, Tsvetaeva, and other lasting impressions that shaped the poet. Instead it ends with a definitive farewell that leaves no regrets. The painful parting with Vladimir Maiakovskii recollects the deliberate separation from a self-centered type of writing that Pasternak had imposed on his 1917 collection of verse, *Poverkh bar'erov* [Over the Barriers]. The romantic hyperbole personified by Maiakovskii and the tragedy that bears his name could not coexist with his own beloved metonymy.

DAŠA ŠILHÁNKOVÁ DI SIMPLICIO

Doctor Zhivago

Doktor Zhivago

Novel, 1957

Pasternak's novel, recognized by many as the greatest Russian novel of the 20th century, was first published in Russian and in Italian translation by the publisher Feltrinelli in Milan in 1957, having been rejected by the Soviet journal *Novyi mir* the previous year. It was translated into English in 1958. Awarded the Nobel Prize for Literature shortly afterwards, Pasternak was immediately subjected to a storm of official Soviet disapproval. He was expelled from the Soviet Writers' Union and forced to give up the prize. The novel, branded in the Soviet Union as anti-socialist, anti-democratic, and anti-historical, was banned for three decades until it appeared in 1988, in the very journal which had originally rejected it.

The notoriety surrounding it quickly earned the novel best-seller status in the west despite critical reservations about its structure, its genre, and its hero. There was never any doubt about the brilliance of its prose and the poignancy of its love story, even though Pasternak's reputation until then had been principally that of a rather esoteric poet. In 1965 the novel was made into a highly successful film directed by David Lean, starring Omar Sharif and Julie Christie, with a screenplay by Robert Bolt.

Multifaceted and many-layered, *Doctor Zhivago* is about both revolution and the making of poetry; it is partly autobiography, partly epic novel; it is partly *sui generis*, partly in the tradition of the great 19th-century novel but without the emphasis on causality; it is about the experiences of the doctor-poet, Iurii Zhivago, from boyhood to death, about his loves and his betrayals, just as it is also a form of latterday Christian hagiography that proclaims an ultimate symbolic victory of life over death in the final 25 poems that comprise Zhivago's testament.

The total chronological span of the fiction encompasses at least 50 years, from 1903 to 1953, and it embraces the worlds both of Zhivago himself and of Lara Guishar, the Tiverzins, the Gromekos, Misha Gordon, Nikki Dudorov, and Antipov-Strelnikov. Opening in 1903 with the death of Zhivago's mother when he is ten years old, it tells how the boy is finally orphaned by the suicide of his father through the malign influence of his lawyer, Komarovskii. Zhivago is then brought up in the Gromeko family; he is awakened to his own gift of life, his poetic vocation, by the death of his adoptive mother and the realization that he should use his gift in the furtherance of healing. Simultaneously, Lara Guishar, "the girl from a different world", as she is called, seduced in her teens by the unscrupulous Komarovskii, marries her boyhood sweetheart Pasha Antipov. Zhivago, who has qualified as a doctor, also marries and has a child, but when he meets Lara during World War I he falls in love with her and recognizes he must choose between her and his wife and family. Returning to Moscow after the October Revolution, he accepts the changes in an affirmative spirit. Growing privation, though, and disillusionment make him and his family decide to leave Moscow for the haven of the Urals.

There, at Varykino, not far from the town of Iuriatin, they live out several seasons of the Civil War and by chance Zhivago encounters Lara again. He succumbs to his love for her and chooses a life with her, only to be ambushed and made captive by local partisans who force him to act as their doctor. Appalled at the rigidity of their revolutionary doctrines, but also forced to realize the ambiguity of his own loyalties in the Civil War, he eventually escapes and makes his way back to Lara. His family, supposing him to be dead, have meanwhile returned to Moscow where they are due to be deported.

In the depth of winter Komarovskii discovers Lara and Zhivago at Varykino and offers them a kind of safe conduct to the east. Lara and her daughter leave with him on the understanding that Zhivago will follow shortly. He remains behind in snow-bound Varykino where he is visited by Lara's former husband, Pasha Antipov, renowned now as Strelnikov, a partisan leader, who commits suicide after acknowledging his disillusionment with the Revolution.

Finally Zhivago returns to Moscow, resumes his career as a doctor and marries again, but his life is increasingly dominated by his poetry. He dies of a weak heart during a protracted tram journey in August 1929. Lara reappears before his burial and delivers a final epitaph to their love, but his real memorial is his poetry, which his friends Gordon and Dudorov are seen studying at the novel's close, some months after Stalin's death.

Inevitably such a digest emphasizes the improbabilities of coincidence that comprise the "moving entireness" (Pasternak's term) of the novel. The greatness of the work resides more certainly in the steely, poetic exactitude of the nature descriptions, in the deeply pondered dialogues, in the poetry so intimately linked with the narrative, and in the impact of the love story played out against the novel's central theme, which is the tragedy of a nation divided by revolution and civil war. This tragedy has personal meaning for Zhivago in that his life becomes irreversibly split. He cannot return to what he was, no more than he can give up his love for Lara. The break occurs in chapter or part 10, the only section of the novel from which he is wholly absent and the moment, structurally, when the historical calendar becomes a fictional calendar. Zhivago becomes superfluous, like the pre-revolutionary intelligentsia as a whole.

Nevertheless, he epitomizes a life-renewing principle (his name derives from *zhivoi*: "living") and he is supported in life by the intervention of both a miracle-working half-brother and a transfiguring Christian ideal received in boyhood. The image of Hamlet (as in his first poem), forced to play the role of Christ is Zhivago's ultimate epitaph and has the power of a parable (implicit in his final poem "Gethsemane") that can surmount his death and the death of his world.

RICHARD FREEBORN

When the Weather Clears

Kogda razguliaetsia

Poetry collection, 1960

Pasternak's last book of poetry, *When the Weather Clears*, was composed through the 1950s. The Proust epigraph, comparing a book to a cemetery, strikes a different chord from his earlier poetry of natural affirmation: "A book is a huge cemetery in which most of the tombstones have names that are effaced and can no longer be read". Such a metaphor has been used by a number of writers at least from the romantic period onwards. Comparing the metapoetics of this epigraph with the Lenau epigraph (to *My Sister-Life*), we find a striking progression. From an artist in the process of composition, we move to a still-life of the end-product: the cemetery or burial ground that is the book. Although the title heralds clarification and illumination, its opaque epigraph hints at the reverse. Given the association in *My Sister-Life* between life, love, creative energy, historical turbulence, and inclement weather, this title presages an end to all that and is, indeed, not without its ambivalence. The Proust epigraph here takes on the quality of a metaphoric expression of "anxiety of influence". Other and arguably greater prior texts have gone into this book's composition; their not being named as such stems from the indecipherability lent by time and imposed by the artist himself.

One poem is frequently linked with the Proust epigraph: "[My] Soul" (*Dusha*). When Pasternak likens his soul to a burial vault (*usypal'nitsa*) or funeral urn (*mogil'naia urna*) containing the remains or ashes of those who "suffered torments when alive" (*zamuchennye zhiv'em*), it is assumed to refer to his poet-contemporaries, Maiakovskii, Mandel'shtam, and Tsvetaeva, who, less fortunate than he, did not survive into the 1950s. Unnamed, they evoke the "effaced names" on the tombstones. As Pasternak frequently identified his soul with his poetry, this poem can also be read as an allegorical tribute to the intertextuality of art. The poet has borne witness to the suffering and persecution of his poet-peers and paid tribute to them through his verses; and their verses too have helped to germinate his. Moreover, the poem's concluding stanza suggests that Pasternak's own remains will be added to the "graveyard compost" (*pogostnyi peregnoi*) that will, in turn, germinate future texts. Thus the spirit of intertextual affirmation complements a spirit of life-affirmation (with religious overtones). The final stanza invites comment; the subject of the imperative verb is, indeed, "my soul": "And keep on grinding / Everything that happened to me / For almost forty years, / Into a churchyard compost". The poet is addressing people and events that have filled his life and germinated his art.

The titles of the following two poems are of interest in terms of personal relationships. "Eve" is a celebration of womankind, or Woman, in Pasternak's life. This archetypal naming of the poem serves to underscore the undifferentiated nature of the poet's tribute to Woman. The next poem, however, is an individualized portrait of an unnamed woman that highlights her personal characteristics and the associated familiar setting. This woman has been "identified" as Ol'ga Ivinskaia; the fact that the poem that pays her such specific tribute is entitled "Bez nazvaniia" ("Untitled" or "Nameless") serves to dramatize her enforced anonymity and yet uniqueness. Thus, the final stanza can be read on more than one plane: "The word love is banal [*poshlo*], you're right. / I'll think up another name [*klichka*] / For you, I'll rename, if you wish, / All the world, all the words." The poet's insistence here that he will rename the universe, if it is her wish, is not without its attendant ironies. Unwilling to name her, he offers to rename everything else in her honour. He thus casts himself as Adam, to whom God granted such a privilege of naming. When the poet, then, (or Adam) offers to rename things for her, he is suggesting that a second creation, or renaming of creation, is in order, whereby she will no longer be Eve, and everything else will be renamed accordingly. Until then, however, anonymity or namelessness must be her badge of distinction.

The overall title affronts the reader with its anticipated, antithetical calm. Most obviously, it evokes the particular period when the book was being completed, namely, the late 1950s: the storm of controversy surrounding the publication of *Doctor Zhivago*, the awarding of the Nobel Prize, and the complexities of Pasternak's private life. It is thus both realistic and optimistic: hope that the weather will clear, but as yet unfulfilled. A more elegiac note is struck, however, beneath these surface melodies, resounding even more loudly when we recall the place of this final book of verse in Pasternak's own chronology: by this time his health was deteriorating. The anticipated "clearing of the weather", evokes, therefore, death's illumination and simplification, rather than its mystery and darkness.

The poet is here the viewer of an animated still-life, namely, the suburban woodland setting of Peredelkino, undergoing transformations of light and colour as the weather changes. The effect produced is to turn nature into a church where a service is in progress. The poet is one of the congregation: "With secret trembling, to the end, / I will thy long and moving service / In tears of happiness attend". The perfective verb *otstoiat'* (translated by Lydia Slater Pasternak as *attend*) means "to stand through something to the end". With nature as church, the peace and stillness, already descending as the weather clears and the sun comes out, acquire a quality of reverence and revelation.

The requirement of being stood through to the end invites speculation as to why this seemingly welcome stillness should necessitate such endurance and conjures up the spectre of what might follow. Evidently, what is invoked is not only the fact of death, but also the process of dying that precedes it: endurance to be "stood through to the end". Also evoked here is the intermediary stage between dying and the darkness beyond the grave: namely, the funeral service that precedes burial. In an extraordinary synthesis, the poet combines an image of himself as a mourner at his own funeral with that of the newly deceased lying in the coffin.

One of the greatest poems in the cycle is a tribute to the artist, entitled "Noch'" ("Night"). "Night" is about a poet who has taken flight and is depicted as a solo pilot on a night flight. Another French writer, Antoine de Saint-Exupéry, may here have left his mark, by providing Pasternak with at least a partial impulse: his novel *Vol de Nuit* (*Night Flight*) published in France in the early 1930s. A detachment is felt here between the poetic persona and the pilot. The poet (who enters the poem only in the concluding stanzas) is very much earthbound, while the pilot emerges as a model. The poet enters as an impersonal presence: "komu-nibud' ne spitsia ..." (someone cannot sleep). Eventually, however, he is addressed as *khudozhnik* (artist). Sleeplessness is a familiar malady in Pasternak, often associated with creativity; given the themes of this collection, such allusions to the irresistibility of sleep are indeed redolent of imminent mortality.

KATHERINE TIERNAN O'CONNOR

Konstantin Georg'evich Paustovskii 1892–1968

Prose writer

Biography

Born in Moscow, 31 May 1892. Attended school in Kiev; Kiev University, 1912–14; Moscow University, 1914. Medical orderly in the Russian Army, 1914–15. Married: 1) Ekaterina Stepanovna Zagorskaia in 1916; 2) Valeriia Vladimirovna Valishevskaia in 1937; 3) Tat'iana Alekseevna Evteeva in 1951; two sons. Reporter in Moscow, Odessa, Taganrog, Caucasus, 1917–23. Settled in Moscow, 1923; frequent travel throughout the Soviet Union. Full-time writer from 1932. War correspondent, 1941–45. For health reasons moved to Tarusa, 1955. Nominated for the Lenin and Nobel Prizes for Literature, 1965. Died in Moscow, 14 July 1968; buried in Tarusa.

Publications

Collected Editions

The Flight of Time: New Stories, translated by Lev Navrozov. Moscow, Foreign Languages Publishing House, 1956.
Sobranie sochinenii, 6 vols. Moscow, 1957–58.
Poteriannye romany [The Lost Novels]. Kaluga, 1962.
Rasskazy/Selected Stories [in Russian], introduction and notes by Peter Henry. Oxford, Pergamon Press, 1967.
Sobranie sochinenii, 8 vols. Moscow, 1967–70.
Selected Stories, translated by Kathleen Cook *et al.* Moscow, Progress, 1970; reprinted 1974.
Sobranie sochinenii, 9 vols. Moscow, 1981–86.
Rainy Dawn and Other Stories, translated by David and Ludmila Matthews. London, Quartet, 1995.

Fiction

Morskie nabroski [Sea Sketches]. Moscow, 1925.
Blistiaiushchie oblaka [Shining Clouds]. Moscow, 1929.
Kara-Bugaz. Moscow, 1932; translated as *The Black Gulf*, by E. Shimanskaya, London, Hutchinson, 1946; reprinted Westport, Connecticut, Hyperion Press, 1979.
Sud'ba Sharlia Lonsevilia [The Destiny of Charles Lonceville]. Moscow, 1933.
Kolkhida. Moscow, 1934; translated as "Colchis", by Kathleen Cook, in *Selected Stories*, 1970.
Romantiki [The Romantics]. Moscow, 1935.
Severnaia povest' [A Northern Tale]. Moscow, 1939.
Meshchorskaia storona [The Meshchora]. Moscow, 1939.
Povest' o lesakh [The Story of Forests]. Moscow, 1948.
Zolotaia roza. Moscow, 1956; translated as *The Golden Rose*, by Susanna Rosenberg, Moscow, Foreign Languages Publishing House, 1957.
Naedine s osen'iu [Alone with Autumn]. Moscow, 1967.
Vo glubine Rossii; translated as "In the Heart of Russia", in *In the Heart of Russia and Other Stories*, Moscow, Raduga, 1986.

Memoirs and Essays

Povest' o zhizni, 2 vols. Moscow, 1964; *Kniga skitanii*, Moscow, 1965; translated as *The Story of a Life*, by Joseph Barnes, 2 vols, New York, Pantheon, 1964; as *Story of a Life (Childhood and Schooldays, Slow Approach of Thunder, In That Dawn, Years of Hope)*, by Michael Duncan and Manya Harari, 4 vols, London, Harvill Press, 1964–68; and as *The Story of a Life, Southern Adventure, The Restless Years*, translated by Kyril FitzLyon, vols 5–6, London, Harvill Press, 1969–74.
Kniga o khudozhnikakh. Moscow, 1966; translated as *A Book about Artists*, by Kathleen Cook, Moscow, Progress, 1978.
Blizkie i dalekie. Literaturnye portrety [Near and Far. Literary Portraits]. Moscow, 1967.

Editor

Literaturnaia Moskva [Literary Moscow]. Moscow, 1956.
Tarusskie stranitsy [Pages from Tarusa]. Moscow, 1961.

Critical Studies

Rannee tvorchestvo K. Paustovskogo 1916–32gg, by Liudmila Sergeevna Achkasova, Kazan, 1960.
"Strana Paustovskogo", by B. Balter, *Literaturnaia Rossiia* (26 February 1965).
"Introduction", by Peter Henry, in *Rasskazy/Selected Stories*, 1967, xi–xxxvii.
Konstantin Paustovskii – novellist, by E.A. Aleksanian, Moscow, 1969.
Der Stil Konstantin Georgievič Paustovskijs, by Wolfgang Kasack, Cologne, Böhlau, 1971.
"Schast'e otkryvat' mir", by Viktor Shklovskii, *Izvestiia* (15 February 1975).
Konstantin Paustovskii. Ocherk tvorchestva, by Lev Levitskii, Moscow, 1977.

Vospominaniia o Konstantine Paustovskom, edited by Lev Levitskii, Moscow, 1983.
Konstantin Paustovskii, master prozy, by G.P. Trefilova, Moscow, 1983.
"Konstantin (Georgievich) Paustovsky", in *Contemporary Literary Criticism*, edited by Daniel G. Marowski, Detroit, Gale, 1986, vol. 40, 357–68.

Bibliography
Russkie sovetskie pisateli prozaiki. Biobibliograficheskii ukazatel', vol. 3. Leningrad, 1964, 524–62.

Konstantin Paustovskii's father, a railway official, was descended from the Zaporozhian Cossacks. Paustovskii went to a classical high school in Kiev where one of his schoolmates was Mikhail Bulgakov. His first story was published in 1912 but, aware that he lacked a knowledge of life, he published nothing for another ten years.

On the outbreak of World War I, after two years at Kiev University, and a short time at Moscow University, he enlisted as a medical orderly. During the Revolution, Civil War – events, in which, as he declared, he was "not a participant, but a profoundly interested witness" – and the 1920s he wandered from place to place in the south of Russia, working as factory worker, fisherman, and reporter. In Taganrog he began his first major work, *Romantiki* [The Romantics] (1916–23; published 1935). In 1917 he was a newspaper reporter in Moscow; in Kiev he was forcibly enrolled in Skoropadski's army and also served briefly in the Red Army. As a journalist on the Odessa newspaper *Moriak*, he was in contact with Babel', Il'f, Shklovskii, and Bagritskii.

In the 1920s he wrote about the romance of the sea, creating an exotic world of gorgeous colours and musical sounds. His characters are sea-captains, artists, composers, and writers dissatisfied with the drab world around them. *Morskie nabroski* [Sea Sketches] and *Blistiaiushchie oblaka* [Shining Clouds] are written in the manner of Aleksandr Grin; Babel' noted affinities with Joseph Conrad. Paustovskii's contributions to the literature of Social Command were the novel *Kara-Bugaz* (*The Black Gulf*), part documentary and part fictional, about explorers east of the Caspian Sea, and a romanticized historical tale, *Sud'ba Sharlia Lonsevilia* [The Destiny of Charles Lonceville]. Other works in that genre are *Kolkhida* (*Colchis*) and *Severnaia povest'* [A Northern Tale]. In the mid-1930s Paustovskii "discovered" Meshchora District, south of Moscow, which provided the setting of numerous short stories, written in a simple, seemingly effortless idiom, part realistic, part lyrical, with nature descriptions unsurpassed in Soviet literature, such as the cycles *Meshchorskaia storona* [The Meshchora] and the later *Povest' o lesakh* [The Story of Forests]. A correspondent during World War II, he wrote no stories about front-line heroism, but a play about Lermontov, a short novel about the rescue of art treasures in Leningrad, and muted love stories – "Sneg" [Snow] (1943), and "Dozhdlivyi rassvet" [A Rainy Dawn] (1945). This did not endear him to Soviet critics, who in spite of his artistic mastery and great popularity from the 1930s onwards either ignored or disparaged his work.

Paustovskii's stories are in the manner of those of Chekhov and Bunin, though less incisive and more sentimental than the latter's. Paustovskii focused on the inherent goodness of people, harmonious relationships, and sensitive attitudes to life and nature. A meticulous stylist, he carefully arranged his material, selected significant details and precise epithets of colour and sound, thereby creating a strong visual impact and a lyrical mood. He also wrote numerous essays, reminiscences, and lyrical novellas about Russian and foreign writers – Bunin, Bulgakov, Olesha, Grin, Heine, Maupassant, Andersen, Kipling, and Oscar Wilde – and about artists and composers – Orest Kiprenskii, Levitan, Pirosmanishvili, Van Gogh, Turner, Grieg, and Tchaikovskii. He wrote frequently on matters of public concern, warning, for example, of the ravages of the countryside – the pollution of forests, rivers, and lakes. He savagely attacked the insincerity, disregard for moral values and timidity of much officially approved writing and linguistic ugliness encountered in literature and in the press (*Literaturnaia gazeta*, 20 May 1959).

In *Zolotaia roza* (*The Golden Rose*) he wrote about the writer's craft, his personal approach to literature and manner of writing, on "the art of seeing the world". He taught creative writing at the Moscow Literary Institute for ten years; his pupils included Iurii Kazakov, Vladimir Tendriakov, and Iurii Bondarev. Largely ignoring the tenets of socialist realism, he insisted on total artistic freedom, on every writer's right to select his own themes and develop his own style. As co-editor of the anthology *Literaturnaia Moskva* [Literary Moscow] and editor of *Tarusskie stranitsy* [Pages from Tarusa] he played a major role in the rehabilitation of Bunin, Tsvetaeva, Olesha, Babel', Grin, Zabolotskii and promoted new writers out of favour with the Establishment like Okudzhava, Korzhavin, and Kazakov. A committed liberal, he defended Dudintsev in 1956, and Daniel' and Siniavskii in 1966.

His most impressive work, the autobiographical *Povest' o zhizni* (*Story of a Life*), earned him international acclaim. In six volumes he covers the period from the turn of the century till the mid-1930s. It is not a panoramic chronicle of the times, but a selective record of happenings in his personal world, into which major events intrude from time to time and only when they affect him directly. Translated into many languages, it is a superbly written series of loosely interrelated episodes.

In the 1950s and 1960s he paid several visits to western Europe (to Britain in 1964) and wrote feuilletons about his impressions and encounters with foreign and Russian émigré writers. Some of his stories have been filmed and turned into effective radio plays. As Veniamin Kaverin wrote in 1967: "In [Paustovskii's] writings there is not a single false line ... He possessed the gift that many have lost – inner freedom".

PETER HENRY

Karolina Karlovna Pavlova 1807–1893

Prose writer and poet

Biography

Born Karolina Karlovna Jänisch in Iaroslavl, 22 July 1807; father professor of physics and chemistry in Moscow. Educated at home; participated in Moscow literary salons, 1820s and 1830s. The Polish poet Adam Mickiewicz proposed to her, 1825, but her family disapproved of the match. Inherited uncle's substantial estate, 1836. Married: Nikolai Filippovich Pavlov in December 1836 or early 1837 (separated 1853), one son. With her husband, hosted well-attended literary salon in Moscow, 1839–44; published poetry in various journals regularly until 1852. Linked with the Slavophiles, who claimed Pavlova as a partisan, but with whom she had philosophical disagreements. Initiated proceedings against husband for risking her estate by excessive gambling, 1852. Forbidden books found in Nikolai Pavlov's library during resulting search: he was arrested 10 January 1853, exiled to Perm. Pavlova moved to St Petersburg, then to Dorpat, 1853. Returned to St Petersburg to settle business matters, 1854–55. Travelled to Italy, Constantinople, Germany, Moscow, and St Petersburg, 1856–58; settled in Dresden, 1858. Corresponded with and translated the works of A.K. Tolstoi; visited Russia occasionally. Died in Dresden, 14 December 1893.

Publications

Collected Editions

Stikhotvoreniia. Moscow, 1863.

Sobranie sochinenii, 2 vols, edited by Valerii Briusov. Moscow, 1915.

Polnoe sobranie stikhotvorenii. Moscow and Leningrad, 1939; 2nd edition 1964.

Fiction

Dvoinaia zhizn'. Moscow, 1848; translated as *A Double Life*, by Barbara Heldt Monter, Ann Arbor, Ardis, 1978; reprinted with an introduction by Barbara Heldt, Oakland, Barbary Coast Books, 1986.

"Za chainym stolom", *Russkii vestnik*, 12 (1859); translated as "At the Tea-Table" by Diana Greene and Mary Zirin, in *An Anthology of Russian Women's Writing, 1777–1992*, edited by Catriona Kelly, Oxford, Oxford University Press, 1994, 30–70 (with two poems translated by Catriona Kelly, 22–29).

Poetry

Das Nordlicht. Proben der neuen russischen Lyrik (German translation). Leipzig, 1833.

Razgovor v Kremle [Conversation in the Kremlin]. St Petersburg, 1854.

"Kadril'" [Quadrille], *Russkii vestnik*, 1859.

"Fantasmagorii" [Phantasmagorias], *Russkoe obozrenie*, 12 (1894).

Das deutsche Werk Karolina Karlovna Pavlovas (German translations), edited by Frank Göpfert. Textsammlung zur ersten deutschen Gesamtausgabe, Universität Potsdam, 1994.

Memoirs and Letters

"Vospominanii", *Russkii arkhiv*, 10 (1875), 222–40; also in *Sobranie sochinenii*, 1915.

"Twelve Unpublished Letters to Alexey Tolstoy", translated by Munir Sendich, *Russian Literature Triquarterly*, 9 (1974), 541–48.

Critical Studies

"Karolina Pavlova", by Valerii Briusov, *Ezhemesiachnye sochineniia*, 11–12 (1903), 273–90.

Karolina Pavlova. Materialy dlia izucheniia zhizni i tvorchestva, by B. Rapgof, Petrograd, 1916.

"The Life and Works of Karolina Pavlova", by Munir Sendich, PhD dissertation, New York, 1968.

"Twofold Life: A Mirror of Karolina Pavlova's Shortcomings and Achievement", by A.D.P. Briggs, *Slavonic and East European Review*, 49 (1971), 1–17.

"Karolina Pavlova: A Survey of Her Poetry", by Munir Sendich, *Russian Literature Triquarterly*, 3 (1972), 229–48.

"Moscow Literary Salons: Thursdays at Karolina Pavlova's", by Munir Sendich, *Welt der Slaven*, 17 (1972), 341–57.

"*Ot Moskvy do Drezdena*: Karolina Pavlova's Unpublished Memoirs", by Munir Sendich, *Russian Language Journal*, 102 (1975), 57–78.

"Karolina Pavlova: The Woman Poet and the Double Life", by Barbara Heldt, introduction to *A Double Life*, Oakland, Barbary Coast Books, 1986.

A History of Russian Women's Writing, 1820–1992, by Catriona Kelly, Oxford and New York, Clarendon Press, 1994, 93–107.

Karolina Pavlova struggled for most of her life to be taken seriously among her male contemporaries and peers as the talented woman poet that she was. Her poetry and translations earned esteem in the 1830s and 1840s, but she was ridiculed for her need to live "as a poet", preoccupied and possessed by her art. By the mid-19th century, when utilitarian interests were beginning to dominate the literary establishment, her poetry was perceived as reflecting an "art for art's sake" attitude and was rather simplistically associated with the Slavophiles' nationalism and philosophy. Both of these judgments reveal more of the popular appraisal of Pavlova as a person – as a woman who insisted on identifying herself primarily as a poet, and who maintained friendships with writers who identified themselves as Slavophiles – than a careful evaluation of her considerable literary talents. Pavlova died forgotten in 1893, but the Symbolists rescued her poetry from obscurity. Valerii Briusov set the tone for a re-evaluation of her work by praising her technique in a critical article and by editing a substantial collection of her poems. Today Pavlova is considered one of the most accomplished poets of her time, and her story stands as a classic embodiment of the plight of the woman writer in Russia.

Karolina Karlovna Jänisch was born in 1807, daughter of a Moscow professor of physics and chemistry. Her parents doted on her; despite the family's straightened circumstances – they were forced to abandon their home when Napoleon's army occupied Moscow in 1812 – they provided their sensitive, impressionable daughter with an excellent home education. They also depended on her to restore the family fortune by inheriting her rich uncle's estate, which she eventually did, though at tremendous cost to her personal life.

In the 1820s Karolina Jänisch frequented the Moscow literary salons. She impressed visitors to the Elagin-Kireevskii home both with her poetry and with her facility in languages (she knew several, and wrote freely in Russian, German, and French). During this decade she received praise from the German naturalist Alexander Humboldt, and nurtured friendships with the poets Iazykov and Viazemskii, all of whose good opinions she valued highly. At the salon of Zinaida Volkonskaia she met the Polish poet Adam Mickiewicz, who tutored her in Polish. This was her first significant romantic attachment; Pavlova treasured the memory of this love throughout her life and continued to draw poetic inspiration from it. Mickiewicz proposed to her, but her benefactor-uncle would not approve the match, and the pair did not marry.

In 1836, after her uncle's death, she contracted what was apparently a marriage of convenience with the writer Nikolai Pavlov. The two respected each other's talents at first – he had just created a sensation with the volume that would be the highlight of his career, *Tri povesti* [Three Tales] – but their marriage eventually became so unhappy that in 1853 Pavlova played a role in having her husband arrested. Shortly after this crisis had damaged her already shaky reputation in society, and after her father had died in a cholera epidemic in St Petersburg, Pavlova left Russia. For the rest of her life she travelled and lived mainly in Germany.

During the 1830s and early 1840s, the Pavlovs hosted one of the most prominent literary salons in Moscow. Various accounts of the Thursday gatherings list a brilliant company of many major Russian literary lights from both of the increasingly hostile literary-philosophical camps: the Westernizers and the Slavophiles. While Nikolai Pavlov became more and more consumed by this social life, and wrote less, Pavlova's literary star was rising. She had begun by publishing collections of translations of Russian poetry into German (her first volume, *Das Nordlicht* [Northern Lights], appeared in 1833) and French, but eventually concentrated on writing original poetry in Russian. Fantasies, ballads, elegies, and narrative poems by Pavlova were featured regularly in the leading journals, and received generally good reviews. Her novella *Dvoinaia zhizn'* (*A Double Life*) was published in 1848. While her early verse had often focused on the higher calling of the poet, the mysteries of the soul, and the power of nature to inspire man, the poetry of this "middle" period of her career increasingly reflects a bitterness with life, and particularly an anger at the lot of the poet and of women in society. This was no doubt a symptom of Pavlova's own frustration at her lack of complete acceptance in literary society. In various memoirs, Pavlova is described without much affection; she is labelled "theatrical" and arrogant, with such a high opinion of her own poetry that her manner was considered unseemly.

In 1853, shortly after her marriage broke up, Pavlova moved to Dorpat, where she met Boris Utin, a young law student with whom she enjoyed the happiest love relationship of her life for the next two years. She experienced a sort of creative renewal and transition, and dedicated a new cycle of poems to their relationship. In 1854 her long poem *Razgovor v Kremle* [Conversation in the Kremlin] appeared to accolades from the conservative literary camp for its treatment of the favourite nationalist Slavophile theme of Russia's history and destiny. In her later poetry, Pavlova develops the theme of the exile who, wandering from place to place, reflects on personal and historical destiny.

After settling in Dresden for good in 1858, Pavlova worked mainly on translations. Her collected poems were published in 1863. She maintained a close relationship with the poet and playwright A.K. Tolstoi, some of whose works she translated into German. She published a fragment of her memoirs in 1875, but no more poetry. She died in Dresden in 1893.

Pavlova's poetry is worthy of mention alongside the work of her more recognized contemporaries – Baratynskii, Iazykov, and others. She wrote beautifully in several forms, concentrating early in her career on lyrical ballads, and later moving to elegies and narrative poetry. Often she mixed forms in an innovative way that was later admired by the Symbolist poets. Pavlova's poetry can be recognized by its linearity and unity. Thematic and formal elements are tightly arranged in an almost classical style. She was extremely skilled at manipulating poetic structure and rhythm, and she has long been recognized for her "strong" and vigorous language. The span of her themes over her entire opus is clearly connected with her own (also somewhat linear) spiritual and emotional development over the course of her life. Nevertheless, Pavlova largely succeeds in what she considered to be the quest of the poet, that of raising the personal to the universal through beautiful language.

CAROLYN JURSA AYERS

A Double Life

Dvoinaia zhizn'

Novella, 1848

Among Pavlova's creative works, *A Double Life* contributes most to earning its author consideration as "the Russian George Sand". In a striking and original format, Pavlova alternates episodes of a society tale, written in a worldly, cynical prose, and philosophical verse interludes to present a highly critical picture of the fate of a sensitive young woman in Moscow high society. The title refers to the tension between the two sides of the heroine, Cecilia. In society, she performs as she has been trained, like a beautiful wind-up doll, dancing unthinkingly through the manoeuvrings of courtship toward a marriage that clearly will bring her little happiness. In the solitude of her room at night, however, she is disturbed by strange, intriguing, poetic voices that speak to her of dreams and unrealized aspirations.

Pavlova worked on this complex novella from 1844 to 1847. A preliminary version of chapter 1 was published in 1845 in the journal *Moskvitianin*, and a verse fragment from chapter 5 appeared in 1847, to mixed reviews. The work got a warm reception from the literary establishment when it was published in its entirety, with the subtitle "Ocherk K. Pavlovoi" [A Sketch by K. Pavlova], in Moscow in 1848. Pavlova's reputation had been based mainly on her translations of poetry to and from Russian, German, and French, and on her own original poetry, so this substantial new offering in prose highlighted a new dimension of her talent. *A Double Life* is now Pavlova's best-known and most appreciated work, both because of its artistic qualities, and because it reveals much of the author's view of life in an age from which we have relatively few recorded female viewpoints.

A Double Life displays the highly organized, logical, and symmetrical structure that is typical of Pavlova's poetry. The work is divided into ten chapters. Each begins with a prose episode, describing a chain of social events in which Cecilia shines as a poised young debutante, the object of the attentions and manipulations of her mother, her friend and rival, and the local eligible young society men. Each episode ends with Cecilia retiring to her room alone, her senses exhausted from the whirl of social activity. There follows a brief transition, as Cecilia yields to the mesmerizing sounds of night and nature that lull her into a dream state. The chapter then shifts to several stanzas of verse, in which voices address Cecilia, making her aware of inner creative impulses and conflicts that she dare not express to the outside world.

Critics of the time responded most favourably to Pavlova's indictment of the hypocrisy and superficiality of high society life. Indeed, in the prose passages Pavlova demonstrates her fine ear for drawing room dialogue, as well as a gift for describing the social configurations and motivations of her characters with the wry and experienced voice of someone who has observed high society at first hand. There are allusions to some of Pavolva's contemporaries; for instance, the poet who reads at Vera Vladimirovna's evening party is recognizable as the Siberian poet Evgenii Mil'keev. These sections also contain some sharp social criticism. Commenting on the practice of arranged marriage, the narrator blames mothers for pushing their daughters to a fate they themselves know to be miserable:

> Haven't these poor women cried? Haven't they ... realized the bitter fruit of this lie that is sown? ... But maybe many haven't! There are unlikely cases and strange exceptions. There have been examples in which people have fallen out of the third floor onto the pavement and remained unharmed; why not give your daughter a shove too?

In contrast to her contemporary, worldly prose, Pavlova's haunting verse passages seem to come from another, unknown realm. These sections incorporate many of Pavlova's favourite romantic motifs, including the night, the stars, and the rustling of leaves, and they reflect the influence on the author of German romantic mysticism.

These conflicting images and modes combine to dramatize the confrontation of voices between the two worlds of Cecilia's consciousness. Associated with the main dichotomy between society and solitude are several related oppositions: the urban, secular world, concerned with superficial appearances and engaged in empty chatter, is challenged by the natural, spiritual world of essences and profound thoughts, which remain unarticulated. While society is concerned only with the present moment, the dream world moves fluidly between the past and the future. The way the two discourses treat death (an ominous presence in both worlds) is telling. The funeral of a young society wife provokes little reaction among the society women besides the desire to avoid a tiresome social occasion; Cecilia's inner voices, meanwhile, dwell on the mysteries of death and the possibilities for eternity.

The idea of a divided self is not only a romantic cliché; it is also characteristic of women's writing, even up to the present time. Writing in a pre-feminist age, however, Pavlova reverses the opposition a modern reader might expect between the male and female spheres. Cecilia's society is dominated by women – besides the struggling poet, the men are all emphatically described as passive and ineffectual. On the other hand, the creative, poetic voices in both worlds are all male, even though some of them come from within Cecilia herself and represent her own creative impulses.

Behind many of these oppositions is the problem of communication, the difficulty of differentiating truth from deception in the voices of others and oneself. The plot of *A Double Life* is motivated by instances of deliberate and accidental misunderstanding in social conversations. But Cecilia's inner voices are by no means any clearer; indeed, after she wakes up she can only recall vague snatches of them. The problem of conflicting motivations remains unsolved, and perhaps unsolvable. In the final verse section, the voice of the poet herself intrudes, as she wrestles with her desire to keep her poetic treasure safe in her own inner world, and the need to bequeath it to an unsympathetic, unlistening world.

CAROLYN JURSA AYERS

Viktor Pelevin 1962 –

Prose writer

Biography

Born in 1962. Attended Aviation College, Moscow. Worked in a design office. Full-time writer since 1991. Recipient: "little" Booker Prize, 1993 for the short-story collection, *Sinii fonar'* (*The Blue Lantern*).

Publications

Collected Editions

Sochineniia, 2 vols. Moscow, 1996.

Zhizn' nasekomykh: romany. Moscow, 1997.

Fiction

Sinii fonar'. Moscow, 1991; translated as *The Blue Lantern and Other Stories*, by Andrew Bromfield, New York, New Directions, 1997.

"Omon Ra", *Znamia*, 5 (1992), 1–63; separate edition Moscow, 1993; extract translated as *Omon Ra*, by Andrew Bromfield, *Glas*, 7 (1994), 58–65; full translation by Andrew Bromfield, London, Harbord, 1994; New York, Farrar Straus and Giroux, 1996.

"Nika", *Iunost'*, 6/7/8 (1992), 123–36.

"Buben verkhnego mira", *Oktiabr'*, 2 (1993), 103–10; translated as "The Tambourine for the Upper World", by James Escombe, *Glas*, 11 (1996), 40–54.

"Zhizn' nasekomykh", *Znamia*, 4 (1993), 6–65; translated as *The Life of Insects*, by Andrew Bromfield, London, Harbord, 1996.

"Zheltaia strela", *Novyi mir*, 7 (1993), 96–121; translated as *The Yellow Arrow*, by Andrew Bromfield, London, Harbord, 1994; New York, New Directions, 1996.

"Tarzanka", translated by J. Mackenzy, *Glas*, 7 (1994), 66–81.

"Papakhi na bashniakh" [Papakhas on the Towers], *Ogonek*, 42 (1995).

"Sviatochnyi kiberpank, ili 'Rozhdestvenskaia Noch'-117.DIR' [Xmas Cyberpunk, or "Christmas Night - 117.DIR"], *Ogonek*, 1 (1996).

"Chapaev i Pustota" [Chapaev and Pustota], *Znamia*, 4–5 (1996).

Critical Studies

"Chistoe pole literatury", by S. Kostyrko, *Novyi mir*, 12 (1992), 250–59.

"Predvoditel' serebristok sharikov", by R. Arbitman, *Literaturnaia gazeta* (14 July 1993), 4.

"Zaratursy i messershmidti", by V. Vial'tsev, *Nezavisimaia gazeta* (31 July 1993), 6.

"Sbyvsheesia nebyvshee", by S. Chuprinin, *Znamia*, 9 (1993), 181–88.

"Na puti k razrushennomu mostu", by A. Egoritsyn, *Moskovskaia pravda* (18 September 1993), 9.

"Peizazh posle bitvy", by N. Ivanova, *Znamia*, 9 (1993), 189–98.

"Samyi modnyi pisatel'", interview by S. Kuznetsov, *Ogonek*, 35 (1996), 52–53.

"Ludic Nonsense or Ludicrous Despair: Viktor Pelevin and Russian Postmodernist Prose", by S. Dalton-Brown, *Slavic and East European Review*, 75/12 (1997), 216–33.

Viktor Pelevin's first collection, *Sinii fonar'* (*The Blue Lantern*), established him as a postmodernist writer whose work is characterized by fragmentation, conscious artificiality (i.e. the construction of "hyperrealities"), and game-playing. Pelevin's texts deal in particular with the relationship of observer to phenomena; do we "create the world around us"? Or perhaps we are "simply the reflection of what surrounds us" ("Deviatyi son Very Pavlovny" [The Ninth Dream of Vera Pavlovna]). Existence is a question of belief: "when a great number of people believe in the reality of a certain object (or process), it begins to manifest itself" ("Oruzhie vozmezdiia" [The Weapon of Retribution]). His work is highly visual, and his texts usually focus on a few well-chosen metaphors – often only one extended metaphor per text, as in *Zheltaia strela* (*The Yellow Arrow*) or "Prints Gosplan" [Prince Stateplan] – which lose their status as created images and become "real", reversing the status of image/phenomenon (or signifier/signified).

Pelevin is also concerned with the nature of the observer. Identity is never a constant in his work; in the story "Mittel' spil'" ("Mid-Game"), all four characters have had sex changes, while humans metamorphose into animals and vice versa in "Problema vervolka v Srednei polose" [Problem of a Werewolf] and *Zhizn' nasekomykh* (*The Life of Insects*). Pelevin often adds a further twist to the problem of what is real by introducing metafictional concepts; his texts constantly remind the reader of their fictiveness. Literary parody is usually present, whether of jargonistic clichés as in *The Life of Insects* or "Papakhi na bashniakh" [Papakhas on the Towers], or of Dostoevskii in his recent work, *Chapaev i Pustota* [Chapaev and Pustota] (1996), in which the KGB raid a literary night club where a bizarre performance of a play entitled "Raskol'nikov and Marmeladov" is taking place.

As the reader finds himself manipulated into the reflexive position occasioned by the conscious artificiality of Pelevin's prose, he realizes that humour has become the main concern. The subject matter veers from the sublimely ridiculous to the serious, the most charming of the stories being "Zhizn' i prikliucheniia saraia Nomer XII" ("The Life and Adventures of Shed XII"), in which a shed whose greatest desire is to be a bicycle finds itself locked in battle with a barrel of pickled cucumbers that attempts to stifle its soul and reduce it to vegetative subconsciousness.

Pelevin's concern with existence and with man as creator and as "created" often has political overtones. The title of "Deviatyi son Very Pavlovny" is deliberately ironic, for instead of the brave new world of Chernyshevskii's Vera, we have the life and thoughts of a lavatory attendant in a story that looks at changes under perestroika through the happenings at a men's toilet. Propaganda is also the main theme of his short novel *Omon Ra* (1992), a text based on the Soviet space programme. The hero, Omon Krivomazov, and his fellow cosmonauts, well-prepared for their technologically challenging mission to the moon from their close study of the works of Lenin, set off, only to discover that they are still on earth and that the entire journey has been a sham. In Pelevin's texts Russian history becomes peopled with characters such as a cocaine-sniffing Red officer guarding the Smolnyi in October 1917 ("Khrustal'nyi mir" ["Crystal World"]), or filled with absurd experiments such as the one described in "Otkrovenie Kregera" [Kroeger's Revelation], based on the idea that the book "Lev Tolstoi as a Mirror of the Revolution" is an encoded prophecy about the progress of socialism. Modern Russia is also strongly satirized; the recent story "Sviatochnyi kiberpank, ili 'Rozhedestvenskaia Noch'-117.DIR' [Xmas Cyberpunk, or "Christmas Night - 117.DIR"] deals with a crooked mayor whose comeuppance occurs by means of a computer virus, while "Papakhi na bashniakh" describes the farcical seizure of the Kremlin by a Chechen group.

The blurred boundary between life and death is a significant theme in Pelevin's ludic and often farcical explorations of the slippery concept of reality. In "Buben verkhnogo mira" ("The Tambourine for the Upper World") he describes corpses being resurrected to be auctioned off as husbands for girls, since there is a local shortage of men. In "Vstroennyi pominatel'" [A Built-in

Reminder] he discusses an avant-garde art movement called "vibrationalism" in which the artists create a lifelike puppet with a "remote destruct and a built-in memory of death", and in "Vesti iz Nepala" ("News from Nepal"), a radio broadcast announces to the assembled characters that they are in fact dead; this story begins and ends with the same words: the characters are caught in an eternal loop. In "The Blue Lantern" the question is asked "how can you tell who's alive and who's dead?", a question that Pelevin rephrases as "how can one know who's awake and who is dreaming?", the premise of "Spi" [Sleep!]. And in the story "Ukhriab" Pelevin offers the meaningless word "ukhriab" as the key to existence, but a key that can only be understood, impossibly "with the help of the symbol itself, that is, the ukhriab", a self-referential icon.

Existence is a journey towards discovery of the ultimately nonsensical nature of reality, its "ukhriab". The human race is depicted as travelling, hopelessly confused, through a universe to which the key has been lost. In *The Yellow Arrow*, life is likened to a train in which we sit backwards. Perhaps all roads lead "nowhere", as Pelevin remarks in his essay on Erofeev and Castaneda ("Ikstlan-Petushki"). Life is a Buddhistic state of transient dream, or a computer game (as in "Prints Gosplan" in which the narrator is simultaneously attempting to ascend all 12 levels of the game, and living a "normal" life in a technical institute). Or perhaps life is a form of Darwinian struggle for survival of the fittest (*The Life of Insects*), a text that is no more, we are told, than "the hallucination of the drug addict Petrov", who is himself the hallucination of a drunken *starshina* (sergeant-major). In his texts Pelevin layers existential doubt upon metafictional uncertainty upon metaphysical questioning to create some of the most fascinating texts in post-perestroika prose: Nabokovian ludic prose transplanted to the new world of computers, drugs, and postmodernist pastiche.

S. Dalton-Brown

Liudmila Stefanovna Petrushevskaia 1938–

Dramatist and prose writer

Biography

Born in Moscow, 26 May 1938. Attended Moscow University. Married; three children. Worked as a journalist, 1961–70. Has worked as a radio reporter, improvisation teacher, editor at a television studio, translator from Polish. First stories appeared in *Avrora*, July, 1972. Shortlisted for the Russian Booker Prize for *Vremia noch'* (*The Time: Night*), 1992.

Publications

Collected Editions

Four ("Love", "Nets and Traps", "Come into the Kitchen", "The Violin"). New York, Institute for Contemporary Drama and Theatre, 1984.

Bessmertnaia liubov'. Moscow, 1988; translated as *Immortal Love*, by Sally Laird, New York, Pantheon, and London, Virago, 1995.

Pesni XX veka [20th-Century Songs]. Moscow, 1988.

Monologi: Temnaia komnata [Monologues: The Dark Room]. Moscow, 1988.

P'esy. Moscow, 1988.

Tri devushki v golubom (sbornik p'es) [Three Girls in Blue]. Moscow, 1989.

Svoi krug (rasskazy) [Our Crowd]. Moscow, 1990.

Cinzano: Eleven Plays, translated by Stephen Mulrine. London, Nick Hern, 1991.

Po doroge boga Erosa [In the Way of the God Eros]. Moscow, 1993.

Taina doma. Povesti i rasskazy [The Secret of the House ...]. Moscow, 1995.

Sobranie sochinenni, 5 vols. Kharkov and Moscow, 1996.

Bal poslednogo cheloveka. Povesti i rasskazy [Last Man's Ball]. Moscow, 1996.

Fiction

"Skripka", *Druzhba narodov*, 10 (1973), 151–53; translated as "The Violin", in *Four*, 1984; and by Marina Artman, in *Balancing Acts*, edited by Helena Goscilo, Bloomington, Indiana University Press, 1989, 122–25.

"Mania", *Druzhba narodov*, 10 (1973), 154–57; translated as "Mania", by Helena Goscilo, in *Balancing Acts*, 1989, 256–60.

"Seti i lovushki", *Avrora*, 4 (1974), 52–55; translated as "Nets and Traps", in *Four*, 1984; also by Stephen Mulrine, in *Cinzano*, 1991; also by Alma Law, in *The Image of Women in Contemporary Soviet Fiction*, edited by Sigrid McLaughlin, London, Macmillan, and New York, St Martin's Press, 1989, 100–10.

"Smotrovaia ploshchadka" [The Observation Platform], *Druzhba narodov*, 1 (1982), 56–70; translated as "The Overlook", by D. Dyrcz-Freeman, in *Soviet Women Writing*, New York, Abbeville Press, 1990; London, John Murray, 1991, 275–99.

"Cherez polia", *Avrora*, 5 (1983), 113–14; translated as "Through the Fields", by Stefani Hoffman, in *The New Soviet Fiction: Sixteen Short Stories*, edited by Sergei Zalygin, New York, Abbeville Press, 1989, 235–38.

"Svoi krug", *Novyi mir*, 1 (1988), 116–30; translated as "Our Crowd", by Helena Goscilo, in *Glasnost': An Anthology of Literature under Gorbachev*, edited by Goscilo and Byron Lindsey, Ann Arbor, Ardis, 1990, 3–24.

"Izolirovannyi boks" [Isolation Ward], *Novyi mir*, 12 (1988), 116–20.
"Novye Robinzony", *Novyi mir*, 8 (1989), 166–72; translated as "A Modern Family Robinson", by George Bird, in *Dissonant Voices: The New Russian Fiction*, edited by Oleg Chukhontsev, London, Harvill Press, 1991, 414–24.
"Skazki dlia vzroslykh" [Fairy-Tales for Grown-Ups], *Iunost'*, 9 (1990), 66–67.
"Pesni vostochnykh slavian" [Songs of the Eastern Slavs], *Novyi mir*, 8 (1990), 7–19.
"Vremia noch'", *Novyi mir*, 2 (1992), 65–110; translated as *The Time: Night*, by Sally Laird, London, Virago, and New York, Pantheon, 1994.
"Skazki dlia vse sem'i" [Fairy Tales for all the Family], *Oktiabr'*, 1 (1993), 3–37.
"V sadakh drugikh vozmozhnostei" [In the Gardens of Other Possibilities], *Novyi mir*, 2 (1993), 105–26.
"Nu, mama, nu. Skazki, rasskazannye detiam" [Come on then, Mama. Fairy Tales Told to Children], *Novyi mir*, 8 (1993), 130–59.
"Karamzin (Derevenskii dnevnik)" [Karamzin (A Country Diary)], *Novyi mir*, 9 (1994), 3–60.
"Most Vaterloo (rasskazy)" [Waterloo Bridge], *Novyi mir*, 3 (1995), 7–26.

Plays

Dva okoshka [Two Windows]. 1975; in *Literaturnaia Armeniia*, 5 (1989), 54–63.
"Prokhodite v kukhniu", in *Odnoaktnye p'esy*, Moscow, 1978; translated as "Come into the Kitchen", in *Four*, 1984.
"Bystro khorosho ne byvaet, ili chemodan chepukhi" [Things Don't Get Better Quickly, or The Suitcase of Nonsense], in *Odnoaktnye p'esy*, Moscow, 1979.
"Liubov'", *Teatr*, 5 (1979), 183–90; translated as "Love", in *Four*, 1984.
"Ozelenenie" [Planting], in *Odnoaktnye p'esy*, 2, Moscow, 1980.
"Uroki muzyki", in *P'esy*, by V. Slavkin and L. Petrushevskaia, Moscow, 1983; translated as "Music Lessons", by Stephen Mulrine, in *Cinzano*, 1991.
"Lestnichnaia kletka", in *P'esy*, by V. Slavkin and L. Petrushevskaia, Moscow, 1983; translated as "The Stairwell", by Stephen Mulrine, in *Cinzano*, 1991.
"Tri devushki v golubom", *Sovremennaia dramaturgiia*, 3 (1983); translated as "Three Girls in Blue", by Stephen Mulrine, in *Cinzano*, 1991.
Cinzano (produced Soviet Union, 1987); translated by Stephen Mulrine, in *Cinzano*, 1991.
Zolotaia boginia (skazka v 2-kh deistviiakh) [The Golden Goddess] (VAAP-INFORM, 1987).
"Kvartira Kolumbiny" [Columbine's Apartment], *Teatr*, 2 (1988).
Zaiachii khvostik (fil'm-skazka dlia detei) [A Hare's Tail] (VTRO, 1988).
"Andante", *Teatr*, 2 (1988).
"Syraia noga, ili Vstrecha druzei", *Sovremennaia dramaturgiia*, 2 (1989), 53–74; translated as "The Meeting", by Stephen Mulrine, in *Cinzano*, 1991.
"I'm for Sweden (Ia boleiu za Shvetsiu)", translated by June Goss and Elena Goreva, *Soviet Literature*, 3 (1989), 79–91.
Stakan vody; translated as "A Glass of Water", by Stephen Mulrine, in *Cinzano*, 1991.

Critical Studies

"In Cinzano Veritas: The Plays of Liudmilla Petrushevskaya", by M.T. Smith, *Slavic and East European Arts Special Issue: Recent Polish and Soviet Drama*, 12, (Winter–Spring 1985), 247–52.
"Trudnye p'esy", by M. Turovskaia, *Novyi mir*, 12 (1985), 247–52.
"Liudmila Petrushevskaia: How the 'Lost People' Live", by Nancy Condee, *Publication of the Institute of Current World Affairs*, 14 (1986), 1–12.
"Khronika odnoi dramy", by R. Doktor and A. Plavinskii, *Literaturnoe obozrenie*, 12 (1986), 88–94.
"'Zvuki My' (o dramaturgii Petrushevskoi)", by N. Agisheva, *Teatr*, 9 (1988), 55–64.
"About Brothers and Sisters, Fathers and Sons", by Victoria Vainer, *Soviet Theatre*, 2 (1988).
"Women Without Men in the Writings of Contemporary Soviet Women Writers", by Adele Barker, in *Russian Literature and Psychoanalysis*, edited by Daniel Rancour-Laferrière, Amsterdam, John Benjamins, 1989, 431–39.
"Liudmila Petrushevskaya", by Sigrid McLaughlin, in *The Image of Women in Contemporary Soviet Fiction*, edited by McLaughlin, London, Macmillan, and New York, St Martin's Press, 1989.
"Ty – chto? Ili vvedenie v teatr Petrushevskoi", by Roman Timenchik, in Petrushevskaia's *Tri devushki v golubom*, Moscow, 1989, 394–98.
"An Interview with Liudmila Petrushevskaya", by Victoria Vainer, *Theater*, 20/3 (1989).
"Zhenskaia Proza and the New Generation of Women Writers", by K.A. Simmons, *Slovo*, 3/1 (1990), 66–78.
"V svoem krugu", by E. Shcheglov, *Literaturnoe obozrenie*, 3 (1990), 19–23.
"Neopalimyi golubok. 'Poshlost'' kak esteticheskii fenomen", by N. Ivanova, *Znamia*, 8 (1991), 211–33.
"The Generic Diversity of Ljudmila Petrushevskaja's Plays", by Nina Kolesnikoff, in *Slavic Drama: The Question of Innovation*, edited by Andrew Donskov *et al.*, Ottawa, University of Ottawa, 1991.
"Lyudmila Petrushevskaya's 'Svoi krug'", by J. Halliday, in *The Wider Europe: Essays on Slavonic Languages and Cultures in Honour of Professor Peter Henry on the Occasion of His Retirement*, edited by J.A. Dunn, Nottingham, Astra Press, 1992.
Plays for the Period of Stagnation: Liudmila Petrushevskaia and the Theatre of the Absurd, by Katy Simmons, Birmingham, Birmingham Slavonic Monographs, 1992.
The Last Years of Soviet Russian Literature: Prose Fiction, 1975–1991, by Deming Brown, Cambridge and New York, Cambridge University Press, 1993, 151–56.
"V chuzhom piru pokhmel'e", by V. Toporov, *Zvezda*, 4 (1993), 188–98.
"Cross(-Dress)ing One's Way to Crisis: Yevgeny Popov and Lyudmila Petrushevskaya and the Crisis of Category in Contemporary Russian Culture", by A.J. Vanchu, *World Literature Today*, 67/1 (Winter 1993), 107–18.
"The Minotaur in the Maze: Remarks on Lyudmila

Petrushevskaya", by J. Woll, *World Literature Today*, 67/1 (Winter 1993), 125–30.
Russia's Alternative Prose, by Robert Porter, Oxford, Berg, 1994, 54–62.
"The Time is Always Night: Liudmila Petrushevskaia's Dark Monologues", by S. Dalton-Brown, *Interface*, 1 (Spring 1995).
Russian Literature 1988–1994: The End of an Era, by N.N. Shneidman, Toronto, University of Toronto Press, 1995, 99–106.
Dehexing Sex: Russian Womanhood During and After Glasnost, by Helena Goscilo, Ann Arbor, University of Michigan Press, 1996.

Liudmila Petrushevskaia is one of the most striking and versatile voices in contemporary prose and drama in Russia today; she is equally well known in the world of cinema, for her scenarios for the internationally award-winning animated film *Skazka skazok* [Tale of Tales] among others. She began to write in the 1960s, but her work soon encountered opposition; three of her stories were to be published in *Novyi mir* in January 1969, but fell foul of the difficulties the journal was then undergoing for being too liberal. Petrushevskaia had to wait for three years to see two of her stories appear in print, while her plays remained largely unseen on the stages of Brezhnevite theatres. Although her work did appear in Germany, only with glasnost has Petrushevskaia at last received recognition in her own country, with her story *Vremia noch'* (*The Time: Night*) being shortlisted for the Russian Booker Prize in 1992.

Petrushevskaia is known for producing texts in which both style and themes are stark and uncompromising; although only overtly political in certain texts, her work generally paints a realistic, extremely black picture of daily life in Russia, including such daily problems as infidelity, isolation, madness, family quarrels, lack of housing space and food, illness, drunken violence, grief, death, the shortage of men, low wages, unwanted pregnancy, abortion. Her work is therefore often categorized as "chernukha", or black realism. Critics have noted a Dostoevskiian element in her work, for her characters' tales are told in darkness and despair, cries from the edge of the abyss.

Petrushevskaia is chiefly concerned not with social problems but with human isolation; her texts, placed in claustrophobic settings and squeezed into short, constricted genres such as the short story, the brief monologue, the one- or two-act play, and the *povest'*, are essentially studies of solipsism and loneliness. Her favourite genre is the monologue; several of her texts are subtitled "monologi", while her other works are studies of characters' inability to conquer their own self-absorption. Her prose texts are often narrated by first-person female narrators, who paradoxically through their *skaz* style draw the reader into a dialogue while simultaneously reminding him or her that communication is in short supply in Petrushevskaia's world. Petrushevskaia appears to believe that life for women in Russia takes the form of a grim struggle for survival in which it is everyone for herself, and in which isolation is the inevitable result.

She frequently describes her characters in terms of animal imagery, or as children, as people reduced by the inhumane conditions under which they live. Petrushevskaia's most chilling depiction of dehumanization occurs in the dialogue "Izolirovannyi boks" [Isolation Ward], a conversation of sorts between two terminally ill cancer patients. The two women, called only "A" and "B", to suggest how dehumanized they have become in the eyes of society, realize that they have been put in an isolation ward or "box" because no one wishes to be "contaminated" by death. The "20th-century songs" (borrowing the title of one of her collected editions) that Petrushevskaia's characters sing are their death-songs, marking the end to hope, to love, to freedom, songs that no one hears, for they are monologues spoken in the dark.

This is most clearly to be seen in Petrushevskaia's *The Time: Night*, a harrowing tale of family disharmony that describes the life of Anna, the acid-tongued protagonist, her disturbed grandson, her abusive layabout son, her daughter, with her three illegitimate children, and her schizophrenic mother. Isolation is the central theme; by the end of the story Anna is alone; her daughter has decamped, taking her children with her; her son has long since left, and her mother has been moved to a distant mental asylum. The final lines of the text fade into the dark abyss of despair created by Anna's grief, as she recites the names of all those she has lost.

Friendship in this dark world is usually found lacking, and love is in short supply. The title given by Petrushevskaia to her first story collection, *Bessmertnaia liubov'* (*Immortal Love*), is clearly an ironic one. The title story deals with a love triangle between the woman Lena, her lover Ivanov, and her husband Al'bert. Ivanov, despite Lena's humbling herself before him on bended knees, abandons her and moves to another town; Lena follows him two months later, but after seven years Al'bert appears and drags her back. Rather than a glorification of illicit passion, the story is typically filled with both grim and mundane details; Lena has a retarded son and an insane mother, for example, and, when Ivanov leaves her, she is too occupied with the mundane task of finding a dacha for the summer to pursue him immediately.

Petrushevskaia does not tackle directly the feminist issue of women defining themselves only in terms of their use to others, most commonly to men (either husbands or male offspring), but she is clearly cynical about whether such devotion can be regarded as positive. In *The Time: Night* she makes the point that the stereotypical maternal relationship between a doting mother and spoilt son is a highly destructive one; Anna's son repays her devotion by threatening her, demanding money, and even by setting fire to her letter-box. His own marriage is clearly a disaster, for this man has never learned to grow up and take responsibility for his actions (oddly enough, Anna's daughter is, by contrast, a victim, not a destroyer; but Anna has no pity for her). In "Svidanie" [A Meeting] a mother seems almost to rejoice when her adult son crumbles and submits to her domination, agreeing that he must be mentally ill, needing to be looked after like a child. The possessive nature of maternal love is perhaps understandable among women who possess so little else; but it is hardly a healthy attitude.

Perhaps the real motivation behind maternal love is the desire for immortality, for the preservation of one's family genes through the generations. *The Time: Night* exposes the fallacy of this belief, for all that is passed on between the generations appears to be the ability to argue – an almost hereditary inability to get on with one's family.

Although Petrushevskaia is best known as a writer of "dark" literature, throughout her texts runs a vein of absurdity, of humour mixed with fantasy; her plays are always blackly amusing. She has also written several plays for children, in which another world appears, one of delightful absurdity, as seen in the brightly illustrated editions of *Zaiachii khvostik* [A Hare's Tail] or *Zolotaia boginia* [The Golden Goddess], with its clowns and nonsense dialogue between a rich man who hires a painter to decorate the town he has bought – down to creating a gold apple tree with the help of some glue, gold paint, and linden trees.

Petrushevskaia's work often implies the presence of two worlds, one dark, the other romantic or fantastic. Recently, her songs have taken on another note, the voice of fairy tales, a genre that implies communication between generations, of old-fashioned lore transmitted between mother and child. In these humorous short pieces, which first appeared in 1990, Petrushevskaia has perhaps found a new, less stark, genre than that of the dark monologue; one that summons the reader not to the abyss but to a childlike, and happier world. Perhaps, if Petrushevskaia continues in this vein, the reader will cease to see her primarily as an author whose work can be summed up by the rather gloomy comment made in "Smotrovaia ploshchadka" [The Observation Platform]: "victories are only temporary phenomena" (p. 70). In the battle with living conditions, one's own nature and with selfish men, Petrushevskaia's characters are always, ultimately, the losers.

S. DALTON-BROWN

Three Girls in Blue

Tri devushki v golubom

Play, 1983

Blue is the Russian colour of hope, but in Petrushevskaia's dramatic universe hope is best abandoned on entry. The "girls" of the title are 30-something and mothers of sons. Petrushevskaia's title thus sets up multiple ironies as a structural principle of her work.

The setting is a dacha outside of Moscow, the *locus communus* of much of the "hyperrealistic" Russian drama of the late 1970s and early 1980s. Although by inheritance, the dacha belongs to three cousins – Svetlana, Tat'iana, and Irina, it stands a house divided. Svetlana and Tat'iana and their families spend the summer rent-free in one half of the dacha; in the other half, Irina (Ira) and her son Pavlik must overstretch her already overextended means to rent a room from the dacha's year-round occupant, Fedorovna. Ira is thus symbolically dispossessed from the play's outset: she has no husband, she is in debt, her son Pavlik is ill, and Pavlik is the butt of the other little boys' pranks. Ira's landlady, Fedorovna, frets more about the fate of the prodigal offspring of her cat Elka than about any of the human inhabitants.

In a Chekhovian manner, Petrushevskaia's dialogue proceeds through juxtaposed monologues of characters who desperately seek to express their needs and desires, but who are incapable of hearing each other. Faintly echoing Irina in Chekhov's *Tri sestry* (*Three Sisters*), Ira is an expert in irrelevant languages – Manx, Welsh, and Cornish, the last of which, she explains, is a dead language. Contemporary Russian, in Petrushevskaia, however, seems equally ill-equipped for communication.

Rambling monologue is particularly the province of the older generation, as the younger women are too consumed with everyday cares. Conflicts borne of the petty details that shape their lives preclude genuine dialogue among the women. In Act one, the over-protective young mothers' interaction sinks to the level of childish scuffles, when Ira accuses the other boys of roughhousing in the river with Pavlik, thereby causing him to fall ill. Svetlana immediately runs to the other two boys to get to the bottom of "who took what off whom" in their underwater struggles. Meanwhile, above these petty squabbles there is the barest hint of a moral, metaphysical dimension in the pathetic and charming fairy tales told in the voice of the unseen child, Pavlik.

Yet, ultimately, it is a "higher" consideration that forces the women in the play to seek resolution to their conflicts – the dacha's roof leaks. Since it is Svetlana/Tat'iana's side that leaks, they press the unsuspecting Ira to exchange with them. There remains, of course, the ineluctable obstacle of finances – how to share Ira's 240-rouble rent and to find someone to do repairs.

While *Three Girls in Blue* is populated mainly by women, their desire for the ever-illusive male moves the action. In comedic tradition, *Three Girls in Blue* centres on a love plot: mother love, however, not romantic love, proves the only real emotion that can sustain life.

Indeed, husbands and lovers are of dubious value. Svetlana's husband is dead, having bequeathed to his widow his mother and young son. Tat'iana's husband Valera is an alcoholic; for any of life's problems, Valera's solution is to run out and buy a bottle of something. Small wonder that the divorced Irina succumbs to the wooing of Nikolai Ivanovich, an *apparatchik* capable of solving domestic dilemmas with a simple phone call to the appropriate authorities. Nikolai Ivanovich wins Ira's heart with a gift, "personally for you" – of an outhouse. This present forces Ira to remember Nikolai fondly every day, "and not just once", as she is quick to point out. Ira recognizes the predatory nature of this man of privilege who pursues her. None the less, she falls for him, explaining "... you unexpectedly turned out to be a good person".

This (albeit debased) romantic hero, all-powerful in the public arena, makes himself hostage to fatherly affections and domestic arrangements. Having induced Ira to abandon the sick Pavlik to fly off to the Black Sea resort of Koktebel, Nikolai Ivanovich callously rejects Irina in order to "protect" his own teenage daughter and ex-wife from the scandal of acknowledging his new mistress's presence on the beach. Among his justifications: Irina has committed a *faux pas* by wandering onto the beach territory of the privileged classes (*nomenklatura*) to steal a glance at her beloved.

So Irina, who had admitted to joy at finding a suitor with his own automobile (so as not to feel her worth equal to the cost of a taxi fare home, as had been the case with a previous lover), must now sell her raincoat for a plane ticket back to Moscow. There, she knows, she will be greeted not only by rain, but by a frightened Pavlik, who has been left alone by his rather hypochondriacal grandmother Maria Philippovna, who has chosen this of all moments to enter the hospital for a long-postponed operation.

Indeed, in Petrushevskaia's world, *babushki*, the old women on whom Soviet society is anchored, play a fatal role in the lives of their daughters and daughters-in-law. Ira's youth has been spent in seeking escape from her querulous mother. Leokadia,

Svetlana's mother-in-law, appears in the final minutes of the play, when the young women at the dacha have finally reconciled their differences, as a *diabola ex machina* comes to announce to the young women that the roof in the "intact" part of the house is also leaking.

Symbolically, Ira's return from straying is paralleled by the return of the stray kitten that was missing at the play's opening. The mother cat Elka is pregnant with her next litter. In both animal and human worlds, the males may come and go, but continuity of the species is through the female.

The first full-length play by this author whose one-acts had already established her as a major voice in Russian-Soviet dramaturgy, *Three Girls in Blue* ably interweaves themes from her earlier works, and launched her on the "official" stage (in a production at the Moscow Lenkom Theatre, directed by Mark Zakharov, with actress Inna Churikova) and in mainstream theatrical publications (*Sovremennaia dramaturgiia*). Petrushevskaia's comedy gathered the collective experience of Russian women of the Brezhnev era. In the words of Maria Arbatova, one outstanding member of the generation of women authors after Petrushevskaia: "this play is about me".

MELISSA T. SMITH

Our Crowd

Svoi krug

Story, 1988

"I'm a hard, harsh person, always with a smile on my full rosy lips and a sneer for everyone." With that smug, purposely provocative opening line the nameless female narrator launches into a monologue ostensibly about herself but in fact about the lives and mores of the Moscow intelligentsia in Brezhnev's Russia. To the extent that one can speak of a plot line in the jagged narration, it revolves around the narrator's realization that she has a terminal illness and her strategy for making certain that her seven-year-old son Aleshka will have a home after her death. That story, however, emerges only in fragments from her casually lurid account of her crowd's lives and especially of the drunken Friday nights that they spend together over the course of many years.

Their hostess on Fridays is Marysha, who was originally married to Serzh, an engineer best known for an idea that he in fact stole. For years everyone viewed Serzh and Marysha as an ideal couple, but then Serzh had an affair and Marysha started showing interest in the narrator's husband, Kolia. As the narrator points out, Serzh and Kolia are best friends, but Kolia and Marysha have started living together nevertheless.

Several other characters figure in the Friday night sprees. Andrei, another engineer, readily admits that he is a police informer at the Institute for Oceanic Research. The beautiful Lenka Marchukaite, formerly a crooked clerk at a record store, now has a position as a laboratory worker in Serzh's department. Valera, a policeman with Stalinist views, came by once to check people's documents and has become a regular.

The years pass, the narrator's parents die, and the narrator comes down with a kidney disease that will first make her blind and then kill her. Since her husband Kolia now lives with Marysha, the question of a home for her son Alesha becomes acute. To resolve it, the narrator invites all the old crowd over to her place the Friday before Easter. At the same time she sends her seven-year-old off to their cottage in the country on his own. As the guests leave, they discover Aleshka cowering on the stairs. The narrator wallops him across the face, and moved by something like pity, Kolia and the others take Aleshka with them. The narrator has planned all of this, because, as she concludes her grisly tale, "I'm smart, I understand things."

Written in 1979 but not published until 1988, "Our Crowd" takes on many Soviet taboos and sacred cows. First, it completely deflates the image of the intelligentsia as a civilized and civilizing force in Soviet Russia. In the world that Petrushevskaia depicts, best friends betray each other on every possible level; highly-educated professionals shun any sort of intellectual or political discussion, revelling in mindlessness; and people's decisions are informed by the crudest kind of pragmatism rather than by any high-minded principles. Across the board, Soviet literature depicts relations between parents and children in a sentimental light. The characters in "Our Crowd" become parents because "it's kind of absurd to live without children" and alternately neglect and abuse their progeny. In short, Petrushevskaia's intelligentsia lives in and contributes to a milieu that degrades and corrupts absolutely everyone and everything.

Second, "Our Crowd" ridicules Soviet science and medicine, two areas that official propaganda consistently treated as evidence of the superiority of the Soviet system. The research institutes where the characters in Petrushevskaia's story work are staffed by charlatans, frauds, informers, and drones. Doctors botch operations, and hospitals become chambers of horrors. At the same time, Petrushevskaia makes clear the utter oppressiveness of the Soviet police state, which portrayed itself as a humane democracy. In short, virtually everything in Soviet life turns out to be sham.

The final taboo that Petrushevskaia shatters concerns the body and its functions. Russian and Soviet culture, prudish in the extreme, have generally averted readers' gazes from the body, but "Our Crowd" presents a gory catalogue of body parts and body functions. The character Nadia has an artificial eye that falls out at odd moments; the policeman and the narrator talk obsessively about flatulence; Marysha "pukes" out the window; Aleshka wets the bed; doctors leave the narrator's mother to die "with an open wound the size of a fist". As Helena Goscilo has noted, in "Our Crowd" bodies speak more eloquently than any of the characters.

Even though she had published short stories as early as the 1970s, Petrushevskaia was primarily known as a dramatist until "Our Crowd" appeared in print. Critics immediately took note of a significant new direction in her work, but there has been little agreement about how to characterize it. For some commentators, "Our Crowd" is a prime example of *chernukha*, that is, unrelentingly gloomy works that perhaps should not be counted as "literature" at all. Others follow Sergei Chuprinin's lead in assigning Petrushevskaia's story to "the other prose", a designation for a body of writing completely divorced from mainstream Soviet literature and that in part takes its inspiration from Formalist experiments in the 1920s. Certainly Petrushevskaia's *skaz* narration, which strives for the illusion of orality and the complete distancing of narrator from author, harks back to such a writer as Mikhail Zoshchenko. The influential critic Natal'ia Ivanova sees "Our Crowd" as an exercise in the grotesque, while other readers stress surrealistic aspects of the story.

Speaking recently at a symposium on her work, Petrushevskaia stated that her model is the stories that Russians tell each other about their lives and work and that blend gossip, urban folklore, invention, and the desire to top all previous stories on a given topic. Certainly Petrushevskaia's remarks offer a key to the style of "Our Crowd". As for the story's tonality, it clearly owes much to Petrushevskaia's own bleak view of the world. In any case, "Our Crowd" is a brilliant and devastating story by a writer at the top of her own distinct form.

DAVID A. LOWE

The Time: Night

Vremia noch'

Novella, 1992

A nuanced, chilling investigation of totalitarian maternal pseudo-nurture, this novella represents Petrushevskaia's supreme achievement to date. Its title primes the reader for psychic devastation in "the heart of darkness" that belongs to Anna Andrianovna. She epitomizes the monster Mother, psychologically eviscerating everyone in her orbit through nurture and narration.

The Time: Night ostensibly recounts 57-year-old Anna Andrianovna's laudable endeavours to sustain, morally and economically, her family members: her mother Sima, son Andrei, daughter Alena, and grandson Timochka. Petrushevskaia distributes among these four generations virtually all of her favourite synecdochic signs of existential horror: Sima, presumably a schizophrenic (though only a fraction more insane than anyone else), has been committed by her daughter to a psychiatric hospital, and when Anna has her transferred to a mental asylum, the incontinent old woman with a persecution mania helplessly urinates where she stands, awaiting transportation. Andrei, after serving a term in prison, where he submits to presumably forcible homosexual advances, brings two women off the street to his mother's room, and there proves his manhood, to the rhythm of Anna's discreet tapping on the door. Permanently maimed through leaping out of a second-story window after an argument with his wife, Andrei is an alcoholic who appeases his craving with money pilfered from his mother. Alena, who abandoned her older child Timochka to her mother's care, inadvertently leaving behind a notebook graphically detailing her sexual encounters with her ex-husband and her married deputy director, now lives with the baby fathered by the latter and expects a third child. Anna alternates between tears of self-pity and vindictive contempt; Andrei steals and drinks; Alena breeds; and Timochka at six has a nervous tic from all of his psychological traumas. Indigent, close to starvation, torn by hysterical jealousy and loathing for each other, the family corroborates Tolstoi's dictum that "each unhappy family is unhappy in its own way". Indeed, references to *Anna Karenina* thickly intersperse the narrative.

Anna Andrianovna promotes her own image as an extraordinary paragon of martyred largesse, a rock of dependability in a morass of appetite-driven, irresponsible self-indulgence. The freighted wording of passages lamenting Andrei's ingratitude, however, diminishes the adult Andrei into a foetus living off the maternal body, part of Anna's comprehensive imaging of her physical, emotional, and verbal self as devoured by her offspring's needs and demands. As she relentlessly reminds everyone, while eking out a pittance through her poetry readings, Anna nevertheless maintains the household, takes in her self-destructive offspring, cooks, launders, and denies herself even minimal necessities for the sake of her beloved grandson. In short, overly conscious self-sacrifice frequently originates in less than admirable drives.

A closer inspection of the text's double-voicing unmasks Anna's vaunted Christian self-abnegation as a mode of unappeasable sadistic control and vampirism – all in the name of love, which she trumpets as the most important thing in life. Beneath her rhetoric we uncover the pre-Oedipal mother, an all-powerful, engulfing figure who theatricalizes the Freudian scenario of the mother/child relationship. Hyperbole and melodrama reduce her comments to verbal gesture. Much like Dostoevskii's two Katerina Ivanovnas (of *Crime and Punishment* and *The Brothers Karamazov*), she dramatizes her role of martyr through tears, clasped hands, overstated entreaties, invidious comparisons between self and others, and extorts a psychological price for all of her "kindnesses," prompted by bottomless pride. An authority on all questions, she deems herself an inspired voice articulating a higher Truth – a function associated with her self-proclaimed role of poet.

In epistemological terms, Anna tirelessly maximizes the subject/object distinction to her advantage. Attributing purely negative motives to all objects of her implacable subjectivity, she not only exempts herself from like judgment, but packages as estimable all her own impulses and actions, including those that patently mirror behaviour she deplores in others. She publicly denounces strangers' behaviour with children, criticizes her adult offsprings' and their spouses' hygiene, sexual habits, and choices of partner. Her narrative testifies to the epistemological and psychological empowerment that automatically accrues to every teller of any tale: this privileged position allows her to manipulate perspective, tone, and emphasis so as to convert at will any phenomenon into its antipode.

Anna thus exercises her narrative prerogative by deploying a full panoply of rhetorical forces, so as to vindicate her conduct and insinuate her superiority on multiple fronts: from beauty and sex appeal, to poetic ability. By dwelling on the near-coincidence of her name with Anna Andreevna Akhmatova's, she implies a commensurability of talent. As mother, however (and possibly as poet), Anna Andrianovna sooner resembles another Anna – Anna Karenina, with whose pre-suicidal inner monologue the narrative mode of the novella resonates. As with Tolstoi's Anna, narration in *The Time: Night* functions primarily as accusatory self-exculpation via defamation.

Incorporating alternate voices into the narration, Petrushevskaia implants clues to Anna's psychological imbalance that multiply as the text progresses and, by constructing her as objectionable object, increasingly undermine her reliability. The nature of her talent comes under question when we discover that children comprise the audience for her poetry readings. Moreover, while her initial silence as to why she lost her job hints at political intrigue, in combination with other revelations it invites less flattering conclusions – subsequently confirmed when she divulges that her romance with a married father of three led to her dismissal. In countless passages Anna unwittingly betrays precisely what her defensive stratagems attempt to mask: her vanity, repressiveness, sexual problems, and, above all, the generational continuity within her family – in particular, the congruence between her own and Alena's amorous misadventures. While proclaiming dissimilarity to mother and daughter alike, Anna demonstrates her ineradicable sameness, the family resemblance recalling the familial traits shared by Anna and Stiva Oblonskii.

Several scenes significantly discredit both Anna's perspective on events and her vaunted perspicacity and magnanimity: when her husband leaves her, she considers leaping from the window – to punish him, à la Karenina; when Alena visits, Anna physically tries to prevent Timochka opening the door to his mother, even when the boy screams in protest; voyeuristically peeping at her daughter through a crack, she likewise resists the child's efforts to pull her away. Finally, can the reader reconcile Anna's advertised role as protector of children with her confession of sinful, carnal ("plotskaia") love for her grandson?

What distinguishes Anna Andrianovna from her doubles is her "telling power", which assumes the tyrannical form of censorship over all narrative within the story. When quoting extracts from her daughter's private diary, she ridicules and ultimately trivializes it through cynical editorial commentary, eliminating the subjective immediacy of Alena's impassioned confessions by interposing her own viewpoint. Furthermore, Anna substitutes her voice for Alena's by writing her daughter's memoirs about her – A.A.! Thus her voice reaches beyond the grave in the manuscript submitted to the publisher by her silenced daughter, who speaks only to find a forum for her mother's voice.

The Time: Night reveals most dramatically Petrushevskaia's profound debt to Dostoevskii's explorations of shadowed niches in the human psyche and his exposé of confession as yet another in a series of psychological violations.

HELENA GOSCILO

Viacheslav Alekseevich P'etsukh 1946–

Prose writer

Biography

Born in Moscow, 1946. Studied history at Moscow Pedagogical Institute, 1970. Taught history in a secondary school until 1982. Member of the editorial board of *Sel'skaia molodezh'*, as an advisor for young authors. Editor-in-chief of *Druzhba narodov* since 1993. Married; one son. Lives in Moscow.

Publications

Collected Editions

Alfavit [Alphabet]. Moscow, 1983.
Veselye vremena [Happy Times]. Moscow, 1988.
Novaia moskovskaia filosofiia [New Moscow Philosophy]. Moscow, 1989.
Predskazanie budushchego [The Future Foretold]. Moscow, 1989.
Ia i prochee [Myself and So On]. Moscow, 1990.
Rommat [Romantic Materialism]. Moscow, 1990.
Tsikly [Cycles]. Moscow, 1991.

Fiction

"Dva rasskaza" ("Bilet" [The Ticket] and "Novyi zavod" [The New Factory]), *Novyi mir*, 6 (1987); translated by Byron Lindsey and Jan Butler, in *The Wild Beach and Other Stories*, edited by Lindsey and Helena Goscilo. Ann Arbor, Ardis, 1992, 264–75; 277–82.
"Tsentral'no-Ermolovskaia voina", *Ogonek*, 3 (1988); translated as "The Central-Ermolaevo War", by Arch Tait in *The Penguin Book of New Russian Writing: Russia's "Fleurs du mal"*, edited by Viktor Erofeev and Andrew Reynolds, Harmondsworth and New York, Penguin, 1995, 237–56.
"Novaia moskovskaia filosofiia", *Novyi mir*, 1 (1989); first part translated in *Soviet Literature*, 1 (1990).
"Anamnes i epikriz", *Novyi mir*, 4 (1990); translated as "Anamnesis and Epicrisis", by Andrew Reynolds, in *Dissonant Voices: The New Russian Fiction*, edited by Oleg Chukhontsev, London, Harvill Press, 1991, 389–413.
"Aleksandr Krestitel'", *Oktiabr'*, 2 (1991).
"Gadanie na kofeinoi gushche" [Fortune-Telling from Coffee Grounds], *Druzhba narodov* (1991).
"Rasskazy" ("Sorok chetyre goda s samim soboi" [44 Years with Oneself]; "Novikov, feodal" [Novikov, the Feudal Lord]; "Posle dozhdichka v chetverg" [After Thursday's Rain]; "Zhertvoprinoshenie" [The Sacrifice]), *Druzhba narodov*, 2 (1992).
"Rasskazy" ("Palata No 7" [Ward No. 7]; "Dramaturgiia" [Dramaturgy]; "Nashi prishli" [Ours Have Come]; "Vor" [The Thief]; "Ia i bessmertie" [Myself and Immortality]), *Oktiabr'*, 1 (1992).
"Zakoldovannaia strana" [The Bewitched Country], *Znamia*, 2 (1992).
"Tuda i obratno" [Return Ticket], *Znamia*, 5 (1993).
"Rasskazy" ("Piatoe dokazatel'stvo" [The Fifth Evidence]; "O prividenii akh" [About Ghosts]; "Piatnitskii, dissident" [Piatnitskii, the Dissident]), *Znamia*, 8 (1994).
Gosudarstvennoe ditia: Povesti i rasskazy [A Child of the State]. Moscow, 1997.

Critical Studies

The Last Years of Soviet Russian Literature: Prose Fiction, 1975–1991, by Deming Brown, Cambridge and New York, Cambridge University Press, 1993, 163–66.

Russian Literature 1988–1994: The End of an Era, by N.N. Shneidman, Toronto, Toronto University Press, 1995, 145–51.

Viacheslav P'etsukh belongs to the generation of "40-year-olds" who, although writing earlier, only emerged with perestroika. He writes novels, novellas, and short stories, in which he tends to parody themes of 19th-century literature and history.

His novel *Novaia moskovskaia filosofiia* [New Moscow Philosophy], published in 1989, won him a reputation as a novelist and prose writer. The plot is both simple and complex: an old lady, Pumpianskaia, disappears from a communal flat; after it was initially thought that she was murdered by one of the flat's occupants who wanted her room, she is finally found frozen to death on a park bench. However, the account is interspersed with cross references to 19th-century characters and ideas, and with pseudo-philosophical debates between two inhabitants of the communal flat. There may be utilitarian ideas and reasons for Pumpianskaia's disappearance, but there is no crime; her death is not caused by physical, but spiritual violence: by negligence and indifference. *Novaia moskovskaia filosofiia* works on a variety of interpretative levels: everyday, meta-literary, and philosophical. On the level of everyday life the novel is a satire on the Soviet state, and its characters represent in their genealogy the history of the Soviet Union. On the meta-literary level P'etsukh rewrites Dostoevskii's *Prestuplenie i nakazanie* (*Crime and Punishment*), setting it in the Moscow of the late 1980s, instead of the St Petersburg of the 1860s; and not in a room, but a communal flat. P'etsukh thus rejects Dostoevskii's setting and distances himself from the "great writer" without idolizing him, but also without elevating himself to Dostoevskii's status, by maintaining an ironic distance to his own work. P'etsukh admits to this ironic distance, and defines his use of references to themes and characters of the literary tradition of the 19th century as parodic. On the philosophical level P'etsukh claims already by his choice of title to belong to the tradition of serious, philosophical writers. He juxtaposes his own work with Chaadaev's "old" Moscow philosophy, which perceived westernism as a positive influence and Russia as retarded. However, P'etsukh misleads the reader with the title, and mocks the philosophical themes in his novel.

Rommat [Romantic Materialism] is a novel in which P'etsukh merges fact and fiction: using the names of historical figures involved in the Decembrist uprising, he debates the background of 19th-century Russian history and its relation to individuals, pondering over the development Russian culture would have taken had the uprising been successful. Philosophical debate usurps a large part of the novel, while the author remains reluctant to develop a full psychological picture of his characters. With his novel *Istoriia goroda Glupova* [The History of Glupov] P'etsukh provides a parodic reading of Saltykov-Shchedrin's *Istoriia odnogo goroda* (*The History of a Town*).

P'etsukh's shorter prose reveals a similar preoccupation with history; in "Novikov, feodal" [Novikov, the Feudal Lord] he investigates the process and effects of the restoration of serfdom in the microcosm of a farm; in "Anamnes i epikriz" ("Anamnesis and Epicrisis") an ongoing debate on Russian history and society between patients in a hospital escalates and causes material damage to the ward. Yet P'etsukh never neglects his concern for moral values, which is especially strong in his shorter prose. "Bilet" ("The Ticket") is set in a Siberian gold-mining settlement, where Novosiltsev's father is buried with a winning lottery ticket in his pocket. After discovering this, the young worker Novosiltsev has the body exhumed, but finds the corpse naked. The suit has been stolen and eventually passes to Pasha, a homeless "beach-comber", who receives it in compensation for his own suit that another beach-comber burnt. Pasha finds the ticket and duly returns it to Novosiltsev; they drink, and a philosophical debate ensues about the way of life and the moral issues of exhumation for material benefit. Pasha is deemed unfit to survive in Novosiltsev's world; but he does not want to, either.

P'etsukh outlines his view of uncompromised moral values, now deemed old-fashioned, which triumph in the philosophical debates over materialist, corrupt and compromised morality. Although P'etsukh sides with morality, the materialists do not abandon their status, but are merely initiated to a process of thinking. P'etsukh's works are often journeys into characters' worlds of imagination, or discussions of morality on the basis of imagined circumstances or situations.

The title of his fable "Potop" [The Deluge] already alludes to the exaggeration contained in the story: an office in central Moscow is flooded when a pipe bursts. While the clerks wait for the plumber, they seek shelter on the tables and watch documents drown. They relate incidents of everyday life in Moscow, such as a bank robbery that failed because the cashier refused to hand the state (and people's) money to the robbers, involving them instead in a debate; or the difficulty of getting rid of a corpse and arranging a burial. Although the incidents seem surreal, they are grotesque and yet perfectly realistic aspects of Soviet life.

In "Tsentral'no-Ermolovskaia voina" ("The Central-Ermolaevo War") a war flares up between two villages after Papa Carlo from Central insulted Petia from Ermolaev. The feud escalates and is terminated with an eclipse of the sun. The feud is described as though it were a Sicilian mafia event, with the narrator, as often in P'etsukh's work, commenting and interfering with biased comments; such a comment is the remark about what will happen after the eclipse of the moon.

P'etsukh always links the action of his plots with the everyday life of contemporary Russia, and always digresses into long philosophical debates. These two elements are not always balanced and integrated, so that, for example, the debate in *Novaia moskovskaia filosofiia* is not serious, either in content or in manner. Often philosophical debates are inappropriate ("Bilet"). But P'etsukh's intention seems twofold: to expose the grotesque elements of everyday life; and to imply that, because of the grotesque nature of this reality, philosophical debates must be empty, and can therefore only be parodied. His works are excursions into the minds and thoughts of today's Russian man.

BIRGIT BEUMERS

Boris Andreevich Pil'niak 1894–1938

Prose writer

Biography

Born Boris Andreevich Vogau in Mozhaisk, 11 October 1894. Educated in Kolomna, Saratov, Bogorodsk, and Nizhnii Novgorod. Completed correspondence course through Moscow Commercial Institute (Marx Institute of Economics), 1921; graduated in economic science. Writing career began seriously, 1915. Married: 1) Mariia Alekseevna Sokolova in 1917 (divorced 1925), one son and one daughter; 2) Ol'ga Sergeevna Shcherbinovksaia in 1925 (divorced 1932); 3) Kira Georg'evna Andronikashvili in 1933, one son. First collection of stories published, 1918; first novel, *Golyi god* (*The Naked Year*), published in 1922. Travelled to Germany, 1922; Great Britain, 1923; North Pole, 1924; by hydroplane through backwater Russia, 1925; Mediterranean, 1925; Japan and China, 1926; the United States, 1931; Scandinavia and Finland, 1934. Elected chairman of Moscow section of All-Russian Union of Writers, 1929. Suffered extended Party defamation campaign, 1929. Arrested 6 October 1937. Date of death erroneously given out as 1937 and 1941; in fact executed 21 April 1938. Official civil rehabilitation, 6 December 1956. Partially republished from 1976; fully published only from the glasnost period.

Publications

Collected Editions

Tales of the Wilderness, translated by F. O'Dempsey. London, Routledge, 1924; New York, Knopf, 1925; reprinted Westport, Connecticut, Hyperion Press, 1973.
Sobranie sochinenii, 8 vols. Moscow and Leningrad, 1929–30.
Izbrannye rasskazy. Moscow, 1935.
"Tale of the Unextinguished Moon" and Other Stories, translated by Beatrice Scott. New York, Washington Square Press, 1967.
Mother Earth and Other Stories, translated by Vera T. Reck and Michael Green. New York, Praeger, 1968.
Izbrannye proizvedeniia. Moscow, 1976.
Tselaia zhizn': Izbrannaia proza [A Whole Life]. Moscow, 1988.
Chinese Story and Other Tales, translated by Vera T. Reck and Michael Green. Norman, University of Oklahoma Press, 1988; reprinted Ann Arbor, Ardis, 1993.
Boris Pil'niak. Povest' nepogashennoi luny i drugie [Boris Pil'niak. The Tale of the Unextinguished Moon and Others]. Moscow, 1989.
Rasplesnutoe vremia [Spilled Time]. Moscow, 1990.
Rasskazy, povesti, romany. Moscow, "Sovetskii pisatel'", 1990.
Chelovecheskii veter. Romany, povesti, rasskasy [Human Wind]. Tbilisi, 1990.
Povesti i rasskazy 1915–29. Moscow, 1991.
Sobranie sochinenii, 3 vols. Moscow, 1994.

Fiction

S poslednim parokhodom i drugie rasskazy [With the Last Steamer and Other Stories]. Moscow, 1918.
Ivan-da-Mar'ia [Ivan and Maria/Cow-Wheat]. Berlin, Grzhebin, 1922.
Byl'e [Bygones]. Revel, 1922.
Golyi god, Berlin, Petrograd, and Moscow, Grzhebin, 1922; reprinted Letchworth, Bradda, 1966; translated as *The Naked Year*, by Alec Brown, New York, Payson and Clarke, and London, Putnam, 1928; also by Alexander Tulloch, Ann Arbor, Ardis, 1975.
"Tret'ia stolitsa" [Third Capital], in *Krug*, book 1, 1923; Berlin, Slovo, 1924.
Povesti o chernom khlebe [Stories about Black Bread]. Moscow and Petrograd, 1923.
Mashiny i volki [Machines and Wolves]. Leningrad, 1925; reprinted Munich, Fink, 1971.
"Mat' syra-zemlia", *Krug*, 4 (1925); translated as "Mother Earth", by Vera T. Reck and Michael Green, in *Mother Earth and Other Stories*, 1968.
"Povest' nepogashennoi luny", *Novyi mir*, 5 (1926); translated as "Tale of the Unextinguished Moon", by Beatrice Scott, in *Tale of the Unextinguished Moon and Other Stories by Boris Pilnyak*, 1967; and as "The Death of the Army Commander", by Helen Colaclides, in *Fifty Years of Russian Prose: From Pasternak to Solzhenitsyn*, edited by Krystyna Pomorska, Cambridge, Massachusetts, MIT Press, 1971, vol. 1, 59–81.
Rasskazy. Moscow, 1927; 2nd edition, 1929.
"Kitaiskaia povest", *Novyi mir*, 6 (1927); translated as "Chinese Story", by Vera T. Reck and Michael Green, in *Chinese Story and Other Tales*, 1988.
"Ivan-Moskva", *Krasnaia nov'*, 6 (1927); translated as *Ivan Moscow*, by A. Schwartzmann, New York, Christopher, 1935; Westport, Connecticut, Hyperion Press, 1973.
Rasplesnutoe vremia. Rasskazy [Spilled Time]. Moscow, 1927; reprinted 1966.
"Shtoss v zhizn'" [A Chance on Life], *Krasnaia nov'*, 10 (1928).
"Krasnoe derevo" in *Krasnoe derevo i drugie*, Berlin, Petropolis, 1929; title story reprinted Ann Arbor, Ardis, n.d.; translated as "Mahogany", by Vera T. Reck and Michael Green, in *Chinese Story and Other Tales*, 1988.
Volga vpadaet v Kaspiiskoe more, Moscow, 1930; translated as *The Volga Falls to the Caspian Sea*, by Charles Malamuth, New York, Farrar and Rinehart, 1931; reprinted, New York, AMS Press, 1970; also translated as *The Volga Flows to the Caspian Sea* [no translator named], London, Peter Davies, 1932.
Rozhdenie cheloveka [The Birth of a Man]. Moscow, 1935.
Sozrevanie plodov [The Ripening of Fruit]. Moscow, 1936.
Dvoiniki [The Doubles]. London, Overseas Publications Interchange, 1983.
Solianoi ambar [The Salt Barn]. (written 1937); published in *Rasplesnutoe vremia*, Moscow, 1990.
Zashtat [Back of Beyond]. 1991.

Travel Sketches

Korni iaponskogo sol'ntsa [Roots of the Japanese Sun]. 1927.

"O'kei: Amerikanskii Roman" [OK: An American Novel], *Novyi mir*, 3–6 (1932).

Critical Studies

Boris Pil'niak. Stat'i i materialy. Leningrad, 1928; reprinted Ann Arbor, Ardis, n.d.
"The Pioneers: Pil'nyak and Ivanov", by Robert Maguire, in his Red Virgin Soil: Soviet Literature in the 1920s, Princeton, Princeton University Press, 1968.
"The Enigma of Pil'njak's *The Volga Falls to the Caspian Sea*", by Kenneth N. Brostrom, *Slavic and East European Journal*, 18 (1974), 271–98.
"The 'Man vs. Machine' Theme in Pilnyak's *Machines and Wolves*", by A.R. Tulloch, *Russian Literature Triquarterly*, 8 (1974), 329–40.
Boris Pilniak: A Soviet Writer in Conflict with the State, by Vera T. Reck, Montreal and London, McGill-Queen's University Press, 1975.
Boris Pil'njaks Geschichts- und Menschenbild, Bibliographische und themtische Untersuchungen, by Reinhard Damerau, Giessen, Schmitz, 1976.
Nature as Code: The Achievement of Boris Pilniak, 1915–1924, by Peter Alberg Jensen, Copenhagen, Rosenkilde and Bagger, 1979.
"Pil'nyak's *Naked Year*: The Problem of Faith", by Kenneth N. Brostrom, *Russian Literature Triquarterly*, 16 (1979), 114–53.
Three Russian Writers and the Irrational: Zamyatin, Pil'nyak and Bulgakov, by T.R.N. Edwards, Cambridge, Cambridge University Press, 1982.
Border Crossings: The West and Russian Identity in Soviet Literature 1917–1934, by Carol Avins, Berkeley, University of California Press, 1983.
Boris Pilniak: Scythian at a Typewriter, by Gary Browning, Ann Arbor, Ardis, 1985.
"A New Soviet Novel for a New Soviet Man?", by Michael Falchikov, *Irish Slavonic Studies*, 8 (1987), 31–47.
"Boris Pil'niak and Modernism: Redefining the Self", by Mary A. Nicholas, *Slavic Review*, 2 (1991), 416–27.
"*Solyanoi ambar*: Pilnyak's Great Soviet Novel?", by Michael Falchikov, *Irish Slavonic Studies*, 14 (1993), 69–86.
"Pil'niak on Writing", by Mary A. Nicholas, *Slavonic and East European Review*, 2 (1993), 217–33.
Boris Pil'niak: opyt segodniashnego prochteniia (po materialam nauchnoi konferentsii posviashchennoi 100-letiiu pisatelia). Moscow, 1995.
The KGB's Literary Archive, by Vitaly Shentalinsky, translated by John Crowfoot, London, Harvill Press, 1995.

Born in 1894 as Boris Andreevich Vogau, Pil'niak began his serious literary career in 1915. By the time of the October Revolution, Pil'niak had written at least 17 short stories, ten of which had been published. His first slim volume of four stories was ready for publication early in 1917, although it appeared only in 1918.

Also in 1918 Pil'niak joined the All-Russian Union of Writers founded that year in Moscow. This union of old and new intelligentsia specialists and "fellow-travellers" provided professional and temporal support for its members. In 1922 Pil'niak was elected a member of the governing board of this Union, and in 1929, the powerful Moscow chairman.

Pil'niak's influential early patrons included the minister of education A. Lunacharskii, the writer Maksim Gor'kii, and the critic A. Voronskii. The latter devoted a long and perceptive article to Pil'niak, published in the journal *Krasnaia tselina* (August 1922). Voronskii wrote of Pil'niak as the "most talented writer of revolutionary *byt* [everyday life]" and "the most important among young artists". When *Golyi god* (*The Naked Year*) appeared in book form in 1922, Pil'niak received robust acclaim from his fellow writers.

Also in 1922 Pil'niak travelled to Germany, the first of many extended trips abroad. Soon after his first trips, Pil'niak began emphasizing a second side to his ideational banner – along with his passion for the elemental and instinctive in nature and life, now arose a growing admiration for civilization and culture, the means to liberate humankind from barbarism.

In *Mashiny i volki* [Machines and Wolves], Pil'niak portrayed the archetypal conflict between the instinctive, natural, anarchic (embodied as the powerful and free wolf) on the one hand with the intellectual ideal of the rational, regulated and immutable, all symbolized, on the other, by the machine. The wild, dangerous wolf genuinely appealed to Pil'niak's deepest emotions, but in moments of reflection he was also convinced that civilization, culture, and technology were saving forces of humankind.

In May 1926 *Povest' nepogashennoi luny* (*Tale of the Unextinguished Moon*) appeared in *Novyi mir*. In this novella Pil'niak, despite his denial, implies that responsibility for the death of the military hero Mikhail Frunze lay with Party leaders, finally with Stalin himself. Zealots never forgot this egregious transgression that haunted Pil'niak until his early death.

In 1929 Pil'niak asserted in the maiden issue of *Literaturnaia gazeta* that, in form, art must be free to follow an experimental course; and, in content, one should not expect writers to conform to externally imposed ideological standards. His recently-published novella *Krasnoe derevo* (*Mahogany*) served well as an example of his own formal and ideological independence. In the politically charged post-NEP climate of "intensified class struggle", a vigorous defamation campaign against Pil'niak (and, to a lesser degree, against others) developed into the most extensive and sustained public attack on an author in the history of Russian literature.

Traditionally, western commentators have excoriated Pil'niak for capitulating to Party demands and abjectly recanting. However, a careful examination of documents suggests that, given the crushing pressures of the time and considering the behaviour of contemporaries, Pil'niak acquitted himself well. An objective analysis of Pil'niak's novel *Volga vpadaet v Kaspiiskoe more* (*The Volga Falls to the Caspian Sea*), into which most of *Mahogany* was incorporated, reveals that Pil'niak not only preserved his significant criticisms of Soviet *byt*, but augmented them, for instance, through an exposé on the Soviet exploitation of women construction workers.

Throughout the 1930s Pil'niak continued to aver the correctness of his course – and the Party watchdogs continued to hound the writer. Articles, conferences, and public speeches denounced him (and, of course, others). Pil'niak became increasingly linked to "Trotskiite friends", Karl Radek and Voronskii who, it was alleged, conspired with Pil'niak to produce the scurrilous *Tale of the Unextinguished Moon*. Pil'niak was arrested in October 1937. His official death date was given as 9 September 1941, now corrected to 21 April 1938.

The vast majority of Pil'niak's works centre on aspects and combinations of four themes: instinct within nature's unchanging life cycle (sexual love and propagation); ideology (relativism and pan-humanism or communism in its ideal theory); the heritage and destiny of Russia; and the power of culture to transform societal and individual barbarism. In essence Pil'niak was a romantic writer, inclined to the exotic, the sensational, the decadent or transcendent, the astonishing and coincidental, and the concealed "truth". Pil'niak's style was frequently self-conscious and mannered. His preferred figures of speech are metonymy and, especially, the implicit allegory. Pil'niak's best-known metonymy is the "leather jacket" image for a Bolshevik.

Many of Pil'niak's critics, most influentially Gor'kii and Mirsky, consider him an unoriginal, fundamentally derivative epigone, principally of Remizov and Belyi. However, Pil'niak was more original than critics realized. Pil'niak's post-revolutionary subject-matter and his deep emotional commitment to the vital, natural life cycle, his greater freedom in stylistic and compositional experimentation, his bold and simultaneous juxtaposition of a broad spectrum of contrasting genres and narrative models, and in all this his brash disregard of time-honoured literary conventions and forms demonstrate his originality even during the first half of the 1920s (the period of greatest Remizov-Belyi influence).

Pil'niak was the acknowledged master of a dominant literary style in Russian literature from 1920 to 1925, "Ornamental Prose". Artists within this tradition focused more on elaborate means of expression than on narrative interest, character portrayal, or message. Prose is distinguished by its intentionally obvious and deliberate artfulness. It is more perceptibly crafted for the effects of euphony, rhythm, and image, and frequently employs alliteration, assonance, and other sound repetitions. Ornamental style not only strikes readers by its poetic musicality, but startles and perplexes them by its stylistic unfamiliarity. Forms of narration change abruptly within a work, and the structure is fragmentary, chaotic, and ostensibly arbitrary. Protruding from this initially bewildering montage, however, are accretive refrains (repeating, incremental, aphoristic leitmotifs) that suggest the author's intended meanings.

GARY BROWNING

The Naked Year

Golyi god

Novel, 1922

Completed late in 1920 but published in its entirety only in 1922, *The Naked Year* attempts to portray diverse post-revolutionary social strata. This 200-page "novel" is a montage of tangentially related but often contradictory and indistinct images and ideas, produced through brief, disjointed scenes without anticipated explanatory comment or clear transitions. In its art the novel corresponds well to the chaotic times of the Revolution and the Civil War. Especially for many young writers and critics, *The Naked Year* provided a surprising resonance despite its formal cacophony.

In *The Naked Year* Pil'niak concentrates on four prominent societal groups: the provincial nobility; mystics and sorcerers; anarchists; and Bolsheviks. The author plumbs each group's intellectual and spiritual depths both at a single historical juncture (revolutionary times) and in the perspective of the immutable natural life cycle (physical love and propagation). In this novel Pil'niak views the Revolution as a purifying fire or a cleansing blizzard that is ridding Russia of foreign encrustations in material and spiritual culture, while opening a space for the reassertion of ancient, native-Russian ideals.

The Ordynin family – generally diseased and in precipitous decline – represents the provincial nobility. The Ordynins' position is virtually hopeless, for they condemn and are rejected by the Revolution; furthermore, the debauched excesses of their fathers have bequeathed hereditary syphilis on the children, thereby making healthy reproduction virtually impossible.

The second group includes those from the realm of the mystical, among them degraded Freemasons and backwater folk sorcerers. Pil'niak ridicules the former, but revels in the exotic beliefs and hoary customs of the white-haired sorcerer, Egorka. This wizard is steeped in pre-Christian folk wisdom, incantations, herbal medicine, and popular superstition. Egorka views the Revolution as a native-Russian rebellion in the spirit of Sten'ka Razin and with sparse ideological or international pretention. With respect to love, Egorka represents the free and spontaneous, found in nature among animal life, as illustrated by his tempestuous affair with the forest girl, Arina. While Egorka is a voice surviving from the misty past and irrelevant to Russia's future, his portrayal is lavish and alluring.

The third important collection of voices belongs to the anarchists, among whom Pil'niak lived for a time in 1918. Through them another alternative of life independent from government and Revolution, a life of robust and unaffected love, finds its place in the polyphony.

The fourth and final major set of voices belongs to the Bolsheviks, a diverse group from the superficial yet menacing opportunists to the vital and self-denying idealists. The former are motivated merely by revenge and greed, and are scorned as barbarians.

The pair that eventually appears capable of best satisfying the criteria of an affirmative attitude toward the renewing revolutionary forces and of a promise of healthy love and family are Natal'ia Ordynina and Arkhip Arkhipov. Natal'ia, the only fit person in her aristocratic family, is a convert to Bolshevism and labours as a doctor in the town hospital. Arkhip, a member of the local Party executive committee, is from a hardy, clever, and honest peasant family. The section that depicts their betrothal Pil'niak entitles "the brightest" chapter in the novel. Merging the purest of the aristocracy with the strongest of the peasantry through the media of revolution and love produces firm expectations of future happiness.

The Naked Year includes many more voices, most of them occasional rather than continual. However, Pil'niak does create a semblance of organization and suggests a thematic convergence and ideological centre through his skilful use of accretive refrains. These refrains recur intact or segmented throughout the novel. The technique is to introduce a motif, then illustrate it through episodes from the life of the times, while at intervals repeating central elements of the refrain. With each repetition the refrain increases in significance and acquires a fuller, more concrete relevance. For example, the "China-town" refrain always recalls the second member in the dichotomies of motion and rest, civilization and primitiveness, progress and stagnation, and order and anarchy. Its appearance reminds the reader of the deep-seated strength of what is banal, petty, stupid, and vicious in Russia.

In the novel, style ranges along a broad spectrum and includes reasonably traditional speech and description. However, the language is more commonly stylized, impressionistic, "dynamic", anecdotal, and allegorical. Pil'niak reveals in speech peculiarities of the trivial, "foreign" communists, the vigorous but incompletely educated "leather jacket" Bolsheviks, a deranged monk, the sorcerer Egorka, and many others. Complementing these literary stylizations are frequent "documentary" materials, often indented or set in distinguishing type fonts. Generally these documents would be considered foreign to belles-lettres: quotations from city government minutes, an ecclesiastical chronicle, a book on Masonry, and another on folk wedding customs, to name a few.

The points of view in *The Naked Year* are legion. The reader encounters alternatively a stylized omniscient, objective-dramatic, first person, lyrical, romantic-ironic narration, and other forms. In all this welter Pil'niak's persona functions as a dramatic narrator, a spirit and oracle of the times, the *Zeitgeist* itself standing on stage among other actors. The spotlight frequently shines on him – then fades. *He* recites the accretive refrains and provides lyrical asides, exclamations, and queries. All of this decelerates the tempo, compels the reader to consider the text itself more carefully, and attracts attention to the dramatic narrator who provides muted clues with which to decode the message.

GARY BROWNING

Tale of the Unextinguished Moon

Povest' nepogashennoi luny

Novella, 1926

First published in 1926, this work attracted political controversy. This is discussed below, but with political considerations no longer a factor, *Tale of the Unextinguished Moon* impresses as one of Pil'niak's most vivid and well-crafted short works.

Unusually for Pil'niak, there is a single, well-defined plot, developed in a reasonably straightforward fashion. The story begins with a train pulling into a city from somewhere in the south. Army Commander Gavrilov emerges from the sleeping-car. After taking a cure in the Caucasus, he has been summoned to the city for a purpose as yet unclear to him. This somewhat remote and forbidding Civil War hero is given a more human dimension by his old comrade Popov, who meets the train. They speak of their past as provincial weavers, turned fighters for the Revolution and we learn, too, that the fear Gavrilov expresses suddenly becomes real, as he reads in the newspapers that he is to undergo an operation for a stomach ulcer.

The second chapter opens with a description of two large public buildings. The first stands at the intersection of the city's two main streets. (Interestingly, "the city" is never actually named as Moscow and its topography remains imprecise). This House No. 1 is clearly the hub of a major power. In an office there sits a man alone, described only as "The Unbending Man". Gavrilov arrives and in the conversation that ensues it becomes clear that orders have already been given for the operation: "You once gave the order to send four thousand men to certain death", the Unbending Man reminds Gavrilov. "You did right." Thus, in House No. 1, Gavrilov appears the willing victim of authority and discipline, contrasting with the life-enhancing spontaneity that he displays in Popov's company.

Next, in a hospital on the edge of the city (House No. 2), a medical consultation appoints two professors to carry out the operation on Gavrilov. The surgeons see Gavrilov only as a remote, rather frightening figure, but his human side emerges again that evening, when he sits in Popov's hotel room, chatting and singing a lullaby to Popov's young daughter, Natasha. At this point, the moon appears for the first time over the city, looking down alike on the two old friends and the Unbending Man alone in his office.

Returning to his sleeping-car, Gavrilov becomes once more the stern commander. As in the opening scene, he turns to Tolstoi's *Detstvo*, *Otrochestvo*, *Iunost'* (*Childhood*, *Boyhood* and *Youth*). In conversation with Popov, he has rejected "revolutionary literature" in favour of the sense of "lived life" he finds in Tolstoi. Then, after writing three letters "to be opened after my death", he orders a car and takes Popov on a crazy, yet life-affirming drive deep into the country, returning to the city at dawn.

Awaiting his operation in House No. 2 the following day, Gavrilov has a last conversation with Popov, in which he refers again to Tolstoi, specifically this time to the section where Tolstoi discusses the concept of *comme il faut*. "Death", Gavrilov muses, "is not *comme il faut*". The operation and the build-up to it are described in some detail. It is apparent that Gavrilov is exceptionally resistant to anaesthetic, taking 47 minutes to go under, but that is what causes his heart to stop, just as Professor Lozovskii lays bare the healed ulcer (a double irony!). Thirty-seven hours later, Gavrilov is officially prononunced dead, Lozovskii having reported in a three-minute conversation to House No. 1, the Unbending Man visits the hospital to say farewell to his old comrade (or is it to check that he is really dead?). Then he, too, goes for a fast drive in the country, ordering his driver to stop at the same spot as Gavrilov and Popov did on their drive. As dawn is breaking, he too returns to the city.

The epilogue follows Gavrilov's funeral. Popov and his daughter are in the hotel room. As he reads his dead friend's letter, Popov watches his daughter looking out at the pale moon, trying to blow it out. But the moon floats on and the city begins to wake.

When *Tale of the Unextinguished Moon* appeared in *Novyi mir*, it was harshly criticized. Pil'niak's "crime", apparently, was to have accused the Party leadership of the medical murder of Army Commander M.F. Frunze, who had recently died during an operation. Furthermore, his depiction of the sympathetic, doomed Gavrilov was somehow deemed an insult to Frunze's memory. The hidden agenda was that, in the Unbending Man, Pil'niak had portrayed the ruthless and unapproachable figure of Stalin, dispensing life and death from his office in the Kremlin.

In his brief preface, Pil'niak disclaims any intention of writing about Frunze, saying that he hardly knew him and urging the reader not to look for real events or people at all. This is a curious introduction, however, and indeed real events are alluded to in the text and the fictional Gavrilov's biography bears some resemblance to that of Frunze. There is evidence, too, that Pil'niak knew something of the circumstances and rumours surrounding Frunze's death. However, in our time, it becomes much easier to view *Tale of the Unextinguished Moon* in a purely literary light. Thus, the central episode of Gavrilov's death now looks like a tragic accident, rather than a medical assassination enacted out of political rivalry (one suggestion being that Stalin's close comrade, Voroshilov, wanted Frunze's job). We see how the "iron discipline" of the Revolution leads the individual to abdicate responsibility and turn his life over completely to the Party, thus reinforcing Gavrilov's inner conflict.

Gavrilov's spontaneity contrasts with the machine-like rigidity of the Unbending Man, a dichotomy often encountered in Pil'niak. There remains, however, the puzzling symbol of the moon and Natasha's attempt to extinguish it. One recent critic, E. Iablokov, sees the moon as another machine. But one might also regard it as a force of nature, transcending ephemeral humanity. So, Natasha's funny, touching action is somehow life-affirming. We are reminded, too, of Gavrilov's preoccupation with Tolstoi and *comme il faut*. Death, Tolstoi says, strips away the false mask of ciivilization we all don. Gavrilov knew this and his spirit lives on in the little girl blowing innocently at the moon.

MICHAEL FALCHIKOV

Mahogany

Krasnoe derevo

Novella, 1929

The Volga Falls to the Caspian Sea

Volga vpadaet v Kaspiiskoe more

Novel, 1930

Mahogany (published in Berlin in 1929) led to a brush with the authorities. Pil'niak was accused of publishing anti-Soviet material abroad. Forced to defend himself in the highly-charged atmosphere of the time, he claimed he had decided to incorporate the story into a larger work about the Five-Year Plan on which he was already embarking. Much of *Mahogany* has indeed found its way into *The Volga Falls to the Caspian Sea* (with some "political" excisions), but, as a separate work, it creates a very different impression. Set in an unnamed provincial town (identifiable as Uglich) it describes, with a mixture of nostalgia and mockery, a society declining economically and morally, but still clinging to the old ways. The Bezdetov brothers, furniture-restorers, visit the town to buy antiques from impoverished families to sell to the new Soviet bourgeoisie. Their chief contact is the 85-year-old Iakov Karpovich Skudrin, homespun philosopher and general fixer. There is a large Skudrin clan, including a brother Ivan, who has renamed himself Ozhogov and who remains true, as he sees it, to the ideals of 1917 and lives in a commune in a brickworks. The moral and political ambivalence of the younger generation is reflected in the itinerant Trotskiite Akim and the pregnant and unmarried Klavdia, who divides her time between getting drunk in a bathhouse with the Bezdetovs and teaching in the local school. The Bezdetovs pass their time in the town buying furniture, drinking, and discussing life with Skudrin and Ozhogov before departing again for Moscow. Although Pil'niak respects the historical continuity of towns like Uglich and writes with feeling of a vanishing way of life and people clinging to the remains of their past, the overriding impression is of a slow drift into decadence. Only Ivan Ozhogov, drunken failure though he may be, retains some idealism for the Revolution and its possibilities, though for him personally it all ended in 1921.

If *Mahogany* showed the Russian provinces on the eve of great upheaval, in *The Volga Falls to the Caspian Sea* the first Five-Year Plan has started. Significantly, Pil'niak opens his novel in Moscow, but transfers the main action to Kolomna. In keeping with the formula of the "production novel", the central event is the construction of a dam at the confluence of the Moskva and Oka to open up a major link with the Volga and also irrigate the area, at a cost of engulfing several villages. The construction project is always in the background (Pil'niak includes some technical discussions and descriptions of the site) but much of the novel is concerned with the lives and relationships of four engineers connected with the project. The setting of Kolomna also incorporates substantial parts of *Mahogany* and most of its characters, especially Skudrin and Ozhogov (but not the Trotskiite Akim, though a couple of references to Trotskii, removed from the 1930 edition, have been restored). By contrast with *Mahogany*, though, the message is unequivocal: the old Russia is on the way out, the new USSR has taken over.

In keeping with the demands of the production genre, there is a wreckers' plot, involving Skudrin and Poltorak, one of the engineers, which is unmasked by Ivan Ozhogov, but it is both unconvincing and peripheral to the novel's development. *The Volga Falls to the Caspian Sea* is structured so that the principal characters all converge on Kolomna for a couple of days as the project is nearing completion and at the same time the intertwining of their personal lives resolves itself. By means of lengthy flashbacks, we learn of the connections between the four engineers – Poletika, Poltorak, Laslo, and Sadykov. Thus, Poletika's wife had left him for his junior Laslo 14 years ago, but Laslo leaves her for Mariia Sadykova, who commits suicide the day before Poletika and Poltorak arrive from Moscow. The four engineers represent various stages in "revolutionary consciousness" and acceptance of the new society. Thus Poltorak enjoys the most privileged existence with a smart Moscow flat and links with "top people". But he is also a self-confessed anti-Bolshevik, follower of Solov'ev, and a compulsive womanizer, who, with rather heavy-handed symbolism, neglects his wife, Sof'ia, for her sister, Vera, and two other young women, Nadezhda and Poletika's daughter, Liubov'. Laslo, a good communist, but an unstable personality is drawn unwittingly into Poltorak's "conspiracy", doomed to self-destruction after his wife's suicide, an event that sparks off a revolt among the women on the construction site. Mariia's funeral is a key episode that leads to the women asserting their right to be treated as equals in the new order. Women, they say, are still oppressed by men, but the Revolution has "taught them what to do". The idea of Revolution as sexual liberation is familiar in Pil'niak – what is new is the strong pitch for women's rights.

The future belongs to the new communist-educated generation – Sadykov, the engineer "from the ranks", and Liubov' Poletika, archaeologist and komsomolka. But it is Liubov''s father, Professor Pimen Poletika, who exemplifies continuity. The oldest of the four engineers, a man whose ideas were formed before 1917, Poletika nevertheless succeeds in reconstructing himself to serve the new regime, thus embodying Pil'niak's idea of integrating the best of pre-revolutionary culture and ideals.

In *The Volga Falls to the Caspian Sea*, Pil'niak seems to have been attempting first to create a longer, more richly-textured work than previously, and second to signal his acceptance of the fundamental shift in Soviet society brought about by the Five-Year Plan. On the whole, he succeeded in both aims. In keeping with the genre, the "plot" is thwarted and the generations come together to build a future in Kolomna – Liubov' and Sadykov, Poletika and his first wife and the younger children. Ivan Ozhogov "a splendid man from the splendid epoch of 1917–21" (and a more heroic figure than in *Mahogany*) dies in the flooding but not before warning, however, that, following the social revolution and now the cultural revolution, "we need a revolution of honour and conscience".

MICHAEL FALCHIKOV

Aleksei Feofilaktovich Pisemskii 1821–1881

Novelist and dramatist

Biography

Born on family estate of Ramene in Chukhloma district, Kostroma, 23 March 1821. Early childhood spent in Vetluga, educated by private tutors; gymnasium in Kostroma, 1835. Studied mathematics at Moscow University, 1840–44. Worked in Kostroma Chamber of State Properties, 1845; promoted to Moscow Chamber, 1845. Returned to Kostroma, 1847. First short stories written, 1847–48. Special agent to military governor of Kostroma province, 1848. Married: Ekaterina Pavlovna Svinina in 1848; three sons. Appointed provincial *assessor*, 1850. Moved to St Petersburg, 1854. Early play, *Ipokhondrik* [The Hypochondriac], staged in St Petersburg and Moscow, 1855. Resigned from civil service; joined the editorial staff of *Biblioteka dlia chteniia*, 1857. Break with radical writers, 1861. Visited western Europe, 1862; moved to Moscow, 1863. Returned to civil service, 1866. Temporarily Vice-Governor of Moscow, 1871–72. Final retirement from civil service, 1872. Second visit to western Europe, 1874, third, invited by Turgenev, 1875. Recipient: Uvarov Prize for drama, jointly with A.N. Ostrovskii, 1860. Died in Moscow, 2 February 1881. Buried in Novodevichii monastery.

Publications

Collected Editions

Sochineniia: Posmertnoe polnoe izdanie, 20 vols. St Petersburg and Moscow, 1883–86.
Sobranie sochinenii, 9 vols. Moscow, 1959.
Nina, The Comic Actor and An Old Man's Sin, translated by Maya Jenkins. Ann Arbor, Ardis, 1988.

Fiction

Nina, in *Syn otechestva*, 7 (1848); translated as "Nina", by Maya Jenkins, in *Nina, The Comic Actor and An Old Man's Sin*, 1988.
Tiufiak, in *Moskvitianin*, 1 (1850); translated as *The Simpleton*, by Ivy Litvinov, Moscow, Foreign Languages Publishing House, 1959.
Ocherki iz krest'ianskogo byta [Stories from Peasant Life]. St Petersburg, 1856.
Boiarshchina, in *Biblioteka dlia chteniia*, 1–2 (1858).
Tysiacha dush, in *Otechestvennye zapiski*, 1–6 (1858); translated as *One Thousand Souls*, by Ivy Litvinov, Moscow, Foreign Languages Publishing House, and New York, Grove Press, 1959.
Starcheskii grekh, in *Biblioteka dlie chteniia*, 1 (1861); translated as "An Old Man's Sin", by Maya Jenkins, in *Nina, The Comic Actor and An Old Man's Sin*, 1988.
Vzbalamuchennoe more [Troubled Seas], in *Russkii vestnik*, 3–8 (1863).
Liudi sorokovykh godov [Men of the 1840s], in *Zaria*, 1–9 (1869).
V vodovorote [In the Whirlpool], *Beseda*, 1–6 (1871).
Masony [The Masons], in *Ogonek*, 3–4 (1880).

Plays

Ipokhondrik [The Hypochondriac], *Moskvitianin*, 1 (1852).
Gor'kaia sud'bina, in *Biblioteka dlia chteniia*, 11 (1859); translated as "A Bitter Fate", by A. Kagan and G.R. Noyes, in *Masterpieces of the Russian Drama*, edited by G.R. Noyes, vol. 2, New York and London, Appleton, 1933.
Byvye sokoli [Former Falcons], in *Vsemirni trud*, 9 (1868).
Khishchniki [Plunderers], *Grazhdanin*, 7–10 (1873).
Vaal, in *Russki vestnik*, 4 (1873); translated as "Baal. A Play", by A. Donskov, *Russian Literature Triquarterly*, 9 (1974), 160–219.
Prosveshchennoe vremia [An Enlightened Age], in *Russkii vestnik*, 1 (1875).
Finansovyi genii [A Financial Genius], in *Gazeta Gattsuka*, 3–4 (1876).
Ptentsy poslednogo poleta [Fledglings of the Last Flight]. 1883–86.

Critical Studies

"Aleksei Filaktovich Pisemskii", by V.V. Zelinskii, in *Polnoe*

sobranie sochinenii, by A.F. Pisemskii, vol. 1, St Petersburg, 1895, xv–clx.
A.F. Pisemskii, by M.P. Eremin, Moscow, 1956.
"Pisemsky's *Bitter Fate*: The First Outstanding Drama of Russian Peasant Life", by Maya Jenkins, *Canadian Slavonic Papers*, 3 (1958), 76–88.
"The Bitter Fate of A.F. Pisemsky", by R.E. Steussy, *Russian Review*, 25 (1966), 170–83.
Pisemsky: A Provincial Realist, by Charles A. Moser, Cambridge, Massachusetts, Harvard University Press, 1969.
"Pisemsky's Talent as a Playwright", by Andrew Donskov, *Russian Literature Triquarterly*, 9 (1974), 486–95.
"A.F. Pisemsky: The Making of a Russian Novelist", by J. Woodhouse, *Forum for Modern Language Studies*, 20 (1984), 49–69.
"A Realist in a Changing Reality: A.F. Pisemsky and *Vzbalamuchennoe more*", by J. Woodhouse, *Slavonic and East European Review*, 64 (1986), 489–505.
Tri eretika, by Lev Anninskii, Moscow, 1988.

Bibliography
Russkie pisateli vtoroi poloviny XIX–nachala XX vv (do 1917 goda): Rekomendatel'nyi ukazatel' literatury, edited by R.N. Krendel and B.A. Peskina, Moscow, 1958.

Aleksei Pisemskii, a prolific novelist, story-writer and dramatist, first appeared in print in 1848 with a slight tale, "Nina", but two years later he began to attract more notice with a novella, *Tiufiak* (*The Simpleton*), whose main theme was to become common in his writings: a young idealist who does not survive the destruction of his dreams when faced by a harsh reality. On the suggestion of Ostrovskii, who, almost alone, was to remain Pisemskii's friend for the rest of his life, he joined the staff of one of the leading literary journals of the early 1850s *Moskvitianin*, which printed his first play, *Ipokhondrik* [The Hypochondriac] in 1852 and then a three-story collection, *Ocherki iz krest'ianskogo byta* [Stories from Peasant Life], which established his early reputation as a portrayer of the life of ordinary people. As Pisemskii came from the provinces, he was soon regarded by his social and intellectual "betters" as a striking example of the coarse peasant with his lack of graces, strong accent, and successive fondness for food and drink. Undeterred, he continued to write and in the mid-1850s joined the periodical *Biblioteka dlia chteniia*, soon to become its editor. The years 1858–61 marked the peak of his literary fame. The novel *Boiarshchina* – a place name – was published in 1858, and related, in a rather complicated way, how Anna Pavlovna, who suffers at the hands of a crude husband, takes up with her former friend N.N. Elchaninov who then deserts her. She is seduced by a heartless nobleman and subsequently dies. It gives a detailed description of provincial life, has impressive character sketches and realistic dialogue. This was followed by his three most enduring works, the four-part novel *Tysiacha dush* (*One Thousand Souls*), the play *Gor'kaia sud'bina* (*A Bitter Fate*) and *Starcheskii grekh* (*An Old Man's Sin*).

One Thousand Souls concerns an extremely ambitious young man, Kalinovich, from the provinces who makes his way to St Petersburg determined to achieve wealth and fame. He deserts his former fiancée and helped by an influential patron, Prince Ivan Ramenskii, (the villain of the piece), marries a rich but unattractive general's daughter and rises rapidly to be vice-governor of the province whence he sprang. On the way he gets involved in many of the prince's illegal activities. The last part of the novel portrays him as a zealous, reforming governor who also attempts to bring the prince to justice but is thwarted by the latter's powerful connections and is forced to resign. Pisemskii's common concerns of loveless marriage, the corruption engendered by the desire for material well-being, the uselessness of ideals in a harsh world, and the malpractices of the bureaucracy all appear in abundance. Pisemskii, however, always lacked the ability to convince without ramming the point home, the level of his arguments is low, and his nature descriptions are flat and factual. It would seem that he was more interested in events than ideas or his characters and, despite some interesting portraits and realistic dialogue, he often failed to attract the readers' sympathy for his creations. Although the last part of the novel is a powerful attack on the evils of serfdom, the above points might well go some way to explaining why his reputation was soon to falter.

His best play, *A Bitter Fate*, has been described as one of only two "realistic tragedies", the other being Tolstoi's *Vlast' tmy* (*The Power of Darkness*), and is in some ways superior to it. During a peasant's absence from the estate, his wife falls in love with the landowner and bears his child. On her return the peasant finds out and in his rage and jealousy kills the baby. Then, full of remorse, he admits his crime, begs forgiveness and accepts his punishment. The play is, however, not the commonplace story of an innocent young girl being seduced by an older and more experienced man, for there is genuine affection on both sides. The critics appreciated both this aspect of the play and its accurate portrayal of some of the negative aspects of Russian life.

An Old Man's Sin is also typical of its author. A lonely bureaucrat falls for the scheming machinations of a beautiful woman, embezzles government money for her, discovers she has no affection for him at all, and in despair commits suicide. It is only scoundrels who succeed and beauty is but a mask for corruption. Pisemskii's pessimistic view of the world is here at its deepest.

In the 1860s Pisemskii broke with the radical critics and the pamphleteering novel, *Vzbalamuchennoe more* [Troubled Seas], was his response. A vast canvas of contemporary life, it attempts to show that the young radicals of the time were just as egoistic and greedy as their elders whom they attacked so vehemently. The outrage that this work provoked led him to return to a period with which he felt more comfortable and he wrote *Liudi sorokovykh godov* [Men of the 1840s]. In spite of it being an impressive picture of the times, the work was not well-received and led to his being disregarded for the rest of his life. Indeed many of his novels and plays passed all but unnoticed.

Although he enjoyed a few years of fame when even the leading radical critic, Pisarev, thought him the equal of Goncharov and in some ways superior to Turgenev, Pisemskii was soon eclipsed by his more gifted contemporaries and his reputation has never recovered, despite being a worthy contributor to what was known as the "literature of exposure". He died a week before Dostoevskii and his modest funeral, in contrast to the latter's (an event of some historical significance), would only have confirmed his pessimism and conviction that Russians were irredeemable and their country was filled only with selfishness, materialism, and a lack of any ideals or consideration for others. His provincialism and conservatism, his unpolished style and his unmitigated jaundiced view of the human condition seem destined to ensure that his reputation will not be resurrected.

A.V. KNOWLES

One Thousand Souls

Tysiacha dush

Novel, 1858

In 1858 Pisemskii was working in the civil service in the provincial city of Kostroma and establishing his reputation as a writer in his off-duty hours, which were plentiful. He was informed that he was to be transferred to Kherson, but, because he lacked the necessary funds to move himself and his family, he resigned his official position and retired to his family estate of Ramene, even deeper in the provinces than Kostroma. This personal dissatisfaction with what he saw as his bitter fate at least had the advantage of allowing him to devote himself for a time entirely to writing. The result was his best work, *One Thousand Souls*; it took him four years to complete, by which time he had moved to St Petersburg. The novel was published from January to June 1858 in the literary journal *Otechestvennye zapiski*, much to the chagrin of the poet and literary editor of *Sovremennik*, N.A. Nekrasov, who had printed some of Pisemskii's earlier works and thought he had bought the new novel for his journal for two thousand roubles. When he heard that Pisemskii had in fact sold it to the rival *Otechestvennye zapiski* for three thousand, his earlier, somewhat negative, view of Pisemskii's literary talents was intensified. "It is astonishing", he told Turgenev, "how little trouble [Pisemskii] experiences in resolving the most difficult of problems. I don't know why, but I cannot think of him in any other way than as a *literary policeman*, who resolves all the problems of life and the heart with a club!"

One Thousand Souls is written in four parts. The first two describe the protagonist, Kalinovich, an ambitious young man and budding author, living in the restricting and lifeless world of a Russian backwater. With boundless self-confidence and unlimited personal aspirations, he has few, if any, scruples about achieving personal success, wealth and the estate with "a thousand souls". He begins a bureaucratic career as an inspector of a small provincial school and proceeds to fall in love with his predecessor's daughter. His life appears to be progressing smoothly and happily, until the arrival of the novel's "villain", Prince Ivan Ramenskii, who decides to become Kalinovich's protector. He arranges a marriage for Kalinovich to Polina, the physically unattractive but wealthy daughter of a general. He also involves him in numerous illegal activities. There is then the amazingly quick rise, from school inspector to special government agent, and then to acting vice-governor of the province from which Kalinovich originated. Pisemskii devotes barely a couple of pages to this series of events, and this passage is, therefore, thought by many to be the novel's main weakness. The fourth and last part shows Kalinovich as the reforming, progressive vice-governor and finally governor. He has achieved, through his marriage, the wealth, and through his work, the power and influence he always craved. In the process, however, he becomes self-righteous and legalistic. The evil-doings of Prince Ramenskii come to public knowledge and, despite the fact that Kalinovich owes almost everything to his former patron, he has him arrested. Ignoring the influence of the prince's powerful connections, Kalinovich is finally forced to resign. His wife leaves him and then loses all her money in helping the prince. With his power in society and his financial security both removed from him, he is left only to drag out a lonely and futile existence.

The first two parts of the novel, and to a lesser extent the third, are faithful to the reality of the setting they describe, the life and customs of provincial existence. The psychology of Kalinovich is convincingly portrayed; he is a talented, ambitious man, thwarted from his early childhood onwards, who turns against the society that he considers to blame. Although honest and decent at heart, he nevertheless is willing to use others to further his aims or be obsequious to those who can assist him. Typical Pisemskii themes of idealism opposed by a cruel reality, of a loveless marriage, of the malevolent effect of seeking and gaining wealth and power, and of the wide corruption of the bureaucracy are all present. In the final part, which in some ways is less than perfectly integrated with the first three and forms a type of epilogue, Pisemskii provides a striking description of the evils prevailing under serfdom. This highlights his ability to portray the more negative aspects of humanity and the generally appalling conditions of Russian life, both physically degrading and morally bare. Kalinovich, who has changed, somewhat unconvincingly, from corrupt, self-seeking egotist to upright, reforming zealot, personifies another of Pisemskii's abiding concerns. How far is it possible, if at all, for a single person, irrespective of his being wealthy and influential, to change the customs and practices of a basically flawed and corrupt society? Pisemskii's response is deeply pessimistic. Once Kalinovich begins to improve conditions for people, once he tries to push people out of the inertia that governs Russian life, his hands are tied and he sinks moodily into resignation. Pisemskii seems to be suggesting that not only is Kalinovich fully aware of his ultimate failure but that it was utterly futile for him even to have hoped for success. While Pisemskii was radical neither in his social or his political views, (let alone revolutionary), he suggests that it is useless to change parts of the system if the system itself remains basically unaltered.

The contemporary critical reaction to *One Thousand Souls* was predictably mixed and the views were, rather unusually for the time, not entirely coloured by the reviewer's political leanings. S.S. Dudyshkin praised both its didacticism and its artistry, while A.V. Druzhinin, albeit critically, suggested it was a worthy addition to the "literature of exposure". P.V. Annenkov, however, saw the characterization of Kalinovich as the novel's main flaw, a hero so negative but equally so predominant over all the other personages that they only existed through him. Dostoevskii could not understand why anyone should enthuse over what he considered a mediocre pastiche of the works of others, and Saltykov-Shchedrin thought that Kalinovich's rise to governor was unrealistic: people got on by hard work, hand-licking (and other parts of the body) and never attained such heights anyway from such a lowly beginning. The most radical critics, while all in favour of works of social comment, did not consider that the novel was true to Russian life. Nor has *One Thousand Souls* survived the test of time. It might contain numerous impressive character sketches and describe in detail much of what was wrong with Russian life, but its plot is decidedly loose, its dialogue somewhat contrived and Kalinovich's motivations and psychology ultimately confused or unconvincing. The novel seems destined for a lower place in the pantheon than those of Pisemskii's contemporaries.

A.V. KNOWLES

Andrei Platonovich Platonov 1899–1951

Prose writer

Biography

Born Andrei Platonovich Klimentov in Voronezh, 1 September 1899. Various manual jobs, from 1912. Completed secondary schooling at evening classes. First publications of verse and prose in local journals, 1918. Joined the Red Army; fought in the Civil War, 1919. Worked for Voronezh newspapers, early 1920s. Graduated from Polytechnical Institute, 1924. Worked as land reclamation specialist; drafted to Commissariat of Agriculture in Moscow, 1926. Stories began to appear regularly in Moscow journals. Worked for journals *Literaturnyi kritik* and *Literaturnoe obozrenie*, 1937–40. Served in the Soviet Army as correspondent for the newspaper *Krasnaia zvezda* during World War II. Contracted tuberculosis, 1944; demobilized, 1946. Published children's stories, 1947–50. Died in Moscow, 5 January 1951, leaving large quantities of his literary output unpublished.

Publications

Collected Editions

Izbrannye rasskazy. Moscow, 1958.
Fro and Other Stories [various translators]. Moscow, Progress, 1972.
Collected Works, translated by Thomas P. Whitney *et al.* Ann Arbor, Ardis, 1978.
Izbrannye proizvedeniia, 2 vols. Moscow, 1978.
Sobranie sochinenii, 3 vols. Moscow, 1984–85.
Povesti i rasskazy (1928–1934 gody). Moscow, 1988.
Gosudarstvennyi zhitel' [The State Inhabitant]. Moscow, 1988.
Zhivia glavnoi zhizn'iu [Light of Life]. Moscow, 1989.
Vzyskanie pogibshikh [Punishment of the Lost Ones]. Moscow, 1995.

Fiction

Elektrifikatsiia [Electrification]. Voronezh, 1921.
Epifanskie shliuzhy. Moscow, 1927; translated as "The Epifan Locks", by Marion Jordan, in *Collected Works*, 1978.
Lugovye mastera [Meadow Craftsmen]. Moscow, 1928.
Sokrovennyi chelovek [Secret Man]. Moscow, 1928.
Proiskhozhdenie mastera [The Making of a Master Craftsman]. Moscow, 1929.
Reka Potudan'. Moscow, 1937; edited by Marilyn Minto, London, Bristol Classical Press, 1995; translated as "The Potudan River", by Alexey A. Kiselev, in *Collected Works*, 1978.
Odukhotvorennye liudi [Inspired People]. Moscow, 1942.
Rasskazy o rodine [Stories about the Motherland]. Moscow, 1943.
Soldatskoe serdtse [A Soldier's Heart]. Moscow, 1946.
Kotlovan. London, Flegon Press, 1969; also in *Novyi mir*, 1987; translated as *The Foundation Pit: A Bilingual Edition*, by Thomas P. Whitney, with a preface by Joseph Brodsky, Ann Arbor, Ardis, 1973, reprinted in *Collected Works*, 1978; also translated by Mirra Ginsburg, New York, Dutton, 1975, reprinted Evanston, Illinois, Northwestern University Press, 1994; and by Robert Chandler and Geoffrey Smith, London, Harvill Press, 1996.
The Fierce and Beautiful World: Stories by Andrey Platonov, with an introduction by Yevgeny Yevtushenko, translated by Joseph Barnes. New York, Dutton, 1970.
Chevengur. Paris, YMCA-Press, 1972 [incomplete]; also in *Druzhba narodov*, 1988; separate edition Moscow, 1989; reprinted Moscow, 1991; translated as *Chevengur*, by Anthony Olcott, Ann Arbor, Ardis, 1978.
"Iuvenil'noe more" [The Sea of Youth], *Ekho*, 4 (1979); *Znamia*, 6 (1986).
Starik i starukha. Poteriannaia proza [The Old Man and the Old Woman. Lost Prose], compiled by F. Levin. Munich, 1984.

Poetry

Golubaia glubina. Kniga stikhov [Blue Depths]. Krasnodar, 1922.

Plays

Volshebnoe sushchestvo [A Magical Being], with R.I. Fraerman. Moscow, 1967.
14 krasnykh izbushek [Fourteen Red Cabins], *Grani*, 86 (1972).
Vysokoe napriazhenie [High Tension]. Moscow, 1974.
Uchenik litseia [Grammar School Boy]. Moscow, 1974.
Sharmanka. Ann Arbor, Ardis, 1975; *Teatr*, 1 (1988); translated as "The Barrel Organ", by Carl R. Proffer, in *Collected Works*, 1978.

Essays and Articles

Razmyshleniia chitatelia. Stat'i. [Musings of a Reader]. Moscow, 1970.
Masterskaia [Workshop]. Moscow, 1977.

Critical Studies

Tvorchestvo A. Platonova, edited by V.P. Skobelev *et al.*, Voronezh, 1970; reprinted Ann Arbor, Ardis, 1986.
Poiski smysla otdel'nogo i obshchego sushchestvovaniia, by A. Shubin, Moscow, 1978.
"O sviazi nizshikh urovnei teksta s vysshimi (Proza Andreia Platonova), by E. Tolstaia-Segal, *Slavica Hierosolymitana*, 2 (1978), 169–212.
Filosofskaia proza A. Platonova, by N.G. Poltavtseva, Rostov-on-Don, 1981.
"Ideologicheskie konteksty Platonova", by E. Tolstaia-Segal, *Russian Literature*, IX (1981), 231–80.
Andrei Platonov v poiskakh schast'ia, by M. Geller, Paris, YMCA-Press, 1982.
Platonov and Fyodorov, by Ayleen Teskey, Amersham, Avebury, 1982.
Chelovek v filosofskoi proze Platonova, by A.P. Fomenko, Kalinin, 1985.
Estetika A. Platonova, by N.M. Malygina, Irkutsk, 1985.
Less than One: Selected Essays, by Joseph Brodsky, New York, Farrar Straus and Giroux, and London, Viking, 1986; Harmondsworth, Penguin, 1987.
Russian Literature (special issue), Amsterdam, 23/4 (1988).
The Shape of Apocalypse in Modern Russian Fiction, by David M. Bethea, Princeton, Princeton University Press, 1989.
"Ispytanie istoriei", by V. Svitel'skii, in Platonov's *Chevengur*, Voronezh, 1989.
"Platonov – tragicheskie paradoksy gumanizma", by V. Vakhrushev, *Volga*, 8 (1989), 166–74.
"Natsional'naia tragediia: utopiia i real'nost'. Roman Andreia Platonova 'Chevengur' v kontekste ego vremeni", by V. Vasil'ev, *Nash sovremennik*, 3 (1989).
Zhanrovye problemy utopii i "Chevengur" A. Platonova, by Hans Gunter, Moscow, Progress, 1991.
"Chevengur i okrestnosti", by Boris Paramonov, *Iskusstvo kino*, 12 (1991).
"A.P. Platonov v vospriiatii zarubezhnykh issledovatelei (Obzor)", by I.V. Savel'zon, *Referativnyi zhurnal. Obshchestvennye nauki v SSSR. Literaturovedenie*, 4 (1991).
"Evnukh dushi", by V. Podoroga, *Paralleli*, 2 (1992).
Andrei Platonov, by Thomas Seifrid, Cambridge, Cambridge University Press, 1992.
Zdes' i teper' (special issue), 3 (1993).
The Seeds of Time, by Fredric Jameson, New York, Columbia University Press, 1994.
Text Counter Text: Rereadings in Russian Literary History, by Alexander Zholkovsky, Stanford, Stanford University Press, 1994.
Andrei Platonov. Materialy dlia biografii 1899–1929 gg, by T. Langerak, Amsterdam, Pegasus, 1995.
The KGB's Literary Archive, by Vitaly Shentalinsky, translated by John Crowfoot, London, Harvill Press, 1995.
"Strana filosofov" Andreia Platonova: Problemy tvorchestva, Moscow, 1995.
Tvorchestvo Andreia Platonova: Issledovaniia i materialy. Bibliografiia, St Petersburg, 1995.
Khudozhestvennyi mir Andreia Platonova, by N.M. Malygina, Moscow, 1995.
"Carnivalization and Populism in the Soviet Modernist Novel: Andrei Platonov and Mikhail Bakhtin", by Craig Brandist, *Essays in Poetics*, 22 (1997), 1–29.
"The Pit and the Tower: Andrei Platonov's Prose Style", by Angela Livingstone, *Essays in Poetics*, 22 (1997), 139–57.

Bibliographies

A.P. Platonov: Materialy k biobibliografii, by N.M. Mitrakova, Moscow, 1969.
"Andrei Platonovich Platonov (1899–1951). Bibliograficheskii ukazatel'", by V. Maramzin *et al.*, *Ekho*, 4 (1979); 1–4 (1980).
Bibliography in *Andrei Platonov*, by Thomas Seifrid, Cambridge, Cambridge University Press, 1992, 250–66.

Andrei Platonov was born into a working-class family in the town of Voronezh. At the age of 13 he was working on a threshing machine, and at 14 he was found a job at the locomotive building factory where his father was a metal worker. Studying in the evenings, he completed his secondary schooling and was awarded a school leaving certificate. Platonov joined the Red Army in 1919 and fought in the Civil War. He enrolled at the Polytechnical Institute and at the same time began to write poetry. His first works (poems, short stories and articles) were published in the newspapers *Voronezhskaia bednota* and *Voronezhskaia kommuna*. A volume of poetry, *Golubaia glubina* [Blue Depths], was published in Krasnodar in 1922. Platonov worked in the offices of the newspapers *Voronezhskaia kommuna, Krasnaia derevnia*, *Ogni*, on the journal *Zheleznyi put'*, and was published in the Moscow journals *Kuznitsa* and *Krasnaia niva*.

After the end of the Civil War Platonov graduated from the Polytechnical Institute (1924) and began working as a land reclamation specialist. In 1926 he was drafted to the Commissariat of Agriculture (Narkomzem) in Moscow. He then went on to publish the books *Epifanskie shliuzy* (*The Epifan Locks*) in 1927, *Lugovye mastera* [Meadow Craftsmen], and *Sokrovennyi chelovek* [Secret Man] in 1928. The following year saw the publication of some of his most famous stories "Gosudarstvennyi zhitel'" [The State Inhabitant] and "Usomnivshiisia Makar" ("Makar the Doubtful"), and in 1931 his novella "Vprok" [To Good Advantage] was published. Platonov now concentrated on purely literary work, and was published in *Krest'ianskaia bednota* and *Izvestiia*. *Proiskhozhdenie mastera* [The Making of a Master Craftsman] and *Reka Potudan'* (*The Potudan River*) had also been published by this time. Many decades later Andrei Mikhalkov-Konchalovsky, an American producer of Russian origin, made a film adaptation of the latter, titled *Maria's Lovers*.

From 1937 to 1940 Platonov was employed by the journals *Literaturnyi kritik* and *Literaturnoe obozrenie*, writing under the pseudonyms of F. Chelovekov and A. Firsov. In 1939 a collection of his articles was typeset for publication by the Sovetskii pisatel' publishing house, but after production of a single proof copy the editor, Sergei Borodin, gave instructions for the type to be broken up. A supplemented edition appeared only in 1970 under the title *Razmyshleniia chitatelia* [Musings of a Reader].

During World War II, Platonov served in the Soviet Army as a special correspondent of the newspaper *Krasnaia zvezda*. His experiences at the front inform the collections *Rasskazy o rodine* [Stories about the Motherland] and *Soldatskoe serdtse* [A

Soldier's Heart], and others. In November 1944 Platonov contracted a virulent form of tuberculosis and returned from the front. He was demobilized in 1946, and in the same year V. Ermilov wrote a denunciatory article about his story *Sem'ia Ivanova* [Ivanov's Family].

Platonov wrote works for children, short stories, and such literary adaptations of folk-tales as *Bashkirskie narodnye skazki* [Bashkir Folk Tales] (1947) and *Volshebnoe kol'tso. Russkie skazki* [The Magic Ring. Russian Tales] (1950). He was also a playwright, writing *14 krasnykh izbushek* [Fourteen Red Cabins], *Vysokoe napriazhenie* [High Tension], *Uchenik litseia* [Grammar School Boy], and *Volshebnoe sushchestvo* [A Magical Being], jointly with R.I. Fraerman. He died on 5 January 1951 in Moscow. At the time of Platonov's death large quantities of his literary output remained unpublished.

In philosophical terms Platonov's writing lies somewhere between those of Sigmund Freud and another, less widely-known genius, Nikolai Fedorov, the "Socrates of Moscow". If Platonov cannot be said to be their disciple, the principal themes of his work manifestly bear the impress of their philosophical ideas. Hans Gunter has attempted to show that his ideas are also linked with the philosophical works of Anatolii Lunacharskii, the first Soviet Commissar of Enlightenment (*Religion and Socialism*).

Fedorov believed in "resurrecting the fathers": that it is the overriding ethical duty of living generations to resurrect, not metaphorically but physically, their dead ancestors. He considered this to be inevitable and that consequently, in an eschatological perspective, the difference between the living and the dead was being eroded. This is why Platonov's heroes are so often asleep, or existing in a state of semi-somnolence. Sleep is, after all, an intermediate state between life and death. This is also the reason why suicide is not seen by Platonov's heroes in the terms of Nikolai Berdiaev (for whom the urge was only a moment of despair that it was essential to experience in order thereafter to continue one's former life). The idea of suicide haunts the engineer Prushevskii, architect of the "all-proletarian club", as well as Serbinov, and the worker Voshchev, who never does find the "meaning of life". Sonia Mandrova attempts to kill herself, while *Chevengur* concludes with the suicide of Aleksandr Dvanov. Finally, in *Kotlovan* (*The Foundation Pit*), after the death of the little girl Nastia, the navvies dig down ever deeper into the foundation pit, never more to emerge. Platonov took the very image of the foundation pit (*kotlovan*) from Fedorov's *Philosophy of the Common Cause*, in which it appears as the hollow (*kotlovina*), and it stands for an aggressive, all-devouring void.

Platonov's prose is the literary ontology of the Russian Revolution, mirroring its most diverse aspects. He succeeded in showing Marxism becoming a new faith, and human enthusiasm turning into a new fanaticism embodied in the totalitarian hierarchy. He saw the essence of this new fanaticism in its striving to destroy culture, to clear the ground for "socialism".

Man in his "fierce and beautiful world" (as one of Platonov's best-known stories is titled) does not adapt machinery to his own needs. On the contrary, many of his heroes are happy to be incorporated into the mechanism and become a component part of it. For Platonov the most apt symbol of revolution is the locomotive, a mechanism perfect, harmonious, and rushing into the future.

Platonov is most attracted by the world of lifeless natural things, infinitely more than by the world of people and living creatures. Among people, however, his favourites are children. The attitude of any political programme or any philosophy towards children seems to him to be its most important attribute. The death of a child is an indictment of the society in which it occurs. The death of children is the central episode in both *The Foundation Pit* and in *Chevengur*. "If children perish, then this society too is not a society of universal happiness", reason his seekers of communism. Platonov's style is typically grotesque, with a capricious fragmentariness that makes his works exceptionally difficult to translate.

BORIS LANIN

The Foundation Pit

Kotlovan

Novel, 1969 (written 1929–30)

The hero of *The Foundation Pit*, Voshchev, has been sacked from his factory job for free-thinking, for allowing his thoughts to wander, instead of concentrating on the socialist task of construction. He spends a night on a site intended for a Proletarian House and is allowed to participate in the digging of its foundations. Nevertheless, he continues to believe that it is impossible to keep the human spirit nourished on labour alone, and finds his body growing weak when he is deprived of truth. The workers he joins are half-dead, "their lips caked dry from silence", their beards "growing sparsely from exhaustion". They do not undress at night for fear of wasting energy that could be spent on production. Of their leaders, only the engineer Prushevskii regrets the lack of excitement in the struggle to build for the collective. The others, from the single-minded labourer Chiklin, the tyrannical slogan-spouter Kozlov, to the ideologist Safronov, are desensitized and brutal. The group that is to benefit from the new world is equally crippled, both mentally and physically. These include the symbol of the socialist future, the young girl Nastia, found next to her dying mother in a derelict tile factory; the fat, toothless, legless Zhachev, who hurtles round the building site on his trolley, masturbating whenever young girls go by; and the most disciplined worker, Misha, who works in the smithy and happens to be a bear.

Misha the bear plays an energetic role in the scenes of collectivization that follow, smelling out the kulaks who had formerly starved him. The flies that everywhere infest rotting carcasses lead him to their homes. The kulaks have killed their livestock and then stuffed themselves with the meat, to avoid donating them to the collective farm. Half-dead cattle are being chewed by dogs, while the stalls are so cramped that the carcasses of dead cows are supported by the living. Kulaks caught slaughtering are despatched downstream on a raft to drown at sea on the instructions of the village activist. He insists peasant women learn politically correct words by rote, beginning with the letter "a", as well as an alphabet that includes a hard sign to make for "harshness and clarity of formulations".

At the collectivization celebrations even the horses neigh and eat in unison. The collective's Utopian plans come to nought however. The Proletarian House has continued to expand so irrationally that all that remains is an ever-increasing pit. The most collectivized worker, the Bear, in his obsession with hard work, beats the molten iron so mindlessly that he continually ruins it. The Activist is broken by ever-changing directives, then killed by Chiklin for showing weakness. Kozlov and Safronov are murdered by the peasants. By the end of the novel, Prushevskii is contemplating suicide, for he cannot stand a life enriched solely by recollections. Voshchev is still wandering around perplexed. Nastia has died from illness and has been buried deep in the foundation pit by Chiklin.

The novel centres on Voshchev's search for the meaning of life. On his journey he does not achieve any understanding of self or the world, nor does he find anything with which to nourish his soul. Everywhere he encounters death and destruction. In this world the only meaningful thought is of the past, the main longing is for forgetfulness, the only consolation for the vulnerable is to nestle together. Even the digging of the pit is "automatic", carried out by half-dead workers.

The picture Voshchev's travels presents is all the more depressing because he is, as Brodskii (1978) has noted, one of the inarticulate masses. When thoughts do come upon him, the narrator articulates them on his behalf. Having failed to find the truth, for example, he assumes that it must have existed once within a plant or vermin, and then been eaten up or trampled by a beggar. The narrator follows this thought through, suggesting that the beggar would probably have died in an autumn ravine, his body blown to nothing by the wind. The tone and themes conveyed in this episode are typical of the novel as a whole. All is entropy, everywhere matter dominates being. Even language has broken down. The confusion, the senselessness is not articulated by the characters, but conveyed by both character and narrator in disturbingly visual episodes, most often connected with dying or death. The bear gives Nastia a dead fly for a present. Chiklin kisses the emaciated face of the mother's fur-covered corpse. Nastia ties a bandage round her dying mother's head to keep her mouth shut. Bones protrude out of the workers' legs. Nastia's playroom and bedroom is a coffin.

As Seifrid (1992) suggests, Platonov may have intended the novel to present both a grotesque inversion of the production novel and of Five-Year Plan intentions, and admiration for real labour and lost socialist ideals. The parodic tone, however, is superseded by philosophical despair, for the novel's conclusion is a dead-end. The future, represented by Nastia, is dead, a victim of the cold. The elements have won, their most telling symbol the sight of black on white, horrid dead flies dotted over the pure snow. The weed-covered wasteground has not been transformed. Intended as a refuge for the proletariat, all the foundation pit can provide is a store for the despised kulaks' coffins, then a burial place for Nastia, for that same young girl who had first appeared in the novel in the "dead-end cemetery of the tile factory". If the pit graveyard symbolizes a temple-museum, Nikolai Fedorov's concept of a storehouse for ancestors' artefacts, it is an empty one. Each object Voshchev collects in his bag as a present for Nastia may represent "an eternal memory of a forgotten human being", but these are only stones and leaves. The ending of this deeply depressing novel illustrates the irreconcilable conflicts in Platonov's thought. Chiklin's wish to preserve Nastia for posterity is reduced to burying her body deep in the bowels of the earth. Throughout the novel matter had dominated being, destroying as it went. It was as though, in this last act, Chiklin was attempting to protect Nastia from matter, and thereby deny all that he had hitherto believed in.

MARILYN MINTO

Chevengur

Novel, 1988 (written 1926–29)

Platonov wrote *Chevengur* between 1926 and 1929. The first part of the novel was published as a novella, *Proiskhozhdenie mastera*. However, when the manuscript was completed it was rejected by the Federatsiia publishing house, and Platonov turned for help to Maksim Gor'kii. He, however, felt the novel was unpublishable primarily on literary grounds: it was too original for the censor, too satirically barbed. The irony of all this was that the satire was at odds with the task Platonov had originally set himself.

Intending initially to write a novel that would extol "our country's builders" (this was actually the original title of *Chevengur*), Platonov ended up producing a work where the Revolution and Civil War are associated with the motifs of death and destruction, famine and ruin, with scenes of mutual destruction, and with a brooding sense of the imminent end of the world. His novel took on a life of its own quite different from the one he had expected, obliging him to fight for the survival of a baby.

The ban on *Chevengur* meant effectively that it played no role in the literary history of the 1920s. Its generic singularity was so marked among the many works about the Revolution being written in those years that it was only to be published in Russia some 60 years later. Love of dead bodies proves stronger than love for the living, and the smell of decay, the sight of a decomposed body does not discomfort the heroes in the least. On the contrary, it proves the only possible link between people.

The affluent town is contrasted in *Chevengur* with the Utopia of war communism and itself becomes an anti-Utopia. Fire fetishes are also present. The "bonfire of class war" is a typical Utopian fire fetish against which the anti-Utopia fights. The struggle of Utopia and anti-Utopia in *Chevengur* is one of the most important themes. The Utopias stand opposed to and confound each other.

Renaming the world, recreating it, conjuring it with a new name or a new word is a typical Utopian characteristic with which anti-Utopias take issue. And when, in Novokhopersk, which has been occupied by the Reds, the hero Dvanov's contemporaries sit in the club on the bazaar square and, heedless of the danger of being shot, calmly get on with reading revolutionary writings, this is a further demonstration of how sacrosanct revolutionary conjurings are. One character, Zakhar Pavlovich, formulates his main idea of how the state should be ordered: "Property needs to be brought low", Zakhar Pavlovich realized. "And people should be left with no one watching them. It will all turn out much better then, God knows!"

In *Chevengur* the family and women are part and parcel of bourgeois acquisitiveness and exploitation. Almost all the pairings in the work are incestuous and outside the norm of the classical family. In Platonov's writings, if somebody longs for a family this is presented as a longing for the past.

The Revolution isolates two norms of living. There is no return to the old norm. The Revolution has cut that off, leaving only an unfruitful future. Rejection of a full-blooded family life, the leading of a life of asceticism are a commandment of the Revolution. To tell stories about the family thus becomes almost a form of ideological subversion. Those who leave Chevengur because they long for a normal life do so after hearing tales about the family. For Platonov the very concept of woman is totally discredited. The most she can achieve in the world of Chevengur is to be the "comrade by the side of man". Meanwhile, she is a hostile element that the proletariat must overcome.

The family thus remains a relic of the past and a battlefield for people still burdened with private property. If the inhabitants of Chevengur intend to be able to switch even the sun on and off at will, "switching off" the family's role in the order of things should be a simple matter. All that remains to link the anti-Utopian world of Utopia realized with the pre-communist past is the image of children. The children are to grow up harmonious, healthy, and happy. It is for their sake, growing up without the concern and supervision of a family, that the inhabitants of Chevengur and the builders of the foundation pit endure the torments of their disordered existence. But in Platonov's fiction children remain children for all time, they never grow up. They die at the most beautiful age, and their death nullifies all the ingenious social engineering of the directors of progress.

The death of a hero in a literary work is always an important signal. In Platonov's context it points up the futility of efforts to replace the warmth of the family with the hot breath of a social class. Platonov touches here on a delicate matter, because in Chevengur the family yields its place to a conventionalized homosexual brotherhood. Boris Paramonov defines *Chevengur* as "a gnostic fantasy on a bedding of homosexual psychology".

Chevengur is in fact misogynistic from start to finish, associating woman with bourgeois fussiness and acquisitiveness. The balance between Eros and Thanatos is expressed in the figures of Kopenkin and Roza Luxemburg, and the triumph of the death wish over the instinct for life is alluded to in the comment of a transient gypsy woman: "You have graves in place of brides". Paramonov's assertion that "The world revealed in *Chevengur* is a world of men without women" can be extended to the entire ideological underpinning of the anti-Utopian genre.

Mikhail Epshtein sees Platonov's heroes as embodying an extraordinary mixture of "the enthusiasm of Ostrovskii's Pavel Korchagin and the sybaritic sensibility of Oblomov". "*Chevengur* is a chivalrous romance", Epshtein claims, "complete with all the obligatory deliriums and feats of valour". Dvanov and Kopenkin are typical chivalrous figures within a chivalrous landscape. Dvanov's suicide is itself a demonstration of the senselessness of chivalrous questing in an era which has lost chivalrous ideals. In *Chevengur*, different generic structures, including Utopian and anti-Utopian elements, coexist and intertwine. Its heterogenerity, its successful alloying of different elements into a unique, harmonious whole, mark it out as a truly outstanding literary work.

BORIS LANIN

Antonii Pogorel'skii 1787–1836

Prose writer

Biography

Born Aleksei Alekseevich Perovskii in Moscow, 1787. Illegitimate son of Count A.K. Razumovskii and Countess Mariia Sobolevskaia. Educated at home and at Moscow University, 1802–07; graduated with doctorate of philosophy in literature. Civil servant, 1807–12. Military service, 1812–16; senior adjutant to Count Repnin, spent two years at his headquarters in Dresden. Worked in the department of religious affairs and foreign denominations, 1816–22. Retired to Pogorel'sk estate, assisted in the education of his nephew, Count Aleksei Tolstoi, 1822–24. Curator of Kharkov district in Ministry of Education, 1825–27. Died while travelling to Italy, 21 July 1836.

Publications

Collected Editions

Sochineniia, 2 vols. St Petersburg, 1853.

Dvoinik, ili moi vechera v Malorossii, Monastyrka [The Double or My Evenings in Little Russia and The Convent Girl], with an introduction by N.L. Stepanov. Moscow, 1960.

Izbrannoe. Moscow, 1985.

Fiction

Dvoinik, ili moi vechera v Malorossii. St Petersburg, 1828; translated as *The Double or My Evenings in Little Russia*, by Ruth Sobel, Ann Arbor, Ardis, 1988.

Chernaia kuritsa, ili Podzemnye zhiteli. St Petersburg, 1829; reprinted 1945; translated as "The Black Hen", by Ruth Sobel, *Russian Literature Triquarterly*, 23 (1989).

Monastyrka. St Petersburg, 1833; translated as "The Convent Girl", by Christine Rydel, in *The Ardis Anthology of Russian Romanticism*, edited by Christine Rydel, Ann Arbor, Ardis, 1984, 267–80.

Critical Studies

The Russian Hoffmannists, by Charles E. Passage, The Hague, Mouton, 1963.

"Zabytyi pisatel' (Antonii Pogorel'skii)", by N.L. Stepanov, in *Poety i prozaiki*, Moscow, 1966.

Antoni Pogorelski, zycie i twórczosc na tle epoki, by J. Smaga, Warsaw, Krakow, Wrocław, 1970.

"A.A. Perovskij (Pogorel'skij): Gentleman and Literateur", by Philip Edward Frantz, PhD dissertation, Michigan, 1981.

"Antony Pogorelsky", by William Edward Brown, in his *A History of Russian Literature of the Romantic Period*, vol. 2, Ann Arbor, Ardis, 1986.

Aleksei Alekseevich Perovskii (pen-name Antonii Pogorel'skii) was born in Moscow in 1787. He was the eldest illegitimate son of Count A.K. Razumovskii and Mariia Sobolevskaia. He spent his childhood at his father's estate Pochep where he and his numerous siblings were educated by private tutors. In 1802 Pogorel'skii enrolled at Moscow University from which he graduated in 1807. A year later he joined the Imperial civil service where he was employed until 1812, the year Napoleon invaded Russia. Pogorel'skii volunteered for the army and served for four years, taking part in several battles; later he was appointed senior adjutant to Count Repnin and spent two years at his headquarters in Dresden. At that time he became acquainted with German literature, especially the works of E.T.A. Hoffmann and other Romantics who were an important influence on his later fiction.

On his return to Russia in 1816 he rejoined the civil service and was appointed to the department of religious affairs and foreign denominations. His career was not progressing well and in 1822 he resigned from his post because of family circumstances. Another important event that considerably influenced his life was the marriage of his sister Anna to Count K.P. Tolstoi, and the birth of his nephew Aleksei Tolstoi, the future writer. Pogorel'skii took care of his nephew until his own death and was like a father to him. For nearly three years (1822–24) he lived on his Ukrainian estate of Pogorel'sk. During this period he made several trips abroad, but in 1825 he rejoined the civil service for the last time and was appointed to the post of curator of the Kharkov district in the Ministry of Education. He left the service for good in 1827.

In his youth Pogorel'skii dabbled in literature and even published a few pieces of both verse and criticism. Towards the end of the 1820s he turned to prose. His first important work, *Dvoinik, ili moi vechera v Malorossii* (*The Double or My Evenings in Little Russia*), appeared in 1828, although one story from this cycle had been published in 1825, in the magazine *Novosti literatury*. *The Double* is a cycle consisting of four tales, a form popular at that time, "held together" by some literary device, for example a single or several narrators, as is the case here. Antonii and his double, who one evening suddenly and mysteriously appears at his house, take turns in telling stories and discussing various subjects, ranging from the existence of ghosts and spirits to rudimentary psychology. The first tale told by Antonii, the sentimental "Isidor i Aniuta" ("Isidor and Aniuta"), is of slight literary merit; it shows the influence of both Karamzin and Bestuzhev-Marlinskii and abounds in melodramatic effects. The tale entitled "Pagubnye posledstviia neobuzdannogo voobrazheniia" ("The Pernicious Effects of an Unbridled Imagination") is a story of a sensitive young man endowed with a lively imagination who falls in love with a doll. The tale ends on a tragic note with the deranged hero committing suicide. The influence of E.T.A. Hoffmann is unmistakable, but Pogorel'skii's tale lacks both the depth and the frisson of his model, largely because of a rather pedestrian explanation of the mystery. Artistically the best tale in the collection is "Lafertovskaia makovnitsa" ("The Poppy-Seed Cake Seller from Lafertovo") that successfully blends realistic descriptions of low life in Moscow with elements of the supernatural. Pogorel'skii's particular achievement, praised by Pushkin, is the portrayal of a cat turned civil servant – Murlykin.

"Puteshestvie v dilizhanse" ("A Journey in a Stagecoach") is a variant on a popular theme – love between man and animal, telling the story of a tender friendship between a giant female ape Toutou and a certain colonel whom she nursed when he was a child and who, as a result of an unfortunate twist of fate, had to kill her. He is so tormented by remorse that he goes off to fight and eventually dies in battle. With this cycle Pogorel'skii made an important contribution to Russian literature, he introduced the figure of the Double as a character and gave this phenomenon a name ("Dvoinik").

Monastyrka (*The Convent Girl*) exploits the hankering after the exotic that was one of the major trends in European literature of that time. For Russian writers the remote regions of the Empire, the Ukraine, the Caucasus, or Siberia supplied the necessary backdrop. The novel tells the story of Aniuta, the Smolny Institute graduate, who returned to the Ukraine and of her subsequent adventures that end in a happy marriage. In this novel Pogorel'skii included many realistic descriptions of the Ukraine, but he did not eschew completely his tendency to Sentimentalism.

Another interesting contribution by Pogorel'skii was the fairy tale *Chernaia kuritsa ...* (*The Black Hen*) which was published in 1829. This fairy tale, written first for his nephew, quickly became a favourite with Russian children and is popular even today. It tells the story of a boy sent to boarding-school who befriends a black hen, and saves her life. Since the hen is an important minister in a secret underground kingdom, the boy is also rewarded for this deed. However, the reward he chooses, a magic seed that enables him never to do any school-work, also proves to be his undoing. In the end he loses both the seed and his friend. The tale is didactic and moralistic, but the descriptions of the festivities in the underground kingdom are lively and entertaining.

After the publication of his novel Pogorel'skii devoted all his efforts to the upbringing of his nephew. He died in 1836 *en route* to Italy.

RUTH SOBEL

Nikolai Alekseevich Polevoi 1796–1846

Novelist, historiographer, critic, and translator

Biography

Born in Irkutsk, 3 July 1796. No formal education. First publication, 1817. Moved to Moscow, 1820. Prominent representative of Russian romanticism. Co-publisher, with his brother Ksenofont Alekseevich, of the journal *Moskovskii telegraf*, 1825–34: journal closed down for political reasons. Moved to St Petersburg, 1834. Thereafter prohibited from editing any journal. Associated with the conservative journals *Syn otechestva* and *Severnaia pchela*; he lost prestige in literary society. Died in St Petersburg, 6 March 1846.

Publications

Collected Editions

Ocherki russkoi literatury [Sketches on Russian Literature], 2 vols. St Petersburg, 1839.
Dramaticheskie sochineniia i perevody [Dramatic Works and Translations], 4 vols. St Petersburg, 1842–43.
Sochineniia, 3 vols. 1903.
Izbrannye proizvedeniia i pis'ma. Leningrad, 1986.
Mechty i zhizn' [Dreams and Life]. Moscow, 1990.

Fiction

Povesti i literaturnye otryvki, 6 vols. Moscow, 1829–30.
Kliatva pri grobe Gospodnem [An Oath on the Lord's Grave]. 1832.
Abbaddonna. 1834.
Povesti Ivana Gudoshnika [Ivan Gudoshnik's Short Stories]. 1843.

Historical Writing

Istoriia russkogo naroda [A History of the Russian People], 6 vols. 1829–33.
Istoriia Napoleona [The History of Napoleon], 5 vols. 1844–48.

Literary Criticism

Literaturnaia kritika [Literary Criticism]. Leningrad, 1990.

Translator

Gamlet [Hamlet], by William Shakespeare, 1837.

Critical Studies

Nikolai Polevoi. Materialy po istorii russkoi literatury i zhurnalistiki tridtsatykh godov, edited by V.N. Orlov, Leningrad, 1934.
"Literaturno-esteticheskie pozitsii *Moskovskogo telegrafa*", by N.A. Guliaev, *Uchennye zapiski Kazanskogo universiteta*, 123/9 (1963), 3–20.
"Literaturno-esteticheskie vzgliady N.A. Polevogo", by N.A. Guliaev, *Voprosy literatury*, 12 (1964), 69–87.
Puti i sud'by, by V.N. Orlov, Leningrad, 1971, 313–504.
"K atributsii proizvedenii N.A. Polevogo v *Moskovskom telegrafe*", by Ia. G. Safnullin, in *Romantizm v russkoi i zarubezhnoi literature*, Moscow, 1974, 144–63.
E.T.A. Gofman i russkaia literatura, by A.B. Botnikova, Voronezh, 1977.
"Khudozhestvennaia proza N.A. Polevogo", by V.M. Shamakhova, *Problemy metoda i zhanra*, Tomsk, 1977, 4, 13–25.
Istoriia russkogo dramaticheskogo teatra, vol. 3, Moscow, 1978, 37–39, 57–61.
Istoricheskie vzgliady N.A. Polevogo, by A.E. Shiklo, Moscow, 1981.
"Zhurnal N.A. Polevogo *Moskovskii telegraf* i chitatel'", by V.G. Berezina, *Vestnik LGU*, 2 (1981), *Istoriia iazyka i literatury*, vol. 1, 38–44.
Russian Romantic Fiction, by John Mersereau, Jr, Ann Arbor, Ardis, 1983.
A History of Russian Literature of the Romantic Period, by William Edward Brown, 4 vols, Ann Arbor, Ardis, 1986.
"Zadushennii talant", by Iu. Alianskii, *Iskusstvo Leningrada*, 1 (1989), 88–93, 102–05.
"Uslyshat' uroki istorii", by A.S. Kurilovin, in *Izbrannaia istoricheskaia proza*, Moscow, 1990, 7–24.

Bibliography

Istoriia russkoi literatury XIX v.: Bibliograficheskii ukazatel', edited by D.D. Muratova, Moscow and Leningrad, 1962.

Nikolai Polevoi came from an old, but impoverished merchant family from Siberia. His pride in his bourgeois origin, his liberal principles and strong patriotism predestined Polevoi to become a leading figure of the 1820s. His encyclopedic journal *Moskovskii telegraf* (1825–34) was contributed to by prominent Russian writers, headed by Pushkin and P.A. Viazemskii, the poet and a leading theoretician of Russian romanticism. The journal was critical of the normative aesthetics of classicism, and on behalf of romanticism proclaimed the freedom of creative literature. Polevoi's strong critical views made him a predecessor of Belinskii. The journal was shut down in 1834 for political reasons. Controversial also was the reception of Polevoi's main historical work, *Istoriia russkogo naroda* [A History of the Russian People], polemically aimed at Nikolai Karamzin, whose *Istoriia gosudarstva Rossiiskogo* [History of the Russian State] (1818–29) Polevoi considered a mere history of rulers, not of the nation. Polevoi's models were the contemporary historians of the French restoration, Guizot and Thiers, whom the author connected with Schelling's philosophical system. Polevoi's encyclopedic orientation is obvious from his attempts to evaluate economic geography, folklore, ethnography, and literature. His *Istoriia russkogo naroda* was only brought up to the year 1505 and not to his own time, as he had intended. Polevoi's interest in Europe is shown in his, also unfinished, five-volume *Istoriia Napoleona* [The History of Napoleon]. *Istoriia Suvorova* [A History of Suvorov] is another of Polevoi's extensive works.

Most of his prose and drama draws on Russian, European or Byzantine history. While the Byzantine theme, which he was the first to use in Russia, takes him back to the early Middle Ages, the setting of his other historical works is the turn of the 14th and 15th centuries. Many interesting features can be found in his novel *Kliatva pri grobe Gospodnem* [An Oath on the Lord's

Grave], which for the first time presents the controversial figure of Ivan Gudoshnik, a type of educated *skomorokh* (entertainer), who travels to Jerusalem to take an oath that he will return independence to the Suzdal principality. Thanks to his particular social status, which enables him to meet common people as well as members of high society, the protagonist manages to influence many an event. Finally, though, he comes to realize that the fratricidal fighting of the apanage principalities brings nothing but destruction to the country. Later on, like Pushkin and Gogol', Polevoi used this character as a central figure around whom to construct a cycle of his shorter historical works (see his *Povesti Ivana Gudoshnika* [Ivan Gudoshnik's Short Stories] 1843). While his historical prose creates, above all, plastic pictures from the past, his prose set in contemporary society develops the psychology of a creative personality in conflict with the world at large. Polevoi, in the spirit of romanticism, is interested in art; thus the heroes of his best works of this genre are artists of non-noble origin. Their love relationships break down, however, and their artistic career is endangered when confronted with reality. The victim is usually the artist himself, or his beloved. This is the case in the novel set in German burgher circles *Abbaddonna* (1834), named after the fallen angel in Klopstock' s tale in verse, *Der Messias* (*The Messiah*). Polevoi's hero in this novel is a dramatist, who enjoys success thanks only to the fact that a prima donna, kept by a theatre patron, loves him. Unlike the novella "Zhivopisets" [Painter], which is built on the model of a romantic tale in verse with its inclination to extemporizing, the novel *Abbaddonna* is a well-balanced work of art, already showing the influence of novels of intrigue, such as were written by Stendhal and others.

In the 1840s Polevoi found himself in a very troublesome situation. After the prohibition of *Moskovskii telegraf*, he was not allowed to edit any other journals. His political compromises and co-operation with the conservative periodicals *Syn otechestva* and *Severnaia pchela* diminished his prestige in society. Polevoi's memoirs provide evidence of his grinding poverty, which forced the writer to work from morning till night, writing novels for Bulgarin's workshop, editing other people's unskilful texts and working on translations. When his outstanding translation of *Hamlet* (1837), as well as his free adaptation of *Ugolina* (1838) – (a play by a German pre-romantic writer H.W. Gerstenberg) – had been successfully staged, Polevoi wrote about 40 historical dramas. They were popular in their time, but were soon forgotten, due to their containing more craft than creative invention.

Polevoi's works of fiction and historical prose are being re-discovered today, since they contain values that can also be appreciated by the modern reader.

DANUŠE KŠICOVA

Simeon Polotskii 1628/29–1680

Poet and theologian

Biography

Born in Polotsk, 1628 or 1629. Baptized Samuil; given monastic name Simeon in 1656; adopted topical surname Polotskii after settling in Moscow, 1664. Educated at Mohyla College, Kiev and possibly at the Vilna Jesuit Academy. Took monastic vows at Epiphany (Bogoiavlenskii) Monastery, Polotsk, 1656. Taught at monastery school. Moved to Zaikonospasskii Monastery, Nikol'skaia Street, Moscow, 1664. Taught Latin to clerks of Bureau of Secret Affairs, c.1665. Established a school at his monastery, c.1666. Took part in Church Council of 1666–67; wrote a rebuttal of Old Believer teachings, *Zhezl pravleniia* [Sceptre of Government], 1667, and an exposition of Christian doctrine, *Venets very* [Crown of Faith], 1670. Preached regularly in Moscow, 1668–74; sermons collected into two volumes, *Obed dushevnyi* [Spiritual Dinner], 1681, and *Vecheria dushevnaia* [Spiritual Supper], 1683. Tutor to Tsarevich Aleksei Alekseevich, 1667–70, and to Tsarevich Fedor Alekseevich from 1670; overseer of Nikita Zotov when latter appointed tutor to Tsarevich Petr Alekseevich (the future Peter I), 1679. Presented verse declamations to court to mark royal events. Established a printing press at the Kremlin, outside the censorship control of the Patriarch, 1679. Died in Moscow, 25 August 1680.

Publications

Collected Editions

Izbrannye sochineniia. Moscow and Leningrad, 1953.
Virshi [Syllabic Verses]. Minsk, 1990.

Single Works

Orel rossiiskii. Tvorenie Simeona Polotskogo [The Russian Eagle], edited by N.A. Smirnov. Obshchestvo liubitelei drevnei pis'mennosti, no. 133, Petrograd, 1915.
"Vertograd mnogotsvetnyi" [Garden of Many Flowers], edited by Anthony Hippisley and L.I. Sazonova, in *Bausteine zur Geschichte der Literatur bei den Slaven*, edited by H.-B. Harder and H. Rothe. Cologne, Böhlau, 1996.

Theological Works

Zhezl pravleniia na pravitel'stvo myslennago stada pravoslavno-rossiiskiia tserkve [Sceptre of Government for the Governance of the Metaphorical Flock of the Russian Orthodox Church]. Moscow, 1667; IDC microfiche 493.

O ezhe ne peti besovskikh pesnei [On Not Singing Devilish Songs]. Moscow, 1668.
O blagogoveinom stoianii v khrame [On Standing Devoutly in Church]. Moscow, 1668.
Predislovie k iunosham uchitisia khotiashchim [Preface to Young Men who Desire to Learn]. Moscow, 1669.

Homiletic Works
Obed dushevnyi [Spiritual Dinner]. Moscow, 1681; IDC microfiche 491.
Vecheria dushevnaia [Spiritual Supper]. Moscow, 1683; IDC microfiche 492.

Metrical Psalms
Psaltyr' rifmotvornaia [Rhyming Psalter]. Moscow, 1680; IDC microfiche 494.

Drama
Istoriia ili deistvie evaggelskiia pritchi o bludnom syne byvaemoe [Story or Play about the Gospel Parable of the Prodigal Son]. Moscow, 1685; IDC microfiche 505.

Pedagogical Works
Bukvar' iazyka slavenska, sirech' nachalo ucheniia detem, khotiashchym uchitisia chteniiu pisanii [Slavonic ABC, or Beginning of Learning for Children who Desire to Learn to Read]. Moscow, 1679.

Works ascribed to Polotskii
Bukvar' [ABC]. Moscow, 1664.
Bukvar' iazyka slovenska, pisanii chteniia uchitisia khotiashchim [Slavonic ABC for Those who Desire to Learn to Read]. Moscow, 1667; reissued 1669.

Critical Studies

Simeon Polostkii: ego zhizn' i deiatel'nost'. Opyt issledovaniia iz istorii prosveshcheniia i vnutrennei tserkovnoi zhizni vo vtoruiu polovinu XVII veka, by I. Tatarskii, Moscow, 1886.
"Simeon Polotskii", by L.N. Maikov, in his *Ocherki iz istorii russkoi literatury XVII i XVIII stoletii*, St Petersburg, 1889, 1–162.
"Poeticheskii stil' Simeona Polotskogo", by I.P. Eremin, *Trudy Otdela drevnerusskoi literatury*, 6 (1948), 125–53; reprinted in his *Literatura drevnei Rusi*, Moscow and Leningrad, 1966, 211–33.
A History of Seventeenth-Century Russian Literature, by William Edward Brown, Ann Arbor, Ardis, 1980.
Simeon Polotskii i ego knigoizdatel'skaia deiatel'nost', edited by A.N. Robinson, Moscow, 1982.
The Poetic Style of Simeon Polotsky, by Anthony Hippisley, Birmingham, Birmingham Slavonic Monographs, no. 16, 1985.
"*Vertograd mnogotsvetnyi* Simeona Polotskogo: dukhovnoe edinstvo knigi", by L.I. Sazonova, in her *Poeziia russkogo barokko*, Moscow, 1991, 187–221.

Simeon Polotskii is one of the most important figures in 17th-century Russian culture. This is largely due to the fact that, having been born in Belorussia and educated in the Ukraine, he then settled in Moscow and pursued intellectual activities that had a generally European, and a specifically Roman Catholic, foundation. While Church leaders in Moscow were quick to detect Polotskii's Latin sympathies the tsar, Aleksei Mikhailovich, respected him for his learning and appointed him tutor, first to his son and heir Aleksei Alekseevich, and later to his second son Fedor Alekseevich. Polostkii enjoyed royal patronage and protection throughout the 16 years of his residence in Moscow, during which time he composed a number of theological works, including two volumes of sermons and a metrical Psalter, wrote two plays, and produced the first corpus of Russian poetry.

Polotskii's poetry falls into two main generic categories. First, he composed a vast number of declamatory poems that were gathered into a 654-leaf volume entitled *Rifmologion, ili stikhoslov* [Rhymology] (extant in one manuscript copy). Some of the poems are panegyrics marking actual events in the royal household (birth, marriage, death, coronation, etc.), the most important and substantial of which are the following: "Blagoprivetstvovanie" [Hearty Welcome] on the birth of Tsarevich Simeon Alekseevich, 23 April 1665; "Orel Rossiiskii" [The Russian Eagle] on the "showing" of Tsarevich Aleksei Alekseevich, 1 September 1667; "Freny ili plachi" [Laments] on the death of Tsaritsa Mariia Miloslavskaia, 29 April 1669; "Privetstvo" [Welcome] on the royal family's taking up residence in the new palace at Kolomenskoe, 1672; "Glas poslednii" [Last Utterance] on the death of Tsar Aleksei Mikhailovich, 29 January 1676; "Gusl' dobroglasnaia" [Euphonious Psaltery] on the coronation of Tsar Fedor Alekseevich, 18 June 1676. Most of the remaining part of *Rifmologion* consists of model poems to be declaimed on specific recurrent occasions such as Church festivals or the recipient's saint's day, which makes the collection a kind of handbook of oratory. Finally, towards the end of *Rifmologion* are Polotskii's two plays: "Komidiia pritchi o bludnem syne" [Comedy of the Parable of the Prodigal Son] and "O Navokhodonosore tsare, o tele zlate i o triekh otrotsekh, v peshchi ne sozhzhennykh" [About Nebuchadnezzar the King, the Golden Calf, and the Three Boys who did not Burn in the Furnace]. The former is a dramatization of the parable told by Jesus in Luke 15. Despite being written in Church Slavonic rather than Latin, it owes its compositional structure to the genre of school drama taught at Jesuit academies as part of the rhetoric course, which Polotskii would have encountered if, as seems probable, he attended the Vilna Academy. It begins with a prologue and closes with an epilogue, it is divided into acts and scenes, and at the end of each act (except the last) the stage directions call for an interlude (*intermedium*), a few minutes of clowning in which a parody of the previous act was usually performed. The theme of the prodigal son was a common one in the tradition of European morality plays because it lent itself to didacticism: an excursion into sin is followed by repentance and a return to the fold. Polotskii adds a new layer of meaning that seems to reflect the mood among some of the younger generation in Moscow. The prodigal uses an argument with his father that is not based on the Gospel account: "What shall I gain at home? What shall I learn? I shall enrich my mind better by travelling. Fathers have sent sons younger than me to foreign lands and not regretted it". The other play is based on the account in the book of Daniel of how the three holy children, Ananias, Azarias and Misael, were cast into the fiery furnace by Nebuchadnezzar for refusing to give up their faith in God. It derives from *Peshchnoe deistvo* [Furnace Play], one of a small number of ritualized dramatizations in the Eastern Orthodox Church that had survived down to the mid-17th century.

Second, Polotskii compiled a collection of poems entitled *Vertograd mnogotsvetnyi* [Garden of Many Flowers] (extant in three manuscript copies varying from 547 to 621 leaves) that are designed to be read rather than recited. They range from two-line aphorisms to narrative poems of several hundred lines, and they draw upon a wide variety of sources of which the most persistent are works of Jesuit homiletics. Many of these poems have a spiritual didactic message, but the colourfulness of the illustrative material makes them instantly attractive and interesting. Polotskii's poetry is immensely rich in symbolic imagery and this, together with other prominent features of his style, mark him as the first and perhaps clearest representative of the baroque in Russian literature. The three manuscripts of *Vertograd mnogotsvetnyi* reveal the evolution of the poet's ideas about the composition of this work: it moves from a collection of large thematic units (e.g., faith, virtue, lust, etc.) based chiefly on the sources with which he was working, to an alphabetized encyclopedia with one or more poems entered under each heading (beginning with "Aaron": four poems, "Abba, Father": one poem, "Abel": four poems, "Absolom": three poems, etc.). *Vertograd mnogotsvetnyi* is the largest collection of poems under a single title in the whole of Russian literature, which is one reason why it has never been published. The critical edition that is about to appear will fill a major gap in the history of Russian poetry.

All Simeon Polotskii's poetry, including the two plays, is written in syllabic verse. This is the form of versification that characterizes Polish poetry of the 16th and 17th centuries, and which Polotskii brought with him to Moscow. Each line of a poem has the same number of syllables, usually either 11 or 13. All rhymes are paired, and all are feminine, which means that the penultimate syllable is stressed. Throughout the rest of the line the stresses on words do not attempt to fit into any meter. The question of matching stress to particular syllables in a line of verse was not resolved until the 18th century, when syllabo-tonic verse was developed by Trediakovskii and Lomonosov. Polotskii's syllabic verse stands at the fountainhead of Russian poetry, and he can deservedly take the title of first Russian poet.

Printing in Russia benefited from Polotskii's theological differences with the Moscow hierarchy. All books published at Pechatnyi dvor (the printing office) had to receive the imprimatur of the Patriarch, which could effectively have nipped in the bud any publishing ambition Polotskii might have had. He therefore persuaded his former pupil Fedor Alekseevich to order the establishment of a new press at the Kremlin in 1679, the Verkhniaia tipografiia. In its four-year existence this press produced seven books (four of which were by Polotskii): *Bukvar' iazyka slavenska* [Slavonic ABC] (1679), *Testament, ili Zavet Vasilia tsaria grecheskago k synu ego Lvu filosofu* [Testament of the Greek Emperor Basil to His Son Leo the Philosopher] (1680), *Psaltyr' khudozhestvom rifmotvornym prelozhennaia* [Psalter Artisitically Translated into Rhyme] (1680), *Istoriia o Varlaame pustynnozhiteli i Ioasafe tsare Indeistem* [History of Barlaam the Hermit and Josaphat King of India] (1680), *Obed dushevnyi* [Spiritual Dinner] (1681), *Schitanie udobnoe* [Simple Counting] (1682), and *Vecheria dushevnaia* [Spiritual Supper] (1683). The *Verkhniaia tipografiia* had made its mark as the first free press in Russia, anticipating the private presses of the 18th century. Polotskii would almost certainly have published his greatest work, *Vertograd mnogotsvetnyi*, at the press, but death intervened in 1680. Of his published works, the ABC book appeared during his life, but the metrical Psalter and the two volumes of sermons were brought out posthumously by his disciple and assistant Sil'vestr Medvedev. After Fedor Alekseevich's death in April 1682 the future of the press looked bleak: in 1683 it was closed down by Patriarch Ioakim and all its publications were declared heretical and were banned. Polotskii's library of more than 500 Latin and Polish books passed at his death to Medvedev, who continued to add to it until he was arrested for political reasons in 1689. Medvedev was executed in 1691 and the collection eventually became part of the Sinodal'naia tipografiia library, remaining almost intact to the present day and thus providing modern students of Polotskii with a valuable insight into his intellectual background.

ANTHONY HIPPISLEY

Nikolai Gerasimovich Pomialovskii 1835–1863

Prose writer

Biography

Born in Malaia Okhta, St Petersburg, 23 April 1835. Attended Aleksandr Nevskii Seminary, St Petersburg; parish school, 1843–45; clerical school (*bursa*), 1845–51; seminary, 1851–57. Teacher at "Sunday School" (Shlisselberg High Road), 1860–62. Became regular contributor to *Sovremennik*, from February 1861. First hospitalization for alcoholism, September 1861. Contributed *Ocherki bursy* (*Seminary Sketches*) to Dostoevskii's journal, *Vremia*, May–September 1862. Second hospitalization for alcoholism, spring 1863. Contributed to the reopened *Sovremennik*, April 1863. Died 17 October 1863.

Publications

Collected Editions

Polnoe sobranie sochinenii, 2 vols. Moscow and Leningrad, 1935.

Sochinenie, 2 vols. Moscow and Leningrad, 1965.

Fiction

"Meshchanskoe schast'e" [Lower-Class Happiness], *Sovremennik*, (February 1861).

"Molotov", *Sovremennik*, (October 1861).

"Ocherki bursy", *Vremia*, (May–September 1862); reprinted Leningrad, 1971; translated as *Seminary Sketches*, by Alfred Kuhn, Ithaca, Cornell University Press, 1973.

Brat i sestra [Brother and Sister]. 1864.

Critical Studies

Realizm Pomialovskogo: voprosy stilia, by N.P. Zhdanovskii, Moscow, 1960.

N.G. Pomialovskii: Lichnost' i tvorchestvo, by I. Iampol'skii, Moscow and Leningrad, 1968.

"An Alternative View of the Peasantry: The 'Raznochintsy' Writers of the 1860s", by Rose Glickman, *Slavic Review*, 32 (1973), 693–704.

"N.G. Pomialovsky's *Seminary Sketches*: Context and Genre", by Carol Apollonio Flath, PhD dissertation, University of North Carolina, 1987.

Nikolai Gerasimovich Pomialovskii was born on 23 April 1835 in a rural suburb of St Petersburg, Malaia Okhta, the third son of a lowly church deacon. The clergy in Russia were virtually a self-contained caste and Pomialovskii was educated at ecclesiastical schools (the *bursa* and the seminary) as one destined to enter the church. Yet it is one of the ironies of Russian life, which Pomialovskii's writings do much to explain, that the seminaries were often the training ground for "nihilists" and revolutionaries. Dobroliubov and Chernyshevskii, with whom Pomialovskii would later be associated, were prominent radicals of the 1860s, who both came from this background.

From the beginning education was one of Pomialovskii's chief interests. He threw himself into the campaign for literacy promoted by the young radicals through "Sunday Schools" for the underprivileged, and his first two short stories, "Vukol" (1859) and an early sketch of *bursa* life, "Dolbnia" (1860) were both published in educational journals. At the beginning of the 1860s Chernyshevskii and Dobroliubov were turning *Sovremennik* into a radical tribune for the ideas of the younger generation. As a result such eminent "gentry" writers as Turgenev and Tolstoi refused to contribute. Pomialovskii's first short novel, *Meshchanskoe schast'e* [Lower-Class Happiness] published by *Sovremennik* in February 1861, was seen as an attempt to fill the vacuum left by their defection. With its country-estate setting and theme of unrequited love *Meshchanskoe schast'e* has the characteristics of a Turgenevan novel, yet the perspective is quite different. Molotov is a plebeian hero who, as a child, has been rescued from his background by a benevolent professor and given a university education. He feels himself the equal of the rural squire who offers him work, but an overheard conversation (another Turgenevan touch) apprises him of his true social standing in the eyes of the family; mortified, he leaves to take up a civil service post. The pride and sensitivity of the plebeian intellectual are very much at issue, and for all that Obrosimov is a liberal with "advanced" ideas on education. Molotov has been brought face to face with the reality of gentry liberalism, as indeed, through the Great Reforms, had the country itself (in the eyes of the young radicals).

Education and women's rights are themes of the 1860s. Molotov's position is complicated by the openly declared love of a young neighbour, Lenochka. Described as the "muslin girl" (*kiseinaia devushka*) – a phrase that has passed into the language, Lenochka is naive, sentimental, and vulnerable. Their relationship has strong echoes of previous accounts of the "superfluous man" in love, and Molotov himself may be seen as a plebeian reinterpretation of this stock figure of gentry literature. He too is rootless, "cosmopolitan" and above all cannot rise to the challenge of love. Lenochka, like Pushkin's Tat'iana, takes the initiative by writing a letter, yet in everything, except maturity, she seems a typical Turgenevan heroine. The relationship highlights the moral ambiguities that beset the "new man". Molotov himself says: "Obrosimov does not want to acknowledge me as a full human being like himself, and I did not want to acknowledge Lenochka fully as a woman". *Meshchanskoe schast'e* appeared a whole year before Turgenev's *Ottsy i deti* (*Fathers and Sons*) and the two works were inevitably compared. To many of the younger generation, incensed by Turgenev's portrayal of one of their number, Molotov was the true representative of their values and sense of dignity.

Pomialovskii's second novel, *Molotov*, appeared in *Sovremennik* in October 1861. We now see the hero in a civil service environment. His love for Nadia Dorogova, the daughter of a civil service colleague, is at first thwarted by her father who wishes to marry her to a general. Yet Molotov finally achieves his "lower-class happiness" promised in the title of the first work and marries Nadia, his intellectual equal, but he realizes that people like him cannot demand too much: "We love to smash, either we become out and out rogues or prosper as I am prospering." In his struggle with Dorogova and the general, Molotov may have "smashed" the convention of marriage as a contract without love, but he has not done so when it comes to the contract of work, and the author's final sentence, "Oh, gentlemen, it is a bit boring", hardly suggests real happiness.

Nevertheless, in the phrase "we love to smash" we have a foretaste of Turgenev's hero Bazarov and it is Cherevanin who represents this strand in the novel with his "graveyard philosophy" (*kladbishchenstvo*) of out and out nihilism. Cherevanin is aware of "terrible thoughts in the realm of ideas", but so far conscience has prevented him from acting on them. Cherevanin seems to provide an ideological link between the ideas of Bazarov and those of Dostoevskii's Raskol'nikov, but in Pomialovskii's last unfinished novel *Brat i sestra* [Brother and Sister], published posthumously in 1864, we have a clear anticipation of Dostoevskii's hero. Potesin has found a rational argument against conscience: wealth, he argues, is like unoccupied land to be claimed by the first person who puts up a flag. In this novel, fragmentary as it is, we move, well in advance of *Prestuplenie i nakazanie* (*Crime and Punishment*) 1866, into a very Dostoevskian world of the lower depths of St Petersburg and the intellectual justification for crime. It is therefore interesting that it was in Dostoevskii's *Vremia* that Pomialovskii published the first two of his *Ocherki bursy* (*Seminary Sketches*) in May and September 1862.

However, 1862 was a difficult year for the young radicals. In May fires broke out in St Petersburg and were attributed to the work of "nihilists". They, however, saw them as government provocation, and an excuse for reaction. In June the Sunday Schools were closed and the journals *Sovremennik* and *Russkoe slovo* were suspended for eight months. In July Chernyshevskii himself was arrested. Pomialovskii reacted badly to these events and, given Dostoevskii's sympathies, refused to contribute further to *Vremia*. The next two *Seminary Sketches* were published in 1863 (March and July) in the newly reopened *Sovremennik*. It was here that in November his last sketch was published posthumously.

The *Seminary Sketches*, with their grim depiction of the squalor and brutality of the ecclesiastical schools, were a deepening of the realistic tradition, established by the Natural School of the 1840s. The focus on education, corrupt institutions and the evils of corporal punishment are, however, typical preoccupations of the 1860s. Pisarev regarded these *bursa* or seminary conditions as worse than Dostoevskii's description of penal settlement. Pomialovskii's seminary is far more realistically portrayed than that of Narezhnyi and Gogol', and he provides a view of childhood radically different from the nobleman's upbringing, depicted by Aksakov, Tolstoi, and Goncharov.

The causes of Pomialovskii's own tragedy are also to be found in childhood. He was forced to drink at the age of seven and chronic alcoholism led to his death on 17 October 1863. Two early stories with educational themes, "Makhilov" and "Danilushka", and various unfinished works were published posthumously. Pomialovskii's talent is more remarkable for its promise, yet he can range from sensitive depiction of psychology and the beauty of the countryside to the most sordid aspects of city and seminary life; at the same time he is a writer with strong intellectual content, who, having applied a new focus to the world of Turgenev, developed in a way that clearly anticipates Dostoevskii.

RICHARD PEACE

Evgenii Anatol'evich Popov 1946–

Prose writer

Biography

Born in Krasnoiarsk, 5 January 1946. Began writing at an early age; first publication in local newspaper, 1962. Studied geology in Moscow, 1963–68. Unsuccessful attempts to enrol at the Gor'kii Literary Institute and the Institute of Cinematography in Moscow, 1972. Worked as geologist in and around Krasnoiarsk, 1968–75. Returned to Moscow, 1975. Two stories published by *Novyi mir* with an introduction by Vasilii Shukshin, 1976. Member of the Writers' Union, 1978. Involved in the *Metropol'* affair, expelled from the Writers' Union, 1979. Unable to publish in Soviet Union, 1979–86. Short story published in *Iunost'*, 1986. Regular publication and public appearances at home and abroad. Lives in Moscow with wife and son.

Publications

Collected Edition

Merry-Making in Old Russia, translated by Robert Porter. London, Harvill Press, 1996; Evanston, Illinois, Northwestern University Press, 1997.

Fiction

"Rasskazy", *Novyi mir*, 4 (1976), 164–72.

"Chertova diuzhina", in *Metropol'*, Ann Arbor, Ardis, 1979; translated as "A Baker's Dozen of Stories", by George Saunders, in *Metropol*, New York, Norton, 1982, 85–153.

Veselie Rusi [The Merriment of Russia]. Ann Arbor, Ardis, 1981.

Zhdu liubvi ne verolomnoi [I Await a Love That's True]. Moscow, 1989.

"Dusha patriota ili razlichnye poslaniia Ferfichkinu", *Volga*, 2 (1989); separate edition with illustrations by Viacheslav Sysoev and verse by Dmitrii Prigov, Moscow, 1994; translated as *The Soul of a Patriot, or Various Epistles to Ferfichkin*, by Robert Porter, London, Harvill Press, and Evanston, Illinois, Northwestern University Press, 1994.

Tikhokhodnaia barka "Nadezhda" [The Slow Barge "Hope"]. Moscow, 1990.

Prekrasnost' zhizni. Glavy iz "romana s gazetoi", kotoryi nikogda ne budet nachat i zakonchen [The Splendour of Life ...]. Moscow, 1990.

Samolet na Kel'n [The Plane to Cologne]. Moscow, 1991.

"Nakanune nakanune" [On the Eve of the Eve], *Volga*, 3 (1993).

Plays

"Avtovokzal" [Bus Station], *Volga*, 10 (1988).

"Palka, ili Pizdets Amerike" [A Stick of Shit to America], in *Zolotoi vek*, 3 (1992).

Critical Studies

"O poeticheskom mire Evgeniia Popova", by A. Vishevskii, *Russian Language Journal*, 45, 151–52 (1991), 185–225; translated as "Creating a Shattered World: Towards the Poetics of Yevgeny Popov", *World Literature Today*, 67/1 (1993), 19–25.

The Last Years of Soviet Russian Literature: Prose Fiction, 1975–1991, by Deming Brown, Cambridge and New York, Cambridge University Press, 1993, 158–63.

"Cross(-Dress)ing One's Way to Crisis: Yevgeny Popov and

Lyudmila Petrushevskaya and the Crisis of Category in Contemporary Russian Culture", by A. Vanchu, *World Literature Today*, 67/1 (1993), 107–18.
Russia's Alternative Prose, by Robert Porter, Oxford, Berg, 1994, 88–137.

Evgenii Popov is one of the best representatives of the "lost" generation of writers associated with Brezhnev's Russia. Such writers were too young to have established a reputation either at home or internationally during the more liberal Khrushchev era that might have assured them some immunity in the "stagnant" years that followed. Yet they continued to write, even though the possibilities of publication were minimal, eventually coming into their own after 1985. Popov gained some small recognition in 1976 with the publication in *Novyi mir* of two short stories, prefaced by the hugely popular Vasilii Shukshin. However, as one of the five editors of the unofficial anthology *Metropol'* (1979), Popov was expelled from the Writers' Union (together with his friend, Viktor Erofeev) after just eight months' membership, and he returned to the twilight zone until the late 1980s. Once he was published on a regular basis in his homeland, he became recognized as one of the brightest talents of the new age.

Popov's dozens of short stories, his novels and occasional plays are characterized nearly always by a comic perception of what is often, but not always, everyday life. At times his narratives teeter on the brink of the macabre or stray into the realms of the fantastic, but usually he deals in routine scenes of domestic life, incidents at the workplace, the factory or the office, encounters in seedy restaurants or over a bottle of vodka. His characters are frequently downgraded in their domestic or professional pursuits to produce a sophisticated form of bathos or irony. Stories set in the author's native Siberia are often a mockery of the heroic achievements claimed by socialist realist hacks, while the grandiose scenery and riches of the area are no more than a backcloth to episodes of drunkenness, wife-beating and petty criminality. Here one detects not so much the obvious parodying of socialist realism as of the school of Village Prose exemplified best by such fellow Siberians as Rasputin and Zalygin. Far from depicting rustic folk as stoical, highly moral and diligent, albeit at times superstitious and uneducated, Popov presents the reader with a gallery of individuals who are headstrong, lustful and violent. In "Kak s'eli petukha" ("How They Ate the Cock") we are treated to two anecdotes – thugs slash a woman's face and blind her, and children are snatched and the blood drained out of them to be sold to the transfusion centre – before we come to the narrative proper: a fight and reconciliation between man and wife over what to eat for New Year.

In many ways Popov can be compared to Zoshchenko, for each specializes in comic dialogue and the use of *skaz* (first-person narration) to establish an informal, conversational rapport with the reader. There is a tension between the lofty claims of the Soviet system and the earthy and thoroughly personalized tones that the characters employ. If Zoshchenko recorded the rift between aspiration and reality as the ordinary Russian entered the Soviet era, Popov performs the same feat as Soviet man re-entered the Russian era. Political satire is there, but Popov is more concerned with the broader issues of human absurdity; political parody is at least equalled by literary parody. There are cross-references of a kind between some of Popov's texts, so that street names and characters' names reappear, the result being that the vastness of the Soviet Union, and Siberia in particular, is reduced to the dimensions of a village. A "catch-phrase" in Popov is "The city of K. which is situated on the two banks of the river E., which flows into the Arctic ocean ..." and, referring as it does to the author's birthplace, has a dual function: first, it provides a light-hearted example of how writers in non-communist quarters and in post-communist times frequently insisted on their own voice rather than kow-towing to a directive from on high; second, it cocks a snook at the pedestrian rhetoric of officialdom.

At times Popov's stories take the form of an inverted fairy story, utilizing motifs like "once upon a time ...", depicting a hero undergoing three ordeals or making three encounters, but there is never a happy ending. An allied device is to be found in the coda that Popov adds to some of his narratives. Sometimes this is in the form of a highly ironic moral or a message – a clarion call concludes his "Piat' pesen o vodke" [Five Stories about Vodka]: "My dear people! Good people! ... I hear the howls of families falling apart and I see little children, their faces contorted with anguish." Sometimes the coda involves a shift in focus to a hitherto minor character, perhaps a muted old woman who witnesses and tolerates all the folly around her yet fails to comprehend – let alone arrest – it. Popov's males are often an excrescence of the eccentric (*chudak* or *chudik*) we find in Shukshin.

Dusha patriota (*The Soul of a Patriot*) apart, Popov's longer narratives are *Prekrasnost' zhizni. Glavy iz "romana s gazetoi", kotoryi nikogda ne budet nachat i zakonchen* [The Splendour of Life ...] and *Nakanune nakanune* [On the Eve of the Eve]. The first of these is an enormous compilation of items from the Soviet press arranged in such as a way as to produce hilarious ironies and absurdities and interlaced with some of Popov's own narratives. The montage technique could be taken as a parody of Dos Passos and even of Solzhenitsyn's *Krasnoe koleso* (*The Red Wheel*), as well as, of course, of the more familiar teleological preoccupations of the Soviet media. The untranslatable pun in the subtitle ("love affair with a newspaper" or "novel together with a newspaper") is a modest example of Popov's considerable linguistic dexterity. Lengthy compound and complex grammatical structures are mobilized to depict the grossest human ineptitudes and passions. *Nakanune nakanune* is a transparent parody of Turgenev's novel, now relocated in the Soviet era to elucidate the tribulations of Popov's generation.

The persistent parody and joking in Popov is fully comprehensible when one notes that for many intellectuals in the Soviet Union public life had itself become a parody of serious policy-making (an ailing gerontocracy presiding over an ailing economy, while making all sorts of boasts to the contrary). Popov's fiction is devoid of any didactic purpose, but it says much about the spirituality and absurdity of modern man.

ROBERT PORTER

The Soul of a Patriot

Dusha patriota

Novel, 1989

The Soul of a Patriot, or Various Epistles to Ferfichkin is ostensibly a series of random letters dashed off by one Evgenii Anatol'evich Popov to a friend, Ferfichkin, with whom the reader never becomes acquainted. What emerges is an anarchic novel reminiscent of Laurence Sterne's *Tristram Shandy* and a number of 20th-century texts in which traditional notions of character and plot go by the board. There is an episodic text describing some of the writer's family history back to before the Revolution, and an account of some of his escapades as a student and then as a proscribed contemporary writer. The whole thing is pulled deftly together by the death of "HIM WHO WAS" (clearly, Leonid Brezhnev). The narrator and his close friend, D.A. Prigov, embark on a series of "funereal wanderings" to try and reach the "epicentre of world history", namely the erstwhile Soviet leader's lying in state in the Hall of Columns in the House of Unions. The work ends with an account in note form of the state funeral as viewed on television by Popov and some of his close acquaintances, and finally an inordinately long toast to all the characters mentioned in the book – with one significant exception, Stalin.

The Soul of a Patriot can be read as a huge literary joke, containing as it does a great many references to Russian, Soviet and foreign classics as well as a degree of "in-joking" among the dispossessed intelligentsia of the late Brezhnev era. Yet it is also a dense text, which has much to say about the Russian psyche and Russian history: HE WHO WAS would be billed as the greatest of patriots by the media, but the narrator, who has had to labour under his dictatorship, seems to display more affection for his homeland and its history. Moreover, the Russian soul can be prone to chauvinism and ignorance. The novel's epigraph is simply: "'... garden ...' Voltaire", as if to imply that the enlightened values that the French writer stood for have barely filtered through to Russia. The book also paints an engrossing picture of the "years of stagnation" under Brezhnev, with some intellectuals licensed to operate, at least within certain limits (Voznesenskii, Evtushenko, Okudzhava), while others spent their time in near-futile negotiation with literary bureaucrats. Several writers (Petrushevskaia, Akhmadulina, Kormer) are designated only by an initial letter, as if to emphasize their twilight existence.

The novel, written quite quickly in late 1982, has proved prophetic. The irony of the long list of "friendly Caucasian peoples" in the very first epistle has become richer with the disintegration of the Soviet Union and the ensuing civil wars in the region. Few novels can have registered so promptly the fact that Brezhnev's death represented a historical watershed. When the narrator and Prigov do get as close as they can to the "epicentre", they swear, as did Herzen and Ogarev on the Sparrow Hills, "not to forget", thus linking the events of 1982 with those of the 1825 Decembrist uprising.

The novel starts with a personal account of a family history and ends on a personal note. The author's professed attempts to record history as it unfolds are constantly interrupted by his private life (domestic altercations, drinking sessions, a blocked-up toilet, having to take his empty bottles back for the deposit). In addition, his encounters with all sorts of colourful acquaintances, for instance the elderly sculptor and labour-camp veteran Nefed Nefedych, who was "forced to leave his wife, since she hindered him in his study of mankind, or more particularly in his study of womankind", distract him from his epistolatory endeavours. Neither is he helped by his self-confessed incompetence, as he gets mixed up and keeps trying to correct himself.

Thus the real epicentre is to be found within the individual, despite all his contradictions. The narrator's tone of voice and style shift from the colloquial and bawdy to the mock heroic, from the rhetorical to the plainly sincere. "You old sod! You shit-bag! You clapped out kulak! You Port Arthur prick!" he can mentally hurl at his Grandad Pasha, a veteran of the campaign against the Japanese in 1905, who inadvertantly stamped on the narrator's pet kitten, which he had as a boy. He can also call for "appeasement, tranquility, freedom, a feeling that life isn't lived for nothing"; and he expresses himself frequently on religion, art, literature and even architecture. Digression and allusion are the chief devices by which the narrator establishes his own set of values, and Russian critics saw the work's merit in its lack of inhibition.

Non-Russian readers might have difficulty registering all the quotations, snatches of poetry and oblique references in *The Soul of a Patriot*, but no one could fail to appreciate the numerous moments of sheer comedy: Uncle Kolia the Second invents a machine that can cut up pine trees automatically, as a result of which he becomes a university professor – until he gets drunk and tries to shoot his wife; Sergei Pauker breaks his leg while drunk at a party, and to avoid expulsion from university for his alcoholic state, is taken by his wife out to the park the next day, the plaster cast is removed and they pretend he has had a skiing accident. The novel also has special visual appeal, with the typography fluctuating from standard print to italics, block capitals and occasionally employing the old orthography. There are two sketch maps that purport to illustrate the narrator's "funereal wanderings"; finally, the text thins out into note form as HE WHO WAS is laid to rest. This visual aspect of the novel was greatly elaborated in the book edition of 1994, which included poems by D.A. Prigov and copious, cartoon-style illustrations by Viacheslav Sysoev. *The Soul of a Patriot* could well stand as one of those short, complex texts (on a par with, say, Pil'niak's *Golyi god* (*The Naked Year*)) that captures the spirit of dislocation, confusion and yet exhilaration that comes with the end of an epoch.

ROBERT PORTER

Povest' o boiaryne Morozovoi *see* Tale of Boiaryna Morozova

Povest' o Frole Skobeeve *see* Frol Skobeev, the Rogue

Povest' o Gore-Zlochastii *see* Tale of Woe-Misfortune

Povest' o Shemiakinom sude *see* Shemiaka's Judgment

Povest' ob Ul'ianii Osor'inoi *see* Tale of Ul'ianiia Osor'ina

Povest' vremennykh let *see* Primary Chronicle

Dmitrii Aleksandrovich Prigov 1940–

Performance poet and artist

Biography

Born in Moscow, 5 November 1940. Trained as an artist at the Stroganov Art Institute, from which he was expelled during Khrushchev's attack on Formalist and Abstractionist artists; reinstated a year later, graduated in 1967. Married: Nadezhda Burova; one son. Recipient: Pushkin Prize established by Friedrich von Schiller Foundation, 1993 (shared with Timur Kibirov).

Publications

Collected Editions

Slezy geral'dicheskoi dushi [Tears of the Heraldic Soul]. Moscow, 1990.

Piat'desiat kapelek krovi [Fifty Drops of Blood]. Moscow, 1993.

Zveri nashei zhizni. Les Fauves de la Vie. Bilingual Selected Poems, translated by Christine Zeytounian-Beloüs. Paris, Triptyque LPS-AMGA, 1994.

Iavlenie stikha posle ego smerti [Appearance of Verse After Its Death]. Moscow, 1995.

Teksty nashei zhizni. Texts of Our Life. Bilingual Selected Poems, edited with an introduction by Valentina Polukhina. Keele, Staffordshire, Essays in Poetics, 1995.

Sobranie stikhov 1963–1974 (vol. 1), Vienna, Wiener Slawistischer Almanach, 1996.

Poetry (in chronological order of composition)

Abramtsevskii sbornik [Abramtsevo Collection].

Dom i byt [Home and Daily Life].

Istoricheskie i geroicheskie pesni [Historical and Heroic Songs].

Kul'turnye pesni [Cultural Songs].

Virshi na kazhdyi den' [Verses for Everyday].

Apofeoz militsioneru [Apotheosis of the Policeman].

Obraz Reigana v sovetskoi literature [An Image of Reagan in Soviet Literature].

"Moskva i Moskvichi" [Moscow and Muscovites], in *Molodaia Poeziia 89*, Moscow, 1989, 423–29.

"Makhrot' vseia Rusi" [Makhrot' of All Russia], in *Vestnik novoi russkoi literatury*, 1 (1990), 90–97.
"Kniga o schast'e v stikhakh i dialogakh" [A Book about Happiness in Verse and Dialogues], *Znamia*, 8 (1994), 71–76.
Piat' sbornikov zhenskoi poezii [Five Collections of Women's Poetry].
Moi milyi laskovyi drug [My Dear Tender Friend].
"Oboroten'" [Werewolf], *Teatr*, 1 (1993), 133–35.
Tam, gde otorvali Mishke lapku [Where the Teddy-Bear's Little Paw was Torn off], extracts in *Novyi dzhentl'men*, Spring (1995), 96–97.

Anthologies containing Prigov's poems in English translation
The Hungry Russian Winter, edited by Victor Kulle. Moscow, 1991, 93–112.
The Poetry of Perestroika, edited by Peter Mortimer and S.J. Litherland. Newcastle upon Tyne, Iron Press, 1991, 82–85.
Third Wave: The New Russian Poetry, edited by Kent Johnson and Stephen M. Ashby. Ann Arbor, University of Michigan Press, 1992, 101–15.
Contemporary Russian Poetry – A Bilingual Anthology, translated by Gerald S. Smith. Bloomington, Indiana University Press, 1993, 212–23.
The Penguin Book of New Russian Writing: Russia's "Fleurs du mal", edited by Viktor Erofeev and Andrew Reynolds. Harmondsworth and New York, Penguin, 1995, 292–99.

Poetry in Periodicals
NBL, Salzburg, 1979–80, 46–65.
Al'manakh katalog, Ann Arbor, Ardis, 1982, 204–34.
Iunost', 1 (1988).
Iskusstvo, 10 (1988), 48–50.
Al'manakh poeziia, 52 (1989), 89–91.
Al'manakh zerkala, 1 (1989), 218–37.
Dekorativnoe iskusstvo, 11 (1989), 21–28.
Vestnik novoi russkoi literatury, 1 (1990), 90–97.
Iskusstvo, 1 (1990), 10–14.
Indeks, Moscow, (1990), 206–12.
Dekorativnoe iskusstvo, 9–10 (1991), 10–12.
Wiener Slawistischer Almanach, 31 (1991), 569–74.
Solo, 2 (1991), 58–60.
Sud'ba teksta, Moscow, (1992), 11–25.
Vestnik novoi russkoi literatury, (1992), 90–97.
Rodnik, Riga, 5 (1992), 22–25.
Novyi mir, 1 (1993), 168–71.
Teatr, 1 (1993), 131–35.
Ogonek, (April 1993), 62.
Znamia, 8 (1994), 21–26.
Novyi zhurnal, 196 (1995), 87–94.

Conceptual Texts
Prizyvy [Appeals].
Obrashcheniia [Exhortations].
Predlozheniia [Resolutions].
"Opisanie predmetov" [Description of Objects] (written 1979), in *Katalog*, Ann Arbor, Ardis, 1982, 226–31.
"Nekrologi" [Obituaries], *Ogonek*, (April 1993), 62.
Stalinskoe [From Stalin]. Moscow, 1994.

Plays
Chernyi pes [Black Dog]; *Glupyi mal'chik* [Silly Boy]; *Ia igraiu na garmoshke* [I Play the Accordion]; *Mesto Boga* [The Place of God]; *Kozel* [Goat]; *Katarsis* [Catharsis].

Critical Studies
Paradoksy novizny. O literaturnom razvitii XIX–XX vekov, by M. Epshtein, Moscow, 1988.
"Zametki o literaturnom kontseptualizme", by I. Bakshtein, in *Russkaia al'ternativnaia poeziia XX veka*, Moscow, 1989, 8–12.
"Iskusstvo predposlednikh istin: Beseda s Dmitriem Prigovym", by P. Vail' and A. Genis, *Al'manakh Panorama*, (February 1989), 17–24.
"Estetizatsiia ideologicheskogo teksta", by Boris Grois, *Sovetskoe iskusstvo okolo 1990 goda; Catalogue*, Cologne, 1990, 31–39.
"Nekotorye drugie ... Variant khroniki: pervaia versiia", by M. Aizenberg, *Teatr*, 4 (1991), 98–118.
"Iskusstvo mezhdu bukv", by E. Degot', in *Lichnoe delo*, Moscow, 1991, 86–145.
"Afterword: Metamorphosis", by M. Epshtein, in *Third Wave: The New Russian Poetry*, edited by Kent Johnson and Stephen M. Ashby, Ann Arbor, University of Michigan Press, 1992, 271–86.
The Total Art of Stalinism: Avant-Garde, Aesthetic Dictatorship, and Beyond, by Boris Grois, translated by Charles Rougle, Princeton, Princeton University Press, 1992, 75–112.
"Utverzhdaia svobodu ... Postmodernizm kak kul'turnoe iavlenie i tip soznaniia. Beseda s D.A. Prigovym", by S. Shapovalov, *Novyi dzhentel'men/New Gentleman*, (Spring 1995), 92–95.
"Groys – Prigow: Dialog, Dmitrij Prigow", in *Arbeiten 1975–1995*, Städtisches Museum Mülheim an der Ruhr, 1995, 16, 81–85.
"Dmitrij Prigov and the Russian Avant-Garde: Then and Now", by Mary A. Nicholas, *Russian Literature*, 39/1 (1996), 13–34.
"'Machrot' vseja Rusi' by Dmitrij Prigov as a Composition of Moscow Conceptualism", by Viktoria A. Olskaia, *Russian Literature*, 39/1 (1996), 39–64.

Bibliography
"Dmitrij Aleksandrovich Prigov: Selected Bibliography", by Mary A. Nicholas, *Russian Literature*, 39/1 (1996), 35–38.

Dmitrii Prigov is the foremost Russian postmodernist poet; he is also a major figure on the contemporary art scene. Thanks to his versatile activity he has gained an extraordinary popularity in Russia: he has written a staggering number of poetry books, among them about 86 *Azbuka* [Alphabets] and dozens of essays; he has exhibited his paintings in numerous galleries in Russian and European cities. In 1991 alone his works were shown at four international exhibitions in Moscow, Berlin, Frankfurt, and Hannover. He has delivered many extraordinary performances and displayed striking installations, has given one-man shows, and has been featured in various magazines; he has also taken part in many international festivals (being a key participant in the ICA *Novostroika* in 1991, one of the first festivals of Russian Art in Britain). He began writing poetry in 1957, but his development as a poet progressed slowly. However, fame was thrust on Prigov before he had published a single poem, a strange, but typical phenomenon in the history of 20th-century Russian poetry. Like the works of many other Russian poets of his generation, Prigov's poems and taped poetry readings were circulated in *samizdat* throughout the country and also in the west. At the time he was also practising graphic art, sculpture, and multi-media installations. The name of this many-sided multi-media artist soon became synonymous with a Russian brand of postmodernism.

The first selection of his poetic works, *Slezy geral'dicheskoi dushi* [Tears of the Heraldic Soul], appeared as late as 1990, a book that includes only a handful of his poems (83 out of the 15,000 written by then). His second book of poetry, *Piat'desiat kapelek krovi* [Fifty Drops of Blood], was published in 1993. Apart from these two collections, the 1990s saw the publication of Prigov's poems in many leading Russian periodicals.

Prigov collects his poems in cycles, each one consisting of ten to 20 poems, arranged in the manner of *samizdat*. So far he has produced more than 150 such "books", or about 21,000 poems, and he is planning to write 3,000 more poems by the end of the millennium. At the same time Prigov displays various styles. He has revived the very rare genre of *Azbuka* based on Church Slavonic alphabetical prayers and filled it with references to contemporary life, both Russian and western. He handles social satire and subtle wit with equal ease. He reverses the gender roles in his poems, and carries his fantasies to the extreme. The reader laughs at the depiction as much as at what is depicted. Since the early 1970s he has been creating visual and manipulative texts, mini books (texts inscribed on cans), window-texts, and telegrammes. "A tireless inventor of new forms on the crossroads of different genres", as Mikhail Aizenberg called him, Prigov, the artist-conceptualist, transplanted some branches of Conceptualism into the rich soil of Russian poetry. Together with Lev Rubinshtein, he revealed and laid bare the gap between the concept of communism and Soviet reality by turning the ideological chimeras of socialism into poems, stories, or pictures. They managed to transgress the laws of poetry by creating it out of the very essence of Soviet life. Prigov had always been fascinated by the phantoms of Soviet reality; his installations, for example, can be seen as "copies of nonexistent reality that are reminiscent of the existing one".

Common, trivial and vulgar, Prigov's texts both pandered to and parodied socialist realist aesthetics, using its sources, its stereotypes and ideological fetishism. His texts mirror Soviet life more faithfully than any documentary by taking to the logical conclusion all the hidden premises of Soviet ideology. This is very rare since neither brutal laughter, nor buffoonery alone are capable of creating a convincing hyperbole of Soviet life in which mediocrity and absurdism have reached their maximum level. It is precisely Prigov's capacity to recreate the past that gives his poems the edge in the present. This Bard of Perestroika, as he's often called, sees himself as a postmodernist poet, presenting an objective view of Russian life; he depicts it in the most condensed and exaggerated forms.

Prigov has developed an unusual skill – making poetry out of "that poor, utterly distorted, monstrous language, Russian newspeak" (Ol'ga Sedakova). He is particularly fond of the language of ideology, with its empty rhetoric, its clichés and party slogans (this was especially typical of his poems written during the 1970s). His work with linguistic clichés is not limited by Russian newspeak but extends to other components of complex linguistic mentality. Prigov would like to claim that the principal character of his poems is not a human being, but rather the Russian language itself, in various forms of its existence, high and low, official and private, literary and colloquial. However, it is only one of the many characters in his grand play peopled by voices and images.

Prigov is cultivating a deliberately primitive poetics: tautological rhymes, repetitive rhythm and syntactic constructions, a lack of punctuation, and an absence of tropes. These features would be obvious weaknesses in any other poet, but Prigov has turned them into his essential strength. With such a simplification of poetic language the composition of the poem takes a leading role. His ability to tell a story in the most concise form is an obvious feature of his work. His poetics has a lot in common with that of the Russian absurdists (Kharms, Vvedenskii, Vaginov, and Zabolotskii): much of his humour derives from a mixture of sense and nonsense as well as from moral incongruity; a great deal of detachment is combined with infantilism and sentimentalism; alogical connections of thought and disjointed events constitute another obvious device. He has also learnt a great deal from folklore as well as from so-called "writings degree zero".

More importantly, Prigov has created a personal style that suits perfectly his own image as a clever God's fool. This wise daftness, as a mood of presentation, is a very Russian phenomenon and has its roots in buffoonery, madness, and carnivals. Its tradition and socio-psychological basis was described by Bakhtin. Prigov has painted it with a postmodernist's cosmetics. Apart from quotations from the classics of Marxism-Leninism (see his dialogues with comrade Stalin) and from popular Soviet songs (see his songs of Soviet villages), his poems are saturated with allusions to Russian poets from Pushkin to Pasternak.

Prigov has abandoned the very idea of a lyric hero and replaced him with various stereotypes of different cultures, including Soviet, conveying the negative and paradoxical nature of the Russian mentality, its sentimentality, its duality and imperial tendencies (for example, his cycle *Moskva i Moskvichi* [Moscow and Muscovites]). His artistic strategy is, it seems, to deconstruct socio-political discourse and socio-cultural behaviour. He claims that he prefers to work "with categories and symbols rather than characters and images", seeing himself as a director rather than an actor. Indeed, his Policeman (or "Pliceman" – *Militsaner*) is a symbol of the State, the Jew is an embodiment of history, Mariia represents love, while Ronald Reagan is depicted as a symbol of the "enemy". He works with the patterns of human behaviour, social, cultural, private. He does not write confessional poetry and would go to any length to avoid self-representation.

As a freelance artist and writer he spends his time between Russia, Germany, and England. He has given many performances and poetry readings and between 1987 and 1989 he lectured widely in the United States. He seems to flourish in a foreign cultural environment, but he is always longing to return to Russia, to the linguistic roots of his poetic consciousness. In one of his interviews Prigov confessed:

> My art is opposed to the mainstream, the establishment. I'm a critic and an outsider in relation to it. There is no immediate danger of my becoming part of the mainstream

in Russia which is still largely traditional with a preference for romantic-confessional types of art.

The new kind of poetry that is now beginning to appear in Russia is opposed to elaborate intellectual style and Prigov, as one of its principal exponents, has a claim to a permanent place in the history of Russian poetry.

VALENTINA POLUKHINA

Primary Chronicle

Anonymous 12th-century chronicle

Editions

Ipat'evskaia letopis'. 2nd edition, St Petersburg, 1908 (*Polnoe sobranie russkikh letopisei*, vol. 2); reprinted Moscow, 1962, cols 1–285.

Lavrent'evskaia letopis'. 2nd edition, Moscow, 1926 (*Polnoe sobranie russkikh letopisei*, vol. 1, facs. 1); reprinted Moscow, 1962.

Povest' vremennykh let [The Tale of Bygone Years], edited by D.S. Likhachev and V.P. Adrianova-Peretts, 2 vols. Moscow and Leningrad, 1950; 2nd revised edition, edited by D.S. Likhachev, St Petersburg, 1996.

Handbuch zur Nestorchronik, edited by L. Müller, 3 vols. Munich, Fink, 1977–86.

"Povest' vremennykh let", in *Pamiatniki literatury Drevnei Rusi. XI–pervaia polovina XII v.* Moscow, 1978, 22–277, 418–51.

Translation

The Russian Primary Chronicle. Laurentian Text, edited and translated by Samuel Hazzard Cross and Olgerd P. Sherbowitz-Wetzor. Cambridge, Massachusetts, Mediaeval Academy of America, 1953; 3rd edition, 1973.

Critical Studies

Razyskaniia o drevneishikh russkikh letopisnykh svodakh, by A.A. Shakhmatov, St Petersburg, 1908.

"'Povest' vremennykh let' i ee istochniki", by A.A. Shakhmatov, *Trudy otdela drevnerusskoi literatury*, 4 (1940), 11–150.

Russkie letopisi i ikh kul'turno-istoricheskoe znachenie, by D.S. Likhachev, Moscow and Leningrad, 1947.

Drevniaia Rus': skazaniia, byliny, letopisi, by B.A. Rybakov, Moscow, 1963, 215–300.

"Die 'Dritte Redaktion' der sogenannten Nestorchronik", by L. Müller, in *Festschrift für M. Woltner zum 70. Geburtstag*, Heidelberg, 1967, 171–86.

Povest' vremennykh let: sud'ba literaturnogo pamiatnika v Drevnei Rusi, by M.Kh. Aleshkovskii, Moscow, 1971.

Otechestvennaia istoriografiia russkogo letopisaniia, by V.I. Buganov, Moscow, 1975.

Leksika "Povesti vremennykh let", by A.S. L'vov, Moscow, 1975.

"Povest' vremennykh let i Nachal'nyi svod. Tekstologicheskii kommentarii", by O.V. Tvorogov, *Trudy otdela drevnerusskoi literatury*, 30 (1976), 3–26.

Nachal'nye etapy drevnerusskogo letopisaniia, by A.G. Kuz'min, Moscow, 1977.

The Great Heritage: The Classical Literature of Old Rus', by D.S. Likhachov [Likhachev], translated by Doris Bradbury, Moscow, Progress, 1981, 44–135.

"Textual Criticism and the *Povest' vremennykh let*: Some Theoretical Considerations", by Donald Ostrowski, *Harvard Ukrainian Studies*, 5 (1981).

"Some Apocryphal Sources of Kievan Russian Historiography", by Simon Franklin, *Oxford Slavonic Papers*, new series, 15 (1982), 1–27.

Leksicheskii sostav "Povesti vremennykh let" (slovoukazateli i chastotnyi slovnik), by O.V. Tvorogov, Kiev, 1984.

"Les premières années byzantines du *Récit des temps passés*", by I. Sorlin, *Revue des Études Slaves*, 63 (1991), 8–18.

"Borrowed Time: Perceptions of the Past in Twelfth-Century Russia", by Simon Franklin, in *The Perception of the Past in Twelfth-Century Europe*, edited by Paul Magdalino, London, Hambledon Press, 1992, 157–71.

Povest' vremennykh let (*Primary Chronicle*) was put together in approximately its extant form in the second decade of the 12th century by a Kievan monk, often (but not securely) identified as Nestor of the Caves monastery. The importance of the *Primary Chronicle* is threefold: it became the central text in the Russian – and Ukrainian – mythology of national origins and identity; it remains the most valuable single source of the early history of the Rus' and of the formation of their polity; and both as a whole and in its component parts it is a focal work for the study of the emergence of East Slavonic literature.

Early Christian and Byzantine chroniclers had charted the history of mankind from the Creation to the notional end of time, showing how Divine Providence manifested itself in temporal affairs. When the Rus' formally adopted Eastern Christianity, one of their tasks was to locate themselves on this imported and unfamiliar map of sacred time and space, to legitimize themselves as part of Providential history, to show that they, too, had their place in the Divine Plan. The *Primary Chronicle* is the most ambitious and influential attempt to do so.

The story begins just after the biblical flood, with an apocryphal tale of how Noah divided all lands and peoples among his three sons. Versions of the same tale were commonly used for the equivalent purpose in chronicles throughout medieval Europe. The *Primary Chronicle* traces the Rus' and the Slavs to the peoples of the north and west, allocated to Noah's third son Japheth. With respectable biblical origins thus established, the narrative narrows to a survey of the various Slav tribes, before focusing on the Poliane of the Kiev region, and eventually on the family who ruled over them: from the Flood to the Kievan Rus'.

From the mid-9th century ethnic history gives way to dynastic history, from the origins of peoples to the origins of the ruling family. Here the form of the chronicle also changes from continuous narrative to annals, in which events are noted year by year. This is the framework for the chronicle's account of native history, perceived above all as the history of the princes of Kiev and their kin. The most prominent episodes have become familiar through countless paraphrases: the summoning of Riurik the Varangian and his kin – the Rus' – to rule in Novgorod; the expansion southwards along the "way from the Varangians to the Greeks", and the establishment of the Rus' dynasty in Kiev; the campaigns of Oleg and Igor' against Constantinople; the guile and piety of Princess Ol'ga; the rugged exploits of Sviatoslav, who smashed the power of the Khazars, pacified the Bulgarians and for a while managed to install himself at a new capital on the Danube, thus threatening (in Byzantine eyes) the integrity and security of the Byzantine Empire itself; the acceptance and imposition of Christianity by Vladimir; the exemplary fraternal submissiveness of the dynastic saints Boris and Gleb; and the triumphal display of Christian culture under Iaroslav.

Thus, in the chronicle's account, Riurik's pagan progeny established a dynastic polity; through Conversion that polity (the Land of the Rus') found its proper place under Divine Providence, and its Christian status and identity were affirmed and manifested through Iaroslav's public patronage and the promotion of naive Christian culture. In the *Primary Chronicle*, therefore, the Land of the Rus' acquires its distinct identity from a synthesis of three elements: the dynasty of the Varangians, the language of the Slavs, and the faith of the "Greeks".

The remainder of the chronicle, from Iaroslav's death in 1054 to the early part of the reign of Vladimir Monomakh (1113–25), shows Iaroslav's sons and grandsons attempting to maintain this legacy while adapting it to changing circumstances. As new rivalries emerged within the princely family, and as new neighbours threatened (in particular the Polovtsy of the southern steppes), the chronicle not only records but also evaluates. Here it is concerned less with the legitimation of the whole than with the legitimacy of specific types of princely action. If in its early sections the chronicle articulated national myth, in its later sections it becomes a kind of handbook of political morality.

The *Primary Chronicle* was copied and re-copied by later chroniclers throughout the Middle Ages. Indeed, it does not actually survive at all as a separate text in any medieval manuscript, but only as a component part of subsequent compilations. Strictly speaking, therefore, the *Primary Chronicle* is no more than a hypothesis, an extrapolation. However, though the detailed readings are in many places debatable, the overall shape and contents of the chronicle are not in much doubt.

Far more problematic and intriguing are the chronicle's sources and components. The compiler could use eye-witness or contemporary native written sources only for the last half-century or so of his narrative. Prior to the mid-11th century it is unlikely that the Rus' produced or preserved any formal written records of their own. The *Primary Chronicle* is one of a series of attempts – by far the most thorough and thoughtful – to reconstitute a distant past that was largely unknown. Traces of previous attempts can be detected in the chronicle itself, as well as in some later compilations, but there are huge gaps because the chronicler's sources of information were fragmentary and heterogeneous. Much of the chronicle is a conscientiously assembled but incomplete mosaic, including translated fragments of Byzantine chronicles, folksy anecdotes and heroic legends, the dry formulae of diplomatic documents (10th-century trade agreements with Byzantium) and the effusive formulae of ecclesiastical rhetoric.

For the historian of facts, all of this is frustrating. It means, crudely, that the *Primary Chronicle* is unreliable. The selection of episodes is subordinate not only to the chronicler's ideological design but also to the vagaries of his own sparse sources. Such basics as dates, places and people are often demonstrably wrong. For the historian of literature and culture, however, the unconcealed compilatory nature of the chronicle is perhaps its most exciting feature. Instead of paraphrasing the various types of source and blending them into a smooth and integrated narrative, the chronicler tended to respect the range of forms and styles. The result is a single text which is also a multitude of texts; a composite genre including valuable specimens of, or evidence for, several types of non-chronicle discourse which in many cases – paradoxically – do not survive from the earliest period except as parts of the chronicle. In a sense, therefore, the *Primary Chronicle* serves as a kind of literary mosaic of the age, although there is occasional dispute as to whether the work as a whole can or should be classed as "literature" by modern definitions.

SIMON FRANKLIN

Mikhail Mikhailovich Prishvin 1873–1954

Prose writer

Biography

Born in Elets district, Orel Province, 4 February 1873, into a family of bankrupt salesman. Attended Elets gymnasium from 1887; excluded for aggressive behaviour toward teacher, Vasilii Rozanov, whose philosophy would later influence him. Attended Tiumen technical high school until 1893; studied in the department of chemistry and agriculture, Riga Polytechnical Institute from 1893 until arrest in 1897 for distribution of illegal literature; studied agronomy at the University of Leipzig, 1900; graduated with diploma in agricultural engineering, 1902. Married: 1) Evrosin'ia Pavlovna Smogaleva in 1903, two sons; 2) his literary secretary Valeriia Dmitrievna Lebedeva in 1940. Agronomist in Klin and Luga until 1905. First non-fiction book published in 1904; first short story, 1905. Expedition to Olonets and Karelia in 1905. Travelled to Norway in 1907, to settlements of Old Believers in the Volga region in 1908, and to the Crimea and Kazakhstan. Associated with Remizov, Rozanov, and Merezhkovskii, 1908–12; member of Religious-Philosophical Society in St Petersburg. Lived in Elets, Aleksino (Smolensk region), after 1917; Iaroslavl from 1925, later in Zagorsk. Published in *Novyi mir* and *Krasnaia nov'*, from the 1920s. Delegate to the First Congress of Soviet Writers, 1934. Moved to Moscow, late 1930s. During World War II, lived near Pereslavl-Zalesskii. Died in Moscow, 16 January 1954.

Publications

Collected Editions

Sobranie sochinenii, 3 vols. Moscow, 1912–14.
Sobranie sochinenii, 7 vols. Moscow, 1927–30.
Sobranie sochinenii, 6 vols. Moscow, 1956–57.
Sobranie sochinenii, 8 vols. Moscow, 1982–86.

Fiction

V kraiu nepuganykh ptits. Ocherki Vygovskogo kraia [In the Land of the Unfrightened Birds. Sketches of the Vygov Country]. St Petersburg, 1907.
Za volshebnym kolobkom. Iz zapisok na Krainem Severe Rossii i Norvegii [Beyond the Enchanted Loaf]. St Petersburg, 1908.
"Chernyi Arab" [The Black Arab], *Russkaia mysl'*, 11 (1910).
Zavoroshka. Otkliki zhizni [Complications. Echoes of Life]. Moscow, 1913; translated in part as *The Black Arab, and Other Stories*, by David Magarshack, London, Hutchinson, 1947.
Kashcheeva tsep' [Kashchei's Chain]. 1924–54; Moscow and Leningrad, 1927.
"Kalendar' prirody", *Krasnaia nov'*, 8 (1925); separate edition as *Rodniki Berendeia*, Moscow and Leningrad, 1936; integral edition in *Sobranie sochinenii*, 1935–39, vol. 3; translated as *The Lake and the Woods, or Nature's Calendar*, by W.L. Goodman, London, Routledge and Kegan Paul, 1951; New York, Pantheon, 1952; reprinted Westport, Connecticut, Greenwood Press, 1975; as *Nature's Diary*, by Lev Navrozov, Moscow, Foreign Languages Publishing House, 1958; New York, Penguin, 1987.
"Zhen'-shen'. Koren' zhizni", *Krasnaia nov'*, 3 (1933); Moscow, 1934; translated as *Jen Sheng: The Root of Life*, by George Walton and Philip Gibons, London, A. Melrose and New York, Putnam, 1936; also as *The Root of Life*, by Alice Stone Nakhimovsky and Alexander Nakhimovsky, New York, Macmillan, and London, Collier Macmillan, 1980.
Zolotoi rog [The Golden Horn]. Leningrad, 1934.
Lesnaia kapel' [Forest Drip]. Moscow, 1943.
Kladovaia solntsa. Moscow, 1946; translated as *The Treasure Trove of the Sun*, by Tatiana Balkoff-Drowne, New York, Viking, 1952; also as *The Sun's Storehouse*, by Ivy Litvinov, Moscow, Progress, 1975.
Moia strana [My Country]. Moscow, 1948.
Boys and Ducklings, translated by Olga Shartse. Moscow, Foreign Languages Publishing House, 1950.
"Korabel'naia chashcha", *Novyi mir*, 5–6 (1954); translated as *Shiptimber Grove*, by David Fry, London, Lawrence and Wishart, 1957.
Osudareva doroga [The Ruler's Path]. Moscow, 1958.
A Selection [no translator named]. Moscow, Raduga, 1985.

Diaries

Moi tetradki [My Notebooks]. Leningrad, 1948.
Dnevniki 1905–54 [Diaries]. Moscow, 1986.
Dnevniki [Diaries]. Moscow, 1991.

Sketch and Letters

Moi ocherk [My Sketch]. Moscow, 1933.
Perepiska M.M. Prishvina s russkimi pisateliami [Correspondence of M.M. Prishvin with Russian Writers]. Moscow, 1991.

Critical Studies

Tvorchestvo Mikhaila Prishvina, by Tamara Khmel'nitskaia, Leningrad, 1959.
Mikhail Prishvin, by Andrei Khailov, Leningrad, 1960.
Mikhail Prishvin, by Igor' Motiashov, Moscow, 1965.
Das Frühwerk Michail Prischwins, by Horst Lampl, Vienna, Notring, 1967.
Mikhail Prishvin, by Grigorii Ershove, Moscow, 1973.
"Questions of Art, Fact and Genre in Mikhail Prishvin", by Ray J. Parrott Jr, *Slavic Review*, 36/3 (1977), 465–77.
"Evolution of a Critical Response: Mikhail Prishvin", by Ray J. Parrott Jr, *Russian Language Journal*, 109 (1977), 101–23.
Prishvin i russkie pisateli XX veka, by Anatolii Kiselev, Kuibyshev, 1985.
Mikhail Prishvin: ocherk tvorchestva, by Valentin Kurbatov, Moscow, 1986.
Tvorchestvo Mikhaila Prishvina: Issledovaniia i materialy. Voronezh, 1986.
Zagadnienia poetyki "Powiesci-bajki" Michala Priszwina, by Franciszek Apanowicz, Wrocław, Zaklad Narodowy im. Ossolinskich, 1988.
Priroda v khudozhestvennom mire Prishvina, by Taisia Grinfel'd-Zingurs, Saratov, 1989.
Vospominaniia o Mikhaile Prishvine, Moscow, 1991.

Bibliography
Mikhail Prishvin: Bibliografiia, by Natal'ia Plekhanova, Orel, 1960.

To this day, Russian mainstream audiences view Mikhail Prishvin as predominantly a children's writer. This absurdly inadequate reputation emerged thanks to the collective efforts of Soviet critics and publishing officials who dwarfed one of the great masters of Russian prose by demoting him to a harmless author of nature stories. Ray Parrott has collected some of the most ludicrous labels coined by critics for Prishvin, among them "poet-agronomist", "poet-hunter", "poet-traveller", and "poet-fisherman". The fact that Prishvin's preferred subject-matter was mistaken for substance, and his stylistic straightforwardness for plain simplicity, shows that his *oeuvre* has received neither appropriate appreciation nor sufficient research. Yet, in spite of this critical misunderstanding and the great number of clichéd writer-and-dog photographs visualizing it, perceptive readers recognized Prishvin during his lifetime as heir to the Russian classical tradition. Praise bestowed on Prishvin by Blok, Gor'kii, and Ivanov-Razumnik created that aura, which even Stalin seems to have sensed; for it was the tyrant in person who granted Prishvin the status of a classic, making him untouchable for the watchdogs of socialist realism.

Certainly, one can value Prishvin as an exemplary case of "inner emigration" under the Soviet regime, as his loyal community of followers were attracted to the literary refuge he presented. Still, there is an enormous contemporary relevance in Prishvin yet to be discovered: his non-aggressive, emphatic approach toward nature, formulated at a time when slogans for conquering and completely remodelling it were in vogue; his uncompromising individualistic position in a Kafkaesque regime; his understanding of the role of literature in communicating with the deepest layers of our mythical consciousness.

The publication of Prishvin's diaries in the late 1980s was a sensation to the Russian literary community: it revealed that the seemingly harmless author of short-stories and semi-fictional essays had been fully aware of the destructive core of communism, that he had never forgiven the regime for its annihilation of the Russian peasantry and that he had tried to do his share in the preservation of Russian language and letters. The niche that he had created to protect himself from official control was but a shrewd disguise, hiding a radically humanistic thinker beneath the mask of a kind and somewhat naive grandfather-storyteller. Read through this lens, the symbolic value of *Kashcheeva tsep'* [Kashchei's Chain], Prishvin's ultimate prose achievement, acquires a dangerous ambiguity; not only does it represent the chain of human isolation, cast as a terrible spell on mankind, it is also the chain of unfreedom that can be broken once the will to break its power is strong enough.

As a matter of fact, Prishvin viewed the diaries that he produced from 1904 until his death as the central work of his life, and he consciously directed his major creative energies into them. Several of his books, such as *Kalendar' prirody* (*Nature's Diary*) were based on his diaries, or rather on the part of them that was publishable during his lifetime. To Prishvin, a diary was not merely a notebook of transient value but a means of self-observation and a source of immediacy and authenticity. Moreover, the diary genre was a subversive challenge to a society in which individualism was condemned as a major deviation from the collectivist norm. The much-debated question of the reasons for his concentration on essays and essay-like short stories can likewise be answered by looking at the two major dimensions of Prishvin's creativity: factual precision and subjective, that is poetic, truth.

Perhaps Prishvin's stubbornly maintained individualism, together with his passionate love for everything natural and organic, untouched by human hands, was part of his family heritage. Prishvin was proud of his roots, and it seems as if the spirit of his mother, a descendant of Old Believers, enabled him to successfully play the role that officialdom had reserved for him and at the same time keep his unique world-view without making the slightest compromises. Such was his tempestuous personal life, as well. In 1902, Prishvin met Varvara Izmalkova in Paris, and his unrequited love for her brought him close to suicide; his claim that it was she who awoke the artist-creator in him and she who left a wound in his heart that was never to heal, is certainly more than sentimentality.

Prishvin's intense interest in ethnography and folklore is well known, yet, a merely descriptive approach toward people and culture always frustrated his searching mind. Truly, the mythological characters populating his works – the sorceress Manefa, Kashchei the Immortal, Mar'ia Morevna, the witch Baba Iaga – are nothing less than lively dramatis personae of his poetic universe. They are not dead or confined to the bookish realm of scholarship. Prishvin seems to say: they live on and surround us, and the energy of myths is ever-present in our environment. Only to a superficial viewer can the combination of practicality and romantic desire that is characteristic of Prishvin's writings and life look paradoxical, for the inner structure of all his works is based on a merger of the factual with the imaginative, the historical with the mythological, of scientific reasoning with poetic speculation. Prishvin's deep respect for the inherent wisdom of the natural order may also account for his aesthetic sensitivity and his attempt to stylize his works according to folkloric models. The poetic truth of his works is, again, authenticated by *skaz*-type narration, an "oral diary", so to speak, in which the author-narrator, an uneducated wanderer, relates his experiences in a seemingly relaxed, conversational manner.

Prishvin's approach to nature was influenced by Greek pantheism, by the works of Goethe, and by those of Knut Hamsun whom he saw as a brother-in-spirit. In his best texts, one can trace the movement from a parallelism between nature and the human soul to the point where the two grow together; for example, in his outstanding short story "Chernyi arab" ("The Black Arab"), which was inspired by a sojourn to the Central Asian steppe.

Not by coincidence, Prishvin's immediate literary teachers were Bunin, Remizov, and Arsen'ev; their attention to the purity and enigmatic riches of the Russian language encouraged him to strive for as much verbal diversity as he could achieve. Major prose texts such as *Osudareva doroga* [The Ruler's Path], a peculiar blend of fairy-tale, autobiography, and historical narrative, are treasures of images, magical word combinations, and myths that combine into works of utmost originality. The value of these works was certainly understated by Prishvin himself when he described his art as "the appearance of the human soul in the images of nature" (1950). More fitting seems

John Updike's admiring statement on Prishvin's mastership, "the vibration of our animal existence is in him, as well as those tentative motions of mind whereby Man began to subdue his magnificent, riddle-filled environment".

PETER ROLLBERG

Anna Semenova Prismanova 1892–1960

Poet and prose writer

Biography

Born Anna Semenova Prisman in Libau, Latvia, 18 September 1892. Daughter of a Russian Jewish dermatologist; brought up in Libau (now Liepaja), Latvia. Moved with family to Moscow, c.1918; joined Gumilev's Union of Poets in 1921. Emigrated to Berlin in early 1920s, where first poems published in 1923. Moved thence to Paris in 1924. Married: the poet and littérateur Aleksandr Ginger in 1926; two sons. Joined the Union of Young Writers; first collection of verse appeared, 1937. Took Soviet citizenship, though remained in Paris, 1937. Began publishing intensively, with collections appearing in 1946, 1949 and 1960. Died of heart disease in Paris, 4 November 1960.

Publications

Collected Edition

Sobranie sochinenii, edited by Petra Couvée. The Hague, Leuxenhoff, 1990.

Poetry

Ten' i telo [Shadow and Body]. Paris, 1937.

Bliznetsy [Twins]. Paris, 1946.

Sol' [Salt]. Paris, 1949.

Vera. Paris, 1960.

Four poems/extracts, translated by Temira Pachmuss, in *A Russian Cultural Revival*, edited by Pachmuss. Knoxville, University of Tennessee Press, 1981.

Two poems, translated by Catriona Kelly, in *An Anthology of Russian Women's Writing, 1777–1992*, edited by Kelly, Oxford, Oxford University Press, 1994.

Prose

"Les coqs", *Cahiers du Sud*, 331 (1942), 436–40.

"Les fleurs et couronnes", *Cahiers du Sud*, 353 (1946), 68–74.

"O gorode i ogorode", *Mosty*, 12 (1966), 39–42; translated as "On Guard and on Town Gardens", by Catriona Kelly, in *An Anthology of Russian Women's Writing, 1777–1992*, edited by Kelly, Oxford, Oxford University Press, 1994.

Critical Studies

"Parizhskie poety", by Mark Slonim, *Novosel'e*, 29/30 (1946), 89–96.

"Pamiati Anny Prismanovoi", by A. Bakhrakh, *Mosty*, 6 (1961), 365–68.

"Rozi ili rozh'?", by E. Tauber, *Novyi zhurnal*, 61 (1964), 151–68.

"Anna Prismanova", by Iurii Terapiano, in *Literaturnaia zhizn' russkogo Parizha za polveka (1924–1974): Esse, vospominaniia, stat'i*, edited by Iurii Terapiano, Paris, Izdatel'stvo Al'batros – Tret'ia volna, 1987, 227–36.

"Introduction", by Petra Couvée, in *Sobranie sochinenii*, by A.S. Prismanova, 1990, 11–31.

"O Sobranii sochinenii Anny Prismanovoi", by Vadim Kreid, *Novyi zhurnal*, 182 (1991), 391–94.

"Anna Semenovna Prismanova", by Petra Couvée, in *Dictionary of Russian Women Writers*, edited by Marina Ledkovsky, Charlotte Rosenthal, and Mary Zirin, Westport, Connecticut, Greenwood Press, 1994, 520–22.

A History of Russian Women's Writing, 1820–1992, by Catriona Kelly, Oxford and New York, Oxford University Press, 1994, 268–69; 276–78.

"Grandfather's Glass Eye: The Poetry of Anna Prismanova", by Catriona Kelly, *New Poetry Quarterly*, 2 (September 1994), 61–64.

As in the cases of several other noted women writers, for example Irina Grekova, Natal'ia Baranskaia and Vera Merkur'eva, Anna Prismanova had a late-developing talent. She began publishing poetry in 1923, when she was 31, and while some of her early work displays extraordinary verbal intricacy and metrical virtuosity (particularly "Na kante mira muza Kantemira" [Kantemir's muse, next the world's cant immured], her 1929 poem addressed to Lomonosov), it was only with her first collection, *Ten' i telo* [Shadow and Body], that Prismanova was to cease eclectic experimentation, and acquire a consistent and individual voice.

The title of Prismanova's first collection, and also that of her second, *Bliznetsy* [Twins], are clear indications of the Neo-platonic dualism that characterized her world-view. Like many Russian poets, she struggled to perceive the "other", spiritual world beyond the material world of fleshly things; typically for Russian culture too, feminine identity is represented by Prismanova as a constant struggle between the earth-bound forces of biology and the spiritual release attainable in mysticism. What makes Prismanova's work stand out is the accuracy with which the physical world is perceived, the originality, indeed eccentricity, of her metaphorical system, and the density of her symbolism, which depends, like Mandel'shtam's, on incantatory, almost obsessive repetition of certain key images (including the salt, sea-water, fish, parts of the human body, especially the bones, the crowing of cocks, and colours, in particular yellow and black) so that the properties of the real world acquire fluctuating signification, which can be personal (references to her Baltic birthplace are identifiable in many works) or general (relating to the purpose of human life itself). The ideas in Prismanova's work are often straightforward, but their artistic realization is not simple-minded; however, it also avoids pretension. In "Sestry" [Sisters], for example, she portrays Martha and Mary, predictably enough, as representatives of alternative possibilities for women. Martha, who has dedicated her life to service for others, and thinks of herself only when preparing to visit church on Sundays, is opposed to Mary, who "plays, while the moon shines, on her lyre", and whose "neglected children" sit in "threadbare short trousers" on the yard fence. While Prismanova's identification with Mary, rather than the self-sacrificing and eventually self-annihilating Martha, is obvious, the poet's choice is dramatized by the poem's conclusion, reproachfully apostrophizing Mary's "bonhomie with dreams" ("s mechtoiu panibratstvo"), and also by the vivid imagery that is applied to both women. Martha, "in a skinny coat with fox-tail tippets", arrives to do her charring "like a bird returning to its own cage"; her face is "dry and grey as steppe grass", and she raised her hands to dust "as though the shelves were guns". For her part, Mary lets her garden-fork "sprout and bud in the shed", while her knitting "has turned to moss". In "Chai" [Tea], the scent of China tea not only provokes a debate on "high things and low things", but also forms part of an extended network of alliteratively-linked associations, from the chain in front of a kennel "Like a Chinaman's pigtail", to Chinese "inscrutability" as a model of the linguistic stoicism that necessarily characterizes all thinking human beings. Furthermore, clusters of imagery are linked by sound analogy (consonance and assonance): the word "Chinese" (*kitaiskii*) suggests in turn *kury* (chickens), *korova* (cow), as well as such phonetically more distant, but semantically more important words as *iabloko* (apple), *verevka* (rope) and *stekla* (glasses). In addition, Prismanova, like other émigré writers, and in particular Tsvetaeva and Nabokov, frequently structures her poetry around visual and verbal puns. "Ryba" [Fish], the second poem of Prismanova's third collection *Sol'* [Salt], first introduces the idea of tears as "living liquid" poured on to, and mixed with, "desiccated words"; the notion of salt water is then turned on its head as a medium in which the fish-like Prismanova, with her "spiny" words and feelings, can herself happily swim. "Azbuka" [Alphabet], from *Bliznetsy*, plays repeatedly on the sound associations of the old names for Russian letters (v, *védi*, becomes *vedí!* lead us!, *buki*, b, *buk*, a beech tree, and so on).

Both in terms of thematics and in terms of language, Prismanova's poetry has close links with the mature work of Marina Tsvetaeva; the latter's narrative poems, such as "Lestnitsa" [Staircase] and "Popytka komnaty" [Attempt at a Room] seem to have suggested certain of Prismanova's images (for example, the images of eyes as "tubs of washing blue" in Prismanova's "Sestry" is probably an appropriation from "Lestnitsa"). However, Prismanova's diction and metrics are very much her own; preferring "classical" metres (in particular iambs) to Tsvetaeva's idiosyncratic forms of accentual verse, she yet treated these with considerable freedom and virtuosity, and off-set sentence and line rhythm with particular skill.

Prismanova was a most accomplished poet even when judged by the high standards that predominated in first-wave Russian émigré poetry. The qualities of her prose fragments, which add a knowing and manipulative narrative technique to the verbal skills evident in her poetry, make one regret the infrequency of her engagement with this genre. Her work is among the most impressive achievements in 20th-century Russian literature. Now available in a substantial one-volume edition, it has, however, yet to attract the sustained critical attention that it deserves.

CATRIONA KELLY

Anatolii Ignat'evich Pristavkin 1931–

Novelist and short-story writer

Biography

Born in Liubertsy, near Moscow, 17 October 1931. War orphan. Lived in "dozens of children's homes". Wandered throughout Russia, during World War II; worked in a canning factory from the age of 12, until his military service began. Literary debut in 1952. Attended the Gor'kii Literary Institute, Moscow; graduated in 1959. First prose sketches published in *Iunost'*, 1959. Worked on Bratsk hydro-electric project. Editorial staff member of the journal *Molodaia gvardiia*, 1963–66. Joined the Communist Party, 1965. Recipient: Writers' Union Prize, 1978. Driving force behind "April" (Aprel') literary movement from 1985. Chair, Union of Russian Writers, 1992. Chair of Clemency Committee (for cases of capital punishment). Lives in Moscow.

Publications

Collected Edition

Kukushata [The Cuckoos]. Moscow, 1995.

Fiction

Strana Lepiia [LEP Country]. Moscow, 1960.

Tri zhizni [Three Lives]. Moscow, 1960.

Malen'kie rasskazy [Little Stories]. Moscow, 1962.
Rozhdennomu zhit' [Who is Born Must Live]. Moscow, 1963; as *Kostry v taige* [Bonfires in the Taiga], 1964.
Sibirskie povesti [Siberian Stories]. Moscow, 1964.
Seliger Seligerovich. Moscow, 1965.
"Golubka" [Little Dove], *Znamia*, 3–6 (1967).
Liricheskaia kniga [Lyrical Book]. Moscow, 1969.
Na Angare [On the Angara]. Moscow, 1975.
Angara-reka [The Angara River]. Moscow, 1977.
Angara. Moscow, 1981.
Vozdelai pole svoe [Cultivate Your Own Field]. Moscow, 1981.
"Gorodok" [Little Town], *Novyi mir*, 1–2 (1983).
Nochevala tuchka zolotaia [A Golden Cloud Rested]. Moscow, 1988 (also contains "Soldat i mal'chik" [The Soldier and the Boy]); "Nochevala tuchka zolotaia", translated as *The Inseparable Twins*, by Michael Glenny, London, Picador, 1991.
Nochevala tuchka zolotaia. Moscow, 1988 (also contains "Ptushen'ka").
"Kukushata, ili zhalobnaia pesn' dlia uspokoeniia serdtsa" [The Cuckoos, or a Sad Song for the Calm of One's Heart], *Iunost'*, 11–12 (1989).
"Riazanka (chelovek s predmest'ia)" [Riazanka (a Person from the Suburbs)], *Znamia*, 3–4 (1991).

Other Writings
Answers to *Voprosy literatury* questionnaire, translated in *Russian Writing Today*, edited by Robin Milner-Gulland and Martin Dewhirst, Harmondsworth, Penguin, 1977, 396–97.

Critical Studies

"Sto tyshch Smirnovykh", by E. Poliakova, *Novyi mir*, 12 (1967), 239–43 (review of "Golubka").
Scenes from Soviet Life: Soviet Life Through Official Literature, by Mary Seton-Watson, London, BBC Publications, 1986.
Inside the Soviet Writers' Union, by John and Carol Garrard, London, Collier Macmillan, and New York, Free Press, 1990.
Russian Literature 1988–1994: The End of an Era, by N.N. Shneidman, Toronto, Toronto University Press, 1995.

Had it not been for his novel *Nochevala tuchka zolotaia* [A Golden Cloud Rested], translated as *The Inseparable Twins*, one of the key documents of the era of glasnost, Anatolii Pristavkin would be regarded as a very minor literary figure. It is significant that he does not rate a mention in Victor Terras's *Handbook of Russian Literature* (1985). However, at least two of his other works attracted critical attention: *Golubka* [Little Dove], published in *Znamia* in 1967, and *Gorodok* [Little Town], completed in the mid-1970s but not published until 1983 in *Novyi mir*. The title of the former, which might be translated as "little dove" or "little darling", alludes punningly both to the surname of the heroine Zhenia Golubeva and the epigraph "It is said that all hopes and renewal come into our world on the wings of a dove". The characters are involved in the building of a hydroelectric power station in Siberia. Siberia is the setting for much of Pristavkin's work, notably his *Sibirskie povesti* [Siberian Stories], *Strana Lepiia* [LEP Country], the title of which derives from an acronym for electric powerlines, and *Kostry v taige* [Bonfires in the Taiga], originally published as *Rozhdennomu zhit'* [Who is Born Must Live] in 1963.

In *Golubka* the relationship between Zhenia and her husband Viktor Smirnov gives the novel its subtitle "a novel about love". There are echoes of pre-war Soviet construction novels such as Valentin Kataev's *Vremia, vpered!* (*Time, Forward!*), although the tone of Pristavkin's descriptions is much more down-to-earth. *Gorodok* is also set in Siberia. The title, which Mary Seton-Watson renders as "The Sub-Town", refers to the settlement of private homes put up by workers building a new town. The policy of the local authorities is for the workers to live in hostels, but the hero of the novel Grigorii Shokhov and his partner Petrukha feel that the workers will only be happy if they have their own homes. Both men are rugged individualists with a belief in hard work and a pride in good workmanship. Inevitably, however, the materials for the new dwellings are filched from the main construction site, so much so that the new unofficial settlement becomes known as "Thieves' town" (*Vor-gorodok*). Ultimately the settlement is demolished at the behest of the authorities. Pristavkin's sympathies clearly lie with Shokhov and Petrukha, a fact confirmed in an interview with the journalist Igor' D'iakov in which Pristavkin asserted that the formulation "the collective is always right" was the biggest hindrance to the development of perestroika. Such a viewpoint was inadmissible in the Brezhnev era and led to the delay in publishing the novel.

Most of Pristavkin's work has a strong autobiographical element. "Ptushen'ka" (1969) is a case in point. The title, a regional form of "ptitsa" (bird), is the nickname of the story's heroine, Aleksandra Egorovna, who was once in love with the narrator's father. The narrator is clearly the young Pristavkin himself – the surname is used – and he and his father return to the Smolensk region in search of the family's ancestral home and graveyard. Ptushen'ka's harrowing wartime experiences, when she was forced to witness the torture and execution of two of her sons, partisan fighters who were betrayed to the Germans by locals, forms the main part of the story. References to pro-German Russians and to the earlier "dekulakization" of successful peasant farmers, whose prosperity stemmed from Stolypin's land reforms in the first decade of the 20th century, make this story uncomfortable reading material for Soviet literary bureaucrats. Pristavkin's heroes are often present or former inmates of children's homes, or they are people who begin work at a very early age. A good example is the novella *Soldat i mal'chik* [The Soldier and the Boy] (1977), in which the Kuz'min twins, heroes of *The Inseparable Twins*, make a brief appearance. Set during World War II, it tells how a gang of boys from a children's home rob a sleeping soldier, only for one of them, Vas'ka Smorchok, to be overcome by conscience. Pristavkin sees himself as belonging to a generation, born between 1923 and 1932, which he dubs the generation of the "era of homelessness" (*besprizorshchina*). He claims that nearly half the speakers at the meeting of the Writers' Union at which *The Inseparable Twins* was discussed were themselves former inmates of children's homes and that the only physical relic he retains from that era was a child-size knuckleduster "which could kill". However, the psychological scars remain. As Pristavkin himself puts it: "You can never tear yourself away from the children's home". The gang warfare between homes, the brutal regimes within homes and resourcefulness needed simply in order to survive, and many other aspects of life in these institutions, are recurrent themes in Pristavkin's work.

Particularly effective is their use in a number of very short stories such as "Chelovecheskii koridor" [The Human Corridor], "Portret ottsa" [A Portrait of Father] and "Mezhdu strok" [Between the Lines].

Much influenced by his teacher at the Literary Institute, the poet Lev Oshanin, Pristavkin confesses to feeling resentment towards the older generation of writers who, he claims, conspicuously failed to help his generation and left the young of the 1970s and 1980s in limbo, caught between a past cloaked in silence and a future holding no promise for them. Pristavkin's role in the literary politics of the Gorbachev era was considerable. As chief spokesman for the "April Committee", an independent pressure group within the Russian Federation branch of the Writers' Union, he attacked the union for its lack of democratic procedures, its lack of accountability in the handling of its *Litfond* (a fund used mainly to sponsor compliant writers) and its silence about its role in the Stalin and Brezhnev eras. In an interview in August 1989 Pristavkin made it clear that he and his fellow "writers for perestroika" were not attempting to abolish the union but rather to reform it from within.

MICHAEL PURSGLOVE

The Inseparable Twins

Nochevala tuchka zolotaia

Short novel, 1988

This short novel by Anatolii Pristavkin is set in 1944. Dated 1981 by the author, it was not published until 1987 in *Znamia* and in book form the following year. The title, the opening line of Lermontov's lyric "Utes" [The Cliff], is referred to several times in the novel, most importantly in chapter 28 when the inseparable twin boys Sashka and Kol'ka Kuz'min (referred to throughout the novel as "the little Kuzmins" – Kuzmenyshi) are separated by Chechen fighters, who murder Sashka. In his grief Kol'ka recalls the one poem he has learned in his orphanage and sees Sashka as the cloud and himself as the grieving cliff that laments the loss of the cloud. The poem also alludes to a recurrent image in the novel, that of the Caucasus mountains, to where the twins have been evacuated. From the "colony" of orphaned children where they live and the jam factory where they work they can see the mountains that come to represent for them the hope of escape to a better life. When, however, after the murder of his brother, Kol'ka finally reaches the mountains in the company of his new "brother", a Chechen boy, they are in a dangerous place, fought over by Soviet troops and Chechen fighters defending their homeland. From the Soviet point of view these fighters are traitors who have sided with Hitler. The retribution exacted by Stalin – the deportation of the entire Chechen people – is viewed through the uncomprehending eyes of the twins. What they see is a guarded train with incomprehensible cries coming from the wagons. Only later does Kol'ka realize that the incomprehensible words are the Chechen word for "water". There are veiled references, too, to Stalin's deportation of other nations when Kol'ka and his Chechen "brother" find themselves in an orphanage alongside a Crimean Tartar child and a Volga German. When Kol'ka's benefactress Regina Petrovna comes to rescue them, she is harshly interrogated by a military official and a civilian who clearly belong to the security organs. They represent the harsh, uncaring face of Stalin's Russia and their actions are contrasted with the kindness of Regina Petrovna, of the orphanage director, who is herself of German descent and of the Russian soldier who rescues Kol'ka and his "brother" when they are on the brink of starvation.

It was the political dimension of the novel that accounted both for the delay in publication and for its success as one of the major works of the era of glasnost. The novel, however, has a more enduring charm. Although the narrative is almost exclusively third-person, the world-view and the language, much of it contained in dialogues, is almost exclusively that of the twins and their fellow orphans who inhabit a world familiar to Pristavkin. So racy is their language that explanations of some of the more obscure words and expressions are given. All the devices of *skaz* are to be found, from folk etymology (the name of the orphanage – Tomilino – is transformed, with a certain aptness, into Tomitel'noe – "Agonizing") to mispronunciation, notably by the "conjurer", who reduces all sibilants to "sh" and the widespread use of non-standard diminutives and other vulgarisms. At one point the master of *skaz*, Mikhail Zoshchenko, is indirectly referred to when the children stage a version of his famous story "Kocherga" [The Poker]. The resourcefulness and resilience of these children, known in Russian as *besprizornye*, gives rise to some richly comic scenes, particularly when, inspired by the twins' example, they organize a massive pilfering operation at the jam factory. Attempts at retribution by the man in charge of the children, the hapless Petr Anisimovich, are foiled when an incriminating document is removed from his ever-present briefcase during a conjuring trick by Mitek, the star turn of the concert given by the "colony" to placate the locals. Further comedy is derived from the fact that the twins are virtually indistinguishable and often assume each other's identity. Even Regina Petrovna, who becomes like a mother to them, cannot tell them apart and her "Who is who?", said in English but spelled in Cyrillic, becomes a comic refrain in the novel. Only Zina, the ill-educated supervisor at the jam factory can distinguish them but Pristavkin himself is at pains to do so. Although they sometimes seem to be one person inhabiting two bodies, Sashka is the "head" (*golova*) while Kol'ka is the "leg" (*noga*), or, as he puts it in the racy slang that is a feature of the writing, "not such an egghead" as his brother. The tragic irony is that the brainy "head" is captured and killed while Kol'ka, displaying considerable native wit, escapes capture and survives. Tragedy and comedy are never far apart in the novel. The comic concert is followed by a scene in which the Chechens attack the town and kill any Russian they meet; Zina's vocabulary is comic (she uses "dvoiniashki" for "twins", a word the twins themselves have never heard before) but her life story is tragic: her daughter and mentally ill sister have been raped by the Germans and then branded traitors for consorting with them.

Pristavkin's novel is given historical perspective by a small number of passages written in the first person. The majority of these appear to be written from the point of view of an inmate of the orphanage, but chapter 30 is written from the point of view of the adult Kol'ka. One first-person passage, in chapter 3, is clearly an authorial statement. In it the author says he has been a published author for 25 years and has repeatedly returned to the theme of orphans in wartime. He laments that he has had no reply and describes this novel as probably his "last cry in the wilderness". Now that events in Chechnia in the 1990s have given additional topicality to the novel, Pristavkin may at last get his answer.

MICHAEL PURSGLOVE

Koz'ma Petrovich Prutkov 1803–1863

Fictitious poet and prose writer

Biography

Fictitious writer created by A.K. Tolstoi (1817–75), and his cousins, Aleksei Zhemchuzhnikov (1821–1908), Aleksandr Zhemchuzhnikov (1826–96), and Vladimir Zhemchuznikov (1830–84). Prutkov's fictitious biography is as follows: Born in St Petersburg, 11 April 1803. Joined the Hussars, 1820, only for the dress uniform. Appointed to the Assay Office of the Ministry of Finance as a civil servant in 1823. Remained in its employ, finally becoming Director, until his death. Recipient: Order of St Stanislav of the First Degree. Married: Antonina Platonovna Proklevetanova in 1828; four daughters and six sons. Literary career began under a pseudonym in 1850. Published under his own name from 1854 onwards. Died 13 January 1863.

Publications

Collected Editions

Polnoe sobranie sochinenii. St Petersburg, 1884.
Polnoe sobranie sochinenii. Moscow, 1949.
Sochineniia Koz'my Prutkova. Leningrad and Moscow, 1965.
Sochineniia. Moscow, 1981.

Poetry

"Twenty Translations from Koz'ma Prutkov", appendix to *Koz'ma Prutkov: The Art of Parody*, translated by Barbara Heldt Monter. The Hague, Mouton, 1972, 121–38.

Prose

"Proekt: o vvedenii edinomysliia v Rossii", *Sovremennik*, 4 (1863); translated in "Project: Towards Creating Uniformity of Opinion in Russia. The Fruits of Meditation: Thoughts and Aphorisms", by L. Senelick, *Russian Literature Triquarterly*, 14 (1976), 297–301.

Plays

Fantaziia. (produced 1851).
Blondy [Silk Lace]. (produced 1852).
Oprometchivyi Turka [The Reckless Turk]. (produced 1854).

Critical Studies

Koz'ma Prutkov – direktor Probirnoi palatki i poet. K istorii russkoi parodii, by P.N. Berkov, Leningrad and Moscow, 1933.
Iazyk i stil' parodii Koz'my Prutkova: Leksiko-stilisticheskii analiz, by I.M. Sukiasova, Tbilisi, 1961.
"Koz'ma Prutkov is More 'Alive' than Ever", by Frank Ingram, *Russian Language Journal*, 91 (1971), 3–9.
Koz'ma Prutkov: The Art of Parody, by Barbara Heldt Monter, The Hague, Mouton, 1972.
Koz'ma Prutkov i ego druz'ia, by D.A. Zhukov, Moscow, 1976; 2nd edition, 1983.
"Koz'ma Prutkov: The Dean of Russian Burlesque Satire", by Frank Ingram, in *Russian Language Journal*, 119 (1980), 67–88.

Koz'ma Prutkov, the fictitious writer and bureaucrat invented in 1852 by Aleksei Tolstoi and his cousins the Zhemchuzhnikov brothers, is one of Russia's most humorous literary creations. Invented during the stifling reaction of Nicholas I's final years as tsar, Prutkov provided his authors with a way of amusing themselves and others in an otherwise gloomy time, as well as giving them the possibility of parodying both the works of their peers and, more generally, the writing of literature and their society as a whole, without, it should be stressed, any ultimate polemical purpose. "Author" of a wide variety of plays, poems, sayings and anecdotes, Prutkov is best remembered, however, for his absurd aphorisms, many of which immediately entered the Russian language and have retained their popularity to this day.

The irony of Prutkov's personality, containing the peculiar combination of romantic artist and dedicated civil servant, clearly owes a debt to his French prototype, Joseph Prudhomme, created in 1830 by Henri Monnier, satirist of the French bourgeoisie, while his name is also partly inspired by that of the Zhemchuzhnikovs' valet Kuz'ma Frolov. As well as a ribald sense of humour, Tolstoi and the Zhemchuzhnikovs, particularly Aleksandr, shared with Monnier a penchant for practical jokes, which is how Prutkov initially came into being, after a successsion of summers spent concocting literary pranks at the family estate. The production of works under the name of Prutkov was not actually the cousins' first collaborative enterprise; the creation of the personage of Koz'ma Prutkov in fact came significantly after the composition of works that were later attributed to his authorship. Thus some of Prutkov's works were performed on stage and published before their author had even been invented. It was only in 1854, when signed pieces started to appear in the literary journals to which the cousins submitted the fruits of their efforts, that Prutkov began to emerge as a visible literary presence.

The first canonical Prutkov work, a farcical comedy about a

pug dog called *Fantaziia* was written in 1850 by Aleksei Zhemchuzhnikov and Aleksei Tolstoi, with the participation of Vladimir Zhemchuzhnikov, who contributed the ending. An irreverent parody of contemporary vaudeville, it shocked its first night audience when it was produced in January 1851 at the Aleksandrinskii Theatre in the presence of Nicholas I and was promptly banned from further performances. Before walking out, the humourless tsar was apparently particularly offended by the "small interlude" in the middle of the comedy featuring the pug dog running across the stage, followed, to the accompaniment of a tune from *The Barber of Seville*, by a bull dog "sniffing its traces". It was after the Zhemchuzhnikov brothers published three parodies of didactic fables the following year that they began to discuss with Tolstoi the idea of writing in a variety of genres under one name. The sheer incongruity in their eyes of creating someone who was a self-righteous, pompous bureaucrat and loyal subject of Nicholas I *and* a poet meant that the personality of Koz'ma Prutkov was comic from the start, and the humour only increased when the fictitious author started producing pretentious but utterly banal poetry and prose. Works signed by Prutkov began to appear in *Sovremennik* and other monthly journals that published parodies and humorous verse from 1854 onwards, and were widely imitated. Prutkov's last piece in *Sovremennik* (which published approximately half of his writings) appeared in 1863, the year of his "death", but Aleksandr Zhemchuzhnikov persisted in publishing "non-canonical" posthumous works for many years afterwards. Although it was generally realized that Prutkov was a piece of literary mystification, the true identity of his literary "guardians", as Tolstoi and the Zhemchuzhnikovs liked to see themselves, remained concealed until 1884, the year that his Collected Works were published.

The impressive stylistic unity of Prutkov's writings is testament to the fact that this was a truly collaborative exercise, for it is difficult to establish the exact authorship of each work. Of the four collaborators, only two of them actually saw themselves as writers, and only Aleksei Tolstoi enjoyed a literary career in his own right (and was indeed the author of humorous writings under his own name). Aleksei Zhemchuzhnikov started publishing the poetry he had been writing all his life in the 1870s after retiring from government service, but was far more successful as a contributor to Prutkov than as a serious poet himself. It was the youngest Zhemchuzhnikov brother Vladimir who seems to have contributed most to Prutkov's literary *oeuvre*. A civil servant like Tolstoi and his brothers, Vladimir devoted his leisure time to editing Prutkov's writings in preparation for the Collected Works (hilariously adding the censor's remarks as footnotes in the case of *Fantaziia*, for example). The final manuscript contained all hitherto published writings and a few new items, plus various biographical documents written by Vladimir specially for the occasion, which reveal the self-satisfied, vain and philistine bureaucrat in all his glory.

Convinced of his talent as a poet purely on the basis of having read the works of others, Prutkov supposedly wrote in the style of his contemporaries, while his verses were in reality a satire of their works. Full of hackneyed romantic clichés and spectacularly tasteless images, Prutkov's poetry parodies the work of writers such as Benediktov, Fet, and Khomiakov. But while many of Prutkov's works (such as his plays) are parodic treatments of popular genres, much of his writing is pure nonsense, and with hindsight it can be seen today that the alogical, surreal literature produced by Daniil Kharms and his fellow *oberiuty* had an important 19th-century antecedent. Thus Prutkov's fables not only lack the customary moral at their conclusion but are totally senseless, his children's alphabet begins nonsensically with "Anton is leading the goat" as a mnemonic for the letter "A", and his famous aphorisms, satires on hoary old proverbs, are preposterous in their complete obviousness and fatuity ("No one can embrace the unembraceable", "Be vigilant!", "Many people are like sausages: the things used to stuff them they have inside themselves", "Buy a picture first, then the frame!").

ROSAMUND BARTLETT

Aleksandr Sergeevich Pushkin 1799–1837

Poet and prose writer

Biography

Born in Moscow, 6 June 1799. Entrusted to nursemaids, French tutors and governesses; learned Russian from household serfs and nanny, Arina Rodionovna. Attended the new *lycée* of Tsarskoe Selo, near St Petersburg, 1811–17. Held an undemanding government post in St Petersburg, and led a dissipated life, 1817–20; tenuous connections with revolutionary-minded young people. Some unpublishable political poems circulated in manuscript: exiled because of them to the south of Russia, thence to Kishinev, 1820. Transferred to Odessa, 1823. Returned north for two further years of exile at parents' estate of Mikhailovskoe, 1824. Released, 1826, but with the tsar, Nicholas I, as his personal censor; returned to dissipated lifestyle. Four-month visit to Transcaucasia, including action with Russian Army against the Turks, 1829. Visited another family estate, Boldino, 1830; stranded by cholera for three months, very productive literary period. Married: Natal'ia Goncharova in 1831. Travelled east to the Urals for historical research, 1833; also a second "Boldino autumn". Unhappy period in St Petersburg, 1833–36:

humiliation in court circles, mounting debts, worries about his wife's possible infidelity. Goaded by scandalous rumours into a duel with Georges D'Anthès, adopted son of Dutch Ambassador; fatally wounded, died 10 February 1837.

Publications

Collected Editions

The Poems, Prose and Plays of Pushkin, edited by Avrahm Yarmolinsky. New York, Random House, 1936.

Polnoe sobranie sochinenii, 17 vols. Moscow and Leningrad, 1937–49; reprinted Moscow, 1994-

Polnoe sobranie sochinenii, 10 vols. Moscow and Leningrad, 1949; 2nd edition, 1956–58.

Selected Verse with Introduction and Prose Translations, translated by John Fennell. Harmondsworth, Penguin, 1964; reprinted Bristol, Bristol Classical Press, 1991.

Complete Prose Tales of Alexander Sergeyevitch Pushkin, translated by Gillon R. Aitken. New York, Norton, 1967; revised edition Salisbury, Michael Russell, 1978.

Pushkin Threefold: Narrative, Lyric, Polemic and Ribald Verse, translated by Walter Arndt. New York, Dutton, 1972.

Complete Prose Fiction, edited and translated by Paul Debreczeny. Stanford, Stanford University Press, 1983.

Epigrams and Satirical Verse, edited and translated by Cynthia Whittaker. Ann Arbor, Ardis, 1984.

Collected Narrative and Lyrical Poetry, translated by Walter Arndt. Ann Arbor, Ardis, 1984.

The Queen of Spades and Other Stories, edited by Andrew Kahn and translated by Alan Myers. Oxford, Oxford University Press, 1997.

Poetry

Ruslan i Liudmila. St Petersburg, 1820; translated as *Ruslan and Liudmila*, by Walter Arndt, Ann Arbor, Ardis, 1974.

Kavkazskii plennik. St Petersburg, 1822; translated as "The Prisoner in the Caucasus", by Jacob Krup, in *Six Poems from Pushkin*, New York, Galleon Press, 1936.

Bakhchisaraiskii fontan. Moscow, 1824; translated as "The Fountain of Bakhchisaray", by Walter Arndt, in *Collected Narrative and Lyrical Poetry*, 1984.

Tsygany. Moscow, 1827; translated as "The Gypsies", by Walter Arndt, in *Collected Narrative and Lyrical Poetry*, 1984.

Graf Nulin. St Petersburg, 1828; translated as "Count Nulin", by Walter Arndt, in *Collected Narrative and Lyrical Poetry*, 1984.

Poltava. St Petersburg, 1829; translated as "Poltava", by Jacob Krup, in *Six Poems from Pushkin*, 1936; and by Walter Arndt, in *Collected Narrative and Lyrical Poetry*, 1984.

Evgenii Onegin. St Petersburg, 1833; translated as *Evgeny Onegin*, by Oliver Elton, London, Pushkin Press, 1937; revised as *Yevgeny Onegin*, by A.D.P. Briggs, London, Everyman, 1995; and by Walter Arndt, New York, Dutton, 1963; 2nd edition, 1981; also as *Eugene Onegin: A Novel in Verse*, by Vladimir Nabokov, 4 vols, New York, Bollingen, 1964; revised edition Princeton, Princeton University Press, 1975; as *Eugene Onegin*, by Charles Johnston, Ilkley, Scolar Press, 1977; New York, Viking, 1978; Harmondsworth, Penguin, 1979; and by James E. Falen, Oxford, Oxford University Press, 1995.

Mednyi vsadnik. St Petersburg, 1841; translated as "The Bronze Horseman", by D.M. Thomas, in *The Bronze Horseman: Selected Poems of Alexander Pushkin*, New York, Viking, 1981; Harmondsworth, Penguin, 1982.

Fiction

Povesti Belkina. St Petersburg, 1831; translated as *The Tales of Belkin*, by Gillon R. Aitken and David Budgen, London, Angel, 1983; also translated by Alan Myers in *The Queen of Spades and Other Stories*, Oxford, Oxford University Press, 1997.

Pikovaia dama, in *Biblioteka dlia chteniia* (1834); translated as "The Queen of Spades", by Rosemary Edmonds, in *The Queen of Spades and Other Stories*, Harmondsworth, Penguin, 1962; also translated by Alan Myers in *The Queen of Spades and Other Stories*, Oxford, Oxford University Press, 1997.

Kapitanskaia dochka, in *Sovremennik*, 4 (1836); translated as "The Captain's Daughter", by Rosemary Edmonds, in *The Queen of Spades and Other Stories*, Harmondsworth, Penguin, 1962; also translated by Alan Myers in *The Queen of Spades and Other Stories*, Oxford, Oxford University Press, 1997.

Travel Writing

Puteshestvie v Arzrum, in *Sovremennik*, 1 (1836); translated as *A Journey to Arzrum*, by Birgitta Ingemanson, Ann Arbor, Ardis, 1974.

Plays

Boris Godunov. St Petersburg, 1831; translated as *Boris Godounov*, by Alfred Hayes, London, Trench Trübner, and New York, Dutton, 1918; reprinted London, Allen Lane, 1982; also as *Boris Godunov*, Russian text with translation and notes by Philip L. Barbour, New York, Columbia University Press, and Oxford, Oxford University Press, 1953; reprinted Westport, Connecticut, Greenwood Press, 1976; also translated by D.M. Thomas, Leamington Spa, Warwickshire, Sixth Chamber Press, 1985; and by Nicholas Rzhevsky, Armonk, New York, M.E. Sharpe, 1997.

Malen'kie tragedii, (written 1830); translated as *Mozart and Salieri: The Little Tragedies*, by Antony Wood, London, Angel, 1983.

Historical Writing

Istoriia Pugacheva. 1833; St Petersburg, 1834; translated as *The History of Pugachev*, by Earl Sampson, Ann Arbor, Ardis, 1983.

Letters and Diaries

The Letters of Alexander Pushkin, edited and translated by J. Thomas Shaw, 3 vols. Bloomington, Indiana University Press, 1963; reprinted in 1 vol., Madison, University of Wisconsin Press, 1967.

Dnevniki. Zapiski [Diaries. Memoirs]. St Petersburg, 1995.

Literary Criticism

Pushkin on Literature, edited and translated by Tatiana Wolff. London, Athlone Press, 1971; revised edition London, Athlone Press, and Stanford, Stanford University Press, 1986.

Critical Studies

Pushkin, by D.S. Mirsky, London, Routledge, 1926; reprinted New York, Dutton, 1963.

Pushkin and Russian Literature, by Janko Lavrin, London, Hodder and Stoughton, 1947.

Pushkin's "Bronze Horseman": The Story of a Masterpiece, by Waclaw Lednicki, Berkeley, University of California Press, 1955.

Pushkin, by Ernest Simmons, New York, Random House, 1964.

Pushkin, by David Magarshack, New York, Grove Press, and London, Chapman and Hall, 1967.

Pushkin: Death of a Poet, by Walter Vickery, Bloomington, Indiana University Press, 1968.

Alexander Pushkin, by Walter Vickery, New York, Twayne, 1970; revised edition, 1992.

Pushkin: A Comparative Commentary, by John Bayley, Cambridge, Cambridge University Press, 1971.

Puškin and His Sculptural Myth, by Roman Jakobson, The Hague, Mouton, 1975; first published in Czech in 1937; reprinted as "The Statue in Puškin's Poetic Mythology", in Jakobson's *Language in Literature*, edited by Krystyna Pomorska and Stephen Rudy, Cambridge, Massachusetts, and London, Belknap Press of Harvard University Press, 1987.

Progulki s Pushkinym, by Abram Terts (A. Siniavskii), London, Overseas Publications Interchange, 1975; St Petersburg, 1993; translated as *Strolls with Pushkin*, by Catherine Theimer Nepomnyashchy and Slava I. Yastremski, New Haven, Yale University Press, 1993.

Alexander Puškin: A Symposium, edited by Andrej Kodjak and Kiril Taranovsky, New York, New York University Press, 1976.

Russian Views of Pushkin, edited and translated by D. Richards and R. Cockrell, Oxford, Meeuws, 1976.

Pushkin's I.P. Belkin, by Andrej Kodjak, Columbus, Ohio, Slavica, 1979.

Alexander Puškin: Symposium II, edited by Andrej Kodjak, Krystyna Pomorska, and Kiril Taranovsky, Columbus, Ohio, Slavica, 1980.

Alexander Pushkin: A Critical Study, by A.D.P. Briggs, London, Croom Helm, 1983; reprinted, Bristol, Bristol Classical Press, 1991.

The Other Pushkin: A Study of Alexander Pushkin's Prose Fiction, by Paul Debreczeny, Stanford, Stanford University Press, 1983.

Pushkin's Prose, by Abram Lezhnev, translated by Roberta Reeder, Ann Arbor, Ardis, 1983.

Pushkin's "Egyptian Nights": The Biography of a Work, by Leslie O'Bell, Ann Arbor, Ardis, 1984.

Ice and Flame: Alexander Pushkin's "Eugene Onegin", by J. Douglas Clayton, Toronto, University of Toronto Press, 1985.

Pushkin: A Concordance to the Poetry, by J. Thomas Shaw, 2 vols, Columbus, Ohio, Slavica, 1985.

A History of Russian Literature of the Romantic Period, by William Edward Brown, vol. 3, Ann Arbor, Ardis, 1986.

Fiction and Society in the Age of Pushkin, by William Mills Todd III, Cambridge, Massachusetts, Harvard University Press, 1986.

Alexander Pushkin, edited by Harold Bloom, New York, Chelsea House, 1987.

Russian Views of Pushkin's "Eugene Onegin", edited by Sona Stephan Hoizington, Bloomington, Indiana University Press, 1988.

Distant Pleasures: Aleksandr Pushkin and the Writing of Exile, by Stephanie Sandler, Stanford, Stanford University Press, 1989.

Eugene Onegin, by A.D.P. Briggs, Cambridge, Cambridge University Press, 1992.

Pushkin Today, edited by David M. Bethea, Bloomington, Indiana University Press, 1993.

Pushkin's "The Queen of Spades", by Neil Cornwell, London, Bristol Classical Press, 1993.

Pushkin, by Robin Edmonds, London, Macmillan, 1994.

Pushkin and Romantic Fashion: Fragment, Elegy, Orient, Irony, by Monika Greenleaf, Stanford, Stanford University Press, 1994.

The Esoteric Tradition in Russian Romantic Literature: Decembrism and Freemasonry, by Lauren G. Leighton, University Park, Pennsylvania State University Press, 1994.

Pushkin's Poetics of the Unexpected: The Nonrhymed Lines in the Rhymed Poetry and the Rhymed Lines in the Nonrhymed Poetry, by J. Thomas Shaw, Columbus, Ohio, Slavica, 1994.

Pushkin, by Iurii Lotman, St Petersburg, 1995.

Pushkin's "Mozart and Salieri": Themes and Psychology, by Robert Reid, Amsterdam, Rodopi, 1995.

Pushkin's "Evgenii Onegin", by S. Dalton-Brown, London, Bristol Classical Press, 1996.

Poetika romana A.S. Pushkina "Evgenii Onegin", by V.N. Turbin, Moscow, 1996.

Pushkin Poems: And Other Studies, by J. Thomas Shaw, Los Angeles, Schlacks, 1996.

Social Functions of Literature: Alexander Pushkin and Russian Culture, by Paul Debreczeny, Stanford, Stanford University Press, 1997.

Bibliographies

Pushkiniana 1900–10. Leningrad, 1929.

Pushkiniana 1911–17. Leningrad, 1937.

Bibliografiia proizvedenii A.S. Pushkina i literatury o nem, 1886–99, Moscow and Leningrad, 1949.

Bibliografiia proizvedenii A.S. Pushkina i literatury o nem. Parts I–VII: 1918–57. Moscow and Leningrad, 1952–60.

"Alexander Pushkin: A Bibliography of Criticism in English: 1920–75", by P.J. and A.I. Wreath, in *Canadian-American Slavic Studies, Special Edition, Pushkin (1)*, (Summer 1976), 279–304.

Universally acknowledged as Russia's greatest poet, Aleksandr Pushkin set the standards and provided models that have formed and directed the national literature ever since his death. Although he died at the age of 37, he left a prolific legacy extending over many genres, with a masterpiece in each of them, and even creating new genres. His lyric and narrative poetry, drama, novels in verse and prose, stories, historical and critical articles, along with his collected letters, comprise the richest single treasure-house in Russian culture.

It is in poetry that Pushkin achieved most, not only creating dozens of lyrics and narratives that are recalled lovingly from memory by all Russian-speakers, but actually changing the Russian language itself. Pushkin brought together all the scattered linguistic potential bequeathed by his predecessors. In his works grand and sonorous Old Slavonic blends into rough vernacular Russian and the two native languages become modernized and civilized by graceful Gallic sensitivity. At the same time the natural flow of everyday language accommodates itself to the hidden rules of literature; vocabulary, syntax, and word order are, as never before in Russian letters, allowed to remain normal and unconstrained. This ability to assimilate and adapt Pushkin applied also to the world's literature, which he knew well and read with remarkable critical discrimination. Examples abound of Pushkin's flirtation with literary models only for him to subvert, parody, improve on or transcend the original; Ovid, Voltaire, Shakespeare, Sterne, Byron, and Scott are only the best-known examples. For all their apparent straightforwardness, Pushkin's writings are very demanding; only an educated and sensitive reader can appreciate the hidden literary subtleties, jokes, and frequent irony.

More than 800 lyrics came from Pushkin's pen, together with a dozen narrative poems. Fairly conventional in form (with a preponderance of the iambic tetrameter, commonly in rhymed quatrains), this poetry is consistent in its rich exploitation of the lovely sounds that characterize the Russian language. Pushkin is famed for the subtle persuasiveness of his assonance and alliteration. His themes are manifold; predominant among them are both the enchantment and travail of love, the proud isolation and responsibility of the poet, the elusiveness of happiness, the loveliness of autumn and winter, and the preciousness of human freedom. His narratives show a clear line of development. *Ruslan i Liudmila* (*Ruslan and Liudmila*) was the first landmark in the poet's career, selling well and making his name. It was, nevertheless, a false start, a kind of fairy story in verse with some thinly-hidden eroticism, impressively fluent and agreeable, but too extensive (with six cantos running to nearly 9,000 lines of verse) and lacking any real point. Under Byron's influence, Pushkin then wrote four exotic "Southern" narratives, the best of which are *Kavkazskii plennik* (*The Prisoner in the Caucasus*) and *Tsygany* (*The Gypsies*). The latter already shows a sharpening of technique; vagueness and relative prolixity (though never anything like that of Byron) give way to greater clarity and conciseness, two qualities that would develop further as the poet matured. If we set aside the disappointing *Poltava*, an excursion into a historical theme (Peter the Great's defeat of Charles XII of Sweden) with a love story inadequately infused into it, Pushkin achieved two unalloyed masterpieces in *Graf Nulin* (*Count Nulin*), a delightful anecdote of flirtation and attempted seduction, which began as a parody of Shakespeare, and *Mednyi vsadnik* (*The Bronze Horseman*), one of his finest achievements, which unites a sense of history and politics with human interest while subtly intimating that our worst fears should centre on malevolent destiny expressing itself through the forces of nature. Pushkin's greatest work, however, is undoubtedly his novel in verse, *Evgenii Onegin*, the fullest expression of all his redoubtable poetic gifts; the unhappy love story of Evgenii Onegin and Tat'iana Larina, and the death of young Lenskii in a duel, are told in 365 enchanting stanzas, an irresistible source of inspiration for Tchaikovskii's well-loved opera.

In drama Pushkin was less successful. His Shakepeare-style history play, *Boris Godunov*, also well known in operatic adaptation (by Musorgskii), contains magnificent poetry but is deemed to lack unity because of its many disparate scenes and characters. (This deficiency has been unnecessarily exaggerated; the play is certainly stageable). *Malen'kie tragedii* (*The Little Tragedies*), brief studies in monomania including the well-known "Motsart i Sal'eri" ("Mozart and Salieri"), although again containing truly memorable verses, cannot be staged successfully because of their brevity and excessive concentration of character and incident.

Pushkin turned mainly to prose in the last years of his life. His historical novel, *Kapitanskaia dochka* (*The Captain's Daughter*), breaks new ground by intermingling real-life and fictional characters and events, and by covering the broadest possible social range from tsarina to servant, but it lacks the solid substantiation expected of the genre. Even more lightweight are his *Povesti Belkina* (*The Tales of Belkin*), a set of amusing anecdotes best read as parodies. Despite such shortcomings, however, the language used in these works is exquisite in its neatness, exactitude, and poetic expressiveness. Pushkin's finest qualities are brought together in his prose *chef d'oeuvre*, *Pikovaia dama* (*The Queen of Spades*), a perfect tale of the supernatural. It provided the source material for yet another famous opera, once again by Tchaikovskii. Pushkin's voluminous literary criticism, and his collected correspondence, remain a delight to read, remarkable acumen combining with enthusiasm, intelligence, good sense, wit, and amusement.

Pushkin is rightly compared to Mozart: the two artists are alike in their instinctively classical spirit that guarantees formal perfection (apparently, but not actually, effortless), spontaneous flow of melodic inventiveness, ostensible simplicity (which in reality hides amazing intricacy), the paradoxical sense of lightness and carefree enjoyment that intermixes painfully with human misery, and an insouciant manner that pretends only to light entertainment but touches more often than not on seriousness and sometimes tragedy.

A.D.P. Briggs

The Gypsies

Tsygany

Narrative poem, 1827 (written 1824)

Early in his career, during the period 1820–24, the heyday of Byronism in Russia, Pushkin wrote four narrative poems (one unfinished), collectively known as his "Southern poems" by analogy with Byron's popular and modish "Eastern" ones. The last of these is *The Gypsies*, a poem that completes Pushkin's movement away from Byron by reducing to a minimum the vagueness, artificiality, self-conscious exoticism, and (by the Russian poet's demanding standards) unnecessary loquacity of the first three. This poem is a good example of transitional art, displaying some of the residual shortcomings of the immature poet as well as many of the fine qualities that would one day produce masterpieces in this genre such as *Count Nulin* and *The Bronze Horseman*.

The story concerns Aleko, a fugitive from some kind of legal or political persecution, who joins up (as Pushkin himself once did in Moldavia) with a troupe of gypsies. He wins the affection of Zemfira and for two years they live happily together; she bears him a child. However, reverting to type, Zemfira finds that she cannot maintain Aleko's alien standards of connubial fidelity. She cannot resist taking a gypsy lover. Aleko's suspicion and jealousy mount steadily, unmitigated by the persuasive stories of Zemfira's old father who will have no truck with revenge or violence even though he was once cruelly betrayed by her mother, Mariula. Surprising the two gypsy lovers together, Aleko stabs them both to death. For this, his only punishment is banishment from the gypsy camp. We leave him as a lonely, now doubly alienated figure, abandoned in the wilderness.

Brevity and formal variety are the hallmarks of this poem. Well under 600 lines long, it consists of ten separate, unnumbered, sections, and an epilogue. Perhaps the sections should be described as scenes, since they include much dialogue, sometimes even accompanied by what look like stage directions, and a couple of songs. These latter depart from the standard iambic tetrameter, in which virtually all of Pushkin's narrative poetry (including *Evgenii Onegin*) is written, by using trochaic and even anapaestic feet (the latter deriving from a Moldavian folk-song). This imaginative updating of narrative poetry in formal terms, together with the sharp accuracy and aptness of Pushkin's language, underwrite the poem's success; it is dramatic, colourful, and always interesting, in both its story-line and its ideas, despite some overstatement of the latter. Except for the odd poetic archaism (such as "Leave, children, your couch of bliss ... "), there are no serious lapses or longueurs.

In Aleko we have Pushkin's response to the traditional Romantic hero, alienated, idealistic, and in search of happiness through absolute freedom. At the time of writing the author was much concerned with questions of personal freedom; he was part-way through a six-year period of exile in one form or another. Pushkin's personal involvement is emphasized by the fact that "Aleko" is a form of his own name and that in the epilogue to this poem he confirms his first-hand experience of gypsy life. The hero of *The Gypsies* is shown to be utterly self-centred, serving no generalized principle of liberty but seeking freedom only for himself. So much for personal idealism. But Pushkin's gypsies (who are not much like real gypsies despite his knowledge of them) are little better in this respect. Zemfira's ready infidelity and indifference to Aleko's suffering have been foreshadowed by her own mother's behaviour in abandoning her baby girl at a moment's notice to follow the demands of passion, with no thought for the unhappiness she was causing. Her father has ended up no less miserable than Aleko, except that he is more passive and fatalistic. Freedom and happiness are shown in this poem to be quite unlike the positive aspirations of earlier romantic dreamers; they are so elusive and short-lived as to be impossible of realization anywhere. The idea that one can run away from corruption and misery is thus entirely debunked. These themes, linked as they are with the ever-present idea of pursuit by a malevolent destiny, are handled with consistency, and their pessimism is perhaps understandable in one who was never to discover freedom or happiness for himself. Less forgivable, in artistic terms, is the obviousness of the ideas expressed. The words "free" and "freedom" crop up dozens of times in the poem, hardly a subtle exposition of the concept of liberty. It is by this deficiency that the astonishing achievement of *The Bronze Horseman*, with its density and understatement, can be measured.

The quality of *The Gypsies* derives not only from the characters and ideas but equally from the poetry, style, and construction of the poem. The beginning and the end are superbly done. As if in anticipation of Eisenstein's magnificent cinematography, the angle of vision swoops down on the encamping gypsies at the outset and soars away at the conclusion, from bird's eye view to intimate involvement and back again. These set pieces are equalled in quality by others, such as the detailed depictions of gypsy life (even if somewhat idealized), the enchanting song of the carefree bird, the old man's story of Ovid in exile, the taunting song of Zemfira and the wonderfully tense scene of confrontation, insult, and resentment in which it appears.

Recent research has shown that Bizet's famous opera, *Carmen*, derives directly from this poem. Prosper Mérimée, the author of the story *Carmen*, revered Pushkin and published a prose translation of this poem under the title *Les Bohémiens*. The story itself probably derives in part from Pushkin; certainly the librettists, including Bizet himself, used not only Mérimée's tale but also the text of *Les Bohémiens* for the book of the opera. The scene-stealing Escamillo and the bull-fighting may have been added, but the main characters, Don José and Carmen, clearly have their origins in Aleko and Zemfira, as does her death by the dagger.

A.D.P. BRIGGS

The Little Tragedies

Malen'kie tragedii

Group of plays, written 1830

The Little Tragedies were part of the group of plays that Pushkin was planning to write in 1827; yet only four plays were eventually written in autumn 1830, in Boldino. Pushkin defined his work as dramatic scenes (initially they were titled dramatic investigations), and they represent an epitomized study of human psychology. There is a conflict at the heart of each play that brings a tragic twist to the plot. The titles of the tragedies suggest a conflict, concealing an oxymoron: "Skupoi rytsar'" ("The Avaricious Knight"), "Motsart i Sal'eri" ("Mozart and Salieri"), "Kamennyi gost'" ("The Stone Guest"), "Pir vo vremia chumy" ("The Feast During the Plague"). Only one of the plays, "Mozart and Salieri", was performed during Pushkin's lifetime. It is generally felt that these plays are for reading rather than staging since they are too condensed and poetic for the theatre. Briusov, for example, observed that: "Pushkin gave in his dramas the elixir of poetry". The form of the diminutive tragedy was borrowed from Barry Cornwall, whom Pushkin greatly admired.

"The Avaricious Knight" was written in October 1830 and published subsequently in April 1836 in the journal *Sovremennik*, under the pseudonym "R". The play was to be staged in the Akeksandrinskii Theatre in 1837, but because of Pushkin's death the authorities banned it, fearing that it could provoke political unrest. Pushkin's play bears the subtitle "Scenes from the tragi-comedy 'The Covetous Knight' by Shenstone", but that was pure mystification: William Shenstone (1714–63) wrote no such play. The most probable motive for such deliberate confusion is Pushkin's desire to disguise the autobiographical elements: his father was a notorious miser, and the play deals with the conflict between a miserly father and his covetous son. Both father and son share a love of money as a means to power. The Baron and Albert are on the point of duelling, but are prevented by the Duke at the end. The short three-act play concludes with the Baron's unexpected death from natural causes. Yet tension is achieved by the symbolic duel fought throughout the play by the two antagonists. Each desires the death of the other: the son is worried that the father might outlive him, and the Baron hates to think that his son "would steal the keys from his corpse" and "would open the chests with a laugh" (the Baron's treasure is hidden in chests in the cellar). The highlight of the play is the Baron's monologue in the second scene: Pushkin compares him to "a young profligate man awaiting a rendezvous" who hastens to "the faithful chests". The consummation of love is achieved through his proclamation of full possession of the gold; he claims, "I am above all desire, I am serene; I know my power!" The imagery of love and death go hand-in-hand throughout the play: the Baron's gesture of inserting the key into the chest is compared to the plunging of a knife into his victim. It is at the same time pleasant and terrifying, and the keys that the knight calls for while dying become the symbol of his inhuman obsession.

"Mozart and Salieri" was written at the end of October 1830, although Pushkin started work on it in 1826, in Mikhailovskoe. The initial title was "Envy". It was staged in January and February 1832 by the Bolshoi Theatre in St Petersburg. The story-line is based on the rumours that Mozart was poisoned by Salieri. It was suggested by some German newspapers that Salieri confessed to the murder just before he died in May 1825. Pushkin's play is a psychological study of envy and of the two different types of artistic personality: Mozart is a reckless genius, who writes the most beautiful music almost half-heartedly, while Pushkin's Salieri is a hard-working devotee whose efforts remain unrewarded. In Pushkin's play Salieri is obsessed with murdering his rival, and he succeeds in killing Mozart with the poison he has been carrying with him for 18 years. He is a man of action, unlike Mozart who is carried away by divine inspiration. The tension of the conflict is reinforced by the fact that Salieri loves Mozart passionately, and he gains short-lived freedom from envy and doubt about his own talent by killing the music itself (Mozart in his eyes was the living spirit of music). "Having destroyed the sounds, / I dissected music, like a corpse", concludes Salieri. Music is used in the play to assert life in the face of death. Mozart is aware of his coming death: the man in black is a symbolic figure who commissions the composer to write a Requiem. It has been suggested by the critic Gershenzon that Pushkin's play is autobiographical, shedding light on Pushkin's split personality. Pushkin poses one of the most fundamental questions: whether evil and genius are compatible. Just before taking the poisonous drink, Mozart addresses Salieri: "He was a genius, / Just like you and me. And genius and evil / Aren't compatible. Are they?". Salieri does not answer the question, but poison's Mozart's drink: "Do you think so? [He throws the poison into Mozart's drink.] Well, have a drink." At the end of the play Salieri returns to this moral dilemma, and doubts again whether Mozart's assertion is true, referring to Napoleon, and to Michelangelo who allegedly killed his model in order to depict the figure of the dying Christ more realistically. Salieri regards himself as the chosen one who is called upon to kill Mozart, "so that by eliminating this monstrous anomaly, the proper order of things will be restored" (Gershenzon). The play reflects Pushkin's concern with envy and resentment and ways of manipulating fate. It illustrates that any attempt to take destiny into one's own hands leads to a tragic outcome. The same metaphysical and moral dilemma is highlighted in Pushkin's story "Vystrel" ("The Shot"), written at the same time.

The demonic theme is replayed on a different note in "The Stone Guest", which is based on the Don Juan legend, and is also used in Molière's play and in Mozart's opera. The plot is similar to other versions of the legend, but the characters are given a different interpretation. Pushkin's Don Juan falls madly in love with Donna Anna, the widow of the Commander killed by him. He meets her at her husband's grave, by the statue of the Commander once famous for his tyrannic jealousy. The autobiographical element is evident in this play too. Don Juan resembles Pushkin (who was famous for his amours) especially because he is also a poet: in the second act Laura sings a song composed by Don Juan. He dies as a true poet with the name of his beloved on his lips; the statue drags him into the abyss, and Don Juan's last utterance is: "I am perishing – that's it – oh, Donna Anna!" He lives up to his word: prior to his unexpected death he confesses to Donna Anna that he is prepared to give up his life "for a sweet moment of endearment". Don Juan invites the statue to witness his meeting with Donna Anna: by endangering himself he pours oil on the flames of his passion. The play reflects Pushkin's own worries at the time; having led the reckless life of a Casanova, he had decided to settle for domesticity, and Donna Anna is rather different from the other female characters who appear in Pushkin's writings: she is pretty and shallow, a symbol of commonplace and virtue, a stereotype of the perfect wife who is faithful to her dead husband. The tragedy of Don Juan is that he discovers the banality of virtue, witnessing the de-romanticization of his goddess; but the Stone Commander, a symbolic figure of justice and of the chastening super-ego, enforces his doom. As Tomashevskii observes, "Like the other *Little Tragedies* of Pushkin, this piece unfolds its characters ... linked to one another by the idea of the pleasures of life (inspiration, love, wealth)".

"The Feast During the Plague" is a translation of parts of a single scene from John Wilson's drama *The City of the Plague* with two original songs incorporated into the text. The comparison between Pushkin's play and the original was undertaken by Victor Terras (see Kodjak and Taranovsky, 1976). The theme of the play is the pleasure derived from being exposed to mortal danger. Its autobiographical background is important: Pushkin himself was forced to spend the autumn of 1930 in Boldino, away from his fiancée Natal'ia Goncharova, because of a cholera epidemic. Walsingham, the Master of Ceremonies, is called on to deliver a Bacchic song, and his hymn in honour of the plague celebrates living dangerously, and (as suggested by Pushkin) the different experiences of mortal danger, labelled by the poet "the breath of the Plague". The conflict lies between the Dionysian approach to life and Christian values; this is conveyed in the play by the priest who condemns the reckless oblivion of the drunken party as an insult to the memory of the dead, beloved ones. The play ends with the scene of Walsingham "submerged in deep contemplation". A sense of despair prevails: his link with the prostitute bars him in his own eyes from communion with true goodness: he recalls his marriage with his deceased wife as the lost paradise. In the death-obsessed world a dissociation of virtue and pleasure has occurred; the world seems to be deceased and disturbed. The moral dilemma is intensified by Mary's song, featuring the prototype of eternal love and faithfulness after the death of one of the partners. The play presents, therefore, a sequence of songs and spontaneous speeches reflecting various attitudes to impending death. It is a play of atmosphere, offering a discourse on the happiness of love and innocence destroyed by an external force beyond human control. The attempt to change the course of fate is crushed in the face of terrifying reality.

These plays develop the strategy, also found in Pushkin's narrative poems, of subverting and modifying readily available propositions and moral commonplaces: the main characters find themselves fatally trapped by false pretensions brought on by freedom and pleasure.

ALEXANDRA SMITH

Boris Godunov

Play, 1831 (written 1824–25)

Pushkin began work on *Boris Godunov* in the autumn of 1824 and completed it in November of the following year. Censorship restrictions prevented the complete work from coming out until the end of 1830 (the volume was dated 1831). The first production (from an incomplete text) was in 1870. Pushkin took the story of Boris's reign largely from Nikolai Karamzin's *Istoriia gosudarstva Rossiiskogo* [History of the Russian State].

Soon after Boris Godunov's election to the throne in 1598, rumours spread that he had killed the rightful heir, Prince Dmitrii. Pushkin, following Karamzin, built his play around Boris's tortured sense of guilt and the successful scheming of one Grigorii Otrep'ev to seize the throne under the pretence that he was Dmitrii and had survived the murder attempt.

The play had a programmatic interest for Pushkin. Although Pushkin had one foot firmly planted in the 18th century, in *Boris Godunov* he allied himself with the Romantic revolt against the stranglehold of French classicism. The theatre of Racine appeared to him and his generation as rule-bound, formalistic, abstractly unhistorical, and aristocratic. His model (and that of his age) was Shakespeare, who was a "national poet", unlike the "court" poet Racine: "... I imitated Shakespeare in his free and broad portrayal of characters, his casual and uncomplicated composing of types". Shakespeare's characters were multi-faceted, while French classicism schematized character into eternal types. Scorning the "affected rules of the French theatre", "a Romantic tragedian accepts as a rule inspiration alone".

"The absence of any rules", which Pushkin proudly asserted, is striking. The traditional unities are dispensed with. The action spreads well over seven years (1598–1605), scenes range through Moscow's Kremlin, Red Square (in old Russian, "Beautiful Square"), medieval monasteries, boyar palaces, a mansion in Krakov, the forests of Russia. Comedy mixes with tragedy, prose with blank verse (an innovation for Russian tragedy), high poetry with conversational language and even vulgarisms (it is the first Russian tragedy in which people speak to each other instead of declaiming). There are no acts, only a string of 23 scenes. The false Dmitrii appears in nine, the eponymous hero in a mere six! Remaining true to the historical record, Pushkin could not allow them to meet, so the two stories – that of the tsar and the pretender – develop independently. Many contemporaries complained of a lack of *any* unity.

Pushkin lacked Shakespeare's grasp of dramatic structure, and *Boris Godunov* has achieved greater renown through Musorgskii's musical genius than it has as a piece of theatre. Instead, it was Shakespeare's historical imagination that caught Pushkin's attention: "Following the example of Shakespeare, I limited myself to the portrayal of an epoch and historical characters, not pursuing scenic effects, romantic pathos, etc.". He originally called the play "a dramatic novella", and the structure of *Boris Godunov* is indeed novelistic. Its accumulation of scenes and the large, diverse cast offer a vivid panorama of a period of Russian history. In classical theatre "character is destiny" it is only partly so in *Boris Godunov*. The fortunes of men are also determined by historical events beyond their control. "History", wrote one of Pushkin's contemporaries, "has become the language of fate ...". If one were to seek analogies, they would not be to future Russian plays, but to a novel like *War and Peace* for its epic sweep and historical placement of individual lives.

The narrative lacks the animated drive of Tolstoi, or for that matter of Pushkin's other works. Pushkin's attempts to imitate the stolid solemnity of Old Russia may have caused an uncharacteristic stasis in many of the scenes and a certain monotony in the blank verse – which also, at times, achieves magnificent resonance. Nevertheless, *Boris Godunov* belongs to a line of Pushkin's works – *Evgenii Onegin* and *The Captain's Daughter* are outstanding examples – which in their fine grasp of historical reality anticipate the Russian novel.

The structure of *Boris Godunov* is loose, but it is coherent, as the play parallels the ascending line of Dmitrii's career against Boris's decline. A host of other characters provide the essence and pressure of the time: plotting boyars, pious churchmen, Polish aristocrats, renegade monks, free Cossacks. The common people, who in 18th-century Russian drama were brought on stage solely for comic relief, are clearly an active agent of history. The play opens with the people's election of Boris, Dmitrii's revolt is predicated on popular discontent, the play ends with the famous final stage direction: "The People are silent". The line is certainly a judgement on Dmitrii and his boyars' murder of Boris's wife and son, and is perhaps a suggestion that someday the people will speak.

The contrast between Boris and Dmitrii is the most fascinating aspect of the play. In their persons two cultures collide. Boris is an enlightened monarch, curious about the world, interested in education, and most important for Pushkin, he values an aristocracy of merit against one of birth. He is also traditionally "Russian": pious, paternal, yet capable of authoritarian repression. His piety is the other side of the coin of his tortured conscience. Dmitrii is a new man of the European west, a kind of 16th-century Gogolian Khlestakov – self-made, footloose, ambitious, without principle, easily dominated by women, unconnected to place, ready to sell his people to Polish Catholicism. The play continually evinces a delicious irony of language: the solemn dignified tones of the Kremlin and the Church, the folksy language of Boris's household, the bawdy invective of a Russian tavern are all set against the courtly elegance of Dmitrii's Polish court. Compare the passionate directness of Boris's speech with the self-conscious literariness of the Pretender:

Dmitrii: I love the blossoms of Parnassus.
I believe the prophecies of poets.
No, not in vain ecstasy seethes in their fiery breasts.
Boris: ... Let me catch my breath
felt the blood rushing to my face and sluggishly receding.
for thirteen years I have dreamed of that murdered child.
Yes, yes. That's it! Now I understand.
But who is he, my terrible enemy?
Who pursues me? An empty name, a shade...

MILTON EHRE

The Tales of Belkin

Povesti Belkina

Collection of tales, 1831

The Tales of the Late Ivan Petrovich Belkin (to give them their full title) were written in late summer 1830 on the author's remote estate of Boldino where he had become stranded because of a cholera outbreak. They consist of an introductory note ("From the Publisher") and five short stories, the whole collection amounting to about 20,000 words. Pushkin decided to publish them anonymously, partly in order to avoid the censor's eye, but perhaps also because he was a little unsure of himself, these being his first completed prose works. Even so the initials A.P. at the end of the "Note" seem to give the game away. The purpose of this little piece has been the subject of much conjecture. While ostensibly provided in order to describe the editor of the stories, Ivan Belkin, and to explain how he came across them, the note clearly has other functions. It lends the collection a much-needed though spurious air of unity, and it gives Pushkin a chance to exploit his talent for comic portraiture; one critic, however, has seen it as a long encoded message addressed to Decembrist sympathizers.

The tales vary in many respects. The first one, "Vystrel" ("The Shot"), has the strongest story-line. Silvio, a saturnine and glamorous officer, amazes his colleagues by not responding to an insult in the traditional manner – by challenging the offender to a duel. It transpires that he cannot do any such thing, since he is half-way through a duel already – he had delayed his own shot when his adversary had seemed offensively indifferent to it – and must not put his own life at risk. Years later the narrator discovers the outcome of these circumstances, when he visits by chance Count B., the very man who had been Silvio's opponent. Silvio had turned up shortly after the Count's marriage, when life had become dear to him, and had gained his satisfaction, not by killing his man, but by seeing him at last show signs of anxiety and alarm.

The second tale, "Metel'" ("The Blizzard"), tells of a young couple who wish to marry without parental approval. They decide to elope, but a snowstorm prevents the groom from getting to the church. Maria, the bride, goes through the ceremony, not knowing that the "bridegroom" is an impostor, Burmin, who had happened to be passing and allowed himself to be hustled through the false marriage as a prank. When, four years later, Maria falls in love with a young officer, this earlier wedding is the only obstacle between them – until they realize that they were indeed the bride and groom who had gone through that secret ceremony.

In "Grobovshchik" ("The Coffin-Maker"), Adrian Prokhorov, an undertaker, drinks too much at a party and returns home, late at night, to find his house full of "guests"; they are the skeletons, in various stages of preservation, of all his past clients, some of them with grievances to complain about. It all turns out to be a dream.

The heroine of "Stantsionnyi smotritel'" ("The Stationmaster") is an attractive young girl, Dunia, who is abducted from her father's posting station by a handsome hussar. Samson Vyrin, the father, follows Dunia to town, only to discover that she is content and does not want to be rescued. He returns to his station, where only the bottle and the grave await him.

The final story is "Baryshnia-Krest'ianka" ("The Peasant Lady"), which tells of two feuding Russian families, one with a son, Aleksei, and the other with a daughter, Liza, both marriageable. They finally come together, but only after a sequence of events that includes a dire misunderstanding when Aleksei falls in love with a peasant girl only to discover it is Liza in disguise.

The literary value of these tales is not easy to assess. Both "The Blizzard" and "The Peasant Lady" suffer so acutely from implausibility that one wonders whether Pushkin should be taken at all seriously. "The Coffin-Maker", however, reads like a good joke, and both "The Shot" and "The Stationmaster" provide both narrative interest and intriguing characterization. Indeed, Samson Vyrin, is seen as the prototype "little man" (a downcast victim of adversity, suffering irredeemably from social discrimination, personal inadequacy and bad luck) whose successors populate many pages of later Russian literature, especially in the works of Gogol' and Dostoevskii. Perhaps the best way to view the stories is to see them as parodies; the only quality they have in common is a clear intention to ridicule the absurdities and excesses of earlier and contemporary European writers in the Romantic period, especially the tales of crossed lovers, ghosts and graveyards, abducted heroines and suffering victims of misunderstanding, disguise, and coincidence. Critics have established beyond all doubt, for example, that the sadly amusing outcome of "The Stationmaster" depends for its effect on the frustration of expectations aroused by close familiarity (guaranteed in Pushkin's readership) with both the biblical parable of the prodigal son (pictures of which hang on the stationmaster's wall) and Karamzin's popular story *Bednaia Liza* (*Poor Liza*). It is clear also that Pushkin has introduced a new style of writing based on his own dictum that "brevity and precision are the first virtues of prose". His succinct, no-nonsense manner comes like a breath of fresh air into Russian letters; there are no wordy descriptions, elaborate conceits, protracted metaphors or passages of purple eloquence. Those that do exist in these stories are so exceptional that they stand out as literary jokes. Humour is another clear aim of the stories; all of them contain amusing situations and good jests.

Pushkin's *Tales of Belkin* still leave much for individual readers to decide for themselves. Dismissed as inconsequential by the author's contemporaries, overvalued by some later critics as outright masterpieces, they remain indeterminate, partly because of the air of experimentation that pervades them. Their marked defects and qualities have yet to be balanced out; perhaps judgement of them will always remain a matter of individual preference.

A.D.P. BRIGGS

Evgenii Onegin

Novel in verse, 1833 (written 1823–31)

This novel in verse, Pushkin's masterpiece and the highest achievement of Russian poetry, was written over an eight-year period (1823–31) in the poet's prime. It tells the story of a bored man-about-town, Evgenii Onegin, who retires to the country on inheriting his uncle's estate. There he meets and apparently befriends a young neighbour, Vladimir Lenskii, who is in love with a local girl, Ol'ga Larina. Her elder sister, Tat'iana, falls in love with Onegin and naively, in a long letter, offers herself to him. Uninterested, he rejects her approach. Invited to Tat'iana's name-day celebration, Onegin monopolizes Ol'ga out of pique, to an insulting degree. Lenskii challenges him to a duel, and is shot dead. Shortly after these events Tat'iana pays a visit to Onegin's castle and, by looking at his possessions and especially his books, comes to see how empty his character is. About three years later Onegin meets Tat'iana again; married to a prince (and general), she has risen by this time to the highest ranks of St Petersburg society. He now declares his love to her, but it is her turn to reject him, saying that she will not betray her husband.

The novel is not long, consisting of about 20,000 words arranged in eight chapters and running to five and a half thousand lines (iambic tetrameters), or 366 stanzas. Despite the use of a shorter line (four feet instead of the more usual five), the stanzas are very much like sonnets; their unvarying rhyme-scheme being AbAbCCddEffEgg (capital letters denoting feminine rhymes). The verse is of exquisite quality, drawing on Pushkin's redoubtable mastery of all the poetic arts and exploiting the full potential of the sound-rich Russian language. Minute analysis of individual stanzas reveals a most intricate system of sound-manipulation; when critics claim that not a syllable could be changed without detriment to the overall effect, they scarcely exaggerate. The whole of the first chapter, an extended portrait of the hero, is particularly inspired. Despite the jaundiced attitude to the world shown by Onegin, here Pushkin positively revels in making good poetry. This is his most sustained tract of accomplished and witty versifying; not a few Russians know the entire chapter by heart. There are many other unforgettable sections, for which poetry could have been the only medium: for example, Tat'iana's declaration of her love for Onegin (chapter 3, stanzas 15–20); the description of winter at the beginning of chapter 5 and the heroine's lurid nightmare (11–20); the duel (6, 29–32), and the final confrontation in the last chapter.

The story and characters are among the best-known in Russian literature. The ending of the novel has remained in the national memory, and the image of a strong young woman ranged against an impractical, indecisive man is one that has been imitated several times by other Russian writers, Ivan Turgenev prominent among them. Tat'iana, in particular, has been regarded as the incarnation of feminine fortitude and moral probity. Onegin, although not much loved, has usually escaped the severest censure; critics have tended to see him as a victim – of the repressive Russian society in which he finds himself, of the high society that he abhors, of Europe-wide *mal du siècle*, of cruel destiny. If such allowances are disregarded, it is hard to see Onegin as anything other than a cynical destroyer of another man's happiness and very existence, for which forgiveness is hard to find. Moreover, some doubt may be cast over the degree of temptation towards infidelity suffered by Tat'iana at the end of the story, given her full knowledge of Onegin's personality and behaviour, and her recent elevation to such a high social station. Debate surrounding the leading characters and their behaviour continues unabated, a tribute to the success of Pushkin's characterization.

The claim of *Evgenii Onegin* to be a novel rather than just a poem is based on this very success, together with its skilful use of dialogue (even in verse) and, most importantly, its incorporation of serious ideas. These latter are ostensibly disavowed by the insouciant narrator who, whatever mood he is in, pretends to a flippancy in which, given the easy flow of the poetry and all its charm, it is all too tempting to believe. No one should be deluded; in point of fact, this novel will make demands on the most educated mind, being full of subtle and overt references to other writers and figures of importance. Its ideas and implications are wide-ranging and thought-provoking; it has much to tell us about human conduct, virtue and morality, and the pursuit of happiness. There are clear lessons in how not to live a life, and thoughts of death abound. Above all, like the rest of Pushkin's work, this beautiful poem is a delightful paradox: seeming to deal with banality, disappointment and tragedy, it asserts the goodness of living through the beauty of language in every stanza and through recurrent incidental glimpses of happiness, particularly in the world of nature. The narrator may be careworn, the subject-matter largely negative, the hero thoroughly jaundiced; nevertheless *Evgenii Onegin* has been properly described by one critic as sparkling "like champagne in sunshine". It has inspired one of the loveliest operas on the world stage, with the libretto carefully compiled, predominantly from Pushkin's words, by the composer, Tchaikovskii himself. Its poetry, characters, and atmosphere have also proved inspirational for generations of Russian writers and ordinary citizens. There is nothing solemn about the status and achievement of *Evgenii Onegin*; this is one of the best-loved works of world literature.

A.D.P. BRIGGS

The Queen of Spades

Pikovaia dama

Story, 1834

Written during the "Boldino autumn" of 1833 and published in 1834, *The Queen of Spades* quickly became both a popular and a critical success; it has been made into an opera by Tchaikovskii, as well as a play and several films. Its plot can be summed up as follows: a young officer in the Engineers, named Germann [Hermann], hears of the Countess Anna Fedotovna's secret formula for winning at cards. Determined to obtain the secret, Germann exploits the Countess's romantic young ward, Lizaveta, in order to gain entrance to the house, and confronts the aged woman in her boudoir. Although the Countess dies of fright without revealing the secret, she later appears to Germann to inform him that he will win if he plays three faro cards, the three, seven and ace, on three successive days. Germann stakes everything and wins twice, but loses on the third day when the winning card turns out not to be the ace, but the queen of spades, uncannily resembling the Countess herself. Instead of winning great fortune, Germann goes mad.

The reader is constantly tantalized by the variety of possible interpretations that can be placed on the text, wondering whether it is a supernatural tale, or whether *The Queen of Spades* is a story of one man's obsession, hallucination, and insanity brought on by alcohol and stress. Or is it a society tale in which Pushkin is chiefly concerned with depicting a jaded aristocracy, preoccupied with wealth and status, and unable to love? Perhaps it is the tragic disappointment of poor Liza, who initially believes that Germann has come to save her from her humiliating position as ward and unpaid servant to the cantankerous old Countess, which the reader finds central. Any summary barely does justice to a story that is marvellously compact, written in the pared, elegant style that marked Pushkin's radical divergence from the elaborate prose of the day.

The Queen of Spades is notable for its complexity; it is a work in which there is nothing extraneous or undeliberate, and "nothing is ever as simple as it might seem" (Cornwell, 1993). The story begins with an epigraph taken "from the latest fortune-telling book", which reads: "the queen of spades signifies secret malice", a hint at the marvellously sinister atmosphere that Pushkin then proceeds to create in the work. The story is presented in the form of six chapters, each prefaced by an intriguingly oblique epigraph, with a brief epilogue completing the text. Pushkin's manipulation of the *fabula* is particularly skilful; the text contains references to events that take place 60 years before the main action, when the Countess is supposedly given the secret of the three cards by the mysterious Count St Germain, and to events that occur after Germann's descent into insanity: Liza's marriage is referred to briefly in the epilogue. The central action, dealing with Germann's decision to win the secret from the Countess, takes place over a 26-day period, described through sophisticated use of retrospectives, inversion, and shifts of point of view.

The story has been exhaustively, perhaps even over-exhaustively, analysed, with some critics even arguing that the story conceals encoded messages of support for the Decembrists. Certainly each word offers the possibility of unlimited discussion, from the choice of the hero's name to the recurrence of the numbers one, three, and seven. Neil Cornwell provides a detailed history of the great variety of critical approaches adopted. These can be somewhat simplistically listed as (increasingly complex, and sometimes overlapping) variations on the following basic approaches: 1) the stylistic: including structural analyses of composition, division of the textual "reality" into various worlds, circles, or oppositional structures, and the (Proppian) focus on fairy-tale elements; 2) the coded: including articles on Freemasonry and numerology (an approach that has been called "exegetical"); 3) the psychological: including the concern with negative erotic elements in a text in which Germann "woos" an aged Countess instead of the fresh young Liza; 4) the socio-cultural: including Lotman's semiotic analysis of the cards; and 5) the literary: dealing with Pushkin's intertextual allusions, literary sources for the text, influences on and of Pushkin, and including the idea of reading the text through subsequent works. Finally, there is the genre approach, in terms of which critics have analysed the interaction of the above-mentioned readings as well as concentrating on issues such as the fantastic element, romantic parody – always a constant delight in Pushkin's prose – and Bakhtinian carnival motifs. Interpretations often ignore the most fundamental aspect of the work, namely its humour; Pushkin mocks his characters, who fall laughably short of the Romantic standard. Germann is no dashing lover, but one who woos money; Liza is a pallid and conventional heroine, yet one who commits the daring step of inviting Germann to her room late at night; and the Countess is a wonderfully egoistic creation, an ex-society beauty clinging obstinately to the trappings of the power such beauty once commanded.

Power is a constant theme of the text, which operates to illustrate how helpless man is in his attempts to halt the passage of time, or to achieve status and freedom. The reader is also drawn into this net of impotence; *The Queen of Spades* is a text in which Pushkin does indeed "play" with his readers. Pushkin has created a textual world in which meaning is the prize; but this is a world in which the game never ends. Like Germann, the reader who believes that he can control – through reasoned analysis – the outcome of the game, is deluding himself. Ultimately, this is a "mirror" text reflecting the readers' own perceptions; a text about that most broad of artistic issues, how man attempts (and fails) to control reality, whether through cards, plans, pacts with supernatural forces, or with the interpretative logic of words.

S. DALTON-BROWN

The Bronze Horseman

Mednyi vsadnik

Narrative poem, 1841 (written 1833)

Pushkin's narrative poem *The Bronze Horseman* although written in 1833 was only published posthumously in a complete edition in 1841. It is based on the flood of 1824 that engulfed the city of St Petersburg. The Introduction is an ode lauding the achievements of Petersburg's founder, Peter the Great. The tsar stands on the banks of the Neva, dreaming of transforming this miserable marshland, won back from the Swedes in 1703, into a powerful city, foreseeing St Petersburg's strategic importance as a "window into Europe". The Introduction ignores the intervening years when the city's construction caused substantial loss of life. It jumps 100 years to the fulfilment of Peter's dream, when a beautiful, seemingly indestructible city stands on the once desolate site. This swift transition from dream to achievement is a powerful reminder that all this was the result of one man's will. Even nature has acceded to his power, the waters contained within granite banks, the swamps replaced by verdant gardens.

The poet's voice then enters the poem, conveying his passion for Petersburg as a beautiful woman, well-formed, pensive, radiant. He loves her frosty winters, the Admiralty spire, the graceful palaces, and particularly her white nights when he can write till dawn. His panegyric ends with the hope that both the conquered natural elements and foes will leave Peter's eternal dream undisturbed. The tone suddenly changes in the last stanza.

The poet draws the readers into the narrative, warning that his tale will be a terrible one.

Part 1 chronicles the horror that follows. St Petersburg, with its warm summer nights, becomes November Petrograd, its harshness echoed in the grating consonants. Nature is disturbed, animated as man and beast. The Neva tosses like a sick man in its bed, the rains angrily beat at windows, the wind howls sadly. Then the poet introduces Evgenii, a minor civil servant. One night he is agitated by personal thoughts: about poverty, the inclement weather that may separate him from his beloved Parasha if the drawbridges are raised, about marrying, raising children, giving them a refuge, being buried by grandchildren. His dreams are interrupted by howling wind, by rain again lashing against the windows. Then follows that most terrible day when the Neva broke its banks, roaring like a lion, seething with the sounds of a boiling cauldron, hurling itself upon the city like an enraged animal. The poem echoes with the rhetorical warning shouts of battle, but the attack is one-sided and pointless. Evil waves creep into the windows like thieves, while gravestones can be seen floating down the streets.

Tsar Alexander looks on sadly, powerless to effect change, unlike Peter. For a moment he is on a level with Evgenii, who can be seen perched on a marble lion in Peter's square, hands crossed on his chest defensively, the lion and the wind more powerful than he. Suddenly Evgenii notices to his horror what appears to be Parasha's tumbledown house floating on the waves. Then his attention is attracted by the idol on its bronze horse, back turned, hand defiantly outstretched (Falconet's statue commissioned by Catherine the Great in the 1760s in praise of Peter).

In Part 2, Evgenii unexpectedly encounters a boatman prepared to ferry him across the still seething Neva to the island where Parasha lives. The rhythm of the short, sharp lines reflects his panic; her house has vanished. Suddenly a terrible laugh escapes from his throat. From now on, he lives like a beggar, beaten by stone-throwing children and coachmen's whips, neither man nor animal, nor even dead ghost. One night he suddenly recalls all the past horror, rushes backwards and forwards, then finds himself in front of the lions with their raised paws and the statue with its hand outstretched. For a moment he feels tremendous strength; gritting his teeth he threatens the statue. As the lines resound with the onomatopoeic rattle of hooves, he imagines the bronze horseman pursuing him through the night. The poem ends, as it began, with a desolate island, poor fishermen, Parasha's tumbledown "black" house. The body of Evgenii has been washed up in front of it, later to be given a pauper's burial.

Topical and universal themes are intertwined throughout. Russia has undoubtedly gained from St Petersburg's strategic position, but at what cost in human suffering? Does the end justify the means? Should interests of state take precedence over those of the individual? Pushkin takes pride in his ancestor's achievements, introducing Peter as "He", a man who needs no name, such is his superhuman status. Had he wished to condemn him, he could have drawn on the details of the statue itself, the stubby hands, the lascivious face, the serpent coiled round the hooves. But this does not prove that Pushkin favours absolutism. He also sympathizes with Evgenii, describing him as "our" hero, a man with simple dreams and thoughts, the antithesis of Peter.

If the fantastic white nights of the Introduction hint at that uncontrollable natural force that will later wreak havoc, the prevailing tone is eulogistic. St Petersburg gives Pushkin physical pleasure, as the synaesthesia and onomatopoeia of the popping corks at balls and the clanging of cannon for national celebrations reveal. Conceivably, Pushkin wished the conflict of state and individual to be interpreted as an elaborate allegory for his complex relationship with Tsar Nicholas. He may also have hoped that Evgenii's undoing would be viewed as a reflection of the Decembrists' fate. Yet he also used the poem's conflicts to investigate disquieting, universal themes. The tumbledown hovels, blackness, poor fishermen, miserable skiffs that appear in both the first and last stanzas, suggest that nothing has changed. For Evgenii, however, the situation has worsened dramatically. Not only is he driven crazy, then destroyed, but the poem ends with his corpse. These scenes echo Lear's predicament, in which wisdom comes with madness. Individuals are left to face their isolation, insignificance and the pointlessness of their endeavours. Peter's arrogance prevented him realizing that even he could not impose order on chaos. It did not occur to him that there might exist another power, destiny. The unexpected ferryman's battle across the waters recalls the crossing of the Styx, while fate apparently brings Parasha's house and Evgenii's corpse together at the end. The one theme that Pushkin states unambiguously, as A.D.P. Briggs (1983) argues, is that nature is an eternal presence that it is arrogance to attempt to dominate.

MARILYN MINTO

R

Aleksandr Nikolaevich Radishchev 1749–1802

Prose writer and poet

Biography

Born in Saratov district, 31 August 1749. Family was well-to-do, cultured, "progressive". Educated first at home, then sent to relatives in Moscow, 1756. Page in Imperial household, 1762, followed Court to St Petersburg, 1764. Sent as part of select group to study law in Leipzig, 1767–71. Joined Masonic lodge "Urania" and the English Club, 1773. Entered College of Commerce, 1777; assistant director of Customs and Excise Department, 1780; director in 1790. Stripped of rank, title, privileges and arrested for sedition by Catherine II for the publication of *Puteshestvie iz Peterburga v Moskvu* (*A Journey from St Petersburg to Moscow*), 1790. Death sentence commuted to Siberian exile, 1790. Permitted move to Kaluga, 1797; remained in exile at Nemtsovo until 1801. Commited suicide, 24 September 1802.

Publications

Collected Editions

Sobranie ostavshikhsia sochinenii. Moscow, 1806–11.
Sochineniia. St Petersburg, 1872.
Polnoe sobranie sochinenii. Moscow, 1907.
Polnoe sobranie sochinenii, 3 vols. Moscow and Leningrad, 1938–52.
Izbrannoe. Moscow, 1976.

Fiction

Puteshestvie iz Peterburga v Moskvu. St Petersburg, 1790; Leningrad, 1974; translated as *A Journey from St Petersburg to Moscow*, by L. Wiener, edited and with an introduction by R.P. Thaler. Cambridge, Massachusetts, Harvard University Press, 1958.
"Dnevnik odnoi nedeli". 1811; translated as "Diary of One Week", by Tanya Page, *Russian Literature Triquarterly*, 20 (1987), 133–38.

Poetry

Vol'nost' [Liberty]. St Petersburg, 1906.
Polnoe sobranie stikhotvorenii. Leningrad, 1940.
Stikhotvoreniia. "Biblioteka poeta", Leningrad. 1975.

Biography

Zhitie Fedora Vasil'evicha Ushakova, s priobshcheniem nekotorykh ego sochinenii [The Life of Fedor Vasil'evich Ushakov ...]. St Petersburg, 1789.

Translator

Razmyshleniia o grecheskoi istorii, ili O prichinakh blagodenstviia i neschastiia grekov [Reflections on Greek History, or On the Reasons for the Prosperity and Misfortune of the Greeks] by Mably, St Petersburg, 1773.
Lessepsovo Puteshestvie po Kamchatke i po iuzhnoi storone Sibiri [Lesseps' Journey via Kamchatka and Southern Siberia] by Lesseps, Moscow, 1801–02.

Critical Studies

Alexander Radishchev. A Russian Humanist of the 18th Century, by Boris Sergeevich Evgeniev, London, Hutchinson, 1946.
Aleksandr Radishchev (1799–1949), by D.D. Blagoi, Moscow, 1949.
A.N. Radishchev.(Ocherk zhizni i tvorchestva), by G.P. Makogonenko, Moscow, 1949.
Radishchev. Stat'i i materialy. Leningrad, 1950.
A.N. Radishchev. (Zhizn' i tvorchestvo), by D.D. Blagoi, Moscow, 1952.
Radishchev i russkaia literatura, by V.N. Orlov, Leningrad, 1952.
Radishchev i ego vremia, by G.P. Makogonenko, Moscow, 1956.
A.N. Radishchev. (Kritiko-biograficheskii ocherk), by L.B. Svetlov, Moscow, 1958.
The First Russian Radical: Alexander Radishchev (1749–1802), by David M. Lang, London, Allen and Unwin, 1959.
The Philosphical Ideas of Alexander Radishchev, by Jesse V. Clardy, New York, Astra Books, 1964.
A Russian Philosophe: Alexander Radishchev 1749–1802, by Allen McConnell, The Hague, Nijhoff, 1964.
Potaennyi Radishchev, by G. Shtorm, Moscow, 1974.
"Kommentarii", edited by L.I. Kulakova and V.A. Zapadov, in Radishchev's *Puteshestvie iz Peterburga v Moskvu*, Leningrad, 1974.
A History of 18th Century Russian Literature, by William Edward Brown, Ann Arbor, Ardis, 1980.
Aleksandr Nikolaevich Radishchev: ego zhizn' i sochineniia (facsimile), edited by V.I. Pokrovskii, Oxford, Meeuws, 1985.
"The *Diary of One Week*: Radishchev's Record of Suicidal Despair", by Tanya Page, *Russian Literature Triquarterly*, 21 (1988), 117–27.

Bibliography
A.N. Radishchev. (K 150-letiiu so dnia smerti). Pamiatka chitateliu. Pskov, 1952.

To his fellow-countrymen Aleksandr Radishchev has always been the first Russian revolutionary, the first radical, and his multifarious activities in the service of anti-despotic, pro-democratic agitation are normally held to focus themselves most clearly in his *Puteshestvie iz Peterburga v Moskvu* (*A Journey from St Petersburg to Moscow*), published clandestinely in 1790 and officially proscribed until 1905. This work is the summation of Radishchev's angry and rebellious apprehension of the state of socio-political affairs in Russia at the time, traversing the space between the new and old Russian capitals with an eye sharply critical of the injustices witnessed *en route*, perpetually interrupting itself to recall anecdotes, interpolate allegories, to bemoan, magniloquently and in high sentimentalist fashion, the evils perpetrated by the powerful upon the vulnerable. By the time of publication, Radishchev had been active as a writer for more than ten years. A voracious reader, he had absorbed in his early days as a firebrand student in Leipzig and later Russia not only the radical political culture of the period (Mably and Freemasonry were pre-eminent influences on him then) but other, "belletristic" voices, and in, for example, the early piece *Dnevnik odnoi nedeli* (*Diary of One Week*), written in the 1770s, one has an extreme example of emotionally wrought Sentimentalism – the distillation, as it were, of the mode. Radishchev knew the exemplars, the Europeans (Richardson, Sterne, Marivaux, the early Goethe) as well as the Russians, and the *Diary*, relatively plot-free as it is, recapitulates the type of the "feeling hero", hypersensitive to the slightest accession of the emotions, morbidly brooding, self-involved to a degree. This meant moral nobility in 18th-century terms, and the sentimental manner was the contemporary way of wielding the fine-bladed scalpel – laying bare the innermost springs of psychology.

A Journey from St Petersburg to Moscow, a manifesto of indignation, is erected on this premise. Melding solipsistic responsiveness with political commentary, it can be seen to some extent to take its cue from Radishchev's earlier pamphlet, *Zhitie Fedora Vasil'evicha Ushakova* [The Life of Fedor Vasil'evich Ushakov]. This is less a biography than an exalting paean to friendship. The late Fedor Ushakov had been a law student with Radishchev in Germany and later Russia, and the essay remembers idealistic conversations about oppression, injustice (often personalized in the character of their harsh governor, a Major Bokum), and world changing. The *Life* is a step forward in terms of characterization: Ushakov comes through not only as a "true son of the fatherland" but an independent personality, with inclinations, moods, quirks, and Radishchev's careful protectiveness of these endearing qualities lies behind the humanitarianism of his attitude towards degrading and oppressing environments.

The *Life*, and other, lesser works similarly inspired, are properly seen as the prelude to *A Journey from St Petersburg to Moscow*. The journey is undertaken by a Radishchevian everyman, the mobilized consciousness of Russia, and each stop on the way adds cumulatively to the weight of social repression witnessed. It inclines to be the encyclopedic sum of everything Radishchev has to say, chapter by chapter: national character and folklore ("Sofiia"), the feudal hierarchy ("Tosna"), the forced labour of the peasantry ("Liubani"), the inhumanity of bureaucratic power ("Chudovo"), autocracy ("Spasskaia polest'"), popular enlightenment ("Podberez'e"), the bourgeoisie ("Novgorod"), religion ("Bronnitsy"), education ("Krestsy"), health and hygiene ("Iazhelbitsy"), prostitution ("Valdai"), the Imperial court and courtiers ("Vydropusk"), censorship ("Torzhok"), the auction of peasants ("Mednoe"), revolutionary poetry ("Tver'"), the press-gang ("Gorodnia"), popular ethics and aesthetics ("Klin"), poverty ("Peshki"), wife-beating ("Chernaia griaz'"), and so on. Further chapters introduce and develop new themes. Anything that provokes Radishchev's ire (and at times there seems to be little of contemporary life that does not) will find its due place. What is required is a type of rational fair-play. Evils must be redressed and wrongs righted wherever one finds them, from the bestial violence of petty landowners right up to the throne itself: at no stage is Radishchev inclined to a nihilistic or anarchistic ground-clearing for its own sake.

The iniquitousness of institutions, and the unconquerable heroism of the small people who suffer by them, are represented by Radishchev by means of close, descriptive characterization, and it is never the groups but the individuals who are thus represented. At the top are the vulpine executors of inequality, the grandees, state officials and landowners, usually benighted, sometimes enlightened, found always in the service of a fundamentally flawed dispensation. Alongside these Radishchev's perpetually scandalized third-person narrator draws the ranks of the victims, the peasants and toilers, the eternally exploited. Intellectuals, independents and freethinkers make up a third category. These chime with Radishchev's exquisitely-tuned champion of freedom, the sort of people with a "project for the future", this latter, however, never extensively sketched out.

Because in *A Journey from St Petersburg to Moscow* Radishchev is trying to do everything – to have the last word – he draws on a bewildering armoury of literary styles and mannerisms, generically and in terms of register. Cobbett-like in intention, he rarely, if ever, attains William Cobbett's lucidity. Intensity of emotion warps coherence on page after page, and the texture of the book disintegrates into inchoate jaggedness. The lexis is now Old Church Slavonic, in portentously biblical periods, now sentimentalistically suave. Pushkin, otherwise an admirer, found Radishchev's style "barbarous". It arises through Radishchev's fear of missing something out. He is a stranger to nuance, not content with suggestion or implication: injustice must be seen to be done. Descriptive detail is there, with greater clarity than any of Radishchev's inflammatory big ideas can be said to possess: the interior of a peasant hut, the manner of dress, of speech, of peasants, all balanced by the narrator in a tense equilibrium. The centre cannot always be guaranteed to hold, and then the extraordinary travelogue falls to pieces, a scatter of angular vignettes.

A labour of hate and love, *A Journey from St Petersburg to Moscow* had to be published by Radishchev anonymously, at his own expense and on his own press. It passed the censor (who had not bothered to read it) and came to the outraged attention of the Empress, Catherine II, who perceived in it a Masonic threat to destabilize her government. There subsequently ensued a depressing string of consequences: mock trial, sentencing to death, commutation to exile, years of distant persecution, recall from exile, threats of further banishment. Crushed, Radishchev swallowed a beaker of sulphuric acid in September 1802 and died a few hours later.

NICHOLAS CROWE

Valentin Grigor'evich Rasputin 1937–

Prose writer

Biography

Born in Ust-Uda, Irkutsk Oblast, 15 March 1937. Attended Irkutsk State University, graduated in literature and history, 1959. Journalist in Siberia, 1959–61. Full-time writer since 1961: leading Village Prose writer. Member of the editorial staff, *Nash sovremennik*, Moscow. Member of the Soviet Writers' Union, 1975; member of the board, 1981. Elected a People's Deputy, 1989. Member of Mikhail Gorbachev's Presidential Council, 1990–91. Recipient: State Prize, 1977, 1987; Hero of Socialist Labour, 1987.

Publications

Collected Editions

Povesti. Moscow, 1976.

Money for Maria, and Borrowed Time: Two Village Tales, translated by Kevin Windle and Margaret Wettlin. St Lucia, University of Queensland Press, and London, Quartet, 1981.

Chetyre povesti [Four Novels]. Leningrad, 1982.

Izbrannye proizvedeniia, 2 vols. Moscow, 1984.

Povesti i rasskazy [Novels and Stories]. Moscow, 1984.

Poslednii srok: Proshchanie s Materoi: povesti i rasskazy. Moscow, 1985.

You Live and Love and Other Stories, translated by Alan Myers. London, Granada, 1985; New York, Vanguard, 1986.

Siberia on Fire: Stories and Essays, translated by Gerald Mikkelson and Margaret Winchell. DeKalb, Illinois, Northern Illinois University Press, 1989.

Pozhar. Povesti [Fire. Tales]. Moscow, 1990.

Fiction

Ia zabyl sprosit' u Aleshki [I Forgot to Ask Leshka], *Angara*, 1 (1961).

Krai vozle samovo neba [The Land at the Edge of Heaven Itself]. Irkutsk, 1966.

Chelovek s etogo sveta [A Man from This World]. Krasnoiarsk, 1967.

Den'gi dlia Marii. Moscow, 1968; translated as *Money for Maria*, with *Borrowed Time*, by Kevin Windle and Margaret Wettlin, 1981.

"Poslednii srok", *Nash sovremennik*, 1970; translated as *Borrowed Time*, with *Money for Maria*, by Kevin Windle and Margaret Wettlin, 1981.

Vniz i vverkh po techeniiu [Down and Up Stream]. Moscow, 1972; translated as "Downstream", by Valentina G. Brougher and Helen C. Poot, in *Contemporary Russian Prose*, edited by Carl and Ellendea Proffer, Ann Arbor, Ardis, 1982, 379–430.

Zhivi i pomni. Moscow, 1975; translated as *Live and Remember*, by Antonina W. Bouis, New York, Macmillan, 1978; reprinted with a foreword by Kathleen Parthé, Evanston, Illinois, Northwestern University Press, 1992.

Proshchanie s Materoi. Moscow, 1976; translated as *Farewell to Matyora*, by Antonina W. Bouis, New York and London, Macmillan, 1979; reprinted Evanston, Illinois, Northwestern University Press, 1992.

Uroki frantsuzskogo. Moscow, 1981; translated as "French Lessons", by Alan Myers, in *You Live and Love and Other Stories*, 1985; and by Gerald Mikkelson and Margaret Winchell, in *Siberia on Fire*, 1989.

Vek zhivi – vek liubi: Rasskazy. Moscow, 1982; 2nd expanded edition Moscow, 1988; translated as "You Live and Love", by Alan Myers, in *You Live and Love and Other Stories*, 1985.

"Pozhar", *Nash sovremennik*, 7 (1985); translated as "The Fire", by Alex Miller, *Soviet Literature*, 7 (1986); and by Gerald Mikkelson and Margaret Winchell, in *Siberia on Fire*, 1989.

Chto peredat' vorone?. Moscow, 1988 (first published in almanac *Sibir'*, 5, 1981); translated as "What Should I Tell the Crow?", by Alan Myers, in *You Live and Love and Other Stories*, 1985; and by Gerald Mikkelson and Margaret Winchell, in *Siberia on Fire*, 1989.

"Sania edet" [Sania is on His Way]; "Rossiia molodaia" [Young Russia]; "V odnom sibirskom gorode" [In a Small Siberian Town], *Moskva*, 7 (1994).

"V bol'nitse" [In Hospital], *Nash sovremennik*, 4 (1995).

"V tu zhe zemliu" [Into that Same Earth], *Nash sovremennik*, 8 (1995).

Stories for Children

Na reke Angare [On the River Angara]. Moscow, 1980.

Zemlia rodiny [The Earth of the Motherland]. Moscow, 1984.

V taige, nad Baikalom [In the Taiga, Above Baikal]. Moscow, 1987.

Memoirs

Vospominaniia sovremennikov [Recollections of Contemporaries]. Moscow, 1990.

Essays

Chto v slove, chto za slovom? [What's in a Word, What's for a Word?]. Irkutsk, 1987.

Essays, with *Valentin Rasputin*, by Nikolai Kotenko, Moscow, Raduga, 1988.

Sibir', Sibir'.... Novosibirsk, 1990; translated as *Siberia, Siberia*, by Margaret Winchell and Gerald Mikkelson, Evanston, Illinois, Northwestern University Press, 1997.

"Vniz po Lene-reke" [Down the Lena River], *Nash sovremennik*, 11 (1993).

"Gde moia derevnia?" [Where is My Village?], *Moskva*, 2 (1995).

Critical Studies

"To Live and to Remember: Comments on Valentin Rasputin's Prose", by E. Starikova, *Soviet Studies in Literature*, 14 (1978).

"For Truth and Goodness: The Stories of Valentin Rasputin", by Vladimir Vasil'ev, *Soviet Studies in Literature*, 14 (1978).

"Valentin Rasputin: A General View", by Deming Brown, in *Russian Literature and Criticism*, edited by Evelyn Bristol, Berkeley, Berkeley Slavic Specialties, 1982.

"Valentin Rasputin's *Proshchanie s Materoi*", by John Dunlop, in *Russian Literature and Emigration*, edited by Evelyn Bristol, Berkeley, Berkeley Slavic Specialties, 1982.

"Religious Symbolism in Valentin Rasputin's Tale *Live and Remember*", by Gerald Mikkelson, in *Studies in Honor of Xenia Gasiorowska*, edited by Lauren G. Leighton, Columbus, Ohio, Slavica, 1982.

"Valentin Rasputin: The Human Race is Not Accidental", by Alexander Afanasyev, *Soviet Literature*, 7/424 (1983).

"Childhood and the Adult World in the Writing of Valentin Rasputin", by David C. Gillespie, *Modern Language Review*, 80/2 (1985).

Die Prosa V.G. Rasputins, by Renate Schäper, Munich, Sagner, 1985.

"Home or Shelter? Notes on Valentin Rasputin's Story 'The Fire'", by Fyodor Chapchakov, *Soviet Literature*, 7/460 (1986).

Valentin Rasputin and Soviet Russian Village Prose, by David C. Gillespie, London, Modern Humanities Research Association, 1986.

"The Mother Theme in Valentin Rasputin", by Robert Porter, in *Canadian Slavonic Papers*, 28/3 (1986).

"Fate?", by Elizabeth Rich, and "Soundness of Moral Character" (in reply to Rich's article), by Nikolai Kotenko, both in *Soviet Literature*, 3/468 (1987).

Valentin Rasputin, by Svetlana Semenova, Moscow, 1987.

"'Live and Love': The Spiritual Path of Valentin Rasputin", by Margaret Winchell, *Slavic and East European Journal*, 31/4 (1987).

Valentin Rasputin, by Nikolai Kotenko, Moscow, 1988; translated into English, Moscow, Raduga, 1988.

The Novellas of Valentin Rasputin: Genre, Language and Style, by Teresa Polowy, New York, Peter Lang, 1989.

Four Contemporary Russian Writers, by Robert Porter, Oxford, Berg, 1989.

"Valentin Rasputin: Then and Now: *Soviet Literature*'s Round Table", *Soviet Literature*, 5/494 (1989).

"Conflicts in the Soviet Countryside in the Novellas of Valentin Rasputin", by Julian Laychuk, *Rocky Mountain Review of Language and Literature*, 47/1–2 (1993).

Spirit of the Totem: Religion and Myth in Soviet Fiction, 1964–1988, by Irena Maryniak, Leeds, W.S. Maney, 1995.

Russian Literature 1988–1994: The End of an Era, by N.N. Shneidman, Toronto, University of Toronto Press, 1995.

Bibliography

"A Bilingual Bibliography of Works by and about Valentin Rasputin", by Suzan K. Burks, *Russian Literature Triquarterly*, 22 (1988).

Valentin Rasputin is best known as a writer for the four novellas (*povesti*) on rural themes published between 1967 and 1976. His writing subsequently, both fiction and non-fiction, has deteriorated aesthetically, and in the mid-1990s bears all the hallmarks of embittered tendentiousness.

His first acclaimed work was *Den'gi dlia Marii* (*Money for Maria*), a deceptively simple tale of rural life in Siberia that succeeds in exploring the bonds that keep a family and a community together, but which may also tear it apart. Rasputin here not only charts the changing morality of the countryside from generation to generation, but also invests the narrative with a range of artistic and symbolic devices: a gallery of peasant character types, the contrast of town and village, the disfiguring modernism of the railway, and the existential drama of simple folk caught up in a crisis not of their doing, and over which they have no control. The appearance of *Poslednii srok* (*Borrowed Time*), however, brought him nationwide acclaim. Again, the plot is relatively simple, and is set in the Siberian countryside: four brother and sisters who have not seen each other for several years meet up at their mother's bedside as she is about to breath her last. Over the few days they spend together, they recall their childhood together, and the urbanized Il'ia and Liusia feel the nostalgic pull of the countryside and the village community. Eventually they all quarrel and go their separate ways; that night, their mother dies. Anna, the old woman, embodies a purity of spirit born of a life spent on the land in harmony with the rhythms of nature, and her spiritual and moral qualities are sorely lacking in her children. Once more Rasputin is lamenting the passing of a way of life and its values.

In *Zhivi i pomni* (*Live and Remember*) and *Proshchanie s Materoi* (*Farewell to Matyora*), Rasputin again invests a straightforward narrative with considerable symbolic and poetic depth. His themes remain the same: the destruction of the rural hearth and the values it imparts, the great moral and spiritual legacy of the Siberian village, and the folly of Russia's headlong rush into industrialization. These themes are further developed in his work of the 1980s and 1990s, although much of this is of a non-fictional nature. There is, nevertheless, a curious hiatus with the publication of four short stories in 1981, where the author moves away from the social processes that have hitherto shaped his fiction and turns inwardly to explore individual consciousness, perception, and the nature of experience. These stories are particularly incisive and startlingly innovative, but their insights are not developed elsewhere. In 1985 the publication of *Pozhar* (*The Fire*) was greeted with some caution, as it seemed a particularly nihilistic tale of death, wholesale destruction and moral and social decay. The action takes place in the large, semi-urban settlement (*poselok*) of Sosnovka, where people from various villages have been resettled following the submerging of their lands as part of one of the local hydro-electric projects. It is thus set chronologically after *Farewell to Matyora*, though within the same geographical area. We learn that people are indifferent to their new home, they have no feeling for the land, they are uprooted, dislocated, and demoralized. As a blaze threatens the community's food supplies in a warehouse, violence erupts as people help themselves to what they can pilfer, especially vodka, and little effort is spent actually tackling the fire. The impression we get of the population, with few exceptions, is of a thoroughly debased people that has lost all vestiges of its humanity, culture or traditions. The main character, Ivan Petrovich, having witnessed mass pillage and even murder, retreats into the depths of the *taiga*, to lose himself in the wilds of nature rather than be in the world of men.

In the late 1980s Rasputin's main writing was devoted to the customs, traditions, history, and people of Siberia, as well as to the environmental dangers threatening Lake Baikal. He also allied himself to various nationalistic causes in the volatile political climate of Gorbachev's and then Yeltsin's Russia, alliances that made him a controversial figure both inside Russia and in the west. His platform has, nevertheless, been consistent: he has always shown concern for Russia and the Russian soul, and what he sees as its degradation in the modern world. The same themes show through in his fiction-barely-disguised-as-propaganda in the mid-1990s. In a series of short stories published in 1994, Rasputin once more decries the modern world, but this time the world is that of post-October 1993. His tone is restrained, almost remorseful, as he feels that he is no longer part of the new world. His picture of youth is aggressively hostile, lambasting their love of western fashions, music, pornography. In "V bol'nitse" [In the Hospital] Rasputin explicitly tries to do for post-Soviet Russia what Solzhenitsyn in *Rakovyi korpus* (*Cancer Ward*) did for the post-Stalin Soviet Union, and fails. Rasputin's picture of modern reality is one of unrelieved gloom, and through the mouths of his two main patients he lines up the various aspects of society to be knocked down: the rise of crime and corruption, permissiveness, sex, television (even the television announcers are satirized for their Barbie-doll hair-styles), and the educational system.

Rasputin remains trapped in a time lock that became closed with the completion of *Farewell to Matyora* in 1976. There he portrayed the end of a world and a whole way of life, the end of a golden age of Russian culture and tradition. Rasputin remains embittered and nostalgic, angry at having become largely redundant in the new Russia, and sad that the Russia he knew and loved (if it existed at all) is no more.

DAVID GILLESPIE

Live and Remember

Zhivi i pomni

Novella, 1975

Published in the nationalist journal *Nash sovremennik* towards the end of 1974 and in book form the following year, *Live and Remember* was well received by Soviet critics who approved of its affirmation of Soviet patriotism, and by western scholars who remarked on the work's religious and symbolic themes. It is something of a departure in Rasputin's writing as it is the only one of his novellas (*povesti*) not set in the present. Instead, it is set in Rasputin's beloved Siberia in 1945, and covers the last months of the war and the first post-war months. Andrei Gus'kov deserts on his way back to the front from a military hospital, and returns home, to his village of Atamanovka. He makes his presence known only to his wife, Nastena, who continues to live in the family house, together with Andrei's mother and father, while he sets up home in a hut in the forest across the river. They resume a semblance of their marriage before it was cut short four years previously, and eventually Nastena gets pregnant. The suspicions of the other villagers, and Andrei's parents, are aroused, although Nastena insists that she was made pregnant by a stranger from outside the village. Ostracized from the community, and driven out of her home, she nevertheless remains faithful to Andrei and tells no-one of his whereabouts. One day in the summer, she crosses the river by boat to warn Andrei that police are in the village, but she is followed. Finally broken by months of guilt and duplicity, she throws herself into the swift-running waters of the Angara river. Her death – and the death of her unborn child – serve also to damn Andrei and finally isolate him from the human community.

The story is not just a symbolic working out of sin and martyrdom, set in and around a remote Siberian village. It is also very much a psychological drama, and the author develops his two characters, and their "new" relationship, with considerable sensitivity and attention to detail. Nastena's life has been one of almost uninterrupted suffering. We learn that she lost both her parents during collectivization, and after her marriage Andrei would beat her up – once with particular brutality, after she suggested that their childlessness was not perhaps her fault, but because of a defect in him. After Andrei's return, though, they develop a loving relationship, Andrei is gentler with her when he learns of her pregnancy – although he thinks nothing of the hardships she has to endure in the village when this begins to show.

We learn also that Andrei's desertion is not caused by cowardice, but rather of a desire to see his home after four years at the front. Indeed, Rasputin is at pains to show that Andrei has done his fair share of fighting: he has been wounded, suffered shell-shock, and been decorated for bravery. He has fought on all the major fronts: Smolensk, Moscow, and Stalingrad. When he is in hospital, recovering from his wounds, he is encouraged by his doctors that he will soon be allowed home for a few days. Instead, he is sent back directly to the front. It is then that he decides to desert, but only to see his home for a few days. As his journey wears on, it becomes obvious to him that he will not return to his unit. Andrei feels himself torn apart by his feelings and his situation, and, although we may feel sympathy for him at the outset, he is finally judged by Nastena's tragic fate.

The theme of the work is consistent with Rasputin's major concern throughout his writing: the human response to crisis, and the exploration of bonds that tie the individual to the community. This theme is largely developed through imagery and symbolism. The first symbol that occurs is when Andrei first visits the bath-house next to his parents' house, and steals his father's axe. The disappearance of the axe portends ill, as Nastena realizes, and it is with this axe that Andrei later kills a four-month-old calf, in front of its mother. Nastena is at this time four months' pregnant. It is both a savage physical act and a symbolic strike against motherhood, and the death of the calf is a portent of the death of Andrei's own child later. Andrei and Nastena live on opposite banks of the Angara river, and this natural divide also assumes a symbolic importance, as Nastena is to die in it. Furthermore, when Nastena crosses the river and the forest to visit him, her movements are hampered as she is accompanied by storms, rain, and darkness. She sees the hut Andrei inhabits as cold, dark, and desolate – just like his soul.

Further symbolism emphasizes the development of the two main characters. Andrei lives like a beast, sleeps during the day and hunts at night, cut off from the human community. He learns how to howl like a wolf, so that even the animals in the forest keep away. He becomes associated with demonic imagery: he kills a goat, and sees reflected in its dying eyes his own head with horns. When Nastena first sees him, ungainly and unkempt in the gloom of the bath-house, she thinks she is being attacked by a werewolf, and she later also sees him as a "wood goblin" (*leshii*) and "the evil spirit" (*nechistaia sila*). Nastena, on the other hand, achieves heights of Christian martyrdom and absolution, and is surrounded by religious imagery. One night she stands naked before the window, and the moon casts the shadow of the pane across her breast in the shape of a cross. Andrei calls her "Holy Mother", and implores her to save his soul. The moment when she discovers her pregnancy is also described as "the threshold of her holy path". In the seconds before she drowns, she hears thousands of church bells.

Rasputin succeeds in creating a human drama, told with restraint and compassion. It is also invested with symbolism, a tragic story with a universal relevance heightened by the author's attention to local detail, such as the speech of his characters, his sense of place, and the lyrical description of forests and rivers he himself knows so well. Together with the rest of his fiction, it is ultimately about man's denial of his roots and identity, and the consequences this entails for the individual's soul.

DAVID GILLESPIE

Farewell to Matyora

Proshchanie s Materoi

Novella, 1976

Published in 1976, this work is generally recognized as bringing to an end the Village Prose movement. Its theme is death: of the village, of Russia, of Mother Nature. It is set in the village of Matera, a 300-year-old island settlement on the Angara river. Matera is soon to be flooded as the whole area is designated to become part of a huge reservoir for the hydro-electric dam constructed up-river. Before it is flooded, all the buildings are to be razed by fire. The villagers will be housed in a new, semi-urban settlement (*poselok*) further down-river. The story, therefore, can be seen in purely publicistic terms as a microcosm of the modernization of society, with all the painful psychological consequences that implies. Rasputin, however, does not restrict his narrative to a plaintive emotional cry on behalf of those who are uprooted and dislocated. The narrative contains symbolic, allegorical, and mythological allusions.

First, it can be seen as a modern allegory of the Apocalypse, and the symbolic dimension is emphasized in the name of the island: Matera, with the word *mat'*, meaning "mother", at its root. The novella is thus not just about the death of a village, but of Mother Russia itself, its old customs, traditions, culture, and history drowned by the forces of reason and materialism in the technological age. The idyll is destroyed by faceless technocrats. It is little wonder that Village Prose had little else to say after this work.

The major characters comprise three generations of the Pinigin family. Dar'ia is 80 years old, and serves as the custodian of the village's values and spirit; her son Pavel, a confused and irresolute man, is charged with clearing the island of its structures before it is submerged; his son Andrei returns to the island to help with its destruction. Andrei wants to be in "the front line" of progress, and repeats the slogans of Soviet rationalism: "Man is the tsar of nature". Dar'ia, with her age-old wisdom and truth, asserts the opposite: "He who has no memory has no life". These words could serve as an epigraph for the whole Village Prose movement. The characters, apart from Pavel, are divided into "positive" and "negative": the former are those who belong to the village, especially the older folk (although some villagers, such as Petrukha, who burns down his own house, are portrayed negatively), while the "negative" characters are those from outside who come to oversee the destruction, such as the chairman of the village soviet Vorontsov, and the bureaucrat Zhuk.

Much of the narrative concentrates on the village's last days, the rhythm of a dying way of life, and the preparations for its destruction. Into this elegy Rasputin introduces folkloric and mythological aspects: one of the inhabitants of the village, Bogodul, is reminiscent of the "holy fool" of Russian folk culture, as he walks around barefoot, uttering obscenities, and is generally held in awe by the villagers. Furthermore, there is a small creature, about the same size as a cat, the Master (*Khoziain*) of the island, that knows every living thing on the island, but which itself cannot be seen. Only Dar'ia, towards the end of the narrative, senses the existence of this creature, which will die when the island dies.

The peasants see the destruction of their home as the "end of the world" (*svetoprestavlen'e*), and the end of the novella seems to reinforce their fears. The only building left on the island is the barrack hut inhabited by Bogodul, and here the last few old people of the village gather as the waters of the river begin to rise. A boat sets out from the shore to collect them, but gets lost in a dense and impenetrable fog, and the story ends with the peasants looking out of the door into the gloom, unsure of the future, unsure, indeed, whether they are dead or alive. The past is lost, the present unsure, the future in the balance.

Rasputin's use of language is also an important part of the narrative, for both the speech of his peasants and the authorial language of the narrative are peppered with local words, Siberian dialecticisms and colloquialisms. Rasputin, like other Village Prose writers, reproduces the local language of real people and real places, unlike Solzhenitsyn, who (in "Matrenin dvor" ("Matryona's House"), for instance) largely invents a peasant idiom of his own. Language has more than an aesthetic function, however; the idiom of the peasants separates them from those representing officialdom, who speak in an impersonal, bureaucratized language of their own.

Farewell to Matyora remains one of the most important works of Soviet literature of the 1970s, as it thoroughly rejects the Marxist-Leninist view of man and his future. Its theme is a rejection of the ethos of Soviet industrialization, that is, the onward rush towards material improvement without any consideration for the people who have to make way. In an age of rapid modernization and dynamic movement, the novella reminds us of the peace and stability of home, and reasserts the human value of progress. It is a lyrical elegy for a culture and way of life, and its inherent value system, which have largely disappeared in Russia. The author also skilfully combines religious, pagan, and mythological elements to show the spiritual and cultural forces that have formed the Siberian mentality. The novella remains a work firmly located in a specific place and time, but with a universal significance and relevance that encapsulate the human dilemma in the late 20th century.

DAVID GILLESPIE

Irina Borisovna Ratushinskaia 1954–

Poet, prose writer, and dissident

Biography

Born in Odessa, 4 March 1954. Attended school in Odessa; Odessa University, 1971–76; degree in physics 1976. Schoolteacher and taught at Odessa Pedagogical Institute. Moved to Kiev, 1979. Married: Igor' Gerashchenko in 1979; twin sons. Human rights campaigner; applied to emigrate, 1980. Arrested in Moscow, 10 December 1981; sentenced to ten days in Butyrki Prison; arrested again near Kiev, September 1982; charged with "preparing and disseminating anti-Soviet materials"; received maximum sentence of seven years in a labour camp plus five years of internal exile. Released in October 1986 after serving four years; permitted to travel to England with her husband, December 1986. Both lost their Soviet citizenship in May 1987. Currently resides in London with her husband and sons. Published in Russia and the Ukraine from 1990.

Publications

Poetry

Stikhi/Poems/Poèmes. Ann Arbor, Hermitage, 1984.
Ia dozhivu [I Shall Live]. New York, Cultural Center for Soviet Refugees, 1986.
Vne limita. Frankfurt, Posev, 1986; translated as *Beyond the Limit: Poems* (bilingual edition), by Frances Padorr Brent and Carol J. Avins, Evanston, Illinois, Northwestern University Press, 1987.
No, I'm Not Afraid, translated by David McDuff. Newcastle upon Tyne, Bloodaxe, 1986.
Stikhi. Chicago, Literary Courier, 1988.
Pencil Letter, various translators. Newcastle upon Tyne, Bloodaxe, 1988; New York, Knopf, 1989.
Dance with a Shadow, translated by David McDuff. Newcastle upon Tyne, Bloodaxe, 1992.

Fiction

Skazka o trekh golovakh / The Tale of the Three Heads (bilingual edition), translated by Diane Nemec Ignashev. Tenafly, New Jersey, Hermitage, 1986.
Odessity. Roman. Moscow, 1996; translated as *The Odessans*, by Geoffrey Smith, London, Sceptre, 1996.

Autobiography

Sery – tsvet nadezhdy, London, Overseas Publications Interchange, 1989; translated as *Grey is the Colour of Hope*, by Alyona Kojevnikov, London, Hodder and Stoughton, and New York, Knopf, 1988; London, Sceptre, 1989.
In the Beginning, translated by Alyona Kojevnikov. London, Hodder and Stoughton, 1990.

Critical Studies

"The Poetry of Irina Ratushinskaya", by Raymond Cooke, *Journal of Russian Studies*, 57 (1987), 48–55.
"What Does a Six-Winged Seraphim Taste Like?", by David Bethea, *Parnassus: Poetry in Review*, 14/2 (1988), 310–23.

Irina Ratushinskaia began to write poetry as a small girl, but only started to take herself seriously as a poet in the late 1970s, partly because of the impact of reading, for the first time, the proscribed works of Akhmatova, Mandel'shtam, Tsvetaeva, Pasternak, and Gumilev, which revealed to her the wealth and political import of the Russian literary heritage. As a Russian of Polish descent living in the Ukraine, she has been dismissive of nationalist prejudices. Baptized a Catholic by her grandmother, Ratushinskaia early embarked on a personal spiritual quest at odds with the atheist ideology that prevailed in her environment. She describes a guiding hand that enables her to choose between right and wrong, a voice that urges her to preserve her moral and intellectual integrity. Well before her imprisonment, her poetry proclaimed her abhorrence of the corrupting, violent, and debasing influence of the Soviet system. The experience of prison and camp, long anticipated as an inevitable destiny, only strengthened her resolve to fulfil with dignity the role of martyr bestowed on her by the Russian poetic tradition. During her incarceration she composed intensively, despite being prevented from preserving the poems in written form. The international campaign that may have helped to bring about her release by Gorbachev, was not only inspired by the outrageous punishment meted out to her for the writing of poetry critical of the State, but also fuelled by the information that, even in the camp, she was sacrificing her health and few privileges in an ongoing battle with the authorities for the rights of her fellow-prisoners. There were times when her ill-treatment and hunger-strikes brought her close to death.

For Ratushinskaia writing is a medium for interpreting and reflecting on immediate experience. Her dated poems chart the course of her life and her different moods to form a lyric diary. One of her earliest known poems, "Odnoklassnik" [My Classmate], imagines the excuses mumbled by an erstwhile classmate instructed to execute her, and deplores, through irony, the petty cowardice that has brought tyranny upon a Soviet people afraid to assume responsibility for its actions. Ratushinskaia's dedication to honour and fearlessness is a recurrent theme of her work. Her poems of the late 1970s speak of her "hateful" native land and the fact that its citizens are all prisoners; they also reflect her sadness as many of her friends, including the man she loved, seized the opportunity available at the time to emigrate. A characteristic feature of her writing, however, is her ability to find solace and humour in the most improbable situations. In prison, Ratushinskaia befriends sparrows and mice to console herself and establishes with them the intimacy her surroundings lack; she is able to transport herself beyond her immediate circumstances through her imagination, which allows her to travel familiar routes with her beloved or anticipate the joy of reunion. She composes letters that will never be sent or received, although she is confident that Igor' Gerashchenko will be capable of "reading between the undelivered lines" (*Pis'mo karandashom* [*Pencil Letter*]). From time to time she evokes the image of Russia as an uncomprehending parent of its children; in more than one poem she reflects wistfully on the children she and her fellow-prisoners may never bear. Childhood is presented as a time of freedom unfettered by adult preoccupations; she recalls the thimble given her as a present that became a prop for all her games of fantasy rather than a prosaic tool ("Kogda mne ispolnilos' sem' ..." ("On my seventh birthday ...")). Some of her work, like the absurdist short stories collected in the volume *Skazka o trekh golovakh* (*The Tale of the Three Heads*), is clearly written with an audience of children in mind. A wry poem composed in prison before she sets off for the labour camp comments on the irony of her situation as a "dangerous subversive" who is actually most troubled at that precise moment by the fact that one of her wisdom teeth is coming through – a sharp object, what's more, such as is prohibited by prison regulations ... ("U izmennitsy i otstupnitsy ..." ("This traitress and apostate ...")). She is strengthened in her defiance and determination to overcome oppression by her religious faith, and expresses the hope that God will redeem her sinful land. After being released and allowed to travel to the west in 1986, Ratushinskaia did not forget the travails of her homeland and urged Russia to find the courage to free itself from darkness – this was from Italy, a land so beautiful that she feels death seems scarcely to reach there ("V Italii barochny oblaka ..." ("In Italy the clouds are baroque ...")).

Ratushinskaia has been thought of as a poet of limited scope; the experiences that feed her work – love, parting, imprisonment – if powerful, are nevertheless in some respects narrow. Some have suggested that the influence of other poets such as Akhmatova in mood and theme (see " – Korol' uekhal v gory ..." (" – The king has left for the hills ...")), or Tsvetaeva in certain formal respects (the exclamatory nature of much of Ratushinskaia's writing and her conscious re-use of Tsvetaeva's typical device of dashes within words, particularly apparent in *Pencil Letter*), is so strong as to indicate a lack of originality. Iosef Brodskii, however, has expressed the view that "Ratushinskaia is a remarkably genuine poet, a poet with faultless pitch, who hears historical and absolute time with equal precision". Viewed as a whole, her poetry impresses by the freshness of her vision, the creative ingenuity of much of her imagery, and the overriding sense the reader gains of her strength and courage. Her reputation has been buttressed by the publication of two highly readable volumes of autobiography, *Sery – tsvet nadezhdy* (*Grey is the Colour of Hope*), which adds to the chronicles of Soviet camp life, and *In the Beginning* (not yet available in Russian), which looks back over her entire life up until the moment when she left the Soviet Union. In 1996 a historical novel, *Odessity* (*The Odessans*), was published, which chronicles the lives of several Odessan families from the 1905 Revolution to Hitler's attack on Russia in June 1941.

J.A.E. Curtis

Evgenii Borisovich Rein 1935–

Poet

Biography

Born in Leningrad, 29 December 1935. Brought up by mother, his father having been killed in World War II. Attended the Leningrad Technological Institute from 1954; expelled in 1957; continued education at the Institute of Industrial Refrigeration, graduating in 1959. Worked as refrigeration engineer, then freelance journalist and screenwriter; moved to Moscow, 1972. Married: 1) Galina Norinskaia, one daughter; 2) Natal'ia Ruvinskaia, one son; 3) Nadezhda Posisaeva in 1989. Writes popular science, journalism, and poetry. Poems appeared in *samizdat* almanac, *Metropol'*, 1979. Slim collection published, 1984; following perestroika, published prolifically from 1989. Recipient: Arion Prize for poetry, 1995.

Publications

Collected Editions

Izbrannoe. Moscow, 1993.

Mne skuchno bez Dovlatova: Novye tseny iz zhizni moskovskoi bogemy: Poemy i rasskazy [I'm Bored Without Dovlatov: New Scenes from Moscow Bohemian Life] (poems and stories). Moscow, 1997.

Poetry

Imena mostov [The Names of the Bridges]. Moscow, 1984.

Pis'mo na Kamchatku [A Letter to Kamchatka] (bilingual edition). Milan, Edizione Shweiler, 1988.

Beregovaia polosa [A Shoreline Strip]. Moscow, 1989.

Temnota zerkal [The Darkness of Mirrors]. Moscow, 1990.

Nepopravimyi den' [An Irretrievable Day]. Moscow, 1991.

Protiv chasovoi strelki [Anti-Clockwise]. Tenafly, New Jersey, Hermitage, 1991.

Nezhnosmo. Moscow, 1992.

Poems in *Twentieth Century Russian Poetry: Silver and Steel. An Anthology*, with an introduction by Yevgeny Yevtushenko, edited by Albert C. Todd and Max Hayward, London, Fourth Estate, and New York, Doubleday, 1993, 852–58.

Poems in *Contemporary Russian Poetry: A Bilingual Anthology*, translated by Gerald S. Smith, Bloomington, Indiana University Press, 1993, 70–85.

Predskazanie [Prediction]. Moscow, 1994.

Sapozhok. Kniga ital'ianskikh stikhov [Boot. Book of Italian Poetry]. Moscow, 1995.

Fiction

Iskry. Roman [Sparks: A Novel]. Tenafly, New Jersey, Hermitage, 1996.

Critical Studies

Review of *Imena mostov*, by Dmitrii Bobyshev, *Kontinent*, 44 (1985), 325–32.

"'Nepopravimyi den' ... O stikhakh Evgeniia Reina", by Aleksandr Mezhirov, *Literaturnaia gazeta*, 24 October 1990.

"Tragicheskii elegik (o poezii Evgenii Reina)", by Iosif Brodskii, *Znamia*, 7 (1991), 180–85.

"Predskazanie izbrannosti", by Aleksei Purin, *Novyi mir*, 12 (1994), 223.

"'Ia vyrastal v zabavneishee vremia' ... O dvukh chetverkakh. Issledovaniia Iu. Lotmana kak kliuch k stikham E. Reina", by Efim Etkind, *Literaturnaia gazeta*, 31 May 1995.

For nearly 30 years Evgenii Rein supported himself by writing commissioned works on cultural and popular science subjects for magazines and film studios and occasionally books for children. As a journalist he travelled widely within the Soviet Union (but never abroad). He continued to write poetry that remained by and large unpublished, either in the Soviet Union or abroad, until 1979, when a dozen poems appeared in *Metropol'*. In 1984 his first, skimpy and unrepresentative collection, *Imena mostov* [The Names of the Bridges], was issued, but genuine, albeit belated, public recognition came to him only a few years later, after perestroika. Ten collections of Rein's poetry were published between 1989 and 1995, his new poetic works began to appear regularly in periodicals, accompanied by a spate of reviews and articles. During the same period he attended a number of international conferences, poetry festivals, and symposia in Europe and the United States.

Rein's sudden rise to fame and to being recognized as one of his country's leading poets was helped by Iosif Brodskii, who, on many occasions following his 1987 Nobel Prize, called Rein his mentor and wrote an appreciative essay about Rein's poetic world. Indeed, some very important aspects of Brodskii's poetic art seem to have been inspired by reading Rein's early works. The future Nobel Laureate and his peers, aspiring young poets and writers in Leningrad of the 1950s and 1960s, were greatly influenced by the colourful personality of Evgenii Rein, then the reincarnation of an archetypal romantic, avant-garde poet, against the grey backdrop of Soviet cultural officialdom. Characteristically, one of Rein's most popular early works was a long poem, "Rembo" [Rimbaud], a not entirely true account of the French poet's life, but a powerful manifesto by a new Russian *poète maudit*. Invited or, more often, uninvited, the young Rein would read his poetry, so different from the prevailing kind, in clubs and bookstores, employing a thundering, exaggeratedly intoned voice and scandalizing audiences by his public behaviour no less than by the unusual poetics and subject-matter. There was, however, one element in the young poet's work and public behaviour usually lacking in a young artistic rebel: the "anxiety of influence". Memoirists often refer to Rein in his early period as a member of the "magic choir", as Anna Akhmatova nicknamed the group of young poets (Bobyshev, Brodskii, Naiman, and Rein) who became close to her during the last years of her life. But Rein was the one who actively sought other cross-generational connections beyond the cherished friendship with Akhmatova. He was an enthusiastic visitor in the homes and studios of older writers and artists, famous or forgotten survivors of the Silver Age and the early Soviet artistic avant-garde. Thus he took upon himself an important cultural role as a collector and transmitter of bohemian lore, the builder of a bridge between forcibly separated epochs. By the 1970s "Dvukh stolits neprikaiannyi zhitel'" ("the restless inhabitant of two capitals") became a staple figure in the bohemian circles of Leningrad and Moscow, more what Russians call a *dusha obshchestva* ("society soul"), a man about town, everybody's friend and a terrific raconteur, rather than the one-time stirrer of literary scandals.

Unlike his Moscow counterparts and personal friends, Bella Akhmadulina, Evgenii Evtushenko, and Andrei Voznesenskii, Rein almost never addressed political themes in his poetry; yet, paradoxically, while their poetry, replete with poignant allegory and *double entendre*, could find its way into print, Rein's apolitical verse turned out to be absolutely unacceptable to Soviet publishers. One might suggest that the Soviet authorities, thanks to a certain institutional intuition, detected in Rein's poetry an encroachment on a fundamental premise of the regime: reality as an ideological construct. Indeed, Rein's lyrical hero lives in a world distinctly recognizable as the Soviet world of his time: he dwells in the wretched rooms of communal apartments, travels in filthy commuter trains, and boozes in garish restaurants; the poet heaps up "realistic" detail – vivid descriptions of clothes, furniture, food, drink, houseware – with gusto, an overabundance more reminiscent of Zola's novels than anything in Russian poetry. The signs and symbols of the Soviet system and communist ideology are not eschewed from this world, but they appear on a par with inclement weather or morbid health. In other words, Rein's lyrical realm is the "real reality", in which the poet and the majority of his compatriots lived. By ignoring ideology, Rein denied it the recognition provided even by those dissident poets who were willing to enter into dialogue with it.

There were other uncompromising poets of the same generation who were inspired by the mundane and the trivial in Soviet life; two illustrious examples are Vladimir Ufland in St Petersburg and Genrikh Sapgir in Moscow. Unlike these two, Rein's poetic expression is not tinted with parody and absurdism, his lyrical emotions exhibit a straightforward pathos. In this respect, his is the most unadulterated voice of his time. Should someone in the future decide to write a sentimental history of Soviet Russia, the poetry of Evgenii Rein could serve as that historian's primary source.

The chief sentiment found in Rein's elegies is an acute sense of place and time. In his essay Brodskii noted that the favourite locale of Rein's lyrical persona is the waterside and explained this preference as a genetic memory of the species, shaped by both Darwinian evolutionism and Christian metaphysics (the fish being an early emblem of the Saviour). It seems that there is another, historically more immediate, message in this recurrent motif: a claustrophobic sense of confinement within the empire's borders and the longing for a cosmopolitan civilization, to which the author feels an affinity and from which he has been forcibly separated. This is why the haven of a Soviet Black Sea resort town is for him "the remotest appendix of the Mediterranean" (*Izbrannoe* [Selected Works]) and Tallin, the capital of Soviet Estonia, "the ugly outskirts of the Hanseatic League". This powerful nostalgia is directed not just spatially but also temporally: Rein presents himself "looking from the pier at time sinking". History, recent and distant, always shines through modern scenes in Rein's poetry. In a poem entitled "Druz'iam v Leningrade" [To Friends in Leningrad], he reckons his fellow Leningrad poets in the company of Derzhavin, Shikhmatov, and Shakhovskoi (Neoclassical poets of the 1800s). In many poems he keenly sees poignant messages affecting his current existence in the architectural styles of city buildings and in antiquarian bagatelles in the apartments of ordinary people.

Rein's sophisticated sense of history accounts also for the roots of his peculiar poetics. Besides continuing the Acmeist tradition, a heritage that he shared with his Leningrad peers, Rein picked up and developed many innovations peculiar to early Soviet "Kiplingesque" poets, such as Nikolai Tikhonov, Eduard Bagritskii, and Vladimir Lugovskoi, whose work was compromised in the eyes of his generation because of their genuine loyalty to the Soviet regime. These features of Rein's poetics include the elegiac ballad as a genre of choice, a diction sparing of verbs and rich in concrete (non-metaphoric) nouns and adjectives, and a style constantly swaying between lofty poeticism and vulgarity.

LEV LOSEFF

Aleksei Mikhailovich Remizov 1877–1957

Prose writer

Biography

Born in Moscow, 6 July 1877. Enrolled at Moscow University in 1894; studied physics and mathematics; arrested and expelled from university for taking part in a demonstration, 1896: imprisoned for two months. Exiled until 1903. During this period he became a professional writer. Worked for Meierkhol'd's theatre company in Kherson as literary consultant, translator, and administrator, 1903–04. Married: Serafima Pavlovna Dovgello in 1903; one daughter. Lived in St Petersburg, 1905–21. Called up for military service, but found to be medically unfit, 1916. After the Revolution was briefly associated with the Scythians, and held various positions in new literary organizations. Emigrated first to Berlin in 1921, then to France in 1923. Recipient: Golden Fleece Prize for the story "Chertik" ("The Devil"), 1906. Died in Paris, 26 November 1957.

Publications

Collected Editions

Sochineniia, 8 vols. St Petersburg, 1910; 2nd edition St Petersburg, 1912; reprinted Munich, Fink, 1971.

The Fifth Pestilence, The History of the Tinkling Cymbal and Sounding Brass: Ivan Semyonovich Stratilatov, translated by Alec Brown. London, Chatto and Windus, 1926; New York, Payson and Clarke, 1928; reprinted Westport, Connecticut, Hyperion Press, 1977.

Izbrannoe. Moscow, 1978.

Selected Prose, edited by Sona Aronian, translated by Aronian *et al*. Ann Arbor, Ardis, 1985.

Povesti i rasskazy. Moscow, 1990.

Izbrannoe. Leningrad, 1991.

Sochineniia, 2 vols. Moscow, 1993.

Izbrannye proizvedeniia. Moscow, 1995.

Works

[Remizov's works are in the main regarded as generically indeterminable]

Posolon' [Sunwise], *Zolotoe runo* (1907); reprinted Paris, Tair, 1930.

Limonar'. Siriech: Lug dukhovnyi [Leimonarium. The Meadow of the Spirit]. St Petersburg, 1907.

Prud [The Pond]. St Petersburg, 1908.

Chasy. St Petersburg, 1908; translated as *The Clock*, by John Cournos, London, Chatto and Windus, and New York, Knopf, 1924.

Chertov log i polunochnoe solntse: Rasskazy i poemy [The Devil's Lair and the Midnight Sun: Stories and Poems]. St Petersburg, 1908.

Rasskazy [Stories]. St Petersburg, 1910.

"Neuemnyi buben" [The Irrepressible Cymbal], in *Al'manakh dlia vsekh*, book 1, St Petersburg, 1910; translated as "The History of the Tinkling Cymbal and Sounding Brass: Ivan Semyonovich Stratilatov", by Alec Brown, in *The Fifth Pestilence* ..., 1926.

Krestovye sestry [Sisters of the Cross], Berlin, Grzhebin, 1910; reprinted Letchworth, Bradda, 1969.

"Piataia iazva", *Literaturno-khudozhestvennyi al'manakh izdatel'stva "Shipovnik"*, 18 (1912); reprinted Letchworth, Bradda, 1970; translated as "The Fifth Pestilence", by Alec Brown, in *The Fifth Pestilence* ..., 1926.

Nikola Milostivy: Nikoliny pritchi [Nicholas's Parables]. Petrograd, 1918.

Sibirskii prianik: bol'shim i dlia malykh rebiat skazki [The Siberian Cookie]. Petrograd, 1919.

Besovskoe deistvo [The Devil's Deed]. Petrograd, 1919.

Tragediia o Iude [The Tragedy of Judas]. Petrograd and Moscow, 1919.

Tsar' Maksimilian [Tsar Maximilian]. Petrograd, 1920.

Shumy goroda [The Noises of the City]. Revel, Bibliofil, 1921.

Ognennaia Rossiia [Fiery Russia]. Revel, Bibliofil, 1921.

Mara [Fata Morgana]. Berlin, Epokha, 1922.

Chakkhchygys-Taasu. Berlin, Skify, 1922.

V pole blakitnom. Berlin, Ogon'ki, 1922; translated as *On a Field of Azure*, by Beatrice Scott, London, Lindsay Drummond, 1946.

Rossiia v pismenakh [Russia in Writ]. Berlin, Gelikon, 1922; reprinted New York, Russica, 1982.

Trava-Murava [Sward-Grass]. Berlin, S. Efron, 1922.

Rusaliia. Berlin, Grzhebin, 1923.

Kukha. Rozanovy pis'ma [Kukha. Rozanov's Letters]. Berlin, Grzhebin, 1923; reprinted New York, Serebrianyi vek, 1978.

Skazki russkogo naroda [Tales of the Russian Folk]. Berlin, 1923.

Zvenigorod oklikannyi [Echoes of Zvenigorod]. Paris, Alatas, 1924.

Zga. Volshebnye rasskazy [Zga: Tales of Wonder]. Prague, Plamia, 1925.

Vzvikhrennaia Rus' [Russia in the Whirlwind]. Paris, Tair, 1927; reprinted London, Overseas Publications Interchange, 1979.

Olia. Paris, Vol, 1927.

Zvezda nadzvezdnaia. Stella Maria Maris [Star above All Stars. Stella Maria Maris]. Paris, YMCA-Press, 1928.

Po karnizam [Along the Cornices]. Belgrade, Russkaia tipografiia, 1929.

Moskovskie liubimye legendy. Tri serpa. [The Three Sickles, 1–2], Paris, Tair, 1929.

Obraz Nikolaia Chudotvortsa, alatyr-kamen' russkoi very [The Image of Nicholas the Miracle Worker]. Paris, YMCA-Press, 1931.

Golubinaia kniga [The Book of the Dove]. Hamburg, Rodnik, 1946.

Pliashushchii demon [The Dancing Demon]. Paris, Tanets i slovo, 1949.

Povest' o dvukh zveriakh. Ikhnelat [The Tale of Two Beasts. Ikhnelat]. Paris, Opleshnik, 1950.

Besnovatye. Savva Grudtsyn i Solomoniia [The Possessed. Savva Grudytsyn i Solomoniia]. Paris, Opleshnik, 1951.

Podstrizhennymi glazami [With Clipped Eyes]. Paris, YMCA-Press, 1951.

Meliuzina. Paris, Opleshnik, 1952.

V rozovom bleske [In a Rosy Light]. New York, Izdatel'stvo imeni Chekhova, 1952; reprinted Letchworth, Bradda, 1969; Moscow, 1990.

Myshkina Dudochka [A Mouse's Fife]. Paris, Opleshnik, 1953.

Ogon' veshchei [The Fire of Things]. Paris, 1954; reprinted Moscow, 1989.

Martyn Zadeka. Paris, Opleshnik, 1954.

Krug schast'ia: legendy o Tsare Solomone [Circle of Happiness: Legends of King Solomon]. Paris, Opleshnik, 1957.

Tristan i Isolda. Bova korolevich [Tristan and Isolda. Prince Bova]. Paris, Opleshnik, 1957.

Vstrechi. Peterburgskii buerak. [Encounters. Petersburg Gully]. Paris, Lev, 1981.

Uchitel' muzyki. Katorzhnaia idilliia [The Music Teacher. Prison Idyll]. Paris, Press Libre, 1983.

Iveren': zagoguliny moei pamiati [Splinters], edited by Olga Raevsky-Hughes. Berkeley, Berkeley Slavic Specialties, 1986.

Critical Studies

"Remizov", by V.N. Il'in, in *O t'me i prosvetlenii: Kniga khudozhestvennoi kritiki: Bunin, Remizov, Shmelev*, Munich, 1959, 79–131.

Aleksei Remizov, by Natalia Kodrianskaia, Paris, n.p., 1959.

A.M. Remizov; Stilstudien, by Katharina Östreich-Geib, Munich, Fink, 1970.

"Remizov's *Prud*: From Symbolism to Neo-Realism", by A.M. Shane, *California Slavic Studies*, 6 (1971), 71–82.
"Aleksej Remizovs Beitrag zum russischen Theater", by Horst Lampl, *Wiener Slavistische Jahrbuch*, 17 (1972), 136–83.
"A Prisoner of Fate: Remizov's Short Fiction", by A.M. Shane, *Russian Literature Triquarterly*, 4 (1972), 303–18.
"Parody in Remizov's 'Pjataja jazva'", by Renate S. Bialy, *Slavic and East European Journal*, 19/4 (1975), 403–10.
"Puti i pereput'ia Alekseia Remizova", by Iurii Andreev, *Voprosy literatury*, 21/5 (1977), 216–43.
"Arkhiv A.M. Remizova", by S.S. Grechishkin, *Ezhegodnik rukopisnogo otdela Pushkinskogo doma na 1975 god*, Leningrad, 1977, 20–45.
Aleksei Remizov v svoikh pis'makh, by Natalia Kodrianskaia, Paris, n.p., 1977.
"Povest' A. M. Remizova 'Savva Grubtsyn' i ee drevnerusskii prototip", by A.M. Gracheva, *Trudy otdela drevnerusskoi literatury*, 33 (1979), 388–400.
Ognennaia pamiat': vospominaniia o Aleksee Remizove, by Nathalie Reznikoff, Berkeley, Berkeley Slavic Specialties, 1980.
"Nadpisi A.M. Remizova na knigakh. Iz moego sobraniia", by Gleb Struve, in *Russkii al'manakh*, edited by Z. Shakovskaia and R. Guerra, Paris, 1981, 429–49.
Russian Literature Triquarterly (special Remizov issue), 18 (1985); 19 (1986).
"Geroi A. M. Remizova i ego prototip", by A.A. Danilevskii, *Uchenye zapiski Tartusskogo gosudarstvennogo universiteta*, 748 (1987), 150–65.
Aleksej Remizov: Approaches to a Protean Writer. Proceedings of the 1985 International Symposium on Remizov, edited by Greta N. Slobin, Columbus, Ohio, Slavica, 1987.
"Aleksei Remizov's Defense of the Russian Language", by Olga Raevsky-Hughes, in *Language, Literature, Linguistics. In Honour of Francis Whitfield on his Seventieth Birthday*, edited by Michael Flier and Simon Karlinsky, Berkeley, Berkeley Slavic Specialties, 1987, 192–211.
"Drevnerusskie povesti v pereskazakh Remizova", by A.M. Gracheva, *Russkaia literatura*, 3 (1988), 110–34.
"Povest' A.M. Remizova 'Solomoniiv' i ee drevnerusskii istochnik", by A.V. Pigin, *Russkaia literatura*, 2 (1989), 114–30.
"Model' remizovskogo ada: Analiz povesti 'Piataia iazva'", by Katalin Szöke, *Studia Slavica*, 35/3–4 (1989), 385–92.
"Aleksei Remizov's *The Clock* and the Russian Symbolist Novel", by C. Dowsett, *Modern Language Review*, 86/2 (1991), 372–86.
Remizov's Fictions, by Greta N. Slobin, DeKalb, Illinois, Northern Illinois University Press, 1991.
"Remizov's Erotic Tales: Stylization and Subversion", by Greta N. Slobin, in *The Short Story in Russia, 1900–17*, edited by Nicholas Luker, Nottingham, Astra, 1991.
"The Life of Peter and Fevroniia: Transformations and Interpretations in Modern Russian Literature and Music", by Lyubomira Parpulova Gribble, *Russian Review*, 52/2 (1993), 184–97.
"Remizov's Judas: Apocryphal Legend into Symbolist Drama", by Edward Manouelian, *Slavic and East European Journal*, 37/1 (1993), 46–66.
"Esenin i Remizov: Otrazhenie russkogo narodnogo samosoznaniia", by Maria Pavlovszky, in *American Contributions to the Eleventh International Congress of Slavists, Bratislava, Slovakia: Literature*, edited by Robert A. Maguire and Alan Timberlake, Columbus, Ohio, Slavica, 1993, 111–29.
Aleksei Remizov: Issledovaniia i materialy, edited by A.M. Gracheva, St Petersburg, 1994.

Bibliographies
Istoriia russkoi literatury kontsa XIX–nachala XX v: Bibliograficheskii ukazatel', Leningrad, 1963.
Bibliographie des oeuvres de Alexis Remizov, by Helène Sinany, Paris, Institut d'Études Slaves, 1978.
"Bemerkungen und Erganzungen zur Bibliographie A.M. Remizovs", by Horst Lampl, *Wiener Slawistische Almanach*, 2 (1978), 31–326.

Aleksei Remizov had a remarkably long and prolific literary career: he started to write in 1896, his first published work appeared in 1902 in *Vestnik* ("Plach devushki pered zamuzhestvom" [Lament of a Maiden before Marriage]) under the pseudonym Nikolai Moldavanov, and he wrote without interruption until his death in 1957, publishing 83 books. Nevertheless he is not well known or widely studied, because of his eccentric, difficult, esoteric, and almost untranslatable literary manner, which may explain the initial unenthusiastic critical responses and his reputation as a writer's writer. His production spans a wide variety of works; it is difficult to tie them to traditional genres. One class includes original works: short and long prose fiction, mystery plays, memoirs, recorded dreams, diaries, and literary criticism; another class includes works derived from pre-existing texts and oral sources, incorporating medieval literary, historical, biblical, apocryphal, and folklore sources. Remizov formally belonged to no movement, although his works are closely related to Symbolism, in terms of both influence and polemics, and other Silver Age trends. The essence of his art is the mingling of modernism with the native literary and non-literary heritage of the past, using a montage technique. Thus, his works exhibit the intangible influence of such diverse phenomena as Christianity (official and popular), occultism, medieval religious mysticism, scientific research, medieval manuscripts, etc. He also incorporated other arts (kinetic, musical, visual) into his works, following the general Silver Age tendency of uniting eclectic art forms. He himself was an artist, a paleocalligrapher; he illustrated his own works and copied them in an ornamental hand, adopting the 17th-century semiuncial and cursive. He wrote predominately prose, although his writing sometimes approaches poetry in its rhythmic or musical compositional principles. His innovative drama was influenced by medieval miracle plays and folklore (*Besovskoe deistvo* [The Devil's Deed]; *Tragediia o Iude* [The Tragedy of Judas]; *Tsar' Maksimilian* [Tsar Maximilian]; *Rusaliia*), and most clearly exemplify his synthesis of the expressive devices of different art forms, combining the theatre with dance, music, and painting.

Six of his novels and novellas were written early in his career: *Prud* [The Pond]; *Chasy* (*The Clock*); *Krestovye sestry* [Sisters of the Cross]; *Neuemnyi buben* (*The History of the Tinkling Cymbal and Sounding Brass: Ivan Semyonovich Stratilatov*); *Piataia iazva* (*The Fifth Pestilence*); and *(Pliachushchaia) kanava ili L'vinyi rov* [The (Weeping) Ditch, or The Den of Lions] (originally published only in excerpts; first full edition 1991). The subject-matter evokes both the Gogolian grotesque and the Dostoevskian tragic world, tempered by Remizov's reinterpretation of certain aspects of human misery, abandonment, the incomprehensibility of existence, the insignificance of man, and the stifling atmosphere of provincial Russian towns through a blend of passion, laughter, grotesquery, and parody. His highly stylized narrative discourse draws on the tradition of Gogol' and Leskov; he employs the *skaz* technique, which blends the narrator's point of view and language with those of the characters, thus creating the illusion of an intimate theatricalized discourse. His novels are saturated with literary allusions introduced as parallels and/or targets for polemics on many levels, parodying the originals or commenting on contemporary issues.

More than a third of his original short stories focus on children. Remizov not only offers piquant observations and lyrical involvement, but also captures their peculiar point of view in such stories as "Slonenok" [The Little Elephant], "Chertik" ("The Little Devil"), "Tsarevna Mymra" [Princess Mymra], and "Petushok" [The Little Cock].

Real success came to Remizov through his retold works, in which he fused pagan and Christian popular myths. The first two were *Posolon'* [Sunwise], in which children's games, holiday celebrations, rituals, and fairy tales are arranged according to the movement of the sun from spring to winter, and *Limonar': Lug dukhovnyi* [Leimonarium: The Meadow of the Spirit], (later extended by the sequel *Paralipomenon*), which was based on Remizov's reworking of canonical and apocryphal texts, oriented more toward religion.

Remizov addressed the same sources many times, revising and rearranging the same material in various ways; thus similar titles, images, and devices recur in several collections, functioning as unifying leitmotifs for his entire *oeuvre*, e.g., his famous adaptions of the popular legends and hagiographies about St Nicholas, the patron saint of Russia, emphasizing the double belief system reflected in the image of the saint (*Nikoliny pritchi* [Nicholas's Parables]; *Zvenigorod oklikannyi* [Echoes of Zvenigorod]; *Tri serpa* [The Three Sickles 1–2]; *Obraz Nikolaia Chudotvortsa* [The Image of Nicholas the Miracle Worker]).

Most of Remizov's works are derived from native sources, especially Old Russian Literature ("Povest' o Petre i Fevronii" [The Tale of Peter and Fevroniia], "Povest' o dvukh zveriakh" [The Tale of Two Beasts], "Besnovatye: Savva Grudytsyn i Solomoniia" [The Possessed: Savva Grudytsyn and Solomoniia]), and certain religious prototypes are ultimately of Byzantine origin. In several works he turns to western sources or the folk heritage of non-western peoples (Zyrians, Georgians, Armenians, Tibetans), but always working with material familiar to Russians, such as, his *Sibirskii prianik* [The Siberian Cookie]; *Chakkhchygys-Taasu*; *Trava-Murava*.

Remizov's reaction to the October Revolution was controversial. Before October 1917, he wrote his prophetic prose-poem "Slovo o pogibeli zemli russkoi" [Oration on the Downfall of the Russian Land], a reworking of the eponymous ancient Russian lament. Remizov foresaw the destruction of ancient Russia and Christianity by impending events and likened them to the Tartar invasion. The atmosphere of St Petersburg during war and revolution is captured in the story cycles *Shumy goroda* [The Noises of the City], and *Mara* [Fata Morgana]. His most significant work about the Revolution and its aftermath is the memoir *Vzvikhrennaia Rus'* [Russia in the Whirlwind], written with a decade's detachment, a subjective montage of disjointed fragments: dreams, tales, reminiscences, literary allusions, lyric digressions, letters. This work pointed in a new artistic direction.

After emigration Remizov wrote no new fiction, although he did revise some previous works, moving toward an eclectic memoir-fiction that strove to evoke a timeless world between dream, legend, faith, and reality. Typical are the surrealistic memoir-biography *Podstrizhennymi glazami* [With Clipped Eyes], which juxtaposes the visions of a wise elder and an untainted child; *Myshkina Dudochka* [A Mouse's Fife]; and *Ogon' veshchei* [The Fire of Things], a volume of essays on major Russian writers oriented around the interpretation of dreams. His interest in visual arts developed further; he compiled albums of drawings, assembled a diary from graphic designs, and even Picasso remarked on his abstract pictures.

His experimental writing influenced the development of Russian prose before and after the Revolution, especially Zamiatin, Prishvin, and Pil'niak. His Russian language style seeks to restore pre-Petrine usage by exterminating foreign influences. Because of his striving to establish a national style, Mirsky calls him "the most naturally Slavophile of modern Russian writers". He attempted to save words from "oblivion" by revitalizing them, assigning to them new meanings. His richly ornate style rests upon simple Slavonic syntax and spoken intonation. His vocabulary is perhaps the widest in Russian literature, as he resurrects layers of Russian forgotten by most of its speakers. His texts are fragmented; the parts are at times interchangable and can be rearranged. Remizov's innovative style, deeply rooted in the Russian national tradition, conveys essential questions about Russia's destiny, its place among other nations, and the national character.

MARIA PAVLOVSZKY

Evdokia Petrovna Rostopchina 1812–1858

Poet and prose writer

Biography

Born Evdokia Petrovna Sushkova in Moscow, 4 January 1812. Brought up by grandparents; educated at home by governesses. Met Pushkin in Moscow, 1829. Published first verses in *Severnye tsvety*, 1831. Married: Count Andrei Rostopchin in 1833; two daughters and one son. Moved to St Petersburg, 1836. Held soirées at St Petersburg home, frequented by Pushkin, Prince Odoevskii, Gogol', Zhukovskii, and Krylov. Good friendship with Lermontov who moved to Moscow, 1841. Travelled with husband to Poland, Italy, France, Germany, and Switzerland, 1845–47. Moved to Moscow, 1847. Organized regular literary soirées, frequented by A.N. Ostrovskii. Visited by Alexandre Dumas who requested that she write her memoirs of Lermontov. Suffered ill health, 1856–58. Died in Moscow, 15 December 1858.

Publications

Collected Editions

Sochineniia, 2 vols. St Petersburg, 1890.
Sobranie sochinenii. St Petersburg, 1910.
Stikhotvoreniia. Proza. Pis'ma. Moscow, 1986.
Talisman. Moscow, 1987.
Schastlivaia zhenshchina [Happy Woman]. Moscow, 1990.

Poetry

"Talisman", *Severnye tsvety*, 1831.
Stikhotvoreniia. St Petersburg, 1841.
Dnevnik devushki. Roman v stikhakh [A Girl's Diary]. St Petersburg, 1866.
"Dom sumasshedshikh v Moskve v 1858g." [Mad House in Moscow in 1858], in *Epigramma i satira: iz istorii literaturnoi bor'by XIX veka (1800–1880)*, Moscow and Leningrad, 1931–32, vol. 2; reprinted Oxford, Meeuws, 1975.

Prose

"Chiny i den'gi" [Ranks and Money]. 1837.
Ocherki bol'shogo sveta [Sketches of High Society]. St Petersburg, 1839.
U pristani. Roman v pis'makh [At the Pier. A Novel in Letters]. St Petersburg, 1857.
"Poedinok" [The Duel], in *Russkaia romanticheskaia novella*, Moscow, 1989.

Plays

Neliudimka [The Recluse]. 1849.
Vozvrat Chatskogo v Moskvu. Prodolzhenie komedii Griboedova "Gore ot uma" [Chatskii's Return to Moscow. A Continuation of Griboedov's Comedy "Woe from Wit"]. St Petersburg, 1856.

Critical Studies

"Grafinia E.P. Rostopchina: Ee zhizn' i lirika", by V. Khodasevich, in his *Stat'i o russkoi poezii*, Petrograd, 1922, 7–42; reprinted Letchworth, Prideaux Press, 1971.
"U pristani: Roman v pis'makh grafini Evdokii Rostopchiny", by N.A. Dobroliubov (1857), in his *Sobranie sochinenii*, 1962, vol. 2.
Russkie poetessy XIX veka [Pavlova i Rostopchina], by A. Zorin, Moscow, 1982, 51–53.
Russian Romantic Fiction, by John Mersereau Jr, Ann Arbor, Ardis, 1983.
V.F. Odoyevsky: His Life, Times and Milieu, by Neil Cornwell, London, Athlone Press, and Athens, Ohio University Press, 1986.
"The Scandal of Countess Rostopchina's Polish-Russian Allegory", by L. Pedrotii, *Slavonic and East European Journal*, 30 (1986).
Pisatel'nitsy pushkinskoi pory, by M.Sh. Fainshtein, Leningrad, 1989.
"Po staromu sledu (o ballade E. Rostopchinoi 'Nasil'nyi brak')", by V.S. Kiselev-Sergenin, *Russkaia literatura*, 3 (1995), 137–51.

In 1812 when Evdokia Rostopchina was less than a year old she was taken by her family from Moscow to the Simbirsk province to escape from the invading French army. Evdokia was six years old when she lost her mother; her father left the family home soon afterwards to run his in-laws' iron foundries, then moved to St Petersburg and eventually to Orenburg. Later he sent for his sons to come and live with him, but left Evdokia in the care of her ageing grandparents in whose house she lived until her marriage in 1833. As was the custom of the times Evdokia was educated by governesses: French, Swiss and one Russian. The curriculum was typical for girls from noble families at that period: French and German, some history and geography, a little maths, music, dancing, etc. From early childhood Evdokia loved poetry and reading. At the age of 11 or 12 she started to write verse.

At the age of 16, she wrote an ode to Charlotte Cordet, the girl who killed Marat; later she dedicated several poems to the Decembrists. At that time she became friendly with Nikolai Ogarev and Mikhail Lermontov, both of whom shared her love of poetry. During one of Pushkin's visits to Moscow, in 1829, Rostopchina made his acquaintance at a ball. The poet was enchanted by her and spent almost the whole evening talking to Evdokia. When she was nearly 20, Baron Del'vig, the editor of *Severnye tsvety*, published her poem "Talisman" given to him by Prince Viazemskii. This was her debut on the literary scene. The poem is very short and its author confesses that the talisman in question is the memory of a lost love.

In 1833 Evdokia married Count Andrei Rostopchin, the son of the Moscow governor, an immensely rich heir who managed to squander his enormous inheritance in 30 years. For the first two years the couple lived in one of their villages, Anna, and then returned to Moscow, finally, in 1836 moving to St Petersburg. Their first daughter, Ol'ga, was born in 1837, the second Lidiia in 1838, and their son Viktor a year later.

After moving to St Petersburg Rostopchina led the typical life of a great society lady: attending and giving balls or receptions. Yet her intellectual interests did not wane and to her soirées came such celebrated authors as Zhukovskii, Pushkin, Prince Odoevskii,

Krylov, Gogol' and many others; the composers Glinka and Dargomyzhskii also frequented her salon.

In 1841 a friend from her childhood, Lermontov, arrived in the capital and their friendship was renewed. That winter they met frequently and, before leaving, Lermontov gave her an album in which he had inscribed his poem dedicated to her that stresses their common fate as poets, saying that they were born under the same star, followed the same path and were deceived by the same dreams. There is no doubt that their friendship was both profound and sincere.

After several years in St Petersburg the Rostopchins left for Europe (1845), where they spent more than two years travelling through Poland, Germany, Italy, France, and Switzerland. Following their return to Russia in the autumn of 1847 they moved to Moscow. After a year in Moscow, Rostopchina began to arrange literary soirées in her house; on Saturdays men of letters would visit her, among whom was the young A.N. Ostrovskii. Although her salon attracted many writers and poets Rostopchina felt less at ease in the intellectual atmosphere of the 1850s. She could accept wholeheartedly neither the extreme views of the Slavophiles nor the Westernizers. It was also difficult for her to find any common language with the new generation of writers. For the last two years of her life, she was gravely ill with cancer; one of the most important events in her life at that time was the meeting with Alexandre Dumas who visited her in Moscow and at whose request she wrote down her reminiscences of Lermontov. She died in her native Moscow, aged almost 47 years.

Although Rostopchina began writing poetry at an early age, she submitted her poems for publication only after her marriage, and the appearance of "Talisman" in 1831 was arranged without her knowledge. Her first book of poems entitled *Stikhotvoreniia*, where she included verse written in 1829–39, was published in 1841. She considered it to be a kind of confession, the outpouring of the innermost feelings and dreams of a young girl. It has often been described as a "lyrical diary". Her first collection of poems was well received by most critics and many of her themes stressed the female angle of her poetry, focusing on women's feelings, reactions, and perceptions. Still earlier, in 1839, she had published anonymously her first prose work entitled "Ocherki bol'shogo sveta" [Sketches of High Society]; a number of her works were well received by the critics.

Rostopchina was often accused by her contemporaries and later critics of focusing too much on feminine topics (some of them trivial, such as balls), but this is not a completely just or unbiased view. She also wrote about nature, about peasant life, and even civic verse. As a woman poet she composed her own *art poétique*, a guide on how women should write poetry, advocating restraint, understatement, and subdued passion; women's poetry should be like the moon hiding behind clouds, shining as if through a veil, yet invisible herself.

In the mid to late 1840s Rostopchina began to turn more and more to prose; she also tried her hand at drama. *Neliudimka* [The Recluse], written in 1849, portrays a rich and beautiful young woman, Zoia, who is an orphan and therefore fairly free from the pressures of family and society. She lives in her village and engages in various occupations, among them memoir-writing and charitable work for her peasants; she also refuses to marry and follow the ordinary path of women born into the gentry. Although the play is not well crafted, it is nevertheless an interesting attempt to point to an alternative path for women: one of choice rather than compulsion.

An interesting foray into comedy is her *Vozvrat Chatskogo v Moskvu* [Chatskii's Return to Moscow] (1856), based on Griboedov's comedy *Gore ot uma* (*Woe from Wit*). In those years of decline she did not completely abandon poetry for prose. She wrote a long poem, "Poeziia i proza zhizni. Roman v stikhakh" [Poetry and Prose of Life. A Novel in Verse], as well as others. However the critics, with rare exceptions, judged her more and more severely. A year before her death she began to publish the collected edition of her poems; the first volume appeared in 1857, the second posthumously.

RUTH SOBEL

Anatolii Naumovich Rybakov 1911–

Novelist

Biography

Born Anatolii Aronov in Chernigov, 14 January 1911. Primary school education in Moscow, completed Lepshinskii commune school in 1928. Stevedore and driver for Dorogomilov chemical factory. Attended Moscow Transport Institute 1930–33. Arrested, 1933: exiled to Kezhma and the Angara region, 1934–36. Married: 1) Anastasiia Alekseevna Tysiachnikova in 1940 (divorced 1953), one son; 2) Maia Maksimovna Davydova in 1955 (divorced 1978), one son; 3) Tat'iana Markovna Vinokurova (née Belenkaia) in 1978. Various jobs in cities throughout Russia, 1936–40. Military service 1941–46, returned to Moscow 1946. Literary debut with *Kortik* [The Sailor's Knife], mystery/adventure story for young readers, 1948. Publication of eight more works primarily for young readers, 1948–75; many produced as feature or television films. Rehabilitated, 1960. Publication of controversial Holocaust novel *Tiazhelyi pesok* (*Heavy Sand*) in 1978; attracted international readership. Speaking tours of the United States in 1986 and 1987. Publication of anti-Stalinist blockbuster *Deti Arbata* (*Children of the Arbat*), 1987. Books 1 and 2 of *Strakh:*

Tridtsat' piatyi i drugie gody (*Fear*) published in *Druzhba Narodov* 1988–90. *Prakh i pepel* (*Dust and Ashes*) (1994) completes a trilogy, portraying Soviet society and Stalin from the mid-1930s through World War II. Currently writing memoirs in Peredelkino and New York.

Publications

Collected Editions

Izbrannye proizvedeniia, 2 vols. Moscow, 1978.
Sobranie sochinenii, 4 vols. Moscow, 1981–82.
Sobranie sochinenii, 7 vols. Moscow, 1995.

Fiction

"Kortik" [The Sailor's Knife], *Detskaia literatura*, 1948.
"Voditeli" [The Drivers], *Oktiabr'*, 1950.
"Ekaterina Voronina", *Novyi mir*, 1955.
"Bronzovaia ptitsa" [The Bronze Bird], *Iunost'*, 1956.
"Prikliucheniia Krosha" [Krosh's Adventures], *Iunost'*, 1960.
"Leto v Sosniakakh" [Summer in Sosniaki], *Novyi mir*, 1964.
"Kanikuly Krosha" [Krosh's Holiday], *Iunost'*, 1966.
"Neizvestnyi soldat" [The Unknown Soldier], *Iunost'*, 9–10 (1970).
"Vystrel" [The Shot], *Iunost'*, 1975.
"Tiazhelyi pesok", *Oktiabr'*, 7–9 (1978); Moscow, 1979; translated as *Heavy Sand*, by Harold Shukman, London, Allen Lane, and New York, Viking, 1981; Harmondsworth, Penguin, 1982.
"Deti Arbata", *Druzhba narodov*, 4–6 (1987); Moscow, 1987; translated as *Children of the Arbat*, by Harold Shukman, Boston, Little Brown, and London, Hutchinson, 1988.
"Tridtsat' piatyi i drugie gody. Kniga pervaia" [1935 and Other Years. Book One], *Druzhba narodov*, 9–10 (1988); "Strakh: tridtsat' piatyi i drugie gody. Kniga vtoraia", *Druzhba narodov*, 9–10 (1990); separate edition, Moscow, 1990; translated as *Fear*, by Antonina Bouis, Boston, Little Brown, 1992.
Prakh i pepel. Moscow, 1994; translated as *Dust and Ashes*, by Antonina Bouis, Boston, Little Brown, and London, Hutchinson, 1996.

Essays

"Dlia detei i dlia vzroslykh" [For Children and Grown-Ups], *Vslukh pro sebia*, compiled by A.I. Vislov and F.E. Ebin. Moscow, 1978, 324–49.

Critical Studies

Anatolii Rybakov, ocherk tvorchestva, by E. Starikova, Moscow, 1977.
"Pamiat' i vymysel", [interview] by L. Bakhnov, *Voprosy literatury*, 5 (1980), 102–24.
"Mify Deminga Brauna" [Deming Brown's Myths], by A. Beliaev, *Inostrannaia literatura*, 2 (1981), 198–212.
"Pochva. Vozdukh. Sud'ba", by L. Anninskii, *Novyi mir*, 1 (1983), 248–58.
"Vol'noe dykhanie", by N. Ivanova, *Voprosy literatury*, 3 (1983), 179–213.
"Ottsy i syny", (under the general heading "*Deti Arbata*: istoriia i sovremennost'"), by L. Anninskii, *Oktiabr'*, 10 (1987), 185–92.
"Protivostoianie" (under the general heading "*Deti Arbata*: istoriia i sovremennost'"), by A. Bocharov, *Oktiabr'*, 10 (1987), 179–84.
"Ottsy i: deti epokhi", by N. Ivanova, *Voprosy literatury*, 11 (1987), 50–83.
"Interview with Anatolij Rybakov", by John Schillinger, *Russian Language Journal*, 41/138–139 (1987), 191–201.
"Problema chelovecheskogo sushchestvovaniia v romane A. Rybakova *Deti Arbata*", by A.A. Ivanova and V.K. Pukhlikov, *Voprosy filosofii*, 11 (1988), 97–112.
"Roman i istoriia (dialog v pis'makh)", by V. Kavtorin and V. Chubinskii, *Neva*, 3 (1988) 156–75.
"My vse gliadim v Napoleony", by A. Lanshchikov, *Nash sovremennik*, 2 (1988), 106–42.
"Peremeny i mneniia", by D. Urnov, *Voprosy literatury*, 8 (1988), 26–47.
"U menia net drugogo vykhoda" interview with L. Bakhnov, *Druzhba narodov*, 9 (1989), 262–70.
Images of Dictatorship: Portraits of Stalin in Literature, by Rosalind Marsh, London and New York, Routledge, 1989.
"Stalin's Revolution", by O.L. Smaryl, *Encounter*, 72 (March 1989), 34–36.
S raznykh tochek zreniia: Deti Arbata Anatoliia Rybakova, edited by Sh.G. Umerov, Moscow, 1990.
"Rybakov's *Deti Arbata*: Reintegrating Stalin into Soviet History", by Sigrid McLaughlin, *Slavic Review*, 50 (Spring 1991), 90–99.
"Socialist Realism and the Holocaust: Jewish Life and Death in Anatoly Rybakov's *Heavy Sand*", by Gary Rosenshield, *PMLA*, 111/2 (1996), 240–55.

Bibliography

"Anatolii Rybakov", by Z. Papernyi, *Russkie sovetskie pisateli prozaiki, Bibliograficheskii ukazatel'*, 4 (1966), 26–32.

Anatolii Naumovich Rybakov was born to Naum Borisovich Aronov, director of the local distillery, and Dina Abramovna Aronova (née Rybakova) on 14 January 1911 in Chernigov. After the Revolution, Rybakov's father became president of a rural *sovkhoz*, but in 1919 the family moved to the Arbat section of Moscow. That same year Rybakov entered School No. 7 on Krivoarbat lane, later enrolling in the Revolution-inspired Lepeshinskii commune school for his final two years. Though the school emphasized practical subjects such as economics and statistics on a Marxist-Leninist background, Rybakov had developed a love of 19th- and 20th-century Russian and French authors in his teens. Like Sasha Pankratov's father in *Deti Arbata* (*Children of the Arbat*), Rybakov's distant and unaffectionate father was a constant negative force, but his decision to live away from the family created a financial strain. Upon completing his ninth year of school in 1928, Rybakov began working at the Dorogomilov chemical factory, first as a stevedore and later a driver.

In 1930 Rybakov enrolled in the Moscow Transport Institute, but his education ended on 5 November 1933 when he was arrested, interrogated in Lubianka prison, and transferred to Butyrka prison charged with anti-Soviet activity. On 9 January he was sentenced to three years of exile which he spent in Kezhma and the Angara region until receiving a temporary passport in 1936. Rybakov spent the next four years moving about Russia working at a variety of jobs, seldom remaining anywhere longer than six months.

In 1939 Rybakov found work on an autobase in Riazan where he met and married his first wife, Anastasiia Alekseevna Tysiachnikova, in 1940. Their son Aleksandr was born that same year. In 1941 Rybakov was called up for army service. Because of his record, he initially served as a second-class soldier posted as a field engineer in the construction division, but in June 1942 he became an officer at the front heading vehicle services for the Fourth Guard Corps. In 1945 he accompanied the first Soviet occupation troops to enter Berlin.

Rybakov was decorated for valour in action during battles in the southern steppe, Briansk, and Belorussia. Hospitalized with a bomb blast contusion from one engagement, Rybakov, on release from the army, received the modest pension of 50 roubles per month awarded to injured veterans. For his exemplary service record Rybakov was found by a military tribunal to be innocent of previous charges in 1945; nevertheless, he was not fully rehabilitated until 1960.

Back in Moscow in 1946 with limited options, Rybakov decided to gamble on his future. Encouraged by his mother's praise of the short sketches he had written earlier, Rybakov felt he might succeed as a writer. Instead of using his pension to supplement the salary from a job as the state intended, Rybakov rented a room in a village outside Moscow, vowing not to return until he had written a book. Throughout his life, the influence of his mother's side of the family far outweighed that of his father's. Given his uncertain civilian status, Rybakov took his mother's maiden name when he submitted the completed work for publication. The result was *Kortik* [The Sailor's Knife] (1948), a children's book that emerged from early notebook sketches in the 1930s and developed further while Rybakov was stationed in Germany.

Set in the years following the Revolution, *Kortik* creatively blended mystery and adventure with historical events to capture the spirit of the times and the imagination of young readers. With his first published work, which for generations of Soviet readers was parallel to Mark Twain's *The Adventures of Tom Sawyer*, the "people's enemy" Anatolii Aronov disappeared forever, and Anatolii Rybakov took his place among the people's best-known authors, soon to join the exclusive Soviet Writers' Union.

In 1953, Rybakov and Anastasiia were divorced after 13 years of marriage. Two years later, he married Maia Maksimovna Davydova, an aspiring writer. Their son, Aleksei, was born in 1960. In 1978 he and Maia divorced, and Rybakov married Tat'iana Markovna Vinokurova (née Belenkaia), a family friend, accomplished editor, and wife of the poet Evgenii Mikhailovich Vinokurov since 1952. Belenkaia's life had also been shattered during Stalin's purges of the 1930s, her childhood spent with relatives following the execution of her father and the labour-camp exile of her mother.

In the 30 years between *Kortik* and *Tiazhelyi pesok* (*Heavy Sand*), Rybakov's works found an avid readership, frequently reaching an extended audience in the form of films for both the cinema and television. Rybakov's stories blended intriguing mysteries with morally instructive plots and characters. Some characters, such as Misha Poliakov from *Kortik*, reappeared in subsequent works. In *Voditeli* [The Drivers], for which Rybakov was named USSR State Prize Laureate, an older Poliakov uncovers bureaucratic misuse of power in the transport industry. In *Bronzovaia ptitsa* [The Bronze Bird], he is a Young Pioneer on a camping trip who solves a mystery reminiscent of that of *The Maltese Falcon* with counter-revolutionary overtones; and in *Vystrel* [The Shot], Misha Poliakov foils a scheme of unscrupulous NEP transport industry profiteers.

Sergei (Krosh) Krasheninnikov is the young hero in yet another series beginning with *Prikliucheniia Krosha* [Krosh's Adventures] (1960), in which Krosh uncovers an autobase scam during an apprenticeship. In *Kanikuly Krosha* [Krosh's Holiday], he uncovers the illegal sale of rare Japanese netsuke figures; and in the last work, *Neizvestnyi soldat* [The Unknown Soldier], Krosh's work with a road construction crew in the 1970s is interspersed with flashbacks to events during World War II as he follows clues to solve the mystery of a roadside grave. An especially popular work, *Neizvestnyi soldat* was produced as *Minuta molchaniia* [A Minute of Silence] (1971) by the Gor'kii film studio, for which Rybakov was recognized as an RSFSR State Prize Laureate.

The two remaining works in this period were more adult oriented. *Ekaterina Voronina* (1955) treated irregularities in the shipping transport industry on the background of a romantic relationship; while *Leto v Sosniakakh* [Summer in Sosniaki], which appeared in *Novyi mir* in 1964, traces a chemical facility suicide to revelations of Stalin-era victimization. Two years later, *Novyi mir* announced the impending publication of Rybakov's *Children of the Arbat*; but it would be more than 20 years before the novel finally appeared in print.

In 1978, on the 30th anniversary of *Kortik*, Rybakov again enjoyed the literary limelight with the appearance of *Heavy Sand*, the first novel in decades by a Soviet author to examine the annihilation of the Jews in the Holocaust. Translated into 39 languages, the controversial *Heavy Sand* gained the attention of western readers and aided the publication of *Children of the Arbat*, the anti-Stalinist blockbuster of the glasnost era that appeared shortly after Rybakov's first speaking tour of the United States in 1986. *Children of the Arbat* and the two novels that followed, *Strakh: tridtsat' piatyi i drugie gody* (translated as *Fear*) – part one of *Fear* appeared in issues of *Druzhba narodov* as *Tridtsat' piatyi i drugie gody* [1935 and Other Years] in 1988, and part two in 1990 as *Strakh: tridtsat' piatyi i drugie gody* – and *Prakh i pepel* (*Dust and Ashes*), 1994, portray Soviet society on two levels, the first through the friends, family, and personal experiences of a fictional Sasha Pankratov as he lives through youth, exile, return to society, and World War II. The second, which interacts with the first, depicts historical figures and events, focusing on the innermost thoughts of an omnipotent and ruthless Stalin whose paranoia and utter amorality enable him to manipulate his country and countrymen through the fear of annihilation and the hope of self-preservation. Evoking the image of "The Lost Tramcar" ("Zabludivshiisia tramvai") in a poem by Nikolai Gumilev, himself executed in 1921 for supposed counter-revolutionary activities, Rybakov's trilogy describes a totalitarian system that has run amok, leaving behind millions of bodies and shattered lives.

The Arbat trilogy completed, Rybakov is currently writing his memoirs in Peredelkino and New York.

JOHN SCHILLINGER

Heavy Sand

Tiazhelyi pesok

Novel, 1978

In the fall of 1986, while Anatolii Rybakov was conducting his first speaking tour of the United States, the members of the university and Jewish émigré communities who largely made up his audiences came to meet the author of *Heavy Sand*, the first Soviet work to depict the Nazi murder of Jews that had appeared in decades. At that time few of Rybakov's listeners were aware of the existence of his controversial Stalin-era novel, *Children of the Arbat*, which after 20 years on the shelf was soon to become a glasnost "blockbuster".

Almost a decade before the publication of *Children of the Arbat*, Rybakov's *Heavy Sand* (the title is taken from the Book of Job, where he describes his grief and calamity as "heavier than the sand of the sea") had been an immediate sensation in the Soviet Union. Rybakov's novel also received considerable attention in the west because of its strikingly moving and colourful depiction of families in a Ukrainian Jewish village prior to the Nazi *Anschluss* of 1941, and its unprecedented portrayal of their courage, self-sacrifice, and heroism during the horrendous period of occupation.

While western reviewers had been generally positive in their appraisal of *Heavy Sand* and had applauded Rybakov's inclusion of negative details such as the collaboration between Nazis and local authorities, they also noted the absence of references to Stalin's equally inhuman treatment of the Jews and an inclination to reflect the behaviour of non-Jewish Ukrainians toward the Jews in a much too positive light. Conventional wisdom also held that the publication of Rybakov's work implied that the author was in collusion with the Party, and as an established member of the Soviet Writers' Union, he was serving his own best interests. For his part, Rybakov maintained that western readers had little idea of what post-revolutionary Jews were really like in the Soviet Union, and that it was no easy matter to publish a book in the Soviet Union that contradicted traditional stereotypes. Consequently, while most who attended Rybakov's campus talks anticipated an evening with an important and controversial new author, some also came to engage him in a discussion of the motives behind the publication of *Heavy Sand* and to challenge his depiction of Jewish villagers.

As his audiences soon learned, at the age of 75 Rybakov was hardly a new author; it had simply taken the overwhelming response to *Heavy Sand* in the Soviet Union (Rybakov received thousands of letters from readers) and the exceptional measure of translating his novel into 39 languages to bring him to their attention. Rybakov had in fact established his reputation in the Soviet Union at one stroke 30 years before publishing *Heavy Sand*, with a phenomenally successful short story for young readers entitled *Kortik*, a work that had delighted generations of Soviet readers.

Given the non-controversial and formulaic nature of the short stories for which he had become so well known, the appearance of *Heavy Sand* in the respected conservative journal *Oktiabr'* came as a complete surprise to his readers. Even though basic moral themes familiar from Rybakov's previous stories could still be found in *Heavy Sand*, this work was quite different. As his background for the novel, Rybakov had drawn upon his own Jewish roots – a far more personal source for his setting and characters – and he had adopted a new authorial voice as well. This change is evident at the very outset, since, uncharacteristically for Rybakov, *Heavy Sand* is told in the first person by a narrator who, following the technique of *skaz* used so memorably by Gogol' and others, takes on a separate identity and addresses the reader in a familiar and conversational tone as if they were friends sitting together in the same room.

Rybakov's narrator, Boris Iakovlevich Ivanovskii, is a former member of the village in which the story is set, and it is through his family history and elements of events he has compiled from interviews with survivors that the tale unfolds. Unlike typical Holocaust works prior to *Heavy Sand* that began with Jews as victims already living in a ghetto, Rybakov's characters are introduced by the narrator in a warm and reflective chronicle of decades of family life and love that gradually changes to a somewhat under-emotionalized and almost surrealistic depiction of the atrocities visited upon the unsuspecting people of the village, among whom more than 7,000 are Jews. Far from the all-too familiar and hackneyed portraits of Jews with comic appearances and devious and contemptuous behaviour, Rybakov's characters perhaps counter productively evoke the heroes and heroines of socialist realism: Boris Ivanovskii's grandfather Abram Rakhlenko is handsome and, physically and morally, a giant of a man, a shoemaker who has earned the respect and awe of the village. His mother Rachel is a Rakhlenko possessed of great beauty, a marvellous voice and tremendous reserves of strength and determination; his uncle Misha rides horses like a Cossack and rises to high rank in the military; his brother Genrikh becomes a celebrated fighter pilot; and Boris's half-Jewish father Jakob forsakes a good and promising intellectual life abroad to work with his hands and raise a family in a Ukrainian village.

Still, not all the Rakhlenkos are so admirable – uncle Iosif the dentist becomes the head of the Judenrat and collaborates with the enemy; but he is shot by Boris's sister Dina before he can betray friends and family. Dina is later crucified – martyred like her grandfather, her grandmother, her father, and her youngest brother for their courageous acts of opposition. Although thousands perish at the hands of the Nazis in the final pages of the novel, the aggressors pay a heavy price during a ghetto uprising; and led by Rachel Rakhlenko in a fantastic/mystic sequence that could never occur in a socialist realist novel, hundreds of villagers escape into the deep forest.

In *Heavy Sand* Rybakov does not portray Jewish victims of the Holocaust but men, women, and children who, counter to stereotype, fight heroically and die with exceptional bravery. In a final tribute to their lives and as an admonition – and here Rybakov refers beyond this novel to centuries of Jewish history – the concluding message of *Heavy Sand* is voiced by Boris Ivanovskii when he returns to his native village and reads an inscription rendered in both Russian and Hebrew on a monument over a mass grave. While the Russian version is a simple platitude honouring the memory of the dead, the Hebrew is more pointed: "Those who spill innocent blood will never be forgiven."

John Schillinger

Children of the Arbat

Deti Arbata

Novel, 1987

Early in 1987, in keeping with a practice that had been familiar even to readers of pre-revolutionary Russian literary journals, an announcement of the impending publication of a novel in three instalments, *Children of the Arbat*, appeared in *Druzhba narodov*, a Soviet "thick" journal founded in 1939 at the end of Stalin's purges. The publication notice sent a wave of excitement through a Soviet readership buoyed up by the new policy of glasnost that came with the Gorbachev era. It was well known that Rybakov, regarded primarily as a writer of adventure stories for Soviet youth, had also penned a decidedly anti-Stalinist novel. People were aware of *Children of the Arbat* because this was an unprecedented third in a series of such publication announcements that had appeared for the book since 1966. The intelligentsia was tantalized by the prospect of witnessing a sensation – the appearance of a book banned twice before, now publicly championed by prominent individuals who stressed the importance of publishing Rybakov's depiction of Stalin and the human tragedies of the era that bears his name.

More than decades earlier, the determination of *Novyi mir* editor Aleksandr Tvardovskii had propitiously connected with Khrushchev's de-Stalinization initiative to make possible the publication of Aleksandr Solzhenitsyn's *One Day in the Life of Ivan Denisovich* (1962). Yet only four years later, after Tvardovskii had informed the public that Rybakov's new novel, *Children of the Arbat*, would appear in forthcoming issues, he was forced by the rapidly changing political climate to halt publication. Twelve years later, in 1978, the editor of the more conservative journal *Oktiabr'* followed suit. With the exception of *One Day in the Life of Ivan Denisovich*, novels such as *Children of the Arbat*, if they were to be printed at all, were destined to appear first in translation in the west.

In effect, Rybakov's novel remained in the desk drawer for over two decades, as was the tradition for such problematic works. In reality, however, Rybakov continued to develop, expand, and rewrite the novel through a seventh version, all the while gathering support for publication from fellow writers and public figures, never abandoning the hope that the work would appear in his lifetime, in Russian, and in his own country before any other. The breakthrough Rybakov had hoped for came not long after he returned to his home in Peredelkino from a speaking tour (ostensibly devoted to discussing *Heavy Sand*) of the United States in 1986. Though even on the tour it had been deemed risky to discuss the book in public, he learned that *Children of the Arbat* once again had been approved for publication. The third time was indeed the charm. When the April issue of *Druzhba narodov* reached the bookstalls, waiting readers promptly bought it out and extra runs of the issue were ordered. Echoing the response to the sensational appearance of *One Day in the Life of Ivan Denisovich* 25 years earlier, copies of the first instalment of *Children of the Arbat* were passed overnight from reader to reader. Emotional letters of reaction were published, further heightening interest and public controversy, and Rybakov's long-awaited work was declared "the blockbuster novel" of the glasnost period.

Set in 1934 shortly before the assassination of Kirov, *Children of the Arbat* addresses the Stalin era on two planes. On the first, Rybakov chronicles the life of Sasha Pankratov, a self-confident and idealistic young Komsomol member who, like the author, grew up in the bohemian Arbat quarter of Moscow. Sasha reflects Rybakov's own childhood, youth, and exile in Siberia when he becomes a victim of the paranoia of the times in the familiar pattern of suspicion, denunciation, and punishment. On this plane too is a vision of Sasha's contemporaries – the other children of the Arbat referred to in the title – reminiscent of the characters in F. Scott Fitzgerald's fiction. Among them are the independent and loyal Var'ia, Sasha's ultimate romantic interest; Lena, the privileged but vulnerable daughter of a military official who suffers a painful abortion; the opportunistic and hedonistic Vika; and Iura, the sellout to the NKVD. The Arbat children give the Fitzgeraldian image of Moscow a purely Stalin-era twist – a new generation finding its way between the cataclysms of the Revolution and the Stalin purges, drawn by what Moscow has to offer the young and the adventurous, yet threatened or seduced by the same forces that trap Sasha.

Industry, architecture, and other themes associated with socialist realist literature are also woven into the novel's fabric, but tend to be associated with flaws, rather than serve as examples of successes of the system. Thus, Sasha's uncle, Mark Riazanov, an official in the industrial sector becomes an object lesson in direct contrast with self-sacrificing Gleb and Dasha in Gladkov's *Tsement* (*Cement*) as his personal ambition leads him to sacrifice family for career opportunity; and Var'ia's work in an architect's office hardly inspires the positive image of enthusiastic co-operation in designing and building for the greater glory of the Soviet people familiar to readers of such works as Vsevolod Kochetov's *Zhurbiny* [The Zhurbins] (1952).

On the second plane looms Stalin, the source of the paranoia, a solitary figure who looks down abstractly and emotionlessly on the plane below, not like the Greek gods who became involved with the mortals they watched over, but like a puppeteer who simply has a sense of ownership or control.

Rybakov's image of Stalin is produced by a combination of anecdotal glimpses of his idiosyncratic behaviour and a considerable amount of eavesdropping on the coldly systematic progression of *his* thoughts. He is aloof; for him people are inanimate objects over whom he maintains and increases his power. Stalin lives for this power, and keeps it by the ruthless elimination of real and imagined opposition. "History", muses Stalin at one point, "gives no simple answer to the question of who was right and who was wrong in the past – the victor is right." Elsewhere he comments, "Death solves all problems. No man, no problems." After repeatedly witnessing his wilful and ruthless destruction of the faceless masses as well as of those closest to him, the ultimate denouement, the assassination of Kirov – clearly implied to be on Stalin's orders, and one can only imagine the impact this clear implication in print would have had on Soviet readers in 1966 – is made all the more believable by the heaping up of incidents and telling interior monologues in Rybakov's almost paint-by-numbers portrait of Stalin.

Rybakov's unembellished style, termed flat by some critics, is familiar to anyone who has read any of his earlier works. There is certain irony in this, since Rybakov was just as straightforward about presenting a morally uplifting adventure tale for Soviet youth as he is in his systematic demythification of Stalin. But this style *is* Rybakov, a no nonsense kind of person and author who finds Dostoevskii's flights of verbosity and fevered introspection unbearable, and prefers the prose of Chekhov and Pushkin, for whom the point was the story, and small details spoke volumes. Rybakov told the story first in his own country, in Russian, and that was the point.

JOHN SCHILLINGER

Kondratii Fedorovich Ryleev 1795–1826

Poet

Biography

Born in Batovo, near St Petersburg, 29 September 1795. Attended the First Cadet Corps College in St Petersburg, from 1801: passed out as ensign in First Cavalry Company, First Reserve Artillery Brigade, 1814; stationed in Paris, 1815; transferred to Ostrogozhsk, Voronezh *guberniia*, 1817; resigned his commission, 1818. Married: N.M. Teviasheva in 1819; one daughter, one son. Moved to St Petersburg, acquainted with Del'vig, Grech, Gnedich, and Pushkin; began to publish; joined Masonic lodge, 1820. Assessor at St Petersburg criminal court from 1821; joined Free Society of Lovers of Russian Literature. Recruited by I.I. Pushchin to the Decembrists' Northern Society, 1823. Joined Russian-American Company as office manager; met P.I. Pestel' in St Petersburg; appointed to the directorate of the Northern Society, 1824. Arrested hours after the uprising of 14 December; imprisoned in Peter and Paul Fortress, 1825. Interrogated by Investigating Commission, tried by Supreme Criminal Court, and hanged in Peter and Paul Fortress, 25 July 1826.

Publications

Collected Editions

The Poems of K.F. Relaieff, translated by T. Hart-Davies. London, Remington, 1887.
Polnoe sobranie stikhotvorenii. Leningrad, 1934.
Polnoe sobranie sochinenii. Moscow and Leningrad, 1934.
Stikhotvoreniia, stat'i, ocherki, dokladnye zapiski, pis'ma. Moscow, 1956.
Polnoe sobranie stikhotvorenii. Leningrad, 1971.
Dumy [Meditations]. Moscow, 1975.
Sochineniia. Leningrad, 1987.

Poetry

Dumy [Meditations]. 1821–23.
Voinarovskii. 1824.
Nalivaiko. 1825.
Poems in *Three Centuries of Russian Poetry*, edited by Nikolai Bannikov. Moscow, Progress, 1980, 139–43.
Poems in *The Ardis Anthology of Russian Romanticism*, edited by Christine Rydel. Ann Arbor, Ardis, 1984, 81–82.

Non-Fiction

"Dekabristy-literatory" [Decembrist Men of Letters], *Literaturnoe nasledstvo*, 59/1 (1954).

Critical Studies

Literaturnaia deiatel'nost' K.F. Ryleeva, by V.I. Maslov, Kiev, 1912.
Tvorchestvo Ryleeva, by A.G. Tseitlin, Moscow, 1955.
"K.F. Ryleev: A Self-Sacrifice for Revolution", by Franklin Walker, *Slavonic and East European Review*, 47 (1969), 436–46.
K.F. Ryleev v Voronezhskom krae, by B.T. Udodov, Voronezh, 1971.
"Ukrainian Themes in Ryleev's Works", by John P. Pauls, *Wiener Slawistisches Jahrbuch*, 17 (1972), 28–42.
O russkom romantizme, by E.A. Maimin, Moscow, 1975.
"Medieval and Eighteenth-Century Themes in the Work of Ryleev", by Patrick O'Meara, *Study Group on Eighteenth-Century Russia: Newsletter*, 8 (1980) 17–20.
K.F. Ryleev. A Political Biography of the Decembrist Poet, by Patrick O'Meara, Princeton, Princeton University Press, 1984; translated into Russian as *K.F. Ryleev. Politicheskaia biografiia poeta-dekabrista*, Moscow, Progress, 1989.
"The Poetry of Kondratii Ryleev: Some Problems of Decembrist Literary Aesthetics", by Patrick O'Meara, in *Russian Thought and Society 1800–1917: Essays in Honour of Eugene Lampert*, edited by R.P. Bartlett, Keele, University of Keele Press, 1984, 1–22.
A History of Russian Literature of the Romantic Period, by William Edward Brown, vol. 2, Ann Arbor, Ardis, 1986.
Hagiography and Modern Russian Literature, by Margaret Ziolkowski, Princeton, Princeton University Press, 1988.
Alexander Bestuzhev-Marlinsky and Russian Byronism, by Lewis Bagby, University Park, Pennsylvania, State University Press, 1995.

Kondratii Ryleev was born in 1795 in Batovo near Petersburg. His father, Fedor Andreevich, was estate manager to a member of the Golitsyn family. Removed early on from his father's overbearing presence, Ryleev was sent by his mother (Anastasiia Matveevna Essen) to the First Cadet Corps College in St Petersburg aged just six. Here he lived for 13 years until February

1814 when he enlisted in the First Cavalry Company of the First Reserve Artillery Brigade with the rank of ensign.

Ryleev's unit participated in the final liberation of Europe from Napoleon, and during 1814 and 1815 saw action in Poland, Germany, and France. Like so many other young Russian officers, he was struck by the contrast between conditions in Russia and those he observed in the west. He was later to attribute his "free-thinking" to his experience of life there. Ryleev resigned his commission in December 1818 and the following month married N.M. Teviasheva, the daughter of a Voronezh landowner. The newly-weds settled near St Petersburg where, from January 1821, Ryleev served as an elected assessor at the criminal court. He acquired an unusual reputation for impartiality and fairness during his three years in the post. Also in St Petersburg, Ryleev joined a Masonic Lodge but remained a member for only a year. He left just months ahead of their closure as potentially conspiratorial hot-beds by Alexander I in 1822. Nevertheless, it was in this milieu that he made some of his earliest literary acquaintances, including Vil'gel'm Kiukhel'beker and Fedor Glinka. And it was around this time that Ryleev began to make his mark in the capital's literary circles. From 1820 his poems began to appear in *Nevskii zritel'*, among them his satirical ode "K vremenshchiku" [To the Favourite], a veiled criticism of the emperor's unpopular chief executive, Count A.A. Arakcheev.

The fusion of poetic inspiration and a deep sense of social accountability led Ryleev to articulate a romantic view of his purpose: "I am not a poet but a citizen." It was a claim ridiculed by his contemporary Aleksandr Pushkin, who nevertheless reacted positively to some of the citizen-poet's work, remained on friendly terms with him, and was to lament his tragic fate.

Much of Ryleev's work, especially the cycle *Dumy* [Meditations] (1821–23), and the two major narrative poems *Voinarovskii* (1824) and *Nalivaiko* (1825), portray prominent historical figures as "civic" heroes set in a romantically evoked, frequently mythologized past. Invariably fired by a deep patriotism, their courageous and selfless pursuit of enlightened goals against impossible odds was to provide Ryleev's readers with edifying role-models. In his poems "Grazhdanskoe muzhestvo" [Civic Courage] (1823) and "Grazhdanin" ("The Citizen") 1824, Ryleev celebrates the individual's opposition to tyranny and salutes liberty. It was in such poems as these that Decembrist poetic oratory reached its zenith, while the romantic fatalism of "Ispoved' Nalivaiki" ("Nalivaiko's Testament") represents, in the words of Aleksandr Herzen, "the quintessential Ryleev".

Ryleev was chiefly influenced by Radishchev, Derzhavin, Gnedich, and Pushkin. Of non-Russian poets, he was impressed above all by Byron to whom he dedicated a poem "Na smert' Beirona" [On the Death of Byron] (1824). His main historical source, which he adapted very freely, was Nikolai Karamzin's *Istoriia gosudarstva rossiiskogo* [History of the Russian State] (1818–29). Together with Aleksandr Bestuzhev (Marlinskii), Ryleev produced the remarkably successful, if short-lived, "civic"-inspired annual, *Poliarnaia zvezda* (1823–25). Belinskii credited *Poliarnaia zvezda* with initiating the "almanac period" of Russian literature.

Ryleev's Decembrist involvement dates from spring 1823 with his recruitment to the Northern Society. As a civilian with good military connections, as a literary figure, and as office manager of the prestigious Russian-American Company, Ryleev sought through his various networks to spread the reformist aspirations of his fellow conspirators and to recruit those ready to commit themselves to their realization. He explored the possibility of uniting the Northern and Southern Societies and the Society of United Slavs, particularly through negotiations with Pavel Pestel, a leading member of the Southern Society. The latter made a generally unfavourable impression on the St Petersburg Decembrists who discerned beneath his insistence on a strictly centralized system of government (and the recourse to regicide) a personal ambition of Napoleonic proportions. Ryleev's meeting with Pestel produced only an agreement to review the matter of a united movement during 1826. In any case, Ryleev himself favoured Nikita Murav'ev's proposal for a United States-type federal system of government.

The unexpected death of Alexander I in November 1825 precipitated a dynastic crisis and a two-week interregnum. Ryleev's role in mobilizing the ill-prepared conspiracy for the uprising of 14 December was crucial. Although the nominal leader was Sergei Trubetskoi, it was Ryleev who effectively took charge. Despite harbouring few illusions about their success he characteristically chose to act and so "to awaken Russia". After the failed uprising, Ryleev was quickly arrested, brought before Nicholas I, and incarcerated in the Peter and Paul Fortress. Here, after a six-month interrogation and a summary trial, he was hanged alongside four of his co-conspirators on 25 July 1826.

Ryleev's maturing understanding of the concept of civil liberty represented an important aspect of the Decembrists' contribution to political thought in 19th-century Russia. His attempt to articulate his ideals in his verse laid the foundations of a new, "civic" tradition in Russian poetry, subsequently more fully developed by Nikolai Nekrasov.

PATRICK O'MEARA

S

Mikhail Evgrafovich Saltykov-Shchedrin 1826–1889

Prose writer

Biography

Born Mikhail Evgrafovich Saltykov in Spas-Ugol, Tver province, 27 January 1826. Attended Moscow Pension for the Nobility and Aleksandr Lycée, St Petersburg, 1838–44. Entered the civil service (War Ministry), 1844. First stories published, 1847–48. Exiled to Viatka for his "subversive" story ("Zaputannoe delo" [A Complicated Business]), 1848–55; served in provincial administration. Returned to St Petersburg, 1856. Married: Elizaveta Apollonovna Boltina in 1856; one daughter and one son. Served in the Ministry of the Interior in St Petersburg from 1856; then as vice-governor of Riazan, 1858–60, and of Tver, 1860–62. Contributor to St Petersburg journals from 1856. Resigned official post and joined the editorial staff of *Sovremennik*, 1862. Returned to state service, 1864; senior posts in provincial administrations of Penza, 1865–66, Tula 1866–67, and Riazan 1867–68. Retired from service (under official pressure) with rank of Actual State Counsellor, and devoted himself full-time to literature as joint-editor, with Nekrasov and Eliseev, of *Otechestvennye zapiski*,1868; chief editor after Nekrasov's death (1878). *Otechestvennye zapiski* suppressed, 1884. Continued writing in other journals 1884–89. Died in St Petersburg, 10 May 1889.

Publications

Collected Editions

Sobranie sochinenii, 20 vols. Moscow, 1965–67.

M.E. Saltykov-Shchedrin: Selected Satirical Writings (in Russian), edited by I.P. Foote. Oxford, Oxford University Press, 1977.

Fiction

Gubernskie ocherki [Provincial Sketches]. 1856–57.

Nevinnye rasskazy [Innocent Tales]. 1857–63.

Satiry v proze [Satires in Prose]. 1859–62.

Priznaki vremeni [Signs of the Times]. 1863–71.

Pompaduri i pompadurshi [Pompadours and Pompadouresses]. 1863–74; translated as *The Pompadours: A Satire on the Art of Government*, by David Magarshack, Ann Arbor, Ardis, 1985.

Pis'ma o provintsii [Letters on the Provinces]. 1868–70.

Istoriia odnogo goroda, in *Otechestvennye zapiski*, 1869–70; translated as *The History of a Town*, by I.P. Foote, Oxford, Meeuws, 1980; also translated as *The History of a Town, or The Chronicle of Foolov*, by Susan Brownsberger, Ann Arbor, Ardis, 1982.

Gospoda Tashkenttsy [Gentlemen of Tashkent]. 1869–72.

Skazki. 1869–86; parts translated as *Fables*, by Vera Volkhovsky, London, Chatto and Windus, 1931; reprinted Westport, Connecticut, Hyperion Press, 1977; also as *Tales from M. Saltykov-Shchedrin*, by Dorian Rottenberg, Moscow, Foreign Languages Publishing, 1956.

Dnevnik provintsiala v Peterburge [Diary of a Provincial in Petersburg]. 1872.

Blagonamerennye rechi [Well-Intentioned Speeches]. 1872–76.

V srede umerennosti i akkuratnosti [In the World of Moderation and Precision]. 1874–77.

Gospoda Golovlevy. 1875–80; translated as *The Gollovlev Family*, by Athelstan Ridgway, London, Jarrold [1916]; also as *The Golovlyov Family*, by Natalie Duddington, New York, Macmillan, and London, Allen and Unwin, 1931; by Samuel D. Cioran, Ann Arbor, Ardis, 1977; and by Ronald Wilks, Harmondsworth, Penguin, 1988; also translated as *The Golovlevs*, by I.P. Foote, Oxford and New York, Oxford University Press, 1986.

Sovremennaia idilliia [A Contemporary Idyll]. 1877–83.

Ubezhishche Mon Repo [The Haven of Mon Repos]. 1878–79.

Kruglyi god [The Year Round]. 1879–80.

Za rubezhom [In Foreign Parts]. 1880–81.

Pis'ma k teten'ke [Letters to Auntie]. 1881–82.

Poshekhonskie rasskazy [Poshekhon'e Tales]. 1883–84.

Nedokonchennye besedy [Unfinished Chats]. 1883–84.

Pestrye pis'ma [Variegated Letters]. 1884–86.

Melochi zhizni [The Trivia of Life]. 1886–87.

Poshekhonskaia starina [Old Times in Poshekhon'e]. 1887–89.

Play

Smert' Pazukhina, 1857; translated as *The Death of Pazukhin*, by J. Leigh, New York, 1924; also translated as "Pazukhin's Death", by L. Senelick, *Russian Literature Triquarterly*, 14 (1976), 321–76.

Critical Studies

Saltykov-Shchedrin. Biografiia, by S.A. Makashin, 4 vols: vol. 1, Moscow, 1949; vol. 2, Moscow, 1972; vol. 3, Moscow, 1984; vol. 4, Moscow, 1989.

Saltykov-Chtchédrine: Sa vie et ses oeuvres, by Kyra Sanine, Paris, Université de Paris Institut d'Études Slaves, 1955.

Satira Saltykova-Shchedrina, by A.S. Bushmin, Moscow and Leningrad, 1959.
Revoliutsionnaia satira Saltykova-Shchedrina, by E. Pokusaev, Moscow, 1963.
Saltykov and the Russian Squire, by Nikander Strelsky, New York, AMS Press, 1966 (original edition, 1940).
"Reaction or Revolution: The Ending of Saltykov-Shchedrin's *History of a Town*", by I.P. Foote, *Oxford Slavonic Papers*, 1 (1968), 105–25.
"M.E. Saltykov-Schchedrin: *The Golovlyov Family*", by I.P. Foote, *Forum for Modern Language Studies*, 4/1 (1968), 53–63.
O proze, by Boris Eikhenbaum, Leningrad, 1969.
"Satiric Form in Saltykov's *Gospoda Golovlevy*", by K.D. Kramer, *Slavic and East European Journal*, 14/4 (1970), 453–64.
"'Istoriia odnogo goroda' M.E. Saltykova-Shchedrina", by D. Nikolaev, in *Tri shedevra russkoi klassiki*, Moscow, 1971.
"The Anti-Hero with a Thousand Faces: Saltykov-Shchedrin's Porfiry Golovlev", by W.M. Todd, *Studies in the Literary Imagination*, 9/1 (1976), 87–105.
"A Classic of Russian Realism: Form and Meaning in *The Golovlyovs*", by Milton Ehre, *Studies in the Novel*, 9 (1977), 3–16.
"Quintessential Saltykov-Shchedrin: *Ubezhishche Mon Repo*", by I.P. Foote, *Oxford Slavonic Papers*, 12 (1979), 84–103.
Smekh Shchedrina, by D. Nikolaev, Moscow, 1988.
Saltykov-Shchedrin i russkaia literatura, edited by V.N. Baskakov and V.V. Prozorov, Leningrad, 1991.
Saltykov-Shchedrin i poetika russkoi literatury vtoroi poloviny XIX veka, by A.P. Auer, Kolomna, 1993.
Techniques of Satire: The Case of Saltykov-Shchedrin, by Emil A. Draitser, Berlin and New York, Mouton de Gruyter, 1994.
The Golovlyovs: A Critical Companion, edited by I.P. Foote, Evanston, Illinois, Northwestern University Press, 1997.

Bibliographies
Bibliografiia literatury o M.E. Saltykove-Shchedrine 1848–1917, by L.M. Dobrovol'skii, Moscow and Leningrad, 1961.
Bibliografiia literatura o M.E. Saltykove-Shchedrine 1918–65, by B.N. Baskakov, Moscow and Leningrad, 1966.
Bibliography by B.N. Baskakov, in *Saltykov-Shchedrin 1826–1976. Stat'i, materialy, bibliografiia*, Leningrad, 1976.
"M.E. Saltykov-Shchedrin in English: A Bibliography", by I.P. Foote, *Oxford Slavonic Papers*, 22 (1989).

Mikhail Saltykov-Shchedrin, a satirist, novelist and journalist, was a major figure on the Russian literary scene in the 1850s–1880s. He was first and foremost a commentator on his times. Most of his writings were concerned with the social and political condition of Russia in that period and are now largely dated for the general reader. However, certain works – *Gospoda Golovlevy* (*The Golovlevs*), *Istoriia odnogo goroda* (*The History of a Town*), *Skazki* (*Fables*) – are of more than local or contemporary significance. His profound insight into the problems of his day was founded on the broad experience he had of Russian life at different levels, particularly as an official in the provinces. The majority of his works were published in the leading radical journals of the time – *Sovremennik* and *Otechestvennye zapiski*; of the latter he was a very proficient editor in the period 1868–84.

Saltykov-Shchedrin began writing seriously in 1856 on his return from exile in Viatka. His cycle *Gubernskie ocherki* [Provincial Sketches] brought him immediate recognition for their pungent and amusing criticism of provincial officialdom. Thereafter his output was prolific. He wrote reviews, polemical articles, surveys of current affairs, and, above all, the numerous satirical sketches for which he is known. Individual sketches appeared monthly, subsequently being gathered into cycles on a particular theme for publication in book form.

The main themes addressed by Saltykov-Shchedrin in his satires were first, the relationship between the Russian state and the people. He showed the state machine to be tyrannical, corrupt, and irrelevant to the needs of the population, whose passivity and lack of political awareness he likewise deplored. The "great reforms" of Alexander II altered nothing: his *Satiry v proze* [Satires in Prose] and *Pompaduri i pompadurshi* (*The Pompadours: A Satire on the Art of Government*) of the 1860s indicated there was no change in the relationship. Saltykov-Shchedrin's definitive judgement was given in *The History of a Town*, which records the administration of Glupov-Russia by a succession of lunatic tyrants, whose only common policy was to "flog the inhabitants". Second, the social and economic condition of Russia and the effects of Alexander's reforms, especially the Emancipation of the Serfs (1861). He cast a backward look at pre-emancipation Russia in the late, semi-autobiographical *Poshekhonskaia starina* [Old Times in Poshekhon'e]. From the 1860s he recorded the continuing misery of the peasants (*passim*, succinctly stated in the fable "Koniaga" ["The Old Nag"]); the degeneration of the landowning class (in *Dnevnik provintsiala v Peterburge* [Diary of a Provincial in Petersburg], *Blagonamerennye rechi* [Well-Intentioned Speeches], *Ubezhishche Mon Repo* [The Haven of Mon Repos], *The Golovlevs*); and the emergence of new social predators, especially the rapacious rural capitalist (*Blagonamerennye rechi*, *Ubezhishche Mon Repo*). Third, the political disposition of Russian society. For the general masses this was passivity based on ignorance (as in *The History of a Town*). From the 1860s Saltykov-Shchedrin examined the responses of the educated classes to the reforms and to the political crisis of the 1870s and 1880s. His main target was the liberals. He attacked the specious liberalism of the reform period (*Satiry v proze*, *The Pompadours*) and, later, the liberals' conformism and abandonment of principles in the face of reaction (*Ubezhishche Mon Repo*, *Sovremennaia idilliia* [A Contemporary Idyll]), *Pis'ma k teten'ke* [Letters to Auntie], *Fables*). He was critical too in the 1880s of the general public's inclination to lie low and avoid the serious issues of the day (*Fables*).

In so far as Saltykov-Shchedrin saw the need for fundamental change in Russia, he was a radical, but he never aligned himself with any particular political programme or faction. In his satires he set out to expose and undermine the rule of "arbitrariness, hypocrisy, lying, rapacity, treachery, and vacuity" that characterized Russian life and to raise the political consciousness of the passive Russian public. Despite the negative tenor of his work, Saltykov-Shchedrin held to the Utopian faith of his youth that a just and rational order would one day be achieved. The key to this belief was *conscience*, which he saw as an indestructible element in man that could survive even in his most debased characters, such as Porfirii Golovlev.

Saltykov-Shchedrin's sketches were of two types: the discursive essay and the narrative. Occasionally he used the dramatic form. His satirical gifts are best displayed in his narratives, in which full play is made of humour, irony, parody, and sarcasm; fantasy and the grotesque are a prominent element in many satires, notably *The History of a Town* and *Fables*. He was particularly skilled in presenting a whole social trend or situation in a single typical episode or character (group or individual). This ability is most strikingly evident in the *Fables*, brief narratives in which the substance of his criticism of society is succinctly stated. Saltykov-Shchedrin had a robust style and was a master of many modes of language. Because of the censorship of the day he employed an Aesopic language of indirect statement and allusion, which poses a further barrier to the modern reader. His power as a descriptive writer is well demonstrated in *The Golovlevs*.

Saltykov-Shchedrin was highly regarded by his contemporaries, although he was criticized by some (notably, Pisarev) for having no clear guiding principle. The topical interest of his work caused him to be neglected for a time after his death, but in the 1930s he was accepted into the Soviet pantheon of 19th-century progressive writers – ironically, since much of what he wrote applied as well to Soviet as to tsarist Russia. He is best known today for *The Golovlevs*, his one recognized novel in the Russian realist tradition.

I.P. FOOTE

The History of a Town

Istoriia odnogo goroda

Novel, 1869–70

The History of a Town, one of Saltykov-Shchedrin's best satires, was published serially in *Otechestvennye zapiski* from January 1869 to September 1870. The first separate edition appeared in 1870, 2nd and 3rd editions (with revisions) in 1879 and 1883.

The History of a Town is a mock chronicle of the town of Glupov (Stupidtown), which symbolizes Russia. The early history is sketched briefly with details drawn from the old Russian chronicle account of the foundation of the Russian state by foreign princes, invited to bring order to the factious tribes incapable of ruling themselves. The core of the work recounts the administration of the town by the 21 governors in office from 1731 to 1826. These are characterized in a summary list; the detailed narrative relates the activities of Brudastyi (the 8th governor) and his successors to the penultimate governor listed (Ugrium-Burcheev). It is a tale of continuous inept tyranny: the townsfolk are taxed, beaten, subdued by force, suffer famine and fire, and are finally compelled to destroy their town and reconstruct it as a military camp. The governors, whatever their individual colourings, are united in one thing: they "all flog the inhabitants". The administration of the town is conducted not *for* but *against* the populace, who can only submit. Only during the rule of inactive governors (e.g. Pryshch) do the Glupovites enjoy temporary relief and prosperity. The relevance of *The History of a Town* to Russia is made obvious in the similarity of particular town-governors to major historical figures of the period in question: the succession of empresses in the 18th century is reflected in the episode of the "six town-governesses"; there is affinity between the governor Negodiaev and the Emperor Paul, between Grustilov and Alexander I, and between Benevolenskii and Ugrium-Burcheev and Alexander's ministers Speranskii and Arakcheev. These connections signal the fact that Glupov should be read as "Russia". The work was not, however, intended as a mere parody of Russia's past. The historical setting was only a convenient means of declaring judgement on the relationship between state and people in Russia at *all* times, not least that when *The History of a Town* was written. Composed at the end of the "reform" decade of the 1860s, *The History of a Town* pointed to the fact that whatever changes might occur in the government of Russia, such changes are superficial and do not alter the fundamental relationship between the power of the state and the powerlessness of the people. "What I had in mind", wrote Saltykov-Shchedrin, "was not an 'historical' satire, but a perfectly ordinary satire aimed at those features of Russian life that make it not altogether comfortable". The timelessness of the satire is indicated too by the fusing of past and present in anachronistic references to events and personages of Saltykov-Shchedrin's own day.

The climax of the work is the destruction of the town on the orders of Ugrium-Burcheev, an "idiot" leveller dedicated to the principle of the straight line, who sets out to convert the town into a military camp and rigidly control every aspect of the life of the townsfolk. However, in this final chapter two telling episodes indicate some measure of hope. In the first Ugrium-Burcheev encounters a force of nature, a river, which defeats his attempt to straighten its courses; in the second, not fully developed, the "chronicler" records the shame of the Glupovites when they see the results of their compliance with the "idiot" governor's orders. The suggestion is that nature and human nature will prove in the end to be indestructible. The satire ends obscurely with the removal of Ugrium-Burcheev by a whirlwind ("It") and "history ceasing its course". Opinions on the significance of the ending vary. Some see it as the onset of a yet more terrible tyranny (the reign of Nicholas I?) earlier predicted by Ugrium-Burcheev; others (mostly Soviet commentators) consider the cleansing force of "It" (improbably) as popular revolution or, more acceptably, as indication of the fact that the status quo is not immutable and even the most entrenched tyranny will one day be destroyed.

In an Appendix, sample administrative works by the governors, for example "On the Agreeable Outward Aspects of Town-Governors", "On the Proper Baking of Pies", illustrate the absurdity of the town's rulers.

In *The History of a Town* Saltykov-Shchedrin demonstrates the full range of his satirical talents. He uses irony (the town prospers when *not* administered; "wars of enlightenment" are waged against the populace – to enforce the use of mustard; the Glupovites rebel *on their knees*), parody (of the Russian chronicles, pedantic editors, bureaucratic documents), and, particularly, fantasy (a governor who flies through the air, another with a truffle-stuffed head that is eaten by a colleague, another an automaton capable of uttering only two phrases – both of them threats).

The History of a Town is one of Saltykov-Shchedrin's most pointed and popular works. Turgenev, in a review (in English) in the London journal *The Academy*, praised it for its humour, "satirical verve", and interest for future historians of Russia. The severest contemporary criticism came from A.S. Suvorin, who complained that the work was ahistorical, and that, in his presentation of the citizens of Glupov, Saltykov-Shchedrin had mocked the Russian people: to the latter objection Saltykov-

Shchedrin responded that, though he recognized the stultification of Glupov-Russia as the effect of long practised tyranny, in his depiction of the Glupovites he simply conformed to the facts of history.

I.P. FOOTE

The Golovlevs

Gospoda Golovlevy

Novel, 1875–80

The Golovlevs originated in sketches forming part of the cycle *Blagonamerennye rechi* (1872–76). The first two chapters appeared in *Otechestvennye zapiski* in 1875, the following four at intervals in 1876, the last in 1880. It was published as a separate edition in 1880 (2nd edition 1883). It is regarded as Saltykov-Shchedrin's greatest work and has been republished many times.

Blagonamerennye rechi was intended by Saltykov-Shchedrin to expose the hollowness of the principles declared to be pillars of Russian society – state, family, and property – which he showed as being systematically violated by those who proclaimed them. In a letter of 1881 to E.A. Utin, Saltykov-Shchedrin stated: "I wrote *The Golovlevs* as an attack on the family principle".

The novel recounts the history of a family of landowners through three generations. Except for a few ancillary figures, all the characters are of the Golovlev family: the parents Vladimir Mikhailovich and Arina Petrovna, their sons Stepan, Pavel, Porfirii, and (deceased) daughter Anna; their grandchildren Vladimir and Petr (sons of Porfirii) and Anna (Annin'ka) and Liubov' (Liubin'ka) (orphaned daughters of Anna). It is a bleak tale of degeneration. All the Golovlevs lead futile, unsatisfactory lives and die wretchedly (assisted in some cases by drink); at the end Annin'ka, a consumptive alcoholic, is the only survivor. The dominant figures are the family tyrants Arina Petrovna and Porfirii, who, despite their pretensions of concern for "the family", are the main agents of its destruction.

There are seven unnumbered chapters. "Semeinyi sud" ("Family Court") introduces the first two generations: the domineering Arina Petrovna, her frivolous husband, their sons – Stepan, a shiftless wastrel, Pavel, "a man bereft of deeds", and "Bloodsucker" Porfirii, nicknamed in the family "Judas" (Iudushka). The destitute Stepan returns to Golovlevo (his "coffin"), is received as an outcast and confined to an outhouse, where he drinks himself to death. In "Po rodstvennomu" ("Kith and Kin"), ten years later, Arina Petrovna, her world overturned by the Emancipation of the Serfs, is in decline. Porfirii usurps her position as family tyrant and machinates to inherit the property of Pavel, who dies in drunken despair. "Semeinye itogi" ("Family Scores") shows Arina Petrovna, five years on, a hanger-on in Porfirii's household. Her granddaughters have "escaped" to become provincial actresses. Porfirii, rejecting appeals for help from his sons, is the indirect cause of their ruin: one commits suicide, the other, convicted for embezzlement, dies on his way to Siberia. In "Plemianushka" ("The Niece") Arina Petrovna is dead. Annin'ka returns to Golovlevo and sees it in its true light. She refuses to stay, preferring the freedom of her seamy life as an actress. "Nedozvolennye semeinye radosti" ("Illicit Family Joys") continues the exposure of Porfirii's villainy. Evpraksiia, his mistress, gives birth to a son, whom Porfirii dispatches to a foundlings' home. In "Vymorochnyi" ("Entailed") Evpraksiia is in open revolt, leaving Porfirii without an audience for his moralizing prattle. He becomes a recluse and submerges himself in a fantasy world of aimless financial calculations and phantoms conjured up from the past. "Raschet" ("The Reckoning") sees Annin'ka back in Golovlevo. The sisters' theatrical career has brought them to moral corruption and degradation. Liubin'ka has committed suicide; Annin'ka returns to Golovlevo to die. Uncle and niece participate in powerful scenes of carousal and recrimination. Finally, Porfirii's conscience is stirred; aware at last of the destructive sterility of his life, he dies on his way to make amends at Arina Petrovna's grave.

The Golovlevs is undoubtedly a savage denunciation of the family principle: between the Golovlevs there is no bond of sympathy or affection, only malice, distrust, or indifference. Lacking any moral foundation, the strong tyrannize and destroy the weak. The family is not, though, the novel's sole concern; it also passes judgement on the land owning gentry as a class. Saltykov-Shchedrin identifies the causes of the Golovlev's degeneration as "idleness, incapacity for work of any kind, and drinking", of which the first two, at least, can be seen as attributes of the gentry class corrupted by generations of serf-owning. Golovlevo (the estate) – in contrast to the civilized gentry nests depicted by Turgenev and Tolstoi – is identified as the symbolic source of the family's malaise, and its pernicious influence is denounced by Annink'a in the novel's finale.

The social-historical interest of *The Golovlevs* is, however, overshadowed by the psychological portrayal of the two main characters, Arina Petrovna and, in particular, Porfirii, whose presence dominates from the third chapter of the novel. Arina Petrovna is stern, energetic, and successful in increasing the Golovlev property "for the family", but, as she comes to see, her activity is an obsessive ritual that brings her dependents deprivation rather than benefit. Porfirii is an outstanding creation, a classic figure of the hypocrite, an empty man devoid of moral substance and concerned only with form. Mean-spirited and vicious, he accompanies his villainies with pious posturing and nauseating streams of moralizing prattle. In "Family Scores" Saltykov-Shchedrin characterized him as a specifically Russian type of hypocrite, a mere gratuitous liar, since Russia lacked the social bases that in the west the hypocrite feigned to accept. The stirrings of Porfirii's conscience at the end, if unexpected (and an improbable outcome in the view of Goncharov), in fact accords with Saltykov-Shchedrin's consistent belief that the human element in man can never be totally suppressed.

The Golovlevs is a grim and powerfully written novel. Saltykov-Shchedrin excels in the conversational duels between the characters and, in particular, the scenes of drunken despair as, one by one, the Golovlevs decline and die. "The gloomiest novel in Russian literature" deserves its status as a classic. Its merits were recognized from the publication of the first chapters and it was the encouraging reception given them by Turgenev, Nekrasov, and others that persuaded Saltykov-Shchedrin to develop the sketches into a novel.

I.P. FOOTE

David Samuilovich Samoilov 1920–1990
Poet

Biography
Born David Samuilovich Kaufman in Moscow, 1 June 1920. Attended school in Moscow; studied at the Institute of Philology, Literature and History (IFLI), 1938–41. Volunteered in 1941 and stayed with the army until 1945. Married: 1) Fogel'son, one son; 2) Galina Morozova, one daughter and two sons. First publication in *Oktiabr'*, 1941. Full-time writer after World War II. Worked for the radio and translated poetry mainly from East European languages. Recipient: State Prize for Literature, 1987, for the poetry collection *Golosa za kholmami* [Voices Beyond the Hills]. Lived mostly in Piarnu, Estonia from mid-1970s. Died in Tallin, 23 February 1990.

Publications
Collected Editions

Izbrannoe: Stikhotvoreniia i poemy. Moscow, 1980.

Izbrannye proizvedeniia, 2 vols, with an introduction by Igor Shaitanov. Moscow, 1989.

Poetry

Blizhnie strany [Close Countries]. Moscow, 1958.

Vtoroi pereval [The Second Crossing]. Moscow, 1963.

Dni [Days]. Moscow, 1970.

Ravnodenstvie [Equinox]. Moscow, 1972.

Kniga o russkoi rifme [Book about Russian Rhythm]. Moscow, 1973; 2nd edition, Moscow, 1982.

Volna i kamen' [Wave and Stone]. Moscow, 1974.

Vest' [News]. Moscow, 1978.

Zaliv [The Bay]. Moscow, 1981.

Vremena [Times]. Moscow, 1983.

Stikhotvoreniia. Moscow, 1985.

Golosa za kholmami [Voices Beyond the Hills]. Tallin, 1987.

Beatrice. Tallin, 1989.

Gorst' [A Handful]. Moscow, 1989.

Snegopad: Moskovskie stikhi [Snowfall: Moscow Poems]. Moscow, 1990.

Memoirs

Pamiatnye zapiski [Memorial Notes]. Moscow, 1995.

Critical Studies
"Poetov nado liubit'", by U. Boldyrev, *Literaturnoe obozrenie*, 2 (1979).

"Neprinuzhdennost' kak svoistvo poezii", by Evgenii Evtushenko, in his *Talant est' chudo nesluchainoe*, Moscow, 1980.

"Muzyka i slovo", by M. Borshchevskaia, *Novyi mir*, 7 (1982).

"Palimpsest", by Igor Shaitanov, *Literaturnoe obozrenie*, 5 (1982).

David Samoilov: Poet i ego pokolenie, by V. Baevskii, Moscow, 1986.

Piarnusskii Al'bom: David Samoilov, by V. Perelygin, Tallin, 1991.

Although David Samoilov's career as a poet was never formally allied to any literary group or movement, he has frequently been labeled by critics as a result of certain facts in his biography. The first such instance took place when he was a student at IFLI, a prestigious centre for the study of humanities, which had replaced the former philological faculty of Moscow University with the aim of fostering an ideological elite. Future captains of Soviet culture were educated there together with future dissidents, intellectuals, and poets. In the IFLI poetic circle Samoilov, more than anybody else, benefited from the high educational standard provided. His cultural and poetic antecedents, though, can be traced even further back to his schooldays, when he absorbed and learned by heart Pasternak and Mandel'shtam.

Most of Samoilov's early poems remained unpublished for decades; when they were eventually printed, they betrayed further poetic preferences: in particular Khlebnikov and Zabolotskii. Slow in movement and intently ponderous, these poems formed a striking contrast in style to the easy flowing, nonchalant diction that Samoilov had become famous for, but they also shed light on the origin of his later attempts to explore the material property of simple things. In 1941 the "IFLI poet" turned over a new page in his biography, to be classified from then on as a poet of "the war generation". Unlike many others, Samoilov never drew greatly from his own memories of the war in terms either of tragedy or of heroism. The prevailing tone of his war recollections is that of the bewilderment experienced by a young man, too young to comprehend or even to be scared.

Samoilov was the last in his generation of poets to have a book of verse published; *Blizhnie strany* [Close Countries] was able to appear in the wake of the Thaw. Although he was never seriously politically engaged, nor an obvious dissident, his poetry was frowned on by the authorities. His tone constantly aroused official suspicion by being too independent and personal, as if unsuspecting of the great issues, and addressed to an intimate circle where a high-flown word could seem comically inappropriate. Samoilov was at his best in momentary glimpses of memory: his parents passing in a horse-drawn carriage through the streets of the still unreconstructed Moscow; or he himself as a child, staying in bed with a sore throat and listening, in tears, to his father singing Pushkin's ballad about Prince Oleg. Pushkin was also part of the poet's intimate world, opposed in this manner to the bronze and gilded monuments of the officially established classical heritage. Samoilov's growing reputation depended to a degree also on his historical scenes and portraits, such as his Tsar Ivan cycle. The historical genre always remained important in Samoilov's poetry, taking the form of either a fleeting fragment or a very short epic, apocryphally unrestrained in the treatment of plots and characters ("Strufian, Son o Gannibale" [Strufian, A Dream about Hannibal]).

Samoilov's reputation was on the rise by the 1960s, despite his relatively few publications in book form. By the time his first small book of collected verse *Ravnodenstvie* [Equinox] appeared in 1972, he could claim a considerable status among Russian poets living in the USSR. Far beyond the range of his personal acquaintance, many readers referred to him affectionately by the diminutive form of his name – "Dezik". Samoilov's rising literary fame and the reviews of each new book, which steadily progressed from approval to enthusiastic applause, did not affect the intimate and ironic nature of his verse, although he was changing under the advance of old age, aggravated by physical infirmities and catastrophically failing eyesight. In the mid-1970s Samoilov bought a house in the small Estonian town of Piarnu and settled there, paying occasional visits to Moscow and elsewhere. His poetry of that period displays evidence of a lonely life on the sea-shore with his failing eyes turned now on nature. This new situation is revealed in the titles of his later books: *Volna i kamen'* [Wave and Stone] (1974); *Zaliv* [The Bay] (1981); *Golosa za kholmami* [Voices Beyond the Hills] (1987); and *Beatrice* (1989).

Paradoxically, it was then, in accordance with a new label forced on him by certain nationalist critics, that he was classed among the "bookish poets" (*knizhnye poety*): alongside Arsenii Tarkovskii, Iunna Morits, and Aleksandr Kushner. The critical assumption made at the time was that these poets were guilty either of reducing tradition to name-and-quotation-dropping, or of allowing it to sink into burlesque, with an over-familiar touch of contemporary speech and sensibility. Samoilov seemed an easy target, counting himself a member of "the latterday Pushkin Pleiad", and proclaiming himself proud of his poetic achievement: "And again I have restored the concept of playing to poetry, as it used to be ...". His unwillingness to compose poetry that was solemn, sublime, and serious was well known. It was a feature both of his moral position and of his poetic vision.

Samoilov made every effort to avoid both straightforward statement and detailed description. He had chosen the path of elusiveness and preferred to view things from a "sidewards-glance". His poetic manner increasingly resembled *poèsie fugitive* because of its intimate spontaneity. As early as the 1950s Samoilov had confessed: "I love ordinary words as unexplored lands ...". Always engaged in exploring the ordinary, he sought to renew perception, to create for the reader the moment of wonder that was unique and, at the same time, resounding in reminiscence. Samoilov could begin a poem with a categorical negation, "Repetitions never occur ...", and then proceed to unravel the argument into a chain of fragile winter impressions, presumed irretrievable, thus subverting the opening statement, to make the whole poem bristle with allusions to Pushkin, Fedor Tiutchev, or V. Sokolov. What might seem passing and momentary in individual life retains, once experienced and written down, an ever-recurring existence within culture.

Samoilov synchronized culture and his efforts were, in due course, associated with the critical metaphor of "*palimpsest*", which was used to qualify his poetry. This may appear to have been prompted by postmodern associations contemporary to his creative work, but opposed to the very ideals of his cultural archaeology: he never dreamt of deconstructing man, and all he wished for was to resist the deconstruction of humanity by a totalitarian state. Elusive as ever, Samoilov made his poetry into a very clear and outspoken argument for cultural values, which he viewed as waning dangerously in the former USSR.

IGOR SHAITANOV

Ol'ga Aleksandrovna Sedakova 1949–

Poet and critic

Biography

Born in Moscow, 26 December 1949. Attended Moscow State University, graduated in 1972; Institute of Slavic and Balkan Studies; PhD, 1983. Married: 1) Aleksandr Lazarevich in 1972 (divorced 1985); 2) Valerii Kotov in 1985 (divorced 1991). Assessor of foreign books at the Institute for Scientific Information, 1986–89. Lecturer, Moscow Literary Institute, 1989–91; senior lecturer, Moscow State University, 1991–93. Reader, Institute of World Culture, since 1993; poet-in-residence, Keele University, England, 1994. Recipient: Andrei Belyi Prize for Poetry, 1980; Paris Prize for a Russian Poet, 1991; Töpfer Schiftung Fund Award, 1993.

Publications

Collected Edition

Stikhi. Moscow, 1994.

Poetry

Iz rannikh stikhov [From the Early Poems]. 1965–73 (a few poems are also in the collection *Stikhi*, 1994).

Dikii shipovnik [Wild Rose]. 1978; also in *Stikhi*, 1994.

Starye pesni [Old Songs]. 1980–82; also in *Kitaiskoe puteshestvie*, 1990.

Poems translated by Andrew Wachtel, *Berkeley Fiction Review*, 6 (1985–86) [double issue], 190–201.

Vrata, Okna, Arki: Izbrannye stikhotvoreniia [Gates, Windows, Arches]. Paris, YMCA-Press, 1986.

"Solovei, Filomena, sud'ba" [The Nightingale, Filomena, Fate], *Druzhba narodov*, 10 (1988), 121–40.

Kitaiskoe puteshestvie [A Chinese Journey]. Moscow, 1990.

Poems translated by Andrew Wachtel, in *Third Wave: The New Russian Poetry*, edited by Kent Johnson and Stephen M. Ashby. Ann Arbor, University of Michigan Press, 1992, 129–36.

Poems translated by Gerald S. Smith, in his *Contemporary*

Russian Poetry: A Bilingual Anthology, Bloomington, Indiana University Press, 1993, 268–79.
Shelk vremeni. The Silk of Time. Bilingual Selected Poems, edited with an introduction by Valentina Polukhina. Keele, Keele University Press, 1994.
The Wild Rose and Selected Poems (bilingual edition), translated by Richard McKane. London, Approach, 1997.

Memoirs, Essays, and Literary Criticism
"Pamiat' slova" [Memory of a Word], *Znanie-sila*, 10 (1975), 27–29.
"O 'bronzovom' veke" [On the Bronze Age], *Grani*, 130 (1983), 274–78.
"Kheddi Luk", *Laterna Magia. Literaturno-khudozhestvennyi, istoriko-kul'turnyi al'manakh*, Moscow, 1990, 261–66.
"O pogibshem literaturnom pokolenii – pamiati Leni Gubanova" [On the Lost Literary Generation – in Memory of Lenia Gubanov], *Volga*, 6 (1990), 135–46; first published in *Vybor*, 2 (1984), 293–334.
"Muzyka glukhogo vremeni (russkaia lirika 70-kh godov)" [Music of the Dead Time: Russian Lyrics of the 70s], *Vestnik novoi literatury*, 2 (1990), 257–65.
"M. Gasparov – O. Sedakova: Dialogi o Bakhtine" [Dialogues on Bakhtin], *Novyi krug*, 1 (1991), 113–17.
"Postmodernizm: Usvoenie otchuzhdeniia" [Postmodernism: Mastering of Alienation], *Moskovskii nabliudatel'*, 5 (1991), 14–16.
"Zametki i vospominaniia o raznykh stikhotvoreniiakh, a takzhe Pokhvala poezii" [Notes and Recollections about Various Poems and also "In Praise of Poetry"], *Volga*, 6 (1991), 135–64.
"Vospominaniia o Venedikte Erofeeve" [Remembering Venedikt Erofeev], *Teatr*, 9 (1991), 98–103.
"Ocherk drugoi poezii. Ocherk pervyi. Viktor Krivulin" [Essay on Other Poetry. Essay One. Viktor Krivulin], *Volga*, 10 (1991), 258–66.
"Pamiati Arseniia Tarkovskogo" [In Memory of Arsenii Tarkovskii], *Volga*, 12 (1991), 174–77.
"Znak, smysl, vest'" [Sign, Meaning, Information], *Nezamechennaia zemlia, Literaturno-khudozhestvennyi al'manakh*, Moscow and St Petersburg, 1991, 249–52.
"*Mednyi vsadnik*: Kompozitsiia konflikta" [The Bronze Horseman: Composition of Conflict], *Rossiia – Russia*, 7 (1991), 39–55.
"Puteshestvie v Briansk" [A Journey to Briansk], *Volga*, 5–6 (1992), 138–57.
"Po russkom imeni ..." [About the Russian Name ...], *Iskusstvo kino*, 10 (1993), 4–7.
"Pritcha i russkii roman" [The Parable and the Russian Novel], *Iskusstvo kino*, 4 (1994), 11–16.

Translator
Izbrannye stikhi, by Paul Claudel, Moscow, 1992.
Izbrannye stikhotvoreniia, by Ezra Pound, Moscow, 1992.

Critical Studies
"Ol'ga Sedakova: Novyi put'", by D.S. (V.A. Saitanov), in Sedakova's *Vrata, Okna, Arki, Izbrannye stikhotvoreniia*, Paris, YMCA-Press, 1986, 113–28.
Paradoksy novizny, by Mikhail Epshtein, Moscow, 1988, 161–64.
"Pis'mo o smerti, liubvi i kotenke", by A.K. Shevchenko, *Filosofskaia i sotsiologicheskaia mysl'*, 9 (1989), 110–14.
"Gore, polnoe do dna", by S.S. Averintsev, in Sedakova's *Stikhi*, Moscow, 1994, 356–63.
A History of Russian Women's Writing, 1820–1992, by Catriona Kelly, Oxford and New York, Clarendon Press, 1994, 423–32.
"Teni slov", by M. Zhazhonian, *Russkaia mysl'*, 7–13 (April 1994), 12.
"Sedakova Brings Silver Age Image to Modern Verse", by A. Smith, *The Moscow Tribune* (14 December 1994), 15.
"Ol'ga Sedakova", by Iana Sverdliuk, *Segodnia* (31 December 1994), 13.
"Thinking Self in the Poetry of Ol'ga Sedakova", by Stephanie Sandler, in *Gender and Russian Literature: New Perspectives*, edited by Rosalind Marsh, Cambridge and New York, Cambridge University Press, 1996.

Ol'ga Sedakova is one of Russia's most admired and respected poets, heir to the tradition of the great Russian poets, Osip Mandel'shtam, Anna Akhmatova, and Velimir Khlebnikov. She began writing poetry while still at school. Her first poems appeared in the students' newspapers of Tartu University (Estonia) and Tbilisi University (Georgia), and also in unofficial journals in Moscow and Leningrad in the late 1980s. After perestroika such prestigious magazines as *Novyi mir*, *Druzhba narodov*, and *Znamia* expressed great interest in Sedakova's poetry. Brought up during the time of sluggishness and stagnation, she swiftly developed her own distinct style. She has already acquired cultural importance in France (where in 1991 she was awarded the Paris Prize for a Russian poet), in Italy and in Germany, where she received a Schiller Fund Award. While in England, she became the first Russian poet in residence at Keele University (1993–94). Sedakova is also an outstanding scholar. She has written many academic articles and essays on Pushkin, Pasternak, Akhmatova, and Khlebnikov as well as on her own contemporaries such as Venedikt Erofeev, Leonid Gubanov, and Viktor Krivulin. One of the special strengths of her essays is a profound and vivid thought process that is conveyed with a touch of irony and dazzling style. In many senses, her prose can be seen as a continuation of her poetry: the same sharpness of observation, the same elegant meditative tone; they are both fed by the same spring.

Her work reflects a profound assimilation of the classics and modern European poetry. She also has a keen sense of history and, it seems, she shares the belief that poets were the inventors of civilization. Her vast knowledge of European poetry and her love of the classics helped to form the foundation of her own poetic vision. She has translated the works of T.S. Eliot, Pound, Hardy, Claudel, Rilke, Petrarch, Horace, and Dante. Their poetry has provided the "context" for some of her poems. Sedakova has also been influenced by modern philosophy and borrowed many motifs from it. Her knowledge of modern music allows her to take delicious liberties with rhythm that plays an important role in the general semantic construction of her verse. Thus, in her "Elegiia osennei vody" [Autumn Water's Elegy] the mixture of long lines and single-word lines portray the freedom of the waters cascading over the hills and refer back to the foundation of poetic inspiration. Her landscapes are visual and vivid.

Sedakova is regarded by many as being primarily a religious poet. But she herself avoids that term because for her Christianity is not only a cultural, a structuralizing, a generative principle; it is not just enlightened conservatism, it could also be a radicalism, a rejection of the world and all its cultures. Nevertheless, she is one of the best confessional Christian poets writing in Russian today. Her poetry provokes metaphysical and theological thoughts and demonstrates the beauty of faith. This perhaps will help Sedakova to realize her greatest ambition to return poetry to the Russian Orthodox Church and to give the Church to poetry. It is also true that religious and secular motifs are inseparable in her poems. Water, earth, air, and fire appear with particular frequency throughout her poetry. These four elements bring with them a whole range of mythical, theological, and symbolic allusions to the origins of our civilization. Like her beloved Mandel'shtam, she takes upon herself the entire civilization in a very unobtrusive way by charging her poems with obvious, obscure, and abeyant cultural references. But this *poeta doctus* has nothing in common with postmodernistic games. Unashamedly traditionalist, she is only too aware of the poet's duty to avoid polluting human memory with trivial and nonsensical images, since a written poem can be memorized.

Sedakova follows Mandel'shtam and Acmeist poetics in her treatment of language: for her, the most important thing in poetry is the word *per se*, the word as name; it is more important, she insists, than syntax, versification or tropes. In her opinion, the poem serves the word, so that each individual word realizes the full range of its potential: both etymological and phonetic, and its potential for ambivalence of meaning. But it is not just words that create the stylistic excellence of her writings; the composition of her poems is another device that deserves attention. The composition is based on the principle of the plastic representation of transience, of the perishable, of achieving a balance between the important and the unimportant, as in the poem "Kuznechik i sverchok" ("The Grasshopper and the Cricket"). She has also exhibited a consummate skill in deploying dreams as a part of the composition. She believes that dreams and premonitions give reality an additional dimension and she uses them as means of communication with another realm. The acoustic splendour of her poems contributes greatly to *le plaisir du texte*: *raz* and *roz* in *razvernesh'sia* and in *mirozdan'ia* announce in advance the appearance of a rose in "Dikii shipovnik" [The Wild Rose]; love for Christ is expressed in the anagram: *i belyi belee liubogo*. "Dikii shipovnik" is an example of a truly poetic transformation; it presents a breathtaking spiritual expansion, taking us beyond the horizon of our vision, indeed, it extends our vision. Two more poets should be mentioned here: Dante and Rilke; they are both, for Sedakova, tantamount to poetry itself. She has learnt from them how to convey the incurable longing of the partial and private for the whole and for holiness. This aspiration gives her poems inner energy.

We notice an ethical and aesthetic self-restraint, a restrained tone and a reluctance to put herself at the centre of her poems. The first-person figure is rare in her verse. The desire to go "beyond oneself" in search of some ultimate meaning is expressed in "Piatye stansy" [Fifth Stanzas]. Many of her poems could be read as a symbol of contemplative life. Her main interest is the knowledge of the spirit, buried deep inside us; to restore the life of the spirit within man is the poet's prime concern. Whether writing about the Song of Hannah or the mysterious story of Saul, Sedakova forces us to rethink our attitude to faith. What is lacking in Sedakova's work is any interest in a feminist literary tradition; the fashionable issue of gender bewilders her. This "deficiency" is more than compensated for by poetic integrity, a rare quality among contemporary poets. Sedakova's poetry embodies a certain nobility and sublime simplicity; her poems give a wonderful sense of proportion and harmony. It is interesting to note that the publication of her collection *Stikhi* in 1994 was seen by a leading Moscow philosopher, V.V. Bibikhin, as a most important cultural event.

VALENTINA POLUKHINA

Lidiia Nikolaevna Seifullina 1889–1954

Prose writer

Biography

Born in Varlamovo (near Magnitogorsk), 3 April 1889. Daughter of a well-educated priest of Tartar origin. Attended a local church school; high school in Omsk. Worked as a teacher in the Mordov region, 1912–15. Politically active in Cheliabinsk, 1918. Attended All-Russian Congress on education in Moscow, 1920, where she heard Lenin speak. Returned to Siberia to help organize one of first Soviet "thick" journals (*Sibirskie ogni*), 1921. First publication, 1922. Settled in Moscow, 1923. Began adapting her stories for the stage. Travelled to Turkey in 1924 and to western Europe in 1927, partly to supervise stage adaptations. Criticized for her apparently lukewarm politics; devoted herself increasingly to the theatre and to journalism from the 1930s. Died 25 April 1954.

Publications

Collected Editions

Sobranie sochinenii, 3 vols. Moscow, 1925.
Sobranie sochinenii, 5 vols. Moscow and Leningrad, 1926–27.

Sobranie sochinenii, 6 vols. Moscow and Leningrad, 1929–31.
Sobranie sochinenii, 4 vols. Moscow, 1968–69.
Sochineniia, 2 vols. Moscow, 1980.

Fiction
"Chetyre glavy" [Four Chapters], *Sibirskie ogni*, 1 (1922).
"Pravonarushitelni", *Sibirskie ogni*, 2 (1922); translated as "The Lawbreakers", by George Reavey and Marc L. Slonim, in *Soviet Literature*, London, Wishart, 1934.
"Peregnoi" [Humus], *Sibirskie ogni*, 5 (1922).
"Virineia", *Krasnaia nov'*, 1924.

Articles and Memoirs
O literature: Stat'i i vospominaniia [On Literature: Articles and Memoirs]. Moscow, 1958.

Critical Studies
Lidiia Seifullina, by N. Ianovskii, Moscow, 1959; 2nd edition 1972.
Dve sud'by: Lidiia Seifullina i ee povest' "Virineia", by V. Kardin, Moscow, 1975.
Izbrannye stat'i o literature, by A. Voronskii, Moscow, 1982.

Lidiia Nikolaevna Seifullina acquired a reputation as a leading writer in the early 1920s. If not exactly a product of the October Revolution, she was very obviously not committed in any major sense to the pre-Soviet world. In a vital respect she was representative of the novelty and freshness that characterized the early years of Soviet writing. First, she brought a woman's point of view to her pictures of the Civil War and revolutionary change without any overbearing feminism or special pleading. Second, the setting of her best work was unusual in that it was Siberia, the region near her birthplace; her themes were also unusual, taken from the lives of the ordinary peasantry of the area rather than from the intelligentsia. Third, and most importantly, her writing, especially dialogue, is bold and full of vigour.

She was not alone, of course, in writing about Siberia. Her contemporary, Vsevolod Ivanov, also set his major work (*Armoured Train 14-69*) there, but Seifullina does not rely on the exoticism of the locale or the quasi-poetic manner characteristic, say, of Belyi to give her work a special appeal. Hers was on the whole a realistic manner that owed much to her reading of Pushkin, Lermontov and Tolstoi, with whose works she became closely acquainted during her schooldays in Omsk. Later her work as a teacher brought her into close contact with the peasantry in remote villages. This experience was invaluable to her not only because it gave her an intimate understanding of peasant life, but also because it helped to foster her self-confidence as a public speaker and as an organizer, qualities that led her to be chosen to attend a pedagogical course in Moscow in 1920. A year later she returned to work in Novosibirsk and helped to organize one of the first leading Soviet journals in Siberia, *Sibirskie ogni*.

Seifullina's literary career as a Soviet writer dates approximately from this time. She had published newspaper articles, a short story and a play previously, but she quickly acquired widespread popularity with such short stories as "Chetyre glavy" [Four Chapters], "Pravonarushiteli" ("The Lawbreakers"), Peregnoi [Humus] and, most popular of all, "Virineia" (published initially in the Moscow journal *Krasnaia nov'* in 1924 after Seifullina had moved to the capital). Her literary reputation was henceforward to be connected with Moscow and was to rest wholly on the work she produced there.

The vigorous shorthand manner so characteristic of Seifullina's work, with its emphasis on pungent, quick-fire exchanges of dialogue, can be seen to good effect in the short story "Chetyre glavy". O. Henry springs to mind as a comparison, and the shadow of Chekhov is always close at hand; but this brief study of Anna, who was loved by a political activist but chose instead a life of bourgeois comfort, is bleak in its implications and rather censorious in its tone. The portrayal of Anna is a good example of Seifullina's capacity for suggesting the meaninglessness of the common run of women's lives. "The Lawbreakers" is, by contrast, a lively and heartwarming short study of "lawless" children (*besprizornye*), victims of the Civil War period, and a teacher who, like Seifullina herself, tried to rehabilitate them and re-introduce them to society. Her sympathies are by no means all on the teacher's side, just as she does not sentimentalize the "lawless" boys. In the end, a touching, rough-and-ready *modus vivendi* is achieved between Martynov, the teacher, and Grishka, the most fully portrayed of the *bezprizornye*.

"Peregnoi" is a more substantial work. It deals in miniature with a whole peasant society shaken by Revolution and Civil War though it remains, in many respects, as backward as before. The "humus" referred to in the title is the peasantry, especially one peasant called Sofron, who attempts to enact, in frequently brutal fashion, the new edicts emanating from Moscow. Arguably such peasant interpreters of Bolshevism could provide the humus in which socialism might take root in rural Russia. In this particular instance the promise is unfulfilled. Cossack counter-revolutionaries snuff it out. "Virineia" tells of a peasant woman, Virineia or Virka (for short), who receives enough of an education from a period of employment in the city to make her literate but prefers to return to her peasant village where she enters into a common-law marriage. Her "husband" is much less intelligent than her and worlds apart when it comes to sensitive awareness and self-will. She falls in love with a visiting engineer; the relationship is shaming and she becomes notorious as a drunken woman of loose morals. Her "husband" dies in prison falsely accused of killing the engineer; the real murderer is the peasant "holy man" Magara who had earlier determined to fulfil what he regarded as his divine destiny – to die, that is to say, in obedience to God's will. Magara discovers to his chagrin that death was not prepared to have him (one of the best and most ironic scenes in this novella). Virineia herself, meanwhile, is attracted to an ex-soldier, Pavel Suslov, under whose influence she begins to find a purpose to her life by helping to support the Bolshevik cause in the Civil War. Supposing herself to be barren, she becomes pregnant by her new lover, only to die a violent death virtually as she gives birth.

The melodramatic qualities of the narrative and the earnestness of Seifullina's intentions tend to detract from the lasting worth of the story in a literary sense. What gives it enduring appeal is the portrait of the heroine. She receives vitality above all from the energy and colourfulness of her colloquial peasant speech. Conceived, one feels, as much in terms of the drama as the short story, it is not surprising that "Virineia" should have enjoyed great success when adapted for the stage. And for most of her subsequent working life Seifullina devoted herself to the theatre.

RICHARD FREEBORN

Aleksandr Serafimovich 1863–1949

Prose writer

Biography

Born Aleksandr Serafimovich Popov in Nizhne-Kumoiarskaia, 19 January 1863, into a Cossack family. Family settled in Ust-Medveditskaia in Don region after father's retirement. Attended the local high school until 1883; St Petersburg University, 1883–87. Met Lenin's elder brother, Aleksandr Ul'ianov. Implicated in an attempt to assassinate Tsar Alexander III, sentenced to five-year exile in Arkhangelsk region, 1887; released in 1890. Moved to Novocherkassk, 1892. Worked for the newspaper *Priazovskii krai* in Mariupol; then to Rostov-on-Don. Moved to Moscow, 1902; became a member of the literary group, *Sreda*. Established as a writer, remained in Moscow and published all major works in central publications. Member of the Communist Party, 1918. Editor-in-chief of the journal, *Oktiabr'*, 1926–29. Recipient: Stalin Prize for literature (jointly with V. Veresaev), 1942. Died 19 January 1949.

Publications

Collected Editions

Sobranie sochinenii, 10 vols. Moscow, 1940–48.
Sobranie sochinenii, 7 vols. Moscow, 1959–60.

Fiction

Ocherki i rasskazy. St Petersburg, 1901.
Gorod v stepi [City in the Steppe], *Sovremennyi mir*, 1–5 (1912).
Zheleznyi potok, *Nedra*, 4 (1924); translated as *The Iron Flood* [no translator named], London, Martin Lawrence, and New York, International Publishers, 1935; Moscow, Progress, 1978.
Sand and Other Stories, translated by George H. Hanna. Moscow, Foreign Languages Publishing House, 1956.

Critical Studies

Russian Literature since the Revolution, by Edward J. Brown, Cambridge, Massachusetts, Harvard University Press, 1963; 2nd edition, 1982, 122–25.
Rozhdenie epopei: Zheleznyi potok A.S. Serafmovicha, by L.A. Gladkovskaia, Moscow and Leningrad, 1963.
Put' pisatelia: Zhizn' i tvorchestvo A. Serafimovicha, by R. Khigerovich, 3rd edition, Moscow, 1963.
Tvorcheskii put' A.S. Serafimovicha, by A. Volkov, 2nd edition, Moscow, 1963.
"A.S. Serafimovich's Forgotten Novel, *City in the Steppe* (1912)", by Vera Lafferty, *Canadian Slavonic Papers*, 16 (1974), 202–20.

Best known for the graphic *Zheleznyi potok* (*The Iron Flood*) 1924, a novella-style work describing an "epic" march by a peasant army down the eastern seaboard of the Black Sea during the Civil War, Aleksandr Serafimovich had already achieved a reputation as a realist writer of the Gor'kii school several decades earlier. *The Iron Flood* has to be considered the climax of his career. Without it, of course, his literary standing would be minor. Its celebration of revolutionary values turned it into a somewhat overrated classic of Soviet literature and led to the neglect of Serafmovich's earlier work. Not that this was wholly unfair. *The Iron Flood* stands out as a very remarkable achievement by any standards. But the descriptive power it exhibits had been anticipated in several outstanding works of the 1890s and first years of the 20th century.

Though older than Maksim Gor'kii, Serafimovich was nevertheless to be considerably influenced by him; but his first role-models as writers were Korolenko, Gleb Uspenskii, and Leonid Andreev. Serafimovich fits more readily into that group of writers than he does into the more committed left-wing group associated with Gor'kii's Znanie publishing house. He chose quite deliberately, it seems, to be aligned with the "realists" and liked to be known, especially during the Soviet period, as a "proletarian" writer. In fact, a certain unfamiliarity and awkwardness informs his studies of proletarian subjects, whereas his touch in dealing with rural, predominantly peasant, milieux is altogether surer. This is in no way to belittle his opposition to capitalism, which became an increasingly significant factor in his writing as his career progressed. But he was not by birthright or upbringing a member of the proletariat and when describing, for example, the Presnia workers' uprising in Moscow during the 1905 Revolution, which he witnessed at first hand (see "Na Presne" [Rebellion in Presnia] 1905), he may have provided a remarkably vivid account, yet it was essentially the account of an eye-witness rather than that of a participant or an avowed sympathizer.

As a young man, however, he had been politically active and was exiled to the Arkhangelsk region for being implicated in the attempt to assassinate Tsar Alexander III in 1887 (for which Lenin's brother was hanged). Though Serafimovich was permitted to leave exile in 1890, the experience in the Arctic provided the setting and material for his first literary work. A brilliant piece of descriptive writing, it is a short study of a seal-hunter who perishes in the Arctic ice-floes ("Na l'dine" [On the Ice] 1889) and it opened the way for a series of sketch-type works, of varying length and importance, which he was to publish over the next 20 years.

Serafimovich did not enjoy substantial success as a writer until after 1905. It is generally accepted that he first attracted widespread praise with his long short-story of 1908 "Peski" ("Sand"). The tale of an elderly proprietor of a water-mill who marries an attractive peasant girl and soon falls victim to her efforts to poison him, it is less about the pettiness of human ageing and greed than about the inexorable encroachment of nature, in the shape of all-consuming sands that invade and gradually destroy the miller's once fertile world. Much the same message lies behind Serafimovich's most important pre-revolutionary work, the novel *Gorod v stepi* [City in the Steppe] 1912. In this case the encroaching evil is more obviously human greed in the shape of capitalist exploitation.

Composed over many years, the novel is episodic and structurally weak, in a manner characteristic of Gor'kii's novels. It is the story of a developing rivalry between the vicious and corrupt capitalist entrepreneur, Koroedov, and the engineer Polynov. They are both jointly responsible for creating the industrial settlement known as "the city in the steppe". Polynov learns to his cost that the association with Koroedov involves moral degradation and total destruction of his intelligentsia ideals. Tacked on, as it were, rather than subtly integrated into this relationship, are issues such as the rights of the workers, their struggle against exploitation and the intelligentsia's hopes for the overthrow of the capitalist system. The most telling indictment is embodied in Koroedov's son, Sergei, the seeming product of an incestuous relationship between father and daughter. Sergei epitomizes in his depraved intelligence the way in which capitalism may seem to contain the seeds of its own destruction.

Serafimovich proved himself particularly adept as a war correspondent during World War I when he reported from the front in Galicia. With the coming of Revolution his left-wing sympathies quickly brought him to prominence as a leading organizer of writers' groups. His bald head, round Cossack features and unremittingly stern expression projected a somewhat forbidding image of militancy appropriate to the role of the writer as a Party activist in the workers' cause. It was an image that received iconic status, the equivalent of Soviet sainthood, once he had published in 1924 his own contribution to the growing literature of revolution and Civil War, *The Iron Flood*.

Daring in its own time as an example of a literary work that drew on cinematic techniques such as montage, which was very popular in the early Soviet cinema, Serafimovich's masterpiece achieved its effects principally through glowing descriptive passages and, despite its episodic character, through suggesting with considerable skill the inexorable and finally unstoppable force of the "iron flood" of peasants fleeing from the White armies. Less convincing, though highly praised in Soviet criticism, was the attempt to demonstrate that such a peasant mass could create for itself a conscious political leadership in the shape of Kozhukh. Fundamentally this was more a case of creating a cult of personality. It anticipated the adulation that was subsequently to be paid to comrade Stalin as the leader, teacher, and friend of the Soviet people.

Serafimovich's reputation has naturally become linked to the Stalin period. He gave every appearance of being devoted to the Soviet dictator and received in return the accolades and privileges commonly accorded to an officially approved writer, even though for the last 25 years of his life he produced nothing of any worth.

RICHARD FREEBORN

The Iron Flood

Zheleznyi potok

Novella, 1924

A classic example of early Soviet literature, this account of a motley peasant army's retreat down the eastern shoreline of the Black Sea during the Civil War received lasting acclaim throughout the Soviet period, but for Serafimovich himself, already over 60 when it was published, it was not an event experienced at first hand and he relied on eye-witnesses for his material. He visited the Caucasus in 1913 and long harboured the wish to write about the area. But World War I intervened and it was not until he met the hero of the event two years after it occurred that he was able to embark on his work; and even then he worked on it only in fits and starts.

To save itself and the mass of peasantry threatened by Cossack forces in the area, the so-called Taman Army found itself obliged in the summer of 1918 to embark on a retreat along the eastern seabord of the Black Sea through Novorossisk to Tuapse and then inland, through the Caucasian mountains, in order to join up with the Red Army in the Kuban on the North Caucasus front. The leadership of such a disparate mass of people was entrusted to E.I. Kovtiukh (who wrote about it in *Ot Volgi do Kubani i obratno* [From the Volga to the Kuban and Back], Moscow, 1926). The enormous trek lasted 33 days and was an exodus of near-biblical proportions. Serafimovich respected the major facts associated with it but introduced certain features – the renaming of the leader as Kozhukh, for instance – in order to mythologize the whole episode and immortalize it as "an iron flood" symbolizing the victory of the peasant masses against all the odds. He was later criticized for failing to show as fully as he should the extent of Party leadership in the event.

The work opens and closes with descriptions of meetings. At the opening meeting Kozhukh is chosen as the leader of the momentous attempt to escape from the encircling White armies, though his antecedents as military leader are unclear. It is easy enough to dismiss him as a marionette figure, of no real depth, but enough of a biographical background is supplied to explain his commitment to the cause of the impoverished and starving peasant masses. The emphasis placed on his iron jaws and gimlet eyes naturally suggests a placard-style portraiture suitably revolutionary in its intent. Claims for him as the first portrayal of a revolutionary leader in Soviet literature can be dismissed as largely propagandist.

The body of the work alternates between passages of vivid nature description, momentary episodes of hectic military activity and sections of dialogue containing a special Ukrainian peasants' argot. A rapid succession of small scenes has a cinematic effect, which is reinforced by minimal characterization and a virtually total absence of any reference to the participants' thoughts. Tension is supplied by a concentration on the vulnerability of the peasant army as it winds snake-like down the coast road, pursued by its enemies and forced to endure the constant torment of intense heat, thirst, and hunger. The impact of the trek is felt most strongly in the sheer descriptive power that Serafimovich exhibits when he depicts landscape, the implacable mountains on the one hand and the azure but clearly hostile sea on the other, all permeated by an ever-present and stiflingly hot sunlight. The enemies – the pursuing Cossacks, German naval vessels, Georgian Mensheviks, White marauders – are on the whole faceless, with the exception of the Georgian Prince Mikheladze who is projected in a somewhat stilted, one-sided characterization. Some episodes are obviously horrific, such as the occasion when the horde is forced to march past the corpses of Maikop workers strung up on telegraph poles; others have a grotesque humour – for instance, a record of clownish laughter played on a gramophone induces waves of equivalent laughter to ripple down the lines of the marchers. Among the horde itself little effort is made to provide detailed portraits. Dialogue reading much like interpolated speech in a silent film conveys the multifaceted experience of the march. The only identifiably articulate character of any consequence is the old crone, Granny Gorbina, whose function is to mix homely diatribe with a blatant, not to say propagandist, chorus element.

What the work as a whole sets out to demonstrate is the transformation of the disparate peasant mass into an "iron flood" united in a single revolutionary purpose. The transformation is achieved by the forging process of the march itself with all its horrors and privations. The image of the horde united in the beating of "a single, inhumanly enormous heart" signifies the ultimate stage of the forging process, when the "iron flood" becomes invincible and succeeds in its aim of joining up with the Red Army in the Kuban. But this image is projected in a more recognizable form in the figure of the leader, Kozhukh. His final address at the meeting, which concludes the work, serves, in its biblical tone, to highlight the way in which the epic march can be seen in retrospect as a kind of latterday Calvary. Simultaneously Kozhukh's own role may be seen as that of a Christ-like saviour of the peasant masses. He cannot fail to acquire in the process the charisma of a cult figure and to suggest that in the end the Revolution may easily give birth to what we now know as Stalin's "cult of personality".

Any assessment of Serafimovich's work must be tempered by the caustic judgement passed on it by Zamiatin, author of the long-banned masterpiece *My* (*We*). He suggested that if a piece of "iron" from *The Iron Flood* were sent to a laboratory for analysis it would turn out to have been rusting for a long time in the cellars of Gor'kii's *Znanie* (a reference to Serafimovich's earlier association with Gor'kii's school of realistic writing). His final estimate of the work and its hero is waspishly wicked: "The thickest overlay of tinsel is reserved for the ending – the apotheosis of the hero, whose figure is assembled in strict conformity to all the known operatic rules."

RICHARD FREEBORN

Igor' Severianin 1887–1941

Poet

Biography

Born Igor' Vasil'evich Lotarev in St Petersburg, 16 May 1887. Father was an army officer. Educated at school and at home, no higher degree. Began to publish in 1904. Founder of "Ego-Futurism" in 1911; achieved remarkable popularity as a performance poet. Moved to Estonia in 1918; changed his name to Severianin-Lotarev. Married: Felissa Kruut in 1921 (separated 1937); one son. Lived with Vera Borisovna Korendi from 1935. Died in Tallin, 20 December 1941.

Publications

Collected Editions

Sobranie poezii, 4 vols. Moscow, 1915–16; reprinted Washington, DC, Kamkin, 1966–70.

Stikhotvoreniia. Leningrad, 1975,

Sobranie sochinenii, 5 vols. St Petersburg, 1995–96.

Poetry

Gromokipiashchii kubok [The Thunder-Seething Goblet], Moscow, 1913; reprinted Washington, DC, Kamkin, 1966.

Zlatolira [The Golden Lyre]. Moscow, 1914.

Ananasy v shampanskom [Pineapples in Champagne]. Moscow, 1915; reprinted Rockville, Maryland, Kamkin, 1970.

Victoria Regia. Moscow, 1915.

Poezoantrakt [Poetry Interval]. Moscow, 1915.

Tost bezotvetnyi [A Silent Toast]. Moscow, 1916.

Poezokontsert [Poetry Concert]. Moscow, 1918.

Vervena. Iurev, Odames, 1920.

Menestrel' [Minstrel]. Berlin, 1921.

Mirrelia. Berlin, 1922.

Feia Eiole. Berlin, 1922.

Paduchaia stremnina [Shooting the Rapids]. Berlin, 1922.

Tragediia Titana [Titan's Tragedy]. Berlin and Moscow, 1923.

Solovei [Nightingale]. Berlin and Moscow, 1923.

Kolokola sobora chuvstv [The Bells of the Sentimental Cathedral], Iurev and Tartu, 1925.

Rosa oranzhevogo chasa [Dew of the Orange Hour]. Iurev and Tartu, 1925.

Klassicheskie rozy [Classical Roses]. Belgrade, 1931.

Adriatika [Adriatic]. Narva, 1932.

Medal'ony [Medallions]. Belgrade, 1934.
Roial' Leandra [Leandra's Piano]. Bucharest, 1935.
Garmoniia kontrastov [A Harmony of Contrasts]. Moscow, 1995.

Letters
Pis'ma k Avguste Baranovoi: 1916–1938 [Letters to Avgust Baranovyi: 1916–1938], edited by Bengt Jangfeldt and Rein Kruus. Stockholm, Almqvist & Wiksell, 1988.

Translator
Poety Estonii [Poets of Estonia]. Tartu, 1929.

Critical Studies
Russian Futurism: A History, by Vladimir Markov, Berkeley, University of California Press, 1968.
"The Life and Outlook of Igor' Severianin as Reflected in His Poetic Work", by E. Boronowski, PhD dissertation, Münster, 1978.
"Maiakovskii i Igor' Severianin", by N. Khardzhiev, *Russian Literature*, 6/4 (1978), 307–46.
"Novye dannye o zhizni i tvorchestve Igoria Severianina", by Rein Kruus, *Uchenye zapiski Tartuskogo Gosudarstvennogo universiteta*, 683 (1986), 79–81.
"Georgii Shengeli ob Igore Severianine", by E. Korkina, *Tallin*, 3 (1987), 89–92.
"Pristat' by mne k rodnomu beregu ...": Igor' Severianin i ego okruzhenie v Estonii, by Iu. Shumakov, Tallin, 1992.

Bibliography
"Igor' Severianin v Estonii: Materialy k bibliografii", by S.G. Isakov, *De Visu*, 9/10 (1993), 64–68.

Igor' Severianin began his literary career with a few slim collections of poetry that were published during 1904 and 1905. They included poems about the Russian-Japanese War. One of the poems, "Gibel' Riurika" [Riurik's death], appeared in the army journal *Dosug i delo* of 1 February 1905. These publications were followed by a number of humorous verses in several St Petersburg almanacs: in *Kolokol'chiki*, for example, his poems published under bizarre pseudonyms such as "The Needle" and "Count Evgraf D'Aksangraf". He began using "Severianin" (meaning northerner) as a pseudonym in 1907. By 1912 he had published 35 collections of poetry, though some of them could be described as mere pamphlets. Severianin proclaimed himself an Ego-Futurist, but later was associated with the Russian Cubo-Futurists. His book *Gromokipiashchii kubok* [The Thunder-Seething Goblet], published in March 1913, included an introduction by Fedor Sologub. At the time Valerii Briusov was also writing favourable essays about Severianin, and this might have helped the latter's rise to fame: in a six-year period *Gromokipiashchii kubok* was republished ten times. It was followed by *Zlatolira* [The Golden Lyre] (1914), *Ananasy v shampanskom* [Pineapples in Champagne] (1915), *Victoria Regia* (1915), and other collections. On 28 January 1918 Severianin moved to Toila in Estonia, but he continued to make visits to Russia. He was labelled "the king of poets" at a recital of his poetry in Moscow in February 1918, thereby outsmarting Maiakovskii. In 1920 Estonia gained independence, and Severianin found himself an émigré in Russia. He returned to Estonia with his mother and his common-law wife, Mariia Vassil'evna Dombrovskaiia. Their marriage did not last; in 1921 he married an Estonian girl, Felissa Kruut. They were separated 15 years later, and Severianin spent the rest of his life, from 1935 to his death on 20 December 1941, with the poet Vera Borisovna Korendi (née Zapol'skaiia) in Tallin. This union was kept a secret from many of his friends and the general public.

Severianin is also known as a translator of Estonian poetry into Russian. His anthology *Poety Estonii* [Poets of Estonia] (1929), together with translations of poetry by Visnapuu and Rannit, secured him a substantial income from the Estonian government in the form of grants in 1926–31 and in 1937–40. Severianin remained a prolific writer all his life. He published a number of narrative poems such as *Kolokola sobora chuvstv* [The Bells of the Sentimental Cathedral] (1925), *Rosa oranzhevogo chasa* [The Dew of the Orange Hour] (1925), and *Roial' Leandra* [Leandra's Piano] (1935). His collection of verse *Klassicheskie rozy* [Classical Roses] was published in Belgrade in 1931 in the prestigious series "The Russian Library". Apart from poetry he wrote memoirs and a book on versification (unpublished). His last collections of poetry – *Nastroika liry* [Tuning of the Lyre], *Litavry solntsa* [Kettledrums of the Sun] and *Ocharovatel'nye razocharovaniia* [Charming Disillusions] – remain unpublished. His late poetry was highly praised by Tsvetaeva; she attended his recital in Paris in March 1931, and according to her impressions, which she described in several letters, Severianin abandoned his earlier eccentric manner of singing his poems and kitsch-style vocabulary in favour of simplicity of expression. Severianin himself was critical of his early work, admitting that it had been infiltrated by "the classical clichés" of the time and "melodism" due to his frequent visits to opera-houses. During his last years Severianin tried to return to Russia, and when he was advised by his friend Shengeli to write a poem to Stalin he wrote several poems in praise of the new regime. Some of his poems and essays about Russian composers appeared in the Soviet press (in *Ogonek*, for example).

Severianin's poetry was very fashionable in the 1910s and 1920s, because of its interesting effects, neologisms, and oxymorons (such as "charming disillusions"). His mix of the trivial and the exotic appealed to an audience with a taste for the erotic and the exciting. The most popular poems, such as "Ia genii – Igor' Severianin" [I am Igor' Severianin, the genius ...] and "Eto bylo u moria, ..." [It was by the sea ...], manifest the love for the new style and pretentiousness. However, perhaps the most appealing aspect of Severianin's early poetry is that it is undemanding and often frivolous. Yet a perceptive reader may sense that it produces a kaleidoscope of masks cleverly constructed by the author to suit different moods and circumstances. Perhaps Severianin's characterization of Alexander IV (*Aleksandr IV*, 1918) as "an idealist in the decadent style" is more serviceable as a self-portrait of the poet. In spite of his numerous trips to Europe, Severianin remained profoundly Russian: he had an idealized vision of Russia that contrasted with pragmatic western culture. This is particularly evident in his poem "Igrai tselyi vecher" [Play for the Whole Evening] (1937): "Play for me something from the "Queen of Spades" / The most moving opera ... Especially in this pragmatically-mean Europe". A collection of Severianin's poetry was published in Leningrad in 1975 and there has been a minor revival of interest in his work in recent years.

Alexandra Smith

Marietta Sergeevna Shaginian 1888–1982

Prose writer and poet

Biography
Born in Moscow, 2 April 1888, to an Armenian father and a Russian mother of Armenian descent. First collection of verse, *Pervye vstrechi* [First Encounters] published in 1909. Studied philosophy at Moscow University, 1908–12; and minerology, 1912–14; also studied in Heidelberg. Interned in Germany in 1914; escaped via Switzerland with help of the Red Cross. Married: Iu.S. Khachatriants in 1917. Began to write prose fiction after 1917. Published several works under pseudonym Jim Dollar. Lived in Leningrad/Petrograd, 1920–27. Member of the board of the Writers' Union, 1934–82. Evacuated to the Urals during World War II. Member of the Communist Party, 1942. Received doctorate for dissertation on Shevchenko, 1944. Recipient: Stalin Prize, 1950; Lenin Prize, 1972, for her cycle of works on Lenin. Died 21 March 1982.

Publications
Collected Editions
Sobranie sochinenii, 6 vols. Moscow, 1956–58.
Sobranie sochinenii, 9 vols. Moscow, 1971–75.
Sobranie sochinenii, 9 vols. Moscow, 1986–89.

Fiction
Svoia sud'ba [One's Own Fate]. Moscow and Petrograd, 1923; revised edition, 1954.
Prikliucheniia damy iz obshchestva [Adventures of a Society Lady], *Krasnaia niva* (1923), 48–51.
Mess-Mend, ili Ianki v Petrograde. Moscow and Leningrad, 1924; translated as *Mess-Mend – Yankees in Petrograd*, by Samuel D. Cioran, Ann Arbor, Ardis, 1991.
Peremena [Change]. Leningrad, 1924.
Kik, in *Zvezda*, 2–3 (1929).
Gidrotsentral' [Hydrocentral], *Novyi mir* (1930–31); Leningrad, 1931.
Sem'ia Ul'ianovykh [The Ulianov Family], 4 vols. Moscow, 1938–70:
1. *Rozhdenie syna* [The Birth of a Son], *Krasnaia nov'* (1938)
2. *Pervaia Vserossiiskaia* [The First All-Russian]. 1965.
3. *Bilet po istorii* [Ticket to History], *Literaturnaia gazeta*, (22 April 1960); Moscow, 1969.
4. *Chetyre uroka u Lenina* [Four Lessons from Lenin]. Moscow, 1970.

Voskreshenie iz mertvykh [Resurrection from the Dead], *Oktiabr'* (1963).

Poetry
Pervye vstrechi. Stikhi [First Encounters]. Moscow, 1909.
Orientalia. Stikhi. Moscow, 1913; 7th edition Berlin, 1922.

Travel Writing, Essays, and Memoirs
Puteshestvie v Veimar [Journey to Weimar]. 1923.
Ural v oborone [The Urals under Defence]. Moscow and Leningrad, 1943–44.
Puteshestvie po Sovetskii Armenii [Journey Through Soviet Armenia]. Moscow, 1950.
Ocherki raznykh let [Sketches of Various Years]. 1977.
Chelovek i vremia [Man and Time]. Moscow, 1980.

Diary
Dnevnik pisatel'ia: 1950–52 [Diary of a Writer]. Moscow, 1953.

Biographies
T.G. Shevchenko. Moscow and Leningrad, 1941.
I.A. Krylov. Erevan, 1944.
I.V. Gete [Goethe]. Moscow, 1950.

Critical Studies
Leninskaia tema v tvorchestve Marietty Shaginian, by R.S. Gol'dina, Erevan, 1969.
Marietta Shagininan – khudozhnik: Zhizn' i tvorchestvo, by L. Skorino, Moscow, 1975; 2nd edition, 1981.
Border Crossings: The West and Russian Identity in Soviet Literature 1917–34, by Carol Avins, Berkeley, University of California Press, 1983.
"Canon Fodder? Problems in the Reading of a Soviet Production Novel", by David Shepherd, in *Discontinuous Discourses in Modern Russian Literature*, edited by Catriona Kelly *et al.*, London, Macmillan, and New York, St Martin's Press, 1989, 39–59.
Beyond Metafiction: Self-Consciousness in Soviet Literature, by David Shepherd, Oxford, Clarendon Press, and New York, Oxford University Press, 1992.

To most contemporary Russians Marietta Shaginian is famous, or notorious, for her massive contribution to literature in the now discredited field of Leniniana. However, her image as a loyal supporter of the system (she became a Hero of Socialist Labour in 1976 and was awarded numerous other decorations) is belied by her literary work in the first two decades of the 20th century. She also worked as a journalist in the period 1909–19, in both Moscow and the Baku area. She first achieved literary success as a poet. Her first collection *Pervye vstrechi* [First Encounters] was strongly influenced by Symbolism in general and by the work of Zinaida Hippius in particular. Indeed, Shaginian moved to St Petersburg in order to be near Hippius and her husband Dmitrii Merezhkovskii. Shaginian was attracted by their philosophy of "god-building" (*bogostroitel'stvo*). The break with Merezhkovskii and his wife came in 1911. In February 1912 Shaginian began a friendship with Sergei Rakhmaninov, who had asked her to select texts for him to set to music. Shaginian signed her letters to Rakhmaninov "Re" and dedicated her second collection of poetry, *Orientalia*, to him. This collection, published in 1913, has been described by Victor Terras as "stylised poems on exotic Moslem Caucasian themes with earthy passions". It won critical approval from Briusov, Gumilev, and Vladimir Narbut. Shaginian followed this success in 1924 with the adventure novel *Mess-Mend* (two words taken at random from an English-Russian dictionary). The work was written under the pseudonym Jim Dollar and cast in her favoured trilogy form. Here, as in most of Shaginian's prose writing, characters can be assigned to either the Old or the New. To the latter category belong the working-class characters, headed by Lori Len and the main hero Mik Tingsmaster, while the old world is exemplified by Gregorio Cice. The old capitalist world collapses in the face of a world revolution. *Mess-Mend* was turned into a film as early as 1925 and a version of it was the first work to be staged by the newly formed Obraztsov Puppet Theatre. Shaginian regarded the first part of the trilogy as her best piece of writing. Many, however, would consider an earlier trilogy to be of more lasting value. This is the trilogy that consists of the novel *Peremena* [Change], the novella *Prikliuchenie damy iz obshchestva* [Adventures of a Society Lady], and the short story "Agitvagon" [Agitwaggon]. Much of the material for this work was gathered by Shaginian in southern Russia during the turbulent period 1917–20.

In 1923 she published yet another novel, *Svoia sud'ba* [One's Own Fate] (a work that was revised in 1954). This novel attacks Freud and, like much of Shaginian's work, exalts the creative force of labour. Her experimental novel *Kik* appeared in 1929 but in 1931, with her novel *Gidrotsentral'* [Hydrocentral], she abandoned experimentalism in favour of a style soon to be dubbed socialist realist. The novel is based on her personal experience of the building of a power station on the River Kamenka (in the book "Mizinka") in Armenia and, with its combination of novelistic plot and a mass of technical detail, it is a typical example of a "production novel". Its industrial themes were anticipated in short stories such as "Kachestvo produktsii" [Quality of Production] (1925), while the Armenian setting is a recurrent feature of Shaginian's work, from some of the *Orientalia* poems ("K Armenii" [To Armenia], "Armianskomu narodu" [To the Armenian People]), to the short story "Vakho" (1927), and the most famous of her many books of travel notes, *Puteshestvie po Sovetskoi Armenii* [Journey Through Soviet Armenia]. She also wrote a very large number of articles devoted to literary, aesthetic, and political themes.

The sketch (*ocherk*) is perhaps the form that suited Shaginian best and her output has been likened by Liudmila Skorino to a "lyrical and philosophical diary". Shaginian herself considered the period 1932–58 as having been dominated by the sketch, dividing her output into into three cycles: 1932–41, 1941–44, and 1944–58. Even the last of her Lenin novels, *Chetyre uroka u Lenina* [Four Lessons from Lenin], is cast in the form of four separate sketches. Shaginian had a flair for investigative journalism and literary research. Her Lenin cycle was the product not only of two visits to Lenin's home town Ul'ianovsk (Simbirsk) but of long work in archives and libraries and of interviews with Nadezhda Krupskaia and other contemporaries of Lenin. The Lenin cycle consists of *Sem'ia Ul'ianovykh* [The Ulianov Family], which ends with the birth of Lenin in 1870, *Pervaia Vserossiiskaia* [The First All-Russian], a reference to the first All-Russian Polytechnic Exhibition held in 1872 and the first version of *Sem'ia Ul'ianovykh*, *Bilet po istorii* [Ticket to History], and *Chetyre uroka u Lenina*. The cycle gave rise to seven articles, written between 1957 and 1973. She wrote a number of literary biographies, notably of Goethe (1950), a figure who continued to fascinate her throughout her life and to whom she devoted the article "Puteshestvie v Veimar" [Journey to Weimar] (1923), and *Pis'ma iz GDR* [Letters from the GDR]. This interest stemmed both from her father and from her friendship with the philosopher E.K. Metner and his brother, the composer Nikolai Metner. Her other major biography is of Taras Shevchenko. Shaginian's skill as a historical novelist is seen at its best in *Voskreshenie iz mertvykh* [Resurrection from the Dead], devoted to the almost forgotten Czech composer Josef Mysliveček (1737–81), once known as "il divino Boemo" and admired by Mozart. In the course of her research Shaginian found the long-lost manuscript of Myslivičeck's first opera and the full text of his last. Shaginian's last major work was her memoirs *Chelovek i vremia* [Man and Time].

Shaginian's odyssey from decadent poet to left-leaning fellow-traveller and then to Marxist chronicler of Lenin is not entirely unprecedented among Russian writers but the sheer volume of her work and the length of her career (79 years if one accepts her assertion that her professional career began at 15) make her case remarkable.

MICHAEL PURSGLOVE

Kik

Novel, 1929

Shaginian's experimental novel *Kik* was first planned in 1924 and first published in *Zvezda* 2 and 3 (1929) and in book form later the same year. In the journal publication the work is described as a "novel" (*roman*) but in the book version it is termed a "novel-complex" (*roman-kompleks*).

It consists of three "episodes". The first details strange events in the town of Amanaus in Dagestan involving the placing of a spurious advertisement for a non-existent film in the local newspaper, *Amanausskaia pravda*. The reader learns of these events through two extracts from the paper and a variety of other documents: letters, minutes of a party meeting, transcribed telephone conversations, official summonses to the local GPU (secret police), interrogation records, and a private letter. Each document has its own distinctive register and, in addition, the extracts from the newspaper exemplify different styles: feuilleton, sketch, article, and leader. From these the reader learns of the appearance in the locality of one Comrade L'vov who makes a speech to the local executive committee of the Ministry of Education and then disappears into the local wilderness on a bison hunt. The fact that he does not return from this can only be gleaned from the second episode. This opens with the news that the local poet Valentin Gorskii has been arrested. It later becomes clear that there have been four more arrests, all of patients in the local sanatorium: the poet A. El', the journalist S. Ivanitskii, the writer Irina Gellers, and Professor Kazankov. The four agree to write their own version of events and these form the bulk of the second episode. All are given shorthand titles by the commandant of the local prison. The first, "Rog Dianyrdi" [The Horn of Diana], is a narrative poem (*poema*) in iambic tetrameter written by the poet El' and prefaced by a quotation from Pushkin; the second, "Trinadsat' trinadsat'" [Thirteen Thirteen], prefaced by a quotation from Tiutchev, consists of three chapters of Ivanitskii's unfinished novella; the third, an unfinished verse melodrama by Irina Gellers, gives its title to the whole book: "Koldun'ia i kommunist – kik" [The Sorceress and the Communist]; while the fourth, Kazankov's "Zemlia i oko – zio" [The Earth and the Eye], is in the form of a science film, complete with instructions to the director. The third episode is put into the mouth of the mysterious L'vov himself and is cast in the form of a "speech given on the ** of August 192* in the commandant's office of the Amanaus reformatory".

In what is clearly a formulation of Shaginian's own views, L'vov criticizes the way in which each of the four detainees has fleshed out the bare details given in two numbers of *Amanausskaia pravda*, involving L'vov, a bison hunt, a mysterious woman, the mineral resources of the Bu-Ul'gen region, and a supposed White Guard plot to steal them. His criticism is two-pronged: on the one hand the four writers have been unduly influenced by 19th-century Russian literature; on the other hand they are united in what they have omitted from the newspaper stories. None of them mentions the textile factory, transport problems or the local workforce. Had they done so they would perforce have included such issues as the impoverishment of the peasantry, the flight from the land, and the growth of mechanization. Anticipating the obvious objection that this is not the stuff of art, L'vov retorts that a Marxist history of art remains to be written. Meanwhile contemporary writers are still living in the past. He defends Glavlit (i.e censorship) the beneficence of which organization renders the four writers' claim to have written uncensored pieces superfluous. In a phrase that signals Shaginian's break with her experimentalist past and her enthusiasm for Goethe and anticipates her adherence to the tenets of socialist realism (*Gidrotsentral'* [Hydrocentral] was published the following year), L'vov announces that "Lenin's words are the art of the future". It falls to L'vov, too, whom Shaginian calls "my hero", to tie up the loose ends of the adventure story. The conjectures of the four authors were all wrong. In fact L'vov's disappearance was engineered in order to flush out the local remnants of the White Guard.

In 1956 Shaginian wrote an important prefatory note to the novel. This opens with an admission that the novel was written in the same way that "one sometimes writes a letter to 'nobody' because you want to write this letter which is essential to your own soul". Although contemporary critics saw the book as an adventure story, this was, says Shaginian, herself the author of a number of adventure stories in the 1920s, merely an "outer wrapping". In reality the book is a statement about writers and writing. Shaginian recalls how, at the time of the book's composition, young writers tended to specialize as novelists, critics, poets, children's writers or young people's writers. The great writers of the 19th century, on the other hand – she cites Turgenev, Goncharov, and Gor'kii – cannot be pigeonholed in this fashion. Herself a strong opponent of over-specialization, Shaginian says that she wrote *Kik* in order to "pass a literacy examination in all genres of literature". That the work is a literary *tour de force* can scarcely be denied. That the author chose to put her undoubted talent at the service of the Soviet state can scarcely be applauded.

Shaginian's work in general has received very little critical attention either in Russia or in the west. In Russia the experimental form of the work and the anti-Bolshevik sentiments placed in the mouths of the four detainees presumably rendered the work unpalatable. Liudmila Skorino's 360-page work on Shaginian the artist (*Marietta Shaginian – khudozhnik*, 1981) does, however, devote some nine pages to *Kik*. In the west the only study of the work can be found in David Shepherd's *Beyond Metafiction: Self-Consciousness in Soviet Literature*.

MICHAEL PURSGLOVE

Aleksandr Aleksandrovich Shakhovskoi 1777–1846

Dramatist and poet

Biography

Born in Bezzaboty, near Smolensk, 5 May 1777. Sent to boarding school in Moscow 1784–86. Served with the Preobrazhenskii Regiment, Guards Sergeant – Staff Captain, 1786–1802. Joined the Imperial Theatre directorate and sent abroad (one year in France) for recruitment of actors, 1802. Established reputation but also aroused much controversy with his play *Novyi Stern* [The New Sterne], 1805. Active member of Shishkov's anti-Karamzin association, the Society of Lovers of the Russian Word. Increased hostility followed *Urok koketkam, ili Lipetskie vody* [A Lesson for Coquettes, or Lipetsk Spa], 1815. Enjoyed great popularity in the 1820–30s, especially following *Kazak-stikhotvorets* [The Cossack Poet]. Decline in energy and ability during the 1830s accompanied by growing conservatism; eclipsed by other writers, especially Gogol'. Died 3 February 1846. Buried in Novodevichii cemetery.

Publications

Collected Edition

Komedii, stikhotvoreniia, edited by A.A. Gozenpud. Leningrad, 1961.

Plays

Novyi Stern. 1805; translated as "The New Sterne. A Comedy in One Act", by J. Eyre, *American Slavic and East European Review*, 4/8–9 (1945), 80–92.

Polubarskie zatei, ili domashnii teatr [Semi-Lordly Escapades, or The House Theatre]. 1808.

Kazak-stikhotvorets [The Cossack Poet]. 1812.

Urok koketam, ili Lipetskie vody [A Lesson for Coquettes, or Lipetsk Spa]. 1815.

Svoia sem'ia, ili zamuzhniaia nevesta [All in the Family, or The Married Fiancée], with Griboedov and Khmel'nitskii, 1817.

Ne lyubo – ne slushai, a lgat' ne meshai [Don't Listen if You Don't Want to, But Don't Interfere with Lying]. 1818.
Aristofan, ili predstavlenie "vsadnikov" [Aristophanes, or the Presentation of "The Horsemen"]. 1825.

Critical Studies

Russian Drama from Its Beginnings to the Age of Pushkin, by Simon Karlinsky, Berkeley, University of California Press, 1985, 228–49.
Tvorchestvo A.A. Shakhovskogo v istoriko-literaturnom protsesse 1800–1840-kh godov, by S.M. Shavrygin, St Petersburg, 1996.

Following a century of undervaluation and neglect Aleksandr Shakhovskoi has emerged in recent decades as one of the most important and influential figures in the rapidly-changing Russian theatre during the first third of the 19th century; he also made a strong impact on the development of Russian poetry and even the language itself. A man of unprepossessing physical appearance and some political ineptness, he courted controversy and all too easily attracted malicious rumour and hostility, none of which precluded simultaneous popularity and admiration. Versatility was his hallmark. There were no aspects of theatrical life in which his talents, originality, and passionate commitment failed to fructify in both theory and practice. More polymath than dilettante, he served Russian dramaturgy as a prolific writer, adapter, translator, impresario, talent-spotter, director, theatre-manager, and eventually a respected doyen of the profession, worthy of a passing mention in Pushkin's *Evgenii Onegin*.

Shakhovskoi's professional activity began early, in 1795, and spanned five decades, though its heyday covered the period 1805–25. His first success was with a 45 minute one-act comedy in prose, *Novyi Stern* (*The New Sterne*), produced in 1805. Even now this neatly-written text is amusing to read; in its day it became both popular and notorious. Intended as a parody of extreme sentimentalism (rather than anything by Sterne himself), the play appeared to go beyond the lampooning of affectation and artificiality and to attack the modernizers of Russian culture, Karamzin prominent among them. Shakhovskoi was well launched on his career of cleverness and controversy.

Within three years he had another success in the full-length (five-act) prose comedy, *Polubarskie zatei, ili domashnii teatr* [Semi-Lordly Escapades, or The House Theatre]. "Semi-lordly" is a good way to describe the hero, a parvenu landlord, Tranzhirin, an ill-bred and uneducated descendant of Molière's Monsieur Jourdain who unwittingly makes fun of himself by attempting to start up a serf theatre without any knowledge of how to go about it. Mikhail Shchepkin made the most of this splendid comic role, and the play did well. Sequels followed, as well as a succession of adaptations of French and German stage works. Continued exposure to French models led to one of Shakhovskoi's most original and far-reaching innovations when, in 1812, he wrote a one-act musical play, described by the author as a "bastard child of comedy and comic opera", entitled *Kazak-stikhotvorets* [The Cossack Poet]. This work has been accepted as the first Russian vaudeville; as such it ushered in an age of theatrical entertainment that lasted for several decades and enjoyed enormous popularity at every level of society.

Shakhovskoi achieved what is generally accepted to be his masterpiece in 1815 with a play that at first sight seems to be irredeemably backward-looking. This work, *Urok koketam, ili Lipetskie vody* [A Lesson for Coquettes, or Lipetsk Spa], reverted to the obsolescent traditional form of a five-act drama written in verse and observing the unities. But its subject-matter was modern; it presented a group of army officers recuperating at a famous spa, fresh from fighting Napoleon. A coquettish countess is foiled, mainly by the cleverness of a servant girl, in her attempt to break up a promising match involving one of these ex-soldiers. The thin, conventional plot was not much more than a vehicle for the author's ideas. Again he castigated the excesses of sentimentalism and romanticism, on this occasion lampooning another venerable figure of the Russian literary establishment, Vasilii Zhukovskii – for which he suffered bitter denunciation in the press. He was on safer ground in attacking hypocrisy, chiefly in the heroine of the play, and also those Russians who respect only that which is foreign. The up-to-date setting, characters, and issues were complemented by an unprecedented naturalness of language. Although contained within an archaic form (an unbroken series of hexameters rhyming in couplets or quatrains and observing every single caesura), Shakhovskoi's lines flow along with an easy spontaneity that seems almost to mock the medium by which they are expressed. Following Ivan Krylov (whose fluent diction had enjoyed the extra advantage of mixing together iambic lines of any length, up to six feet), Shakhovskoi almost for the first time in Russian poetry used normal words in their normal order over long tracts of verse. The agreeable effect that these lines must have had on his listening public may be gauged by the ease with which one may still read, or declaim, them today. This play, which exemplifies many of the problems and paradoxes of a transitional age, is in itself a pleasing hybrid of the old and new.

Shakhovskoi was to write for another quarter of a century, though without reaching quite the same heights of achievement. The one later play of some distinction to which he can lay claim is a collaborative work three-quarters his, *Svoia sem'ia, ili zamuzhniaia nevesta* [All in the Family, or The Married Fiancée], to which Aleksandr Griboedov was also a contributor. The collation was so scrupulously edited (by Shakhovskoi) that the joints and insertions cannot be detected. The result is another comedy in hexameters, though now in three acts; its story is, for once, of real interest. The heroine, Natasha, married in secret to a young man, Liubim, has to win the approval of his entire family in order for him to gain his inheritance. This is achieved by her changing character in the presence of each relative, with varying styles of ingratiation. By turns she has to appear penny-pinching, tearfully sensitive, serious-minded and well-informed, mindlessly simple, and flippantly fun-loving. Needless to say, the ploy works – and much to the advantage of any capable young actress given the role.

Shakhovskoi wrote (or adapted) well over a hundred plays. His overall contribution to the development of Russian dramaturgy during the first two or three decades of the 19th century is outstanding. Equally so is his use of ordinary, natural language in poetry, which foreshadows fundamental change for which exclusive credit is commonly given to Aleksandr Pushkin.

A.D.P. Briggs

Varlam Tikhonovich Shalamov 1907–1982

Poet and prose writer

Biography

Born in Vologda, Northern Russia, 1 July 1907. Attended school in Vologda, 1914–23. Moved to Kuntsevo, Moscow District to work as leather-tanner. Entered Law Faculty, Moscow University, 1926. Wrote poetry and participated in literary life; involved in political opposition to Stalin, culminating in arrest and three-year sentence for distributing Lenin's suppressed letter to the 12th Party Congress, 1929. Served sentence in Vishera Camp, Northern Urals. Returned to Moscow, 1932. Worked for industrial and technical journals, 1933–37. Married: 1) Galina Ignat'evna Gudz' in 1934, one daughter; 2) Ol'ga Sergeevna Nekliudova (divorced 1966). Arrested and condemned to five years' hard labour for "counter-revolutionary Trotskiite activity", 1937; served in various camps in Kolyma, Siberia. Sentence extended, 1942; given further ten years for anti-Soviet agitation (describing Ivan Bunin as "a Russian classic"), 1943. Trained as a paramedic, 1946. Wrote the verses *Kolymskie tetradi* [Kolyma Notebooks], 1949–50. Released from the camp, 1951, but stayed on as "free worker" until 1953 (leaving Kolyma after 16 years). Allowed to visit Moscow briefly, 1953; met Boris Pasternak with whom he had corresponded. Employed in turf-producing industry in Kalinin District, 1953–56. Began writing *Kolymskie rasskazy* (*Kolyma Tales*), 1954. Formally "rehabilitated" and moved to Moscow, 1956. Poems appeared in *Znamia*, 1957. Seriously ill, 1957–58. Slim volumes of poetry and occasional essays appeared, 1961–77. Failed to find a publisher for *Kolyma Tales*. Met Solzhenitsyn, 1962. Piecemeal publication of *Kolyma Tales* began in émigré periodicals, 1966; objected in *Literaturnaia gazeta* to such publication and declared that the problems raised were no longer relevant, 1972. Moved to a home for the aged and infirm, 1979; lost hearing and sight. Recipient: Freedom Prize of the French Section of PEN, 1980. Transferred to psychiatric hospital and died a few days later on 17 January 1982. *Kolyma Tales* published in Moscow journal, 1988; his books published in Russia from 1989.

Publications

Collected Editions

Voskreshenie listvennitsy [Resurrection of the Daurian Larch]. Paris, YMCA-Press, 1985.

Neskol'ko moikh zhiznei: Proza, poeziia, esse [My Several Lives: Prose, Verse and Essays]. Moscow, 1996.

Fiction

Kolymskie rasskazy. London, Overseas Publications Interchange, 1978; 2nd and 3rd editions, Paris, YMCA-Press, 1982, 1985; Moscow, 1989; 2 vols, Moscow, 1992 [fullest selection of the various cycles up to that point]; selections published as *Kolyma Tales*, by John Glad, New York, Norton, 1980; Harmondsworth, Penguin, 1990; and as *Graphite*, by John Glad, New York, Norton, 1981; both selections together under the title *Kolyma Tales*, Harmondsworth, Penguin, 1994.

Voskreshenie listvennitsy [Resurrection of the Daurian Larch]. Moscow, 1989 (includes selections from *Kolymskie rasskazy*).

Levyi bereg [Left Bank]. Moscow, 1989.

Vishera: Antiroman [Vishera: An Anti-Novel]. Moscow, 1989.

Perchatka ili KR-2 [The Glove or KT-2]. Moscow, 1990 [includes *Vishera: Antiroman*].

Poetry

Ognivo [Fire-Steel]. Moscow, 1961.

Shelest list'ev [A Rustle of Leaves]. Moscow, 1964.

Doroga i sud'ba [Road and Destiny]. Moscow, 1967.

Moskovskie oblaka [Moscow Clouds]. Moscow, 1972.

Tochka kipeniia [Boiling Point]. Moscow, 1977.

Stikhotvoreniia [Poems]. Moscow, 1988.

Kolymskie tetradi [Kolyma Notebooks], edited by I.P. Sirotinskaia. Moscow, 1994; Vologda, 1994.

Play

"Anna Ivanovna", *Russian Literature Triquarterly*, 19 (1986), 327–64; *Teatr*, 1 (1989).

Memoirs and Notebooks

"Chetvertaia Vologda" [The Fourth Vologda] (1971), *Voskreshenie listvennitsy* (Paris), 1985; *Lad* (Vologda), 3–10 (1991); separate edition, Vologda, 1994; in *Neskol'ko moikh zhiznei*, 305–62.

"Oskolki dvadtsatykh godov" [Fragments of the Twenties], *A, Ia* (Paris), 1 (1985), 124–51; as "Dvadtsatye gody: zametki studenta MGU" [The Twenties: Notes of a Student from MGU], *Iunost'*, 11–12 (1987), 37–45; 28–38.

"Vospominaniia" [Memoirs] (1970s), *Znamia*, 4 (1993), 114–70; reprinted in *Shalamovskii sbornik*.

Essays and Notes

"Tablitsa umnozheniia dlia molodykh poetov" [Multiplication Table for Young Poets], *Iunost'*, 3 (1987), 62–63.

"Iskusstvo lisheno prava na propoved'" [Art is Deprived of the Right to Preach], *Moscow News* (4 December 1988), 16 [in both Russian- and English-language issues of the newspaper].

"O proze" [On Prose], in *Levyi bereg*, 544–54; *Neskol'ko moikh zhiznei*, 425–33.

"Iz tvorcheskogo naslediia: Poeziia – vseobshchii iazyk", *Literaturnoe obozrenie*, 1 (1989), 100–03.

"Varlam Shalamov o literature", *Voprosy literatury*, 5 (1989), 225–48.

"O moei proze" [On My Prose], letter to I.P. Sirotinskaia, *Novyi mir*, 12 (1989), 58–66.

"Sekrety stikhov ili stikhi stikhov" [The Secrets of Poetry or The Poetry of Poetry], *Oktiabr'*, 7 (1991), 169–76; also in *Neskol'ko moikh zhiznei*, 434–41.

"Kriticheskie zametki. Esse. Vospominaniia" [Critical Notes. Essays. Memoirs], *Oktiabr'*, 7 (1991), 169–85.

"Iz zapisnykh knizhek ..." [Extracts from Notebooks], *Znamia*, 6 (1995), 134–75.

"Chto ia videl i ponial" [What I Saw and Understood], *Krasnyi sever* (13 June 1996), 6.

Letters
"Razgovory o samom glavnom ...: Perepiska B.L. Pasternaka i V.T. Shalamova" [Conversations about the Most Important Matters ...: The Correspondence of B.L. Pasternak and V.T. Shalamov], *Iunost'*, 10 (1988), 54–67.
"Pis'ma A. Solzhenitsynu" [Letters to A. Solzhenitsyn], edited and annotated by I.P. Sirotinskaia, *Znamia*, 7 (1990), 62–89; reprinted in *Shalamovskii sbornik*, issue 1, 63–103.
"Perepiska s N. Mandel'shtam" [Correspondence with N. Mandel'shtam], *Znamia*, 2 (1992), 158–77.
"Iz perepiski" [Correspondence with A. Dobrovol'skii *et al.*], *Znamia*, 5 (1993).
Correspondence avec Alexandre Soljenitsyne et Nadejda Mandelstam [and others], translated by Francine Andreieff. Lagrasse, Editions Verdier, 1995.

Critical Studies
"Ognivo vysekaet ogon'", by Boris Slutskii, *Literaturnaia gazeta* (5 October 1961), 3.
"Vtoraia vstrecha s poetom", by Vera Inber, *Literaturnaia gazeta* (23 June 1964), 3.
"Les cercles de l'enfer, Varlam Chalamov, Alexandre Soljenitsyne", by Michel (Mikhail) Geller in his *Le monde concentrationnaire et la littérature soviétique*, Lausanne, L'Âge d'Homme, 1974, 216–36; revised Russian version in his *Kontsentratsionnyi mir i sovetskaia literatura*, London, Overseas Publications Interchange, 1974, 281–99.
"Art out of Hell: Shalamov of Kolyma", by John Glad, *Survey*, 107 (1979), 45–50.
"The Ultimate Circle of the Stalinist Inferno", by Geoffrey Hosking, *New Universities Quarterly* (Spring 1980), 161–68.
"Beyond Bitterness", by Irving Howe, *New York Review of Books* (14 August 1980), 36–37.
"The Chekhov of the Camps", by Geoffrey Hosking, *Times Literary Supplement* (17 October 1980), 1163.
"V.T. Shalamov i A.I. Solzhenitsyn (sravnitel'nyi analiz nekotorykh proizvedenii)", by Anna Shur, *Novyi zhurnal*, 155 (1984), 92–101.
"Shalamov, Solzhenitsyn and the Mission of Memory", by Matt F. Oja, *Survey*, 29/2 (Summer 1985), 62–69.
"Emu udalos' ne slomat'sia", by Iu.A. Shreider, *Sovetskaia bibliografiia*, 3 (1988), 61–68.
"Stories from Kolyma: The Sense of History", by Leona Toker, *Hebrew University Studies in Literature and the Arts*, 17 (1989), 188–220.
"V kruge poslednem: Varlam Shalamov i Aleksandr Solzhenitsyn", by Vladimir Frenkel', *Daugava*, 4 (1990), 79–82.
Varlam Shalamov, by E.A. Shklovskii, Moscow, 1991.
"Poetika lagernoi prozy", by L. Timofeev, *Oktiabr'*, 3 (1991), 182–95.
"A Tale Untold: Varlam Shalamov's 'A Day Off'", by Leona Toker, *Studies in Short Fiction*, 28/1 (1991), 1–8.
"Varlam Shalamov's 'New Prose'", by C. Hollosi, *Rusistika*, 6 (1992), 19–24.
Shalamovskii sbornik, issue 1, edited by V.V. Esipov, Vologda, 1994 [an excellent source of primary and secondary materials].

Bibliographies
"K bibliografiiu V.T. Shalamova" [publications 1957–88], compiled by A.V. Ratner and A.I. Suetnov, *Sovetskaia bibliografiia*, 3 (1988), 61–70.
"Varlam Shalamov: Mezhdu Visheroi i Kolymoi" [publications 1932–37], compiled by I.P. Sirotinskaia, *Sovetskaia bibliografiia*, 6 (1990), 93–95.
"Shalamov na zapade", by Michael Nicholson, *Sovetskaia bibliografiia*, 6 (1990), 96–99; reprinted in *Shalamovskii sbornik*, issue 1, 211–15.

There are few talented Russian writers of the 20th century who have been so consistently battered and cheated by fate as Varlam Shalamov, and whose legacy is so disturbing. The terse official announcement of his death in 1982 identified him as a "well-known Soviet poet", alluding to that carefully sifted portion of his verse that had been considered publishable, and ignoring some 150 *Kolymskie rasskazy* (*Kolyma Tales*), on which his reputation now principally rests. In the west, where his verse was and remains largely unknown, the stories found an admiring, if narrow audience, but a decade of piecemeal publication blunted their impact and the delay cast them as an appendage of the sensational labour-camp literature of previous decades. Even now French and German readers have access to far more of Shalamov's prose than their English-speaking counterparts. Since the late 1980s the bulk of Shalamov's writings has been published in his homeland, but works that would have stunned his compatriots in the 1960s and 1970s had to jostle for attention in the boisterous marketplace of post-perestroika Russia, or were caught up in the polemics between his post-modernist admirers and the representatives of an allegedly outmoded "humanistic" tradition.

Overshadowing all other contours of Shalamov's biography are the 16 years he spent in the Gulag, first as a *zek* (prisoner), then as a notionally "free" worker. His unassailable seniority among labour-camp writers is based not solely on the length of his confinement, but on its location in the Kolyma region of Siberia, a byword for savagery and hopelessness within the camp system. Shalamov spent years close to the edge of survival and at times teetered on its very brink. This lends a chilling authority and authenticity to his evocations of the Gulag ethos: Solzhenitsyn, for instance, acknowledges "with respect that it fell to him, rather than to me to plumb the depths of brutalization and despair towards which the camp world was dragging us all". An abiding motif in Shalamov's works is the unredeemed negativity of the camp experience. The camps were not a place where, despite atrocity and danger, the moral fibre of the individual could yet be tested and toughened. They were a place where 99 per cent failed that test, a soulless world that no living eye should see.

This does not mean that Shalamov's verse and stories are an unmediated scream from the abyss. In the 1930s, with one sentence behind him, but before his fateful consignment to Kolyma, he had enjoyed a prolific and successful literary apprenticeship: several of his short stories as well as dozens of journalistic pieces appeared in the Soviet press and hundreds of unpublished poems of these years were lost after his arrest. This was a writer who, in the 1920s, had been close to the Left Front of Art movement, who had heard Maiakovskii recite his verse and was familiar with the ideas of the Constructivists, with Brik, Aseev, and other literary contemporaries. He recalls drawing sustenance in Kolyma, years later, from the poetry memorized in his youth, but it was not until the late 1940s that he began to write the poems of his *Kolymskie tetradi* [Kolyma Notebooks], when his near-miraculous elevation to the status of paramedical orderly offered a precarious foothold on life and the temporary security of a dispensary in which to preserve his creations. Much of the power of his Kolyma poetry and the verses that followed right up to his death derives from the collision of a cultured literariness with the wariness, the physical immediacy, and bleak minimalism of the survivor. His first, hand-stitched book of verse was smuggled back to Moscow in 1952 and found an enthusiastic admirer in Boris Pasternak.

Shalamov's verse occasionally describes the experience of the camps directly. His ironic "Toast to the River Aian-Uriakh" juxtaposes the expiring *zeks*' blue lips and scurvied gums with the leering teeth of the dogs guarding them; in "Funeral" the poet dies "without tears", and a handful of rock is thrown in his face for want of soil, "closing the circle of sickly nights and anxious days". More often, attention is focused on manifestations of nature, notably the ice, snow, rock, and hardy vegetation of the far North. "Verses in Honour of the Pine" is transparent in its allegory and anthropomorphization: memories of hearth and home fade, the touch of naked corpses extinguishes "for ever" the star above, but the poet is saved by a lone pine tree, more compassionate than a wife, who rearms him for the fray and returns to him the gift of anger and of speech. Effective in its very elusiveness is "Warming His Frozen Fingers" (the most typical, in his eyes, of the Kolyma poems). In it the poet is seen trying to make poetic sense of a patch of unfrozen water glimpsed in an ice-bound stream and of the strange power it exerts. For every defiant stanza in Shalamov's verse ("I know myself this is no game, but death, / Yet for the sake of life itself I shall, / Like Archimedes, cling fast to my pen / and never crumple up this open page") is another dominated by despair ("I dread to take a step ahead, / As if into a pit, a forest black, / Where memory will take me by the hand, / And skies have fled"). Confidence in the power of memory to resurrect the past gives way to impotence before the onrush of oblivion. Love lyrics are to be found, but more often love and faith figure as casualties ("All that is human has passed and gone / And all that was has been in vain"). "In trees", by contrast, "there is no ugliness", and "only minerals are immortal". Literary and classical allusions abound, interwoven with elements of nature and the deadly serious, life-preserving business of writing itself. Shalamov's tolerance of technical vocabulary (rhyming *avtomashine* "motor vehicle" with *vershinu* "summit", for instance), of the primitive, ungainly, even bathetic, though the subject of criticism, has to be seen as part of a conscious aesthetic.

The image of Shalamov as congenitally short-winded was fostered not only by his usually terse lyrics, but also by the brevity of the *Kolyma Tales*, which he began writing immediately after his release. It is worth noting, however, that he produced a detailed outline for a novel about Berzin, the Secret Police officer charged with opening up the Kolyma goldfields, and wrote various memoirs, including the outstanding *Chetvertaia Vologda* [The Fourth Vologda], his attempt late in life to reconstruct the cultural and psychological landscape of his childhood. In addition, he continued to write essays after Kolyma and finished one of several plays he had planned.

When the doors of Soviet publishing-houses opened in the early 1960s to admit a trickle of anti-Stalinist and labour-camp writings, Shalamov failed to squeeze through. While others were hailed as the poets of the camps, he stalked the editorial offices of Moscow like the Ancient Mariner – a living reproach, ill, deaf, and cantankerous. But the futility of Shalamov's efforts to force through his own word, of which he was fiercely proud, added to his suffering and sense of isolation. Whereas in 1966 he had penned one of the most effective responses to the trial of the writers Siniavskii and Daniel', his contempt for the rituals and mores of "progressive humanity" grew, far exceeding any inclinations to political dissidence. In 1972, with his latest collection of poetry held up at the press, he consented to denounce his émigré publishers in the west, and in so doing wrote little short of a public disavowal of his own *Kolyma Tales*. His stalled volume was duly published.

Embittered bravado was as much a part of Shalamov's ravaged make-up as was his suspicion that the camps had left him stunted and crippled. Even his most vulnerable and inconsistent gestures emerged against the background of a stubborn integrity, and in conditions of sickness, poverty, and lonely frustration that left few able to judge him with an easy mind. His achievement is least of all a political one. It rests on the attempt to render through literature, but without belletrization, the moral void left after Auschwitz, Hiroshima, Kolyma, to convey the death of humanism, of culture – and of literature itself.

MICHAEL NICHOLSON

Kolyma Tales

Kolymskie rasskazy

Short-story collection, 1978 (written 1954–73)

"How does one show that death of the spirit sets in earlier than physical death? ... How does one derive the law of this disintegration? The law of resistance to it? How can one express in words ... what is the final boundary beyond which everything human is lost?" Twenty years after his release from Kolyma, Shalamov was still struggling to find a genre in which literary form and convention would not smother the fading truth of his camp experience. The fruits of this 20-year endeavour were some 150 short stories, loosely known as the *Kolyma Tales*. In fact, Shalamov went to some trouble to group his stories into six distinct cycles, of which "Kolyma Tales" (1954–62) is only the first, followed by "Artist lopaty" [Artist of the Shovel] (1959–65), "Levyi bereg" [Left Bank] (1959–65), "Voskreshenie listvennitsy" [Resurrection of the Daurian Larch] (1966–67), "Ocherki prestupnogo mira" [Sketches from the Criminal World] (1959), and "Perchatka, ili KR-2" [The Glove or KT-2] (1970–73), "KT" standing for "Kolyma Tales". A further cycle, "Vishera: Antiroman" [Vishera: An Anti-Novel] (1961), is set not in Kolyma but in a camp in the Urals and evokes the period of Shalamov's first, comparatively light sentence.

Shalamov was concerned that the language of any written narrative must inevitably be richer and more elaborate than the primal grunting of the prisoner *in extremis*. He saw it as his task to minimize that disparity. The "new prose" to which he aspired called for "laconic, succinct writing, devoid of everything canonized". Retrospective motivation, exogenous logic and moralizing had no place. "Art is deprived of the right to preach", he later wrote. "Nobody has the right to teach anyone. Art does not ennoble or improve people." Early readers were struck by the economy of the stories, the spareness of their style, the disquieting dispassionate recording of atrocity. In "A Day Off" the prisoner and former priest Zamiatin is tricked by criminals into eating the puppy he has befriended, in the belief that they are serving him mutton. Starving though he is, he cannot hold the meal down once he learns the truth, and we leave him standing outside the hut, vomiting and angry. The makings of an allegorical ending – compassion and generosity asserting themselves involuntarily over cynicism and betrayal – are undercut by the final exchange between narrator and priest: "'What bastards', I said. 'Yes, of course', said Zamiatin. 'But the meat did taste good. Just as good as mutton.'" Again, in the story "On Tick" the narrator records the casual murder of a companion, who has refused to hand over his sweater, a parting gift from his wife, in order that a criminal can settle a gambling debt. The closing lines read: "Taking care not to smear his fingers with blood, Sevochka put the sweater away in his plywood suitcase. The game was over and I could go home. Now I would have to find another partner to saw firewood with." Although this disturbing moral neutrality prompted early comparisons with the stories of Isaak Babel', Shalamov has nothing in common with the "ornamental" stylistic flourishes that characterize Babel''s prose style. Each of his stories, he held, was a "slap in the face", bound by laws of muscular contraction, finished in its way, but not polished.

One of the finest of the Kolyma stories is "Sententious", an almost programmatic attempt to capture the true "succession of sensations" as the *zek* approaches extinction. The narrator feels first indifference and then malice, "the last human feeling". And as death recedes, he drifts back through apathy to envy of the well-fed and the fortunate dead, and apprehension lest worse befall. The word "sententious", so incongruous in the harsh, monosyllabic world of the camp, floats by chance into his mind and helps draw him back to life, just as poetry became a lifeline for Shalamov himself. Even pity for animals is restored to the narrator with time. But, we are told, love for humans comes back last of all – "or rather, does it ever return?"

For a new generation of Russian writers and critics, it is Shalamov, with his sense of the corroding power of evil, and his distrust of absolutes and rejection of didacticism who has best captured the essence of the Gulag experience and of the modern condition that it epitomizes. At the same time, Shalamov himself draws attention to "the detail as symbol, the detail as sign, shifting the entire story onto a different plane and giving it a 'subtext'". A belief in the ultimate triumph of humanist values may yet, as Leona Toker puts it, be "formulated in the course of the reader's pursuit of meaning in the chinks between paragraphs and lines". Certainly commentators have been drawn time and again to the paradox that the Kolyma stories – not least by the very act of their creation – challenge the prevailing spiritual desolation of their setting.

MICHAEL NICHOLSON

Shemiaka's Judgment

Anonymous 17th-century prose work

Manuscripts

Russian National Library (RNB), St Petersburg (and the major libraries).

Editions

Shemiakin sud. St Petersburg, 1780; reprinted as *Starinnaia russkaia povest' "Sud Shemiakin" s basniami v litzakh*, Moscow, 1794 and 1801.

"Shemiakin sud (po rukopisi XVII v.)", *Istoricheskii vestnik*, 1 (1890), 102–14.

Shemiakin sud. Komediia o nepravednom sud'ie Shemiake, muzhike bogatom, muzhike gorbatom i o muzhike ubogom. V odnom deistvii. Iz starinnogo skazaniia. Moscow, 1900; 2nd edition, Moscow, 1910.

Shemiakin sud. Komediia v 8 epizodakh dlia kukol'nogo teatra. Po starinnym lubochnym kartinam, pozdneishim literaturnym variantam, materialam fol'klora i komedii Popova. Moscow, 1936.

"Povest' o Shemiakinom sude", in *Russkaia povest' XVII veka*, edited by I.P. Eremin. Leningrad, 1954, 140–42; also in *Russkaia demokraticheskaia satira XVII veka*, Moscow, 1977, 17–25; in *Satira XI–XVII vekov*, Moscow, 1987, 153–56; in *Pamiatniki literatury Drevnei Rusi. XVII vek*, (2), Moscow, 1989, 182–84.

Translations

"Shemiaka's Judgment", in *The Seventeenth-Century Popular "Satires": Annotated Translations and a Survey of Critical Approaches*, by Richard H. Marshall, *Dissertation Abstracts International* 33: 5686A. Columbia.

"Shemiaka's Judgment", translated by Serge A. Zenkovsky, in his *Medieval Russia's Epics, Chronicles, and Tales*. New York, Dutton, 1963, 449–52.

Critical Studies

"Povest' o sude Shemiaki i sudebnaia praktika vtoroi poloviny

XVII v", by I.P. Lapitskii, in *Trudy Otdela Drevnerusskoi Literatury*, 6 (Moscow and Leningrad 1948), 79–99.

History of Early Russian Literature, by N.K. Gudzii, translated by Susan Wilbur Jones, New York, Macmillan, 1949, 476–79.

"Povest' o Shemiakinom sude", by I.P. Lapitskii, in *Russkaia povest' XVII veka*, Leningrad, 1954, 441–51.

History of Russian Literature from the Eleventh Century to the End of the Baroque, by Dmitrij Čiževskij, The Hague, Mouton, 1960; reprinted 1971, 343–44.

Early Russian Literature, by John Fennell and Antony Stokes, Berkeley, University of California Press, and London, Faber, 1974, 262–63.

A History of Seventeenth-Century Russian Literature, by William Edward Brown, Ann Arbor, Ardis, 1980, 58–60.

A History of Old Russian Literature, by V.V. Kuskov, Moscow, Progress, 1980, 299–300.

Smekh v Drevnei Rusi, by D.S. Likhachev, A.M. Panchenko, and N.V. Ponyrko, Leningrad, 1984.

A History of Russian Literature, 11th–17th Centuries, by D.S. Likhachev, translated by K.M. Cook-Horujy, Moscow, Raduga, 1989, 491–93.

Bibliographies

Bibliografiia drevnerusskoi povesti, by V.P. Adrianova-Peretts and V.F. Pokrovskaia, Moscow and Leningrad, 1940.

Literatura i kul'tura Drevnei Rusi. Slovar'-spravochnik, edited by V.V. Kuskov, Moscow, 1994, 134–35.

Povest' o Shemiakinom sude (*Shemiaka's Judgment*) is a short satirical narrative, written in the second part of the 17th century. Some scholars call it a tale or novella. It exists as a prose narrative in manuscripts dating from the 17th and 18th centuries. Later in the 18th century the story was rearranged in syllabic verse. In this version the story is longer, but there is no difference in the plot. The main episodes from the prose version form the basis for the *lubok* (chapbook form, in wood-cuts) text of *Shemiaka's Judgment*. The second verse version of this work appeared in a tonic verse system that only exists in one manuscript, dating from the 19th century. Apart from these prose and verse texts of *Shemiaka's Judgment* there is also a drama with the same plot.

Shemiaka's Judgment is one of the so-called "Russian democratic satires" of institutional and social mores. The two main themes of the story are the venality of the judge, considered typical of the entire judicial system, and the triumph of the Poor Person (the hero of the story) whom the corrupt judge exonerates by mistake. The first part of the story consists of three tragicomic episodes, which we can consider as anecdotes. The Poor Person plucks a tail from a horse that he has borrowed from his rich brother to bring firewood from the forest. The brother lends his horse, but no harness, so the Poor Person has to tie the sledge to the horse's tail. The Rich Brother decides to take the matter to court. On their way to town the brothers spend one night in a priest's house where the protagonist falls from the raised platform (*polati*) onto a child – the son of the priest – and kills him. The priest accordingly joins the previous plaintiff and the three of them continue on to town for the trial. Approaching the town this procession has to cross a bridge. The Poor Person falls into despair at his situation and tries to commit suicide. He jumps off the bridge, over a dry ditch. At that moment a townsman is taking his sick father to the bath-house. So the protagonist, instead of taking his own life, kills the sick man by landing on him. So yet another plaintiff joins the original procession.

The critic Dmitrii Likhachev considers this first part of the story to be a separate tale:

> These three episodes can be regarded as "simple forms", as unfinished anecdotes or an exposition. In themselves they are amusing but not complete, for they lack a denouement. The denouement awaits the reader in the second part of the tale, where the unfair judge Shemiaka appears, a cunning and mercenary pettifogger. This part is more complex in composition. It is divided into the judge's verdicts and the "framework", which has an independent and complete plot of its own.

The "framework" tells how the Poor Person deceives the judge Shemiaka, a bribetaker and pettifogger, by showing him a stone wrapped in a cloth. Shemiaka supposes the bundle to be a bribe (a bag full of money) and pronounces judgment in the Poor Person's favour. When Shemiaka discovers that it is not a bribe he is not too upset, because he suspects the Poor Person will send the stone flying at his head if he makes the wrong decision. Shemiaka thankfully prays, for he has "judged according to God".

Shemiaka's verdicts are reflections of the Poor Person's misadventures and this provides the comic effect. Shemiaka asks the rich brother to give his horse to the poor one and to wait until the horse grows a new tail. Shemiaka orders the priest to surrender his wife to the Poor Person until they beget a baby to replace the dead one. In the third case the judge follows the same pattern: he tells the plaintiff to jump off the bridge himself and kill the defendant, as he had killed his father. Naturally none of the plaintiffs is satisfied with the verdicts and they prefer to pay the Poor Person money in order to avoid Shemiaka's orders.

Scholars have noticed that 17th-century Russians understood *Shemiaka's Judgment* as a satire, in that they could compare such episodes with contemporary legal practice. According to the legal code of 1649, punishment reflected the crime, so this story can be understood as a parody of the medieval Russian legal system. Possibly the name of the judge had certain connotations but, if so, these remain obscure. Indeed, the name Shemiaka can be traced to the middle of the 15th century when Dmitrii Shemiaka, prince of the northern city of Galich (not to be confused with Galich, capital of the southwestern province of Galicia), waged an endless feud against his cousin, Vasilii III, Great Prince of Muscovy. The proper name Shemiaka however, subsequently became quite popular in Muscovite Russia, and there is no definite indication that the hero of the tale can be identified with Prince Dmitrii Shemiaka or any other historical figure.

The origins of *Shemiaka's Judgment* remain unclear even now. Some specialists (for example, N.S. Tikhonravov) considered the story to be a translation from Polish, having drawn attention to a note in one of the manuscripts, saying: "... copied from Polish books". We can now say that such a story was not original even to Polish literature. A.N. Afanas'ev took it to be a literary version of a Russian folk-tale about "The Rich and the Poor Brothers". A.N. Veselovskii suggested some similarities with Eastern legends on the same theme. Many Russian, Belorussian, and Ukrainian folk and fairy-tales about an unjust judge commonly employ motifs of crime and depict court decisions similar to those found in this tale. Scholars have also found parallels in Tibetan, Indian and Persian folk-tales and legends and even in the Bible. Finally, D.S. Likhachev has drawn attention to the "complication" of the plot that follows from generic specifications (of the Russian novella).

No one has been able, however, to reveal the direct sources of these Russian tales (or novellas). In all cases we can speak only of general resemblance and of analogous plots, but not of direct textual dependence. In the history of the novella the origin of such works is not of decisive importance. The "simple forms", jokes, witticisms and anecdotes out of which novellas developed cannot be considered the property of any one people. They travelled from country to country or, given the similarity of everyday happenings, arose in different places, often at one and the same time. The poetic laws of such tales are universal, and thus it is problematic to distinguish between borrowed and original texts.

EKATERINA ROGACHEVSKAIA

Mariia Mikhailovna Shkapskaia 1891–1952
Poet

Biography
Born Mariia Mikhailovna Andreevskaia in St Petersburg, 15 October 1891. First poem published, 1910. Married in 1910; two sons and one daughter. Expelled from medical school in St Petersburg, served part of term of exile in France. Graduated in philology from faculty of letters at Toulouse University, 1914. Returned to Russia, 1916. Joined the Petrograd Poets' Union, 1920; published first book, 1921. Several volumes of poetry published by 1925; visited Berlin. Worked exclusively as a journalist and an editor, from 1925. Moved to Moscow, 1937. Died in Moscow, 7 September 1952.

Publications
Collected Editions

Stikhi, edited by Boris Filippov and Evgeniia Zhiglevich. London, Overseas Publications Interchange, 1979.

Mariya Shkapskaya: The Mother and the Stern Master. Selected Poems (bilingual edition), translated by Sandra Shaw Bennett. Nottingham, Astra Press, 1998.

Poetry

Mater dolorosa. Petrograd and Berlin, 1921; 2nd edition Revel, 1922.

Chas vechernii. Stikhi (1913–1917 gg.) [Evening Hour]. Petrograd, 1922.

Baraban strogogo gospodina. Stikhi [A Stern Master's Drum]. Berlin, Ogon'ki, 1922.

Krov'-ruda. Stikhi [Blood-Ore]. Petrograd, 1922; 2nd edition Moscow, 1925.

Iav': Poema [Reality]. Moscow, 1923; in *An Anthology of Russian Women's Writing*, 1777–1992, edited by Catriona Kelly, Oxford, Oxford University Press, 1994, 437–41; translated as "No Dream", by Catriona Kelly, 237–42.

Tsa-tsa-tsa (kitaiskaia poema) [Tsa-tsa-tsa (A Chinese Poem)]. Berlin, 1923.

Kniga o Lukavom Seiatele [Book about the Shrewd Sower]. Moscow, 1923.

"Chelovek idet na Pamir: Poema" [A Man Goes to the Pamyres], *Zvezda*, 5 (1924), 102–07.

Zemnye remesla [Stikhi] [A Mundane Profession]. Moscow, 1925.

Documentary Sketches

Piatnadtsat' i odin [Fifteen and One]. Leningrad, 1930.

Voda i veter [Water and Wind]. Leningrad, 1931.

Sama po sebe [By Myself]. Leningrad, 1932.

Chelovek rabotaet khorosho [A Man Works Well]. Leningrad, 1932; 2nd edition, 1938.

Eto bylo na samom dele. 1942; translated as *It Actually Happened: A Book of Facts* [no translator named], Moscow, Foreign Languages Publishing House, 1954.

Puti i poiski [Journeys and Searchings]. Moscow, 1968.

Critical Studies
"Sredi stikhov", by Valerii Briusov, *Pechat' i revoliutsiia*, 2 (1922), 143–49; 1 (1923), 70–78.

"Vspominaia Shkapskuiu", by Aleksandr Bakhrakh, *Novoe russkoe slovo* (9 December 1979).

"O zamolchannoi", by Boris Filippov, in Shkapskaia's *Stikhi*, 1979, 7–17.

"Mariia Shkapskaia, *Stikhi*. London, 1979" (anonymous review), *Kontinent*, 23 (1980).

"Mariia Shkapskaia", by V.Iu. Bobretsov, *Russkaia literatura*, 3 (1991), 219.

"Chernaia pchela", by M.L. Gasparov, *Oktiabr'*, 2 (1992), 168–71; 172–78 (includes several previously unpublished poems).

"Motherhood in a Cold Climate: The Poetry and Career of Maria Shkapskaya", by Barbara Heldt, in *Sexuality and the Body in Russian Culture*, edited by Jane T. Costlow, Stephanie Sandler, and Judith Vowles, Stanford, Stanford University Press, 1993, 237–54; originally published in *Russian Review*, 51/2 (1992), 160–71.

"Shkapskaia, Mariia Mikhailovna", by Barbara Heldt, in *Dictionary of Russian Women Writers*, edited by Marina Ledkovsky, Charlotte Rosenthal, and Mary Zirin, Westport, Connecticut, Greenwood Press, 1994, 591–93.

Mariia Shkapskaia was born Mariia Mikhailovna Andreevskaia

in St Petersburg on 15 October 1891, the oldest of five children, Russian on her father's side and German on her mother's. Her father was a minor government official; his mother was born a serf. For understandable reasons, Shkapskaia's later autobiographical writings emphasize the family's poverty and low origins, but both her poetry and other family records suggest that they lived comfortably enough on her father's pension. Her mother suffered from paralysis, and her father had retired because of mental illness – the poem "Vstala zhenoiu Lota" [I Stood like Lot's Wife] describes a harrowing visit to him in an asylum. Shkapskaia graduated from the gymnasium with distinction in 1910. In the same year she published her first poetry and married, taking her husband's name and so became a rare, well-known, Silver Age woman-poet who did not publish under her maiden name or a pseudonym. She started medical school and took part in demonstrations and the distribution of illegal Socialist Revolutionary literature. Arrested and imprisoned in 1912, she was then expelled and denied the right to study in any educational institution of the Empire. She and her husband were allowed to go abroad rather than spend their terms of exile in the provinces; in Paris she met Vladimir Korolenko, Maksimilian Voloshin, and Il'ia Erenburg. While studying, she began to publish journalistic articles as well as poetry in Russian papers in Paris and Petrograd.

Shkapskaia graduated from the faculty of philology at Toulouse University in 1914. She returned to Russia in 1916 and spent the rest of her exile in the provinces, writing for *Den'* until it was closed down in 1918. The family witnessed both Red and White terror during the Civil War, and by 1919 they had two sons. In 1920 Shkapskaia was accepted into the Petrograd Poets' Union, and in 1921 she worked with Aleksandr Blok. Her first volume of poetry, *Mater dolorosa*, was published in 1921. In 1923, when travel across the Soviet border was still easy, she visited the lively Russian community in Berlin and placed some of her work with publishers there.

Like most poetry at the time, Shkapskaia's came out in slender volumes. The earlier work (some published in the 1922 volume *Chas vechernii* [Evening Hour], was traditional in form and often paradoxical or impersonal in theme, but her mature poetry is unique in Russian letters for concentrating on maternity and such taboo topics as pregnancy, childbirth, miscarriage, and abortion. Such different readers as Maksim Gor'kii and Father Pavel Florenskii praised Shkapskaia for this and for her peculiar religiosity (Mary-centred and often assertively critical of God). Some scholars have compared her to Vasilii Rozanov, because of her blend of religious issues and attention to the flesh. She reclaims blood, the fruit of violence, as a mark of fertile childbirth and powerful vehicle of heredity; one of her collections of poetry bears the title *Krov'-ruda* [Blood-Ore]. Her maternal position rises above the divisions of her time to mourn all victims of violence, especially children, regardless of class, politics, or descent. Her long poem "Chelovek idet na Pamir" [A Man Goes to the Pamyres] polemically describes the burden man's technological and historical progress places on women and children as well as on nature, the groaning mother earth.

In form, Shkapskaia's mature poetry retains traditional rhyme and metrical schemes but often replaces line-ended stanzas with paragraphs that conceal the rhymes until a poem is read. She was evidently shy and reserved about her work and sensed that her critical view of technological progress and of the Revolution's cost in human lives irritated the emerging literary bureaucracy. Russian squeamishness towards her innovative topics and approaches, both political and "gynaecological", echoes even in descriptions of her work as "decadent" or "so harsh" in the late 1980s and early 1990s. After 1925 her poems were no longer printed in the Soviet Union, except one final selection in 1929, though she was by then an established writer. Instead, she expanded her work as a journalist. Her third child, a daughter, was born in 1928. Shkapskaia worked for the Leningrad *Vecherniaia krasnaia gazeta* as a traveling correspondent and feuilletonist, writing about weavers in Samarkand, cotton growers in Tadzhikistan, or "On the Rubber Front", and thus escaped the literary politics of urban centres. From 1932 to 1936 she took part in Maksim Gor'kii's mammoth project on factory history, which was never wholly published. Shkapskaia moved to Moscow in 1937. After World War II she worked as an editor for the Anti-Fascist Committee of Soviet Women, suffering from ill health, overwork, and accidental injuries. Her younger son, taken prisoner during the war, was sent to a camp in 1950; Shkapskaia died on 7 September 1952, too soon to see his release.

Unlike many poets of her generation who established their reputations before the Revolution, Shkapskaia seems to have lost all confidence in her poetic voice in the mid-1920s, faced with hard-line criticism from the likes of *Krasnaia nov'*. None of the unpublished poems in her archive are dated after 1925. In personal letters she criticized her poetry in the same ideological terms that were applied to other poets; after all, she and the class with which she identified had received tangible rewards from the Revolution. Hoping that her poetry would remain for the future, Shkapskaia chose to abandon it, not trying to write according to prescription or "for the drawer". The fates of old Socialist Revolutionary acquaintances and fear for her children must have influenced her decision to remake herself into the kind of writer the Soviet Union valued, and even to retouch her life story. Her new chosen genre of the sketch (*ocherk*), unlike the aristocratic genre of lyric poetry, had a politically sound pedigree reaching back to Belinskii and the 19th-century realists. Today, however, it is Shkapskaia's poetry that attracts readers, and she has re-emerged as a major if neglected poet of Russia's Silver Age.

SIBELAN FORRESTER

Mikhail Aleksandrovich Sholokhov 1905–1984

Prose writer

Biography

Born in Kruzhilin, near Veshenskaia stanitsa, the Don Military Region, 24 May 1905. Attended schools in Kargin, Moscow, Boguchar, and Veshenskaia, 1912–19. Served in Soviet educational, government, and food-procurement agencies in the Upper Don area, 1920–22. Unskilled labourer, longshoreman, stonemason, and accountant in Moscow, 1922–24. Began to publish, 1923; full-time writer from 1924. Married: Mariia Petrovna Gromoslavskaia in 1924; two daughters and two sons. Joined the Communist Party, 1934; delegate to All-Party Congresses from 1939; member of the Party Central Committee, 1961–84. Member of the governing board of the Soviet Writers' Union, 1934–84. Delegate to the USSR Supreme Soviet, 1937–84. Member of the Soviet Academy of Sciences, 1939. Reporter for the newspapers *Krasnaia zvezda* and *Pravda* during World War II. Recipient: Stalin Prize for Literature, first class, 1941; Lenin Prize, 1960; Nobel Prize for Literature, 1965. Honorary degrees: St Andrew's University, Scotland, 1962; universities of Rostov-on-Don and Leipzig, 1965. Hero of Socialist Labour, 1967, 1980. Died 21 January 1984.

Publications

Collected Editions

Sobranie sochinenii, 8 vols. Moscow, 1956–58.
Early Stories, translated by Robert Daglish and Yelena Altshuler. Moscow, Progress, 1966.
Collected Works, translated by Robert Daglish. 8 vols, Moscow, Progress, 1984.
Sobranie sochinenii, 8 vols. Moscow, 1985.

Fiction

Lazorevaia step': Rasskazy [The Tulip Steppe]. Moscow, 1926.
Donskie rasskazy. Moscow, 1926; selection in Russian as *Selected Tales from the Don*, edited by C.G. Bearne, Oxford, Pergamon Press, 1966; translated as *Tales from the Don*, by H.C. Stevens, London, Putnam, 1961; reprinted London, Abacus, 1983.
Tikhii Don, 4 vols. 1928–40; revised versions 1953 and 1956; translated as *And Quiet Flows the Don*, by Stephen Garry, London, Putnam, 1934; Harmondsworth, Penguin, 1967; and *The Don Flows Home to the Sea*, by Stephen Garry, London, Putnam, 1940; Harmondsworth, Penguin, 1970; also translated as "Quiet Flows the Don", by Robert Daglish, in *Collected Works*, 1984; reprinted in 2 vols, Moscow, Raduga, and Wellingborough, Collets, 1988; revised edition, edited by Brian Murphy, London, Dent, 1996; reprinted 1997.
Podniataia tselina, vol. 1. Moscow, 1932; translated as *Virgin Soil Upturned*, by Stephen Garry, London, Putnam, 1935; and *Seeds of Tomorrow*, New York, Knopf, 1935; reprinted Harmondsworth, Penguin, 1977.
"Podniataia tselina", vol. 2, *Neva*, 7 (1959), 3–52; 1 (1960), 3–66; translated as *Harvest on the Don*, by H.C. Stevens, London, Putnam, 1960; reprinted Harmondsworth, Penguin, 1978; also as *Virgin Soil Upturned*, by Robert Daglish, Moscow, Progress, 1961.
Podniataia tselina, 2 vols. Moscow, 1960; as *Virgin Soil Upturned*, by Robert Daglish, 2 vols, Moscow, Progress, 1979.
"Nauka nenavisti", *Pravda* (22 June 1942); translated as *Hate* [no translator named], Moscow, Foreign Languages Publishing House, 1942; and *The Science of Hatred* [no translator named], New York, New Age Publishers, 1943.
"Sud'ba cheloveka", *Pravda*, 31 December 1956 and 1 January 1957; translated as *The Fate of a Man*, by Robert Daglish, Moscow, Progress, 2nd revised edition, 1967; also as "One Man's Destiny", in *One Man's Destiny and Other Stories, Articles, and Sketches, 1923–1963*, by H.C. Stevens, London, Putnam, 1967; reprinted London, Abacus, 1984.
"Oni srazhalis' za rodinu", *Roman-gazeta*, 1 (1959), *Pravda*, 12–15 March 1969; translated as "They Fought for Their Country", by Robert Daglish, *Soviet Literature*, 7 (1959), 3–56; 8 (1959), 3–72; 10 (1959), 3–39.

Essays

Po veleniiu dushi: Stat'i, ocherki, vystupleniia, dokumenty. Moscow, 1970; translated as *At the Bidding of the Heart: Essays, Sketches, Speeches, Papers* (abridged), by Olga Shartse, Moscow, Progress, 1973.

Letters

"Sholokhov i Stalin: Perepiska nachala 30-kh godov" [Sholokhov and Stalin: Correspondence from the Early 1930s], *Voprosy istorii*, 3 (1994), 3–25.

Critical Studies

Put' Sholokhova, by I. Lezhnev, Moscow, 1958.
Russian Fiction and Soviet Ideology: Introduction to Fedin, Leonov, and Sholokhov, by Ernest Simmons, New York, Columbia University Press, 1958.
Zhizn' i tvorchestvo M.A. Sholokhova, by L. Iakimenko, Moscow, 1964; 2nd edition, 1970; 3rd edition, 1977; translated as *Sholokhov: A Critical Appreciation* (abridged), by Brian Bean, Moscow, Progress, 1973.
Mikhail Sholokhov: A Critical Introduction, by D.H. Stewart, Ann Arbor, University of Michigan Press, 1967.
Sholokhov, by C.G. Bearne, Edinburgh, Oliver and Boyd, 1969.
The World of Young Sholokhov: Vision of Violence, by Michael Klimenko, North Quincy, Massachusetts, Christopher, 1972.
Stremia "Tikhogo Dona": Zagadki romana, by "D", Paris, YMCA-Press, 1974.
Problems in the Literary Biography of Mikhail Sholokhov, by Roy A. Medvedev, translated by A.D.P. Briggs, Cambridge, Cambridge University Press, 1977.
Mikhail Sholokhov and His Art, by Herman Ermolaev, Princeton, Princeton University Press, 1982.
The Authorship of the Quiet Don, by Geir Kjetsaa *et al.*, Oslo, Solum, and Atlantic Highlands, New Jersey, Humanities Press, 1984.
"Istoriia odnogo posviashcheniia. Neizvestnaia perepiska M. Sholokhova", by L. Kolodny, *Znamia*, 10 (1987).

"Istok 'Tikhogo Dona'", by L. Kolodny, *Moskovskaia pravda*, 20 May 1990.
"Plagiator li Sholokhov? Otvet opponentam", by G. Kh'etso [Kjetsaa], *Scando-Slavica*, 41 (1995).
Tainaia zhizn' Mikhaila Sholokhova. Dokumental'naia khronika bez legend, by V. Osipov, Moscow, 1995.
Kto napisal "Tikhii Don": khronika odnogo poiska, by L.E. Kolodnyi, Moscow, 1995.
Sholokhov's "Tikhii Don": A Commentary, by A.B. Murphy, V.P. Butt, and Herman Ermolaev, 2 vols, Birmingham, Birmingham Slavonic Monographs, 1997.

Bibliographies
M.A. Sholokhov: Seminarii, by V.V. Gura and F.A. Abramov, 2nd edition, Leningrad, 1962.
"Mikhail Aleksandrovich Sholokhov", in *Russkie sovetskie pisateli prozaiki: Biobibliograficheskii ukazatel'*, vol. 6, part 2, Moscow, 1969, 3–163.

Mikhail Aleksandrovich Sholokhov, Soviet novelist and the author of the greatest epic about the Cossacks, was not a Cossack by origin. He was the son of a lower-middle-class Russian, who had no steady occupation, and of an illiterate maid of Ukrainian peasant stock. Sholokhov had to give up his formal education half way through secondary school when his native Don region became a scene of bitter Civil-War fighting. For the greater part of the war he lived in or near the battle zone and witnessed the anti-Bolshevik uprising of the Upper Don Cossacks in the spring of 1919. In the early years of the Soviet regime he served in his native area as a teacher, clerk, and tax inspector. As a member of food-requisitioning and punitive detachments he took part in fighting anti-Soviet partisans. Much of what he saw or experienced during the 1918–22 period was reflected in his works.

From October 1922 to May 1924 Sholokhov lived in Moscow, trying, without success, to continue his education. On his return to the Don region, he lived almost all his life in Veshenskaia. Between 1923 and 1927 Sholokhov wrote at least 30 short stories. Most of them, beginning with "Ispytanie" [The Test] (1923), were first published in newspapers and magazines and then appeared in the collections entitled *Donskie rasskazy* (*Tales from the Don*), and *Lazorevaia step'* [The Tulip Steppe]. As a rule the stories focus on the vicious socio-political struggle within the Cossack villages and families during the Civil War and the early 1920s. Cruelty and suffering are presented with epic calmness. The author sympathizes with the Soviets, but a number of stories are unbiased and devoted to purely human problems. Although the stories are artistically uneven, they attest to Sholokhov's rapid development from an imitative apprentice into an original craftsman with a sharp eye for detail, a predilection for dramatic collisions, an earthy sense of humour, and complete mastery of the juicy Cossack dialect. *Tales from the Don* carried an enthusiastic foreword by Aleksandr Serafimovich, a venerable proletarian writer and a Don Cossack. In 1925 Sholokhov began to work on his epic masterpiece *Tikhii Don* (*Quiet Flows the Don*).

During collectivization and the Great Terror Sholokhov showed rare courage and concern for the people. In April 1933 he wrote a detailed letter to Stalin about the brutal mistreatment of collective farmers and the famine in the Upper Don area. Stalin sent grain to the area and thousands of lives were saved. In the spring of 1938 Sholokhov wrote to Stalin about the mass arrests and tortures of innocent people by the security police in the Rostov Province. Several months later the security police contrived a treason case against Sholokhov, an act that could have been hardly possible without Stalin's preliminary approval. But the dictator apparently changed his mind and spared Sholokhov to promote him as a symbol of Soviet cultural accomplishments. From the late 1930s Sholokhov was officially regarded as the top Soviet writer. He received the highest literary awards and held influential positions in the Communist Party.

Sholokhov's second novel, *Podniataia tselina* (*Virgin Soil Upturned*), depicts collectivization in a Don Cossack village. Volume 1, written while collectivization was still in progress, displays the immediacy of an eyewitness report. The dramatic events of the early months of collectivization – stormy debates about collective farming, the dispossession of "class enemies", the murder of a Cossack couple, the slaughter of cattle, and a riot by Cossack women – follow each other in rapid sequence, generating tension and suspense. The novel's heroes are dedicated communists who must cope with the Cossacks' hostility to collective farming and with a conspiracy organized by former White Army officers. The local communists and Cossacks cut convincing and colourful figures, while the protagonist, an industrial communist worker from Leningrad, is rather flat. The enemies are presented predominantly in dark colours. The political climax of volume 1 is the appearance of Stalin's article "Golovokruzhenie ot uspekhov" ("Dizzy with Success"), which blames local authorities for the excesses of collectivization and seemingly offers the peasant a choice between private and collective farming. Sholokhov, however, lets two of his characters expose the deceptiveness of Stalin's article.

Published in 1960, volume 2 of *Virgin Soil Upturned* bespeaks Sholokhov's artistic decline, attributable to his growing adherence to official interpretations of events, alcoholism, and the exhaustion of his creativity. Volume 2 does not go beyond the summer of 1930, avoiding the repression and famine of the years 1932–33. The narrative is static and filled with various stories and anecdotes told by the author and by the characters, with a strong admixture of the comical element. Sholokhov's faith in the historically determined victory of socialism and his identification of the people's interests with those of the Party make volume 2 a typical work of socialist realism. The critical reaction to both volumes of the novel was overwhelmingly favourable.

During World War II Sholokhov produced several agitational sketches and a story, *Nauka nenavisti* (*The Science of Hatred*), showing real and imagined atrocities of the German army. He also started the war novel *Oni srazhalis' za rodinu* (*They Fought for Their Country*), which remains unfinished. Its published chapters describe a battle in the Don region and provide flashbacks into the characters' past. To judge from what was printed, the novel promised to be politically orthodox, aesthetically undistinguished, and philosophically shallow. Sholokhov's last completed work, the story, *Sud'ba cheloveka* (*The Fate of a Man*) 1957, blends Soviet patriotic propaganda with the theme of personal grief caused by the German invasion.

In most of his speeches and journalistic writings, Sholokhov followed the official policy of the day. He praised the Party's guidance over literature and viciously attacked western leaders and dissident Soviet writers.

Sholokhov is a controversial figure. He is both a standard-bearer and a victim of the Soviet regime. But above all he is the creator of *Quiet Flows the Don*, an original and powerful work treating the eternal themes of morality, love, and death.

HERMAN ERMOLAEV

Quiet Flows the Don

Tikhii Don

Novel, 1928–40

In 1925 Sholokhov was not yet 20 when he began the first two books of his epic novel, *Quiet Flows the Don*. They both caused a sensation when they appeared in 1928; the third book's frank account of communist ill treatment of the Cossacks caused the journal *Oktiabr'* to suspend publication in 1929. Permission to resume was only accorded after reference to Stalin himself. Book 4 did not appear in complete form until 1940, 15 years after the young author had first conceived the early scenes.

For their part in suppressing the rebellions of 1905 the Cossacks had been regarded as cruel barbarians by many Russians. Sholokhov sought to redress the balance. He showed his people as having a higher standard of living and better systems of farming than the peasants of central Russia. Book 1 set out first the pre-war scenes of life in a Cossack village, and then Cossack cavalry going into action against the Germans in 1914. Book 2 shows the Cossacks refusing to support the monarchist Kornilov against the liberals in the Provisional Government and recounts the beginning of the deadly feud between Reds and Whites in the Don territory. The year 1919 brought the crucial clash with the Bolsheviks, whom the Cossacks to this day accuse of practising genocide against them. The novel is woven from a number of strands, but the main theme that emerges is the conflict between communist dogma and the Cossacks' reluctance to give up their land or abandon the old village organization that had been the basis of their prosperity.

The character of Grigorii Melekhov, the main hero of *Quiet Flows the Don*, is based on a historical prototype, Kharlampii Ermakov – one of the first Cossacks to rise against the communists in 1919 and one of the rebels' most successful commanders. Six years after the Soviets had pacified the Don area, Ermakov was imprisoned under a new wave of Red terror and in 1927 was shot without any proper trial. Listening to Ermakov's story in the months before his execution made Sholokhov realize that this popular leader had many of the best qualities of the Cossacks and could personify their heart-searchings and doubts in the struggle with the Soviet regime. The novel remained faithful to its aim of showing a balanced picture of the Civil War, but during the long period before it could be completed its structure underwent a fundamental change. Sholokhov had started with the concept of a polyphonic epic, to show a wide range of social types, including not only simple villagers, but also aristocrats such as the Listnitskiis, besides the merchant Mokhov and his pseudo-intellectual, nymphomaniac daughter. These secondary story lines fade out in books 3 and 4 as Sholokhov focuses attention on Grigorii, who has remained one of the most memorable characters in Soviet fiction.

Like many figures of classical tragedy Grigorii is destroyed by his own virtues. Out of joint with his time, he refuses to adhere blindly to the doctrine of any one faction. Books 3 and 4 centre on his struggle to retain basic human decency against the callous fanaticism of the Civil War. Even in the most desperate circumstances, Grigorii retains a certain nobility and hates the cruel excesses practised by those around him who have been brutalized by war. Grigorii's independent spirit is also marked out by his constant attachment to another man's wife, in defiance of the patriarchal traditions of Cossack society. His love of Aksin'ia develops from a carefree *amour goût* into a bond of total devotion.

After the White collapse in 1920 Grigorii tries to redeem his past by serving with the Red Army. When he comes back at the end of the year he is driven from his home and destroyed by the hardline communism of a former friend who believes that any ruthlessness is justified in the struggle to establish Soviet power.

The Russian title of the novel, *Tikhii Don*, is the traditional appellation for the river. In it Sholokhov has used the connotation "quiet" and the great slow flowing stream to symbolize the perpetual succession of the seasons. The vain tumult of human aspirations is seen as transient against the imperturbable processes of nature. Many similes in the text make comparisons between human actions and natural phenomena.

By reading *Quiet Flows the Don*, we can learn much truth about the October Revolution as a crucial turning-point in Russian history. The work has held its place as a great classic of Soviet literature that unfolds its story before our eyes in a series of vividly compelling scenes. Each single episode has an almost tactile realism. Even the minor characters are clearly differentiated by some physical feature or mannerism of speech. Most of them use their local dialect with pithy wit, and the author's own narrative is coloured by the South Russian speech of the Don and the folklore of the villagers among whom he lived.

Confusion has been caused over the English versions by a translation of books One and Two appearing in 1934 with the title *And Quiet Flows the Don*, while books 3 and 4 were translated in 1940 as *The Don Flows Home to the Sea*. Those who wish to read the novel in English should seek out the Dent paperback edition of 1997, which is based on the translation by Robert Daglish.

Sholokhov made wide use of historical sources and took much from first-hand accounts of the Civil War, talking to those who had survived the terrible years when the Don territory lost half its population. Since the first parts of the novel were published rumours have circulated that Sholokhov plagiarized the work of some other writer. Solzhenitsyn, Tomashevskaia, and other ingenious critics have exercised their talents in attempting to lend substance to these rumours. Against them should be weighed Kjetsaa's positive computer-study of the text and some two thousand pages of manuscript dicovered in 1987 and authenticated as being Sholokhov's holograph. Unless some solid evidence is produced to the contrary, Sholokhov must be considered the true author.

A.B. MURPHY

Vasilii Makarovich Shukshin 1929–1974

Prose writer, film director, and actor

Biography

Born in Srostki, Altai region of Siberia, 25 July 1929. Attended village school, 1937–44; Biisk Automobile Technical College, 1944–45. Worked on kolkhoz in Srostki, 1945–46; held various casual labouring jobs throughout the USSR. Served in the Navy, 1949–52: declared unfit for active service on account of a stomach ulcer. Returned to Srostki to recover; also obtained school leaving certificate. Teacher of Russian language and literature at Srostki Youth College. Married: 1) Mariia Shumskaia in 1954, one daughter; 2) Lidiia Nikolaevna Fedoseeva in 1964, two daughters. Moved to Moscow, 1954; attended All-Union Institute of Cinematography, 1954–60; graduated from faculty for Directors. Member of the Communist Party, 1955. First publication in journal, *Smena*, 1958. First collection, *Sel'skie zhiteli* [Village Dwellers] published, 1963; first feature film, *Zhivet takoi paren'* [There Lives Such a Lad], 1964, which won Golden Lion Award at Venice Film Festival. Recipient: Brothers Vasil'ev Prize, 1967; USSR State Prize, 1971; Lenin Prize, 1976 (posthumously). Died in Kletskii, Volgograd, 2 October 1974. Buried in Novodevich'ii cemetery.

Publications

Collected Editions

Izbrannye proizvedeniia, 2 vols. Moscow, 1976.
I Want to Live: Short Stories by Vasilii Shukshin, translated by Robert Daglish. Moscow, Progress, 1978.
Snowball Berry Red and Other Stories [various translators], edited by Donald M. Fiene. Ann Arbor, Ardis, 1979.
Sobranie sochinenii, 3 vols. Moscow, 1984–85.
Roubles in Words, Kopeks in Figures and Other Stories, translated by Natasha Ward and David Iliffe. London, Marion Boyars, 1985.
Short Stories [various translators]. Moscow, Raduga, 1990.
Sobranie sochinenii, 5 vols. Ekaterinburg, 1992.
Sobranie sochinenii, 5 vols. Moscow, 1996.
Stories from a Siberian Village, translated by Laura Michael and John Givens. DeKalb, Northern Illinois University Press, 1996.

Fiction

Sel'skie zhiteli [Village Dwellers]. Moscow, 1963.
Liubaviny [The Liubavins] (part 1). Moscow, 1965.
Tam, vdali [There, Far Away]. Moscow, 1968.
"Ia prishel dat' vam voliu" [I Came to Give You Freedom], *Iskusstvo kino*, 6 (1968) [screenplay]; *Sibirskie ogni*, 1–2 (1971) [novel]; separate edition Moscow, 1974, 1982, 1984.
Zemliaki [Countrymen]. Moscow, 1970.
Kharaktery [Characters]. Moscow, 1973.
Besedy pri iasnoi lune [Conversations under a Clear Moon]. Moscow, 1974.
Brat moi [My Brother]. Moscow, 1975.
Rasskazy. Moscow, 1975.
Osen'iu [In the Autumn]. Barnaul, 1976.
Do tret'ikh petukhov. Moscow, 1976; title story translated as "Before the Cock Crows Thrice", by Natasha Ward, in *Roubles in Words, Kopeks in Figures and Other Stories*, 1985.
Okhota zhit'. Kazan, 1977; title story translated as "I Want to Live", by Robert Daglish, in *I Want to Live: Short Stories by Vasilii Shukshin*, 1978.
Tochka zreniia [A Point of View]. Moscow, 1979.
Rasskazy. Moscow, 1979.
"Liubaviny" [The Liubavins] (part 2), *Druzhba narodov*, 1–2 (1987).

Screenplays

Zhivet takoi paren' [There Lives Such a Lad]. Moscow, 1964.
"Kalina krasnaia", *Nash sovremennik*, 4 (1973); edited by David Holohan, London, Bristol Classical Press, 1996; translated as "Snowball Berry Red", by Donald M. Fiene, in *Snowball Berry Red and Other Stories*, 1979.
Kinopovesti [Screenplays]. Moscow, 1975; revised edition, 1988.

Play

"Energichnye liudi", *Literaturnaia Rossiia*, 7 June 1974, 18–19; 14 June 1974, 12–13; 21 June 1974, 18–20; translated as "Energetic People", by Natasha Ward and David Iliffe, in *Roubles in Words, Kopeks in Figures and Other Stories*, 1985.

Essays and Articles

Nravstvennost' est' pravda [Morality is Truth]. Moscow, 1979.
Voprosy samomu sebe [Questions to Myself]. Moscow, 1981.
Vasily Shukshin: Articles, edited by Eduard Yefimov, translated by Avril Pyman. Moscow, Raduga, 1986.

Critical Studies

"The Remarkable Art of Vasily Shukshin", by Donald M. Fiene and B.N. Peskin, *Russian Literature Triquarterly*, 11 (1975), 174–78.
Beyond Socialist Realism: Soviet Fiction since "Ivan Denisovich", by Geoffrey Hosking, London, Granada, and New York, Holmes and Meier, 1980, chapter 8, 162–79.
Kharaktery Vasiliia Shukshina, by Viktor Gorn, Barnaul, 1981.
Talantlivaia zhizn', by Valentina Karpova, Moscow, 1986.
"Shukshin's Women: An Enduring Stereotype", by Lyndall Morgan, *Australian Slavonic and East European Studies*, 1/2 (1987), 137–46.
Tvorcheskaia evoliutsiia Vasiliia Shukshina, by Galina Pavlovna Binova, Brno, Univerzita J.E. Purkyne, 1988.
"The Art of Vasilij Šukšin: Volja Through Song", by Diane Nemec Ignashev, *Slavic and East European Journal*, 32 (1988), 415–27.
"Vasily Shukshin's *Srezal* and the Question of Transition", by Diane Nemec Ignashev, *Slavonic and East European Review*, 66 (1988), 337–56.
"Trial by Truth", by Natal'ia Ivanova, *Studies in Soviet Literature*, 24/3 (1988), 5–57.

Vasilii Shukshin, by Vladimir Korobov, Moscow, 1988.
Vasilii Shukshin: Lichnost', knigi, by Viktor Gorn, Barnaul, 1990.
Vasilii Shukshin i russkoe dukhovnoe vozrozhdenie, by Evgenii Vertlib, New York, Effect, 1990.
"The Subversive Sub-text: Allegorical Elements in the Short Stories of Vasilii Shukshin", by Lyndall Morgan, *Australian Slavonic and East European Studies*, 5/1 (1991), 59–76.
V.M. Shukshin: Zhizn' i tvorchestvo, edited by A.A. Chuvakin *et al.*, Barnaul, 1992.
"Siberia as *Volia*: Vasilii Shukshin's Search for Freedom", by John Givens, in *Between Heaven and Hell: The Myth of Siberia in Russian Culture*, edited by G. Diment and Iu. Slezkine, New York, St Martin's Press, 1993.
Introduction by David Holohan, in *Kalina krasnaia/Snowball Berry Red*, London, Bristol Classical Press, 1996, vii–xxvii.
"Vasilii Shukshin and the Russian Fairy Tale: A Study of 'Until the Cock Crows Thrice'", by Nicole Christian, *Modern Language Review*, 92/2 (1997), 392–400.
"Manifestations of the Eccentric in the Works of Vasilii Shukshin", by Nicole Christian, *Slavonic and East European Review*, 75/2 (1997), 201–15.

Vasilii Shukshin is not easily categorized as a writer. He has often been labelled a *derevenshchik* (Village Prose writer), the rural settings and themes of his work contributing to this image. However, Shukshin displays a degree of versatility and a sense of irony uncommon among the traditional *derevenshchiki*. He represents a halfway-house between Village Prose's reverence for the traditions of rural Russia, and the total irreverence displayed by more recent writers such as Evgenii Popov.

Shukshin began his literary career while still a student at the All-Union State Institute of Cinematography in Moscow. He learned how to write concisely and evocatively under the tutelage of the film director Mikhail Romm and was first published in the journal *Smena* in 1958. His early works are simple village vignettes dealing with everyday rural life. Yet even at this stage he displayed an interest in the unusual villager, the eccentric or *chudak*. This figure was to recur in various forms throughout Shukshin's literary and cinematic career.

Shukshin's eccentric is always male and stands in stark contrast to the female characters, who are invariably stereotypes: either idealized mother-figures, the typical love-interest, or caricatures of the nagging wife. The *chudak* is an eternal dreamer, searching for an escape from the monotony of real life. This escape manifests itself in different ways. The hero of the short story "Odni" ("Alone") 1963, forgets the drudgery of the working day by playing his balalaika. His wife, however, considers his musical interests to be a distraction from his work as a harness-maker, and tries to prevent him from playing whenever she can. So he is forced to wait until she leaves the house before he can enjoy the sense of transcendence he attains with his music. In the later story "Mil' pardon, madam!" ("Mille pardons, madame!") 1968, the protagonist, Bron'ka Pupkov, finds his escape in telling a particular tall tale. Bron'ka regularly accompanies visiting city people on hunting trips and likes to tell the story of his failed assassination attempt on Hitler during World War II. The story has no basis in reality, and, perhaps for that reason, affords its teller a sense of release from ordinary life, the opportunity to dream out loud in front of an audience. In "Srezal" ("Cut Down to Size") 1970, one villager, Gleb Kapustin, takes particular delight in humiliating visiting intellectuals from the city. His wish is to be heard and regarded as a force to be reckoned with, despite his rural background. Yet, his knowledge of current issues is drawn from magazines, television and radio shows and is consequently patchy. Gleb, however, is oblivious to this minor detail, and achieves his sense of escape when he baffles the city folk with – what he believes to be – his superior knowledge.

Although Shukshin's literary forte is generally considered to be the short story, he also wrote successful novellas and cine-novellas, the most important of which is *Kalina krasnaia* (*Snowball Berry Red*). This tale of an eccentric ex-convict, who tries to escape his old lifestyle and start afresh away from the city, is probably Shukshin's best-known work. As a film it enjoyed huge success in the Soviet Union as well as some acclaim abroad. Other novellas include *Do tret'ikh petukhov* (*Before the Cock Crows Thrice*), an extravagant parody of the Russian fairy tale, and *Tochka zreniia* [A Point of View], which describes a matchmaking from four different points of view. The latter two works represent Shukshin's mature *oeuvre*; in later years he displayed a marked shift from the realities of everyday life to an interest in the fantastic, the unreal. He developed a talent for satire and parody, and an increased sense of irony. This new style is also apparent in his only play, *Energichnye liudi* (*Energetic People*).

Aside from his shorter works, Shukshin wrote two historical novels, neither of which received great acclaim. It has been argued that Shukshin was not an accomplished novelist; his longer works, in particular *Liubaviny* [The Liubavins], resemble a series of short episodes strung together, lacking cohesion and structure. *Liubaviny* tells of a Siberian family and their difficulties in coming to terms with the new Soviet regime being enforced in their village in the early 1920s. It follows more than one generation of the family and spans several decades. The novel was written in two stages, the second half of which lay unnoticed in Shukshin's archive for 13 years and was only published in 1987. His other novel, *Ia prishel dat' vam voliu* [I Came to Give You Freedom], is a reinterpretation of the Sten'ka Razin legend. The novel covers the build-up to, and carrying out of, the Cossack and peasant rebellion led by Razin in the 17th century. The work was to become an obsession for its author as he battled with the authorities to have it accepted as a film project. Thwarted by censors and ill health, he never achieved his dream of writing, directing, and starring in the film version. Shukshin died in 1974, at the age of 45, leaving more than one unfinished project.

During his lifetime, Shukshin's works were given a mixed reception in the Soviet Union. While some critics admired the refreshing style and humour of his works, others were appalled by his frank depictions of village life. Shukshin tried to maintain a dialogue with his readers and film-goers, publishing a number of articles in answer to criticism from the public and established critics. Following Shukshin's premature death, critics were able to interpret the author's works as they wished and there was a deluge of books and articles, underlining his supposed Soviet orthodoxy. In death Shukshin took on the role of popular hero; poems were dedicated to his memory, a book of Shukshin's sayings was published, and a Shukshin museum was opened in his home village. In the Soviet Union of the 1970s and 1980s he was virtually canonized; in Russia today, although still respected, he is considered somewhat *passé*. His reception in the west has been muted by comparison. Chapters in text books of Soviet literature are devoted to him (see Geoffrey Hosking, for instance), and there has been a small number of journal articles and American PhD dissertations over the years. A significant figure in the development of Russia's literary and cinematic traditions, Shukshin now deserves serious re-evaluation.

NICOLE CHRISTIAN

Snowball Berry Red

Kalina krasnaia

Cine-novella, 1973

Snowball Berry Red was first published in 1973 in *Nash sovremennik* and attracted limited interest. However, when the film version (in which Shukshin starred) was completed in early 1974 and screened in the spring, it caused a furore in the world of Russian cinema. The critic Lev Anninskii regarded this work as Shukshin's "creative testament".

The story begins with the release of Egor Prokudin from prison. The hero relishes his new-found freedom and enjoys the fact that it coincides with the coming of spring. Egor manages to get a lift into town and *en route* discusses poetry, happiness, and world outlook with the morose driver. Instead of making a fresh start on his arrival in the city, Egor returns to his old criminal gang. He encounters a mixed reception; Guboshlep (Fat Lip), the gang-leader, is frosty and disapproves of Egor's post-prison exuberance. Lucienne, a former flame, is the only gang member who is truly pleased to see him. The meeting is soon broken up when the police try to raid their hideout. Egor escapes after receiving some money from Guboshlep and unsuccessfully tries to find refuge with former girlfriends. Then he remembers his prison penfriend, Liuba Baikalova (in the film version, played by Shukshin's wife, Lidiia Fedoseeva), and he decides to visit her. On first meeting they form an instant understanding. Egor accompanies her to her family's house and, after an initial uneasiness, the parents and brother accept him. Egor is anxious to make a good impression and appreciates their hospitality. The next day, however, their country kindness becomes too stifling for Prokudin and he escapes to town where he spends a great deal of money on an attempt at an orgy of pleasure. This too fails and Egor decides to return to Liuba and make a genuine fresh start. He finds a job on the collective farm as a tractor driver and his life begins to take on a semblance of normality; this is soon to be shattered by two events. One evening, Egor goes with Liuba to visit an old woman (he claims he is doing a prison friend a favour). Egor wears dark glasses and asks Liuba to pretend they have come from the social services to check up on the woman's situation. After the meeting Egor admits that the woman is his mother. His guilt at having abandoned her without word and then leading a criminal life is overwhelming, and he breaks down. Second, Egor receives a threatening visit from one of Guboshlep's men, urging him to return to the gang. Egor refuses, but the gang soon catches up with him and the consequences are fatal. Guboshlep comes in search of him, interrupting his work in the fields, and Egor Prokudin meets his death at the hands of his former friend and leader.

One of the most prominent themes of the work is Egor's search for a sense of release. His release from prison is merely a step in the right direction, his main wish is to find release for his soul. He coins the term "festival of the soul" ("prazdnik dushi") and tries to achieve this dream throughout the story. These fine words, however, do not ring true, as Egor's attempts to fulfil his dream are steeped in confusion. He tries to create his festival on the one hand through honest, hard work supported by the love of a good woman, and on the other by flirting with every attractive young woman, and organizing an (unsuccessful) orgy of drinking and debauchery. In creating a rural idyll with Liuba Baikalov, Egor makes a significant advance in his personal renaissance. However, it cannot last; Egor realizes that he will not escape his past. The persistence of his gang forms only one proof of his irrepressible past. The visit to his mother allows him to comprehend the impossible nature of his situation. Shukshin explained his hero's thoughts: "... when he saw his mother, he understood everything in an instant: in life, he would never find that festival, that peace, there was no way he could ever atone for his sins before his mother – it would torment his conscience forever". Perhaps for this reason, it has been suggested that Prokudin meets his death willingly, voluntarily, as though in this manner justice will be served.

The depiction of criminality and an underworld life were quite a novelty in Soviet literature of the 1960s and 1970s. The publication of Solzhenitsyn's *Odin den' Ivana Denisovicha* (*One Day in the Life of Ivan Denisovich*) in 1962 caused considerable controversy, and few writers wished to tempt fate with similar works for a number of years thereafter. When it became clear that the hero of *Snowball Berry Red* was an ex-convict, discussions ensued. Certain officials were undecided about the suitability of the subject-matter for a film. However, plans went ahead, if in a somewhat sanitized form, and the criminal, Egor Prokudin, became not only widely known, but also immensely popular in Russia.

In spite of the serious issues addressed in the work – the criminal underworld, rehabilitation of an ex-convict, the search for spiritual release in a faithless society, and death – Shukshin's talent for comedy shines through. Prokudin appealed to the public by virtue of his humour, his zest for life, the scrapes he finds himself in and his ingenious ways of getting out of them.

While the publication of the story aroused little interest, the film provoked a good deal of debate. It was considered worthy of coverage by the journal *Voprosy literatury*, which invited a number of critics to comment on both film and scenario. Two camps emerged: those who criticized its sentimentality, the banality of the characters and the unbelievable nature of certain scenes; and those who appreciated the warmth of the characters, the serious issues addressed and the emphasis on faith. In spite of the harsh criticism, the work won the approval of the public. Paradoxically, Shukshin's untimely death in October 1974 contributed to its success; the public linked Egor's tragedy with that of Shukshin and the author achieved the status of a national hero. If the work is at times marred by moral platitudes or melodramatic overtones, the overwhelming impression is of a varied and pacy story-line. More significantly, Shukshin made a valid point about the loss of spirituality in Soviet Russia. He noticed a void that the deprivation of religion created, which could not be filled by communist doctrine.

NICOLE CHRISTIAN

Elena Andreevna Shvarts 1948–

Poet

Biography

Born in Leningrad, 1948. Father died when she was an infant. Grew up in Leningrad with mother, the artistic director of the Bolshoi Dramaticheskii Theatre. Began writing poetry in her early teens. Studied for a year at the philological faculty of Leningrad State University, then transferred to the Theatrical Institute where she graduated as an external student. Published in *samizdat* journals in 1970s and 1980s (*37*, *Obvodnyi kanal*, *Chasy*). Member of Leningrad unofficial writers' group, Club-81. Member of the Writers' Union, 1991. Married: Mikhail Sheinker, the critic and editor of *Vestnik novoi literatury*.

Publications

Poetry

Tantsuiushchii David [Dancing David]. New York, Russica, 1980.
Trudy i dni Lavinii, monakhini iz ordena obrezaniia serdtsa [The Works and Days of the Nun Lavinia]. Ann Arbor, Ardis, 1987.
Stikhi. Paris, Beseda, 1987.
Storony sveta [Four Corners of the World]. Leningrad, 1989.
Stikhi. Leningrad, 1990.
Lotsiia nochi [Sailing Directions at Night]. St Petersburg, 1993.
Paradise: Selected Poems, translated by Michael Molnar and Catriona Kelly. Newcastle upon Tyne, Bloodaxe, 1993.
Pesnia ptitsy na dne morskom [Birdsong at the Bottom of the Sea]. Moscow, 1995.
Mundus imaginalis (kniga otvetvlenii) [Mundus imaginalis (A Book of Offshoots)]. St Petersburg, 1996.
Zapadno-vostochnyi veter: Novye stikhotvoreniia [A Western-Eastern Wind]. St Petersburg, 1997.

Critical Studies

"The Poetry of Elena Shvarts", by Barbara Heldt, *World Literature Today*, Summer (1989), 381–83.
"Misticheskaia geografiia 'Storon sveta'", by Viktor Krivulin, *Russkaia mysl'*, 3784 (14 July 1989), 11.
"Bez bytiia", by Ol'ga Nikolaeva, *Novyi mir*, 10 (1991), 244–48.

During two decades working in Leningrad's "second culture", Elena Shvarts gained a reputation as one of the leading poets of the post-war generation. Her poems appeared in *samizdat* journals, her readings were highly acclaimed and always to full houses. She offered her audiences a blend of *faux-naïf* humour and quirky mysticism that was a powerful antidote to a certain type of proclamatory verse that she mocks in her mischievous "Kinfiia" ("Cynthia") cycle:

> Why do you, Septimus, importune the Muse?
> In vain you intone, in vain you belabour the air
> Beating the rhythm. You have inflicted mortal
> Boredom on Calliope and Euterpe ...

Her lightness of touch is the craft of a *chansonneuse* adept at switching roles without sacrificing her own intonations. Each of her long poem-cycles displays various aspects of a mutable poetic persona, one of whose attractions is its refusal to pontificate or freeze into any fixed shape. Her role-playing beguiles and distances the reader who is constantly shuttled between mockery and sympathy. She is able to infuse emotional depth into eccentric and grotesque characters. *Trudy i dni Lavinii* [The Works and Days of the Nun Lavinia] presents a deranged nun from the phantasmic and heterodox "convent of the circumcision of the heart". Knockabout humour rides a strong religious current; the laughter or irony is a play of light on a surface that occasionally opens to reveal a species of Plotinian mysticism: "Alive, I have become a tomb / And I will fly to God alone."

On the appearance of her first Soviet collection in 1989, her fellow Leningrad poet Viktor Krivulin greeted the publication as a critical moment in contemporary Russian poetry, and as decisive evidence of a break with the past and the portent of a new literary audience. If her work was previously unpublishable, this was not only because of its religious themes, but because it was so singularly a-social. Her obsessions are solitude, pain, death, and the path of the sinful soul yearning for salvation.

But it would be misleading to categorize Shvarts simply as a religious poet, and not just because humour and irony leavens the high seriousness of her themes, but also because she remains outside the certainties of church or institutional faith that her personae appear to desire. Her idiosyncratic and eclectic juggling with religious concepts can shock and offend the more orthodox, as can be seen, for instance, in the review of her work by Ol'ga Nikolaeva in *Novyi mir* (1991).

If the sovereign characteristic of her poetic personae is solitude, it is not so much the proud isolation of the self-sufficient as the permanent insecurity of the tormented, exposed to the eddying of their own capricious fears and desires: "No one of a more changeable nature than mine / Has ever been born in Rome ..." ("Cynthia").

Her cosmos (in so far as it can be deduced, for she refrains from intellectualizing) is as much mythical and gnostic as Christian, and finds its most complete expression in the four "Elegii na storony sveta" ("Elegies on the Cardinal Points"), which chart a soul's travels and travails through a spectral universe inhabited by angels, saints, the Antichrist, mythical and biblical figures, and even fragments of shattered bodies: "In the heavens ethereal fires blaze / And a flight of eyes wings to the South."

Phantasmagoric images of shattered bodies are leitmotifs in her poetry: the poet is even reduced at one point to a "gouged eye on a bloody thread, for a moment filled / with all the pain and glory of the world". ("Podrazhanie Bualo" [Imitation of Boileau]). A primordial catastrophe has shattered the universe and her poetry is saturated with the sense of unattainable harmony. At one level this manifests itself in terms of karma – "But why are we resurrected / From pain to pain?" ("Chernaia Paskha" [Black Easter]): at another it expresses itself as a morbid fascination with blood, pain, and physical torment, or as a hypersensitive consciousness recoiling from its own corporeality: "In anguish here before my God I stand / Holding my skull in a trembling hand" ("Elegiia na rentgenovskii snimok moego cherepa" [Elegy on an X-Ray Photo of My Skull]).

In his introduction to her Soviet collection, the Leningrad poet

Aleksandr Kushner noted her rapid variations of rhythm and mood, a patter and skittishness of form and content alike that he termed an "infantile intonation" in her verse. Yet this magisterial phrase clearly implies a pseudo-classical concept of poetry, and one that Shvarts just as clearly does not share. In this clash of viewpoints the unconfronted question of femininity is latent. Barbara Heldt has hailed her work for its resolute opposition to a prevailing patriarchal culture (Heldt, 1989). Yet this femininity never emerges as feminism. Her work is equally shocking to all political activists, whether feminist, Soviet or Russian Orthodox, for its indifference to any form of *sobornost'* or social activity.

If as a poet she has assumed a cause, then Elena Shvarts has chosen not a political one but a particular vein of contemporary Russian culture. One of her roles is as a voice for St Petersburg and its history and this is undoubtedly one reason for her wider appeal, since St Petersburg can often serve as a Russian microcosm, epitomizing as it does a persistent theme in post-Petrine Russia, namely the interplay of Slavophile and westernizing forces. Elena Shvarts's concern is with the concomitant undercurrents, personal and cultural, and with the question posed by the mystical aspects of Russian Orthodoxy. Her poetry patches together a quilt out of the various myths and anecdotes that cling round Peter the Great's "Paradise", which, in her verse, becomes a "city laid out like a carcass" ("Detskii sad cherez tridtsat' let" [Kindergarten: Thirty Years On]). Although highly individual, her poetical mythmaking is founded on a collective folklore; consequently its appeal is far-reaching and it may even serve as subliminal echo to the social drama now being acted out by archaic national and religious concepts.

MICHAEL MOLNAR

Evgenii L'vovich Shvarts 1896–1958

Dramatist

Biography

Born in Kazan, 21 October 1896. Attended Moscow University, but abandoned studies in 1915. Married: 1) an actress from the Rostov theatre troupe (divorced); 2) Ekaterina Ivanovna. Moved to Rostov-on-Don and worked as an actor for P.K. Veisbrem's experimental theatre, 1919; moved with the company to Petrograd, 1921; after two seasons mostly gave up acting and turned to writing humorous articles and sketches for the "House of Arts" writers' club. Moved to Bakhmut, in the Donbass region; staff member of a newspaper, 1923–24. Returned to Leningrad, and worked on Samuil Marshak's magazines *Ezh* and *Chizh* for the children's department of Gosizdat, the State publishing house. Remained in Leningrad during World War II and the siege; worked as defence warden, leaving only in 1942. Lived in the Komarovo artists' community near Leningrad in later years. Died in Leningrad, 15 January 1958.

Publications

Collected Editions

"Ten'" i drugie p'esy ["The Shadow" and Other Plays]. Leningrad, 1956.
Kukol'nyi gorod. P'esy dlia kukol'nogo teatra [Toy Town. Plays for the Puppet Theatre]. 1959.
P'esy. Leningrad, 1960.
P'esy i kinostsenary. Leningrad, 1962.
Skazki; Povesti; P'esy. Leningrad, 1969.
P'esy. Leningrad, 1972.
Three Plays: Golyi korol'; Ten'; Drakon, edited by Avril Pyman. Oxford, Pergamon Press, 1972.
The Naked King; The Shadow; The Dragon, translated by Elisaveta Fen. London, Marion Boyars, 1976.
Klad [The Treasure, etc.] (10 plays). Leningrad, 1982.

Plays

Undervud [Underwood] (produced 1929). Leningrad, 1930.
Pustiaki [Trifles] (puppet play; produced 1932). Leningrad, 1932.
Klad [The Treasure] (produced 1933), in *P'esy*, 1960.
"Prikliucheniia Gogenshtaufen" [The Adventures of Hohenstaufen], *Zvezda*, 1934.
Golyi korol'. 1934; in *P'esy*, 1960; translated as "The Naked King", by F.D. Reeve, in *Contemporary Russian Drama*, New York, Pegasus, 1968; and by Sally Pullinger, London, Ginn, 1972; also by Elisaveta Fen, in *The Naked King*, 1976.
Brat i sestra [Brother and Sister] (produced 1936). Leningrad, 1936.
Krasnaia Shapochka [Little Red Riding Hood] (produced 1939). Leningrad, 1936; in *P'esy*, 1972.
Snezhnaia koroleva [The Snow Queen] (produced 1939), in *"Ten'" i drugie p'esy*, 1956.
Kukol'nyi gorod [Toy Town] (produced 1939), in *Kukol'nyi gorod: P'esy dlia kukol'nogo teatra*, Leningrad, 1959.
Nashe gostepriimstvo [Our Hospitality]. 1939.
Skazka o poteriannom vremeni [A Tale about Wasted Time] (puppet play; produced 1940). 1948.
"Ten'" (produced 1940), *Literaturnyi sovremennik*, 1940; also in *"Ten'" i drugie p'esy*, 1956; translated as "The Shadow", by Elisaveta Fen, in *The Naked King*, 1976.
Odna noch' [One Night]. 1942; in *"Ten'" i drugie p'esy*, 1956.
Pod lipami Berlina [Under the Berlin Lindens] (produced 1942).
Dalekii krai [Distant Land] (produced 1943). 1950.
Drakon (produced 1944). 1944; translated as *The Dragon*, by Elizabeth Reynolds Hapgood, New York, Theatre Arts

Books, 1963; London, Heinemann, 1969; and by Max Hayward and Harry Shukman, in *Three Soviet Plays*, Harmondsworth, Penguin, 1966; reprinted as *The Golden Age of Soviet Theatre*, Harmondsworth, Penguin, 1981.
Dva klena (produced 1954); in *"Ten'" i drugie p'esy*, 1960; translated as "The Two Maples", in *Russian Plays for Young Audiences*, edited and translated by Miriam Morton, Rowayton, Connecticut, New Plays Books, 1977.
Obyknovennoe chudo [An Ordinary Miracle] (produced 1956); in *"Ten'" i drugie p'esy*, 1960.
Zolushka [Cinderella], in *"Ten'" i drugie p'esy*, 1956.
Povest' o molodykh suprugakh [Tale of the Newlyweds] (produced 1957); in *P'esy*, 1960.

Screenplays
Zolushka [Cinderella]. 1947.
Snezhnaia koroleva [The Snow Queen]. 1950.
Don Quixote, from Bulgakov's adaptation, 1957; in *P'esy*, 1960.
"Tsar' Vodokrut", in *P'esy i kinostsenary*, 1962.
Kain XVIII [Cain XVIII], completed by Nikolai Erdman. 1963.

Fiction
Rasskaz staroi balalaiki [Story of the Old Balalaika]. 1925.

Memoirs
Memuary [Memoirs]. Paris, La Presse Libre, 1982.
Zhivu bespokoino: Iz dnevnikov [I Live Uneasily: From My Diaries]. Leningrad, 1990.
Telefonnaia knizhka [The Telephone Book]. Moscow, 1997.

Critical Studies
Evgenii Shvarts: Kritika – Bibliograficheskii ocherk, by Sergei Tsimbal, Leningrad, 1961.
My znali Evgeniia Shvartsa. Leningrad and Moscow, 1966.
"Evgenij Svarc: Dramatist, Satirist, Wizard", by Lionel R. Simard, in *Symbolae in honorem Georgii Y. Shevelov*, edited by William E. Harkins *et al.*, Munich, 1971.
Evgenii Swarz, Mensch und Schatten, edited by L. Debürer, Berlin, 1972.
"The Theatre of E.L. Shvarts: An Introduction", by J. Douglas Clayton, *Études Slaves et Est-Européennes*, 19 (1974), 24–43.
"Evgeny L'vovich Shvarts: A Biographical Sketch", by Irina H. Corten, *Russian Literature Triquarterly*, 16 (1979), 222–43.
"Evgeny Shvarts and the Uses of Fantasy in the Soviet Theatre", by Felicia H. Londré, *Research Studies* (Washington State University), 47 (1979).
Evgenii Shvarts and His Fairy-Tales for Adults, by Amanda J. Metcalf, Birmingham, Birmingham Slavonic Monographs, 1979.
Twentieth-Century Russian Drama: From Gorky to the Present, by Harold B. Segel, New York, Columbia University Press, 1979.
On the Beneficence of Censorship: Aesopian Language in Modern Russian Literature, by Lev Loseff, translated by Jane Bobko, Munich, Sagner, 1984.
"The Undervud Affair. A Case Study of Pedagogies, Pioneers and Politics in the Soviet Children's Theatre of 1929", by Amanda Metcalf, *Irish Slavonic Studies*, 8 (1987).
Epicheskii teatr Evgeniia Shvartsa, by V.E. Golovchinev, Tomsk, 1992.

Bibliography
"Evgenii L'vovich Shvarts: A Selected Bibliography", by Irina H. Corten, *Russian Literature Triquarterly*, 16 (1979), 333–39.

Evgenii Shvarts's literary career spanned nearly 40 years, most of it largely devoted to the theatre. His theatrical career began just as Soviet literature and society were entering the Stalin era, and he only lived a few years into the Thaw that followed Stalin's death. It is therefore surprising that his output includes such a large amount of extremely unorthodox material. As is common with many Soviet authors during (and after) the Stalin era, he wrote many more plays than have been produced. A number of those not staged are none the less memorable for other reasons (whether by virtue of literary quality or as a *cause célèbre*) and merit at least a mention.

His plays can be divided into four main categories: realistic plays for children, fairy tales for children, realistic plays for adults and fairy tales for adults. Of his fairy tales, some are adaptations of existing tales (often those by Hans Christian Andersen), while others are original tales using fairy tale themes and characters.

His realistic plays for children, since they usually relate to particular times and themes, are among the more minor and transient of Shvarts's works. By contrast to the realistic plays, the fairy tales for children include some of the most popular and long-lasting staples of the Soviet children's theatre. *Undervud* [Underwood] is superficially a realistic play about the adventures of a Young Pioneer and her friends in foiling the plots of a wicked speculator, but was conceived by the author, and accepted by the critics as a disguised fairy tale, at a time when the fairy tale was not approved by Soviet educationalists. *Krasnaia Shapochka* [Little Red Riding Hood], was an adaptation from Perrault's traditional tale of Little Red Riding Hood, expanded with additional characters and action. It was still being staged to enthusiastic young audiences long after Shvarts's death. *Snezhnaia koroleva*, adapted from Hans Christian Andersen's *The Snow Queen*, subsequently became one of the mainstay productions of the Central Children's Theatre in Moscow. Three relatively short-lived puppet plays of the 1940s were: *Kukol'nyi gorod* [Toy Town], a wartime (but pre-war in Soviet terms) play about the struggle between a community of toys, under the direction of the old toy-maker, against an army of rats and their allies; *Skazka o poteriannom vremeni* [A Tale about Wasted Time], a cautionary tale about the effects of time-wasting (young children becoming prematurely aged because a group of magicians is stealing the time they waste and using it to become younger themselves); *Novaia skazka* [New Tale], which features children, evacuated from a former war zone, who return to their old house to rescue it from the various "goblins" associated with war damage.

The smallest group of Shvarts's works is that of realistic plays for adults; very few, even of these non fairy-tale plays, were staged. Those which were not, include: *Telefonnaia trubka* [Telephone Receiver] (1932), a workplace play dealing with the unmasking of bad work attitudes among staff; *Nashe gostepriimstvo* [Our Hospitality], one of the wave of "defence plays" common in the late 1930s, which despite much discussion at the time, fell foul of the censor because, since Soviet borders had been officially declared inviolable, its basic premise – the landing of an alien plane on Soviet territory – was impossible. *Pod lipami Berlina* [Under the Berlin Lindens], a short-lived light comedy revue, satirizing the Nazi regime, was staged at the Comedy Theatre in Leningrad during the early days of the war. *Odna noch'* [One Night] is the best of this category of plays; set in Leningrad during the blockade, and detailing the events of one night in a block of flats, it is a realistic study of ordinary people facing extraordinary conditions. *Povest' o molodykh suprugakh* [Tale of the Newlyweds], a story of the first year's ups and downs in the life of a newlywed couple, could be included among the fairy-tale plays, owing to the presence of a large doll and a teddy bear who act as a Chorus to the action, but, since they do not interact with the characters, it fits better with the realistic plays. *Don Kikhot* [Don Quixote] is a thoughtful adaptation of Cervantes that follows the action of the original, but uses Shvarts's own dialogue.

Shvarts's best-known plays in the west are his fairy tales for adults – although, again, few of these reached the stage at the time of writing. *Prikliucheniia Gogenshtaufena* [The Adventures of Hohenstaufen], written for a short-lived experimental music-hall workshop and published but never staged, is an amusing semi-realistic fairy-tale-plus-message, involving workers in a Soviet business, some of whom also have a magic streak compatible with their respective work attitudes (a vampire, a good fairy, and so on). *Golyi korol'* (*The Naked King*) is a delightful and lively satire aimed explicitly at the early days of the Nazi era (and implicitly at totalitarian militaristic regimes in general), adapted from Andersen's tale of *The Emperor's New Clothes*. *Ten'* (*The Shadow*), in which a man's shadow acquires a life of its own and sets out to try to destroy its master, is another of Shvarts's adaptations of Andersen, although the latter's story of the same title has the opposite ending (Andersen's Shadow wins and has its former master, the Scholar, beheaded: Shvarts's Shadow loses and has to disappear to save himself). *Drakon* (*The Dragon*), the tale of the rescue of a whole community labouring under the oppressive totalitarian rule of a dragon, was staged by the Comedy Theatre in Moscow in 1944, was immediately banned and revived only in 1962. *Obyknovennoe chudo* [An Ordinary Miracle], a rather sentimental fairy tale play, reverses the idea of the person bewitched into an animal. Here we have an animal (in this case a bear) turned into a handsome young prince, who will reluctantly revert to being a bear if kissed by a princess. This leads to all kinds of romantic complications before the dilemma is resolved.

There are certain features common to Shvarts's fairy tales, which are also to be found in the realistic plays. They demonstrate the classic struggle between good and evil, but Shvarts has his own (somewhat Soviet, but also personally characteristic) slant on the features displayed by each side. The side of "Good" is usually represented by people who build, or work, while those on the side of "Evil" frequently show themselves to be either destructive, or lazy; those on the side of "Good" work together as a team, often winning over, and obtaining help from those on the fringes of "Evil", whereas those at the heart of the "Evil" side are selfish, and mistrust and alienate even their own supporters.

A feature peculiar to Shvarts is his "fairy-tale logic" – the development of a fairy-tale cliché or theme to a technically logical, but sometimes unexpected, conclusion (such as the complaint of the maker of "hats of invisibility" that he never sees how well his creations suit the wearer). A classic illustration of this drives the climax of *The Shadow*: the defeat of the Shadow occurs because, when the hero is beheaded, the Shadow also (quite logically) loses his own head. His allies then have to have the real man restored with the Water of Life in order to restore the Shadow, although the latter's power is broken. Many of his plays contain a strong female character, often a lively young heroine – note his choice of such fairy tales as Little Red Riding Hood, Cinderella, and the Snow Queen for adaptation. His heroines in these plays are, if anything, even more vital and dynamic than their originals – his Cinderella, for example, does not sit and cry in the ashes, but cheers up and gets on with her work. The character of the dynamic heroine Annunziata (unknown to Hans Christian Andersen), the driving force behind the otherwise passive hero of *The Shadow*, and the very lively daughter of the king in *The Naked King* demonstrate his preference for a certain type of character. Only El'sa, from *The Dragon*, is a more passive type, and at least she has the excuse of carrying 400 years of oppression in her cultural baggage. Shvarts's plays also demonstrate a "third age of woman" – the mother. From Marfa Vasil'eva in *Odna noch'* (making her way through enemy lines into besieged Leningrad looking for her under-age son who has run away to join the army) to Vasilisa-rabotnitsa in *Dva klena* (*The Two Maples*) (seeking her two runaway sons to save them from *baba-yaga*), and even the occasional inescapable mothers in the realistic school and pioneer plays of the 1930s, they are strong, kind, hard-working, and wise.

Shvarts's plays were always well received by his immediate circle and usually by anyone else permitted to see them who did not have a Stalinist political or pedagogical axe to grind. Unfortunately, during his lifetime, most of those on whom the fortunes of his work depended fell into the latter category.

AMANDA METCALF

The Dragon

Drakon

Play, 1944

The Dragon, arguably Shvarts's best play, was written in 1943 and premiered in 1944 in Dushanbe, the capital city of Tadzhikistan, by the Leningrad Comedy Theatre, temporarily in residence there as a result of the blockade of their home city. The director was Nikolai Akimov. It was first presented in Moscow in the same year and although, according to Akimov, Glavrepertkom (effectively the Party censorship committee for the theatre) had initially raised no objections, "a certain super-alert high-up of the time saw something in the play that was completely absent from it". Consequently it was immediately banned from Soviet repertory. It was briefly revived in 1962 and scheduled for production again in 1968. However the events in Prague in the August of that year rehardened the Party line and the play, although produced outside the USSR, remained largely unknown to Russian theatre-goers until the post-glasnost period. It is now well known all over the world. A musical version composed by Efim Adler with libretto by N. Orlova and Iu. Riashentsev was published in Moscow in 1985.

Like most of Shvarts's work, the play is based on an existing legend or folk-tale, in this case that of St George and the Dragon, but without any immediately obvious religious significance. Typically Shvarts's hero is the unsaintly, mild-mannered, unassuming, slightly world-weary, very human Lancelot, coolly blasé about his profession of hero and monster-slayer. On his arrival in an unnamed town at the opening of the play he is told about the dragon by a somewhat cynical and worldly-wise cat; the latter finds it particularly depressing that the town's citizens, forced to make an annual sacrifice of a young maiden to the dragon who rules their lives, accept this with almost cheerful resignation. The conversation takes place in the house of Charlemagne, Keeper of the Town Archives, whose daughter, El'za, is due to be handed over to the dragon on the following day. Charlemagne tells Lancelot that the dragon has lived in the area for the past 400 years and has, in fact, occasionally been quite helpful, using his fiery breath to boil water at the time of a cholera epidemic and saving the town from "the horrible gypsies". The dragon itself appears in the unlikely temporary shape of a slightly deaf middle-aged man. He is about to kill Lancelot on the spot, but Charlemagne reminds him of the contract he signed 382 years ago that prevents him so doing. The town Mayor, who appears to be mentally unstable, tries to dissuade Lancelot from his dragon-slaying mission, since he believes a live dragon is preferable to the chaos that may well ensue if it is slain. Indeed, all the characters seem to resent the hero's intrusion into the regular routine that has been established over the years.

The Mayor reluctantly gives Lancelot his "weapons": a barber's bowl for his helmet, a tin tray for his shield, a piece of paper to certify that his lance is under repair. Three "drovers" give him a magic carpet, a hat to make him invisible and a self-playing musical instrument, seemingly symbolic of the power of art to work miracles. The fight then begins in the sky above the town. Henry, the Mayor's son, a scheming and ambitious young man, gives a commentary. He reports that the dragon is winning, although a small child can see otherwise. The dragon is slain, his three heads falling to earth one after the other. Lancelot is so exhausted by the combat that he seems likely to die.

In Act III the Mayor, claiming to have slain the dragon himself, has become president, aided and abetted by Henry. The citizens readily accept the changed situation, although there are signs of some underground resistance to it. The Mayor deals ruthlessly with any possible opposition and plans to marry El'za himself. The wedding ceremony begins. El'za, unwilling to go through with it, appeals to the townsfolk to wake up to the reality of the situation, but in vain. Lancelot, miraculously recovered from his ordeal, makes a dramatic entrance, rebukes the citizens for their time-serving hypocrisy and orders the Mayor and Henry to be thrown into jail.

On the play's first appearance during World War II it was seen primarily as a satirical attack on Hitler's Germany. Tsimbal, in *Evgenii Shvarts* (Leningrad, 1961), described it as "a lampoon of the fascist state of Hitler's beastly philosophy of war and destruction, the base and blinkered apathy that turned its back on Hitler as he rose to power". But this is a simplistic interpretation. It is true that there are elements easily connected with Nazi Germany: the anti-gypsy prejudice (anti-Semitism), Henry as Goebbels telling lies about the way the war is going, the underground resistance movement. But *The Dragon* has deeper implications and is relevant for Stalin and Khrushchev's Russia, even for Thatcher's Britain, indeed for any political system anywhere, right- or left-wing, since it focuses on the basic human tendency to become passively compliant under persuasion. It might even be argued that, in its comparatively light-hearted way, it relates to the question raised by Dostoevskii in "The Legend of the Grand Inquisitor" in *The Brothers Karamazov*: how do human beings reconcile their need for security with their need for individual freedom? In *The Dragon* the citizens "learn to live" with their dragon, and when it is killed they are all too ready to create another one, however unlikely their material. The Mayor and Henry take full advantage of this, aware that ordinary people seem to need a "Big Brother" however unpleasant he might be. Lancelot tells El'za at the end of the play: "We cannot leave. There's still a little job to do. Worse than needlework. The dragon in each of them has to be killed." The Gardener reminds him that he will need to be patient. People are like plants: they have to be treated gently and not have their roots damaged.

This ending might be seen as sentimentally optimistic and therefore unconvincing, but it reflects the generally positive view of life that Shvarts managed to retain in spite of the stress and strain of his career as a writer in Stalin's Russia. And the universal theme of *The Dragon* should ensure that it remains permanently in world repertory.

John Goodliffe

Simeon Polotskii *see* Polotskii

Konstantin Mikhailovich Simonov 1915–1979

Prose writer and poet

Biography

Born in Petrograd, 28 November 1915. Father served in the tsarist army. Worked as a lathe operator until 1935. First poem published in 1934. Attended Gor'kii Literary Institute, Moscow, 1934–38. First collection of stories published in 1938. Witnessed the Battle of Khalkin-Gol against the Japanese, summer 1939. Worked for the army newspaper *Geroicheskaia krasnoarmeiskaia* in Mongolia; war correspondent for *Krasnaia zvezda*, 1941–45. Wrote war poems, the most famous of which was "Zhdi menia" [Wait for Me]. Reported a large part of the Battle of Stalingrad. Deputy general secretary of the Writers' Union, 1946–54, and Secretary from 1967. Editor-in-chief of *Novyi mir*, 1946–50, and 1954–58. Corresponding member of Central Committee of the Communist Party, 1952–56. *Zhivye i mertvye* (*The Living and the Dead*) published in 1959. Supported the publication of Solzhenitsyn's work; however, his signed letter was published in *Pravda* (31 August 1973) condemning Solzhenitsyn. Recipient: Stalin Prize in 1941, 1942, 1943–44, 1946, 1948, 1949; Order of the Red Banner; Order of the Fatherland (twice); Military Cross of Czechoslovakia. Died in Moscow, 28 August 1979.

Publications

Collected Editions

Rasskazy. Moscow, 1946.

Stikhi. P'esy. Rasskazy. Leningrad, 1949.

Sobranie sochinenii, 6 vols. Moscow, 1966–70.

Sobranie sochinenii, 11 vols [10+1]. Moscow, 1979–85.

Fiction

Russkie liudi. 1942; translated as *The Russians*, by A. Zeltser, Southport, "A to Z" Publishers, 1943.

Stalingrad Fights On, translated by D.L. Fromberg. Moscow, Foreign Languages Publishing House, 1942.

Dni i nochi. 1944; translated as *Days and Nights*, by J. Fineberg, London, Hutchinson, 1945; and by John Barnes, New York, Simon and Schuster, 1945.

"Tovarishchi po oruzhiiu" [Comrades to Arms], *Novyi mir*, 10–12 (1952), 9–121; 43–182; 28–138.

Zhivye i mertvye. 1959; translated as *The Living and the Dead*, by R. Ainsztein, New York, Doubleday, 1962; retitled as *Victims and Heroes*, London, Hutchinson, 1963; also translated as *The Living and the Dead*, by Alex Miller, Moscow, Progress, 1975.

"Soldatami ne rozhdaiutsia" [Soldiers Are Made, Not Born], *Znamia*, 8–11 (1963), 13–69; 3–71; 3–64; 3–44; 1–5 (1964), 3–52; 3–57; 13–67; 20–59; 79–122.

Ot Khalkhingola do Berlina [From Khalkin-Gol to Berlin]. Moscow, 1973.

Dvadtsat' dnei bez voiny. Iz zapisok Lopatina [Twenty Days Without War. From Lopatin's Notes]. Moscow, 1973.

Poetry

Stikhotvoreniia i poemy. Moscow, 1945.

Voennaia lirika. 1936–1956 [Lyric War Poetry]. Moscow, 1968.

Essays, Memoirs, Letters, and Travel Writing

On the Petsamo Road. Notes of a War Correspondent [no translator named]. Moscow, Foreign Language Publishing House, 1942.

Ostaius' zhurnalistom. Putevye ocherki, zametki, reportazhi, pis'ma, 1958–1967 [I Remain a Journalist. Travel Sketches, Notes, Reports, Letters]. Moscow, 1968.

Daleko na vostoke. Khalkhin-gol'skie zapisi [It's a Long Way to the East]. Moscow, 1969.

Razgovor s tovarishchami. Vospominaniia, stat'i, literaturnye zametki, o sobstvennoi rabote [A Conversation with Comrades. Memoirs, Articles, Literary Criticism, On My Own Work]. Moscow, 1970.

Raznye dni voiny: Dnevnik pisatelia [Various Days in the Wartime Diary of a Writer]. Moscow, 1977.

Glazami cheloveka moego pokoleniia, razmyshleniia o I.V. Staline [Through the Eyes of a Man of My Generation, Thoughts on I.V. Stalin]. Moscow, 1990.

Critical Studies

Dramaturgiia K. Simonova, by L. Lazarev, Moscow, 1952.

Konstantin Simonov, ocherk tvorchestva, by I. Vishnevskaia, Moscow, 1966.

Tvorchestvo Konstantina Simonova, by S.Ia. Fradkina, Moscow, 1968.

Voennaia proza Konstantina Simonova, by L. Lazarev, Moscow, 1974.

Vremia ne vlastno. Pistaeli na fronte, by D. Ortenberg, Moscow, 1975.

Konstantin Simonov, tvorcheskii put', by L. Fink, Moscow, 1979.

Written with the Bayonet: Soviet Russian Poetry of World War Two, by Katharine Hodgson, Liverpool, Liverpool University Press, 1996.

Bibliography

K.M. Simonov bibliograficheskii ukazatel', by D.A. Berman and B.M. Tolochinskaia, Moscow, 1985.

Konstantin Simonov was one of a number of writers who successfully combined a career as a writer and as an influential member of the Soviet literary establishment. Although he wrote on a wide range of themes both before and after the period 1941–45, Simonov is best known as a war writer and poet. The atmosphere of the 1930s, when Simonov made his literary debut, was undoubtedly a formative influence. Germany had already begun to cast off the clauses of the Treaty of Versailles. By the end of the decade Nazis and communists were embroiled in the Spanish Civil War. In the Far East an expansionist Japan posed a clear threat to Soviet interests. A series of military crises seemed to be moving inexorably towards resolution.

As a war correspondent Simonov witnessed the Japanese

defeat, which was planned and executed by Zhukov at the Battle of Khalkin-Gol in 1939. Zhukov's performance against the Japanese created quite a different impression of Soviet military competence from the debacle of the winter war against Finland. Simonov's fictional characters are often participants in the Khalkin-Gol campaign, the author's vote of confidence in their military abilities.

Simonov was a prolific and versatile writer whose work extended well beyond regular pieces for *Krasnaia zvezda* and *Pravda*. One of the avowed aims of Soviet war-time literature in all its forms was to fan the flames of Russian patriotism. To this end poetry proved to be a powerful medium, and Simonov's poems, such as "Zhdi menia" [Wait for Me] (1941), "Rodina" [Motherland] (1941), "Ubei ego" [Kill Him] (1942), "Bezymiannoe pole" [An Anonymous Field] (1942), are some of the best exemplars of the genre. Much of the poetry of the period lacks technical virtuosity, but this is more than compensated for by the author's evident sincerity. War-time poetry in the Soviet Union was the spontaneous outpouring of a nation's terrible grief and suffering. Simonov's popularity as a war-time poet stems from his relative indifference to politics, a quality shared to a lesser extent by Ol'ga Berggol'ts and Vera Inber. Printed literally in millions, "Zhdi menia" can stake a claim to being the most famous poem of the war. Simonov's themes – essentially apolitical – are home, work, rest, and the bonds of love. Repeated like a liturgical chant, the title expresses an almost mystical faith in the power of hope.

Hope matured into something more tangible as the German attempt to seize Stalingrad faltered in the late summer of 1942. Simonov covered the Soviet operation from start to finish, and *Dni i nochi* (*Days and Nights*) is one of a number of Soviet works dedicated to this all-important victory. By the standards of war-time writing Simonov's style is restrained, the realism gritty, and the novel comes across well in translation. The success of the Soviet counter-attack that was launched in November 1942 depended on the defenders holding the Germans. *Days and Nights* looks to this defensive phase, and tries to explain the tenacity with which the Russians resisted the German onslaught. Numerous participants in the battle – among them Grossman, Nekrasov, and Zaitsev – have stressed the simple and stark fact that the Volga marked the beginning of Asia; that the final reckoning with the Germans could be delayed no longer. The reflections of Simonov's hero, Saburov, on the Russianness of the Volga are convincing, even moving. Implicit in Saburov's thoughts is the question of why the Germans were allowed to get as far as they did in the first place.

With the war against Hitler won, the Soviet Union rejected further co-operation with its former western allies. Anti-western propaganda was stepped up. The importance of ideology was reasserted. Andrei Zhdanov, Stalin's Commissar of Culture, initiated a systematic purge of Soviet intellectual life that lasted until Stalin's death in 1953. Simonov's play, *Russkii vopros* [The Russian Question], is a typical propagandist piece of the time. Published in December 1946, the play sets out to show that the American press is no more than a compliant tool of the government, that the west is responsible for the Cold War. After Stalin's death, attempts were made to build bridges with the west. Well known in left-wing, western intellectual circles, Simonov, along with Il'ia Erenburg and Aleksandr Fadeev, played an active role in efforts to influence western politicians and to win support for Soviet foreign policy initiatives.

Present at some of the crucial battles on the Eastern front, and a competent exponent in various genres, Simonov was undoubtedly one of the Soviet Union's leading war writers. But Simonov's writing in the post-war era remains disappointing. One feels that he was never able to realize his considerable potential. There are moments when this undeniable talent is on display. True, his fiction becomes progressively more critical and revealing of certain Soviet aspects of the war *Zhivye i mertvye* (*The Living and the Dead*) and *Soldatami ne rozhdaiutsia* [Soldiers Are Made, Not Born] are good examples. Unlike, however, the newer writers who were being published from the mid-1950s onwards – Baklanov, Bykov, Nekrasov, and Bondarev – the artist in Simonov always seems to take second place to the aspiring, literary bureaucrat. Simonov's well-crafted war story will never attain even flawed greatness, since one foot remains firmly on the ground, and a watchful eye is always glancing over his shoulder.

Simonov's memoirs, which were published in *Znamia* (1988) at the height of glasnost, lend support to this assessment of his writing. They provide a large amount of detail concerning the workings of the Soviet literary machine, especially the extraordinary extent to which Stalin personally involved himself in literary matters. For instance, Simonov reveals that his story *Dym otechestva* [Smoke of the Fatherland] was given a favourable review by a cultural official of the Central Committee. Stalin, however, decided the book was bad. The favourable review was withdrawn, a hostile one was duly written. With their many fascinating and bizarre insights into the Soviet establishment, the memoirs show the author to be an accomplished survivor. Simonov was acutely sensitive to what was required by his political masters, and skilfully weathered several changes in the Soviet leadership. By the time of his death in 1979 he was something of an official elder statesman in Soviet letters.

FRANK ELLIS

The Living and the Dead

Zhivye i mertvye

Novel, 1959

Although it lacks the pace and harsher realism of Grigorii Baklanov's *Iul' 1941* [July 1941], *The Living and the Dead* is a thoroughly readable account of Russia's desperate struggle for survival in the summer of 1941. Simonov's narrative carefully records the landmark dates in the first few months of the war: 22 June 1941 (the day of the invasion); 3 July 1941 (Stalin's radio address to the people); 16 October 1941 (the panic in the Moscow area); and 7 November 1941 (Stalin's address on Red Square). While these details enhance the illusion that what we are being offered is faction – to use a modern term – rather than pure fiction, they also draw attention to various lacunae in the narrative. There is, for example, no mention of the notorious TASS communiqué, promulgated on 13 June 1941, in which rumours of war were flatly denied. Thus, the false assumptions and wishful thinking stemming from the Ribbentrop-Molotov Pact, as well as the pact itself, are simply ignored by Simonov. As a result, there is no serious discussion as to why Germany has attacked the Soviet Union.

Simonov offers various technical reasons for Soviet failure: lack of sub-machine-guns; insufficient numbers of the latest tanks and aircraft; and the tactical advantage of surprise enjoyed by the Germans. The question of why the Germans achieved tactical surprise, a consequence of the Soviet-German pact, is studiously ignored. Then there was the evident failure of Soviet pre-war propaganda. One of the novel's heroes recalls reading an account of a fictional Russo-German war that was won by the Soviet side within three days. No title or author is given, but it is highly likely that the book in question is Nikolai Shpanov's *Pervyi udar, povest' o predstoiashchei voiny* [The First Blow, The Story of the Forthcoming War] (1939). The irony of the book is that the techniques supposedly used by the Soviet armed forces to rout their enemy – skilful use of airborne troops, effective bombing and use of armour – were the very techniques used to crush the Russians. Soldiers who during the 1930s had been sold the idea of Soviet invincibility now had to come to terms with the brutal realities of the Wehrmacht's Blitzkrieg. In the air war, Stalin's falcons, the 1930s heroes of Soviet aviation, are painfully outmatched by the Luftwaffe.

On another level *The Living and the Dead* may be seen as a Soviet Bildungsroman. The two main characters, the junior political instructor Sintsov and the infantry general, Serpilin, undergo a series of trials, not all of which are directly related to the German invasion. Like many of his senior commanders, Sintsov is on leave when news of the invasion reaches him, a telling point from Simonov on the readiness of the Soviet army. In the ensuing chaos Sintsov attempts to reach his unit. Along the way he observes a miscellany of incidents that illuminate the collapse of the Red Army. Two quite different struggles are being waged simultaneously: one by a disorganized and demoralized Russia against the German invader; a second internal one against the many idiocies of the Party, variously represented by the NKVD and zealous commissars.

Symptomatic of this latter struggle are the constant demands for proof of identity. Carrying identity documents could result in summary execution in the event of capture, especially if the holder was a party member or commissar. Since capture was likely as whole armies were outflanked and encircled, it made sense either to destroy or to hide documents. Mindful perhaps of the purges, the Party regarded such precautions as treachery, the prelude to desertion. Thus, the ability to produce these documents on demand was more important as a test of loyalty to the system than a standard article of military discipline.

Sintsov's ordeal begins with the loss of these documents. Unbeknown to him a comrade has removed them while he was concussed, as well his badges of rank. Having broken through the ring of German encirclement, Sintsov must now convince a sequence of petty officials that he is no deserter, but a loyal soldier. So powerful is the fear of not having documents that a fellow officer wants nothing to do with him. This is a legacy of the purges. Moreover, Sintsov's dogged determination to defend Moscow stands in stark contrast to the shameful flight of Party officials who flee the city as the Germans advance. After a seemingly endless series of grotesque bureaucratic indignities, Sintsov joins a militia battalion. By chance his story is corroborated and he rejoins the ranks of the living, as it were.

With Serpilin the conflict between military common sense and Party bureaucracy stems from the purges. Arrested for over-emphasizing the strength of German military power – now painfully evident – he survives the camps. As with so many former prisoners, Serpilin refuses to blame Soviet power for his arrest, seeing it as an "absurdity". This bizarre justification of a period in which millions perished appears utterly baffling. However such psychology is not peculiar to Simonov. Soviet fiction contains enough examples of those who believed the Party had made a mistake, or that Stalin did not know what was going on.

Serpilin's military professionalism enables him to bring his unit through the German cordon. With more generals like Serpilin, Simonov suggests, the Germans would not be having things all their own way. Other officers do not measure up to these standards. During the retreat a colonel Baranov, dressed in a private's uniform, is brought before Serpilin. The change in uniform points to an attempt to blend in among the mass of disorganized soldiers, to shirk the responsibilities of leadership. This is the same Baranov who denounced Serpilin in 1937. Once again the link between the purges and military disaster is made: the careerist who mouths the latest slogan and denounces his fellow officers in 1937 cannot be trusted in battle in 1941. Serpilin sums up this type well: "No faith, no honour, no conscience".

As the military situation at the front stabilizes in the winter campaign of 1941, so the personal fortunes of Sintsov and Serpilin improve. The coincidence is symbolic. The German defeat before Moscow not only marks the beginning of the long road to military victory, but the end of the corrosive self-doubt and fear engendered by the purges of the 1930s. A line has been drawn under the past, or so it would seem.

FRANK ELLIS

Andrei Donatovich Siniavskii 1925–1997

Prose writer, essayist, and critic

Biography

Born in Moscow, 8 October 1925. Wrote much of his fiction and criticism as Abram Terts [Tertz]. Attended Moscow University; graduated in 1949, candidate of philological sciences, 1952. Served in the Soviet Army. Married: Mariia Rozanova-Kruglikova; one son. Junior, then senior, research fellow, Gor'kii Literary Institute, Moscow, until 1965; lecturer in Russian literature, Moscow University, until 1960; lecturer at the Theatre Studio of the Moscow Arts Theatre, until 1965. Arrested for alleged anti-Soviet writings, with Iulii Daniel', September 1965, sentenced to seven years' hard labour, 1966; released from prison, 1971. Permitted to emigrate to France, 1973. Active co-editor of the journal and the publishing house *Sintaksis* (founded by Mariia Rozanova). Assistant Professor, then Professor of Slavic Studies, the Sorbonne, Paris, from 1973 until his retirement in 1994. Russian citizenship restored in 1990. Died in Paris, 25 February 1997.

Publications

Collected Editions

The Trial Begins and On Socialist Realism, translated by Max Hayward and George Dennis. New York, Vintage, 1965.

Fantasticheskii mir Abrama Tertsa. New York, Inter-Language Literary Associates, 1967.

Abram Terts/Andrei Siniavskii, *Sobranie sochinenii*, 2 vols. Moscow, 1992.

Fiction

"Sud idet", *Kultura* (Paris), 1960; translated as *The Trial Begins*, by Max Hayward, New York, Pantheon, and London, Collins and Harvill, 1960; London, Fontana, 1977.

Fantasticheskie povesti. Paris, Instytut Literacki, 1961; translated as *Fantastic Stories*, by Max Hayward and Ronald Hingley, New York, Pantheon, 1963; reprinted Evanston, Illinois, Northwestern University Press, 1986; also translated as *The Icicle, and Other Stories*, London, Collins and Harvill, 1963.

Liubimov; in Polish as *Lubimow*, Paris, Instytut Literacki, 1963; in Russian, Washington, DC, Filipoff, 1964; translated as *The Makepeace Experiment*, by Manya Harari, New York, Pantheon, and London, Collins and Harvill, 1965; London, Fontana, 1977; reprinted Evanston, Illinois, Northwestern University Press, 1989.

"Pkhentz", translated by Jeremy Biddulph, in *Soviet Short Stories: Volume 2*, edited by Peter Reddaway. Harmondsworth, Penguin, 1968.

Kroshka Tsores. Paris, Sintaksis, 1980; translated as *Little Jinx*, by Larry P. Joseph and Rachel May, Evanston, Illinois, Northwestern University Press, 1992; London, Quartet, 1993.

Spokoinoi nochi. Paris, Sintaksis, 1984; translated as *Goodnight!*, by Richard Lourie, New York, Penguin, 1989; London, Viking, 1990; Harmondsworth, Penguin, 1991.

Literary Criticism, Essays, and Letters

"Chto takoe sotsialisticheskii realizm?", *L'Esprit* (February 1959); translated as *On Socialist Realism*, by George Dennis, New York, Pantheon, 1961; Paris, Sintaksis, 1988.

"Poeziia Pasternaka", in *Stikhotvoreniia i poemy*, by Boris Pasternak. Moscow and Leningrad, 1965; translated as "Boris Pasternak", in *Pasternak, Modern Judgements*, edited by Donald Davie and Angela Livingstone, London, Macmillan, 1969; also translated by Laszlo Tikos and Murray Peppard, in *For Freedom of Imagination*, New York, Holt Rinehart and Winston, 1971; and as "Pasternak's Poetry", in *Pasternak: A Collection of Critical Essays*, edited by Victor Erlich, Englewood Cliffs, New Jersey, Prentice-Hall, 1978.

Mysli vrasplokh. New York, Rausen, 1966; translated as "Thought Unaware", *New Leader* (19 July 1965); also as *Unguarded Thoughts*, by Manya Harari, London, Collins Harvill, 1972.

For Freedom of Imagination, translated by Laszlo Tikos and Murray Peppard. New York, Holt Rinehart and Winston, 1971.

Golos iz khora. London, Stenvalley, 1973; translated as *A Voice from the Chorus*, by Kyril FitzLyon and Max Hayward, New York, Farrar Straus and Giroux, and London, Collins Harvill, 1976; reprinted New Haven, Yale University Press, 1995.

"Literaturnyi protsess v Rossii", *Kontinent*, 1 (1974); translated as "The Literary Process in Russia", by Michael Glenny, in *Kontinent*, New York, Doubleday, 1976.

Progulki s Pushkinym. London, Overseas Publications Interchange, 1975; translated as *Strolls with Pushkin*, by Catharine Theimer Nepomnyashchy and Slava I. Yastremski, New Haven, Yale University Press, 1993.

V teni Gogolia [In the Shadow of Gogol']. London, Overseas Publications Interchange, 1975; reprinted Paris, Sintaksis, 1981.

"Opavshie list'ia" V.V. Rozanova [V.V. Rozanov's Fallen Leaves]. Paris, Sintaksis, 1982; excerpts translated as "Rozanov", in *Ideology in Russian Literature*, edited by Richard Freeborn and Jane Grayson, London, Macmillan, and New York, St Martin's Press, 1990.

Osnovy sovetskoi tsivilizatsii; in French as *La Civilisation soviétique*, Paris, Albin Michel, 1989; as *Soviet Civilization: A Cultural History*, translated by Joanne Turnbull, New York, Arcade, 1990.

The Russian Intelligentsia, translated by Lynn Visson, New York, Columbia University Press, 1997.

Biography

Pikasso [Picasso], with I.N. Golomshtok. Moscow, 1960.

Critical Studies

"Abram Tertz's Ordeal by Mirror", by Andrew Field, in Siniavskii's *Mysli vrasplokh*, New York, Rausen, 1966, 7–42.

On Trial: The Case of Sinyavsky (Tertz) and Daniel (Arzhak),

edited by Leopold Labedz and Max Hayward, New York, Harper, and London, Collins and Harvill, 1967; revised edition, Westport, Connecticut, Greenwood Press, 1980.
Russian Themes, by Mikhailo Mikhailov, New York, Farrar Straus and Giroux, 1968.
"The Art of Andrei Sinyavsky", by Deming Brown, *Slavic Review*, 29/4 (1970), 662–81; reprinted in *Major Soviet Writers: Essays in Criticism*, edited by Edward J. Brown, London, Oxford University Press, 1973; and in *Soviet Russian Literature since Stalin*, by Deming Brown, Cambridge, Cambridge University Press, 1978.
"Sinyavsky in Two Worlds: Two Brothers Named Chénier", by Richard Pevear, *Hudson Review*, 25 (1972), 375–402.
Andrei Siniavskii and Julii Daniel', Two Soviet "Heretical" Writers, by Margaret Dalton, Würzburg, Jal, 1973.
"Andrei Siniavskii: The Chorus and the Critic", by Walter F. Kolonosky, *Canadian-American Slavic Studies*, 9 (1975), 352–60.
"The Sense of Purpose and Socialist Realism in Tertz's *The Trial Begins*", by W.J. Leatherbarrow, *Forum for Modern Language Studies*, 11 (1975), 268–79.
Letters to the Future: An Approach to Sinyavsky-Tertz, by Richard Lourie, Ithaca, Cornell University Press, 1975.
"The Bible and the Zoo in Andrey Sinyavsky's *The Trial Begins*", by Richard L. Chapple, *Orbis Litterarum*, 33 (1978), 349–58.
"Narrator, Metaphor and Theme in Sinjavskij's *Fantastic Tales*", by Andrew R. Durkin, *Slavic and East European Journal*, 24 (1980), 133–44.
Sovremennaia russkaia proza, by Aleksandr Genis and Petr Vail', Ann Arbor, Hermitage, 1982.
"Inherent and Ulterior Design in Sinjavskij's 'Pxenc'", by Walter F. Kolonosky, *Slavic and East European Journal*, 26 (1982), 329–37.
"Andrei Sinyavsky's 'You and I': A Modern Day Fantastic Tale", by Catharine Theimer Nepomnyashchy, *Ulbandus Review*, 2/2 (1982), 209–30.
Writers in Russia, 1917–1978, by Max Hayward, London, Harvill Press, and San Diego, Harcourt Brace Jovanovich, 1983.
"The Writer as Alien in Sinjavskij's 'Pkhenc'", by Ronald E. Peterson, *Wiener Slawistischer Almanach*, 12 (1983), 47–53.
The Third Wave: Russian Literature in Emigration, edited by Olga Matich and Michael Henry Heim, Ann Arbor, Ardis, 1984.
"Conflicting Imperatives in the Model of the Russian Writer: The Case of Tertz/Sinyavsky", by Donald Fanger, in *Literature and History: Theoretical Problems and Russian Case Studies*, edited by Gary Saul Morson, Stanford, Stanford University Press, 1986, 111–24.
"Spokojnoj noci: Andrej Sinjavskij's Rebirth as Abram Terc", by Olga Matich, *Slavic and East European Journal*, 33/1 (1989), 50–63.
"Literary Selves: The Tertz-Sinyavsky Dialogue", by Andrew J. Nussbaum, in *Autobiographical Statements in Twentieth-Century Russian Literature*, edited by Jane Gary Harris, Princeton, Princeton University Press, 1990, 238–59.
"The Triumph of Abram Tertz", by Joseph Frank, *New York Review of Books* (27 June 1991), 35–43.
"The Transfiguring of Context in the Work of Abram Terts", by Beth C. Holmgren, *Slavic Review*, 50/4 (1991), 965–77.
"Siniavskii's Alternative Autobiography: *A Voice from the Chorus*", by Marcus C. Levitt, *Canadian Slavonic Papers*, 33/1 (1991), 46–61.
"Sex, Death and Nation in the *Strolls with Pushkin* Controversy", by Stephanie Sandler, *Slavic Review*, 51 (1992), 294–308.
Russian Experimental Fiction: Resisting Ideology after Utopia, by Edith W. Clowes, Princeton, Princeton University Press, 1993.
"At the Circus with Olesha and Siniavskii", by Neil Cornwell, *Slavonic and East European Review*, 71 (1993), 1–13.
Abram Tertz and the Poetics of Crime, by Catharine Theimer Nepomnyashchy, New Haven and London, Yale University Press, 1995.

For some four decades Andrei Siniavskii pursued two separate, but complementary writing careers – one under his own name and the other under the pseudonym Abram Terts. Beginning in 1950 and up until his arrest in 1965, Siniavskii published literary scholarship and criticism openly in his homeland. Early recognized as a promising young literary scholar, he came into his own during the Khrushchev Thaw. In the late 1950s and early 1960s, Siniavskii participated in the three-volume *History of Soviet Literature* put out by the Academy of Sciences, published articles in the most important journal of the period, *Novyi mir*, and co-authored books on early Soviet poetry and on Picasso. He also wrote a substantive introduction to the first volume of Pasternak's poetry to be published in the USSR after the appearance of *Doctor Zhivago* in the west.

At the same time as he established a reputation as a liberal voice in Soviet letters, Siniavskii embarked on a clandestine parallel literary course. In 1956, he began to have works he did not believe could pass the Soviet censorship smuggled abroad for publication in the west. The first of these works to appear, *Chto takoe sotsialisticheskii realizm?* (*On Socialist Realism*), was published in French translation in the journal *L'Esprit* in February 1959. A second work, the novel *Sud idet* (*The Trial Begins*) was published in Paris in Polish translation. Russian editions and English translations of both works soon appeared, attributed to "Abram Terts". The essay, which remains Siniavskii's best-known work, constitutes a literary manifesto for the writings of Terts. Deploying the device of irony to discredit the basic premises of socialist realism, in the concluding paragraphs of the essay Siniavskii calls for "a phantasmagoric art with hypotheses instead of a purpose, and grotesque in place of realistic descriptions of everyday life". *The Trial Begins* recasts the central arguments made in the essay in fictional form, serving as an illustration of this "phantasmagoric art", which the writer later termed alternatively "fantastic realism" and "exaggerated prose". In succeeding years, the first two works were followed by six "fantastic tales", a novel entitled *Liubimov* (translated into English as *The Makepeace Experiment*), and a collection of aphorisms, *Mysli vrasplokh* (*Unguarded Thoughts*). Terts's other early fiction, like *The Trial Begins*, seeks, as Siniavskii put it in *On Socialist Realism*, "to be truthful with the help of absurd fantasy". On a superficial level, these works, which hark back to Gogol' and to the ornamental prose of the 1920s, may be read as political satire. Yet, in a deeper sense, the concerns Siniavskii broaches from the very beginning in his works published as Terts are quintessentially literary: the relationship between representation and reality, the nature of meaning, the recasting of self into text. As Siniavskii later remarked, his differences with the Soviet literary establishment were above all "stylistic".

The appearance of the Terts works created a sensation in western literary circles. The author's anonymity gave rise to speculation about his true identity. While some commentators maintained that the Terts pseudonym must mask an already well-known writer of the older generation, the majority accepted the assumption that Terts represented a new, probably younger voice in Soviet literature and thus stood as evidence that a potentially vibrant literary culture was re-emerging in Russia after the bleak years of Stalinism.

The Soviet authorities' attempts to decipher Terts's true identity were less academic. In October 1965, Siniavskii was arrested along with the writer Iulii Daniel', who, with Siniavskii's help, had also published works abroad under the pseudonym Nikolai Arzhak. The two writers were placed on trial in February 1966 and condemned to hard labour for having engaged in "anti-Soviet propaganda". While Siniavskii's and Daniel''s respective seven- and five-year sentences were certainly a foregone conclusion, the defendants' refusal to plead guilty to the charges against them marked a radical departure from the show trials of the Stalin years. The case of Siniavskii and Daniel' became a *cause célèbre* in the west and a rallying point for the incipient dissident movement in the USSR. Characteristically, however, during his questioning and in his closing words to the court, Siniavskii tried to draw a distinction between political opposition and literary experimentation: "In my unpublished story 'Pkhents' there is a sentence I consider autobiographical: 'You think that if I am simply different, you must immediately curse me ...' So there it is: I am different. But I do not regard myself as an enemy, and my works are not hostile works." While challenging the Soviet hegemony over culture by trying to remove literature from the realm of politics, Siniavskii, in his concluding statement, distinguished between the language of literature and the language of the law: "You, jurists, deal with terms which, the narrower they are, the more precise. In contrast to the term, the meaning of the artistic image is more precise the broader it is." Siniavskii thus implicitly enunciated what is perhaps the fundamental underlying principle of his later Terts writings: the liberation of the reader from the tyranny of authorship and the text.

Siniavskii continued to write during his years of incarceration in various labour camps in the Dubrovlag system in Mordovia. While imprisoned, he wrote what was to become his most controversial book, *Progulki s Pushkinym* (*Strolls with Pushkin*), which he sent out in letters to his wife. He also wrote the first chapter of a book on Gogol', *V teni Gogolia* [In the Shadow of Gogol']. After his release and subsequent return to Moscow in 1971, he gathered together fragments from other prison letters to his wife to make the book *Golos iz khora* (*A Voice from the Chorus*). After his emigration to France in 1973, all three books were published in the west under the Terts pseudonym. During the years he has spent in emigration, Siniavskii has also published articles, a novella entitled *Kroshka Tsores* (*Little Jinx*), and the "autobiographical novel" *Spokoinoi nochi* (*Goodnight!*) under the Terts pseudonym, while at the same time signing more overtly political and conventionally scholarly articles and books, notably *Opavshie list'ia V.V. Rozanova* [V.V. Rozanov's Fallen Leaves] and *Osnovy sovetskoi tsivilizatsii* (*Soviet Civilization: A Cultural History*), with his real name. Siniavskii's continued use of the Terts pseudonym after it had lost its practical function of concealing his identity highlights the importance of the figure of Abram Terts as a metaphor for the author's conception of writing as crime. Borrowed from the legendary Jewish outlaw Abrashka Terts celebrated in a thieves' song, popular in Odessa in the 1920s, the pseudonym exemplifies the challenge to conventional linguistic and generic boundaries posed by the Terts texts.

Siniavskii remains perhaps the most controversial Russian literary figure of his generation. At first welcomed by the mainstream of the Russian emigration, publishing in early issues of the journal *Kontinent*, Siniavskii soon broke with the journal and, after 1978, published his works primarily in the journal *Sintaksis* and with the publishing house of the same name founded by Mariia Rozanova. His articles attacking chauvinistic and anti-Semitic tendencies in the emigration placed him at odds with the powerful Russophile faction headed by Aleksandr Solzhenitsyn. More sensationally, Siniavskii's playful book mocking the official canonization of Pushkin in Soviet culture, *Strolls with Pushkin*, was wrongly taken as a "Russophobic" attack on Pushkin – and, by extension, all of Russian culture – by Russian nationalists, first after its publication in the west in 1975 and again after the appearance of an excerpt in the Soviet journal *Oktiabr'* in 1989. Despite continued attacks on his political stance and despite the relative inaccessibility of the linguistically complicated writings to a mass readership, Siniavskii has been increasingly recognized both in the west and in Russia as one of the most significant Russian literary figures of the post-Stalin period.

CATHARINE THEIMER NEPOMNYASHCHY

Fantastic Stories

Fantasticheskie povesti

Short-story collection, 1961

Siniavskii's *Fantastic Stories* were written under the pseudonym of Abram Terts between 1955 and 1961, published in Paris in 1961 and in English translation in 1963. "Pkhentz", not in the original collection and not published until 1966 (also abroad and under the same pseudonym), was in fact written in 1957 and is now normally regarded as one of the series.

During the period of their composition, Siniavskii, then aged between 30 and 36, was also establishing his reputation as a leading literary critic. Like other intellectuals of the time, he was also reacting to the shock of the Thaw and Khrushchev's denunciation of Stalin in 1956. His own father, arrested on a trumped-up charge in 1951, was released from prison in 1956 but died soon afterwards. Though the *Fantastic Stories* are set in contemporary Soviet society, they are less explicitly polemical than the other two early works *The Trial Begins* (1960) and *On Socialist Realism* (1959), and they focus more on philosophical and psychological problems and on the individual's relationship with society.

In his study of socialist realism, Siniavskii wrote of the need for "a phantasmagoric art ... Such an art would correspond to the best spirit of our time." Along with *The Trial Begins*, the *Fantastic Stories* were an attempt by Siniavskii to translate this prescription into practice. Though their subject-matter ranges widely, the unifying theme is the need for each central figure to escape from the intolerable pressures of his existence. Sinoavskii's literary works formed part of the charges against him at his trial, and they contain much satire and ironical treatment of Soviet life. But this is only one dimension in a complex series of literary works. The title recalls E.T.A. Hoffmann's stories and there are other references to western literature, but their form belongs to the Soviet writing of the 1950s while their spirit lies in the questioning and doubt of 19th-century literature. Underlining this are frequent references to Chekhov, Gogol', and Dostoevskii: the latter two were particularly influential in the composition of the stories.

Though Siniavskii acknowledged only "Pkhentz" as having autobiographical reference, all the stories describe the circumstances of Moscow life that would have been familiar to him. In order of composition, the earliest is "V tsirke" ("At the Circus") 1955. The central figure, Konstantin Petrovich, acquires magical powers from a magician in a circus. These powers enable him to pick pockets with supernatural dexterity. Financed by this means, he embarks on a new and grander life. But some compulsion leads him to attempt a burglary, during which he encounters and kills the magician from whom he had acquired his powers. The magic powers disappear; Konstantin is sent to prison and is shot trying to escape. At the moment of his death he is "gripped by a feeling akin to inspiration" and strains for the "supernatural power that would hurl him up into the air in a mighty leap". But instead comes the bullet that ends his life, as well as the symbolic striving to rise above its constraints.

"Pkhentz", now the best known of the stories, was the last of Siniavskii's works to be sent out of the Soviet Union for publication under the Terts pseudonym before his arrest in 1965. It is the journal of a strange creature who arrived on earth from somewhere in the solar system 32 years previously (Siniavskii was 32 when he wrote the story). It describes his life in Moscow in the adopted persona of Andrei Kazimirovich Sushinskii (evoking Siniavskii's own name), his inhuman number of arms forced against his body and hidden in human clothing, giving him the appearance of a hunchback. It is a poignant striving for self-expression and for spiritual refreshment, symbolized by the creature's longing to soak his limbs in water (an evocation of Christian baptism). He is trapped in a world that would regard him as a freak if it discovered his true nature; and his power to communicate in his native language is atrophying. His eventual despairing decision is to return to Siberia, where he first landed, and die there.

In "Ty i ia" ("You and I") (written in 1959), the paranoia endemic in Soviet society under Stalin is taken to an extreme in a fantasy of entrapment. Resorting to a feigned love affair as a means of escape, the central figure's obsessive belief in a conspiracy against him forces the disintegration and eventual destruction of his personality, portrayed in Dostoevskian split form. The same year saw the composition of *Kvartiranti* [Tenants], written at a time when Siniavskii himself was living in a communal appartment of the kind described in the story. Like "Pkhentz", it is in the form of a monologue; like "Pkhentz" too it is about the desire to escape. The narrator is a *domovoi*, a wood demon who has been driven out of the countryside and into the city by the forces of industrialization. His companions in the communal apartment, who are intent on his destruction, are at first identified with, then become, other creatures of folklore: a witch, a devil and a forest spirit (who has a job in the forest ministry). The story's framework derives from the folkloric pattern of a repeating cycle of events. The personality of the actual tenants merges with that of their folkloric *alter egos* and the evil witches crowd round to destroy the wood demon.

"Grafomani" ("The Graphomaniacs") was written in 1960 and describes the desperate life of unpublished writers. Censorship and the tyranny of the publishers leave them only their fantasies of greatness while official literature is dominated by mediocrities. The central figure, Pavel Ivanovich Straustin (this name being aptly derived from the Russian word *straus* for ostrich), is the author of the unpublished and unpublishable "In Search of Joy"; he is convinced of his own genius and of the mediocrity of the "graphomaniacs" who scribble away incessantly around him, driven by a feverish need for self-expression. Graphomania is a disease that drives Straustin to abandon his family and leads him to the point of madness. He becomes convinced that all contemporary works have plagiarized his own unpublished manuscript. Though blind to the derivative quality of his own book, Straustin sees the lunatic obsessiveness of his fellow graphomaniacs and recognizes the damage he is doing to his own family; but the disease is too strong. The story concludes with Straustin settling down, his soul "full of inspiration", to write as his notional swan-song this very story about graphomaniacs. The subtitle, "A Story from My Life", is an ironical reference to Siniavskii himself and his own writings, inside and outside the official system.

"Gololeditsa" ("The Icicle"), written in 1961, is substantially the longest story. Through the force of his love for Natasha, Vasilii acquires the power of second sight, a metaphor for the transcending of the self that characterizes love. This enables him to look forward and back in time in both his own and other people's lives, an ability much prized by the state when he is eventually arrested and interrogated. His power enables him to foresee Natasha's death from an icicle falling on her own head but denies him the ability to prevent her death. The title, meaning icy conditions in Russian, may be an ironical contrasting reference to Il'ia Erenburg's famous post-Stalin novel, *Ottepel'* (*The Thaw*). Siniavskii's *Fantastic Stories* now stand as a key "unofficial" work of Thaw literature.

CHARLES BLAND

The Makepeace Experiment

Liubimov

Novel, 1964

Liubimov was written between 1961 and 1962 and was first published in Polish in 1963. It appeared in Russian in 1964 and in English as *The Makepeace Experiment* in 1965. It was published under the pseudonym Abram Terts and was one of the three books that formed the basis of charges against Siniavskii at his trial in 1965.

The Makepeace Experiment is an allegory of the Soviet Union over the 50 years since the Revolution. The central figure is Lenny Makepeace, a dreamy bicycle-repair mechanic whose obsession is inventing a perpetual motion machine. His character contains elements of various Soviet leaders; his surname in Russian (Tikhomirov) means world peace while his first name may evoke the Russian words for wood demon and laziness, as well as the name of Lenin himself.

The setting is the imaginary city of Liubimov, a dull, provincial city of undefined location but with characteristics from both before and after the Revolution. Its church was destroyed after the Revolution and a bakery built on the site but the influence of religion persists. To Liubimov comes a captivating beauty, Serafima Kozlova. Her arrival symbolizes the impact on Russia of communism: she "came straight from Leningrad to teach a foreign language". Though she has a pure Russian name and though he is entranced by her, Lenny cannot rid himself of the feeling that there is something alien about her; indeed he eventually discovers that she has a child by an earlier marriage and that she was born with a German name.

Serafima is at first indifferent to Lenny, the Russian archetype. But he acquires a mysterious magical power, described as magnetism, which enables him to control others by willpower, convincing them of anything he wants by the power of suggestion. This power enables him to compel the Secretary of the city Party Committee to instruct the townspeople to proclaim Lenny supreme ruler. It is the ultimate peaceful coup, reinforced by his ability to convince his people of the prospect of unlimited material well-being. Soon both Serafima and the whole of Liubimov are at his feet. Only the dogs of the town are not deceived.

Lenny's power derives from his ancestor, Samson Samsonovich Proferansov, who embodies the 19th-century liberal intellectual tradition. He lived on his estate and despised the court and all its works. He occupied himself with Russian literature and scientific experiments and brought the secret of magnetism from India. With his eccentricities and associations with other intellectuals, Proferansov represents a ghostly composite of the Russian intellectual traditions that interacted with imported Marxist ideology to produce the uniquely Soviet course of the Revolution and its aftermath.

Back in Liubimov, Lenny celebrates his accession to power and his union with Serafima with a bravura display of the power of suggestion. A lavish feast is laid out for the townspeople: it is in fact made up of red peppers and toothpaste but they are convinced that they are eating rich delicacies. Mineral water becomes alcohol and the river runs with champagne. The evocation here of the marriage feast at Cana is a reminder of the resonance between the pure ideals of Christianity and communism. But there is also an ironical reference to the political fault of "voluntarism", of which Khrushchev was accused by his successors: i.e. the belief that problems could be solved merely by the application of will-power.

Soon Liubimov is under threat from the forces of repression who believe that a counter-revolutionary coup has taken place. Spies penetrate the city's defences, one in the shape of an American journalist who suggests that Liubimov should join NATO and, reflecting western incomprehension of communist aspirations, offers to buy Lenny's secret of magnetism for a huge amount of money. Lenny shows how the people of Liubimov have risen beyond the need of money by pointing to walls papered in 100-rouble notes.The spies are won over to support Lenny and his ideals of world peace. But other forces of repression, this time in the form of the regional Soviet authorities, including an hilarious characterization of Khrushchev in the person of Comrade O ("The minute I get started on the Vatican or the struggle for peace, I see red, I could tear them all to pieces with my own hands"). The authorities send out soldiers to reassert their authority. The power of magnetism defeats them, however, and they retreat, lost and in confusion.

Lenny's magical power enables him to make Liubimov invisible, to withdraw it from the surrounding world. The era of intensive Soviet industrialization is evoked in labour units bent on exceeding their norms. A breathing space will enable Liubimov's economy to outstrip those of Holland and Belgium; then "we can begin to think about territorial expansion and the propagation of our ideas on a mass scale". The period of forced collectivization is seen in the picture of an old peasant woman passionate to become a tractor driver and hand over her animals to the collective. Lenny presides over all this, managing the defence and development of Liubimov, aided only by the power of magnetism and a dreamy commitment to world peace. The lunatic tyranny of Soviet government and policy is evoked in the light but devastating satire. But Lenny is not just a satirical figure; he is a Russian tsar full of love for his people and tries to protect them and bring them happiness. (The derivation of the name of the city from the Russian word for beloved reflects this idea.) He is a tyrant without cruelty whose undoing is the idealism of his aims and the cynical self-interest of those who oppose him. The verdict on the Soviet Union is clear: pure ideals have been corrupted. Lenny's mother, a recurring figure, embodies in her peasant simplicity the eternal qualities of the Russian character that were so valued in 19th-century literature and thought: the true heroes of the work are the Russian people themselves.

Outside Liubimov the forces of repression step up their attack and eventually succeed in breaking through. Lenny's power fades, not without some surreal final effects, and Liubimov is overwhelmed. The experiment is at an end and Lenny escapes as a destitute refugee towards Siberia.

The Makepeace Experiment is a short work, dense with symbolism and with Soviet imagery. Though it is lightly written and often very funny in its characterizations and references to Soviet reality, it constitutes a relentless challenge to the ideological rigidities of orthodox Marxist-Leninist Utopianism. But it has broader application too in its study of the relationship between the ruler and the ruled and of the effects of totalitarianism on the individual citizen.

CHARLES BLAND

Little Jinx

Kroshka Tsores

Novella, 1980

Little Jinx was originally conceived as a part of *Goodnight!*, but subsequently developed into a work of its own.

There are few works written by Siniavskii that more clearly bear the stamp of his underground *alter ego* Abram Terts. *Little Jinx*, with its elements of horror, the fantastic and the grotesque, fully corresponds to Terts's credo of the "phantasmagoric" in art. At one stage Tsores comments that "some kind of abnormality has crept into reality. A kind of dislocation." The real name of the hero nicknamed Kroshka Tsores is Siniavskii, and, although he is entirely fictitious, the author has suggested that Abram Terts is here "making fun" of the "contemplative, honest, ... a little bit boring" Siniavskii by identifying him with the dwarfish hero of this Soviet-style fairy tale. The storyline is borrowed from Hoffmann's *Klein Zaches, genannt Zinnober* (1819), and then inverted: in Hoffmann's tale an unpleasant, dwarf-like child is credited with the good actions of others and enjoys a magical rise to the post of Minister, until his humble origins are revealed and his downfall results. Siniavskii's Tsores, on the other hand, wishes no evil but unwittingly causes the death of his five half-brothers. Tsores's alienation from his environment is emphasized by the fact that his five victims are firmly located in Soviet society and pursue the respected professions of sea captain, agronomist, border guards officer, surgeon, and highly-placed bureaucrat. There is here a certain degree of social comment – the five half-brothers (with the exception of the officer) are portrayed unsympathetically, along with the world of Stalinist *meshchanstvo* (petty bourgeoisie) that they represent.

But *Little Jinx* is not primarily about Stalinist society. In this short work Siniavskii once again pursues his favourite theme – that of writing and the writer. Tsores stutters as a small child until he is cured by his "good fairy" Dora Aleksandrovna, the paediatrician. From this moment the boy immerses himself in language: "I dreamt of nothing more than that my speech should resound and flow unimpeded, winging from my lips in perfect octaves". It cannot be a coincidence that his disastrous jinx apparently also dates from this time. For Siniavskii the writer is always an outsider, a breaker of taboos who is regarded with suspicion by those around him. Tsores's marginal status is underlined by his uncertain parentage: he never discovers who his father is and bears a different name to that of his half-brothers. In school he is a misfit, but his passion for writing develops further. He claims he could "build a new city in two paragraphs". His aesthetic sense forms rapidly. For example, he notices the way that water flows from a tap in "convoluted spirals" and concludes defiantly that "nothing unartistic exists at all". His identity as a writer remains significant to the very end. In the final chapter, after he has recounted all the disasters he has indirectly caused, he begins a narrative where he meets Dora Aleksandrovna in a grocery store many years after she cured him of his speech defect. In the fantastic sequence that develops from this encounter Tsores marries Dora Aleksandrovna and sees at the dinner-table his five half-brothers who are discussing him as if *he* has died, not they. In the morning, at dawn, he finds Dora has disappeared, but he is left with "the ream of pages written throughout the night" as tangible evidence of his imaginative powers.

As in *Goodnight!*, where Siniavskii is regarded by the camp authorities as a more dangerous criminal than even the most violent murderer, the writer-hero Tsores is held responsible for events in a way that an ordinary being could never be. Yet Siniavskii's exploration of Tsores's blameless guilt does not just relate to the artist's predicament, but also raises more general moral questions. In this work Siniavskii playfully continues his struggle against moral complacency and dogmatism. Tsores advances arguments for shared guilt: "Were we not evil and guilty, neither Hitler nor Stalin could have surfaced from among us." He is also able to admit that he is not necessarily any better than the people who shun him: when his school-friend Vadim confesses to him that he has accidentally shot his little sister with an air-pistol, Tsores, who by this time has two deaths on his conscience, decides never to have anything more to do with him. In Siniavskii's imaginative presentation, good and evil appear to be dictated by chance. "Evil is merely a by-product of the good we tarry for ...". Siniavskii is no relativist (he is not afraid to call evil by its name), but he presents evil as something that can afflict any of us at any time. It is therefore unwise to attempt to sit in judgement over others. As a horrifying illustration of the random nature of evil, here is one "episode" related by Tsores in shockingly dead-pan style: a little boy accidentally kills a neighbour's rooster with a rock; she locks him up in the pig-pen, where he is eaten by a sow. When the boy's father discovers this, he murders the neighbour with an axe. Tsores comments that "the culprit is triviality, stupidity, some natural error, the invisible jinx". There are indeed cases which might drive people to "organize a protest demonstration at the Last Judgement". Grotesque, fantastic, thought-provoking, darkly humorous, *Little Jinx* is perhaps the most concentrated example of Siniavskii's main stylistic and thematic particularities.

STEPHEN LOVELL

Goodnight!

Spokoinoi nochi

Novel, 1984

Goodnight! was first published in Paris in 1984. It was written about a decade after emigration and bears all the marks of Siniavskii's deep reflection on his own life, on a broad stretch of Soviet history, on the role of the writer and the nature of literature, and on a range of ethical questions. It is simultaneously an artist's spiritual autobiography and a chronicle of his times. However, Siniavskii gives this traditional undertaking of the Russian writer his own twist. In this work, as in his controversial studies of Pushkin and Gogol', Siniavskii challenges intellectual rigidity and moral complacency without ever losing his good humour.

Siniavskii called *Goodnight!* a novel, and that raises the question of the relationship between fact and fiction. It becomes clear from the very first pages that Siniavskii is aiming to transform his own experience into an imaginative structure that has all the force of myth. He makes no apologies for the anecdotal quality and non-linear chronology of his narrative. He speaks of his "effort of memory to bring hero and author into a significant unity, to bind a variety of parts into a harmonious chain of causality where real time is not too binding". It is Siniavskii's firm belief that "the past cannot be grasped in sequence": he maintains that the imaginative patterns of a work of art can render reality more faithfully than a simple chronological account.

The narrative is divided into five chapters. The first begins with Siniavskii's arrest in 1965 and goes on to tell the story of his interrogation, trial, and journey to the camps. Siniavskii, true to his artistic principles, turns his duels with the interrogator Pakhomov into a "fairy-tale play" entitled "Zerkalo" ("The Mirror"). This dialogue illustrates well the emotionally based logic and psychology of Pakhomov and others who perform similar functions.

Camp life is the theme of the second section. The main location is the "public house" where prisoners once a year have the right to meet and spend a couple of days with their wives. Siniavskii darts back in time to the long period before his arrrest when the Soviet secret service was trying to hunt down the mysterious Abram Terts. He also relates a few prison episodes, for example the horrific shooting down of the simple-minded Klaus. But Siniavskii never aims just to shock. Instead he is able to sound almost upbeat about the experience:

> There's a voluptuous pleasure in slipping into this torture garden full of marvellous creatures that, in some strange way, are a continuation of my own capricious ideas, my own long, slippery snake-mask.

Here Siniavskii shows some affinity with other works of Russian literature where imprisonment and suffering represent not death but the beginning of resurrection. This is a typically Russian Orthodox idea which, true to form, Siniavskii problematizes somewhat by placing his "resurrection" (chapter 2) before his "fall" (chapter 5). The second chapter ends with a moving passage on the "ancient pantomime" of sex. Siniavskii sees the sexual act in symbolic terms as "a prayer for help, a confession, and an incantation all at the same time". For the prisoner and his wife brought together just for one night, the "cadences and spasms of the genitals" have a special meaning. Siniavskii concludes that conception is "not so much a matter of genes. Or molecules. But of understanding and memory ...".

Siniavskii steps outside the chronology of his own life in chapter 3 for a portrait of his father. A Socialist Revolutionary in his youth, his father managed to stay out of political life thereafter and survived the Terror of the 1930s. In 1951, however, his past caught up with him: his contact with an American famine-relief organization in 1922 was dug up as evidence against him and he was accused of spying. The climax of the chapter is Siniavskii's visit to his father in exile. Siniavskii is shocked that this fearless and strong-willed man should now be convinced that a super-powerful brain scanner from Moscow is tapping into his thoughts. Father and son have become remote from each other. It is no accident that this chapter occupies the privileged central position in the novel. In it we find some of Siniavskii's most important insights on memory, history, and art. The forest where the conversation with his father takes place is transformed in his mind into a metaphor for the written text. The forest/text is a separate domain where the writer operates "without thinking about anything". Siniavskii defends his right to "stories" against the demands of "heroic epics and art's relationship to reality".

Chapter 4 is imbued with the atmosphere of late Stalinism. In Siniavskii's imaginative version the Stalin myth is associated with the supernatural and the occult. The actress A. receives a visitation from Stalin, who appears before her as "the positive expression of an ultimate negation". On the day Stalin's death is announced huge crowds rush off, as if guided by a magical force, to the Hall of Columns where Stalin's body is lying in state. Siniavskii's response to the announcement is telling: he heads for the Lenin Library and immerses himself in 17th-century Russian history. He is able to fit the Time of Troubles and Stalin's death into the same mythical framework: "For the first time, history was revealed to me as a field and equation of supernatural forces."

In chapter 5 Siniavskii goes even further back in time and introduces us to the informer S. (or Sergei), whom he has known since his school-days. At that time Sergei's tastes in poetry and painting were more precocious than Siniavskii's, indeed Siniavskii maintains that he owes his earliest aesthetic education to Sergei. But Sergei's artistic sensibilities were always accompanied by shocking moral cowardice and inhumanity. A career as an informer was always a natural choice for him. It is typical of Siniavskii's refusal to seize the moral high ground that against the background of the perfidious Sergei he relates his own brief career as an informer. In the late 1940s the KGB enlisted his help in monitoring his close friend Hélène, daughter of a French naval attaché in Moscow. When dispatched to Vienna in 1952 to ensnare her in an obscure KGB plot, Siniavskii tells Hélène what is afoot from the outset, but he regards this inability to betray her not as evidence of his own moral superiority, but instead as a "miracle" in which his conscious agency played no part.

Siniavskii is no conventional moralist, just as *Goodnight!* is no conventional novel. He does none the less have strong moral convictions that are tied to an artistic vision. *Goodnight!* is a highly complex and wide-ranging work, but it is still possible to find a reassuringly firm base to Siniavskii's world view: "Art is stronger and more enduring, and, if you will, more alive, than destructive life. That is why it is both healing and always moral, but independent of foolish morality".

STEPHEN LOVELL

Skazanie o Borise i Glebe *see* Legend of Boris and Gleb

Slovo o polku Igoreve *see* Lay of Igor's Campaign

Boris Abramovich Slutskii 1919–1986

Poet

Biography

Born in Slaviansk, Ukraine, 7 May 1919. Attended school in Kharkov. Studied at the Moscow Institute of Jurisprudence, 1937–41; simultaneously studied at Gor'kii Literary Institute, from which he graduated in 1941. Literary debut, May 1941. Volunteered for active service, November 1941; wounded and became *politruk* (a political instructor). Joined the Communist Party, 1943. Married: Tat'iana Dashkovskaia (died in 1977). Worked for All-Union Radio, 1948–52. Died 22 February 1986.

Publications

Collected Editions

Izbrannaia lirika. Moscow, 1965.
Stikhi raznykh let: iz neizdannogo. Moscow, 1988.
Stikhotvoreniia. Moscow, 1989.
Sobranie sochinenii, 3 vols. Moscow, 1991.

Poetry

Pamiat' [The Memorial]. 1957.
Vremia [Time]. Moscow, 1959.
Segodnia i vchera [Today and Yesterday]. Moscow, 1961.
Rabota [Work]. 1964.
Sovremennye istorii [Contemporary Stories]. Moscow, 1969.
Godovaia strelka [The Year Hand]. Moscow, 1971.
Dobrota dnia [The Kindness of Day]. Moscow, 1973.
Prodlennyi polden' [A Prolonged Midday]. Moscow, 1975.
Neokonchennye spory [Unfinished Quarrels]. Moscow, 1978.
Ruka i dusha [Hand and Soul]. 1981.
Unizhenie vo sne [Humiliation in a Dream]. 1981.
Sroki [Times]. Moscow, 1984.
Ia istoriiu izlagaiu [I Set Forth a Story]. Moscow, 1990.
"Iz poslednei zapisnoi knizhki" [From the Last Notebook], *Znamia*, 5 (1994), 3–5.

Memoirs

"Zarubki pamiati (iz knigi *Zapiski o voine*)" [Notches of Memory (from the Book, Notes on the War)], *Voprosy literatury*, 3 (1995), 38–82.

Critical Studies

"Stikhi i rabota", by A. Urban, *Zvezda*, 1 (1965).
"Kogda proza stanovitsia poeziei", by L. Lazarev, *Voprosy literatury*, 1 (1967).
"Drug i sopernik", by David Samoilov, *Oktiabr'*, 9 (1992), 178–90.
"B.A. Slutskii. Kharakter i sud'ba", by Inna Prussakova, *Neva*, 4 (1994), 273–78.

Having published his first poems during World War II, Boris Slutskii did not publish his next poem, "Pamiatnik" [The Memorial], until 1953 and it was a further four years before his first collection was published. Evtushenko reports in his *Autobiografiia* (*Precocious Autobiography*) that at the age of 35, Slutskii had still not been admitted to the Writers' Union. The reason for his belated acceptance by the literary establishment was almost certainly his studiedly anti-heroic stance in his descriptions of war and his muted criticism of Stalin's post-war policies in poems such as "1945" (1963). His work consists entirely of short poems, of which he wrote more than 750 in his lifetime. In "Tvorcheskii metod" [Creative Method] he claims that poets are distinguished from other people by their devotion to directness and brevity. "Pamiatnik" exemplifies this aphorism. The verb in the very first line is colloquial and the poem is characterized by the bitterly ironic contrast between the reality of the soldier's death and the idealized monument that is erected on the spot.

Very few of Slutskii's poems are marked with a date and many have clearly been worked on for a considerable time. World War II remains the dominant theme in his work and in two famous poems, "Kak ubivali moiu babku" [How They Killed My Granny] and "Vse slabeli, baby – ne slabeli" [Everyone Grew Weak. Only the Women Did Not], he highlights the suffering of women in war. This theme, which might so easily have seemed hackneyed, is given additional poignancy by the autobiographical element in the first poem (Slutskii's grandmother was among a group of Ukrainian Jews executed by the Nazis and their local collaborators) and by the stark, unemotional language in the second poem, dedicated to Ol'ga Berggol'ts. The war informs much of Slutskii's imagery. Good examples are "Moi tovarishchi" [My Comrades], with its brutal first line, "My comrades burnt to death in the tanks" and "Gora" [The Hill], with its typically prosaic diction. Even poems on other themes, such as "Kak delaiut stikhi" [How Verses Are Made], are full of military imagery. The prosaic nature of Slutskii's verse is so marked that, in 1965, some Soviet journals wondered aloud whether Slutskii's verses were really poetry; certainly their earthy, conversational idiom, the grim tone and "diary-like" quality (*dnevnikovost'*) give Slutskii a unique and unmistakable voice. Two of his most controversial works were "Bog" [God] and "Khoziain" [The Boss] (1954). The first, with its repeated line "My vse khodili pod bogom" [We all went with God's guidance], ironically likens Stalin to God. Stalin is simply "cleverer and more evil" than Jehovah and, unlike Him, travels in five-car motorcades along the Arbat. The second poem again refers to Stalin who, like all "bosses", is unaware of the love and devotion he inspires in his minions. More than that, the "Boss" is afraid of them and actively loathes them. Both poems contain a personal element that undoubtedly adds to their strength. After the publication of "Khoziain" in *Literaturnaia gazeta* in 1962, neither poem was published again in Russia until 1990. These two works form part of a remarkable group of poems that deal with the phenomenon of Stalin and Stalinism. These include "Slava" [Glory] dated Autumn 1956, which comments on the contrast between Lenin's enduring fame and Stalin's tarnished reputation. Others in this group include "Tovarishch Stalin pis'mennyi" [Comrade Stalin in Written Form], the confessional "Ia ros pri Staline ..." [I Grew up Under Stalin's Rule ...], "Vozhd' byl kak dozhd'" [The Leader was like Rain], "Generala legko poniat'" [It's Easy to Understand the General], which explores the psychology of a military man who, even after 1956, continues to revere Stalin, "Razgovor" [Conversation] and "Paiats" [The Clown]. One poem that does not even feature in the 1990 collection is the one written in the wake of the furore stirred up by the publication of Evtushenko's "Babii Iar'" in 1961. Here Evtushenko's manifest sympathy with the plight of persecuted Jews led to accusations from the far Right that either the poet was Jewish or he had no right to speak on their behalf. Shortly afterwards a 12-line poem was widely circulated full of crudely anti-Jewish sentiments that ends by denying the existence of the Holocaust. The words are those of a typical Russian anti-Semite, the crassness of whose statements condemn him out of his own mouth. Slutskii, a Jew, was widely believed to be the author, though he himself always refused to confirm or deny this. Slutskii's credentials as a liberal were confirmed by his contributing four poems to the liberal almanac *Tarusskie stranitsy*, but there is another side to him. He contributed to the anti-Pasternak campaign of 1957–59 and some critics talk dismissively of "the fundamentally publicistic nature of his poetry" and "a certain spiritual poverty" (Terras, 1987). There are certainly publicistic poems, for example "Gudki" [Hooters], on the death of Lenin or "Kak menia prinimali v partiiu" [How I Was Accepted into the Party], but they are in a minority. Slutskii has also tackled many other themes, notably the role of the poet. The most famous of these is probably "Fiziki i Liriki" [Physicists and Lyricists] (1965), which laconically records the fact that physicists are held in greater exteem than lyricists. Others include "Chitatel' otvechaet za poeta" [The Reader Answers for the Poet] and "Chistota stikha" [Purity of Verse]. Many of his poems are addressed to fellow poets – Nikolai Aseev, Vladimir Maiakovskii, Velemir Khlebnikov, and Pavel Kogan among others. Discussing art in more general terms, Slutskii attacks those who deny religion as a basis for artistic expression in his "K diskussii ob Andree Rubleve" [Discussion on Andrei Rublev] (1962). If, ideologically, Slutskii is more liberal than conservative, technically, he is fairly conservative although he does use accentual metres on occasion, as, for instance, in "Moi kombat Nazarov" [My Battalion Commander Nazarov]. Deming Brown (1978) comments that "his rhymes seem so bad as to seem intentionally grotesque" but claims this is in keeping with Slutskii's concept of beauty.

Slutskii's last poems date from early 1977 and include moving verses about his wife, who died that year. Slutskii himself fell ill in May 1977 and wrote nothing more.

MICHAEL PURSGLOVE

Nadezhda Stepanovna Sokhanskaia 1823–1884

Prose writer

Biography

Born in Korocha, Kursk province, 1 March 1823 (some sources 1825). Attended boarding school in Kharkov. Moved to the family property Makarovka in the Kupianskii region, Kharkov province, 1840. Also wrote under the pseudonyms Kokhanovskaia, Makarovskaia, and Nadezhda ***. First work "Maior Smagin" [Major Smagin], published in 1844. Encouraged by Petr Pletnev, the editor of *Sovremennik*, to write her autobiography, 1847–48 (published posthumously 1896); attracted attention with story "Gaika" [The Nut], 1856. Contributed to Slavophile journals, 1858–62. First trip to St Petersburg, 1862. Artistic publication dwindled, critical and publicistic publication continued. Play staged in Moscow, 1873. Unsuccessfully attempted to organize a Slavophilic brotherhood in the southwest region of the Ukraine. Died of cancer at the family estate, 15 December 1884.

Publications

Collected Edition

Povesti, 2 vols. Moscow, 1863.

Fiction

"Maior Smagin" [Major Smagin], *Syn otechestva*, 1844.

"Grafiniia D***" [Countess D...], *Otechestvennye zapiski*, 61, 12 (1848).

"Gaika" [The Nut], first part published, *Panteon*, 1856; full version in *Russkoe slovo*, 4 (1860); translated as *The Rusty Linchpin*, with *Luboff Archipovna*, Boston, Lothrop, 1887.

"Posle obeda v gostiakh" [After-Dinner Guests], *Russkii vestnik*, 1858; translated as *Luboff Archipovra*, with *The Rusty Linchin*, Boston, Lothrop, 1887; as "A Conversation After Dinner", in *Russian Women's Shorter Fiction: An Anthology 1835–1860*, translated by Joe Andrew, Oxford, Clarendon Press, 1996, 378–459.

"Iz provintsialnoi gallerei portretov" [From a Provincial Portrait Gallery], *Russkii vestnik*, 5 (1859).

"Stepnaia baryshnia sorokovykh godov" [A Young Lady of the Steppes of the 1840s], *Rus'*, 3–6 (1885).

Autobiography

"Avtobiografiia", *Russkoe obozrenie*, 6–12 (1896); separate edition, Moscow, 1896.

Critical Studies

"O povestiakh g-zhi Kokhanovskoi", by M. DePule, *Russkoe slovo*, 12 (1859), 1–36.

"O novoi povesti g-zhi Kokhanovskoi", by N.P. Giliarov-Platonov, *Russkaia beseda*, 3 (1859), 65–86.
"Povestei Kokhanovskoi", by N. Chernyshevskii, *Sovremennik*, 9 (1863).
"G-zha Kokhanovskaia i ee povesti", by V. Ostrovskii, *Biblioteka dlia chteniia*, 7 (1869).
Zhizn' i trudy M.P. Pogodina, by Nikolai Platonovich Barsukov, 1888–1910, vol. 19, 392–416.
"Novye dannye dlia biografiia Kokhanovskoi", by A. Pypin, *Vestnik evropy*, 12 (1896), 717–748.
"Neudachnye predpriatiia narodoliubki", by F. Kudrinskii, *Kievskaia stat'ia*, 10/1 (1900), 83–122; separate edition Kiev, 1900.
"*Russkii vestnik* 1858 goda", by D.I. Pisarev, in his *Sochineniia. Polnoe sobranie*, 5th edition, St Petersburg, 1909, vol. 1, 74–81.
Kokhanovskaia (N. S. Sokhanskaia), 1823–1884. Biograficheskii ocherk. S portretom, by N.N. Platonova, St Petersburg, 1909.
"Sokhanskaia, Nadezhda Stepanova", in *The Bloomsbury Guide to Women's Literature*, edited by Claire Buck, London, Bloomsbury, and New York, Prentice Hall, 1992.
"Sokhanskaia, Nadezhda Stepanova", by Mary Zirin, in *Dictionary of Russian Women Writers*, edited by Marina Ledkovsky, Charlotte Rosenthal, and Mary Zirin, Westport, Connecticut, Greenwood Press, 1994, 613–16.
"Women's Prose Fiction in the Age of Realism", by Mary Zirin, in *Women Writers in Russian Literature*, edited by Toby W. Clyman and Diana Greene, Westport, Connecticut, Greenwood Press, 1994, 82–84.
A History of Russian Women's Writing, 1820–1992, by Catriona Kelly, Oxford and New York, Clarendon Press, 1994.

Bibliographies
Bibliograficheskii slovar' russkikh pisatelnits, by N.N. Golitsyn, St Petersburg, 1889; reprinted Leipzig, 1974, 233–36.
Istoriia russkoi literatury XIX veka. Bibliograficheskii ukazatel', Moscow and Leningrad, 1962.

Born into an impoverished provincial noble family, Nadezhda Sokhanskaia was left in the care of her mother and aunts after her father's early death. In 1834 she was placed at a boarding school in Kharkov, where despite her deficient educational foundation and the embarrassment of her poverty, she eventually graduated with high honours. During this time she was influenced by the institute's teacher of Russian language and literature, Mikhail Ivanovich Ilenko, and some of her poems were read at the graduation commencement in 1840.

After completing her studies at the institute, Sokhanskaia settled at the estate of her mother and aunts in Kharkov province, Makarovka. Frustrated by the lack of intellectual stimulation in her steppe village, she went through a period of depression that she overcame through religion. A wealthy neighbour began supplying her with literary journals, the contents of which did not satisfy her, and so Sokhanskaia began to write herself. In 1844 her first story, "Maior Smagin" [Major Smagin], was published in *Syn otechestva*, but the editor did not pay her or respond to her letters. She entered into correspondence with Petr Pletnev, editor of *Sovremennik* in 1846. Pletnev encouraged Sokhanskaia to strengthen her literary skills by writing her autobiography. She finished the work in 1848, but it was not published until after her death. Sokhanskaia also received professional advice from her neighbour, the writer Grigorii Danilevskii.

Sokhanskaia's early works received little notice, but the first part of the story "Gaika" [The Nut], published in 1856 in the journal *Panteon*, attracted attention. In it Sokhanskaia depicts a romance between an independent girl and an estate owner. As a result of the positive critical reception of the story, A.V. Druzhinin and M.N. Katkov invited Sokhanskaia to contribute to their journals. From 1858 to 1862 she published several works, and in 1863 her stories appeared in a separate edition. Her best work is considered to be "Posle obeda v gostiakh" [After-Dinner Guests], in which the main character, Liubov, Arkhipovna, recounts the tale of an unhappy love affair and her acceptance of a loveless marriage to a merchant.

Sokhanskaia's works focus on life in the Ukrainian provinces, are frequently drawn from family history, use folklore and peasant idiom, and have a strong regional flavour. Critics recognized her deep knowledge of peasant life, and her mastery of narration and peasant language. Her emphasis on the peasantry and her tendency to idealize the past united her with the Slavophile movement. Although Sokhanskaia frequently depicted the common abuses of power in rural life, her victims always resign themselves to their fate, even considering themselves guilty in their insubordination and disrespect and frequently finding comfort in religion. Liberal critics recognized her artistic talent but criticized Sokhanskaia for social indifference and idealization of a way of life that had been abolished by the Emancipation of the Serfs in 1861.

After 1863, Sokhanskaia's fictional output diminished, although her letters on contemporary issues from the provinces and collections of folk-songs were published. She did not fulfil the expectations of those who had championed her; her sensitivity to criticism led to strained relations with editors and other writers, and the deaths of the Slavophile leaders Khomiakov (1860) and Konstantin Aksakov (1862) left her without a literary home.

Sokhanskaia further alienated liberals with her support for societies organized to propagate and protect the Orthodox Church in the southwestern Ukraine, and for her anti-Semitic inclinations. She spent her final years in her village, and her final publication was a response to Lev Tolstoi's *Ispoved'* (*A Confession*), published in the journal *Grazhdanin* in 1884, the year of her death. After her death, several of her letters to literary figures were published, as well as the autobiography she wrote in her youth.

KARLA THOMAS SOLOMON

Sasha Sokolov 1943–

Prose writer

Biography

Born Aleksandr Vsevolodovich Sokolov in Ottawa, Ontario, Canada, 6 November 1943. Attended the Military Institute of Foreign Languages, Moscow, 1962–65; Moscow University: BA in journalism, 1971. Married; one daughter. Worked for the journals *Novorossiiskii rabochii*, 1967, *Kolkhoznaia pravda*, Morky, 1967–68, *Literaturnaia Rossiia*, Moscow, 1969–71, *Studencheskii meridian*, summers 1970–71, and *Leninskaia pravda*, Georgievsk, 1974. Went on hunger-strike to obtain an exit visa from Soviet authorities following ban on his marriage. Emigrated to Canada in 1976; writer-in-residence and instructor in Russian, Grand Valley State College, Allendale, Michigan, from 1977. Returned to Russia, 1989–90. Currently resides in Canada.

Publications

Fiction

Shkola dlia durakov. Ann Arbor, Ardis, 1976; translated as *A School for Fools*, by Carl R. Proffer, Ann Arbor, Ardis, 1977; reprinted New York, Four Walls Eight Windows, 1988.

Mezhdu sobakoi i volkom [Between Dog and Wolf]. Ann Arbor, Ardis, 1980.

Palisandriia. Ann Arbor, Ardis, 1985; Moscow, 1992; translated as *Astrophobia*, by Michael Henry Heim, New York, Grove Weidenfeld, 1989.

Critical Studies

"*Škola dlja durakov*. Versuch über Saša Sokolov", by Felix Philip Ingold, *Wiener Slawistischer Almanach*, 3 (1979), 93–124.

"A Structural Analysis of Sasha Sokolov's *School for Fools*: A Paradigmatic Novel", by D. Barton Johnson, in *Fiction and Drama in Eastern and Southeastern Europe: Evolution and Experiment in the Postwar Period*, edited by Henrik Birnbaum and Thomas Eekman, Columbus, Ohio, Slavica, 1980, 207–37.

"Zaitil'shchina", by Vadim Kreid, *Dvadtsat' dva*, 19 (1981), 213–18.

"Sasha Sokolov's *Between Dog and Wolf* and the Modernist Tradition", by D. Barton Johnson, in *Russian Literature in Emigration: The Third Wave*, edited by Olga Matich and Michael Henry Heim, Ann Arbor, Ardis, 1984, 208–17.

"Sasha Sokolov's *Palisandrija*", by D. Barton Johnson, *Slavic and East European Journal*, 30 (1986), 389–403.

"Sasha Sokolov's Twilight Cosmos: Themes and Motifs", by D. Barton Johnson, *Slavic Review*, 45 (1986), 639–49.

"Sasha Sokolov's *Palisandriia*: History and Myth", by Olga Matich, *Russian Review*, 45 (1986), 415–26.

"Cohesion and Coherence in Pathological Discourse and Its Literary Representation in Saša Sokolov's *Škola dlja durakov*", by Cynthia Simmons, *International Journal of Slavic Linguistics and Poetics*, 33 (1986), 71–96.

"Sasha Sokolov and Vladimir Nabokov", by D. Barton Johnson, *Russian Language Journal*, 138–39 (1987), 415–26.

Canadian-American Slavic Studies (special Sokolov issue), 21/3–4 (1987).

"Sasha Sokolov: The New Russian Avant-Garde", by D. Barton Johnson, *Critique: Studies in Modern Fiction*, 30 (1989).

"The Galoshes Manifesto: A Motif in the Novels of Sasha Sokolov", by D. Barton Johnson, *Oxford Slavonic Papers*, 22 (1989).

"Incarnations of the Hero Archetype in *School for Fools*", by Cynthia Simmons, in *The Supernatural in Slavic and Baltic Literature: Essays in Honor of Victor Terras*, edited by Amy Mandelker and Roberta Reeder, Columbus, Ohio, Slavica, 1989, 275–89.

"Nasylaiushchii veter", by Andrei Zorin, *Novyi mir*, 12 (1989), 250–53.

"Aberration or the Future: The Avant-Garde Novels of Sasha Sokolov", by Arnold McMillin, in *From Pushkin to "Palisandriia": Essays on the Russian Novel in Honour of Richard Freeborn*, edited by McMillin, London, Macmillan, and New York, St Martin's Press, 1990, 229–43.

Their Fathers' Voice: Vassily Aksyonov, Venedikt Erofeev, Eduard Limonov and Sasha Sokolov, by Cynthia Simmons, Bern and New York, Peter Lang, 1993.

"Saša Sokolov's *Škola dlia durakov*: Aesopian Language and Intertextual Play", by Ludmilla L. Litus, *Slavic and East European Journal*, 41/1 (1997), 114–34.

Bibliography

Canadian-American Slavic Studies, 21/3–4 (1987).

Sasha Sokolov is the author of three novels, a little poetry and several short stories. Until the late 1980s he was widely regarded as one of the most outstanding Russian prose writers of today, but he has not produced any major work since 1985, and, indeed, seems to have given up writing altogether. Even if this is the case, however, his ambitious novels will ensure him a lasting position in Russian postmodernist prose. Each of these three works displays an almost completely different aspect of his talent. The first, *Shkola dlia durakov* (*A School for Fools*), reveals most clearly the influence of Nabokov in its psychological portrait of a schizophrenic youth attending a special school in a settlement near Moscow, a world that is both confused and confusing and yet above all lyrically poetic. The 20-year-old narrator recalls his thoughts and feelings some two years earlier through a stream of consciousness that takes various forms: sometimes a dialogue with his *alter ego*, sometimes reminiscences and reflections, and sometimes purely imaginary dialogues with characters who may be either dead or inaccessible in some other way – as in Sokolov's other novels, the boundaries between life and death are blurred or even dissolved here. The main themes arising from this subtle and sensitive mind's seemingly unfocused discourse are the – also fluid – boundaries between madness and sanity, the normal adolescent longing for individuality, acceptance and sex, and the selective memory that is associated with madness.

Time in *A School for Fools*, as in all Sokolov's writing, is unconventional, and the suspension of monolinear chronology represents a constant theme in the novel as well as a basic element in the text's structure. This most lyrical of modern novels requires of the reader close reading to disentangle the many interwoven strands of thought, but is immensely rewarding in its charming whimsicality, psychological insights, and unforced lyric symphony. This novel will probably prove to be Sokolov's most lasting monument.

The second and most dificult of the novels, *Mezhdu sobakoi i volkom* [Between Dog and Wolf], consists of both prose and poetry; it has been described by D. Barton Johnson, the most perceptive of Sokolov's critics, as "a quantum leap, leaving behind many ... readers". Unlike *A School for Fools*, which has appeared in many languages, or Sokolov's third novel, of which there exists at least one English version, *Mezhdu sobakoi i volkom* appears to have defied translation, perhaps because of the complete dissolution of reality in the novel (be it in geography, human relations, or personality), and the extreme complexity of its language, which is partially the native, uncorrupted, almost folkloric lexicon and syntax of remote Central Russia for the main narration, and a semi-literate stream of confused and passionate consciousness for the novel's letters; the verse sections, which are far more readily comprehensible than the prose, present a different potential trap for translators on account of their highly referential, parodic nature.

The novel is set in a remote, semi-mythical part of the Upper Volga region where crippled, deranged, and deformed people lead lives of cruelty and bestiality, their physical squalor matched by almost total spiritual emptiness. It appears to retell the Oedipus legend in an exceptionally grotesque and obscure form (little in the book is graspable without the closest of imaginative reading). A series of dimly perceived, often horrifying, adventures, murders and other extremes of behaviour follow from the barely human characters' loves, jealousy, and desire for revenge. An important part of *Mezhdu sobakoi i volkom* comprises the rambling, confused letters to the public prosecutor by the (probably dead) hero Il'ia, and 37 poems by his son (and, quite possibly, murderer) Iakov, which mainly comprise parodies of such early 19th-century classics as Pushkin, Lermontov, and Gogol'. The book has met muted critical rapture, but was acclaimed by an underground Leningrad journal as the best prose of 1981.

Sokolov's third novel, *Palisandriia* (*Astrophobia*), differs as much from its predecessors as they do from each other. Lighter in tone, and with an outrageous plot of sorts, it comprises a series of improbable and extravagant picaresque episodes that appear to parody the émigré taste for writing historical novels, as well as the quasi-pornography to which several fellow writers in exile have devoted themselves. Political treatises and science fiction are among other genres guyed, but the endemic element of self-parody throughout this work blurs the lines of genre distinction. In this respect at least *Astrophobia* is no less modern a text than the earlier novels.

The book was ostensibly written in the year 2757 by a biographer-cum-editor, and comprises the memoirs of one Palisandr Dal'berg, a grand nephew of Beria and great grandson of Rasputin who is, moreover, the heir to the Russian throne during Brezhnev's period of stagnation. An oversexed, bald, and cross-eyed hermaphrodite with seven fingers on each hand, he rampages around the Kremlin in a series of wild erotic adventures, later moving on to Moscow itself and Europe where his necrophiliac passions (the result of rape as a child) are indulged alongside an active career as bisexual prostitute, pornographer, and Nobel Prize-winning advocate of hermaphrodite rights. At the end of the book he collects all the graves of exiled Russians before returning to assume the throne of Russia. For all its scabrous episodes, however, *Astrophobia* is almost entirely free from lexical vulgarisms, being written in a quasi-chivalric style, reminiscent of Russia's Silver Age. Indeed, self-referentiality and an obsession with Russian literature of all periods are major features of this exuberant but essentially lightweight text.

Sokolov's short prose and verses are less important than the novels, and his reputation now seems likely to rest principally on the subtle grace, charm, and lyrical profundity of *A School for Fools*.

ARNOLD MCMILLIN

A School for Fools

Shkola dlia durakov

Novel, 1976

A School for Fools, Sokolov's first novel, was written in the Soviet Union but published in 1976 shortly after his emigration. Hailed by Vladimir Nabokov as "an enchanting, tragic, and touching book", it was an immediate critical success. The modernist novel is a journey through the mental landscape of a nameless, schizophrenic adolescent told with the assistance of an author-persona who may be the boy's older self. Through the kaleidoscope of the teenager's schizoid mind, we see incidents reflecting his bizarre perceptions and his attempts to come to terms with the surrounding world.

The boy's aberration has two primary features: doubling, and the absence of linear time. Always referring to himself as "we", he perceives himself and several other characters as two distinct but related persons, each with his or her own name. Much of the narrative is an interior dialogue between the two halves of the boy's mind, or interior monologues directed toward unidentified persons. The boy does not perceive time in any fixed chronological order. Past, present, and future are random and intermixed. These peculiarities determine the unorthodox form of the novella. There is, in the ordinary sense, no plot. It is replaced by an ever-swirling verbal collage whose parts are linked by key sound segments.

The hero's remembered experiences arise from his relationships with his parents, with residents of the summer dacha community, with his doctor, and staff members of the School for Fools that he attends. His prosecutor father is a cavilling misanthrope, genus "Homo sovieticus". The son has spent time in a mental institution where he is treated by Dr Zauze who seeks to cure him by uniting the two halves of his personality. Allied with Dr Zauze in the boy's mind are Perillo, the petty tyrant in charge of the school, and his deputy, Sheina Trachtenberg, who ominously stalks the corridors dragging her club foot.

Two other characters, both teachers at the school, play major roles in the boy's fantasy life. Both own summer dachas near that of the boy's family. The first is Veta Acatova, his biology teacher whom he loves and fantasizes as his bride-to-be. One of the story's two main, albeit very tenuous narrative threads, is the boy's imaginary romance with Veta. The second thread involves the boy's adored geography teacher, the free-spirited Pavel (who is also called Savl) Norvegov, who has died at some point in the boy's school years. Most of the hero's conversations with him postdate the teacher's death and are entirely imaginary, as are his conversations with Veta's father. The two teachers serve as focal points for the disturbed adolescent's efforts to grasp the fundamental human experiences of sex and death.

Much of the narrative (with its many free-floating digressions) is set within two very long, disjointed, intermittent, imagined dialogues to which the boy returns again and again. One is with Norvegov from whom the boy attempts to learn about sex. The other is with Veta Acatova's father in which the boy, a winter butterfly collector, seeks to apprentice himself to the old entomologist and to ask for Veta's hand in marriage. These conversations are interspersed with other fantasies such as the hero's rendezvous with Veta, and with the distorted memories of real events such as visits to his grandmother's grave and to his accordion teacher.

The boy's thought processes and narrative are so chaotic that any résumé of events is hazardous. The first chapter, "Nimfeia" ("Nymphea"), opens with the two halves of the boy's mind arguing over stylistic questions in the description of the summer house district: the suburban train station, pond, and wooded paths. On the train platform we meet the barefooted Norvegov, who has died two years earlier, but is still very much alive in the boy's mind. Through this, we learn of the boy's "timelessness" and his inability to grasp the unidirectionality of death. We also learn of his "selective memory" and tendency to lose his identity, to dissolve into objects of natural beauty. Sitting in a rowboat, he picks a white water lily and becomes so engrossed that he merges with it, assuming its Latin name Nymphea Alba. After numerous digressions, the young hero sets off on a night journey to the dacha of his unsuspecting love, Veta Acatova.

The Veta theme is continued in the "Savl" chapter which, however, focuses on Norvegov and the hated School for Fools with its trivial regimentation (the slipper system) and its deceitful goal of turning its "special" students into good Soviet engineers. The following chapter, "Skirly" ("Skeerly"), takes sex as its theme. The boy visits his prospective father-in-law and through the folk-tale "Skeerly" expresses his anxiety over his sexual ignorance. A second imaginary conversation, this one with Savl in the school's lavatory, addresses the sexual question somewhat more directly, although Savl (already deceased) is more interested in trying to recall his own fate. "Zaveshchanie" ("Testament"), the last chapter, tells of Savl's skeleton that he has bequeathed to the school biology classroom. Here we learn of the geography teacher's illness, suspension, and death. In the final pages the author-persona steps forward. After discussing a title and the possible inclusion of new episodes, the author and his hero wander arm-in-arm down the street to buy more writing paper.

Russian literature has a long tradition linking rationalism with political and social authoritarianism, and artistic sterility. The irrational, on the other hand, is identified with social and personal freedom, and creativity. It is not by chance that all Sokolov's negative characters (with their conspicuously non-Russian names) are the representatives of a rigidly rationalized institutionalized society. His positive characters, however, bear names connected with nature: Nymphea Alba, Veta Acatov, Norvegov, etc. These names are phonetically linked to the Russian word *veter*, "wind", which in the form of the "Ill-boding Wind" represents the forces of nature, devastating to the enemies of freedom but nourishing to its children – all of whom bear traces of its name in their own. The eccentric iconoclast Norvegov, mentor to the young hero, is known as the "Winddriver", and is the prophet of the wind of creative freedom. Sokolov's *A School for Fools* was one of the first works to reaffirm the long submerged tradition of the avant-garde.

D. BARTON JOHNSON

Mezhdu sobakoi i volkom

Between Dog and Wolf

Novel, 1980

Mezhdu sobakoi i volkom, Sokolov's second novel, is an extremely complex surrealist text in prose and verse which, perhaps for that reason, has not found so much favour with readers as his other novels, although it has attracted a number of enterprising academic studies. Written in 1980 and published in America, it was declared "the best prose of 1981" by the Leningrad *samizdat* journal *Chasy*. To date it has not been translated into any foreign language.

The title is drawn from Pushkin's *Evgenii Onegin* and not only reflects two animals that figure in the book, but also the temporal and moral twilight zone of an unbelievably god-forsaken area of the Upper Volga region inhabited by crippled, crazy, and deformed people with no sense of morality or decency, who live lives of unrelieved physical squalor and spiritual emptiness. The novel, we know from extrinsic evidence, is set in the year Sokolov spent in this region, although there is no element of reportage. It appears, however, that some of the horrific events invented for the novel have subsequently been enacted there.

As always with Sokolov, chronology has an unconventional and important role. In this novel a legendary hunter compares chronology to a river, moving fast in a town, slowly in a village, and standing still in the forests. There seems to be no causality as such, the border between life and death is eroded, and there is no distinction in status between different versions of the same event. The lack of a single teleological linear plot is ironically underlined by an obscure arrangement of sections of text with arabic and roman numbers, providing further evidence of Sokolov's distrust of chronology and causality.

The river Itil' (an old Tartar word for the Volga) divides the living from the dead, and the novel's characters pass from one side to the other over the ice. On one bank is the settlement of Bydgoshch inhabited by the dead, and on the other is Gorodnishche, a town of beggars, thieves, cripples, and otherwise grotesquely deformed and defective citizens whose existence is as vicious as it is bleak. Like many of Dostoevskii's novels, *Mezhdu sobakoi i volkom* is a story of adventures, jealousy, revenge, love, murder and other passionate extremes, but there the resemblance ends, for Sokolov has no interest in plot as such, and the task of finding out what is in fact happening requires sophisticated investigative skills. Nor, with all the obscuring intercutting, changing of tense, backtracking, and frequent periods of narrative limbo, can there be the slightest certainty that any single reading is a correct "solution".

The main character, Il'ia Zynzyrela, a crippled itinerant knife-grinder, is killed precisely because he fails to distinguish between a dog and a wolf. Staggering home drunk down the frozen river after a wake, he imagines he is being followed by a wolf, engages it in a savage struggle, and kills what turns out to be the dog of the drunken gamekeeper Iakov Palamakhterov who in revenge steals Il'ia's crutches. The feud grows apace, with Il'ia killing two of the gamekeeper's dogs, and in consequence being drowned by Iakov and his friends. This and much more can only be ascertained from obscure hints and allusions in a series of illiterate letters from Il'ia (who, it slowly emerges, is already dead) to the criminal investigator Pozhilykh. From these waffling and unfocused scribblings the reader, as in an advanced intelligence test, has to ascertain the relationship between Il'ia and Iakov; among other possibilities, the latter may in fact be Il'ia's son, although neither of them suspects it. The third character in this disturbing and depressing novel is Orina (also known as Marina), Il'ia's debauched and unfaithful wife who had herself died in a belated attempt to save Il'ia when he had been tied to railway lines by some of her many lovers (he only lost a leg). Like the women in Sokolov's other novels, she appears in various incarnations, including that of a crazy girl whom both Iakov and Il'ia love. This may well be the most obscure and squalid version of the Oedipus myth in all literature.

As always with Sokolov, language and style are all-important. Il'ia's outpourings are in a language that is both ungrammatical and steeped in an ancient linguistic tradition preserved in central Russia far away from western influences of all kinds. In this use of "pure", authentic language, Sokolov resembles Solzhenitsyn or, indeed, the Village Prose writers (*derevenshchiki*), popular in the Soviet Union during the previous two decades. The other main part of the book, the verse, interspersed with the apparently prose text is also a linguistic *tour de force* (and considerably more comprehensible), comprising some 37 orderly, consequential, and structured poems by the widely read but untutored and tasteless Iakov in which Sokolov indulges in parody of, among other things, the great figures of early 19th-century Russian prose, Pushkin, Lermontov, and Gogol', reflecting Iakov's own struggle to find a link between poetry and prose. Several poems are also inset in the unparagraphed prose sections, and it may thus be said that, in pursuing his aim of raising prose to the level of poetry, Sokolov has written a text that combines poetic prose with prosaic poetry.

Though maximally remote from the realistic tradition, this is a very typically Russian novel, both in the obvious literary allusions, in the mixing of prose and poetry traditions (Pushkin, Gogol', Nabokov, and Pasternak all come to mind) and, above all, in the richly colloquial, quasi-folkloric prose. Sokolov's apparent indifference to philosophical and moral questions set him apart from both 19th-century and Soviet traditions. In a sophisticated, highly worked, deliberately irrational modernistic style Sokolov has painted a grim but fascinating picture of life at its most primitive. The philosophy of this novel, if it has one, is of unrelieved pessimism in the human condition. Its comprehensive analysis and assessment as a literary text lie some way in the future.

ARNOLD MCMILLIN

Astrophobia

Palisandriia

Novel, 1985

Astrophobia, Sokolov's third novel, is a rambling quasi-historical fantasy. It differs from its predecessors in many ways, not least in that it has an overt plot, although the latter's purpose seems more to link a series of wild and colourful episodes than to pursue a credible or consistent story, or, indeed, develop a strong idea. The genre is extravagant comic picaresque with some elements of the mock-epic, and there are several echoes of traditional folk themes, as well as innumerable references to world culture and Russian literature in particular. More accessible than its predecessors, *Astrophobia* is, however, no shallow romp, and represents a feat of great creative imagination.

Ostensibly produced in the year 2757 by a biographer-cum-editor, it consists of the memoirs of Palisandr Dal'berg, a grand nephew of Lavrentii Beria and great-grandson of Grigorii Rasputin, who is heir-apparent to the throne of Russia, after Beria's suicide. The ensuing period, in which a Council of Guardians is presided over by a Brezhnev figure, is known as the Period of Timelessness, and at the start of the memoirs the young but far from innocent Palisandr is steward of the Government Massage Parlour, situated in the most famous monastery in Moscow. We learn that he has been banished here for his part in a jape that frightened Stalin to death, but the post seems to suit him, for he is, it emerges, an oversexed hermaphrodite, bald as a coot, seven-fingered and cross-eyed, who was sadistically raped as a boy and who has an abiding quasi-necrophiliac passion for old or dead women; his pursuit of this passion is described in some detail (but in chaste language) in the course of the book.

Having just learned from a newspaper that an old couple in the Duchy of Belvedere are advertising for a grandson and heir, Palisandr is informed by Andropov that Russia is being secretly ruled by a (perhaps Masonic) group from abroad, indeed from Belvedere. Palisandr is instructed to infiltrate and spy on them, gaining credibility by killing Brezhnev (his rival, incidentally, for the favours of his employer, Shagane, madame of the massage parlour). The assassination attempt fails, and our hero is imprisoned and eventually airlifted by balloon to Belvedere where he suffers hard times, a fate made no easier by the discovery (which he had previously concealed from himself and the world) that he is both old and a hermaphrodite. He falls into the clutches of Majorette, the woman who had sadistically corrupted him in his youth. She (or her reincarnation) is now ensconced in a former Romanov estate in France that she has converted into a sex den disguised as an old people's home. Raped by her again, Palisandr flees abroad and takes up a new international career as a bisexual prostitute, author of pornographic books, and Nobel-Prize winning advocate of hermaphrodite rights. Now wealthy and famous, he engages in the collection of the graves of all the distinguished Russians who have died in exile. Many years later he is invited to bring them back to their fatherland and to assume his own rightful place on the throne of Russia.

A summary of the contents of this extravagantly sprawling novel gives an idea of its genre: comic picaresque with some elements of the mock-epic, and a strong admixture of folk themes. The narrator is loquacious and unreliable, and time in the novel is anything but linear (both the latter features are prominent in Sokolov's earlier novels). The main single element in this book, however, is undoubtedly parody, and its principal objects may be seen to be the most popular genres of third-wave Russian émigré literature: history, first of all; particularly the type of historical writing, epitomized by Solzhenitsyn, which seeks to correct the distortions of official history (Sokolov, it should be noted, regards all historical writing as "simply an addition to the collective myth"). Other objects of parody in the novel include the erotic or pornographic novel, science fiction, political treatises and detective writing. More striking than any of them, however, are the constant references to classical and modern mythology, to world literature, and particularly to Russian literature of the 19th and 20th centuries, not least that of other expatriate writers. The book is almost saturated with literary allusions and reminiscences, far from all of which play an obvious role.

Astrophobia is more than anything else a book about literature, and the language in which it is written calls attention to itself. Palisandr's meandering memoirs are, intermittently, in a quasi-chivalric style, ranging from the pompous loftiness of Russian Neoclassicism via Gogol''s labyrinthine wordiness to the refinement and somewhat recherché elegance of the early 20th-century Silver Age. Despite all the sexual escapades there is almost no use of the vulgar lexicon so popular with many émigré writers. Instead Sokolov/Dal'berg chooses elaborate and sometimes exquisite circumlocutions both for genital parts and for various erotic functions and techniques; in this he clearly recalls Nabokov, a writer he greatly admires. Sokolov's novel is also unusual in that it does not make great play with distortions of Soviet speech and slogans, despite the prominent part played in its early pages by a range of prominent representatives of communist power. Only, perhaps, in Palisandr's graphomania is there a hint at the Soviet leaders' loquaciousness in both speeches and memoirs.

Astrophobia does not seem to have produced a great impact on either Russian or western readers, despite (or perhaps because) of its having a hero combining elements of Don Juan, Oedipus, Dracula and others, and a plot that parodies both Russian historical memoirs and a traditional mythological quest, with myriad references to literature and politics. Most readers, understandably, prefer the much more organically whole and formally polished *A School for Fools*, while those who see the reading of literature as a game prefer *Mezhdu sobakoi i volkom*. None the less *Astrophobia* is an absurdist epic of great energy whose many layers of irony and grotesque fantasy can provide rich entertainment as well as cerebral satisfaction. It is to be hoped that with his third novel Sokolov, silent for a decade, has not written himself out.

ARNOLD MCMILLIN

Vladimir Aleksandrovich Sollogub 1813–1882

Prose writer

Biography

Born in St Petersburg, 20 August 1813, of Polish descent. Educated at home then at Dorpat University, graduated in 1834. Met Pushkin in 1831. Became official in the Ministry of the Interior, 1835. Literary debut, 1837. Married: Sof'ia Mikhailovna Viel'gorskaia in 1840. Visited Nice and met Gogol' in 1843. Court historiographer, 1856. Sent abroad to study European theatre, 1858. Died in Hamburg, 17 June 1882.

Publications

Collected Edition

Sochineniia, 5 vols. St Petersburg, 1855–56.

Fiction

Tarantas: Putevye vpechatleniia. 1845; facsimile of 1845 edition, Moscow, 1982; translated as *The Tarantas: Travelling Impressions of Young Russia*, London, Chapman and Hall, 1850; also as *The Tarantas: Impressions of a Journey*, by William Edward Brown, Ann Arbor, Ardis, 1989.

Povesti i rasskazy. Moscow and Leningrad, 1962.

Tri povesti. Moscow, 1978.

Povesti i rasskazy. Moscow, 1988.

Memoirs

Vospominaniia. 1887.

Vospominaniia. Moscow and Leningrad, 1931.

Plays

Bukety [Bouquets] (produced 1845).

His Hat and Cane: A Comedy in One Act, translated by members of The Bellevue Dramatic Club of Newport, Boston, Baker, 1902.

Vodevili [Vaudevilles]. Moscow, 1937.

Critical Studies

"Tarantas" (review, 1845), by V.G. Belinskii, in his *Polnoe sobranie sochinenii*, vol. 9, 1955, 75–117.

"Sochineniia grafa V.A. Solloguba" (review, 1857), by N.A. Dobroliubov, in his *Sobranie sochinenii*, 1961, vol. 1, 520–43.

Vladimir Sollogub i ego glavnaia kniga, by A.S. Nemzer,

Moscow, 1982 (issued with facsimile edition of *Tarantas*, 1982).

"V.A. Sollogub and *High Society*", by Michael Pursglove, in *The Society Tale in Russian Literature: From Odoevskii to Tolstoi*, edited by Neil Cornwell, Amsterdam, Rodopi, 1998, 59–72.

Vladimir Sollogub's first short stories, "Tri zhenikha" [Three Bridegrooms] and "Dva studenta" [Two Students], appeared in the journal *Sovremennik* in 1837. Thereafter his work appeared mainly in *Otechestvennye zapiski*, where it attracted the attention of Vissarion Belinskii. He wrote society novellas, such as "Lev" [The Lion],1841 and "Bol'shoi svet" [High Society], 1840 which describe the emptiness and vanity of St Petersburg life. "Sobachka" [The Dog], the theme of which was theatrical life and provincial boredom, was Sollogub's contribution to the Natural School, while "Povest' o dvukh kaloshakh" [The History of Two Galoshes] (1839) was a popular sentimental tear-jerker. "Vospitanitsa" [The Ward] (1846) is cast in the form of the memoirs of a wandering actor and, appropriately perhaps, is overlong and melodramatic. In the 1845–46 season his play *Bukety* [Bouquets] was produced with considerable success in St Petersburg. Based on the visit of leading Italian opera singers to St Petersburg the previous year and the practice of throwing flowers on to the stage, it has a vaudeville plot concerning a minor official, Triapka (i.e. Rag), who throws flowers on to the stage on behalf of his superior. Unfortunately he chooses the wrong singer to compliment in this manner and is dismissed. The work was attacked by the reactionary journal *Severnaia pchela* for its disrespectful attitude to officialdom. It also caused its author great problems with the censor, having incurred the displeasure of the future Alexander II. Sollogub also had a play, *Preuve d'amitie*, produced in Paris in 1859 and wrote an anti-nihilist poem "Nigilist" [The Nihilist] (1865). His memoirs describe his relations with Pushkin, with whom he almost fought a duel and for whom he was to have acted as second in an aborted duel with Dantes in 1836. Pushkin encouraged Sollogub's early literary efforts. The memoirs are witty and full of such incidents as the one that gave rise to *Anton-Goremyka* by D.V. Grigorovich, whose father worked on the Sollogub estate near Simbirsk. However, Sollogub's fame rests almost entirely on *Tarantas: Putevye vpechatleniia* (*The Tarantas: Impressions of a Journey*), which appeared in part in 1840 and in full in 1845. The title alludes to a type of carriage, owned by the corpulent, somewhat hen-pecked, tea-swilling, down-to-earth landowner Vasilii Ivanovich. He is returning from Moscow via Kazan to his estate and is joined on the journey by another landowner, 30 years his junior, the talkative Ivan Vasil'evich, who is familiar with western Europe and now wants to inspect Russia in the light of that experience. As their mirror-image names suggest, the two men are complete opposites, rather in the manner of Gogol''s two Ivans. There are echoes of Gogol' everywhere in *The Tarantas*, from a reference to *Revizor* (*The Government Inspector*) to the obvious influence of *Mertvye dushi* (*Dead Souls*): the carriage itself; the travelling hamper (*pogrebets*); the agglomeration of detail in, for example, the second chapter; the "homunculus" on the opening page – a tailor who has had a sign saying "Newly arrived from Petersburg" for the last 40 years; the use of synecdoche – at one point Vasilii Ivanovich becomes his tarantas; the delayed biographies of the two main characters. The journey was, in fact, based on a real journey made in 1839 by the author and G.G. Gagarin, a future president of the Academy of Arts. Gagarin illustrated the text and the wood-cuts made from his sketches, over 50 in all, were regarded by many as the highlight of the book, not least by Belinskii who devoted a quarter of his review to discussing them. There are interesting differences between the seven chapters (1–3, 5, 8, 9, and 18 in the final version) that appeared in *Otechestvennye zapiski* in 1840 and the 1845 edition, which consists of an expanded version of these chapters plus a further 13 chapters. To assign this book to a particular literary genre is difficult. The subtitle is "impressions of a journey" and the inclusion of a chapter devoted entirely to a description of the Monastery of the Caves in Nizhnii Novgorod, which the author has visited but his fictional characters have not, reinforces the impression that this is a travelogue. On the other hand, it might equally well be regarded as a novel, held together structurally by the "journey" device. The narrative is twice interrupted in novellistic fashion (chapters 7 and 9) by "tales" told by episodic characters. In his short review of *The Tarantas* Belinskii points out the difficulty of classifying the work: "It is not a novel, not a novella, not a travelogue, not a philosophical tract, not a journal article but all these things rolled into one." He concedes that the book is "original and interesting", that it is "lively, colourful, inspired, and variegated". He goes on to say that it is "a book which raises questions in the soul of the reader" and terms it a "colourful kaleidoscope of paradoxes". In his subsequent long article devoted to the book, Belinskii spells out what the questions are and comes to the conclusion that the book is not, after all, paradoxical. The question revolves round the views expressed by Ivan Vasil'evich, which, at the beginning of chapter 6, are characterized as a desire to "put his native land back again into pre-Petrine antiquity", and the extent to which they reflect Sollogub's own views. Belinskii concludes that they do not, any more than Chichikov's views reflect those of Gogol'. The way in which the most portentous utterances of Ivan Vasil'evich are undercut by Vasilii Ivanovich seems to bear out this view. A good example is provided by the end of chapter 6, where Ivan Vasil'evich's views on literature provoke nothing but sleep in his interlocutor. However, the tone of the book is uneven, with the 1840 chapters being much lighter in tone than the rest. Perhaps because Sollogub's own ideological position is predictably unclear – he was more renowned for his wit than his commitment – the book did, indeed provoke questions, particularly on the nature of Slavophilism. The Slavophile critic Iurii Samarin devoted a long review to the book in 1846.

MICHAEL PURSGLOVE

Fedor Kuz'mich Sologub 1863–1927

Prose writer, poet, and dramatist

Biography

Born Fedor Kuz'mich Teternikov in St Petersburg, 1 March 1863. Graduated from the Teachers' Training Institute, 1882. Taught mathematics at provincial schools, 1882[-]92. Returned to St Petersburg, continued to teach mathematics until 1907. From 1892 became known as modernist poet. His novel, *Melkii bes* (*The Petty Demon*) published in 1907. Married: Anastasia Chebotarevskaia in 1908 (committed suicide in 1921). Became one of most popular living Russian poets of his time; a 12-volume edition of his works was published, 1909[-]12, and a 20-volume edition was planned, 1913. Significant figure of the Symbolist movement. Requested permission from Lenin to travel abroad, 1921: request denied. A further eight small volumes of his poetry were published, 1921[-]23. Chairman of the Leningrad Writers' Union, 1927. Died in Leningrad, 5 December 1927.

Publications

Collected Editions

Sobranie sochinenii, 12 vols. St Petersburg, 1909[-]12.
Sobranie sochinenii, vols 1, 3, 5, 6, 9, 11[-]20, St Petersburg, 1913[-]14.
The Sweet-Scented Name and Other Fairy-Tales, Fables and Stories, edited by Stephen Graham. London, Constable, and New York, Putnam, 1915.
The Old House and Other Tales, translated by John Cournos. London, Martin Secker, 1916; Westport, Connecticut, Greenwood Press, 1974.
Izbrannoe. Chicago, Russian Language Specialties, 1965.
Stikhotvoreniia. "Biblioteka poeta", Leningrad, 1975.
The Kiss of the Unborn and Other Stories, translated by Murl G. Barker. Knoxville, University of Tennessee Press, 1977.
Rasskazy. Berkeley, University of California Press, 1979.
Neizdannoe i nesobrannoe. Munich, Sagner, 1989.
Izbrannoe. Moscow, 1990.
Sobranie sochinenii, vol. 1 (*Rasskazy 1894–1908*), edited by Ulrich Steltner. Munich, Sagner, 1992; vol. 2 (*Rasskazy 1909–1921*), Munich, Sagner, 1997.
Neizdannyi Fedor Sologub. Moscow, 1997.

Fiction

Tiazhelye sni, in *Severnyi vestnik*, 7–12 (1895); translated as *Bad Dreams*, by Vassar W. Smith, Ann Arbor, Ardis, 1978.
Teni [Shadows], *Severnyi vestnik*, 12 (1896).
Zhalo smerti [The Sting of Death], *Skorpion* (1904).
Melkii bes. St Petersburg, 1908; reprinted Letchworth, Bradda, 1966; translated as *The Little Demon*, by John Cournos and Richard Aldington, London, Martin Secker, and New York, Knopf, 1916; and by Ronald Wilks, London, New English Library, 1962 [incomplete text]; Harmondsworth, Penguin, 1994; as *The Petty Demon*, by Andrew Field, New York, Random House, 1962; Bloomington, Indiana University Press, 1970; and by Samuel Cioran, Ann Arbor, Ardis, 1983; London, Quartet, 1990.
Kniga ocharovanii [A Book of Charms]. 1909.
Tvorimaja legenda. Eine Legende im Werden. Nachdruck der Bde XVIII–XX der Gesamtausgabe der Werke Sologubs, St Petersburg, 1914; reprinted with an introduction by Johannes Holthusen, Munich, Fink, 1972; *Tvorimaia legenda*, 2 vols, edited by Lev Sobolev, Moscow, 1991; translated as *The Created Legend*, by John Cournos, New York, Stokes, 1916; and by Samuel D. Cioran, 3 vols, Ann Arbor, Ardis, 1979.

Poetry

Rasskazy i stikhi. St Petersburg, 1896.
Rodine [To the Homeland]. St Petersburg, 1906.
Plamennyi krug [The Fiery Circle]. Moscow, 1908; Berlin, Grzhebin, 1922.
Voina: Stikhi [War], *Otechestvo* (1915).
Fimiamy. Petrograd, 1921; reprinted Letchworth, Bradda, 1972.
Nebo goluboe [The Blue Sky]. 1921; reprinted Letchworth, Bradda, 1972.
Sobornyi blagovest [The Cathedral Bell-Ringing]. Petrograd, 1921.
Charodeinaia chasha [The Magical Cup]. Petrograd, 1922; reprinted Letchworth, Bradda, 1970.
Koster dorozhnyi [The Roadside Bonfire]. Moscow, 1922; reprinted Letchworth, Bradda, 1980.
Stikhi. 1923.

Plays

Dar mudrykh pchel [The Gift of the Wise Bees]. 1907.
Pobeda smerti [Conquest of Death]. 1907.
Nochnye plaski [Nocturnal Dances]. 1908.
Van'ka kliuchnik i pazh Zhan [Johnny the Butler and Jean the Page]. 1908.

Critical Studies

"Plamennyi krug", by A. Gornfel'd, in *Zarnitsy. Literaturno-politicheskii sbornik*, no. 2, St Petersburg, 1909, 53–88.
O F. Sologube: Kritika, stat'i i zametki, edited by Anastasia Chebotarevskaia, St Petersburg, 1911; reprinted Ann Arbor, Ardis, 1983.
Fedor Sologubs Roman-trilogie (Tvorimaja legenda). Aus der Geschichte des russischen Symbolismus, by Johannes Holthusen, The Hague, Mouton, 1960.
Prekhitraia viaz', by Galina Selegen', Washington, DC, Kamkin, 1968.
"Trirodov among the Symbolists: From the Drafts for Sologub's *Tvorimaja legenda*", by Henryk Baran, in *Neue Russische Literatur*, Almanach 2–3, Salzburg, University of Salzburg, 1979–80, 179–202.
Sologub's Literary Children: Keys to a Symbolist Prose, by Stanley J. Rabinowitz, Columbus, Ohio, Slavica, 1980.
"Fedor Sologub and the Critics: The Case of *Nav'i čary*", by Henryk Baran, in *Studies in 20th Century Russian Prose*, edited by Nils Åke Nilsson, Stockholm, Almqvist & Wiksell, 1982, 26–58.
Fedor Sologub 1884–1984: Texte Aufsätze, Bibliographie, edited by Berhard Lauer, Munich, Sagner, 1984.

Insidious Intent: An Interpretation of Fedor Sologub's "The Petty Demon", by Diana Greene, Columbus, Ohio, Slavica, 1986.
Fiodor Sologub 1863–1927, by Nina Denisoff, Paris, Minard, 1987.
Poetika russkoi literatury nachala XX veka, by Henryk Baran, Moscow, 1993, 211–63.
"Fyodor Sologub: A Critical Biography", by V.W. Smith, PhD dissertation, California, Stanford University, 1993.
"Transformation as Revelation: Sologub, Schopenhauer and the Little Man", by Eric Laursen, *Slavic and East European Journal*, 39/4 (1995), 552[-]67.
"Plotting Against Abstraction in Russian Literature's Provincial Hell: Fedor Sologub's Aesthetics of Embodiment", by Stephen Hutchings, *Modern Language Review*, 91 (1996), 655–76.

The most versatile of the Russian "decadents" and Symbolists, Fedor Sologub fought his way up from obscurity. His father, a tailor and footman, died when Sologub was four, and the poet was brought up by his mother, a strong-minded, but illiterate and often cruel laundry woman. Sologub's childhood was a hell of thrashings, from which Teachers' Training Institute and books – above all *Don Quixote* – saved him. From 1882 to 1892, with his mother and sister, he taught in obscure provincial schools, beginning his finest novel, *Melkii bes* (*The Petty Demon*), a hallucinatory product of these years, on his return in 1892 to St Petersburg. By 1889 Sologub had begun to translate the poetry of Verlaine and had mastered Symbolist, as well as naturalistic modes in literature. From 1892 he made a reputation as a modernist poet, pursuing musicality and longing for the unearthly and unattainable. The journal *Severnyi vestnik* invented his pseudonym, presumably to protect his official career as a schoolteacher and inspector (deputy head) from his decadent notoriety. His first novel was published as *Tiazhelye sny* (*Bad Dreams*) in 1895, anticipating his major trilogy *Tvorimaia legenda* (*The Created Legend*) 1908–12. The philosophy of Schopenhauer (in the Russian translation by the poet Afanasii Fet) sharpened Sologub's vision in the late 1890s; social concerns and civic awareness give way to existential despair, which is lightened only by a demonic rebellion inspired by his reading of Nietzsche and Dostoevskii.

A happy marriage to the writer (of critiques on art and of children's stories) Anastasia Chebotarevskaia – quite apart from Sologub's correct formal attire "a brick in a frock-coat" – belied his decadent writings, and brought into his work a fervent sympathy with the child and adolescent: this warmth makes his short stories about children unique in their empathy, but the novels sometimes hint of paedophilia. Children represent innocence, but also the ingenuous sexual explorations of Daphnis and Chloe, which can make a modern reader uncomfortable. Sologub's poetry develops the childlike myth (out of Lermontov's poem "Angel") that our souls have been delivered to the wrong planet, that we belong to the planet Oile and the star Maira – a myth that Nabokov developed in his novel *Ada*, where the characters are stranded on Antiterra, receiving only telepathic messages from Terra. This childlike science fiction becomes Sologub's main pathos from 1898: "Everything we lack here, / Everything which the sinful earth dreams, / Has flowered and shone on you, / O blessed fields of Ligoia!"

Sologub's development was interrupted by brief moments of civic concern in the 1905 Revolution and the first years of World War I; the agonizing death of his sister in 1907 sent him back to his tragic invented world and led him for the rest of his life to take Don Quixote as the example of a poet who lives by an invented ideal, turning "sweaty" Aldonsas into pure Dulcineas. From 1907 Sologub became a dramatist; although his plays had limited success in production, *Dar' mudrykh pchel* [The Gift of the Wise Bees], and *Van'ka kliuchnik i pazh Zhan* [Johnny the Butler and Jean the Page] are the most viable of Russian Symbolist dramas. In 1908 Sologub's best verse was collected in *Plamennyi krug* [The Fiery Circle]. From now on he classified his verse by quality (and price per line), a cynicism that reflected his objective editorial abilities. Sologub managed his image and his work in order to impress and to shock. In 1909 his Collected Works began to appear in three separate editions and he became, with Andreev, Kuprin, and Gor'kii one of the four best-known living Russian writers (both in Russia and abroad), although from 1913 until 1920 he showed little development. In 1920 Sologub fought for permission to leave Russia; the strain drove Anastasia Chebotarevskaia to drown herself. Sologub could not accept her death and in the last seven years of his life led a stoic solitary life. He published a great deal in the 1920s, partly earlier verse, but a body of poems that are his greatest (and most desolate): "Whatever they give you, even vomit on a plate, / Eat it and don't bare your teeth". Despite his hostility to the times, he was elected to represent Leningrad's writers in 1926. The month of his death fulfilled his prediction of 1913: "December's dark will destroy me".

Sologub still awaits a complete edition of his work. Despite the unevenness, the existing edition includes the finest and most terrifying of short stories, such as "Svet i Teni" [Light and Shadows] (1895), where a mother is drawn into her son's insane obsession with shadow-puppets, or "Soediniaushchii dushi" [The Uniter of Souls] (1906), where two complementary men are united, to leave not the perfect human being, but only a tiny pool on the carpet. *The Petty Demon* is, with Belyi's *Petersburg*, the most powerful novel of the Silver Age – it develops from Chekhov's stories of degenerate schoolteachers in nameless provincial hell-holes and from Gogol''s dead souls a grey, bureaucratic inferno, with a parody of Symbolist eternal feminine in the fiery "untouchable" (*nedotykomka*) and the vile servant-girl, Varvara, who both lead the schoolteacher to paranoia and murder and provoke the town's inhabitants to riot and scandal. The many Don Quixote lyrics are magical in their despair: "Forgotten are wine and merriment, / Abandoned are armour and sword. / Alone he descends to the dungeon / And refuses to light a lamp." Quite apart from the extensive and fine translation from French Symbolists and Greek classics, when Sologub's best original work is extracted from his dross, he will be seen as the greatest of the Russian Symbolists.

DONALD RAYFIELD

The Petty Demon

Melkii bes

Novel, 1908

Sologub's most successful work, and his only fully satisfying novel, *The Petty Demon*, was conceived in his years as a provincial schoolteacher, and completed ten years later in 1902. A major episode (chapters 18 to 23), from the hero's first dementia to his marriage, was serialized in 1905, but not until 1907 did the novel make Sologub a household name. It merges several traditions. One clear influence comes from Chekhov – Peredonov, the grammar-school teacher reduced to a subhuman paranoiac by his provincial existence under a repressive state, recalls the "Chelovek v futliare" ("Man in a Case"), Belikov, with his denunciations, and "Uchitel' slovesnosti" ("The Literature Teacher"), in his degradation by marriage. The grotesque series of town officials who govern Peredonov's life and to whom he denounces his colleagues and pupils are direct descendants of Gogol''s civil servants, while the scandalous ball, which is the novel's most successful climax, with its rioting and fire, reminds one of the fête for distressed governesses in Dostoevskii's *Besy* (*The Devils* or *The Possessed*). There is also a considerable debt to Saltykov-Shchedrin's horrific study of moral degeneration, *Gospoda Golovlevy* (*The Golovlevs*). In a more modern vein, the fiery spirit, the *nedotykomka* ("untouchable") that appears to Peredonov in his madness and leads him to arson and to murder, is a typically Decadent mutant of the Eternal Feminine common to most of the Russian Symbolists. Sologub himself claimed that the novel was a realistic portrayal of the hell of the provinces from which he fortuitously emerged into literary St Petersburg. It was for him not just a personal, but a social hell: "No, my dear contemporaries," he wrote, in the same vein as Gogol', "it was about you that I wrote my novel about the Petty Demon and its horrific 'untouchable'." The very name of the hero, Peredonov, "the very bottom", suggests a harrowing hellish world. The school at which Peredonov unaccountably rises so high in rank (he is a "state councillor") is run by a benign, wise, but impotent headmaster, Khripach ("the hoarse"), who closely resembles the wise author in his perceptions and kindliness, while the contrast of sensitive, vulnerable children and adolescents with gross, vile adults is a typical standpoint of Sologub the pedagogue.

The Petty Demon is also convincing, like many Chekhov stories, as a fictional record of the progress of a disease. Peredonov's ambitious, cowardly, devious, but gullible nature is gradually driven by frustration into paranoia; his nastiness (as he trashes his landlady's house) degenerates into cruelty and finally bloody violence; his sensitiveness to the opinions of others develops into persecution mania. In the thrall of illusory voices, Peredonov can be seen not only as the victim of disease, but of inspiration – an association common enough in Sologub's work.

Like Sologub's best stories, the work is child-centred not only in its creation of a childlike counterbalance but in its direct, simplified narration. The nightmarish atmosphere is built on the basis of short sentences, uncomplicated narration, which may owe a great deal to the techniques of Sologub's wife, Anastasia Chebotarevskaia, a skilful writer for children. Sologub's child world does not strike every reader as a healthy counter-balance to his depraved adults. The sub-plot (in which Sasha Pylnikov, whom Peredonov has singled out to bully, is captivated by the Rutilov sisters, who engage in endless but inconclusive foreplay with him) has a pornographic resonance to a modern reader, and we are left with no illusions about the innocence of Liudmila and Sasha's games when Sasha is dressed up as a geisha for the ball scene. The experimentation with perfumes and transvestism to corrupt Sasha reminds one of episodes in J.-K. Huysmans's *À Rebours (Against Nature)* and forces one to classify *The Petty Demon* as a Decadent work, for all its protests about exploitation of children. The novel was singled out for criticism in a study of 1909, *The Pornographic Element in Russian Literature*, by G.S. Nezlobin.

The female emerges in *The Petty Demon* as a repulsive, threatening force. Peredonov's mistress, the kitchen-maid Varvara, tricks him into marriage by promising that her former employer will make him school inspector if he marries her; their neighbours, for instance Grushina, are little more than malevolent witches, while in the riot of the ball, it is the women who show the greatest savagery in assaulting the transvestite Sasha. The novel is hardly a psychological work: male and female are driven by incoherent urges. They act mechanically, and many scenes are constructed around a scenario more suited for a puppet-theatre than a novel of motivation. By mingling elements of traditional realism with Decadence and puppet-theatre, Sologub has inadvertently anticipated Samuel Beckett's dismal and repetitive universe.

In 1909 Sologub dramatized his novel as a five-act tragedy. He deliberately altered the tone and focus of the novel, declaring: "In the novel Peredonov is depicted more vile than weak; in the drama the reverse". The play was performed in ten cities in the following winter, but it was torn to shreds by the critics – "a beautiful poem has died on stage ... a cruel and unnecessary operation" – and then dropped from the repertoire, scarcely to be published in Russia (until 1988); the excisions (largely of erotic fantasies from the Liudmila/Sasha sub-plot) arguably improved the work and protected Sologub from accusations of prurience.

DONALD RAYFIELD

Plamennyi krug

The Fiery Circle

Poetry collection, 1908

Two collections of Sologub's verse bear this title: a 1908 edition published in Moscow by the Symbolist journal *Zolotoe runo* and a 1922 edition, nearly identical in content, put out in Berlin by the émigré publisher Z.I. Grzhebin. In terms of Sologub's literary development, the original volume played a major role. It brought together more than 150 poems, almost all of which had previously appeared in various periodicals and anthologies; among those included were a number of texts that Sologub and his contemporaries valued very highly. The collection was regarded not only as a distillation of Sologub's achievement in the realm of poetry up to that point, but also as a kind of synthesis of his idiosyncratic poetic *Weltanschauung*.

In the brief foreword to *Plamennyi krug*, Sologub underscores the panchronic quality of the collection and of his vision: "Born not for the first time, and not for the first time in the process of completing the circle of external metamorphoses, I open up my soul calmly and simply. I open it for I wish that the intimate become universal". At the same time, he quotes in the foreword from one of his solipsistic texts: "For I am everything and in everything, and only I, and there is not, was not and will not be another". The two formulations neatly complement each other, and provide the starting and end points for the collection.

The idea of metempsychosis motivates the various lyric

personae assumed by the poet; beneath the "masks of life experiences" ("Lichiny perezhivanii" – the title of the initial, keynote section) we are asked to see the "I" of the poet, who shares with the reader the experience of past incarnations. His lyric journey into former times and cultures begins as Adam in the Garden ("Ia byl odin v moem raiu ..." [I was alone within my Paradise]) and includes appearances of such figures as the celebrated 4th-century BC Athenian hetaera Phryne ("Nasytiv ochi nagotoiu" [After filling my eyes with the naked beauty]), an assassin doomed to painful death in ancient Rome ("Neron skazal bogam derzhavnym" [Nero told to the sovereign gods]), and a hangman in the medieval city of Nuremberg, whose assertion of quasi-existential boredom contrasts with the blood-thirst that leads him to torment his own son ("Niurembergskii palach" – one of Sologub's finest poems). On occasion, Sologub goes even further by having his protagonist assume the form of a dog (e.g., "Vysoka luna Gospodnia" [High above is God's moon]: that such risky anthropomorphism results in moving lyric experiences is a tribute to his brilliance as a poet.

Each section in the collection highlights a central theme. These are the constant elements of Sologub's private mythology: earthly existence as a prison ("My – plenennye zveri" [We are captive beasts]), death as a friend whose arrival brings welcome release, the attraction of evil, etc. Some of these are not fully reconcilable within the framework of a single ontology: while in one part of the volume Sologub vaunts the power of dream, of imagination, to build a private cosmos superior to Nature ("A sinful youth, he lived alone, / In dreams and fairy-tales flowered his soul"), elsewhere, especially in the section "Tikhaia dolina" [A Quiet Valley], he echoes Lermontov and Tiutchev in creating exquisite landscapes, celebrating the beauty of the natural world, and emphasizing the underlying isomorphism of Nature and the human psyche. By helping to relieve the volume's tendency towards schematism, such tensions actually prove beneficial.

The expression "the flaming circle" is associated with different meanings. There is, first, the notion that human existence, painful in and of itself, is tied to the constantly revolving wheel of birth and rebirth. At the same time, a circle may be used in sorcerous rites, and the theme of sorcery recurs throughout the collection, where the poet, making good though restrained use of Russian popular beliefs and rituals, often assumes the guise of a seeker after forbidden knowledge, at once drawn to and threatened by the world of the occult. Flame imagery is further linked to sexuality, generally presented as evil, poisonous, yet inescapable (Innokentii Annenskii commented: "Sologub's love is lustful and tender, but one perceives in it a bit of decay, a bit of something almost Karamazov-like, a kind of constant likelihood of crime"). Significantly, the realms of magic and Eros are frequently conjoined – in texts that succeed in evoking the realm of folklore while, simultaneously, functioning within the context of a Symbolist (Decadent) poetics.

The original edition of *Plamennyi krug* appeared when Russian Symbolism was at the peak of its influence, and when Sologub himself, thanks largely to *The Petty Demon* and a notorious lyric cycle devoted to sadomasochist thematics, had become one of its most prominent and avidly discussed representatives. During this period, sensation-seeking journalists and critics perused each new work to come from his pen for clues to his personality. The verse collection, with its explicit (and misleading) avowal of revealing the author's innermost secrets, seemed designed to meet such demands, though in fact Sologub forbore from including in it some of his most audacious texts. Still, the aura of scandal that habitually surrounded him was heightened when the Moscow censorship office, suspecting sacrilegious references to the Virgin Mary in one of the poems, briefly held up sales of his book.

The reception of *Plamennyi krug* was generally very favourable. According to Aleksandr Blok, Sologub had never before reached "such perfection in his verse"; in the same vein, Georgii Chulkov listed several texts in the volume which "have now become classic and which one must know by heart". For his part, Valerii Briusov saw the collection as containing "the most profound, the most euphonious of Sologub's creations", though he noted instances of the poet's formal carelessness, and declared Sologub's philosophy of "extreme solipsism" to be unoriginal and uncompelling. This last point was challenged by Sergei Gorodetskii, who claimed that it was precisely Sologub's philosophy that "forms the life and meaning of his creations", that "renders his image within a crowd of other poets, and against the background of our contemporary life, tragic and solitary".

HENRYK BARAN

The Created Legend

Tvorimaia legenda

Novel, 1914

The third, and by far the most controversial, of Sologub's novels exists in two major versions in Russian.The first of these, with the overall title *Nav'i chary* [The Spells of the Dead], appeared in several parts over a period of seven years: *Tvorimaia legenda* (*The Created Legend*) 1907, *Kapli krovi* (*Drops of Blood*) 1908, *Koroleva Ortruda* (*Queen Ortruda*) 1909, and *Dym i pepel* (*Smoke and Ashes*) 1912–13. A second, revised version, now entitled *The Created Legend*, came out in 1914, at the tail end of the 20-volume "Sirin" *Sobranie sochinenii* (vol. 18 – *Kapli krovi*, vol. 19 – *Koroleva Ortruda*, vol. 20 – *Dym i pepel*). In it, responding in part to reviewers' comments, Sologub substantially modified the style of his narrative and eliminated or shifted certain episodes (stricter censorship rules also were a factor); these changes were not always felicitous. The "Sirin" edition is regarded as definitive, and was used in a Fink Verlag reprint and as the basis of the 1991 reissue of the novel in Russia. In fact, however, the most complete text of the novel exists not in Russian but in an authorized German translation that was free of censorship and was based on a manuscript copy provided by Sologub himself. There are two translations into English. John Cournos's 1916 translation preserves a certain authenticity (due in part to his having moved in Symbolist circles), but covers only the first part of the trilogy. Samuel D. Cioran published a complete translation in 1979 of the second redaction, restoring deleted episodes from the initial version. While there is some justification for his decision, the result is problematic synthesis that ignores authorial will and disregards the issue of stylistic divergence between the first and second versions of the trilogy.

The novel's opening proclaims the author's method:

> I take a piece of life, coarse and barren, and from it I create an exquisite legend, for I am a poet. Whether life, dull and

> common, stagnates in the gloom, or bursts forth in a raging fire, I, the poet, will erect above you, life, my legend which is being created, my legend of the enchanting and the beautiful.

The Created Legend (literally, *A Legend in Creation*) represents a major departure in Sologub's approach to the genre of the novel. The tightly plotted *Tiazhelye sny* (*Bad Dreams*) and *Petty Demon*, with their depiction of brutish provincial mores in the manner of Gogol' and Saltykov-Shchedrin, give way to a heterogeneous composition that leaves realist tradition far behind, where the principal character suggests that "perhaps you and I are not at all living people, but only the acting personages of a novel, and the author of this novel is not at all inhibited by any concern with external verisimilitude". There are two main, mutually mirroring plot lines: the first is set in Russia during the revolutionary year 1905 and centres on Georgii Trirodov and his beloved Elisaveta; the other takes place in a fictitious Mediterranean kingdom (the United Isles), ruled by the passionate, unhappy Queen Ortruda (an analogue of Elisaveta – one of many such structural doublets in the novel). Although the basic premises of the world depicted in these two story-lines appear to be realistic, this assumption is regularly subverted by such elements as supernatural occurrences and magical ceremonies, a drug-induced vision of the Utopian planet Oile, a science-fiction-derived flight into space, and numerous references to and quotations from contemporary events, personalities, ideas, and literary and publicistic works (some explicit, others – more carefully hidden). Materials for early drafts show that Sologub considered including in the novel certain other episodes, such as a parody on Symbolist literary salons and the bloody suppression of a rebellion by Russian authorities. The text's openness, its potential for absorbing new situations and motifs, goes hand in hand with the lack of resolution of some of its narrative threads, as if the author, underscoring the artificiality of literary creation, deliberately did not tie up the loose ends of the plot, thus leaving open the possibility – real or suggested – of further developments.

Trirodov – chemist, educational reformer, political activist, mage, and decadent poet – not only resembles Sologub in some details of physical appearance, not only displays some of the author's private obsessions (as in other of his works, Sologub tantalizes us with glimpses of his psyche, while, simultaneously, denying that he does so), but also acts as *porte-parole* for the latter's most cherished ideas. Throughout *The Created Legend*, we find numerous quotations from Sologub's verse and prose on his and other characters' lips (Kornei Chukovskii termed the novel a "museum of Sologub's past experiences"). In line with Sologub's avowal of art's power to transform reality (a major component of his world-view during the period 1905–10), Trirodov is shown as a strong, active individual, marked by being able to accept the unresolved dichotomies of Sologub's universe (irony / lyric, Aldonsa / Dulcinea, life / death, etc.) without losing his ability to act. Throughout the novel, he clashes with and triumphs over – be it by his intellect, his mysterious powers, or thanks to his aristocratic connections – provincial, often reactionary Russian society, epitomized by the figure of Peredonov (mysteriously revived and elevated to the rank of vice-governor). At the end, Sologub's *alter ego* escapes a Black Hundred pogrom with his family, friends, and residents of his educational colony, reaching the less oppressive, though not untroubled United Isles. There, elected monarch following Ortruda's death, he will have the chance to attempt to put into practice on a large scale some of his visionary ideas.

Nav'i chary was eagerly awaited by readers and the press, and became one of the most controversial works of its time (especially the novel's initial sections). For the most part, the reaction was negative, with only modernist critics responding favourably to Sologub's cavalier treatment of realist canons. In general, the novel received a superficial reading (publication delays were a contributing factor). It was derided for the seemingly unmotivated semantic heterogeneity of its fictional world; in a typical comment, one reviewer noted that it "creates the impression of something confused, unnecessary, of combining striking realism with unneeded, uninteresting, organically unattached symbolism". There was extensive discussion, largely unfavourable, of Sologub's prose style, especially his reliance on abbreviated sentences, subjectless constructions, and syntactic inversions (all this modified in the "Sirin" version); these features were an easy target for several clever parodies. Those whose sympathies lay with the recent Revolution of 1905 were incensed by Sologub's treatment of political matters: the Marxist critic Vorovskii termed the novel an instance of "literary scavenging". Finally, thanks in part to Sologub's prior reputation as the "incomparable Russian pornographer", there was widespread criticism of the text's sado-masochist thematics (a love scene, involving Trirodov and the Social Democrat teacher Alkina, provoked Gor'kii's outburst in a letter to Lunacharskii), as well as ironic speculation about Trirodov and the mysterious "quiet boys" in his school (leading the author to defend his protagonist in a newspaper interview against the charge of pederasty).

In assessing this critical *furor*, we must bear in mind that it was prompted by the first redaction of the novel. When the final volumes of the "Sirin" edition appeared, they were almost completely ignored. Still, in 1916 Sologub negotiated for a film version of the novel, and Vsevolod Meierkhol'd worked on its script (preliminary materials for this production are extant).

Though modern readers can look at *The Created Legend* more objectively than did Sologub's contemporaries, its flaws are quite apparent. The text tantalizes with its hints and riddles (e.g. a possible layer of occultist references), but these are of interest primarily to commentators. Trirodov, though interesting as a quasi-self-portrait of Sologub, is too remote, too self-contained a figure to engage the reader's interest. The novel succeeds best when it comes close to the manner of *The Petty Demon*, or when it blends the fantastic with the everyday; the middle part, devoted to the United Isles, is often dull.

Despite these problems, *The Created Legend* retains its importance, not only as a central text among Sologub's works, but as a major example of Symbolist prose. Looking at it from a broader perspective, we can recognize in the trilogy's untrammelled mixture of reality and fancy, of culture, science, folklore, and everyday life, in its encyclopedism and intertextuality, in its play with the conventions of narrative, an early venture in a series of narrative experiments that, by the end of our century, have come to constitute the body of postmodern fiction.

HENRYK BARAN

Vladimir Alekseevich Soloukhin 1924–1997

Prose writer, poet, and essayist

Biography

Born in Alepino Stavrovskii, Vladimir region, 14 June 1924. Attended the Vladimir Engineering Technicum, 1938–42; Gor'kii Literary Institute, Moscow, 1946–51. Married: Rosa Soloukhin. Served in the army until 1945. Magazine feature writer for *Ogonek*. Joined the Communist Party, 1952. Member of the board of the Soviet Writers' Union, from 1959–75. Member of the editorial staff, Molodaia gvardiia publishing house, Moscow, 1964–81. Recipient: State Prize for Literature, 1979. Died 4 April 1997.

Publications

Collected Edition

Sobranie sochinenii, 10 vols. Moscow, 1995 –

Fiction

Kaplia rosy [A Drop of Dew]. Moscow, 1960.
Liricheskie povesti. Rasskazy [Lyrical Tales. Stories]. Moscow, 1961.
Mat'-machekha [Coltsfoot]. Moscow, 1966.
Zakon nabata [The Law of the Alarm]. Moscow, 1971.
Med na khlebe. Moscow, 1978; translated as *Honey on Bread* [various translators], Moscow, Progress, 1982.
Bedstvie s golubiami: Rasskazy i ocherki [Misfortune with Doves: Stories and Essays]. Moscow, 1984.
Scenes from Russian Life, translated by David Martin. London, Peter Owen, 1989.
Smekh za levym plechom. Moscow, 1989; translated as *Laughter Over the Left Shoulder*, by David Martin, London, Peter Owen, 1990.
Lugovaia gvozdichka [Meadow Carnations]. Moscow, 1989.
Posledniaia stupen'. Roman [The Last Step. A Novel]. Moscow, 1995.

Poetry

Dozhd' v stepi [Rain on the Steppe]. Moscow, 1953.
Zhuravlikha [Cranes]. Moscow, 1959.
Zhit' na zemle [To Live on Earth]. Moscow, 1965.
Izbrannaia lirika. Moscow, 1970.
Sedina [Grey Hair]. Moscow, 1977.
Stikhotvoreniia. Moscow, 1982.
Stikhotvoreniia. Moscow, 1990.
Derevo [Tree]. Moscow, 1991.

Essays and Nature Writing

Vladimirskie proselki. Moscow, 1958; translated as *A Walk in Rural Russia*, by Stella Miskin, London, Hodder and Stoughton, 1966; New York, Dutton, 1967.
S liricheskikh pozitsii [From Lyrical Points of View]. Moscow, 1965.
Pis'ma iz russkogo muzeia; Chernye doski; Vremia sobirat' kamni [Letters from the Russian Museum; Blackboards; Time to Collect Stones]. Moscow, 1966; *Chernye doski* translated as *Searching for Icons in Russia*, by Paul Falla, London, Harvill Press, 1971; New York, Harcourt Brace, 1972.
Tret'ia okhota [Third Hunt]. Moscow, 1968.
Slovo zhivoe i mertvoe (o vremeni i o sebe) [The Word Living and Dead (About Time and Self)]. Moscow, 1976.
Kameshki na ladoni [A Handful of Pebbles], 3 vols. Moscow, 1977–88.
Chitaia Lenina [Reading Lenin]. Frankfurt, Posev, 1989.
Rasstavanie s idolom [Parting with the Idol]. Moscow, 1991.
A Time to Gather Stones: Essays, translated by Valerie Z. Nollan. Evanston, Illinois, Northwestern University Press, 1993.

Translator

Moi Dagestan [My Dagestan], by R. Gamzatov, Moscow, 1972.
Slomannaia podkova [A Broken Shoe], by A. Keshokov, Moscow, 1973.

Critical Studies

A History of Post-War Soviet Writing: The Literature of Moral Opposition, by Grigori Svirskii, edited and translated by Robert Dessaix and Michael Ulman, Ann Arbor, Ardis, 1981.
"A Brief Survey of Vladimir Soloukhin's Works", by N.G. Kosachov, *Russian Language Journal* (1981), 121–22.
"Energy and Talent", by Andrei Turkov, *Soviet Literature*, 6/435 (1984).
Russian Village Prose: The Radiant Past, by Kathleen F. Parthé, Princeton, Princeton, University Press, 1992.
"Reinterpreting the Soviet Period of Russian History: Vladimir Soloukhin's Poetic Cycle *Druz'iam*", by Valerie Z. Nollan, *Slavic and East European Journal*, 41/1 (1997), 74–93.

Vladimir Soloukhin is clearly associated with the Village Prose movement, and his themes, concerns and even his literary style have much in common with the likes of Vasilii Belov, Fedor Abramov, Valentin Rasputin, Evgenii Nosov, Boris Mozhaev, Viktor Astaf'ev, and Aleksandr Solzhenitsyn. Above all, he is linked to the other *derevenshchiki* (Village Prose writers) in his preoccupation with personal memory, especially the memory of his own rural childhood.

Soloukhin first came to prominence in the 1950s, and was the first of the Village Prose writers to direct the reader's attention away from the dire economic plight of the collective farm, as was the trend in the publicistic writing of the time, and toward the freshness and beauty of the Russian countryside. This was in his now celebrated essay *Vladimirskie proselki* (*A Walk in Rural Russia*), a seminal work for the evolution of Village Prose's lyrical and environmental concerns. Not only does it purport to "rediscover" nature, in the form of various plants, trees, shrubs, animals and birds, all enumerated and discussed lovingly at length, but also reminds the reader of the Russian past, as exemplified by churches and monuments (especially that of Bagration, hero of the war with Napoleon) that have fallen into disrepair.

These twin themes remain constant in Soloukhin's writing up to the late 1980s, when he is able to become more forthright in his espousal of environmental concerns and the pull of history, and is also able to apportion blame for past mistakes. Another feature of Soloukhin's writing evident here that imbues most of his work is the first-person author/narrator (a notable exception is the autobiographical novel *Mat'-machekha* [Coltsfoot], written as a third-person narrative). Soloukhin consistently engages the reader in a personal dialogue, or rather monologue, where the reader becomes the writer's confidant and is expected to accept and support all his arguments and occasional indictments. In subsequent collections of non-fictional writings such as *Pis'ma iz russkogo muzeia* [Letters from the Russian Museum], *Chernye doski* (*Searching for Icons in Russia*), and *Vremia sobirat' kamni* (*A Time to Gather Stones*) he concludes his celebration of the glorious heritage of Russian art (such as icons and church art and music), architecture and culture, but also criticizes officialdom for consciously seeking to destroy this focus of Russian national identity. In these works he also offers a positive assessment of Christianity: the essay entitled "A Time to Gather Stones", thus giving its name to the collection, is a compelling account of the Optina Pustyn' monastery, made famous by Dostoevskii in *Brat'ia Karamozovy* (*The Brothers Karamazov*) and subsequently destroyed during the Soviet period.

In the late 1980s Soloukhin was able to be more forthright in his criticism of Marxism-Leninism and the Stalinist onslaught on the Russian village. But he did not stop there, and, in the essays *Chitaia Lenina* [Reading Lenin] and *Rasstavanie s idolom* [Parting with the Idol], he was one of the first in Gorbachev's Russia to point the finger at Lenin himself. Devoutly religious, Soloukhin clearly loves the Russian cultural and spiritual heritage, although his espousal of nationalistic causes has made him the butt of jokes by his contemporaries (most notably Grigorii Svirskii). He remains one of the most influential publicists of the nationalist school in Russia in the 1990s.

It would be wrong to assume, however, that Soloukhin's nationalism is virulently anti-western or xenophobic, as is the case with some of his compatriots and literary bed-fellows. Rather, his is a restrained, often lyrical voice. In both his poetry and his prose Soloukhin is content to affirm the joys of nature, the Russian countryside and the Russian cultural heritage. His anger is directed not at foreigners, "non-Russians" intent on destroying the Russian soul, but at faceless bureaucrats driven by ideology (he was, nevertheless, a member of the Communist Party from 1952). Indeed, many of his sketches are positive and enthusiastic accounts of his trips to foreign lands. His writing is infused with nostalgia and sadness at the passing of a way of life, and his fiction contains many wholesome peasant types we associate with the stock characters of Village Prose.

It is likely that Soloukhin's best work will remain *Smekh za levym plechom* (*Laughter Over the Left Shoulder*), in many ways a re-writing of his autobiographical novels *Mat'-machekha* and especially *Kaplia rosy* [A Drop of Dew]. Both *Laughter Over the Left Shoulder* and *Kaplia rosy* concern Soloukhin's own childhood, and cover essentially the same period and events. In the later work, though, Soloukhin "fills in" the blanks left by apparent gaps in his memory, in particular regarding collectivization and the threat to his own family in being labelled as kulaks. *Kaplia rosy* gives more emphasis to the lyricism of a rural childhood; *Laughter Over the Left Shoulder* is more interested in settling accounts with those who pursued collectivization. Curiously, *Laughter Over the Left Shoulder* was first published abroad; back in 1958 Soloukhin had taken part in the campaign of vilification against Pasternak, attacking him above all for publishing *Doctor Zhivago* abroad.

Soloukhin is a writer whose fictional and non-fictional genres fused into one: his concerns remained consistent over 40 years: the Russian past, Russian culture, the Russian countryside and its inhabitants. He continued arguing for their preservation and for greater governmental concern to maintain the Russian cultural heritage.

DAVID GILLESPIE

Vladimir Sergeevich Solov'ev 1853–1900

Poet and religious philosopher

Biography

Born in Moscow, 28 January 1853. Son of the eminent historian, Sergei Mikhailovich Solov'ev. Studied natural sciences, philosophy, and history at Moscow University, 1869–73; Moscow Theological Academy, 1873–74; defended master's thesis, 1874; doctoral thesis, 1880. Favourable reception of his theses led to lectureship, St Petersburg University. Studied at the British Museum, London, 1875; travelled to Egypt, November 1875–March 1876. Gave a series of public lectures, 1877–81: in one lecture made plea for Alexander II's assassins to be treated justly; reprimanded by the Minister of Public Education and as a result voluntarily resigned lectureship and abandoned his academic career. Full-time writer from 1881. Editor (also contributor) of the philosophical sections of the Brockhaus-Efron Encyclopedia from 1891. Travelled again to Europe and Egypt, 1898. Suffered from arterial sclerosis and kidney failure. Died near Moscow, 13 August 1900.

Publications

Collected Editions

Sobranie sochinenii, 2nd edition, 10 vols. St Petersburg, 1911–14; reprinted Brussels, Foyer Oriental Chrétien, 1966–70.

A Solovyov Anthology, edited by S.L. Frank, translated by Natalie Duddington. London, SCM Press, and New York, Scribner, 1950.
Stikhotvoreniia i shutochnye p'esi. "Biblioteka poeta", Leningrad, 1974.
Sochineniia, 2 vols. Moscow, 1989.
Izbrannoe. Moscow, 1990.
Stikhotvoreniia, estetika, literaturnaia kritika. Moscow, 1990.

Philosophical and Theological Writing
Chteniia o Bogochelovechestve, 1877–81; translated as *Lectures on Godmanhood*, by Peter Zouboff, London, Dennis Dobson, 1948; revised edition as *Lectures on Divine Humanity*, edited by Boris Jakim, Hudson, New York, Lindisfarne Press, 1995.
L'Idée russe. Belgium, 1888; translated into Russian, 1909.
La Russie et l'église universelle. 1889; translated into Russian, 1911; translated as *Russia and the Universal Church*, by Herbert Rees, London, Geoffrey Bles, 1948.
Opravdanie dobra. 1897; Moscow, 1996; translated as *The Justification of the Good: An Essay in Moral Philosophy*, by Natalie Duddington, London, Constable, 1918.
Tri razgovora [Three Conversations]. 1900; reprinted New York, Izdatel'stvo imeni Chekhova, 1954; translated as *War, Progress, and the End of History*, by Alexander Bakshy, London, London University Press, 1915.
Dogmaticherkoe razvitie tserkvi, v sviazi s voprosom o soedinenii tserkvei [The Dogmatic Development of the Church, in Connection with the Question of Unification of Churches], St Petersburg, 1994.

Poetry
Tri svidaniia [Three Meetings]. 1898.

Play
Alsin. 1876–78.

Critical Studies
"The Successors of Vladimir Solovyev", by Nicholas Lossky, *Slavonic and East European Review* (June 1924), 92–105.
V.S. Solov'ev, by Konstantin Mochul'skii, Paris, 1936; 2nd edition, Paris, YMCA-Press, 1951.
The Frenzied Poets: Andrey Bely and the Russian Symbolists, by Oleg Maslenikov, Berkeley, University of California Press, 1952.
A History of Russian Philosophy, by V.V. Zenkovsky, translated by George L. Kline, vol. 2, New York, Columbia University Press, 1953, 469–531.
The Poets of Russia 1890–1930, by Renato Poggioli, Cambridge, Massachusetts, Harvard University Press, 1960.
Die Lyrik Vl. Solov'evs und ihre Nachwirkung bei A. Belyi und A. Blok, by Armin Knigge, Amsterdam, Hakkert, 1973.
Vladimir Soloviev and the Knighthood of the Divine Sophia, by Samuel D. Cioran, Waterloo, Ontario, Wilfred Laurier University Press, 1977.
Zhizn' i tvorcheskaia evoliutsiia Vladimira Solov'eva, by Sergei Mikhailovich Solov'ev, Brussels, Zhizn' s Bogom, 1977.
"Russian Religious Thought", by George L. Kline, in *Nineteenth Century Religious Thought in the West*, vol. 2, edited by Ninian Smart *et al.* Cambridge and New York, Cambridge University Press, 1985, 208–17.
The Religious Philosophy of Vl. Solovyov: Towards a Reassessment, by Jonathan Sutton, London, Macmillan, and New York, St Martin's Press, 1988.
Kniga o Vladimire Solov'eve, edited by B. Averin and D. Bazanova, Moscow, 1991.
Gogol'. Solov'ev. Dostoevskii, by K. Mochul'skii, edited by V.M. Tolmachev, Moscow, 1995.
Dostoevsky and Soloviev: The Art of Integral Vision, by Marina Kostalevsky, New Haven, Yale University Press, 1997.

The only major Russian thinker qualified by west European criteria to be a professor of philosophy, Vladimir Solov'ev was the son of Russia's greatest historian, Sergei Mikhailovich Solov'ev. He developed precociously, passing through a materialist phase in his early teens, but switching from biology to philology at Moscow university and gaining a Master's degree with a critique of pagan mythology and of western philosophy at the age of 20. His doctorate, "Kritika otvlechennykh nachal" [A Criticism of Abstract Principles] 1880, won him fame and a lectureship at St Petersburg University. The theocratic nature of his arguments and something ambivalent, even provocatively roguish, in his character are said to have given Dostoevskii material for the ideas and personality of Ivan Karamazov. Despite his brilliance, Solov'ev was refused a university chair, and, after giving a lecture calling for the assassins of Alexander II to be reprieved, was denounced by government ministers as a "psychopath". Dislike of teaching, as much as official disfavour, led him to abandon the University. He became a writer, primarily of religious and philosophical works, but also of poetry that led the way to Russian Symbolism. Inspired by visions of Sophia Divine Wisdom, he went to study in the British Museum and then to the Egyptian desert near Thebes. His mysticism alternated with bouts of very sane scepticism, but one *idée fixe* was the ecumenical idea, in defence of which he published a number of brochures, notably *L'Idée russe* in Belgium (1888). This was the sole aspect of his work that antagonized the Russian state and censorship. An early Utopian view of positive Christianity as an ideology for a universal theocratic state gave way to increasingly pessimistic views. He was scrupulously fair to his predecessors (notably in the many articles he contributed to the Brockhauz-Efron Encyclopedia) and was responsible for restoring the reputation of the brilliant reactionary and obscurantist Konstantin Leont'ev from oblivion. Solov'ev's own private life was unhappily contrived, being marked by unrequited love (for unattainable women). He suffered from kidney failure and arterial sclerosis as premature as his academic brilliance. After his 600-page philosophical and theological master-work, *Opravdanie dobra* (*The Justification of the Good*), he produced his most imaginative and frightening work, a combination of Plato and Nostradamus, of satire and vision, *Tri razgovora* (translated as *War, Progress, and the End of History*), whose last part has proven to have remarkable predictive accuracy. Barely 47 years old, he died, troubled by what he felt were satanic tricks: "mystics" who proclaimed themselves Sophia Divine Wisdom and him as Jesus Christ. His shadow stretched over the new century and over the whole apocalyptic Russian Symbolist movement.

The idea of the Eternal Feminine, Sophia Divine Wisdom

"Soul of the World", unites Solov'ev to Goethe's romanticism, to the cult of the Virgin Mary in Catholicism and to mystic or Neoplatonic Christianity (such as Rosicrucianism or Anthroposophy); it also combines the religious thinker with the idealistic poet, and develops the idea of Providence, of a *logos* become reality, so central to earlier Russian historiosophists. Solov'ev's analytical intellect, however, prevented him from prolonged self-delusion. He rejected the Slavophile view of Russia as the herald of the Second Coming. He held the schism between the churches to be the greatest sin, and, even though God might work by opposites, he declared the separateness of Orthodoxy to be as helpful to man's redemption as the betrayal of Judas was to Christ's resurrection. In 1896 Solov'ev appears to have converted to Catholicism (considering, however, that he was still a member of the Orthodox Church). But his hopes in the Roman Catholic church as a reunifying force weakened. His residual optimism was to view Kant's "Categorical Imperative" as a biologist might and by this inherited force for good, beauty, and truth to hope that mankind might yet become spirit. Unperverted instinct, he felt, coincided with scriptural and mystic revelation. Naturally, the most convincing part of any philosopher's work is the denunciation of his predecessors: Solov'ev's "Kritika otvlechennykh nachal'", like his demolition of the new anti-materialists such as Nietzsche, is far more convincing than his mapping out of the triumph of idealism and the good. Likewise, in his poetry, the discursive *Tri svidaniia* [Three Meetings], recreating three visions of the Eternal Feminine, in church at the age of nine, in the reading room of the British Museum and in the Egyptian desert, convinces us by its light irony and self-deprecation far more than the more solemn evocations in verse of the supernatural or the speculation on how man can become God. Both Andrei Belyi and Aleksandr Blok were formed by Solov'ev's poetry – as much by its Finnish scenery as by its cult of the Eternal Feminine. It is all the more disconcerting that Solov'ev was also a wicked parodist of Valerii Briusov's collection, *Russkie simvolisty* [Russian Symbolists]. Solov'ev had an acute ear for falsity, pretentiousness, and sanctimoniousness – hence his power as a critic, literary and ideological. In *Tri razgovora* he very effectively demolishes conservative, Tolstoian and revolutionary ideas on combating the evil in the world, whether by prisons, non-resistance or subversion, thus leaving us only with a Mr Z's manuscript, an apocalyptic tale of the Antichrist that sets out the eventual triumph of the universal church after a terrible Armageddon in which all other ideologies and their adherents perish. In Solov'ev's last analysis, not theocracy but satanocracy will precede the Second Coming. Forty years of history after his death seem to prove him right.

DONALD RAYFIELD

Aleksandr Isaevich Solzhenitsyn 1918–

Prose writer, dramatist, and poet

Biography

Born in Kislovodsk, 11 December 1918, son of a tsarist artillery officer. Attended school at Rostov-on-Don; studied mathematics and physics at Rostov University, 1936–41; correspondence course in literature, Moscow Institute of Philosophy, Literature, and History, 1939–41. Married: 1) Natal'ia Alekseevna Reshetovskaia in 1940 (divorced 1950), remarried in 1957 (divorced 1972), three sons; 2) Natal'ia Dmitrievna Svetlova in 1973, one stepson. Physics teacher, Morozovsk secondary school, 1941. Served in the Soviet Army, 1941–45: captain of artillery, twice decorated. Arrested at the East Prussian front for having written a letter containing disparaging remarks about Stalin, 1945 and given an eight-year sentence for anti-Soviet agitation. Served in camps and prisons near Moscow, and camp in Ekibastuz, Kazakhstan, 1945–53; exiled to South Kazakhstan village of Kok-Terek, 1953–56; worked as mathematics and physics teacher, and wrote in secret. Gravely ill with cancer, but successfully treated in Tashkent, 1954–55. Released from exile, 1956. "Rehabilitated" and settled in Riazan as teacher, 1957. His first work, *Odin den' Ivana Denisovicha* (*One Day in the Life of Ivan Denisovich*), brought overnight fame, 1962. Became full-time writer, four more stories published, 1963–66, including "Matrenin dvor" ("Matryona's House"). Candidacy for a Lenin Prize controversially rejected, 1963. KGB confiscated the novel *V kruge pervom* (*The First Circle*) and other writings, 1965. Circulated open letter to Fourth Congress of the Writers' Union, 1967. Unpublished works were smuggled to the west, including *The First Circle* and *Rakovyi korpus* (*Cancer Ward*), 1968. Expelled from the Writers' Union, 1969. Recipient: Nobel Prize for Literature, 1970. Authorized publication in the west of *Avgust chetyrnadtsatogo* (*August 1914*), 1971, and *Arkhipelag GULag* (*The Gulag Archipelago*), 1974, precipitated arrest for treason and forcible deportation to Frankfurt. Lived in Zurich, 1974–76; then Cavendish, Vermont, 1976–94. Received many prizes and awards, but alienated western liberal opinion with broadcasts and speeches, including the Harvard Commencement Address, 1978. Worked on the historical epic *Krasnoe koleso* (*The Red Wheel*) in the 1970s and 1980s. With perestroika the publication of his works resumed in Russia, notably *The Gulag Archipelago*, 1989; reinstated in the Writers' Union, 1989; Soviet citizenship restored and programmatic essay *Kak nam obustroit' Rossiiu* (*Rebuilding Russia*) widely published, 1990; treason charges formally dropped, 1991. After sensational whistle-stop tour through Siberia, settled in Moscow; received by President Yeltsin and gave address to

Russian Duma, 1994. Announced the establishment of the Solzhenitsyn Prize for Russian writing, 1997.

Publications

Collected Editions

We Never Make Mistakes: Two Short Novels by Alexander Solzhenitsyn ("An Incident at Krechetovka Station" and "Matryona's House"), translated by Paul W. Blackstock. Columbia, University of South Carolina Press, 1963; New York, Norton, 1971; London, Sphere, 1972.

Dva rasskaza [Two Stories]. London, Flegon Press, 1963.

Izbrannoe. Chicago, Russian Language Specialties, 1965.

Sochineniia. Frankfurt, Posev, 1966.

Sobranie sochinenii, 6 vols. Frankfurt, Posev, 1969–70; 2nd edition, 1973.

Stories and Prose Poems, translated by Michael Glenny. London, Bodley Head, and New York, Farrar Straus and Giroux, 1971; Harmondsworth, Penguin, 1973; retitled as *Matryona's House and Other Stories*, from 1975.

Rasskazy (authorized edition). Frankfurt, Posev, 1976.

Sobranie sochinenii (authorized edition), 20 vols. Vermont and Paris, YMCA-Press, 1978–91.

Rasskazy, Moscow. 1990.

Maloe sobranie sochinenii (based on the YMCA-Press edition, 1978–91), 7 vols. Moscow, 1991.

Kak zhal' i drugie rasskazy ["What a Pity" and Other Stories], edited by Gennady Barabtarlo. London, Bristol Classical Press, 1996.

Fiction

"Odin den' Ivana Denisovicha", *Novyi mir*, 11 (1962), 9–74; Moscow, 1963; translated as *One Day in the Life of Ivan Denisovich*, by Ronald Hingley and Max Hayward, London, Pall Mall, and New York, Praeger, 1963; also translated by Ralph Parker, London, Gollancz, and New York, Dutton, 1963; authorized text first in *Odin den' Ivana Denisovicha; Matrenin dvor*, Paris, YMCA-Press, 1973, 9–121; also in *Sobranie sochinenii*, 1978, vol. 3; also translated by Gillon Aitken, London, Bodley Head, and New York, Farrar Straus and Giroux, 1971; and by H.T. Willetts, London, Harvill Press, and New York, Farrar Straus and Giroux, 1991.

"Matrenin dvor", *Novyi mir*, 1 (1963), 42–63; translated as "Matryona's House", by Paul W. Blackstock, in *We Never Make Mistakes*, 1963; and by Michael Glenny, in *Stories and Prose Poems*, 1971; authorized Russian text in *Odin den' Ivana Denisovicha; Matrenin dvor*, 1973, 125–61; and in *Sobranie sochinenii*, 1978, vol. 3.

"Sluchai na stantsii Krechetovka", *Novyi mir*, 1 (1963), 9–42; with restored title "Sluchai na stantsii Kochetovka", in *Rasskazy*, 1976; and in *Sobranie sochinenii*, 1978, vol. 3; translated as "An Incident at Krechetovka Station", by Paul W. Blackstock, in *We Never Make Mistakes*, 1963; and by Michael Glenny, in *Stories and Prose Poems*, 1971.

"Dlia pol'zy dela", *Novyi mir*, 7 (1963), 58–90; revised editions in *Rasskazy*, 1976; and in *Sobranie sochinenii*, 1978, vol. 3; translated as *For the Good of the Cause*, by David Floyd and Max Hayward, London, Pall Mall, and New York, Praeger, 1964; London, Sphere, 1971; also by Michael Glenny, in *Stories and Prose Poems*, 1971.

"Etiudy i krokhotnye rasskazy", first 15 in *Grani*, 56 (1964), i–xi; in *Sochineniia*, 1966; and as *Krokhotnye rasskazy*, Paris, Librairie des cinq continents, 1970; two more in *Grani*, 80 (1971), 8–9; complete Russian edition, in *Sobranie sochinenii*, 1978; vol. 3; translated (16 only), by Michael Glenny, in *Stories and Prose Poems*, 1971.

"Zakhar-kalita", *Novyi mir*, 1 (1966), 69–76; authorized text first in *Rasskazy*, 1976; translated as "Zakhar-the-Pouch", by Michael Glenny, in *Stories and Prose Poems*, 1971.

Rakovyi korpus, 2 vols. London, Bodley Head, and Frankfurt, Posev, 1968; authorized text in *Sobranie sochinenii*, 1979, vol. 4; translated as *Cancer Ward*, by Nicholas Bethell and David Burg, London, Bodley Head, 2 vols, 1968–69; in 1 vol. 1970; New York, Farrar Straus and Giroux, 1969; Harmondsworth, Penguin, 1971; reprinted 1997; also translated by Rebecca Frank, New York, Dial Press, 1968.

V kruge pervom. Frankfurt, Posev, 1968 [imprimature: Belgrade, Marija Čudina *et al.*]; Frankfurt, Fischer, New York, Harper and Row, and London, Flegon Press, 1968; as *V pervom krugu*, New York, Harper and Row, and Paris, YMCA-Press, 1969; authorized text in *Sobranie sochinenii*, 1978, vols. 1–2; translated as *The First Circle*, by Thomas Whitney, New York, Harper and Row, 1968; and by Michael Guybon, London, Collins Harvill, 1969.

Krasnoe koleso: Povestvovan'e v otmerennykh srokakh [The Red Wheel: A Narrative in Discrete Periods of Time], in *Sobranie sochinenii*, 1983–91, vols 11–20; revised edition, 10 vols, Moscow, 1993 (comprises four "knots"):

1. *Avgust chetyrnadtsatogo*. Paris, YMCA-Press, 1971; unauthorized reprint, London, Flegon Press, 1971; translated as *August 1914*, by Michael Glenny, London, Bodley Head, and New York, Farrar Straus and Giroux, 1972; Harmondsworth, Penguin, and New York, Bantam, 1974; expanded version first in *Sobranie sochinenii*, 1983, vols. 11[-]12; translated as *The Red Wheel: A Narrative in Discrete Periods of Time*, by H.T. Willetts, London, Bodley Head, and New York, Farrar Straus and Giroux, 1989; Harmondsworth, Penguin, 1990.
2. *Oktiabr' shestnadtsatogo* [October 1916], 2 vols. 1984.
3. *Mart semnadtsatogo* [March 1917], 4 vols. 1986–88.
4. *Aprel' semnadtsatogo* [April 1917], 2 vols. 1991.

Lenin v Tsiurikhe. Paris, YMCA-Press, 1975; translated as *Lenin in Zurich*, by H.T. Willetts, London, Bodley Head, and New York, Farrar Straus and Giroux, 1976; and Harmondsworth, Penguin, 1977 (comprises a chapter excised from the already published first "knot" [*uzel*] of the preceding item, together with chapters from two subsequent "knots" [*uzly*]).

"Ego"; "Na kraiakh" [Ego; At the Edge], *Novyi mir*, 5 (1995), 12–50.

"Dvuchastnye rasskazy" [Tales in Two Parts] ("Molodniak" [Younger Generation]; "Nasten'ka" [Little Nastia]; "Abrikosovoe varen'e" [Apricot Preserves]), *Novyi mir*, 10 (1995), 3–34; "Vse ravno" [Makes No Difference], *Literaturnaia gazeta*, 33 (16 August 1995), 5–6; "Na izlomakh" [Twists and Turns], *Novyi mir*, 6 (1996), 3–25.

Poetry

Prusskie nochi. Paris, YMCA-Press, 1974; *Prussian Nights* (bilingual edition), translated by Robert Conquest, London,

Collins Harvill, and New York, Farrar Straus and Giroux, 1977.

Plays

"Svecha na vetru", *Student*, 11–12 (1968); *Grani*, 71 (1969), 15–77; authorized text as *Svet, kotoryi v tebe (Svecha na vetru)*, in *Sobranie sochinenii*, vol. 8, 1981, 351–417; translated as *Candle in the Wind*, by Keith Armes, Minnesota, Minnesota University Press, and London, Bodley Head and Oxford University Press, 1973; Harmondsworth, Penguin, 1976.

"Olen' i shalashovka", *Grani*, 73 (1969), 3–95; reprinted London, Flegon Press, 1969 [dated 1968]; translated as *The Love Girl and the Innocent*, by Nicholas Bethell and David Burg, London, Bodley Head, and New York, Farrar Straus and Giroux, 1969; Harmondsworth, Penguin, and New York, Bantam, 1971; authorized edition as *Respublika truda* [Republic of Labour], in *Sobranie sochinenii*, vol. 8, 1981, 251–349.

Pir pobeditelei, in *Sobranie sochinenii*, vol. 8, 1981, 7–124; translated as *Victory Celebrations*, by Helen Rapp and Nancy Williams, London, Bodley Head, and New York, Farrar Straus and Giroux, 1983.

"Plenniki", in *Sobranie sochinenii*, vol. 8, 1981, 125–250; translated as *Prisoners*, by Helen Rapp and Nancy Williams, London, Bodley Head, and New York, Farrar Straus and Giroux, 1983.

Artistic Research

Arkhipelag GULag 1918–1956: Opyt khudozhestvennogo issledovaniia, 3 vols. Paris, YMCA-Press, 1973–76; and in *Sobranie sochinenii*, vols 5–7, 1980; as separate edition, 3 vols, Moscow, 1989; translated as *The Gulag Archipelago 1918–1956: An Experiment in Literary Investigation*, by Thomas Whitney (vols 1 and 2) and H.T. Willetts (vol. 3), London, Collins Harvill, and New York, Harper and Row, 1974–78; London, Fontana, 1974–78; New York, Perennial Library, 1974–79; single condensed volume, London, Collins, 1986.

Essays, Publicistic Writings, and Speeches

Solzhenitsyn: A Documentary Record, edited by Leopold Labedz. London, Allen Lane, 1970; New York, Harper and Row, 1971; Harmondsworth, Penguin, 1972; 2nd expanded edition, Bloomington, Indiana University Press (Midland Books), 1973; Harmondsworth, Penguin, 1974 [most complete edition].

Amerikanskie rechi. Paris, YMCA-Press, 1974; translated as *The Voice of Freedom*, Washington, DC, American Federation of Labor and Congress of Industrial Organizations, 1975; and as *Warning to the West* (includes two BBC interviews of 1976), New York, Farrar Straus and Giroux, 1976; and as *Alexander Solzhenitsyn Speaks to the West* (includes the Harvard Commencement Address), by Harris L. Coulter and Nataly Martin, London, Bodley Head, 1978; and as *Détente: Prospects for Democracy and Dictatorship* (includes the Harvard Address), New Brunswick, Transaction Books, 1976; 2nd edition, 1980.

A World Split Apart: Commencement Address Delivered at Harvard University, June 8, 1978 (bilingual edition), translated by I.I. Alberti, New York, Harper, 1978; and as *Solzhenitsyn at Harvard*, Washington, DC, Ethics and Public Policy Center, 1980.

East and West (includes the Nobel Lecture, Letter to Soviet Leaders and the Harvard Address), various translators. New York, Harper and Row, 1980.

The Mortal Danger: How Misconceptions about Russia Imperil America, translated by Michael Nicholson and Alexis Klimoff. New York, Harper and Row, and London, Bodley Head, 1981.

"Kak nam obustroit' Rossiiu", *Komsomol'skia pravda*, and *Literaturnaia gazeta* (18 September 1990); separate edition, Paris, YMCA-Press, 1990; translated as *Rebuilding Russia: Reflections and Tentative Proposals*, by Alexis Klimoff, New York, Farrar Straus and Giroux, and London, Harvill Press, 1991.

Russkie pisateli-Laureaty Nobelevskoi premii: Aleskandr Solzhenitsyn (contains four early stories, the Nobel Lecture and documents from *The Oak and the Calf*), edited with an introduction by A. Arkhangel'skii, Moscow, 1991.

"Russkii vopros k kontsu XX veka", *Novyi mir*, 7 (1994), 135–76; as separate edition, Moscow, 1995; translated as *The Russian Question at the End of the 20th Century* (includes the 1993 Address to the International Academy of Philosophy, Leichtenstein), by Yermolai Solzhenitsyn, New York, Farrar Straus and Giroux, and London, Harvill Press, 1995.

Po minute v den' [A Minute a Day] (Television broadcasts and speeches). Moscow, 1995.

Publitsistika v trekh tomakh. Iaroslavl [2 vols published], vol. 1, "Stat'i i rechi", 1995; vol. 2, "Obshchestvennye zaiavleniia, pis'ma, interv'iu", 1996.

Editor

Iz-pod glyb: Sbornik statei. Paris, YMCA-Press, 1974; translated as *From Under the Rubble*, by Michael Scammell *et al.*, Boston, Little Brown, and London, Harvill Press, 1975; New York, Bantam, and London, Fontana, 1976.

Dictionary

Russkii slovar' iazykovogo rasshireniia [A Russian Dictionary of Lexical Augmentation]. Moscow, 1990.

Memoirs

Bodalsia telenok s dubom: Ocherki literaturnoi zhizni. Paris, YMCA-Press, 1975; revised and expanded edition (includes *Nevidimki*), Moscow, 1996; translated as *The Oak and the Calf: Sketches of Literary Life in the Soviet Union*, by H.T. Willetts, London, Collins and Harvill Press, and New York, Harper and Row, 1980.

Skvoz' chad [Through the Fumes], from the Sixth Supplement to *The Oak and the Calf*. Paris, YMCA-Press, 1979.

Nevidimki, from the Fifth Supplement to *The Oak and the Calf*, *Novyi mir*, 11–12 (1991), 119–46; 5–76 (1991); translated as *Invisible Allies*, by Alexis Klimoff and Michael Nicholson, Washington, DC, Counterpoint, 1995.

Ugodilo zernyshko promezh dvukh zhernovov: ocherki izgnaniia [A Grain Landed Between Two Milestones: Essays from Exile]. 1996.

Critical Studies

Solschenizyn, by Georg Lukács, Neuwied and Berlin, Luchterhand, 1970; translated as *Solzhenitsyn*, by William David Graf, London, Merlin Press, 1970; Cambridge, Massachusetts, MIT Press, 1971.

Alexander Solsjenitsyn: Biografi och dokument, by Hans Björkegren, Stockholm, Wahlström and Widstrand, 1971; translated as *Aleksandr Solzhenitsyn: A Biography*, by Kaarina Eneberg, New York, Third Press, 1972; Henley, Aidan Ellis, 1973.

Canadian Slavonic Papers (special Solzhenitsyn issue), 13/2–3 (1971).

Solženicyn, by Giovanni Grazzini, Milan, Longanesi, 1971; translated as *Solzhenitsyn*, by Eric Mosbacher, London, Michael Joseph, and New York, Dell, 1973; London, Sphere, 1974.

Soljénitsyne, edited by Georges Nivat and Michel Aucouturier, Paris, L'Herne, 1971.

Aleksandr Solzhenitsyn: The Major Novels, by Abraham Rothberg, Ithaca, Cornell University Press, 1971.

Solzhenitsyn: A Biography, by David Burg and George Feifer, New York, Stein and Day, and London, Hodder and Stoughton, 1972; London, Abacus, 1973.

Tvorets i podvig: Ocherki po tvorchestvu Aleskandra Solzhenitsyna, by L. Rzhevskii, Frankfurt, Posev, 1972; translated as *Solzhenitsyn: Creator and Heroic Deed*, by Sonja Muller, Tuscaloosa, University of Alabama Press, 1978.

Aleksandr Solzhenitsyn: Critical Essays and Documentary Materials, edited by John B. Dunlop, Richard Haugh, and Alexis Klimoff, Belmont, Massachusetts, Nordland, 1973; 2nd expanded edition, New York and London, Collier Macmillan, 1975.

Desiat' let posle "Odnogo dnia Ivana Denisovicha", by Zhores A. Medvedev; translated as *10 Years After Ivan Denisovich*, by Hilary Sternberg, London, Macmillan, 1973; Harmondsworth, Penguin, 1975.

Solzhenitsyn, by Christopher Moody, Edinburgh, Oliver and Boyd, 1973; expanded edition, New York, Barnes and Noble, 1976.

L'esprit de Soljénitsyne, by Olivier Clément, Paris, Stock, 1974; translated as *The Spirit of Solzhenitsyn*, by Sarah Fawcett and Paul Burns, London, Search Press, 1976; New York, Barnes and Noble, 1977.

Solzhenitsyn: A Pictorial Autobiography, New York, Noonday Press, 1974; and as *Solzhentisyn: A Pictorial Record*, London, Bodley Head, 1974.

The Last Circle, by I. Solovyov *et al.*, Moscow, 1974.

V spore s vremenem, by Natal'ia Reshetovskaia, Moscow, 1975 [with extensive Novosti/KGB editing]; translated as *Sanya: My Life with Aleksandr Solzhenitsyn*, by Elena Ivanoff, Indianapolis, Bobbs-Merrill, 1975; also as *Sanya: My Husband Aleksandr Solzhenitsyn*, London, Hart-Davis, 1977; her authorized memoirs issued as *Aleksandr Solzhenitsyn i chitaiushchaia Rossiia*, Moscow, 1990; *Razryv*, Irkutsk, 1992; *Otluchenie: Iz zhizni Aleksandra Solzhenitsyna: Vospominaniia zheny*, Moscow, 1994.

Solzhenitsyn: A Collection of Critical Essays, edited by Kathryn Feuer, Englewood Cliffs, New Jersey, Prentice-Hall, 1976.

Solzhenitsyn: Politics and Form, by Francis Barker, London, Macmillan, and New York, Holmes and Meier, 1977.

The Politics of Solzhenitsyn, by Stephen Carter, London, Macmillan, 1977.

"Solzhenitsyn, Tvardovskii i «Novyi mir»", by Vladimir Lakshin, in *Dvadtsatyi vek: Obshchestvenno-politicheskii i literaturnyi al'manakh*, edited by Roy Medvedev, no. 2, London, TCD Publications, 1977, 151–218; translated as *Solzhenitsyn, Tvardovsky and "Novy Mir"*, by Michael Glenny, Cambridge, Massachusetts, MIT Press, 1980.

Modern Fiction Studies (special Solzhenitsyn issue), 23/1 (1977).

Alexander Solzhenitsyn, by Steven Allaback, New York, Taplinger, 1978.

Solzhenitsyn and the Secret Circle, by Olga Carlisle, New York, Holt Rinehart and Winston, and London, Routledge and Kegan Paul, 1978.

Alexander Solzhenitsyn, by Andrej Kodjak, Boston, Twayne, 1978.

Solzhenitsyn: The Moral Vision, by Edward E. Ericson, Grand Rapids, Michigan, Eerdmans, 1980.

Solzhenitsyn and Dostoevsky: A Study in the Polyphonic Novel, by Vladislav Krasnov, Athens, University of Georgia Press, and London, George Prior, 1980.

Soljénitsyne, by Georges Nivat, Paris, Seuil, 1980; translated into Russian as *Solzhenitsyn*, by Simon Markish and the author, London, Overseas Publications Interchange, 1984; Moscow, 1992.

Vokrug Solzhenitsyna, by A. Flegon, 2 vols, London, Flegon Press, 1981; abridged translation as *A. Solzhenitsyn: Myth and Reality*, London, Flegon Press, 1986.

Solzhenitsyn's Traditional Imagination, by James M. Curtis, Athens, University of Georgia Press, 1984.

Solzhenitsyn: A Biography, by Michael Scammell, New York, Norton, 1984; London, Hutchinson, 1985.

Aleksandr Solzhenitsyn: Ocherki tvorchestva, by Mariia Shneerson, Frankfurt, Posev, 1984.

Solzhenitsyn in Exile: Critical Essays and Documentary Materials, edited by John B. Dunlop, Richard S. Haugh, and Michael Nicholson, Stanford, Hoover Institution Press, 1985.

Materialy konferentsii «A.I. Solzhenitsyn i ego tvorchestvo», edited by Aleksandr Glezer, Paris and New York, Tret'ia volna, 1988.

Gorodu i miru: O publitsistike A.I. Solzhenitsyna, by Dora Shturman, Paris and New York, Tret'ia volna, 1988.

Aleksandr Solzhenitsyn: Putevoditel', by Petr Palamarchuk, Moscow, 1991.

The Great Reversal: Politics and Art in Solzhenitsyn, by Paul N. Siegel, San Francisco, Walnut, 1991.

Solzhenitsyn and the Modern World, by Edward E. Ericson, Washington, DC, Regnery Gateway, 1993.

Aleksandr Solzhenitsyn. Lichnost'. Tvorchestvo. Vremia, by Iu.A. Meshkov, Ekaterinburg, 1993.

Aleksandr Solzhenitsyn: Zhizn' i tvorchestvo: Kniga dlia uchashchikhsia, by V.A. Chalmaev, Moscow, 1994.

Zvezda (special Solzhenitsyn issue), 6 (1994).

Ot Gor'kogo do Solzhenitsyna: Posobie po literature dlia postupaiushchikh v vuzy, by L.Ia. Shteinberg and I.V. Kondakov, Moscow, 1994; expanded edition, 1995.

Ot Bloka do Solzhenitsyna: Sud'by Russkoi literatury XX veka

(posle 1917 goda): Novyi konspekt-putevoditel', by V.M. Akimov, St Petersburg, 1994.
Kremlevskii samosud: Sekretnye dokumenty politbiuro o pisatele A. Solzhenitsyne, edited by A.V. Korotkov *et al.*, Moscow, 1994; translated as *The Solzhenitsyn Files: Secret Documents Reveal One Man's Fight Against the Monolith*, under the supervision of Catherine A. Fitzpatrick, edited by Michael Scammell, Chicago, Edition Q, 1995.
One Day in the Life of Ivan Denisovich: A Critical Companion, edited by Alexis Klimoff, Evanston, Illinois, Northwestern University Press, 1997.
Solzhenitsyn's "One Day in the Life of Ivan Denisovich", by Robert Porter, London, Bristol Classical Press, 1997.

Bibliographies
Alexander Solzhenitsyn: An International Bibliography of Writings by and about Him, 1962–1973, by Donald M. Fiene, Ann Arbor, Ardis, 1973.
Alexander Solschenizyn: Eine Bibliographie seiner Werke, by Werner Martin, Hildesheim, Georg Olms, 1977.
"Solzhenitsyn in 1981: A Bibliographical Reorientation", by Michael Nicholson, in *Solzhenitsyn in Exile: Critical Essays and Documentary Materials*, edited by John B. Dunlop *et al.*, Stanford, Hoover Institution Press, 1985, 351–412.
Solzhenitsyn Studies: A Quarterly Survey (Colgate University, New York), 1/1–2 (1980); (Lancaster University, England) 1/3–4 (1980); 2/1 (1981).
Aleksandr Solzhenitsyn: Bibliograficheskii ukazatel', Avgust 1988–1990, compiled by N.G. Levitskaia, Moscow, 1991.

Among the literary juvenilia on which Aleksandr Solzhenitsyn embarked as a student in the late 1930s, his most ambitious venture was a historical narrative recreating the Russian defeat at Tannenberg in 1914 and aspiring to reveal the origins of the October Revolution. Solzhenitsyn tackled this precursor of *Avgust chetyrnadtsatogo* (*August 1914*) and its parent cycle *Krasnoe koleso* [The Red Wheel] with the determination and intense mental focus that would mark his entire career as a writer. It was not in itself an unorthodox undertaking: Solzhenitsyn was at the time a Komsomol enthusiast and convinced Leninist, and epic belletrizations of the Revolution were very much in fashion. At the same time, the scope and ambition of the project, as well as its fusion of documentary and autobiographical materials with *belles-lettres*, anticipate much that was to come. Indeed, Solzhenitsyn would return to his epic at the end of the 1960s and devote some 20 years of his life to reworking and continuing it.

The more immediate subject-matter that the war thrust before the young subaltern and would-be writer was abruptly displaced in its turn by his experience of arrest and imprisonment. His years in the camps left him with a consuming urge to commemorate and keep faith with the millions of Gulag dead, to expose not just the myrmidons of the Gulag system, but its architects, Lenin as much as Stalin, and the ideology that impelled them. Solzhenitsyn's rejection of socialism and embrace of Christianity and Russian patriotism were not instantaneous. At the same time, accounts of his development based on the sequence of publication of his writings can easily mislead. In particular, *Odin den' Ivana Denisovicha* (*One Day in the Life of Ivan Denisovich*), the work that marked his debut, did not stand at the beginning of his post-Gulag writing. In camp at Ekibastuz he had kept himself sane by composing and memorizing some 12,000 lines of an autobiographical narrative poem incorporating one complete play in verse – *Pir pobeditelei* (*Victory Celebrations*) 1951 – and scenes from another – *Plenniki* (*Prisoners*) 1952–53. Although poetry commended itself primarily for mnemonic purposes, Solzhenitsyn did, as his *Prusskie nochi* (*Prussian Nights*) attests, produce vigorous and highly competent narrative verse in the tradition of Tvardovskii and Nekrasov. But his commitment to drama, as a means of unburdening his memory and conscience was a considered choice and rested on a long-standing affection for the theatre. The first new work composed after his release, *Respublika truda* (*Republic of Labour*) was a four-act drama with more than 50 speaking parts, including representatives of all strata of labour-camp life. The naturalistic staging called for prisoners to be unloaded from a truck, a vigorous knife-fight, and a foundry complete with furnace. This series of plays was followed, in the mid-1950s, by the first versions of the long prison-novel *V kruge pervom* (*The First Circle*). Short stories would come later, but for now Solzhenitsyn's need to testify appeared to demand capacious structures, large casts, and overt dramatization of historical events. The tendency reached its apogee in a scathing exploration of the labour-camp universe, the hugely influential *Arkhipelag GULag* (*Gulag Archipelago*). This 1800-page *tour de force*, part historical, part rhetorical and forensic, was conceived in 1958, though circumstance prevented its completion for ten years.

What links Solzhenitsyn's historical project with his labour-camp writing is anamnesis, the resurrection of memory, be it memory of atrocity or memory of stifled national identity and language. Teleological commitment is an inseparable part of his literary endeavour, and imparts characteristic strengths and weaknesses. It is axiomatic for him that a writer has a civic duty and that the truth of art is no different from truth in any other occupation. With no time for relativism, paradox or avant-garde aestheticism, he tends to favour a traditional psychological realism, in which allegorical patterns and moments of lyrical tranquillity intimate a universal plane of meaning beyond the grim struggles in the microcosm. Since God has not fled from the ravaged fictional worlds of the mature Solzhenitsyn, the dynamic of his texts characteristically sets defeat and frustration in the historically concrete setting against a victory of conscience and spirit in the world beyond: at the end of *The First Circle* the zeks are cast into the deadly outer circles of the Gulag, but they are at peace with themselves and freer than ever their captors will be. In *Rakovyi korpus* (*Cancer Ward*) Kostoglotov limps back to his desert exile alone on the "last day of creation", uncured, probably impotent, but with conscience intact. In *August 1914* Colonel Vorotyntsev, ignominiously ejected from the Supreme Headquarters after vainly attempting to tell the truth about the calamitous mishandling of the war, is yet liberated and elevated by his intervention on behalf of martyred Russia.

Rejecting the ideology of his youth, Solzhenitsyn came to believe that the struggle between good and evil cannot be resolved among parties, classes, doctrines or nations, but is waged within the individual human heart and conscience on the basis of an intuitive, and divinely ordained, sense of absolute right and wrong. So unacceptable was this essentially traditional Christian morality to his communist critics that it lent a flavour of radical daring to works seeking publication in the 1960s and 1970s. The Tolstoian question "What do men live by?" could appear deeply subversive in the setting of a Tashkent cancer ward soon after the death of Stalin. With the collapse of communism and Russia's accelerated acquaintance with the polysemantic world of postmodernism, Solzhenitsyn's art would be dismissed in some quarters as obsolete, as determined, even in its heroic opposition, by the mendacious, monumental socialist realism that it reviled. Such generalizations neglect the formal and generic struggles that impart to his better works a salutary tension and dynamism.

Bombarded with a mass of personal and factual material, and aware of his vulnerability when venturing into more abstract settings, as in the play *Svecha na vetru* (*Candle in the Wind*), Solzhenitysn wrestled over the years with problems of narrative time and space. Although he was sensitive as a writer to the charms of the short form, his need to testify drew him away from it, and only since his return to Russia has he turned back to the short story. Behind his use of long and hybrid genres lies not thoughtless prolixity, but a calculated effort to restrict, limit and compress his overwhelming material. Reflected most obviously in the single day and restricted location accorded Ivan Denisovich, this concern is no less alive in the topographical and symbolic circles of *The First Circle*, where the narrative present covers barely four days. It is at work, too, in *Cancer Ward*, where disease radiates outwards to link the patient in his bed, with wider geographical, national, and universal human spheres, and where in order to show the progress of the illness, Solzhenitsyn chose not to extend the linear chronology, but instead split the work into two temporally compact parts with an interval between. It is active again in the "knot" structure of his vast *Krasnoe koleso*. Apart from the threat of data overload, Solzhenitsyn has shown himself more sensitive than he is often given credit for to the potential tyranny of the direct, moralizing voice. He has attempted to restrict his narrative function to the perspective and intonations of individual characters, aiming in the longer works for a proliferation of major secondary heroes and a corresponding multi-voiced effect. Moreover, revisions of his works have included the removal of portentous or sententious utterances.

As emerges vividly from his autobiographical *Nevidimki* (*Invisible Allies*), Solzhenitsyn produced the bulk of his works in conditions so charged and abnormal that it is difficult to imagine how he found the time and peace of mind to complete any of them. The intemperateness and stridency that critics have sometimes deplored are inseparable from the single-mindedness that allowed him to survive not just the camps and illness, but some seven years of open confrontation with the Soviet authorities. Solzhenitsyn's finest writing is attained when the unconditional truths of cause and mission come up against the exigencies of literary form and expression. The power of *One Day in the Life of Ivan Denisovich* rests not on the *absence* of the didactic, sermonizing voice, but on its constraint: the verbal and intellectual limitations of Ivan Denisovich and the detailed quotidian routine of his world are made to contain and enhance the universalizing, symbolizing impulse that racks the text. Not all of Solzhenitsyn's attempts to mediate the authorial voice were as felicitous, but his successes were sufficient to warrant his unique place in the literature of post-Stalinist Russia.

MICHAEL NICHOLSON

One Day in the Life of Ivan Denisovich

Odin den' Ivana Denisovicha

Novel, 1962

When *One Day in the Life of Ivan Denisovich* appeared in 1962 it produced an extraordinary range of responses. Ex-prisoners commented on the authenticity of what Solzhenitsyn described, while some die-hard Stalinists were outraged by the author's negative portrayal of Soviet life. The mainstream reviewers, broadly speaking, saw the work as a necessary exercise in exorcism, so that the Soviet system might continue on its path of democratization under Khrushchev. While it is right and proper to read the work primarily as an exposé of Stalin's crimes, to leave it at that would be to rank Solzhenitsyn as no more than a highly competent journalist. *One Day in the Life of Ivan Denisovich*'s literary qualities have moved generations of readers from all round the world, and its special features endow the work with a universality that rises above political demarcation lines.

We follow Ivan Denisovich Shukhov throughout the day from reveille at 5 o'clock to lights out, from his bunk, to the guard-house floor he has to wash, to the mess-hall, the sick-bay, then as he is marched out of the camp for the day's work, his return, the evening meal, and excursion to a neighbouring barracks hut to buy tobacco and then back to his own hut. Much of the story is told in an adapted form of *skaz*, whereby the narrator reports Ivan's thought processes and perceptions in his own peasant speech, while occasionally employing a more neutral, "omniscient narrator" tone and viewpoint. Solzhenitsyn was most keen that his hero should be an uneducated peasant, unable to verbalize fully, let alone rationalize, his predicament. Thus he comes across as a thoroughly credible type, not like the somewhat contrived peasant philosophers that Tolstoi sometimes produced.

There is a strong Tolstoian element in the work, though. With an economical use of formal description and snatches of dialogue, the author creates a vast array of characters, all with their idiosyncrasies, despite the dehumanizing conformity of their lives: guards and prisoners alike are slaves to routine and they all wear uniforms. Naturally the prisoners are most subject to uniformity, but even here the wayward human spirit breaks through, bestowing a degree of individuality and dignity: "Fetiukov was one of the lowliest members of the gang – even Shukhov was a cut above him. Outwardly the gang all looked the same but there were big differences." Ivan is slightly amused by the heroic protest of Buinovskii when the prisoners are made to undo their shirts to be searched, a futile gesture that earns the former sea captain ten days in the punishment cell. Ivan, by contrast, is much more resourceful and experienced, never missing an opportunity, for example, to earn an extra scrap of food from the better-off prisoners who might receive food parcels. He starts the day badly, feeling unwell and unable to be placed on the sick list, but he grows in mind and body as the hours pass, so that by the afternoon and early evening he is working flat out on the brick-laying to which he has been assigned. His motivation at this point has nothing to do with any a priori material considerations, and in the closing sentences of the story he recalls the enjoyment he found in his work. Elsewhere too, we see that the human impulse springs not always from the quest for material survival: "He ate every bit of every fish, gills, tails, even eyes if they were where they should be, but if they had boiled out of the head and were floating loose in the bowl – big fish-eyes goggling at him – he wouldn't eat them. The others laughed at him for it." In Ivan's survival and in the impression the reader has of a vast and self-contained world – which is both temporal and geographical – there is something of the epic.

Ivan has memories of his life on the collective farm before the war and he is unable to comprehend what his wife tells him in her twice-yearly letters, for instance about some of the peasants now making healthy sums of money by stencilling patterns on cheap material to sell as carpets. The hero is more superstitious than religious, telling Buinovskii that in his village the peasants believed that God broke up the moon each month to make stars. There are more unequivocal illustrations of religious devotion, notably in the figure of Aleshka, the Baptist. Ivan is unable to relate to the world of intellectuals, and indeed intellectuals do not take notice of him; witness the scene where he takes Tsezar''s dinner to him and overhears the latter's argument with Kh-123 about Eisenstein. None of the characters finds himself where he truly belongs, and in this, *One Day in the Life of Ivan Denisovich* is about dislocation and alienation.

For a work that aspires through flesh and blood characters to epic proportions, the text has a curious modernist flavour to it, seeking as it does to establish an entire universe within the parameters of one day and one psyche. Here is a world in which nearly all actions are explained and yet one that has no overall *raison d'être* – there is only one oblique reference to Stalin, and the charges brought against the various prisoners are spurious in the extreme. Foreign critics were quick to see the labour camp as a microcosm of Soviet society as a whole. Max Hayward went further, seeing the work as a comment on modern man in general and arguing that in it the Kafkaesque nightmare had become the reality. Certainly, the world that Ivan Denisovich accepts so matter-of-factly ("almost a happy day" the hero reflects at the end) leaves the reader disorientated and outraged. The mixture of dialect, prison slang, and obscenity – such a contrast to the prudish Sovietese of the time – plays no small part in the shock tactics. However, some subtler devices are at work too, not least in the references to the natural elements, which, despite their harshness, provide a link to a more normal world: at times even this natural order seems threatened, as when the camp searchlights make the stars look dim; yet at other times the natural world provides, irrationally, spiritual sustenance: "Aleshka gazed at the sun and a happy smile spread from his eyes to his lips ... what had he got to be happy about?" *One Day in the Life of Ivan Denisovich* describes the horrors of labour-camp life, but ultimately it is more subversive in its quiet dismissal of materialist philosophy.

ROBERT PORTER

Matryona's House

Matrenin dvor

Story, 1963

This story fits into the genre of Village Prose: it is set in the immediate post-Stalin era, in 1953, in an isolated collective farm village. The story is virtually documentary; it was written in 1957–59 and based on actual events. In the Brezhnev era the story was initially criticized for not following the tenets of socialist realism: it depicts the gloomy side of material and spiritual reality and in general portrays rural life as a worthy milieu, entirely distinct from city life and even superior to it. Solzhenitsyn addresses social problems such as the official abuse of the peasantry and the corruption of the whole system, especially in the realm of education. The story's setting in the heart of Russia, in a village surrounded by unspoiled nature, exemplifies both present-day backwardness and the value system of the pre-revolutionary peasantry.

The story comprises three chapters together with a prologue that briefly foreshadows the closing drama and frames the story. The narrator, however, alludes only obliquely to the concluding disaster, maintaining an atmosphere of mystery. The narrator returns to provincial Russia from exile in Central Asia, and takes a room with Matryona, a seriously ill but hard-working, loving, elderly peasant woman. Her greedy relatives tear down part of her house for timber; they intend to use it for building purposes in another location. The timber is then hauled away; *en route* to their destination they must cross a railway line, and Matryona, who is helping, is struck by a train and killed. Subsequently, the narrator compares her selflessness to the selfishness of all the others who surround her: relatives, neighbours, and government officials.

Like other works by Solzhenitsyn, this story continues the great tradition of 19th-century Russian moralistic prose: the constant contrasting of positive and negative moral values, and the narrator's manifest sensitivity to human suffering metonymically reinforce the story's message. The time period of the narrative (from the summer of 1953 to February 1954), when the narrator actually knew Matryona, expands to envelop her entire life. Thus the narrative space symbolically widens: Matryona's "dvor" (peasant homestead) encompasses not only her farmstead, but a whole domain; the village stands for Russia and all its possibilities.

The narrator is close to Solzhenitsyn, and lives within the world of the characters. He regained his freedom after exile in 1953, and becomes the witness and hagiographer of Matryona's life. The narrative avoids any objectivized moralizing. Matryona apparently dies an unnecessary death after an unsuccessful life, but the symbolic meaning of her existence shines forth in the form of truth revealed to the narrator.

Against the backdrop of the realistic setting, the story focuses on the life of the central peasant character Matryona, a personification of old Mother Russia. All her life is devoted to the service of others, without thought of her personal needs. Matryona's figure is iconic; in keeping with the Russian Slavophile literary tradition, her female strength represents the moral cornerstone of the Russian national type, evincing an uncorrupted elemental force that reflects a Christian archetype. The corruption and alienation from the nation's roots engendered by civilization, symbolized by her body's mutilation by the train, also echoes the Russian literary heritage (Dostoevskii, Tolstoi, Esenin). The train makes repeated appearances at the beginning of the story as a foreshadowing of events to come; subsequently we learn that Matryona is afraid of trains. Her household lacks another technical achievement of her time: there is no radio. The new world confronts her mythopoeic existence outwardly, while the dark forces within her old world confront it inwardly, as symbolized by Faddei, who represents another Russian peasant archetype. She is afraid of not only the train but other elemental forces such as lightning, fire, unclean spirits (traditional subjects of folk superstition); the disappearance of her pot during a church ritual is an ominous event shortly before her death. As a result of her superstitions, she is characterized by her neighbours as a heathen. Her faith mirrors the ancient double-belief system of the Russian peasantry, based on coexistence of Christian and pagan views in the popular consciousness. Matryona does not follow the external aspect of the official religion, but she lives by its spirit; she never prayed the traditional way, although her life is one long summons to God.

Matryona's personality centres on Truth, Goodness, Charity, and Beauty; she is a living expression of the beatitudes. She is burdened by external circumstances: age, illness, poverty, loneliness, the hardship of everyday life; everything has gone wrong in her life. When the narrator meets her at the age of 60, she is abandoned, misunderstood, laughed at, and despised; she is a poor, sick, lonely widow – her countenance has only one attractive feature: the radiant smile on her roundish face reflects her inner state, spiritual health, and the serenity within her ailing body. She is blessed with Christian virtues: she is unselfconsciously righteous and pious, and a hard worker – work is her source of joy and spiritual balance. She is indifferent toward earthly possessions, and is respectful and kind to all God's creatures, at one with nature; her companions are a lame cat, a dirty white goat, mice, cockroaches, and rubber plants. She bears no bitterness or anger toward anyone, but she patiently endures whatever misery befalls her. She endures God's plans with considerable strength, accepting even injustices with humility and equanimity. Her tragic end fits into this paradigm: she perishes while helping her relatives, death brought upon her by those who despise her and are blinded by their own vices to her true worth. She attains inner freedom through these New Testament values, which are traditionally associated with the Russian national character and the kenotic model of sainthood. The story is constructed as a model for contemporary hagiography; these virtues could and should be transplanted and thus preserved in the Soviet context. But Matryona is a Don Quixote figure, a holy fool, the only preserver of the spiritual traditions of Old Russia among the mass-produced individuals of the Soviet state; her life is necessarily tragic, standing not only as an ideal, but as a warning that this type is destined to perish under the totalitarian regime. Her disfigured, martyred body stands as a symbol for the country, its life and history.

Distortion envelops all levels of the story. Even the language is corrupted, as reflected in the name of the village Torfprodukt ("Peat Product"), but nevertheless the narrator is touched by Matryona, a woman of the people, through the life-giving mellifluousness of her native tongue, which recreates the fairy-tale magic of age-old Russia. The narration is almost in the *skaz* style: the educated narrator often lapses into Matryona's speech pattern, and thus the linguistic resources of the story dwell on the freshening and reviving potency of peasant speech.

As reassurance for the future of Russia, the story ends with panegyric for Matryona, referring to her as "the righteous one without whom, as the proverb says, no village can stand. Nor any city. Nor our land." This passage directly recalls the biblical episode when Abraham bargains with the Lord to save Sodom, if at least one righteous man can be found there (Genesis 18: 24–33).

MARIA PAVLOVSZKY

Cancer Ward

Rakovyi korpus

Novel, 1968

Using a term first coined by Bakhtin in his examination of Dostoevskii's novels, Solzhenitsyn in the 1960s stated that his preferred method as a novelist was "polyphonic". In his definition this involves the author lending his weight to each of his main characters in turn, so that no single voice predominates. Polyphony is certainly in evidence in *Cancer Ward*. It was the Marxist critic Georg Lukács who detected a similarity between Solzhenitsyn's novel and Thomas Mann's *Der Zauberberg* (*The Magic Mountain*), for each of these works uses a hospital setting to draw together a wide range of characters who would not, under normal circumstances, interact so uninhibitedly, even if they met at all. The combination of polyphony and liberating circumstance is the key to *Cancer Ward*.

The geographical and historical setting of the novel ("Cancer Wing, or Block" would be a more accurate translation of the title) is all-important. It is a state-run hospital in an unnamed city in Central Asia in the early months of 1955 (Solzhenitsyn was treated in Tashkent in 1954). The structure of the work is episodic rather than dramatic, and there is little of the preoccupation with time that one finds in several of the author's other works. The action takes place over some six weeks and the fates of a good many characters are left undecided at the end. The relatively relaxed, yet still oppressive, atmosphere permits the characters, now confronted with disease and possible death, to reflect on their lives and their own values. The patients argue about life and philosophy, politics, history and literature, about medicine, education and sex. They have nothing to lose in expressing themselves so candidly, for the awareness of imminent death has liberated them from fear of human retribution and the hospital ward has stripped them of any social constraint.

The hero, Oleg Kostoglotov, bears some resemblance to his creator, but should not be taken as his *porte-parole*; he is forthright in his condemnation of Stalinism, being a veteran of the camps himself, but at times he is tongue-tied as he listens to others' views; moreover, like so many of the main characters, he is caught in a web of ironies and self-contradictions. At last he is free to marry, and indeed becomes loosely attached to two of the female medical staff, just at a time when he should undergo hormone therapy that will destroy his sexuality. He insists on the patient's right to know and to decide matters for himself, if necessary by flying in the face of medical advice, but he refuses to enlighten a fellow patient as to his inoperable condition. The dedicated and thoroughly decent specialist Liudmila Dontsova, a great advocate of the public health system, contracts cancer herself, but instead of relying on the official procedures she turns to her old tutor, a private practitioner.

There is a strong literary debate running throughout the book, which starts with a discussion of Tolstoi's *Chem liudi zhivy* (*What Men Live By*) and later takes in the post-Stalinist thaw (Pomerantsev's article "On Sincerity in Literature" of 1953 in particular), as well as the Russian classics. This debate, as much as anything else, highlights the differences between the various characters. The hero's arch-enemy in the ward is Pavel Rusanov, a high-ranking functionary, much disturbed by the political changes following Stalin's death. In a novel that is consistently realistic, Rusanov runs dangerously close to caricature at times. A more intriguing foil to Kostoglotov is Aleksei Shulubin, a man (an Everyman?) who has persistently made compromises with his conscience in order to survive materially ("They executed people like you, but they made us stand up and applaud the verdicts as they were announced"); now confronted with major surgery, he feels able to speak his mind. Referring to Francis Bacon's "idols" and sundry other thinkers and writers, including Kropotkin, Solov'ev, and Herwegh, he propounds a philosophy of "ethical socialism"; but it would be wrong to take this as Solzhenitsyn's "message", given the novel's polyphony and ubiquitous irony.

The scientific debate in the novel is similarly highly charged. The frequent passages concerned with radiotherapy, blood transfusions and the like are more than counter-balanced by the patients' reliance on their more home-spun cures. Kostoglotov's recourse to the mandrake root from Issyk-Kul is taken directly from Solzhenitsyn's biography. Of more importance still, for the dynamics of the novel, is the unremitting questioning of scientific practice altogether, and in this there are echoes of Dostoevskii's Underground Man. As the hero tells Dontsova: "Man is a complicated being, why should he be explainable by logic ... I don't want to be saved at any price!"

At the back of Kostoglotov's intellectual and moral searchings, one detects a degree of simple Russian stoicism, an ability to suffer – though not, in his case, in silence – which derives from the world of nature. Dontsova is comforted more by the appearance of a St Bernard dog than by science. On being discharged, the hero visits the zoo, where each of the animals symbolizes something for him: "Oleg stood there for five minutes and departed in admiration. The goat had not even stirred. That was the sort of character a man needed to get through life"; but this image is offset by the squirrel frantically running inside its wheel to no purpose. The tiger reminds the hero of Stalin. However, it is the one absent animal – the monkey, blinded by "an evil man" – which lingers longest in Kostoglotov's consciousness. The burden of this image is that though evil may never be defeated, moral rejuvenation is possible when evil, unclouded by Stalinist jargon, can at least be identified for what it is.

Cancer Ward has been read by some as pure allegory (cancer = communism); but equally it invites comparison with Tolstoi's *Smert' Ivana Il'icha* (*The Death of Ivan Ilych*), given its emphasis on moral and spiritual health (it is suggested by one patient that a clear conscience is necessary for full physical recovery), and it is a novel of the Thaw in several ways: it depicts a society that is making some attempt to come to terms with its past; there is a prima facie cause for optimism in the figure of the sympathetic official with whom Kostoglotov has to register on his release from hospital; the young, honest communist, Vadim, and the gallery of positive heroes among many of the medical staff and some of the patients would not look out of place in accepted Soviet literature; there is, of course, the allegorical transition from winter to spring. The novel came close to being published in the mid-1960s, before the Brezhnevite winter started to bite. Together with *The First Circle*, it stands as Solzhenitsyn's most successful long work of fiction, eschewing one-sided polemics and didacticism, while voicing in the most powerful terms mankind's deepest concerns.

ROBERT PORTER

The First Circle

V kruge pervom

Novel, 1968

There are two Russian versions of the novel *The First Circle*: the 87-chapter version – Solzhenitsyn refers to it as *K* (for *Krug* = Circle) *87* – prepared in the vain hope of having it published in the Soviet Union, which is structurally the tighter and neater, and the 96-chapter version (*K96*), which structurally is flabbier but politically sharper and more vital. Only *K87* has been translated and is known to non-Russian readers all over the world.

In an afterword printed in volume 2 of the 1978 Russian edition of his complete works, Solzhenitsyn writes that "the *sharashka* [prison research institute] Marfino itself, and almost all of its inhabitants, are copied from nature". This confirms the view that Solzhenitsyn belongs to that kind of writer whose fiction is based on the author's own life experience. The characters Nemov, Nerzhin, Kostoglotov, and Alex – in *Olen' i shalashkova* (*The Love Girl and the Innocent*), *The First Circle*, *Cancer Ward*, and *Candle in the Wind* respectively – re-create, as it were, Solzhenitsyn's life from the time of his arrest to his return from prison and exile.

The *K87* version was not only "lightened" in an endeavour to pass the censorship, but, as Solzhenitsyn says, "dismantled brick by brick and put together again". This resulted, on the negative side, in a number of sharp, mainly political passages being removed, some secondary characters having depth, and some of Solzhenitsyn's views about the state of Stalinist society and about its future being left out. On the positive side, Solzhenitsyn made it easier to visualize and understand life under Stalin by adding details that helped to explain it.

The plot of the novel is rather thin and fragmented: a telephone call made by a councillor in the Ministry of Foreign Affairs is intercepted by the secret police and considered to be treacherous. The prisoners in the telecommunication research institute, who work on the theory, designedly invented by them, that human voices can be distinguished by mechanically recording and measuring the amplitude of individual sounds, are given three tape recordings of voices and ordered to identify the caller, who is then promptly arrested. The strength of the novel lies partly in the locale – a "privileged" prison inhabited by brilliant scientists who work for the secret police and live with the hope of not being sent to an "ordinary" prison camp, and mainly in the study of the characters and their relationships in the Stalinist post-World War II society. The action covers 70 hours, from 4:05 in the afternoon of Saturday 24 December, to 2:30 in the afternoon on Tuesday 27 December, 1949. It describes in detail the life and behaviour of the prisoners, to a lesser extent of their guards, of their "free" wives, of some of the leaders of the country including Stalin himself, and of the few persons only tangentially connected with the prisoners of the research institute.

There are three main characters, all prisoners. Gleb Nerzhin is the author's *alter ego* who seeks to experience fully the hell of the Gulag in order to find the true meaning of life; he refuses to take part in what he considers to be a morally unacceptable task of delivering another human being into the hands of an inhuman authority and is therefore sent from what is, in the prisoners' view, the equivalent of the first circle in Dante's Hell to the yawning abyss of the Gulag's penal camps. Lev Rubin, Nerzhin's close friend, is a former university teacher, a generous and kind scholar, who remains a true Marxist believer in spite of having had the "misadventure" of being classified an enemy of the regime. It is he who, by means of his pseudo-scientific "phonoscopy", identifies the speaker of the treasonable telephone call. Dmitrii Sologdin, also Nerzhin's close friend, a brilliant engineer and ardent right-wing nationalist, hopes to exchange his successful solution of the technical problems connected with the construction of a foolproof voice encoder for his release from the prison. Both Rubin and Sologdin have their known prototypes. They are Lev Kopelev and Dmitrii Panin; both survived their imprisonment and emigrated in the 1970s to the west: Kopelev to take up university work in Germany, and Panin to settle in France and to produce a number of politico-philosophical works that have enjoyed posthumous success in the present-day Russia. These three characters encapsulate, as it were, three types of members of the Soviet intelligentsia: the seeker of truth in the middle, flanked on the left by an ideologically honest believer in the validity of the Soviet experiment, and on the right by an ardent nationalist who, in the name of "Russianness", totally rejects this experiment. Solzhenitsyn passes judgement on, and repudiates, two of these representatives of educated Russia: Rubin, whose faithfulness to ideology forces him to perpetrate a morally unacceptable act of delivering a potentially innocent man (*Innokentii*) to the murderous secret police; and Sologdin, whose selfish arrogance permits him morally to compromise with his own haughtily proclaimed principles.

There are two important invented characters in the novel: Innokentii Volodin, who makes the fateful telephone call and is arrested; the description of his first 24 hours in prison shows this spoilt member of the Soviet elite, who has just taken the first steps into hell, to be made of unexpectedly strong stuff; and Spiridon, the *sharashka* janitor, who personifies the wisdom and the moral strength of the Russian peasant. He is the predecessor of Ivan Denisovich, the hero of Solzhenitsyn's best-known work, and, as Lev Tolstoi's Platon Karataev to Pierre Bezukhov, he is a kind of mentor to Nerzhin. It remains, however, unclear what this wisdom and moral strength is, and so Nerzhin, the main hero of the novel, fashioned after the author himself and depicted as being tough and decisive in his actions, turns out to be ideologically blurred. This is a vexing weakness in what is otherwise one of the greatest works of Russian prose fiction in the second half of the 20th century.

GLEB ŽEKULIN

Krasnoe koleso

The Red Wheel

Tetralogy, 1971–91

Solzhenitsyn's tetralogy *Krasnoe koleso* spans and culminates the author's entire career. Although most of it was completed between 1976 and 1991 during Solzhenitsyn's exile in the United States, the author says that the initial idea came to him in 1937, and the first edition of *August 1914* was published abroad while the author was still in the USSR. The tetralogy's sections (called "knots", defined as "the full and thick exposition of events in condensed chunks of time, but with total breaks between them") are themselves complex, multi-volume works: *August 1914*, *Oktiabr' shestnadtsatogo* [October 1916] (2 vols, 1984), *Mart semnadtsatogo* [March 1917] (4 vols, 1986–88), and *Aprel' semnadtsatogo* [April 1917] (2 vols, 1991). This sprawling mixture of fiction and history deals with the collapse of Russia during World War I and explicates, from Solzhenitsyn's idiosyncratic viewpoint, the causes of the Revolution and the origins of the Bolshevik state. In many respects the cycle is as original and compelling as *Gulag Archipelago*, and read in conjunction these two monumental works provide a panorama of the central tragedies of 20th-century Russian history. However, at some 6,000 pages, *Krasnoe koleso* is probably the largest work in the Russian tradition, and its sheer size as well as its unconventional narrative structure have limited its appeal.

Each of the four knots contains chapters devoted to the lives of fictional characters and chapters featuring historical figures. In combining historical and fictional narrative Solzhenitsyn is clearly working in a Russian tradition whose most famous exemplar is Tolstoi with *Voina i mir* (*War and Peace*). Predictably, most of the criticism devoted to the tetralogy has focused on the influence of Tolstoi, and Solzhenitsyn has generally been considered to have failed to equal his supposed model. In fact, despite the references to Tolstoi, particularly in *August 1914*, Solzhenitsyn's work is not very close to that of Tolstoi.

From the beginning of the tetralogy it is clear that Solzhenitsyn's relationship to the Tolstoian tradition is ambiguous. The first knot chronicles the reactions of a variety of individual Russians and of Russian society as a whole to the events of August, 1914. Some of these personages are fictional and, as in Tolstoi's epic, a number of the central characters are based on the author's family. Solzhenitsyn's book is more "democratic" however, in that he depicts not a single class, but a wide spectrum of classes. Like Tolstoi, only more frequently and to a greater extent, Solzhenitsyn freely mixes chapters devoted to historical figures (treated novelistically) with those concerning invented characters, and he imports undigested contemporary documents into his text. From time to time he employs an absolute "authorial" voice that is able to interpret the overall course of history. Finally, he includes two long historical digressions – biographies of Stolypin and of Nicholas II – to provide the reader with sufficient historical background and to "correct" previous accounts.

Still, Solzhenitsyn emphasizes his differences with Tolstoi in both subtle and not so subtle ways. Most obviously, he radically disagrees with Tolstoi's concept of history. For Solzhenitsyn, it is not the mass but the individual who makes history, and for that reason *Krasnoe koleso* concentrates on individuals and emphasizes their personal role in, and responsibility for, the flow of history. What is more, Solzhenitsyn's language is deliberately heavy and archaic, filled with Slavonicisms, in sharp contrast to Tolstoi's crisp, Gallicized Russian. Ultimately, it is better to see

Solzhenitsyn's work, particularly the later knots, as an attempt to break with the Tolstoian tradition rather than a clumsy imitation of it.

Solzhenitsyn brings a number of innovations to his work. First and foremost is a re-orientation of the spatio-temporal axes of narrative. Where previous writers were primarily interested in the interrelationships of one or a few characters over time to each other and to the historical process, Solzhenitsyn wants to show how the actions and ideas of a large number of people shape the historical moment. In order to do so, he presents a multitude of characters united only by their temporal coexistence. The result is a dizzying series of compelling narrative fragments, each told from an individual point of view in the present tense with no overt narrative control or commentary. Solzhenitsyn makes no distinction between his presentation of the thoughts, dreams, and inner lives of his created characters and those of, say, Nicholas II or Lenin. As a result the fictional is thoroughly historicized, while the historical is thoroughly fictionalized.

The overall structure of the work is no less original than the presentation of its parts. In most novels one expects that the created characters will interact. Solzhenitsyn, however, provides some 20 separate narratives that are related to each other only in so far as they unfold simultaneously. The unit of narrative interest is neither the fictional story (with its conventional beginning, middle, and end) nor the historical event, but rather the month. The only overt organizing principle is chronology; if something happened in the month of the knot then it is eligible to be included – from the most momentous occurrence to the most trivial detail. Symptomatic of the author's desire to refocus narrative interest is the avoidance of a string of chapters devoted to the same character. In *August 1914*, Solzhenitsyn may follow a single character in three or four successive chapters. This creates the illusion that he is writing a more or less standard, if fragmented, novel. But by *Aprel' semnadtsatogo* no two successive chapters are devoted to the same individual, which greatly increases the sense of fragmentariness and emphasizes the strictly chronological principle governing the selection of fictional and historical material.

For readers expecting a "normal" novel, this method is maddening. It is difficult to follow 20 plot lines developing simultaneously, and one keeps waiting for the plot twists that will tie up the narrative knots, but they never come. Furthermore, even individual stories are never told in their entirety: the dramatic action develops in the life of a character, but the narrative switches to another character and the month frequently ends without returning to the individual with whom we had begun to empathize. The illusion is that we have relived the experience of a cross-section of a society at a selected moment rather than followed the full life story of randomly chosen individuals.

Although at first Solzhenitsyn's exclusively temporal concerns seem entirely innovative, for a Russian reader there exists an obvious model for this kind of prose: the Russian chronicles, historical works whose principle of organization is temporal. In theory each chronicle entry is shaped not by the "logical" contours of a complete story, but rather by a chronological unit: the year. What Solzhenitsyn has done in *Krasnoe koleso* is to turn his back on the entire modern period of Russian historiography and fiction and to create instead a new Russian chronicle. In this respect, Solzhenitsyn can be seen not as an imitator of Tolstoi, but rather as a radical conservative, an orientation that is completely consistent with his overall world-view. It remains to be seen whether Solzhenitsyn's conservative experiment will ever find a reading public. It may be that the size, complexity, and experimental nature of *Krasnoe koleso* will ensure that it remains a failure. If so, it will certainly be the most grandiose failure in the Russian literary tradition.

ANDREW BARUCH WACHTEL

Song of Igor's Campaign *see* Lay of Igor's Campaing

Vladimir Georgievich Sorokin 1955–

Prose writer

Biography

Born in the Moscow region, 1955. Graduated as chemical engineer from the Moscow Oil and Gas Institute. Worked subsequently as a graphic artist and as a stage designer. Associated with the Conceptualist movement in Russian avant-garde art, as represented in the poetry of Dmitrii Prigov. Began writing in the 1970s, remained unpublished in Russia until the early 1990s. Married; two daughters.

Publications

Fiction

Ochered', Paris, "Sintaksis", 1985; extract in *Ogonek*, 46

(1991), 10–12; translated as *The Queue*, by Sally Laird, New York and London, Readers International, 1988.

"Zasedanie zavkoma", *Strelets*, 3 (1991), 122–35; translated as "Next Item on the Agenda", by Andrew Reynolds, in *The Penguin Book of New Russian Writing: Russia's "Fleurs du mal"*, edited by Reynolds and Viktor Erofeev, Harmondsworth and New York, Penguin, 1995, 321–44.

Norma [The Norm]. extracts in *Volga*, 9 (1991), 29–34; *Literaturnaia gazeta* (6 March 1991), 12; Moscow, 1994.

Mesiats v Dakhau [A Month in Dachau], n.p., Gräfeling, n.d. [1992].

Sbornik rasskazov [Collection of Short Stories]. Moscow, 1992.

Roman. Moscow, 1994.

"Serdtsa chetyrekh" [The Hearts of the Four], in *Konets veka: Nezavisimyi al'manakh*, edited by A. Nikishin, Moscow, 1994, 5–116.

Tridtsataia liubov' Mariny [The Thirtieth Love of Marina]. Moscow, 1995.

Russkii Bog Trubetskoi [The Russian God, Trubetskoi]. Moscow, 1996.

Play

"Doverie: P'esa v piati aktakh" [Trust], *Siuzhety*, 9 (1990), 83–138.

Essays

"Igra s prostranstvom kul'tury" [Game with an Expanse of Culture], *Moskovskie novosti*, 18 October 1992, 22–23.

"V.G. Sorokin – V.V. Sorokin: Obraz bez podobiia" [V.G. Sorokin – V.V. Sorokin: An Image Without Similarity], *Iskusstvo kino*, 6 (1994), 35–44.

"Eroticheskoi literatury ne sushchestvuet" [Erotic Literature Does Not Exist], *Novyi dzhentl'men* (Spring 1995), 104–07.

Critical Studies

The Total Art of Stalinism: Avant-garde, Aesthetic Dictatorship and Beyond, by Boris Groys, Princeton, Princeton University Press, 1992, 99–102.

Russia's Alternative Prose, by Robert Porter, Oxford, Berg, 1994, 38–42.

"Antisovetchik Vladimir Sorokin", by Bakhyt Kenzheev, *Znamia*, 4 (1995), 202–05.

"Stripping Socialist Realism of Its Seamless Dress: Vladimir Sorokin's Deconstruction of Soviet Utopia and the Art of Representation", by Serafima Roll, *Russian Literature*, 39/1 (1996), 65–78.

"Sex, Violence and the Video Nasty: The Ferocious Prose of Vladimir Sorokin", by David Gillespie, *Essays in Poetics*, 22 (1997), 158–75.

Vladimir Sorokin is the author of the novels *Ochered'* (*The Queue*), *Norma* [The Norm], *Roman*, *Serdtsa chetyrekh* [The Hearts of the Four], *Tridtsataia liubov' Mariny* [The Thirtieth Love of Marina]; he has also written the novella *Mesiats v Dakhau* [A Month in Dachau], the play *Doverie* [Trust] and has published a book of short stories. His works are published both in Russia and the west, and *The Queue* has been translated into eight languages. A common feature of all his works is the desire to shock and disgust, both in his use of language and in the breaking down of all sexual and social taboos. Clearly influenced by the absurdist writings of the OBERIU writers of the 1920s, Sorokin extends their preoccupation with irrationality and senseless violence to chart the breakdown of public morality and the collapse of a society. At the same time, Sorokin is adept at parodying the style and content of socialist realist writing and, especially in *Roman*, reveals considerable talent for writing in the spirit and style of the 19th-century Russian classical tradition.

The subject-matter of Sorokin's fiction does not make for pleasant reading. His works contain many scenes of merciless killing, sadism, torture, cannibalism, amputation, coprophagy, gratuitous sex, sexual abuse of minors, and extreme verbal abuse and profanity. Very often apoplexy and violence extend to the text itself, as grammar and syntax implode, and the narrative trails off in nonsensical collocations. Sorokin can be obscene, occasionally pornographic, but he can also be extremely funny. He can unerringly reproduce the oaths and profanities of everyday speech, but he can equally delight the reader with lyrical nature description or sensitive accounts of emotional relationships.

Sorokin consistently challenges the reader's aesthetic sensibilities, and seems determined to outrage. Thus, *Tridtsataia liubov' Mariny* contains many detailed erotic descriptions of sexual coupling, and, indeed, the novel is ultimately no more than the sum of these parts. *Serdtsa chetyrekh* amounts to a catalogue of killing and violence in a parody of the detective thrillers that flooded the Russian market in the 1990s (of which Fridrikh Neznanskii and Eduard Topol' would seem to be the prime exponents). However, Sorokin is also capable of great subtlety and humour.

The Queue concerns nothing more than the excruciatingly slow movement of a queue as hundreds, perhaps thousands, of people line up to buy American denims. There is no third-person narrative, no authorial presence, the novel consists only of snatches of street dialogue as those in the queue debate issues from their immediate surroundings, be they the course of the current football World Cup (this is 1982), western pop music or the "order" in society that existed under Stalin. *Norma* comprises several chapters, all written in a particular stylistic key, and all with a separate theme. The first chapter consists of a series of vignettes, episodes from everyday life in the Soviet Union, with scenes involving lovers (both heterosexual and homosexual), criminals, parents and children, the petty jealousies of the intelligentsia, and the relatively luxurious lifestyle of the Communist Party elite. All are united in their love of the *norma*, a piece of attractively packaged excrement that is the staple diet of the masses. In another chapter we get a novel within a novel in *Padezh* [Case], a short account of the cruelty and sadism subjected on the countryside by the authorities, resulting in the annihilation, and physical decomposition, of those classes of people regarded as hostile to the Party. In both these chapters Sorokin literalizes the abuse heaped on society to create ferocious parodies of the Russian anti-Utopia.

The first 300 pages of *Roman* are written in the classic literary style, set in a timeless landscape of rural dwellers, peasants, intellectuals, and hunters. No mention is made of the modern world, of technology, of political or historical events. The way of life of the main characters is slow and deliberate, revolving around celebrations, tea-drinking and earnest discussions on philosophical or spiritual themes. Roman, the main character (the Russian title is thus a pun), is then bitten by a wolf while out picking mushrooms in the forest, is nursed back to health by Tat'iana, and, with her help, in the last hundred or so pages, massacres and mutilates the entire neighbourhood, including children, and then dies himself. If, in his other works, Sorokin destroys the Soviet world and its values, here he definitively brings the 19th century to an end.

Sorokin deconstructs the cultural myths of a society, and subjects to merciless attack the symbols of authority and power of that society. He not only charts the degradation of a society and a way of life, but also the revolt of the sons against the fathers. The sheer viscerality of his prose will undoubtedly alienate many readers accustomed to homilies and smug semi-truths, but he metaphorically rips away the flesh of a society based on falsehood, hypocrisy, and expediency. His dominant motifs are of death, degradation and decay, for he is indeed writing for the post-Dachau world. It remains to be said that Sorokin's works are about ends, and not new beginnings. It may well be, in the chaotic Russia of the mid-1990s, that his writings offer not so much an aesthetic signpost, as a psychological one, where the traumas of destruction and upheaval remain dominant in the Russian cultural consciousness.

DAVID GILLESPIE

Sergei Georg'evich Stratanovskii 1944–

Poet

Biography

Born in Leningrad, 5 December 1944, into a family of well-known scholars. Studied French, then Russian literature at Leningrad University, 1962–68. Worked as guide in the Hermitage and Pushkin Museum; bibliographer in the Russian National Library. Married: Valentina Sannikova. Recipient: "Tsarskoe Selo" Prize in 1994 for the collection *Stikhi*.

Publications

Collected Edition

Stikhi. St Petersburg, 1993.

Poetry (poems appear in following publications):

Apollon-77, Paris (1977).
Vestnik russkogo khristianskogo dvizheniia, Paris, 121 (1977).
Ekho, Paris, 4 (1978).
Tret'ia volna, Paris, 17 (1984).
Beseda, Paris, 2 (1984).
Krug, Leningrad (1985).
Rodnik, 6 (1988).
Neva, 9 (1989).
Nezamechennaia zemlia, Moscow and Leningrad (1991).
Vestnik novoi literatury, 3 (1991).
Strelets, 1 (1991); 4 (1994).
Poslednii ekzempliar, 1 (1993).
Zvezda, 1 (1993); 2 (1994); 6 (1995).
Twentieth Century Russian Poetry: Silver and Steel. An Anthology, with an introduction by Yevgeny Yevtushenko, edited by Albert C. Todd and Max Hayward, New York, Doubleday, and London, Fourth Estate, 1993; as *Strafy veka: Antologiia russkoi poezii XX veka*, Moscow, 1994.
V Peterburge my soidemsia snova, Leningrad (1994).
Arion, 1 (1994).
Soglasie, 5 (1995).
Znamia, 1 (1996).

Essays and Literary Criticism

"Chto takoe rusofobiia" (Razmyshlenie nad stat'ei I.R. Shifarevicha "Rusofobiia") [What is Russophobia? ...], *Zvezda*, 4 (1990).
"Beseda": Obzor parizhskogo religiozno-filosofskogo zhurnala [Survey of the Parisian Religious-Philosophical Journal, "Beseda"], *Zvezda*, 11 (1991).
"Poet i revoliutsiia: Opyt sovremennogo prochteniia poemy Bloka 'Dvenadtsat'" [Poet and Revolution: Attempt at a Contemporary Reading of Blok's "The Twelve"], *Zvezda*, 11 (1991).
"V plenu illiuzii: Zametki o smenovekhovstve" [A Captive of Illusion: Notes on the Changing Landmarks Movement], *Volga*, 8 (1991).
"Predislovie k publikatsii memuarov F. Stepuna 'Byvshee i nesbyvsheesia'" [Foreword to F. Stepun's Memoirs], *Volga*, 8 (1991).
"Za belym klobukom: Russkaia ideia v sovremennykh sporakh" [Behind the White Cowl: The Russian Idea in Contemporary Discussions], *Volga*, 1 (1992).
"'I putnik ustalyi na Boga roptal': Motiv neobratimosti vremeni v tvorchestve A.S. Pushkina" ["And the Weary Traveller Grumbled at God": The Motif of Irreversibility in the Work of A.S. Pushkin], *Pushkinskaia epokha i khristianskaia kul'tura*, St Petersburg, 1993.
"Religioznye motivy v sovremennoi russkoi poezii" [Religious Motifs in Contemporary Russian Poetry], *Volga*, 4–6, 8 (1993).

Critical Studies

"Predislovie k podborke stikhotvorenii", by Viktor Krivulin, in *37 (samizdat)*, 7–8 (1977).
"Stikhi Stratanovskogo", by K. Mamontov (K.M. Butyrin), *Obvodnoi kanal*, 1 (1981); also in *Chasy (samizdat)*, 34 (1981).
"Stratanovskii i leningradskaia poeticheskaia shkola", by V. Kreid, *Novyi zhurnal*, 156 (1984).

"V poiskakh utrachennogo begemota: O sovremennoi leningradskoi religioznoi poezii", by E. Pazukhin, *Beseda*, 2 (1984).
"Dlia neizvestnoi literatury nastali novye vremena", by E. Gollerbakh (interview with Stratanovskii), *Chas pik* (25 June 1990), 7.
"Nekotorye drugie", by M. Aizenberg, *Teatr*, 4 (1991).
"Predislovie k publikatsii", by M. Sh., *Arion*, 4 (1994).
"Prizraki i dushi", by S. Shapovalov (interview with Stratanovskii), *Moskovskie novosti*, 15 (1994).
"Retsenziia", by Iu. Kublanovskii, *Novyi mir*, 2 (1995).
"Dvukhgolovaia teoditseia s posleduiushchim ee oproverzheniem", by A. Levin, *Znamia*, 7 (1995).

Sergei Stratanovskii is a St Peterburg poet, philologist, dramatist, bibliographer, editor of *samizdat* journals, and from 1970 to 1980 was one of the major figures of unofficial culture in Leningrad. Born into the family of a famous Hellenist and translator of Josephus Flavius and Herodotus, he began writing poetry in childhood. From 1959 to 1961 he attended the youth poetry studio in the Pioneers' Palace. The first poem that he recited in public was devoted to the victims of Auschwitz. It was the only way to remind the audience about Stalin's camps and prisons, where his father spent several years. In 1962 Stratanovskii entered the department of Romance languages of Leningrad University, but soon transferred to the Russian department. He studied folklore, under V.Ia. Propp's supervision, and poetry of the Silver Age with D.E. Maksimov. During his university years he continued writing poetry and soon developed his own unique poetic style. He took active part in a philological circle of like-minded students discussing classical and contemporary literature. Many of the members of this circle became famous academics, critics, translators, poets – Sergei Grechishkin, Aleksandr Lavrov, Georgii Levinton, Kiril Buturin, Aleksandr Zhidkov, to name but a few. The Soviet invasion of Prague on 21 August 1968 made a great impact on Stratanovskii's moral and aesthetic position and brought absurdity and bitter irony to his poetry.

His most intensive creative period was from 1968 to 1973, when Stratanovskii attended the so-called Leningrad "Lito" under the supervision of Gleb Semenov together with Elena Shvarts, Oleg Okhapkin, Aleksandr Mironov, and other talented young poets. By the middle of the 1970s his poetry had reached unusually broad horizons and a relatively big audience although, before 1977, he was published only in *samizdat*. His first *samizdat* collection, *V strakhe i trepete* [In Fear and Trembling] (1979) was highly appreciated both in dissident circles and among poetry lovers in Moscow and Leningrad. From 1975 Stratanovskii actively participated in an unofficial religious-philosophical seminar. From 1976 onwards he was one of the most significant authors of the *samizdat* journals *37*, *Chasy*, and *Severnaia pochta*, where his poems, reviews and essays were published. After these journals ceased publication, in 1981, Stratanovskii together with Kiril Butyrin published the literary and socio-philosophical journal *Obvodnoi kanal*. From 1977 his poems began to appear in the émigré press. In 1981 he became one of the editors of *Club-81*, which brought together the best unofficial writers in Leningrad. The year 1991 saw his first official publication in Russia in the collection *Krug*. Since the collapse of communism Stratanovskii's poems and essays have been in great demand by such journals as *Zvezda*, *Neva*, *Volga*, *Znamia*, and *Novyi mir*. He is also author of a monumental poetic drama devoted to one of the most tragic events in contemporary Russian history – the construction of the White Sea-Baltic Canal.

Stratanovskii's poems are metaphysical in the sense that they tell us not so much about actual changes as about what is left in the world after all these changes have taken place and how they affect man. The main themes of his poetry are death and moral suffering in the totalitarian world, the modern city and eros, and the eternal questions addressed in fear and trembling by Job to God. The relationship between God and man is Stratanovskii's major concern: God in his poems is unattainable, He dooms man to failure and does not guarantee salvation. It is precisely man's defencelessness that provides the purity for his art. Man's creative power is seen as compensation for his suffering: it brings happiness even to the weak and helpless. An almost stoic resistance to the world's calamities through art constitutes Stratanovskii's ethical position. Stratanovskii has a tendency to treat abstract concepts as real facts. His perception of the world is existential and tragic. He is truly a poet-philosopher, perhaps the only one left now in Russia. His poems demonstrate his profound knowledge of contemporary philosophy, from Husserl, Heidegger, Sartre and the post-structuralists to Russian religious philosophy. He also often turns to history, as in his poems about the great Russian military leader A.V. Suvorov and about the Ukrainian mystic philosopher Grigorii Skovoroda. Both poems, "Suvorov" and "Skovoroda", include a great deal of absurdity as well as the classic ode tradition. They can be seen as models of historical and philosophical contemporary Russian poetry.

Many of his works are devoted to the failure of social and religious Utopias. On the eve of perestroika Stratanovskii published a cycle of poems, which depict futuristic scenes based on Nikolai Fedorov's ideas, realized with the support of computer technology. This is not anti-Utopia or satire; it is a melancholy meditation about the future, which is for the poet like a pre-historic and pre-Christian past. Now, when so many Russian writers and poets are dancing on the grave of the communist Utopia, there is a danger that some of Stratanovskii's poems could be read through the prism of the influential Moscow Conceptualists' poetry and could lose some of their charm and essence. Although he works in the same virtual space as D.A. Prigov and L. Rubinshtein, that is the space of Soviet Utopian language, Stratanovskii carries the basic elements of the "Russian Global Myth" to the point of absurdity. His style is close to Platonov's prose. An existentialist and absurdist, Stratanovskii often merges biblical motifs with Soviet cliché, imitating Christian and communist Utopias. This tendency is reflected in his vocabulary, which is coloured by many neologisms: "chelovekokoni", "temnotel'nyi", "babatara", which are based on Soviet abbreviations. Sometimes his poetry reminds us of a landscape after a battle, or most likely an unfinished grand Soviet construction, with a half-destroyed church on the horizon. The most important element in this landscape is the tiny figure of a man, rushing about, now disappearing from sight, now vanishing altogether. The decomposition of Stalin's empire is a long and painful process which is still going on. It has its own aesthetic and its own attraction. But like any empire, it has its own parks, including the tsar's summer palace park, which is the source of Stratanovskii's inspiration.

VIKTOR KRIVULIN

Arkadii Natanovich and Boris Natanovich Strugatskii

Science fiction writers

Arkadii Natanovich Strugatskii 1925–1991

Biography

Born in Batumi, Georgia, 28 August 1925. Served in the Soviet Army, 1943–55: senior lieutenant. Attended the Military Institute for Foreign Languages, graduated, 1949. Married: Elena Oshanina in 1955; one stepdaughter. Editor, Institute for Technical Information, Goslitizdat, 1959–61; editor, Detgiz, 1961–64; freelance writer and translator from English and Japanese, from 1964. Died 23 October 1991.

Boris Natanovich Strugatskii 1933 –

Biography

Born in Leningrad, 15 April 1933. Studied astronomy at Leningrad University, graduated, 1956. Married: Adelaida Karpeliuk in 1957; one son. Astronomer and computer mathematician at the Pulkovo Astronomical Observatory, near Leningrad, 1956–64. Freelance writer from 1964.
Recipients: Second Award of Ministry of Education for *Strana bagrovykh tuch* [The Land of the Red Clouds], 1959; Aelita Prize for *Zhuk v muraveinike* (*The Beetle in the Anthill*), 1981; European Association of Science Fiction Writers Award, Jules Verne Society of Sweden Award, John Campbell Award, World Science Fiction Conference 1987 Award.

Publications

Collected Edition

Sobranie sochinenii, 12 vols. Moscow, 1990–93.

Fiction

"Spontannyi refleks", *Znanie-sila*, 8 (1958), 32–38; translated as "Spontaneous Reflex", by Violet L. Dutt, in *Soviet Science Fiction*, New York, Collier, 1962.

Strana bagrovykh tuch [The Land of the Red Clouds]. Moscow, 1959; translated as *Atomvulkan Golkonda*, Berlin, Kultur und Fortschritt, 1961.

"Noch'iu na Marse", *Znanie-sila*, 6 (1960), 32–36; translated as "Night on Mars", by Patrick L. McGuire, in *Noon: 22nd Century*, New York, Macmillan, 1978; London, Collier, 1979.

Put' na Amal'teiu, Moscow, 1960; translated as "Destination: Amaltheiea" [no translator named], in *Destination: Amaltheiea*, Moscow, Foreign Languages Publishing House, 1962.

"Pol'den': 22-ii vek", chapters in *Ural*, 6 (1961), 13–89; as *Vozvraschchenie (Pol'den': 22-ii vek)*, Moscow, 1962; revised and expanded edition, *Pol'den', XXII vek (Vozvrashchenie)*, Moscow, 1967; translated as *Noon: 22nd Century*, by Patrick L. McGuire, New York, Macmillan, 1978; London, Collier, 1979.

"Popytka k begstvu", in *Fantastika. 1962 god*, Moscow, 1962; translated as *Escape Attempt*, by Roger DeGaris, New York, Macmillan, and London, Collier, 1982.

"Dalekaia raduga", in *Novaia signal'naia*, Moscow, 1963; translated as *Far Rainbow*, by Alan Myers, Moscow, Mir, 1967; also translated by Antonina W. Bouis, New York, Macmillan, and London, Collier, 1980.

Trudno byt' bogom. Moscow, 1964; translated as *It's Hard to Be a God*, by Wendayne Ackerman, New York, DAW, 1974.

Khishchnie veshchi veka. Moscow, 1965; translated as *The Final Circle of Paradise*, by Leonid Reinen, New York, DAW, 1976; London, Dobson, 1979.

Ponedel'nik nachinaetsia v subbotu. Moscow, Detskaia literatura, 1965; translated as *Monday Begins on Saturday*, by Leonid Reinen, New York, DAW, 1977.

"Kandid" [part of *Ulitka na sklone*], in *Ellinskii sekret*, Leningrad, 1966; "Pepper" [part of *Ulitka na sklone*], *Baikal*, 1–2 (1968); first full edition in Estonian, Tallin, Periodika, 1971; first full edition in Russian, *Smena*, 11–16 (1988); translated as *The Snail on the Slope*, by Alan Myers [misprinted as Meyers], London, Gollancz, and New York, Bantam, 1980.

"Vtoroe nashestvie marsian", *Baikal*, 1 (1967), 54–109; also in *Stazhery – Vtoroe nashestvie marsian*, Moscow, 1968; translated as "The Second Martian Invasion", in *Vortex: New Soviet Science Fiction*, edited by C.G. Bearne, London, MacGibbon and Kee, 1970; New York, Macmillan, 1973; also translated as *The Second Invasion from Mars*, by Gary Kern, New York, Macmillan, and London, Collier, 1980.

"Skazka o troike", *Angara*, 4–5 (1968); translated as "Tale of the Troika", by Antonina W. Bouis, in *Roadside Picnic – Tale of the Troika*, New York and London, Macmillan, 1977.

"Obitaemyi ostrov", *Neva*, 3–5 (1969); Moscow, 1971; translated as *Prisoners of Power*, by Helen Saltz Jacobson, New York and London, Macmillan, 1977; Harmondsworth, Penguin, 1983.

"Piknik na obochine", *Avrora*, 7–10 (1972); translated as *Roadside Picnic*, by Antonina W. Bouis, New York and London, Macmillan, 1977; Harmondsworth, Penguin, 1979.

Gadkie lebedi, Frankfurt, Posev, 1972 [unauthorized edition]; as "Vremia dozhdia", *Daugava*, 1–7 (1987); also in *Priroda i chelovek*, 9–12 (1988); 1–6 (1989); translated as *The Ugly Swans*, by Alice Stone Nakhimovsky and Aleksander Nakhimovsky, New York, Macmillan, 1979; later designated as the "inner part" of *Khromaia sud'ba*.
"Za milliard let do kontsa sveta", *Znanie-sila*, 9–12 (1976); 1 (1977); translated as *Definitely Maybe*, by Antonina W. Bouis, New York, Macmillan, and London, Collier, 1978.
"Zhuk v muraveinike", *Znanie-sila*, 9–12 (1979); 1–6 (1980); translated as *The Beetle in the Anthill*, by Antonina W. Bouis, New York, Macmillan, 1980.
"Volny gasiat veter", *Znanie-sila*, 6–12 (1985); 1–3 (1986); translated as *The Time Wanderers*, by Antonina W. Bouis, New York, Richardson and Steirman, 1986.
"Khromaia sud'ba" [Lame Fate], *Neva*, 8–9 (1986); published with *Gadkie lebedi*, as *Khromaia sud'ba*, Moscow, 1989; translated as *Das lahme Shicksal*, by Erika Pietrass and Helga Gutsche, Berlin, Das Neue Berlin, 1990.
"Grad obrechennyi" [The Doomed City], *Znanie-sila*, 12 (1987); 1 (1988); also *Neva*, 9–10 (1988); 2–3 (1989); translated as *Stadt der verdammte*, Frankfurt and Berlin, Ullstein, 1993.
"Otiagoshchennye zlom, ili sorok let spustia" [Burdened by Evil, or 40 Years Later], *Iunost'*, 6 (1988), 8–42.
"Bednye zlye liudi" [Poor Evil People], *Zheleznodorozhnik Povolzh'ia* (22 November 1989).
"Zhidy goroda Pitera, ili neveselye besedy pri svechakh (Komediia)" [The Jews of the Town of Peter, or Unhappy Candlelit Conversations (A Comedy)], *Neva*, 9 (1990), 92–115.

Critical Studies
"Introduction", by D. Suvin, in *The Snail on the Slope*, translated by Alan Myers, London, Gollancz, and New York, Bantam, 1980, 1–20.
"Future History, Soviet Style: The Work of the Strugatsky Brothers", by Patrick L. McGuire, in *Critical Encounters II: Writers and Themes in Science Fiction*, edited by Tom Staicar, New York, Ungar, 1982.
"About the Strugatskys' *Roadside Picnic*", by Stanisław Lem, in *Microworlds: Writings on Science Fiction and Fantasy*, edited by Franz Rottensteiner, San Diego, Harcourt Brace Jovanovich, 1984; London, Secker and Warburg, 1985.
"Towards the Last Fairy Tale: On the Fairy-Tale Paradigm in the Strugatskys' Science Fiction 1963–72", by I. Csicsery-Ronan, *Science-Fiction Studies*, 13 (1986), 1–41.
"Chtoby ne nastupil konets sveta!", by Iu. Andreev, in *Povesti*, Leningrad, 1988, 481–95.
"Models and Anti-Models in Soviet Science Fiction: Ivan Efremov and the Strugatsky Brothers", by Gary Kern, in *Shelters of the Infinite: The Science Fiction of Arkady and Boris Strugatsky*, edited by G.E. Slusser and Gary Kern, Mercer, Washington, 1988.
"Tri veka skitanii v mire utopii", by V. Serbinenko, *Novyi mir*, 5 (1989), 242–55.
"Structures of Apprehension: Lem, Heinlein and the Strugatskys", by G.E. Slusser, *Science-Fiction Studies*, 16/1 (1989), 1–37.
"Change and the Individual in the Work of the Strugatskys", by Christopher Pike, in *Science Fiction, Social Conflict and War*, edited P.J. Davies, Manchester, Manchester University Press, 1990, 85–97.
Apocalyptic Realism: The Science Fiction of Arkady and Boris Strugatsky, by Yvonne Howell, New York, Peter Lang, 1994.

Bibliographies
"Criticism of the Strugatsky Brothers' Work", by D. Suvin, *Canadian-American Slavic Studies*, 2 (Summer 1972), 286–307.
"The Literary Opus of the Strugatsky Brothers", by D. Suvin, *Canadian-American Slavic Studies*, 3 (Fall 1974), 454–63.
"Bibliografiia", *Sovetskaia bibliografiia*, 3 (May–June 1988).

The Strugatskii brothers were, until the death of Arkadii in 1991, Russia's leading science-fiction writers, with more than a dozen major long works, many short stories (some interlinked in collections), a comedy, and six film scripts (including an adaptation of their novel *Piknik na obochine* [*Roadside Picnic*] 1972 for Tarkovskii's *Stalker*) to their credit. They began their writing career in the late 1950s with the publication of several stories that already bore the hallmarks of the mature Strugatskii text, with its humour, intensity, fast-pacing and, in particular, love for enigmas. Among these early publications, "Noch'iu na Marse" ("Night on Mars"), for example, deals with a mysterious beast that poses a danger to two doctors crossing the Martian terrain to attend the birth of the first human child on the planet. The beast is never clearly described, but remains a typical Strugatskii device for increasing suspense and heightening an atmosphere of mystery, a method that reaches its apogee in their *Ulitka na sklone* (*The Snail on the Slope*), in which the central image of the forest is an elusive metaphor for unseen, barely comprehended forces.

With the appearance of *Trudno byt' bogom* (*It's Hard to Be a God*), in 1964, the Strugatskiis attained their rightful place as leaders of the Russian science-fiction field, the combination of Boris's scientific expertise and Arkadii's knowledge of western texts imparting to their work both technological innovation and a "western" outlook that has rendered their work particularly accessible to audiences abroad (they are Russia's most widely-translated science-fiction writers). Adulation at home was to be a short-lived phenomenon, however, as the brothers' increasing tendency to utilize the science-fiction genre as a vehicle for social satire rather than fantasy brought them into conflict with the censors in 1969, when *Gadkie lebedi* (*The Ugly Swans*) did not immediately find a publisher. Its unauthorized appearance in Germany in 1972 turned the Strugatskiis, despite their official "protest" against the publication, from writers acclaimed by the establishment into semi-outcasts who were to face increasing difficulty in publishing until the advent of glasnost. During the five years from 1985 to 1990, however, five major works have appeared, including *Khromaia sud'ba* [Lame Fate], the "extended" version of *The Ugly Swans*.

The Strugatskiis' artistic and philosophical creed is one of independence at all costs. A constant theme of their prose is that of propaganda. People are shown to be brainwashed by unscrupulous governments, as in *Khishchnie veshchi veka* (translated as *The Final Circle of Paradise*) in that the inhabitants of this so-called Utopia are shown to be victims of electric wave psychotechnics that impart pleasing dreams and keep the populace docile and mindlessly hedonistic. In *Obitaemyi ostrov* (*Prisoners of Power*) the government again uses transmissions to numb the critical faculties of the people into accepting its lies.

The latter is one of the texts that follows the fortunes of Maksim Kammerer, one of the many characters who reappear in the Strugatskiis' work, providing interlinked accounts of the future galactic civilization with its mixture of backward, usually barbarian regimes, and allegedly more enlightened societies engaged in exploration and, often, in infiltration. The so-called "Wanderers" to whom the authors refer in several texts are supermen with their own, not altogether clear, reasons for interfering in human social uplift, usually without reward. The Strugatskiis introduce the theme of xenophobia into texts such as *Volny gasiat veter* (*The Time Wanderers*), in which the supermen conduct experiments on mankind in order to single out those able to welcome the introduction of the alien into their lives. Xenophobia is also introduced into *Zhuk v muraveinike* (*The Beetle in the Anthill*), in which the alien who goes by the name of Lev Abalkin meets an ambiguous but tragic end.

The Strugatskiis constantly return to the theme of ignorance; whether as a result of propaganda, conservatism, or fear of the uncontrolled unknown, it provides the cause, if not the rationale, for man's cruel and instinctively egotistic behaviour. The Strugatskiis have amply demonstrated that their texts go beyond the didactic concern with social injustice. Their work transcends genre boundaries, containing parable and folktale elements as well as those of science fiction and the dystopia. Their texts are Gogolian analyses of man's innate lack of spirituality, his tendency to cling to the conformist tedium of bureaucratese, his hubris, and self-deception.

As well as a deep concern with the individual, usually that of an outcast or critic of society, who must develop his true identity and come to terms with his surroundings, the Strugatskiis have demonstrated their interest in the expected themes of science fiction. Technology and its dangers are constantly referred to, and the threat to a planet's ecology presented strongly. Concerned with man's ability to control forces that he is as yet (in evolutionary terms) unable to manage wisely, the Strugatskiis fill their texts with animal images that underline man's unfitness to be "gods". "Animals stood by the door", the penultimate sentence to *The Beetle in the Anthill*, provides an elliptic image of man's aspiration and of the impediment to attaining that aspiration, crossing that threshold: his bestiality, his unthinking reaction to events. Without knowledge, rationality and control, men will never be free, but will forever be "prisoners of power". The Strugatskiis' work is dedicated to such freedom.

S. DALTON-BROWN

It's Hard to Be a God

Trudno byt' bogom

Novel, 1964

Arkadii and Boris Strugatskii began publishing in 1958, achieving a degree of success with *Vozvrashchenie (Pol'den': 22-ii vek)* (translated as *Noon: 22nd Century*) in 1962. *It's Hard to Be a God*, published in 1964, was however the text that brought them recognition as serious writers, whose genre is not merely that of entertaining science fiction, but rather that of the dystopian novel. In *It's Hard to Be a God* "Utopian ethics are put to the test of anti-Utopian darkness, of an inhuman and apparently irresistible wave of destruction" (Suvin). An immensely popular text, it establishes the conventions and concerns that dominate the later Strugatskii texts, and which allow the latter to take their rightful place among the ranks of writers of serious science fiction/dystopian fiction such as Philip K. Dick and Ursula K. Le Guin.

"Life in the Strugatskii's books is always a battle" (Vasiuchenko), and *It's Hard to Be a God* demonstrates this statement adequately. A group of historians from a future, and technologically advanced, Earth (*Terra*) visit a medieval planet in order to observe its historical development. The novel centres on one such historian, Anton, whose medieval pseudonym is "Don Rumata". While living in the city of Arkanar, he observes with growing unease the increasing tension and repression in the city as the weak, snivelling king accedes more and more power to the Minister for Security, Don Reba, who is organizing violent pogroms among the members of the intelligentsia – for the state needs no clever people, only loyalty. Any literate man is liable for instant execution by Reba's Grey Soldiers, unless Rumata, using his technological superiority, is able to effect a rescue first.

Eventually there is a coup, the king is poisoned, the heir slain, and Reba comes to power, revealing himself now as the head of a holy order; his "black monks" begin a systematic purging of the populace. Rumata, left in peace by the new rulers, suffers the loss of his mistress, Kyra; it is hinted that in a fit of rage he kills Reba, before being hurriedly repatriated to Earth.

The plot is lively, and the Strugatskiis handle suspense well; the medieval atmosphere is skilfully evoked through the narrative perspective of the fastidious Rumata, the "god" of the title, who observes with distaste the brutality, amorality, drunkenness, ignorance and lack of hygiene common among the inhabitants of this backward society. The strength of the text lies in its depiction of the frustration felt by a good man (Rumata) at being forced to be merely a spectator of violent events. Even though he does contravene the Terran Historical Institute's directive of non-interference by helping dissidents to escape from Arkanar, Rumata feels he has become tainted by passivity to the point where he loses his god-like objectivity. Swinging from one emotional extreme to the other, he vacillates between hatred for these barbarous people, and a feeling of brotherly love towards them. Both emotions come to a head in the sub-plot dealing with Kyra, whom he loves and whose loss drives him finally from the heights of god-like impassivity to barbarous rage.

Can man be a god? "A fine god you are", Rumata tells himself, enraged at losing his gold coins to a pickpocket; "you've become a beast" (chapter 3). The Strugatskiis are, through the title of the work, arguing both a religious point and a psychological one. Firstly, can – or should – a god permit evil? The Dostoevskian issue of the god who hears not the tears of the children is hinted at when Rumata asks, "Is a god entitled to any other feelings besides pity?" (chapter 5). The Strugatskiis also ponder the question of whether man can be a god; social evil cannot be eradicated, until man frees his own soul from the evil lust for power; man's greatest enemy is himself. Power leads to tyranny; passivity and ignorance to enslavement. Rumata at one stage gives the following advice to a citizen who asks whether the best thing would be simply to live quietly and not bother others: "Oh no. Those who remain quiet will be the first ones to be slaughtered" (chapter 8). However, this is also the reason why Rumata must remain a spectator; when asked by the rebel leader Arata for "thunderbolts", he realizes that he cannot supply such weapons, for the people must free themselves.

The authors have a particular point to make about artistic passivity. The poet Gur, terrorized by the state, burns his work and now recites only ultra-patriotic pap, but is still tortured by his unquenchable need to write original work; to produce hack work violates the fundamental nature of his being. Artistic repression violates, too, the natural development of the state. "Without art and culture, a state will lose its capacity for self-criticism", states Rumata (chapter 6), presumably voicing the Strugatskii's own defiant credo.

Other aspects of the Strugatskiis' satire against Soviet society include a "doctors' plot", forced confessions, historical re-interpretation and leader worship – all aspects of Stalinism. The Strugatskiis add further images from Nazi Germany to consolidate their black picture of a fascist state; there is a "night of the long knives". Propaganda is much in evidence; the "Tower of Joy" is in fact the prison, torture chamber, and Security headquarters where graduates of the "School for Patriots" discuss their efforts at torture. There is also a "Boulevard of Overwhelming Gratitude", a nice dig at Soviet road-naming habits.

The novel has a certain fatalistic note to it, despite the energy with which medieval drinking, wenching, and sword-fights are described (no doubt the reason for its popularity on the mass literature market). The image with which the book opens and closes is that of the "anisotropic" road – the one-way road of history. There is no way back along this road; if one tries, all that one finds is a "chained skeleton". Despite the blood and chaos the people encounter on the road of history, there can be no turning back.

S. Dalton-Brown

Roadside Picnic

Piknik na obochine

Novel, 1972

First published in serial form in the journal *Avrora* in 1972, *Roadside Picnic* has proven to be one of the Strugatskiis' most successful and popular short novels. In *Roadside Picnic*, the authors use a stereotypical science-fiction situation – first contact with an alien "super-civilization" – in order to subvert many of the assumptions and clichés of Utopian fiction and thought. At the same time, the novel can be read as a critique of the ethical solipsism of individualism, a study of the obsession with the promise of technology, or the need to believe in miracles. In its sensitive probing of psychology, its elements of political allegory, and its philosophical and ethical relevance, *Roadside Picnic* transcends the genre of science fiction and demands to be read alongside the best works of fantastic realism in modern Russian literature.

The general situation of the novel is summed up in the introduction, an excerpt from a radio interview with Professor Pilman, one of the scientists involved in studying the visitation: aliens have, apparently, visited several different places on the earth 13 years ago and left behind various bits of "space litter," weird (and dangerous) objects that seem to hold the promise of revolutionizing human science and technology. Despite well-intentioned efforts to internationalize the study of these objects, their seemingly limitless potential has attracted the interest of various military-industrial complexes and given birth to a lively black market trade. Redrick Schuhart, the novel's main character and the narrator of three of the text's four parts, is a stalker, that is, a smuggler of space objects from the "zone" for sale to the highest bidder. Schuhart is an honest criminal, a hard-boiled loner in the manner of Hemingway or Chandler, who, despite his gruff exterior and his affected individualism, is one of the few characters capable of real friendship, love, and loyalty. In the novel's climactic final pages, he experiences what can only be called a transcendent vision of universal love and pity for all of suffering humanity.

Typical of the Strugatskiis' unusual treatment of the theme of contact with an extra-terrestrial civilization is the low-key approach of Professor Pilman, who first suggests the simile of a roadside picnic as a possible explanation of the space garbage strewn all over the zone of visitation. Pilman's equally unpopular opinion that the visitation is important not because the secrets of alien technology will revolutionize human science, but because it offers conclusive proof that we are not alone in the universe, holds the key to the meaning of the novel's perplexing final scene, and the ethical meaning of the text as a whole. Schuhart and Arthur Burbridge, the son of a disabled stalker, search the zone for the fabled "golden ball", which supposedly has the power to make one's deepest desires come true. Schuhart dreams of curing his mutant daughter, while Arthur would restore his father to health. When they catch sight of the golden ball lying at the base of a little hill, Arthur dances towards it, singing about happiness and freedom for everybody, when he is suddenly and without warning killed by one of the invisible dangers of the zone. It turns out that Schuhart was planning all along to sacrifice Arthur in order to discover a safe passage to the golden ball. Nevertheless, in a surprising reversal, Schuhart rejects the solipsistic logic of egoism that led him to dispose of Arthur's life, and the novel ends with his repeating Arthur's final plea for universal happiness: "Happiness for everybody, free, and no one will go away unsatisfied!" By rediscovering the ethical imperative of caring for others, Schuhart transforms Pilman's cosmological "we are not alone" into an ethical principle. In other words, the Strugatskiis have transformed the science fiction/Utopian element of the search for a dream machine into a meditation on the competing demands of individualism and community. In so doing, they provide a surprising gloss to the epigraph from Robert Penn Warren, with which the novel begins: "You have got to make the good out of the bad because that is all you have got to make it out of."

For much of the 1970s and early 1980s, publication of works by and about the Strugatskiis was consistently blocked by the censor. In fact, *Roadside Picnic* was not published in book form in the Soviet Union for almost 20 years after its initial journal publication. In recent post-Soviet criticism, the works of the Strugatskiis, including *Roadside Picnic*, are usually read in the context of the anti-Utopian tradition in Russian literature. One of the most interesting and unusual critical responses to the work was published by Stanisław Lem (whose own brand of philosophical science fiction is close to that of the Strugatskiis), as the afterword to the Polish translation of 1977. Lem's enormously learned article, which has since appeared in German and English translations, puts the Strugatskiis' text into the context of science fiction's repeated attempts to imagine contact with a rational alien civilization and attempts to solve the riddle of the real nature of the alien visitation. Although he is ultimately critical of some elements of the Strugatskiis' treatment of the alien contact, Lem describes *Roadside Picnic* as a work that "surpass[es] the canon established by [H.G.] Wells" and "transcend[s] the science-fiction tradition".

Andrei Tarkovskii used several motifs from *Roadside Picnic* (the zone, the stalker, the dream machine) as the starting-point for his 1987 film *Stalker*, a complex personal allegory about the paradoxical nature of desire that, ultimately, has little to do with the Strugatskiis' novel.

ANTHONY ANEMONE

Aleksandr Petrovich Sumarokov 1717–1777

Dramatist

Biography

Born 25 November 1717 into an ancient noble family. Educated at home by his father and foreign governesses; and at newly founded Cadet School for the nobility in Moscow, 1732–40. Served as adjutant to Count Golovkin from 1740; and then to Count Razumovskii, one of the favourites of the Empress Elizabeth, rising to the rank of brigadier. Appointed director of the newly opened Russian Theatre, 1756; retired from this post, following constant conflict with the court office in charge of the theatre, 1761; thereafter devoted himself entirely to his literary activity. A difficult, impulsive, and irascible man, quarrelled with most of those around him. Died alone and in penury, 12 October 1777.

Publications

Collected Editions

Polnoe sobranie vsekh sochinenii, 10 vols. Moscow, 1781–82; 2nd edition 1787.
Stikhotvoreniia. Leningrad, 1953.
Izbrannye proizvedeniia. Leningrad, 1957.
Selected Tragedies of A.P. Sumarokov, translated by Richard and Raymond Fortune. Evanston, Illinois, Northwestern University Press, 1970.

Plays

Khorev. 1747; translated by Richard and Raymond Fortune, in *Selected Tragedies of A.P. Sumarokov*, 1970.
Gamlet. 1748; translated as "Hamlet", by Richard and Raymond Fortune, in *Selected Tragedies of A.P. Sumarokov*, 1970.
Sinav i Truvor [Sinav and Truvor]. 1750.
Artistona [Artystone]. 1750.
Tresotinius. 1750.
Ssora muzha s zhenoi [A Husband's Quarrel with His Wife]. 1750; reworked as *Pustaia ssora* [A Pointless Quarrel].
Chudovishchi [Monsters]. 1750.
Semira. 1751; translated by Richard and Raymond Fortune, in *Selected Tragedies of A.P. Sumarokov*, 1970.
Dimiza. 1758; reworked as *Iaropolk i Dimiza* [Iaropolk and Dimiza].
Opekun [The Guardian]. 1765.
Vysheslav. 1768.
Likhoimets [The Usurer]. 1768.
Iadovityi [The Poison-Tongued]. 1768.
Tri brata sovmestniki [Three Brothers as Rivals]. 1768.
Pridanoe obmanom [A Dowry by Deceit]. 1769.
Nartsiss [Narcissus]. 1769.
Dimitrii samozvanets. 1771; translated as "Dmitrii the Imposter", in *The Literature of Eighteenth-Century Russia*, edited by Harold B. Segel, 2 vols, New York, Dutton, 1967; and by Richard and Raymond Fortune, in *Selected Tragedies of A.P. Sumarokov*, 1970.
Mat' – sovmestnitsa docheri [A Mother, Her Daughter's Rival]. 1772.
Vzdorshchitsa [The Quarrelsome Lady]. 1772.
Rogonosets po voobrazheniiu [The Imaginary Cuckold]. 1772.
Mstislav. 1774.

Critical Studies

"Sumarokov's 'Hamlet'. A Misjudged Russian Tragedy of the 18th Century", by David M. Lang, *Modern Language Review*, 43 (1948), 67–72.
"Boileau and Sumarokov: The Manifesto of Russian Classicism", by David M. Lang, *Modern Language Review*, 43 (1948), 500–06.
Aleksandr Petrovich Sumarokov, 1717–1777, by Pavel N. Berkov, Leningrad, 1949.
Russian Comedy 1765–1823, by David J. Welsh, Mouton, The Hague, 1966.
"The Simile in the Poetry of Sumarokov, Karamzin and Derzhavin", by Zita D. Dabars, *Russian Literature Triquarterly*, 1 (1973), 389–406.
A History of 18th Century Russian Literature, by William Edward Brown, Ann Arbor, Ardis, 1980.
Russian Drama from Its Beginnings to the Age of Pushkin, by Simon Karlinsky, Berkeley, University of California Press, 1985 (chapters 3 and 4).

"Trediakovsky on Sumarokov: The Critical Issues", by Karen Rosenberg, *Russian Literature Triquarterly*, 21 (1988), 49–60.
"The Eighteenth Century: Neo-Classicism and the Enlightenment, 1730–90", by Ilya Serman, in *The Cambridge History of Russian Literature*, edited by Charles A. Moser, Cambridge and New York, Cambridge University Press, 1989; revised edition, 1992 (chapter 2).
"Aleksandr Sumarokov's *Ody torźestvennye* (Toward a History of the Russian Lyric Sequence in the Eighteenth Century), by Ronald Voon, *Zeitscrift für Slavische Philologie*, 55/2 (1995–96), 223–63.

Aleksandr Sumarokov is notable in Russian literary history as the father of Russian drama and – in his tragedies at least – as a major representative of the Neoclassical manner. He wrote in many genres, producing odes, idylls, eclogues, sonnets, ballads, madrigals, epigrams, satires (for example "O blagorodstve" [On Nobility], probably written in 1771), choruses ("Khor ko prevratnomu svetu" [Chorus to a Perverse World] 1763), fables (among them veiled satires against court favourites, corrupt officials, and literary opponents), and elegies and songs notable for their feeling. He also contributed to the emergence of journalism: he edited *Trudoliubivaia pchela* in 1759. However, the principal part of his *oeuvre* is his drama. He was the creator of a national repertoire that could be performed in place of the French Neoclassical plays staged in Russia in the reign of Elizabeth by foreign troupes.

Sumarokov wrote nine tragedies: *Khorev*, *Gamlet* (*Hamlet*), *Sinav i Truvor* [Sinav and Truvor], *Artistona* [Artystone], *Semira*, *Dimiza* (subsequently reworked as *Iaropolk i Dimiza* [Iaropolk and Dimiza]), *Vysheslav*, *Dimitrii samozvanets* (*Dmitrii the Impostor*), and *Mstislav*. These tragedies are intended to conform to the classical aesthetic, modelled to a considerable extent on Nicolas Boileau's *L'Art poétique* (*The Art of Poetry*) 1674, which Sumarokov had adumbrated in two epistles written in 1747 and published in 1748, "O russkom iazyke" [On the Russian Language] and "O stikhotvorstve" [On the Composition of Poetry]. This aesthetic envisaged that the playwright would incline the spectator to virtue by showing him, in theatrical representation, events that affect his feelings. This objective is pursued by the depiction of characters of high social rank who are afflicted by an inner struggle between reason and passion. The spectator's attention is sharply focused by elimination of peripheral material. Thus the three unities of action, time, and place are observed; the drama unfolds over five acts, each with its precisely conceived function ranging from exposition to denouement; the cast of characters is small and includes a confidant or confidante to whom the main character may unburden himself or herself; important events take place off stage; diction is elevated and refined and the 13-syllable French alexandrine with its rhyming couplets is emulated.

At the same time Sumarokov's tragedies differ from those of Corneille and Racine in that they deal not with subject-matter from classical antiquity but with native historical subjects that are closer to the audience and with matters of contemporary political significance such as conceptions of kingship and nobility. Sumarokov contrasted the image of a just monarch with that of the despot (which, by the time he wrote his last tragedies, Sumarokov and others believed Catherine had become). This concern to promote enlightened monarchy is apparent in *Vysheslav*, with its depiction of a monarch who has overcome his passions, but it is most striking in Sumarokov's most famous play, *Dmitrii the Impostor*.

Based loosely on events in the Time of Troubles at the beginning of the 17th century, *Dmitrii the Impostor* portrays the pretender Otrep'ev as an evil tyrant, in love as well as kingship, whose attempt to subdue Russia to the Catholic Poles is thwarted by patriotic Russians and – in the background at least – by the restless mob. The classical conventions are observed. And yet Sumarokov does not attempt to distance his subject from the audience as the Neoclassical tragedian should; on the contrary there is copious reference both to Moscow, in which the play is set, and to events and themes with topical resonance in the Russia of Catherine II, particularly the contempt of the monarch for law and for the well-being of the people, and conflict between Russians and Poles. The audience can have no sympathy with or admiration for this representative of the institution of monarchy – although it is lack of virtue rather than lack of royal lineage that renders Dmitrii illegitimate in Sumarokov's eyes – and his suicide at the end of the play brings the audience not catharsis but relief.

Sumarokov also wrote 12 comedies, eight of them of only one act each, the remaining four of three acts each: *Tresotinius*, which lampoons Trediakovskii, *Ssora muzha s zhenoi* [A Husband's Quarrel with His Wife] (subsequently renamed *Pustaia ssora* [A Pointless Quarrel], a satire on Gallomania and dandyism), and *Chudovishchi* [Monsters], all first published in 1750; *Opekun* [The Guardian] (1765); *Likhoimets* [The Usurer], *Iadovityi* [The Poison-Tongued] and *Tri brata sovmestniki* [Three Brothers as Rivals], all published in 1768; *Nartsiss* [Narcissus] and *Pridanoe obmanom* [A Dowry by Deceit], of 1769; *Mat' – sovmestnitsa docheri* [A Mother, Her Daughter's Rival], *Vzdorshchitsa* [The Quarrelsome Lady], and *Rogonosets po voobrazheniiu* [The Imaginary Cuckold], all composed in 1772. The last of these comedies is usually considered the best; it is a critical depiction of the mores of the provincial gentry influenced by Fonvizin's ground-breaking *Brigadir* (*The Brigadier*). The purpose of comedy is conceived by Sumarokov as correction of morals through mockery. The comedies are written in prose and in much more colloquial, even demotic, language than the tragedies, and they hold up to ridicule some recognizably Russian characters as well as the universal butts of comedy such as the fop, the idler, and the spendthrift. In the later comedies, as in some of the fables, some sympathy for the oppressed and awareness of cruelty to serfs are apparent, although Sumarokov elsewhere defended social inequality and the privileged position of the nobility.

While Sumarokov was highly regarded by contemporaries such as Novikov and Radishchev, his reputation quickly faded and he came to be seen as a talentless imitator of foreign models, the creator of implausible character and stilted verse. His view of himself as a Russian Racine seems absurdly inflated. However, what his plays lack in aesthetic merit, they make up for in terms of their literary historical interest. Sumarokov deserves some credit both for his contribution to the creation of a dramatic tradition in Russia and to the attempt on the part of the enlightened section of the 18th-century nobility to bring morality into social and political life.

DEREK OFFORD

T

The Tale of Boiaryna Morozova

Anonymous prose narrative, written in 1675

Editions

"Povest' o boiaryne Morozovoi", in *Povest' o boiaryne Morozovoi: podgotovka tekstov i issledovanie*, by A.I. Mazunin. Leningrad, 1979, 127–207.

Translation

"A Biography of Boyarina Morozova" (abridged), translated by Basil Dmytryshyn, in his *Medieval Russia: A Source Book, 850–1700*. 3rd edition, Fort Worth, Texas, Holt Rinehart and Winston, 1991, 489–97.

Critical Studies

"Povest' o boiaryne Morozovoi", by M.O. Skripil', in *Istoriia russkoi literatury*, vol. 2, Moscow, 1948, 329–32.

Povest' o boiaryne Morozovoi: podgotovka tekstov i issledovanie, by A.I. Mazunin, Leningrad, 1979.

"Narrative Patterning in the Seventeenth-Century Old Believer Lives of Bojarynja Morozova and Gregory Neronov", by J. Alissandratos, in *Gattung und Narration in den alteren slavischen Literaturen*, edited by K-D. Seeman, Munich, 1984, 29–46.

Violent religious schism in Russia during the second half of the 17th century was precipitated by opposition to Patriarch Nikon's attempts to reform the practices and rituals of the Orthodox Church. This produced countless martyrs and many literary records of their suffering. One of the leading figures in the Old Believer movement, comprising those who fought to preserve the ancient traditions of the Orthodox Church, was the Archpriest Avvakum Petrovich (1620–82), and his most active female disciple was the Boiaryna Feodosiia Prokopiovich Morozova. *Povest' o boiaryne Morozovoi* [The Tale of Boiaryna Morozova] is a significant historical document pertaining to the time of the schism and the intolerance and brutal methods by which the dissenting Old Believers were suppressed by the authorities. It is also a powerfully emotive narrative and one of the earliest works in native Russian literature to portray a strong and intelligent female protagonist in highly realistic detail.

Feodosiia was born on 21 May 1632 into the noble Muscovite family of the Sokovnins. Married in 1649 to an influential aristocrat Gleb Ivanovich Morozov, to whom she bore a son Ivan, she was widowed in 1662. Feodosiia served as a royal courtier during the reign of Tsar Aleksei, and is depicted as a loyal, warm and highly intelligent woman whose powers of debate and conversation were widely admired. She was instructed in spiritual matters by Archpriest Avvakum and steadfastly refused to accept Nikon's reforms, despite much persuasion from her family, the tsar and Archimandrite Ioakim. This determined adherence to the Old Believers' faith was to bring sustained persecution from the authorities. The tale recounts how Feodosiia becomes the spiritual pupil of Mother Melaniia from the Zhuba Convent near Belov, under whose instruction Feodosiia takes her solemn vows. Although continuing to live in the secular world, she withdraws from all possible official court duties and devotes her life to ascetic practices such as fasting, praying and charity, as well as to the support and defence of fellow Old Believers. She is joined in faith by her sister Princess Evdokiia. Greatly increased official persecution, however, rapidly follows Feodosiia's refusal to attend the tsar's second marriage. Neither the boyars nor the highest Church authorities can find a way of persuading Feodosiia to change her convictions and finally she is removed from her home by force, and placed under arrest together with Evdokiia. The sisters are subjected to a long and harsh regime of imprisonment in various monasteries, where they stoically endure long hours of gruelling interrogation of their religious beliefs and often terrible torture. Finally Tsar Aleksei orders Feodosiia to be removed from Moscow and taken to an underground dungeon in the fort of Borovsk, where she undergoes further torture and punishment, including starvation. She dies, still imprisoned, on 11 September 1672.

The tale is essentially anonymous, although the familiarity with Feodosiia's everyday routine and the very personal detail revealed in her characterization suggest that the author was very close to her and someone who even participated in some of the events. A strong candidate for authorship is one of Feodosiia's household butlers, Andrei, himself an Old Believer and known to have been literate. Her long struggle to uphold the ancient Russian Orthodox traditions rendered Feodosiia an ever-lasting martyr to the Old Believer faith, and her life-story an exemplary model of tenacity in the face of those who sought to eradicate the Old Believers. The tale was clearly written with the aim of didactic inspiration for future generations of Old Believers. Feodosiia has, of course, never been canonized as the official Russian Orthodox Church still regards the Old Believer movement as heretical.

No original manuscript of the tale (composed as early as the end of 1675) has been preserved, but it is believed to have been the principal source for the oldest of the three remaining extant redactions – the extended redaction. This redaction provides the fullest account of Feodosiia's sufferings, incorporating many lengthy passages of debate between Feodosiia and a wide range of secondary figures, in which Feodosiia is made repeatedly to refute all challenges to her faith in a confident and convincing manner. Never before in the history of Russian literature has such sagacity and coherent skill in debating spiritual affairs been attributed to a female character. Nor has such a realistic portrayal of the many aspects of medieval womanhood appeared in one central protagonist prior to this Tale: Feodosiia is shown in the context of her family as a loving and devoted mother and wife, even if her religious convictions differed from those of her husband; she is a loyal courtier and appears to agonize over her decision to refuse the tsar's wishes on the grounds of her faith; she is shown as highly intelligent, perceptive and capable of arguing theological matters with men of great learning and knowledge, both secular and ecclesiastical; finally, she is depicted as possessing an insurmountable determination which carries her through the agonies of persecution and shows her ultimately as being a far stronger character and triumphing psychologically, if not physically, over the brutality of her spiritual enemies.

The second and third redactions of the tale, the abbreviated and the short, differ significantly from the extended redaction in terms of emphasis and style. They show a conscious effort on the author's part to intensify the images of Feodosiia's suffering and determination through selective editing and, where desirable, even rearrangement of the original order of the narrative content in order to place renewed emphasis on Feodosiia as the central character, with the secondary figures in the work becoming far more insignificant. Both abridged redactions also show a marked increase in traditional hagiographical *topoi*.

Generic classification of this work has proved difficult: while most critics during the Soviet period labelled it a purely secular biography, much research has also been carried out on the hagiographical features of the tale. The stylistic and thematic content, including traditional *topoi*, biblical allegory and linguistic structures all strongly indicate that the tale was indeed intended as a hagiographical *zhitie* in honour of an extraordinarily courageous religious martyr. It continues in the tradition of the *Povest' ob Ul'ianiia Osor'inoi* [The Tale of Ul'ianiia Osor'ina], playing an important role in the evolution of hagiography as well as challenging social attitudes to women.

ROSALIND MCKENZIE

Tale of Frol Skoveev *see* Frol Skoveev, the Rogue

Tale of the Campaign of Igor *see* Lay of Igor's Campaign

The Tale of Ul'ianiia Osor'ina

17th-century prose narrative

Editions

"Povest' ob Ul'ianii Osor'inoi (Kommentarii i teksty)", in *Trudy otdela drevnerusskoi literatury*. Vol. 6, 1948, 276–323 (includes short and extended redactions [versions 1 and 2]).

"Povest' o Iulianii Lazarevskoi", in *Khrestomatiia po drevnei russkoi literature XI–XVII vekov*, edited by N.K. Gudzii. Moscow, 1962, 345–51.

Translation

"The Life of Yuliania Lazarevskaia", translated by Serge A. Zenkovsky, in his *Medieval Russia's Epics, Chronicles, and Tales*. New York, Dutton, 1963, 312–20.

Critical Studies

"Povest' ob Ul'ianii Osor'inoi (Kommentarii i teksty)", by M.O.

Skripil', in *Trudy otdela drevnerusskoi literatury*, vol. 6, 1948, 256–76.
"Iulianiya Lazarevskaya", by T.A. Greenan, *Oxford Slavonic Papers*, 15 (1982), 28–45.
"New Approaches to the Problem of Identifying the Genre of the Life of Julijana Lazarevskaja", by J. Alissandratos, *Cyrillomethodianum*, 7 (1983), 235–43.

Povest' ob Ul'ianii Osor'inoi, translated as *The Life of Yuliania Lazarevskaia*, is the life story of Ul'ianiia Iustinovna Osor'ina, commonly known as Ul'ianiia Lazarevskaia after the village of Lazarevo, near Murom, which belonged to her husband. The tale was composed no earlier than 1614 and probably no later than 1630 by Ul'ianiia's son Kalistrat Druzhina Osor'in (1570–1640), an Officer of the Peace in Murom, and therefore was not, strictly speaking, anonymous. Genealogical detail is plentiful and historical documentation helps accurately to reconstruct and identify the Osor'in family tree. As Kalistrat Osor'in is not otherwise to be considered a writer, this work is grouped among the "anonymous works".

Although Ul'ianiia has never been officially canonized, she is venerated on a widespread local basis. The tale is a highly significant work in the evolution of Russian hagiography: not only is the "saint" a laywoman of non-aristocratic origin (the first such venerated woman in Russia), but the author was her own son, likewise a layman, who adapted the familiar patterns and topoi of traditional hagiography to recount what may in some respects be considered his own family chronicle with a warmth and intimacy unknown to earlier *zhitie* (biography) composition.

Born during the reign of Ivan IV, Ul'ianiia was orphaned at the age of six and brought up by relatives. She was an exceptionally pious, obedient and humble child. There were no churches in the district where she lived and so she received no formal religious instruction until the age of 16, when she was married to the wealthy and virtuous Georgii Osor'in. After the marriage Osor'in was frequently absent from home for several years at a time on military service in Astrakhan, leaving Ul'ianiia to manage and run the entire household and estate, which she did with great diligence and skill. She successfully brought her family and household through times of severe famine and devastating plague, while still offering protection and help to those less fortunate than herself. Of her 13 children, six died in infancy, the eldest son was killed during an argument with a serf and one more son lost his life on a military campaign. Following the death of her sons, Ul'ianiia begged her husband to allow her to retreat to a convent, but he persuaded her that her Christian duty was to remain with and care for the rest of her family. Ul'ianiia accepted his decision and compromised with a life of complete chastity, poverty and prayer, unceasingly mortifying her flesh. Osor'in died ten years later, leaving Ul'ianiia to withdraw ever more from the world and gradually distribute all her material wealth and possessions among the poor. Towards the end of her life there was another terrible famine throughout which she gave vital support to the poor. She died on 2 January 1604 and was buried eight days later beside her husband in the town of Lazarevo.

All extant manuscripts of the tale have been shown to belong to one of two basic redactions, short or extended, both apparently composed by Kalistrat. No copy of Kalistrat's original composition has been preserved, although it is generally accepted that the short redaction is closest to the original, chronologically followed by the first version of the extended redaction, and finally the second version of the extended redaction. An interesting process of gradual hagiographical embellishment emerges in each successive redaction and version of the tale: the short redaction recounts the story of Ul'ianiia's life in the most factual and unadorned fashion, although it does include several typically hagiographical topoi and is the only version to claim that the myrrh found at Ul'ianiia's grave had miraculous curative powers. The first version of the extended redaction contains detailed and lengthy narrative concerning the attainment of Christian salvation in the secular world, and many biblical quotations, although lacking the posthumous miracles. The second version of the extended redaction is stylistically far closer to traditional hagiographical style and content, although this version likewise makes no mention of posthumous miracles.

There has been much debate over the generic classification of this work: one argument heralds the tale as the tentative beginnings of a truly secular *povest'* genre in Russian literature; while there is equal support for the work to be recognized simply as an unusual and original hagiographical *zhitie*. While some claim that Kalistrat knew no other stylistic genre than hagiographical composition through which to recount his mother's life-story, others claim that there is no episode in the work which does not deliberately seek to portray Ul'ianiia as an extraordinary example of Christian virtue, and that there are no examples of purely descriptive narrative – the overriding theme is Ul'ianiia's sanctity. The tale does include many typically hagiographical motifs (such as St Nikolai protecting Ul'ianiia from the demons who plague her; Ul'ianiia's miraculous transformation of treebark and goosefoot into the sweetest-tasting bread during famine; as well as posthumous preservation of her body and miracles), although in the absence of the most important structural conventions of hagiography (*exordium*, eulogy and *conclusio*), classification of the work as a *zhitie* is far from automatic.

Clarification appears to lie in the ideological undercurrent of the work. There are many passages in the tale of a distinctly anti-clerical nature which would appear alien in a purely hagiographical work. There are many clear indications, however, that this was intentional, for Kalistrat is believed to have been a follower of the Transvolgan hermit movement, the so-called Non-possessors, who did not hold with many of the established Russian Orthodox Church practices, including the concept of true salvation being attainable only through monastic orders and official Orthodoxy. The Non-possessors believed that a pious secular life dedicated to charity and selfless love of God was an equally worthy path to salvation: and this is how Kalistrat has portrayed Ul'ianiia by emphasizing her humility, obedience, extreme life-long asceticism and her dedication to helping the poor and needy while remaining firmly in the secular world.

The tale thus emerges as one of the most important 17th-century Russian hagiographical works, marking the acceptance of a real and openly secular character as saintly protagonist, while subtly challenging the authority of the Orthodox Church.

ROSALIND MCKENZIE

Tale of Woe-Misfortune

Anonymous 17th-century prose narrative

Editions

"Povest' o Gore-Zlochastii", *Pamiatniki literatury drevnei Rusi. XVII vek. Kniga pervaia.* Moscow, 1988, 28–39.

Translation

"Misery-Luckless-Plight", translated by Serge A. Zenkovsky, in his *Medieval Russia's Epics, Chronicles, and Tales.* New York, Dutton, 1963; reprinted 1974, 489–501.

Critical Studies

"Povest' o Gore i Zlochastii i pesni o Gore", by V.F. Rzhiga, *Slavia* (Prague), 10 (1931), 40–66, 288–315.

"Gore Zlochastie. Malheur-Mauvais Destin", by André Mazon, *Révue des Études Slaves*, 28 (1951), 17–42.

"Russian Folk Ballads and the Tale of Misery and Ill Fortune", by W.E. Harkins, *American Slavic and East European Review*, 13 (1954), 402–13.

"The Pathetic Hero in Russian Seventeenth-Century Literature", by W.E. Harkins, *American Slavic and East European Review*, 14 (1955), 512–27.

"Parody in *Povest' o Gore i Zlochastii*", by N.W. Ingham, *Slavic and East European Journal*, 27/2 (1983), 141–57.

"Russian Literature in the Seventeenth Century: A Historiographical Problem", by Jostein Børtnes, in her *Visions of Glory: Studies in Early Russian Hagiography*, Atlantic Highlands, New Jersey, Humanities Press International, 1988, 194–227.

Bibliography

"Povest' o Gore-Zlochastii (Bibliografiia)", by V.L. Vinogradova, *Trudy otdela drevnerusskoi literatury*, vol. 12, Moscow, 622–41.

Discovered by A.N. Pypin in 1856, this anonymous tale belongs to the most remarkable works of the 17th-century transitional period of Russian literature. Extant in only one 18th-century manuscript, it exemplifies works of an unofficial literature, most of which have been preserved by chance, as the authorities fervently attempted to suppress it. Commonly assigned to the domain of folk poetry, and often included in the general body of 17th-century satirical tales, the original title of this hybrid work, *Povest' o Gore i Zlochastii, kak Gore-Zlochastie dovelo molodtsa vo inocheskii chin* [Tale of Woe-Misfortune, How Woe-Misfortune Brought the Young Man to the Monastic Order], points at a characteristic duality of elements belonging to both the folkloric and religious traditions.

The tale tells the story of a youth who, having been instructed by his parents, leaves his home, but then strays from the right path, gives in to drink, wastes his patrimony, and indulges in a dissipated lifestyle. The youth's boasting arouses the Woe-Misfortune, his evil spirit and the incarnation of death, which pursues him relentlessly until he is saved by entering a monastery where he can be spiritually reborn.

The work has a traditional tripartite structure. Styled in the manner of medieval cosmology, the proem presents a general (albeit original) view of the human condition in the story of the Creation and the Fall of mankind through disobedience. Shaped as a parable of the prodigal son, the central narrative section takes up the theme of disobedience, depicting the fall of the individual sinner. The work ends with a conclusion in the form of a three-line prayer for deliverance from torment after death. Written in the unrhymed lines of the folk epic (*bylina*), the didactic tale appears to be a literary transcription of an oral composition close to the genre of "penitential songs", and can be seen as a total negation of the medieval ideas about the compulsory unity of subject, form and style.

Moreover, a peculiar mix of biblical motifs and adventure story, the tale is a central text to a special group of *povesti* where laughter mingles with tears. In contrast to the merry, recreational parody in such satires as *Povest' o Shemiakin sud* (*Shemiaka's Judgment* and the *Povest' o Karpe Sutulove* [Tale about Karp Sutulov], where the hero/heroine outwits the negative figures, in this group of *povesti* the protagonist is an anti-hero who clashes with his environment, only to end up as an outcast devoid of any social status. Drawn from the lower social levels, the nameless youth in the tale thus marks a fall in the hero's status, signifying a shift in both literary decorum and world vision.

With its duality of the folkloric/oral and the religious/literary, the tale can be seen as an example of the growing influence of folk poetry on literature, and as such, the "democratization" of the latter. Among the folk elements are such tropes and figures as paronomasia, tautological and copulative compounds, fixed semantic and syntactical repetitions. Familiar formulaic phrases and imagery abound, and, as is often the case in folk songs, the hero wanders to "a foreign land", all characters remain nameless, and time and place are not designated. Among the aspects relating to the written and religious tradition are the instruction of the hero's parents, the admonitions of the guests at a feast, the proem and the theme of the prodigal son. Furthermore, a combination of a folkloric concept with a Christian one, the personification of Woe-Misfortune is in itself ambiguous. Going back to representations in the Slavonic apocrypha of "khmel" (humulus) as an animate creature and the devil's helper, in folk lyrics the often personified figure of Woe-Misfortune can be the result of a particular action or attitude on the part of a passive protagonist. Following an individual from birth to death, it cannot be broken. In the Christian tradition, however, representing the idea of punishments for sinful behaviour, Woe-Misfortune pursues an "active" hero for his disobedience to his parents, and the spell *can* be broken, though not with repentance alone. The unique combination of various aspects of literary/religious and oral/folk traditions as exemplified in the tale, can be said to reveal the full potential of 17th-century Russian literary art, in which, as Victor Terras noted, it was possible "to create literary works comparable in quality and analogous creations of the western baroque literature".

Whereas the official literature would have condemned any breach with the established order, interestingly, the anonymous author of the "unofficial" tale appears to side with his anti-hero, showing that in his misery the youth still has in him the potential for good. With the shift of perspective as seen in the hero's renouncing the world and becoming a monk, his abasement becomes a transitional stage between the world and all its evil on the one hand, and his new life in the monastery on the other. Moreover, the universe of the tale is no longer defined by the contrast between the established order and the underworld, but between the transcience of this world and the kingdom to come. In this negation of reality, the fundamental message of the old genres has lost its function and become a mere cliché invested with new meaning, by which another reality (of *the Wholly Other*) is set forth. The satire in the tale differs from the modern understanding of the term, for at its root lies a tragic vision of a world dominated by evil and where those who govern society no longer represent the will of God, but have become a vehicle for the power of evil (Jostein Børtnes). Thus, showing how two or more world visions and the bringing together of different styles and genres create a new, "transitional" work of literature, the tale marks an early stage of the distance travelled by 17th-century Russian literature towards a more modern national prose fiction.

KNUT GRIMSTAD

Teffi 1872–1952

Prose writer, dramatist, and poet

Biography

Born Nadezhda Aleksandrovna Lokhvitskaia in St Petersburg, 21 May 1872, into distinguished gentry family. Sister of the poet Mirra Lokhvitskaia. Educated at home and at secondary school in St Petersburg. Married: the Polish aristocrat Vladislav Buchinskii c.1890 (divorced c.1900); two daughters and one son. Lived in Takhvin, then Mogilev Province. Left her husband and settled in St Petersburg; embarked on a career as a writer. Began to publish, 1901; worked for leading newspapers and magazines in St Petersburg and Moscow, 1905–18. Fled Russia via Constantinople and settled in Paris, 1919. Contributed to the émigré press until her death. Died in Paris, 6 October 1952.

Publications

Collected Editions

Rasskazy. Moscow, 1971.
Nostal'giia: Rasskazy, vospominanii [Nostalgia]. Leningrad, 1989.
Iumoristicheskie rasskazy [Humorous Stories]. Moscow, 1990.
Smeshnoe v pechal'nom [The Funny Aspect in Sadness]. Moscow, 1992.
Demonicheskaia zhenshchina [The Demonic Woman]. Moscow, 1995.

Fiction

Iumoristicheskie rasskazy [Humorous Stories], 2 vols. St Petersburg, 1910–11.
I stalo tak ... [And So It Came to Be]. St Petersburg, 1912.
Karusel' [The Carousel]. St Petersburg, 1913.
Dym bez ognia [Smoke Without Fire]. St Petersburg, 1914.
Nichego podobnogo [Nothing of the Sort]. Petrograd, 1915.
Nezhivoi zver' [The Un-Living Animal]. Petrograd, 1916.
Rys' [Trot]. Berlin, 1923.
Vechernii den' [The Nocturnal Day]. Prague, 1924.
Provorstvo ruk [Dexterity]. Moscow and Leningrad, 1926.
Gorodok [The Small Town]. Paris, 1927.
Tango smerti [Tango of Death]. Moscow and Leningrad, 1927.
Kniga iiun' [The June Book]. Belgrade, 1931.
"Avantiurnyi roman" [Adventure Novel], *Vozrozhdenie*, Paris (17 August–28 December 1930); Paris, 1932.
Ved'ma [The Witch]. Paris, 1936.
O nezhnosti [About Tenderness]. Paris, 1938.
Zigzag. Paris, Russkiia Zapiski, 1939.
Vse o liubvi. Paris, La Presse Française et Étrangère, 1946[?]; translated as *All about Love*, by Darra Goldstein, Ann Arbor, Ardis, 1983.
Zemnaia raduga [The Earthly Rainbow]. New York, Izdatel'stvo imeni Chekhova, 1952.
"Za stenoi", translated as "Walled Up", by Catriona Kelly, in *An Anthology of Russian Women's Writing, 1777–1992*, edited by Kelly, Oxford, Oxford University Press, 1994, 193–201.

Plays

Vosem' miniatiur [Eight Miniatures]. St Petersburg, 1913; "Zhenskii vopros", translated as "The Woman Question", by Elizabeth Neatrour, in *An Anthology of Russian Women's Writing, 1777–1992*, edited by Catriona Kelly, Oxford, Oxford University Press, 1994, 174–92.
P'esy [Plays]. Paris, 1934.

Poetry

Sem' ognei [Seven Fires]. St Petersburg, 1910.
Passiflora [The Passion Flower]. Berlin, 1923.
Shamram, pesni vostoka [Shamram, Songs of the East]. Berlin, 1923.

Memoirs

"Vospominanii", *Vozrozhdenie* (16 December 1928–15 December 1929); separate edition, Paris, 1931.

Critical Studies

"Miniatures of Russian Literature at Home and in Emigration: The Life and Works of N.A. Teffi", by Elizabeth B. Neatrour, PhD dissertation, Indiana University, 1973.

"Nadezhda Teffi", by Edythe Haber, *Russian Literature Triquarterly*, 9 (1974), 454–72.

Women Writers in Russian Modernism: An Anthology, by Temira Pachmuss, Urbana, Illinois University Press, 1978.

A Russian Cultural Revival: A Critical Anthology of Émigré Literature before 1939, by Temira Pachmuss, Knoxville, University of Tennessee Press, 1981, 106–31.

"Teffi's *Adventure Novel*", by Edythe Haber, in *Studies in Russian Literature in Honor of Vsevolod Setchkarev*, edited by Julian W. Connolly and Sonia I. Ketchian, Columbus, Ohio, Slavica, 1986, 140–52.

"Introduction", by Elizabeth B. Neatrour, to *Nostal'giia*, Leningrad, 1989.

"N. Teffi, Publikatsiia V.V. Zoshchenko", by M.M. Zoshchenko, *Ezhegodnik rukopisnogo otdela IRLI*, Leningrad, 1992.

"Introduction", by Boris Averin and Elizabeth Neatrour, to *Smeshnoe v pechal'nom*, Moscow, 1992.

A History of Russian Women's Writing, 1820–1992, by Catriona Kelly, Oxford and New York, Clarendon Press, 1994, 195–205.

During the decade preceding the 1917 Revolution and subsequently for more than 30 years in emigration, Teffi was one of the most popular writers among the Russian reading public. Her feuilletons and short stories were widely read. Before the Revolution, her name was known throughout the nation. People repeated her sayings; perfume and candy bore her name. Although – like Chekhov whose influence she acknowledged – she first won recognition as a talented humourist, from the very outset, the comic and the serious formed a union in her art. Teffi's published literary legacy is amazing in quantity and diversity: more than 500 short stories and feuilletons, plays, poetry, a novel, memoirs, essays on well-known contemporaries, and travel notes.

Growing up in an old gentry family that treasured literature, Teffi observed that all the children tried their hand at writing. Her older sister Mirra was twice awarded the Pushkin Prize and was considered a leading poet at the turn of the century; her younger sisters Varvara and Elena had their sketches published in periodicals and their plays performed in various theatres. Teffi's own professional career began in 1901 with the publication of a poem in the journal *Sever* and then a short story in *Niva* under her maiden name, Nadezhda Lokhvitskaia. Later, seeking the attention of publishers, she began to use the pseudonym Teffi (English "Taffy"). Like other members of the St Petersburg intelligentsia in 1905, she found herself engulfed by the revolutionary spirit. That same year she joined Nikolai Minskii and Zinaida Vengerova on the staff of the legal Bolshevik newspaper *Novaia zhizn'*. Later she would dismiss these early political works lightly. Her career was firmly established when she became a regular contributor to such famous satirical weeklies as *Satirikon* and *Novyi satirikon* and to such prestigious newspapers as *Birzhevye vedomosti*, *Rech'*, and, particularly, *Russkoe slovo*. Her first volumes of poetry, *Sem' ognei* [Seven Fires], and prose, *Iumoristicheskie rasskazy* [Humorous Stories], appeared in 1910, the latter going through many editions. Like the first, subsequent collections of stories such as *I stalo tak ...* [And So It Came to Be], *Karusel'* [The Carousel], and *Dym bez ognia* [Smoke Without Fire] were also bestsellers. At the same time that her satirical verses, weekly feuilletons, and books of short stories were bringing her renown, she was also gaining fame as a dramatist. Enthusiastically received, her one-act plays, mainly satirical miniatures such as "Zhenskii vopros" ("The Woman Question") were staged in St Petersburg theatres and in the cabaret theatre Crooked Mirror. She continued to write poetry and participated in a number of literary circles, including Viacheslav Ivanov's Wednesdays and Sologub's Sundays, where she would repeat or sing her exotic poems between readings by Blok, Kuzmin, and Remizov. It is likely that some of these verses were included in two volumes published in Berlin in 1923: *Shamram, pesni vostoka* [Shamram, Songs of the East], dedicated to Teffi's close companion in St Petersburg and emigration, P.A. Tikston, and *Passiflora* [The Passion Flower] containing her best poetry. Some verses in the former recall the exoticism of the 1910 collection; those in the latter echo Symbolist longings for a spiritual realm beyond the material world and include her widely praised "Serebrianyi korabl'" [The Silver Ship]. Whereas reviews of Teffi's prose and drama during her lifetime were always positive, those about her poetry were mixed.

The October Revolution of 1917 and the closing of *Russkoe slovo* forced her to flee first to Kiev, Crimea, then through Constantinople to Paris. In the French capital, she immediately took an active leadership role, organizing a literary salon early in 1920 and contributing weekly prose pieces to leading émigré periodicals, a practice she continued – with rare exceptions-for two decades up to World War II. Her first feuilleton published in Paris, "Ke fer?" (a pun on "que faire"), became a slogan in all the émigré colonies. Her first volumes published in emigration (1920–21, Shanghai, Berlin, and Stockholm) consisted of stories that had appeared earlier in Russia. Her plays, for which she professed a special pride, were performed throughout the Diaspora. Except for periods of ill health exacerbated by the deprivations of the war years spent in Paris, Teffi continued writing and making extremely popular public appearances until her death.

There is a remarkable unity in Teffi's art from her earliest works to the last collection, but emigration marks an expansion of themes and further development of her bitter-sweet style. The comic voice remains, but the notes of sadness are intensified. The melancholy and poignancy pervading the best pre-revolutionary collection, *Nezhivoi zver'* [The Un-Living Animal], with its fine title story, recur in *Rys'* [Trot], *Vechernii den'* [The Nocturnal Day], *Gorodok* [The Small Town], *Kniga iiun'* [The June Book], and *Zigzag*. These volumes centre on three main themes: the tragic plight of the émigrés, absurd aspects of life in general, and comic situations resulting from emigration. Familiar types from Teffi's gallery – braggarts, clowns, coquettes, failures – reappear, but the scope of pathetic characters widens to include helpless émigrés who feel lost in their new milieu or who are enveloped in deceit and illusion. Some stories are light-hearted in tone, focusing on comical linguistic problems and displaying what Zoshchenko once called Teffi's mastery of the "secret of amusing words". Hallmarks of her stories continue to be concision, keen observation, deft portraiture, lively dialogue, sparkling wit, and elegant style.

Themes familiar from pre-revolutionary collections – child psychology, lonely old age, and alienation – recur in an émigré setting. Among Teffi's most successful stories are those about children. Their keen imagination and directness provide respite from the weary posing of adults. Children figure prominently in a number of collections, including *Ved'ma* [The Witch] – Teffi's most distinctive collection and one particularly admired by Bunin, Kuprin, and Merezhkovskii – where gossip, nostalgic childhood memories, customs, figures from Russian folklore, and an interest in the supernatural blend together to form excellent stories.

Although the theme of love recurs throughout Teffi's prose, poetry, and drama, it is most concentrated in the volumes *O nezhnosti* [About Tenderness] and *Vse o liubvi* (*All about Love*). In Teffi's world, romantic love is synonymous with deceit and victimizing. For her, the highest values are tenderness, devotion, and self-sacrifice. Like many of Teffi's characters, the heroine of her long work, *Avantiurnyi roman* [Adventure Novel], is a victim caught up in the absurd whirl of deception spun by a younger man for whom she feels maternal love. More successful than the novel is Teffi's other long work, *Vospominaniia* [Memoirs]. This fine narrative, spanning a few months during 1918–19, weaves together glimpses of well-known literary figures, comical and absurd situations, and philosophical reflections.

Whether in poetry, prose or drama, and whether in comic or serious works, Teffi's vision remained consistent throughout her career. Her unhappy and pathetic characters seem trapped like puppets in the absurd whirl of their empty lives. Viewing them with sadness and irony, Teffi suggests that an escape is possible to a better world through religion and compassion for others.

Over the past few years, there has been a resurgence of interest in Teffi in Russia. Her works published in emigration, largely banned for 40 years in her native land, are now becoming accessible; and her place in Russian literature is being reassessed.

ELIZABETH B. NEATROUR

Vladimir Fedorovich Tendriakov 1923–1984

Prose writer

Biography

Born in Makarovskaia, Vologda district, 5 December 1923. Son of a public prosecutor. Left school, 1941; immediately sent to the Front. Active service in World War II, wounded in 1943: invalided out of the army. Worked as a schoolteacher and Komsomol official. Moved to Moscow. Studied at the Institute of Cinematography, 1945; transferred to Gor'kii Literary Institute, 1946–51. Joined the Communist Party, 1948. Began publishing, 1947; worked as journalist 1951–53. Came to public attention in post-Stalin Thaw. Editor of *Literaturnaia Moskva*, 1958. Writers' Union official, 1960s–70s. Died in Moscow, 3 August 1984.

Publications

Collected Editions

Three Novellas, with an introduction and notes by J.G. Garrard. Oxford and New York, Pergamon Press, 1967.
Three, Seven, Ace and Other Stories, translated by David Alger *et al.* London, Harvill Press, and New York, Harper and Row, 1973.
A Topsy-Turvy Spring, translated by Alex Miller and Avril Pyman. Moscow, Progress, 1978.
Sobranie sochinenii, 4 vols. Moscow, 1978–80.
Sobranie sochinenii, 5 vols. Moscow, 1987–89.
Neizdannoe [Unpublished Works]. Moscow, 1995.

Fiction

"Padenie Ivana Chuprova" [The Fall of Ivan Chuprov], *Novyi mir*, 11 (1953), 104–34.
"Ukhaby" [Potholes], *Nash sovremennik*, 2 (1956), 43–69.
"Sasha otpravliaetsia v put'" [Sasha Sets Off] (later published under the title "Tugoi uzel" [A Tight Knot]), *Novyi mir*, 2–3 (1956), 25–88, 79–133.
"Chudotvornaia" [The Miracle-Working Icon], *Znamia*, 5 (1958), 3–55.
"Za begushchim dnem" [Beyond the Current Day], *Molodaia gvardiia*, 10–12 (1959).
"Troika, semerka, tuz", *Novyi mir*, 3 (1960), 3–31; translated as "Three, Seven, Ace", by David Alger *et al.*, in *Three, Seven, Ace and Other Stories*, 1973.
"Sud" [The Trial], *Novyi mir*, 3 (1961), 15–60; translated as "Justice", by Olive Stevens, in *Three, Seven, Ace and Other Stories*, 1973; also translated as "The Trial", by Alex Miller, in *A Topsy-Turvy Spring*, 1978.
"Chrezvychainoe" [An Exceptional Event]. 1961.
"Svidanie s Nefertiti" [A Meeting with Nefertiti], *Moskva*, 10–12 (1964), 4–78; 62–130; 3–119.
"Nakhodka". 1965; translated as "The Find", by Alex Miller, in *A Topsy-Turvy Spring*, 1978.
"Podenka-vek korotkii" [Ephemera Are Short-Lived], *Novyi mir*, 5 (1965), 95–141; translated as "Creature of a Day", by Paul Falla, in *Three, Seven, Ace and Other Stories*, 1973.
"Konchina" [The Death of the Boss], *Moskva*, 3 (1968), 3–138.
"Apostol'skaia komandirovka" [On Apostolic Business], *Nauka i religiia*, 8–10 (1969), 69–87; 53–69; 77–95.
"Vesennie perevertyshi", *Novyi mir*, 1 (1973), 118–71; translated as "A Topsy-Turvy Spring", by Avril Pyman, in *A Topsy-Turvy Spring*, 1978.

"Noch' posle vypuska" [The Night After Graduation], *Novyi mir*, 9 (1974), 82–130.
"Zatmenie" [The Eclipse], *Druzhba narodov*, 5 (1977), 15–150.
"Rasplata" [Atonement], *Novyi mir*, 3 (1979), 6–99.
"Chistye vody Kitezha" [The Clear Waters of Kitezh], *Druzhba narodov*, 8 (1986), 129–71.
"Pokushenie na mirazhi" [Shooting at Mirages], *Novyi mir*, 4–5 (1987), 59–116, 89–164.
"Para gnedykh; Khleb dlia sobaki; Parania; Donna Anna" [A Pair of Bay Horses; Bread for a Dog ...], *Novyi mir*, 3 (1988), 3–61; "Donna Anna", translated by Lila H. Wangler and Helena Goscilo, in *The Wild Beach: An Anthology of Contemporary Russian Short Stories*, edited by Goscilo, Ann Arbor, Ardis, 1992, 191–217.
"Na blazhennom ostrove kommunizma", *Novyi mir*, 9 (1988), 2–37; translated as "On the Blessed Island of Communism", by Michael Duncan, in *Dissonant Voices: The New Russian Fiction*, edited by Oleg Chukhontsev, London, Harvill Press, 1991, 76–102.
"Okhota" [The Hunt], *Znamia*, 9 (1988), 87–124.
Liudi ili neliudi. Povesti i rasskazy [People or Animals]. Moscow, 1990.

Play
"Pozhar" [The Fire], *Sovremennaia dramaturgiia*, 2 (1985), 189–218.

Essays
"Den', vytesnivshii zhizn'", *Druzhba narodov*, 1 (1985), 31–67; translated as "A Day That Ousted a Life", by Robert Daglish, *Soviet Literature*, 9 (1985), 3–54.
"Lichnost' i kommunizm" [The Individual and Communism], *Zvezda*, 8 (1989), 96–121.
"Metamorfozy sobstvennosti" [Metamorphoses of Property], *Zvezda*, 3–4 (1990), 123–38, 137–60.
"Revoliutsiia! Revoliutsiia! Revoliutsiia!" [Revolution! ...], *Oktiabr'*, 9 (1990), 3–65.

Critical Studies

"Vladimir Tendrjakov", by J.G. Garrard, *Slavic and East European Journal*, 9/1 (1965), 1–18.
"Vladimir Tendryakov", by Geoffrey Hosking, in his *Beyond Socialist Realism: Soviet Fiction since "Ivan Denisovich"*, London, Granada, and New York, Holmes and Meier, 1980, 84–100.
Scenes from Soviet Life: Soviet Life Through Official Literature, by Mary Seton-Watson, London, BBC Publications, 1986.
"A Begrudging Testament: The Christ Who Wouldn't Go Away", by Richard Chapple, *Australian Slavonic and East European Studies*, 2/1 (1988), 55–68.
Soviet Literature in the 1980s: Decade of Transition, by N.N. Shneidman, Toronto, University of Toronto Press, 1989.
"Glasnost' in Literature", by Margaret Ziolkowski, *Michigan Quarterly Review*, 28 (1989), 639–47.
"Introduction", by Peter Doyle, to *The Trial*, edited by Doyle, Oxford, Blackwell, 1990, xi–xxv.
Russian Village Prose: The Radiant Past, by Kathleen F. Parthé, Princeton, Princeton University Press, 1992, 113–19.
The Last Years of Soviet Russian Literature: Prose Fiction, 1975–1991, by Deming Brown, Cambridge and New York, Cambridge University Press, 1993.
Russian Literature 1988–1994: The End of an Era, by N.N. Shneidman, Toronto, University of Toronto Press, 1995.

Vladimir Tendriakov began publishing in the late 1940s, but attracted attention in the immediate post-Stalin years as a writer concerned with rural issues. In his writings of the mid-1950s, such as "Padenie Ivana Chuprova" [The Fall of Ivan Chuprov] and "Tugoi uzel" [A Tight Knot] (1956), Tendriakov was one of a number of like-minded writers who criticized the Stalinist management of collective farms, and the resulting waste, inefficiency and demoralization of the peasantry. In his later novel, "Konchina" [The Death of the Boss], the author is at pains to decry the Stalinist mismanagement of agriculture, in particular the policy of collectivization in the late 1920s and early 1930s, and the resultant famine in the countryside in 1933. This novel also investigates the psychology of tyranny, and can be seen as an allegory of the reign of Stalin. In other works, such as "Ukhaby" [Potholes], "Troika, semerka, tuz" ("Three, Seven, Ace"), and "Sud" ("The Trial"), he also gained a reputation for emphasizing the individual's need to heed his own conscience, rather than Party dictates. In the late 1950s and early 1960s Tendriakov was reprimanded by the Writers' Union for his anti-Stalinist writings, in particular his participation in the second volume of *Literaturnaia Moskva*, 1956.

Although a Party member, Tendriakov obviously felt the need for a moral revitalization of society following Stalin's death, and the spiritual regeneration of the individual. To this end he also published works that dealt with religion, such as "Chudotvornaia" [The Miracle-Working Icon], and "Apostol'skaia komandirovka" [On Apostolic Business]. In the latter work Tendriakov points to the spiritual vacuum in Soviet society as individuals search for meaning in their lives through Christianity. His awareness of the loss of values led him in the 1970s to look at the way values are actually instilled in children. His interest in the educational process, and its contribution towards the individual's moral integrity, is reflected in his novel *Za begushchim dnem* [Beyond the Current Day], and further in "Vesennie perevertyshi" ("A Topsy-Turvy Spring") and "Noch' posle vypuska" [The Night After Graduation].

Tendriakov's fiction of the late 1970s shows an increasing preoccupation with individual psychology, but also shows his deepening concern for the moral make-up of Soviet society. "Zatmenie" [The Eclipse] once again discusses religious faith, and "Rasplata" [Atonement] explores the broader moral and spiritual implications when a teenager kills his father. Tendriakov's reputation as a writer who challenged the prevailing moral standards will no doubt ultimately rest on his works written "for the drawer" throughout the "stagnation years", and published only after 1986. These include short stories, novellas, and novels. In short stories such as "Para gnedykh" [A Pair of Bay Horses] and "Khleb dlia sobaki" [Bread for a Dog], Tendriakov confronts the horrors of collectivization in the countryside in a bolder and more forthright manner than in his previously published fiction. Published in 1988, these stories were actually written 1969–71, as was "Donna Anna", set in wartime. Tendriakov's first short stories of the late 1940s were about World War II, but here he took a more uncompromising anti-Stalinist stance, condemning the fear and terror within the ranks of the Soviet soldiers as they fought near Stalingrad. "Liudi ili neliudi" [People or Animals], written 1975–76 but first published in 1989, also touches on the war in its depiction of atrocities committed on prisoners by both German and Russian troops, but also, and more substantially, contains the author's own reflections on the relationship of the writer to authority in Soviet Russia and man's capacity for cruelty and violence generally. The mood of the work is sombre, and reflects the deepening despair Tendriakov experienced towards the end of the 1970s.

In "Liudi ili neliudi" Tendriakov often engages in a dialogue with himself on the nature of evil, and also condemns his own perfidious actions in the past, such as when he stole bread from his hungry comrades in wartime. Much space is also devoted to the Soviet writer's fate under a totalitarian system. In other memoir-like works, such as "Okhota" [The Hunt], written in 1971, and "Na blazhennom ostrove kommunizma" ("On the Blessed Island of Communism"), written in 1961 (both works were published in 1988), Tendriakov further discusses the contemporary literary situation. In the former, the setting is the anti-cosmopolitan purges of the late 1940s, and the role of Aleksandr Fadeev, while the latter is set in 1960 and attacks the sycophancy of the literary intelligentsia towards the then Soviet leader, Nikita Khrushchev.

All of these works published in 1988 have an eye-witness authenticity, and testify to the fact that the work Tendriakov managed to publish during the Thaw and stagnation years only partly revealed his attitudes towards his society and its prevailing ideology. Like other writers whose best work has only been made available since glasnost (such as Fedor Abramov), Tendriakov retained his integrity by committing his real feelings and thoughts to private writings, that is, those written "for the drawer". Perhaps his best works are the two longer pieces published in 1986 and 1987, but written towards the end of the 1970s. "Chistye vody Kitezha" [The Clear Waters of Kitezh] is a bitterly satirical attack both on journalistic double standards and the indifference and aloofness of time-serving authorities, but it also offers a sad comment on the population's fear of authority and capacity for apathy. "Pokushenie na mirazhi" [Shooting at Mirages] combines Tendriakov's pronounced interest in the moral upbringing of young people, as seen in earlier works, with deliberations on the nature of history and the role of the individual in historical development.

Taken as a whole, the literary legacy of Vladimir Tendriakov shows that he, like other writers of his time, such as Fedor Abramov and Iurii Trifonov, was a writer profoundly concerned and disturbed by the spiritual and moral bankruptcy of his society, and the cynicism of its leaders.

DAVID GILLESPIE

The Trial

Sud

Novella, 1961

"The Trial" was first published in *Novyi mir* in 1961, at a time when the post-Stalin Thaw was approaching its apogee. It first appeared in book form in the second volume of Tendriakov's *Izbrannye proizvedeniia* [Selected Works] in 1963. The first eight of the 25 chapters comprise a typical Russian "hunting story", a genre with a pedigree going back at least as far as Aksakov and Turgenev in the 19th century. Many of the familiar ingredients are present: the experienced old hunter, Semen Teterin, described as a man "used to the forest, to solitude and to silence"; the novice, the medical orderly Mitiagin, whose inexperience threatens the whole operation; the technical hunting vocabulary; the evocation of the forest, in this case, of its sounds; the respect of the hunter for his quarry; the bond between man and dog and between man and Nature, the sense of continuity with the past. In chapter 8, however, the book changes direction when tragedy strikes the hunting party. In attempting to shoot their quarry, a bear, a young man is killed by a stray bullet. Teterin finds irrefutable evidence that the fatal shot was fired by the third member of the hunting party, Dudyrev, the influential head of a huge local construction site, but it is Mitiagin who is brought to trial. The vital evidence is destroyed by Teterin and the case against Mitiagin is dropped. The novella ends with Teterin and his favourite dog Kalinka. The dog has been injured by the bear and is now no use for hunting. Teterin is injured psychologically, having allowed an innocent man to stand trial. Now he is left to wrestle with his conscience for, as the final, sententious words of the story put it: "There is no heavier judgment than the judgment of one's own conscience". Here Tendriakov puns on the Russian word "sud", meaning both "trial" and "judgment". In its former sense the word alludes to the trial of Mitiagin that could be regarded as portraying the fairness of Soviet justice, with its unrelenting search for the truth personified in the persons of the investigating detective Ditiatichev and the prosecutor Testov. This reading of the story marks it out as a typical work of the Thaw. There are, however, other echoes. The presence of the third hunter and the reaching of the right verdict for the wrong reasons are strongly reminiscent of Dostoevskii's *The Brothers Karamazov*. So, too, is the conclusion arrived at by Ditiatichev in chapter 16 that all three hunters are equally guilty. These references to Russian classical literature are reinforced by the fact that Testov, a bibliophile, can quote Blok and Esenin from memory, and he characterizes Dudyrev's frankness and willingness to assume responsibility for the accident as reminiscent of Cervantes's (and Turgenev's) Don Quixote and Tolstoi's self- sacrificing hero Nekhliudov from *Voskresenie* (*Resurrection*).

Like Tolstoi, Tendriakov makes effective use of contrast. The way in which the roles of Teterin and Dudyrev are reversed once they leave the hunting environment is a good example. Teterin, so adept at finding his way in the forest, gets lost on the construction site (chapter 14) and the terminology of the hunt is now applied to Dudyrev's world of the construction site. In the opening sentence of chapter 6 we read that, as the hunt for the bear reaches its climax, Dudyrev "stopped being a normal man and turned into a wild animal humself – malign, bloodthirsty, patient". In chapter 14 it is the machines controlled by Dudyrev in his other life – a bulldozer and a digger – to which the term "animal" (*zverina*) is applied, while in chapter 12 the term "boss" (*khoziain*), used by hunters to refer to a bear, is now applied to Teterin himself. Elsewhere Tendriakov contrasts the private and public lives of his characters. Dudyrev is the obvious example of this, but there is also the trial judge Tepliakova who is well known to Teterin simply as "a quiet woman, permanently worried and with a large family".

In this, in many ways, typically Soviet work there are nevertheless hints of the posthumously published works in which Tendriakov was extremely critical of Soviet reality. That a prosecutor could, at the scene of the tragedy, announce that someone will go to jail for what has happened, that the investigator could allege to a witness (Teterin) that, while there is no direct evidence against Mitiagin, there are "oblique" (*kosvennye*) clues pointing to his guilt, or that a piece of material evidence – Mitiagin's bullet that actually killed the bear – could simply be handed back to Teterin can be taken as a comment on the total absence of legality (as distinct from laws) in the Soviet Union.

Whatever the ambiguities of its content, the story is extremely competently written. Tendriakov employs a wide range of devices, including flashback in chapter 4 and *skaz* (first-person narration) in chapter 11. He has an excellent ear for the speech rhythms and vocabulary of provincial Russia, in this case his home province of Vologda, some 300 miles north-east of Moscow. A number of recurrent motifs – darkness, life, death, the latter reinforced by the repetition of the adjective "sprawled out" (*rasplastannyi*) – lend unity to the narrative. The depiction of the accident itself is extremely skilful. The victim is simply a "lad" with an accordion on his way to see his girlfriend. Only later do we learn that he has a name – Pashka Lyskov – and that he is the last surviving son of his parents. The scene in which the boy's body is taken home by Teterin and the boy's stoical father, Mikhailo, is all the more moving for being understated.

A film based on the novel appeared in 1962 and an English version under the title "Justice" was published in *Three, Seven, Ace and Other Stories* in 1973. An edition of the Russian text by Peter Doyle was published in 1990.

MICHAEL PURSGLOVE

A Topsy-Turvy Spring

Vesennie perevertyshi

Novella, 1973

This novella was first published in *Novyi mir* (No. 1, 1973) and in English translation in *Soviet Literature* (No. 12, 1973). The story centres on 13-year-old Diushka Tiagunov who lives in the undistinguished settlement of Kudelino. Two events combine to turn Diushka's world upside down. First he refuses to join in a cruel game devised by the epitome of evil in the story, the school bully San'ka Erakha. Having amused himself by tying a piece of string to a cat and then seeing who can throw it furthest, San'ka replaces the cat with a frog and devises a game that involves dashing the frog against a wall. To defend himself against future attacks by San'ka, Diushka takes to carrying a brick in his briefcase. This fact is duly discovered and Diushka is questioned by the school's headteacher. In a scene (chapter 19) reminiscent of the trial scene in "The Trial", the difficulty of establishing the truth and the misleading nature of apparently damning evidence is highlighted. The second upset in Diushka's life comes when he convinces himself that Natal'ia Goncharova, the famous beauty who became Pushkin's wife, has been reincarnated in the person of a fellow pupil, Rimka Brateneva. This conviction brings Diushka closer to the 15-year-old Levka Gaizer, who becomes both his protector and his mentor. Levka lends Diushka a book that provides a third major change in his life by opening his eyes to the mystery of the atom and of Einsteinian physics. The hitherto undistinguished schoolboy now becomes the star pupil. Diushka's willingness to admit change in his life leads ultimately to changes in the lives of the adults in the story. Diushka's father, an engineer, is a severely practical man who dismisses his son's speculations about reincarnation. However, not having bought flowers for his wife for 15 years, he now travels many miles to the nearest town to do so. His wife, a doctor, has seen death many times but when one of her patients, Stepan Grinchenko, now recovered, comes to visit the family, he confesses that not only is he cured physically, he is also cured spiritually. The mathematics teacher Vasilii Vasil'evich Vasil'ev, known inevitably as "Vasia cubed", believes that "everybody has talent, but they don't know it". His belief in Diushka's "hidden talent" for mathematics at first "poisons" the boy's life but proves to be correct, although it is Levka rather than the teacher who reveals it. The most interesting of the adults is Nikolai Bolotov, the father of Diushka's slightly younger protégé, Min'ka. We first hear of him through Min'ka, who weeps at the tension between his mother and father. Paradoxically he regards his father as both good and bad. Nikolai Bolotov turns out to be a former journalist who, tired of hack work, takes on an undemanding office job in order to concentrate on his poetry. He loves his wife, who does not love him and yearns to escape from Kudelino and to see the sea. Bolotov quotes Pasternak ("To love other people is a heavy burden") and is referred to as "the Dante of Kudelino, singing the praises of his Beatrice". Such literary references permeate this work as they do "The Trial". Surprisingly it is Nikita Bogatov who rescues Diushka from San'ka.

Geoffrey Hosking, in his study of the work in *Beyond Socialist Realism* (1980), sets this story in the context of Tendriakov's work as a whole, pointing out his progression from a belief in the possibility of a "positive hero", expressed in a number of works dating from the early 1950s, to a position in which the most basic assumptions of life and death are challenged. He also notes Tendriakov's growing interest in religious questions, raised in this story by Diushka's grandmother Klimovna. N.N. Shneidman, in his *Soviet Literature in the 1980s*, links "A Topsy-Turvy Spring" with another novella from the same year *Tri meshka sornoi pshenitsy* [Three Bags of Weedy Wheat], and underlines the educational theme in the story. It is a theme that runs right through Tendriakov's work and is linked with his search for the "positive hero". In "A Topsy-Turvy Spring" the picture of the school is not unsympathetic. Both "Vasia cubed" and the young head teacher Anna Petrovna are dedicated, enlightened intelligent people, and the attitude to violence in the school is summed up by the words of the young teacher Zoia Petrovna, "How horrible!". The story, then, is permeated with more optimism than pessimism. It is set against the traditional harbinger of hope, the coming of spring but this is an ambiguous spring which, as well as bringing the promise of new and, possibly, better life, also, through San'ka's torture of the frogs, brings out the latent evil in Man. The basic theme of the story, enshrined in the title, is alluded to explicitly throughout the work, notably in its last sentence. It is also alluded to symbolically in, for example, the image of the crane that has dominated the village for so long that Diushka regards it as a friend, and is said by his father to have been placed on soft ground that will ensure its eventual collapse. Even the frog, dangling upside down on the end of San'ka's string, suggests the overturning of accepted ideas and values that Diushka is about to experience. A key moment for this comes at the end of chapter 4 when Diushka finds a portrait of Natal'ia Goncharova in a volume of Pushkin. The chapter ends with the last two lines of Pushkin's sonnet "Madonna". The Madonna, for Pushkin, resembles Natal'ia Goncharova, just as Rimka Barten'eva resembles Natal'ia in Diushka's eyes. It is immediately after this, at the beginning of chapter 5, that Diushka is struck by the feeling that he alone survives among the world of men and that the remaining inhabitants of Kudelino have been replaced by the rooks, the arrival of which, as Savrasov's painting reminds us, traditionally heralds the beginning of spring.

MICHAEL PURSGLOVE

Terts *see* Siniavskii

Fedor Ivanovich Tiutchev 1803–1873

Poet

Biography

Born in Ovstug, near Briansk, 23 November 1803. Educated at home in Ovstug and in Moscow, 1812–19. First poem published, 1819. Attended Moscow University, 1819–21, graduated in philology, 1821. Served in the diplomatic corps, 1822–41. Married: 1) Eleonore Peterson (née von Bothmer) in 1826, three daughters; 2) Ernestine von Dörnberg (née von Pfeffel) in 1839, one daughter and two sons; also had one daughter and two sons by his mistress, Elena Aleksandrovna Denis'eva. Position as Second Secretary in Munich, 1828–37. Poems published in Pushkin's *Sovremennik*, 1836–40. First Secretary, 1837–39, and Chargé d'Affaires, 1838–39, both in Turin; dismissed from Ministry of Foreign Affairs, 1841; reinstated in 1845. Published pan-Slav articles in French, 1844–54. Senior censor in special section of Ministry of Foreign Affairs, 1848–58. Corresponding member of the Academy of Sciences (Russian language and literature section), 1857–73. Chairman of the Committee of Foreign Censorship, 1858–73. Member of Society of Lovers of Russian Literature, 1859–73. Died at Tsarskoe Selo, 15 July 1873.

Publications

Collected Editions

Polnoe sobranie sochinenii. St Petersburg, 1912.

Polnoe sobranie stikhotvorenii, 2 vols. Moscow, 1933–34; reprinted Moscow, 1994.

Polnoe sobranie stikhotvorenii. Leningrad, 1957.

Versions from Fyodor Tyutchev. 1803–1873, translated by Charles Tomlinson. London and New York, Oxford University Press, 1960.

Lirika, 2 vols. 2nd edition, Moscow, 1966.

Poems and Political Letters of F.I. Tyutchev, translated with an introduction by Jesse Zeldin. Knoxville, University of Tennessee Press, 1973.

Poems of Night and Day. Fyodor Tyutchev, translated by Eugene Kayden. Boulder, University of Colorado Press, 1974.

Sochineniia, 2 vols. Moscow, 1984.

On the Heights of Creation: The Lyrics of Fedor Tiutchev (includes complete translations of Tiutchev's poetry), by Anatoly Liberman. Greenwich, Connecticut, Jai Press, n.d.

O, veshchaia dusha moia! [Oh, My Prophetic Soul!]. Moscow, 1995.

Essays and Witticisms

Tiutcheviana. Epigrammy, aforizmy i ostroty F.I. Tiutcheva [Tiutcheviana. Epigrams, Aphorisms and Witticisms by F.I. Tiutchev], edited by Georgii Chulkov. Moscow, 1922; Oxford, Meeuws, 1976.

Politicheskie stat'i [Political Articles]. Paris, YMCA-Press, 1976.

Critical Studies

Letopis' zhizni i tvorchestva F.I. Tiutcheva, by Georgii Chulkov, Moscow and Leningrad, 1933.

La Poésie et l'idéologie de Tiouttchev, by Dmitrii Strémooukhoff, Paris, Societé d'Édition Les Belles Lettres, 1937.

F.I. Tjutcev. Persönlichkeit und Dichtung, by Rolf Kemp, Göttingen, Göttingen University Press, 1956.

Zhizn' i tvorchestvo F.I. Tiutcheva, by Kirill Pigarev, Moscow, 1962; revised edition as *F.I. Tiutchev i ego vremia*, Moscow, 1978.

Fedor Tiutchev: The Evolution of a Poet, by Richard Gregg, New York, Columbia University Press, 1965.

Tjutcevs Kurzlyrik. Traditionszusammenhänge und Interpretationen, by Almut Schulze, Munich, Fink, 1968.

Poeticheskoe mirovozzrenie Tiutcheva, by Vera Kasatkina, Saratov, 1969.

"Russia and the Revolution in Tiutchev's Poetry: Some Poems of 1828–1830", by Ronald Lane, *Slavonic and East European Review*, 51 (1973), 214–30.
A Concordance to the Russian Poetry of Fedor I. Tiutchev, by Boris Bilokur, Providence, Rhode Island, Brown University Press, 1975.
"Tiutchev in Russian Fiction", by Ronald Lane, *New Zealand Slavonic Journal*, 2 (1975), 17–32.
"Tiutchev's Place in the History of Russian Literature", by Ronald Lane, *Modern Language Review*, 71 (1976), 344–56.
"Temporal and Spatial Enclosures in the Poetry of Tiutchev", by R. Byrns, *Slavic and East European Journal*, 21 (1977), 180–90.
"Tiutchev and Writing", by Albert T. Wehrle, *Russian Language Journal*, 116 (1979), 69–84.
Poeziia Tiutcheva. Posobie po Spetskursu, by Oleg Orlov, Moscow, 1981.
"Tiutchev in the 1820s–1840s: An Unpublished Correspondence of 1874–75", by Ronald Lane, *Irish Slavonic Studies*, 3 (1982), 2–13.
The Political Poetry and Ideology of F.I. Tiutchev, by Roger Conant, Ann Arbor, Ardis, 1983.
The Semantics of Chaos in Tiutčev, by Sarah Pratt, Munich, Sagner, 1983.
Russian Metaphysical Romanticism: The Poetry of Tiutchev and Boratynskii, by Sarah Pratt, Stanford, Stanford University Press, 1984.
"Tiutchev's Role as Mediator Between the Government and M.N. Katkov (1863–66)", by Ronald Lane, *Russian Literature*, 12 (1985), 111–26.
Tiutchev, by Vadim Kozhinov, Moscow, 1988.
Literaturnoe nasledstvo, vol. 97, books 1–2, Fedor Tiutchev, Moscow, 1988–89.
Tiutchev segodnia: Materialy IV Tiutchevskikh chtenii, Moscow, 1995.

Bibliographies
F.I. Tiutchev. Bibliograficheskii ukazatel' proizvedenii i literatury o zhizni i deiatel'nosti, 1818–73, edited by Kirill Pigarev, Moscow, 1978.
Bibliography of Works by and about F.I. Tiutchev to 1985, edited by Ronald Lane, Nottingham, Astra Press, 1987.

In 1833 Fedor Tiutchev destroyed un unknown quantity of poems, including some of his best. The surviving canon (including a few poems in French) comprises 400 mostly short pieces. In terms of bulk, it divides into 1) translations or adaptations, 2) occasional/ society pieces, 3) political verse, and 4) lyrics. Apart from a few translations, the last two categories contain the core of his distinguished *oeuvre*. In his own verse he cultivated only the lyric and short occasional poem. Apart from juvenile years (1813–21) and final illness (1873), the poetry falls into the periods 1822–38 and 1848–72.

The years 1813–21 produced a variety of experimental subjects and forms, influenced by what can be termed the hedonism of his tutor (the poet-translator Raich) and Horace, and by the introspection of Derzhavin, Pascal, and Lamartine. In 1822–30 the impact mainly of Schelling and Goethe continued the first tendency, that of Heine and, again, Goethe prolonging the second.

Tiutchev's political verse of quality divides into groups: 1) "manifesto"-like poems (chiefly 1848–50), proclaiming a conservative, Slavophile, pan-Slav ideology; 2) three pieces (1848–53) concerned with the conflict of revolutionary west and conservative Russia (the wit and rhetoric of these groups are impressive); 3) four poems (1850–57) sympathetically attuned to the peasants' humble, "holy" suffering (only these equal the best lyrics in inspiration).

Tiutchev's lyrics appear to be products of instants in which a concrete experience and his constant search for insight and understanding crystallize in a revelation of meaning based on an analogy, usually between nature and human life; like the best of his puns (he is a celebrated wit and *causeur*), they are simple and profound. The main themes are love, nature, physical well-being, night, time, and fate. In poems from the period 1822–38 innocent, young love, expressed in striking conceits, soon gives way to sensuality, cynicism, suffering, and insensitivity to the woman's feelings. As for nature, there are a few objective vignettes and rather more mythological illustrations and manifestos of panvitalism (a more accurate term than "pantheism"). Nature is treated as part mother, part almost mistress. Increasingly he uses her as a book of parables of the human condition. Bodily well-being emphasizes pleasurable languor and sensitivity to warmth and coolness: circulation and respiration in nature and human are fused. Night is connected with the unconscious, dreams, and disquiet. Tiutchev is acutely aware of fragile stability and changefulness in nature, where passage of time dominates. Increasingly this is linked to messages of ephemerality, mortality, vulnerability, and anxiety.

In 1848–72 the love-poetry lost the arch artifices, becoming more direct, natural, and psychologically realistic. The "Denis'eva cycle" is justly famous for the combination of emotional conflicts, tenderness, happiness, suffering, guilt, and poignancy of Tiutchev's "last love". In the nature verse panvitalism becomes less strident and explicit; mythology and mountains in spring/ summer are replaced by reality and plains in autumn. Bodily well-being becomes less prominent, while time and fate dominate increasingly. This takes shape in nihilism, a catalogue of woes, almost a cult of suffering, which, despite consciousness of sin, finds little comfort in Christianity and leaves only a stubborn rearguard action against fate, based on affinity with fellow-sufferers.

A remarkable cyclicity can be observed. Within both main periods (first youth, 1822–30; second youth, 1848–50) Tiutchev experiences revelation of the supernatural in the natural world, miraculously combining love, nature, bodily well-being, timelessness, and trust in the universe and fate: he is happy, secure, unselfconscious. The vision then disintegrates (1830–38, 1850–64): the supernatural is lost, and faced with a hostile world, he becomes unhappy, insecure, self-conscious. There was a minor lyrical surge in 1864–66 and then gradual decline.

Formally, most lyric poems are no longer than 20 lines. Stanzaic structure and rhyme-schemes are predominantly regular and conventional, providing a tight, tidy framework: occasionally an extra, penultimate line delays the ending masterfully. The metres are largely unadventurous: like most Russian contemporaries he favours the four-foot iamb. But the verse is rhythmically rich, with skilful use of spondee and pyrrhic. Generally the form is unobtrusively effective.

Stylistically, Tiutchev uses euphonic devices to enhance

meaning and "orchestrate" atmosphere. His vocabulary is both archaic and modern. His modern lexicon is as "pregnant" and saturated as possible, consisting largely of symbols for exploring inner space – terms for circulation, respiration, bliss, paradise, plenitude, divinity, purity, sleep/dream, magic, enchantment, captivation, miracle, mystery, secrecy, etc. He uses grammatical comparatives to intensify emotional and atmospheric effect. His syntax is also archaic and modern: antiquated word-order, paraphrase and rhetoric give way to impressionism (e.g. absence of verbs), melodic intonations, and refrains. He employs parallelism, daring similes and metaphors that compare known with unknown. Many poem-endings introduce unexpected features, opening new perspectives. While most lyrics seem to stem from specific personal experiences, they are seldom obscure and bring out a universal dimension.

Tiutchev's attitude to his poems was puzzlingly ambivalent. While eagerly publishing political and society pieces, he avoided discussing the lyrics, scorned them, was indifferent to their fate and yet continued writing them. The first substantial group appeared (on others' initiative) only in 1836: it was largely ignored. The first book edition appeared in 1854, with a second in 1868: in both he took little part. In an age of prose he was largely forgotten, to be rediscovered by the Symbolists. Largely neglected under socialist realism, he now receives much attention both within and outside Russia.

Tiutchev had no poetic career as such, participated in no "school" and had no disciples or immediate successors. Isolated in Europe from the mainstream of Russian poetry until 1844, he developed his lyrics, based on German idealistic romantic thought, particularly Friedrich Schelling's *Naturphilosophie*, rather than French models or Byronism. He was a lyric genius whose potential remained largely unfulfilled. Silent for ten years, he wrote desultorily, destroyed many poems, neglected others, squandered his gift on political and society versifying and spent an inordinate amount of time philandering and socializing. He did not systematically develop his unique receptivity to thrilling revelations of the mystical unity-in-variety of all natural things. "Silentium" and "Son na more" [A Dream at Sea] remain among the most admired lyrics in the language, while "a thought expressed becomes a lie" is one of the most frequently quoted sayings from 19th-century Russia. There are, unfortunately, relatively few priceless gems from a long life. But with Tiutchev small is beautiful.

RONALD LANE

Viktoriia Samoilovna Tokareva 1937–

Prose writer and scriptwriter

Biography

Born in Leningrad, 20 November 1937. Attended the Leningrad music school. Student in the scriptwriting department at the State Institute of Cinematography in Moscow, 1963: graduated, 1969. First story published in 1964; full-time writer. Author also of 15 film scripts. Married; has one daughter. Lives in Moscow.

Publications

Collected Editions

Letaiuschchie kacheli. Nichego osobennogo [Flying Swans. Nothing Special]. Moscow, 1987.

The Talisman and Other Tales, translated by Rosamund Bartlett. London, Picador, 1993.

Kheppi end. Moscow, 1995.

Shla sobaka po roialiu [The Dog Walked Across the Piano], 2 vols. Moscow, 1995.

Sobranie sochinenii, 3 vols. Moscow, 1996.

Rimskie kanikuly [Roman Holidays]. Moscow, 1996.

Loshadi s kryl'iami. Povesti, rasskazy [Horses with Wings]. Moscow, 1996.

Koshka na doroge: Povesti, rasskazy [The Cat on the Road]. Moscow, 1997.

Nakhal: Rasskazy, povesti [Cheekie So-and-So]. Moscow, 1997.

Fiction

O tom, chego ne bylo [About That, Which Didn't Happen]. Moscow, 1969.

Kogda stalo nemnozhko teplee [When It Got a Bit Warmer]. Moscow, 1972.

Zanuda [The Bore]. Tallin, 1977.

Letaiushchie kacheli [Flying Swings]. Moscow, 1978.

"Samyi schastlivyi den'". 1980; translated as "The Happiest Day of My Life", by Sigrid McLaughlin, in *The Image of Women in Contemporary Soviet Fiction: Selected Short Stories from the USSR*, edited by McLaughlin, London, Macmillan, and New York, St Martin's Press, 1989, 161–83.

Nichego osobennogo. Moscow, 1983; the title story translated as "Nothing Special", by Helena Goscilo, in *Balancing Acts: Contemporary Stories by Russian Women*, edited by Goscilo, Bloomington, Indiana University Press, 1989, 49–78.

"Mezhdu nebom i zemlei". 1985; translated as "Between Heaven and Earth", by Helena Goscilo, in *Balancing Acts: Contemporary Stories by Russian Women*, edited by Goscilo, Bloomington, Indiana University Press, 1989, 273–84.

"Thou Shalt Not Create", translated by Vladimir Korotky, *Soviet Literature*, 3 (1989), 48–68.

"Pervaia popytka". 1989; translated as "Dry Run", by Michael Glenny, *Granta*, 33 (1990), 77–112.

"Piat' figur na postamente". 1989; translated as "Five Figures

on a Pedestal", by Debra Irving, in *Soviet Women Writing: Fifteen Short Stories*, New York, Abbeville Press, and London, John Murray, 1990, 153–201.
"Hello!", translated by Paul David Gould, *Soviet Literature*, 8 (1990), 40–49.
"Centre of Gravity", translated by Michael Glenny, *Granta*, 35 (1990), 92–105.
"Ia est'. Ty est'. On est'" [I Am. You Are. He Is], *Novyi mir*, 9 (1991), 129–51.
Skazat' – ne skazat' [Tell, Don't Tell]. Moscow, 1991.
Korrida [Corrida]. Moscow, 1993.
Vmesto menia [Instead of Me]. Moscow, 1995.

Film, Television, and Theatre Scripts
Dzhentel'meni udachi [Gentlemen of Success]. Moscow, 1971.
Sovsem propashchii [Completely Hopeless], with G. Daneliia. Moscow, 1972.
Mimino: Kinostsenarii, with G. Daneliia and R.L. Gabriliadze. Moscow, 1978.
Eksprompt-fantaziia [Improvisation-Fantasy]. Moscow, 1982.

Critical Studies

"Fantaziia na temu liubvi: Eksprompt-fantaziia", by I. Marinova, *Sovietskii teatr*, 1–2 (1983), 10–12.
"An Interview with Viktoria Tokareva", by Sigrid McLaughlin, *Canadian Women Studies*, 10/4 (1989).
"Mezhdu nebom i obstoiatel'stvami", by M. Prorokov, *Oktiabr'*, 4 (1989), 202–04.
"Happy Never After: The Work of Viktoriia Tokareva and *Glasnost*", by Richard Chapple in *Fruits of Her Plume: Essays on Contemporary Russian Women's Culture*, edited by Helena Goscilo, New York, M.E. Sharpe, 1993, 185–204.
The Last Years of Soviet Russian Literature: Prose Fiction, 1975–1991, by Deming Brown, Cambridge and New York, Cambridge University Press, 1993, 137–40.
"Tokareva, Viktoriia Samoilovna", by Sigrid McLaughlin, in *Dictionary of Russian Women Writers*, edited by Marina Ledkovsky, Charlotte Rosenthal, and Mary Zirin, Westport, Connecticut, Greenwood Press, 1994, 649–51.
Russian Literature 1988–1994: The End of an Era, by N.N. Shneidman, Toronto, Toronto University Press, 1995, 109–11.

Viktoriia Tokareva, one of Russia's most widely-read and successful living authors, is an unusual writer whose popularity not only stayed at a consistently high level during the last decades of Soviet rule, but has remained undiminished since the collapse of the Communist regime. Since 1992, her readership has, if anything, increased.

Tokareva's secondary education at a specialist musical school in Leningrad, the city where she was born and grew up, seemed to destine her for further studies at a conservatoire and a career in music, but her desire to become an actress led her instead to enroll as a student at the State Institute of Cinematography in Moscow after some time spent teaching singing. It was in the screenwriting department, however, that she found her niche. At the same time she discovered she also had creative talents in another sphere: that of prose fiction. Her first short story, "Den' bez vran'ia" [A Day Without Lies], was published while she was a second-year student at the Institute in 1964, and brought her instant acclaim. Although she has written the occasional novella, the short story has remained Tokareva's preferred medium. Since her first collection, *O tom, chego ne bylo* [About That, Which Didn't Happen], appeared in 1969, she has gone on to publish seven others. One recent collection, *Korrida* [Corrida], was issued in 1993, and contains stories published in Russia's leading literary and popular journals in the late 1980s and early 1990s. At the same time, Tokareva has also enjoyed success as a screenwriter. She is the author of 13 film scripts, several of which have won awards (including the Golden Prize for *Mimino* at the 1977 Moscow International Film Festival). She has also adapted the writings of others for the screen, most notably I. Grekova's *Vdovii parokhod* (*The Ship of Widows*). But it is on her work as a short-story writer that her reputation rests.

Since graduating from the Institute of Cinematography, Tokareva has continued to live in Moscow, the setting for most of her stories, all of which have a contemporary and specifically Russian focus. Like Chekhov, the writer whom she most admires and on whom she models herself (his name crops up in many of her stories), Tokareva likes to write about ordinary men and women and the vicissitudes of their day-to-day lives in a prose that is unpretentious, concise, often witty and sometimes poignant. Although there is much that differentiates the two writers, Tokareva's stories exhibit certain traits that indeed align her with Russia's most famous author of short fiction, namely: a highly developed sense of irony that is nevertheless concomitant with a deep compassion for her struggling characters, and a rich vein of humour that precludes her work from ever becoming too moribund or sentimental. A major concern with loneliness and insensitive behaviour links Tokareva and Chekhov thematically, as well as a general preoccupation with the complexities of male-female interaction. Many of Tokareva's stories feature men and women in whose lives there is an absence or insufficiency of love, often causing them to behave in a selfish way. Whether single, divorced, locked in stale marriages or at an impasse in dead-end relationships, Tokareva's characters tend to be unfulfilled, miserable people leading a mundane existence. Convinced that life has passed them by, they are unable to see a way of changing the state of affairs. Occasionally the reader's expectations are confounded and a character's dreams (which are usually of a highly conventional nature) come true, perhaps taking the story almost into the realm of fantasy, as in "Odin kubik nadezhdy" [A Cubic Centimetre of Hope] and "Zigzag", but, more often than not, the situation remains the same. The most positive outcome occurs when an unexpected event causes her characters to gain insight into the deficiencies of their behaviour, or to come to terms with the limitations of their life, as in "Iaponskii zontik" [The Japanese Umbrella] or "Ia est'. Ty est'. On est'." [I Am. You Are. He Is]. Sometimes a sudden insight into another, even more unfortunate, character's point of view means that only the reader goes through this mental process, and the characters themselves experience no such epiphany, see, for example, "Plokhoe nastroenie" [Bad Mood].

Iurii Nagibin describes Tokareva as looking "at the world as if other eyes have not seen it yet, as if she was given the chance of discovering nature and the essence of things first". At best Tokareva's stories contain perceptive and original authorial statements about the human condition that are all the more effective for being masked by her detached and insouciant narrative voice; at worst, however, they verge on triteness, as wit sometimes comes at the expense of depth. It could be argued that the price of success in Soviet times was a certain superficiality. Although the stories Tokareva has written since the introduction of glasnost all take place against a background of Russia as it really is, the style and content of her writing has not essentially changed. Tokareva may now write more openly about corruption than before, her female characters may have abortions, and her male characters may be irresponsible alcoholics, yet it is the search for love and the frequent absurdity of human behaviour in this sphere that remains her uppermost concern. This is combined sometimes with a wry and wickedly accurate retrospective portrayal of the idiosyncracies of Soviet behaviour; an example of this can be found in "Sentimental'noe puteshestvie" [Sentimental Journey], one of her later stories, a hilarious but also rather sad tale about a group of Soviet tourists visiting Italy in the late 1970s. Not as trenchant in her portrayal of the brutalities of Russian life as Liudmila Petrushevskaia, nor as linguistically rich as Tat'iana Tolstaia, Viktoriia Tokareva is not as artistically ambitious as either of these writers, yet her ability to produce consistently entertaining and highly readable stories should not be underestimated.

ROSAMUND BARTLETT

Tat'iana Nikitinichna Tolstaia 1951–

Prose writer

Biography

Born in Leningrad, 3 May 1951 (one of seven children). Great-grandniece of Lev Tolstoi, granddaughter of Aleksei Nikolaevich Tolstoi and the poet Natal'ia Vasil'evna Krandievskaia. Studied classics at Leningrad State University, 1968–74. Married: Andrei Lebedev in 1974; two sons. Junior editor in the Eastern Literature Division of Nauka publishing house, 1974–83. Began to write, January 1983; first story appeared in *Avrora*, August, 1983. First collected edition of her stories, *Na zolotom kryl'tse sideli* (*On the Golden Porch*), 1987. Writer-in-residence, University of Richmond, Virginia, 1988; senior lecturer in Russian literature at University of Texas at Austin, 1989; writer-in-residence, Texas Tech University in Lubbock, 1990.

Publications

Collected Editions

Na zolotom kryl'tse sideli, Moscow, 1987; translated as *On the Golden Porch*, by Antonina W. Bouis, New York, Knopf, 1989; Harmondsworth, Penguin, 1990.

Sleepwalker in a Fog, translated by Jamey Gambrell. New York, Knopf, and London, Virago, 1992; Harmondsworth, Penguin, 1993.

Three Stories/Tri rasskaza, edited by S. Dalton-Brown. London, Bristol Classical Press, 1996.

Fiction

"Na zolotom kryl'tse sideli", *Avrora*, 8 (1983), 94–101; translated as "On the Golden Porch", by Antonina W. Bouis, in *On the Golden Porch*, 1989.

"Svidanie s ptitsei", *Oktiabr'*, 12 (1983), 52–57; translated as "Rendezvous with a Bird", by Antonina W. Bouis, in *On the Golden Porch*, 1989.

"Uta-monogatari", *Voprosy literatury*, 2 (1984), 259–64.

"Sonia", *Avrora*, 10 (1984), 77–83; also in *Rasskaz: 1984*, Moscow, 1984, 373–80); translated as "Sonya", by Antonina W. Bouis, in *On the Golden Porch*, 1989.

"Chistyi list", *Neva*, 12 (1984), 116–25; translated as "A Clean Sheet", by Antonina W. Bouis, in *On the Golden Porch*, 1989.

"Milaia Shura", "Okhota na mamonta", *Oktiabr'*, 12 (1985), 113–21; translated as "Sweet Shura" and "Hunting the Woolly Mammoth", by Antonina W. Bouis, in *On the Golden Porch*, 1989.

"Reka Okkervil'", *Avrora*, 3 (1985), 137–46; translated as "Okkervil River", by Antonina W. Bouis, in *On the Golden Porch*, 1989.

"Peters", *Novyi mir*, 1 (1986) ,123–31; translated as "Peters", by Antonina W. Bouis, in *On the Golden Porch*, 1989.

"Spi spokoino, synok", *Avrora*, 4 (1986), 94–101; translated as "Sweet Dreams, Son", by Antonina W. Bouis, in *On the Golden Porch*, 1989.

"Ogon' i pyl'", "Samaia liubimaia", *Avrora*, 10 (1986), 82–110; translated as "Fire and Dust", by Antonina W. Bouis, in *On the Golden Porch*, 1989.

"Poet i muza", "Serafim", "Fakir", *Novyi mir*, 12 (1986), 113–33; translated as "The Poet and the Muse", and "Serafim", by Jamey Gambrell, in *Sleepwalker in a Fog*, 1992; "Fakir" translated as "The Fakir", by Antonina W. Bouis, in *On the Golden Porch*, 1989.

"Liubish' – ne liubish'", "Noch'", "Krug", *Oktiabr'*, 4 (1987), 89–104; "Liubish' ..." and "Krug" translated as "Loves Me, Loves Me Not" and "The Circle", by Antonina W. Bouis, in *On the Golden Porch*, 1989; "Noch'" translated as "Night", by Jamey Gambrell, in *Sleepwalker in a Fog*, 1992.

"Vyshel mesiats iz tumana", *Krest'ianka*, 4 (1987), 32–35; translated as "The Moon Came Out", by Jamey Gambrell, in *Sleepwalker in a Fog*, 1992.

"Plamen' nebesnyi", *Avrora*, 11 (1987), 130–39; translated as "Heavenly Flame", by Jamey Gambrell, in *Sleepwalker in a Fog*, 1992.

"Somnambula v tumane", *Novyi mir*, 7 (1988), 8–26; translated as "Sleepwalker in a Fog", by Jamey Gambrell, in *Sleepwalker in a Fog*, 1992.
"Limpopo", *Znamia*, 11 (1991), 45–70; also in *Sintaksis*, 27 (1990); translated as "Limpopo", by Jamey Gambrell, in *Sleepwalker in a Fog*, 1992.

Critical Studies

"Eta prekrasnaia zhizn'", by E. Nevzgliadova, *Avrora*, 10 (1986), 111–20.
"S vysoty svoego kurgana", by V. Bushin, *Nash sovremennik*, 8 (1987), 182–85.
"Motivy i fantomy", by M. Zolotonosov, *Literaturnoe obozrenie*, 4 (1987), 58–61.
"Tat'iana Tolstaia's 'Dome of Many-Coloured Glass': The World Refracted Through Multiple Perspectives", by Helena Goscilo, *Slavic Review*, 47/2 (Summer 1988), 280–90.
"Are Women Writing Women's Writing in the Soviet Union Today? Tolstaya and Grekova", by Adele Barker, *Studies in Comparative Communism*, 21/303 (Autumn–Winter 1988), 357–64.
"Rastochitel'nost' talanta", by I. Grekova, *Novyi mir*, 1 (1988), 252–56.
"Uroki zazerkal'ia", by S. Piskunova and V. Piskunov, *Oktiabr'*, 8 (1988), 188–98.
"Nich'i babushki na zolotom kryl'tse", by R. Shishkova, *Kontinent*, 56 (1988), 398–402.
"Otkroite knigu molodykh", by E. Bulin, *Molodaia gvardiia*, 3 (1989), 237–48.
"Sto let zhenskoi odinochestva", by N. Startseva, *Don*, 3 (1989), 58–65.
"The Human Spirit is Androgynous" (interview), *Index on Censorship*, 9 (1990), 29–30.
"Tolstajan Love as Surface Text", by Helena Goscilo, *Slavic and East European Journal*, 34/1 (1990), 40–51.
"Paradise, Purgatory and Post-Mortems in the World of Tat'iana Tolstaia", by Helena Goscilo, *Indiana Slavic Studies*, 5 (1990), 97–113.
"Gorodok v tabakerke", by P. Vail and A. Genis, *Zvezda*, 8 (1990), 147–50.
"Tolstaian Times: Traversals and Transfers", by Helena Goscilo, in *New Directions in Soviet Literature – Selected Papers from the Fourth World Congress for Soviet and East European Studies, Harrogate, 1990*, edited by Sheelagh Duffin Graham, New York, St Martin's Press, and London, Macmillan, 1992.
"Tvortsy raspada'", by E. Ovanesian, *Molodaia gvardiia* (3 April 1992), 249–62.
"Interview", *World Literature Today*, 67/1 (Winter 1993), 49–53.
"Na iskhode real'nosti", by A. Aleksandrova, *Grani*, 168 (1993), 302–17.
"Perspective in Tatyana Tolstaya's Wonderland of Art", by Helena Goscilo, *World Literature Today*, 67/1 (Winter 1993), 80–90.
Fruits of Her Plume: Essays on Contemporary Russian Women's Culture, edited by Helena Goscilo, New York, M.E. Sharpe, 1993.
"Monsters Monomaniacal, Marital, and Medical: Tat'iana Tolstaia's Regenerative Use of Gender Stereotypes", by Helena Goscilo, in *Sexuality and the Body in Russian Culture*, edited by Jane T. Costlow, Stephanie Sandler, and Judith Vowles, Stanford, Stanford University Press, 1993.
Russia's Alternative Prose, by Robert Porter, Oxford, Berg, 1994, 63–71.
"Violence in the Garden: A Work by Tolstaja in Kleinian Perspective", by Daniel Rancour-Laferrière, Vera Loseva, and Aleksej Lunkov, *Slavic and East European Journal*, 39/4 (1995).
Russian Literature 1988–1994: The End of an Era, by N.N. Shneidman, Toronto, Toronto University Press, 1995, 160–64.
"A Map of the Human Heart: Tatyana Tolstaya's Topographies", by S. Dalton-Brown, *Essays in Poetics*, 21 (1996), 1–18.
Dehexing Sex: Russian Womanhood During and After Glasnost, by Helena Goscilo, Ann Arbor, University of Michigan Press, 1996.
TNT: The Explosive World of Tatyana N. Tolstaya's Fiction, by Helena Goscilo, New York, M.E. Sharpe, 1996.
"Carnivalization of the Short Story: Tatyana Tolstaya's *The Poet and the Muse*", by Erika Greber, *Essays in Poetics*, 21 (1996), 50–78.

When, in 1987, a book containing 13 stories entitled *Na zolotom kryl'tse sideli* (*On the Golden Porch*) appeared in the book kiosks, it was sold out within an hour. Tat'iana Tolstaia was soon to be hailed as one of the two most prominent women writers in Russia today (the other being Liudmila Petrushevskaia); she is the acknowledged master of the short-story genre among contemporary Russian writers. Her reputation at first glance seems unwarranted, based as it is on only 21 stories; yet Tolstaia's work shows an extraordinarily high degree of craftmanship. Her work is notable more for its stylistic brilliance than for its themes, although she has her point to make about the age-old romantic conflict between ideas and reality.

Tolstaia herself in an interview in 1987 stated that her interest was in "unfortunates"; the first thing the reader notes in a story by Tolstaia is the central character, usually a person unfortunate in love, of unprepossessing appearance, confused, trapped, unhappy, childlike, and alone. These are people whom Tolstaia calls "normal", for it is the essence of the human condition to be unhappy, as she suggested during an interview in *Moskovskie novosti* in 1987. Her male characters are usually beset by old age, or facing a mid-life crisis, like Simeonov in "Reka Okkervil'" ("Okkervil River"), Vasilii Mikhailovich in "Krug" ("The Circle"), the depressed Ignatev in "Chistyi list" ("A Clean Sheet"), or the pensive Denisov in "Somnambula v tumane" ("Sleepwalker in a Fog"); her female characters are equally dissatisfied, filled with longing for interesting places and events, as in the case of Rimma in "Ogon' i pyl'" ("Fire and Dust"), who dreams of the warm south, or the spinster Natasha in "Vyshel mesiats iz tumana" ("The Moon Came Out") who stands by the window listening to life pass her by. They do also, however, long for domestic bliss, as in "Okhota na mamonta" ("Hunting the Woolly Mammoth") in which the "heroine", Zoia, demonstrates an obsessive desire for a husband and a comfortable routine.

Tolstaia's characters spend their lives attempting to escape from the dissatisfying quotidian, seeking the alchemical word that will turn dross into gold. This is the reason for the combination of physical, tawdry, and unpleasant detail with images of enchanting beauty in her work. Tolstaia's work is classifiable as magic realism, a generic tradition rarely found in 20th-century Russian writing, but one that has its similarities with Gogolian realism of the previous century. Her texts tell the reader very little about modern Russia, being, with the exception of "Limpopo", which comments indirectly on racism, apolitical, but they have a great deal to say about another world – that of the imagination.

Tolstaia's style is intensely visual; in her awareness of the colour and shape of the people and objects she describes (and, at times, the texture and odour) critics have labelled her work "iridescent, and luxurious", even "kaleidoscopic". At first glance, it appears that Tolstaia's style is a cluttered one, with clause piled upon clause, list of images upon list. The flow of clauses and the use of alliteration, assonance, and anaphora combine to create an essentially poetic and musical prose line that has an almost incantatory effect. Tolstaia combines such sentences with *skaz* (first-person narration) devices to represent the meandering, excited, or fragmented speech of her characters. The stream-of-consciousness narration that Tolstaia employs (often wandering between this form and the third-person mode) permits each character's mind to be "emptied", like a box of mementos, before the reader, who finds many curious conjunctions among the objects listed, images that yoke together unlikely epithets and nouns, metaphors that sparkle like strange bits of glass, hidden among dust and old photographs. The image of the treasure chest appears in "Fire and Dust", in which women eagerly search through a pile of clothing, silks, and ribbons of diaphanous splendour – only to find that everything is too small, too ridiculous, or too short. The magic treasure chest turns out ultimately to be no more than a rubbish bin.

Yet all is not dross. The cluttered world from which characters long to escape, the "enchanted" world in which characters sleep while their surroundings rust and grow shabby, is often replaced by another topography, infinitely more desirable, and usually described in terms of exotic scenery, as in "Sleepwalker in a Fog", in which Denisov dreams of New Guinea, or as in "Fire and Dust", in which Rimma dreams of a far-off place with parrots and surf. Certain characters have such appeal precisely because they remind the protagonist of exotic lands, because they appear to have the power to transform and transport. These are characters such as the singer Vera Vasil'evna in "Okkervil River", with her siren voice, who represents to the ageing Simeonov an ideal love, or the luscious Faina to the socially inept "hero" of "Peters"; or Filin, the "fakir" of the story of that name, who can "transform the world"; or Uncle Pasha, like "a Solomon holding a cornucopia" in the eyes of the children in "Na zolotom kryl'tse sideli" ("On the Golden Porch"), or Isol'da in "The Circle", who represents to Vasilii Mikhailovich his salvation.

Vasilii, however, gets bored with Isol'da and goes back to his wife; all the other characters find that another person, however loved and admired, cannot provide the alchemical force necessary to escape this world. Love seldom brings happiness, and is always thwarted, left behind, or abused, leaving the characters feeling foolish, lost and trapped, catching at beauty where they can; in colours, in flowers, in the flight of a bird, and in fruit (all of which make frequent appearances in Tolstaia's prose). Animal imagery is also prominent, and people are often described in terms of such, reminding the reader that, as in a fairy tale, people may sometimes be animals in disguise. One of the many paradoxes of Tolstaia's work may be that, for her characters, transformation has already taken place; but it has left its victims bewildered and unsure, inhabiting a limbo half-way between the world of animals (nasty, brutish, and dominated by hunger, whether for food or love) and a fairy-tale world in which frogs can become princes. Her characters, like magpies, gather objects and people to line their nests, hoping for magic rings that will enchant the wearer and allow them to find their heart's desire – to escape. Tolstaia tantalizes the reader with glimpses of something beyond this life, something inscribed in images of flame and darkness, but possibly containing the promise of salvation. Do Tolstaia's characters remain chained and imprisoned, waiting until siren voices wake them from the long sleep of the soul that life imposes on its servants; and, if they awaken, what awaits them?

S. DALTON-BROWN

On the Golden Porch

Na zolotom kryl'tse sideli

Short-story collection, 1987

Sleepwalker in a Fog

Somnambula v tumane

Short-story collection, 1992

Tat'iana Tolstaia began her career in 1983 with the publication in the journal *Avrora* of "On the Golden Porch", from which the title of her 1987 collection of 13 stories was taken. The collection was translated into English, appearing in 1989. *On the Golden Porch* gained for Tolstaia both international acclaim and a year's teaching in America. A second collection in English, *Sleepwalker in a Fog*, followed in 1992. Between them, these collections include all Tolstaia's stories, 21 in all (only her untranslatable parody of Japanese poetry, *Uta-monogatari*, has, unsurprisingly, not appeared in the west).

Lauded for her Nabokovian, intricate style, refreshingly modern (to the Russian critical establishment) in terms of its magic realism, Tolstaia has proved particularly skilled at producing a prose of defeated passion. Her characters, who are often tired urban professionals, or children adrift in a confusing world, long for a better place, a realm beyond the domination of time or space. Whether such a world is attainable is doubtful; Tolstaia is more certain when describing life as anti-triumph, than as Utopia; at conveying a sense of deep and frustrated longing than at depicting contentment.

Critics have devoted attention to the most striking aspect of Tolstaia's work, her complex, allusive, and ironic style. She is usually discussed in conjunction with Liudmila Petrushevskaia, but the two are stylistically quite different; Tolstaia's ornamental mode of writing is more akin to that of Belyi or Babel', than to the style of her contemporaries. Her themes, however, do bear some resemblance to those of Petrushevskaia. Tolstaia's central concern has been summed up in various ways by critics as the conflict between ideas and reality (Bakhnov), man's relationship to reality (Spivak), childhood and its foe, time (Vail and Genis,

Zolotonosov, Shiskova), life (Nevgliadova), spiritual poverty (Stepanian), death (Ivanova), cruel reality (Zorin), or romanticism (Dark, Mihailov; Helena Goscilo has also written on love and personality).

Such summations point to the prevalence of an on-going struggle in Tolstaia's work between people and their environment, which confuses, ages, and entraps. Escapism is the inevitable result. Journeys are frequently mentioned; most of Tolstaia's characters are travelling – or, rather, trying to flee: "everyone's running, running away from himself or in search of himself" ("Limpopo"). In her stories we find landscapes repeated, enabling a broad categorization of topographies and their emotional co-efficients. The city stands for a feeling of disillusionment and confinement; the sea, or river, suggests a longing to escape, a longing for beauty; while the garden, or lushly vegetative landscape, refers to childhood, usually depicted as a golden, exotic land, an Eden to which the characters passionately desire to return.

The search for the magical word that will unfetter the characters from this world of disappointments is Tolstaia's main preoccupation; her texts strive for alliterative, incantatory rhythms, seeking for the magical phrase that will transform the mundane, if only for an instant, into the magical. In "Vyshel mesiats iz tumana" ("The Moon Came Out"), children, while playing nonsense games, find a word that unlocks the gates of time and causality, and "for a second the horrific wheel of the world stopped running, stood rooted to the spot, the iron gates locked open, the fetters unfastened".

The need to escape is great; Tolstaia's characters usually inhabit a cramped, domestic world, dominated, as critics have noted, by objects. Her characters are, whether they know it or not, "penned" by the clutter of everyday life like the "mammoth", Vladimir, in "Okhota na mamonta" ("Hunting the Woolly Mammoth"), whom the marriage-obsessed Zoia finally nooses and tames with slippers and sorrowful glances. Tolstaia describes life as a closed circle in which her characters are trapped like sleepers under enchantment, or she sees existence as a tunnel, with only one way out – through death ("The Circle"). The characters desperately seek a way out of this cluttered, verbally elaborate world, described in labyrinthine sentences and tightly-turned phrases; where is the door, the crack in the wall, the unnoticed secret passage ("Milaia Shura" ["Sweet Shura"]), the way back to a golden childhood or forward to a far-off or fabled land?

Tolstaia's characters, it seems, cannot discover the way out to that desired place because their own selves are largely undiscovered. The world to most of Tolstaia's characters is a labyrinth akin to that in their own minds, a world cluttered with feelings, objects, people (few people have souls "smooth as a pipe", like the character Zhenechka in "Samaia liubimaia" ("Most Beloved")). An authorial concern with lack of identity is a supporting theme to the central preoccupation with escape. Longing to scratch their names on the boundless walls of infinity, Tolstaia's characters have first to find their names or identities (as suggested perhaps in the epigraph to *On the Golden Porch*, describing a children's game in which characters have to say who they are). Without names, Tolstaia's characters will find that escape may result in a different kind of entrapment, within a boundless, disorientating space, which frightens and perhaps even causes insanity, like that experienced by Lora's father (*Sleepwalker in a Fog*). Tolstaia's characters are often emotionally undeveloped like Peters ("Peters"), poseurs like Filin ("Fakir"), strangers or alien beings like Judy ("Limpopo") or the winged Serafim ("Serafim"), capable of excess like the frenzied Lizaveta who scratches her paintings with her fingernails ("Poet i muza" ("The Poet and the Muse")), and many more. These are not so much human beings as stylistic marvels, as beautifully or grotesquely painted as antique dolls.

It is doubtful whether Tolstaia's characters, her "sleepwalkers in the fog", ever attain Eden; and yet, in the story of that name, the sleepwalker is finally seen running along a road over open ground towards the light, an image with highly symbolic connotations of epiphany and salvation. However, Tolstaia tends to mix her occasional religious imagery with fairy-tale motifs. Perhaps the belief that "man is immortal, that youth can return, that a candle once lit will never go out, and that virtue, whatever we may think of it, will eventually be rewarded" ("Most Beloved") may indeed be no more than the stuff of fairy tales.

S. Dalton-Brown

Aleksei Konstantinovich Tolstoi 1817–1875

Prose writer, dramatist, and poet

Biography

Born in St Petersburg, 5 September 1817. Educated at home in the Ukraine, and then in St Petersburg after 1826. First trip abroad to Karlsbad, Dresden, and Weimar, 1827, followed by trip to Italy, 1831. Studied at the Moscow Archives of Ministry of Foreign Affairs, 1834; at the same time received tuition from Moscow University professors, graduated, 1835. Lived abroad rom 1836; attached to the Russian Embassy in Frankfurt. Returned to Russia in 1840; took up appointment in the Second Section of the Imperial Chancellery in St Petersburg. Published first story in 1841 and first lyric poetry in 1851. Master of Ceremonies at the Imperial Court, 1851. Served in the Russian Army, 1855–56: resigned, 1861. Full-time writer from 1861. Married: Sof'ia Andreevna Miller in 1863. Died in Krasnyi Rog, 10 October 1875.

Publications

Collected Editions

Stikhotvoreniia. Berlin, 1922.

Stikhotvoreniia. Leningrad, 1936.

Sobranie sochinenii, 4 vols, edited by I.G. Iampol'skii. Moscow, 1963–64.

Polnoe sobranie stikhotvorenii, 2 vols. Leningrad, 1984.

Fiction

Upyr'. St Petersburg, 1841; translated as "The Vampire", by Fedor Nikanov, in *Vampires: Stories of the Supernatural*, New York, Hawthorn Books, 1969; and as "Vampire", by Olga Shartse, in *Russian 19th-Century Gothic Tales*, Moscow, Raduga, 1984.

Kniaz' Serebrianyi. St Petersburg, 1862; translated as *A Prince of Outlaws*, by Cornelius A. Manning, New York, Knopf, 1927.

"La famille de Vourdalac" (written in French). 1884; translated as "The Family of Vourdalak", by Christopher Frayling, in his *Vampyres: Lord Byron to Count Dracula*, London, Faber, 1992.

Poetry

Ioann Damaskin [John Damascene]. 1858.

Plays

Smert' Ioanna Groznogo. St Petersburg, 1866; translated as "The Death of Ivan the Terrible", by G.R. Noyes, in his *Masterpieces of Russian Drama*, New York, Dover, 1961, vol. 2, 457–546.

Tsar' Fedor Ioannovich. St Petersburg 1868; translated as *Czar Fyodor Ivanovich*, by A. Hayes, London, Paul, 1924.

Tsar' Boris. St Petersburg, 1870.

Critical Studies

Le poète Alexis Tolstoi. L'homme et l'oeuvre, by André Lirondelle, Paris, Hachette, 1912.

A. K. Tolstoy: Russian Humorist, by Thomas Edwin Berry, Bethany, West Virginia, Bethany College Press, 1971.

A.K. Tolstoy, by Margaret Dalton, New York, Twayne, 1972.

Serdtse polno vdokhnoveniia: Zhizn' i tvorchestvo A.K. Tolstogo, by G.I. Stafeev, Moscow, 1979.

"Rhyme and Reason: An Aspect of A.K. Tolstoy's Poetic Technique", by S. Graham, *Essays in Poetics*, 4/1 (1979).

Aleksei Konstantinovich Tolstoi, by Dmitrii Zhukov, Moscow, 1982.

The Lyric Poetry of A.K. Tolstoi, by Sheelagh Duffin Graham, Amsterdam, Rodopi, 1985.

A gifted and versatile writer, Count Aleksei Tolstoi's modest but unique contribution to the 19th-century Russian literary canon is sometimes unfairly overlooked. Best known for his trilogy of plays and a novel, all on historical subjects, Tolstoi was also a lyric poet of note, and a parodist of distinction. His place in the annals of Russian literary history should be assured on the strength of his humorous verse alone, some of which is brilliantly inspired and has direct links to the 20th-century Russian literature of the absurd, as exemplified in the works of Daniil Kharms and others.

Tolstoi's birth into a wealthy aristocratic family was both a help and a hindrance to him. While it gave him the advantages of a fine education and the possibility of extensive travel in Europe, his family's close connections to the Imperial family (he knew Alexander II from childhood) obliged him to fulfil duties at court, duties he found arduous, and from which he was only able to resign in 1861. Thus for most of his adult life Tolstoi was unable to devote himself fully to literature, which he felt was his real calling. Tolstoi began writing poetry at an early age, but it was as a prose writer that he first entered the Russian literary arena, with the publication of a story called *Upyr'* (*The Vampire*) in 1841. A romantic horror tale with a convoluted plot, it was followed by a further six stories (three more Gothic tales of the supernatural, two hunting sketches written in a more realistic vein, and a humorous piece), all of which were written in the late 1830s and early 1840s. Tolstoi's only novel, *Kniaz' Serebrianyi* (*A Prince of Outlaws*), set in the times of Ivan the Terrible, is his most significant prose work. Although begun in the late 1840s, Tolstoi broke off work on it for several years in order to devote himself to poetry, and by the time it was published in 1862 the vogue for the romantic historical novel, which had developed initially under the inspiration of Walter Scott's works in this genre, and peaked in Russia in the 1830s, had of course long since passed. With its patriotic sentiment and dramatic qualities, however, it is a work that nevertheless enjoyed a degree of popularity with the Russian public, and continued to be read with enthusiasm during Soviet times. Although his background made him conservative in many ways, Tolstoi was very much a liberal-minded Westernizer in his wholehearted embrace of European culture and in his antipathy towards despotism in any form, particularly as existed under Ivan the Terrible in 16th-century Muscovy. In his novel, Tolstoi contrasts the Oriental despot Ivan with the noble young boyar hero, who epitomizes the chivalrous and European spirit of old Russia during the Kievan period, which the author intended to idealize.

It was the times of Ivan the Terrible that formed the subject of Tolstoi's three tragic dramas, on which his reputation as Russia's most important 19th-century historical dramatist rests. Tolstoi had developed an interest in this period while attached as a student to the Moscow Archives in the 1830s, and, as he had done for *A Prince of Outlaws*, he was able to draw on Karamzin's monumental history of Russia as his primary source material. The first play, *Smert' Ioanna Groznogo* (*The Death of Ivan the Terrible*), written in blank verse, was completed in 1863, published three years later and first performed in St Petersburg in 1867. It was followed by *Tsar' Fedor Ioannovich* (*Czar Fyodor Ivanovich*), and *Tsar' Boris*, both of which were written in a mixture of blank verse and prose, following Pushkin's *Boris Godunov*, which, along with the plays of Shakespeare and Schiller, was one of Tolstoi's main models. For censorship and other reasons neither were performed in Tolstoi's lifetime. The great merit of these three plays is their depth and complexity of psychological characterization, and their unity of theme and time period.

An exceptionally wide-ranging writer, Tolstoi's poetic *oeuvre* embraces many genres, including love lyrics (all of which were addressed to his wife), polemical poems, among which the most important is "Protiv techeniia" [Against the Current] (1867), and narrative verse, which he called ballads; the most highly regarded in this category is his *Ioann Damaskin* [John Damascene]. It is perhaps in the sphere of lyric poetry that Tolstoi's work is most in need of reassessment, however. Tolstoi's mystical approach to art as religion, his notion that the artist had a duty to serve the ideal of beauty and his longing for unity are fully consonant with the central precepts of German romanticism. Tolstoi in fact spent much of his time in Germany, translated the works of Goethe and Heine, and was one of many Russian writers who became fascinated by Schopenhauer. Although there is much in his work that links it with the second-generation Russian Symbolists, who were also deeply inspired by German romanticism, it was Tolstoi's misfortune to start writing his transcendental poetry in the 1840s, when realistic and ideologically-minded prose was becoming the dominant artistic form. Tolstoi believed in literature as a force in moral education, but, as an apologist of pure art, was firmly opposed to it becoming a vehicle for any kind of propaganda. His first collection appeared in 1867, and received little attention from critics and public alike. Although traditional from the metrical point of view, Tolstoi's lyric poetry was innovative in its exploration of unusual rhyme. Often very musical (Musorgskii, Rachmaninov, Tchaikovskii and others made many settings of his poems), his major weakness as a lyric poet is a tendency towards sentimentality. Yet, remarkably, Tolstoi was also a literary parodist *par excellence*. Along with his cousins, the Zhemchuzhnikov brothers, Tolstoi was one of the creators of one of Russia's most humorous satirical figures, the fictional poet-bureaucrat Koz'ma Prutkov (see separate entry), and he also produced an important corpus of literary parodies and nonsense verse of his own (including the famous *Son Popova* [The Dream of Popov] in 1874), in which realm he was without peer.

ROSAMUND BARTLETT

Aleksei Nikolaevich Tolstoi 1883–1945

Novelist

Biography

Born in Nikolaevsk, Samara Province, 10 January 1883. Educated at home, and then at secondary school in Samara, 1894–1901; attended St Petersburg Technological Institute, 1901–08. War correspondent for the newspaper *Russkie vedomosti*, several visits to the Front line, also to England and France, 1914–16; worked for General Denikin's propaganda section, 1917. Emigrated to Paris, 1918 and then Berlin, 1921; returned to the Soviet Union, 1923. Elected Chairman of the Writers' Union, 1936; deputy to the Supreme Soviet, 1937. Participated in anti-fascist congresses in Paris and London, 1935–36; took part in the 2nd International Congress of Writers in Madrid at the height of the Spanish Civil War. Elected member of the Soviet Academy of Sciences, 1939. Recipient: Stalin Prize in 1941 for *Khozhdenie po mukam* (*Road to Calvary*), in 1942 for *Petr Pervyi* (*Peter the First*), and in 1944 for *Ivan Groznyi* [Ivan the Terrible]; Order of Lenin and numerous other orders and medals. Died in Moscow, 23 February 1945.

Publications

Collected Editions

Sochineniia, 2 vols. St Petersburg, 1910–12.

Sochineniia, 6 vols. Moscow, 1912–18.

Povesti i rasskazy 1910–1943. Moscow, 1944.

Polnoe sobranie sochinenii, 15 vols. Moscow, 1946–53.

Sobranie sochinenii, 10 vols. Moscow, 1958–61.

Sobranie sochinenii, 8 vols. Moscow, 1972.

Collected Works, 6 vols, translated by Ivy and Tatiana Litvinova. Moscow, Progress, 1982.

Fiction

"Nedelia v Tureneve" ("Petushok"), *Apollon*, 4 (1910); translated as "A Week in Turenovo", by George Reavey, in *A Week in Turenovo and Other Stories*, New York, Grove Press, 1958.

Chudaki [The Eccentrics]. St Petersburg, 1911.

Povesti i rasskazy A. Tolstogo. St Petersburg, 1912.

"Soroch'i skazki" [Tales of a Magpie], in *Sochineniia*, Moscow, 1912–18, vol. 4.

Khromoi barin [The Lame Prince]. St Petersburg, 1912.

Khozhdenie po mukam [Tour of Hell: Trilogy]. 1943; translated as *Road to Calvary*, by Edith Bone, London, Hutchinson, 1945; New York, Knopf, 1946; also translated as *Ordeal*, by Ivy and Tatiana Litvinov, Moscow, Foreign Languages Publishing House, 1953; in part as *Darkness at Dawn*, by Edith Bone and Emile Burns, New York, Longman Green, 1936; reprinted Westport, Connecticut, Greenwood Press, 1977.

1. "Sestry", *Sovremennye zapiski*, 1–6 (1920–21); Berlin, 1922.
2. *Vosemnadtsatyi god*. Moscow and Leningrad, 1929.
3. *Khmuroe utro*. Tashkent, 1942.

Detstvo Nikity (original title "Povest' o mnogikh prevoskhodnykh veshchakh"). Moscow and Berlin, 1922; translated as *Nikita's Childhood*, by Violet Dutt, London, Hutchinson, 1945.

Aelita (Zakat Marsa). Moscow and Petrograd, 1923; translated as *Aelita*, by Antonina W. Bouis, New York, Macmillan, 1981; and as *Aelita, or The Decline of Mars*, by Leland Fetzer, Ann Arbor, Ardis, 1985.

"Golubye goroda" [Blue Towns], *Krasnaia nov'*, 4 (1925).
"Giperboloid Inzhenera Garina", *Krasnaia nov'*, 7–9 (1925); 4–7 (1926); translated as *The Death Box*, by B.G. Guerney, London, Methuen, 1936; and as *The Garin Death Ray*, by George Hanna, Moscow, Foreign Languages Publishing House, 1955.
"Chernoe zoloto" ("Emigranty") [Black Gold (The Émigrés)], *Novyi mir*, 1–12 (1931).
"Petr Pervyi", *Novyi mir*, 7–11 (1929), 1–7 (1930); 2–12 (1933), 1–4 (1934); 3–9 (1944), 1 (1945); translated as *Peter the Great*, by Edith Bone and Emile Burns, London, Gollancz, 1936; and as *Peter the First*, by Tatiana Shebunina, London, Lawrence and Wishart, 1956; New York, Macmillan, 1959.
Khleb. Moscow, 1937; translated as *Bread*, by S. Garry, London, Gollancz, 1938.
Russkie skazki. Moscow and Leningrad, 1940; translated as *Russian Tales for Children*, by Evgenia Shimanskaya, London, Routledge, 1944; New York, Dutton, 1947.
"Rodina", *Pravda* (7 November 1941); translated as *My Country*, by D.L. Fromberg, London, Hutchinson, 1943.
"Rasskazy Ivana Sudareva" [Stories of Ivan Sudarev], published, with the exception of the last story "Russkii kharakter" [The Russian Character], in *Povesti i rasskazy 1910–1943*, Moscow, 1944.
Russkie narodnye skazki v obrabotke A. Tolstogo [Russian Folktales, reworked by A. Tolstoi]. Moscow, 1944.

Poetry
Lirika [Lyrics]. 1907.
Za sinimi rekami [Beyond the Blue Rivers]. 1911.

Plays
Liubov' kniga zolotaia [Love. The Golden Book]. Berlin, 1922.
Zagovor imperatritsy [The Conspiracy of the Empress]. Leningrad, 1926.
"Chudesa v reshete" [Miracle in a Sieve], *30 dnei*, 12 (1926).
Na dybe: Istoricheskie p'esy [On the Rack: Historical Plays]. Moscow and Leningrad, 1929.
"Petr Pervyi" [Peter the First], *Molodaia gvardiia*, 3 (1938).
P'esy [Plays]. Moscow and Leningrad, 1940.
Ivan Groznyi [Ivan the Terrible]. Moscow, 1944.

Letters
Perepiska A.N. Tolstogo [The Correspondence of A.N. Tolstoi]. Moscow, 1989.

Critical Studies

Alexei Tolstoy: kritisch-biographische Skizze, by W. Stscherbina, Weimar, Buhlaus, 1954.
Tvorchestvo A.N. Tolstogo, by A.V. Alpatov, Moscow, 1956.
Istoricheskii roman A.N. Tolstogo "Petr Pervyi", by V.G. Beliaev, Kiev, 1956.
A.N. Tolstoi. Tvorcheskii put', by V. Shcherbina, Moscow, 1956.
Aleksei Tolstoi – master istoricheskogo romana, by A.V. Alpatov, Moscow, 1958.
A.N. Tolstoi. Zhizn' i tvorchestvo, by Iu.A. Krestinskii, Moscow, 1960.
Aleksei Tolstoi – khudozhnik, by L.M. Poliak, Moscow, 1964.
Soviet Russian Literature: Writers and Problems, 1917–67, by Marc Slonim, New York and Oxford, Oxford University Press, 1967; revised edition, 1977.
Trilogiia A.N. Tolstogo "Khozhdenie po mukam", by G.M. Smirnova, Leningrad, 1969.
Russian Literature under Lenin and Stalin, 1917–53, by Gleb Struve, London, Routledge, 1972.
Vospominaniia ob A.N. Tolstom, edited by Z.A. Nikitina and L.I. Tolstaia, Moscow, 1973; 1982.
Aleksei Tolstoi, by V. Petelin, Moscow, 1978.
The Images of Peter the Great in Russian Fiction, by Xenia Gasiorowska, Madison, University of Wisconsin Press, 1979.
Sud'ba khudozhnika: Ocherk zhizni i tvorchestva A.N. Tolstogo, by V.V. Petelin, Moscow, 1979.
A.N. Tolstoi – master istoricheskoi dramaturgii, by L.I. Zvereva, L'vov, 1982.
Poetika prozy A.N. Tolstogo, by E.G. Mushchenko, Voronezh, 1983.
Aleksei Tolstoi. Stranitsy zhizni i tvorchestva, by Sergei Borovikov, Moscow, 1984.
A.N. Tolstoi: Materialy i issledovaniia, edited by A.M. Kriukova, Moscow, 1985.
A.N. Tolstoi. Problemy tvorchestva. Mezhvuzovskii sbornik nauchnykh trudov, edited by I.E. Kharitonov, Voronezh, 1990.
Stil istoriiske proze A.N. Tolstoia, by Branimir Chovich, Novi Sad, Institut za strane jezike i književnosti Filozofskog fakulteta Univerziteta u Novom Sadu, 1991.
A.N. Tolstoi: Novye materialy i issledovaniia. Moscow, 1995.

Bibliography
"Aleksei Nikolaevich Tolstoi", in *Russkie sovetskie pisateli: Prozaiki. Bibliograficheskii ukazatel'*, 5 (1968), 27–190.

Straddling the pre-revolutionary and Soviet eras Aleksei Nikolaevich Tolstoi was a versatile, successful and prolific writer, the author of many stories, more than 40 plays and a number of major novels. Tolstoi grew up not knowing his real father, Nikolai Aleksandrovich Tolstoi, a member of the elite of Russian society and a titled landowner possessing a number of large estates in the Samara region. Even before Aleksei was born, his mother Aleksandra Leont'evna (née Turgeneva) had left her husband and three children, having fallen in love with the man who was to become Aleksei's stepfather, Aleksei Apollonovich Bostrom. Shortly after Aleksei's birth his mother moved to a farm in the steppe land some distance from Samara. Here Aleksei led a solitary childhood, receiving no formal education, other than from the occasional tutor, until the age of 13. From an early age he avidly read the classics of Russian literature.

After graduating from high school in 1901 Tolstoi went to St Petersburg where he later enrolled as a student in the Department of Mechanics. His first literary experiments revealed the strong influence of the Symbolist movement. *Za sinimi rekami* [Beyond the Blue Rivers] showed also his interest in Russian folklore and Slavonic myth. At the same time he was beginning to write prose tales with a more realistic slant, including one of his best early works, *Nedelia v Tureneve* (*A Week in Turenovo*), and a whole series of stories, *Soroch'i skazki* [Tales of a Magpie], recreating his childhood experiences. The two novels *Khromoi barin* [The Lame Prince] and *Chudaki* [The Eccentrics] brought this period of early reminiscences to a close.

During World War I Tolstoi served as a war correspondent and wrote a number of essays and stories reflecting his experiences. At the same time he wrote five plays, all of which were produced on the stage. Initially unable to accept the Bolshevik Revolution, Tolstoi moved with his family to Paris, where he wrote *Detstvo Nikity* (*Nikita's Childhood*), a lyrical and memorable story interweaving autobiographical elements with a realistic yet affectionate portrayal of life in a Russian village. Here, too, he embarked on the novel that was subsequently to become the first part of his trilogy, *Khozhdenie po mukam* (*Road to Calvary*), and which was not to be finally completed until 1941. In 1922, a deep sense of nostalgia for Russia, coupled with a change in his political beliefs, expressed particularly in his letter to the leader of the White émigré movement, N.V. Chaikovskii, led to his decision to return to his homeland.

After an initial uneasy period, during which he was treated with some suspicion because of his aristocratic origins, Tolstoi swiftly became established as a leading Soviet writer. Shortly after his return to Soviet Russia his science-fiction fantasy *Aelita*, which he had written while still in Berlin, was published. Unevenly written and somewhat didactic in tone, the novel tells the story of a Soviet expedition to Mars with the aim of establishing communism. Another novel written in the same vein, although with greater conviction, was *Giperboloid Inzhenera Garina* (*The Garin Death Ray*). During the mid to late 1920s Tolstoi wrote several other stories and a number of plays, including adaptations of works by Eugene O'Neill and Karel Čapek.

Although many of these works reflected, in one way or another, contemporary Soviet reality, Tolstoi's interest in Russia's history remained as strong as ever. In 1927 he returned to the depiction of his country's immediate past with work on the second volume of *Road to Calvary*. Three years later he began work on *Petr Pervyi* (*Peter the First*), a wide-ranging novel portraying the life of the tsar who ruled from 1696 to 1725 and who is regarded as the founder of modern Russia. By 1934 the first two parts of this work had been written, covering the years from 1682 to 1704, but Tolstoi died before he was able to complete the third part. The author himself claimed that the idea for *Peter the First* had arisen not because he intended it to be a foil to contemporary Soviet life, but because of his desire to convey the "unembellished creative forces that were inherent in the life of those times, when the Russian character revealed itself with particular vividness". This may be a little disingenuous, for it is difficult to believe that Tolstoi did not have Stalin in mind when creating the figure of Peter. Nevertheless, this richly imaginative and multifaceted novel fully deserves its reputation as one of the masterpieces of 20th-century Russian literature. Tolstoi portrays Peter as an idiosyncratic but immensely powerful and talented figure embodying Russia's creative forces and energies. Apart from Peter himself, the novel contains a whole galaxy of characters, portrayed, almost without exception, with vitality and conviction. The author is equally at ease depicting significant historical events, such as the founding and construction of the Russian navy in the shipyards of Voronezh and its emergence into the Black Sea, the start of the war with Sweden, the crushing defeat of the Russian army at Narva and the first Russian military victories; or, the complex inner life of his characters, a dimension that is particularly evident in the novel's second part. Although Tolstoi made extensive use of archival sources and memoirs while writing the novel, the work overall is as striking for its freshness and sense of immediacy as for its historical authenticity. The novel's qualities are even more remarkable when we take into account the fact that it is unfinished; Tolstoi saw the first two parts as forming only an exposition of themes that were to be taken up and fully developed in the final part.

Tolstoi's reputation in the west has undoubtedly suffered as a result of his espousal of the Bolshevik cause. The fact, however, that he was responsible for such crudely propagandist works as *Chernoe zoloto* [Black Gold], renamed *Emigranty* [The Émigrés], or *Khleb* (*Bread*), an unashamedly hagiographical account of Stalin's role in the Civil War, should not be allowed to overshadow the achievements of an extraordinarily gifted writer.

ROGER COCKRELL

Road to Calvary

Khozhdenie po mukam

Novel trilogy, 1920–42

Aleksei Tolstoi's *Road to Calvary* ("Tour of Hell" might arguably have been a more apt translation) is a trilogy of epic proportions covering the course of events in Russia's history from the eve of World War I to Bolshevik victory at the end of the Civil War. As yet uncommitted to Bolshevism, Tolstoi started work on what was subsequently to become the first part of the trilogy during his stay in Paris in 1919, completing it two years later. The novel was first published in the émigré journal *Sovremennye zapiski* (1–6, 1920–21) and as a separate edition in Berlin in 1922. On his return to Russia in 1923 he introduced a number of significant amendments to the text, with the first Soviet edition appearing in 1925. Some two years later Tolstoi set to work on another novel that was to form the second part of the trilogy, with the title *Vosemnadtsatyi god* (*The Year 1918*); this was to be published, together with the amended first part, in Leningrad in 1929. After a gap of ten years, during which Tolstoi was preoccupied with the writing of *Peter the First* and *Bread*, he began work on the final part of the trilogy, *Khmuroe utro* (*Bleak Morning*); this was completed on 22 June 1941, the very day Hitler's troops invaded Russia. The entire trilogy first appeared in 1943, with the first part renamed *Sestry* (*Sisters*), and the original title *Road to Calvary* being used for the opus as a whole.

Tolstoi himself defined the theme of his trilogy as that of his native land, which had been "lost and once again restored". This theme is reflected in the epigraph to *Sisters*, "Oh, Russian land! ...", a quotation from Russia's most famous medieval epic poem, *Slovo o polku Igoreve* (*The Lay of Igor's Campaign*). This epigraph establishes the trilogy's ideological focus and, with its more than faint echo of Pushkin's epigraph to chapter 2 of *Evgenii Onegin* ("O Rus'!"), Tolstoi's links with earlier Russian literature. Whereas, however, Pushkin's epigraph is punning (on Horace's "o rus") and ironic in tone, Tolstoi's reflects a deeply serious purpose: to convey through his novel his love for Russia and his admiration for its suffering people with their extraordinary resilience and ability to endure and to survive no matter how difficult and horrific the circumstances.

Road to Calvary is a traditional work, written in a realistic mode that remains largely impervious to modernism. At the centre of the novel lie four people and the relationships between them: two sisters, Dasha and Katia, and the two men, Telegin and Roshchin, with whom they fall in love. Artistically speaking, the first part, *Sisters*, covering the years up to the Bolshevik Revolution is by far the most successful. Tolstoi provides his readers with a portrayal of pre-revolutionary Russian society that combines a powerful indictment of the sterile politics and hypertrophic decadence of the upper classes and "liberal" thinkers of the time, with a sensitive and close understanding of those who are apparently irrevocably trapped in a way of life that holds out no hope for the future. This is most poignantly illustrated in the lives of the sisters: Dasha is unable to reconcile her deep and instinctive need for honesty, purity, and truth with her sexuality and the attraction, taking the form almost of an illness, which she feels for the decadent poet Bessonov, whom she despises; Katia, caught in a loveless marriage to a sententious barrister, one of whose literary antecedents is clearly Lev Tolstoi's Karenin, possesses everything that she could possibly need in a materialist sense but, as she herself admits, is living a life of no purpose and has become like a phantom in a mirage. When Katia leaves her husband to live in Paris, Dasha remains on the edge of the abyss, sustained only by her growing feeling for the uncomplicated and trustworthy Telegin, who represents all the qualities that she sees as lacking in the others around her.

All this is seen through the eyes of an omniscient narrator in a manner that holds out few surprises other than questions of plot. Characters and events, both large-scale and small-scale, are evenly illuminated, leaving no dead ground or mysterious, unexplained shadows. As a result the reader knows, for example, precisely what Dasha is feeling, what motivates Bessonov to act in a particular way, and whether or not the author intends the reader to approve of this or that character. This pattern is maintained in the other two parts of the trilogy, *The Year 1918* and *Bleak Morning*, with the author's voice remaining in careful control, even when events such as the description of the battle for Tsaritsyn (later to be renamed Stalingrad) during the Civil War are at their most confused.

Road to Calvary is, in its own way, a 20th-century *War and Peace*. Apart from the controlling voice of the author, the trilogy has many points in common with the earlier novel, including the interlocking of personal and domestic matters with traumatic historical events, and the manner in which relatively unimportant men and women can help to shape a nation's destiny. Although, however, there can be little doubt concerning the trilogy's many qualities and its significance and place in Russian literature, its overall impact is less than fully satisfying. For, as it proceeds, yet another theme, which hitherto has remained largely implicit, becomes more and more prominent: that of the moral superiority of the communists and of the inevitability of a Bolshevik victory. The balance between art and propaganda tilts firmly in favour of the latter, so that even the major characters, with whose destinies we have become so involved, take on a somewhat contrived and mechanical air. In the final analysis, however, we cannot be totally certain that Tolstoi actually believed in the Bolshevik ideas that are promoted in the last two parts of *Road to Calvary*. Perhaps the very fact that the pre-revolutionary world depicted in *Sisters* is artistically more convincing suggests a deeper ambivalence within an author who was himself shaped by its values.

ROGER COCKRELL

Peter the First

Petr Pervyi

Novel, 1929–45

Peter the First is a historical novel written from 1929 to 1945, with a screenplay appearing in 1935; in 1941 Tolstoi was awarded a Stalin Prize for this work.

The novel consists of two parts. Its action starts in the Russian provinces, at the home of the Brovkin family. Gloomy scenes depict the depth of Russia's social degeneration and the tyranny of a handful of noblemen. The first part shows the young Peter's life among the foreigners in Nemetskaia Sloboda, where he met several important persons (F. Lefort, the English merchant Hamilton who had left his native country because of Cromwell's dictatorship, Colonel Gordon, Mons, and others). He had to face many court intrigues and was a witness to the sharp contradictions between hostile political forces ending in the rebellion of riflemen (*strel'tsy*) who often organized palace revolutions. The riflemen were hanged, and the execution was so cruel that even brutal soldiers refused to participate. A country littered with corpses trembled. Then, in the March wind, vague silhouettes of merchant ships appeared off the Baltic coast. The second part of the novel describes the Great Northern War between Russia and Sweden, culminating in the siege and capture of Narva.

The idea of writing a novel of the life and times of Peter the Great arose at the end of the 1920s when Tolstoi had published the second volume of his trilogy *Road to Calvary*, describing the cruel fate of the Russian intelligentsia before World War I, during the two revolutions and the years of Civil War, and in the early post-revolutionary period. Russian readers were awaiting the third volume of the trilogy (which should have been called *Deviatnadsatyi god* [1919]), but he decided to start work on a short story going back to the years of Peter's reforms. Work on the novel was very complicated, not only because he was trying also to finish his trilogy, but because of the social order (*obshchestvennyi zakaz*) covering this kind of literature. At the end of the 1920s it was clear that the communist Revolution had won only in Russia. Stalin's model of political power differed from those of Lenin and Trotskii; it was largely based on the revival of national consciousness, going back to the nationalistic feeling of tsarist Russia. It was also necessary to unearth "useful" heroes from the past, so as to justify the violence associated with Stalin's policies of industrialization and collectivization. Tolstoi, with his aristocratic ancestry, his disillusioned sojourn in Berlin, and as an émigré author who had produced short stories dealing with Peter's time, was the appropriate figure to take up the subject. Later he met other political demands of the time and wrote *Ivan Groznyi* [Ivan the Terrible] (1942–43). Apart from a tendency towards historical prose, current in the 1930s (as in works by A. Novikov-Priboi, O. Forsh, and Iu. Tynianov), Tolstoi's interest in the historical novel was also occasioned by an interest in the eternal questions concerning Russia's history and its position between Europe and Asia. Tolstoi's own fate after the October Revolution provided a specific answer to the question widely asked by the Russian intelligentsia of that time: does the Bolshevik Revolution represent the betrayal of Russia's national interests, the destruction of the deep roots of Russian national life and thought ("the road to Calvary"), or is it a new national revival? The crucial problem of Russia's identity centres on Peter's personality and on the inner contradictions between the barbarous east and the utilitarian west. Many hints in the novel suggest that Peter's reign was a sort of experiment that started among the Moscow foreigners in Nemetskaia Sloboda and ended in the Battle of Poltava, which completely changed the political map of Europe. The experimental character of Russia's history, mentioned by the first modern Russian thinker Petr Chaadaev in the 1830s, is highlighted by the structure of the novel, presenting a peculiarly panoramic picture of Russia in all its complexity, from poor farmers to cruel noblemen (boyars) fighting with each other for power and glory.

In Tolstoi's earlier prose depicting Peter's reign, which appeared during the Russian Civil War, there is a concern with Dostoevskii's "damned questions" ("prokliatye voprosy") over the price to be paid for any revolution or *coup d'état*. Peter's severity reminded Tolstoi then of the cruelty and revolutionary radicalism of victorious Bolsheviks. Even later, in his drama *Na dybe* [On the Rack] (1929), Peter the Great is depicted as a contradictory figure. In *Peter the First* the Emperor of Russia emerges out of the blind and chaotic historical forces that had driven social disorder. Thus, *Peter the First* belongs to a cluster of unfinished Russian prose works that depict the eternal and insoluble questions raised by Lev Tolstoi in *War and Peace*, Dostoevskii in *The Brothers Karamazov*, Gor'kii in *Zhizn' Klima Samgina* (*The Life of Klim Samgin*), Bulgakov in *The Master and Margarita* and Pasternak in *Doctor Zhivago*.

Peter the First represents an original synthesis in Tolstoi's novelistic technique. His novels, including *Peter the First*, usually disintegrated into a number of autonomous spatio-temporal entities. This time Tolstoi tried to overcome this problem by presenting a panoramic vision of reality. The polyphonic structure of the novel evokes Peter's personality from different, often contradictory angles. Consequently, narrative style is the most important factor. The author evoked the historical atmosphere by utilizing moderate archaisms with the narrator standing as an impersonal spokesman for public opinion. The dominant features of Tolstoi's style are the accumulation of artistic detail, the use of monologue, dialogue, and scenes of local colour. Fragments of the text are sometimes borrowed from historical sources and documents, including texts from old Russian literature (*The Life of Avvakum*). From this point of view, *Peter the First* is a complex intertext consisting of linguistic and stylistic borrowings that nevertheless form a diversified unity.

Tolstoi's approach to historical facts, however, was a realistic one, based on a detailed depiction of social life. He is said to have visited the Hermitage just to see the form of the buttons on Peter's uniform and to smell the air of the past. In this sense, Tolstoi's craft of fiction, tending towards a presentation of universal meaning through the detailed depiction of reality, belongs to the 19th-century tradition, and is comparable to Lev Tolstoi's *War and Peace* and Gustave Flaubert's *Salammbô*.

IVO POSPÍŠIL

Lev Nikolaevich Tolstoi 1828–1910

Prose writer, dramatist, essayist, and religious writer

Biography

Born in Iasnaia Poliana, near Tula, 9 September 1828, the fourth of five children. Educated by private tutors; attended Kazan University first in the Faculty of Eastern Languages, then Faculty of Law, 1844–47: did not graduate; studied law for a brief period at St Petersburg University, 1849. Travelled to the Caucasus with his brother Nikolai, 1851. Served in the Russian Army, 1852–56: saw action in Caucasus where he was nearly killed by grenade, 1852, and at Sebastopol: retired as lieutenant. Began to publish, 1852. Participated in St Petersburg intellectual life, 1855–59. First serious romance, with V.V. Arsen'eva, 1856. Travelled to western Europe twice, 1857, 1860–61. Torrid affair with Aksinia Bazykina, one of the peasants on his estate, 1858: possibly continued to marriage, at least one child. Established a school at Iasnaia Poliana for the children of his serfs, 1859–62. Beloved eldest brother Nikolai died, 1860. Married: Sof'ia [Sonia] Andreevna Behrs (1844–1919) in 1862; 13 children (nine survived to adulthood). Lived continuously at Iasnaia Poliana throughout 1860s and 1870s, with occasional summer trips to Samara from 1871. Re-opened school at Iasnaia Poliana, 1872. Wrote and compiled materials for a complete elementary education course: published it as the primer *Azbuka*, 1872, revised and reissued as *Novaia azbuka*, 1875 (ran to 28 editions in his lifetime). Petitioned the new tsar asking him to pardon the assassins of Alexander II; took up winter residence, Moscow, 1881. Took part in Moscow census, 1882. Met V.G. Chertkov, subsequently his closest disciple, 1883. First attempt to leave home, 1884. Founded popular press, "Posrednik" (Intermediary), 1885. After unsuccessful attempts, finally gave up meat, alcohol, and tobacco, 1888. In 1892 he renounced his copyright on works published after 1881. Famine relief in Riazan Province, 1891–93. Published novel *Voskresenie* (*Resurrection*) to raise money for Dukhobors, 1899. International Tolstoi Society founded, 1900. Excommunicated from the Orthodox Church, 1901; serious illness and recuperation in Crimea, 1901. Left home, 1910. Died at Astapovo railway station, 7 November 1910. Buried at Iasnaia Poliana, 20 November 1910.

Publications

Collected Editions

Polnoe sobranie sochinenii, 90 vols. Moscow and Leningrad, 1928–58.

The Centenary Edition of Tolstoy, 21 vols, translated by Louise and Aylmer Maude. Tolstoy Society for Oxford University Press, London, Charles Milford, 1928–37.

Sobranie sochinenii, 20 vols. Moscow, 1960–65.

Leo Tolstoy: The Death of Ivan Ilych and Other Stories, translated by Aylmer Maude. New York, Signet, 1960.

The Cossacks, Happy Ever After, The Death of Ivan Ilyich, translated by Rosemary Edmonds, Harmondsworth, Penguin, 1960.

Leo Tolstoy: Short Stories, 2 vols, edited by Ernest Simmons, translated by Aylmer and Louise Maude *et al.* New York, Random House, 1964.

Short Novels: Stories of Love, Seduction and Peasant Life, 2 vols, edited by Ernest Simmons, translated by Aylmer and Louise Maude *et al.* New York, Random House, 1965.

Great Short Works of Leo Tolstoy, with an introduction by John Bayley, translated by Aylmer and Louise Maude *et al.* New York, Harper and Row, 1967.

Master and Man and Other Stories, translated by Paul Foote. Harmondsworth and New York, Penguin, 1977.

The Portable Tolstoy, edited by John Bayley, translated by Aylmer Maude and George L. Kline. New York, Viking Press, and Harmondsworth, Penguin, 1978.

The Raid and Other Stories, edited by P.N. Furbank, translated by Louise and Aylmer Maude. Oxford, Oxford University Press, 1982.

A Prisoner in the Caucasus and Other Stories, translated by Yu. Zelenkov. Moscow, Raduga, 1983.

The Kreutzer Sonata and Other Stories, translated by David McDuff. Harmondsworth and New York, Penguin, 1985.

Father Sergius and Other Stories [various translators]. Moscow, Raduga, 1988.

The Death of Ivan Ilych and Other Stories, translated by Rosemary Edmonds, Harmondsworth, Penguin, 1989.

Tolstoy's Short Fiction: Revised Translations, Background and Sources; Criticism, edited by Michael R. Katz. New York, Norton, 1991.

How Much Land Does a Man Need? and Other Stories, with an introduction by A.N. Wilson, translated by Ronald Wilks. Harmondsworth and New York, Penguin, 1993.

Tolstoy: Plays, 2 vols (vol. 1, 1856–1886; vol. 2, 1886–1889), translated by Marvin Kantor with Tanya Tulchinsky. Evanston, Illinois, Northwestern University Press, 1994–96.

Fiction

"Detstvo", as "Istoriia moego detstva", *Sovremennik*, 9 (1852), 5–104; translated as "Childhood", in *Childhood, Boyhood, Youth*, translated by Rosemary Edmonds, Harmondsworth, Penguin, 1964.

"Nabeg", *Sovremennik*, 3 (1853); translated as "The Raid".

"Otrochestvo", *Sovremennik*, 9 (1854), 81–146; translated as "Boyhood", in *Childhood, Boyhood, Youth*, translated by Rosemary Edmonds, Harmondsworth, Penguin, 1964.

"Sevastopol'skie rasskazy", *Sovremnnik*, 6/9 (1855), 1 (1856); translated as *The Sebastopol Sketches*, by David McDuff, Harmondsworth, Penguin, 1985.

"Utro pomeshchika", *Otechestvennye zapiski*, 12 (1856); translated as "A Landowner's Morning".

"Iunost'", *Sovremennik*, 1 (1857), 13–163; translated as "Youth", in *Childhood, Boyhood, Youth*, translated by Rosemary Edmonds, Harmondsworth, Penguin, 1964.

"Semeinoe schast'e", *Russkii vestnik*, 7/8 (1859); translated as "Family Happiness"; also as "Happy Ever After".

"Kazaki", *Russkii vestnik*, 1 (1863); translated as "The Cossacks".

Voina i mir, in *Russkii vestnik* (1865–66) and (1868–69); translated as *War and Peace*, by Rosemary Edmonds, Harmondsworth and New York, Penguin, 1957; also translated by Louise and Aylmer Maude, edited by George Gibian, New York, Norton, 1966; also by Louise and Aylmer Maude, edited by Henry Gifford, Oxford, Oxford University Press, 1991.

Anna Karenina, in *Russki vestnik* (1875–77); translated as *Anna Karenin*, by Rosemary Edmonds, Harmondsworth, Penguin, 1954; also translated as *Anna Karenina*, by Louise and Aylmer Maude, edited by George Gibian, New York, Norton, 1970; also by Louise and Aylmer Maude, edited by John Bayley, Oxford, Oxford University Press, 1980.

"Smert' Ivana Il'icha", in *Sochineniia grafa L. N. Tolstogo*, vol. 12, Moscow, 1886; translated as "The Death of Ivan Ilych".

Mnogo li cheloveku zemli nuzhno, L. N. Tolstoy. Tri skazki, Moscow, 1886; translated as "How Much Land Does a Man Need?".

"Kreitserova sonata", in *Sochineniia L.N. Tolstogo*, vol. 13, Moscow, 1890; translated as "The Kreutzer Sonata".

"Khoziain i rabotnik", *Severnyi vestnik*, 3 (1895); translated as "Master and Man".

Voskresenie, 1899; translated as *Resurrection*, by Rosemary Edmonds, Harmondsworth and New York, Penguin, 1966; also translated by Louise Maude, edited by Richard F. Gustafson, Oxford, Oxford University Press, 1993.

"D'iavol", in *Posmertnye khudozhestvennye proizvedeniia L. N. Tolstogo*, vol. 1, Moscow, 1911; translated as "The Devil".

"Otets Sergei", in *Posmertnye khudozhestvennye proizvedeniia L. N. Tolstogo*, vol. 2, Moscow, 1911; translated as "Father Sergius".

"Posle bala", in *Posmertnye khudozhestvennye proizvedeniia L. N. Tolstogo*, vol. 1, Moscow, 1911; translated as "After the Ball".

"Khadzhi-murat", in *Posmertnye khudozhestvennye proizvedeniia L. N. Tolstogo*, vol. 3, Moscow, 1912; translated as "Hadji Murad"; "Hadj Murat".

Plays

Pervyi vinokur, ili kak chertenok kraiushku zasluzhil, Moscow, 1886; translated as "The First Distiller", by Louise and Aylmer Maude, in *The Centenary Edition of Tolstoy*, 1928–37, vol. 17.

Vlast' t'my, ili korotok uviaz, vsei ptichke propast' (produced Paris, 1888); translated as "The Power of Darkness", by Louise and Aylmer Maude, in *The Centenary Edition of Tolstoy*, 1928–37, vol. 17.

"Plody prosveshcheniia", in *V pamiat' S. A. Iureva. Sbornik, izdannyi druzi'ami pokoinogo*, Moscow, 1891; translated as

The Fruits of Enlightenment, by Michael Frayne, London, Eyre Methuen, 1979.

"Zhivoi trup" (unfinished), written 1900, published posthumously, *Russkoe slovo*, 23 September 1911; translated as "The Live Corpse", by Louise and Aylmer Maude, in *The Centenary Edition of Tolstoy*, 1928–37, vol. 17.

Letters, Memoirs, and Diaries

Recollections and Essays, translated by Louise and Aylmer Maude (vol. 21 of *The Centenary Edition of Tolstoy*). London, Oxford University Press, 1961.

Tolstoy's Letters, 2 vols, edited and translated by R.F. Christian. London, Athlone Press, and New York, Scribner, 1978.

Tolstoy's Diaries, edited and translated by R.F. Christian. London, Athlone Press, and New York, Scribner, 1985.

Essays

Azbuka [The Alphabet]. St Petersburg, 1872; revised as *Novaia azbuka i russkie knigi dlia chteniia* [The New Alphabet and Russian Books for Reading]. 1875.

"Chem liudi zhivy", *Detskii otdykh*, 12 (1885); translated as "What Men Live By".

Chto takoe iskusstvo? 1897; translated as "What is Art?", by Aylmer Maude, in *Tolstoy on Art*, New York, Haskell House, 1973; edited by W. Gareth Jones, London, Bristol Classical Press, 1994; also by Richard Pevear and Larissa Volkhonsky, Harmondsworth, Penguin, 1995.

Ne mogu molchat'. 1908; translated as "I Cannot Be Silent", in *I Cannot Be Silent: Selected Non-Fiction*, edited by W. Gareth Jones, Bristol, Bristol Classical Press, 1989.

Why Do Men Stupefy Themselves? and Other Writings, translated by Aylmer Maude, Hankins, New York, Strength Books, 1975.

Tolstoy on Education: Tolstoy's Educational Writings, 1861–1862, edited by Alan Pinch and Michael Armstrong. Rutherford, New Jersey, Fairleigh Dickinson University Press, and London, Athlone Press, 1982.

Writings on Civil Disobedience and Non Violence, translated by Aylmer Maude and Ronald Sampson. Philadelphia, New Society, 1988.

Religious Writing

Ispoved'. 1879–81; translated as "A Confession", by Jane Kentish, in *A Confession and Other Religious Writings*, Harmondsworth and New York, Penguin, 1987; also by Aylmer Maude, in *Fyodor Dostoyevsky, "Notes from Underground"/Lev Tolstoy, "A Confession"*, edited by A.D.P. Briggs, London, Everyman, 1994.

The Lion and the Honeycomb: The Religious Writings of Tolstoy, edited and with an introduction by A.N. Wilson, translated by Robert Chandler. London, Collins, and San Francisco, Harper and Row, 1987.

The Gospel According to Tolstoy, edited and translated by David Patterson. Tuscaloosa, University of Alabama Press, 1992.

Biographical Materials

Lev Nikolaevich Tolstoi: Materialy k biografii s 1828 po 1855 god, by N.N. Gusev, Moscow, 1954.

Lev Nikolaevich Tolstoi: Materialy k biografii s 1855 po 1869 god, by N.N. Gusev, Moscow, 1957.

Letopis' zhizni i tvorchestva L'va Nikolaevicha Tolstogo, 1828–1890, by N.N. Gusev, Moscow, 1958.

Letopis' zhizni i tvorchestva L'va Nikolaevicha Tolstogo, 1890–1910, by N.N. Gusev, Moscow, 1960.

Lev Nikolaevich Tolstoi: Materialy k biografii s 1870 po 1881 god, by N.N. Gusev, Moscow, 1963.

Lev Nikolaevich Tolstoi: Materialy k biografii s 1886 po 1892 god, by L.D. Opul'skaia, Moscow, 1979.

Critical Studies

Tolstoi as Man and Artist with an Essay on Dostoievski, by Dmitri Merejkowski [D.S. Merezhkovskii], London, Constable, 1902; reprinted, Westport, Connecticut, Greenwood Press, 1970.

The Life of Tolstoy, by Aylmer Maude, 2 vols, London, Constable, 1908–10; reprinted Oxford, Oxford University Press, 1987.

Analiz, stil', i veianie: o romanakh gr. L.N. Tolstogo, by K. Leontev, 1912; reprinted, with a foreword by Donald Fanger, Providence, Rhode Island, Brown University Press, 1965.

Reminiscences of Tolstoy, Chekhov, and Andreyev, by Maxim Gorky, translated by Katherine Mansfield, S.S. Koteliansky, and Leonard Woolf, London, Hogarth Press, 1934; New York, Viking Press, 1959.

Leo Tolstoy, by E.J. Simmons, Boston, Little Brown, 1946; reprinted New York, Vintage, 1960.

The Hedgehog and the Fox: An Essay on Tolstoy's View of History, by Isaiah Berlin, London, Weidenfeld and Nicolson, and New York, Simon and Schuster, 1953; reprinted in his *Russian Thinkers*, Harmondsworth, Penguin, 1979.

Tolstoy and Shakespeare, by George Gibian, The Hague, Mouton, 1957.

Tolstoy or Dostoevsky: An Essay in the Old Criticism, by George Steiner, New York, Knopf, 1959; London, Faber, 1960; Harmondsworth, Penguin, 1967; Chicago, University of Chicago Press, 1985.

Tolstoy's "War and Peace": A Study, by R.F. Christian, Oxford, Clarendon Press, 1962.

Tolstoy Between War and Peace, by Waclaw Lednicki, The Hague, Mouton, 1965.

Tolstoy and the Novel, by John Bayley, New York, Viking Press, and London, Chatto and Windus, 1966; Chicago, University of Chicago Press, 1988.

Tolstoy: A Collection of Critical Essays, edited by Ralph Matlaw, Englewood Cliffs, New Jersey, Prentice-Hall, 1967.

Tolstoy, by Henri Troyat, translated by Nancy Amphoux, New York, Doubleday, 1967; Harmondsworth, Penguin, 1970.

Tolstoy: A Critical Introduction, by R.F. Christian, Cambridge, Cambridge University Press, 1969.

Leo Tolstoy: A Critical Anthology, by Henry Gifford, Harmondsworth, Penguin, 1971.

The Young Tolstoi, by Boris Eikhenbaum, translated and edited by Gary Kern, Ann Arbor, Ardis, 1972.

Women in Tolstoy: The Ideal and the Erotic, by Ruth Crego Benson, Urbana, University of Illinois Press, 1973.

Tolstoy: The Making of a Novelist, by Edward Crankshaw, New York, Viking Press, and London, Weidenfeld and Nicolson, 1974.

The Architecture of "Anna Karenina": A History of Its Writing, Structure, Message, by Elisabeth Stenbock-Fermor, Lisse, Peter de Ridder Press, 1975.
Tolstoy: The Comprehensive Vision, by E.B. Greenwood, London, Dent, and New York, St Martin's Press, 1975.
Tolstoy, by T.G.S. Cain, London, Paul Elek, and New York, Barnes and Noble, 1977.
New Essays on Tolstoy, edited by Malcolm Jones (with a bibliographical survey of Tolstoy studies in Great Britain by Garth M. Terry), Cambridge, Cambridge University Press, 1978.
Tolstoy: The Critical Heritage, edited by A.V. Knowles, London, Routledge and Kegan Paul, 1978.
Lev Tolstoy, by Victor Shklovsky, Moscow, Progress, 1978.
Tolstoy's Major Fiction, by Edward Wasiolek, Chicago, University of Chicago Press, 1978.
A Guide to the Russian Texts of Tolstoy's "War and Peace", by Edgar H. Lehrman, Ann Arbor, Ardis, 1979.
Tolstoy in Prerevolutionary Russian Criticism, by Boris Sorokin, Columbus, Ohio State University Press, 1979.
Tolstoi in the Sixties, by Boris Eikhenbaum, translated by Duffield White, Ann Arbor, Ardis, 1982.
Tolstoi in the Seventies, by Boris Eikhenbaum, translated by Albert Kaspin, Ann Arbor, Ardis, 1982.
Tolstoy, by Henry Gifford, Oxford, Oxford University Press, 1982.
The Structure of Anna Karenina, by Sydney Schultze, Ann Arbor, Ardis, 1982.
Tolstoy and the Russians: Reflections on a Relationship, by Alexander Fodor, Ann Arbor, Ardis, 1984.
The Diaries of Sophia Tolstoy, edited by O.A. Golinenko, translated by Cathy Porter, New York, Random House, 1985.
Leo Tolstoy: Modern Critical Views, edited by Harold Bloom, New York, Chelsea House, 1986.
Leo Tolstoy: Resident and Stranger; A Study in Fiction and Theology, by Richard F. Gustafson, Princeton, Princeton University Press, 1986.
Leo Tolstoy, by William W. Rowe, Boston, Twayne, 1986.
Critical Essays on Tolstoy, edited by Edward Wasiolek, Boston, G.K. Hall, 1986.
Leo Tolstoy's "Anna Karenina", edited by Harold Bloom, New York, Chelsea House, 1987.
Hidden in Plain View: Narrative and Creative Potentials in "War and Peace", by Gary Saul Morson, Stanford, Stanford University Press, 1987.
Leo Tolstoy: Anna Karenina, by Anthony Thorlby, Cambridge, Cambridge University Press, 1987.
The Unsaid Anna Karenina, by Judith Armstrong, London, Macmillan, and New York, St Martin's Press, 1988.
Leo Tolstoy's "War and Peace", edited by Harold Bloom, New York, Chelsea House, 1988.
Tolstoy, by A.N. Wilson, London, Hamish Hamilton, 1988; New York, Ballantine, 1989.
Reflecting on Anna Karenina, by Mary Evans, London, Routledge, 1989.
In the Shade of the Giant: Essays on Tolstoy, edited by Hugh McLean, Berkeley, University of California Press, 1989.
Anna Karenina: The Bitterness of Ecstasy, by Gary Adelman, Boston, Twayne, 1990.
The Influence of Tolstoy on Readers of His Work, by Gareth Williams, Lewiston, New York, and Lampeter, Wales, Edwin Mellen Press, 1990.
On Psychological Prose, by Lidiia Ginzburg, edited and translated by Judson Rosengrant, Princeton, Princeton University Press, 1991.
Tolstoy's Aesthetics and His Art, by Rimvydas Silbajoris, Columbus, Ohio, Slavica, 1991.
Zhivaia zhizn': O Dostoevskom i L've Tolstom, Apollon i Dionis (o Nitsshe), by V.V. Veresaev, Moscow, 1991.
The Death of Ivan Ilich: An Interpretation, by Gary R. Jahn, New York, Twayne, 1993.
Tolstoy's Art and Thought, 1847–1880, by Donna Tussing Orwin, Princeton, Princeton University Press, 1993.
A Psychological Study of Tolstoy's "Anna Karenina", by Anthony Piraino, San Francisco, EmText, 1993.
Tolstoy's Pierre Bezukhov: A Psychoanalytical Study, by Daniel Rancour-Laferrière, London, Bristol Classical Press, 1993.
Framing "Anna Karenina": Tolstoy, the Woman Question and the Victorian Novel, by Amy Mandelker, Columbus, Ohio State University Press, 1994.
Anna Karenina Companion, by C.J.G. Turner, Waterloo, Ontario, Wilfred Laurier University Press, 1994.
"War and Peace": Tolstoy's Mirror of the World, by Rimvydas Silbajoris, New York, Twayne, 1995.
Tolstoy's "Childhood", by Gareth Williams, London, Bristol Classical Press, 1995.
L.N. Tolstoy and D.H. Lawrence, by Dorthe G.A. Engelhardt, Frankfurt and New York, Peter Lang, 1996.
Tolstoy and the Genesis of "War and Peace", by Kathryn B. Feuer, edited by Robin Feuer Miller and Donna Tussing Orwin, Ithaca, Cornell University Press, 1996.
The Presentation of Death in Tolstoy's Prose, by Josef Metzele, Frankfurt and New York, Peter Lang, 1996.
Tolstoy, by John Bayley, Plymouth, Northcote House, 1997.
Tolstoy, Woman and Death: A Study of "War and Peace" and "Anna Karenina", by David Holbrook, Madison, New Jersey, Fairleigh Dickinson University Press, 1997.

Bibliographies

Bibliografiia literatury o L.N. Tolstom, 1917–1958, edited by N.G. Sheliapina *et al.*, Moscow, 1960.
Khudozhestvennye proizvedeniia L.N. Tolstogo v perevodakh na innostrannye iazyki, edited by T.I. Motyleva *et al.*, Moscow, 1961.
Bibliografiia literatury o L.N. Tolstom, 1959–1961, edited by N.G. Sheliapina *et al.*, Moscow, 1965.
Bibliografiia literatury o L.N. Tolstom, 1962–1967, edited by N.G. Sheliapina *et al.*, Moscow, 1972.
Bibliografiia literatury o L.N. Tolstom, 1968–1973, edited by N.G. Sheliapina *et al.*, Moscow, 1978.
Leo Tolstoy: An Annotated Bibliography of English Language Sources to 1978, edited by David R. Egan and Melinda A. Egan, Metuchen, New Jersey, Scarecrow Press, 1979.
Bibliografiia literatury o L.N. Tolstom, 1974–1978, edited by N.G. Sheliapina *et al.*, Moscow, 1990.

Count Lev Nikolaevich Tolstoi was one of the greatest of all novelists. An aristocrat, proud and patriotic, he grew up under the stifling regime of Nicholas I. He came to manhood in the

1840s and 1850s, just as Russians were struggling to define themselves as a modern people, and his works contributed to that project of national identity.

The "Russian soul" that Tolstoi helped create was, paradoxically and significantly, a product of self-analysis. Tolstoi's fiction grew originally out of his diaries, in which he tried to understand his own feelings and actions so as to control them. This focus on psychological minutiae made Tolstoi's writing open-ended, with a tendency toward big forms in order to accommodate detail. It also kept him honest: he had always to check moral conclusions against the facts of his own inner life.

As an artist, the young Tolstoi may be said to have had two goals: to recreate reality and to order it according to higher moral truth. He believed that truth resides in individual experience, and hence that what he learned from himself could be applied to humankind in general. This premise underlies all his early writing, including his first great work, the trilogy *Detstvo, Otrochestvo, Iunost'* (*Childhood, Boyhood, Youth*), in which he attempted to recapitulate the first three stages of life. The fourth stage is described in the other masterpiece of Tolstoi's youth, *Kazaki* (*The Cossacks*), which was originally entitled "Molodost'" [Young Manhood]. This work sets the stage for *Voina i mir* (*War and Peace*) by systematically exploring the relation between man and nature. In the 1850s, Tolstoi also wrote a series of stories based on his military experience. (These, along with *Childhood* and *Boyhood*, made his early reputation). Drawing on his own addiction, he wrote a short study of gambling called "Zapiski markera" ("Notes of a Billiard Marker"). He published "Utro pomeshchika" ("A Landowner's Morning"): a fragment of a never-completed self-described didactic novel that fictionalizes his own unsuccessful attempt to help his serfs. He borrowed from his romance with V.V. Arsen'eva to create *Semeinoe schast'e* (*Family Happiness*), his first in-depth investigation of feminine psychology. He wrote an interesting if unsuccessful work, "Albert", on the psychology of the artist; and "Dva gusara" ("Two Hussars"), his only published attempt (before *War and Peace*) at a historical narrative. (The other was "Dekabristy" ("The Decembrists"), an unfinished novel published only in 1884). In "Metel'" ("The Snowstorm"), also based on a personal experience, he explored the effect of natural necessity (the storm) on psychic life. His first trip abroad yielded "Liutsern" ("Lucerne"), a lyrical tirade attacking (English) civilization and arguing for the morality of nature.

The young Tolstoi read copiously, both in literature and philosophy. In the Caucasus he read Plato and Rousseau (the latter for the second time), Dickens and Sterne; through the 1850s he also read and admired Goethe, Stendhal, Thackeray, and George Eliot; and of course he knew and learned from his Russian predecessors and contemporaries. He worked on a style that would place the reader within a scene or character by appealing to the reader's own sense, perceptions, and memories. He also developed an impersonal authoritative narrative voice to structure his vivid realism, a voice first heard thundering in the *Sevastopol'skie rasskazy* (*The Sebastopol Sketches*). Returning in 1855 directly from the Sebastopol front to St Petersburg, Tolstoi made the acquaintance of a group of friends who introduced him to the philosophical debates of the 1840s and involved him in the clash between an older German idealism and the newer materialist generation headed by N.G. Chernyshevskii. Under the influence of these debates the uniquely Tolstoian blend of realism and idealism continued to take shape. The writer of "Lucerne" also penned "Tri smerti" ("Three Deaths") and "Polikushka", which seemed unbearably naturalistic to contemporaries.

In the late 1850s Tolstoi withdrew from life in the capital and founded a school at his estate at Iasnaia Poliana. He married in 1862, and the first years of his marriage were the happiest of his life. He wrote his most ambitious work, *War and Peace*, in which he successfully united the principles of happiness and virtue in the person of Pierre Bezukhov. *Anna Karenina*, written in the 1870s, marked the beginnings of a fatal split between virtue and happiness that led to the spiritual crisis depicted in *Ispoved'* (*A Confession*) in the early 1880s. If *War and Peace* had been written in the spirit of Rousseau and Goethe, *Anna Karenina* reflected a more modern and Dostoevskian mix of Schopenhauer and Kant.

In the second half of Tolstoi's life, beginning in the early 1880s, he saw himself more as a sage and moral leader than an artist. He turned against his class and the ideal of family life that he had inculcated in his young wife (who by then had borne him ten children). He used his immense prestige as a writer to champion various causes, and most of his artistic works from this 30-year period are written in their service. He believed that the way to establish the Kingdom of God on earth was through individual moral reform. His teachings influenced Gandhi in India, and the kibbutz movement in Palestine, and in Russia his moral authority rivalled that of the tsar.

The early Tolstoi believed that natural reality itself was good and moral, and needed only to be fully expressed in art. The later Tolstoi believed less in natural goodness and used art to convey a moral lesson from his narrator. His most typical later art was, therefore, more naturalistic and more moralistic at the same time. On one end of the spectrum of these later didactic works, there are realistic stories with clear-cut morals like "Fal'shivyi kupon" ("The False Coupon"), and on the other, there are modern parables like "Assiriiskii tsar' Asarkadon" ("Esarhaddon") and "Razrushenie ada i vosstanovlenie ego" ("The Restoration of Hell") that display elements of Bunyanesque allegory or the medieval morality play, illustrating moral points.

In his fascinating treatise, *Chto takoe iskusstvo?* (*What is Art?*), the later Tolstoi tried to specify the role of art in ethics. Without denying what he now regarded as art's essential amorality, he defined it as a conveyor of feelings, good and bad, from the artist to others. Through feeling, the artist "infects" another with the desire to act well or badly. Of all his previous works, Tolstoi singled out only two short stories, "Kavkazskii plennik" ("A Prisoner in the Caucasus") and "Bog pravdu vidit, da ne skoro skazhet" ("God Sees the Truth but Waits"), as "good" art. These two stories, composed in a new terse style derived from Homer, the Russian chronicles, and Pushkin, are the first and among the best of a series of works that Tolstoi wrote for the people. *Vlast' t'my* (*The Power of Darkness*), the best of Tolstoi's few plays, was also written for peasants, to dramatize the forces of evil in their lives.

Although Tolstoi rejected his own earlier prose as elitist, he did in fact write a number of long psychological studies. His first such work after 1880 was *Smert' Ivana Il'icha* (*The Death of Ivan Ilych*), about the death-denying hypocrisy of the upper classes. He attacked sex and pride in *Kreitserova sonata* (*The Kreutzer

Sonata) and *Otets Sergei* (*Father Sergius*). "Kholstomer" ("Strider"), narrated by a gelding, exposes the unnaturalness of ownership, and denouces passion, especially sexual passion.

Tolstoi's artistically successful later works reflect his moral concerns but achieve a satisfying complexity that makes them perhaps the greatest art generated by the 19th-century "Victorian" obsession with duty. This is true to a surprising extent of most of the works already mentioned and most definitely of the three masterpieces of Tolstoi's old age. Of these, *Khoziain i rabotnik* (*Master and Man*), the artistic work in which he best succeeded in expressing his later positive vision, ends with a blending in death of self-sacrifice and happiness; while in the novel *Voskresenie* (*Resurrection*), a powerful, indeed revolutionary indictment of the old regime, his hero Nekhliudov learns that duty, not personal happiness, is the goal of life. The final work, *Khadzhi-murat* (*Hadji Murad*), is an elegiac reprise of the dominant themes of Tolstoi's life and art. Its hero, a noble savage, passes between civilized and savage life and tries to juggle his natural desire for happiness and his sense of duty. Laconic in style, the work is constructed from short vivid chapters each comprising a snapshot of some part of Hadji Murad's world or character. Framing these chapters, which aspire to a Homeric objectivity, is a lyrical narrative structure in which Tolstoi describes himself as an old man, who, having seen a mangled thistle in a ploughed field, creates the tale of Hadji Murad out of memory and imagination. The narrative structure puts Hadji Murad in his place, explaining his flaws through the rational consciousness of the narrator. But at the same time Hadji Murad is a tragic hero, whose quest for glory does not diminish his stature.

DONNA TUSSING ORWIN

Childhood, Boyhood, Youth

Detstvo, Otrochestvo, Iunost'

Prose works, 1852–57

In 1852 the famous St Petersburg literary journal *Sovremennik* published under the initials L.N. a short prose work entitled *Childhood*. This lyrical, almost completely plotless, first-person narrative was the debut work of a 24-year-old army officer by the name of Lev Nikolaevich Tolstoi. Although it was initially conceived as the first part of a tetralogy, only *Boyhood* (1854) and *Youth* (1857), were eventually finished.

Taken together, the trilogy describes the coming of age and examines the emotional world of a young gentry boy: Nikolai Irten'ev. Irten'ev is, to a certain extent, an autobiographical character, but Tolstoi went to great lengths to avoid an overly close relationship with his main character. Indeed, in the final version, autobiographical and novelistic impulses are held in delicate equipoise: on the one hand, the narrative is particular and individualized; the autobiographer Irten'ev recounts experiences that relate to him and to him alone. On the other, the lyrical tone that pervades the whole, coupled with the fact that Irten'ev is a fictional creation, lend it a feeling of generality: it seems as if Irten'ev's childhood could have belonged to anyone.

Childhood begins on the narrator's tenth birthday and describes, through a series of flashbacks, three central days in his life. We meet the major influences in the child's existence – father, mother, tutor, nurse, and the rural world of the Russian estate – and the book ends with the traumatic death of Irten'ev's mother. The over-arching message in *Childhood* is that childhood is an idyllic period; the child is still curious, innocent, and unaware of adult problems. This does not exclude the possibility of unhappy moments, of course, but the overall impression of childhood is – and Tolstoi implies should be – one of joyous innocence. The narrator's nostalgic desire and his ability to summon up a past, happy world, coupled with the realization that the world thus recreated is only an illusion, lies at the very core of *Childhood*.

The periods of boyhood and youth, by contrast, are far less idyllic. After the death of his mother, Irten'ev moves to Moscow, and it is here that he slowly loses his youthful innocence. The young Irten'ev interacts with the world outside his family, attends school, makes friends, experiences his first serious sexual awakenings, and begins to doubt in the goodness of the world around him. Eventually, Irten'ev is, at least externally, thoroughly corrupted both by his own weakness and by that of the world around him. That this loss of childhood innocence is inevitable does not make it any less bitter, and although the adult narrator Irten'ev can still point to happy times in *Boyhood* and *Youth*, the tone of these two volumes is bitter compared to that of *Childhood*. Nevertheless, Irten'ev never entirely loses the desire to be good that characterized him from his childhood, and the trilogy ends on an optimistic note as he struggles to find his moral center.

Formally, the trilogy is the first Russian example of a narrative type that combines the immediacy of autobiography with the creative freedom of the novel: the pseudo-autobiography. The pseudo-autobiography is an autobiographically-based work that imitates the autobiography in all respects but one: its author and narrator are not the same person. For both author and reader the lack of identity between author and narrator means that the work is to be treated as fiction, read and judged by a set of criteria different from those applied to non-fiction.

The pseudo-autobiography, which Tolstoi adapted from European models, allows for a complex interplay of narrative voices. The first voice here is that of the child Irten'ev, expressing the impressions of his life as they seemed to him at the time of their occurrence. Of course, the reader knows consciously that the text was written by an adult writer, and that it is impossible for the narrator to remember exactly conversations or events that occurred years before. Nevertheless, Tolstoi successfully captures the feeling of the unmediated voice of the child, boy or youth. The second voice is that of the older Irten'ev, the narrator and putative writer of the text; he explains the actions of his protagonist (his younger self) and comments on them. Finally, there is an authorial voice that usually resembles the voice of Tolstoi himself as we know it from the diaries and his later work. This voice makes generalizing comments that go far beyond the commentary provided by Irten'ev. The success of the trilogy in Tolstoi's day was due to the author's ability to balance these three voices, and through them to delve into the mind of his protagonist.

There are two compelling, although unrelated, reasons for valuing Tolstoi's trilogy today. First, as Tolstoi's earliest finished work, it can be seen as a laboratory for the concerns and literary techniques that the writer would later perfect in such masterpieces as *War and Peace* and *Anna Karenina*. Already in *Childhood* we see the microscopic and merciless psychological analysis – what Chernyshevskii dubbed his knowledge of the "dialectic of the soul" – that would become one of the author's trademarks. In Irten'ev we find the same search for moral purity, and the same difficulties in achieving it, that will be characteristic of Tolstoi's heroes from Olenin in *The Cossacks*, through Pierre Bezukhov in *War and Peace* and Levin in *Anna Karenina* as well as in Tolstoi himself.

It would be a mistake, however, to look at the trilogy as nothing more than a preliminary to Tolstoi's later, admittedly greater fiction. Of equal importance is the influence that the trilogy had in opening up an entirely new subject for Russian literature and culture – childhood – and in providing a model for understanding childhood in Russian culture. *Childhood* was the first work of Russian literature to have a child as the central character, and writers as disparate as Aksakov, Gor'kii, Belyi, Bunin, and Nabokov, as well as generations of gentry autobiographers recalled and rewrote their childhoods incorporating both Tolstoi's literary technique and his overall mythology of childhood. In this respect *Childhood* (and to a lesser extent *Boyhood* and *Youth*) remained paradigmatic for Russian culture even as it was overshadowed by the literary achievements of Tolstoi's mature period.

ANDREW BARUCH WACHTEL

War and Peace

Voina i mir

Novel, 1865–69

At the beginning of the 1860s Tolstoi had almost decided to give up literature. In his opinion, the sort of fiction he wrote was little better than a perversion practised by the cultured elite. Before the end of the decade, however, he had completed *War and Peace*, his most famous novel and a work which, perhaps above all others, symbolizes 19th-century Russian literature to the world at large.

Tolstoi had intended to publish *War and Peace* in serial form and the public first saw the novel in the journal *Russkii vestnik* in 1865, under the title *Tysiacha vosem'sot piatyi god* (*The Year 1805*). Tolstoi soon felt that this serial form imposed severe restrictions; he withdrew the novel from *Russkii vestnik* and started to publish it himself, introducing changes to the earlier sections. The first two complete editions were published almost simultaneously, and then a third followed with considerable corrections. The first two editions included long passages of French as part of the original text – French being the language of polite society. Tolstoi reduced this in the third edition. He also decided to cut down the historical digressions, much of which were removed to an appendix. The fifth edition of 1886 put back the French conversation of the original, but the sixth edition translated those passages into Russian. Eventually the Jubilee Edition (which took from 1928 to 1964 to produce) established what had been the fifth edition as the definitive text.

Tolstoi's original intention had been to write a novel on the Decembrists (in the wake of the release of the survivors from their Siberian exile after the death of Nicholas I), but he soon found himself drawn back to the Napoleonic period. The story therefore begins in 1805. On the initiative of Alexander I, a coalition had been formed (consisting of England, Russia, Sweden, Austria, and Hanover), in order to resist Napoleon. The wise heads in Madame Scherer's salon, in the opening scene of the novel, concluded that Napoleon's ensuing machinations had made war between France and Russia almost inevitable. This, then, is the setting for the opening of Tolstoi's epic novel.

The young Nikolai (Nicholas) Rostov is just beginning to fledge his wings, intending to go into the army. His father, Count Il'ia Rostov, is a convivial elderly member of the gentry who spends more than he can afford on hospitality. Other prominent characters are soon presented, including Nikolai's vivacious sister, Natasha. At the same time in Moscow, the immensely wealthy Count Bezukhov is dying, with no direct legitimate descendants. His only heir seems to be the young man who has just arrived from Switzerland, whom everyone calls M'sieur Pierre. Subsequently we are introduced to members of the other main families, the Kuragins and the Bolkonskiis, as well as to historical figures from court and army: and so the fictional and historical levels of the work are set in motion.

At the beginning of the novel the reader is not given any particular impression as to Tolstoi's basically determinist ideas on history. The conversation in Madame Scherer's salon suggests that history is created in the schemes and plans of clever people in such very salons. Interpretation of individual actions can make those talked about seem unduly significant and, in the process, can also inflate the role of the raconteur. The *habitués* of Madame Scherer's salon identify with and subscribe to this type of personal history. As we follow Nikolai Rostov through his early training and into action, however, we see the way in which Tolstoi transforms a mass of men into an authentic unit. This process then carries on when the same men arrive in battle situations. Progressive exploitation of fictional and historical situations exposes the impact (or often the lack thereof) of the individual on military or historical crisis points, as well as the general ineffectiveness of the high command. A major problem facing Tolstoi, therefore, in the narration of *War and Peace* centred on finding techniques for the communication in a convincing manner of large amounts of historical material. One device employed was a realistic depiction of military parades: when the reader had been convinced once or twice by these, Tolstoi's artistic battle was well on the way to being won.

From such beginnings, Tolstoi proceeds to construct a massive fictional and historical edifice. Love affairs, family fortunes, and individual careers are juxtaposed with immense historical and political upheaval. Natasha grows up, gets engaged to Prince Andrei (Andrew) Bolkonskii, is all but ruined by Anatole Kuragin, and finally marries Pierre Bezukhov. Nikolai survives the war, to make an unlikely marriage with Andrei's sister, Mar'ia (Princess Mary). Pierre and Andrei (the twin Tolstoian self-projections) each pursue their personal intellectual quests and resolve, or succumb to, their own brands of Tolstoian fate. The doomed peasant captive, Platon Karataev, preaches the Tolstoian message of resignation in the face of adversity; somewhat incongruously (and ahistorically, it might be said), General Kutuzov re-enacts this policy in the political and military arena. By the end of the novel, some 1500 pages on, Pierre and Natasha, together with Nikolai and Mar'ia, their respective children and Andrei's son, continue to work out their destinies in the post-Napoleonic era. We are still some years from Tolstoi's original intended starting point – the Decembrist uprising of 1825 (in which Pierre might have been a participant).

Meanwhile inter-familial rivalry and strife has paralleled the diplomacy and warfare between nations. The salon, the ballroom, and the country estate have alternated with the parade ground, the battlefield, and the council of war. A gigantic cast of fictional characters has mingled with the leading historical and political figures of the epoch (Napoleon, Alexander I, Speranskii, Kutuzov and many more). Tolstoi has produced a formidable theoretical tract on the philosophy of history, while simultaneously endeavouring to illustrate its detailed workings in fictional form.

Tolstoi's vast experiment in fiction with history, designed above all to portray the Russian nobility in its finest hour, did not please all contemporary reviewers, while Henry James later termed it "a loose and baggy monster". As has recently been pointed out (Morson, 1987), Tolstoi's great epic work seems to contain three coexisting books: "Peace", "War" and "Historical-Philosophical Essays"; and to incorporate three parallel genres: the novel, fictionalized history, and the non-fictional essay. Criticism, even at the end of the 20th century, still strives to determine and clarify the underlying structural principles of this celebrated huge and hybrid work.

GARETH WILLIAMS

Anna Karenina

Novel, 1875–77

Anna Karenina was regarded by Tolstoi as his first genuine novel. Alongside Flaubert's *Madame Bovary* and Fontane's *Effi Briest*, it stands as perhaps the most prominent 19th-century European novel of adultery; but it is, both in reality and in reputation, rather more than that. F.R. Leavis, indeed, rated Tolstoi "an incomparably representative European" and *Anna Karenina* as "surely, *the* European novel". Other prominent cultural commentators to have singled out this work for special attention include Matthew Arnold, D.H. Lawrence, Thomas Mann, Vladimir Nabokov, Georg Lukács, and Vladimir Il'ich Lenin. Like *War and Peace*, *Anna Karenina* has frequently attracted the attention of film and television studios; perhaps the most famous adaptation remains Clarence Brown's Hollywood version of 1935, starring Greta Garbo.

Anna Karenina is the last work to have been written in Tolstoi's "middle", or mature period of composition: following *War and Peace*, which had made his reputation as a writer of major, if hybrid, fiction on a European plane; it just preceded (and indeed heralded) the "spiritual crisis", that produced *A Confession* (1879–81) and all but finished Tolstoi's career as a writer of fiction, at least for quite some years. Strong traces of the later anti-sexual preachings of Tolstoi (who was always at very least something of a moralist) colour *Anna Karenina*; the late Tolstoi, when he did return to fiction, was capable of the fundamentalist extremism of *The Kreutzer Sonata* (1890). By then it had become impossible to separate Tolstoi the preacher from Tolstoi the artist, except in his ultra-late and final masterpiece, *Hadji Murad* (1904).

No mere novel of adultery, then, *Anna Karenina* juxtaposes crises of family life with the quest for the meaning of life in a society drama with a contemporary backdrop. As the seasons rotate, the settings alternate (the urban and the rural, the Russian and the European, Moscow and St Petersburg, capital and provinces), and the themes likewise: despair and spiritual resurrection, birth and death, unhealthy passion and healthy love. Something of the epic scope of *War and Peace* does survive into *Anna Karenina*, but on a reduced scale. Historical treatise gives way to a lesser airing of topical socio-political issues, although, as before, a philosophical second layer of Tolstoian soul-searching is provided, in effect to offset the more dramatic primary narrative.

Anna Karenina is a novel of two parallel plots, linked to one major and several minor sub-plots. The story of Anna's passionate and protracted love affair with Vronskii, and the consequent break-up of the Karenin family home, proceeds in counterpoint, and at virtually equal length, to Levin's courtship and marriage to Kitty Shcherbatskaia (the Shcherbatskii family serving here as something of a successor to the Rostovs of *War and Peace*) and the saga of his personal spiritual quest (the name "Levin" [intended to be pronounced "Lyovin"] being based, it is thought, on Tolstoi's first name, Lev [pronounced "Lyov"]). Linking these two plotlines, both thematically and by familial relationships, is the principal sub-plot, that of the checkered marriage of Dolly (Kitty's sister) and Stiva Oblonskii (Anna's brother). Further links are inbuilt by means of recurring imagery and symbolism. Tolstoi himself mentioned an (unspecified) overarching "keystone", pivotal to the novel's construction. The motifs of the "accident", trains, the recurrent dream and death are frequently held here to be of major significance. Further minor sub-plots, all of thematic relevance, extend the architectural pattern. The by now perfected and widely acclaimed Tolstoian narrative techniques – of narration both by telling and by showing (often most effectively through dialogue), plus a developed use of free indirect discourse and interior monologue – are all on full display in *Anna Karenina*.

The tragic saga of Anna, the overall precedence of which is confirmed in the novel's title, is in large measure what has endowed *Anna Karenina* with its mighty reputation. There can be little doubt that an independent novel concentrating on "Konstantin Levin" would have found a significantly smaller readership. Contemporay reviewers did in fact question the wisdom of the inclusion of part 8, considering that the novel was effectively over with Anna's suicide. Modern criticism, however, has generally enhanced appreciation of the inter-linking structural devices and the narrative and societal reach of Tolstoi's fiction, thus perceiving, in *Anna Karenina* in particular, a satisfying totality, in preference to the "fluid pudding" school of thought, earlier advanced by Henry James.

The reputation of *Anna Karenina* as a European classic has long been unassailable. Nevertheless, criticism continues to debate the degree and the effects of authorial tendentiousness within Tolstoi's art and still endeavours to apportion the blame for Anna's fate. In the view of Nabokov, "his art was so powerful, so tiger bright, so original and universal that it easily transcends the sermon". However, the biblical epigraph ("Vengeance is mine, and I shall repay") sets the Pauline Christian tone of Tolstoi's absolute view of marriage, even of the arranged variety. Furthermore, Anna and Stiva (as Oblonskiis) cannot maintain the approved moral standards of the Shcherbatskiis: shades of the Kuragins *vis-à-vis* the Rostovs; as John Bayley has put it, for Tolstoi, "irrespective of social level, some families are like this, some like that". Does the selection and presentation of material load the dice against Anna throughout?

Does Anna's ultimate disaster stem from an overbearing and illicit passion, from a tragic inevitability, or really more from a series of chance misunderstandings? Is blame to be laid at the door of uncontrolled female sexuality, or of an intolerant and hypocritical social code? For some, Anna – much as we, and even perhaps Tolstoi, may feel for her – gets nothing more than her just deserts; for others, her catastrophe is the outcome of a brilliantly crafted and tragic inexorability; for yet others, Anna was doomed to suicide as such, and under a train in particular, more by the initial conception of the book, by the fate of the woman near Tolstoi's estate in 1870 (which provided the novel's impulse), and by the necessity under Tolstoian law to punish the guilty adulteress (as with *la belle Hélène* in *War and Peace*).

Some criticism (Gustafson for example) prefers to see Tolstoi simply as a representative of Eastern Christianity, writing extended parables of the right and the wrong way to live; such a stripping away of the novel's ambiguity, in the words of Gary Adelman, "denies the fact that Anna takes the book away from Levin". While, in recent years, gender and Freudian studies have begun to contribute significantly to discussions of *Anna Karenina* (see the studies by Judith Armstrong, Mary Evans, and Edward Wasiolek), a full feminist critique of Tolstoi's *oeuvre* is still awaited.

NEIL CORNWELL

The Death of Ivan Ilych

Smert' Ivana Il'icha

Story, 1886

To many of his contemporaries *The Death of Ivan Ilych* was the most powerful story Tolstoi ever wrote, and the composer Tchaikovskii even went so far as to say that its author was "the greatest author-painter of all". And it still retains its force, honesty, and conviction today. While Tolstoi frequently externalized many of his own concerns in his fiction, the one that troubled him most was that of death. This is apparent from his first published work, *Childhood* (1852), where the young boy's innocent love of life is overshadowed by the agonizing death of his mother and his, and others' reaction to it. The realization that the event could arouse horror in him filled him with despair. By contrast the death of the simple-hearted nurse and housekeeper strikes him as more bearable. Although she welcomed death as a blessing, "she accomplished the greatest and best thing in life – she died without fear or regret". How to face the grim reality of death recurs again and again, most notably with Prince Andrei Bolkonskii in *War and Peace*; his gradual rejection of all life's values, both negative and positive is told, as it were, from within. It was a matter of regret to Tolstoi that the two most momentous events in human existence, one's own birth and death, could not be described, but then he came close to it.

In the second half of his writing career, Tolstoi became even more of an iconoclast and non-conformist, but the problem of death never ceased to plague him. He became convinced that the only way to overcome the fear of it was to lead a better life beforehand. This idea might have struck many as rather unorthodox; after all, it was argued, should not one try to lead a better life anyway, for all sorts of reasons, rather than simply to be able to face death with equanimity? Yet two of his later stories are mightily convincing arguments in his favour, *Master and Man* and particularly *The Death of Ivan Ilych*.

When the short novel was published in 1886, the reading public hailed it with enthusiasm. Tolstoi had published little of note since finishing *Anna Karenina* some nine years before and it appeared that he had again returned to his *métier*. Although clearly a tale with a definite moral, gone is any trace of the didacticism that occasionally marred some of his other works. He reverts to the best realistic style of his earlier novels and stories. The reader is spared none of the horrors of disease and death and Tolstoi's acclaimed psychological insight has lost none of its power. Put simply, *The Death of Ivan Ilych* is the story of an ordinary, even commonplace, man who is devastated by an event that destroys all his former values. An apparently simple mishap, a fall when fixing some curtains, proves to be fatal. He is forced to look back over his life, which to all intents and purposes has been successful, at least in the material sense, but he finds that not to be the case. Only when he realizes this, does he understand how he should have behaved, and then he can accept the inevitability of his death with some composure. His life, wrote Tolstoi, had been the most simple and most ordinary and therefore the most terrible. As a magistrate he had been honest, but extremely strict, in carrying out his duties. These duties he interpreted as being what his superiors told him. He is punctillious at the trials he has to judge. He will hear of no consideration other than the letter of the law. There is no room for understanding, let alone pity. It is only ironic that when during his illness, he asks the doctor whether the complaint is dangerous, he is told to limit himself to the questions put to him or "I shall be obliged to have you removed from the court". Throughout his long, increasingly painful illness, he, like Tolstoi, tries to overcome the irrationality of death and to find some justification for what he had formerly considered to have been a good life that should not end in such an unjust way. But, as critics have always pointed out, Tolstoi has no pity whatsoever for those of his characters he finds wrong-headed or worse. This implies, of course, that they do not fit in with what was Tolstoi's own scheme of things. Readers have always felt that Ivan Ilych hardly deserves the death Tolstoi inflicts on him. Ivan's realization that he has not lived as he ought is made even clearer to him by seeing the sincere grief of his young son and its contrast with those who either shut their eyes to his suffering or find it an extreme inconvenience. The only understanding sympathy comes largely from the quarter where he least expected to find it, from the almost cheerful self-sacrifice of his simple, kind-hearted servant Gerasim. As in *Master and Man*, while the end draws ever closer, Ivan, like the selfish, materialist Brekhunov, undergoes a mystical transformation. Without the Christian undertones of the later work, Ivan discovers that man's essence lies in the spirit. Death is indeed an awakening. Ivan bids farewell to his family and asks for their forgiveness. His death is not only a relief from his suffering, but is accepted, even welcomed. Unlike Prince Andrei, who seems to those caring for him to die actually long before his final breath, Ivan sees the light at the bottom of the "black sack". He is at peace with those around him and with himself.

A.V. KNOWLES

The Power of Darkness

Vlast' t'my

Play, 1888

The Power of Darkness is a five-act tragedy of Russian peasant life written by Tolstoi in late 1886 with an overtly didactic purpose. His aim was to draw attention to the disgusting primitivism of rural Russia three decades after reform, and while doing so to proclaim a Christian message about the exponential infectiousness of evil behaviour. Clear indication of the latter is given by both the subtitle ("If a claw gets caught the bird is lost") and the epigraph, from St Matthew (V, 28–29). Read to the tsar in 1887, it was accepted by him as an artistic success and unofficially approved for stage performance, but permission was rapidly withdrawn following the intervention of Count Pobedonostsev (Procurator of the Holy Synod) who deemed it to be vulgar, brutal, and immoral. The play was banned at home on the eve of its planned premiere, though it was soon published and saw its first performance in France at the Théâtre Antoine (1888). Produced at last in Russia in 1895, it was taken up by the Moscow Arts Theatre in 1902 and soon became permanently established in the Russian repertory. The Russian theatre, which has next to no successful tragedies to be proud of, must count this play as one of its finest.

The story tells of Nikita Chilikin, a peasant workman who has an affair with his sick master's wife, Aksin'ia. His evil mother, Matrena, sees good prospects here, though his father, Akim, wants him to marry Marina, whom he has also seduced. At the instigation of Matrena, the master (Petr) is poisoned by Aksin'ia, who then marries Nikita, only for him to seduce and impregnate her 16-year-old daughter, Akulina. Months later the new-born baby is crushed to death and buried in the cellar. In the concluding scene Nikita, worn down by the burden of his guilt, uses the occasion of Akulina's (enforced) wedding celebration to confess the crimes before the whole village community. These events are taken from a real-life occurrence, except for the poisoning, the burial in a cellar and much of the character of Matrena, all of which seem to derive from Leskov's tale *Ledi Makbet mtsenskogo uezda* (*Lady Macbeth of the Mtsensk District*). A curious feature of the play is that it offers an alternative ending to the fourth act. In case the presentation of infanticide on stage should appear too gruesome, another possibility is offered by which a good workman and a small girl discuss the baby and overhear Matrena and Nikita talking about the murder. Both scenes are full of agonizing pathos making for a rich theatrical experience; it will always be difficult for directors to choose between them, but they should go for the nasty original.

A strong story-line and powerful action are the hallmarks of this play, which generates a truly horrifying atmosphere through its inexorable progression down the path of evil selfishness and violence as human greed and uncontrolled sexual desire tighten their grip on the characters. The structure is remorselessly logical, as in classical drama, and the succession of personal crises, increasing all the time in significance and intensity, are guaranteed to hold an audience in appalled fascination. In his day the author was criticized for the brutality of his realism, an excess of sanguinary detail and a disconcerting tendency to indulge in dialect and linguistic vulgarity. None of these charges seems to stand up now. The ghastly realism is justified by the subject-matter and vindicated both by the artistic merit of the piece and its elevated didactic purpose. The rough language seems nicely in character and should on no account be adulterated by blandness in translation.

Besides the stark appeal of its story, this play presents a full range of well-authenticated characters. Seven ages of humanity are represented, from birth and infancy through each decade until the age of 60, in children and adults, women and men, 22 characters in all, plus extras. Among them are three or four outstanding roles. Nikita is the very model of human susceptibility, physically attractive but without personality, a victim of his own weaknesses and other people's manipulation. His parents appear like archetypes of evil and good, but only in retrospect. While ever the action is moving Matrena is all too convincing, as dreadful to behold as her usual comparator, Lady Macbeth; the depths of her awfulness in goading others into the vilest behaviour suggest irredeemable wickedness brought about by personal deficiencies bordering on madness, rather than the deprivations to which all the other characters were subjected. Akim, her husband, is a great triumph of Tolstoian characterization. All through the play he attempts to prevent or offset evil actions by good words. This might have seemed simplistically pious if the author had not had the clever idea of giving the old chap a stammer. As it is, his well-meant utterances, endearingly comical and only half-comprehensible when spoken, build up a fund of relevance and value that brings about the strange last-act climax and allows it to ring as true on these pages as its real-life prototype must have done. Tolstoi here enjoys one of his rare post-conversion successes in blending nobility of spirit with sympathy and verisimilitude. On page or stage these characters have everything necessary to convince and disturb an audience.

However unlikely it may seem, *The Power of Darkness* has proved strangely successful in achieving something like the concept of a *Macbeth* with repentance in the last act. It is a play with important ideas, which are not forced upon us; the story and characters always hold sway. Tolstoi's socio-political criticism of contemporary life is presented so obliquely that some critics have denied that there is any. His Christian message has greater clarity, but even that, since most of it comes from the lips of a likeable bumbling innocent, is filtered down into a gentle stream of reasonable recommendations for our moral improvement. This is Tolstoi at his most persuasive and effective in matters of ethical and spiritual indoctrination. This is, through art, the power of enlightenment.

A.D.P. Briggs

The Kreutzer Sonata

Kreitserova sonata

Story, 1890

According to Tolstoi's wife Sonia, the idea for the story about the evil effect of sexual relations was given to Tolstoi by the actor V.N. Andreev-Burlak during a visit to the Tolstoi's home at Iasnaia Poliana in June 1887. The actor had told him that on a train journey a man had complained of the unhappiness his wife's infidelity had caused him. Tolstoi wished to examine the theme and began to write soon afterwards, but it was not until the autumn of 1889 that he completed it. The fact that it was widely distributed in manuscript copies and was given many private readings in some ways delayed its publication. Tolstoi agreed to let it appear in a *Festschrift* for the editor of the journal *Russkaia mysl'*, but the censor, well aware of its contents, refused publication. Their decision was reaffirmed when there were plans to include it in an edition of Tolstoi's Collected Works because it contained, among other things, "unsuitable expressions". Sonia appealed directly to Tsar Alexander III who permitted it to be included in the collection in 1890. It appeared separately later that year.

For many years Tolstoi had been concerned with the problems, as he saw it, of married life. In 1888 he wrote to his friend and disciple V.G. Chertkov, "The question of sexual relations between husband and wife, and to what extent they are justified is one of the most important ... I think that for the good of mankind both men and women should strive for absolute chastity". When it was pointed out that such forbearance would lead to the extinction of the human race, Tolstoi responded, "What will die out is man the animal. What a terrible misfortune that would be! Just as the animals of prehistoric times died out, so, probably will the human animal ... Let it. I am no more sorry for this two-legged animal than I am for the ichthyosaurs etc." The question of man, the animal, had been treated by Tolstoi just before with "Strider" in 1886, where human beings are seen as being inferior to the rest of the animal kingdom.

In the spring of 1888 an amateur performance of Beethoven's *Kreutzer Sonata* took place in Tolstoi's home and it made a particularly strong emotional and, according to his daughter, physical impression on him, and he returned to an idea he had had in the 1860s. Further encouraged by the writings of an American doctor, especially the chapter "Chastity in the Marriage Relation" in her book *Tokology – A Book for Every Woman*, and by reading about the American Shaker community who preached absolute chastity, he set to completing his story. Its nine drafts were assiduously copied out by his wife, who became increasingly disturbed, believing Tolstoi was writing about their own marriage and terrified that, her husband being what he was, she would fall pregnant. All these various drafts were copied and widely distributed. They caused a sensation. The critic and publisher Strakhov told Tolstoi that people no longer asked each other when they met how they were, but "Have you read *The Kreutzer Sonata*?" Tolstoi was accused of preaching immorality and attempting to deprave the young; many thought he had gone mad. Pobedonostsev, Chief Procurator of the Holy Synod, was horrified that such a book could be openly purchased by schoolgirls. He wrote personally to the tsar, and this marks the formal beginning of the process that led ultimately to Tolstoi's excommunication. Upset by all the misunderstandings the book caused, Tolstoi was forced to write a postscript (1890) in which he attempted to explain his unorthodox views.

Written in the form of a frame-story, a style much favoured by Turgenev but used rarely by Tolstoi, *The Kreutzer Sonata* is set on a train. Readers of *Anna Karenina* would know of the author's attitude to railways and might well expect that the events about to be unfolded would not have a happy outcome. The conversations among the passengers develop into a discussion of the institution of marriage, the relations between the sexes, and of women's inferior position in society. The most outspoken opinions are clearly Tolstoi's own. The story develops into a long conversation, or rather a series of monologues by the chief character, Pozdnyshev, with a few comments from the unnamed narrator. Pozdnyshev tells of his youth, his first visits to brothels, and his subsequent remorse and self-disgust. Ten years or so of "debauchery" follow, before he decides to get married. After a brief engagement, he and his wife spend a disastrous honeymoon in Paris, giving Tolstoi a further opportunity to attack certain aspects of western European life that he found repugnant. Back at home in Russia the marriage develops into arguments, animosity and mutual hatred, interspersed with ever-decreasing periods of reconciliation. While he is away on business his wife is seemingly seduced by a musician, and on his return Pozdnyshev finds the couple together. Jealousy, shame, and hatred turn into uncontrollable anger and he tries to strangle his wife and then stabs her to death with a dagger. Pozdnyshev blames the whole sorry story on society and on women, who, with nothing else to do and with the aid of the dressmaker, corsetière and cosmetician, simply inflame men's animal instincts. The only solution is absolute chastity.

Never before in Russian literature had marriage, and the sexual relations it implied, been so openly and frankly discussed. Yet what might have become a dry tract on celibacy and an attack on various other of Tolstoi's *bêtes noires*, is saved by the extraordinary artistic tact and the compelling psychological insight it contains. The story is an outstanding example of Tolstoi's perhaps unique ability to propound a moral idea of his own through forceful, convincing narrative.

A.V. KNOWLES

Resurrection

Voskresenie

Novel, 1899

Resurrection was Tolstoi's last "big" novel. Called *The Awakening* in the earliest American translations, it is a thesis novel, informed throughout by Tolstoi's religious, social, and moral insights and driven by his desire to communicate those insights to his readers as forcefully and convincingly as possible. Although artistically inferior to *Anna Karenina* and *War and Peace*, lacking their breadth of vision and multiplicity of design, it had a far greater immediate social impact both within Russia and internationally than any of his previous works. Tolstoi worked on the material in three distinct periods (1889–90, 1895–96 and 1898–99), doing so with a sense of guilty exhilaration, for it represented a return to fiction that he had long since attempted to renounce in favour of more "useful" writing. He only completed the novel, working under great duress of time throughout 1899, so as to raise money for the Dukhobors, a fundamentalist, Christian pacifist sect, whose members were being persecuted by the Russian authorities on account of their refusal to bear arms and were seeking to emigrate to Canada. The novel was first published simultaneously in two Russian editions, one serialized and heavily censored in the St Petersburg weekly journal *Niva* between March and December 1899 and the other, uncensored, by Vladimir Chertkov's Svobodnoe slovo publishing house in England. It also appeared at the same time in a number of hastily produced translations of varying length and accuracy both in Europe and America, being rapidly reprinted in a variety of different editions. The most authoritative and long-lasting translation into English was the version by Louise Maude, published in book form by Francis Henderson in London in 1900 and by Dodd Mead in New York. This translation was also incorporated (volume 19, 1928) in the 21-volume Centenary Edition of Tolstoi's works published by Oxford University Press (1928–37) under the editorship of Aylmer Maude. The novel's social impact was greatly enhanced by 33 specially commissioned illustrations by Leonid Osipovich Pasternak.

The stimuli for the novel's story were both internal and external, for it is based on a combination of Tolstoi's own experiences as a young man, and an incident drawn from the legal practice of his friend, the lawyer A.F. Koni. Interest concentrates on the unequal relationship between the 30-year-old nobleman, Prince Dmitrii Ivanovich Nekhliudov and the prostitute, Ekaterina (Katiusha, alias Liubka) Maslova, aged 26, whom Nekhliudov, as a young man, had got with child and abandoned to her fate. The relationship is portrayed almost exclusively from Nekhliudov's perspective: he is the subject, the observer, the instigator of the action. Maslova is the recipient, the object, generally passive and observed. Structurally and thematically *Resurrection* is based on juxtaposition and contrast: between the rich and the poor, the free and the unfree, darkness and light, town and country, the natural and the artificial, the spiritual and the physical, male and female, the individual and the institutional, above all on the antithesis between good and evil, where greed and gluttony are associated with privilege and power and, like all exclusive concentration on the pursuit of physical pleasure, lead inexorably to brutality, moral turpitude, and a total lack of compassion.

This multiplicity of contrasts is clear from the start. The novel begins (significantly on a bright morning in spring) with Maslova in her filthy female prison being called to court on charges of murdering a client, while Nekhliudov, ignorant of what awaits him, proceeds from his delicately perfumed bed-chamber to the same court where he will be required to sit in judgement over her as a member of the jury. Nekhliudov recognizes Maslova and, during an interval in the proceedings, recollects in flashback their earlier relationship, moving swiftly from the bright innocence of early love to the dark, sordid, early-morning seduction and fall. Once back in court Nekhliudov himself stands accused. Not publicly, although he understandably fears exposure, but in the eyes of the reader and in the court of his own conscience. Whereas initially he had been obliged by his role as juror to participate on the side of law and order in the official processes of trial and judgement, he now suddenly finds himself on trial as well as Maslova.

Immediately after the sentence Nekhliudov embarks on a campaign to "rescue" the victim of his youthful passion and thereby to bring about his own and her moral resurrection. His sense of guilt and responsibility for her predicament is heightened by the fact that, due to an oversight by the judge and a lack of attention on the part of the jury, Maslova is wrongly sentenced to four years' penal servitude in Siberia. What begins as a campaign to rectify a single miscarriage of justice, and as a quest for purely personal salvation, rapidly becomes a far more generalized, socially significant undertaking. Seeking truth and justice, Nekhliudov is persuaded by Maslova and her fellow-prisoners to present ever more petitions on their behalf. This not only takes him into places of privilege and power, but also, for the first time, into society's "lower depths" where he encounters not only the results of man's inhumanity to man, but also genuine feelings and a sense of comradeship. He meets common criminals, gaolers, political prisoners and all manner of other social types far removed from the polite, upper-class environment in which he had previously moved. Despite Maslova's refusal of his offer of marriage – she eventually draws close to a young vegetarian revolutionary – Nekhliudov follows her convoy to Siberia, eventually obtaining commutation of her sentence from hard labour with common criminals to exile with the "politicals".

Nekhliudov's campaign for Maslova's release becomes a voyage of discovery, both for him and for the reader, and enables Tolstoi to put the law itself on trial, passing in review all those negative aspects of contemporary Russian society to which he so earnestly sought to direct public attention. Nekhliudov's perception of the apparatus of the state changes as he goes further than any previous Tolstoian hero and attempts to find freedom by breaking with his class. Declaring war on his past, he is drawn into an all-embracing struggle against the whole social order. Like Tolstoi, he comes to see it as a corrupt system based on violence, or the threat of violence, and upheld by a venal judicial apparatus in which misguided, but not necessarily evil, men and women arrogate to themselves the right to sit in judgement over their fellows. Being far from perfect themselves, they create institutions that are evil and totally devoid of compassion and moral authority. Finally, taking the Sermon on the Mount as his guide, he comes, like Tolstoi, to the realization that only when men acknowledge their guilt before God, refuse to judge others and seek to forgive rather than to punish, will the vicious circle be broken and the kingdom of heaven be established on earth. Tolstoi has no time to reveal how Nekhliudov puts his new-found belief into practice, but he finds freedom as he awakens into a new perception of life's purpose.

Resurrection affirms Tolstoi's belief in the primacy of the individual conscience over the collective morality of the group. An intense, impatient, deeply disturbing novel in which biting satire alternates with great compassion, and detailed physical description with conjecture and abstraction, it proclaims the urgent need for the spiritual rebirth of the individual and, through the individual, of society as a whole.

MICHAEL J. DE K. HOLMAN

Vasilii Vasil'evich Trediakovskii 1703–1769

Poet, translator, and literary theorist

Biography

Born in Astrakhan, 5 March 1703, to an Orthodox clergyman's family. Initial education by Cappucine monks. Married: 1) Fedosii'ia Fadeeva (died of cholera in 1728); 2) Mar'ia Sibileva in 1742; one son. Departed Astrakhan, leaving his first wife. Continued his education at the Slavo-Greco-Latin Academy in Moscow, 1723–25; travelled to western Europe, spent two years at the Hague; studied mathematics, philosophy, and linguistics at the University of Paris and the Sorbonne, 1726–30. Translator at St Petersburg Imperial Academy of Sciences; appointed Secretary of the Academy, 1732. Home and possessions destroyed in a fire, 1736; avoided creditors by leaving St Petersburg for a year, lived in the provinces, 1738; public beating at court by the Minister Artemii Volynskii, 1740. Lived in Moscow, 1741. Professor at the Academy in St Petersburg, 1745; polemic with Aleksandr Sumarokov and Mikhail Lomonosov, translation competition of "Psalm 143", house burned down, destroying manuscript of his translations of Rollins, 1748. Quarrel with the Academy who ceased to publish his works; serious disputes with Lomonosov, 1757; dismissed from the Academy for unknown reasons, 1759. Publication of *Tilemakhida*, 1766. Lived in increasing solitude and poverty. Died 17 August 1769.

Publications

Collected Editions

Sochineniia i perevody kak stikhami tak i prozoiu, 2 vols. St Petersburg, 1752.

Sochineniia Trediakovskogo, 3 vols. St Petersburg, 1849.

Stikhotvoreniia. "Biblioteka poeta", Leningrad, 1935.

Izbrannye proizvedeniia. Moscow and Leningrad, 1963.

Poetry

Argenida, povest' geroicheskaia (verse rendering of *Argenis*, by John Barclay), 2 vols. St Petersburg, 1751.

Psalter (adaptation in verse of the Psalter, composed 1753), edited by A. Levitsky. Paderborn, 1989 (first full publication).

Feoptiia [Theoptia]. 1754.

Essays and Literary Theory

Novyi i kratkii sposob k slozheniiu rossiiskikh stikhov, 1735; translated as "A New and Brief Method for Composing Russian Verse" (1735), in *Russian Versification: The Theories of Trediakovsky, Lomonosov and Kantemir*, by Rimvydas Silbajoris, New York, Columbia University Press, 1968, 36–68.

Razgovor mezhdu chuzhestrannym chelovekom i rossiiskiim ob ortografii starinnoi i novoi i o vsem chto prinadlezhit i sei materii [Conversation Between a Foreigner and a Russian about Old and New Orthography]. St Petersburg, 1748.

Translator

Ezda v ostrov liubvi [*Voyage de L'Isle d'Amour*], by Paul Tallemant, 1730.

Tilemakhida (translation/adaptation of *Télémaque*), by François Fénelon, 1765.

Critical Studies

"Trediakovskii", by L.V. Pumpianskii, in *Istoriia russkoi literatury*, 1941, vol. 3, part 1, 215–63.

A History of the Russian Hexameter, by Richard Burgi, Hamden, Connecticut, Shoe String Press, 1954.

"Literaturnaia polemika Lomonosova i Trediakovskogo", by L.B. Modzalevskii, *XVIII vek*, 4 (1959), 45–65.

"Trochaic Metres in Early Russian Syllabo-Tonic Poetry", by C.L. Drage, *Slavonic and East European Review*, 37/19 (1960), 361–79.

Russian Versification: The Theories of Trediakovskij, Lomonosov and Kantemir, by Rimvydas Silbajoris, New York, Columbia University Press, 1968.

Die Feoptija V.K. Trediakovskijs: Ein phsyiko-theologisches Lehrgedicht in Russland des 18 Jahrhunderets, by W. Breitschah, Munich, 1973.

"Trediakovskii i Iansenisty", by A.B. Shishkin and B.A. Uspenskii, *Simvol*, 23 (1980), 105–262.

V.K. Trediakovskii – perevodchik: Stanovlenie klassitsisticheskogo perevoda v Rossii, by A.A. Deriugin, Saratov, 1985.

"Trediakovsky on Sumarokov: The Critical Issues", by Karen Rosenberg, *Russian Literature Triquarterly*, 21 (1988), 49–60.

Vasilii Trediakovsky: The Fool of the "New" Russian Literature, by Irina Reyfman, Stanford, Stanford University Press, 1990.

Trediakovskij und die "Argenida", by Capucine Carrier, Munich, Sagner, 1991.

Poet, translator, dramatist, theoretician of Russian versification and linguistics, Vasilii Trediakovskii's contributions to all these fields were the object of controversy in his lifetime. In the 1750s fundamental differences in their approach to the literary language and questions of poetics caused an irreconcilable rift with Mikhail Lomonosov and Aleksandr Sumarokov, expressed in a series of satirical epigrams and plays. In the 1760s Trediakovskii's prolific output failed to find a readership, and his reputation was eclipsed by the greater influence and fame of Lomonosov, whose poetic system and reform of the literary language had exercised a decisive impact, especially at Moscow University. Subsequently, the turbulent biography of this quixotic figure has come to overshadow dispassionate assessment of his achievements; he left an impressive body of published and unpublished works that still await a scholarly edition.

After a period of travel and study in Europe in the late 1720s when he was almost certainly on a secret mission for the Jansenists, Trediakovskii returned to Russia full of designs for the modernization of Russian literature. In 1730 he published his first book, *Ezda v ostrov liubvi*, a translation of Paul Tallemant's novel *Voyage de L'Isle d'Amour* (Paris, 1663). In the first in a long series of steps toward transplanting European literary culture Trediakovskii made available for the first time to the Russian reader the precious language of the salon. Trediakovskii's other efforts to introduce western literary models in Russian were various, including a verse rendering of the Latin novel, *Argenis*, by John Barclay; numerous French lyrics offering first generic models for poetic forms like the sonnet, the *rondeau*, the elegy and, most importantly, the epic. It is in *Tilemakhida* (1765), his translation-cum-imitation of Fénelon's *Télémaque*, that Trediakovskii's style is at its most impressive, replete with orotund sound-orchestration and novel compound-epithets. Composed in the heroic hexameter in imitation of Greek epic, the work is a metrical *tour de force*. Trediakovskii also put a premium on direct absorption of the ancients; his devotion to antiquity climaxes in his translations in 1761 and 1767, respectively, of Charles Rollin's *Histoire romaine* and *Histoire ancienne*, an achievement that earned no popular response.

From 1732 as Secretary at the Academy of Sciences Trediakovskii supervised numerous translations. In a speech to the Academy in 1735 Trediakovskii expressed his enormous ambitions to codify the new literary language by establishing a standard prescriptive grammar, a reliable dictionary, a rhetoric, all intended to foment the development of a true Russian literary language based on its historical usage. Arguably his most important idea was that the translator of western literature had the additional obligation of acting as the medium for transmittting European culture and knowledge to Russian society. Toward the end of the 1730s the Academy's efforts resulted in the compilation of a dictionary listing 60,000 Russian words, many of them new in the language, with their French and Latin equivalents. This unpublished work served as the basis for the Dictionary of the Russian Academy published in six volumes in 1789–94.

The nature of the Russian literary language was also a preoccupation. According to Trediakovskii the vernacular Russian and Slavonic were two separate languages, and at this time in his career he was adamant that the literary language should be based on the spoken language. In breaking with the ecclesiastical linguistic culture Trediakovskii sought to create in Russia a situation similar to that of Europe, where the language of the Church was Latin, but the vernacular served for secular texts. In the 1748 *Razgovor mezhdu chuzhestrannym chelovekom i rossiiskiim ob ortografii starinnoi i novoi i o vsem chto prinadlezhit i sei materii* [Conversation Between a Foreigner and a Russian about Old and New Orthography], Trediakovskii had written that the position of Slavonic *vis-à-vis* Russian was not the same as that of Latin to French, Italian and Spanish. The speakers of those modern European languages had to study Latin in order to understand it while Russians understood the Slavonic language without having studied it.

Hence from the mid-1740s Trediakovskii's linguistic orientation changed direction. Whereas in his earlier period he advocated the use of a literary language that cultivated the virtues of speech, directness, and simplicity unadorned by Slavonicisms, in time he came to insist that Slavonic and Russian were but two sides of a single language. In his view the writer's duty was not to return to the past and revitalize Slavonic, but rather to create a new literary language in which the two are fused, based on the liturgical tradition. The two chief works that reflected this new tendency were his adaptation in verse of the Psalter in 1753, published in full for the first time only in 1989, and the theological poem *Feoptiia* [Theoptia]. In translating the Psalms Trediakovskii's purpose, as he stated in the preface, was to provide alternative models to the Ancient poets; it was also an attempt to renew the significance of the Psalms.

As a scholar, Trediakovskii followed European fashion when he directed his attention to questions of rhetoric and poetics. His handbook on versification, his essays on eloquence, comedy, the epic and the ode attempted to explain the origin, goals, and rules of verbal art. His treatise on orthography treated questions of grammar; though his conclusions were rejected, they stimulated important linguistic speculation and thought. While it is now clear that neither Trediakovskii nor Lomonosov were the first to write syllabo-tonic verse in Russian, Trediakovskii's *Novyi i kratkii sposob k slozheniiu rossiiskikh stikhov* (*A New and Brief Method for Composing Russian Verse*) breaks new ground as the first systematic explication of the new Russian syllabo-tonic versification in which the regular alternation of stressed and unstressed syllables organizes word-placement. According to Trediakovskii, the new verse line must consist of bisyllabic feet and cannot admit ternary meters or trisyllabic feet, such as the dactyl or anapest. The best line contained purely trochaic feet. For Trediakovskii the best line preserved the 13-syllable length traditionally employed by writers of syllabic verse. None of these features was preserved in the more successful system that Lomonosov promulgated in 1739.

Despite his large and impressive output, it is difficult to place Trediakovskii in the literary world of the 18th century since his gifts as a linguist and theoretician outstripped his abilities as a poet. His rules of versification and prosody entailed syntax of a baffling intricacy totally at odds with the flow of the spoken language. At his best, however, as in *Tilemakhida* and the Psalms, his verse attains great stature.

ANDREW KAHN

Iurii Valentinovich Trifonov 1925–1981

Prose writer

Biography

Born in Moscow, 28 August 1925. His father, Valentin, an old Bolshevik and long-time Communist Party member, was arrested in June 1937 and executed as an "enemy of the people". Mother was also arrested and exiled; Trifonov and his sister were raised by their grandmother (mother returned to Moscow 1946). Evacuated to Tashkent, 1941; completed schooling there, 1942. Returned to Moscow, worked as labourer, fitter, and part-time fireman. Attended the Gor'kii Literary Institute, Moscow, 1944–49. Married: 1) Nina Nelina in 1951 (died 1966); 2) Alla Pastukhova in 1972; 3) Ol'ga Miroshnichenko in 1979; two children. Began to publish, 1947. Full-time writer and occasional journalist from 1950. Member of the Writers' Union, 1957. Travelled extensively in Turkmenia, 1950s; also to the west, 1950s–60s, as a sports journalist. Achieved international fame with the publication of "Moscow" stories late 1960s–70s; associated with the journal *Novyi mir* under the editorship of Tvardovskii in the 1960s. Recipient: Stalin Prize, 1950. Died in Moscow, 28 March 1981.

Publications

Collected Editions

Izbrannye proizvedeniia, 2 vols. Moscow, 1978; reprinted 1990.

The Long Goodbye: Three Novellas, Ann Arbor, Ardis, 1978.

Another Life and The House on the Embankment, translated by Michael Glenny. New York, Simon and Schuster, 1983.

Sobranie sochinenii, 4 vols. Moscow, 1985–87.

The Exchange and Other Stories, translated by Ellendea Proffer *et al.*, Ann Arbor, Ardis, 1991.

Fiction

"Studenty. Povest'", *Novyi mir*, 10–11 (1950), 56–175, 49–182; translated as *Students. A Novel*, by Margaret Wettlin and Ivy Litvinova, Moscow, Foreign Languages Publishing House, 1953.

"Puti v pustyne. Rasskazy" [Paths into the Desert], *Znamia*, 2 (1959), 70–99.

"Utolenie zhazhdy. Roman", *Znamia*, 4–7 (1963), 81–118; 3–39; 3–68; 3–88; translated as *Thirst Aquenched*, by Ralph Parker, in *Soviet Literature*, 1 (January 1964).

Otblesk kostra [Fireglow]. Moscow, 1966.

"Dva rasskaza: Vera i Zoika; Byl letnii polden'" [Vera and Zoika; One Summer's Noon], *Novyi mir*, 12 (1966), 75–91.

"Dva rasskaza: Samyi malen'kii gorod; Golubinaia gibel'" [The Smallest City; Death of a Dove], *Novyi mir*, 1 (1968), 74–88.

"Obmen. Povest'", *Novyi mir*, 12 (1969), 29–65; published separately as *Obmen*, edited by Robert Russell, Oxford, Blackwell, 1990; translated as "The Exchange", by Ellendea Proffer, in *The Long Goodbye: Three Novellas*, Ann Arbor, Ardis, 1978.

"Predvaritel'nye itogi", *Novyi mir*, 12 (1970), 101–40; translated as "Taking Stock", by Helen P. Burlingame, in *The Long Goodbye: Three Novellas*, Ann Arbor, Ardis, 1978.

"Dolgoe proshchanie", *Novyi mir*, 8 (1971), 53–107; translated as "The Long Goodbye", by Helen P. Burlingame, in *The Long Goodbye: Three Novellas*, Ann Arbor, Ardis, 1978.

"Neterpenie. Roman", *Novyi mir*, 3–5 (1973), 44–116; 35–112; 8–90; translated as *The Impatient Ones*, by Robert Daglish, Moscow, Progress, 1978.

"Drugaia zhizn'. Povest'", *Novyi mir*, 8 (1975), 7–99; translated as *Another Life*, by Michael Glenny, in *Another Life and House on the Embankment*, New York, Simon and Schuster; 1983; published separately, London, Abacus, 1985.

"Dom na naberezhnoi. Povest'", *Druzhba narodov*, 1 (1976), 83–167; Ann Arbor, Ardis, 1983; translated as *The House on the Embankment*, by Michael Glenny, in *Another Life and House on the Embankment*, New York, Simon and Schuster, 1983; published separately, London, Abacus, 1985.

"Starik. Roman", *Druzhba narodov*, 3 (1978), 27–153; translated as *The Old Man*, by Jacqueline Edwards and Mitchell Schneider, New York, Simon and Schuster, 1984.

"Oprokinutyi dom. Rasskazy" [The Overturned House], *Novyi mir*, 7 (1981), 58–87.

"Vremia i mesto. Roman" [Time and Place], *Druzhba narodov*, 9–10 (1981), 72–148, 22–108.

Vechnye temy. Romany, povesti [Eternal Themes]. Moscow, 1984.

"Ischeznovenie. Roman", *Druzhba narodov*, 1 (1987), 6–95; translated as *Disappearance*, by David Lowe, Ann Arbor, Ardis, 1991; reprinted Evanston, Illinois, Northwestern University Press, 1997.

Plays

Teatr pisatelia. Tri povesti dlia teatra [The Writer's Theatre. Three Stories for the Theatre] (includes *Beskonechnye*, *Obmen*, *Dom na naberezhnoi*). Moscow, 1982.

Articles

Iadro pravdy: Stat'i, interv'iu [The Core of Truth: Articles, Interviews]. Moscow, 1987.

Critical Studies

"Kakoi ei byt', zhizni?", by G. Bazhenov, *Oktiabr'*, 12 (1975), 210–12.

"Stoit li umirat' ran'she vremeni?", by V. Dudintsev, *Literaturnoe obozrenie*, 4 (1976), 52–57.

"Problema avtora i put' pisatelia", by V. Kozhinov, in *Kontekst – 1977*, edited by N. Gei, Moscow, 1978, 23–47.

"Vremia i mesto prozy Iu. Trifonova", by S. Eremina and V. Piskunov, *Voprosy literatury*, 5 (1982), 34–65.

"Jurij Trifonov's *House on the Embankment*: Narration and Meaning", by Sigrid McLaughlin, *Slavic and East European Journal*, 26/4 (1982), 419–33.

Obzor tvorchestva Iuriia Trifonova, by T. Patera, Ann Arbor, Ardis, 1983.

Proza Iuriia Trifonova, by Natal'ia Ivanova, Moscow, 1984.

"Trifonov's *Starik*: The Truth of the Past", by Josephine Woll, *Russian Literature Triquarterly*, 19 (1986), 243–58.

Iurii Trifonov: Portret-vospominanie, by Iurii Oklianskii, Moscow, 1987.
"Time and Place in the Works of Iurii Trifonov", by Robert Russell, *Forum*, 24/1 (1988).
"The Theme of Terror in *Starik*", by Herman Ermolaev, in *Aspects of Modern Russian and Czech Literature: Selected Papers of the Third World Congress for Soviet and East European Studies*, edited by Arnold McMillin, Columbus, Ohio, Slavica, 1989, 96–109.
"Yury Trifonov's Male Protagonists in the 'Test of Life'", by J.L. Laychuk, *New Zealand Slavonic Journal*, (1989–90), 109–25; 113–16.
Trifonov and the Drama of the Russian Intelligentsia, by Caroline De Maegd-Soëp, Ghent, Ghent State University, 1990.
"The Temporal and Narrative Structure of Trifonov's Novel *Starik*", by N. Kolesnikoff, *Russian Literature*, 28/1 (1990), 23–32.
Yury Trifonov's The Moscow Cycle, by Colin Partridge, Lewiston, New York, and Lampeter, Wales, Edwin Mellen Press, 1990.
"Trifonov's *Dom na naberezhnoi* and the Fortunes of Aesopian Speech", by T. Seifrid, *Slavic Review*, 49/4 (1990), 611–24.
Yury Trifonov: A Critical Study, by Nina Kolesnikoff, Ann Arbor, Ardis, 1991.
Invented Truth: Soviet Reality and the Literary Imagination of Iurii Trifonov, by Josephine Woll, Durham, North Carolina, Duke University Press, 1991.
Iurii Trifonov: Unity Through Time, by David Gillespie, Cambridge, Cambridge University Press, 1992.
"Creating a Sense of Time: Some Aspects of Style in Iurii Trifonov's Mature Prose", by S. Dalton-Brown, *Modern Language Review*, 88 (1993), 706–17.

Iurii Trifonov became an overnight success with the publication of his first novel, *Studenty* (*Students*). Obviously based on his own experience, it can be seen as a typical product of socialist realism, with clear-cut "good" and "bad" characters and an affirmation of the idealism and political commitment of the younger generation. After this, however, he struggled to find his theme, and, after publishing some short stories in the late 1950s, his next novel, *Utolenie zhazhdy* (*Thirst Aquenched*), appeared in 1963. This was about the building of the Kara-Kum canal in Turkmenia, and combines features of the typical Soviet production novel, with considerable description of the workings of land-moving equipment and discussion of the most efficient means of building the canal, with the spirit of the post-Stalin Thaw.

It was only in the late 1960s, with the publication in 1969 in Tvardovskii's *Novyi mir* of *Obmen* (*The Exchange*), and subsequent stories of contemporary Moscow life – *Predvaritel'nye itogi* (*Taking Stock*), *Dolgoe proshchanie* (*The Long Goodbye*), *Drugaia zhizn'* (*Another Life*) – that Trifonov became well known both in the Soviet Union and abroad. These stories concentrated on the morality – or lack of it – of the modern Russian intelligentsia, the compromises that are made in order to guarantee some material benefit, and the betrayal of old values. Furthermore, they are characterized by Soviet critics as being concerned with *byt* – the minutiae of everyday life, set in communal apartments, research or historical institutes, or in the writing milieu. At the same time, Trifonov demonstrated his interest in the passage of time and its effects on individuals and societies, and tried to place his modern, often fragmented, narrative within a historical framework.

Trifonov's interest in Russian and Soviet history had first become apparent in his 1965 publication *Otblesk kostra* [Fireglow]. Significantly expanded in the book edition of 1966, it purports to tell the story of his father, Valentin Trifonov, to put the historical record straight on his services to the Revolution, and to serve as a rehabilitation of his entire generation. Although in the book Iurii never questions the values and idealism of that generation, he does pass a damning indictment of Stalin and his destruction of a generation. In 1973 he published a historical novel, *Neterpenie* (*The Impatient Ones*), about the People's Will terrorists of the 1880s, and their assassination of Tsar Alexander II. In part a straightforward historical narrative, in part an analogy with the intellectual and political climate in Brezhnev's Russia, the novel also hints at a connection between the terrorists of the 1880s and the ruthlessness of the Bolsheviks in the Civil War.

By the late 1970s Trifonov was becoming bolder in his investigation of the recent Soviet past, and more experimental in his narrative technique. *Dom na naberezhnoi* (*The House on the Embankment*) has two distinct narrative voices, and the action takes place both in the present and (as recalled) in the past. A similar pattern of twin narrative planes is established in *Starik* (*The Old Man*) where the events of the Civil War are recalled 50 years later by the protagonist, Pavel Evgrafovich Letunov. By now Trifonov was working in the genre of what he termed later "the novel of consciousness", a version of "stream of consciousness" writing deemed acceptable for socialist realism. The novel *Vremia i mesto* [Time and Place] and the cycle of stories *Oprokinutyi dom* [The Overturned House] both appeared shortly after Trifonov's death in 1981, and show a further evolution, both in his choice of subject-matter and his stylistic treatment. In these works Trifonov is more concerned with the figure of the writer himself, his role in society and his inner development. *Vremia i mesto* is an ambitious portrayal of a writer, Sasha Antipov, beginning in his childhood years in the 1930s and ending with him in middle age in the late 1970s. Trifonov's writing, up to and including *Vremia i mesto*, concentrates on an individual at the moment, frozen in time, when he is forced to make a decision, to choose between maintaining or abandoning his integrity. Antipov, unusually for Trifonov's anti-heroes, makes his choice and remains true to himself.

Antipov shares many characteristics with Trifonov himself, and in *Oprokinutyi dom* Trifonov drops the pretence of a fictional protagonist and places himself in the forefront of the narrative. The stories relate Trifonov's travels in Italy, Finland, the United States, Austria, and France, and contain his reflections on the writer's integrity and honesty, the past, his sense of home and identity. Here, more than in any other work, Trifonov lays bare his soul, and the writer's persona confronts his age. *Ischeznovenie* (*Disappearance*), although apparently written in the 1970s, was published only in 1987. Its main plot is about the purges, and includes a detailed description of the search of an arrested man's apartment by the NKVD, but it is also about the loss of childhood. Significantly, there are several characters and details in this work that coincide with those from his own childhood. More fundamentally, it is also about the destruction of the old Bolsheviks, the generation that brought about the Revolution and of which Valentin Trifonov was an eminent representative.

Trifonov began his writing career responding to his times, be they the last years of Stalin or the Thaw, but increasingly came to examine closely not only contemporary Soviet society, but also its historical roots and its intellectual development, going back to the radical terrorists of 100 years ago. In his mature works he also begs questions of Russian statehood, tracing the use of terror as a means of government back to Ivan the Terrible. Throughout his writing Trifonov makes extensive use of his own experiences, especially those of his childhood, and so it comes as no great surprise that, towards the end of his life, he writes about himself and his own "time and place". In conclusion, it should be noted that Trifonov explored themes of moral compromise and historical truth at a time of considerable repression and censorship, and published his work many years, sometimes decades, before Gorbachev's policy of glasnost made it both possible and fashionable to pursue such themes.

DAVID GILLESPIE

The Exchange

Obmen

Novella, 1969

The novella opens in Moscow in the 1970s, where Viktor Dmitriev's mother, Ksenia Fedorovna, has been diagnosed with terminal cancer (she is unaware of the prognosis). Dmitriev's wife, Lena, dislikes her mother-in-law intensely but suddenly suggests that they and their daughter should live together with Ksenia Fedorovna. The proposal appalls Dmitriev because of its crassness.

At this early point in the tale some clarification is essential for readers unfamiliar with the housing situation in the Soviet Union. Apartments were allotted by the state, and the number of rooms depended initially on family size. A later move to another apartment could be accomplished legally only as an exchange, a tedious bureaucratic procedure. Viktor, Lena, and their daughter live in a one-room ("studio") apartment. Lena knows that, because of the housing rules, their best chance to move to a larger apartment is if they can trade theirs and Ksenia Fedorovna's for one where they will all live together. Dmitriev understands only too well what Lena does not need to say: that after his mother's imminent death they will have the whole apartment to themselves.

A series of flashbacks traces the stormy history of the relations between Dmitriev's family and that of Lena. In the person of his grandfather, an old revolutionary, Dmitriev's family represents a dying breed: what Trifonov sees as the idealistic, self-sacrificing, ascetic intelligentsia that waged a revolution against bourgeois values. Lena's parents, the Lukianovs, are members of a new, pragmatic class of professionals that Stalin created and that to a large extent set the tone for the Brezhnev era. Not surprisingly, the families do not get along at all, and Dmitriev is caught in the middle.

Giving in to Lena, Dmitriev suggests the exchange to his mother. In the novella's most pointed line, she tells her son that he has already made an exchange (by which she means that he has adopted his in-laws' values). In a surprising development, Ksenia Fedorovna none the less agrees to the exchange. The last-minute bureaucratic procedures take their toll on Dmitriev, as does his mother's death shortly thereafter, and he ends up in hospital suffering from hypertension.

The Exchange is the earliest of a group of narratives that have come to be called Trifonov's Moscow novellas. They generally focus on what seem at first to be the exclusively domestic trials and tribulations of a middle-aged man. As the novellas progress, however, the protagonist's personal and family history turn out to be inextricably linked to larger issues of Soviet social and political history. In this regard, the title of *The Exchange* works on several levels, referring both to families trading apartments as well as to individuals and a whole society trading values over time. In *The Exchange* the present and the past, private history and social history, meet in the pages devoted to the Dmitriev family's dacha at Pavlinovo, where much of the novella's action transpires.

Dmitriev's father received the dacha by joining a co-operative. Over the years the family and their neighbours – people like them – proved unable or unwilling to keep up the property and the co-operative. After Dmitriev's marriage, Lena quickly refurnishes the dacha, offending in-laws in the process, and her parents use their connections to have the cesspool fixed and a telephone installed. The details have an allegorical function in addition to a realistic one: they symbolize the triumph of a new generation of pragmatists over an old-fashioned intelligentsia that sometimes prided itself on its impracticality. By the end of the novella the dacha at Pavlinovo has been torn down to make way for a new stadium: Brezhnev's USSR, where culture boils down to sports, has swept away another reminder of a now irrelevant revolutionary intelligentsia.

Critics and readers alike recognized that *The Exchange*, first published in 1969, was quite unlike anything that Trifonov had written earlier. Until then he had been a rather conventional Soviet writer, but with his Moscow novellas Trifonov became an unconventional Soviet author. Orthodox Soviet critics denigrated *The Exchange* and the other Moscow tales for their allegedly excessive attention to *byt*, the texture of daily life. What the critics actually meant, but did not dare state openly, was that Trifonov's portrait of the Soviet present and past in no way flattered the Soviet regime. Dissident Soviet writers of the 1970s were wary of Trifonov, who managed to remain a Soviet writer in good standing with officialdom even as he published works that would have been denounced as anti-Soviet had they rolled off underground or western presses.

The Exchange demonstrates several features of Trifonov's mature artistry. The novella is Chekhovian in its use of telling detail, hint, and allusion. The subtle narrative technique allows readers to see Dmitriev alternately from the inside and the outside. All in all, the gift for characterization is phenomenal.

The moral issues in *The Exchange* are more complex than they initially appear. Nearly all the characters in the novella defy easy categorization with regard to their ethics and their relationship to any truth. Ksenia Fedorovna's high ideals and self-sacrifice owe more than a bit to her desire to project a certain image and in that sense are not entirely sincere. Lena's family is associated with crassness, crudeness, venality, mistrust, and even violence, yet they accomplish deeds that are objectively "good". In the final analysis, Dmitriev comes off as a rather pathetic figure not because he has traded a "good" set of values for a "bad" set, but because he himself seems so wishy-washy, so utterly without principles. Not that Dmitriev does not have goals. Above all he desires peace and quiet in his domestic life, and *The Exchange* dramatizes the messy personal and societal consequences of a willingness to pay any price for domestic tranquillity.

DAVID A. LOWE

Another Life

Drugaia zhizn'

Novella, 1975

Another Life, which appeared in the journal *Novyi mir* in 1975, is the fourth and penultimate in Trifonov's cycle of Moscow tales. All five texts fall into the genre of urban *byt* prose; they deal with the disillusionment and moral dilemmas of middle-aged *intelligenty* (members of the intelligentsia) trapped in a domestic *zamknutyi mirok* (closed world). Trifonov's mastery of the genre, which has been less ably emulated by Trifonov's "followers" such as Ruslan Kireev and other *sorokaletnie* (40-year-old) writers, is revealed principally in his style. Trifonov's Chekhovian tales of dreary lives and inevitable disappointments are complex and oblique, written in "dotted lines", in hints and nuances, requiring the reader to fill in the gaps left by the author.

Harshly criticized by Soviet critics during the 1970s for his non-judgmental, ironic attitude to his characters, Trifonov created texts intended to make the reader look inwards, at his own faults, rather than permit complacent judgements of the characters. *Another Life* is primarily a text about limited viewpoint, a penetrating study of one woman's inability to transcend her own egoism. Trifonov describes the attempt by Ol'ga Vasil'evna, a biochemist, to look back at her life and to understand its significance, an undertaking triggered by the recent death of her husband, Sergei. Trifonov skilfully uses his favoured narrative method of *nesobstvenno-priamaia rech'* (free indirect discourse) to indicate to the reader that Ol'ga's view of her dead husband is by no means complete, and that she is bent on self-vindication rather than on self-knowledge.

An idealistic character, unable to compromise, Sergei is an historian engaged in researching the activities of the tsarist secret police in the period before the February Revolution. He obtains a list of these informers, including, it is hinted, names of people still alive and in government positions; one reason why his colleagues are so anxious to impede his work. Sergei, however, will not bend under pressure to leave this topic alone. He ultimately breaks, dying of a heart attack at the early age of 42. To his wife, however, Sergei is a failure. Despite her (patently untrue) claim that she neither demanded anything from her husband, nor reproached him for his lack of material success, Ol'ga is clearly disappointed in her "irresponsible" spouse. Her jealous possessiveness translates itself into the belief that he cannot manage without her; casting him in the role of child and buffoon, Ol'ga inevitably sees him as an inadequate husband and father. She wonders why he cannot be more successful in his career, even if this means pandering to unpleasant types such as Kislovskii, or the aptly named Genital'ich Klimuk. The latter are only two examples of many such philistine and careerist types in Trifonov's texts, characters who oppose more idealistic figures such as Sergei's mother, Aleksandra Prokof'evna, formerly a typist in the political department of the Red Army and now working as an unpaid legal adviser.

The repeated introduction of such characters as old "revolutionaries" and philistines into his work has lead many Soviet critics to label Trifonov's Moscow tales, somewhat simplistically, as texts about the conflict between idealism and *meshchanstvo* (philistinism). Ol'ga herself belongs to the latter pole of the dichotomy. Like her forerunners, Lena in *The Exchange*, or Rita in *Taking Stock*, she is an at times amusing, at times admirably strong-minded, yet ultimately inflexible female tyrant who cannot see that her materialistic doctrine of pragmatic expediency might be at all unsound or, at least, limited.

Despite being one of the lesser-known of the cycle (critics have tended to concentrate on *The Exchange* and *The House on the Embankment*), *Another Life* demonstrates Trifonov's continued interest in themes such as man's capacity for self-deception, time and history, and the post-Stalinist expedient mentality. Trifonov describes a new generation of Soviet citizens; those who, often without knowing it, have succumbed to an ideology that has encouraged them to forget their principles. A secondary character in *Another Life*, the painter Georgii Maksimovich (based on the artist A.M. Niurenburg, father of Trifonov's first wife), whom Sergei describes as a "businessman", provides one such example of a man who has sacrificed integrity for material success. Others have forgotten not only ideals, but have turned their backs on their past, on the legacy of political courage entrusted to them by their revolutionary forebears. The strong presence of this theme makes *Another Life* one of the most personal of Trifonov's texts, hinting as it does at the author's own long battle to come to terms with his father's status as a revolutionary and victim of Stalinism. *Another Life* indirectly poses a question: do men and women ultimately "resemble their time more than their fathers", as Trifonov stated in an interview in Germany (*Frankfurter Rundschau*, 19 April 1975), or can they free themselves from the prevailing ideology, and remain faithful to their heritage?

Trifonov offers the reader an indirect criticism of the Stalinist legacy that birthed a generation afraid to enquire too closely into dark corners of history, or to question their own ethics. Sergei is not merely an historian, but a detective looking for one of the many corpses buried in the unmarked graves of Soviet history. He is also something of a philosopher, with a view of history that appears to borrow in general terms from Nikolai Fedorov's concept of memory as a resurrective force. Sergei tries to recreate the threads of history, which, broken by Stalinist violence, cannot act any longer as conduits through which certain "indestructible elements" can be genetically passed to subsequent generations. Such elements appear to be the traits of independence, courage, and idealism; the characteristics that Sergei's own forebears possessed in abundance. His historical research is not only an attempt to find truth by "filling in the gaps" of history (just as the reader fills in the gaps created in the text by an elusive author), but is a means towards discovering his own identity through "resurrecting" his ancestors.

Trifonov's text is about time, about the attempt to rediscover the past, and, paradoxically, to break free of it. At the end of the text, Ol'ga begins a new relationship. Whether this will be more successful than her marriage is open to doubt; in typical fashion, Trifonov allows the reader to decide whether Ol'ga has learned anything from her own historical "research" into her past life. Does she remain trapped, fated to repeat past mistakes in her new relationship, or will another life truly begin for her?

S. DALTON-BROWN

The House on the Embankment

Dom na naberezhnoi

Novella, 1976

Published in the journal *Druzhba narodov* in 1976, *The House on the Embankment* met with a hostile reception by official critics. It is a structurally complex novella that is also a powerful indictment of the generation that prospered under Stalin. The central character is Vadim Glebov, whom we first see in middle age attempting to buy an item of antique furniture. As the result of a chance meeting with a childhood friend, Levka Shulepnikov, while negotiating this purchase, Glebov begins to recall his past, beginning with his childhood, and in particular his student years at the Moscow Literary Institute in the late 1940s.

In terms of plot, it is largely a re-writing of Trifonov's Stalin Prize-winning novel *Students*. In both works the central character becomes engaged in a campaign against a professor at the Institute, resulting in both cases in his dismissal. In both works the downturn in the professor's fortunes is matched by the upturn in those of the protagonist. But there the similarity ends. Whereas in the first novel the emphasis is on the political correctness of the students' stance against their backward-looking professor, in *The House on the Embankment* psychological motivation is usually based on envy, greed, lust, or careerism. Whereas the first novel ends on a triumphant note affirming the dominance of Soviet internationalism and young people's faith in the future, *The House on the Embankment* ends in death and recriminations. There are few "positive" characters, and even they – Anton Ovchinnikov, Sonia Ganchuk, Kuno Ivanovich – submit to stronger and darker forces. The atmosphere of fear and denunciation is ever-present, even in school, where pupils are openly encouraged to inform on one another. At the end of the work we see what has become of Levka and Professor Ganchuk in the 1970s, a quarter of a century after the main events, and the reader is struck by their demoralization and vacuity. Significantly, the final scene begins in a cemetery where Sonia Ganchuk is buried, and where Levka, one of the dead souls of Soviet society, is the watchman. In the character of Glebov, Trifonov succeeds in giving a convincing picture of the Soviet academic's path to success, the fate of those he brushes aside on the way, and the inner price he has to pay. Trifonov also thus succeeds in providing an allegory for the moral and spiritual development of the Soviet intelligentsia over the past 50 years.

The figure of Professor Ganchuk is important in this respect. In his youth a fearless fighter for the Red cause during the Civil War, and subsequently a literary theoretician who regarded a debate as more of a battle designed to "kill off" the enemy – in other words a maker of history – he becomes, in later life, a victim of the times he has helped to create. Once a devoted admirer of Gor'kii, the "founder of socialist realism and originator of Soviet literature" (as described in the official Soviet *Brief Literary Encyclopedia*), he briefly rejects him and turns to Dostoevskii as a key to understanding the depths of evil in the human soul.

In terms of its structure and style, the work, unlike its simplistic predecessor, is highly complex. The key to Glebov's character and his past is provided not by Glebov himself, whose efforts to recall people and events from 30 years previously are really an attempt to forget, but by an unseen and unnamed character who assumes the first-person narration. It is the narrator who provides information Glebov is unwilling to face, such as his actual part in the denunciation of Ganchuk at a special meeting held in the Institute. It is also the narrator who passes judgement on Glebov's character, calling him a "nonentity", but, like all nonentities, likely to go far. More significantly, the author goes into Glebov's mind. When Glebov suffers bouts of remorse and tries to rationalize his actions by blaming "the times", we know that the blame cannot be shifted that easily. "The times" are actually created by people, and Glebov is himself one of those people. Glebov may be a moral cripple, but he is entirely representative of his generation.

Therefore, the narrative is not only divided into the action of the present, and memories of the past, but also into two complementary narrative standpoints. Trifonov further complicates matters when he shows the workings of Glebov's own mind, allowing Glebov to justify himself in his own tortured words. An element of *skaz* (first-person narration) serves to confuse the narrative voices, so that the reader is at times unsure who is speaking, Glebov or the author. Trifonov's style is sometimes breathtakingly compressed, with long sentences punctuated by many subordinate or relative clauses, so that even sentence structure and syntax follow the flow of time in Trifonov's prose. The narrative covers almost 40 years, and whereas whole decades can be glossed over, crucial moments, even seconds, in the life of a character are dwelt on in detail. Time itself becomes one of the dramatis personae, and there are many passages in the work devoted to its fluidity and its effects on individuals. *The House on the Embankment* offers not just a bleak commentary on the Stalin years, especially the late 1940s, but also shows how the consequences of the decisions and moral choices made during those years live on in the present.

DAVID GILLESPIE

The Old Man

Starik

Novel, 1978

Published in the journal *Druzhba narodov* in 1978, and Trifonov's last work to appear in his lifetime, *The Old Man* courted controversy as it was the first work of Soviet literature since *Tikhii Don* (*Quiet Flows the Don*) to discuss Bolshevik atrocities during the Civil War. The novel begins in 1973 when Pavel Evgrafovich Letunov, a veteran of the Civil War, receives a letter from Asia Igumnova, whom he has not seen for over half a century. Five years previously Letunov had written an article on Sergei Migulin, a Cossack commander who fought on the side of the Reds but who was executed by them. Letunov's article effectively rehabilitated Migulin. With the arrival of Asia's letter Letunov returns in his mind to the past, at first to his life in St

Petersburg before the Revolution, when he knew Asia as a young girl, and then the bloody, bitter years of the Civil War on the Don. Asia was Migulin's wife at the time. Letunov wants to know the answer to the question: why did Migulin move his forces, against orders, to the front? Was he attempting to change sides, as he was later accused, and for which he was executed? Or, consigned to the rear but eager to take part in the battle, was his action a desperate gamble? Trifonov supplies no answer, for that is no longer the point. The point is that Letunov gave evidence against Migulin at his trial in 1921, something he himself had forgotten about. As in *The House on the Embankment*, Trifonov writes here about history, memory, and the present, and how, alongside the human victims, perhaps the greater casualty is truth.

With Letunov's memories of the Civil War, Trifonov paints a picture of brutality, ideological fanaticism, and even genocide. Bolshevik commanders such as Braslavskii and Shigontsev enforce the policy of "de-Cossackization" with great zeal, execute innocent hostages, and promise to destroy villages "like Carthage". Indeed, we learn that Bolshevik policy towards the Cossacks was to exterminate the entire upper strata of the Cossackry, although Trifonov is at pains to exonerate Lenin or the Bolshevik leadership for this decision. Historical parallels abound, as the Don rebellion is likened to the rising of the Vendée against the new French republic's National Convention in 1793, and Bolshevik leaders consistently use the French Revolution as a frame of reference for their use of terror. Terror is "justified" when it is committed by "the new, progressive class, sweeping away from its path the remnants of feudalism and popular ignorance". Trifonov, on the other hand, uses parallels with the 19th-century Nihilist and terrorist Sergei Nechaev, thus providing a different, far from "historically expedient" justification for murderous violence. Terrorism cannot lead to a brave new world of justice and freedom, because the end cannot justify the means. Elsewhere in the narrative, as characters in the 1970s discuss Russian history, events in Russia under Ivan the Terrible are juxtaposed with events in contemporary France, in particular the massacre of the Huguenots. Violence and murder are not limited to Russia.

Moreover, Trifonov returns to the territory previously traversed in *Otblesk kostra* [Fireglow], for Migulin is based on the charismatic and popular Don Cossack leader Fillip Mironov, and his wise and far-seeing commissar Danilov is based on Trifonov's own father. Indeed, almost the whole of the second half of *Otblesk kostra* is devoted to Mironov, a Cossack leader who was popular and respected by his men, but suspected and resented by Bolshevik leaders and politicians. Mironov was executed in unexplained circumstances in the Butyrki prison in Moscow in 1921, and only rehabilitated in 1960. There is, however, a significant development. In the earlier book the idealism of Valentin Trifonov and his generation is unimpaired, and they become the victims of "the cult of personality". In *The Old Man* Danilov's good judgement and fairness come to nought as Migulin is executed, destroyed by fanatics and demagogues long before Stalin came to power.

The events of the Civil War, however, are mere memories. The actual present is represented by the sordid squabble over a neighbouring dacha that is desired both by Letunov's son, Ruslan, basically a decent man, and the odious Oleg Kandaurov. Kandaurov is a career bureaucrat, opportunistic and totally cynical, and will stop at nothing to get what he wants, be this the dacha or a prestigious posting abroad. Although in middle age, he keeps himself physically fit, has a young mistress, and lies to everyone. This mundane struggle – the very stuff of *byt* – is contrasted greatly with the titanic struggle of ideas and ideals that Letunov recalls of the Civil War. The past has been betrayed and debased, and the current generation is lost in a spurious materialism. The younger generation, furthermore, no longer understands the values of Letunov, and, indeed, his daughter brings doctors to see him inconspicuously to decide if he is going senile. Significantly, Kandaurov is diagnosed as suffering from a terminal illness, and the whole dacha settlement is soon to be razed to the ground. All, it seems, is vanity, and returns to dust.

In *The Old Man* Trifonov gives us a pessimistic picture of Soviet society, both its present and its past. The present is spiritually and morally barren, and the past built on terror and lies: the values of the Revolution – idealism, freedom, justice – were destroyed during the Civil War, when men of principle and vision were physically annihilated or sidelined. Trifonov shows in his posthumous novel *Disappearance* that the men who were victorious in 1921 were also those who killed off the old Bolsheviks in 1937. In other words, this is a society based on terror and coercion, so it is little wonder that those who do well in the present, are those who "know how to live" and who "exert all their power" to get what they want. Trifonov states in *Otblesk kostra* that he is interested in the Civil War period not only because of his father's participation in it, but also because this is when Soviet society began. By looking at its historical roots, and telling as much of the truth as possible in a repressive age, Trifonov did a great service both to his own people, and to future writers and historians who could examine the period in greater freedom.

DAVID GILLESPIE

Marina Ivanovna Tsvetaeva 1892–1941

Poet and prose writer

Biography

Born in Moscow, 8 October 1892. Attended schools in Switzerland and Germany, and at the Sorbonne, Paris. Married: Sergei Efron in 1912 (executed 1939); two daughters and one son. Trapped in Moscow for five years after the 1917 Revolution; emigrated to Berlin, 1922, and then Prague; settled in Paris, 1925. Returned to the USSR in 1938; officially ostracized and unable to publish. Evacuated from Moscow. Died (suicide by hanging) in Elabuga, 31 August 1941. Her reputation has grown greatly since the 1970s.

Publications

Collected Editions

Izbrannoe. Moscow, 1961.
Izbrannye proizvedeniia. Moscow, 1965; 2nd edition Moscow, 1991.
Stikhotvoreniia. Letchworth, Bradda, 1969.
Selected Poems, translated by Elaine Feinstein. London, Oxford University Press, 1971; revised edition Oxford, Oxford University Press, 1981; Harmondsworth, Penguin, 1986.
Neizdannoe: Stikhi, teatr, proza. Paris, YMCA-Press, 1976.
Izbrannaia proza 1917–1937, edited by Alexander Sumerkin, 2 vols. New York, Russica, 1979.
Stikhotvoreniia i poemy. Moscow, 1980.
Sochineniia, 2 vols. Moscow, 1980.
Stikhotvoreniia i poemy, edited by Alexander Sumerkin and Viktoria Schweitzer, 5 vols. New York, Russica, 1980–90.
Selected Poems, translated by David McDuff. Newcastle upon Tyne, Bloodaxe, 1987.
"Poklonis' Moskvu ..." [Worship Moscow ...] (poetry, prose, diaries, letters). Moscow, 1989.
Sobranie sochinenii, poem i dramaticheskikh proizvedenii, 3 vols. Moscow, 1990.
Poemy. Dramaticheskie proizvedeniia. 1992.
Sobranie sochinenii, 7 vols. Moscow, 1994–95.

Poetry

Vechernii al'bom [Evening Album]. Moscow, 1910.
Volshebnyi fonar' [Magic Lantern]. Moscow, 1912; reprinted Paris, YMCA-Press, 1979.
Iz dvukh knig [From Two Books]. Moscow, 1913.
Versty [Mileposts]. Moscow, 1921; 2nd edition, 1922.
Versty, Vypusk I [Mileposts: Book One]. Moscow, 1922; reprinted Ann Arbor, Ardis, 1972.
Razluka [Separation]. Berlin, 1922; reprinted Paris, Lev, 1975.
Stikhi k Bloku [Poems to Blok]. Berlin, 1922; reprinted Letchworth, Prideaux Press, 1978.
Tsar'-devitsa [The Tsar-Maiden]. Petrograd, 1922; reprinted Letchworth, Prideaux Press, 1971.
Remeslo [Craft]. Berlin, 1923; reprinted Oxford, Meeuws, 1981.
Psikheia [Psyche]. Berlin, 1923; reprinted Paris, Lev, 1979.
Molodets [The Swain]. Prague, 1924; reprinted Letchworth, Prideaux Press, 1971.
Krysolov [The Ratcatcher]. Paris, 1925; reprinted Letchworth, Prideaux Press, 1978.
Posle Rossii: 1922–1925. Paris, 1928; reprinted Paris, 1976; translated as *After Russia* (bilingual edition), by Michael M. Naydan, Ann Arbor, Ardis, 1992.
Lebedinyi stan. Munich, 1957; translated as *The Demesne of the Swans* (bilingual edition), by Robin Kemball, Ann Arbor, Ardis, 1980.
Prosto serdtse [Simply the Heart]. 1967.
Stikhotvoreniia i poemy. Leningrad, 1979.
Three Russian Women Poets: Anna Akhmatova, Marina Tsvetaeva, Bella Akhmadulina, edited and translated by Mary Maddock. Trumansburg. New York, Crossing Press, 1983.
Stikhotvoreniia. Izbrannaia lirika 1908–1939. Moscow, 1986.
In the Inmost Hour of the Soul, translated by Nina Kossman. Clifton, New Jersey, Humana Press, 1989.
V polemike s vekom [Polemics with the Century]. Moscow, 1991.
Sivilla [Seville]. Moscow, 1991.

Plays

Konets Kazanovy [Casanova's End]. 1922.
Metel'. Prikliuchenie. Ariadna. P'esy [The Blizzard. Adventure. Ariadne. Plays]. Letchworth, Bradda, 1978.
Teatr [Theatre]. Moscow, 1988.

Fiction

Proza [Prose]. New York, Izdatel'stvo imeni Chekhova, 1953.
Proza [Prose]. Letchworth, Bradda, 1969.
A Captive Spirit: Selected Prose, edited and translated by J. Marin King. Ann Arbor, Ardis, 1980; London, Virago, 1983; revised edition, New York, Vintage, 1994.

Letters

Pis'ma k Anne Teskovoi [Letters to Anna Teskovoi], edited by V. Morkovin. Prague, Academiia, 1969; Jerusalem, Versty, 1982.
Pis'ma k raznym litsam [Letters to Various Persons]. 1969.
Neizdannye pis'ma [Unpublished Letters], edited by Gleb and Nikita Struve. Paris, YMCA-Press, 1972.
Rainer Maria Rilke, Marina Zwetajewa, Boris Pasternak: Briefwechsel, edited by Yevgeny Pasternak, Yelena Pasternak, and Konstantin M. Azadovsky. Frankfurt, Insel, 1983; translated as *Boris Pasternak, Marine Tsevtaeva, Rainer Maria Rilke: Letters, Summer 1926*, by Margaret Wettlin and Walter Arndt, San Diego, Harcourt Brace Jovanovich 1985; London, Jonathan Cape, 1986; Oxford, Oxford University Press, 1988.
Pis'ma k Ariadne Berg (1934–1939) [Letters to Ariadna Berg]. Paris, YMCA-Press, 1990.
Pis'ma k docheri. Dnevnikovye zapisi [Letters to a Daughter ...]. Moscow, 1995.
Pis'ma k Anatoliiu Shteigeru [Letters to Anatolii Shteiger]. Moscow, 1995.

Autobiography
Avtobiograficheskaia proza [Autobiographical Prose]. Moscow, 1991.

Essays and Literary Criticism
Moi Pushkin [My Pushkin]. Moscow, 1967.
Gde otstypaetsia liubov' ... [Where Love Renounces ...]. Moscow, 1991.
Ob iskusstve: Marina Tsvetaeva [On Art: Marina Tsvetaeva]. Moscow, 1991.
Art in the Light of Conscience: Eight Essays on Poetry, translated by Angela Livingstone. London, Bristol Classical Press, and Cambridge, Massachusetts, Harvard University Press, 1992.

Critical Studies
Marina Cvetaeva: Her Life and Art, by Simon Karlinsky, Berkeley, University of California Press, 1966.
"Logaoedic Metres in the Lyric Poetry of Marina Tsvetaeva", by Gerald S. Smith, *Slavonic and East European Review*, 53/132 (1975), 330–54.
Marina Tsvetaeva, Fotobiografiia, compiled by Ellendea Proffer, Ann Arbor, Ardis, 1980.
Nightingale Fever: Russian Poets in Revolution, by Ronald Hingley, New York, Knopf, 1981; London, Weidenfeld and Nicolson, 1982.
Marina Zwetajewa. Mythos und Wahrheit, by Marina Razumovsky, Vienna, Karolinger, 1981; translated as *Marina Tsvetayeva: A Critical Biography*, by Aleksey Gibson, Newcastle upon Tyne, Bloodaxe, 1994.
Poets of Modern Russia, by Peter France, Cambridge, Cambridge University Press, 1982.
Vospominaniia, by Anastasia Tsvetaeva, 3rd edition, Moscow, 1983.
Mifologizm i teologizm Tsvetaevoi, by Jerzy Faryno, Vienna, Wiener Slawistischer Almanach, 1985.
Marina Tsvetaeva: The Woman, Her World and Her Poetry, by Simon Karlinsky, Cambridge, Cambridge University Press, 1985.
Marina Tsvetaeva: Stranitsy zhizni i tvorchestva (1910–1922), by Anna Saakiants, Moscow, 1986.
A Captive Lion: The Life of Marina Tsvetayeva, by Elaine Feinstein, London, Hutchinson, and New York, Dutton, 1987.
Terrible Perfection: Women and Russian Literature, by Barbara Heldt, Bloomington, University of Indiana Press, 1987.
Marina Tsvetaeva: Un itinéraire poétique, by Véronique Lossky, Paris, Solin, 1987.
Byt i bytie Mariny Tsvetaevoi, by Viktoria Schweitzer, Paris, Sintaksis, 1988; translated as *Tsvetaeva*, by Robert Chandler, H.T. Willetts, and Peter Norman, London, Harvill Press, 1992.
O Marine Tsvetaevoi: Vospominaniia docheri, by Ariadna Efron, Moscow, 1989.
A Life Through Poetry: Marina Tsvetaeva's Lyric Diary, by Jane A. Taubman, Columbia, Ohio, Slavica, 1989.
Poeziia Mariny Tsvetaevoi: Lingvisticheskii aspekt, by L.V. Zubova, Moscow, 1989.
Marina Tsvetaeva: Trudy 1-ogo mezhdunarodnogo simpoziuma (Lozanna, 30. vi–3. vii 1982), edited by Robin Kemball, Bern, Peter Lang, 1991.
Nebesnaia arka: Marina Tsvetaeva i Rainer Mariia Ril'ke, edited by K.M. Azadovskii, St Petersburg, 1992.
"Bells and Cupolas: The Formative Role of the Female Body in Marina Tsvetaeva's Poetry", by Sibelan Forrester, *Slavic Review*, 51/2 (1992), 232–46.
Marina Tsvetaeva v Moskve, by Iudif Kagan, Moscow, 1992.
Vospominaniia [Reminiscences], edited by L.A. Mnukhin and L.M. Turchinskii, Moscow, 1992.
Marina Tsvetaeva: Stat'i i teksty, edited by L.A. Mnukhin, Vienna, Wiener Slawistischer Almanach, 1992.
Marina Tsvetaeva: Poetics of Appropriation, by Michael Makin, Oxford, Clarendon Press, 1993.
Marina Tsvetaeva: The Double Beat of Heaven and Hell, by Lily Feiler, Durham, North Carolina, Duke University Press, 1994.
Gibel' Mariny Tsvetaevoi, by I. Kudrova, Moscow, 1995.
The Song of the Mocking Bird: Pushkin in the Work of Marina Tsvetaeva, by Alexandra Smith, Bern, Peter Lang, 1995.
Tsvetaeva's Orphic Journeys to the Worlds of the Word, by Olga Peters Hasty, Evanston, Illinois, Northwestern University Press, 1996.
Slovar' poeticheskogo iazyka Mariny Tsvetaevoi, 4 vols, Moscow, 1996–

Bibliography
Bibliographie des oeuvres de Tsvetayeva, by Tatiana Gladkova and Lev Mnukhin, Paris, Institut d'Études Slaves, 1982; 2nd edition, 1993.

Although Marina Tsvetaeva is now universally acknowledged as one of the most original of 20th-century Russian poets, her reputation among both critics and readers has not always been so high. Her first collection, *Vechernii al'bom* [Evening Album] (1910), was favourably, though not uncritically, reviewed by Voloshin, Gumilev, Briusov, and Shaginian, but the other work Tsvetaeva published before the Revolution, for all its technical accomplishment, was widely seen as failing to outgrow her early adolescent themes and a predilection for romantic clichés. By the time she published *Versty* [Mileposts] and *Versty, Vypusk I* [Mileposts: Book One], the first manifestation of what has been called the "real Tsvetaeva", in 1921 and 1922, the critical community in Russia that might have promoted her had fallen victim to the Revolution and the Civil War. In the Soviet Union she became *persona non grata* for her impassioned support of the White cause, while the conservative émigré communities of Berlin, Prague, and Paris tended to treat her work with suspicion because of its formal unorthodoxy. Such support as it did afford her was forfeited when it became clear in the late 1930s that her husband, once a White Army officer, had been working for the NKVD. When Tsvetaeva died in 1941 she was isolated and unpublished; her literary rehabilitation began only in the mid-1960s.

Part of the reason for Tsvetaeva's failure to promote her work during her lifetime lies in the fact that she belonged to no recognized school of poetry and had no literary colleagues or disciples. Her work lacks the philosophical underpinnings of Symbolism or Acmeism and is distant too from the passionate espousal of the modern that characterized the Futurists. Tsvetaeva's work defies categorization, but she is, if anything, a belated (and highly original) romantic; her main theme is the isolation of the individual in an uncaring world, and especially the tension between women's private emotions and their public roles.

The dominant principle of Tsvetaeva's verse, on both a thematic and a formal plane, is energy itself, above any individual manifestation of it. This leads her to a cult of the romantic hero, particularly in her early work, and to the adoption of a strikingly wide range of stylistic masks: lower-class Moscow women; characters from Russian folklore and history, from the Bible and classical mythology, and from works of both high and popular literature. She chooses, for example, such figures as Phaedra, Ariadne, Rachel, Ophelia, and Manon Lescaut, whose experience can be seen to epitomize her central theme of personal drama. Emotion in Tsvetaeva's writing frequently manifests itself as an assertion of individual independence or of freedom in love. On other occasions it is seen as a withdrawal from the world into homesickness or the celebration of everyday objects or the world of literature.

When she writes about poetry itself, Tsvetaeva's image of the poet is of a rebel or an outcast and she expresses her admiration for the independence of her own poetic teachers – Pushkin, Akhmatova, Blok – in a series of eulogistic cycles. At various times Tsvetaeva's poetry also treats contemporary political events, and it is for its martial energy as much as anything that she praises the White Army in *Lebedinyi stan* (*The Demesne of the Swans*). Her much later *Stikhi k Chekhii* [Poems to the Czechs], on the other hand, focus on the plight of a small country in the face of the Nazi invasion, and valorize its unique cultural identity much as the historical continuity of Moscow had been foregrounded in *Versty*.

The language of Tsvetaeva's poetry is the perfect medium for the expression of the impassioned commitment of her thematics. She strikingly juxtaposes words from different semantic registers: archaisms, vulgarisms, and neologisms appear in otherwise lexically standard texts. There is much use of ellipsis, particularly of verbs and pronouns, which has the effect of intensifying the sentiments expressed. There is much word-play, especially of the sort that emphasizes the separate meanings of word roots and derives complex associative chains from deliberate misunderstandings or from misplaced word-stress. There is extensive use of hyperbole and of semantic parallelism and of the clustering of multiple images around a central idea. Each of these techniques increases the inherent tension of Tsvetaeva's verse.

Tsvetaeva's early books show her facility with the five traditional metres of Russian versification, but with *Versty* she begins to experiment with *dol'niki*, and with *Remeslo* [Craft] and *Posle Rossii* (*After Russia*), the fusion of binary and ternary metres and the use of adjacent stressed syllables become the norm. Tsvetaeva's rhymes are generally unadventurous, but she shows particular inventiveness in the elaboration of stanzaic forms. Enjambment, particularly across stanzas, provides yet another source of tension.

Tsvetaeva's writing was by no means confined to lyric poetry. Her narrative poems of the early 1920s – notably *Tsar'-devitsa* [The Tsar-Maiden] and *Molodets* [The Swain] – make use of folkloric models in their plots, language, and imagery to continue Tsvetaeva's lyric programme on a broader scale. In the late 1920s Tsvetaeva published several satirical works, including the lengthy *Krysolov* [The Ratcatcher], and her attacks on middle-class complacency complement her glorification of the romantic hero. Tsvetaeva's interest in the heroines of Greek literature and their emotional sufferings, which is particularly strong in her later books of poetry, reaches a climax in her verse plays *Tezei-Ariadne* [Theseus-Ariadne] and *Fedra* [Phaedra].

During the last ten years of her life Tsvetaeva turned increasingly to prose. Much of it is autobiographically inspired and offers an impressionistic mythologization of the life of the Poet as manifested in Tsvetaeva's own experience in her personal and professional relationships with figures such as Voloshin and Belyi. Pushkin is treated as a contemporary and linked with Tsvetaeva's own development as a poet in *Moi Pushkin* [My Pushkin]; he is also an important subject of Tsvetaeva's literary criticism. These prose works, like Tsvetaeva's verse, have, through their emotional and rhetorical power, proved an inspiration to later generations of Russian writers.

DAVID N. WELLS

Tsar'-devitsa

The Tsar-Maiden

Narrative poem, 1922

This fairy-tale poem was written in summer 1920 and published in 1922 in Moscow and in Berlin. Its sources of inspiration include Derzhavin's *Tsar'-devitsa* [King-Maiden], Afanas'ev's *Narodnye russkie skazki* [Popular Russian Tales], Polonskii's lyric *Tsar'-devitsa*, Ershov's *Konek-gorbunok* [The Hunch-Backed Horse]; and *byliny* (Russian traditional heroic poems). It signifies Tsvetaeva's turn from dramatic to narrative poetry.

One possible reason for Tsvetaeva's attraction to narrative poetry and Russian folklore was suggested by her daughter: Ariadna Efron's memoirs recall the great impression made on Tsvetaeva by Blok's recitals of his poetry in May 1920. According to Efron, after reading Blok's *Dvenadtsat'* (*The Twelve*), Tsvetaeva felt ashamed as a poet for overlooking popular culture and the "element of the revolution" ("stikhiia revoliutsii", in Blok's words). Tsvetaeva's tale is covert political commentary in the style of Pushkin's "Skazka o zolotom petushke" ("The Tale of the Golden Cockerel"). Unlike Blok, Tsvetaeva sees dark forces woken by the Revolution: her tale is full of scenes of drunken orgies, erotic revelry, witchcraft, spells, and chaos. In conjunction with Tsvetaeva's pro-monarchist cycle *The Demesne of the Swans*, which she wrote at the same time, some passages of *Tsar'-devitsa* can be read as a direct political comment:

Let's look how the country
Suffers and cry,
How it copes with the night
Without the Tsar.

Images from *The Demesne of the Swans* reappear in *Tsar'-devitsa*, such as the image of white bolituses.

Korkina defines all Tsvetaeva's narrative poems as part of one cycle featuring the conflict between an egocentric rebel who reviles conventions, a character representing a demoniac force; and the victim seeking a union with a superior force, who is prepared to abandon mundane duties.

The plot is focused on the rivalry between the characters of the King-Maiden and the stepmother over the tsarevich's heart. When the 18-year-old tsarevich plays the Psalter the sound of his music enchants the King-Maiden, and she sails across the sea to meet him. He is also an object of the illicit attention of his young stepmother disillusioned with her drunken, aged husband. She asks the tsarevich's lecherous tutor to use a magic spell so that the tsarevich is asleep on the three mornings when the King-Maiden plans to meet him. On successive nights the stepmother rewards the tutor with her affection, and attempts to seduce the tsarevich. In a drunken revel that takes place on the third night, the tsar orders his son and wife to commit incest so as to entertain him. The description of this orgy suggests that the stepmother is a witch. As in many folk-tales she has dark hair matching her evil nature. This presents a contrast to the fair-haired and good-natured protagonist, embodied here by the King-Maiden. When the King-Maiden meets the tsarevich for the third time, she discovers a long black hair on his tunic, which belongs to her rival. The King-Maiden breaks her sword in distress, tears her heart out of her chest and casts it into the sea. She calls on the wind to fill the hole in her breast, and then disappears. The tutor lifts his magic spell from the tsarevich and the young man wakes up to see the three meetings with the King-Maiden depicted in a cloud like a reflection in a mirror. He finds her abandoned armour with a message:

I am nowhere.
I've vanished in no land.
Nobody catches up with me.
Nothing will bring me back.

The evil stepmother is duly punished at the end: the Wind takes her on a stormy ride, and eventually drops her back down to earth; she reappears on the ground in the form of a snake. The tale concludes with the uprising of the populace; the tsar is overthrown and Red Russia prevails. The final definition of the state as "Rus' kulashnaia – kalashnaia – kumashnaia" an untranslatable evocation of both medieval and modern Russia.

The composition of the tale is well structured: there is an introduction; four sections describing night scenes at the royal palace separated from each other by three scenes depicting morning meetings between the King-Maiden and the tsarevich; and the final scene of the popular revolt concludes the narration. The symmetrical composition used by Tsvetaeva, together with the blend of historical allusions and elements of the fantastic, resembles the narrative techniques found in a Russian *bylina*.

Tsar'-devitsa has received considerable attention from scholars. The critical responses vary from discussion of the sources of inspiration and intertextual links (Karlinsky, Makin, Pauli, Poliakova), analysis of the characters and of Tsvetaeva's subversion of sexual stereotypes (Smith, Kroth), to discussion of Tsvetaeva's links with Slav folklore and mythology (Faryno, Korkina). Tsvetaeva's tale can be classified as another example of *belles-lettres*, since there are references to Greek mythology, to Pushkin's tales and to Gor'kii's verse in prose. It can be argued that at times Tsvetaeva uses folklore imagery and motifs to motivate political commentary and parody. There is also a vivid cosmogonic mythology embedded in *Tsar'-devitsa* that enables readers to interpret the historic events to which the tale alludes in terms of mythological and natural cycles. There are references to winter, and the deep sleep of the tsarevich can be seen as a state of hibernation or near death that will be followed by resurrection in a new form. The work conveys Tsvetaeva's favourite motif of spiritual awakening and the fight against the temptations of the material world. The tsarevich is a singer and a Psalter-player, making him similar to other characters in Tsvetaeva's poetry who embark on journeys to spiritual realms. In many ways the imagery of the tale resembles the cycle *Stikhi k Bloku* [Poems to Blok], in which Tsvetaeva compares Blok to Orpheus, to a sleepy and dead person (before his actual death), and then to the new sun. Her laments over his body are similar to the King-Maiden's attempts to shed tears over the tsarevich in order to "fertilize" him with new life. Tsvetaeva's "Poema vozdukha" [Poem to the Air], written in 1931, develops some of the themes and images of *Tsar'-devitsa*. However, the mystical experience of the later poem's lyric heroine is dominated by tragic overtones, more typical of Tsvetaeva's later work.

ALEXANDRA SMITH

Remeslo

Craft

Poetry collection, 1923

Remeslo was published in Berlin in 1923; it includes 104 poems written during 1921–22, and a narrative poem, "Pereulochki" [Sidestreets]. The title of the collection conceals Tsvetaeva's homage to Karolina Pavlova with her phrase "my sacred craft". Vera Lur'e called it Tsvetaeva's masterpiece. Bakhrakh, Rozhdestvenskii, Struve, and Bobrov highly praised it. Recent scholarship points out its complexity. In Etkind's words, "the reader moves from poems that are transparent in meaning toward enigmatic and obscure ones".

The book includes several cycles: "Uchenik" [Pupil], "Marina", "Razluka" [Separation], "Georgii" [St George], "Blagaia vest'" [Joyful News], "Otrok" [Young Man], "Khanskii polon" [Khan's Captivity], "Vifleem" [Bethlehem], "Novogodniaia" [New Year's Eve Song], "Doch' Iaira" [Jairus's Daughter]. The collection deals with a great variety of subjects and images: poetry as craft and magic; love and separation; Christian and pagan; the White Army resistance; the rebirth of Russia; the Orphic myth; and femininity. One of the cycles, "Razluka", was published earlier as a separate book (Berlin, 1922) and inspired Belyi to call Tsvetaeva "a poet-composer" and "a poet-singer".

"Uchenik" is dedicated to Volkonskii, an aristocrat, who symbolized the old world for Tsvetaeva. One of the best poems of this cycle, "Est' nekii chas" [There is a special hour ...], contains allusions to Tiutchev's poetry; it reaches a profound vision of wisdom and solitude, inevitable in the career of a true poet. The fourth poem of the cycle depicts two people climbing a hill to experience divine beauty and closeness to God. The image of the cloak permeates the cycle, identifying the boundaries between the humdrum and the divine. The poem "Dusha, ne znaiushchaia" [The soul which knows no limit] portrays a heretic. It seems that the rest of the book is tested against the ideals declared at the beginning. In the cycle "Marina", the theme of pride expressed at the beginning of the collection is represented by the Polish princess whom Tsvetaeva accuses of being "pseudo-Marina". Her evil beauty is dismissed.

"Bessonnitsa" [Insomnia] is dedicated to T.F. Shlietser, Skriabin's second wife, with whom Tsvetaeva was infatuated in 1920. It alludes to Derzhavin's "Lastochka" [Swallow], in which the soul of his dead wife is immortalized as a swallow. Tsvetaeva calls Skriabina (who died in April 1922) "my swallow"; insomnia and erotic imagery entwined with the image of a sweet drink and pearls at the bottom of a glass bring to mind Gumilev's collection of poems *Zhemchuga* [Pearls], in which the narrator seeks to experience a last pleasure before death.

"Razluka" is a lyrical diary reflecting Tsvetaeva's thoughts on her separation from her husband, whom she considered to be dead. The poem "Vestniku" [To the Messenger] is based on reality: Tsvetaeva asked Erenburg to take a letter for her husband, Efron, on his visit to Berlin in case he could be found there. In the cycle "Georgii", Tsvetaeva produces the mythologized portrayal of her husband as St George the protector of Moscow. The rhetorical devices employed by Tsvetaeva in the cycle suggest close links with the title: here her poetic techniques are turned into the art of persuasion; she appeals to her readers to praise the White Army officer as a true Russian hero. The "Blagaia vest'" cycle develops the same autobiographical themes; but in "Otrok" Tsvetaeva's heroine adopts the role of Sibyl. Recurrent images in the collection (eyes as mirrors, azure space, seductive music) appear here once again. The poem "Tak plyli: golova i lira ..." [Thus they floated: Head and Lyre] is a homage to Blok whom Tsvetaeva saw as the embodiment of Orpheus in 20th-century Russia. It touches on Tsvetaeva's favourite theme, the immortality of the poetic voice. There is also a poem about Amazons, who were admired by the author for their knight-like qualities: Tsvetaeva's heroine is faced with many obstacles in her spiritual quest; her activities involve not only a battle of the sexes, but battles between darkness and light, and the spiritual and the mundane. The curious reference to God's army and Soviet mass culture (in the poem "Tak govoriu ..." [That's What I Say]) is a hint at Tsvetaeva's blasphemy in both the religious and political senses. Towards the end of the collection the motif of rebellion and heresy becomes ever more prominent. The new political regime is compared to the regime of Genghis Khan.

The narrative poem "Pereulochki" concludes Tsvetaeva's meditation on poetic craft and Russia's destiny. It is loosely based on an oral folk poem (*bylina*) about Dobrynia Nikitich and the sorceress Marina Ignatevna. Tsvetaeva adds to the main storyline her own details: Dobrynia is transformed into an abstract male protagonist; the heroine seduces him with more challenging temptations; and after taking him to spiritual heights she turns him into a bison. In Karlinsky's words, it is "a work of great verbal virtuosity, it strikes the reader as one vast incantation". Faryno regards this narrative poem as one of Tsvetaeva's most original works, standing out not as another version of the folk-poem but as a new cosmogonic myth: Tsvetaeva is extending her vision of craft to archaic forms of spells, to withcraft. "Pereulochki" can be compared also to the Eleusinian mysteries of Demetre and Kore, derived from the agrarian festivals that celebrated the fertility of nature. Tsvetaeva's poem shares with them the belief in an enlightening power of initiation, as well as the belief that the cycle of nature relates directly to human life. In the mysteries death came to all the divine forces of nature but finally life was victorious: Kore returned from the realm of Hades; Dionysus vivified his worshippers; the Mithraic bull provided life for the world. Dionysus was described as a divine bull and became linked with the cult of devotion to a divine mother.

At the very end of Tsvetaeva's poem the bison with its golden horns suggests new life: the male protagonist transforms into the divine bull (implied by the colour of the horns). As in the mystery, the female heroine acts as a hierophant. The visual images of the azure space are intensified in the poem, so the beholder is enlightened with knowledge of the end of life as well as of its Zeus-given beginnings. The references in "Pereulochki" to sacrifices made to God, non-Christian rituals, visual spectacles, vegetation and plantation, and death and rebirth, all suggest Tsvetaeva's appropriation of the ancient source. In this respect, her vision of poetry as the craft of reviving ancient myth and tradition displays its very evident roots in Russian Symbolist culture.

ALEXANDRA SMITH

Molodets

The Swain

Narrative poem, 1924

In the spring of 1922 Tsvetaeva wrote a plan for her second fairy tale in verse – *Molodets* – and completed it in Czechoslovakia during Christmas 1922. The book was widely reviewed by the émigré press with sympathetic responses from D.S. Mirsky and Khodasevich. Khodasevich's article (*Poslednie novosti*, 11 June 1925) claimed that the folklore element prevails over the literary in Tsvetaeva's tale, and that she enhanced the genre with the verse and narrative techniques of folk songs. Other critics did not know what to make of *Molodets*. Aikhenval'd, for example, complained about the obscurity of the language and the complexity of the narration, arguing that fairy tales are normally transparent. The story itself is based on Afanas'ev's version of the folk-tale *Upyr'* [The Vampire], although it does echo other vampire tales found in European culture and Russian literature (for example, Pushkin's "Vurdalak" and Zhukovskii's "Svetlana").

Tsvetaeva faithfully recreates the outline of Afanas'ev's story, which featured a village girl, Marusia, who becomes betrothed to a lad she meets at a local festival. After their next meeting Marusia follows her fiancé and to her horror observes him in the churchyard eating a corpse. She runs home, keeping her discovery a secret. She is persuaded to spend an evening with the young man, and in conversation with him denies seeing him acting as a vampire. He foretells the death of her father the following day. After her bereavement they meet again, and once more Marusia denies knowing his real character. He then predicts the death of her mother. The events repeat themselves, and finally he predicts Marusia's own death. Acting on the advice of her grandmother, Marusia instructs the village priest that should she die her body is to be carried out of the house and buried at the crossroads. The vampire's prediction is fulfilled. Later a young nobleman passes down this road and falls in love with the tree flowering on Marusia's grave. He digs up the tree and takes it home. One day his servant is shocked to observe the flower turn into a girl who wanders around the house and helps herself to food. On the second occasion the nobleman captures the girl and asks her to marry him. She agrees on the condition that for four years she will not have to go into a church. After some years the nobleman boasts to his guests about his wife's beauty and they insist she must be baptized. She unwillingly follows her husband to church where she meets the vampire once again. The usual interrogation follows, and her refusal to admit that she saw him eating the dead results in the loss of her husband and son. On the third meeting with the monster, Marusia admits seeing his vampire acts and manages to splash him with holy water and he is destroyed. Marusia revives her husband and son with the holy water, giving the story an apparently happy ending. In adapting the plot Tsvetaeva brushes aside obscure details of the story's source and adds greater momentum.

Molodets consists of two parts each with five cantos. The first part treats Marusia's encounters with the vampire, leading to the death of her family and her own burial. The second part features Marusia and the nobleman. Tsvetaeva adds psychological motivation, implying that Marusia loved the vampire and risked her life by not naming him. The sexual myth, present in many literary versions of the story, is subverted by Tsvetaeva. Marusia finds herself being damned and so prefers the vampire to her nobleman. Finally she flies off with him into the blue realm. Thus Tsvetaeva's heroine rebels against the conventions of familial and social order.

The narrative techniques also differ from the original source. Tsvetaeva's tale is one of the best examples of polyphony: the narrative voice is often submerged by other voices, some belonging to characters in the story while others remain unidentified. The final canto (Cherubic) is full of disembodied voices of spirits fighting for possession of the heroine. This is the culminative point of Tsvetaeva's story where Marusia forsakes her husband and son, and against the background of Church Slavonic liturgy and readings from the Book of Psalms she flies with the vampire toward heaven, characterized in the text as "ogn'-sin'" (fire-azure). Tsvetaeva's use of the church service, featuring the preparation for the Eucharist and images of sacred flight from the Cherubic hymn, provides a dramatic twist. The ending of the story is blasphemous: the flight of Marusia with the vampire symbolizes the victory of pagan forces. The theme of evil attraction and the pagan nature of inspiration in art are also found in Tsvetaeva's prose and essays of the 1930s ("Iskusstvo pri svete sovesti" [Art in the Light of Conscience], for example). Teletova compares Tsvetaeva's tale to Goethe's *Faust*, Byron's *Cain*, and Remizov's "Drevniaia zloba" [The Ancient Anger]. The imagery and symbolism of *Molodets* is more easily traced, however, to Briusov's novel, *Ognennyi angel* (*The Fiery Angel*), and to Belyi's *Zoloto v lazuri* [Gold in Azure]. Tsvetaeva's symbolic description of the other-worldly realm in fiery-golden tones submerged by the azure derive directly from Belyi's connotations of the surreal and spiritual world lying beyond ordinary perception. Marusia stands out as a double of Tsvetaeva herself, who was faithful to Symbolist ideals and themes. Tsvetaeva also follows Briusov's steps in creating her own story of diabolic love. While Briusov turned his attention to German medieval legends and folklore, Tsvetaeva explored similar motifs and images in Russian popular culture.

In 1929 Tsvetaeva and Natal'ia Goncharova, who drew a series of illustrations for this fairy tale, tried in vain to publish *Molodets* in French. Tsvetaeva wrote a new poem in French, *Le Gars*, based on her Russian work. Extracts from this poem were published by Efim Etkind in Paris in 1986. Some references to the battle of the sexes and to the Amazon in *Le Gars* were particularly welcomed by French feminists, who read Tsvetaeva's work in terms of the liberation of feminine sexuality.

ALEXANDRA SMITH

Krysolov

The Ratcatcher

Narrative poem, 1925

This work was begun in 1925 in Czechoslovakia and finished in Paris. According to Marie-Luise Bott (who translated it into German), Tsvetaeva was familiar with versions of the Pied Piper of Hamelin legend in German literary tradition. Tsvetaeva's satire mocks philistinism and those who want to impose materialistic values on literature. Some parody of contemporary Soviet literature is present in the text. The phonetic richness and stylistic inventiveness in this poem can be compared to Robert Browning's "The Pied Piper of Hamelin".

There are six cantos; the atmosphere of the German legend is mimicked by Tsvetaeva in the proper names and in the mixture of German and Russian phrases in some passages. For example, in the following passage:

Cl-o-ose your Bible, Dad.
Housewife, put your bonnet on.
Hus-band, your nightcap.
"Morgen ist ..."

Tsvetaeva's version repeats the basic tale of the plague of rats charmed away by the mysterious Piper, whose work goes unrewarded by the burghers of the town. In revenge he takes away their children. The strong mark of Tsvetaeva's poetics can be seen in the poem's emphasis and in many of its details.

The first chapter, "Gorod Gammel'n" [The City of Hamelin], describes the boring life of the citizens. In this canto there is an ironic account of the moral value of the button, and a likeness is established between the creative artists, paupers, and convicts who are all out of place in the wealthy "paradise-town". The second canto, "Sny" [Dreams], describes the prosaic dreams of the citizens. Its irony, aimed at established order and clichés, resembles that of European romanticism. However, some of the couplets sound like a parody of Maiakovskii's socialist realist poetry. For example:

As stitches go smoothly along a knitting needle
Peter sees Paul (what else?).
And Paul sees Peter.

The third canto, "Napast'" [Attack], portrays the market scene and the invasion of the rats, who sound like revolutionaries. Tsvetaeva's sarcastic narration suggests that the rat plague is caused by the moral decay of a populace concerned only with obtaining an abundance of food and wealth. The revolutionary takeover of the city by rats recalls Heinrich Heine's "Die Wanderratten"; in one of her letters of this period Tsvetaeva admits that her poem is a homage to Heine. The bureaucratic jargon of Soviet Russia makes the rats' language sound strikingly modern; especially names like "Glavkhvost" (The Department of Tails), and "Narkomchert" (People's Commissariat of Devils). The council announces that the person who can free the town of the rats will be granted the right to marry the burgomaster's daughter. The arrival of the unremarkable musician in green carrying the flute is then described.

The fourth canto, "Uvod" [Removal], describes the embourgeoisement and indulgence of the rats that follows their seizure of the town. This chapter alludes to Russia under NEP. (The poem was first published in full in Russia only in 1990.) The piper enchants the rats with the music of his flute and leads them to the nearest lake where they drown. In the fifth canto, "V ratushe" [At the Town Council], the piper learns to his disappointment that he will not receive the reward for his deed. The council are suspicious of music, believing it leads to revolution and anarchy, and decides to present the piper with a case for his flute rather than with the burgomaster's daughter Greta. The piper refuses their offer.

In the final canto, "Detskii rai" [Children's Paradise], the piper takes his revenge: early in the morning the children are enchanted by the magic sound of the flute, which promises the fulfilment of everyone's dreams, and they follow the piper out of the town. The narration contains a polyphony of voices: some children seek their paradise, some an escape from corporal punishment at school, some girls are hoping to find husbands, etc. They are deceived by the piper just like the rats before them who drowned in the nearest lake. Tsvetaeva's lengthy description of the drowning children aroused controversy among the critics, but Mirsky claimed that "it is a serious political (in the broadest sense of this term) and ethical satire that is perhaps destined to play a role in the growth of consciousness in all of us". Tsvetaeva's sympathy in *Krysolov* is neither with the degenerate burghers nor with the revolutionary rats, but with the musician who rebels against philistines and all who lack spirituality. It is also permeated with a passion for individual freedom and choice; Tsvetaeva proclaims art to be free of all social orders and established canons (this theme is reinforced in "Iskusstvo pri svete sovesti" [Art in the Light of Conscience], written in 1931).

Etkind discusses in detail the rhythmic and stylistic richness of Tsvetaeva's work, employing intertextual analysis. *Krysolov* contains numerous examples of the distortion brought into the Russian language by the Revolution; it is a remarkable allegory of the ugly and inhumane life of contemporary Russia. The ending of the poem has a philosophical twist that can be traced to Heraclitus' ideas of universal change and hidden destiny (which Tsvetaeva often referred to in her work). According to Heraclitus, all material things are like flames, a combustion that develops in accordance with natural law and destiny; one should strive to understand intuitively the thought that steers everything on its course. Tsvetaeva's image of the Pied Piper, the true ruler of the world, resembles Heraclitus' vision of the Great Man, who is worth more than ten thousand ordinary men.

ALEXANDRA SMITH

Poem of the Mountain

Poema gory

Poem of the End

Poema kontsa

Narrative poems, 1926

Poema gory ("Poem of the Mountain") first appeared in *Versty*, in 1926, in Prague. Together with *Poema kontsa* ("Poem of the End"), and various poems of this period, it was inspired by Tsvetaeva's affair with Konstantin Rodzevich (1895–1988), an ex-Red Army officer who was captured by the White Army and fled to Prague, where he graduated as a lawyer in 1926. He moved to Paris where he was an active member of various pro-communist organizations; from 1936–38 he fought in Spain, and later joined the French resistance. He spent two years in captivity in Germany during the war. From 1945 until his death he lived in Paris. In 1960 he sent his Tsvetaeva archive to Moscow. According to Rodzevich himself, Tsvetaeva created a beautiful "myth" out of their affair. Tsvetaeva's husband, Sergei Efron, was deeply hurt by the affair and wanted to leave his wife, but eventually their marriage was saved. The prototype of Tsvetaeva's hill was Petřín Hill in Prague. Often in Tsvetaeva's work hills and mountains are symbols of spiritual heights; she liked to compare poets to mountain-climbers (see her essay "Poet-al'pinist" [Poet-Alp-Climber]).

The narration is in the first person; the principal hero of the poem is the Hill that is animated and personified. The poem contains ten cantos, a brief introduction, and an epilogue. The epigraph, from a poem of Hölderlin, indicates Tsvetaeva's preoccupation with German romanticism. The first canto is dominated by the theme of marriage made in heaven and the suggestion that God takes revenge on humans who experience divine happiness. The second canto is a short lyric monologue about the heroine's vision of the hill. The third canto provides a metonymic description of the couple running to the hill and making love. The fourth canto is a reference to Persephone with whom the lyric heroine identifies. The fifth canto suggests the rebirth of both characters; Tsvetaeva's neologism "heaven-dwellers of love" is an expressive description of their emotional state. In the sixth canto the mountain speaks about the punishment awaiting the lovers for their sin, suggesting that their love was a practical joke played on them by demons. The seventh canto drifts into generalization, claiming that "all love stories are the same". This encompasses Tsvetaeva's favourite theme that love's end is predestined. There is a powerful contrast between the characters' romantic attraction and the murky reality that they have to face on their descent. The hill takes a sympathetic view of the two lovers, who "must go down – Separately, through the mud / Into the life known to everyone as: Scum place / market place / barracks ...". The image of the ancient Gordian knot of duty and passion resembles the style of the classical tragedies. (Tsvetaeva's tragedy *Ariadna* belongs to the same period.) In the eighth canto the lyric heroine refers to her affair as an experience of the past, blaming the mountain for all her present misfortunes. The ninth chapter is the most autobiographical. It offers a discourse on the future of the mountain, which will turn into a common village filled with hundreds of philistines who dream of conventional order and happiness. The heroine's dream-place will be turned into plots of land. Tsvetaeva talks on many occasions about her hatred for convention and humdrum existence. The tenth canto puts the plot of the love story into perspective. It is a rebellious outcry from the heroine who refuses to accept the wisdom of the Ten Commandments, and casts a spell on the mountain so that it becomes an unhappy place for others: "I curse you, ants, Not to be happy on my mountain!" In the epilogue the narrator addresses her lover, saying that he is no more than a separate part of their experience of true love. It ends with the revenge of memory: "I can see you with no one / That's my memory's trick".

"Poem of the End" was first published in *Kovčea*, Prague, in 1926. It continues the theme of romantic love expressed in "Poem of the Mountain", with the focus on the parting of two lovers forced by circumstances to separate. The main feature of the poem is a dialogue between the lyric heroine and the male character interwoven into the simple story-line. They meet at a café, and then part on a bridge. The account of the urban landscape of Prague is very realistic, and can be easily reconstructed. The poem was written between 1 February and 9 June 1924. It is based on oxymorons; they can be defined as love-poetry, connection-separation, life-death. Thus the concept of love is viewed differently by the heroine and her lover. For example, he claims it is a bond, she argues it is "a streched bow: separation"; he suggests eloping and living together somewhere else, she proposes they die together so they can become one spirit. The poem defends the romantic notion of love immortalized only through death. The heroine also prefers to commit suicide than to face life without her lover. There are numerous allusions to the Bible, classical mythology, and Russian and German literary sources. In spite of the unbalanced state of mind of the heroine, emotions are concealed in verbal structures that are clear and logical. There are recurrent refrains, images and variations of the same themes and syntactic structures.

The unprecedented metres, the elliptical style, the theatrical quality of the poem won the admiration of Pasternak, Aseev, and Kirsanov. Pasternak wrote to Tsvetaeva in March 1926 saying that he was deeply moved by the poem that "draws its readers to its world like tragedy", and praised Tsvetaeva as an artist of extraordinarily great talent. However, many émigré readers of the poems were shocked by Tsvetaeva's implied public admission of her extra-marital affair. In 1911 Briusov wrote about Tsvetaeva's first book, remarking on the fact that her poetry was inspired by her biography. According to him, this revealed incredible intimacy, to the extent "that readers feel embarrassed as if they had peeped through drawn curtains and witnessed a scene not meant for someone else's eyes"; Briusov hoped that Tsvetaeva would shift away from family album poetry to synthetic images and universal symbols. "Poem of the End" merges the symbolic and the autobiographical, and stands out as an allegory of the cursed human race that has moved away from the divine and natural.

ALEXANDRA SMITH

After Russia

Posle Rossii

Poetry collection, 1928

After Russia comprises poems written in Berlin and Prague. In Karlinsky's words "it represents a successful synthesis of several of her previous styles and is the most mature and perfect of her collections". The reaction among Tsvetaeva's contemporaries was mixed. Adamovich, for example, complained about the unusual words and the syntax, but concluded his review with the praise that "Tsvetaeva is a genuine and rare poet". The book's print run was very small; 100 numbered copies of the collection were sold by special subscription. It was Tsvetaeva's last collection of lyric poetry. Initially she intended to title it "Umysly" [Intentions] – which would have been a direct reference to Montaigne's maxim on fantasies about the past. The book comprises two parts, Notebooks 1 and 2. Both parts are preceded by epigraphs: one is from Trediakovskii's work "An Opinion on the Origin of Poetry and Verse in General"; another is taken from from Montaigne's essay "On Solitude". Michael Naydan, translator of this book into English, remarks that it resembles a chronicle more than a lyrical diary, especially because of its numerous allusions to historical chronicles (to the Bible and to *The Iliad*, for example). The poems are arranged chronologically, but they are also centred on Tsvetaeva's experiences of friendship and love with various people (Vishniak, Pasternak, and Teskova just to name a few). Karlinsky identifies Neoclassical tendencies in the style of many of the poems; the language employed by Tsvetaeva is often elevating and rhetorical. The most explicit expression of 20th-century Neoclassicism, according to Karlinsky, is the second poem from the cycle, "Provoda" ("Wires"), in which the lyric persona tells her addressee that all the works of Racine and Shakespeare would not be enough to describe her unhappiness. The most innovative feature of Tsvetaeva's collection is that she merges two tendencies prevalent in Russian poetry at that time: urban/modern images and language as favoured by the Futurists; and the classical style rediscovered by the Acmeists. In the poem "Chtob vyskazat' tebe ..." ("In Order to Express It to You") the allusions to Phaedra and Hyppolitus, Ariadna and Theseus are used as a backdrop for the expression of the heroine's own tragedy: it is impossible for her to be united with her beloved one, and she is pictured weeping by the telegraph pole, implying that her poem is a telegram. There is no method of communication that can allow her to recover her loss. In "Wires" Tsvetaeva creates a mythologized image of the voice that can act as a wire, as a pulling force capable of bringing Eurydice back to life; the long vowels used in the cycle produce the effect of physicality in the voice: "The distance: pi-ity", "A telegraphic fa-are-well", etc.

The first part of the collection comprises the most philosophical cycles of the book: "Derev'ia" ("Trees") and "Bog" ("God"). The cycle about trees contains a mosaic of different visions of trees, with references to the Tree of Life and to other images found in the Bible and, perhaps, to expressionist paintings. It is one of the most beautiful and moving cycles in Russian poetry, which awakens readers spiritually through visual and verbal stimulation. For example: "Upward where the mountain ash / Prettier than King David!", "The woods! My Elisium!", "Whole nations / On an exodus! – To please and to anger! / Vide! – Abide!- Remember! /... A few trees running / Up the hill, in the evening." The imagery thrusts forward the basic Christian principles and archaic forms of communion with nature, which the cycle contrasts with urban modernity. The cycle was dedicated to Anna Teskova, the Czech writer, translator, and theosoph. The cycle was perhaps inspired by their conversations on theosophical subjects.

Another prominent cycle in the book, "Wires", is dedicated to Pasternak, whom Tsvetaeva considered to be her *alter ego* in poetry. The cycle conveys great emotional intensity; in spite of the mutual admiration and infatuation expressed in their letters to each other, they were not able to fulfil their intention of meeting in Berlin in 1923.

The cycle "God" reveals Tsvetaeva's vision of the Absolute: she sees God as a divine spirit, unconfined by physical shape; her notion of the poet as Cain who challenges God and seeks divine knowledge is strongly pronounced in the cycle "Poety" ("Poets"). Despite several references to Russian themes, the book stands out as a homage to European culture; Tsvetaeva's attempt "to correct" Shakespeare is of particular interest. Her Ophelia gives a speech in defence of the Queen: her argument, sound and straightfoward, implies that it is not for the virgin to be the judge of passion. Furthermore, at the end of "Ofeliia – v zashchitu Korolevy Fedra" ("Ophelia in defence of the Queen"), Ophelia teases Hamlet, threatening to rise to defend her queen, and calls herself his immortal passion. The assertiveness of female sexuality is also central to the cycle "Fedra" ("Phaedra"). These cycles would be of particular interest to feminist critics as an example of the hysteric discourse, "the woman's masculine language" (J. Mitchell).

After Russia offers a number of poems of great innovative quality. The poem "Ras-stoianie: versty, mili ..." ("Distance: mileposts, miles ..."), for example, is constructed from different connotations of the prefix dis-: two lovers are dis-located, dis-placed, dis-embodied (metaphorically), made to dis-agree, and so on. The volume concludes with greetings from the lyric heroine to the Russian rye. According to Tsvetaeva's numerous statements, Russia borders land that is the embodiment of God; it can be suggested, therefore, that the meditative tone of many poems from the collection comes from the transcending human experience of her past and from the broadening of her spiritual and cultural horizons.

ALEXANDRA SMITH

Evgeniia Tur 1815–1892

Prose writer and translator

Biography

Born Elizaveta Vasil'evna Sukhovo-Kobylina in Moscow, 24 August 1815. Educated by tutors at home. Her translations began to appear anonymously from 1834. Married: the French count Salhias de Tournemire in 1837; three children. Published first prose under the pseudonym Evgeniia Tur in *Sovremennik*, 1849. Began publishing literary criticism in *Russkii vestnik*, 1856; worked closely with editors of that journal, 1856–60. Travelled to France, 1858. Honorary member of the Society of Lovers of Russian Letters. Left *Russkii vestnik*, 1860; founder and editor of *Russkaia rech'*, 1861–62. Lived in France, 1861–72. Wrote historical, religious stories for children, 1860–88. Died in Warsaw, Poland, 27 March 1892.

Publications

Collected Edition

Povesti i rasskazy, 4 vols. Moscow, 1859–60.

Fiction

"Oshibka" [The Mistake], *Sovremennik*, 10 (1849), 137–284.

"Plemiannitsa" [The Niece], *Sovremennik*, 1–4 (1850), 51–130; 161–210; 5–51; 125–66; translated in part as *Antonina*, by Michael R. Katz, Evanston, Illinois, Northwestern University Press, 1996.

"Dolg" [The Debt], *Sovremennik*, 11 (1850), 4–60.

Tri pory zhizni [Three Seasons of Life]. 1853.

Essays

"Miss Bronte, ee zhizn' i sochineniia" [Miss Brontë, Her Life and Works], *Russkii vestnik*, 12 (1858), 501–75.

"Zhenshchina i liubov' po poniatiiam g. Mishle" [Woman and Love According to Mr Michelet], *Russkii vestnik*, 6 (1859), 461–500.

Travel Writing

"Parizhskie pis'ma" [Paris Letters], *Russkii vestnik*, 1858.

Stories for Children

Katakomby [Catacombs]. Moscow, 1866.

Semeistvo Shalonskikh [The Shalonskii Family]. St Petersburg, 1880.

Kniazhna Dubrovina [Princess Dubrovina]. Moscow, 1886.

Memoirs

"Vospominaniia" (incomplete), *Poliarnaia zvezda*, 1881.

Critical Studies

"Oshibka", review by A.N. Ostrovskii, *Moskvitianin*, 7 (1850), 89–99.

"Plemiannitsa", review by I.S. Turgenev, *Sovremennik*, 1 (1852), 1–14.

"Tri pory zhizni", review by N.G. Chernyshevskii, *Sovremennik*, 5 (1854), 1–12.

Obzor zhizni i trudov pokoinykh russkikh pisatelei i pisatel'nits umershikh v 1892, by D.D. Iazykov, St Petersburg, 1912.

"Speaking the Sorrow of Women: Turgenev's 'Neschastnaia' and Evgeniia Tur's 'Antonina'", by Jane Costlow, *Slavic Review*, 2 (1991), 328–35.

"Evgeniia Tur, in *Dictionary of Russian Women Writers*, edited by Marina Ledkovsky, Charlotte Rosenthal, and Mary Zirin, Westport, Connecticut, Greenwood Press, 1994.

Bibliographies

Bibliograficheskii slovar' russkikh pisatel'nits, edited by N.N. Golitsyn, St Petersburg, 1889.

Istoriia russkoi literatury XIX v, edited by K.D. Muratova, Moscow and Leningrad, 1962.

Evgeniia Tur (Elizaveta Vasil'evna Sukhovo-Kobylina) was born into the well-off and prominent Sukhovo-Kobylin family in Moscow. Tur's sister, Sof'ia, was later a celebrated painter, and her brother Aleksandr, a well-known writer. One of five children, Tur was educated at home by private tutors including the poet S.E. Raikh, the historian and future professor at Moscow University, N.I. Nadezhdin, and the future editor of *Moskvitianin*, M.P. Pogodin. In 1834–35, Tur anonymously published several translations in Nadezhdin's journal, *Teleskop*. At the insistence of her mother, Tur went to Paris in 1837 where her mother arranged for her to marry the French count Salhias de Tournemire. They returned to Russia where, during the 1840s and 1850s, Tur hosted a literary salon and was friendly with such luminaries as I.S. Turgenev, T.N. Granovskii, A.N. Afanas'ev, and others. Financial hardship compelled Tur to embark on a literary career after her husband, himself destitute, squandered her substantial dowry. Her first story, "Oshibka" [The Mistake], appeared in 1849 in the journal *Sovremennik* and was very well received. It is a society tale that tells of the sad fate of a young girl from a poor family. She is abandoned by a man who had long sought permission from his wealthy family to marry her, but who, upon finally receiving it, realizes he no longer loves her. Tur's second endeavour, the four-part novella *Plemiannitsa* [The Niece], was so eagerly awaited that publication of Nikolai Nekrasov's "Mertvoe ozero" [Dead Lake] was said to have been postponed so it could be published. *Plemiannitsa* also won considerable acclaim. It was most notably but ambiguously reviewed by Turgenev, who, while conceding the novel's merit, attacked Tur's "unnecessary discourse", and "chatter", as well as her subjectivity. The limitations of woman's inescapable position in the family and society, and the misery that results therefrom, constitute important themes in these and other works by Tur. Such themes were not uncommon in fiction written by men and women during this period.

Though Tur's sympathetic but complex portrayal of female characters has been considered a significant achievement, her subsequent works of fiction, including *Tri pory zhizni* [Three Seasons of Life] and "Starushka" [The Old Woman] (1856), were less successful than her first two works. By 1856, Tur began writing articles of a more journalistic nature, many of which broached questions regarding the role of women in society. She worked closely with *Russkii vestnik* from 1856 to 1860, where she published reviews of George Sand's *Histoire de ma vie* (*Story of My Life*), the historian Jules Michelet's *L'Amour*, Elizabeth Gaskell's *The Life of Charlotte Brontë*, and others. Her *Parizhskie pis'ma* [Paris Letters], penned and published while Tur was in France in 1858, were among the articles about France which "were and are constantly read hungrily" by Russian readers, according to the poet and editor of *Sovremennik*, N.A. Nekrasov. Tur's critical reviews and essays were published primarily in *Russkii vestnik*, but also in *Otechestvennye zapiski*, and *Severnaia pchela* among others.

A quarrel with M.N. Katkov, editor of *Russkii vestnik*, precipitated her break with that journal in 1860. In 1861, she founded and edited her own journal, *Russkaia rech'*, whose subtitle proclaimed it to be "a review of literature, history, art and social life in the west and in Russia". Although *Russkaia rech'* displayed conservative tendencies, it did not have a clearly defined ideological direction, and profited by the participation of a variety of talented writers, such as N.S. Leskov, A.I. Zabelin, N.A. Nekrasov, V.A. Sleptsov, and others. Tur made repeated attempts to have Turgenev's works published in *Russkaia rech'*, but to no avail. Tur herself wrote a great many critical works for the journal, including articles about M.V. Adveev, V. Krestovskii (pseudonym of N. Khvoshchinskaia), and Dostoevskii, as well as a critique of Turgenev's *Ottsy i deti* (*Fathers and Sons*). After its 39th issue, *Russkaia rech'* merged with *Moskovskii vestnik*, and published 66 more issues on a twice-weekly basis until it ceased publication early in 1862.

Shortly thereafter, Tur began to turn her attention and efforts toward literature for children and adolescents. For over two decades, until just a few years before her death in 1892, she wrote and translated primarily historical and religious works of a morally edifying character, such as *Katakomby* [Catacombs], based on Cardinal Wiseman's popular novel *Fabiola* (1854), *Semeistvo Shalonskikh* [The Shalonskii Family], a young girl's wartime memories; *Kniazhna Dubrovina* [Princess Dubrovina]; "Ocherk zhizni i deianii Innokentiia mitropolita Moskovskogo" [A Sketch of the Life and Acts of Innokentii, Metropolitan of Moscow] (1884); and the translation *Poslednie dni Pompei* [The Last Days of Pompeii] (1882). Tur gained respect and renown for her work in children's literature, which was more structured and succinct than her earlier prose, and continued to publish until 1888. In 1881, she began writing and publishing her memoirs in *Poliarnaia zvezda*, a short-lived journal founded by her son, Evgenii Andreevich, himself then a novelist of some renown. His journal, however, folded in 1882, and Tur's memoirs were never completed.

JENNIFER LONERGAN

Ivan Sergeevich Turgenev 1818–1883

Prose writer and dramatist

Biography

Born in Orel, 9 November 1818. Attended Moscow University, 1833–34; St Petersburg University, 1834–37; University of Berlin, 1838–41: completed master's exam in St Petersburg, 1842. Worked for the Ministry of the Interior, 1843–45. Thereafter concentrated on country pursuits, writing, and travel. Intimate relationship with the singer Pauline Garcia Viardot; travelled to France with her and her husband, 1845–46 and 1847–50. Coined the phrase "superfluous man" in a story of 1850. Arrested and confined to his country estate for writing a commemorative article on Gogol''s death, 1852–53. Left Russia to live in western Europe, 1856: first in Baden-Baden, then Paris with the Viardots, 1871–83. Corresponding member of the Imperial Academy of Sciences, 1860. Doctor of Civil Laws, Oxford University, 1879. Died in Bougival, near Paris, 3 September 1883.

Publications

Collected Editions

The Novels of Turgenev. 15 vols, translated by Constance Garnett. New York, Macmillan, and London, Heinemann, 1894–99.

Novels and Stories, 13 vols, translated by Isabel F. Hapgood. New York, Scribner, 1903–04.

Plays, translated by M.S. Mandell. London, Macmillan, 1924; New York, Russell and Russell, 1970.

Three Famous Plays, translated by Constance Garnett. New York, Scribner, and London, Duckworth, 1951.

Polnoe sobranie sochinenii i pisem [Complete Works and Letters], 28 vols. Moscow and Leningrad, 1960–68.

Five Short Novels, translated by F.D. Reeve. New York, Bantam, 1961.

Polnoe sobranie sochinenii i pisem, 30 vols. Moscow, 1978.

The Mysterious Tales, translated by Robert Dessaix. Canberra. Australian National University, 1979.

Love and Death, translated by Richard Freeborn. London, Folio Society, 1983; retitled as *First Love and Other Stories*, Oxford, Oxford University Press, 1989.

The Essential Turgenev, edited by Elizabeth Cheresh Allen. Evanston, Illinois, Northwestern University Press, 1994.

Fiction

Dnevnik lishnego cheloveka. 1850; translated as *The Diary of a Superfluous Man*, by Constance Garnett, in *The Novels of Turgenev*, 1894–99; by F.D. Reeve, in *Five Short Novels*, 1961; by David Patterson, New York, Norton, 1984; and by Richard Freeborn, in *First Love and Other Stories*, 1989.

Zapiski okhotnika. 1852; translated as *Russian Life in the Interior*, by James D. Meiklejohn, Edinburgh, A. and C. Black, 1855; as *A Sportsman's Sketches*, by Constance Garnett, in *The Novels of Turgenev*, 1894–99; as *Sketches from a Hunter's Album*, by Richard Freeborn, Harmondsworth, Penguin, 1967; complete edition, 1990; also as *A Sportman's Notebook*, by Charles and Natasha Hepburn, London, Cresset Press, 1950; reprinted, London, Everyman, and New York, Knopf, 1992.

Rudin. 1856; edited by Patrick Waddington, London, Bristol Classical Press, 1994; translated by Constance Garnett, in *The Novels of Turgenev*, 1894–99; by F.D. Reeve, in *Five Short Novels*, 1961; and by Richard Freeborn, Harmondsworth, Penguin, 1975.

Asia. 1858; edited by F.G. Gregory, London, Bristol Classical Press, 1992; translated as *Acia*, by Constance Garnett, in *King Lear of the Steppes and Other Stories*, London, Heinemann, 1898; and as "Asya", by Richard Freeborn, in *First Love and Other Stories*, 1989.

Dvorianskoe gnezdo. 1859; translated as *A Nest of Gentlefolk*, 1869; as *Lisa*, 1872; also translated as *A House of Gentlefolk*, by Constance Garnett, in *The Novels of Turgenev*, 1894–99; as *A Nest of Hereditary Legislators*, 1913; as *A Nest of the Gentry*, by Bernard Isaacs, 1947; also as *Home of the Gentry*, translated by Richard Freeborn, Harmondsworth, Penguin, 1970.

Nakanune. 1860; translated as *On the Eve*, by Constance Garnett, in *The Novels of Turgenev*, 1894–99; and by Gilbert Gardiner, Harmondsworth, Penguin, 1950.

Pervaia liubov'. 1860; edited by F.G. Gregory, London, Bristol Classical Press, 1991; translated as *First Love* (with *Rudin*), by Isaiah Berlin, London, Hamish Hamilton, 1950; Harmondsworth, Penguin, 1978; by F.D. Reeve, in *Five Short Novels*, 1961; and by Richard Freeborn, in *First Love and Other Stories*, 1989.

Ottsy i deti. 1862; edited by E.R. Sands, London, Bristol Classical Press, 1992; numerous translations, including as *Fathers and Children*, by Constance Garnett, in *The Novels of Turgenev*, 1894–99; and by Avril Pyman, London, Everyman, 1991; as *Fathers and Sons*, by Rosemary Edmunds, Harmondsworth, Penguin, 1965; and edited by Ralph E. Matlaw, New York, Norton, 1966, 2nd edition, 1989; by Richard Freeborn, Oxford, Oxford University Press, 1991; and by Michael R. Katz, New York, Norton, 1994.

Dym. 1867; translated as *Smoke*, by Constance Garnett, in *The Novels of Turgenev*, 1894–99.

Stepnoi Korol' Lir. 1870; as *A King Lear of the Steppes*, by F.D. Reeve, in *Five Short Novels*, 1961; and by Richard Freeborn, in *First Love and Other Stories*, 1989.

Veshnie vody. 1872; translated as *The Torrents of Spring*, by Constance Garnett, in *The Novels of Turgenev*, 1894–99; by David Magarshack, New York, Vintage, 1959; as *Spring Torrents*, by F.D. Reeve, in *Five Short Novels*, 1961; and by Leonard Shapiro, Harmondsworth, Penguin, 1972.

Nov'. 1877; translated as *Virgin Soil*, by Constance Garnett, in *The Novels of Turgenev*, 1894–99.

Pesn' torzhestvuiushchei liubvi. 1881; translated as *The Song of Triumphant Love*, by Jessica Morelle, Upton on Severn, SPA, 1990.

Klara Milich. 1882; translated by Robert Dessaix, in *The Mysterious Tales*, 1979.

Plays
"Neostorozhnost'" [Carelessness], *Otechestvenye zapiski*, 1843.
Bezdenezh'e (produced 1852). 1846; translated as *The Poor Gentleman*, by Constance Garnett, in *Three Famous Plays*, 1951.
Gde tonko, tam i rvetsia (produced 1851). 1848; translated as *Where It's Thin, There It Tears*, by M.S. Mandell, in *Plays*, 1924.
Zavtrak u predvoditelia [Lunch at the Marshal of the Nobility's] (produced 1849). 1856.
Kholostiak. 1849; translated as *The Bachelor*, by M.S. Mandell, in *Plays*, 1924.
Razgovor na bol'shoi doroge (produced 1850). 1851; translated as *A Conversation on the Highway*, by M.S. Mandell, in *Plays*, 1924.
Provintsialka (produced 1851). 1851; translated as *The Provincial Lady*, by M.S. Mandell, in *Plays*, 1924; and as *A Provincial Lady*, by Constance Garnett, in *Three Famous Plays*, 1951.
Mesiats v derevne (produced 1872); in *Sovremennik*, 1855; in *Sobranie sochinenii*, 1869; edited by T.A. Greenan, London, Bristol Classical Press, 1992; translated as *A Month in the Country*, by M.S. Mandell, in *Plays*, 1924; by Constance Garnett, in *Three Famous Plays*, 1951; by Isaiah Berlin, Harmondsworth, Penguin, 1981; and by Richard Freeborn, Oxford, Oxford University Press, 1991.
Nakhlebnik (produced 1862). 1857; translated as *The Family Charge*, by M.S. Mandell, in *Plays*, 1924.
Vecher v Sorrente (produced 1882). 1891; translated as *An Evening in Sorrento*, by M.S. Mandell, in *Plays*, 1924.

Poetry
Parasha. 1843.
Razgovor [The Conversation]. 1845.
Andrei. 1846.
Pomeshchik [The Landowner]. 1846.
Senilia. 1878; as *Stikhotvoreniia v proze*, 1882; translated as *Poems in Prose* [no translator named], Boston, Cupples, Upham, 1883; also as *Senilia: Poems in Prose*, by S.J. Macmullan, Bristol, Arrowsmith, 1890; and as *Poems in Prose in Russian and English* (bilingual edition), by Constance Garnett and Roger Rees, Oxford, Blackwell, 1951.

Memoirs
Literaturnye i zhiteiskie vospominaniia. 1874; revised edition, 1880; translated as *Literary Reminiscences and Autobiographical Fragments*, by David Magarshack, New York, Farrar Straus and Cudahy, 1958; London, Faber, 1959; reprinted 1984.

Letters
Nouvelle correspondance inédite, edited by Alexandre Zviguilsky, 2 vols. Paris, 1971–72.
Lettres inédites de Tourguenev à Pauline Viardot et à sa famille, edited by Alexandre Zviguilsky and Henri Granjard. Lausanne, L'Âge d'Homme, 1972.
Letters to an Actress: The Story of Ivan Turgenev and Marya Gavrilovna Savina, translated by Nora Gottlieb and Raymond Chapman. Athens, Ohio University Press, and London, Allison and Busby, 1973.
Turgenev's Letters, edited by A.V. Knowles. London, Athlone Press, and New York, Scribner, 1983.
Letters, edited by David Lowe, 2 vols. Ann Arbor, Ardis, 1983.
Flaubert and Turgenev: A Friendship in Letters: The Complete Correspondence, edited and translated by Barbara Beaumont. London, Athlone Press, and New York, Norton, 1985.

Critical Studies
Turgenev: The Man, His Art, and His Age, by Avraham Yarmolinsky, London, Hodder and Stoughton, 1926; 2nd edition, New York, Orion, 1959; New York, Octagon, 1977.
Ivan Tourguénev et les courants politiques et sociaux de son temps, by Henri Granjard, 2nd edition, Paris, Institut d'Études Slaves, 1954.
Turgenev: A Life, by David Magarshack, New York, Grove Press, and London, Faber, 1954.
Turgenev: The Novelist's Novelist: A Study, by Richard Freeborn, Oxford, Oxford University Press, 1960; reprinted Westport, Connecticut, Greenwood Press, 1978.
I.S. Turgenev v vospominaniiakh sovremennikov, 2 vols. Moscow, 1969.
Ivan Turgenev, by Charles A. Moser, New York, Columbia University Press, 1972.
The Other Turgenev: From Romanticism to Symbolism, by Marina Ledkovsky, Würzburg, Jal, 1973.
The Portrait Game, with illustrations by Turgenev, edited and translated by Marion Mainwaring, London, Chatto and Windus, 1973.
Hamlet and Don Quixote: Turgenev's Ambivalent Vision, by Eva Kagan-Kans, The Hague, Mouton, 1975.
The Clement Vision: Poetic Realism in Turgenev and James, by Dale E. Peterson, Port Washington, New York, Kennikat Press, 1976.
The Gentle Barbarian: The Life and Work of Turgenev, by V.S. Pritchett, New York, Random House, and London, Chatto and Windus, 1977.
Turgenev: His Life and Times, by Leonard Schapiro, New York, Random House, and Oxford, Oxford University Press, 1978.
Turgenev: The Quest for Faith, by Robert Dessaix, Canberra, Australian National University, 1980.
Dialogue in Turgenev's Novels: Speech-Introductory Devices, by Ludmila Hellgren, Stockholm, Almqvist & Wiksell, 1980.
Turgenev's Russia: From "Notes of a Hunter" to "Fathers and Sons", by Victor Ripp, Ithaca, Cornell University Press, 1980.
Turgenev's Early Works: From Character Sketches to a Novel, by Walter Smyrniw, Oakville, Ontario, Mosaic, 1980.
Turgenev and England, by Patrick Waddington, London, Macmillan, 1980; New York, New York University Press, 1981.
Turgenev and George Sand: An Improbable Entente, by Patrick Waddington, London, Macmillan, 1981.
I.S. Turgenev i russkii realisticheskii roman XIX veka, by V.M. Markovich, Leningrad, 1982.
Turgenev, by Lev Shestov, Ann Arbor, Ardis, 1982.
Nikolai Gogol and Ivan Turgenev, by Nick Worrall, London, Macmillan, 1982.
Ivan Turgenev. Zhizn' i tvorchestvo, by M.M. Dunaev, Moscow, 1983.

Turgenev's Fathers and Sons, by David Lowe, Ann Arbor, Ardis, 1983.
Ivan Turgenev, by A.V. Knowles, Boston, Twayne, 1988.
Turgenev: A Biography, by Henri Troyat, translated by Nancy Amphoux, New York, Dutton, and London, W.H. Allen, 1988.
Worlds Within Worlds: The Novels of Ivan Turgenev, by Jane T. Costlow, Princeton, Princeton University Press, 1990.
Metaphysical Conflict: A Study of the Major Novels of Ivan Turgenev, by James Woodward, Munich, Sagner, 1990.
Turgenev: A Reading of His Fiction, by Frank F. Seeley, Cambridge, Cambridge University Press, 1991.
Beyond Realism: Turgenev's Poetics of Secular Salvation, by Elizabeth Cheresh Allen, Stanford, Stanford University Press, 1992.
Turgenev and the Context of English Literature 1850–1900, by Glyn Turton, London and New York, Routledge, 1992.
Fathers and Sons: Russia at the Cross-Roads, by Edward Wasiolek, New York, Twayne, 1993.
Turgenev and Britain, edited by Patrick Waddington, Oxford, Berg, 1995.
Character in the Short Prose of Ivan Sergeevič Turgenev, by Sander Brouwer, Amsterdam, Rodopi, 1996.
Turgenev's "Fathers and Sons", by James Woodward, London, Bristol Classical Press, 1996.

Bibliographies
Turgenev in English: A Checklist of Works by and about Him, by Rissa Yachnin and David H. Stam, New York, New York Public Library, 1962.
A Bibliography of Writings by and about Turgenev Published in Great Britain Up to 1900, by Patrick Waddington, Wellington, New Zealand, Department of Russian, Victoria University of Wellington, 1985.
Turgenev: A Bibliography of Books 1843–1982 by and about Ivan Turgenev, with a Check-List of Canadian Library Holdings, by Nicholas G. Zekulin, Calgary, Alberta, Calgary University Press, 1985.

Although Ivan Turgenev has been overshadowed in the 20th century by his two great contemporaries Dostoevskii and Tolstoi, he remains indisputably one of the major figures of 19th-century Russian literature. Certainly his fiction is more limited than theirs in its scope and pretensions and his imagination is less fertile, but the comparison also illuminates the qualities that give his art its unique appeal: the beauty of his language, the classical sense of form and measure, the economy and subtlety of detail, and the artful blend of realistic narration, lyricism, and elegiac nostalgia that is his hallmark. Preferring observation to invention, he was a great writer of "surfaces", but he was also a subtle psychologist and a penetrating commentator on the human condition. Lacking the religious faith of his two great compatriots and distrusting "systems of thought", he was an artist torn between his emotional and intellectual responses to life. He celebrated the beauty of youth, love, nature, and art, but he saw life as brutal, callous, and devoid of meaning. Exultation and pessimism continually alternate, imbuing his art with its characteristic ambivalence.

The lyricism of Turgenev's prose is a constant reminder that he began his literary career as a poet, as a writer mainly of lyric poetry in the romantic vein, but also of a few narrative poems and the dramatic poem *Steno* (1834), based on Byron's *Manfred*. By 1843, however, he had already switched his attention to the theatre, and during the next nine years he wrote ten plays. They included seven one-acters and, more notably, the five-act "comedy" *Mesiats v derevne* (*A Month in the Country*), in which he provided the first intimation of those skills that were to distinguish the novelist – above all, of the remarkable subtlety that was to characterize his mature psychological portraiture. A "comedy" in the Chekhovian sense written ten years before Chekhov's birth, the play also anticipated Turgenev's novels with its "situation" (the settled society of a gentry estate thrown into confusion by the arrival of an outsider), and with its structural pattern (a sequence of closed dramatic scenes, each usually involving two characters). In the figure of Rakitin it presented an early example of the type that was to recur in both the novels and the stories: the type of highly civilized and sensitive intellectual debilitated by self-analysis whom Turgenev saw as most characteristic of his generation and to whom he gave the names "the superfluous man" and "the Hamlet type".

The "superfluous man" had already made his first appearance in Turgenev's first story, "Andrei Kolosov" (1844), as had the device, employed both in *A Month in the Country* and in the novels, of contrasting him in a love triangle with a strong, "natural" rival. He also reappears in *Dnevnik lishnego cheloveka* (*The Diary of a Superfluous Man*), 1850 and "Gamlet Shchigrovskogo uezda" ("Hamlet of the Shchigrovsky District"), 1849, the latter being one of 22 sketches written between 1846 and 1851 that were combined in 1852 to form *Zapiski okhotnika* (*Sketches from a Hunter's Album*), the work with which Turgenev made his first major impact on the Russian public (and the Russian government). Representing, he claimed, the fulfilment of his "Hannibalic oath" to wage war on the evils of serfdom, the volume acquires its power less from the direct exposure of these evils than by simply presenting the serf as a human being. It is the humanity of the portraits, combined with the magnificent landscapes framing them, which give this early work its justified eminence in Turgenev's *oeuvre*.

In the decade 1853–62 Turgenev's fiction arrived at its full artistic maturity. He wrote some of his finest stories and novellas during this period and also the first four of his six novels: *Rudin* 1856, *Dvorianskoe gnezdo* (*A Nest of the Gentry*) 1859, *Nakanune* (*On the Eve*) 1860, and *Ottsy i deti* (*Fathers and Sons*) 1862. In two of the stories, "Mumu", 1855 and *Postoialyi dvor* (*The Inn*) 1856, he continued the attack on serfdom, but love (or, more precisely, the "superfluous man's" failures in love) is his dominant theme in the shorter genres, recurring in *Zatish'e* [A Backwater] 1854, *Perepiska* (*A Correspondence*) 1854, *Faust* 1856, and *Asia* 1858. The series culminates in the autobiographical *Pervaia liubov'* (*First Love*) 1860, a masterpiece of poetic evocation in which the 16-year-old narrator's infatuation with the enchanting and flirtatious Zinaida is ironically contrasted with her mature, passionate, and tragic love for the boy's father. Typically "Turgenevan" in these tales are the paradoxical view of love as at once the key to life and a crippling sickness, the conception of happiness in love as ineluctably transient, the connection between love and death, and the attitude of stoic resignation expressed by the hero of *Faust*. Reflecting the unhappiness of Turgenev's personal life during this period (of his relationship, that is, with Pauline

Viardot), they also reaffirm his disillusionment with the Romantic generation to which he belonged.

Turgenev's novels, of which *Fathers and Sons* is usually considered the best, are distinguished from his novellas chiefly by their broader social canvas. They are critical examinations of the ideas and ideals advanced by successive generations of the Russian intelligentsia over a period of some 40 years, from the 1830s to the 1870s. Above all, they reflect Turgenev's search for "positive heroes", for those who will liberate Russia from her backwardness and oppression, for men and women endowed with the "superfluous man's" intelligence, but also with the faith, will-power, and capacity for action which, in his essay "Gamlet i Don Kikhot" [Hamlet and Don Quixote] (1860), he identified with Cervantes's hero. At the heart of each novel lies the love story, in which the hero's response to the challenge represented by the heroine expresses Turgenev's judgement on him and on the ideas which he embodies. Rarely do Turgenev's own views (his passionate westernism and opposition to revolution) obtrude. The "superfluous man" and his rebellious successors are dispassionately assessed, and they are ultimately found wanting. For Turgenev the future belonged to their more moderate and sober rivals, to the kind of slow, methodical, confident builder represented in *Nov'* (*Virgin Soil*) by the engineer Solomin.

The stories and novellas of Turgenev's last period, spent mainly in Baden-Baden and Paris, are divisible into two main groups: the so-called "tales of mystery", which are commonly viewed as anticipating modernism and the last two of which, *Pesn' torzhestvuiushchei liubvi* (*The Song of Triumphant Love*), 1881 and *Klara Milich*, 1882, are perhaps the most remarkable, and the so-called "tales of reminiscence", in which episodes from the past are recalled for the purpose of illuminating the mysteries of the "Russian soul". To the latter group belong the novellas *Stepnoi Korol' Lir* (*A King Lear of the Steppes*) 1870, and *Veshnie vody* (*Spring Torrents*) 1872, which rank with *First Love* as his finest achievements in the genre. His last published work was the collection of meditations, portraits, anecdotes, and landscapes entitled *Poemy v proze* (*Poems in Prose*) 1883.

JAMES WOODWARD

Sketches from a Hunter's Album

Zapiski okhotnika

Short-story cycle, 1852

Sketches from a Hunter's Album constitutes a cycle of 25 short prose works, purporting to describe the narrator's experiences and encounters during hunting trips. Most of the sketches were written and published in the period 1847–51, a period towards the end of the reign of Nicholas I (ruled 1825–55) that was characterized in Russia by grim repression and a general dearth of major works of imaginative literature. Turgenev added a few more sketches to the cycle towards the end of his life.

The sketches are of interest as literary experiments by a writer who had begun his career with narrative poems but who by the late 1840s – when the reading public, under the influence of the by then radical critic Belinskii, had begun to demand topical content in literature – was beginning to explore the possibilities of prose. With their treatment of the peasant as a legitimate subject for imaginative literature and as a human being deserving of sympathy, the sketches have much in common with other works of the so-called "Natural School" of writers nurtured by Belinskii at that period (for example, Grigorovich, Butkov, Nekrasov, and the early Dostoevskii) who dwell in their works on the plight of the urban and rural poor. Above all, though, Turgenev's sketches are notable for their humanity and their artistry.

A number of the sketches, particularly those written at the time when Turgenev was personally close to Belinskii (1847), carry an implicit plea for the liberation, or at least the civilized treatment, of the serf. This plea finds expression in two main ways. First, Turgenev portrays the peasant as a human being with a character, feelings, and a sensibility of his own, and he thereby implicitly undermines the legitimacy of an order in which the serf can be treated as chattel by his master. In the sketch "Khor' i Kalinych" ("Khor' and Kalinych"), for example, the two peasants to whom the title refers are examined as representative of general human types, the former industrious, thrifty and rational, the latter less far-sighted but more carefree and with a fuller spirit. Repeatedly in the sketches the peasants show good sense and exhibit composure and useful skills that the pampered nobleman lacks. Such traits are revealed, for example, by the narrator's guide Ermolai in the course of hunting or when he steers the narrator ashore after their boat has sunk in a lake (in the sketch "L'gov") and by the peasant Erofei, who in the sketch "Kas'ian s Krasivoi Mechi" ("Kas'ian from the Beautiful Lands") repairs the broken axle of the narrator's carriage. In the same sketch the narrator is shamed too by the moral purity of the eponymous hero, Kasian, a pious man who loves God's world and abhors the blood-lust that sets the hunter at war with nature. Second, the peasant's noble master, by contrast, is frequently depicted as brutal and is implicitly degraded by the power he cruelly wields – as had Turgenev's own mother – over fellow human beings. In the sketch "Ermolai i mel'nichikha" ("Ermolai and the Miller's Wife"), for example, the landowner Zverkov (the name implies bestiality) describes to the narrator how he has punished a domestic serf, the maid Arina. She had the temerity to fall in love while serving his wife, and so Zverkov sells her to the miller, whom she does not love. In "Burmistr" ("The Bailiff") Turgenev depicts a landowner, Penochkin, who behind a thin veneer of western cultivation is a barbaric tyrant; he orders the flogging of a servant who has served wine at the wrong temperature and entrusts a village on his estate to a brutal bailiff from among the ranks of the peasants themselves. Landowners of this sort have no sense of responsibility towards their serfs and think only of themselves: when the carriage in which Penochkin's cook is travelling is overturned, injuring the cook, Penochkin's sole concern is that his cook's ability to feed him should not be impaired. In the sketch "Dva pomeshchika" ("Two Landowners") it is argued by one of the landowners that the serfs are like children who need to be treated firmly for their own good.

As a form of humanitarian tract that may be traced back to Radishchev's *Puteshestvie iz Peterburga v Moskvu* (*A Journey from St Petersburg to Moscow*) 1790, Turgenev's cycle of sketches had great power. It was even said that it moved Alexander, who became tsar in 1855, to undertake the Emancipation of the Serfs, a measure implemented by the edict of February 1861. All the same one may question whether

Turgenev, for all his undoubted humaneness and his abhorrence of serfdom, was moved to write the sketches primarily by a desire to improve the lot of his fellow men. The wretchedness of peasants, and in particular serfs, does not feature prominently in a large proportion of the sketches. Arguably Turgenev's paramount concern is artistic. We find him in the cycle experimenting with methods of characterization and deploying skills and techniques that will later be employed to good effect in his novels. For instance, he is learning to sketch character by nuance and implication rather than laboured exposition. Thus Penochkin's superficiality and falsity are suggested by the fact that he sings a few operatic parts through his teeth while playing cards and that the French books and newspapers to which he subscribes are unread by him. Again, atmosphere is deftly evoked in "Bezhin lug" ("Bezhin Lea"), in which peasant boys frighten each other around the camp fire with tales of spirits. Turgenev is also able already to endow a work with unity. The apparently disparate components of "Ermolai and the Miller's Wife" (a description of nature and the hunt; a portrait of the hunter's assistant, the coarse peasant Ermolai; a description of Ermolai's dog, Valetka; the story of Arina's treatment by Zverkov and his wife; the concluding passage in which the hunter settles down for the night) form a beautifully harmonious cameo revealing a natural order in which all humans, indeed creatures, struggle to survive as best they can and behave brutally to those below them in the scale of things.

Finally, Turgenev broaches what are to become major themes in his work. Most notably, in "Pevtsy" ("The Singers"), in which he describes a singing contest witnessed by the narrator in the inn of a god-forsaken village, he conveys a sense of the transience of beauty. Amid passages describing the ugly, arid environment and the commonplace characters with their prosaic nicknames, Turgenev evokes the moving beauty of a peasant song. And yet try as he might, by leaving the inn as soon as the contest is over, the narrator cannot preserve the beauty Iakov has created; the sketch ends with sounds of drunken revelry and with a coarse voice calling for a child to come to be thrashed. The sketches reflect too the author's love of nature that provides a backdrop to the hunter's experience; and yet nature for Turgenev is indifferent to man's suffering. This we see in "Svidanie" ("The Meeting"), in which a peasant girl is jilted by her lover, a valet, or in "Ermolai and the Miller's Wife", in which the sad story of Arina's plight is distanced from the reader by a closing reference to the natural world at dusk.

DEREK OFFORD

A Month in the Country

Mesiats v derevne

Play, 1855

Before becoming a novelist Turgenev served a long literary apprenticeship in the course of which he wrote ten plays; *A Month in the Country*, the seventh of them, stands out from the rest by its acknowledged quality and its enduring success in stage peformance. Written in 1848–50, it was rejected at first by the censor, then published in 1855. The first performance was delayed until 1872 (in the Moscow Malyi Theatre), and even after that the play never became popular in its author's lifetime. Following a celebrated Stanislavskii version at the Moscow Arts Theatre in 1909, it became established at last in the Russian repertory and soon gained popularity abroad, especially in England.

The action of the play occurs over a four-week period on the country estate of the Islaev family who have hired a summer tutor, the 21-year-old Aleksei Beliaev, for their small son. Beliaev, for all his youth and innocence, has a tremendous effect on the whole family. Neglected by her busy husband, Mme Islaeva (Natal'ia Petrovna) finds herself falling in love with him, to her own chagrin, and reduced to competing for his affection with her own 17-year-old ward, Vera. The young girl is easily outmanoeuvred and directed eventually into an unwanted marriage with a ridiculous middle-aged neighbour, Bolshintsov. Brought to a sudden understanding of his unintended impact on the two women, Beliaev departs for the town, leaving emotional devastation in his wake. This extends even to a long-time friend of Natal'ia's, Rakitin (whose lonely bachelorhood reflects that of the author himself); suspected of impropriety by Islaev, he too has to leave. The only two characters who emerge happily from the turbulent developments are Dr Shpigelskii and Lizaveta Bogdanovna (Natal'ia's companion), whose fearfully pragmatic, but successful, courtship is a source of much humour. Everyone else suffers disappointment or worse.

Turgenev, always readier to accommodate negative criticism than to back his own judgement, accepted that *A Month in the Country* was a failure. "This is not really a comedy", he wrote, "It is a novel in dramatic form. One thing is clear – it's no good for the stage". This disclaimer is the reverse of the truth, in two senses. The play has now proved itself beyond any doubt, and in any case Turgenev's finest qualities as a novelist – the creation of atmosphere, character, and convincing dialogue – are essentially theatrical; his lack of imagination in manipulating events or sustaining narrative interest does not suggest natural affinity for the novel. His misfortune was to have written not a bad play, but one that was decades ahead of its time. Europe, let alone Russia, was not yet ready for psychological drama, in which there is little on-stage activity, though the emotional or spiritual turmoil of the characters is abundantly clear to the onlookers, especially at the end of a play when it becomes clear that personal destinies have been radically altered. Turgenev had moved too rapidly for contemporary taste away from the depiction of larger-than-life characters engaged in remarkable activites to the presentation of inconsequential provincial people doing little more than make a mess of their humdrum lives. The mature Ibsen and Chekhov lay decades in the future.

Psychological drama, so little reliant on incident, opens up broad possibilities for characterization, in which *A Month in the Country* is remarkably successful. All 13 characters are fully authenticated; one or two of them develop and mature perceptibly during the action of the play without any risk to credulity. Particularly poignant are the two leading female roles. Vera is forced through a brutal progression from innocent adolescence to adult cynicism; her resignation to a hopeless future, at least for some years ahead, gives her something near to the status of a tragic heroine. Natal'ia, by contrast, looks at first sight like an out-and-out villain, willing to destroy a young life in pursuit of her own interests, though this superficial view needs considerable adjustment. Her behaviour has much to do with a growing sense of desperation; stuck in a boring marriage she can see her youth and beauty beginning to slip away, and in any case she finds the power of erotic attraction simply too devastating to control. Any condemnation of her attitudes and actions must be tempered with a sensitive understanding of her panicky trepidation; her role calls for an actress of some subtlety. The other parts are strongly differentiated. Beliaev is the incarnation of youthful energy and innocence. Islaev plods along, always one move behind events. Rakitin's sense of sadness and failure is brought to painful maturity. Several sadly comic characters help in their different ways to distract from the main action and vary the tone of the play, steering it away from obsessiveness. *A Month in the Country*, with its straightforward realism, calls for understated acting of the kind achievable by sensitive non-specialist performers; for this reason it is as well suited to the amateur as to the professional stage. On both it should be played more for gentle comic effect than for tragedy or pathos; the underlying unpleasantness will speak for itself.

Many critics have made passing references to similarities between this play and much of Chekhov's drama. Chekhov himself denied any influence from this quarter, but recent research has disclosed parallels – especially between *A Month in the Country* and *Uncle Vania* – which can scarcely be coincidental. It is no exaggeration to claim that Chekhov's settings and moods, as well as some of his characters, their actions, speech, and preoccupations, owe more to Turgenev than has yet been acknowledged. The astonishing fact is that his one truly successful play, anticipating a method that would enjoy widespread popularity two generations later, was written ten years before Chekhov was even born.

A.D.P. BRIGGS

Rudin

Novel, 1856

From an artistic point of view *Rudin* is a somewhat flawed work, but it is of considerable importance as Turgenev's first attempt at the genre of the novel and as the first of his portraits of the typical representative of the Russian educated class in the period c.1840–60.

Like all Turgenev's major novels, *Rudin* is set in the Russian countryside where a way of life that has proceeded quietly for generations is disrupted by some outside influence. In this case the disruption lies in the person of the nomadic impoverished eponymous hero, who brings ill-defined but inspiring notions (of mainly Germanic origin) of duty, self-sacrifice, and service to some noble cause. The first two chapters serve, through a series of rather contrived encounters, to introduce the secondary characters who frequent the household of Dar'ia Mikhailovna Lasunskaia, a cold, pretentious, self-centred old woman, on whose estate the main action of the novel takes place. These characters include the kind-hearted widow Aleksandra Lipina; the dour, practical neighbouring landowner Lezhnev; Volyntsev, the limited suitor for the hand of Lasunskaia's daughter, the heroine Natal'ia; the toady and parasite Pandalevskii; Basistov, the idealistic and impressionable tutor to Lasunskaia's younger children; and Pigasov, another neighbouring landowner and an inveterate cynic. Rudin himself arrives at Lasunskaia's in place of an expected guest, in chapter 3. He easily discredits Pigasov and inspires some of the company with his apparent ardent idealism. To Lasunskaia he seems a useful embellishment to her provincial salon, and he remains in the household as a guest. The main body of the novel, from chapters 5 to 9, traces the relationship that develops between Rudin and Natal'ia. Rudin awakens in Natal'ia a deep love, and as this love develops she is transformed from a self-effacing girl to a strong, mature young woman. Rudin, however, is unable to respond to this love; for all his intellectual ardour and theoretical altruism he is at heart a cold egoist who is incapable of conducting warm and natural human relationships. His shortcomings are exposed in a number of trysts with Natal'ia, culminating in chapter 9 when he fails to agree to Natal'ia's suggestion that they elope and, in defence of his weakness, lapses into a patronising and even spiteful attitude towards her. By now their relationship has in any case been reported to Lasunskaia by Pandalevskii, who in chapter 7 has spied on one of their meetings, and in chapter 11 Rudin leaves the household in disgrace to resume his wanderings. Chapter 12 depicts a world in which, two years on, order has been restored. Against a summer setting reminiscent of the tranquillity of the opening passage of the novel, Turgenev shows Lezhnev and Lipina embarking on a happy family life that points up the sort of personal fulfilment, prosaic but substantial, which may be achieved if one develops in harmony with life's seasons. Rudin, by contrast, remains at the age of 35 an immature, unpractical "poet".

In terms of theme, characterization, and literary technique there is much in this novel that is typical of Turgenev's fiction, and much to admire. The novel conveys a keen, tragic sense of the frailty of human relationships, the elusiveness of happiness, and the transitoriness of those deep feelings, expressed above all in love between a man and woman, through which people reach beyond themselves. The hero is feckless and fails to find fulfilment. On the other hand, the heroine, who eventually settles for marriage to Volyntsev, shows strength of character and moral purity, and through the emotional storm she undergoes she reaches a state in which she will bring happiness to others and find a form of satisfaction of her own.

The true nature and feelings of characters are deftly portrayed by certain observations, such as Lasunskaia's habit of turning all conversations to herself. Strands of imagery, notably relating to man's need for refuge and to fruitfulness, are profitably deployed and ultimately turned against Rudin himself, who towards the end of the novel is portrayed as having gone to seed. There is a rich sub-text of allusion to Pushkin, and in particular to his seminal work *Evgenii Onegin*, on which Turgenev draws both thematically and in terms of characterization.

The most important flaws of the novel relate to its balance and structure. They may be explained not only by Turgenev's inexperience in the genre of the novel, but also by the circumstances in which *Rudin* was written. Turgenev began work on what was originally conceived as a *povest'* or novella in the summer of 1855 while in exile on the estate he had inherited from his mother in Orel Province. He only completed it in late 1855 and early 1856 after his return to St Petersburg. At that late stage he inserted: flashbacks in chapters 5 and 6, in which Lezhnev describes Rudin's student days; chapter 12, in which Lezhnev tries to assess Rudin's strengths and weaknesses and his significance for his country; and the long first epilogue, in which Lezhnev, some years after the main action, meets Rudin by coincidence and hears his account of his various failed undertakings (in estate management, as an entrepreneur attempting to make a river navigable, and as a teacher of Russian literature). The effect of these insertions is to increase the topical significance of the work at a time when the Russian intelligentsia, following the death of Nicholas I in 1855 and the country's defeat in the Crimean War (1853–56), was beginning to anticipate greater freedom and reform after decades of repression.

Rudin may be seen, therefore, as an attempt on Turgenev's part, at the beginning of a new age of Russian history, to give a balanced assessment of the typical humane, educated man of his generation, whose time was now past. That type, the "superfluous man", could be condemned for his failure to put undoubted talents to practical use and for moral weakness; but he also deserved credit, in Turgenev's interpretation, for his idealism and his capacity to inspire others, for sowing "good seeds". In order to create this balanced picture, though, Turgenev is heavily reliant on the interpolations of Lezhnev, who by chapter 5 has developed from the unimpressive "sack of flour", as Lipina describes him in chapter 1, to an authoritative commentator in league with the narrator. It is also arguable that the narrative goes on for too long. Turgenev fails convincingly to demonstrate through his examination of Rudin's unsuccessful relationship with Natal'ia what perhaps ultimately becomes his main point: the "superfluous man" lacks the ability to be of practical use to his country, with the result that the writer is forced to attempt to complete his meaning in cumbersome appendages to the novel's action.

The short second epilogue, in which Rudin dies on the Parisian barricades in 1848, was written in 1860. In showing Rudin to be capable of dying for a cause, it serves as a partial vindication of the "man of the 1940s" in the face of the criticism by then being levelled at him by the militant young radical wing of the intelligentsia.

DEREK OFFORD

A Nest of the Gentry

Dvorianskoe gnezdo

Novel, 1859

Set in 1842, Turgenev's second novel opens in a provincial capital at the home of the widow Mar'ia Dmitrievna Kalitina and her three children. Mar'ia Dmitrievna's guests this day include Lavretskii, the novel's central hero, and Panshin, a flashy young bachelor.

As in the majority of his works, Turgenev follows the introductory exposition with the hero's biography. The son of a gentry father and a serf mother, Lavretskii met his wife, Varvara Petrovna, while a student at Moscow University. At her urging, the couple eventually took up residence in Paris, where Varvara Petrovna moved in the highest social circles and Lavretskii devoted his days to not very clearly defined studies. After discovering his wife's infidelity, Lavretskii left her in Paris and eventually returned to Russia to one of his family's estates near the town where the Kalitins live.

Although Lavretskii has resolved to forget about women and to take up useful action, he none the less finds himself attracted to Mar'ia Dmitrievna's daughter, Liza, and has come to their house today to invite mother and daughter to visit him. Accepting, the religious Liza asks Lavretskii how he could have left his wife, since God had brought them together.

The Kalitins' visit passes most agreeably. Not long after their departure, Lavretskii reads a notice of his wife's death in a Paris newspaper. He is thus suddenly free to marry Liza, but she is seriously considering a proposal from Panshin, partly because her mother approves of the match, and partly because her faith persuades her that happiness on earth depends on submitting to God's will.

Late one night on a walk Lavretskii wanders into the Kalitins' garden. Liza, unable to sleep, is there too, and in response to his avowal of love she embraces him. The very next day Varvara Petrovna, very much alive, turns up with their daughter at Lavretskii's house in town. He refuses to forgive her for her past behaviour but installs her on one of his estates on the condition that she never leave it. Liza then declines Panshin's proposal and retires to a monastery as penance for her and Lavretskii's having dared to court happiness. Lavretskii goes back to Moscow.

In an epilogue set eight years later Lavretskii makes a nostalgic visit to the Kalitins' home, where Mar'ia Dmitrievna's son and his family now live. Watching the lively children at play, Lavretskii addresses an elegiac mental blessing to them. In the final lines of the novel, the narrator mentions a rumour that Lavretskii also visited the monastery to which Liza had retreated. There they allegedly caught sight of each other briefly: "What did they think? What did they both feel? Who can know? Who can say? There are certain moments in life, certain feelings ... One can only point them out – and pass on by".

Written in the years 1856–58 and first published in 1859, *A Nest of the Gentry* has most of the typical features of a Turgenev novel. It is short – really an overgrown novella; it is hero-centred; and it revolves around a love story that has philosophical and at times socio-political overtones. Turgenev perceives a conflict between personal happiness and duty, particularly duty to society and humanity. For Liza the primary issue at stake is a religious one, while Lavretskii sees it as a philosophical one lacking any possible resolution. At best he seems to hope that the coming generation will know both happiness and socially useful activity.

A Nest of the Gentry reveals at least two major literary influences. The first is Pushkin's verse novel *Evgenii Onegin*. Like Pushkin's main character, Lavretskii seems virtually a stranger to the milieu into which he comes, and like Pushkin's Tat'iana, the strong, highly moral Liza poses a love test for him. Unlike Onegin and most Turgenev heroes, however, he passes the test. Unfortunately, fate smiles on neither him nor Liza.

Goncharov's novel *Obryv* (*The Precipice*) provides the second major literary stimulus for *A Nest of the Gentry*. Goncharov did not finish the novel until 1869, but Turgenev knew the general outlines of the work from conversations with the author. The bits that Turgenev indisputably appropriated from Goncharov led the latter to conclude that Turgenev had plagiarized his work. The charge is excessive but not entirely groundless.

Lavretskii represents one of the "superfluous men" who populate Russian novels of the 19th century. Unable to realize themselves in either their private or public lives, these exclusively male characters mirror male writers' frustration with oppressive Russian governmental policies and practices, additionally demonstrating the confusion of the personal and social in 19th-century Russian culture. On the biographical level, the figure of Lavretskii contains a great deal of Turgenev himself. The description of Lavretskii's estate resembles Turgenev's own Spasskoe, and Lavretskii's return from Europe reflects Turgenev's own meditations on Russian life and culture and his doubts about the suitability for Russia of the German philosophy that he had imbibed in Berlin in the 1830s.

Liza and Varvara Petrovna are variations on the Madonnas and whores who seem to provide the only two options for female characters in the Russian realist novel. The amoral Varvara Petrovna stands in a line of adultresses that culminates in Tolstoi's Anna Karenina. Liza is a typical "Turgenev maiden" – chaste, modest, self-sacrificing, and morally superior to the men surrounding her. Contemporary non-Russian feminist criticism has shown what an ambiguous legacy the classic Russian realist portraits of women represent for Russians today.

Almost all the critics greeted *A Nest of the Gentry* enthusiastically when it first appeared, and the work remained Turgenev's most popular novel throughout his life. The 20th century has come to see *Fathers and Sons* as Turgenev's most masterful novel, but the poetry of *A Nest of the Gentry* has not lost its potency. Certain scenes etch themselves in the reader's memory, for they seem to capture ethereal, transcendental moments. Moreover, Turgenev's compassion and fondness for the major characters in *A Nest of the Gentry* strike a balance between objectivity and sentiment that he would never again attain.

DAVID A. LOWE

First Love

Pervaia liubov'

Novella, 1860

First Love was first published in *Biblioteka dlia chtenia* in 1860. It is widely regarded as one of Turgenev's finest achievements, especially in the shorter mode, as well as among the most autobiographical of his works. The story was also one of which the author himself was particularly fond. Towards the end of his life, he wrote: "It is the only thing that still gives me pleasure, because it is life itself, it was not made up ... *First Love* is part of my experience." He is also reported as saying: "There is only one story I reread with pleasure. That is *First Love*. It is perhaps my favourite work. In the others there is, if only a little, some invention, while in *First Love* is described a real event without the slightest decoration and when I reread it, the characters arise before me as if alive."

Like the similar and nearly contemporary *Asia*, the story is narrated by a middle-aged man who recalls a powerful, transcendent, erotic experience of his youth. In both tales the central male character relates a moment in his life that was never to be repeated and in which an enthralling young woman was the focal point. In *First Love* the main thread of the story is provided by the encounter between the young (16-year-old) hero, Vladimir, and the enigmatic, alluring Zinaida, five years his senior, and the main engine of the plot is his attempts to solve the riddle of her existence. In so doing he uncovers an even darker mystery.

The story proper begins when young Vladimir moves to the suburbs of Moscow one May in 1833, that is, nearly 30 years before the tale itself was written, and when Turgenev was himself 15: at once autobiographical resonances are established. Next to his parents' summer villa live two princesses, mother and daughter. Before long Vladimir has encountered the bewitching Zinaida, and almost at once becomes infatuated. She is surrounded by a strange entourage of men, with whom she flirts, teases, and torments. Vladimir is soon one of their number and he declares "My real torments began from that day." Gradually, however, Zinaida's power and authority seem to weaken, and she enters a decline, now appearing pale and unwell, as opposed to her earlier vivacious and captivating self. At the same time, Vladimir comes to realize that Zinaida is seriously in love with another man, none other than his own father! (Indeed, it is probable that this dangerous liaison had existed before the story begins, and this is precisely why Vladimir's family had moved to this particular house.) The full secret of the relationship between his father and Zinaida is revealed when Vladimir witnesses an encounter between them that culminates in the father striking Zinaida with a whip. At the end of this fateful summer, they return to Moscow, and Vladimir goes to university. His father soon dies, having broken off his affair with Zinaida, probably under pressure from his wife, Vladimir's mother. Four years later Zinaida dies in childbirth, and the middle-aged Vladimir, who recounts the dramatic events of this far-away summer, has never married.

First Love was published at a time of great tension in Russian literary critical circles, appearing as it did just one year before the long-awaited Emancipation of the Serfs. Even more crucially, it came out almost immediately after Turgenev's controversial political novel *On the Eve*. Consequently, even though the story itself is not at all political in its thematics, it received a decidedly mixed reaction, both from the critics, and in private correspondence. But its lasting reputation has been almost universally positive. The leading British authority on Turegenev in recent times, Richard Freeborn, has noted that "Alongside *Fathers and Children* one must place that most enchanting and brilliant of his stories, *First Love*."

Freeborn is also not alone in seeing the story as a light-filled evocation of youthful passion, when he remarks: "*First Love* traces the gestation of love in subtler, brighter and more lucid ways [than *Asia*]". Certainly, the story, opening as it does in early May begins with evocations of a lost, golden age. The narrator comments: "I shall never forget the first weeks I spent in the country. The weather was magnificent." Within his body, he feels great expectancy and "shoots of happy feeling, of young and surging life". Looking at the story as a whole, there is much to attract the reader, and it has retained great poularity as one of Turgenev's most accessible works. The characterization is vivid and dynamic, and the story intensely dramatic and involving. The evocation of the torments love can bring is certainly powerfully drawn, and, as one would expect from such a painstaking stylist as Turgenev, it is all beautifully written.

Yet the lasting impressions for the reader are rather darker. For example, the image of the heroine, Zinaida, may start as that of a strong, positive woman, but gradually she declines from this position of authority, first into an iconically ailing and sad victim, before bearing the brunt of her lover's whip, only to depart the stage in the traditionally female scene of death in childbirth. The view in the story of love, both first and last, is also ultimately negative. In Russian, as in Latin, the word for "passion" ("strast'") is derived from the word "to suffer" ("stradat'"), and the picture that develops is that sexual love is indeed a passion, a "storm" (to use another metaphor from the story) that must be endured. As elsewhere in Turgenev, moreover, the close link between *eros* and *thanatos* becomes apparent. Both Zinaida and Vladimir's father die, and the latter sums up this theme very chillingly. On the day of the stroke that is to kill him, he writes to Vladimir: "My son ... beware a woman's love, beware this happiness, this poison." Love, whether first, only or last, may appear to bring happiness, but it will be brief, and involve mutual torment and suffering. More particularly, the love of a woman is poison.

JOE ANDREW

On the Eve

Nakanune

Novel, 1860

On the Eve is set between the summer of 1853 and spring of 1854 and tells the story of Elena Stakhova, the strong-willed and impulsive daughter of aristocratic parents. Two friends, Bersenev, a student of philosophy, and Shubin, a sculptor, both vie good-humouredly for her affection. Elena initially feels a certain fondness towards Bersenev, but she soon falls in love with Insarov, a Bulgarian student wholeheartedly devoted to the liberation of his country from Turkish oppression. As tension mounts in the Balkans, Insarov prepares to leave for Bulgaria with Elena, but falls seriously ill. Bersenev nurses him to a partial recovery, and Insarov and Elena marry in secret, but her parents find out and are horrified. However, as Elena and Insarov leave Moscow for Bulgaria, Elena's father arrives to give them his blessing. On reaching Venice, Insarov suffers a relapse and soon dies. Elena sends a letter to her parents informing them of her intention to cross the Adriatic Sea to Zara, where she will bury Insarov's body and then become a nurse for the Slav soldiers. Her subsequent fate remains uncertain.

Turgenev first began working on his third novel, *On the Eve*, at the beginning of 1858 when he wrote a list of the main characters. During the first months of 1859 he worked on a detailed plan of the novel and completed it in April of that year at his estate, Spasskoe. He began writing it in Vichy on Tuesday 28 June 1859, and completed it at Spasskoe on Sunday 6 November 1859. In January 1860 *On the Eve* was first published in the journal *Russkii vestnik*.

Although work on the novel began in 1858, the idea of writing it came to Turgenev as early as 1853. The character of Elena, whom Turgenev intended to be, in his own words, "a new type in Russian life", was already sketched out in his mind, but the character of a man to whom his resolute heroine could devote herself still eluded him. The solution to this problem was provided by one of his neighbours, a certain Vasilii Karateev, with whom Turgenev became friends while serving out his internal exile at Spasskoe in 1852. Karateev left Russia in 1855 to fight in the Crimean War, but, before leaving, gave Turgenev a clumsily fictionalized account of one of his experiences at Moscow University. While there Karateev fell in love with a Russian girl who, after initially returning his love, subsequently gave her affections to a Bulgarian student called Katranov, a poet and patriot. She went with Katranov to Bulgaria where he died soon after. On reading Karateev's story, Turgenev immediately recognized in Katranov the hero he had been searching for, and he based his novel on this account. The writing of *On the Eve*, however, was delayed by several years while Turgenev worked on the novels *Rudin* and *A Nest of the Gentry*.

Although a love story stands at the centre of its plot, *On the Eve* is first and foremost a novel of ideas. In it Turgenev obliquely explores the theme of Russia's future and the kind of leaders needed to deliver her from oppression. As in his contemporaneous article, "Gamlet i Don-Kikhot" [Hamlet and Don Quixote], Turgenev discredits the Hamlet-like irresolution of the Russian "superfluous man", seeing in that Quixotic sense of commitment with which Insarov is imbued the key to salvation. The portrayal of Elena as a woman capable of independent thought and action also represents a landmark in Russian literature, yet ultimately Elena's fate is dependent on that of a man, and the question of women's position in society is subordinate to the wider themes of the book.

Turgenev, in view of the topical issues that his novel raised, was somewhat naive in his surprise at the volume of criticism that *On the Eve* attracted in the leading journals of the day, and he was also stung by its general hostility. Conservative journals were almost unanimous in their disapproval of the allegedly dangerous political message it preached, especially in the light of the impending Emancipation of the Serfs, and of what they perceived to be immoral conduct on the part of Elena. Criticism from liberal and radical journals was more diverse. While there was a certain amount of praise for the novel's literary qualities, the dominant tone was one of antipathy towards the character of Insarov. Dobroliubov's critique of the novel, which was published in *Sovremennik* against the wishes of Turgenev, was highly influential. While he welcomed the appearance of a new kind of hero, and indeed heroine, so dedicated to virtuous struggle, he was critical of Turgenev's failure to show Insarov engaged in any kind of action. If, as Dobroliubov surmised, Turgenev hoped to show in his contrast of Insarov with Bersenev and Shubin the inadequacy of Russians for Quixotic heroism, then Insarov's ineffectuality could hardly serve as a slap in the face to Russians, much less as an example of the New Man to be followed.

In truth Dobroliubov's critique was motivated more by his own political ends than by any purely literary considerations, and was essentially manipulative. Turgenev's vision in *On the Eve* was of a new type of leader who could unite the educated classes with the masses in the cause of enlightenment and freedom, and as such its message was more optimistic than either of his previous two novels. However, the hallmark of Turgenev's most successful works is the absence of any subjectivity, while *On the Eve* is fundamentally a *roman à thèse*. In addition, the novel depends to a large extent on the portrayal of Insarov, and his superficiality undermines many positive aspects of the novel, such as the characterization of Elena. In artistic terms *On the Eve* represents something of a low point in Turgenev's career and may be viewed as a prelude to his masterpiece of two years later, *Fathers and Sons*. In the context of the 19th-century Russian novel as a socio-political phenomenon, however, *On the Eve* can claim its place alongside *Fathers and Sons* and Chernyshevskii's

Chto delat'? (*What is to Be Done?*) as a work that exerted a strong influence on Russian radicals of the 1860s and subsequent decades.

ROBERT LAGERBERG

Fathers and Sons

Ottsy i deti

Novel, 1862

Conceived during a visit to the Isle of Wight in August 1860 and first published in 1862, *Fathers and Sons*, the fourth of Turgenev's six novels, is generally recognized as his *chef d'oeuvre* and as one of the major works of Russian literature. It is also one of the most controversial, raising issues that divided contemporary Russian society and posing questions about its meaning that have fuelled one of the most heated and durable debates in Russian literary studies.

Turgenev's subject in the novel is the conflict of ideologies that split the Russian intelligentsia during the six-year period of social ferment. This period began with Russia's defeat in the Crimean War and culminated in the Emancipation of the Serfs. Like the subsequent novels of Dostoevskii, the work was a response, in particular, to the appearance on the social scene during this period of a new, more aggressive type of intellectual of lower-class origin (most notably represented by the publicists Chernyshevskii and Dobroliubov), who was fully prepared to embrace the idea of revolution. In the figure of his hero, the young medical student Evgenii Bazarov, who has been described as the "first Bolshevik" in Russian literature, Turgenev embodies the distinctive characteristics of these young radicals: their uncompromisingly rational approach to life based on study of the natural sciences, their ruthlessly iconoclastic approach to traditional values, and their socialist, materialist, and utilitarian convictions to which he gives the name "nihilism". His aims in the novel were to present a dispassionate assessment of these "new men" (the "sons") and to illuminate the differences of view and outlook that divided them from the liberal gentry of the older generation (the "fathers"), to whom he himself belonged and who are represented in the work by the landowner Nikolai Petrovich Kirsanov and his brother Pavel. He confronts the old with the new, the abstract, impractical idealism of the "fathers" with the harsh rationalism and empiricism of the new iconoclasts, and the result was the first Russian ideological novel, a dramatization of the clash of ideas, generations, and social classes to which its title alludes.

Dominated by the figure of its hero, the novel hinges structurally on his journeys between four locations and the confrontations that result from them. His first journey at the beginning of the work brings him to the Kirsanov estate, Mar'ino, as the guest of his young university friend Arkadii, Nikolai's son, and the scene is thus set for his debates with Pavel in chapters 6 and 10 that lie at the heart of *Fathers and Sons* as a social and ideological novel. With his indictment of the gentry's inertia, his damning exposure of social injustice, and his resolute commitment to remedial action he emerges from these debates unquestionably the victor. Turgenev acknowledges here the justice of the criticism that the "sons" levelled against his own generation and pays full tribute to their strength of will and purpose. But he also prepares the ground for the criticism of the "sons" that his novel presents. He does so by examining the implications of their nihilism and by thus introducing a more fundamental conflict between the characters that cuts across and ultimately eclipses the class, generational, and ideological differences that divide them. Converting the social novel into a philosophical novel, it involves different conceptions of man's relation to the world in which he lives.

Turgenev's criticism of the "sons" takes the form of a challenge to the assumptions from which they derived their strength: to their unlimited faith in the powers of human reason and to their consequent view of man as self-sufficient, as nature's master and as the maker of his own destiny. His rejection of these assumptions is conveyed in three different ways: by the negative attributes of his hero that he ascribes to them (his arrogant, dogmatic extremism, his crudely utilitarian measure of value, his indifference to the beauty of nature and art, his cynical attitude to love and human relationships, and, above all, his proud solitude); by the contrast with the emotional responsiveness and instinctive "openness" to life and people of Nikolai and Arkadii; and, most conclusively, by the change that takes place in Bazarov as a result of his infatuation with, and rejection by, the beautiful landowner Anna Odintsova. Performing the role that it always plays in the Turgenevan novel as a "test" to which the hero's ideas are subjected, the love story in *Fathers and Sons* has the effect of undermining the entire system of values on which Bazarov's supreme self-confidence had previously rested. Exposing the impotence of reason, the experience of love deprives his life of the only purpose and meaning that it had for him.

The concluding ten chapters of the novel record the process of Bazarov's decline, the main stages of which are signalled by his flirtation with the young peasant-girl Fenechka, Nikolai's mistress and the mother of his child, his consequent duel with Pavel, and his death, which results from his failure to cauterize a cut that he suffers while performing an autopsy on a peasant who has died from typhus. For all the anguish, embitterment, and aimlessness that he displays in these chapters, however, Bazarov presents himself in decline as an immensely more engaging and heroic figure. The collapse of his convictions does not change his posture of proud defiance. Though now acknowledging man's subordination to powers beyond his control, he refuses to submit. The revolutionary who had challenged Russian society in the name of human reason is now replaced by a rebel who challenges life ("the laws of nature") in the name of human freedom and dignity. Irrationally he pits his will against the "laws" that have confounded his reason, even challenging death to do its worst. In the novel's conclusion his defiance and death are contrasted with Nikolai's and Arkadii's unquestioning affirmation of life, which receives fitting expression in their marriages to Fenechka and Odintsova's sister, Katia. It is to them, to the ability of their hearts to find a meaning in life that is inaccessible to the hero's reason, that Turgenev grants the victory. Yet it is a victory overshadowed by the hero's tragedy, which Turgenev invests with all the power that derived from his own despair, from his own futile search for a rational meaning in life. For the conflict between head and heart was Turgenev's own conflict, and it is *this* conflict that the novel ultimately dramatizes, acquiring as a result its disturbing ambivalence that continues to stimulate the critical debate.

JAMES WOODWARD

Aleksandr Trifonovich Tvardovskii 1910–1971

Poet and editor

Biography

Born in Zagor'e village, Smolensk, 21 June 1910. Attended Smolensk Pedagogical Institute; graduated from Moscow Institute of Philosophy, Literature and History in 1939. Worked as journalist in 1930s. Served in the Red Army, 1939–40. Reporter during World War II. Poet and editor. Married: Mari'a Tvardovskaia (died in 1992); one daughter. Member of the Communist Party. Editor-in-chief of *Novyi mir*, 1950–54, 1958–70. Secretary of the Board of the Soviet Writers' Union, 1950–54, 1959–71. Deputy of Supreme Soviet of USSR, 1950–60s. Recipient: Stalin Prize in 1941, 1946, 1947; Lenin Prize in 1961; State Prize in 1971. Died in Krasnaia Parkha village, near Moscow, 18 December 1971.

Publications

Collected Editions

Sobranie sochinenii, 4 vols. Moscow, 1959–60.
Sobranie sochinenii, 5 vols. Moscow, 1966–71.
Proza. Stat'i. Pis'ma. Moscow, 1974.
Tyorkin and the Stovemakers: Poetry and Prose, translated by Anthony Rudolf. Cheadle, Carcanet Press, 1974.
Sobranie sochinenii, 6 vols. Moscow, 1976–83.
Selected Poetry. Moscow, Progress, 1981.
Izbrannye sochineniia. Moscow, 1981.
Stikhotvoreniia i poemy, edited by M.I. Tvardovskaia. Leningrad, 1986.
Iz rannikh stikhotvorenii (1925–35) [From the Early Poems (1925–35)], edited by M.I. Tvardovskaia. Moscow, 1987.
Poemy: "Strana Muraviia", "Vasilii Terkin", "Dom u dorogi", "Za dal'iu dal'", "Terkin na tom svete", "Po pravu pamiati" [Poems: "The Land of Muravia", "Vasilii Terkin", "House by the Road", "Distance Beyond Distance", "Terkin in the Other World", "By Right of Memory"]. Moscow, 1988.

Poetry

Put' k sotsializmu [The Road to Socialism]. 1931.
Strana Muraviia [The Land of Muravia]. Moscow, 1935.
Dom u dorogi [The House on the Road]. Moscow, 1945.
Vasilii Terkin. Moscow, 1945; translated as *Vassili Tyorkin: A Book about a Soldier*, by Alex Miller, Moscow, Progress, 1975.
Za dal'iu dal' [Distance Beyond Distance]. Moscow, 1953.
Terkin na tom svete. Moscow, 1963; translated (in part) as "Tyorkin in the Other World", in *Post-War Russian Poetry*, edited by Daniel Weissbort, Harmondsworth, Penguin, 1974, 69–71.
Iz liriki etikh let: 1959–67 [From the Lyrics of Those Years: 1959–67]. Moscow, 1967.
Kniga liriki [Book of Lyrics]. Moscow, 1967.
"Po pravu pamiati" [By Right of Memory], *Znamia*, 2 (1987).

Prose

Dnevnik predsedatelia kolkhoza [Diary of a Collective Farm Chairman]. Moscow, 1932.

Literary Criticism

Stat'i i zametki o literature [Articles and Notes on Literature]. Moscow, 1973.

Letters, Speeches, and Autobiography

"Perepiska A.T. Tvardovskogo i V.V. Ovechkina, 1946–68" [Correspondence Between A.T. Tvardovskii and V.V. Ovechkin, 1946–68], *Sever*, 10 (1979); 2 (1980).
Zapakh ognia, zalog tepla ... [The Smell of the Fire, the Pledge of Warmth ...]. Moscow, 1983.
Pis'ma o literature: 1930–70 [Letters on Literature: 1930–70]. Moscow, 1985.

Critical Studies

Aleksandr Tvardovskii, by P.S. Vykhodtsev, Moscow, 1958.
Russian Literature since the Revolution, by Edward J. Brown, Cambridge, Massachusetts, Harvard University Press, 1963; 2nd edition, 1982.
Aleksandr Tvardovskii, by P.F. Roshchin, Moscow, 1966.
Aleksandr Tvardovskii, by A. Turkov, 2nd edition, Moscow, 1970.
Alexander Twardowski Allein der Wahrheit Verplichtet, edited by Robert Von Herausgegeben, S.J. Hotz, and Konrad Farmer, vol. 1, Bern, Peter Lang, 1972.
Desiat' let posle "Odnogo dnia Ivana Denisovicha", by Zh. Medvedev, translated by Hilary Sternberg, London, Macmillan, 1973; reprinted Harmondsworth, Penguin, 1975.
A. Tvardovskii, by A.I. Kondratovich, Moscow, 1978; 2nd edition, 1985.
Solzhenitsyn, Tvardovsky and "Novy mir", by Vladimir Lakshin, translated by Michael Glenny, Cambridge, Massachusetts, MIT Press, 1980.
Novy mir: A Case Study in the Politics of Literature, 1952–1958, by Edith Rogovin Frankel, Cambridge, Cambridge University Press, 1981.
Tvorcheskii put' Tvardovskogo, by A.V. Makedonov, Moscow, 1981.
"Vasilii Terkin" Aleksandra Tvardovskogo, by A.L. Grishunin, Moscow, 1987.
Tvorchestvo Aleksandra Tvardovskogo: Issledovaniia i materialy, edited by P.S. Vykhodtsev and A. Groznova, Leningrad, 1989.
Written with the Bayonet: Soviet Russian Poetry of World War Two, by Katharine Hodgson, Liverpool, Liverpool University Press, 1996.

Aleksandr Tvardovskii was born into the family of a wealthy peasant (kulak) blacksmith, who fell victim to Stalin's collectivization. Tvardovskii's early poems appeared in the Smolensk newspapers in 1925. He studied at the Pedagogical Institute (in Smolensk) and at the Moscow Institute of Philosophy, Literature and History, graduating in 1939. Between 1930 and 1936 he worked as a poet and a reporter for various Smolensk newspapers. In 1939 he was drafted, serving in Belorussia; he was demobilized, but soon redrafted, working as a war journalist during the Finnish War (1940) and World War II. During this period he wrote his famous narrative poem *Vasilii Terkin*. This created a new type of folk hero with whom Soviet soldiers could easily identify. Tvardovskii also wrote sketches, essays and lyric poetry; but he is better known for his editorial work and for his narrative poems.

His early narrative poems include *Put' k sotsializmu* [The Road to Socialism] (1931), and *Strana Muraviia* [The Land of Muravia] (1935). Both poems deal with life on a collective farm. *Strana Muraviia* was awarded the Stalin Prize for literary achievements in 1941. It is a story about a peasant, Nikita Morgunok, who is opposed to collectivization; he embarks on a journey in search of Utopia where he can have his own farm. Failing to find such a land, he returns to his village and is happy to join the collective farm. The poem alludes to the epic poems of Nekrasov; yet elements of the fairy tale prevail over realistic description. In 1947 Tvardovskii was awarded his third Stalin Prize for the epic poem *Dom u dorogi* [House on the Road]; written during 1942–45, it creates a portait of Russian life under Nazi occupation. In 1961 his other narrative poem, *Za dal'iu dal'* [Distance Beyond Distance] was awarded the Lenin Prize; the narrator talks about his train journey through Siberia, on which he meets a friend returning home after 17 years in labour camps. Tvardovskii's criticism of Stalin, however, did not extend beyond the remarks made by Khrushchev at the 20th Congress of the Communist Party. His scornful look at Soviet reality was continued in the poem *Terkin na tom svete* (*Terkin in the Other World*), published in 1963. It is a humorous and bitter story of Terkin's visit to hell, a satirical allegory of the inhuman bureaucratism of the Stalinist period. Another poem of critical nature, *Po pravu pamiati* [By Right of Memory] (written 1967–69), was banned from publication. It is an autobiographical work that revealed the fate of Tvardovskii's father who had suffered under Stalin. Published in Russia only in 1987 (with a previous appearance in Germany in 1969), Tvardovskii's last work displays courage and honesty, as he openly confesses his guilt towards his exiled father. It contains a warning for future generations not to abandon moral values in favour of swimming with the political tide.

In many ways Tvardovskii is closely associated with the period of liberalization in Soviet culture, often labelled as the Thaw. Tvardovskii used his influence in literary circles (he was on the board of the Writers' Union, and for a while was its chairman) to promote the most revealing and liberal literature. As editor-in-chief he managed to introduce readers of *Novyi mir* to the works of Solzhenitsyn, Voinovich, Siniavskii, Grekova, Pasternak, Tsvetaeva, Babel', Mandel'shtam, Akhmatova, and many others whose significance had been ignored during the Stalinist era. In spite of being awarded the State Prize in 1971 for a lyric poetry collection that was published in 1967, his liberalism was constantly attacked by the conservatives; in 1970 he was forced to resign his editorial post. Tvardovskii died in December 1971 in his house in Krasnaia Parkha, not far from Moscow.

Tvardovskii's impact on the development of Soviet literature is immense. His epic poems continued the democratization of literature that had started in the 19th century: these poems encompass folkloric themes with a richness of colloquial language and moral values, which left their mark on the prose writers of the 1960s and 1970s.

ALEXANDRA SMITH

Vasilii Terkin

Narrative poem, 1945

Terkin in the Other World

Terkin na tom svete

Narrative poem, 1963

Vasilii Terkin was written during World War II (1941–45), and became the most popular long narrative poem in Soviet literary history. Following its partial publication in Soviet newspapers, it was awarded the Stalin Prize of the first rank for literary achievement. It tells the story of the everyday life of a soldier, Vasilii Terkin, whose straightforward manner and humour conquered the hearts of the public. He is a folk-like hero, to whom hundreds of Russian soldiers felt they could easily relate. The style and metre are balladic, conveying different episodes from Terkin's life in a manner that links him to characters from popular Russian fairy tales, medieval epics, and Russian history. The historical perspective is achieved by constant references to the heroic past: there are allusions to the 1920s and 1940s, suggestive of traditions passed from fathers to sons, for instance:

These lads are marching already,
They're soldiers living through war,
Just like, let's say, in 1920
Their comrade-fathers did.

They follow the same severe path,
Which Russian toiler-soldier
Took two hundred years ago,
Holding his flintlock gun.

One of the most tense and profound chapters of the poem, "Pereprava" ("River Crossing"), describes a battle with numerous casualties on the Russian side; thus the young soldiers, Terkin's contemporaries, witness death for the first time. The scene resembles Tolstoi's descriptions of war in *War and Peace*, but in more laconic manner. Tvardovskii is just as disgusted by the mess and absurdity of war as was Tolstoi: "There is confusion in the cross-fire / Where are ours? Who is where? Where is the line?" The survivors feel morally responsible for those who died. The sense of overwhelming despair, however, is partially lifted by a miracle: Terkin, believed to be dead, reappears, as indestructable as ever, and faith in the grand holy battle for life is restored: "The holy and fair battle is on; / Mortal battle, not for fame, / But for the life on earth." In this narrative Tvardovskii reveals his firsthand experience of war, when he worked as a war correspondent for several newspapers. In his autobiography Tvardovskii designates *Vasilii Terkin* as the most important work of the period: "it was my lyric poetry, my journalism, my songs and my instructions, my anecdotes and my maxims, my intimate conversations and my comments on various events". All these genres are happily blended in the narrative, giving the poem its true epic quality. Needless to say, it is one of the most typical pieces of socialist realist writing, portraying a positive super-hero and conveying the sense of moral victory for the socialist notion of "collective man".

Terkin in the Other World is not a continuation of the earlier *Vasilii Terkin*, but it uses the same narrative structure – a book about a soldier – to bring into play satirical and documentary perspectives. It is Tvardovskii's major post-Stalinist work, written in 1954–63, a poetic response to the anti-Stalinist campaign promoted by the 20th and 22nd Party Congresses. The poem was begun and more or less completed in 1954, and it circulated in *samizdat* from 1957 until it was published in *Izvestiia* in 1963. The circumstances of its publication are rather curious. In August 1963 Khrushchev was anxious to establish closer ties with the west and he invited a large group of foreign writers to his villa in the Crimea where he gave a long speech on Russian history followed by an unusual cultural entertainment: he invited Tvardovskii to read aloud his satirical poem *Terkin in the Other World*. The effect was confusing as it was impossible for western writers to grasp all the peasant idioms and untranslatable colloquial expressions, but the political implications were clear: the poem, similar in its condemnation of Stalinism to Solzhenitsyn's *Odin den' Ivana Denisovicha* (*One Day in the Life of Ivan Denisovich*), appeared to have been personally approved by the Soviet leader. Three days later it was published in Moscow.

In Tvardovskii's own words, "it is a fairy tale in verse, telling a story about a character who finds himself in the next world, symbolizing in a satirical way all the negative aspects of our reality which prevent us from moving forward, I mean conservatism, bureaucracy, formalism". The plot of the poem suggests that Terkin dismisses the next world, that his life-asserting qualities help him to overcome all the obstacles and hardships of his adventures there – so he comes back to life for another 100 years or so.

There is a semi-veiled reference to Stalin towards the end of the poem: Terkin learns from his friend (whom he encounters in the other world) that the leader ("whose name was on the lips of every soldier plunging into attack") is the Chief of Personnel in the world of the dead, and discipline is very strict thanks to him. The poem informs us that Stalin enjoys a double status: he is only partially dead and manages to influence the minds of many of the living while scrutinizing the inhabitants of the other world:

– He manages everything,
There isn't one more superior than he is.
– Well, but is he alive?
– Alive, too.
Partially.

He's a real father for living ones,
Their law, their banner,
And for us, dead ones, he's one of us -
So he is both with them
And with us.
You still can't get
That he governs the living ones,
But he has been erecting monuments to himself
For quite some time ...

Tvardovskii's satire is also aimed at Soviet society of his day; he dismisses bureaucratism, censorship, and lack of respect for the individual. In this respect *Terkin in the Other World* offers a polemical touch, with the first narrative poem promoting a close bond between the individual and society. It is far from being optimistic, sounding bitter in places and reflecting the state of post-Stalinist ideology. Thus Terkin learns that even in the other world there is a division between socialist and capitalist society; that censors have higher wages than authors; that the health service barely cares for common folk; that pornographic films are shown only for highly placed officials; that the *nomenklatura* outlives the labourers; and so on. Some of the parts resemble satirical folk couplets; for example, Terkin compares the bureaucratic machine to an ambulance: "like an ambulance: it cuts you, it runs over you, and it provides you with first-aid". Undoubtedly, this narrative poem is one of the most profound writings of the period of the Thaw and is charged with far-reaching criticism. Yet after Tvardovskii was dismissed from editorial work on *Novyi mir* (for his promotion of Solzhenitsyn's writings), it was never mentioned in the Soviet press or by literary historians. Following Tvardovskii's death on 18 December 1971, the obituaries and many articles on his work hardly mentioned his editorship of *Novyi mir* and his controversial poems *Terkin in the Other World* and *Po pravu pamiati* [By Right of Memory].

In 1966 the Moscow Theatre of Satire staged a dramatization of Tvardovskii's *Terkin in the Other World*; it was produced by V. Pluchek, and the leading character was played by A. Papanov. The play was widely criticized for its pessimistic and grotesque depiction of Soviet reality. The poem itself was defined by the author as a fairy tale, and its readership was inclined to accept Terkin's escape from the other world as typical for a fairy tale's happy ending. Tvardovskii, however, praised the production for illuminating the poem's meaning and artistic devices; in his words, "the poem appeared on the stage in the most accessible form ... reinforced by the talent of the producer and the brilliant performance of the actors involved".

ALEXANDRA SMITH

Iurii Nikolaevich Tynianov 1894–1943

Literary theorist and historical novelist

Biography

Born in Vitebsk province, 18 October 1894. Attended school in Vitebsk; studied history and philology at Petrograd University, 1915–18. Worked as French interpreter for Comintern, 1918–21. Professor of literature at Petrograd Institute of Art History, 1921–30. One of the leading figures of Russian Formalism. Lived in Perm during World War II; suffered from illness. Poetry editor for the Sovetskii pisatel' publishing house, from 1931. Died in Moscow, 20 December 1943.

Publications

Collected Editions

Sochineniia, 3 vols. Moscow and Leningrad, 1959.
Sochineniia, 2 vols. Leningrad, 1985.
Lieutenant Kizhe and Young Vitushishnikov, translated by Mirra Ginsburg. Boston, Eridanos, 1990.
Sochineniia, 3 vols. Moscow, 1994.

Fiction

Kiukhlia. 1925.
Smert' Vazir-Mukhtara [The Death of Vazir-Mukhtar]. 1928; Moscow, 1995; translated as *Death and Diplomacy in Persia*, by Alec Brown, London, Boriswood, 1938; reprinted Westport, Connecticut, Hyperion Press, 1975.
"Podporuchik Kizhe", *Krasnaia nov'*, 1928; reprinted 1930; translated as "Lieutenant Kizhe", by Mirra Ginsburg, in *Lieutenant Kizhe and Young Vitushishnikov*, 1990.
"Voskovaia persona" [The Wax Figure], *Zvezda*, 1–2 (1932).
"Maloletnii Vitushishnikov", *Literaturnyi sovremennik*, 7 (1933); translated as "Young Vitushishnikov", by Mirra Ginsburg, in *Lieutenant Kizhe and Young Vitushishnikov*, 1990.
Pushkin. Leningrad, 1936–59; separate edition Leningrad, 1974.

Literary Criticism

Gogol' i Dostoevskii: K teorii parodii [Gogol' and Dostoevskii: Towards a Theory of Parody]. Petrograd, 1921.
Problema stikhotvornogo iazyka. Petrograd, 1924; translated as *The Problem of Verse Language*, by Michael Sosa and Brent Harvey, with an afterword by Roman Jakobson, Ann Arbor, Ardis, 1981.
Arkhaisty i novatory [Archaists and Innovators]. Moscow, 1929; reprinted Munich, Fink, 1967; Ann Arbor, Ardis, 1985.
Pushkin i ego sovremenniki [Pushkin and His Contemporaries]. Moscow, 1969.
Poetika. Istoriia literatury. Kino [Poetics. Literary History. Cinema]. Moscow, 1977.

Critical Studies

Iurii Tynianov, by Arkadii Belinkov, Moscow, 1960; 1965.
Iurii Tynianov: Pisatel' i uchenyi, edited by V. Kaverin, Moscow, 1966.
"Soviet Views of Parody: Tynianov and Morozov", by J. Douglas Clayton, *Canadian Slavonic Studies*, 7 (1973), 485–93.
"Truth and Design: Technique in Tynjanov's *Smert' Vazir-Muchtara*", by Evelyn Jasiulko Harden, *Mnemozina: Studia litteraria russica in honorem Vsevolod Setchkarev*, edited by Joachim T. Baer and Norman W. Ingham, Munich, Fink, 1974, 171–84.
"U istokov sovetskogo istoricheskogo romana", by Anna Tamarchenko, *Neva*, 10 (1974), 179–87.
Vospominaniia o Iu. Tynianove. Portrety i vstrechi. Moscow, 1983.
"Neosushchestvlennye zamysly Tynianova", by E.A. Toddes, in *Tynianovskii sbornik*, Riga, 1984, 25–45.
"On Tynjanov the Writer and His Use of Cinematic Technique in *The Death of the Wazir Mukhtar*", by Dmitri N. Breschinsky and A. Zinaida, *Slavic and East European Journal*, 29/1 (1985), 1–17.
"Tvorchestvo Iuriia Tynianova", by Boris Eikhenbaum, in *O proze. O poezii. Sbornik statei*, Leningrad, 1986, 186–223.
"Istochniki i podteksty romana 'Smert' Vazira-Mukhtara'", by G.A. Levinton, in *Tynianovskii sbornik. Tret'ie Tynianovskie chteniia*, Riga, 1988, 6–14.
"Griboedovskie podteksty v romane 'Smert' Vazira-Mukhtara'", by G.A. Levinton, in *Tynianovskii sbornik. Chetvertye Tynianovskie chteniia*, Riga, 1990, 21–34.
"Fact and Fiction in Tynjanov's *Smert' Vazir-Muchtara*: Paradoxes of a 'Scientific Novel'", by Angela Brintlinger, *Russian Literature*, 39/3 (1996), 273–302.

Iurii Tynianov is well known as a prose writer and an influential literary and film critic. His father was a doctor. He graduated from the Department of History and Philology at Petrograd University, and between 1921 and 1930 he was a professor at the Institute of Art History in Petrograd, lecturing on literary history. He was appointed an editor of the prestigious "Biblioteka poeta" series in the Sovetskii pisatel' publishing house in 1931, a position he held until his death.

In the 1920s Tynianov became one of the most prominent adherents of the Formalist school; his ideas had an impact on the work of contemporary and more recent scholars (such as Lukács, Lotman and Todorov, to name but a few). His most famous works include *Problemy stikhotvornogo iazyka* (*The Problem of Verse Language*) and *Arkhaisty i novatory* [Archaists and Innovators]. Tynianov's main theoretical notion was based on the idea of literary dynamism. This implied a consequentiality of literary styles, an ever-changing perception of literary work, and a dynamism within the poetic text triggered by the conflict between the suppressed elements of poetic speech and the more advanced ones. He studied the styles of Pushkin, Tiutchev, Nekrasov, Dostoevskii, Briusov, Blok, and Khlebnikov. He was also well known as a translator of Heinrich Heine's poetry. However, his contribution to Russian historical fiction remains unsurpassed. Tynianov's second career as a writer can also be partly explained by the fact that the Formalist school of thought became oppressed towards the end of the 1920s.

His first historical novel, *Kiukhlia*, was devoted to Pushkin's childhood friend, Vil'gel'm Kiukhel'beker, an author of civic poetry and patriotic odes who was exiled to Siberia for participating in the Decembrist uprising. It has been noted by scholars that Tynianov advanced a rather arguable point that Kiukhel'beker was the prototype of Lenskii from Pushkin's *Evgenii Onegin*; reversing this, Tynianov modelled his fictional hero on Lenskii. In his historical novels Tynianov translated documentary evidence into metaphorical language, using montage techniques (which led to chronological shifts and compressions) and focusing on a realistic psychological portrayal of literary and historical figures. The tone of Tynianov's prose is ironic, and, in places, sarcastic. For example, in the story *Podporuchik Kizhe* (*Lieutenant Kizhe*) he depicts the absurd state of the bureaucracy under Tsar Paul I, and the main character is merely a fictional creation. In *Maloletnii Vitushishnikov* (*Young Vitushishnikov*) Tynianov criticizes the political regime under Nicholas I, and in *Voskovaia persona* [The Wax Figure] the metaphoric portrayal of Peter the Great turning into a wax sculpture is merciless. Aside from the important historical problems discussed in the novel, the issue of creativity is highly significant: being true craftsmen, Peter the Great and Rasstrelli were opposed to a society of the mediocre. In Belinkov's view, Tynianov's historical prose illuminates the conflict between an extraordinary personality and society. This is especially true of the novels about Griboedov and Pushkin.

In *Smert' Vazir-Mukhtara* (abridged and translated into English as *Death and Diplomacy in Persia*) Griboedov, the dramatist, composer and diplomat, represents a whole generation of people who contributed to the development of liberal thought in Russia but became disillusioned with the outcome of the Decembrist uprising and had to adapt to the new historical situation. Griboedov was killed in Teheran while on a diplomatic mission. The suggestiveness of the style and the occasional factual distortion and metaphoric hyperbolism in the novel were often criticized by Soviet scholars. Tynianov attempted to project his own image of Griboedov as the "saddest personality of the 1820s" (as he described him to Gor'kii in 1926). A similar clash between a talented poet and society shaped the framework for Tynianov's unfinished novel, *Pushkin* (some fragments were published in *Literaturnyi sovremennik*, 1935–36). The novel deals with Pushkin's childhood and youth, including the early scenes of exile in the Crimea. The novel reveals Tynianov's in-depth knowledge of the period; the literary polemic between the archaists and the innovators is incorporated into the text as it might have been perceived by the young Pushkin. The emphasis of this work is once again on the study of a highly talented individual at odds with his background.

Tynianov's prose is very experimental; its symbolism and fragmented structure can be compared to the writings of Belyi and Zamiatin. It may be argued that his novels are double-edged in places: the characteristic situation of a politically dangerous atmosphere forcing people not to trust anyone and to spend their time quietly in the provinces sounded ambiguously allusive to the Stalinist regime.

In 1934 Tynianov was elected to the board of the Writers' Union. During World War II he lived in Perm, suffering from a long illness. After his death in 1943, his name vanished into oblivion until the late 1950s, when Kaverin attempted to give Tynianov and Bulgakov their legitimate place in Russian literature. Tynianov's last novel about the liberally-minded Pushkin reflects dissatisfaction with the political regime of his own time.

ALEXANDRA SMITH

Smert' Vazir-Mukhtara

The Death of Vazir-Mukhtar

Novel, 1928

"Griboedov is wonderful," wrote Maksim Gor'kii in a letter to Iurii Tynianov about his 1928 novel, *Smert' Vazir-Mukhtara*, "although I did not expect to find him quite like that. But you showed him so convincingly, that he must have been that way, and if not, he will be now." Wonderful, convincing, and yet unexpected: such was the hero of Tynianov's novel to some contemporary readers. Others found Tynianov's Griboedov an exact and truthful portrait; still others thought the literary-scholar-and-theorist-turned-novelist tampered too much with the facts in his fictional treatment of the famous poet-martyr. Debates on the veracity and sources of the portrait continue to this day. But Gor'kii's assessment is perhaps the most perceptive and even prophetic; Tynianov, using the conventional myth of Griboedov in his novel, created a new myth that superseded all previous images of the 19th-century poet.

Aleksandr Griboedov was one of the most vague figures of his epoch; his date of birth, his talent as a poet and diplomat, his allegiances and values are all subject to debate. But in Tynianov's rendition, Griboedov becomes a new mythical figure, a representative of his epoch. Questions of myth notwithstanding, Boris Eikhenbaum's term for *Smert' Vazir-Mukhtara*, a "scientific" or "scholarly novel," can be fully substantiated; Tynianov mined Griboedov's personal and official correspondence as well as other primary documents and memoirs for material, plot and even intonation. Yet he perpetrated enough changes and twisting of these sources to suggest that myth-making, and possibly historical allegory, were indeed his goals. In the novel, Griboedov is constantly tortured by thoughts of his unstaged masterpiece, *Gore ot uma* (*Woe from Wit*), and by fears that his literary talent has dried up. At the same time, he is elated at his diplomatic triumph with the Persian peace treaty and certain that he can outsmart Nicholas I and his ministers and convince them to allow him to create an East India Company-like structure for the Caucasus region, which he, as director, will rule like a king. When he is instead appointed minister to Persia, he senses that he is being sent to his death, and, despite a few other attempts to escape this fate, ultimately gives in to the inexorable progression of events that ends in the massacre of virtually the whole Russian mission in Teheran. Relations between Griboedov and important literary, military and governmental figures feature prominently in the novel; Tynianov portrays an entire cross-section of Russian society, from Ermolov to Pushkin, from Chaadaev to former Decembrists and their hangmen, from the ballerina Katia Teleshova to the journalists Bulgarin and Senkovskii. Thus this "biographical" novel offers a wide panorama of Russian society in the 1820s.

The most important portion of the novel is arguably the prologue, which sets the scene at the premature dawn of a new decade following the 1825 Decembrist revolt. Tynianov suggests that the unsuccessful uprising created a "break in time" and, indeed, a break within people themselves. Men of the 1820s, the narrator claims, had a spring in their step; they were susceptible to love, poetry, adventure, ideas and excitement, and indeed sought them. Men of the 1830s, in contrast, were driven by money and production, executing with "deaf faces" and bustling motions the will of the state machine. The new epoch had new, different blood, and the worst fate, asserts the narrator, fell to those in whom the blood of epochs became mixed: the transformed, metamorphosed. The metamorphosis of Griboedov and his society is, indeed, the main theme of the novel.

Contemporary critics found the novel too "formalist" and found the author too focused on paradoxes in Griboedov's life and epoch and too ready to distort the traditional image of Griboedov. But, as Eikhenbaum pointed out, the title of Tynianov's novel already alerts the reader that this is no ordinary biographical novel; instead, it is about the disappearance of the man, Griboedov, into his post, Vazir-Mukhtar (Persian for minister plenipotentiary) and the subsequent death and dismemberment of the body and even the name, as the story of Pushkin's famous meeting with the fragments of Griboedov's body and name ("Griboed") on the road back to Moscow vividly testifies. Through his carefully constructed novel Tynianov gives us a portrait of a man caught between epochs and careers, lost, and ultimately unable to exert his own will against the circumstances of his fate.

One of the numerous ways to view this novel is as an Aesopian treatment of post-revolutionary Soviet Russia. Indeed, particularly in the prologue, where the narrator explicitly identifies himself as a writer looking back over the decades, such a parallel between the turn of the decade in the 19th and 20th centuries virtually asks to be drawn: both epochs, as many of Tynianov's readers sensed, were identified by a pervasive metamorphosis, by deceit and spying and betrayal, by the "emptiness" leading into Nicholas I's reaction and Stalin's reign of terror. Even the fact of Griboedov's tragic death at the hands of an angry mob in Teheran had resonance for the 20th century, when in 1919 and 1920 the Russian embassy in Teheran was attacked again, ultimately resulting once more in the death of the ambassador.

A fascinating novel, *Smert' Vazir-Mukhtara* is also a literary *pièce de résistance*, the most intricately executed and complex of Tynianov's fictional works, more challenging than the essentially straightforward *Kiukhlia*, a biographical novel about Vil'gel'm Kiukhel'beker, and more meticulously crafted than the weighty and unfinished *Pushkin*. The author uses colour imagery, extended metaphors, and interesting descriptive techniques (such as cinematic montage), often creating an estranging effect (in Formalist terms, *ostranenie*) with abrupt sentence structures that force the reader to pay careful attention not just to the adventure-novel-like plot, but to the construction of the novel as well. The English-language reader should be warned that the 1938 British translation by Alec Brown is heavily abridged, omitting, in the translator's words, "mainly material interesting only to Russian readers or to those who are reasonably well acquainted with Russian literature," including the essential prologue. Perhaps well-intentioned, Brown's cuts emasculate the novel; let his title-change to *Death and Diplomacy in Persia* serve as a caution to the reader that, in true British Raj fashion, Brown turned the work into a Middle East novel of intrigue. The "wonderful" and "convincing" Griboedov of Tynianov's original, the new myth of the poet-martyr, has yet to make it into the English language.

ANGELA BRINTLINGER

Lieutenant Kizhe

Podporuchik Kizhe

Novella, 1928

More widely known as a critic and theorist (in particular as one of the leaders of the Formalist school in Russian literature), Tynianov also created artistic works based on Russian history. "While remaining a literary historian", he wrote in his autobiography, "I became a writer of fiction".

Lieutenant Kizhe, written in 1927 and published the following year in the journal *Krasnaia nov'*, exemplifies its author's conviction that literature differs from history not by "invention" but by a greater and more vital understanding of people and events. The writer of fiction must look a lot more deeply, guess, and resolve a lot more, and then comes the final thing in art – the feeling of authentic truth: it could have been this way, perhaps it was this way.

Set in the age of Paul I, *Lieutenant Kizhe* was the first of three novellas on historical themes, the others being *Voskovaia persona* [The Wax Figure], written in 1930 and set in the age of Peter I, and *Young Vitushishnikov* of 1933 relating to the age of Nicholas I. (Tynianov also wrote a trilogy of novels about well-known literary figures: *Kiukhla*, 1925, about Kiukhel'beker; *Smert' Vazir-Mukhtara*, about Griboedov; and *Pushkin*). *Lieutenant Kizhe*, however, remains the best-known of all Tynianov's literary works, first because of its theme – that of a man created by a bureaucratic error who subsequently takes on a life of his own – and, perhaps more importantly, because it gave rise to Sergei Prokofiev's popular "Lieutenant Kizhe Suite", created for Aleksandr Faintsimmer's film version of the novella in 1934. The five movements of this suite generalize the life that the fictitious Kizhe is presumed to have had: "Birth of Kizhe", "Romance" (Kizhe's courtship), "Kizhe's Wedding", "Troika" (a drinking song with the bells of a troika as background) and "Burial of Kizhe".

The novella, however, is more complex, and is based on not one but two anecdotes relating to the time of Paul (published in *Pavel I. Sobranie anekdotov, otzyvov, kharakteristik, kazov i pr.*, St Petersburg, 1901). According to the first, a clerk accidentally combined the "-ki" ending of the word for lieutenants with the following emphatic particle "zh", creating a new name "Kizh". The Emperor Paul then also assumed this was a real lieutenant and with time promoted him through the ranks to general; when told that Kizh had died, Paul's reaction was: "Pity, he was a good officer". According to the second, an officer was mistakenly declared dead and excluded from the service, and his commanding officer did not dare to certify that he was in fact alive. The officer now had no rights at all, and his subsequent petition to be reinstated was denied, "for the same reason". Tynianov expanded on both stories, creating the non-existent Kizhe, whom everyone pretends is alive once the Emperor has signed the order, and the real Lieutenant Siniukhaev, who is unable to convince anyone he is not dead.

The novella is first and foremost a satire of bureaucracy, where an official order has greater weight than the evidence of one's own eyes: for many, the invisible Kizhe really does exist and Siniukhaev does not. Indeed, Siniukhaev doubts his own existence and thinks there must be something wrong with him, because he is still wandering around. While he finally disappears "without trace, crumbling into dust, as though he had never existed", the fictitious Kizhe in contrast has an event-filled life: being sent to Siberia because of the Emperor's displeasure; returning to be married to a lady-in-waiting who was in love with him; giving birth to a son (his wife has, of course, taken lovers); receiving promotions and gifts of land from the Emperor; and finally being given a state funeral when he dies.

The story was popular in the Soviet Union, where it could readily be accepted as critical of the former tsarist society. But it does not take too great a stretch of the imagination to see it as satire on the bureaucracy within Soviet society too, where there was always a tendency to quote theory as though it were fact and ordinary people would similarly deny the evidence of what was plainly visible. Historically, the novella creates a vivid picture of tsarism at the turn of the 18th and 19th centuries, and of the Emperor's court in particular. The portrait of Paul is the traditional one: with his hatred of his mother (Catherine the Great), his determination to undo everything she created, and his unbalanced personality bordering on insanity. He is shown as alternating between great anger and fear of everyone around him, leading to reliance on the secret police and ruthless repression – which, of course, is reflected in the fear and subservience of his subordinates. At the same time, he wishes to be loved by his subjects and has a box put outside his palace for complaints, which serves only for an impolite letter. His eventual selection of Kizhe as a trusted officer to have by him – a man who does not exist – reflects the paranoia of his final years before his murder. Other historical figures include his confidante, Ekaterina Nelidova, whose influence at this time is on the wane; the poet and courtier Neledinskii-Meletskii; the cautious and reactionary Commandant of St Petersburg, Count Arakcheev; and the leader of the plot against Paul, the Count fon Palen. But some of the fictional characters are equally memorable: the army clerk, the adjutants, ordinary soldiers, the lady-in-waiting who becomes Kizhe's wife, Siniukhaev's surgeon father, and Siniukhaev himself in his struggle for his very existence.

A delightfully comic and yet human story, *Lieutenant Kizhe* reflects the absurd in human society.

A. COLIN WRIGHT

U

Gleb Ivanovich Uspenskii 1843–1902

Prose writer

Biography

Born in Tula, 25 October 1843. Attended schools in Tula and Chernigov, 1853–61; studied law at St Petersburg University, 1861: expelled within a year because of student disorders and his inability to pay, which also restricted studies at Moscow University, 1862. Made his literary debut, 1862; encouraged by his cousin N.V. Uspenskii. First major work, *Nravy Rasteriaevoi ulitsy* [Manners of Rasteriaeva Street] published in Nekrasov's *Sovremennik* in 1866. Later published in Saltykov-Shchedrin's *Otechestvennye zapiski*. Met Turgenev in Paris, 1875; thereafter remained friends with the older writer, who much admired his work. Contributed to the liberal journals, *Russkie vedomosti* and *Russkaia mysl'*, after 1884. Collected Works published, 1883–86. Visited Siberia, 1888–89. Suffered from schizophrenia in his last years. Died in St Petersburg, 6 April 1902. Buried in Volkovo cemetery.

Publications

Collected Editions

Polnoe sobranie sochinenii, 14 vols. Moscow and Leningrad, 1940–54.

Sobranie sochinenii, 9 vols. Moscow, 1955–57.

Fiction

"Mikhalych", *Iasnaia Poliana*, 1862.

Nravy Rasteriaevoi ulitsy [Manners of Rasteriaeva Street], *Sovremennik* (1866).

Razoren'e – nabliudeniia Mikhaila Ivanovicha [Ruin – Observations of Mikhail Ivanovich], *Otechestvennye zapiski* (1869).

Tishe vody, nizhe travy [Meak and Mild], *Otechestvennye zapiski* (1870).

Nabliudeniia provintsial'nogo lentiaia [Observations of a Lazy Man], *Otechestvennye zapiski* (1871).

Novye vremena, novye zaboty [New Times, New Anxieties], *Otechestvennye zapiski* (1873–78).

Iz derevenskogo dnevnika [From a Village Diary], *Otechestvennye zapiski* (1877–80).

Krest'ianin i krest'ianskii trud [The Peasant and Peasant Labour], *Otechestvennye zapiski* (1880).

Vlast' zemli [The Power of the Soil], *Otechestvennye zapiski* (1882).

Zhivye tsifry [Living Numbers], *Severnyi vestnik* (1888).

Travel Writing

Pis'ma iz Serbii [Letters from Serbia], *Sankt-Peterburgskie vedomosti* and *Otechestvennye zapiski* (1876).

Essays

Vypriamila [Straightened Out]. *Russkaia mysl'* (1885).

Critical Studies

Gleb Ivanovič Uspensky et le populisme russe, by Jean Lothe, Leiden, E.J. Brill, 1963.

G.I. Uspenskii: Zhizn' i tvorchestvo, by N.I. Sokolov, Leningrad, 1968.

Gleb Uspensky, by N.I. Prutskov, New York, Twayne, 1972.

G. Uspenskii, by Iu.A. Bel'chikov, Moscow, 1979.

Gleb Uspenskii was the most influential of the Populist writers, a group which included Pavel Zasodimskii, Filipp Nefedov, S. Karonin, and Nikolai Zlatovratskii. The dominant subject for these writers was the Russian village following the Emancipation of the Serfs in 1861. The Tula area, where Uspenskii was born, gave the world many writers, most notably Lev Tolstoi and Ivan Turgenev. Uspenskii was close to both, publishing his first story, "Mikhalych", in Tolstoi's own journal, *Iasnaia Poliana*, in 1862. Unlike these writers, however, Uspenskii was not of aristocratic origin but was instead a *raznochinets* (literally: "other-ranker"). Although he once contemplated writing a novel based on the life of a fellow Populist, A. Lopatin, Upenskii adopted as the basic unit of his writing the *ocherk* or sketch, which he arranged in cycles and linked through a central character. Within the sketch Uspenskii makes extensive use of dialogue and there are unexpected flashes of humour. Although Tolstoi accused him of writing in Tula dialect, his use of dialectisms is, in fact, very restrained.

His first major work, *Nravy Rasteriaevoi ulitsy* [Manners of Rasteriaeva Street], is set in a fictional street in the working-class district of the town of "T". The reference to Tula is clear, the more so since the characters in the sketches are all *kaziuki*, workers in the booming metal-working industry of Tula in the years immediately before the Emancipation. Uspenskii coins the word *rasteriaevshchina* (roughly: Rasteriaeva-itis) to denote the all-pervasive moral corruption, compounded by drunkenness and illiteracy that pervades the street. Nowhere is this more evident than in the character who dominates the first four sketches, Prokhor Porfirych. Beginning as an apprentice, Prokhor stops at nothing to move upwards socially. The same disease infects other main characters: the servile official Tolokonnikov demands limitless respect and acts in a brutal and arbitrary manner; Khripushin, a quack doctor, is the epitome of ignorance. *Nravy Rasteriaevoi ulitsy*, which was given its final shape in 1883, is written in a lively satirical vein that owes much to Herzen, Sleptsov, Saltykov-Shchedrin and, beyond them, to Gogol'.

In the 1870s Uspenskii increasingly concerned himself with rural themes. As he wrote in his autobiography: "The genuine truth of life drew me to its source, that is to the peasant." The overall impression of Uspenskii's peasant sketches is, in contrast to the Tula sketches, one of dogged worthiness. In the 1870s Uspenskii devoted two cycles to peasant problems, *Novye vremena, novye zaboty* [New Times, New Anxieties] and *Iz derevenskogo dnevnika* [From a Village Diary]. These were followed by the two best-known cycles, *Krest'ianin i krest'ianskii trud* [The Peasant and Peasant Labour] (1880) and *Vlast' zemli* [The Power of the Soil] (1882). In the latter he chronicles the total dependence of the peasant on the land. What makes these sketches more than a mere statement of the obvious is Uspenskii's refusal to accept a moral code based on such dependency. Here, as throughout his work, Uspenskii refuses to paint an idealized portrait of the peasant commune (*mir*) in particular or peasant life in general.

He was critical of the "going to the people" of the 1870s, seeing this as mere self-indulgence on the part of the intelligentsia. His thesis was that, only with what he called the "awakening of thought" in the countryside, a process to be encouraged by the active involvement of the intelligentsia and the spread of education, would the problems of the Russian village be solved. These problems included the development in the countryside of a particularly brutal form of capitalism. The power of money is a recurrent theme in Uspenskii's work and he intended to write a cycle of sketches entitled *Vlast' kapitala* [The Power of Capital]. The project was never completed but some of the sketches intended for it became part of the cycle *Zhivye tsifry* [Living Numbers] (1888).

His sketches of the 1880s are more journalistic and less artistic than his earlier works and he increasingly lived out at first hand the problems he wrote about, settling in the depths of the countryside at Chudovo in Novgorod Province. It was his inability to influence the situation personally, allied to a feeling that his work did not reach the people – the peasants and the *raznochintsy* – for whom it was intended, which led to his mental breakdown. Uspenskii also wrote *povesti*, the most important of which are *Razoren'e – nabliudeniia Mikhaila Ivanovicha* [Ruin – Observations of Mikhail Ivanovich] (1869), *Tishe vody, nizhe travy* [Meek and Mild] (1870), and *Nabliudeniia provint-sial'nago lentiaia* [Observations of a Lazy Man] (1871), later collected as a trilogy under the title of the first sketch. The eponymous Mikhail Ivanovich is a Tula metal-worker who rebels against the harsh conditions of his life. *Tishe vody, nizhe travy* is cast in the form of the diary of a *raznochinets* and the whole trilogy underscores the gap between the reforming or revolutionary aspirations of the intelligentsia and the realities of peasant life. In addition to his fictional and semi-fictional writings, Uspenskii wrote travel notes, such as *Pis'ma iz Serbii* [Letters from Serbia] (1876), and tracts on aesthetics, the most important of which, *Vypriamila* [Straightened Out] (1885), reopened the debate over "art for art's sake" by attacking Afanasii Fet's interpretation of the Venus de Milo in his poem of the same name ("Venera Milosskaia", 1856).

Uspenskii was highly regarded in his day, especially in left-wing intellectual and literary circles, two of the most celebrated representatives of which were Maksim Gor'kii and Vladimir Korolenko. Echoing Uspenskii's own desire to do something about the problems he wrote about, Gor'kii asserted that "after reading the work of Gleb Uspenskii one wishes to do something decisive". Today, however, Uspenskii is little read, being remembered only for a few individual sketches, such as "Chetvert' loshadi" [A Quarter of a Horse] (1885), and "Budka" [The Sentry Box] (1868), the chief character of which, the brutal policeman Mymretsov, became famous for his slogan: "Drag them in and don't let them go".

MICHAEL PURSGLOVE

V

Konstantin Konstantinovich Vaginov 1899–1934

Poet and prose writer

Biography

Born Konstantin Konstantinovich Vagengeim in St Petersburg, 16 April 1899. Attended Gurevich Gymnasium, 1908–17; studied law at St Petersburg University, 1917–18; Poetry Seminar, Dom iskusstv, 1921; State Institute for the History of the Arts, 1923–26. Served in the Red Army, 1918–22. First publication in 1921; full-time writer from 1921. Married: Aleksandra Fedorov in 1926. Associated with the literary groups Abbatstvo gaerov, Kol'tso poetov, Zvuchashchaia rakovina, Tsekh poetov, Soiuz poetov, Ostrovitiane, Emotsionalisty, OBERIU. Died of tuberculosis in Leningrad, 26 April 1934.

Publications

Collected Editions

Sobranie stikhotvorenii, edited by Leonid Chertkov. Munich, Sagner, 1982.

Kozlinaia pesn'. Trudy i dni Svistonova. Bambochada [The Satyr Song. The Work and Days of Svistonov. Bambochada], edited by Tat'iana Nikol'skaia. Moscow, 1989.

Kozlinaia pesn'. Romany [The Satyr Song], edited by Tat'iana Nikol'skaia. Moscow, 1991.

Poetry

Puteshestvie v khaos [A Journey into Chaos]. Petrograd, 1921; reprinted, Ann Arbor, Ardis, 1978.

Stikhi. Leningrad, 1926; reprinted Ann Arbor, Ardis, 1978.

Opyty soedineniia slov posredstvom ritma [Experiments in Connecting Words Through Rhythm]. Leningrad, 1931; reprinted Moscow, 1991.

Fiction

Kozlinaia pesn' [The Satyr Song]. Leningrad, 1928; reprinted New York, Serebriannyi vek, 1978.

Trudy i dni Svistonova [The Works and Days of Svistonov]. Leningrad, 1929; reprinted New York, Serebriannyi vek, 1984.

Bambochada. Leningrad, 1931.

Garpagoniada. Ann Arbor, Ardis, 1983.

Critical Studies

"Left Art in Leningrad: The OBERIU Declaration", by Robin Milner-Gulland, *Oxford Slavonic Papers*, 3 (1970), 65–75.

"Petrogradskie bibliofily. Po stranitsam satiricheskikh romanov K. Vaginova", by Ivan Martynov and A. Blium, *Al'manakh bibliofilov*, 4 (1977), 217–35.

"La letteratura e la vita nel romanze di Vaginov", by L. Paleari, *Rassegne Sovietica*, 5 (1981), 153–70.

"Literatura kak okhrannaia gramota", by Dmitrii Segal, *Slavica Hierisolymitana*, 5–6 (1981), 151–244.

"Poezijia Konstantina Vaginova", by Leonid Chertkov, in Vaginov's *Sobranie stikhotvorenii*, 1982, 213–30.

"K.K. Vaginov: Kanva biografii i tvorchestva", by Tat'iana Nikol'skaia, in *Chetvertye Tynianovskie chteniia: Tezisy dokladov i materialy dlia obsuzhdeniia*, Riga, 1988, 67–88.

"Discrowning the Writer: Konstantin Vaginov", by David Shepherd, in his *Beyond Metafiction: Self-Consciousness in Soviet Literature*, Oxford, Clarendon Press, 1992, 90–121.

The Last Soviet Avant-Garde: OBERIU — Fact, Fiction, Metafiction, by Graham Roberts, Cambridge, Cambridge University Press, 1997.

Bibliography

Bibliography, by Tat'iana Nikol'skaia, in *Chetvertye Tynianovskie chteniia: Tezisy dokladov i materialy dlia obsuzhdeniia*, Riga, 1988, 83–88.

Konstantin Vaginov's life and career can be taken as broadly representative of the experience of an entire generation of Russian writers, educated in the last decades of tsarist Russia, yet forced to make a career in the radically different social and cultural atmosphere of Soviet power. Between 1921 and 1934, Vaginov participated in a series of literary groups that span the history of post-Symbolist literature in St Petersburg, from Ego-Futurism to Acmeism, expressionism to imaginism, absurdism to the literature of fact and the "social demand." In this frenzied search for a new poetics, we can observe the response of Vaginov's generation to the political and artistic crisis of the avant-garde in the 1920s: was it possible for the avant-garde to serve both the modernist and the political revolution? If Vaginov's early poetry attempts to assimilate and synthesize characteristic elements of Symbolism (language and themes), Acmeism (attitude towards cultural tradition, architectural images), and Futurism (phonetic experiment), all of his writings show an awareness of the political revolution's threat to traditional culture.

The early poetry of *Puteshestvie v khaos* [A Journey into Chaos] is characterized by emphatic musicality and sound orchestration, imagery motivated more by phonetic resemblances and associations than by logical semantic connections, and free shifts (*sdvigi*) of time and space. Its central theme, developed in *Stikhi* (1926), *Opyty soedineniia slov posredstvom ritma* [Experiments in Connecting Words Through Rhythm], as well as in his first novel *Kozlinaia pesn'* [The Satyr Song], is a myth of the Russian Revolution as an ambivalent apocalypse of Russian culture. In a reaction common to many Russian intellectuals of the period, Vaginov originally welcomed the Revolution as a purifying breath of fresh air in the stifling atmosphere of tsarist Russia. He soon realized, however, that the political revolution that had put an end to the hated tsarist regime also threatened to replace the Judaeo-Christian cultural tradition (of which he was a product) with a civilization that was profoundly alien to him. Applying the then influential theories of historical cycles and eternal recurrence associated with Nietzsche, Spengler, and Russian disciples such as Danilevskii and Merezhkovskii, to Russian history, Vaginov viewed the Bolshevik Revolution as an inevitable yet ambivalent tragedy because, although it threatened the destruction of the old culture, it carried within itself the possibility of the future rebirth of a new and, perhaps, superior culture.

As in the poetry of Blok, Belyi, Mandel'shtam, Akhmatova, Khodasevich and others, St Petersburg, traditionally a symbol of the triumph of art and order over the chaos and formlessness of nature, becomes in Vaginov's works a metonymy for Russian culture threatened by the Bolshevik cultural revolution. St Petersburg as a concrete symbol of Russia's connection to the legacy of classical antiquity is also central to Vaginov's poetics. Yet Vaginov's pessimistic fascination with the world of Roman decadence is closer to C.P. Cavafy's love of Decadent Alexandria than to the "Joyful Hellenism" of Viacheslav Ivanov and Mandel'shtam. The poet's *alter ego*, Philostratus, at once an obscure Greek author of the 2nd century AD, a representative of the ideal lyric poet who lives in the timeless realm of synchronous culture, and the personification of Vaginov's poetics of historical anachronism, moves back and forth between the classical past and the Soviet present, foregrounding the relevant historical and cultural parallels.

Although already known as the promising author of several collections of avant-garde poems, in the mid-1920s Vaginov turned from poetry to prose, undergoing a kind of literary rebirth as a satirical novelist. Between 1926 and his death in 1934, Vaginov wrote four satirical novels, the last of which was left incomplete at his death and was not published until almost 50 years after its author's death. Vaginov's prose is typical of the literature of the 1920s in its focus on the fate of the pre-revolutionary intelligentsia in Soviet society. His own metamorphosis from visionary poet to ironic prose writer serves as a metaphor for the transformation of Soviet society and, specifically, of the Russian artistic intelligentsia in the 1920s: from the apocalyptic and heroic mode of the revolution and Civil War, characterized by a high sense of historical mission and popular solidarity born of shared privation and sufferings, to the "prosaic" and individualistic New Economic Policy, in which social and economic differentiation and narrow self-interest became increasingly dominant. Set against a background of triumphant vulgarity and philistinism, *Kozlinaia pesn'* and *Trudy i dni Svistonova* [The Works and Days of Svistonov] trace their heroes' disillusionment with the Revolution, with themselves, with high culture, and their eventual reconciliation with the reality of Soviet *byt*.

The central figures of Vaginov's last two novels (*Bambochada* and *Garpagoniada*) are obsessive collectors who tend to replace reality with the ephemeral objects of their collections, a symbol for cultural production in the Soviet world. Vaginov's caricatures become more marked, his satire broader, the obsession with accumulation becomes increasingly trivialialized, and the characters themselves are increasingly demonized. Despite the obvious signs of fetishism and madness, there is a certain Faustian quality to the obsession with recreating a lost world through amassing and classifying a collection. Collecting, what Walter Benjamin called a "dangerous though domesticated passion", is an intensely ambivalent activity for Vaginov: if it can represent a heroic defence of cultural continuity at a time of revolutionary cultural shift, it also exhibits a tendency towards hypertrophy or obsession that threatens to eclipse reality itself.

Vaginov's satirical prose is often seen as his most important contribution to the legacy of the absurdist literary group, the OBERIU, the Association of Real Art (*Ob"edinenie real'nogo iskusstva*), with which he was associated in the late 1920s. Despite many differences in style and substance, Vaginov and the OBERIU used the grotesque and the absurd as a way of forcing the reader to confront the conventional absurdities of everyday life in the early Soviet period. What unites Vaginov and the *oberiuty* is their rejection of purely linguistic experiments associated with pre-revolutionary futurism (*zaum'*) and their movement towards a cognitive and ethical exploration of modern Russian life in the specific social and historical context of Soviet Russia in the 1920s and 1930s. Vaginov's final years were marked by serious illness and vicious reviews of his works by intolerant Soviet critics, for whom Vaginov's satirical irony was a sign of an unacceptable alienation from Soviet life.

ANTHONY ANEMONE

Aleksandr Valentinovich Vampilov 1937–1972

Dramatist

Biography

Born in Kutulik, Siberia, 19 August 1937. Attended Irkutsk University, graduated in 1960. Married; one daughter. Sketch writer; editor of a newspaper in Irkutsk, 1960–64; moved to Moscow; studied at the Gor'kii Literary Institute. *Proshchanie v iiune* (*Farewell in June*), his first play, was staged in 1966. Member of the Writers' Union, 1965. Died in a boating accident on Lake Baikal, Siberia, 17 August 1972.

Publications

Collected Editions

Izbrannoe. Moscow, 1975; revised edition, 1984.

Proshchanie v iiune [Farewell in June]. Moscow, 1977; reprinted 1984; translated as *Farewell in June: Four Russian Plays*, by Kevin Windle and Amanda Metcalf, St Lucia, University of Queensland Press, 1983; New York, Gordon and Breach, 1996.

Belye goroda [White Cities]. Moscow, 1979.

Bilet na Ust'-Ilim [Ticket to Ust-Ilim]. Moscow, 1979.

Ia s vami, liudi [I Am with You, People]. Moscow, 1988.

Duck-Hunting. Last Summer in Chulimsk, translated by Patrick Miles. Nottingham, Bramcote Press, 1994.

The Major Plays, edited and translated by Alma Law. Reading, Harwood Academic, 1996.

Plays

"Schast'e Kati Kozlovoi" [Katia Kozlova's Happiness], in *Odnoaktnye p'esy*, Moscow, 1959.

"Tikhaia zavod'" [The Silent Bay], *Volzhskii al'manakh*, 13 (1960).

"Dom oknami v pole", *Teatr*, 11 (1964); separate edition, Irkutsk, 1982; translated as "The House with a View on the Field", *Soviet Literature*, 3 (1980).

"Proshchanie v iiune", *Teatr*, 8 (1966); translated as "Farewell in June", by Kevin Windle and Amanda Metcalf, in *Farewell in June: Four Russian Plays*, St Lucia, University of Queensland Press, 1983.

"Predmest'e" [The Suburb], *Angara*, 2 (1968); revised version, as "Starshii syn", 1970; translated as "The Elder Son", by Kevin Windle and Amanda Metcalf, in *Farewell in June: Four Russian Plays*, St Lucia, University of Queensland Press, 1983.

"Dvadtsat' minut s angelom" [Twenty Minutes with an Angel], *Angara* 4 (1970); also in *Provintsial'nye anekdoty*, 1971.

"Utinaia okhota", *Angara*, 6 (1970); translated as *Duck Hunting*, by Alma H. Law, New York, Dramatic Play Service, 1980; also translated by Patrick Miles, in *Duck-Hunting. Last Summer in Chulimsk*, 1994.

"Istoriia s metranpazhem" [Incident with a Paginator], in *Provintsial'nye anekdoty*, 1971.

"Nesravnennyi Nakonechnikov" [The Incomparable Nakonechnikov] (unfinished). 1972; also in *Ia s vami, liudi*, 1988.

"Proshlym letom v Chulimske", *Sibir'*, 3 (1973); separate edition, 1974; translated as "Last Summer in Chulimsk", in *Nine Modern Soviet Plays*, by Geil Vroon *et al.*, Moscow, Progress, 1977; also translated by Patrick Miles, in *Duck-Hunting. Last Summer in Chulimsk*, 1994.

"Voron'ia roshcha" [The Rooky Wood], *Sovremennaia dramaturgiia*, 1 (1986).

"Uspekh" [The Success], *Sovremennaia dramaturgiia*, 1 (1986).

Fiction

Stechenie obstoiatel'stv [Coincidence], published under the pseudonym A. Sanin. Irkutsk, 1961.

Critical Studies

"Vremia v p'esakh molodykh", by L. Bulgak, *Teatr*, 5 (1972), 91–102.

"Zametki o dramaturgii Vampilova", by A. Demidov, *Teatr*, 3 (1974), 63–72.

"Teatr Vampilova", by Iurii Smel'kov, *Literaturnoe obozrenie*, 3 (1975), 92–96.

"Teatr Aleksandra Vampilova", by V. Sakharov, *Nash sovremennik*, 3 (1976), 179–84.

"Po tu storonu vymysla: Zametki o dramaturgii Aleksandra Vampilova", by Konstantin Rudnitskii, *Voprosy literatury*, 10 (1976), 28–72.

"Estestvennost' i teatral'nost': Dramaturgiia Aleksandra Vampilova", *Nash sovremennik*, 3 (1978), 162–77.

Twentieth-Century Russian Drama from Gorky to the Present, by Harold B. Segel, New York, Columbia University Press, 1979; revised edition, Baltimore, Johns Hopkins University Press, 1993.

"Chto kazalos' shutkoi: Proza Aleksandra Vampilova", by Elena Strel'tsova, *Literaturnoe obozrenie*, 10 (1979), 36–40.

"Alexandr Vampilov und Traditionen der russischen Vorrevolutionären und sowjetischen Dramatik", by Gudrun Düwel, *Wissenschaftliche Zeitschrift der Friedrich Schiller Universität*, 29/1 (1980).

"Ein Talent, aber schwierig, eigenwillig... Das Theater Alexander Wampilows", by Gudrun Düwel, in *Was kann ein Dichter auf Erden*, edited by A. Hiersche and E. Kowalski, Berlin, Aufbau, 1982, 56–82.

"Il teatro russo: Aleksandr Vampilov: Una voce della Siberia", by Milli Martinelli, *Lingua e Letteratura*, 1 (1983).

Ethik des Alltags: Die Mehrakter Aleksandr Wampilovs, by Angelika Germ Wilkiewicz, Mainz, Liber, 1986.

Aleksandr Vampilov: Razmyshleniia ob ideinykh korniakh, problematike, khudozhestvennom metode i sud'be tvorchestva dramaturga, by Boris Sushkov, Moscow, 1989.

Aleksandr Vampilov: Ocherk tvorchestva, by Elena Gushanskaia, Leningrad, 1990.

"Aleksandr Vampilov: A Playwright Whose Time is Now", by Patrick Miles, *British East-West Journal*, December (1994), 7–8.

Aleksandr Vampilov: The Major Plays, by Alma Law, London, Harwood Academic, 1996.

Aleksandr Vampilov was without doubt the most popular

playwright in the Soviet Union during the 1970s. In 1973 alone, over 70 theatres had at least one of his plays in their repertoire. His reputation as a dramatist largely overshadowed his work as a prose writer.

In his plays Vampilov challenges a social type that manifested its presence in the 1960s and 1970s; that is, an egoist and materialist, lacking any moral values. Indeed, a comparison with the heroes of Iurii Trifonov's stories may be more appropriate than the frequent comparison with Chekhov. Vampilov's heroes are passive, dissatisfied with their environment, and infected with a sense of *mal du siècle*. They may be able to cope with everyday life, but they are caught up in extraordinary and unusual situations that they cannot handle. In such moments, they reveal – to themselves more than to others – their true self. This type, who is usually male, is contrasted with a person who possesses all the qualities he lacks. Vampilov belongs, with Rozov, Arbuzov, and Volodin, to the new generation of playwrights in the post-war Soviet Union, who, benefiting from the Thaw, exposed the conflicts of contemporary man with society, with the past, and with himself. Critics have noted a parallel between Vampilov's characters and the "superfluous man" of 19th-century literature.

Vampilov's early play, *Dom oknami v pole* (*The House with a View on the Field*), written in 1964, centres on a young man who realizes that he is in love with a local girl just as he is about to leave the village where he has spent three years on a teaching assignment. His egoism has prevented him from seeing life around him, and his realization comes at a turning-point in his life as a "late awakening". *Proshchanie v iiune* (*Farewell in June*) investigates the theme of corruption: what price is the hero prepared to pay for his career? The student Kolesov, who has some minor conflict with the law, is threatened by the dean, Repnikov, with expulsion from the institute. When recognizing his daughter Tania's support for Kolesov, Repnikov blackmails Kolesov by assuring him of his degree only if he will break off his relationship with Tania. Although Kolesov agrees, he later tears up the degree certificate. His career is the price for his (belated) sincerity. Soviet critics have distorted the meaning of the play by defending Repnikov's behaviour and accusing Kolesov of flippant and thoughtless actions. In a sub-plot Vampilov conducts an experiment about corruption: when the speculator Zolotuev is discovered by an inspector, he tries – and fails – to bribe him; Zolotuev fails to understand that this man cannot be bought. Vampilov exposes the detrimental effects of the social system on human behaviour and morality.

In *Starshii syn* (*The Elder Son*) the self-betrayal is of a materialistic nature: a medical student, Busygin, pretends to be the illegitimate son of Sarafanov in order to shelter from the cold after missing the last train. Busygin compromises his honesty and sincerity when he falls in love with Sarafanov's daughter but fails to abandon his false identity: although the idea of leaving crosses his mind, he fails to make a decision in time to keep a way open from his pretentious involvement with the family's problems. *Provintsial'nye anekdoty* [Provincial Anecdotes] is a collection of two short plays, *Istoriia s metranpazhem* [Incident with a Paginator] and *Dvadtsat' minut s angelom* [Twenty Minutes with an Angel]. In the first, a hotel administrator ejects an unknown guest, but, when learning that he may be a journalist from Moscow, becomes so frightened that he suffers a heart attack, from which he recovers only to learn that the guest was merely a paginator. In the second, two travellers in need of money are selflessly offered the required sum by a man, whom they subsequently subject to an interrogation to find out the reasons for his generosity. Both plays reveal clear Gogolian overtones in their choice of theme: the mistaken official, and suspicion that leads to an obsession with clarification and explanation.

Vampilov's last two major plays, *Utinaia okhota* (*Duck-Hunting*) and *Proshlym letom v Chulimske* (*Last Summer in Chulimsk*), are undoubtedly his best and most popular plays. They continue his preoccupation with ethics, with symbols and images, and with language. *Last Summer in Chulimsk* is a two-act play, set in a tea-room that is a microcosm for the lives of the characters, both locals and outsiders. Valentina, who serves in the tea-room, never considers leaving her job or the village; she is constantly preoccupied with the repair of the fence around the tea-room, trying to ensure that nobody destroys what has always existed and breaks with tradition. She secretly loves Shamanov, the judge from town, who is, however, already involved in an affair and is prevented by his mistress from meeting Valentina once he realizes her affection. Shamanov is indifferent, inactive, incapable of making any decision, but thereby causes unhappiness and misfortune for the people around him. At the same time, the landlady's illegitimate son Pashka, an outsider to the community and harassed by his mother for reminding her of her guilt (she had not waited for her fiancé to return from the war) perceives Valentina as an object for possession: Pashka rapes Valentina. Eventually, Valentina remains in the village, while both Shamanov and Pashka leave: for her, life resumes the status quo.

Underlying Vampilov's plays is a critical view of Soviet society in the 1960s: he attacks the corruption allowed by the system; the bureaucracy that takes no account of individuals; and the suspicion that infects man who is himself subjected to suspicion. Vampilov employs language and register in a subtle and varied way, largely as a means of characterization. Words or phrases recur, and structures are repeated. The word becomes a weapon when one character uses another's manner of speech to attack or parody him. Vampilov's prose is short, concise, and humorous. His stories direct an ironic blow at some aspect of human selfishness or lack of moral standards. While his plays often tend towards the serious and pessimistic side, his stories are always funny and anecdotal, but invariably include an incisive criticism of human behaviour.

BIRGIT BEUMERS

Duck-Hunting

Utinaia okhota

Play, 1970

Duck-Hunting is a three-act play, and probably one of Vampilov's finest. Written in 1970, it was first produced in Riga, Latvia; in 1979 it was performed at the Moscow Arts Theatre.

The play has a complex dramatic structure. Throughout the entire action the protagonist, Zilov, recalls the events that led up to his present situation: he has spent the night drinking, wakes up with a hangover, and finds that his friends have played a joke on him: they have sent him a wreath for his own funeral. Zilov imagines his friends mourning him; this projected fantasy contrasts with his recollection of events later in the play through the use of music: while funeral music reflects the serious, tragic atmosphere of the memory, the same funeral march is varied to a frivolous, clownish tune to accompany Zilov's fantasy. Throughout all three acts Zilov sits in his room making telephone calls, between which he brings the memory of the past alive.

In his memory, Zilov runs through a variety of randomly selected incidents, all leading up to the crucial scene, which in turn is the reason for his present state. The first series of reminiscences is about Zilov and his colleague Saiapin meeting in a café (with the revealing name "Forget-me-not") with Zilov's ex-girlfriend Vera and their boss Kushak. Thanks to Kushak, Zilov and his wife Galina have been allocated a flat; during the house-warming Kushak is encouraged to have an affair with Vera, but Zilov's ploy at rewarding his boss fails when Vera falls in love with his colleague Kuziakov. At work, Zilov signs a plan for the reconstruction of a factory as though it were a report on the completed reorganization, and gets involved with an accidental visitor to the office, Irina. Subsequently Zilov and Galina's relationship breaks down, and Galina has an abortion, realizing that she is neither loved nor supported by her husband; the fake report is discovered, and while Saiapin realizes that his chances of getting a flat have now vanished, Zilov receives the news of his father's death. Yet instead of leaving for the funeral, he meets up with Irina. Eventually, Galina leaves Zilov, who has already started an affair with Irina. In the last scene of recollection, Zilov invites all his friends to the café, where he provokes and insults them: he accuses them of a loose lifestyle, of sleeping around, of wanting only material benefit, and of being stupid. The following morning they send him a wreath to punish him for his bad behaviour. Once Zilov has completed his reminiscences, he phones his friends and invites them to the funeral wake. In the meantime he prepares to kill himself, but is interrupted by the premature arrival of Saiapin and his colleague. He asks them to leave, threatens them with the gun, but once they have gone, he abandons his suicide plan and decides to go duck hunting.

Zilov's permanent concern is the duck hunt, which he plans with the waiter of the café, Dima. The duck hunt becomes an obsession, and it is the only preoccupation he has in the present, when between reminiscences he phones either Dima (to check on the time they will depart), or the met office (to find out the weather forecast, and when it will stop raining). The hunt represents Zilov's longing for solitude, peace of mind, and harmony with nature, of which he is incapable: Zilov has no talent for hunting, since he is much too excited, nervous, and drunk to shoot. If Zilov is unable to shoot a duck, then his suicide attempt in the last scene must carry ironic overtones. The duck hunt is a recurrent motif, reinforcing the circular structure of the play: both at the beginning and at the end Zilov prepares for the hunt; his intentions have not changed.

Although Zilov is a negative character, an anti-hero who is passive, insincere, ruthless, and poses a constant threat to the psychological balance of the characters around him, there are worse types: the waiter Dima beats the drunken Zilov; Dima really only wants to use Zilov's boat for the hunt, and exploits him; he also chases Zilov's friends away when they might be most needed. In contrast to the negative characters stand a number of positive ones, mainly women: Galina and Irina are both generous, good-hearted people who genuinely love Zilov despite his egoism and his affairs with other women. They both leave town in the end: there is no room for them in Zilov's world. Saiapin and Kuziakov may worry about obtaining a flat or sustaining a relationship, but this is not their ultimate goal, but simply a means to a better life. Zilov lacks any sense of responsibility: he does not care about Irina, whom he rejects although she stands by him after he insulted his friends; nor about Galina, who wants to have a family, but recognizes that Zilov's irresponsibility would make that impossible; nor about Vera, whom he exploits, having a relationship with her and then pushing her off to his boss (who might, after all, be instrumental in procuring furniture for the new flat); nor for Dima, whose principle not to drink at work he permanently challenges; nor for Saiapin, whose career he puts at risk by signing the fake report; nor about his father, whose telegram asking him to come he chooses to ignore, and whose funeral he misses while preoccupied with a rendezvous. He lacks not only character, responsibility, and sincerity, but also the courage to kill himself.

The telephone is one of the very few props required in the stage directions, and it acquires a symbolic meaning. Zilov uses it constantly between the flashbacks, to call Dima, the met office, Irina's institute, and his friends. Zilov depends on the telephone for contact with the outside world. He insists on having one installed in the new flat, although Galina dislikes telephones and is suspicious of them: they allow Zilov to avoid telling the truth, since it is difficult to lie to somebody straight to their face, but easier to do so over the phone.

Vampilov uses language to characterize people: speech can be hesitant; simple and unimaginative (the phrase used by Vera, addressing everybody as "alik"); or repetitive and meaningless (Kushak's phrase "not that I'm narrow-minded"). Zilov uses his knowledge about people's mannerisms of speech to provoke his friends at the café.

Zilov is not active in the present, but merely communicates over the phone with the outside world. This contrasts with his activity as regards women, where words are shallow; but it corresponds to his passivity concerning decisions: actions rarely happen, decisions are avoided while the word becomes a powerful weapon for destruction and deceit. Words create realities, while physical actions rarely do.

BIRGIT BEUMERS

Aleksandr Fomich Vel'tman 1800–1870

Prose writer

Biography

Born in St Petersburg, 20 July 1800. Son of a member of Swedish gentry who adopted Russian citizenship in 1786. Family moved to Moscow in 1803, evacuated for a short time to Kostroma in 1812. Educated at home, then at various Moscow boarding schools until 1816; graduated with rank of ensign from Moscow officer school, 1817. Spent 12 years in Bessarabia in military surveying and map-making unit, reaching rank of senior adjutant. Awarded Order of Vladimir (2nd class) for bravery in the Russo-Turkish War, 1828–29: retired with rank of colonel, 1831. Married: 1) his second cousin, A.P. Veidel in 1832 (died 1847); 2) the writer Elena Ivanovna Kube in 1850 (died 1868). Assistant director of the Kremlin Armoury, 1842; director from 1852. Editor of official publications of Imperial Society of History and Russian Antiquities; co-editor, with M.P. Pogodin, of the conservative monthly *Moskvitianin*, contributing many articles, 1849–50. Elected corresponding member of Academy of Science, 1854. Reached rank of Full State Counsellor, 1859. Died in Moscow, 23 January 1870.

Publications

Collected Editions

Povesti. Moscow, 1836–37.

Povesti. St Petersburg, 1843.

Povesti i rasskazy 1835–50. Moscow, 1979.

Romany. Moscow, 1985.

Fiction

Beglets: Povest' v stikhakh [The Runaway: A Tale in Verse]. Moscow, 1831.

Muromskie Lesa: Povesti v stikhakh [The Forests of Murom: Tales in Verse]. Moscow, 1831.

Strannik [The Wanderer]. Moscow, 1831–32, 1840; reprinted "Literaturnye pamiatniki", Moscow, 1978.

Koshchei bessmertnyi: Bylina starogo vremeni [Koshchei the Immortal: An Heroic Tale of Old]. Moscow, 1833; reprinted 1985.

MMMCDXLVIII god: Rukopis' Martyna-Zadyka [3448 AD: Martyn-Zadek's Manuscript]. Moscow, 1833.

Lunatik: Sluchai [The Somnambulist: An Incident]. Moscow, 1834.

Sviatoslavich: Vrazhii pitomets: Divo vremen Krasnogo Solntsa Vladimira [Sviatoslavich: A Child of the Devil: A Wondrous Tale of the Times of Vladimir, the Red Sun]. Moscow, 1835; reprinted 1985.

Erotida. Moscow, 1835; reprinted 1985.

Predki Kalimosera: Aleksandr Filippovich Makedonskii [The Forebears of Kalimoser: Alexander Filippovich of Macedon]. Moscow, 1836.

Virginiia, ili poezdka v Rossiiu [Virginia, or A Journey to Russia]. Moscow, 1837.

Serdtse i dumka: Prikliuchenie [Heart and Mind: An Adventure]. Moscow, 1838; reprinted 1986.

General Kalomeros: Roman [General Kalomeros: A Novel]. Moscow, 1840.

Raina, Korolevna Bolgarskaia [Raina, Queen of Bulgaria]. Moscow, 1843; reprinted 1985.

Novy Emelia, ili prevrashcheniia: Roman [The New Emile, or Transformations: A Novel]. Moscow, 1845.

Troian i Angelitsa: Povest', rasskazannaia svetloi Dennitsei iasnomu Mesiatsu (v stikhakh) [Trojan and Angelitsa: A Tale Told by the Radiant Star of Morning to the Bright Moon]. Moscow, 1846.

Prikliucheniia pocherpnutye iz moria zhiteiskogo [Adventures Drawn from the Sea of Life], 4 vols. Moscow, 1848–63; reprinted Moscow and Leningrad, 1933; Moscow, 1957:

1. *Salomeia* [Salome]. Moscow, 1848.
2. *Chudodei* [The Miracle-Worker]. Moscow, 1856.
3. *Vospitanitsa Sara* [Sara, a Ward]. Moscow, 1862.
4. *Schast'e – neschast'e* [Fortune-Misfortune]. Moscow, 1863.

Plays

Ratibor kholmogradskii (istoricheskaia drama v stikhakh) [Ratibor of Kholmograd, An Historical Drama in Verse]. Moscow, 1841.

Kolumb [Columbus]. Moscow, 1842.

Volshebnaia noch': Dramaticheskaia fantaziia [Enchanted Night: A Dramatic Fantasy]. Moscow, 1844.

Historical and Religious Writing and Essays

Nachertanie drevnei istorii Bessarabii [Outline of the Ancient History of Bessarabia]. Moscow, 1828.

O gospodine Novgorode Velikom [On Lord Novgorod the Great]. Moscow, 1834.

Attila i Rus' IV i V v [Attila and Rus' in the 4th and 5th Centuries]. Moscow, 1858.

Pervobytnoe verovanie v Buddizm [Primitive Belief in Buddhism]. Moscow, 1864.

"Travel Impressions and among Other Things, a Pot of Geraniums", translated by J. Gerhard, in *Russian Romantic Prose*, edited by Carl R. Proffer, Ann Arbor, Translation Press, 1979, 102–36.

Critical Studies

Russian Romantic Fiction, by John Mersereau, Jr, Ann Arbor, Ardis, 1983, 230–40.

"Vel'tman's Earliest Novels", by B.Ia. Bukhshtab, in *Russian Prose*, edited by B.M. Eikhenbaum and Iu. Tynianov, translated by Ray Parrott, Ann Arbor, Ardis, 1985, 151–80.

A History of Russian Literature of the Romantic Period, by William Edward Brown, Ann Arbor, Ardis, 1986, vol. 2, 241–58.

In one of the few 20th-century articles on Aleksandr Vel'tman's works, B.Ia. Bukhshtab wrote: "In the history of Russian literature there is no other writer who, having enjoyed as much popularity in his own time as Vel'tman, so rapidly disappeared into complete oblivion." D.S. Mirsky (*A History of Russian Literature*, 1949), calling him "Alexey Weltmann" and giving his death year as 1860, briefly referred to his "delightfully readable style ... blend of imagination and playfully irresponsible humour". More recently in the chapter on Russian romanticism, 1810–40, in *The Cambridge History of Russian Literature* (1989), John Mersereau Jr used the adjectives "amusing", "far-fetched" and "prolific" in the only comment he made about Vel'tman, apropos of his "society tale" *Erotida* (1835), the only story mentioned. On the other hand V.F. Pereverzev, the so-called "vulgar sociologist" Soviet critic, went so far as virtually to claim that without Vel'tman there would have been no *Crime and Punishment* or *The Brothers Karamazov*.

Vel'tman was certainly prolific, both as a writer of prose fiction and as historian, antiquarian, archaeologist, and linguist. His literary career may be conveniently divided into four periods. The first, 1818–31, covers his military service, mostly in Bessarabia, an experience on which he drew substantially for his fiction. The next, 1831–42, marks the flowering of his literary talent as both poet and writer of prose of a highly imaginative and entertaining variety that his contemporaries, including Pushkin, recognized and admired, but regarded as somewhat shallow. His best work, *Strannik* [The Wanderer], belongs to these years. In the third period, 1842–52, Vel'tman was still energetic as editor, journalist, and fiction-writer, publishing seven prose stories, three longish novels, an adaptation of Shakespeare's *A Midsummer Night's Dream* (1844), and two folk-tales in verse, as well as writing opera libretti and publishing material related to his work at the Kremlin Armoury. In the last period, 1852–70, Vel'tman was less active as a writer. His popularity, such as it was, waned rapidly and the few works he published in the 1860s were generally received with scorn and contempt, especially by the self-styled progressive critics of St Petersburg. Vel'tman was now seen as a relic of the past. He, for his part, felt quite out of sympathy with new trends in thought and literature. His wife died in 1868 and this may well have hastened his own death.

Contemporary critics and later literary historians are in general agreement that the two works that best exemplify his original talent are *Strannik* and *Koshchei bessmertnyi* [Koshchei the Immortal]. *Koshchei bessmertnyi* is partly a parody of the kind of historical novel that enjoyed popularity with Russian readers in the 1830s. Its chief character is the slow-witted Iva Olelkovich Puta-Zarev, who bears a superficial resemblance to Don Quixote, his wits addled not by tales of knightly derring-do, but by over-exposure to the fantastic world of Russian folklore. His ancestry is described, with a good deal of long-winded digression and pseudo-historical speculation. He marries and imagines or dreams that his bride has been captured by Koshchei, the traditional evil-doer of folklore. After various unlikely adventures the pair are reunited. Vel'tman indulges in cheerful leaps through space and time, happy to be sidetracked down the byways of history and folk-tale. Contemporary critics tended to see the work as unduly playful, frivolous and undisciplined, probably taking it more seriously than necessary.

Lunatik [The Somnambulist] is a love story set against the background of the events of 1812. Here Vel'tman draws on his boyhood experiences of Napoleon's invasion and the burning of Moscow. The somnambulist is a university student who undergoes a series of hair-raising adventures as he searches for his lady-love, only to discover in the end that she is his sister. Vel'tman uses this plot as an excuse for digression into, for example, descriptions of provincial life à la Gogol', ideas on education, and philosophical speculation about Napoleon. Pereverzev saw the student, like Iva in *Koshchei Bessmertnyi*, living half in the real world, half in a dream world, as a precursor of Dostoevkii's "doubles".

Sviatoslavich: Vrazhii pitomets [Sviatoslavich: A Child of the Devil], like *Koshchei bessmertnyi*, is a mixture of fact, fantasy, and history. Set in a period shortly after Kiev Rus' adopted Christianity, it features as its hero Prince Vladimir of Novgorod (son of Sviatoslav) and he too has a double, the "Devil's Child" of the title, his evil genius from the world of fantasy. The conflict between the two embodies the clash between Christianity and paganism and the work is correspondingly more serious than *Koshchei Bessmertnyi*. Pereverzev saw this story as an anticipation of *The Brothers Karamazov*.

Virginiia and *Serdtse i dumka* [Heart and Mind], both with a contemporary setting, mark something of a turning-point in Vel'tman's writing career. Henceforth he exercised greater control over his plots and style, curbing his earlier fondness for extravagant digression and verbal play. The simple love-plot of *Virginiia* is unoriginal, but the work is enlivened by a series of letters, supposedly written by the heroine's lover, which satirize traditional foreign attitudes towards Russia. *Serdtse i dumka* is a kind of fairy-tale allegory with a psychological basis. The heart and mind of the title belong to the heroine, Zoia Romanovna, and their adventures illustrate the perennial split in human consciousness between what one feels and what one thinks.

General Kalomeros was the first of Vel'tman's works to be subtitled "roman", obviously in the sense of "romance", since it is about Napoleon (alias General Kalomeros) fathering a son with a Russian girl during his time in Russia. Again there is a conflict between love and duty.

In 1848 Vel'tman began to publish his cycle of novels, *Prikliucheniia pocherpnutye iz moria zhiteiskogo* [Adventures Drawn from the Sea of Life], on which he was to work for most of the rest of his life. This is set in the contemporary world of Moscow "middle-class" society: state servants, merchants, tradespeople – the world of the "natural school". By this time Dostoevskii had begun his literary career and, in a sense, Vel'tman was overtaken by the new tide of "realism".

Vel'tman's contribution to Russian literature is worth attention in that it bridged the romanticism of the 1830s with the growing realism of the 1840s in a way that is unique to him. Lack of space has precluded covering more than a representative sample of his large output. His merits are mostly to be found in the earlier stories where he allowed his whimsical fancy free rein. In the aftermath of socialist realism, with a renewal of interest among Russian writers and readers in matters of form, Vel'tman has been partly rescued from the long oblivion to which he was consigned earlier.

JOHN GOODLIFFE

Strannik

The Wanderer

Novel, 1831–32

The early chapters of *Strannik* were written in the summer of 1830 when Vel'tman was still serving in the Russian Army in

Moldavia in the aftermath of the Russo-Turkish War, 1828–29. They were first published in the journal *Moskovskii telegraf* at the end of 1830. In January 1831 Vel'tman was discharged from the army on medical grounds and he continued to publish excerpts from the work in almanacs published in that year. The last excerpt to appear in a periodical was chapter 290, an imaginary conversation between Octavius Augustus and Ovid. In book form Part I was published in March, Part II in October 1831, and Part III in December 1832. A second edition appeared in 1840. Since that time only excerpts were published until 1977 when it appeared, fully edited and annotated by Iu.M. Akutin, as a volume in the prestigious "Literaturnye Pamiatniki" Series. This contains the complete text of *Strannik* and other works by Vel'tman, mostly excerpted. The publication history of *Strannik* well illustrates Vel'tman's rapid plunge into literary oblivion after his popularity in the 1830s, and the 1978 edition demonstrates why it is this work that is his greatest claim to literary fame.

Each of the three parts of the work is divided into 15 "days", and each day divided into chapters of varying length, some extremely short, some of one sentence only and two non-existent, their omission part of Vel'tman's playfulness. The total number of chapters is 325. The narrative is in the first person, ostensibly by Vel'tman himself, mainly in prose, but with frequent switches into verse. Some chapters, like 290, consist entirely of dialogue. Only a small proportion of the work is straight narrative, since Vel'tman takes every opportunity to digress into descriptions, miniature essays, and general musings on all manner of topics, relevant or not.

The skeleton hidden beneath this heavy mound of flesh is an account based on the author's actual experiences in Bessarabia as a surveyor in the tsarist army. His expertise as topographer and mapmaker is used to good effect, as too is his interest in the history of Bessarabia. In April 1828 at the outbreak of hostilities with Turkey the Russian Army crossed the river Prut near Fălciu (now in Romania) and advanced towards the Danube, aiming to liberate the Slavs and Greeks in that area from the Turkish yoke, their ultimate objective was the town of Varna. Vel'tman was actively involved in these operations and in *Strannik* we can, in a limited way, follow the progress of the Russian Army up to the capture of Varna in Part III, Day 37, and Vel'tman's return to Moscow in the final chapter of the book. But this journey is merely a framework covered up by what the author himself calls "intellectual ballast".

Vel'tman's use (or abuse) of digressions may be connected with A.S. Pushkin's comment in a letter of 1825: "a novel needs chatter". In *Strannik* the "chatter" swamps almost everything else. The title suggests a wanderer in both the physical and mental sense, as well as implying eccentricity (*strannost'*). Thus the interest of the work lies almost entirely in its form, an unusual phenomenon in 19th-century Russian prose. In chapter 26 there is reference to "the multicoloured pebbles of a kaleidoscope", and the writer's task to play with these pebbles and create interesting patterns.

Much of the "pebble-play" makes fun of the conventional travel account, a genre which by 1830 in Russia seemed to have worn itself out. Vel'tman delights in confusing the reader over whether the journey he describes is real or imaginary, the "traveller" merely tracing his route on a map. For example on Day 4 what at first appears to be an actual flood in Spain and France proves to be the contents of a glass of water spilt over the map on the traveller's table.

The division of the work into days and chapters is used as a device to mock the kind of travel account, of which there had been many examples in Russian literature, where on certain days, although nothing of importance happens, the traveller none the less feels obliged to write something, however trite. For instance, Day 40, chapter 283 is sandwiched between two chapters containing verse and simply reads: "We went into the tent". Almost every day ends with a reference to going to bed, however inappropriately this matches what it precedes or follows. Vel'tman continually reminds his reader that what he writes is purely a matter of fanciful choice: "At this point, appropriately or inappropriately, for reasons known to me or for no reason at all, purely at my own whim, which frequently happens in this world, I have to or, never mind that, just feel like making the following observation." There follow three brief irrelevant notes about Alexander of Macedon, probably Vel'tman's favourite character, and then, tersely, "That is all I wanted to say today". (chapter 27)

Vel'tman "wanders" through a wide variety of literary styles both in prose and verse, now waxing rhetorical or lyrical, now being drily factual or briskly businesslike. These styles are often juxtaposed for maximum effect. Thus Day 22, chapter 168 is an account of military movements in the language of an official logbook while chapter 170 is a mock lyrical description of a 180-pound mortar, concluding with "etc". Vel'tman mocks most literary conventions of his day, including the epigraph. The main epigraph after the title is from *Strannik* itself. Epigraphs to various chapters are in Russian, Latin, Greek, French, English, Moldavian, German, or Italian. Occasionally they are meaningless: chapter 236: "2 x 2 = 4".

As a polyglot and lover of words, Vel'tman indulges himself to the full. Apart from the languages mentioned above, *Strannik* contains snatches of Yiddish, Turkish, Ukrainian, Romanian, and Bulgarian. In chapter 157 the traveller imagines himself surrounded by a crowd of servants and tradespeople who bombard him with exclamations in a weird variety of languages. In chapter 326 he attempts to reproduce the bizarre speech of a character who addresses him in an incongruous mixture of Greek, Moldavian, and Russian. He likes lists: of strangely named birds, of Greek historians, or exotic places. B.Ia. Bukhshtab dubbed him the greatest punster in Russian literature, with the possible exception of Leskov. The word-jokes often rely on treating a metaphorical image as if it were concrete and physical: thus the "steed" of the author's imagination keeps changing into a "real" horse to carry him further on his way. Most of the best puns are inevitably untranslatable.

In chapter 224 of *Strannik* Vel'tman comments that harmony can only be properly appreciated if it is contrasted with disharmony and chaos, and the overall effect of the work is certainly chaotic. Indeed the contemporary critic N.I. Nadezhdin (1804–56) dismissed it as "incoherent ridiculous gibberish". It tends to become more incoherent as it continues so that in Part III the tenuous thread of the real-life journey vanishes almost without trace, leaving a hotch-potch of disconnected oddments. Vel'tman had clearly let the joke go on too long.

In his later career as a writer Vel'tman became more orthodox and moved away from eccentric fantasy towards a more serious and concrete depiction of real life. Thus the evolution of his work is analogous with the general development of Russian prose in the period 1830–50. The few literary historians who have written about him are in general agreement that his forte is fantasy and verbal pyrotechnics. B.M. Eikhenbaum put him in a kind of junior league of Russian literature along with writers like V.I. Dal', N.S. Leskov, A.M. Remizov, and M.A. Kuzmin, all of whom share his fondness for linguistic tricks. The appearance of *Strannik* at a time when Russian prose fiction was in its embryonic stage makes it of more significance for the development both of language and literature than its essential lightweightedness might suggest. It also serves as a reminder that, for some 19th-century Russian writers at least, literature could be sheer fun.

JOHN GOODLIFFE

Dmitrii Vladimirovich Venevitinov 1805–1827

Poet

Biography

Born in Moscow, 26 September 1805. Educated by private tutors; granted free attendance at Moscow University lectures from 1822. Passed entrance examination, 1823; gained qualifications in literature and philosophy enabling him to work in the Moscow Foreign Ministry archive, 1824. Founding member of philosophical group of "Wisdom Lovers" (*Liubomudry*), 1823–25; Aleksandr Pushkin, his distant cousin, visited the group in 1826. Moved to St Petersburg and arrested on arrival, October 1826. Died of unknown causes, 27 March 1827.

Publications

Collected Editions

Polnoe sobranie sochinenii. Leningrad, 1934.
Polnoe sobranie stikhotvorenii. Leningrad, 1960.
"Complete Poetry. 35 Poems", translated by Donald R. Boucher and Larry Andrews. *Russian Literature Triquarterly*, 8 (1974), 84–130.
Stikhotvoreniia. Proza. Moscow, 1980.

Essays

"Three Essays", translated by Larry Andrews, *Russian Literature Triquarterly*, 11 (1975), 179–85. [Sculpture, Painting and Music; Morning, Midday, Evening and Night; Anaxagoras: A Platonic Dialogue].

Critical Studies

"Opyt filosofskoi liriki (Venevitinov)", by L.Ia. Ginzburg, *Poetika*, 5 (1929), 72–104.
Dmitrij Vladimirovič Venevitinov als Dichter der russischen Romantik, by Günther Wytrzens, Graz-Cologne, Böhlau, 1962.
"Zametki o Dmitrii Venevitinove", by I.I. Gribushin, *Russkaia literatura*, 1 (1968), 191–201.
"D.V. Venevitinov: A Sketch of His Life and Work", by Larry Andrews, *Russian Literature Triquarterly*, 8 (1974), 373–84.
Dmitrii Venevitinov (Lichnost'. Mirovozzrenie. Tvorchestvo), by L. Tartakovskaia, Tashkent, 1974.
"Byron and Venevitinov", by Arnold McMillin, *Slavonic and East European Review*, 53/131 (1975), 188–201.
Moskovskii kruzhok liubomudrov, by Z.A. Kamenskii, Moscow, 1980, 68–140.
"Venevitinov und Goethe. Zur Geschichte der frühen russischen Romantik", by Arnold McMillin, in *Goethe und die Welt der Slawen*, edited by H.B. Harder and H. Rothe, Giessen, Schmitz, 1981, 147–57.
"Tjutčev et Venevitinov", by F. Cornillot, *Slavia Gandensia*, 11 (1984), 43–56.
"Dmitry Venevitinov and His Role in the Early Development of Russian Philosophical Romanticism", by Arnold McMillin, in *Problems of Russian Romanticism*, edited by Robert Reid, Aldershot, Hampshire and Brookfield, Vermont, Gower, 1986, 49–63.
A History of Russian Literature of the Romantic Period, by William Edward Brown, Ann Arbor, Ardis, 1986, vol. 3, 347–63.

Dmitrii Venevitinov has variously been described as "the Russian Keats", a prophet of Schellingian philosophy, and an almost paradigmatic romantic poet, while specific links with such disparate figures as Byron, Goethe, Novalis, and Tiutchev have also been well attested. Poet, critic, philosopher, translator, artist and musician, he achieved much in the course of a tragically short life, and his name for many decades retained a sentimentally exotic aura. He is now remembered for what might have been and for his contribution to the Russian romantic movement.

In childhood Venevitinov enjoyed excellent private tuition, and in time he was able to move in the leading literary, musical, and social circles of his day. Even for one with such a privileged background, his classical and modern erudition was exceptional, and he immersed himself particularly in German romantic idealist philosophy, and especially the *Naturphilosophie* of Friedrich Schelling. He quickly became the founder, chief inspiration and leader of a group of like-minded young intellectuals, mostly colleagues from the Oriental Section of the Foreign Ministry archive, who called themselves "Wisdom Lovers" (*Liubomudry*) in contradistinction to the adherents of French philosophy predominant at that time. By propagating romantic idealist aesthetics, they, in effect, started the metaphysical trend in Russian romantic poetry. Later Venevitinov was to take a keen interest in plans for a new journal, *Moskovskii vestnik*, which, however, he did not live to see. At the time of his death he was working on a prose novel under the title *Vladimir Parenskii*.

Venevitinov's great erudition first came to public notice in an article of 1825, "Razbor rassuzhdeniia g. Merzliakova: o nachale i dukhe drevnei tragedii i proch., napechatannogo pri izdanii ego podrazhanii i perevodov iz grecheskikh i latinskikh stikhotvortsev" [A Critique of Mr Merzliakov's Views on the Principles and Nature of Ancient Tragedy ...], in which he attacked the conservative Neoclassical aesthetics of his teacher, Professor A.F. Merzliakov. His most important piece of literary criticism was an article on the first chapter of *Evgenii Onegin* in which he took issue with critics who diminished Pushkin's originality by casual comparisons with Byron; he himself was far from adulatory, however, finding the novel frivolous, but a later note shows that he greatly preferred the second chapter. For his part, Pushkin described Venevitinov's observations as the only worthwhile criticism of his novel. Venevitinov also wrote a critique of a scene from *Boris Godunov*.

His other main prose works, all remarkable for their intellectual clarity, include "Anaksagor. Beseda Platona" ("Anaxagoras. A Platonic Dialogue") (1825), a philosophical dialogue in the spirit of German natural philosophy in which Plato seems to advance the ideas of Schelling's *Systems des transzendental Idealismus* (*System of Transcendental Idealism*). The same ideas are developed in "Utro, polden', vecher i noch'" ("Morning, Midday, Evening and Night"), and a further exposition of German philosophy is to be found in "Pis'mo grafine NN" [A Letter to Countess NN] (1826). Venevitinov saw the projected *Moskovskii vestnik* as a monument to "Wisdom Loving" (*Liubomudrie*) that would raise the low level of education in Russia, and this is the burden of his most important philosophical essay, "Neskol'ko myslei v plan zhurnala" [A Few Thoughts on the Plan of a Journal] (1826), which was to have been called "On the State of Enlightenment in Russia", and was published only posthumously in 1833.

The ten-page fragment of a novel, *Vladimir Parenskii*, describes a brilliant youth visiting Goethe, and it is the German poet who provides most of the originals for Venevitinov's translations (which also include some weak Ossianic poems and a few versions of light French poetry). Not surprisingly, he chooses the romantic rather than classical side of Goethe's work: *Künstlers Erdewallen* and *Künstlers Apotheose*, and some well-known passages from the first part of *Faust*, such as Faust's monologue from the "Wald und Höhle" scene, part of "Vor dem Tor", and "Gretchen am Spinnrade".

Venevitinov's original verse was conventional in theme, trope and vocabulary, and his great promise hardly fulfilled. Far from the rebelliousness of the Decembrist poets with whom he has sometimes been associated, his verses, particularly in the Moscow period, are frequently elegiac, with a longing for escape to exotic places, and a near-despair at the banality of society. His unrequited love for society beauty Zinaida Volkonskaia infuses several lyrics, but with more passion than originality. Venevitinov is very central in all his poetry, offering a lofty view of the poet's role, but his persona is less that of a lyric hero than a programmatic Schellingian poet, presenting poetry as the highest form of cognition and reconciliation of opposites, the concept of genius as the highest creative power. His other major thematic area concerns Russia and its fate; here, as in his prose, Venevitinov shows a strong Slavophile tendency. All his poetry suffers to some extent from excessive adherence to the poetic dialect inherited from Zhukovskii, Batiushkov, and, in part, Pushkin, compounded by over-reliance on the iambic tetrameter (87.7 per cent of his original lines). For Venevitinov, however, thought always preceded rather than accompanied writing, and his aim, as Belinskii noted, was not so much originality but lucidity and the perfection of existing forms for the transmission of ideas.

Venevitinov's best original verse belongs to what is usually called his Petersburg cycle, and among the most notable lyrics are the programmatic "Poet", a dramatic verse, "Novgorod", dedicated to Princess Trubetskaia, a philosophical reflection, "Zhizn'" [Life], and the best of his friendly epistles, to R(ozhali)n. Outstanding among the love lyrics are "Zaveshchanie" [Testimony], "K moemu perstniu" [To My Ring], "Italiia" [Italy], and "K moei bogine" [To My Goddess]. Also notable is "Poet i drug" [The Poet and His Friend], which ends with the telling line: "How much he knew! How little he lived!".

Venevitinov did not reach the poetic heights of other philosophical poets like Baratynskii and Tiutchev, but he was undoubtedly a pioneer, and it is remarkable – as with the "Wisdom Lovers" as a whole – how much influence he exerted in such a short period of time.

ARNOLD MCMILLIN

Anastasiia Alekseevna Verbitskaia 1861–1928

Prose writer

Biography

Born Anastasiia Alekseevna Ziablova in Voronezh, 23 February 1861. Attended Elizavetin Women's Institute, Moscow, 1870–77. Worked as a private teacher, 1877–79; studied singing at the Moscow Conservatoire, 1879–81. Married: A.V. Verbitskii in 1882; three sons. Singing teacher at a Moscow girls' school, 1882–1901. Copy-editor for the newspaper *Russkii kur'er*, from 1893; compiler of political surveys for *Zhizn'*. Began to publish fiction, 1887; full-time writer from 1894. Became publisher of own works, from 1899. Member of the Moscow Society of Mutual Aid for Intellectual Professions, 1899–1901; closed "for extreme anti-government activity", 1901. Chair of the Society for Improvement of Lot of Women, 1905. Harboured revolutionary sympathies; put her house at disposal of the "Moscow Committee" of Bolsheviks, during the 1905 Revolution. Achieved unprecedented popularity for best-selling novels, 1909–13. Failed to emigrate, 1917; novels banned for alleged pornographic, anti-Semitic, and reactionary tendencies, 1919. Cleared by a commission of State Publishing House; but her name remained on Index of banned authors, 1924. Wrote children's books under pseudonyms, 1920s. Attempts by Olminskii, Lunacharskii, and other prominent Bolsheviks to intervene on her behalf failed. Died in Moscow, 16 January 1928.

Publications

Fiction

"Razlad" [Discord], *Russkaia mysl'*, 6 (1887); as *Pervye lastochki* [First Swallows]. Moscow, 1900.

Osvobodilas! [Liberated!]. Moscow, 1898.

Vavochka. Moscow, 1898; translated as *Wenn die Tuberosen blühen. (Frühlingserwachen)*, in *Roman aus dem Leben der russischen Demivierges*, 2, Berlin, Auflage, 1910.

Sny zhizni [Life's Dreams]. Moscow, 1899.

Prestuplenie Mar'i Ivanovny [Mar'ia Ivanovna's Crime]. Moscow, 1899.

Ch'ia vina [Whose Fault is It?]. Moscow, 1900.

Po-novomu: Roman uchitel'nitsy [In a New Way]. Moscow, 1902.

Istoriia odnoi zhizni [History of a Life]. Moscow, 1903.

Zlaia rosa [Evil Dew]. Moscow, 1904.

Schast'e: Novye rasskazy [Happiness: New Stories]. Moscow, 1905.

Dukh vremeni [The Spirit of the Times]. Moscow, 1907; translated as *Aus Sturmeszeit. Roman*, by Frieda von Stock, Berlin, 1910.

Kliuchi schast'ia [The Keys to Happiness], 6 vols. Moscow, 1909–13; reprinted 2 vols, St Petersburg, 1993; shortened revised version, Moscow, 1993; translated as *Manja. Roman*, by Frieda von Stock, Frankfurt, 1910.

Igo liubvi [The Yoke of Love], Parts 1 and 2, Moscow, 1914–16; Part 3, 1920, unpublished, in Russian archives, TsGALI, f.1042.

Plays

Besplodnye zhertvy. Semeistvo Volginykh [Futile Sacrifices. The Volginyi Family]. Moscow, 1906.

Mirazhi. Moscow, 1909; translated as "Mirages" (extract), by Temira Pachmuss, in *Women Writers in Russian Modernism: An Anthology*, edited by Pachmuss, Urbana, Illinois University Press, 1978.

Screenplay

Pobediteli i pobezhdennie (Kliuchi schast'ia). Drama v 7-i chastiakh s prologom. (Stsenarii avtora) [The Victors and the Vanquished (The Keys to Happiness)]. Moscow, 1917.

Autobiography

Moemu chitateliu. Avtobiograficheskie ocherki s dvumia portretami [To My Readers. Autobiographical Sketches with Two Portraits]. Moscow, 1908.

Avtobiograficheskie ocherki s portretom avtora i semeinymi portretami (Detstvo, gody ucheniia) [Autobiographical Sketches with a Portrait of the Author and Family Portraits (Childhood, Years of Study)]. Moscow, 1911.

Moi vospominaniia. Iunost', Grezy [My Memoirs. Youth, Day-Dreams]. Moscow, 1911.

Critical Studies

"Umiraiushchie illiuzii. (Semeinyi vopros v sovremennoi belletristike)", by E. Koltunovskaia, *Obrazovanie*, 1/3 (1903), 73–80.

Zhenskie tipy v proizvedeniiakh Verbitskoi. Opyt kriticheskogo razbora ee proizvedenii, by Ia. Chimishliiskii, St Petersburg, 1904.

A. Verbitskaia i ee romany "Kliuchi schast'ia" i "Dukh vremeni", by V. Dadonov, Moscow, 1911.

V mire idei i obrazov, by V. Kranikhfeld, 1912, vol. 2, 155–81.

"Verbitskaia", by Kornei Chukovskii, in *Kniga o sovremennykh pisateliakh*, St Petersburg, 1914, 7–21.

Po literaturnym voprosam, by M. Olminskii, Moscow and Leningrad, 1932, 52–55.

Women Writers in Russian Modernism: An Anthology, edited by Temira Pachmuss, Urbana, Illinois University Press, 1978, 114–19.

When Russia Learned to Read: Literacy and Popular Literature, 1861–1917, by Jeffrey Brooks, Princeton, Princeton University Press, 1985, 153–60.

Der Russischen Frauenroman (1890–1912). Exemplarische Untersuchungen, by Tatjana Antalovsky, Munich, Sagner, 1987.

"The Birth, Death and Rebirth of Feminist Writing in Russia", by Rosalind Marsh, in *Textual Liberation: European Feminist Writing in the Twentieth Century*, edited by Helena Forsås-Scott, London and New York, Routledge, 1991.

The Keys to Happiness: Sex and the Search for Modernity in Fin de Siècle Russia, by Laura Engelstein, Ithaca, Cornell University Press, 1992, 404–14.

"Russkoe Nitssheanstvo i Zhenskii Roman Nachala XX Veka",

by Alla Gracheva, in *Gender Restructuring in Russian Studies*, edited by Marianne Liljeström, Eila Mäntysaari, and Arja Rosenholm, Helsinki, Slavica Tamperensia II, 1993, 87–98.

A History of Russian Women's Writing, 1820–1992, by Catriona Kelly, Oxford and New York, Clarendon Press, 1994.

"Verbitskaia, Anastasiia Aleksandrovna", by Alla Gracheva, in *Dictionary of Russian Women Writers*, edited by Marina Ledkovsky, Charlotte Rosenthal, and Mary Zirin, Westport, Connecticut, Greenwood Press, 1994, 703–05.

"Achievement and Obscurity: Women's Prose in the Silver Age", by Charlotte Rosenthal, in *Women Writers in Russian Literature*, edited by Toby W. Clyman and Diane Greene, Westport, Connecticut, Greenwood Press, 1994, 153–54, 157–58.

"Anastasiia Verbitskaia Reconsidered", by Rosalind Marsh, in *Gender and Russian Literature: New Perspectives*, edited by Marsh, Cambridge and New York, Cambridge University Press, 1996.

Anastasiia Verbitskaia usually receives critical censure as an exponent of "women's prose" (*zhenskaia proza*), a literature of trivial or sensational themes, obsessed by sentiment and romance, and couched in a weak or hysterical style. Some modern critics have simply accepted the opinions of the hostile male critics of her own day, notably Kornei Chukovskii, possibly without re-reading all her works, most of which have not been reprinted in Russia.

However, Verbitskaia's career merits reassessment. Her novels played a progressive role in the Russian women's movement, even if they cannot be regarded as "great art"; and her activities as writer and publisher rendered her an important role model for Russian women and an influential popularizer of contemporary feminist ideas. Moreover, Verbitskaia deserves attention because she was such a phenomenon in her day: her later works *Dukh vremeni* [The Spirit of the Times], *Igo liubvi* [The Yoke of Love] and especially *Kliuchi schast'ia* [The Keys to Happiness] were bestsellers, more sought-after in public lending libraries than those of Tolstoi.

Verbitskaia's early work follows the tradition of Russian feminist writing initiated by Nikolai Chernyshevskii and women writers of the previous generation, such as Ol'ga Shapir and Nadezhda Khvoshchinskaia. Verbitskaia emphasizes the value of employment and education as means of changing women's lives, and contributes to the contemporary debate about women's sexual and economic independence. The distinctiveness of her novels resides in her acute psychological analysis of her heroines, who are writers, teachers, actresses, and women on medical courses attempting to forge independent careers for themselves; and her ability to convey feminist ideas in simple, highly readable form.

Many of Verbitskaia's early works highlight a lone woman's struggle against recalcitrant Russian reality. *Osvobodilas!* [Liberated!] portrays a professor's wife, Lizaveta Mel'gunova, who, while enjoying comfortable circumstances as the estranged wife of an adulterous professor, chooses to give lessons to gain economic independence. Although Lizaveta's struggle ends in suicide, Verbitskaia's intention is to depict a strong woman fighting for self-determination, who is ultimately crushed by the constraints of her society and the contradictions of her own personality. Similarly, *Pervye lastochki* [First Swallows] contains an interesting autobiographical depiction of a proud young widow's doomed attempt to feed her three children and make a career as a writer and translator in the Moscow literary world. *Istoriia odnoi zhizni* [History of a Life] presents another independent woman, Ol'ga Devich, whose cherished aim of attending a medical course in St Petersburg is defeated by the feminine side of her nature. Verbitskaia provides a realistic analysis of the failure of Ol'ga's marriage with the charming, but worthless Charnetskii, and of her struggle to bring up her child alone in dire poverty. This novel is less didactic than many of her others; Verbitskaia provides no easy answers to the conflict between Ol'ga's passion and her ambition.

A new departure for Verbitskaia was the portrayal of an anti-heroine, the eponymous *Vavochka*, an egoistic parasite whose only interest in life is to find a rich man to marry. Verbitskaia implies that Vavochka is typical of her generation, and that patriarchal Russian society is responsible for creating ill-educated slave women who are prepared to trade their freedom for a rich life.

A work subjected to considerable criticism was *Ch'ia vina?* [Whose Fault is It?], which provides a new permutation on Verbitskaia's favourite theme of female independence, while also raising the perennial question of divorce and its effect on children. Through her portrait of Vera, who leaves her child to become a famous singer, Verbitskaia suggests that nothing, not even her children's welfare, should fetter a woman's freedom and creativity.

Po-novomu [In a New Way] analyses the attempt of a dedicated teacher, Mar'ia Vasilevna, to establish a new type of marriage, in which both partners have their own room, which the other may not enter without permission, and are able to live their own personal life. Verbitskaia suggests that Mar'ia's programme is untenable, partly because her husband finds it intolerable, but primarily because Russian society is too backward to countenance such advanced ideas.

As Verbitskaia's ambitions grew, the faults in her fiction became more marked. She proved to be less successful at depicting the "new man" influenced by Nietzschean philosophy in her novel *Zlaia rosa* [Evil Dew], or a radical individualist involved in the 1905 Revolution in *Dukh vremeni*, than at painting realistic pictures of the lives and problems of professional Russian women. Although Verbitskaia herself attached more significance to her enormously popular later works, her real talent lay in portraying women trapped in unsatisfactory relationships or conventional family life, or in pointing to the conflict between love and work, between the desire for fulfilment and the oppressive, humdrum reality of Russian women's lives.

In recent years, a derogatory view of Verbitskaia has been perpetuated by critics who still tend to focus almost exclusively on her later blockbusters. However, even these works deservedly evoke some sympathy from feminist critics, who point out that Verbitskaia's heroines are actresses and ballerinas making their own way in the world, and that she was only advocating a sexual freedom for women that men had enjoyed for centuries.

Verbitskaia's work, particularly her neglected early novels, made a valuable contribution to the "feminist phase" of women's literature from the 1880s to the 1920s, a tradition largely forgotten in Soviet Russia. Although Verbitskaia did not create anything of lasting aesthetic value, her unpretentious early works, with their gripping plots, lively dialogue and frequently subtle analysis of female psychology, sexual relationships and the social milieu of pre-revolutionary Russia, deserve to be better known, and to occupy an honourable place in the history of Russian feminist writing. Only Aleksandra Kollontai in her fiction of the 1920s has gone as far as Verbitskaia in suggesting that the key to becoming truly liberated is a woman's own efforts to rid herself of excessive economic and emotional dependence on men, while recognizing that such a change of focus will be agonizingly difficult.

ROSALIND MARSH

Kliuchi schast'ia

The Keys to Happiness

Novel, 1909–13

Whatever view one takes of Verbitskaia's writing, her novel *Kliuchi schast'ia* deserves attention because of its immense popularity in pre-revolutionary Russia. Its exciting plot, sensational themes, and popular treatment of topical political and cultural questions made it a bestseller: its print-run of 280,000 copies was huge for that time; and in 1913 it was made into a film, directed by V. Gardin and Ia. Protazanov, based on Verbitskaia's screenplay. Its popularity was also attested by the number of "sequels" and parodies it spawned, notably by Count Amori (1915).

The heroine of *Kliuchi schast'ia*, Mania Eltseva, is a sexually liberated ballerina who is devoted to her work, but also loves two men and feels no compunction about sleeping with them both. Verbitskaia displays the influence of modernism and Nietzschean philosophy in her interpretation of individualism as the freedom of the creative personality, and of female emancipation as the demand for full freedom in sexual matters. Mania's two lovers are Baron Steinbach, a sensitive, cultured Jewish millionaire, and Nelidov, a Nietzschean superman and member of the anti-Semitic Black Hundreds, who rejects Mania for fear that she has inherited her mother's insanity. This melodramatic plot allows Verbitskaia to explore such topical subjects as heredity, national characteristics, and role reversal on the part of both men and women. Mania is presented as "masculine" in her sexual behaviour; the author suggests that she has a right to follow her passions, while implying that she should behave even more like a man, regarding love as only part of life and not the whole. The "keys to happiness" are bequeathed to Mania by her first lover, the revolutionary Jan: "Your body, your feelings, your life belong to you alone. And you are competent to do with them what you will. But don't give your soul up to love".

Verbitskaia's novel has received a hostile reception by critics, predominantly male, both in her own day, and in more recent times. Whereas her first works had been well received, *Kliuchi schast'ia* was lambasted by contemporary critics for its artistic faults, pseudo-intellectualism, predilection for luxurious interiors, and exotic locations known only through guidebooks, over-simplified treatment of social problems, and allegedly pornographic content. Particularly harsh criticism came from "Tan" (V.G. Bogoraz) who referred to her as "Sanin in a skirt"; and by V.P. Kranikhfeld, who complained of her "lively dialogues, in which the most fashionable issues of the day are touched upon", which venture "no further than the repetition of clichés, but presented in an elevated, exalted tone". Yet perhaps the most influential denunciation published in her lifetime was a witty article of 1910 by the critic Kornei Chukovskii, who at that time was a supporter of the liberal Kadet (Constitutional Democratic) party and hence could not be expected to be sympathetic to her revolutionary leanings. Chukovskii discredits Verbitskaia's blockbuster on aesthetic grounds, pointing to the number of times she uses such expressions as: "she flushes", "her eyes sparkle", "incrustation", "abyss" and "blood". His criticism, which picks an easy target and says nothing about the feminist themes in *Kliuchi schast'ia*, has been more influential than Verbitskaia's writing itself, and bears considerable responsibility for the scorn with which the term "women's prose" (*zhenskaia proza*) has subsequently been regarded in Russia. Arguments by western feminist critics that "women's literature" is a popular artefact that does not automatically deserve a critical reception, since it may contain progressive elements or be of therapeutic value to women readers, would still fall on deaf ears in Russia.

After the Revolution, Verbitskaia's novel was condemned for its "decadence", advocacy of sexual libertinism and so-called "bourgeois feminism"; while critics who identified the author with her hero, Nelidov, unfairly accused her of reactionary, anti-Semitic tendencies. Towards the end of the 1920s, however, an attempt was made to rehabilitate Verbitskaia by the prominent Bolsheviks Lunacharskii and Olminskii, who noted the "democratic" nature of her work and suggested that her novel had played a progressive political role in influencing young people.

In recent years, a derogatory view of Verbitskaia's novel has been perpetuated by historians of Russian popular culture and women's writing; although the novel has evoked some sympathy from feminist critics, who point out that Verbitskaia challenged the false morals of Russian society and the position of women within it. *Kliuchi schast'ia* did not merely, in the words of the critic Dadonov, fulfil the function of creating "rest" and "cheerfulness" for ordinary people; rather, Verbitskaia's depiction of a talented woman running her own life, however extravagant and neurasthenic the heroine may be, could not but exert some influence on her numerous female readers. Even though Mania finally chooses fatal passion with the despotic Nelidov and commits suicide it could be argued that the subordination of Verbitskaia's heroine corresponds more closely to the reality of Russian life in her day, when very few Russian women had the opportunity to attain complete economic independence from men. Contrary to the opinion of Jeffrey Brooks, the denouement of *Kliuchi schast'ia* does not invalidate the feminist "message" of much of the text. Indeed, Mania's self-destructive behaviour could be interpreted as highlighting the greater wisdom of her earlier, more enlightened decision to live for her vocation and her daughter, while choosing friendship then marriage with her patron Steinbach, who takes an interest in her art.

Verbitskaia's *Kliuchi schast'ia* possesses considerable interest as a striking illustration of the way in which Russian popular culture contributed to the first-wave feminist movement and to women's discovery of their own sexuality. The neglect and hostility that Verbitskaia's work provoked cannot be entirely explained by critics' sensitivity to its artistic shortcomings; it also undoubtedly stemmed from her passionate advocacy of equality, self-assertion, and material independence for women, and her exposure of the hypocritical "double standard" in male morality – feminist ideas that were ahead of their time.

ROSALIND MARSH

Petr Andreevich Viazemskii 1792–1878

Poet and literary critic

Biography

Born in Moscow, 23 July 1792. Educated at home and at a Jesuit Pension in St Petersburg. His brother-in-law, Nikolai Karamzin, introduced him to literary circles. Met Pushkin, 1810. Married: Princess Vera Fedorovna Gagarina; five sons and three daughters (all children but one died prematurely). Fought the French in the Battle of Borodino, 1812. Joined Pushkin's Arzamas group, 1815. Forced to work in various official positions after losing half a million roubles in a card game. Fired from a post in Warsaw on account of his liberal sympathies, 1821. Served in the Ministry of Finance for 20 years. Head of censorship, 1856–58; forced to resign by both radicals and reactionaries. Spent time abroad because of ill health and because he was out of favour with Tsar Nicholas I. Ever-decreasing popularity in Russia; outlived his contemporaries and readers. Died in Baden-Baden, Germany, 22 November 1878.

Publications

Collected Editions

Polnoe sobranie sochinenii, 12 vols. St Petersburg, 1878–96.
Stikhotvoreniia. Leningrad, 1958; reprinted 1986.
Sochinenie, 2 vols. Moscow, 1982.

Literary Criticism

Zapisnye knizhki: 1813–1848 [Note Books]. Moscow, 1963.
Estetika i literaturnaia kritika [Aesthetics and Literary Criticism]. Moscow, 1984.
"On *The Captive of the Caucasus*", in *Russian Romantic Criticism: An Anthology*, translated by Lauren G. Leighton, New York, Greenwood Press, 1987, 47–54.

Letters

"The Vyazemsky-Turgenev Correspondence", in *The Ardis Anthology of Russian Romanticism*, edited by Christine Rydel, Ann Arbor, Ardis, 1984, 490–509.

Critical Studies

Pamiati kniazia Viazemskogo, by S.I. Ponomarev, St Petersburg, 1880.
"P.A. Viazemskii i dvizhenie dekabristov", *Uchenye zapiski Tartuskogo gos-universiteta*, vol. 98, 1960, 24–142.
P.A. Vjazemskij, by G. Wytrzens, Vienna, Notring der Wissenschaftlichen Verbande Osterreichs, 1961.
"The Anecdote in Russia: Puškin, Vyazemsky, and Davydov", by Lauren G. Leighton, *Slavic and East European Journal*, 10 (1966), 155–66.
P.A. Viazemskii: Zhizn' i tvorchestvo, by M.I. Gillel'son, Leningrad, 1969.
"Vyazemsky and Romanticism", by J.M. Meijer, in *Dutch Contributions to the Seventh International Congress of Slavists*, edited by A. van Holk, The Hague, Mouton, 1973, 271–304.
"Viazemskii – perevodchik 'Negodovaniia'", by I.A. Paperno and Iu.M. Lotman, *Uchenye zapiski Tartuskogo gos-universiteta*, vol. 369, 1975.
"Vyazemsky as a Critic of Pushkin", by T.E. Little, in *Russian and Slavic Literature*, edited by Richard Freeborn *et al.*, Cambridge, Massachusetts, Slavica, 1976, 1–16.
"P.A. Vyazemsky as a Critic of Gogol'", by T.E. Little, *New Zealand Slavonic Journal*, 1 (1978), 47–58.
Poety Pushkinskoi pory, by V.I. Korovin, Moscow, 1980.
"Vyazemsky – Man of Letters", by L. Ginzburg, in *Russian Prose*, edited by B.M. Eikhenbaum and Iu. Tynianov, translated by Ray Parrott, Ann Arbor, Ardis, 1985, 87–108.
"The Younger Innovators: Prince Pyotr Vyazemsky", by William Edward Brown, in his *A History of Russian Literature of the Romantic Period*, Ann Arbor, Ardis, 1986, vol. 2, 59–83.

The poet Petr Viazemskii's aristocratic Russian breeding was tempered by his Irish mother (O'Reilly) and Swedish great-grandmother. He inherited his father's Voltairean ideas and substantial French library. The historian Karamzin often stayed at the family home, Ostaf'evo, and virtually became Viazemskii's guardian and tutor. Viazemskii also mixed with poets who were to be Pushkin's mentors and precursors – Vasilii Pushkin, Batiushkov, the young Zhukovskii. In 1810 he met Pushkin and, joining the Arzamas group in 1815 as "Asmodeus", Viazemskii became part of the Pushkinian pleiad. The cult of poetry as a brotherly communion, as precise enunciation of moderate thought, remained with Viazemskii long after he had outlived all the other *Arzamastsy*. Viazemskii, however, took up polemics very early (in defence of Karamzin) and thus determined his future as a disgruntled outsider battling with injustice, illusion, and ignobility. He experienced real war in the Battle of Borodino, by which time (1811) he had married Princess Vera Fedorovna Gagarina, who gave birth to five sons and three daughters and lived until 1886. The Viazemskiis' tragedy was the premature death of all their children except one son, the literary historian Pavel (1820–88). In the 1810s Viazemskii lost half a million roubles at cards and was forced to take up the first of a long series of official positions, an experience of government at more and more senior levels that reinforced his general disillusion with progress and with Russia, for all his liberal and national feelings. Apart from his poetry, his private letters (which he assumed the secret police intercepted) gave vent to this dissidence. Intransigence alternating with indigence forced him to resign and retract. The shock of Pushkin's death, chronic illness and Tsar Nicholas I's hatred led him to spend more time abroad. His travels inspired a number of interesting, but forgotten prose articles as well as poetry. Viazemskii was effectively written off (although appreciated) in Gogol''s great essay of 1846 "What is Actually the Essence of Russian Poetry and What is Its Particularity?":

> The absence of a great or full work is Prince Viazemskii's disease, and this can be sensed in his poems. They show an absence of inner harmonious concord in their separate parts, a discord ... next to a verse which is stronger and firmer than any other poet's we find another sort, quite unlike the first; at one moment he will show the pain of living flesh ripped from the heart, at another he will repel with a sound that is almost alien to the heart, which is quite out of tune with the subject; you can feel his lack of inner consistency, a life which is not filled with strength.

Public opinion followed Gogol' and relegated Viazemskii to a living fossil, curious only as the unique survivor (together with Tiutchev) of the Golden Age of Russian poetry. His nostalgic memoirs, published in the late 1860s and 1870s, aroused mild antiquarian interest. In his notebooks he confessed his failure: "I can't find myself in these fragments ... God gave me no full-face, just a few profiles."

The 12 volumes of Viazemskii's Collected Works, published around the time of his death, have never been reprinted, but show a considerable writer not just in quantity and range. Once we allow that his prose lacks vision and his poetry lacks musicality or joy, that he seems stylistically uninnovative, we can appreciate the qualities that have been undervalued ever since the Pushkinian pleiad broke up. First, Viazemskii's permanent and unique state of feeling was disgruntlement, and no Russian poet has expressed this state with such direct and telling force. Second, his acute intelligence found unforgettable metaphors for the poet's and his homeland's moral ills: a number of images in the Russian language, notably "The Russian God" and "The Dressing Gown" [*khalat*], were created by Viazemskii. A well-chosen anthology would rehabilitate Viazemskii entirely and place him on a level comparable to Baratynskii. His motto might well be that of a poem of 1837, "Ia perezhil" [I have survived], where the deaths of Pushkin, Dmitr'ev and five of Viazemskii's children entitle him to his bleak view:

> You may find the trace of yesterday in me.
> But there is nothing now of tomorrow.
> Life has reneged on me; it cannot
> Give me back what it has taken,
> What the earth in its deaf graves
> Has pitilessly buried for ever.

Disinherited, Viazemskii felt free to attack his inheritance and heirs. Even Pushkin, as his junior, was not immune to criticism. For some time Viazemskii, however, spared his readers the vicious wit of his "Russkii Bog" [Russian God]; written in 1828, it was published as a daringly unpatriotic gesture in the middle of the Crimean War:

> God of drooping breasts and buttocks,
> God of bark sandals and swollen feet,
> Of bitter faces and sour cream,
> That is him, the Russian God ...
> Full of grace for the stupid,
> Mercilessly strict to the clever,
> God of everything unneeded,
> That is him, the Russian God ...
> God of vagrant foreigners,
> Who have strayed across our threshhold
> God especially of Germans
> That is him, the Russian God.

The other image of Russia, as an Asiatic dressing gown, pursued Viazemskii all his life. His first assignment as a civil servant to Warsaw he evoked as a "Proshchanie s khalatom" [Farewell to his Dressing Gown] (1817): only if disillusioned by Europe will he return to its comfort: "O my gown, welcoming as of old, / Take me then in your embrace ... / And, reborn in the magical ecstasy of sweet dreams, / Let me find oblivion / Of everything I have seen while awake". Sixty years later, possibly his last and his best poem sees the dressing gown with more ironic affection and imbues the garment with all the significance of being Russian: "Our life in old age is a worn-out dressing gown; / You're ashamed to wear it but loth to abandon it; / The two of us have long since grown together, like brothers; / We can't be repaired or renovated".

Intelligence and lack of pretence compensate for Viazemskii's aridity. Pushkin's comment of 1826: "Your verse is too clever. Poetry, God forgive me, has to be a bit stupid" is telling, but Viazemskii was true to himself:

> I shall never sacrifice my thoughts to sound. In verse I want to say what I want to say; I don't care or think about my neighbour's ears. ... Cows can be beautiful, but saddles don't suit them. A thought, saddled with a verse, may be useless. My stubbornness, my violence sometimes give my verse prosaic limpness, sometimes artificiality.

DONALD RAYFIELD

Georgii Nikolaevich Vladimov 1931–

Novelist

Biography

Born Georgii Nikolaevich Volosevich in Kharkov, 19 February 1931. Attended Suvorov school, Leningrad, where his mother was a teacher; studied law at Leningrad University, 1948–53. Began writing while still a student. Worked in the prose section of *Novyi mir*, 1956–59. Married: 1) Larisa Isarova in 1958, one daughter; 2) Natal'ia Kuznetsova in 1965. Addressed the 4th Congress of Soviet Writers in support of Solzhenitsyn, 1967. Left the Writers' Union voluntarily on ideological grounds, 1977. Worked for the Moscow branch of Amnesty International and supported other human rights campaigns. Under threat of trial and repression, left USSR for West Germany, 1983. Editor of *Grani*, 1984–86. Recipient: Russian Booker Prize for *General i ego armiia* [The General and His Army], 1995. Lives near Frankfurt.

Publications

Fiction

Bol'shaia ruda. Moscow, 1962; translated as *The Great Ore*, by Andrew R. MacAndrew, New York, Bantam, 1965.

"Tri minuty molchaniia", *Novyi mir*, 7–9 (1969); Moscow, 1976; complete edition, Frankfurt, Posev, 1982; translated as *Three Minutes' Silence*, by Michael Glenny, London, Quartet, 1985.

Vernyi Ruslan: Istoriia kavaul'noi sobaki, Frankfurt, Posev, 1975; translated as *Faithful Ruslan: The Story of a Guard Dog*, by Michael Glenny, London, Jonathan Cape, and New York, Simon and Schuster, 1979.

Ne obrashchaite vnimanie, maestro. Frankfurt, Posev, 1983; translated as "Pay No Attention, Maestro", by Roger Keys, *Literary Review*, 59 (1983), 39–55.

"General i ego armiia", *Znamia*, 4–5 (1994), 3–71; 6–49; excerpt translated as "A General and His Army", by Arch Tait, *Glas: New Russian Writing*, 11 (1996), 169–82.

Play

"Shestoi soldat" [The Sixth Soldier], *Grani*, 121 (1981), 5–106.

Critical Studies

"Khudozhestvennoe svoeobrazie prozy G. Vladimova", by A.A. Kots, *Uchenye zapiski Permskogo universiteta*, 241 (1970).

"Gibel' geroev: O tvorchestve Georgiia Vladimova", by V. Cherniavskii, *Grani*, 106 (1977), 204–28.

Beyond Socialist Realism: Soviet Fiction since "Ivan Denisovich", by Geoffrey Hosking, London, Granada, and New York, Holmes and Meier, 1980, 154–61.

"Georgii Vladimov: Literary Path into Exile", by J. Mozur, *World Literature Today*, 59 (1985), 21–26.

"Sekret shedevra", by E. Tudorovskaia, *Strelets*, 8 (1985), 22–24.

Scenes from Soviet Life: Soviet Life Through Official Literature, by Mary Seton-Watson, London, BBC Publications, 1986.

"Strogost' i iasnost'", by A. Arkhangel'skii, *Novyi mir*, 7 (1989), 262–64.

"V poiskakh utrachennoi chelovechnosti", by A. Nemzer, *Oktiabr'*, 8 (1989), 184–94.

Four Contemporary Russian Writers, by Robert Porter, Oxford, Berg, 1989, 129–70.

"Vladimov's *Three Minutes of Silence* and the Soviet Production Novel", by J. Mozur, in *Oregon Studies in Chinese and Russian Culture*, edited by Albert Leong, New York, Peter Lang, 1990, 277–92.

"Liudi i zveri. Po knige G. Vladimova *Vernyi Ruslan (Istoriia karaul'noi sobaki)*", by Abram Terts, *Voprosy literatury*, 1 (1990), 61–86.

Georgii Vladimov's first prose work was *Bol'shaia ruda* (*The Great Ore*). The action takes place in one of the "construction sites of communism" in the Kursk region. The novella contains all the main elements of a Soviet production novel, but its sense and spirit are completely contrary to the official genre. The hero of this work, Proniakin, a lorry driver, is prepared to perform heroic feats in order to create for himself a pleasant, affluent and carefree life, rather than for the triumph of the socialist economy. Disregarding the danger, he goes to work in rainy weather with an overloaded lorry and dies in an accident at the plant. The story was very favourably received by readers and critics alike. The latter, however, reacted quite differently to Vladimov's second novel, *Tri minuty molchaniia* (*Three Minutes' Silence*), about life on a boat from the Murmansk fishing fleet, and in particular about a charming and feckless sailor, Senia Shalai, who in the course of one short voyage learns about mortality, the price of risk, and the value of the warm love of a woman. The novel first appeared in heavily censored form in *Novyi mir* (1969) and in a full edition in Germany in 1982.

Vladimov's third and most important work, *Vernyi Ruslan* (*Faithful Ruslan*), was written, like most of this author's works, over many years. This story of an Alsatian prison-camp guard dog, or – more broadly – of the country as a whole, was strictly forbidden by the censor. After publication in the west it was translated into many European languages, and was only officially published in Russia in 1989.

A comedy in two acts, *Shestoi soldat* [The Sixth Soldier], was published in *Grani* in 1981, shortly before Vladimov's emigration from the USSR. The action takes place in an undefined geographical space that none the less closely resembles a small provincial Soviet town. It treats questions of human relations, love, and treachery under appalling political conditions.

The year 1983 saw the separate publication of Vladimov's satirical story, *Ne obrashchaite vnimanie, maestro* (*Pay No Attention, Maestro*), which recreates the atmosphere surrounding the political harassment of a writer. The story describes the interference in the writer's private life of the secret police who have set up an observation point in the house opposite his flat. The story describes many aspects of the everyday absurdity of Soviet life; much in the narration is clearly autobiographical. One particular object of mockery is the strained, even hostile relations between the competing organizations of the KGB and the militia; it is clear that in this situation the author's preference lies with the militia.

Vladimov's recent work, published in the Russian journal *Znamia* in 1994, *General i ego armiia* [The General and His Army], is devoted to events of World War II. The main events take place in Ukraine, where the attacking Soviet Army is preparing to take Kiev (called Predslavl' in the novel). The work is based on fact and most of the characters have real prototypes; a few, like Nikita Khrushchev and Marshal Zhukov, are given their own names. The novel touches on some of the most sensitive points of the war period: the incompetent Soviet conduct of the war, the cruelty to troops in the name of prestigious victories, careerism and civil cowardice among the highest military ranks, the irreconcilable national conflict between Russians and Ukrainians. The basic plot of the book describes the fact that the Russian general Kobrisov (real name Chibisov) was not permitted, despite the clear advantage of his position, to liberate Predslavl (Kiev) which, for the sake of national glory, was given to the Ukrainian general Tereshchenko (Moskalenko). A very important part of the novel is concerned with the work of the military counter-intelligence organization, Smersh, which terrorized not the enemy but its own army. A separate strand of the plot deals with the contradictory and tragic story of General Vlasov's army. Vladimov was awarded the *Znamia* Prize for the best novel of 1994 and the Russian Booker Prize the following year.

Georgii Vladimov is a very important figure in post-war Russian literature. His masterly prose and exceptional civil courage and honesty have given him the reputation of a "knight" of Russian letters.

SVETLANA SHNITMAN-MCMILLIN

Three Minutes' Silence

Tri minuty molchaniia

Novel, 1969

Three Minutes' Silence was first published in *Novyi mir* in 1969. After the success of *The Great Ore* this was the second, and long-awaited work by Vladimov. The book's origin lies in a journey made by Vladimov as a sailor on fishing trawler, the "Vsadnik", in the North Atlantic.

The novel provoked accusations and criticism of both the author and the journal in which it was published. Those who wanted the editor of *Novyi mir*, Aleksandr Tvardovskii, to leave used the novel as an excuse for the journal to be crushed. Colourful headlines appeared in the newspapers: "In a crooked mirror", "The shallows and reefs of thought", "Are Murmansk sailors really like that?" and so on. Vladimov himself took this criticism lightly, saying that "the most interesting thing in all this nonsense were the titles of the articles." But severe consequences soon followed: book publication of the novel was held up for seven years. Paradoxically, it was only after the appearance in the west in 1975 of *Faithful Ruslan* that the authorities decided to allow Vladimov to reach a Soviet audience, finally permitting the book to be published by the publishing house Sovremennik, albeit with many censorial cuts. A full version of Vladimov's text was published in the west by Posev in 1982.

The action of the novel, which is set on a deep-sea fishing boat in the 1960s, begins in the port of Murmansk and continues at sea. Murmansk, the biggest fishing port in northern Russia, is a typical port: set amid the quiet charm of the northern landscape, it is a busy town full of restaurants, prostitutes, and speculators, with a high crime rate and *bichi*, namely homeless sailors who have taken to drink and gone to seed, living mainly on the generosity of other sailors and petty theft. The hero of the novel, Senia Shalai, becomes stuck in the port after performing his national service at sea. It is a familiar story. The north exerts a pull, and Senia is a homeless and lonely creature. Somewhere in the depths of Russia he has a mother and sister but he has left home and is no longer inclined to return. In the north, on the other hand, they pay a bonus for the unhealthy climate, and Senia's dream, from one voyage to the next, is to earn enough money to make a comfortable life for himself somewhere in the centre or south of Russia. But every time he decides to say farewell to the north he spends so much money on the farewell that he has to go on another voyage to earn enough for the move south. This time, however, the decision has been firmly taken and the money he has earned carefully hidden in an inside pocket. Senia bids farewell to the bay as he walks around the port that he has got to know so well. But suddenly the ubiquitous scourges appear in front of him, and little by little Senia is drawn into a familiar game. He is persuaded by the *bichi* to buy a fashionable Norwegian jacket of uncertain origin, the purchase has to be celebrated, and then events take their course: a visit to a restaurant, an evening binge, a drunken fight, an unsuccessful visit to his beloved, theft of the money, and a night at the police station. Having squandered and lost in one day all the financial reserves on which his hopes for the future depended, Senia sets out on another voyage.

This trip is to change Senia Shalai's inner world as well as his external circumstances. Having got into a critically dangerous situation, the captain of the trawler, thinking only of his career, and with typical Soviet arrogance, decides to continue sailing out to sea, as a result of which the boat comes within an ace of being lost. Only a miracle saves the sailors from drowning, and this brush with death makes Senia and his fellow-sailors understand afresh the value of life. The dramatic meeting with Norwegian sailors and the colourful description of life in a little fishing village of an unknown country were also a great novelty for readers of the novel behind the closed frontiers of the Soviet Union.

Senia's affair with Liliia, who works in a research institute, comes to an end without any particular event, words, thoughts or feelings. An unexpectedly sudden wave of love drives him to the waitress Klavka, a temperamental, forceful, experienced, and vivid beauty. And instead of the circle of a lonely, carefree existence, the novel ends with the beginning of a new stage in Senia's life: "I would have told you both how we spent our first day and what happened later, but that is the start of a whole new story ..."

The description of the sailors' life, the harsh conditions, bad equipment, absence of special clothing, are described by Vladimov in vivid language. The authenticity of the story is a result of the author's own experience and practical knowledge of his subject-matter. But, as Vladimov himself said, "... the trustful author took too literally the calls from the comrades in control for a realistic and comprehensive study of life". Instead of the familiar and noble picture of stern daily labour in the name of the

Land of the Soviets' radiant future, Vladimov painted a quite different scene: drunkenness, fecklessness, general bad organization, poverty, a joyless existence in which each tries to struggle with the most elementary aspects of life. Nor do the images of the women, the laundress Ninka and waitress Klavka, have anything in common with the pure Komsomol goddesses, the inspiration of sailors who had hitherto lived in the "sea stories" of Soviet writers. The figure of the "Grandfather", the mechanic Babilov, who had fought on the northern front and then been repressed "on suspicion of spying", was also new in Soviet literature. This man feels fatherly love for Senia and he serves as the moral core of the novel. His presence in the novel makes it clear that the people who sent him for trial (Stalin's lickspittles) are still in their high positions.

There was nothing explicitly "anti-Soviet" in Vladimov's *Three Minutes' Silence*. He merely described faithfully the life of people whom the ideologists of the Soviet state took such care to ignore. Thus it was that the book provoked such a storm of official criticism. It remains none the less one of the most vivid portrayals of life in the northern regions to have appeared in Russian literature since the World War II.

SVETLANA SHNITMAN-MCMILLIN

Faithful Ruslan

Vernyi Ruslan

Novella, 1975

Dogs have long played a role in Russian literature. Among the best-known examples are the dogs in Gogol''s "Zapiski sumasshedshego" ("Diary of a Madman"), Turgenev's "Mumu", Chekhov's "Kashtanka", and Bunin's "Sny Changa" ("The Dreams of Chang"). In the 20th century, after Bulgakov's satire on new Soviet man, *Sobach'e serdtse* (*The Heart of a Dog*), dogs entered the thick of politics. Vladimov's novella *Faithful Ruslan* is undoubtedly the peak of Soviet literature that features dogs. The book belongs to the genre of prison-camp writing that developed in Soviet literature after the Solzhenitsyn's *Odin den' Ivana Denisovicha* (*One Day in the Life of Ivan Denisovich*). Although, following the publication of Solzhenitsyn's novel, the genre virtually disappeared in official literature, and many works on Stalin's Terror circulated in *samizdat*, such as the works of Shalamov, Chukovskaia, Evgeniia Ginzburg, Nadezhda Mandel'shtam, and others. Written in the 1960s, *Faithful Ruslan* was banned from publication in the USSR for three decades. The first editions of it appeared in the west, and it was only in 1989 that this work was first published in Russia, producing an exceptionally strong reaction from the reading public, critics, and press alike.

Faithful Ruslan concerns the shock produced by the first perestroika (or the Thaw) when, following Stalin's death, the whole seemingly indestructible system of ideology and prison camps started to crack. Among the oral tales of the camps that began to circulate at that time, one in particular stood out: the story of trained guard dogs released into unfamiliar freedom as the camps were closed. Released because they were no longer needed for state service, these magnificent, degenerate beasts could find no place for themselves in "normal" life. This restructuring was too complicated for their mental powers: as both oppressors and victims, they were doomed to perish. Their fate forms the subject of Vladimov's novella.

One winter's morning Ruslan, an Alsatian guard dog, is led by his master, out into the snow as usual, but the beast is horrified to see that the zone is empty. For Ruslan the camp had been the embodiment of universal harmony, the "crown" of man's creation. In his eyes the collapse of this microcosmos assumes apocalyptic proportions: the barracks are black "with grief", the unoccupied watchtower is "blinded", the searchlight has "lost its mind". The post holding the barbed wire has been overturned and lies as if crucified "with arms thrown wide apart". Ruslan quickly thinks up his own version of what has happened: a mass breakout! Everyone has run away, masters and prisoners alike, and now Ruslan and his master have to find and bring back to this, the best of worlds, all the "stinking, struggling, crazy herd". Only gradually does the dog begin to sense that his master is not bringing him out into the sparkling morning snow to work. An order has been given to shoot the dogs. Something stirs in the terrible heart of the master, a man who has shot defenceless prisoners without thinking, but who is alarmed at the thought of this dog's blood as a hint of possible retribution. For the first time in his life he ignores an order and releases Ruslan and all his "comrades in service".

Apart from the camp, the only other place the dogs know is the railway station platform at the nearest village where new prisoners were delivered. As if by command, the dogs run there to meet the "fortunate" new arrivals and bring them to the prison-camp heaven in "happy, orderly columns". They wait, but the train does not come, and their masters no longer bring them food. Gradually the dogs wander off, each adapting to "civilian" life according to their individual resourcefulness, quick-wittedness, or bloody-mindedness. Of all the dogs, Ruslan finds adapting to life outside the camp the hardest. Solid in character and faithful by training, he has mastered the science of camp life as a just and happy gospel. And being unable to imagine life without service, he attaches himself to a former prisoner and begins to "look after" him. The shabby man, as this nameless character is called in the book, understands that the dog is "on guard", but, mentally exhausted by the camp, he accepts this terrible and absurd game. In this way the meta-world of the Gulag, which imprisons them both, fills the dog's existence with absurd pseudo-meaning.

Ruslan, however, continues to await real service, and finally a long-awaited train arrives at the station. A cellophane plant is to be built on the site of the camp, and a merry crowd of volunteer workers pours out of the coaches onto the platform. The camp guard dogs appear from all directions to form a convoy of this irresponsible crowd. But something strange has happened: none of the masters has come onto the platform to explain to the new arrivals "that any step to the side will be regarded as an attempt to escape and the guard will fire without warning". The ignorant Komsomol workers on the way to their new quarters eagerly head for a beer stall, whereupon a fierce battle breaks out between them and the guard dogs who are trying to keep them in columns. The description of this battle is among the most powerful and terrible passages of Russian prose. In the battle Ruslan is killed, his spine broken. He is killed because his universe, his meta-world of the Gulag has been destroyed. The guard dog has no place in civilian life.

The hero of the novella, faithful Ruslan, is an idealist, a knight of the prison-camp system, *canis sovieticus*. The work is written from a deliberately narrow "canine" point of view. The dog is a limited creature, by nature incapable of abstraction and analysis. And at the same time he is naively keen, full of the undying flame of life. The narrator relates events as seen through Ruslan's eyes. The shifts of style and perspective he makes when changing to "human" narration only underline the conditional nature of the "canine" view on the unfolding events. This conditional nature stresses the novel's main theme: murderous political manipulation and total distortion of values. As Vladimov has written of the dogs' life, "They had made an agreement with man that they had to love their master and defend him, even with their own life, but the idea of 'guarding two-legged sheep' was not there, but cunningly added later".

Ruslan the Alsatian guard dog is the involuntary oppressor and also victim of the monstrous system that gave rise to the prison camps. The story of the fate of this unhappy creature is one of the most powerful and revealing works about Stalinist totalitarianism.

SVETLANA SHNITMAN-MCMILLIN

A General and His Army

General i ego armiia

Novel, 1994

Vladimov began writing *General i ego armiia* (translated in part as *A General and His Army*) after ghost-writing the memoirs of leading Soviet generals about the conduct of World War II. The KGB soon took an interest, and his manuscripts were confiscated on a number of occasions. Persistent rumours were spread that he was writing a novel that would attempt to rehabilitate General Vlasov, commander of the Russian Liberation Army that fought on the German side against Stalin. Vladimov was expelled from the Soviet Union in 1983 for "anti-Soviet activities". In fact, he describes the main concern of his novel as being the phenomenon of large numbers of Russians, variously estimated at between 400,000 and two million, taking up arms against their motherland. Vlasov makes only a relatively peripheral appearance.

Vladimov is a skilled writer in the style of classical Russian realism and the influence of Tolstoi can be detected in the characters, from Major Donskoi, Kobrisov's adjutant, who tries unsuccessfully to model himself on Prince Andrei Bolkonskii, to the German tank commander Heinz Guderian who reads and re-reads *War and Peace*, trying to fathom the mentality of his Russian foe. The major theme of the novel is the relationship between the traditional Russian mentality and the despotism of Stalin and his secret police in the context of war. Khrushchev is present as a prominent Party representative on the Ukrainian front, and Brezhnev figures as a character so insignificant that no one can remember his name. The novel is densely written, with constant allusion to events past and future, and gives a completely original perspective on the Russian conduct of World War II as an ambiguous history of criminal brutality, incompetence, and heroism. At the same time, Vladimov concedes great shrewdness to Stalin in his understanding of the people over whom he ruled.

The novel is framed by the fictitious General Kobrisov's never accomplished return to GHQ, Moscow, after his recall from the Ukrainian front. (Kobrisov appears to be based on General Sevostianov). Travelling with him in his jeep are his driver Sirotin, his batman Shesterikov, and his aide Donskoi. The characters variously visualize how they will be received at GHQ, none of them realizing that this is in fact located deeper than Hitler's bunker at the Kirovskaia metro station in Moscow. The three occupants also have in common the fact that they have been questioned by Major Svetlookov of Smersh who, for reasons that seem logical to him at least, has been taking a close interest in the psychology of the commander of the 38th Army. The behaviour of Smersh forms a recurrent theme in the novel – the way the secret police inveigles Kobrisov's assistants into informing on him; its pernicious influence in the army and on the conduct of the war; the nature of the people who choose to join Smersh and their power over the military at every level. The naive driver Sirotin is a reluctant but ultimately easy prey. The batman Shesterikov, who once saved Kobrisov's life, gives nothing away but fails to warn his master of the fact of his having been approached. The ineffectual Major Donskoi finds Tolstoian morality no defence against the plebeian brutality of Smersh.

There is a flashback to the day when Kobrisov accidentally blunders into a village occupied by the Germans, is shot in the stomach, and is dragged to safety by Shesterikov. Shesterikov then has to find a way of getting the wounded general to hospital in Moscow, along a road full of demoralized Russian deserters who are heading into town ahead of the (in fact no less demoralized) Germans. His contact with Vlasov comes when the latter hijacks fresh Siberian troops intended to reinforce his own army, and drives the Germans back with them, breaking the encirclement of Moscow. Vlasov's disciplined troops enable the wounded general to be put on a sleigh back to the capital.

This same day Heinz Guderian, commander of the tank army moving on Moscow from the south, finds himself humiliatingly stranded when his tank falls into a shallow ravine. Hitler's decision to divert the *blitzkrieg* towards Kiev (captured) and Leningrad (unsuccessfully besieged) delays the advance on Moscow until the cold of winter wreaks havoc on the ill-equipped troops. Finally returning to his headquarters at Tolstoi's estate of Iasnaia Poliana, Guderian writes out the order for German troops to retreat from Moscow for the winter.

The next flashback is to the autumn of 1943 when Kobrisov, who has now formed the 38th Army, has established a bridgehead on the right bank of the River Dnieper in the Ukraine. He finds himself outmanoeuvred at a war council chaired by Marshal Zhukov, where it is decided that a Ukrainian general should liberate the first major Ukrainian city to be recaptured, Predslavl. Unlike Zhukov or his fellow generals, he has an acute awareness of the value of human lives and cannot reconcile himself to the "four-layer theory" of Russian warfare, whereby three armies pave the way for a fourth to advance over their corpses. (Zhukov was to sacrifice 300,000 Russian lives in the attempt to get to Berlin by May Day 1945 and without the aid of Eisenhower.)

In order to delay Kobrisov's advance on Predslavl he is instructed to encircle and capture Myriatin, a town he has left alone because he knows most of its defenders to be Russians fighting against Stalin. He fails to present a plan of campaign to his superior and is sent back to Moscow to "recuperate". Just as he reaches the capital the radio broadcasts news of the fall of Myriatin to the 38th Army and of the decoration of Kobrisov and his promotion to Lieutenant General. He gets very drunk as he looks down on Moscow, and recalls how, just before the outbreak of war, he was arrested by the GPU on a charge of attempting to assassinate Stalin (two of his tanks had broken down in front of the Mausoleum during the November parade), but was saved by the outbreak of war. He imagines the mass executions that Smersh will now be instigating in Myriatin. The mistake in decorating him as commander of the 38th Army (or has Stalin deliberately disregarded the decision to send him away?) allows him now to turn away from Moscow and return to the front to fight on.

ARCH TAIT

Vladimir Nikolaevich Voinovich 1932–

Prose writer

Biography

Born in Dushanbe, Tadzhikistan, 26 September 1932. Attended Moscow Pedagogical Institute, 1957–59. Served in the Soviet Army, 1951–55. Married: 1) Valentina in 1957, one daughter and one son; 2) Irina Braude in 1965, one daughter. Worked as a herdsman, factory hand, locksmith, construction and railroad worker, carpenter, aircraft mechanic, and director of radio programmes. Freelance writer in Moscow, from 1956. Expelled from the Writers' Union, 1974. Emigrated to West Germany, 1980; deprived of Soviet citizenship, 1981. Taught Russian literature, Princeton University, 1982–83; Soviet citizenship restored, 1990. Lives in both Munich and Moscow.

Publications

Collected Editions

Povesti [Novellas]. Moscow, 1972.

Putem vzaimnoi perepiski [By Means of Mutual Correspondence]. Paris, YMCA-Press, 1979.

In Plain Russian: Stories, translated by Richard Lourie. New York, Farrar Straus and Giroux, 1979; London, Jonathan Cape, 1980.

Maloe sobranie sochinenii, 5 vols. Moscow, 1993–95.

Fiction

"My zdes' zhivem" [We Live Here], *Novyi mir*, 1 (1961).

"Khochu byt' chestnym: Povesti", *Novyi mir*, 2 (1963); as separate edition, Moscow, 1989; translated as "I'd Be Honest if They'd Let Me", by Andrew R. MacAndrew, in *Four Soviet Masterpieces*, Toronto, Bantam, 1963.

"Dva tovarishcha" [Two Comrades], *Novyi mir*, 1 (1967).

"Vladychitsa" [The Sovereign], *Nauka i religiia*, 4–5 (1969).

Zhizn' i neobychainye prikliucheniia soldata Ivana Chonkina. Part 1 published in *Grani*, 72 (1969); parts 1 and 2 published Paris, YMCA-Press, 1975; translated as *The Life and Extraordinary Adventures of Private Ivan Chonkin*, by Richard Lourie, New York, Farrar Straus and Giroux, and London, Jonathan Cape, 1977; Harmondsworth, Penguin, 1978; reprinted Evanston, Illinois, Northwestern University Press, 1995.

Stepen' doveriia [A Degree of Trust]. Moscow, 1972.

"Putem vzaimnoi perepiski" [By Means of Mutual Correspondence], *Grani*, 87–88 (1973); edited by Robert Porter, London, Bristol Classical Press, 1996; translated as "From an Exchange of Letters", by Richard Lourie, in *In Plain Russian*, 1979.

Pretendent na prestol: Novye prikliucheniia soldata Ivana Chonkina. Paris, YMCA-Press, 1979; translated as *Pretender to the Throne: The Further Adventures of Private Ivan Chonkin*, by Richard Lourie, New York, Farrar Straus and Giroux, and London, Jonathan Cape, 1981; reprinted Evanston, Illinois, Northwestern University Press, 1995.

Moskva 2042. Ann Arbor, Ardis, 1986; translated as *Moscow 2042*, by Richard Lourie, San Diego, Harcourt Brace, 1987; London, Picador, 1989.

"Skazka o glupom Galilee" [The Tale of Stupid Galileo], *Strana i mir*, 3 (1988).

Shapka. London, Overseas Publications Interchange, 1988; translated as *The Fur Hat*, by Susan Brownsberger, San Diego, Harcourt Brace, 1989; London, Jonathan Cape, 1990.

Skazki dlia vzroslykh [Fairy Tales for Grown-Ups]. Moscow, 1996.

Plays

"Fiktivnii brak" [Fictitious Wedding], *Vremia i my*, 72 (1983).

Tribunal: Sudebnaia komediia v trekh deistviiakh. London, Overseas Publications Interchange, 1985.

Essays and Autobiographical Writing

"Proisshestvie v 'Metropole'" [Incident in the Metropol], *Kontinent*, 5 (1975).

Ivan'kiada: Ili rasskaz o vselenii pisatelia Voinovicha v novuiu kvartiru. Ann Arbor, Ardis, 1976; translated as *The Ivankiad: The Tale of the Writer Voinovich's Installation in His New Apartment*, by David Lapeza, New York, Farrar Straus and Giroux, 1977; London, Jonathan Cape, 1978; Harmondsworth, Penguin, 1979.

Antisovetskii sovetskii soiuz. Ann Arbor, Ardis, 1985; translated as *The Anti-Soviet Soviet Union*, by Richard Lourie, San Diego, Harcourt Brace, 1986.

Nulevoe reshenie [Zero Decision]. Moscow, 1990.

"Delo no. 34840" [File No. 34840], *Znamia*, 12 (1993).

"Zamysel" [The Design], *Znamia*, 10–11 (1994); Moscow, 1996.

Critical Studies

Beyond Socialist Realism: Soviet Fiction since "Ivan

Denisovich", by Geoffrey Hosking, London, Granada, and New York, Holmes and Meier, 1980.
"Vladimir Voinovich and the Comedy of Innocence", by Robert Porter, *Forum for Modern Language Studies* (April 1980).
"Vladimir Voynovich and the Rules of the Game", by Neil Cornwell, *Essays in Poetics*, 7/1 (1982), 84–100.
"Vladimir Voinovich's *Pretender to the Throne*", by John B. Dunlop, in *Literature and American Critics: In Honor of Deming B. Brown*, edited by Kenneth N. Brostrom, Ann Arbor, University of Michigan Press, 1984.
Images of Dictatorship: Portraits of Stalin in Literature, by Rosalind Marsh, London and New York, Routledge, 1989.
"Vladimir Voynovich: The Joker", by Robert Porter, in his *Four Contemporary Russian Writers*, Oxford, Berg, 1989.
"From Incompetence to Satire: Voinovich's Image of Stalin as Castrated Leader of the Soviet Union in 1941", by Daniel Rancour-Laferrière, *Slavic Review*, 50 (1991), 36–47.
Russkaia antiutopiia XX veka, by B.A. Lanin and M.M. Borizhanskaia, Moscow, 1994.
"Voinovich's *Moskva 2042* as Literary Parody", by Karen L. Ryan-Hayes, *Russian Literature*, 36 (1994), 453–80.
"Castratory Imagery in Voinovich's *Moscow 2042*", by Daniel Rancour-Laferrière, *Russian Language Journal*, 49/162–64 (1995), 193–204.
Contemporary Russian Satire: A Genre Study, by Karen L. Ryan-Hayes, Cambridge, Cambridge University Press, 1995.

Vladimir Nikolaevich Voinovich first came to public attention in 1960 by writing the song that later became the unofficial hymn of the Soviet cosmonauts, and which was sung by Khrushchev himself from the mausoleum platform. His next contribution to Soviet literature was "My zdes' zhivem" [We Live Here], a story about a naive young Muscovite writer visiting the virgin lands, published in the first volume of *Novyi mir* in 1961, but it was criticized for failing to uphold the spirit of socialist realism.

In 1962 Voinovich wrote the story that he later called his personal manifesto, the wryly optimistic "Khochu byt' chestnym" ("I'd Be Honest if They'd Let Me"), in which the theme of conflict between the individual's integrity and the expectations of the group is highlighted. This work was criticized for its "unheroic" hero, as was the play based on the book, and a film script was later abandoned.

In 1963 *Novyi mir* announced but did not actually publish the first instalment of Voinovich's masterpiece, *Zhizn' i neobychainye prikliucheniia soldata Ivana Chonkina* (*The Life and Extraordinary Adventures of Private Ivan Chonkin*), on which he was to work from 1963 to 1970. In this satirical novel the eponymous hero, styled on the Russian folk character Ivan-the-fool, innocently brings chaos to World War II simply by being himself in a world distorted by the rules of the totalitarian game.

The year 1967 saw the publication of *Dva tovarishcha* [Two Comrades] and the performance of a play of the same name, an urban tale of youthful friendship, betrayal and self-deceit that was attacked for its uninspiringly ordinary hero. In the same year *Chonkin* was published abroad without the author's permission in the émigré journal *Grani*, which compounded the difficulties he experienced as a result of supporting the dissidents, Siniavskii and Daniel' in 1966 and Ginsburg and Galanskov in 1968. Voinovich's plays were suspended and his writing became more satirical, including works unpublishable at the time, such as *Putem vzaimnoi perepiski* (*From an Exchange of Letters*), a horrific moral tale set in an anti-romantic countryside, in which the unlucky hero falls foul of the power of his own words.

In 1969, the allegory *Vladychitsa* [The Sovereign] appeared, developing the theme of personal responsibility within the State, concluding that the people generally get the rulers they deserve. This theme features increasingly in Voinovich's work, thrown into relief by the alienated figure of the fictional or actual writer. In 1969 and 1970 the first two parts of *Chonkin* were published in Paris, this time with Voinovich's knowledge, leading to further conflict with the Writers' Union, as did his protests in support of Solzhenitsyn in 1969.

In 1972 Voinovich published *Stepen' doveriia* [A Degree of Trust], a novel about the revolutionary Vera Figner. While this went some way towards placating the literary establishment, at the same time he was working on the continuation of the Chonkin story, *Pretendent na prestol: Novye prikliucheniia soldata Ivana Chonkina* (*Pretender to the Throne: The Further Adventures of Private Ivan Chonkin*). In 1974 Voinovich was expelled from the Writers' Union, but continued to write, publishing "Proisshestvie v 'Metropole'" ("Incident at the Metropol") in an émigré journal in 1975. This documents, immediately after the event, the KGB's alleged attempt to poison him with doctored cigarettes. This was followed by publication in the US in 1976 of the epic story of Voinovich's battle for his rightful apartment, *Ivan'kiada: Ili rasskaz o vselenii pisatelia Voinovicha v novuiu kvartiru* (*The Ivankiad: The Tale of the Writer Voinovich's Installation in His New Apartment*).

In 1979 *Pretender to the Throne* was published in Paris, and in 1980 Voinovich voiced an appeal on behalf of Sakharov. On 21 December 1980, after threats of internal exile or imprisonment, Voinovich and his family left the Soviet Union for Munich.

His first major work in emigration was *Antisovietskii sovietskii soiuz* (*The Anti-Soviet Soviet Union*), a collection of essays broadcast on Radio Liberty recounting the absurdities of Soviet life. Voinovich continued to write exclusively in Russian for a Russian readership, so the problem of his dislocation from contemporary Russian life soon became acute, and he turned next to science fiction in *Moskva 2042* (*Moscow 2042*). In this novel he sends his hero, an exiled Russian writer, to Moscow 60 years in the future, warning that the trends of the present will be extrapolated into the future unless the warnings of the past are heeded. Another solution to the problem of topical accuracy was to write allegories, the most notable being "Skazka o glupom Galilee" [The Tale of Stupid Galileo], written in 1988 and based on the life of the astronomer Galileo, who was unwise enough to publicly announce that the world was not flat at a time when this counts as heresy. Everyone else knows him to be right, but no one else is foolish enough to attract the attention of the ideologues, waiting instead for the earth to turn on its axis until the "right time" comes round. Galileo in old age counts the cost of his honesty, much as Voinovich in emigration must have counted the cost of his chronological, as well as ideological and geographical exiles.

Voinovich first revisited Moscow in 1989, and since having his citizenship restored in 1990 has spent an increasing proportion of each year there. In the new market economy, with stiff competition from imported pulp fiction, Voinovich has demonstrated his versatility by writing social and political journalism and a soap opera, as well as a review of his KGB files relating to the *Metropol'* incident, and being involved in the production of a film of *Chonkin*. His main work, however, published in 1994 after a long period of incubation, is the retrospective and unsatirical *Zamysel* [The Design], intended to be a blend of *Chonkin* and his own autobiography, cemented by the theme that it is the task of every individual to understand the grand design for his life that lies within him. For Voinovich this *zamysel* has been the imperative to write, and the question arises as to what will become of the satirist in a commercial world with no more taboos to break nor static targets at which to shoot.

RACHEL S. FARMER

The Life and Extraordinary Adventures of Private Ivan Chonkin

Zhizn' i neobychainye prikliucheniia soldata Ivana Chonkina

Novel, 1975 (written 1963–70)

The first part of a planned trilogy, this novel is regarded by many as Voinovich's masterpiece, a richly comic satire on army life, false science, propaganda, corruption, innumerable other human foibles, and, above all, the inane absurdity of official thinking in a monolithic communist state. Written in the period 1963–70, widely circulated in *samizdat*, and first published abroad, the novel was one of the principal causes of its author's expulsion from the Soviet Union in 1980.

Described as a novel-anecdote, *The Life and Extraordinary Adventures of Private Ivan Chonkin* describes the experiences of a latter-day Ivan Durachok, the holy fool of Russian folklore, who, on the eve of the German invasion of Russia, is sent to guard a plane that has crash-landed. Easily the most dispensible member of his unit, he is forgotten by the army, and settles down to village life, living happily for a while with the only slightly less simple village postmistress. Those who are in positions of power, such as the collective farm chairman, suspect him of being a secret investigator (there are several deliberate echoes of Gogol' in the novel), but it is the absurd rumour that Chonkin is leading a diversionary anti-Soviet gang that brings special troops to dislodge him. They are, however, repulsed, for Chonkin is endowed with a clear conscience and doubt-free common sense as well as a capacity for strenuous effort, all of which qualities are notably absent in his would-be captors, as indeed among most of the village people of Krasnoe (Red) (formerly Griaznoe – Dirty). Chonkin is eventually captured, and his subsequent fate forms the subject of the novel's sequel.

Ivan Chonkin is not only a physically comic figure (bow-legged and with protruding ears – all the admirable heroes had already been snatched up by other writers, Voinovich tells us apologetically in the opening pages) – but he is also one of Russian literature's great positive heroes. Indeed, like the admirably resolute men of socialist realism with whom he is ironically compared, he wins the love of his woman, cultivates the land successfully, and overcomes greatly superior forces – the fact that they are Soviet rather than German is irrelevant to the anecdote. The catalyst for most of the comedy in this novel is Chonkin's naivety or innocence: if society is deeply absurd, then a completely honest, innocent nature, taking everything at face value, is an ideal medium for revealing this absurdity with maximum clarity. Ivan Chonkin, simply by being who he is, highlights the fantastic edifice of Soviet newspeak and propaganda in all its grotesqueness; totally oblivious to the rules of the game being played by almost everyone else, he wins hands down. In this he differs from the good soldier Švejk to whom he has sometimes been compared, for if the latter pretended to be simple in order to undermine a ridiculous and corrupt system, Chonkin unconsciously achieves the same effect by an unfeigned simplicity that carries him virtually unscathed through the hazards of cynical Soviet chicanery and bureaucracy.

The novel is written in a very readable, light style, as befits a humorous anecdote, with numerous asides, extended (sometimes almost autonomous) metaphors, dreams, magic, cameo portraits, and farcical episodes bound together by a strong story-line throughout. The characters of this fast-moving narrative have been described as cartoon figures, and indeed many are little more, although few are exaggerated or caricatured. Chonkin and Niura, however, go well beyond the inhuman masks of cartoons, Niura achieving pathos by her loyalty and her intimacy with the natural, particularly animal, world, Ivan by his sterling values, revealed only when he gets away from the alien and artificial atmosphere of army indoctrination into the simpler world of tilling the land and other physical tasks. But it is the episodes and anecdotes with their myriad minor figures, as much as the heroes and central action, that make this a hugely entertaining novel. The text is studded with many gems, such as, for example, the bullying police-chief Miliaga (Captain Nice – comic names abound) who, under interrogation himself, thinks he is dealing with the invading Germans, declaring "Ich bin arbeiten in Russisch Gestapo" and "Ich liebe Genosse Hitler", "Heil Hitler! Stalin kaput!"; the pathetic but fierce jealousy of Ivan (who had himself wooed Niura almost silently, like an animal) towards his beloved's pet pig Borka (an affair between them had been rumoured by malicious villagers); the Jew who escapes routine persecution (from the Soviet side) by virtue of his name being Stalin, and so on. This immensely fecund book abounds in such characters and situations, as if Voinovich was for the first time able to relate in print his accumulated stock of funny stories, and to give free rein to a host of richly comic images and portraits.

Chonkin's friend, the pretentious village wise man Gladyshev, is one of the book's most memorable creations, an enthusiast for popular science, he lords it over the other villagers, and indulges in various bogus experiments, such as crossing a potato with a tomato (grandly entitled "puks", an acronym of "the path to socialism", but also a childish word for "fart"), or making alcohol from all manner of excrement, to the despair of his wife, who especially resents having her peasant name replaced by Aphrodite when her house is full of stinking jars and bottles. In a sense Gladyshev (who is the first to report his friend to the authorities) represents the falsity of Stalinist society at least as much as the editor or collective farm chairman for whom deception is a long-established way of life.

Voinovich is notable as a comic writer for being able to combine serious satirical targets with a rich vein of broad but not vulgar humour. For many, though not all, readers this makes him a natural heir to Gogol', and contributes to the status of *The Life and Extraordinary Adventures of Private Ivan Chonkin* as one of the great comic novels of the 20th century.

ARNOLD MCMILLIN

Pretender to the Throne

Pretendent na prestol

Novel, 1979

Pretender to the Throne, the second part of a projected trilogy, follows on from where *The Life and Extraordinary Adventures of Private Ivan Chonkin* leaves off. In a Russian edition of 1990, however, it is presented as the second part of *Chonkin* under the same title, with what was previously known as *Chonkin* now titled "Neprikosnovennoe litso" [An Inviolable Person]. First published in 1979, *Pretender to the Throne* is quite different from the earlier work, with the focus less directly on Chonkin and Niura, no strong plot line, and the atmosphere decidedly less comic. Having absolutely no hope of publishing it in the Soviet Union, Voinovich here writes with a fierce and open satire that centres on the image of Stalin's Russia as a Dantesque hell, and of its official characters as innately and irredeemably two-faced. The influence of Gogol' is still to be felt, but the tone of *Pretender to the Throne* is also reminiscent of Orwell and Kafka. There are many comic moments, but Voinovich also presents a very serious message about the workings of a totalitarian society.

The novel begins with an absurd official correspondence about a soap allowance for Ivan Chonkin who has been imprisoned as a dangerous element. Both the Soviets and the Germans take a strong interest in him, and this gives Voinovich the chance to highlight many similarities between communist and fascist thinking. For Hitler, Chonkin is a blond Aryan aristocrat; for Stalin, he is the peasant embodiment of Soviet achievements. In the course of the novel naive country lad Vania Chonkin is transformed by turn into so-called Chonkin, White-Guardist Chonkin, Chonkin-Golitsyn, and Golitsyn-Chonkin, finally by a stroke of NKVD chief Beria's pen, turning into simply Prince Golitsyn, scion of one of Russia's most noble families and pretender to the throne. The mystery of Chonkin's identity brings the German and Soviet forces to his village of Krasnoe, but at the end of the novel the chaos of war allows him to escape execution and to disappear into the forests of Russia, whence, no doubt, Voinovich intended to – and may yet – return him for the third part of the trilogy.

A major role in *Pretender to the Throne* is taken by the interrogators of the security services. Niura makes brave attempts to secure her beloved's release, and much humour is derived from her simple incomprehension of the interrogators' thinking: when asked by Evpraksein what Chonkin has been arrested for, she says, with accuracy, "For nothing"; to an ironic enquiry whether there is Soviet power in Krasnoe, she replies in the negative, on the grounds that the village soviet is in another village over the river. Like Chonkin's victorious simplicity earlier, so her genuine failure to understand the newspeak and twisted thought of Stalinism floors prosecutor Evpraksein. The latter, unlike some of his colleagues, is endowed with a conscience, which makes him both funny and pathetic: drunk, he repents of his cruelty, but on sobering up resumes his role as a ruthless pursuer of enemies of the State. Conscience seems to be the beginning of the end for Stalinist *apparatchiks* (member of Party or governmental machine), including Evpraksein, but even his suicide is tragi-comic. The book's overall impression, however, is less of individuals than of a total system of absurdity and evil, comparable to that chronicled by Solzhenitsyn (whose *V kruge pervom* [*First Circle*], incidentally, is gently parodied in *Pretender to the Throne*).

The endless hellish corridors of Soviet establishments that Niura paces with a crowd of other petitioners are "illuminated by a constant twilight, always raw and cold", and the figures of authority she meets come to seem all the same to her, "like Chinese". The chasm between the authorities and the people is constantly underlined in this work: District Party Secretary Revkin, for instance, meets an old woman with a huge sack of peas on her back, trudging towards town, in order to help her starving family; having ascertained this, and marvelling at the self-sacrifice of the Russian people, Revkin gets back in his limousine and drives on. At a lower level, Niura's boss, sacking her for her liaison with Chonkin, looks at the wall, with the words "As a woman I sympathize with you, but as a communist I cannot tolerate [such behaviour]".

Much of the satire is set in the remote district town of Dolgov and directed against those members of the creative intelligentsia who cravenly support this grotesque system, not least the civic poet Serafim Butylko and editor Boris Ermolkin. The latter's newspaper *Bolshevik Tempos* causes consternation with an article suggesting that the teaching of Marx, Engels, Lenin, and Stalin will eventually lead to the emergence of long-skulled rather than round-skulled people; assuming a coup by a long-skulled leader to be imminent, the intelligentsia frantically search for ways of artificially lengthening their skulls. Ermolkin, who has built his career on the printing of lies, comes to grief by overlooking a misprint that makes Stalin into a gelding (*merin*) rather than a yardstick (*merilo*) for Soviet society. Another parodic gem is Butylko's absurd panegyric epitaph to the late Captain Miliaga, which is made still more grotesque by Party advice that it be "more optimistic" and "more in a major key". Intellectuals are a particular target of Voinovich's satire, and the special language that maintains the gross edifice of Stalinism is ridiculed extensively.

Nodding off during the prosecutor's speech at his trial, Chonkin sees Niura in the form of mischievous mermaid who asks whether he knows any devilish words. Having confessed that he does not, he is overjoyed when Niura recites, "Communism, capitalism, fascism, idealism, cataclysm", and wakes up shouting the demonic "Clism, clism", only to hear the prosecutor asking that he be sentenced to "the highest measure of proletarian humaneness", that is, to execution. Newspeak is everywhere. In prison Chonkin meets a former aristocrat who has learned to speak "their way" (Voinovich quotes some characteristic distortions) and made a political career, but who incautiously quotes a few Latin phrases at a Party banquet and is promptly arrested as a Latin spy. NKVD Major Figurin keeps for posterity a notebook of aphorisms such as "The arrest of the accused is sufficient and exhaustive proof of his guilt" and "The Soviet regime is objectively so good that anyone who does not like it in full or in part is insane".

The cruel and artificial Stalinist apparatus is contrasted with the simple, animal-like Ivan and Niura who, against such a background, become heroic figures, holding out some hope for the future. Voinovich in *Pretender to the Throne* is far less genially comic than in *Chonkin*, but here he has achieved a new thematic profundity.

ARNOLD MCMILLIN

Moscow 2042

Moskva 2042

Novel, 1986

Moscow 2042 was Voinovich's first novel to be written entirely in the west, and it was also his first venture into the future, but his keen satirical eye and unfailing sense of the absurd are no less evident in a dystopian environment than in the utterly Soviet settings of the *Chonkin* novel(s). Begun in 1982 and first published in 1986, it was quickly followed by the first Gorbachev-induced cracks in the Soviet edifice, but only at one level has the book been overtaken by events, for the main objects of its satire include political ambition, religious fanaticism, the psychology of dissidence and emigration, western materialism, and many other universal targets, in addition to specifically Soviet absurdities. It is an inventive and witty comic romp that should certainly be read and savoured long after 2042.

The first-person narrator of *Moscow 2042*, Vasilii Kartsev is also an expatriate writer living, by chance, in exactly the same German village in which Voinovich settled after leaving Russia. At the start of the novel Kartsev learns that Lufthansa are offering clandestine time travel and, funded by a New York newspaper, sets off to report back on what he finds in his native country 60 years hence. An additional task is to transport from Canada 36 suppressed volumes by megalomaniac Sim Simych Karnavalov (the delightfully inappropriate name of a Solzhenitsyn look-alike), leader of a pious group of right-wing tsarist dissidents, to whom Kartsev makes a hilariously uncomfortable visit before setting off for the future.

Voinovich's narrator is intermittently scathing about science fiction as a literary genre, and the physical aspects of his flight into the future are not for the literal-minded. More brain-teasing complications follow quickly. In the city state of Moscow, where communists still hang on to power, he is handed a copy of his own novel, *Moscow 2042* (not to be written, of course, until his return to Germany in 1986). The new-style communists of the next century, however, are already familiar with its contents; he is lionized as a classic of Preliminary Literature, that is, literature written before the Great August Revolution when the Genialissimo began building communism in One City. The authorities are particularly concerned about its prophecy of the triumphal return to Russia of the fanatical Sim Simych in the guise of Tsar Serafim the First. Here Voinovich's premise gains a new dimension, as Kartsev is badgered to cancel Karnavalov from history by cutting him out of his book, thus reducing himself to the moral level of those who for decades distorted Russian history and art to prop up Marxism, the very thing against which his original dissidence had been directed. Kartsev moreover is not sure whether it was for refusing to tinker with precisely this book that he was labelled a dissident in the first place. The dizzying circles of meaning continue indefinitely.

Kartsev is successful in preserving the odiously self-important Sim Simych in his novel, and the latter is soon installed in the Kremlin, where he sets about establishing a fundamentalist anti-communist regime which, however, seems unlikely to reduce the misery of ordinary Russians. The narrator is given a second audience, parallelling his earlier unfriendly reception in Karnavalov's Canadian fortress.

Within this overall structure the book is divided into short episodic sections, sometimes anecdotes or cameos, each with its own heading, and progress is, indeed, episodic, as Kartsev encounters the curiously familiar new world. Technology now allows Moscow citizens to lie on their backs and watch "Dallas", but they receive little joy from the various "rings of hostility" that surround the city state. The main export to these rings appears to be excrement, known as "secondary matter", and Kartsev is led to some postmodernist reflections on the nature of art and reality. (Which comes first in the process of consumption and creation?) Ramifications of this are explored through the city state's food distribution system: in 2042 Muscovites have to exchange their waste products for tokens entitling them to receive food, encouraged by a poster of a sinewy worker confidently brandishing a large pot, with the sub-Maiakovskian jingle, "Everyone who hands in secondary matter / Will feast on primary, served on a platter".

The narrator, though acclaimed as a great Russian writer, is a very likeable, sensual fellow, relishing sex, vodka and, particularly, the absurdities of life in the future. Some things, however, do not seem to have changed much, beginning with the flight to the future, where Kartsev finds himself sitting next to an idealistic asylum-seeking terrorist (who is promptly tortured by the regime when he arrives), the supply of miniatures of spirits on the plane is limited by the slowness of the serving staff, and so on. In Moscow, 60 years on, the portmanteau words and acronyms so beloved of communists have proliferated even further: the ruling Party is now known as the KPGB (Communist Party of the State Security); *pukomrasy* (strongly resonant of *mrakobesy* – obscurantists) which are points of communal distribution in accordance with service to the collective – a direct descendent of the much-resented Soviet *raspredeliteli* or closed retail establishments. Word play and macaronic invention are relished (not least in the Canadian sections), as are some of the less arduous conundrums such as, for example, Kartsev's disingenuous protestations that Sim Simych was only the creation of his novelist's imagination: Voinovich's picture of the future tsar, predictably, provoked annoyance among some émigrés who saw in it a caricature of their revered moral leader. It seems to be the fate of this jocular, ebullient author to upset both Soviet and émigré sensibilities.

Voinovich's dystopian satire may also be read as a satire on the genre itself, as well as on science fiction. He certainly raises major political and moral issues, not least that of the ability of totalitarian states to rewrite their own history and future, but does so in an eminently readable whirlwind of comic narration. Writing at a time of fierce debate on the negative effects of emigration on literature, Voinovich has given a clear personal answer with his felicitous combination of imagination and humour. *Moscow 2042* occupies an important and unique place both within its genre and in this writer's *oeuvre* as a whole.

ARNOLD MCMILLIN

Maksimilian Aleksandrovich Voloshin 1877–1932

Poet

Biography

Born Maksimilian Aleksandrovich Kir'enko-Voloshin in Kiev, 28 May 1877, into an aristocratic family, descendants of Cossacks and russified Germans. Father was a lawyer. Attended schools in Moscow and Theodosiia, Crimea; graduated in 1897; studied law at Moscow University: expelled in 1899. Spent a year in Germany, also visited France, Italy, and Switzerland. Lived in Paris, occasionally spent time in the Crimea, St Petersburg, and Moscow, 1901–16. Joined the Parisian Society of Russian Artists. Prominent Symbolist poet, critic, and translator of French poetry. Married: 1) the artist Margarita Vasil'evna Sabashnikova in 1906 (separated 1907); 2) Mar'ia Zabolotskaia in 1927. Settled in Koktebel, Crimea, 1917. Lectured extensively on art, drama, and poetry during the 1920s. Member of the Crimean History Society, from 1927. Died from pneumonia in Koktebel, 11 August 1932.

Publications

Collected Editions

Stikhotvoreniia. Leningrad, 1977.

Stikhotvoreniia i poemy, 2 vols. Paris, YMCA-Press, 1982–84.

Stikhotvoreniia. Stat'i. Vospominaniia sovremennikov. Moscow, 1991.

Poetry

Stikhotvoreniia: 1900–10. Moscow, 1910.

Anno mundi ardentis. 1915. Moscow, 1916.

Iverni. Moscow, 1918.

Demony glukhonemye [Deaf-Mute Demons]. Kharkov, 1919; 2nd edition Berlin, 1923; reprinted London, Flegon Press, 1965.

Stikhi o terrore [Poems on the Terror]. Berlin, 1923.

Fiction

"Rasskaz o Cherubine de Gabriak" [Story about Cherubina de Gabriak], in *Pamiatniki kul'tury: Novye otkrytiia*. Moscow, 1989, 41–61.

Autobiography, Memoirs, and Essays

Liki tvorchestva [Masks of Creativity]. Book 1, St Petersburg, 1914; edited by V.A. Manuilov *et al*. Leningrad, 1988.

Putnik po vselennym [Traveller of the Universe] (autobiographical prose, memoirs, essays; most previously unpublished), with an introduction and notes by V. Kupchenko and Z. Davydova. Moscow, 1990.

Critical Studies

Pisatel'skaia sud'ba Maksimiliana Voloshina, by E. Lann, Moscow, 1927.

"Zhivoe o zhivom", by Marina Tsvetaeva, in her *Proza*, New York, Izdatel'stvo imeni Chekhova, 1953.

Die grüne Schlange, by Margarita Woloschin, Stuttgart, 1954; translated into Russian by M.N. Zhemchuzhnikova, Moscow, 1993.

Sud'ba poeta, Lichnost' i poeziia M. Voloshina, by I.T. Kupriianov, Kiev, 1978.

Maksimilian Voloshin als Künstler und Kritiker, by Claudia Wallrafen, Munich, Sagner, 1982.

M.A. Voloshin: Artist-Poet. A Study of the Synaesthetic Aspects of His Poetry, by Cynthia Marsh, Birmingham, Birmingham Slavonic Monographs, No. 14, 1983.

Vospominaniia o M. Voloshine, Moscow, 1990.

Stranstvie Maksimiliana Voloshina: Dokumental'noe povestvovanie, by V.P. Kupchenko, St Petersburg, 1996.

Maksimilian Voloshin was a poet, an artist, and an art critic. He studied in several gymnasiums in Moscow and in Theodosiia, completing his studies in 1897. Voloshin started to write poetry at the age of 12; and his talent as a painter was spotted by Aivazovskii, a famous seascape artist who often visited the gymnasium in Theodosiia. Despite his artistic inclinations Voloshin went to Moscow University to study law, but he attended additional lectures at the philological department (especially those given by Veselovskii and Fortunatov). In February 1899 Voloshin was expelled from the University for attending revolutionary demonstrations; as a result he was not allowed to live in Moscow for one year. In September 1899 he went abroad. He attended some lectures at the University of Berlin, and in Paris he translated Heinrich Heine's *Deutschland: Ein Wintermärchen* (*Germany: A Winter's Tale*). In May 1900 he published his first review, in which he criticized Bal'mont's translations of Gerhart Hauptmann. In the same year he passed his second-year exams at the University of Moscow, then travelled to Germany, Italy, and Switzerland. On his return to Russia he was arrested for declarations and a politically dangerous poem, "Predvestiia" [Prediction], and spent a short time in prison; he was banned from continuing his studies at the University. In September 1900 he went to Tashkent, where he managed to publish essays and articles on travel and art, as well as his own translations.

From Spring 1901 until 1916 Voloshin spent most of his time in Paris, where he became a secretary of the Montparnasse society of Russian artists. In 1910 he published his first substantial collection of verse, *Stikhotvoreniia: 1900–10* [Poems: 1900–10], which was very well reviewed by Briusov. This volume, in particular the cycle "Parizh" [Paris] and the poem "Ruanskii sobor" [Rouen Cathedral], reflect Voloshin's interest in French poetry and history. Most of the poems in this book are written in the impressionist manner, and were praised by Russian Symbolists as truly Decadent. The period of 1903–07 was marked by Voloshin's infatuation with Margarita Vasil'evna Sabashnikova (1882–1973), a Symbolist poet, painter, and theosophist. Her influence on Voloshin's outlook was immense; she introduced him to Rudolf Steiner, for example. They were married in 1906, but soon after, in May 1907, they separated. (Her memoirs provide a good insight into Voloshin's personality). In November 1909 Voloshin and a young poet, E. Dmitrieva, played a practical joke on Makovskii, editor of *Apollon*. They created a non-existent Catholic girl, Cherubina de

Gabriak, who was allegedly madly in love with Makovskii, according to her numerous letters to him, and whose poems were published in the second issue of this prestigious journal. The hoax had tragic implications: Gumilev was in love with Dmitrieva and subsequently duelled with Voloshin over her involvement; Annenskii, the forerunner of Acmeism, died from a heart attack after learning *Apollon* had rejected publication of his poems in favour of the work of Cherubina de Gabriak. In 1910 Voloshin befriended the young poet Marina Tsvetaeva and became her spiritual guru. In 1911 he turned to journalism for a while and worked as Paris correspondent for *Moscow News*. His second book of verse, *Anno mundi ardentis 1915*, was published in 1916.

During the October Revolution Voloshin lived in the Crimea; Soviet rule came to the capital Theodosiia in January 1918 and Voloshin's perception of the historical events as a tragedy is reflected in the poems "Rus' glukhonemaia" [Deaf and Dumb Russia], "Iz bezdny" [From the Abyss], and the narrative poem *Avvakum*. (Needless to say, all were banned from publication in Russia until the end of the 1980s.) His third collection of verse, *Iverni*, was published in Moscow in May 1918. During the Civil War Voloshin gave refuge to both Red Army and White Army officers; his poetry of the period dismissed terror of any kind. Voloshin tried to help many distressed and starving friends, and his poem "Dom poeta" [The Poet's House] reflects on his charitable activities. His *Stikhi o terrore* [Verses on the Terror], a poetic testimony to the tragic events, appeared in Berlin in 1923. He remained an opponent of the communist regime, but survived due to the protection of his influential friends. Voloshin's watercolours, poems, and essays of the period reveal his mystical outlook and his perception of history in cosmogonic and teleological ways.

At the end of 1920 Voloshin was given the post of inspector of the national heritage, which involved reporting to the Department of Education in Theodosiia on the state of the monuments and private libraries in the Crimea. During this period he took part in several theatrical productions, gave lectures, and recited poetry in various locations. He joined the Union of All-Russian Poets in May 1921. For most of the period 1921–22 he lived in the house of A.I. Aivazovskii. At this time he wrote his narrative poem *Putiami Kaina* [Following Cain]. In spring 1922 he met his future second wife, Mar'ia Zabolotskaia (1887–1976). The following year Zabolotskaia moved into his house in Koktebel as his wife. In the summer his house, full of visitors as ever, became a holiday place for Zamiatin, Shkapskaia, Chukovskii, and many others – in the summer of 1923 there were more than 60 guests. In March 1924 he was granted permission from Lunacharskii to turn his house into a free *pension* for Russian writers. Over the next two years his watercolours were exhibited in various places, including Moscow. In April 1927 he was elected honorary member of the Crimean History Society and member of the French Astronomical Society. In March of the same year he was officially married to Zabolotskaia. He continued writing poetry and in 1929 composed the narrative poem *Sviatoi Serafim* [Saint Seraphim]. In 1930, Voloshin began to write his autobiography and experienced periods of depression; he also applied for a state pension at this time. In 1931, after donating part of his house to the All-Russian Union of Writers, he was granted the pension. The following year he was beset by illness, but was still able to write his memoirs. His asthma worsened with the onset of pneumonia. After his death, his body was buried on the rock Kuchuk-Enishary, often called Voloshin's rock. His house became a place of pilgrimage for thousands of people interested in his poetry and watercolours, and a work place for many Soviet writers. The first collection of his verse appeared in the Soviet Union only in 1977.

Voloshin became a legend in his lifetime, because of his remarkable ability to blend with writers and artists, actors and ballet dancers regardless of their aesthetic and political views. His eccentricity and interest in ancient cultures as well as theosophy and Christianity made him popular with many cultural communities, both at home and abroad. His poetry reveals not so much a great craftsman, as profound ideas, a grasp of historical issues, as well as successful imitations of Dante, Byron, and above all the French Symbolists, which appealed to many of his contemporaries (Gertsyk, Briusov, Tsvetaeva, Belyi, and Ellis, for example). His poems are full of apocalyptic and religious images and revelations, which resemble the controversial ideas and passions of the philosopher, Nikolai Berdiaev's writings. Voloshin's collection of essays on art, theatre, and literature, entitled *Liki tvorchestva* [Masks of Creativity], are of particular interest as they help in restoring a picture of Russia's cultural life in the first three decades of the 20th century.

ALEXANDRA SMITH

Iuliia Nikolaevna Voznesenskaia 1940–

Prose writer and poet

Biography

Born in Leningrad, 14 September 1940. Spent some years with her parents in the German Democratic Republic, 1945–49. Made an attempt to escape from the Soviet Union as a young woman. Married: 1) Vladimir Okulov, two sons; 2) Vladimir Kromas in 1985. Attended the Leningrad Institute of Theatre, Music, and Drama. Arrested for "resisting the authorities" (assaulting a policeman) and sentenced to one year's corrective factory labour, 1964. Her apartment became a centre for poetry readings and unofficial publishing endeavours during the 1970s. Involved in human rights activities, 1976. Arrested, offered the opportunity to emigrate, which she refused, and re-arrested on the charge of "slandering the Soviet state"; sentenced to five years' internal exile; commuted to two years in a labour camp, 1977. Participated in the feminist almanac *Zhenshchina i Rossiia* [Woman and Russia], and the religious group the Maria Club in Leningrad, 1979. Emigrated to West Germany, where she worked for the journals *Posev* and *Grani*, 1980; worked for Radio Liberty, based in Munich, from 1985. Visited the Soviet Union in 1990.

Publications

Fiction

Zhenskii dekameron. Tel-Aviv, Zerkalo, 1987; Moscow, 1992; translated as *The Women's Decameron*, by W.B. Linton, London, Quartet, and Boston, Atlantic Monthly Press, 1986.

Zvezda Chernobyl'. New York, Liberty, 1987; translated as *The Star Chernobyl*, by Alan Myers, London, Quartet, 1987.

Rusalka v basseine [The Mermaid in the Swimming Pool]. Moscow, 1994.

Documentary and Autobiographical Writing

"Pis'mo iz Novosibirska", in *Al'manakh zhenshchinam o zhenshchinakh*, Leningrad, 1979; translated as "Letter from Novosibirsk", by The Women and Eastern Europe Group [no individual translator named], in *Woman and Russia*, London, Sheba, 1980.

"Zapiski iz rukava" [Notes from the Cuff], continued as "Romashka belaia" [White Camomile], *Poiski*, 1 (1979), 149–206; 4 (1982), 153–82; and 5–6 (1983), 303–35; also extracts in *Iunost'*, 1–3 (1991), 81–88; 65–69; 45–47.

"Zhenskii lager'" [The Women's Camp], *Grani*, 117 (1980), 204–31.

Letters of Love: Women Political Prisoners in Exile and the Camps, edited by Voznesenskaia, translated by Roger and Angela Keys. London, Quartet, 1989.

Poetry

"Stikhi iz tsikla 'Kniga razluk'" [Poems from the Cycle, "Book of Partings"], *Grani*, 108 (1978), 31–38.

"Stikhi", *Tret'ia volna*, 6 (1979), 35–40.

"Iz tsikla 'Kniga razluk': Stikhi", *Grani*, 111–12 (1979), 224–29.

"Stikhi", *Vestnik*, 128 (1979), 145–46.

"Iz 'Knigi razluk'", *Mariia*, 1 (1981), 13–18.

Critical Study

The Blue Lagoon Anthology of Modern Russian Poetry, edited by Konstantin K. Kuzminsky and Gregory L. Kovalev, vol. 5B, Newtonville, Massachusetts, Oriental Research Partners, 1986 (devoted almost entirely to materials on Voznesenskaia).

Iuliia Voznesenskaia started writing poetry as a child and has completed at least two unpublished volumes of poetry as well as a long poem on the invasion of Czechoslovakia in 1968, and a cycle of fairy-tale poems for children. It represents an important part of her life, even if she is modest about her talents as a poet. Her political views became radicalized during the 1970s as the "Second Culture" (which she initially distinguished from dissidence) came under increasing pressure from the KGB. Her uncompromising stance and courage during her interrogations and trial in 1976 were bolstered by her unswerving faith as a Christian.

Voznesenskaia's observations of her fellow-prisoners helped to focus her attention on the theme of women's lives, and her memoirs of this period interweave her own experiences with many anecdotes of the lives of others. The radical western brand of feminist thought embraced by Tat'iana Mamonova and other contributors to *Zhenshchina i Rossiia* (*Woman and Russia*) was not wholly to her taste, and she felt more at ease in the Maria Club. This group published its own journal, *Mariia*, to express a shared religious faith that held Mary, Mother of God, as a sacred ideal; they sought to counter the materialism and godlessness of Soviet society with the feminine values of sacrifice and unselfish love. This feminine culture would represent a true democracy, unlike the false democracies of masculinity. On the whole, Voznesenskaia has preferred to call herself a women's writer than a feminist writer.

In 1986 Voznesenskaia published her first novel, *The Women's Decameron* (*Zhenskii dekameron*, originally referred to as *Damskii dekameron*), in English and other languages, although it appeared in Russian only a year later. As in Boccaccio's *Decameron*, itself a work largely narrated by and for women, the storytellers are in quarantine, here in a maternity hospital; and they while away the time by recounting funny, sad, and sometimes sexually frank episodes from their lives. The work enters hitherto uncharted waters in Soviet literature in documenting the intimate domestic, sexual, social, and economic pressures of their day-to-day existence. The novel's patchwork of tales is unified by the psychological development of its characters as women of widely differing backgrounds (an air-stewardess, a Party official, a dissident, a drop-out, etc.) come to understand that as women there is more to unite them than divides them on political or class grounds. The novel portrays weariness and scepticism rather than outright subversion: the women make the best of things and remain full of laughter despite their burdens. It is simply implied that, if power had resided in the hands of women, Soviet society would surely have developed in much more humane directions.

In *Zvezda Chernobyl'* (*The Star Chernobyl*) Voznesenskaia

draws on the documentary materials available to her at Radio Liberty from radio broadcasts and printed sources relating to the 1986 Chernobyl catastrophe to chart the disinformation and criminally inadequate reporting of the disaster within the Soviet Union, despite Gorbachev's professed dedication to glasnost. The chapters of the novel are divided by selected extracts from actual items from the media of the day. Highlighting the government's cynicism with regard to the welfare of its citizens, Voznesenskaia shows that individuals were thrown back on their own resources. As the émigré Anna watches helplessly from abroad, it is the Party stalwart Anastasia who has to battle her way to Chernobyl to discover their younger sister's fate; along the way she loses all her illusions about the Soviet authorities as she meets obstruction at every turn. Once again the suggestion is made that the headlong pursuit of scientific knowledge, like the desire for political power, is an essentially masculine trait.

Since *The Star Chernobyl* Voznesenskaia has published documentary texts, such as a volume of interviews with Russian émigrés about the Germans, and a book that came out in 1987 under the title *Letters of Love – Women Political Prisoners in Exile and the Camps*. This consists of an anthology of letters written to and from labour camps, some of which are patently her own. Since then she has been working on a series of crime novels featuring an aristocratic detective heroine, Countess Apraksina, born in the year of the Revolution and determined to outlive the corrupt Soviet state. Only the first book, a story about illegal immigrants from Russia in Germany, *Rusalka v basseine* [The Mermaid in a Swimming Pool], has been published.

When we survey Voznesenskaia's writings it is striking that almost all of them are in some sense fragmentary in character. In this respect her work is akin to that of her close friend, the writer Svetlana Aleksevich from Belarussia. To a certain extent this was a matter of necessity: in exile Voznesenskaia declared that she had decided to record her Odyssey in the form of brief notes, since this made it easier to remember and to conceal them, or smuggle them to the outside world. Diary entries, correspondence, short lyrics, the hundred stories that make up *The Women's Decameron*, autobiographical prose that is larded with poems and accounts of individual episodes from other people's lives, journalistic articles, and the snippets of documentary text that frame the narrative of *The Star Chernobyl* – all of these reflect her instinct, and her gift, for combining small parts to create a kaleidoscopic whole. This mosaic of documentary material, which captures the reality of women's lives, is characteristic of the closely focused and relatively small-scale scope of much Soviet women's writing in general, where the fabric of everyday and concrete existence is brought into literature to subversive effect in a literature and a culture where the problems of reality have for so long been ignored.

J.A.E. CURTIS

Andrei Andreevich Voznesenskii 1933–

Poet

Biography

Born in Moscow, 12 May 1933. Attended the Institute of Architecture, Moscow, graduated, 1957. Married: Zoia Boguslavskaia in 1965; one son. Writer and painter. Member of the board of the Writers' Union, since 1967; chair, Commission on the Legacy of Pasternak, 1987; vice-president, Soviet PEN club, from 1989. Recipient: International Award for distinguished achievement in poetry, 1978; State Prize, 1978; State Prize for poetry, 1979; Order of the Red Banner of Labour. Member of the American Academy, 1972; Bavarian Academy of Fine Arts; and French Académie Mérimée.

Publications

Collected Editions

Selected Poems, translated by Anselm Hollo. New York, Grove Press, 1964.

Selected Poems, translated by Herbert Marshall. New York, Hill and Wang, and London, Methuen, 1966.

Izbrannoe. Alma-Ata, 1981.

Sobranie sochinenii, 3 vols. Moscow, 1983–84.

An Arrow in the Wall: Selected Poetry and Prose (bilingual edition), edited by F.D. Reeve and William Jay Smith. New York, Holt, and London, Secker and Warburg, 1987.

On the Edge: Poems and Essays from Russia, translated by Richard McKane. London, Weidenfeld and Nicolson, 1991.

Poetry

Mastera [The Masters]. 1957.

Mozaika [Mosaic]. Vladimir, 1960.

Parabola. Moscow, 1960.

Pishetsia kak liubitsia [I Write as I Love] (in Russian and Italian). Milan, Feltrinelli, 1962.

40 liricheskikh otstuplenii iz poemy "Treugol'naia grusha" [40 Lyrical Digressions from the Poem "The Triangular Pear"]. Moscow, 1962.

Menia pugaiut formalizmom [They Frighten Me with Formalism]. London, Flegon Press, 1963.

Antimiry (contains *Oza*). Moscow, 1964; translated as *Antiworlds*, by W.H. Auden *et al.*, edited by Patricia Blake and Max Hayward, New York, Basic Books, 1966; London, Oxford University Press, 1967; augmented edition, as *Antiworlds and The Fifth Ace* (bilingual edition), edited by

Patricia Blake and Max Hayward, New York, Doubleday, 1967; London, Oxford University Press, 1968.
Akhillesovo serdtse [An Achilles Heart]. Moscow, 1966.
Moi liubovnyi dnevnik [My Diary of Love]. London, Flegon Press, 1966.
Stikhi. Moscow, 1967.
Rossiia – rodina moia [Russia is My Native Land]. 1967.
Svetovye gody [Light Years]. Riga, 1968.
Ten' zvuka [The Shadow of Sound]. Moscow, 1969.
Vzgliad [The Look]. Moscow, 1972.
Dogalypse. San Francisco, City Lights, 1972.
Little Woods: Recent Poems, translated by Geoffrey Dutton and Igor Mezhakoff-Koriakin, with an introduction by Evgenii Evtushenko. Melbourne, Sun, 1972.
Vypusti ptitsu! [Release the Bird]. Moscow, 1974.
Integral ot sireni [Integral from Lilac]. Tallin, 1974.
Dubovyi list violonchel'nyi [Violincello Oak Leaf]. Moscow, 1975.
Vitrazhnykh del master [Maker of Stained-Glass Windows]. Moscow, 1976.
Nostalgia for the Present, translated by Robert Bly *et al.*, edited by Vera Dunham and Max Hayward. New York, Doubleday, 1978; London, Oxford University Press, 1980.
Izbrannaia lirika [Selected Lyrics]. Moscow, 1979.
Soblazn [Temptation]. Moscow, 1979.
Nebom edinym [By Heaven Above]. Minsk, 1980.
Bezotchetnoe [Unaccountable]. Moscow, 1981.
Proraby dukha [Clerks of Works to the Spirit]. Moscow, 1984.
Iverskii svet [Iberian Light]. 1984.
Rov: Dukhovnyi protsess [The Ditch: A Spiritual Trial]. Moscow, 1987.
Aksioma samoiska [Axiom]. Moscow, 1990.
Rossiia [Russia]. Moscow, 1991.
Stikhotvoreniia. Moscow, 1991.
Videomy. Moscow, 1992.
Gadanie po knige [Telling by the Book]. Moscow, 1994.

Plays
Beregite vashi litsa [Save Your Faces] (produced Moscow, 1971–72).
Juno and Avos (for television), music by Alexei Rybnikov, translated by Adrian Mitchell. 1983.

Fiction
Povest' pod parusami. 1971; translated as *Story under Full Sail*, by Stanley Kunitz *et al.* New York, Doubleday, 1974.
"O. Povest'", *Novyi mir*, 11 (1982).
Petrovo gnezdo [Peter's Nest]. Leningrad, 1990.

Letters and Memoirs
"Pis'mo v redaktsii gazetu 'Pravda'" [A Letter to the Editor of the Newspaper "Pravda"], *Grani*, 66 (1967).
"Mne chetyrnadtsat' let" [I'm Fourteen], *Novyi mir*, 9 (1980), 155–74.

Editor
Poeziia Evropy [Poetry of Europe], 3 vols. Moscow, 1978–79.

Critical Studies

"*Antiworlds* by Andrei Voznesensky on the Stage of the Moscow Theatre", by Tatiana Skianczenko, *Drama and Theatre*, 7 (1969).
"A Look Around: The Poetry of Andrey Voznesensky", by W.G. Jones, in *Major Soviet Writers: Essays in Criticism*, edited by Edward J. Brown, London, Oxford University Press, 1973.
"The Verse of Andrej Voznesenskij as an Example of Present-Day Russian Versification", by James Bailey, *Slavic and East European Journal*, 17 (1974).
"Voznesensky's Dystopia", by J.A. Harvie, *New Zealand Slavonic Journal*, 2 (1974).
"The Functions of Tonality and Grammar in a Voznesenskii Poem", by Dennis Ward, *International Journal of Slavic Linguistics and Poetics*, 17 (1974).
"Andrey Voznesensky: Between Pasternak and Mayakovsky", by R.D.B. Thomson, *Slavonic and East European Review*, 54 (1976).
"Perchance to Freeze. Two *Poemy* by Andrej Voznesenskij", by Michael Pursglove, *Scando-Slavica*, 25 (1979), 83–92.
"The Many Faces of Voznesensky's *Oza*", by Gerald Janecek, *Canadian-American Slavic Studies*, 14 (1980), 449–65.
"On the Art of Linguistic Opportunism", by Dennis Mickiewicz, *Russian Literature*, 8 (1980).
"Refresh My Tongue, Contemporary Muse", by Valeri Dementyev, *Soviet Literature*, 5/422 (1983).
"Andrei Voznesensky: The Poet as 'Tightrope-Walker'", by R. Kearney, *The Crane Bag*, Dublin, 7 (1983), 41–48.
"Oliver Friggieri Talks to Andrej Voznesenskij" (interview), *Skylark* (India), 64 (1988).
"Finding the Proper Equivalent: Translating the Poetry of Andrei Voznesensky", by William Jay Smith, in *Translating Poetry: The Double Labyrinth*, edited by Daniel Weissbort, Iowa City, University of Iowa Press, and London, Macmillan, 1989.
"A Russian Poet Finds a New Poetry in Collage", by John Russell, *New York Times* (30 June 1991), 27–29.
"Decoding Voznesenskii's 'Goiia'", by Cynthia Marsh, in *Symbolism and After: Essays on Russian Poetry in Honour of Georgette Donchin*, edited by Arnold McMillin, London, Bristol Classical Press, 1992, 186–97.
"'Menya pugayut formalizmom': Voznesensky's Poetic Art since 1980", by Michael Pushkin, *Essays in Poetics*, 18/1 (1993), 1–17.

Andrei Voznesenskii is one of the major poets of post-Stalinist Russia. His place in modern Russian literary history is controversial in relation to both the form and the subject-matter of his poetry. A trained architect, a disciple of Pasternak in his formative years, he had developed his own distinctive manner by the late 1950s.

His work, centred on lyric poetry, has a wide generic range. His output includes many narrative poems, from *Mastera* [The Masters] (1957) to *Rov* [The Ditch] (1987). His prose writings are extensive, with autobiographical memoirs, such as "Mne chetyrnadtsat' let" [I'm Fourteen], about his early years and friendship with Pasternak, critical essays, such as "O", with its commentaries on writers and artists, and maxims exploring spirituality, such as "Krestiki" [Little Crosses]. Some of the narrative poems, such as *Oza* (1964) and *Rov*, blend verse and prose, with the prose conveying factual or fantastic content.

He has composed a number of works of fiction. He has a long-standing interest in the theatre, with theatrical performances based on recitations of his verse, such as *Antimiry* (*Antiworlds*) at the Taganka Theatre, plays (such as the suppressed *Beregite vashi litsa* [Save Your Faces]), and operas ("Dama tref" [The Queen of Clubs] – a "detective opera"; *Iunona i Avos* [Juno and Avos] – a rock opera). Architecture has played an increasing role in his work, through his prose reminiscences and experimental architectural designs, such as "Poetarkh" (1983). His visual art has taken both sculptural and pictorial form. He designed the Georgian monument on Tishinskaia Square in Moscow; in 1993 his "Easter installation" on the theme of Russia's rebirth included a large plaster-of-Paris Easter egg representing the globe. Graphic design is a significant feature of his poetry. *Ten' zvuka* [The Shadow of Sound] contains an illustrated essay on visual poetry entitled "Izopy" ("izobrazitel'naia poeziia" [Graphic Poetry]). His 1993 exhibition in Moscow's Pushkin Museum was based on his book of collage-like designs (*Videomy*) published at the end of 1992.

As early as 1958 Voznesenskii suffered accusations of "Formalism" ("Vecher na stroike" [An Evening on a Building-Site]). He views his main task as the pursuit of "poetry as such", and has always asserted the right to formal experimentation. His primary poetic influences are associated with the post-revolutionary avant-garde, stylistically if not always politically: Pasternak, with his profoundly metaphorical approach; Maiakovskii, who combined moral imperatives with formal innovation; and Tsvetaeva, whose rhythmical complexity and lexical heterogeneity mirror his own. Voznesenskii's poetry has always been metrically varied. His lines are mostly rhymed, with a preference for assonantal rhymes; blank verse is occasionally encountered.

His work is characterized by extreme metaphorical density, with frequent juxtaposition of discrete phenomena: natural and artificial; technical and spiritual; ancient and contemporary. His lexis is correspondingly extensive, ranging across widely differing registers: literary, colloquial, scientific, religious, historical, political. The graphic aspect of his poetry is expressed verbally through visual imagery. Other sense-perceptions are frequently intermingled synaesthetically with the visual. The metaphorical burden is often borne by word-association, especially by verbal puns and, more recently, through the exploration of visual correspondences in his *Videomy*. The ease and ubiquity of his puns has led to accusations of superficiality. Other criticisms include experimentation for its own sake, name-dropping, and simplistic moral rhetoric. His artistic detractors include both pro-Soviet conservatives and anti-communist radicals.

Voznesenskii has also had a major public role as a civic poet. One prominent theme is the relationship between politics, technology and the human and natural environment. He often refers to the balance between the constructive potential of technology and its risks. These include not only physical dangers, such as nuclear irradiation (*Oza*), nuclear winter ("Iz Bairona" [From Byron] 1984), or the ozone hole ("Ne poniat' pri etoi zhizni" [There's No Understanding Life When This Happens] 1994), but also human and social standardization, through robotization ("Zombi zabveniia" [Zombie of Oblivion] 1982) or totalitarianism (*Oza*). In 1973 he welcomed technology, but made clear that his approval was conditional on intellectual and spiritual freedom ("NTR").

Universal questions of morality and evil, religion and spirituality, are an increasing preoccupation; there are marked mystical tendencies in the 1990s. He has become fascinated by coincidence and fatalism, as expressed in *Videomy*; his recent collection, *Gadanie po knige* [Telling by the Book], is constructed around fortune-telling. The fundamental spatial and temporal co-ordinates of the universe often act as a framework for these concerns ("O proportsiiakh" [On Proportions] 1983).

The contemporary situation of poetry has been a recurrent theme. Poetry readings to huge crowds in stadia in the 1960s were justified by their relative freedom from censorship. During the Brezhnev period dangerous messages had to be communicated indirectly through Aesopian language. Voznesenskii is aware of the possible decline of the book in the face of technological development and contemplates a computerized form for his next publication.

Universal themes have coexisted in his work with more parochial responses to Russian social and political issues. Underdogs and occupants of the underworld have populated his poems since the 1950s ("Posledniaia elektrichka" [The Last Train] 1958). His women are abused but increasingly fight back. The social victims of rapid economic change in contemporary Russia, the poor and homeless, and the physical victims of organized crime or political murder, all make their appearance in his recent work. He suggests links between organized crime and political power. In his poetry he has voiced his objections to the Soviet interventions in Georgia, Lithuania, and Afghanistan and to Russian involvement in Chechnia.

Yet the major debate about Voznesenskii concerns the authenticity of his commitment, despite the public attacks by Khrushchev, his open letters to the authorities, his defence of the theatre from the censors, the periodic withdrawal of travel rights, the accusations that he was a CIA spy. Some have criticized the stridency of his moral rhetoric about conscience, speaking of journalism rather than poetry. His emotional content is seen as intellectualized, his spiritual interests as superficial, with little presentation of inner experience. Advocates of open opposition have challenged the ambiguities of his position on Aesopian language and on literature as the art of the possible. Others respond that Voznesenskii was a beacon of freedom in difficult times ("Ne otrekus'" [I Shall Not Give Up] 1975), using his art to question official ideology and to assert the primacy of human values.

MICHAEL PUSHKIN

Oza

Narrative poem, 1964

Oza is a complex and generically ambiguous narrative poem. The overt subject is the scientific and technical revolution, particularly the danger posed to humanity by the advent of nuclear power and nuclear weapons. Behind these concerns lies an awareness of the suppression of individuality in modern society, with clear allusions to the Soviet political system.

The poem consists of 14 loosely alternating cantos of verse and prose, the poems representing the free creative human spirit and the prose passages describing the soulless world of programmed robots. Two cantos (the second and seventh) are exclusively prose. The tenth canto is prose, but contains a prayer in verse. The fourth canto is divided almost equally between verse and prose. There are several differences between the various published versions, but in only two cases is the order of the cantos affected. When Voznesenskii read the poem in England in 1965, he transposed the ninth canto of Soviet editions to the beginning and placed the introductory poem last.

Voznesenskii's authorial identity overlaps with that of the fictional author of the poem, which is described at the outset as "a notebook found on the bedside table of a hotel in Dubna". The interplay of narratorial levels is to some extent conveyed graphically, through alterations in font and layout. Several characters intervene with monologues, including a scientist, a historian, and a raven. The protagonist, the focus of the poem's pathos, hardly speaks at all. She is Zoia, a physicist at the nuclear research establishment at Dubna, near Moscow. She recklessly enters a forbidden zone and is irradiated. Her grasp on normal human existence is broken by the excesses of science. In the process her name is anagrammatically transformed from Zoia (life) to the scientifically evocative Oza.

Oza's vulnerability, representative of the physical and spiritual fragility of human existence, is conveyed through the ambiguity of her depiction as well as through direct assertion. Four cantos end with the question "Perhaps her name is Oza?" She is identified with Dante's Beatrice, possibly with St Anne, mother of the Virgin Mary, and implicitly with Christ. The poet cannot rescue her from her fate, yet it was she who had saved him when others had jeered at or betrayed him. Zoia/Oza's multiple identities are compounded by puns on her name: Oza, Roza (Rose), *stervoza* (whore), *metamorfoza*. Her slippers remind him of doves in a tank's path, delicate, eggshell-like.

The dehumanized world of robots is embodied in the figure of the scientist, referred to in the text as "the experimenter". This destroyer of human identity is nameless, his only identification being the soundless and now almost functionless Russian hard sign. He appears in the tenth canto as the toastmaster at his god-daughter Zoia's birthday party at the Berlin restaurant in Moscow. The nameless scientist cannot even remember her name. He has a passion for experimentation. In the second canto he proposes rearranging human anatomy and physiology, sacrificing psyche and poetry to create robots. The globe itself could be rearranged, cut in half like an eggshell, with one half turned upside-down and placed inside the other. Half of the human race would perish, but the other half would enjoy the experiment.

The ambiguities of vulnerability and new life, of death and resurrection, implicit in the image of the eggshell, were given tangible expression recently by Voznesenskii. He designed a large globe of the world in the form of a plaster eggshell as the centrepiece of his open-air celebration of Russia's potential for rebirth, held during Easter 1993 in the square in front of the Church of the Resurrection on Nezhdanova Street in Moscow.

The prose sections devoted to the "inside-out world" of the experimenter are grotesquely surreal. People queue passively for reassembly, emerging with ears screwed to foreheads or hearts left out. The members of the Presidium of the Quasi-Art Section all resemble identical translucent eggs, except the member whose legs protrude periscope-like above the table instead of his torso. The slogans and arrows pointing forward to the glorious future are undermined by the speaker's back-to-front head, prompting the narrator's question "Which way is forward?"

Temporality assumes both metaphysical and political significance in *Oza*. The ninth canto (the introduction in Voznesenskii's reading) addresses the problem of immortality. In a Dostoevskian spirit he asserts the primacy of organic continuity over a historical full-stop, when time stands still. Together with the frequent accompaniment of Oza's name by the Latin greeting *Ave* and incantation of the word "soul", this metaphysical concern reinforces the poem's religious overtones. The poem has also been seen as an anti-Utopian tract in the tradition of the romantic revolt against reason, with Russian antecedents by Baratynskii, Dostoevskii, and Zamiatin.

Equally significant, though more rarely recognized, are the political resonances. The historian in the fourth canto sees history as proceeding backwards from old age to youth, echoing the slogan that "Communism is the youth of the world". In the future all dreams will come true with the aid of technology in good hands. In the original *Molodaia gvardiia* version of *Oza*, the historian's monologue is interrupted by a very different alternative historical scenario in the form of a six-stanza satirical poem about Stalin, reminiscent of that of Mandel'shtam. The first to be published in the Soviet Union, it was omitted from subsequent Soviet editions. Stalin is "the Great Engineer", oblivious to human beings, his grey moustaches of state tinged red with blood. The sixth canto is a parody of Edgar Allan Poe's "The Raven", featuring a conversation between the poet and his *alter ego*, the raven. To the poet's Utopian fantasies of godlike domination over nature and democratic transformation, the raven retorts that the poet is enslaved to standardization, free without freedom, racing along in a car with no steering-wheel.

Voznesenskii meets accusations of infatuation with technology by apologizing for that reputation in the twelfth canto. He asserts instead that all progress is retrograde if man is destroyed in the process, a slogan chanted at the end of the Taganka Theatre's production of his work. He considers himself to have been committed throughout his career to the human vision expressed in *Oza* and sees the poem as a landmark in his development, an appropriate reply in 1964 to Khrushchev's political campaign against him the previous year.

MICHAEL PUSHKIN

Rov: Dukhovnyi protsess

The Ditch: A Spiritual Trial

Narrative poem, 1987

Rov is a long and complex narrative poem based on a double crime. In 1941 12,000 Jews were shot by the Nazis in a ditch near Simferopol. In 1985 several men were imprisoned for stealing valuables, including gold tooth fillings, from the graves. Voznesenskii wrote a poem about the incident, then entitled *Alch'* [Greed]. On 7 April 1986 he visited the scene for the first time and discovered fresh excavations and heaps of human skulls, which prompted a revised version of the poem, now renamed *Rov*.

The work consists of some three dozen sections, of which eight are in prose and the remainder in verse. The text as originally published (*Iunost'*, 4, 1986) differs somewhat from the second version in the volume entitled *Rov* (1987). The latter includes two new poems ("Okovy dev" [The Maidens' Fetters] and "Reaktsiia gosmuzha" [The Reaction of the Husband of State]). Four poems are omitted ("Tochka" [Full Stop], "Venskaia povest'" [Vienna Tale], "Skorpomoshch'" [Ambulance] and "Letiat vorony" [The Crows are Flying]). Otherwise the sections proceed in the same order, except that the factual and statistical prose account "Delo" [The Trial], which in *Iunost'* is in two parts separated by two poems, is consolidated in the *Rov* edition.

The poem's subtitle, *Dukhovnyi protsess* [A Spiritual Trial], is designed to draw attention away from the legal towards the spiritual dimensions of the affair. The poem entitled "Vstuplenie" [Introduction] is preceded, with characteristic structural perversity, by a "Posleslovie" [Afterword] in prose describing the poet's visit and response to the scene of the crime. Mentioned here for the first time is the earlier neologistic title *Alch'*, which implies both greed and hunger. This "spiritual epidemic" of greed is the sickness that is the poem's subject.

The "Introduction" itself is replete with associative patterns. One of the central images is that of the skull, linked directly with Hamlet in several sections, and implicitly here through quotation of Hamlet's "The time is out of joint". The concluding quatrain identifies the moral demand of the 12,000 pairs of Jewish eyes with the moral imperatives posed by his huge audiences in the Luzhniki stadium during the early 1960s. The victims' Jewishness, still unmentionable in print at the time (it was referred to in the 1987 edition), was eloquently conveyed by repetition of the word "genocide" in the title poem "Rov". Its accompaniment by the epithet "pogromist", with its tsarist associations, emphasized the affair's Russian antecedents.

Much of Voznesenskii's work is based on contrastive imagery. The antithesis to greed here is speech, by which Voznesenskii means human culture in general. The reader is prepared for the contrast in the poem "Legenda" [A Legend]. In an allusion to Pushkin's [Prophet], instead of a winged seraph tearing out his tongue, the poet is rendered speechless by the sole survivor of the massacre, Valia Perekhodnik, leading him into the ditch. The eyes of the dead endow the living with the wound of "new sight" or "a new way of seeing". The poem entitled "Alch'. Prezhnii prolog" [Greed. Original Prologue] develops the concept of sickness with startlingly physical imagery (organism, bile, hypodermic). In spiritual epidemics cross-infection by metastasis destroys not neighbouring organs but one's own comrades.

The patterns of contrast encompass positive heroes and a gallery of 1980s anti-heroes. In a society where novelty is prized, the "new novel" and "new cinema" are complemented by the "new thief", who steals souls. The acquisitive spirit finds its natural home in the "Skupoi rytsar' NTR" [Covetous Knight of the Scientific and Technical Revolution], typified by the venal deputy minister with his Volvo, and detached house and garden where videos hang from the branches. Voznesenskii conflates current obsessions with computers, sport, and sexual display by inventing the "Displayboy" (whose program eventually breaks down altogether). Voznesenskii blames spiritual sickness rather than capitalism. The root of the sickness may be spiritual but its effects are all too physical, as the pollution of Lake Baikal and the Chernobyl disaster demonstrate.

The "new way of seeing" is expressed in the poem of the same name, one of several in which positive heroes emerge, including his familiar "clerks of the works of the spirit", seen in "Ozero" [The Lake] campaigning for Baikal to be turned into a nature reserve, or for the restoration of the Tret'iakov Gallery and its surroundings. Alongside them are the helicopter pilots who flew over Chernobyl and the American bone marrow surgeon who flew in to tend its victims ("Chelovek" [Man] and "Bol'nitsa" [Hospital]).

In "Skhvatka" [The Fight] the heroes and anti-heroes are artistically integrated through the image of the spade, the implement of the diggers of both Simferopol and Chernobyl. The former dig up corpses, but are themselves moral corpses. The latter save lives but risk their own. In the "Epilog" [Epilogue], the poet hopes piously that greed will burn out and be forgotten.

The critical response to *Rov* has concentrated primarily on its generic ambiguity. There has been some discussion of its status as a unified narrative poem, with the work alternatively defined as a cycle. The introduction of prose passages has prompted much argument. Voznesenskii himself sees the work primarily as a publicistic attempt to bring an anti-Semitic outrage into the open. In this way he justifies the bare factual quality of the prose passages, distinguishing them from those in *Oza*, which were by turns lyrical and surreal. The rich variety of genres, verse forms, and voices has led some critics to dub the work "polyphonic", but others see it as "polyphonic journalism". The factography of the prose and the moral outrage of the verse are seen as vitiated by repetition, emotional and vocal extremism, and lack of a sense of measure. In the words of one critic, "the theme masks the poetry". The contrastive images of good and evil are viewed by some as simplistic. Yet the use of rhyme for semantic contrast is at times genuinely inventive: Nobel/Chernobyl, for example. The poem's lexis, as in much of his work, abounds in jokey modernistic inventions, such as "Hitchcock kitsch", "windsurfing seraph", "pop-*alch'*", "*alch'-nuovo*" and "corpse aerobics". The language is denounced as populist, unserious and tasteless, dependent on that same debased "new" culture that the poet abhors: the language undermines the message.

The poem's impact is indicated by the very different response it evoked from the neo-fascist society *Pamiat'*, in the form of threatening phone-calls and letters. They occupied 200 of the front seats at a poetry reading and passed an obscene anti-Semitic message and drawing to him.

MICHAEL PUSHKIN

Aleksandr Ivanovich Vvedenskii 1904–1941

Poet and dramatist

Biography

Born in St Petersburg, 6 December 1904. Attended the L.D. Lentovskaia gymnasium, St Petersburg; studied law at Petrograd University, then Chinese, 1921–23: did not graduate. Worked briefly as clerk, before becoming full-time writer. Married: 1) Tamara A. Meier; 2) Anna Semenovna Ivanter; 3) G.B. Viktorova in 1936, one son. Formed the Chinari philosophical circle, 1922; collaborated with the poet Igor' Terent'ev on a research project at the Institute of Artistic Culture, 1923–26; member of the Leningrad All-Russian Union of Poets, 1924, published two poems in Union anthologies, 1926; member of Aleksandr Tufanov's group, "Orden Zaumnikov, DSO", 1925–26. Worked with the experimental theatre group "Radiks", 1926; founder-member of group which, from 1927 to 1930, was known as OBERIU. Published children's literature in S. Marshak's journals *Ezh*, 1928–35, and *Chizh*, 1930–41. Excluded from the Leningrad Poets' Union, 1929; arrested 1931; imprisoned in Leningrad, released June 1932, exiled to Kursk and Vologda, July–November, 1932; admitted into the newly-organized Writers' Union, 1934; moved to Kharkov, 1936; arrested again, died in uncertain circumstances during evacuation from Kharkov, late 1941. Rehabilitated, 1956. Published gradually from 1970s, mainly in the west. "Complete Works" first published in Russia in 1993.

Publications

Collected Editions

Russia's Lost Literature of the Absurd: A Literary Discovery. Selected Works of Daniil Kharms and Alexander Vvedensky, edited and translated by George Gibian. Ithaca, Cornell University Press, 1971; revised version as *The Man with the Black Coat – Russia's Literature of the Absurd: Selected Works of Daniil Kharms and Alexander Vvedensky*, Evanston, Illinois, Northwestern University Press, 1987; reprinted 1997.

Izbrannoe, edited by Wolfgang Kasack. Munich, Sagner, 1974.

Polnoe sobranie sochinenii, 2 vols, edited by Mikhail Meilakh. Ann Arbor, Ardis, 1980–84.

Polnoe sobranie proizvedenii v dvukh tomakh, 2 vols, edited by Mikhail Meilakh and Vladimir Erl'. Moscow, 1993.

Poetry

Sobranie stikhotvorenii. 1926.

Koster [Bonfire]. 1927.

Plays

Elka u Ivanovykh [Christmas at the Ivanovs'], *Grani*, 81 (1971).

"Potets", *Russian Literature Triquarterly*, 11 (1975).

Minin i Pozharskii [Minin and Pozharskii], Munich, Sagner, 1978.

Critical Studies

"Tvorchestvo Aleksandra Vvedenskogo", by A. Aleksandrov and Mikhail Meilakh, in *Materialy XXII nauchnoi studencheskoi konferentsii: Poetika. Istoriia literatury. Lingvistika*, edited by A.B. Roginskii and G.G. Superfin, Tartu, 1967, 105–10.

"'Left Art' in Leningrad: the OBERIU Declaration", by Robin Milner-Gulland, *Oxford Slavonic Papers*, 3 (1970), 65–74.

Absurde Literatur in Russland: Entstehung und Entwicklung, by Bertram Müller, Munich, Sagner, 1978.

"Kachestvennaia i funktsional'naia kharakteristika vremeni v poezii A. I. Vvedenskogo", by O.G. Revzina, *Russian Literature*, 6/4 (1978), 397–401.

"About Vvedensky's *Conversations*", by Alice Stone Nakhimovsky, *Ulbandus Review*, 1/1 (1979), 106–37 (includes a translation of the *Conversations*, 112–37).

"Vvedenskii: Text and Subtext", by Il'ia Levin, *Neue Russische Literatur*, 4–5 (1981–82), 189–201.

Laughter in the Void: An Introduction to the Writings of Daniil Kharms and Aleksandr Vvedenskii, by Alice Stone Nakhimovsky, Vienna, Wiener Slawistischer Almanach, 5, 1982.

"I poemi drammatici di Aleksandr Vvedenskij *Minin i Pozharskij* e *Krugom vozmozhno Bog*", by Rozanna Giaquinta, *Annali di Ca' Foscari*, 22/1–2 (1983), 67–81.

"'Kovarnye stikhi': Notes on Daniil Kharms and Aleksandr Vvedensky", by Robin Milner-Gulland, *Essays in Poetics*, 9/1 (1984), 16–37.

"Tradition in the Topsy-Turvey World of Parody: Analysis of Two Oberiu Plays", by Anatoly Vishevsky, *Slavic and East European Journal*, 30/3 (1986), 355–66.

"Oberiu (problema smeshnogo)", by Anna Gerasimova, *Voprosy literatury*, 4 (1988), 48–79.

"Vvedenskii i Blok: Materialy k poeticheskoi predystorii Oberiu", by A.A. Kobrinskii and Mikhail Meilakh, *Blokovskii sbornik*, 10 (1991), 72–80.

"Diabolical Discourse or Divine Discourse? A Study of *Nekotoroe kolichestvo razgovorov* by Aleksandr Vvedensky", by Graham Roberts, *Essays in Poetics*, 16/2 (1991), 24–49.

Teatr (special OBERIU issue), 11 (1991).

The Last Soviet Avant-Garde: OBERIU — Fact, Fiction, Metafiction, by Graham Roberts, Cambridge, Cambridge University Press, 1997.

Although the earliest works written by the poet and dramatist Aleksandr Vvedenskii date from before the October Revolution, the first important event of Vvedenskii's literary career occurred in 1919, when, together with Leonid Lipavskii and A. Alekseev, he composed *Byk Buddy* [The Buddha's Bull], a parody of Futurism. In 1922, he formed the Chinari circle with Lipavskii, Tamara Meier, and the mathematician, philosopher, and musicologist Iakov Druskin. This group, which was joined in 1925 by Daniil Kharms and the poet Nikolai Oleinikov, met on a regular basis virtually until Vvedenskii's death in 1941 to discuss a broad range of ethical, linguistic, and aesthetic questions.

Between 1923 and 1926, Vvedenskii worked with the poet Igor' Terent'ev at the phonology department of Kasimir Malevich's Institute of Artistic Culture. Here, Terent'ev and

Vvedenskii would read lists of *zaum'* (trans-rational) words to poets and artists (such as Tatlin, Filonov, and Matiushin) as part of a project exploring the relationship between discursive and pictorial representation.

It is for his creative friendship with Kharms, however, that Vvedenskii is best known. Between 1925 and 1926 they were both members of "Orden Zaumnikov DSO", the group of *zaum'* poets headed by Aleksandr Tufanov, and in 1926 both worked with the "Radiks" experimental theatre group. Vvedenskii and Kharms co-wrote a play, *Moia mama vsia v chasakh* [My Mummy All in Watches], which was performed by "Radiks" in 1926. In the same year Vvedenskii and Kharms, together with Igor' Bakhterev, Nikolai Zabolotskii, Konstantin Vaginov, Boris-Doivber Levin, and Sergei Tsimbal, formed the nucleus of an experimental literary group which went through a number of changes in name and personnel, eventually to become, between December 1927 and April 1930, OBERIU (a distorted acronym for "The Association of Real Art" (*Ob"edinenie real'nogo iskusstva*)). In the group's aesthetic "manifesto", read out during the "Three Left Hours" performance at the Leningrad Press Club on 24 January 1928, Vvedenskii was described as being "at the extreme left of our association", as a writer who "breaks the object down into parts ... [and] action down into fragments".

By the time criticism in the Soviet press forced OBERIU to disband, in April 1930, Vvedenskii was writing for the children's magazines *Ezh* and *Chizh*, as he continued to do throughout the last decade of his life (his children's writing is generally considered to be inferior to that of Kharms). Even this relatively safe pursuit could not guarantee him immunity from arrest, which finally came in December 1931. After a brief period of exile, Vvedenskii moved to Kharkov in 1936. It was here, during the last years of his life, that he wrote what are held to be his best works, including *Nekotoroe kolichestvo razgovorov* [A Certain Quantity of Conversations] (1936–37) and *Elka u Ivanovykh* [Christmas at the Ivanovs'] (1938).

Vvedenskii's work, of which only about a quarter survives, consists of poems, dramatized dialogues, and plays. It is the sheer difficulty of his writing, rather than the paucity of extant texts, however, which perhaps best explains why Vvedenskii has attracted relatively little critical attention, compared to contemporaries such as Zabolotskii and Kharms. In the studies that have been written, adjectives such as "surreal", "grotesque", "phantasmagoric", "illogical", even "absurd" have been used to describe Vvedenskii's *oeuvre* (thereby echoing the reception of Kharms's work).

Part of the difficulty with this self-styled "Autho-rity of Meaninglessness" (*Avto-ritet bessmyslitsy*) comes from the different ways in which he disrupts established modes of thought and language. Concepts such as time, space, and identity are fluid in his texts. Disembodied voices engage in fragments of dialogue where the boundaries between the concrete and the abstract, and the real and the imaginary are frequently blurred (as, for example, in *Fakt, teoriia i Bog* [Fact, Theory and God] 1930). Vvedenskii's characters indulge in a whole host of "language games", although Vvedenskii tends to defamiliarize language at the level of semantics or syntax (and, in his early work, punctuation), largely eschewing the phonetic-based *zaum'* of poets such as Tufanov. Vvedenskii's interest in language is, like Kharms's, primarily cognitive. Where Vvedenskii differs from his fellow *oberiut*, however, is the extent to which his particular cognitive project is theological and eschatological. Much of Vvedenskii's extant opus is united by one tripartite theme, namely that of time, death, and God, and the impossibility of expressing these concepts satisfactorily using conventional human language, with its basis in rational thought.

From his early poems right through to late works such as *Nekotoroe kolichestvo razgovorov*, Vvedenskii dramatizes the "fallen" nature of human language, underlining the inadequacy of such language when faced with the ineffably discontinuous nature of time. In one of his earliest texts, *Minin i Pozharskii* [Minin and Pozharskii] (1926), Vvedenskii ridicules the discursive construct of history, which assumes time as a continuum stretching from the past through the present to the future. This text, typically for Vvedenskii, is highly fragmented; various characters from a variety of historical epochs and countries appear and then disappear with bewildering rapidity.

For Vvedenskii only death can truly be said to exist in time, since death represents the moment of transition from the infinitely small time of human life to the infinitely great time of eternity and God. Many of Vvedenskii's texts contain dialogues of the dead, a feature they share with the tradition of "Menippean Satire". Such dialogues can be found, for example, in *Minin i Pozharskii*, and in another important work, *Krugom vozmozhno Bog* [All Around Maybe God] (1931), a text that deals with the death and after-life of a certain "EF" (in a way which, once again, subverts "logical" notions of time). Time, death, and language are also central to *Chetyre opisaniia* [Four Descriptions] (1931–34), in which four characters, identified only as "dy(ing)" ("umir[aiushchii]"), and numbered one to four, recount their own deaths.

Among the discourses that Vvedenskii posits as alternatives to human language is the "language" of nature, as, for example, in his play *Elka u Ivanovykh*. This work, a parody of Chekhov's drama, which contains many features of German Expressionism, mixes sex and death in equal measure in its depiction of the bourgeois household of the Puzyrev family, whose members all die suddenly one Christmas Eve. One of the scenes takes place in the forest and contains a "lesson" on time and death given by a giraffe, a wolf, a lion, and a piglet (this links Vvedenskii to Zabolotskii, who was also writing about nature at this time, although in a somewhat different vein). *Nekotoroe kolichestvo razgovorov*, on the other hand, contains discourse of another sort. This text, which follows three inmates of a mental asylum through suicide to what appears to be discursive unity with God, fuses the language of the "insane", with a Heideggerean "holy silence" (in *Potets*, 1936–37, a similar "terrible silence" is associated with the apocalypse). In the two extant works from the 1940s, *Elegiia* [An Elegy] (1940), and *Gde, kogda* [When, Where] (1941), yet another voice can be heard. Here Vvedenskii, quoting a number of his earlier works and implicitly associating himself with Pushkin, looks forward in an intensely personal and moving way to his own death.

With his deep scepticism towards established modes of discourse and cognition, and his search for a new, authentic language, Vvedenskii belongs to a tradition in Russian literature that includes Khruchenykh, Khlebnikov, and Kharms, as well as (more recently) the poet, dramatist, and prose writer Vladimir Kazakov, and the Russian Conceptualist poets of the 1980s.

GRAHAM ROBERTS

Vladimir Semenovich Vysotskii 1938–1980

Poet and songwriter

Biography

Born in Moscow, 25 January 1938. Lived in Eberswalde, East Germany, 1947–49. Graduated from the Moscow Arts Theatre studio, 1960. Married: 1) the actress Iza Zhukova; 2) the actress Liudmila Abramova, two sons; 3) the actress Marina Vlady (Poliakova) in 1966. Worked at the Pushkin Theatre and the Theatre of Miniatures. Joined the Taganka Theatre company, where he established his reputation as a stage actor, 1964. Performed throughout the Soviet Union, from 1966; France, 1977; and the United States, 1979. Died in Moscow, 25 July 1980. Buried in Vagankovo Cemetery, Moscow. Posthumously awarded the State Prize of the USSR, 1987.

Publications

Collected Editions

Pesni russkikh bardov [Songs of the Russian Bards], vols 1–4. Paris, YMCA-Press, 1977–78.

Metropol'. Literaturnyi al'manakh (contains 25 poems by Vysotskii). Ann Arbor, Ardis, 1979; translated as *Metropol: Literary Almanac*, by Kevin Klose, New York, Norton, 1982.

Nerv [Nerve]. Moscow, 1981.

Pesni i stikhi [Songs and Poems], edited by Boris Berest, 2 vols. New York, *Literaturnoe zarubezh'e*. 1981–83.

Vladimir Vysotskii: Stikhi i pesni [Poems and Songs]. Moscow, 1988.

Izbrannoe. Moscow, 1988.

Sobranie stikhov i pesen, 3 vols. New York, Apollon Foundation and Russica, 1988.

Poeziia i proza. Moscow, 1989.

Vladimir Vysotsky: Hamlet with a Guitar, edited by Yuri Andreyev and Iosif Boguslavsky, translated by Sergei Roy. Moscow, Progress, 1990.

Sochineniia, 2 vols. Moscow, 1991.

Sobranie sochinenii, 5 vols. Tula, 1993–

Critical Studies

"Modern Russian Underground Song: An Introductory Survey", by Gerald S. Smith, *Journal of Russian Studies*, 28 (1974), 3–12.

"Horace's Heirs: Beyond Censorship in the Soviet Songs of the *magnitizdat*", by Rosette C. Lamont, *World Literature Today*, 53 (1979), 220–27.

"O Vysotskom", by Natal'ia Krymova, *Avrora*, 8 (1981).

Vladimir Vysotskii i drugie, by Pavel Leonidov, New York, New York Russian Publishing, 1983.

Songs to Seven Strings: Russian Guitar Poetry and Soviet "Mass Song", by Gerald S. Smith, Bloomington, Indiana University Press, 1984.

Das sowjetrussische Autorenlied: Eine Untersuchung am Beispiel des Schaffens von Aleksandr Galič, Bulat Okudžava und Vladimir Vysockij, by Dagmar Boss, Munich, Sagner, 1985.

Vladimir ou le vol arrêté, by Marina Vlady, Paris, Fayard, 1987; as *Vladimir ili prervannyi polet*, Moscow, Progress, 1989.

Chetyre chetverti puti, edited by Andrei Krylov, Moscow, 1988.

Ia, konechno, vernus'..., edited by Natal'ia Krymova, Moscow, 1988.

Zhivaia zhizn', edited by Valeria Perevozchikova, Moscow, 1988.

"Vladimir Vysotskii: Epizody tvorcheskoi sud'by", by Boris Akimov and Oleg Terent'ev, *Studencheskii meridian*, 10–12 (1988) and 1–3 (1990).

Vladimir Vysotskii, kakim znaiu i liubliu, by Alla Demidova, Moscow, 1989.

Chetyre vechera s Vladimirom Vysotskim, edited by Eldar Riazanov, Moscow, 1989; accompanied a four-part television series on Vysotskii.

Vspominaia Vladimira Vysotskogo, edited by A. Safonov, Moscow, 1989.

Vladimir Vysotskii: Chelovek, poet, akter, edited by Iu. Andreev and I. Boguslavskii, Moscow, 1989.

Pisatel' Vladimir Vysotskii v soiuze pisatelei ne sostoial ..., by Vladimir Novikov, Moscow, 1990.

Vladimir Vysotskii: Mir i slovo, by A. Skobelev and S. Shaulov, Voronezh, 1991.

Vse v zhertvu pamiati tvoei, by Valerii Zolotukhin, Moscow, 1992.

Textbeziehungen im dichterischen Werk Vladimir Vysockijs, by Heinrich Pfandl, Munich, Sagner, 1993.

Staratel': Eshche o Vysotskom, edited by Andrei Krylov and Iurii Tyrin, Moscow, 1994.

Problema tragicheskogo v poezii V.S. Vysotskogo, by N.M. Rudnik, Kursk, 1995.

Bibliographies

"Zhizn' i tvorchestvo Vladimira Semenovicha Vysotskogo", edited by Iurii Rybal'chenko, in *Avrora*, 6–7 (1988), 99; 146–47.

Vladimir Semenovich Vysotskii: alfavitnyi, khronologicheskii i bibliograficheskii ukazatel'-spravochnik, compiled by L. Tomenchuk, edited by A. Skobolev, Voronezh, 1990, 66–84.

Vladimir Semenovich Vysotskii: bibliograficheskii spravochnik 1960–1990gg: chto? gde? kogda?, edited by A. Epshtein, Kharkov, 1992.

Vladimir Vysotskii grew up in the backstreets of central Moscow with the exception of a two-year period spent in East Germany when his father was posted to Eberswalde as an army officer. His childhood experience exerted a long-lasting effect on his later career; he would always remain loyal to the use of colloquial language, underground jargon, and alcohol – things he imbibed during those formative years.

While training as an actor, Vysotskii began to write poems, which he sang to his own guitar accompaniment. He was one of the bards or "guitar poets", and his hoarse voice soon became his trademark. Vysotskii's songs and poems deal with themes incompatible with socialist realist art: alcoholism, Stalinism, authentic street life, prostitution. Since he addressed the people and their problems, he received popular veneration, but was never officially recognized as a poet during his lifetime. Very few of his poems and songs were published in the Soviet Union, but most were circulated on private tapes (*magnitizdat*).

Vysotskii started performing his songs around 1960, initially to friends, and only later to large audiences. These songs can be grouped according to different themes. There are "street" or "criminal" songs, which stylize the young Vysotskii's experience of life in the Moscow streets. He explicitly referred to those aspects of Soviet life that were taboo subjects: eroticism and promiscuity in "Ninka" or "Navodchitsa" ("The Lady Nark"); prostitution and theft in "Grustnyi romans" ("Sad Romance"); or alcoholism in "Militseiskii protokol" ("Militia Report"). He used colloquial language, right down to the vulgar slang of Moscow's streets. He parodied fairy tales and folk legends, such as "Lukomor'ia bol'she net" ("The Sea-Cove's Gone for Good"), which is a skit on Pushkin's *Ruslan and Liudmila* juxtaposing "conventional folk phraseology" with "vulgar urban slang" (Smith).

A number of Vysotskii's poems concern everyday Soviet life, which he treats in ordinary language. He mocked lifestyles, past and present: "Dialog u televizora" ("Dialogue in Front of the TV") is an understanding, yet parodic report of an everyday conversation of a couple in front of the television set, which he sang parodying the speakers' voices. In "Nezhnaia Pravda" ("Tender Truth") he attacks the pseudo-objectivity of the Soviet press, echoing the unjust and uninformed campaign a Soviet paper (*Sovetskaia Rossiia*) had launched against him in 1968. He investigated the everyday problems of the average citizen: flight delays and cancellations, the formalities and surveillance associated with travel abroad, overcrowded transport, discussions with the telephone operator. There are also several songs about sport that offer an ironic perspective on the Soviet obsession with fitness and physical exercises, such as "Utrenniaia gimnastika" ("a.m. P.T.") with its mockery of the daily morning exercises on radio, or "O sentimental'nom boksere" ("The Sentimental Boxer") where the movements of the boxer carry political undertones.

Songs about the war form an important part of Vysotskii's work: although he did not experience it first-hand, his songs reveal a deep understanding of individual suffering. He expressed an unorthodox attitude by rejecting the war heroism prevailing in descriptions of the Great Patriotic War in favour of an emphasis on the individual and human sacrifice involved in the struggle. In "Serezha Fomin" he challenges the heroic principles of the Soviet Union when he reports that Fomin has been made a Hero of the Soviet Union although he has avoided the draft and never fought during the war; meanwhile the little man goes without any reward. In "On ne vernulsia iz boia" ("He Didn't Come Back") he mourns the death of a friend during battle, underlining the feeling of personal loss. "Na neitral'noi polose" ("In No-Man's Land") describes the attempt of a Soviet and a Turkish frontier guard to pick flowers for their beloved ones on neutral land, and asks why borders exist at all. Vysotskii's songs about war are descriptive and mournful, sad but without explicit reproach. His stance, nevertheless, was essentially a pacifist one.

A major theme throughout Vysotskii's career was the role of the poet in society: his delicate and fragile position, his loneliness, his responsibility are reflected in such songs as "Natianutyi kanat" ("The Tightrope"), or "Koni priveredlivye" ("Unruly Horses"). Later the poet was preoccupied with the theme of death, first in a humorous form, "O fatal'nykh datakh i tsifrakh" ("On Fatal Dates and Figures"), later gloomily anticipating an early death in "Mne sud'ba" ("It's My Fate") and "Ia iz dela ushel" ("I Retired").

His most famous song is undoubtedly "Okhota na volkov" ("Wolf Hunt"), where he identifies with a wolf, doomed to be hunted by the huntsmen (the Soviet system), but finally breaks with all conventions and escapes. This song reflects a poem by Sergei Esenin in which the latter also identified with a hunted wolf – who is killed. Its only hope is that somebody will write a song about him; Vysotskii fulfilled that request, and he replaced Esenin as Russia's most genuinely popular poet.

Vysotskii's poems were not published in the Soviet Union during his lifetime; he attempted publication when he participated in the almanac *Metropol'* in 1979, which was later published abroad.

Vysotskii's fame as a bard and poet was complemented by his reputation as an actor, both in film and on the stage. He starred in films such as Muratova's *Korotkie vstrechi* [Brief Encounters], Stolper's *Zhivye i mertvye* [Living and Dead] (1963), and *Chetvertyi* [The Fourth Man] (1972), and Shveitser's *Malen'kie tragedii* [Little Tragedies] (1980, as Don Juan). On the stage of the Taganka Theatre under the director Iurii Liubimov he created the parts of Brecht's Galileo, Dostoevskii's Svidrigailov, and Esenin's Khlopusha. Most important, however, was his performance as Hamlet: he turned the Danish prince into a man from the street, allowing the little man to understand Hamlet's ethical dilemma, and started the performance with a recital to guitar accompaniment of Pasternak's poem "Hamlet" from *Doctor Zhivago* (then unpublished). He composed a number of songs for theatre productions and for films, and often performed his songs on the stage.

His death in 1980 marked one of the greatest losses for the Taganka Theatre; for the majority of Muscovites it was a far more important event than the Olympic Games that were held in Moscow during that summer. Vysotskii was a man of the people, an individual in constant contact with his social environment, and also an actor who was part of an ensemble. His songs belong to the modern urban folk tradition. In 1981 the Taganka Theatre created a production in homage to Vysotskii, which remained banned until 1988. His grave in Moscow's Vagankovo Cemetery has become a place of pilgrimage.

BIRGIT BEUMERS

Yesenin *see* Esenin

Yevtushenko *see* Evtushenko

Z

Nikolai Alekseevich Zabolotskii 1903–1958
Poet

Biography

Born in Kazan district, 7 May 1903. Grew up in remote Viatka province. Father was an agronomist; mother was a schoolteacher. Attended Urzhum secondary school; studied medicine in Moscow; studied literature at the Herzen Institute in Petrograd, graduated in 1925. Associated with Leningrad avant-garde artistic groupings. Worked for the children's publishing house, OGIZ, under Samuil Marshak. Began to publish in 1927. Arrested in 1938; spent six and a half years in prison and two in exile. Began to re-establish literary career in Moscow, 1946. Rehabilitated after the death of Stalin. Died of a heart attack in Moscow, 14 October 1958.

Publications

Collected Editions

Stikhotvoreniia. Washington, DC, Inter-Language Literary Associates, 1965.

Stikhotvoreniia i poemy. "Biblioteka poeta", Moscow and Leningrad, 1965.

Izbrannye proizvedeniia, 2 vols. Moscow, 1972.

Sobranie sochinenii, 3 vols. Moscow, 1983–84.

"Ogon', mertsaiushchii v sosude ..." ["A Light Flickering in the Vessel ..."], edited by N.N. Zabolotskii. Moscow, 1995.

Poetry

Stolbtsy. Leningrad, 1929; translated as *Scrolls: Selected Poems*, by Daniel Weissbort, London, Jonathan Cape, 1971.

"Torzhestvo zemledeliia" [The Triumph of Agriculture], *Zvezda*, 2–3 (1933).

Vtoraia kniga [The Second Book]. Leningrad, 1937.

Stikhotvoreniia. Moscow, 1948.

Stikhotvoreniia. Moscow, 1957.

Poems in *Post-War Russian Poetry*, edited by Daniel Weissbort. Harmondsworth, Penguin, 1974, 45–60.

Memoirs

"The Story of My Imprisonment", edited and translated by Robin Milner-Gulland, *Times Literary Supplement* (9 October 1981); as "Istoriia moego zakliucheniia", *Chistye prudy*, 2 (1988).

Critical Studies

"N.A. Zabolockij 1903–1958", by V. Sandomirsky, *Russian Review* (1960).

"Surrealism in Twentieth-Century Russian Poetry: Churilin, Zabolotskii, Poplavsky", by Simon Karlinsky, *Slavic Review*, 26 (1967).

Nikolai Zabolotskii. Zhizn'. Tvorchestvo. Metamorfozy, by A. Makedonov, Leningrad, 1968.

"Zabolotsky: Philosopher-Poet", by Robin Milner-Gulland, *Soviet Studies* (April 1971).

"Stolbcy" by Nikolai Zabolotsky: Analyses, by F. Björling, Stockholm, Almqvist & Wiksell, 1973.

"Some Themes and Motifs in N. Zabolockij's *Stolbcy*", by I. Masing-Delic, *Scando-Slavica*, 20 (1974).

"Zabolotsky and the Reader: Problems of Approach", by Robin Milner-Gulland, *Russian Literature Triquarterly*, 8 (1974).

"*Ofort* by Nikolaj Zabolockij. The Poem and the Title", by F. Björling, *Scando-Slavica*, 23 (1975).

Vospominaniia o N. Zabolotskom. Moscow, 1977; 2nd edition, Moscow, 1984.

"Zabolotsky's *Vremya*", by Robin Milner-Gulland, *Essays in Poetics*, 6/1 (1981).

Nikolai Zabolotskii, by A.M. Turkov, Moscow, 1981.

"Zabolotsky's 'The Triumph of Agriculture': Satire or Utopia?", by I. Masing-Delic, 42 (1983).

"Antithesis and Completion: Zabolockij responds to Tiutčev", by Sarah Pratt, *Slavic and East European Journal*, 27/2 (1983).

Nikolai Zabolotskii, by I.I. Rostovtseva, Moscow, 1984.

"'The Chickens also Want to Live': A Motif in Zabolockij's *Columns*", by I. Masing-Delic, *Slavic and East European Journal*, 31/3 (1987).

Nikolai Zabolotsky: Play for Mortal Stakes, by Darra Goldstein, Cambridge, Cambridge University Press, 1993.

The Life of Zabolotsky, by N.N. Zabolotsky, edited and translated by Robin Milner-Gulland, Cardiff, University of Wales Press, 1994.

The life and work of Nikolai Zabolotskii provide a remarkable example of the power of the literary – specifically poetic – vocation. He emerged not from the Moscow or St Petersburg literary intelligentsia, but from a family that had only just risen above its peasant origins, in what was even for Russia the exceptionally out-of-the-way and rural Viatka province. There were books in the house, and by the age of seven, apparently, Zabolotskii had chosen his future career. He got a good but unremarkable rural secondary education, and became an indigent student in Moscow, then in Petrograd, during the famine-stricken years immediately after the Revolution. Though briefly tempted by academic life, he was determined to be (and with some hardships became) a professional writer. Thereafter he pursued his mission with an innate stubbornness that eventually jeopardized his life and probably saved it too: he was arrested in 1938, but after prison and exile (perhaps uniquely) managed to re-establish himself afterwards as a writer. Personally unobtrusive, courteous and fastidious, of clerkly demeanour, the very opposite of the popular notion of the inspired bohemian, he was driven until, literally, his last day of life by the overwhelming sense of what he could do, and what it was his responsibility to do, in poetry.

Since Zabolotskii's manner of writing changed more than once, apparently abruptly and mysteriously, to the extent that one (well-disposed) critic could assert that "unlike Akhmatova or Mandel'shtam, Zabolotskii is moved by nothing other than the desire to write", his consistent single-mindedness of purpose deserves further scrutiny. His aims seem to have been at all periods fundamentally cognitive: poetry was to him a special kind of, or route to, knowledge. In his last full year of life he wrote notes (probably for lectures) that state the writer's purpose in terms that would not have been inappropriate for the Formalists of the 1920s:

> ... the genuine artist strips objects and phenomena of their everyday coverings and speaks to the reader: "Those things that you have become used to seeing daily, over whose surfaces your habituated and indifferent gaze slides, are really far from ordinary, far from everyday, but full of inexplicable delight ..."

To achieve his purposes:

> the poet works with all his being simultaneously: with reason, heart, soul, and muscles. He works with all his organism, and the more harmoniously integrated this work, the higher its quality. For thought to triumph he embodies it in images. For language to work he draws from it all its musical might. Thought – Image – Music: that is the ideal trinity towards which the poet strives.

The cognitive purpose and method remained constant: the objects of cognition and the stylistic means employed for its realization underwent remarkable transformations. (Perhaps this is appropriate, since transformation or "metamorphoses" – title of a fine poem of 1937 – are among Zabolotskii's constant themes). A frequent catalyst for changes of style or subject-matter would be encounters with writers, thinkers or their works: "as far as people and books are concerned, I have struck very lucky", as he wrote. The most crucial early encounter came in the mid-1920s when he met Daniil Kharms and Aleksandr Vvedenskii, with whom in 1928 he founded the OBERIU group of writers and performers. He rejected his early work, imitating as he said now Blok, now Akhmatova, now Maiakovskii, now Esenin, and sank himself in the composition of a cycle of highly idiosyncratic, fragmented, grotesque pictures of Leningrad life under NEP, that were to become the central element of his slim first book, *Stolbtsy* (*Scrolls*), which propelled him into instant notoriety. At that stage press criticism could be shrugged off; less than a decade later it might lead to arrest, even (perhaps particularly) in the case of a fundamentally apolitical writer such as Zabolotskii. In the 1920s his fantastical imagination brought him (and his friends) an invitation from the poet Samuil Marshak to work in children's literature, which provided his means of livelihood until translations, above all from Georgian, took over. As for OBERIU – whose manifesto Zabolotskii largely wrote – it was effectively snuffed out in 1930, though its members and supporters continued to meet informally (in Leonid Lipavskii's "Club of Semi-Literate Scholars", a curious discussion-group that gave rise to Zabolotskii's poem *Vremia* [Time]) for some years.

Zabolotskii's early work is often described as "belated Futurism", though he was choosy among his contemporaries (he admired in particular Khlebnikov and Mandel'shtam, later Pasternak, but rejected Maiakovskii and his followers, not to mention the whole of Symbolism, peasant poetry etc.). He was at home among classically-minded figures of the past: Tiutchev, Baratynskii, Pushkin, Goethe (he knew German), and 18th-century writing, particularly the dialogues of Skovoroda. But visual artists were just as important to him, and the greatest personal example was set by Pavel Filonov (1883–1941), the ascetic, obsessive, and charismatic painter whose theory of "madeness" led to an utterly individual yet self-abnegating art of intense analysis. Following his father's interests he was equally concerned with the natural sciences (particularly biology and ecology): here the major influence was another ascetic eccentric, Konstantin Tsiolkovskii (father of Russian rocket technology and cosmology), with whom he corresponded. In the 1930s urban grotesquerie was displaced in his work by a concern with the natural world, the ordering of mankind's place in it, the metamorphoses between animate and inanimate being, and the meaning of death. It led to a more ordered poetic texture (though without eliminating strangenesses of diction and perception): among several long poems *Torzhestvo zemledeliia* [The Triumph of Agriculture] caused a particular stir (it was taken as a lampoon on collectivization, and was partly responsible for his arrest).

Many Leningrad writers were arrested early in 1938 in connection with a supposed counter-revolutionary plot "led" by N. Tikhonov (who actually remained at liberty). Zabolotskii was lucky to escape with his life, after serious maltreatment and a spell in a prison psychiatric ward. He refused to confess or make any denunciations, and was sentenced to five years in the camps (such sentences were nearly always extended during World War II). He and his family never stopped trying to get the sentence revoked, and this may have assisted his eventual release (it was some time thereafter until he secured permission to live in Moscow). He wrote a sober yet hair-raising account of his arrest and interrogation ("Istoriia moego zakliucheniia" ["The Story of My Imprisonment"] – a classic of its kind), not published until long after his death. He survived imprisonment partly through getting a job as a draughtsman on the new BAM railway in the Far East, but hard labour in the Kazakh steppe permanently undermined his health.

Imprisonment virtually stopped his poetic activity, but on release (while still in exile) he resumed translation work on his classic version of the medieval *Slovo o polku Igoreve* (*The Lay of Igor's Campaign*), and in the late 1940s wrote some fine original poems still in the mode of his work of the late 1930s. Then he fell silent for the final Stalin years. He always found it hard to get his work published, and much did not appear in print in his lifetime; Soviet literary officialdom did its best to ignore the existence of his disturbing and obscure early work. In the Thaw of the mid-1950s, however, he found a new and fluent voice, and a small measure of public acclaim; in 1957 he was invited on his one visit abroad, to Italy. His late poems seem lucid and formally conventional. Social and personal themes appear (there is even a cycle of unusual love-poems, *Posledniaia liubov'* [Last Love]), but the old strangenesses of perception, and quest for cognition, are not far beneath the surface. His last major work is the cycle *Rubruk v Mongolii* [Rubruk in Mongolia], based on the journey of the historical 13th-century monk Rubrucius, witty and ironical while essentially serious, reminding us that for all his sobriety of countenance and formality in behaviour this enigmatic figure was full of fun, and had indeed written some of the wittiest light and occasional verse in Russian (little of which, alas, has survived). Underrated and often mocked – in Russia and abroad – during his lifetime, Zabolotskii is now generally understood to be among the great luminaries of Russian modernism, to have set a personal example few could match, and to be one of the main influences on the generation of Russian writers to have come to maturity in the last couple of decades.

ROBIN MILNER-GULLAND

Scrolls

Stolbtsy

Poetry collection, 1929

Zabolotskii's first volume of poetry, which appeared in 1929, contains 22 poems written between 1926 and 1928. The collection was revised and enlarged for subsequent actual and projected republications, but it remains in the fullest sense a work of the 1920s. On one level *Scrolls* is a satirical description of life in Leningrad during the NEP period, focusing particularly on the conspicuous materialism of the *nouveaux riches*. The title of the collection itself (*Stolbtsy*, meaning newspaper columns, scrolls) underlines its role as a chronicle of its times.

The first poem, "Krasnaia Bavariia" ("Red Bavaria"), catalogues the dubious attractions of a night-time bar, and from here the reader is taken on a tour of the city, visiting, for example, a market and a bakery; attending a football match, a funeral and a wedding; and observing the mechanical and philistine behaviour of the generic "Ivanovs" who are the city's inhabitants. Zabolotskii's gaze is fixed on a grotesque world beneath the veneer of social custom. In "Novyi byt" ("The New Way of Life"), the new order is personified as a typical NEP-man who goes through life rejecting the values of his elders and of religion and seeking only to satisfy his own appetite.

Zabolotskii's presentation of his material is determined by the programme set down for poetry in the OBERIU declaration of 1928. His aim is "to broaden and deepen the sense of the object and the word" and to present the "concrete object, stripped bare of its literary and everyday shell". Just as the fragmented "analytical" art of Pavel Filonov, which Zabolotskii much admired, creates a new and surprising vision of the world through the unexpected juxtaposition of images, so the discourse of *Scrolls* exploits the power of metaphor and particularly metonymy to produce similar displacements in perception.

The poetry of *Scrolls* is predominantly noun-based, reflecting Zabolotskii's concern for the "concrete object", and has even been compared with 17th-century genre painting in its affinity for cameo scenes. Yet Zabolotskii's images are characterized by a confusion of categories that undermines this stasis. For example, the description of a wedding feast in "Svad'ba" ("Wedding") includes a section told from the point of view of a chicken before it is eaten. The animate is often seen in terms of the inanimate, and normally insentient objects regularly acquire feelings and a life of their own. Laughter may take flight as a parrot, people become trees, a primus stove is seen as a dwarf, and often these associations are elaborated at length.

Zabolotskii's extensive use of reference to earlier works of literature is another instrument of displacement. The dominant allusion is the St Petersburg tradition of Gogol' and Dostoevskii in which the ordered public face of the city conceals an unpredictable and frequently sordid hyperreality. In "Belaia noch'" ("White Night"), for example, which begins with the teasing phrase, "Look, it is not a ball, not a masquerade", the romantic associations of summer nights are contrasted with the prosaic and drunken activities of actual lovers. The poem's title, of course, evokes the evanescent St Petersburg of Dostoevskii's novel *Belye nochi* (*White Nights*). Echoes of classical Russian poetry – Pushkin, Derzhavin, Blok – are also heard in Zabolotskii's verse, often with parodic intent. As in Gogol''s view of the city, nothing is quite what it seems.

A further tension is produced in Zabolotskii's poetry by the contrast between his dislocated imagery and satirical perspective and the formal properties of his versification. *Scrolls* is written using traditional metres, predominantly a very regular iambic tetrameter, and with conservative rhymes. Moreover, there is little use of enjambment. The "doggerel" effect thus produced is calculated to throw the poems' unconventional patterns of perception into especial relief.

While from one point of view *Scrolls* condemns humankind for failing to live up to its own ideals, from another perspective human behaviour can be seen to form part of a universal pattern of creation in which every entity is of equal importance. The confusion of categories that has been noted certainly contributes to a sense of the grotesque, but it also implies an essential equivalence between all members of the natural world, between animate and inanimate objects. A particular link is established between humans and the rest of creation by a persistent emphasis on death, the ultimate phenomenon in which the two are united. Death comes most strikingly to the soccer player hero of "Futbol" ("Football") and the singing "Cherkesenka" ("Circassian Girl"), just as it comes to the chicken of "Wedding". The imagery of death is often used too in Zabolotskii's description of nature.

The philosophical approach to the natural world and to the role of humans in it that can be discerned in *Scrolls* is more apparent in some of Zabolotskii's poems of the 1920s, which do not include the social satire elements of the *Scrolls* poems and were not included in their number. "Litso konia" [A Horse's Face], for example, celebrates the superior beauty and wisdom of horses in a world where only humans have the gift of speech. In this light *Scrolls* can be seen to look forward to Zabolotskii's post-war poetry where his interest in the philosophy of nature assumes a much more central role.

The publication of *Scrolls* in 1926 provoked heated debate in literary circles. Several prominent journals printed favourable reviews and praised Zabolotskii for the creation of his unique idiom. However, as the Communist Party began to assert its authority over literature in the late 1920s, Zabolotskii was attacked for concentrating on the depiction of vulgarity rather than praising the building of Soviet society. This line of argument was used increasingly against Zabolotskii in the years that followed, and although *Scrolls* is now recognized as among the most important works of late Russian modernism, it was never reprinted during its author's lifetime.

DAVID N. WELLS

Zadonshchina

Anonymous prose epic, c.1390

Editions

Povesti o Kulikovskoi bitve, edited by L.A. Dmitriev *et al.* Moscow, 1959.
Sofonija's Tale of the Russian-Tatar Battle on the Kulikovo Field, edited by Roman Jakobson and Dean S. Worth. The Hague, Mouton, 1963.
"Teksty *Zadonshchiny*", edited by R.P. Dmitrieva, in *Slovo o polku Igoreve: Pamiatniki Kulikovskogo tsikla*, edited by D.S. Likhachev and L.A. Dmitriev. Moscow and Leningrad, 1966.
Zadonshchina: drevnerusskaia pesnia-povest' o Kulikovskoi bitve, edited by A.A. Zimin. Tula, 1980.
Skazaniia i povesti o Kulikovskoi bitve, edited by L.A. Dmitriev *et al.* Leningrad, 1982.

Translation

"Sofony of Riazan: Zadonshchina", translated by Serge A. Zenkovsky, in his *Medieval Russia's Epics, Chronicles, and Tales*. New York, Dutton, 1963, 185–98.

Critical Studies

"La Zadonshchina": Réhabilitation d'une Oeuvre", by André Mazon, in *Le Slovo d'Igor*, Paris, 1940, 5–40.
La Zadonshchina, épopée russe du xv siècle, by A. Vaillant, Paris, 1967.
"Zadonshchina", by D.S. Likhachev, in his *Izbrannye raboty*, vol. 2, Leningrad, 1987, 263–72.

Zadonshchina [The Battle Beyond the Don] is an epic work in prose commemorating the victory of Grand Prince Dmitrii of Moscow over the Tartar leader Mamai at Kulikovo Field in 1380. The title, probably not affixed by the author, refers to the scope of battle across the Don region. The *Zadonshchina* is one of a cycle works written within a century of this historic event that include both short and long chronicle accounts, and several versions of an extensive tale called the *Skazanie o Mamaevom poboishche* [The Legend of the Rout of Mamai]. Neither the authorship nor the date of composition of the *Zadonshchina* can be fixed on the basis of the manuscript tradition. Yet unlike the *Slovo o polku Igoreve* (*The Lay of Igor's Campaign*), which has attracted so much controversy concerning its authenticity, the *Zadonshchina* is unquestionably a medieval work, dating either from the 1390s or the early part of the 15th century. It survives in six manuscripts ranging from a 15th-century copy to the most complete version preserved in the Undol'skii manuscript from the 17th century. These versions divide into two main branches and preserve the bulk of the text and its structure. The texts differ considerably, sometimes on major points and frequently on the level of detail where wording and spelling vary. Such discrepancies have made it extremely difficult to establish a standard text. Presently the most widely used reconstructions of the prototype are by Roman Jakobson and Dean Worth and the text established by L.A. Dmitriev.

The question of authorship has proven equally vexing. Two of the six manuscripts that are grouped together and form one branch of the textual tree, refer to Sofonii of Riazan in their heading and suggest that he is the writer. Elsewhere, in three manuscripts defining another branch, the heading fails to mention Sofonii; in contradistinction to the other manuscripts these copies refer to him in the text. While initially these references seemed to solve the question of attribution, the Russian scholar Rufina Dmitrieva has persuasively argued that in these copies the author is citing Sofonii as a predecessor, on the model of the writer of *The Lay of Igor's Campaign*, who cites Boian as his artistic paradigm. If Sofonii were the author he would hardly refer to himself in this manner. Thus the identity of the author remains open to conjecture.

Apart from its intrinsic merit and the light it sheds on the literary culture of medieval Russia late into the Tartar occupation, the *Zadonshchina* is of historical interest in the relation it bears to *The Lay of Igor's Campaign*. The works share a common lexicon, set of images and identical phrases, making it clear that there has been wholesale imitation. When the Undolskii version first appeared in 1852 the remarkable number of borrowings were taken as proof of the authenticity of *The Lay of Igor's Campaign*. It was argued that the writer of the *Zadonshchina*, whether he was working in the 1390s or somewhat later, must have had a copy of the earlier epic before him. Following this argument it became almost automatic to praise *The Lay of Igor's Campaign* as a work of original genius and, correspondingly, to disparage the *Zadonshchina* as an imperfect, derivative work of admirable patriotism but clumsy technique. In the 1930s the French scholar André Mazon ignited controversy by making a counter-claim. While not questioning the premise that in literary history an imitation is inferior to the model, Mazon argued that in many respects the *Zadonshchina* was superior artistically to *The Lay of Igor's Campaign* and therefore bound to be the earlier composition. In so far as his convictions demonstrated the subjectivity of the claims that had been made on the evidence of artistic merit, Mazon succeeded in invalidating this as criterion for dating. If his arguments have not met with wide assent, they have at least emphasized the importance of the *Zadonshchina* as a work in its own right; it is not only considered to be of interest on account of its similarity to *The Lay of Igor's Campaign*.

The *Zadonshchina* begins with an introduction in which Prince Dmitrii and his brother Prince Volodimir learn, during a feast, that the Tartar Mamai has invaded. In a lyrical moment Prince Dmitrii imagines an ascent to the mountains of Kiev and conjures the panorama of Russia before him. This leads to a meditation on the plight of Russia: Dmitrii recalls the defeat of Rus' 160 years earlier at the River Kaiala when the Tartar yoke was imposed. At this point the author's voice intrudes, and conflates the defeat at Kaiala with the defeat Igor' suffered at the river Kala in 1185, thus extending the chain of misfortune and foreign domination. A transitional passage likens the two princes to soaring eagles. There follows the convocation by Dmitrii of allied princes, who show their unity against the enemy, (one of the key themes of the *Zadonshchina*). Instead of chronicling their procession, the writer inserts a highly evocative piece of description in which images from the world of nature anticipate the parallel landscape of the battlefield. Prince Dmitrii leads the charge against the Tartars and encounters defeat. The narrator once again steps in, eulogizing and heroicizing the dead. His own plaint is echoed by the lamentation of the wives of the fallen in a traditional *plach* (lament). There follows the second, and now successful, attack by the Russian forces. The enemy Mamai is put to flight. The work ends as Prince Dmitrii extols the heroism of the Russian princes, enumerates the extensive list of fallen, and thanks God for punishing the arrogant Tartar and saving the Russian land.

The *Zadonshchina* is less unified stylistically than *The Lay of Igor's Campaign*. In the nature descriptions and the high pathos of its laments the author employs a high poetic style that apparently owes much to *The Lay of Igor's Campaign*. If, in the more descriptive passages the author lifted phrases from his predecessor, the nature passages are none the less more dynamic and effusive, proof of occasional original inspiration. This is particularly visible in the extensive ornithological imagery. Elsewhere, and particularly in the descriptions of battle, the author prefers a dry matter-of-fact prose style, more in keeping with chronicle writing. The author characterizes the work as a *zhalost'* (lament) and *pokhvala* (eulogy). As in *The Lay of Igor's Campaign*, the lament represents a turning-point as victory displaces defeat. Just as Igor' eventually returns from captivity, Dmitrii also saves the day after initial disaster. Whether or not one accepts the suggestion of Jakobson and Worth that the two works comprise a diptych, it is clear that they are closely related not only on the level of style and structure but also thematically. While *The Lay of Igor's Campaign* records the disastrous effects of disunity among the Russian princes, the *Zadonshchina* hails the national unity shown at Kulikovo as an end to the foreign domination of Russia and the restoration of former independence.

ANDREW KAHN

Mikhail Nikolaevich Zagoskin 1789–1852

Novelist and dramatist

Biography

Born 25 August 1789. Fought in the 1812 conflict: much decorated. Entered the civil service and was elevated subsequently to a succession of posts, culminating with appointment as Director of Moscow Theatres. Died in Moscow, 5 July 1852.

Publications

Collected Editions

Polnoe sobranie sochinenii, 10 vols. Moscow, 1898.

Sochinenii, 2 vols. Moscow, 1987.

Askol'dova mogila. Iurii Miloslavskii [Askol'd's Grave. Iurii Miloslavskii]. Moscow, 1994.

Fiction

Iurii Miloslavskii, ili Russkie v 1612 godu [Iurii Miloslavskii, or the Russians in 1612]. Moscow, 1829; Paris, YMCA-Press, 1954; Moscow, 1956; translated as *The Young Muscovite, or the Poles in Russia*, by Frederic Chamier, 3 vols, New York, Harper, and London, Cochrane, 1834.

Roslavlev, ili Russkie v 1812 godu [Roslavlev, or the Russians in 1812]. Moscow, 1831.

Askol'dova mogila [Askold's Grave]. Moscow, 1833.

Brynskii les [Brynskii Forest]. Moscow, 1846.

Tales of Three Centuries, translated by Jeremiah Curtin. Boston, Little Brown, 1891.

Play

Stikhotvornaia komediia kontsa XVIII i nachala XIX veka [Comedy in Verse of the End of the 18th Century and Beginning of the 19th], edited and with an introductory article by M.O. Iankovskii. Moscow and Leningrad, 1964.

Critical Studies

"Istoricheskii roman", by S.M. Petrov, in *Istoriia russkogo romana v dvukh tomakh*, edited by G.M. Fridlender, 2 vols, Moscow and Leningrad, 1962, vol. 1, 203–50.

"M.N. Zagoskin as a Historical Novelist", by Miriam G. Schwartz, PhD dissertation, Columbus, Ohio State University, 1978.

Russian Romantic Fiction, by John Mersereau, Jr, Ann Arbor, Ardis, 1983, 102–11.

A History of Russian Literature of the Romantic Period, by William Edward Brown, Ann Arbor, Ardis, 1986, vol. 2, 280–87.

Pre-eminent among writers of historical fiction in the first decades of the 19th century, Mikhail Zagoskin belonged to a corps of novelists who supplied a recently engendered need in Russia for full-length adventure tales that dramatize great moments of national historical pride. This was a loose confraternity of novelists that include, among others, Bulgarin, Lazhechnikov, Masal'skii, Polevoi, Vel'tman, and Zotov. Unfurled panoramically across broad novelistic canvases, these works chimed with an eagerly discovered sense of national consciousness. Feeding into this particularly were memories of the war in 1812 and the concomitant awakening of interest in the largest moments of the turbulent national past, captured by such as Zagoskin in a highly-coloured and dramatic, rather than meditatively antiquarian, frame of reference. His epic, stirring fictions represent a novelization of the "great men" interpretation of history, and are today apt to be seen as the keystones of the new Russian prose genre of the historical novel.

Zagoskin continued writing novels of a popularly acceptable standard up until his death in 1852, but it is his first example of the form – and the first example, indeed, in Russia – which consolidated the validity of this type of fiction in the eyes of critic and general reader alike. *Iurii Miloslavskii, ili Russkie v 1612 godu* [Iurii Miloslavskii, or the Russians in 1612, translated as *The Young Muscovite, or the Poles in Russia*] appeared in 1829 to considerable critical acclaim. Zagoskin had set out with high hopes of becoming a playwright, and it was Pushkin, in a review of the new novel, who first demonstrated the essentially dramaturgical wellsprings of its composition. The period of the "Time of Troubles" is vividly illuminated by tense collisions of dramatic characterization, a proliferating cast of dramatis personae, an eye for sharply apprehended visual symbolism, and a sense at once for immediacy and archaic distance, served by a scrupulous avoidance of anachronism and a credibly contemporary-sounding lexis in terms of dialogue and reported speech.

Zagoskin's dialogue, which preponderates over descriptive passages, is laconic, even at times urgent: that this does not detract from the irresistible sweep of the narrative is a genuine achievement, rarely attained by those who were caught imitatively in the novelist's wake. The dialogue is also, to its credit, socially as well as historically verisimilar. Pushkin, whose own dramatic recapitulation of the period, *Boris Godunov*, had appeared four years earlier, adverted by no means critically to the monumental edifice of patriarchal security that the novel appears to support, articulated through the interrelations of tsar, boyars, cossacks, monks, and the fractious groundswell of the people, the *narod*. Zagoskin's notion of national unity depends upon this willed symbiosis of rulers and ruled, a divinely ordained dispensation that is ever the agency by which Rus' (or Russia) must come into her own. This sentiment is focused most strongly in the novel among the feudal aristocracy, the boyars, whose fictional spokesman, Iurii Miloslavskii, is the hero of the work. He is the organizing genius of Russia's glory and greatness at a time of massive disruption, internecine strife, interregnum, occupation by Polish forces, and he is thus eligible for elevation to quasi-mythical status. Naturally the novel was destined for success: Zhukovskii and Krylov were among numerous celebrated voices joining the rather over-enthusiastic chorus of approbation, and the public ensured that the novel went through four editions in three years. The buoyant suprematism of the narrative has reserved a favourable attitude towards it in the more recent criticism of the Soviet period, which is by no means usual for prose writing of this vintage, although the feudalistic value-system advocated by Zagoskin – the glamorous overlords set alongside the lumpen ovine masses unaware of their need to be pulled into shape – has generally had to be pushed into the background.

Almost from its publication *Iurii Miloslavskii* has been compared to the prose fiction of Walter Scott, whose star was still waxing in Russia at the time, and more specifically with Scott's *A Legend of Montrose*. There is little doubt that the (unacknowledged) debt owed to Scott, not only in this but in Zagoskin's other novels, would include the methodology involved in representing convincingly the passage of historical time, and the usefulness of an interplay of real and imaginary characters, which permits the author to maintain basic historical fidelities while using character and psychology, rather than concrete events, to express this or that aspect of the flux of history. This is a romantic (or more accurately "pre-romantic") interpretation of historical contexts that had been famously practised across the turn of the century by the lyrical ballads of Zhukovskii, singing the psychological "moment", or the prose work of Karamzin, whose stories present history, as it were, expressed through the character, rather than the character slotting into the history.

Such compositional features recur throughout Zagoskin's later fiction, successful still, but progressively diminishing in imaginative strength. The title of his second historical foray recalls his first: *Roslavlev, ili Russkie v 1812 godu* [Roslavlev, or the Russians in 1812]. Zagoskin argues that what will perpetuate the spiritual superiority of Russia is "unshakeable loyalty to the throne, an attachment to the faith of our ancestors, and love for our native land." As a veteran of 1812 Zagoskin was here able to substitute memory for research, and approximate more nearly to the popular notion of the idealized virtuous warrior-hero, deriving originally from the Old Russian myth-kitty but speaking to the readers of the day in the magniloquent, modern idiom.

Zagoskin's later, weaker novels continue to be thus inspirited. *Askol'dova mogila* [Askold's Grave] and *Brynskii les* [Brynskii Forest] perform the Zagoskin treatment respectively on the Kievan Russia of Prince Vladimir and the expanding progressivistic Russia of Peter the Great. Historical baggage is unapologetically discarded whenever it is at odds with the patriotic afflatus that Zagoskin is perpetually seeking to invoke. Dramatically orchestrated derring-do governs the technique, as always. The imperial favour that Zagoskin thus earned for himself is largely the cause of his prominent position within a canon of variously forgettable writers, but it is not to be overlooked that at its inception the form was his own.

NICHOLAS CROWE

Boris Konstantinovich Zaitsev 1881–1972

Prose writer and dramatist

Biography

Born in Orel, 10 February 1881. Son of mining engineer of noble extraction. Attended school in Kaluga, 1892–98; technical school, Moscow, 1898–99: expelled for participation in student disorders; Mining Institute in St Petersburg, 1899–1901; studied law at Moscow University, 1902–06: did not graduate. Literary debut, 1901. Married: Vera Alekseevna Smirnova (née Oreshnikova) after her divorce from her first husband in 1912; one daughter. Chairman of the Moscow section of the All-Russian Writers' Union, 1921. Emigrated to Paris, 1922; lived in Germany and Italy before settling in Paris, 1924. Died in Paris, 28 January 1972. Buried in cemetery of Sainte Geneviève-des-Bois.

Publications

Collected Editions

Sobranie sochinenii, 7 vols. Berlin, Grzhebin, 1922–23.
Izbrannoe. New York, Put' zhizni, 1973.
Sochineniia, 3 vols. Moscow, 1993.

Fiction

Dal'nii krai [A Distant Region]. 1913.
Zemnaia pechal' [Earthly Sorrow]. 1916; reprinted Leningrad, 1990.
Putniki [Travellers]. 1919.
Ulitsa Sv. Nikolaia [St Nicholas Street]. Berlin, 1923; reprinted Moscow, 1989.
Strannoe puteshestvie [Strange Journey]. 1924; reprinted Moscow, 1996.
Zolotoi uzor [The Golden Pattern]. Prague, 1926.
Anna. Paris, 1929; translated as *Anna*, by Natalie Duddington, London, Allen and Unwin, and New York, Holt, 1937.
Dom v Passi [The House in Passy]. Berlin, 1935.
Puteshestvie Gleba [Gleb's Journey], 4 vols. 1937–53.

1. *Zaria* [Dawn]. Berlin, Petropolis, 1937.
2. *Tishina* [Stillness]. Paris, Vozrozhdenie, 1948.
3. *Iunost'* [Youth]. Paris, YMCA-Press, 1950.
4. *Drevo zhizni* [The Tree of Life]. New York, Izdatel'stvo imeni Chekhova, 1953.

Moskva [Moscow]. Munich, TSOPE, 1960.

Essays and Articles

Afon [Athos]. Paris, YMCA-Press, 1928.
Dalekoe. Stat'i [Far Away. Articles]. Washington, DC, Inter-Language Literary Associates, 1965.
Moi sovremenniki [My Contemporaries]. London, Oversesas Publications Interchange, 1988.
Dni [Days]. Moscow and Paris, YMCA-Press, 1995.

Biographies

Prepodobnyi Sergii Radonezhskii. Paris, YMCA-Press, 1926.
Zhizn' Turgeneva. Biografiia [The Life of Turgenev]. Paris, YMCA-Press, 1932; 2nd edition, 1949.
Zhukovskii. Paris, YMCA-Press, 1951.
Chekhov. Literaturnaia biografiia [Chekhov. A Literary Biography]. New York, Izdatel'stvo imeni Chekhova, 1954.

Critical Studies

Sikrety russkikh pisatelei, by Iu. Aikhenval'd, Berlin, 1923; reprinted The Hague, Mouton, 1969.
"La place de B. Zaitsev dans la littérature russe du XXe siècle", by N. Pervouchine, *Études Slaves et Est-Europeénnes*, 14 (1969), 121–28.
Boris Zaitsev i ego belletrizovannye biografii, by A. Shiliaeva, New York, 1971.
A Russian Cultural Revival, by Temira Pachmuss, Knoxville, University of Tennessee Press, 1981.

Bibliography

Bibliographie des oeuvres de Boris Zaitsev, by René Guerra, Paris, Institut d'Études Slaves, 1982.

Although he had a literary career spanning more than 60 years, 50 of them spent in emigration, Boris Zaitsev will probably be best remembered for a handful of short stories published in the first two decades of the 20th century. In all he published six collections of short stories during this period. In a brief autobiographical piece, "O sebe" [About Myself] (1943) Zaitsev asserts that he "began with impressionism" and goes on to maintain that he did not attain artistic maturity until after his emigration in 1922. The dominant qualities of the early stories are lyricism, musicality, plotlessness, a gentle melancholy, a preoccupation with death, and a painterly quality that sometimes gives individual stories a particular colouration. Thus "Volki" [The Wolves] is suffused with whites and greys, "Mif" [The Myth] with gold and "Chernye vetry" [Black Winds] with reds and blacks. Unwilling to be closely allied with any literary grouping, Zaitsev managed to remain on good terms with most of them, from Symbolists, such as Blok and other members of the Zori group, to realists such as Leonid Andreev and other members of the Muscovite Sereda group. He acted as a mediator between Ivan Bunin, with whom he remained in close touch in emigration, and the Symbolists. In his old age Zaitsev emphasized his unique position: "I was my own man. In my youth I was a loner and that's what I remained". His work also shows the strong influence of both Russian classical literature and European literature. He was particularly interested in the work of Maupassant, and the Belgian writers Maurice Maeterlinck, Georges Rodenbach and Emile Verhaeren. Among Russian classical authors the influence of Dostoevskii, Gogol', and especially Chekhov is easily discernible. Gogol''s *Nevskii Prospekt* is reflected in Zaitsev's story "Ulitsa *Sv.* Nikolaia" [St Nicholas Street] (1923), while Chekhov is one of three authors of whom Zaitsev wrote biographies (*Chekhov*, 1954). The other subjects for Zaitsev's biographical writing are Turgenev (1932) and Zhukovskii (1951). His play *Usad'ba Laninykh* [The Lanins' Estate] (1914), which enjoyed considerable success, also clearly derives from Chekhov, as does his story "Agrafena", widely regarded as his best work.

By contrast, Zaitsev's novel *Dal'nii krai* [A Distant Region] (1913) was not a critical success. Like many of his short stories it is markedly autobiographical. The heroine is a thinly disguised portrait of Zaitsev's wife, Vera Alekseevna. In *Zemnaia pechal'* [Earthly Sorrow] (1916) and *Putniki* [Travellers] (1919), on the other hand, the heroines are reminiscent of the heroines of Ivan Turgenev. The main theme of these stories is tragic love and there are strong echoes of the early stories of A.N. Tolstoi. Another strong influence was Vladimir Solov'ev, who introduced Zaitsev to Orthodox Christianity. Religious themes became an important part of Zaitsev's work and indeed some of his fictional works have as their basis the *zhitie*, or life of a saint. In emigration Zaitsev wrote lives of St Sergii Radonezhskii (*Prepodobnyi Sergii Radonezhskii*, 1926 and *Afon*, 1928), an account of his visit to the monastic communities on Mount Athos. In emigration the main theme of Zaitsev's work, perhaps inevitably, became his native land. In 1938, to mark the 950th anniversary of the coming of Christianity to Russia, Zaitsev published *Slovo o rodine* [The Story of My Homeland]. He claimed to detect three Russias, a Holy Russia, an Artistic Russia and a Military Russia, epitomized for him in the persons of St Sergii, Turgenev, and Suvorov. All his post-emigration fictional work, with the exception of the novel *Dom v Passi* [The House in Passy] (1935), is set in pre-revolutionary Russia. It includes the novels *Zolotoi uzor* [The Golden Pattern] (1926) and the tetralogy *Puteshestvie Gleba* [Gleb's Journey], which comprises *Zaria* [Dawn] (1937), *Tishina* [Stillness] (1948), *Iunost'* [Youth] (1950) and *Drevo zhizni* [The Tree of Life] (1953). This work, part novel, part chronicle and part narrative poem was viewed by the critic Gleb Struve as a pendant to Ivan Bunin's *Zhizn' Arsen'eva* (*The Life of Arsen'ev*). Zaitsev's post-1922 work is also characterized, like much of the best literature published within the Soviet Union, by a constant tension between the Old and the New, seen to best effect in his trio of short stories "Strannoe puteshestvie" [Strange Journey] (1924), "Avdot'ia-smert'" [Avdotia-Death] (1927), and "Anna" (1929).

Zaitsev wrote more than 500 reviews and other short pieces and played an active role in the Russian émigré press in Paris. He was also a skilled translator. While still resident in Russia he translated Flaubert's *La Tentation de Saint Antoine* (*The Temptation of Saint Anthony*) 1907 and *Un Coeur Simple* (*A Simple Heart*) 1910, and William Beckford's 18th-century oriental story *Vathek* (1912). His major translation, however, was of Dante's *Inferno*, completed in 1918 but not published until 1961. This work exemplifies Zaitsev's lifelong love of Italy, a country he visited for the first time in 1904, to which he returned several times in the period 1907–11, and where he lived briefly in emigration. In 1918, together with M. Osorgin, I. Novikov, B. Griftsov, P.P. Muratov and A. Dzhivelegov, he formed the Studio Italiano in Moscow. Zaitsev's impressions of Italy, which owe much to Gogol', were gathered in one volume of his Collected Works, but apart from these impressions, Italian themes can be found in the short stories "Izgnanie" [Exile], "Vechernii chas" [Evening Hour] and "Raphael", and the novels *Dal'nii krai*, *Zolotoi uzor*, *Iunost'*, and *Drevo zhizni*.

Zaitsev will probably ultimately be remembered as a stylist. Boris Filippov has written perceptively of the "water-colour quality" (*akvarel'nost'*) of his style. He is a master of the thumb-nail sketch and his portraits of his contemporaries, while never cruel, are always pithy. Thus Bal'mont is described as "victoriously capricious", a "magnificent chanticleer greeting the day", while Pil'niak is a "gingerish *littérateur*" and Esenin "a Russian without restraint". Probably the best epitaph on Zaitsev was bestowed on him as early as 1917 by Andrei Belyi: "A remarkable man and a small talent".

MICHAEL PURSGLOVE

Sergei Pavlovich Zalygin 1913–

Prose writer and literary critic

Biography

Born in Ufa province, Siberia, 6 December 1913. Family moved to Barnaul in Altai mountain range, 1920. Entered Agricultural Technical Institute in Barnaul, 1928; worked as an agronomist. Completed studies in hydrology and land reclamation at Omsk Agricultural Institute, 1939; began writing in Omsk. First story published, 1940. Hydrologist in north-western Siberia during World War II. Defended dissertation, 1948; professor in Omsk Agricultural Institute. Moved to Novosibirsk in 1955, then to Moscow in 1968. Secretary of the RSFSR Writers' Union, 1970; secretary of the USSR Writers' Union, 1986. Editor-in-chief of *Novyi mir*, 1986; published previously forbidden works by Nabokov and Solzhenitsyn, and Pasternak's *Doktor Zhivago*, late 1980s. Has devoted himself to ecological issues from the 1980s. Recipient: State Prize for Literature, 1968.

Publications

Collected Editions

Izbrannye proizvedeniia, 2 vols. Moscow, 1973.
Sobranie sochinenii, 4 vols. Moscow, 1979–81.
Sobranie sochinenii, 6 vols. Moscow, 1989–91.

Fiction

Ocherki i rasskazy. Moscow, 1955.
"Tropy Altaia" [Altai Paths], *Novyi mir*, 1–3 (1962), 3–77; 65–131; 49–129.

"Na Irtyshe (iz khroniki sela Velikie Luki)" [On the Irtysh ...], *Novyi mir*, 2 (1964), 3–80.
"Solenaia Pad'" [Salt Hollow], *Novyi mir*, 4–6 (1967), 3–94; 22–89; 5–116.
"Iuzhno-amerikanskii variant", *Nash sovremennik*, 1–2 (1973), 2–79, 81–139; translated as *The South American Variant*, by Kevin Windle, St Lucia, University of Queensland Press, 1979.
"Komissiia", *Nash sovremennik*, 9–11 (1975), 11–111, 44–121, 11, 13–105; translated as *The Commission*, by David Gordon Wilson, DeKalb, Northern Illinois University Press, 1993.
"Posle buri" [After the Storm], *Druzhba narodov*, 4–5 (1980), 5–59; 32–236; 5 (1982), 7–115; 7–9 (1985), 3–70; 80–132; 7–107.
"Novosti ekonomiki" [News of the Economy], *Novyi mir*, 7 (1991), 29–60.
"Kak-nibud'" [Somehow], *Novyi mir*, 11 (1992), 121–37.
"Ekologicheskii roman" [An Ecological Novel], *Novyi mir*, 12 (1993), 3–106.

Literary Criticism
Literaturnye zaboty [Literary Concerns]. Moscow, 1972; revised editions 1979, 1982.
Sobesedovaniia [Discussions]. Moscow, 1982.
"Literatura i priroda" [Literature and Nature], *Novyi mir*, 1 (1991), 10–17.
"Trifonov, Shukshin i my" [Trifonov, Shukshin and Us], *Novyi mir*, 11 (1991), 221–30.

Editor
The New Soviet Fiction: Sixteen Short Stories. New York, Abbeville Press, 1989.

Critical Studies
"A New Approach to Old Problems: The Contemporary Prose of Sergej Zalygin", by N.N. Shneidman, *Russian Language Journal*, 30 (1976), 115–29.
Sergei Zalygin: Stranitsy zhizni, stranitsy tvorchestva, by I. Dedkov, Moscow, 1985.
Sergei Zalygin, by A. Gorshenin, Novosibirsk, 1986.
"Sergey Zalygin and the 'Zhenskiy Vopros'", by Anne Hughes, *Journal of Russian Studies*, 50 (1986), 38–44.

As a writer Sergei Zalygin has tried his hand at many genres, but it is as a historical novelist that he has produced his major work. Zalygin's first attempts at short fiction were based on his own experiences working as a hydrologist and land reclamation engineer in Siberia. His first major long work, *Tropy Altaia* [Altai Paths] (1962), also touched on this professional experience as, within the plot framework of a scientific expedition into the Altai mountains, it confronts topical post-Stalin issues such as soulless careerism, the search for truth and man's relationship with nature. These themes are pursued in his next major work, *Na Irtyshe* [On the Irtysh]. This was the first Soviet novel to attack Stalin's policy of the collectivization of agriculture, and paved the way for further, and more substantial, critical works by Vasilii Belov and Boris Mozhaev in the 1980s. His novel *Solenaia Pad'* [Salt Hollow] is another historical work set in Siberia, this time during the years of the Civil War. Solenaia Pad' is the name of a village in the centre of bitter fighting between Whites and Reds in autumn 1919, and the central plot of the novel focuses not on the conflict of the two opposing forces, as expected, but on the two main Red leaders. Here Zalygin shows himself to be one of the first Soviet writers to describe a Stalinist type characterized by cunning and brutality, a ruthless careerist determined to destroy the "good" Bolshevik, the man of the people, and to attain power at all costs.

Very much a sequel to *Solenaia pad'*, *Komissiia* (*The Comission*), also set in Siberia during the Civil War, similarly criticizes by its very subject-matter the Party's official interpretation of this period. Once more the central character is an honest peasant, a man of the people who is destroyed by his times, but in this novel Zalygin interweaves ecological and even religious strands to construct a philosophical meditation on the fate of Russia in the 20th century. *The Commission* is Zalygin's most ambitious novel. *Posle buri* [After the Storm] is similarly vast in scope and intention, and continues Zalygin's historical interests. It is set in the NEP years following the Civil War, and attempts to portray a panorama of characters trying to adjust to the new Soviet reality after the "storm" of social upheaval. The novel also discusses in detail Lenin's policy of NEP that was intended to restore the USSR's shattered economy. It can therefore be seen as anticipating the economic and social debates that were to mark Soviet public life in the late 1980s.

Zalygin's most controversial work, however, has nothing to do with his rather bold interpretations of recent Russian history. *Iuzhno-amerikanskii variant* (*The South American Variant*) contributed to the contemporary discussion of male-female relationships in literature as it presented an assertive woman attempting to control her own life and desires. Here again, Zalygin was one of the first Soviet writers to portray sympathetically a woman intent on escaping from her established routine; he also painted a negative picture of the personal lives of many urban-based intellectuals. The novel was applauded by Soviet critics on the one hand for its realistic depiction of personal relationships, but was criticized on the other for its inability to portray the female psyche convincingly.

Sergei Zalygin has also written many essays of literary criticism, and much of his most significant work has been on the work of Chekhov, Platonov, Rasputin, Shukshin, and Trifonov. He continues to write in the 1990s, as well as following his editorial and ecological interests, but, as a writer of fiction, is most likely to be remembered for his series of historical novels, set in the early Soviet period, that challenged the established political interpretation, and in many ways anticipated the revisionist tendencies of glasnost.

DAVID GILLESPIE

Na Irtyshe

On the Irtysh

Novel, 1964

Published in *Novyi mir* under the full title "Na Irtyshe (iz khroniki sela Velikie Luki)" [On the Irtysh (From the Chronicle of the Village of Velikie Luki)], this work met with a mixed response from critics that mirrored the fortunes of de-Stalinization at that time. On the one hand, there were some who appreciated the novel's honest and far-reaching social criticism, whereas others were reluctant to see any departure from the socialist realist depiction of characters and historical events.

The events of the novel take place in the Siberian village of Krutye Luki in March 1931, that is, after dekulakization and the collectivization of agriculture, and following Stalin's article "Golovokruzhenie ot uspekhov" ("Dizzy with Success"), which put a stop to some of the excessive violence that accompanied the campaign. The central character is the peasant Stepan Chauzov, whom we first see heroically putting out a blaze in the village's grain store, risking his life for the common good. He thus serves as the peasant community's moral leader. The fire has been started by the kulak Udartsev, who disappears from the village, deserting his wife and children who are then looked after by Chauzov. This is one of the reasons for Chauzov's later downfall.

Chauzov possesses great courage and integrity; he is honest, hard-working, and prosperous, without exploiting the labour of others. His political loyalty should not be doubted: he fought against the Whites during the Civil War, and has joined the kolkhoz (collective farm). But the same positive qualities that make him stand out in the community also earn him the suspicions of the political activists. They see him as "a bearer of individualism and love of property", someone who has to be "isolated from the masses". Chauzov naively takes in and cares for the family of a kulak, a class enemy; he refuses to hand over his private grain to the collective farm as he now has extra mouths to feed, and he has stopped his wife Klavdiia from becoming an activist. In the end, Chauzov is categorized as a kulak and driven from the village because of his innate desire for prosperity and to live well, a desire that is evidently incompatible with the Stalinist vision of the future.

Other characters in the novella are not particularly developed, but rather represent particular types or viewpoints. Thus, Udartsev is a kulak, recognizable as such in his antipathy towards the new order, and similar to other such negative figures in the works of Stalinist "kolkhoz prose". The peasant Nechaev speaks with foreboding on the future bureaucratization and impersonality of agriculture and village life. Gilev is an *agent provocateur*, himself an exploiter of labour as his mute brother toils in the fields and his sister trades at the railway station; he is able to ingratiate himself with the authorities and it is he who is directly responsible for Chauzov's eventual exile as a kulak. Young Mitia also condemns Chauzov, a crime all the more damnable as Mitia had grown up in Chauzov's house, and in his betrayal we can see a symbolic representation of the village turning on itself and tearing itself apart. Pechura is the Party representative and kolkhoz chairman, a man wise enough to see that Chauzov is doomed unless he can become part of the system, rather than draw attention to himself by standing outside it. He wants Chauzov to become the kolkhoz chairman, then join the Party.

Perhaps the most significant character is Koriakin, the activist and former poor peasant, now living in the city, who sees everything and everyone in purely ideological terms, and whose merciless logic bears no relation to objective reality. It is Koriakin who embodies the state's desire to control and manipulate the peasantry, to establish political hegemony over the village, but he is also portrayed as being driven by jealousy and a selfish desire to get even. For the first time in Soviet literature, the state's instrument in enforcing party policy in the village was seen as a negative influence and, more importantly, wrong in his judgments.

The action of *Na Irtyshe* takes place over four days and the author succeeds in investing the narrative with tension and drive. The novella also contains many lyrical and descriptive passages and, throughout, human life and fortunes are viewed as a part of the natural cycle. The author clearly has an ear for authentic Siberian peasant dialogue and contrasts this colourful and vivid speech with the crass and bureaucratic language of the activists. Above all, he brings to bear a clear distinction, or rather a gulf, between the world of the peasant, his aspirations and expectations, and the machinations of his political masters.

Zalygin has not only shown the injustices of the policy of collectivization (we also learn, almost as an authorial aside, that many peasants leave the kolkhoz after the appearance of Stalin's article), but also the persecution of a good, honest man by blinkered and scheming officials. Once again in Zalygin's fiction the State destroys the man of the soil, the true representative of the people. As an allegory, the work can be seen as a statement on the destruction of a whole way of life based on stability and harmony. Because of the time in which it was written, its message is necessarily understated and occasionally oblique, but its themes were taken up by other "Village Prose writers" in the more propitious times of glasnost, in works where the crimes of the state before the people could no longer be even half-concealed.

DAVID GILLESPIE

Evgenii Ivanovich Zamiatin 1884–1937

Prose writer

Biography

Born in Lebedian, 1 February 1884. Attended Progymnasium, Lebedian, 1892–96; gymnasium in Voronezh 1896–1902. Studied naval engineering at St Petersburg Polytechnic Institute, 1902–08. Joined the Bolshevik Party while still a student; arrested and exiled for political activity, 1906. Naval engineer, 1908–11; lecturer at St Petersburg Polytechnic Institute, from 1911; sent to England to supervise the construction of ice-breakers, 1916–17. Associated with the Serapion Brothers literary group, from 1921. Editor of the journals *Dom Iskusstva*, 1921, *Sovremennyi zapad*, 1922–24, and *Russkii sovremennik*, 1924. Worked for the World Literature publishing house. Served on the board of numerous literary organisations. Removed from the leadership of the All-Russian Writers' Union; his works were banned and he was unable to publish, late 1920s. Left the Soviet Union, 1931; settled in Paris, 1932. Died in Paris, 10 March 1937.

Publications

Collected Editions

Sobranie sochinenii, 4 vols. 1929.

The Dragon: Fifteen Stories, edited and translated by Mirra Ginsburg. New York, Random House, 1966; London, Gollancz, 1972; reprinted as *The Dragon and Other Stories*, Harmondsworth, Penguin, 1975.

Povesti i rasskazy. Letchworth, Bradda, 1969.

Sochineniia, 4 vols. Munich, Neimanis, 1970–88.

Islanders and The Fisher of Men, translated by Sophie Fuller and Julian Sacchi. London, Salamander Press, 1984.

Povesti. Rasskazy. Voronezh, 1986.

Sochineniia. Moscow, "Iz literaturnogo nalsediia", 1988.

My: Romany, povesti, rasskazy, skazki. Moscow, 1989.

Izbrannye proizvedeniia. Moscow, 1989.

Izbrannye proizvedeniia. Moscow, 1990.

Izbrannye proizvedeniia, 2 vols. Moscow, 1990.

Fiction

Uezdnoe, in *Zavety*, 5 (May 1913); translated as "A Provincial Tale", by Mirra Ginsburg, in *The Dragon: Fifteen Stories*, 1966.

Na kulichkakh, in *Zavety*, 3 (March 1914); translated as *A Godforsaken Hole*, by Walker Foard, Ann Arbor, Ardis, 1988.

Ostrovitiane, in *Skify* (1918); translated as "The Islanders", by T.S. Berczynski, *Russian Literature Triquarterly*, 2 (1972), 1–46; reprinted in *Evgeny Zamyatin, The Islanders / Vsevolod Ivanov, Armoured Train 14–69*, Ann Arbor, Trilogy, 1978; also translated as "Islanders", by Sophie Fuller and Julian Sacchi, in *Islanders and The Fisher of Men*, 1984.

Mamai, in *Dom iskusstv*, 1 (1921); translated as "Mamai", by Neil Cornwell, *Stand*, 4 (1976).

Lovets cheloveka, in *Dom iskusstv*, 2 (1921); translated as "The Fisher of Men", by Sophie Fuller and Julian Sacchi, in *Islanders and The Fisher of Men*, 1984.

Peshchera, in *Zapiski mechtatelej*, 5 (1922); translated as "The Cave", by Mirra Ginsburg, in *The Dragon: Fifteen Stories*, 1966.

Bol'shim detiam skazki [Fairy Tales for Grown-Up Children]. 1922.

My: Roman, in *Volja Rossii*, 2 (February 1927); separate edition, New York, Izdatel'stvo imeni Chekhova, 1952; New York, Inter-Language Literary Associates, 1967; London, Bristol Classical Press, 1994; translated as *We*, by Gregory Zilboorg, New York, Dutton, 1924; by B.G. Guerney, London, Jonathan Cape, 1970; Harmondsworth, Penguin, 1972; by Mirra Ginsburg, New York, Viking, 1972; by Alex Miller, Moscow, Raduga, 1991; and by Clarence Brown, Harmondsworth and New York, Penguin, 1993.

Rasskaz o samom glavnom, in *Russkii sovremennik*, 1 (1924); translated as "A Story about the Most Important Thing", by Mirra Ginsburg, in *The Dragon: Fifteen Stories*, 1966.

Nechestivye rasskazy [Impious Stories]. 1927; reprinted Ann Arbor, Ardis, 1978.

Zhitie blokhi ot dnia chudesnogo ee rozhdeniia ... [The Life of a Flea from the Day of Its Miraculous Birth ...]. 1929.

"Navodnenie", *Zemlia i fabrika* (Leningrad), 4 (1929); Leningrad, 1930; reprinted Ann Arbor, Ardis, 1976; Letchworth, Prideaux Press, 1978; translated as "The Flood", by Mirra Ginsburg, in *The Dragon: Fifteen Stories*, 1966.

Bich Bozhii [Scourge of God]. 1937.

Plays

Ogni sviatogo Dominika [The Fires of St Dominic]. Berlin, 1922; reprinted Würzburg, Jal, 1973.

Blokha [The Flea] (produced 1925). Leningrad, 1926.

Obshchestvo pochotnykh zvonarei [The Society of Honorable Bellringers] (produced 1925). Leningrad, 1926.

Sensatsiia, from the play *The Front Page* by Ben Hecht and Charles MacArthur (produced 1930).

"Atilla", and "Afrikanskii gost'" [The African Guest], *Novyi zhurnal*, 24 (1950); and 73 (1963).

Screenplays

Severnaia liubov' [Northern Love]. 1928.

Les Bas-Fonds [The Lower Depths]. 1936.

Biographies

Robert Maier. Berlin, Grzhebin, 1922.

Gerbert Uells [H.G. Wells]. Petrograd, 1922.

Essays

Litsa [Faces]. New York, Izdatel'stvo imeni Chekhova, 1955; New York, Inter-Language Literary Associates, 1967; translated as *A Soviet Heretic: Essays*, by Mirra Ginsburg, Chicago, University of Chicago Press, 1970; London, Quartet, 1991; Evanston, Illinois, Northwestern University Press, 1992.

Critical Studies
Zamyatin: A Soviet Heretic, by David J. Richards, London, Bowes and Bowes, 1962.
The Life and Works of Evgenii Zamjatin, by Alex M. Shane, Berkeley, University of California Press, 1968 (includes bibliography).
Evgenij Zamjatin: An Interpretative Study, by Christopher Collins, The Hague, Mouton, 1973.
"Literature and Revolution in *We*", by Robert Russell, *Slavonic and East European Review*, 51 (1973), 36–46.
Brave New World, 1984, and We: An Essay on Anti-Utopia, by Edward J. Brown, Ann Arbor, Ardis, 1976.
"A Modernist's Palette: Color in the Fiction of Evgenij Zamjatin", by Julian W. Connolly, *Russian Language Journal*, 33/115 (1979), 82–97.
"The Imagination and the "I" in Zamjatin's *We*", by Gary Rosenshield, *Slavic and East European Journal*, 23/1 (1979), 51–62.
Three Russian Writers and the Irrational: Zamyatin, Pil'nyak, and Bulgakov, by T.R.N. Edwards, Cambridge, Cambridge University Press, 1982.
"Adam and the Ark of Ice: Man and Revolution in Zamyatin's *The Cave*", by Andrew Barratt, *Irish Slavonic Studies*, 4 (1983), 20–37.
"The First Entry of 'We': an Explication", in *The Structural Analysis of Russian Narrative Fiction*, edited by Joe Andrew, Keele, Essays in Poetics Publications, [1984].
"Revolution as Collusion: The Heretic and the Slave in Zamyatin's *My*", by Andrew Barratt, *Slavonic and East European Review*, 62 (1984), 344–61.
Evgenij Zamjatin: Sein Weltbild und seine literarische Thematik, by Leonore Scheffler, Cologne, Böhlau, 1984.
"The X-Factor in Zamyatin's *We*", by Andrew Barratt, *Modern Language Review*, 80/3 (1985), 659–72.
Zamyatin's 'We': A Collection of Critical Essays, edited by Gary Kern, Ann Arbor, Ardis, 1988 (includes bibliography).
Autour de Zamiatine: suivi de E. Zamiatine, "Ecrits oubliés", edited by Leonid Heller, Lausanne, L'Âge d'Homme, 1989.
"Zamyatin's 'Friendship' with Gogol", by Julian Graffy, *Scottish Slavonic Review*, 14 (1990), 139–80.
The Literary Underground: Writers and the Totalitarian Experience, 1900–1950, by John Hoyles, New York and London, Harvester Wheatsheaf, 1991.
"The Last Utopia: Entropy and Revolution in the Poetics of Evgeny Zamjatin", by Efraim Sicher, *History of European Ideas*, 13/3 (1991), 225–37.
"Ornamental'nyi tekst i mificheskoe myshlenie v rasskaze E. Zamiatina 'Navodnenie'", by Wolf Schmidt [Vol'f Shmid], *Russkaia literatura*, 2 (1992), 56–67.
"Evgenii Zamiatin in Newcastle: The Green Wall and the Pink Ticket", by Alan Myers, *Slavonic and East European Review*, 71 (1993), 416–27.
"K 'dopechatnoi' istorii romana E.I. Zamiatina 'My' (1921–1924)", by A. Galushkin, *Stanford Slavic Studies*, 8 (1994), 366–74.
"'Moi deti – moi knigi' – from Evgenii Zamiatin's Letters", by Julian Graffy and Andrey Ustinov, *Stanford Slavic Studies*, 8 (1994), 343–65.
Russkaia antiutopia XX veka, by B.A. Lanin and M.M. Borishanskaia, Moscow, 1994.
The Twentieth-Century Russian Novel: An Introduction, by David Gillespie, Oxford, Berg, 1996.
Zamiatin's "We", by Robert Russell, London, Bristol Classical Press, 1998.

Despite his sober and respectable appearance (he affected an English style of dressing after a trip to Britain in 1916 and was consequently dubbed "The Englishman" by friends and colleagues), Evgenii Zamiatin was one of Russia's most flamboyant, colourful, and talented writers of the 20th century. By turn professional writer, lecturer, translator, literary journalist, dramatist, and scriptwriter, he belongs generally to the Gogol'-Leskov-Remizov tradition in Russian literature, a tradition characterized by ceaseless experimentation and innovation, an impish sense of humour, a strong satirical and erotic bent, a flair for parody and grotesque exaggeration, an extraordinary gift for metaphor, and an expert knowledge of the Russian language in its colloquial and historical forms. His fiction was banned from the time of his emigration in 1931 until 1986, representing as it did a modernist and avant-garde tendency that Soviet authors were not permitted to explore for ideological reasons.

Zamiatin was born in 1884 in the small town of Lebedian, Tambov province, to religious and conservative parents (his father was a priest at the local church). After finishing secondary school in Voronezh in 1902, he studied naval engineering in St Petersburg. In 1905, returning from a study trip in the Near East, he witnessed the Potemkin mutiny in Odessa; later the same year, having joined the Bolshevik Party, he was arrested and briefly jailed for sedition. Subsequent years saw him living illegally in and around the capital and gravitating politically towards the Socialist-Revolutionary (SR) Party. His literary debut occurred in 1908 with "Odin" [Alone], a fictionalized account of his time spent in prison; and recognition as an extraordinary new talent followed in 1913 with publication of his third story, "Uezdnoe" ("A Provincial Tale"), in the Socialist-Revolutionary Party's cultural almanac, *Zavety*. Further notoriety was attained with his satirical account of army garrison life in Vladivostok, *Na kulichkakh* (*A Godforsaken Hole*), which led to the confiscation of the relevant issue of the journal in 1914.

Zamiatin was despatched to England in March 1916 to supervise the construction of ice-breakers at the Armstrong-Whitworth shipyards in Newcastle upon Tyne. Returning to Russia in September 1917, he found himself in Petrograd for the Bolshevik *coup d'état* ; however, despite his radical past, Zamiatin's response to the new Soviet government was cautious. Writing under a pseudonym for the opposition SR newspaper, *Delo naroda*, he criticized the barbarism and violence of the new regime, the flagrant disregard for human rights and the growing political intolerance. At the same time, he worked closely with Maksim Gor'kii on state-funded initiatives aimed at bringing culture to the masses, including translation studios and lectures in the techniques of creative writing at the Petrograd House of Arts during 1919 and 1920. Zamiatin was a sardonic, sarcastic and provocative polemicist, and his firm belief in the virtues of heretical thought led to brief periods of arrest in 1919 and 1922. Difficulties with getting his works published in the 1920s led him to try his hand at writing plays and film scenarios based on his own stories; however, increasing official intolerance of non-conformist artists and independent thinkers culminated in a vicious campaign of vilification in 1929 over the publication abroad of his dystopian novel, *My* (*We*). Zamiatin refused to recant; yet surprisingly, after a well-framed and courageous letter of complaint to Stalin himself (no doubt aided by Gor'kii's assiduous intervention behind the scenes on his behalf), he was given permission to travel abroad in 1931. He died in exile in Paris in March 1937, still holding his Soviet passport.

Zamiatin was by nature an innovator who constantly developed his methods and devices. His first stories are set in the provinces and feature a highly colloquial, crude, and expressive mode of narration, almost as if the author is hiding behind the mask of a provincial narrator whose language, outlook, and social position are markedly different from his own. Impossible to translate adequately into English, the language of these stylizations is full of dialect, ellipses, and violent syntactical inversions. Zamiatin believed that popular speech should be enfranchised within literary prose for an effect of vigour, dynamism, and spontaneity. His fiction at this stage incorporates materials from the imaginative world of the "folk", such as oral literature, customs and rituals, superstitions, popular songs, ballads and saints' lives; yet his attitude towards this world is ironic and subversive. The exploration of the darker side of provincial reality, especially the suffocation, stifling tedium, and violent brutality that characterized the lives of the peasantry and lumpen proletariat, was nothing new in Russian literature; but Zamiatin's poetic gifts, and the harsh, euphonic instrumentation of his prose were highly idiosyncratic. For many, the stories of this period are his special contribution to Russian literature.

His time spent in Britain resulted in a radical development of his prose style and the appearance of themes and devices that characterize his mature period. In "Ostrovitiane" ("The Islanders") and "Lovets chelovekov" ("The Fisher of Men") to compensate for the radical change of class and milieu depicted, coarseness and harshness give way to an impression of sophistication and mellifluousness. Zamiatin's "English" stories are densely packed with inventive and brilliantly observed metaphors, much in the manner of Charles Dickens. His target, like that of Dickens in *Hard Times*, is the machine-like regularity, conformity, and predictability of middle-class surburban life; yet this orderly, repressive existence is constantly in the process of disruption in the form of primitive and irrational instincts, such as sexual love. This energy-entropy opposition forms the vital link between Zamiatin's experience in Britain and the development of his artistic philosophy *vis-à-vis* the October Revolution. The growing cult of the machine among proletarian poets, Constructivists and Futurists, as well as his interest in the science-fiction novels of H.G. Wells, gave rise to *We*, a dazzling but ultimately over-formulaic expression of his fears regarding a technological, collectivized future. A further experiment in the fantastic genre, this time intersecting the story of a dying star on a collision course with Earth with the final hours of a "reactionary" insurgent facing execution during the Civil War, was attempted in 1924 with *Rasskaz o samom glavnom* ("A Story about the Most Important Thing")

The notoriety of *We* has tended to overshadow his other achievements: the *Skazki pro Fitu* [Tales of Theta], a series of miniature satires that attempt the first literary lampoon of Lenin; "Drakon" ("The Dragon"), a surreal, pseudo-apocalyptic vignette about Red Army brutality in the wintry hell-fire of the Revolution; "Mamai", a sharp Gogolian comedy about an insurance-seller's obsessional love of books during the early months of revolution; "Peshchera" ("The Cave"), a tragic story about the desperate struggle to preserve dignity and morality in the famine-struck, ice-bound capital; and lastly the two hagiographical parodies, *O tom, kak istselen byl otrok Erazm* ("The Healing of the Novice Erasmus") 1922 and *O chude, proisshedshem v Pepel'nuiu Sredu* ("The Miracle of Ash Wednesday") 1926. Although Zamiatin's prose output diminished towards the end of the 1920s as his attention was drawn towards theatre and film, he did produce one masterpiece, "Navodnenie" ("The Flood"), a perfectly executed, Dostoevskian tale about a woman whose desperate desire to have a child leads her to commit an axe murder.

While abroad after 1931, Zamiatin devoted himself almost exclusively to screenplay versions of Russian classics; yet his only real success came with Jean Renoir's *Les Bas-Fonds* [The Lower Depths], which was adapted from Gor'kii's classic play of the same title and released in December 1936.

PHILIP CAVENDISH

The Islanders

Ostrovitiane

Story, 1918

This story, written in 1917, depicts life in England as experienced by Zamiatin when he worked in Newcastle, Sunderland, and South Shields. In his autobiography Zamiatin recollects writing "The Islanders" during World War I in England while being bombed by the German warplanes; hearing the news about the February Revolution in Russia:

> when the newspapers had been saturated with headlines such as "Revolution in Russia", "Abdication of Russian Tsar", it became intolerable to stay in England, and in September 1917 I took an old English boat back home (it was so old that nobody would have cared if it had been shot up by Germans).

The story was published in 1918 in a collection, compiled and edited by Zamiatin's friend, Ivanov-Razumnik. Reflecting on his work in England as ship-designer and writer, he commented that his ice-breaker ("Aleksandr Nevskii") and his story ("The Islanders") were both successful.

"The Islanders" may be seen as a satirical description of English life: the small town stands out as a hyperbolical symbol of the small-mindedness of its inhabitants. It develops some of the themes and imagery of Zamiatin's prose, revealing disturbing aspects of life in rural Russia. Zamiatin's talent of stylization is particularly evident in his "English" prose; "The Islanders" may be easily mistaken for a translation from English. It deals with the conflict also featured in other Zamiatin's writings between the individual and society. The main character of the story, young Lord Kemble [or Campbell], falls in love with an actress of disrepute who is getting divorced from her husband. Lord Kemble's mother, the local priest Dooley, and the parish are shocked by his intention to marry a woman of lower social standing. They plot to enter her apartment so as to allow the young Kemble to witness a love-making scene between the actress and the barrister O'Kelly, Kemble's boss. Kemble is shocked by the revelation of betrayal, and following the episode he shoots O'Kelly. He gives himself up to the police and is subsequently imprisoned and executed. The execution is depicted by Zamiatin as one of those spectacles – like boxing – which does not disturb the peaceful and boring routine of the community. Zamiatin's use of metonymy is particularly forceful at the end of the story, when after the execution he draws a landscape bathed in glorious sunshine:

> It was not possible to hear anything else: the scales were rotating vigorously, variegated with scarves and shouts. The sun, pink and indifferent, was triumphant. The Salvation Army trumpets were playing a slow hymn. Some began kneeling with relief – to pray for the soul of the murderer.

The narrative is permeated with ironic remarks and a merciless description of a society that runs like clockwork. Zamiatin's irony is strongly felt in the scene portraying a crowd annoyed by the delay of the execution:

> Hamburger-like, red-faced regulars of boxing and racing were glued to their watches. The Salvation Army trumpets were shining indifferently. The red-faced, plump, triumphant sun was rolling out slowly ... The moment was tense and glass-still, but nothing followed. The bell was silent ... The whole crowd felt offended, including all these fans of boxing and racing, and the defenders of culture.

Love is presented in Zamaitin's prose as an expression of the individual and the unconventional; however, any break with the established routine and order leads his characters to death. Perhaps Zamiatin's vision of civilized society is grotesque. It is disturbing since it tries to impose rationalized forms of being onto a natural environment, pushing mankind ever more into an artificial world where chaos and emotions are strictly controlled. The vicar Dooley is the most vivid representative of the civilized outlook in "The Islanders". He preaches on the necessity of parliamentary ratification of the bill he calls The Legacy of Salvation – in order that salvation "should become mathematically inevitable" for every member of civilized society. The end of the story suggests that Dooley's vision of salvation will soon be forced upon everyone. In "The Islanders" the image of a scientifically organized society, operating with abstract values, foreshadows Zamiatin's novel *We*, the work that is thought to have influenced George Orwell.

Metonymy helps Zamiatin to reveal the signs of mechanization of members of society. We learn that the pince-nez is the main and the most dominant part of Mrs Dooley's body, that Lady Kemble's lips move like worms (the narrator avoids mentioning the word "lips", referring instead to a "slight movement of worms" on her face), that Didi's dog is a marble-like pet, that Kemble's chin is a tractor, and that an electric iron is in his view the embodiment of homeliness and happiness. In some ways Zamiatin's story echoes the problems raised in H.G. Wells's writing, advancing the idea of the reorganization of society. His true sympathy, however, lies in the opposite direction: with those like the young lord Kemble who follow moral beliefs and irrational impulses.

The story contains 16 short chapters; the titles of each chapter highlight one particular detail or episode that is projected like a cinematic "close up". Some scholars point out the structural similarities of "The Islanders" with the montage technique employed in film-making. Remizov claimed that in Russian literature only Belyi and Zamiatin could produce narratives so solidly structured. Yet the narrative structure of the story is far from being linear. As Leonid Geller observes, the style of the story is elliptical: the reader is forced "to reconstruct the omitted episode, to guess the thoughts and emotions of the characters by just one gesture, to imagine how the interrupted conversation would have ended". It clearly reflects Zamiatin's dissatisfaction with the traditional plot-building adopted by 19th-century realists that forced him to experiment with the Symbolist style of writing. One of the chapters, "Litso kul'turnogo cheloveka" ("The Face of the Civilized Person"), is intended to tease readers: it claims that a "civilized person ought to have no face whatsoever. It should look just like the face of other (civilized) people, and certainly it should never in any circumstances change its expression". Zamiatin's story combines detailed insights with the symbolic, the paradoxical with straightforward abrupt dialogues, and fantastic elements with satirical down-to-earth observations. The title implements a sense of estrangement, but the plot is presented in a way that evokes and shocks at the same time. It is one of the first Russian anti-Utopian works of the 20th century to be inspired by H.G. Wells, whose novels fascinated Zamiatin in their capacity as new "urban fairy tales".

ALEXANDRA SMITH

We

My

Novel, 1924

We, substantially written in 1920 and completed in 1921, is Zamiatin's most celebrated work. The author hoped to have it published either by one of the companies with which he had connections or in the journal *Russkii sovremennik*, which he edited, but these plans came to nothing and the novel remained unpublished in Russia (although it was well known in literary circles since Zamiatin allowed the manuscript to be widely circulated and he himself frequently read extracts in public). Unusually for a work that has come to be recognized as a masterpiece, it was first published not in the language of composition, but in English translation in 1924. Extracts from the Russian text were published in Prague in 1927, but the full Russian version appeared as late as 1952 in New York and the first publication in Russia itself was in 1988, more than 50 years after Zamiatin's death.

Zamiatin described *We* as his "most jocular and most serious piece". Set at least 1000 years in the future in OneState, an organized and rational society run by a dictator called the Benefactor, the novel takes the form of a diary kept by D-503, an engineer and chief constructor of a spaceship called the Integral that is intended to spread OneState's message of total control and "mathematically infallible happiness" to other planets. At first the diary is intended as a hymn of praise to the Benefactor and the State, but D-503 falls in love with I-330, a female member of a revolutionary group called the MEFI, and under the influence of passion his diary entries are transformed into a record of his increasing irrationality and rebellion, culminating in a visit to the MEFI outside the Green Wall that surrounds and protects OneState and an unsuccessful attempt to hijack the Integral during its maiden flight. The Benefactor responds, however, with a compulsory operation to remove the imagination – a fantasectomy – and D-503 becomes once again a fanatical supporter of OneState, able to watch dispassionately as I-330 is tortured prior to execution. As the novel ends, the outcome of the MEFI revolt is still uncertain. D-503 asserts that "reason must conquer", but fighting is continuing in the western suburbs, and in any case D-503's former lover, O-90, has escaped beyond the Wall in order to have their baby, so there is a continuing guarantee of revolution.

Despite its brevity (it consists of 40 fairly short diary entries occupying in most editions fewer than 200 pages), *We* is a densely packed compendium of Zamiatin's philosophical and artistic ideas as well as a highly influential example of the 20th-century anti-Utopian novel. It is particularly revealing to compare *We* with some of the articles that Zamiatin wrote in the early 1920s in which he sets out succinctly many of the ideas explored in the novel. "O literature, revoliutsii i entropii" ("On Literature, Revolution and Entropy") 1923, for example, deals with the theme of eternal movement on a universal scale (associated with energy), and presents any attempt to stand still, to believe in absolute truths, as ill-founded. From this follows the need for heretics to speak out against the accepted "truths" of any society: "Heretics are the only (bitter) medicine against the entropy of human thought". In *We* the supporters of OneState believe that they have almost reached perfection, and that some day – with the abolition of the remaining "Personal Hours" – no further movement will be necessary or possible; a paradise of total happiness will have been attained. It is against this notion of static perfection that the heretical I-330 and the MEFI rebel, drawing D-503 into their revolution.

The fact that *We* was not published in Russia during Zamiatin's lifetime was undoubtedly because of the many satirical references to aspects of early Soviet society. Zamiatin's contemporaries could not have failed to recognize the allusions to the theory and practice of the Proletkul't, with its emphasis on communality, to the Cheka, those early guardians of Bolshevik purity, and even to Lenin himself in the figure of the bald-headed Benefactor. For all that it seems to anticipate aspects of a later, more unequivocally totalitarian age, the novel's roots in Civil War Russia should not be ignored.

Zamiatin draws on a very wide range of sources for *We*, not only literary but also philosophical, scientific, and artistic. There are references, both explicit and implicit, to Lobachevskii, Einstein, the German physicist Robert Maier, the British mathematicians Brook Taylor and Colin Maclaurin, the American specialist in the organization of labour Frederick Taylor; to Plato, the Pythagoreans, Hegel and Nietzsche; to the Bible, particularly the Book of Genesis; to Milton and Goethe; to Pushkin, Chernyshevskii, and, especially, to Dostoevskii. The quantity and diversity of intertextual references adds greatly to the meaning of *We*, and the reader is drawn into an intriguing intellectual labyrinth. The links with some of Dostoevskii's ideas are particularly productive. The vision of paradise put forward by Shigalev (*Besy* [*The Devils*]), "The Legend of the Grand Inquisitor" (*The Brothers Karamazov*), and the Underground Man's rebellion against rationalism all find parallels in Zamiatin's novel.

We is the most fully-developed example of Zamiatin's modernist aesthetic, which he himself called "synthetism" or "Neorealism" and which he presented as analogous to the dynamic and revolutionary thought of Einstein. If, at first, D-503's prose appears to be the very model of clarity and stability, it soon becomes the antithesis of these qualities as it reflects the diarist's increasingly emotional and irrational state of mind. Sudden and unusual shifts of perspective abound, as do striking metaphors, many of which are the "extended" or "mother" images that serve as psychological leitmotifs and which are a central aesthetic principle in Zamiatin's mature work. Through his original use of language as much as through any of his actions, D-503 reveals himself to be a revolutionary. For Zamiatin, all true artists were, of necessity, heretics, and he underlines the link by tracing D-503's double journey from conventional citizen to revolutionary on the one hand and from mere copier from the State Gazette to original writer on the other. The use of colour and shape is particularly interesting and subtle, and indicates Zamiatin's empathy with contemporary artistic trends, including Cubism and the Suprematism of Malevich.

We has been read in many different ways: as a satire on Proletkul't, as a prophetic warning against the evils of totalitarianism, as a philosophical work, as a key text of Russian modernism, as archetypal myth. Zamiatin's multi-faceted novel supports all of these interpretations and more, and is now generally recognized as one of the major works of 20th-century Russian fiction.

ROBERT RUSSELL

The Flood

Navodnenie

Story, 1929

Zamiatin's last story to be published in the Soviet Union is representative of his later works, moving toward purity and simplicity, and preserving his prevailing tragic conception of life. A married couple takes in an orphaned teenage girl. After a time, the man begins a sexual relationship with the girl. His barren wife endures this situation until, following a major flood of the Neva River, she attacks the girl with an axe and chops her into pieces. Immediately thereafter the wife becomes pregnant, and as her pregnancy advances, so do her feelings of guilt and confusion. After giving birth to a daughter, she becomes convinced that she is dying and confesses her crime; however, she does not die, and the story closes with a policeman taking notes on her story.

Zamiatin's writing changed from his earlier ornate style to a less exuberant and more chaste prose; the narration is more objective, balanced, and classically restrained; satire is completely absent. This story was published when Zamiatin was already under attack, and until quite recently it was mentioned in histories of Russian literature only as a specimen of a certain "reprehensible tendency": i.e., Zamiatin's "primitivism" in characterization made the story "a most vile lampoon on the socialist epoch and its creators". Lately the story has begun to be published in anthologies as a masterpiece of Zamiatin's Neorealism.

The story echoes 19th-century Russian prose by continuing the St Petersburg mythopoeic tradition as well as the emphasis on character psychology. The composition follows the traditional pattern of a short story, and the theme of the flood takes on mythical dimensions under Zamiatin's pen. The story is perhaps the most intensely psychological of Zamiatin's stories, alluding to Dostoevskii's *Crime and Punishment* as a narrative about transgressing the threshold, committing an axe murder, confessing, and moving toward punishment. The story does not focus directly on the reality of the 1920s, although it alludes to the slow normalization of life through well-chosen details: Trofim Ivanych resumes shaving daily, the observation that nobody eats horsemeat any more, and so on. Outward reality appears obliquely through the prism of the characters' consciousness, and is reflected in selective details of everyday life, such as the shortage of bread, the deteriorating quality of coal, the silent machines, or the new game "Kolchak" played by the children. The theme of lawlessness and evil fostered by the Revolution is transferred indirectly on the psychology of the individual (people governed by base instincts, turned into savages). The characters' consciousness operates on the primordial mythical level, a step backward from the two thousand years of Christianity. The world of the story is tragically marred not only by violation of the laws of nature, but also by the lack of the redemptive force of love.

The plot centres on primitive and base human passions, sensual love, and jealousy, culminating in murder; it establishes a direct parallel between the inner events of the human soul and outward appearances. Zamiatin explored a similar theme in the 1913 short story "Chrevo" ("The Womb"), but these elements take a more complex form in "The Flood". Zamiatin wrote: "... the integral image of the flood is followed through on two planes. The actual flood in St Petersburg is reflected in the spiritual flood, and all the basic images of the story flow into their common channel". A natural disaster (a violent elemental force in the macrocosm) is mirrored on the level of smaller units, most obviously in the inner flood within the body (the microcosm of nature) and the soul of Sof'ia. Her actions rise through primordial gut sensations, the stomach and the subconscious, to the heart and mind. This inner process is linked to the psychological reaction triggering the action; thus all the compositional elements are linked by the circular and linear motion of the flood. In this way Zamiatin recreates the primordial mythological unity between humans and nature. The motivating force within the characters revolves around sexuality and natural reproductive urges, especially a woman's desire to bear a child, and the sins of child abuse, adultery, and jealousy culminate in the crime of murder.

The story is structured as a rising movement up to the murder and then a spreading movement. The imagery is built on a system of dichotomies (wet/dry, open/shut, up/down, barrenness/fertility, interior/exterior, victim/perpetrator, etc.), the conscious versus the subconscious, and recurring sensual perceptions (taste, smell, touch, vision/colour, sound). The colour pattern reflects a shift from black to white after Gan'ka's burial: a progression from dark anger, hatred, and death toward purification. The essence of the characters is conveyed through visual leitmotifs: a fly; Trofim Ivanych's teeth flashing like accordion keys set against his coal-black hair; Gan'ka's black birthmark on her lips and the lock of hair over her forehead; her hot, sweetish odour, round knees and other images that suggest fertility. The two female characters, whose hostile relationship is based on that of both mother-daughter and sexual rivals, undergo a partial metamorphosis into animals: Sof'ia is a bird and Gan'ka a cat, reversing their traditional roles in the story. These leitmotifs also introduce a fatalistic sense of foreboding through the parallelism of dream and reality. Many metaphors are linked to the cyclical, mythical movement of time, as in *Genesis*, day and night: "This was at night. Then came the day, and evening once again"; the seasons: as the story moves from spring to a hot, dry summer, on to autumn and then to a new summer, Sof'ia acts in accordance with these seasons. Another layer of archetypal images is related to the cycle of life-death-new life, centring on fertility, such as the *terra mater*, the life-giving sun circling above the earth; the clouds and the glass – a barrier; an empty pit parallels Sof'ia's barrenness. After Sof'ia slays Gan'ka, an inner flood of pent-up anger and hatred is released in her: she experiences relief and a sense of a fresh start, just as confession frees the suppressed self. This feeling is expressed in the independence of her hands and eyes, and in the act of freeing a caged bird from the intent stare of a cat. The natural cycle by which a seed dies in order to engender new life is altered by the violence of murder, just as the violence of the Revolution is reflected in the distortion of human personality and the natural way of life. Once the soil has been filled with Gan'ka's body and moisturized by blood instead of rain (the clouds are dry and barren), this fertilization extends to Sof'ia's womb as well: she is now able to conceive. Thus, she has conquered the guilt and shame of her barrenness; her masculine violence brings forth new life – a recreation of Gan'ka (she knows in advance that she gives birth to a baby girl). With the growth of the child in her womb, the urge to come to terms with her crime also increases. Finally, she empties herself physically through the physical pain of childbirth while the Neva River spills over its banks in a flood. Spiritually, in her subconscious post-natal confession (with the help of her recurring vision of the fly) she identifies the murderous hands as her own and experiences the freeing of her real self, reaching inner peace without ever reflecting on the ethical plane.

MARIA PAVLOVSZKY

Ivan Fedorovich Zhdanov 1948–
Poet

Biography
Born in Usti-Tulatinka, Altai, 16 January 1948. Attended Moscow State University, Faculty of Journalism, 1967; graduated from State Pedagogical Institute of Barnaul, Department of Russian Philology, 1976. Resident in Moscow since 1977. Has had a variety of jobs including: factory worker, land-surveyor, drill-operator, stage-hand, lift-operator, and editor. Member of the Soviet Writers' Union, from 1986. Member of Russian PEN club, from 1990. Participated in international poetry festivals and meetings of writers in Europe and the United States, 1988–95.

Publications
Poetry

Portret [Portrait]. Moscow, 1982.
Poèmes. Paris, Centre International des Lettres, 1986.
Tavsneds hvide frugs/ The White Raft of Silence. Copenhagen, Huseds, 1988.
Nerazmennoe nebo [Unchangeable Sky]. Moscow, 1990.
Mesto zemli [The Place of the Earth]. Moscow, 1991.
Poems translated by Gerald S. Smith, in *Contemporary Russian Poetry: A Bilingual Anthology*, Bloomington, Indiana University Press, 1993, 258–67.
Fotorot zapretnogo mira: Stikhotvoreniia [Photocopying the Forbidden World]. St Petersburg, 1997.

Critical Study
"Metamorfoza", by Mikhail Epshtein, in his *Paradoksy novizny*, Moscow, 1988, 139–76.

The first book of poetry by Ivan Zhdanov, *Portret* [Portrait], was published in the last year of the Brezhnev era, at the very height of social and cultural stagnation. It turned out to be quite an event. As a justification for such a strange and vague volume of poetry, which was well outside the context of official literature (being meditative or even mystical in content), the publishers carefully emphasized (on the cover) the peasant origins and proletarian career of the author. That was sufficient to satisfy the censorship of the time. Perhaps no one else from the so-called "second culture" (ie. the authors of *samizdat*) could provide such a social alibi. Thus, Zhdanov's book was the first public example of this type of radical, non-conformist art. The very lack of any political themes and nuances in it was indicative: the artists of the 1970s hated the political bravado and the rhetoric of the previous generation, the "men of the 1960s".

This first book was astonishing in its maturity; it contains a number of poems that undoubtedly can be considered masterpieces of Russian poetry. *Portret* had nothing in common with any of the trends of contemporary official poetry, either traditionalist or modernist (with the exception of Arsenii Tarkovskii, the last of the old masters of Russian verse). The collection demonstrated its links with Mandel'shtam, Khlebnikov, and other authors of Russian poetry's Silver Age, and one could recognize in it too echoes of 20th-century French and Spanish, German, and English poetry. Zhdanov utilized mythological and musical references; his metaphors were frequently based on archetypal and scientific images. All this was more than strange to the Soviet tradition. Yet more strange is the irrational semantics of these verses: they sound like a sort of puzzle, needing a philosophical or philological commentary. Zhdanov made no effort to be comprehensible to everyone, as this would have been the first pretence of the loyal Soviet writer. The critics invented especially for him – and for some other new poets, whose debuts followed that of Zhdanov (A. Parshchikov, A. Eremenko, I. Kutik) – the terms "meta-metaphorist" or "metarealist".

It would be wrong, however, to see Zhdanov as just an erudite poet. The profound originality of his Muse is of another order. Closest to him is perhaps the case of Dylan Thomas: the elementary innate power of his imagination, the liturgical solemnity of tone, the Orphic darkness of metaphor, the mighty and somewhat monotone rythmical sequences of stanza and, above all, the sonoric quality that tends toward magical incantation and which is highly impressive in authorial readings. All of these are Zhdanov's trademarks. Furthermore, his later poetry has become more and more inventive and sophisticated in its formal devices, even tending towards a loss of original integrity and freshness, just as with Dylan Thomas.

Zhdanov avoids autobiographical themes. His lyrical self is an epic one; all personal emotions are deeply transformed. Even grammatically, he tries to eliminate the pronoun "I" and prefers to speak in the second or third person. Nevertheless, the reader can clearly grasp the spiritual biography of the poet and his dramatic relations with the world: the vivid feeling of its providential beauty and wholeness, the shock of its corrupt and estranged actual state (which includes a sense of personal guilt and wickedness), an eschatological lust for a new heaven and a new earth, and heavy doubts about the very possibility of a better world. His early poems are full of hope, which can be called a paradoxical hope: "But you mustn't obey what you can yet open yourself to ...".

The later poems demonstrate an increasingly desperate attitude. Zhdanov's religious sensibility, with all the Christian references he employed (among his central and constant themes are the Crucifixion and prayer to the mother of God, the Protectress of all the world), is far from traditional Orthodoxy; it resembles a sort of Gnostic experience, extremely personal and deeply rooted in the Jungian subconscious. This strong flow of irrational imagery displays a considerable debt to Mandel'shtam. However, in contradistinction to the refined and ascetic forms of Mandel'shtam, Zhdanov is eclectic; he mixes high poetic, archaic, scientific and everyday realities without imposing any hierarchy. His manner may be called "polystylistic": perhaps its real nature is "counter-stylistic". He aims to create a new kind of mythology out of modern – technological – reality ("the mechanical Archne"). Even more interesting is his "natural mythology", with its "heroes": rain, frost, stones, trees, water, hills, houses, birds and animals, and pure spatial forms (the niche, the vertical, the column).

The composition of his poems, which tend toward the

monumental even when their scale is small, comes close to musical improvisation. Zhdanov is well aware of the crisis of traditional form in modern Russian verse. His experiments deal with new rythmical patterns – a kind of French *verset* and other types of free or semi-free verse.

Zhdanov's poetry is to be seen as one of the real achievements of the new wave of Russian poetry; its influence is now recognizable in many younger poets. Along with his contemporaries – Iosif Brodskii, Elena Shvarts, Viktor Krivulin and others – Zhdanov has changed the very notions of the terms "poetry" and "poetical" among a new generation of Russian readers.

OLGA SEDAKOVA

Mariia Semenovna Zhukova 1804–1855

Prose writer

Biography

Born in Zevakina, Nizhnii Novgorod province in 1804. Childhood spent in Arzamas and on father's small estate in Tambov province. Educated at home, possibly by local deacon. Possibly brought up as ward in Korsakov and Golitsyn households. Married: Razumnik Vasil'evich Zhukov, a minor landowner, no later than 1822 (separated at an early stage); one son. Began publishing in 1837. Suffered from ill health: for the rest of her life spent winters in southern Russia and the Mediterranean. Published actively between 1838 and 1842, thereafter less and less, almost ceasing publication in 1844. Acquainted with Elena Gan's mother; possibly met Gan. Died in Saratov, 26 April 1855.

Publications

Collected Editions

Vechera na Karpovke [Evenings by the Karpovka], 2 vols. St Petersburg, 1837–38; also Moscow 1986; sections translated by Joe Andrew, in his *Short Fiction by Russian Women Writers, 1835–1860*, Oxford, Oxford University Press, 1996, 122–44.

Povesti, 2 vols. St Petersburg, 1840.

Fiction

"Baron Reichman", 1837; in *Russkaia romanticheskaia povest'*, edited by V.I. Sakharov, Moscow, 1980, 519–52; translated as "Baron Reichman", by Joe Andrew, in his *Short Fiction by Russian Women Writers, 1835–1860*, Oxford, Oxford University Press, 1996, 145–80.

"Medal'on", 1837; translated as "The Locket", by Joe Andrew, in his *Short Fiction by Russian Women Writers, 1835–1860*, Oxford, Oxford University Press, 1996, 181–219.

"Samopozhertvovanie", 1840; translated as "Self-Sacrifice", by Joe Andrew, in his *Short Fiction by Russian Women Writers, 1835–1860*, Oxford, Oxford University Press, 1996, 398–459.

"Dacha na Petergovskoi doroge" [The Dacha on the Peterhof Road], in *Otechestvennye zapiski*, 39 (1845), 225–326; also in *Dacha na Petergovskoi doroge: proza russkikh pisatel'nits pervoi poloviny XIX veka*, edited by V.V. Uchenova, Moscow, 1986, 246–322.

Travel Writing

Ocherki iuzhnoi Frantsii i Nitstsy [Sketches of Southern France and Nice], 2 vols. St Petersburg, 1844.

Critical Studies

Mothers and Daughters: Women of the Intelligentsia in Nineteenth Century Russia, by Barbara Alpern Engel, Cambridge, Cambridge University Press, 1983.

Narrative and Desire in Russian Literature, 1822–49: The Feminine and the Masculine, by Joe Andrew, London, Macmillan, and New York, St Martin's Press, 1993, 139–83.

A History of Russian Women's Writing, 1820–1992, by Catriona Kelly, Oxford and New York, Oxford University Press, 1994, 79–91.

"The Society Tale as Pastiche: Mariia Zhukova's Heroines Move to the Country", by Hilde Hoogenboom, in *The Society Tale in Russian Literature: From Odoevskii to Tolstoi*, edited by Neil Cornwell, Amsterdam, Rodopi, 1998, 85–97.

Mariia Zhukova was one of the cohort of women writers who, along with Nadezhda Durova, Elena Gan, Karolina Pavlova, and others, entered the male bastion of the Russian literary world in the 1830s and not only offered the first, however tentative, explorations of the "woman question", but also played an important part, hitherto "hidden from history", in the generic experimentation and other developments that were to lead to the "Great Tradition of the realist novel" in the middle of the century. Less radical than Gan, Zhukova was the more consummate artist, and had perhaps a more realistic approach in her conservative answers to the questions of gender raised in her work.

Zhukova's career marks "a turning-point in the history" (Kelly) of female Russian writers. She was the first woman writer to produce a large, varied corpus; unlike most writers of the period she wrote exclusively in prose; at least in part for financial reasons she began her publishing career in book form, rather than in the more customary journal outlets. Consequently, her work was reviewed widely from the outset, and she became the first woman writer in Russia to be accorded significant praise and honour. Because of personal circumstances (separation from her husband), she regarded writing as a profession. This led to great productivity for a time: when her future – and, more significantly, that of her son – seemed assured, her output diminished dramatically, although this may also have been because of failing health.

Like most writers in the 1830s, male as well as female, Zhukova's forte was the society tale: many of the sections of her debut work, *Vechera na Karpovke* [Evenings by the Karpovka] are broadly within this genre, as is perhaps her most important work, *Dacha na Petergovskoi doroge* [The Dacha on the Peterhof Road]. This genre enabled her to explore her main concern, the psychology of social behaviour, especially that of women. Indeed, a number of her works are more extended portraits of the female character, rather than well-structured narratives ("Medal'on" [The Locket], for example). Her career is a microcosm of literary development in the 1830s and 1840s: she began with shorter fiction, moving to longer tales, such as *Samopozhertvovanie* (*Self-Sacrifice*). She also displayed some generic variation, both in *Vechera na Karpovke*, and by turning to travel sketches in her later development (*Ocherki iuzhnoi Frantsii i Nitstsy* [Sketches of Southern France and Nice]. Her work is mainly set among the lower and middle gentry, with *Inok* [The Monk] being a rare excursion into the merchant class. This work also shows Zhukova's willingness to move into historical narratives, as does *Nemaia* [The Dumb Girl]. Setting is also reasonably varied, ranging from St Petersburg, to the countryside, to abroad: see *Provintsial'ka* [The Provincial Girl] in particular. Zhukova played her part in the literary polemics of the day, as in the frame sections of *Vechera na Karpovke*: indeed, the very title and structure of this work put her at the centre of developments in this decade. At the same time, her work suffered from the same kinds of contrivance and artifice that were to bedevil even the most successful of the transitional works of this period, including Lermontov's novel *Geroi nashego vremeni* (*A Hero of Our Time*).

Thematically, Zhukova's work is again quite varied. She tackled the subject of madness (*Dacha na Petergovskoi doroge*); male honour (*Baron Reichman*); nature, and religion (see *Medal'on*). She also touches on such popular concerns of the period as education and reading, as well as the dangers of trusting superficial appearances. But first and last, her central concern is women, especially their inner world, and their relationships with men. She sees women very much in the social context, and the implication is that the social forces which constrain women are much the same in all societies and in all ages. By and large she takes a conservative, even pessimistic view of female destiny. She is aware of the strength of "patriarchal power" as she terms it in *Inok*, but believes that tight social constraints are necessary to control the dangers of passion and other powerful emotions. Occasionally she will endorse the behaviour of outsiders, even of transgressors, but usually they are shown to be wrong (*Baron Reichman*, *Dacha na Petergovskoi ulitse*). Women are shown to have more depth and resources than men, who are usually either peripheral or weak. She shows great interest in the *vospitannitsa* (ward) situation, and her treatment of older women is much more interesting and more positive than in virtually all male writers of the period. But she was not able or willing to take the implications of her writing further. Nowhere does she really envisage a career or field of female activity beyond the traditional roles, and the ideal for a woman is a successful marriage. This does not mean a love match: indeed, it often seems that love and marriage are incompatible and the positive treatment of the marriage market and of arranged matches is a feature of Zhukova's work. At the same time, however, her picture of marriage is generally pessimistic: a happy marriage may be her ideal, but it was neither a reality for the writer herself, nor for her heroines.

In her day Zhukova was, from her first published work through to her later output, both generally well received by the critics and a popular author. Belinskii was generally positive, and Grech put her almost on a par with Lermontov, while *Ocherki iuzhnoi Frantsii i Nitstsy* was welcomed with unanimous warmth. Almost immediately after her death, however, she slipped from view and received very little mention anywhere until the 1980s. In the last 15 years she has been rediscovered and is now rightly regarded as an important, if second-rank, writer of the 1830s and 1840s, and as one of the two most important women prose writers of the period.

JOE ANDREW

Vasilii Andreevich Zhukovskii 1783–1852

Poet and translator

Biography

Born in the village of Mishenskoe, Belev district, Tula province, 9 February 1783, the illegitimate child of a landowner, Afanasii Bunin, and a captive Turkish woman; given the surname of his godfather. Enlisted (fictitiously) in army; "promoted" (ensign), received the status of nobleman, "retired", 1789. Attended private boarding school in Tula, 1790; central public school, Tula, 1792; Pensionnat for the Nobility at Moscow University, 1797–1800. Began to publish, 1797. Member of The Friendly Literary Society from 1801. Entered service in the Moscow office of the salt industry; "arrested" for negligence, retired, 1801. Became acquainted with Karamzin; worked as private tutor, 1802–07; editor of *Vestnik Evropy*; 1808–11. Took part in "Patriotic War" against Napoleon, 1812: lieutenant, promoted to junior captain, decorated; retired, 1813. Moved to St Petersburg, 1813; permanent secretary to the "Arzamas" society, 1815. Held various Court posts, including tutor to the Heir to the throne (the future Alexander II), 1826–41. Close associate of Karamzin, Viazemskii, Pushkin, Gogol' (1820–30s). Travelled in Russia and western Europe (with the heir), 1837–39. Moved to Germany. Married: Elizabeth Reutern in 1841; one daughter and one son. Died in Baden-Baden, Germany, 24 April 1852.

Publications

Collected Editions

Stikhotvoreniia, 2 vols. St Petersburg, 1815–16; 2nd edition 3+1 vols, 1818; 3rd edition, 3 vols, 1824; 4th edition, 9 vols, 1835–44; 5th edition 13 vols, 1849–57.

Ballady i povesti [Ballads and Tales], 2 vols. St Petersburg, 1831.

Polnoe sobranie sochinenii, 12 vols. St Petersburg, 1902.

Sobranie sochinenii, 4 vols. Moscow and Leningrad, 1959–60.

Zarubezhnaia poeziia v perevodakh V.A. Zhukovskogo [Foreign Poetry in Translations of V.A. Zhukovskii], 2 vols. Moscow, 1985.

Poetry

Dvenadtsat' spiashchikh dev, starinnaia povest' [The Twelve Sleeping Maidens: An Ancient Tale]. St Petersburg, 1817.

Für Wenige. Dlia nemnogikh [For the Few], nos. 1–5. St Petersburg, 1818 (in German and Russian).

Shil'onskii uznik, poema lorda Bairona [The Prisoner of Chillon: A Poem of Lord Byron]. St Petersburg, 1822.

Prose

Opyty v proze [Essays in Prose]. St Petersburg and Moscow, 1818 [vol. 4 of the 1818 collection].

Sochineniia v proze [Works in Prose]. 2nd edition, St Petersburg, 1826.

Literary Criticism

Estetika i kritika [Aesthetics and Criticism]. Moscow, 1985.

Letters and Diaries

Pis'ma V.A. Zhukovskogo k Aleksandru Ivanovichu Turgenevu [V.A. Zhukovskii's Letters to Aleksandr Ivanovich Turgenev]. Moscow, 1895.

Dnevniki [Diaries]. St Petersburg, 1903.

Editor

Sobraniie russkikh stikhotvorenii [Collected Russian Poems], 5 vols. Moscow, 1810–11.

Critical Studies

V.A. Zhukovskii: Poeziia chuvstva i "serdechnogo voobrazheniia", by A.N. Veselovskii, St Petersburg, 1904; 2nd edition, Petrograd, 1918.

O lirike, by Lidiia Ginzburg, Leningrad, 1964.

"The Simile in Batyushkov and Zhukovsky", by Doris Johnson, *Russian Literature Triquarterly*, 7 (1973), 407–24.

"Vasily Andreevich Zhukovsky", by William Edward Brown, *Russian Literature Triquarterly*, 8 (1974), 295–328.

Vasily Zhukovsky, by Irina M. Semenko, Boston, Twayne, 1976.

The Literary Ballad in Early Nineteenth-Century Russian Literature, by Michael R. Katz, Oxford, Oxford University Press, 1976.

"Zhukovskii's World of Fleeting Visions", by S. Senderovich, *Russian Literature*, 12 (1985), 203–20.

A History of Russian Literature of the Romantic Period, by William Edward Brown, Ann Arbor, Ardis, 1986, vol. 1.

Zhukovskii i russkaia kul'tura, edited by R.V. Iezuitova *et al.*, Leningrad, 1987.

Zhukovskii i literatura kontsa XVIII–XIX veka, edited by V.Iu. Troitskii, Moscow, 1988.

Zhukovskii i ego vremia, by R.V. Iezuitova, Leningrad, 1989.

The name of Vasilii Zhukovskii, that of an epoch-making poet, has become emblematic of Russian romanticism. He developed a wide range of poetic genres: the meditative elegy, the elegized epistle, the song and the literary ballad (1800–20s), patriotic lyrics (1810s), the romantic narrative poem and tragedy (1820s), verse tales (1830s), and epic poetry (1830–40s). His last period included a complete hexametric translation of the *Odyssey* (1842–49). In effect, most of his works are translations (from German, English and French) or, more usually, free versions. It was Zhukovskii who gave the Russian audience access to German (pre)romanticism; however, his role was not that of a passive intermediary: his borrowings were creative and transformative. Zhukovskii made a fundamental reform in poetic language. Essentially, the role of the epithet was changed: the modifier-substantive links tended now to be based on the emotive (rather than the cognitive) aspect of meaning, expressing the poet's subjective mood (rather than "objective" relations). Accordingly, the significance of asemiotic aspects of the verse (non-imitative alliteration, melody etc.) considerably increased. For him, "the sound was as precious as the word" (Nikolai Polevoi). Zhukovskii became the initiator of the melodic (as opposed to the declamatory and conversational) type of Russian lyric poetry (Eikhenbaum); his translations often reproduce phono-prosodic features of the original rather than its denotative content. Zhukovskii's editorial and journalistic work is also indispensable for the history of Russian culture; as an essayist he contributed a great deal to literary theory, translation studies, and the moral philosophy of that time.

The education of Zhukovskii the artist is marked by his relations with Andrei Turgenev and Nikolai Karamzin. A striving for moral self-perfection and a great attention to nuances of sentiment continued to determine his outlook on life and art for the rest of his career. His apprenticeship was intensive and fairly short (1797–1801). Zhukovskii's translation of Thomas Gray's elegy – "Country Churchyard" ("Sel'skoe kladbishche") (1801–02) – which appeared in 1802, was immediately accepted as an outstanding work. The meditative elegy was further developed in "Vecher" [Evening] (1806), "Slavianka" (1815), and "Tsvet zaveta" [The Flower of the Covenant] (1819).

The year 1806 was extraordinarily productive; Zhukovskii attempted the most diverse of genres (fables, epigrams, inscriptions etc.). It was to be two more years, however, before he found his new genre and became, to his contemporaries, a "balladier". "Liudmila", a Russian ballad, imitated from Bürger's "Lenore", followed by another reworking of the same source, "Svetlana" (published 1813), confirmed Zhukovskii's reputation as a leading poet. (As with Gray's elegy, he returned to Bürger's model ballad for the third time: "Lenora", 1831; these successive versions clearly stand as new and self-sufficient poems). In 1810 Zhukovskii gave his theoretical definition of the genre: ballads belong to "epico-lyric" poetry, being "narrative" in content but "lyrical" in form. In 1808–14 he composed 13 ballads, among them translations of Schiller's "Cassandra" ("Kassandra") and "The Cranes of Ibycus" ("Ivikovy zhuravli"), Southey's "Rudiger" (translated as "Adel'stan"), "Lord William" (as "Varvik") and "The Old Woman of Berkeley" (as "Ballada, v kotoroi ..."; not permitted by the censors until 1831), as well as original ballads, "Akhill" [Achilles] and "Eolova arfa" [Aeolian Harp]. With them, Zhukovskii found new approaches to the literary assimilation of European and Russian folklore and created precedents for romantic re-interpretation of themes of Ancient Greece. Another genre of great importance was that of "songs and romances" which formed a special section in Zhukovskii's collections (characteristically, the originals of some translated texts were not, in fact, "songs"). Among them are versions (1811–12) of Schiller's "Longing" ("Zhelanie") and "The Ideals" ("Mechty"), Matthisson's "Elysium" ("Elizium") or non-translated romances, such as "Pevets" [The Singer]. Zhukovskii himself thought that he had introduced into Russian literature not only novel sentiments, but also new ideas. The duality of his poetic world (rejection of the earthly *here* and aspiration for the celestial *there*) was one of the most important features that made Belinskii claim Zhukovskii introduced "romanticism" to Russia. Zhukovskii's poems on the events of the "Patriotic War" further revealed his versatility. He made his first attempt at the martial hymn with his "Song of the Bard" as early as 1806, but it was "Pevets vo stane russkikh voinov" [A Bard in the Camp of the Russian Warriors] (1812) that made him the poet of the nation. Followed by epistles to Kutuzov and Alexander I, it marked the creation of the civic poetry of the post-classical era. Later Zhukovskii became the author of a new national anthem (1833).

The 1815–24 period is known for such masterpieces as: a verse translation of C.H. Spiess's novel of horror, *The Twelve Sleeping Maidens* (*Dvenadtsat' spiashchikh dev*) 1817; almanacs *Für Wenige* (1818), which included versions of Goethe's "The Fisherman" ("Rybak") and "Elf-king" ("Lesnoi tsar'"), Schiller's "The Count of Hapsburg" ("Graf Gapsburgskii") and "The Knight of Toggenburg" ("Rytsar' Togenburg"), Hebel's idylls etc.; sensational translations of Byron's *The Prisoner of Chillon* (*Shil'onskii uznik*) (1821–22), and Schiller's *The Maid of Orleans* (*Orleanskaia deva*) 1824, with their (respectively) iambic tetrameters with masculine rhymes and unrhymed iambic pentameters; also, original poems, among which was Zhukovskii's poetic credo, "Nevyrazimoe" [The Inexpressible]. His work from the mid-1820s to the 1840s may be defined as that of a translator-experimentalist-enlightener. His later ballads (from Walter Scott, Schiller, Southey, and Uhland) are typified by a partially increased accuracy in translation and the translator's intentions to represent the "exemplary works" of the genre. When experimenting with different forms of narrative poetry, he versified Friedrich de la Motte Fouqué's *Undine* (1831–36) and Mérimée/Chamisso's *Matteo Falcone* (1843). Zhukovskii's interest in national epics revealed itself as early as the mid-1810s; in the 1840s, using German intermediate versions, he translated episodes from *Mahabharata* and *Shah-Nameh*. Preceded by his extracts from the *Aeneid*, *Metamorphoses* and the *Iliad* (1820s), Zhukovskii's *Odyssey* crowned his epic projects and, though it was made from a German interlinear translation, it formed, together with the *Iliad* of Gnedich, the standard Russian Homer.

IGOR PILSHCHIKOV

Zinovii Zinik 1945–

Prose writer and literary critic

Biography

Born in Moscow, 1945. Studied painting at a Moscow art school and later topology at Moscow University. Began writing prose in the mid-1960s, and contributed to the journal *Teatr*. Emigrated to Israel, 1975; directed a Russian-language student theatre group at the Hebrew University in Jerusalem. Moved to Britain to work for the BBC Russian Service, 1976; freelance critic and lecturer since the 1980s; editor and producer of the Russian Service's arts magazine *West End*. Regular contributor to the *Times Literary Supplement* and other British and American newspapers. British citizen. Married; two children. Lives in London.

Publications

Fiction

"Izveshchenie" [The Notification], *Vremia i my*, 6 (1976).

Peremeshchennoe litso [Displaced Person]. Paris, Albin Michel, 1981 (in French); New York, Russica, 1986 (in Russian).

"Uklonenie ot povinnosti" [Dereliction of Duty], *Vremia i my*, 69 (1982).

Russkaia sluzhba [Russian Service]. Paris, Sintaksis, 1983; *Rodnik*, 5–9 (1990); and in *Russkaia sluzhba i drugie istorii*, Moscow, 1993; Paris, Albin Michel, 1984 (in French).

Nisha v Panteone [A Niche in the Pantheon]. Paris, Sintaksis, 1985; Paris, Albin Michel, 1986 (in French); Tel-Aviv, Am Oved, 1989 (in Hebrew).

Russofobka i fungofil. London, Russian Roulette Press, 1986; Moscow, 1991; translated as *The Mushroom Picker*, by Michael Glenny, London, Heinemann, 1987; New York, St Martin's Press, 1988.

Lord i eger'. Moscow, 1991; translated as *The Lord and the Gamekeeper*, by Alex De Jonge, London, Heinemann, 1991.
One-Way Ticket, translated by Frank Williams *et al.*, London, Harbord, 1995.
"The Moth", translated by Bernard Meares, *Glas: New Russian Writing*, 11 (1996), 87–122.

Literary Criticism and Essays
"Emigratsiia kak literaturnyi priem" [Emigration as a Literary Device], *Sintaksis*, 11 (1983), 167–87.
"Voobrazhaemoe interv'iu s Vladimirom Nabokovym" [An Imaginary Interview with Vladimir Nabokov], *Sintaksis*, 15 (1986), 178–87.
"Goticheskii roman uzhasov emigratsii" [The Gothic Romance of the Horrors of Emigration], *Sintaksis*, 16 (1986), 34–70.
"The Hero in Search of an Author", in *Under Eastern Eyes: The West as Reflected in Recent Russian Émigré Writing*, edited by Arnold McMillin, London, Macmillan, 1991, 12–16; New York, St Martin's Press, 1992.

Critical Studies

Review of *Russkaia sluzhba*, by Alex De Jonge, *Times Literary Supplement*, 4182 (1983), 538.
Review of *The Mushroom Picker*, by T.J. Lewis, *World Literature Today*, 64/1 (1990), 147–48.
Review of *The Lord and the Gamekeeper*, by Simon Franklin, *Times Literary Supplement*, 4599 (1991), 20.
"Esli ne liubit', ne znachit – gad", by Ol'ga Timofeeva, *Nezavisimaia gazeta* (14 April 1992), 7.
"Outsider's View of an Incomer", by Tom Birchenough (review of *The Mushroom Picker*), *The Times* (28 January 1993), 38.
"Bilingualism and Word Play in the Work of Russian Writers of the Third Wave of Emigration: The Heritage of Nabokov", by Arnold McMillin, *Modern Language Review*, 89/3 (1994), 417–26.
Emigration als literarisches Verfahren bei Zinovij Zinik, by Anja Pülsch, Munich, Sagner, 1995.
"Nikakoi Derzhavin menia ne blagoslovlial", by Zinovii Zinik, *Literaturnaia gazeta* (22 November 1995), 5.
"Zinovii Zinik's Gothic Suburbia", by Robert Porter, in *Reconstructing the Canon: Russian Writing in the 1980s*, edited by Arnold McMillin, New York and London, Harwood Academic, 1998.

All the works Zinovii Zinik has written since his departure from Russia examine aspects of the duality and duplicity of émigré existence, with its clash of east and west, past and present. Zinik was one of the first writers of the third wave of emigration to set his work in the western world, with his émigré heroes reassessing their Soviet past from a new viewpoint. He follows the tradition of Conrad and Nabokov (whose examples he readily acknowledges) and, like them, manages to blend the style and traditions of both Russian and English literature. The title of one of his first essays to be published in the west was "Emigration as a Literary Device": "The life you leave behind you becomes a completed picture", he commented.

Zinik's writing in Moscow, more than 3,000 pages of complicated Joycean prose, was smuggled to the west through the good offices of the Dutch Embassy. "When I opened the suitcase in Jerusalem, I realised that it was completely dead: it was only readable in particular circumstances, at a certain time and within a certain set of people". Simultaneously philosophical and comic, Zinik's prose is now about role playing and identity crises, about a sense of displacement and betrayal; it is also about the dictatorial rule of received ideas and dogmas over our lives. He remains, in his own words, a hybrid; a spy with a Jewish soul, Russian brains, and an English heart.

Originally written in Russian, his novels *Peremeshchennoe litso* [Displaced Person] and *Nisha v Panteone* [A Niche in the Pantheon] first appeared in French translation. In the former, a middle-aged professor of Street Culture in Old Russia, who was at the centre of a dissident circle that met in cafés around Pushkin Square in Moscow, has to come to terms with the finality of his emigration and a new understanding of the unhappy reality of his relationships with his nearest and dearest in Russia. In the latter a professor of mathematical logic succumbs to paranoia in a tenement block in the outskirts of Jerusalem. Convinced of his psychic power to change the course of history, he unwisely re-crosses the Soviet border and, in a bid to be a proof-reader in Moscow, becomes an equally despised corrector and modernizer of émigré announcers' pronunciation in the Russian Service of the BBC in London. His life in England then spawns horrid parallels to his tribulations in Russia. *Russofobka i fungofil* (*The Mushroom Picker*) was published in English in 1987 and dramatized for BBC television in 1993. His novel *Lord i eger'* (*The Lord and the Gamekeeper*) and a collection of short stories, *One-Way Ticket*, have now also appeared in English.

Zinik has a predilection in his fiction for the macabre, a fondness for the word "monster" (frequently *monstr*, but also *urod*, *chudovishche* and their cognates), and for occasional forays into violent, bloody scenes. His depiction of these hovers curiously between the humorous (à la Tom Sharpe) and the macabre. Near the beginning of the novel *Nisha v Panteone*, he describes an encounter in Israel with a former acquaintance from Russia (such meetings in themselves constitute a recurrent theme in Zinik): a trick of the light makes the acquaintance appear to the narrator like a King Kong figure – a giant towering over high rise buildings – when he is in fact just a down-at-heel mortal in a cemetery, whom the narrator has been talking to not a minute before.

In *Russkaia sluzhba* [Russian Service] the Gothic element is grounded very much in fact. Almost two years after Zinik began to work for the BBC Russian Service, the Bulgarian defector, Georgi Markov, who also worked there, was murdered by the Bulgarian secret service with a poisoned umbrella. The novel tells the story of Narator, an employee of a Soviet Ministry, who comes to England to make contact with the man behind the voice he listens to on the mysterious External Broadcasting Corporation. The External Broadcasting Corporation is a somewhat surreal amalgamation of all the foreign stations to which the hero tunes in: the Voice of America, Radio Liberty, and the BBC. Narator could be construed as a parody of Gogol''s Akakii Akakevich: 40 years old, balding, sexually inexperienced, and engrossed in his work as a corrector of misprints. Gothic motifs can be glimpsed in his being told to chew garlic to ward off revolutionary infections when he is participating in a film version of John Reed's *Ten Days that Shook the World*; or the fact that he becomes unsure as to when his birthday is, given that he was reared by his grandmother who did not recognize New Style dating. Like a good many of Zinik's heroes, Narator has difficulty perceiving and then coming to terms with the realia around him. Back in Moscow he was very slow even to learn of the existence of foreign broadcasting stations; and when he started listening to them, suddenly there were two "truths". In England his limited grasp of the language does not so much present a barrier as generate all manner of strange associations. Thus we are treated to a series of puns and neologisms: Waterloo Station as *Vaterklozet* is one of the more chaste. All this underscores the serious question of identity.

The story "Kriket" [Cricket], unlike *Russkaia sluzhba* and *The Mushroom Picker*, is a work that is almost entirely liberated from the stereoptypes thrown up during the Cold War era, yet it illustrates some traditional English vices, such as xenophobia, superficiality, and the pre-eminence of form over content. Taking this story in the context of all Zinik's works, one might be tempted to ask if the notions it presents contributed as much to the Cold War as did the surface political debates and actions of that era. In what purports to be a civilized and educated stratum of English society, the mutual misreadings and hostilities are almost endless.

The first-person narrator is a Russian expatriot of 15 years' standing, who is still referred to by a female friend, Joanna, as "my Russian", and who always introduces him as coming from Moscow. For her he will always be a foreigner. The game of cricket, notoriously difficult for foreigners to comprehend, is something quintessentially English for which he acquires some understanding and empathy initially. These are blasted away by an encounter with a man called Ricketts at the match, who abuses him in anti-Semitic tones. The narrator feels like a monster from outer space. However, he is later to regain a sense of belonging. Much of Zinik's fiction can be read as an attempt to illustrate and overcome the Gothic horror that bubbles beneath the apparently civilized veneer of English suburban life.

Apart from English and French, Zinik's work has been translated into Hebrew, Dutch, Polish, Hungarian, and Estonian. His work was blacklisted after his emigration in 1975, but editions of his novels have now appeared in Russia to critical and public acclaim.

ROBERT PORTER

The Mushroom Picker

Russofobka i fungofil

Novel, 1986

The plot of *The Mushroom Picker* is anchored in an English dinner party threatened by rain in a tiny garden in a London suburb where Cleo, a secretary recently married to the Russian Kostia, is entertaining her boss, homosexual CND supporter Anthony, and his bisexual Trotskiite wife Margot, who is Kostia's lover. Cleo is a vegetarian with unoriginal left-wing views borrowed from Margot, while Kostia is a cleaver-wielding meat-eater who once wrote a treatise called *Russian Cuisine: A History of Terror and Cannibalism*, on culinary relations between Russia and the west.

The plot flashes back as Cleo remembers how, under the influence of Margot, she had gone to Moscow to observe the life of the Russian workers at first hand and how, at a New Year's party, she found herself abruptly and unanimously ostracized by the assembled dissident collective for mouthing her memorized left-wing slogans. Zinik conveys the linguistic fog of incomprehension through which Cleo struggles to make sense of this baffling new world. She finds herself suddenly so appalled by the squalor of the flat and her own isolation that:

> ... if she had then made one further mental effort, taken one further step towards admitting to herself how completely she was defeated by the world, she might then have liberated herself from the importunate garbage of other people's words and slogans and begun to live life on her own account, without always glancing over her shoulder, without Margot, and without Russia.

The situation had been saved (or lost) by the arrival of Kostia.

Cleo recalls also one of the few erotic episodes in her life. Anthony's youthful protégé at work, a certain Colin, appeared to develop a crush on her and, lying in wait for her after the firm's Christmas party, attempted rather ineptly to rape her. Later it seemed to her that the episode was probably an effort on Colin's part to get even with Anthony for abandoning him.

Prompted at least in part by a desire to bring an element of excitement into her drab life, Cleo subsequently returned to live in Moscow for a year and married Kostia. Life in Moscow reached crisis point when the disabled and impotent husband of Tonia, with whom Cleo has been sharing Kostia, discovered the lovers *in flagrante* and beat his wife to death with his wooden leg. Cleo, after a particularly disastrous series of attempts to prise sour cream from the Soviet retail network for Kostia's cooking, tore up his manuscript; Kostia had meanwhile been beaten up by the KGB for pointing out to a Party propagandist the obvious fact that matzo bread mixed with the blood of Christian babies would not be kosher. Supposing the destruction of his manuscript to be the work of the KGB, he leaves with Cleo for England.

Kostia retires from the meal in the garden to the kitchen, and is joined by a Polish neighbour, Pan Tadeusz who, as a fellow Slav, supports his enthusiasm for those mushrooms that most Englishmen, including Anthony, consider to be poisonous toadstools. The wimpish Anthony is initiated, after simpering protest, into how to drink vodka like a man, his enthusiasm for unilateral disarmament a thinly disguised desire to bare himself before the phallic rocketry of Russia. In Kostia, and in the Russians he meets in Moscow, unilateralist Anthony encounters only an ironic and exploitative recognition of his sexual inferiority. His whining provokes Kostia into unbuttoning his flies and ejaculating into Anthony's mouth in a scene in which a grotesque word-play is woven around the members of the Politburo, Stalin's will of iron, fluttering red banners and vaginal labia, pumped up balloons and Kostia's testicles.

A climactic storm breaks, Cleo observes Kostia sharpening a double-edged knife that she supposes is intended for her and, as Margot and Anthony drive off in their Jaguar, flees to seek the protection of Pan Tadeusz. It is, however, not murder but mushrooms that are on Kostia's mind and, as he drives off, Pan Tadeusz is only too willing to help Cleo to trail him.

The trail leads to a top-secret British nuclear missile site where, in the middle of the night, the three of them are apprehended by the security forces. Unfortunately Kostia is in possession of a map that appears to designate the location of different types of missiles but which in fact indicates the location of different types of mushrooms. As Kostia rushes towards Cleo with the unsheathed knife, but in fact intent only on saving his mushrooms, the crazed figure of Colin, who has been obsessively stalking Cleo, ineptly leaps from the bushes to defend her and is impaled fatally on the knife. At this moment a large anti-nuclear protest march arrives, headed by Anthony.

The plot might seem to have run its course, but at this point the author intervenes to tell us that he was asked by the defence counsel at Kostia's trial to give an expert literary assessment of a novel he had written. It describes how a rootless émigré professor is researching the biography of a Russian serf sold to an English ambassador who became a famed cook and free man in England, but chose to return to Russia, to his old sadistic master, in order to belong. "Zinovii Zinik" ironically notes in this novel some of his own weaknesses: the intrusive culinary symbolism, the endless philosophical digressions.

Zinik shifts the perspective on the novel just read by referring to this alternative novel that Kostia might have written about the same experiences. More, when Zinik goes to meet Kostia in prison, it transpires that he is acquainted with the writer's own essays, and he perceptively criticizes the strengths and weakness of his style (which the reader has doubtless been dissecting as he read). He is told (fairly) that he is a "neophyte of emigration" with an exaggerated interest in parallels and contrasts between east and west, a tendency to over-extended metaphors, and more than a touch of influence from "that Poseidon of the three waves of emigration, Nabokov". (For a Russian reader Zinik also offers a treasury of lore on such English oddities as garden gnomes, and the grisly ritual of the office Christmas party).

Kostia now acts as Zinik's ironical mouthpiece as he muses that the Soviet Union has an irresistible appeal to any who are unsure of their values: it takes away the sovereignty and responsibilities of the individual. Zinik goes on to reflect intimately on his predicament as an émigré writer, the small deceptions he has practised to construct himself an identity acceptable to his new country, and how the "reality" of Kostia has disrupted this. "He was insisting on his right to belong to a world from which I had been scandalously divorced and whose death I desired with all my heart". It is a confession worthy of Jean-Jacques Rousseau whose *Confessions* is a leitmotif of western individualism and personal isolation throughout the novel.

Zinik's characters are grotesques, and yet he characterizes Cleo's sad, chilled English loneliness, or her muddled journalistically-inspired notions of social relations in the Soviet Union with devastating precision. He pushes situations over the top into absurdity, and indulges in absurdist word-play and intellectual set pieces.

ARCH TAIT

The Lord and the Gamekeeper

Lord i eger'

Novel, 1991

Like Zinik's other major novel *The Mushroom Picker*, *The Lord and the Gamekeeper* concerns itself with the varying (mis) perceptions that the east and the west have of each other. The mirror-like qualities, as in the previous novel, are structured around a scene unfolding in a garden, which fans out into a series of lengthy flashbacks. Thus, what is a perfectly ascertainable string of events is deliberately convoluted and has the reader guessing at almost every turn. The purpose is simply to illustrate how erroneous first, second, and third impressions, can be. *The Lord and the Gamekeeper* is a comic romp through the clichés of both English and Russian life, with delightful excursions into the reasoning (or otherwise) at the back of individuals' prejudices and passions. While surface events may be fixed, the identities of the characters, their motivations and values, remain mercurial. Beneath the comfort and stability of the English way of life there lurks disorientation and alienation; and ultimately, the characters are masters of their own misery. Political and philosophical platforms have rotting and dangerous planks.

Feliks, Viktor, and Silva, three Russian émigrés, are on the lawn of a charitable clinic, funded by one Lord Edward who is receiving therapy at the hands of Dr Genoni. These chapters are entitled "Asylum", and the authorial aside on the ambiguity of the term in English (lunatic and political) is only one example of Zinik's delight in bilingual word-play. The *ménage à trois* that the characters formed in Moscow has been reproduced in South London and old jealousies are revived. As one reviewer of the English translation put it, the novel is "about translation", and by this one understands translation from one society to another, from one language to another, perhaps even from one identity to another. Feliks is an expert on English drama and has come to England (via Jerusalem) to translate Pushkin's "Feast in the Time of Plague" into English, but the questions arise as to whether Pushkin was merely a plagiarist, adapting part of *The City of the Plague* by the Scottish poet John Wilson for one of his *Little Tragedies*, and should Feliks simply reproduce the original rather than translate from the Russian adaptation. Viktor is a political dissident (his surname, Karvalanov, is a cheeky allusion to Luis Corvalan, the Chilean communist, swapped in December 1976 for Vladimir Bukovskii, the Soviet dissident – this being just one of several political "in-jokes"), whom Lord Edward has managed to bring to the west. Silva is in England since she is able to claim kinship with a Scottish family (a Lermontov connection).

Zinik's talent in this novel, as elsewhere in his fiction, is to combine a stream-of-consciousness, free-association manner with a taut plot-line. There is the motif of plague, underscored by where the Russians live, Blackheath, reputedly a former burial ground for plague victims, and with this comes the image of rats and émigrés scurrying for shelter, or leaving sinking ships. The east-west divide is spelled out by the proximity of Greenwich and its meridian. When Viktor encounters someone he thinks is Lord Edward on the estate (most likely in fact it is the gamekeeper) he finds him to be a virtual prisoner in his own home, and there are poignant parallels between the Soviet and English experience: "They're holding me here as if in exile. I'm an internal émigré. I'm a stranger in my own country, almost an enemy of the people", the "Lord" tells the Russian dissident. At the back of his anguish is a feeling of guilt and past crimes, redolent of the 19th-century Russian intellectual. It emerges that the gamekeeper's father had been accidentally killed by the previous Lord of the manor during a pheasant shoot. However, the gamekeeper's son, Edmund, now passing himself off as Lord Edward, was also in part to blame for the accident. He has become an animal rights activist, protecting pheasants and was instrumental in bringing Viktor's dog to the west – at least as difficult as bringing his dissident master to the west, given the British fears about rabies. Hence, the motif of madness. Dr Genoni feels that Edmund would be cured if a reconstruction of the pheasant shoot could be staged, giving the

Russians various roles. At Viktor's shot Edmund collapses with a heart attack. While awaiting his recovery the three Russians agree to therapy.

Readers of the novel with a political axe to grind may balk at the recurrent equation of the Soviet and western systems ("Lewisham combined all the disadvantages of western democracy with all the horrors of a Soviet labour camp"), but Zinik's business, one feels, is ultimately *anti*-political. He stresses the human inadequacies of all his characters and thus renders them equal – the lord is interchangeable with the gamekeeper, and even at the end of the book we are not sure if we have encountered the real Lord Edward. At one point Viktor listens to Edward/Edmund "like a psychiatrist". The moral superiority in which the Russians bask at the beginning of the novel is utterly undermined at the end, and they are left humble and self-doubting. This time they have nowhere to emigrate to and any personal and moral solutions must be found within themselves. In this connection, and similarly in *The Mushroom Picker*, there is no one central character, let alone "hero" in the conventional sense. Feliks seems to dominate the first half of the novel, Viktor holds centre stage later on, while a kind of rickety equalitarian *sobornost'* obtains in the "asylum chapters".

Typical of much contemporaneous Russian fiction, *The Lord and the Gamekeeper* is shot through with literary parody, not to disparage the classics of world literature, but rather to attempt self-definition through good-natured reference and even self-reference. Allusions great and small to such as Defoe, Joyce, Pirandello, Shakespeare, Pushkin, and Blok are topped off at the end with allusion to Zinovii Zinik; and one detects in the passages on John Wilson – ranked far higher in his day than in Zinik's – a combination, none too common in literary circles, especially Russian ones, of self-esteem and humility on the author's part.

ROBERT PORTER

Aleksandr Aleksandrovich Zinov'ev 1922–

Prose writer and philosopher

Biography

Born in the village of Pakhtino, Chukhloma district in the region of Kostroma, 29 October 1922. Educated in Moscow. Arrested by the NKVD in 1939, escaped, spent a year on the run. Joined the Soviet Army without papers as a volunteer in 1940: served initially as a cavalry officer, then as fighter pilot; wounded in action, decorated several times. Married: 1) Nina Kalinin in 1943, one son; 2) Tamara Filat'ev in 1951, one daughter; 3) Ol'ga Mironovna Sorokin in 1967, two daughters. After demobilization enrolled in the Faculty of Philosophy at Moscow University; graduated in 1951. Appointed as junior staff member in the Department of Philosophy; pursued academic career at Moscow University and at the Academy of Sciences Institute of Philosophy from 1951: Professor and Head of Department of Logic, 1964–74. Refused to write for the journal *Kommunist* or to sack two dissident lecturers, leading to difficulties; became marginalized. Embarked on a new career as writer and commentator on Soviet life. Expelled with his wife and daughter in 1978, took up residence in Munich. Lost Soviet citizenship. Wrote 30 books on Soviet communism and the west, 1976–92. Soviet citizenship restored in 1990. Continues to comment on events in Russia. Recipient: Prix Medicis, 1978; Prix Tocqueville, 1982; Premio Internationale Tevere, 1992. Elected Member of the Russian Academy of Social Sciences, 1994.

Publications

Fiction

Ziiaiushchie vysoty. Lausanne, L'Âge d'Homme, 1976; translated as *The Yawning Heights*, by Gordon Clough, London, Bodley Head, and New York, Random House, 1979; Harmondsworth, Penguin, 1981.

Svetloe budushchee. Lausanne, L'Âge d'Homme, 1978; translated as *The Radiant Future*, by Gordon Clough, New York, Random House, 1980; London, Bodley Head, 1981.

Zapiski nochnogo storozha [Notes of a Night-Watchman]. Lausanne, L'Âge d'Homme, 1979.

V preddverii raia [On the Threshold of Paradise]. Lausanne, L'Âge d'Homme, 1979.

Zheltyi dom, 2 vols. Lausanne, L'Âge d'Homme, 1980; translated as *The Madhouse*, by Michael Kirkwood, London, Gollancz, 1986.

Gomo sovetikus. Lausanne, L'Âge d'Homme, 1982; translated as *Homo Sovieticus*, by Charles Janson, London, Gollancz, and Boston, Atlantic Monthly Press, 1985.

Nashei iunosti polet [Flight of Our Youth]. Lausanne, L'Âge d'Homme, 1983.

Idi na Golgofu [Go to Calvary]. Lausanne, L'Âge d'Homme, 1985.

Para bellum. Lausanne, L'Âge d'Homme, 1986.

Der Staatsfreier. Zurich, Diogenes, 1986.

Zhivi! [Live!]. Lausanne, L'Âge d'Homme, 1989.

Tsarville. Paris, PLON, 1992.

Poetry

Moi dom – moia chuzhbina [My House – My Foreign Land]. Lausanne, L'Âge d'Homme, 1982.

Evangelie dlia Ivana [Gospel for John]. Lausanne, L'Âge d'Homme, 1984.

Play
"Ruka Kremlia" [The Hand of the Kremlin], *Kontinent*, 47 (1986), 137–84.

Essays, Articles, and Interviews
Bez illiuzii [Without Illusions]. Lausanne, L'Âge d'Homme, 1979.
Kommunizm kak real'nost'. Lausanne, L'Âge d'Homme, 1981; translated as *The Reality of Communism*, by Charles Janson, London, Gollancz, and New York, Schocken, 1984.
My i Zapad [The West and Us]. Lausanne, L'Âge d'Homme, 1981.
Ni svobodu, ni ravenstva, ni bratstva [Neither Liberty, Nor Equality, Nor Fraternity]. Lausanne, L'Âge d'Homme, 1983.
Die Diktatur der Logik. Munich, Piper, 1985.
Die Macht des Unglaubens. Munich, Piper, 1986.
Gorbachevizm. New York, Liberty, 1988.
Les Confessions d'un Homme en trop. Paris, Olivier Orban, 1990.
Il superpotere in URSS: il comunismo e' veramente tramontato? Milan, Sugar Co Edizioni, 1990.
Katastroika: Povest' o perestroike v Partgrade. Lausanne, L'Âge d'Homme, 1990; translated as *Katastroika: Legend and Reality of Gorbachevism*, by Charles Janson, London, Claridge Press, 1990.
Perestroika et contre-perestroika. Paris, Olivier Orban, 1991; translated as *Perestroika in Partygrad*, by Charles Janson, London, Peter Owen, 1992.
Zapad: Fenomen zapadnizma, Moscow, 1995.

Biography
Mon Tchekhov. Brussels, Editions Complexe, 1989.

Critical Studies

"Elements of Structure in Zinov'ev's *Zheltyi dom*", by Michael Kirkwood, *Essays in Poetics*, 7/2 (1982).
Alexandre Zinoviev: Résistance et lucidité, by Claude Schwab, Lausanne, L'Âge d'Homme, 1984.
Alexander Zinoviev as Writer and Thinker: An Assessment, edited by Philip Hanson and Michael Kirkwood, London, Macmillan, and New York, St Martin's Press, 1988.
Alexandre Zinoviev; Les fondements scientifiques de la sociologie, by Fabrice Fassio, Paris, La Pensée Universelle, 1988.
La nature du communisme selon Alexandre Zinoviev, by Fabrice Fassio, Lion-sur-mer, Arcane-Beauvieux, 1991.
"Vniz po rechke po Ibanke", by Boris Lanin, *Khronika*, 8 (1992).
"Vy chto, boites' Zinov'eva?", by V. Tolstykh, *Nezavisimaia gazeta* (29 September 1992).
Alexander Zinoviev: An Introduction to His Work, by Michael Kirkwood, London, Macmillan, 1993.
"On Translating Zinoviev", by Michael Kirkwood, *Essays in Poetics*, 20 (1995), 102–32.

Aleksandr Aleksandrovich Zinov'ev was born in the year the Soviet Union was founded (1922) and it may be that history will show that, whereas he was probably the sharpest critic of the Soviet system, he ceased to be important as a writer about the time that the Soviet Union ceased to exist (1991). Certainly there are those who believe that his talent has been greatly exaggerated. On the other hand, there have equally been those who have ranked Zinov'ev with writers of the calibre of Apuleius, Sterne, Rabelais, Swift, Kafka, and Orwell. Furthermore, he has been awarded a series of prestigious prizes: the Prix Medicis in 1978 for his work *Svetloe budushchee* (*The Radiant Future*), the Tocqueville Prize in 1982 for *Kommunizm kak real'nost'* (*The Reality of Communism*) and the Premio Internationale Tevere in 1992 for *Zhivi!* [Live!]. He will probably be best remembered for his monumental *Ziiaiushchie vysoty* (*The Yawning Heights*), an allegory of the Soviet Union set in mythical Ibansk. Few literary critics have thought that it was a work of serious literary art. Few, apart from Zinov'ev himself, have thought any of the 30 or so books that he has written since *The Yawning Heights* will be of lasting literary value. Why, then, does he merit inclusion in a reference guide to Russian literature?

The answer is that he is unique as a chronicler of the Soviet system. Like no other writer, he portrays in merciless and repetitive detail the tedium and monotony, the irrationality and make-believe "reality" of everyday Soviet life. There is no one who can match Zinov'ev in his distillation of the essence of "Soviet-ness", not even Solzhenitsyn. To find out what makes the Soviet countryside "Soviet", or what is "Soviet" about a Soviet factory or what it is like to be a "Soviet" soldier at war, one should read Zinov'ev, not Rasputin or Fadeev or Tvardovskii or Gladkov. Zinov'ev writes apparently disconnected, or at best loosely connected short texts, some in verse, some in prose, some in the form of dramatic dialogue, series of which are gathered together and published between a set of covers as a "novel" (e.g. *The Radiant Future*), a "play" (*Ruka Kremlia* [The Hand of the Kremlin]), a "novel in verse" (*Moi dom – moia chuzhbina* [My House – My Foreign Land]), or a collection of essays (*The Reality of Communism*). All his works have a kaleidoscopic quality that makes them difficult to categorize. Conventional genre labels fail to capture their structural essence. It is difficult, indeed impossible, to determine at what point Zinov'ev is speaking as himself or through the mouth of one of his characters (or, more accurately, caricatures).

Zinov'ev's literary output of some 30 books and countless articles essentially spans the period between 1976 and 1992. What is fascinating is the transformation of the author's attitude to his subject-matter over that period. Zinov'ev's twin themes are Soviet communism and the west's inability to understand it. His earliest works reflect his view that the west is the guardian of civilization, that communism is a cancerous growth on the surface of the planet and likely to spread, largely because of Soviet opportunism on the one hand and western incomprehension and self-deception on the other. Experience of life in the west, however, together with political developments in the Soviet Union effect a radical change in his outlook, albeit not immediately. During the early 1980s Zinov'ev published a large number of books with the intention of teaching the west how to defend itself against the communist menace. Collections of articles and lectures (*My i Zapad* [The West and Us] 1981, *Bez illiuzii* [Without Illusions] 1979, *Ni svobody, ni ravenstva, ni bratstva* [Neither Liberty, Nor Equality, Nor Fraternity] 1983) reinforced in more succinct form the underlying message of his earlier works. Other books were designed to teach the west how to interpret Soviet rhetoric and ideology (*Die Diktatur der Logik*

1985, *Die Macht des Unglaubens* 1986). He was appalled at what he considered to be western unpreparedness for war and the influence of the various peace movements. He tried to stiffen western resolve and counteract what he regarded as a mixture of self-deception and cowardice with books such as *Gomo sovetikus* (*Homo Sovieticus*), published in 1982, *Moi dom – moia chuzhbina* (1982), *Para bellum* (1986) and *Der Staatsfreier* (1986).

By 1986, of course, Gorbachev had come to power and perestroika was about to get under way in earnest. Zinov'ev's attitude to perestroika underwent a steady transition from lofty derision of Gorbachev and his attempts to reform the system, to outright hatred when it became clear that the system was in steep decline and conceivably heading for destruction. (No one, it should be remembered, predicted the collapse of the Soviet system). This transition can be charted in the books he produced between 1986 and 1991: *Gorbachevizm* (1988), *Katastroika* (1990), *Les Confessions d'un Homme en trop* (1990), *Il superpotere in URSS: il comunismo e' veramente tramontato?* (1990), *Perestroika et contre-perestroika* (1991), *Tsarville* (1992).

Interest in Zinov'ev's work in the west, in the words of Philip Hanson, "peaked early". The critical literature devoted to the study of the man and his works would occupy much less space than that required for his own writings. To date there have been very few books written about him and many of his works have been entirely ignored. The vast bulk of what is available is devoted directly or indirectly to *The Yawning Heights*. Much of it is polemical, for Zinov'ev is a controversial figure, whether within Russian émigré circles during the 1980s or within Russia itself in the 1990s. It is probably true to say that people writing about Zinov'ev have been attracted more by his socio-political and philosophical views than by his literary talent, although studies, notably those of Wolf Moskovitch and Michael Kirkwood, have shown that he is a master of satire and skilful in his use of parody.

Zinov'ev is a controversial figure because of a combination of qualities: incisive intelligence, caustic wit, a natural tendency to be provocative, apparent indifference to what people think of him. At his best Zinov'ev is unrivalled in his ability to reveal important insights into the nature of Soviet society, almost literally at the stroke of a pen. His natural talent as a gifted cartoonist is paralleled by his ability to produce "cartoons" in verbal form. Two factors, however, are unfavourable to him. The first is the sheer volume of his, at first sight, uniform output. Few readers have kept pace with his writing. The second factor is the demise of the Soviet system. The bulk of Zinov'ev's output describes a system which, despite his prediction that it would last as long as the kingdom of the Pharaohs, lasted a mere 70 years or so. His description, however, is detailed and insightful. It will have lasting documentary value. The exception is *The Yawning Heights*. Its allegorical form ensures it a lasting place in the literature of Utopias and anti-Utopias. Ibansk has been seen as an anti-Utopia to date. Whether it continues to be seen as such, given the present state of Russia, will perhaps increasingly be a matter for debate.

MICHAEL KIRKWOOD

The Yawning Heights

Ziiaiushchie vysoty

Novel, 1976

Written in the remarkably short time of six months during the summer and autumn of 1974, *The Yawning Heights* was smuggled piecemeal out of the Soviet Union by the author's friends and published in Paris in 1976. Its reception in the west was enthusiastic and it was instantly translated into the major European languages. An English-language translation appeared in 1979.

Zinov'ev's stylistic "trade-mark" is the short, free-standing text varying in length from a few lines to a few pages. Some of these texts contain, or are composed of, verse. Each text has an accompanying title. Varying numbers of these texts are strung together, apparently without order, and published as "books". *The Yawning Heights* contains 600. Research has shown that the texts can, in fact, be ordered in sequences or "chains" containing a number of thematic links. The role of the title is two-fold: it topicalizes a given text; it links texts together that share the same title. Zinov'ev can thus deal with a particular topic in several ways. He can "pepper" a particular topic from various points of view by simply juxtaposing texts or he can treat it in depth by devoting a particular number of texts to it.

These twin devices of short text and title were chosen by Zinov'ev for practical as much as aesthetic reasons, but they have turned out to be enormously powerful. Zinov'ev wrote *The Yawning Heights* at a time when he was under surveillance by the KGB. He feared confiscation of his manuscript and wanted to ensure that the shape and approach of his analytical system survived. He thus wrote in kaleidoscopic fashion, sending portions of his text abroad when they were ready, thereby ensuring that the contours of his system and the essence of his views were known. However, he has retained these twin devices in his later works, when there was no longer any pragmatic requirement to do so. The fact that Zinov'ev has chosen the fictitious location of Ibansk and set his anti-Utopia at a time in the far distant future ensures that *The Yawning Heights* will occupy a niche in the international literary canon, even though the system it describes has foundered. It will do so because many of the themes that Zinov'ev treats are universal and recurrent. His point, however, is that they take a particularly virulent form in a totalitarian system.

Ibansk is a miserable location, with a miserable social system that the people have built themselves and with which they are now stuck. The word "Ibansk" is untranslatable since it is a pun based on the Russian word *ebat'* ("to fuck"), but it suggests Jean-Paul Sartre's *Huis clos* (*No Exit*) grossed up to the size of a country. Perhaps the most arresting image of the essence of Ibansk is Zinov'ev's famous painting depicting two rats tied to each other by their tails shaking each other simultaneously by the hand and the throat. Life is grey, monotonous, and uneventful. Above all, it is irrational. No one is particularly important or essentially different from anyone else. There is no need, therefore, for people to have different names. They are all called "Iban Ibanovich Ibanov" (clearly it is a male-dominated society!). Mediocrity is the engine of upward social mobility. Superior intellect ensures a position on the margins. Thus "leading figures" in Ibansk society have nicknames such as "Sociologist", "Thinker", "Member". These are all nonentities. The real thinkers have nicknames such as "Schizophrenic", "Chatterer", "Slanderer", "Bawler". The former acquire all the honours and prestige, often by plagiarizing the ideas of the latter.

The work is divided into six parts, each of which contains important "chains" of texts. These chains explore various themes. Moreover, the work is structured on two planes, the synchronic and diachronic. Zinov'ev thus provides himself with a means of giving both a sociological account of the Soviet system as it existed and an account of how it developed. Many of the themes that were first treated by Zinov'ev in *The Yawning Heights* receive book-length treatment in later works. In one sense, therefore, *The Yawning Heights* can be seen as the fountainhead of the vast, uninterrupted out-pouring of writing that ensued after 1976 and lasted until 1992 before slackening off.

A brief listing of some of the major themes in *The Yawning Heights* indicates the range and depth of the author's analysis: Shizophrenic's "tract" on the laws governing human society; his other "tract" telling of his war experiences; Ibansk history; the battle between the "radicals" and the "reactionaries"; the experimental rat-colony; Slanderer's notes on ideology; Chatterer's theses on the nature of Ibansk art; life in a penal battalion; the naivety of foreigners; "lectures" on the State, government, and the "Brotherhood" (Ibansk's equivalent of the CPSU); childhood in Ibansk; the ubiquity of the queue and its socio-political significance.

The range and variety of themes is matched by a similar range of stylistic treatment. Virtually every register is represented, together with their parodies. Some texts are written in the form of an academic treatise. The issues in those texts receive satirical treatment in others. Pervading the whole work is an authorial voice that says: Ibansk is dreadful, it is irrational, it is grotesque. An adequate description must replicate these features. Thus certain underlying socio-political or socio-economic laws can be described in an appropriate social-science idiom. The irrational and the grotesque, however, cannot be described rationally. An adequate description will contain examples of the irrational and the grotesque. This explains the rich variety of styles.

As noted above, *The Yawning Heights* is assured a place in satirical world literature. A major aspect that is lost in translation is the texture of the Russian, since Zinov'ev has managed to produce a text that is saturated in allusion to Soviet rhetoric. Furthermore, the density of the book, together with its fragmentary nature, means that it is difficult for the casual reader. For these reasons, translations of this monumental work are inevitably defective. However, despite these handicaps, and despite the fact that Zinov'ev demands effort on the part of his readers, in the case of *The Yawning Heights* that effort is well worth making.

MICHAEL KIRKWOOD

The Madhouse

Zheltyi dom

Novel, 1980

The Madhouse is a novel in four parts, published in two volumes in 1980. It occupies a central position in Zinov'ev's *oeuvre*, straddling as it does his last year in the Soviet Union and his first year in the west. It was also the first work that the author was able to revise from start to finish before sending it to his publisher, his previous works having been written piecemeal and smuggled abroad.

The compositional history of *The Madhouse* is interesting in other respects. It is not the case that Zinov'ev wrote the first volume in the Soviet Union and the second after his arrival in the west. Zinov'ev's "unit of composition" is the short, free-standing text accompanied by a title. *The Madhouse* consists of 824 of them. Zinov'ev worked on all four parts of his novel simultaneously, completing about half the total number of texts before leaving Moscow and the other half in Munich. But despite Zinov'ev's opportunity to revise the total manuscript before submitting it to his publisher, the novel contains a major structural flaw. Part 3 of the novel sits awkwardly between parts 2 and 4. It could be excised completely without making any difference whatsoever to the development of the, admittedly, scarcely visible plot. Moreover, if the reader has failed to read the introduction to the novel, he or she will find it very difficult to account for the presence of part 3 at all.

Part 3 does, however, contain some of Zinov'ev's funniest writing. Much of the action takes place on a Soviet collective farm near Moscow during the "battle for the harvest". Zinov'ev is unbeatable when it comes to showing what makes the Soviet countryside "Soviet". One only has to cite his description of a gaggle of Moscow intellectuals standing in the rain, up to their knees in mud, listening to a political lecture on the need to harvest the cabbages because of the international political situation. The cabbages, when collected, are then "stored" in a hole in the same muddy field, the materials for the construction of a "vegetable store" having "fallen off" a series of lorries on the way to the site. These intellectuals are from the Institute of Ideology of the Academy of Sciences (a thinly veiled allusion to the Institute of Philosophy of the Academy of Sciences) and are billeted in a ramshackle barn belonging to Matrena Dura. She, of course, is Zinov'ev's answer to Solzhenitsyn's Matrena as depicted in "Matrenin dvor" ("Matryona's House").

The Madhouse is quite heavily autobiographical. Much of the "action" takes place in the Institute of Ideology, which is an allusion to an institution in which Zinov'ev worked as a Junior Research Assistant for some years. The "hero" of *The Madhouse* is a young Junior Research Fellow (JRF), who, Zinov'ev assures us, is not based on the author. The JRF wishes to conform but is congenitally incapable of doing so. He is a reluctant renegade. Despite his attempts to integrate with his collective at the Institute, he is gradually marginalized and finally removed from the Institute and society at large. The major theme of the novel, then, is the conflict between individualism and collectivism.

If the setting in part 3 is largely a Soviet collective farm, parts 1 and 2 are set in Moscow and the Academy of Sciences Institute of Ideology, and part 4 is set partly in Moscow and partly in a rest home (*dom otdykha*) near the capital. Part 1 is shown from the perspective of JRF. The 190 texts in prose and verse reveal his thoughts about Soviet life in general, about life in the Institute of Ideology, his work and his colleagues. His aim is to get onto the reserve list of candidates for Party membership. His head is full of "voices", his "*alter egos*" of which he has an inordinate number. Zinov'ev cleverly lets his hero assign names to many of these "*egos*", such as "Lenin", "Stalin", "Marx", "Beria", "Dzerzhinskii", etc. The hero accordingly has many conversations with these egos, allowing Zinov'ev the opportunity to make a series of penetrating but also hilarious comments about the discrepancies between Soviet life as it actually is and how it was envisaged by the "founding fathers". The texts in part 2 are from the perspective of the narrator. JRF is referred to in the third person, but there are many texts containing his "voices", making a link with part 1. In part 2 a KGB file is opened on JRF. Since he is very intelligent and outspoken, it would suit many of his colleagues were he to disappear. Many of his "friends" therefore collaborate willingly with the authorities. Part 2 ends with JRF being given leave to spend a month in a sanatorium outside Moscow while the investigation continues.

Zinov'ev uses the rest home as a metaphor for communism under conditions of abundance. The inmates want for nothing. Their material, physical, and spiritual needs are catered for. Yet life's "eternal problems" still recur. It is a neat demolition of the idea that it is possible to build paradise on earth.

The canvas of *The Madhouse* is thus wide and varied. We have the contrast between the inner world of individuals (JRF in part 1) and the external behaviour of these individuals (JRF as observed by others in parts 2–4), life in the town, life in the countryside, life at work, life at "rest". Many of the themes have recurred in earlier works but receive further treatment in *The Madhouse*. Some of Zinov'ev's most humorous writing is to be found in this work, particularly some of his verses such as JRF's "epistles" to the Russian People and his "collective", his "Loser's Lament" and the "Hymn to the Marxist quote". But the sad fact is that few have read this monumental work. By the time it appeared in translation, the "Zinov'ev effect" had begun to wear off.

MICHAEL KIRKWOOD

Lidiia Zinov'eva-Annibal 1866–1907

Prose writer and dramatist

Biography

Born in Kogore, 1 March 1866. Early years spent in St Petersburg, educated at home and in private schools, from which she was expelled for rebellious and disrespectful behaviour. Married: 1) her history tutor, Konstantin Semenovich Shvarsalon in 1884 (divorced 1899), two sons and one daughter; 2) Viacheslav Ivanov in 1899, one daughter. First publication, 1889. Left Russia with her children in the early 1890s. Travelled throughout Europe (met Viacheslav Ivanov in Rome, 1893). Returned with Ivanov to St Petersburg, 1905. Published in various genres, 1904–07. Set up, with Ivanov, the Wednesday salon, known as "The Tower", which was a major circle for the Symbolist cultural elite, 1905–07. Died of scarlet fever in Zagor'e, Mogilev, 30 October 1907.

Publications

Fiction

Tridtsadt' tri uroda. St Petersburg, 1907; translated as "Thirty-Three Abominations", by Samuel D. Cioran, *Russian Literature Triquarterly*, 9 (1974), 94–116.

Tragicheskii zverinets [The Tragic Menagerie]. St Petersburg, 1907; Tomsk, 1997.

Net! [No!]. Petrograd, 1918.

Plays

Kol'tsa [The Rings]. Moscow, 1904.

"Pevuchii osel. Trilogii pervaia chast' i altsvet'" [The Singing Ass], in *Tsvetnik or Koshnitsa pervaia: Stikhotvoreniia*, St Petersburg, 1907, 121–69.

Critical Studies

"Vvedenie", by Olga Deschartes, in *Sobranie sochinenii*, by Viacheslav Ivanov, Brussels, 1971.

"Women Writers in Russian Decadence", by Temira Pachmuss, *Journal of Contemporary History*, 17 (1982), 111–36.

"Tvorcheskii put' L.D. Zinov'evoi-Annibal", by T.L. Nikol'skaia, *Blokovskii sbornik*, Tartu, 1988, vol. 8, 123–37.

Vospominaniia: kniga ob ottse, by Lidiia Ivanova, Paris, Atheneum, 1990.

"'My – dva grozoi zazhzhennye stvola': Erotika v russkoi poezii – ot simvolistov do oberiutov", by N.A. Bogomolov, in *Erotika v russkoi literature: Ot Barkova do nashikh dnei*, Moscow, 1992, 56–65.

"Laid Out in Lavender: Perceptions of Lesbian Love in Russian Literature and Criticism of the Silver Age, 1893–1917", by Diana Burgin, in *Sexuality and the Body in Russian Culture*, edited by Jane T. Costlow, Stephanie Sandler, and Judith Vowles, Stanford, Stanford University Press, 1993, 177–203.

"Strasti po Lidii. Tvorcheskii portret L. Zinov'evoi-Annibal", by Mariia Mikhailova, *Preobrazhenie: Russkii feministskii zhurnal*, 2 (1994), 144–57.

"The Fate of Women Writers in Literature at the Beginning of the Twentieth Century: 'A. Mire', Ann Mar, Lidiia Zinov'eva-Annibal", by Mariia Mikhailova, in *Gender and Russian Literature: New Perspectives*, edited by Rosalind Marsh, Cambridge and New York, Cambridge University Press, 1996, 141–54.

"Lidiia Zinov'ev-Annibal's *The Singing Ass*: A Woman's View of Men and Eros", by Pamela Davidson, in *Gender and Russian Literature: New Perspectives*, edited and translated by Rosalind Marsh, Cambridge, Cambridge University Press, 1996, 155–83.

In the space of her relatively brief career as a writer Lidiia Zinov'eva-Annibal wrote and published in a broad range of genres: she was the author of Symbolist plays, including *Kol'tsa* [The Rings] and *Pevuchii osel* [The Singing Ass] (of which only the first act was ever published), the novella *Tridtsat' tri uroda* (*Thirty-Three Abominations*), the autobiographical novel *Tragicheskii zverinets* [The Tragic Menagerie] and numerous short stories, many published only after her death, in the collection entitled *Net!* [No!]. In addition she wrote several critical essays. Born into an aristocratic family and educated for a life in society, Zinov'eva-Annibal was throughout her life a rebel and nonconformist: expelled from boarding schools; most deeply happy as a child when she summered in the country; infatuated with Populist ideas and the tutor who instilled them in her; married to the tutor only to find him no match for her own convictions. It was while travelling in Europe in 1895 that she met the man who was to play a decisive role in her emotional and artistic fate. Her meeting with Viacheslav Ivanov was for both of them profoundly transformative. It was in the wake of their meeting that Zinov'eva-Annibal began to write in earnest and together they played a pivotal role in Russian Symbolism. From 1905 until her death Zinov'eva-Annibal was a crucial figure at their Wednesday salons (known by the name of their apartment, "The Tower"), where she and her husband received many of the luminaries of the St Petersburg Silver Age. Memoirists of the period recall her unconventional dress and intense, ecstatic behavior; Ivanov thought of her as the living embodiment of the Dionysian principle, the spirit of eros and tragedy through which he longed to reconcile Christianity and the ancient world. Much of Zinov'eva-Annibal's own work reflects the milieu of which she was so vivid a part, and her career as a writer can perhaps be seen as an extended struggle to negotiate the influence of her husband (he himself referred to this struggle).

While her dramatic work is of interest to students of Russian Symbolism (*Kol'tsa* is her attempt at a Symbolist mystery play), two prose works have particular resonance for contemporary readers, and a more than historical significance: *Thirty-Three Abominations*, a novella that deals explicitly if problematically with lesbianism; and *Tragicheskii zverinets*, Zinov'eva-Annibal's finest work, an autobiographical novel of the author's childhood. Both works were published in 1907, the year of her death.

The novella *Thirty-Three Abominations* recounts in diary form the romantic relationship between two women, the actress Vera and her unnamed lover, whose words we read. Exploiting the clichés of Decadence and *fin-de-siècle* homophobia (the women's relationship is characterized by prolonged bouts of tears and narcissistic gazing into a mirror; they are celebrants of an intimate cult of body and beauty), the story none the less raises enduring aesthetic and psychological issues. Its plot is simple: initially secluded in their romantic bower (where they are perpetually in reclining positions), the actress Vera ultimately succumbs to her desire to have an eternal image of her lover: to this end she "gives" her lover as model to a group of 33 male artists. Apparently driven to this act by her desire to arrest the flow of time, she realizes only after the fact that her gift has been an act of betrayal. One of the story's central concerns seems to lie in this opposition of dramatic and visual art: Zinov'eva-Annibal juxtaposes mortality and change with the apparent timelessness of the image. Whether performance implies a kind of "prostitution"; whether art can represent the self (or whether such representation is possible only in the eyes of the beloved); whether submission to a powerful "male gaze" inevitably entails the loss of female community – these are some of the issues that the story poses.

Tragicheskii zverinets was hailed by numerous critics as the author's strongest work; Aleksandr Blok referred to its "elemental realism", thus suggesting its striking departure from Zinov'eva-Annibal's other fiction and dramatic work. While most critics refer to *Tragicheskii zverinets* as a "group of stories", it is perhaps best understood as a unified Bildungsroman, a feminine version of Tolstoi's *Detstvo*, *Otrochestvo*, *Iunost'* (*Childhood*, *Boyhood*, *Youth*) – a comparison which at least one contemporary critic suggested in reviewing the novel. In this novel of girlhood, the heroine Vera (as Zinov'eva-Annibal names her surrogate) moves from the near-Edenic wildness of summers on a Baltic estate, through emerging consciousness of social inequality, into the hell of an urban boarding school. She moves from intimacy with a series of wild animals (the novel's first chapters are entitled "The Bear Cubs", "The Young Crane", "The Wolves") and awkward affection for girls who are her social inferiors, into the milieu of the school – where she becomes something of an adolescent decadent, rivalling the worst excesses of Sologub's petty demons. Vera's journey into her own version of the lower depths is resolved in an epiphanic moment (after her expulsion from school) on the Italian seashore: in an extended passage of powerful lyrical prose, Zinov'eva-Annibal describes her heroine's intuition of a mode of being that involves neither violence nor the will to power. *Tragicheskii zverinets* raises important ethical issues regarding the relationship of human beings to the animal world; it also investigates the psychology of violence and intimacy in the character of a young girl estranged from the world of nature that had nurtured and sustained her. In its movement "through" decadence toward an epiphany of reconciliation with nature, *Tragicheskii zverinets* represents an important articulation of the modernist revision of traditional values. It is, moreover, a work that resonates powerfully with late 20th-century ecological thinking and feminism, bodies of thought that aim to expose and critique the devastations of hypertrophied rationalism and repressive gender arrangements. While undoubtedly influenced by her husband's philosophy of Dionysian ecstasy and sacrifice, the novel is its own deeply realized statement of experience and belief, working towards more embodied, narrative revelations where Ivanov's system of thought found expression in philosophical and poetic discourse.

JANE COSTLOW

Mikhail Mikhailovich Zoshchenko 1895–1958

Prose writer and dramatist

Biography

Born in St Petersburg, 10 August 1895. Attended St Petersburg 8th gymnasium; studied law at the Imperial St Petersburg University, 1913–14: left university because of financial difficulties. Served as an officer in the tsarist Army, 1914–17: rose to the rank of captain; decorated for bravery five times. Had a number of jobs including: post-office worker, cobbler, telephone operator, policeman, instructor in poultry husbandry, 1917–20. Volunteered for the Red Army, 1919; decommissioned for health reasons in the same year. Married: Vera Vladimirovna Kerbits in 1920; one son. Member of Serapion Brothers. Rocketed to fame in the early 1920s for his short stories. Recipient: Banner of Red Labour medal, 1939; medal for "Valorous Labour during the Great Patriotic War", April 1946. Joined the editorial board of *Zvezda*, June 1946. Attacked by Resolution of the Central Committee of the Communist Party "On the Journals *Zvezda* and *Leningrad*", 14 August 1946. Expelled from the Writers' Union, 4 September 1946. Literary activity and access to publication under own name greatly limited, from 1946. Re-admitted to the Writers' Union, but not rehabilitated, 23 June 1953. Died of poor health aggravated by severe depression, in Sestroretsk, 22 July 1958. CPSU Resolution of 1946 repealed by Politburo, 20 October 1988.

Publications

Collected Editions

Sobranie sochinenii, 6 vols. Leningrad, 1929–31.
Izbrannye proizvedeniia 1923–1945. Leningrad, 1946.
Rasskazy i povesti 1923–1956. Leningrad, 1956.
Izbrannoe. Ann Arbor, University of Michigan Press, 1960.
Rasskazy, fel'etony, komedii, neizdannye proizvedeniia. Moscow and Leningrad, 1963.
Izbrannye proizvedeniia, 2 vols. Leningrad, 1968.
Neizdannyi Zoshchenko, edited by Vera von Wiren. Ann Arbor, Ardis, 1976.
Sobranie sochinenii, 3 vols. Leningrad, 1986–87.
Uvazhaemye grazhdane: Parodii. Rasskazy. Fel'etony. Satiricheskie zametki. Pis'ma k pisateliu. Odnoaktnye p'esy [Dear Citizens: Parodies. Short Stories. Feuilletons. Satirical Articles. Letters to a Writer. One-act Plays]. Moscow, 1991.
Sobranie sochinenii, 5 vols. Moscow, 1994.

Fiction

Rasskazy Nazara Il'icha, gospodina Sinebriukhova [Stories of Nazar Il'ich, Mr Bluebelly]. Leningrad, 1922; 2nd edition, 1926.
Uvazhaemye grazhdane [Dear Citizens]. Moscow and Leningrad, 1926; 2nd–10th editions, 1928.
Nervnye liudi. Kharkov, 1927; 2nd–3rd editions, 1928; translated as "Nervous People", by Maria Gordon and Hugh McLean, in *Nervous People and Other Satires*, edited by Hugh McLean, London, Gollancz, and New York, Pantheon, 1963.
O chem pel solovei. Sentimental'nye povesti [What the Nightingale Sang About. Sentimental Stories]. Leningrad and Moscow, 1927 (2 editions); 3rd edition, 1929.
Nad kem smeetes' [Who Are You Laughing At]. Moscow and Leningrad, 1928 (3 editions); 4th edition, 1929.
"Vozvrashchennaia molodost'", *Zvezda*, nos 6, 8, 10 (1933); translated as *Youth Restored*, by Joel Stern, Ann Arbor, Ardis, 1984.
"Golubaia kniga" [A Skyblue Book], *Krasnaia nov'*, 3/10 (1934); 6–7, 10 (1935).
"Chernyi prints" [The Black Prince], *Iunyi proletarii*, 4–5, 7–9 (1936).
Istoricheskie rasskazy [Historical Stories]. Moscow, 1936.
Rasskazy o Lenine [Stories about Lenin]. Moscow and Leningrad, 1939; 1941 (2 editions).
"Talisman. Shestaia povest' Belina" [Talisman. Belin's Sixth Story], *Zvezda*, 1 (1937).
"Vozmezdie" [Retribution], *Novyi mir*, 10, (1937).
"Besslavnyi konets / Kerenskii" [An Inglorious Ending / Kerenskii], *Literaturnyi sovremennik*, 1 (1938).
"Taras Shevchenko", *Literaturnyi sovremennik*, 2–3 (1939).
"Pered voskhodom solntsa", *Oktiabr'*, 6–7, 8–9 (1943); *Zvezda*, 3 (1972) as "Povest' o razume"; separate edition, New York, Izdatel'stvo imeni Chekhova, 1967, 2nd editon, 1973; translated as *Before Sunrise*, by Gary Kern, Ann Arbor, Ardis, 1974.
Scenes from the Bathhouse and Other Stories of Communist Russia, translated by Sidney Monas. Ann Arbor, University of Michigan Press, 1962.
A Man is Not a Flea: Stories, translated by Serge Shishkoff. Ann Arbor, Ardis, 1989.

Plays

"Uvazhaemyi tovarishch" [Dear Comrade], *30 dnei*, 9 (1930).
Kul'turnoe nasledie [Cultural Legacy]. Leningrad, 1933.
"Prestuplenie i nakazanie" [Crime and Punishment], *Krasnaia nov'*, 3 (1933).
"Svad'ba" [The Wedding], *Krasnaia nov'*, 3 (1933).
Estrada [The Stage]. Leningrad and Moscow, 1940.
"Opasnye sviazi" [Dangerous Liaisons], *Zvezda*, 2 (1940).
"Ochen' priiatno" [Delighted], *Leningrad*, 1–2 (1946).

Essays and Letters

Veselye proekty [Merriment of Design]. Leningrad, 1928.
Pis'ma k pisateliu [Letters to a Writer]. Leningrad, 1929.
Schastlivye idei [Happy Ideas]. Leningrad, 1931.

Critical Studies

Mastera sovremennoi literatury, edited by B.V. Kazanskii and Iu.N. Tynianov, Leningrad, 1928.
"The Tragedy of a Soviet Satirist: The Case of Zoshchenko", by Rebecca Domar, in *Through the Glass of Soviet Literature*, edited by Ernest J. Simmons, New York, Columbia University Press, 1953.
"On Zoshchenko and Major Literature", by V. Shklovsky, *Russian Literature Triquarterly*, 14 (1976), 407–14.

Mikhail Zoshchenko. Ocherk tvorchestva, by Dmitrii Moldavskii, Leningrad, 1977.
Poetika Mikhaila Zoshchenko, by M.O. Chudakova, Moscow, 1979.
Mikhail Zoshchenko v vospominaniiakh sovremennikov, edited by A. Smolian and N. Iurgeneva, Moscow, 1981.
Mikhail Zoshchenko: A Literary Profile, by A.B. Murphy, Oxford, Meeuws, 1981.
Tekhnika komicheskogo u Zoshchenko, by Mikhail Kreps, Vermont, Chalidze, 1986.
Mikhail Zoshchenko. Sud'ba khudozhnika, by Anatolii Starkov, Moscow, 1990.
Vspominaia Mikhaila Zoshchenko, edited by Iurii Tomashevskii, Leningrad, 1990.
"Kniga o Zoshchenko", by Tsezar' Vol'pe, in *Iskusstvo nepokhozhesti*, Moscow, 1991 (reprint of two 1941 articles).
The Pragmatics of Insignificance: Chekhov, Zoshchenko, Gogol, by Cathy Popkin, Stanford, Stanford University Press, 1993.
Mikhail Zoshchenko: Evolution of a Writer, by Linda Hart Scatton, Cambridge, Cambridge University Press, 1993.
Litso i maska Mikhaila Zoshchenko, edited by Iurii Tomashevskii, Moscow, 1994.
Vospominaniia o Mikhaile Zoshchenko. Moscow, 1995.
Inventsii, by Aleksandr Zholkovskii, Moscow, 1995.
"The Speaking Author: *Skaz* in Mikhail Zoshchenko's *Sentimental Tales*", by Rose France, *Essays in Poetics*, 21 (1996), 35–49.

Bibliographies
Russkie sovetskie pisateli prozaiki, 2, Leningrad, 1964, 78–114.
Mikhail Zoshchenko: Evolution of a Writer, by Linda Hart Scatton, Cambridge, Cambridge University Press, 1993, 259–66; 280–91.
Litso i maska Mikhaila Zoshchenko, edited by Iurii Tomashevskii, Moscow, 1994, 340–65.

Mikhail Zoshchenko is best known for the satirical, very short stories he wrote in the 1920s and 1930s and for his unfortunate role as co-target (with Anna Akhmatova) of a post-World War II Soviet crackdown on the arts. From his first published efforts in 1922 until he was effectively silenced by a Resolution of the Communist Party Central Committee in 1946, Zoshchenko experimented with a number of different prose genres. However, it was his riotous short stories that made him a household name in the first decades of Soviet rule. They were so popular that the absurdities of daily life under the new regime were often characterized as "straight out of Zoshchenko".

Joining other young writers like Kaverin, Fedin, Lunts, Polonskaia, and Slonimskii in Leningrad, he was one of the original Serapion Brothers, a short-lived but illustrious and highly productive group that espoused an independent role for the arts. Zoshchenko's unique talent enabled him to work within a genre disrespected at that time (the very short story, vignette, anecdote), and turn it into a high art form. He accomplished this through his use of language, narrative technique, and elusive, subtly ironic tone. Zoshchenko's satirical sketches are at once descendants of Anton Chekhov's humorous and poignant short stories and Nikolai Gogol''s absurdist tales.

Although Zoshchenko himself had roots in the gentry and his early, unpublished literary attempts reveal rather conventional language and plot, he found immediate success with the publication of stories in which the first-person narrator is a man of the people – uneducated, bumbling, but stridently confident of his own worth and opinions. The narrator exposes his ignorance through his views and his language, which is full of incorrectly used words, Soviet bureaucratese, neologisms, and colloquialisms. Brilliant and idiosyncratic, Zoshchenko's prose is almost as difficult to translate as poetry. He is regarded as one of Russian literature's finest practitioners of *skaz*, a literary technique that offers the illusion of oral speech through a form of narrative that differs markedly from the accepted literary norm. The resulting stylistic distance and dissonance between author and narrator, not to mention the reader, often serve to cast doubt on the narrator's judgement.

In 1922 Zoshchenko published his first book, *Rasskazy Nazara Il'icha, gospodina Sinebriukhova* [Stories of Nazar Il'ich, Mr Bluebelly], which provoked at once serious critical attention and some questions regarding the political allegiance of its author. Its narrator is a former peasant, now a demobilized soldier, who recounts in cocky, mock-heroic tones tales of war and the return to civilian life. Having found his narrative voice with Mr Bluebelly, and wanting to reach a newly literate audience that was not accustomed to buying books or literary magazines ("thick journals"), Zoshchenko turned to publishing stories and feuilletons in the numerous humorous magazines of the day. His short works appeared in these inexpensive, mass-market publications, where he took as his subject-matter the challenges of day-to-day existence in the Soviet Union, namely securing housing, using a public bath, buying illegally distilled liquor, visiting the doctor, sharing a communal apartment, learning how to use new-fangled equipment, attending the theatre. The language and subject-matter were such a far cry from the serious literature of 19th-century Russia that they were seen to capture the spirit, if not the ideology, of the regime, and the reading public embraced the writer with gusto.

Critical reception of Zoshchenko was less positive: his use of substandard language and irony, as well as the ideological imprecision that underlies his tales, were often disparaged by contemporary critics. However, he did have strong supporters among writers and critics as disparate as Maksim Gor'kii, Viktor Shklovskii, Kornei Chukovskii, Osip Mandel'shtam, and Aleksei Voronskii.

At the same time that he was gaining renown for his short stories, he also published novellas with what seemed to be more traditional plots and language. However, these *Sentimental'nye povesti* [Sentimental Stories] were intended as parodies of 20th-century imitations of 19th-century Russian masters such as Gogol' and Dostoevskii. His goal in these tales was to show incontrovertibly that both the style and thematics of classical Russian literature of the 19th century were inappropriate for the new era and deserved to be abandoned.

By the end of the decade Zoshchenko's Collected Works were issued in six small-format volumes (1929–31). Testimony of his readers' wild enthusiasm for his stories is provided by an unusual book he published in 1929, which consists of selected letters to him from his readers: *Pis'ma k pisateliu* [Letters to a Writer].

A life-long depressive, Zoshchenko gradually came to believe that humour and irony were among the vices of which he must cure himself, and he set about gradually removing these elements from his writing. At the same time, in the literary politics of the 1930s, writers were being encouraged to devote themselves to non-fiction, to compose serious, positive works, to abandon satire as a genre because it was argued that the ideal nature of Soviet society left little to satirize. This confluence of internal and external pressures steered Zoshchenko's writings in new directions. While continuing to produce his trademark short stories and feuilletons, and frequently to reissue them in anthologies, he also tried his hand at biography, autobiography, children's literature, and comedy. The most successful of these are his children's stories, in particular the thinly-veiled autobiographical *Lelia and Min'ka* tales (1938–40), a series of first-person childhood reminiscences with clear moral teachings.

Zoshchenko also began in the 1930s to gather and reshape his stories into book-like works, combining fiction and non-fiction into hybrid genres. *Vozvrashchennaia molodost'* (*Youth Restored*), *Golubaia kniga* [A Skyblue Book], and *Pered voskhodom solntsa* (*Before Sunrise*) together form his trilogy, each one an attempt to fashion connecting and over-arching structures around new and existing stories in such a way as to make the end result greater than the sum of its parts. *Youth Restored* combines a novella-like story of a disaffected intellectual with an extensive, separate, scholarly apparatus on the subject of senescence and ways to combat it. *Youth Restored* was the first hint for his readers that their favourite humourist had a serious side. *Golubaia kniga* organizes and recasts some of Zoshchenko's best-known short stories around the themes of money, love, treachery, failure, and remarkable events. It represented for the writer another experiment in integrating fictional and documentary material; the narrator links the stories to one another by offering a series of historical facts and curiosities.

Before Sunrise is at once an investigation by its author/narrator into the reasons for his depression and a recounting of the method he has found for curing himself. However, the 1943 publication of this innovative, serious, and personal work in the journal *Zvezda* was halted after only the first half had appeared. (The second half was published posthumously in 1972). Zoshchenko was not to be forgiven by Party leaders for such self-absorption during wartime, and the post-war attack on him ostensibly provoked by his children's story, "Prikliucheniia obez'ianki" [Adventures of a Monkey], was in reality a settling of scores over *Before Sunrise*. Zoshchenko's literary experiments with short forms came to a bitter end after Andrei Zhdanov, Stalin's Cultural Commissar, targeted him for vilification in 1946. He was expelled from the Writers' Union, shunned by friends and colleagues, and produced little of note from then until his death in 1958.

LINDA HART SCATTON

Before Sunrise

Pered voskhodom solntsa

Autobiographical work, 1943–72

Before Sunrise is the last major work written by Zoshchenko. Unlike much of his earlier output, it is a serious and deeply personal book, a sort of autobiography, which recounts the author's life as the story of painfully achieved insight into, and ultimately mastery over, chronic depression. Focusing on progressively deepening insight, it is thus an unusual autobiographical work, because the events of main interest to the narrator are internal (insights, sudden recollections of long-forgotten events, theoretical understanding derived from research). The external events described (childhood, love, war, career) function either as raw material to be sifted in arriving at therapeutic insights, or as illustrations of theoretical points once insight is gained. The priority of the mental is signalled immediately, in the preface: the narrator reports that his theme, the necessity of reason, far from making the book untimely, makes it especially pertinent during the war with Nazi Germany, which despised reason. From this thought flows the decision to finish and publish his book without waiting for the end of the war – a fateful decision, as it turned out.

After describing his initial attempts at rationalizing his misery (depression is the result of great intellectual gifts) and then at curing it (with medicines and water cures), Zoshchenko begins his struggle in earnest with the thought that his depression is not some inexplicable curse but rather the result of forgotten, traumatic events. The central sections of the book chronicle the search for the causes of his depression. Resolving to try to recall those events, the narrator produces over 100 first-person, mostly page-long vignettes, or "photographs", which purport to relate the sharpest recollections preserved in his memory. For some readers, these sections, the most traditionally autobiographical and the most literary, are the most successful in the book.

Nevertheless, the search of conscious memory, however rewarding artistically, does not succeed in identifying the precipitating trauma, which, the narrator concludes, must have occurred before the sunrise of reason, before the age of two. In order to penetrate those earliest experiences, he pursues the traumatic cause through dream interpretation. These sections read like a psychological detective story, with Zoshchenko's mind investigating itself. In this investigation, Freudian ideas are fundamental, most notably those of the unconscious, dream symbolism and interpretation, and the aetiology of neurosis in childhood trauma. Nevertheless, because psychoanalysis was officially taboo in the Soviet Union in 1943, Zoshchenko conceals much of his dependence on Freud by criticizing him very often (sometimes reasonably, sometimes not).

In part to provide his argument with additional cover, he also makes heavy use of Pavlov's theory of conditioned reflexes to explain his illness as the association of fear and displeasure with certain key objects, and then to account for the cure as the severing of those associations using logic and understanding. On locating the traumatic early childhood events that connected the realities of food, water, and women with fearful and unpleasant feelings, Zoshchenko asserts that he became a different person, for whom "every hour, every minute of my life was filled with some sort of rapture, happiness, joy". The book concludes with sections devoted to verifying his Freudian-Pavlovian approach to depression and to arguing generally for the necessity of reason in everyday life (by which he means rationality rather than adherence to some lofty, Kantian standard of judgement).

Despite Zoshchenko's strenuous attempts to connect his very personal book with the ruling Soviet orthodoxies, the publication of the first half of *Before Sunrise*, in October 1943, elicited an official campaign of denunciation, halting publication of the text midway and criticizing the book for its detailed concern with private pathology at a time of national emergency. Though the fatal blow was not to fall until three years later, when Andrei Zhdanov placed on Zoshchenko the equivalent of official Soviet anathema. His career as a writer was effectively ended with the truncated publication of what he called "my main book."

Like its author, *Before Sunrise* has also needed time to recover from its early traumas. The second half of the text was published for the first time only in 1972 and the complete text in 1973, a full 30 years after the publication of the first half. On top of official repudiation, the book also suffered initially from readers' incomprehension that a writer normally identified with humour and satire would write such a serious book about such personal matters. Furthermore, encompassing so many genres – short sketch, popular scientific article, Bildungsroman, and autobiography – *Before Sunrise* is impossible to classify, a fact that also delayed comprehension and acceptance. In the past 15 years, though, serious interpretation has begun. Scholars have seen in it the influences of Pushkin, Belyi, Stephan Zweig, Nietzsche, and Nikolai Fedorov (a Utopian philosopher). Several scholars have interpreted it as a conversion tale similar to Augustine's *Confessions*, with reason substituting for God. Most critics, however, agree on one thing: the cure announced by Zoshchenko ("I became an entirely different person") does not ring true. In spite of this, it still remains to explain the power of this moving book. The key to its enduring value lies in its dramatizing so vividly the mind's attempt to understand itself. It is as if Freud described his self-analysis, or as if one of his patients, possessing great literary gifts, wrote up his own case history. Unlike so many contemporary accounts of conquering psychological torment, Zoschenko's reader feels privileged to witness the writer's dire combat with his demons. If the cure rings false, the painful search for insight does not. In *Before Sunrise* the most popular Soviet writer of his day used all his narrative skill, and knowingly risked his career, to put on paper an account of his most intimate struggle with himself.

RICHARD B. GROSE

TITLE INDEX

The name(s) in parentheses will direct the reader to the appropriate entry, where full publication information is given. The date given is that of first publication. Revised titles and English-language translations, if different from the original, are listed, with their appropriate dates. Titles in **bold** are subjects of individual essays.

Brat moi (Shukshin), 1975
Bratets (Khvoshchinskaia), 1858
Brat'ia (Fedin), 1928
Brat'ia i sestry (Abramov), 1958
Brat'ia Karamazovy (Dostoevskii), 1879–80
Bratsk Station (Evtushenko), 1966
Bratskaia GES (Evtushenko), 1965
Bratskie pesni (Kliuev), 1912
Bread (A.N. Tolstoi), 1938
Breaking-Point (Artsybashev), 1915
Breakup (G. Ivanov), 1975
Bred (Aldanov), 1954–57
Bride (Chekhov)
Brigadier (Fonvizin), 1968
Brigadir (Fonvizin), 1780
Brigantina podnimaet parusa (Gladilin), 1959
Brityi chelovek (Mariengof), 1984
Bronepoezd 14–69 (V.V. Ivanov), 1922
Bronze Horseman (Pushkin), 1981
Bronzovaia ptitsa (Rybakov), 1956
Brothers Karamazov (Dostoevskii), 1912
Brute (Chekhov), 1958
Brynskii les (Zagoskin), 1846
Buben verkhnego mira (Pelevin), 1993
Bud' zdorov, shkoliar (Okudzhava), 1961
Buddha's Return (Gazdanov), 1951
Budem kak solntse (Bal'mont), 1903
Buian-ostrov (Mariengof), 1920
Bukety (Sollogub), 1845
Bukhtiny vologodskie zaviral'nye v shesti temakh (Belov), 1969
Bukvar' (Polotskii), 1664
Bukvar' iazyka slavenska (Polotskii), 1679
Bukvar' iazyka slovenska, pisanii chteniia uchitisia khotiashchim (Polotskii), 1667
Bumazhnyi peizazh (Aksenov), 1983
Buntashnyi ostrov (Nagibin), 1994
Burelom (Gladkov), 1921
Buria (Erenburg), 1948
Burn (Aksenov), 1984
Burnaia zhizn' Lazika Roitshvanetsa (Erenburg), 1928
Burned Ruins (Kliuev), 1977
Bursak (Narezhnyi), 1824
Byl letnii polden' (Trifonov), 1966
Byl mesiats mai (Baklanov), 1971
Byl'e (Pil'niak), 1922
Byloe i dumy (Herzen), 1855–69
Bystander (Gor'kii), 1930
Bystro khorosho ne byvaet (Petrushevskaia), 1979
Byvye sokoli (Pisemskii), 1868

Cabal of Hypocrites (Bulgakov), 1972
Camera Obscura (Nabokov), 1936
Cancer Ward (Solzhenitsyn), 1968–69
Candle in the Wind (Solzhenitsyn), 1973
Captain Dikshtein (Kuraev), 1990
Captain's Daughter (Pushkin), 1962
Captive of the Caucasus (Makanin), 1996
Captive Spirit (Tsvetaeva), 1980
Carpenter's Yarns (Belov), 1983
Carriage (Gogol'), 1995
Cathedral Folk (Leskov), 1924
Cavalry Maid (Durova), 1988
Cavalry Maiden (Durova), 1988
Cave (Zamiatin), 1966
Celebration (Chekhov), 1958
Cement (Gladkov), 1929
Central-Ermolaevo War (P'etsukh), 1995
Centre of Gravity (Tokareva), 1990
Chaepitie na Arbate (Okudzhava), 1996
Chaika (Chekhov), 1896
Chakkhchygys-Taasu (Remizov), 1922
Chapaev (Furmanov), 1923
Chapaev i Pustota (Pelevin), 1996
Chapayev (Furmanov), 1955
Charodeinaia chasha (Sologub), 1922
Chas slova (Aitmatov), 1988
Chas vechernii (Shkapskaia), 1922
Chasha iarosti (Maksimov), 1982
Chasha zhizni (Bunin), 1915
Chast' rechi (Brodskii), 1977
Chasy (Remizov), 1908
Chatsky (Griboedov), 1972
Cheekbones, a Nose and a Gully (Viktor Erofeev), 1991
Chefs d'oeuvre (Briusov), 1895
Chekhov s nami (Kuraev), 1990
Chekhov, Stendhal (Erenburg), 1962
Chelovecheskii veter (Pil'niak), 1990
Chelovek (V.I. Ivanov), 1939
Chelovek (Maiakovskii), 1918
Chelovek i ego okrestnosti (Iskander), 1993
Chelovek i vremia (Shaginian), 1980
Chelovek idet na Pamir (Shkapskaia), 1924
Chelovek rabotaet khorosho (Shkapskaia), 1932
Chelovek s etogo sveta (Rasputin), 1967
Chelovek s fronta (Nagibin), 1943
Chelovek svity (Makanin), 1982
Chelovek v futliare (Chekhov), 1898
Chelovek v peizazhe (Bitov), 1988
Chelovek za pismennym stolom (L. Ginzburg), 1989
Chem liudi zhivy (L. Tolstoi), 1885
Chemodan (Dovlatov), 1986
Chemu raven iks? (Baranskaia), 1974
Cheremukha (Astaf'ev), 1978
Cherez Moskvu proezdom (Kurchatkin), 1981
Cherez polia (Petrushevskaia), 1983
Chernaia kniga (Erenburg), 1980
Chernaia kuritsa (Pogorel'skii), 1829
Chernaia metallurgiia (Fadeev), 1951–56
Chernoe more (Bulgakov), 1988
Chernoe po belomu (Hippius), 1908
Chernoe zoloto (A.N. Tolstoi), 1931
Chernovik cheloveka (Kaverin), 1931
Chernye doski (Soloukhin), 1966
Chernye maski (Andreev), 1908
Chernyi Arab (Prishvin), 1910
Chernyi god (Narezhnyi), 1829
Chernyi monakh (Chekhov), 1894
Chernyi pes (Prigov)
Chernyi prints (Zoshchenko), 1936
Cherry Orchard (Chekhov), 1908
Chert i rechetvortsy (Kruchenykh), 1913
Chertov log i polunochnoe solntse (Remizov), 1908
Chertova diuzhina (Popov), 1979
Chertova kukla (Hippius), 1911
Chetki (Akhmatova), 1914
Chetvertaia meshchanskaia (Evtushenko), 1959
Chetvertaia proza (O. Mandel'shtam), 1930
Chetvertaia Vologda (Shalamov), 1971
Chetvertyi Rim (Kliuev), 1922
Chetyre apologa (V.F. Odoevskii), 1824
Chetyre dnia (Grossman), 1936
Chetyre foneticheskikh romana (Kruchenykh), 1927
Chetyre glavy (Seifullina), 1922
4338-oi god (V.F. Odoevskii), 1926
Chetyre simfonii (Belyi), 1917
Chetyre stikhtvoreniia (Gorbanevskaia), 1976
Chetyre temperamenta (Aksenov), 1979
Chetyre uroka u Lenina (Shaginian), 1970
14 krasnykh izbushek (Platonov), 1972
14 Dekabria (Merezhkovskii), 1918
Chevengur (Platonov), 1988
Ch'ia vina (Verbitskaia), 1900
Chik and His Friends (Iskander), 1984
Childhood (L. Tolstoi), 1964
Childhood and Schooldays (Paustovskii), 1964
Childhood and Youth (Erenburg), 1962
Childhood of Luvers (Pasternak), 1945
Childhood Years of Bagrov Grandson (Aksakov), 1984
Childhood, Youth and Exile (Herzen), 1979
Children of the Arbat (Rybakov), 1988
Children of the Sun (Gor'kii), 1988
Chinese Story (Pil'niak), 1988
Chiny i den'gi (Rostopchina), 1837
Chistye prudy (Nagibin), 1961
Chistye vody Kitezha (Tendriakov), 1986
Chistyi list (Tolstaia), 1984
Chitaia Lenina (Soloukhin), 1989
Choice (Bondarev), 1983
Choice of a Tutor (Fonvizin), 1916
Choosing a Location, Georgian Album (Bitov), 1992
Chortov most (Aldanov), 1925
Chrezvychainoe (Tendriakov), 1961
Christened Chinaman (Belyi), 1991
Chteniia o Bogochelovechestve (Solov'ev), 1877–81
Chto delat'? (Chernyshevskii), 1863
Chto delat' russkoi emigratsii (Hippius), 1930
Chto ia videl i ponial (Shalamov), 1996
Chto peredat' vorone? (Rasputin), 1988
Chto takoe iskusstvo? (L. Tolstoi), 1897
Chto takoe rusofobiia (Stratanovskii), 1990
Chto takoe sotsialisticheskii realizm? (Siniavskii), 1959
Chto v slove, chto za slovom? (Rasputin), 1987
Chudaki (Gor'kii), 1910
Chudaki (Kniazhnin), 1793
Chudaki (A.N. Tolstoi), 1911
Chudesa v reshete (A.N. Tolstoi), 1926
Chudesnaia zhizn' Iosifa Bal'zamo (Kuzmin), 1919
Chudesnyi desant (Loseff), 1985
Chudodei (Vel'tman), 1856
Chudotvornaia (Tendriakov), 1958
Chudovishche (Katerli), 1983
Chudovishchi (Sumarokov), 1750

Free Love (Kollontai), 1932
Freedom and the Tragic Life (V.I. Ivanov), 1952
Fregat Nadezhda (Marlinskii), 1833
Fregat Pallada (Goncharov), 1858
French Lessons (Rasputin), 1985
Fro (Platonov), 1972
Frol Skobeev, the Rogue
From an Exchange of Letters (Voinovich), 1979
From the Other Shore (Herzen), 1956
From the Reminiscences of Private Ivanov (Garshin), 1988
From Two to Five (Chukovskii), 1963
Front prikhodit k nam (Okudzhava), 1967
Front-Line Stalingrad (V.P. Nekrasov), 1962
Fruits of Enlightenment (L. Tolstoi), 1979
Frunze (Furmanov), 1925
FSSR Frantsuzskaia Sovetskaia Sotsialisticheskaia Respublika (Gladilin), 1985
Fur Hat (Voinovich), 1989
Für Wenige (Zhukovskii), 1818

Gadanie na kofeinoi gushche (P'etsukh), 1991
Gadanie po knige (Voznesenskii), 1994
Gadkie lebedi (A. and B. Strugatskii), 1972
Gaika (Sokhanskaia), 1856
Galereia zamechatel'neishikh romanov (Druzhinin), 1850
Gambler (Dostoevskii), 1916
Gamblers (Gogol'), 1927
Gambrinus (Kuprin), 1970
Gamlet (Sumarokov), 1748
Garden (Akhmadulina), 1990
Garin Death Ray (A.N. Tolstoi), 1955
Garkusha (Narezhnyi), 1950
Garmoniia kontrastov (Severianin), 1995
Garpagoniada (Vaginov), 1983
Gde i kogda (Gorbanevskaia), 1985
Gde moi dom? (Bal'mont), 1924
Gde moia derevnia? (Rasputin), 1995
Gde nebo skhodilos' s kholmami (Makanin), 1984
Gde otstypaetsia liubov' (Tsvetaeva), 1991
Gde tebia zhdut, angel? (Maksimov), 1993
Gde tonko, tam i rvetsia (Turgenev), 1851
Gde-to gremit voina (Astaf'ev), 1967
General and His Army (Vladimov), 1996
General i ego armiia (Vladimov), 1994
General Kalomeros (Vel'tman), 1840
General'naia repetitsiia (Galich), 1974
Generations of Winter (Aksenov), 1994
Gentle Creature (Dostoevskii), 1995
Gentle Spirit (Dostoevskii), 1917
Gentleman from San Francisco (Bunin), 1922
Geroi nashego vremeni (Barkova), 1992
Geroi nashego vremeni (Lermontov), 1840
Gibel' Evropy na Strastnoi ploshchadi (Erdman), 1924
Gibel' senatora (Peterburg) (Belyi), 1986
Gibel' Zheleznoi (V.V. Ivanov), 1928
Gidrotsentral' (Shaginian), 1930–31
Gift (Nabokov), 1963
Gil'otina (Kurchatkin), 1989
Gimnaziia (Chukovskii), 1938
Giperboloid Inzhenera Garina (A.N. Tolstoi), 1925
Girl of My Dreams (Okudzhava), 1988
Glas (Mariengof), 1991
Glass of Water (Petrushevskaia), 1991
Glavy iz Blokadnoi knigi (Granin), 1977
Glazami cheloveka moego pokoleniia (Simonov), 1990
Glazami ekstsentrika (Venedikt Erofeev), 1982
Glinianye golubki (Kuzmin), 1914
Glory (Nabokov), 1971
Glossolaliia (Belyi), 1922
Glotok svobody (Okudzhava), 1971
Glubinka (Berggol'ts), 1932
Glück auf! (Grossman), 1934
Glupyi mal'chik (Prigov)
Go West! (Lunts), 1975
Goatibex Constellation (Iskander), 1975
God chuda i pechali (Borodin), 1981
God velikogo pereloma (Belov), 1989
God zhizni v Peterburge (Durova), 1838
Godforsaken Hole (Zamiatin), 1988
Godovaia strelka (Slutskii), 1971
Gody voiny (Grossman), 1946
Gogol' i chert (Merezhkovskii), 1906
Going Under (Chukovskaia), 1972
Golden Calf (Il'f and Petrov), 1953
Golden Rose (Paustovskii), 1957
Gollovlev Family (Saltykov-Shchedrin), 1916
Golodniak (Kruchenykh), 1922
Gologor (Borodin), 1982
Golos (Kushner), 1978
Golos iz khora (Siniavskii), 1973
Golosa (Kharitonov), 1990
Golosa (Makanin), 1980
Golosa za kholmami (Samoilov), 1987
Golovlevs (Saltykov-Shchedrin), 1986
Golovlyov Family (Saltykov-Shchedrin), 1931
Golubaia glubina (Platonov), 1922
Golubaia kniga (Zoshchenko), 1934
Goluben' (Esenin), 1918
Golubi mira (V.V. Ivanov), 1939
Golubinaia gibel' (Trifonov), 1968
Golubinaia kniga (Remizov), 1946
Golubka (Pristavkin), 1967
Goluboe i krasnoe (Makanin), 1983
Goluboe i zelenoe (Kazakov), 1963
Goluboi i v polosku (Loseff), 1974
Golubye goroda (A.N. Tolstoi), 1925
Golubye peski (V.V. Ivanov), 1922–23
Golyi god (Pil'niak), 1922
Golyi korol' (E.L. Shvarts), 1934
Gomo sovetikus (Zinov'ev), 1982
Gondla (Gumilev), 1917
Good Mentor (Fonvizin), 1974
Goodbye, Schoolboy (Okudzhava), 1971
Goodnight! (Siniavskii), 1989
Gooseberries (Chekhov)
Gora Zvezdy (Briusov), 1975
Gorbachevizm (Zinov'ev), 1988
Gordost' (Gladkov), 1935
Gore ot uma (Griboedov), 1825
Goriachii sneg (Bondarev), 1969
Goriashchie zdaniia (Bal'mont), 1900
Gor'kaia sud'bina (Pisemskii), 1859
Gor'kii sredi nas (Fedin), 1943
Gornitsa (G. Ivanov), 1914
Gornye tropy (Iskander), 1957
Gornyi put' (Nabokov), 1923
Gorod na zare (Galich), 1940
Gorod pravdy (Lunts), 1924
Gorod v podarok (Kushner), 1976
Gorod v stepi (Serafimovich), 1912
Goroda i gody (Fedin), 1924
Gorodok (Pristavkin), 1983
Gorodok (Teffi), 1927
Gorodok Okurov (Gor'kii), 1910
Gorodok v tabakerke (V.F. Odoevskii), 1834
Gorst' (Samoilov), 1989
Gory i liudi (Libedinskii), 1947
Gospel According to Chegem (Iskander), 1984
Gospoda Golovlevy (Saltykov-Shchedrin), 1875–80
Gospoda Tashkenttsy (Saltykov-Shchedrin), 1869–72
Gospodin iz San-Frantsisko (Bunin), 1916
Gosudarstvennoe ditia (P'etsukh), 1997
Gosudarstvennyi zhitel' (Platonov), 1988
Government Inspector (Gogol'), 1927
Govnososka (Viktor Erofeev), 1989
Govorit Leningrad (Berggol'ts), 1964
Govorit Moskva (Daniel'), 1962
Grad obrechennyi (A. and B. Strugatskii), 1987
Graf Nulin (Pushkin), 1828
Grafiniia D*** (Sokhanskaia), 1848
Grammatika liubvi (Bunin), 1915
Graphite (Shalamov), 1981
Grass of Oblivion (Kataev), 1969
Grasshopper (Chekhov)
Grazhdane, poslushaite menia (Evtushenko), 1989
Grazhdanin ubegaiushchii (Makanin), 1984
Great Love (Kollontai), 1929
Great Ore (Vladimov), 1965
Grecheskie stikhotvoreniia N. Shebriny (Druzhinin), 1850
Green Ring (Hippius), 1920
Grekh da beda na kogo ne zhivet (A.N. Ostrovskii), 1863
Grey is the Colour of Hope (Ratushinskaia), 1988
Gromokipiashchii kubok (Severianin), 1913
Groza (A.N. Ostrovskii), 1859
Grozd' (Nabokov), 1922
Grunia (Mikhailov), 1847
Gruzinskii al'bom (Bitov), 1985
Gubernskie ocherki (Saltykov-Shchedrin), 1856–57
Gudiat provoda (Belov), 1978
Gudishki (Durova), 1839
Guillotine (Kurchatkin), 1990
Gulag Archipelago (Solzhenitsyn), 1974–78
Gypsies (Pushkin), 1984

Hadji Murad (L. Tolstoi)
Half Way to the Moon (Aksenov), 1963
Hamlet (Sumarokov), 1970
Hand, or The Confession of an Executioner (Aleshkovskii), 1989

NOTES ON ADVISERS AND CONTRIBUTORS

Aizlewood, Robin. Senior Lecturer, School of Slavonic and East European Studies, University of London. Author of *Verse Form and Meaning in the Poetry of Vladimir Maiakovskii*, 1989 and articles on Daniil Kharms. **Essays:** *Incidents* (Kharms); Maiakovskii; *Cloud in Trousers* (Maiakovskii).

Andrew, Joe. Professor of Russian Literature, Keele University. Author of several books on Russian literature and society, and on women in 19th-century Russian literature, including *Narrative and Desire in Russian Literature, 1822–49: The Feminine and the Masculine*, 1993. Founder editor of the journal, *Essays in Poetics*. **Essays:** Gan; *Naprasnyi dar* (Gan); "Diary of a Madman" (Gogol'); *Who is to Blame?* (Herzen); *First Love* (Turgenev); Zhukova.

Anemone, Anthony. Associate Professor of Russian, College of William and Mary, Williamsburg, Virginia. Specialist on the *oberiuty* and on 20th-century literary theory. **Essays:** *Roadside Picnic* (Arkadii and Boris Strugatskii); Vaginov.

Ayers, Carolyn Jursa. Post-doctoral Research Fellow, University of Groningen, The Netherlands. Doctoral dissertation on the Russian society tale (University of Chicago, 1994). **Essays:** Durova; Pavlova; *A Double Life* (Pavlova).

Bache, Joy H. Doctoral student in medieval Russian literature, School of Slavonic and East European Studies, University of London; part-time Lecturer, Birkbeck College, University of London (Extra-Mural Centre). **Essay:** Monomakh.

Bagby, Lewis. Professor of Russian Language and Literature, University of Wyoming. Author of *Alexander Bestuzhev-Marlinsky and Russian Byronism*, 1995. **Essays:** *Tsyganka* (Baratynskii); Marlinskii.

Baïkovitch, Gilda. Doctoral student, University of Bath: completing dissertation on Fedor Abramov. **Essays:** Abramov; *Two Winters and Three Summers* (Abramov).

Balasubramanian, Radha. Assistant Professor, Department of Modern Languages, University of Nebraska, Lincoln. Author of *The Poetics of Korolenko's Fiction*, 1997. **Essay:** Korolenko.

Baran, Henryk. Associate Professor, Department of Germanic and Slavic Languages and Literatures, State University of New York, Albany. Specialist on early 20th-century Russian poetry, whose essays are collected in his *Poetika russkoi literatury nachala XX veka*, 1993. **Essays:** *Ka* (Khlebnikov); *Night Search* (Khlebnikov); *Plamennyi krug* (Sologub); *The Created Legend* (Sologub).

Barratt, Andrew. Associate Professor, Department of Slavonic Languages and Literatures, University of Otago, New Zealand. Author of *Yurii Olesha's Envy*, 1981; *Between Two Worlds: A Critical Introduction to "The Master and Margarita"*, 1987; and *The Early Fiction of Maksim Gorky*, 1993. Co-editor and co-translator (with Barry Scherr) of Gor'kii's *Selected Letters*, 1997. **Essays:** *My Childhood, My Apprenticeship, My Universities* (Gor'kii); *Envy* (Olesha).

Bartlett, Rosamund. Lecturer, University of Manchester. Author of *Wagner and Russia*, 1995; co-author (with Anna Benn) of *Literary Russia: A Guide*, 1997. **Essays:** Prutkov; Tokareva; A.K. Tolstoi.

Basker, Michael. Senior Lecturer in Russian Studies, University of Bristol. Has written widely on Nikolai Gumilev and Anna Akhmatova. **Essays:** *Poem Without a Hero* (Akhmatova); *Requiem* (Akhmatova); *Zoloto v lazuri* (Belyi); Gumilev; *Ognennyi stolp* (Gumilev); Kuzmin.

Beresford, Michael. Formerly Senior Lecturer in Russian, University of Manchester. Author of *Complete Russian Course for Scientists*, 1965 and *Complete Russian Course for Beginners*, 1978. Editor of a major edition of Gogol''s *Revizor*, 1996. **Essay:** *The Government Inspector* (Gogol').

Bethea, David M. Vilas Research Professor of Russian Literature, University of Wisconsin, Madison. Author of *Khodasevich: His Life and Art*, 1983; *The Shape of Apocalypse in Modern Russian Fiction*, 1989; and *Joseph Brodsky and the Creation of Exile*, 1994. Editor of *Pushkin Today*, 1993. **Introductory Essay:** Aleksandr Pushkin: From Byron to Shakespeare. **Essay:** Brodskii.

Beumers, Birgit. Lecturer in Russian Studies, University of Bristol. Author of *Yury Lyubimov at the Taganka Theatre*, 1997. **Introductory Essay:** Post-Revolutionary Russian Theatre. **Essays:** Erdman; *The Suicide* (Erdman); Galich; P'etsukh; Vampilov; *Duck-Hunting* (Vampilov); Vysotskii.

Bland, Charles. Civil servant; private scholar, and translator. **Essays:** *Fantastic Stories* (Siniavskii); *The Makepeace Experiment* (Siniavskii).

Brandist, Craig. HRB Research Fellow, Bakhtin Centre, University of Sheffield. Author of *Carnival Culture and the Soviet Modernist Novel*, 1996. **Essay:** Olesha.

Briggs, A.D.P (Adviser). Professor of Russian, University of Birmingham. Author of *Alexander Pushkin: A Critical Study*, 1983; *Eugene Onegin*, 1992; and numerous publications on 19th-century Russian literature. Editor and translator of editions of Pushkin's *Eugene Onegin*, 1995 and verse, 1997. **Introductory Essay:** Pre-Revolutionary Russian Theatre. **Essays:** Fonvizin; *Oblomov* (Goncharov); *Woe from Wit* (Griboedov); Ozerov; Pushkin; *The Gypsies* (Pushkin); *The Tales of Belkin* (Pushkin); *Evgenii Onegin* (Pushkin); Shakhovskoi; *The Power of Darkness* (Lev Tolstoi); *A Month in the Country* (Turgenev).

Brintlinger, Angela. Assistant Professor, Department of Slavic and East European Languages and Literatures, Ohio State University, Columbus. **Essay:** *Smert' Vazir-Mukhtara* (Tynianov).

Browning, Gary. Professor of Russian, Brigham Young University, Provo, Utah. Author of *Boris Pilniak: Scythian at a Typewriter*, 1985. **Essays:** *The Place of the Skull* (Aitmatov); Pil'niak; *The Naked Year* (Pil'niak).

Burgin, Diana Lewis. Professor of Russian and Chair of the Department of Modern Languages, University of Massachusetts, Boston. Fellow of the Russian Research Center, Harvard University. Author of *Sophia Parnok: The Life and Work of Russia's Sappho*, 1994. Co-translator (with Katherine Tiernan O'Connor) of Bulgakov's *The Master and Margarita*, 1995. **Essay:** Parnok.

Carrick, Neil. Has lectured in Russian at the University of Edinburgh and Trinity College, Dublin. Author of studies on Daniil Kharms. **Essays:** *Elizaveta Bam* (Kharms); *The Old Woman* (Kharms).

Cavendish, Philip. Lecturer in Russian, School of Slavonic and East European Studies, University of London. Doctoral dissertation on Evgenii Zamiatin (University of London, 1997). **Essay:** Zamiatin.

Chances, Ellen (Adviser). Professor of Russian Literature and Culture, Princeton University. Author of *Conformity's Children: An Approach to the Superfluous Man in Russian Literature*, 1978 and *Andrei Bitov: The Ecology of Inspiration*, 1993. **Introductory Essay:** The Superfluous Man in Russian Literature. **Essays:** Bitov; "Life in Windy Weather" (Bitov).

Christian, Nicole. Associate editor of the current volume. Doctoral dissertation on Vasilii Shukshin (University of Bristol, 1997). Author of articles on Shukshin. **Essays:** Shukshin; *Snowball Berry Red* (Shukshin).

Clark, Katerina. Professor of Comparative Literature, Yale University. Author of *The Soviet Novel: History as Ritual*, 1981 and *St. Petersburg: Crucible of Cultural Revolution*, 1995; co-author (with Michael Holquist) of *Mikhail Bakhtin*, 1984. **Introductory Essay:** Socialist Realism in Soviet Literature.

Cockrell, Roger. Senior Lecturer in Russian, University of Exeter. Co-editor of *Russian Views of Pushkin*, 1976 and *The Voice of a Giant: Essays on Seven Russian Prose Classics*, 1985. Editor of an edition of Aleksandr Fadeev's *Razgrom / The Rout*, 1995. **Essays:** *The Rout* (Fadeev); Furmanov; *Chapaev* (Furmanov); Gladkov; Vsevolod Ivanov; *Armoured Train 14–69* (Vsevolod Ivanov); Kaverin; A.N. Tolstoi; *Road to Calvary* (A.N. Tolstoi).

Connolly, Julian W. Professor of Slavic Languages and Literatures, University of Virginia, Charlottesville. Author of *Ivan Bunin*, 1982 and *Nabokov's Early Fiction*, 1992. **Essays:** *Evenings on a Farm Near Dikanka* (Gogol'); *The Defence* (Nabokov); *Despair* (Nabokov).

Cooke, Olga. Associate Professor, Department of Modern and Classical Languages, Texas A & M University. Has written widely on Andrei Belyi; editor of *The Andrej Belyj Society Newsletter*. **Essays:** *The Silver Dove* (Belyi); *Moscow* (Belyi); Evgeniia Ginzburg.

Cornwell, Neil. Editor of the current volume. Professor of Russian and Comparative Literature, University of Bristol. His books on 19th- and 20th-century literature include *The Life, Times, and Milieu of V.F. Odoyevsky, 1804–1869*, 1986; *Daniil Kharms and the Poetics of the Absurd* (as editor), 1991; *Pushkin's "The Queen of Spades"*, 1993; and *Vladimir Odoevsky and Romantic Poetics*, 1998. Series editor of Russian Texts and Critical Studies in Russian Literature for Bristol Classical Press. **Essays:** Vladimir Odoevskii; *Russian Nights* (Vladimir Odoevskii); *Anna Karenina* (Lev Tolstoi).

Costlow, Jane. Associate Professor of Russian, Bates College, Lewiston, Maine. Author of *Worlds Within Worlds: The Novels of Turgenev*, 1990. Co-editor of *Sexuality and the Body in Russian Culture*, 1993. **Essay:** Zinov'eva-Annibal.

Crone, Anna Lisa (Adviser). Associate Professor, Department of Slavic Languages and Literatures, University of Chicago. Author of *Rozanov and the End of Literature*, 1978 and *New Studies in Russian Language and Literature*, 1986. **Essay:** Derzhavin.

Cross, Anthony. Professor of Slavonic Studies, University of Cambridge. Author of *"By the Banks of the Thames": Russians in Eighteenth-Century Britain*, 1980; *Anglo-Russica: Aspects of Cultural Relations Between Great Britain and Russia in the Eighteenth and Early Nineteenth Centuries*, 1993; and *"By the Banks of the Neva": Chapters from the Lives and Careers of the British in Eighteenth-Century Russia*, 1997. Editor, *Newsletter of Study Group on Eighteenth-Century Russia*, 1973–. General editor of Anglo-Russian Affinities Series for Berg, 1992–. **Essays:** Karamzin; "Poor Liza" (Karamzin).

Crowe, Nicholas. Former Research Fellow, St John's College, Oxford. Wrote doctoral dissertation on 18th-century Russian literature. **Essays:** Chulkov; Dashkova; Emin; *Iabeda* (Kapnist); Kniazhnin; *Khvastun* (Kniazhnin); Narezhnyi; Aleksandr Odoevskii; Radishchev; Zagoskin.

Curtis, J.A.E. Lecturer in Russian and Fellow of Wolfson College, Oxford. Author of *Bulgakov's Last Decade: The Writer as Hero*, 1987 and *Manuscripts Don't Burn: Mikhail Bulgakov, A Life in Letters and Diaries*, 1991. **Essays:** *The Heart of a Dog* (Bulgakov); Ratushinskaia; Voznesenskaia.

Dalton-Brown, S. Lecturer in Russian, University of Exeter. Co-author of a study on Leont'ev, 1993 and a monograph on *Evgenii Onegin*, 1997. **Essays:** Grekova; *The Bathhouse* (Maiakovskii); Makanin; Pelevin; Petrushevskaia; *The Queen of Spades* (Pushkin); Arkadii and Boris Strugatskii; *It's Hard to Be a God* (Arkadii and Boris Strugatskii); Tolstaia; *On the Golden Porch* and *Sleepwalker in a Fog* (Tolstaia); *Another Life* (Trifonov).

Davidson, Pamela. Lecturer in Russian, School of Slavonic and East European Studies, University of London. Author of *The Poetic Imagination of Vyacheslav Ivanov*, 1989 and *Viacheslav Ivanov: A Reference Guide*, 1996. **Essay:** Viacheslav Ivanov.

Dewhirst, Martin. Lecturer in Russian, University of Glasgow. Specialist on post-war and contemporary Soviet and Russian literature. Co-editor of *The Soviet Censorship*, 1973 and *Russian Writing Today*, 1977. **Introductory Essay** (with Alla Latynina): Russian Literature in the Post-Soviet Period.

Dienes, Laszlo. Associate Professor, Department of Slavic Languages and Literatures, University of Massachusetts, Amherst. Specialist on Gaito Gazdanov and Russian émigré literature. Author of *Russian Literature in Exile: The Life and Work of Gajto Gazdanov*, 1982. **Essay:** Gazdanov.

Di Simplicio, Daša Šilhánková. Researcher and translator; formerly Lecturer in Russian, University of Siena. Author of *La nascita di un poeta: Boris Pasternak*, 1990. Currently editing Italian edition of Pasternak's correspondence. **Essays:** *The Childhood of Luvers* (Pasternak); *Safe Conduct* (Pasternak).

Doyle, Peter. Formerly, Lecturer in Russian, University of Manchester. Specialist on 20th-century Russian literature. **Essays:** Baranskaia; "A Week Like Any Other" (Baranskaia); Dombrovskii; *The Keeper of Antiquities* (Dombrovskii); *The Faculty of Useless Knowledge* (Dombrovskii).

Dryzhakova, Elena. Associate Professor, Department of Slavic Languages and Literatures, University of Pittsburgh. Specialist in 19th-century Russian intellectual history. **Essays:** Herzen; *My Past and Thoughts* (Herzen); Ogarev.

Ehre, Milton. Professor of Slavic Languages and Literatures, University of Chicago. Author of *Oblomov and His Creator: The Life and Art of Ivan Goncharov*, 1973 and *Isaac Babel*, 1986. Editor and translator of works by Gogol' and by Chekhov. **Essays:** *A Common Story* (Goncharov); *The Precipice* (Goncharov); *The Forest* (Aleksandr Ostrovskii); *Boris Godunov* (Pushkin).

Ellis, Frank. Lecturer in Russian and Media Studies, University of Leeds. Author of *Vasiliy Grossman: The Genesis and Evolution of a Russian Heretic*, 1994. **Essays:** Baklanov; *The Foothold* (Baklanov); Bondarev; *Silence* (Bondarev); Grossman; *Forever Flowing* (Grossman); *Life and Fate* (Grossman); Simonov; *The Living and the Dead* (Simonov).

Elsworth, John. Professor of Russian Studies, University of Manchester. Author of *Andrey Bely*, 1972 and *Andrey Bely: A Critical Study of the Novels*, 1983. Editor of *The Silver Age of Russian Literature*, 1992. **Essay:** Kushner.

Ermolaev, Herman. Professor of Russian and Soviet Literature, Princeton University. Author of *Soviet Literary Theories, 1917–1934*, 1963; *Mikhail Sholokhov and His Art*, 1982; and *Censorship in Soviet Literature, 1917–1991*, 1997. Co-author of *Sholokhov's "Tikhii Don": A Commentary in 2 Volumes*, 1997. Editor and translator of Gor'kii's *Untimely Thoughts*, 1995. **Essays:** Fadeev; Sholokhov.

Falchikov, Michael. Senior Lecturer in Russian, University of Edinburgh. Specialist in 20th-century Russian literature. Co-translator of Viktor Nekrasov's *Postscripts*, 1991. **Essays:** "The Gentleman from San Francisco" (Bunin); *The Unknown Artist* (Kaverin); Viktor Nekrasov; *Front-Line Stalingrad* (Viktor Nekrasov); *Tale of the Unextinguished Moon* (Pil'niak); *Mahogany* and *The Volga Falls to the Caspian Sea* (Pil'niak).

Farmer, Rachel S. Graduate teaching assistant, Department of Slavonic Studies, University of Nottingham. Doctoral dissertation on Vladimir Voinovich (University of Nottingham, 1997). Author of *Teach Yourself Beginner's Russian*, 1996. **Essay:** Voinovich.

Foote, I.P. Formerly University Lecturer in Russian; Emeritus Fellow of Queen's College, Oxford. Editor and translator of various editions of works by Mikhail Saltykov-Shchedrin. Joint editor, *Oxford Slavonic Papers*, 1972–91 and *Slavonic and East European Review*, 1980–90. **Essays:** Saltykov-Shchedrin; *The History of a Town* (Saltykov-Shchedrin); *The Golovlevs* (Saltykov-Shchedrin).

Forrester, Sibelan. Assistant Professor of Russian, Swarthmore College, Pennsylvania. Co-editor of *Engendering Slavic Literatures*, 1996. **Essays:** Chukovskii; Lokhvitskaia; Shkapskaia.

France, Peter. Endowment Fellow and Emeritus Professor of French, University of Edinburgh. Fellow of the British Academy. Author of *Poets of Modern Russia*, 1982. Translator of poetry by Aigi, Blok, and Pasternak. **Essay:** Aigi.

Franklin, Simon. Lecturer in Slavonic Studies, University of Cambridge. Co-author of *The Emergence of Rus, 750–1200*, 1996. Translator of *Sermons and Rhetoric of Kievan Rus'*, 1991. **Essays:** *Dead Souls* (Gogol'); *The Lay of Igor's Campaign*; *Primary Chronicle*.

Freeborn, Richard. Emeritus Professor of Russian Literature, University of London. Author of *Turgenev: The Novelist's Novelist*, 1960; *The Rise of the Russian Novel*, 1973; and *The*

Russian Revolutionary Novel, 1982. Translator of works by Turgenev and by Dostoevskii. **Introductory Essay:** The Classic Russian Novel. **Essays:** *Cities and Years* (Fedin); Gor'kii; "Twenty-Six Men and a Girl" (Gor'kii); *Wings* (Kuzmin); Libedinskii; *Doctor Zhivago* (Pasternak); Seifullina; Serafimovich; *The Iron Flood* (Serafimovich).

French, Jacqueline. Doctoral student, University of Bristol: completing dissertation on contemporary Russian fiction. **Essays:** Borodin; Kuraev.

Friedrich, Paul. Professor of Anthropology, Linguistics and Social Thought, and Associate Professor of Slavic Languages and Literatures, University of Chicago. Author of many books on linguistic and anthropological topics, including *Language, Context, and the Imagination*, 1979; *The Language Parallax*, 1986; and *The Princes of Naranja*, 1986. **Essay:** Krylov.

Gheith, Jehanne M. Assistant Professor of Russian Literature, Duke University, Durham, North Carolina. Specialist in Russian women's writing. **Essay:** Khvoshchinskaia.

Gillespie, David. Reader in Russian, University of Bath. Author of *Valentin Rasputin and Soviet Russian Village Prose*, 1986; *Iurii Trifonov: Unity Through Time*, 1992; and *The Twentieth-Century Russian Novel: An Introduction*, 1996. Editor of the Slavonic section, *Modern Language Review*. **Introductory Essay:** Thaws, Freezes, and Wakes: Russian Literature, 1953–1991. **Essays:** Astaf'ev; Nikolai Ostrovskii; Rasputin; *Live and Remember* (Rasputin); *Farewell to Matyora* (Rasputin); Soloukhin; Sorokin; Tendriakov; Trifonov; *The House on the Embankment* (Trifonov); *The Old Man* (Trifonov); Zalygin; *Na Irtyshe* (Zalygin).

Goodliffe, John. Senior Lecturer in Russian, University of Canterbury, New Zealand. Editor and translator of *These Fortunate Isles: Some Russian Perceptions of New Zealand in the Nineteenth and Early Twentieth Centuries*, 1992. **Essays:** *The Dragon* (Evgenii Shvarts); Vel'tman; *Strannik* (Vel'tman).

Goscilo, Helena. Associate Professor and Chair, Department of Slavic Languages and Literatures, University of Pittsburgh. Author of several books on contemporary Russian literature and gender studies, including *Dehexing Sex: Russian Womanhood During and After Glasnost*, 1996 and *TNT:The Explosive World of Tatyana N. Tolstaya's Fiction*, 1996. Translator of contemporary Russian writing. **Essays:** "The Ladies' Hairdresser" (Grekova); *The Ship of Widows* (Grekova); Katerli; *The Time: Night* (Petrushevskaia).

Grimstad, Knut. Lecturer in Russian, University of Trondheim. Currently working on the rhetoric of Nikolai Leskov. **Essays:** Nestor; *Tale of Woe-Misfortune*.

Grose, Richard B. Independent researcher. Has written on Zoshchenko and Nietzsche. **Essay:** *Before Sunrise* (Zoshchenko).

Grossman, Joan Delaney. Professor, Department of Slavic Languages and Literatures, University of California, Berkeley. Author of *Edgar Allan Poe in Russia*, 1973 and *Valery Bryusov and the Riddle of Russian Decadence*, 1985. Co-editor of *Creating Life: The Aesthetic Utopia of Russian Modernism*, 1994. **Essays:** Briusov; *Urbi et orbi* (Briusov); Konevskoi.

Harris, Jane Gary. Professor of Russian Literature, University of Pittsburgh. Author of *Osip Mandelstam*, 1988. Editor and co-translator of *Mandelstam: The Complete Critical Prose and Letters*, 1979 (as *The Collected Critical Prose and Letters*, 1991); editor of *Autobiographical Statements in Twentieth-Century Russian Literature*, 1990, and special Lidiia Ginzburg issue of *Canadian-American Slavic Studies*, 1994. **Essay:** Lidiia Ginzburg.

Henry, Peter. Emeritus Professor of Slavonic Languages and Literatures, University of Glasgow. Author of *A Hamlet of His Time: Vsevolod Garshin, The Man, His Works, and His Milieu*, 1983. Editor of translations and editions of works by Garshin, Chekhov, and Bunin. Founding editor, *Scottish Slavonic Review*, 1983–93; co-editor, *Slavonica*, 1993–. **Essays:** Bunin; *The Village* (Bunin); Garshin; "The Red Flower" (Garshin); Paustovskii.

Hippisley, Anthony. Lecturer in Russian, University of St Andrews. Specialist in 17th-century Russian literature. Author of *The Poetic Style of Simeon Polotsky*, 1985. **Essay:** Polotskii.

Hodgson, Katharine. Lecturer in Russian, University College of North Wales, Bangor. Author of *Written with the Bayonet: Soviet Russian Poetry of World War Two*, 1996. **Essay:** Berggol'ts.

Holman, Michael J. de K. Professor of Russian and Slavonic Studies, University of Leeds. Series editor of Blackwell Russian Texts, 1985–91. Specialist on Tolstoi and Tolstoianism. **Essay:** *Resurrection* (Lev Tolstoi).

Holohan, David M. Formerly Lecturer in Russian, University of Surrey. Doctoral dissertation on Mozhaev. Editor of an edition of Vasilii Shukshin's *Snowball Berry Red*, 1996. **Essays:** Mozhaev; *Muzhiki i baby* (Mozhaev).

Howells, D.L.L. Assistant Librarian, Taylor Institution Library, Oxford. Author of numerous bibliographical publications. **Essay:** Ivan IV.

Hutchings, Stephen. Lecturer in Russian, University of Surrey. Author of *A Semiotic Analysis of the Short Stories of Leonid Andreev, 1900–1909*, 1990. **Essays:** Andreev; *The Seven That Were Hanged* (Andreev).

Janecek, Gerald J. Professor and Chair, Department of Russian and Eastern Studies, University of Kentucky, Lexington. Author of *The Look of Russian Literature*, 1984. Editor and translator of works by and on Andrei Belyi. **Essays:** *Kotik Letaev* (Belyi); Kruchenykh.

Johnson, D. Barton. Emeritus Professor of Russian, University of California, Santa Barbara. Author of *Worlds in Regression: Some Novels of Vladimir Nabokov*, 1985; also writes on Sokolov. Founding editor of *Nabokov Studies*. **Essay:** *A School for Fools* (Sokolov).

Jones, Malcolm V. Emeritus Professor of Slavonic Studies, University of Nottingham. Author of *Dostoyevsky: The Novel of Discord*, 1976 and *Dostoyevsky after Bakhtin: Readings in Dostoevsky's Fantastic Realism*, 1990. Editor of collections of essays on Tolstoi and Dostoevskii. General editor, Cambridge Studies in Russian Literature, 1985–. President, International Dostoevsky Society, 1995–. **Essays:** *The Idiot* (Dostoevskii); *The Devils /The Possessed* (Dostoevskii).

Jones, W. Gareth. Professor of Russian, University College of North Wales, Bangor. Author of *Nikolay Novikov: Enlightener of Russia*, 1984. Editor of various publications by and on Tolstoi. **Introductory Essay:** Russian Literature in the 18th Century.

Kahn, Andrew. University Lecturer in Russian and Fellow of St Edmund Hall, Oxford. Specialist in 18th-century Russian literature. Editor of an edition of M.N. Murav'ev's *Institutiones Rhetoricae: A Treatise of a Russian Sentimentalist*, 1995 and of Pushkin's *The Queen of Spades and Other Stories*, 1997. **Essays:** Avvakum; Lomonosov; Trediakovskii; *Zadonshchina*.

Kalbouss, George. Associate Professor, Department of Slavic and East European Languages and Literatures, Ohio State University, Columbus. Author of *Russian Culture*, 1979; *The Plays of the Russian Symbolists*, 1982; and *A Study Guide to Russian Culture*, 1991. **Essay:** *The First Encounter* (Belyi).

Kelly, Catriona (Adviser). Lecturer in Russian and Fellow of New College, Oxford. Author of *A History of Russian Women's Writing*, 1994. Editor of *An Anthology of Russian Women's Writing*, 1994; co-editor of *An Introduction to Russian Cultural Studies*, 1998. **Introductory Essay:** Women's Writing in Russia. **Essays:** Barkova; Letkova; Prismanova.

Ketchian, Sonia I. Research Fellow, Russian Research Center, Harvard University. Author of *The Poetry of Anna Akhmatova: A Conquest of Time and Space*, 1986 and *The Poetic Craft of Bella Akhmadulina*, 1993. Editor of *Anna Akhmatova, 1889–1989*, 1993. **Essays:** Akhmadulina; *Skazka o dozhde* (Akhmadulina); *Taina* (Akhmadulina); *Evening* (Akhmatova); *Chetki* (Akhmatova).

Keys, R.J. Lecturer in Russian, University of St Andrews. Author of *The Reluctant Modernist: Andrei Belyi and the Development of Russian Fiction, 1902–1914*, 1996. **Essay:** Belyi.

Kirkwood, Michael. Professor of Slavonic Languages and Literatures, University of Glasgow. Author of *Alexander Zinoviev: An Introduction to His Work*, 1993. Co-editor of *Alexander Zinoviev as Writer and Thinker*, 1988; editor of *Language Planning in the Soviet Union*, 1989. Translator of Zinov'ev's *The Madhouse*, 1986. **Essays:** Zinov'ev; *The Yawning Heights* (Zinov'ev); *The Madhouse* (Zinov'ev).

Knapp, Shoshana Milgram. Associate Professor of English, Virginia Polytechnic Institute and State University, Blacksburg, Virginia. Has written several articles on comparative literary topics. **Essay:** Kollontai.

Knowles, A.V. Senior Lecturer in Russian and Soviet Studies and Director of Combined Honours (Arts), University of Liverpool. Author of *Ivan Turgenev*, 1988. Editor of *Tolstoy: The Critical Heritage*, 1978; editor and translator of *Turgenev's Letters*, 1983. **Essays:** Goncharov; Griboedov; Il'f and Petrov; *The Twelve Chairs* and *The Golden Calf* (Il'f and Petrov); Kapnist; Aleksandr Ostrovskii; Pisemskii; *One Thousand Souls* (Pisemskii); *The Death of Ivan Ilych* (Lev Tolstoi); *The Kreutzer Sonata* (Lev Tolstoi).

Krivulin, Viktor. Russian poet. See his own entry. **Essay:** Stratonovskii.

Kšicova, Danuše. Professor of Russian Literature, Masaryk University, Brno, Czech Republic. Author of studies on Russian poetry and romanticism. Co-editor of *Litteraria Humanitas* I–II, 1991–93. **Essay:** Polevoi.

Lagerberg, Robert. Lecturer in Russian, University of Auckland. **Essay:** *On the Eve* (Turgenev).

Lane, Ronald. Lecturer in Russian, University of Durham. Author of *Bibliography of Works by and about F.I. Tiutchev to 1985*, 1987, and of numerous articles on Tiutchev. **Essay:** Tiutchev.

Lanin, Boris. Senior Research Fellow, Academy of Education of Russia, Moscow. Author of numerous books on 20th-century Russian literature. Editor-in-chief of *Slovesnik*, 1991–93. **Introductory Essay:** Experiment and Emigration: Russian Literature, 1917–1953. **Essays:** Gladilin; Platonov; *Chevengur* (Platonov).

Latynina, Alla. Leading contemporary Moscow critic of modern Russian literature; columnist for *Literaturnaia gazeta*. Author of *Vsevolod Garshin*, 1986 and books on the recent Russian literary scene. First chair of the Russian Booker Prize. **Introductory Essay** (with Martin Dewhirst): Russian Literature in the Post-Soviet Period.

Laursen, Eric. Assistant Professor of Russian, University of Utah, Salt Lake City. Associate editor of the journal, *The Silver Age of Russian Literature and Culture*. **Essays:** *Cement* (Gladkov); Georgii Ivanov.

Leach, Robert. Senior Lecturer in Drama, University of Birmingham. Author of *Vsevolod Meyerhold*, 1989 and *Revolutionary Theatre*, 1994. Co-editor of the forthcoming *The Cambridge History of Russian Theatre*. **Essays:** *He Who Gets Slapped* (Andreev); *Masquerade* (Lermontov); *The Storm* (Aleksandr Ostrovskii).

Leatherbarrow, W.J. Professor of Russian, University of Sheffield. Author of *Fedor Dostoevsky*, 1981; *Fedor Dostoevsky: A Reference Guide*, 1990; and *Fyodor Dostoyevsky: "The Brothers Karamazov"*, 1992. Editor of *Dostoevskii and Britain*, 1995. **Essays:** Dostoevskii; *Crime and Punishment* (Dostoevskii); *The Brothers Karamazov* (Dostoevskii).

Lee, C. Nicholas. Professor of Russian, Department of Germanic and Slavic Languages and Literatures, University of Colorado, Boulder. Author of *The Novels of Mark Aleksandrovich Aldanov*, 1969 and various articles. **Essay:** Aldanov.

Lonergan, Jennifer. Teacher of English language and literature. Doctoral dissertation on Mikhailov (University of Bristol, 1996). **Essays:** Chernyshevskii; *What is to Be Done?* (Chernyshevskii); Druzhinin; *Polinka Saks* (Druzhinin); Mikhailov; Tur.

Longan, Nathan. Assistant Professor, Department of Modern Languages and Literatures, Oakland University, Rochester, Michigan. **Essays:** *Tales of the Mountains and Steppes* (Aitmatov); *The White Steamship* (Aitmatov); *The Day Lasts More than a Hundred Years* (Aitmatov); Okudzhava.

Loseff, Lev. Russian poet. See his own entry. **Essay:** Rein.

Lovell, Stephen. Doctoral student and former Temporary Lecturer in Russian, School of Slavonic and East European Studies, University of London. Writing dissertation on culture under Gorbachev. **Essays:** *Little Jinx* (Siniavskii); *Goodnight!* (Siniavskii).

Lowe, David A. Associate Professor of Slavic Languages and Literatures, Vanderbilt University, Nashville, Tennessee. Author of *Turgenev's "Fathers and Sons"*, 1983 and *Russian Writing since 1953*, 1987. Co-editor and co-translator of Dostoevskii's *Complete Letters*, 5 vols, 1988–91; translator of Trifonov's *Disappearance*, 1991. **Essays:** "Our Crowd" (Petrushevskaia); *The Exchange* (Trifonov); *A Nest of the Gentry* (Turgenev).

Luck, Christopher. Deputy Head Teacher, Davison School, Worthing, Sussex. Author of *Figures of War and Fields of Honour: Isaak Babel's Red Cavalry*, 1995. Editor of edition of *Konarmiia/Red Cavalry*, 1994. **Essays:** Babel'; *Red Cavalry* (Babel').

Luker, Nicholas. Senior Lecturer in Russian, University of Nottingham. Author of *Alexander Grin*, 1973; *Alexander Kuprin*, 1978; and *Aleksandr Grin: The Forgotten Visionary*, 1980. Editor of various anthologies and collections of essays on 20th-century Russian literature. **Essays:** Artsybashev; Grin; *Scarlet Sails* (Grin); Kuprin.

McKenzie, Rosalind. Doctoral student, School of Slavonic and East European Studies, University of London. Working on a dissertation on the hagiographical tradition in medieval Russian literature. **Essays:** *Frol Skobeev, the Rogue*; *The Legend of Boris and Gleb*; *The Tale of Boiaryna Morozova*; *The Tale of Ul'ianiia Osor'ina*.

McMillin, Arnold (Adviser). Professor of Russian Literature, School of Slavonic and East European Studies, University of London. Author of *A History of Byelorussian Literature from Its Origins to the Present Day*, 1977 and numerous articles on Russian and Belorussian literature. Editor of various collections of essays on Russian literature. Chairman of Editorial Committee of *The Slavonic and East European Review*, 1995–. **Essays:** Aksenov; *A Ticket to the Stars* (Aksenov); *The Island of Crimea* (Aksenov); Aleshkovskii; *Tales of Odessa* (Babel'); Belov; Daniel'; *The Double* (Dostoevskii); *The Duel* (Kuprin); Sokolov; *Mezhdu sobakoi i volkom* (Sokolov); *Astrophobia* (Sokolov); Venevitinov; *The Life and Extraordinary Adventures of Private Ivan Chonkin* (Voinovich); *Pretender to the Throne* (Voinovich); *Moscow 2042* (Voinovich).

McNair, John. Senior Lecturer and Head, Department of Russian, University of Queensland, Australia. Co-editor of *Russia and the Fifth Continent: Aspects of Russian-Australian Relations*, 1992. **Essays:** Aksakov; *The Family Chronicle* (Aksakov).

McVay, Gordon. Professor of Russian Literature, University of Bristol. Author of *Esenin: A Life*, 1976; *Isadora and Esenin*, 1980; *Chekhov's "Three Sisters"*, 1995; and numerous articles on Russian literature and theatre. Editor and translator of *Anton Chekhov: A Life in Letters*, 1994. **Essays:** Chekhov; *The Seagull* (Chekhov); *The Cherry Orchard* (Chekhov); Esenin; Mariengof.

Marsh, Cynthia. Senior Lecturer in Russian and Drama, University of Nottingham. Author of *M.A. Voloshin: Artist-Poet*, 1983 and *File on Gorky*, 1993. **Essays:** *The Lower Depths* (Gor'kii); *Enemies* (Gor'kii).

Marsh, Rosalind. Professor of Russian Studies, University of Bath. Author and editor of several books on Russian literature of the post-Stalin period, including *History and Literature in Contemporary Russia*, 1995. Editor and translator of *Gender and Russian Literature: New Perspectives*, 1996 and *Women in Russia and Ukraine*, 1996. **Essays:** Granin; Verbitskaia; *Kliuchi schast'ia* (Verbitskaia).

Martin, David W. Lecturer in Russian, University of Wales, Swansea. Translator of two collections of works by Soloukhin. Author of several essays on Chekhov. **Essay:** Lermontov.

Metcalf, Amanda. Administrator and formerly Tutor in Slavonic Languages, Australian National University, Canberra. Author of *Evgenii Shvarts and His Fairy-Tales for Adults*, 1979. **Essay:** Evgenii Shvarts.

Meyer, Priscilla. Professor of Russian Language and Literature, Wesleyan University, Middletown, Connecticut. Author of *Find What the Sailor Has Hidden: Vladimir Nabokov's "Pale Fire"*, 1988. Co-editor of *Essays on Gogol: Logos and the Russian Word*, 1992. **Essay:** *The Burn* (Aksenov).

Míkulašek, Miroslav. Professor of Russian, Masaryk University, Brno, Czech Republic. Author of a book on Soviet comedy, 1962 and studies of Maiakovskii, 1975 and 1982. **Essay:** Lunts.

Milne, Lesley. Reader in Modern Russian Literature, University of Nottingham. Author of *The Master and Margarita: A Comedy of Victory*, 1977 and *Mikhail Bulgakov: A Critical Biography*, 1990. Editor of *Bulgakov: The Novelist-Playwright*, 1995. **Essays:** Bulgakov; *The White Guard* (Bulgakov); *The Master and Margarita* (Bulgakov); Iskander.

Milner-Gulland, Robin (Adviser). Professor of Russian and European Studies, University of Sussex. Author of *The* Russians, 1997; co-author of *Cultural Atlas of Russia and the Soviet Union*, 1989; has written numerous articles on Russian poetry and culture. Editor and co-translator of *The Life of Zabolotsky*, 1994. **Introductory Essay:** Old Russian Literature. **Essays:** Oleinikov; Zabolotskii.

Minto, Marilyn. Senior Lecturer in Russian and formerly Dean of Arts and Social Sciences, University College of North Wales, Bangor. Author of *Windows into Heaven: An Introduction to the Russian Icon*, 1996. Editor and translator of *Russian Tales of the Fantastic*, 1994. Editor of an edition of Platonov, 1995. **Essays:** *Poor Folk* (Dostoevskii); *Mother* (Gor'kii); *The Foundation Pit* (Platonov); *The Bronze Horseman* (Pushkin).

Molnar, Michael. Research Director, The Freud Museum, London. Author of *Body of Words: A Reading of Belyi's "Kotik Letaev"*, 1987. Editor and translator of *The Diary of Sigmund Freud, 1929–1939*, 1992. Translator of contemporary Russian poetry. **Essays:** Dragomoshchenko; Krivulin; Parshchikov; Elena Shvarts.

Mozur, Joseph P., Jr. Associate Professor, Department of Foreign Languages and Literatures, University of South Alabama, Mobile. Author of *Parables from the Past: The Prose Fiction of Chingiz Aitmatov*, 1995. **Essay:** Aitmatov.

Muckle, James. Special Lecturer, University of Nottingham. Author of *Nikolai Leskov and the "Spirit of Protestantism"*, 1978 and books about education in Russia. Translator of works by Leskov. Former editor, *Journal of Russian Studies*. **Essays:** *Childhood Years of Bagrov Grandson* (Aksakov); Leskov; *Lady Macbeth of Mtsensk* (Leskov).

Murphy, A.B. Professor Emeritus of Russian, University of Ulster. Author of various studies of Russian language and literature; co-author of *Sholokhov's "Tikhii Don": A Commentary*, 2 vols, 1997. **Essay:** *Quiet Flows the Don* (Sholokhov).

Neatrour, Elizabeth B. Professor of Russian, James Madison University, Harrisonburg, Virginia. Has written widely on the work of Teffi. **Essay:** Teffi.

Nepomnyashchy, Catharine Theimer. Associate Professor, Slavic Department, Barnard College, New York. Author of *Abram Tertz and the Poetics of Crime*, 1995. Co-translator of Siniavskii's *Strolls with Pushkin*, 1993. Formerly editor of the *Ulbandus Review*. **Essay:** Siniavskii.

Nicholson, Michael. University Lecturer and Fellow of University College, Oxford. Has written widely on Solzhenitsyn. Co-editor of *Solzhenitsyn in Exile: Critical Essays and Documentary Materials*, 1985. Editor of *Solzhenitsyn Studies*, 1980–81. **Essays:** Shalamov; *Kolyma Tales* (Shalamov); Solzhenitsyn.

O'Connor, Katherine Tiernan. Associate Professor, Department of Modern Foreign Languages and Literatures, Boston University. Author of *Pasternak's "My Sister-Life"*, 1988. Co-translator (with Diana Lewis Burgin) of Bulgakov's *The Master and Margarita*, 1995. **Essays:** "A Boring Story" (Chekhov); *My Sister-Life* (Pasternak); *When the Weather Clears* (Pasternak).

Offord, Derek. Professor of Russian, University of Bristol. Author of *Portraits of Early Russian Liberals*, 1985; *The Russian Revolutionary Movement in the 1880s*, 1986; *Modern Russian: An Advanced Grammar Course*, 1993; and *Using Russian: A Guide to Contemporary Usage*, 1996. Editor of *The Golden Age of Russian Literature and Thought*, 1992. **Essays:** Belinskii; *The Minor* (Fonvizin); Kantemir; Sumarokov; *Sketches from a Hunter's Album* (Turgenev); *Rudin* (Turgenev).

O'Meara, Patrick. Head, Department of Russian, Fellow and formerly Senior Lecturer (Pro-VC Academic), Trinity College, Dublin. Author of *K.F. Ryleev: A Political Biography of the Decembrist Poet*, 1984. **Essay:** Ryleev.

Orwin, Donna Tussing. Senior Resident, Center for Russian and East European Studies and Visiting Professor, Slavic Department, University of Toronto. Author of *Tolstoy's Art and Thought*, 1847–1880, 1993. Co-editor of Kathryn B. Feuer's *Tolstoy and the Genesis of "War and Peace"*, 1996. **Essay:** Lev Tolstoi.

O'Toole, Michael. Professor of Communication Studies, Murdoch University, Perth, Australia. Author of *Structure, Style and Interpretation in the Russian Short Story*, 1982 and *The Language of Displayed Art*, 1994. Co-editor of *Functions of Style*, 1988. Co-editor, *Russian Poetics in Translation*, 1975–81. **Introductory Essay:** Russian Literary Theory: From the Formalists to Lotman.

Pachmuss, Temira A. Professor of Russian Literature and Comparative Literatures, University of Illinois, Champaign-Urbana. Author of *Zinaida Hippius: An Intellectual Profile*, 1971; *Russian Literature in the Baltic Between the Wars*, 1987; and *D.S. Merezhkovsky in Exile*, 1990. Editor of editions of the works of Hippius and various anthologies. **Essays:** Hippius; *Chertova kukla* and *Roman-Tsarevich* (Hippius).

Parsons, Neil. Lecturer in Russian, University of Glasgow. Editor and translator of Korolenko's *The History of My Contemporary*, 1972. **Essay:** Nadson.

Parthé, Kathleen (Adviser). Associate Professor, Department of Modern Languages and Cultures, University of Rochester, New York. Author of *Time, Backward! Memory and the Past in Soviet Russian Village Prose*, 1987 and *Russian Village Prose: The Radiant Past*, 1992.

Pavlovszky, Maria. Associate Instructor, Department of Foreign Languages, Indiana University-Purdue University, Indianapolis. Has written widely on Sergei Esenin. **Essays:** *Petersburg* (Belyi); *Na pole Kulikovom* (Blok); *All Souls' Day* (Esenin); *Moskva kabatskaia* (Esenin); *Cor Ardens* (Viacheslav Ivanov); *Winter Sonnets* and *De profundis amavi* (Viacheslav Ivanov); Kliuev; Nikitin; Remizov; "Matryona's House" (Solzhenitsyn); "The Flood" (Zamiatin).

Peace, Richard. Emeritus Professor, University of Bristol. Author of *Dostoyevsky: An Examination of the Major Novels*, 1971; *The Enigma of Gogol*, 1981; *Chekhov: A Study of the Four Major Plays*, 1983; *Oblomov: A Critical Examination of Goncharov's Novel*, 1991; and *Dostoyevsky's "Notes from Underground"*, 1993. **Essays:** *Notes from Underground* (Dostoevskii); Gogol'; Pomialovskii.

Pedrick, Thomas. Completed Master's dissertation on Dovlatov,

School of Slavonic and East European Studies, University of London. **Essay:** Dovlatov.

Pilkington, Anna. Lecturer in Russian, Queen Mary and Westfield College, University of London. Author of *Traveller's Russian*, 1990. **Essay:** Panova.

Pilshchikov, Igor. Formerly Lector in Russian, Keele University. Editor of the Moscow journal, *Philologica*. Author of various articles on Russian romantic poetry. **Essays:** Baratynskii; *Sumerki* (Baratynskii); Batiushkov; Zhukovskii.

Polukhina, Valentina. Professor of Russian Literature, Keele University. Specialist in modern Russian poetry. Author, editor, and co-editor of several books on Brodskii, including *Joseph Brodsky: A Poet for Our Time*, 1989 and *Brodsky Through the Eyes of His Contemporaries*, 1992. **Essays:** *A Part of Speech* (Brodskii); *To Urania* (Brodskii); Loseff; Prigov; Sedakova.

Porter, Robert. Reader in Russian, University of Bristol. Author of *Four Contemporary Russian Writers*, 1989; *Russia's Alternative Prose*, 1994; and *Solzhenitsyn's "One Day in the Life of Ivan Denisovich"*, 1997. Translator of works by Popov. **Essays:** Popov; *The Soul of a Patriot* (Popov); *One Day in the Life of Ivan Denisovich* (Solzhenitsyn); *Cancer Ward* (Solzhenitsyn); Zinik; *The Lord and the Gamekeeper* (Zinik).

Pospíšil, Ivo. Professor of Russian Literature and Head of Institute of Slavonic Studies, Masaryk University, Brno, Czech Republic. Author of several studies in modern Russian literature. **Essays:** *Dvoinoi portret* (Kaverin); *Peter the First* (A.N. Tolstoi).

Pursglove, Michael. Senior Lecturer in Russian, University of Exeter. Author of *D.V. Grigorovich: The Man Who Discovered Chekhov*, 1987. Editor of *The New Russia*, 1995 and several editions of 19th-century texts. **Essays:** Dudintsev; *Not by Bread Alone* (Dudintsev); Evtushenko; *Winter Station* (Evtushenko); Fet; Grigorovich; *Anton-Goremyka* (Grigorovich); Kazakov; Kol'tsov; Nagibin; Pristavkin; *The Inseparable Twins* (Pristavkin); Shaginian; *Kik* (Shaginian); Slutskii; Sollogub; "The Trial" (Tendriakov); "A Topsy-Turvy Spring" (Tendriakov); Uspenskii; Zaitsev.

Pushkin, Michael. Lecturer, Department of Russian Language and Literature, University of Birmingham. Has written on Russian social history and on modern Russian poetry. **Essays:** Voznesenskii; *Oza* (Voznesenskii); *Rov: Dukhovnyi protsess* (Voznesenskii).

Pyman, Avril. Emeritus Reader in Russian Literature, University of Durham. Author of *The Life of Aleksandr Blok*, 2 vols, 1979–80; *A History of Russian Symbolism*, 1994; and numerous articles on the Symbolists. Editor and translator of various texts from modern Russian literature. **Essays:** Blok; *The Puppet Show* (Blok); *The Twelve* (Blok).

Ransome, Michael. Head of Modern Languages, Bristol Grammar School. Author of articles on Nikolai Nekrasov and co-author of Russian language textbooks. **Essays:** Nikolai Nekrasov; "Red-Nosed Frost" (Nikolai Nekrasov); *Who Can Be Happy and Free in Russia?* (Nikolai Nekrasov).

Rayfield, Donald. Professor of Russian and Georgian, Queen Mary and Westfield College, University of London. Author of *Chekhov: The Evolution of His Art*, 1975; *"The Cherry Orchard": Catastrophe and Comedy*, 1994; *The Literature of Georgia: A History*, 1994; *Chekhov's "Uncle Vania" and "The Wood Demon"*, 1995; and *Anton Chekhov: A Life*, 1997. Translator of works by Osip Mandel'shtam. **Essays:** *The Cypress Chest* (Annenskii); *Vozmezdie* (Blok); "The Steppe" (Chekhov); *Uncle Vania / The Wood Demon* (Chekhov); "Ward Six" (Chekhov); "The Lady with the Dog" (Chekhov); *Three Sisters* (Chekhov); Del'vig; *Gondla* (Gumilev); Iazykov; *Sandro of Chegem* (Iskander); *Zangezi* (Khlebnikov); Khodasevich; Khomiakov; Kiukhel'beker; Nadezhda Mandel'shtam; *The Voronezh Notebooks* (Osip Mandel'shtam); Nabokov; *The Gift* (Nabokov); Sologub; *The Petty Demon* (Sologub); Solov'ev; Viazemskii.

Reid, Robert. Senior Lecturer in Russian, Keele University. Author of *Pushkin's "Mozart and Salieri"*, 1995 and various studies of Lermontov including *Lermontov's "A Hero of Our Time"*, 1997. Editor of *Problems of Russian Romanticism*, 1986. Co-editor, *Essays in Poetics*. **Essays:** *Mtsyri* (Lermontov); *A Hero of Our Time* (Lermontov); *The Demon* (Lermontov).

Reynolds, Andrew. Lecturer in Russian and Fellow, Selwyn College, Cambridge. Specialist on Osip Mandel'shtam. Co-editor (with Viktor Erofeev) of *The Penguin Book of New Russian Writing*, 1995. Translator of works by Viktor Erofeev. **Essays:** Viktor Erofeev; Osip Mandel'shtam.

Roberts, Graham. Lecturer in Russian Studies, University of Strathclyde. Specialist on the *oberiuty*. Author of *The Last Soviet Avant-Garde, OBERIU*, 1997 and of articles on Kharms and Vvedenskii. **Essays:** Kharms; Vvedenskii.

Rogachevskaia, Ekaterina. Senior Research Fellow, Department of Medieval Russian Literature, Institute of World Literature, Moscow. Has published widely on medieval Russian topics. **Essay:** *Shemiaka's Judgment*.

Rogachevskii, Andrei. Doctoral student and part-time tutor, Department of Slavonic Languages and Literatures, University of Glasgow. Author of a monograph on the rhetorical tradition in Pushkin, 1994. **Essay:** *About This* (Maiakovskii).

Rollberg, Peter. Associate Professor, Department of Slavic Languages and Literatures, George Washington University, Washington, DC. Editor of *Festschrift in Honor of Charles A. Moser*, 1996 and several volumes on modern Russian literature (published in Germany). Editor (from vol. 10) of *The Modern Encyclopedia of East Slavic, Baltic and Eurasian Literatures*. **Essays:** Erenburg; *Julio Jurenito* (Erenburg); *The Thaw* (Erenburg); *A White Sail Gleams* (Kataev); *Almaznyi moi venets* (Kataev); Maksimov; *The Seven Days of Creation* (Maksimov); Prishvin.

Rosengrant, Judson. Independent scholar and translator. Formerly holder of various Visiting Professorships and Fellowships. Editor and translator of Olesha's *No Day Without a Line*, 1979; of Lidiia Ginzburg's *On Psychological Prose*, 1991; and the forthcoming *On Lyric Poetry*. **Essay:** *No Day Without a Line* (Olesha).

Rosslyn, Wendy. Reader in Russian Literature, University of Nottingham. Author of *The Prince, the Fool and the Nunnery: The Religious Theme in the Early Poetry of Anna Akhmatova*, 1984 and *Anna Bunina (1774–1829) and the Origins of Women's Poetry in Russia*, 1997. Editor of *The Speech of Unknown Eyes: Akhmatova's Readers on Her Poetry*, 1990. **Essays:** Akhmatova; Bagritskii; Bunina.

Russell, Robert. Professor of Russian, University of Sheffield. Specialist in modern Russian Prose and drama. Author of *Valentin Kataev*, 1981 and *Russian Drama of the Revolutionary Period*, 1988. **Essays:** Kataev; *The Bedbug* (Maiakovskii); *We* (Zamiatin).

Scatton, Linda Hart. Assistant Provost for Graduate Studies and Research, State University of New York, Albany. Author of *Mikhail Zoshchenko: Evolution of a Writer*, 1993. **Essay:** Zoshchenko.

Schillinger, John. Professor and Chair, Department of Language and Foreign Studies, The American University, Washington, DC. Specialist in 20th-century Russian literature. Advisory Editor, *Russian Language Journal*. **Essays:** Rybakov; *Heavy Sand* (Rybakov); *Children of the Arbat* (Rybakov).

Schwartz, Marian. Freelance translator, including works by Berberova. **Essay:** Berberova.

Sedakova, Olga. Russian poet and Senior Lecturer, Institute of World Culture, Moscow University. See her own entry. **Essays:** Ilarion of Kiev; Zhdanov.

Shaitanov, Igor. Professor of Comparative Literature, Russian University for Humanities, Moscow. Has published books and articles on Russian and English poetry. **Essays:** Aseev; Samoilov.

Sheinker, Mikhail. Editor, *Vestnik novoi literatury*; also literary critic. **Essays:** Bobyshev; Livshits.

Shnitman-McMillin, Svetlana. Associate lecturer in Russian, University of Westminster, London. Author of *Venedikt Erofeev, "Moskva-Petushki" ili "The Rest is Silence"*, 1989; contributor to *Neue Zürcher Zeitung* and *Schweizerische Beiträge zum XI Internationalen Slavistenkongress in Bratislava*. **Essays:** Chukovskaia; *Sof'ia Petrovna* (Chukovskaia); *Going Under* (Chukovskaia);Venedikt Erofeev; *Moscow Circles* (Venedikt Erofeev); Vladimov; *Three Minutes' Silence* (Vladimov); *Faithful Ruslan* (Vladimov).

Smith, Alexandra. Lecturer in Russian, University of Canterbury, Christchurch, New Zealand. Author of *The Song of the Mocking Bird: Pushkin in the Work of Marina Tsvetaeva*, 1995. **Essays:** *Budem kak solntse* (Bal'mont); Bednyi; *The Fiery Angel* (Briusov); Chukhontsev; Fedin; *The Life of Klim Samgin* (Gor'kii); *Tiazhelaia lira* (Khodasevich); Merezhkovskii; *The Little Tragedies* (Pushkin); Severianin; *Tsar'-devitsa* (Tsvetaeva); *Remeslo* (Tsvetaeva); *Molodets* (Tsvetaeva); *Krysolov* (Tsvetaeva); "Poem of the End" and "Poem of the Mountain" (Tsvetaeva); *After Russia* (Tsvetaeva); Tvardovskii; *Vasilii Terkin* and*Terkin in the Other World* (Tvardovskii); Tynianov; Voloshin; "The Islanders" (Zamiatin).

Smith, Melissa T. Associate Professor of Russian, Youngstown State University, Ohio. Specialist on modern Russian women's writing. Editor-in-chief of special issue, *Ivan Elagin: In Memoriam, Canadian-American Slavic Studies*, 1993. **Essay:** *Three Girls in Blue* (Petrushevskaia).

Sobel, Ruth. Honorary Senior Lecturer, Ministry of Defence School of Languages, Beaconsfield. Author of *Gogol's Forgotten Book*, 1981. Translator of Pogorel'skii's *The Double*, 1988. **Essays:** *Mirgorod* (Gogol'); "The Nose" (Gogol'); Panaeva; Pogorel'skii; Rostopchina.

Sokol, Elena. Associate Professor and Chair, Department of Russian Studies, College of Wooster, Ohio. Author of *Russian Poetry for Children*, 1984. **Essay:** Marshak.

Solomon, Karla Thomas. Doctoral student, University of Kansas, Lawrence. **Essay:** Sokhanskaia.

Spieker, Sven. Assistant Professor, Department of Germanic, Slavic and Semitic Studies, University of California, Santa Barbara. Author of *Figures of Memory and Forgetting in Andrej Bitov's Prose*, 1996. **Essays:** *Pushkin House* (Bitov); "Pushkin's Photograph" (Bitov).

Sullivan, John. Senior Lecturer in Russian, University of St Andrews. Has written articles on history of the Russian language. **Essay:** *Domostroi.*

Tait, Arch. Senior Lecturer, Department of Russian Language and Literature, University of Birmingham. Author of a monograph on Lunacharskii, 1984. Translator of contemporary Russian prose. Co-editor, *Glas: New Russian Writing*. **Essays:** Kharitonov; Kurchatkin; Lipkin; *Uprazdnennyi teatr* (Okudzhava); *A General and His Army* (Vladimov); *The Mushroom Picker* (Zinik).

Tejerizo, Margaret. Lecturer, Department of Slavonic Languages and Literatures, University of Glasgow. Editor of *Rusistika*. **Essay:** Gorbanevskaia.

Thomson, Francis J. Professor, University of Antwerp. Author of more than 60 articles on early Slav literature and culture. **Essay:** Maxim the Greek.

Thomson, R.D.B. Professor, Department of Slavic Languages and Literatures, University of Toronto. Author of two books on Russian culture and society, 1972 and 1978. Editor of *Canadian Slavonic Papers*, 1980–86. **Essays:** Leonov; *The Thief* (Leonov); *The Russian Forest* (Leonov).

Tilly, Helen L. Research student, University of Bristol, working on Chukovskaia. **Essays:** Limonov; *It's Me, Eddie!* (Limonov).

Timenchik, Roman. Professor of Russian Literature, Hebrew

University, Jerusalem. Author of numerous publications on early 20th-century Russian poetry. **Essay:** Annenskii.

Wachtel, Andrew Baruch. Professor, Department of Slavic Languages and Literatures, Northwestern University, Evanston, Illinois. Author of *The Battle for Childhood*, 1990 and *An Obsession with History: Russian Writers Confront the Past*, 1994. **Essays:** *The Life of Arsen'ev* (Bunin); *Krasnoe koleso* (Solzhenitsyn); *Childhood, Boyhood, Youth* (Lev Tolstoi).

Wells, David N. Librarian, Curtin University of Technology Library, Perth, Australia. Author of *Akhmatova and Pushkin*, 1994 and *Anna Akhmatova: Her Poetry*, 1996. **Essays:** *White Flock* (Akhmatova); Bal'mont; *Stikhi o prekrasnoi dame* (Blok); *Ostanovka v pustyne* (Brodskii); Khlebnikov; *Stone* (Osip Mandel'shtam); *Tristia* (Osip Mandel'shtam); Pasternak; Tsvetaeva; *Scrolls* (Zabolotskii).

Weststeijn, Willem G. Professor of Slavic Literature, University of Amsterdam. Author of *Velimir Chlebnikov and the Development of Poetical Language in Russian Symbolism and Futurism*, 1983. Series editor, Studies in Slavic Literature and Poetics, Rodopi, Amsterdam. **Essay:** Kibirov.

Whitehead, Claire. Doctoral student, University of Bristol, working on the fantastic in Russian and French literature of the first half of the 19th century. **Essay:** *Pestrye skazki* (Vladimir Odoevskii).

Wigzell, Faith. Senior Lecturer in Russian Language and Literature, School of Slavonic and East European Studies, University of London. Author (as Faith C.M. Kitch) of *The Literary Style of Epifanij Premudryj: "Pletenie sloves"*, 1976. Editor of *Russian Writers on Russian Writers*, 1994. **Essays:** Epifanii Premudryi; Kirill of Turov; *The Cathedral Folk* (Leskov); *The Enchanted Wanderer* (Leskov).

Williams, Gareth. Senior Lecturer in Russian, University College of Wales, Swansea. Author of *The Influence of Tolstoy on Readers of His Works*, 1990 and *Tolstoy's "Childhood"*, 1995. **Essay:** *War and Peace* (Lev Tolstoi).

Woodward, James. Professor of Russian, University College of Wales, Swansea. Author of *Metaphysical Conflict: A Study of the Major Novels of Ivan Turgenev*, 1990; *Form and Meaning: Essays on Russian Literature*, 1993; and *Turgenev's "Fathers and Sons"*, 1996. **Essays:** Turgenev; *Fathers and Sons* (Turgenev).

Wright, A. Colin. Professor, Department of Russian Studies, Queens University, Kingston, Ontario. Author of *Mikhail Bulgakov: Life and Interpretations*, 1978. **Essays:** *Flight* (Bulgakov); *Lieutenant Kizhe* (Tynianov).

Wyllie, Barbara. Doctoral student, University College London. Writing dissertation on Nabokov and postmodern American fiction. **Essays:** *The Return of Chorb* (Nabokov); *Mary* (Nabokov); *Invitation to a Beheading* (Nabokov).

Žekulin, Gleb. Professor Emeritus, University of Toronto. Has written on various aspects of modern Russian literature. **Essays:** "The Overcoat" (Gogol'); *The First Circle* (Solzhenitsyn).

Zinik, Zinovii. Russian novelist and critic. See his own entry. **Essays:** Aizenburg; Ioffe.

Zohrab, Irene. Senior Lecturer in Russian, Victoria University, Wellington, New Zealand. Specialist on Russian intellectual history. Editor, *New Zealand Slavonic Journal*. **Essay:** *Without a Dowry* (Aleksandr Ostrovskii).